SECOND EDITION

Computer Organization and Design

THE HARDWARE/SOFTWARE INTERFACE

T R A D E M A R K S

The following trademarks are the property of the following organizations:

TeX is a trademark of Americal Mathematical Society.

Apple II and Macintosh are trademarks of Apple Computers, Inc.

CDC 6600, CDC 7600, CDC STAR-100, CYBER-180, CYBER-180/990, and CYBER-205 are trademarks of Control Data Corporation.

The Cosmic Cube is a trademark of California Institute of Technology.

CP3100 is a trademark of Conner Peripherals.

Cray, CRAY-1, CRAY J90, CRAY T90, CRAY X-MP/416, and CRAY Y-MP are trademarks of Cray Research.

Alpha, AlphaServer, AlphaStation, DEC, DECsystem, DECsystem 3100, DECstation, PDP-8, PDP-11, Unibus, VAX, VAX 8700, and VAX11/780 are trademarks of Digital Equipment Corporation.

MP2361A, Super Eagle, VP100, VP200, and VPP300 are trademarks of Fujitsu Corporation.

Gnu C Compiler is a trademark of Free Software Foundation.

Goodyear MPP is a trademark of Goodyear Tire and Rubber Co., Inc.

Apollo DN 300, Apollo DN 10000, Convex, HP, HP Precision Architecture, HPPA, HP850, HP 3000, HP 300/70, PA-RISC, and Precision are registered trademarks of Hewlet-Packard Company.

432, 960 CA, 4004, 8008, 8080, 8086, 8087, 8088, 80186, 80286, 80386, 80486, Delta, iAPX 432, i860, Intel, Intel486, Intel Hypercube, iP-SC/2, MMX, Multibus, Multibus II, Paragon, and Pentium are trademarks of Intel Corporation. Intel Inside is a registered trademark of Intel Corporation.

360, 360/30, 360/40, 360/50, 360/65, 360/85, 360/91, 370, 370/158, 370/165, 370/168, 370-XA, ESA/370, 701, 704, 709, 801, 3033, 3080, 3080 series, 3080 VF, 3081, 3090, 3090/100, 3090/200, 3090/400, 3090/600, 3090/600S, 3090 VF, 3330, 3380, 3380D, 3380 Disk Model AK4, 3380J, 3390, 3880-23, 3990, 7090, 7094, IBM, IBM PC, IBM PC-AT, IBM SVS, ISAM, MVS, PL.8, PowerPC, POWERstation, RT-PC, RAMAC, RS/6000, Sage, Stretch, System/360, Vector Faility, and VM are trademarks of International Business Machines Corporation. POWERserver, RISC System/6000, and SP2 are registered trademarks of International Business Machines Corporation.

ICL DAP is a trademark of International Computers Limited.

Inmos and Transputer are trademarks of Inmos.

FutureBus is a trademark of the Institute of Electrical and Electronic Engineers.

KSR-1 is a trademark of Kendall Square Research.

MASPAR MP-1 and MASPAR MP-2 are trademarks of MasPar Corporation.

MIPS, R2000, R3000, and R10000 are registered trademarks of MIPS Technology, Inc.

Windows is a trademark of Microsoft Corporation.

NuBus is a trademark of Massachusetts Institute of Technology.

Delta Series 8608, System V/88 R32V1, VME bus, 6809, 68000, 68010, 68020, 68030, 68881, 68882, 88000, 88000 1.8.4m14, 88100, and 88200 are trademarks of Motorola Corporation.

Ncube and nCube/ten are trademarks of Ncube Corporation.

NEC is a registered trademark of NEC Corporation.

Network Computer is a trademark of Oracle Corporation.

Parsytec GC is a trademark of Parsytec, Inc.

Imprimis, IPI-2, Sabre, Sabre 97209, Seagate, and Wren IV are trademarks of Seagate Technology, Inc.

NUMA-Q, Sequent, and Symmetry are trademarks of Sequent Computers.

Power Challenge, Silicon Graphics, Silicon Graphics 43/240, Silicon Graphics 4D/60, Silicon Graphics 4D/240, and Silicon Graphics 4D Series are trademarks of Silicon Graphics. Origin2000 is a registered trademark of Silicon Graphics.

SPEC is a registered trademark of the Standard Performance Evaluation Corporation.

Spice is a trademark of University of California at Berkeley.

Enterprise, Java, Sun, Sun Ultra, Sun Microsystems, and Ultra are trademarks of Sun Microsystems, Inc. SPARC and UltraSPARC are registered trademarks of SPARC International, Inc., licensed to Sun Microsystems, Inc.

Connection Machine, CM-2, and CM-5 are trademarks of Thinking Machines.

Burroughs 6500, B5000, B5500, D-machine, UNIVAC, UNIVAC I, and UNIVAC 1103 are trademarks of UNISYS.

Alto, PARC, Palo Alto Research Center, and Xerox are trademarks of Xerox Corporation.

The UNIX trademark is licensed exclusively through X/Open Company Ltd.

All other product names are trademarks or registered trademarks of their respective companies. Where trademarks appear in this book and Morgan Kaufmann Publishers was aware of a trademark claim, the trademarks have been printed in initial caps or all caps.

SECOND EDITION

Computer Organization and Design

THE HARDWARE/SOFTWARE INTERFACE

John L. Hennessy
Stanford University

David A. Patterson
University of California, Berkeley

With a contribution by
James R. Larus
University of Wisconsin

Morgan Kaufmann Publishers, Inc.
San Francisco, California

Sponsoring Editor   Denise Penrose
Production Manager   Yonie Overton
Production Editor   Julie Pabst
Editorial Coordinator   Jane Elliott
Text and Cover Design   Ross Carron Design
Illustration   Alexander Teshin Associates, with second edition modifications by Dartmouth Publishing, Inc.
Chapter Opener Illustrations   Canary Studios
Copyeditor   Ken DellaPenta
Composition   Nancy Logan
Proofreader   Jennifer McClain
Indexer   Steve Rath
Printer   Courier Corporation

Morgan Kaufmann Publishers, Inc.
Editorial and Sales Office:
340 Pine Street, Sixth Floor
San Francisco, CA 94104-3205
USA

Telephone   415/392-2665
Facsimile   415/982-2665
Email   *mkp@mkp.com*
WWW   *http://www.mkp.com*
Order toll free   800/745-7323

Advice, Praise, and Errors: Any correspondence related to this publication or intended for the authors should be sent electronically to *cod2bugs@mkp.com.* Information regarding error sightings is encouraged. Any error sightings that are accepted for correction in subsequent printings will be rewarded by the authors with a payment of $1.00 (U.S.) per correction at the time of their implementation in a reprint.

Library of Congress Cataloging-in-Publication Data
Patterson, David A.
      Computer organization and design : the hardware/software interface
      / David A. Patterson, John L. Hennessy.—2nd ed.
            p.   cm.
      Includes bibliographical references and index.
      ISBN 1-55860-428-6 (cloth).—ISBN 1-55860-491-X (paper)
      1. Computer organization. 2. Computers—Design and construction.
            3. Computer interfaces.   I. Hennessy, John L.   II. Title
            QA76.9.C643H46   1997
            004.2'2—dc21   97-16050

TO LINDA AND ANDREA

Foreword

by John H. Crawford
Intel Fellow, Director of Microprocessor Architecture
Intel Corporation, Santa Clara, California

Computer design is an exciting and competitive discipline. The microprocessor industry is on a treadmill where we double microprocessor performance every 18 months and double microprocessor complexity—measured by the number of transistors per chip—every 24 months. This unprecedented rate of change has been evident for the entire 25-year history of the microprocessor, and it promises to continue for many years to come as the creativity and energy of many people are harnessed to drive innovation ahead in spite of the challenge of ever-smaller dimensions. This book trains the student with the concepts needed to lay a solid foundation for joining this exciting field. More importantly, this book provides a framework for thinking about computer organization and design that will enable the reader to continue the lifetime of learning necessary for staying at the forefront of this competitive discipline.

The text focuses on the boundary between hardware and software and explores the levels of hardware in the vicinity of this boundary. This boundary is captured in a computer's architecture specification. It is a critical boundary for a successful computer product: an architect must define an interface that can be efficiently implemented by hardware and efficiently targeted by compilers. The interface must be able to retain these efficiencies for many generations of hardware and compiler technology, much of which will be unknown at the time the architecture is specified. This boundary is central to the discipline of computer design: it is where compilation (in software) ends and interpretation (in hardware) begins.

This book builds on introductory programming skills to introduce the concepts of assembly language programming and the tools needed for this task: the assembler, linker, and loader. Once these prerequisites are completed, the remainder of the book explores the first few levels of hardware below the architectural interface. The basic concepts are motivated and introduced with clear and intuitive examples, then elaborated into the "real stuff" used in today's modern microprocessors. For example, doing the laundry is used as an analogy in Chapter 6 to explain the basic concepts of pipelining, a key technique used in all modern computers. In Chapter 4, algorithms for the basic floating-point arithmetic operators such as addition, multiplication, and division are first explained in decimal, then in binary, and finally they are elaborated into the best-known methods used for high-speed arithmetic in today's computers.

New to this edition are sections in each chapter entitled "Real Stuff." These sections describe how the concepts from the chapter are implemented in commercially successful products. These provide relevant, tangible examples of the concepts and reinforce their importance. As an example, the Real Stuff in Chapter 6, Enhancing Performance with Pipelining, provides an overview of a dynamically scheduled pipeline as implemented in both the IBM/Motorola PowerPC 604 and Intel's Pentium Pro microprocessor.

The history of computing is woven as a thread throughout the book to reward the reader with a glimpse of key successes from the brief history of this young discipline. The other side of history is reported in the Fallacies and Pitfalls section of each chapter. Since we can learn more from failure than from success, these sections provide a wealth of learning!

The authors are two of the most admired teachers, researchers, and practitioners of the art of computer design today. John Hennessy has straddled both sides of the hardware/software boundary, providing technical leadership for the legendary MIPS compiler as well as the MIPS hardware products through many generations. David Patterson was one of the original RISC proponents: he coined the acronym RISC, evangelized the case for RISC, and served as a key consultant on Sun Microsystem's SPARC line of processors. Continuing his talent for marketable acronyms, his next breakthrough was RAID (Redundant Arrays of Inexpensive Disks), which revolutionized the disk storage industry for large data servers, and then NOW (Networks of Workstations).

Like other great "software" products, this second edition went through an extensive beta testing program: 13 beta sites tested the draft manuscript in classes to "debug" the text. Changes from this testing have been incorporated into the "production" version.

Patterson and Hennessy have succeeded in taking the first edition of their excellent introductory textbook on computer design and making it even better. This edition retains all of the good points of the original, yet adds significant new content and some minor enhancements. What results is an outstanding introduction to the exciting field of computer design.

Contents

6 **Enhancing Performance with Pipelining** 434

7 **Large and Fast: Exploiting Memory Hierarchy** 538

8 **Interfacing Processors and Peripherals** 636

9 | **Multiprocessors** 710

A P P E N D I C E S

A | **Assemblers, Linkers, and the SPIM Simulator** A-2

by James R. Larus, University of Wisconsin

Worked Examples

Chapter 5: The Processor: Datapath and Control

Chapter 6: Enhancing Performance with Pipelining

Chapter 7: Large and Fast: Exploiting Memory Hierarchy

Chapter 8: Interfacing Processors and Peripherals

Computer Organization and Design Online

All of the following resources are available at *http://www.mkp.com/cod2e.htm*.

Web Extensions

These materials are extensions of the book's content.

Web Extension I: Survey of RISC Architectures

Supplies current detailed information for several RISC architectures.

- Desktop RISC Architectures (Alpha, PA-RISC, MIPS, PowerPC, SPARC)
- Embedded RISC Architectures (ARM, Hitachi SH4, MIT M32R, MIPS 16, Thumb)

Web Extension II: Introducing C to Pascal Programmers

Provides Pascal programmers with a quick reference for understanding the C code in the text.

- Variable Declarations
- Assignment Statements
- Relational Expressions and Conditional Statements
- Loops
- Examples to Put It All Together
- Exercises

Web Extension III: Another Approach to Instruction Set Architecture—VAX

Presents an example of a CISC computer architecture for comparison with the MIPS architecture described in the text.

- VAX Operands and Addressing Modes
- Encoding VAX Instructions
- VAX Operations
- An Example to Put it All Together: swap

- A Longer Example: sort
- Fallacies and Pitfalls
- Historical Perspective and Further Reading
- Exercises

Supplements

This electronic support package includes files that can be viewed and downloaded in a number of formats.

Lecture slides

Electronic versions of text figures

Instructors Manual

Links to course home pages from selected schools

Instructions for using new DOS and Windows versions of PCspim simulators

Links to SPIM simulators (see page xviii)

Resources

Multiprocessors Page

Extends Chapter 9's coverage of real machines by providing links to companies that manufacture current multiprocessor machines.

Discussion Group

Provides readers with the opportunity to exchange ideas and information related to the book.

The SPIM Simulator

Developed by James R. Larus, the SPIM S20 is a software simulator that runs assembly language programs for the MIPS R2000/R3000 RISC computers. It can read and run MIPS a.out files (when compiled and running on a system containing a MIPS processor). SPIM is a self-contained system that contains a debugger and an interface to the operating system.

SPIM is portable; it has run on a DECStation 31000/51000, Sun 3, Sun 4, PC/RT, IBM RS/6000, HP Bobcat, HP Snake, and Sequent. Students can generate code for a simple, clean, orthogonal computer, regardless of the machine used. SPIM comes with complete source code and documentation of all instructions.

SPIM can be downloaded in versions for DOS, Windows, and UNIX, either from *www.mkp.com/cod2e.htm* or by direct ftp.

Retrieval of SPIM by ftp

SPIM is available for anonymous ftp from *ftp.cs.wisc.edu* in the file *pub/spim/spim.tar.Z* (this is a compressed tar file).

For those who are unfamiliar with command-line anonymous ftp, here are the steps to follow to get a copy of your preferred version of SPIM.

1. ftp to *ftp.cs.wisc.edu* from your computer:

    ```
    % ftp ftp.cs.wisc.edu
    ```

2. The ftp server will respond and ask you to log in. Log in as anonymous and use your email address as a password:

    ```
    Name (ftp.cs.wisc.edu:larus): anonymous
    331 Guest login ok, send login or email address as password
    Password:
    ```

3. The server will then print a welcome message. Change to the directory containing spim:

    ```
    ftp> cd pub/spim
    ```

4. Set binary mode for the transfer (since the file is compressed):

    ```
    ftp> binary
    ```

5. Choose the file appropriate for your machine and copy:

    ```
    ftp> get spim.tar.Z (UNIX)
    ftp> get PCspim.zip (Windows)
    ftp> get PCspim-dos.zip (DOS)
    ```

6. Exit the ftp program:

    ```
    ftp> quit
    ```

7. Uncompress and untar the file:

    ```
    % uncompress spim.tar.Z
    % tar xvf spim.tar
    ```

    If the uncompression fails, you probably forgot to set binary (step 4). Try again. There are directions in the file README.

Preface

The most beautiful thing we can experience is the mysterious.
It is the source of all true art and science.

Albert Einstein, *What I Believe*, 1930

About This Book

We believe that learning in computer science and engineering should reflect the current state of the field, as well as introduce the principles that are shaping computing. We also feel that readers in every specialty of computing need to appreciate the organizational paradigms that determine the capabilities, performance, and, ultimately, the success of computer systems.

Modern computer technology requires professionals of every computing specialty to understand both hardware and software. The interaction between hardware and software at a variety of levels also offers a framework for understanding the fundamentals of computing. Whether your primary interest is computer science or electrical engineering, the central ideas in computer organization and design are the same. Thus, our emphasis in this book is to show the relationship between hardware and software and to focus on the concepts that are the basis for current computers.

Traditionally, the competing influences of assembly language, organization, and design have encouraged books that consider each area as a distinct subset. In our view, such distinctions have increasingly lost meaning as computer technology has advanced. To truly understand the breadth of our field, it is important to understand the interdependencies among these topics.

The audience for this book includes those with little experience in assembly language or logic design who need to understand basic computer organization as well as readers with backgrounds in assembly language and/or logic design who want to learn how to design a computer or understand how a system works and why it performs as it does.

Changes for the Second Edition

We had six major goals for the second edition: tie the ideas from the book more closely to the real world; enhance how well the book works for beginners; extend the book material using the World Wide Web; improve quality; improve pedagogy; and finally, update the technical content to reflect changes in the industry since the publication of the first edition in 1994—the conventional reason for a new edition.

First, to make the examples in the book even more concrete and connected with the real world, in each chapter we explained how the ideas were realized in the latest microprocessors from Intel or from IBM/Motorola. Hence you can learn how the mechanisms discussed are used in the computer on your desktop. Each chapter has a new section called "Real Stuff" that ties the ideas you read about to the machine you probably use everyday.

Second, we wanted the book to work better for readers interested in an overview of computer organization. Each chapter now has a list of the key terms discussed in the chapter, and we added a glossary of more than 300 definitions. We also rely on analogies from everyday life to explain subtleties of computers:

- commercial airplanes to show how performance differs if measured as bandwidth or latency
- the stealth of spies to explain procedure invocation and nesting
- plumbing to show how carry-lookahead logic works
- the laundry room to explain pipeline execution and hazards
- a desk in a library to demonstrate principles of memory hierarchy
- the management overhead as committees grow to illustrate the difficulty of achieving high performance in large-scale multiprocessors

More specifically, we added more assembly language programming examples and more explanation in each example to help the beginner understand assembly language programming in Chapters 3 and 4. We also added an introductory section to the pipelining chapter (Chapter 6) that allows understanding of the important ideas and issues in pipeline design without having to delve into the details of a pipelined datapath and control.

Our third goal was to go beyond the limitations of a printed book by adding descriptions and links on the World Wide Web. Throughout this book, you will often see the "Web Enhanced" icon shown at the left. Wherever this icon appears, you can go to *http://www.mkp.com/cod2e.htm* to find materials related to the text.

The WWW lets us give examples of recent, relevant machines so that you can see the latest versions of the ideas in the book. For example, we've added a new online appendix (Web Extension I) comparing RISC architectures. Other examples include links for specific references in the book to other sites; instructions on how to use PCspim, the new DOS and Windows versions of the SPIM simulator, as well as links to all the versions of SPIM; access to all the figures from the book; lecture slides; links to instructors' home pages; and an online Instructors Manual. We also included some appendices from the first edition (Web Extensions II and III) that you may find valuable. We intend to update these pages periodically to make new and better links.

Fourth, we wanted to significantly reduce the flaws that creep into a book during the revision process. The first edition of the book used beta testing to see which ideas worked well and which did not, and we were very happy with the improvements as a result. We did the same with the second edition. To further reduce the chances of bugs in the book, we gave ourselves a longer development cycle and involved many more computer architects in its preparation. First, Tod Amon completely revised all exercises, in part based on suggestions of exercises by a dozen instructors. The book now has 30% new exercises and another 30% that have been reworked for a total of 400. We believe that they are much more clearly worded than before and that there is sufficient variety for a broader group of students. Second, Kent Wilken carefully read the beta edition, suggesting hundreds of improvements. After we revised the beta edition, George Adams gave another very careful read of our revision, again making hundreds of useful suggestions. Finally, we reviewed the copyedit and read the page proof to try to catch mistakes that can creep in during the book production process. Although we are sure there must still be bugs for which you can get rewards, we believe this edition is far cleaner than the first.

The fifth goal was to improve the exposition of the ideas in the book, based on difficulties mentioned by readers of the first edition. We expanded the section of Chapter 3 explaining procedures, showing the procedure infrastructure in a longer sequence of examples. Chapter 4 has a longer description of carry lookahead and carry save adders. We simplified the explanation of the multicycle datapath in Chapter 5 by adding several registers. Chapter 6 actually got a good deal shorter by adding an overview section, since it allowed us to reduce the number of examples in the detailed pipelining sections. We also made numerous changes in the pipeline diagrams to make them easier to understand and more consistent. Chapter 7 was reorganized to put all caches together before moving to virtual memory and then translation buffers, coming back to the commonalities at the end. We also changed the emphasis from virtual memory as simply another level of the hierarchy to the hardware enforcer of protection. Chapter 8 was refocused to be more quantitative and design oriented. Chapter 9 was completely rewritten and retitled, reflecting the dramatic change in the parallel processing industry since 1994.

Finally, in the interval since the first edition of this book, a computer has run a program at the rate of 1 teraFLOPS—a trillion floating-point operations per second or a million floating-point operations per *microsecond,* another computer has played better chess than the best human being, and the whole world is more closely connected thanks to the World Wide Web. These events occurred in part because computer designers have first improved performance of a single computer by a factor of 100 in the last 10 years and then harnessed together many of them to achieve even greater performance. We have included descriptions of new ideas that helped make these miracles occur, such as branch prediction and out-of-order execution in Chapter 6, multilevel and nonblocking caches in Chapter 7, switched networks and new buses in Chapter 8, and nonuniform-memory-access, shared-memory multiprocessors and clusters in Chapter 9.

Supplements and Web Extensions

A directory of the Web supplements, extensions, and resources appears on page xvi. In it you'll find a complete electronic supplements package, as well as a variety of materials and resources designed to support this text, that you can access on the publisher's World Wide Web site at *www.mkp.com/ cod2e.htm*. Included in the supplements package is an online Instructors Manual. The Instructors Manual contents are available from the Web site with the exception of the solutions. Instructors should contact the publisher directly to obtain access to solutions.

If they prefer, instructors may choose a printed Instructors Manual that includes chapter objectives, teaching hints, and critical points for each chapter as well as solutions to the exercises. Instructors should contact the publisher directly to obtain the printed Instructors Manual.

Relationship to CA:AQA

Some readers may be familiar with *Computer Architecture: A Quantitative Approach*. Our motivation in writing that book was to describe the principles of computer architecture using solid engineering fundamentals and quantitative cost/performance trade-offs. We used an approach that combined examples and measurements, based on commercial systems, to create realistic design experiences. Our goal was to demonstrate that computer architecture could be learned using scientific methodologies instead of a descriptive approach.

A majority of the readers for *Computer Organization and Design: The Hardware/Software Interface* do not plan to become computer architects. The performance of future software systems will be dramatically affected, however, by how well software designers understand the basic hardware techniques at work in a system. Thus, compiler writers, operating system designers, database programmers, and most other software engineers need a firm grounding in the principles presented in this book. Similarly, hardware designers must understand clearly the effects of their work on software applications.

Thus, we knew that this book had to be much more than a subset of the material in *Computer Architecture*. We've approached every topic in a new way. Topics shared between the books were written anew for this effort, while many other topics are presented here for the first time. To further ensure the uniqueness of *Computer Organization and Design*, we exchanged the writing responsibilities we assigned to ourselves for *Computer Architecture*. The topics that Hennessy covered in the first book were written by Patterson in this one, and vice versa. Several of our reviewers suggested that we call this book "Computer Organization: A Conceptual Approach" to emphasize the significant differences from our other book. It is our hope that the reader will find new insights in every section, as well as a more tractable introduction to the abstractions and principles at work in a modern computer.

We were so happy with *Computer Organization and Design* that the second edition of *Computer Architecture* was revised to remove most of the introductory material, hence there is much less overlap today than with the first editions of both books.

Learning by Evolution

It is tempting for authors to present the latest version of a hardware concept and spend considerable time explaining how these often sophisticated ideas work. We decided instead to present each idea from its first principles, emphasizing the simplest version of an idea, how it works, and how it came to be. We believe that presenting the fundamental concepts first offers greater insight into why machines look the way they do today, as well as how they might evolve as technology changes.

To facilitate this approach, we have based the book upon the MIPS processor. It offers an easy-to-understand instruction set and can be implemented in a simple, straightforward manner. This allows readers to grasp an entire machine organization and to follow exactly how the machine implements its instructions. Throughout the text, we present the concepts before the details, building from simpler versions of ideas to more complex ones. Examples of this approach can be found in almost every chapter. Chapter 3 builds up to MIPS assembly language starting with one simple instruction type. The concepts and algorithms used in modern computer arithmetic are built up starting from the familiar grade school algorithms in Chapter 4. Chapters 5 and 6 start from the simplest possible implementation of a MIPS subset and build to a fully pipelined version. Chapter 7 illustrates the abstractions and concepts in memory hierarchies by starting with the simplest possible cache, then extending it, and then covering virtual memory and TLBs using the same ideas.

This evolutionary process is used extensively in Chapters 5 and 6, where the complete datapath and control for a processor are presented. Since learning is a visual process, we have included sequences of figures that contain progressively more detail or show a sequence of events within the machine. We have also used a second color to help readers follow the figures and sequences of figures.

Learning from this Book

Our objective of demonstrating first principles through the interrelationship of hardware and software is enhanced by several features found in each chapter. The Hardware/Software Interface sections are used to highlight these relationships. We've also included Big Picture sections for each chapter to remind readers of the major insights. And as mentioned above, each chapter has a Real Stuff section to tie concepts to mechanisms found in current desktop computers. We hope that these elements reinforce our goal of making this book equally valuable as a foundation for further study in both hardware and software courses.

To illustrate the relationship between high-level language and machine language and to describe the hardware algorithms, we have chosen C. It is widely used in compiler and operating system courses, it is widely used by computer professionals, and several facilities in the language make it suitable for describing hardware algorithms. For those who are familiar with Pascal rather than C, Web Extension II, found at *www.mkp.com/cod2e.htm* provides a quick introduction to C for Pascal programmers and should be sufficient to understand the code sequences in the text.

We have tried to manage the pace of the presentation for readers of varying experience. Ideas that are not essential to a newcomer, but which may be of interest to the more advanced reader, are set off from the main text and presented as elaborations. When appropriate, advanced concepts have been saved for the exercise sets and enhanced with additional discussion as In More Depth sections. In addition, we found that the extent of background that students have in logic design varies widely. Thus, Appendix B provides all the necessary background for those readers not versed in the basics of logic design, as well as some slightly more sophisticated material for the more advanced student. Within a course, this material can be used in supplementary lectures or incorporated into the mainstream of the course, depending on the background of the students and the goals of the instructor.

We have also found that readers enjoy learning the history of the field, so the Historical Perspective sections include many photographs of important machines and little known stories about the ideas behind them. We hope that the perspective offered by these anecdotes and photographs will add a new dimension for our readers.

Course Syllabi and this Book

One particularly difficult issue facing instructors is the balance of assembly language programming with computer organization. We have written this book so that readers will learn more about organization and design, while still providing a complete introduction to assembly language. By using a RISC architecture, students can learn the basics of an instruction set and assembly language programming in less time than is typically reserved in the curriculum for CISC-based assembly courses. Many instructors have also found that using a simulator, rather than running in native mode on a real machine, provides the experience of assembly language programming in substantially less time (and with less pain for the student).

SPIM is the simulator of the MIPS processor developed by James R. Larus. The publisher's Web site at *www.mkp.com/cod2e.htm* has links to spim and xspim, which were developed by Larus to run on UNIX, and to PCspim (DOS) and PCspim (Windows), which were adapted from the Unix versions by David Carley. Although not identical to the Unix versions, the DOS and Windows versions offer the same general functionality. PCspim (Windows) will run under Windows 3.1, Windows 95, and Windows NT. We feel this will enhance student opportunities for learning about computer organization (see Appendix A). Finally, stepwise derivation of assembly from a high-level language takes less study time than learning it from the ground up. Chapter 3 and Appendix A may be used together or separately, depending upon the reader's background. Chapter 3 provides the basics and can be supplemented with additional detail from Appendix A for a complete introduction to modern assembly language programming. In the end, we hope this approach offers a more efficient treatment of assembly for most readers, while being sufficiently broad to support detailed lecture or laboratory coverage if an instructor wants more emphasis on assembly language programming.

For those courses intended to expose students to the important principles of computer organization, the chapters from 4 to 9 explain the key ideas. Chapter 4 explains the idea of number representation for both integers and floating-point numbers and shows how arithmetic algorithms work. Chapters 5 and 6 introduce key ideas in control and pipelining and can be covered at several levels. Chapter 7 introduces the principles of memory hierarchies, unifying the ideas of caching and virtual memory. Chapter 8 shows how I/O systems are organized and controlled, explaining the cooperative relationship between the hardware and the operating system. Finally, Chapter 9 uses examples to introduce the key principles used in multiprocessors.

For readers who want a greater emphasis on computer design, Chapters 4 through 8, together with Appendices B and C, provide that opportunity. For example, Chapter 4 explains a number of techniques used by computer designers to speed up addition and multiplication. Chapters 5 and 6 derive complete implementations of a MIPS subset using the arithmetic elements from Chapter 4 and a number of common datapath elements (such as register files and memories) that are explained in detail in Appendix B. Chapter 5 starts with a very simple implementation; a complete datapath and control unit are constructed for this organization. The implementation is then modified to derive a faster version where each instruction can take differing numbers of clock cycles. The control for this multicycle implementation is designed using two different methods in Chapter 5. Appendix C shows in detail how the control specifications are implemented using structured logic blocks. Chapter 6 builds on the single-clock cycle implementation created in Chapter 5 to show how pipelined machines are designed. The design is extended to show how hazards can be handled and how control for interrupts works. The student interested in computer design is not only exposed to three different designs for the same instruction set, but can also see how these designs compare in terms of advantages and disadvantages.

Chapter Organization and Overview

Using these plans as the core, we developed the other chapters to introduce and support that core.

Many students remarked that they appreciated learning about the continuing rapid change in speed and capacity of hardware, as well as some of the history of computer development. This material is the focus of Chapter 1. It provides a perspective on how software or hardware will need to scale during the coming decades. Chapter 1 also introduces topics to be covered in later chapters.

Chapter 2 shows that time is the only safe measure of computer performance. It also relates common measurements used by hardware and software designers to the reliable measurement of time. The material in this chapter motivates the techniques discussed in Chapters 5, 6, and 7 and provides a framework for evaluating them.

Chapter 3 builds on the knowledge of a programming language to derive an assembly language, offering several rules of thumb that guide the designer of the assembly language. We chose the instruction set of a real computer, in this case MIPS, so that real compilers could be used by students to see the code that would be generated. We hide the delayed branch and load until Chapter 6 for pedagogical reasons. Fortunately, the MIPS assembler schedules both delayed branches and loads so the assembly language programmer can ignore these complexities without danger. Readers can see a very different approach to instruction set design in the Intel 80x86, which is covered in this chapter as well.

Although there is no consensus on what should be covered or what should be skipped in learning about computer arithmetic, we couldn't write Chapter 4 without reaching some conclusions of our own! Our solution is to introduce all the central ideas in the chapter and to provide some additional background for more advanced topics in the exercises. This allows one instructor to cover more advanced topics and assign exercises based on them, while another instructor may skip the material.

Chapters 5 and 6 show a realistic example of a processor in detail. Most readers appreciate having a real example to study, and a complete example provides the insight needed to see how all the pieces of a processor fit together for a pipelined and nonpipelined machine. To facilitate skipping some details on hardware implementation of control, we have included much of this material in Appendix C.

Just as Chapters 2 through 6 provide important background for readers with an interest in compilers, Chapters 7 and 8 provide vital background to anyone pursuing further work in operating systems or databases. Chapter 7 describes the principles of memory hierarchies, focusing on the commonality between virtual memory and caching. Chapter 7 also emphasizes the role of the operating system and its interaction with the memory system.

Topics as diverse as operating systems, databases, graphics, and networking require an understanding of I/O systems organization as well as the major technical characteristics of devices that influence this organization. Chapter 8 focuses on the topic of how I/O systems are organized starting with bus organizations, working up to communication between the processor and I/O device, and finally to the management role of the operating system. While we emphasize the interfacing issues, especially between hardware and software, several other important topics are introduced. Many of these topics are useful not only in computer organization but as background in other areas. For example, the handshaking protocol, used to interface asynchronous I/O devices, has applications in any distributed system.

For some readers, this book may be their only overview of computer systems, so we have included a survey of multiprocessing. Rather than the traditional catalog of characteristics for many parallel machines, we have tried to describe the underlying principles that will drive the designs of parallel processors for the next decade. This section includes a small running example to show different versions of the same program for different parallel architectures. And as mentioned above, we have linked many example multiprocessors from the real world on the book's WWW page at *www.mkp.com/cod2e.htm*.

Because the book is intended as an introduction for readers with a variety of interests, we tried to keep the presentation flexible. The appendices on assembly language and logic design are one of the principle vehicles to allow such flexibility, as these are easily skipped by more advanced readers. The presence of the appendices has made it possible to use this book in a course that mixes EE and CS majors with fairly different backgrounds in logic design and software.

Assembly language programming is best learned by doing and in many cases will be done with the use of the simulator available with this book. Because of this, we invited Jim Larus, the creator of the SPIM simulator, to join us as contributor of Appendix A. Appendix A describes the SPIM simulator and provides further details of the MIPS assembly language. In addition, it describes assemblers and linkers, which handle the translation of assembly language programs to executable machine language.

The logic design appendix is intended as a supplement to the material on computer organization rather than a comprehensive introduction to logic design. While many EE students in a computer organization course will have already had a course on logic design or digital electronics, we have found that CS majors in many institutions have not had much exposure to this area. The first few sections of Appendix B provide the necessary background. We include some material, such as the organization of memories and finite state machine control of a processor, in the mainstream material, since it is crucial to understanding computer organization.

Selection of Material

If you had no prior background and wanted to read from cover-to-cover, the following order makes sense: Chapters 1 and 2, Web Extension III (if needed),

Chapter 3, Chapter 4, Appendix A and Web Extension II (if interested), Appendix B, Chapter 5, Appendix C, Chapters 6, 7, 8, and 9. Clearly, most readers skip material. We have worked to provide readers with flexibility in their approach to the material, without making the discussions redundant. The chapters have been written as self-contained units with cross-references to other chapters when related text or figures should be considered. The book has been used successfully in a variety of courses with different goals and student backgrounds.

Concluding Remarks

In *Computer Architecture* we alternated the gender of a pronoun chapter by chapter. In this book we believe we have removed all such pronouns, except of course for specific people.

If you read the following acknowledgments section, you will see that we went to great lengths to correct mistakes. Since a book goes through many printings, we have the opportunity to make even more corrections. If you uncover any remaining, resilient bugs, please contact the publisher by electronic mail at *cod2bugs@mkp.com* or by low-tech mail using the address found on the copyright page. The first person to report a technical error will be awarded a $1.00 bounty upon its implementation in future printings of the book!

Finally, like the last book, there is no strict ordering of the authors' names. About half the time you will see Hennessy and Patterson, both in this book and in advertisements, and half the time you will see Patterson and Hennessy. You'll even find it listed both ways in bibliographic publications such as *Books in Print*. This again reflects the true collaborative nature of this book: Together we brainstormed about the ideas and method of presentation, then individually wrote about one-half of the chapters and acted as reviewer for every draft of the other. The page count suggests we again wrote almost exactly the same number of pages. Thus, we equally share the blame for what you are about to read.

Acknowledgments for the Second Edition

We'd like to again express our appreciation to **Jim Larus** for his willingness in contributing his expertise on assembly language programming, as well as for welcoming readers of this book to use the simulator he developed and maintains at the University of Wisconsin. PCspim (DOS) and PCspim (Windows) versions of the simulator were developed by **David Carley**.

Tod Amon of Southwest Texas State University was the exercise editor, creating and editing many new exercises. He also incorporated exercises donated by

Doug Clark, Princeton; **Richard Fateman**, University of California, Berkeley; **Max Hailperin**, Gustavus Adolphus College; **Robert Kline**, West Chester University; **Gandhi Puvvada**, University of Southern California; **Hamzeh Roumani**, York University; **Mike Smith**, Harvard University; and **Gregory Weber**, Indiana University.

The following people helped with solutions of the exercises:

> **George Adams,** Purdue University, and the following students: **Pritpal Ahuja**, Princeton; **Alan Alpert**, Southwest Texas State University; **Charles Fraleigh**, Stanford; **Bob Heath**, University of Kentucky; **Scott Karlin**, Princeton; **Bill Poucher**, Stanford; and **Xiang Yu**, Princeton.

Marc Zimmerman, a student of Kent Wilken at the University of California at Davis, worked out solutions to the exercises to help Tod Amon evaluate the clarity of the exercise text. Thanks to the good work by all these people, we have a much richer and more clearly written set of exercises.

The beta edition was released for class testing in the fall of 1996 by the following instructors and institutions:

> **Mike Clancy**, University of California, Berkeley; **Doug Clark**, Princeton; **David Culler**, University of California, Berkeley; **Max Hailperin**, Gustavus Adolphus College; **Richard Hughey**, University of California at Santa Cruz; **Mary Jane Irwin**, Pennsylvania State University; **Truman Joe**, Stanford University; **Robert Kline**, West Chester University; **Everald Mills** and **Kosuke Imamura**, Seattle University; **Gandhi Puvvada**, University of Southern California; **Mike Smith**, Harvard University; **Steve Taylor**, Worcester Polytechnical University; and **Bob Wood**, Florida State University.

We would like to thank these instructors and their students for their help.

We would especially like to acknowledge the careful reviewing by **Kent Wilken** of University of California at Davis and **George Adams** of Purdue University. We are grateful to both for their efforts in making this edition as clean and clear as possible.

We wish to thank the extended Morgan Kaufmann family for agreeing to publish this book again, this time under the able leadership of **Denise Penrose**. She found imaginative ways to balance our workload, had excellent ideas for realizing the goals of the second edition, and kept our feet to the fire of a demanding schedule. **Julie Pabst** managed the entire book production process, from the beta edition to the final second edition that you hold today. **Jane Elliott** coordinated the beta test, ran the bug extermination program, and created the first draft of the glossary among many other tasks. **Jennifer Mann** started the development process by surveying users of the first edition and finding beta testers. We thank also the many freelance vendors who contributed to this volume, especially **Nancy Logan**, our compositor.

The contributions of the scores of people we mentioned here and hundreds of others who participated in the beta testing and surveys have made this second edition our best book yet. Enjoy!

David A. Patterson   **John L. Hennessy**

1

Computer Abstractions and Technology

Civilization advances by extending the number of important operations which we can perform without thinking about them.

Alfred North Whitehead
An Introduction to Mathematics, 1911

1.1 Introduction

Welcome to this book! We're delighted to have this opportunity to convey the excitement of the world of computer systems. This is not a dry and dreary field, where progress is glacial and where new ideas atrophy from neglect. No! Computer systems have a vital and synergistic relationship to an important industry—responsible for 5% to 10% of the gross national product of the United States—and this unusual industry embraces innovation at a breathtaking rate. Since 1985 there have been a half-dozen new machines whose introduction appeared to revolutionize the computing industry; these revolutions were cut short only because someone else built an even better computer.

This race to innovate has led to unprecedented progress since computing's inception in the late 1940s. Had the transportation industry kept pace with the computer industry, for example, today we could travel coast to coast in 5 seconds for 50 cents. Take just a moment to contemplate how such an improvement would change society—living in Tahiti while working in San Francisco, going to Moscow for an evening at the Bolshoi Ballet—and you can appreciate the implications of such a change.

Computers have led to a third revolution for civilization, with the information revolution taking its place alongside the agricultural and the industrial revolutions. The resulting multiplication of humankind's intellectual strength and reach naturally has affected the sciences as well. There is now a new vein of scientific investigation, with computational scientists joining theoretical and experimental scientists in the exploration of new frontiers in astronomy, biology, chemistry, physics, . . .

The computer revolution continues. Each time the cost of computing improves by another factor of 10, the opportunities for computers multiply. Applications that were economically infeasible suddenly become practical. In the recent past, the following applications were "computer science fiction."

- *Automatic teller machines:* A computer placed in the wall of banks to distribute and collect cash was a ridiculous concept in the 1950s, when the cheapest computer cost at least $500,000 and was the size of a car.

- *Computers in automobiles:* Until microprocessors improved dramatically in price and performance in the early 1980s, computer control of cars was ludicrous. Today, computers reduce pollution and improve fuel efficiency via engine controls and increase safety through the prevention of dangerous skids and through the inflation of air bags to protect occupants in a crash.

- *Laptop computers:* Who would have dreamed that advances in computer systems would lead to laptop computers, allowing students to bring computers to coffeehouses and on airplanes?

- *Human genome project:* The cost of computer equipment to map human DNA sequences will be hundreds of millions of dollars. It's unlikely that anyone would have considered this project had the computer costs been 10 to 100 times higher, as they would have been 10 to 20 years ago.

- *World Wide Web:* Not in existence at the time of the first edition of this book, currently the World Wide Web is transforming our society. Among its uses are distributing news, sending flowers, buying from online catalogues, taking electronic tours to help pick vacation spots, finding others who share your esoteric interests, and even more mundane topics like finding the lecture notes of the authors of your textbooks.

Clearly, advances in this technology now affect almost every aspect of our society. Hardware advances have allowed programmers to create wonderfully useful software, and explain why computers are omnipresent. Tomorrow's science fiction computer applications are the cashless society, automated intelligent highways, and genuinely ubiquitous computing: no one carries computers because they are available everywhere.

Successful programmers have always been concerned about the performance of their programs because getting results to the user quickly is critical in creating successful software. In the 1960s and 1970s, a primary constraint on computer performance was the size of the computer's memory. Thus programmers often followed a simple credo: Minimize memory space to make programs fast. In the last decade, advances in computer design and memory technology have greatly reduced the importance of small memory size. Programmers interested in performance now need to understand the issues that have replaced the simple memory model of the 1960s: the hierarchical nature of memories and the parallel nature of processors. Programmers who seek to build competitive versions of compilers, operating systems, databases, and even applications will therefore need to increase their knowledge of computer organization.

We are honored to have the opportunity to explain what's inside this revolutionary machine, unraveling the software below your program and the hardware under the covers of your computer. By the time you finish this book, you will understand the secrets of programming a computer in its native tongue, the internal organization of computers and how it affects performance of your programs, and even how you could go about designing a computer of your very own.

This first chapter lays the foundation for the rest of the book. It introduces the basic ideas and definitions, places the major components of software and hardware in perspective, and introduces integrated circuits, the technology that fuels the computer revolution.

1.2 Below Your Program

In Paris they simply stared when I spoke to them in French; I never did succeed in making those idiots understand their own language.

Mark Twain, *The Innocents Abroad*, 1869

To actually speak to an electronic machine, you need to send electrical signals. The easiest signals for machines to understand are *on* and *off*, and so the machine alphabet is just two letters. Just as the 26 letters of the English alphabet do not limit how much can be written, the two letters of the computer alphabet do not limit what computers can do. The two symbols for these two letters are the numbers 0 and 1, and we commonly think of the machine language as numbers in base 2, or *binary numbers*. We refer to each "letter" as a *binary digit* or *bit*. Computers are slaves to our commands; hence, the name for an individual command is *instruction*. Instructions, which are just collections of bits that the computer understands, can be thought of as numbers. For example, the bits

```
1000110010100000
```

tell one computer to add two numbers. Chapter 3 explains why we use numbers for instructions *and* data; we don't want to steal that chapter's thunder, but using numbers for both instructions and data is a foundation of computing.

The first programmers communicated to computers in binary numbers, but this was so tedious that they quickly invented new notations that were closer to the way humans think. At first these notations were translated to binary by hand, but this process was still tiresome. Using the machine to help program the machine, the pioneers invented programs to translate from symbolic notation to binary. The first of these programs was named an *assembler*. This program translates a symbolic version of an instruction into the binary version. For example, the programmer would write

```
add A,B
```

and the assembler would translate this notation into

```
1000110010100000
```

This instruction tells the computer to add the two numbers A and B. The name coined for this symbolic language, still used today, is *assembly language*.

Although a tremendous improvement, assembly language is still far from the notation a scientist might like to use to simulate fluid flow or that an accountant might use to balance the books. Assembly language requires the programmer to write one line for every instruction that the machine will follow, forcing the programmer to think like the machine.

Such low-level thinking inspired a simple question: If we can write a program to translate from assembly language to binary instructions to simplify programming, what prevents us from writing a program that translates from some higher-level notation down to assembly language?

The answer was: nothing. Although more challenging to create than an assembler, this higher-level translator was plausible.

Programmers today owe their productivity—and their sanity—to this observation. Programs that accept this more natural notation are called *compilers*, and the languages they *compile* are called *high-level programming languages*. They enable a programmer to write this high-level language expression:

```
A + B
```

The compiler would compile it into this assembly language statement:

```
add A,B
```

The assembler would translate this statement into the binary instruction that tells the computer to add the two numbers A and B:

```
1000110010100000
```

Figure 1.1 shows the relationships among these programs and languages.

High-level
language
program
(in C)

```
swap(int v[], int k)
{int temp;
    temp = v[k];
    v[k] = v[k+1];
    v[k+1] = temp;
}
```

C compiler

Assembly
language
program
(for MIPS)

```
swap:
    muli $2, $5,4
    add  $2, $4,$2
    lw   $15, 0($2)
    lw   $16, 4($2)
    sw   $16, 0($2)
    sw   $15, 4($2)
    jr   $31
```

Assembler

Binary machine
language
program
(for MIPS)

```
00000000101000010000000000011000
00000000100011100001100000100001
10001100011000100000000000000000
10001100111100100000000000000100
10101100111100100000000000000000
10101100011000100000000000000100
00000011111000000000000000001000
```

FIGURE 1.1 C program compiled into assembly language and then assembled into binary machine language. Although the translation from high-level language to binary machine language is shown in two steps, some compilers cut out the middleman and produce binary machine language directly. These languages and this program are examined in more detail in Chapter 3. (Web Extension III, available at *www.mkp.com/cod2e.htm*, explains C to Pascal programmers.)

High-level programming languages offer several important benefits. First, they allow the programmer to think in a more natural language, using English words and algebraic notation, resulting in programs that look much more like text than like tables of cryptic symbols (see Figure 1.1). Moreover, they allow languages to be designed according to their intended use. Hence, Fortran was designed for scientific computation, Cobol for business data processing, Lisp for symbol manipulation, and so on.

The second advantage of programming languages is improved programmer productivity. One of the few areas of widespread agreement in software development is that it takes less time to develop programs when they are written in languages that require fewer lines to express an idea. Conciseness is a clear advantage of high-level languages over assembly language.

The final advantage is that programming languages allow programs to be independent of the computer on which they were developed, since compilers and assemblers can translate high-level language programs to the binary instructions of any machine. These three advantages are so strong that today little programming is done in assembly language.

As programming matured, many of its practitioners saw that reusing programs was much more efficient than writing everything from scratch. Hence programmers began to pool potentially widely used routines into libraries. One of the first of these *subroutine libraries* was for inputting and outputting data, which included, for example, routines to control printers, such as ensuring paper is in the printer before printing can begin. Such software controlled other input/output devices, such as magnetic disks, magnetic tapes, and displays.

It soon became apparent that a set of programs could be run more efficiently if there was a separate program that supervised running those programs. As soon as one program completed, the supervising program would start the next program in the queue, thereby avoiding delays. These supervising programs, which soon included the input/output subroutine libraries, are the basis for what we call *operating systems* today. Operating systems are programs that manage the resources of a computer for the benefit of the programs that run on that machine.

Software came to be categorized by its use. Software that provides services that are commonly useful is called *systems software*. Operating systems, compilers, and assemblers are examples of systems software. In contrast to programs aimed at programmers, *applications software,* or just *applications,* is the name given to programs aimed at computer users, such as spreadsheets or text editors. Figure 1.2 shows the classical drawing mapping the hierarchical layers of software and hardware.

This simplified view has some problems. Should we really place compilers in the systems software level in Figure 1.2? Compilers produce programs at both the applications *and* the systems level, and applications programs don't normally call on the compiler while they are running. A more realistic view of the nature of systems appears in Figure 1.3. It shows that software does not consist of monolithic layers, but is composed of many programs that build on one another. Like the strands of a thick rope, each time you look carefully at what appears to be a single strand, you find it is really composed of many finer components.

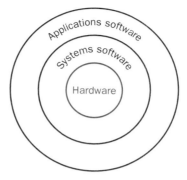

FIGURE 1.2 **A simplified view of hardware and software as hierarchical layers, classically shown as concentric rings building up from the core of hardware to the software closest to the user.**

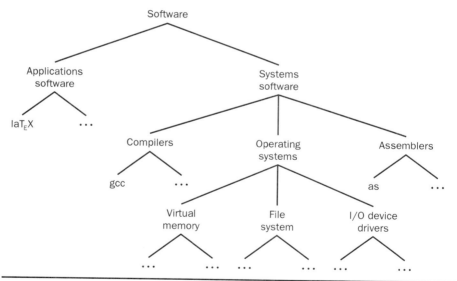

FIGURE 1.3 **An example of the decomposability of computer systems.** The terms in the middle of the chart, such as laT$_E$X and gcc, are examples of Unix programs. The terms lower in the chart, such as virtual memory, will be introduced in Chapters 7 and 8.

1.3   Under the Covers

Now that we have looked below your program to uncover the underlying software, let's open the covers of the computer to learn about the underlying hardware.

Figure 1.4 shows a typical desktop computer with keyboard, mouse, screen, and a box containing even more hardware. What is not visible in the photograph is a network that connects the computer to printers and disks. This photograph reveals two of the key components of computers: *input devices*, such as the keyboard and mouse, and *output devices*, such as the screen and printers. As the names suggest, input feeds the computer and output is the result of computation sent to the user. Some devices, such as networks and disks, provide both input and output to the computer.

Chapter 8 describes input/output (I/O) devices in more detail, but let's take an introductory tour through the computer hardware, starting with the external I/O devices.

FIGURE 1.4   A desktop computer. The cathode ray tube (CRT) screen is the primary output device, and the keyboard and mouse are the primary input devices.

Anatomy of a Mouse

I got the idea for the mouse while attending a talk at a computer conference. The speaker was so boring that I started daydreaming and hit upon the idea.

Doug Engelbart

Although many users now take mice for granted, the idea of a pointing device such as a mouse was invented 30 years ago. Engelbart showed the first demonstration of a system with a mouse on a research prototype in 1967. The Alto, which was the inspiration for all workstations as well as for the Macintosh, included a mouse as its pointing device in 1973. By the 1980s, all workstations and many personal computers included this device, and new user interfaces based on graphics displays and mice became popular. The mouse is actually quite simple, as the photograph in Figure 1.5 shows.

The mechanical version consists of a large ball that is mounted in such a way that it makes contact with a pair of wheels, one positioned on the x-axis and the other on the y-axis. These wheels either turn mechanical counters or turn a slotted wheel, through which a light-emitting diode (LED) shines on a photosensor. In either scheme, moving the mouse rolls the large ball, which turns the x-wheel or the y-wheel or both, depending on whether the mouse is moved in the vertical, horizontal, or diagonal direction. Although there are many styles of interfaces for these pointing devices, moving each wheel essentially increments or decrements counters somewhere in the system. The counters serve to record how far the mouse has moved and in which direction.

FIGURE 1.5 **The inside of a mechanical mouse.** Mouse courtesy of Logitech.

Through the Looking Glass

Through computer displays I have landed an airplane on the deck of a moving carrier, observed a nuclear particle hit a potential well, flown in a rocket at nearly the speed of light and watched a computer reveal its innermost workings.

Ivan Sutherland, the "father" of computer graphics, quoted in
"Computer Software for Graphics," *Scientific American*, 1984

The most fascinating I/O device is probably the graphics display. Based on television technology, a *raster cathode ray tube* (CRT) *display* scans an image one line at a time, 30 to 75 times per second (Figure 1.6). At this *refresh rate*, people don't notice a flicker on the screen.

The image is composed of a matrix of picture elements, or *pixels*, which can be represented as a matrix of bits, called a *bit map*. Depending on the size of the screen and the resolution, the display matrix ranges in size from 512×340 to 1560×1280 pixels. The simplest display has 1 bit per pixel, allowing it to be black or white. For displays that support 256 different shades of black and white, sometimes called *gray-scale* displays, 8 bits per pixel are required. A color display might use 8 bits for each of the three primary colors (red, blue, and green), for 24 bits per pixel, permitting millions of different colors to be displayed.

Portable computers often use *liquid crystal displays* (LCDs) instead of CRTs to get a thin, low-power display. The main difference is that the LCD pixel is not the source of light. A typical LCD includes rod-shaped molecules in a liquid that form a twisting helix that bends light entering the display, typically from a light source behind the display. The rods straighten out when a current is applied and no longer bend the light. The active matrix LCD has a tiny switch at each pixel to precisely control current and thus make sharper images.

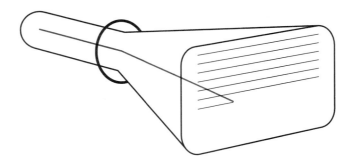

FIGURE 1.6   A CRT display. A beam is shot by an electronic gun through the vacuum onto a phosphor-coated screen. The steering coil at the neck of the CRT aims the gun. Raster scan systems, used in television and in almost all computers, paint the screen a line at a time as a series of dots, or pixels. The screen is refreshed 30 to 70 times per second.

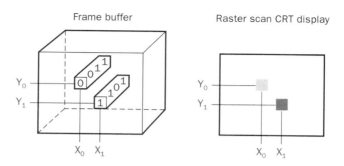

FIGURE 1.7   Each coordinate in the frame buffer on the left determines the shade of the corresponding coordinate for the raster scan CRT display on the right. Pixel (X_0, Y_0) contains the bit pattern 0011, which is a lighter shade of gray on the screen than the bit pattern 1101 in pixel (X_1, Y_1).

No matter what the display, the computer hardware support for graphics consists mainly of a *raster refresh buffer*, or *frame buffer*, to store the bit map. The image to be represented on-screen is stored in the frame buffer, and the bit pattern per pixel is read out to the graphics display at the refresh rate. Figure 1.7 shows a frame buffer with 4 bits per pixel.

The goal of the bit map is to faithfully represent what is on the screen. The challenges in graphics systems arise because the human eye is very good at detecting even subtle changes on the screen. For example, when the screen is being updated, the eye can detect the inconsistency between the portion of the screen that has changed and that which hasn't.

Opening the Box

If we open the box containing the computer, we see a fascinating board of thin green plastic, covered with dozens of small gray or black rectangles. Figure 1.8 shows the contents of the desktop computer in Figure 1.4. This *motherboard* is shown vertically in the back, with a floppy disk drive and power supplies shown on the left.

The small rectangles on the motherboard contain the devices that drive our advancing technology, *integrated circuits* or *chips*. The board is composed of three pieces: the piece connecting to the I/O devices mentioned above, the memory, and the processor. The I/O devices are connected via the two large boards attached perpendicularly to the motherboard toward the middle on the right-hand side.

The *memory* is where the programs are kept when they are running; it also contains the data needed by the running programs. In Figure 1.8, memory is found on the two small boards that are attached perpendicularly toward the middle of the motherboard. Each small memory board contains eight integrated circuits.

FIGURE 1.8   Inside a personal computer. The vertical board in the back is a printed circuit board (PC board), called the *motherboard* in a PC, that contains most of the electronics of the computer; Figure 1.11 is an overhead photograph of that board, rotated 90 degrees. The processor is the large black rectangle in the lower-right corner of the board. (Figure 1.9 is a photograph of the processor before it is placed in the black package.) The two large boards attached perpendicularly in the top third of the motherboard on the right contain input/output interfaces to the Ethernet local area network and a video card for a CRT. The two small boards attached perpendicularly to the middle of the motherboard contain the memory chips. The large box to the lower left contains the power supply, and above it are a hard magnetic disk drive and a floppy disk drive.

The *processor* is the active part of the board, following the instructions of a program to the letter. It adds numbers, tests numbers, signals I/O devices to activate, and so on. The processor is the large square below the memory boards in the lower-right corner of Figure 1.8. Occasionally, people call the processor the *CPU*, for the more bureaucratic-sounding *central processor unit*.

Descending even lower into the hardware, Figure 1.9 reveals details of the processor in Figure 1.8. The processor comprises two main components: datapath and control, the respective brawn and brain of the processor. The *datapath* performs the arithmetic operations, and *control* tells the datapath, memory, and I/O devices what to do according to the wishes of the instructions of the program. Chapter 5 explains the datapath and control for a straightforward implementation, and Chapter 6 describes the changes needed for a higher-performance design.

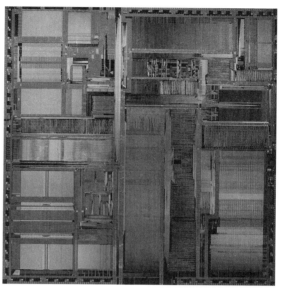

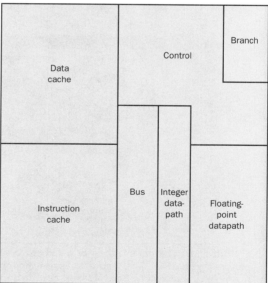

FIGURE 1.9 Inside the processor chip used on the board shown in Figure 1.8. This chip is the Intel Pentium: the upper photo is a close-up of the chip and the lower drawing identifies major blocks. The die area is 91 mm^2, and it contains about 3.3 million transistors. Cache memory occupies almost 1 million of those transistors. Chapter 7 explains why so much of the resources are spent on caches. Other components of the chip are described in later chapters: branch prediction is covered in Chapter 6 and buses in Chapter 8. Photo courtesy of Intel.

We have now identified the major components of any computer. When we come to an important point in this book, a point so important that we hope you will remember it forever, we emphasize it by identifying it as a "Big Picture" item. We have about a dozen Big Pictures in this book, with the first being the five components of a computer.

The Big Picture

The five classic components of a computer are input, output, memory, datapath, and control, with the last two sometimes combined and called the processor. Figure 1.10 shows the standard organization of a computer. This organization is independent of hardware technology: You can place every piece of every computer, past and present, into one of these five categories. To help you keep all this in perspective, the five components of a computer are shown on the front page of the following chapters, with the portion of interest to that chapter highlighted.

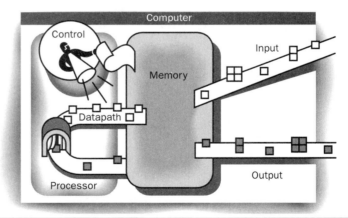

FIGURE 1.10 The organization of a computer, showing the five classic components. The processor gets instructions and data from memory; input writes data to memory and output reads data from memory. Control sends the signals that determine the operations of the datapath, memory, input, and output.

Descending into the depths of any component of the hardware reveals insights into the machine. We have done this for the processor, so let's try memory. The board in Figure 1.11 contains two kinds of memories: DRAM and cache. *DRAM* stands for *dynamic random access memory*. Several DRAMs are used together to contain the instructions and data of a program. In contrast to sequential access memories such as magnetic tapes, the *RAM* portion of the

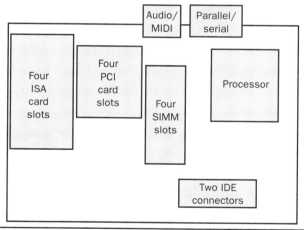

FIGURE 1.11 Close-up of PC motherboard. This board uses the Intel Pentium Pro processor, which is located on the right upper edge of the board. It is covered by tall black metal points, called *heat sinks*, which help cool the chip. The Pentium Pro package contains high-speed cache memories. The main memory is contained on the two small boards that are perpendicular to the motherboard in the middle. The DRAM chips are mounted on these boards (called *SIMMs*, for single inline memory modules) and then plugged into the connectors. Much of the rest of the board comprises connectors for external I/O devices: audio/MIDI and parallel/serial at the top edge, four PCI card slots below them, four ISA card slots to the left, and two IDE connectors on the lower right. Such cards connect the board to printers, speakers, CRTs, local area networks, disks, and so on.

term DRAM means that memory accesses take the same amount of time no matter what portion of the memory is read. *Cache memory* consists of a small, fast memory that acts as a buffer for the DRAM memory. (The nontechnical definition of *cache* is a safe place for hiding things.)

You may have noticed a common theme in both the software and the hardware descriptions: delving into the depths of hardware or software reveals more information or, conversely, lower-level details are hidden to offer a simpler model at higher levels. The use of such layers, or *abstractions,* is a principal technique for designing very sophisticated computer systems.

One of the most important abstractions is the interface between the hardware and the lowest-level software. Because of its importance, it is given a special name: the *instruction set architecture,* or simply *architecture,* of a machine. The instruction set architecture includes anything programmers need to know to make a binary machine language program work correctly, including instructions, I/O devices, and so on. (The components of an architecture are discussed in Chapters 3, 4, 7, and 8.)

This standardized interface allows computer designers to talk about functions independently from the hardware that performs them. For example, we can talk about the functions of a digital clock (keeping time, displaying the time, setting the alarm) independently from the clock hardware (quartz crystal, LED displays, plastic buttons). Computer designers distinguish architecture from an *implementation* of an architecture along the same lines: an implementation is hardware that obeys the architecture abstraction. These ideas bring us to another Big Picture.

> **The Big Picture**
>
> Both hardware and software consist of hierarchical layers, with each lower layer hiding details from the level above. This principle of *abstraction* is the way both hardware designers and software designers cope with the complexity of computer systems. One key interface between the levels of abstraction is the *instruction set architecture*: the interface between the hardware and low-level software. This abstract interface enables many *implementations* of varying cost and performance to run identical software.

Macintosh users understand the impact of changing instruction set architectures: programs designed for the PowerPC architecture do not run on the 68000-based machines, and 68000-based programs do not run well on the PowerPC. The Intel 80x86 family, in contrast, offers several implementations of the same architecture: programs written for the original 8086 in 1978 can be run on the latest Pentium Pro. As Chapter 3 points out, Intel has added features over the years, but all succeeding generations are still constrained to run old programs and run them well.

A Safe Place for Data

I think Silicon Valley was misnamed. If you look back at the dollars shipped in products in the last decade, there has been more revenue from magnetic disks than from silicon. They ought to rename the place Iron Oxide Valley.

Al Hoagland, one of the pioneers of magnetic disks, 1982

Thus far we have seen how to input data, compute using the data, and display data. If we were to lose power to the computer, however, everything would be lost because the memory inside the computer is *volatile*; that is, when it loses power, it forgets. In contrast, a cassette tape for a stereo doesn't forget the recorded music when you turn off the power because the tape is magnetic and is thus a *nonvolatile* memory technology.

To distinguish between the memory used to hold programs while they are running and this nonvolatile memory used to store programs between runs, the term *primary memory* or *main memory* is used for the former, and *secondary memory* for the latter. DRAMs have dominated main memory since 1975, but magnetic disks have dominated secondary memory since 1965.

There are two major types of magnetic disks: floppy disks and hard disks. The basic concept at work in these disks is the same: a rotating platter coated with a magnetic recording material. The primary differences arise because the floppy disk is made of a mylar substance that is flexible, while the hard disk uses metal. Floppy disks can be removed and carried around, while most hard disks today are not removable. Floppy disk capacity ranges from 1.44 MB in low-cost floppy disks to 100 MB in the Zip floppy disks.

Another removable medium is the optical compact disk, or CD, which can be cheaper but slower than magnetic disk. At the bottom of the performance barrel is magnetic tape, used for backing up disks; it can take seconds to find data on a magnetic tape.

As Figure 1.12 shows, a magnetic hard disk consists of a collection of platters, which rotate on a spindle at 3600 to 7200 revolutions per minute. The metal platters are covered with magnetic recording material on both sides, similar to the material found on a cassette tape. To read and write information on a hard disk, a movable *arm* containing a small electromagnetic coil called a *read/write head* is located just above each surface. By borrowing disk heads and media stabilization from hard disk technology, Zip drives come closer to the performance and capacity of hard disks than of traditional floppy disks.

Diameters of hard disks vary by about a factor of 5 today, from 1.3 to 5.25 inches, and have been shrunk over the years to fit into new products; workstation servers, personal computers, laptops, and palmtops have all inspired new disk form factors. Traditionally, the widest disks have the highest performance, the smallest disks have the lowest unit cost, and the best cost per megabyte is usually a disk in between.

FIGURE 1.12   A disk showing 10 disk platters and the read/write heads. Photo courtesy of Storage Technology Corp.

The use of mechanical components means that access times for magnetic disks are much slower than for DRAMs: disks typically take 5 to 20 milli-seconds, while DRAMs take 50 to 100 nanoseconds—making DRAMs about 100,000 times faster. Yet disks have much lower costs than DRAM for the same storage capacity because the production costs for a given amount of disk stor-age are lower than for the same amount of integrated circuit. In 1997, the cost per megabyte of disk is about 50 times less expensive than DRAM's cost per megabyte.

Thus there are three primary differences between magnetic disks and main memory: disks are nonvolatile because they are magnetic; they have a slower access time because they are mechanical devices; and they are cheaper per megabyte because they have very high storage capacity at a modest cost.

Communicating to Other Computers

We've explained how we can input, compute, display, and save data, but there is still one missing item found in today's computers: computer networks. Just as the processor shown in Figure 1.10 on page 16 is connected to memory and I/O devices, networks connect whole computers, allowing computer users to extend the power of computing by including communication. Networks have become so popular that they are the backbone of current computer systems; a new machine without an optional network interface would be ridiculed. Networked computers have several major advantages:

- *Communication:* Information is exchanged between computers at high speeds.

- *Resource sharing:* Rather than each machine having its own I/O devices, devices can be shared by computers on the network.

- *Nonlocal access:* By connecting computers over long distances, users need not be near the computer they are using.

Networks vary in length and performance, with the cost of communication increasing according to both the speed of communication and the distance that information travels. Perhaps the most popular network is the *Ethernet*. Its length is limited to about a kilometer, and the most popular version takes at least a second to send 1 million bytes of data. Its length and speed make the Ethernet useful to connect computers on the same floor of a building; hence, it is an example of what is generically called a *local area network*. *Wide area networks*, which cross continents, are the backbone of the Internet, which supports the World Wide Web. They are typically based on optical fibers and are leased from telecommunication companies.

Integrated Circuits: Fueling Innovation

I thought [computers] would be a universally applicable idea, like a book is. But I didn't think it would develop as fast as it did, because I didn't envision we'd be able to get as many parts on a chip as we finally got. The transistor came along unexpectedly. It all happened much faster than we expected.

J. Presper Eckert, co-inventor of ENIAC, speaking in 1991

Processors and memory have improved at an incredible rate because computer designers have long embraced the latest in electronic technology to try to win the race of designing a better computer. Figure 1.13 shows the technologies that have been used over time, with an estimate of the relative

Year	Technology used in computers	Relative performance/unit cost
1951	Vacuum tube	1
1965	Transistor	35
1975	Integrated circuit	900
1995	Very large-scale integrated circuit	2,400,000

FIGURE 1.13 Relative performance per unit cost of technologies used in computers over time. Source: Computer Museum, Boston.

performance per unit cost for each technology. This section explores the technology that has fueled the computer industry since 1975 and will continue to do so for the foreseeable future. Since this technology shapes what computers will be able to do and how quickly they will evolve, we believe all computer professionals should be familiar with the basics of integrated circuits.

A *transistor* is simply an on/off switch controlled by electricity. The *integrated circuit* combined dozens to hundreds of transistors into a single chip. To describe the tremendous increase in the number of transistors from hundreds to millions, the adjective *very large scale* is added to the term, creating the abbreviation *VLSI*, for *very large-scale integrated circuit.*

This rate of increasing integration has been remarkably stable. Figure 1.14 shows the growth in DRAM capacity since 1977. The industry has consistently quadrupled capacity every 3 years, resulting in an increase in excess of 16,000 times in just over 20 years! This remarkable rate of advance in cost/ performance and capacity of integrated circuits governs the design of hardware *and* software, underscoring the need to understand this technology.

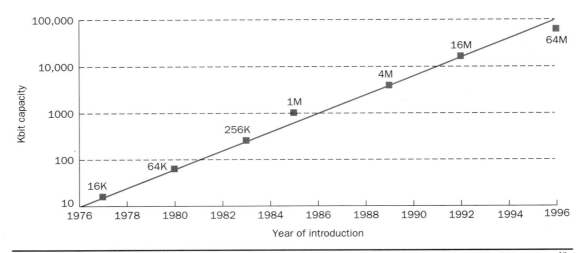

FIGURE 1.14 Growth of capacity per DRAM chip over time. The y-axis is measured in Kbits, where $K = 1024$ (2^{10}). The DRAM industry has quadrupled capacity every 3 years, a 60% increase per year, for almost 20 years. One exception was the 1-Mbit DRAM, which arrived a year earlier than expected; another was the 64-Mbit DRAM, which arrived a year late. This "four times every three years" rule of thumb is called the *DRAM growth rule.*

Let's start at the beginning. The manufacture of a chip begins with *silicon*, a substance found in sand. Because silicon does not conduct electricity well, it is called a *semiconductor*. With a special chemical process, it is possible to add materials to silicon that allow tiny areas to transform into one of three devices:

- Excellent conductors of electricity (similar to copper or aluminum wire)

- Excellent insulators from electricity (like plastic sheathing or glass)

- Areas that can conduct *or* insulate under special conditions (as a switch)

Transistors fall in the last category. A VLSI circuit, then, is just millions of combinations of conductors, insulators, and switches manufactured in a single, small package.

The manufacturing process for integrated circuits is critical to the cost of the chips and hence important to computer designers. Figure 1.15 shows that process. The process starts with a silicon crystal ingot, which looks like a giant sausage. Today, ingots are 6–12 inches in diameter and about 12–24 inches long. An ingot is finely sliced into *wafers* no more than 0.1 inch thick. These wafers then go through a series of processing steps, during which patterns of chemicals are placed on each wafer, creating the transistors, conductors, and insulators discussed above.

A single microscopic flaw in the wafer itself or in one of the dozens of patterning steps can result in that area of the wafer failing. These *defects*, as they are called, make it virtually impossible to manufacture a perfect wafer. To cope with imperfection, several strategies have been used, but the simplest is to place many independent components on a single wafer. The patterned wafer is then chopped up, or *diced*, into these components, called *dies* and more informally known as *chips*. Dicing enables you to discard only those dies that were unlucky enough to contain the flaws, rather than the whole wafer. This concept is quantified by the *yield* of a process, which is defined as the percentage of good dies from the total number of dies on the wafer.

Once you've found good dies, they are connected to the input/output pins of a package, using a process called *bonding*. These packaged parts are tested a final time, since mistakes can occur in packaging, and then they are shipped to customers.

Elaboration: We occasionally insert elaborations to include ideas that are not essential to the newcomer, but which may be of interest if you are more advanced.

One new issue in computer design is energy efficiency. Not only is it vital for computers used in portable applications to extend battery life, it is a consideration for desktop computers as single-chip computers increase in clock rate. For example, the Alpha 21264 microprocessor dissipates an amazing 72 watts at 600 MHz. Power may become an issue that limits performance.

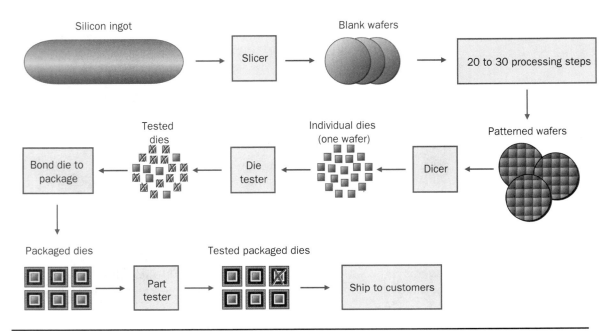

FIGURE 1.15   The chip manufacturing process. After being sliced from the silicon ingot, blank wafers are put through 20 to 30 steps to create patterned wafers (see Figure 1.17). These patterned wafers are then diced into dies (see Figure 1.18) and each die is tested. In this figure, one wafer produced 20 dies, of which only 6 passed testing. (*X* means the die is bad.) The yield of good dies in this case was 6/20, or 30%. These good dies are then bonded into packages (see Figure 1.19) and tested one more time before shipping the packaged parts to customers. One bad packaged part was found in this final test.

1.5   Real Stuff: Manufacturing Pentium Chips

Each chapter has a section entitled "Real Stuff" that ties the concepts in the book with the computer you may use every day. These sections always cover the technology underlying the IBM PC and will often include the technology of the Apple Macintosh as well. For this chapter, we tie the integrated circuit concepts of the prior section to the chips that drive the IBM PC.

Figure 1.16 is a photograph of a wafer containing single-chip processors before they have been diced. It contains copies of the chip shown in the close-up in Figure 1.9. Figure 1.17 is a photograph of a wafer of Pentium Pros, the Pentium's successor. Figure 1.18 shows an individual die of the Pentium Pro.

Note that there are many more of the smaller dies per wafer than the larger dies: there are 196 Pentium dies in the 8-inch diameter wafer in Figure 1.16 but

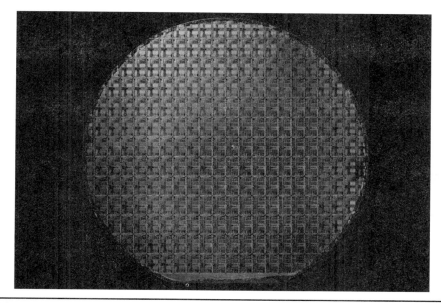

FIGURE 1.16 An 8-inch (200-mm) diameter wafer containing Intel Pentium processors. The number of Pentium dies per wafer at 100% yield is 196. The die area is 91 mm^2, and it contains about 3.3 million transistors. Figure 1.9 on page 15 is a photomicrograph of one of these Pentium dies. The several dozen partially rounded chips at the boundaries of the wafer are useless; they are included because it's easier to create the masks used to pattern the silicon. Photo courtesy of Intel.

only 78 of the larger Pentium Pro dies in the wafer in Figure 1.17. Since a wafer costs about the same no matter what is on it, fewer dies mean higher costs. Costs are increased further because a larger die is much more likely to contain a defect and thus fail to work.

Hence die costs rise very fast with increasing die area. (Exercises 1.46 through 1.53 explore die costs in more detail.) Clearly, computer designers must be familiar with the technology they are using to be sure that the added cost of larger chips is justified by enhanced performance.

FIGURE 1.17   An 8-inch (200-mm) diameter wafer containing Intel Pentium Pro processors. The number of Pentium Pro dies per wafer at 100% yield is 78. The die is 306 mm^2, and it contains about 5.5 million transistors. Figure 1.18 is a photomicrograph of one of these dies. Wafer courtesy of Intel.

Figure 1.19 shows the packaged parts for both dies. Note that the Pentium Pro package actually contains two dies! Rather than have an even larger die size for the Pentium Pro, Intel engineers decided to go with a second die. As the exercises show, two small dies can be cheaper than one large die. The second die is an external cache chip, described in Chapter 7.

Computer designers must know both hardware *and* software technologies to build competitive computers. Silicon is the medium in which computer designers work, so they must understand the foundations of integrated circuit costs and performance. Designers must also learn the principles of the software that most strongly affects computer hardware, namely, compilers and operating systems.

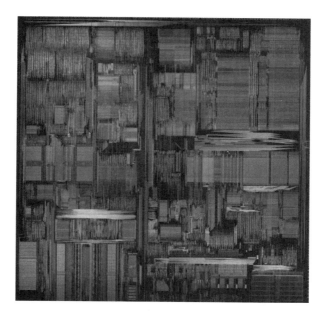

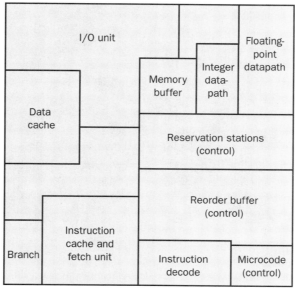

FIGURE 1.18 A Pentium Pro die: the photo (top) is a close-up of the chip, and the drawing (bottom) identifies major blocks. The die area is 306 mm^2, and it contains about 5.5 million transistors. Cache memory is a smaller fraction of the die area—just 1 million of 5.5 million transistors—because the Pentium Pro is packaged with an external cache with 31 million transistors. The blocks in the Pentium Pro die are described in later chapters: microcode is described in Chapter 5; instruction decode, reservation stations, reorder buffer, and branch prediction in Chapter 6; and caches and memory buffers in Chapter 7. Photo courtesy of Intel.

a.

b.

FIGURE 1.19   A package containing the Pentium die (a) and a package of the Pentium Pro die (b). The Pentium uses 296 pins and the Pentium Pro uses 387 pins. The extra pins allow a wider path between the main memory and the processor, allowing faster transfers of data and the addressing of larger memories. The second die in the Pentium Pro package is an external cache (see Figure 7.32 on page 612 for another view). Photos courtesy of Intel.

1.6 Fallacies and Pitfalls

Science must begin with myths, and the criticism of myths.

Sir Karl Popper, *The Philosophy of Science,* 1957

The purpose of a section on fallacies and pitfalls, which will be found in every chapter, is to explain some commonly held misconceptions that you might encounter. We call such misbeliefs *fallacies*. When discussing a fallacy, we try to give a counterexample. We also discuss *pitfalls*, or easily made mistakes. Often pitfalls are generalizations of principles that are true in a limited context. The purpose of these sections is to help you avoid making these mistakes in the machines you may design or use.

Fallacy: Computers have been built in the same, old-fashioned way for far too long, and this antiquated model of computation is running out of steam.

For an antiquated model of computation, it surely is improving quickly. Figure 1.20 plots the top performance per year of workstations between 1987 and 1997. (Chapter 2 explains the proper way to measure performance.) The graph shows a line indicating an improvement of 54% per year, or doubling performance approximately every 18 months. In contrast to the statement above, computers are improving in performance faster today than at any time in their history—a hundredfold improvement between 1987 and 1997!

Pitfall: Ignoring the inexorable progress of hardware when planning a new machine.

Suppose you plan to introduce a machine in three years, and you claim the machine will be a terrific seller because it's three times as fast as anything available today. Unfortunately, the machine will probably sell poorly because the average performance growth rate for the industry will yield machines with the same performance. For example, assuming a 50% yearly growth rate in performance, a machine with performance x today can be expected to have performance $1.5^3 x = 3.4x$ in three years. Your machine would have no performance advantage! Many projects within computer companies are canceled, either because they ignore this rule or because the project is completed late and the performance of the delayed machine is below the industry average. This phenomenon may occur in any industry, but rapid improvements in cost/performance make it a major concern in the computer industry.

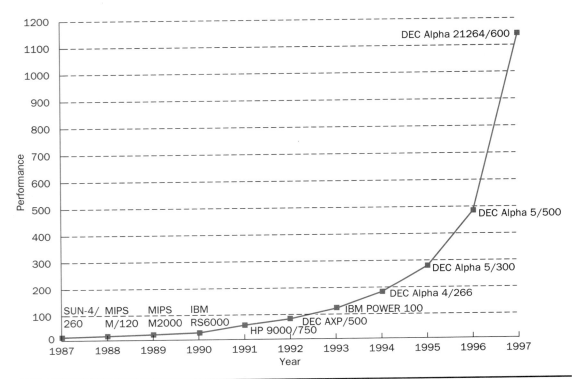

FIGURE 1.20 Performance increase of workstations, 1987–1997. Here performance is given as approximately the number of times faster than the VAX-11/780, which was a commonly used yardstick. The rate of performance improvement is about 1.54 per year, or doubling every 1.6 years. These performance numbers are for the integer SPEC92 benchmarks (SPECbase_int92); see Chapter 2, section 2.6 for more details on SPEC. As these points are becoming more difficult to see over time, here are the machines, with performance ratings in parentheses, starting in 1987: Sun-4/260 (9), MIPS M/120 (13), MIPS M2000 (18), IBM RS6000/540 (24), HP 9000/750 (51), Digital 3000 AXP/500 (80), IBM POWERstation 100 (117), Digital Alphastation 4/266 (183), Digital Alphastation 5/300 (280), Digital Alphastation 5/500 (481), and a machine based on the 600-MHz Alpha 21264 microprocessor (1140). The later two machines were based on SPECin95base and multiplied by a factor to estimate SPECbase92 performance.

1.7   Concluding Remarks

Where . . . the ENIAC is equipped with 18,000 vacuum tubes and weighs 30 tons, computers in the future may have 1,000 vacuum tubes and perhaps weigh just 1¹/₂ tons.

Popular Mechanics, March 1949

Although it is difficult to predict exactly what level of cost/performance computers will have in the future, it's a safe bet that they will be much better than they are today. To participate in these advances, computer designers and programmers must understand a wider variety of issues.

Both hardware and software designers construct computer systems in hierarchical layers, with each lower layer hiding details from the level above. This principle of abstraction is fundamental to understanding today's computer systems, but it does not mean that designers can limit themselves to knowing a single technology. Perhaps the most important example of abstraction is the interface between hardware and low-level software, called the *instruction set architecture*. Maintaining the instruction set architecture as a constant enables many implementations of that architecture—presumably varying in cost and performance—to run identical software. On the downside, the architecture may preclude introducing innovations that require the interface to change.

Key technologies for modern processors are compilers and silicon. Clearly, to participate you must understand some of the characteristics of both. Equal in importance to an understanding of integrated circuit technology is an understanding of the expected rates of technological change. One example of this relationship is the DRAM tradition of a fourfold capacity increase every three years. While silicon fuels the rapid advance of hardware, new ideas in the organization of computers have improved price/performance. Two of the key ideas are exploiting parallelism in the processor, typically via pipelining, and exploiting locality of accesses to a memory hierarchy, typically via caches.

Road Map for This Book

At the bottom of these abstractions are the five classic components of a computer: datapath, control, memory, input, and output (refer back to Figure 1.10). These five components also serve as the framework for the rest of the chapters in this book:

- *Datapath:* Chapters 4, 5, and 6
- *Control:* Chapters 5 and 6
- *Memory:* Chapter 7
- *Input:* Chapter 8
- *Output:* Chapter 8

Chapter 6 describes how processor pipelining exploits parallelism, and Chapter 7 describes how the memory hierarchy exploits locality. The remaining chapters provide the introduction and the conclusion to this material. Chapter 2 covers performance and thus describes how to evaluate the whole computer. Chapter 3 describes instruction sets—the interface between compilers and the machine—and emphasizes the role of compilers and programming languages in using the features of the instruction set. Chapter 9 concludes this coverage with a discussion on multiprocessors.

Historical Perspective and Further Reading

An active field of science is like an immense anthill; the individual almost vanishes into the mass of minds tumbling over each other, carrying information from place to place, passing it around at the speed of light.

Lewis Thomas, "Natural Science," in *The Lives of a Cell*, 1974

A section devoted to a historical perspective closes each chapter in the text. We may trace the development of an idea through a series of machines or describe some important projects, and we provide references in case you are interested in probing further. This section provides historical background on some of the key ideas presented in this opening chapter. Its purpose is to give you the human story behind the technological advances and to place achievements in their historical context. By understanding the past, you may be better able to understand the forces that will shape computing in the future.

The First Electronic Computers

J. Presper Eckert and John Mauchly at the Moore School of the University of Pennsylvania built what is widely accepted to be the world's first operational electronic, general-purpose computer. This machine, called ENIAC (Electronic Numerical Integrator and Calculator), was funded by the United States Army and became operational during World War II, but was not publicly disclosed until 1946. ENIAC was a general-purpose machine used for computing artillery firing tables. This U-shaped computer was 80 feet long by 8.5 feet high and several feet wide (Figure 1.21). Each of the 20 10-digit registers was 2 feet long. In total, ENIAC used 18,000 vacuum tubes.

In size, ENIAC was two orders of magnitude bigger than machines built today, yet it was more than four orders of magnitude slower, performing 1900 additions per second. ENIAC provided conditional jumps and was programmable, clearly distinguishing it from earlier calculators. Programming was done manually by plugging cables and setting switches, and data was entered on punched cards. Programming for typical calculations required from half an hour to a whole day. ENIAC was a general-purpose machine, limited primarily by a small amount of storage and tedious programming.

In 1944, John von Neumann was attracted to the ENIAC project. The group wanted to improve the way programs were entered and discussed storing programs as numbers; von Neumann helped crystallize the ideas and wrote a memo proposing a stored-program computer called EDVAC (Electronic Discrete Variable Automatic Computer). Herman Goldstine distributed the

FIGURE 1.21   ENIAC, the world's first general-purpose electronic computer. Note the court tag in the lower-right corner; this is from the patent case mentioned on page 34. Photo courtesy of Charles Babbage Institute, University of Minnesota.

memo and put von Neumann's name on it, much to the dismay of Eckert and Mauchly, whose names were omitted. This memo has served as the basis for the commonly used term *von Neumann computer*. Several early pioneers in the computer field believe that this term gives too much credit to von Neumann, who wrote up the ideas, and too little to the engineers, Eckert and Mauchly, who worked on the machines. For this reason, the term does not appear elsewhere in this book.

In 1946, Maurice Wilkes of Cambridge University visited the Moore School to attend the latter part of a series of lectures on developments in electronic computers. When he returned to Cambridge, Wilkes decided to embark on a project to build a stored-program computer named EDSAC (for Electronic Delay Storage Automatic Calculator). EDSAC, shown in Figure 1.22, became operational in 1949 and was the world's first full-scale, operational, stored-program computer [Wilkes 1985]. (A small prototype called the Mark-I, built at the University of Manchester in 1948, might be called the first operational stored-program machine.) Section 3.4 in Chapter 3 explains the stored-program concept.

FIGURE 1.22 EDSAC in 1949 was the first full-scale stored-program computer. Wilkes is the person in the front, kneeling and wearing glasses. Photo courtesy of the Computer Museum, Boston.

In 1947, Eckert and Mauchly applied for a patent on electronic computers. The dean of the Moore School, by demanding that the patent be turned over to the university, may have helped Eckert and Mauchly conclude that they should leave. Their departure crippled the EDVAC project, delaying completion until 1952.

Goldstine left to join von Neumann at the Institute for Advanced Study (IAS) at Princeton in 1946. Together with Arthur Burks, they issued a report based on the memo written earlier [Burks, Goldstine, and von Neumann 1946]. The paper was incredible for the period; reading it today, you would never guess this landmark paper was written more than 50 years ago because it discusses most of the architectural concepts seen in modern computers. This paper led to the IAS machine built by Julian Bigelow. It had a total of 1024 40-bit words and was roughly 10 times faster than ENIAC. The group thought about uses for the machine, published a set of reports, and encouraged visitors. These reports and visitors inspired the development of a number of new computers.

Recently, there has been some controversy about the work of John Atanasoff, who built a small-scale electronic computer in the early 1940s. His machine, designed at Iowa State University, was a special-purpose computer that was never completely operational. Mauchly briefly visited Atanasoff before he built ENIAC. The presence of the Atanasoff machine, together with delays in filing the ENIAC patents (the work was classified and patents could not be filed until after the war) and the distribution of von Neumann's EDVAC paper, were used to break the Eckert-Mauchly patent. Though controversy still rages over Atanasoff's role, Eckert and Mauchly are usually given credit for building the first working, general-purpose, electronic computer [Stern 1980].

Another early machine that deserves some credit was a special-purpose machine built by Konrad Zuse in Germany in the late 1930s and early 1940s. Although Zuse had the design for a programmable computer ready, the German government decided not to fund scientific investigations taking more than two years because the bureaucrats expected the war would be won by that deadline.

Across the English Channel, during World War II special-purpose electronic computers were built to decrypt the intercepted German messages. A team at Bletchley Park, including Alan Turing, built the Colossus in 1943. The machines were kept secret until 1970; after the war, the group had little impact on commercial British computers.

While work on ENIAC went forward, Howard Aiken was building an electromechanical computer called the Mark-I at Harvard (a name that Manchester later adopted for its machine). He followed the Mark-I with a relay machine, the Mark-II, and a pair of vacuum tube machines, the Mark-III and Mark-IV. In contrast to earlier machines like EDSAC, which used a single memory for instructions and data, the Mark-III and Mark-IV had separate memories for instructions and data. The machines were regarded as reactionary by the advocates of stored-program computers; the term *Harvard architecture* was coined to describe machines with separate memories. Paying respect to history, this term is used today in a different sense to describe machines with a single main memory but with separate caches for instructions and data.

The Whirlwind project was begun at MIT in 1947 and was aimed at applications in real-time radar signal processing. Although it led to several inventions, its most important innovation was magnetic core memory. Whirlwind had 2048 16-bit words of magnetic core. Magnetic cores served as the main memory technology for nearly 30 years.

Commercial Developments

In December 1947, Eckert and Mauchly formed Eckert-Mauchly Computer Corporation. Their first machine, the BINAC, was built for Northrop and was shown in August 1949. After some financial difficulties, their firm was acquired by Remington-Rand, where they built the UNIVAC I (Universal Automatic Computer), designed to be sold as a general-purpose computer (Figure 1.23). First delivered in June 1951, UNIVAC I sold for about $1 million and was the first successful commercial computer—48 systems were built! This early machine, along with many other fascinating pieces of computer lore, may be seen at the Computer Museum in Boston, Massachusetts, and the Computer History Center in Mountain View, California.

IBM had been in the punched card and office automation business but didn't start building computers until 1950. The first IBM computer, the IBM 701, shipped in 1952, and eventually 19 units were sold. In the early 1950s, many people were pessimistic about the future of computers, believing that the market and opportunities for these "highly specialized" machines were quite limited.

FIGURE 1.23   UNIVAC I, the first commercial computer in the United States. It correctly predicted the outcome of the 1952 presidential election, but its initial forecast was withheld from broadcast because experts doubted the use of such early results. Photo courtesy of the Charles Babbage Institute, University of Minnesota.

In 1964, after investing $5 billion, IBM made a bold move with the announcement of the System/360. An IBM spokesman said the following at the time:

We are not at all humble in this announcement. This is the most important product announcement that this corporation has ever made in its history. It's not a computer in any previous sense. It's not a product, but a line of products . . . that spans in performance from the very low part of the computer line to the very high.

Moving the idea of the architecture abstraction into commercial reality, IBM announced six implementations of the System/360 architecture that varied in price and performance by a factor of 25. Figure 1.24 shows four of these

a.

c.

b.

d.

FIGURE 1.24 IBM System/360 computers: models 40, 50, 65, and 75 were all introduced in 1964. These four models varied in cost and performance by a factor of almost 10; it grows to 25 if we include models 20 and 30 (not shown). The clock rate, range of memory sizes, and approximate price for only the processor and memory of average size: (a) Model 40, 1.6 MHz, 32 KB–256 KB, and $225,000; (b) Model 50, 2.0 MHz, 128 KB–256 KB, and $550,000; (c) Model 65, 5.0 MHz, 256 KB–1 MB, and $1,200,000; and (d) Model 75, 5.1 MHz, 256 KB–1 MB, $1,900,000. Adding I/O devices typically increased the price by factors of 1.8 to 3.5, with higher factors for cheaper models. Photos courtesy of IBM.

models. IBM bet its company on the success of a *computer family,* and IBM won. The System/360 and its successors dominated the large computer market.

About a year later Digital Equipment Corporation (DEC) unveiled the PDP-8, the first commercial *minicomputer,* shown in Figure 1.25. This small machine was a breakthrough in low-cost design, allowing DEC to offer a computer for under $20,000. Minicomputers were the forerunners of microprocessors, with Intel inventing the first microprocessor in 1971—the Intel 4004, shown in Figure 1.26 as a microphotograph.

FIGURE 1.25   The DEC PDP-8, the first commercial minicomputer, announced in 1965. Among other uses, the PDP-8 was used to stage the musical *A Chorus Line.* Photo courtesy of Digital Equipment Corporation, Corporate Photo Library.

FIGURE 1.26   Microphotograph of the Intel 4004 from 1971, the first microprocessor. Contrast this microprocessor, with just 2300 transistors and 0.3 by 0.4 cm in size, with the microprocessor in Figure 1.18 on page 27. Photo courtesy of Intel.

In 1963 came the announcement of the first *supercomputer*. This announcement came not from the large companies nor even from the high tech centers. Seymour Cray led the design of the Control Data Corporation CDC 6600 in Minnesota. This machine included many ideas that are beginning to be found in the latest microprocessors. Cray later left CDC to form Cray Research, Inc., in Wisconsin. In 1976 he announced the Cray-1 (Figure 1.27). This machine was simultaneously the fastest in the world, the most expensive, and the computer with the best cost/performance for scientific programs. But 1996 saw the passing of Cray Research into the hands of Silicon Graphics, which means there are no longer any stand-alone supercomputer companies.

FIGURE 1.27 Cray-1, the first commercial vector supercomputer, announced in 1976. This machine had the unusual distinction of being both the fastest computer for scientific applications and the computer with the best price/performance for those applications. Viewed from the top, the computer looks like the letter C. Seymour Cray passed away in 1996 as a result of injuries sustained in an automobile accident. At the time of his death, this 70-year-old computer pioneer was working on his vision of the next generation of supercomputers. (See the Cray link at *www.mkp.com/books_catalog/cod/links.htm* for more details.) Photo courtesy of Cray Research, Inc.

While Seymour Cray was creating the world's most expensive computer, other designers around the world were looking at using the microprocessor to create a computer so cheap that you could have it at home. There is no single fountainhead for the *personal computer*, but in 1977 the Apple II (Figure 1.28) of Steve Jobs and Steve Wozniak set standards for low cost, high volume, and high reliability that defined the personal computer industry. But even with a four-year head start, Apple's personal computers finished second in popularity. The IBM Personal Computer, announced in 1981, became the best-selling computer of any kind; its success gave Intel the most popular microprocessor and Microsoft the most popular operating system. Today, the most popular CD is the Microsoft operating system, even though it costs many times more than a music CD!

FIGURE 1.28   The Apple IIC. Designed by Steve Wozniak, its success defined the personal computer industry in 1977 and set standards of cost and reliability for the industry. Photo courtesy of Apple Computer, Inc.

While the general-purpose computer is the focus of attention in this book, computers are used as well inside other products without the owner being aware what is inside. These embedded processors are increasingly popular. For example, the table below shows the most popular microprocessors in 1995. For MIPS, only 300,000 of the 5,500,000 are used in computers: the rest of the microprocessors are embedded in video games, laser printers, and so on.

Instruction set	Number
80x86	50,000,000
MIPS	5,500,000
PowerPC	3,300,000
SPARC	700,000
HP PA-RISC	300,000
DEC Alpha	200,000

Computer Generations

Since 1952, there have been thousands of new computers using a wide range of technologies and having widely varying capabilities. To put these developments in perspective, the industry has tended to group computers into generations. This classification is often based on the implementation technology used in each generation, as shown in Figure 1.29. Traditionally, each *computer generation* is 8 to 10 years in length, although the length and birth years—especially of recent generations—are debated. By convention, the first generation is taken to be commercial electronic computers, rather than the mechanical or electromechanical machines that preceded them.

The success of the microprocessor has considerably extended the fourth generation, to almost as long as the prior three. Success has been sustained by rapid but evolutionary improvements. Computer generations aren't commonly mentioned today as a result of the long-standing domination of the industry by the VLSI microprocessor. With no revolutionary technology on the horizon, it is unclear when a fifth generation will appear.

Figure 1.30 summarizes the key characteristics of some machines mentioned in this section. After adjusting for inflation, price/performance has improved by about 240 million in 45 years, or about 54% per year.

Readers interested in computer history should consult *Annals of the History of Computing,* a journal devoted to the history of computing. Several books describing the early days of computing have also appeared, many written by the pioneers themselves.

Generation	Dates	Technology	Principal new product
1	1950–1959	Vacuum tubes	Commercial electronic computer
2	1960–1968	Transistors	Cheaper computers
3	1969–1977	Integrated circuit	Minicomputer
4	1978–?	LSI and VLSI	Personal computers and workstations

FIGURE 1.29   Computer generations are usually determined by the change in dominant implementation technology. Typically, each generation offers the opportunity to create a new class of computers and to create new computer companies.

Year	Name	Size (cu. ft.)	Power (watts)	Performance (adds/sec)	Memory (KB)	Price	Price/ performance vs. UNIVAC	Adjusted price (1996 $)	Adjusted price/ performance vs. UNIVAC
1951	UNIVAC I	1000	124,500	1,900	48	$1,000,000	1	$4,996,749	1
1964	IBM S/360 model 50	60	10,000	500,000	64	$1,000,000	263	$4,140,257	318
1965	PDP-8	8	500	330,000	4	$16,000	10,855	$66,071	13,135
1976	Cray-1	58	60,000	166,000,000	32,768	$4,000,000	21,842	$8,459,712	51,604
1981	IBM PC	1	150	240,000	256	$3,000	42,105	$4,081	154,673
1991	HP 9000/ model 750	2	500	50,000,000	16,384	$7,400	3,556,188	$8,156	16,122,356
1996	Intel PPro PC (200 MHz)	2	500	400,000,000	16,384	$4,400	47,846,890	$4,400	239,078,908

FIGURE 1.30 Characteristics of key commercial computers since 1950, in actual dollars and in 1996 dollars adjusted for inflation. In contrast to Figure 1.24, in this figure the price of the IBM S/360 model 50 includes I/O devices. Source: The Computer Museum, Boston, and Producer Price Index for Industrial Commodities.

To Probe Further

Bell, C. G. [1984]. "The mini and micro industries," *IEEE Computer* 17:10 (October) 14–30.

An insider's personal view of the computing industry, including computer generations.

Bell, C. G. [1996]. *Computer Pioneers and Pioneer Computers*, ACM and the Computer Museum, videotapes.

Two videotapes on the history of computing, produced by Gordon and Gwen Bell, including the following machines and their inventors: Harvard Mark-I, ENIAC, EDSAC, IAS machine, and many others.

Burks, A. W., H. H. Goldstine, and J. von Neumann [1946]. "Preliminary discussion of the logical design of an electronic computing instrument," Report to the U.S. Army Ordnance Department, p. 1; also appears in *Papers of John von Neumann*, W. Aspray and A. Burks, eds., MIT Press, Cambridge, MA., and Tomash Publishers, Los Angeles, 1987, 97–146.

A classic paper explaining computer hardware and software before the first stored-program computer was built. We quote extensively from it in Chapter 3. It simultaneously explained computers to the world and was a source of controversy because the first draft did not give credit to Eckert and Mauchly.

Campbell-Kelly, M., and W. Aspray [1996]. *Computer: A History of the Information Machine*, Basic Books, New York.

Two historians chronicle the dramatic story. The New York Times *calls it well written and authoritative.*

Goldstine, H. H. [1972]. *The Computer: From Pascal to von Neumann*, Princeton University Press, Princeton, NJ.

A personal view of computing by one of the pioneers who worked with von Neumann.

Hennessy, J. L., and D. A. Patterson [1996]. Sections 1.4 and 1.5 of *Computer Architecture: A Quantitative Approach,* second edition, Morgan Kaufmann Publishers, San Francisco.

These sections contain much more detail on the cost of integrated circuits and explain the reasons for the difference between price and cost.

Public Broadcasting System [1992]. *The Machine that Changed the World,* videotapes.

These five one-hour programs include rare footage and interviews with pioneers of the computer industry.

Slater, R. [1987]. *Portraits in Silicon,* MIT Press, Cambridge, MA.

Short biographies of 31 computer pioneers.

Stern, N. [1980]. "Who invented the first electronic digital computer?" *Annals of the History of Computing* 2:4 (October) 375–76.

A historian's perspective on Atanasoff vs. Eckert and Mauchly.

Wilkes, M. V. [1985]. *Memoirs of a Computer Pioneer,* MIT Press, Cambridge, MA.

A personal view of computing by one of the pioneers.

1.9   Key Terms

A list of key terms appears at the end of each chapter and appendix. These terms reflect the key ideas discussed in each chapter or appendix. If you're unsure of the meaning of any of the terms listed below, please refer to the Glossary at the back of the book. Each key term is fully defined there.

abstraction
assembler
assembly language
binary digit or bit
cache memory
central processor unit (CPU)
chip
compiler
computer generation
control
datapath
defect
die
die area
dynamic random access memory (DRAM)
floppy disk
general-purpose electronic computer
gigabyte
hard disk

high-level programming language
implementation
input device
instruction set architecture
integrated circuit
kilobyte
magnetic disk
megabyte
memory
motherboard
nonvolatile memory
operating system
output device
personal computer
pipelining
pixel
primary or main memory
raster cathode ray tube (CRT) display
secondary memory

semiconductor
sequential access memory
silicon
silicon crystal ingot
single in-line memory module (SIMM)
subroutine library
supercomputer
systems software
terabyte
transistor
vacuum tube
vector supercomputer
very large-scale integrated circuit (VLSI)
volatile memory
wafer
wide area network
yield

Exercises

The relative time ratings of exercises are shown in square brackets after each exercise number. On average, an exercise rated [10] will take you twice as long as one rated [5]. Sections of the text that should be read before attempting an exercise will be given in angled brackets; for example, <§1.4> means you should have read section 1.4, "Integrated Circuits: Fueling Innovation," to help you solve this exercise. If the solution to an exercise depends on others, they will be listed in curly brackets; for example, {Ex. 1.51} means that you should answer Exercise 1.51 before trying this exercise.

Exercises 1.1 through 1.26 Find the word or phrase from the list below that best matches the description in the following questions. Use the letters to the left of words in the answer. Each answer should be used only once.

a	abstraction	n	DRAM (dynamic random access memory)
b	assembler	o	implementation
c	binary number	p	instruction
d	bit	q	instruction set architecture
e	cache	r	integrated circuit
f	central processor unit (CPU)	s	memory
g	chip	t	operating system
h	compiler	u	processor
i	computer family	v	semiconductor
j	control	w	supercomputer
k	datapath	x	transistor
l	defect	y	VLSI (very large-scale integrated circuit)
m	die	z	yield

1.1 [2] Specific abstraction that the hardware provides the low-level software.

1.2 [2] Active part of the computer, following the instructions of the programs to the letter. It adds numbers, tests numbers, and so on.

1.3 [2] Another name for processor.

1.4 [2] Approach to the design of hardware or software. The system consists of hierarchical layers, with each lower layer hiding details from the level above.

1.5 [2] Base 2 number.

1.6 [2] Binary digit.

1.7 [2] Collection of implementations of the same instruction set architecture. They are available at the same time and vary in price and performance.

1.8 [2] Component of the processor that performs arithmetic operations.

1.9 [2] Component of the processor that tells the datapath, memory, and I/O devices what to do according to the instructions of the program.

1.10 [2] Hardware that obeys the instruction set architecture abstraction.

1.11 [2] High-performance machine, costing more than $1 million.

1.12 [2] Individual command to a computer.

1.13 [2] Integrated circuit commonly used to construct main memory.

1.14 [2] Integrates dozens to hundreds of transistors into a single chip.

1.15 [2] Integrates hundreds of thousands to millions of transistors into a single chip.

1.16 [2] Location of programs when they are running, containing the data needed as well.

1.17 [2] Microscopic flaw in a wafer.

1.18 [2] Nickname for a die or integrated circuit.

1.19 [2] On/off switch controlled by electricity.

1.20 [2] Percentage of good dies from the total number of dies on the wafer.

1.21 [2] Program that manages the resources of a computer for the benefit of the programs that run on that machine.

1.22 [2] Program that translates a symbolic version of an instruction into the binary version.

1.23 [2] Program that translates from a higher-level notation to assembly language.

1.24 [2] Rectangular component that results from dicing a wafer.

1.25 [2] Small, fast memory that acts as a buffer for the main memory.

1.26 [2] Substance that does not conduct electricity well.

Exercises 1.27 through 1.44   Using the categories in the list below, classify the following examples. Use the letters to the left of the words in the answer. Unlike the previous exercises, answers in this group may be used more than once.

a	applications software	f	output device
b	high-level programming language	g	personal computer
c	input device	h	semiconductor
d	integrated circuit	i	supercomputer
e	minicomputer	j	systems software

1.27 [1] Assembler

1.28 [1] C++

1.29 [1] Cathode ray tube display

1.30 [1] Compiler

1.31 [1] Cray-1

1.32 [1] DEC Alpha

1.33 [1] DRAM

1.34 [1] IBM PC

1.35 [1] Keyboard

1.36 [1] Macintosh

1.37 [1] Microprocessor

1.38 [1] Mouse

1.39 [1] Operating system

1.40 [1] Pascal

1.41 [1] Printer

1.42 [1] Silicon

1.43 [1] Spreadsheet

1.44 [1] Text editor

1.45 [10] <§1.3> In a magnetic disk, the disks containing the data are constantly rotating. On average it should take half a revolution for the desired data on the disk to spin under the read/write head. Assuming that the disk is rotating at 5400 revolutions per minute, what is the average time for the data to rotate under the disk head? What is the average time if the disk is spinning at 7200 revolutions per minute?

1.46 [5] <§§1.4, 1.5> Assume that wafer A has twice as many dies on it as wafer B and that the same fabrication process is used for both wafers (thus, defects per unit area is a constant). Will one of the dies be likely to cost twice as much as the other one, or will the difference be greater? Provide an informal explanation of your answer (do not rely on the formulas used for Exercises 1.48 through 1.53).

1.47 [5] <§§1.4, 1.5> Estimate the number of transistors that could be placed in the period at the end of this sentence using the fabrication processes that produced the dies in Figures 1.9 and 1.18.

In More Depth

Integrated Circuit Cost

Our approach in this book is to include optional sections—called "In More Depth"—in the exercises, leaving it up to the instructor whether to cover the material in class, have students read it on their own, or skip the material altogether. This first such section gives more information on the cost of integrated circuits and is used in Exercises 1.48 through 1.53.

The cost of an integrated circuit can be expressed in three simple equations:

$$\text{Cost per die} = \frac{\text{Cost per wafer}}{\text{Dies per wafer} \times \text{yield}}$$

$$\text{Dies per wafer} \approx \frac{\text{Wafer area}}{\text{Die area}}$$

$$\text{Yield} = \frac{1}{(1 + (\text{Defects per area} \times \text{Die area}/2))^2}$$

The first equation is straightforward to derive. The second is an approximation, since it does not subtract the area near the border of the round wafer that cannot accommodate the rectangular dies. The final equation is based on years of empirical observations of yields at integrated circuit factories, with the exponent related to the number of critical processing steps in the manufacturing process.

1.48 [5] <§§1.4, 1.5> What is the approximate relationship between cost and die area? The approximate relationship can be described as

$$\text{Cost} = f((\text{Die area})^x)$$

for some x. You don't have to determine f, but you can determine x by first writing

$$\text{Dies per wafer} = f((\text{Die area})^y)$$

$$\text{Yield} = f((\text{Die area})^z)$$

and then examining how these two equations impact the first one (you need to figure out what y and z are). What implications does this have for designers?

1.49 [15] <§§1.4, 1.5> Compare the estimate of the number of dies per wafer calculated in the formula above to the actual number given in the caption of Figure 1.16 on page 25. Propose a formula that gives a more accurate estimate of the number of dies per wafer, and give an explanation of your formula.

1.50 [10] <§§1.4, 1.5> What is the approximate cost of a die in the wafer shown in Figure 1.16 on page 25? Assume that an 8-inch wafer costs $1000 and that the defect density is 1 per square centimeter. Use the number of dies per wafer given in the figure caption.

Exercises 1.51 through 1.53 DRAM chips have significantly increased in die size with each generation, yet yields have stayed about the same (43% to 48%). Figure 1.31 shows key statistics for DRAM production over the years.

Year	Capacity (Kbits)	Die area (sq. cm)	Wafer diameter (inches)	Yield
1980	64	0.16	5	48%
1983	256	0.24	5	46%
1985	1024	0.42	6	45%
1989	4096	0.65	6	43%
1992	16384	0.97	8	48%

FIGURE 1.31 History of DRAM capacity, die size, wafer size, and yield. Source: Howard Dicken of DM Data Inc., of Scottsdale, Arizona.

1.51 [5] <§§1.4, 1.5> Given the increase in die area of DRAMs, what parameter (see the equations) must improve to maintain yield?

1.52 [10] <§§1.4, 1.5> {Ex. 1.51} Derive a formula for the improving parameter found in Exercise 1.51 from the other parameters.

1.53 [10] <§§1.4, 1.5> {Ex. 1.51, 1.52} Using the formula in the answer to Exercise 1.52, what is the calculated improvement in that parameter between 1980 and 1992?

1.54 [8] <§§1.1–1.5> This book covers abstractions for computer systems at many different levels of detail. Pick another system with which you are familiar and write one or two paragraphs describing some of the many different levels of abstraction inherent in that system. Some possibilities include automobiles, homes, airplanes, geometry, the economy, and the government. Be sure to identify both high-level and low-level abstractions.

1.55 [15] <§§1.1–1.5> A less technically inclined friend has asked you to explain how computers work. Write a detailed, one-page description for your friend.

1.56 [10] <§§1.1–1.5> In what ways do you lack a clear understanding of how computers work? Are there levels of abstraction with which you are particularly unfamiliar? Are there levels of abstraction with which you are familiar but still have specific questions about? Write at least one paragraph addressing each of these questions.

2

The Role of
Performance

Time discovers truth.

Seneca
Moral Essays, 22 A.D.

The Five Classic Components of a Computer

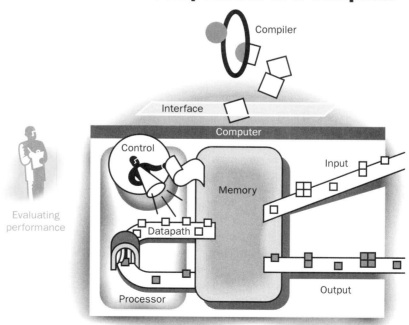

2.1   Introduction

This chapter discusses how to measure, report, and summarize performance and describes the major factors that determine the performance of a computer. A primary reason for examining performance is that hardware performance is often key to the effectiveness of an entire system of hardware and software.

Assessing the performance of such a system can be quite challenging. The scale and intricacy of modern software systems, together with the wide range of performance improvement techniques employed by hardware designers, have made performance assessment much more difficult. It is simply impossible to sit down with an instruction set manual and a significant software system and determine how fast the software will run on the machine. In fact, for different types of applications, different performance metrics may be appropriate and different aspects of a computer system may be the most significant in determining overall performance.

Of course, in trying to choose among different computers, performance is almost always an important attribute. Accurately measuring and comparing different machines is critical to purchasers, and therefore to designers. The people selling computers know this as well. Often, salespeople would like you to see their machine in the best possible light, whether or not this light accurately reflects the needs of the purchaser's application. In some cases, claims are made about computers that don't provide useful insight for any real applications. Hence, understanding how best to measure performance and the limitations of performance measurements is important in selecting a machine.

Our interest in performance, however, goes beyond issues of assessing performance only from the outside of a machine. To understand why a piece of software performs as it does, why one instruction set can be implemented to perform better than another, or how some hardware feature affects performance, we need to understand what determines the performance of a machine. For example, to improve the performance of a software system, we may need to understand what factors in the hardware contribute to the overall system performance and the relative importance of these factors. These factors may include how well the program uses the instructions of the machine, how well the underlying hardware implements the instructions, and how well the memory and I/O systems perform. Understanding how to determine the performance impact of these factors is crucial to understanding the motivation behind the design of particular aspects of the machine, as we will see in the chapters that follow.

Airplane	Passenger capacity	Cruising range (miles)	Cruising speed (m.p.h.)	Passenger throughput (passengers x m.p.h.)
Boeing 777	375	4630	610	228,750
Boeing 747	470	4150	610	286,700
BAC/Sud Concorde	132	4000	1350	178,200
Douglas DC-8-50	146	8720	544	79,424

FIGURE 2.1   The capacity, range, and speed for a number of commercial airplanes. The last column shows the rate at which the airplane transports passengers, which is the capacity times the cruising speed (ignoring range and takeoff and landing times).

The rest of this section describes different ways in which performance can be determined. In section 2.2, we describe the metrics for measuring performance from the viewpoint of both a computer user and a designer. In section 2.3, we look at how these metrics are related and present the classical processor performance equation, which we will use throughout the text. Sections 2.4 and 2.5 describe how best to choose benchmarks to evaluate machines and how to accurately summarize the performance of a group of programs. Section 2.6 describes one set of commonly used CPU benchmarks and examines measurements for a variety of Intel processors using those benchmarks. Finally, in section 2.7, we'll examine some of the many pitfalls that have trapped designers and those who analyze and report performance.

Defining Performance

When we say one computer has better performance than another, what do we mean? Although this question might seem simple, an analogy with passenger airplanes shows how subtle the question of performance can be. Figure 2.1 shows some typical passenger airplanes, together with their cruising speed, range, and capacity. If we wanted to know which of the planes in this table had the best performance, we would first need to define performance. For example, considering different measures of performance, we see that the plane with the highest cruising speed is the Concorde, the plane with the longest range is the DC-8, and the plane with the largest capacity is the 747.

Let's suppose we define performance in terms of speed. This still leaves two possible definitions. You could define the fastest plane as the one with the highest cruising speed, taking a single passenger from one point to another in the least time. If you were interested in transporting 450 passengers from one point to another, however, the 747 would clearly be the fastest, as the last column of the figure shows. Similarly, we can define computer performance in several different ways.

If you were running a program on two different workstations, you'd say that the faster one is the workstation that gets the job done first. If you were running a computer center that had two large timeshared computers running jobs submitted by many users, you'd say that the faster computer was the one that completed the most jobs during a day. As an individual computer user, you are interested in reducing *response time*—the time between the start and completion of a task—also referred to as *execution time*. Computer center managers are often interested in increasing *throughput*—the total amount of work done in a given time.

Throughput and Response Time

Example

To illustrate the application of new ideas, specific examples are used throughout this text. We highlight the example and then provide an answer. Try working out the answer yourself, or—if you feel unsure about the material—just follow along. The examples that appear are similar in type to the problems that you will have an opportunity to tackle in the exercises at the end of each chapter. Here's our first example:

Do the following changes to a computer system increase throughput, decrease response time, or both?

1. Replacing the processor in a computer with a faster version

2. Adding additional processors to a system that uses multiple processors for separate tasks—for example, handling an airline reservations system

Answer

Decreasing response time almost always improves throughput. Hence, in case 1, both response time and throughput are improved. In case 2, no one task gets work done faster, so only throughput increases. If, however, the demand for processing in the second case was almost as large as the throughput, the system might force requests to queue up. In this case, increasing the throughput could also improve response time, since it would reduce the waiting time in the queue. Thus, in many real computer systems, changing either execution time or throughput often affects the other.

In discussing the performance of machines, we will be primarily concerned with response time for the first few chapters. (In Chapter 8, on input/output systems, we will discuss throughput-related measures.) To maximize performance, we want to minimize response time or execution time for some task. Thus we can relate performance and execution time for a machine X:

$$\text{Performance}_X = \frac{1}{\text{Execution time}_X}$$

This means that for two machines X and Y, if the performance of X is greater than the performance of Y, we have

$$\text{Performance}_X > \text{Performance}_Y$$

$$\frac{1}{\text{Execution time}_X} > \frac{1}{\text{Execution time}_Y}$$

$$\text{Execution time}_Y > \text{Execution time}_X$$

That is, the execution time on Y is longer than that on X, if X is faster than Y.

In discussing a computer design, we often want to relate the performance of two different machines quantitatively. We will use the phrase "X is n times faster than Y" to mean

$$\frac{\text{Performance}_X}{\text{Performance}_Y} = n$$

If X is n times faster than Y, then the execution time on Y is n times longer than it is on X:

$$\frac{\text{Performance}_X}{\text{Performance}_Y} = \frac{\text{Execution time}_Y}{\text{Execution time}_X} = n$$

Relative Performance

Example

If machine A runs a program in 10 seconds and machine B runs the same program in 15 seconds, how much faster is A than B?

Answer

We know that A is n times faster than B if

$$\frac{\text{Performance}_A}{\text{Performance}_B} = n$$

or

$$\frac{\text{Execution time}_B}{\text{Execution time}_A} = n$$

Thus the performance ratio is

$$\frac{15}{10} = 1.5$$

and A is therefore 1.5 times faster than B.

In the above example, we could also say that machine B is 1.5 times *slower than* machine A, since

$$\frac{\text{Performance}_A}{\text{Performance}_B} = 1.5$$

means that

$$\frac{\text{Performance}_A}{1.5} = \text{Performance}_B$$

For simplicity, we will normally use the terminology *faster than* when we try to compare machines quantitatively. Because performance and execution time are reciprocals, increasing performance requires decreasing execution time. To avoid the potential confusion between the terms *increasing* and *decreasing*, we usually say "improve performance" or "improve execution time" when we mean "increase performance" and "decrease execution time."

2.2   Measuring Performance

Time is the measure of computer performance: the computer that performs the same amount of work in the least time is the fastest. Program *execution time* is measured in seconds per program. But time can be defined in different ways, depending on what we count. The most straightforward definition of time is called *wall-clock time, response time,* or *elapsed time.* These terms mean the total time to complete a task, including disk accesses, memory accesses, input/output (I/O) activities, operating system overhead—everything.

Computers are often timeshared, however, and a processor may work on several programs simultaneously. In such cases, the system may try to optimize throughput rather than attempt to minimize the elapsed time for one program. Hence, we often want to distinguish between the elapsed time and the time that the processor is working on our behalf. *CPU execution time* or simply *CPU time,* which recognizes this distinction, is the time the CPU spends computing for this task and does not include time spent waiting for I/O or running other programs. (Remember, though, that the response time experienced by the user will be the elapsed time of the program, not the CPU time.) CPU time can be further divided into the CPU time spent in the program, called *user CPU time,* and the CPU time spent in the operating system performing tasks on behalf of the program, called *system CPU time.* Differentiating between system and user CPU time is difficult to do accurately because it is often hard to assign responsibility for operating system activities to one user program rather than another.

The breakdown of the elapsed time for a task is reflected in the Unix `time` command, which, for example, might return the following:

`90.7u 12.9s 2:39 65%`

User CPU time is 90.7 seconds, system CPU time is 12.9 seconds, elapsed time is 2 minutes and 39 seconds (159 seconds), and the percentage of elapsed time that is CPU time is

$$\frac{90.7 + 12.9}{159} = 0.65$$

or 65%. More than a third of the elapsed time in this example was spent waiting for I/O, running other programs, or both.

Sometimes we ignore system CPU time when examining CPU execution time because of the inaccuracy of operating systems' self-measurement and the inequity of including system CPU time when comparing performance between machines with different operating systems. On the other hand, system code on some machines is user code on others, and no program runs without some operating system running on the hardware, so a case can be made for using the sum of user CPU time and system CPU time as the measure of program execution time.

For consistency, we maintain a distinction between performance based on elapsed time and that based on CPU execution time. We will use the term *system performance* to refer to elapsed time on an unloaded system, and use *CPU performance* to refer to user CPU time. We will concentrate on CPU performance in this chapter, although our discussions of how to summarize performance can be applied to either elapsed time or to CPU time measurements.

Although as computer users we care about time, when we examine the details of a machine it's convenient to think about performance in other metrics. In particular, computer designers may want to think about a machine by using a measure that relates to how fast the hardware can perform basic functions. Almost all computers are constructed using a clock that runs at a constant rate and determines when events take place in the hardware. These discrete time intervals are called *clock cycles* (or ticks, clock ticks, clock periods, clocks, cycles). Designers refer to the length of a *clock period* both as the time for a complete *clock cycle* (e.g., 2 nanoseconds, or 2 ns) and as the *clock rate* (e.g., 500 megahertz, or 500 MHz), which is the inverse of the clock period. In the next section, we will formalize the relationship between the clock cycles of the hardware designer and the seconds of the computer user.

2.3   Relating the Metrics

Users and designers often examine performance using different metrics. If we could relate these different metrics, we could determine the effect of a design change on the performance as seen by the user. Since we are confining our-selves to CPU performance at this point, the bottom-line performance measure is CPU execution time. A simple formula relates the most basic metrics (clock cycles and clock cycle time) to CPU time:

$$\text{CPU execution time for a program} = \text{CPU clock cycles for a program} \times \text{Clock cycle time}$$

Alternatively, because clock rate and clock cycle time are inverses,

$$\text{CPU execution time for a program} = \frac{\text{CPU clock cycles for a program}}{\text{Clock rate}}$$

This formula makes it clear that the hardware designer can improve performance by reducing either the length of the clock cycle or the number of clock cycles required for a program. As we will see in this chapter and later in Chapters 5, 6, and 7, the designer often faces a trade-off between the number of clock cycles needed for a program and the length of each cycle. Many techniques that decrease the number of clock cycles also increase the clock cycle time.

Improving Performance

Example   Our favorite program runs in 10 seconds on computer A, which has a 400-MHz clock. We are trying to help a computer designer build a machine, B, that will run this program in 6 seconds. The designer has determined that a substantial increase in the clock rate is possible, but this increase will affect the rest of the CPU design, causing machine B to require 1.2 times as many clock cycles as machine A for this program. What clock rate should we tell the designer to target?

Answer   Let's first find the number of clock cycles required for the program on A:

$$\text{CPU time}_A = \frac{\text{CPU clock cycles}_A}{\text{Clock rate}_A}$$

$$10 \text{ seconds} = \frac{\text{CPU clock cycles}_A}{400 \times 10^6 \frac{\text{cycles}}{\text{second}}}$$

$$\text{CPU clock cycles}_A = 10 \text{ seconds} \times 400 \times 10^6 \frac{\text{cycles}}{\text{second}} = 4000 \times 10^6 \text{cycles}$$

CPU time for B can be found using this equation:

$$\text{CPU time}_B = \frac{1.2 \times \text{CPU clock cycles}_A}{\text{Clock rate}_B}$$

$$6 \text{ seconds} = \frac{1.2 \times 4000 \times 10^6 \text{cycles}}{\text{Clock rate}_B}$$

$$\text{Clock rate}_B = \frac{1.2 \times 4000 \times 10^6 \text{cycles}}{6 \text{ seconds}} = \frac{800 \times 10^6 \text{cycles}}{\text{second}} = 800 \text{ MHz}$$

Machine B must therefore have twice the clock rate of A to run the program in 6 seconds.

Hardware Software Interface

Throughout this text, you will see sections called "Hardware Software Interface." These sections highlight major interactions between some aspect of the software (typically a program, a compiler, or an operating system) and some hardware aspect of a computer. In addition to highlighting such interactions, these sections are reminders that hardware and software design interact in many ways.

The equations in our previous examples do not include any reference to the number of instructions needed for the program. However, since the compiler clearly generated instructions to execute, and the machine had to execute the instructions to run the program, the execution time must depend on the number of instructions in a program. One way to think about execution time is that it equals the number of instructions executed multiplied by the average time per instruction. Therefore, the number of clock cycles required for a program can be written as

$$\text{CPU clock cycles} = \text{Instructions for a program} \times \frac{\text{Average clock cycles}}{\text{per instruction}}$$

The term *clock cycles per instruction*, which is the average number of clock cycles each instruction takes to execute, is often abbreviated as CPI. Since different instructions may take different amounts of time depending on what they do, CPI is an average of all the instructions executed in the program. CPI provides one way of comparing two different implementations of the same instruction set architecture, since the instruction count required for a program will, of course, be the same.

Using the Performance Equation

Example

Suppose we have two implementations of the same instruction set architecture. Machine A has a clock cycle time of 1 ns and a CPI of 2.0 for some program, and machine B has a clock cycle time of 2 ns and a CPI of 1.2 for the same program. Which machine is faster for this program, and by how much?

Answer

We know that each machine executes the same number of instructions for the program; let's call this number I. First, find the number of processor clock cycles for each machine:

$$\text{CPU clock cycles}_A = I \times 2.0$$

$$\text{CPU clock cycles}_B = I \times 1.2$$

Now we can compute the CPU time for each machine:

$$\text{CPU time}_A = \text{CPU clock cycles}_A \times \text{Clock cycle time}_A$$

$$= I \times 2.0 \times 1 \text{ ns} = 2 \times I \text{ ns}$$

Likewise, for B:

$$\text{CPU time}_B = I \times 1.2 \times 2 \text{ ns} = 2.4 \times I \text{ ns}$$

Clearly, machine A is faster. The amount faster is given by the ratio of the execution times:

$$\frac{\text{CPU performance}_A}{\text{CPU performance}_B} = \frac{\text{Execution time}_B}{\text{Execution time}_A} = \frac{2.4 \times I \text{ ns}}{2 \times I \text{ ns}} = 1.2$$

We can conclude that machine A is 1.2 times faster than machine B for this program.

We can now write this basic performance equation in terms of instruction count (the number of instructions executed by the program), CPI, and clock cycle time:

$$\text{CPU time} = \text{Instruction count} \times \text{CPI} \times \text{Clock cycle time}$$

or

$$\text{CPU time} = \frac{\text{Instruction count} \times \text{CPI}}{\text{Clock rate}}$$

These formulas are particularly useful because they separate the three key factors that affect performance. We can use these formulas to compare two different implementations or to evaluate a design alternative if we know its impact on these three parameters.

The Big Picture

Figure 2.2 shows the basic measurements at different levels in the computer and what is being measured in each case. We can see how these factors are combined to yield execution time measured in seconds:

$$\text{Time} = \frac{\text{Instructions}}{\text{Program}} \times \frac{\text{Clock cycles}}{\text{Instruction}} \times \frac{\text{Seconds}}{\text{Clock cycle}}$$

Always bear in mind that the only complete and reliable measure of computer performance is time. For example, changing the instruction set to lower the instruction count may lead to an organization with a slower clock cycle time that offsets the improvement in instruction count. Similarly, because CPI depends on instruction mix, the code that executes the fewest number of instructions may not be the fastest.

Components of performance	Units of measure
CPU execution time for a program	Seconds for the program
Instruction count	Instructions executed for the program
Clock cycles per instruction (CPI)	Average number of clock cycles per instruction
Clock cycle time	Seconds per clock cycle

FIGURE 2.2   The basic components of performance and how each is measured.

How can we determine the value of these factors in the performance equation? We can measure the CPU execution time by running the program, and the clock cycle time is usually published as part of the documentation for a machine. The instruction count and CPI can be more difficult to obtain. Of course, if we know the clock rate and CPU execution time, we need only one of the instruction count or the CPI to determine the other.

We can measure the instruction count by using software tools that profile the execution or by using a simulator of the architecture. Alternatively, we can use hardware counters, which have been included on some processors, to record a variety of measurements, including the number of instructions executed. Since the instruction count depends on the architecture, but not on the exact implementation, we can measure the instruction count without knowing all the details of the implementation. The CPI, however, depends on a wide variety of design details in the machine, including both the memory system and the processor structure (as we will see in Chapters 5, 6, and 7), as well as on the mix of instruction types executed in an application. Thus CPI varies by application, as well as among implementations with the same instruction set.

Designers often obtain CPI by a detailed simulation of an implementation or by combining hardware counters and simulation. Sometimes it is possible to compute the CPU clock cycles by looking at the different types of instructions and using their individual clock cycle counts. In such cases, the following formula is useful:

$$\text{CPU clock cycles} = \sum_{i=1}^{n} (\text{CPI}_i \times \text{C}_i)$$

where C_i is the count of the number of instructions of class i executed, CPI_i is the average number of cycles per instruction for that instruction class, and n is the number of instruction classes. Remember that overall CPI for a program will depend on both the number of cycles for each instruction type and the frequency of each instruction type in the program execution.

Comparing Code Segments

Example

A compiler designer is trying to decide between two code sequences for a particular machine. The hardware designers have supplied the following facts:

Instruction class	CPI for this instruction class
A	1
B	2
C	3

For a particular high-level-language statement, the compiler writer is considering two code sequences that require the following instruction counts:

Code sequence	Instruction counts for instruction class		
	A	B	C
1	2	1	2
2	4	1	1

Which code sequence executes the most instructions? Which will be faster? What is the CPI for each sequence?

Answer

Sequence 1 executes $2 + 1 + 2 = 5$ instructions. Sequence 2 executes $4 + 1 + 1 = 6$ instructions. So sequence 1 executes fewer instructions.

We can use the equation for CPU clock cycles based on instruction count and CPI to find the total number of clock cycles for each sequence:

$$\text{CPU clock cycles} = \sum_{i=1}^{n} (\text{CPI}_i \times \text{C}_i)$$

This yields

$$\text{CPU clock cycles}_1 = (2 \times 1) + (1 \times 2) + (2 \times 3) = 2 + 2 + 6 = 10 \text{ cycles}$$

$$\text{CPU clock cycles}_2 = (4 \times 1) + (1 \times 2) + (1 \times 3) = 4 + 2 + 3 = 9 \text{ cycles}$$

So code sequence 2 is faster, even though it actually executes one extra instruction. Since code sequence 2 takes fewer overall clock cycles but has more instructions, it must have a lower CPI. The CPI values can be computed by

$$\text{CPI} = \frac{\text{CPU clock cycles}}{\text{Instruction count}}$$

$$\text{CPI}_1 = \frac{\text{CPU clock cycles}_1}{\text{Instruction count}_1} = \frac{10}{5} = 2$$

$$\text{CPI}_2 = \frac{\text{CPU clock cycles}_2}{\text{Instruction count}_2} = \frac{9}{6} = 1.5$$

The above example shows the danger of using only one factor (instruction count) to assess performance. When comparing two machines, you must look at all three components, which combine to form execution time. If some of the factors are identical, like the clock rate in the above example, performance can be determined by comparing all the nonidentical factors. Since CPI varies by instruction mix, both instruction count and CPI must be compared, even if clock rates are identical. Exercises 2.18 through 2.24 explore this further by asking you to evaluate a series of machine and compiler enhancements that affect clock rate, CPI, and instruction count. In the next section, we'll examine a common performance measurement that does not incorporate all the terms and can thus be misleading.

2.4 Choosing Programs to Evaluate Performance

A computer user who runs the same programs day in and day out would be the perfect candidate to evaluate a new computer. The set of programs run would form a *workload*. To evaluate two computer systems, a user would simply compare the execution time of the workload on the two machines. Most users, however, are not in this situation. Instead, they must rely on other methods that measure the performance of a candidate machine, hoping that the methods will reflect how well the machine will perform with the user's workload. This alternative is usually followed by evaluating the machine using a set of *benchmarks*, which are programs specifically chosen to measure performance. The benchmarks form a workload that the user hopes will predict the performance of the actual workload.

Today, it is widely understood that the best type of programs to use for benchmarks are real applications. These may be applications that the user employs regularly or simply applications that are typical. For example, in an environment where the users are primarily engineers, you might use a set of benchmarks containing several typical engineering or scientific applications. If the user community were primarily software development engineers, the best benchmarks would probably include such applications as a compiler or document processing system. Using real applications as benchmarks makes it much more difficult to find trivial ways to speed up the execution of the benchmark. Furthermore, when techniques are found to improve performance, such techniques are much more likely to help other programs in addition to the benchmark.

The use of benchmarks whose performance depends on very small code segments encourages optimizations in either the architecture or compiler that target these segments. The compiler optimizations might recognize special code fragments and generate an instruction sequence that is particularly efficient for this code fragment. Likewise, a designer might try to make some sequence of instructions run especially fast because the sequence occurs in a benchmark. Recently, several companies have introduced compilers with special-purpose optimizations targeted at specific benchmarks. Often these optimizations must be explicitly enabled with a specific compiler option, which would not be used when compiling other programs. Whether the compiler would produce good code, or even *correct* code, if a real application program used these switches, is unclear. Sometimes in the quest to produce highly optimized code for benchmarks, engineers introduce erroneous optimizations. For example, in late 1995, Intel published a new performance rating for the integer SPEC benchmarks (see sections 2.6 and 2.9 for a further discussion of SPEC) running on a Pentium processor and using an internal compiler, not used outside of Intel. Unfortunately, the code produced for one of the benchmarks was wrong, a fact that was discovered when a competitor read through the binary to understand how Intel had sped up one of the programs in the benchmark suite so dramatically. In January of 1996, Intel admitted the error and restated the performance.

Small programs or programs that spend almost all their execution time in a very small code fragment are especially vulnerable to such efforts. For example, the SPEC processor benchmark suite was chosen to use primarily real applications. Unfortunately, the first release of the SPEC suite in 1989 included a benchmark called matrix300, which consists solely of a series of matrix multiplications. In fact, 99% of the execution time is in a single line of this benchmark. The fact that so much time is spent in one line doing the same computation many times has led several companies to purchase or develop special compiler technology to improve the running time of this benchmark. Figure 2.3 shows the performance ratios (inverse to execution time) for one machine with two different compilers. The enhanced compiler has essentially no effect on the running time of 8 of the 10 benchmarks, but it improves performance on matrix300 by a factor of more than nine. On matrix300, the program runs 729.8 times faster using the enhanced compiler than the reference time obtained from a VAX-11/780—but the more typical performance of the machine is much slower. The other programs run from just over 30 times faster to just over 140 times faster. A user expecting a program to run 700 times faster than it does on a VAX-11/780 would likely be very disappointed! In the 1992 release of the SPEC benchmark suite, matrix300 was dropped.

So why doesn't everyone run real programs to measure performance? One reason is that small benchmarks are attractive when beginning a design, since they are small enough to compile and simulate easily, sometimes by hand. They are especially tempting when designers are working on a novel machine because compilers may not be available until much later in the design. Small benchmarks are also more easily standardized than large programs; hence numerous published performance results are available for small benchmarks.

Although the use of such small benchmarks early in the design process may be justified, there is no valid rationale for using them to evaluate working computer systems. In the past, it was hard to obtain large applications that could

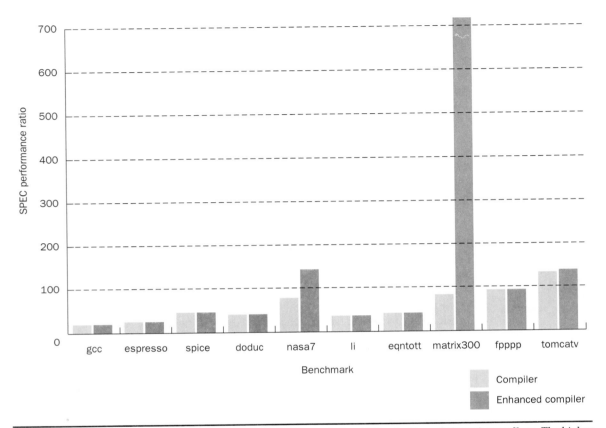

FIGURE 2.3   SPEC89 performance ratios for the IBM Powerstation 550 using two different compilers. The higher numbers on matrix300 (and nasa7) result from applying an optimization technique to these two kernel-oriented benchmarks. For the enhanced compiler, special flags are passed to the compiler for both nasa7 and matrix300, which are not used for the other benchmarks. In both programs, the compiler transforms the program by blocking the matrix operations that are in the inner loops. These blocking transformations substantially lower the number of memory accesses required and transform the inner loops from having high cache miss rates to having almost negligible cache miss rates. Interestingly, the original motivation for including matrix300 was to exercise the computer's memory system; however, this optimization basically reorganizes the program to minimize memory usage. This data appeared in two SPEC reports during the fall and winter of 1991. The susceptibility of this benchmark to compiler optimization, and the relatively uninteresting behavior of the benchmark after optimization, led to the elimination of matrix300 from the 1992 release of the SPEC benchmarks.

be easily ported to a machine, but this is no longer true. Using small programs as benchmarks was an attempt to make fair comparisons among different machines, but use of anything less than real programs after initial design studies is likely to give misleading results and lure the designer astray.

Once we have selected a set of suitable benchmarks and obtained performance measurements, we can write a performance report. The guiding principle in reporting performance measurements should be *reproducibility*—we should list everything another experimenter would need to duplicate the results. This list must include the version of the operating system, compilers, and the input, as well as the machine configuration. As an example, we include the system description section of a SPEC benchmark report in Figure 2.4.

Hardware	
Model number	Powerstation 550
CPU	41.67-MHz POWER 4164
FPU	Integrated
Number of CPUs	1
Cache size per CPU	64K data/8K instruction
Memory	64 MB
Disk subsystem	2 400-MB SCSI
Network interface	NA
Software	
OS type and rev	AIX v3.1.5
Compiler rev	AIX XL C/6000 Ver. 1.1.5
	AIX XL Fortran Ver. 2.2
Other software	None
File system type	AIX
Firmware level	NA
System	
Tuning parameters	None
Background load	None
System state	Multiuser (single-user login)

FIGURE 2.4 System description of the machine used to obtain the higher performance results in Figure 2.3. A footnote attached to the entry for the Fortran compiler states: "AIX XL Fortran Alpha Version 2.2 used for testing." Although no tuning parameters are indicated, additional footnotes describe a number of special flags passed to the compilers for the benchmarks.

2.5

Comparing and Summarizing Performance

Once we have selected programs to use as benchmarks and agreed on whether we are measuring response time or throughput, you might think that performance comparison would be straightforward. However, we must still decide how to summarize the performance of a group of benchmarks.

	Computer A	Computer B
Program 1 (seconds)	1	10
Program 2 (seconds)	1000	100
Total time (seconds)	1001	110

FIGURE 2.5   Execution times of two programs on two different machines. Taken from Figure 1 of Smith [1988].

Although summarizing a set of measurements results in less information, marketers and even users often prefer to have a single number to compare performance. The key question is, How should a summary be computed? Figure 2.5, which is abstracted from an article about summarizing performance, illustrates some of the difficulties facing such efforts.

Using our definition of *faster*, the following statements hold for the program measurements in Figure 2.5:

- A is 10 times faster than B for program 1.
- B is 10 times faster than A for program 2.

Taken individually, each of these statements is true. Collectively, however, they present a confusing picture—the relative performance of computers A and B is unclear.

Total Execution Time: A Consistent Summary Measure

The simplest approach to summarizing relative performance is to use total execution time of the two programs. Thus

$$\frac{\text{Performance}_B}{\text{Performance}_A} = \frac{\text{Execution time}_A}{\text{Execution time}_B} = \frac{1001}{110} = 9.1$$

That is, B is 9.1 times faster than A for programs 1 and 2 together.

This summary is directly proportional to execution time, our final measure of performance. If the workload consists of running programs 1 and 2 an equal number of times, this statement would predict the relative execution times for the workload on each machine.

The average of the execution times that is directly proportional to total execution time is the *arithmetic mean* (AM):

$$AM = \frac{1}{n}\sum_{i=1}^{n} Time_i$$

where $Time_i$ is the execution time for the ith program of a total of n in the workload. Since it is the mean of execution times, a smaller mean indicates a smaller average execution time and thus improved performance.

The arithmetic mean is proportional to execution time, assuming that the programs in the workload are each run an equal number of times. Is that the right workload? If not, we can assign a weighting factor w_i to each program to indicate the frequency of the program in that workload. If, for example, 20% of the tasks in the workload were program 1 and 80% of the tasks in the workload were program 2, then the weighting factors would be 0.2 and 0.8. By summing the products of weighting factors and execution times, we can obtain a clear picture of the performance of the workload. This sum is called the *weighted arithmetic mean*. One method of weighting programs is to choose weights so that the execution time of each benchmark is equal on the machine used as the base. The standard arithmetic mean is a special case of the weighted arithmetic mean where all weights are equal. We explore the weighted mean in more detail in Exercises 2.29 and 2.30.

2.6   Real Stuff: The SPEC95 Benchmarks and Performance of Recent Processors

The most popular and comprehensive set of CPU benchmarks is the SPEC (System Performance Evaluation Cooperative) suite of benchmarks. SPEC was created by a set of computer companies in 1989 to improve the measurement and reporting of CPU performance through a better controlled measurement process and the use of more realistic benchmarks. A more detailed history is contained in section 2.9.

The latest release of the SPEC benchmarks is the SPEC95 suite, which consists of 8 integer and 10 floating-point programs, as shown in Figure 2.6. Separate summaries are reported for each set. The execution time measurements are first normalized by dividing the execution time on a Sun SPARCstation 10/40 by the execution time on the measured machine; this normalization yields a measure, called the *SPEC ratio*, which has the advantage that bigger numeric results indicate faster performance (i.e., SPEC ratio is the inverse of execution time). A SPECint95 or SPECfp95 summary measurement is obtained by taking the geometric mean of the SPEC ratios. (See the fallacy on page 81 of the next section for a discussion of trade-offs in using geometric mean.)

Benchmark	Description
go	Artificial intelligence; plays the game of Go
m88ksim	Motorola 88K chip simulator; runs test program
gcc	The Gnu C compiler generating SPARC code
compress	Compresses and decompresses file in memory
li	Lisp interpreter
ijpeg	Graphic compression and decompression
perl	Manipulates strings and prime numbers in the special-purpose programming language Perl
vortex	A database program
tomcatv	A mesh generation program
swim	Shallow water model with 513 x 513 grid
su2cor	Quantum physics; Monte Carlo simulation
hydro2d	Astrophysics; Hydrodynamic Naiver Stokes equations
mgrid	Multigrid solver in 3-D potential field
applu	Parabolic/elliptic partial differential equations
turb3d	Simulates isotropic, homogeneous turbulence in a cube
apsi	Solves problems regarding temperature, wind velocity, and distribution of pollutant
fpppp	Quantum chemistry
wave5	Plasma physics; electromagnetic particle simulation

FIGURE 2.6   The SPEC95 CPU benchmarks. The 8 integer benchmarks in the top half of the table are written in C, while the 10 floating-point benchmarks in the bottom half are written in Fortran 77. For more information on SPEC and on the SPEC benchmarks, see the link to the SPEC Web pages at *www.mkp.com/books_catalog/cod/links.htm.*

For a given instruction set architecture, increases in CPU performance can come from three sources:

1. Increases in clock rate

2. Improvements in processor organization that lower the CPI

3. Compiler enhancements that lower the instruction count or generate instructions with a lower average CPI (e.g., by using simpler instructions)

To illustrate such performance improvements, Figures 2.7 and 2.8 show the SPECint95 and SPECfp95 measurements for a series of Intel Pentium processors (as implemented in the Intel XXpress system) and Pentium Pro processors (as implemented in the Intel Alder system). Since SPEC requires that the benchmarks be run on real hardware and the memory system has a significant effect on performance, other systems with these processors may produce different performance levels. The Intel machines measured here have aggressive memory systems and compilers (as opposed to the standard third-party compilers in broad use), and most systems delivered with these processors will have lower performance for the SPEC benchmarks.

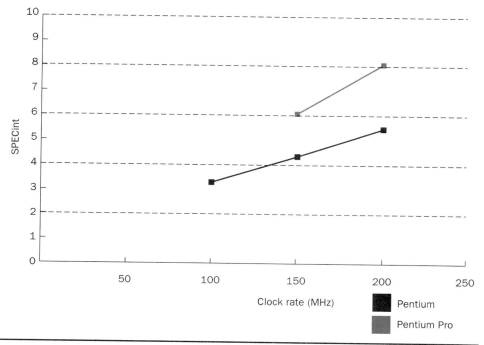

FIGURE 2.7 The SPECint95 ratings for the Pentium and Pentium Pro processors at different clock speeds. SPEC requires two sets of measurements: one that allows aggressive optimization with benchmark-specific switches, and one that allows only the standard optimization switches (called SPECint_base95). For the integer benchmarks on these processors, the results are the same. The link to these results can be found at *www.mkp.com/books_catalog/cod/links.htm.*

There are several important observations from these two performance graphs. The most obvious is the performance enhancement offered by the Pentium Pro over the Pentium: at the same clock rate the SPECint95 measure shows that the Pentium Pro is 1.4 to 1.5 times faster, and the SPECfp95 measure shows that the Pentium Pro is 1.7 to 1.8 times faster. Although there are specific compiler enhancements for each processor, the majority of the performance improvement comes from organizational enhancements to the Pentium Pro; we will see some of these enhancements when we examine pipelining in Chapter 6 and the memory system in Chapter 7.

The other major observation is that when the clock rate is increased by a certain factor, the processor performance increases by a lower factor. For example, when the clock rate of the Pentium doubles from 100 MHz to 200 MHz, the SPECint95 performance improves by only 1.7 and the SPECfp95 performance improves by only 1.4! The reason for this is performance loss in the memory

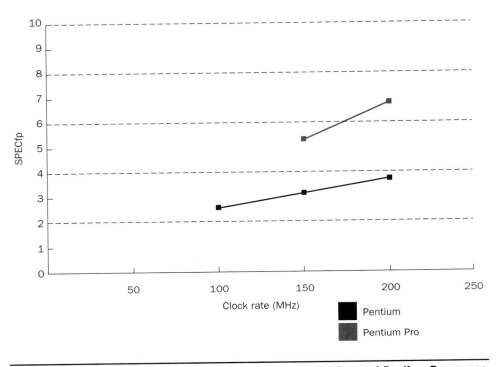

**FIGURE 2.8   The SPECfp95 ratings for the Pentium and Pentium Pro proces-
sors at different clock speeds.** These results can be found via the link to SPEC at
www.mkp.com/books_cataog/cod/links.htm.

system. In general, since the speed of the main memory is not increased, increasing the processor speed will exacerbate the bottleneck at the memory system. This effect is most acute on the floating-point benchmarks, since they are
larger. This behavior is an example of a general principle, called *Amdahl's law,*
which we examine in more detail in the next section.

In comparison, the Pentium Pro processor performance scales somewhat
better with increases in clock rate, though still not as fast as the clock rate. For
example, the SPECfp95 improvement in going from 150 MHz to 200 MHz is
1.24, while the Pentium processor shows a smaller improvement of 1.18 for the
same increase in clock rate.

In Chapter 7, we will see how the memory systems on these processors are
designed and how designers minimize the memory system losses as processor
performance improves. Section 7.6 describes some techniques that the Pentium Pro uses to reduce performance lost in the memory system, which explain
why its performance scales better with clock rate than a Pentium.

2.7 Fallacies and Pitfalls

Cost/performance fallacies and pitfalls have ensnared many a computer architect, including us. Accordingly, this section suffers no shortage of relevant examples. We start with a pitfall that has trapped many designers and reveals an important relationship in computer design.

> *Pitfall: Expecting the improvement of one aspect of a machine to increase performance by an amount proportional to the size of the improvement.*

This pitfall has visited designers of both hardware and software. A simple design problem illustrates it well. Suppose a program runs in 100 seconds on a machine, with multiply operations responsible for 80 seconds of this time. How much do I have to improve the speed of multiplication if I want my program to run five times faster?

The execution time of the program after I make the improvement is given by the following simple equation:

Execution time after improvement

$$= \left(\frac{\text{Execution time affected by improvement}}{\text{Amount of improvement}} + \text{Execution time unaffected} \right)$$

For this problem:

$$\text{Execution time after improvement} = \frac{80 \text{ seconds}}{n} + (100 - 80 \text{ seconds})$$

Since we want the performance to be five times faster, the new execution time should be 20 seconds, giving

$$20 \text{ seconds} = \frac{80 \text{ seconds}}{n} + 20 \text{ seconds}$$

$$0 = \frac{80 \text{ seconds}}{n}$$

That is, there is no amount by which we can enhance multiply to achieve a fivefold increase in performance, if multiply accounts for only 80% of the workload. The performance enhancement possible with a given improvement is limited by the amount that the improved feature is used. This concept is referred to as *Amdahl's law* in computing, or the law of diminishing returns in everyday life. We'll see some other implications of this relationship in Exercises 2.41 through 2.46.

A common theme in hardware design is a corollary of Amdahl's law: *Make the common case fast*. This simple guideline reminds us that in many cases the frequency with which one event occurs may be much higher than another. Amdahl's law reminds us that the opportunity for improvement is affected by how much time the event consumes. Thus making the common case fast will tend to enhance performance better than optimizing the rare case. Ironically, the common case is often simpler than the rare case and hence is often easier to enhance.

Fallacy: Hardware-independent metrics predict performance.

Because accurately predicting and comparing performance is so difficult, many designers and researchers have tried to devise methods to assess performance that do not rely on measurements of execution time. These methods are frequently employed when designers compare different instruction sets to factor out the effects of different implementations or software systems and arrive at conclusions about the performance obtainable for different instruction sets.

One such method, which has been used in the past, is to use code size as a measure of speed. With this method, the instruction set architecture with the smallest program is fastest. The size of the compiled program is, of course, important when memory space is at a premium, but it is not the same as performance. In fact, today, the fastest machines tend to have instruction sets that lead to larger programs but can be executed faster with less hardware.

Evidence of the fallacy of using code size to measure speed can be found on the cover of a book published in 1973, shown in Figure 2.9. The figure clearly shows the lack of a direct relationship between code size and execution time. For example, the CDC 6600's programs are over three times as big as those on the Burroughs B5500, yet the CDC machine runs Algol 60 programs almost six times *faster* than the B5500, a machine designed specifically for Algol 60.

Compiler writers sometimes use code size to choose between two different code segments on the same architecture. While this is less misleading than trying to compare code size across architectures, the accuracy of predicting performance from code size can vary widely.

Pitfall: Using MIPS as a performance metric.

A number of popular measures have been devised in attempts to create a standard and easy-to-use measure of computer performance. One result has been that simple metrics, valid in a limited context, have been heavily misused. All proposed alternatives to the use of time as the performance metric have led eventually to misleading claims, distorted results, or incorrect interpretations.

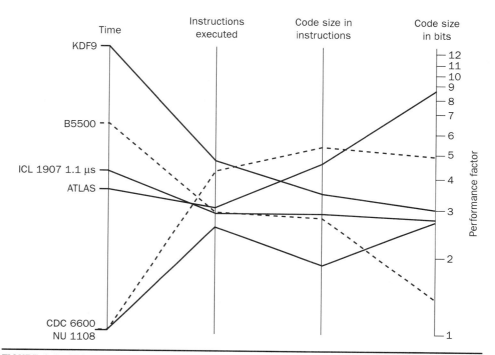

FIGURE 2.9 This graph is from the cover of *Algol 60 Compilation and Assessment* by B. A. Wichmann (published in 1973). The graph shows relative execution time, instructions executed, and code size in both instructions and bits for a set of programs written in Algol 60 and run on six different machines. The results are normalized to a reference machine, with a higher number indicating more execution time, larger instruction counts, or larger code size. The graph clearly shows that abstract measures such as code size bear little relationship to performance measures such as execution time or instructions executed. Despite the evidence that code size and execution time could be totally unrelated, many designers continued to emphasize code size throughout the 1980s. Graph redrawn with permission from Academic Press.

One alternative to time as the metric is MIPS (million instructions per second). For a given program, MIPS is simply

$$\text{MIPS} = \frac{\text{Instruction count}}{\text{Execution time} \times 10^6}$$

This MIPS measurement is also called *native MIPS* to distinguish it from some alternative definitions of MIPS that we discuss in section 2.9.

Since MIPS is an instruction execution rate, MIPS specifies performance inversely to execution time; faster machines have a higher MIPS rating. The good news about MIPS is that it is easy to understand, and faster machines mean bigger MIPS, which matches intuition.

There are three problems with using MIPS as a measure for comparing machines. First, MIPS specifies the instruction execution rate but does not take into account the capabilities of the instructions. We cannot compare computers with different instruction sets using MIPS, since the instruction counts will certainly differ. Second, MIPS varies between programs on the same computer; thus a machine cannot have a single MIPS rating for all programs. Finally and most importantly, MIPS can vary inversely with performance! There are many examples of this anomalous behavior; one is given below.

MIPS as a Performance Measure

Example

Consider the machine with three instruction classes and CPI measurements from the last example on page 64. Now suppose we measure the code for the same program from two different compilers and obtain the following data:

Code from	Instruction counts (in billions) for each instruction class		
	A	B	C
Compiler 1	5	1	1
Compiler 2	10	1	1

Assume that the machine's clock rate is 500 MHz. Which code sequence will execute faster according to MIPS? According to execution time?

Answer

First we find the execution time for the two different compilers using the following equation:

$$\text{Execution time} = \frac{\text{CPU clock cycles}}{\text{Clock rate}}$$

We can use an earlier formula for CPU clock cycles:

$$\text{CPU clock cycles} = \sum_{i=1}^{n}(\text{CPI}_i \times \text{C}_i)$$

$$\text{CPU clock cycles}_1 = (5 \times 1 + 1 \times 2 + 1 \times 3) \times 10^9 = 10 \times 10^9$$

$$\text{CPU clock cycles}_2 = (10 \times 1 + 1 \times 2 + 1 \times 3) \times 10^9 = 15 \times 10^9$$

Now, we find the execution time for the two compilers:

$$\text{Execution time}_1 = \frac{10 \times 10^9}{500 \times 10^6} = 20 \text{ seconds}$$

$$\text{Execution time}_2 = \frac{15 \times 10^9}{500 \times 10^6} = 30 \text{ seconds}$$

So, we conclude that compiler 1 generates the faster program, according to execution time. Now, let's compute the MIPS rate for each version of the program, using

$$\text{MIPS} = \frac{\text{Instruction count}}{\text{Execution time} \times 10^6}$$

$$\text{MIPS}_1 = \frac{(5 + 1 + 1) \times 10^9}{20 \times 10^6} = 350$$

$$\text{MIPS}_2 = \frac{(10 + 1 + 1) \times 10^9}{30 \times 10^6} = 400$$

So, the code from compiler 2 has a higher MIPS rating, but the code from compiler 1 runs faster!

As examples such as this show, MIPS can fail to give a true picture of performance—even when comparing two versions of the same program on the same machine. In section 2.9, we discuss other uses of the term *MIPS,* and how such usages can also be misleading.

Fallacy: Synthetic benchmarks predict performance.

Synthetic benchmarks are artificial programs that are constructed to try to match the characteristics of a large set of programs. The goal is to create a single benchmark program where the execution frequency of statements in the benchmark matches the statement frequency in a large set of benchmarks. Whetstone and Dhrystone are the most popular synthetic benchmarks. Whetstone was based on measurements of Algol programs in a scientific and engineering environment. It was later converted to Fortran and became popular. Dhrystone, which was inspired by Whetstone, was created as a benchmark for systems programming environments and was based on a set of published frequency measurements. Dhrystone was originally written in Ada and later converted to C, after which it became popular.

One major drawback of synthetic benchmarks is that no user would ever run a synthetic benchmark as an application because these programs don't compute anything a user would find remotely interesting. Furthermore, because synthetic benchmarks are not real programs, they usually do not reflect program behavior, other than the behavior considered when they were created. Finally, compiler and hardware optimizations can inflate performance of these benchmarks, far beyond what the same optimizations would achieve on real programs. Of course, because these benchmarks are not natural programs, they may not reward optimizations of behavior that occur in real programs. Here are some examples of how Dhrystone may distort the importance of various optimizations:

- Optimizing compilers can easily discard 25% of the Dhrystone code; examples include loops that are executed only once, making the loop overhead instructions unnecessary. To address these problems, the authors of the benchmark "require" both optimized and unoptimized code to be reported. In addition, they "forbid" the practice of inline procedure expansion optimization because Dhrystone's simple procedure structure allows elimination of all procedure calls at almost no increase in code size.

- One C compiler appears to include optimizations targeted just for Dhrystone. If the proper option flag is set at compile time, the compiler turns the portion of the C version of this benchmark that copies a variable-length string of bytes (terminated by an end-of-string symbol) into a loop that transfers a fixed number of words. The compiler also assumes that the source and destination of the string is word-aligned in memory. Although an estimated 99.70% to 99.98% of typical string copies could *not* use this optimization, this single change can make a 20% to 30% improvement in Dhrystone's overall performance.

The small size and simplistic structure of synthetic benchmarks makes them especially vulnerable to this type of activity.

Pitfall: Using the arithmetic mean of normalized execution times to predict performance.

This pitfall has trapped many researchers, including one of the authors of this book. An inviting method of presenting machine performance is to normalize execution times to a reference machine, just as is done to obtain a SPEC ratio, and then take the average of the normalized execution times. However, if we average the normalized execution time values with an arithmetic mean, the result will depend on the choice of the machine we use as the reference. For example, in Figure 2.10, the execution times from Figure 2.5 are normalized to both A and B, and the arithmetic mean is computed. When we normalize to A, the arithmetic mean indicates that A is faster than B by 5.05/1, which is the inverse ratio of the execution times. When we normalize to B, we conclude that *B is faster by exactly the same ratio.* Clearly, both these results cannot be correct!

			Normalized to A		Normalized to B	
	Time on A	Time on B	A	B	A	B
Program 1	1	10	1	10	0.1	1
Program 2	1000	100	1	0.1	10	1
Arithmetic mean of time or normalized time	500.5	55	1	5.05	5.05	1
Geometric mean of time or normalized time	31.6	31.6	1	1	1	1

FIGURE 2.10 Execution times from Figure 2.5 normalized to each machine. The means are computed for each column. While the arithmetic means vary when we normalize to either A or B, the geometric means are consistent, independent of normalization.

The difficulty arises from the use of the arithmetic mean of ratios. Instead, normalized results should be combined with the *geometric* mean. The formula for the geometric mean is

$$\sqrt[n]{\prod_{i=1}^{n} \text{Execution time ratio}_i}$$

where Execution time ratio$_i$ is the execution time, normalized to the reference machine, for the ith program of a total of n in the workload, and

$$\prod_{i=1}^{n} a_i \text{ means the product } a_1 \times a_2 \times \ldots \times a_n$$

The geometric mean is independent of which data series we use for normalization because it has the property

$$\frac{\text{Geometric mean}(X_i)}{\text{Geometric mean}(Y_i)} = \text{Geometric mean}\left(\frac{X_i}{Y_i}\right)$$

meaning that taking either the ratio of the means or the means of the ratios produces the same results. Thus the geometric mean produces the same relative result whether we normalize to A or B, as we can see in the bottom row of Figure 2.10. When execution times are normalized, only a geometric mean can be used to consistently summarize the normalized results. Unfortunately, as we show in the exercises, geometric means do not track total execution time and thus cannot be used to predict relative execution time for a workload.

Fallacy: The geometric mean of execution time ratios is proportional to total execution time.

The advantage of the geometric mean is that it is independent of the running times of the individual programs, and it doesn't matter which machine is used for normalization. The drawback to using geometric means of execution times is that they violate our fundamental principle of performance measurement—they do not predict execution time. The geometric means in Figure 2.10 suggest that for programs 1 and 2 the performance is the same for machines A and B. Yet, the arithmetic mean of the execution times, which we know is proportional to total execution time, suggests that machine B is 9.1 times faster than machine A! If we use total execution time as the performance measure, A and B would have the same performance only for a workload that ran the first program 100 times more often than the second program!

In general, no workload for three or more machines will match the performance predicted by the geometric mean of normalized execution times. The ideal solution is to measure a real workload and weight the programs according to their frequency of execution. If this can't be done, normalizing so that equal time is spent on each program on some machine at least makes the relative weightings explicit and predicts execution time of a workload with that mix. If results must be normalized to a specific machine, first summarize performance with the proper weighted measure, and then do the normalizing.

The Big Picture

Execution time is the only valid and unimpeachable measure of performance. Many other metrics have been proposed and found wanting. Sometimes these metrics are flawed from the start by not reflecting execution time; other times a metric valid in a limited context is extended and used beyond that context or without the additional clarification needed to make it valid.

Similarly, any measure that summarizes performance should reflect execution time. Weighted arithmetic means summarize performance while tracking execution time. Through the use of weights, a weighted arithmetic mean can adjust for different running times, balancing the contribution of each benchmark to the summary.

2.8   Concluding Remarks

Although we have focused on performance and how to evaluate it in this chapter, designing only for performance without considering cost is unrealistic. All computer designers must balance performance and cost. Of course, there exists a domain of *high-performance design,* in which performance is the primary goal and cost is secondary. Much of the supercomputer industry designs in this fashion. At the other extreme is *low-cost design,* where cost takes precedence over performance. Computers like the low-end IBM PC clones belong here, as do most embedded computers. Between these extremes is *cost/performance design*, in which the designer balances cost against performance. Examples from the workstation industry typify the kinds of trade-offs that designers in this region must live with.

We have seen in this chapter that there is a reliable method of determining and reporting performance, using the execution time of real programs as the metric. This execution time is related to other important measurements we can make by the following equation:

$$\frac{\text{Seconds}}{\text{Program}} = \frac{\text{Instructions}}{\text{Program}} \times \frac{\text{Clock cycles}}{\text{Instruction}} \times \frac{\text{Seconds}}{\text{Clock cycle}}$$

We will use this equation and its constituent factors many times. Remember, though, that individually the factors do not determine performance: Only the product, which equals execution time, is a reliable measure of performance.

Of course, simply knowing this equation is not enough to guide the design or evaluation of a computer. We must understand how the different aspects of a design affect each of these key parameters. This insight involves a wide variety of issues, from the effects of instruction set design on dynamic instruction count, to the impact of pipelining and memory systems on CPI, to the interaction between the technology and organization that determine the clock rate. The art of computer design lies not in plugging numbers into a performance equation, but in accurately determining how design alternatives will affect performance and cost.

Most computer users care about both cost and performance. While understanding the relationship among aspects of a design and its performance is challenging, determining the cost of various design features is often a more difficult problem. The cost of a machine is affected not only by the cost of the components, but by the costs of labor to assemble the machine, of research and development overhead, of sales and marketing, and of the profit margin. Finally, because of the rapid change in implementation technologies, the most cost-effective choice today is often suboptimal in six months or a year.

Computer designs will always be measured by cost and performance, and finding the best balance will always be the art of computer design, just as in any engineering task.

2.9 Historical Perspective and Further Reading

From the earliest days of computing, designers have specified performance goals—ENIAC was to be 1000 times faster than the Harvard Mark-I, and the IBM Stretch (7030) was to be 100 times faster than the fastest machine then in existence. What wasn't clear, though, was how this performance was to be measured.

The original measure of performance was the time required to perform an individual operation, such as addition. Since most instructions took the same execution time, the timing of one was the same as the others. As the execution times of instructions in a machine became more diverse, however, the time required for one operation was no longer useful for comparisons.

To take these differences into account, an *instruction mix* was calculated by measuring the relative frequency of instructions in a computer across many programs. Multiplying the time for each instruction by its weight in the mix gave the user the *average instruction execution time*. (If measured in clock cycles, average instruction execution time is the same as average CPI.) Since instruction sets were similar, this was a more precise comparison than add times. From average instruction execution time, then, it was only a small step to MIPS. MIPS had the virtue of being easy to understand; hence it grew in popularity.

MIPS, MOPS, and Other FLOPS

One particularly misleading definition of MIPS that has been occasionally popular is *peak MIPS*. Peak MIPS is obtained by choosing an instruction mix that minimizes the CPI, even if that instruction mix is totally impractical. In the example above, the peak MIPS ratings are the same for both machines: 500 MIPS. To achieve a 500-MIPS rating with a 500-MHz clock, the CPI for the program must be 1. But the only program that can have a CPI of 1 is a program consisting solely of type A instructions!

In practice, processors are sometimes marketed by touting the peak MIPS rating, which can distort the real picture of performance. When the Intel i860 was announced in February 1989, the product announcement used the peak performance of the processor to compare performance against other machines. The i860 was able to execute up to two floating-point operations and one integer operation per clock. With a clock rate target of 50 MHz, the i860 was claimed to offer 100 MFLOPS and 150 MOPS (millions of operations per second). The first i860-based systems (using 40-MHz parts) became available for benchmarking during the first quarter of 1991. By comparison, a MIPS machine based on a 33-MHz R3000 processor, available at about the same time, had a peak performance of about 16 MFLOPS and 33 MOPS. Although the peak performance claims might suggest that the i860-based machine was more than five times faster than the R3000-based machine, the SPEC benchmarks showed that the R3000-based machine was actually about 15% faster! Although peak MIPS is an essentially useless measure, computer manufacturers still occasionally announce products using peak MIPS as a metric, often neglecting to include the word "peak"!

One attempt to retain the use of the term MIPS, but to make it useful among different instruction sets, was to choose a definition of MIPS that is relative to some agreed-upon reference machine, similar to the SPEC ratio measurement. *Relative MIPS,* the term used for this measure, has been defined as follows:

$$\text{Relative MIPS} = \frac{\text{Time}_{\text{reference}}}{\text{Time}_{\text{unrated}}} \times \text{MIPS}_{\text{reference}}$$

where

$\text{Time}_{\text{reference}}$ = Execution time of a program on the reference machine

$\text{Time}_{\text{unrated}}$ = Execution time of the same program on machine to be rated

$\text{MIPS}_{\text{reference}}$ = Agreed-upon MIPS rating of the reference machine

Relative MIPS is proportional to execution time *only* for a given program and a given input. Even when these are identified, it becomes harder to find a reference machine on which to run programs as the machine ages. (In the 1980s the dominant reference machine was the VAX-11/780, which was called a 1-MIPS machine, for a reason we will discuss shortly, and is now hard to find in operation.) Moreover, should the older machine be run with the newest release of the compiler and operating system, or should the software be fixed so the reference machine does not become faster over time? There is also the temptation to generalize from a relative MIPS rating obtained using one benchmark to a general statement about relative performance, even though there can be wide variations in performance of two machines across a complete set of benchmarks.

The development of relative MIPS as a popular performance measurement demonstrates that benchmarking does not necessarily evolve in a logical fashion. In the 1970s, MIPS was being used as a way to compare the performance of IBM 360/370 implementations. Because the measure was used to compare identical architectures (and hence identical instruction counts), it was a valid metric. The notion of relative MIPS came along as a way to extend the easily understandable MIPS rating. In 1977, when the VAX-11/780 was ready to be announced, DEC ran small benchmarks that were also run on an IBM 370/158. IBM marketing referred to the 370/158 as a 1-MIPS computer and, since the programs ran at the same speed, DEC marketing called the VAX-11/780 a 1-MIPS computer.

The popularity of the VAX-11/780 made it a popular reference machine for relative MIPS, especially since relative MIPS for a 1-MIPS reference machine is easy to calculate. If a machine was five times faster than the VAX-11/780, its rating for that benchmark would be 5 relative MIPS. The 1-MIPS rating was widely believed for four years, until Joel Emer of DEC measured the VAX-11/780 under a timesharing load. Emer found that the actual VAX-11/780 MIPS rate was 0.5. Subsequent VAXs that run 3 million VAX instructions per second for some benchmarks were therefore called 6-MIPS machines because they run six times faster than the VAX-11/780.

The 1970s and 1980s marked the growth of the supercomputer industry, which was defined by high performance on floating-point-intensive programs. Average instruction time and MIPS were clearly inappropriate metrics for this industry—hence the invention of MFLOPS (millions of floating-point operations per second). Unfortunately, customers quickly forgot the program used for the rating, and marketing groups decided to start quoting peak MFLOPS in the supercomputer performance wars. The usage of MFLOPS and problems associated with it are discussed starting on page 99 in the exercises.

The Quest for an Average Program

As processors were becoming more sophisticated and relied on memory hierarchies (the topic of Chapter 7) and pipelining (the topic of Chapter 6), a single execution time for each instruction no longer existed; neither execution time nor MIPS, therefore, could be calculated from the instruction mix and the manual. While it might seem obvious today that the right thing to do would have been to develop a set of real applications that could be used as standard benchmarks, this was a difficult task until relatively recent times. Variations in operating systems and language standards made it hard to create large programs that could be moved from machine to machine simply by recompiling. Instead, the next step was benchmarking using synthetic programs. The Whetstone synthetic program was created by measuring scientific programs written in Algol 60 (see Curnow and Wichmann's [1976] description). This program was converted to Fortran and was widely used to characterize scientific program performance. Whetstone performance is typically quoted in Whetstones per second—the number of executions of one iteration of the Whetstone benchmark! Dhrystone was developed much more recently (see Weicker's [1984] description and methodology).

About the same time Whetstone was developed, the concept of *kernel benchmarks* gained popularity. Kernels are small, time-intensive pieces from real programs that are extracted and then used as benchmarks. This approach was developed primarily for benchmarking high-end machines, especially supercomputers. Livermore Loops and Linpack are the best-known examples. The Livermore Loops consist of a series of 21 small loop fragments. Linpack consists of a portion of a linear algebra subroutine package. Kernels are best used to isolate the performance of individual features of a machine and to explain the reasons for differences in the performance of real programs. Because scientific applications often use small pieces of code that execute for a long period of time, characterizing performance with kernels is most popular in this application class. Although kernels help illuminate performance, they often overstate the performance on real applications. For example, today's supercomputers often achieve a high percentage of their peak performance on such kernels. However, when executing real applications, the performance often is only a small fraction of the peak performance.

The Quest for a Simple Program

Another misstep on the way to developing better benchmarking methods was the use of toy programs as benchmarks. Such programs typically have between 10 and 100 lines of code and produce a result the user already knows before running the toy program. Programs like Sieve of Erastosthenes, Puzzle, and Quicksort were popular because they are small, easy to compile, and run on almost any computer. These programs became quite popular in the early 1980s, when universities were engaged in designing the early RISC machines. The small size of these programs made it easy to compile and run them on simulators. Unfortunately, we have to admit that we played a role in popularizing such benchmarks, by using them to compare performance and even collecting sets of such programs for distribution. Even more unfortunately, some people continue to use such benchmarks—much to our embarrassment! However, we can report that we have learned our lesson and we now understand that the best use of such programs is as beginning programming assignments.

Summarizing Can Be Tricky

Almost every issue that involves measuring and reporting performance has been controversial, including the question of how to summarize performance. The methods used have included the arithmetic mean of normalized performance, the harmonic mean of rates, the geometric mean of normalized execution time, and the total execution time. Several references listed at the end of this section discuss this question, including Smith's [1988] article, whose proposal is the approach used in section 2.5.

SPECulating about Performance

An important advance in performance evaluation was the formation of the System Performance Evaluation Cooperative (SPEC) group in 1988. SPEC comprises representatives of many computer companies—the founders being Apollo/Hewlett-Packard, DEC, MIPS, and Sun—who have agreed on a set of real programs and inputs that all will run. It is worth noting that SPEC couldn't have come into being before portable operating systems and the popularity of high-level languages. Now compilers, too, are accepted as a proper part of the performance of computer systems and must be measured in any evaluation.

History teaches us that while the SPEC effort may be useful with current computers, it will not meet the needs of the next generation without changing. In 1991, a throughput measure was added, based on running multiple versions of the benchmark. It is most useful for evaluating timeshared usage of a uniprocessor or a multiprocessor. Other system benchmarks that include OS-intensive and I/O-intensive activities have also been added. Another change, motivated in part by the kind of results shown in Figure 2.3, was the decision to drop matrix300 and to add more benchmarks. One result of the difficulty in finding benchmarks was that the initial version of the SPEC benchmarks (called SPEC89) contained six floating-point benchmarks but only four integer benchmarks. Calculating a single summary measurement using the geometric mean of execution times normalized to a VAX-11/780 meant that this measure favored machines with strong floating-point performance.

In 1992, a new benchmark set (called SPEC92) was introduced. It incorporated additional benchmarks, dropped matrix300, and provided separate means (SPECint and SPECfp) for integer and floating-point programs. In addition, the SPECbase measure, which disallows program-specific optimization flags, was added to provide users with a performance measurement that would more closely match what they might experience on their own programs. The SPECfp numbers show the largest increase versus the base SPECfp measurement, typically ranging from 15% to 30% higher.

In 1995, the benchmark set was once again updated, adding some new integer and floating-point benchmarks, as well as removing some benchmarks that suffered from flaws or had running times that had become too small given the factor of 20 or more performance improvement since the first SPEC release. SPEC95 also changed the base machine for normalization to a Sun SPARCstation 10/40, since operating versions of the original base machine were becoming difficult to find!

SPEC has also added additional benchmark suites beyond the original suites targeted at CPU performance. The SDM (Systems Development Multitasking) benchmark contains two benchmarks that are synthetic versions of development workloads (edits, compiles, executions, system commands). The SFS (System-level File Server) benchmark set is a synthetic workload for testing performance as a file server. Both these benchmark sets include significant I/O and operating systems components, unlike the CPU tests. The most recent addition to SPEC is the SPEChpc96 suite, two benchmarks aimed at testing performance on high-end scientific workloads. For the future, SPEC is exploring benchmarks for new functions, such as Web servers.

Creating and developing such benchmark sets has become difficult and time consuming. Although SPEC was initially created as a good faith effort by a group of companies, it became important to competitive marketing and sales efforts. The selection of benchmarks and the rules for running them are made by representatives of the companies that compete by advertising test results.

Conflicts between the companies' perspectives and those of consumers naturally arise. Perhaps in the future the decisions about such performance benchmarks should be made by, or at least include, a more representative group.

To Probe Further

Curnow, H. J., and B. A. Wichmann [1976]. "A synthetic benchmark," *The Computer J.* 19 (1):80.

Describes the first major synthetic benchmark, Whetstone, and how it was created.

Flemming, P. J., and J. J. Wallace [1986]. "How not to lie with statistics: The correct way to summarize benchmark results," *Comm. ACM* 29:3 (March) 218–21.

Describes some of the underlying principles in using different means to summarize performance results.

McMahon, F. M. [1986]. "The Livermore FORTRAN kernels: A computer test of numerical performance range," Tech. Rep. UCRL-55745, Lawrence Livermore National Laboratory, Univ. of California, Livermore (December).

Describes the Livermore Loops—a set of Fortran kernel benchmarks.

Smith, J. E. [1988]. "Characterizing computer performance with a single number," *Comm. ACM* 31:10 (October) 1202–06.

Describes the difficulties of summarizing performance with just one number and argues for total execution time as the only consistent measure.

SPEC [1989]. *SPEC Benchmark Suite Release 1.0*, SPEC, Santa Clara, CA, October 2.

Describes the SPEC benchmark suite. For up-to-date information, see the SPEC Web page via a link at www.mkp.com/books_catalog/cod/links.htm.

Weicker, R. P. [1984]. "Dhrystone: A synthetic systems programming benchmark," *Comm. ACM* 27:10 (October) 1013–30.

Describes the Dhrystone benchmark and its construction.

2.10 Key Terms

This chapter has introduced the basics of performance evaluation, measurement, and analysis. A variety of new terms were introduced, and they are listed below. These key terms are defined in the Glossary at the back of the book.

Amdahl's law
arithmetic mean
clock cycle or tick, clock tick,
    clock period, clock, cycle
clock cycles per instruction
    (CPI)
clock rate
CPU execution time
geometric mean

harmonic mean of rates
instruction mix
kernel benchmark
million floating-point
    operations per second
    (MFLOPS)
million instructions per
    second (MIPS)
response or execution time

speedup
system CPU time
System Performance
    Evaluation Cooperative
    (SPEC) benchmark
user CPU time
weighted arithmetic mean
workload

Exercises

2.1 [5] <§2.1> We wish to compare the performance of two different machines: M1 and M2. The following measurements have been made on these machines:

Program	Time on M1	Time on M2
1	10 seconds	5 seconds
2	3 seconds	4 seconds

Which machine is faster for each program and by how much?

2.2 [5] <§2.1> Consider the two machines and programs in Exercise 2.1. The following additional measurements were made:

Program	Instructions executed on M1	Instructions executed on M2
1	200×10^6	160×10^6

Find the instruction execution rate (instructions per second) for each machine when running program 1.

2.3 [5] <§§2.2–2.3> If the clock rates of machines M1 and M2 in Exercise 2.1 are 200 MHz and 300 MHz, respectively, find the clock cycles per instruction (CPI) for program 1 on both machines using the data in Exercises 2.1 and 2.2.

2.4 [5] <§§2.2–2.3> {Ex. 2.3} Assuming the CPI for program 2 on each machine in Exercise 2.1 is the same as the CPI for program 1 found in Exercise 2.3, find the instruction count for program 2 running on each machine using the execution times from Exercise 2.1.

2.5 [5] <§2.1> Suppose that M1 in Exercise 2.1 costs $10,000 and M2 costs $15,000. If you needed to run program 1 a large number of times (i.e., if you were concerned with throughput instead of response time), which machine would you buy in large quantities? Why?

2.6 [10] <§2.1> Suppose you had many more machines to consider besides M1 and M2 described in Exercises 2.1 and 2.5 (each with a cost and an execution time for program 1, which you need to run a large number of times). Could you use the cost divided by the execution time as a metric to help you in your purchasing decision? How about the cost multiplied by the execution time? If either of the two formulas cannot be used, present a simple example that demonstrates why not.

2.7 [5] <§2.1> {Ex. 2.6} If we wanted our metric (call it cost-effectiveness) to be similar to performance in that a larger number should indicate a better cost-effectiveness, what formula would we use?

2.8 [5] <§2.1> Another user is concerned with the throughput of the machine in Exercise 2.1, as measured with an equal workload of programs 1 and 2. Which machine has better performance for this workload? By how much? Which machine is more cost-effective for this workload? By how much?

2.9 [10] <§2.1> Yet another user has the following requirements for the machines discussed in Exercise 2.1: program 1 must be executed 200 times each hour. Any remaining time can be used for running program 2. If the machine has enough performance to execute program 1 the required number of times per hour, performance is measured by the throughput for program 2. Which machine is faster for this workload? Which machine is more cost-effective?

2.10 [5] <§§2.2–2.3> Consider two different implementations, M1 and M2, of the same instruction set. There are four classes of instructions (A, B, C, and D) in the instruction set.

M1 has a clock rate of 500 MHz. The average number of cycles for each instruction class on M1 is as follows:

Class	CPI for this class
A	1
B	2
C	3
D	4

M2 has a clock rate of 750 MHz. The average number of cycles for each instruction class on M2 is as follows:

Class	CPI for this class
A	2
B	2
C	4
D	4

Assume that peak performance is defined as the fastest rate that a machine can execute an instruction sequence chosen to maximize that rate. What are the peak performances of M1 and M2 expressed as instructions per second?

2.11 [10] <§§2.2–2.3> If the number of instructions executed in a certain program is divided equally among the classes of instructions in Exercise 2.10, how much faster is M2 than M1?

2.12 [5] <§§2.2–2.3> {Ex. 2.11} Assuming the CPI values from Exercise 2.10 and the instruction distribution from Exercise 2.11, at what clock rate would M1 have the same performance as the 750-MHz version of M2?

2.13 [10] <§§2.2–2.3> Consider two different implementations, M1 and M2, of the same instruction set. There are three classes of instructions (A, B, and C) in the instruction set. M1 has a clock rate of 400 MHz, and M2 has a clock rate of 200 MHz. The average number of cycles for each instruction class on M1 and M2 is given in the following table:

Class	CPI on M1	CPI on M2	C1 usage	C2 usage	Third-party usage
A	4	2	30%	30%	50%
B	6	4	50%	20%	30%
C	8	3	20%	50%	20%

The table also contains a summary of how three different compilers use the instruction set. C1 is a compiler produced by the makers of M1, C2 is a compiler produced by the makers of M2, and the other compiler is a third-party product. Assume that each compiler uses the same number of instructions for a given program but that the instruction mix is as described in the table. Using C1 on both M1 and M2, how much faster can the makers of M1 claim that M1 is compared with M2? Using C2 on both M2 and M1, how much faster can the makers of M2 claim that M2 is compared with M1? If you purchase M1, which compiler would you use? If you purchase M2, which compiler would you use? Which machine would you purchase if we assume that all other criteria are identical, including costs?

2.14 [5] <§§2.2, 2.3, 2.7> For the following set of variables, identify all of the subsets that can be used to calculate execution time. Each subset should be minimal; that is, it should not contain any variable that is not needed.

{CPI, clock rate, cycle time, MIPS, number of instructions in program, number of cycles in program}

2.15 [10] <§§2.2, 2.3, 2.7> We are interested in two implementations of a machine, one with and one without special floating-point hardware.

Consider a program, P, with the following mix of operations:

floating-point multiply	10%
floating-point add	15%
floating-point divide	5%
integer instructions	70%

Machine MFP (Machine with Floating Point) has floating-point hardware and can therefore implement the floating-point operations directly. It requires the following number of clock cycles for each instruction class:

floating-point multiply	6
floating-point add	4
floating-point divide	20
integer instructions	2

Machine MNFP (Machine with No Floating Point) has no floating-point hardware and so must emulate the floating-point operations using integer instructions. The integer instructions all take 2 clock cycles. The number of integer instructions needed to implement each of the floating-point operations is as follows:

floating-point multiply	30
floating-point add	20
floating-point divide	50

Both machines have a clock rate of 1000 MHz. Find the native MIPS ratings for both machines.

2.16 [10] <§§2.2, 2.3, 2.7> If the machine MFP in Exercise 2.15 needs 300 million instructions for this program, how many integer instructions does the machine MNFP require for the same program?

2.17 [5] <§§2.2, 2.3, 2.7> {Ex. 2.16} Assuming the instruction counts from Exercise 2.16, what is the execution time (in seconds) for the program in Exercise 2.15 run on MFP and MNFP?

2.18 [10] <§§2.2–2.3> You are the lead designer of a new processor. The processor design and compiler are complete, and now you must decide whether to produce the current design as it stands or spend additional time to improve it.

You discuss this problem with your hardware engineering team and arrive at the following options:

a. *Leave the design as it stands.* Call this base machine *Mbase*. It has a clock rate of 500 MHz, and the following measurements have been made using a simulator:

Instruction class	CPI	Frequency
A	2	40%
B	3	25%
C	3	25%
D	5	10%

b. *Optimize the hardware.* The hardware team claims that it can improve the processor design to give it a clock rate of 600 MHz. Call this machine *Mopt*. The following measurements were made using a simulator for Mopt:

Instruction class	CPI	Frequency
A	2	40%
B	2	25%
C	3	25%
D	4	10%

What is the CPI for each machine?

2.19 [5] <§§2.2, 2.3, 2.7> {Ex. 2.18} What are the native MIPS ratings for Mbase and Mopt in Exercise 2.18?

2.20 [10] <§§2.2–2.3> {Ex. 2.18} How much faster is Mopt than Mbase in Exercise 2.18?

2.21 [5] <§§2.2–2.3> The compiler team has heard about the discussion to enhance the machine discussed in Exercises 2.18 through 2.20. The compiler team proposes to improve the compiler for the machine to further enhance performance. Call this combination of the improved compiler and the base machine *Mcomp*. The instruction improvements from this enhanced compiler have been estimated as follows:

Instruction class	Percentage of instructions executed vs. base machine
A	90%
B	90%
C	85%
D	95%

For example, if the base machine executed 500 class A instructions, Mcomp would execute $0.9 \times 500 = 450$ class A instructions for the same program. What is the CPI for Mcomp?

2.22 [5] <§§ 2.2–2.3> {Ex. 2.18, 2.21} Using the data of Exercise 2.18, how much faster is Mcomp than Mbase?

2.23 [10] <§§2.2–2.3> {Ex. 2.18, 2.21, 2.22} The compiler group points out that it is possible to implement both the hardware improvements of Exercise 2.18 and the compiler enhancements described in Exercise 2.21. If *both* the hardware and compiler improvements are implemented, yielding machine *Mboth*, how much faster is Mboth than Mbase?

2.24 [10] <§§2.2–2.3> {Ex. 2.18, 2.21, 2.22, 2.23} You must decide whether to incorporate the hardware enhancements suggested in Exercise 2.18 or the compiler enhancements of Exercise 2.21 (or both) to the base machine described in Exercise 2.18. You estimate that the following time would be required to implement the optimizations described in Exercises 2.18, 2.21, and 2.23:

Optimization	Time to implement	Machine name
Hardware	6 months	Mopt
Compiler	6 months	Mcomp
Both	8 months	Mboth

Recall from Chapter 1 that CPU performance improves by approximately 50% per year, or about 3.4% per month. Assuming that the base machine has performance equal to that of its competitors, which optimizations (if any) would you choose to implement?

2.25 [10] <§§2.4, 2.6> Look at the current list of SPEC programs in Figure 2.6 on page 72. Does it include applications that match the ways you typically use your computer? What classes of programs are irrelevant or missing? Why do you think they were or were not included in SPEC? What would have to be done to include/exclude such programs in the next SPEC release?

2.26 [5] <§2.5> The table below shows the number of floating-point operations executed in two different programs and the runtime for those programs on three different machines:

Program	Floating-point operations	Execution time in seconds		
		Computer A	Computer B	Computer C
Program 1	10,000,000	1	10	20
Program 2	100,000,000	1000	100	20

Which machine is fastest according to total execution time? How much faster is it than the other two machines?

2.27 [5] <§§2.5, 2.7> You wonder how the performance of the three machines in Exercise 2.26 would compare using other means to normalize performance. Which machine is fastest by the geometric mean?

2.28 [15] <§§2.5, 2.7> {Ex. 2.27} Find a workload for the two programs of Exercise 2.26 that will produce the same performance summary using total execution time of the workload as the geometric mean of performance, as computed in Exercise 2.27. Give the workload as a percentage of executions of each program for the pairs of machines: A and B, B and C, and A and C.

2.29 [15] <§§2.5, 2.7> One user has told you that the two programs in Exercise 2.26 constitute the bulk of his workload, but he does not run them equally. The user wants to determine how the three machines compare when the workload consists of different mixes of these two programs. (You know you can use the arithmetic mean to find the relative performance.)

Suppose the total number of FLOPS executed in the workload is equally divided among the two programs. That is, program 1 is run 10 times as often as program 2. Find which machine is fastest for this workload and by how much. How does this compare with the total execution time for a workload with equal numbers of program executions?

2.30 [15] <§§2.5, 2.7> An alternative weighting to that of Exercise 2.29 is to assume that equal amounts of time will be spent running each program on some machine. Which machine is fastest using the data of Exercise 2.26 and assuming a weighting that generates equal execution time for each benchmark on machine A? Which machine is fastest if we assume a weighting that generates equal execution time for each benchmark on machine B? How do these results compare with the unweighted performance summaries?

2.31 [5] <§2.7> Assume that multiply instructions take 12 cycles and account for 10% of the instructions in a typical program and that the other 90% of the instructions require an average of 4 cycles for each instruction. What percentage of time does the CPU spend doing multiplication?

2.32 [5] <§2.7> {Ex. 2.31} Your hardware engineering team has indicated that it would be possible to reduce the number of cycles required for multiplication to 6 in Exercise 2.31, but this will require a 20% increase in the cycle time. Nothing else will be affected. Should they proceed with the modification?

2.33 [10] <§§2.1–2.7> Consider the following hypothetical news release:

"The company will unveil the industry's first 800-MHz version of the chip, which offers a 20% performance boost over the company's former speed champ, which runs at 666 MHz. The new chip can be plugged into system boards for the older original chip (which ran at 400 MHz) to provide a 70% performance boost."

Comment on the definition (or definitions) of performance that you believe the company used. Do you think the news release is misleading?

2.34 [3 hours] <§2.5> Pick two computers, A and B, and run the Dhrystone benchmark and some substantial C program, such as the C compiler, calling this program P. Try running the two programs using no optimization and maximum optimization. Then calculate the following performance ratios:

a. Unoptimized Dhrystone on machine A versus unoptimized Dhrystone on machine B.

b. Unoptimized P on A versus unoptimized P on B.

c. Optimized Dhrystone on A versus optimized Dhrystone on B.

d. Optimized P on A versus optimized P on B.

e. Unoptimized Dhrystone versus optimized Dhrystone on machine A.

f. Unoptimized P versus optimized P on A.

g. Unoptimized Dhrystone versus optimized Dhrystone on B.

h. Unoptimized P versus optimized P on B.

We want to explore whether Dhrystone accurately predicts the performance of other C programs. If Dhrystone does predict performance, then the following equations should be true about the ratios:

(a) = (b) and (c) = (d)

If Dhrystone accurately predicts the value of compiler optimizations for real programs, then

(e) = (f) and (g) = (h)

Determine which of the above relationships hold. For the situations where the relationships are not close, try to find the explanation. Do features of the machines, the compiler optimizations, or the differences between P and Dhrystone explain the answer?

2.35 [3 hours] <§2.5> Perform the same experiment as in Exercise 2.34, replacing Dhrystone with Whetstone and choosing a floating-point program written in Fortran to replace P.

2.36 [4 hours] <§§2.4, 2.7> Devise a program in C or Pascal that determines the peak MIPS rating for a computer. Run it on two machines to calculate the peak MIPS. Now run a real C or Pascal program such as a compiler on the two machines. How well does peak MIPS predict performance of the real program?

2.37 [indefinite] <§§2.1–2.7> Collect a set of articles that you believe contain incorrect analyses of performance or use misleading performance metrics to try to persuade readers. For example, an article in the *New York Times* (April 20, 1994, p. D1) described a video game player "that will surpass the computing power of even the most powerful personal computers" and presented the following chart to support the argument that "video game machines may be the supercomputers of tomorrow":

Machine	Approximate number of instructions per second	Price
1975 IBM Mainframe	10,000,000	$10,000,000
1976 Cray-1	160,000,000	$20,000,000
1979 Digital VAX	1,000,000	$200,000
1981 IBM PC	250,000	$3,000
1984 Sun 2	1,000,000	$10,000
1994 Pentium-chip PC	66,000,000	$3,000
1995 Sony PCX video game	500,000,000	$500
1995 Microunity set-top	1,000,000,000	$500

The article never discussed how the nature of the instructions should impact the definition of "powerful." For each article you collect, describe why you think it is misleading or incorrect. Good places to look for material include the business or technology sections of newspapers, magazines (both articles and ads), and the Internet (newsgroups and the Web).

In More Depth

MFLOPS as a Performance Metric

Another popular alternative to execution time is *million floating-point operations per second*, abbreviated *megaFLOPS* or *MFLOPS* but always pronounced "megaflops." The formula for MFLOPS is simply the definition of the acronym:

$$\text{MFLOPS} = \frac{\text{Number of floating-point operations in a program}}{\text{Execution time} \times 10^6}$$

A *floating-point operation* is an addition, subtraction, multiplication, or division operation applied to a number in a single or double precision floating-point representation. Such data items are heavily used in scientific calculations and are specified in programming languages using key words like *float*, *real*, *double*, or *double precision*.

Clearly, a MFLOPS rating is dependent on the program. Different programs require the execution of different numbers of floating-point operations (see Exercise 2.38 for an example). Since MFLOPS were intended to measure floating-point performance, they are not applicable outside that range. Compilers, as an extreme example, have a MFLOPS rating near 0 no matter how fast the machine is, because compilers rarely use floating-point arithmetic.

Because it is based on operations in the program rather than on instructions, MFLOPS has a stronger claim than MIPS to being a fair comparison between different machines. The key to this claim is that the same program running on different computers may execute a different number of instructions but will always execute the same number of floating-point operations. Unfortunately, MFLOPS is not dependable because the set of floating-point operations is not consistent across machines, and the number of actual floating-point operations performed may vary. For example, the Cray-2 has no divide instruction, while the Motorola 68882 has divide, square root, sine, and cosine. Thus several floating-point operations are needed on the Cray-2 to perform a floating-point division, whereas on the Motorola 68882, a call to the sine routine, which would require performing several floating-point operations on most machines, would require only one operation.

Another potential problem is that the MFLOPS rating changes according not only to the mixture of integer and floating-point operations but to the mixture of fast and slow floating-point operations. For example, a program with 100% floating-point adds will have a higher rating than a program with 100% floating-point divides. The solution to both these problems is to define a method of counting the number of floating-point operations in a high-level language program. This counting process can also weight the operations, giving more complex operations larger weights, allowing a machine to achieve a high MFLOPS rating even if the program contains many floating-point divides. These MFLOPS might be called *normalized MFLOPS*. Of course, because of the counting and weighting, these normalized MFLOPS may be very different from the actual rate at which a machine executes floating-point operations.

Like any other performance measure, the MFLOPS rating for a single program cannot be generalized to establish a single performance metric for a computer. The use of the same term to refer to everything from peak performance (the maximum MFLOPS rate possible for any code segment), to the MFLOPS rate for one benchmark, to a normalized MFLOPS rating, only increases the confusion. The worst of these variants of MFLOPS, peak MFLOPS, is unrelated to actual performance; the best variant is redundant with execution time, our principal measure of performance. Yet, unlike execution time, it is tempting to characterize a machine with a single MFLOPS rating without naming the program or input.

2.38 [5] <§2.2> Find the MFLOPS ratings for each of the two programs on each machine in Exercise 2.26, assuming that each floating-point operation counts as 1 FLOP. How do the MFLOPS ratings for programs 1 and 2 compare for each machine? Does the example illustrate one of the problems discussed above?

2.39 [15] <§2.5> If performance is expressed as a rate, such as MFLOPS, then a higher rating and a higher average indicate better performance. When performance is expressed as a rate, the average that tracks total execution time is the *harmonic mean* (HM):

$$HM = \frac{n}{\sum\limits_{i=1}^{n} \frac{1}{Rate_i}}$$

Each Rate$_i$ is 1/Time$_i$, where Time$_i$ is the execution time for the ith of n programs in the workload. Prove that the harmonic mean of a set of rates tracks execution time by showing that it is the inverse of the arithmetic mean of the corresponding execution times.

2.40 [4 hours] <§2.4> Devise a program in C or Fortran that determines the peak MFLOPS rating for a computer. Run it on two machines to calculate the peak MFLOPS. Now run a real floating-point program on both machines. How well does peak MFLOPS predict performance of the real floating-point program?

In More Depth

Amdahl's Law

Amdahl's law is sometimes given in another form that yields the speedup. *Speedup* is the measure of how a machine performs after some enhancement relative to how it performed previously. Thus, if some feature yields a speedup ratio of 2, performance with the enhancement is twice what it was before the enhancement. Hence, we can write

$$\text{Speedup} = \frac{\text{Performance after improvement}}{\text{Performance before improvement}}$$

$$= \frac{\text{Execution time before improvement}}{\text{Execution time after improvement}}$$

The earlier version of Amdahl's law was given as

Execution time after improvement

$$= \left(\frac{\text{Execution time affected by improvement}}{\text{Amount of improvement}} + \text{Execution time unaffected} \right)$$

2.41 [5] <§2.7> Suppose we enhance a machine to make all floating-point instructions run five times faster. Let's look at how speedup behaves when we incorporate the faster floating-point hardware. If the execution time of some benchmark before the floating-point enhancement is 10 seconds, what will the speedup be if half of the 10 seconds is spent executing floating-point instructions?

2.42 [10] <§2.7> We are looking for a benchmark to show off the new floating-point unit described in Exercise 2.41, and we want the overall benchmark to show a speedup of 3. One benchmark we are considering runs for 100 seconds with the old floating-point hardware. How much of the initial execution time would floating-point instructions have to account for to show an overall speedup of 3 on this benchmark?

2.43 [10] <§2.7> Assuming that we enhance the floating-point unit as described in Exercise 2.41, plot the speedup obtained, versus the fraction of time in the original program spent doing floating-point operations, on a graph of the following form:

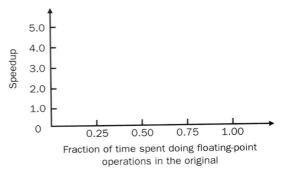

2.44 [5] <§2.7> You are going to enhance a machine, and there are two possible improvements: either make multiply instructions run four times faster than before, or make memory access instructions run two times faster than before. You repeatedly run a program that takes 100 seconds to execute. Of this time, 20% is used for multiplication, 50% for memory access instructions, and 30% for other tasks. What will the speedup be if you improve only multiplication? What will the speedup be if you improve only memory access? What will the speedup be if both improvements are made?

2.45 [5] <§2.7> {Ex. 2.44} You are going to change the program described in Exercise 2.44 so that the percentages are not 20%, 50%, and 30% anymore. Assuming that none of the new percentages is 0, what sort of program would result in a tie (with regard to speedup) between the two individual improvements? Provide both a formula and some examples.

2.46 [20] <§2.7> Amdahl's law is often written in terms of overall speedup as a function of two variables: the size of the enhancement (or amount of improvement) and the fraction of the original execution time that the enhanced feature is being used. Derive this form of the equation from the two equations above.

Instructions: Language of the Machine

I speak Spanish to God,
Italian to women,
French to men,
and German to my horse.

Charles V, King of France
1337–1380

The Five Classic Components of a Computer

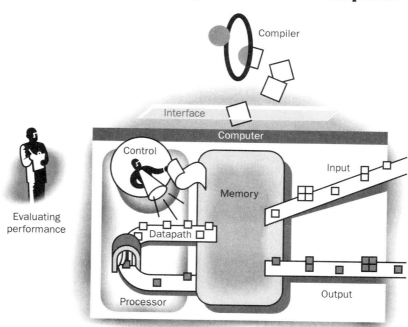

3.1   Introduction

To command a computer's hardware, you must speak its language. The words of a machine's language are called *instructions*, and its vocabulary is called an *instruction set*. In this chapter you will see the instruction set of a real computer, both in the form written by humans and in the form read by the machine. Starting from a notation that looks like a restricted programming language, we refine it step-by-step until you see the real language of a real computer.

You might think that the languages of machines would be as diverse as those of humans, but in reality machine languages are quite similar, more like regional dialects than like independent languages. Hence once you learn one, it is easy to pick up others. This similarity occurs because all computers are constructed from hardware technologies based on similar underlying principles and because there are a few basic operations that all machines must provide. Moreover, computer designers have a common goal: to find a language that makes it easy to build the hardware and the compiler while maximizing performance and minimizing cost. This goal is time-honored; the following quote was written before you could buy a computer, and it is as true today as it was in 1947.

> *It is easy to see by formal-logical methods that there exist certain [instruction sets] that are in abstract adequate to control and cause the execution of any sequence of operations. . . . The really decisive considerations from the present point of view, in selecting an [instruction set], are more of a practical nature: simplicity of the equipment demanded by the [instruction set], and the clarity of its application to the actually important problems together with the speed of its handling of those problems.*

> Burks, Goldstine, and von Neumann, 1947

The "simplicity of the equipment" is as valuable a consideration for the machines of the 2000s as it was for those of the 1950s. The goal of this chapter is to teach an instruction set that follows this advice, showing both how it is represented in the hardware and the relationship between high-level programming languages and this more primitive one. We are using the C programming language. (If you are familiar with Pascal, you may wish to refer to Web Extension III, available at *www.mkp.com/cod2e.htm,* for a short comparison of C with Pascal.)

By learning how instructions are represented, you will also discover the secret of computing: the stored-program concept. And you will exercise your "foreign language" skills by writing programs in the language of the machine and running them on the simulator that comes with this book. We conclude with a look at the historical evolution of instruction sets and an overview of other machine dialects.

The chosen instruction set comes from MIPS, used by NEC, Nintendo, Silicon Graphics, and Sony, among others, and is typical of instruction sets designed since the early 1980s. We reveal the MIPS instruction set a piece at a time, giving the rationale along with the machine structures. This step-by-step tutorial weaves the components with their explanations, making assembly language more palatable. To keep the overall picture in mind, each section ends with a figure summarizing the MIPS instruction set revealed thus far, highlighting the portions presented in that section.

3.2 Operations of the Computer Hardware

There must certainly be instructions for performing the fundamental arithmetic operations.

Burks, Goldstine, and von Neumann, 1947

Every computer must be able to perform arithmetic. The MIPS assembly language notation

```
add a, b, c
```

instructs a computer to add the two variables b and c and to put their sum in a.

This notation is rigid in that each MIPS arithmetic instruction performs only one operation and must always have exactly three variables. For example, suppose we want to place the sum of variables b, c, d, and e into variable a. (In this section we are being deliberately vague about what a "variable" is; in the next section we'll give a more detailed and realistic picture.)

The following sequence of instructions adds the variables:

```
add a, b, c  # The sum of b and c is placed in a.
add a, a, d  # The sum of b, c, and d is now in a.
add a, a, e  # The sum of b, c, d, and e is now in a.
```

Thus it takes three instructions to take the sum of four variables.

The words to the right of the sharp symbol (#) on each line above are *comments* for the human reader, and they are ignored by the computer. Note that unlike other programming languages, each line of this language can contain at most one instruction. Another difference is that comments always terminate at the end of a line.

The natural number of operands for an operation like addition is three: the two numbers being added together and a place to put the sum. Requiring every instruction to have exactly three operands, no more and no less, conforms to the philosophy of keeping the hardware simple: hardware for a variable number of operands is more complicated than hardware for a fixed number. This situation illustrates the first of four underlying principles of hardware design:

Design Principle 1: Simplicity favors regularity.

We can now show, in the two examples that follow, the relationship of programs written in higher-level programming languages to programs in this more primitive notation. Figure 3.1 summarizes the portions of MIPS assembly language described in this section.

Compiling Two C Assignment Statements into MIPS

Example

This segment of a C program contains the five variables a, b, c, d, and e:

```
a = b + c;
d = a - e;
```

The translation from C to MIPS assembly language instructions is performed by the *compiler*. Show the MIPS code produced by a C compiler.

Answer

A MIPS instruction operates on two source operands and places the result in one destination operand. Hence the two simple C statements above compile directly into these two MIPS assembly language instructions:

```
add a, b, c
sub d, a, e
```

MIPS assembly language

Category	Instruction	Example	Meaning	Comments
Arithmetic	add	add a,b,c	a = b + c	Always three operands
	subtract	sub a,b,c	a = b - c	Always three operands

FIGURE 3.1   MIPS architecture revealed in section 3.2. The real machine operands will be unveiled in the next section. Highlighted portions in such summaries show MIPS assembly language structures introduced in this section; for this first figure, all is new.

Compiling a Complex C Assignment into MIPS

Example

A somewhat complex C statement contains the five variables f, g, h, i, and j:

```
f = (g + h) - (i + j);
```

What would a C compiler produce?

Answer

The compiler must break this C statement into several assembly instructions since only one operation is performed per MIPS instruction. The first MIPS instruction calculates the sum of g and h. We must place the result somewhere, so the compiler creates a temporary variable, called t0:

```
add t0,g,h  # temporary variable t0 contains g + h
```

Although the next C operation is subtract, we need to calculate the sum of i and j before we can subtract. Thus the second instruction places the sum i and j in another temporary variable created by the compiler, called t1:

```
add t1,i,j  # temporary variable t1 contains i + j
```

Finally, the subtract instruction subtracts the second sum from the first and places the result in the variable f, completing the compiled code:

```
sub f,t0,t1 # f gets t0 - t1, which is (g + h)-(i + j)
```

These instructions are symbolic representations of what the MIPS processor actually understands. In the next few sections we will evolve this symbolic representation into the real language of MIPS, with each step making the symbolic representation more concrete.

3.3   Operands of the Computer Hardware

Unlike programs in high-level languages, the operands of arithmetic instructions cannot be any variables; they must be from a limited number of special locations called *registers*. Registers are the bricks of computer construction, for registers are primitives used in hardware design that are also visible to the programmer when the computer is completed. The size of a register in the MIPS architecture is 32 bits; groups of 32 bits occur so frequently that they are given the name *word* in the MIPS architecture.

One major difference between the variables of a programming language and registers is the limited number of registers, typically 32 on current computers. MIPS has 32 registers. (See section 3.15 for the history of the number of registers.) Thus, continuing in our stepwise evolution of the symbolic representation of the MIPS language, in this section we have added the restriction that the three operands of MIPS arithmetic instructions must each be chosen from one of the 32 32-bit registers.

The reason for the limit to 32 registers may be found in the second of our four underlying design principles of hardware technology:

Design Principle 2: Smaller is faster.

A very large number of registers would increase the clock cycle time simply because it takes electronic signals longer when they must travel farther.

Guidelines such as "smaller is faster" are not absolutes; 31 registers may not be faster than 32. Yet the truth behind such observations causes computer designers to take them seriously. In this case, the designer must balance the craving of programs for more registers with the designer's desire to keep the clock cycle fast.

Chapters 5 and 6 show the central role that registers play in hardware construction; as we shall see in this chapter, effective use of registers is key to program performance.

Although we could simply write instructions using numbers for registers, from 0 to 31, the MIPS convention is to use two character names following a dollar sign to represent a register. Section 3.6 will explain the reasons behind these names. For now we will use $s0, $s1, ... for registers that correspond to variables in C programs and $t0, $t1, ... for temporary registers needed to compile the program into MIPS instructions.

Compiling a C Assignment Using Registers

Example   It is the compiler's job to associate program variables with registers. Take, for instance, the C assignment statement from our earlier example:

```
f = (g + h) - (i + j);
```

The variables f, g, h, i, and j can be assigned to the registers $s0, $s1, $s2, $s3, and $s4, respectively. What is the compiled MIPS assembly code?

Answer   The compiled program is very similar to the prior example, except we replace the variables with the registers mentioned above plus two temporary registers, $t0 and $t1, which correspond to the temporary variables above:

```
add $t0,$s1,$s2  # register $t0 contains g + h
add $t1,$s3,$s4  # register $t1 contains i + j
sub $s0,$t0,$t1  # f gets $t0 - $t1, which is (g + h)-(i + j)
```

Programming languages have simple variables that contain single data elements as in these examples, but they also have more complex data structures such as arrays. These complex data structures can contain many more data elements than there are registers in a machine. How can a computer represent and access such large structures?

Recall the five components of a computer introduced in Chapter 1 and depicted on page 105. The processor can keep only a small amount of data in registers, but computer memory contains millions of data elements. Hence data structures, such as arrays, are kept in memory.

As explained above, arithmetic operations occur only on registers in MIPS instructions; thus MIPS must include instructions that transfer data between memory and registers. Such instructions are called *data transfer* instructions. To access a word in memory, the instruction must supply the memory *address*. Memory is just a large, single-dimensional array, with the address acting as the index to that array, starting at 0. For example, in Figure 3.2, the address of the third data element is 2, and the value of Memory[2] is 10.

The data transfer instruction that moves data from memory to a register is traditionally called *load*. The format of the load instruction is the name of the operation followed by the register to be loaded, then a constant and register used to access memory. The memory address is formed by the sum of the constant portion of the instruction and the contents of the second register. The actual MIPS name for this instruction is `lw`, standing for *load word*.

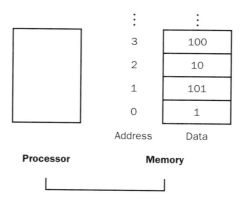

FIGURE 3.2 Memory addresses and contents of memory at those locations. This is a simplification of the MIPS addressing; Figure 3.3 shows MIPS addressing for sequential words in memory.

Compiling an Assignment When an Operand Is in Memory

Example

Let's assume that A is an array of 100 words and that the compiler has associated the variables g and h with the registers $s1 and $s2 as before. Let's also assume that the starting address, or *base address*, of the array is in $s3. Translate this C assignment statement:

```
g = h + A[8];
```

Answer

Although there is a single operation in this C assignment statement, one of the operands is in memory, so we must first transfer A[8] to a register. The address of this array element is the sum of the base of the array A, found in register $s3, plus the number to select element 8. The data should be placed in a temporary register for use in the next instruction. Based on Figure 3.2, the first compiled instruction is

```
lw   $t0,8($s3) # Temporary reg $t0 gets A[8]
```

(On the next page we'll make a slight adjustment to this instruction, but we'll use this simplified version for now.) The following instruction can operate on the value in $t0 (which equals A[8]) since it is in a register. The instruction must add h ($s2) to A[8] ($t0) and put the sum in the register corresponding to g ($s1):

```
add   $s1,$s2,$t0 # g = h + A[8]
```

The constant in a data transfer instruction is called the *offset*, and the register added to form the address is called the *base register*.

Hardware Software Interface

In addition to associating variables with registers, the compiler allocates data structures like arrays and structures to locations in memory. The compiler can then place the proper starting address into the data transfer instructions.

Since 8-bit *bytes* are useful in many programs, most architectures address individual bytes. Therefore the address of a word matches the address of one of the 4 bytes within the word. Hence, addresses of sequential words differ by 4. For example, Figure 3.3 shows the actual MIPS addresses for Figure 3.2; the byte address of the third word is 8.

Words must always start at addresses that are multiples of 4 in MIPS. This requirement is called an *alignment restriction*, and many architectures have it. (Chapter 5 suggests why alignment leads to faster data transfers.)

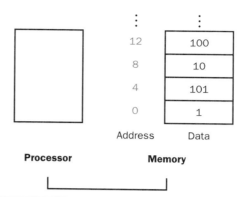

FIGURE 3.3 Actual MIPS memory addresses and contents of memory for those words. The changed addresses are highlighted to contrast with Figure 3.2. Since MIPS addresses each byte, word addresses are multiples of four (there are four bytes in a word).

Machines with byte addresses are split into those that use the address of the leftmost or "big end" byte as the word address versus those that use the rightmost or "little end" byte. MIPS is in the *Big Endian* camp. (Appendix A, page A-48, shows the two options to number bytes in a word.)

Byte addressing also affects the array index. To get the proper byte address in the code above, **the offset to be added to the base register** $s3 **must be** 4×8, **or 32**, so that the load address will select A[8] and not A[8/4].

The instruction complementary to load is traditionally called *store*; it transfers data from a register to memory. The format of a store is similar to that of a load: the name of the operation, followed by the register to be stored, then offset to select the array element, and finally the base register. Once again, the MIPS address is specified in part by a constant and in part by the contents of a register. The actual MIPS name is sw, standing for *store word*.

Compiling Using Load and Store

Example

Assume variable h is associated with register $s2 and the base address of the array A is in $s3. What is the MIPS assembly code for the C assignment statement below?

```
A[12] = h + A[8];
```

Answer

Although there is a single operation in the C statement, now two of the operands are in memory, so we need even more MIPS instructions. The first two instructions are the same as the prior example, except this time we use the proper offset for byte addressing in the load word instruction to select A[8], and the add instruction places the sum in $t0:

```
lw   $t0,32($s3)    # Temporary reg $t0 gets A[8]
add  $t0,$s2,$t0    # Temporary reg $t0 gets h + A[8]
```

The final instruction stores the sum into A[12], using 48 as the offset and register $s3 as the base register.

```
sw   $t0,48($s3)    # Stores h + A[8] back into A[12]
```

Arrays are often accessed with variables instead of constants, so that the array element being selected can change while the program is running.

Compiling Using a Variable Array Index

Example

Here is an example of an array with a variable index:

```
g = h + A[i];
```

Assume A is an array of 100 elements whose base is in register $s3 and that the compiler associates the variables g, h, and i with the registers $s1, $s2, and $s4. What is the MIPS assembly code corresponding to this C segment?

Answer

Before we can load A[i] into a temporary register, we need to have its address. Before we can add i to the base of array A to form the address, we must multiply the index i by 4 due to the byte addressing problem. We will see a multiply instruction in the next chapter; for now we will get the effect of multiplying i by 4 by first adding i to itself ($i + i = 2i$) and then adding that sum to itself ($2i + 2i = 4i$):

```
add $t1,$s4,$s4    # Temp reg $t1 = 2 * i
add $t1,$t1,$t1    # Temp reg $t1 = 4 * i
```

To get the address of A[i], we need to add $t1 and the base of A in $s3:

```
add $t1,$t1,$s3    # $t1 = address of A[i] (4 * i + $s3)
```

Now we can use that address to load A[i] into a temporary register:

```
lw   $t0,0($t1)  # Temporary reg $t0 = A[i]
```

The final instruction adds A[i] and h, and places the sum in g:

```
add  $s1,$s2,$t0 # g = h + A[i]
```

Hardware Software Interface

Many programs have more variables than machines have registers. Consequently, the compiler tries to keep the most frequently used variables in registers and places the rest in memory, using loads and stores to move variables between registers and memory. The process of putting less commonly used variables (or those needed later) into memory is called *spilling* registers.

The hardware principle relating size and speed suggests that memory must be slower than registers since registers are smaller. This is indeed the case; data accesses are faster if data is kept in registers instead of memory.

Moreover, data is more useful when in a register. A MIPS arithmetic instruction can read two registers, operate on them, and write the result. A MIPS data transfer instruction only reads one operand or writes one operand, without operating on it.

Thus MIPS registers take both less time to access *and* have higher throughput than memory—a rare combination—making data in registers both faster to access and simpler to use. To achieve highest performance, MIPS compilers must use registers efficiently.

Figure 3.4 summarizes the portions of the symbolic representation of the MIPS instruction set described in this section. Load word and store word are the instructions that transfer words between memory and registers in the MIPS architecture. Other brands of computers use instructions in addition to load and store to transfer data. An architecture with such alternatives is the Intel 80x86, described in section 3.12.

Elaboration: The offset plus base register addressing is an excellent match to structures as well, since the register can point to the beginning of the structure and the offset can select the desired element. We'll see such an example in section 3.10.

The register in the data transfer instructions was originally invented to hold an index of an array with the offset used for the starting address of an array. Thus the base register is also called the *index register*. Today's memories are much larger and the software model of data allocation is more sophisticated, so the base address of the array is normally passed in a register since it won't fit in the offset, as we shall see.

MIPS operands

Name	Example	Comments
32 registers	$s0, $s1, . . . , $t0, $t1, . . .	Fast locations for data. In MIPS, data must be in registers to perform arithmetic.
2^{30} memory words	Memory[0], Memory[4], . . . , Memory[4294967292]	Accessed only by data transfer instructions in MIPS. MIPS uses byte addresses, so sequential words differ by 4. Memory holds data structures, such as arrays, and spilled registers.

MIPS assembly language

Category	Instruction	Example	Meaning	Comments
Arithmetic	add	add $s1,$s2,$s3	$s1 = $s2 + $s3	three operands; data in registers
	subtract	sub $s1,$s2,$s3	$s1 = $s2 – $s3	three operands; data in registers
Data transfer	load word	lw $s1,100($s2)	$s1 = Memory[$s2 + 100]	Data from memory to register
	store word	sw $s1,100($s2)	Memory[$s2 + 100] = $s1	Data from register to memory

FIGURE 3.4   MIPS architecture revealed through section 3.3. Highlighted portions show MIPS assembly language structures introduced in section 3.3.

3.4   Representing Instructions in the Computer

We are now ready to explain the difference between the way humans instruct machines and the way machines see instructions. But first, let's quickly review how a machine represents numbers.

Humans are taught to think in base 10, but numbers may be represented in any base. For example, 123 base 10 = 1111011 base 2.

Numbers are kept in computer hardware as a series of high and low electronic signals, and so they are considered base 2 numbers. (Just as base 10 numbers are called *decimal* numbers, base 2 numbers are called *binary* numbers.) A single digit of a binary number is thus the "atom" of computing, since all information is composed of binary digits or *bits*. This fundamental building block can be one of two values, which can be thought of as several alternatives: high or low, on or off, true or false, or 1 or 0.

Instructions are also kept in the computer as a series of high and low electronic signals and may be represented as numbers. In fact, each piece of an instruction can be considered as an individual number, and placing these numbers side by side forms the instruction.

Since registers are part of almost all instructions, there must be a convention to map register names into numbers. In MIPS assembly language, registers $s0 to $s7 map onto registers 16 to 23, and registers $t0 to $t7 map onto registers 8 to 15. Hence $s0 means register 16, $s1 means register 17, $s2 means register 18, . . . , $t0 means register 8, $t1 means register 9, and so on. We'll describe the convention for the rest of the 32 registers in the following sections.

Translating a MIPS Assembly Instruction into a Machine Instruction

Example

Let's do the next step in the refinement of the MIPS language as an example. We'll show the real MIPS language version of the instruction represented symbolically as

```
add $t0,$s1,$s2
```

first as a combination of decimal numbers and then of binary numbers.

Answer

The decimal representation is

0	17	18	8	0	32

Each of these segments of an instruction is called a *field*. The first and last fields (containing 0 and 32 in this case) in combination tell the MIPS computer that this instruction performs addition. The second field gives the number of the register that is the first source operand of the addition operation (17 = $s1) and the third field gives the other source operand for the addition (18 = $s2).The fourth field contains the number of the register that is to receive the sum (8 = $t0). The fifth field is unused in this instruction, so it is set to 0. Thus this instruction adds register $s1 to register $s2 and places the sum in register $t0.

This instruction can also be represented as fields of binary numbers as opposed to decimal:

000000	10001	10010	01000	00000	100000
6 bits	5 bits	5 bits	5 bits	5 bits	6 bits

To distinguish it from assembly language, we call the numeric version of instructions *machine language* and a sequence of such instructions *machine code*.

This layout of the instruction is called the *instruction format*. As you can see from counting the number of bits, this MIPS instruction takes exactly 32 bits—the same size as a data word. In keeping with our design principle that simplicity favors regularity, all MIPS instructions are 32 bits long.

MIPS Fields

MIPS fields are given names to make them easier to discuss:

op	rs	rt	rd	shamt	funct
6 bits	5 bits	5 bits	5 bits	5 bits	6 bits

Here is the meaning of each name of the fields in MIPS instructions:

- *op*: Basic operation of the instruction, traditionally called the *opcode*.
- *rs*: The first register source operand.
- *rt*: The second register source operand.
- *rd*: The register destination operand, it gets the result of the operation.
- *shamt*: Shift amount. (This term is explained in Chapter 4 when we see the shift instructions; it will not be used until then, and hence the field contains zero.)
- *funct*: Function. This field selects the specific variant of the operation in the op field, and is sometimes called the *function code*.

A problem occurs when an instruction needs longer fields than those shown above. For example, the load word instruction must specify two registers and a constant. If the address were to use one of the 5-bit fields in the format above, the constant within the load word instruction would be limited to only 2^5 or 32. This constant is used to select elements from large arrays or data structures, and it often needs to be much larger than 32. This 5-bit field is too small to be useful.

Hence we have a conflict between the desire to keep all instructions the same length and the desire to have a single instruction format. This leads us to the third hardware design principle:

Design Principle 3: Good design demands good compromises.

The compromise chosen by the MIPS designers is to keep all instructions the same length, thereby requiring different kinds of instruction formats for different kinds of instructions. For example, the format above is called *R-type* (for register) or *R-format*. A second type of instruction format is called *I-type* or *I-format* and is used by the data transfer instructions. The fields of I-format are

op	rs	rt	address
6 bits	5 bits	5 bits	16 bits

The 16-bit address means a load word instruction can load any word within a region of $\pm 2^{15}$ or 32,768 bytes (2^{13} or 8192 words) of the address in the base register rs.

Let's take a look at the load word instruction from page 114:

```
lw    $t0,32($s3)    # Temporary reg $t0 gets A[8]
```

Here, 19 (for $s3) is placed in the rs field, 8 (for $t0) is placed in the rt field, and 32 is placed in the address field. Note that the meaning of the rt field has changed for this instruction: in a load word instruction, the rt field specifies the *destination* register, which receives the result of the load.

Although multiple formats complicate the hardware, we can reduce the complexity by keeping the formats similar. For example, the first three fields of the R-type and I-type formats are the same size and have the same names; the fourth field in I-type is equal to the length of the last three fields of R-type.

In case you were wondering, the formats are distinguished by the values in the first field: each format is assigned a distinct set of values in the first field (op) so that the hardware knows whether to treat the last half of the instruction as three fields (R-type) or as a single field (I-type). Figure 3.5 shows the numbers used in each field for the MIPS instructions covered through section 3.3.

Instruction	Format	op	rs	rt	rd	shamt	funct	address
add	R	0	reg	reg	reg	0	32	n.a.
sub (subtract)	R	0	reg	reg	reg	0	34	n.a.
lw (load word)	I	35	reg	reg	n.a.	n.a.	n.a.	address
sw (store word)	I	43	reg	reg	n.a.	n.a.	n.a.	address

FIGURE 3.5 MIPS instruction encoding. In the table above, "reg" means a register number between 0 and 31, "address" means a 16-bit address, and "n.a." (not applicable) means this field does not appear in this format. Note that add and sub instructions have the same value in the op field; the hardware uses the funct field to decide the variant of the operation: add (32) or subtract (34).

Translating MIPS Assembly Language into Machine Language

Example

We can now take an example all the way from what the programmer writes to what the machine executes. Assuming that $t1 has the base of the array A and that $s2 corresponds to h, the C assignment statement

```
A[300] = h + A[300];
```

is compiled into

```
lw   $t0,1200($t1) # Temporary reg $t0 gets A[300]
add  $t0,$s2,$t0   # Temporary reg $t0 gets h + A[300]
sw   $t0,1200($t1) # Stores h + A[i] back into A[300]
```

What is the MIPS machine language code for these three instructions?

Answer

For convenience, let's first represent the machine language instructions using decimal numbers. From Figure 3.5 we can determine the three machine language instructions:

op	rs	rt	rd	address/shamt	funct
35	9	8		1200	
0	18	8	8	0	32
43	9	8		1200	

The lw instruction is identified by 35 (see Figure 3.5) in the first field (op). The base register 9 ($t1) is specified in the second field (rs), and the destination register 8 ($t0) is specified in the third field (rt). The offset to select A[300] (1200 = 300 × 4) is found in the final field (address).

The add instruction that follows is specified with 0 in the first field (op) and 32 in the last field (funct). The three register operands (18, 8, and 8) are found in the second, third, and fourth fields and correspond to $s2, $t0, and $t0.

The sw instruction is identified with 43 in the first field. The rest of this final instruction is identical to the lw instruction.

The binary equivalent to the decimal form is the following (1200 in base 10 is 0000 0100 1011 0000 base 2):

100011	01001	01000	0000 0100 1011 0000		
000000	10010	01000	01000	00000	100000
101011	01001	01000	0000 0100 1011 0000		

Note the similarity of the binary representations of the first and last instructions. The only difference is found in the third bit from the left.

Figure 3.6 summarizes the portions of MIPS assembly language described in this section. As we shall see in Chapters 5 and 6, the similarity of the binary representations of related instructions simplifies hardware design. These instructions are another example of regularity in the MIPS architecture.

Elaboration: Representing decimal numbers in base 2 gives an easy way to represent positive integers in computer words. Chapter 4 explains how negative numbers can be represented, but for now take it on faith that a 32-bit word can represent integers between -2^{31} and $+2^{31} -1$ or $-2,147,483,648$ to $+2,147,483,647$. Such integers are called *two's complement* numbers.

MIPS operands

Name	Example	Comments
32 registers	$s0, $s1 , . . . , $s7 $t0, $t1 , . . . , $t7	Fast locations for data. In MIPS, data must be in registers to perform arithmetic. Registers $s0–$s7 map to 16–23 and $t0–$t7 map to 8–15.
2^{30} memory words	Memory[0], Memory[4], . . . , Memory[4294967292]	Accessed only by data transfer instructions in MIPS. MIPS uses byte addresses, so sequential words differ by 4. Memory holds data structures, such as arrays, and spilled registers.

MIPS assembly language

Category	Instruction	Example	Meaning	Comments
Arithmetic	add	add $s1,$s2,$s3	$s1 = $s2 + $s3	Three operands; data in registers
	subtract	sub $s1,$s2,$s3	$s1 = $s2 - $s3	Three operands; data in registers
Data transfer	load word	lw $s1,100($s2)	$s1 = Memory[$s2 + 100]	Data from memory to register
	store word	sw $s1,100($s2)	Memory[$s2 + 100] = $s1	Data from register to memory

MIPS machine language

Name	Format	Example						Comments
add	R	0	18	19	17	0	32	add $s1,$s2,$s3
sub	R	0	18	19	17	0	34	sub $s1,$s2,$s3
lw	I	35	18	17	100			lw $s1,100($s2)
sw	I	43	18	17	100			sw $s1,100($s2)
Field size		6 bits	5 bits	5 bits	5 bits	5 bits	6 bits	All MIPS instructions 32 bits
R-format	R	op	rs	rt	rd	shamt	funct	Arithmetic instruction format
I-format	I	op	rs	rt	address			Data transfer format

FIGURE 3.6 MIPS architecture revealed through section 3.4. Highlighted portions show MIPS machine language structures introduced in section 3.4. The two MIPS instruction formats so far are R and I. The first 16 bits are the same: both contain an *op* field, giving the base operation; an *rs* field, giving one of the sources; and the *rt* field, which specifies the other source operand, except for load word, where it specifies the destination register. R-format divides the last 16 bits into an *rd* field, specifying the destination register; *shamt* field, which is unused in Chapter 3 and hence always is 0; and the *funct* field, which specifies the specific operation of R-format instructions. I-format keeps the last 16 bits as a single *address* field.

The Big Picture

Today's computers are built on two key principles:

1. Instructions are represented as numbers.

2. Programs can be stored in memory to be read or written just like numbers.

These principles lead to the *stored-program* concept; its invention let the computing genie out of its bottle. Figure 3.7 shows the power of the concept; specifically, memory can contain the source code for an editor program, the corresponding compiled machine code, the text that the compiled program is using, and even the compiler that generated the machine code.

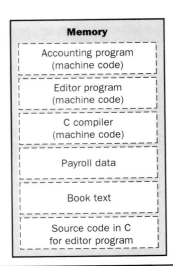

FIGURE 3.7   The stored-program concept. Stored programs allow a computer that performs accounting to become, in the blink of an eye, a computer that helps an author write a book. The switch happens simply by loading memory with programs and data and then telling the computer to begin executing at a given location in memory. Treating instructions in the same way as data greatly simplifies both the memory hardware and the software of computer systems. Specifically, the memory technology needed for data can also be used for programs, and programs like compilers, for instance, can translate code written in a notation far more convenient for humans into code that the machine can understand.

3.5   Instructions for Making Decisions

The utility of an automatic computer lies in the possibility of using a given sequence of instructions repeatedly, the number of times it is iterated being dependent upon the results of the computation. When the iteration is completed a different sequence of [instructions] is to be followed, so we must, in most cases, give two parallel trains of [instructions] preceded by an instruction as to which routine is to be followed. This choice can be made to depend upon the sign of a number (zero being reckoned as plus for machine purposes). Consequently, we introduce an [instruction] (the conditional transfer [instruction]) which will, depending on the sign of a given number, cause the proper one of two routines to be executed.

Burks, Goldstine, and von Neumann, 1947

What distinguishes a computer from a simple calculator is its ability to make decisions. Based on the input data and the values created during the computation, different instructions are executed. Decision making is commonly represented in programming languages using the *if* statement, sometimes combined with *go to* statements and labels. MIPS assembly language includes two decision-making instructions, similar to an *if* statement with a *go to*. The first instruction is

```
beq register1, register2, L1
```

This instruction means go to the statement labeled L1 if the value in register1 equals the value in register2. The mnemonic beq stands for *branch if equal*. The second instruction is

```
bne register1, register2, L1
```

It means go to the statement labeled L1 if the value in register1 does *not* equal the value in register2. The mnemonic bne stands for *branch if not equal*. These two instructions are traditionally called *conditional branches*.

Compiling an *If* Statement into a Conditional Branch

Example

In the following C code segment, f, g, h, i, and j are variables:

```
          if (i == j) go to L1;
          f = g + h;
L1:       f = f - i;
```

Assuming that the five variables f through j correspond to the five registers $s0 through $s4, what is the compiled MIPS code?

Answer

The first C statement compares for equality and then branches to the subtract operation. Since both the operands are in registers, this maps exactly to a branch if equal instruction (we'll define the label L1 later):

```
beq $s3,$s4, L1   # go to L1 if i equals j
```

The following C assignment statement performs a single operation, and if all the operands are allocated to registers, it is just one instruction:

```
add $s0,$s1,$s2   # f = g + h (skipped if i equals j)
```

The final statement can again be compiled into a single instruction. The problem is how to specify its address so that the conditional branch can skip the add instruction above.

Instructions are stored in memory in stored-program computers; hence instructions must have memory addresses just like other words in memory. The last instruction simply appends the label L1 that was forward-referenced by the beq instruction.

```
L1:        sub $s0,$s0,$s3  # f = f - i (always executed)
```

The label L1 thus corresponds to the address of the subtract instruction.

Notice that the assembler relieves the compiler or the assembly language programmer from the tedium of calculating addresses for branches, just as it does for calculating data addresses for loads and stores (see section 3.9).

Hardware Software Interface

Compilers frequently create branches and labels where they do not appear in the programming language. Avoiding the burden of writing explicit labels and branches is one benefit of writing in high-level programming languages and is a reason coding is faster at that level.

Compiling *if-then-else* into Conditional Branches

Example

Using the same variables and registers from the previous example, compile this C *if* statement:

```
if (i == j) f = g + h; else f = g - h;
```

Answer

Figure 3.8 is a flowchart of what the MIPS code should do. The first C expression compares for equality, so it would seem that we would want the beq as before. In general the code will be more efficient if we test for the opposite condition to branch over the code that performs the subsequent *then* part of the *if* (the label Else is defined below):

```
bne $s3,$s4,Else   # go to Else if i ≠ j
```

The next C assignment statement performs a single operation, and if all the operands are allocated to registers, it is just one instruction:

```
add $s0,$s1,$s2    # f = g + h (skipped if i ≠ j)
```

We now need to go to the end of the *if* statement. This example introduces another kind of branch, often called an *unconditional branch*. This instruction says that the machine always follows the branch. To distinguish between conditional and unconditional branches, the MIPS name for this type of instruction is *jump*, abbreviated as j (the label Exit is defined below).

```
j Exit          # go to Exit
```

The assignment statement in the *else* portion of the *if* statement can again be compiled into a single instruction. We just need to append the label Else to this instruction. We also show the label Exit that is after this instruction, showing the end of the *if-then-else* compiled code:

```
Else:    sub $s0,$s1,$s2 # f = g - h (skipped if i = j)
Exit:
```

Loops

Decisions are important both for choosing between two alternatives—found in *if* statements—and for iterating a computation—found in loops. The same assembly instructions are the building blocks for both cases.

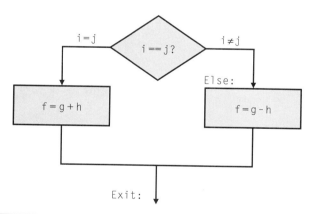

FIGURE 3.8 Illustration of the options in the *if* statement above. The left box corresponds to the *then* part of the *if* statement, and the right box corresponds to the *else* part.

Compiling a Loop with Variable Array Index

Example

Here is a loop in C:

```
Loop:    g = g + A[i];
         i = i + j;
         if (i != h) goto Loop;
```

Assume that A is an array of 100 elements and that the compiler associates the variables g, h, i, and j with the registers $s1, $s2, $s3, and $s4, respectively. Let's assume that the base of the array A is in $s5. What is the MIPS assembly code corresponding to this C loop?

Answer

The first step is to load A[i] into a temporary register. We borrow the code from the similar example that starts on page 114. We need only add the label Loop to the first instruction so that we can branch back to that instruction at the end of the loop:

```
Loop:    add $t1,$s3,$s3     # Temp reg $t1 = 2 * i
         add $t1,$t1,$t1     # Temp reg $t1 = 4 * i
         add $t1,$t1,$s5     # $t1 = address of A[i]
         lw  $t0,0($t1)      # Temporary reg $t0 = A[i]
```

The next two instructions add A[i] to g and then j to i:

```
         add $s1,$s1,$t0     # g = g + A[i]
         add $s3,$s3,$s4     # i = i + j
```

The final instruction branches back to Loop if i ≠ h:

```
         bne $s3,$s2, Loop   # go to Loop if i ≠ h
```

Since the body of the loop modifies i, we must multiply its value by 4 each time through the loop. (Section 3.11 shows how to avoid these "multiplies" when writing loops like this one.)

Hardware Software Interface

Such sequences of instructions that end in a branch are so fundamental to compiling that they are given their own buzzword: a *basic block* is a sequence of instructions without branches, except possibly at the end, and without branch targets or branch labels, except possibly at the beginning. One of the first early phases of compilation is breaking the program into basic blocks.

Compiling a *while* Loop

Example

Of course, programmers don't normally write loops with *go to* statements, so it is up to the compiler to translate traditional loops into MIPS language. Here is a traditional loop in C:

```
while (save[i] == k)
        i = i + j;
```

Assume that i, j, and k correspond to registers $s3, $s4, and $s5 and the base of the array save is in $s6. What is the MIPS assembly code corresponding to this C segment?

Answer

The first step is to load save[i] into a temporary register. It starts with code similar to the prior example:

```
Loop:    add $t1,$s3,$s3    # Temp reg $t1 = 2 * i
         add $t1,$t1,$t1    # Temp reg $t1 = 4 * i
         add $t1,$t1,$s6    # $t1 = address of save[i]
         lw  $t0,0($t1)     # Temp reg $t0 = save[i]
```

The next instruction performs the loop test, exiting if save[i] ≠ k:

```
         bne $t0,$s5, Exit  # go to Exit if save[i] ≠ k
```

The next instruction adds j to i:

```
         add  $s3,$s3,$s4   # i = i + j
```

The end of the loop branches back to the *while* test at the top of the loop. We just add the Exit label after it, and we're done:

```
         j    Loop          # go to Loop
  Exit:
```

(See Exercise 3.9 for an optimization of this sequence.)

The test for equality or inequality is probably the most popular test, but sometimes it is useful to see if a variable is less than another variable. For example, a *for* loop may want to test to see if the index variable is less than 0. Such comparisons are accomplished in MIPS assembly language with an instruction that compares two registers and sets a third register to 1 if the first is less than the second; otherwise, it is set to 0. The MIPS instruction is called *set on less than*, or slt. For example,

```
slt   $t0, $s3, $s4
```

means that register $t0 is set to 1 if the value in register $s3 is less than the value in register $s4; otherwise, register $t0 is set to 0.

Hardware Software Interface	MIPS compilers use the slt, beq, bne, and the fixed value of 0 always available by reading register $zero to create all relative conditions: equal, not equal, less than, less than or equal, greater than, greater than or equal. (As you might expect, register $zero maps to register 0.)

Compiling a Less Than Test

Example

What is the code to test if variable a (corresponding to register $s0) is less than variable b (register $s1) and then branch to label Less if the condition holds?

Answer

The first step is to use the set on less than instruction and a temporary register:

```
slt $t0,$s0,$s1          # $t0 gets 1 if $s0 < $s1 (a < b)
```

Register $t0 is set to 1 if a is less than b. Hence, a branch to see if register $t0 is not equal to 0 will give us the effect of branching if a is less than b. Register $zero always contains 0, so this final test is accomplished using the bne instruction and comparing register $t0 to register $zero:

```
bne $t0,$zero, Less    # go to Less if $t0 ≠ 0
                       #   (that is, if a < b)
```

This pair of instructions, slt and bne, implements branch on less than.

Heeding von Neumann's warning about the simplicity of the "equipment," the MIPS architecture doesn't include branch on less than because it is too complicated; either it would stretch the clock cycle time or this instruction would take extra clock cycles per instruction. Two faster instructions are more useful.

Case/Switch Statement

Most programming languages have a *case* or *switch* statement that allows the programmer to select one of many alternatives depending on a single value. One way to implement *switch* is via a sequence of conditional tests, turning the *switch* statement into a chain of *if-then-else* statements. But sometimes the alternatives may be efficiently encoded as a table of addresses of alternative instruction sequences, called a *jump address table*, and the program needs only to index into the table and then jump to the appropriate sequence. The jump table is then just an array of words containing addresses that correspond to labels in the code.

To support such situations, computers like MIPS include a *jump register* instruction (jr), meaning an unconditional jump to the address specified in a register. The program loads the appropriate entry from the jump table into a register, and then it jumps to the proper address using a jump register.

Compiling a *switch* Statement by Using a Jump Address Table

Example

This C version of a *case* statement is called a *switch* statement. The following C code chooses among four alternatives depending on whether k has the value 0, 1, 2, or 3.

```
switch (k) {
      case 0:  f = i + j; break; /* k = 0 */
      case 1:  f = g + h; break; /* k = 1 */
      case 2:  f = g - h; break; /* k = 2 */
      case 3:  f = i - j; break; /* k = 3 */
}
```

Assume the six variables f through k correspond to six registers $s0 through $s5 and that register $t2 contains 4. What is the corresponding MIPS code?

Answer

We use the *switch* variable k to index a jump address table, and then jump via the value loaded. We first test k to be sure it matches one of the cases (0 ≤ k ≤ 3); if not, the code exits the *switch* statement.

```
slt  $t3,$s5,$zero    # Test if k < 0
bne  $t3,$zero,Exit    # if k < 0, go to Exit
slt  $t3,$s5,$t2      # Test if k < 4
beq  $t3,$zero,Exit    # if k >= 4, go to Exit
```

Since we are using the variable k to index into this table of words, we must first multiply by 4 to turn k into its byte address:

```
add   $t1,$s5,$s5    # Temp reg $t1 = 2 * k
add   $t1,$t1,$t1    # Temp reg $t1 = 4 * k
```

Assume that four sequential words in memory, starting at an address contained in $t4, have addresses corresponding to the labels L0, L1, L2, and L3. We can now load the proper jump address this way:

```
add   $t1,$t1,$t4    # $t1 = address of JumpTable[k]
lw    $t0,0($t1)     # Temp reg $t0 = JumpTable[k]
```

A jump register instruction jumps via the register to the address from the jump table.

```
jr    $t0            # jump based on register $t0
```

The first three *switch* cases in this example are the same: a label, a single instruction performing the *case* statement, and then a jump to exit the *switch* statement:

```
L0:  add   $s0,$s3,$s4    # k = 0 so f gets i + j
     j     Exit           # end of this case so go to Exit
L1:  add   $s0,$s1,$s2    # k = 1 so f gets g + h
     j     Exit           # end of this case so go to Exit
L2:  sub   $s0,$s1,$s2    # k = 2 so f gets g - h
     j     Exit           # end of this case so go to Exit
```

A more complex example might have several instructions for each case.

For the final case we drop the jump to exit (since this is the last instruction of the switch code) and append an Exit label afterwards to mark the end of the switch statement:

```
L3:  sub   $s0,$s3,$s4    # k = 3 so f gets i - j
Exit:                     # end of switch statement
```

Figure 3.9 summarizes the portions of MIPS assembly language described in this section. This step along the evolution of the MIPS language has added branches and jumps to our symbolic representation, and fixes the useful value 0 permanently in a register.

Elaboration: If you have heard about *delayed branches*, covered in Chapter 6, don't worry: The MIPS assembler makes them invisible to the assembly language programmer. Also, for C programmers not familiar with the infinitely abusable go to statement, it transfers control from wherever it appears to the label.

MIPS operands

Name	Example	Comments
32 registers	$s0, $s1,..., $s7 $t0,$t1,...,$t7, $zero	Fast locations for data. In MIPS, data must be in registers to perform arithmetic. Registers $s0–$s7 map to 16–23 and $t0–$t7 map to 8–15. MIPS register $zero always equals 0.
2^{30} memory words	Memory[0], Memory[4], . . . , Memory[4294967292]	Accessed only by data transfer instructions in MIPS. MIPS uses byte addresses, so sequential words differ by 4. Memory holds data structures, such as arrays, and spilled registers.

MIPS assembly language

Category	Instruction	Example	Meaning	Comments
Arithmetic	add	add $s1,$s2,$s3	$s1 = $s2 + $s3	Three operands; data in registers
	subtract	sub $s1,$s2,$s3	$s1 = $s2 – $s3	Three operands; data in registers
Data transfer	load word	lw $s1,100($s2)	$s1 = Memory[$s2 + 100]	Data from memory to register
	store word	sw $s1,100($s2)	Memory[$s2 + 100] = $s1	Data from register to memory
Conditional branch	branch on equal	beq $s1,$s2,L	if ($s1 == $s2) go to L	Equal test and branch
	branch on not equal	bne $s1,$s2,L	if ($s1 != $s2) go to L	Not equal test and branch
	set on less than	slt $s1,$s2,$s3	if ($s2 < $s3) $s1 = 1; else $s1 = 0	Compare less than; used with beq, bne
Unconditional jump	jump	j 2500	go to 10000	Jump to target address
	jump register	jr $t1	go to $t1	For *switch* statements

MIPS machine language

Name	Format	Example						Comments
add	R	0	18	19	17	0	32	add $s1,$s2,$s3
sub	R	0	18	19	17	0	34	sub $s1,$s2,$s3
lw	I	35	18	17	100			lw $s1,100($s2)
sw	I	43	18	17	100			sw $s1,100($s2)
beq	I	4	17	18	25			beq $s1,$s2,100
bne	I	5	17	18	25			bne $s1,$s2,100
slt	R	0	18	19	17	0	42	slt $s1,$s2,$s3
j	J	2	2500					j 10000 (see section 3.8)
jr	R	0	9	0	0	0	8	jr $t1
Field size		6 bits	5 bits	5 bits	5 bits	5 bits	6 bits	All MIPS instructions 32 bits
R-format	R	op	rs	rt	rd	shamt	funct	Arithmetic instruction format
I-format	I	op	rs	rt	address			Data transfer, branch format

FIGURE 3.9   MIPS architecture revealed through section 3.5. Highlighted portions show MIPS structures introduced in section 3.5. The J-format, used for jump instructions, is explained in section 3.8. Section 3.8 also explains the proper values in address fields of branch instructions.

3.6   Supporting Procedures in Computer Hardware

A procedure or subroutine is one tool programmers use to structure programs, both to make them easier to understand and to allow code to be reused. Procedures allow the programmer to concentrate on just one portion of the task at a time, with parameters acting as a barrier between the procedure and the rest of the program and data, allowing it to be passed values and return results.

You can think of a procedure like a spy who leaves with a secret plan, acquires resources, performs the task, covers his tracks, and then returns to the point of origin with the desired result. Nothing else should be perturbed once the mission is complete. Moreover, a spy operates on only a "need to know" basis, so the spy can't make assumptions about his employer.

Similarly, in the execution of a procedure, the program must follow these six steps:

1. Place parameters in a place where the procedure can access them.

2. Transfer control to the procedure.

3. Acquire the storage resources needed for the procedure.

4. Perform the desired task.

5. Place the result value in a place where the calling program can access it.

6. Return control to the point of origin.

As mentioned above, registers are the fastest place to hold data in a computer, so we want to use them as much as possible. Hence MIPS software allocates the following of its 32 registers for procedure calling:

- $a0–$a3: four argument registers in which to pass parameters

- $v0–$v1: two value registers in which to return values

- $ra: one return address register to return to the point of origin

In addition to allocating these registers, MIPS assembly language includes an instruction just for the procedures: it jumps to an address and simultaneously saves the address of the following instruction in register $ra. The *jump-and-link* instruction (jal) is simply written

```
jal ProcedureAddress
```

The *link* portion of the name means that an address or link is formed that points to the calling site to allow the procedure to return to the proper address. This "link," stored in register $ra, is called the *return address*. The return address is needed because the same procedure could be called from several parts of the program.

Implicit in the stored-program idea is the need to have a register to hold the address of the current instruction being executed. For historical reasons, this register is almost always called the *program counter*, abbreviated *PC* in the MIPS architecture, although a more sensible name would have been *instruction address register*. The `jal` instruction saves PC + 4 in register $ra to link to the following instruction to set up the procedure return.

We already have an instruction to do the return jump:

```
jr    $ra
```

The jump register instruction, which we used above in the *switch* statement, jumps to the address stored in register $ra—which is just what we want. Thus the calling program, or *caller*, puts the parameter values in $a0–$a3, and uses `jal X` to jump to procedure X (sometimes named the *callee*). The callee then performs the calculations, places the results in $v0–$v1, and returns control to the caller using `jr $ra`.

Using More Registers

Suppose a compiler needs more registers for a procedure than the four argument and two return value registers. Since we are supposed to cover our tracks after our mission is complete, any registers needed by the caller must be restored to the values that they contained *before* the procedure was invoked. This situation is an example in which we need to spill registers to memory, as mentioned in the Hardware Software Interface section on page 115.

The ideal data structure for spilling registers is a *stack*—a last-in-first-out queue. A stack needs a pointer to the most recently allocated address in the stack to show where the next procedure should place the registers to be spilled or where old register values can be found. The stack pointer is adjusted by one word for each register that is saved or restored. Stacks are so popular that they have their own buzzwords for transferring data to and from the stack: placing data onto the stack is called a *push*, and removing data from the stack is called a *pop*.

MIPS software allocates another register just for the stack: the *stack pointer* ($sp), used to save the registers needed by the callee. By historical precedent, stacks "grow" from higher addresses to lower addresses. This convention means that you push values onto the stack by subtracting from the stack pointer. Adding to the stack pointer shrinks the stack, thereby popping values off the stack.

Compiling a Procedure that Doesn't Call Another Procedure

Example

Let's turn the example on page 109 into a procedure:

```
int leaf_example (int g, int h, int i, int j)
{
    int f;

    f = (g + h) - (i + j);
    return f;
}
```

For the rest of this section we assume we can add or subtract constants like 4, 8, or 12. (Section 3.8 reveals how constants are handled in MIPS assembly language.) What is the compiled MIPS assembly code?

Answer

The parameter variables g, h, i, and j correspond to the argument registers $a0, $a1, $a2, and $a3, and f corresponds to $s0. The compiled program starts with the label of the procedure:

```
leaf_example:
```

The next step is to save the registers used by the procedure. The C assignment statement in the procedure body is identical to the example on page 109, which uses two temporary registers. Thus we need to save three registers: $s0, $t0, and $t1. We create space for three words on the stack and then store the old values:

```
sub $sp,$sp,12    # adjust stack to make room for 3 items
sw  $t1, 8($sp)   # save register $t1 for use afterwards
sw  $t0, 4($sp)   # save register $t0 for use afterwards
sw  $s0, 0($sp)   # save register $s0 for use afterwards
```

Figure 3.10 shows the stack before, during, and after the procedure call. The next three statements correspond to the body of the procedure, which follows the example on page 109:

```
add $t0,$a0,$a1   # register $t0 contains g + h
add $t1,$a2,$a3   # register $t1 contains i + j
sub $s0,$t0,$t1   # f = $t0 - $t1, which is (g + h)-(i + j)
```

To return the value of f, we copy it into a return value register:

```
add $v0,$s0,$zero  # returns f ($v0 = $s0 + 0)
```

Before returning, we restore the old values of the registers we saved and then "pop" the stack to its original value:

```
lw   $s0, 0($sp)     # restore register $s0 for caller
lw   $t0, 4($sp)     # restore register $t0 for caller
lw   $t1, 8($sp)     # restore register $t1 for caller
add $sp,$sp,12       # adjust stack to delete 3 items
```

The procedure ends with a jump register using the return address:

```
jr   $ra             # jump back to calling routine
```

In the example above we used temporary registers and assumed their old values must be saved and restored. To avoid saving and restoring a register whose value is never used, which might happen with a temporary register, MIPS software offers two classes of registers:

- $t0–$t9: 10 temporary registers that are *not* preserved by the callee (called procedure) on a procedure call

- $s0–$s7: 8 saved registers that must be preserved on a procedure call (if used, the callee saves and restores them)

This simple convention reduces register spilling. In the example above, since the caller (procedure doing the calling) does not expect registers $t0 and $t1 to be preserved across a procedure call, we can drop two stores and two loads from the code. We still must save and restore $s0, since the callee must assume that the caller needs its value.

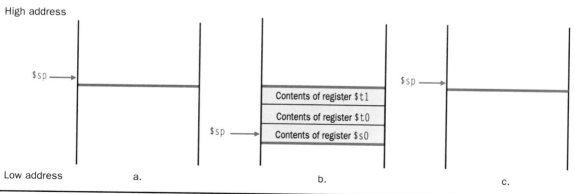

FIGURE 3.10   The values of the stack pointer and the stack (a) before, (b) during, and (c) after the procedure call. The stack pointer always points to the "top" of the stack, or the last word in the stack in this drawing.

Nested Procedures

Procedures that do not call others are called *leaf* procedures. Life would be simple if all procedures were leaf procedures, but they aren't. Just as a spy might employ other spies as part of a mission, who in turn might use even more spies, so do procedures invoke other procedures. Moreover, recursive procedures even invoke "clones" of themselves. Just as we need to be careful when using registers in procedures, more care must also be taken when invoking non-leaf procedures.

For example, suppose that the main program calls procedure A with an argument of 3, by placing the value 3 into register $a0 and then using jal A. Then suppose that procedure A calls procedure B via jal B with an argument of 7, also placed in $a0. Since A hasn't finished its task yet, there is a conflict over the use of register $a0. Similarly, there is a conflict over the return address in register $ra, since it now has the return address for B. Unless we take steps to prevent the problem, this conflict will eliminate procedure A's ability to return to its caller.

One solution is to push all the other registers that must be preserved onto the stack, just as we did with the saved registers. The caller pushes any argument registers ($a0–$a3) or temporary registers ($t0–$t9) that are needed after the call. The callee pushes the return address register $ra and any saved registers ($s0–$s7) used by the callee. The stack pointer $sp is adjusted to account for the number of registers placed on the stack. Upon the return, the registers are restored from memory and the stack pointer is readjusted.

Compiling a Recursive Procedure, Showing Nested Procedure Linking

Example

Let's tackle a recursive procedure that calculates factorial:

```
int fact (int n)
{
    if (n < 1) return (1);
        else return (n * fact(n-1));
}
```

Assume that you can add or subtract constants like 1 or 8, as we will show in section 3.8. What is the MIPS assembly code?

Answer

The parameter variable n corresponds to the argument register $a0. The compiled program starts with the label of the procedure and then saves two registers on the stack, the return address and $a0:

```
fact:
        sub     $sp,$sp,8    # adjust stack for 2 items
        sw      $ra, 4($sp)  # save the return address
        sw      $a0, 0($sp)  # save the argument n
```

The first time fact is called, sw saves an address in the program that called fact. The next two instructions test if n is less than 1, going to L1 if n ≥ 1.

```
        slt     $t0,$a0,1    # test for n < 1
        beq     $t0,$zero,L1 # if n >= 1, go to L1
```

If n is less than 1, fact returns 1 by putting 1 into a value register: it adds 1 to 0 and places that sum in $v0. It then pops the two saved values off the stack and jumps to the return address:

```
        add     $v0,$zero,1  # return 1
        add     $sp,$sp,8    # pop 2 items off stack
        jr      $ra          # return to after jal
```

Before popping two items off the stack, we could have loaded $a0 and $ra. Since $a0 and $ra don't change when n is less than 1, we skip those instructions.

If n is not less than 1, the argument n is decremented and then fact is called again with the decremented value:

```
L1:     sub     $a0,$a0,1    # n >= 1: argument gets (n - 1)
        jal     fact         # call fact with (n - 1)
```

The next instruction is where fact returns. Now the old return address and old argument are restored, along with the stack pointer:

```
    lw  $a0, 0($sp)    # return from jal: restore argument n
    lw  $ra, 4($sp)    # restore the return address
    add $sp, $sp,8     # adjust stack pointer to pop 2 items
```

Next, the value register $v0 gets the product of old argument $a0 and the current value of the value register. We assume a multiply instruction is available, even though it is not covered until Chapter 4:

```
        mul     $v0,$a0,$v0  # return n * fact (n - 1)
```

Finally, fact jumps again to the return address:

```
        jr      $ra              # return to the caller
```

Preserved	Not preserved
Saved registers: $s0–$s7	Temporary registers: $t0–$t9
Stack pointer register: $sp	Argument registers: $a0–$a3
Return address register: $ra	Return value registers: $v0–$v1
Stack above the stack pointer	Stack below the stack pointer

FIGURE 3.11 What is and what is not preserved across a procedure call. If the software relies on the frame pointer register or on the global pointer register, discussed in the following sections, they are also preserved.

Figure 3.11 summarizes what is preserved across a procedure call. Note that several schemes are used to preserve the stack. The stack above $sp is preserved simply by making sure the callee does not write above $sp; $sp is itself preserved by the callee adding exactly the same amount that was subtracted from it, and the other registers are preserved by saving them on the stack (if they are used) and restoring them from there. These actions also guarantee that the caller will get the same data back on a load from the stack as it put into the stack on a store: because the callee promises to preserve $sp and because the callee also promises not to modify the caller's portion of the stack, that is, the area above the $sp at the time of the call.

Allocating Space for New Data

The final complexity is that the stack is also used to store variables that are local to the procedure that do not fit in registers, such as local arrays or structures. The segment of the stack containing a procedure's saved registers and local variables is called a *procedure frame* or *activation record*. Figure 3.12 shows the state of the stack before, during, and after the procedure call.

Some MIPS software uses a *frame pointer* ($fp) to point to the first word of the frame of a procedure. A stack pointer might change during the procedure, and so references to a local variable in memory might have different offsets depending on where they are in the procedure, making the procedure harder to understand. Alternatively, a frame pointer offers a stable base register within a procedure for local memory references. Note that an activation record appears on the stack whether or not an explicit frame pointer is used. We've been avoiding $fp by avoiding changes to $sp within a procedure: in our examples, the stack is adjusted only on entry and exit of the procedure.

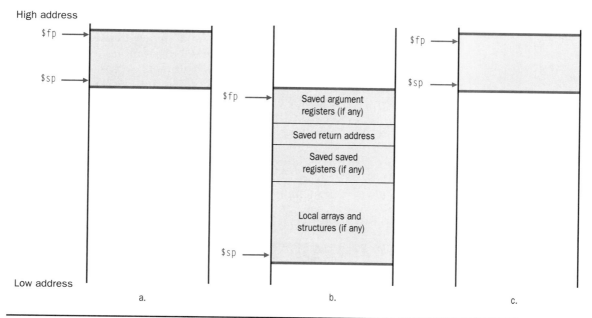

FIGURE 3.12   Illustration of the stack allocation (a) before, (b) during, and (c) after the procedure call. The frame pointer ($fp) points to the first word of the frame, often a saved argument register, and the stack pointer ($sp) points to the top of the stack. The stack is adjusted to make room for all the saved registers and any memory-resident local variables. Since the stack pointer may change during program execution, it's easier for programmers to reference variables via the stable frame pointer, although it could be done just with the stack pointer and a little address arithmetic. If there are no local variables on the stack within a procedure, the compiler will save time by *not* setting and restoring the frame pointer. When a frame pointer is used, it is initialized using the address in $sp on a call, and $sp is restored using $fp.

Figure 3.13 summarizes the register conventions for the MIPS assembly language, and Figure 3.14 summarizes the parts of the MIPS instruction set described so far.

Elaboration: What if there are more than four parameters? The MIPS convention is to place the extra parameters on the stack just above the frame pointer. The procedure then expects the first four parameters to be in registers $a0 through $a3 and the rest in memory, addressable via the frame pointer.

As mentioned in the caption of Figure 3.12, the frame pointer is convenient because all references to variables in the stack within a procedure will have the same offset. The frame pointer is not necessary, however. The GNU MIPS C compiler uses a frame pointer, but the C compiler from MIPS/Silicon Graphics does not; it uses register 30 as another save register ($s8).

Elaboration: jal actually saves the address of the instruction that *follows* jal into register $ra, thereby allowing a procedure return to be simply jr $ra.

| **Hardware Software Interface** | A C variable is a location in storage, and its interpretation depends both on its *type* and *storage class*. Types are discussed in detail in Chapter 4, but examples include integers and characters. C has two storage classes: *automatic* and *static*. Automatic variables are local to a procedure and are discarded when the procedure exits. Static variables exist across exits from and entries to procedures. C variables de- |

clared outside all procedures are considered static, as are any variables declared using the keyword static. The rest are automatic. To simplify access to static data, MIPS software reserves another register, called the *global pointer*, or $gp.

We will see where in memory the static data is allocated in section 3.9.

Name	Register number	Usage	Preserved on call?
$zero	0	the constant value 0	n.a.
$v0–$v1	2–3	values for results and expression evaluation	no
$a0–$a3	4–7	arguments	yes
$t0–$t7	8–15	temporaries	no
$s0–$s7	16–23	saved	yes
$t8–$t9	24–25	more temporaries	no
$gp	28	global pointer	yes
$sp	29	stack pointer	yes
$fp	30	frame pointer	yes
$ra	31	return address	yes

FIGURE 3.13   MIPS register convention. Register 1, called $at, is reserved for the assembler (see section 3.9), and registers 26–27, called $k0–$k1, are reserved for the operating system.

MIPS operands

Name	Example	Comments
32 registers	$s0–$s7, $t0–$t9, $zero,$a0–$a3, $v0–$v1, $gp, $fp, $sp, $ra	Fast locations for data. In MIPS, data must be in registers to perform arithmetic. MIPS register $zero always equals 0. $gp (28) is the global pointer, $sp (29) is the stack pointer, $fp (30) is the frame pointer, and $ra (31) is the return address.
2^{30} memory words	Memory[0], Memory[4], . . . , Memory[4294967292]	Accessed only by data transfer instructions. MIPS uses byte addresses, so sequential words differ by 4. Memory holds data structures, such as arrays, and spilled registers, such as those saved on procedure calls.

MIPS assembly language

Category	Instruction	Example	Meaning	Comments
Arithmetic	add	add $s1,$s2,$s3	$s1 = $s2 + $s3	Three operands; data in registers
	subtract	sub $s1,$s2,$s3	$s1 = $s2 – $s3	Three operands; data in registers
Data transfer	load word	lw $s1,100($s2)	$s1 = Memory[$s2 + 100]	Data from memory to register
	store word	sw $s1,100($s2)	Memory[$s2 + 100] = $s1	Data from register to memory
Conditional branch	branch on equal	beq $s1,$s2,L	if ($s1 == $s2) go to L	Equal test and branch
	branch on not equal	bne $s1,$s2,L	if ($s1 != $s2) go to L	Not equal test and branch
	set on less than	slt $s1,$s2,$s3	if ($s2 < $s3) $s1=1; else $s1 = 0	Compare less than; for beq, bne
Unconditional jump	jump	j 2500	go to 10000	Jump to target address
	jump register	jr $ra	go to $ra	For switch, procedure return
	jump and link	jal 2500	$ra = PC + 4; go to 10000	For procedure call

MIPS machine language

Name	Format	Example						Comments
add	R	0	18	19	17	0	32	add $s1,$s2,$s3
sub	R	0	18	19	17	0	34	sub $s1,$s2,$s3
lw	I	35	18	17	100			lw $s1,100($s2)
sw	I	43	18	17	100			sw $s1,100($s2)
beq	I	4	17	18	25			beq $s1,$s2,100
bne	I	5	17	18	25			bne $s1,$s2,100
slt	R	0	18	19	17	0	42	slt $s1,$s2,$s3
j	J	2	2500					j 10000 (see section 3.8)
jr	R	0	31	0	0	0	8	jr $ra
jal	J	3	2500					jal 10000 (see section 3.8)
Field size		6 bits	5 bits	5 bits	5 bits	5 bits	6 bits	All MIPS instructions 32 bits
R-format	R	op	rs	rt	rd	shamt	funct	Arithmetic instruction format
I-format	I	op	rs	rt	address			Data transfer, branch format

FIGURE 3.14   MIPS architecture revealed through section 3.6. Highlighted portions show MIPS assembly language structures introduced in section 3.6. The J-format, used for jump and jump-and-link instructions, is explained in section 3.8. This section also explains why putting 25 in the address field of beq and bne machine language instructions is equivalent to 100 in assembly language.

3.7   Beyond Numbers

Computers were invented to crunch numbers, but as soon as they became commercially viable they were used to process text. Most computers today use 8-bit bytes to represent characters, with the American Standard Code for Information Interchange (ASCII) being the representation that nearly everyone follows. Figure 3.15 summarizes ASCII.

A series of instructions can be used to extract a byte from a word, so load word and store word are sufficient for transferring bytes as well as words. Because of the popularity of text in some programs, however, MIPS provides special instructions to move bytes. Load byte (lb) loads a byte from memory, placing it in the rightmost 8 bits of a register. Store byte (sb) takes a byte from the rightmost 8 bits of a register and writes it to memory. Thus we copy a byte with the sequence

```
lb $t0,0($sp)   # Read byte from source
sb $t0,0($gp)   # Write byte to destination
```

ASCII value	Character	ASCII value	Character	ASCII value	Character	ASCII value	Character	ASCII value	Character	ASCII value	Character
32	space	48	0	64	@	80	P	96	`	112	p
33	!	49	1	65	A	81	Q	97	a	113	q
34	"	50	2	66	B	82	R	98	b	114	r
35	#	51	3	67	C	83	S	99	c	115	s
36	$	52	4	68	D	84	T	100	d	116	t
37	%	53	5	69	E	85	U	101	e	117	u
38	&	54	6	70	F	86	V	102	f	118	v
39	'	55	7	71	G	87	W	103	g	119	w
40	(	56	8	72	H	88	X	104	h	120	x
41	)	57	9	73	I	89	Y	105	i	121	y
42	*	58	:	74	J	90	Z	106	j	122	z
43	+	59	;	75	K	91	[	107	k	123	{
44	,	60	<	76	L	92	\	108	l	124		
45	-	61	=	77	M	93	]	109	m	125	}
46	.	62	>	78	N	94	^	110	n	126	~
47	/	63	?	79	O	95	_	111	o	127	DEL

FIGURE 3.15   ASCII representation of characters. Note that upper- and lowercase letters differ by exactly 32; this observation can lead to shortcuts in checking or changing upper- and lowercase. Values not shown include formatting characters. For example, 9 represents a tab character and 13 represents a carriage return. Other useful ASCII values are 8 for backspace and 0 for Null, the value the programming language C uses to mark the end of a string.

Characters are normally combined into strings, which have a variable number of characters. There are three choices for representing a string: (1) the first position of the string is reserved to give the length of a string, (2) an accompanying variable has the length of the string (as in a structure), or (3) the last position of a string is indicated by a character used to mark the end of a string. C uses the third choice, terminating a string with a byte whose value is 0 (named null in ASCII). Thus the string "Cal" is represented in C by the following 4 bytes, shown as decimal numbers: 67, 97, 108, 0.

Compiling a String Copy Procedure, Showing How to Use C Strings

Example

The procedure `strcpy` copies string `y` to string `x` using the null byte termination convention of C:

```
void strcpy (char x[], char y[])
{
    int i;

    i = 0;
    while ((x[i] = y[i]) != 0) /* copy and test byte */
        i = i + 1;
}
```

What is the MIPS assembly code?

Answer

Below is the basic MIPS assembly code segment. We again assume we can add or subtract constants like 1 or 4, which we cover in section 3.8. Assume that base addresses for arrays `x` and `y` are found in `$a0` and `$a1`, while `i` is in `$s0`. `strcpy` adjusts the stack pointer and then saves the saved register `$s0` on the stack:

```
strcpy:
    sub    $sp,$sp,4     # adjust stack for 1 more item
    sw     $s0, 0($sp)   # save $s0
```

To initialize `i` to 0, the next instruction sets `$s0` to 0 by adding 0 to 0 and placing that sum in `$s0`:

```
    add    $s0,$zero,$zero    # i = 0 + 0
```

This is the beginning of the loop. The address of `y[i]` is first formed by adding `i` to `y[]`:

```
L1: add    $t1,$a1,$s0   # address of y[i] in $t1
```

Note that we don't have to multiply `i` by 4 since `y` is an array of *bytes* and not of words, as in prior examples.

To load the character in y[i], we use load byte, which puts the character into $t2:

```
lb      $t2, 0($t1)  # $t2 = y[i]
```

A similar address calculation puts the address of x[i] in $t3, and then the character in $t2 is stored at that address.

```
add     $t3,$a0,$s0  # address of x[i] in $t3
sb      $t2, 0($t3)  # x[i] = y[i]
```

Next we increment i and loop back if the character was not 0; that is, if this is not the last character of the string.

```
add     $s0,$s0,1    # i = i + 1
bne     $t2,$zero,L1 # if y[i] != 0, go to L1
```

If we don't loop back, it was the last character of the string; we restore $s0 and the stack pointer, and then return.

```
lw      $s0, 0($sp)  # y[i] == 0: end of string;
                     # restore old s0
add     $sp,$sp,4    # pop 1 word off stack
jr      $ra          # return
```

String copies are usually done with pointers instead of arrays in C to avoid the operations on i in the code above. See section 3.11 for an explanation of arrays versus pointers.

Since the procedure strcpy above is a leaf procedure, the compiler could allocate i to a temporary register and avoid saving and restoring $s0. Hence, instead of thinking of the $t registers as being just for temporaries, we can think of them as registers that the callee should use whenever convenient. When a compiler finds a leaf procedure, it exhausts all temporary registers before using the registers it must save.

Elaboration: There is a universal encoding of the characters of most human languages called *Unicode*, which needs 16 bits to represent a character. The programming language Java, for example, uses Unicode. The full MIPS instruction set has explicit instructions to load and store 16-bit quantities, called *halfwords*. We skip halfword instructions in this book to keep the instruction set as easy to understand as possible, although section A.10 starting on page A-49 includes the full instruction set.

Also, MIPS software tries to keep the stack aligned to word addresses, allowing the program to always use lw and sw (which must be aligned) to access the stack. This convention means that a char variable allocated on the stack will be allocated 4 bytes, even though it needs just 1 byte. A string variable or an array of bytes *will* pack 4 bytes per word, however.

Other Styles of MIPS Addressing

Designers of the MIPS architecture provided two more ways of accessing operands. The first is to make it faster to access small constants, and the second is to make branches more efficient.

Constant or Immediate Operands

Many times a program will use a constant in an operation—for example, incrementing an index to point to the next element of an array, counting iterations of a loop, or adjusting the stack in a nested procedure call. In fact, in two programs, more than half of the arithmetic instructions have a constant as an operand: in the C compiler gcc, 52% of arithmetic operations involve constants; in the circuit simulation program spice, it is 69%.

Using only the instructions in Figure 3.14, we would have to load a constant from memory to use it. (The constants would have been placed in memory when the program was loaded.) For example, to add the constant 4 to register $sp, we could use the code

```
lw     $t0, AddrConstant4($zero) # $t0 = constant 4
add    $sp,$sp,$t0               # $sp = $sp + $t0 ($t0 == 4)
```

assuming that AddrConstant4 is the memory address of the constant 4.

An alternative that avoids memory accesses is to offer versions of the arithmetic instructions in which one operand is a constant, with the novel constraint that this constant is kept inside the *instruction* itself. Following the recommendation urging regularity, we use the same format for these instructions as for the data transfer and branch instructions. In fact, the *I* in the name of the I-type format is for *immediate*, the traditional name for this type of operand. The MIPS field containing the constant is 16 bits long.

Translating Assembly Constants into Machine Language

Example

The add instruction that has one constant operand is called *add immediate* or addi. To add 4 to register $sp, we just write

```
addi     $sp,$sp,4    # $sp = $sp + 4
```

The op field value for addi is 8. Try to guess the rest of the corresponding MIPS machine instruction.

Answer   This instruction is the following machine code (using decimal numbers):

op	rs	rt	immediate
8	29	29	4

(Figure 3.13 on page 140 shows that register 29 corresponds to $sp.) In binary addi is

001000	11101	11101	0000 0000 0000 0100

Immediate or constant operands are also popular in comparisons. Since register $zero always has 0, we can already compare to 0. To compare to other values, there is an immediate version of the set on less than instruction. To test if register $s2 is less than the constant 10, we can just write

```
slti $t0,$s2,10   # $t0 = 1 if $s2 < 10
```

Similar to the earlier example on page 128 (Hardware Software Interface), this instruction can be followed by bne $t0,$zero to branch if register $s2 is less than the constant 10.

Immediate addressing illustrates the final hardware design principle, first mentioned in Chapter 2:

Design Principle 4: Make the common case fast.

Constant operands occur frequently, and by making constants part of arithmetic instructions, they are much faster than if they were loaded from memory.

Although constants are frequently short and fit into the 16-bit field, sometimes they are bigger. The MIPS instruction set includes the instruction *load upper immediate* (lui) specifically to set the upper 16 bits of a constant in a register, allowing a subsequent instruction to specify the lower 16 bits of the constant. Figure 3.16 shows the operation of lui.

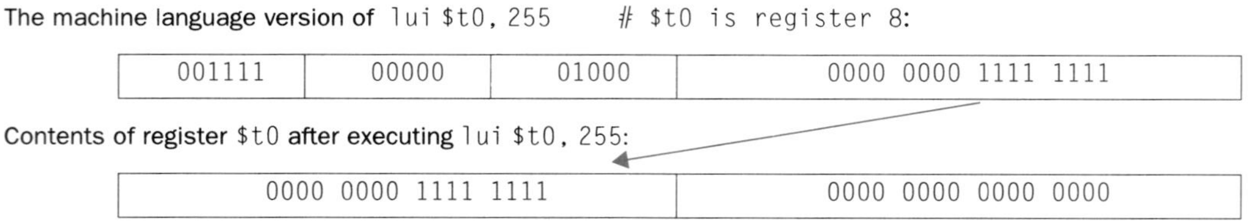

The machine language version of lui $t0, 255   # $t0 is register 8:

001111	00000	01000	0000 0000 1111 1111

Contents of register $t0 after executing lui $t0, 255:

0000 0000 1111 1111	0000 0000 0000 0000

FIGURE 3.16 The effect of the lui instruction. The instruction lui transfers the 16-bit immediate constant field value into the leftmost 16 bits of the register, filling the lower 16 bits with 0s. As we shall see in Chapter 4, this instruction is like multiplying the constant by 2^{16} before loading it into the register.

Loading a 32-Bit Constant

Example	What is the MIPS assembly code to load this 32-bit constant into register $s0?

```
0000 0000 0011 1101 0000 1001 0000 0000
```

Answer	First we would load the upper 16 bits, which is 61 in decimal, using `lui`:

```
lui $s0, 61    # 61 decimal = 0000 0000 0011 1101 binary
```

The value of register $s0 afterward is

```
0000 0000 0011 1101 0000 0000 0000 0000
```

The next step is to add the lower 16 bits, whose decimal value is 2304:

```
addi $s0, $s0, 2304 # 2304 decimal = 0000 1001 0000 0000
```

The final value in register $s0 is the desired value:

```
0000 0000 0011 1101 0000 1001 0000 0000
```

Hardware Software Interface

Either the compiler or the assembler must break large constants into pieces and then reassemble them into a register. As you might expect, the immediate field's size restriction may be a problem for memory addresses in loads and stores as well as for constants in immediate instructions. If this job falls to the assembler, as it does for MIPS software, then the assembler must have a temporary register available in which to create the long values. This is a reason for the register $at, which is reserved for the assembler.

Hence the symbolic representation of the MIPS machine language is no longer limited by the hardware, but to whatever the creator of an assembler chooses to include (see section 3.9). We stick close to the hardware to explain the architecture of the machine, noting when we use the enhanced language of the assembler that is not found in the machine.

Elaboration: We need to be careful about creating 32-bit constants. The instruction `addi` will copy the leftmost bit of the 16-bit immediate field of the instruction into the upper 16 bits of a word. An instruction we will see in the next chapter, `ori`, for *logical or immediate*, loads 0s into the upper 16 bits and hence is used by the assembler in conjunction with `lui` to create 32-bit constants.

Addressing in Branches and Jumps

The simplest addressing is found in the MIPS jump instructions. They use the final MIPS instruction format, called the *J-type*, which consists of 6 bits for the operation field and the rest of the bits for the address field. Thus,

```
j    10000   # go to location 10000
```

is assembled into this format:

2	10000
6 bits	26 bits

where the value of the jump opcode is 2 and the jump address is 10000.

Unlike the jump instruction, the conditional branch instruction must specify two operands in addition to the branch address. Thus,

```
bne $s0,$s1,Exit    # go to Exit if $s0 ≠ $s1
```

is assembled into this instruction, leaving only 16 bits for the branch address:

5	16	17	Exit
6 bits	5 bits	5 bits	16 bits

If addresses of the program had to fit in this 16-bit field, it would mean that no program could be bigger than 2^{16}, which is far too small to be a realistic option today. An alternative would be to specify a register that would always be added to the branch address, so that a branch instruction would calculate the following:

$$\text{Program counter} = \text{Register} + \text{Branch address}$$

This sum allows the program to be as large as 2^{32} and still be able to use conditional branches, solving the branch address size problem. The question is then, which register?

The answer comes from seeing how conditional branches are used. Conditional branches are found in loops and in *if* statements, so they tend to branch to a nearby instruction. For example, almost half of all conditional branches in gcc and spice go to locations less than 16 instructions away. Since the program counter (PC) contains the address of the current instruction, we can branch within $\pm 2^{15}$ words of the current instruction if we use the PC as the register to be added to the address. Almost all loops and *if* statements are much smaller than 2^{16} words, so the PC is the ideal choice.

This form of branch addressing is called *PC-relative addressing*. As we shall see in Chapter 5, it is convenient for the hardware to increment the PC early to point to the next instruction. Hence the MIPS address is actually relative to the address of the following instruction (PC + 4) as opposed to the current instruction (PC).

Like most recent machines, MIPS uses PC-relative addressing for all conditional branches because the destination of these instructions is likely to be close to the branch. On the other hand, jump-and-link instructions invoke procedures that have no reason to be near the call, and so they normally use other forms of addressing. Hence the MIPS architecture offers long addresses for procedure calls by using the J-type format for both jump and jump-and-link instructions.

Showing Branch Offset in Machine Language

Example

The *while* loop on page 127 was compiled into this MIPS assembler code:

```
Loop:  add $t1,$s3,$s3    # Temp reg $t1 = 2 * i
       add $t1,$t1,$t1    # Temp reg $t1 = 4 * i
       add $t1,$t1,$s6    # $t1 = address of save[i]
       lw  $t0,0($t1)     # Temp reg $t0 = save[i]
       bne $t0,$s5, Exit  # go to Exit if save[i] ≠ k
       add $s3,$s3,$s4    # i = i + j
       j   Loop           # go to Loop
Exit:
```

If we assume that the loop is placed starting at location 80000 in memory, what is the MIPS machine code for this loop?

Answer

The assembled instructions and their addresses would look like this:

80000	0	19	19	9	0	32
80004	0	9	9	9	0	32
80008	0	9	22	9	0	32
80012	35	9	8		0	
80016	5	8	21		8	
80020	0	19	20	19	0	32
80024	2	80000				
80028	. . .					
80012	35	9	8		0	

Remember that MIPS instructions use byte addresses, so addresses of sequential words differ by four, the number of bytes in a word. The bne instruction on the fifth line adds 8 bytes to the address of the *following* instruction (80020), specifying the branch destination relative to that instruction (8) instead of the current instruction (12) or using the full destination address (80028). The jump instruction on the last line does use the full address (80000), corresponding to the label Loop.

Since all MIPS instructions are 4 bytes long, MIPS stretches the distance of the branch by having PC-relative addressing refer to the number of *words* to the next instruction instead of the number of bytes. Thus the 16-bit field can branch four times as far by interpreting the field as a relative word address rather than as a relative byte address. Hence the address field in the bne instruction at location 80016 in the example above should have 2 instead of 8. (Relative word addressing is the reason that the machine language versions of beq and bne in Figures 3.9 and 3.14 have 25 in their address fields instead of 100, as in the assembly language versions.)

Hardware Software Interface	Nearly every conditional branch is to a nearby location, but occasionally it branches far away, farther than can be represented in the 16 bits of the conditional branch instruction. The assembler comes to the rescue just as it did with large addresses or constants: it inserts an unconditional jump to the branch target, and the condition is inverted so that the branch decides whether to skip the jump.

Branching Far Away

Example

Given a branch on register $s0 being equal to register $s1,

```
        beq    $s0,$s1, L1
```

replace it by a pair of instructions that offers a much greater branching distance.

Answer

It can be replaced by these instructions:

```
        bne    $s0,$s1, L2
        j      L1
    L2:
```

Elaboration: The 26-bit field in jump instructions is also a word address, meaning that it represents a 28-bit byte address. Since the PC is 32 bits, 4 bits must come from someplace else. The MIPS jump instruction replaces only the lower 28 bits of the PC, leaving the upper 4 bits of the PC unchanged. The loader and linker (section 3.9) must be careful to avoid placing a program across an address boundary of 256 MB (64 million instructions), for otherwise a jump must be replaced by a jump register instruction preceded by other instructions to load the full 32-bit address into a register.

MIPS Addressing Mode Summary

We have seen two new forms of addressing in this section. Multiple forms of addressing are generically called *addressing modes*. The MIPS addressing modes are the following:

1. *Register addressing*, where the operand is a register

2. *Base* or *displacement addressing*, where the operand is at the memory location whose address is the sum of a register and a constant in the instruction

3. *Immediate addressing*, where the operand is a constant within the instruction itself

4. *PC-relative addressing*, where the address is the sum of the PC and a constant in the instruction

5. *Pseudodirect addressing*, where the jump address is the 26 bits of the instruction concatenated with the upper bits of the PC

Note that a single operation can use more than one addressing mode. Add, for example, uses both immediate (addi) and register (add) addressing. Figure 3.17 shows how operands are identified for each addressing mode. Section 3.12 expands this list to show addressing modes found in other styles of computers.

Hardware Software Interface

Although we show the MIPS architecture as having 32-bit addresses, nearly all microprocessors (including MIPS) have 64-bit address extensions. (See Web Extension I at *www.mkp.com/cod2e.htm.*) These extensions were in response to the needs of software for larger programs. The process of instruction set extension allows architectures to be expanded in a way that lets software move compatibly upward to the next generation of architecture.

Decoding Machine Language

Sometimes you are forced to reverse-engineer machine language to create the original assembly language. One example is when looking at a core dump. Figure 3.18 shows the MIPS encoding of the fields for the MIPS machine language. This figure can be used to translate by hand between assembly language and machine language.

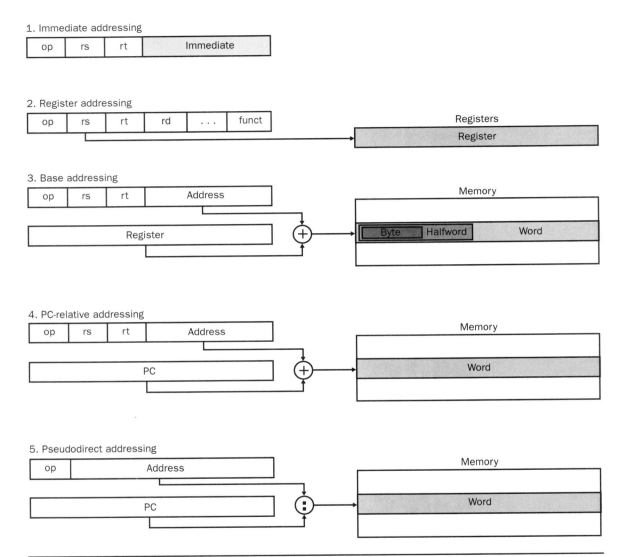

FIGURE 3.17   Illustration of the five MIPS addressing modes. The operands are shaded in color. The operand of mode 3 is in memory, whereas the operand for mode 2 is a register. Note that versions of load and store access bytes, half-words, or words. For mode 1 the operand is 16 bits of the instruction itself. Modes 4 and 5 are used to address instructions in memory, with mode 4 adding a 16-bit address to the PC and mode 5 concatenating a 26-bit address with the upper bits of the PC.

op(31:26)								
28–26 31–29	0(000)	1(001)	2(010)	3(011)	4(100)	5(101)	6(110)	7(111)
0(000)	R-format	Bltz/gez	jump	jump & link	branch eq	branch ne	blez	bgtz
1(001)	add immediate	addiu	set less than imm.	sltiu	andi	ori	xori	load upper imm
2(010)	TLB	FlPt						
3(011)								
4(100)	load byte	lh	lwl	load word	lbu	lhu	lwr	
5(101)	store byte	sh	swl	store word			swr	
6(110)	lwc0	lwc1						
7(111)	swc0	swc1						

op(31:26)=010000 (TLB), rs(25:21)								
23–21 25–24	0(000)	1(001)	2(010)	3(011)	4(100)	5(101)	6(110)	7(111)
0(00)	mfc0		cfc0		mtc0		ctc0	
1(01)								
2(10)								
3(11)								

op(31:26)=000000 (R-format), funct(5:0)								
2–0 5–3	0(000)	1(001)	2(010)	3(011)	4(100)	5(101)	6(110)	7(111)
0(000)	sll		srl	sra	sllv		srlv	srav
1(001)	jump reg.	jalr			syscall	break		
2(010)	mfhi	mthi	mflo	mtlo				
3(011)	mult	multu	div	divu				
4(100)	add	addu	subtract	subu	and	or	xor	nor
5(101)			set l.t.	sltu				
6(110)								
7(111)								

FIGURE 3.18 MIPS instruction encoding. This notation gives the value of a field by row and by column. For example, in the top portion of the figure load word is found in row number 4 (100_{two} for bits 31–29 of the instruction) and column number 3 (011_{two} for bits 28–26 of the instruction), so the corresponding value of the op field (bits 31–26) is 100011_{two}. Underscore means the field is used elsewhere. For example, R-format in row 0 and column 0 (op = 000000_{two}) is defined in the bottom part of the figure. Hence subtract in row 4 and column 2 of the bottom section means that the funct field (bits 5–0) of the instruction is 100010_{two} and the op field (bits 31–26) is 000000_{two}. The FlPt value in row 2, column 1 is defined in Figure 4.48 on page 292 in Chapter 4. Bltz/gez is the opcode for four instructions found in Appendix A: bltz, bgez, bltzal, and bgezal. Instructions given in full name using color are described in Chapter 3, while instructions given in mnemonics using color are described in Chapter 4. Appendix A covers all instructions.

Decoding Machine Code

| Example |

What is the assembly language corresponding to this machine instruction?

(Bits: *31   28   26   5   2   0)*
                0000 0000 1010 1111 1000 0000 0010 0000

| Answer |

The first step is to look at the op field to determine the operation. Referring to Figure 3.18, when bits 31–29 are 000 and bits 28–26 are 000, it is an R-format instruction. Let's reformat the binary instruction into R-format fields, listed in Figure 3.19:

op	rs	rt	rd	shamt	funct
000000	00101	01111	10000	00000	100000

The bottom portion of Figure 3.18 determines the operation of an R-format instruction. In this case, bits 5–3 are 100 and bits 2–0 are 000, which means this binary pattern represents an add instruction.

We decode the rest of the instruction by looking at the field values. The decimal values are 5 for the rs field, 15 for rt, 16 for rd (shamt is unused). Figure 3.13 on page 140 says these numbers represent registers $a1, $t7, and $s0. Now we can show the assembly instruction:

    add $s0,$a1,$t7

Figure 3.20 shows the MIPS assembly language revealed in Chapter 3; the remaining hidden portion of MIPS instructions deals mainly with arithmetic, covered in the next chapter.

Name	Fields						Comments
Field size	6 bits	5 bits	5 bits	5 bits	5 bits	6 bits	All MIPS instructions 32 bits
R-format	op	rs	rt	rd	shamt	funct	Arithmetic instruction format
I-format	op	rs	rt	address/immediate			Transfer, branch, imm. format
J-format	op	target address					Jump instruction format

FIGURE 3.19   MIPS instruction formats in Chapter 3. Highlighted portions show instruction formats introduced in this section.

MIPS operands

Name	Example	Comments
32 registers	$s0–$s7, $t0–$t9, $zero, $a0–$a3, $v0–$v1, $gp, $fp, $sp, $ra, $at	Fast locations for data. In MIPS, data must be in registers to perform arithmetic. MIPS register $zero always equals 0. Register $at is reserved for the assembler to handle large constants.
2^{30} memory words	Memory[0], Memory[4], . . . , Memory[4294967292]	Accessed only by data transfer instructions. MIPS uses byte addresses, so sequential words differ by 4. Memory holds data structures, such as arrays, and spilled registers, such as those saved on procedure calls.

MIPS assembly language

Category	Instruction	Example		Meaning	Comments
Arithmetic	add	add	$s1,$s2,$s3	$s1 = $s2 + $s3	Three operands; data in registers
	subtract	sub	$s1,$s2,$s3	$s1 = $s2 - $s3	Three operands; data in registers
	add immediate	addi	$s1,$s2,100	$s1 = $s2 + 100	Used to add constants
Data transfer	load word	lw	$s1,100($s2)	$s1 = Memory[$s2 + 100]	Word from memory to register
	store word	sw	$s1,100($s2)	Memory[$s2 + 100] = $s1	Word from register to memory
	load byte	lb	$s1,100($s2)	$s1 = Memory[$s2 + 100]	Byte from memory to register
	store byte	sb	$s1,100($s2)	Memory[$s2 + 100] = $s1	Byte from register to memory
	load upper immediate	lui	$s1,100	$s1 = 100 * 2^{16}	Loads constant in upper 16 bits
Conditional branch	branch on equal	beq	$s1,$s2,25	if ($s1 == $s2) go to PC + 4 + 100	Equal test; PC-relative branch
	branch on not equal	bne	$s1,$s2,25	if ($s1 != $s2) go to PC + 4 + 100	Not equal test; PC-relative
	set on less than	slt	$s1,$s2,$s3	if ($s2 < $s3) $s1 = 1; else $s1 = 0	Compare less than; for beq, bne
	set less than immediate	slti	$s1,$s2,100	if ($s2 < 100) $s1 = 1; else $s1 = 0	Compare less than constant
Uncondi-tional jump	jump	j	2500	go to 10000	Jump to target address
	jump register	jr	$ra	go to $ra	For switch, procedure return
	jump and link	jal	2500	$ra = PC + 4; go to 10000	For procedure call

FIGURE 3.20 MIPS assembly language revealed in Chapter 3. Highlighted portions show portions from sections 3.7 and 3.8.

3.9   Starting a Program

This section describes the four steps in transforming a C program in a file on disk into a program running on a computer. Figure 3.21 shows the translation hierarchy. Some systems combine these steps to reduce translation time, but these are the logical four phases that all programs go through. This section follows this translation hierarchy.

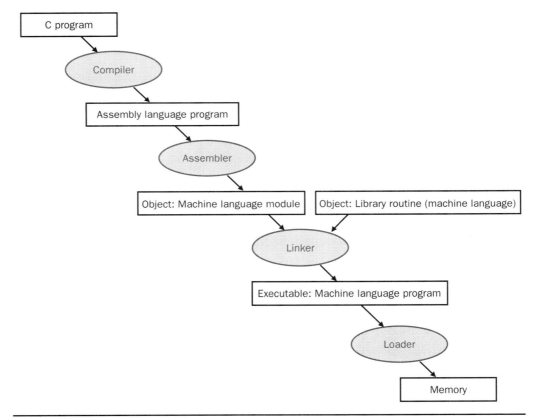

FIGURE 3.21   A translation hierarchy. A high-level-language program is first compiled into an assembly language program and then assembled into an object module in machine language. The linker combines multiple modules with library routines to resolve all references. The loader then places the machine code into the proper memory locations for execution by the processor. To speed up the translation process, some steps are skipped or combined together. Some compilers produce object modules directly, and some systems use linking loaders that perform the last two steps. To identify the type of file, Unix follows a suffix convention for files: C source files are named x.c, assembly files are x.s, object files are named x.o, and an executable file by default is called a.out. MS-DOS uses the suffixes .TXT, .ASM, .OBJ, and .EXE to the same effect.

Compiler

The compiler transforms the C program into an *assembly language program*, a symbolic form of what the machine understands. High-level-language programs take many fewer lines of code than assembly language, so programmer productivity is much higher.

In 1975 many operating systems and assemblers were written in assembly language because memories were small and compilers were inefficient. The 16,000-fold increase in memory capacity per DRAM chip has reduced program size concerns, and optimizing compilers today can produce assembly language programs nearly as good as an assembly language expert, and sometimes even better for large programs.

Assembler

As mentioned on page 147, since assembly language is the interface to higher-level software, the assembler can also treat common variations of machine language instructions as if they were instructions in their own right. These instructions need not be implemented in hardware; however, their appearance in assembly language simplifies translation and programming. Such instructions are called *pseudoinstructions*.

For example, the MIPS hardware makes sure that register $zero always has the value 0. That is, whenever register $zero is used, it supplies a 0, and the programmer cannot change the value of register $zero. Register $zero is used to create the assembly language instruction move that copies the contents of one register to another. Thus the MIPS assembler accepts this instruction even though it is not found in the MIPS architecture:

```
move $t0,$t1        # register $t0 gets register $t1
```

The assembler converts this assembly language instruction into the machine language equivalent of the following instruction:

```
add  $t0,$zero,$t1  # register $t0 gets 0 + register $t1
```

The MIPS assembler also converts blt (branch on less than) into the two instructions slt and bne mentioned in the example on page 128. Other examples include bgt, bge, and ble. It also converts branches to faraway locations into a branch and jump. As mentioned above, the MIPS assembler can even allow 32-bit constants to be loaded into a register despite the 16-bit limit of the immediate instructions.

In summary, pseudoinstructions give MIPS a richer set of assembly language instructions than those implemented by the hardware. The only cost is reserving one register, $at, for use by the assembler. If you are going to write assembly programs, use pseudoinstructions to simplify your task. To understand the MIPS architecture and to be sure to get best performance, however, study the real MIPS instructions found in Figures 3.18 and 3.20.

Assemblers will also accept numbers in a variety of bases. In addition to binary and decimal, they usually accept a base that is more succinct than binary yet can easily be converted to a bit pattern. MIPS assemblers use base 16, called *hexadecimal*; we use the subscript "hex" to indicate a hexadecimal number. The hexadecimal digits are 0 to 9 for the first 10 digits and then the letters *a* to *f* for the last 6 digits. For example, the bit pattern from the example on page 154 is shown as both binary and hexadecimal numbers:

$$0000\ 0000\ 1010\ 1111\ 1000\ 0000\ 0010\ 0000_{two} = 00af\ 8020_{hex}$$

Such features are convenient, but the primary task of an assembler is assembly into machine code. The assembler turns the assembly language program into an *object file*, which is a combination of *machine language* instructions, data, and information needed to place instructions properly in memory.

To produce the binary version of each instruction in the assembly language program, the assembler must determine the addresses corresponding to all labels. Assemblers keep track of labels used in branches and data transfer instructions in a *symbol table*. As you might expect, the table contains pairs of symbol and address.

The object file for Unix systems typically contains six distinct pieces:

- The *object file header* describes the size and position of the other pieces of the object file.

- The *text segment* contains the machine language code.

- The *data segment* contains whatever data that comes with the program: either *static data*, which is allocated throughout the program, or *dynamic data*, which can grow or shrink as needed by the program.

- The *relocation information* identifies instructions and data words that depend on absolute addresses when the program is loaded into memory.

- The *symbol table* contains the remaining labels that are not defined, such as external references.

- The *debugging information* contains a concise description of how the modules were compiled so that a debugger can associate machine instructions with C source files and make data structures readable.

The next subsection shows how to attach such routines that have already been assembled, such as library routines.

Linker

What we have presented so far suggests that a single change to one line of one procedure requires compiling and assembling the whole program. Complete retranslation is a terrible waste of computing resources. This repetition is particularly wasteful for standard library routines because programmers would be compiling and assembling routines that by definition almost never change. An alternative is to compile and assemble each procedure independently, so that a change to one line would require compiling and assembling only one procedure. This alternative requires a new systems program, called a *link editor* or *linker*, that takes all the independently assembled machine language programs and "stitches" them together.

There are three steps for the linker:

1. Place code and data modules symbolically in memory.

2. Determine the addresses of data and instruction labels.

3. Patch both the internal and external references.

The linker uses the relocation information and symbol table in each object module to resolve all undefined labels. Such references occur in branch instructions, jump instructions, and data addresses, so the job of this program is much like that of an editor: It finds the old addresses and replaces them with the new addresses. Editing is the origin of the name "link editor," or linker for short. The reason a linker makes sense is that it is much faster to patch code than it is to recompile and reassemble.

If all external references are resolved, the linker next determines the memory locations each module will occupy. Figure 3.22 shows the MIPS convention for allocation of program and data to memory. Since the files were assembled in isolation, the assembler could not know where a module's instructions and data will be placed relative to other modules. When the linker places a module in memory, all *absolute* references, that is, memory addresses that are not relative to a register, must be *relocated* to reflect its true location.

The linker produces an *executable file* that can be run on a computer. Typically, this file has the same format as an object file, except that it contains no unresolved references, relocation information, symbol table, or debugging information. It is possible to have partially linked files, such as library routines, which still have unresolved addresses and hence result in object files.

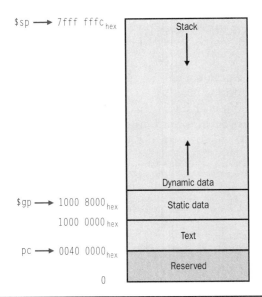

FIGURE 3.22 The MIPS memory allocation for program and data. Starting top down, the stack pointer is initialized to $7fff\ fffc_{hex}$ and grows down toward the data segment. At the other end, the program code ("text") starts at $0040\ 0000_{hex}$. The static data starts at $1000\ 0000_{hex}$. Dynamic data, allocated by malloc in C, is next and grows up toward the stack. The global pointer, $gp, is set to an address to make it easy to access data. It is initialized to $1000\ 8000_{hex}$ so that it can access from $1000\ 0000_{hex}$ to $1000\ ffff_{hex}$ using the positive and negative 16-bit offsets from $gp (see two's complement addressing in Chapter 4).

Linking Object Files

Example

Link the two object files below. Show updated addresses of the first few instructions of the completed executable file. We show the instructions in assembly language just to make the example understandable; in reality, the instructions would be numbers.

Note that in the object files we have highlighted the addresses and symbols that must be updated in the link process: the instructions that refer to the addresses of procedures A and B and the instructions that refer to the addresses of data words X and Y.

Object file header			
	Name	Procedure A	
	Text size	100_{hex}	
	Data size	20_{hex}	
Text segment	Address	Instruction	
	0	lw $a0, 0($gp)	
	4	jal 0	
	...	...	
Data segment	0	(X)	
	...	...	
Relocation information	Address	Instruction type	Dependency
	0	lw	X
	4	jal	B
Symbol table	Label	Address	
	X	–	
	B	–	
Object file header			
	Name	Procedure B	
	Text size	200_{hex}	
	Data size	30_{hex}	
Text segment	Address	Instruction	
	0	sw $a1, 0($gp)	
	4	jal 0	
	...	...	
Data segment	0	(Y)	
	...	...	
Relocation information	Address	Instruction type	Dependency
	0	sw	Y
	4	jal	A
Symbol table	Label	Address	
	Y	–	
	A	–	

Procedure A needs to find the address for the variable labeled X to put in the load instruction and to find the address of procedure B to place in the jal instruction. Procedure B needs the address of the variable labeled Y for the store instruction and the address of procedure A for its jal instruction.

Executable file header		
	Text size	300_{hex}
	Data size	50_{hex}
Text segment	Address	Instruction
	$0040\ 0000_{hex}$	lw $a0, 8000_{hex}($gp)
	$0040\ 0004_{hex}$	jal 40 0100_{hex}
	...	...
	$0040\ 0100_{hex}$	sw $a1, 8020_{hex}($gp)
	$0040\ 0104_{hex}$	jal 40 0000_{hex}
	...	...
Data segment	Address	
	$1000\ 0000_{hex}$	(X)
	...	...
	$1000\ 0020_{hex}$	(Y)
	...	...

From Figure 3.22 we know that the text segment starts at address $40\ 0000_{hex}$ and the data segment at $1000\ 0000_{hex}$. The text of procedure A is placed at the first address and its data at the second. The object file header for procedure A says that its text is 100_{hex} bytes and its data is 20_{hex} bytes, so the starting address for procedure B text is $40\ 0100_{hex}$, and its data starts at $1000\ 0020_{hex}$.

Now the linker updates the address fields of the instructions. It uses the instruction type field to know the format of the address to be edited. We have two types here:

1. The jals are easy because they use pseudodirect addressing. The jal at address $40\ 0004_{hex}$ gets $40\ 0100_{hex}$ (the address of procedure B) in its address field, and the jal at $40\ 0104_{hex}$ gets $40\ 0000_{hex}$ (the address of procedure A) in its address field.

2. The load and store addresses are harder because they are relative to a base register. In this example, the global pointer is used as the base register. Figure 3.22 shows that $gp is initialized to $1000\ 8000_{hex}$. To get the address $1000\ 0000_{hex}$ (the address of word X), we place 8000_{hex} in the address field of lw at address $40\ 0000_{hex}$. Chapter 4 explains 16-bit two's complement computer arithmetic, which is why 8000_{hex} in the address field yields $1000\ 0000_{hex}$ as the address. Similarly, we place 8020_{hex} in the address field of sw at address $40\ 0100_{hex}$ to get the address $1000\ 0020_{hex}$ (the address of word Y).

Loader

Now that the executable file is on disk, the operating system reads it to memory and starts it. It follows these steps in Unix systems:

1. Reads the executable file header to determine size of the text and data segments.

2. Creates an address space large enough for the text and data.

3. Copies the instructions and data from the executable file into memory.

4. Copies the parameters (if any) to the main program onto the stack.

5. Initializes the machine registers and sets the stack pointer to the first free location.

6. Jumps to a start-up routine that copies the parameters into the argument registers and calls the main routine of the program. When the main routine returns, the start-up routine terminates the program with an `exit` system call.

Sections A.3 and A.4 in Appendix A describe linkers and loaders in more detail.

3.10 An Example to Put It All Together

One danger of showing assembly language code in snippets is that you will have no idea what a full assembly language program looks like. In this section and the next, we derive the MIPS code from two procedures written in C: one to swap array elements and one to sort them.

The Procedure swap

Let's start with the code for the procedure `swap` in Figure 3.23. This procedure simply swaps two locations in memory. When translating from C to assembly language, we follow these general steps:

1. Allocate registers to program variables.

2. Produce code for the body of the procedure.

3. Preserve registers across the procedure invocation.

This section describes the `swap` procedure in these three pieces, concluding by putting all the pieces together.

```
swap(int v[], int k)
{
  int temp;
  temp = v[k];
  v[k] = v[k+1];
  v[k+1] = temp;
}
```

FIGURE 3.23   A C procedure that swaps two locations in memory. This procedure will be used in the sorting example in the next section. Web Extension III at *www.mkp.com/cod2e.htm* shows the C and Pascal versions of this procedure side by side.

Register Allocation for swap

As mentioned on page 132, the MIPS convention on parameter passing is to use registers $a0, $a1, $a2, and $a3. Since swap has just two parameters, v and k, they will be found in registers $a0 and $a1. The only other variable is temp, which we associate with register $t0 since swap is a leaf procedure (see page 144). This register allocation corresponds to the variable declarations in the first part of the swap procedure in Figure 3.23.

Code for the Body of the Procedure swap

The remaining lines of C code in swap are

```
temp = v[k];
v[k] = v[k+1];
v[k+1] = temp;
```

Recall that the memory address for MIPS refers to the *byte* address, and so words are really 4 bytes apart. Hence we need to multiply the index k by 4 before adding it to the address. *Forgetting that sequential word addresses differ by 4 instead of by 1 is a common mistake in assembly language programming.* Hence the first step is to get the address of v[k] by multiplying k by 4:

```
add    $t1, $a1,$a1    # reg $t1 = k * 2
add    $t1, $t1,$t1    # reg $t1 = k * 4
add    $t1, $a0,$t1    # reg $t1 = v + (k * 4)
                       # reg $t1 has the address of v[k]
```

Now we load v[k] using $t1, and then v[k+1] by adding 4 to $t1:

```
lw     $t0, 0($t1)     # reg $t0 (temp) = v[k]
lw     $t2, 4($t1)     # reg $t2 = v[k + 1]
                       # refers to next element of v
```

Next we store $t0 and $t2 to the swapped addresses:

```
sw     $t2, 0($t1)     # v[k] = reg $t2
sw     $t0, 4($t1)     # v[k+1] = reg $t0 (temp)
```

Procedure body			
swap:	add	$t1, $a1, a1	# reg $t1 = k * 2
	add	$t1, $t1, t1	# reg $t1 = k * 4
	add	$t1, $a0, $t1	# reg $t1 = v + (k * 4)
			# reg $t1 has the address of v[k]
	lw	$t0, 0($t1)	# reg $t0 (temp) = v[k]
	lw	$t2, 4($t1)	# reg $t2 = v[k + 1]
			# refers to next element of v
	sw	$t2, 0($t1)	# v[k] = reg $t2
	sw	$t0, 4($t1)	# v[k+1] = reg $t0 (temp)

Procedure return		
jr	$ra	# return to calling routine

FIGURE 3.24   MIPS assembly code of the procedure swap **in Figure 3.23.**

Now we have allocated registers and written the code to perform the operations of the procedure. The only missing code is the code that preserves for the caller the saved registers that are used within swap. Since we are not using saved registers in this leaf procedure, there is nothing to preserve.

The Full swap Procedure

We are now ready for the whole routine, which includes the procedure label and the return jump. To make it easier to follow, we identify in Figure 3.24 each block of code with its purpose in the procedure.

The Procedure sort

To ensure that you appreciate the rigor of programming in assembly language, we'll try a second, longer example. In this case, we'll build a routine that calls the swap procedure. This program sorts an array of integers. Figure 3.25 shows the C version of the program. Once again we present this procedure in several steps, concluding with the full procedure.

Register Allocation for sort

The two parameters of the procedure sort, v and n, are in the parameter registers $a0 and $a1, and we assign register $s0 to i and register $s1 to j.

Code for the Body of the Procedure sort

The procedure body consists of two nested *for* loops and a call to swap that includes parameters. Let's unwrap the code from the outside to the middle.

The first translation step is the first *for* loop:

```
for (i = 0; i < n; i = i + 1) {
```

```
sort (int v[], int n)
{
    int i, j;
    for (i = 0; i < n; i = i + 1) {
        for (j = i - 1; j >= 0 && v[j] > v[j + 1]; j = j - 1) { swap(v,j);
        }
    }
}
```

FIGURE 3.25 A C procedure that performs a sort on the array v. In case you are unfamiliar with C, the three parts of the first *for* statement are the initialization that happens before the first iteration (i = 0), the test if the loop should iterate again (i < n), and the operation that happens at the end of each iteration (i = i + 1). Web Extension II at *www.mkp.com/cod2e.htm* shows the C and Pascal versions of this procedure side by side.

Recall that the C *for* statement has three parts: initialization, loop test, and iteration increment. It takes just one instruction to initialize i to 0, the first part of the *for* statement:

```
        move  $s0, $zero      # i = 0
```

(Remember that move is a pseudoinstruction provided by the assembler for the convenience of the assembly language programmer; see page 157.) It also takes just one instruction to increment i, the last part of the *for* statement:

```
        addi  $s0, $s0, 1     # i = i + 1
```

The loop should be exited if i < n is *not* true, or, said another way, should be exited if i ≥ n. The set on less than instruction sets register $t0 to 1 if $s0 < $a1 and 0 otherwise. Since we want to test if $s0 ≥ $a1, we branch if register $t0 is 0. This test takes two instructions:

```
for1tst: slt  $t0, $s0, $a1  # reg $t0 = 0 if $s0 ≥ $a1 (i≥n)
         beq  $t0, $zero,exit1 # go to exit1 if $s0≥$a1 (i≥n)
```

The bottom of the loop just jumps back to the loop test:

```
         j    for1tst         # jump to test of outer loop
exit1:
```

The skeleton code of the first *for* loop is then

```
         move $s0, $zero      # i = 0
for1tst: slt  $t0, $s0, $a1  # reg $t0 = 0 if $s0 ≥ $a1 (i≥n)
         beq  $t0, $zero,exit1 # go to exit1 if $s0≥$a1 (i≥n)
         . . .
         (body of first for loop)
         . . .
         addi $s0, $s0, 1     # i = i + 1
         j    for1tst         # jump to test of outer loop
exit1:
```

Voila! Exercise 3.9 explores writing faster code for similar loops.

The second *for* loop looks like this in C:

```
for (j = i - 1; j >= 0 && v[j] > v[j + 1]; j = j - 1) {
```

The initialization portion of this loop is again one instruction:

```
addi   $s1, $s0, -1       # j = i - 1
```

The decrement of j at the end of the loop is also one instruction:

```
addi   $s1, $s1, -1       # j = j - 1
```

The loop test has two parts. We exit the loop if either condition fails, so the first test must exit the loop if it fails (j < 0):

```
for2tst: slti  $t0, $s1, 0 # reg $t0 = 1 if $s1 < 0 (j < 0)
         bne   $t0, $zero, exit2 # go to exit2 if $s1<0 (j < 0)
```

This branch will skip over the second condition test. If it doesn't skip, j ≥ 0.

The second test exits if v[j] > v[j + 1] is *not* true, or exits if v[j] ≤ v[j + 1]. First we create the address by multiplying j by 4 (since we need a byte address) and add it to the base address of v:

```
add    $t1, $s1,$s1       # reg $t1 = j * 2
add    $t1, $t1,$t1       # reg $t1 = j * 4
add    $t2, $a0,$t1       # reg $t2 = v + (j * 4)
```

Now we load v[j]:

```
lw     $t3, 0($t2)        # reg $t3   = v[j]
```

Since we know that the second element is just the following word, we add 4 to the address in register $t2 to get v[j + 1]:

```
lw     $t4, 4($t2)        # reg $t4   = v[j + 1]
```

The test of v[j] ≤ v[j + 1] is the same as v[j + 1] ≥ v[j], so the two instructions of the exit test are

```
slt    $t0, $t4, $t3      # reg $t0 = 0 if $t4   ≥ $t3
beq    $t0, $zero,exit2   # go to exit2 if $t4   ≥ $t3
```

The bottom of the loop jumps back to the inner loop test:

```
j      for2tst            # jump to test of inner loop
```

Combining the pieces together, the skeleton of the second *for* loop looks like this:

```
       addi  $s1, $s0, -1     # j = i - 1
for2tst: slti $t0, $s1, 0     #  reg $t0 = 1 if $s1 < 0 (j<0)
       bne   $t0, $zero,exit2 # go to exit2 if $s1 < 0 (j<0)
       add   $t1, $s1,$s1     # reg $t1 = j * 2
```

```
add    $t1, $t1,$t1      # reg $t1 = j * 4
add    $t2, $a0,$t1      # reg $t2 = v + (j * 4)
lw     $t3, 0($t2)       # reg $t3   = v[j]
lw     $t4, 4($t2)       # reg $t4   = v[j + 1]
slt    $t0, $t4, $t3     #  reg $t0 = 0 if $t4  ≥ $t3
beq    $t0, $zero,exit2  # go to exit2 if $t4   ≥ $t3

       . . .
       (body of second for loop)
       . . .
addi   $s1, $s1, -1      # j = j - 1
j      for2tst           # jump to test of inner loop
exit2:
```

The Procedure Call in sort

The next step is the body of the second *for* loop:

```
swap(v,j);
```

Calling swap is easy enough:

```
jal    swap
```

Passing Parameters in sort

The problem comes when we want to pass parameters because the sort procedure needs the values in registers $a0 and $a1, yet the swap procedure needs to have its parameters placed in those same registers. One solution is to copy the parameters for sort into other registers earlier in the procedure, making registers $a0 and $a1 available for the call of swap. (This copy is faster than saving and restoring on the stack.) We first copy $a0 and $a1 into $s2 and $s3 during the procedure:

```
move   $s2, $a0   # copy parameter $a0 into $s2
move   $s3, $a1   # copy parameter $a1 into $s3
```

Then we pass the parameters to swap with these two instructions:

```
move   $a0, $s2   # first swap parameter is v
move   $a1, $s1   # second swap parameter is j
```

Preserving Registers in sort

The only remaining code is the saving and restoring of registers. Clearly we must save the return address in register $ra, since sort is a procedure and is called itself. The sort procedure also uses the saved registers $s0, $s1, $s2, and $s3, so they must be saved. The prologue of the sort procedure is then

```
addi    $sp,$sp,-20   # make room on stack for 5 regs
sw      $ra,16($sp)   # save $ra on stack
sw      $s3,12($sp)   # save $s3 on stack
sw      $s2, 8($sp)   # save $s2 on stack
sw      $s1, 4($sp)   # save $s1 on stack
sw      $s0, 0($sp)   # save $s0 on stack
```

The tail of the procedure simply reverses all these instructions, then adds a jr to return.

The Full Procedure sort

Now we put all the pieces together in Figure 3.26, being careful to replace references to registers $a0 and $a1 in the *for* loops with references to registers $s2 and $s3. Once again to make the code easier to follow, we identify each block of code with its purpose in the procedure. In this example, 9 lines of the sort procedure in C became the 35 lines in the MIPS assembly language.

Elaboration: One optimization that would work well in this example is *procedure inlining*. Instead of passing arguments in parameters and invoking the code with a jal instruction, the compiler would copy the code from the body of the swap procedure where the call to swap appears in the code. Inlining would avoid four instructions in this example. The downside of the inlining optimization is that the compiled code would be bigger, assuming that the inlined procedure is called from several locations. Such a code expansion might turn into *lower* performance if it increased the cache miss rate; see Chapter 7.

The MIPS compilers always save room on the stack for the arguments in case they need to be stored, so in reality they always decrement $sp by 16 to make room for all 4 argument registers (16 bytes). One reason is that C provides a vararg option that allows a pointer to pick, say, the third argument to a procedure. When the compiler encounters the rare vararg, it copies the registers onto the stack into the reserved locations.

		Saving registers		
	sort:	addi	$sp,$sp, -20	# make room on stack for 5 registers
		sw	$ra, 16($sp)	# save $ra on stack
		sw	$s3,12($sp)	# save $s3 on stack
		sw	$s2, 8($sp)	# save $s2 on stack
		sw	$s1, 4($sp)	# save $s1 on stack
		sw	$s0, 0($sp)	# save $s0 on stack
			Procedure body	
Move parameters		move	$s2, $a0	# copy parameter $a0 into $s2 (save $a0)
		move	$s3, $a1	# copy parameter $a1 into $s3 (save $a1)
Outer loop		move	$s0, $zero	# i = 0
	for1tst:slt		$t0, $s0, $s3	# reg $t0 = 0 if $s0 ≥ $s3 (i ≥ n)
		beq	$t0, $zero, exit1	# go to exit1 if $s0 ≥ $s3 (i ≥ n)
Inner loop		addi	$s1, $s0, -1	# j = i - 1
	for2tst:slti		$t0, $s1, 0	# reg $t0 = 1 if $s1 < 0 (j < 0)
		bne	$t0, $zero, exit2	# go to exit2 if $s1 < 0 (j < 0)
		add	$t1, $s1, $s1	# reg $t1 = j * 2
		add	$t1, $t1, $t1	# reg $t1 = j * 4
		add	$t2, $s2, $t1	# reg $t2 = v + (j * 4)
		lw	$t3, 0($t2)	# reg $t3 = v[j]
		lw	$t4, 4($t2)	# reg $t4 = v[j + 1]
		slt	$t0, $t4, $t3	# reg $t0 = 0 if $t4 ≥ $t3
		beq	$t0, $zero, exit2	# go to exit2 if $t4 ≥ $t3
Pass parameters and call		move	$a0, $s2	# 1st parameter of swap is v (old $a0)
		move	$a1, $s1	# 2nd parameter of swap is j
		jal	swap	# swap code shown in Figure 3.24
Inner loop		addi	$s1, $s1, -1	# j = j - 1
		j	for2tst	# jump to test of inner loop
Outer loop	exit2:	addi	$s0, $s0, 1	# i = i + 1
		j	for1tst	# jump to test of outer loop
			Restoring registers	
	exit1:	lw	$s0, 0($sp)	# restore $s0 from stack
		lw	$s1, 4($sp)	# restore $s1 from stack
		lw	$s2, 8($sp)	# restore $s2 from stack
		lw	$s3,12($sp)	# restore $s3 from stack
		lw	$ra,16($sp)	# restore $ra from stack
		addi	$sp,$sp, 20	# restore stack pointer
			Procedure return	
		jr	$ra	# return to calling routine

FIGURE 3.26   MIPS assembly version of procedure sort **in Figure 3.25 on page 166.**

3.11 Arrays versus Pointers

A challenging topic for any new programmer is understanding pointers. Comparing assembly code that uses arrays and array indices to the assembly code that uses pointers offers insight into that difference. This section shows C and MIPS assembly versions of two procedures to clear a sequence of words in memory: one using array indices and one using pointers. Figure 3.27 shows the two C procedures.

> **Hardware Software Interface**
>
> People used to be taught to use pointers in C to get greater efficiency than available with arrays: "Use pointers, even if you can't understand the code." The procedure clear2 in Figure 3.27 is such an example. Modern optimizing compilers can produce just as good code for the array version of the code. The purpose of this section is to show how pointers map into MIPS instructions, and not to endorse a questionable style.

```
clear1(int array[], int size)
{
  int i;
  for (i = 0; i < size; i = i + 1)
      array[i] = 0;
}

clear2(int *array, int size)
{
  int *p;
  for (p = &array[0]; p < &array[size]; p = p + 1)
      *p = 0;
}
```

FIGURE 3.27 Two C procedures for setting an array to all zeros. Clear1 uses indices, while clear2 uses pointers. The second procedure needs some explanation for those unfamiliar with C. The address of a variable is indicated by & and referring to the object pointed to by a pointer is indicated by *. The declarations declare that array and p are pointers to integers. The first part of the *for* loop in clear2 assigns the address of the first element of array to the pointer p. The second part of the *for* loop tests to see if the pointer is pointing beyond the last element of array. Incrementing a pointer by one, in the last part of the *for* loop, means moving the pointer to the next sequential object of its declared size. Since p is a pointer to integers, the compiler will generate MIPS instructions to increment p by four, the number of bytes in a MIPS integer. The assignment in the loop places 0 in the object pointed to by p.

Array Version of Clear

Let's start with the array version, clear1, focusing on the body of the loop and ignoring the procedure linkage code. We assume that the two parameters array and size are found in the registers $a0 and $a1, and that i is allocated to register $t0.

The initialization of i, the first part of the *for* loop, is straightforward:

```
move $t0,$zero      # i = 0 (register $t0 = 0)
```

To set array[i] to 0 we must first get its address. Start by multiplying i by 4 to get the byte address:

```
loop1: add  $t1,$t0,$t0    # $t1 = i * 2
       add  $t1,$t1,$t1    # $t1 = i * 4
```

Since the starting address of the array is in a register, we must add it to the index to get the address of array[i] using an add instruction:

```
       add  $t2,$a0,$t1    # $t2 = address of array[i]
```

(This example is an ideal situation for indexed addressing; see page 175.) Finally we can store 0 in that address:

```
       sw   $zero, 0($t2)  # array[i] = 0
```

This instruction is the end of the body of the loop, so the next step is to increment i:

```
       addi $t0,$t0,1      # i = i + 1
```

The loop test checks if i is less than size:

```
       slt  $t3,$t0,$a1     # $t3 = (i < size)
       bne  $t3,$zero,loop1 # if (i < size) go to loop1
```

We have now seen all the pieces of the procedure. Here is the MIPS code for clearing an array using indices:

```
       move $t0,$zero       # i = 0
loop1: add  $t1,$t0,$t0     # $t1 = i * 2
       add  $t1,$t1,$t1     # $t1 = i * 4
       add  $t2,$a0,$t1     # $t2 = address of array[i]
       sw   $zero, 0($t2)   # array[i] = 0
       addi $t0,$t0,1       # i = i + 1
       slt  $t3,$t0,$a1     # $t3 = (i < size)
       bne  $t3,$zero,loop1 # if (i < size) go to loop1
```

(This code works as long as size is greater than 0.)

Pointer Version of Clear

The second procedure that uses pointers allocates the two parameters array and size to the registers $a0 and $a1 and allocates p to register $t0. The code for the second procedure starts with assigning the pointer p to the address of the first element of the array:

```
move    $t0,$a0     # p = address of array[0]
```

The next code is the body of the *for* loop, which simply stores 0 into p:

```
loop2:  sw      $zero,0($t0) # Memory[p] = 0
```

This instruction implements the body of the loop, so the next code is the iteration increment, which changes p to point to the next word:

```
addi    $t0,$t0,4   # p = p + 4
```

Incrementing a pointer by 1 means moving the pointer to the next sequential object in C. Since p is a pointer to integers, each of which use 4 bytes, the compiler increments p by 4.

The loop test is next. The first step is calculating the address of the last element of array. Start with multiplying size by 4 to get its byte address:

```
add $t1,$a1,$a1     # $t1 = size * 2
add $t1,$t1,$t1     # $t1 = size * 4
```

and then we add the product to the starting address of the array to get the address of the first word *after* the array:

```
add $t2,$a0,$t1     # $t2 = address of array[size]
```

The loop test is simply to see if p is less than the last element of array:

```
slt $t3,$t0,$t2     # $t3 = (p<&array[size])
bne $t3,$zero,loop2 # if (p<&array[size]) go to loop2
```

With all the pieces completed, we can show a pointer version of the code to zero an array:

```
        move $t0,$a0        # p = address of array[0]
loop2:  sw   $zero,0($t0)   # Memory[p] = 0
        addi $t0,$t0,4      # p = p + 4
        add $t1,$a1,$a1     # $t1 = size * 2
        add $t1,$t1,$t1     # $t1 = size * 4
        add $t2,$a0,$t1     # $t2 = address of array[size]
        slt $t3,$t0,$t2     # $t3 = (p<&array[size])
        bne $t3,$zero,loop2 # if (p<&array[size]) go to loop2
```

As in the first example, this code assumes size is greater than 0.

Note that this program calculates the address of the end of the array every iteration of the loop, even though it does not change. A faster version of the code moves this calculation outside the loop:

```
        move $t0,$a0          # p = address of array[0]
        add  $t1,$a1,$a1      # $t1 = size * 2
        add  $t1,$t1,$t1      # $t1 = size * 4
        add  $t2,$a0,$t1      # $t2 = address of array[size]
loop2:  sw   $zero,0($t0)     # Memory[p] = 0
        addi $t0,$t0,4        # p = p + 4
        slt  $t3,$t0,$t2      # $t3 = (p<&array[size])
        bne  $t3,$zero,loop2  # if (p<&array[size]) go to loop2
```

Comparing the Two Versions of Clear

Comparing the two code sequences side by side illustrates the difference between array indices and pointers (the changes introduced by the pointer version are highlighted):

```
        move $t0,$zero   # i = 0                      move $t0,$a0     # p = & array[0]
loop1:  add  $t1,$t0,$t0 # $t1 = i * 2               add  $t1,$a1,$a1 # $t1 = size * 2
        add  $t1,$t1,$t1 # $t1 = i * 4               add  $t1,$t1,$t1 # $t1 = size * 4
        add  $t2,$a0,$t1 # $t2 = &array[i]           add  $t2,$a0,$t1 # $t2 = &array[size]
        sw   $zero, 0($t2)# array[i] = 0    loop2:   sw   $zero,0($t0)# Memory[p] = 0
        addi $t0,$t0,1   # i = i + 1                 addi $t0,$t0,4   # p = p + 4
        slt  $t3,$t0,$a1 # $t3 = (i < size)          slt  $t3,$t0,$t2 # $t3=(p<&array[size])
        bne  $t3,$zero,loop1# if () go to loop1      bne  $t3,$zero,loop2# if () go to loop2
```

The version on the left must have the "multiply" and add inside the loop because i is incremented and each address must be recalculated from the new index; the memory pointer version on the right increments the pointer p directly. The pointer version reduces the instructions executed per iteration from 7 to 4. Many modern compilers will optimize the C code in clear1 to produce code similar to the assembly code above on the right-hand side.

Elaboration: The C compiler would add a test to be sure that size is greater than 0. One way would be to add a jump just before the first instruction of the loop to the slt instruction.

3.12 Real Stuff: PowerPC and 80x86 Instructions

Beauty is altogether in the eye of the beholder.

Margaret Wolfe Hungerford, *Molly Bawn*, 1877

Designers of instruction sets sometimes provide more powerful operations than those found in MIPS. The goal is generally to reduce the number of instructions executed by a program. The danger is that this reduction can occur at the cost of simplicity, increasing the time a program takes to execute because the instructions are slower. This slowness may be the result of a slower clock cycle time or of requiring more clock cycles than a simpler sequence (see section 2.8 on page 82).

The path toward operation complexity is thus fraught with peril. To avoid these problems, designers have moved toward simpler instructions. Section 3.13 demonstrates the pitfalls of complexity.

The IBM/Motorola PowerPC

The PowerPC, made by IBM and Motorola and used in the Apple Macintosh, shares many similarities to MIPS: both have 32 integer registers, instructions are all 32 bits long, and data transfer is possible only with loads and stores. The primary difference is two more addressing modes plus a few operations.

Indexed Addressing

In the examples above we saw cases where we needed one register to hold the base of the array and the other to hold the index of the array. PowerPC provides an addressing mode, often called *indexed addressing*, that allows two registers to be added together. The MIPS code

```
add    $t0,$a0,$s3   # $a0 has base of an array, $s3 is index
lw     $t1,0($t0)    # reg $t1 gets Memory[$a0+$s3]
```

could be replaced by the following single instruction in PowerPC:

```
lw     $t1,$a0+$s3   # reg $t1 gets Memory[$a0+$s3]
```

Using the same notation as Figure 3.17, Figure 3.28 shows indexed addressing. It is available with both loads and stores.

Update Addressing

Imagine the case of a code sequence marching through an array of words in memory, such as in the array version of clear1 on page 172. A frequent pair

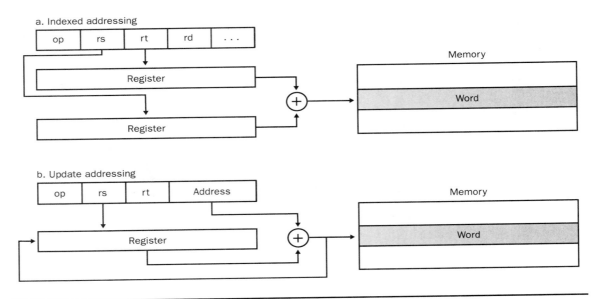

FIGURE 3.28 Illustration of indexed and update addressing mode. The operand is shaded in color.

of operations would be loading a word and then incrementing the base register to point to the next word. The idea of *update addressing* is to have a new version of data transfer instructions that will automatically increment the base register to point to the next word each time data is transferred. Since the MIPS architecture uses byte addresses and words are 4 bytes, this new form would be equivalent to this pair of MIPS instructions:

```
lw      $t0,4($s3)    # reg $t0 gets Memory[$s3+4]
addi    $s3,$s3,4     # $s3 = $s3 + 4
```

The PowerPC includes an instruction like this:

```
lwu     $t0,4($s3)    # reg $t0=Memory[$s3+4]; $s3 = $s3+4
```

That is, the register is updated with the address calculated as part of the load. Figure 3.28 also shows update addressing. PowerPC has update addressing options for both base and indexed addressing, and for both loads and stores.

Unique PowerPC Instructions

The PowerPC instructions follow the same architecture style as MIPS, largely relying on fast execution of simple instructions for performance. Here are a few exceptions.

The first is load multiple and store multiple. These can transfer up to 32 words of data in a single instruction and are intended to make fast copies of locations in memory by using load multiple and store multiple back to back. They also save code size when saving or restoring registers.

A second example is loops. The PowerPC has a special counter register, separate from the other 32 registers, to try to improve performance of a *for* loop.

Suppose we wanted to execute the following C code:

```
for (i = n; i != 0; i = i - 1)
    {. . .};
```

If we want to decrement a register, compare to 0, and then branch as long as the register is not 0, we could use the following MIPS instructions:

```
Loop:   ...
        addi    $t0,$t0,-1      # $t0 = $t0 - 1
        bne     $t0,$zero, Loop # if $t0 != 0 go to Loop
```

In PowerPC we could use a single instruction instead:

```
        bc      Loop,ctr!=0     # $ctr = $ctr - 1;
                                # if $ctr != 0 go to Loop
```

Hardware Software Interface
In addition to going against the advice of simplicity, such sophisticated operations may not *exactly* match what the compiler needs to produce. For example, suppose that instead of decrementing by one, the compiler wanted to increment by four, or instead of branching on not equal zero, the compiler wanted to branch if the index was less than or equal to the limit. Then the instruction just described would be a mismatch. When faced with such objections, the instruction set designer might then generalize the operation, adding another operand to specify the increment and perhaps an option on which branch condition to use. Then the danger is that a common case, say, incrementing by one, will be slower than a sequence of simple operations.

The Intel 80x86

MIPS was the vision of a single small group in 1985; the pieces of this architecture fit nicely together, and the whole architecture can be described succinctly. Such is not the case for the 80x86; it is the product of several independent groups who evolved the architecture over almost 20 years, adding new features to the original instruction set as someone might add clothing to a packed bag. Here are important 80x86 milestones:

- **1978**: The Intel 8086 architecture was announced as an assembly-language-compatible extension of the then-successful Intel 8080, an 8-bit microprocessor. The 8086 is a 16-bit architecture, with all internal registers 16 bits wide. Unlike MIPS, the registers have dedicated uses, and hence the 8086 is not considered a *general-purpose register* architecture.

- **1980**: The Intel 8087 floating-point coprocessor is announced. This architecture extends the 8086 with about 60 floating-point instructions. Instead of using registers, it relies on a stack (see section 3.15 and section 4.9).

- **1982**: The 80286 extended the 8086 architecture by increasing the address space to 24 bits, by creating an elaborate memory-mapping and protection model (see Chapter 7), and by adding a few instructions to round out the instruction set and to manipulate the protection model.

- **1985**: The 80386 extended the 80286 architecture to 32 bits. In addition to a 32-bit architecture with 32-bit registers and a 32-bit address space, the 80386 added new addressing modes and additional operations. The added instructions make the 80386 nearly a general-purpose register machine. The 80386 also added paging support in addition to segmented addressing (see Chapter 7). Like the 80286, the 80386 has a mode to execute 8086 programs without change.

- **1989–95**: The subsequent 80486 in 1989, Pentium in 1992, and Pentium Pro in 1995 were aimed at higher performance, with only four instructions added to the user-visible instruction set: three to help with multiprocessing (Chapter 9) and a conditional move instruction.

- **1997**: After the Pentium and Pentium Pro were shipping, Intel announced that it would expand the Pentium and the Pentium Pro architectures with MMX. This new set of 57 instructions uses the floating-point stack to accelerate multimedia and communication applications. MMX instructions typically operate on multiple short data elements at a time, in the tradition of single instruction, multiple data (SIMD) architectures (see Chapter 9).

This history illustrates the impact of the "golden handcuffs" of compatibility on the 80x86, as the existing software base at each step was too important to jeopardize with significant architectural changes.

Whatever the artistic failures of the 80x86, keep in mind that there are more instances of this architectural family than of any other in the world, perhaps 300 million in 1997. Nevertheless, this checkered ancestry has led to an architecture that is difficult to explain and impossible to love.

Brace yourself for what you are about to see! Do *not* try to read this section with the care you would need to write 80x86 programs; the goal instead is to give you familiarity with the strengths and weaknesses of the world's most popular architecture.

Rather than show the entire 16-bit and 32-bit instruction set, in this section we concentrate on the 32-bit subset that originated with the 80386, as this portion of the architecture will be increasingly dominant over time. We start our explanation with the registers and addressing modes, move on to the integer operations, and conclude with an examination of instruction encoding.

80x86 Registers and Data Addressing Modes

The evolution of the instruction set can be seen in the registers of the 80386 (Figure 3.29). The 80386 basically extended all 16-bit registers (except the segment registers) to 32 bits, prefixing an *E* to their name to indicate the 32-bit version. We'll refer to them generically as GPRs (general-purpose registers). The 80386 contains only eight GPRs. This means MIPS programs can use four times as many.

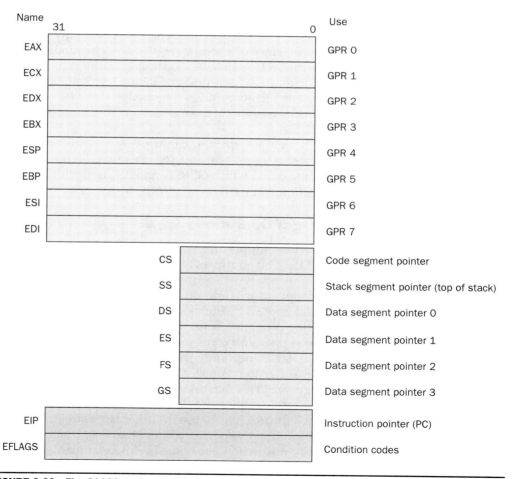

FIGURE 3.29   The 80386 register set. Starting with the 80386, the top eight registers were extended to 32 bits and could also be used as general-purpose registers.

Source/destination operand type	Second source operand
Register	Register
Register	Immediate
Register	Memory
Memory	Register
Memory	Immediate

FIGURE 3.30   Instruction types for the arithmetic, logical, and data transfer instructions.
The 80x86 allows the combinations shown. The only restriction is the absence of a memory-memory mode. Immediates may be 8, 16, or 32 bits in length; a register is any one of the 14 major registers in Figure 3.29 (not EIP or EFLAGS).

The arithmetic, logical, and data transfer instructions are two-operand instructions that allow the combinations shown in Figure 3.30. There are two important differences here. The 80x86 arithmetic and logical instructions must have one operand act as both a source and a destination; MIPS allows separate registers for source and destination. This restriction puts more pressure on the limited registers, since one source register must be modified. The second important difference is that one of the operands can be in memory. Thus virtually any instruction may have one operand in memory, unlike MIPS and PowerPC.

The seven data memory-addressing modes, described in detail below, offer two sizes of addresses within the instruction. These so-called *displacements* can be 8 bits or 32 bits.

Although a memory operand can use any addressing mode, there are restrictions on which *registers* can be used in a mode. Figure 3.31 shows the 80x86 addressing modes and which GPRs cannot be used with that mode, plus how you would get the same effect using MIPS instructions.

80x86 Integer Operations

The 8086 provides support for both 8-bit (*byte*) and 16-bit (*word*) data types. The 80386 adds 32-bit addresses and data (*double words*) in the 80x86. The data type distinctions apply to register operations as well as memory accesses. Almost every operation works on both 8-bit data and on one longer data size. That size is determined by the mode, and is either 16 bits or 32 bits.

Clearly some programs want to operate on data of all three sizes, so the 80386 architects provide a convenient way to specify each version without expanding code size significantly. They decided that most programs would be dominated by either 16-bit or 32-bit data, and so it made sense to be able to set a default large size. This default data size is set by a bit in the code segment register. To override the default data size, an 8-bit *prefix* is attached to the instruction to tell the machine to use the other large size for this instruction.

The prefix solution was borrowed from the 8086, which allows multiple prefixes to modify instruction behavior. The three original prefixes override the

Mode	Description	Register restrictions	MIPS equivalent
Register indirect	Address is in a register.	not ESP or EBP	`lw $s0,0($s1)`
Based mode with 8- or 32-bit displacement	Address is contents of base register plus displacement.	not ESP or EBP	`lw $s0,100($s1) # ≤16-bit` `              # displacement`

Base plus scaled index	The address is
	Base + (2^{Scale} x Index)
	where Scale has the value 0, 1, 2, or 3.
		Base: any GPR
		Index: not ESP
			`mul $t0,$s1,4`
			`add $t0,$t0,$s1`
			`lw  $s0,0($t0)`

Base plus scaled index with 8- or 32-bit displacement	The address is
	Base + (2^{Scale} x Index) + displacement
	where Scale has the value 0, 1, 2, or 3.
		Base: any GPR
		Index: not ESP
			`mul $t0, $s1,4`
			`add $t0, $t0,$s1`
			`lw  $s0, 100($t0) # ≤16-bit`
			`                  # displacement`

FIGURE 3.31   80x86 32-bit addressing modes with register restrictions and the equivalent MIPS code. The Base plus Scaled Index addressing mode, not found in MIPS or the PowerPC, is included to avoid the multiplies by four (scale factor of 2) to turn an index in a register into a byte address (see Figures 3.24 and 3.26). A scale factor of 1 is used for 16-bit data, and a scale factor of 3 for 64-bit data. Scale factor of 0 means the address is not scaled. If the displacement is longer than 16 bits in the second or fourth modes, then the MIPS equivalent mode would need two more instructions: a `lui` to load the upper 16 bits of the displacement and an `add` to sum the upper address with the base register $s1. (Intel gives two different names to what is called Based addressing mode—Based and Indexed—but they are essentially identical and we combine them here.)

default segment register, lock the bus to support a semaphore (see Chapter 9), or repeat the following instruction until the register ECX counts down to 0. This last prefix was intended to be paired with a byte move instruction to move a variable number of bytes. The 80386 also added a prefix to override the default address size.

The 80x86 integer operations can be divided into four major classes:

1. Data movement instructions, including move, push, and pop

2. Arithmetic and logic instructions, including test and integer and decimal arithmetic operations

3. Control flow, including conditional branches, unconditional jumps, calls, and returns

4. String instructions, including string move and string compare

The first two categories are unremarkable, except that the arithmetic and logic instruction operations allow the destination to either be a register or a memory location. Figure 3.32 shows some typical 80x86 instructions and their functions.

Conditional branches on the PowerPC and the 80x86 are based on *condition codes* or *flags*. Condition codes are set as a side effect of an operation; most are used to compare the value of a result to 0. Branches then test the condition codes. The argument for condition codes is that they occur as part of normal operations and are faster to test than it is to compare registers as MIPS does for

Instruction	Function
JE name	if equal(condition code) {EIP=name}; EIP-128 ≤ name < EIP+128
JMP name	EIP=name
CALL name	SP=SP-4; M[SP]=EIP+5; EIP=name;
MOVW EBX,[EDI+45]	EBX=M[EDI+45]
PUSH ESI	SP=SP-4; M[SP]=ESI
POP EDI	EDI=M[SP]; SP=SP+4
ADD EAX,#6765	EAX= EAX+6765
TEST EDX,#42	Set condition code (flags) with EDX and 42_{hex}
MOVSL	M[EDI]=M[ESI]; EDI=EDI+4; ESI=ESI+4

FIGURE 3.32 Some typical 80x86 instructions and their functions. A list of frequent operations appears in Figure 3.33. The CALL saves the EIP of the next instruction on the stack. (EIP is the Intel PC.)

beq and bne. The argument against condition codes is that the compare to 0 extends the time of the operation, since it uses extra hardware after the operation, and that often the programmer must use compare instructions to test a value that is not the result of an operation. Also, PC-relative branch addresses must be specified in the number of bytes, since unlike MIPS, 80386 instructions are not all 4 bytes in length.

String instructions are part of the 8080 ancestry of the 80x86 and are not commonly executed in most programs. They are often slower than equivalent software routines (see the fallacy on page 185).

Figure 3.33 lists some of the integer 80x86 instructions. Many of the instructions are available in both byte and word formats.

80x86 Instruction Encoding

Saving the worst for last, the encoding of instructions in the 8086 is complex, with many different instruction formats. Instructions for the 80386 may vary from 1 byte, when there are no operands, up to 17 bytes.

Figure 3.34 shows the instruction format for several of the example instructions in Figure 3.32. The opcode byte usually contains a bit saying whether the operand is 8 bits or 32 bits. For some instructions the opcode may include the addressing mode and the register; this is true in many instructions that have the form "register = register op immediate." Other instructions use a "postbyte" or extra opcode byte, labeled "mod, reg, r/m," which contains the addressing mode information. This postbyte is used for many of the instructions that address memory. The base plus scaled index mode uses a second postbyte, labeled "sc, index, base."

Instruction	Meaning
Control	**Conditional and unconditional branches**
JNZ, JZ	Jump if condition to EIP + 8-bit offset; JNE (for JNZ), JE (for JZ) are alternative names
JMP	Unconditional jump—8-bit or 16-bit offset
CALL	Subroutine call—16-bit offset; return address pushed onto stack
RET	Pops return address from stack and jumps to it
LOOP	Loop branch—decrement ECX; jump to EIP + 8-bit displacement if ECX ≠ 0
Data transfer	**Move data between registers or between register and memory**
MOV	Move between two registers or between register and memory
PUSH, POP	Push source operand on stack; pop operand from stack top to a register
LES	Load ES and one of the GPRs from memory
Arithmetic, logical	**Arithmetic and logical operations using the data registers and memory**
ADD, SUB	Add source to destination; subtract source from destination; register-memory format
CMP	Compare source and destination; register-memory format
SHL, SHR, RCR	Shift left; shift logical right; rotate right with carry condition code as fill
CBW	Convert byte in 8 rightmost bits of EAX to 16-bit word in right of EAX
TEST	Logical AND of source and destination sets condition codes
INC, DEC	Increment destination, decrement destination; register-memory format
OR, XOR	Logical OR; exclusive OR; register-memory format
String	**Move between string operands; length given by a repeat prefix**
MOVS	Copies from string source to destination by incrementing ESI and EDI; may be repeated
LODS	Loads a byte, word, or double word of a string into the EAX register

FIGURE 3.33   Some typical operations on the 80x86. Many operations use register-memory format, where either the source or the destination may be memory and the other may be a register or immediate operand.

Figure 3.35 shows the encoding of the two postbyte address specifiers for both 16-bit and 32-bit mode. Unfortunately, to fully understand which registers and which addressing modes are available, you need to see the encoding of all addressing modes and sometimes even the encoding of the instructions.

80x86 Conclusion

Intel had a 16-bit microprocessor two years before its competitors' more elegant architectures, such as the Motorola 68000, and this head start led to the selection of the 8086 as the CPU for the IBM PC. Intel engineers generally acknowledge that the 80x86 is more difficult to build than machines like MIPS, but the much larger market means Intel can afford more resources to help overcome the added complexity. What the 80x86 lacks in style is made up in quantity, making it beautiful from the right perspective.

The saving grace is that the most frequently used 80x86 architectural components are not too difficult to implement, as Intel has demonstrated by rapidly improving performance of integer programs since 1978. To get that performance, compilers must avoid the portions of the architecture that are hard to implement fast.

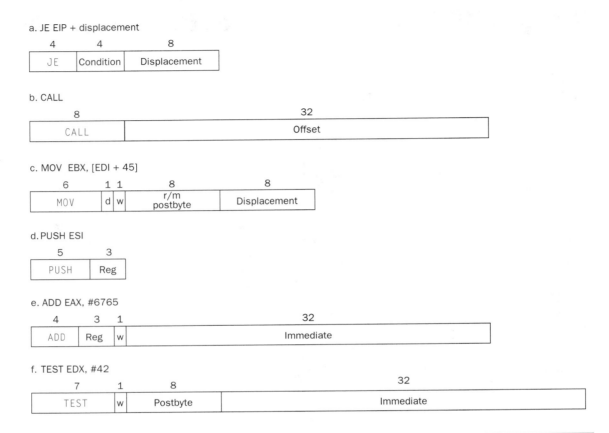

a. JE EIP + displacement

b. CALL

c. MOV EBX, [EDI + 45]

d. PUSH ESI

e. ADD EAX, #6765

f. TEST EDX, #42

FIGURE 3.34   Typical 80x86 instruction formats. The encoding of the postbyte is shown in Figure 3.35. Many instructions contain the 1-bit field w, which says whether the operation is a byte or double word. The d field in MOV is used in instructions that may move to or from memory and shows the direction of the move. The ADD instruction requires 32 bits for the immediate field because in 32-bit mode the immediates are either 8 bits or 32 bits. The immediate field in the TEST is 32 bits long because there is no 8-bit immediate for test in 32-bit mode. Overall, instructions may vary from 1 to 17 bytes in length. The long length comes from extra 1-byte prefixes, having both a 4-byte immediate and a 4-byte displacement address, using an opcode of 2 bytes, and using the scaled index mode specifier, which adds another byte.

reg		w = 0	w = 1	r/m	mod = 0		mod = 1		mod = 2		mod = 3
		16b	32b		16b	32b	16b	32b	16b	32b	
0	AL	AX	EAX	0	addr=BX+SI	=EAX	same	same	same	same	same
1	CL	CX	ECX	1	addr=BX+DI	=ECX	addr as	addr as	addr as	addr as	as
2	DL	DX	EDX	2	addr=BP+SI	=EDX	mod=0	mod=0	mod=0	mod=0	reg
3	BL	BX	EBX	3	addr=BP+SI	=EBX	+ disp8	+ disp8	+ disp16	+ disp32	field
4	AH	SP	ESP	4	addr=SI	=(sib)	SI+disp8	(sib)+disp8	SI+disp8	(sib)+disp32	"
5	CH	BP	EBP	5	addr=DI	=disp32	DI+disp8	EBP+disp8	DI+disp16	EBP+disp32	"
6	DH	SI	ESI	6	addr=disp16	=ESI	BP+disp8	ESI+disp8	BP+disp16	ESI+disp32	"
7	BH	DI	EDI	7	addr=BX	=EDI	BX+disp8	EDI+disp8	BX+disp16	EDI+disp32	"

FIGURE 3.35 The encoding of the first address specifier of the 80x86, "mod, reg, r/m." The first four columns show the encoding of the 3-bit reg field, which depends on the w bit from the opcode and whether the machine is in 16-bit mode (8086) or 32-bit mode (80386). The remaining columns explain the mod and r/m fields. The meaning of the 3-bit r/m field depends on the value in the 2-bit mod field and the address size. Basically, the registers used in the address calculation are listed in the sixth and seventh columns, under mod = 0, with mod = 1 adding an 8-bit displacement and mod = 2 adding a 16-bit or 32-bit displacement, depending on the address mode. The exceptions are r/m = 6 when mod = 1 or mod = 2 in 16-bit mode selects BP plus the displacement; r/m = 5 when mod = 1 or mod = 2 in 32-bit mode selects EBP plus displacement; and r/m = 4 in 32-bit mode when mod ≠ 3, where (sib) means use the scaled index mode shown in Figure 3.31 on page 181. When mod = 3, the r/m field indicates a register, using the same encoding as the reg field combined with the w bit.

3.13 Fallacies and Pitfalls

Fallacy: More powerful instructions mean higher performance.

Part of the power of the Intel 80x86 is the prefixes that can modify the execution of the following instruction. One prefix can repeat the following instruction until a counter counts down to 0. Thus, to move data in memory, it would seem that the natural instruction sequence is to use move with the repeat prefix to perform 32-bit memory-to-memory moves. On a 133-MHz Pentium (with the Triton chip set, 60-ns EDO DRAM, 256-KB cache), this user-level program can move data at about 40 MB/sec.

An alternative method, which uses the standard instructions found in all computers, is to load the data into the registers and then store the registers back to memory. This second version of this program, with the code replicated so as to reduce loop overhead, copies at about 60 MB/sec on the same machine, or 1.5 times faster. A third version, which used the larger floating-point registers instead of the integer registers of the 80x86, copies at about 80 MB/sec, or 2.0 times faster than the complex instruction.

Fallacy: Write in assembly language to obtain the highest performance.

At one time compilers for programming languages produced naive instruction sequences; the increasing sophistication of compilers means the gap between compiled code and code produced by hand is closing fast. In fact, to compete with current compilers, the assembly language programmer needs to thoroughly understand the concepts in Chapters 6 and 7 on processor pipelining and memory hierarchy.

This battle between compilers and assembly language coders is one situation in which humans are losing ground. For example, C offers the programmer a chance to give a hint to the compiler about which variables should be kept in registers versus spilled to memory. When compilers were poor at register allocation, such hints were vital to performance. In fact, some C textbooks spent a fair amount of time giving examples that effectively use register hints. Today's C compilers generally ignore such hints because the compiler does a better job at allocation than the programmer.

As a specific counterexample, we ran the MIPS assembly language programs in Figures 3.24 and 3.26 to compare performance to the C programs in Figures 3.23 and 3.25. Figure 3.36 shows the results. As you can see, the compiled program is 1.5 times faster than the assembled program. The compiler generally was able to create assembly language code that was tailored exactly to these conditions, while the assembly language program was written in a slightly more general fashion to make it easier to modify and understand. The specific improvements of the C compiler were a more streamlined procedure linkage convention and changing the address calculations to move the multiply outside the inner loop.

Even *if* writing by hand resulted in faster code, the dangers of writing in assembly language are longer time spent coding and debugging, the loss in portability, and the difficulty of maintaining such code. One of the few widely accepted axioms of software engineering is that coding takes longer if you write more lines, and it clearly takes many more lines to write a program in assembly language than in C. And once it is coded, the next danger is that it will become a popular program. Such programs always live longer than expected, meaning that someone will have to update the code over several years and make it work with new releases of operating systems and new models of ma-

Language	Time
Assembly	37.9 seconds
C	25.3 seconds

FIGURE 3.36   Performance comparison of the C and assembly language versions of the sort **and** swap **procedures in section 3.10.** The size of the array to be sorted was increased to 10,000 elements. The programs were run on a DECsystem 5900 with 128 MB of main memory and a 40-MHz R3000 processor using version 4.2a (Revision 47) of the Ultrix operating system. The C compiler was run with the –O option.

chines. Writing in higher-level language instead of assembly language not only allows future compilers to tailor the code to future machines, it also makes the software easier to maintain and allows the program to run on more brands of computers.

Pitfall: Forgetting that sequential word addresses in machines with byte addressing do not differ by one.

Many an assembly language programmer has toiled over errors made by assuming that the address of the next word can be found by incrementing the address in a register by one instead of by the word size in bytes. Forewarned is forearmed!

Pitfall: Using a pointer to an automatic variable outside its defining procedure.

A common mistake in dealing with pointers is to pass a result from a procedure that includes a pointer to an array that is declared local to that procedure. Following the stack discipline, in Figure 3.12 on page 139, the memory that contains the local array will be reused as soon as the procedure returns. Pointers to automatic variables can lead to chaos.

Concluding Remarks

Less is more.

Robert Browning, *Andrea del Sarto*, 1855

The two principles of the *stored-program* computer are the use of instructions that are indistinguishable from numbers and the use of alterable memory for programs. These principles allow a single machine to aid environmental scientists, financial advisers, and novelists in their specialties. The selection of a set of instructions that the machine can understand demands a delicate balance among the number of instructions needed to execute a program, the number of clock cycles needed by an instruction, and the speed of the clock. Four design principles guide the authors of instruction sets in making that delicate balance:

1. *Simplicity favors regularity.* Regularity motivates many features of the MIPS instruction set: keeping all instructions a single size, always requiring three register operands in arithmetic instructions, and keeping the register fields in the same place in each instruction format.

2. *Smaller is faster.* The desire for speed is the reason that MIPS has 32 registers rather than many more.

3. *Good design demands good compromises.* One MIPS example was the compromise between providing for larger addresses and constants in instructions and keeping all instructions the same length.

4. *Make the common case fast.* Examples of making the common MIPS case fast include PC-relative addressing for conditional branches and immediate addressing for constant operands.

Above this machine level is assembly language, a language that humans can read. The assembler translates it into the binary numbers that machines can understand, and it even "extends" the instruction set by creating symbolic instructions that aren't in the hardware. For instance, constants or addresses that are too big are broken into properly sized pieces, common variations of instructions are given their own name, and so on. The MIPS instructions we have covered so far (both real and pseudo) are listed in Figure 3.37.

These instructions are not born equal; the popularity of the few dominates the many. For example, Figure 3.38 shows the popularity of each class of instructions for two programs, gcc and spice. The varying popularity of instructions plays an important role in the chapters on performance, datapath, control, and pipelining.

Each category of MIPS instructions is associated with constructs that appear in programming languages:

■ The arithmetic instructions correspond to the operations found in assignment statements.

■ Data transfer instructions are most likely to occur when dealing with data structures like arrays or structures.

■ The conditional branches are used in *if* statements and in loops.

■ The unconditional jumps are used in procedure calls and returns and also for *case/switch* statements.

More of the MIPS instruction set is revealed in Chapter 4, after we explain computer arithmetic.

MIPS instructions	Name	Format	Pseudo MIPS	Name	Format
add	add	R	move	move	R
subtract	sub	R	multiply	mult	R
add immediate	addi	I	multiply immediate	multi	I
load word	lw	I	load immediate	li	I
store word	sw	I	branch less than	blt	I
load byte	lb	I	branch less than or equal	ble	I
store byte	sb	I	branch greater than	bgt	I
load upper immediate	lui	I	branch greater than or equal	bge	I
branch on equal	beq	I			
branch on not equal	bne	I			
set less than	slt	R			
set less than immediate	slti	I			
jump	j	J			
jump register	jr	R			
jump and link	jal	J			

FIGURE 3.37 The MIPS instruction set covered so far, with the real MIPS instructions on the left and the pseudoinstructions on the right. Appendix A (section A.10 on page A-49) describes the full MIPS architecture. Figure 3.18 on page 153 shows more details of the MIPS architecture revealed in this chapter.

Instruction class	MIPS examples	HLL correspondence	Frequency	
			gcc	spice
Arithmetic	add, sub, addi	operations in assignment statements	48%	50%
Data transfer	lw, sw, lb, sb, lui	references to data structures, such as arrays	33%	41%
Conditional branch	beq, bne, slt, slti	*if* statements and loops	17%	8%
Jump	j, jr, jal	procedure calls, returns, and *case/switch* statements	2%	1%

FIGURE 3.38 MIPS instruction classes, examples, correspondence to high-level program language constructs, and percentage of MIPS instructions executed by category for two programs, gcc and spice. Figure 4.54 on page 311 shows the percentage of the individual MIPS instructions executed.

3.15 Historical Perspective and Further Reading

accumulator: Archaic term for register. On-line use of it as a synonym for "register" is a fairly reliable indication that the user has been around quite a while.

Eric Raymond, *The New Hacker's Dictionary*, 1991

Accumulator Architectures

Hardware was precious in the earliest stored-program computers. As a consequence, computer pioneers could not afford the number of registers found in today's machines. In fact, these machines had a single register for arithmetic instructions. Since all operations would accumulate in a single register, it was called the *accumulator*, and this style of instruction set is given the same name. For example, EDSAC in 1949 had a single accumulator.

The three-operand format of MIPS suggests that a single register is at least two registers shy of our needs. Having the accumulator as both a source operand *and* as the destination of the operation fills part of the shortfall, but it still leaves us one operand short. That final operand is found in memory. Accumulator machines have the memory-based operand-addressing mode suggested earlier. It follows that the add instruction of an accumulator instruction set would look like this:

```
add    200
```

This instruction means add the accumulator to the word in memory at address 200 and place the sum back into the accumulator. No registers are specified because the accumulator is known to be both a source and a destination of the operation.

Compiling an Assignment Statement into Accumulator Instructions

Example   What is the accumulator-style assembly code for this C code?

```
A = B + C;
```

Answer   It would be translated into the following instructions in an accumulator instruction set:

```
load    AddressB # Acc = Memory[AddressB], or Acc = B
add     AddressC # Acc = B + Memory[AddressC],or Acc = B + C
store   AddressA # Memory[AddressA] = Acc, or A = B + C
```

All variables in a program are allocated to memory in accumulator machines, instead of normally to registers as we saw for MIPS. One way to think about this is that variables are always spilled to memory in this style of machine. As you may imagine, it takes many more instructions to execute a program with a single-accumulator architecture. (See Exercise 3.19 for another example.)

The next step in the evolution of instruction sets was the addition of registers dedicated to specific operations. Hence, registers might be included to act as indices for array references in data transfer instructions, to act as separate accumulators for multiply or divide instructions, and to serve as the top-of-stack pointer. Perhaps the best-known example of this style of instruction set is found in the Intel 8086, the computer at the core of the IBM Personal Computer. This style of instruction set is labeled *extended accumulator, dedicated register,* or *special-purpose register*. Like the single-register accumulator machines, one operand may be in memory for arithmetic instructions. Like the MIPS architecture, however, there are also instructions where all the operands are registers.

General-Purpose Register Architectures

The generalization of the dedicated-register machine allows all the registers to be used for any purpose, hence the name *general-purpose register*. MIPS is an example of a general-purpose register machine. This style of instruction set may be further divided into those that allow one operand to be in memory as found in accumulator machines, called a *register-memory* architecture, and those that demand that operands always be in registers, called either a *load-store* or a *register-register* machine. Figure 3.39 shows a history of the number of registers in some popular computers.

Machine	Number of general-purpose registers	Architectural style	Year
EDSAC	1	accumulator	1949
IBM 701	1	accumulator	1953
CDC 6600	8	load-store	1963
IBM 360	16	register-memory	1964
DEC PDP-8	1	accumulator	1965
DEC PDP-11	8	register-memory	1970
Intel 8008	1	accumulator	1972
Motorola 6800	2	accumulator	1974
DEC VAX	16	register-memory, memory-memory	1977
Intel 8086	1	extended accumulator	1978
Motorola 68000	16	register-memory	1980
Intel 80386	8	register-memory	1985
MIPS	32	load-store	1985
HP PA-RISC	32	load-store	1986
SPARC	32	load-store	1987
PowerPC	32	load-store	1992
DEC Alpha	32	load-store	1992

FIGURE 3.39 Number of general-purpose registers in popular machines over the years.

The first load-store machine was the CDC 6600 in 1963, considered by many to be the first supercomputer. MIPS is a more recent example of a load-store machine.

The 80386 is Intel's attempt to transform the 80x86 into a general-purpose register-memory instruction set. Perhaps the best-known register-memory instruction set is the IBM 360 architecture, first announced in 1964. This instruction set is still at the core of IBM's mainframe computers—responsible for a large part of the business of the largest computer company in the world. Register-memory architectures were the most popular in the 1960s and the first half of the 1970s.

Digital Equipment Corporation's VAX architecture took memory operands one step further in 1977. It allowed any combination of registers and memory operands to be used in an instruction. A style of machine in which all operands can be in memory is called *memory-memory*. (In truth the VAX instruction set, like almost all other instruction sets since the IBM 360, is a hybrid since it also has general-purpose registers.)

Compiling an Assignment Statement into Memory-Memory Instructions

Example   What is the memory-memory style assembly code for this C code?

```
A = B + C;
```

Answer   It would be translated into the following instructions in a memory-memory instruction set:

```
add      AddressA,AddressB,AddressC
```

(See Exercise 3.19 for another example.)

Although MIPS has a single add instruction with 32-bit operands, the Intel 80x86 has many versions of a 32-bit add to specify whether an operand is in memory or is in a register. In addition, the memory operand can be accessed with more than seven addressing modes. This combination of address modes and register/memory operands means that there are dozens of variants of an 80x86 add instruction. Clearly this variability makes 80x86 implementations more challenging.

Compact Code and Stack Architectures

When memory is scarce, it is also important to keep programs small, so machines like the Intel 80x86, IBM 360, and VAX had variable-length instructions, both to match the varying operand specifications and to minimize code size. Intel 80x86 instructions are from 1 to 17 bytes long; IBM 360 instructions are 2, 4, or 6 bytes long; and VAX instruction lengths are anywhere from 1 to 54 bytes. If instruction memory space becomes precious once again, such techniques could return to popularity.

In the 1960s, a few companies followed a radical approach to instruction sets. In the belief that it was too hard for compilers to utilize registers effectively, these companies abandoned registers altogether! Instruction sets were based on a *stack model* of execution, like that found in the older Hewlett-Packard handheld calculators. Operands are pushed on the stack from memory or popped off the stack into memory. Operations take their operands from the stack and then place the result back onto the stack. In addition to simplifying compilers by eliminating register allocation, stack machines lent themselves to compact instruction encoding, thereby removing memory size as an excuse not to program in high-level languages.

Compiling an Assignment Statement into Stack Instructions

Example

What is the stack-style assembly code for this C code?

```
A = B + C;
```

Answer

It would be translated into the following instructions in a stack instruction set:

```
push    AddressC    # Top=Top+4;Stack[Top]=Memory[AddressC]
push    AddressB    # Top=Top+4;Stack[Top]=Memory[AddressB]
add                 # Stack[Top-4]=Stack[Top]
                    # + Stack[Top-4];Top=Top-4;
pop     AddressA    # Memory[AddressA]=Stack[Top];
                    #   Top=Top-4;
```

To get the proper byte address, we adjust the stack by 4. The downside of stacks as compared to registers is that it is hard to reuse data that has been fetched or calculated without repeatedly going to memory. (See Exercise 3.19 for another example.)

Memory space may be precious again for the heralded Network Computer (NC), both because memory space is limited to keep costs low and because programs must be downloaded over the Internet, and smaller programs take less time to transmit. Hence compactness in instruction set encoding is desired for the NC. Such arguments have been used to justify building a hardware interpreter for the Java intermediate language, which is based on a stack. Time will tell whether these arguments have technical versus marketing merit.

High-Level-Language Computer Architectures

In the 1960s, systems software was rarely written in high-level languages. For example, virtually every commercial operating system before Unix was programmed in assembly language, and more recently even OS/2 was originally programmed at that same low level. Some people blamed the code density of the instruction sets rather than the programming languages and the compiler technology.

Hence a machine-design philosophy called *high-level-language computer architecture* was advocated, with the goal of making the hardware more like the programming languages. More efficient programming languages and compilers, plus expanding memory, doomed this movement to a historical footnote. The Burroughs B5000 was the commercial fountainhead of this philosophy, but today there is no significant commercial descendent of this 1960s radical.

Reduced Instruction Set Computer Architectures

This language-oriented design philosophy was replaced in the 1980s by *RISC (reduced instruction set computer)*. Improvements in programming languages, compiler technology, and memory cost meant that less programming was being done at the assembly level, so instruction sets could be measured by how well compilers used them as opposed to how well assembly language programmers used them.

Virtually all new instruction sets since 1982 have followed this RISC philosophy of fixed instruction lengths, load-store instruction sets, limited addressing modes, and limited operations. MIPS, Sun SPARC, Hewlett-Packard PA-RISC, IBM PowerPC, and DEC Alpha are all examples of RISC architectures.

A Brief History of the 80x86

The ancestors of the 80x86 were the first microprocessors, produced late in the first half of the 1970s. The Intel 4004 and 8008 were extremely simple 4-bit and 8-bit accumulator-style machines. Morse et al. [1980] describe the evolution of the 8086 from the 8080 in the late 1970s in an attempt to provide a 16-bit machine with better throughput. At that time, almost all programming for microprocessors was done in assembly language—both memory and compilers were in short supply. Intel wanted to keep its base of 8080 users, so the 8086 was designed to be "compatible" with the 8080. The 8086 was *never* object-code compatible with the 8080, but the machines were close enough that translation of assembly language programs could be done automatically.

In early 1980, IBM selected a version of the 8086 with an 8-bit external bus, called the 8088, for use in the IBM PC. They chose the 8-bit version to reduce the cost of the machine. This choice, together with the tremendous success of the IBM PC, has made the 8086 architecture ubiquitous. The success of the IBM

PC was due in part because IBM opened the architecture of the PC and enabled the PC-clone industry to flourish. As discussed in section 3.12, the 80286, 80386, 80486, Pentium, and Pentium Pro have extended the architecture and provided a series of performance enhancements.

Although the 68000 was chosen for the Macintosh, the Mac was never as pervasive as the PC, partly because Apple did not allow Mac clones based on the 68000, and the 68000 did not acquire the same software leverage that the 8086 enjoys. The Motorola 68000 may have been more significant *technically* than the 8086, but the impact of the selection by IBM and IBM's open architecture strategy dominated the technical advantages of the 68000 in the market.

Some argue that the inelegance of the 80x86 instruction set is unavoidable, the price that must be paid for rampant success by any architecture. We reject that notion. Obviously no successful architecture can jettison features that were added in previous implementations, and over time some features may be seen as undesirable. The awkwardness of the 80x86 begins at its core with the 8086 instruction set, and was exacerbated by the architecturally inconsistent expansions found in the 8087, 80286, 80386, and MMX.

A counterexample is the IBM 360/370 architecture, which is much older than the 80x86. It dominates the mainframe market just as the 80x86 dominates the PC market. Due undoubtedly to a better base and more compatible enhancements, this instruction set makes much more sense than the 80x86 more than 30 years after its first implementation.

Hewlett-Packard and Intel will announce a new, common instruction set architecture in about 1998. It will be upwards compatible with the 80x86, and thus the 80x86 instruction will be available in some form in computers of the next century.

Instruction set anthropologists of the 21st century will peel off layer after layer from such machines until they uncover artifacts from the first microprocessor. Given such a find, how will they judge 20th-century computer architecture?

To Probe Further

Bayko, J. [1996]. "Great Microprocessors of the Past and Present," available at *www.mkp.com/books_catalog/cod/links.htm.*

A personal view of the history of representative or unusual microprocessors, from the Intel 4004 to the Patriot Scientific ShBoom!

Kane, G., and J. Heinrich [1992]. *MIPS RISC Architecture,* Prentice Hall, Englewood Cliffs, NJ.

This book describes the MIPS architecture in greater detail than Appendix A.

Levy, H., and R. Eckhouse [1989]. *Computer Programming and Architecture: The VAX,* Digital Press, Boston.

This book concentrates on the VAX, but also includes descriptions of the Intel 80x86, IBM 360, and CDC 6600.

Morse, S., B. Ravenal, S. Mazor, and W. Pohlman [1980]. "Intel Microprocessors—8080 to 8086," *Computer* 13:10 (October).

The architecture history of the Intel from the 4004 to the 8086, according to the people who participated in the designs.

Wakerly, J. [1989]. *Microcomputer Architecture and Programming,* Wiley, New York.

The Motorola 680x0 is the main focus of the book, but it covers the Intel 8086, Motorola 6809, TI 9900, and Zilog Z8000.

3.16   Key Terms

The terms listed below reflect the key ideas discussed in this chapter. If you're unsure of the meaning of any of these terms, refer to the Glossary for a full definition.

activation record	general-purpose register (GPR)	opcode
address	global pointer	PC-relative addressing
addressing mode	immediate addressing	procedure
base or displacement addressing	instruction format	procedure frame
basic block	instruction set	program counter (PC)
callee	jump address table	pseudoinstruction
caller	jump-and-link instruction	register addressing
conditional branch	linker or link editor	return address
data transfer instruction	load-store or register-register machine	stack
executable file	loader	stack pointer
frame pointer	object program	stored-program computer
		stored-program concept
		word

3.17   Exercises

Appendix A describes the MIPS simulator, which is helpful for these exercises. Although the simulator accepts pseudoinstructions, try not to use pseudoinstructions for any exercises that ask you to produce MIPS code. Your goal should be to learn the real MIPS instruction set, and if you are asked to count instructions, your count should reflect the actual instructions that will be executed and not the pseudoinstructions.

There are some cases where pseudoinstructions must be used (for example, the `la` instruction when an actual value is not known at assembly time). In many cases they are quite convenient and result in more readable code (for example, the li and move instructions). If you choose to use pseudoinstructions for these reasons, please add a sentence or two to your solution stating which pseudoinstructions you have used and why.

3.1 [5] <§§3.3, 3.5, 3.8> Add comments to the following MIPS code and describe in one sentence what it computes. Assume that $a0 is used for the input and initially contains n, a positive integer. Assume that $v0 is used for the output.

```
begin:    addi $t0, $zero, 0
          addi $t1, $zero, 1
loop:     slt  $t2, $a0, $t1
          bne  $t2, $zero, finish
          add  $t0, $t0, $t1
          addi $t1, $t1, 2
          j    loop
finish:   add  $v0, $t0, $zero
```

3.2 [12] <§§3.3, 3.5, 3.8> The following code fragment processes an array and produces two important values in registers $v0 and $v1. Assume that the array consists of 5000 words indexed 0 through 4999, and its base address is stored in $a0 and its size (5000) in $a1. Describe in one sentence what this code does. Specifically, what will be returned in $v0 and $v1?

```
          add  $a1, $a1, $a1
          add  $a1, $a1, $a1
          add  $v0, $zero, $zero
          add  $t0, $zero, $zero
outer:    add  $t4, $a0, $t0
          lw   $t4, 0($t4)
          add  $t5, $zero, $zero
          add  $t1, $zero, $zero
inner:    add  $t3, $a0, $t1
          lw   $t3, 0($t3)
          bne  $t3, $t4, skip
          addi $t5, $t5, 1
skip:     addi $t1, $t1, 4
          bne  $t1, $a1, inner
          slt  $t2, $t5, $v0
          bne  $t2, $zero, next
          add  $v0, $t5, $zero
          add  $v1, $t4, $zero
next:     addi $t0, $t0, 4
          bne  $t0, $a1, outer
```

3.3 [10] <§§3.3, 3.5, 3.8> Assume that the code from Exercise 3.2 is run on a machine with a 500-MHz clock that requires the following number of cycles for each instruction:

Instruction	Cycles
add,addi,slt	1
lw, bne	2

In the worst case, how many seconds will it take to execute this code?

3.4 [5] <§3.8> Show the single MIPS instruction or minimal sequence of instructions for this C statement:

```
a = b + 100;
```

Assume that a corresponds to register $t0 and b corresponds to register $t1.

3.5 [10] <§3.8> Show the single MIPS instruction or minimal sequence of instructions for this C statement:

```
x[10] = x[11] + c;
```

Assume that c corresponds to register $t0 and the array x has a base address of 4,000,000$_{ten}$.

3.6 [10] <§§ 3.3, 3.5, 3.8> The following program tries to copy words from the address in register $a0 to the address in register $a1, counting the number of words copied in register $v0. The program stops copying when it finds a word equal to 0. You do not have to preserve the contents of registers $v1, $a0, and $a1. This terminating word should be copied but not counted.

```
loop:   lw      $v1,0($a0)      # Read next word from source
        addi    $v0,$v0,1       # Increment count words copied
        sw      $v1,0($a1)      # Write to destination
        addi    $a0,$a0,1       # Advance pointer to next source
        addi    $a1,$a1,1       # Advance pointer to next dest
        bne     $v1,$zero,loop  # Loop if word copied ≠ zero
```

There are multiple bugs in this MIPS program; fix them and turn in a bug-free version. Like many of the exercises in this chapter, the easiest way to write MIPS programs is to use the simulator described in Appendix A. (Go to *www.mkp.com/cod2e.htm* to get a copy of this program.)

3.7 [15] <§3.4> Using the MIPS program in Exercise 3.6 (with bugs intact), determine the instruction format for each instruction and the decimal values of each instruction field.

3.8 [10] <§§3.2, 3.3, 3.5, 3.8> {Ex. 3.6} Starting with the corrected program in the answer to Exercise 3.6, write the C code segment that might have produced this code. Assume that variable source corresponds to register $a0, variable destination corresponds to register $a1, and variable count corresponds to register $v0. Show variable declarations, but assume that source and destination have been initialized to the proper addresses.

3.9 [10] <§3.5> The C segment

```
while (save[i] == k)
    i = i + j;
```

on page 127 uses both a conditional branch and an unconditional jump each time through the loop. Only poor compilers would produce code with this loop overhead. Rewrite the assembly code so that it uses at most one branch or jump each time through the loop. How many instructions are executed before and after the optimization if the number of iterations of the loop is 10 (i.e., save[i + 10 * j] do not equal k and save[i], . . . , save[i + 9 * j] equal k)?

3.10 [25] <§3.9> As discussed on page 157 and summarized in Figure 3.37, pseudoinstructions are not part of the MIPS instruction set but often appear in MIPS programs. For each pseudoinstruction in the following table, produce a minimal sequence of actual MIPS instructions to accomplish the same thing. You may need to use $at for some of the sequences. In the following table, big refers to a specific number that requires 32 bits to represent and small to a number that can be expressed using 16 bits.

Pseudoinstruction	What it accomplishes
move $t5, $t3	$t5 = $t3
clear $t5	$t5 = 0
li $t5, small	$t5 = small
li $t5, big	$t5 = big
lw $t5, big($t3)	$t5 = Memory[$t3 + big]
addi $t5, $t3, big	$t5 = $t3 + big
beq $t5, small, L	if ($t5 = small) go to L
beq $t5, big, L	if ($t5 = big) go to L
ble $t5, $t3, L	if ($t5 <= $t3) go to L
bgt $t5, $t3, L	if ($t5 > $t3) go to L
bge $t5, $t3, L	if ($t5 >= $t3) go to L

3.11 [30] <§3.5> Consider the following fragment of C code:

```
for (i=0; i<=100; i=i+1) {a[i] = b[i] + c;}
```

Assume that a and b are arrays of words and the base address of a is in $a0 and the base address of b is in $a1. Register $t0 is associated with variable i and register $s0 with c. Write the code for MIPS. How many instructions are executed during the running of this code? How many memory data references will be made during execution?

3.12 [5] <§§3.8, 3.9> Given your understanding of PC-relative addressing, explain why an assembler might have problems directly implementing the branch instruction in the following code sequence:

```
here:    beq $t1, $t2, there
 . . .
there:   add $t1, $t1, $t1
```

Show how the assembler might rewrite this code sequence to solve these problems.

3.13 [10] <§3.12> Consider an architecture that is similar to MIPS except that it supports update addressing (like the PowerPC) for data transfer instructions. If we run gcc using this architecture, some percentage of the data transfer instructions shown in Figure 3.38 on page 189 will be able to make use of the new instructions, and for each instruction changed, one arithmetic instruction can be eliminated. If 25% of the data transfer instructions can be changed, which will be faster for gcc, the modified MIPS architecture or the unmodified architecture? How much faster? (You can assume that both architectures have CPI values as given in Exercise 3.16 and that the modified architecture has its cycle time increased by 10% in order to accommodate the new instructions.)

3.14 [10] <§3.14> When designing memory systems, it becomes useful to know the frequency of memory reads versus writes as well as the frequency of accesses for instructions versus data. Using the average instruction-mix information for MIPS for the program gcc in Figure 3.38 on page 189, find the following:

a. The percentage of *all* memory accesses that are for data (vs. instructions).

b. The percentage of *all* memory accesses that are reads (vs. writes). Assume that two-thirds of data transfers are loads.

3.15 [10] <§3.14> Perform the same calculations as for Exercise 3.14, but replace the program gcc with spice.

3.16 [15] <§3.14> Suppose we have made the following measurements of average CPI for instructions:

Instruction	Average CPI
Arithmetic	1.0 clock cycles
Data transfer	1.4 clock cycles
Conditional branch	1.7 clock cycles
Jump	1.2 clock cycles

Compute the effective CPI for MIPS. Average the instruction frequencies for gcc and spice in Figure 3.38 on page 189 to obtain the instruction mix.

3.17 [20] <§3.10> In this exercise, we'll examine quantitatively the pros and cons of adding an addressing mode to MIPS that allows arithmetic instructions to directly access memory, as is found on the 80x86. The primary benefit is that fewer instructions will be executed because we won't have to first load a register. The primary disadvantage is that the cycle time will have to increase to account for the additional time to read memory. Consider adding a new instruction:

```
addm $t2, 100($t3)  # $t2 = $t2 + Memory[$t3+100]
```

Assume that the new instruction will cause the cycle time to increase by 10%. Use the instruction frequencies for the gcc benchmark from Figure 3.38 on page 189, and assume that two-thirds of the data transfers are loads and the rest are stores. Assume that the new instruction affects only the clock speed, not the CPI. What percentage of loads must be eliminated for the machine with the new instruction to have at least the same performance?

3.18 [10] <§3.10> Using the information in Exercise 3.17, write a multiple-instruction sequence in which a load of $t0 followed immediately by the use of $t0—in, say, an add—could *not* be replaced by a single instruction of the form proposed.

In More Depth

Comparing Instruction Sets of Different Styles

For the next two exercises, your task is to compare the memory efficiency of four different styles of instruction sets for two code sequences. The architecture styles are the following:

- *Accumulator.*
- *Memory-memory*: All three operands of each instruction are in memory.

- *Stack*: All operations occur on top of the stack. Only push and pop access memory, and all other instructions remove their operands from the stack and replace them with the result. The implementation uses a stack for the top two entries; accesses that use other stack positions are memory references.

- *Load-store*: All operations occur in registers, and register-to-register instructions have three operands per instruction. There are 16 general-purpose registers, and register specifiers are 4 bits long.

Consider the following C code:

```
a = b + c;    # a, b, and c are variables in memory
```

Section 3.15 contains the equivalent assembly language code for the different styles of instruction sets. For a given code sequence, we can calculate the instruction bytes fetched and the memory data bytes transferred using the following assumptions about all four instruction sets:

- The opcode is always 1 byte (8 bits).

- All memory addresses are 2 bytes (16 bits).

- All data operands are 4 bytes (32 bits).

- All instructions are an integral number of bytes in length.

- There are no optimizations to reduce memory traffic.

For example, a register load will require four instruction bytes (one for the opcode, one for the register destination, and two for a memory address) to be fetched from memory along with four data bytes. A memory-memory add instruction will require seven instruction bytes (one for the opcode and two for each of the three memory addresses) to be fetched from memory and will result in 12 data bytes being transferred (eight from memory to the processor and four from the processor back to memory). The following table displays a summary of this information for each of the architectural styles for the code appearing above and in section 3.15:

Style	Instructions for a = b + c	Code bytes	Data bytes
Accumulator	3	3 + 3 + 3	4 + 4 + 4
Memory-memory	1	7	12
Stack	4	3 + 3 + 1 + 3	4 + 4 + 0 + 4
Load-store	4	4 + 4 + 3 + 4	4 + 4 + 0 + 4

3.19 [20] <§3.15> For the following C code, write an equivalent assembly language program in each architectural style (assume all variables are initially in memory):

```
a = b + c;
b = a + c;
d = a - b;
```

For each code sequence, calculate the instruction bytes fetched and the memory data bytes transferred (read or written). Which architecture is most efficient as measured by code size? Which architecture is most efficient as measured by total memory bandwidth required (code + data)? If the answers are not the same, why are they different?

3.20 [5] <§3.15> Sometimes architectures are characterized according to the typical number of memory addresses per instruction. Commonly used terms are 0, 1, 2, and 3 addresses per instruction. Associate the names above with each category.

3.21 [10] <§3.7> Compute the decimal byte values that form the null-terminated ASCII representation of the following string:

```
A byte is 8 bits
```

3.22 [30] <§§3.6, 3.7> Write a program in MIPS assembly language to convert an ASCII decimal string to an integer. Your program should expect register $a0 to hold the address of a null-terminated string containing some combination of the digits 0 through 9. Your program should compute the integer value equivalent to this string of digits, then place the number in register $v0. Your program need not handle negative numbers. If a nondigit character appears anywhere in the string, your program should stop with the value –1 in register $v0. For example, if register $a0 points to a sequence of three bytes 50_{ten}, 52_{ten}, 0_{ten} (the null-terminated string "24"), then when the program stops, register $v0 should contain the value 24_{ten}. (The subscript "ten" means base 10.)

3.23 [20] <§§3.6, 3.7> Write a procedure, bfind, in MIPS assembly language. The procedure should take a single argument that is a pointer to a null-terminated string in register $a0. The bfind procedure should locate the first b character in the string and return its address in register $v0. If there are no b's in the string, then bfind should return a pointer to the null character at the end of the string. For example, if the argument to bfind points to the string "imbibe," then the return value will be a pointer to the third character of the string.

3.24 [20] <§§3.6, 3.7> {Ex. 3.23} Write a procedure, bcount, in MIPS assembly language. The bcount procedure takes a single argument, which is a pointer to a string in register $a0, and it returns a count of the total number of b characters in the string in register $v0. You must use your bfind procedure in Exercise 3.23 in your implementation of bcount.

3.25 [30] <§§3.6, 3.7> Write a procedure, itoa, in MIPS assembly language that will convert an integer argument into an ASCII decimal string. The procedure should take two arguments: the first is an integer in register $a0; the second is the address at which to write a result string in register $a1. Then itoa should convert its first argument to a null-terminated decimal ASCII string and store that string at the given result location. The return value from itoa, in register $v0, should be a count of the number of non-null characters stored at the destination.

In More Depth

Tail Recursion

Some recursive procedures can be implemented iteratively without using recursion. Iteration can significantly improve performance by removing the overhead associated with procedure calls. For example, consider a procedure used to accumulate a sum:

```
int sum (int n, int acc) {
   if (n > 0)
       return sum(n - 1, acc + n);
   else
       return acc;
}
```

Consider the procedure call sum(3,0). This will result in recursive calls to sum(2,3), sum(1,5), and sum(0,6), and then the result 6 will be returned four times. This recursive call of sum is referred to as a *tail call*, and this example use of tail recursion can be implemented very efficiently (assume $a0 = n and $a1 = acc):

```
sum:     beq  $a0, $zero, sum_exit # go to sum_exit if n is 0
         add  $a1, $a1, $a0        # add n to acc
         addi $a0, $a0, -1         # subtract 1 from n
         j sum                     # go to sum
sum_exit:
         move $v0, $a1             # return value acc
         jr   $ra                  # return to caller
```

3.26 [30] <§3.6> Write a MIPS procedure to compute the *n*th Fibonacci number F(n) where

```
F(n) = 0,       if n = 0;
       1,       if n = 1;
       F(n-1) + F(n-2), otherwise.
```

Base your algorithm on the straightforward but hopelessly inefficient procedure below, which generates a recursive process:

```
int fib(int n){
   if (n == 0)
      return 0;
   else if (n == 1)
      return 1;
   else
return fib(n-1) + fib(n-2);
```

3.27 [30] <§3.6> Write a program as in Exercise 3.26, except this time base your program on the following procedure and optimize the tail call so as to make your implementation efficient:

```
int fib_iter (int a, int b, int count) {
   if (count == 0)
      return b;
   else
      return fib_iter(a + b, a, count - 1);
```

Here, the first two parameters keep track of the previous two Fibonacci numbers computed. To compute F(n) you have to make the procedure call fib_iter(1, 0, n).

3.28 [20] <§3.6> Estimate the difference in performance between your solution to Exercise 3.26 and your solution to Exercise 3.27.

In More Depth

The Single Instruction Computer

The computer architecture used in this book, MIPS, has one of the simpler instruction sets in existence. However, it is possible to imagine even simpler instruction sets. In this assignment, you are to consider a hypothetical machine called SIC, for Single Instruction Computer. As its name implies, SIC has only one instruction: subtract and branch if negative, or sbn for short. The sbn instruction has three operands, each consisting of the address of a word in memory:

```
sbn a,b,c # Mem[a] = Mem[a] - Mem[b];if (Mem[a]<0) go to c
```

The instruction will subtract the number in memory location b from the number in location a and place the result back in a, overwriting the previous value. If the result is greater than or equal to 0, the computer will take its next instruction from the memory location just after the current instruction. If the result is less than 0, the next instruction is taken from memory location c. SIC has no registers and no instructions other than sbn.

Although it has only one instruction, SIC can imitate many of the operations of more complex instruction sets by using clever sequences of sbn instructions. For example, here is a program to copy a number from location a to location b:

```
start:  sbn temp,temp,.+1    # Sets temp to zero
        sbn temp,a,.+1       # Sets temp to -a
        sbn b,b,.+1          # Sets b to zero
        sbn b,temp,.+1       # Sets b to -temp, which is a
```

In the program above, the notation .+1 means "the address after this one," so that each instruction in this program goes on to the next in sequence whether or not the result is negative. We assume temp to be the address of a spare memory word that can be used for temporary results.

3.29 [10] <§3.15> Write a SIC program to add a and b, leaving the result in a and leaving b unmodified.

3.30 [20] <§3.15> Write a SIC program to multiply a by b, putting the result in c. Assume that memory location one contains the number 1. Assume that a and b are greater than 0 and that it's OK to modify a or b. (Hint: What does this program compute?)

```
c = 0; while (b > 0) {b = b - 1; c = c + a;}
```

4

Arithmetic for Computers

*Numerical precision
is the very soul
of science.*

Sir D'arcy Wentworth Thompson
On Growth and Form, 1917

The Five Classic Components of a Computer

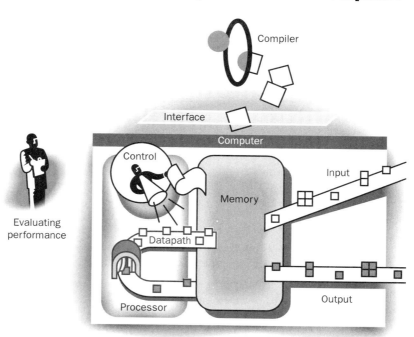

Introduction

Computer words are composed of bits; thus words can be represented as binary numbers. Although the natural numbers 0, 1, 2, and so on can be represented either in decimal or binary form, what about the other numbers that commonly occur? For example:

- How are negative numbers represented?
- What is the largest number that can be represented in a computer word?
- What happens if an operation creates a number bigger than can be represented?
- What about fractions and real numbers?

We could also ask, What is the inside story about the infamous bug in the Pentium? And underlying all these questions is a mystery: How does hardware really add, subtract, multiply, or divide numbers?

The goal of this chapter is to unravel this mystery, including representation of numbers, arithmetic algorithms, hardware that follows these algorithms, and the implications of all this for instruction sets. These insights may even explain quirks that you have already encountered with computers. (If you are familiar with signed binary numbers, you may wish to skip the next section and go to section 4.3 on page 220.)

Signed and Unsigned Numbers

Numbers can be represented in any base; humans prefer base 10 and, as we examined in Chapter 3, base 2 is best for computers. Because we will frequently be dealing with both decimal and binary numbers, to avoid confusion we will subscript decimal numbers with *ten* and binary numbers with *two*.

In any number base, the value of *i*th digit *d* is

$$d \times \text{Base}^i$$

where *i* starts at 0 and increases from right to left. This leads to an obvious way to number the bits in the word: Simply use the power of the base for that bit. For example,

$$1011_{\text{two}}$$

represents

$$(1 \times 2^3) + (0 \times 2^2) + (1 \times 2^1) + (1 \times 2^0)_{ten}$$
$$= (1 \times 8) + (0 \times 4) + (1 \times 2) + (1 \times 1)_{ten}$$
$$= \quad 8 \quad + \quad 0 \quad + \quad 2 \quad + \quad 1_{ten}$$
$$= 11_{ten}$$

Hence the bits are numbered 0, 1, 2, 3, . . . from *right to left* in a word. The drawing below shows the numbering of bits within a MIPS word and the placement of the number 1011_{two}:

31 30 29 28	27 26 25 24	23 22 21 20	19 18 17 16	15 14 13 12	11 10 9 8	7 6 5 4	3 2 1 0
0 0 0 0	0 0 0 0	0 0 0 0	0 0 0 0	0 0 0 0	0 0 0 0	0 0 0 0	1 0 1 1

(32 bits wide)

Since words are drawn vertically as well as horizontally, leftmost and rightmost may be unclear. Hence, the phrase *least significant bit* is used to refer to the rightmost bit (bit 0 above) and *most significant bit* to the leftmost bit (bit 31).

The MIPS word is 32 bits long, so we can represent 2^{32} different 32-bit patterns. It is natural to let these combinations represent the numbers from 0 to $2^{32} - 1$ ($4{,}294{,}967{,}295_{ten}$):

$$0000\ 0000\ 0000\ 0000\ 0000\ 0000\ 0000\ 0000_{two} = \qquad\qquad 0_{ten}$$
$$0000\ 0000\ 0000\ 0000\ 0000\ 0000\ 0000\ 0001_{two} = \qquad\qquad 1_{ten}$$
$$0000\ 0000\ 0000\ 0000\ 0000\ 0000\ 0000\ 0010_{two} = \qquad\qquad 2_{ten}$$
$$. . .\qquad\qquad\qquad\qquad\qquad\qquad\qquad\qquad\qquad . . .$$
$$1111\ 1111\ 1111\ 1111\ 1111\ 1111\ 1111\ 1101_{two} = 4{,}294{,}967{,}293_{ten}$$
$$1111\ 1111\ 1111\ 1111\ 1111\ 1111\ 1111\ 1110_{two} = 4{,}294{,}967{,}294_{ten}$$
$$1111\ 1111\ 1111\ 1111\ 1111\ 1111\ 1111\ 1111_{two} = 4{,}294{,}967{,}295_{ten}$$

Hardware Software Interface

Base 2 is not natural to human beings; we have 10 fingers and so find base 10 natural. Why didn't computers use decimal? In fact, the first commercial computer *did* offer decimal arithmetic. The problem was that the computer still used on and off signals, so a decimal digit was simply represented by several binary digits. Decimal proved so inefficient that subsequent machines reverted to all binary, converting to base 10 only for the infrequent input/output events.

ASCII versus Binary Numbers

Example

We could represent numbers as strings of ASCII digits instead of as two's complement integers (see Figure 3.15 on page 142). What is the expansion in storage if the number 1 billion is represented in ASCII versus a 32-bit integer?

Answer

One billion is 1 000 000 000, so it would take 10 ASCII digits, each 8 bits long. Thus the storage expansion would be $(10 \times 8)/32$ or 2.5. In addition to the expansion in storage, the hardware to add, subtract, multiply, and divide such numbers is also difficult. Such difficulties explain why computing professionals are raised to believe that binary is natural and that the occasional decimal machine is bizarre.

Keep in mind that the binary bit patterns above are simply *representatives* of numbers. Numbers really have an infinite number of digits, with almost all being 0 except for a few of the rightmost digits. We just don't normally show leading 0s.

As we shall see in sections 4.5 through 4.7, hardware can be designed to add, subtract, multiply, and divide these binary bit patterns. If the number that is the proper result of such operations cannot be represented by these rightmost hardware bits, *overflow* is said to have occurred. It's up to the operating system and program to determine what to do if overflow occurs.

Computer programs calculate both positive and negative numbers, so we need a representation that distinguishes the positive from the negative. The most obvious solution is to add a separate sign, which conveniently can be represented in a single bit; the name for this representation is *sign and magnitude*.

Alas, sign and magnitude representation has several shortcomings. First, it's not obvious where to put the sign bit. To the right? To the left? Early machines tried both. Second, adders for sign and magnitude may need an extra step to set the sign because we can't know in advance what the proper sign will be. Finally, a separate sign bit means that sign and magnitude has both a positive and negative zero, which can lead to problems for inattentive programmers. As a result of these shortcomings, sign and magnitude was soon abandoned.

In the search for a more attractive alternative, the question arose as to what would be the result for unsigned numbers if we tried to subtract a large number from a small one. The answer is that it would try to borrow from a string of leading 0s, so the result would have a string of leading 1s.

Given that there was no obvious better alternative, the final solution was to pick the representation that made the hardware simple: leading 0s mean positive, and leading 1s mean negative. This convention for representing signed binary numbers is called *two's complement* representation:

$$0000\ 0000\ 0000\ 0000\ 0000\ 0000\ 0000\ 0000_{two} = 0_{ten}$$
$$0000\ 0000\ 0000\ 0000\ 0000\ 0000\ 0000\ 0001_{two} = 1_{ten}$$
$$0000\ 0000\ 0000\ 0000\ 0000\ 0000\ 0000\ 0010_{two} = 2_{ten}$$

. . .   . . .

$$0111\ 1111\ 1111\ 1111\ 1111\ 1111\ 1111\ 1101_{two} = 2{,}147{,}483{,}645_{ten}$$
$$0111\ 1111\ 1111\ 1111\ 1111\ 1111\ 1111\ 1110_{two} = 2{,}147{,}483{,}646_{ten}$$
$$0111\ 1111\ 1111\ 1111\ 1111\ 1111\ 1111\ 1111_{two} = 2{,}147{,}483{,}647_{ten}$$
$$1000\ 0000\ 0000\ 0000\ 0000\ 0000\ 0000\ 0000_{two} = -2{,}147{,}483{,}648_{ten}$$
$$1000\ 0000\ 0000\ 0000\ 0000\ 0000\ 0000\ 0001_{two} = -2{,}147{,}483{,}647_{ten}$$
$$1000\ 0000\ 0000\ 0000\ 0000\ 0000\ 0000\ 0010_{two} = -2{,}147{,}483{,}646_{ten}$$

. . .   . . .

$$1111\ 1111\ 1111\ 1111\ 1111\ 1111\ 1111\ 1101_{two} = -3_{ten}$$
$$1111\ 1111\ 1111\ 1111\ 1111\ 1111\ 1111\ 1110_{two} = -2_{ten}$$
$$1111\ 1111\ 1111\ 1111\ 1111\ 1111\ 1111\ 1111_{two} = -1_{ten}$$

The positive half of the numbers, from 0 to $2{,}147{,}483{,}647_{ten}$ ($2^{31}-1$), use the same representation as before. The following bit pattern ($1000 \ldots 0000_{two}$) represents the most negative number $-2{,}147{,}483{,}648_{ten}$ (-2^{31}). It is followed by a declining set of negative numbers: $-2{,}147{,}483{,}647_{ten}$ ($1000 \ldots 0001_{two}$) down to -1_{ten} ($1111 \ldots 1111_{two}$).

Two's complement does have one negative number, $-2{,}147{,}483{,}648_{ten}$, that has no corresponding positive number. Such imbalance was a worry to the inattentive programmer, but sign and magnitude had problems for both the programmer *and* the hardware designer. Consequently, every computer today uses two's complement binary representations for signed numbers.

Two's complement representation has the advantage that all negative numbers have a 1 in the most significant bit. Consequently, hardware needs to test only this bit to see if a number is positive or negative (with 0 considered positive). This particular bit is often called the *sign bit*. By recognizing the role of the sign bit, we can represent positive and negative numbers in terms of the bit value times a power of 2 (here xi means the *i*th bit of *x*):

$$(x31 \times -2^{31}) + (x30 \times 2^{30}) + (x29 \times 2^{29}) + \ldots + (x1 \times 2^1) + (x0 \times 2^0)$$

The sign bit is multiplied by -2^{31}, and the rest of the bits are then multiplied by positive versions of their respective base values.

Binary to Decimal Conversion

Example

What is the decimal value of this 32-bit two's complement number?

1111 1111 1111 1111 1111 1111 1111 1100$_{two}$

Answer

Substituting the number's bit values into the formula above:

$$(1 \times -2^{31}) + (1 \times 2^{30}) + (1 \times 2^{29}) + \ldots + (1 \times 2^2) + (0 \times 2^1) + (0 \times 2^0)$$
$$= -2^{31} + 2^{30} + 2^{29} + \ldots + 2^2 + 0 + 0$$
$$= -2{,}147{,}483{,}648_{ten} + 2{,}147{,}483{,}644_{ten}$$
$$= -4_{ten}$$

We'll see a shortcut to simplify conversion soon.

Hardware Software Interface

Signed versus unsigned applies to loads as well as to arithmetic. The *function* of a signed load is to copy the sign repeatedly to fill the rest of the register—called *sign extension*—but its *purpose* is to place a correct representation of the number within that register. Unsigned loads simply fill with 0s to the left of the data, since the number represented by the bit pattern is unsigned.

When loading a 32-bit word into a 32-bit register, the point is moot; signed and unsigned loads are identical. MIPS does offer two flavors of byte loads: *load byte* (`lb`) treats the byte as a signed number and thus sign extends to fill the 24 leftmost bits of the register, while *load byte unsigned* (`lbu`) works with unsigned integers. Since programs almost always use bytes to represent characters rather than consider bytes as short signed integers, `lbu` is used practically exclusively for byte loads.

Just as an operation on unsigned numbers can overflow the capacity of hardware to represent the result, so can an operation on two's complement numbers. Overflow occurs when the leftmost retained bit of the binary bit pattern is not the same as the infinite number of digits to the left (the sign bit is incorrect): a 0 on the left of the bit pattern when the number is negative or a 1 when the number is positive.

Hardware Software Interface

Unlike the numbers discussed above, memory addresses naturally start at 0 and continue to the largest address. Put another way, negative addresses make no sense. Thus, programs want to deal sometimes with numbers that can be positive or negative and sometimes with numbers that can be only positive. Programming languages reflect this distinction. C, for example, names the former *integers* (declared as `int` in the program) and the latter *unsigned integers* (`unsigned int`).

Comparison instructions must deal with this dichotomy. Sometimes a bit pattern with a 1 in the most significant bit represents a negative number and, of course, is less than any positive number, which must have a 0 in the most significant bit. With unsigned integers, on the other hand, a 1 in the most significant bit represents a number that is *larger* than any that begins with a 0.

MIPS offers two versions of the set on less than comparison to handle these alternatives. *Set on less than* (`slt`) and *set on less than immediate* (`slti`) work with signed integers. Unsigned integers are compared using *set on less than unsigned* (`sltu`) and *set on less than immediate unsigned* (`sltiu`).

Signed versus Unsigned Comparison

Example

Suppose register `$s0` has the binary number

$$1111\ 1111\ 1111\ 1111\ 1111\ 1111\ 1111\ 1111_{two}$$

and that register `$s1` has the binary number

$$0000\ 0000\ 0000\ 0000\ 0000\ 0000\ 0000\ 0001_{two}$$

What are the values of registers `$t0` and `$t1` after these two instructions?

```
slt     $t0, $s0, $s1 # signed comparison
sltu    $t1, $s0, $s1 # unsigned comparison
```

Answer

The value in register `$s0` represents −1 if it is an integer and $4,294,967,295_{ten}$ if it is an unsigned integer. The value in register `$s1` represents 1 in either case. Then register `$t0` has the value 1, since $-1_{ten} < 1_{ten}$, and register `$t1` has the value 0, since $4,294,967,295_{ten} > 1_{ten}$.

Before going on to addition and subtraction, let's examine a few useful shortcuts when working with two's complement numbers.

The first shortcut is a quick way to negate a two's complement binary number. Simply invert every 0 to 1 and every 1 to 0, then add one to the result. This shortcut is based on the observation that the sum of a number and its inverted representation must be $111 \ldots 111_{two}$, which represents -1. Since $x + \bar{x} \equiv -1$, therefore $x + \bar{x} + 1 = 0$ or $\bar{x} + 1 = -x$.

Negation Shortcut

Example

Negate 2_{ten}, and then check the result by negating -2_{ten}.

Answer

$$2_{ten} = 0000\ 0000\ 0000\ 0000\ 0000\ 0000\ 0000\ 0010_{two}$$

Negating this number by inverting the bits and adding one,

$$
\begin{aligned}
&\quad 1111\ 1111\ 1111\ 1111\ 1111\ 1111\ 1111\ 1101_{two} \\
+ &\quad\hphantom{1111\ 1111\ 1111\ 1111\ 1111\ 1111\ 1111\ 110}1_{two} \\
\hline
= &\quad 1111\ 1111\ 1111\ 1111\ 1111\ 1111\ 1111\ 1110_{two} \\
= &\quad {-2}_{ten}
\end{aligned}
$$

Going the other direction,

$$1111\ 1111\ 1111\ 1111\ 1111\ 1111\ 1111\ 1110_{two}$$

is first inverted and then incremented:

$$
\begin{aligned}
&\quad 0000\ 0000\ 0000\ 0000\ 0000\ 0000\ 0000\ 0001_{two} \\
+ &\quad\hphantom{0000\ 0000\ 0000\ 0000\ 0000\ 0000\ 0000\ 000}1_{two} \\
\hline
= &\quad 0000\ 0000\ 0000\ 0000\ 0000\ 0000\ 0000\ 0010_{two} \\
= &\quad 2_{ten}
\end{aligned}
$$

The second shortcut tells us how to convert a binary number represented in n bits to a number represented with more than n bits. For example, the immediate field in the load, store, branch, add, and set on less than instructions contains a two's complement 16-bit number, representing $-32,768_{ten}$ (-2^{15}) to $32,767_{ten}$ ($2^{15}-1$). To add the immediate field to a 32-bit register, the machine must convert that 16-bit number to its 32-bit equivalent. The shortcut is to take the most significant bit from the smaller quantity—the sign bit—and replicate it to fill the new bits of the larger quantity. The old bits are simply copied into the right portion of the new word. This shortcut is commonly called *sign extension*.

Sign Extension Shortcut

Example

Convert 16-bit binary versions of 2_{ten} and -2_{ten} to 32-bit binary numbers.

Answer

The 16-bit binary version of the number 2 is

$$0000\ 0000\ 0000\ 0010_{two} = 2_{ten}$$

It is converted to a 32-bit number by making 16 copies of the value in the most significant bit (0) and placing that in the left-hand half of the word. The right half gets the old value:

$$0000\ 0000\ 0000\ 0000\ 0000\ 0000\ 0000\ 0010_{two} = 2_{ten}$$

Let's negate the 16-bit version of 2 using the earlier shortcut. Thus,

$$0000\ 0000\ 0000\ 0010_{two}$$

becomes

$$
\begin{array}{r}
1111\ 1111\ 1111\ 1101_{two} \\
+\qquad\qquad\qquad\qquad 1_{two} \\
\hline
=\quad 1111\ 1111\ 1111\ 1110_{two}
\end{array}
$$

Creating a 32-bit version of the negative number means copying the sign bit 16 times and placing it on the left:

$$1111\ 1111\ 1111\ 1111\ 1111\ 1111\ 1111\ 1110_{two} = -2_{ten}$$

This trick works because positive two's complement numbers really have an infinite number of 0s on the left and those that are negative two's complement numbers have an infinite number of 1s. The binary bit pattern representing a number hides leading bits to fit the width of the hardware; sign extension simply restores some of them.

A final shortcut, which we previewed in Chapter 3, is that we can save reading and writing long binary numbers by using a higher base than binary that converts easily into binary. Since almost all computer data sizes are multiples of 4, *hexadecimal* (base 16) numbers are popular. Since base 16 is a power of 2, we can trivially convert by replacing each group of four binary digits by a single hexadecimal digit, and vice versa. Figure 4.1 shows the hexadecimal Rosetta stone. We will use either the subscript *hex* or the C notation, which uses 0x*nnnn*, for hexadecimal numbers.

Hexadecimal	Binary	Hexadecimal	Binary	Hexadecimal	Binary	Hexadecimal	Binary
0_{hex}	0000_{two}	4_{hex}	0100_{two}	8_{hex}	1000_{two}	c_{hex}	1100_{two}
1_{hex}	0001_{two}	5_{hex}	0101_{two}	9_{hex}	1001_{two}	d_{hex}	1101_{two}
2_{hex}	0010_{two}	6_{hex}	0110_{two}	a_{hex}	1010_{two}	e_{hex}	1110_{two}
3_{hex}	0011_{two}	7_{hex}	0111_{two}	b_{hex}	1011_{two}	f_{hex}	1111_{two}

FIGURE 4.1   The hexadecimal-binary conversion table. Just replace one hexadecimal digit by the corresponding four binary digits, and vice versa. If the length of the binary number is not a multiple of four, go from right to left.

Binary-to-Hexadecimal Shortcut

Example

Convert the following hexadecimal and binary numbers into the other base:

$$\text{eca8 } 6420_{hex}$$
$$0001\ 0011\ 0101\ 0111\ 1001\ 1011\ 1101\ 1111_{two}$$

Answer

Just a table lookup one way:

$$\text{eca8 } 6420_{hex}$$
$$1110\ 1100\ 1010\ 1000\ 0110\ 0100\ 0010\ 0000_{two}$$

And then the other direction:

$$0001\ 0011\ 0101\ 0111\ 1001\ 1011\ 1101\ 1111_{two}$$
$$1357\ 9bdf_{hex}$$

Summary

The main point of this section is that we need to represent both positive and negative integers within a computer word, and although there are pros and cons to any option, the overwhelming choice since 1965 has been two's complement. Figure 4.2 shows the additions to the MIPS assembly language revealed in this section. (The MIPS machine language is also illustrated on the back endpapers of this book.)

MIPS operands

Name	Example	Comments
32 registers	`$s0-$s7, $t0-$t9, $gp, $fp, $zero, $sp, $ra, $at`	Fast locations for data. In MIPS, data must be in registers to perform arithmetic. MIPS register `$zero` always equals 0. Register `$at` is reserved for the assembler to handle large constants.
2^{30} memory words	Memory[0], Memory[4], . . . , Memory[4294967292]	Accessed only by data transfer instructions. MIPS uses byte addresses, so sequential words differ by 4. Memory holds data structures, such as arrays, and spilled registers, such as those saved on procedure calls.

MIPS assembly language

Category	Instruction	Example	Meaning	Comments
Arithmetic	add	`add $s1,$s2,$s3`	$s1 = $s2 + $s3	Three operands
	subtract	`sub $s1,$s2,$s3`	$s1 = $s2 - $s3	Three operands
	add immediate	`addi $s1,$s2,100`	$s1 = $s2 + 100	+ constant
Data transfer	load word	`lw $s1,100($s2)`	$s1 = Memory[$s2 + 100]	Word from memory to register
	store word	`sw $s1,100($s2)`	Memory[$s2 + 100] = $s1	Word from register to memory
	load byte unsigned	`lbu $s1,100($s2)`	$s1 = Memory[$s2 + 100]	Byte from memory to register
	store byte	`sb $s1,100($s2)`	Memory[$s2 + 100] = $s1	Byte from register to memory
	load upper immediate	`lui $s1,100`	$s1 = 100 * 2^{16}	Loads constant in upper 16 bits
Conditional branch	branch on equal	`beq $s1,$s2,25`	if ($s1 == $s2) go to PC + 4 + 100	Equal test; PC-relative branch
	branch on not equal	`bne $s1,$s2,25`	if ($s1 != $s2) go to PC + 4 + 100	Not equal test; PC-relative
	set on less than	`slt $s1,$s2,$s3`	if ($s2 < $s3) $s1 = 1; else $s1 = 0	Compare less than; two's complement
	set less than immediate	`slti $s1,$s2,100`	if ($s2 < 100) $s1 = 1; else $s1 = 0	Compare < constant; two's complement
	set less than unsigned	`sltu $s1,$s2,$s3`	if ($s2 < $s3) $s1 = 1; else $s1 = 0	Compare less than; unsigned numbers
	set less than immediate unsigned	`sltiu $s1,$s2,100`	if ($s2 < 100) $s1 = 1; else $s1 = 0	Compare < constant; unsigned numbers
Unconditional jump	jump	`j 2500`	go to 10000	Jump to target address
	jump register	`jr $ra`	go to $ra	For switch, procedure return
	jump and link	`jal 2500`	$ra = PC + 4; go to 10000	For procedure call

FIGURE 4.2 MIPS architecture revealed thus far. Color indicates portions from this section added to the MIPS architecture revealed in Chapter 3 (Figure 3.20 on page 155). MIPS machine language is listed in the back endpapers of this book.

Elaboration: Two's complement gets its name from the rule that the unsigned sum of an n-bit number and its negative is 2^n, hence the complement or negation of a two's complement number x is $2^n - x$.

A third alternative representation is called *one's complement*. The negative of a one's complement is found by inverting each bit, from 0 to 1 and from 1 to 0, which helps explain its name since the complement of x is $2^n - x - 1$. It was also an attempt to be a better solution than sign and magnitude, and several scientific computers did use the notation. This representation is similar to two's complement except that it also has two 0s: $00 \ldots 00_{two}$ is positive 0 and $11 \ldots 11_{two}$ is negative 0. The most negative number $10 \ldots 000_{two}$ represents $-2{,}147{,}483{,}647_{ten}$, and so the positives and negatives are balanced. One's complement adders did need an extra step to subtract a number, and hence two's complement dominates today.

A final notation, which we will look at when we discuss floating point, is to represent the most negative value by $00 \ldots 000_{two}$ and the most positive value represented by $11 \ldots 11_{two}$, with 0 typically having the value $10 \ldots 00_{two}$. This is called a *biased* notation, for it biases the number such that the number plus the bias has a non-negative representation.

Addition and Subtraction

Subtraction: Addition's Tricky Pal

> No. 10, Top Ten Courses for Athletes at a Football Factory,
> David Letterman et al., *Book of Top Ten Lists*, 1990

Addition is just what you would expect in computers. Digits are added bit by bit from right to left, with carries passed to the next digit to the left, just as you would do by hand. Subtraction uses addition: The appropriate operand is simply negated before being added.

Binary Addition and Subtraction

Example Let's try adding 6_{ten} to 7_{ten} in binary and then subtracting 6_{ten} from 7_{ten} in binary.

Answer

$$
\begin{array}{rll}
  & 0000\,0000\,0000\,0000\,0000\,0000\,0000\,0111_{two} & = \; 7_{ten} \\
+ & 0000\,0000\,0000\,0000\,0000\,0000\,0000\,0110_{two} & = \; 6_{ten} \\
\hline
= & 0000\,0000\,0000\,0000\,0000\,0000\,0000\,1101_{two} & = \; 13_{ten}
\end{array}
$$

The 4 bits to the right have all the action; Figure 4.3 shows the sums and carries. The carries are shown in parentheses, with the arrows showing how they are passed.

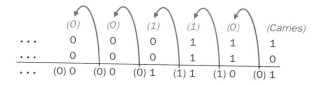

FIGURE 4.3   Binary addition, showing carries from right to left. The rightmost bit adds 1 to 0, resulting in the sum of this bit being 1 and the carry out from this bit being 0. Hence, the operation for the second digit to the right is 0 + 1 + 1. This generates a 0 for this sum bit and a carry out of 1. The third digit is the sum of 1 + 1 + 1, resulting in a carry out of 1 and a sum bit of 1. The fourth bit is 1 + 0 + 0, yielding a 1 sum and no carry.

Subtracting 6_{ten} from 7_{ten} can be done directly:

$$
\begin{array}{lllll}
 & 0000\ 0000\ 0000\ 0000\ 0000\ 0000\ 0000\ 0111_{two} & = & 7_{ten} \\
- & 0000\ 0000\ 0000\ 0000\ 0000\ 0000\ 0000\ 0110_{two} & = & 6_{ten} \\
\hline
= & 0000\ 0000\ 0000\ 0000\ 0000\ 0000\ 0000\ 0001_{two} & = & 1_{ten}
\end{array}
$$

or via addition using the two's complement representation of −6:

$$
\begin{array}{lllll}
 & 0000\ 0000\ 0000\ 0000\ 0000\ 0000\ 0000\ 0111_{two} & = & 7_{ten} \\
+ & 1111\ 1111\ 1111\ 1111\ 1111\ 1111\ 1111\ 1010_{two} & = & -6_{ten} \\
\hline
= & 0000\ 0000\ 0000\ 0000\ 0000\ 0000\ 0000\ 0001_{two} & = & 1_{ten}
\end{array}
$$

We said earlier that overflow occurs when the result from an operation cannot be represented with the available hardware, in this case a 32-bit word. When can overflow occur in addition? When adding operands with different signs, overflow cannot occur. The reason is the sum must be no larger than one of the operands. For example, −10 + 4 = −6. Since the operands fit in 32 bits and the sum is no larger than an operand, the sum must fit in 32 bits as well. Therefore no overflow can occur when adding positive and negative operands.

There are similar restrictions to the occurrence of overflow during subtract, but it's just the opposite principle: When the signs of the operands are the *same*, overflow cannot occur. To see this, remember that $x - y = x + (-y)$ because we subtract by negating the second operand and then add. So, when we subtract operands of the same sign we end up by *adding* operands of *different* signs. From the prior paragraph, we know that overflow cannot occur in this case either.

Having examined when overflow cannot occur in addition and subtraction, we still haven't answered how to detect when it does occur. Overflow occurs when adding two positive numbers and the sum is negative, or vice versa. Clearly, adding or subtracting two 32-bit numbers can yield a result that needs

33 bits to be fully expressed. The lack of a 33rd bit means that when overflow occurs the sign bit is being set with the *value* of the result instead of the proper sign of the result. Since we need just one extra bit, only the sign bit can be wrong. This means a carry out occurred into the sign bit.

Overflow occurs in subtraction when we subtract a negative number from a positive number and get a negative result, or when we subtract a positive number from a negative number and get a positive result. This means a borrow occurred from the sign bit. Figure 4.4 shows the combination of operations, operands, and results that indicate an overflow. (Exercise 4.42 gives a shortcut for detecting overflow more simply in hardware.)

We have just seen how to detect overflow for two's complement numbers in a machine. What about unsigned integers? Unsigned integers are commonly used for memory addresses where overflows are ignored.

The machine designer must therefore provide a way to ignore overflow in some cases and to recognize it in others. The MIPS solution is to have two kinds of arithmetic instructions to recognize the two choices:

- Add (add), add immediate (addi), and subtract (sub) cause exceptions on overflow.

- Add unsigned (addu), add immediate unsigned (addiu), and subtract unsigned (subu) do *not* cause exceptions on overflow.

Because C ignores overflows, the MIPS C compilers will always generate the unsigned versions of the arithmetic instructions addu, addiu, and subu no matter what the type of the variables. The MIPS Fortran compilers, however, pick the appropriate arithmetic instructions, depending on the type of the operands.

Operation	Operand A	Operand B	Result
$A + B$	≥ 0	≥ 0	< 0
$A + B$	< 0	< 0	≥ 0
$A - B$	≥ 0	< 0	< 0
$A - B$	< 0	≥ 0	≥ 0

FIGURE 4.4   Overflow conditions for addition and subtraction.

Hardware Software Interface

The machine designer must decide how to handle arithmetic overflows. Although some languages like C leave the decision up to the machine designer, languages like Ada and Fortran require that the program be notified. The programmer or the programming environment must then decide what to do when overflow occurs.

MIPS detects overflow with an *exception,* also called an *interrupt* on many computers. An exception or interrupt is essentially an unscheduled procedure call. The address of the instruction that overflowed is saved in a register, and the computer jumps to a predefined address to invoke the appropriate routine for that exception. The interrupted address is saved so that in some situations the program can continue after corrective code is executed. (Section 5.6 covers exceptions in more detail; Chapters 7 and 8 describe other situations where exceptions and interrupts occur.)

MIPS includes a register called the *exception program counter* (*EPC*) to contain the address of the instruction that caused the exception. The instruction *move from system control* (mfc0) is used to copy EPC into a general-purpose register so that MIPS software has the option of returning to the offending instruction via a jump register instruction.

Summary

The main point of this section is that, independent of the representation, the finite word size of computers means that arithmetic operations can create results that are too large to fit in this fixed word size. It's easy to detect overflow in unsigned numbers, although these are almost always ignored because programs don't want to detect overflow for address arithmetic, the most common use of natural numbers. Two's complement presents a greater challenge, yet some software systems require detection of overflow, so today all machines have a way to detect it. Figure 4.5 shows the additions to the MIPS architecture from this section.

Elaboration: MIPS can trap on overflow, but unlike many other machines there is no conditional branch to test overflow. A sequence of MIPS instructions can discover overflow. For signed addition, the sequence is the following (see the In More Depth section on page 329 for the definition of the xor and nor instructions):

```
addu  $t0, $t1,  $t2            # $t0 = sum, but don't trap
xor   $t3, $t1,  $t2            # Check if signs differ
slt   $t3, $t3,  $zero          # $t3 = 1 if signs differ
bne   $t3, $zero, No_overflow   # $t1, $t2 signs ≠, so no overflow
xor   $t3, $t0,  $t1            # signs =; sign of sum match too?
                               # $t3 negative if sum sign different
slt   $t3, $t3,  $zero          # $t3 = 1 if sum sign different
bne   $t3, $zero, Overflow      # All three signs ≠; go to overflow
```

MIPS operands

Name	Example	Comments
32 registers	$s0–$s7, $t0–$t9, $gp, $fp, $zero, $sp, $ra, $at	Fast locations for data. In MIPS, data must be in registers to perform arithmetic. MIPS register $zero always equals 0. Register $at is reserved for the assembler to, for example, handle large constants.
2^{30} memory words	Memory[0], Memory[4], . . . , Memory[4294967292]	Accessed only by data transfer instructions. MIPS uses byte addresses, so sequential words differ by 4. Memory holds data structures, such as arrays, and spilled registers, such as those saved on procedure calls.

MIPS assembly language

Category	Instruction	Example		Meaning	Comments
Arithmetic	add	add	$s1,$s2,$s3	$s1 = $s2 + $s3	Three operands; overflow detected
	subtract	sub	$s1,$s2,$s3	$s1 = $s2 – $s3	Three operands; overflow detected
	add immediate	addi	$s1,$s2,100	$s1 = $s2 + 100	+ constant; overflow detected
	add unsigned	addu	$s1,$s2,$s3	$s1 = $s2 + $s3	Three operands; overflow undetected
	subtract unsigned	subu	$s1,$s2,$s3	$s1 = $s2 – $s3	Three operands; overflow undetected
	add immediate unsigned	addiu	$s1,$s2,100	$s1 = $s2 + 100	+ constant; overflow undetected
	move from coprocessor register	mfc0	$s1,$epc	$s1 = $epc	Used to copy Exception PC plus other special registers
Data transfer	load word	lw	$s1,100($s2)	$s1 = Memory[$s2 + 100]	Word from memory to register
	store word	sw	$s1,100($s2)	Memory[$s2 + 100] = $s1	Word from register to memory
	load byte unsigned	lbu	$s1,100($s2)	$s1 = Memory[$s2 + 100]	Byte from memory to register
	store byte	sb	$s1,100($s2)	Memory[$s2 + 100] = $s1	Byte from register to memory
	load upper immediate	lui	$s1,100	$s1 = 100 * 2^{16}	Loads constant in upper 16 bits
Conditional branch	branch on equal	beq	$s1,$s2,25	if ($s1 == $s2) go to PC + 4 + 100	Equal test; PC-relative branch
	branch on not equal	bne	$s1,$s2,25	if ($s1 != $s2) go to PC + 4 + 100	Not equal test; PC-relative
	set on less than	slt	$s1,$s2,$s3	if ($s2 < $s3) $s1 = 1; else $s1 = 0	Compare less than; two's complement
	set less than immediate	slti	$s1,$s2,100	if ($s2 < 100) $s1 = 1; else $s1 = 0	Compare < constant; two's complement
	set less than unsigned	sltu	$s1,$s2,$s3	if ($s2 < $s3) $s1 = 1; else $s1 = 0	Compare less than; unsigned numbers
	set less than immediate unsigned	sltiu	$s1,$s2,100	if ($s2 < 100) $s1 = 1; else $s1 = 0	Compare < constant; unsigned numbers
Unconditional jump	jump	j	2500	go to 10000	Jump to target address
	jump register	jr	$ra	go to $ra	For switch, procedure return
	jump and link	jal	2500	$ra = PC + 4; go to 10000	For procedure call

FIGURE 4.5   MIPS architecture revealed thus far. Color indicates the portions revealed since Figure 4.2 on page 219. MIPS machine language is also listed on the back endpapers of this book.

For unsigned addition ($t0 = $t1 + $t2), the test is

```
addu  $t0, $t1, $t2    # $t0 = sum
nor   $t3, $t1, $zero  # $t3 = NOT $t1
                       # (2's comp - 1: 2^32 - $t1 - 1)
sltu  $t3, $t3, $t2    # (2^32 - $t1 - 1) < $t2
                       # ⟹ 2^32 - 1 < $t1 + $t2
bne   $t3,$zero, Overflow # if (2^32 - 1 < $t1 + $t2) go to overflow
```

Elaboration: In the preceding text, we said that you copy EPC into a register via mfc0 and then return to the interrupted code via jump register. This leads to an interesting question: Since you must first transfer EPC to a register to use with jump register, how can jump register return to the interrupted code *and* restore the original values of *all* registers? You either restore the old registers first, thereby destroying your return address from EPC that you placed in a register for use in jump register, or you restore all registers but the one with the return address so that you can jump—meaning an exception would result in changing that one register at any time during program execution! Neither option is satisfactory.

To rescue the hardware from this dilemma, MIPS programmers agreed to reserve registers $k0 and $k1 for the operating system; these registers are *not* restored on exceptions. Just as the MIPS compilers avoid using register $at so that the assembler can use it as a temporary register (see the Hardware Software Interface section on page 147 in Chapter 3), compilers also abstain from using registers $k0 and $k1 to make them available for the operating system. Exception routines place the return address in one of these registers and then use jump register to restore the instruction address.

4.4 Logical Operations

"Contrariwise," continued Tweedledee, "if it was so, it might be; and if it were so, it would be; but as it isn't, it ain't. That's logic."

Lewis Carroll, *Alice's Adventures in Wonderland*, 1865

Although the first computers concentrated on full words, it soon became clear that it was useful to operate on fields of bits within a word or even on individual bits. Examining characters within a word, each of which are stored as 8 bits, is one example of such an operation. It follows that instructions were added to simplify, among other things, the packing and unpacking of bits into words.

One class of such operations is called *shifts*. They move all the bits in a word to the left or right, filling the emptied bits with 0s. For example, if register $s0 contained

0000 0000 0000 00000 000 0000 0000 0000 1101$_{two}$

and the instruction to shift left by eight was executed, the new value would look like this:

0000 0000 0000 0000 0000 0000 1101 0000 0000$_{two}$

The dual of a shift left is a shift right. The actual name of the two MIPS shift instructions are called *shift left logical* (sll) and *shift right logical* (srl). The following instruction performs the operation above, assuming that the result should go in register $t2:

    sll $t2,$s0,8 # reg $t2 = reg $s0 << 8 bits

We delayed explaining the *shamt* field in the R-format in Chapter 3. It stands for *shift amount* and is used in shift instructions. Hence, the machine language version of the instruction above is

op	rs	rt	rd	shamt	funct
0	0	16	10	8	0

The encoding of sll is 0 in both the op and funct fields, rd contains $t2, rt contains $s0, and shamt contains 8. The rs field is unused, and thus is set to 0.

Another useful operation that isolates fields is *AND*. (We capitalize the word to avoid confusion between the operation and the English conjunction.) AND is a bit-by-bit operation that leaves a 1 in the result only if both bits of the operands are 1. For example, if register $t2 still contains

0000 0000 0000 0000 0000 1101 0000 0000$_{two}$

and register $t1 contains

0000 0000 0000 0000 0011 1100 0000 0000$_{two}$

then, after executing the MIPS instruction

    and $t0,$t1,$t2 # reg $t0 = reg $t1 & reg $t2

the value of register $t0 would be

0000 0000 0000 0000 0000 1100 0000 0000$_{two}$

As you can see, AND can be used to apply a bit pattern to a set of bits to force 0s where there is a 0 in the bit pattern. Such a bit pattern in conjunction with AND is traditionally called a *mask*, since the mask "conceals" some bits.

To place a value into one of these seas of 0s, there is the dual to AND, called *OR*. It is a bit-by-bit operation that places a 1 in the result if *either* operand bit is a 1. To elaborate, if the registers $t1 and $t2 are unchanged from the preceding example, the result of the MIPS instruction

```
or $t0,$t1,$t2 # reg $t0 = reg $t1 | reg $t2
```

is this value in register $t0:

0000 0000 0000 0000 0011 1101 0000 0000$_{two}$

Figure 4.6 shows the logical C operations and the corresponding MIPS instructions. Constants are useful in logical operations as well as in arithmetic operations, so MIPS also provides the instructions *and immediate* (andi) and *or immediate* (ori). This section describes the logical operations AND, OR, and shift found in every computer today. The logical instructions are highlighted in Figure 4.7, which summarizes the MIPS instructions seen thus far.

Logical operations	C operators	MIPS instructions
Shift left	<<	sll
Shift right	>>	srl
Bit-by-bit AND	&	and, andi
Bit-by-bit OR	|	or, ori

FIGURE 4.6 Logical operations and their corresponding operations in C and MIPS.

Hardware Software Interface

C allows *bit fields* or *fields* to be defined within words, both allowing objects to be packed within a word *and* to match an externally enforced interface such as an I/O device. All fields must fit within a single word. Fields are unsigned integers that can be as short as 1 bit. C compilers insert and extract fields using logical instructions in MIPS: and, or, sll, and srl.

MIPS operands

Name	Example	Comments
32 registers	$s0–$s7, $t0–$t9, $gp, $fp, $zero, $sp, $ra, $at	Fast locations for data. In MIPS, data must be in registers to perform arithmetic. MIPS register $zero always equals 0. Register $at is reserved for the assembler to handle large constants.
2^{30} memory words	Memory[0], Memory[4], . . . , Memory[4294967292]	Accessed only by data transfer instructions. MIPS uses byte addresses, so sequential words differ by 4. Memory holds data structures, such as arrays, and spilled registers, such as those saved on procedure calls.

MIPS assembly language

Category	Instruction	Example		Meaning	Comments
Arithmetic	add	add	$s1,$s2,$s3	$s1 = $s2 + $s3	Three operands; overflow detected
	subtract	sub	$s1,$s2,$s3	$s1 = $s2 – $s3	Three operands; overflow detected
	add immediate	addi	$s1,$s2,100	$s1 = $s2 + 100	+ constant; overflow detected
	add unsigned	addu	$s1,$s2,$s3	$s1 = $s2 + $s3	Three operands; overflow undetected
	subtract unsigned	subu	$s1,$s2,$s3	$s1 = $s2 – $s3	Three operands; overflow undetected
	add immediate unsigned	addiu	$s1,$s2,100	$s1 = $s2 + 100	+ constant; overflow undetected
	move from coprocessor register	mfc0	$s1,$epc	$s1 = $epc	Used to copy Exception PC plus other special registers
Logical	and	and	$s1,$s2,$s3	$s1 = $s2 & $s3	Three reg. operands; bit-by-bit AND
	or	or	$s1,$s2,$s3	$s1 = $s2 | $s3	Three reg. operands; bit-by-bit OR
	and immediate	andi	$s1,$s2,100	$s1 = $s2 & 100	Bit-by-bit AND reg with constant
	or immediate	ori	$s1,$s2,100	$s1 = $s2 | 100	Bit-by-bit OR reg with constant
	shift left logical	sll	$s1,$s2,10	$s1 = $s2 << 10	Shift left by constant
	shift right logical	srl	$$s1,$s2,10	$s1 = $s2 >> 10	Shift right by constant
Data transfer	load word	lw	$s1,100($s2)	$s1 = Memory[$s2 + 100]	Word from memory to register
	store word	sw	$s1,100($s2)	Memory[$s2 + 100] = $s1	Word from register to memory
	load byte unsigned	lbu	$s1,100($s2)	$s1 = Memory[$s2 +100]	Byte from memory to register
	store byte	sb	$s1,100($s2)	Memory[$s2 + 100] = $s1	Byte from register to memory
	load upper immediate	lui	$s1,100	$s1 = 100 * 2^{16}	Loads constant in upper 16 bits
Conditional branch	branch on equal	beq	$s1,$s2,25	if ($s1 != $s2) go to PC + 4 + 100	Equal test; PC-relative branch
	branch on not equal	bne	$s1,$s2,25	if ($s1 == $s2) go to PC + 4 + 100	Not equal test; PC-relative
	set on less than	slt	$s1,$s2,$s3	if ($s2 < $s3) $s1 = 1; else $s1 = 0	Compare less than; two's complement
	set less than immediate	slti	$s1,$s2,100	if ($s2 < 100) $s1 = 1; else $s1 = 0	Compare < constant; two's complement
	set less than unsigned	sltu	$s1,$s2,$s3	if ($s2 < $s3) $s1 = 1; else $s1 = 0	Compare less than; natural numbers
	set less than immediate unsigned	sltiu	$s1,$s2,100	if ($s2 < 100) $s1 = 1; else $s1 = 0	Compare < constant; natural numbers
Unconditional jump	jump	j	2500	go to 10000	Jump to target address
	jump register	jr	$ra	go to $ra	For switch, procedure return
	jump and link	jal	2500	$ra = PC + 4; go to 10000	For procedure call

FIGURE 4.7   MIPS architecture revealed thus far. Color indicates the portions introduced since Figure 4.5 on page 224. MIPS machine language is also listed on the back endpapers of this book.

C Bit Fields

The following C code allocates three fields with a word labeled `receiver`: a 1-bit field named `ready`, a 1-bit field named `enable`, and an 8-bit field named `receivedByte`. It copies `receivedByte` into `data`, sets `ready` to 0, and sets `enable` to 1.

```
int data;
struct
{
    unsigned int ready:        1;
    unsigned int enable:       1;
    unsigned int receivedByte: 8;
}receiver;
. . .
    data = receiver.receivedByte;
    receiver.ready = 0;
    receiver.enable = 1;
```

What is the compiled MIPS code? Assume `data` and `receiver` are allocated to $s0 and $s1.

The fields look like this in a word (C right-aligns fields):

31	. . .	10	9		2	1		0
				receivedByte		enable		ready

The first step is to isolate the 8-bit field (`receivedByte`) by first shifting it as far to the left as possible and then as far to the right as possible:

```
sll    $s0, $s1, 22 # move 8-bit field to left end
srl    $s0, $s0, 24 # move 8-bit field to right end
```

The third instruction clears the least significant bit with the mask $fffe_{hex}$ and the last instruction sets its neighbor bit to 1:

```
andi   $s1, $s1, fffe_hex # bit 0 set to 0
ori    $s1, $s1, 0002_hex # bit 1 set to 1
```

Elaboration: In the example this alternative sequence works as well:

```
srl    $s0, $s1, 2
andi   $s0, $s0, 0x00ff
```

The field is in the lower 16 bits of the word and we want 0s in the upper bits of the result of the `andi`. In general, a shift left of $32 - (n + m)$ followed by a shift right by $32 - n$ will isolate any n-bit field whose least significant bit is in bit m.

Since `addi` and `slti` are intended for signed numbers, it is not surprising that their immediate fields are sign-extended before use. Branch and data transfer address fields are sign-extended as well.

Perhaps it *is* surprising that `addiu` and `sltiu` also sign-extend their immediates, but they do. The u stands for unsigned, but in reality `addiu` is often used simply as an add instruction that cannot overflow, and hence we often want to add negative numbers. It's much harder to come up for an excuse that `sltiu` does not sign extend its immediate.

Since `andi` and `ori` normally work with unsigned integers, the immediates are treated as unsigned integers as well, meaning that they are expanded to 32 bits by padding with leading 0s instead of sign extension. Thus if the bit fields in the third line of the example above extended beyond the 16 least significant bits, the `andi` instruction would need a 32-bit constant to avoid clearing the upper portion of the fields.

The MIPS assembler creates 32-bit constants with the pair of instructions `lui` and `ori`; see Chapter 3, page 147 for an example of creating 32-bit constants using `lui` and `addi`.

4.5 Constructing an Arithmetic Logic Unit

*ALU n. [**A**rthritic **L**ogic **U**nit or (rare) **A**rithmetic **L**ogic **U**nit] A random-number generator supplied as standard with all computer systems.*

Stan Kelly-Bootle, *The Devil's DP Dictionary*, 1981

The *arithmetic logic unit* or *ALU* is the brawn of the computer, the device that performs the arithmetic operations like addition and subtraction or logical operations like AND and OR. This section constructs an ALU from the four hardware building blocks shown in Figure 4.8 (see Appendix B for more details on these building blocks). Cases 1, 2, and 4 in Figure 4.8 all have two inputs. We will sometimes use versions of these components with more than two inputs, confident that you can generalize from this simple example. In any case, Appendix B provides examples with more inputs. (You may wish to review sections B.1 through B.3 before proceeding further.)

Because the MIPS word is 32 bits wide, we need a 32-bit-wide ALU. Let's assume that we will connect 32 1-bit ALUs to create the desired ALU. We'll therefore start by constructing a 1-bit ALU.

A 1-Bit ALU

The logical operations are easiest, because they map directly onto the hardware components in Figure 4.8.

1. AND gate (c = a · b)

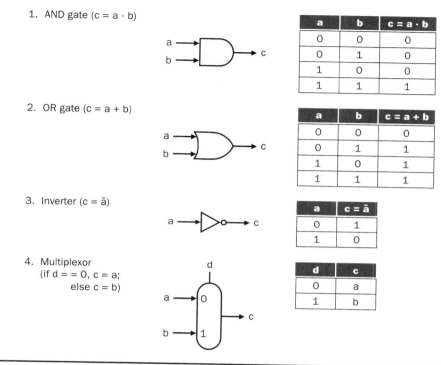

a	b	c = a · b
0	0	0
0	1	0
1	0	0
1	1	1

2. OR gate (c = a + b)

a	b	c = a + b
0	0	0
0	1	1
1	0	1
1	1	1

3. Inverter (c = ā)

a	c = ā
0	1
1	0

4. Multiplexor
(if d == 0, c = a;
else c = b)

d	c
0	a
1	b

FIGURE 4.8 Four hardware building blocks used to construct an arithmetic logic unit.
The name of the operation and an equation describing it appear on the left. In the middle is the
symbol for the block we will use in the drawings. On the right are tables that describe the outputs
in terms of the inputs. Using the notation from Appendix B, a • b means "a AND b," a + b means
"a OR b," and a line over the top (e.g., ā) means invert.

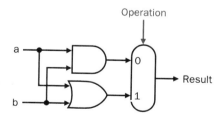

FIGURE 4.9 The 1-bit logical unit for AND and OR.

The 1-bit logical unit for AND and OR looks like Figure 4.9. The multiplexor on the right then selects a AND b or a OR b, depending on whether the value of *Operation* is 0 or 1. The line that controls the multiplexor is shown in color to distinguish it from the lines containing data. Notice that we have renamed the control and output lines of the multiplexor to give them names that reflect the function of the ALU.

The next function to include is addition. From Figure 4.3 on page 221 we can deduce the inputs and outputs of a single-bit adder. First, an adder must have two inputs for the operands and a single-bit output for the sum. There must be a second output to pass on the carry, called *CarryOut*. Since the CarryOut from the neighbor adder must be included as an input, we need a third input. This input is called *CarryIn*. Figure 4.10 shows the inputs and the outputs of a 1-bit adder. Since we know what addition is supposed to do, we can specify the outputs of this "black box" based on its inputs, as Figure 4.11 demonstrates.

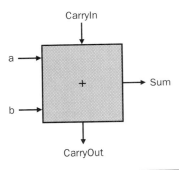

FIGURE 4.10   A 1-bit adder. This adder is called a full adder; it is also called a (3,2) adder because it has 3 inputs and 2 outputs. An adder with only the a and b inputs is called a (2,2) adder or half adder.

Inputs			Outputs		
a	**b**	**CarryIn**	**CarryOut**	**Sum**	**Comments**
0	0	0	0	0	$0 + 0 + 0 = 00_{two}$
0	0	1	0	1	$0 + 0 + 1 = 01_{two}$
0	1	0	0	1	$0 + 1 + 0 = 01_{two}$
0	1	1	1	0	$0 + 1 + 1 = 10_{two}$
1	0	0	0	1	$1 + 0 + 0 = 01_{two}$
1	0	1	1	0	$1 + 0 + 1 = 10_{two}$
1	1	0	1	0	$1 + 1 + 0 = 10_{two}$
1	1	1	1	1	$1 + 1 + 1 = 11_{two}$

FIGURE 4.11   Input and output specification for a 1-bit adder.

From Appendix B, we know that we can express the output functions Carry-Out and Sum as logical equations, and these equations can in turn be implemented with the building blocks in Figure 4.8. Let's do CarryOut. Figure 4.12 shows the values of the inputs when CarryOut is a 1.

We can turn this truth table into a logical equation, as explained in Appendix B. (Recall that a + b means "a OR b" and that a · b means "a AND b.")

$$\text{CarryOut} = (b \cdot \text{CarryIn}) + (a \cdot \text{CarryIn}) + (a \cdot b) + (a \cdot b \cdot \text{CarryIn})$$

If a · b · CarryIn is true, then one of the other three terms must also be true, so we can leave out this last term corresponding to the fourth line of the table. We can thus simplify the equation to

$$\text{CarryOut} = (b \cdot \text{CarryIn}) + (a \cdot \text{CarryIn}) + (a \cdot b)$$

Figure 4.13 shows that the hardware within the adder black box for CarryOut consists of three AND gates and one OR gate. The three AND gates correspond exactly to the three parenthesized terms of the formula above for CarryOut, and the OR gate sums the three terms.

Inputs		
a	b	CarryIn
0	1	1
1	0	1
1	1	0
1	1	1

FIGURE 4.12 **Values of the inputs when CarryOut is a 1.**

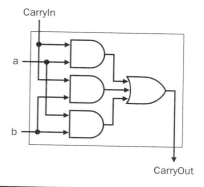

FIGURE 4.13 **Adder hardware for the carry out signal.** The rest of the adder hardware is the logic for the Sum output given in the equation above.

The Sum bit is set when exactly one input is 1 or when all three inputs are 1. The Sum results in a complex Boolean equation (recall that $\bar{a}$ means NOT a):

$$\text{Sum} = (a \cdot \bar{b} \cdot \overline{\text{CarryIn}}) + (\bar{a} \cdot b \cdot \overline{\text{CarryIn}}) + (\bar{a} \cdot \bar{b} \cdot \text{CarryIn}) + (a \cdot b \cdot \text{CarryIn})$$

The drawing of the logic for the Sum bit in the adder black box is left as an exercise (see Exercise 4.43).

Figure 4.14 shows a 1-bit ALU derived by combining the adder with the earlier components. Sometimes designers also want the ALU to perform a few more simple operations, such as generating 0. The easiest way to add an operation is to expand the multiplexor controlled by the Operation line and, for this example, to connect 0 directly to the new input of that expanded multiplexor.

A 32-Bit ALU

Now that we have completed the 1-bit ALU, the full 32-bit ALU is created by connecting adjacent "black boxes." Using xi to mean the ith bit of x, Figure 4.15 shows a 32-bit ALU. Just as a single stone can cause ripples to radiate to the shores of a quiet lake, a single carry out of the least significant bit (Result0) can ripple all the way through the adder, causing a carry out of the most significant bit (Result31). Hence, the adder created by directly linking the carries of 1-bit adders is called a *ripple carry* adder. We'll see a faster way to connect the 1-bit adders starting on page 241.

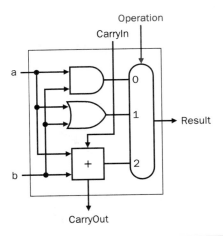

FIGURE 4.14   A 1-bit ALU that performs AND, OR, and addition (see Figure 4.13).

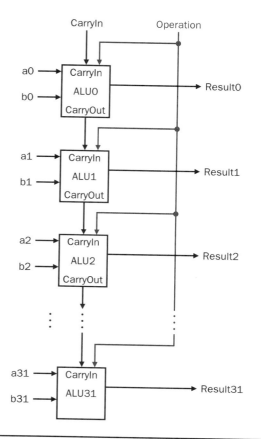

FIGURE 4.15 A 32-bit ALU constructed from 32 1-bit ALUs. CarryOut of the less significant bit is connected to the CarryIn of the more significant bit. This organization is called ripple carry.

Subtraction is the same as adding the negative version of an operand, and this is how adders perform subtraction. Recall that the shortcut for negating a two's complement number is to invert each bit (sometimes called the *one's complement* as explained in the elaboration on page 219) and then add 1. To invert each bit, we simply add a 2:1 multiplexor that chooses between b and $\bar{b}$, as Figure 4.16 shows.

Suppose we connect 32 of these 1-bit ALUs, as we did in Figure 4.15. The added multiplexor gives the option of b or its inverted value, depending on Binvert, but this is only one step in negating a two's complement number. Notice that the least significant bit still has a CarryIn signal, even though it's unnecessary for addition. What happens if we set this CarryIn to 1 instead of 0?

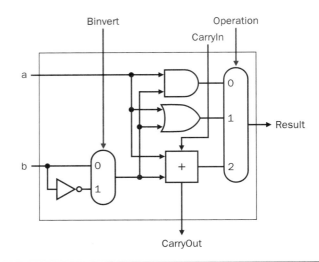

FIGURE 4.16   A 1-bit ALU that performs AND, OR, and addition on a and b or a and b̄. By selecting b (Binvert = 1) and setting CarryIn to 1 in the least significant bit of the ALU, we get two's complement subtraction of b from a instead of addition of b to a.

The adder will then calculate a + b + 1. By selecting the inverted version of b, we get exactly what we want:

$$a + \overline{b} + 1 = a + (\overline{b} + 1) = a + (-b) = a - b$$

The simplicity of the hardware design of a two's complement adder helps explain why two's complement representation has become the universal standard for integer computer arithmetic.

Tailoring the 32-Bit ALU to MIPS

This set of operations—add, subtract, AND, OR—is found in the ALU of almost every computer. If we look at Figure 4.7 on page 228, we see that the operations of most MIPS instructions can be performed by this ALU. But the design of the ALU is incomplete.

One instruction that still needs support is the set on less than instruction (slt). Recall that the operation produces 1 if rs < rt, and 0 otherwise. Consequently, slt will set all but the least significant bit to 0, with the least significant bit set according to the comparison. For the ALU to perform slt, we first need to expand the three-input multiplexor in Figure 4.16 to add an input for the slt result. We call that new input *Less*, and use it only for slt.

The top drawing of Figure 4.17 shows the new 1-bit ALU with the expanded multiplexor. From the description of slt above, we must connect 0 to the Less input for the upper 31 bits of the ALU, since those bits are always set to 0. What remains to consider is how to compare and set *the least significant bit* for set on less than instructions.

What happens if we subtract b from a? If the difference is negative, then a < b since

$$(a - b) < 0 \Rightarrow ((a - b) + b) < (0 + b)$$
$$\Rightarrow a < b$$

We want the least significant bit of a set on less than operation to be a 1 if a < b; that is, a 1 if a − b is negative and a 0 if it's positive. This desired result corresponds exactly to the sign-bit values: 1 means negative and 0 means positive. Following this line of argument, we need only connect the sign bit from the adder output to the least significant bit to get set on less than.

Unfortunately, the Result output from the most significant ALU bit in the top of Figure 4.17 for the slt operation is *not* the output of the adder; the ALU output for the slt operation is obviously the input value Less.

Thus, we need a new 1-bit ALU for the most significant bit that has an extra output bit: the adder output. The bottom drawing of Figure 4.17 shows the design, with this new adder output line called *Set,* and used only for slt. As long as we need a special ALU for the most significant bit, we added the overflow detection logic since it is also associated with that bit.

Alas, the test of less than is a little more complicated than just described because of overflow; Exercise 4.23 on page 326 explores what must be done. Figure 4.18 shows the 32-bit ALU.

Notice that every time we want the ALU to subtract, we set both CarryIn and Binvert to 1. For adds or logical operations, we want both control lines to be 0. We can therefore simplify control of the ALU by combining the CarryIn and Binvert to a single control line called *Bnegate.*

To further tailor the ALU to the MIPS instruction set, we must support conditional branch instructions. These instructions branch either if two registers are equal or if they are unequal. The easiest way to test equality with the ALU is to subtract b from a and then test to see if the result is 0 since

$$(a - b = 0) \Rightarrow a = b$$

Thus, if we add hardware to test if the result is 0, we can test for equality. The simplest way is to OR all the outputs together and then send that signal through an inverter:

$$\text{Zero} = \overline{(\text{Result31} + \text{Result30} + \ldots + \text{Result2} + \text{Result1} + \text{Result0})}$$

Figure 4.19 shows the revised 32-bit ALU. We can think of the combination of the 1-bit Bnegate line and the 2-bit Operation lines as 3-bit control lines for

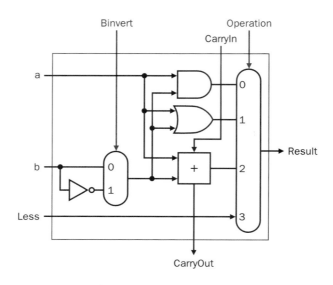

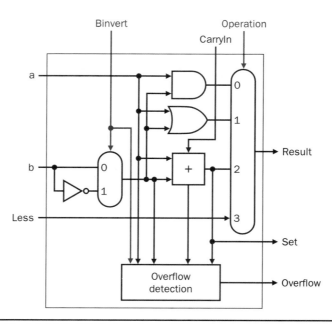

FIGURE 4.17 **(Top) A 1-bit ALU that performs AND, OR, and addition on a and b or b̄, and (bottom) a 1-bit ALU for the most significant bit.** The top drawing includes a direct input that is connected to perform the set on less than operation (see Figure 4.18); the bottom has a direct output from the adder for the less than comparison called Set. (Refer to Exercise 4.42 to see how to calculate overflow with fewer inputs.)

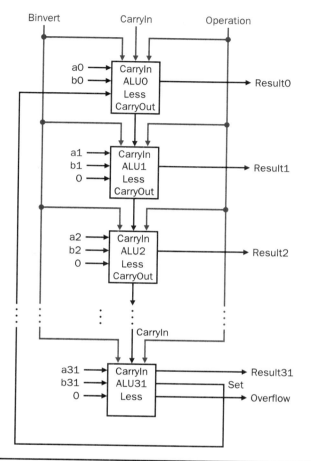

FIGURE 4.18 A 32-bit ALU constructed from the 31 copies of the 1-bit ALU in the top of Figure 4.17 and one 1-bit ALU in the bottom of that figure. The Less inputs are connected to 0 except for the least significant bit, and that is connected to the Set output of the most significant bit. If the ALU performs $a - b$ and we select the input 3 in the multiplexor in Figure 4.17, then Result $= 0 \ldots 001$ if $a < b$, and Result $= 0 \ldots 000$ otherwise.

the ALU, telling it to perform add, subtract, AND, OR, or set on less than. Figure 4.20 shows the ALU control lines and the corresponding ALU operation.

Finally, now that we have seen what is inside a 32-bit ALU, we will use the universal symbol for a complete ALU, as shown in Figure 4.21.

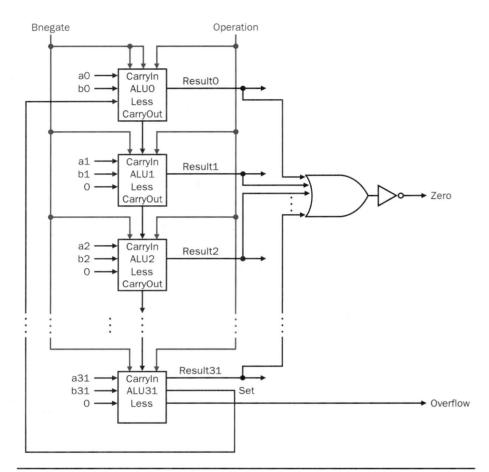

FIGURE 4.19   The final 32-bit ALU. This adds a Zero detector to Figure 4.18.

ALU control lines	Function
000	and
001	or
010	add
110	subtract
111	set on less than

FIGURE 4.20   The values of the three ALU control lines Bnegate and Operation and the corresponding ALU operations.

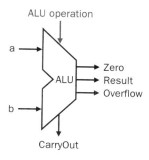

FIGURE 4.21   The symbol commonly used to represent an ALU, as shown in Figure 4.19. This symbol is also used to represent an adder, so it is normally labeled either with ALU or Adder.

Carry Lookahead

The next question is, How quickly can this ALU add two 32-bit operands? We can determine the a and b inputs, but the CarryIn input depends on the operation in the adjacent 1-bit adder. If we trace all the way through the chain of dependencies, we connect the most significant bit to the least significant bit, so the most significant bit of the sum must wait for the *sequential* evaluation of all 32 1-bit adders. This sequential chain reaction is too slow to be used in time-critical hardware.

There are a variety of schemes to anticipate the carry so that the worst-case scenario is a function of the $\log_2$ of the number of bits in the adder. These anticipatory signals are faster because they go through fewer gates in sequence, but it takes many more gates to anticipate the proper carry.

A key to understanding fast carry schemes is to remember that, unlike software, hardware executes in parallel whenever inputs change.

Fast Carry Using "Infinite" Hardware

Appendix B mentions that any equation can be represented in two levels of logic. Since the only external inputs are the two operands and the CarryIn to the least significant bit of the adder, in theory we could calculate the CarryIn values to all the remaining bits of the adder in just two levels of logic.

For example, the CarryIn for bit 2 of the adder is exactly the CarryOut of bit 1, so the formula is

$$\text{CarryIn2} = (b1 \cdot \text{CarryIn1}) + (a1 \cdot \text{CarryIn1}) + (a1 \cdot b1)$$

Similarly, CarryIn1 is defined as

$$\text{CarryIn1} = (b0 \cdot \text{CarryIn0}) + (a0 \cdot \text{CarryIn0}) + (a0 \cdot b0)$$

Using the shorter and more traditional abbreviation of ci for CarryIni, we can rewrite the formulas as

$$c2 = (b1 \cdot c1) + (a1 \cdot c1) + (a1 \cdot b1)$$
$$c1 = (b0 \cdot c0) + (a0 \cdot c0) + (a0 \cdot b0)$$

Substituting the definition of c1 for the first equation results in this formula:

$$c2 = (a1 \cdot a0 \cdot b0) + (a1 \cdot a0 \cdot c0) + (a1 \cdot b0 \cdot c0)$$
$$+ (b1 \cdot a0 \cdot b0) + (b1 \cdot a0 \cdot c0) + (b1 \cdot b0 \cdot c0) + (a1 \cdot b1)$$

You can imagine how the equation expands as we get to higher bits in the adder; it grows exponentially with the number of bits. This complexity is reflected in the cost of the hardware for fast carry, making this simple scheme prohibitively expensive for wide adders.

Fast Carry Using the First Level of Abstraction: Propagate and Generate

Most fast carry schemes limit the complexity of the equations to simplify the hardware, while still making substantial speed improvements over ripple carry. One such scheme is a *carry-lookahead adder*. In Chapter 1, we said computer systems cope with complexity by using levels of abstraction. A carry-lookahead adder relies on levels of abstraction in its implementation.

Let's factor our original equation as a first step:

$$ci+1 = (bi \cdot ci) + (ai \cdot ci) + (ai \cdot bi)$$
$$= (ai \cdot bi) + (ai + bi) \cdot ci$$

If we were to rewrite the equation for c2 using this formula, we would see some repeated patterns:

$$c2 = (a1 \cdot b1) + (a1 + b1) \cdot ((a0 \cdot b0) + (a0 + b0) \cdot c0)$$

Note the repeated appearance of $(ai \cdot bi)$ and $(ai + bi)$ in the formula above. These two important factors are traditionally called *generate* (gi) and *propagate* (pi):

$$gi = ai \cdot bi$$
$$pi = ai + bi$$

Using them to define $ci+1$, we get

$$ci+1 = gi + pi \cdot ci$$

To see where the signals get their names, suppose gi is 1. Then

$$ci+1 = gi + pi \cdot ci = 1 + pi \cdot ci = 1$$

That is, the adder *generates* a CarryOut ($ci+1$) independent of the value of CarryIn (ci). Now suppose that gi is 0 and pi is 1. Then

$$ci+1 \ = \ gi + pi \cdot ci \ = \ 0 + 1 \cdot ci \ = \ ci$$

That is, the adder *propagates* CarryIn to a CarryOut. Putting the two together, CarryIn$i+1$ is a 1 if either gi is 1 or both pi is 1 and CarryIni is 1.

As an analogy, imagine a row of dominoes set on edge. The end domino can be tipped over by pushing one far away provided there are no gaps between the two. Similarly, a carry out can be made true by a generate far away provided all the propagates between them are true.

Relying on the definitions of propagate and generate as our first level of abstraction, we can express the CarryIn signals more economically. Let's show it for 4 bits:

$$c1 \ = \ g0 + (p0 \cdot c0)$$

$$c2 \ = \ g1 + (p1 \cdot g0) + (p1 \cdot p0 \cdot c0)$$

$$c3 \ = \ g2 + (p2 \cdot g1) + (p2 \cdot p1 \cdot g0) + (p2 \cdot p1 \cdot p0 \cdot c0)$$

$$c4 \ = \ g3 + (p3 \cdot g2) + (p3 \cdot p2 \cdot g1) + (p3 \cdot p2 \cdot p1 \cdot g0)$$
$$+ \ (p3 \cdot p2 \cdot p1 \cdot p0 \cdot c0)$$

These equations just represent common sense: CarryIni is a 1 if some earlier adder generates a carry and all intermediary adders propagate a carry. Figure 4.22 uses plumbing to try to explain carry lookahead.

Even this simplified form leads to large equations and, hence, considerable logic even for a 16-bit adder. Let's try moving to two levels of abstraction.

Fast Carry Using the Second Level of Abstraction

First we consider this 4-bit adder with its carry-lookahead logic as a single building block. If we connect them in ripple carry fashion to form a 16-bit adder, the add will be faster than the original with a little more hardware.

To go faster, we'll need carry lookahead at a higher level. To perform carry lookahead for 4-bit adders, we need propagate and generate signals at this higher level. Here they are for the four 4-bit adder blocks:

$$P0 = p3 \cdot p2 \cdot p1 \cdot p0$$
$$P1 = p7 \cdot p6 \cdot p5 \cdot p4$$
$$P2 = p11 \cdot p10 \cdot p9 \cdot p8$$
$$P3 = p15 \cdot p14 \cdot p13 \cdot p12$$

That is, the "super" propagate signal for the 4-bit abstraction (Pi) is true only if each of the bits in the group will propagate a carry.

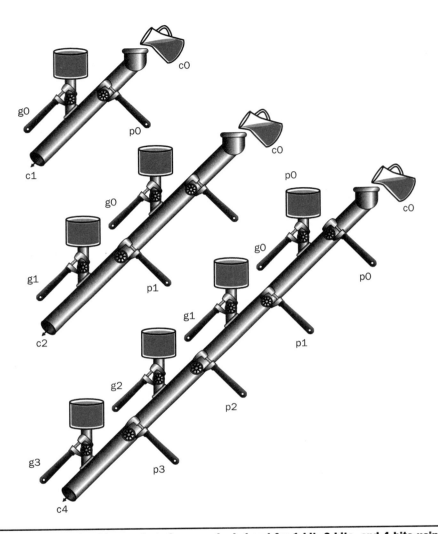

FIGURE 4.22   A plumbing analogy for carry lookahead for 1 bit, 2 bits, and 4 bits using water, pipes, and valves. The wrenches are turned to open and close valves. Water is shown in color. The output of the pipe (c_{i+1}) will be full if either the nearest generate value (g_i) is turned on or if the i propagate value (p_i) is on and there is water further upstream, either from an earlier generate, or propagate with water behind it. CarryIn (c_0) can result in a carry out without the help of any generates, but with the help of *all* propagates.

For the "super" generate signal (G_i), we care only if there is a carry out of the most significant bit of the 4-bit group. This obviously occurs if generate is true for that most significant bit; it also occurs if an earlier generate is true *and* all the intermediate propagates, including that of the most significant bit, are also true:

$$G0 = g3 + (p3 \cdot g2) + (p3 \cdot p2 \cdot g1) + (p3 \cdot p2 \cdot p1 \cdot g0)$$

$$G1 = g7 + (p7 \cdot g6) + (p7 \cdot p6 \cdot g5) + (p7 \cdot p6 \cdot p5 \cdot g4)$$

$$G2 = g11 + (p11 \cdot g10) + (p11 \cdot p10 \cdot g9) + (p11 \cdot p10 \cdot p9 \cdot g8)$$

$$G3 = g15 + (p15 \cdot g14) + (p15 \cdot p14 \cdot g13) + (p15 \cdot p14 \cdot p13 \cdot g12)$$

Figure 4.23 updates our plumbing analogy to show P0 and G0.

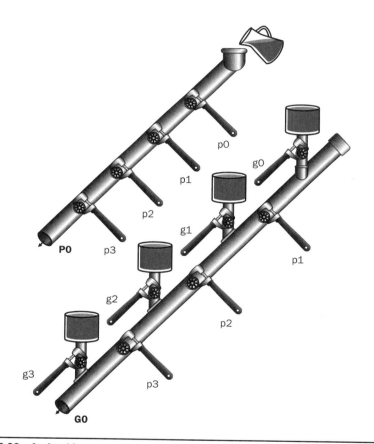

FIGURE 4.23 A plumbing analogy for the next-level carry-lookahead signals P0 and G0. P0 is open only if all four propagates (pi) are open, while water flows in G0 only if at least one generate (gi) is open and all the propagates downstream from that generate are open.

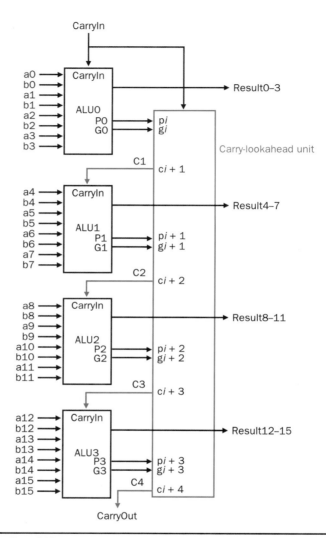

FIGURE 4.24 Four 4-bit ALUs using carry lookahead to form a 16-bit adder. Note that the carries come from the carry-lookahead unit, not from the 4-bit ALUs.

Then the equations at this higher level of abstraction for the carry in for each 4-bit group of the 16-bit adder (C1, C2, C3, C4 in Figure 4.24) are very similar to the carry out equations for each bit of the 4-bit adder (c1, c2, 3, c4) on page 243:

$$C1 = G0 + (P0 \cdot c0)$$

$$C2 = G1 + (P1 \cdot G0) + (P1 \cdot P0 \cdot c0)$$

$$C3 = G2 + (P2 \cdot G1) + (P2 \cdot P1 \cdot G0) + (P2 \cdot P1 \cdot P0 \cdot c0)$$

$$C4 = G3 + (P3 \cdot G2) + (P3 \cdot P2 \cdot G1) + (P3 \cdot P2 \cdot P1 \cdot G0)$$
$$+ (P3 \cdot P2 \cdot P1 \cdot P0 \cdot c0)$$

Figure 4.24 shows 4-bit adders connected with such a carry lookahead unit. Exercises 4.44 through 4.48 explore the speed differences between these carry schemes, different notations for multibit propagate and generate signals, and the design of a 64-bit adder.

Both Levels of the Propagate and Generate

Example

Determine the gi, pi, Pi, and Gi values of these two 16-bit numbers:

```
a:        0001 1010 0011 0011 two
b:        1110 0101 1110 1011 two
```

Also, what is CarryOut15 (C4)?

Answer

Aligning the bits makes it easy to see the values of generate gi $(ai \cdot bi)$ and propagate pi $(ai + bi)$:

```
a:        0001 1010 0011 0011
b:        1110 0101 1110 1011
gi:       0000 0000 0010 0011
pi:       1111 1111 1111 1011
```

where the bits are numbered 15 to 0 from left to right. Next, the "super" propagates (P3, P2, P1, P0) are simply the AND of the lower-level propagates:

$$P3 = 1 \cdot 1 \cdot 1 \cdot 1 = 1$$

$$P2 = 1 \cdot 1 \cdot 1 \cdot 1 = 1$$

$$P1 = 1 \cdot 1 \cdot 1 \cdot 1 = 1$$

$$P0 = 1 \cdot 0 \cdot 1 \cdot 1 = 0$$

The "super" generates are more complex, so use the followinge quations:

$G0$ = $g3 + (p3 \cdot g2) + (p3 \cdot p2 \cdot g1) + (p3 \cdot p2 \cdot p1 \cdot g0)$
  = $0 + (1 \cdot 0) + (1 \cdot 0 \cdot 1) + (1 \cdot 0 \cdot 1 \cdot 1) = 0 + 0 + 0 + 0 = 0$

$G1$ = $g7 + (p7 \cdot g6) + (p7 \cdot p6 \cdot g5) + (p7 \cdot p6 \cdot p5 \cdot g4)$
  = $0 + (1 \cdot 0) + (1 \cdot 1 \cdot 1) + (1 \cdot 1 \cdot 1 \cdot 0) = 0 + 0 + 1 + 0 = 1$

$G2$ = $g11 + (p11 \cdot g10) + (p11 \cdot p10 \cdot g9) + (p11 \cdot p10 \cdot p9 \cdot g8)$
  = $0 + (1 \cdot 0) + (1 \cdot 1 \cdot 0) + (1 \cdot 1 \cdot 1 \cdot 0) = 0 + 0 + 0 + 0 = 0$

$G3$ = $g15 + (p15 \cdot g14) + (p15 \cdot p14 \cdot g13) + (p15 \cdot p14 \cdot p13 \cdot g12)$
  = $0 + (1 \cdot 0) + (1 \cdot 1 \cdot 0) + (1 \cdot 1 \cdot 1 \cdot 0) = 0 + 0 + 0 + 0 = 0$

Finally, CarryOut15 is

$C4$ = $G3 + (P3 \cdot G2) + (P3 \cdot P2 \cdot G1) + (P3 \cdot P2 \cdot P1 \cdot G0)$
  $+ (P3 \cdot P2 \cdot P1 \cdot P0 \cdot c0)$

  = $0 + (1 \cdot 0) + (1 \cdot 1 \cdot 1) + (1 \cdot 1 \cdot 1 \cdot 0) + (1 \cdot 1 \cdot 1 \cdot 0 \cdot 0)$
  = $0 + 0 + 1 + 0 + 0 = 1$

Hence there *is* a carry out when adding these two 16-bit numbers.

The reason carry lookahead can make carries faster is that all logic begins evaluating the moment the clock cycle begins, and the result will not change once the output of each gate stops changing. By taking a shortcut of going through fewer gates to send the carry in signal, the output of the gates will stop changing sooner, and hence the time for the adder can be less.

To appreciate the importance of carry lookahead, we need to calculate the relative performance between it and ripple carry adders.

Speed of Ripple Carry versus Carry Lookahead

Example

One simple way to model time for logic is to assume each AND or OR gate takes the same time for a signal to pass through it. Time is estimated by simply counting the number of gates along the longest path through a piece of logic. Compare the number of *gate delays* for the critical paths of two 16-bit adders, one using ripple carry and one using two-level carry lookahead.

Answer

Figure 4.13 on page 233 shows that the carry out signal takes two gate delays per bit. Then the number of gate delays between a carry in to the least significant bit and the carry out of the most significant is $16 \times 2 = 32$.

For carry lookahead, the carry out of the most significant bit is just C4, defined in the example. It takes two levels of logic to specify C4 in terms of Pi and Gi (the OR of several AND terms). Pi is specified in one level of logic (AND) using pi, and Gi is specified in two levels using pi and gi, so the worst case for this next level of abstraction is two levels of logic. pi and gi are each one level of logic, defined in terms of ai and bi. If we assume one gate delay for each level of logic in these equations, the worst case is $2 + 2 + 1 = 5$ gate delays.

Hence for 16-bit addition a carry-lookahead adder is six times faster, using this simple estimate of hardware speed.

Summary

The primary point of this section is that the traditional ALU can be constructed from a multiplexor and a few gates that are replicated 32 times. To make it more useful to the MIPS architecture, we expand the traditional ALU with hardware to test if the result is 0, detect overflow, and perform the basic operation for set on less than.

Carry lookahead offers a faster path than waiting for the carries to ripple through all 32 1-bit adders. This faster path is paved by two signals, generate and propagate. The former creates a carry regardless of the carry input, and the other passes a carry along. Carry lookahead also gives another example of how abstraction is important in computer design to cope with complexity.

Elaboration: We have now accounted for all but one of the arithmetic and logical operations for the core MIPS instruction set: the ALU in Figure 4.21 omits support of shift instructions. It would be possible to widen the ALU multiplexor to include a left shift by 1 bit or right shift by 1 bit. But hardware designers have created a circuit called a *barrel shifter*, which can shift from 1 to 31 bits in no more time than it takes to add two 32-bit numbers, so shifting is normally done outside the ALU.

Elaboration: The logic equation for the Sum output of the full adder on page 234 can be expressed more simply by using a more powerful gate than AND and OR. An *exclusive OR* gate is true if the two operands disagree; that is,

$$x \neq y \Rightarrow 1 \text{ and } x == y \Rightarrow 0$$

In some technologies, exclusive OR is more efficient than two levels of AND and OR gates. Using the symbol $\oplus$ to represent exclusive OR, here is the new equation:

$$\text{Sum} = a \oplus b \oplus \text{CarryIn}$$

Also, we have drawn the ALU the traditional way, using gates. Computers are designed today in CMOS transistors, which are basically switches. CMOS ALU and barrel shifters take advantage of these switches and have many fewer multiplexors than shown in our designs, but the design principles are similar.

4.6   Multiplication

Multiplication is vexation,
Division is as bad;
The rule of three doth puzzle me,
And practice drives me mad.

Anonymous, Elizabethan manuscript, 1570

With the construction of the ALU and explanation of addition, subtraction, and shifts, we are ready to build the more vexing operation of multiply.

But first let's review the multiplication of decimal numbers in longhand to remind ourselves of the steps and the names of the operands. For reasons that will become clear shortly, we limit this decimal example to using only the digits 0 and 1. Multiplying 1000_{ten} by 1001_{ten}:

Multiplicand	1000_{ten}
Multiplier	$\times \quad 1001_{ten}$
	1000
	0000
	0000
	1000
Product	1001000_{ten}

The first operand is called the *multiplicand* and the second the *multiplier*. The final result is called the *product*. As you may recall, the algorithm learned in grammar school is to take the digits of the multiplier one at a time from right to left, multiplying the multiplicand by the single digit of the multiplier and shifting the intermediate product one digit to the left of the earlier intermediate products.

The first observation is that the number of digits in the product is considerably larger than the number in either the multiplicand or the multiplier. In fact, if we ignore the sign bits, the length of the multiplication of an n-bit multiplicand and an m-bit multiplier is a product that is $n + m$ bits long. That is, $n + m$ bits are required to represent all possible products. Hence, like add, multiply must cope with overflow because we frequently want a 32-bit product as the result of multiplying two 32-bit numbers.

In this example we restricted the decimal digits to 0 and 1. With only two choices, each step of the multiplication is simple:

1. Just place a copy of the multiplicand ($1 \times$ multiplicand) in the proper place if the multiplier digit is a 1, or

2. Place 0 ($0 \times$ multiplicand) in the proper place if the digit is 0.

Although the decimal example above happened to use only 0 and 1, multiplication of binary numbers must always use 0 and 1, and thus always offers only these two choices.

Now that we have reviewed the basics of multiplication, the traditional next step is to provide the highly optimized multiply hardware. We break with tradition in the belief that you will gain a better understanding by seeing the evolution of the multiply hardware and algorithm through three generations. The rest of this section presents successive refinements of the hardware and the algorithm until we have a version used in some computers. For now, let's assume that we are multiplying only positive numbers.

First Version of the Multiplication Algorithm and Hardware

The initial design mimics the algorithm we learned in grammar school; the hardware is shown in Figure 4.25. We have drawn the hardware so that data flows from top to bottom to more closely resemble the paper-and-pencil method.

Let's assume that the multiplier is in the 32-bit Multiplier register and that the 64-bit Product register is initialized to 0. From the paper-and-pencil example above, it's clear that we will need to move the multiplicand left one digit each step as it may be added to the intermediate products. Over 32 steps a

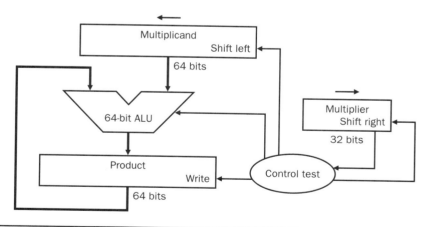

FIGURE 4.25 First version of the multiplication hardware. The Multiplicand register, ALU, and Product register are all 64 bits wide, with only the Multiplier register containing 32 bits. The 32-bit multiplicand starts in the right half of the Multiplicand register, and is shifted left 1 bit on each step. The multiplier is shifted in the opposite direction at each step. The algorithm starts with the product initialized to 0. Control decides when to shift the Multiplicand and Multiplier registers and when to write new values into the Product register.

32-bit multiplicand would move 32 bits to the left. Hence we need a 64-bit Multiplicand register, initialized with the 32-bit multiplicand in the right half and 0 in the left half. This register is then shifted left 1 bit each step to align the multiplicand with the sum being accumulated in the 64-bit Product register.

Figure 4.26 shows the three basic steps needed for each bit. The least significant bit of the multiplier (Multiplier0) determines whether the multiplicand is

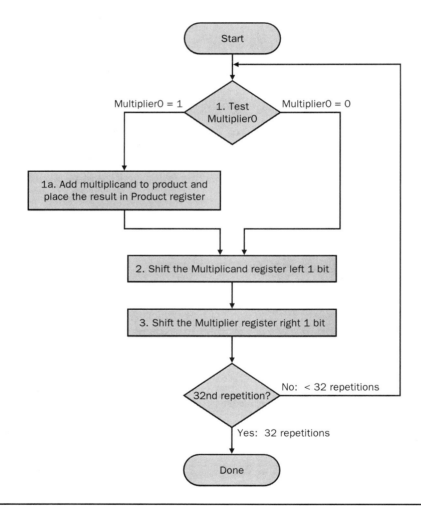

FIGURE 4.26 The first multiplication algorithm, using the hardware shown in Figure 4.25. If the least significant bit of the multiplier is 1, add the multiplicand to the product. If not, go to the next step. Shift the multiplicand left and the multiplier right in the next two steps. These three steps are repeated 32 times.

added to the Product register. The left shift in step 2 has the effect of moving the intermediate operands to the left, just as when multiplying by hand. The shift right in step 3 gives us the next bit of the multiplier to examine in the following iteration. These three steps are repeated 32 times to obtain the product.

First Multiply Algorithm

Example

Using 4-bit numbers to save space, multiply $2_{ten} \times 3_{ten}$, or $0010_{two} \times 0011_{two}$.

Answer

Figure 4.27 shows the value of each register for each of the steps labeled according to Figure 4.26, with the final value of $0000\ 0110_{two}$ or 6_{ten}. Color is used to indicate the register values that change on that step, and the bit circled is the one examined to determine the operation of the next step.

Iteration	Step	Multiplier	Multiplicand	Product
0	Initial values	0011①	0000 0010	0000 0000
1	1a: 1 ⟹ Prod = Prod + Mcand	0011	0000 0010	0000 0010
	2: Shift left Multiplicand	0011	0000 0100	0000 0010
	3: Shift right Multiplier	0001①	0000 0100	0000 0010
2	1a: 1 ⟹ Prod = Prod + Mcand	0001	0000 0100	0000 0110
	2: Shift left Multiplicand	0001	0000 1000	0000 0110
	3: Shift right Multiplier	0000⓪	0000 1000	0000 0110
3	1: 0 ⟹ no operation	0000	0000 1000	0000 0110
	2: Shift left Multiplicand	0000	0001 0000	0000 0110
	3: Shift right Multiplier	0000⓪	0001 0000	0000 0110
4	1: 0 ⟹ no operation	0000	0001 0000	0000 0110
	2: Shift left Multiplicand	0000	0010 0000	0000 0110
	3: Shift right Multiplier	0000	0010 0000	0000 0110

FIGURE 4.27 Multiply example using first algorithm in Figure 4.26. The bit examined to determine the next step is circled in color.

If each step took a clock cycle, this algorithm would require almost 100 clock cycles to multiply. The relative importance of arithmetic operations like multiply varies with the program, but addition and subtraction may be anywhere from 5 to 100 times more popular than multiply. Accordingly, in many applications, multiply can take multiple clock cycles without significantly affecting performance. Yet Amdahl's law (see Chapter 2, page 75) reminds us that even a moderate frequency for a slow operation can limit performance.

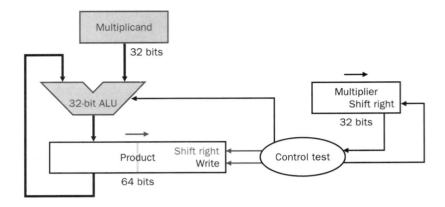

FIGURE 4.28 Second version of the multiplication hardware. Compare with the first version in Figure 4.25. The Multiplicand register, ALU, and Multiplier register are all 32 bits wide, with only the Product register left at 64 bits. Now the product is shifted right. These changes are highlighted in color.

Second Version of the Multiplication Algorithm and Hardware

Computer pioneers recognized that half of the bits of the multiplicand in the first algorithm were always 0, so only half could contain useful bit values. A full 64-bit ALU thus seemed wasteful and slow since half of the adder bits were adding 0 to the intermediate sum.

The original algorithm shifts the multiplicand left with 0s inserted in the new positions, so the multiplicand cannot affect the least significant bits of the product after they settle down. Instead of shifting the multiplicand left, they wondered, what if we shift the *product right*? Now the multiplicand would be fixed relative to the product, and since we are adding only 32 bits, the adder need be only 32 bits wide. Figure 4.28 shows how this change halves the widths of both the ALU and the multiplicand.

Figure 4.29 shows the multiply algorithm inspired by this observation. This algorithm starts with the 32-bit Multiplicand and 32-bit Multiplier registers set to their named values and the 64-bit Product register set to 0. This algorithm only forms a 32-bit sum, so only the left half of the 64-bit Product register is changed by the addition.

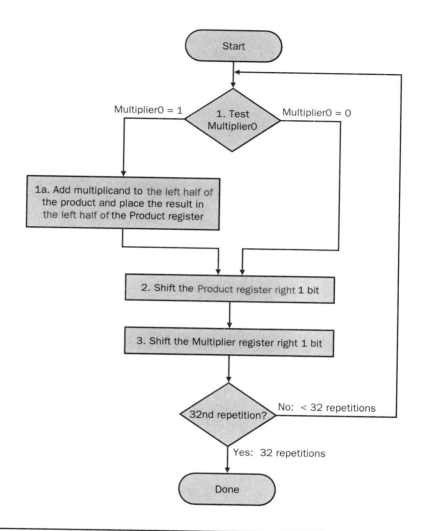

FIGURE 4.29 The second multiplication algorithm, using the hardware in Figure 4.28. In this version, the Product register is shifted right instead of shifting the multiplicand. Color type shows the changes from Figure 4.26.

Second Multiply Algorithm

Example

Multiply $0010_{two} \times 0011_{two}$using the algorithm in Figure 4.29.

Answer

Figure 4.30 shows the revised 4-bit example, again giving a product of $0000\ 0110_{two}$.

Iteration	Step	Multiplier	Multiplicand	Product
0	Initial values	0011	0010	0000 0000
1	1a: 1 => Prod = Prod + Mcand	0011	0010	0010 0000
	2: Shift right Product	0011	0010	0001 0000
	3: Shift right Multiplier	0001	0010	0001 0000
2	1a: 1 => Prod = Prod + Mcand	0001	0010	0011 0000
	2: Shift right Product	0001	0010	0001 1000
	3: Shift right Multiplier	0000	0010	0001 1000
3	1: 0 => no operation	0000	0010	0001 1000
	2: Shift right Product	0000	0010	0000 1100
	3: Shift right Multiplier	0000	0010	0000 1100
4	1: 0 => no operation	0000	0010	0000 1100
	2: Shift right Product	0000	0010	0000 0110
	3: Shift right Multiplier	0000	0010	0000 0110

FIGURE 4.30   Multiply example using second algorithm in Figure 4.29. The bit examined to determine the next step is circled in color.

Final Version of the Multiplication Algorithm and Hardware

The final observation of the frugal computer pioneers was that the Product register had wasted space that matched exactly the size of the multiplier: As the wasted space in the product disappears, so do the bits of the multiplier. In response, the third version of the multiplication algorithm combines the right-most half of the product with the multiplier. Figure 4.31 shows the hardware. The least significant bit of the 64-bit Product register (Product0) now is the bit to be tested.

The algorithm starts by assigning the multiplier to the right half of the Product register, placing 0 in the upper half. Figure 4.32 shows the new steps.

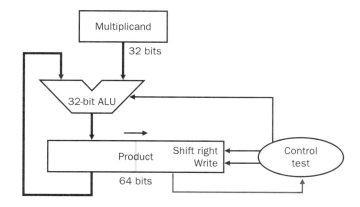

FIGURE 4.31   Third version of the multiplication hardware. Comparing with the second version in Figure 4.28 on page 254, the separate Multiplier register has disappeared. The multiplier is placed instead in the right half of the Product register.

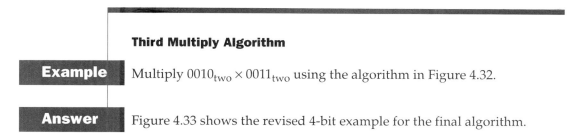

Third Multiply Algorithm

Example

Multiply $0010_{two} \times 0011_{two}$ using the algorithm in Figure 4.32.

Answer

Figure 4.33 shows the revised 4-bit example for the final algorithm.

Signed Multiplication

So far we have dealt with positive numbers. The easiest way to understand how to deal with signed numbers is to first convert the multiplier and multiplicand to positive numbers and then remember the original signs. The algorithms should then be run for 31 iterations, leaving the signs out of the calculation. As we learned in grammar school, we need negate the product only if the original signs disagree.

It turns out that the last algorithm will work for signed numbers provided that we remember that the numbers we are dealing with have infinite digits, and that we are only representing them with 32 bits. Hence the shifting steps would need to extend the sign of the product for signed numbers. When the algorithm completes, the lower word would have the 32-bit product.

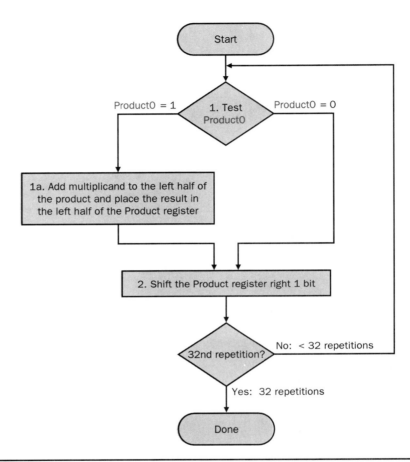

FIGURE 4.32   The third multiplication algorithm. It needs only two steps because the Product and Multiplier registers have been combined. Color type shows changes from Figure 4.29.

Iteration	Step	Multiplicand	Product
0	Initial values	0010	0000 0011
1	1a: 1 => Prod = Prod + Mcand	0010	0010 0011
	2: Shift right Product	0010	0001 0001
2	1a: 1 => Prod = Prod + Mcand	0010	0011 0001
	2: Shift right Product	0010	0001 1000
3	1: 0 => no operation	0010	0001 1000
	2: Shift right Product	0010	0000 1100
4	1: 0 => no operation	0010	0000 1100
	2: Shift right Product	0010	0000 0110

FIGURE 4.33   Multiply example using third algorithm in Figure 4.32. The bit examined to determine the next step is circled in color.

Booth's Algorithm

A more elegant approach to multiplying signed numbers than above is called *Booth's algorithm*. It starts with the observation that with the ability to both add and subtract there are multiple ways to compute a product. Suppose we want to multiply 2_{ten} by 6_{ten}, or 0010_{two} by 0110_{two}:

```
              0010 two
    x         0110 two

    +         0000   shift (0 in multiplier)
    +         0010   add   (1 in multiplier)
    +         0010   add   (1 in multiplier)
    +         0000   shift (0 in multiplier)

          00001100 two
```

Booth observed that an ALU that could add or subtract could get the same result in more than one way. For example, since

$$6_{ten} \quad = - 2_{ten} + 8_{ten}$$

or

$$0110_{two} \quad = - 0010_{two} + 1000_{two}$$

we could replace a string of 1s in the multiplier with an initial subtract when we first see a 1 and then later add when we see the bit *after* the last 1. For example,

```
              0010 two
    x         0110 two

    +         0000 shift (0 in multiplier)
    −         0010 sub   (first 1 in multiplier)
    +         0000 shift (middle of string of 1s)
    +         0010 add   (prior step had last 1)

          00001100 two
```

Booth invented this approach in a quest for speed because in machines of his era shifting was faster than addition. Indeed, for some patterns his algorithm would be faster; it's our good fortune that it handles signed numbers as well, and we'll prove this later. The key to Booth's insight is in his classifying groups of bits into the beginning, the middle, or the end of a run of 1s:

Of course, a string of 0s already avoids arithmetic, so we can leave these alone.

If we are limited to looking at just 2 bits, we can then try to match the situation in the preceding drawing, according to the value of these 2 bits:

Current bit	Bit to the right	Explanation	Example
1	0	Beginning of a run of 1s	00001111000_{two}
1	1	Middle of a run of 1s	00001111000_{two}
0	1	End of a run of 1s	00001111000_{two}
0	0	Middle of a run of 0s	00001111000_{two}

Booth's algorithm changes the first step of the algorithm in Figure 4.32—looking at 1 bit of the multiplier and then deciding whether to add the multiplicand—to looking at 2 bits of the multiplier. The new first step, then, has four cases, depending on the values of the 2 bits. Let's assume that the pair of bits examined consists of the current bit and the bit to the right—which was the current bit in the previous step. The second step is still to shift the product right. The new algorithm is then the following:

1. Depending on the current and previous bits, do one of the following:

    00: Middle of a string of 0s, so no arithmetic operation.

    01: End of a string of 1s, so add the multiplicand to the left half of the product.

    10: Beginning of a string of 1s, so subtract the multiplicand from the left half of the product.

    11: Middle of a string of 1s, so no arithmetic operation.

2. As in the previous algorithm, shift the Product register right 1 bit.

Now we are ready to begin the operation, shown in Figure 4.34. It starts with a 0 for the mythical bit to the right of the rightmost bit for the first stage. Figure 4.34 compares the two algorithms, with Booth's on the right. Note that

Itera-tion	Multi-plicand	Original algorithm		Booth's algorithm	
		Step	**Product**	**Step**	**Product**
0	0010	Initial values	0000 0110⓪	Initial values	0000 0110⓪ ⓪
1	0010	1: 0 ⟹ no operation	0000 0110	1a: 00 ⟹ no operation	0000 0110 0
	0010	2: Shift right Product	0000 001①	2: Shift right Product	0000 001①⓪
2	0010	1a: 1 ⟹ Prod = Prod + Mcand	0010 0011	1c: 10 ⟹ Prod = Prod − Mcand	1110 0011 0
	0010	2: Shift right Product	0001 000①	2: Shift right Product	1111 000①①
3	0010	1a: 1 ⟹ Prod = Prod + Mcand	0011 0001	1d: 11 ⟹ no operation	1111 0001 1
	0010	2: Shift right Product	0001 100⓪	2: Shift right Product	1111 100⓪①
4	0010	1: 0 ⟹ no operation	0001 1000	1b: 01 ⟹ Prod = Prod + Mcand	0001 1000 1
	0010	2: Shift right Product	0000 1100	2: Shift right Product	0000 1100 0

FIGURE 4.34 Comparing algorithm in Figure 4.32 and Booth's algorithm for positive numbers. The bit(s) examined to determine the next step is circled in color.

Booth's operation is now identified according to the values in the 2 bits. By the fourth step, the two algorithms have the same values in the Product register.

The one other requirement is that shifting the product right must preserve the sign of the intermediate result, since we are dealing with signed numbers. The solution is to extend the sign when the product is shifted to the right. Thus, step 2 of the second iteration turns 1110 0011 0_{two} into 1111 0001 1_{two} instead of 0111 0001 1_{two}. This shift is called an *arithmetic right shift* to differentiate it from a logical right shift.

Booth's Algorithm

Example

Let's try Booth's algorithm with negative numbers: $2_{ten} \times -3_{ten} = -6_{ten}$, or $0010_{two} \times 1101_{two} = 1111\ 1010_{two}$.

Answer

Figure 4.35 shows the steps.

Our example multiplies one bit at a time, but it is possible to generalize Booth's algorithm to generate multiple bits for faster multiplies (see Exercise 4.53).

Iteration	Step	Multiplicand	Product
0	Initial values	0010	0000 1101 0
1	1c: 10 ⟹ Prod = Prod – Mcand	0010	1110 1101 0
	2: Shift right Product	0010	1111 0110 1
2	1b: 01 ⟹ Prod = Prod + Mcand	0010	0001 0110 1
	2: Shift right Product	0010	0000 1011 0
3	1c: 10 ⟹ Prod = Prod – Mcand	0010	1110 1011 0
	2: Shift right Product	0010	1111 0101 1
4	1d: 11 ⟹ no operation	0010	1111 0101 1
	2: Shift right Product	0010	1111 1010 1

FIGURE 4.35 Booth's algorithm with negative multiplier example. The bits examined to determine the next step are circled in color.

Hardware Software Interface

Replacing arithmetic by shifts can also occur when multiplying by constants. Some compilers replace multiplies by short constants with a series of shifts, adds, and subtracts. Because one bit to the left represents a number twice as large in base 2, shifting the bits left has the same effect as multiplying by a power of 2, so almost every compiler will substitute a left shift for a multiply by a power of 2.

Multiply by 2^i via Shift

Example

Let's multiply 5_{ten} by 2_{ten} using a left shift by 1.

Answer

Given that

$$101_{two} = (1 \times 2^2) + (0 \times 2^1) + (1 \times 2^0)_{ten} = 4 + 0 + 1_{ten} = 5_{ten}$$

if we shift left 1 bit, we get

$$1010_{two} = (1 \times 2^3) + (0 \times 2^2) + (1 \times 2^1) + (0 \times 2^0)_{ten}$$
$$= 8 + 0 + 2 + 0_{ten} = 10_{ten}$$

and

$$5 \times 2^1{}_{ten} = 10_{ten}$$

Hence the MIPS sll instruction can be used for multiplies by powers of 2.

Now that we have seen Booth's algorithm work, we are ready to see *why* it works for two's complement signed integers. Let a be the multiplier and b be the multiplicand and we'll use a_i to refer to bit i of a. Recasting Booth's algorithm in terms of the bit values of the multiplier yields this table:

a_i	a_{i-1}	Operation
0	0	Do nothing
0	1	Add b
1	0	Subtract b
1	1	Do nothing

Instead of representing Booth's algorithm in tabular form, we can represent it as the expression

$$(a_{i-1} - a_i)$$

where the value of the expression means the following actions:

$$
\begin{aligned}
0: & \quad \text{do nothing} \\
+1: & \quad \text{add } b \\
-1: & \quad \text{subtract } b
\end{aligned}
$$

Since we know that shifting of the multiplicand left with respect to the Product register can be considered multiplying by a power of 2, Booth's algorithm can be written as the sum

$$
\begin{aligned}
& (a_{-1} - a_0) \times b \times 2^0 \\
+ \; & (a_0 - a_1) \times b \times 2^1 \\
+ \; & (a_1 - a_2) \times b \times 2^2 \\
\cdots & \qquad \cdots \\
+ \; & (a_{29} - a_{30}) \times b \times 2^{30} \\
+ \; & (a_{30} - a_{31}) \times b \times 2^{31}
\end{aligned}
$$

We can simplify this sum by noting that

$$-a_i \times 2^i + a_i \times 2^{i+1} = (-a_i + 2a_i) \times 2^i = (2a_i - a_i) \times 2^i = a_i \times 2^i$$

recalling that $a_{-1} = 0$ and by factoring out b from each term:

$$b \times ((a_{31} \times -2^{31}) + (a_{30} \times 2^{30}) + (a_{29} \times 2^{29}) + \ldots + (a_1 \times 2^1) + (a_0 \times 2^0))$$

The long formula in parentheses to the right of the first multiply operation is simply the two's complement representation of a (see page 213.) Thus the sum is further simplified to

$$b \times a$$

Hence Booth's algorithm does in fact perform two's complement multiplication of a and b.

Multiply in MIPS

MIPS provides a separate pair of 32-bit registers to contain the 64-bit product, called *Hi* and *Lo*. To produce a properly signed or unsigned product, MIPS has two instructions: multiply (mult) and multiply unsigned (multu). To fetch the integer 32-bit product, the programmer uses *move from lo* (mflo). The MIPS assembler generates a pseudoinstruction for multiply that specifies three general-purpose registers, generating mflo and mfhi instructions to place the product into registers.

> **Hardware Software Interface**
>
> Both MIPS multiply instructions ignore overflow, so it is up to the software to check to see if the product is too big to fit in 32 bits. To avoid overflow, Hi must be 0 for multu or must be the replicated sign of Lo for mult. The instruction *move from hi* (mfhi) can be used to transfer Hi to a general-purpose register to test for overflow.

Summary

Multiplication is accomplished by simple shift and add hardware, derived from the paper-and-pencil method learned in grammar school. Compilers even use shift instructions for multiplications by powers of two. Signed multiplication is more challenging, with Booth's algorithm rising to the challenge with essentially a clever factorization of the two's complement number representation of the multiplier.

Elaboration: The original reason for Booth's algorithm was speed because early machines could shift faster than they could add. The hope was that this encoding scheme would increase the number of shifts. This algorithm is sensitive to particular bit patterns, however, and may actually increase the number of adds or subtracts. For example, bit patterns that alternate 0 and 1, called *isolated 1s*, will cause the hardware to add or subtract at each step. Looking at more bits to carefully avoid isolated 1s can reduce the number of adds in the worst case. Greater advantage comes from performing multiple bits per step, which we explore in Exercise 4.53.

Even faster multiplications are possible by essentially providing one 32-bit adder for each bit of the multiplier: one input is the multiplicand ANDed with a multiplier bit and the other is the output of a prior adder. When adding such a large column of numbers, a *carry save adder* is useful (see Exercises 4.49 to 4.52).

Elaboration: The replacement of a multiply by a shift, as in the example on page 262, is an instance of a general compiler optimization strategy called *strength reduction*.

4.7 Division

Divide et impera.

Latin for "Divide and rule," ancient political maxim cited by Machiavelli, 1532

The reciprocal operation of multiply is divide, an operation that is even less frequent and even more quirky. It even offers the opportunity to perform a mathematically invalid operation: dividing by 0.

Let's start with an example of long division using decimal numbers to recall the names of the operands and the grammar school division algorithm. For reasons similar to those in the previous section, we limit the decimal digits to just 0 or 1. The example is dividing $1{,}001{,}010_{ten}$ by 1000_{ten}:

$$
\begin{array}{r}
1001_{ten} \quad \text{Quotient} \\
\text{Divisor } 1000_{ten} \,\overline{)\,1001010_{ten}} \quad \text{Dividend} \\
-1000 \\
\overline{10} \\
101 \\
1010 \\
-1000 \\
\overline{10_{ten}} \quad \text{Remainder}
\end{array}
$$

The two operands (*dividend* and *divisor*) and the result (*quotient*) of divide are accompanied by a second result called the *remainder*. Here is another way to express the relationship between the components:

$$\text{Dividend} = \text{Quotient} \times \text{Divisor} + \text{Remainder}$$

where the remainder is smaller than the divisor. Infrequently, programs use the divide instruction just to get the remainder, ignoring the quotient.

The basic grammar school division algorithm tries to see how big a number can be subtracted, creating a digit of the quotient on each attempt. Our carefully selected decimal example uses only the numbers 0 and 1, so it's easy to figure out how many times the divisor goes into the portion of the dividend: it's either 0 times or 1 time. Binary numbers contain only 0 or 1, so binary division is restricted to these two choices, thereby simplifying binary division.

Let's assume that both the dividend and divisor are positive and hence the quotient and the remainder are nonnegative. The division operands and both results are 32-bit values, and we will ignore the sign for now. Rather than make

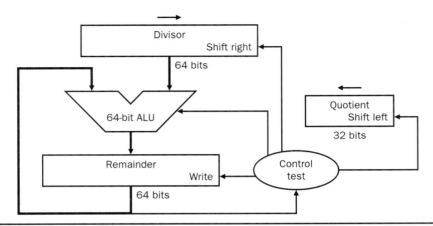

FIGURE 4.36 First version of the division hardware. The Divisor register, ALU, and Remainder register are all 64 bits wide, with only the Quotient register being 32 bits. The 32-bit divisor starts in the left half of the Divisor register and is shifted right 1 bit on each step. The remainder is initialized with the dividend. Control decides when to shift the Divisor and Quotient registers and when to write the new value into the Remainder register.

each of the three evolutionary steps explicit with drawings and examples, as we did for multiply, we will save space by giving a sketch for the two intermediate steps and then give the final algorithm in detail.

First Version of the Division Algorithm and Hardware

Figure 4.36 shows hardware to mimic our grammar school algorithm. We start with the 32-bit Quotient register set to 0. Each step of the algorithm needs to move the divisor to the right one digit, so we start with the divisor placed in the left half of the 64-bit Divisor register and shift it right 1 bit each step to align it with the dividend. The Remainder register is initialized with the dividend.

Figure 4.37 shows three steps of the first division algorithm. Unlike a human, the computer isn't smart enough to know in advance whether the divisor is smaller than the dividend. It must first subtract the divisor in step 1; remember that this is how we performed the comparison in the set on less than instruction. If the result is positive, the divisor was smaller or equal to the dividend, so we generate a 1 in the quotient (step 2a). If the result is negative, the next step is to restore the original value by adding the divisor back to the remainder and generate a 0 in the quotient (step 2b). The divisor is shifted right and then we iterate again. The remainder and quotient will be found in their namesake registers after the iterations are complete.

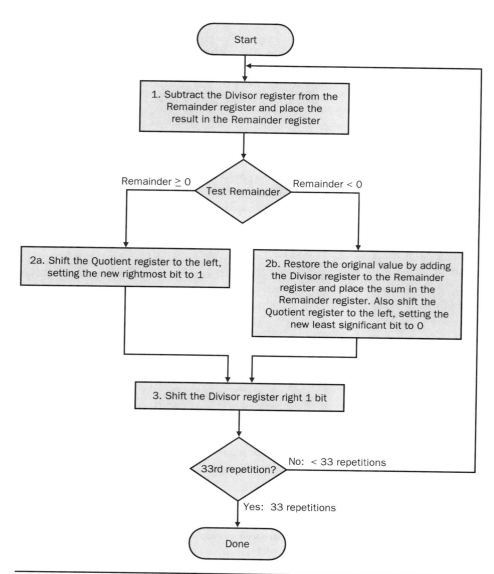

FIGURE 4.37 The first division algorithm, using the hardware in Figure 4.36. If the Remainder is positive, the divisor did go into the dividend, so step 2a generates a 1 in the quotient. A negative Remainder after step 1 means that the divisor did not go into the dividend, so step 2b generates a 0 in the quotient and adds the divisor to the remainder, thereby reversing the subtraction of step 1. The final shift, in step 3, aligns the divisor properly, relative to the dividend for the next iteration. These steps are repeated 33 times; the reason for the apparent extra step will become clear in the next version of the algorithm.

First Divide Algorithm

Example

Using a 4-bit version of the algorithm to save pages, let's try dividing 7_{ten} by 2_{ten}, or $0000\ 0111_{two}$ by 0010_{two}.

Answer

Figure 4.38 shows the value of each register for each of the steps, with the quotient being 3_{ten} and the remainder 1_{ten}. Notice that the test in step 2 of whether the remainder is positive or negative simply tests whether the sign bit of the Remainder register is a 0 or 1. The surprising requirement of this algorithm is that it takes $n + 1$ steps to get the proper quotient and remainder.

Iteration	Step	Quotient	Divisor	Remainder
0	Initial values	0000	0010 0000	0000 0111
1	1: Rem = Rem – Div	0000	0010 0000	①110 0111
	2b: Rem < 0 ⟹ +Div, sll Q, Q0 = 0	0000	0010 0000	0000 0111
	3: Shift Div right	0000	0001 0000	0000 0111
2	1: Rem = Rem – Div	0000	0001 0000	①111 0111
	2b: Rem < 0 ⟹ +Div, sll Q, Q0 = 0	0000	0001 0000	0000 0111
	3: Shift Div right	0000	0000 1000	0000 0111
3	1: Rem = Rem – Div	0000	0000 1000	①111 1111
	2b: Rem < 0 ⟹ +Div, sll Q, Q0 = 0	0000	0000 1000	0000 0111
	3: Shift Div right	0000	0000 0100	0000 0111
4	1: Rem = Rem – Div	0000	0000 0100	⓪000 0011
	2a: Rem ≥ 0 ⟹ sll Q, Q0 = 1	0001	0000 0100	0000 0011
	3: Shift Div right	0001	0000 0010	0000 0011
5	1: Rem = Rem – Div	0001	0000 0010	⓪000 0001
	2a: Rem ≥ 0 ⟹ sll Q, Q0 = 1	0011	0000 0010	0000 0001
	3: Shift Div right	0011	0000 0001	0000 0001

FIGURE 4.38   Division example using first algorithm in Figure 4.37. The bit examined to determine the next step is circled in color.

Second Version of the Division Algorithm and Hardware

Once again the frugal computer pioneers recognized that, at most, half of the divisor has useful information, and so both the divisor and ALU could potentially be cut in half. Shifting the remainder to the left instead of shifting the divisor to the right produces the same alignment and accomplishes the goal of simplifying the hardware necessary for the ALU and the divisor. Figure 4.39 shows the simplified hardware for the second version of the algorithm.

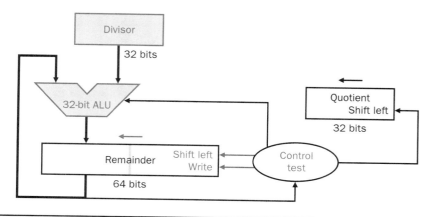

FIGURE 4.39 **Second version of the division hardware.** The Divisor register, ALU, and Quotient register are all 32 bits wide, with only the Remainder register left at 64 bits. Compared to Figure 4.36, the ALU and Divisor registers are halved and the remainder is shifted left. These changes are highlighted.

Another change comes from noticing that the first step of the current algorithm cannot produce a 1 in the quotient bit; if it did, then the quotient would be too large for the register. By switching the order of the operations to shift and then subtract, one iteration of the algorithm can be removed. When the algorithm terminates, the remainder will be found in the left half of the Remainder register.

Final Version of Division Algorithm and Hardware

With the same insight and motivation as in the third version of the multiplication algorithm, computer pioneers saw that the Quotient register could be eliminated by shifting the bits of the quotient into the Remainder instead of shifting in 0s as in the preceding algorithm. Figure 4.40 shows the third version of the algorithm.

We start the algorithm by shifting the Remainder left as before. Thereafter, the loop contains only two steps because the shifting of the Remainder register shifts both the remainder in the left half and the quotient in the right half (see Figure 4.41). The consequence of combining the two registers and the new order of the operations in the loop is that the remainder will be shifted left one time too many. Thus the final correction step must shift back only the remainder in the left half of the register.

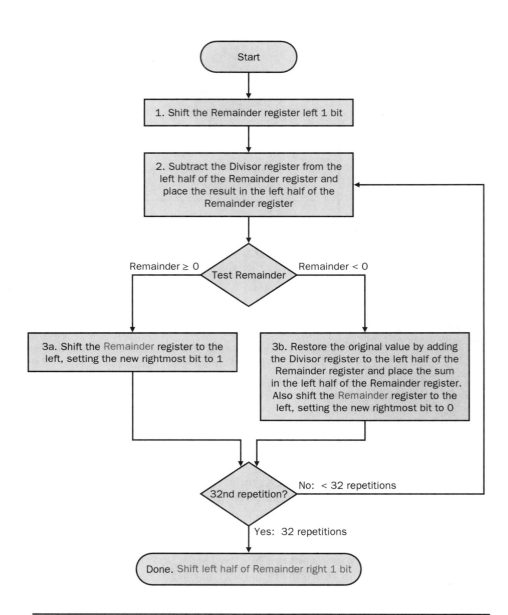

FIGURE 4.40   The third division algorithm has just two steps. The Remainder register shifts left.

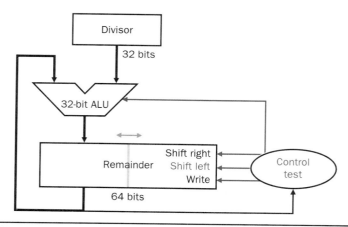

FIGURE 4.41 Third version of the division hardware. This version combines the Quotient register with the right half of the Remainder register.

Third Divide Algorithm

Example

Use the third version of the algorithm to divide $0000\ 0111_{two}$ by 0010_{two}.

Answer

Figure 4.42 shows how the quotient is created in the bottom of the Remainder register and how both are shifted left in a single operation.

Iteration	Step	Divisor	Remainder
0	Initial values	0010	0000 0111
	Shift Rem left 1	0010	0000 1110
1	2: Rem = Rem – Div	0010	①110 1110
	3b: Rem < 0 ⟹ + Div, sll R, R0 = 0	0010	0001 1100
2	2: Rem = Rem – Div	0010	①111 1100
	3b: Rem < 0 ⟹ + Div, sll R, R0 = 0	0010	0011 1000
3	2: Rem = Rem – Div	0010	⓪001 1000
	3a: Rem ≥ 0 ⟹ sll R, R0 = 1	0010	0011 0001
4	2: Rem = Rem – Div	0010	⓪001 0001
	3a: Rem ≥ 0 ⟹ sll R, R0 = 1	0010	0010 0011
	Shift left half of Rem right 1	0010	0001 0011

FIGURE 4.42 Division example using third algorithm in Figure 4.40. The bit examined to determine the next step is circled in color.

Signed Division

So far we have ignored signed numbers in division. The simplest solution is to remember the signs of the divisor and dividend and then negate the quotient if the signs disagree.

The one complication is that we must also set the sign of the remainder. Remember that the following equation must always hold:

$$\text{Dividend} = \text{Quotient} \times \text{Divisor} + \text{Remainder}$$

To understand how to set the sign of the remainder, let's look at the example of dividing all the combinations of $\pm7_{ten}$ by $\pm2_{ten}$. The first case is easy:

$$+7 \div +2: \text{ Quotient} = +3, \text{ Remainder} = +1$$

Checking the results:

$$7 = 3 \times 2 + (+1) = 6 + 1$$

If we change the sign of the dividend, the quotient must change as well:

$$-7 \div +2: \text{ Quotient} = -3$$

Rewriting our basic formula to calculate the remainder:

$$\text{Remainder} = (\text{Dividend} - \text{Quotient} \times \text{Divisor})$$
$$= -7 - (-3 \times +2) = -7 - (-6) = -1$$

So,

$$-7 \div +2: \text{ Quotient} = -3, \text{ Remainder} = -1$$

Checking the results again:

$$-7 = -3 \times 2 + (-1) = -6 - 1$$

The reason the answer isn't a quotient of -4 and a remainder of $+1$, which would also fit this formula, is that the absolute value of the quotient would then change depending on the sign of the dividend and the divisor! Clearly if

$$-(x \div y) \neq (-x) \div y$$

programming would be an even greater challenge. This anomalous behavior is avoided by following the rule that the dividend and remainder must have the same signs, no matter what the signs of the divisor and quotient.

We calculate the other combinations by following the same rule:

$$+7 \div -2: \text{ Quotient} = -3, \text{ Remainder} = +1$$

$$-7 \div -2: \text{ Quotient} = +3, \text{ Remainder} = -1$$

Thus the correctly signed division algorithm negates the quotient if the signs of the operands are opposite and makes the sign of the nonzero remainder match the dividend.

Divide in MIPS

You may have already observed that the same hardware can be used for both multiply and divide. The only requirement is a 64-bit register that can shift left or right and a 32-bit ALU that adds or subtracts. For example, MIPS uses the 32-bit Hi and 32-bit Lo registers for both multiply and divide. As we might expect from the algorithm above, Hi contains the remainder, and Lo contains the quotient after the divide instruction completes.

To handle both signed integers and unsigned integers, MIPS has two instructions: *divide* (div) and *divide unsigned* (divu). The MIPS assembler allows divide instructions to specify three registers, generating the mflo or mfhi instructions to place the desired result into a general-purpose register.

Hardware Software Interface	MIPS divide instructions ignore overflow, so software must determine if the quotient is too large. In addition to overflow, division can also result in an improper calculation: division by 0. Some machines distinguish these two anomalous events. MIPS software must check the divisor to discover division by 0 as well as overflow.

Summary

The common hardware support for multiply and divide allows MIPS to provide a single pair of 32-bit registers that are used both for multiply and divide. Figure 4.43 summarizes the additions to the MIPS architecture for the last two sections.

Elaboration: The reason for needing an extra iteration for the first algorithm and the early shift in the second and third algorithms involves the placement of the dividend in the Remainder register. We expect to have a 32-bit quotient and a 32-bit divisor, but each is really a 31-bit integer plus a sign bit. The product would be 31+31, or 62 bits plus a single sign bit; the hardware can then support only a 63-bit dividend. Given that registers are normally powers of 2, this means we must place the 63-bit dividend properly in the 64-bit Remainder register. If we place the 63 bits to the right, we need to run the algorithm for an extra step to get to that last bit. A better solution is to shift early, thereby saving a step of the algorithm.

An even faster algorithm does not immediately add the dividend back if the remainder is negative. It simply *adds* the dividend to the shifted remainder in the following step since $(r + d) \times 2 - d = r \times 2 + d \times 2 - d = r \times 2 + d$. This *nonrestoring* division algorithm, which takes 1 clock per step, is explored further in Exercise 4.54; the algorithm here is called *restoring* division.

MIPS operands

Name	Example	Comments
32 registers	$s0–$s7, $t0–$t9, $gp, $fp, $zero, $sp, $ra, $at, Hi, Lo	Fast locations for data. In MIPS, data must be in registers to perform arithmetic. MIPS register $zero always equals 0. Register $at is reserved for the assembler to handle large constants. Hi and Lo contain the results of multiply and divide.
2^{30} memory words	Memory[0], Memory[4], . . . , Memory[4294967292]	Accessed only by data transfer instructions. MIPS uses byte addresses, so sequential words differ by 4. Memory holds data structures, such as arrays, and spilled registers, such as those saved on procedure calls.

MIPS assembly language

Category	Instruction	Example		Meaning	Comments
Arithmetic	add	add	$s1,$s2,$s3	$s1 = $s2 + $s3	Three operands; overflow detected
	subtract	sub	$s1,$s2,$s3	$s1 = $s2 − $s3	Three operands; overflow detected
	add immediate	addi	$s1,$s2,100	$s1 = $s2 + 100	+ constant; overflow detected
	add unsigned	addu	$s1,$s2,$s3	$s1 = $s2 + $s3	Three operands; overflow undetected
	subtract unsigned	subu	$s1,$s2,$s3	$s1 = $s2 − $s3	Three operands; overflow undetected
	add immediate unsigned	addiu	$s1,$s2,100	$s1 = $s2 + 100	+ constant; overflow undetected
	move from coprocessor register	mfc0	$s1,$epc	$s1 = $epc	Used to copy Exception PC plus other special registers
	multiply	mult	$s2,$s3	Hi, Lo = $s2 × $s3	64-bit signed product in Hi, Lo
	multiply unsigned	multu	$s2,$s3	Hi, Lo = $s2 × $s3	64-bit unsigned product in Hi, Lo
	divide	div	$s2,$s3	Lo = $s2 / $s3, Hi = $s2 mod $s3	Lo = quotient, Hi = remainder
	divide unsigned	divu	$s2,$s3	Lo = $s2 / $s3, Hi = $s2 mod $s3	Unsigned quotient and remainder
	move from Hi	mfhi	$s1	$s1 = Hi	Used to get copy of Hi
	move from Lo	mflo	$s1	$s1 = Lo	Used to get copy of Lo
Logical	and	and	$s1,$s2,$s3	$s1 = $s2 & $s3	Three reg. operands; logical AND
	or	or	$s1,$s2,$s3	$s1 = $s2	$s3	Three reg. operands; logical OR
	and immediate	andi	$s1,$s2,100	$s1 = $s2 & 100	Logical AND reg, constant
	or immediate	ori	$s1,$s2,100	$s1 = $s2	100	Logical OR reg, constant
	shift left logical	sll	$s1,$s2,10	$s1 = $s2 << 10	Shift left by constant
	shift right logical	srl	$s1,$s2,10	$s1 = $s2 >> 10	Shift right by constant
Data transfer	load word	lw	$s1,100($s2)	$s1 = Memory[$s2+100]	Word from memory to register
	store word	sw	$s1,100($s2)	Memory[$s2 + 100] = $s1	Word from register to memory
	load byte unsigned	lbu	$s1,100($s2)	$s1 = Memory[$s2 + 100]	Byte from memory to register
	store byte	sb	$s1,100($s2)	Memory[$s2 + 100] = $s1	Byte from register to memory
	load upper immediate	lui	$s1,100	$s1 = 100 * 2^{16}	Loads constant in upper 16 bits
Condi-tional branch	branch on equal	beq	$s1,$s2,25	if ($s1 == $s2) go to PC + 4 + 100	Equal test; PC-relative branch
	branch on not equal	bne	$s1,$s2,25	if ($s1 != $s2) go to PC + 4 + 100	Not equal test; PC-relative
	set on less than	slt	$s1,$s2,$s3	if ($s2 < $s3) $s1 = 1; else $s1 = 0	Compare less than; two's complement
	set less than immediate	slti	$s1,$s2,100	if ($s2 < 100) $s1 = 1; else $s1=0	Compare < constant; two's complement
	set less than unsigned	sltu	$s1,$s2,$s3	if ($s2 < $s3) $s1 = 1; else $s1=0	Compare less than; natural numbers
	set less than immediate unsigned	sltiu	$s1,$s2,100	if ($s2 < 100) $s1 = 1; else $s1 = 0	Compare < constant; natural numbers
Uncondi-tional jump	jump	j	2500	go to 10000	Jump to target address
	jump register	jr	$ra	go to $ra	For switch, procedure return
	jump and link	jal	2500	$ra = PC + 4; go to 10000	For procedure call

FIGURE 4.43 MIPS architecture revealed thus far. Color indicates the portions revealed since Figure 4.7 on page 228. MIPS machine language is listed on the back endpapers of this book. *(page 274)*

4.8   Floating Point

Speed gets you nowhere if you're headed the wrong way.

American proverb

In addition to signed and unsigned integers, programming languages support numbers with fractions, which are called *reals* in mathematics. Here are some examples of reals:

$3.14159265\ldots_{\text{ten}}$ (π)

$2.71828\ldots_{\text{ten}}$ (e)

0.000000001_{ten} or $1.0_{\text{ten}} \times 10^{-9}$ (seconds in a nanosecond)

$3{,}155{,}760{,}000_{\text{ten}}$ or $3.15576_{\text{ten}} \times 10^{9}$ (seconds in a typical century)

Notice that in the last case, the number didn't represent a small fraction, but it was bigger than we could represent with a 32-bit signed integer. The alternative notation for the last two numbers is called *scientific notation*, which has a single digit to the left of the decimal point. A number in scientific notation that has no leading 0s is called a *normalized* number, which is the usual way to write it. For example, $1.0_{\text{ten}} \times 10^{-9}$ is in normalized scientific notation, but $0.1_{\text{ten}} \times 10^{-8}$ and $10.0_{\text{ten}} \times 10^{-10}$ are not.

Just as we can show decimal numbers in scientific notation, we can also show binary numbers in scientific notation:

$1.0_{\text{two}} \times 2^{-1}$

To keep a binary number in normalized form, we need a base that we can increase or decrease by exactly the number of bits the number must be shifted to have one nonzero digit to the left of the decimal point. Only a base of 2 fulfills our need. Since the base is not 10, we also need a new name for decimal point; *binary point* will do fine.

Computer arithmetic that supports such numbers is called *floating point* because it represents numbers in which the binary point is not fixed, as it is for integers. The programming language C uses the name *float* for such numbers. Just as in scientific notation, numbers are represented as a single nonzero digit to the left of the binary point. In binary, the form is

$1.xxxxxxxxx_{\text{two}} \times 2^{yyyy}$

(Although the computer represents the exponent in base 2 as well as the rest of the number, to simplify the notation we'll show the exponent in decimal.)

A standard scientific notation for reals in normalized form offers three advantages. It simplifies exchange of data that includes floating-point numbers; it simplifies the floating-point arithmetic algorithms to know that numbers will always be in this form; and it increases the accuracy of the numbers that can be stored in a word, since the unnecessary leading 0s are replaced by real digits to the right of the binary point.

Floating-Point Representation

The designer of a floating-point representation must find a compromise between the size of the significand and the size of the exponent because a fixed word size means you must take a bit from one to add a bit to the other. This trade-off is between accuracy and range: Increasing the size of the significand enhances the accuracy of the significand, while increasing the size of the exponent increases the range of numbers that can be represented. As our design guideline from Chapter 3 reminds us, good design demands good compromises.

Floating-point numbers are usually a multiple of the size of a word. The representation of a MIPS floating-point number is shown below, where *s* is the sign of the floating-point number (1 meaning negative), *exponent* is the value of the 8-bit exponent field (including the sign of the exponent), and *significand* is the 23-bit number in the fraction. This representation is called *sign and magnitude*, since the sign has a separate bit from the rest of the number.

31	30	29	28	27	26	25	24	23	22	21	20	19	18	17	16	15	14	13	12	11	10	9	8	7	6	5	4	3	2	1	0
s		exponent							significand																						
1 bit		8 bits							23 bits																						

In general, floating-point numbers are of the form

$$(-1)^S \times F \times 2^E$$

F involves the value in the significand field and E involves the value in the exponent field; the exact relationship to these fields will be spelled out soon.

These chosen sizes of exponent and significand give MIPS computer arithmetic an extraordinary range. Fractions as small as $2.0_{ten} \times 10^{-38}$ and numbers as large as $2.0_{ten} \times 10^{38}$ can be represented in a computer. Alas, extraordinary differs from infinite, so it is still possible for numbers to be too large. Thus, overflow interrupts can occur in floating-point arithmetic as well as in integer arithmetic. Notice that *overflow* here means that the exponent is too large to be represented in the exponent field.

Floating point offers a new kind of exceptional event as well. Just as programmers will want to know when they have calculated a number that is too large to be represented, they will want to know if the nonzero fraction they are calculating has become so small that it cannot be represented; either event could result in a program giving incorrect answers. This situation occurs when the negative exponent is too large to fit in the exponent field. To distinguish it from overflow, people call this event *underflow*.

One way to reduce chances of underflow or overflow is to use a notation that has a larger exponent. In C this is called *double*, and operations on doubles are called *double precision* floating-point arithmetic; *single precision* floating point is the name of the earlier format.

The representation of a double precision floating-point number takes two MIPS words, as shown below, where s is still the sign of the number, *exponent* is the value of the 11-bit exponent field, and *significand* is the 52-bit number in the fraction.

31	30	29	28	27	26	25	24	23	22	21	20	19	18	17	16	15	14	13	12	11	10	9	8	7	6	5	4	3	2	1	0
s					exponent												significand														

1 bit   11 bits   20 bits

significand (continued)
32 bits

MIPS double precision allows numbers almost as small as $2.0_{ten} \times 10^{-308}$ and almost as large as $2.0_{ten} \times 10^{308}$. Although double precision does increase the exponent range, its primary advantage is its greater accuracy because of the large significand.

These formats go beyond MIPS. They are part of the *IEEE 754 floating-point standard*, found in virtually every computer invented since 1980. This standard has greatly improved both the ease of porting floating-point programs and the quality of computer arithmetic.

To pack even more bits into the significand, IEEE 754 makes the leading 1 bit of normalized binary numbers implicit. Hence, the significand is actually 24 bits long in single precision (implied 1 and a 23-bit fraction), and 53 bits long in double precision (1+52). Since 0 has no leading 1, it is given the reserved exponent value 0 so that the hardware won't attach a leading 1 to it.

Thus $00 \ldots 00_{two}$ represents 0; the representation of the rest of the numbers uses the form from before with the hidden 1 added:

$$(-1)^S \times (1 + \text{Significand}) \times 2^E$$

where the bits of the significand represent the fraction between 0 and 1 and E specifies the value in the exponent field, to be given in detail shortly. If we number the bits of the significand from *left to right* s1, s2, s3, . . . , then the value is

$$(-1)^S \times (1 + (s1 \times 2^{-1}) + (s2 \times 2^{-2}) + (s3 \times 2^{-3}) + (s4 \times 2^{-4}) + \ldots) \times 2^E$$

The designers of IEEE 754 also wanted a floating-point representation that could be easily processed by integer comparisons, especially for sorting. This desire is why the sign is in the most significant bit, allowing a test of less than, greater than, or equal to 0 to be performed quickly.

Placing the exponent before the significand also simplifies sorting of floating-point numbers using integer comparison instructions, since numbers with bigger exponents look larger than numbers with smaller exponents, as long as both exponents have the same sign. (It's a little more complicated than a simple integer sort, since this notation is essentially sign and magnitude rather than two's complement.)

Negative exponents pose a challenge to simplified sorting. If we use two's complement or any other notation in which negative exponents have a 1 in the most significant bit of the exponent field, a negative exponent will look like a big number. For example, $1.0_{two} \times 2^{-1}$ would be represented as

31	30	29	28	27	26	25	24	23	22	21	20	19	18	17	16	15	14	13	12	11	10	9	8	7	6	5	4	3	2	1	0
0	1	1	1	1	1	1	1	1	0	0	0	0	0	0	0	0	0	0	0	0	0	0	0	0	0	0	0	.	.	.	

(Remember that the leading 1 is implicit in the significand.) The value $1.0_{two} \times 2^{+1}$ would look like the smaller binary number

31	30	29	28	27	26	25	24	23	22	21	20	19	18	17	16	15	14	13	12	11	10	9	8	7	6	5	4	3	2	1	0
0	0	0	0	0	0	0	0	1	0	0	0	0	0	0	0	0	0	0	0	0	0	0	0	0	0	0	0	.	.	.	

The desirable notation must therefore represent the most negative exponent as $00 \ldots 00_{two}$ and the most positive as $11 \ldots 11_{two}$. This convention is called *biased notation*, with the bias being the number subtracted from the normal, unsigned representation to determine the real value.

IEEE 754 uses a bias of 127 for single precision, so -1 is represented by the bit pattern of the value $-1 + 127_{ten}$, or $126_{ten} = 0111\ 1110_{two}$, and $+1$ is represented by $1 + 127$, or $128_{ten} = 1000\ 0000_{two}$. Biased exponent means that the value represented by a floating-point number is really

$$(-1)^S \times (1 + \text{Significand}) \times 2^{(\text{Exponent} - \text{Bias})}$$

The exponent bias for double precision is 1023.

Thus IEEE 754 notation can be processed by integer compares to accelerate sorting of floating-point numbers. Let's show the representation.

Floating-Point Representation

Example

Show the IEEE 754 binary representation of the number -0.75_{ten} in single and double precision.

Answer

The number -0.75_{ten} is also

$$-3/4_{ten} \text{ or } -3/2^2{}_{ten}$$

It is also represented by the binary fraction:

$$-11_{two}/2^2{}_{ten} \text{ or } -0.11_{two}$$

In scientific notation, the value is

$$-0.11_{two} \times 2^0$$

and in normalized scientific notation, it is

$$-1.1_{two} \times 2^{-1}$$

The general representation for a single precision number is

$$(-1)^S \times (1 + \text{Significand}) \times 2^{(\text{Exponent} - 127)}$$

and so when we add the bias 127 to the exponent of $-1.1_{two} \times 2^{-1}$, the result is

$$(-1)^1 \times (1 + .1000\ 0000\ 0000\ 0000\ 0000\ 000_{two}) \times 2^{(126 - 127)}$$

The single precision binary representation of -0.75_{ten} is then

31	30	29	28	27	26	25	24	23	22	21	20	19	18	17	16	15	14	13	12	11	10	9	8	7	6	5	4	3	2	1	0
1	0	1	1	1	1	1	1	0	1	0	0	0	0	0	0	0	0	0	0	0	0	0	0	0	0	0	0	0	0	0	0

1 bit   8 bits   23 bits

The double precision representation is

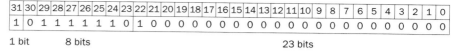

$$(-1)^1 \times (1 + .1000\ 0000\ 0000\ 0000\ 0000\ 0000\ 0000\ 0000\ 0000\ 0000\ 0000\ 0000\ 0000_{two}) \times 2^{(1022-1023)}$$

31	30	29	28	27	26	25	24	23	22	21	20	19	18	17	16	15	14	13	12	11	10	9	8	7	6	5	4	3	2	1	0
1	0	1	1	1	1	1	1	1	1	1	0	1	0	0	0	0	0	0	0	0	0	0	0	0	0	0	0	0	0	0	0

1 bit   11 bits   20 bits

0	0	0	0	0	0	0	0	0	0	0	0	0	0	0	0	0	0	0	0	0	0	0	0	0	0	0	0	0	0	0	0

32 bits

Now let's try going the other direction.

Converting Binary to Decimal Floating Point

Example

What decimal number is represented by this word?

31	30	29	28	27	26	25	24	23	22	21	20	19	18	17	16	15	14	13	12	11	10	9	8	7	6	5	4	3	2	1	0
1	1	0	0	0	0	0	0	1	0	1	0	0	0	0	0	0	0	0	0	0	0	0	0	0	0	0	0	0	0	.	. .

Answer

The sign bit is 1, the exponent field contains 129, and the significand field contains $1 \times 2^{-2} = 1/4$, or 0.25. Using the basic equation,

$$(-1)^S \times (1 + \text{Significand}) \times 2^{(\text{Exponent} - \text{Bias})} = (-1)^1 \times (1 + 0.25) \times 2^{(129 - 127)}$$
$$= -1 \times 1.25 \times 2^2$$
$$= -1.25 \times 4$$
$$= -5.0$$

In the next sections we will give the algorithms for floating-point addition and multiplication. At their core, they use the corresponding integer operations on the significands, but extra bookkeeping is necessary to handle the exponents and normalize the result. We first give an intuitive derivation of the algorithms in decimal, and then give a more detailed, binary version in the figures.

Elaboration: In an attempt to increase range without removing bits from the significand, some computers before the IEEE 754 standard used a base other than 2. For example, the IBM 360 and 370 mainframe computers use base 16. Since changing the IBM exponent by one means shifting the significand by 4 bits, "normalized" base 16 numbers can have up to 3 leading bits of 0s! Hence hexadecimal digits mean that up to 3 bits must be dropped from the significand, which leads to surprising problems in the accuracy of floating-point arithmetic, as noted in section 4.12.

Floating-Point Addition

Let's add numbers in scientific notation by hand to illustrate the problems in floating-point addition: $9.999_{\text{ten}} \times 10^1 + 1.610_{\text{ten}} \times 10^{-1}$. Assume that we can store only four decimal digits of the significand and two decimal digits of the exponent.

Step 1. To be able to add these numbers properly, we must align the decimal point of the number that has the smaller exponent. Hence, we need a form of the smaller number, $1.610_{ten} \times 10^{-1}$, that matches the larger exponent. We obtain this by observing that there are multiple representations of an unnormalized floating-point number in scientific notation:

$$1.610_{ten} \times 10^{-1} = 0.1610_{ten} \times 10^{0} = 0.01610_{ten} \times 10^{1}$$

The number on the right is the version we desire, since its exponent matches the exponent of the larger number, $9.999_{ten} \times 10^{1}$. Thus the first step shifts the significand of the smaller number to the right until its corrected exponent matches that of the larger number. But we can represent only four decimal digits so, after shifting, the number is really:

$$0.016_{ten} \times 10^{1}$$

Step 2. Next comes the addition of the significands:

$$
\begin{array}{r}
9.999_{ten} \\
+ \quad 0.016_{ten} \\
\hline
10.015_{ten}
\end{array}
$$

The sum is $10.015_{ten} \times 10^{1}$.

Step 3. This sum is not in normalized scientific notation, so we need to correct it. Again, there are multiple representations of this number; we pick the normalized form:

$$10.015_{ten} \times 10^{1} = 1.0015_{ten} \times 10^{2}$$

Thus, after the addition we may have to shift the sum to put it into normalized form, adjusting the exponent appropriately. This example shows shifting to the right, but if one number were positive and the other were negative, it would be possible for the sum to have many leading 0s, requiring left shifts. Whenever the exponent is increased or decreased, we must check for overflow or underflow—that is, we must make sure that the exponent still fits in its field.

Step 4. Since we assumed that the significand can be only four digits long (excluding the sign), we must round the number. In our grammar school algorithm, the rules truncate the number if the digit to the right of the desired point is between 0 and 4 and add 1 to the digit if the number to the right is between 5 and 9. The number

$$1.0015_{ten} \times 10^{2}$$

is rounded to four digits in the significand to

$$1.002_{ten} \times 10^{2}$$

since the fourth digit to the right of the decimal point was between 5 and 9. Notice that if we have bad luck on rounding, such as adding 1 to a string of 9s, the sum may no longer be normalized and we would need to perform step 3 again.

Figure 4.44 shows the algorithm for binary floating-point addition that follows this decimal example. Steps 1 and 2 are similar to the example just discussed: adjust the significand of the number with the smaller exponent and then add the two significands. Step 3 normalizes the results, forcing a check for overflow or underflow. The test for overflow and underflow in step 3 depends on the precision of the operands. Recall that the pattern of all zero bits in the exponent is reserved and used for the floating-point representation of zero. Also, the pattern of all one bits in the exponent is reserved for indicating values and situations outside the scope of normal floating-point numbers (see the elaboration on page 300). Thus, for single precision, the maximum exponent is 127 and the minimum exponent is −126. The limits for double precision are 1023 and −1022.

For simplicity, we assume truncation in step 4, one of four rounding options in IEEE 754 floating point. The accuracy of floating-point calculations depends a great deal on the accuracy of rounding, so although it is easy to follow, truncation leads away from accuracy.

Decimal Floating-Point Addition

Example

Try adding the numbers 0.5_{ten} and -0.4375_{ten} in binary using the algorithm in Figure 4.44.

Answer

Let's first look at the binary version of the two numbers in normalized scientific notation, assuming that we keep 4 bits of precision:

$$0.5_{ten} = 1/2_{ten} = 1/2^1{}_{ten}$$
$$= 0.1_{two} = 0.1_{two} \times 2^0 = 1.000_{two} \times 2^{-1}$$
$$-0.4375_{ten} = -7/16_{ten} = -7/2^4{}_{ten}$$
$$= -0.0111_{two} = -0.0111_{two} \times 2^0 = -1.110_{two} \times 2^{-2}$$

Now we follow the algorithm:

Step 1. The significand of the number with the lesser exponent ($-1.11_{two} \times 2^{-2}$) is shifted right until its exponent matches the larger number:

$$-1.110_{two} \times 2^{-2} = -0.111_{two} \times 2^{-1}$$

Step 2. Add the significands:

$$1.0_{two} \times 2^{-1} + (-0.111_{two} \times 2^{-1}) = 0.001_{two} \times 2^{-1}$$

Step 3. Normalize the sum, checking for overflow or underflow:

$$0.001_{two} \times 2^{-1} = 0.010_{two} \times 2^{-2} = 0.100_{two} \times 2^{-3}$$
$$= 1.000_{two} \times 2^{-4}$$

Since $127 \geq -4 \geq -126$, there is no overflow or underflow. (The biased exponent would be $-4 + 127$, or 123, which is between 1 and 254, the smallest and largest unreserved biased exponents.)

Step 4. Round the sum:

$$1.000_{two} \times 2^{-4}$$

The sum already fits exactly in 4 bits, so there is no change to the bits due to rounding.

This sum is then

$$1.000_{two} \times 2^{-4} = 0.0001000_{two} = 0.0001_{two}$$
$$= 1/2^4_{ten} = 1/16_{ten} = 0.0625_{ten}$$

This sum is what we would expect from adding 0.5_{ten} to -0.4375_{ten}.

Many machines dedicate hardware to run floating-point operations as fast as possible. Figure 4.45 sketches the basic organization of hardware for floating-point addition.

Floating-Point Multiplication

Now that we have explained floating-point addition, let's try floating-point multiplication. We start by multiplying decimal numbers in scientific notation by hand: $1.110_{ten} \times 10^{10} \times 9.200_{ten} \times 10^{-5}$. Assume that we can store only four digits of the significand and two digits of the exponent.

Step 1. Unlike addition, we calculate the exponent of the product by simply adding the exponents of the operands together:

New exponent = 10 + (−5) = 5

Let's do this with the biased exponents as well to make sure we obtain the same result: $10 + 127 = 137$, and $-5 + 127 = 122$, so

New exponent = 137 + 122 = 259

This result is too large for the 8-bit exponent field, so something is amiss! The problem is with the bias because we are adding the biases as well as the exponents:

New exponent = (10 + 127) + (−5 +127) = (5 + 2 × 127) = 259

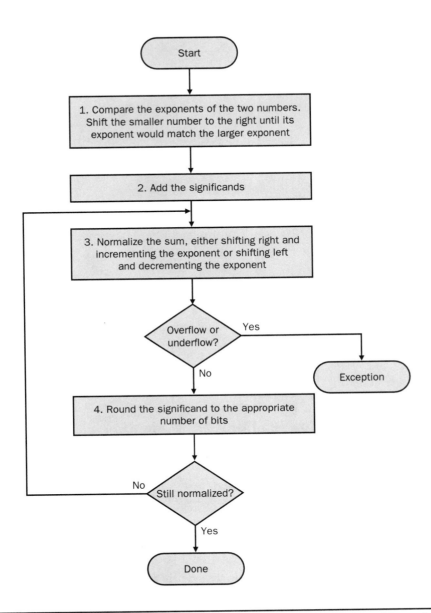

FIGURE 4.44 Floating-point addition. The normal path is to execute steps 3 and 4 once, but if rounding causes the sum to be unnormalized, we must repeat step 3.

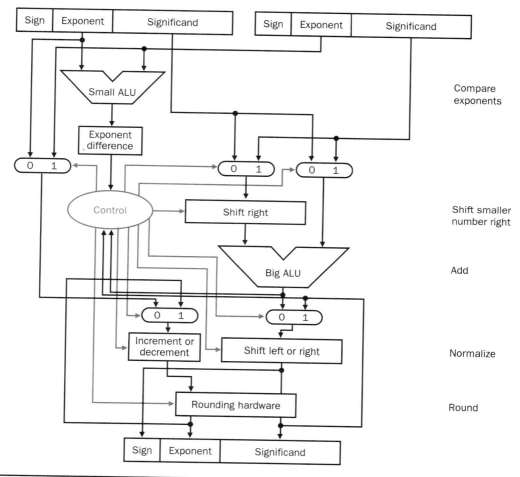

FIGURE 4.45 Block diagram of an arithmetic unit dedicated to floating-point addition. The steps of Figure 4.44 correspond to each block, from top to bottom. First the exponent of one operand is subtracted from the other using the small ALU to determine which is larger and by how much. This difference controls the three multiplexors; from left to right, they select the larger exponent, the significand of the smaller number, and the significand of the larger number. The smaller significand is shifted right and then the significands are added together using the big ALU. The normalization step then shifts the sum left or right and increments or decrements the exponent. Rounding then creates the final result, which may require normalizing again to produce the final result.

Accordingly, to get the correct biased sum when we add biased numbers, we must subtract the bias from the sum:

New exponent = 137 + 122 − 127 = 259 − 127 = 132 = (5 + 127)

and 5 is indeed the exponent we calculated initially.

Step 2.   Next comes the multiplication of the significands:

$$
\begin{array}{r}
1.110_{ten} \\
\times \quad 9.200_{ten} \\
\hline
0000 \\
0000 \\
2220 \\
9990 \\
\hline
10212000_{ten}
\end{array}
$$

There are three digits to the right of the decimal for each operand, so the decimal point is placed six digits from the right in the product significand:

$$10.212000_{ten}$$

Assuming that we can keep only three digits to the right of the decimal point, the product is 10.212×10^5.

Step 3.   This product is unnormalized, so we need to correct it. Again, there are multiple representations of this number, so we must pick the normalized form:

$$10.212_{ten} \times 10^5 = 1.0212_{ten} \times 10^6$$

Thus, after the multiplication, the product can be shifted right one digit to put it in normalized form, adding 1 to the exponent. At this point, we can check for overflow and underflow. Underflow may occur if both operands are small—that is, if both have large negative exponents.

Step 4.   We assumed that the significand is only four digits long (excluding the sign), so we must round the number. The number

$$1.0212_{ten} \times 10^6$$

is rounded to four digits in the significand to

$$1.021_{ten} \times 10^6$$

Step 5.   The sign of the product depends on the signs of the original operands. If they are both the same, the sign is positive; otherwise it's negative. Hence the product is

$$+1.021_{ten} \times 10^6$$

The sign of the sum in the addition algorithm was determined by addition of the significands, but in multiplication the sign of the product is determined by the signs of the operands.

Once again, as Figure 4.46 shows, multiplication of binary floating-point numbers is quite similar to the steps we have just completed. We start with calculating the new exponent of the product by adding the biased exponents, being sure to subtract one bias to get the proper result. Next is multiplication of significands, followed by an optional normalization step. The size of the exponent is checked for overflow or underflow, and then the product is rounded. If rounding leads to further normalization, we once again check for exponent size. Finally, set the sign bit to 1 if the signs of the operands were different (negative product) or to 0 if they were the same (positive product).

Decimal Floating-Point Multiplication

Example

Let's try multiplying the numbers 0.5_{ten} and -0.4375_{ten} using the steps in Figure 4.46.

Answer

In binary, the task is multiplying $1.000_{two} \times 2^{-1}$ by $-1.110_{two} \times 2^{-2}$.

Step 1. Adding the exponents without bias:

$$-1 + (-2) = -3$$

or, using the biased representation:

$$(-1 + 127) + (-2 + 127) - 127 = (-1 - 2) + (127 + 127 - 127)$$
$$= -3 + 127 = 124$$

Step 2. Multiplying the significands:

```
                1.000_two
        X       1.110_two
              ──────────
                0000
               1000
              1000
             1000
        ──────────────
             1110000_two
```

The product is $1.110000_{two} \times 2^{-3}$, but we need to keep it to 4 bits, so it is $1.110_{two} \times 2^{-3}$.

Step 3. Now we check the product to make sure it is normalized, and then check the exponent for overflow or underflow. The product is already normalized and, since $127 \geq -3 \geq -126$, there is no overflow or underflow. (Using the biased representation, $254 \geq 124 \geq 1$, so the exponent fits.)

Step 4.   Rounding the product makes no change:

$$1.110_{two} \times 2^{-3}$$

Step 5.   Since the signs of the original operands differ, make the sign of the product negative. Hence the product is

$$-1.110_{two} \times 2^{-3}$$

Converting to decimal to check our results:

$$-1.110_{two} \times 2^{-3} = -0.001110_{two} = -0.00111_{two}$$
$$= -7/2^5{}_{ten} = -7/32_{ten} = -0.21875_{ten}$$

The product of 0.5_{ten} and -0.4375_{ten} is indeed -0.21875_{ten}.

Floating-Point Instructions in MIPS

MIPS supports the IEEE 754 single-precision and double-precision formats with these instructions:

- Floating-point *addition, single* (add.s) and *addition, double* (add.d)
- Floating-point *subtraction, single* (sub.s) and *subtraction, double* (sub.d)
- Floating-point *multiplication, single* (mul.s) and *multiplication, double* (mul.d)
- Floating-point *division, single* (div.s) and *division, double* (div.d)
- Floating-point *comparison, single* (c.x.s) and *comparison, double* (c.x.d), where x may be *equal* (eq), *not equal* (neq), *less than* (lt), *less than or equal* (le), *greater than* (gt), or *greater than or equal* (ge)
- Floating-point *branch, true* (bc1t) and *branch, false* (bc1f)

Floating-point comparison sets a bit to true or false, depending on the comparison condition, and a floating-point branch then decides whether or not to branch, depending on the condition.

The MIPS designers decided to add separate floating-point registers—called $f0, $f1, $f2, . . .—used either for single precision or double precision. Hence they included separate loads and stores for floating-point registers: lwc1 and swc1. The base registers for floating-point data transfers remain integer registers. The MIPS code to load two single precision numbers from memory, add them, and then store the sum might look like this:

```
lwc1    $f4,x($sp)    # Load 32-bit F.P. number into F4
lwc1    $f6,y($sp)    # Load 32-bit F.P. number into F6
add.s   $f2,$f4,$f6   # F2 = F4 + F6 single precision
swc1    $f2,z($sp)    # Store 32-bit F.P. number from F2
```

A double precision register is really an even-odd pair of single precision registers, using the even register number as its name.

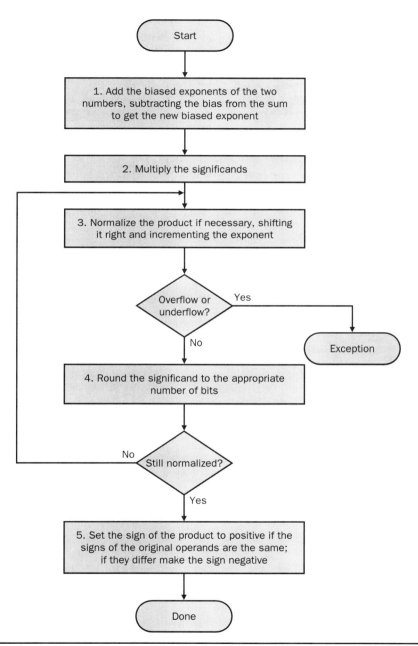

FIGURE 4.46 Floating-point multiplication. The normal path is to execute steps 3 and 4 once, but if rounding causes the sum to be unnormalized, we must repeat step 3.

**Hardware
Software
Interface**

One issue that computer designers face in supporting floating-point arithmetic is whether to use the same registers used by the integer instructions or to add a special set for floating point. Because programs normally perform integer operations and floating-point operations on different data, separating the registers will only slightly increase the number of instructions needed to execute a program. The major impact is to create a separate set of data transfer instructions to move data between floating-point registers and memory.

The benefits of separate floating-point registers are having twice as many registers without using up more bits in the instruction format, having twice the register bandwidth by having separate integer and floating-point register sets, and being able to customize registers to floating point; for example, some machines convert all sized operands in registers into a single internal format.

Figure 4.47 summarizes the floating-point portion of the MIPS architecture revealed in Chapter 4, with the additions to support floating point shown in color. Similar to Figure 3.18 on page 153 in Chapter 3, we show the encoding of these instructions in Figure 4.48.

MIPS floating-point operands

Name	Example	Comments
32 floating-point registers	$f0, $f1, $f2, . . . , $f31	MIPS floating-point registers are used in pairs for double precision numbers.
2^{30} memory words	Memory[0], Memory[4], . . . , Memory[4294967292]	Accessed only by data transfer instructions. MIPS uses byte addresses, so sequential words differ by 4. Memory holds data structures, such as arrays, and spilled registers, such as those saved on procedure calls.

MIPS floating-point assembly language

Category	Instruction	Example	Meaning	Comments
Arithmetic	FP add single	add.s $f2,$f4,$f6	$f2 = $f4 + $f6	FP add (single precision)
	FP subtract single	sub.s $f2,$f4,$f6	$f2 = $f4 − $f6	FP sub (single precision)
	FP multiply single	mul.s $f2,$f4,$f6	$f2 = $f4 × $f6	FP. multiply (single precision)
	FP divide single	div.s $f2,$f4,$f6	$f2 = $f4 / $f6	FP divide (single precision)
	FP add double	add.d $f2,$f4,$f6	$f2 = $f4 + $f6	FP add (double precision)
	FP subtract double	sub.d $f2,$f4,$f6	$f2 = $f4 − $f6	FP sub (double precision)
	FP multiply double	mul.d $f2,$f4,$f6	$f2 = $f4 × $f6	FP multiply (double precision)
	FP divide double	div.d $f2,$f4,$f6	$f2 = $f4 / $f6	FP divide (double precision)
Data transfer	load word copr. 1	lwc1 $f1,100($s2)	$f1 = Memory[$s2 + 100]	32-bit data to FP register
	store word copr. 1	swc1 $f1,100($s2)	Memory[$s2 + 100] = $f1	32-bit data to memory
Conditional branch	branch on FP true	bc1t 25	if (cond == 1) go to PC + 4 + 100	PC-relative branch if FP cond.
	branch on FP false	bc1f 25	if (cond == 0) go to PC + 4 + 100	PC-relative branch if not cond.
	FP compare single (eq,ne,lt,le,gt,ge)	c.lt.s $f2,$f4	if ($f2 < $f4) cond = 1; else cond = 0	FP compare less than single precision
	FP compare double (eq,ne,lt,le,gt,ge)	c.lt.d $f2,$f4	if ($f2 < $f4) cond = 1; else cond = 0	FP compare less than double precision

MIPS floating-point machine language

Name	Format	Example						Comments	
add.s	R	17	16	6	4	2	0	add.s	$f2,$f4,$f6
sub.s	R	17	16	6	4	2	1	sub.s	$f2,$f4,$f6
mul.s	R	17	16	6	4	2	2	mul.s	$f2,$f4,$f6
div.s	R	17	16	6	4	2	3	div.s	$f2,$f4,$f6
add.d	R	17	17	6	4	2	0	add.d	$f2,$f4,$f6
sub.d	R	17	17	6	4	2	1	sub.d	$f2,$f4,$f6
mul.d	R	17	17	6	4	2	2	mul.d	$f2,$f4,$f6
div.d	R	17	17	6	4	2	3	div.d	$f2,$f4,$f6
lwc1	I	49	20	2	100			lwc1	$f2,100($s4)
swc1	I	57	20	2	100			swc1	$f2,100($s4)
bc1t	I	17	8	1	25			bc1t	25
bc1f	I	17	8	0	25			bc1f	25
c.lt.s	R	17	16	4	2	0	60	c.lt.s $f2,$f4	
c.lt.d	R	17	17	4	2	0	60	c.lt.d $f2,$f4	
Field size		6 bits	5 bits	5 bits	5 bits	5 bits	6 bits	All MIPS instructions 32 bits	

FIGURE 4.47 MIPS floating-point architecture revealed thus far. See Appendix A, section A.10, on page A-49, for more detail.

op(31:26):								
28–26 \ 31–29	0(000)	1(001)	2(010)	3(011)	4(100)	5(101)	6(110)	7(111)
0(000)	Rfmt	Bltz/gez	j	jal	beq	bne	blez	bgtz
1(001)	addi	addiu	slti	sltiu	andi	ori	xori	lui
2(010)	TLB	FlPt						
3(011)								
4(100)	lb	lh	lwl	lw	lbu	lhu	lwr	
5(101)	sb	sh	swl	sw			swr	
6(110)	lwc0	lwc1						
7(111)	swc0	swc1						

op(31:26) = 010001 (FlPt), (rt(16:16) = 0 => c = f, rt(16:16) = 1 => c = t), rs(25:21):								
32–21 \ 25–24	0(000)	1(001)	2(010)	3(011)	4(100)	5(101)	6(110)	7(111)
0(00)	mfc1		cfc1		mtc1		ctc1	
1(01)	bc1.c							
2(10)	f = single	f = double						
3(11)								

op(31:26) = 010001 (FlPt), (f above: 01000 => f = s, 01001 => f = d), funct(5:0):								
2–0 \ 5–3	0(000)	1(001)	2(010)	3(011)	4(100)	5(101)	6(110)	7(111)
0(000)	add.f	sub.f	mul.f	div.f		abs.f	mov.f	neg.f
1(001)								
2(010)								
3(011)								
4(100)	cvt.s.f	cvt.d.f			cvt.w.f			
5(101)								
6(110)	c.f.f	c.un.f	c.eq.f	c.ueq.f	c.olt.f	c.ult.f	c.ole.f	c.ule.f
7(111)	c.sf.f	c.ngle.f	c.seq.f	c.ngl.f	c.lt.f	c.nge.f	c.le.f	c.ngt.f

FIGURE 4.48 MIPS floating-point instruction encoding. This notation gives the value of a field by row and by column. For example, in the top portion of the figure lw is found in row number 4 (100_{two} for bits 31–29 of the instruction) and column number 3 (011_{two} for bits 28–26 of the instruction), so the corresponding value of the op field (bits 31–26) is 100011_{two}. Underscore means the field is used elsewhere. For example, FlPt in row 2 and column 1 (op = 010001_{two}) is defined in the bottom part of the figure. Hence sub.f in row 0 and column 1 of the bottom section means that the funct field (bits 5–0) of the instruction) is 000001_{two} and the op field (bits 31–26) is 010001_{two}. Note that the 5-bit rs field, specified in the middle portion of the figure, determines whether the operation is single precision (f = s so rs = 10000) or double precision (f = d so rs = 10001). Similarly, bit 16 of the instruction determines if the bc1.c instruction tests for true (bit 16 = 1 =>bc1.t) or false (bit 16 = 0 =>bc1.f). Rfmt and TLB instruction encodings are found in Figure 3.18 on page 153. Instructions in color are described in Chapters 3 or 4, with Appendix A covering all instructions.

Compiling a Floating-Point C Program into MIPS Assembly Code

Example

Let's convert a temperature in Fahrenheit to Celsius:

```
float f2c (float fahr)
    {
        return ((5.0/9.0) * (fahr - 32.0));
    }
```

Assume that the floating-point argument fahr is passed in $f12 and the result should go in $f0. (Unlike integer registers, floating-point register 0 can contain a number.) What is the MIPS assembly code?

Answer

We assume that the compiler places the three floating-point constants in memory within easy reach of the global pointer $gp. The first two instructions load the constants 5.0 and 9.0 into floating-point registers:

```
f2c:
    lwc1  $f16,const5($gp)    # $f16 = 5.0 (5.0 in memory)
    lwc1  $f18,const9($gp)    # $f18 = 9.0 (9.0 in memory)
```

They are then divided to get the fraction 5.0/9.0:

```
    div.s $f16, $f16, $f18   # $f16 = 5.0 / 9.0
```

(Many compilers would divide 5.0 by 9.0 at compile time and save the single constant 5.0/9.0 in memory, thereby avoiding the divide at runtime.) Next we load the constant 32.0 and then subtract it from fahr ($f12):

```
    lwc1   $f18, const32($gp)# $f18 = 32.0
    sub.s  $f18, $f12, $f18  # $f18 = fahr - 32.0
```

Finally, we multiply the two intermediate results, placing the product in $f0 as the return result, and then return:

```
    mul.s  $f0,  $f16, $f18  # $f0 = (5/9)*(fahr - 32.0)
    jr     $ra               # return
```

Now let's perform floating-point operations on matrices, code commonly found in scientific programs.

Compiling Floating-Point C Procedure with Two-Dimensional Matrices into MIPS

Example

Most floating-point calculations are performed in double precision. Let's perform matrix multiply of X = Y * Z. Let's assume X, Y, and Z are all square matrices with 32 elements in each dimension.

```
void mm (double x[][], double y[][], double z[][])
{
    int i, j, k;

    for (i = 0; i! = 32; i = i + 1)
        for (j = 0; j! = 32; j = j + 1)
            for (k = 0; k! = 32; k = k + 1)
                x[i][j] = x[i][j] + y[i][k] * z[k][j];
}
```

The array starting addresses are parameters, so they are in $a0, $a1, and $a2. Assume that the integer variables are in $s0, $s1, and $s2, respectively. What is the MIPS assembly code for the body of the procedure?

Answer

Note that x[i][j] is used in the innermost loop above. Since the loop index is k, the index does not affect x[i][j], so we can avoid loading and storing x[i][j] each iteration. Instead, the compiler loads x[i][j] into a register outside the loop, accumulates the sum of the products of y[i][k] and z[k][j] in that same register, and then stores the sum into x[i][j] upon termination of the innermost loop.

We keep the code simpler by using the assembly language pseudoinstructions li (which loads a constant into a register), and l.d and s.d (which the assembler turns into a pair of data transfer instructions, lwc1 or swc1, to a pair of floating-point registers).

The body of the procedure starts with saving the loop termination value of 32 in a temporary register and then initializing the three *for* loop variables:

```
mm:...
        li    $t1, 32   # $t1 = 32 (row size/loop end)
        li    $s0, 0    # i = 0; initialize 1st for loop
L1:     li    $s1, 0    # j = 0; restart 2nd for loop
L2:     li    $s2, 0    # k = 0; restart 3rd for loop
```

To calculate the address of x[i][j], we need to know how a 32×32, two-dimensional array is stored in memory. As you might expect, its layout is the same as if there were 32 single-dimension arrays, each with 32 elements. So the first step is to skip over the i "single-dimensional arrays," or rows, to get the one we want. Thus we multiply the index in the first dimension by the size of the row, 32. Since 32 is a power of 2, we can use a shift instead (see page 262):

```
sll    $t2, $s0, 5    # $t2 = i * 2^5 (size of row of x)
```

Now we add the second index to select the jth element of the desired row:

```
addu  $t2, $t2, $s1  # $t2 = i * size(row) + j
```

To turn this sum into a byte index, we multiply it by the size of a matrix element in bytes. Since each element is 8 bytes for double precision, we can instead shift left by 3:

```
sll    $t2, $t2, 3    # $t2 = byte offset of [i][j]
```

Next we add this sum to the base address of x, giving the address of x[i][j], and then load the double precision number x[i][j] into $f4:

```
addu  $t2, $a0, $t2  # $t2 = byte address of x[i][j]
l.d    $f4, 0($t2)    # $f4 = 8 bytes of x[i][j]
```

The following five instructions are virtually identical to the last five: calculate the address and then load the double precision number z[k][j].

```
L3:  sll    $t0, $s2, 5    # $t0 = k * 2^5 (size of row of z)
     addu  $t0, $t0, $s1  # $t0 = k * size(row) + j
     sll    $t0, $t0, 3    # $t0 = byte offset of [k][j]
     addu  $t0, $a2, $t0  # $t0 = byte address of z[k][j]
     l.d    $f16, 0($t0)  # $f16 = 8 bytes of z[k][j]
```

Similarly, the next five instructions are like the last five: calculate the address and then load the double precision number y[i][k].

```
sll    $t2, $s0, 5    # $t0 = i * 2^5 (size of row of y)
addu  $t0, $t0, $s2  # $t0 = i * size(row) + k
sll    $t0, $t0, 3    # $t0 = byte offset of [i][k]
addu  $t0, $a1, $t0  # $t0 = byte address of y[i][k]
l.d    $f18, 0($t0)  # $f18 = 8 bytes of y[i][k]
```

Now that we have loaded all the data, we are finally ready to do some floating-point operations! We multiply elements of y and z located in registers $f18 and $f16, and then accumulate the sum in $f4.

```
mul.d $f16, $f18, $f16# $f16 = y[i][k] * z[k][j]
add.d $f4, $f4, $f16  # f4 = x[i][j] + y[i][k] * z[k][j]
```

The final block increments the index k and loops back if the index is not 32. If it is 32, and thus the end of the innermost loop, we need to store the sum accumulated in $f4 into x[i][j].

```
addiu  $s2, $s2, 1      # $k k + 1
bne    $s2, $t1, L3     # if (k != 32) go to L3
s.d    $f4, 0($t2)      # x[i][j] = $f4
```

Similarly, these final four instructions increment the index variable of the middle and outermost loops, looping back if the index is not 32 and exiting if the index is 32.

```
addiu  $s1, $s1, 1      # $j = j + 1
bne    $s1, $t1, L2     # if (j != 32) go to L2
addiu  $s0, $s0, 1      # $i = i + 1
bne    $s0, $t1, L1     # if (i != 32) go to L1
. . .
```

Elaboration: The array layout discussed in the example, called *row major order,* is used by C and many other programming languages. Fortran instead uses *column major order,* whereby the array is stored column by column.

Only 16 of the 32 MIPS floating-point registers can be used for single precision operations: $f0, $f2, $f4, . . . , $f30. Double precision is computed using pairs of these registers. The odd-numbered floating-point registers are used only to load and store the right half of 64-bit floating-point numbers. A later version of the MIPS instruction set, MIPS II, added l.d and s.d to the hardware instruction set. An even later version, MIPS IV, added indexed addressing for floating-point data transfers, removing the need for the fourth instruction of the five-instruction load sequences above.

Another reason for separate integers and floating-point registers is that microprocessors in the 1980s didn't have enough transistors to put the floating-point unit on the same chip as the integer unit. Hence the floating-point unit, including the floating-point registers, were optionally available as a second chip. Such optional accelerator chips are called *coprocessors,* and explain the acronym for floating-point loads in MIPS: lwc1 means load word to coprocessor 1, the floating-point unit. (Coprocessor 0 deals with virtual memory, described in Chapter 7.) Since the early 1990s, microprocessors have integrated floating point (and just about everything else) on chip, and hence the term "coprocessor" joins "accumulator" and "core memory" as quaint terms that date the speaker.

Elaboration: Although there are many ways to throw hardware at floating-point multiply to make it go fast, floating-point division is considerably more challenging to make fast and accurate. Slow divides in early computers led to removal of divides from many algorithms, but parallel computers have inspired rediscovery of divide-intensive algorithms that work better on these machines. Hence we may need faster divides.

One technique to leverage a fast multiplier is *Newton's iteration,* where division is recast as finding the zero of a function to find the reciprocal $1/x$, which is then multiplied by the other operand. Iteration techniques *cannot* be rounded properly without calculating many extra bits. A TI chip solves this problem by calculating an extra-precise reciprocal, and IBM relies on fused multiply-add to solve it (see section 4.9).

The *SRT division* technique instead tries to guess several quotient bits per step, using a table lookup based on the upper bits of the dividend and remainder, relying on subsequent steps to correct wrong guesses. A Cyrix chip uses this technique to generate 16 bits per step!

Accurate Arithmetic

Unlike integers, which can represent exactly every number between the smallest and largest number, floating-point numbers are normally approximations for a number they can't really represent. The reason is that an infinite variety of real numbers exists between, say, 0 and 1, but no more than 2^{53} can be represented exactly in double precision floating point. The best we can do is get the floating-point representation close to the actual number. Thus, IEEE 754 offers several modes of rounding to let the programmer pick the desired approximation.

Rounding sounds simple enough, but to round accurately requires the hardware to include extra bits in the calculation. In the preceding examples, we were vague on the number of bits that an intermediate representation can occupy, but clearly if every intermediate result had to be truncated to the exact number of digits, there would be no opportunity to round. IEEE 754, therefore, always keeps 2 extra bits on the right during intermediate calculations, called *guard* and *round*, respectively. Let's do a decimal example to illustrate the value of these extra digits.

Rounding with Guard Digits

Example

Add $2.56_{ten} \times 10^0$ to $2.34_{ten} \times 10^2$, assuming that we have three significant decimal digits. Round to the nearest decimal number with three significant decimal digits, first with guard and round digits, and then without them.

Answer

First we must shift the smaller number to the right to align the exponents, so $2.56_{ten} \times 10^0$ becomes $0.0256_{ten} \times 10^2$. Since we have guard and round digits, we are able to represent the two least significant digits when we align exponents. The guard digit holds 5 and the round digit holds 6. The sum is

$$
\begin{array}{r}
2.3400_{ten} \\
+ \quad 0.0256_{ten} \\
\hline
2.3656_{ten}
\end{array}
$$

Thus the sum is $2.3656_{ten} \times 10^2$. Since we have two digits to round, we want values 0 to 49 to round down and 51 to 99 to round up, with 50 being the tiebreaker. Rounding the sum up with three significant digits yields $2.37_{ten} \times 10^2$.

Doing this *without* guard and round digits drops two digits from the calculation. The new sum is then

$$
\begin{array}{r}
2.34_{ten} \\
+ \quad 0.02_{ten} \\
\hline
2.36_{ten}
\end{array}
$$

The answer is $2.36_{ten} \times 10^2$, off by 1 in the last digit from the sum obtained above.

Since the worst case for rounding would be when the actual number is half-way between two floating-point representations, accuracy in floating point is normally measured in terms of the number of bits in error in the least significant bits of the significand; the measure is called the number of *units in the last place*, or *ulp*. If a number was off by 2 in the least significant bits, it would be called off by 2 ulps. Provided there is no overflow, underflow, or invalid operation exceptions, IEEE 754 guarantees that the computer uses the number that is within one-half ulp.

Elaboration: Although the example above really needed just one extra bit, multiply can need two. A binary product may have one leading 0 bit, hence the normalizing step must shift the product 1 bit left. This shifts the guard digit into the least significant bit of the product, leaving the round bit to help accurately round the product.

The goal of the extra rounding bits is to allow the machine to get the same results as if the intermediate results were calculated to infinite precision and then rounded. Thus the standard has a third bit in addition to guard and round; it is set whenever there are nonzero bits to the right of the round bit. This *sticky bit* allows the computer to see the difference between $0.50 \ldots 00_{ten}$ and $0.50 \ldots 01_{ten}$ when rounding. The sticky bit may be set, for example, during addition, when the smaller number is shifted to the right.

Summary

The Big Picture below reinforces the stored-program concept from Chapter 3; the meaning of the information cannot be determined just by looking at the bits, for the same bits can represent a variety of objects. This section shows that computer arithmetic is finite and thus can disagree with natural arithmetic. For example, the IEEE 754 standard floating-point representation

$$(-1)^S \times (1 + \text{Significand}) \times 2^{(\text{Exponent} - \text{bias})}$$

is almost always an approximation of the real number. Computer systems must take care to minimize this gap between computer arithmetic and arithmetic in the real world, and programmers at times need to be aware of the implications of this approximation.

The Big Picture

Bit patterns have no inherent meaning. They may represent signed integers, unsigned integers, floating-point numbers, instructions, and so on. What is represented depends on the instruction that operates on the bits in the word.

The major difference between computer numbers and numbers in the real world is that computer numbers have limited size, hence limited precision; it's possible to calculate a number too big or too small to be represented in a word. Programmers must remember these limits and write programs accordingly.

Hardware Software Interface

In the last chapter we presented the storage classes of the programming language C (see the Hardware Software Interface section on page 140). The following table shows some of the C data types together with the MIPS data transfer instructions and instructions that operate on those types that appear in Chapters 3 and 4.

C type	Data transfers	Operations
int	lw, sw, lui	addu, addiu, subu, mult, div, and, andi, or, ori, slt, slti
unsigned int	lw, sw, lui	addu, addiu, subu, multu, divu, and, andi, or, ori, sltu, sltiu
char	lb, sb, lui	addu, addiu, subu, multu, divu, and, andi, or, ori, sltu, sltiu
bit field	lw, sw, lui	and, andi, or, ori, sll, srl
float	lwc1, swc1	add.s, sub.s, mult.s, div.s, c.eq.s, c.lt.s, c.le.s
double	lwc1, swc1	add.d, sub.d, mult.d, div.d, c.eq.d, c.lt.d, c.le.d

Elaboration: The IEEE 754 floating-point standard is filled with little widgets to help the programmer try to maintain accuracy. We'll cover a few here, but take a look at the references at the end of section 4.12 to learn more.

There are four rounding modes: always round up (toward $+\infty$), always round down (toward $-\infty$), truncate, and round to nearest even. The final mode determines what to do if the number is exactly halfway in between. The Internal Revenue Service always rounds 0.50 dollars up, possibly to the benefit of the IRS. A more equitable way would be to round up this case half the time and round down the other half. IEEE 754 says that if the least significant bit retained in a halfway case would be odd, add one; if it's even, truncate. This method always creates a 0 in the least significant bit, giving the rounding mode its name. This mode is the most commonly used.

Other features of IEEE 754 are special symbols to represent unusual events. For example, instead of interrupting on a divide by 0, software can set the result to a bit pattern representing $+\infty$ or $-\infty$; the largest exponent is reserved for these special symbols. When the programmer prints the results, the program will print an infinity symbol. (For the mathematically trained, the purpose of infinity is to form topological closure of the reals.)

IEEE 754 even has a symbol for the result of invalid operations, such as 0/0 or subtracting infinity from infinity. This symbol is *NaN*, for *Not a Number*. The purpose of NaNs is to allow programmers to postpone some tests and decisions to a later time in the program when it is convenient. To accommodate comparisons that may include NaNs, the standard includes *ordered* and *unordered* as options for compares. Hence the full MIPS instruction set has many flavors of compares to support NaNs.

Finally, in an attempt to squeeze every last bit of precision from a floating-point operation, the standard allows some numbers to be represented in unnormalized form. Rather than having a gap between 0 and the smallest normalized number, IEEE allows *denormalized numbers* (also known as *denorms* or *subnormals*). They have the same exponent as zero but a nonzero significand. They allow a number to degrade in significance until it becomes 0, called *gradual underflow*. For example, the smallest single precision normalized number is

$$1.0000\ 0000\ 0000\ 0000\ 0000\ 000_{two} \times 2^{-126}$$

but the smallest single precision denormalized number is

$$0.0000\ 0000\ 0000\ 0000\ 0000\ 001_{two} \times 2^{-126},\ \text{or}\ 1.0_{two} \times 2^{-149}$$

For double precision, the denorm gap goes from 1.0×2^{-1022} to 1.0×2^{-1074}.

The possibility of an occasional unnormalized operand has given headaches to floating-point designers who are trying to build fast floating-point units. Hence many computers cause an exception if an operand is denormalized, letting software complete the operation. Although software implementations are perfectly valid, their lower performance has lessened the popularity of denorms in portable floating-point software. Also, if programmers do not expect denorms, their programs may be surprised.

Here are the encodings of IEEE 754 floating-point numbers, with the sign bit determining the sign:

Single precision		Double precision		Object represented
Exponent	Significand	Exponent	Significand	
0	0	0	0	0
0	nonzero	0	nonzero	± denormalized number
1–254	anything	1–2046	anything	± floating-point number
255	0	2047	0	± infinity
255	nonzero	2047	nonzero	NaN (Not a Number)

4.9 Real Stuff: Floating Point in the PowerPC and 80x86

Both the PowerPC and 80x86 have regular multiply and divide instructions that operate entirely on registers, unlike the reliance on Hi and Lo in MIPS. (In fact, later versions of the MIPS instruction set have added similar instructions.)

The main differences are found in floating-point instructions. PowerPC is like MIPS except for one novel instruction and twice as many registers: PowerPC offers 32 single precision and 32 double precision floating-point registers. The 80x86 floating-point architecture, on the other hand, is completely different from all other computers in the world.

The Multiply-Add Instruction of the PowerPC

The matrix multiply on page 294 relied on a multiply operation and an add operation, which is typical of many matrix and vector operations. Hence the PowerPC has a "fused" multiply-add instruction: a single instruction reads three operands, multiplies two operands and adds the third to the product, and writes the sum in the result operand. Hence the two MIPS floating-point instructions in the matrix multiply example would be replaced by one in PowerPC. This instruction can increase peak floating-point performance.

Fused multiply-add also performs the two operations and *then* rounds, unlike separate multiply and add instructions, which would round after each operation. The instructions also calculate extra bits for intermediate results to improve accuracy. Besides being potentially faster, the extra accuracy of fused multiply-add can also be helpful for calculating divide and square root, and in software libraries that calculate at higher precision than 64 bits. In fact, PowerPC hardware uses fused multiply-add hardware to calculate divide, and accurate division was the motivation for skipping the round between the two operations.

The 80x86 Floating-Point Architecture

The Intel 8087 floating-point coprocessor was announced in 1980. This architecture extended the 8086 with about 60 floating-point instructions.

Intel provided a stack architecture with its floating-point instructions: loads push numbers onto the stack, operations find operands in the two top elements of the stacks, and stores can pop elements off the stack. Intel supplemented this stack architecture with instructions and addressing modes that allow the architecture to have some of the benefits of a register-memory model. In addition to finding operands in the top two elements of the stack, one operand can be in memory or in one of the seven registers on-chip below the top of the stack. Thus a complete stack instruction set is supplemented by a limited set of register-memory instructions.

This hybrid is still a restricted register-memory model, however, in that loads always move data to the top of the stack while incrementing the top-of-stack pointer and stores can only move the top of stack to memory. Intel uses the notation ST to indicate the top of stack, and ST(i) to represent the ith register below the top of stack.

Another novel feature of this architecture is that the operands are wider in the register stack than they are stored in memory, and all operations are performed at this wide internal precision. Unlike the maximum of 64 bits on the MIPS and PowerPC, the 80x86 floating-point operands on the stack are 80 bits wide. Numbers are automatically converted to the internal 80-bit format on a load and converted back to the appropriate size on a store. This *double extended precision* is not supported by programming languages, although it has been useful to programmers of mathematical software.

Memory data can be 32-bit (single precision) or 64-bit (double precision) floating-point numbers. The register-memory version of these instructions will then convert the memory operand to this Intel 80-bit format before performing the operation. The data transfer instructions also will automatically convert 16- and 32-bit integers to floating point, and vice versa, for integer loads and stores.

The 80x86 floating-point operations can be divided into four major classes:

1. Data movement instructions, including load, load constant, and store

2. Arithmetic instructions, including add, subtract, multiply, divide, square root, and absolute value

3. Comparison, including instructions to send the result to the integer processor so that it can branch

4. Transcendental instructions, including sine, cosine, log, and exponentiation

Figure 4.49 shows some of the 60 floating-point operations. We use the curly brackets {} to show optional variations of the basic operations: {I} means there is an integer version of the instruction, {P} means this variation will pop one operand off the stack after the operation, and {R} means reverse the order of the operands in this operation.

Not all combinations suggested by the notation are provided. Hence

        F{I}SUB{R}{P}

represents these instructions found in the 80x86:

        FSUB, FISUB, FSUBR, FISUBR, FSUBP, FSUBRP

For the integer subtract instructions, there is no pop (FISUBP) or reverse pop (FISUBRP).

Note that we get even more combinations when including the operand modes for these operations. Figure 4.50 shows the many options for floating-point add, even ignoring the integer and pop versions of the instruction.

The floating-point instructions are encoded using the ESC opcode of the 8086 and the postbyte address specifier (see Figure 3.35 on page 185). The memory operations reserve 2 bits to decide whether the operand is a 32- or 64-bit floating point or a 16- or 32-bit integer. Those same 2 bits are used in versions that do not access memory to decide whether the stack should be popped after the operation and whether the top of stack or a lower register should get the result.

Data transfer	Arithmetic	Compare	Transcendental
F{I}LD mem/ST(i)	F{I}ADD{P} mem/ST(i)	F{I}COM{P}{P}	FPATAN
F{I}ST{P} mem/ST(i)	F{I}SUB{R}{P} mem/ST(i)	F{I}UCOM{P}{P}	F2XM1
FLDPI	F{I}MUL{P} mem/ST(i)	FSTSW AX/mem	FCOS
FLD1	F{I}DIV{R}{P} mem/ST(i)		FPTAN
FLDZ	FSQRT		FPREM
	FABS		FSIN
	FRNDINT		FYL2X

FIGURE 4.49   The floating-point instructions of the 80x86. The first column shows the data transfer instructions, which move data to memory or to one of the registers below the top of the stack. The last three operations in the first column push constants on the stack: pi, 1.0, and 0.0. The second column contains the arithmetic operations described above. Note that the last three operate only on the top of stack. The third column is the compare instructions. Since there are no special floating-point branch instructions, the result of the compare must be transferred to the integer CPU via the FSTSW instruction, either into the AX register or into memory, followed by an SAHF instruction to set the condition codes. The floating-point comparison can then be tested using integer branch instructions. The final column gives the higher-level floating-point operations.

Instruction	Operands	Comment
FADD		Both operands in stack; result replaces top of stack.
FADD	ST(i)	One source operand is *i*th register below the top of stack; result replaces the top of stack.
FADD	ST(i), ST	One source operand is the top of stack; result replaces *i*th register below the top of stack.
FADD	mem32	One source operand is a 32-bit location in memory; result replaces the top of stack.
FADD	mem64	One source operand is a 64-bit location in memory; result replaces the top of stack.

FIGURE 4.50   The variations of operands for floating-point add in the 80x86.

Floating-point performance of the 80x86 family has traditionally lagged far behind other computers. It is hard to tell whether it is simply a lack of attention by Intel engineers, a disinterest by customers of PCs, if the fault lies with its architecture, or most likely some combination. We can say that many new architectures have been announced since 1980, and none have followed in Intel's footsteps.

4.10   Fallacies and Pitfalls

Thus mathematics may be defined as the subject in which we never know what we are talking about, nor whether what we are saying is true.

Bertrand Russell, *Recent Words on the Principles of Mathematics*, 1901

Arithmetic fallacies and pitfalls generally stem from the difference between the limited precision of computer arithmetic and the unlimited precision of natural arithmetic.

Fallacy: Floating-point addition is associative; that is, $x + (y + z) = (x + y) + z$.

Given the great range of numbers that can be represented in floating point, problems occur when adding two large numbers of opposite signs plus a small number. For example, suppose $x = -1.5_{ten} \times 10^{38}$, $y = 1.5_{ten} \times 10^{38}$, and $z = 1.0$, and that these are all single precision numbers. Then

$$
\begin{aligned}
x + (y + z) &= -1.5_{ten} \times 10^{38} + (1.5_{ten} \times 10^{38} + 1.0) \\
&= -1.5_{ten} \times 10^{38} + (1.5_{ten} \times 10^{38}) = 0.0 \\
(x + y) + z &= (-1.5_{ten} \times 10^{38} + 1.5_{ten} \times 10^{38}) + 1.0 \\
&= (0.0_{ten}) + 1.0 \\
&= 1.0
\end{aligned}
$$

Since floating-point numbers have limited precision and result in approximations of real results, $1.5_{ten} \times 10^{38}$ is so much larger than 1.0_{ten} that $1.5_{ten} \times 10^{38} + 1.0$ is still $1.5_{ten} \times 10^{38}$. That is why the sum of x, y, and z is 0.0 or 1.0, depending on the order of the floating-point additions, and hence floating-point add is *not* associative.

Fallacy: Just as a left shift instruction can replace an integer multiply by a power of 2, a right shift is the same as an integer division by a power of 2.

Recall that a binary number x, where xi means the ith bit, represents the number

$$\ldots + (x3 \times 2^3) + (x2 \times 2^2) + (x1 \times 2^1) + (x0 \times 2^0)$$

Shifting the bits of x right by n bits would seem to be the same as dividing by 2^n. And this *is* true for unsigned integers. The problem is with signed integers. For example, suppose we want to divide -5_{ten} by 4_{ten}; the quotient should be -1_{ten}. The two's complement representation of -5_{ten} is

$$1111\ 1111\ 1111\ 1111\ 1111\ 1111\ 1111\ 1011_{two}$$

According to this fallacy, shifting right by two should divide by 4_{ten} (2^2):

$$0011\ 1111\ 1111\ 1111\ 1111\ 1111\ 1111\ 1110_{two}$$

With a 0 in the sign bit, this result is clearly wrong. The value created by the shift right is actually $1{,}073{,}741{,}822_{ten}$ instead of -1_{ten}.

A solution would be to have an arithmetic right shift (see page 261) that extends the sign bit instead of shifting in 0s. A 2-bit arithmetic shift right of -5_{ten} produces

$$1111\ 1111\ 1111\ 1111\ 1111\ 1111\ 1111\ 1110_{two}$$

The result is -2_{ten} instead of -1_{ten}; close, but no cigar.

The PowerPC, however, does have a fast shift instruction (*shift right algebraic*) that in conjunction with a special add (add with carry) gives the same answer as dividing by a power of 2.

Pitfall: The MIPS instruction add immediate unsigned `addiu` *sign-extends its 16-bit immediate field.*

Despite its name, `addiu` is used to add constants to signed integers when we don't care about overflow. MIPS has no subtract immediate instruction and negative numbers need sign extension, so the MIPS architects decided to sign-extend the immediate field.

Fallacy: Only theoretical mathematicians care about floating-point accuracy.

Newspaper headlines of November 1994 prove this statement is a fallacy (see Figure 4.51). The following is the inside story behind the headlines.

The Pentium uses a standard floating-point divide algorithm that generates multiple quotient bits per step, using the most significant bits of divisor and dividend to guess the next 2 bits of the quotient. The guess is taken from a look-

FIGURE 4.51   A sampling of newspaper and magazine articles from November 1994, including the *New York Times*, *San Jose Mercury News*, *San Francisco Chronicle*, and *Infoworld*. The Pentium floating-point divide bug even made the "Top 10 List" of the *David Letterman Late Show* on television. Intel eventually took a $300 million write-off to replace the buggy chips.

up table containing –2, –1, 0, +1, or +2. The guess is multiplied by the divisor and subtracted from the remainder to generate a new remainder. Like nonrestoring division (see Exercise 4.54), if a previous guess gets too large a remainder, the partial remainder is adjusted in a subsequent pass.

Evidently there were five elements of the table from the 80486 that Intel thought could never be accessed, and they optimized the PLA to return 0 instead of 2 in these situations on the Pentium. Intel was wrong: while the first 11 bits were always correct, errors would show up occasionally in bits 12 to 52, or the 4th to 15th decimal digits.

The following is a time line of the Pentium bug morality play:

■ *July 1994:* Intel discovers the bug in the Pentium. The actual cost to fix the bug was several hundred thousand dollars. Following normal bug fix procedures, it will take months to make the change, reverify, and put the corrected chip into production. Intel planned to put good chips into production in January 1995, estimating that 3 to 5 million Pentiums would be produced with the bug.

- *September 1994:* A math professor at Lynchburg College in Virginia, Thomas Nicely, discovers the bug. After calling Intel technical support and getting no official reaction, he posts his discovery on the Internet. It quickly gained a following, and some pointed out that even small errors become big when multiplying by big numbers: the fraction of people with a rare disease times the population of Europe, for example, might lead to the wrong estimate of the number of sick people.

- *November 7, 1994: Electronic Engineering Times* puts the story on its front page, which is soon picked up by other newspapers.

- *November 22, 1994:* Intel issues a press release, calling it a "glitch." The Pentium "can make errors in the ninth digit. . . . Even most engineers and financial analysts require accuracy only to the fourth or fifth deci- mal point. Spreadsheet and word processor users need not worry. . . . There are maybe several dozen people that this would affect. So far, we've only heard from one. . . . [Only] theoretical mathemati- cians (with Pentium machines purchased before the summer) should be concerned." What irked many was that customers were told to describe their application to Intel, and then *Intel* would decide whether or not their application merited a new Pentium without the divide bug.

- *December 5, 1994:* Intel claims the flaw happens once in 27,000 years for the typical spreadsheet user. Intel assumes a user does 1000 divides per day and multiplies the error rate assuming floating-point numbers are random, which is one in 9 billion, and then gets 9 million days, or 27,000 years. Things begin to calm down, despite Intel neglecting to explain why a typical customer would access floating-point numbers randomly.

- *December 12, 1994:* IBM Research Division disputes Intel's calculation of the rate of errors (you can access this article by visiting *www.mkp.com/books_catalog/cod/links.htm*). IBM claims that common spreadsheet programs, recalculating for 15 minutes a day, could produce Pentium-related errors as often as once every 24 days. IBM assumes 5000 divides per second, 15 minutes, yielding 4.2 million di- vides per day, and does not assume random distribution of numbers, in- stead calculating the chances as one in 100 million. As a result, IBM immediately stops shipment of all IBM personal computers based on the Pentium. Things heat up again for Intel.

- *December 21, 1994:* Intel releases the following, signed by Intel's presi- dent, chief executive officer, chief operating officer, and chairman of the board: "We at Intel wish to sincerely apologize for our handling of the recently publicized Pentium processor flaw. The Intel Inside symbol means that your computer has a microprocessor second to none in qual- ity and performance. Thousands of Intel employees work very hard to ensure that this is true. But no microprocessor is ever perfect. What Intel continues to believe is technically an extremely minor problem has taken on a life of its own. Although Intel firmly stands behind the quality of the current version of the Pentium processor, we recognize that many users have concerns. We want to resolve these concerns. Intel will exchange the current version of the Pentium processor for an updated version, in which this floating-point divide flaw is corrected, for any owner who requests it, free of charge anytime during the life of their computer."Analysts estimate that this recall cost Intel $300 million.

This story brings up a few points for everyone to ponder. How much cheaper would it have been to fix the bug in July 1994? What was the cost to repair the damage to Intel's reputation? And what is the corporate responsibility in disclosing bugs in a product so widely used and relied upon as a microprocessor?

In April 1997 another floating-point bug was revealed in the Pentium Pro and Pentium II microprocessors. When the floating-point-to-integer store instructions (`fist`, `fistp`) encounter a negative floating-point number that is too large to fit in a 16- or 32-bit word after being converted to integer, they set the wrong bit in the FPO status word (precision exception instead of invalid operation exception). To Intel's credit, this time they publicly acknowledged the bug and offered a software patch to get around it—quite a different reaction from what they did in 1994.

4.11   Concluding Remarks

Computer arithmetic is distinguished from paper-and-pencil arithmetic by the constraints of limited precision. This limit may result in invalid operations through calculating numbers larger or smaller than the predefined limits. Such anomalies, called "overflow" or "underflow," may result in exceptions or interrupts, emergency events similar to unplanned subroutine calls. Chapter 5 discusses exceptions in more detail.

Floating-point arithmetic has the added challenge of being an approximation of real numbers, and care needs to be taken to ensure that the computer number selected is the representation closest to the actual number. The challenges of imprecision and limited representation are part of the inspiration for the field of numerical analysis.

Over the years, computer arithmetic has become largely standardized, greatly enhancing the portability of programs. Two's complement binary integer arithmetic and IEEE 754 binary floating-point arithmetic are found in the vast majority of computers sold today. For example, every desktop computer sold since this book was first printed follows these conventions.

A side effect of the stored-program computer is that bit patterns have no inherent meaning. The same bit pattern may represent a signed integer, unsigned integer, floating-point number, instruction, and so on. It is the instruction that operates on the word that determines its meaning.

With the explanation of computer arithmetic in this chapter comes a description of much more of the MIPS instruction set. One point of confusion is the instructions covered in these chapters versus instructions executed by MIPS chips versus the instructions accepted by MIPS assemblers. The next two figures try to make this clear.

Figure 4.52 lists the MIPS instructions covered in Chapters 3 and 4. We call the set of instructions on the left-hand side of the figure the *MIPS core*. The instructions on the right we call the *MIPS arithmetic core*. On the left of Figure 4.53 are the instructions the MIPS processor executes that are not found in Figure 4.52. We call the full set of hardware instructions *MIPS I*. On the right of Figure 4.53 are the instructions accepted by the assembler that are not part of MIPS I. We call this set of instructions *Pseudo MIPS*.

MIPS core instructions	Name	Format	MIPS arithmetic core	Name	Format
add	add	R	multiply	mult	R
add immediate	addi	I	multiply unsigned	multu	R
add unsigned	addu	R	divide	div	R
add immediate unsigned	addiu	I	divide unsigned	divu	R
subtract	sub	R	move from Hi	mfhi	R
subtract unsigned	subu	R	move from Lo	mflo	R
and	and	R	move from system control (EPC)	mfc0	R
and immediate	andi	I	floating-point add single	add.s	R
or	or	R	floating-point add double	add.d	R
or immediate	ori	I	floating-point subtract single	sub.s	R
shift left logical	sll	R	floating-point subtract double	sub.d	R
shift right logical	srl	R	floating-point multiply single	mul.s	R
load upper immediate	lui	I	floating-point multiply double	mul.d	R
load word	lw	I	floating-point divide single	div.s	R
store word	sw	I	floating-point divide double	div.d	R
load byte unsigned	lbu	I	load word to floating-point single	lwc1	I
store byte	sb	I	store word to floating-point single	swc1	I
branch on equal	beq	I	branch on floating-point true	bc1t	I
branch on not equal	bne	I	branch on floating-point false	bc1f	I
jump	j	J	floating-point compare single	c.x.s	R
jump and link	jal	J	(x = eq, neq, lt, le, gt, ge)		
jump register	jr	R	floating-point compare double	c.x.d	R
set less than	slt	R	(x = eq, neq, lt, le, gt, ge)		
set less than immediate	slti	I			
set less than unsigned	sltu	R			
set less than immediate unsigned	sltiu	I			

FIGURE 4.52 The MIPS instruction set covered so far. This book concentrates on the instructions in the left column.

Figure 4.54 gives the popularity of the MIPS instructions for two programs: gcc and spice. All instructions are listed that were responsible for at least 0.5% of the instructions executed. The table following summarizes that information:

Instruction subset	gcc	spice
MIPS core	95%	45%
MIPS arithmetic core	0%	49%
Remaining MIPS I	5%	6%

Note that although programmers and compiler writers may use MIPS I to have a richer menu of options, MIPS core instructions dominate gcc execution, and the integer core plus arithmetic core dominate spice.

Remaining MIPS I	Name	Format	Pseudo MIPS	Name	Format
exclusive or ($rs \oplus rt$)	xor	R	move	move	rd,rs
exclusive or immediate	xori	I	absolute value	abs	rd,rs
nor ($\neg(rs \vee rt)$)	nor	R	not ($\neg rs$)	not	rd,rs
shift right arithmetic	sra	R	negate (signed or unsigned)	neg*s*	rd,rs
shift left logical variable	sllv	R	rotate left	rol	rd,rs,rt
shift right logical variable	srlv	R	rotate right	ror	rd,rs,rt
shift right arith. variable	srav	R	mult. & don't check oflw (signed or uns.)	mul*s*	rd,rs,rt
shift right arith. variable	srav	R	multiply & check oflw (signed or uns.)	mulo*s*	rd,rs,rt
move to Hi	mthi	R	divide and check overflow	div	rd,rs,rt
move to Lo	mtlo	R	divide and don't check overflow	divu	rd,rs,rt
load halfword	lh	I	remainder (signed or unsigned)	rem*s*	rd,rs,rt
load halfword unsigned	lhu	I	load immediate	li	rd,imm
store halfword	sh	I	load address	la	rd,addr
load word left (unaligned)	lwl	I	load double	ld	rd,addr
load word right (unaligned)	lwr	I	store double	sd	rd,addr
store word left (unaligned)	swl	I	unaligned load word	ulw	rd,addr
store word right (unaligned)	swr	I	unaligned store word	usw	rd,addr
branch on less than zero	bltz	I	unaligned load halfword (signed or uns.)	ulh*s*	rd,addr
branch on less or equal zero	blez	I	unaligned store halfword	ush	rd,addr
branch on greater than zero	bgtz	I	branch	b	Label
branch on $\geq$ zero	bgez	I	branch on equal zero	beqz	rs,L
branch on $\geq$ zero and link	bgezal	I	branch on $\geq$ (signed or unsigned)	bge*s*	rs,rt,L
branch on < zero and link	bgezal	I	branch on > (signed or unsigned)	bgt*s*	rs,rt,L
jump and link register	jalr	R	branch on $\leq$ (signed or unsigned)	ble*s*	rs,rt,L
return from exception	rfe	R	branch on < (signed or unsigned)	blt*s*	rs,rt,L
system call	syscall	R	set equal	seq	rd,rs,rt
break (cause exception)	break	R	set not equal	sne	rd,rs,rt
move from FP to integer	mfc1	R	set greater or equal (signed or unsigned)	sge*s*	rd,rs,rt
move to FP from integer	mtc1	R	set greater than (signed or unsigned)	sgt*s*	rd,rs,rt
FP move (underline{s} or underline{d})	mov.*f*	R	set less or equal (signed or unsigned)	sle*s*	rd,rs,rt
FP absolute value (underline{s} or underline{d})	abs.*f*	R	set less than (signed or unsigned)	sle*s*	rd,rs,rt
FP negate (underline{s} or underline{d})	neg.*f*	R	load to floating point (underline{s} or underline{d})	l.*f*	rd,addr
FP convert (underline{w}, underline{s}, or underline{d})	cvt.*f.f*	R	store from floating point (underline{s} or underline{d})	s.*f*	rd,addr
FP compare un (underline{s} or underline{d})	c.xn.*f*	R			

FIGURE 4.53   Remaining MIPS I and "Pseudo MIPS" instruction sets. Appendix A describes all these instructions. f means single (s) and double precision (d) versions of the floating-point instruction, and s means signed and unsigned (u) versions.

Core MIPS	Name	gcc	spice	Arithmetic core + MIPS I	Name	gcc	spice
add	add	0%	0%	FP add double	add.d	0%	4%
add immediate	addi	0%	0%	FP subtract double	sub.d	0%	3%
add unsigned	addu	9%	10%	FP multiply double	mul.d	0%	5%
add immediate unsigned	addiu	17%	1%	FP divide double	div.d	0%	2%
subtract unsigned	subu	0%	1%	load word to FP single	l.s	0%	24%
and	and	1%	0%	store word to FP single	s.s	0%	9%
and immediate	andi	2%	1%	branch on FP true	bclt	0%	1%
shift left logical	sll	5%	5%	branch on FP false	bclf	0%	1%
shift right logical	srl	0%	1%	FP compare double	c.x.d	0%	1%
load upper immediate	lui	2%	6%	move to FP	mtc1	0%	2%
load word	lw	21%	7%	move from FP	mfc2	0%	2%
store word	sw	12%	2%	convert float integer	cut	0%	1%
load byte	lb	1%	0%	shift right arithmetic	sra	2%	0%
store byte	sb	1%	0%	load half	lh	1%	0%
branch on equal (zero)	beq	9%	3%	branch less than zero	bltz	1%	0%
branch on not equal (zero)	bne	8%	2%	branch greater or equal zero	bgez	1%	0%
jump and link	jal	1%	1%	branch less or equal zero	blez	0%	1%
jump register	jr	1%	1%				
set less than	slt	2%	0%				
set less than immediate	slti	1%	0%				
set less than unsigned	sltu	1%	0%				
set less than imm. uns.	sltiu	1%	0%				

FIGURE 4.54 The frequency of the MIPS instructions for two programs, gcc and spice. Calculated from "pixie" output of the full MIPS I. (Pixie is an instruction measurement tool from MIPS.) All instructions that accounted for at least 0.5% of the instructions executed in either gcc or spice are included in the table. Thus the integer multiply and divide instructions are not listed because they were responsible for less than 0.5% of the instructions executed. Pseudoinstructions are converted into MIPS I before execution, and hence do not appear here.

For the rest of the book, we concentrate on the MIPS core instructions—the integer instruction set excluding multiply and divide—to make the explanation of computer design easier. As we can see, the MIPS core includes the most popular MIPS instructions, and be assured that understanding a computer that runs the MIPS core will give you sufficient background to understand even more ambitious machines.

4.12   Historical Perspective and Further Reading

Gresham's Law ("Bad money drives out Good") for computers would say, "The Fast drives out the Slow even if the Fast is wrong."

W. Kahan, 1992

At first it may be hard to imagine a subject of less interest than the correctness of computer arithmetic or its accuracy, and harder still to understand why a subject so old and mathematical should be so controversial. Computer arithmetic is as old as computing itself, and some of the subject's earliest notions, like the economical reuse of registers during serial multiplication and division, still command respect today. Maurice Wilkes [1985] recalled a conversation about that notion during his visit to the United States in 1946, before the earliest stored-program machine had been built:

> . . . a project under von Neumann was to be set up at the Institute of Advanced Studies in Princeton. . . . Goldstine explained to me the principal features of the design, including the device whereby the digits of the multiplier were put into the tail of the accumulator and shifted out as the least significant part of the product was shifted in. I expressed some admiration at the way registers and shifting circuits were arranged . . . and Goldstine remarked that things of that nature came very easily to von Neumann.

There is no controversy here; it can hardly arise in the context of exact integer arithmetic so long as there is general agreement on what integer the correct result should be. However, as soon as approximate arithmetic enters the picture, so does controversy, as if one person's "negligible" must be another's "everything."

The First Dispute

Floating-point arithmetic kindled disagreement before it was ever built. John von Neumann was aware of Konrad Zuse's proposal for a computer in Germany in 1939 that was never built, probably because the floating point made it appear too complicated to finish before the Germans expected World War II to end. Hence von Neumann refused to include it in the machine he built at Princeton. In an influential report coauthored in 1946 with H. H. Goldstine and A. W. Burks, he gave the arguments for and against floating point. In favor:

> . . . to retain in a sum or product as many significant digits as possible and . . . to free the human operator from the burden of estimating and inserting into a problem "scale factors"—multiplication constants which serve to keep numbers within the limits of the machine.

Floating point was excluded for several reasons:

There is, of course, no denying the fact that human time is consumed in arranging for the introduction of suitable scale factors. We only argue that the time consumed is a very small percentage of the total time we will spend in preparing an interesting problem for our machine. The first advantage of the floating point is, we feel, somewhat illusory. In order to have such a floating point, one must waste memory capacity which could otherwise be used for carrying more digits per word. It would therefore seem to us not at all clear whether the modest advantages of a floating binary point offset the loss of memory capacity and the increased complexity of the arithmetic and control circuits.

The argument seems to be that most bits devoted to exponent fields would be bits wasted. Experience has proved otherwise.

One software approach to accommodate reals without floating-point hardware was called *floating vectors*; the idea was to compute at runtime one scale factor for a whole array of numbers, choosing the scale factor so that the array's biggest number would barely fill its field. By 1951, James H. Wilkinson had used this scheme extensively for matrix computations. The problem proved to be that a program might encounter a very large value, and hence the scale factor must accommodate these rare large numbers. The common numbers would thus have many leading 0s, since all numbers had to use a single scale factor. Accuracy was sacrificed because the least significant bits had to be lost on the right to accommodate leading 0s. This wastage became obvious to practitioners on early machines that displayed all their memory bits as dots on cathode ray tubes (like TV screens) because the loss of precision was visible. Where floating point deserved to be used, no practical alternative existed.

Thus true floating-point hardware became popular because it was useful. By 1957, floating-point hardware was almost ubiquitous. A decimal floating-point unit was available for the IBM 650; and soon the IBM 704, 709, 7090, 7094 . . . series would offer binary floating-point hardware for double as well as single precision.

As a result, everybody had floating point, but every implementation was different.

Diversity versus Portability

Since roundoff introduces some error into almost all floating-point operations, to complain about another bit of error seems picayune. So for 20 years nobody complained much that those operations behaved a little differently on different machines. If software required clever tricks to circumvent those idiosyncrasies and finally deliver results correct in all but the last several bits, such tricks were deemed part of the programmer's art. For a long time, matrix computations mystified most people who had no notion of error analysis; perhaps this continues to be true. That may be why people are still surprised that numerically stable matrix computations depend upon the quality of arithmetic in so few places, far fewer than are generally supposed. Books by Wilkinson and widely used software packages like Linpack and Eispack sustained a false impression, widespread in the early 1970s, that a modicum of skill sufficed to produce *portable* numerical software.

Portable here means that the software is distributed as source code in some standard language to be compiled and executed on practically any commercially significant machine, and that it will then perform its task as well as any other program performs that task on that machine. Insofar as numerical software has often been thought to consist entirely of machine-independent mathematical formulas, its portability has often been taken for granted; the mistake in that presumption will become clear shortly.

Packages like Linpack and Eispack cost so much to develop—over a hundred dollars per line of Fortran delivered—that they could not have been developed without U.S. government subsidy; their portability was a precondition for that subsidy. But nobody thought to distinguish how various components contributed to their cost. One component was algorithmic—devise an algorithm that deserves to work on at least one computer despite its roundoff and over/underflow limitations. Another component was the software engineering effort required to achieve and confirm portability to the diverse computers commercially significant at the time; this component grew more onerous as ever more diverse floating-point arithmetics blossomed in the 1970s.

And yet scarcely anybody realized how much that diversity inflated the cost of such software packages.

A Backward Step

Early evidence that somewhat different arithmetics could engender grossly different software development costs was presented in 1964. It happened at a meeting of SHARE, the IBM mainframe users' group, at which IBM announced System/360, the successor to the 7094 series. One of the speakers described the tricks he had been forced to devise to achieve a level of quality for the S/360 library that was not quite so high as he had previously achieved for the 7094.

Part of the trouble could have been foretold by von Neumann had he still been alive. In 1948 he and Goldstine had published a lengthy error analysis so difficult and so pessimistic that hardly anybody paid attention to it. It did predict correctly, however, that computations with larger arrays of data would probably fall prey to roundoff more often. IBM S/360s had bigger memories than 7094s, so data arrays could grow bigger, and they did. To make matters worse, the S/360s had narrower single precision words (32 bits versus 36) and used a cruder arithmetic (hexadecimal or base 16 versus binary or base 2) with consequently poorer worst-case precision (21 significant bits versus 27) than old 7094s. Consequently, software that had almost always provided (barely) satisfactory accuracy on 7094s too often produced inaccurate results when run on S/360s. The quickest way to recover adequate accuracy was to replace old codes' single precision declarations with double precision before recompilation for the S/360. This practice exercised S/360 double precision far more than had been expected.

The early S/360s' worst troubles were caused by lack of a guard digit in double precision. This lack showed up in multiplication as a failure of identities like $1.0 * x = x$ because multiplying x by 1.0 dropped x's last hexadecimal digit (4 bits). Similarly, if x and y were very close but had different exponents, subtraction dropped off the last digit of the smaller operand before computing $x - y$. This last aberration in double precision undermined a precious theorem that single precision then (and now) honored: If $1/2 \leq x/y \leq 2$, then no rounding error can occur when $x - y$ is computed; it must be computed exactly.

Innumerable computations had benefited from this minor theorem, most often unwittingly, for several decades before its first formal announcement and proof. We had been taking all this stuff for granted.

The identities and theorems about exact relationships that persisted, despite roundoff, with reasonable implementations of approximate arithmetic were not appreciated until they were lost. Previously, all that had been thought to matter were precision (how many significant digits were carried) and range (the spread between over/underflow thresholds). Since the S/360s' double precision had more precision and wider range than the 7094s', software was expected to continue to work at least as well as before. But it didn't.

Programmers who had matured into program managers were appalled at the cost of converting 7094 software to run on S/360s. A small subcommittee of SHARE proposed improvements to the S/360 floating point. This committee was surprised and grateful to get a fair part of what they asked for from IBM, including all-important guard digits. By 1968, these had been retrofitted to S/360s in the field at considerable expense; worse than that was customers' loss of faith in IBM's infallibility (a lesson learned by Intel 30 years later). IBM employees who can remember the incident still shudder.

The People Who Built the Bombs

Seymour Cray was associated for decades with the CDC and Cray computers that were, when he built them, the world's biggest and fastest. He always understood what his customers wanted most: *speed*. And he gave it to them even if, in so doing, he also gave them arithmetics more "interesting" than anyone else's. Among his customers have been the great government laboratories like those at Livermore and Los Alamos, where nuclear weapons were designed. The challenges of "interesting" arithmetics were pretty tame to people who had to overcome Mother Nature's challenges.

Perhaps all of us could learn to live with arithmetic idiosyncrasy if only one computer's idiosyncrasies had to be endured. Instead, when accumulating different computers' different anomalies, software dies the Death of a Thousand Cuts. Here is an example from Cray's machines:

```
if (x == 0.0)    y = 17.0 else y = z/x
```

Could this statement be stopped by a divide-by-zero error? On a CDC 6600 it could. The reason was a conflict between the 6600's adder, where x was compared with 0.0, and the multiplier and divider. The adder's comparison examined x's leading 13 bits, which sufficed to distinguish zero from normal nonzero floating-point numbers x. The multiplier and divider examined only 12 leading bits. Consequently, tiny numbers existed that were nonzero to the adder but zero to the multiplier and divider! To avoid disasters with these tiny numbers, programmers learned to replace statements like the one above by

```
if (1.0*x == 0.0)    y = 17.0 else y = z/x
```

But this statement is unsafe to use in would-be portable software because it malfunctions obscurely on other computers designed by Cray, the ones marketed by Cray Research, Inc. If x is so huge that $2.0 * x$ would overflow, then $1.0 * x$ may overflow too! Overflow happens because Cray computers check the product's exponent *before* the product's exponent has been normalized, just to save the delay of a single AND gate.

In case you think the statement above is safe to use now for portable software, since computers of the CDC 6600 era are no longer commercially significant, you should be warned that it can lead to overflow on a Cray computer even if z is almost as tiny as x; the trouble here is that the Cray computes not z/x but $z * (1/x)$, and the reciprocal can overflow even though the desired quotient is unexceptionable. A similar difficulty troubles the Intel i860s used in its massively parallel computers. The would-be programmer of portable code faces countless dilemmas like these whenever trying to program for the full range of existing computers.

Rounding error anomalies that are far worse than the over/underflow anomaly just discussed also affect Cray computers. The worst error comes from the lack of a guard digit in add/subtract, an affliction of IBM S/360s. Further bad luck for software is occasioned by the way Cray economized his multiplier; about one-third of the bits that normal multiplier arrays generate have been left out of his multipliers because they would contribute less than a unit to the last place of the final Cray-rounded product. Consequently, a Cray's multiplier errs by almost a bit more than might have been expected. This error is compounded when division takes three multiplications to improve an approximate reciprocal of the divisor and then multiply the numerator by it. Square root compounds a few more multiplication errors.

The fast way drove out the slow, even though the fast was occasionally slightly wrong.

Making the World Safe for Floating Point, or Vice Versa

William Kahan was an undergraduate at the University of Toronto in 1953 when he learned to program its Ferranti-Manchester Mark-I computer. Because he entered the field early, Kahan became acquainted with a wide range of devices and a large proportion of the personalities active in computing; the numbers of both were small at that time. He has performed computations on slide rules, desktop mechanical calculators, tabletop analog differential analyzers, and so on; he used all but the earliest electronic computers and calculators mentioned in this book.

Kahan's desire to deliver reliable software led to an interest in error analysis that intensified during two years of postdoctoral study in England, where he became acquainted with Wilkinson. In 1960, he resumed teaching at Toronto, where an IBM 7090 had been acquired, and was granted free rein to tinker with its operating system, Fortran compiler, and runtime library. (He denies that he ever came near the 7090 hardware with a soldering iron but admits asking to do so.) One story from that time illuminates how misconceptions and numerical anomalies in computer systems can incur awesome hidden costs.

A graduate student in aeronautical engineering used the 7090 to simulate the wings he was designing for short takeoffs and landings. He knew such a wing would be difficult to control if its characteristics included an abrupt onset of stall, but he thought he could avoid that. His simulations were telling him otherwise. Just to be sure that roundoff was not interfering, he had repeated many of his calculations in double precision and gotten results much like those in single; his wings had stalled abruptly in both precisions. Disheartened, the student gave up.

Meanwhile Kahan replaced IBM's logarithm program (ALOG) with one of his own, which he hoped would provide better accuracy. While testing it, Kahan reran programs using the new version of ALOG. The student's results changed significantly; Kahan approached him to find out what had happened.

The student was puzzled. Much as the student preferred the results produced with the new ALOG—they predicted a gradual stall—he knew they must be wrong because they disagreed with his double precision results. The discrepancy between single and double precision results disappeared a few days later when a new release of IBM's double precision arithmetic software for the 7090 arrived. (The 7090 had no double precision hardware.) He went on to write a thesis about it and to build the wings; they performed as predicted. But that is not the end of the story.

In 1963, the 7090 was replaced by a faster 7094 with double precision floating-point hardware but with otherwise practically the same instruction set as the 7090. Only in double precision and only when using the new hardware did the wing stall abruptly again. A lot of time was spent to find out why. The 7094 hardware turned out, like the superseded 7090 software and the subsequent early S/360s, to lack a guard bit in double precision. Like so many programmers on those machines and on Cray's, the student discovered a trick to compensate for the lack of a guard digit; he wrote the expression $(0.5 - x) + 0.5$ in place of $1.0 - x$. Nowadays we would blush if we had to explain why such a trick might be necessary, but it solved the student's problem.

Meanwhile the lure of California was working on Kahan and his family; they came to Berkeley and he to the University of California. An opportunity presented itself in 1974 when accuracy questions induced Hewlett-Packard's calculator designers to call in a consultant. The consultant was Kahan, and his work dramatically improved the accuracy of HP calculators, but that is another story. Fruitful collaboration with congenial co-workers, however, fortified him for the next and crucial opportunity.

It came in 1976, when John F. Palmer at Intel was empowered to specify the "best possible" floating-point arithmetic for all of Intel's product line. The 8086 was imminent, and an 8087 floating-point coprocessor for the 8086 was contemplated. (A *coprocessor* is simply an additional chip that accelerates a portion of the work of a processor; in this case, it accelerated floating-point computation.)

Palmer had obtained his Ph.D. at Stanford a few years before and knew whom to call for counsel of perfection—Kahan. They put together a design that obviously would have been impossible only a few years earlier and looked not quite possible at the time. But a new Israeli team of Intel employees led by Rafi Navé felt challenged to prove their prowess to Americans and leaped at an opportunity to put something impossible on a chip—the 8087.

By now, floating-point arithmetics that had been merely diverse among mainframes had become chaotic among microprocessors, one of which might be host to a dozen varieties of arithmetic in ROM firmware or software. Robert G. Stewart, an engineer prominent in IEEE activities, got fed up with this anarchy and proposed that the IEEE draft a decent floating-point standard. Simultaneously, word leaked out in Silicon Valley that Intel was going to put on one chip some awesome floating point well beyond anything its competitors had in mind. The competition had to find a way to slow Intel down, so they formed a committee to do what Stewart requested.

Meetings of this committee began in late 1977 with a plethora of competing drafts from innumerable sources and dragged on into 1985 when IEEE Standard 754 for Binary Floating Point was made official. The winning draft was very close to one submitted by Kahan, his student Jerome T. Coonen, and Harold S. Stone, a professor visiting Berkeley at the time. Their draft was based on the Intel design, with Intel's permission of course, as simplified by Coonen. Their harmonious combination of features, almost none of them new, had at the outset attracted more support within the committee and from outside experts like Wilkinson than any other draft, but they had to win nearly unanimous support within the committee to win official IEEE endorsement, and that took time.

The First IEEE 754 Chips

In 1980, Intel became tired of waiting and released the 8087 for use in the IBM PC. The floating-point architecture of the companion 8087 had to be retrofitted into the 8086 opcode space, making it inconvenient to offer two operands per instruction as found in the rest of the 8086. Hence the decision for one operand per instruction using a stack: "The designer's task was to make a Virtue of this Necessity." (Kahan's [1990] history of the stack architecture selection for the 8087 is entertaining reading.)

Rather than the classical stack architecture, which has no provision for avoiding common subexpressions from being pushed and popped from memory into the top of the stack found in registers, Intel tried to combine a flat register file with a stack. The reasoning was that the restriction of the top of stack as one operand was not so bad since it only required the execution of an FXCH instruction (which swapped registers) to get the same result as a two-operand instruction, and FXCH was much faster than the floating-point operations of the 8087.

Since floating-point expressions are not that complex, Kahan reasoned that eight registers meant that the stack would rarely overflow. Hence he urged that the 8087 use this hybrid scheme with the provision that stack overflow or stack underflow would interrupt the 8086 so that interrupt software could give the illusion to the compiler writer of an unlimited stack for floating-point data.

The Intel 8087 was implemented in Israel, and 7500 miles and 10 time zones made communication difficult from California. According to Palmer and Morse (*The 8087 Primer*, J. Wiley, New York, 1984, p. 93):

> *Unfortunately, nobody tried to write a software stack manager until after the 8087 was built, and by then it was too late; what was too complicated to perform in hardware turned out to be even worse in software. One thing found lacking is the ability to conveniently determine if an invalid operation is indeed due to a stack overflow. . . . Also lacking is the ability to restart the instruction that caused the stack overflow . . .*

The result is that the stack exceptions are too slow to handle in software. As Kahan [1990] says:

> *Consequently, almost all higher-level languages' compilers emit inefficient code for the 80x87 family, degrading the chip's performance by typically 50% with spurious stores and loads necessary simply to preclude stack over/underflow. . . .*

> *I still regret that the 8087's stack implementation was not quite so neat as my original intention. . . . If the original design had been realized, compilers today would use the 80x87 and its descendents more efficiently, and Intel's competitors could more easily market faster but compatible 80x87 imitations.*

In 1982, Motorola announced its 68881, which found a place in Sun 3s and Macintosh IIs; Apple had been a supporter of the proposal from the beginning. Another Berkeley graduate student, George S. Taylor, had soon designed a high-speed implementation of the proposed standard for an early supermini-computer (ELXSI 6400). The standard was becoming de facto before its final draft's ink was dry.

An early rush of adoptions gave the computing industry the false impression that IEEE 754, like so many other standards, could be implemented easily by following a standard recipe. Not true. Only the enthusiasm and ingenuity of its early implementors made it look easy.

In fact, to implement IEEE 754 correctly demands extraordinarily diligent attention to detail; to make it run fast demands extraordinarily competent ingenuity of design. Had the industry's engineering managers realized this, they might not have been so quick to affirm that, as a matter of policy, "We conform to all applicable standards."

IEEE 754 Today

Today the computing industry is enmeshed in a host of standards that evolve continuously as technology changes. The floating-point standards IEEE 754/854 (they are practically the same) stand in somewhat splendid isolation only because nobody wishes to repeat the protracted wrangling that surrounded their birth, when, with unprecedented generosity, the representatives of hardware interests acceded to the demands of those few who represented the interests of mathematical and numerical software.

Unfortunately, the compiler-writing community was not represented adequately in the wrangling, and some of the features didn't balance language and compiler issues against other points. That community has been slow to make IEEE 754's unusual features available to the applications programmer. Humane exception handling is one such unusual feature; directed rounding another. Without compiler support, these features have atrophied.

The successful parts of IEEE 754 are that it is a widely implemented standard with a common floating-point format, it requires minimum accuracy to one-half ulp in the least significant bit, and that operations must be commutative.

At present, IEEE 754/854 have been implemented to a considerable degree of fidelity in at least part of the product line of every North American computer manufacturer. The only significant exceptions are the DEC VAX, IBM S/370 descendants, and Cray Research vector supercomputers, and all three are being replaced by compliant machines. Even Cray Research, now a division of Silicon Graphics, announced that successors to the T90 vector computer will conform "to some degree" to ease the transfer of data files and portable software between Crays and the desktop computers through which Cray users have come to access their machines nowadays.

In 1989, the Association for Computing Machinery, acknowledging the benefits conferred upon the computing industry by IEEE 754, honored Kahan with the Turing Award. On accepting it, he thanked his many associates for their diligent support, and his adversaries for their blunders.

So . . . not all errors are bad.

To Probe Further

If you are interested in learning more about floating point, two publications by David Goldberg [1991, 1995] are good starting points; they abound with pointers to further reading. Several of the stories told above come from Kahan [1972, 1983]. The latest word on the state of the art in computer arithmetic is often found in the *Proceedings* of the latest IEEE-sponsored Symposium on Computer Arithmetic, held every two years; the 13th was held in 1997.

Burks, A. W., H. H. Goldstine, and J. von Neumann [1946]. "Preliminary discussion of the logical design of an electronic computing instrument," *Report to the U.S. Army Ordnance Dept.*, p. 1; also in *Papers of John von Neumann*, W. Aspray and A. Burks, eds., MIT Press, Cambridge, MA, and Tomash Publishers, Los Angeles, 97–146, 1987.

This classic paper includes arguments against floating-point hardware.

Goldberg, D. [1991]. "What every computer scientist should know about floating-point arithmetic," *ACM Computing Surveys* 23(1), 5–48.

Another good introduction to floating-point arithmetic by the same author, this time with emphasis on software.

Goldberg, D. [1995]. "Computer arithmetic," *Appendix A of Computer Architecture: A Quantitative Approach*, second edition, J. L. Hennessy and D. A. Patterson, Morgan Kaufmann Publishers, San Francisco.

A more advanced introduction to integer and floating-point arithmetic, with emphasis on hardware. It covers sections 4.6–4.8 of this book in just 10 pages, leaving another 45 pages for advanced topics.

Kahan, W. [1972]. "A survey of error-analysis," in *Info. Processing 71* (Proc. IFIP Congress 71 in Ljubljana), vol. 2, pp. 1214–39, North-Holland Publishing, Amsterdam.

This survey is a source of stories on the importance of accurate arithmetic.

Kahan, W. [1983]. "Mathematics written in sand," *Proc. Amer. Stat. Assoc. Joint Summer Meetings of 1983, Statistical Computing Section*, pp. 12–26.

The title refers to silicon and is another source of stories illustrating the importance of accurate arithmetic.

Kahan, W. [1990]. "On the advantage of the 8087's stack," unpublished course notes, Computer Science Division, University of California at Berkeley.

What the 8087 floating-point architecture could have been.

Kahan, W. [1997]. Available via a link to Kahan's homepage at *www.mkp.com/books_catalog/cod/links.htm.*

A collection of memos related to floating point, including "Beastly Numbers" (another less famous Pentium bug), "Notes on the IEEE Floating Point Arithmetic" (including comments on how some features are atrophying), and "The Baleful Effects of Computing Benchmarks" (on the unhealthy preoccupation on speed versus correctness, accuracy, ease of use, flexibility, . . .).

Koren, I. [1993]. *Computer Arithmetic Algorithms*, Prentice Hall, Englewood Cliffs, NJ.

A textbook aimed at seniors and first-year graduate students that explains fundamental principles of basic arithmetic, as well as complex operations such as logarithmic and trigonometric functions.

Wilkes, M. V. [1985]. *Memoirs of a Computer Pioneer*, MIT Press, Cambridge, MA.

This computer pioneer's recollections include the derivation of the standard hardware for multiply and divide developed by von Neumann.

4.13   Key Terms

These terms reflect the key ideas in the chapter. Check the Glossary for definitions of the terms you are unsure of.

AND gate	floating point	round
AND operation	guard	scientific notation
arithmetic logic unit (ALU)	hexadecimal	significand
biased notation	least significant bit	single precision
Booth's algorithm	most significant bit	sticky bit
divisor	normalized	underflow
double precision	overflow	units in the last place (ulp)
exclusive OR gate	quotient	
exponent	remainder	

4.14   Exercises

Never give in, never give in, never, never, never—in nothing, great or small, large or petty—never give in.

Winston Churchill, address at Harrow School, 1941

4.1 [3] <§4.2> Convert 512_{ten} into a 32-bit two's complement binary number.

4.2 [3] <§4.2> Convert $-1,023_{ten}$ into a 32-bit two's complement binary number.

4.3 [5] <§4.2> Convert $-4,000,000_{ten}$ into a 32-bit two's complement binary number.

4.4 [5] <§4.2> What decimal number does this two's complement binary number represent: $1111\,1111\,1111\,1111\,1111\,1110\,0000\,1100_{two}$?

4.5 [5] <§4.2> What decimal number does this two's complement binary number represent: $1111\,1111\,1111\,1111\,1111\,1111\,1111\,1111_{two}$?

4.6 [5] <§4.2> What decimal number does this two's complement binary number represent: $0111\,1111\,1111\,1111\,1111\,1111\,1111\,1111_{two}$?

4.7 [5] <§4.2> What binary number does this hexadecimal number represent: $7fff\,fffa_{hex}$? What decimal number does it represent?

4.8 [5] <§4.2> What hexadecimal number does this binary number represent: $1100\,1010\,1111\,1110\,1111\,1010\,1100\,1110_{two}$?

4.9 [5] <§4.2> Why doesn't MIPS have a subtract immediate instruction?

4.10 [10] <§4.2> Find the shortest sequence of MIPS instructions to determine the absolute value of a two's complement integer. Convert this instruction (accepted by the MIPS assembler):

```
abs     $t2,$t3
```

This instruction means that register $t2 has a copy of register $t3 if register $t3 is positive, and the two's complement of register $t3 if $t3 is negative. (Hint: It can be done with three instructions.)

4.11 [10] <§4.2> Two friends, Harry and David, are arguing. Harry says, "All integers greater than zero and exactly divisible by six have exactly two 1s in their binary representation." David disagrees. He says, "No, but all such numbers have an even number of 1s in their representation." Do you agree with Harry or with David, or with neither? (Hint: Look for counterexamples.)

4.12 [15] <§4.4> Consider the following code used to implement the instruction

```
sllv $s0, $s1, $s2
```

which uses the least significant 5 bits of the value in register $s2 to specify the amount register $s1 should be shifted left:

```
            .data
mask:       .word  0xfffff83f
            .text
start:      lw     $t0, mask
            lw     $s0, shifter
            and    $s0,$s0,$t0
            andi   $s2,$s2,0x1f
            sll    $s2,$s2,6
            or     $s0,$s0,$s2
            sw     $s0, shifter
shifter:    sll    $s0,$s1,0
```

Add comments to the code and write a paragraph describing how it works. Note that the two lw instructions are pseudoinstructions that use a label to specify a memory address that contains the word of data to be loaded. Why do you suppose that writing "self-modifying code" such as this is a bad idea (and oftentimes not actually allowed)?

4.13 [10] <§4.2> If A is a 32-bit address, typically an instruction sequence such as

```
lui $t0, A_upper
ori $t0, $t0, A_lower
lw $s0, 0($t0)
```

can be used to load the word at A into a register (in this case, $s0). Consider the following alternative, which is more efficient:

```
lui $t0, A_upper_adjusted
lw $s0, A_lower($t0)
```

Describe how A_upper is adjusted to allow this simpler code to work. (Hint: A_upper needs to be adjusted because A_lower will be sign-extended.)

4.14 [15] <§§3.4, 4.2, 4.8> The Big Picture on page 299 mentions that bits have no inherent meaning. Given the bit pattern:

1000 1111 1110 1111 1100 0000 0000 0000

what does it represent, assuming that it is

    a. a two's complement integer?

    b. an unsigned integer?

    c. a single precision floating-point number?

    d. a MIPS instruction?

You may find Figures 3.18 (page 153), 4.48 (page 292), and A.18 (page A-50) useful.

4.15 [10] <§§4.2, 4.4, 4.8> This exercise is similar to Exercise 4.14, but this time use the bit pattern

0000 0000 0000 0000 0000 0000 0000 0000

4.16 [10] <§4.3> One of the differences between Sun's SPARC architecture and the MIPS architecture we've been studying is that the load word instruction on the SPARC can specify the address either as the sum of two registers'

contents or as one register's contents plus a constant offset (i.e., the way MIPS does). The paper "An analysis of MIPS and SPARC instruction set utilization on the SPEC benchmarks" (R. F. Cmelik, S. I. Kong, D. R. Ditzel, and E. J. Kelly, *Fourth International Conference on Architectural Support for Programming Languages and Operating Systems,* Santa Clara, CA, April 1991) reports that on the SPARC, the gcc benchmark has 15% of its loads use the register + register version (with neither register being $zero). Assume that the same would be true on the MIPS, if it were modified to have this extra addressing option for lw instructions. Using the data from Figure 4.54, what percentage of gcc's instructions could be eliminated with this architectural modification? Why?

4.17 [10] <§4.3> Find the shortest sequence of MIPS instructions to determine if there is a carry out from the addition of two registers, say, registers $t3 and $t4. Place a 0 or 1 in register $t2 if the carry out is 0 or 1, respectively. (Hint: It can be done in two instructions.)

4.18 [15] <§4.3> {Ex. 4.17} Find the shortest sequence of MIPS instructions to perform double precision integer addition. Assume that one 64-bit, two's complement integer is in registers $t4 and $t5 and another is in registers $t6 and $t7. The sum is to be placed in registers $t2 and $t3. In this example, the most significant word of the 64-bit integer is found in the even-numbered registers, and the least significant word is found in the odd-numbered registers. (Hint: It can be done in four instructions.)

4.19 [15] <§4.3> Suppose that all of the conditional branch instructions except beq and bne were removed from the MIPS instruction set along with slt and all of its variants (slti, sltu, sltui). Show how to perform

```
slt $t0, $s0, $s1
```

using the modified instruction set in which slt is not available. (Hint: It requires more than two instructions.)

4.20 [10] <§4.4> The following MIPS instruction sequence could be used to implement a new instruction that has two register operands. Give the instruction a name and describe what it does. Note that register $t0 is being used as a temporary.

```
srl  $s1, $s1, 1    #
sll  $t0, $s0, 31   # These 4 instructions accomplish
srl  $s0, $s0, 1    # "new $s0 $s1"
or   $s1, $s1, $t0  #
```

4.21 [5] <§4.4> Instead of using a special hardware multiplier, it is possible to multiply using shift and add instructions. This is particularly attractive when multiplying by small constants. Suppose we want to put five times the value of $s0 into $s1, ignoring any overflow that may occur. Show a minimal sequence of MIPS instructions for doing this without using a multiply instruction.

4.22 [15] <§4.4> Some computers have explicit instructions to extract an arbitrary field from a 32-bit register and to place it in the least significant bits of a register. The figure below shows the desired operation:

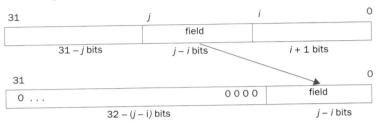

Find the shortest sequence of MIPS instructions that extracts a field for the constant values $i = 7$ and $j = 19$ from register $s0 and places it in register $s1. (Hint: It can be done in two instructions.)

4.23 [15] <§4.5> The ALU supported set on less than (slt) using just the sign bit of the adder. Let's try a set on less than operation using the values -7_{ten} and 6_{ten}. To make it simpler to follow the example, let's limit the binary representations to 4 bits: 1001_{two} and 0110_{two}.

$$1001_{two} - 0110_{two} = 1001_{two} + 1010_{two} = 0011_{two}$$

This result would suggest that $-7 > 6$, which is clearly wrong. Hence we must factor in overflow in the decision. Modify the 1-bit ALU in Figure 4.17 on page 238 to handle slt correctly. Make your changes on a photocopy of this figure to save time.

4.24 [20] <§4.6> Find the shortest sequence of MIPS instructions to perform double precision integer multiplication. Try to do it in 35 instructions or less. Assume that one 64-bit, *unsigned* integer is in registers $t4 and $t5 and another is in registers $t6 and $t7. The 128-bit product is to be placed in registers $t0, $t1, $t2, and $t3. In this example, the most significant word is found in the lower-numbered registers, and the least significant word is found in the higher-numbered registers. (Hint: Write out the formula for $(a \times 2^{32} + b) \times (c \times 2^{32} + d)$.)

4.25 [5] <§4.8> Show the IEEE 754 binary representation for the floating-point number 10_{ten} in single and double precision.

4.26 [5] <§4.8> This exercise is similar to Exercise 4.25, but this time replace the number 10_{ten} with 10.5_{ten}.

4.27 [10] <§4.8> This exercise is similar to Exercise 4.25, but this time replace the number 10_{ten} with 0.1_{ten}.

4.28 [10] <§4.8> This exercise is similar to Exercise 4.25, but this time replace the number 10_{ten} with the decimal fraction $-2/3$.

4.29 [10] <§4.8> Write a simple C program that inputs a floating-point number and shows its bit representation in hexadecimal.

4.30 [10] <§4.8> Write a simple C++ program that inputs a floating-point number and shows its bit representation in hexadecimal.

4.31 [10] <§4.8> A single precision IEEE number is stored in memory at address X. Write a sequence of MIPS instructions to multiply the number at X by 2 and store the result back at X. Accomplish this without using any floating-point instructions (don't worry about overflow).

4.32 [10] <§4.11> For the program gcc (Figure 4.54 on page 311), find the 10 most frequently executed MIPS instructions. List them in order of popularity, from most used to least used. Show the rank, name, and percentage of instructions executed for each instruction. If there is a tie for a given rank, list all instructions that tie with the same rank, even if this results in more than 10 instructions.

4.33 [10] <§4.11> This exercise is similar to Exercise 4.32, but this time replace the program gcc with the program spice.

4.34 <§4.11> {Ex. 4.32, 4.33} These questions examine the relative frequency of instructions in different programs.

a. [5] Which instructions are found both in the answer to Exercise 4.32 and in the answer to Exercise 4.33?

b. [5] What percentage of gcc instructions executed is due to the instructions identified in Exercise 4.34a?

c. [5] What percentage of gcc instructions executed is due to the instructions identified in Exercise 4.32?

d. [5] What percentage of spice instructions executed is due to the instructions identified in Exercise 4.34a?

e. [5] What percentage of spice instructions executed is due to the instructions identified in Exercise 4.33?

4.35 [10] <§4.11> {Ex. 4.32–4.34} If you were designing a machine to execute the MIPS instruction set, what are the five instructions that you would try to make as fast as possible, based on the answers to Exercises 4.32 through 4.34? Give your rationale.

4.36 [15] <§§2.3, 4.11> Using Figure 4.54 on page 311, calculate the average clock cycles per instruction (CPI) for the program gcc. Figure 4.55 gives the average CPI per instruction category, taking into account cache misses and other effects. Assume that instructions omitted from the table have a CPI of 1.0.

Instruction category	Average CPI
Loads and stores	1.4
Conditional branch	1.8
Jumps	1.2
Integer multiply	10.0
Integer divide	30.0
Floating-point add and subtract	2.0
Floating-point multiply, single precision	4.0
Floating-point multiply, double precision	5.0
Floating-point divide, single precision	12.0
Floating-point divide, double precision	19.0

FIGURE 4.55   CPI for MIPS instruction categories.

4.37 [15] <§§2.3, 4.11> This exercise is similar to Exercise 4.36, but this time replace the program gcc with the program spice.

4.38 [2 weeks] Write a simulator for a subset of the MIPS instruction set using MIPS instructions and the SPIM simulator described in Appendix A. Your simulator should execute hand-assembled programs that are located in the data segment of the SPIM simulator and should use $v0 and $v1 for input and output. Other portions of the data segment can be used for storing the memory contents and register values of your virtual machine. Your implementation can use any of the MIPS instructions, but your simulator need only support a smaller subset of the instruction set (e.g., the instructions appearing in Chapters 5 and 6). (Additional details regarding this assignment are available at *www.mkp.com/cod2e.htm*.)

4.39 [1 week] {Ex. 4.38} Add an exception handler to the simulator you developed for Exercise 4.38. Your simulator should generate a simulated exception if a misaligned word is accessed via an `lw`, `sw`, or `jr` instruction. The exception handler should print out an error message identifying the offending address (within the simulation) and then realign the access, perform the instruction, and resume executing the simulated program. (Additional details regarding this assignment are available at *www.mkp.com/cod2e.htm*.)

In More Depth

Logical Instructions

The full MIPS instruction set has two more logical operations not mentioned thus far: xor and nor. The operation xor stands for exclusive OR, and nor stands for not OR. The table that follows defines these operations on a bit-by-bit basis. These instructions will be useful in the following two exercises.

A	B	A xor B	A nor B
0	0	0	1
0	1	1	0
1	0	1	0
1	1	0	0

4.40 [15] <§4.4> Show the minimal MIPS instruction sequence for a new instruction called swap that exchanges two registers. After the sequence completes, the Destination register has the original value of the Source register, and the Source register has the original value of the Destination register. Convert this instruction:

```
swap $s0,$s1
```

The hard part is that this sequence *must use only these two registers!* (Hint: It can be done in three instructions if you use the new logical instructions. What is the value of (A xor B xor A)?)

4.41 [5] <§4.4> Show the minimal MIPS instruction sequence for a new instruction called not that takes the one's complement of a Source register and places it in a Destination register. Convert this instruction (accepted by the MIPS assembler):

```
not $s0,$s1
```

(Hint: It can be done in one instruction if you use the new logical instructions.)

4.42 [20] <§4.5> A simple check for overflow during addition is to see if the CarryIn to the most significant bit is *not* the same as the CarryOut of the most significant bit. Prove that this check is the same as in Figure 4.4 on page 222.

4.43 [10] <§4.5> Draw the gates for the Sum bit of an adder, given the equation on page 234.

4.44 [5] <§4.5> Rewrite the equations on page 247 for a carry-lookahead logic for a 16-bit adder using a new notation. First use the names for the CarryIn signals of the individual bits of the adder. That is, use c4, c8, c12, . . . instead of C1, C2, C3, ... Also, let $P_{i,j}$ mean a propagate signal for bits i to j, and $G_{i,j}$ mean a generate signal for bits i to j. For example, the equation

$$C2 = G1 + (P1 \cdot G0) + (P1 \cdot P0 \cdot c0)$$

can be rewritten as

$$c8 = G_{7,4} + (P_{7,4} \cdot G_{3,0}) + (P_{7,4} \cdot P_{3,0} \cdot c0)$$

This more general notation is useful in creating wider adders.

4.45 [15] <§4.5> {Ex. 4.44} Write the equations for the carry-lookahead logic for a *64-bit* adder using the new notation from Exercise 4.44 and using 16-bit adders as building blocks. Include a drawing similiar to Figure 4.24 in your solution.

4.46 [10] <§4.5> Now calculate the relative performance of adders. Assume that hardware corresponding to any equation containing only OR or AND terms, such as the equations for pi and gi on page 242, takes one time unit T. Equations that consist of the OR of several AND terms, such as the equations for c1, c2, c3, and c4 on page 243, would thus take two time units, 2T, because it would take T to produce the AND terms and then an additional T to produce the result of the OR. Calculate the numbers and performance ratio for 4-bit adders for both ripple carry and carry lookahead. If the terms in equations are further defined by other equations, then add the appropriate delays for those intermediate equations, and continue recursively until the actual input bits of the adder are used in an equation. Include a drawing of each adder labeled with the calculated delays and the path of the worst-case delay highlighted.

4.47 [15] <§4.5> This exercise is similar to Exercise 4.46, but this time calculate the relative speeds of a 16-bit adder using ripple carry only, ripple carry of 4-bit groups that use carry lookahead, and the carry-lookahead scheme on page 242.

4.48 [15] <§4.5> {Ex. 4.45} This exercise is similar to Exercises 4.46 and 4.47, but this time calculate the relative speeds of a 64-bit adder using ripple carry only, ripple carry of 4-bit groups that use carry lookahead, ripple carry of 16-bit groups that use carry lookahead, and the carry-lookahead scheme from Exercise 4.45.

4.49 [10] <§4.5> There are times when we want to add a collection of numbers together. Suppose you wanted to add four 4-bit numbers (A,B, E, F) using 1-bit full adders. Let's ignore carry lookahead for now. You would likely connect the 1-bit adders in the organization in the top of Figure 4.56. Below the traditional organization is a novel organization of full adders. Try adding four numbers using both organizations to convince yourself that you get the same answer.

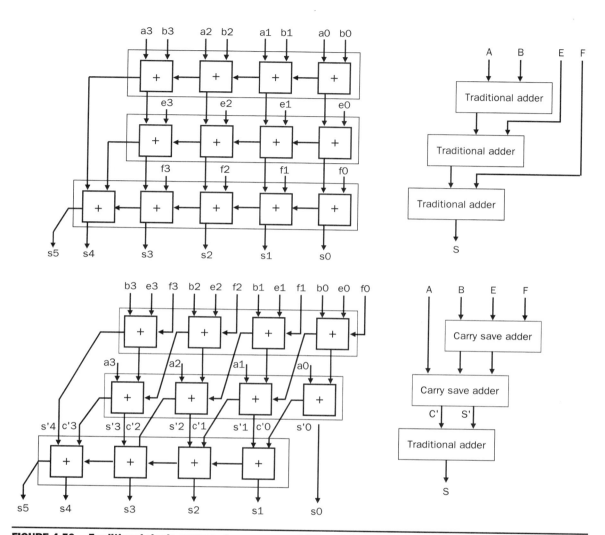

FIGURE 4.56   Traditional ripple carry and carry save addition of four 4-bit numbers. The details are shown on the left, with the individual signals in lowercase, and the corresponding higher-level blocks are on the right, with collective signals in uppercase. Note that the sum of four n-bit numbers can take $n+2$ bits.

4.50 [5] <§4.5> {Ex. 4.49} Assume that the time delay through each 1-bit adder is 2T. Calculate the time of adding four 4-bit numbers to the organization at the top versus the organization in the bottom in Figure 4.56.

In More Depth

Carry Save Adders

Exercises 4.49 and 4.50 motivate an organization that uses the 1-bit adder in Figure 4.10 on page 232 in a way it was not intended. Although this piece of hardware is simple and fast, the problem comes from trying to get the CarryIn signal calculated in a timely fashion across several adders.

We can think of the adder instead as a hardware device that can add three inputs together (ai, bi, ci) and produce two outputs (s, $ci+1$). When we are just adding two numbers together, there is little we can do with this observation, but when we are adding more than two operands, it is possible to reduce the cost of the carry. The idea is to form two independent sums, called S' (sum bits) and C' (carry bits). At the end of the process, we need to add C' and S' together using a normal adder. This technique of delaying carry propagation until the end of a sum of numbers is called *carry save addition*. The block drawing on the lower right of Figure 4.56 shows the organization, with two levels of carry save adders connected by a single normal adder.

4.51 [10] <§4.5> {Ex. 4.47, 4.50} Calculate the delays to add four 16-bit numbers using full carry-lookahead adders versus carry save with a carry-lookahead adder forming the final sum. (The time unit T in Exercises 4.46 and 4.50 is the same.)

4.52 [20] <§4.5, 4.6> {Ex. 4.47} Perhaps the most likely case of adding many numbers at once in a computer would be when trying to multiply more quickly by using many adders to add many numbers in a single clock cycle. Compared to the multiply algorithm in Figure 4.32 on page 258, a carry save scheme with many adders could multiply more than 10 times faster.

This exercise estimates the cost and speed of a combinational multiplier to multiply two positive 16-bit numbers. Assume that you have 16 intermediate terms M15, M14, . . . , M0, called *partial products*, that contain the multiplicand ANDed with multiplier bits m15, m14, . . . , m0.

The idea is to use carry save adders to reduce the n operands into $2/3n$ in parallel groups of three, and do this repeatedly until you get two large numbers to add together with a traditional adder.

First show the block organization of the 16-bit carry save adders to add these 16 terms, as shown on the right in Figure 4.56. Then calculate the delays to add these 16 numbers. Compare this time to the iterative multiplication scheme in Figure 4.32 on page 258 but only assume 16 iterations using a 16-bit adder that has full carry lookahead whose speed was calculated in Exercise 4.47.

4.53 [30] <§4.6> The original reason for Booth's algorithm was to reduce the number of operations by avoiding operations when there were strings of 0s and 1s. Revise the algorithm on page 260 to look at 3 bits at a time and compute the product 2 bits at a time. Fill in the following table to determine the 2-bit Booth encoding:

Current bits		Previous bit	Operation	Reason
a_{i+1}	a_i	a_{i-1}		
0	0	0		
0	0	1		
0	1	0		
0	1	1		
1	0	0		
1	0	1		
1	1	0		
1	1	1		

Assume that you have both the multiplicand and 2 × multiplicand already in registers. Explain the reason for the operation on each line, and show a 6-bit example that runs faster using this algorithm. (Hint: Try dividing to conquer; see what the operations would be in each of the eight cases in the table using a 2-bit Booth algorithm, and then optimize the pair of operations.)

4.54 [30] <§4.6, 4.7> The division algorithm in Figure 4.40 on page 270 is called *restoring division*, since each time the result of subtracting the divisor from the dividend is negative you must add the divisor back into the dividend to restore the original value. Recall that shift left is the same as multiplying by two. Let's look at the value of the left half of the Remainder again, starting with step 3b of the divide algorithm and then going to step 2:

$$(\text{Remainder} + \text{Divisor}) \times 2 - \text{Divisor}$$

This value is created from restoring the Remainder by adding the Divisor, shifting the sum left, and then subtracting the Divisor. Simplifying the result we get

$$\text{Remainder} \times 2 + \text{Divisor} \times 2 - \text{Divisor} = \text{Remainder} \times 2 + \text{Divisor}$$

Based on this observation, write a *nonrestoring division* algorithm using the notation of Figure 4.40 that does not add the Divisor to the Remainder in step 3b. Show that your algorithm works by dividing $0000\ 0111_{two}$ by 0010_{two}.

4.55 [5] <§4.8> Add $6.42_{ten} \times 10^1$ to $9.51_{ten} \times 10^2$, assuming that you have only three significant digits, first with guard and round digits and then without them.

4.56 [5] <§4.8> This exercise is similar to Exercise 4.55, but this time use the numbers $8.76_{ten} \times 10^1$ and $1.47_{ten} \times 10^2$.

4.57 [25] <§4.8> Derive the floating-point algorithm for division as we did for addition and multiplication on pages 280 through 288. First divide $1.110_{ten} \times 10^{10}$ by $1.100_{ten} \times 10^{-5}$, showing the same steps that we did in the example starting on page 282. Then derive the floating-point division algorithm using a format similar to the multiplication algorithm in Figure 4.46 on page 289.

4.58 [30] <§4.8> The elaboration on page 300 explains the four rounding modes of IEEE 754 and the extra bit, called the *sticky bit*, needed in addition to the 2 bits called *guard* and *round*. Guard is the first bit, round is the second bit, and sticky represents whether the remaining bits are 0 or not. Fill in the following table with logical equations that are functions of guard (g), round (r), and sticky (s) for the result of a floating-point addition that creates Sum. Let p be the proper number of bits in the significand for a given precision and Sum_p be the pth most significant bit of Sum. A blank box means that the p most significant bits of the sum are correctly rounded. If you place an equation in a box, a false equation means that the p bits are correctly rounded; a true equation means add 1 to the pth most significant bit of Sum.

Rounding mode	Sum $\geq$ 0	Sum < 0
Toward $-\infty$		
Toward $+\infty$		
Truncate		
Nearest even		

4.59 [30] <§4.8> The elaboration on page 300 mentions that IEEE 754 has two special symbols that are floating-point operands: infinity and Not a Number (NaN). There are also small numbers called *denorms*, which are not normalized. Because these special symbols and numbers are not used very frequently, implementations that employ a mix of both hardware and software techniques are sometimes used. For example, instead of using complicated hardware to handle these special cases, an exception is generated and they are handled in software. Many implementation options exist, each of which has unique performance characteristics. Your task is to benchmark several different machines for floating-point operations as the operands vary from normal numbers to these special cases. Be sure to state your conclusions by comparing the performance of different machines with one another and describing their similarities and differences. What impact are your results likely to have on software designers who must choose whether or not to make use of the special features in the IEEE 754 standard?

4.60 [30] <§4.5> If you have access to a computer containing a MIPS processor, write a loop in assembly language that sets registers $k0 ($26) and $k1 ($27) to an initial value, and then loop for several seconds, checking the contents of these registers. Print the values if they change. See the elaboration on page 225 for an explanation of why they change. Can you find a reason for the particular values you observe?

The Processor: Datapath and Control

In a major matter,
no details are small.

French Proverb

The Five Classic Components of a Computer

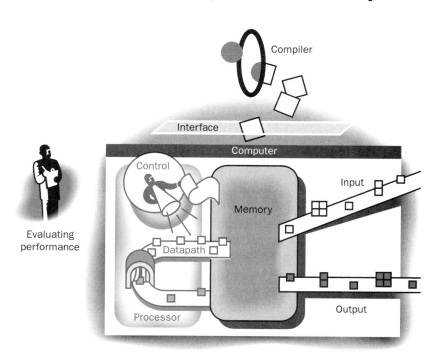

5.1 | Introduction

In Chapter 2, we saw that the performance of a machine was determined by three key factors: instruction count, clock cycle time, and clock cycles per instruction (CPI). The compiler and the instruction set architecture, which we examined in Chapters 3 and 4, determine the instruction count required for a given program. However, both the clock cycle time and the number of clock cycles per instruction are determined by the implementation of the processor. In this chapter, we construct the datapath and control unit for two different implementations of the MIPS instruction set.

We will be designing an implementation that includes a subset of the core MIPS instruction set:

- The memory-reference instructions load word (lw) and store word (sw)
- The arithmetic-logical instructions add, sub, and, or, and slt
- The instructions branch equal (beq) and jump (j), which we add last

This subset does not include all the integer instructions (for example, multiply and divide are missing), nor does it include any floating-point instructions. However, the key principles used in creating a datapath and designing the control will be illustrated. The implementation of the remaining instructions is similar.

In examining the implementation, we will have the opportunity to see how the instruction set architecture determines many aspects of the implementation, and how the choice of various implementation strategies affects the clock rate and CPI for the machine. Many of the key design principles introduced in Chapter 3 can be illustrated by looking at the implementation, such as the guidelines *Make the common case fast* and *Simplicity favors regularity*. In addition, most concepts used to implement the MIPS subset in this chapter and the next are the same basic ideas that are used to construct a broad spectrum of computers, from high-performance machines to general-purpose microprocessors to special-purpose processors, which are used increasingly in products ranging from VCRs to automobiles.

An Overview of the Implementation

In Chapters 3 and 4, we looked at the core MIPS instructions, including the integer arithmetic-logical instructions, the memory-reference instructions, and the branch instructions. Much of what needs to be done to implement these instructions is the same, independent of the exact class of instruction. For every instruction, the first two steps are identical:

1. Send the program counter (PC) to the memory that contains the code and fetch the instruction from that memory.

2. Read one or two registers, using fields of the instruction to select the registers to read. For the load word instruction we need to read only one register, but most other instructions require that we read two registers.

After these two steps, the actions required to complete the instruction depend on the instruction class. Fortunately, for each of the three instruction classes (memory-reference, arithmetic-logical, and branches), the actions are largely the same, independent of the exact opcode.

Even across different instruction classes there are some similarities. For example, all instruction classes use the arithmetic-logical unit (ALU) after reading the registers. The memory-reference instructions use the ALU for an address calculation, the arithmetic-logical instructions for the operation execution, and branches for comparison. As we can see, the simplicity and regularity of the instruction set simplifies the implementation by making the execution of many of the instruction classes similar.

After using the ALU, the actions required to complete the different instruction classes differ. A memory-reference instruction will need to access the memory either to write data for a store or read data for a load. An arithmetic-logical instruction must write the data from the ALU back into a register. Lastly, for a branch instruction, we may need to change the next instruction address based on the comparison.

Figure 5.1 shows the high-level view of a MIPS implementation. In the remainder of the chapter, we refine this view to fill in the details, which requires that we add further functional units, increase the number of connections between units, and, of course, add a control unit to control what actions are taken for different instruction classes. Before we begin to create a more complete implementation, we need to discuss a few principles of logic design.

A Word about Logic Conventions and Clocking

To discuss the design of a machine, we must decide how the logic implementing the machine will operate and how the machine is clocked. This section reviews a few key ideas in digital logic that we will use extensively in this chapter. If you have little or no background in digital logic, you will find it helpful to read through Appendix B before continuing. Section B.9 presents the key terms introduced in Appendix B and is useful as a quick check-up if you want to review your logic design background.

When designing logic, it is often convenient for the designer to change the mapping between a logically true or false signal and the high or low voltage level. Thus, in some parts of a design, a signal that is logically asserted may actually be an electrically low signal, while in others an electrically high signal is asserted. To maintain consistency, we will use the word *asserted* to indicate a signal that is logically high and *assert* to specify that a signal should be driven logically high.

The functional units in the MIPS implementation consist of two different types of logic elements: elements that operate on data values and elements that contain state. The elements that operate on data values are all *combinational*, which means that their outputs depend only on the current inputs. Given the same input, a combinational element always produces the same output. The ALU shown in Figure 5.1 and discussed in detail in Chapter 4 is a combinational element. Given a set of inputs, it always produces the same output because it has no internal storage.

Other elements in the design are not combinational, but instead contain *state*. An element contains state if it has some internal storage. We call these elements *state elements* because, if we pulled the plug on the machine, we could restart it by loading the state elements with the values they contained before

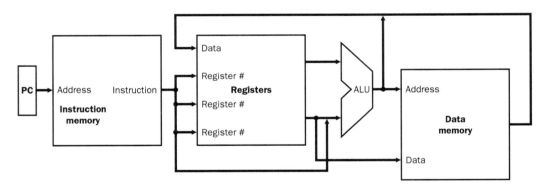

FIGURE 5.1   An abstract view of the implementation of the MIPS subset showing the major functional units and the major connections between them. All instructions start by using the program counter to supply the instruction address to the instruction memory. After the instruction is fetched, the register operands used by an instruction are specified by fields of that instruction. Once the register operands have been fetched, they can be operated on to compute a memory address (for a load or store), to compute an arithmetic result (for an integer arithmetic-logical instruction), or a compare (for a branch). If the instruction is an arithmetic-logical instruction, the result from the ALU must be written to a register. If the operation is a load or store, the ALU result is used as an address to either store a value from the registers or load a value from memory into the registers. The result from the ALU or memory is written back into the register file. Branches require the use of the ALU output to determine the next instruction address, which requires some control logic, as we will see.

we pulled the plug. Furthermore, if we saved and restored the state elements, it would be as if the machine had never lost power. Thus, these state elements completely characterize the machine. In Figure 5.1, the instruction and data memories as well as the registers are all examples of state elements.

A state element has at least two inputs and one output. The required inputs are the data value to be written into the element, and the clock, which determines when the data value is written. The output from a state element provides the value that was written in an earlier clock cycle. For example, one of the logically simplest state elements is a D-type flip-flop (see Appendix B), which has exactly these two inputs (a value and a clock) and one output. In addition to flip-flops, our MIPS implementation also uses two other types of state elements: memories and registers, both of which appear in Figure 5.1. The clock is used to determine when the state element should be written; a state element can be read at any time.

Logic components that contain state are also called *sequential* because their outputs depend on both their inputs and the contents of the internal state. For example, the output from the functional unit representing the registers depends both on the register numbers supplied and on what was written into the registers previously. The operation of both the combinational and sequential elements and their construction are discussed in more detail in Appendix B.

Clocking Methodology

A *clocking methodology* defines when signals can be read and when they can be written. It is important to specify the timing of reads and writes because, if a signal is written at the same time it is read, the value of the read could correspond to the old value, the newly written value, or even some mix of the two! Needless to say, computer designs cannot tolerate such unpredictability. A clocking methodology is designed to prevent this circumstance.

For simplicity, we will assume an *edge-triggered* clocking methodology. An edge-triggered clocking methodology means that any values stored in the machine are updated only on a clock edge. Thus, the state elements all update their internal storage on the clock edge. Because only state elements can store a data value, any collection of combinational logic must have its inputs coming from a set of state elements and its outputs written into a set of state elements. The inputs are values that were written in a previous clock cycle, while the outputs are values that can be used in a following clock cycle.

Figure 5.2 shows the two state elements surrounding a block of combinational logic, which operates in a single clock cycle: All signals must propagate from state element 1, through the combinational logic, and to state element 2 in the time of one clock cycle. The time necessary for the signals to reach state element 2 defines the length of the clock cycle.

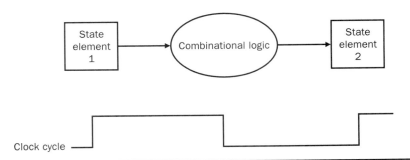

FIGURE 5.2   Combinational logic, state elements, and the clock are closely related. In a synchronous digital system, the clock determines when elements with state will write values into internal storage. Any inputs to a state element must reach a stable value (that is, have reached a value from which they will not change until after the clock edge) before the active clock edge causes the state to be updated. All state elements, including memory, are assumed to be edge-triggered.

For simplicity, we do not show a write control signal when a state element is written on every active clock edge. In contrast, if a state element is not updated on every clock, then an explicit write control signal is required. Both the clock signal and the write control signal are inputs, and the state element is changed only when the write control signal is asserted and a clock edge occurs.

An edge-triggered methodology allows us to read the contents of a register, send the value through some combinational logic, and write that register in the same clock cycle, as shown in Figure 5.3. It doesn't matter whether we assume that all writes take place on the rising clock edge or on the falling clock edge, since the inputs to the combinational logic block cannot change except on the chosen clock edge. With an edge-triggered timing methodology, there is *no* feedback within a single clock cycle, and the logic in Figure 5.3 works correctly. In Appendix B we briefly discuss additional timing constraints (such as set-up and hold times) as well as other timing methodologies.

Nearly all of these state and logic elements will have inputs and outputs that are 32 bits wide, since that is the width of most of the data handled by the processor. We will make it clear whenever a unit has an input or output that is other than 32 bits in width. The figures will indicate *buses*, which are signals wider than 1 bit, with thicker lines. At times we will want to combine several buses to form a wider bus; for example, we may want to obtain a 32-bit bus by combining two 16-bit buses. In such cases, labels on the bus lines will make it clear that we are concatenating buses to form a wider bus. Arrows are also added to help clarify the direction of the flow of data between elements. Finally, color indicates a control signal as opposed to a signal that carries data; this distinction will become clearer as we proceed through this chapter.

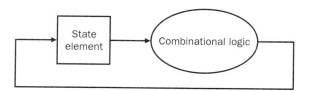

FIGURE 5.3 An edge-triggered methodology allows a state element to be read and written in the same clock cycle without creating a race that could lead to indeterminate data values. Of course, the clock cycle still must be long enough so that the input values are stable when the active clock edge occurs. Feedback cannot occur within 1 clock cycle because of the edge-triggered update of the state element. If feedback were possible, this design could not work properly. Our designs in this chapter and the next rely on the edge-triggered timing methodology and structures like the one shown in this figure.

The MIPS Subset Implementation

We will start with a simple implementation that uses a single long clock cycle for every instruction and follows the general form of Figure 5.1. In this first design, every instruction begins execution on one clock edge and completes execution on the next clock edge.

While easier to understand, this approach is not practical, since it would be slower than an implementation that allows different instruction classes to take different numbers of clock cycles, each of which could be much shorter. After designing the control for this simple machine, we will look at an implementation that uses multiple clock cycles for each instruction. This implementation is more realistic but also requires more complex control.

In this chapter, we will take the specification of the control to the level of logic equations or finite state machine specifications. From either representation, a modern computer-aided design (CAD) system can synthesize a hardware implementation; Appendix C shows how this is done. Before closing the chapter, we will discuss how exceptions, mentioned in Chapter 4, are implemented.

5.2 Building a Datapath

A reasonable way to start a datapath design is to examine the major components required to execute each class of MIPS instruction. Let's start by looking at which datapath elements each instruction needs and build up the sections of the datapath for each instruction class from these elements. When we show the datapath elements, we will also show their control signals.

The first element we will need is a place to store the instructions of a program. A memory unit, which is a state element, is used to hold and supply instructions given an address, as shown in Figure 5.4. The address of the instruction must also be kept in a state element, which we call the *program counter* (PC), also shown in Figure 5.4. Lastly, we will need an adder to increment the PC to the address of the next instruction. This adder, which is combinational, can be built from the ALU we designed in the last chapter simply by wiring the control lines so that the control always specifies an add operation. We will draw such an ALU with the label *Add*, as in Figure 5.4, to indicate that it has been permanently made an adder and cannot perform the other ALU functions.

To execute any instruction, we must start by fetching the instruction from memory. To prepare for executing the next instruction, we must also increment the program counter so that it points at the next instruction, 4 bytes later. The datapath for this step, shown in Figure 5.5, uses the three elements from Figure 5.4.

Now let's consider the R-format instructions (see Figure 3.19 on page 154). They all read two registers, perform an ALU operation on the contents of the registers, and write the result. We call these instructions either *R-type instructions* or *arithmetic-logical instructions* (since they perform arithmetic or logical

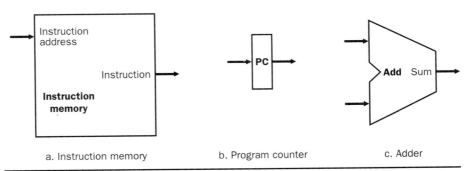

a. Instruction memory   b. Program counter   c. Adder

FIGURE 5.4   Two state elements are needed to store and access instructions, and an adder is needed to compute the next instruction address. The state elements are the instruction memory and the program counter. The instruction memory need only provide read access because the datapath does not write instructions. Since the instruction memory is only reads, we treat it as combinational logic: the output at any time reflects the contents of the location specified by the address input, and no read control signal is needed. (We will need to write the instruction memory when we load the program; this is not hard to add, and we ignore it for simplicity.) Since the instruction memory unit can only be read, we do not include a read control signal; this simplifies the design. The program counter is a 32-bit register that will be written at the end of every clock cycle and thus does not need a write control signal. The adder is an ALU wired to always perform an add of its two 32-bit inputs and place the result on its output.

operations). This instruction class includes add, sub, and slt, which were introduced in Chapter 3, as well as and and or, which were introduced in Chapter 4. Recall that a typical instance of such an instruction is add $t1,$t2,$t3, which reads $t2 and $t3 and writes $t1.

The processor's 32 registers are stored in a structure called a *register file*. A register file is a collection of registers in which any register can be read or written by specifying the number of the register in the file. The register file contains the register state of the machine. In addition, we will need an ALU to operate on the values read from the registers.

Because the R-format instructions have three register operands, we will need to read two data words from the register file and write one data word into the register file for each instruction. For each data word to be read from the registers, we need an input to the register file that specifies the register number to be read and an output from the register file that will carry the value that has been read from the registers. To write a data word, we will need two inputs: one to specify the *register number* to be written and one to supply the *data* to be written into the register. The register file always outputs the contents of whatever register numbers are on the Read register inputs. Writes, however, are controlled by the write control signal, which must be asserted for a write to occur at the clock edge. Thus, we need a total of four inputs (three for register

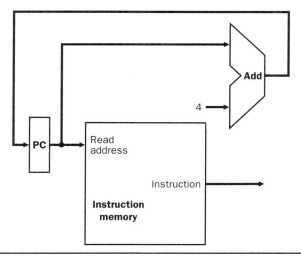

FIGURE 5.5   A portion of the datapath used for fetching instructions and incrementing the program counter. The fetched instruction is used by other parts of the datapath.

numbers and one for data) and two outputs (both for data), as shown in Figure 5.6. The register number inputs are 5 bits wide to specify one of 32 registers ($32 = 2^5$), whereas the data input and two data output buses are each 32 bits wide.

The ALU, shown in Figure 5.6, is controlled by the 3-bit signal described in Chapter 4. The ALU takes two 32-bit inputs and produces a 32-bit result.

The datapath for these R-type instructions, which uses the register file and the ALU of Figure 5.6, is shown in Figure 5.7. Since the register numbers come from fields of the instruction, we show the instruction, which comes from Figure 5.5, as connected to the register number inputs of the register file.

Next, consider the MIPS load word and store word instructions, which have the general form: lw $t1,offset_value($t2) or sw $t1,offset_value ($t2). These instructions compute a memory address by adding the base reg-

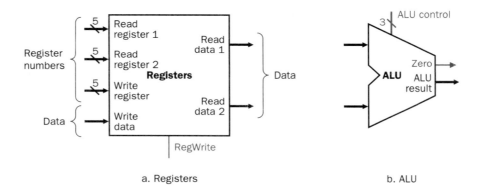

a. Registers   b. ALU

FIGURE 5.6 The two elements needed to implement R-format ALU operations are the register file and the ALU. The register file contains all the registers and has two read ports and one write port. The design of multiported register files is discussed in section B.5 of Appendix B. The register file always outputs the contents of the registers corresponding to the Read register inputs on the outputs; no other control inputs are needed. In contrast, a register write must be explicitly indicated by asserting the write control signal. Remember that writes are edge-triggered, so that all the write inputs (i.e., the value to be written, the register number, and the write control signal) must be valid at the clock edge. Since writes to the register file are edge-triggered, our design can legally read and write the same register within a clock cycle: the read will get the value written in an earlier clock cycle, while the value written will be available to a read in a subsequent clock cycle. The inputs carrying the register number to the register file are all 5 bits wide, whereas the lines carrying data values are 32 bits wide. The operation to be performed by the ALU is controlled with the ALU operation signal, which will be 3 bits wide, using the ALU designed in the previous chapter (see Figure 4.19 on page 240). We will use the Zero detection output of the ALU shortly to implement branches. The overflow output will not be needed until section 5.6, when we discuss exceptions; we omit it until then.

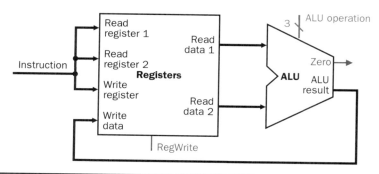

FIGURE 5.7 The datapath for R-type instructions. The ALU discussed in Chapter 4 can be controlled to provide all the basic ALU functions required for R-type instructions.

ister, which is $t2, to the 16-bit signed offset field contained in the instruction. If the instruction is a store, the value to be stored must also be read from the register file where it resides in $t1. If the instruction is a load, the value read from memory must be written into the register file in the specified register, which is $t1. Thus, we will need both the register file and the ALU shown in Figure 5.6.

In addition, we will need a unit to sign-extend the 16-bit offset field in the instruction to a 32-bit signed value, and a data memory unit to read from or write to. The data memory must be written on store instructions; hence, it has both read and write control signals, an address input, as well as an input for the data to be written into memory. Figure 5.8 shows these two elements.

Figure 5.9 shows how to combine these elements to build the datapath for a load word or a store word instruction, assuming that the instruction has already been fetched. The register number inputs for the register file come from fields of the instruction, as does the offset value, which after sign extension becomes the second ALU input.

The beq instruction has three operands, two registers that are compared for equality, and a 16-bit offset used to compute the branch target address relative to the branch instruction address. Its form is beq $t1,$t2,offset. To implement this instruction, we must compute the branch target address by adding the sign-extended offset field of the instruction to the PC. There are two details in the definition of branch instructions (see Chapter 3) to which we must pay attention:

- The instruction set architecture specifies that the base for the branch address calculation is the address of the instruction following the branch.

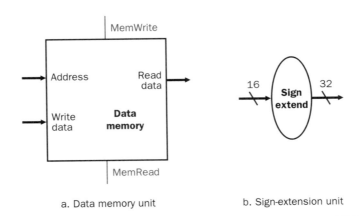

a. Data memory unit

b. Sign-extension unit

FIGURE 5.8   The two units needed to implement loads and stores, in addition to the register file and ALU of Figure 5.6, are the data memory unit and the sign extension unit. The memory unit is a state element with inputs for the address and the write data, and a single output for the read result. There are separate read and write controls, although only one of these may be asserted on any given clock. The sign extension unit has a 16-bit input that is sign-extended into a 32-bit result appearing on the output (see Chapter 4, page 216). We assume the data memory is edge-triggered for writes. Standard memory chips actually have a write enable signal that is used for writes. Although the write enable is not edge-triggered, our edge-triggered design could easily be adapted to work with real memory chips. See section B.5 of Appendix B for a further discussion of how real memory chips work.

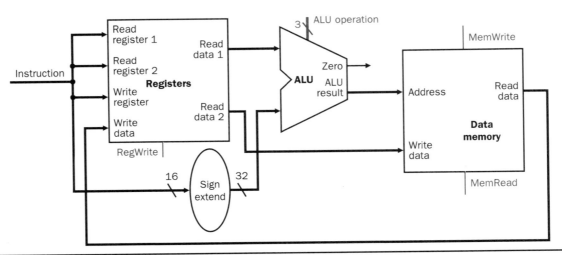

FIGURE 5.9   The datapath for a load or store does a register access, followed by a memory address calculation, then a read or write from memory, and a write into the register file if the instruction is a load.

Since we compute PC + 4 (the address of the next instruction) in the instruction fetch datapath, it is easy to use this value as the base for computing the branch target address.

- The architecture also states that the offset field is shifted left 2 bits so that it is a word offset; this shift increases the effective range of the offset field by a factor of four.

To deal with the latter complication, we will need to shift the offset field by two.

In addition to computing the branch target address, we must also determine whether the next instruction is the instruction that follows sequentially or the instruction at the branch target address. When the condition is true (i.e., the operands are equal), the branch target address becomes the new PC, and we say that the branch is *taken*. If the operands are not equal, the incremented PC should replace the current PC (just as for any other normal instruction); in this case, we say that the branch is *not taken*.

Thus, the branch datapath must do two operations: compute the branch target address and compare the register contents. (Branches also require that we modify the instruction fetch portion of the datapath, which we will deal with shortly.) Figure 5.10 shows the branch datapath. To compute the branch target address, the branch datapath includes a sign extension unit, just like that in Figure 5.8, and an adder. To perform the compare, we need to use the register file shown in Figure 5.6 to supply the two register operands (although we will not need to write into the register file). In addition, the comparison can be done using the ALU we designed in Chapter 4. Since that ALU provides an output signal that indicates whether the result was 0, we can send the two register operands to the ALU with the control set to do a subtract. If the Zero signal out of the ALU unit is asserted, we know that the two values are equal. Although the Zero output always signals if the result is 0, we will be using it only to implement the equal test of branches. Later, we will show exactly how to connect the control signals of the ALU for use in the datapath.

The jump instruction operates by replacing the lower 28 bits of the PC with the lower 26 bits of the instruction shifted left by 2 bits. This shift is accomplished simply by concatenating 00 to the jump offset (as described in the elaboration in Chapter 3, page 150).

Now that we have examined the datapaths needed for the individual instruction classes, we can combine them into a single datapath and add the control to complete the implementation. The datapaths shown in Figures 5.5, 5.7, 5.9, and 5.10 will be the building blocks for two different implementations. In the next section, we will create an implementation that uses a single long clock cycle for every instruction. In section 5.4, we will look at an implementation that uses multiple shorter clock cycles for every instruction.

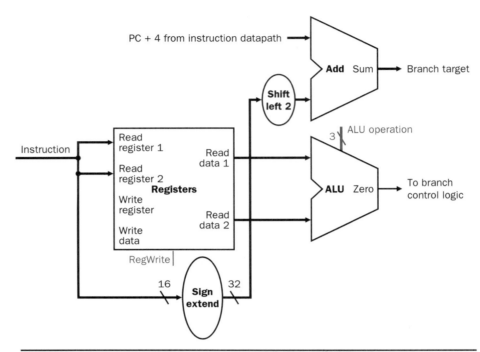

FIGURE 5.10 The datapath for a branch uses the ALU to evaluate the branch condition and a separate adder to compute the branch target as the sum of the incremented PC and the sign-extended, lower 16 bits of the instruction (the branch displacement), shifted left 2 bits. The unit labeled *Shift left 2* is simply a routing of the signals between input and output that adds 00_{two} to the low-order end of the sign-extended offset field; no actual shift hardware is needed, since the amount of the "shift" is constant. Since we know that the offset was sign-extended from 16 bits, the shift will throw away only "sign bits." Control logic is used to decide whether the incremented PC or branch target should replace the PC, based on the Zero output of the ALU.

Elaboration: In the MIPS instruction set, branches are *delayed*, meaning that the instruction immediately following the branch is always executed, *independent* of whether the branch condition is true or false. When the condition is false, the execution looks like a normal branch. When the condition is true, a delayed branch first executes the instruction immediately following the branch before jumping to the specified branch target address. The motivation for delayed branches arises from how pipelining affects branches (see section 6.6). For simplicity, we ignore delayed branches in this chapter and implement a nondelayed beq instruction.

A Simple Implementation Scheme

In this section, we look at what might be thought of as the simplest possible implementation of our MIPS subset. We build this simple datapath and its control by assembling the datapath segments of the last section and adding control lines as needed. This simple implementation covers load word (lw), store word (sw), branch equal (beq), and the arithmetic-logical instructions add, sub, and, or, and set on less than. We will later enhance the design to include a jump instruction (j).

Creating a Single Datapath

Suppose we were going to build a datapath from the pieces we looked at in Figures 5.5, 5.7, 5.9, and 5.10. The simplest datapath might attempt to execute all instructions in 1 clock cycle. This means that no datapath resource can be used more than once per instruction, so any element needed more than once must be duplicated. We therefore need a memory for instructions separate from one for data. Although some of the functional units will need to be duplicated when the individual datapaths of the previous section are combined, many of the elements can be shared by different instruction flows.

To share a datapath element between two different instruction classes, we may need to allow multiple connections to the input of an element and have a control signal select among the inputs. This selection is commonly done with a device called a *multiplexor*, although this device might better be called a *data selector*. The multiplexor, which was introduced in the last chapter (Figure 4.8 on page 231), selects from among several inputs based on the setting of its control lines.

Composing Datapaths

Example

The arithmetic-logical (or R-type) instruction datapath of Figure 5.7 on page 347 and the memory instruction datapath of Figure 5.9 on page 348 are quite similar. The key differences are the following:

- The second input to the ALU unit is either a register (if it's an R-type instruction) or the sign-extended lower half of the instruction (if it's a memory instruction).

- The value stored into a destination register comes from the ALU (for an R-type instruction) or the memory (for a load).

Show how to combine the two datapaths using multiplexors, without duplicating the functional units that are in common in Figures 5.7 and 5.9. Ignore the control of the multiplexors.

Answer

To combine the two datapaths and use only a single register file and an ALU, we must support two different sources for the second ALU input, as well as two different sources for the data stored into the register file. Thus one multiplexor is placed at the ALU input and another at the data input to the register file. Figure 5.11 shows the combined datapath.

The instruction fetch portion of the datapath, shown in Figure 5.5 on page 345, can easily be added to the datapath in Figure 5.11. Figure 5.12 shows the result. The combined datapath includes a memory for instructions and a separate memory for data. This combined datapath requires both an adder and an ALU, since the adder is used to increment the PC while the other ALU is used for executing the instruction in the same clock cycle.

Now we can combine all the pieces to make a simple datapath for the MIPS architecture by adding the datapath for branches from Figure 5.10 on page 350. Figure 5.13 on page 354 shows the datapath we obtain by composing the separate pieces. The branch instruction uses the main ALU for comparison of the register operands, so we must keep the adder in Figure 5.10 for computing the branch target address. An additional multiplexor is required to select either the sequentially following instruction address (PC + 4) or the branch target address to be written into the PC.

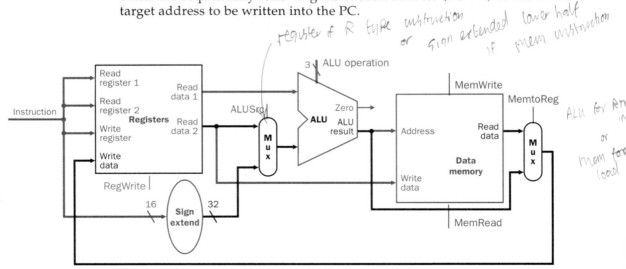

FIGURE 5.11   Combining the datapaths for the memory instructions and the R-type instructions. This example shows how a single datapath can be assembled from the pieces in Figures 5.7 and 5.9 by adding multiplexors. The added multiplexors and connections have been highlighted. The control lines for the multiplexors are also shown.

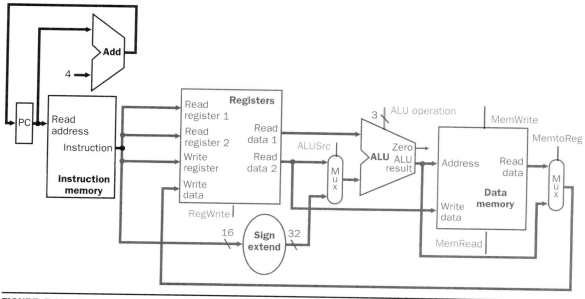

FIGURE 5.12 **The instruction fetch portion of the datapath from Figure 5.5 is appended to the datapath of Figure 5.11 that handles memory and ALU instructions.** The addition is highlighted. The result is a datapath that supports many operations of the MIPS instruction set—branches and jumps are the major missing pieces.

Now that we have completed this simple datapath, we can add the control unit. The control unit must be able to take inputs and generate a write signal for each state element, the selector control for each multiplexor, and the ALU control. The ALU control is different in a number of ways, and it will be useful to design it first before we design the rest of the control unit.

The ALU Control

Recall from Chapter 4 that the ALU has three control inputs. Only five of the possible eight input combinations are used. Figure 4.20 on page 240 showed the five following combinations:

ALU control input	Function
000	AND
001	OR
010	add
110	subtract
111	set on less than

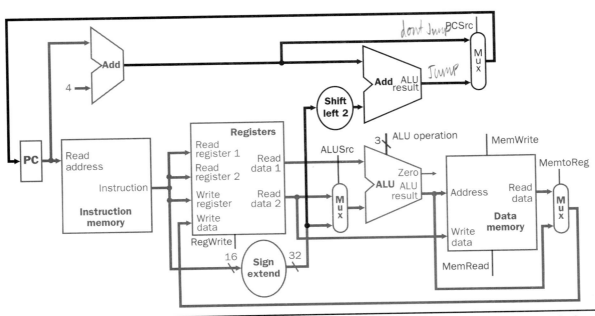

FIGURE 5.13 The simple datapath for the MIPS architecture combines the elements required by different instruction classes. This datapath can execute the basic instructions (load/store word, ALU operations, and branches) in a single clock cycle. The additions to Figure 5.12, which are all highlighted, are used to implement branches. The datapath components for branches come from Figure 5.10. A multiplexor is also needed, since the value written into the PC can be either the sequentially incremented PC or the branch target PC. The support for jumps will be added later.

Depending on the instruction class, the ALU will need to perform one of these five functions. For load word and store word instructions, we use the ALU to compute the memory address by addition. For the R-type instructions, the ALU needs to perform one of the five actions (AND, OR, subtract, add, or set on less than), depending on the value of the 6-bit funct (or function) field in the low-order bits of the instruction (see Chapter 3, page 118). For branch equal, the ALU must perform a subtraction.

We can generate the 3-bit ALU control input using a small control unit that has as inputs the function field of the instruction and a 2-bit control field, which we call ALUOp. ALUOp indicates whether the operation to be performed should be add (00) for loads and stores, subtract (01) for beq, or determined by the operation encoded in the funct field (10). The output of the ALU control unit is a 3-bit signal that directly controls the ALU by generating one of the five 3-bit combinations shown previously.

In Figure 5.14, we show how to set the ALU control inputs based on the 2-bit ALUOp control and the 6-bit function code. For completeness, the relationship between the ALUOp bits and the instruction opcode is also shown. Later in this chapter we will see how the ALUOp bits are generated from the main control unit.

This style of using multiple levels of decoding (i.e., the main control unit generates the ALUOp bits, which then are used as input to the ALU control that generates the actual signals to control the ALU unit) is a common implementation technique. Using multiple levels of control can reduce the size of the main control unit. Using several smaller control units may also potentially increase the speed of the control unit. Such optimizations are important, since the control unit is often performance-critical.

There are several different ways to implement the mapping from the 2-bit ALUOp field and the 6-bit funct field to the three ALU operation control bits. Because only a small number of the 64 possible values of the function field are of interest and the function field is used only when the ALUOp bits equal 10, we can use a small piece of logic that recognizes the subset of possible values and causes the correct setting of the ALU control bits.

As a step in designing this logic, it is useful to create a truth table for the interesting combinations of the function code field and the ALUOp bits, as we've done in Figure 5.15; this truth table shows how the 3-bit ALU control is set depending on these two input fields. Since the full truth table is very large (2^8 = 256 entries) and we don't care about the value of the ALU control for many of these input combinations, we show only the truth table entries for which the ALU control must have a specific value. Throughout this chapter, we will use

Instruction opcode	ALUOp	Instruction operation	Funct field	Desired ALU action	ALU control input
LW	00	load word	XXXXXX	add	010
SW	00	store word	XXXXXX	add	010
Branch equal	01	branch equal	XXXXXX	subtract	110
R-type	10	add	100000	add	010
R-type	10	subtract	100010	subtract	110
R-type	10	AND	100100	and	000
R-type	10	OR	100101	or	001
R-type	10	set on less than	101010	set on less than	111

FIGURE 5.14 How the ALU control bits are set depends on the ALUOp control bits and the different function codes for the R-type instruction. The opcode, listed in the first column, determines the setting of the ALUOp bits. All the encodings are shown in binary. Notice that when the ALUOp code is 00 or 01, the output fields do not depend on the function code field; in this case, we say that we "don't care" about the value of the function code, and the funct field is shown as XXXXXX. When the ALUOp value is 10, then the function code is used to set the ALU control input.

ALUOp		Funct field						Operation
ALUOp1	**ALUOp0**	**F5**	**F4**	**F3**	**F2**	**F1**	**F0**	
0	0	X	X	X	X	X	X	010
X	1	X	X	X	X	X	X	110
1	X	X	X	0	0	0	0	010
1	X	X	X	0	0	1	0	110
1	X	X	X	0	1	0	0	000
1	X	X	X	0	1	0	1	001
1	X	X	X	1	0	1	0	111

FIGURE 5.15   The truth table for the three ALU control bits (called Operation). The inputs are the ALUOp and function code field. Only the entries for which the ALU control is asserted are shown. Some don't-care entries have been added. For example, the ALUOp does not use the encoding 11, so the truth table can contain entries 1X and X1, rather than 10 and 01. Also, when the function field is used, the first two bits (F5 and F4) of these instructions are always 10, so they are don't-care terms and are replaced with XX in the truth table.

this practice of showing only the truth table entries that must be asserted and not showing those that are all zero or don't care. (This practice has a disadvantage, which we discuss in section C.2 of Appendix C.)

Because in many instances we do not care about the values of some of the inputs and to keep the tables compact, we also include "don't-care" terms. A don't-care term in this truth table (represented by an X in an input column) indicates that the output does not depend on the value of the input corresponding to that column. For example, when the ALUOp bits are 00, as in the first line of the table in Figure 5.15, we always set the ALU control to 010, independent of the function code. In this case, then, the function code inputs will be don't cares in this line of the truth table. Later, we will see examples of another type of don't-care term. If you are unfamiliar with the concept of don't-care terms, see Appendix B for more information.

Once the truth table has been constructed, it can be optimized and then turned into gates. This process is completely mechanical. Thus, rather than show the final steps here, we describe the process and the result in section C.2 of Appendix C.

Designing the Main Control Unit

Now that we have described how to design an ALU that uses the function code and a 2-bit signal as its control inputs, we can return to looking at the rest of the control. To start this process, let's identify the fields of an instruction and the control lines that are needed for the datapath we constructed in Figure 5.13 on page 354. To understand how to connect the fields of an instruction to the datapath, it is useful to review the formats of the three instruction classes: the R-type, branch, and load/store instructions. These formats are shown in Figure 5.16.

Field	0	rs	rt	rd	shamt	funct
Bit positions	31–26	25–21	20–16	15–11	10–6	5–0

a. R-type instruction

Field	35 or 43	rs	rt	address
Bit positions	31–26	25–21	20–16	15–0

b. Load or store instruction

Field	4	rs	rt	address
Bit positions	31–26	25–21	20–16	15–0

c. Branch instruction

FIGURE 5.16   The three instruction classes (R-type, load and store, and branch) use two different instruction formats. The jump instructions use another format, which we will discuss shortly. (a) Instruction format for R-format instructions, which all have an opcode of 0. These instructions have three register operands: rs, rt, and rd. Fields rs and rt are sources, and rd is the destination. The ALU function is in the funct field and is decoded by the ALU control design in the previous section. The R-type instructions that we implement are add, sub, and, or, and slt. The shamt field is used only for shifts; we will ignore it in this chapter. (b) Instruction format for load (opcode = 35_{ten}) and store (opcode = 43_{ten}) instructions. The register rs is the base register that is added to the 16-bit address field to form the memory address. For loads, rt is the destination register for the loaded value. For stores, rt is the source register whose value should be stored into memory. (c) Instruction format for branch equal (opcode = 4). The registers rs and rt are the source registers that are compared for equality. The 16-bit address field is sign-extended, shifted, and added to the PC to compute the branch target address.

There are several major observations about this instruction format that we will rely on:

- The op field, also called the *opcode*, is always contained in bits 31–26. We will refer to this field as Op[5-0].

- The two registers to be read are always specified by the rs and rt fields, at positions 25–21 and 20–16. This is true for the R-type instructions, branch equal, and for store.

- The base register for load and store instructions is always in bit positions 25–21 (rs).

- The 16-bit offset for branch equal, load, and store is always in positions 15–0.

- The destination register is in one of two places. For a load it is in bit positions 20–16 (rt), while for an R-type instruction it is in bit positions 15–11 (rd). Thus we will need to add a multiplexor to select which field of the instruction is used to indicate the register number to be written.

Using this information, we can add the instruction labels and extra multiplexor (for the Write register number input of the register file) to the simple datapath. Figure 5.17 shows these additions plus the ALU control block, the write signals for state elements, the read signal for the data memory, and the

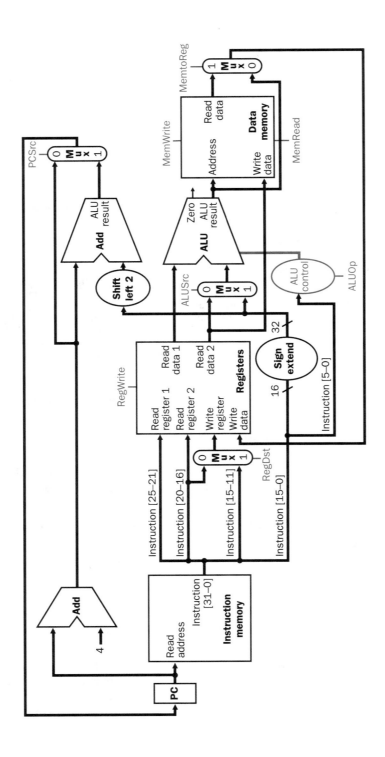

FIGURE 5.17 The datapath of Figure 5.13 with all necessary multiplexors and all control lines identified. The control lines are shown in color. The ALU control block has also been added. The PC does not require a write control, since it is written once at the end of every clock cycle; the branch control logic determines whether it is written with the incremented PC or the branch target address.

Signal name	Effect when deasserted	Effect when asserted
RegDst	The register destination number for the Write register comes from the rt field (bits 20–16).	The register destination number for the Write register comes from the rd field (bits 15–11).
RegWrite	None	The register on the Write register input is written with the value on the Write data input.
ALUSrc	The second ALU operand comes from the second register file output (Read data 2).	The second ALU operand is the sign-extended, lower 16 bits of the instruction.
PCSrc	The PC is replaced by the output of the adder that computes the value of PC + 4.	The PC is replaced by the output of the adder that computes the branch target.
MemRead	None	Data memory contents designated by the address input are put on the Read data output.
MemWrite	None	Data memory contents designated by the address input are replaced by the value on the Write data input.
MemtoReg	The value fed to the register Write data input comes from the ALU.	The value fed to the register Write data input comes from the data memory.

FIGURE 5.18 The effect of each of the seven control signals. When the 1-bit control to a two-way multiplexor is asserted, the multiplexor selects the input corresponding to 1. Otherwise, if the control is deasserted, the multiplexor selects the 0 input. Remember that the state elements all have the clock as an implicit input and that the clock is used in controlling writes. The clock is never gated externally to a state element, since this can create timing problems. (See Appendix B for further discussion of this problem.)

control signals for the multiplexors. Since all the multiplexors have two inputs, they each require a single control line.

Figure 5.17 shows seven single-bit control lines plus the 2-bit ALUOp control signal. We have already defined how the ALUOp control signal works, and it is useful to define what the seven other control signals do informally before we determine how to set these control signals during instruction execution. Figure 5.18 describes the function of these seven control lines.

Now that we have looked at the function of each of the control signals, we can look at how to set them. The control unit can set all but one of the control signals based solely on the opcode field of the instruction. The PCSrc control line is the exception. That control line should be set if the instruction is branch on equal (a decision that the control unit can make) *and* the Zero output of the ALU, which is used for equality comparison, is true. To generate the PCSrc signal, we will need to AND together a signal from the control unit, which we call *Branch*, with the Zero signal out of the ALU.

These nine control signals (seven from Figure 5.18 and two for ALUOp) can now be set on the basis of six input signals to the control unit, which are the opcode bits. The datapath with the control unit and the control signals are shown in Figure 5.19.

Before we try to write a set of equations or a truth table for the control unit, it will be useful to try to define the control function informally. Because the setting of the control lines depends only on the opcode, we define whether each control signal should be 0, 1, or don't care (X), for each of the opcode values.

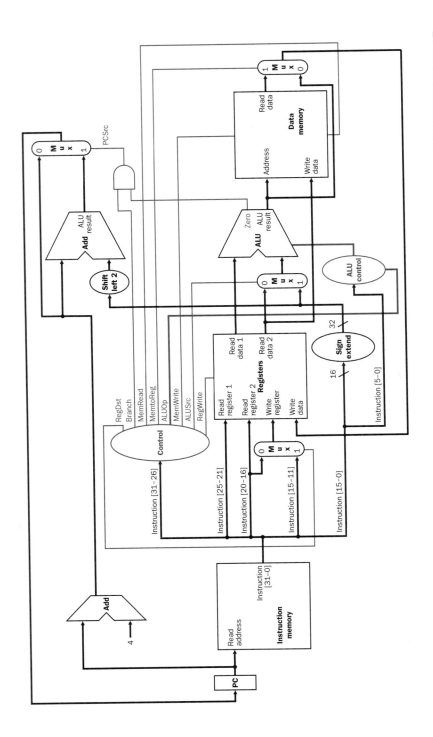

FIGURE 5.19 The simple datapath with the control unit. The input to the control unit is the 6-bit opcode field from the instruction. The outputs of the control unit consist of three 1-bit signals that are used to control multiplexors (RegDst, ALUSrc, and MemtoReg), three signals for controlling reads and writes in the register file and data memory (RegWrite, MemRead, and MemWrite), a 1-bit signal used in determining whether to possibly branch (Branch), and a 2-bit control signal for the ALU (ALUOp). An AND gate is used to combine the branch control signal and the Zero output from the ALU; the AND gate output controls the selection of the next PC. Notice that PCSrc is now a derived signal, rather than one coming directly from the control unit. Thus we drop the signal name in subsequent figures.

Figure 5.20 defines how the control signals should be set for each opcode; this information follows directly from Figures 5.14, 5.18, and 5.19.

Operation of the Datapath

With the information contained in Figures 5.18 and 5.20, we can design the control unit logic, but before we do that, let's look at how each instruction uses the datapath. In the next few figures, we show the flow of three different instruction classes through the datapath. The asserted control signals and active datapath elements are highlighted in each of these. Note that a multiplexor whose control is 0 has a definite action, even if its control line is not highlighted. Multiple-bit control signals are highlighted if any constituent signal is asserted.

Let's begin with an R-type instruction, such as add $t1,$t2,$t3. Rather than looking at the entire datapath as one piece of combinational logic, it is easier to think of an instruction executing in a series of steps, focusing our attention on the portion of the datapath associated with each step. There are four steps to execute an R-type instruction:

1. An instruction is fetched from the instruction memory and the PC is incremented. Figure 5.21 shows this first step. The active units and asserted control lines are highlighted; those that are asserted in later steps of an R-type instruction are in gray, and those in light gray are those not active for an R-type instruction in any step. The same format is followed for the next three steps.

Instruction	RegDst	ALUSrc	Memto-Reg	Reg Write	Mem Read	Mem Write	Branch	ALUOp1	ALUOp0
R-format	1	0	0	1	0	0	0	1	0
lw	0	1	1	1	1	0	0	0	0
sw	X	1	X	0	0	1	0	0	0
beq	X	0	X	0	0	0	1	0	1

FIGURE 5.20   The setting of the control lines is completely determined by the opcode fields of the instruction. The first row of the table corresponds to the R-format instructions (add, sub, and, or, and slt). For all these instructions, the source register fields are rs and rt and the destination register field is rd; this defines how the signals ALUSrc and RegDst are set. Furthermore, an R-type instruction writes a register (RegWrite = 1), but neither reads nor writes data memory. When the Branch control signal is 0, the PC is unconditionally replaced with PC + 4; otherwise, the PC is replaced by the branch target if the Zero output of the ALU is also high. The ALUOp field for R-type instructions is set to 10 to indicate that the ALU control should be generated from the funct field. The second and third rows of this table give the control signal settings for lw and sw. These ALUSrc and ALUOp fields are set to perform the address calculation. The MemRead and MemWrite are set to perform the memory access. Finally, RegDst and RegWrite are set for a load to cause the result to be stored into the rt register. The branch instruction is similar to an R-format operation, since it sends the rs and rt registers to the ALU. The ALUOp field for branch is set for a subtract (ALU control = 01), which is used to test for equality. Notice that the MemtoReg field is irrelevant when the RegWrite signal is 0—since the register is not being written, the value of the data on the register data write port is not used. Thus, the entry MemtoReg in the last two rows of the table is replaced with X for don't care. Don't cares can also be added to RegDst when RegWrite is 0. This type of don't care must be added by the designer, since it depends on knowledge of how the datapath works.

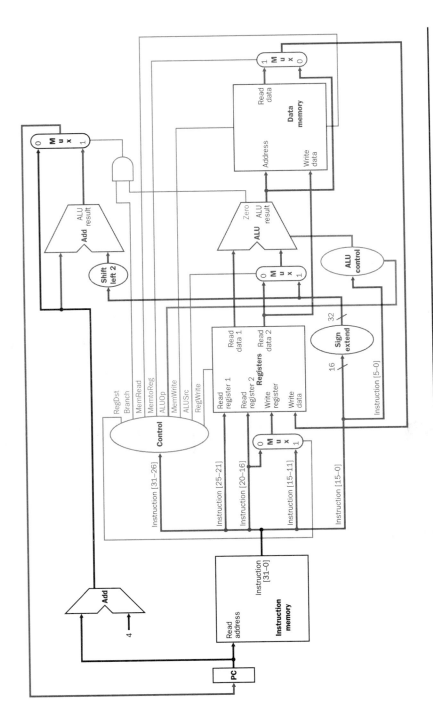

FIGURE 5.21 The first step of an R-type instruction performs a fetch from instruction memory and increments the PC. The portions active in this step are highlighted; the light portions are not active at this step, though some will be active later in the cycle.

2. Two registers, $t2 and $t3, are read from the register file as shown in Figure 5.22 on page 364. The main control unit computes the setting of the control lines during this step also.

3. The ALU operates on the data read from the register file, using the function code (bits 5–0, which is the funct field, of the instruction) to generate the ALU function. Figure 5.23 on page 365 shows the operation of this step.

4. The result from the ALU is written into the register file using bits 15–11 of the instruction to select the destination register ($t1). Figure 5.24 on page 366 shows the final step added to the previous three.

Remember that this implementation is combinational. That is, it is not really a series of four distinct steps. The datapath really operates in a single clock cycle, and the signals within the datapath can vary unpredictably during the clock cycle. The signals stabilize roughly in the order of the steps given above because the flow of information follows this order. Thus, Figure 5.24 shows not only the action of the last step, but essentially the operation of the entire datapath when the clock cycle actually ends.

We can illustrate the execution of a load word, such as

```
lw $t1, offset($t2)
```

in a style similar to Figure 5.24. Figure 5.25 on page 368 shows the active functional units and asserted control lines for a load. We can think of a load instruction as operating in five steps (similar to the R-type executed in four):

1. An instruction is fetched from the instruction memory and the PC is incremented.

2. A register ($t2) value is read from the register file.

3. The ALU computes the sum of the value read from the register file and the sign-extended, lower 16 bits of the instruction (offset).

4. The sum from the ALU is used as the address for the data memory.

5. The data from the memory unit is written into the register file; the register destination is given by bits 20–16 of the instruction ($t1) .

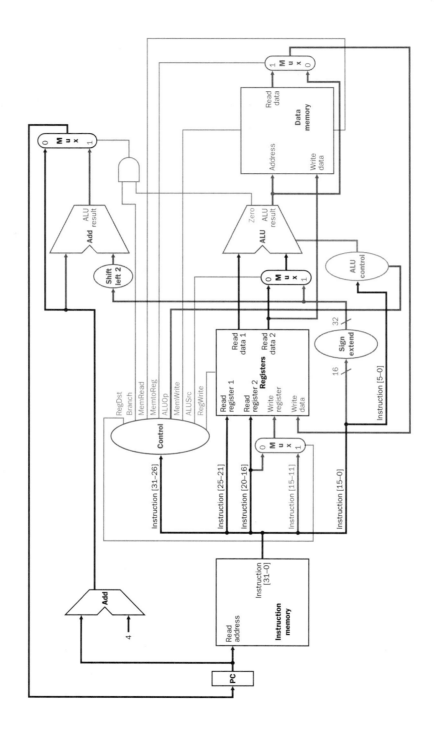

FIGURE 5.22 The second phase in the execution of R-type instructions reads the two source registers from the register file. The main control unit also uses the opcode field to determine the control line setting. These units become active in addition to the units active during the instruction fetch portion, shown in Figure 5.21.

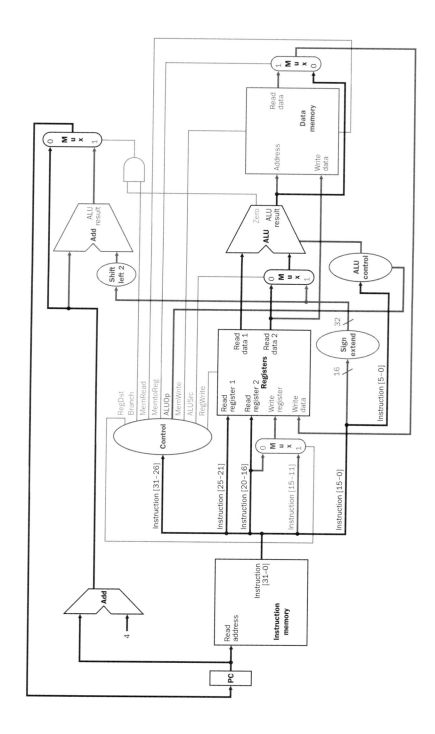

FIGURE 5.23 The third phase of execution for R-type instructions involves the ALU operating on the register data operands. The control line values are all set, and the ALU control has been computed. The ALU operates on the data.

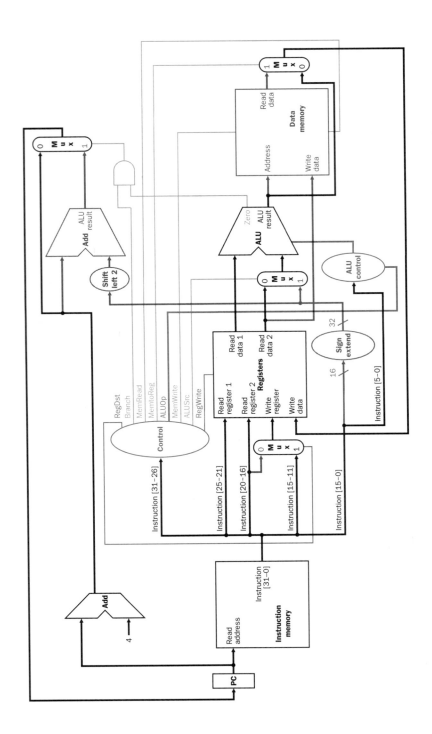

FIGURE 5.24 The final step in an R-type instruction, writing the result, is added to the active units shown for the previous three steps in Figure 5.23. The PC is also updated at the end of this phase. Because the datapath is combinational, this step shows all the active units and asserted control lines when they are stable. Observe that if the instruction is one that uses the same register as both an input and output (such as add R1, R1, R1) it works correctly: the value read from the registers is the value of R1 written at the end of some earlier clock cycle, while the value to be written into the registers by the instruction is not actually written into the register until the clock edge at the end of the current clock cycle.

Finally, we can show the operation of the branch-on-equal instruction, such as beq $t1,$t2,offset, in the same fashion. It operates much like an R-format instruction, but the ALU output is used to determine whether the PC is written with PC + 4 or the branch target address. Figure 5.26 shows the four steps in execution:

1.   An instruction is fetched from the instruction memory and the PC is incremented.

2.   Two registers, $t1 and $t2, are read from the register file.

3.   The ALU performs a subtract on the data values read from the register file. The value of PC + 4 is added to the sign-extended, lower 16 bits of the instruction (offset) shifted left by two; the result is the branch target address.

4.   The Zero result from the ALU is used to decide which adder result to store into the PC.

In the next section, we will examine machines that are truly sequential, namely, those in which each of these steps is a distinct clock cycle.

Finalizing the Control

Now that we have seen how the instructions operate in steps, let's continue with the control implementation. The control function can be precisely defined using the contents of Figure 5.20 on page 361. The outputs are the control lines, the input is the 6-bit opcode field, Op [5–0]. Thus we can create a truth table for each of the outputs. Before doing so, let's write down the encoding for each of the opcodes of interest in Figure 5.20, both as a decimal number and as a series of bits that are input to the control unit:

Name	Opcode in decimal	Opcode in binary					
		Op5	Op4	Op3	Op2	Op1	Op0
R-format	0_{ten}	0	0	0	0	0	0
lw	35_{ten}	1	0	0	0	1	1
sw	43_{ten}	1	0	1	0	1	1
beq	4_{ten}	0	0	0	1	0	0

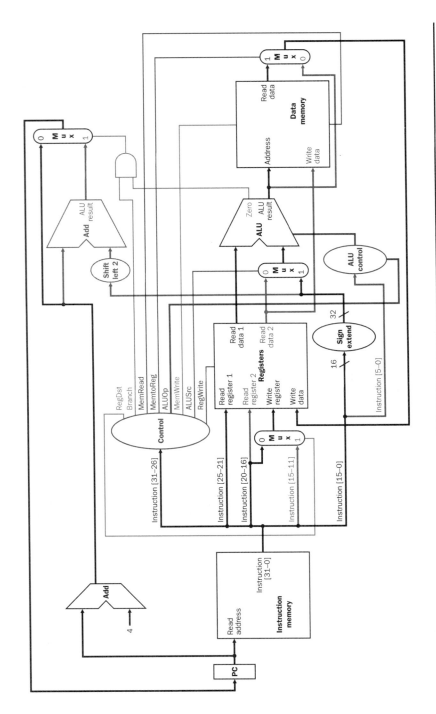

FIGURE 5.25 The operation of a load instruction with the simple datapath control scheme. A store instruction would operate very similarly. The main difference would be that the memory control would indicate a write rather than a read, the second register value read would be used for the data to store, and the operation of writing the data memory value to the register file would not occur.

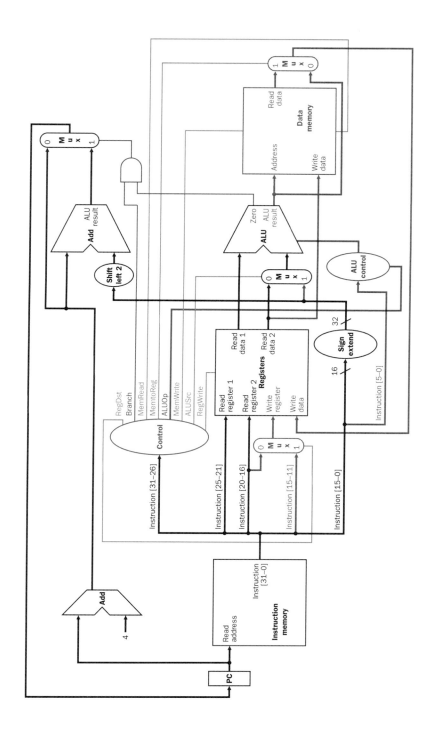

FIGURE 5.26 The datapath in operation for a branch equal instruction. After using the register file and ALU to perform the compare, the Zero output is used to select the next program counter from between the two candidates.

Input or output	Signal name	R-format	lw	sw	beq
Inputs	Op5	0	1	1	0
	Op4	0	0	0	0
	Op3	0	0	1	0
	Op2	0	0	0	1
	Op1	0	1	1	0
	Op0	0	1	1	0
Outputs	RegDst	1	0	X	X
	ALUSrc	0	1	1	0
	MemtoReg	0	1	X	X
	RegWrite	1	1	0	0
	MemRead	0	1	0	0
	MemWrite	0	0	1	0
	Branch	0	0	0	1
	ALUOp1	1	0	0	0
	ALUOp0	0	0	0	1

FIGURE 5.27 The control function for the simple single-cycle implementation is completely specified by this truth table. The top half of the table gives the combinations of input signals that correspond to the four opcodes that determine the control output settings. (Remember that Op [5–0] corresponds to bits 31–26 of the instruction, which is the op field.) The bottom portion of the table gives the outputs. Thus, the output RegWrite is asserted for two different combinations of the inputs. If we consider only the four opcodes shown in this table, then we can simplify the truth table by using don't cares in the input portion. For example, we can detect an R-format instruction with the expression $\overline{Op5} \cdot \overline{Op2}$, since this is sufficient to distinguish the R-format instructions from lw, sw, and beq. We do not take advantage of this simplification, since the rest of the MIPS opcodes are used in a full implementation.

Using this information, we can now describe the logic in the control unit in one large truth table that combines all the outputs, as in Figure 5.27. It completely specifies the control function, and we can implement it directly in gates in an automated fashion. We show this final step in section C.2 in Appendix C.

Now, let's add the jump instruction to show how the basic datapath and control can be extended to handle other instructions in the instruction set.

Implementing Jumps

Example

Figure 5.19 on page 360 shows the implementation of many of the instructions we looked at in Chapter 3. One class of instructions missing is that of the jump instruction. Extend the datapath and control of Figure 5.19 to include the jump instruction. Describe how to set any new control lines.

Field	2	address
Bit positions	31–26	25–0

FIGURE 5.28 Instruction format for the jump instruction (opcode = 2). The destination address for a jump instruction is formed by concatenating the upper 4 bits of the current PC + 4 to the 26-bit address field in the jump instruction and adding 00 as the 2 low-order bits.

Answer

The jump instruction looks somewhat like a branch instruction but computes the target PC differently and is not conditional. Like a branch, the low-order 2 bits of a jump address are always 00_{two}. The next lower 26 bits of this 32-bit address come from the 26-bit immediate field in the instruction, as shown in Figure 5.28. The upper 4 bits of the address that should replace the PC come from the PC of the jump instruction plus four. Thus, we can implement a jump by storing into the PC the concatenation of

- the upper 4 bits of the current PC + 4 (these are bits 31–28 of the sequentially following instruction address)
- the 26-bit immediate field of the jump instruction
- the bits 00_{two}

Figure 5.29 shows the addition of the control for jump added to Figure 5.19. An additional multiplexor is used to select the source for the new PC value, which is either the incremented PC (PC + 4), the branch target PC, or the jump target PC. One additional control signal is needed for the additional multiplexor. This control signal, called *Jump*, is asserted only when the instruction is a jump—that is, when the opcode is 2.

Why a Single-Cycle Implementation Is Not Used

Although the single-cycle design will work correctly, it would not be used in modern designs because it is inefficient. To see why this is so notice that the clock cycle must have the same length for every instruction in this single-cycle design, and the CPI (see Chapter 2) will therefore be 1. Of course, the clock cycle is determined by the longest possible path in the machine. This path is almost certainly a load instruction, which uses five functional units in series: the instruction memory, the register file, the ALU, the data memory, and the register file. Although the CPI is 1, the overall performance of a single-cycle implementation is not likely to be very good, since several of the instruction classes could fit in a shorter clock cycle.

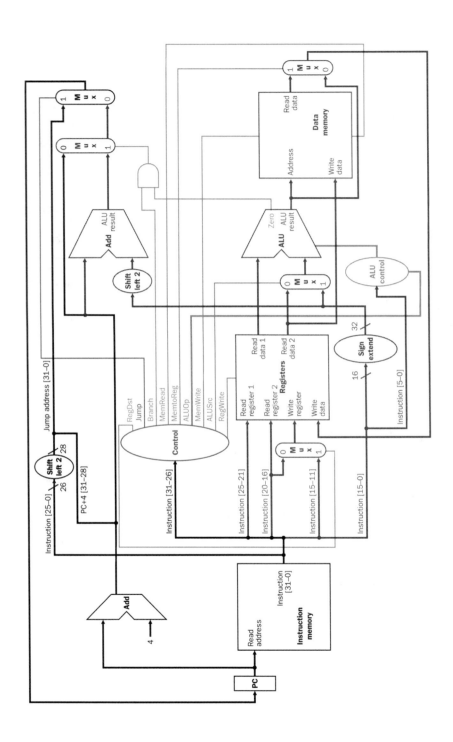

FIGURE 5.29 The simple control and datapath are extended to handle the jump instruction. An additional multiplexor (at the upper right) is used to choose between the jump target and either the branch target or the sequential instruction following this one. This multiplexor is controlled by the jump control signal. The jump target address is obtained by shifting the lower 26 bits of the jump instruction left 2 bits, effectively adding 00 as the low-order bits, and then concatenating the upper 4 bits of PC + 4 as the high-order bits, thus yielding a 32-bit address.

Performance of Single-Cycle Machines

Example

Assume that the operation time for the major functional units in this implementation are the following:

- Memory units: 2 nanoseconds (ns)
- ALU and adders: 2 ns
- Register file (read or write): 1 ns

Assuming that the multiplexors, control unit, PC accesses, sign extension unit, and wires have no delay, which of the following implementations would be faster and by how much?

1. An implementation in which every instruction operates in 1 clock cycle of a fixed length.

2. An implementation where every instruction executes in 1 clock cycle using a variable-length clock, which for each instruction is only as long as it needs to be. (Such an approach is not terribly practical, but it will allow us to see what is being sacrificed when all the instructions must execute in a single clock of the same length.)

To compare the performance, assume the following instruction mix: 24% loads, 12% stores, 44% R-format instructions, 18% branches, and 2% jumps.

Answer

Let's start by comparing the CPU execution times. Recall from Chapter 2 that

$$\text{CPU execution time} = \text{Instruction count} \times \text{CPI} \times \text{Clock cycle time}$$

Since CPI must be 1, we can simplify this to

$$\text{CPU execution time} = \text{Instruction count} \times \text{Clock cycle time}$$

We need only find the clock cycle time for the two implementations, since the instruction count and CPI are the same for both implementations. The critical path for the different instruction classes is as follows:

Instruction class	Functional units used by the instruction class				
R-format	Instruction fetch	Register access	ALU	Register access	
Load word	Instruction fetch	Register access	ALU	Memory access	Register access
Store word	Instruction fetch	Register access	ALU	Memory access	
Branch	Instruction fetch	Register access	ALU		
Jump	Instruction fetch				

Using these critical paths, we can compute the required length for each instruction class:

Instruction class	Instruction memory	Register read	ALU operation	Data memory	Register write	Total
R-format	2	1	2	0	1	6 ns
Load word	2	1	2	2	1	8 ns
Store word	2	1	2	2		7 ns
Branch	2	1	2			5 ns
Jump	2					2 ns

The clock cycle for a machine with a single clock for all instructions will be determined by the longest instruction, which is 8 ns. (This timing is approximate, since our timing model is quite simplistic. In reality, the timing of modern digital systems is complex, often allowing time to be borrowed from one clock cycle for use in the next.)

A machine with a variable clock will have a clock cycle that varies between 2 ns and 8 ns. We can find the average clock cycle length for a machine with a variable-length clock using the information above and the instruction frequency distribution.

Thus, the average time per instruction with a variable clock is

$$\text{CPU clock cycle} = 8 \times 24\% + 7 \times 12\% + 6 \times 44\% + 5 \times 18\% + 2 \times 2\%$$

$$= 6.3 \text{ ns}$$

Since the variable clock implementation has a shorter average clock cycle, it is clearly faster. Let's find the performance ratio:

$$\frac{\text{CPU performance}_{\text{variable clock}}}{\text{CPU performance}_{\text{single clock}}} = \frac{\text{CPU execution time}_{\text{single clock}}}{\text{CPU execution time}_{\text{variable clock}}}$$

$$= \frac{\text{IC} \times \text{CPU clock cycle}_{\text{single clock}}}{\text{IC} \times \text{CPU clock cycle}_{\text{variable clock}}}$$

$$= \frac{\text{CPU clock cycle}_{\text{single clock}}}{\text{CPU clock cycle}_{\text{variable clock}}}$$

$$= \frac{8}{6.3} = 1.27$$

The variable clock implementation would be 1.27 times faster. Unfortunately, implementing a variable-speed clock for each instruction class is extremely difficult, and the overhead for such an approach could be larger than any advantage gained. As we will see in the next section, an alternative is to use a shorter clock cycle that does less work and then vary the number of clock cycles for the different instruction classes.

The penalty for using the single-cycle design with a fixed clock cycle is significant, but might be considered acceptable for this small instruction set. However, if we tried to implement the floating-point unit or an instruction set with more complex instructions, this single-cycle design wouldn't work well at all. Let's look at an example with floating point.

Performance of a Single-Cycle CPU with Floating-Point Instructions

Example

Suppose we have a floating-point unit that requires 8 ns for a floating-point add and 16 ns for a floating-point multiply. All the other functional unit times are as in the previous example, and a floating-point instruction is like an arithmetic-logical instruction, except that it uses the floating-point ALU rather than the main ALU. Using the instruction distribution for spice from Chapter 4, Figure 4.54 on page 311, find the performance ratio between an implementation in which the clock cycle is different for each instruction class and an implementation in which all instructions have the same clock cycle time. Assume the following:

- All loads take the same time and comprise 31% of the instructions.
- All stores take the same time and comprise 21% of the instructions.
- R-format instructions comprise 27% of the mix.
- Branches comprise 5% of the instructions, while jumps comprise 2%.
- FP add and subtract take the same time and together total 7% of the instructions.
- FP multiply and divide take the same time and together total 7% of the instructions.

Answer

From the previous example, we know that

$$\frac{\text{CPU performance}_{\text{variable clock}}}{\text{CPU performance}_{\text{single clock}}} = \frac{\text{CPU clock cycle}_{\text{single clock}}}{\text{CPU clock cycle}_{\text{variable clock}}}$$

The cycle time for the single-cycle machine will be equal to the longest instruction time, which is floating-point multiply. The time for a floating-point multiply, and thus the clock cycle, is $2 + 1 + 16 + 1 = 20$ ns.

Consider a machine whose instructions have different cycle times. The time for a floating-point add instruction is $2 + 1 + 8 + 1 = 12$ ns. Multiplying the cycle times by the instruction frequencies tells us that the average clock length will be

$$\text{CPU clock cycle} = 8 \times 31\% + 7 \times 21\% + 6 \times 27\% + 5 \times 5\%$$

$$+ 2 \times 2\% + 20 \times 7\% + 12 \times 7\% = 7.0 \text{ ns}$$

The improvement in performance is

$$\frac{\text{CPU performance}_{\text{variable clock}}}{\text{CPU performance}_{\text{single clock}}} = \frac{\text{CPU clock cycle}_{\text{single clock}}}{\text{CPU clock cycle}_{\text{variable clock}}}$$

$$= \frac{20}{7} = 2.9$$

A variable clock would allow us to improve performance by 2.9 times.

Similarly, if we had a machine with more powerful operations and addressing modes, instructions could vary from three or four functional unit delays to tens or even hundreds of functional unit delays. In addition, because we must assume that the clock cycle is equal to the worst-case delay for all instructions, we can't use implementation techniques that reduce the delay of the common case but do not improve the worst-case cycle time. A single-cycle implementation thus violates our key design principle of making the common case fast.

In addition, with this single-cycle implementation, each functional unit can be used only once per clock; therefore, some functional units must be duplicated, raising the cost of the implementation. A single-cycle design is inefficient both in its performance and in its hardware cost!

We can avoid these difficulties by using implementation techniques that have a shorter clock cycle—derived from the basic functional unit delays—and that require multiple clock cycles for each instruction. The next section explores this alternative implementation scheme. In Chapter 6, we'll look at another implementation technique, called pipelining, that uses a datapath very similar to the single-cycle datapath, but is much more efficient. Pipelining gains efficiency by overlapping the execution of multiple instructions, increasing hardware utilization and improving performance.

5.4 A Multicycle Implementation

In an earlier example, we broke each instruction into a series of steps corresponding to the functional unit operations that were needed. We can use these steps to create a *multicycle implementation*. In a multicycle implementation, each *step* in the execution will take 1 clock cycle. The multicycle implementation allows a functional unit to be used more than once per instruction, as long as it is used on different clock cycles. This sharing can help reduce the amount of hardware required. The ability to allow instructions to take different numbers of clock cycles and the ability to share functional units within the execution of a single instruction are the major advantages of a multicycle design. Figure 5.30 shows the abstract version of the multicycle datapath. Comparing this to the datapath for the single-cycle version shown in Figure 5.13 on page 354, we can see the following differences:

- A single memory unit is used for both instructions and data.

- There is a single ALU, rather than an ALU and two adders.

- One or more registers are added after every major functional unit to hold the output of that unit until the value is used in a subsequent clock cycle.

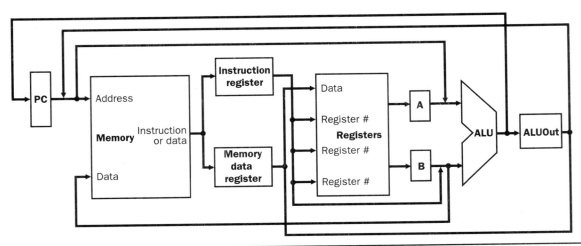

FIGURE 5.30   The high-level view of the multicycle datapath. This picture shows the key elements of the datapath: a shared memory unit, a single ALU shared among instructions, and the connections among these shared units. The use of shared functional units requires the addition or widening of multiplexors as well as new temporary registers that hold data between clock cycles of the same instruction. The additional registers are the Instruction register (IR), the Memory data register (MDR), A, B, and ALUOut.

At the end of a clock cycle, all data that are used in subsequent clock cycles must be stored in a state element. Data used by *subsequent instructions* in a later clock cycle is stored into one of the programmer-visible state elements (i.e., the register file, the PC, or the memory). In contrast, data used by the *same instruction* in a later cycle must be stored into one of these additional registers.

Thus the position of the additional registers is determined by the two factors: what combinational units will fit in a clock cycle and what data are needed in later cycles implementing the instruction. In this multicycle design, we assume that the clock cycle can accommodate at most one of the following operations: a memory access, a register file access (two reads or one write), or an ALU operation. Thus any data produced by one of these three functional units (the memory, the register file, or the ALU) must be saved into a temporary register for use on a later cycle.

The following temporary registers are added to meet these requirements:

- The Instruction register (IR) and the Memory data register (MDR) are added to save the output of the memory for an instruction read and a data read, respectively. Two separate registers are used, since, as will be clear shortly, both values are needed during the same clock cycle.

- The A and B registers are used to hold the register operand values read from the register file.

- The ALUOut register holds the output of the ALU.

All the registers except the IR hold data only between a pair of adjacent clock cycles and will thus not need a write control signal. The IR needs to hold the instruction until the end of execution of that instruction, and thus will require a write control signal. This distinction will become more clear when we show the individual clock cycles for each instruction.

Because several functional units are shared for different purposes, we need both to add multiplexors and to expand existing multiplexors. For example, since one memory is used for both instructions and data, we need a multiplexor to select between the two sources for a memory address, namely the PC (for instruction access) and ALUOut (for data access).

Replacing the three ALUs of the single-cycle datapath by a single ALU means that the single ALU must accommodate all the inputs that used to go to the three different ALUs. Handling the additional inputs requires two changes to the datapath:

1. An additional multiplexor is added for the first ALU input. The multiplexor chooses between the A register and the PC.

2. The multiplexor on the second ALU input is changed from a two-way to a four-way multiplexor. The two additional inputs to the multiplexor are the constant 4 (used to increment the PC) and the sign-extended and shifted offset field (used in the branch address computation).

Figure 5.31 shows the details of the datapath with these additional multiplexors. By introducing a few registers and multiplexors, we are able to reduce the number of memory units from two to one and eliminate two adders. Since registers and multiplexors are fairly small compared to a memory unit or ALU, this could yield a substantial reduction in the hardware cost.

Because the datapath shown in Figure 5.31 takes multiple clock cycles per instruction, it will require a different set of control signals. The programmer-visible state units (the PC, the memory, and the registers) as well as the IR will need write control signals. The memory will also need a read signal. We can use the ALU control unit from the single-cycle datapath (see Figures 5.15 and Appendix C) to control the ALU here as well. Finally, each of the two-input multiplexors requires a single control line, while the four-input multiplexor requires two control lines. Figure 5.32 shows the datapath of Figure 5.31 with these control lines added.

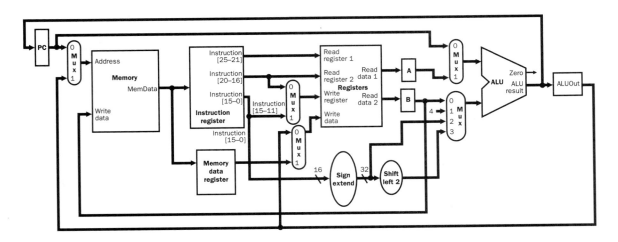

FIGURE 5.31   Multicycle datapath for MIPS handles the basic instructions. Although this datapath supports normal incrementing of the PC, a few more connections and a multiplexor will be needed for branches and jumps; we will add these shortly. The additions versus the single-clock datapath include several registers (IR, MDR, A, B, ALUOut), a multiplexor for the memory address, a multiplexor for the top ALU input, and expanding the multiplexor on the bottom ALU input into a four-way selector. These small additions allow us to remove two adders and a memory unit.

The multicycle datapath still requires additions to support branches and jumps; after these additions, we will see how the instructions are sequenced and then generate the datapath control.

With the jump instruction and branch instruction, there are three possible sources for the value to be written into the PC:

1. The output of the ALU, which is the value PC + 4 during instruction fetch. This value should be stored directly into the PC.

2. The register ALUOut, which is where we will store the address of the branch target after it is computed.

3. The lower 26 bits of the Instruction register (IR) shifted left by two and concatenated with the upper 4 bits of the incremented PC, which is the source when the instruction is a jump.

As we observed when we implemented the single-cycle control, the PC is written both unconditionally and conditionally. During a normal increment and jumps, the PC is written unconditionally. If the instruction is a conditional branch, the incremented PC is replaced with the value in ALUOut only if the two designated registers are equal. Thus the control needs two PC write signals, which we will call PCWrite and PCWriteCond.

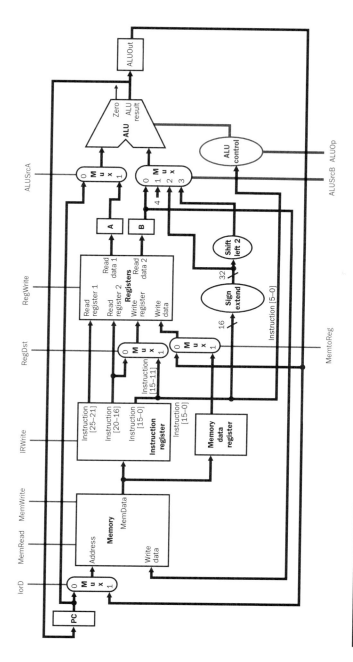

FIGURE 5.32 **The multicycle datapath from Figure 5.31 with the control lines shown.** The signals ALUOp and ALUSrcB are 2-bit control signals, while all the other control lines are 1-bit signals. Neither register A nor B requires a write signal, since their contents are only read on the cycle immediately after it is written. The memory data register has been added to hold the data from a load when the data returns from memory. Data from a load returning from memory cannot be written directly into the register file since the clock cycle cannot accommodate the time required for both the memory access and the register file write. The MemRead signal has been moved to the top of the memory unit to simplify the figures. The full set of datapaths and control lines for branches will be added shortly.

We need to connect these two control signals to the PC write control. Just as we did in the single-cycle datapath, we will use a few gates to derive the PC write control signal from PCWrite, PCWriteCond, and the Zero signal of the ALU, which is used to detect if the two register operands of a beq are equal. To determine whether the PC should be written during a conditional branch, we AND together the Zero signal of the ALU with the PCWriteCond. The output of this AND gate is then ORed with PCWrite, which is the unconditional PC write signal. The output of this OR gate is connected to the write control signal for the PC.

Figure 5.33 shows the complete multicycle datapath and control unit, including the additional control signals and multiplexor for implementing the PC updating.

Before examining the steps to execute each instruction, let us informally examine the effect of all the control signals (just as we did for the single-cycle design in Figure 5.18 on page 359). Figure 5.34 shows what each control signal does when asserted and deasserted.

Elaboration: To reduce the number of signal lines interconnecting the functional units, designers can use *shared buses*. A shared bus is a set of lines that connect multiple units; in most cases, they include multiple sources that can place data on the bus and multiple readers of the value. Just as we reduced the number of functional units for the datapath, we can reduce the number of buses interconnecting these units by sharing the buses. For example, there are six sources coming to the ALU; however, only two of them are needed at any one time. Thus, a pair of buses can be used to hold values that are being sent to the ALU. Rather than placing a large multiplexor in front of the ALU, a designer can use a shared bus and then ensure that only one of the sources is driving the bus at any point. Although this saves signal lines, the same number of control lines will be needed to control what goes on the bus. The major drawback to using such bus structures is a potential performance penalty, since a bus is unlikely to be as fast as a point-to-point connection.

Breaking the Instruction Execution into Clock Cycles

Given the datapath in Figure 5.33, we now need to look at what should happen in each clock cycle of the multicycle execution, since this will determine what additional control signals may be needed, as well as the setting of the control signals. Our goal in breaking the execution into clock cycles should be to balance the amount of work done in each cycle, so that we minimize the clock cycle time. We can begin by breaking the execution of any instruction into a series of steps, each taking 1 clock cycle, which will be roughly balanced in length. For example, we will restrict each step to contain at most one

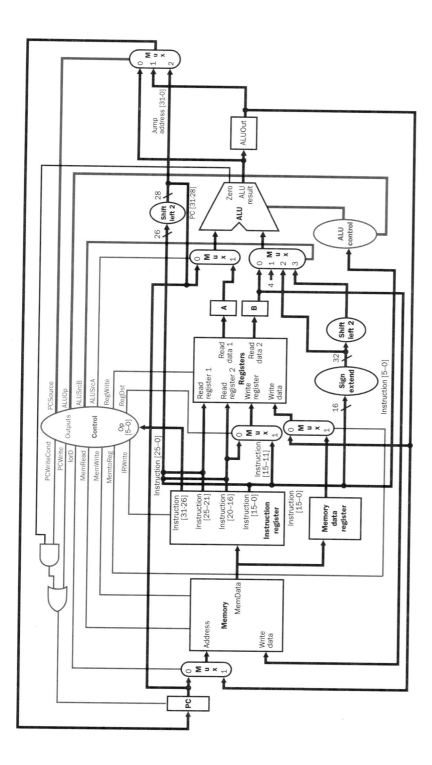

FIGURE 5.33 The complete datapath for the multicycle implementation together with the necessary control lines. The control lines of Figure 5.32 are attached to the control unit, and the control and datapath elements needed to effect changes to the PC are included. The major additions from Figure 5.32 include the multiplexor used to select the source of a new PC value (at the top right); two gates used to combine the PC write signals (top left); and the control signals PCSource, PCWrite, and PCWriteCond. The PCWriteCond signal is ANDed with the Zero output of the ALU to decide whether a branch should be taken; the resulting signal is ORed with the control signal PCWrite to generate the actual write control signal for the PC. In addition, the output of the IR is rearranged to send the lower 26 bits (the jump address) to the logic used to select the next PC. These 26 bits are shifted to the left by two, adding 2 low-order 0 bits; these 28 bits are then concatenated with the high-order 4 bits of the PC, which has already been incremented.

Actions of the 1-bit control signals

Signal name	Effect when deasserted	Effect when asserted
RegDst	The register file destination number for the Write register comes from the rt field.	The register file destination number for the Write register comes from the rd field.
RegWrite	None	The general-purpose register selected by the Write register number is written with the value of the Write data input.
ALUSrcA	The first ALU operand is the PC.	The first ALU operand comes from the A register.
MemRead	None	Content of memory at the location specified by the Address input is put on Memory data output.
MemWrite	None	Memory contents at the location specified by the Address input is replaced by value on Write data input.
MemtoReg	The value fed to the register file Write data input comes from ALUOut.	The value fed to the register file Write data input comes from the MDR.
IorD	The PC is used to supply the address to the memory unit.	ALUOut is used to supply the address to the memory unit.
IRWrite	None	The output of the memory is written into the IR.
PCWrite	None	The PC is written; the source is controlled by PCSource.
PCWriteCond	None	The PC is written if the Zero output from the ALU is also active.

Actions of the 2-bit control signals

Signal name	Value	Effect
ALUOp	00	The ALU performs an add operation.
	01	The ALU performs a subtract operation.
	10	The funct field of the instruction determines the ALU operation.
ALUSrcB	00	The second input to the ALU comes from the B register.
	01	The second input to the ALU is the constant 4.
	10	The second input to the ALU is the sign-extended, lower 16 bits of the IR.
	11	The second input to the ALU is the sign-extended, lower 16 bits of the IR shifted left 2 bits.
PCSource	00	Output of the ALU (PC + 4) is sent to the PC for writing.
	01	The contents of ALUOut (the branch target address) are sent to the PC for writing.
	10	The jump target address (IR[25–0] shifted left 2 bits and concatenated with PC + 4[31–28]) is sent to the PC for writing.

FIGURE 5.34   The action caused by the setting of each control signal in Figure 5.33 on page 383. The top table describes the 1-bit control signals, while the bottom table describes the 2-bit signals. Only those control lines that affect multiplexors have an action when they are deasserted. This information is similar to that in Figure 5.18 on page 359 for the single-cycle datapath, but adds several new control lines (IRWrite, PCWrite, PCWriteCond, ALUSrcB, and PCSource) and removes control lines that are no longer used or have been replaced (PCSrc, Branch, and Jump).

ALU operation, or one register file access, or one memory access. With this restriction, the clock cycle could be as short as the longest of these operations.

Recall that at the end of every clock cycle any data values that will be needed on a subsequent cycle must be stored into a register, which can be either one of the major state elements (e.g., the PC, the register file, or the memory), a temporary register written on every clock cycle (e.g., A, B, MDR, or ALUOut), or a temporary register with write control (e.g., IR). Also remember that because our design is edge-triggered, we can continue to read the current value of a register; the new value does not appear until the next clock cycle.

In the single-cycle datapath, each instruction uses a set of datapath elements to carry out its execution. Many of the datapath elements operate in series, using the output of another element as an input. Some datapath elements operate in parallel; for example, the PC is incremented and the instruction is read at the same time. A similar situation exists in the multicycle datapath. All the operations listed in one step occur in parallel within 1 clock cycle, while successive steps operate in series in different clock cycles. The limitation of one ALU operation, one memory access, and one register file access determines what can fit in one step.

Notice that we distinguish between reading from or writing into the PC or one of the stand-alone registers and reading from or writing into the register file. In the former case, the read or write is part of a clock cycle, while reading or writing a result into the register file takes an additional clock cycle. The reason for this distinction is that the register file has additional control and access overhead compared to the single stand-alone registers. Thus keeping the clock cycle short motivates dedicating separate clock cycles for register file accesses.

The potential execution steps and their actions are given below. Each instruction needs from three to five of these steps:

1. Instruction fetch step

Fetch the instruction from memory and compute the address of the next sequential instruction:

```
IR = Memory[PC];
PC = PC + 4;
```

Operation: Send the PC to the memory as the address, perform a read, and write the instruction into the Instruction register (IR), where it will be stored. Also, increment the PC by four. To implement this step, we will need to assert the control signals MemRead and IRWrite, and set IorD to 0 to select the PC as the source of the address. We also increment the PC by four in this stage, which requires setting the ALUSrcA signal to 0 (sending the PC to the ALU), the ALUSrcB signal to 01 (sending 4 to the ALU), and ALUOp to 00 (to make the ALU add). Finally, we will also want to store the incremented instruction address back into the PC, which requires setting PCWrite. The increment of the PC and the instruction memory access can occur in parallel. The new value of the PC is not visible until the next clock cycle. (The incremented PC will also be stored into ALUOut, but this action is benign.)

2.   Instruction decode and register fetch step

In the previous step and in this one, we do not yet know what the instruction is, so we can perform only actions that are either applicable to all instructions (such as fetching the instruction in step 1) or are not harmful, in case the instruction isn't what we think it might be. Thus, in this step we can read the two registers indicated by the rs and rt instruction fields, since it isn't harmful to read them even if it isn't necessary. The values read from the register file may be needed in later stages, so we read them from the register file and store the values into the temporary registers A and B.

We will also compute the branch target address with the ALU, which also is not harmful because we can ignore the value if the instruction turns out not to be a branch. The potential branch target is saved in ALUOut.

Performing these "optimistic" actions early has the benefit of decreasing the number of clock cycles needed to execute an instruction. We can do these optimistic actions early because of the regularity of the instruction formats. For instance, if the instruction has two register inputs, they are always in the rs and rt fields; and if the instruction is a branch, the offset is always the low-order 16 bits:

```
A = Reg[IR[25-21]];
B = Reg[IR[20-16]];
ALUOut = PC + (sign-extend (IR[15-0]) << 2);
```

Operation: Access the register file to read registers rs and rt and store the results into the registers A and B. Since A and B are overwritten on every cycle, the register file can be read on every cycle with the values stored into A and B. This step also computes the branch target address and stores the address in ALUOut, where it will be used on the next clock cycle if the instruction is a branch. This requires setting ALUSrcA to 0 (so that the PC is sent to the ALU), ALUSrcB to the value 11 (so that the sign-extended and shifted offset field is sent to the ALU), and ALUOp to 00 (so the ALU adds). The register file accesses and computation of branch target occur in parallel.

After this clock cycle, determining the action to take can depend on the instruction contents.

3.   Execution, memory address computation, or branch completion

This is the first cycle during which the datapath operation is determined by the instruction class. In all cases, the ALU is operating on the operands prepared in the previous step, performing one of three functions, depending on the instruction class. We specify the action to be taken depending on the instruction class:

Memory reference:

```
ALUOut = A + sign-extend (IR[15-0]);
```

Operation: The ALU is adding the operands to form the memory address. This requires setting ALUSrcA to 1 (so that the first ALU input is register A) and setting ALUSrcB to 10 (so that the output of the sign extension unit is used for the second ALU input). The ALUOp signals will need to be set to 00 (causing the ALU to add).

Arithmetic-logical instruction (R-type):

```
ALUOut = A op B;
```

Operation: The ALU is performing the operation specified by the function code on the two values read from the register file in the previous cycle. This requires setting ALUSrcA = 1 and setting ALUSrcB = 00 (together causing the registers A and B to be used as the ALU inputs). The ALUOp signals will need to be set to 10 (so that the funct field is used to determine the ALU control signal settings).

Branch:

```
if (A == B) PC = ALUOut;
```

Operation: The ALU is used to do the equal comparison between the two registers read in the previous step. The Zero signal out of the ALU is used to determine whether or not to branch. This requires setting ALUSrcA = 1 and setting ALUSrcB = 00 (so that the register file outputs are the ALU inputs). The ALUOp signals will need to be set to 01 (causing the ALU to subtract) for equality testing. The PCCondWrite signal will need to be asserted to update the PC if the Zero output of the ALU is asserted. By setting PCSource to 01, the value written into the PC will come from ALUOut, which holds the branch target address computed in the previous cycle. For conditional branches that are taken, we actually write the PC twice: once from the output of the ALU (during the Instruction decode/register fetch) and once from ALUOut (during the Branch completion step). The value written into the PC last is the one used for the next instruction fetch.

Jump:

```
PC = PC [31-28] || (IR[25-0]<<2)
```

Operation: The PC is replaced by the jump address. PCSource is set to direct the jump address to the PC, and PCWrite is asserted to write the jump address into the PC.

4. Memory access or R-type instruction completion step

During this step, a load or store instruction accesses memory and an arithmetic-logical instruction writes its result. When a value is retrieved from memory it is stored into the memory data register (MDR), where it must be used on the next clock cycle.

Memory reference:

        MDR = Memory [ALUOut];

or

        Memory [ALUOut] = B;

Operation: If the instruction is a load, a data word is retrieved from memory and is written into the MDR. If the instruction is a store, then the data is written into memory. In either case, the address used is the one computed during the previous step and stored in ALUOut. For a store, the source operand is saved in B. (B is actually read twice, once in step 2 and once in step 3. Luckily, the same value is read both times, since the register number—which is stored in IR and used to read from the register file—does not change.) The signal MemRead (for a load) or MemWrite (for store) will need to be asserted. In addition, for loads, the signal IorD is set to 1 to force the memory address to come from the ALU, rather than the PC. Since MDR is written on every clock cycle, no explicit control signal need be asserted.

Arithmetic-logical instruction (R-type):

        Reg[IR[15-11]] = ALUOut;

Operation: Place the contents of ALUOut, which corresponds to the output of the ALU operation in the previous cycle, into the Result register. The signal RegDst must be set to 1 (to force the rd (bits 15–11) field to be used to select the register file entry to write). RegWrite must be asserted, and MemtoReg must be set to 0 (so that the output of the ALU is written, as opposed to the memory data output).

5. Memory read completion step

During this step, loads complete by writing back the value from memory.

Load:

        Reg[IR[20-16]] = MDR;

Operation: Write the load data, which was stored into MDR in the previous cycle, into the register file. To do this, we set MemtoReg = 1 (to write the result from memory), assert RegWrite (to cause a write), and we make RegDst = 0 to choose the rt (bits 20–16) field as the register number.

Step name	Action for R-type instructions	Action for memory-reference instructions	Action for branches	Action for jumps
Instruction fetch	IR = Memory[PC] PC = PC + 4			
Instruction decode/register fetch	A = Reg [IR[25–21]] B = Reg [IR[20–16]] ALUOut = PC + (sign-extend (IR[15–0]) << 2)			
Execution, address computation, branch/ jump completion	ALUOut = A op B	ALUOut = A + sign-extend (IR[15–0])	if (A == B) then PC = ALUOut	PC = PC [31–28] || (IR[25–0]<<2)
Memory access or R-type completion	Reg [IR[15–11]] = ALUOut	Load: MDR = Memory[ALUOut] or Store: Memory [ALUOut] = B		
Memory read completion		Load: Reg[IR[20–16]] = MDR		

FIGURE 5.35 Summary of the steps taken to execute any instruction class. Instructions take from three to five execution steps. The first two steps are independent of the instruction class. After these steps, an instruction takes from one to three more cycles to complete, depending on the instruction class. The empty entries for the Memory access step or the Memory read completion step indicate that the particular instruction class takes fewer cycles. In a multicycle implementation, a new instruction will be started as soon as the current instruction completes, so these cycles are not idle or wasted. As mentioned earlier, the register file actually reads every cycle, but as long as the IR does not change, the values read from the register file are identical. In particular, the value read into register B during the Instruction decode stage, for a branch or R-type instruction, is the same as the value stored into B during the Execution stage and then used in the Memory access stage for a store word instruction.

This five-step sequence is summarized in Figure 5.35. From this sequence we can determine what the control must do on each clock cycle.

Defining the Control

Now that we have determined what the control signals are and when they must be asserted, we can implement the control unit. To design the control unit for the single-cycle datapath, we used a set of truth tables that specified the setting of the control signals based on the instruction class. For the multicycle datapath, the control is more complex because the instruction is executed in a series of steps. The control for the multicycle datapath must specify both the signals to be set in any step and the next step in the sequence.

In this subsection and in section 5.5, we will look at two different techniques to specify the control. The first technique is based on finite state machines that are usually represented graphically. The second technique, called *microprogramming*, uses a programming representation for control. Both of these techniques represent the control in a form that allows the detailed implementation—using gates, ROMs, or PLAs—to be synthesized by a CAD system. In this chapter, we will focus on the design of the control and its representation in these two forms. If you are interested in how these control specifications are translated into actual hardware, Appendix C continues the development of this chapter, translating the multicycle control unit to a detailed hardware implementation. The key ideas of control can be grasped from this chapter without examining the material in Appendix C. However, if you want to get down to the bits, Appendix C can show you how to do it!

The first method we use to specify the multicycle control is a *finite state machine*. A finite state machine consists of a set of states and directions on how to change states. The directions are defined by a *next-state function*, which maps the current state and the inputs to a new state. When we use a finite state machine for control, each state also specifies a set of outputs that are asserted when the machine is in that state. The implementation of a finite state machine usually assumes that all outputs that are not explicitly asserted are deasserted. The correct operation of the datapath depends on the fact that a signal that is not explicitly asserted is deasserted, rather than acting as a don't care. For example, the RegWrite signal should be asserted only when a register file entry is to be written; when it is not explicitly asserted, it must be deasserted.

Multiplexor controls are slightly different, since they select one of the inputs whether they are 0 or 1. Thus, in the finite state machine, we always specify the setting of all the multiplexor controls that we care about. When we implement the finite state machine with logic, setting a control to 0 may be the default and thus may not require any gates. A simple example of a finite state machine appears in Appendix B, and if you are unfamiliar with the concept of a finite state machine, you may want to examine Appendix B before proceeding.

The finite state control essentially corresponds to the five steps of execution shown on pages 385 through 388; each state in the finite state machine will take 1 clock cycle. The finite state machine will consist of several parts. Since the first two steps of execution are identical for every instruction, the initial two states of the finite state machine will be common for all instructions. Steps 3 through 5 differ, depending on the opcode. After the execution of the last step for a particular instruction class, the finite state machine will return to the initial state to begin fetching the next instruction.

Figure 5.36 shows this abstracted representation of the finite state machine. To fill in the details of the finite state machine, we will first expand the instruction fetch and decode portion, then we will show the states (and actions) for the different instruction classes.

We show the first two states of the finite state machine in Figure 5.37 using a traditional graphic representation. We number the states to simplify the explanation, though the numbers are arbitrary. State 0, corresponding to step 1, is the starting state of the machine.

The signals that are asserted in each state are shown within the circle representing the state. The arcs between states define the next state and are labeled

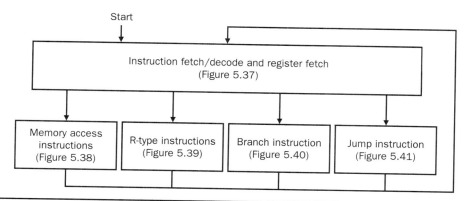

FIGURE 5.36 The high-level view of the finite state machine control. The first steps are independent of the instruction class; then a series of sequences that depend on the instruction opcode are used to complete each instruction class. After completing the actions needed for that instruction class, the control returns to fetch a new instruction. Each box in this figure may represent one to several states. The arc labeled *Start* marks the state in which to begin when the first instruction is to be fetched.

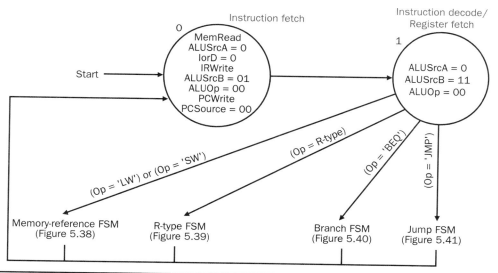

FIGURE 5.37 The instruction fetch and decode portion of every instruction is identical. These states correspond to the top box in the abstract finite state machine in Figure 5.36. In the first state we assert two signals to cause the memory to read an instruction and write it into the Instruction register (MemRead and IRWrite), and we set IorD to 0 to choose the PC as the address source. The signals ALUSrcA, ALUSrcB, ALUOp, PCWrite, and PCSource are set to compute PC + 4 and store it into the PC. (It will also be stored into ALUOut, but never used from there.). In the next state, we compute the branch target address by setting ALUSrcB to 11 (causing the shifted and sign-extended lower 16 bits of the IR to be sent to the ALU), setting ALUSrcA to 0 and ALUOp to 00; we store the result in the ALUOut register, which is written on every cycle. There are four next states that depend on the class of the instruction, which is known during this state. The control unit input, called Op, is used to determine which of these arcs to follow.

with conditions that select a specific next state when multiple next states are possible. After state 1, the signals asserted depend on the class of instruction. Thus, the finite state machine has four arcs exiting state 1, corresponding to the four instruction classes: memory reference, R-type, branch on equal, and jump. This process of branching to different states depending on the instruction is called *decoding*, since the choice of the next state, and hence the actions that follow, depend on the instruction class.

Figure 5.38 shows the portion of the finite state machine needed to implement the memory-reference instructions. For the memory-reference instructions, the first state after fetching the instruction and registers computes the memory address (state 2). To compute the memory address, the ALU input multiplexors must be set so that the first input is the A register, while the second input is the sign-extended displacement field; the result is written into the ALUOut register. After the memory address calculation, the memory should be read or written; this requires two different states. If the instruction opcode is lw, then state 3 (corresponding to the step Memory access) does the memory read (MemRead is asserted). The output of the memory is always written into MDR. If it is sw, state 5 does a memory write (MemWrite is asserted). In states 3 and 5, the signal IorD is set to 1 to force the memory address to come from the ALU. (This is not needed for stores, since the write address uses a different input into the memory.) After performing a write, the instruction sw has completed execution, and the next state is state 0. If the instruction is a load, however, another state (state 4) is needed to write the result from the memory into the register file. Setting the multiplexor controls MemtoReg = 1 and RegDst = 0 will send the loaded value in the MDR to be written into the register file, using rt as the register number. After this state, corresponding to the Memory read completion step, the next state is state 0.

To implement the R-type instructions requires two states corresponding to steps 3 (Execute) and 4 (R-type completion). Figure 5.39 shows this two-state portion of the finite state machine. State 6 asserts ALUSrcA and sets the ALUSrcB signals to 00; this forces the two registers that were read from the register file to be used as inputs to the ALU. Setting ALUOp to 10 causes the ALU control unit to use the function field to set the ALU control signals. In state 7, RegWrite is asserted to cause the register file to write, RegDst is asserted to cause the rd field to be used as the register number of the destination, and MemtoReg is deasserted to select ALUOut as the source of the value to write into the register file.

For branches, only a single additional state is necessary, because they complete execution during the third step of instruction execution. During this state, the control signals that cause the ALU to compare the contents of registers A and B must be set, and the signals that cause the PC to be written conditionally with the address in the ALUOut register are also set. To perform the

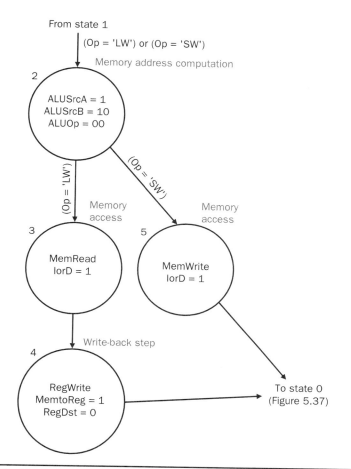

FIGURE 5.38 The finite state machine for controlling memory-reference instructions has four states. These states correspond to the box labeled "Memory access instructions" in Figure 5.36. After performing a memory address calculation, a separate sequence is needed for load and for store. The setting of the control signals ALUSrcA, ALUSrcB, and ALUOp is used to cause the memory address computation in state 2. Loads require an extra state to write the result from the MDR (where the result is written in state 3) into the register file.

comparison requires that we assert ALUSrcA and set ALUSrcB to 00, and set the ALUOp value to 01 (forcing a subtract). (We use only the Zero output of the ALU, not the result of the subtraction.) To control the writing of the PC, we assert PCWriteCond and set PCSource = 01, which will cause the value in the

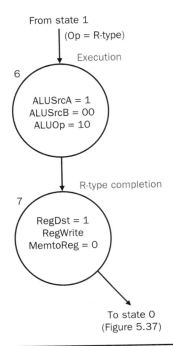

FIGURE 5.39   R-type instructions can be implemented with a simple two-state finite state machine. These states correspond to the box labeled "R-type instructions" in Figure 5.36. The first state causes the ALU operation to occur, while the second state causes the ALU result (which is in ALUOut) to be written in the register file. The three signals asserted during state 7 cause the contents of ALUOut to be written into the register file in the entry specified by the rd field of the Instruction register.

ALUOut register (containing the branch address calculated in state 1, Figure 5.37 on page 391) to be written into the PC if the Zero bit out of the ALU is asserted. Figure 5.40 shows this single state.

The last instruction class is jump; like branch, it requires only a single state (shown in Figure 5.41) to complete its execution. In this state, the signal PCWrite is asserted to cause the PC to be written. By setting PCSource to 10, the value supplied for writing will be the lower 26 bits of the Instruction register with 00_{two} added as the low-order bits concatenated with the upper 4 bits of the PC.

We can now put these pieces of the finite state machine together to form a specification for the control unit, as shown in Figure 5.42. In each state, the signals that are asserted are shown. The next state depends on the opcode bits of the instruction, so we label the arcs with a comparison for the corresponding instruction opcodes.

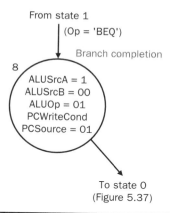

FIGURE 5.40 The branch instruction requires a single state. The first three outputs that are asserted cause the ALU to compare the registers (ALUSrcA, ALUSrcB, and ALUOp), while the signals PCSource and PCWriteCond perform the conditional write if the branch condition is true. Notice that we do not use the value written into ALUOut; instead, we use only the Zero output of the ALU. The branch target address is read from ALUOut, where it was saved at the end of state 1.

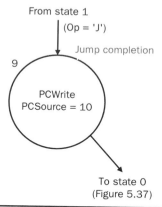

FIGURE 5.41 The jump instruction requires a single state that asserts two control signals to write the PC with the lower 26 bits of the Instruction register shifted left 2 bits and concatenated to the upper 4 bits of the PC of this instruction.

Given this implementation, and the knowledge that each state requires 1 clock cycle, we can find the CPI for a typical instruction mix.

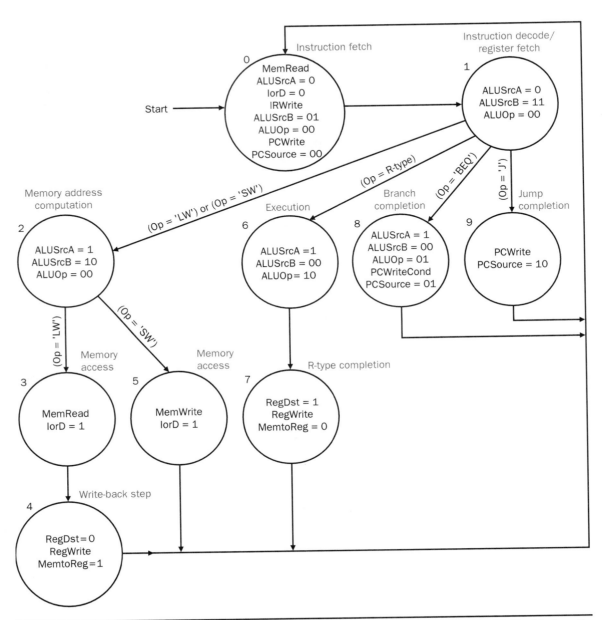

FIGURE 5.42   The complete finite state machine control for the datapath shown in Figure 5.33. The labels on the arcs are conditions that are tested to determine which state is the next state; when the next state is unconditional, no label is given. The labels inside the nodes indicate the output signals asserted during that state; we always specify the setting of a multiplexor control signal if the correct operation requires it. Hence, in some states a multiplexor control will be set to 0. In Appendix C, we examine how to turn this finite state machine into logic equations and look at how to implement those logic equations.

CPI in a Multicycle CPU

Example

Using the control shown in Figure 5.42 and the gcc instruction mix shown in the example starting on page 373, what is the CPI, assuming that each state requires 1 clock cycle?

Answer

The mix is 22% loads, 11% stores, 49% R-format operations, 16% branches, and 2% jumps. From Figure 5.42, the number of clock cycles for each instruction class is the following:

- Loads: 5
- Stores: 4
- R-format instructions: 4
- Branches: 3
- Jumps: 3

The CPI is given by the following:

$$\text{CPI} = \frac{\text{CPU clock cycles}}{\text{Instruction count}} = \frac{\sum \text{Instruction count}_i \times \text{CPI}_i}{\text{Instruction count}}$$

$$= \sum \frac{\text{Instruction count}_i}{\text{Instruction count}} \times \text{CPI}_i$$

The ratio

$$\frac{\text{Instruction count}_i}{\text{Instruction count}}$$

is simply the instruction frequency for the instruction class i. We can therefore substitute to obtain

$$\text{CPI} = 0.22 \times 5 + 0.11 \times 4 + 0.49 \times 4 + 0.16 \times 3 + 0.02 \times 3$$

$$= 1.1 + 0.44 + 1.96 + 0.48 + 0.06 = 4.04$$

This CPI is better than the worst-case CPI would have been if all the instructions took the same number of clock cycles (5).

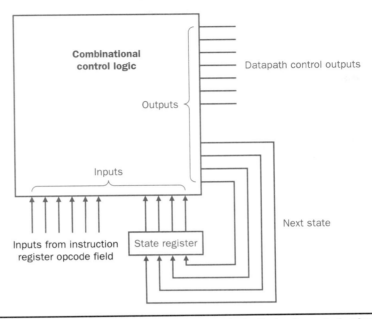

FIGURE 5.43   Finite state machine controllers are typically implemented using a block of combinational logic and a register to hold the current state. The outputs of the combinational logic are the next-state number and the control signals to be asserted for the current state. The inputs to the combinational logic are the current state and any inputs used to determine the next state. In this case, the inputs are the instruction register opcode bits. Notice that in the finite state machine used in this chapter, the outputs depend only on the current state, not on the inputs. The following elaboration explains this in more detail.

A finite state machine can be implemented with a temporary register that holds the current state and a block of combinational logic that determines both the datapath signals to be asserted as well as the next state. Figure 5.43 shows how such an implementation might look. Appendix C describes in detail how the finite state machine is implemented using this structure. In section C.3, the combinational control logic for the finite state machine of Figure 5.42 is implemented both with a ROM (read-only memory) and a PLA (programmable logic array). (Also see Appendix B for a description of these logic elements.) In the next section of this chapter, we consider another way to represent control. Both of these techniques are simply different representations of the same control information.

Elaboration: The style of finite state machine in Figure 5.43 is called a Moore machine, after Edward Moore. Its identifying characteristic is that the output depends only on the current state. For a Moore machine, the box labeled combinatorial control logic can be split into two pieces. One piece has the control output and only the state input, while the other has only the next-state output.

An alternative style of machine is a Mealy machine, named after George Mealy. The Mealy machine allows both the input and the current state to be used to determine the output. Moore machines have potential implementation advantages in speed and size of the control unit. The speed advantages arise because the control outputs, which are needed early in the clock cycle, do not depend on the inputs, but only on the current state. In Appendix C, when the implementation of this finite state machine is taken down to logic gates, the size advantage can be clearly seen. The potential disadvantage of a Moore machine is that it may require additional states. For example, in situations where there is a one-state difference between two sequences of states, the Mealy machine may unify the states by making the outputs depend on the inputs.

5.5 Microprogramming: Simplifying Control Design

For the control of our simple MIPS subset, a graphical representation of the finite state machine, as in Figure 5.42, is certainly adequate. We can draw such a diagram on a single page and translate it into equations (see Appendix C) without generating too many errors. Consider instead an implementation of the full MIPS instruction set, which contains over 100 instructions (see Appendix A). In one implementation, instructions take from 1 clock cycle to over 20 clock cycles. Clearly, the control function will be much more complex. Or consider an instruction set with more instructions of widely varying classes: The control unit could easily require thousands of states with hundreds of different sequences. For example, the Intel 80x86 instruction set has many more addressing mode combinations, as well as a much larger set of opcodes.

In such cases, specifying the control unit with a graphical representation will be cumbersome, since the finite state machine can contain hundreds to thousands of states, and even more arcs! The graphical representation—although useful for a small finite state machine—will not fit on a page, let alone be understandable, when it becomes very large. Programmers know this phenomenon quite well: As programs become large, additional structuring techniques (for example, procedures and modules) are needed to keep the programs comprehensible. Of course, specifying complex control functions directly as equations, without making any mistakes, becomes essentially impossible.

Can we use some of the ideas from programming to help create a method of specifying the control that will make it easier to understand as well as to design? Suppose we think of the set of control signals that must be asserted in a state as an instruction to be executed by the datapath. To avoid confusing the instructions of the MIPS instruction set with these low-level control instructions, the latter are called *microinstructions*. Each microinstruction defines the set of datapath control signals that must be asserted in a given state. Executing a microinstruction has the effect of asserting the control signals specified by the microinstruction.

In addition to defining which control signals must be asserted, we must also specify the sequencing—what microinstruction should be executed next? In the finite state machine shown in Figure 5.42 on page 396, the next state is determined in one of two different ways. Sometimes a single next state follows the current state unconditionally. For example, state 1 always follows state 0, and the only way to reach state 1 is via state 0. In other cases, the choice of the next state depends on the input. This is true in state 1, which has four different successor states.

When we write programs, we also have an analogous situation. Sometimes a group of instructions should be executed sequentially, and sometimes we need to branch. In programming, the default is sequential execution, while branching must be indicated explicitly. In describing the control as a program, we also assume that microinstructions written sequentially are executed in sequence, while branching must be indicated explicitly. The default sequencing mechanism can still be implemented using a structure like the one in Figure 5.43 on page 398; however, it is often more efficient to implement the default sequential state using a counter. We will see how such an implementation looks at the end of this section.

Designing the control as a program that implements the machine instructions in terms of simpler microinstructions is called *microprogramming*. The key idea is to represent the asserted values on the control lines symbolically, so that the microprogram is a representation of the microinstructions, just as assembly language is a representation of the machine instructions. In choosing a syntax for an assembly language, we usually represent the machine instructions as a series of fields (opcode, registers, and offset or immediate field); likewise, we will represent a microinstruction syntactically as a sequence of fields whose functions are related.

Defining a Microinstruction Format

The microprogram is a symbolic representation of the control that will be translated by a program to control logic. In this way, we can choose how many fields a microinstruction should have and what control signals are affected by each field. The format of the microinstruction should be chosen so as to simplify the representation, making it easier to write and understand the microprogram. For example, it is useful to have one field that controls the ALU and a set of three fields that determine the two sources for the ALU operation as well as the destination of the ALU result. In addition to readability, we would also like the microprogram format to make it difficult or impossible to write inconsistent microinstructions. A microinstruction is inconsistent if it requires that a given control signal be set to two different values. We will see an example of how this could happen shortly.

To avoid a format that allows inconsistent microinstructions, we can make each field of the microinstruction responsible for specifying a nonoverlapping set of control signals. To choose how to make this partition of the control signals for this implementation into microinstruction fields, it is useful to re-examine two previous figures:

- Figure 5.33, on page 383, which shows all the control signals and how they affect the datapath
- Figure 5.34, on page 384, which shows the function of each datapath control signal

Signals that are never asserted simultaneously may share the same field. Figure 5.44 shows how the microinstruction can be broken into seven fields and defines the general function of each field. The first six fields of the micro-instruction control the datapath, while the Sequencing field (the seventh field) specifies how to select the next microinstruction.

Microinstructions are usually placed in a ROM or a PLA (both described in Appendix B and used to implement control in Appendix C), so we can assign addresses to the microinstructions. The addresses are usually given out sequentially, in the same way that we chose sequential numbers for the states in the finite state machine. Three different methods are available to choose the next microinstruction to be executed:

1. Increment the address of the current microinstruction to obtain the address of the next microinstruction. This sequential behavior is indicated in the microprogram by putting Seq in the Sequencing field. Since sequential execution of instructions is encountered often, many micro-programming systems make this the default.

Field name	Function of field
ALU control	Specify the operation being done by the ALU during this clock; the result is always written in ALUOut.
SRC1	Specify the source for the first ALU operand.
SRC2	Specify the source for the second ALU operand.
Register control	Specify read or write for the register file, and the source of the value for a write.
Memory	Specify read or write, and the source for the memory. For a read, specify the destination register.
PCWrite control	Specify the writing of the PC.
Sequencing	Specify how to choose the next microinstruction to be executed.

FIGURE 5.44 Each microinstruction contains these seven fields. The values for each field are shown in Figure 5.45.

2. Branch to the microinstruction that begins execution of the next MIPS instruction. We will label this initial microinstruction (corresponding to state 0) as `Fetch` and place the indicator `Fetch` in the Sequencing field to indicate this action.

3. Choose the next microinstruction based on the control unit input. Choosing the next microinstruction on the basis of some input is called a *dispatch*. Dispatch operations are usually implemented by creating a table containing the addresses of the target microinstructions. This table is indexed by the control unit input and may be implemented in a ROM or in a PLA. There are often multiple dispatch tables; for this implementation, we will need two dispatch tables, one to dispatch from state 1 and one to dispatch from state 2. We indicate that the next microinstruction should be chosen by a dispatch operation by placing `Dispatch i`, where i is the dispatch table number, in the Sequencing field.

Figure 5.45 gives a description of the values allowed for each field of the microinstruction and the effect of the different field values. Remember that the microprogram is a symbolic representation. This microinstruction format is just one example of many potential formats.

Elaboration: The basic microinstruction format may allow combinations that cannot be supported within the datapath. Typically, a microassembler will perform checks on the microinstruction fields to ensure that such inconsistencies are flagged as errors and corrected. An alternative is to structure the microinstruction format to avoid this, but this might make the microinstruction harder to read. Most microprogramming systems choose readability and require the microcode assembler to detect inconsistencies.

Creating the Microprogram

Now let's create the microprogram for the control unit. We will label the instructions in the microprogram with symbolic labels, which can be used to specify the contents of the dispatch tables (see section C.5 in Appendix C for a discussion of how the dispatch tables are defined and assembled). In writing the microprogram, there are two situations in which we may want to leave a field of the microinstruction blank. When a field that controls a functional unit or that causes state to be written (such as the Memory field or the ALU dest field) is blank, no control signals should be asserted. When a field *only* specifies the control of a multiplexor that determines the input to a functional unit, such as the SRC1 field, leaving it blank means that we do not care about the input to the functional unit (or the output of the multiplexor).

Field name	Values for field	Function of field with specific value
Label	Any string	Used to specify labels to control microcode sequencing. Labels that end in a 1 or 2 are used for dispatching with a jump table that is indexed based on the opcode. Other labels are used as direct targets in the microinstruction sequencing. Labels do not generate control signals directly but are used to define the contents of dispatch tables and generate control for the Sequencing field.
ALU control	Add	Cause the ALU to add.
	Subt	Cause the ALU to subtract; this implements the compare for branches.
	Func code	Use the instruction's funct field to determine ALU control.
SRC1	PC	Use the PC as the first ALU input.
	A	Register A is the first ALU input.
SRC2	B	Register B is the second ALU input.
	4	Use 4 for the second ALU input.
	Extend	Use output of the sign extension unit as the second ALU input.
	Extshft	Use the output of the shift-by-two unit as the second ALU input.
Register control	Read	Read two registers using the rs and rt fields of the IR as the register numbers, putting the data into registers A and B.
	Write ALU	Write the register file using the rd field of the IR as the register number and the contents of ALUOut as the data.
	Write MDR	Write the register file using the rt field of the IR as the register number and the contents of the MDR as the data.
Memory	Read PC	Read memory using the PC as address; write result into IR (and the MDR).
	Read ALU	Read memory using ALUOut as address; write result into MDR.
	Write ALU	Write memory using the ALUOut as address; contents of B as the data.
PCWrite control	ALU	Write the output of the ALU into the PC.
	ALUOut-cond	If the Zero output of the ALU is active, write the PC with the contents of the register ALUOut.
	Jump address	Write the PC with the jump address from the instruction.
Sequencing	Seq	Choose the next microinstruction sequentially.
	Fetch	Go to the first microinstruction to begin a new instruction.
	Dispatch i	Dispatch using the ROM specified by i (1 or 2).

FIGURE 5.45 Each field of the microinstruction has a number of values that it can take on. The second column gives the possible values that are legal for the field, and the third column defines the effect of that value. Each field value, other than the label field, is mapped to a particular setting of the datapath control lines; this mapping is described in Appendix C, section C.5. That section also shows how the label field is used to generate the dispatch tables. As we will see, the microcode implementation will differ slightly from the finite state machine control, but only in ways that do not affect instruction semantics.

The easiest way to understand the microprogram is to break it into pieces that deal with each component of instruction execution, just as we did when we designed the finite state machine.

The first component of every instruction execution is to fetch the instructions, decode them, and compute both the sequential PC and branch target PC. These actions correspond directly to the first two steps of execution described on pages 385 through 388. The two microinstructions needed for these first two steps are shown below:

Label	ALU control	SRC1	SRC2	Register control	Memory	PCWrite control	Sequencing
Fetch	Add	PC	4		Read PC	ALU	Seq
	Add	PC	Extshft	Read			Dispatch 1

To understand what each microinstruction does, it is easiest to look at the effect of a group of fields. In the first microinstruction, the fields asserted and their effects are the following:

Fields	Effect
ALU control, SRC1, SRC2	Compute PC + 4. (The value is also written into ALUOut, though it will never be read from there.)
Memory	Fetch instruction into IR.
PCWrite control	Causes the output of the ALU to be written into the PC.
Sequencing	Go to the next microinstruction.

The label field, containing the label Fetch, will be used in the Sequencing field when the microprogram wants to start the execution of the next instruction.

For the second microinstruction, the operations controlled by the microinstruction are the following:

Fields	Effect
ALU control, SRC1, SRC2	Store PC + sign extension (IR[15–0]) << 2 into ALUOut.
Register control	Use the rs and rt fields to read the registers placing the data in A and B.
Sequencing	Use dispatch table 1 to choose the next microinstruction address.

We can think of the dispatch operation as a *case* or *switch* statement with the opcode field and the dispatch table 1 used to select one of four different microinstruction sequences with one of four different labels (all ending in "1"):

■ Mem1 for memory-reference instructions

■ Rformat1 for R-type instructions

■ BEQ1 for the branch equal instruction

■ JUMP1 for the jump instruction

The microprogram for memory-reference instructions has four microinstructions, as shown below. The first instruction does the memory address calculation. A two-instruction sequence is needed to complete a load (memory read followed by register file write), while the store requires only one microinstruction after the memory address calculation:

Label	ALU control	SRC1	SRC2	Register control	Memory	PCWrite control	Sequencing
Mem1	Add	A	Extend				Dispatch 2
LW2					Read ALU		Seq
				Write MDR			Fetch
SW2					Write ALU		Fetch

Let's look at the fields of the first microinstruction in this sequence:

Fields	Effect
ALU control, SRC1, SRC2	Compute the memory address: Register (rs) + sign-extend (IR[15–0]), writing the result into ALUOut.
Sequencing	Use the second dispatch table to jump to the microinstruction labeled either LW2 or SW2.

The first microinstruction in the sequence specific to lw is labeled LW2, since it is reached by a dispatch through table 2. This microinstruction has the following effect:

Fields	Effect
Memory	Read memory using the ALU output as the address and writing the data into the MDR.
Sequencing	Go to the next microinstruction.

The next microinstruction completes execution with a microinstruction that has the following effects:

Fields	Effect
Register control	Write the contents of the MDR into the register file entry specified by rt.
Sequencing	Go to the microinstruction labeled Fetch.

The store microinstruction, labeled `SW2`, operates similarly to the load microinstruction labeled `LW2`:

Fields	Effect
Memory	Write memory using contents of ALUOut as the address and the contents of B as the value.
Sequencing	Go to the microinstruction labeled `Fetch`.

The microprogram sequence for R-type instructions consists of two microinstructions: the first does the ALU operation (and is labeled `Rformat1` for dispatch purposes), while the second writes the result into the register file:

Label	ALU control	SRC1	SRC2	Register control	Memory	PCWrite control	Sequencing
`Rformat1`	`Func code`	`A`	`B`				`Seq`
				`Write ALU`			`Fetch`

You might think that because the fields of these two microinstructions do not conflict (i.e., each uses different fields), you could combine them into one. Indeed, microcode optimizers perform such operations when compiling microcode. In this case, however, the result of the ALU instruction is written into the register ALUOut, and the written value cannot be read until the next clock cycle; hence we cannot combine them into one microinstruction. (If you did combine them, you'd end up writing the wrong thing into the register file!) You could try to remove the ALUOut register to allow the two microinstructions to be combined, but this would require lengthening the clock cycle to allow the register file write to occur in the same clock cycle as the ALU operation.

The first microinstruction initiates the ALU operation:

Fields	Effect
ALU control, SRC1, SRC2	The ALU operates on the contents of the A and B registers, using the function field to specify the ALU operation.
Sequencing	Go to the next microinstruction.

The second microinstruction causes the ALU output to be written in the register file:

Fields	Effect
Register control	The value in ALUOut is written into the register file entry specified by the rd field.
Sequencing	Go to the microinstruction labeled `Fetch`.

Because the immediately previously executed microinstruction computed the branch target address, the microprogram sequence for branch, labeled with BEQ, requires just one microinstruction:

Label	ALU control	SRC1	SRC2	Register control	Memory	PCWrite control	Sequencing
BEQ1	Subt	A	B			ALUOut-cond	Fetch

The asserted fields of this microinstruction are the following:

Fields	Effect
ALU control, SRC1, SRC2	The ALU subtracts the operands in A and B to generate the Zero output.
PCWrite control	Causes the PC to be written using the value already in ALUOut, if the Zero output of the ALU is true.
Sequencing	Go to the microinstruction labeled Fetch.

The jump microcode sequence also consists of one microinstruction:

Label	ALU control	SRC1	SRC2	Register control	Memory	PCWrite control	Sequencing
JUMP1						Jump address	Fetch

Only two fields of this microinstruction are asserted:

Fields	Effect
PCWrite control	Causes the PC to be written using the jump target address.
Sequencing	Go to the microinstruction labeled Fetch.

The entire microprogram appears in Figure 5.46. It consists of the 10 microinstructions appearing above. This microprogram matches the 10-state finite state machine we designed earlier, since they were both derived from the same five-step execution sequence for the instructions. In more complex machines, the microprogram sequence might consist of hundreds or thousands of microinstructions and would be the representation of choice for the control. Datapaths of more complex machines typically require additional scratch registers used for holding intermediate results when implementing complex multicycle instructions. Registers A and B are like such scratch registers, but datapaths for more complex instruction sets often have a larger number of such registers

Label	ALU control	SRC1	SRC2	Register control	Memory	PCWrite control	Sequencing
Fetch	Add	PC	4		Read PC	ALU	Seq
	Add	PC	Extshft	Read			Dispatch 1
Mem1	Add	A	Extend				Dispatch 2
LW2					Read ALU		Seq
				Write MDR			Fetch
SW2					Write ALU		Fetch
Rformat1	Func code	A	B				Seq
				Write ALU			Fetch
BEQ1	Subt	A	B			ALUOut-cond	Fetch
JUMP1						Jump address	Fetch

FIGURE 5.46   The microprogram for the control unit. Recall that the labels are used to determine the targets for the dispatch operations. Dispatch 1 does a jump based on the IR to a label ending with a 1, while Dispatch 2 does a jump based on the IR to a label ending with 2.

with a richer set of interconnections to other datapath elements. These registers are available to the microprogrammer and make the analogy of implementing the control as a programming task even stronger.

Implementing the Microprogram

Translating a microprogram into hardware involves two aspects: deciding how to implement the sequencing function and choosing a method of storing the main control function. The microprogram can be thought of as a text representation of a finite state machine, and implemented in exactly the same way we would implement a finite state machine: using a PLA to encode both the sequencing function as well as the main control (see Figure 5.43 on page 398). Often, however, both the implementation of the sequencing function, as well as the implementation of the main control function, are done differently, especially for large microprograms.

The alternative form of implementation involves storing the control function in a read-only memory (ROM) and implementing the sequencing function separately. Figure 5.47 shows this different way to implement the sequencing function: using an incrementer to choose the next control instruction. In this type of implementation, the microcode store would determine the value of the datapath control lines, as well as *how to select* the next state (as opposed to *specifying* the next state, as in our finite state machine implementation). The address select logic would contain the dispatch tables, implemented in ROMs or PLAs, and would, under the control of the address select outputs, determine the next microinstruction to execute. The advantage of this implementation of the sequencing function is that it removes the logic to implement normal

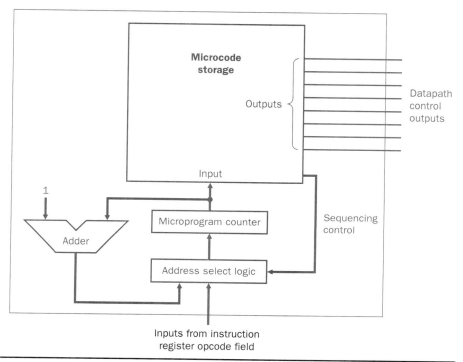

FIGURE 5.47 A typical implementation of a microcode controller would use an explicit incrementer to compute the default sequential next state and would place the microcode in a read-only memory. The microinstructions, used to set the datapath control, are assembled directly from the microprogram. The microprogram counter, which replaces the state register of a finite state machine controller, determines how the next microinstruction is chosen. The address select logic contains the dispatch tables as well as the logic to select from among the alternative next states; the selection of the next microinstruction is controlled by the sequencing control outputs from the control logic. The combination of the current microprogram counter, incrementer, dispatch tables, and address select logic forms a sequencer that selects the next microinstruction. The microcode storage may consist either of read-only memory (ROM) or may be implemented by a PLA. PLAs may be more efficient in VLSI implementations, while ROMs may be easier to change. Further discussions of the advantages of these two alternatives can be found in section 5.9 and in Appendix C.

sequencing of microinstructions, implementing such sequencing with a counter. Thus, in cases where there are long sequences of microinstructions, the explicit sequencer can result in less logic in the microcode controller.

In Figure 5.47, the main control function could be implemented in ROM, rather than implemented in a PLA. With a ROM implementation, the microprogram is assembled and stored in microcode storage and is addressed by the microprogram counter, in much the same way as a normal program is stored in program memory and the next instruction is chosen by the program counter.

This analogy with programming is both the origin of the terminology (micro-code, microprogramming, etc.) and the initial method by which micropro-grams were implemented (see section 5.10).

Although the type of sequencer shown in Figure 5.47 is typically used to im-plement a microprogram control specification, it can also be used to implement a finite state specification. Section C.4 of Appendix C describes how to gener-ate such a sequencer in more detail. Section C.5 describes how a microprogram can be translated to such an implementation. Similarly, Appendix C shows how the control function can be implemented in either a ROM or a PLA and discusses the trade-offs. In total, Appendix C shows how to go from the sym-bolic representations of finite state machines or microprograms shown in this chapter to either bits in a memory or entries in a PLA. If you are interested in detailed implementation or the translation process, you may want to proceed to Appendix C.

The choice of which way to represent the control (finite state diagram versus microprogram) and how to implement control (PLA versus ROM and encoded state versus explicit sequencer) are independent decisions, affected by both the structure of the control function and the technology used to implement the control. We return to these issues briefly in section 5.9, but before we do that we need to look at one of the hardest aspects of control: exceptions.

5.6   Exceptions

Control is the most challenging aspect of processor design: it is both the hard-est part to get right and the hardest part to make fast. One of the hardest parts of control is implementing *exceptions* and *interrupts*—events other than branches or jumps that change the normal flow of instruction execution. An exception is an unexpected event from within the processor; arithmetic over-flow is an example of an exception. An interrupt is an event that also causes an unexpected change in control flow but comes from outside of the proces-sor. Interrupts are used by I/O devices to communicate with the processor, as we will see in Chapter 8.

Many architectures and authors do not distinguish between interrupts and exceptions, often using the older name *interrupt* to refer to both types of events. We follow the MIPS convention, using the term *exception* to refer to *any* unex-pected change in control flow without distinguishing whether the cause is in-ternal or external; we use the term *interrupt* only when the event is externally caused. The Intel 80x86 architecture uses the word *interrupt* for all these events, while the PowerPC architecture uses the word *exception* to indicate that an un-usual event has occurred and *interrupt* to indicate the change in control flow.

Interrupts were initially created to handle unexpected events like arithmetic overflow and to signal requests for service from I/O devices. The same basic mechanism was extended to handle internally generated exceptions as well. Here are some examples showing whether the situation is generated internally by the processor or externally generated:

Type of event	From where?	MIPS terminology
I/O device request	External	Interrupt
Invoke the operating system from user program	Internal	Exception
Arithmetic overflow	Internal	Exception
Using an undefined instruction	Internal	Exception
Hardware malfunctions	Either	Exception or interrupt

Many of the requirements to support exceptions come from the specific situation that causes an exception to occur. Accordingly, we will return to this topic in Chapter 7, when we discuss memory hierarchies, and in Chapter 8, when we discuss I/O, and we better understand the motivation for additional capabilities in the exception mechanism. In this section, we deal with the control implementation for detecting two types of exceptions that arise from the portions of the instruction set and implementation that we have already discussed.

Detecting exceptional conditions and taking the appropriate action is often on the critical timing path of a machine, which determines the clock cycle time and thus performance. Without proper attention to exceptions during design of the control unit, attempts to add exceptions to a complicated implementation can significantly reduce performance, as well as complicate the task of getting the design correct.

How Exceptions Are Handled

The two types of exceptions that our current implementation can generate are execution of an undefined instruction and an arithmetic overflow. The basic action that the machine must perform when an exception occurs is to save the address of the offending instruction in the exception program counter (EPC) and then transfer control to the operating system at some specified address.

The operating system can then take the appropriate action, which may involve providing some service to the user program, taking some predefined action in response to an overflow, or stopping the execution of the program and reporting an error. After performing whatever action is required because of the exception, the operating system can terminate the program or may continue its execution, using the EPC to determine where to restart the execution of the program. In Chapter 7, we will look more closely at the issue of restarting the execution.

For the operating system to handle the exception, it must know the reason for the exception, in addition to the instruction that caused it. There are two main methods used to communicate the reason for an exception. The method used in the MIPS architecture is to include a status register (called the *Cause register*), which holds a field that indicates the reason for the exception.

A second method is to use *vectored interrupts*. In a vectored interrupt, the address to which control is transferred is determined by the cause of the exception. For example, to accommodate the two exception types listed above, we might define the following:

Exception type	Exception vector address (in hex)
Undefined instruction	C0 00 00 00$_{hex}$
Arithmetic overflow	C0 00 00 20$_{hex}$

The operating system knows the reason for the exception by the address at which it is initiated. The addresses are separated by 32 bytes or 8 instructions, and the operating system must record the reason for the exception and may perform some limited processing in this sequence. When the exception is not vectored, a single entry point for all exceptions can be used, and the operating system decodes the status register to find the cause.

We can perform the processing required for exceptions by adding a few extra registers and control signals to our basic implementation and by slightly extending the finite state machine. Let's assume that we are implementing the exception system used in the MIPS architecture. (Implementing vectored exceptions is no more difficult.) We will need to add two additional registers to the datapath:

- *EPC:* A 32-bit register used to hold the address of the affected instruction. (Such a register is needed even when exceptions are vectored.)

- *Cause:* A register used to record the cause of the exception. In the MIPS architecture, this register is 32 bits, although some bits are currently unused. Assume that the low-order bit of this register encodes the two possible exception sources mentioned above: undefined instruction = 0 and arithmetic overflow = 1.

We will need to add two control signals to cause the EPC and Cause registers to be written; call these *EPCWrite* and *CauseWrite*. In addition, we will need a 1-bit control signal to set the low-order bit of the Cause register appropriately; call this signal *IntCause*. Finally, we will need to be able to write the *exception address*, which is the operating system entry point for exception handling, into the PC; let's assume that this address is C0000000$_{hex}$. Currently, the PC is fed from the output of a three-way multiplexor, which is controlled by the signal

PCSource (see Figure 5.33 on page 383). We can change this to a four-way multiplexor, with additional input wired to the constant value C0000000$_{hex}$. Then PCSource can be set to 11_{two} to select this value to be written into the PC.

Because the PC is incremented during the first cycle of every instruction, we cannot just write the value of the PC into the EPC, since the value in the PC will be the instruction address plus four. However, we can use the ALU to subtract four from the PC and write the output into the EPC. This requires no additional control signals or paths, since we can use the ALU to subtract, and the constant 4 is already a selectable ALU input. The data write port of the EPC, therefore, is connected to the ALU output. Figure 5.48 shows the multicycle datapath with these additions needed for implementing exceptions.

Using the datapath of Figure 5.48, the action to be taken for each different type of exception can be handled in one state apiece. In each case, the state sets the Cause register, computes and saves the original PC into the EPC, and writes the exception address into the PC. Thus, to handle the two exception types we are considering, we will need to add only the two states shown in Figure 5.49.

To connect this finite state machine to the finite state machine of the main control unit, we must determine how to detect exceptions and add arcs that transfer control from the main execution machine to this exception-handling finite state machine.

How Control Checks for Exceptions

Now we have to design a method to detect these exceptions and to transfer control to the appropriate state in the exception states shown in Figure 5.49. Each of the two possible exceptions is detected differently:

- *Undefined instruction*: This is detected when no next state is defined from state 1 for the op value. We handle this exception by defining the next-state value for all op values other than lw, sw, 0 (R-type), j, and beq as state 10. We show this by symbolically using *other* to indicate that the op field does not match any of the opcodes that label arcs out of state 1. A modified finite state diagram is shown in Figure 5.50.

- *Arithmetic overflow*: Chapter 4 included logic in the ALU to detect overflow, and a signal called *Overflow* is provided as an output from the ALU. This signal is used in the modified finite state machine to specify an additional possible next state for state 7, as shown in Figure 5.50.

Figure 5.50 represents a complete specification of the control for this MIPS subset with two types of exceptions. Remember that the challenge in designing the control of a real machine is to handle the variety of different interactions between instructions and other exception-causing events in such a way that

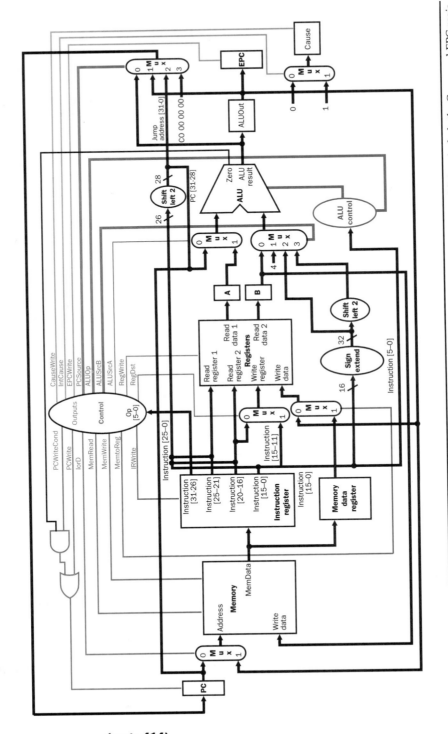

FIGURE 5.48 The multicycle datapath with the addition needed to implement exceptions. The specific additions include the Cause and EPC registers, a multiplexor to control the value sent to the Cause register, an expansion of the multiplexor controlling the value written into the PC, and control lines for the added multiplexor and registers.

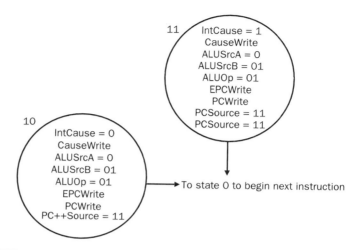

FIGURE 5.49 This pair of states handles the necessary actions for the two different exceptions we are considering. Each state provides control for three actions: setting the Cause register, getting the address of the offending instruction into the EPC, and setting the PC to the exception vector address. Both state 10 and state 11 represent the starting point for an exception. Control is transferred to one of these two states when an exception occurs. After either state 10 or state 11 is completed, control is transferred to state 0, and a new instruction is fetched.

the control logic remains both small and fast. The complex interactions that are possible are what make the control unit the most challenging aspect of hardware design.

Elaboration: If you examine the finite state machine in Figure 5.50 closely, you can see that some problems could occur in the way the exceptions are handled. For example, in the case of arithmetic overflow, the instruction causing the overflow completes writing its result because the overflow branch is in the state when the write completes. However, it's possible that the architecture defines the instruction as having no effect if the instruction causes an exception; this is what the MIPS instruction set architecture specifies. In Chapter 7, we will see that certain classes of exceptions require us to prevent the instruction from changing the machine state, and that this aspect of handling exceptions becomes complex and potentially limits performance.

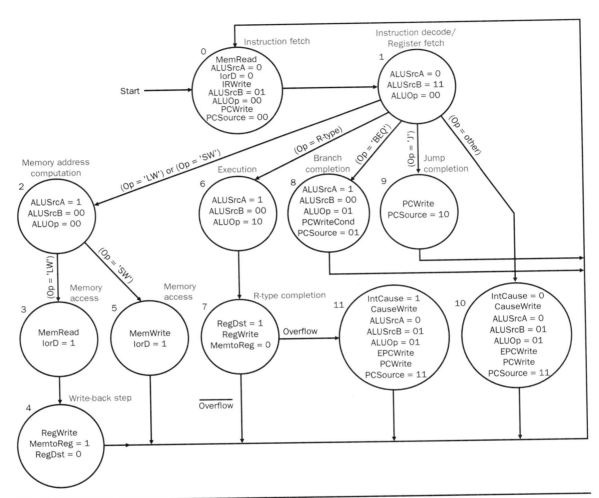

FIGURE 5.50   This shows the finite state machine with the additions to handle exception detection. States 10 and 11 come from Figure 5.49 on page 415. The branch out of state 1 labeled (*Op = other*) indicates the next state when the input does not match the opcode of any of lw, sw, 0 (R-type), j, or beq. The branch out of state 7 labeled *Overflow* indicates the action to be taken when the ALU signals an overflow.

5.7   Real Stuff: The Pentium Pro Implementation

The techniques described in this chapter for building datapaths and control units are at the heart of every computer. All recent computers, however, go beyond the techniques of this chapter and use pipelining. *Pipelining*, which is the subject of the next chapter, improves performance by overlapping the execution of multiple instructions, achieving throughput close to one instruction per clock cycle (like our single-cycle implementation) with a clock cycle time determined by the delay of individual functional units rather than the entire execution path of an instruction (like our multicycle design). The last Intel 80x86 processor without pipelining was the 80386 introduced in 1985; the very first MIPS processor, the R2000, also introduced in 1985, was pipelined.

Recent Intel 80x86 processors (the 80486, Pentium, and Pentium Pro) employ successively more sophisticated pipelining approaches. These processors, however, are still faced with the challenge of implementing control for the complex 80x86 instruction set, described in Chapter 3. The basic functional units and datapaths in use in modern processors, while significantly more complex than those described in this chapter, have the same basic functionality and similar types of control signals. Thus the task of designing a control unit builds on the same principles used in this chapter.

Challenges Implementing More Complex Architectures

Unlike the MIPS architecture, the 80x86 architecture contains instructions that are very complex and can take tens, if not hundreds, of cycles to execute. For example, the string move instruction (MOVS) requires calculating and updating two different memory addresses as well as loading and storing a byte of the string. The larger number and greater complexity of addressing modes in the 80x86 architecture complicates implementation of even simple instructions similar to those on MIPS. Fortunately, a multicycle datapath is well structured to adapt to variations in the amount of work required per instruction that are inherent in 80x86 instructions. This adaptability comes from two capabilities:

1. A multicycle datapath allows instructions to take varying numbers of clock cycles. Simple 80x86 instructions that are similar to those in the MIPS architecture can execute in three or four clock cycles, while more complex instructions can take tens of cycles.

2. A multicycle datapath can use the datapath components more than once per instruction. This is critical to handling more complex addressing modes, as well as implementing more complex operations, both of which are present in the 80x86 architecture. Without this capability the datapath would need to be extended to handle the demands of the more complex instructions without reusing components, which would be completely impractical. For example, a single-cycle datapath, which doesn't reuse components, for the 80x86 would require several data memories and a very large number of ALUs.

Using the multicycle datapath and a microprogrammed controller provides a framework for implementing the 80x86 instruction set. The challenging task, however, is creating a high-performance implementation, which requires dealing with the diversity of the requirements arising from different instructions. Simply put, a high-performance implementation needs to ensure that the simple instructions execute quickly, and that the burden of the complexities of the instruction set penalize primarily the complex, less frequently used, instructions.

To accomplish this goal, every Intel implementation of the 80x86 architecture since the 486 has used a combination of hardwired control to handle simple instructions, and microcoded control to handle the more complex instructions. For those instructions that can be executed in a single pass through the datapath (i.e., those with complexity similar to a MIPS instruction), the hardwired control generates the control information and executes the instruction in one pass through the datapath that takes a small number of clock cycles. Those instructions that require multiple datapath passes and complex sequencing are handled by the microcoded controller that takes a larger number of cycles and multiple passes through the datapath to complete the execution of the instruction. The benefit of this approach is that it enables the designer to achieve low cycle counts for the simple instructions without having to build the enormously complex datapath that would be required to handle the full generality of the most complex instructions.

The Structure of the Pentium Pro Implementation

Both the Pentium and Pentium Pro processors are capable of executing more than one instruction per clock, using an advanced pipelining technique, called *superscalar*. We describe how a superscalar processor works in the next chapter. The important thing to understand here is that executing more than one instruction per clock requires duplicating the datapath resources. The simplest way to think about this is that the processor has multiple datapaths, though these are tailored to handle one class of instructions: say, loads and stores, ALU operations, or branches. In this way, the processor is able to execute a load or store in the same clock cycle that it is also executing a branch and an ALU operation. The Pentium allows up to two such instructions to be executed in a clock cycle, while the Pentium Pro allows up to four.

The datapaths of the Pentium Pro actually execute simple microinstructions (or microoperations in Intel terminology), similar to MIPS instructions. These microinstructions are fully self-contained operations that are initially 72 bits wide. The control of datapath to implement these microinstructions is completely hardwired. This last level of control expands up to four 72-bit microinstructions into 120 control lines for the integer datapaths and 285 control lines for the floating-point datapath. This last step of expanding the microinstructions into control lines is very similar to the control generation for the single-cycle datapath or for the ALU control.

These microinstructions are generated from the 80x86 instructions either by hardwired control or by microprogrammed control. For 80x86 instructions that require less than four microinstructions to implement the 80x86 instruction, the 80x86 instruction is directly decoded into one to four microinstructions by a set of PLAs. These PLAs can generate a total of 1200 different microinstructions. If an 80x86 instruction requires more than four microinstructions, the control dispatches to a microcode control store and uses a traditional microcode sequencer to generate a sequence of five or more microinstructions. The microcode ROM provides a total of about 8000 microinstructions, with a number of sequences being shared among 80x86 instructions.

The use of simple low-level hardwired control and simple datapaths for handling the microinstructions allows the Pentium Pro to achieve impressive clock rates, similar to those for microprocessors implementing simpler instruction set architectures. Furthermore, the translation process, which combines direct hardwired control for simple instructions with microcoded control for complex instructions, allows the Pentium Pro to execute the simple, high-frequency instructions in the 80x86 instruction set at a high rate, yielding a low, and very competitive, CPI for integer instructions.

5.8 Fallacies and Pitfalls

Pitfall: Implementing a complex instruction with microcode may not be faster than a sequence using simpler instructions.

Most machines with a large and complex instruction set are implemented, at least in part, using a microcode stored in ROM. Surprisingly, on such machines, sequences of individual simpler instructions are sometimes as fast as or even faster than the custom microcode sequence for a particular instruction.

How can this possibly be true? At one time, microcode had the advantage of being fetched from a much faster memory than instructions in the program. Since caches came into use in 1968, microcode no longer has such a consistent edge in fetch time. Microcode does, however, still have the advantage of using internal temporary registers in the computation, which can be helpful on machines with few general-purpose registers. The disadvantage of microcode is that the algorithms must be selected before the machine is announced and can't be changed until the next model of the architecture. The instructions in a program, on the other hand, can utilize improvements in its algorithms at any time during the life of the machine. Along the same lines, the microcode sequence is probably not optimal for all possible combinations of operands.

One example of such an instruction in the 80x86 implementations is the move string instruction (MOVS) used with a repeat prefix that we discussed in Chapter 3. This instruction is often slower than a loop that moves words at a time, as we saw earlier in the Fallacies and Pitfalls (see page 185).

Another example involves the LOOP instruction, which decrements a register and branches to the specified label if the decremented register is not equal to zero. This instruction is similar to the PowerPC instruction "branch conditional to count register" (bcctr) discussed in Chapter 3. These instructions are designed to be used as the branch at the bottom of loops that have a fixed number of iterations (e.g., many *for* loops). Such an instruction, in addition to packing in some extra work, has benefits in minimizing the potential losses from the branch in pipelined machines (as we will see when we discuss branches in the next chapter).

Unfortunately, on all recent Intel 80x86 implementations, the LOOP instruction is always slower than the macrocode sequence consisting of simpler individual instructions (assuming that the small code size difference is not a factor). Thus, optimizing compilers focusing on speed never generate the LOOP instruction. This, in turn, makes it hard to motivate making LOOP fast in future implementations, since it is so rarely used!

Fallacy: If there is space in control store, new instructions are free of cost.

One of the benefits of a microprogrammed approach is that control store implemented in ROM is not very expensive, and as transistor budgets grew, extra ROM was practically free. The analogy here is that of building a house and discovering, near completion, that you have enough land and materials left to add a room. This room wouldn't be free, however, since there would be the costs of labor and maintenance for the life of the home. The temptation to add "free" instructions can occur only when the instruction set is not fixed, as is likely to be the case in the first model of a computer. Because upward compatibility of binary programs is a highly desirable feature, all future models of this machine will be forced to include these so-called free instructions, even if space is later at a premium.

During the design of the 80286, many instructions were added to the instruction set. The availability of more silicon resource and the use of microprogrammed implementation made such additions seem painless. Possibly the largest addition was a sophisticated protection mechanism, which is largely unused, but still must be implemented in newer implementations. This addition was motivated by a perceived need for such a mechanism and the desire to enhance microprocessor architectures to provide functionality equal to that of larger computers. Likewise, a number of decimal instructions were added to provide decimal arithmetic on bytes. Such instructions are rarely used today because using binary arithmetic on 32 bits and converting back and forth to decimal representation is considerably faster. Like the protection mechanisms, the decimal instructions must be implemented in newer processors even if only rarely used.

5.9 Concluding Remarks

As we have seen in this chapter, both the datapath and control for a processor can be designed starting with the instruction set architecture and an understanding of the basic characteristics of the technology. In section 5.2, we saw how the datapath for a MIPS processor could be constructed based on the architecture and the decision to build a single-cycle implementation. Of course, the underlying technology also affects many design decisions by dictating what components can be used in the datapath, as well as whether a single-cycle implementation even makes sense. Along the same lines, in the first portion of section 5.4, we saw how the decision to break the clock cycle into a series of steps led to the revised multicycle datapath. In both cases, the top-level organization—a single-cycle or multicycle machine—together with the instruction set, prescribed many characteristics of the datapath design.

Similarly, the control is largely defined by the instruction set architecture, the organization, and the datapath design. In the single-cycle organization, these three aspects essentially define how the control signals must be set. In the multicycle design, the exact decomposition of the instruction execution into cycles, which is based on the instruction set architecture, together with the datapath, define the requirements on the control.

Control is one of the most challenging aspects of computer design. A major reason is that designing the control requires an understanding of how all the components in the processor operate. To help meet this challenge, we examined two techniques for specifying control: finite state diagrams and microprogramming. These control representations allow us to abstract the specification of the control from the details of how to implement it. Using abstraction in this fashion is the major method we have to cope with the complexity of computer designs.

Once the control has been specified, we can map it to detailed hardware. The exact details of the control implementation will depend on both the structure of the control and on the underlying technology used to implement it. Abstracting the specification of control is also valuable because the decisions of how to implement the control are technology-dependent and likely to change over time.

Trade-offs in Control Approaches

Much has changed since Wilkes [1953] wrote the first paper on microprogramming. The most important changes are the following:

- Control units are implemented as integral parts of the processor, often on the same silicon die. They cannot be changed independent of the rest of the processor. Furthermore, given the right computer-aided design tools, the difficulty of implementing a ROM or a PLA is the same.

- ROM, which was used to hold the microinstructions, is no longer faster than RAM, which holds the machine language program. A PLA implementation of a control function is often much smaller than the ROM implementation, which may have many duplicate or unused entries. If the PLA is smaller, it is usually faster.

- Instruction sets have become much simpler than they were in the 1960s and 1970s, leading to reduced complexity in the control.

- Computer-aided design tools have improved so that control can be specified symbolically and, by using much faster computers, thoroughly simulated before hardware is constructed. This improvement makes it plausible to get the control logic correct without the need for fixes later.

These changes have blurred the distinctions among different implementation choices. Certainly, using an abstract specification of control is helpful. How that control is then implemented depends on its size, the underlying technology, and the available CAD tools.

The Big Picture

Control may be designed using one of several initial representations. The choice of sequence control, and how logic is represented, can then be determined independently; the control can then be implemented with one of several methods using a structured logic technique. Figure 5.51 shows the variety of methods for specifying the control and moving from the specification to an implementation using some form of structured logic.

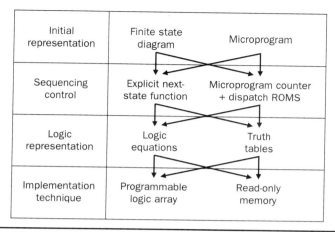

FIGURE 5.51   Alternative methods for specifying and implementing control. The arrows indicate possible design paths: any path from the initial representation to the final implementation technology is viable. Traditionally, "hardwired control" means that the techniques on the left-hand side are used, and "microprogrammed control" means that the techniques on the right-hand side are used.

5.10   Historical Perspective and Further Reading

Maurice Wilkes learned computer design in a summer workshop from Eckert and Mauchly and then went on to build the first full-scale, operational, stored-program computer—the EDSAC. From that experience he realized the difficulty of control. He thought of a more centralized control using a diode matrix and, after visiting the Whirlwind computer in the United States, wrote [Wilkes 1985]:

> I found that it did indeed have a centralized control based on the use of a matrix of diodes. It was, however, only capable of producing a fixed sequence of eight pulses— a different sequence for each instruction, but nevertheless fixed as far as a particular instruction was concerned. It was not, I think, until I got back to Cambridge that I realized that the solution was to turn the control unit into a computer in miniature by adding a second matrix to determine the flow of control at the microlevel and by providing for conditional micro-instructions.

Wilkes [1953] was ahead of his time in recognizing that problem. Unfortunately, the solution was also ahead of its time: To provide control, microprogramming relies on fast memory that was not available in the 1950s. Thus Wilkes's ideas remained primarily academic conjecture for a decade, although he did construct the EDSAC 2 using microprogrammed control in 1958 with ROM made from magnetic cores.

IBM brought microprogramming into the spotlight in 1964 with the IBM 360 family. Before this event, IBM saw itself as a cluster of many small businesses selling different machines with their own price and performance levels, but also with their own instruction sets. (Recall that little programming was done in high-level languages, so that programs written for one IBM machine would not run on another.) Gene Amdahl, one of the chief architects of the IBM 360, said that managers of each subsidiary agreed to the 360 family of computers only because they were convinced that microprogramming made it feasible. To be sure of the viability of microprogramming, the IBM vice president of engineering even visited Wilkes surreptitiously and had a "theoretical" discussion of the pros and cons of microcode. IBM believed that the idea was so important to its plans that it pushed the memory technology inside the company to make microprogramming feasible.

Stewart Tucker of IBM was saddled with the responsibility of porting software from the IBM 7090 to the new IBM 360. Thinking about the possibilities of microcode, he suggested expanding the control store to include simulators, or interpreters, for older machines. Tucker [1967] coined the term *emulation* for this, meaning full simulation at the microprogrammed level. Occasionally, emulation on the 360 was actually faster than on the original hardware.

Once the giant of the industry began using microcode, the rest soon followed. (IBM was over half of the computer industry in 1964, measured in revenue.) One difficulty in adopting microcode was that the necessary memory technology was not widely available, but that was soon solved by semiconductor ROM and later RAM. The microprocessor industry followed the same history, with the limited resources of the earliest chips forcing hardwired control. But as the resources increased, the advantages of simpler design, ease of change, and the ability to use a wide variety of underlying implementations persuaded many to use microprogramming.

In the 1960s and 1970s, microprogramming was one of the most important techniques used in implementing machines. Through most of that period, machines were implemented with discrete components or MSI (medium-scale integration—fewer than 1000 gates per chip), and designers had to choose between two types of implementations: *hardwired control* or *microprogrammed control*. Hardwired control was characterized by finite state machines using an explicit next state and implemented primarily with random logic. In this era, microprogrammed control used microcode to specify control that was then implemented with a microprogram sequencer (a counter) and ROMs. Hardwired control received its name because the control was implemented in hardware and could not be easily changed. Microprograms implemented in ROM were also called *firmware* because they could be changed somewhat more easily than hardware, but not nearly as easily as software.

The reliance on standard parts of low- to medium-level integration made these two design styles radically different. Microprogrammed approaches were attractive because implementing the control with a large collection of low-density gates was extremely costly. Furthermore, the popularity of relatively complex instruction sets demanded a large control unit, making a ROM-based implementation much more efficient. The hardwired implementations were faster, but too costly for most machines. Furthermore, it was very difficult to get the control correct, and changing ROMs was easier than replacing a random logic control unit. Eventually, microprogrammed control was implemented in RAM, to allow changes late in the design cycle, and even in the field after a machine shipped.

With the increasing popularity of microprogramming came more sophisticated instruction sets. Over the years, most microarchitectures became more and more dedicated to support the intended instruction set, so that reprogramming for a different instruction set failed to offer satisfactory performance. With the passage of time came much larger control stores, and it became possible to consider a machine as elaborate as the VAX with more than 300 different instruction opcodes and more than a dozen memory-addressing modes. The use of RAM to store the microcode also made it possible to debug the microcode and even fix some bugs once machines were in the field. The VAX architecture represented the high-water mark for instruction set architectures based on microcode implementations. Typical implementations of the full VAX instruction set required 400 to 500 Kbits of control store.

The VAX architecture has been laid to rest and replaced by the Alpha architecture. This new architecture is based on the same principles of design used in other RISC architectures, including the MIPS, SPARC, IBM PowerPC, and the HP Precision architecture. With the disappearance of the VAX, traditional microprogramming, in which the control is implemented with one major control store, will largely disappear from conventional microprocessor designs. Even processors such as the Intel Pentium and Pentium Pro are employing large amounts of hardwired control, at least for the central core of the processor.

Of course, control unit design will continue to be a major aspect of all computers, and the best way to specify and implement the control will vary, just as computers will vary, from streamlined RISC architectures with simple control, to special-purpose processors with potentially large amounts of more complex and specialized control. One recent movement in this direction is an announcement by Sun that they will build processors designed to interpret Java. Whether such an approach is competitive with compilation, whether there is a significant market for more specialized processors, and what role microcode will play are questions that will be answered in the next few years.

To Probe Further

Kidder, T. [1981]. *Soul of a New Machine*, Little, Brown, and Co., New York.

Describes the design of the Data General Eclipse series that replaced the first DG machines such as the Nova. Kidder records the intimate interactions among architects, hardware designers, microcoders, and project management.

Levy, H. M., and R. H. Eckhouse, Jr. [1989]. *Computer Programming and Architecture: The VAX*, Second ed., Digital Press, Bedford, MA.

Good description of the VAX architecture and several different microprogrammed implementations.

Patterson, D. A. [1983]. "Microprogramming," *Scientific American* 248:3 (March) 36–43.

Overview of microprogramming concepts.

Tucker, S. G. [1967]. "Microprogram control for the System/360," *IBM Systems J.* 6:4, 222–41.

Describes the microprogrammed control for the 360, the first microprogrammed commercial machine.

Wilkes, M. V. [1985]. *Memoirs of a Computer Pioneer*, MIT Press, Cambridge, MA.

Intriguing biography with many stories about industry pioneers and the trials and successes in building early machines.

Wilkes, M. V., and J. B. Stringer [1953]. "Microprogramming and the design of the control circuits in an electronic digital computer," *Proc. Cambridge Philosophical Society* 49:230–38. Also reprinted in D. P. Siewiorek, C. G. Bell, and A. Newell, *Computer Structures: Principles and Examples*, McGraw-Hill, New York, 158–63, 1982, and in "The Genesis of Microprogramming," in *Annals of the History of Computing* 8:116.

These two classic papers describe Wilkes's proposal for microcode.

5.11 Key Terms

This section lists the variety of major new terms introduced in this chapter, which range from elements of the datapath, to clocking methodologies, to control mechanisms, to logic structures used for control. These terms are defined in the Glossary.

branch not taken	exception or interrupt	multicycle or multiple clock
branch taken	firmware	cycle implementation
branch target address	hardwired control	sign-extend
control signal	macroinstruction	single-cycle implementation
datapath element	microcode	superscalar
delayed branch	microinstruction	vectored interrupt
dispatch	microprogram	
don't-care term	microprogrammed control	

5.12 Exercises

5.1 [5] <§5.3> Describe the effect that a single stuck-at-0 fault (i.e., regardless of what it should be, the signal is always 0) would have on the multiplexors in the single-cycle datapath in Figure 5.19 on page 360. Which instructions, if any, would still work? Consider each of the following faults separately: RegDst = 0, ALUSrc = 0, MemtoReg = 0, Zero = 0.

5.2 [5] <§5.3> This exercise is similar to Exercise 5.1, but this time consider stuck-at-1 faults (the signal is always 1).

5.3 [5] <§5.4> This exercise is similar to Exercise 5.1, but this time consider the effect that the stuck-at-0 faults would have on the multiplexors in the multiple-cycle datapath in Figure 5.32 on page 381. Consider each of the following faults: RegDst = 0, MemtoReg = 0, IorD = 0, ALUSrcA = 0.

5.4 [5] <§5.3> This exercise is similar to Exercise 5.3, but this time consider stuck-at-1 faults (the signal is always 1).

5.5 [15] <§5.3> We wish to add the instruction addi (add immediate) to the single-cycle datapath described in this chapter. Add any necessary datapaths and control signals to the single-cycle datapath of Figure 5.19 on page 360 and show the necessary additions to Figure 5.20 on page 361. You can photocopy these figures or download them from *www.mkp.com/cod2e.htm* to make it faster to show the additions.

5.6 [15] <§5.3> This question is similar to Exercise 5.5 except that we wish to add the instruction jal (jump and link), which is described in Chapter 3 on page 132. You may find it easier to modify the datapath in Figure 5.29 on page 372.

5.7 [8] <§5.3> This question is similar to Exercise 5.5 except that we wish to add the instruction bne (branch if not equal), which is described in Chapter 3.

5.8 [15] <§5.3> This question is similar to Exercise 5.5 except that we wish to add a variant of the lw (load word) instruction, which sums two registers to obtain the address of the data to be loaded (see Exercise 4.16) and uses the R-format.

5.9 [5] <§5.3> Explain why it is not possible to modify the single-cycle implementation to implement the swap instruction described in Exercise 4.40 without modifying the register file.

5.10 [5] <§§5.3, 5.4> A friend is proposing that the control signal MemtoReg be eliminated. The multiplexor that has MemtoReg as an input will instead use the control signal MemRead. Will your friend's modification work? Consider both datapaths.

5.11 [10] <§5.3> This exercise is similar to Exercise 5.10 but more general. Determine whether any of the control signals (other than MemtoReg) in the single-cycle implementation can be eliminated and replaced by another existing control signal. Why or why not?

5.12 [15] <§5.3> Consider the following idea: Let's modify the instruction set architecture and remove the ability to specify an offset for memory access instructions. Specifically, all load-store instructions with nonzero offsets would become pseudoinstructions and would be implemented using two instructions. For example:

```
addi    $at, $t1, 104   # add the offset to a temporary
lw      $t0, $at        # new way of doing lw $t0, 104 ($t1)
```

What changes would you make to the single-cycle datapath and control if this simplified architecture were to be used?

5.13 [10] <§5.3> {Ex. 5.12} If the modifications described in Exercise 5.12 are implemented, there are some definite trade-offs with regard to performance. Specifically, the cycle time may be affected, and all load-store instructions with nonzero offsets would now require an extra addi instruction (a good compiler might find ways to reduce the need for extra addi instructions, but you can ignore this). If there are too many load-store instructions with nonzero offsets, it is likely that the modification would not improve performance. Assuming delays as specified on page 373, what is the highest percentage of load-store instructions with offsets that could be tolerated (i.e., that would still result in the modification having a positive impact on performance)?

5.14 [10] <§5.3> In estimating the performance of the single-cycle implementation, we assumed that only the major functional units had any delay (i.e., the delay of the multiplexors, control unit, PC access, sign extension unit, and wires was considered to be negligible). Assume that we change the delays specified on page 373 such that we use a different type of adder for simple addition:

- ALU: 2 ns
- adder for PC + 4: X ns
- adder for branch address computation: Y ns

a. What would the cycle time be if $X = 3$ and $Y = 3$?

b. What would the cycle time be if $X = 5$ and $Y = 5$?

c. What would the cycle time be if $X = 1$ and $Y = 8$?

5.15 [15] <§5.4> We wish to add the instruction addi (add immediate) to the multicycle datapath described in this chapter. This instruction is described in Chapter 3 on page 145. Add any necessary datapaths and control signals to the multicycle datapath of Figure 5.33 on page 383 and show the necessary modifications to the finite state machine of Figure 5.42 on page 396. You may find it helpful to examine the execution steps shown on pages 385 through 388 and consider the steps that will need to be performed to execute the new instruction. You can photocopy existing figures or download figures from *www.mkp.com/cod2e.htm* to make it easier to show your modifications. Try to find a solution that minimizes the number of clock cycles required for the new instruction. Please explicitly state how many cycles it takes to execute the new instruction on your modified datapath and finite state machine.

5.16 [5] <§§5.5, 5.8> {Ex. 5.15 } Write the microcode sequences for the addi instruction. If you need to make any changes to the microinstruction format or field contents, indicate how the new format and fields will set the control outputs.

5.17 [15] <§5.4> This question is similar to Exercise 5.15 except that we wish to add the instruction jal (jump and link), which is described in Chapter 3.

5.18 [15] <§5.4> This question is similar to Exercise 5.15 except that we wish to add the swap instruction described in Exercise 4.40. Do not modify the register file. Since the instruction format for swap has not yet been defined, you are free to define it however you wish.

5.19 [15] <§5.4> This question is similar to Exercise 5.15 except that we wish to add a new instruction, wai (where am I), which puts the instruction's location (the value of the PC when the instruction was fetched) into a register specified by the rt field of the machine language instruction. Assume that the datapath hasn't changed and that, as usual, the clock cycle is too short to allow an ALU operation and a register file access in a single clock cycle if one of them is dependent on the results of the other.

5.20 [15] <§5.4> This question is similar to Exercise 5.15 except that we wish to add a new instruction, jm (jump memory). Its instruction format is similar to that of load word except that the rt field is not used because the data loaded from memory is put in the PC instead of the target register.

5.21 [20] <5.4> This question is similar to Exercise 5.15 except that we wish to add support for four-operand arithmetic instructions such as add3, which adds three numbers together instead of two:

```
add3 $t5, $t6, $t7, $t8    # $t5 = $t6 + $t7 + $t8
```

Assume that the ISA is modified by introducing a new instruction format similar to the R-format except that bits [0–4] are used to specify the additional register (we still use rs, rt, and rd) and of course a new opcode is used. Your solution should not rely on adding additional read ports to the register file, nor should a new ALU be used.

5.22 [10] <§5.4> Show how the jump register instruction (described on pages 129 and A-65) can be implemented simply by making changes to the finite state machine of Figure 5.42 on page 396. (It may help you to remember that $0 = $zero = 0.)

5.23 [15] <§5.4> Consider a change to the multiple-cycle implementation that alters the register file so that it has only one read port. Describe (via a diagram) any additional changes that will need to be made to the datapath in order to support this modification. Modify the finite state machine to indicate how the instructions will work, given your new datapath.

5.24 [15] <§§5.1–5.4> For this problem, use the gcc data from Figure 4.54 on page 311. Assume that there are three machines:

- M1: The multicycle datapath of Chapter 5 with a 500-MHz clock.

- M2: A machine like the multicycle datapath of Chapter 5, except that register updates are done in the same clock cycle as a memory read or ALU operation. Thus, in Figure 5.42 on page 396, states 6 and 7 and states 3 and 4 are combined. This machine has a 400-MHz clock, since the register update increases the length of the critical path.

- M3: A machine like M2, except that effective address calculations are done in the same clock cycle as a memory access. Thus, states 2, 3, and 4 can be combined, as can 2 and 5, as well as 6 and 7. This machine has a 250-MHz clock because of the long cycle created by combining address calculation and memory access.

Find out which machine is fastest. Are there instruction mixes that would make another machine faster, and if so, what are they?

5.25 [20] <§5.4> Your friends at C^3 (Creative Computer Corporation) have determined that the critical path that sets the clock cycle length of the multicycle datapath is memory access for loads and stores (*not* for instructions). This has caused their newest implementation of the MIPS 30000 to run at a clock rate of 500 MHz rather than the target clock rate of 750 MHz. However, Clara at C^3 has a solution. If all the cycles that access memory are broken into two clock cycles, then the machine can run at its target clock rate. Using the gcc mixes shown in Chapter 4 (Figure 4.54 on page 311), determine how much faster the machine with the two-cycle memory accesses is compared with the 500-MHz machine with single-cycle memory access. Assume that all jumps and branches take the same number of cycles and that the set instructions and arithmetic immediate instructions are implemented as R-type instructions.

5.26 [20] <§5.4> Suppose there were a MIPS instruction, called bcp, that copied a block of words from one address to another. Assume that this instruction requires that the starting address of the source block is in register $t1 and the destination address is in $t2, and that the number of words to copy is in $t3 (which is ≥ 0). Furthermore, assume that the values of these registers as well as register $t4 can be destroyed in executing this instruction (so that the registers can be used as temporaries to execute the instruction).

Write the MIPS assembly language program to implement block copy. How many instructions will be executed to perform a 100-word block copy? Using the CPI of the instructions in the multicycle implementation, how many cycles are needed for the 100-word block copy?

5.27 [30] <§5.5> {Ex 5.26} Microcode has been used to add more powerful instructions to an instruction set; let's explore the potential benefits of this approach. Devise a strategy for implementing the bcp instruction described in Exercise 5.26 using the multicycle datapath and microcode. You will probably need to make some changes to the datapath in order to efficiently implement the bcp instruction. Provide a description of your proposed changes and describe how the bcp instruction will work. Are there any advantages that can be obtained by adding internal registers to the datapath to help support the bcp instruction? Estimate the improvement in performance that you can achieve by implementing the instruction in hardware (as opposed to the software solution you obtained in Exercise 5.26) and explain where the performance increase comes from.

5.28 [30] <§5.5> {Ex. 5.27} Using the strategy you developed in Exercise 5.27, modify the MIPS microinstruction format described in Figure 5.45 on page 403 and provide the complete microprogram for the bcp instruction. Describe in detail how you extended the microcode so as to support the creation of more complex control structures (such as a loop) within the microcode. Has support for the bcp instruction changed the size of the microcode? Will other instructions besides bcp be affected by the change in the microinstruction format?

5.29 [15] <§5.6> We wish to add the instruction rfe (return from exception) to the multicycle datapath described in this chapter. A primary task of the rfe instruction is to copy the contents of the EPC to the PC (the exception mechanisms require several additional capabilities that we will discuss in Chapter 7). Add any necessary datapaths and control signals to the multicycle datapath of Figure 5.48 on page 414 and show the necessary modifications to the finite state machine of Figures 5.49 and 5.50 on pages 415 and 416. You can photocopy the figures or download them from *www.mkp.com/cod2e.htm* to make it easier to show your modifications.

5.30 [1 week] <§§5.2, 5.3> Using a hardware simulation language such as Verilog, implement a functional simulator for the single-cycle version. Build your simulator using an existing library of parts, if such a library is available. If the parts contain timing information, determine what the cycle time of your implementation will be.

5.31 [1 week] <§§5.2, 5.4, 5.5> Using a hardware simulation language such as Verilog, implement a functional simulator for the multicycle version of the design. Build your simulator using an existing library of parts, if such a library is available. If the parts contain timing information, determine what the cycle time of your implementation will be.

5.32 [2–3 months] <§§5.1–5.3> Using standard parts, build a machine that implements the single-cycle machine in this chapter.

5.33 [2–3 months] <§§5.1–5.8> Using standard parts, build a machine that implements the multicycle machine in this chapter.

5.34 [Discussion] <§§5.5, 5.8, 5.9> Hypothesis: If the first implementation of an architecture uses microprogramming, it affects the instruction set architecture. Why might this be true? Can you find an architecture that will probably always use microcode? Why? Which machines will never use microcode? Why? What control implementation do you think the architect had in mind when designing the instruction set architecture?

5.35 [Discussion] <§§5.5, 5.10> Wilkes invented microprogramming in large part to simplify construction of control. Since 1980, there has been an explosion of computer-aided design software whose goal is also to simplify construction of control. This has made control design much easier. Can you find evidence, based either on the tools or on real designs, that supports or refutes this hypothesis?

5.36 [Discussion] <§5.10> The MIPS instructions and the MIPS microinstructions have many similarities. What would make it difficult for a compiler to produce MIPS microcode rather than macrocode? What changes to the microarchitecture would make the microcode more useful for this application?

Enhancing Performance with Pipelining

Thus times do shift,
each thing his turn does hold;
New things succeed,
as former things grow old.

Robert Herrick
Hesperides: Ceremonies for Christmas Eve, 1648

The Five Classic Components of a Computer

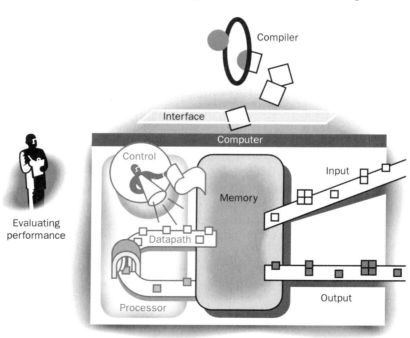

6.1   An Overview of Pipelining

Never waste time.

American proverb

Pipelining is an implementation technique in which multiple instructions are overlapped in execution. Today, pipelining is key to making processors fast.

This section relies heavily on one analogy to give an overview of the pipelining terms and issues. If you are interested in just the big picture, you should concentrate on this section and then skip to section 6.8 to see how pipelining works and its implications on program performance. If you are interested in exploring the anatomy of a pipelined computer, you will find this section referred to repeatedly in sections 6.2 through 6.7.

Anyone who has done a lot of laundry has intuitively used pipelining. The *nonpipelined* approach to laundry would be:

1. Place one dirty load of clothes in the washer.

2. When the washer is finished, place the wet load in the dryer.

3. When the dryer is finished, place the dry load on a table and fold.

4. When folding is finished, ask your roommate to put the clothes away.

When your roommate is done, then start over with the next dirty load.

The *pipelined* approach takes much less time, as Figure 6.1 shows. As soon as the washer is finished with the first load and placed in the dryer, you load the washer with the second dirty load. When the first load is dry, you place it on the table to start folding, move the wet load to the dryer, and the next dirty load into the washer. Next you have your roommate put the first load away, you start folding the second load, the dryer has the third load, and you put the fourth load into the washer. At this point all steps—called *stages* in pipelining—are operating concurrently. As long as we have separate resources for each stage, we can pipeline the tasks.

The pipelining paradox is that the time from placing a single dirty sock in the washer until it is dried, folded, and put away is not shorter for pipelining; the reason pipelining is faster for many loads is that everything is working in parallel, so more loads are finished per hour. If all the stages take about the same amount of time and there is enough work to do, then the speedup due to pipelining is equal to the number of stages in the pipeline.

Pipelined laundry is potentially four times faster than nonpipelined: 20 loads would take about 5 times as long as 1 load, while 20 loads of sequential laundry takes 20 times as long as 1 load. It's only 2.3 times faster in Figure 6.1 because we only show 4 loads.

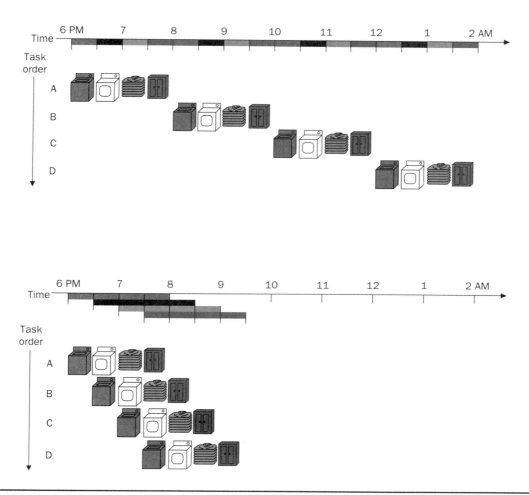

FIGURE 6.1 The laundry analogy for pipelining. Ann, Brian, Cathy, and Don each have dirty clothes to be washed, dried, folded, and put away. The washer, dryer, "folder," and "storer" each take 30 minutes for their task. Sequential laundry takes 8 hours for four loads of wash, while pipelined laundry takes just 3.5 hours. We show the pipeline stage of different loads over time by showing copies of the four resources on this two-dimensional timeline, but we really have just one of each resource.

The same principles apply to processors where we pipeline instruction execution. MIPS instructions classically take five steps:

1. Fetch instruction from memory.

2. Read registers while decoding the instruction (the format of MIPS instructions allows reading and decoding to occur simultaneously).

3. Execute the operation or calculate an address.

4. Access an operand in data memory.

5. Write the result into a register.

Hence the MIPS pipeline we explore in this chapter has five stages. The following example shows that pipelining speeds up instruction execution just as it speeds up the laundry.

Single-Cycle versus Pipelined Performance

Example

To make this discussion concrete, let's create a pipeline. In this example, and in the rest of this chapter, we limit our attention to eight instructions: load word (lw), store word (sw), add (add), subtract (sub), and (and), or (or), set-less-than (slt), and branch-on-equal (beq).

Compare the average time between instructions of a single-cycle implementation, in which all instructions take 1 clock cycle, to a pipelined implementation. The operation times for the major functional units in this example are 2 ns for memory access, 2 ns for ALU operation, and 1 ns for register file read or write. (As we said in Chapter 5, in the single-cycle model every instruction takes exactly 1 clock cycle, so the clock cycle must be stretched to accommodate the slowest instruction.)

Answer

The time required for each of the eight instructions is shown in Figure 6.2. The single-cycle design must allow for the slowest instruction— in Figure 6.2 it is lw—so the time required for every instruction is 8 ns. Similarly to Figure 6.1, Figure 6.3 compares nonpipelined and pipelined execution of three load word instructions. Thus, the time between the first and fourth instructions in the nonpipelined design is 3×8 ns or 24 ns.

All the pipeline stages take a single clock cycle, so the clock cycle must be long enough to accommodate the slowest operation. Just as the single-cycle design must take the worst-case clock cycle of 8 ns even though some instructions can be as fast as 5 ns, the pipelined execution clock cycle must have the worst-case clock cycle of 2 ns even though some stages take only 1 ns. Pipelining still offers a fourfold performance improvement: the time between the first and fourth instructions is 3×2 ns or 6 ns.

We can turn the pipelining speedup discussion above into a formula. If the stages are perfectly balanced, then the time between instructions on the pipelined machine—assuming ideal conditions—is equal to

$$\text{Time between instructions}_{\text{pipelined}} = \frac{\text{Time between instructions}_{\text{nonpipelined}}}{\text{Number of pipe stages}}$$

Instruction class	Instruction fetch	Register read	ALU operation	Data access	Register write	Total time
Load word (lw)	2 ns	1 ns	2 ns	2 ns	1 ns	8 ns
Store word (sw)	2 ns	1 ns	2 ns	2 ns		7 ns
R-format (add, sub, and, or, slt)	2 ns	1 ns	2 ns		1 ns	6 ns
Branch (beq)	2 ns	1 ns	2 ns			5 ns

FIGURE 6.2   Total time for eight instructions calculated from the time for each component. This calculation assumes that the multiplexors, control unit, PC accesses, and sign extension unit have no delay.

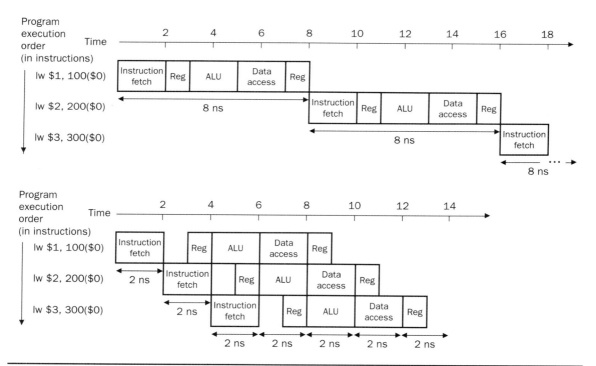

FIGURE 6.3   Single-cycle, nonpipelined execution in top vs. pipelined execution in bottom. Both use the same hardware components, whose time is listed in Figure 6.2. In this case we see a fourfold speedup on average time between instructions, from 8 ns down to 2 ns. Compare this figure to Figure 6.1. For the laundry, we assumed all stages were equal. If the dryer were slowest, then the dryer stage would set the stage time. The computer pipeline stage times are limited by the slowest resource, either the ALU operation or the memory access. We assume the write to the register file occurs in the first half of the clock cycle and the read from the register file occurs in the second half. We use this assumption throughout this chapter.

Under ideal conditions, the speedup from pipelining equals the number of pipe stages; a five-stage pipeline is five times faster.

The formula suggests that a five-stage pipeline should offer a fivefold improvement over the 8 ns nonpipelined time, or a 1.6-ns clock cycle. The example shows, however, that the stages may be imperfectly balanced. In addition, pipelining involves some overhead. Thus the time per instruction in the pipelined machine will exceed the minimum possible, and speedup will be less than the number of pipeline stages.

Moreover, even our claim of fourfold improvement for our example is not reflected in the total execution time for the three instructions: it's 14 ns versus 24 ns. To see why total execution time is less important, what would happen if we increased the number of instructions? We start by extending the previous figures to 1003 instructions. We would add 1000 instructions in the pipelined example; each instruction adds 2 ns to the total execution time. The total execution time would be 1000×2 ns + 14 ns, or 2,014 ns. In the nonpipelined example, we would add 1000 instructions, each taking 8 ns, so total execution time would be 1000×8 ns + 24 ns, or 8,024 ns. Under these ideal conditions, the ratio of total execution times for real programs on nonpipelined to pipelined machines is close to the ratio of times between instructions:

$$\frac{8{,}024 \text{ ns}}{2{,}014 \text{ ns}} = 3.98 \approx \frac{8 \text{ ns}}{2 \text{ ns}}$$

Pipelining improves performance by *increasing instruction throughput, as opposed to decreasing the execution time of an individual instruction,* but instruction throughput is the important metric because real programs execute billions of instructions.

Designing Instruction Sets for Pipelining

Even with this simple explanation of pipelining, we can get insight into the design of the MIPS instruction set, which was designed for pipelined execution.

First, all MIPS instructions are the same length. This restriction makes it much easier to fetch instructions in the first pipeline stage and to decode them in the second stage. In an instruction set like the 80x86, where instructions vary from 1 byte to 17 bytes, pipelining is considerably more challenging.

Second, MIPS has only a few instruction formats, with the source register fields being located in the same place in each instruction. This symmetry means that the second stage can begin reading the register file at the same time that the hardware is determining what type of instruction was fetched. If MIPS instruction formats were not symmetric, we would need to split stage 2, resulting in six pipeline stages. (We will shortly see the downside of longer pipelines.)

Third, memory operands only appear in loads or stores in MIPS. This restriction means we can use the execute stage to calculate the memory address and then access memory in the following stage. If we could operate on the operands in memory, as in the 80x86, stages 3 and 4 would expand to an address stage, memory stage, and then execute stage.

Fourth, operands must be aligned in memory (see the Hardware/Software Interface section on page 112 in Chapter 3). Hence we need not worry about a single data transfer instruction requiring two data memory accesses; the requested data can be transferred between processor and memory in a single pipeline stage.

Pipeline Hazards

There are situations in pipelining when the next instruction cannot execute in the following clock cycle. These events are called *hazards*. We explain the three types of hazards, using our analogy first, and then give the computer equivalent problem and solution.

Structural Hazards

The first hazard is called a *structural hazard*. It means that the hardware cannot support the combination of instructions that we want to execute in the same clock cycle. A structural hazard in the laundry room would occur if we used a washer-dryer combination instead of a separate washer and dryer, or if our roommate was busy doing something else and wouldn't put clothes away. Our carefully scheduled pipeline plans would then be foiled.

As we said above, the MIPS instruction set was designed to be pipelined, making it fairly easy for designers to avoid structural hazards when designing a pipeline. Suppose, however, that we had a single memory instead of two memories. If the pipeline in Figure 6.3 had a fourth instruction, we would see that in 1 clock cycle that the first instruction is accessing data from memory while the fourth instruction is fetching an instruction from that same memory. Without two memories, our pipeline could have a structural hazard.

Control Hazards

The second hazard is called a *control hazard*, arising from the need to make a decision based on the results of one instruction while others are executing.

Suppose our laundry crew was given the happy task of cleaning the uniforms of a football team. Given how filthy the laundry is, we need to determine whether the detergent and water temperature setting we select is strong enough to get the uniforms clean but not so strong that the uniforms wear out sooner. In our laundry pipeline, we have to wait until the second stage to examine the dry uniform to see if we need to change the washer setup or not. What to do?

Here are two solutions to control hazards in the laundry room and two computer equivalents.

> *Stall*: Just operate sequentially until the first batch is dry and then repeat until you have the right formula. This conservative option certainly works, but it is slow.

The equivalent decision task in a computer is the branch instruction. If the computer were to stall on a branch, then it would have to pause before continuing the pipeline. Let's assume that we put in enough extra hardware so that we can test registers, calculate the branch address, and update the PC during the second stage (see section 6.6 for details). Even with this extra hardware, the pipeline involving conditional branches would look like Figure 6.4. The lw instruction, executed if the branch fails, is stalled one extra 2-ns clock cycle before starting. This figure shows an important pipeline concept, officially called a *pipeline stall*, but often given the nickname *bubble*. We shall see stalls elsewhere in the pipeline.

Stall on Branch Performance

Example
Estimate the impact on the clock cycles per instruction (CPI) of stalling on branches. Assume all other instructions have a CPI of 1.

Answer
Figure 3.38 on page 189 in Chapter 3 shows conditional branches being 17% of the instructions executed for gcc. Since other instructions run have a CPI of 1 and branches took one extra clock cycle for the stall, then we would see a CPI of 1.17 and hence a slowdown of 1.17 versus the ideal case. (Since Figure 3.38 includes slt and slti as branch instructions, and they would not stall, this CPI result is appproximate.)

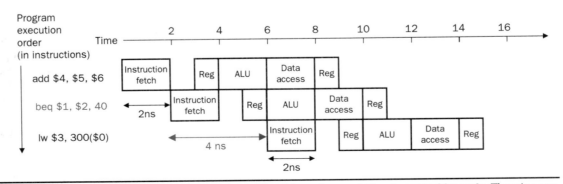

FIGURE 6.4   Pipeline showing stalling on every conditional branch as solution to control hazards. There is a one-stage pipeline stall, or bubble, after the branch.

If we cannot resolve the branch in the second stage, as is often the case for longer pipelines, then we'd see an even larger slowdown if we stall on branches. The cost of this option is too high for most computers to use and motivates a second solution to the control hazard:

> *Predict*: If you're pretty sure you have the right formula to wash uniforms, then just predict that it will work and wash the second load while waiting for the first load to dry. This option does not slow down the pipeline when you are correct. When you are wrong, however, you need to redo the load that was washed while guessing the decision.

Computers do indeed use prediction to handle branches. One simple approach is to always predict that branches will fail. When you're right, the pipeline proceeds at full speed. Only when branches succeed does the pipeline stall. Figure 6.5 shows such an example.

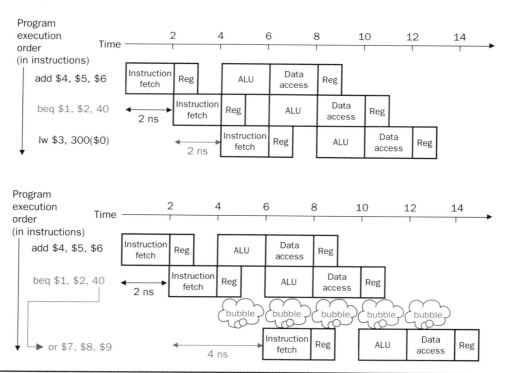

FIGURE 6.5 Predicting that branches are not taken as a solution to control hazard. The top drawing shows the pipeline when the branch is not taken. The bottom drawing shows a taken branch.

A more sophisticated version of branch prediction would have some predicted as branching (*taken*) and some not branching (*untaken*). In our analogy, the dark or home uniforms might take one formula while the light or road uniforms might take another. As a computer example, at the bottom of loops are branches that jump back to the top of the loop. Since they are likely to be taken and they branch backwards, we could always predict taken for branches that jump to an earlier address.

Such rigid approaches to branch prediction rely on stereotypical behavior and don't account for the individuality of a specific branch instruction. *Dynamic* hardware predictors, in stark contrast, make their guesses depending on the behavior of each branch and may change predictions for a branch over the life of a program. Following our analogy, in dynamic prediction a person would look at how dirty the uniform was and guess at the formula, adjusting the next guess depending on the success of recent guesses. One popular approach to dynamic prediction in computers is keeping a history for each branch as taken or untaken, and then using the past to predict the future. Such hardware has about a 90% accuracy (see section 6.6). When the guess is wrong, the pipeline control must ensure that the instructions following the wrongly guessed branch have no effect and must restart the pipeline from the proper branch address.

As in the case of all other solutions to control hazards, longer pipelines exacerbate the problem, in this case by raising the cost of misprediction. Solutions to control hazards are described in more detail in section 6.6.

Elaboration: There is a third approach to the control hazard, called *delayed decision*. In our analogy, whenever you are going to make such a decision about laundry, just place a load of nonfootball clothes in the washer while waiting for football uniforms to dry. As long as you have enough dirty clothes that are not affected by the test, this solution works fine.

Called the *delayed branch* in computers, this is the solution actually used by the MIPS architecture. The delayed branch always executes the next sequential instruction, with the branch taking place *after* that one instruction delay. It is hidden from the MIPS assembly language programmer because the assembler can automatically arrange the instructions to get the branch behavior desired by the programmer. MIPS software will place an instruction immediately after the delayed branch instruction that is not affected by the branch, and a taken branch changes the address of the instruction that *follows* this safe instruction. In our example, the add instruction before the branch in Figure 6.4 does not affect the branch, so in Figure 6.6 we move it to the *delayed branch slot* following the branch.

Compilers typically fill about 50% of the branch delay slots with useful instructions. If the pipeline is longer than five stages, then we may get more branch delay slots, which are even harder to fill.

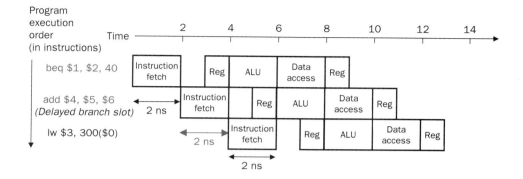

FIGURE 6.6   Pipeline delayed branch as solution to control hazard. The pipe bubble has been replaced by add.

Data Hazards

Returning to the laundry room, suppose that you are folding a load that is mostly socks. You realize that through bad luck the mate of every sock in this load is in another load that is still in the washer. You can't match the socks and put them away until that load is done. Hence you must stall the pipeline. This problem in computers is called a *data hazard*: an instruction depends on the results of a previous instruction still in the pipeline.

For example, suppose we have an add instruction followed immediately by a subtract instruction that uses the sum ($s0):

```
add    $s0, $t0, $t1
sub    $t2, $s0, $t3
```

Without intervention, a data hazard could severely stall the pipeline. The add instruction doesn't write its result until the fifth stage, meaning that we would have to add three bubbles to the pipeline.

Although we could try to rely on compilers to avoid such data hazards, we would fail. These dependencies happen just too often and the delay is just too long to expect the compiler to rescue us from this dilemma.

The primary solution is based on the observation that we don't need to wait for the instruction to complete before trying to resolve the data hazard. For the code sequence above, as soon as the ALU creates the sum for the add, we can supply it as an input for the subtract. Getting the missing item early from the internal resources is called *forwarding* or *bypassing*.

Forwarding with Two Instructions

Example

For the two instructions above, show what pipeline stages would be connected by forwarding. Use the drawing in Figure 6.7 to represent the datapath during the five stages of the pipeline. Align a copy of the datapath for each instruction, similar to the laundry pipeline in Figure 6.1.

Answer

Figure 6.8 shows the connection to forward the value in $s0 after the execution stage of the add instruction as input to the execution stage of the sub instruction.

In this graphical representation of events, forwarding paths are valid only if the destination stage is later in time than the source stage. For example, there cannot be a valid forwarding path from the output of the memory access stage in the first instruction to the input of the execution stage of the following, since that would mean going backwards in time.

Forwarding works very well, and is described in detail in section 6.4. It cannot prevent all pipeline stalls, however. For example, suppose the first instruction were a load of $s0 instead of an add. As we can imagine from looking at Figure 6.8, the desired data would be available only *after* the fourth stage of the first instruction in the dependence, which is too late for the *input* of the third stage of sub. Hence, even with forwarding, we would have to stall one stage for a *load-use data hazard*, as Figure 6.9 shows. Section 6.5 shows how pipelining hardware handles hard cases like these.

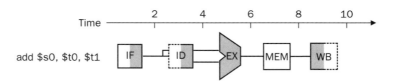

FIGURE 6.7   Graphical representation of the instruction pipeline, similar in spirit to the laundry pipeline in Figure 6.1 on page 437. Here we use symbols representing the physical resources with the abbreviations for pipeline stages used throughout the chapter. The symbols for the five stages: *IF* for the instruction fetch stage, with the box representing instruction memory; *ID* for the instruction decode/register file read stage, with the drawing showing the register file being read; *EX* for the execution stage, with the drawing representing the ALU; *MEM* for the memory access stage, with the box representing data memory; and *WB* for the write back stage, with the drawing showing the register file being written. The shading indicates the element is used by the instruction. Hence MEM has a white background because add does not access the data memory. Shading on the right half of the register file or memory means the element is read in that stage, and shading of the left half means it is written in that stage. Hence the right half of ID is shaded in the second stage because the register file is read, and the left half of WB is shaded in the fifth stage because the register file is written.

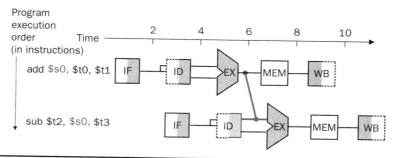

FIGURE 6.8 Graphical representation of forwarding. The connection shows the forwarding path from the output of the EX stage of add to the input of the EX stage for sub, replacing the value from register $s0 read in the second stage of sub.

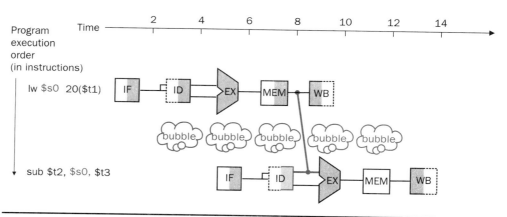

FIGURE 6.9 We need a stall even with forwarding when an R-format instruction following a load tries to use the data. Without the stall, the path from memory access stage output to execution stage input would be going backwards in time, which is impossible.

Reordering Code to Avoid Pipeline Stalls

Example

Find the hazard in this code from the body of the swap procedure, from Figure 3.23 on page 164:

```
                            # reg $t1 has the address of v[k]
    lw      $t0, 0($t1)     # reg $t0 (temp) = v[k]
    lw      $t2, 4($t1)     # reg $t2 = v[k+1]
    sw      $t2, 0($t1)     # v[k] = reg $t2
    sw      $t0, 4($t1)     # v[k+1] = reg $t0 (temp)
```

Reorder the instructions to avoid pipeline stalls.

Answer   The hazard occurs on register $t2 between the second lw and the first sw. Swapping the two sw instructions removes this hazard:

```
                      # reg $t1 has the address of v[k]
    lw    $t0, 0($t1)  # reg $t0 (temp) = v[k]
    lw    $t2, 4($t1)  # reg $t2 = v[k+1]
    sw    $t0, 4($t1)  # v[k+1] = reg $t0 (temp)
    sw    $t2, 0($t1)  # v[k] = reg $t2
```

Note that we do not create a new hazard because there is still one instruction between the write of register $t0 by the load and the read of register $t0 in the store. Thus, on a machine with forwarding, the reordered sequence takes 4 clock cycles.

Hardware Software Interface   In an example of the trade-off between compiler and hardware complexity, the original MIPS processors avoided hardware to stall the pipeline by requiring software to follow a load with an instruction independent of that load. Such loads are called *delayed loads*.

Forwarding yields another insight into the MIPS architecture, in addition to the four mentioned on page 440. Each MIPS instruction writes a single result and does so at the end of its execution. Forwarding is harder if there are multiple results to forward per instruction or they need to write before the end of the instruction. For example, the PowerPC's load instructions may use update addressing (page 175 in Chapter 3), so the processor must be able to forward two results per load instruction.

Pipeline Overview Summary

Pipelining is a technique that exploits parallelism among the instructions in a sequential instruction stream. It has the substantial advantage that, unlike some speedup techniques (see Chapter 9), it is fundamentally invisible to the programmer.

In the next sections of this chapter, we cover the concept of pipelining using the MIPS instruction subset lw, sw, add, sub, and, or, slt, and beq (same as Chapter 5) and a simplified version of its pipeline. We then look at the problems that pipelining introduces and the performance attainable under typical situations.

> **The Big Picture**
>
> Pipelining increases the number of simultaneously executing instructions and the rate at which instructions are started and completed. Pipelining does not reduce the time it takes to complete an individual instruction: the five-stage pipeline still takes 5 clock cycles for the instruction to complete. In the terms used in Chapter 2, page 56, pipelining improves instruction *through-put* rather than individual instruction *execution time*.
>
> Instruction sets can either simplify or make life harder for pipeline designers, who must already cope with structural, control, and data hazards. Branch prediction, forwarding, and stalls help make a computer fast while still getting the right answers.

If you wish to take a more casual approach, we believe that after finishing this section, you have sufficient background to skip to sections 6.8 and 6.9 to familiarize yourself with advanced pipelining concepts, such as superscalar and dynamic pipelining, and to see how pipelining works in recent microprocessors.

Or if you are more dedicated, after finishing this section and Chapter 5, you are ready to understand the changes needed for pipelining in the datapath, explained in section 6.2, and the control lines, explained in section 6.3. You should be able to follow the datapath and control modifications for forwarding in section 6.4, and similar changes for stalls to resolve load-use hazards in section 6.5. You can then read section 6.6 to learn more details about solutions to branch hazards, and then see how exceptions are handled in section 6.7.

Elaboration: The name "forwarding" comes from the idea that the result is passed forward from an earlier instruction to a later instruction. "Bypassing" comes from passing the result by the register file to the desired unit.

6.2 A Pipelined Datapath

Figure 6.10 shows the single-cycle datapath from Chapter 5. The division of an instruction into five stages means a five-stage pipeline, which in turn means that up to five instructions will be in execution during any single clock cycle. Thus we must separate the datapath into five pieces, with each piece named corresponding to a stage of instruction execution:

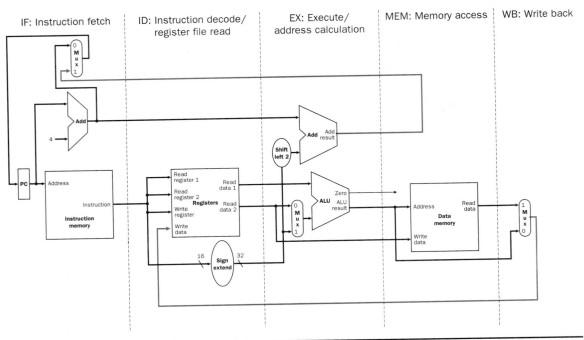

FIGURE 6.10   The single-cycle datapath from Chapter 5 (similar to Figure 5.17 on page 358). Each step of the instruction can be mapped onto the datapath from left to right. The only exceptions are the update of the PC and the write-back step, shown in color, which sends either the ALU result or the data from memory to the left to be written into the register file. (Normally we use color lines for control, but these are data lines.)

1. IF: Instruction fetch

2. ID: Instruction decode and register file read

3. EX: Execution or address calculation

4. MEM: Data memory access

5. WB: Write back

In Figure 6.10, these five components correspond roughly to the way the datapath is drawn; instructions and data move generally from left to right through the five stages as they complete execution. Going back to our laundry analogy, clothes get cleaner, drier, and more organized as they move through the line, and they never move backwards.

There are, however, two exceptions to this left-to-right flow of instructions:

■ The write-back stage, which places the result back into the register file in the middle of the datapath

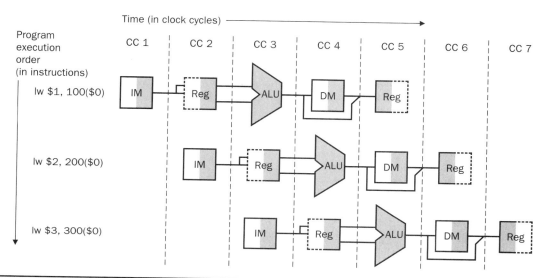

FIGURE 6.11 Instructions being executed using the single-cycle datapath in Figure 6.10, assuming pipelined execution. Similar to Figures 6.7 through 6.9, this figure pretends that each instruction has its own datapath, and shades each portion according to use. Unlike those figures, each stage is labeled by the physical resource used in that stage, corresponding to the portions of the datapath in Figure 6.10. *IM* represents the instruction memory and the PC in the instruction fetch stage, *Reg* stands for the register file and sign extender in the instruction decode/register file read stage (ID), and so on. To maintain proper time order, this stylized datapath breaks the register file into two logical parts: registers read during register fetch (ID) and registers written during write back (WB). This dual use is represented by drawing the unshaded left half of the register file using dashed lines in the ID stage, when it is not being written, and the unshaded right half in dashed lines in the WB stage, when it is not being read. As before, we assume the register file is written in the first half of the clock cycle and the register file is read during the second half.

- The selection of the next value of the PC, choosing between the incremented PC and the branch address from the MEM stage

Data flowing from right to left does not affect the current instruction; only later instructions in the pipeline are influenced by these reverse data movements. Note that the first right-to-left arrow can lead to data hazards and the second leads to control hazards.

One way to show what happens in pipelined execution is to pretend that each instruction has its own datapath, and then to place these datapaths on a timeline to show their relationship. Figure 6.11 shows the execution of the instructions in Figure 6.3 by displaying their private datapaths on a common timeline. We use a stylized version of the datapath in Figure 6.10 to show the relationships in Figure 6.11.

Figure 6.11 seems to suggest that three instructions need three datapaths. In Chapter 5, we added registers to hold data so that portions of the datapath

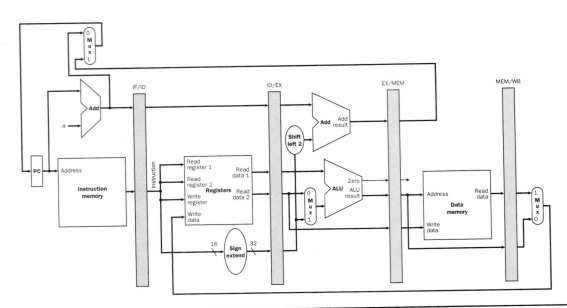

FIGURE 6.12   The pipelined version of the datapath in Figure 6.10. The pipeline registers, in color, separate each pipeline stage. They are labeled by the stages that they separate; for example, the first is labeled *IF/ID* because it separates the instruction fetch and instruction decode stages. The registers must be wide enough to store all the data corresponding to the lines that go through them. For example, the IF/ID register must be 64 bits wide because it must hold both the 32-bit instruction fetched from memory and the incremented 32-bit PC address. We will expand these registers over the course of this chapter, but for now the other three pipeline registers contain 128, 97, and 64 bits, respectively.

could be shared during instruction execution; we use the same technique here to share the multiple datapaths. For example, as Figure 6.11 shows, the instruction memory is used during only one of the five stages of an instruction, allowing it to be shared by other instructions during the other four stages.

To retain the value of an individual instruction for its other four stages, the value read from instruction memory must be saved in a register. Similar arguments apply to every pipeline stage, so we must place registers wherever there are dividing lines between stages in Figure 6.10. (This change is similar to the registers added in Chapter 5 when we went from a single-cycle to a multicycle datapath.) Returning to our laundry analogy, we might have a basket between each stage to hold the clothes for the next step.

Figure 6.12 shows the pipelined datapath with the pipeline registers highlighted. All instructions advance during each clock cycle from one pipeline register to the next. The registers are named for the two stages separated by that register. For example, the pipeline register between the IF and ID stages is called IF/ID.

Notice that there is no pipeline register at the end of the write-back stage. All instructions must update some state in the machine—the register file, memory, or the PC—so a separate pipeline register is redundant to the state that is updated. For example, a load instruction will place its result in 1 of the 32 registers, and any later instruction that needs that data will simply read the appropriate register. (Sections 6.4 and 6.5 describe what happens when there are data hazards between pipelined instructions; ignore them for now.)

To show how the pipelining works, throughout this chapter we show sequences of figures to demonstrate operation over time. These extra pages would seem to require much more time for you to understand. Fear not; the sequences take much less time than it might appear because you can compare them to see what changes in each clock cycle.

Figures 6.13 through 6.15, our first sequence, show the active portions of the datapath highlighted as a load instruction goes through the five stages of pipelined execution. We show a load first because it is active in all five stages. As in Figures 6.7 through 6.12, we highlight the *right half* of registers or memory when they are being *read* and highlight the *left half* when they are being *written*. We show the instruction abbreviation lw with the name of the pipe stage that is active in each figure. The five stages are the following:

1. *Instruction fetch:* The top portion of Figure 6.13 shows the instruction being read from memory using the address in the PC and then placed in the IF/ID pipeline register. (The IF/ID pipeline register is similar to the Instruction register in Figure 5.30 on page 378.) The PC address is incremented by 4 and then written back into the PC to be ready for the next clock cycle. This incremented address is also saved in the IF/ID pipeline register in case it is needed later for an instruction, such as beq. The computer cannot know which type of instruction is being fetched, so it must prepare for any instruction, passing potentially needed information down the pipeline.

2. *Instruction decode and register file read:* The bottom portion of Figure 6.13 shows the instruction portion of the IF/ID pipeline register supplying the 16-bit immediate field, which is sign-extended to 32 bits, and the register numbers to read the two registers. All three values are stored in the ID/EX pipeline register, along with the incremented PC address. We again transfer everything that might be needed by any instruction during a later clock cycle.

3. *Execute or address calculation:* Figure 6.14 shows that the load instruction reads the contents of register 1 and the sign-extended immediate from the ID/EX pipeline register and adds them using the ALU. That sum is placed in the EX/MEM pipeline register.

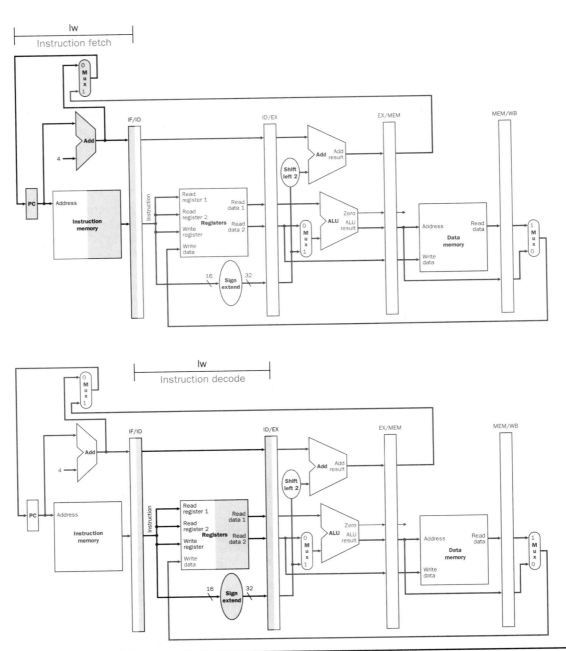

FIGURE 6.13   IF and ID: first and second pipe stages of an instruction, with the active portions of the datapath in Figure 6.12 highlighted. The highlighting convention is the same as that used in Figure 6.7. As in Chapter 5, there is no confusion when reading and writing registers because the contents change only on the clock edge. Although the load needs only the top register in stage 2, the processor doesn't know what instruction is being decoded, so it sign-extends the 16-bit constant and reads both registers into the ID/EX pipeline register. We don't need all three operands, but it simplifies control to keep all three.

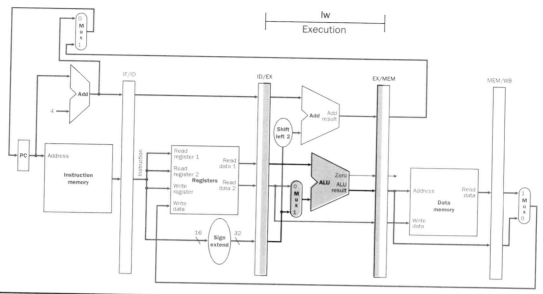

FIGURE 6.14 EX: the third pipe stage of a load instruction, highlighting the portions of the datapath in Figure 6.12 used in this pipe stage. The register is added to the sign-extended immediate, and the sum is placed in the EX/MEM pipeline register.

4. *Memory access:* The top portion of Figure 6.15 shows the load instruction reading the data memory using the address from the EX/MEM pipeline register and loading the data into the MEM/WB pipeline register.

5. *Write back:* The bottom portion of Figure 6.15 shows the final step: reading the data from the MEM/WB pipeline register and writing it into the register file in the middle of the figure.

This walk-through of the load instruction shows that any information needed in a later pipe stage must be passed to that stage via a pipeline register. Walking through a store instruction shows the similarity of instruction execution, as well as passing the information for later stages. Here are the five pipe stages of the store instruction:

1. *Instruction fetch:* The instruction is read from memory using the address in the PC and then is placed in the IF/ID pipeline register. This stage occurs before the instruction is identified, so the top portion of Figure 6.13 works for store as well as load.

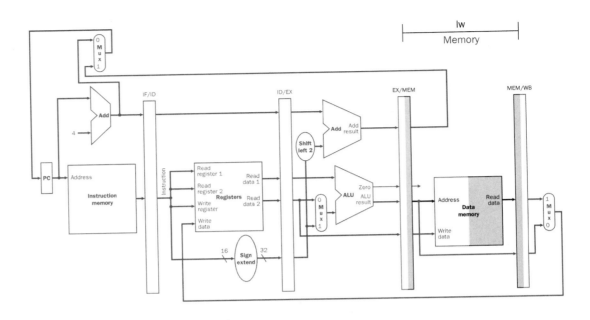

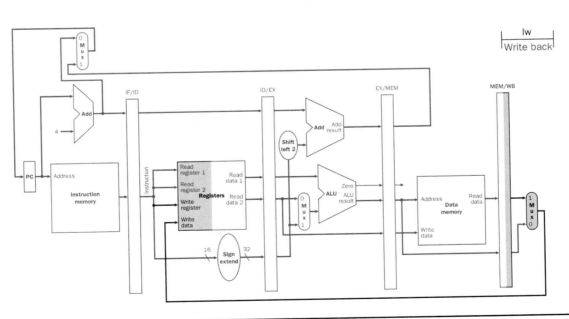

FIGURE 6.15 MEM and WB: the fourth and fifth pipe stages of a load instruction, highlighting the portions of the datapath in Figure 6.12 used in this pipe stage. Data memory is read using the address in the EX/MEM pipeline registers, and the data is placed in the MEM/WB pipeline register. Next, data is read from the MEM/WB pipeline register and written into the register file in the middle of the datapath.

2. *Instruction decode and register file read:* The instruction in the IF/ID pipeline register supplies the register numbers for reading two registers and extends the sign of the 16-bit immediate. These three 32-bit values are all stored in the ID/EX pipeline register. The bottom portion of Figure 6.13 for load instructions also shows the operations of the second stage for stores. These first two stages are executed by all instructions, since it is too early to know the type of the instruction.

3. *Execute and address calculation:* Figure 6.16 shows the third step; the effective address is placed in the EX/MEM pipeline register.

4. *Memory access:* The top portion of Figure 6.17 shows the data being written to memory. Note that the register containing the data to be stored was read in an earlier stage and stored in ID/EX. The only way to make the data available during the MEM stage is to place the data into the EX/MEM pipeline register in the EX stage, just as we stored the effective address into EX/MEM.

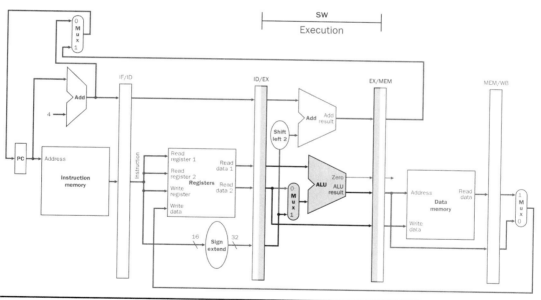

FIGURE 6.16 EX: the third pipe stage of a store instruction. Unlike the third stage of the load instruction in Figure 6.14, the second register value is loaded into the EX/MEM pipeline register to be used in the next stage. Although it wouldn't hurt to always write this second register into the EX/MEM pipeline register, we write the second register only on a store instruction to make the pipeline easier to understand.

5. *Write back:* The bottom portion of Figure 6.17 shows the final step of the store. For this instruction, nothing happens in the write-back stage. Since every instruction behind the store is already in progress, we have no way to accelerate those instructions. Hence an instruction passes through a stage even if there is nothing to do because later instructions are already progressing at the maximum rate.

The store instruction again illustrates that to pass something from an early pipe stage to a later pipe stage, the information must be placed in a pipeline register; otherwise, the information is lost when the next instruction enters that pipeline stage. For the store instruction we needed to pass one of the registers read in the ID stage to the MEM stage, where it is stored in memory. The data was first placed in the ID/EX pipeline register and then passed to the EX/MEM pipeline register.

Load and store illustrate a second key point: each logical component of the datapath—such as instruction memory, register read ports, ALU, data memory, and register write port—can be used only within a *single* pipeline stage. Otherwise we would have a *structural hazard* (see page 441). Hence these components, and their control, can be associated with a single pipeline stage.

Now we can uncover a bug in the design of the load instruction. Did you see it? Which register is changed in the final stage of the load? More specifically, which instruction supplies the write register number? The instruction in the IF/ID pipeline register supplies the write register number, yet this instruction occurs considerably *after* the load instruction!

Hence, we need to preserve the destination register number in the load instruction. Just as store passed the register *contents* from the ID/EX to the EX/MEM pipeline registers for use in the MEM stage, load must pass the register *number* from the ID/EX through EX/MEM to the MEM/WB pipeline register for use in the WB stage. Another way to think about the passing of the register number is that, in order to share the pipelined datapath, we needed to preserve the instruction read during the IF stage, so each pipeline register contains a portion of the instruction needed for that stage and later stages.

Figure 6.18 shows the correct version of the datapath, passing the write register number first to the ID/EX register, then to the EX/MEM register, and finally to the MEM/WB register. The register number is used during the WB stage to specify the register to be written. Figure 6.19 is a single drawing of the corrected datapath, highlighting the hardware used in all five stages of the load word instruction in Figures 6.13 through 6.15. (See section 6.6 for an explanation of how to make the branch instruction work as expected.)

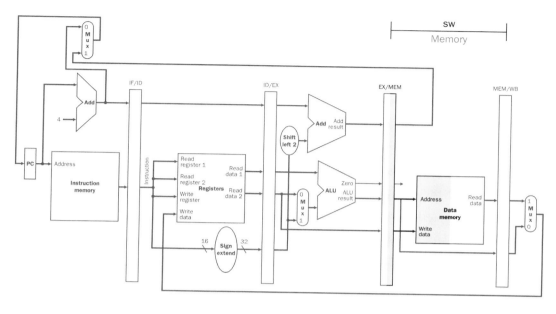

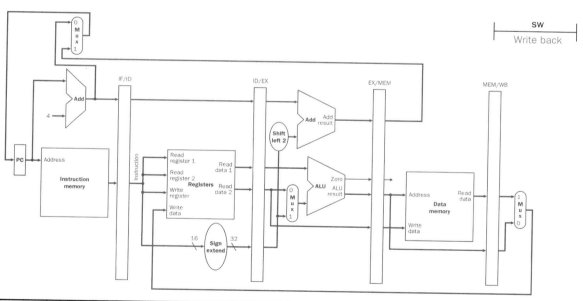

FIGURE 6.17 MEM and WB: the fourth and fifth pipe stage of a store instruction. In the fourth stage, the data is written into data memory for the store. Note that the data comes from the EX/MEM pipeline register and that nothing is changed in the MEM/WB pipeline register. Once the data is written in memory, there is nothing left for the store instruction to do, so nothing happens in stage 5.

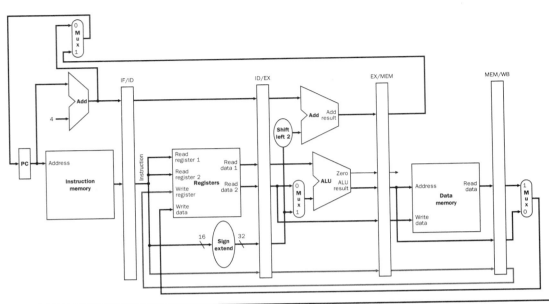

FIGURE 6.18 The corrected pipelined datapath to properly handle the load instruction. The write register number now comes from the MEM/WB pipeline register along with the data. The register number is passed from the ID pipe stage until it reaches the MEM/WB pipeline register, adding 5 more bits to the last three pipeline registers. This new path is shown in color.

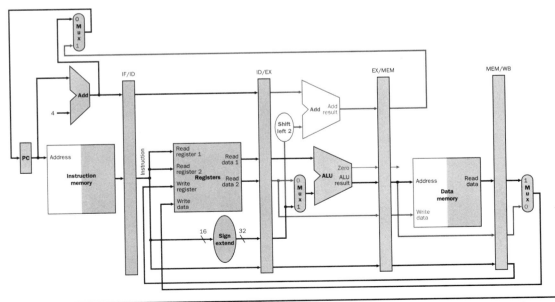

FIGURE 6.19 The portion of the datapath in Figure 6.18 that is used in all five stages of a load instruction.

Graphically Representing Pipelines

Pipelining can be difficult to understand, since many instructions are simultaneously executing in a single datapath in every clock cycle. To aid understanding, there are two basic styles of pipeline figures: *multiple-clock-cycle pipeline diagrams*, such as Figure 6.11 on page 451, and *single-clock-cycle pipeline diagrams*, such as Figures 6.13 through 6.17. Let's try showing a sequence of instructions using both styles of pipeline diagrams for this two-instruction sequence:

```
lw   $10, 20($1)
sub  $11, $2, $3
```

Figure 6.20 shows the multiple-clock-cycle pipeline diagram for these instructions. Time advances from left to right across the page in these diagrams, and instructions advance from the top to the bottom of the page, similar to the laundry pipeline in Figure 6.1 on page 437. A representation of the pipeline stages is placed in each portion along the instruction axis, occupying the proper clock cycles. These stylized datapaths represent the five stages of our pipeline, but a rectangle naming each pipe stage works just as well. Figure 6.21 shows the more traditional version of the multiple-clock-cycle pipeline diagram. Note that Figure 6.20 shows the physical resources used at each stage, while Figure 6.21 uses the *name* of each stage. We use multiple-clock-cycle diagrams to give overviews of pipelining situations.

Single-clock-cycle pipeline diagrams show the state of the entire datapath during a single clock cycle, and usually all five instructions in the pipeline are identified by labels above their respective pipeline stages. We use this type of figure to show the details of what is happening within the pipeline during each clock cycle; typically, the drawings appear in groups to show pipeline operation over a sequence of clock cycles. Figures 6.22 through 6.24 show the single-clock-cycle pipeline diagrams for these two instructions.

These two views of the pipeline are equivalent, of course. One confusing aspect is the order of instructions in the two diagrams: the newest instruction is at the *bottom and to the right* of the multiple-clock-cycle pipeline diagram, and it is on the *left* in the single-clock-cycle pipeline diagram.

Taking a one-clock vertical slice from a multiple-clock-cycle diagram shows the state of the pipeline in a single-clock-cycle diagram. Converting from a sequence of single-clock-cycle pipeline diagrams to one multiple-clock-cycle pipeline diagram is harder. Because the newest instruction must be on the bottom, you rotate each single-clock drawing 90 degrees counterclockwise. The rotated diagrams are then placed side-by-side, each offset by one clock cycle, so that the datapaths of all five stages of each instruction are aligned to occupy a single horizontal line. (See Exercise 6.8.)

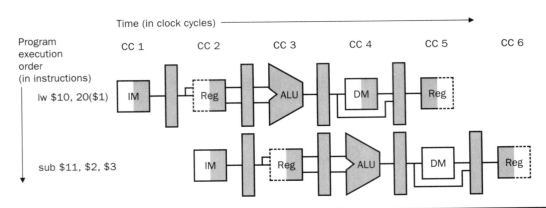

FIGURE 6.20   Multiple-clock-cycle pipeline diagram of two instructions. This style of pipeline representation shows the complete execution of instructions in a single figure. Instructions are listed in instruction execution order from top to bottom, and clock cycles move from left to right. Unlike Figure 6.7, here we show the pipeline registers between each stage. Figure 6.21 shows the traditional way to draw this diagram.

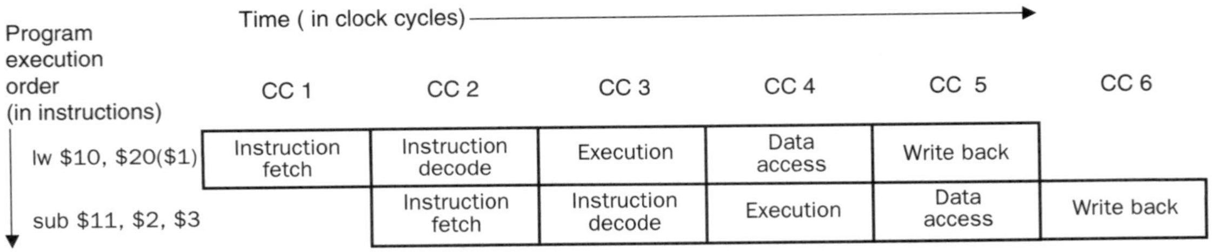

Time (in clock cycles)

Program execution order (in instructions)

	CC 1	CC 2	CC 3	CC 4	CC 5	CC 6
lw $10, $20($1)	Instruction fetch	Instruction decode	Execution	Data access	Write back	
sub $11, $2, $3		Instruction fetch	Instruction decode	Execution	Data access	Write back

FIGURE 6.21   Traditional multiple-clock-cycle pipeline diagram of two instructions in Figure 6.20.

Elaboration: Because the program counter communicates information between two instructions, as opposed to within a single instruction, diagrams such as Figure 6.22 show the PC as an explicit register. You could consider it as a pipeline register before the instruction fetch stage, or equivalently between the write-back stage of one instruction and the instruction fetch of the next instruction. The PC would then be drawn as an elongated rectangle, like the other pipeline registers.

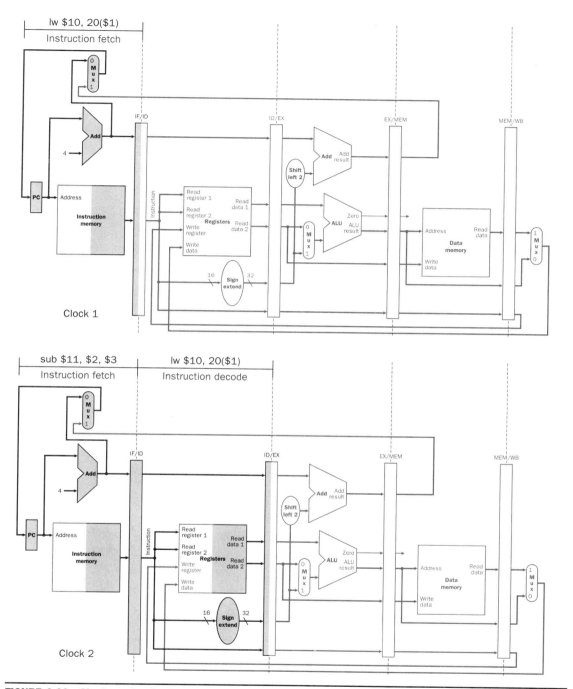

FIGURE 6.22 Single-cycle pipeline diagrams for clock cycles 1 (top diagram) and 2 (bottom diagram). This style of pipeline representation is a snapshot of every instruction executing during 1 clock cycle. Our example has but two instructions, so at most two stages are identified in each clock cycle; normally, all five stages are occupied. The highlighted portions of the datapath are active in that clock cycle. The load is fetched in clock cycle 1 and decoded in clock cycle 2, with the subtract fetched in the second clock cycle. To make the figures easier to understand, the other pipeline stages are empty, but normally there is an instruction in every pipeline stage. *(page 463)*

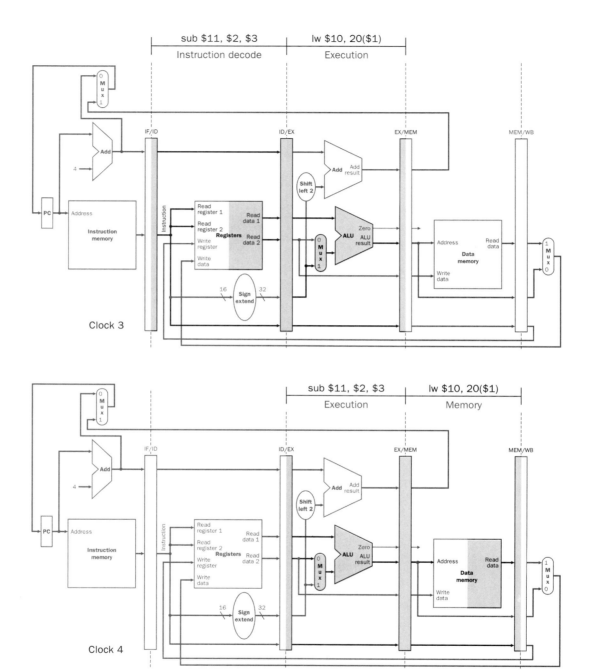

FIGURE 6.23 Single-cycle pipeline diagrams for clock cycles 3 (top diagram) and 4 (bottom diagram). In the third clock cycle in the top diagram, lw enters the EX stage. At the same time, sub enters ID. In the fourth clock cycle (bottom datapath), lw moves into MEM stage, reading memory using the address found in EX/MEM at the beginning of clock cycle 4. At the same time, the ALU subtracts and then places the difference into EX/MEM at the end of the clock cycle. *(page 464)*

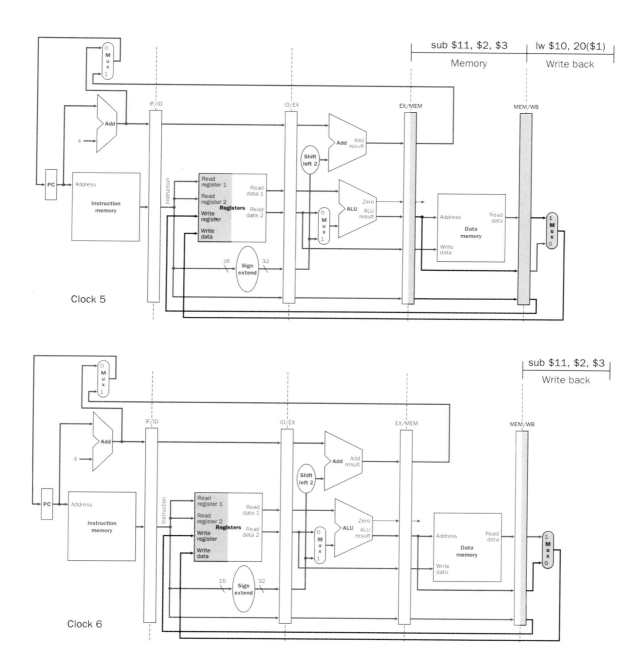

FIGURE 6.24 Single-cycle pipeline diagrams for clock cycles 5 (top diagram) and 6 (bottom diagram). In clock cycle 5, lw completes by writing the data in MEM/WB into register 10, and sub sends the difference in EX/MEM to MEM/WB. In the next clock cycle, sub writes the value in MEM/WB to register 11.

6.3   Pipelined Control

In the 6600 Computer, perhaps even more than in any previous computer, the control system is the difference.

James Thornton, *Design of a Computer:*
The Control Data 6600, 1970

Just as we added control to the simple datapath in section 5.2, we now add control to the pipelined datapath. We start with a simple design that views the problem through rose-colored glasses; in sections 6.4 through 6.8, we remove these glasses to reveal the hazards of the real world.

The first step is to label the control lines on the existing datapath. (Figure 6.25 shows those lines.) We borrow as much as we can from the control for the simple datapath in Figure 5.17 on page 358. In particular, we use the same ALU control logic, branch logic, destination-register-number multiplexor, and control lines. These functions are defined in Figure 5.14 on page 355, Figure 5.18 on page 359, and Figure 5.20 on page 361. (We reproduce the key information in Figures 6.26 through 6.28 to make the remaining text easier to follow.)

As for the single-cycle implementation discussed in Chapter 5, we assume that the PC is written on each clock cycle, so there is no separate write signal for the PC. By the same argument, there are no separate write signals for the pipeline registers (IF/ID, ID/EX, EX/MEM, and MEM/WB), since the pipeline registers are also written during each clock cycle.

To specify control for the pipeline, we need only set the control values during each pipeline stage. Because each control line is associated with a component active in only a single pipeline stage, we can divide the control lines into five groups according to the pipeline stage:

1. *Instruction fetch:* The control signals to read instruction memory and to write the PC are always asserted, so there is nothing special to control in this pipeline stage.

2. *Instruction decode/register file read:* As in the previous stage, the same thing happens at every clock cycle, so there are no optional control lines to set.

3. *Execution/address calculation:* The signals to be set are RegDst, ALUOp, and ALUSrc (see Figures 6.26 and 6.27). The signals select the Result register, the ALU operation, and either Read data 2 or a sign-extended immediate for the ALU.

4. *Memory access:* The control lines set in this stage are Branch, MemRead,

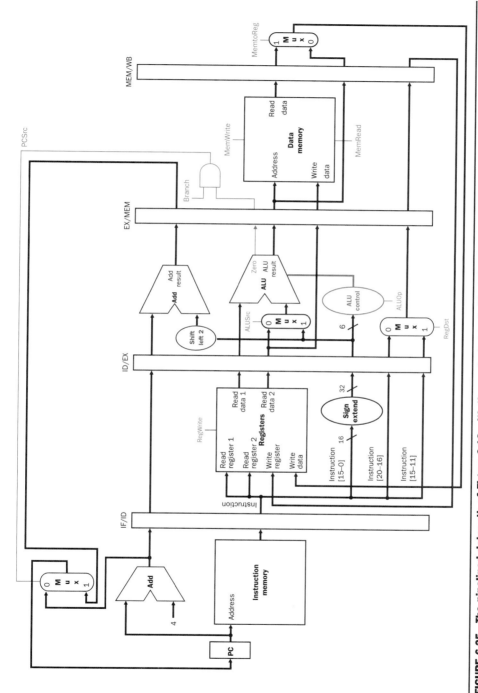

FIGURE 6.25 The pipelined datapath of Figure 6.18 with the control signals identified. This datapath borrows the control logic for PC source, register destination number, and ALU control from Chapter 5. Note that we now need the 6-bit funct field (function code) of the instruction in the EX stage as input to ALU control, so these bits must also be included in the ID/EX pipeline register. Recall that these 6 bits are also the 6 least significant bits of the immediate field in the instruction, so the ID/EX pipeline register can supply them from the immediate field since sign extension leaves these bits unchanged.

Instruction opcode	ALUOp	Instruction operation	Function code	Desired ALU action	ALU control input
LW	00	load word	XXXXXX	add	010
SW	00	store word	XXXXXX	add	010
Branch equal	01	branch equal	XXXXXX	subtract	110
R-type	10	add	100000	add	010
R-type	10	subtract	100010	subtract	110
R-type	10	AND	100100	and	000
R-type	10	OR	100101	or	001
R-type	10	set on less than	101010	set on less than	111

FIGURE 6.26   A copy of Figure 5.14 from page 355. This figure shows how the ALU control bits are set depending on the ALUOp control bits and the different function codes for the R-type instruction.

Signal name	Effect when deasserted (0)	Effect when asserted (1)
RegDst	The register destination number for the Write register comes from the rt field (bits 20–16).	The register destination number for the Write register comes from the rd field (bits 15–11).
RegWrite	None	The register on the Write register input is written with the value on the Write data input.
ALUSrc	The second ALU operand comes from the second register file output (Read data 2).	The second ALU operand is the sign-extended, lower 16 bits of the instruction.
PCSrc	The PC is replaced by the output of the adder that computes the value of PC + 4.	The PC is replaced by the output of the adder that computes the branch target.
MemRead	None	Data memory contents designated by the address input are put on the Read data output.
MemWrite	None	Data memory contents designated by the address input are replaced by the value on the Write data input.
MemtoReg	The value fed to the register Write data input comes from the ALU.	The value fed to the register Write data input comes from the data memory.

FIGURE 6.27   A copy of Figure 5.18 from page 359. The function of each of seven control signals is defined. The ALU control lines (ALUOp) are defined in the second column of Figure 6.26. When a 1-bit control to a two-way multiplexor is asserted, the multiplexor selects the input corresponding to 1. Otherwise, if the control is deasserted, the multiplexor selects the 0 input. Note that PCSrc is controlled by an AND gate in Figure 6.25. If the Branch signal and the ALU Zero signal are both set, then PCSrc is 1; otherwise, it is 0. Control sets the Branch signal only during a `beq` instruction; otherwise, PCSrc is set to 0.

and MemWrite. These signals are set by the branch equal, load, and store instructions, respectively. Recall that PCSrc in Figure 6.27 selects the next sequential address unless control asserts Branch and the ALU result was zero.

5. *Write back*: The two control lines are MemtoReg, which decides between sending the ALU result or the memory value to the register file, and RegWrite, which writes the chosen value.

Instruction	Execution/Address Calculation stage control lines				Memory access stage control lines			Write-back stage control lines	
	Reg Dst	ALU Op1	ALU Op0	ALU Src	Branch	Mem Read	Mem Write	Reg Write	Mem to Reg
R-format	1	1	0	0	0	0	0	1	0
lw	0	0	0	1	0	1	0	1	1
sw	X	0	0	1	0	0	1	0	X
beq	X	0	1	0	1	0	0	0	X

FIGURE 6.28 The values of the control lines are the same as in Figure 5.20 on page 361, but they have been shuffled into three groups corresponding to the last three pipeline stages.

Since pipelining the datapath leaves the meaning of the control lines unchanged, we can use the same control values as before. Figure 6.28 has the same values as in Chapter 5, but now the nine control lines are grouped by pipeline stage.

Implementing control means setting the nine control lines to these values in each stage for each instruction. The simplest way to do this is to extend the pipeline registers to include control information.

Since the control lines start with the EX stage, we can create the control information during instruction decode. Figure 6.29 shows that these control signals are then used in the appropriate pipeline stage as the instruction moves down the pipeline, just as the destination register number for loads moves down the pipeline in Figure 6.18 on page 460. Figure 6.30 shows the full datapath with the extended pipeline registers and with the control lines connected to the proper stage.

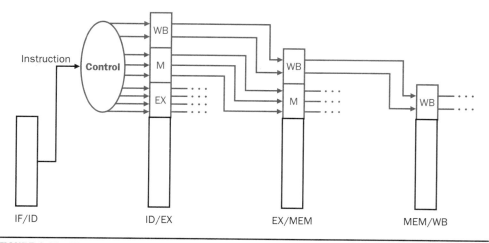

FIGURE 6.29 The control lines for the final three stages. Note that four of the nine control lines are used in the EX phase, with the remaining five control lines passed on to the EX/MEM pipeline register extended to hold the control lines; three are used during the MEM stage, and the last two are passed to MEM/WB for use in the WB stage.

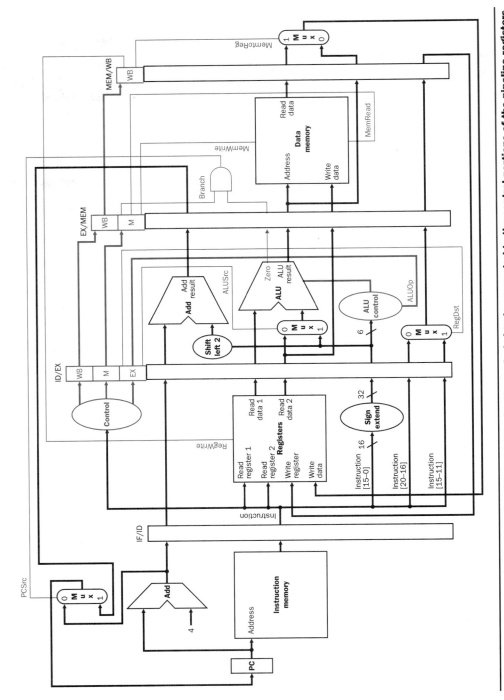

FIGURE 6.30 The pipelined datapath of Figure 6.25, with the control signals connected to the control portions of the pipeline registers. The control values for the last three stages are created during the instruction decode stage and then placed in the ID/EX pipeline register. The control lines for each pipe stage are used, and remaining control lines are then passed to the next pipeline stage.

Labeled Pipeline Execution, Including Control

Show these five instructions going through the pipeline:

```
lw     $10, 20($1)
sub    $11, $2, $3
and    $12, $4, $5
or     $13, $6, $7
add    $14, $8, $9
```

Label the instructions in the pipeline that precede the `lw` as before <1>, before <2>, ..., and the instructions after the `add` as after <1>, after <2>,....

Figures 6.31 through 6.35 show these instructions proceeding through the nine clock cycles it takes them to complete execution, highlighting what is active in a stage and identifying the instruction associated with each stage during a clock cycle.

Reviewing these figures carefully will give you insight into how pipelines work. A few items you may notice:

- In Figure 6.33 you can see the sequence of the destination register numbers from left to right at the bottom of the pipeline registers. The numbers advance to the right during each clock cycle, with the MEM/WB pipeline register supplying the number of the register written during the WB stage.

- When a stage is inactive, the values of control lines that are deasserted, are shown as 0 or X (for don't care).

- In contrast to Chapter 5, where sequencing of control required special hardware, sequencing of control is embedded in the pipeline structure itself. First, all instructions take the same number of clock cycles, so there is no special control for instruction duration. Second, all control information is computed during instruction decode, and then passed along by the pipeline registers.

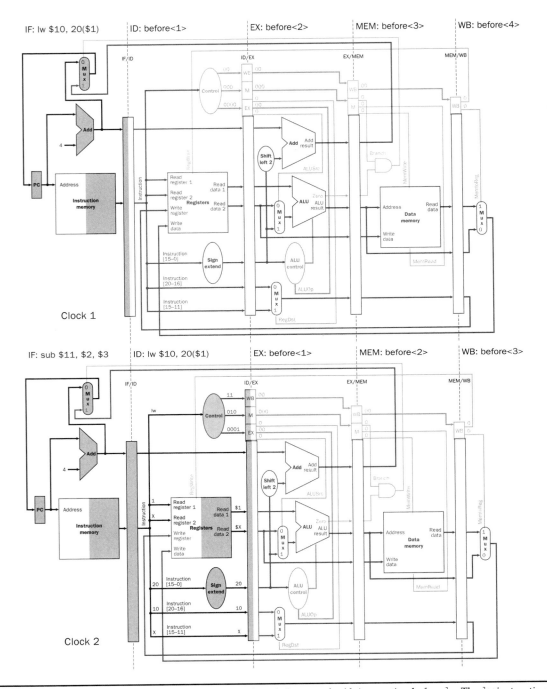

FIGURE 6.31 Clock cycles 1 and 2. The phrase "before<*i*>" means the *i*th instruction before lw. The lw instruction in the top datapath is in the IF stage. At the end of the clock cycle, the lw instruction is in the IF/ID pipeline registers. In the second clock cycle, seen in the bottom datapath, the lw moves to the ID stage, and sub enters in the IF stage. Note that the values of the instruction fields and the selected source registers are shown in the ID stage. Hence register $1 and the constant 20, the operands of lw, are written into the ID/EX pipeline register. The number 10, representing the destination register number of lw, is also placed in ID/EX. Bits 15–11 are 0, but we use *X* to show that a field plays no role in a given instruction. The top of the ID/EX pipeline register shows the control values for lw to be used in the remaining stages. These control values can be read from the lw row of the table in Figure 6.28 on page 469. *(page 472)*

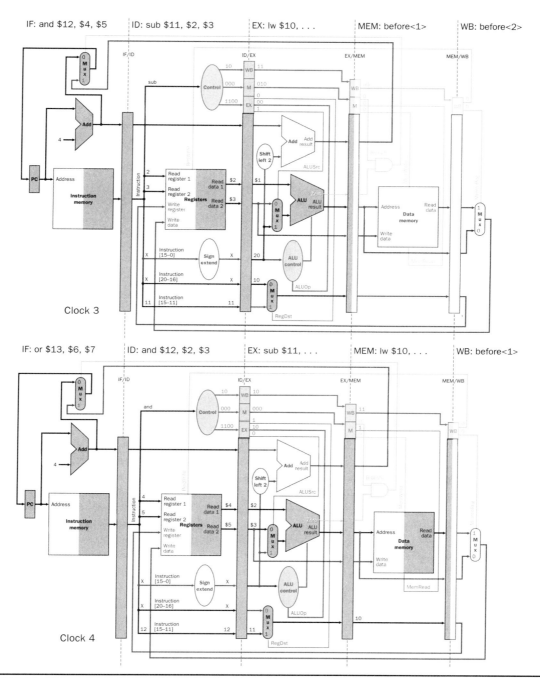

FIGURE 6.32 Clock cycles 3 and 4. In the top diagram, lw enters the EX stage in the third clock cycle, adding $1 and 20 to form the address in the EX/MEM pipeline register. (The lw instruction is written lw $10, . . . upon reaching EX because the identity of instruction operands is not needed by EX or the subsequent stages. In this version of the pipeline, the actions of EX, MEM, and WB depend only on the instruction and its destination register or its target address.) At the same time, sub enters ID, reading registers $2 and $3, and the and instruction starts IF. In the fourth clock cycle (bottom datapath), lw moves into MEM stage, reading memory using the value in EX/MEM as the address. In the same clock cycle, the ALU subtracts $3 from $2 and places the difference into EX/MEM, and reads registers $4 and $5 during ID, and the or instruction enters IF. The two diagrams show the control signals being created in the ID stage and peeled off as they are used in subsequent pipe stages. *(page 473)*

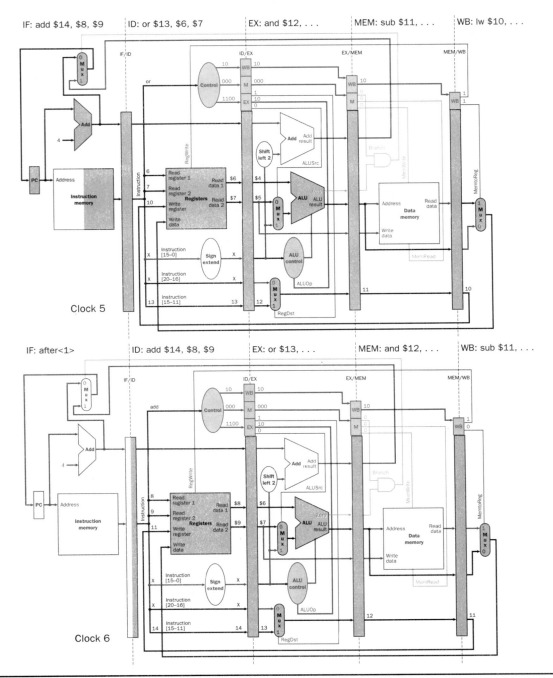

FIGURE 6.33 Clock cycles 5 and 6. With add, the final instruction in this example, entering IF in the top datapath, all instructions are engaged. By writing the data in MEM/WB into register 10, lw completes; both the data and the register number are in MEM/WB. In the same clock cycle sub sends the difference in EX/MEM to MEM/WB, and the rest of the instructions move forward. In the next clock cycle, sub selects the value in MEM/WB to write to register number 11, again found in MEM/WB. The remaining instructions play follow-the-leader: the ALU calculates the OR of $6 and $7 for the or instruction in the EX stage, and registers $8 and $9 are read in the ID stage for the add instruction. The instructions after add are shown as inactive just to emphasize what occurs for the five instructions in the example. The phrase "after<i>" means the ith instruction after add. *(page 474)*

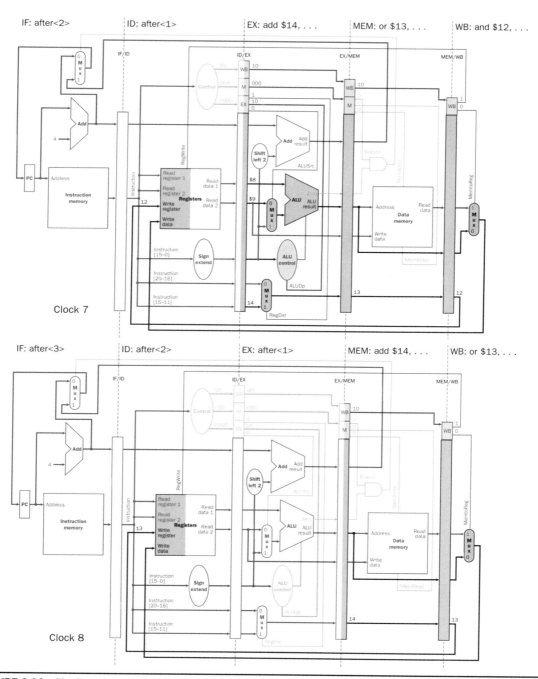

FIGURE 6.34 Clock cycles 7 and 8. In the top datapath, the add instruction brings up the rear, adding the values corresponding to registers $8 and $9 during the EX stage. The result of the or instruction is passed from EX/MEM to MEM/WB in the MEM stage, and the WB stage writes the result of the and instruction in MEM/WB to register $12. Note that the control signals are deasserted (set to 0) in the ID stage, since no instruction is being executed. In the following clock cycle (lower drawing), the WB stage writes the result to register $13, thereby completing or, and the MEM stage passes the sum from the add in EX/MEM to MEM/WB. The instructions after add are shown as inactive for pedagogical reasons.

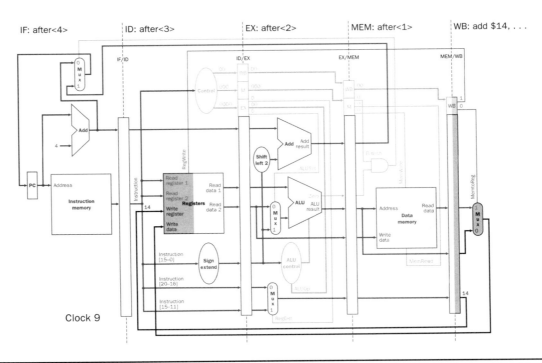

FIGURE 6.35   Clock cycle 9. The WB stage writes the sum in MEM/WB into register $14, completing add and the five-instruction sequence. The instructions after add are shown as inactive for pedagogical reasons.

6.4   Data Hazards and Forwarding

There is less in this than meets the eye.

Tallulah Bankhead, remark to Alexander Wollcott, 1922

The examples in the previous section show the power of pipelined execution and how the hardware performs the task. It's now time to take off the rose-colored glasses and look at what happens with real programs. The instructions in Figures 6.31 through 6.35 were independent; none of them used the results calculated by any of the others. Yet in section 6.1 we saw that data hazards are obstacles to pipelined execution.

Let's look at a sequence with many dependencies, shown in color:

```
sub   $2, $1,    $3    # Register $2 written by sub
and   $12,$2,    $5    # 1st operand($2) depends on sub
or    $13,$6,    $2    # 2nd operand($2) depends on sub
add   $14,$2,    $2    # 1st($2) & 2nd($2) depend on sub
sw    $15,100($2)      # Base ($2) depends on sub
```

The last four instructions are all dependent on the result in register $2 of the first instruction. If register $2 had the value 10 before the subtract instruction and −20 afterwards, the programmer intends that −20 will be used in the following instructions that refer to register $2.

How would this sequence perform with our pipeline? Figure 6.36 illustrates the execution of these instructions using a multiple-clock-cycle pipeline representation. To demonstrate the execution of this instruction sequence in our current pipeline, the top of Figure 6.36 shows the value of register $2 at the beginning of each clock cycle.

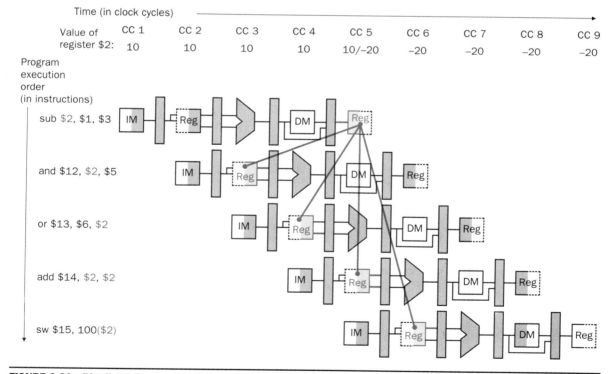

FIGURE 6.36 Pipelined dependencies in a five-instruction sequence using simplified datapaths to show the dependencies. All the dependent actions are shown in color, and "CC *i*" at the top of the figure means clock cycle *i*. The first instruction writes into $2, and all the following instructions read $2. This register is written in clock cycle 5, so the proper value is unavailable before clock cycle 5. (Our register file will read the value written in that clock cycle.) The colored lines from the top datapath to the lower ones show the dependencies. Those that must go backwards in time are *pipeline data hazards*.

One potential hazard can be resolved by the design of the register file hardware: what happens when a register is read and written in the same clock cycle? We assume that the write is in the first half of the clock cycle and the read is in the second half, so the read delivers what is written. As is the case for many implementations of register files, we have no data hazard in this case.

Figure 6.36 shows that the values read for register $2 would *not* be the result of the sub instruction unless the read occurred during clock cycle 5 or later. The instructions that would get the correct value of –20 are add and sw; and and or would get the incorrect value 10. Using this style of drawing, such problems become apparent when a dependence line goes backwards in time. Thus, in Figure 6.36, we see problems with and and or instructions because they are dependent on a value written later.

<table>
<tr><td>**Hardware Software Interface**</td><td>We'll shortly see hardware schemes for resolving data hazards. One alternative strategy is to legislate data hazards out of existence: the compiler is forbidden to generate sequences such as the five instructions above. For example, the compiler would insert two independent instructions between the sub and the and instructions, thereby making the hazard disappear. When no such instructions can be</td></tr>
</table>

found, the compiler inserts instructions guaranteed to be independent: nop instructions. The abbreviation stands for "no operation," because nop neither modifies data nor writes a result. The code below uses nop instructions to get the proper result:

```
sub    $2,   $1, $3
nop
nop
and    $12,  $2, $5
or     $13,  $6, $2
add    $14,  $2, $2
sw     $15,  100($2)
```

Although this code works properly for this pipeline, these two nops occupy 2 clock cycles that do no useful work. As we said in section 6.1, these dependencies happen too often to rely on compilers to come to the rescue.

We must first detect a hazard and then *forward* the proper value to resolve the hazard (see page 446). On closer inspection, when an instruction tries to read a register in its EX stage that an earlier instruction intends to write in its WB stage, we actually need the values as inputs to the ALU.

A notation that names the fields of the pipeline registers allows for a more precise notation of dependencies. For example, "ID/EX.RegisterRs" refers to the number of one register whose value is found in the pipeline register ID/EX; that is, the one from the first read port of the register file. The first part of the name, to the left of the period, is the name of the pipeline register; the second part is the name of the field in that register. Using this notation, the two pairs of hazard conditions are

1a.   EX/MEM.RegisterRd = ID/EX.RegisterRs
1b.   EX/MEM.RegisterRd = ID/EX.RegisterRt
2a.   MEM/WB.RegisterRd = ID/EX.RegisterRs
2b.   MEM/WB.RegisterRd = ID/EX.RegisterRt

The first hazard in the sequence on page 477 is on register $2, between the result of sub $2,$1,$3 and the first read operand of and $12,$2,$5. This hazard can be detected when the and instruction is in the EX stage and the prior instruction is in the MEM stage, so this is hazard 1a:

EX/MEM.RegisterRd = ID/EX.RegisterRs = $2.

Dependency Detection

Example

Classify the dependencies in this sequence from page 477:

```
sub     $2,     $1, $3   # Register $2 set by sub
and     $12,    $2, $5   # 1st operand($2) set by sub
or      $13,    $6, $2   # 2nd operand($2) set by sub
add     $14,    $2, $2   # 1st($2) & 2nd($2) set by sub
sw      $15,    100($2)  # Index($2) set by sub
```

Answer

As mentioned above, the sub-and is a type 1a hazard. The remaining hazards are

■ The sub-or is a type 2b hazard:

MEM/WB.RegisterRd = ID/EX.RegisterRt = $2;

■ The two dependencies on sub-add are not hazards because the register file supplies the proper data during the ID stage of add.

■ There is no data hazard between sub and sw because sw reads $2 the clock cycle *after* sub writes $2.

Because some instructions do not write registers, this policy is inaccurate; sometimes it would forward when it was unnecessary. One solution is simply to check to see if the RegWrite signal will be active: examining the WB control field of the pipeline register during the EX and MEM stages determines if RegWrite is asserted. Also, MIPS requires that every use of $0 as an operand must yield an operand value of zero. In the event that an instruction in the pipeline has $0 as its destination (for example, sll $0, $1, 2), we want to avoid forwarding its possibly nonzero result value. Not forwarding results destined for $0 frees the assembly programmer and the compiler of any requirement to avoid using $0 as a destination. The conditions above thus work properly as long we add EX/MEM.RegisterRd ≠ 0 to the first hazard condition and MEM/WB.RegisterRd ≠ 0 to the second.

Now that we can detect hazards, half of the problem is resolved—but we must still forward the proper data.

Figure 6.37 shows the dependencies between the pipeline registers and the inputs to the ALU for the same code sequence as in Figure 6.36. The change is that the dependency begins from a *pipeline* register rather than waiting for the WB stage to write the register file. Thus the required data exists in time for later instructions, with the pipeline registers holding the data to be forwarded.

If we can take the inputs to the ALU from *any* pipeline register rather than just ID/EX, then we can forward the proper data. By adding multiplexors to the input of the ALU and with the proper controls, we can run the pipeline at full speed in the presence of these data dependencies.

For now, we will assume the only instructions we need to forward are the four R-format instructions: add, sub, and, and or. Figure 6.38 shows a close-up of the ALU and pipeline register before and after adding forwarding. Figure 6.39 shows the values of the control lines for the ALU multiplexors that select either the register file values or one of the forwarded values.

This forwarding control will be in the EX stage, because the ALU forwarding multiplexors are found in that stage. Thus we must pass the operand register numbers from the ID stage via the ID/EX pipeline register to determine whether to forward values. We already have the rt field (bits 20–16). Before forwarding, the ID/EX register had no need to include space to hold the rs field. Hence rs (bits 25–21) is added to ID/EX.

Let's now write both the conditions for detecting hazards and the control signals to resolve them (we highlight the small differences):

1. EX hazard:

   if (EX/MEM.RegWrite
   and (EX/MEM.RegisterRd ≠ 0)
   and (EX/MEM.RegisterRd = ID/EX.RegisterRs)) ForwardA = 10

   if (EX/MEM.RegWrite
   and (EX/MEM.RegisterRd ≠ 0)
   and (EX/MEM.RegisterRd = ID/EX.RegisterRt)) ForwardB = 10

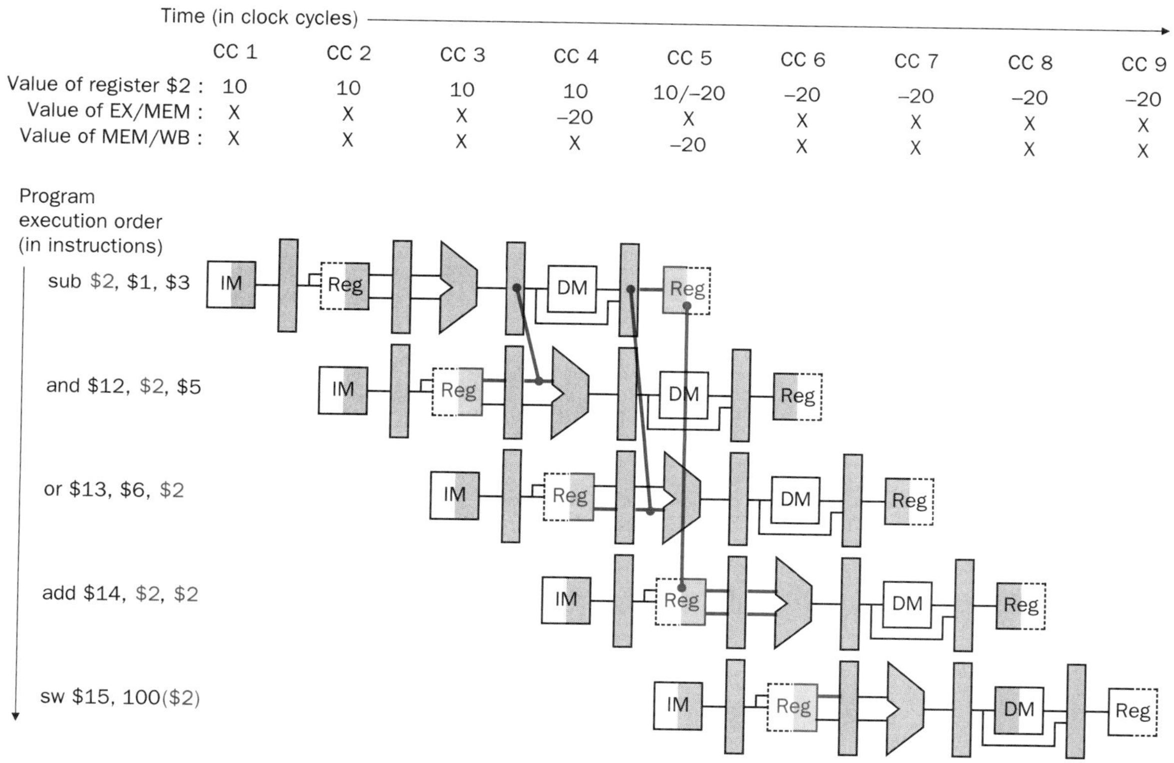

	CC 1	CC 2	CC 3	CC 4	CC 5	CC 6	CC 7	CC 8	CC 9
Value of register $2 :	10	10	10	10	10/–20	–20	–20	–20	–20
Value of EX/MEM :	X	X	X	–20	X	X	X	X	X
Value of MEM/WB :	X	X	X	X	–20	X	X	X	X

FIGURE 6.37 The dependencies between the pipeline registers move forward in time, so it is possible to supply the inputs to the ALU needed by the and **instruction and** or **instruction by forwarding the results found in the pipeline registers.** The values in the pipeline registers show that the desired value is available before it is written into the register file. We assume that the register file forwards values that are read and written during the same clock cycle, so the add does not stall, but the values come from the register file instead of a pipeline register. Register file "forwarding"—that is, the read gets the value of the write in that clock cycle—is why clock cycle 5 shows register $2 having the value 10 at the beginning and –20 at the end of the clock cycle.

This case forwards the result from the previous instruction to either input of the ALU. If the previous instruction is going to write to the register file and the write register number matches the read register number of ALU inputs A or B, provided it is not register 0, then steer the multiplexor to pick the value instead from the pipeline register EX/MEM.

2. MEM hazard:

if (MEM/WB.RegWrite
and (MEM/WB.RegisterRd ≠ 0)
and (MEM/WB.RegisterRd = ID/EX.RegisterRs)) ForwardA = 01

if (MEM/WB.RegWrite
and (MEM/WB.RegisterRd ≠ 0)
and (MEM/WB.RegisterRd = ID/EX.RegisterRt)) ForwardB = 01

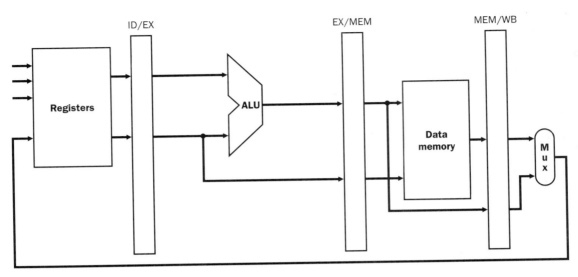

a. No forwarding

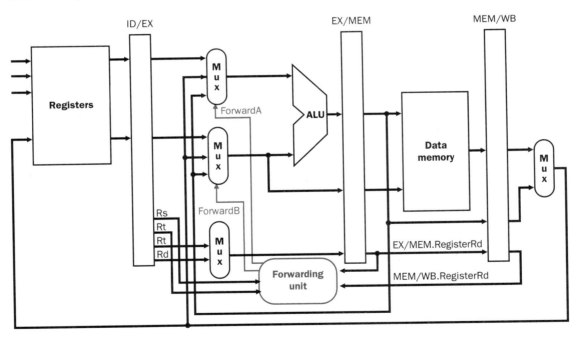

b. With forwarding

FIGURE 6.38   On the top are the ALU and pipeline registers before adding forwarding. On the bottom, the multiplexors have been expanded to add the forwarding paths, and we show the forwarding unit. The new hardware is shown in color. This figure is a stylized drawing, however, leaving out details from the full datapath such as the sign extension hardware. Note that the ID/EX.RegisterRt field is shown twice, once to connect to the mux and once to the forwarding unit, but it is a single signal.

Mux control	Source	Explanation
ForwardA = 00	ID/EX	The first ALU operand comes from the register file.
ForwardA = 10	EX/MEM	The first ALU operand is forwarded from the prior ALU result.
ForwardA = 01	MEM/WB	The first ALU operand is forwarded from data memory or an earlier ALU result.
ForwardB = 00	ID/EX	The second ALU operand comes from the register file.
ForwardB = 10	EX/MEM	The second ALU operand is forwarded from the prior ALU result.
ForwardB = 01	MEM/WB	The second ALU operand is forwarded from data memory or an earlier ALU result.

FIGURE 6.39 The control values for the forwarding multiplexors in Figure 6.38. The signed immediate that is another input to the ALU is described in the elaboration at the end of this section.

As mentioned above, there is no hazard in the WB stage, because we assume that the register file supplies the correct result if the instruction in the ID stage reads the same register written by the instruction in the WB stage. Such a register file performs another form of forwarding, but it occurs within the register file.

One complication is potential data hazards between the result of the instruction in the WB stage, the result of the instruction in the MEM stage, and the source operand of the instruction in the ALU stage. For example, when summing a vector of numbers in a single register, a sequence of instructions will all read and write to the same register:

```
add $1,$1,$2;
add $1,$1,$3;
add $1,$1,$4;
 . . .
```

In this case, the result is forwarded from the MEM stage because the result in the MEM stage is the more recent result. Thus the control for the MEM hazard would be (with the additions highlighted)

if (MEM/WB.RegWrite
and (MEM/WB.RegisterRd ≠ 0)
and (EX/MEM.RegisterRd ≠ ID/EX.RegisterRs)
and (MEM/WB.RegisterRd = ID/EX.RegisterRs)) ForwardA = 01

if (MEM/WB.RegWrite
and (MEM/WB.RegisterRd ≠ 0)
and (EX/MEM.RegisterRd ≠ ID/EX.RegisterRt)
and (MEM/WB.RegisterRd = ID/EX.RegisterRt)) ForwardB = 01

Figure 6.40 shows the hardware necessary to support forwarding.

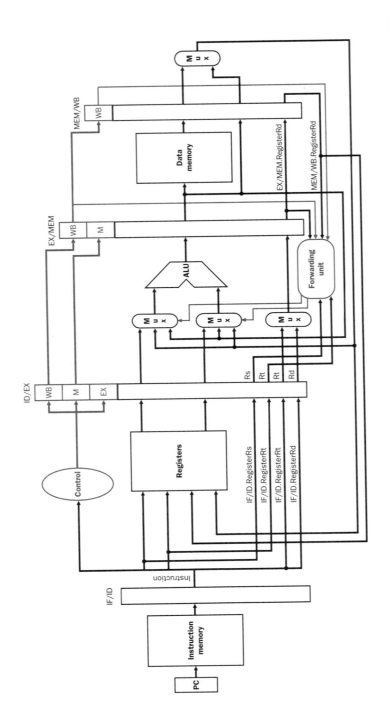

FIGURE 6.40 The datapath modified to resolve hazards via forwarding. Compared with the datapath in Figure 6.30 on page 470, the additions are the multiplexors to the inputs to the ALU. This figure is a more stylized drawing, however, leaving out details from the full datapath such as the branch hardware and the sign extension hardware.

Forwarding

Example

Show how forwarding works with this instruction sequence (with dependencies highlighted):

```
sub    $2, $1, $3
and    $4, $2, $5
or     $4, $4, $2
add    $9, $4, $2
```

Answer

Figures 6.41 and 6.42 show the events in clock cycles 3–6 in the execution of these instructions. In clock cycle 4, the forwarding unit sees the writing by the sub instruction of register $2 in the MEM stage, while the and instruction in the EX stage is reading register $2. The forwarding unit selects the EX/MEM pipeline register instead of the ID/EX pipeline register as the upper input to the ALU to get the proper value for register $2. The following or instruction reads register $4, which is written by the and instruction, and register $2, which is written by the sub instruction. Thus in clock cycle 5 the forwarding unit selects the EX/MEM pipeline register for the upper input to the ALU and the MEM/WB pipeline register for the lower input to the ALU. The following add instruction reads both register $4, the target of the and instruction, and register $2, which the sub instruction has already written. Notice that the prior two instructions both write register $4, so the forwarding unit must pick the immediately preceding one (MEM stage). In clock cycle 6, the forwarding unit thus selects the EX/MEM pipeline register, containing the result of the or instruction, for the upper ALU input but uses the non-forwarding register value for the lower input to the ALU.

Elaboration: Because hazards are officially defined with respect to a particular hardware datapath, instruction sequences with result dependencies are no longer considered hazards when forwarding resolves the dependencies. Hence the name is forwarding unit rather than hazard forwarding unit.

A second point is that an alternative to the explanation of forwarding in this section is to determine the control of the multiplexors on the ALU inputs during the ID stage, setting those values in new control fields of the ID/EX pipeline register. The hardware may then be faster because the time to select the ALU inputs is likely to be on the critical path.

The MIPS nop instruction mentioned on page 478 is represented by all 0s. It represents sll $0, $0, 0, which shifts the register 0 left 0 places. It does nothing to register 0, which can't be changed in any case, and hence is used as a nop by MIPS software.

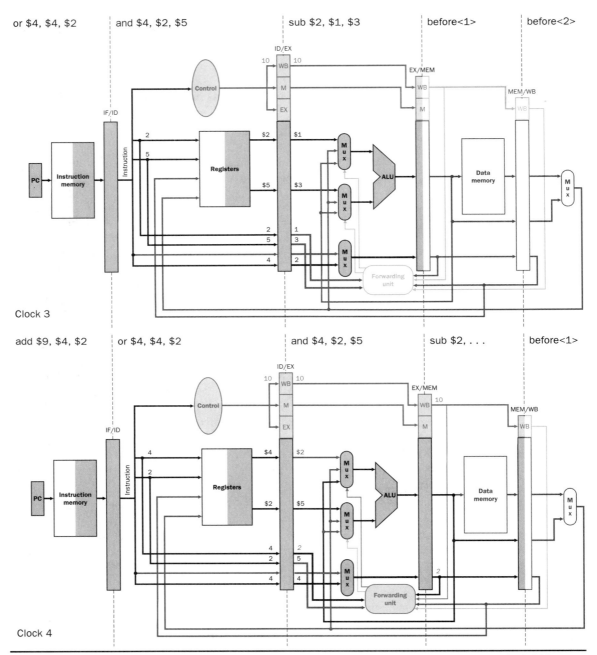

FIGURE 6.41 Clock cycles 3 and 4 of the instruction sequence in the example on page 485. The bold lines are those active in a clock cycle, and the italicized register numbers in color indicate a hazard. The forwarding unit is highlighted by shading it when it is forwarding data to the ALU. The instructions before sub are shown as inactive just to emphasize what occurs for the four instructions in the example. Operand names are used in EX for control of forwarding, thus they are included in the instruction label for EX. Operand names are not needed in MEM or WB, so . . . is used. Compare this with Figures 6.32 through 6.35 showing the datapath without forwarding where ID is the last stage to need operand information.

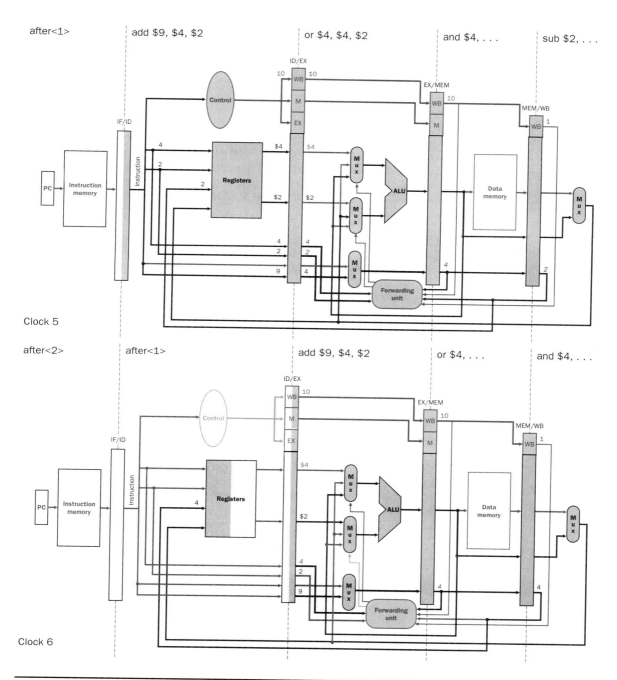

FIGURE 6.42 Clock cycles 5 and 6 of the instruction sequence in the example on page 485. The forwarding unit is highlighted when it is forwarding data to the ALU. The two instructions after add are shown as inactive just to emphasize what occurs for the four instructions in the example. The bold lines are those active in a clock cycle, and the italicized register numbers in color indicate a hazard.

Elaboration: Forwarding can also help with hazards when store instructions are dependent on other instructions. Since they use just one data value during the MEM stage, forwarding is easy. But consider loads immediately followed by stores. We need to add more forwarding hardware to make memory-to-memory copies run faster. If we were to redraw Figure 6.37 on page 481, replacing the sub and and instructions by lw with an sw, we would see that it is possible to avoid a stall, since the data exists in the MEM/WB register of a load instruction in time for its use in the MEM stage of a store instruction. We would need to add forwarding into the memory access stage for this option. Exercise 6.20 examines the changes to the datapath to avoid this hazard.

The signed-immediate input to the ALU, needed by loads and stores, is missing from the datapath in Figure 6.40 on page 484. Since central control decides between register and immediate, and since the forwarding unit chooses the pipeline register for a register input to the ALU, the easiest solution is to add a 2:1 multiplexor that chooses between the ForwardB multiplexor output and the signed immediate. Figure 6.43 shows this addition. Note that this solution differs from what we learned in Chapter 5, where the multiplexor controlled by line ALUSrcB was expanded to include the immediate input. This solution also solves store forwarding by connecting the forwarding multiplexor output—containing store data in this case—to the EX/MEM pipeline register.

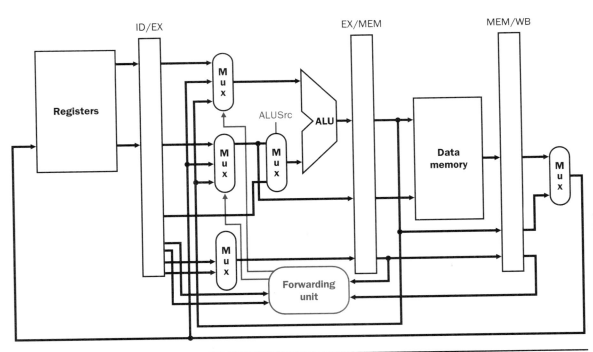

FIGURE 6.43   A close-up of the datapath in Figure 6.38 on page 482 shows a 2:1 multiplexor, which has been added to select the signed immediate as an ALU input.

Data Hazards and Stalls

If at first you don't succeed, redefine success.

Anonymous

As we said in section 6.1, one case where forwarding cannot save the day is when an instruction tries to read a register following a load instruction that writes the same register. Figure 6.44 illustrates the problem. The data is still being read from memory in clock cycle 4 while the ALU is performing the operation for the following instruction. Something must stall the pipeline for the combination of load followed by an instruction that reads its result.

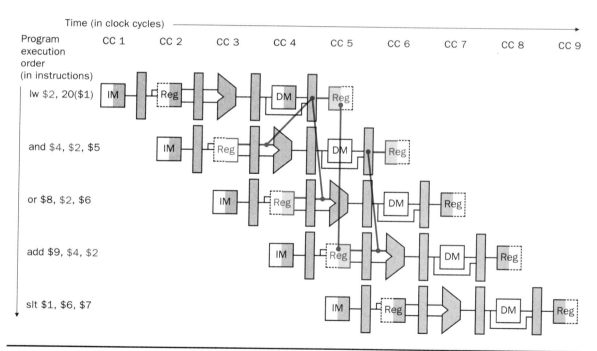

FIGURE 6.44 A pipelined sequence of instructions. Since the dependence between the load and the following instruction (and) goes backwards in time, this hazard cannot be solved by forwarding. Hence, this combination must result in a stall by the hazard detection unit.

Hence, in addition to a forwarding unit, we need a *hazard detection unit*. It operates during the ID stage so that it can insert the stall between the load and its use. Checking for load instructions, the control for the hazard detection unit is this single condition:

> if (ID/EX.MemRead and
>   ((ID/EX.RegisterRt = IF/ID.RegisterRs) or
>   (ID/EX.RegisterRt = IF/ID.RegisterRt)))
>   stall the pipeline

The first line tests to see if the instruction is a load: the only instruction that reads data memory is a load. The next two lines check to see if the destination register field of the load in the EX stage matches either source register of the instruction in the ID stage. If the condition holds, the instruction stalls 1 clock cycle. After this 1-cycle stall, the forwarding logic can handle the dependency and execution proceeds. (If there were no forwarding, then the instructions in Figure 6.44 would need another stall cycle.)

If the instruction in the ID stage is stalled, then the instruction in the IF stage must also be stalled; otherwise, we would lose the fetched instruction. Preventing these two instructions from making progress is accomplished simply by preventing the PC register and the IF/ID pipeline register from changing. Provided these registers are preserved, the instruction in the IF stage will continue to be read using the same PC, and the registers in the ID stage will continue to be read using the same instruction fields in the IF/ID pipeline register. Returning to our favorite analogy, it's as if you restart the washing machine with the same clothes and let the dryer continue tumbling empty.

To stall the pipeline, we need to get the same effect as inserting nop instructions, as in the Hardware/Software Interface section on page 478, but this time the nop "instructions" begin in the EX pipeline stage. In Figure 6.28 on page 469, we see that deasserting all nine control signals (setting them to 0) in the EX, MEM, and WB stages will create a "do nothing" instruction. By identifying the hazard in the ID stage, we can insert a bubble into the pipeline by changing the EX, MEM, and WB control fields of the ID/EX pipeline register to 0. These benign control values are percolated forward at each clock cycle with the proper effect: no registers or memories are written if the control values are all 0.

Figure 6.45 shows what really happens in the hardware. The hazard forces the and and or instructions to repeat in clock cycle 4 what they did in clock cycle 3: and reads registers and decodes, and or is refetched from instruction memory. Such repeated work is what a stall looks like, but its effect is to stretch the time of the and and or instructions and delay the fetch of the add instruction. Like an air bubble in a water pipe, a stall bubble delays everything behind it and proceeds down the instruction pipe until it exits at the end.

Figure 6.46 highlights the pipeline connections for both the hazard detection unit and the forwarding unit. As before, the forwarding unit controls the

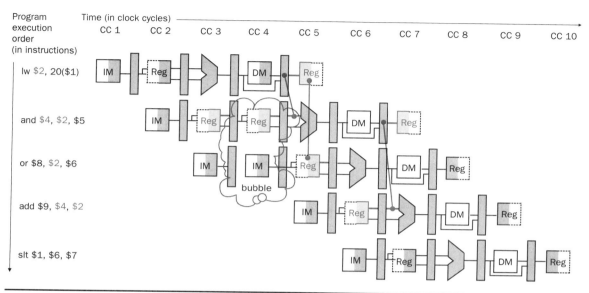

FIGURE 6.45   The way stalls are really inserted into the pipeline. Since the dependencies go forward in time, there are no data hazards.

ALU multiplexors to replace the value from a general-purpose register with the value from the proper pipeline register. The hazard detection unit controls the writing of the PC and IF/ID registers plus the multiplexor that chooses between the real control values and all 0s. The hazard detection unit stalls and deasserts the control fields if the load-use hazard test above is true.

Figures 6.47 to 6.49 show the single-cycle diagram for clocks 2 to 7 for the same example as before, but this time a load replacing the subtract instruction.

The Big Picture

Although the hardware may or may not rely on the compiler to resolve hazard dependencies to ensure correct execution, the compiler must understand the pipeline to achieve the best performance. Otherwise, unexpected stalls will reduce the performance of the compiled code.

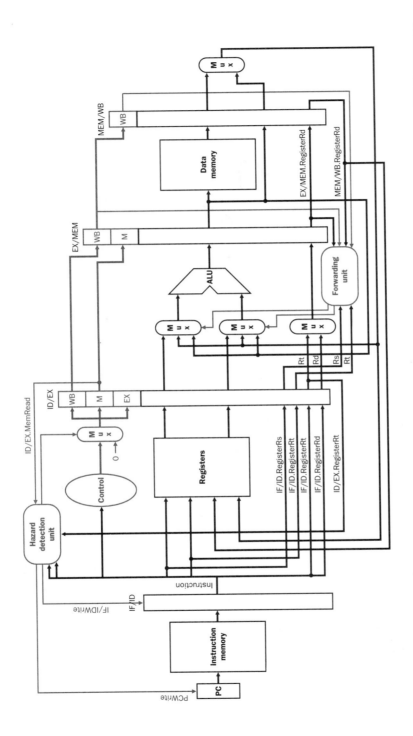

FIGURE 6.46 Pipelined control overview, showing the two multiplexors for forwarding, the hazard detection unit, and the forwarding unit. Although the ID and EX stages have been simplified—the sign-extended immediate and branch logic are missing—this drawing gives the essence of the forwarding hardware requirements.

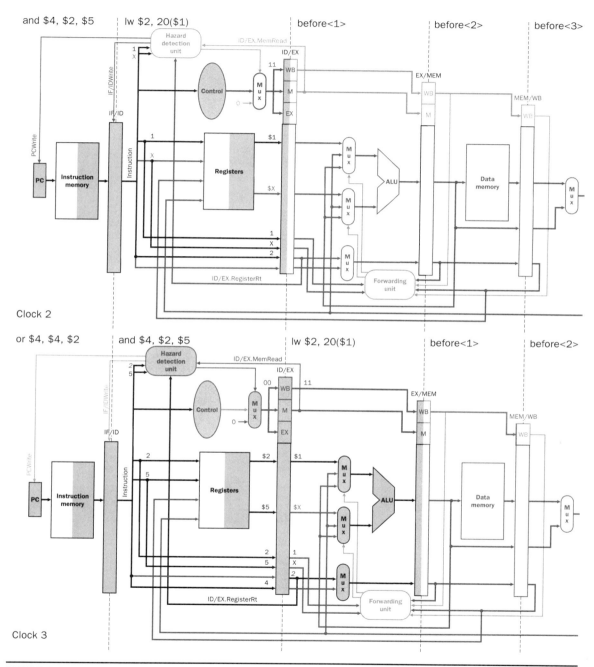

FIGURE 6.47 Clock cycles 2 and 3 of the instruction sequence in the example on page 485 with a load replacing sub**.** The bold lines are those active in a clock cycle, the italicized register numbers in color indicate a hazard, and the . . . in the place of operands means that their identity is information not needed by that stage. The values of the significant control lines, registers, and register numbers are labeled in the figures. The and instruction wants to read the value created by the lw instruction in clock cycle 3, so the hazard detection unit stalls the and and or instructions. Hence the hazard detection unit is highlighted. *(page 493)*

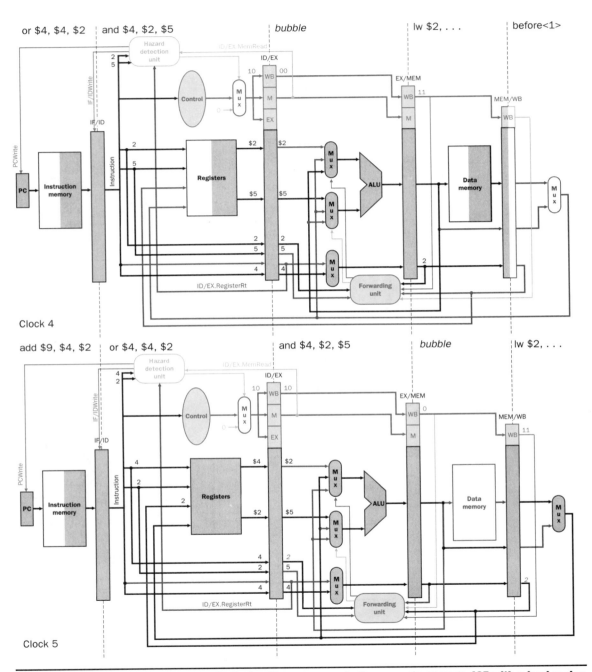

FIGURE 6.48   Clock cycles 4 and 5 of the instruction sequence in the example on page 485 with a load replacing sub. The bubble is inserted in the pipeline in clock cycle 4, and then the and instruction is allowed to proceed in clock cycle 5. The forwarding unit is highlighted in clock cycle 5 because it is forwarding data from lw to the ALU. Note that in clock cycle 4 the forwarding unit forwards the address of the lw as if it were the contents of register $2; this is rendered harmless by the insertion of the bubble. The bold lines are those active in a clock cycle, and the italicized register numbers in color indicate a hazard.

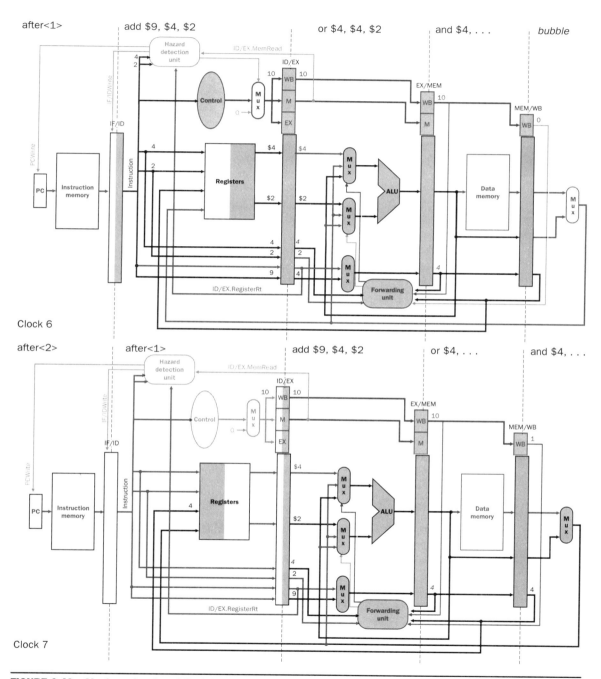

FIGURE 6.49 Clock cycles 6 and 7 of the instruction sequence in the example on page 485 with a load replacing sub. Note that unlike in Figure 6.42, the stall allows the lw to complete, and so there is no forwarding from MEM/WB in clock cycle 6. Register $4 for the add in the EX stage still depends on the result from or in EX/MEM so the forwarding unit passes the result to the ALU. The bold lines show ALU input lines active in a clock cycle, and the italicized register numbers indicate a hazard. The instructions after add are shown as inactive for pedagogical reasons.

Elaboration: Regarding the remark earlier about setting control lines to 0 to avoid writing registers or memory: only the signals RegWrite and MemWrite need be 0, while the other control signals can be don't cares.

6.6   Branch Hazards

There are a thousand hacking at the branches of evil to one who is striking at the root.

Henry David Thoreau, *Walden*, 1854

Thus far we have limited our concern to hazards involving arithmetic operations and data transfers. But as we saw in section 6.1, there are also pipeline hazards involving branches. Figure 6.50 shows a sequence of instructions and indicates when the branch would occur in this pipeline. An instruction must be fetched at every clock cycle to sustain the pipeline, yet in our design the decision about whether to branch doesn't occur until the MEM pipeline stage. As mentioned in section 6.1, this delay in determining the proper instruction to fetch is called a *control hazard* or *branch hazard*, in contrast to the *data hazards* we have just examined.

This section on control hazards is shorter than the previous sections on data hazards. The reasons are that control hazards are relatively simple to understand, they occur much less frequently than data hazards, and there is nothing as effective against control hazards as forwarding is for data hazards. Hence we use simpler schemes. We look at two schemes for resolving control hazards and one optimization to improve these schemes.

Assume Branch Not Taken

As we saw in section 6.1, stalling until the branch is complete is too slow. A common improvement over branch stalling is to assume that the branch will not be taken and thus continue execution down the sequential instruction stream. If the branch is taken, the instructions that are being fetched and decoded must be discarded. Execution continues at the branch target. If branches are untaken half the time, and if it costs little to discard the instructions, this optimization halves the cost of control hazards.

To discard instructions, we merely change the original control values to 0s, much as we did to stall for a load-use data hazard. The difference is that we must also change the three instructions in the IF, ID, and EX stages when the branch reaches the MEM stage; for load-use stalls, we just changed control to

Program execution order (in instructions)

Time (in clock cycles)

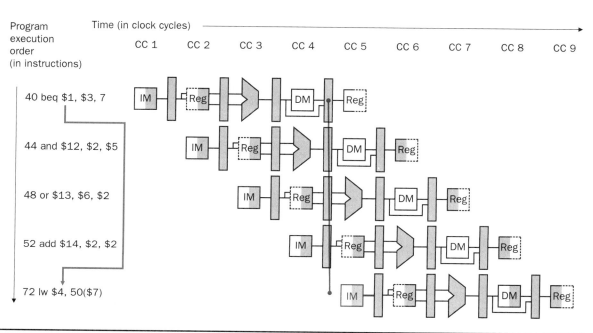

FIGURE 6.50 The impact of the pipeline on the branch instruction. The numbers to the left of the instruction (40, 44, . . .) are the addresses of the instructions. Since the branch instruction decides whether to branch in the MEM stage—clock cycle 4 for the beq instruction above—the three sequential instructions that follow the branch will be fetched and begin execution. Without intervention, those three following instructions will begin execution before beq branches to lw at location 72. (Figure 6.4 on page 442 assumed extra hardware to reduce the control hazard to 1 clock cycle; Figure 6.50 uses the non-optimized datapath.)

0 in the ID stage and let them percolate through the pipeline. Discarding instructions, then, means we must be able to flush instructions in the IF, ID, and EX stages of the pipeline.

Reducing the Delay of Branches

One way to improve branch performance is to reduce the cost of the taken branch. If we move the branch execution earlier in the pipeline, then fewer instructions need be flushed.

Thus far we have assumed the next PC for a branch is selected in the MEM stage. We could save 1 clock cycle of penalty by selecting the branch address at the end of the EX stage instead: if we move the branch decision even earlier in the pipeline, then only one instruction need be flushed. Many MIPS implementations move the branch execution to the ID stage. Figure 6.51 shows the revised datapath.

The easy part of this change is to move up the branch address calculation. We already have the PC value and the immediate field in the IF/ID pipeline register, so we just move the branch adder from the MEM stage to the ID stage.

The harder part is the branch decision itself. For branch equal, we would compare the two registers read during the ID stage to see if they are equal. Equality can be tested by first exclusive-ORing their respective bits and then ANDing all the results. This approach is much faster than using the ALU to subtract and then test if the output is zero, since there are no carries for exclusive-OR. Moving the branch test to the ID stage implies copying the forwarding and hazard detection hardware as well, since a branch dependent on a result still in the pipeline must still work properly with this optimization. By moving the branch execution to the ID stage, there is only one instruction to flush if the branch is taken, the one currently being fetched.

To flush instructions in the IF stage, we add a control line, called IF.Flush, that zeros the instruction field of the IF/ID pipeline register. Clearing the register transforms the fetched instruction into a nop, an instruction that does no operation to change state (see the Elaboration on 485).

Pipelined Branch

Example

Show what happens when the branch is taken in this instruction sequence, assuming the pipeline is optimized for branches that are not taken and that we moved the branch execution to the ID stage:

```
36    sub $10, $4, $8
40    beq $1, $3,  7 # PC-relative branch to 40 + 4 + 7*4 = 72
44    and $12, $2, $5
48    or  $13, $2, $6
52    add $14, $4, $2
56    slt $15, $6, $7
  . . .
72    lw  $4, 50($7)
```

Answer

Figure 6.52 shows what happens when a branch is taken. Unlike Figure 6.50, there is only one pipeline bubble on a taken branch.

Dynamic Branch Prediction

Assuming a branch is not taken is one crude form of *branch prediction*. In that case, we predict that branches are untaken, flushing the pipeline when we are wrong. As we mentioned in section 6.1, with more hardware it is possible to try other schemes of branch prediction.

One approach is to look up the address of the instruction to see if a branch was taken the last time this instruction was executed, and, if so, to begin fetching new instructions from the same place as the last time.

One implementation of that approach is a *branch prediction buffer* or *branch history table*. A branch prediction buffer is a small memory indexed by the

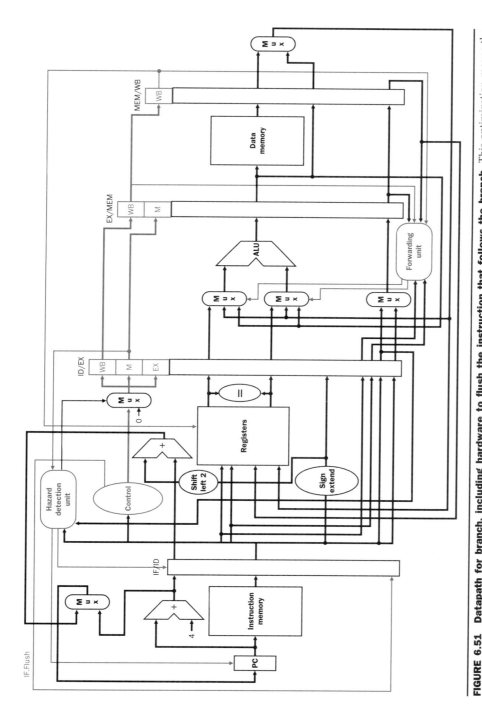

FIGURE 6.51 Datapath for branch, including hardware to flush the instruction that follows the branch. This optimization moves the branch decision from the fourth pipeline stage to the second; only one instruction that follows the branch will be in the pipe at that time. The control line IF.Flush turns the fetched instruction into a `nop` by zeroing the IF/ID pipeline register. Although the flush line is shown coming from the control unit in this figure, in reality it comes from hardware that determines if a branch is taken, labeled with an equal sign to the right of the registers in the ID stage. The forwarding muxes and paths must also be added to this stage, but are not shown to simplify the figure.

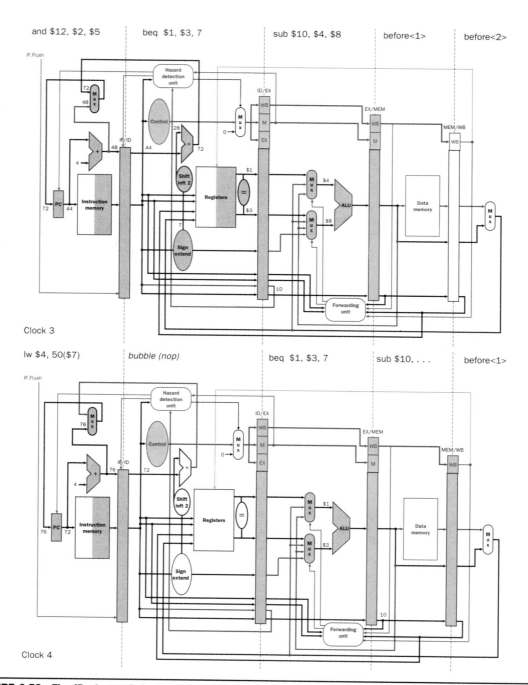

FIGURE 6.52 The ID stage of clock cycle 3 determines that a branch must be taken, so it selects 72 as the next PC address and zeros the instruction fetched for the next clock cycle. Clock cycle 4 shows the instruction at location 72 being fetched and the single bubble or nop instruction in the pipeline as a result of the taken branch. (Since the nop is really or $0, $0, 0, it's arguable whether or not the ID stage in clock 4 should be highlighted.)

lower portion of the address of the branch instruction. The memory contains a bit that says whether the branch was recently taken or not.

This is the simplest sort of buffer; we don't know, in fact, if the prediction is the right one—it may have been put there by another branch that has the same low-order address bits. But this doesn't affect correctness. Prediction is just a hint that is assumed to be correct, so fetching begins in the predicted direction. If the hint turns out to be wrong, the prediction bit is inverted and stored back, and the proper sequence is executed.

This simple 1-bit prediction scheme has a performance shortcoming: even if a branch is almost always taken, we will likely predict incorrectly twice, rather than once, when it is not taken. The following example shows this dilemma.

Loops and Prediction

Example

Consider a loop branch that branches nine times in a row, then is not taken once. What is the prediction accuracy for this branch, assuming the prediction bit for this branch remains in the prediction buffer?

Answer

The steady-state prediction behavior will mispredict on the first and last loop iterations. Mispredicting the last iteration is inevitable since the prediction bit will say taken: the branch has been taken nine times in a row at that point. The misprediction on the first iteration happens because the bit is flipped on prior execution of the last iteration of the loop, since the branch was not taken on that exiting iteration. Thus, the prediction accuracy for this branch that is taken 90% of the time is only 80% (two incorrect predictions and eight correct ones).

Ideally, the accuracy of the predictor would match the taken branch frequency for these highly regular branches. To remedy this weakness, 2-bit prediction schemes are often used. In a 2-bit scheme, a prediction must be wrong twice before it is changed. Figure 6.53 shows the finite state machine for a 2-bit prediction scheme.

A branch prediction buffer can be implemented as a small, special buffer accessed with the instruction address during the IF pipe stage. If the instruction is predicted as taken, fetching begins from the target as soon as the PC is known; as mentioned on page 497, it can be as early as the ID stage. Otherwise, sequential fetching and executing continue. If the prediction turns out to be wrong, the prediction bits are changed as shown in Figure 6.53.

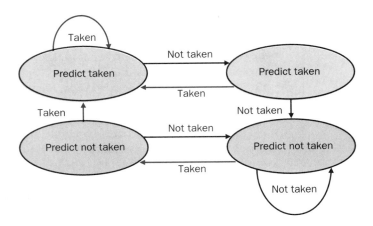

FIGURE 6.53   The states in a 2-bit prediction scheme. By using 2 bits rather than 1, a branch that strongly favors taken or not taken—as many branches do—will be mispredicted only once. The 2 bits are used to encode the four states in the system.

Elaboration: As we described in section 6.1, in a five-stage pipeline we can make the control hazard a feature by redefining the branch. A delayed branch always executes the following instruction, but the second instruction following the branch will be affected by the branch.

Compilers and assemblers try to place an instruction that always executes after the branch in the *branch delay slot*. The job of the software is to make the successor instructions valid and useful. Figure 6.54 shows the three ways in which the branch delay slot can be scheduled.

The limitations on delayed-branch scheduling arise from (1) the restrictions on the instructions that are scheduled into the delay slots and (2) our ability to predict at compile time whether a branch is likely to be taken or not.

Delayed branching is losing popularity. As machines go to both longer pipelines and issuing multiple instructions per clock cycle (see section 6.8), a single delay slot does not offer much help. Moreover, dynamic predictors increase in popularity as the transistors per chip increase.

Elaboration: A side effect of moving branch decision to the decode pipeline stage is that we have to copy the muxes and control for forwarding and stalling to the decode stage too. That is, an add or load followed by a branch that tests the result of the instruction must still work correctly and efficiently even if we change the pipeline.

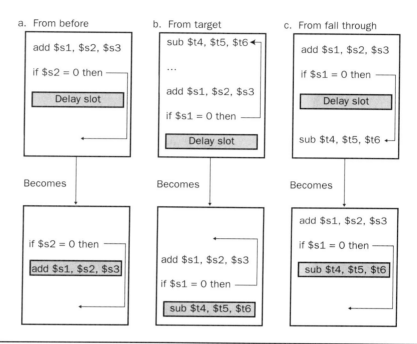

FIGURE 6.54   Scheduling the branch delay slot. The top box in each pair shows the code before scheduling; the bottom box shows the scheduled code. In (a), the delay slot is scheduled with an independent instruction from before the branch. This is the best choice. Strategies (b) and (c) are used when (a) is not possible. In the code sequences for (b) and (c), the use of $s1 in the branch condition prevents the add instruction (whose destination is $s1) from being moved into the branch delay slot. In (b) the branch-delay slot is scheduled from the target of the branch; usually the target instruction will need to be copied because it can be reached by another path. Strategy (b) is preferred when the branch is taken with high probability, such as a loop branch. Finally, the branch may be scheduled from the not-taken fall-through as in (c). To make this optimization legal for (b) or (c), it must be OK to execute the sub instruction when the branch goes in the unexpected direction. By "OK" we mean that the work is wasted, but the program will still execute correctly. This is the case, for example, if $t4 were an unused temporary register when the branch goes in the unexpected direction.

Pipeline Summary

Thus far we have seen three models of execution: single cycle, multicycle, and pipelined. Pipelined control strives for 1 clock cycle per instruction, like single cycle, but also for a fast clock cycle, like multicycle. Let's revisit the example from page 375.

Comparing Performance of Several Control Schemes

Example

Compare performance for single-cycle, multicycle, and pipelined control using the instruction mix for gcc from Figure 4.54. The operation times for the major functional units in this example are 2 ns for memory access, 2 ns for ALU operation, and 1 ns for register file read or write. For pipelined execution, assume that half of the load instructions are immediately followed by an instruction that uses the result, that the branch delay on misprediction is 1 clock cycle, and that one-quarter of the branches are mispredicted. Assume that jumps always pay 1 full clock cycle of delay, so their average time is 2 clock cycles.

Answer

The instruction mix for gcc is 22% loads, 11% stores, 49% R-format operations, 16% branches, and 2% jumps (see Answer on page 397). For the pipelined design, loads take 1 clock cycle when there is no load-use dependency and 2 when there is. Hence the average clock cycles per load instruction is 1.5. Stores take 1 clock cycle, as do the R-format instructions. Branches take 1 when predicted correctly and 2 when not, so the average clock cycles per branch instruction is 1.25. The jump CPI is 2. Hence the average CPI is

$$1.5 \times 22\% + 1 \times 11\% + 1 \times 49\% + 1.25 \times 16\% + 2 \times 2\% = 1.17$$

We multiply 1.17 by the 2-ns clock cycle time of a pipelined machine to get the average instruction time in nanoseconds, yielding 2.34 ns. From before, we know that the average instruction time for the multicycle is 4.04×2 ns or 8.08 ns, and 8 ns for single cycle. Hence pipelined control is about 3.4 times faster than multicycle or single-cycle control.

6.7 Exceptions

To make a computer with automatic program-interruption facilities behave [sequentially] was not an easy matter, because the number of instructions in various stages of processing when an interrupt signal occurs may be large.

Fred Brooks Jr., *Planning a Computer System:*
Project Stretch, 1962

Another form of control hazard involves exceptions. For example, suppose the following instruction

    add $1,$2,$1

has an arithmetic overflow. We need to transfer control to the exception routine at location 4000 0040$_{hex}$ (see Chapter 5, page 410) immediately after this instruction because we wouldn't want this invalid value to contaminate other registers or memory locations.

Just as we did for the taken branch in the previous section, we must flush the instructions that follow the add instruction from the pipeline and begin fetching instructions from the new address. We will use the same mechanism we used for taken branches, but this time the exception causes the deasserting of control lines.

We already saw how to flush the instruction in the IF stage by turning it into a nop. To flush instructions in the ID stage, we use the multiplexor already in the ID stage that zeros control signals for stalls. A new control signal, called ID.Flush, is ORed with the stall signal from the Hazard Detection Unit to flush during ID. To flush the instruction in the EX phase, we use a new signal called EX.Flush to cause new multiplexors to zero the control lines. To start fetching instructions from location 4000 0040$_{hex}$, we simply add an additional input to the PC multiplexor that sends 4000 0040$_{hex}$ to the PC. Figure 6.55 shows these changes.

This example points out a problem with exceptions: If we do not stop execution in the middle of the instruction, the programmer will not be able to see the original value of register $1 that helped cause the overflow because it will be clobbered as the destination register of the add instruction. Because of careful planning, the overflow exception is detected during the EX stage; hence we can use the EX.Flush signal to prevent the instruction in the EX stage from writing its result in the WB stage.

The final step is to save the address of the offending instruction in the Exception Program Counter (EPC), as we did in Chapter 5. In reality, we save the address + 4, so the exception handling routine must first subtract 4 from the saved value. Figure 6.55 shows a stylized version of the datapath, including the branch hardware and necessary accommodations to handle exceptions.

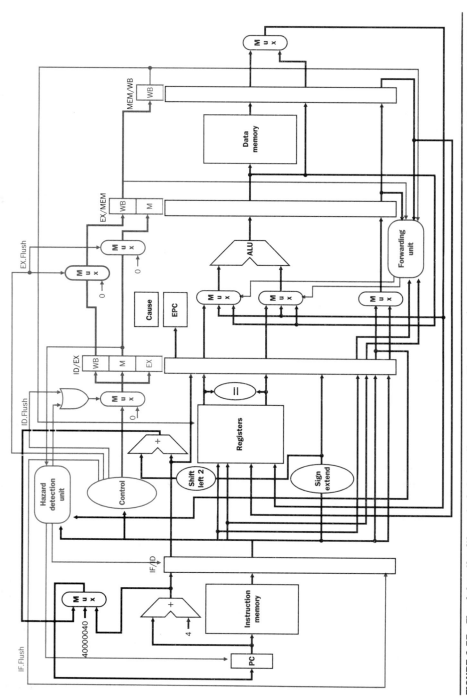

FIGURE 6.55 The datapath with controls to handle exceptions. The changes from Figure 6.51 include a new input, with the value 4000 0040$_{hex}$ in the multiplexor that supplies the new PC value; a Cause register to record the cause of the exception; and an Exception PC register to save the address of the instruction that caused the exception. The 4000 0040$_{hex}$ input to the multiplexor is the initial address to begin fetching instructions in the event of an exception. Although not shown, the ALU overflow signal is an input to the control unit.

(page 506)

Exception in a Pipelined Computer

Example

Given this instruction sequence,

```
40hex    sub     $11, $2, $4
44hex    and     $12, $2, $5
48hex    or      $13, $2, $6
4Chex    add      $1, $2, $1
50hex    slt     $15, $6, $7
54hex    lw      $16, 50($7)
. . .
```

assume the instructions to be invoked on an exception begin like this:

```
40000040hex    sw      $25, 1000($0)
40000044hex    sw      $26, 1004($0)
. . .
```

Show what happens in the pipeline if an overflow exception occurs in the add instruction.

Answer

Figure 6.56 shows the events, starting with the add instruction in the EX stage. The overflow is detected during that phase, and $4000\ 0040_{hex}$ is forced into the PC. Clock cycle 6 shows that the add and following instructions are flushed, and the first instruction of the exception code is fetched. Note that the address of the instruction *following* the add is saved: $4C_{hex} + 4 = 50_{hex}$.

Chapter 5 lists some other causes of exceptions:

- I/O device request
- Invoking an operating system service from a user program
- Using an undefined instruction
- Hardware malfunction

With five instructions active in any clock cycle, the challenge is to associate an exception with the appropriate instruction. Moreover, multiple exceptions can occur simultaneously in a single clock cycle. The normal solution is to prioritize the exceptions so that it is easy to determine which is serviced first; this strategy works for pipelined machines as well. In most MIPS implementations, the hardware sorts exceptions so that the earliest instruction is interrupted.

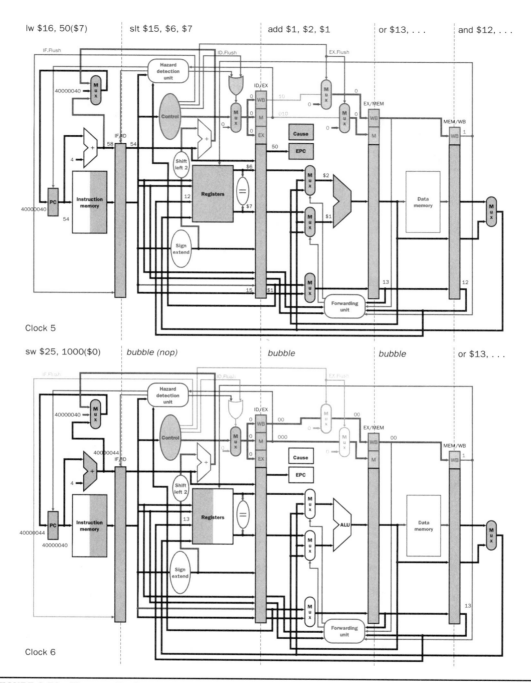

FIGURE 6.56 The result of an exception due to arithmetic overflow in the add instruction. The overflow is detected during the EX stage of clock 5, saving the address following the add in the EPC register (4C + 4 = 50$_{hex}$). Overflow causes all the Flush signals to be set near the end of this clock cycle, deasserting control values (setting them to 0) for the add. Clock cycle 6 shows the instructions converted to bubbles in the pipeline plus the fetching of the first instruction of the exception routine—sw $25,1000($0)—from instruction location 4000 0040$_{hex}$. Note that the and and or instructions, which are prior to the add, still complete.   Although not shown, the ALU overflow signal is an input to the control unit.   *(page 508)*

I/O device requests and hardware malfunctions are not associated with a specific instruction, so the implementation has some flexibility as to when to interrupt the pipeline. The hardware should pick the simplest instruction to associate with the I/O exception, but because the hardware is unstable when a malfunction happens, it may be wise to stop as soon as possible.

The EPC captures the address of the interrupted instructions, and the MIPS Cause register records all possible exceptions in a clock cycle, so the exception software must match the exception to the instruction. An important clue is knowing in which pipeline stage a type of exception can occur. For example, an undefined instruction is discovered in the ID stage, and invoking the operating system occurs in the EX stage. Exceptions are collected in the Cause register so that the hardware can interrupt based on later exceptions, once the earliest one has been serviced.

Hardware Software Interface

The machine and the operating system must work in conjunction so that exceptions behave as you would expect. The hardware contract is normally to stop the offending instruction in midstream, let all prior instructions complete, flush all following instructions, set a register to show the cause of the exception, save the address of the offending instruction, and then jump to a prearranged address. The operating system contract is to look at the cause of the exception and act appropriately. For an undefined instruction, hardware malfunction, or arithmetic overflow exception, the operating system normally kills the program and returns an indicator of the reason. For an I/O device request or an operating system service call, the operating system saves the state of the program, performs the desired task, and then restores the program to continue execution.

The difficulty of always associating the correct exception with the correct instruction in pipelined computers has led some computer designers to relax this requirement in noncritical cases. Such machines are said to have *imprecise interrupts* or *imprecise exceptions*. In the example above, PC would normally have 58_{hex} at the start of the clock cycle after the exception is detected, even though the offending instruction is at address $4C_{hex}$. A machine with imprecise exceptions might put 58_{hex} into EPC and leave it up to the operating system to determine which instruction caused the problem. MIPS and the vast majority of machines today support *precise interrupts* or *precise exceptions*. (One reason is to support virtual memory, which we shall see in Chapter 7.)

6.8   Superscalar and Dynamic Pipelining

Be forewarned that sections 6.8 and 6.9 are brief overviews of fascinating but advanced topics. If you want to learn more details, you should consult our more advanced book, *Computer Architecture: A Quantitative Approach,* second edition.

In the interest of even faster processors, there have been three major directions in which the simple pipelines of this chapter have been extended. The first is sometimes called *superpipelining,* but it simply means longer pipelines. Since the ideal maximum speedup from pipelining is related to the number of pipeline stages, some recent microprocessors have gone to pipelines with eight or more stages.

Using our laundry analogy, we could divide our washer into three machines that perform the wash, rinse, and spin steps of a traditional machine. We would then move from a four-stage to a six-stage pipeline. To get the full speedup, we need to rebalance the remaining steps so they are the same length, in processors or in laundry.

The second trend is to replicate the internal components of the computer so that it can launch multiple instructions in every pipeline stage. The buzzword *superscalar* is applied to this technique. A superscalar laundry would replace our household washer and dryer with, say, three washers and three dryers. You would also have to recruit more assistants to fold and put away three times as much laundry in the same amount of time. The downside is the extra work to keep all the machines busy and transferring the loads to the next pipeline stage.

Launching multiple instructions per stage allows the instruction execution rate to exceed the clock rate or, stated alternatively, for the CPI to be less than 1. (Some wags have even flipped the metric, calling it *IPC,* or *instructions per clock cycle!*) Hence a 1000-MHz four-way superscalar microprocessor can execute a peak rate of four billion instructions per second, and have a best case CPI of 0.25. Today's superscalar machines try to find two to six instructions to execute in every pipeline stage. If the instructions in the instruction stream are dependent or don't meet certain criteria, however, only the first few instructions in the sequence are issued, or perhaps even just the first instruction.

The third trend is *dynamic pipeline scheduling* or *dynamic pipelining* by the hardware to avoid pipeline hazards. So far, our pipeline stalls when waiting for a hazard to be resolved, even if the later instructions are ready to go. For example, in the code sequence

```
lw     $t0, 20($s2)
addu   $t1, $t0, $t2
sub    $s4, $s4, $t3
slti   $t5, $s4, 20
```

even though the `sub` and `slti` instructions are ready to execute, they must wait for the `lw` and `addu` to complete first, which might take many clock cycles if memory is slow. (Chapter 7 explains caches, the reason that memory accesses are sometimes very slow.) Dynamic pipelining is normally combined with extra hardware resources so later instructions can proceed in parallel.

The cost is much more complicated pipeline control, and a more complicated instruction execution model than the simple linear timeline in Figure 6.1.

Superscalar MIPS

What would a MIPS machine look like as a superscalar implementation? Let's assume that two instructions are issued per clock cycle. One of the instructions could be an integer ALU operation or branch, and the other could be a load or store.

Issuing two instructions per cycle will require fetching and decoding 64 bits of instructions. To keep the decoding simple, we could require that the instructions be paired and aligned on a 64-bit boundary, with the ALU or branch portion appearing first. The alternative is to examine the instructions and possibly swap them before they are sent to the ALU or memory unit; however, this introduces additional requirements for hazard detection. In either case, the second instruction can be issued only if the first instruction can be issued. Figure 6.57 shows how the instructions look as they go into the pipeline in pairs. Remember that the hardware makes this decision dynamically, issuing only the first instruction if the conditions are not met.

To issue an ALU and a data transfer operation in parallel, the first need for additional hardware—beyond the usual hazard detection logic—is extra ports in the register file (see Figure 6.58). In 1 clock cycle we may need to read two

Instruction type	Pipe stages							
ALU or branch instruction	IF	ID	EX	MEM	WB			
Load or store instruction	IF	ID	EX	MEM	WB			
ALU or branch instruction		IF	ID	EX	MEM	WB		
Load or store instruction		IF	ID	EX	MEM	WB		
ALU or branch instruction			IF	ID	EX	MEM	WB	
Load or store instruction			IF	ID	EX	MEM	WB	
ALU or branch instruction				IF	ID	EX	MEM	WB
Load or store instruction				IF	ID	EX	MEM	WB

FIGURE 6.57 Superscalar pipeline in operation. The ALU and data transfer instructions are issued at the same time.

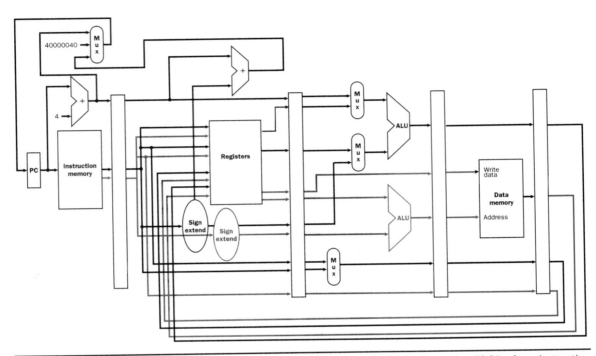

FIGURE 6.58   A superscalar datapath. The superscalar additions are highlighted: another 32 bits from instruction memory, two more read ports and one more write port on the register file, and another ALU. Assume the bottom ALU handles address calculations for data transfers and the top ALU handles everything else.

registers for the ALU operation and two more for a store, and also one write port for an ALU operation and one write port for a load. Since the ALU is tied up for the ALU operation, we also need a separate adder to calculate the effective address for data transfers. Without these extra resources, our superscalar pipeline would be hindered by structural hazards.

There is another difficulty that may limit the effectiveness of a superscalar pipeline. In our simple MIPS pipeline, loads have a latency of 1 clock cycle, which prevents one instruction from using the result without stalling. In the superscalar pipeline, the result of a load instruction cannot be used on the next *clock cycle*. This means that the next *two* instructions cannot use the load result without stalling. To effectively exploit the parallelism available in a superscalar processor, more ambitious compiler or hardware scheduling techniques are needed, as well as more complex instruction decoding.

Simple Superscalar Code Scheduling

Example

How would this loop be scheduled on a superscalar pipeline for MIPS?

```
Loop:   lw      $t0, 0($s1)     # $t0=array element
        addu    $t0,$t0,$s2     # add scalar in $s2
        sw      $t0, 0($s1)     # store result
        addi    $s1,$s1,-4      # decrement pointer
        bne     $s1,$zero,Loop  # branch $s1!=0
```

Reorder the instructions to avoid as many pipeline stalls as possible.

Answer

The first three instructions have data dependencies, and so do the last two. Figure 6.59 shows the best schedule for these instructions. Notice that just one pair of instructions executes in superscalar mode. It takes 4 clocks per loop iteration; at 4 clocks to execute 5 instructions, we get the disappointing CPI of 0.8 versus the best case of 0.5.

	ALU or branch instruction	Data transfer instruction	Clock cycle
Loop:		lw $t0, 0($s1)	1
	addi $s1,$s1,-4		2
	addu $t0,$t0,$s2		3
	bne $s1,$zero,Loop	sw $t0, 4($s1)	4

FIGURE 6.59 The scheduled code as it would look on a superscalar MIPS.

One technique to get more performance from loops that access arrays is *loop unrolling*; as the name suggests, multiple copies of the loop body are made, and instructions from different iterations are scheduled together.

Loop Unrolling for Superscalar Pipelines

Example

See how well loop unrolling and scheduling work in the example above. Assume that the loop index is a multiple of four.

Answer

To schedule the loop without any delays, it turns out that we need to make four copies of the loop body. After unrolling, the loop will contain four copies each of lw, addu, and sw, plus one addi and one bne. The unrolled and scheduled code is shown in Figure 6.60.

Notice now that 12 of the 14 instructions in the loop execute in superscalar mode. It takes 8 clocks for four loop iterations, or 2 clocks per iteration. Loop unrolling and scheduling with superscalar execution gave us a factor of two improvement, partly from reducing the loop control instructions and partly from superscalar execution. The cost of this performance improvement is using four temporary registers rather than one.

	ALU or branch instruction		Data transfer instruction		Clock cycle
Loop:	addi	$s1,$s1,-16	lw	$t0, 0($s1)	1
			lw	$t1,12($s1)	2
	addu	$t0,$t0,$s2	lw	$t2, 8($s1)	3
	addu	$t1,$t1,$s2	lw	$t3, 4($s1)	4
	addu	$t2,$t2,$s2	sw	$t0, 0($s1)	5
	addu	$t3,$t3,$s2	sw	$t1,12($s1)	6
			sw	$t2, 8($s1)	7
	bne	$s1,$zero,Loop	sw	$t3, 4($s1)	8

FIGURE 6.60   The unrolled and scheduled code of Figure 6.59 as it would look on a superscalar MIPS. Since the first pair decrements $s1 by 16, the addresses loaded are the original value of $s1, then that address minus 4, minus 8, and minus 12.

The Big Picture

Both pipelining and superscalar execution increase peak instruction throughput. Longer pipelines and wider superscalar issue put even more pressure on the compiler to deliver on the performance potential of the hardware. But data and control dependencies in programs, together with instruction latencies, offer an upper limit on delivered performance because the processor must sometimes wait for a dependency to be resolved, such as with mispredicted branch.

While striving for the highest performance, hardware designers must also ensure correct execution of all instruction sequences. Compiler writers may or may not be asked to participate by limiting the types of sequences generated, but they *must* understand the pipeline to achieve best performance, and then to generate the appropriate code.

Dynamic Pipeline Scheduling

Dynamic pipeline scheduling goes past stalls to find later instructions to execute while waiting for the stall to be resolved. Typically, the pipeline is divided into three major units: an instruction fetch and issue unit, execute units, and a commit unit. Figure 6.61 shows the model. The first unit fetches instructions, decodes them, and sends each instruction to a corresponding functional unit of the execute stage. There might be 5 to 10 functional units. Each functional unit has buffers, called *reservation stations*, that hold the operands and the operation. As soon as the buffer contains all its operands and the functional unit is ready to execute, the result is calculated. It is then up to the commit unit to decide when it is safe to put the result into the register file or (for a store) into memory.

The basic model is multiple independent state machines performing instruction execution: one unit fetching and decoding instructions, several functional units performing the operations, and one unit deciding when instructions are complete so that the results can be committed. To make programs behave as if they were running on a simple nonpipelined computer, the instruction fetch and decode unit is required to issue instructions in order, and the commit unit is required to write results to registers and memory in

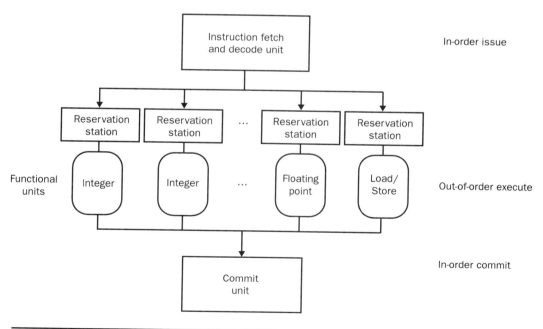

FIGURE 6.61 The three primary units of a dynamically scheduled pipeline.

program execution order. This conservative mode is called *in-order completion*. Hence, if an exception occurs, the computer can point to the last instruction executed, and the only registers updated will be all those written by instructions before the exceptional instruction. The functional units, however, are free to start and finish whenever they want. A more radical approach, which typically introduces imprecise interrupts, is to allow the commit to be out of order. This liberal mode is called *out-of-order completion*.

Dynamic pipelining is more complicated than the traditional or *static pipelining*, and getting the bugs out of such hardware is a challenge. Part of the difficulty is that dynamic scheduling is normally combined with branch prediction, so the commit unit must be able to discard all the results in the execution unit that were due to instructions executed after a mispredicted branch. Combining dynamic scheduling with branch prediction is called *speculative execution*. A second reason for complexity is that dynamic scheduling is also typically combined with superscalar execution, so each unit may be issuing or committing four to six instructions each clock cycle.

In summary, such dynamic machines are predicting program flow, looking at the instructions in multiple segments to see which to execute next, and then speculatively executing instructions based on the prediction and the instruction dependencies. The motivations for dynamic execution are threefold:

1. Hide memory latency, a major issue for computers described in Chapter 7.

2. Avoid stalls that the compiler could not schedule, often due to potential dependencies between store and load.

3. Speculatively execute instructions while waiting for hazards to be resolved.

A microprocessor that follows all three trends—deep pipelines, superscalar, and dynamic pipelining—is the DEC Alpha 21264. This superscalar machine fetches four instructions per clock cycle—but can issue up to six instructions—and uses out-of-order execution and in-order completion. The pipeline takes nine stages for simple integer and floating-point operations, yielding a clock rate of 600 MHz in 1997.

Putting this rate into perspective, the 1997 clock rate of the Cray T-90 supercomputer is just 455 MHz. Chapter 2 reminds us that clock rate is only one of three key performance parameters, but this is still an impressive achievement.

Elaboration: A commit unit controls updates to the register file *and* memory. Some dynamically scheduled machines update the register file immediately during execution. Other machines have a copy of the register file, and the actual update to the register file occurs later as part of the commit. For memory, there is normally a *store buffer*, also called a *write buffer* (see Chapter 7). The commit unit allows the store to write to memory from the buffer when the buffer has a valid address and valid data, and when the store is no longer dependent on predicted branches.

Elaboration: Memory accesses benefit from *nonblocking caches*, which continue servicing cache accesses during a cache miss (see Chapter 7). Out-of-order execution processors need nonblocking caches to allow instructions to execute during a miss.

Real Stuff: PowerPC 604 and Pentium Pro Pipelines

Dynamically scheduled pipelines are used in both the PowerPC 604 and the Pentium Pro. They have such similar pipeline organizations that we use a single generic drawing, Figure 6.62, to describe both. Figure 1.18 on page 27 shows the silicon area required by dynamic pipelining in the Pentium Pro.

The instruction cache fetches 16 bytes of instructions and sends them to an instruction queue: four instructions for the PowerPC and a variable number of instructions for the Pentium Pro. Next, several instructions are fetched and decoded. Both processors use a 512-entry branch history table to predict branches and speculatively execute instructions after the predicted branch. The dispatcher unit sends each instruction and its operands to the reservation station of one of the six functional units. The dispatcher also places an entry for the instruction in the reorder buffer of the commit unit. Thus an instruction cannot issue unless there is space available in both an appropriate reservation station and in the reorder buffer.

With so many instructions executing at the same time, we can run out of places to keep results. Both processors have extra internal registers, called *rename buffers* or *rename registers,* that are used to hold results while waiting for the commit unit to commit the result to one of the real registers. The decode unit is where rename buffers get assigned, thereby reducing hazards on register numbers. Whenever an entry in the reservation station has all its operands and the associated functional unit is available, the operation is performed.

The commit unit keeps track of all the pending instructions in its reorder buffer. Because both machines use branch prediction, an instruction isn't finished until the commit unit says it is. When the branch functional unit determines whether or not a branch was taken, it informs both the branch prediction unit, so that it can update its state machine, and the commit unit, so that it can decide the fate of pending instructions. If the prediction was accurate, the results of the instructions after the branch are marked valid and thus can be placed in the programmer-visible registers and memory. If a misprediction occurred, then all the instructions after the branch are marked invalid and discarded from the reservation stations and reorder buffer.

The commit unit can commit several instructions per clock cycle. To provide precise behavior during exceptions, the commit unit makes sure the instruc-

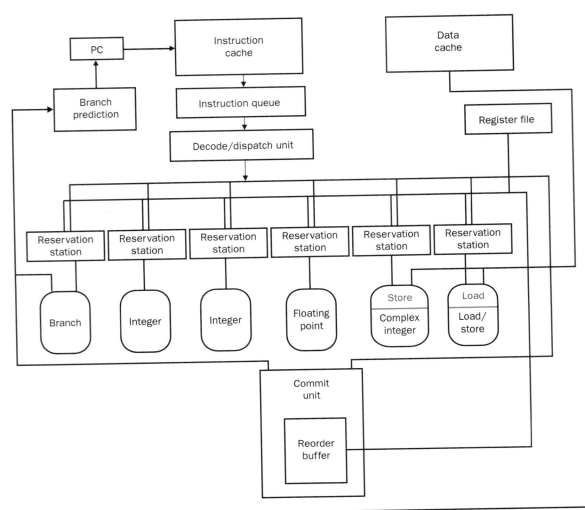

FIGURE 6.62 The generic pipeline organization of the Intel Pentium Pro and the PowerPC 604. Both have six functional units, and the first four have the same responsibilities. For the Pentium Pro, the last two functional units are Store and Load (in color), and the PowerPC 604 has Complex Integer and Load/Store functional units. The figure shows that every functional unit has its own path to a reservation station, but the Pentium Pro has a single central reservation station that can be used for any functional units with one bus shared by the branch and one of the integer units, one bus shared by the other integer unit and floating-point unit, and separate buses for the rest of the functional units. The names for the major units on the Pentium Pro are Fetch/Decode Unit, Dispatch/Execute Unit, and Retire Unit, and the functional units are called Jump Execution Unit (EU), Integer EU, Floating Point EU, Store Address Generation Unit (AGU), and Load AGU. The real names for the major units on the PowerPC are Instruction Unit, Functional Units, and Completion Unit, and the functional units are called Branch Processing Unit, Single-Cycle Integer Unit, Floating Point Unit, Multi-Cycle Integer Unit, and Load/Store Unit.

tions commit in the order they were issued. Thus the commit unit cannot commit an instruction until the operation is finished in the functional unit, all branches on which it might depend are resolved, and all instructions issued before it have committed.

Figure 6.63 lists the specific parameters for the PowerPC 604 and Pentium Pro pipelines. Many of the differences between the Pentium Pro and the PowerPC 604 are cosmetic. The largest difference, not surprisingly, is in decode and dispatch. As described in section 5.7, rather than try to pipeline variable-length 80x86 instructions, the Pentium Pro decode unit translates the Intel instructions into 72-bit, fixed-length microoperations, and then sends these microoperations to the reorder buffer and reservation stations. This translation takes 1 clock cycle to determine the length of the 80x86 instructions and then 2 more to create the microoperations.

As discussed in Chapter 5, these microoperations have two source registers and one destination register, and are similar to MIPS instructions. Most 80x86 instructions are translated into one to four microoperations, but the really complex 80x86 instructions are executed by a conventional microprogram that issues long sequences of microoperations.

Parameter name	PowerPC 604	Pentium Pro
Maximum number of instructions issued per clock cycle	4	3
Maximum number of instructions completing execution per clock cycle	6	5
Maximum number of instructions committed per clock cycle	6	3
Number of bytes fetched from instruction cache	16	16
Number of bytes in instruction queue	32	32
Number of instructions in reorder buffer	16	40
Number of entries in branch table buffer	512	512
Number of history bits per entry in branch history buffer	2	4
Number of rename buffers	12 integer + 8 FP	40
Total number of reservation stations	12	20
Total number of functional units	6	6
Number of integer functional units	2	2
Number of complex integer operation functional units	1	0
Number of floating-point functional units	1	1
Number of branch functional units	1	1
Number of memory functional units	1 for both load and store	1 for load + 1 for store

FIGURE 6.63   Specific parameters of the PowerPC 604 and Pentium Pro in Figure 6.62.

6.10   Fallacies and Pitfalls

Fallacy: Pipelining is easy.

Our books testify to the subtlety of correct pipeline execution. Our advanced book had a pipeline bug in its first edition, despite its being reviewed by more than 100 people and being class-tested at 18 universities. The bug was uncovered only when someone tried to build the computer in that book. Similarly, the alpha version of the first edition of this book had a bug involving forwarding and store instructions, and this bug escaped the scrutiny of many reviewers and students. Beware!

Fallacy: Pipelining ideas can be implemented independent of technology.

When the number of transistors on-chip and speed of transistors made a five-stage pipeline the best solution, then the delayed branch (see elaborations on pages 444 and 502) was a simple solution to control hazards. With longer pipelines, superscalar execution, and dynamic branch prediction, it is now redundant. In the early 1990s, dynamic pipeline scheduling took too many resources and was not required for high performance, but as transistor budgets continued to double and logic became much faster than memory, then multiple functional units and dynamic pipelining made more sense.

Pitfall: Failure to consider instruction set design can adversely impact pipelining.

Many of the difficulties of pipelining arise because of instruction set complications. Here are some examples:

- Widely variable instruction lengths and running times can lead to imbalance among pipeline stages, causing other stages to back up. They can also severely complicate hazard detection and the maintenance of precise exceptions.

- Sophisticated addressing modes can lead to different sorts of problems. Addressing modes that update registers, such as update addressing (see page 175 in Chapter 3), complicate hazard detection. Other addressing modes that require multiple memory accesses substantially complicate pipeline control and make it difficult to keep the pipeline flowing smoothly.

Perhaps the best example is the DEC Alpha and the DEC NVAX. In comparable technology, the new instruction set architecture of the Alpha allowed an implementation whose performance is more than twice as fast as NVAX. In another example, Bhandarkar and Clark [1991] compared the MIPS M/2000 and the VAX 8700 by counting clock cycles of the SPEC benchmarks; they

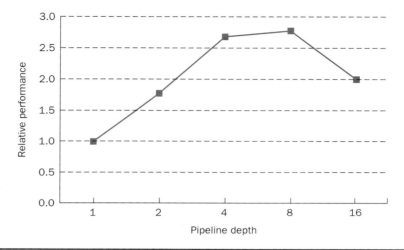

FIGURE 6.64 The depth of pipelining versus the speedup obtained. The x axis shows the number of stages in the EX portion of the floating-point pipeline. A single-stage pipeline corresponds to 32 levels of logic, which might be appropriate for a single FP operation. This data is based on Table 2 in S. R. Kunkel and J. E. Smith, "Optimal pipelining in supercomputers," *Proc. 13th Symposium on Computer Architecture* (June 1986), pages 404–414.

concluded that, although the MIPS M/2000 executes more instructions, the VAX on average executes 2.7 times as many clock cycles, so the MIPS is faster.

Fallacy: Increasing the depth of pipelining always increases performance.

Three factors combine to limit the performance improvement gained by pipelining. First, data hazards in the code mean that increasing the pipeline depth increases the time per instruction because a larger percentage of the cycles become stalls. Second, control hazards mean that increasing pipeline depth results in slower branches, thereby increasing the clock cycles for the program. Finally, pipeline register overhead can limit the decrease in clock period obtained by further pipelining. Figure 6.64 shows the trade-off between pipeline depth and performance for a floating-point pipeline.

Concluding Remarks

Nine-tenths of wisdom consists of being wise in time.

American proverb

This chapter started in the laundry room, showing principles of pipelining in an everyday setting. Using that analogy as a guide, we explain instruction pipelining step by step, starting with the single-cycle datapath and then adding pipeline registers, forwarding paths, data hazard detection, branch prediction, and flushing instructions on exceptions. Figure 6.65 shows the final evolved datapath and control.

Pipelining improves the average execution time per instruction. Depending on whether you start with a single-cycle or multiple-cycle datapath, this reduction can be thought of as decreasing the clock cycle time or as decreasing the number of clock cycles per instruction (CPI). We started with the simple single-cycle datapath, so pipelining was presented as reducing the clock cycle time of the simple datapath. Figure 6.66 shows the effect on CPI and clock rate for each of the datapaths from Chapters 5 and 6, with pipelining offering both a low CPI and a fast clock rate.

Pipelining improves throughput, but not the inherent execution time, or *latency*, of instructions; the latency is similar in length to the multi-cycle approach. Unlike that approach, which uses the same hardware repeatedly during instruction execution, pipelining starts an instruction every clock cycle by having dedicated hardware. Figure 6.67 shows the datapaths from Figure 6.66 placed according to the amount of sharing of hardware and instruction latency.

Latency introduces difficulties due to dependencies in programs because a dependency means the machine must wait the full instruction latency for the hazard to be resolved. The cost of data dependencies can be reduced through the use of forwarding hardware, and the frequency of control dependencies can be reduced through both branch prediction hardware and compiler scheduling.

The switch to longer pipelines, superscalar instruction issue, and dynamic scheduling has recently sustained the 60% per year processor performance increase that we have benefited from since 1986. In the past, it appeared that the choice was between the highest clock rate processors and the most sophisticated superscalar processors. The Alpha 21264—which issues six instructions per clock cycle, does out-of-order execution, and in 1997 has a 600-MHz clock rate—proved that it is possible to do both. Not surprisingly, this 15-million-transistor chip also has the best SPEC95 performance.

With remarkable advances in processing, Amdahl's law suggests that another part of the system will become the bottleneck. That bottleneck is the topic of the next chapter: the memory system.

An alternative to pushing uniprocessors to automatically exploit parallelism at the instruction level is trying multiprocessors, which exploit parallelism at much coarser levels. Parallel processing is the topic of Chapter 9.

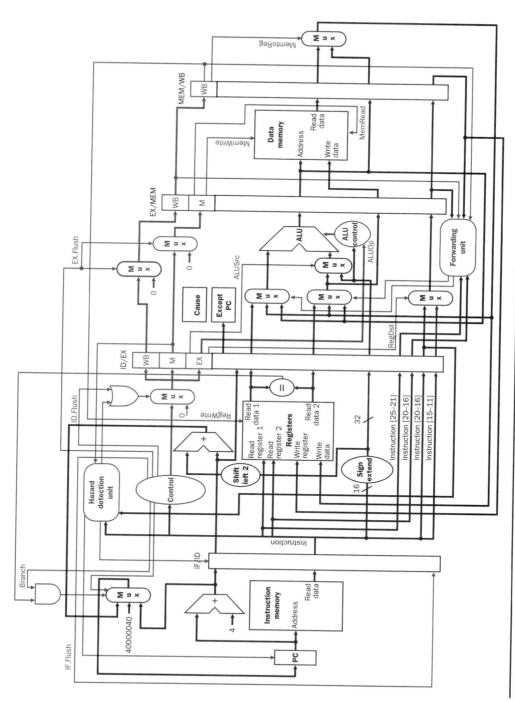

FIGURE 6.65 The final datapath and control for this chapter.

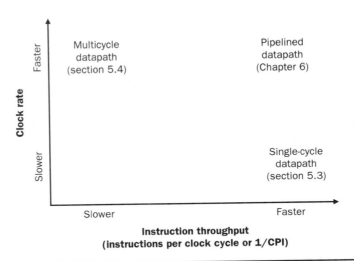

FIGURE 6.66   The performance consequences of simple (single-cycle) datapath and multicycle datapath from Chapter 5 and the pipelined execution model in Chapter 6. Although the instructions per clock cycle (instruction throughput) is slightly larger in the simple datapath, the pipelined datapath is close and it uses a clock rate as fast as the multicycle datapath.

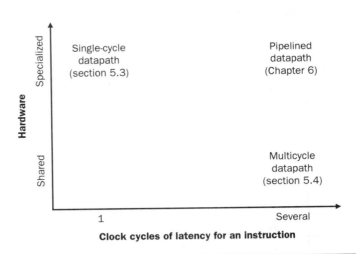

FIGURE 6.67   The basic relationship between the datapaths in Figure 6.66. The pipelined datapath is shown as multiple clock cycles for instruction latency because the execution time of an instruction is not shorter; it's the instruction throughput that is improved.

6.12 Historical Perspective and Further Reading

supercomputer: Any machine still on the drawing board.

Stan Kelly-Bootle, *The Devil's DP Dictionary*, 1981

This section describes some of the major advances in pipelining. It is generally agreed that one of the first general-purpose pipelined machines was Stretch, the IBM 7030 (Figure 6.68). Stretch followed the IBM 704 and had a goal of being 100 times faster than the 704. The goals were a "stretch" of the state of the art at that time—hence the nickname. The plan was to obtain a factor of 1.6 from overlapping fetch, decode, and execute, using a four-stage pipeline; apparently the rest was to come from much more hardware and faster logic. Stretch was also a training ground for both the architects of the IBM 360, Gerrit Blaauw and Fred Brooks Jr., and the architect of the IBM RS/6000, John Cocke.

FIGURE 6.68   The Stretch computer, one of the first pipelined computers. Photo courtesy of IBM.

Control Data Corporation (CDC) delivered what is considered to be the first supercomputer, the CDC 6600, in 1964 (Figure 6.69). The core instructions of Cray's subsequent computers have many similarities to those of the original CDC 6600. The CDC 6600 was unique in many ways. The interaction between pipelining and instruction set design was understood, and the instruction set was kept simple to promote pipelining. The CDC 6600 also used an advanced packaging technology. Thornton's book [1970] provides an excellent description of the entire machine, from technology to architecture, and includes a foreword by Seymour Cray. (Unfortunately, this book is currently out of print.) Both Cray and Thorton have won the ACM Eckert-Mauchly Award.

The IBM 360/91 introduced many new concepts, including dynamic detection of memory hazards, generalized forwarding, and reservation stations (Figure 6.70). The approach is normally named *Tomasulo's algorithm*, after an engineer who worked on the project. The team that created the 360/91 was led by Michael Flynn, who was given the 1992 ACM Eckert-Mauchly Award, in part for his contributions to the IBM 360/91, and in 1997 the same award went to Robert Tomasulo, for his pioneering work on out-of-order processing.

The internal organization of the 360/91 shares many features with the PowerPC 604 and the Pentium Pro. One major difference was that there was no branch prediction and hence no speculation. Another major difference was

FIGURE 6.69   The CDC 6600, the first supercomputer. Photo courtesy of Charles Babbage Institute, University of Minnesota.

FIGURE 6.70 The IBM 360/91 pushed the state of the art in pipelined execution when it was unveiled in 1966. Photo courtesy of IBM.

that there was no commit unit, so once the instructions finished execution, they updated the registers. Out-of-order instruction commit led to *imprecise interrupts*, which proved to be unpopular and led to the commit units in dynamically scheduled pipelined machines since that time.

The RISC machines refined the notion of compiler-scheduled pipelines in the early 1980s. The concepts of delayed branches and delayed loads—common in microprogramming—were extended into the high-level architecture. In fact, the Stanford machine that led to the commercial MIPS architecture was called Microprocessor without Interlocked Pipelined Stages because it was up to the assembler or compiler to avoid data hazards.

IBM did pioneering work on multiple issue. In the 1970s, a project called ACS was underway. It included multiple-instruction issue concepts, but never reached product stage. The earliest proposal for a superscalar processor that dynamically makes issue decisions was by John Cocke; he described the key ideas in several talks in the mid-1980s and coined the name *superscalar*. This original design was named America. The IBM Power-1 architecture, used in the RS/6000 line, is based on these ideas, and the PowerPC is a variation of the Power-1 architecture. Cocke won the Turing Award for his architecture work, the highest award in computer science and engineering.

An approach that predated superscalar that relies on similar compiler technology is called *long instruction word* (LIW) or sometimes *very long instruction word* (VLIW). In this approach, several instructions are issued during each clock cycle as in the superscalar case, but in LIW the compiler guarantees that there are no dependencies between instructions that issue at the same time and that there are sufficient hardware resources to execute them, thereby simplifying the instruction decoding and issuing logic. A very practical advantage of superscalar over LIW designs is that superscalar processors can run without changing binary machine programs that run on more traditional architectures; LIW works well when the source code for the programs is available so that the programs can be recompiled.

To Probe Further

Bhandarkar, D., and D. W. Clark [1991]. "Performance from architecture: Comparing a RISC and a CISC with similar hardware organizations," *Proc. Fourth Conf. on Architectural Support for Programming Languages and Operating Systems*, IEEE/ACM (April), Palo Alto, 310–19.

A quantitative comparison of RISC and CISC written by scholars who argued for CISCs as well as built them; they conclude that MIPS is between 2 and 4 times faster than a VAX built with similar technology, with a mean of 2.7.

Hennessy, J. L., and D. A. Patterson [1996]. *Computer Architecture: A Quantitative Approach*, Second Edition, Morgan Kaufmann, San Francisco.

Chapters 3 and 4 go into considerably more detail about pipelined machines, including dynamic hardware scheduling and superscalar machines.

Jouppi, N. P., and D. W. Wall [1989]. "Available instruction-level parallelism for superscalar and superpipelined machines," *Proc. Third Conf. on Architectural Support for Programming Languages and Operating Systems*, IEEE/ACM (April), Boston, 272–82.

A comparison of superpipelined and superscalar systems.

Kogge, P. M. [1981]. *The Architecture of Pipelined Computers*, McGraw-Hill, New York.

A formal text on pipelined control, with emphasis on underlying principles.

Russell, R. M. [1978]. "The CRAY-1 computer system," *Comm. of the ACM* 21:1 (January) 63–72.

A short summary of a classic computer, which uses vectors of operations to remove pipeline stalls.

Smith, A., and J. Lee [1984]. "Branch prediction strategies and branch target buffer design," *Computer* 17:1 (January) 6–22.

An early survey on branch prediction.

Smith, J. E., and A. R. Plezkun [1988]. "Implementing precise interrupts in pipelined processors," *IEEE Trans. on Computers* 37:5 (May) 562–73.

Covers the difficulties in interrupting pipelined computers.

Thornton, J. E. [1970]. *Design of a Computer: The Control Data 6600*, Scott, Foresman, Glenview, IL.

A classic book describing a classic machine, considered the first supercomputer.

Key Terms

These terms reflect the key ideas discussed in the chapter. Please refer to the Glossary at the back of the book for definitions of any terms you might be unsure of.

branch delay slot
branch or control hazard
branch prediction
branch prediction buffer or
    branch history table
commit unit
data dependencies
data hazard or pipeline data
    hazard
delayed load
dynamic pipeline scheduling
flush (instructions)

forwarding or bypassing
imprecise interrupt or
    exception
in-order commit
in-order execution
instruction latency
latency (pipeline)
load-use data hazard
loop unrolling
multiple-instruction issue
nop
out-of-order commit

out-of-order execution
pipeline stall
pipelining stage
precise interrupt or exception
rename buffer or register
reorder buffer
reservation station
speculative execution
structural hazard
superpipelining
superscalar pipelining

Exercises

6.1 [5] <§6.1> If the time for an ALU operation were actually 4 ns instead of 2 ns (as described in Figure 6.2 on page 439), how would this affect the speedup obtained from pipelining a single-cycle implementation?

6.2 [5] <§6.1> Using a drawing similar to Figure 6.8 on page 447, show the forwarding paths needed to execute the following three instructions:

```
add $2, $3, $4
add $4, $5, $6
add $5, $3, $4
```

6.3 [5] <§6.1> How could we modify the following code to make use of a delayed branch slot?

```
Loop: lw   $2, 100($3)
      addi $3, $3, 4
      beq  $3, $4, Loop
```

6.4 [10] <§6.1> Identify all of the data dependencies in the following code. Which dependencies are data hazards that will be resolved via forwarding?

```
add $2, $5, $4
add $4, $2, $5
sw  $5, 100($2)
add $3, $2, $4
```

6.5 [5] <§6.2> For each pipeline register in Figure 6.25 on page 467, label each portion of the pipeline register with the name of the value that is loaded into the register. Determine the length of each field in bits. For example, the IF/ID pipeline register contains two fields, one of which is an instruction field that is 32 bits wide.

6.6 [15] <§§4.8, 6.2> Using Figure 4.42 on page 271 as your foundation, figure out a reasonable pipelined datapath structure for floating-point addition, and integrate the floating-point registers and the data memory into your picture to produce a figure similar to Figure 6.12 on page 452, except that your diagram should also contain an alternative pipeline for floating-point add instructions. Don't worry too much about the delays associated with each of the functions in Figure 4.42. You should simply assume that the sum of the delays is fairly large, and thus requires you to use 2 or 3 cycles to perform floating-point addition. The addition should be pipelined so that a new floating-point add instruction can be started every cycle, assuming that there are no dependencies (you can ignore dependencies for this problem).

6.7 [10] <§6.2> Using Figure 6.25 on page 467 as a guide, use colored pens or markers to show which portions of the datapath are active and which are inactive in each of the five stages of the add instruction. We suggest that you use five photocopies of Figure 6.25 to answer this exercise. (We hereby grant you permission to violate the Copyright Protection Act in doing the exercises in Chapters 5 and 6!) You could also download the figure from *www.mkp.com/cod2e.htm*. Be sure to include a legend to explain your color scheme.

6.8 [15] <§6.3> To be sure you understand the relationship between the two styles of drawing pipelines, draw the information in Figures 6.31 through 6.35 on pages 472 through 476 in the style of Figure 6.36 on page 477. Be sure to highlight the active portions of the datapaths in this simpler figure.

6.9 [20] <§6.3> Figure 6.71 is similar to Figure 6.33 on page 474, but the instructions are unidentified. Your task is to determine as much as you can about the five instructions in the five pipeline stages. If you cannot fill in a field of an instruction, state why. For some fields it will be easier to decode the machine instructions into assembly language, using Figure 3.18 on page 153 and Figure A.18 on page A-50 as references. For other fields it will be easier to look at the

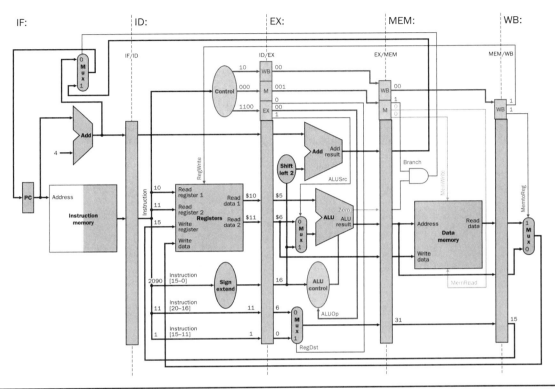

FIGURE 6.71 The pipelined datapath for Exercise 6.9. Use the numeric labels to determine as many fields of each of the five instructions in the pipeline as possible.

values of the control signals, using Figures 6.26 through 6.28 on pages 468 and 469 as references. You may need to carefully examine Figures 6.31 through 6.35 to understand how collections of control values are presented (i.e., the leftmost bit in one cycle will become the uppermost bit in another cycle). For example, the EX control value for the subtract instruction, 1100, computed during the ID stage of cycle 3 in Figure 6.32, becomes three separate values specifying RegDst (1), ALUOp (10), and ALUSrc (0) in cycle 4.

6.10 [40] <§6.3> Using Figure 6.33 on page 474, determine the value of *every* field in the four pipeline registers in clock cycle 5. (These are the values at the beginning of the clock cycle.) Assume that before the instructions are executed, the state of the machine was as follows:

- The PC has the value 500_{ten}, the address of the lw instruction.

- Every register has the initial value 10_{ten} plus the register number (e.g., register $8 has the initial value 18_{ten}).

■ Every memory word accessed as data has the initial value 1000_{ten} plus the byte address of the word (e.g., Memory[8] has the initial value 1008_{ten}).

Determine the value of every field, including those unidentified in the figure and those unnecessary for a specific instruction. If you believe a field value is impossible to determine from the information provided, explain why.

6.11 [5] <§§6.4, 6.5> Consider executing the following code on the pipelined datapath of Figure 6.46 on page 492:

```
add    $1,  $2,  $3
add    $4,  $5,  $6
add    $7,  $8,  $9
add    $10, $11, $12
add    $13, $14, $15
```

At the end of the fifth cycle of execution, which registers are being read and which register will be written?

6.12 [5] <§§6.4, 6.5> {Ex. 6.11} With regard to the program in Exercise 6.11, explain what the forwarding unit is doing during the fifth cycle of execution. If any comparisons are being made, mention them.

6.13 [5] <§§6.4, 6.5> {Ex. 6.11} With regard to the program in Exercise 6.11, explain what the hazard detection unit is doing during the fifth cycle of execution. If any comparisons are being made, mention them.

6.14 [5] <§6.5> Consider a program consisting of 100 lw instructions (don't worry about whether this is good code) and in which each instruction is dependent upon the instruction before it. What would the actual CPI be if the program were run on the pipelined datapath of Figure 6.45 on page 491?

6.15 [5] <§6.4, 6.5> Consider executing the following code on the pipelined datapath of Figure 6.46 on page 492:

```
add    $5, $6, $7
lw     $6, 100($7)
sub    $7, $6, $8
```

How many cycles will it take to execute this code? Draw a diagram like that of Figure 6.44 on page 489 that illustrates the dependencies that need to be resolved, and provide another diagram like that of Figure 6.45 on page 491 that illustrates how the code will actually be executed (incorporating any stalls or forwarding) so as to resolve the identified problems.

6.16 [15] <§6.5> List all the inputs and outputs of the forwarding unit in Figure 6.46 on page 492. Give the names and the number of bits for each input and output.

6.17 [30] <§6.5, Appendix C> {Ex. 6.16} Using Appendix C and the answer to Exercise 6.16, design the hardware to implement the forwarding unit. (Hint: To decide if register numbers are equal, try using an exclusive OR gate. See the elaboration on page 249 of Chapter 4 or the In More Depth section on page 329 of Chapter 4.)

6.18 [20] <§6.5> The forwarding unit could be moved to the ID stage and forwarding decisions could be made earlier. The results of these decisions would need to be passed along with the instruction and used in the EX stage when actual forwarding would take place. This modification would speed up the EX stage and might allow for possible cycle-time improvement. Perform the modification. Provide a revised datapath and a description of the necessary changes. How has the ID/EX register changed? Provide new forwarding equations to replace those appearing on pages 480–483.

6.19 [10] <§§6.4, 6.5> The following code contains a "read after write" data hazard that is resolved by forwarding:

```
add    $2, $3, $4
add    $5, $2, $6
```

Consider the similar situation in which a memory read occurs after a memory write:

```
sw    $7, 100($2)
lw    $8, 100($2)
```

Write a paragraph describing how this situation differs from the one involving registers, and describe how the potential "read after write" problem is resolved.

6.20 [20] <§§6.4, 6.5> Consider an instruction sequence used for a memory-to-memory copy:

```
lw    $2, 100($5)
sw    $2, 200($6)
```

The elaboration starting on page 488 of the text discusses this situation and states that additional forwarding hardware can improve its performance. Show the necessary additions to the datapath of Figure 6.43 to allow code like this to run without stalling. Include forwarding equations (such as the ones appearing on pages 480–483) for all of the control signals for any new or modified multiplexors in your datapath. Finally, rewrite the stall formula on page 490 so that this code sequence won't stall.

6.21 [15] <§§6.2–6.5> In Exercise 5.12, the ability to specify an offset for load and store instructions was removed. How would this modification to the instruction set architecture affect a pipelined implementation? Describe changes to the datapath and how performance would be impacted. Be sure to include a discussion of forwarding in your answer.

6.22 [10] <§§6.2–6.5> Exercise 3.23 described an instruction, addm, that allows arithmetic instructions to directly access memory, as is found in the 80x86. Write a paragraph or two explaining why it would be hard to add this instruction to the MIPS pipeline described in this chapter.

6.23 [10] <§§6.4–6.6> The example on page 447 shows how to *maximize* performance on our pipelined datapath with forwarding and stalls on a use following a load. Rewrite the following code to *minimize* performance on this datapath—that is, reorder the instructions so that this sequence takes the *most* clock cycles to execute while still obtaining the same result.

```
lw    $3,    0($5)
lw    $4,    4($5)
add   $7,    $7,    $3
add   $8,    $8,    $4
add   $10,   $7,    $8
sw    $6,    0($5)
beq   $10,   $11,   Loop
```

6.24 [15] <§6.6> Using the example on page 498, rewrite the code to be as fast as possible using a new instruction beqd, which means a branch equal instruction with a single-branch delay slot.

6.25 [10] <§6.6> {Ex. 6.24} Using the answer to Exercise 6.24, draw the execution of the instructions as in Figure 6.52 on page 500. Once again, photocopying or downloading from *www.mkp.com/cod2e.htm* may save time.

6.26 [20] <§6.6> Consider the pipelined datapath in Figure 6.51 on page 499. Can an attempt to flush and an attempt to stall occur simultaneously? If so, do they result in conflicting actions and/or cooperating actions? If there are any cooperating actions, how do they work together? If there are any conflicting actions, which should take priority? Is there a simple change you can make to the datapath to ensure the necessary priority? You may want to consider the following code sequence to help you answer this question:

```
        beq $1, $2,    TARGET # assume that the branch is taken
        lw  $3, 40($4)
        add $3, $3,    $3
        sw  $3, 40($4)
TARGET: or  $10,$11,   $12
```

6.27 [30] <§6.6> In which stage must the branch decision be made to reduce the branch delay to a single instruction? Redraw the datapath using new hardware that will reduce the branch delay to one cycle.

6.28 [10] <§6.6> One extension of the MIPS instruction set architecture has two new instructions called movn (move if not zero) and movz (move if zero). For example, the instruction

```
movn $8, $11, $4
```

copies the contents of register 11 into register 8, provided that the value in register 4 is nonzero (otherwise it does nothing). The movz instruction is similar but copying takes place only if the register's value is zero. Show how to use the new instructions to put whichever is larger, register 8's value or register 9's value, into register 10. If the values are equal, copy either into register 10. You may use register 1 as an extra register for temporary use. Do not use any conditional branches.

6.29 [10] <§6.6> {Ex. 6.28} The solution to Exercise 6.28 should involve the execution of fewer instructions than would be required using conditional branches. Sometimes, however, rewriting code to use movn and movz rather than conditional branches doesn't reduce the number of instructions executed. Nonetheless, even if the use of movn and movz doesn't reduce the number of instructions executed, it can still make the program faster if it is being executed on a pipelined datapath. Explain why.

6.30 [10] <§6.8> In this exercise, which is similar to the example on page 513, we consider the benefits of performing loop unrolling on code that is executed on the standard MIPS pipeline developed in sections 6.2–6.6. Specifically, consider the following code that has been unrolled but not yet scheduled. In this case, the code has been unrolled once under the assumption that the loop index is a multiple of two (i.e., $s1 is a multiple of eight):

```
Loop:   lw      $t0, 0($s1)
        addu    $t0, $t0, $s2
        sw      $t0, 0($s1)
        lw      $t1, -4($s1)
        addu    $t1, $t1, $s2
        sw      $t1, -4($s1)
        addi    $s1, $s1, -8
        bne     $s1, $zero, Loop
```

First schedule this code for fast execution on the standard MIPS pipeline (assume that it supports addi and addu instructions). Taking into account any necessary stalls, compare the difference in performance between the original unrolled code, which appears on page 513, and your code, which has been unrolled and then scheduled.

6.31 [20] <§6.8> This exercise is similar to Exercise 6.30, except this time the code should be unrolled twice (creating three copies of the code). However, it is not known that the loop index is a multiple of three, and thus you will need to invent a means of ensuring that the code still executes properly. (Hint: Consider adding some code to the beginning or end of the loop that takes care of the cases not handled by the loop.)

6.32 [20] <§6.9> Modifying complex processors such as the PowerPC 604 and the Pentium Pro in order to improve performance involves complex decisions that often can be answered only with the aid of extensive simulation. Assume that technology improvements have increased your "transistor budget" and that you can increase some of the parameters in Figure 6.63 on page 519. What assumptions might cause you to choose specific parameters to improve? How are some of the parameters interrelated?

6.33 [30] <§6.9> New processors are introduced more quickly than new versions of textbooks. To keep your textbook current, investigate some of the latest developments in this area and write a one-page elaboration to insert at the end of section 6.9. You might want to visit the MIPS site via the link at *www.mkp.com/books_catalog/cod/links.htm* as a starting point.

6.34 [1 week] <§§6.4, 6.5> Using the simulator provided with this book, collect statistics on data hazards for a C program (supplied by either the instructor or with the software). You will write a subroutine that is passed the instruction to be executed, and this routine must model the five-stage pipeline in this chapter. Have your program collect the following statistics:

- Number of instructions executed.
- Number of data hazards.
- Number of hazards that result in stalls.
- If the MIPS C compiler that you are using issues nop instructions to avoid hazards, count the number of nop instructions as well.

Assuming that the memory accesses always take 1 clock cycle, calculate the average number of clock cycles per instruction. Classify nop instructions as stalls inserted by software, then subtract them from the number of instructions executed in the CPI calculation.

6.35 [1 month] <§§5.3, 6.3–6.7> If you have access to a simulation system such as Verilog or ViewLogic, first design the single-cycle datapath and control from Chapter 5. Then evolve this design into a pipelined organization, as we did in this chapter. Be sure to run MIPS programs at each step to ensure that your refined design continues to operate correctly.

Large and Fast: Exploiting Memory Hierarchy

*Ideally one would desire an indefinitely large
memory capacity such that any particular . . .
word would be immediately available. . . .
We are . . . forced to recognize the possibility
of constructing a hierarchy of memories, each
of which has greater capacity than the
preceding but which is less quickly accessible.*

A. W. Burks, H. H. Goldstine, and J. von Neumann
*Preliminary Discussion of the Logical Design of an Electronic Computing
Instrument,* 1946

The Five Classic Components of a Computer

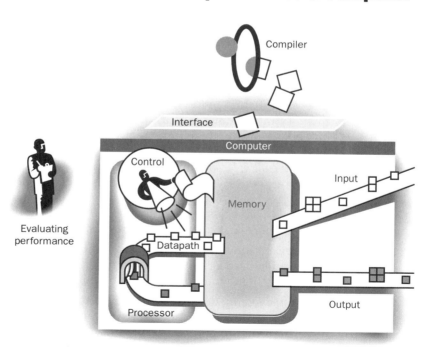

7.1   Introduction

From the earliest days of computing, programmers have wanted unlimited amounts of fast memory. The topics we will look at in this chapter all focus on aiding programmers by creating the illusion of unlimited fast memory. Before we look at how the illusion is actually created, let's consider a simple analogy that illustrates the key principles and mechanisms that we use.

Suppose you were a student writing a term paper on important historical developments in computer hardware. You are sitting at a desk in the engineering or math library with a collection of books that you have pulled from the shelves and are examining. You find that several of the important machines that you need to write about are described in the books you have, but there is nothing about the EDSAC. So, you go back to the shelves and look for an additional book. You find a book on early British computers that covers EDSAC. Once you have a good selection of books on the desk in front of you, there is a good probability that many of the topics you need can be found in them, and you may spend a great deal of time just using the books on the desk without going back to the shelves. Having several books on the desk in front of you saves time compared to having only one book there and constantly having to go back to the shelves to return it and take out another.

The same principle allows us to create the illusion of a large memory that we can access as fast as a very small memory. Just as you did not need to access all the books in the library at once with equal probability, a program does not access all of its code or data at once with equal probability. Otherwise, it would be impossible to make most memory accesses fast and still have large amounts of memory in machines, just as it would be impossible for you to fit all the library books on your desk and still have a chance of finding what you wanted quickly.

This *principle of locality* underlies both the way in which you did your work in the library and the way that programs operate. The principle of locality states that programs access a relatively small portion of their address space at any instant of time, just as you accessed a very small portion of the library's collection. There are two different types of locality:

- *Temporal locality* (locality in time): If an item is referenced, it will tend to be referenced again soon. If you recently brought a book to your desk to look at, you will probably need to look at it again soon.

- *Spatial locality* (locality in space): If an item is referenced, items whose addresses are close by will tend to be referenced soon. For example, when you brought out the book on early computers in England to find out about EDSAC, you also noticed that there was another book shelved next to it about early mechanical computers, so you also brought back that book and, later on, found something useful in that book. Books on the same topic are shelved together in the library to increase spatial locality. We'll see how spatial locality is used in memory hierarchies a little later in this chapter.

Just as accesses to books on the desk naturally exhibit locality, locality in programs arises from simple and natural program structures. For example, most programs contain loops, so instructions and data are likely to be accessed repeatedly, showing high amounts of temporal locality. Since instructions are normally accessed sequentially, programs show high spatial locality. Accesses to data also exhibit a natural spatial locality. For example, accesses to elements of an array or a record will naturally have high degrees of spatial locality.

We take advantage of the principle of locality by implementing the memory of a computer as a *memory hierarchy*. A memory hierarchy consists of multiple levels of memory with different speeds and sizes. The fastest memories are more expensive per bit than the slower memories and thus are usually smaller.

Today, there are three primary technologies used in building memory hierarchies. Main memory is implemented from DRAM (dynamic random access memory), while levels closer to the CPU (caches) use SRAM (static random access memory). DRAM is less costly per bit than SRAM, although it is substantially slower. The price difference arises because DRAM uses significantly less area per bit of memory, and DRAMs thus have larger capacity for the same amount of silicon; the speed difference arises from several factors described in section B.5 of Appendix B. The final technology, used to implement the largest and slowest level in the hierarchy, is magnetic disk. The access time and price per bit vary widely among these technologies, as the table below shows, using typical values for 1997:

Memory technology	Typical access time	$ per MByte in 1997
SRAM	5–25 ns	$100–$250
DRAM	60–120 ns	$5–$10
Magnetic disk	10–20 million ns	$0.10–$0.20

Because of these differences in cost and access time, it is advantageous to build memory as a hierarchy of levels, with the faster memory close to the processor and the slower, less expensive memory below that, as shown in Figure 7.1. The goal is to present the user with as much memory as is available in the cheapest technology, while providing access at the speed offered by the fastest memory.

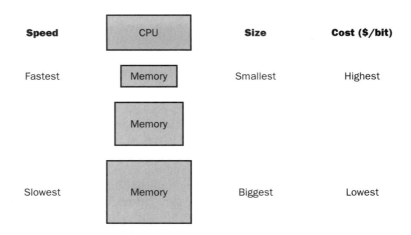

Speed		Size	Cost ($/bit)
	CPU		
Fastest	Memory	Smallest	Highest
	Memory		
Slowest	Memory	Biggest	Lowest

FIGURE 7.1   The basic structure of a memory hierarchy. By implementing the memory system as a hierarchy, the user has the illusion of a memory that is as large as the largest level of the hierarchy, but can be accessed as if it were all built from the fastest memory.

The memory system is organized as a hierarchy: a level closer to the processor is a subset of any level further away, and all the data is stored at the lowest level. By comparison, the books on your desk form a subset of the library you are working in, which is in turn a subset of all the libraries on campus. Furthermore, as we move away from the processor, the levels take progressively longer to access, just as we might encounter in a hierarchy of campus libraries.

A memory hierarchy can consist of multiple levels, but data is copied between only two adjacent levels at a time, so we can focus our attention on just two levels. The upper level—the one closer to the processor—is smaller and faster (since it uses more expensive technology) than the lower level. The minimum unit of information that can be either present or not present in the two-level hierarchy is called a *block*, as shown in Figure 7.2; in our library analogy, a block of information is one book.

If the data requested by the processor appears in some block in the upper level, this is called a *hit* (analogous to your finding the information in one of the books on your desk). If the data is not found in the upper level, the request is called a *miss*. The lower level in the hierarchy is then accessed to retrieve the block containing the requested data. (Continuing our analogy, you get up from your desk and go over to the shelves to look for the desired information.) The *hit rate*, or *hit ratio*, is the fraction of memory accesses found in the upper level; it is often used as a measure of the performance of the memory hierarchy. The *miss rate* (1 – hit rate) is the fraction of memory accesses not found in the upper level.

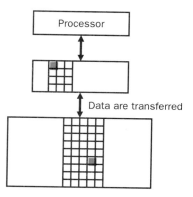

FIGURE 7.2   Every pair of levels in the memory hierarchy can be thought of as having an upper and lower level. Within each level, the unit of information that is present or not is called a *block*. Usually we transfer an entire block when we copy something between levels.

Since performance is the major reason for having a memory hierarchy, the speed of hits and misses is important. *Hit time* is the time to access the upper level of the memory hierarchy, which includes the time needed to determine whether the access is a hit or a miss (that is, the time needed to look through the books on the desk). The *miss penalty* is the time to replace a block in the upper level with the corresponding block from the lower level, plus the time to deliver this block to the processor (or, the time to get another book from the shelves and place it on the desk). Because the upper level is smaller and built using faster memory parts, the hit time will be much smaller than the time to access the next level in the hierarchy, which is the major component of the miss penalty. (The time to examine the books on the desk is much smaller than the time to get up and go look for something in a book on the shelves.)

As we will see in this chapter, the concepts used to build memory systems affect many other aspects of a computer, including how the operating system manages memory and I/O, how compilers generate code, and even how applications use the machine. Of course, because all programs spend much of their time accessing memory, the memory system is necessarily a major factor in determining performance. The reliance on memory hierarchies to achieve performance has meant that programmers, who used to be able to think of memory as a flat, random access storage device, now need to understand how memory hierarchies work to get good performance. We show how important this understanding is with an example in the Fallacies and Pitfalls section.

Since memory systems are so critical to performance, computer designers have devoted a lot of attention to these systems and developed sophisticated mechanisms for improving the performance of the memory system. In this chapter we will see the major conceptual ideas, although many simplifications and abstractions have been used to keep the material manageable in length and complexity. We could easily have written hundreds of pages on memory systems, as a number of recent doctoral theses have demonstrated.

The Big Picture   Programs exhibit both temporal locality, the tendency to reuse recently accessed data items, and spatial locality, the tendency to reference data items that are close to other recently accessed items. Memory hierarchies take advantage of temporal locality by keeping more recently accessed data items closer to the processor. Memory hierarchies take advantage of spatial locality by moving blocks consisting of multiple contiguous words in memory to upper levels of the hierarchy.

A memory hierarchy uses smaller and faster memory technologies close to the processor, as shown in Figure 7.3. Thus accesses that hit in the highest level of the hierarchy can be processed quickly. Accesses that miss go to lower levels of the hierarchy, which are larger but slower. If the hit rate is high enough, the memory hierarchy has an effective access time close to that of the highest (and fastest) level and a size equal to that of the lowest (and largest) level.

In most systems, the memory is a true hierarchy, meaning that data cannot be present in level i unless it is present in level $i + 1$.

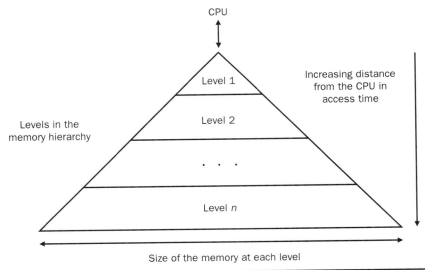

FIGURE 7.3 This diagram shows the structure of a memory hierarchy: as the distance from the CPU increases, so does the size. This structure with the appropriate operating mechanisms allows the CPU to have an access time that is determined primarily by level 1 of the hierarchy and yet have a memory as large as level n. Maintaining this illusion is the subject of this chapter.

7.2 The Basics of Caches

Cache: a safe place for hiding or storing things.

Webster's New World Dictionary of the American Language,
Third College Edition (1988)

In our library example, the desk acted as a cache—a safe place to store things (books) that we needed to examine. *Cache* was the name chosen to represent the level of the memory hierarchy between the CPU and main memory in the first commercial machine to have this extra level. Today, although this remains the dominant use of the word *cache*, the term is also used to refer to any storage managed to take advantage of locality of access. Caches first appeared in research machines in the early 1960s and in production machines later in that same decade; virtually every general-purpose machine built today, from the fastest to the slowest, includes a cache.

In this section, we begin by looking at a very simple cache in which the processor requests are each one word and the blocks also consist of a single word. Figure 7.4 shows such a simple cache, before and after requesting a data item that is not initially in the cache. Before the request, the cache contains a collection of recent references $X1, X2, \ldots, Xn - 1$, and the processor requests a word Xn that is not in the cache. This request results in a miss, and the word Xn is brought from memory into cache.

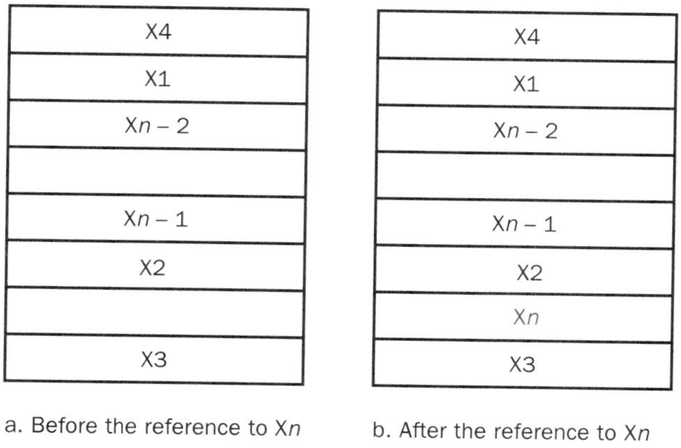

a. Before the reference to Xn b. After the reference to Xn

FIGURE 7.4 The cache just before and just after a reference to a word Xn that is not initially in the cache. This reference causes a miss that forces the cache to fetch Xn from memory and insert it into the cache.

Looking at the scenario in Figure 7.4, we can see that there are two questions we must answer: How do we know if a data item is in the cache? And, if it is, how do we find it? The answers to these two questions are related. If each word can go in exactly one place in the cache, then we will know how to find the word if it is in the cache. The simplest way to assign a location in the cache for each word in memory is to assign the cache location based on the address of the word in memory. This cache structure is called *direct mapped*, since each memory location is mapped to exactly one location in the cache. The typical mapping between addresses and cache locations for a direct-mapped cache is usually simple. For example, almost all direct-mapped caches use the mapping:

(Block address) modulo (Number of cache blocks in the cache)

This mapping is attractive because if the number of entries in the cache is a power of two, then modulo can be computed simply by using only the low-order $\log_2$ (cache size in blocks) bits of the address; hence the cache may be accessed directly with the low-order bits. For example, Figure 7.5 shows a direct-mapped cache of eight words and the memory addresses between 1_{ten} (00001_{two}) and 29_{ten} (11101_{two}) that map to locations 1_{ten} (001_{two}) and 5_{ten} (101_{two}) in the cache.

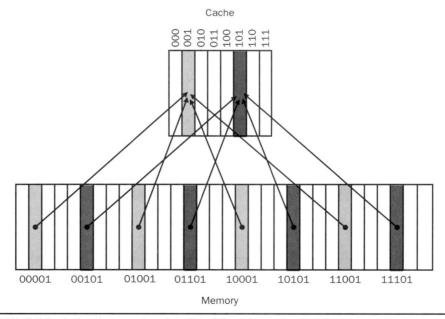

FIGURE 7.5 A direct-mapped cache with eight entries showing the addresses of memory words between 0 and 31 that map to the same cache locations. Because there are eight words in the cache, an address X maps to the cache word X modulo 8. That is, the low-order $\log_2(8) = 3$ bits are used as the cache index. Thus, addresses 00001_{two}, 01001_{two}, 10001_{two}, and 11001_{two} all map to entry 001_{two} of the cache, while addresses 00101_{two}, 01101_{two}, 10101_{two}, and 11101_{two} all map to entry 101_{two} of the cache.

Because each cache location can contain the contents of a number of different memory locations, how do we know whether the data in the cache corresponds to a requested word? That is, how do we know whether a requested word is in the cache or not? We can plan for this by adding a set of *tags* to the cache. The tags contain the address information required to identify whether a word in the cache corresponds to the requested word. The tag needs only to contain the upper portion of the address, corresponding to the bits that are not used as an index into the cache. The reason for this is that the bits corresponding to the index are used to select the unique entry in the cache corresponding to the supplied address, and thus we only need to ensure that the upper portion of the supplied address matches the tag. For example, in Figure 7.5 we need only have 2 of the 5 address bits in the tag, since the lowest 3 bits of the address select the block.

We also need a way to recognize that a cache block does not have valid information. For instance, when a processor starts up, the cache will be empty, and the tag fields will be meaningless. Even after executing many instructions, some of the cache entries may still be empty, as in Figure 7.4. Thus we need to know that the tag should be ignored for such entries. The most common method is to add a *valid bit* to indicate whether an entry contains a valid address. If the bit is not set, there cannot be a match for this block.

For the rest of this section, we will focus on explaining how reads work in a cache and how the cache control works for reads. In general, handling reads is a little simpler than handling writes, since reads do not have to change the contents of the cache. After seeing the basics of how reads work and how cache misses can be handled, we'll examine the cache designs for two real machines and detail how these caches handle writes.

Accessing a Cache

Figure 7.6 shows the contents of an eight-word direct-mapped cache as it responds to a series of requests from the processor. Since there are eight blocks in the cache, the low-order 3 bits of an address give the block number. Here is the action for each reference:

Decimal address of reference	Binary address of reference	Hit or miss in cache	Assigned cache block (where found or placed)
22	10110_{two}	miss (7.5b)	$(10110_{two} \bmod 8) = 110_{two}$
26	11010_{two}	miss (7.5c)	$(11010_{two} \bmod 8) = 010_{two}$
22	10110_{two}	hit	$(10110_{two} \bmod 8) = 110_{two}$
26	11010_{two}	hit	$(11010_{two} \bmod 8) = 010_{two}$
16	10000_{two}	miss (7.5d)	$(10000_{two} \bmod 8) = 000_{two}$
3	00011_{two}	miss (7.5e)	$(00011_{two} \bmod 8) = 011_{two}$
16	10000_{two}	hit	$(10000_{two} \bmod 8) = 000_{two}$
18	10010_{two}	miss (7.5f)	$(10010_{two} \bmod 8) = 010_{two}$

Index	V	Tag	Data
000	N		
001	N		
010	N		
011	N		
100	N		
101	N		
110	N		
111	N		

a. The initial state of the cache after power-on

Index	V	Tag	Data
000	N		
001	N		
010	N		
011	N		
100	N		
101	N		
110	Y	10_{two}	Memory(10110_{two})
111	N		

b. After handling a miss of address (10110_{two})

Index	V	Tag	Data
000	N		
001	N		
010	Y	11_{two}	Memory (11010_{two})
011	N		
100	N		
101	N		
110	Y	10_{two}	Memory (10110_{two})
111	N		

c. After handling a miss of address (11010_{two})

Index	V	Tag	Data
000	Y	10_{two}	Memory (10000_{two})
001	N		
010	Y	11_{two}	Memory (11010_{two})
011	N		
100	N		
101	N		
110	Y	10_{two}	Memory (10110_{two})
111	N		

d. After handling a miss of address (10000_{two})

Index	V	Tag	Data
000	Y	10_{two}	Memory (10000_{two})
001	N		
010	Y	11_{two}	Memory (11010_{two})
011	Y	00_{two}	Memory (00011_{two})
100	N		
101	N		
110	Y	10_{two}	Memory (10110_{two})
111	N		

e. After handling a miss of address (00011_{two})

Index	V	Tag	Data
000	Y	10_{two}	Memory (10000_{two})
001	N		
010	Y	10_{two}	Memory (10010_{two})
011	Y	00_{two}	Memory (00011_{two})
100	N		
101	N		
110	Y	10_{two}	Memory (10110_{two})
111	N		

f. After handling a miss of address (10010_{two})

FIGURE 7.6 The cache contents are shown after each reference request that *misses*, with the index and tag fields shown in binary. The cache is initially empty, with all valid bits (V entry in cache) turned off (N). The processor requests the following addresses: 10110_{two} (miss), 11010_{two} (miss), 10110_{two} (hit), 11010_{two} (hit), 10000_{two} (miss), 00011_{two} (miss), 10000_{two} (hit), and 10010_{two} (miss). The figures show the cache contents after each miss in the sequence has been handled. When address 10010_{two} (18) is referenced, the entry for address 11010_{two} (26) must be replaced, and a reference to 11010_{two} will cause a subsequent miss. The tag field will contain only the upper portion of the address. The full address of a word contained in cache block i with tag field j for this cache is $j \times 8 + i$, or equivalently the concatenation of the tag field j and the index i. For example, in cache f above, index 010 has tag 10 and corresponds to address 10010.

When the word at address 18 (10010_{two}) is brought into cache block 2 (010_{two}), the word at address 26 (11010_{two}), which was in cache block 2 (010_{two}), must be replaced by the newly requested data. This behavior allows a cache to take advantage of temporal locality: recently accessed words replace less recently referenced words. This situation is directly analogous to needing a book from the shelves and having no more space on your desk—some book already on your desk must be returned to the shelves. In a direct-mapped cache, there is only one place to put the newly requested item and hence only one choice of what to replace.

We know where to look in the cache for each possible address: the low-order bits of an address can be used to find the unique cache entry to which the address could map. Figure 7.7 shows how a referenced address is divided into

- a cache index, which is used to select the block

- a tag field, which is used to compare with the value of the tag field of the cache

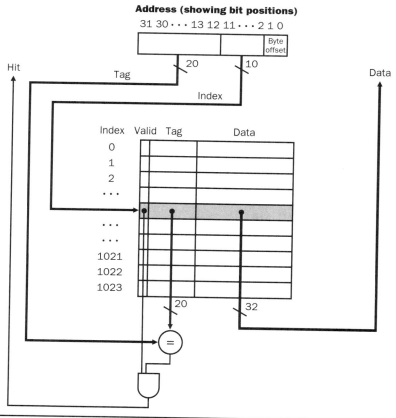

FIGURE 7.7 For this cache, the lower portion of the address is used to select a cache entry consisting of a data word and a tag. The tag from the cache is compared against the upper portion of the address to determine whether the entry in the cache corresponds to the requested address. Because the cache has 2^{10} (or 1024) words, and a block size of 1 word, 10 bits are used to index the cache, leaving $32 - 10 - 2 = 20$ bits to be compared against the tag. If the tag and upper 20 bits of the address are equal and the valid bit is on, then the request hits in the cache, and the word is supplied to the processor. Otherwise, a miss occurs.

Because a given address can appear in exactly one location, the tag need only correspond to the upper portion of the address, which is not used to index the cache. Thus, the index of a cache block, together with the tag contents of that block, uniquely specify the memory address of the word contained in the cache block. Because the index field is used as an address to access the cache and because an n-bit field has 2^n values, the total number of entries in the cache must be a power of two. In the MIPS architecture, the least significant 2 bits of every address specify a byte within a word and are not used to select the word in the cache.

The total number of bits needed for a cache is a function of the cache size and the address size because the cache includes both the storage for the data and for the tags. Assuming the 32-bit byte address, a direct-mapped cache of size 2^n words with one-word (4-byte) blocks will require a tag field whose size is $32 - (n + 2)$ bits, because 2 bits are used for the byte offset and n bits are used for the index. The total number of bits in a direct-mapped cache is $2^n \times (\text{block size} + \text{tag size} + \text{valid field size})$. Since the block size is one word (32 bits) and the address size is 32 bits, the number of bits in such a cache is $2^n \times (32 + (32 - n - 2) + 1) = 2^n \times (63 - n)$.

Bits in a Cache

Example

How many total bits are required for a direct-mapped cache with 64 KB of data and one-word blocks, assuming a 32-bit address?

Answer

We know that 64 KB is 16K words, which is 2^{14} words, and, with a block size of one word, 2^{14} blocks. Each block has 32 bits of data plus a tag, which is $32 - 14 - 2$ bits, plus a valid bit. Thus the total cache size is

$$2^{14} \times (32 + (32 - 14 - 2) + 1) = 2^{14} \times 49 = 784 \times 2^{10} = 784 \text{ Kbits}$$

or 98 KB for a 64-KB cache. For this cache, the total number of bits in the cache is over 1.5 times as many as needed just for the storage of the data.

Handling Cache Misses

Before we look at the cache of a real system, let's see how the control unit deals with cache misses. The control unit must detect a miss and process the miss by fetching the data from memory (or a lower-level cache). If the cache reports a hit, the machine continues using the data as if nothing had happened. Consequently, we can use the same basic control that we developed in

Chapter 5 and enhanced to accommodate pipelining in Chapter 6. The memories in the datapath used in Chapters 5 and 6 are simply replaced by caches.

Modifying the control of a processor to take a hit into account is trivial; misses, however, require some extra work. The basic approach is to stall the CPU, freezing the contents of all the registers. A separate controller handles the cache miss, fetching the data into the cache from memory. Once the data is present, execution is restarted at the cycle that caused the cache miss. The cache miss handling is done with the processor control unit and with a separate controller that initiates the memory access and refills the cache. The processing of a cache miss creates a stall, similar to the pipeline stalls discussed in Chapter 6, as opposed to an interrupt, which would require saving the state of all registers. For a cache miss, we can stall the entire machine, essentially freezing the contents of the temporary and programmer-visible registers, while we wait for memory. In contrast, pipeline stalls, discussed in Chapter 6, are more complex because we must continue executing some instructions while we stall others.

Let's look a little more closely at how instruction misses are handled for either the multicycle or pipelined datapath; the same approach can be easily extended to handle data misses. If an instruction access results in a miss, then the contents of the Instruction register are invalid. To get the proper instruction into the cache, we must be able to instruct the lower level in the memory hierarchy to perform a read. Since the program counter is incremented in the first clock cycle of execution in both the pipelined and multicycle processors, the address of the instruction that generates an instruction cache miss is equal to the value of the program counter minus four. We can compute this value using the ALU, although we may need additional temporary storage in the pipelined implementation. Once we have the address, we need to instruct the main memory to perform a read. We wait for the memory to respond (since the access will take multiple cycles), and then write the word into the cache.

We can now define the steps to be taken on an instruction cache miss:

1. Send the original PC value (current PC – 4) to the memory.

2. Instruct main memory to perform a read and wait for the memory to complete its access.

3. Write the cache entry, putting the data from memory in the data portion of the entry, writing the upper bits of the address (from the ALU) into the tag field, and turning the valid bit on.

4. Restart the instruction execution at the first step, which will refetch the instruction, this time finding it in the cache.

The control of the cache on a data access is essentially identical: on a miss, we simply stall the processor until the memory responds with the data. In the rest of this section we describe two different caches from real machines, and we examine how they handle both reads and writes. In section 7.5, we will describe the handling of writes in more detail.

Elaboration: To reduce the penalty of cache misses, designers employ two techniques, one of which we discuss here and another that we will discuss later. To reduce the number of cycles that a processor is stalled for a cache miss, we can allow a processor to continue executing instructions while the cache miss is handled. This strategy does not help for instruction misses because we cannot fetch new instructions to execute. In the case of data misses, however, we can allow the machine to continue fetching and executing instructions until the loaded word is required. Hence the name for this technique: *stall on use*. While this additional effort may save cycles, it will probably not save very many cycles because the loaded data will likely be needed very shortly and because other instructions will need access to the cache. A more sophisticated technique is used in some modern processors; we describe it in section 7.6.

An Example Cache: The DECStation 3100

The DECStation 3100 was a workstation that used a MIPS R2000 as the processor and a very simple cache implementation. Near the end of the chapter, we will examine the cache design of a more recent computer, but we start with this simple, yet real, example for pedagogical reasons.

This processor has a pipeline similar to that discussed in Chapter 6. When operating at peak speed, the processor requests both an instruction word and a data word on every clock. To satisfy the demands of the pipeline without stalling, separate instruction and data caches are used. Each cache is 64 KB, or 16K words, with a one-word block. Figure 7.8 shows the organization of the DECStation 3100 data cache.

Read requests for the cache are straightforward. Because there are separate data and instruction caches, separate control signals will be needed to read and write each cache. (Remember that we need to write into the instruction cache when a miss occurs.) Thus the steps for a read request to either cache are as follows:

1. Send the address to the appropriate cache. The address comes either from the PC (for an instruction read) or from the ALU (for a data access).

2. If the cache signals hit, the requested word is available on the data lines. If the cache signals miss, we send the address to the main memory. When the memory returns with the data, we write it into the cache.

Writes work somewhat differently. Suppose on a store instruction, we wrote the data into only the data cache (without changing main memory); then, after

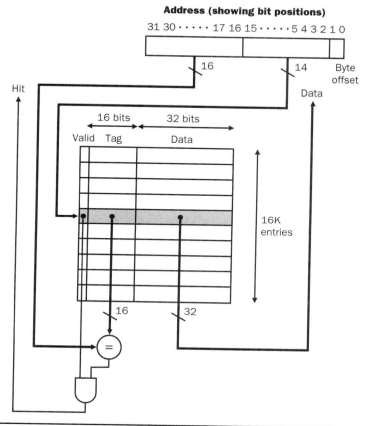

FIGURE 7.8   The caches in the DECStation 3100 each contain 16K blocks with one word per block. This means that the index is 14 bits and that the tag contains 16 bits.

the write into the cache, memory would have a different value from that in the cache. In such a case, the cache and memory are said to be *inconsistent*. The simplest way to keep the main memory and the cache consistent is to always write the data into both the memory and the cache. This scheme, which the DEC-Station 3100 uses, is called *write-through*.

The other key aspect of writes is what occurs on a write miss. Because the data word in the cache is being written by the processor, there is no reason to read a word from memory; it would just be overwritten by the processor. In fact, for this simple cache we can always just write the word into the cache, updating both the tag and data. We do not need to consider whether a write hits or misses in the cache. This observation leads to the following simple scheme for processing writes, used on the DECStation 3100:

1. Index the cache using bits 15–2 of the address.

2. Write bits 31–16 of the address into the tag, write the data word into the data portion, and set the valid bit.

3. Also write the word to main memory using the entire address.

Although this design handles writes very simply, it would not provide very good performance. With a write-through scheme, every write causes the data to be written to main memory. These writes will take a long time and could slow down the machine considerably. In gcc, for example, 13% of the instructions are stores. In the DECStation 3100, the CPI without cache misses for a program like gcc is about 1.2, so spending 10 cycles on every write would lead to a CPI of $1.2 + 10 \times 13\% = 2.5$, reducing performance by more than a factor of two.

One solution to this problem is to use a *write buffer*. A write buffer stores the data while it is waiting to be written to memory. After writing the data into the cache and into the write buffer, the processor can continue execution. When a write to main memory completes, the entry in the write buffer is freed. If the write buffer is full when the processor reaches a write, the processor must stall until there is an empty position in the write buffer. Of course, if the rate at which the memory can complete writes is less than the rate at which the processor is generating writes, no amount of buffering can help because writes are being generated faster than the memory system can accept them.

The rate at which writes are generated may also be *less* than the rate at which the memory can accept them, and yet stalls may still occur. This can happen when the writes occur in bursts. To reduce the occurrence of such stalls, machines usually increase the depth of the write buffer beyond a single entry. For example, the DECStation 3100 write buffer is four words deep. As the difference between the rate at which programs can generate writes and the rate at which the memory system can accept them increases, even deeper write buffers (e.g., 10 entries) are appropriate.

The alternative to a write-through scheme is a scheme called *write-back*. In a write-back scheme, when a write occurs, the new value is written only to the block in the cache. The modified block is written to the lower level of the hierarchy when it is replaced. Write-back schemes can improve performance, especially when processors can generate writes as fast or faster than the writes can be handled by main memory; a write-back scheme is, however, more complex to implement than write-through.

What sort of cache miss rates are attained with a cache structure like that used by the DECStation 3100? Figure 7.9 shows the miss rates for the instruction and data caches for two programs, which we have seen before. The com-

Program	Instruction miss rate	Data miss rate	Effective combined miss rate
gcc	6.1%	2.1%	5.4%
spice	1.2%	1.3%	1.2%

FIGURE 7.9 Instruction and data miss rates for the DECStation 3100 when executing two different programs. The combined miss rate is the effective miss rate seen for the combination of the 64-KB instruction cache and 64-KB data cache. It is obtained by weighting the instruction and data individual miss rates by the frequency of instruction and data references. Remember that data misses include only data reads because writes cannot miss in the DECStation 3100 cache.

bined miss rate is the effective miss rate per reference for each program after accounting for the differing frequency of instruction and data accesses.

Remember that although miss rate is an important characteristic of cache designs, the ultimate measure will be the effect of the memory system on program execution time; we'll see how miss rate and execution time are related shortly. First we must explore how the memory system can take advantage of spatial locality.

Elaboration: A combined cache of the total size equal to the sum of the two split caches will usually have a better hit rate. This higher rate occurs because the combined cache does not rigidly divide the number of entries that may be used by instructions from those that may be used by data. Nonetheless, many machines use a split instruction and data cache to increase the *bandwidth* from the cache.

Here are some measurements for the DECStation 3100 for the program gcc, and for a combined cache whose size is equal to the total of the two caches on the 3100:

- Total cache size: 128 KB
- Split cache effective miss rate: 5.4%
- Combined cache miss rate: 4.8%

The miss rate of the split cache is only slightly worse.

For many systems, the advantage of doubling the cache bandwidth, by supporting both an instruction and data access simultaneously, easily overcomes the disadvantage of a slightly increased miss rate. This observation is another reminder that we cannot use miss rate as the sole measure of cache performance.

Taking Advantage of Spatial Locality

The cache we have described so far, while simple, does nothing to take advantage of spatial locality in requests, since each word is in its own block. As we noted in section 7.1, spatial locality exists naturally in programs. To take advantage of spatial locality, we want to have a cache block that is larger than one word in length. When a miss occurs, we will then fetch multiple words that are adjacent and carry a high probability of being needed shortly.

Figure 7.10 shows a cache that holds 64 KB of data, but with blocks of four words (16 bytes) each. Compared with Figure 7.8 on page 553, which shows the same total size cache with a one-word block, an extra block index field occurs in the address of the cache in Figure 7.10. This block index field is used to control the multiplexor (shown at the bottom of the figure), which selects the requested word from the four words in the indexed block. The total number of tags and valid bits in the cache with a multiword block is smaller because each tag and valid bit is used for four words. This sharing of tags improves the efficiency of memory use in the cache.

How do we find the cache block for a particular address? We can use the same mapping that we used for a cache with a one-word block:

(Block address) modulo (Number of cache blocks)

The block address is simply the word address divided by the number of words in the block (or equivalently, the byte address divided by the number of bytes in the block).

Mapping an Address to a Multiword Cache Block

Example

Consider a cache with 64 blocks and a block size of 16 bytes. What block number does byte address 1200 map to?

Answer

The block is given by

(Block address) modulo (Number of cache blocks)

Where the address of the block is

$$\frac{\text{Byte address}}{\text{Bytes per block}}$$

Notice that this block address is the block containing all addresses between

$$\left\lfloor \frac{\text{Byte address}}{\text{Bytes per block}} \right\rfloor \times \text{Bytes per block}$$

and

$$\left\lfloor \frac{\text{Byte address}}{\text{Bytes per block}} \right\rfloor \times \text{Bytes per block} + (\text{Bytes per block} - 1)$$

Thus, with 16 bytes per block, byte address 1200 is block address

$$\left\lfloor \frac{1200}{16} \right\rfloor = 75$$

which maps to cache block number (75 modulo 64) = 11.

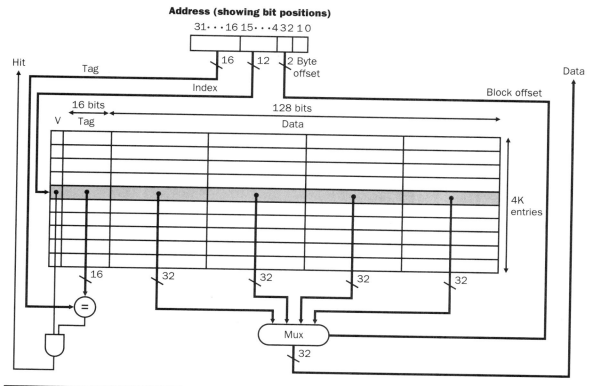

FIGURE 7.10 **A 64-KB cache using four-word (16-byte) blocks.** The tag field is 16 bits wide and the index field is 12 bits wide, while a 2-bit field (bits 3–2) is used to index the block and select the word from the block using a 4-to-1 multiplexor. In practice, the low-order bits of the address (bits 2 and 3 in this case) are used to enable only those RAMs that contain the desired word, eliminating the need for the multiplexor. Another way to eliminate the multiplexor is to have a large RAM for the data (with the tags stored separately) and use the block offset to supply 2 address bits for the RAM. The RAM must be 32 bits wide and have four times as many words as blocks in the cache.

Read misses are processed the same way for a multiword block as for a single-word block; a miss always brings back the entire block. Write hits and misses, however, must be handled differently than they were in the DECStation 3100 cache. Because the block contains more than a single word, we cannot just write the tag and data. To see why this is true, assume that there are two memory addresses, X and Y, that both map to cache block C, which is a four-word block that currently contains Y. Now consider writing to address X by simply overwriting the data and tag in cache block C. After the write, block C will have the tag for X, but the data portion of block C will contain one word of X and three words of Y!

Program	Block size in words	Instruction miss rate	Data miss rate	Effective combined miss rate
gcc	1	6.1%	2.1%	5.4%
	4	2.0%	1.7%	1.9%
spice	1	1.2%	1.3%	1.2%
	4	0.3%	0.6%	0.4%

FIGURE 7.11 The miss rates for gcc and spice with a cache like that in the DECStation 3100 with a block size of either one word or four words. With the four-word block, we include write misses, which do not incur any penalty for the one-word block and are not included in that case. If write misses were included in both cases, the difference in miss rate would be slightly larger than shown.

We can solve this problem for a write-through cache by writing the data while performing a tag comparison, just as if the request were a read. If the tag of the address and the tag in the cache entry are equal, we have a write hit and can continue. If the tags are unequal, we have a write miss and must fetch the block from memory. After the block is fetched and placed into the cache, we can rewrite the word that caused the miss into the cache block. Unlike the case with a one-word block, write misses with a multiword block will require reading from memory.

The reason for increasing the block size was to take advantage of spatial locality to improve performance. So how does a larger block size affect performance? In general, the miss rate falls when we increase the block size. This trend is easiest to see with an example. Suppose the following byte addresses are requested by a program: 16, . . . , 24, . . . , 20 and none of these addresses is in the cache. Spatial locality tells us that some pattern of this form is highly probable, although the order of the references may vary. If the cache has a four-word block, then the miss to address 16 will cause the block containing addresses 16, 20, 24, and 28 to be loaded into the cache. Only one miss is encountered for the three references, provided that an intervening reference doesn't bump the block out of the cache. With a one-word block, two additional misses are required because each miss brings in only a single word.

Figure 7.11 shows the miss rates for the programs gcc and spice with one- and four-word blocks. The instruction cache miss rates drop at a rate that is nearly equal to the increase in block size; this larger decrease in the instruction versus data miss rate occurs because the instruction references have better spatial locality.

The miss rate may actually go up if the block size becomes a significant fraction of the cache size because the number of blocks that can be held in the cache will become small, and there will be a great deal of competition for those blocks. As a result, a block will be bumped out of the cache before many of its words are accessed. As Figure 7.12 shows, increasing the block size usually decreases the miss rate. However, the spatial locality among the words in a block decreases with a very large block; consequently, the improvements in the miss rate become smaller—and the miss rate can eventually even increase.

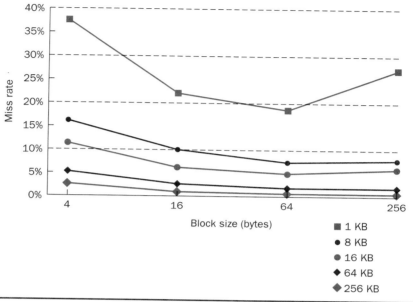

FIGURE 7.12 Miss rate versus block size. For a small 1-KB cache, a large 256-byte block size causes a higher miss rate than the smaller block sizes. This data was collected for a direct-mapped cache using traces (SAVE0) collected by Agarwal for the VAX. More details can be found in A. Agarwal, *Analysis of Cache Performance for Operating Systems and Multiprogramming*, Ph.D. thesis, Stanford Univ., Tech. Rep. No. CSL-TR-87-332 (May 1987).

A more serious problem associated with just increasing the block size is that the cost of a miss increases. The miss penalty is determined by the time required to fetch the block from the next lower level of the hierarchy and load it into the cache. The time to fetch the block has two parts: the latency to the first word and the transfer time for the rest of the block. Clearly, unless we change the memory system, the transfer time—and hence the miss penalty—will increase as the block size grows. Furthermore, the improvement in the miss rate starts to decrease as the blocks become larger. The result is that the increase in the miss penalty overwhelms the decrease in the miss rate for large blocks, and cache performance thus decreases. Of course, if we design the memory to transfer larger blocks more efficiently, we can increase the block size and obtain further improvements in cache performance. We discuss this topic in the next section.

Elaboration: The major disadvantage of increasing the block size is that the cache miss penalty increases. Although it is hard to do anything about the latency component of the miss penalty, we may be able to hide some of the transfer time so that the miss penalty is effectively smaller. The simplest method for doing this, called *early restart*, is simply to resume execution as soon as the requested word of the block is returned, rather than wait for the entire block. Many machines use this technique for instruction access, where it works best. Instruction accesses are largely sequential, so if the memory system can deliver a word every clock cycle, the processor may be able to restart operation when the requested word is returned, with the memory system delivering new instruction words just in time. This technique is usually less effective for data caches because it is likely that the words will be requested from the block in a less predictable way, and the probability that the processor will need another word from a different cache block before the transfer completes is high. If the processor cannot access the data cache because a transfer is ongoing, then it must stall.

An even more sophisticated scheme is to organize the memory so that the requested word is transferred from the memory to the cache first. The remainder of the block is then transferred, starting with the address after the requested word and wrapping around to the beginning of the block. This technique, called *requested word first*, or *critical word first*, can be slightly faster than early restart, but it is limited by the same properties that limit early restart.

Designing the Memory System to Support Caches

Cache misses are satisfied from main memory, which is constructed from DRAMs. In section 7.1, we saw that DRAMs are designed with the primary emphasis on density rather than access time. Although it is difficult to reduce the latency to fetch the first word from memory, we can reduce the miss penalty if we increase the bandwidth from the memory to the cache. This reduction allows larger block sizes to be used while still maintaining a low miss penalty, similar to that for a smaller block.

To understand the impact of different organizations for memory, let's define a set of hypothetical memory access times:

- 1 clock cycle to send the address
- 15 clock cycles for each DRAM access initiated
- 1 clock cycle to send a word of data

If we have a cache block of four words and a one-word-wide bank of DRAMs, the miss penalty would be $1 + 4 \times 15 + 4 \times 1 = 65$ clock cycles. Thus the number of bytes transferred per clock cycle for a single miss would be

$$\frac{4 \times 4}{65} = 0.25$$

Figure 7.13 shows three options for designing the memory system. The first option follows what we have been assuming so far: memory is one word wide, and all accesses are made sequentially. The second option increases the bandwidth to memory by widening the memory and the buses between the processor and memory; this allows parallel access to all the words of the block.

The third option increases the bandwidth by widening the memory but not the interconnection bus. Thus we still pay a cost to transmit each word, but we can avoid paying the cost of the access latency more than once. Let's look at how much these other two options improve the 65-cycle miss penalty that we would see for the first option (Figure 7.13a).

Increasing the width of the memory and the bus will increase the memory bandwidth proportionally, decreasing both the access time and transfer time portions of the miss penalty. With a main memory width of two words, the miss penalty drops from 65 clock cycles to $1 + 2 \times 15 + 2 \times 1 = 33$ clock cycles. With a four-word-wide memory, the miss penalty is just 17 clock cycles. The bandwidth for a single miss is then 0.48 (almost twice as high) bytes per clock cycle for a memory that is two words wide, and 0.94 bytes per clock cycle when the memory is four words wide (almost four times higher). The major costs of this enhancement are the wider bus and the potential increase in cache access time due to the multiplexor and control logic between the CPU and cache.

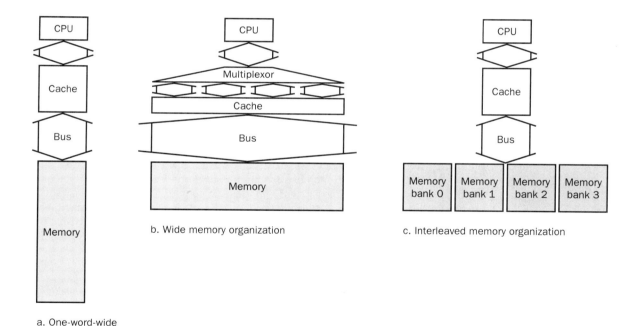

a. One-word-wide
memory organization

b. Wide memory organization

c. Interleaved memory organization

FIGURE 7.13 The primary method of achieving higher memory bandwidth is to increase the physical or logical width of the memory system. In this figure, there are two ways in which the memory bandwidth is improved. The simplest design, (a), uses a memory where all components are one word wide; (b) shows a wider memory, bus, and cache; while (c) shows a narrow bus and cache with an interleaved memory. In (b), the logic between the cache and CPU consists of a multiplexor used on reads and control logic to update the appropriate words of the cache on writes.

Instead of making the entire path between the memory and cache wider, the memory chips can be organized in banks to read or write multiple words in one access time rather than reading or writing a single word each time. Each bank could be one word wide so that the width of the bus and the cache need not change, but sending an address to several banks permits them all to read simultaneously. This scheme, which is called *interleaving*, retains the advantage of incurring the full memory latency only once. For example, with four banks, the time to get a four-word block would consist of 1 cycle to transmit the address and read request to the banks, 15 cycles for all four banks to access memory, and 4 cycles to send the four words back to the cache. This yields a miss penalty of $1 + 1 \times 15 + 4 \times 1 = 20$ clock cycles. This is an effective bandwidth per miss of 0.80 bytes per clock, or about three times the bandwidth for the one-word-wide memory and bus. Banks are also valuable on writes. Each bank can write independently, quadrupling the write bandwidth and leading to fewer stalls in a write-through cache. As we will see, there is an alternative strategy for writes that makes interleaving even more attractive.

Elaboration: As capacity per memory chip increases, there are fewer chips in the same-sized memory system. Memory chips are organized to produce a small number of output bits, usually 1 to 16, with 4 and 8 being the most popular in 1997. We describe the organization of a RAM as $d \times w$, where d is the number of addressable locations (the depth) and w is the output (or width of each location). Thus, the most popular 16-Mbit DRAMs are 4M x 4. As memory chip densities grow, the width of a memory chip remains constant (or grows slowly), but the depth increases (see Appendix B for further discussion of DRAMs). Because of this, multiple banks become less attractive, because the minimum memory configuration increases. For example, a 64-MB main memory built using 4-Mbit x 1 chips can be organized into four banks, each 32 bits wide, and holding a total of 128 DRAMs. If we use 16-Mbit x 1 memory chips instead of 4-Mbit x 1 chips, our 64-MB memory can contain only one bank that is 32 bits wide, since the entire memory needs only 32 DRAMs. Of course, four banks could be constructed if we used 4-Mbit x 4 chips rather than 16-Mbit x 1 chips. Likewise, a 64-MB memory with four banks using 64-Mbit chips would require 4-Mbit x 16 DRAMs. This potential requirement for increased width in DRAM chips is the main disadvantage of interleaved memory banks. Another possibility for improving the rate at which we transfer data from the memory to the caches is to take advantage of the structure of DRAMs. DRAMs are logically organized as square arrays, and access time is divided into row access and column access. DRAMs buffer a row of bits inside the DRAM for column access. They also come with optional timing signals that allow repeated accesses to the buffer without a row-access time. One common version of this capability is called *page mode*, which has gone through a series of enhancements, the most recent called EDO (Extended Data Out) RAMs. In page mode, the buffer acts like an SRAM; by changing column address, random bits can be accessed in the buffer until the next row access. This capability changes the access time significantly, since the access time to bits in the row is much lower. For example, the total row and column access times without page mode is about 120 ns; basic page mode provides 60-ns access to data in the page, while EDO mode provides 25-ns access to data in the page. Figure 7.14 shows how the density, cost, and access time of DRAMS have changed over the years.

Year introduced	Chip size	$ per MB	Total access time to a new row/column	Column access time to existing row
1980	64 Kbit	1500	250 ns	150 ns
1983	256 Kbit	500	185 ns	100 ns
1985	1 Mbit	200	135 ns	40 ns
1989	4 Mbit	50	110 ns	40 ns
1992	16 Mbit	15	90 ns	30 ns
1996	64 Mbit	10	60 ns	20 ns

FIGURE 7.14 DRAM size increases by multiples of four approximately once every three years. The improvements in access time have been slower but continuous, and cost almost tracks density improvements, although cost is often affected by other issues, such as availability and demand. Column access time usually determines the time to perform a page mode access. DRAMs are almost always available in narrower configurations initially (e.g., 4 Mbit x 4). Wider configurations (e.g., 1 Mbit x 16) usually track availability of the narrower configuration, and they cost more. Reasons for this are that both the testing cost and package cost for the narrower configuration are slightly cheaper, the narrower configuration is usually the commodity product, and the die size of the narrower configuration is slightly smaller.

The newest development are SDRAMs (synchronous DRAMs). SDRAMs provide for a burst access to data from a series of sequential locations in the DRAM. An SDRAM is supplied with a starting address and a burst length. The data in the burst is transferred under control of a clock signal, which in 1997 can run at up to 100 MHz. The two key advantages of SDRAMs are the use of a clock that eliminates the need to synchronize and the elimination of the need to supply successive addresses in the burst. Together these advantages help lower the time between successive bits from 25 ns for an EDO RAM to 8–10 ns for an SDRAM.

The advantage of these optimizations is that they use the circuitry already largely on the DRAMs, adding little cost to the system while achieving a significant improvement in bandwidth. (The same is true of interleaving.) Furthermore, these DRAM options allow us to increase the bandwidth without incurring system disadvantages in terms of expandability and minimum memory size that are associated with wider memories or interleaving. The internal architecture of DRAMs and how these optimizations are implemented are described in section B.5 of Appendix B.

Summary

We began the previous section by examining the simplest of caches: a direct-mapped cache with a one-word block. In such a cache, both hits and misses are simple, since a word can go in exactly one location and there is a separate tag for every word. To keep the cache and memory consistent, a write-through scheme can be used, so that every write into the cache also causes memory to be updated. The alternative to write-through is a write-back scheme that copies a block back to memory when it is replaced; we'll discuss this scheme further in upcoming sections.

To take advantage of spatial locality, a cache must have a block size larger than one word. The use of a larger block decreases the miss rate and improves the efficiency of the cache by reducing the amount of tag storage relative to the amount of data storage in the cache. Although a larger block size decreases the miss rate, it can also increase the miss penalty. If the miss penalty increased linearly with the block size, larger blocks could easily lead to lower performance. To avoid this, the bandwidth of main memory is increased to transfer cache blocks more efficiently. The two common methods for doing this are making the memory wider and interleaving. In both cases, we reduce the time to fetch the block by minimizing the number of times we must start a new memory access to fetch a block, and, with a wider bus, we can also decrease the time needed to send the block from the memory to the cache.

7.3 Measuring and Improving Cache Performance

In this section, we begin by looking at how to measure and analyze cache performance; we then explore two different techniques for improving cache performance. One focuses on reducing the miss rate by reducing the probability that two different memory blocks will contend for the same cache location. The second technique reduces the miss penalty by adding an additional level to the hierarchy. This technique, called *multilevel caching*, first appeared in high-end machines selling for over $100,000 in 1990; since then it has become common on desktop computers selling for less than $3,000!

CPU time can be divided into the clock cycles that the CPU spends executing the program and the clock cycles that the CPU spends waiting for the memory system. Normally, we assume that the cost of cache accesses that are hits are part of the normal CPU execution cycles. Thus,

$$\text{CPU time} = (\text{CPU execution clock cycles} + \text{Memory-stall clock cycles}) \times \text{Clock cycle time}$$

The memory-stall clock cycles come primarily from cache misses, and we make that assumption here. We also restrict the discussion to a simplified model of the memory system. In real processors, the stalls generated by reads and writes can be quite complex, and accurate performance prediction usually requires very detailed simulations of the processor and memory system.

Memory-stall clock cycles can be defined as the sum of the stall cycles coming from reads plus those coming from writes:

$$\text{Memory-stall clock cycles} = \text{Read-stall cycles} + \text{Write-stall cycles}$$

The read-stall cycles can each be defined in terms of the number of read accesses per program, the miss penalty in clock cycles for a read, and the read miss rate:

$$\text{Read-stall cycles} = \frac{\text{Reads}}{\text{Program}} \times \text{Read miss rate} \times \text{Read miss penalty}$$

Writes are more complicated. For a write-through scheme, we have two sources of stalls: write misses, which usually require that we fetch the block before continuing the write (see the elaboration on page 607 for more details on dealing with writes), and write buffer stalls, which occur when the write buffer is full when a write occurs. Thus, the cycles stalled for writes equals the sum of these two:

$$\text{Write-stall cycles} = \left(\frac{\text{Writes}}{\text{Program}} \times \text{Write miss rate} \times \text{Write miss penalty} \right) + \text{Write buffer stalls}$$

Because the write buffer stalls depend on the timing of writes, and not just the frequency, it is not possible to give a simple equation to compute such stalls. Fortunately, in systems with a reasonable write buffer depth (e.g., four or more words) and a memory capable of accepting writes at a rate that significantly exceeds the average write frequency in programs (e.g., by a factor of two), the write buffer stalls will be small, and we can safely ignore them. If a system did not meet these criteria, it would not be well designed; instead the designer should have used either a deeper write buffer or a write-back organization.

Write-back schemes also have potential additional stalls arising from the need to write a cache block back to memory when the block is replaced. We will discuss this more in section 7.5.

In most write-through cache organizations, the read and write miss penalties are the same (the time to fetch the block from memory). If we assume that the write buffer stalls are negligible, we can combine the reads and writes by using a single miss rate and the miss penalty:

$$\text{Memory-stall clock cycles} = \frac{\text{Memory accesses}}{\text{Program}} \times \text{Miss rate} \times \text{Miss penalty}$$

We can also write this as

$$\text{Memory-stall clock cycles} = \frac{\text{Instructions}}{\text{Program}} \times \frac{\text{Misses}}{\text{Instruction}} \times \text{Miss penalty}$$

Let's consider a simple example to help us understand the impact of cache performance on machine performance.

Calculating Cache Performance

Example   Assume an instruction cache miss rate for gcc of 2% and a data cache miss rate of 4%. If a machine has a CPI of 2 without any memory stalls and the miss penalty is 40 cycles for all misses, determine how much faster a machine would run with a perfect cache that never missed. Use the instruction frequencies for gcc from Chapter 4, Figure 4.54, on page 311.

Answer   The number of memory miss cycles for instructions in terms of the Instruction count (I) is

$$\text{Instruction miss cycles} = I \times 2\% \times 40 = 0.80 \times I$$

The frequency of all loads and stores in gcc is 36%. Therefore, we can find the number of memory miss cycles for data references:

$$\text{Data miss cycles} = I \times 36\% \times 4\% \times 40 = 0.56 \times I$$

The total number of memory-stall cycles is $0.80\,I + 0.56\,I = 1.36\,I$. This is more than 1 cycle of memory stall per instruction. Accordingly, the CPI with memory stalls is $2 + 1.36 = 3.36$. Since there is no change in instruction count or clock rate, the ratio of the CPU execution times is

$$\frac{\text{CPU time with stalls}}{\text{CPU time with perfect cache}} = \frac{I \times \text{CPI}_{\text{stall}} \times \text{Clock cycle}}{I \times \text{CPI}_{\text{perfect}} \times \text{Clock cycle}}$$

$$= \frac{\text{CPI}_{\text{stall}}}{\text{CPI}_{\text{perfect}}} = \frac{3.36}{2}$$

The performance with the perfect cache is better by $\dfrac{3.36}{2} = 1.68$.

What happens if the processor is made faster, but the memory system stays the same? The amount of time spent on memory stalls will take up an increasing fraction of the execution time; Amdahl's law, which we examined in Chapter 2, reminds us of this fact. A few simple examples show how serious this problem can be. Suppose we speed up the machine in the previous example by reducing its CPI from 2 to 1 without changing the clock rate, which might be done with an improved pipeline. The system with cache misses would then have a CPI of $1 + 1.36 = 2.36$, and the system with the perfect cache would be

$$\frac{2.36}{1} = 2.36 \text{ times faster}$$

The amount of execution time spent on memory stalls would have risen from

$$\frac{1.36}{3.36} = 41\%$$

to

$$\frac{1.36}{2.36} = 58\%$$

Similarly, increasing the clock rate without changing the memory system also increases the performance lost due to cache misses, as the next example shows.

Cache Performance with Increased Clock Rate

Example

Suppose we increase the performance of the machine in the previous example by doubling its clock rate. Since the main memory speed is unlikely to change, assume that the absolute time to handle a cache miss does not change. How much faster will the machine be with the faster clock, assuming the same miss rate as the previous example?

Answer

Measured in the faster clock cycles, the new miss penalty will be twice as long, or 80 clock cycles. Hence:

Total miss cycles per instruction $= (2\% \times 80) + 36\% \times (4\% \times 80) = 2.75$

Thus the faster machine with cache misses will have a CPI of $2 + 2.75 = 4.75$, compared to a CPI with cache misses of 3.36 for the slower machine.

Using the formula for CPU time from the previous example, we can compute the relative performance as

$$\frac{\text{Performance with fast clock}}{\text{Performance with slow clock}} = \frac{\text{Execution time with slow clock}}{\text{Execution time with fast clock}}$$

$$= \frac{IC \times CPI \times \text{Clock cycle}}{IC \times CPI \times \frac{\text{Clock cycle}}{2}}$$

$$= \frac{3.36}{4.75 \times \frac{1}{2}} = 1.41$$

Thus the machine with the faster clock is about 1.4 times faster rather than 2 times faster, which it would have been without the increased effect of cache misses.

As these examples illustrate, relative cache penalties increase as a machine becomes faster. Furthermore, if a machine improves both clock rate and CPI, it suffers a double hit:

1. The lower the CPI, the more pronounced the impact of stall cycles.

2. The main memory system is unlikely to improve as fast as processor cycle time. When calculating CPI, the cache miss penalty is measured in CPU clock cycles needed for a miss. Therefore, if the main memories of two machines have the same absolute access times, a higher CPU clock rate leads to a larger miss penalty.

Thus the importance of cache performance for CPUs with low CPI and high clock rates is greater, and consequently the danger of neglecting cache behavior in assessing the performance of such machines is greater. As we will see in section 7.6, the use of fast, pipelined processors in desktop PCs and workstations has led to the use of sophisticated cache systems even in computers selling for a few thousand dollars.

The previous examples and equations assume that the hit time is not a factor in determining cache performance. Clearly, if the hit time increases, the total time to access a word from the memory system will increase, possibly causing an increase in the processor cycle time. Although we will see additional examples of what can increase hit time shortly, one example is increasing the cache size. A larger cache could clearly have a longer access time, just as if your desk in the library was very large (say, 3 square meters), it would take longer to locate a book on the desk. At some point, the increase in hit time for a larger cache could dominate the improvement in hit rate, leading to a decrease in processor performance.

The next subsection discusses alternative cache organizations that decrease miss rate but may sometimes increase hit time; additional examples appear in the Fallacies and Pitfalls (section 7.7).

Reducing Cache Misses by More Flexible Placement of Blocks

So far, when we place a block in the cache, we have used a simple placement scheme: A block can go in exactly one place in the cache. This placement scheme is called *direct mapped* because there is a direct mapping from any block address in memory to a single location in the upper level of the hierarchy. There are actually a whole range of schemes for placing blocks. At one extreme is direct mapped, where a block can be placed in exactly one location.

At the other extreme is a scheme where a block can be placed in *any* location in the cache. Such a scheme is called *fully associative* because a block in memory may be associated with any entry in the cache. To find a given block in a fully associative cache, all the entries in the cache must be searched because a block can be placed in any one. To make the search practical, it is done in parallel with a comparator associated with each cache entry. These comparators significantly increase the hardware cost, effectively making fully associative placement practical only for caches with small numbers of blocks.

The middle range of designs between direct mapped and fully associative is called *set associative*. In a set-associative cache, there are a fixed number of locations (at least two) where each block can be placed; a set-associative cache with *n* locations for a block is called an *n*-way set-associative cache. An *n*-way set-associative cache consists of a number of sets, each of which consists of *n* blocks. Each block in the memory maps to a unique *set* in the cache given by the index field, and a block can be placed in *any* element of that set. Thus a set-associative placement combines direct-mapped placement and fully associative placement: a block is directly mapped into a set, and then all the blocks in the set are searched for a match.

Remember that in a direct-mapped cache, the position of a memory block is given by

$$\text{(Block number) modulo (Number of cache blocks)}$$

In a set-associative cache, the set containing a memory block is given by

$$\text{(Block number) modulo (Number of sets in the cache)}$$

Since the block may be placed in any element of the set, *all the elements of the set* must be searched. In a fully associative cache, the block can go anywhere and *all the blocks in the cache* must be searched. For example, Figure 7.15 shows where block 12 can be placed in a cache with eight blocks total, according to the block placement policy for direct-mapped, two-way set-associative, and fully associative caches.

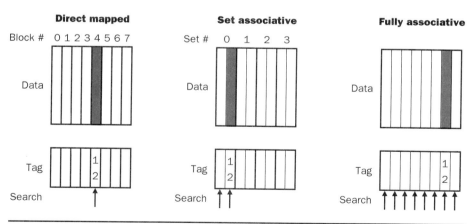

FIGURE 7.15 The location of a memory block whose address is 12 in a cache with eight blocks varies for direct-mapped, set-associative, and fully associative placement. In direct-mapped placement, there is only one cache block where memory block 12 can be found, and that block is given by (12 modulo 8) = 4. In a two-way set-associative cache, there would be four sets, and memory block 12 must be in set (12 mod 4) = 0; the memory block could be in either element of the set. In a fully associative placement, the memory block for block address 12 can appear in any of the eight cache blocks.

We can think of every block placement strategy as a variation on set associativity. A direct-mapped cache is simply a one-way set-associative cache: each cache entry holds one block and forms a set with one element. A fully associative cache with m entries is simply an m-way set-associative cache; it has one set with m blocks, and an entry can reside in any block within that set. Figure 7.16 shows the possible associativity structures for an eight-block cache.

The advantage of increasing the degree of associativity is that it usually decreases the miss rate, as the next example shows. The main disadvantage, which we discuss in more detail shortly, is an increase in the hit time.

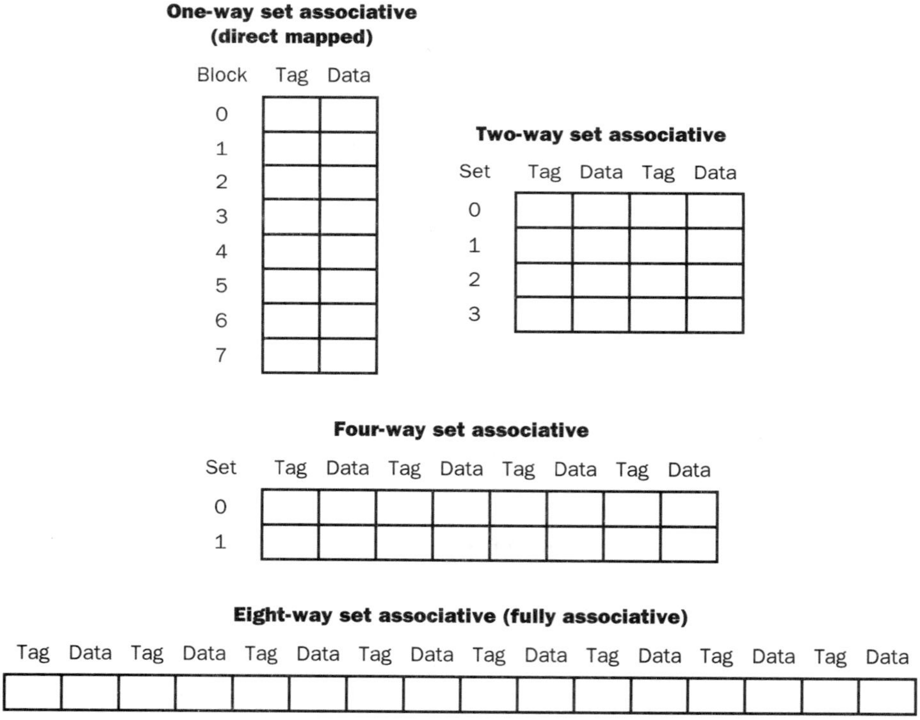

FIGURE 7.16 An eight-block cache configured as direct mapped, two-way set associative, four-way set associative, and fully associative. The total size of the cache in blocks is equal to the number of sets times the associativity. Thus, for a fixed cache size, increasing the associativity decreases the number of sets, while increasing the number of elements per set. With eight blocks, an eight-way set-associative cache is the same as a fully associative cache.

Associativity in Caches

Example

There are three small caches, each consisting of four one-word blocks. One cache is fully associative, a second is two-way set associative, and the third is direct mapped. Find the number of misses for each cache organization given the following sequence of block addresses: 0, 8, 0, 6, 8.

Answer

The direct-mapped case is easiest. First, let's determine to which cache block each block address maps:

Block address	Cache block
0	(0 modulo 4) = 0
6	(6 modulo 4) = 2
8	(8 modulo 4) = 0

Now we can fill in the cache contents after each reference, using a blank entry to mean that the block is invalid and a colored entry to show a new entry added to the cache for the associate reference:

Address of memory block accessed	Hit or miss	Contents of cache blocks after reference			
		0	**1**	**2**	**3**
0	miss	Memory[0]			
8	miss	Memory[8]			
0	miss	Memory[0]			
6	miss	Memory[0]		Memory[6]	
8	miss	Memory[8]		Memory[6]	

The direct-mapped cache generates five misses.

The set-associative cache has two sets (with indices 0 and 1) with two elements per set. Let's first determine to which set each block address maps:

Block address	Cache set
0	(0 modulo 2) = 0
6	(6 modulo 2) = 0
8	(8 modulo 2) = 0

Because we have a choice of which entry in a set to replace on a miss, we need a replacement rule. Set-associative caches usually replace the least recently used block within a set; that is, the block that was used furthest in the past is replaced. (We will discuss replacement rules in more detail shortly.) Using this replacement rule, the contents of the set-associative cache after each reference looks like this:

Address of memory block accessed	Hit or miss	Contents of cache blocks after reference			
		Set 0	Set 0	Set 1	Set 1
0	miss	Memory[0]			
8	miss	Memory[0]	Memory[8]		
0	hit	Memory[0]	Memory[8]		
6	miss	Memory[0]	Memory[6]		
8	miss	Memory[8]	Memory[6]		

Notice that when block 6 is referenced, it replaces block 8, since block 8 has been less recently referenced than block 0. The two-way set-associative cache has a total of four misses, one less than the direct-mapped cache.

The fully associative cache has four cache blocks (in a single set); any memory block can be stored in any cache block. The fully associative cache has the best performance, with only three misses:

Address of memory block accessed	Hit or miss	Contents of cache blocks after reference			
		Block 0	Block 1	Block 2	Block 3
0	miss	Memory[0]			
8	miss	Memory[0]	Memory[8]		
0	hit	Memory[0]	Memory[8]		
6	miss	Memory[0]	Memory[8]	Memory[6]	
8	hit	Memory[0]	Memory[8]	Memory[6]	

For this series of references, three misses is the best we can do because three unique block addresses are accessed. Notice that if we had eight blocks in the cache, there would be no replacements in the two-way set-associative cache (check this for yourself), and it would have the same number of misses as the fully associative cache. Similarly, if we had 16 blocks, all three caches would have the same number of misses. This change in miss rate shows us that cache size and associativity are not independent in determining cache performance.

How much of a reduction in the miss rate is achieved by associativity? Figure 7.17 shows the improvement for the programs gcc and spice with a pair of 64-KB caches (split instruction and data) with a four-word block, and associativity ranging from direct mapped to four-way. On gcc, going from one-way to two-way associativity improves the effective combined miss rate by about 20%, but there is no further improvement in going to four-way associativity. The low miss rates for spice leave little opportunity for improvement by increasing associativity.

Locating a Block in the Cache

Now, let's consider the task of finding a block in a cache that is set associative. Just as in a direct-mapped cache, each block in a set-associative cache includes an address tag that gives the block address. The tag of every cache block within the appropriate set is checked to see if it matches the block address from the CPU. Figure 7.18 shows how the address is decomposed. The index value is used to select the set containing the address of interest, and the tags of all the blocks in the set must be searched. Because speed is of the essence, all the tags in the selected set are searched in parallel. As in a fully associative cache, a serial search would make the hit time of a set-associative cache too slow.

If the total size is kept the same, increasing the associativity increases the number of blocks per set, which is the number of simultaneous compares needed to perform the search in parallel: each increase by a factor of two in associativity doubles the number of blocks per set and halves the number of sets. Accordingly, each factor-of-two increase in associativity decreases the size of

Program	Associativity	Instruction miss rate	Data miss rate	Effective combined miss rate
gcc	1	2.0%	1.7%	1.9%
gcc	2	1.6%	1.4%	1.5%
gcc	4	1.6%	1.4%	1.5%
spice	1	0.3%	0.6%	0.4%
spice	2	0.3%	0.6%	0.4%
spice	4	0.3%	0.6%	0.4%

FIGURE 7.17 The miss rates for gcc and spice with a cache like that in the DECStation 3100 but with a block size of four words and associativity varying from one-way to four-way.

Tag	Index	Block Offset

FIGURE 7.18 The three portions of an address in a set-associative or direct-mapped cache. The index is used to select the set, then the tag is used to choose the block by comparison with the blocks in the selected set. The block offset is the address of the desired data within the block.

the index by 1 bit and increases the size of the tag by 1 bit. In a fully associative cache, there is effectively only one set, and all the blocks must be checked in parallel. Thus there is no index, and the entire address, excluding the block off-set, is compared against the tag of every block. In other words, we search the entire cache without any indexing.

In a direct-mapped cache, such as that shown in Figure 7.7 on page 549, only a single comparator is needed, because the entry can be in only one block, and we access the cache simply by indexing. In a four-way set-associative cache, shown in Figure 7.19, four comparators are needed, together with a 4-to-1

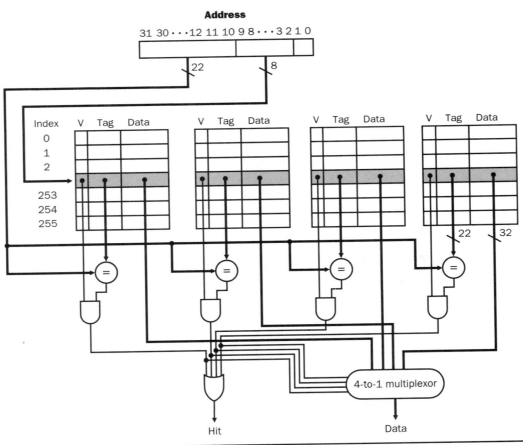

FIGURE 7.19 The implementation of a four-way set-associative cache requires four comparators and a 4-to-1 multiplexor. The comparators determine which element of the selected set (if any) matches the tag. The output of the comparators is used to select the data from one of the four blocks of the indexed set, using a multiplexor with a decoded select signal. In some implementations, the Output enable signals on the data portions of the cache RAMs can be used to select the entry in the set that drives the output. The Output enable signal comes from the comparators, causing the element that matches to drive the data outputs. This organization eliminates the need for the multiplexor.

multiplexor to choose among the four potential members of the selected set. The cache access consists of indexing the appropriate set and then searching the elements of the set. The costs of an associative cache are the extra comparators and any delay imposed by having to do the compare and select from among the elements of the set.

Size of Tags versus Set Associativity

Example

Increasing associativity requires more comparators, as well as more tag bits per cache block. Assuming a cache of 4K blocks and a 32-bit address, find the total number of sets and the total number of tag bits for caches that are direct mapped, two-way and four-way set associative, and fully associative.

Answer

The direct-mapped cache has the same number of sets as blocks, and hence 12 bits of index, since $\log_2(4K) = 12$; hence the total number of tag bits is $(32 - 12) \times 4K = 80$ Kbits.

Each degree of associativity decreases the number of sets by a factor of two and thus decreases the number of bits used to index the cache by one and increases the number of bits in the tag by one. Thus, for a two-way set-associative cache, there are 2K sets, and the total number of tag bits is $(32 - 11) \times 2 \times 2K = 84$ Kbits. For a four-way set-associative cache, the total number of sets is 1K, and the total number of tag bits is $(32 - 10) \times 4 \times 1K = 88$ Kbits.

For a fully associative cache, there is only one set with 4K blocks, and the tag is 32 bits, leading to a total of $32 \times 4K \times 1 = 128K$ tag bits.

The choice among direct-mapped, set-associative, or fully associative mapping in any memory hierarchy will depend on the cost of a miss versus the cost of implementing associativity, both in time and in extra hardware.

Choosing Which Block to Replace

When a miss occurs in a direct-mapped cache, the requested block can go in exactly one position, and the block occupying that position must be replaced. In an associative cache, we have a choice of where to place the requested block, and hence a choice of which block to replace. In a fully associative cache, all blocks are candidates for replacement. In a set-associative cache, we must choose among the blocks in the selected set.

The most commonly used scheme is *least recently used (LRU)*, which we used in the previous example. In an LRU scheme the block replaced is the one that has been unused for the longest time. LRU replacement is implemented by keeping track of when each element in a set was used relative to the other elements in the set. For a two-way set-associative cache, tracking when the two elements were used can be implemented by keeping a single bit in each set and setting the bit to indicate an element whenever that element is referenced. As associativity increases, implementing LRU gets harder; in section 7.5, we will see an alternative scheme for replacement.

Reducing the Miss Penalty Using Multilevel Caches

All modern computers make use of caches. In most cases, these caches are implemented on the same die as the microprocessor that forms the CPU. To further close the gap between the fast clock rates of modern processors and the relatively long time required to access DRAMs, high-performance microprocessors support an additional level of caching. This second-level cache, which often is off-chip in a separate set of SRAMs, is accessed whenever a miss occurs in the primary cache. If the second-level cache contains the desired data, the miss penalty will be the access time of the second-level cache, which will be much less than the access time of main memory. If neither the primary nor secondary cache contains the data, a main memory access is required, and a larger miss penalty is incurred.

How significant is the performance improvement from the use of a secondary cache? The next example shows us.

Performance of Multilevel Caches

Example

Suppose we have a processor with a base CPI of 1.0, assuming all references hit in the primary cache, and a clock rate of 500 MHz. Assume a main memory access time of 200 ns, including all the miss handling. Suppose the miss rate per instruction at the primary cache is 5%. How much faster will the machine be if we add a secondary cache that has a 20-ns access time for either a hit or a miss and is large enough to reduce the miss rate to main memory to 2%?

Answer

The miss penalty to main memory is

$$\frac{200 \text{ ns}}{2\dfrac{\text{ns}}{\text{clock cycle}}} = 100 \text{ clock cycles}$$

The effective CPI with one level of caching is given by

Total CPI = Base CPI + Memory-stall cycles per instruction

For the machine with one level of caching,

Total CPI = 1.0 + Memory-stall cycles per instruction = $1.0 + 5\% \times 100 = 6.0$

With two levels of cache, a miss in the primary (or first-level) cache can be satisfied either in the secondary cache or in main memory. The miss penalty for an access to the second-level cache is

$$\frac{20 \text{ ns}}{2\dfrac{\text{ns}}{\text{clock cycle}}} = 10 \text{ clock cycles}$$

If the miss is satisfied in the secondary cache, then this is the entire miss penalty. If the miss needs to go to main memory, then the total miss penalty is the sum of the secondary cache access time and the main memory access time.

Thus, for a two-level cache, total CPI is the sum of the stall cycles from both levels of cache and the base CPI:

Total CPI = 1 + Primary stalls per instruction
            + Secondary stalls per instruction
            = $1 + 5\% \times 10 + 2\% \times 100 = 3.5$

Thus the machine with the secondary cache is faster by

$$\frac{6.0}{3.5} = 1.7$$

Alternatively, we could have computed the stall cycles by summing the stall cycles of those references that hit in the secondary cache $((5\% - 2\%) \times 10 = 0.3)$ and those references that go to main memory, which must include the cost to access the secondary cache as well as the main memory access time $(2\% \times (10 + 100) = 2.2)$.

The design considerations for a primary and secondary cache are significantly different because the presence of the other cache changes the optimal choice versus a single-level cache. In particular, a two-level cache structure allows the primary cache to focus on minimizing hit time to yield a shorter clock cycle, while allowing the secondary cache to focus on miss rate to reduce the penalty of long memory access times.

The interaction of the two caches permits such a focus. The miss penalty of the primary cache is significantly reduced by the presence of the secondary cache, allowing the primary to be smaller and have a higher miss rate. For the secondary cache, access time becomes less important with the presence of the primary cache, since the access time of the secondary cache affects the miss penalty of the primary cache, rather than directly affecting the primary cache hit time or the CPU cycle time.

The effect of these changes on the two caches can be seen by comparing each cache to the optimal design for a single level of cache. In comparison to a single-level cache, the primary cache of a multilevel cache is often smaller. Furthermore, the primary cache often uses a smaller block size, to go with the smaller cache size and reduced miss penalty. In comparison, the secondary cache will often be larger than in a single-level cache, since the access time of the secondary cache is less critical. With a larger total size, the secondary cache often will use a larger block size than appropriate with a single-level cache.

Elaboration: There are a number of complications that arise when multilevel caches are used. One of these is that there are now several different types of misses and corresponding miss rates. In the example above, we saw the primary cache miss rate and the *global miss rate*, that is, the fraction of references that missed in all levels. There is also a miss rate for the secondary cache that is given by the ratio of all misses in the secondary cache divided by the number of accesses. This miss rate is called the *local miss rate* of the secondary cache. Because the primary cache filters accesses, especially those with good spatial and temporal locality, the local miss rate of the secondary cache is much higher than the global miss rate. For the example above, we can compute the local miss rate of the secondary cache as: 2%/5% = 40%! Luckily, it is the combined miss rate that dictates how often we must access the main memory! Additional complications arise because the caches will likely have different block sizes to match the larger or smaller total size. Likewise, the associativity of the cache may change. On-chip primary caches are often built with associativity of two to four, while off-chip caches rarely have associativity of greater than two. These changes in block size and associativity introduce complications in the modeling of the caches, which typically means that both levels need to be simulated together to understand the behavior.

Summary

In this section, we focused on three topics: cache performance, using associativity to reduce miss rates, and the use of multilevel cache hierarchies to reduce miss penalties.

Since the total number of cycles spent on a program is the sum of the processor cycles and the memory-stall cycles, the memory system can have a significant effect on program execution time. In fact, as processors get faster (either by lowering CPI or by increasing the clock rate), the relative effect of the memory-stall cycles increases, making a good memory system critical to achieving high performance. The number of memory-stall cycles depends on both the miss rate and the miss penalty. The challenge, as we will see in section 7.5, is to reduce one of these factors without significantly affecting other critical factors in the memory hierarchy.

To reduce the miss rate, we examined the use of associative placement schemes. Such schemes can reduce the miss rate of a cache by allowing more flexible placement of blocks within the cache. Fully associative schemes allow blocks to be placed anywhere, but also require that every block in the cache be searched to satisfy a request. This search is usually implemented by having a comparator per cache block and searching the entries in parallel. The cost of the comparators makes large fully associative caches impractical. Set-associative caches are a practical alternative, since we need only search among the elements of a unique set that is chosen by indexing. Set-associative caches yield an improvement in hit rate but are slightly slower to access, because of the cost of the comparisons and the selection from among the elements of a set. Whether a direct-mapped cache or a set-associative cache yields better performance depends on both the technology and the details of the implementation.

Finally, we looked at multilevel caches as a technique to reduce the miss penalty by allowing a larger secondary cache to handle misses to the primary cache. Second-level caches have become commonplace as designers find that limited silicon and the goals of high clock rates prevent primary caches from becoming large. The secondary cache, which is often 10 or more times larger than the primary cache, catches many accesses that miss in the primary cache. In such cases, the miss penalty is that of the access time to the secondary cache (typically < 10 cycles) versus the access time to memory (typically > 40 cycles). As with associativity, the design trade-offs between size of the secondary cache and its access time depend on a number of aspects of the implementation.

7.4 Virtual Memory

. . . a system has been devised to make the core drum combination appear to the programmer as a single level store, the requisite transfers taking place automatically.

Kilburn et al., "One-level storage systems," 1962

In the previous section, we saw how caches served as a method for providing fast access to recently used portions of a program's code and data. Similarly, the main memory can act as a "cache" for the secondary storage, usually implemented with magnetic disks. This technique is called *virtual memory*. There are two major motivations for virtual memory: to allow efficient and safe sharing of memory among multiple programs and to remove the programming burdens of a small, limited amount of main memory.

Consider a collection of programs running at once on a machine. The total memory required by all the programs may be much larger than the amount of main memory available on the machine, but only a fraction of this memory is actively being used at any point in time. Main memory need contain only the active portions of the many programs, just as a cache contains only the active portion of one program. This allows us to efficiently share the processor as well as the main memory. Of course, to allow multiple programs to share the same memory, we must be able to protect the programs from each other, ensuring that a program can only read and write the portions of main memory that have been assigned to it.

We cannot know which programs will share the memory with other programs when we compile them. In fact, the programs sharing the memory change dynamically while the programs are running. Because of this dynamic interaction, we would like to compile each program into its own *address space*, that is, a separate range of memory locations accessible only to this program. Virtual memory implements the translation of a program's address space to physical addresses. This translation process enforces protection of a program's address space from other programs.

A second motivation for virtual memory is to allow a single user program to exceed the size of primary memory. Formerly, if a program became too large for memory, it was up to the programmer to make it fit. Programmers divided programs into pieces and then identified the pieces that were mutually exclusive. These *overlays* were loaded or unloaded under user program control during execution, with the programmer ensuring that the program never tried to access an overlay that was not loaded and that the overlays loaded never exceeded the total size of the memory. Overlays were traditionally organized as modules, each containing both code and data. Calls between procedures in different modules would lead to overlaying of one module with another.

As you can well imagine, this responsibility was a substantial burden on programmers. Virtual memory, which was invented to relieve programmers of this difficulty, automatically manages the two levels of the memory hierarchy represented by main memory (sometimes called *physical memory* to distinguish it from virtual memory) and secondary storage.

Although the concepts at work in virtual memory and in caches are the same, their differing historical roots have led to the use of different terminology. A virtual memory block is called a *page*, and a virtual memory miss is called a *page fault*. With virtual memory, the CPU produces a *virtual address*, which is translated by a combination of hardware and software to a *physical address*, which in turn can be used to access main memory. Figure 7.20 shows the virtual addressed memory with pages mapped to main memory. This process is called *memory mapping* or *address translation*. Today, the two memory hierarchy levels controlled by virtual memory are DRAMs and magnetic disks (see Chapter 1, pages 19–20). If we return to our library analogy, we can think of a virtual address as the title of a book and a physical address as the location of that book in the library, such as might be given by the Library of Congress call number.

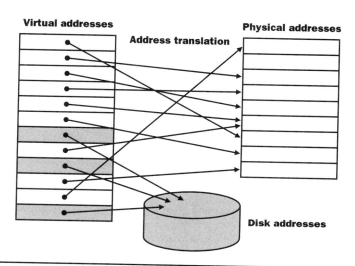

FIGURE 7.20 In virtual memory, blocks of memory (called pages) are mapped from one set of addresses (called virtual addresses) to another set (called physical addresses). The processor generates virtual addresses while the memory is accessed using physical addresses. Both the virtual memory and the physical memory are broken into pages, so that a virtual page is really mapped to a physical page. Of course, it is also possible for a virtual page to be absent from main memory and not be mapped to a physical address, residing instead on disk. Physical pages can be shared by having two virtual addresses point to the same physical address. This capability is used to allow two different programs to share data or code.

Virtual memory also simplifies loading the program for execution by providing *relocation*. Relocation maps the virtual addresses used by a program to different physical addresses before the addresses are used to access memory. This relocation allows us to load the program into any location in main memory. Furthermore, all virtual memory systems in use today relocate the program as a set of fixed-size blocks (pages), thereby eliminating the need to find a contiguous block of memory to allocate to a program; instead, the operating system need only find a sufficient number of pages in main memory. Formerly, relocation problems required special hardware and special support in the operating system; today, virtual memory also provides this function.

In virtual memory, the address is broken into a *virtual page number* and a *page offset*. Figure 7.21 shows the translation of the virtual page number to a *physical page number*. The physical page number constitutes the upper portion of the physical address, while the page offset, which is not changed, constitutes the lower portion. The number of bits in the page offset field determines the page size. The number of pages addressable with the virtual address need not match the number of pages addressable with the physical address. Having a larger number of virtual pages than physical pages is the basis for the illusion of an essentially unbounded amount of virtual memory.

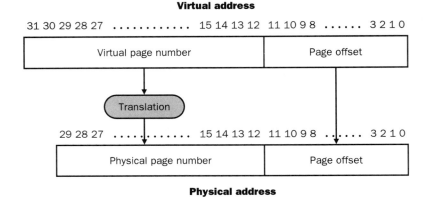

FIGURE 7.21 Mapping from a virtual to a physical address. The page size is 2^{12} = 4 KB. The number of physical pages allowed in memory is 2^{18}, since the physical page number has 18 bits in it. This means that main memory can have at most 1 GB, while the virtual address space is 4 GB.

Many design choices in virtual memory systems are motivated by the high cost of a miss, which in virtual memory is traditionally called a *page fault*. A page fault will take millions of cycles to process. (The table on page 541 shows the relative speeds of main memory and disk.) This enormous miss penalty, dominated by the time to get the first word for typical page sizes, leads to several key decisions in designing virtual memory systems:

- Pages should be large enough to amortize the high access time. Sizes from 4 KB to 16 KB are typical today, with new systems being developed to support 32-KB and 64-KB pages, and 4-KB pages are being phased out.

- Organizations that reduce the page fault rate are attractive. The primary technique used here is to allow fully associative placement of pages.

- Page faults can be handled in software because the overhead will be small compared to the access time to disk. Furthermore, software can afford to use clever algorithms for choosing how to place pages because even small reductions in the miss rate will pay for the cost of such algorithms.

- Using write-through to manage writes in virtual memory will not work, since writes take too long. Instead, virtual memory systems use write-back.

The next few sections address these factors in virtual memory design.

Elaboration: The discussion of virtual memory in this book focuses on paging, which uses fixed-size blocks. There is also a variable-size block scheme called *segmentation*. In segmentation, an address consists of two parts: a segment number and a segment offset. The segment register is mapped to a physical address, and the offset is *added* to find the actual physical address. Because the segment can vary in size, a bounds check is also needed to make sure that the offset is within the segment. The major use of segmentation is to support more powerful methods of protection and sharing in an address space. Most operating system textbooks contain extensive discussions of segmentation compared to paging and of the use of segmentation to logically share the address space. The major disadvantage of segmentation is that it splits the address space into logically separate pieces that must be manipulated as a two-part address: the segment number and the offset. Paging, in contrast, makes the boundary between page number and offset invisible to programmers and compilers.

Segments have also been used as a method to extend the address space without changing the word size of the machine. Such attempts have been unsuccessful because of the awkwardness and performance penalties inherent in a two-part address of which programmers and compilers must be aware.

Many architectures divide the address space into large fixed-size blocks that simplify protection between the operating system and user programs and increase the efficiency of implementing paging. Although these divisions are often called "segments," this mechanism is much simpler than variable block size segmentation and is not visible to user programs; we discuss it in more detail shortly.

Placing a Page and Finding It Again

Because of the incredibly high penalty for a page fault, designers would like to reduce the number of page faults by optimizing the page placement. If we allow a virtual page to be mapped to any physical page, the operating system can then choose to replace any page it wants when a page fault occurs. For example, the operating system can use a sophisticated algorithm and complex data structures, which track page usage, to try to choose a page that will not be needed for a long time. The ability to use a clever and flexible replacement scheme is actually the primary motivation for using fully associative placement of pages. Of course, fully associative placement also reduces the page fault rate.

As we mentioned earlier, the difficulty in using fully associative placement is in locating an entry, since it can be anywhere in the upper level of the hierarchy. A full search is impractical. In virtual memory, we locate pages by using a full table that indexes the memory; this structure is called a *page table*. A page table, which resides in memory, is indexed with the page number from the virtual address and contains the corresponding physical page number. Each program has its own page table, which maps the virtual address space of that program to main memory. In our library analogy, the page table corresponds to a mapping between book titles and library locations. Just as the card catalog may contain entries for books in another library on campus rather than the local branch library, we will see that the page table may contain entries for pages not present in memory. To indicate the location of the page table in memory, the hardware includes a register that points to the start of the page table; we call this the *page table register*. Assume for now that the page table is in a fixed and contiguous area of memory.

Figure 7.22 uses the page table register, the virtual address, and the indicated page table to show how the hardware can form a physical address. A valid bit is used in each page table entry, just as we did in a cache. If the bit is off, the

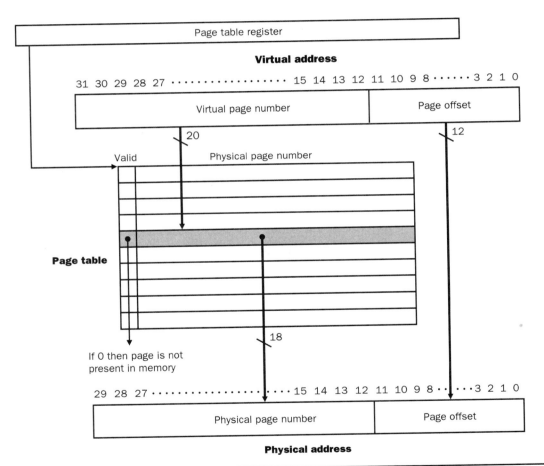

FIGURE 7.22 The page table is indexed with the virtual page number to obtain the corresponding portion of the physical address. The starting address of the page table is given by the page table pointer. In this figure, the page size is 2^{12} bytes, or 4 KB. The virtual address space is 2^{32} bytes, or 4 gigabytes, and the physical address space is 2^{30} bytes, which allows main memory of up to 1 gigabyte. The number of entries in the page table is then 2^{20}, or 1 million entries. The valid bit for each entry indicates whether the mapping is legal. If it is off, then the page is not present in memory. Although the page table entry shown here need only be 19 bits wide, it would typically be rounded up to 32 bits for ease of indexing. The extra bits would be used to store additional information that needs to be kept on a per page basis, such as protection.

page is not present in main memory and a page fault occurs. If the bit is on, the page is valid and the entry contains the physical page number.

Because the page table contains a mapping for every possible virtual page, no tags are required. In cache terminology, the index, which is used to access the page table, consists of the full block address, which is the virtual page number.

Hardware Software Interface

The page table, together with the program counter and the registers, specifies the state of a program. If we want to allow another program to use the CPU, we must save this state. Later, after restoring this state, the program can continue execution. We often refer to this state as a *process*. The process is considered *active* when it is in possession of the CPU; otherwise, it is considered *inactive*. The operating system can make a process active by loading the process's state, including the program counter, which will initiate execution at the value of the saved program counter.

The process's address space, and hence all the data it can access in memory, is defined by its page table, which resides in memory. Rather than save the entire page table, the operating system simply loads the page table register to point to the page table of the process it wants to make active. Each process has its own page table, since different processes use the same virtual addresses. The operating system is responsible for allocating the physical memory and updating the page tables, so that the virtual address spaces of different processes do not collide. As we will see shortly, the use of separate page tables also provides protection of one process from another.

Page Faults

If the valid bit for a virtual page is off, a page fault occurs. The operating system must be given control. This transfer is done with the exception mechanism, the details of which we discuss later in this section. Once the operating system gets control, it must find the page in the next level of the hierarchy (usually magnetic disk) and decide where to place the requested page in main memory.

The virtual address alone does not immediately tell us where the page is on disk. Returning to our library analogy, we cannot find the location of a library book on the shelves just by knowing its title. Instead, we go to the catalog and look up the book, obtaining an address for the location on the shelves, such as the Library of Congress call number. Likewise, in a virtual memory system, we must keep track of the location on disk of each page in the virtual address space.

Because we do not know ahead of time when a page in memory will be chosen to be replaced, the operating system usually creates the space on disk for all the pages of a process when it creates the process. At that time, it also creates a data structure to record where each virtual page is stored on disk. This data structure may be part of the page table or may be an auxiliary data structure indexed in the same way as the page table. Figure 7.23 shows the organization when a single table holds either the physical page number or the disk address.

The operating system also creates a data structure that tracks which processes and which virtual addresses use each physical page. When a page fault occurs, if all the pages in main memory are in use, the operating system must choose a page to replace. Because we want to minimize the number of page faults, most operating systems try to choose a page that they hypothesize will not be needed in the near future. Using the past to predict the future,

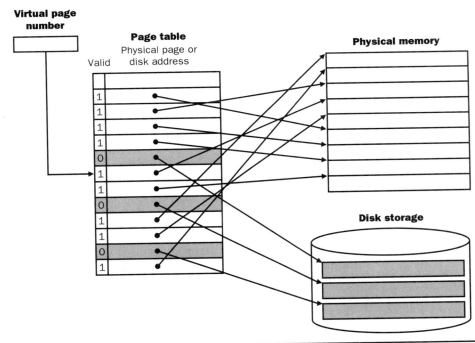

FIGURE 7.23   The page table maps each page in virtual memory to either a page in main memory or a page stored on disk, which is the next level in the hierarchy. The virtual page number is used to index the page table. If the valid bit is on, the page table supplies the physical page number (i.e., the starting address of the page in memory) corresponding to the virtual page. If the valid bit is off, the page currently resides only on disk, at a specified disk address. In many systems, the table of physical page addresses and disk page addresses, while logically one table, is stored in two separate data structures. Dual tables are justified in part because we must keep the disk addresses of all the pages, even if they are currently in main memory. Remember that the pages in main memory and the pages on disk are identical in size.

operating systems follow the least recently used (LRU) replacement scheme, which we mentioned earlier. The operating system searches for the least recently used page, making the assumption that a page that has not been used in a long time is less likely to be needed than a more recently accessed page.

For example, suppose the most recent page references (in order) were 10, 12, 9, 7, 11, 10, and then we referenced page 8, which was not present in memory. The LRU page is page 12; in LRU replacement, we would replace page 12 in main memory with page 8. If the next reference also generated a page fault, we would replace page 9, since it would then be the LRU among the pages present in memory.

Hardware Software Interface

Implementing a completely accurate LRU scheme is too expensive, since it requires updating a data structure on *every* memory reference. Instead, most operating systems approximate LRU by keeping track of which pages have and which pages have not been recently used. To help the operating system estimate the LRU pages, some machines provide a *use bit* or *reference bit*, which is set whenever a page is accessed. The operating system periodically clears the reference bits and later records them so it can determine which pages were touched during a particular time period. With this usage information, the operating system can select a page that is among the least recently referenced (detected by having its reference bit off). If this bit is not provided by the hardware, the operating system must find another way to estimate which pages have been accessed.

Elaboration: With a 32-bit virtual address, 4-KB pages, and 4 bytes per page table entry, we can compute the total page table size:

$$\text{Number of page table entries} = \frac{2^{32}}{2^{12}} = 2^{20}$$

$$\text{Size of page table} = 2^{20} \text{ page table entries} \times 2^2 \frac{\text{bytes}}{\text{page table entry}} = 4 \text{ MB}$$

That is, we would need to use 4 MB of memory for each program in execution at any time. On a machine with tens to hundreds of active programs and a fixed-size page table, most or all of the memory would be tied up in page tables!

A range of techniques are used to reduce the amount of storage required for the page table. The five techniques below aim at reducing the total maximum storage required as well as minimizing the main memory dedicated to page tables:

1. The simplest technique is to keep a bounds register that limits the size of the page table for a given process. If the virtual page number becomes larger than

the contents of the limit register, entries must be added to the page table. This technique allows the page table to grow as a process consumes more space. Thus, the page table will only be large if the process is using many pages of virtual address space. This technique requires that the address space expand in only one direction.

2. Allowing growth in only one direction is not sufficient, since most languages require two areas whose size is expandable: one area holds the stack and the other area holds the heap. Because of this duality, it is convenient to divide the page table and let it grow from the highest address down, as well as from the lowest address up. This means that there will be two separate page tables and two separate limits. The use of two page tables breaks the address space into two segments. The high-order bit of an address usually determines which segment and thus which page table to use for that address. Since the segment is specified by the high-order address bit, each segment can be as large as one-half of the address space. A limit register for each segment specifies the current size of the segment, which grows in units of pages. This type of segmentation is used by many architectures, including the MIPS architecture. Unlike the type of segmentation discussed in the elaboration on page 583, this form of segmentation is invisible to the application program, although not to the operating system. The major disadvantage of this scheme is that it does not work well when the address space is used in a sparse fashion rather than as a contiguous set of virtual addresses.

3. Another approach to reducing the page table size is to apply a hashing function to the virtual address so that the page table data structure need be only the size of the number of *physical* pages in main memory. Such a structure is called an *inverted page table*. Of course, the lookup process is slightly more complex with an inverted page table because we can no longer just index the page table.

4. Multiple levels of page tables can also be used to reduce the total amount of page table storage. The first level maps large fixed-size blocks of virtual address space, perhaps 64 to 256 pages in total. These large blocks are sometimes called segments, and this first-level mapping table is sometimes called a segment table, though the segments are invisible to the user. Each entry in the segment table indicates whether any pages in that segment are allocated and, if so, points to a page table for that segment. Address translation happens by first looking in the segment table, using the highest-order bits of the address. If the segment address is valid, the next set of high-order bits is used to index the page table indicated by the segment table entry. This scheme allows the address space to be used in a sparse fashion (multiple noncontiguous segments can be active) without having to allocate the entire page table. Such schemes are particularly useful with very large address spaces and in software systems that require noncontiguous allocation. The primary disadvantage of this two-level mapping is the more complex process for address translation.

5. To reduce the actual main memory tied up in page tables, most modern systems also allow the page tables to be paged. Although this sounds tricky, it works by using the same basic ideas of virtual memory and simply allowing the page tables to reside in the virtual address space. In addition, there are some small but critical problems, such as a never-ending series of page faults, that must be

avoided. How these problems are overcome is both very detailed and typically highly machine-specific. In brief, these problems are avoided by placing all the page tables in the address space of the operating system and placing at least some of the page tables for the system in a portion of main memory that is physically addressed and is always present and never on disk.

What about Writes?

The difference between the access time to the cache and main memory is tens of cycles, and write-through schemes can be used, although we need a write buffer to hide the latency of the write from the processor. In a virtual memory system, writes to the next level of the hierarchy (disk) take millions of processor clock cycles; therefore, building a write buffer to allow the system to write through to disk would be completely impractical. Instead, virtual memory systems must use write-back, performing the individual writes into the page in memory and copying the page back to disk when it is replaced in the memory. This copying back to the lower level in the hierarchy is the source of the other name for this technique of handling writes, namely *copy back*.

Hardware Software Interface

A write-back scheme has another major advantage in a virtual memory system. Because the disk transfer time is small compared with its access time, copying back an entire page is much more efficient than writing individual words back to the disk. A write-back operation, although more efficient than transferring individual words, is still costly. Thus, we would like to know whether a page *needs* to be copied back when we choose to replace it. To track whether a page has been written since it was read into the memory, a *dirty bit* is added to the page table. The dirty bit is set when the page is first written. If the operating system chooses to replace the page, the dirty bit indicates whether the page needs to be written out before its location in memory can be given to another page.

Making Address Translation Fast: The TLB

Since the page tables are stored in main memory, every memory access by a program can take at least twice as long: one memory access to obtain the physical address and a second access to get the data. The key to improving access performance is to rely on locality of reference to the page table. When a translation for a virtual page number is used, it will probably be needed again in the near future because the references to the words on that page have both temporal and spatial locality.

Accordingly, modern machines include a special cache that keeps track of recently used translations. This special address translation cache is traditionally referred to as a *translation-lookaside buffer (TLB)*. The TLB corresponds to that little piece of paper we typically use to record the location of a set of books we look up in the card catalog; rather than continually searching the entire catalog, we record the location of several books and use the scrap of paper as a cache.

A TLB is a cache that holds only page table mappings. Thus, each tag entry in the TLB holds a portion of the virtual page number, and each data entry of the TLB holds a physical page number. Because we will no longer access the page table on every reference, instead accessing the TLB, the TLB will need to include other bits, such as the reference and the dirty bit. Figure 7.24 shows how the TLB acts as a cache for the page table references.

On every reference, we look up the virtual page number in the TLB. If we get a hit, the physical page number is used to form the address, and the corresponding reference bit is turned on. If the processor is performing a write, the dirty bit is also turned on. If a miss in the TLB occurs, we must determine whether it is a page fault or merely a TLB miss. If the page exists in memory, then the TLB miss indicates only that the translation is missing. In such cases, the CPU can handle the TLB miss by loading the translation from the page table into the TLB and then trying the reference again. If the page is not present in memory, then the TLB miss indicates a true page fault. In this case, the CPU invokes the operating system using an exception. Because the TLB has many fewer entries than the number of pages in main memory, TLB misses will be much more frequent than true page faults.

TLB misses can be handled either in hardware or software. In practice, there is little performance difference between the two approaches because the basic operations that must be performed are the same in either case.

After a TLB miss occurs and the missing translation has been retrieved from the page table, we will need to select a TLB entry to replace. Because the reference and dirty bits are contained in the TLB entry, we need to copy these bits back to the page table entry when we replace an entry. These bits are the only portion of the TLB entry that can be changed. Using a write-back strategy (that is, copying these entries back at miss time rather than whenever they are written) is very efficient, since we expect the TLB miss rate to be small. Some systems use other techniques to approximate the reference and dirty bits, eliminating the need to write into the TLB except to load a new table entry on a miss.

Some typical values for a TLB might be

- TLB size: 32–4,096 entries
- Block size: 1–2 page table entries (typically 4–8 bytes each)
- Hit time: 0.5–1 clock cycle
- Miss penalty: 10–30 clock cycles
- Miss rate: 0.01%–1%

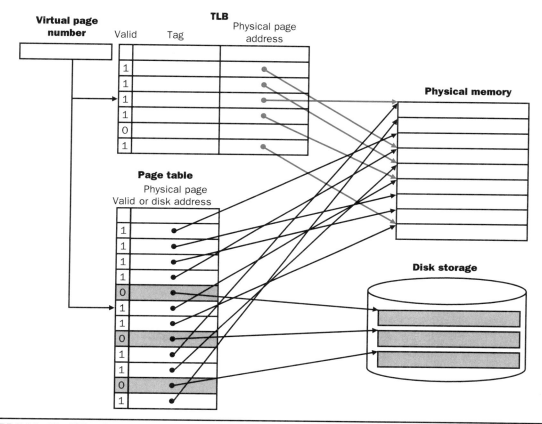

FIGURE 7.24 The TLB acts as a cache on the page table for the entries that map to physical pages only. The TLB contains a subset of the virtual-to-physical page mappings that are in the page table. The TLB mappings are shown in color. Because the TLB is a cache, it must have a tag field. If there is no matching entry in the TLB for a page, the page table must be examined. The page table either supplies a physical page number for the page (which can then be used to build a TLB entry) or indicates that the page resides on disk, in which case a page fault occurs. Since the page table has an entry for every virtual page (it is *not* a cache, in other words), no tag field is needed.

Designers have used a wide variety of associativity in TLBs. Some systems use small, fully associative TLBs because a fully associative mapping has a lower miss rate; furthermore, since the TLB is small, the cost of a fully associative mapping is not too high. Other systems use large TLBs, often with no or small associativity. With a fully associative mapping, choosing the entry to replace becomes tricky since implementing a hardware LRU scheme is too expensive. Furthermore, since TLB misses are much more frequent than page faults and must be handled more cheaply, we cannot afford an expensive software algorithm, as we can for page faults. As a result, many systems provide some support for randomly choosing an entry to replace. We'll examine replacement schemes in a little more detail in section 7.5.

The MIPS R2000 TLB

To see how these ideas work in practice, let's take a closer look at the TLB of the MIPS R2000, which was used in the DECStation 3100. This TLB, while extremely simple, exhibits most of the characteristics in more recent TLBs. The memory system uses 4-KB pages and a 32-bit address space; thus the virtual page number is 20 bits long, as shown in Figure 7.22 on page 584. The physical address is the same size as the virtual address. The TLB contains 64 entries, is fully associative, and is shared between the instruction and data references. Each entry is 64 bits wide and contains a 20-bit tag (which is the virtual page number for that TLB entry), the corresponding physical page number (also 20 bits), a valid bit, a dirty bit, and several other bookkeeping bits.

Figure 7.25 shows the TLB and one of the caches, while Figure 7.26 shows the steps in processing a read or write request. When a TLB miss occurs, the MIPS hardware saves the page number of the reference in a special register and generates an exception. The exception invokes the operating system, which handles the miss in software. To find the physical address for the missing page, the TLB miss routine indexes the page table using the page number of the virtual address and the page table register, which indicates the starting address of the active process page table. Using a special set of system instructions that can update the TLB, the operating system places the physical address from the page table into the TLB. A true page fault occurs if the page table entry does not have a valid physical address. A TLB miss can take as few as 10 cycles, but on average takes about 16 cycles. The hardware maintains an index that indicates the recommended entry to replace; the recommended entry is chosen randomly.

There is an extra complication for write requests: namely, the write access bit in the TLB must be checked. This bit prevents the program from writing into pages for which it has only read access. If the program attempts a write and the write access bit is off, an exception is generated. The write access bit forms part of the protection mechanism, which we discuss shortly.

Integrating Virtual Memory, TLBs, and Caches

Under the best of circumstances, a virtual address is translated by the TLB and sent to the cache where the appropriate data is found, retrieved, and sent back to the CPU. In the worst case, a reference can miss in all three components of the memory hierarchy: the TLB, the page table, and the cache. The following example illustrates these interactions in more detail.

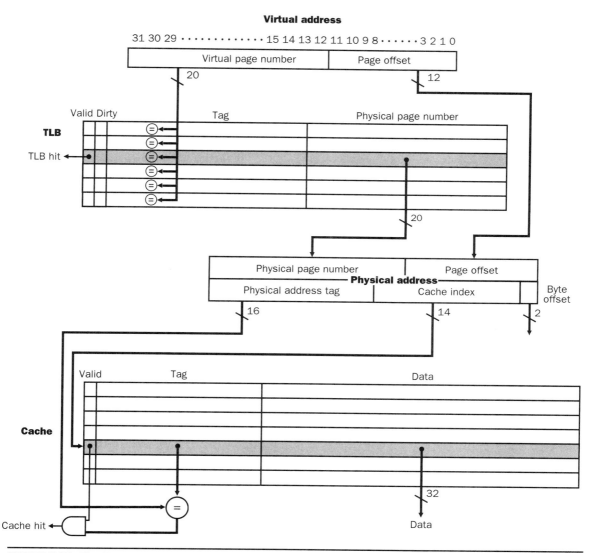

FIGURE 7.25 The TLB and cache implement the process of going from a virtual address to a data item in the DECStation 3100. This figure shows the organization of the TLB and one of the caches in the DECStation 3100. This diagram focuses on a read; Figure 7.26 describes how to handle writes. While the cache is direct mapped, the TLB is fully associative. Implementing a fully associative TLB requires that every TLB tag be compared against theT index value, since the entry of interest can be anywhere in the TLB. If the valid bit of the matching entry is on, the access is a TLB hit, and the page number together with the page offset forms the index that is used to access the cache.

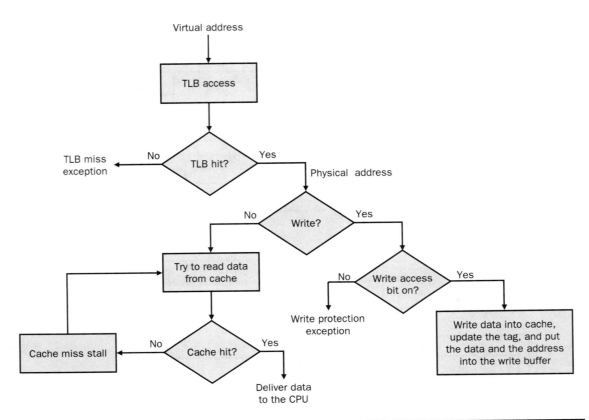

FIGURE 7.26   Processing a read or a write through the DECStation 3100 TLB and cache. If the TLB generates a hit, the cache can be accessed with the resulting physical address. If the operation is a write, the cache entry is overwritten and the data is sent to the write buffer; remember, though, that a cache write miss cannot occur for the DECStation 3100 cache, which uses one-word blocks and a write-through cache. For a read, the cache generates a hit or miss and supplies the data or causes a stall while the data is brought from memory. In actuality, the TLB does not contain a true dirty bit; instead, it uses the write access bit to detect the first write and then set the dirty bit in the page table. Notice that a TLB hit and a cache hit are independent events, and that the cache access is not even tried when a TLB miss occurs. Furthermore, a cache hit can only occur after a TLB hit occurs, which means that the data must be present in memory. The relationship between TLB misses and cache misses is examined further in the exercises at the end of this chapter.

Example   **Overall Operation of a Memory Hierarchy**

In a memory hierarchy like that of Figure 7.25 that includes a TLB and a cache organized as shown, a memory reference can encounter three different types of misses: a cache miss, a TLB miss, and a page fault. Consider all the combinations of these three events with one or more occurring (seven possibilities). For each possibility, state whether this event can actually occur and under what circumstances.

Answer   Figure 7.27 shows the possible circumstances and whether they can arise in practice or not.

Our virtual memory and cache systems work together as a hierarchy, so that data cannot be in the cache unless it is present in main memory. The operating system plays an important role in maintaining this hierarchy by flushing the contents of any page from the cache, when it decides to migrate that page to disk. At the same time, the OS modifies the page tables and TLB, so that an attempt to access any data on the page will generate a page fault.

Elaboration: Figure 7.27 assumes that all memory addresses are translated to physical addresses before the cache is accessed; Figure 7.25 shows such a memory system organization. In this organization, the cache is *physically indexed* and *physically tagged* (both the cache index and tag are physical, rather than virtual, addresses). In such a system, the amount of time to access memory, assuming a cache hit, must accommodate both a TLB access and a cache access; of course, these accesses can be pipelined.

Cache	TLB	Virtual memory	Possible? If so, under what circumstance?
miss	hit	hit	Possible, although the page table is never really checked if TLB hits.
hit	miss	hit	TLB misses, but entry found in page table; after retry, data is found in cache.
miss	miss	hit	TLB misses, but entry found in page table; after retry, data misses in cache.
miss	miss	miss	TLB misses and is followed by a page fault; after retry, data must miss in cache.
miss	hit	miss	Impossible: cannot have a translation in TLB if page is not present in memory.
hit	hit	miss	Impossible: cannot have a translation in TLB if page is not present in memory.
hit	miss	miss	Impossible: data cannot be allowed in cache if the page is not in memory.

FIGURE 7.27   The possible combinations of events in the TLB, virtual memory system, and cache. Three of these combinations are impossible, and one is possible (TLB hit, virtual memory hit, cache miss) but never detected.

Alternatively, the CPU can index the cache with an address that is completely or partially virtual. This is called a *virtually addressed cache,* and it uses tags that are virtual addresses, hence such a cache is *virtually indexed* and *virtually tagged.* In such caches, the address translation hardware (e.g., the TLB) is unused during the normal cache access, since the cache is accessed with a virtual address that has not been translated to a physical address. When a cache miss occurs, however, the processor needs to translate the address to a physical address so that it can fetch the cache block from main memory.

When the cache is accessed with a virtual address and pages are shared between programs (which may access them with different virtual addresses), there is the possibility of *aliasing.* Aliasing occurs when the same object has two names—in this case, two virtual addresses for the same page. This ambiguity creates a problem because a word on such a page may be cached in two different locations, each corresponding to different virtual addresses. This would allow one program to write the data without the other program being aware that the data had changed. Completely virtually addressed caches introduce either design limitations on the cache and TLB to reduce aliases or require the operating system, and possibly the user, to take steps to ensure that aliases do not occur.

A common compromise between these two design points are caches that are virtually indexed (sometimes using just the page offset portion of the address, which is really a physical address since it is untranslated), but use physical address tags. The cache and the TLB are accessed in parallel, and the physical address tags from the cache are compared against the physical address from the TLB. These designs, which are virtually indexed but physically tagged, attempt to achieve the performance advantages of virtually indexed caches with the architecturally simpler advantages of a physically addressed cache.

Implementing Protection with Virtual Memory

One of the most important functions for virtual memory is to allow sharing of a single main memory by multiple processes, while providing memory protection among these processes and the operating system. The protection mechanism must ensure that although multiple processes are sharing the same main memory, one renegade process cannot write into the address space of another user process or into the operating system either intentionally or unintentionally. For example, if the program that maintains student grades is running on a machine at the same time as the programs of the students in the first programming course, we wouldn't want the errant program of a beginner to write over someone's grades. The write access bit in the TLB can protect a page from being written.

We also want to prevent one process from reading the data of another process. For example, we wouldn't want one student program to read the grades while they were in the processor's memory. Once we begin sharing main memory, we must provide the ability for a process to protect its data from both reading and writing by another process; otherwise, sharing the main memory will be a mixed blessing!

Remember that each process has its own virtual address space. Thus, if the operating system keeps the page tables organized so that the independent virtual pages map to disjoint physical pages, one process will not be able to access another's data. Of course, this also requires that a user process be unable to change the page table mapping. The operating system can assure safety if it prevents the user process from modifying its own page tables. Yet the operating system must be able to modify the page tables. Placing the page tables in the address space of the operating system satisfies both requirements.

Hardware Software Interface

To enable the operating system to implement protection in the virtual memory system, the hardware must provide at least the three basic capabilities summarized below.

1. Support at least two modes that indicate whether the running process is a user process or an operating system process, variously called a *kernel* process, a *supervisor* process, or an *executive* process.

2. Provide a portion of the CPU state that a user process can read but not write. This includes the user/supervisor mode bit, which dictates whether the processor is in user or supervisor mode, the page table pointer, and the TLB. To write these elements the operating system uses special instructions that are only available in supervisor mode.

3. Provide mechanisms whereby the CPU can go from user mode to supervisor mode, and vice versa. The first direction is typically accomplished by a *system call* exception, implemented as a special instruction (*syscall* in the MIPS instruction set) that transfers control to a dedicated location in supervisor code space. As with any other exception, the program counter from the point of the system call is saved, and the CPU is placed in supervisor mode. The return to user mode from the exception, using the *return from exception* (RFE) instruction, will restore the state of the process that generated the exception.

By using these mechanisms and storing the page tables in the operating system's address space, the operating system can change the page tables while preventing a user process from changing them, ensuring that a user process can access only the storage provided to it by the operating system.

When processes want to share information in a limited way, the operating system must assist them, since accessing the information of another process requires changing the page table of the accessing process. The write access bit can be used to restrict the sharing to just read sharing, and, like the rest of the page table, this bit can be changed only by the operating system. To allow another process, say P1, to read a page owned by process P2, P2 would ask the operating system to create a page table entry for a virtual page in P1's address space that points to the same physical page that P2 wants to share. The operating system could use the write protection bit to prevent P1 from writing the data, if that was P2's wish. Any bits that determine the access rights for a page must be included in both the page table and the TLB because the page table is accessed only on a TLB *miss*.

Elaboration: When the operating system decides to change from running process P1 to running process P2 (called a *context switch* or *process switch*), it must ensure that P2 cannot get access to the page tables of P1 because that would compromise protection. If there is no TLB, it suffices to change the page table register to point to P2's page table (rather than to P1's); with a TLB, we must clear the TLB entries that belong to P1—both to protect the data of P1 and to force the TLB to load the entries for P2. If the process switch rate were high, this could be quite inefficient. For example, P2 might load only a few TLB entries before the operating system switched back to P1. Unfortunately, P1 would then find that all its TLB entries were gone and would have to go through TLB misses to reload them. This problem arises because the virtual addresses used by P1 and P2 are the same, and we must clear out the TLB to avoid confusing these addresses.

A common alternative is to extend the virtual address space by adding a *process identifier* or *task identifier*. This small field identifies the currently running process; it is kept in a register loaded by the operating system when it switches processes. The process identifier is concatenated to the tag portion of the TLB, so that a TLB hit occurs only if both the page number *and* the process identifier match. This combination eliminates the need to clear the TLB, except on rare occasions.

Similar problems can occur for a cache, since on a process switch the cache will contain data from the running process. These problems arise in different ways for physically addressed and virtually addressed caches, and a variety of different solutions, such as process identifiers, are used to ensure that a process gets its own data.

Handling Page Faults and TLB Misses

Although the translation of virtual to physical addresses with a TLB is straightforward when we get a TLB hit, handling TLB misses and page faults is more complex. A TLB miss occurs when no entry in the TLB matches a virtual address. A TLB miss can indicate one of two possibilities:

1. The page is present in memory, and we need only create the missing TLB entry.

2. The page is not present in memory, and we need to transfer control to the operating system to deal with a page fault.

How do we know which of these two circumstances has occurred? When we process the TLB miss, we will look for a page table entry to bring into the TLB; if the matching page table entry has a valid bit that is turned off, then the corresponding page is not in memory and we have a page fault, rather than just a TLB miss. If the valid bit is on, we can simply retrieve the physical page number from the page table entry and use it to create the TLB entry. A TLB miss can be handled in software or hardware because it will require only a short sequence of operations to copy a valid page table entry from memory into the TLB.

Handling a page fault requires using the exception mechanism to interrupt the active process, transferring control to the operating system, and later resuming execution of the interrupted process. A page fault will be recognized sometime during the clock cycle used to access memory. To restart the instruction after the page fault is handled, the program counter of the instruction that caused the page fault must be saved. Just as in Chapters 5 and 6, the exception program counter (EPC) is used to hold this value.

In addition, the page fault exception must be asserted by the end of the same clock cycle that the memory access occurs, so that the next clock cycle will begin exception processing rather than continue normal instruction execution. If the page fault was not recognized in this clock cycle, a load instruction could overwrite a register, and this could be disastrous when we try to restart the instruction. For example, consider the instruction lw $1,0($1): the machine must be able to prevent the write-back operation from occurring; otherwise, it could not properly restart the instruction, since the contents of $1 would have been destroyed. A similar complication arises on stores. We must prevent the write into memory from actually completing when there is a page fault; this is usually done by deasserting the write control line to the memory.

Once the process that generated the page fault has been interrupted and the operating system has control, it uses the exception Cause register to diagnose the cause of the exception. Because the exception is a page fault, the operating system knows that extensive processing will be required. Thus it saves the entire state of the active process. This state includes all the general-purpose and floating-point registers, the page table address register, the EPC, and the exception Cause register. The virtual address that caused the fault depends on whether the fault was an instruction or data fault. The address of the instruction that generated the fault is in the EPC. If it was an instruction page fault, the EPC contains the virtual address of the faulting page; otherwise, the faulting virtual address can be computed by examining the instruction (whose address is in the EPC) to find the base register and offset field.

Once the operating system knows the virtual address that caused the page fault, it must complete three steps:

1. Look up the page table entry using the virtual address and find the location of the referenced page on disk.

2. Choose a physical page to replace; if the chosen page is dirty, it must be written out to disk before we can bring a new virtual page into this physical page.

3. Start a read to bring the referenced page from disk into the chosen physical page.

Of course, this last step will take millions of processor clock cycles (so will the second if the replaced page is dirty); accordingly, the operating system will usually select another process to execute in the CPU until the disk access completes. Because the operating system has saved the state of the process, it can freely give control of the processor to another process.

When the read of the page from disk is complete, the operating system can restore the state of the process that originally caused the page fault and execute the instruction that returns from the exception. This instruction will reset the processor from kernel to user mode, as well as restore the program counter. The user process then reexecutes the instruction that faulted, accesses the requested page successfully, and continues execution.

Page fault exceptions that occur for data accesses are difficult to implement because of a combination of three characteristics: they occur in the middle of instructions; the instruction cannot be completed before handling the exception; and, after handling the exception, the instruction must be restarted as if nothing had occurred.

Making instructions *restartable*, so that the exception can be handled and the instruction later continued, is relatively easy in an architecture like the MIPS. Because each instruction writes only one data item and this write occurs at the end of the instruction cycle, we can simply prevent the instruction from completing (by not performing the write) and restart the instruction at the beginning.

For machines with much more complex instructions that may touch many memory locations and write many data items, making instructions restartable is much harder. Processing one instruction may generate a number of page faults in the middle of the instruction. For example, some machines have block move instructions that touch thousands of data words. In such machines, instructions often cannot be restarted from the beginning, as we do for MIPS instructions. Instead, the instruction must be interrupted and later continued midstream in its execution. Resuming an instruction in the middle of its execution usually requires saving some special state, processing the exception, and restoring that special state. Making this work properly requires careful and detailed coordination between the exception-handling code in the operating system and the hardware.

**Hardware
Software
Interface**

Between the time we begin executing the exception handler in the operating system and the time that the operating system has saved all the state of the process, the
operating system is particularly vulnerable. For example,
if another exception occurred when we were processing
the first exception in the operating system, the control unit
would overwrite the exception program counter, making it
impossible to return to the instruction that caused the page fault! We can
avoid this disaster by providing the ability to disable and enable exceptions.
When an exception first occurs, we set a bit that disables all other exceptions;
this could happen at the same time we set the supervisor mode bit. The operating system will then save just enough state to allow it to recover if another
exception occurs (namely, the exception program counter and Cause register).
The operating system can then reenable exceptions. These steps make sure
that exceptions will not cause the processor to lose any state and thereby be
unable to restart execution of the interrupting instruction.

**Hardware
Software
Interface**

Because the TLB is the subset of the page table that is
accessed on every cycle, protection violations are also seen
as TLB exceptions. The operating system can handle these
with the same basic hardware that it uses to deal with TLB
misses and page faults. A special set of values in the Cause
register may be used to indicate protection violations (e.g.,
attempt to perform a write when the write access bit is off),
as opposed to a TLB miss. The operating system can access the TLB or page
table entry that matched the virtual page so that it can examine the process's
access rights and report the appropriate error.

Elaboration: Handling TLB misses in software is analogous to handling page
faults: both a TLB miss and a page fault are signaled by the same event in the MIPS
R2000 TLB. To speed up processing of a simple TLB miss that will be much more frequent than a true page fault, two different values for the MIPS Cause register are generated by a TLB miss. One setting indicates that there was no matching TLB entry, while
another setting indicates that the TLB entry exists but that the page is not present in
memory (the TLB valid bit really contains the page table valid bit). On a MIPS
R2000/3000 processor, these two events are distinguished. Because the exception for
TLB entry missing is much more frequent, the operating system loads the TLB from the

page table without examining the entry and restarts the instruction when such an exception occurs. If the entry is invalid, another exception occurs, and the operating system recognizes that a page fault has occurred. This method makes the frequent case of a TLB miss fast, at a slight performance penalty for the infrequent case of a page fault.

Summary

Virtual memory is the name for the level of memory hierarchy that manages caching between the main memory and disk. Virtual memory allows a single program to expand its address space beyond the limits of main memory. More importantly in recent computer systems, virtual memory supports sharing of the main memory among multiple, simultaneously active processes, which together require far more total main memory than exists. To support this sharing, virtual memory also provides mechanisms for memory protection.

Managing the memory hierarchy between main memory and disk is challenging because of the high cost of page faults. Several techniques are used to reduce the miss rate:

1. Blocks, called pages, are made large to take advantage of spatial locality and to reduce the miss rate.

2. The mapping between virtual addresses and physical addresses, which is implemented with a page table, is made fully associative so that a virtual page can be placed anywhere in main memory.

3. The operating system uses techniques, such as LRU and a reference bit, to choose which pages to replace.

Writes to disk are also expensive, so virtual memory uses a write-back scheme and also tracks whether a page is unchanged (with a dirty bit) to avoid writing unchanged pages back to disk.

The virtual memory mechanism also provides address translation from a virtual address used by the program to the physical address space used for accessing memory. This address translation allows protected sharing of the main memory and provides several additional benefits, such as simplifying memory allocation. To ensure that processes are protected from each other requires that only the operating system can change the address translations, which is implemented by preventing user programs from changing the page tables. Controlled sharing of pages among processes can be implemented with the help of the operating system and access bits in the page table that indicate whether the user program has read or write access to a page.

If a CPU had to access a page table resident in memory to translate every access, virtual memory would have too much overhead. Instead, a TLB acts as a cache for translations from the page table. Each address is then translated from a virtual address to a physical address using the translations in the TLB.

Caches, virtual memory, and TLBs all rely on a common set of principles and policies. The next section discusses this common framework.

7.5   A Common Framework for Memory Hierarchies

By now, you've recognized that the different types of memory hierarchies share a great deal in common. Although many of the aspects of memory hierarchies differ quantitatively, many of the policies and features that determine how a hierarchy functions are similar qualitatively. Figure 7.28 shows how some of the quantitative characteristics of memory hierarchies can differ. In the rest of this section, we will discuss the common operational aspects of memory hierarchies and how these determine their behavior. We will examine these policies as a series of four questions that apply between any two levels of a memory hierarchy, although for simplicity we will primarily use terminology for caches.

Question 1: Where Can a Block Be Placed?

We have seen that block placement in the upper level of the hierarchy can use a range of schemes, from direct mapped to set associative to fully associative. As mentioned above, this entire range of schemes can be thought of as variations on a set-associative scheme where the number of sets and the number of blocks per set varies:

Scheme name	Number of sets	Blocks per set
Direct mapped	Number of blocks in cache	1
Set associative	$\dfrac{\text{Number of blocks in cache}}{\text{Associativity}}$	Associativity (typically 2–8)
Fully associative	1	Number of blocks in the cache

Feature	Typical values for caches	Typical values for paged memory	Typical values for a TLB
Total size in blocks	1000–100,000	2000–250,000	32–4,000
Total size in kilobytes	8–8,000	8000–8,000,000	0.25–32
Block size in bytes	16–256	4000–64,000	4–32
Miss penalty in clocks	10–100	1,000,000–10,000,000	10–100
Miss rates	0.1%–10%	0.00001%–0.0001%	0.01%–2%

FIGURE 7.28 The key quantitative design parameters that characterize the three major memory hierarchies in a machine. These are typical values for these levels as of 1997. Although the range of values is wide, this is partially because many of the values that have shifted over time are related; for example, as caches become larger to overcome larger miss penalties, block sizes also grow.

The advantage of increasing the degree of associativity is that it usually decreases the miss rate. The improvement in miss rate comes from reducing misses that compete for the same location. We will examine both of these in more detail shortly. First, let's look at how much improvement is gained. Figure 7.29 shows the data for a workload consisting of the SPEC92 benchmarks with caches of 1 KB to 128 KB, varying from direct mapped to eight-way set associative. The largest gains are obtained in going from direct mapped to two-way

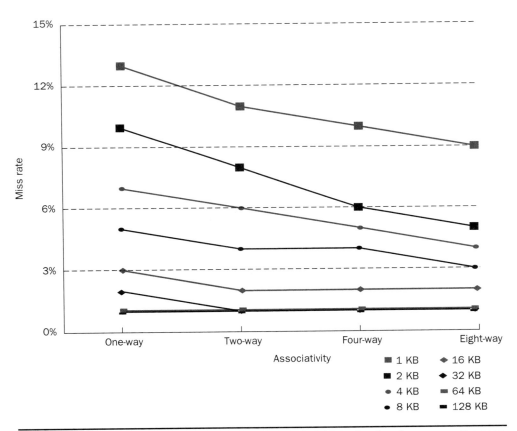

FIGURE 7.29 The miss rates for each of eight cache sizes improve as the associativity increases. While the benefit of going from one-way (direct mapped) to two-way set associative is significant, the benefits of further associativity are smaller (e.g., 8%–16% going from two-way to four-way versus 20%–30% improvement going from one-way to two-way). There is even less improvement in going from four-way to eight-way set associative, which, in turn, comes very close to the miss rates of a fully associative cache. Smaller caches obtain a significantly larger absolute benefit from associativity because the base miss rate of a small cache is larger. This data was generated using the SPEC92 integer and floating-point benchmarks with a 32-byte block size for all caches. This data was collected by Mark Hill and his students and is available online via a link at *www.mkp.com/books_catalog/cod/links.htm.*

set associative, which yields between a 20% and 30% reduction in the miss rate. As cache sizes grow, the relative improvement from associativity is constant or increases slightly; since the overall miss rate of a larger cache is lower, however, the opportunity for improving the miss rate decreases and the absolute improvement in the miss rate from associativity shrinks significantly. The potential disadvantages of associativity, as we mentioned earlier, are increased cost and slower access time.

Question 2: How Is a Block Found?

The choice of how we locate a block depends on the block placement scheme, since that dictates the number of possible locations. We can summarize the schemes as follows:

Associativity	Location method	Comparisons required
Direct mapped	index	1
Set associative	index the set, search among elements	degree of associativity
Full	search all cache entries	size of the cache
	separate lookup table	0

The choice among direct-mapped, set-associative, or fully associative mapping in any memory hierarchy will depend on the cost of a miss versus the cost of implementing associativity, both in time and in extra parts. In general, implementing a high degree of associativity in caches is not worthwhile because the cost in comparators continues to grow, while the miss rate improvements are small. Fully associative caches are prohibitive except for small sizes, where the cost of the comparators is not overwhelming and where the absolute miss rate improvements are greatest.

In virtual memory systems, a separate mapping table (the page table) is kept to index the memory. In addition to the storage required for the table, using an index table requires an extra memory access. The choice of full associativity and the extra table is motivated by four facts:

1. Full associativity is beneficial, since misses are *very* expensive.

2. Full associativity allows software to use sophisticated replacement schemes that are designed to reduce the miss rate. We'll examine these in more detail shortly.

3. The full map can be easily indexed with no extra hardware and no searching required.

4. The large page size means the page table size overhead is relatively small. (The use of a separate lookup table, like a page table for virtual memory, is not practical for a cache because the table would be much larger than a page table and could not be accessed quickly.)

Therefore, virtual memory systems always use fully associative placement.

Set-associative placement is often used for caches and TLBs, where the access combines indexing and the search of a small set. Many recent systems have used direct-mapped caches because of their advantage in access time and simplicity. The advantage in access time occurs because finding the requested block does not depend on a comparison. Such design choices depend on many details of the implementation, such as whether the cache is on-chip or off-chip, the technology used for implementing the cache, and the critical role of cache access time in determining the processor cycle time.

Question 3: Which Block Should Be Replaced on a Cache Miss?

When a miss occurs in an associative cache, we must decide which block to replace. In a fully associative cache, all blocks are candidates for replacement. If the cache is set associative, we must choose among the blocks in the set. Of course, replacement is easy in a direct-mapped cache because there is only one candidate.

We have already mentioned the two primary strategies for replacement in set-associative or fully associative caches:

- *Random:* Candidate blocks are randomly selected, possibly using some hardware assistance.

- *Least recently used (LRU):* The block replaced is the one that has been unused for the longest time.

In practice, LRU is too costly to implement for hierarchies with more than a small degree of associativity (two to four, typically), since tracking the information is costly. Even for four-way set associativity, LRU is often approximated—for example, by keeping track of which of a pair of blocks is LRU (which requires 1 bit), and then tracking which block in each pair is LRU (which requires 1 bit per pair). For larger associativity, LRU is either approximated or random replacement is used. In caches, the replacement algorithm is in hardware, which means that the scheme should be easy to implement. Random replacement is simple to build in hardware, and for a two-way set-associative cache, random replacement has a miss rate about 1.1 times higher than LRU replacement. As the caches become larger, the miss rate for both replacement strategies falls, and the absolute difference becomes small. In fact, random replacement is sometimes better than simple LRU approximations that can be easily implemented in hardware.

In virtual memory, some form of LRU is always approximated since even a tiny reduction in the miss rate can be important when the cost of a miss is enormous. Reference bits or equivalent functionality is often provided to make it easier for the operating system to track a set of less recently used pages. Because misses are so expensive and relatively infrequent, approximating this information primarily in software is acceptable.

Question 4: What Happens on a Write?

A key characteristic of any memory hierarchy is how it deals with writes. We have already seen the two basic options:

- *Write-through*: The information is written to both the block in the cache and to the block in the lower level of the memory hierarchy (main memory for a cache). The caches in section 7.2 used this scheme.

- *Write-back* (also called *copy-back*): The information is written only to the block in the cache. The modified block is written to the lower level of the hierarchy only when it is replaced. Virtual memory systems always use write-back, for the reasons discussed in section 7.4.

Both write-back and write-through have their advantages. The key advantages of write-back are the following:

- Individual words can be written by the processor at the rate that the cache, rather than the memory, can accept them.

- Multiple writes within a block require only one write to the lower level in the hierarchy.

- When blocks are written back, the system can make effective use of a high bandwidth transfer, since the entire block is written.

Write-through has these advantages:

- Misses are simpler and cheaper because they never require a block to be written back to the lower level.

- Write-through is easier to implement than write-back, although to be practical in a high-speed system, a write-through cache will need to use a write buffer.

In virtual memory systems, only a write-back policy is practical because of the long latency of a write to the lower level of the hierarchy (disk). As CPUs continue to increase in performance at a faster rate than DRAM-based main memory, the rate at which writes are generated by a processor will exceed the rate at which the memory system can process them, even allowing for physically and logically wider memories. As a consequence, more and more caches are using or will use a write-back strategy in the future.

Elaboration: Writes introduce several complications into caches that are not present for reads. Here, we discuss two of them: the policy on write misses and efficient implementation of writes in write-back caches.

> **The Big Picture**
>
> While caches, TLBs, and virtual memory may initially look very different, they rely on the same two principles of locality and can be understood by looking at how they deal with four questions:
>
> **Question 1:** Where can a block be placed?
> **Answer:** One place (direct mapped), a few places (set associative), or any place (fully associative).
>
> **Question 2:** How is a block found?
> **Answer:** There are four methods: indexing (as in a direct-mapped cache), limited search (as in a set-associative cache), full search (as in a fully associative cache), and a separate lookup table (as in a page table).
>
> **Question 3:** What block is replaced on a miss?
> **Answer:** Typically, either the least recently used or a random block.
>
> **Question 4:** How are writes handled?
> **Answer:** Each level in the hierarchy can use either write-through or write-back.

Consider a miss in a write-through cache. The strategy followed in most write-through cache designs, called *fetch-on-miss*, *fetch-on-write*, or sometimes *allocate-on-miss*, allocates a cache block to the address that missed and fetches the rest of the block into the cache before writing the data and continuing execution. Alternatively, we could either allocate the block in the cache but not fetch the data (called *no-fetch-on-write*), or even not allocate the block (called *no-allocate-on-write*). Another name for these strategies that do not place the written data into the cache is *write-around*, since the data is written around the cache to get to memory. The motivation for these schemes is the observation that sometimes programs write entire blocks of data before reading them. In such cases, the fetch associated with the initial write miss may be eliminated. There are a number of subtle issues involved in implementing these schemes in multiword blocks, including complicating the handling of write hits by requiring mechanisms similar to those used for write-back caches, which we discuss in the next paragraph. Notice that the DEC 3100 cache is a special case, since the one-word block size allows the cache to implement allocate-on-write without having to do a fetch.

Actually implementing stores efficiently in a cache that uses a write-back strategy is more complex than in a write-through cache. In a write-back cache, we must write the block back to memory if the data in the cache is dirty and we have a cache miss. If we simply overwrote the block on a store before we knew whether the store had hit in the cache (as we could for a write-through cache), we would destroy the contents of the block, which is not backed up in memory. A write-through cache can write the data into the cache and read the tag; if the tag mismatches, then a miss occurs. Because the cache is write-through, the overwriting of the block in the cache is irrelevant.

In a write-back cache, because we cannot overwrite the block, stores either require two cycles (a cycle to check for a hit followed by a cycle to actually perform the write) or require an extra buffer, called a *store buffer*, to hold that data—effectively allowing the store to take only one cycle by pipelining it. When a store buffer is used, the processor does the cache lookup and places the data in the store buffer during the normal cache access cycle. Assuming a cache hit, the data is written from the store buffer into the cache on the next unused cache access cycle.

By comparison, in a write-through cache, writes can always be done in one cycle. There are some extra complications with multiword blocks, however, since we cannot simply overwrite the tag when we write the data. Instead, we read the tag and write the data portion of the selected block. If the tag matches the address of the block being written, the processor can continue normally, since the correct block has been updated. If the tag does not match, the processor generates a write miss to fetch the rest of the block corresponding to that address. Because it is always safe to overwrite the data, write hits still take one cycle.

The Three Cs: An Intuitive Model for Understanding the Behavior of Memory Hierarchies

In this section, we look at a model that provides good insight into the sources of misses in a memory hierarchy and how the misses will be affected by changes in the hierarchy. We will explain the ideas in terms of caches, although the ideas carry over directly to any other level in the hierarchy. In this model, all misses are classified into one of three categories (the three Cs):

- *Compulsory misses*: These are cache misses caused by the first access to a block that has never been in the cache. These are also called *cold-start misses*.

- *Capacity misses*: These are cache misses caused when the cache cannot contain all the blocks needed during execution of a program. Capacity misses occur because of blocks being replaced and later retrieved when accessed.

- *Conflict misses*: These are cache misses that occur in set-associative or direct-mapped caches when multiple blocks compete for the same set. Conflict misses are those misses in a direct-mapped or set-associative cache that are eliminated in a fully associative cache of the same size. These cache misses are also called *collision misses*.

Figure 7.30 shows how the miss rate divides into the three sources. These sources of misses can be directly attacked by changing some aspect of the cache design. Since conflict misses arise directly from contention for the same cache block, increasing associativity reduces conflict misses. Associativity, however, may slow access time, leading to lower overall performance.

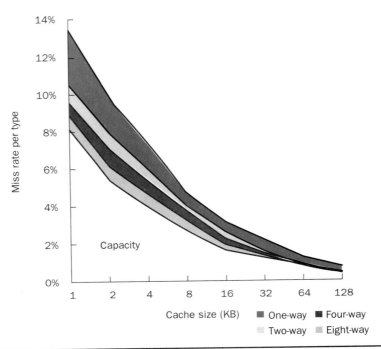

FIGURE 7.30   The miss rate can be broken into three sources of misses. This graph shows the total miss rate and its components for a range of cache sizes. This data is for the SPEC92 integer and floating-point benchmarks and is from the same source as the data in Figure 7.29. The compulsory miss component, which for the long runs seen in the SPEC92 benchmarks and the 32-byte block size is only 0.2%, cannot be seen in this graph. The next component is the capacity miss rate, which depends on cache size. The conflict portion, which depends both on associativity and on cache size, is shown for a range of associativities from one-way to eight-way. In each case, the labeled section corresponds to the increase in the miss rate that occurs when the associativity is changed from the next higher degree to the labeled degree of associativity. For example, the section labeled *two-way* indicates the additional misses arising when the cache has associativity of two rather than four. Thus the difference in the miss rate incurred by a direct-mapped cache versus a fully associative cache of the same size is given by the sum of the sections marked *eight-way*, *four-way*, *two-way*, and *one-way*.

Capacity misses can easily be reduced by enlarging the cache; indeed, caches have been growing steadily larger for many years. Of course, when we make the cache larger we must also be careful about increasing the access time, which could lead to lower overall performance.

Because compulsory misses are generated by the first reference to a block, the primary way for the cache system to reduce the number of compulsory misses is to increase the block size. This will reduce the number of references required to touch each block of the program once because the program will consist of fewer cache blocks. Increasing the block size too much can have a negative effect on performance because of the increase in the miss penalty.

The decomposition of misses into the three Cs is a useful qualitative model. In real cache designs, many of the design choices interact, and changing one cache characteristic will often affect several components of the miss rate. Despite such shortcomings, this model is a useful way to gain insight into the performance of cache designs.

The Big Picture

The challenge in designing memory hierarchies is that every change that potentially improves the miss rate can also negatively affect overall performance, as Figure 7.31 summarizes. This combination of positive and negative effects is what makes the design of a memory hierarchy challenging.

Design change	Effect on miss rate	Possible negative performance effect
Increase size	decreases capacity misses	may increase access time
Increase associativity	decreases miss rate due to conflict misses	may increase access time
Increase block size	decreases miss rate for a wide range of block sizes	may increase miss penalty

FIGURE 7.31 Memory hierarchy design challenges.

7.6 Real Stuff: The Pentium Pro and PowerPC 604 Memory Hierarchies

In this section, we will look at the memory hierarchy in two modern microprocessors: the Intel Pentium Pro (PPro) and the PowerPC (PPC) 604. In 1997, the PPro is used in a variety of high-end PC desktops and servers from a variety of manufacturers, including Dell, DEC, Gateway, HP, Intergraph, and Micron; clock rates range from 150 to 250 MHz. In 1997, the PPC 604 is used in several Apple Macintosh models (7600, 8500, and 9500) and several IBM RS/6000 workstations (41 and 42 series products) at clock rates ranging from 100 to 250 MHz.

Both the PPro and PPC 604 offer support for secondary caches off the main CPU die. The PPro is somewhat unique because it uses a 256-KB or 512-KB secondary cache that is a separate die integrated into the same package, as shown in Figure 7.32. This organization allows a reduced access time to the secondary cache and also reduces the number of pins from the package, since the secondary cache pins remain inside the package. The PPC uses more conventional SRAMs that are separately packaged. The Apple Power Macintosh 7600 and 8500 series use 256-KB secondary caches, while the 9500 series uses a 512-KB secondary cache. The L2 cache organizations are somewhat flexible, with the sizes mentioned here being typical.

Additional Techniques to Reduce Miss Penalties

Both the Pentium Pro and PowerPC 604 have additional optimizations that allow them to reduce the miss penalty. The first of these is the return of the requested word first on a miss, as described in the elaboration on page 559. In addition, the PPC 604 implements optimizations similar to those described on pages 552 and 559, which allow the processor to continue executing instructions during cache misses and to resume execution as soon as the critical word is delivered back to the cache.

The PPro goes a step further than these optimizations, allowing the processor to continue to execute instructions that access the data cache during a cache miss, as opposed to the simpler schemes (early restart and stall on use) that allow only instructions that do not use the data cache to be executed. This technique, called a *nonblocking cache*, is becoming widespread as designers attempt to hide the cache miss latency. The PPro implements both flavors of nonblocking. *Hit under miss* allows additional cache hits during a miss, while *miss under miss* allows multiple outstanding cache misses. The first of these two aims at hiding some of the miss latency with other work, while the second aims at overlapping the latency of two different misses.

FIGURE 7.32   An Intel Pentium Pro showing the secondary cache chip (on the left) packaged together with the processor (on the right). Photo courtesy of Intel.

The Memory Hierarchies of the Pentium Pro and PowerPC 604

The PPro and PPC 604 differ in their address translation, and these differences carry over into the TLB hardware, as shown in Figure 7.33. The PowerPC architecture has a much larger 52-bit virtual address versus the PPro's 32-bit address space.

At the primary cache level, the PPC 604 and PPro differ in size and in the optimizations to reduce the miss penalty, which we discussed earlier. Other than these differences, the primary caches for the two processors are very similar, as shown in Figure 7.34.

Characteristic	Intel Pentium Pro	PowerPC 604
Virtual address	32 bits	52 bits
Physical address	32 bits	32 bits
Page size	4 KB, 4 MB	4 KB, selectable, and 256 MB
TLB organization	A TLB for instructions and a TLB for data Both four-way set associative Pseudo-LRU replacement Instruction TLB: 32 entries Data TLB: 64 entries TLB misses handled in hardware	A TLB for instructions and a TLB for data Both two-way set associative LRU replacement Instruction TLB: 128 entries Data TLB: 128 entries TLB misses handled in hardware

FIGURE 7.33 Address translation and TLB hardware for the Pentium Pro and PowerPC 604. Both machines provide support for large pages, which are used for things like the operating system or mapping a frame buffer. The large-page scheme avoids committing a large number of entries to map a single object that is always present. The PPC 604 also provides a variable page size to enable the use of larger pages (still powers of two).

Characteristic	Intel Pentium Pro	PowerPC 604
Cache organization	Split instruction and data caches	Split instruction and data caches
Cache size	8 KB each for instructions/data	16 KB each for instructions/data
Cache associativity	Four-way set associative	Four-way set associative
Replacement	Approximated LRU replacement	LRU replacement
Block size	32 bytes	32 bytes
Write policy	Write-back	Write-back or write-through

FIGURE 7.34 First-level caches in the Pentium Pro and PowerPC 604. The primary caches in both machines are physically indexed and tagged, like all the other caches we have examined in this chapter; for a discussion of the alternatives, see the elaboration on page 595. The second-level caches for the PPro and PowerPC 604 contain both code and data and are either 256 KB or 512 KB.

The sophisticated memory hierarchies of the PowerPC 604 and Pentium Pro show the significant design effort expended to try to keep the gap between processor cycle times and memory cycle times under control. Future advances in processor pipelines, together with the increased use of multiprocessing (which presents its own problems in memory hierarchies), will provide lots of new challenges for designers.

Elaboration: There are many challenges facing the designers of memory systems for high-performance processors. In this elaboration, we discuss three challenges faced in the PPro and/or PPC 604: supporting multiple memory accesses per clock, taking advantage of nonblocking caches, and efficient implementation of write-back caches.

One of the most significant challenges facing cache designers is to support processors that want to execute more than one memory instruction per clock cycle. For example, the pipeline structure of the Pentium Pro allows both a load and store to be executed on every clock cycle. Multiple requests can be supported in the first-level cache by two different techniques. The cache can be multiported (as our register file is), allowing more than one simultaneous access to the same cache block. Multiporting the cache, however, is often too expensive, since the RAM cells in a multiported memory must be much larger than single-ported cells. Thus this approach is only used for very small caches (tens of entries). The alternative scheme, which is used in the Pentium Pro, is to break the cache into banks and allow multiple, independent accesses (one load and one store), provided the accesses are to two different banks. When a conflict occurs, the load takes priority over the store, since it is most often critical. When such conflicts occur, a buffer for stores allows the processor to avoid stalling, similar to the way a write buffer works.

A second major challenge is integrating and benefiting from the use of nonblocking caches. Obtaining significant performance from nonblocking caches, as in the PPro, requires the use of out-of-order instruction execution, described in the last chapter. Without such a capability, the processor could not hide much of the miss latency, since it would stall for the instruction using the data shortly after detecting the miss. With out-of-order execution, the processor can execute other instructions during the miss time. This ability to continue execution can both hide the miss latency (relying on hit under miss) and find additional misses (relying on miss under miss). To overlap a large fraction of the miss times for two outstanding misses requires a high-bandwidth memory system capable of handling multiple misses in parallel. In desktop systems, the memory may only take small advantage of this capability, but large servers and multiprocessors often have memory systems capable of handling more than one outstanding miss in parallel.

As write-back caches become the norm, implementing them efficiently becomes increasingly important. When we discussed write-through caches, we described the need for write buffers to make such caches practical. Many write-back caches also include write buffers that are used to reduce the miss penalty when a miss requires replacing a dirty block. In such a case, rather than first write out the dirty block to memory and then read the requested block (forcing the processor to stall for two memory access cycles), the dirty block is moved to a write-back buffer associated with the cache, the requested block is read from memory, and execution is resumed (with a stall of only one memory access cycle). The write-back buffer is then written back to memory. Assuming another miss does not occur immediately, this technique halves the miss penalty when a dirty block must be replaced. The Intel PPro uses such write-back buffers for both the primary and secondary caches.

7.7 Fallacies and Pitfalls

As one of the most naturally quantitative aspects of the computer architecture, memory hierarchy would seem to be less vulnerable to fallacies and pitfalls. Not only have there been many fallacies propagated and pitfalls encountered, but some have led to major negative outcomes. We start with a pitfall that often traps students in exercises and exams.

Pitfall: Forgetting to account for byte addressing or the cache block size in simulating a cache.

When simulating a cache (by hand or machine), we need to make sure we account for the effect of byte addressing or multiword blocks in determining which cache block a given address maps into. For example, if we have a 32-byte, direct-mapped cache with a block size of 4 bytes, the byte address 36 maps into block 1 of the cache, since byte address 36 is block address 9 and (9 modulo 8) = 1. On the other hand, if address 36 is a word address, then it maps into block (36 mod 8) = 4. Make sure the problem clearly states the base of the address.

In like fashion, we must account for the block size. Suppose we have a cache with 256 bytes and a block size of 32 bytes. Which block does the byte address 300 fall into? Byte address 300 is block address

$$\left\lfloor \frac{300}{32} \right\rfloor = 9$$

The number of blocks in the cache is

$$\left\lfloor \frac{256}{32} \right\rfloor = 8$$

Block number 9 falls into cache block number (9 modulo 8) = 1.

This mistake catches many people, including authors (in earlier drafts) and instructors who forget whether they intended the addresses to be in words, bytes, or block numbers. Remember this pitfall when you tackle the exercises.

Pitfall: Using miss rate as the only metric for evaluating a memory hierarchy.

As we just discussed, miss rate can be a misleading metric when other cache parameters are ignored. Let's consider a specific example. Suppose that we were running the workload used for the measurements in Figure 7.29 on page 604. Increasing the direct-mapped cache size from 16 KB to 32 KB reduces the miss rate from 3.0% to about 2.0% for a two-way set-associative cache. Suppose the machine with the larger cache has a clock cycle time of 2 ns, while the machine with the smaller cache has a clock cycle time of 1.6 ns, and we assume that the CPI without memory stalls is the same. If the miss penalty to the secondary cache is 20 ns and there are 1.5 memory references per instruction (1 instruction reference and 0.5 data references), the machine with the larger cache is actually slower, despite its superior cache hit rate. To see this, use the following equation:

$$\text{CPU time} = (\text{CPU execution clock cycles} + \text{Memory-stall clock cycles}) \times \text{Clock cycle time}$$

where the memory-stall cycles are given using the equation from page 565:

$$\text{Memory-stall clock cycles} = \frac{\text{Instructions}}{\text{Program}} \times \frac{\text{Misses}}{\text{Instruction}} \times \text{Miss penalty}$$

The term *misses per instruction* combines the instruction and data miss rates into a single term:

$$\frac{\text{Misses}}{\text{Instruction}} = \text{Instruction miss rate} + \left(\text{Data miss rate} \times \frac{\text{Data references}}{\text{Instruction}} \right)$$

For the smaller cache (using I to stand for *instructions per program*),

$$\text{Memory-stall clock cycles} = I \times (3\% \times 1.5) \ \times \left\lceil \frac{\text{Absolute miss penalty}}{\text{Clock cycle time}} \right\rceil$$

$$\text{Memory-stall clock cycles} = I \times 0.045 \times \left\lceil \frac{20}{1.6} \right\rceil = 0.585 \times I$$

For the machine with the larger cache,

$$\text{Memory-stall clock cycles} = I \times (2\% \times 1.5) \ \times \left\lceil \frac{\text{Absolute miss penalty}}{\text{Clock cycle time}} \right\rceil$$

$$\text{Memory-stall clock cycles} = I \times 0.030 \times \left\lceil \frac{20}{2} \right\rceil = 0.30 \times I$$

Now we can put these pieces into the CPU time equation. Let the CPI without memory stalls be C. Then the number of CPU execution clock cycles is $C \times I$. This leads to the following CPU execution time for the machine with the smaller cache:

$$\text{CPU time} = (\text{CPU execution clock cycles} + \text{Memory-stall clock cycles}) \times \text{Clock cycle time}$$

$$\text{CPU time} = ((C \times I) + (0.585 \times I)) \times 1.6 \text{ ns} = (1.6C + 0.936) \times I$$

Now, for the larger cache we obtain

$$\text{CPU time} = ((C \times I) + (0.30 \times I)) \times 2 \text{ ns} = (2C + 0.6) \times I$$

Thus the machine with the larger cache is faster if $(1.6C + 0.936) > (2C + 0.6)$, which is true only if $(C < 0.84)$. So for machines with a pipelined CPI greater than 0.84, the machine with the smaller cache is faster.

Although it seems obvious that focusing on cache miss rate, and ignoring the impact of the cache design on the clock cycle time, would be a mistake, many designers have focused primarily on miss rate in the past, ignoring implications on cycle time.

Pitfall: Ignoring memory system behavior in writing programs or in generating code in a compiler.

This could have easily be written as a fallacy: "Programmers can ignore memory hierarchies in writing code." We illustrate an example that shows this using matrix multiply, but there are many examples we could use.

Here is the inner loop of the version of matrix multiply from Chapter 4:

```
for (i=0; i!=500; i=i+1)
    for (j=0; j!=500; j=j+1)
        for (k=0; k!=500; k=k+1)
            x[i][j] = x[i][j] + y[i][k] * z[k][j];
```

When run with inputs that are 500×500 double precision matrices, the CPU runtime of the above loop on a Silicon Graphics Challenge L containing a MIPS R4000 with a 1-MB secondary cache is 77.2 seconds. If the loop order is changed to k,j,i (so i is innermost), the runtime drops to 44.2 seconds! The only difference is how the program accesses memory and the ensuing effect on the memory hierarchy. Further compiler optimizations using a technique called *blocking* can result in a runtime that is under 10 seconds for this code! This optimization was the basis for the matrix300 results we discussed in Chapter 2.

Pitfall: Extending an address space by adding segments on top of an unsegmented address space.

During the 1970s, many programs grew so large that not all the code and data could be addressed with just a 16-bit address. Machines were then revised to offer 32-bit addresses, either through an unsegmented 32-bit address space (also called a *flat address space*) or by adding 16 bits of segment to the existing 16-bit address. From a marketing point of view, adding segments that were programmer-visible and that forced the programmer and compiler to decompose programs into segments could solve the addressing problem. Unfortunately, there is trouble any time a programming language wants an address that is larger than one segment, such as indices for large arrays, unrestricted pointers, or reference parameters. Moreover, adding segments can turn every address into two words—one for the segment number and one for the segment offset—causing problems in the use of addresses in registers. As this book is being completed, the limits of 32-bit addresses are being reached. Some architectures, such as the MIPS R4000, DEC Alpha, and Sun SPARC, have chosen to support 64-bit flat address spaces. Others, such as HP PA-RISC, are providing an extended address space via segmentation, as a temporary solution. Still other architectures, such as the 80x86, are expected to be replaced by a new 64-bit architecture.

7.8   Concluding Remarks

The difficulty of building a memory system to keep pace with faster CPUs is underscored by the fact that the raw material for main memory, DRAMs, is essentially the same in the fastest computers as it is in the slowest and cheapest. It is the principle of locality that gives us a chance to overcome the long latency of memory access—and the soundness of this strategy is demonstrated at all levels of the memory hierarchy. Although these levels of the hierarchy look quite different in quantitative terms, they follow similar strategies in their operation and exploit the same properties of locality.

Because CPU speeds continue to increase faster than either DRAM access times or disk access times, memory will increasingly be the factor that limits performance. Processors continue to increase in performance at a spectacular rate, and DRAMs show signs of continuing their fourfold improvement in density every three years. The *access time* of DRAMs, however, is improving at a much slower rate—about 9% per year. Figure 7.35 plots optimistic and pessimistic processor cycle time estimates against the steady 9% annual performance improvement in DRAM speeds. This data includes only the effect of decreasing processor cycle times. Processors have also been reducing the CPI component of performance, leading to more memory access per cycle and a relatively larger penalty for long memory access times.

Recent enhancements in DRAM technology (synchronous DRAMs and related techniques) have led to increases in potential memory bandwidth. This potentially higher memory bandwidth has enabled designers to increase cache block sizes with smaller increases in the miss penalty. In the future, such enhancements and design trade-offs will be critical to limiting the performance loss in the memory system.

Recent Trends

The challenge in designing memory hierarchies to close this growing gap, as we noted in the Big Picture on page 611, is that all the hardware design choices for memory hierarchies have both a positive and negative effect on performance. This means that for each level of the hierarchy there is an opti-

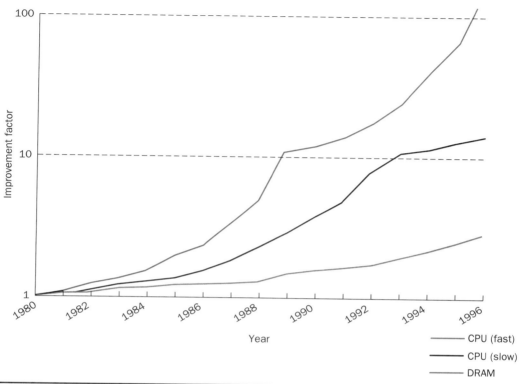

FIGURE 7.35   Using their 1980 performance as a baseline, the access time of DRAMs versus the cycle time of processors is plotted over time. The DRAM baseline is 64 KB in 1980, and the average improvement in access time per year is 9%. Both the fast and slow processor performance lines are based on typical processors produced during this time. The slow processor line shows a 15% improvement per year in cycle time until 1985 and a 25% improvement thereafter. The fast processor line shows a 25% performance improvement per year in clock rate between 1980 and 1985 and 40% per year thereafter. Of course, processor performance has increased by more than just cycle time. Reductions in CPI have yielded an additional factor of 15–20 in performance for the fast CPUs over the period shown in the graph. This reduction in CPI further enlarges the losses due to memory system performance, although the increasing CPI gap may not lead to larger access times for a cache hit. Note that the vertical axis must be on a logarithmic scale to record the size of the processor-DRAM performance gap.

mal performance point, which must include some misses. If this is the case, how can we overcome the growing gap between CPU speeds and lower levels of the hierarchy? This question is currently the topic of much research.

On-chip first-level caches have helped close the gap that was growing between CPU clock cycle time and off-chip SRAM cycle time. To narrow the gap between the small on-chip caches and DRAM, second-level caches became widespread. Today, all mid-range and high-end desktop machines use second-level caches. In fact, high-end servers are using second-level caches of 1–16 MB! Second-level caches also make it possible to more easily use other optimizations for two reasons. First, the design parameters of a second-level cache are different than a first-level cache. For example, because a second-level cache will be much larger, it is possible to use larger block sizes. Second, a second-level cache is not constantly being used by the CPU, as a first-level cache is. This allows us to consider having the second-level cache do something when it is idle that may be useful in preventing future misses; we will see an example of this in just a bit.

Another attempt to reduce the processor-DRAM performance gap is to re-assess the interface on the DRAM chips. Several efforts are under way to redesign that interface to offer much higher bandwidth than standard DRAMs, in part by supplying a clock to DRAM chips to synchronize transfers and in part by increasing the number of pins on the DRAMS. These techniques make it easier to justify increasing the block size, since the transfer time component of the miss penalty can be made smaller. Although such DRAMs currently have a price premium (10%–30%, typically), it appears that, at least in some environments, designers are willing to pay these higher costs. A related development has been the use of synchronous SRAMs, which are being used for secondary caches, and which help reduce the time to transfer a block from the secondary to the primary cache. Synchronous SRAMs are becoming the default for secondary caches.

Another possible direction is to seek software help. Efficiently managing the memory hierarchy using a variety of program transformation and hardware facilities is a major focus of research in compilers. Two different ideas are being explored. One idea is to reorganize the program to enhance its spatial and temporal locality. This approach focuses on loop-oriented programs that use large arrays as the major data structure; large linear algebra problems are a typical example. By restructuring the loops that access the arrays, substantially improved locality—and, therefore, cache performance—can be obtained. The example on page 617 showed how effective even a simple change of loop structure could be.

Another direction is to try to use compiler-directed *prefetching*. In prefetching, a block of data is brought into the cache before it is actually referenced. The compiler tries to identify data blocks needed in the future and, using special instructions, tells the memory hierarchy to move the blocks into the cache. When the block is actually referenced, it is found in the cache, rather than causing a cache miss. The use of secondary caches has made prefetching even more attractive, since the secondary cache can be involved in a prefetch, while the primary cache continues to service processor requests.

As we will see in Chapter 9, memory systems are also a central design issue for parallel processors. The growing importance of the memory hierarchy in determining system performance in both uniprocessor and multiprocessor systems means that this important area will continue to be a focus of both designers and researchers for some years to come.

7.9   Historical Perspective and Further Reading

. . . the one single development that put computers on their feet was the invention of a reliable form of memory, namely, the core memory. . . . Its cost was reasonable, it was reliable and, because it was reliable, it could in due course be made large.

Maurice Wilkes,
Memoirs of a Computer Pioneer, 1985

The developments of most of the concepts in this chapter have been driven by revolutionary advances in the technology we use for memory. Before we discuss how memory hierarchies were developed, let's take a brief tour of the development of memory technology. In this section, we focus on the technologies for building main memory and caches; Chapter 8 will provide some of the history of developments in disk technology.

The ENIAC had only a small number of registers (about 20) for its storage and implemented these with the same basic vacuum tube technology that it used for building logic circuitry. However, the vacuum tube technology was far too expensive to be used to build a larger memory capacity. Eckert came up with the idea of developing a new technology based on mercury delay lines. In this technology, electrical signals were converted into vibrations that were sent down a tube of mercury, reaching the other end, where they were read out and recirculated. One mercury delay line could store about 0.5 Kbits. Although these bits were accessed serially, the mercury delay line was about a hundred times more cost-effective than vacuum tube memory. The first known working mercury delay lines were developed at Cambridge for the EDSAC. Figure 7.36 shows the mercury delay lines of the EDSAC, which had 32 tanks and a total of 512 36-bit words.

Despite the tremendous advance offered by the mercury delay lines, they were terribly unreliable and still rather expensive. The breakthrough came with the invention of core memory by J. Forrester at MIT as part of the Whirlwind project, in the early 1950s (see Figure 7.37). Core memory uses a ferrite core, which can be magnetized, and once magnetized, acts as a store (just as a magnetic recording tape stores information). A set of wires running through

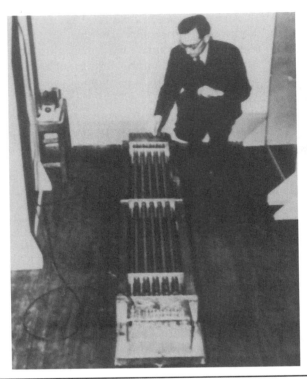

FIGURE 7.36   The mercury delay lines in the EDSAC. This technology made it possible to build the first stored-program computer. The young engineer in this photograph is none other than Maurice Wilkes, the lead architect of the EDSAC. Photo courtesy of the Computer Museum, Boston.

the center of the core, which had a dimension of 0.1–1.0 millimeters, make it possible to read the value stored on any ferrite core. The Whirlwind eventually included a core memory with 2048 16-bit words, or a total of 32 Kbits. Core memory was a tremendous advance: It was cheaper, faster, much more reliable, and had higher density. Core memory was so much better than the alternatives that it became the dominant memory technology only a few years after its invention and remained so for nearly 20 years.

The technology that replaced core memory was the same one that we now use both for logic and memory: the integrated circuit. While registers were built out of transistorized memory in the 1960s, and IBM machines used transistorized memory for microcode store and caches in 1970, building main

FIGURE 7.37 A core memory plane from the Whirlwind containing 256 cores arranged in a 16 x 16 array. Core memory was invented for the Whirlwind, which was used for air defense problems, and is now on display at the Smithsonian. (Incidentally, Ken Olsen, the founder and president of Digital for 20 years, built the machine that tested these core memories; it was his first computer.) Photo courtesy of the Computer Museum, Boston.

memory out of transistors remained prohibitive until the development of the integrated circuit. With the integrated circuit, it became possible to build a DRAM (dynamic random access memory—see Appendix B for a description). The first DRAMS were built at Intel in 1970, and the machines using DRAM memories (as a high-speed option to core) came shortly thereafter; they used 1-Kbit DRAMs. In fact, computer folklore says that Intel developed the microprocessor partly to help sell more DRAM. Figure 7.38 shows an early DRAM board. By the late 1970s, core memory became a historical curiosity. Just as core memory technology had allowed a tremendous expansion in memory size, DRAM technology allowed a comparable expansion. In the 1990s, many personal computers have as much memory as the largest machines using core memory ever had.

Nowadays, DRAMs are typically packaged with multiple chips on a little board called SIMM (single inline memory module) or DIMM (dual inline memory module). The SIMM shown in Figure 7.39 contains a total of 1 MB and sells for about $5 in 1997. In 1997, SIMMs and DIMMs are available with up to 64 MB. While DRAMs will remain the dominant memory technology for some time to come, dramatic innovations in the packaging of DRAMs to provide both higher bandwidth and greater density are ongoing.

FIGURE 7.38   An early DRAM board. This board uses 18-Kbit chips. Photo courtesy of IBM.

FIGURE 7.39   A 1-MB SIMM, built in 1986, using 1-Mbit chips. This SIMM, used in a Macintosh, sells for about $5/MB in 1997. In 1997, most main memory is packed in either SIMMs or DIMMs similar to this, though using much higher-density memory chips (16-Mbit or 64-Mbit). Photo courtesy of MIPS Technology, Inc.

The Development of Memory Hierarchies

Although the pioneers of computing foresaw the need for a memory hierarchy and coined the term, the automatic management of two levels was first proposed by Kilburn and his colleagues and demonstrated at the University of Manchester with the Atlas computer, which implemented virtual memory. This was the year *before* the IBM 360 was announced. IBM planned to include virtual memory with the next generation (System/370), but the OS/360 operating system wasn't up to the challenge in 1970. Virtual memory was announced for the 370 family in 1972, and it was for this machine that the term *translation-lookaside buffer* was coined. The only computers today without virtual memory are a few supercomputers, and even they may add this feature in the near future.

The problems of inadequate address space have plagued designers repeatedly. The architects of the PDP-11 identified a small address space as the only architectural mistake that is difficult to recover from. When the PDP-11 was designed, core memory densities were increasing at a very slow rate, and the competition from 100 other minicomputer companies meant that DEC might not have a cost-competitive product if every address had to go through the 16-bit datapath twice. Hence the decision to add just 4 more address bits than the predecessor of the PDP-11. The architects of the IBM 360 were aware of the importance of address size and planned for the architecture to extend to 32 bits of address. Only 24 bits were used in the IBM 360, however, because the low-end 360 models would have been even slower with the larger addresses. Unfortunately, the expansion effort was greatly complicated by programmers who stored extra information in the upper 8 "unused" address bits.

Running out of address space has often been the cause of death for an architecture, while other architectures have managed to make the transition to a larger address space. For example, the PDP-11, a 16-bit machine, was replaced by the 32-bit VAX. The 80386 extended the 80286 architecture from 16 bits to 32 bits. Several recent RISC instruction sets have made the transition from 32-bit addressing to 64-bit addressing by providing a compatible extension of their instruction sets. Intel has announced a plan to develop a new instruction set jointly with HP. This new instruction set will provide 64-bit addressing.

Many of the early ideas in memory hierarchies originated in England. Just a few years after the Atlas paper, Wilkes [1965] published the first paper describing the concept of a cache, calling it a "slave:"

The use is discussed of a fast core memory of, say, 32,000 words as slave to a slower core memory of, say, one million words in such a way that in practical cases the effective access time is nearer that of the fast memory than that of the slow memory.

This two-page paper describes a direct-mapped cache. Although this was the first publication on caches, the first implementation was probably a direct-mapped instruction cache built at the University of Cambridge by Scarrott and described at the 1965 IFIP Congress. It was based on tunnel diode memory, the fastest form of memory available at the time.

Subsequent to that publication, IBM started a project that led to the first commercial machine with a cache, the IBM 360/85. Gibson at IBM recognized that memory-accessing behavior would have a significant impact on performance.

He described how to measure program behavior and cache behavior and showed that the miss rate varies between programs. Using a sample of 20 programs (each with 3 million references—an incredible number for that time), Gibson analyzed the effectiveness of caches using average memory access time as the metric. Conti, Gibson, and Pitkowsky described the resulting performance of the 360/85 in the first paper to use the term *cache* in 1968. Since this early work, it has become clear that caches are one of the most important ideas not only in computer architecture, but in software systems as well. The idea of caching has found applications in operating systems, networking systems, databases, and compilers, to name a few. There are thousands of papers on the topic of caching, and it continues to be an important area of research.

Protection Mechanisms

Architectural support for protection has varied greatly over the past 20 years. In early machines, before virtual memory, protection was very simple at best. In the 1970s, more elaborate mechanisms that supported different protection levels (called *rings*) were invented. In the late 1970s and early 1980s, very elaborate mechanisms for protection were devised and later built; these mechanisms supported a variety of powerful protection schemes that allowed controlled instances of sharing, in such a way that a process could share data while controlling exactly what was done to the data. The most powerful method, called *capabilities*, created a data object that described the access rights to some portion of memory. These capabilities could then be passed to other processes, thus granting access to the object described by the capability. Supporting this sophisticated protection mechanism was both complex and costly because creation, copying, and manipulation of capabilities required a combination of operating system and hardware support. Recent machines all support a simpler protection scheme based on virtual memory, similar to that discussed in section 7.4.

To Probe Further

Conti, C., D. H. Gibson, and S. H. Pitowsky [1968]. "Structural aspects of the System/360 Model 85, part I: General organization," *IBM Systems J.* 7:1, 2–14.

Describes the first commercial machine to use a cache and its resulting performance.

Hennessy, J., and D. Patterson [1996]. Chapter 5 in *Computer Architecture: A Quantitative Approach*, Second edition, Morgan Kaufmann Publishers, San Francisco.

For more in-depth coverage of a variety of topics including protection, improving write performance, virtually addressed caches, multilevel caches, additional latency tolerance mechanisms, and cache coherency.

Kilburn, T., D. B. G. Edwards, M. J. Lanigan, and F. H. Sumner [1962]. "One-level storage system," *IRE Transactions on Electronic Computers* EC-11 (April) 223–35. Also appears in D. P. Siewiorek, C. G. Bell, and A. Newell, *Computer Structures: Principles and Examples*, McGraw-Hill, New York, 135–48, 1982.

This classic paper is the first proposal for virtual memory.

Przybylski, S. A. [1990]. *Cache and Memory Hierarchy Design: A Performance-Directed Approach*, Morgan Kaufmann Publishers, San Francisco.

A thorough exploration of multilevel memory hierarchies and their performance.

Silberschatz, A., and P. Galvin [1994]. *Operating System Concepts*, Addison-Wesley, Reading, MA.

An operating systems textbook with a thorough discussion of virtual memory, processes and process management, and protection issues.

Smith, A. J. [1982]. "Cache memories," *Computing Surveys* 14:3 (September) 473–530.

The classic survey paper on caches. This paper defined the terminology for the field and has served as a reference for many computer designers.

Tanenbaum, A. [1991]. *Operating Systems Principles*, Addison-Wesley, Reading, MA.

An operating system textbook with a good discussion of virtual memory.

Wilkes, M. [1965]. "Slave memories and dynamic storage allocation," *IEEE Trans. Electronic Computers* EC-14:2 (April) 270–71.

The first, classic paper on caches.

7.10 Key Terms

Designers have developed a wide variety of strategies that rely on locality to overcome the gap between processor and main memory, leading to a large amount of terminology to describe these schemes.

address translation or mapping
aliasing
block
cache miss
capacity miss
compulsory or cold start miss
conflict or collision miss
context switch
exception or direct-mapped cache
fully associative cache
global miss rate
hit rate
hit time
interrupt enable
kernel or supervisor mode

least recently used (LRU)
local miss rate
memory hierarchy
miss penalty
miss rate
multilevel cache
nonblocking cache
page fault
page table
physical address
physically addressed cache
prefetching
protection
reference or use bit
restartable instruction
segmentation
set-associative cache

spatial locality
split cache
system call
tag
temporal locality
three Cs model
translation-lookaside buffer (TLB)
valid bit
virtual address
virtual memory
virtually addressed cache
write-back
write buffer
write-through

7.11 Exercises

7.1 [10] <§7.2> Describe the general characteristics of a program that would exhibit very little temporal and spatial locality with regard to data accesses. Provide an example program (pseudocode is fine).

7.2 [10] <§7.2> Describe the general characteristics of a program that would exhibit very high amounts of temporal locality but very little spatial locality with regard to data accesses. Provide an example program (pseudocode is fine).

7.3 [10] <§7.2> Describe the general characteristics of a program that would exhibit very little temporal locality but very high amounts of spatial locality with regard to data accesses. Provide an example program (pseudocode is fine).

7.4 [10] <§7.2> Describe the general characteristics of a program that would exhibit very little temporal and spatial locality with regard to instruction fetches. Provide an example program (pseudocode is fine).

7.5 [10] <§7.2> Describe the general characteristics of a program that would exhibit very high amounts of temporal locality but very little spatial locality with regard to instruction fetches. Provide an example program (pseudocode is fine).

7.6 [10] <§7.2> Describe the general characteristics of a program that would exhibit very little temporal locality but very high amounts of spatial locality with regard to instruction fetches. Provide an example program (pseudocode is fine).

7.7 [10] <§7.2> Here is a series of address references given as word addresses: 1, 4, 8, 5, 20, 17, 19, 56, 9, 11, 4, 43, 5, 6, 9, 17. Assuming a direct-mapped cache with 16 one-word blocks that is initially empty, label each reference in the list as a hit or a miss and show the final contents of the cache.

7.8 [10] <§7.2> Using the series of references given in Exercise 7.7, show the hits and misses and final cache contents for a direct-mapped cache with four-word blocks and a *total size* of 16 words.

7.9 [10] <§7.2> Compute the total number of bits required to implement the cache in Figure 7.10 on page 557. This number is different from the size of the cache, which usually refers to the number of bytes of data stored in the cache. The number of bits needed to implement the cache represents the total amount of memory needed for storing all of the data, tags, and valid bits.

7.10 [10] <§7.2> Find a method to eliminate the AND gate on the valid bit in Figure 7.7 on page 549. (Hint: You need to change the comparison.)

7.11 [10] <§7.2> Consider a memory hierarchy using one of the three organizations for main memory shown in Figure 7.13 on page 561. Assume that the cache block size is 16 words, that the width of organization b of the figure is four words, and that the number of banks in organization c is four. If the main memory latency for a new access is 10 cycles and the transfer time is 1 cycle, what are the miss penalties for each of these organizations?

7.12 [10] <§7.2> {Ex. 7.11} Suppose a processor with a 16-word block size has an effective miss rate per instruction of 0.5%. Assume that the CPI without cache misses is 1.2. Using the memories described in Figure 7.13 on page 561 and Exercise 7.11, how much faster is this processor when using the wide memory than when using narrow or interleaved memories?

7.13 [15] <§7.2> Cache C1 is direct-mapped with 16 one-word blocks. Cache C2 is direct-mapped with 4 four-word blocks. Assume that the miss penalty for C1 is 8 clock cycles and the miss penalty for C2 is 11 clock cycles. Assuming that the caches are initially empty, find a reference string for which C2 has a lower miss rate but spends more cycles on cache misses than C1. Use word addresses.

7.14 [15] <§7.2> For the caches in Exercise 7.13, find a series of references for which C2 has more misses than C1. Use word addresses.

In More Depth

Average Memory Access Time

To capture the fact that the time to access data for both hits and misses affects performance, designers often use average memory access time (AMAT) as a way to examine alternative cache designs. Average memory access time is the average time to access memory considering both hits and misses and the frequency of different accesses; it is equal to the following:

$$AMAT = \text{Time for a hit} + \text{Miss rate} \times \text{Miss penalty}$$

AMAT is useful as a figure of merit for different cache systems.

7.15 [5] <§7.2> Find the AMAT for a machine with a 2-ns clock, a miss penalty of 20 clock cycles, a miss rate of 0.05 misses per instruction, and a cache access time (including hit detection) of 1 clock cycle. Assume that the read and write miss penalties are the same and ignore other write stalls.

7.16 [5] <§7.2> {Ex. 7.15} Suppose we can improve the miss rate to 0.03 misses per reference by doubling the cache size. This causes the cache access time to increase to 1.2 clock cycles. Using the AMAT as a metric, determine if this is a good trade-off.

7.17 [10] <§7.2> [Ex. 7.16} If the cache access time determines the processor's clock cycle time, which is often the case, AMAT may not correctly indicate whether one cache organization is better than another. If the machine's clock cycle time must be changed to match that of a cache, is this a good trade-off? Assume the machines are identical except for the clock rate and the number of cache miss cycles; assume 1.5 references per instruction and a CPI without cache misses of 2. The miss penalty is 20 cycles for both machines.

7.18 [10] <§§7.2, B.5> You have been given 18 32K × 8-bit SRAMs to build an instruction cache for a processor with a 32-bit address. What is the largest size (i.e., the largest size of the data storage area in bytes) direct-mapped instruction cache that you can build with one-word (32-bit) blocks? Show the breakdown of the address into its cache access components (for an example, see Figure 7.8) and describe how the various SRAM chips will be used. (Hint: You may not need all of them.)

7.19 [10] <§§7.2, B.5> This exercise is similar to Exercise 7.18, except that this time you decide to build a direct-mapped cache with four-word blocks as in Figure 7.10. Once again show the breakdown of the address and describe how the chips are used.

7.20 [10] <§7.3> Using the series of references given in Exercise 7.7, show the hits and misses and final cache contents for a two-way set-associative cache with one-word blocks and a *total size* of 16 words. Assume LRU replacement.

7.21 [10] <§7.3> Using the series of references given in Exercise 7.7, show the hits and misses and final cache contents for a fully associative cache with one-word blocks and a *total size* of 16 words. Assume LRU replacement.

7.22 [10] <§7.3> Using the series of references given in Exercise 7.7, show the hits and misses and final cache contents for a fully associative cache with four-word blocks and a *total size* of 16 words. Assume LRU replacement.

7.23 [5] <§7.3> Associativity usually improves the miss ratio, but not always. Give a short series of address references for which a two-way set-associative cache with LRU replacement would experience more misses than a direct-mapped cache of the same size.

7.24 [15] <§7.3> Suppose a computer's address size is k bits (using byte addressing), the cache size is S bytes, the block size is B bytes, and the cache is A-way set-associative. Assume that B is a power of two, so $B = 2^b$. Figure out what the following quantities are in terms of *S, B, A, b,* and *k*: the number of sets in the cache, the number of index bits in the address, and the number of bits needed to implement the cache (see Exercise 7.9).

7.25 [10] <§7.3> This exercise concerns caches of unusual sizes. Can you make a fully associative cache containing exactly 3K words of data? How about a set-associative cache or a direct-mapped cache containing exactly 3K words of data? For each of these, describe how or why not. Remember that $1K = 2^{10}$.

7.26 [10] <§7.3> This exercise is similar to Exercise 7.25, except replace 3K with 300. Remember that $300 = 3 * 10^2$.

7.27 [20] <§7.3> Consider three machines with different cache configurations:

- *Cache 1:* Direct-mapped with one-word blocks
- *Cache 2:* Direct-mapped with four-word blocks
- *Cache 3:* Two-way set associative with four-word blocks

The following miss rate measurements have been made:

- *Cache 1:* Instruction miss rate is 4%; data miss rate is 8%.
- *Cache 2:* Instruction miss rate is 2%; data miss rate is 5%.
- *Cache 3:* Instruction miss rate is 2%; data miss rate is 4%.

For these machines, one-half of the instructions contain a data reference. Assume that the cache miss penalty is 6 + Block size in words. The CPI for this workload was measured on a machine with cache 1 and was found to be 2.0. Determine which machine spends the most cycles on cache misses.

7.28 [5] <§7.3> {Ex. 7.27} The cycle times for the machines in Exercise 7.27 are 2 ns for the first and second machines and 2.4 ns for the third machine. Determine which machine is the fastest and which is the slowest.

7.29 [10] <§§7.2, 7.3> The following C program is run (with no optimizations) on a machine with a cache that has four-word (16-byte) blocks and holds 256 bytes of data:

```
int i,j,c,stride,array[256];
...
for (i=0; i<10000; i++)
  for (j=0; j<256; j=j+stride)
    c = array[j]+5;
```

If we consider only the cache activity generated by references to the array and we assume that integers are words, what is the expected miss rate when the cache is direct-mapped and stride = 132? How about if stride = 131? Would either of these change if the cache were two-way set associative?

7.30 [10] <§§7.3, B.5> This exercise is similar to Exercise 7.18, except that this time you decide to build a three-way set-associative cache with one-word blocks. Once again show the breakdown of the address (see Figure 7.19 for an example of a four-way set-associative cache) and describe how the chips are used. Note that each SRAM will only perform a single read per cache access.

7.31 [5] <§§7.2–7.4> Rank each of the possible event combinations appearing in the example on page 595 according to how frequently you think they would occur.

7.32 [15] <§7.4> Consider a virtual memory system with the following properties:

- 40-bit virtual byte address
- 16-KB pages
- 36-bit physical byte address

What is the total size of the page table for each process on this machine, assuming that the valid, protection, dirty, and use bits take a total of 4 bits and that all the virtual pages are in use? (Assume that disk addresses are not stored in the page table.)

7.33 [15] <§7.4> Assume that the virtual memory system of Exercise 7.32 is implemented with a two-way set-associative TLB with a total of 256 TLB entries. Show the virtual-to-physical mapping with a figure like Figure 7.25 on page 593. Make sure to label the width of all fields and signals.

7.34 [15] <§7.3> Assume that the cache for the system described in Exercise 7.32 is two-way set associative and has eight-word blocks and a total size of 16 KB. Show the cache organization and access using the same format as Figure 7.19 on page 574.

7.35 [15] <§7.4> Page tables require fairly large amounts of memory (as described in the elaboration on page 587), even if most of the entries are invalid. One solution is to use a hierarchy of page tables. The virtual page number, as described in Figure 7.21 on page 582, can be broken up into two pieces, a "page table number" and a "page table offset." The page table number can be used to index a first-level page table that provides a physical address for a second-level page table, assuming it resides in memory (if not, a first-level page fault will occur and the page table itself will need to be brought in from disk). The page table offset is used to index into the second-level page table to retrieve the physical page number. One obvious way to arrange such a scheme is to have the second-level page tables occupy exactly one page of memory. Assuming a 32-bit virtual address space with 4-KB pages and 4 bytes per page table entry, how many bytes will each program need to use to store the first-level page table (which must always be in memory)? Provide figures similar to Figures 7.20, 7.21, and 7.22 (pages 581–584) that demonstrate your understanding of this idea.

7.36 [15] <§7.4> Assuming that we use the two-level hierarchical page table described in Exercise 7.35 and that exactly one second-level page table is in memory and exactly half of its entries are valid, how many bytes of memory in our virtual address space actually reside in physical memory? (Hint: The second-level page table occupies exactly one page of physical memory.)

7.37 [10] <§7.4> Some programs, such as complex simulations of weather patterns, are loaded into a computer where they will run, uninterrupted, for long periods of time. Expensive supercomputers are often purchased for these applications. Discuss some of the reasons why virtual memory may or may not be desirable for machines designed for these types of applications. Would a cache be necessary?

7.38 [5] <§§7.5> If all misses are classified into one of three categories—compulsory, capacity, or conflict (as discussed on page 609)—which misses are likely to be reduced when a program is rewritten so as to require less memory? How about if the clock rate of the machine that the program is running on is increased? How about if the associativity of the existing cache is increased?

7.39 [5] <§7.5> The following C program could be used to help construct a cache simulator. Many of the data types have not been defined, but the code accurately describes the actions that take place during a read access to a direct-mapped cache.

```
word ReadDirectMappedCache(address a)
  static Entry cache[CACHE_SIZE_IN_WORDS];
  Entry e = cache[a.index];
  if (e.valid == FALSE !! e.tag != a.tag) {
    e.valid = true;
    e.tag = a.tag;
    e.data = load_from_memory(a);
  }
  return e.data;
```

Your task is to modify this code to produce an accurate description of the actions that take place during a read access to a direct-mapped cache with multiple-word blocks.

7.40 [8] <§7.5> This exercise is similar to Exercise 7.39, except this time write the code for read accesses to an *n*-way set-associative cache with one-word blocks. Note that your code will likely suggest that the comparisons are sequential in nature when in fact they would be performed in parallel by actual hardware.

7.41 [8] <§7.5> {Ex. 7.39} Extend your solution to Exercise 7.39 by including the specification of a new procedure for handling write accesses, assuming a write-through policy. Be sure to consider whether or not your solution for handling read accesses needs to be modified.

7.42 [8] <§7.5> {Ex. 7.39} Extend your solution to Exercise 7.39 by including the specification of a new procedure for handling write accesses, assuming a write-back policy. Be sure to consider whether or not your solution for handling read accesses needs to be modified.

7.43 [8] <§7.5> {Ex. 7.40} This exercise is similar to Exercise 7.41, but this time extend your solution to Exercise 7.40. Assume that the cache uses random replacement.

7.44 [8] <§7.5> {Ex. 7.40} This exercise is similar to Exercise 7.42, but this time extend your solution to Exercise 7.40. Assume that the cache uses random replacement.

7.45 [5] <§§7.7–7.8> Why might a compiler perform the following optimization?

```
/* Before */
for (j = 0; j < 20; j++)
   for (i = 0; i < 200; i++)
    x[i][j] = x[i][j] + 1;
/* After */
for (i = 0; i < 200; i++)
   for (j = 0; j < 20; j++)
    x[i][j] = x[i][j] + 1;
```

7.46 [3 hours] <§7.2> Use a cache simulator to simulate several different cache organizations for the first 1 million references in a trace of gcc. Both dinero (a cache simulator) and the gcc traces are available—see the preface of this book for information on how to obtain them. Assume an instruction cache of 32 KB and a data cache of 32 KB using the same organization. You should choose at least two kinds of associativity and two block sizes. Draw a diagram like that in Figure 7.19 on page 574 that shows the data cache organization with the best hit rate.

7.47 [4 hours] <§§7.2–7.4> We want to use a cache simulator to simulate several different TLB and virtual memory organizations. Use the first 1 million references of gcc for this evaluation. We want to know the TLB miss rate for each of the following TLBs and page sizes:

 1. 64-entry TLB with full associativity and 4-KB pages

 2. 32-entry TLB with full associativity and 8-KB pages

3. 64-entry TLB with eight-way associativity and 4-KB pages

4. 128-entry TLB with four-way associativity and 4-KB pages

7.48 [1 day] <§7.2> You are commissioned to design a cache for a new system. It has a 32-bit physical byte address and requires separate instruction and data caches. The SRAMs have an access time of 1.5 ns and a size of 32K × 8 bits, and you have a total of 16 SRAMs to use. The miss penalty for the memory system is 8 + 2 × Block size in words. Using set associativity adds 0.2 ns to the cache access time. Using the first 1 million references of gcc, find the best I and D cache organizations, given the available SRAMs.

8

Interfacing
Processors
and Peripherals

*I/O certainly has been lagging
in the last decade.*

Seymour Cray
Public lecture, 1976

The Five Classic Components of a Computer

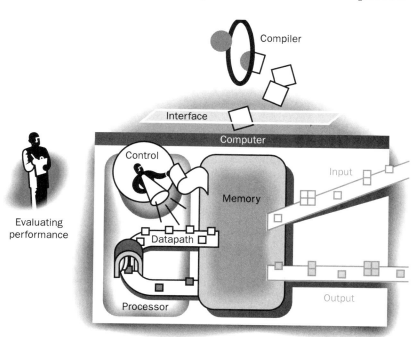

8.1 Introduction

As in processors, many of the characteristics of input/output (I/O) systems are driven by technology. For example, the properties of disk drives affect how the disks should be connected to the processor, as well as how the operating system interacts with the disks. I/O systems, however, differ from processors in several important ways. Although processor designers often focus primarily on performance, designers of I/O systems must consider issues such as expandability and resilience in the face of failure as much as they consider performance. Second, performance in an I/O system is a more complex characteristic than for a processor. For example, with some devices we may care primarily about access latency, while with others throughput is crucial. Furthermore, performance depends on many aspects of the system: the device characteristics, the connection between the device and the rest of the system, the memory hierarchy, and the operating system. Figure 8.1 shows the structure of a system with its I/O. All of the components, from the individual I/O devices to the processor to the system software, will affect the performance of tasks that include I/O.

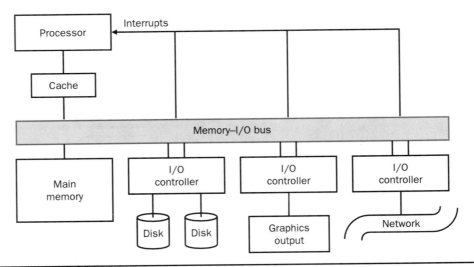

FIGURE 8.1 Typical collection of I/O devices. The connections between the I/O devices, processor, and memory are usually called *buses*. Communication among the devices and the processor use both protocols on the bus and interrupts, as we will see in this chapter.

The difficulties in assessing and designing I/O systems have often relegated I/O to second-class status. Research focuses on processor design; companies present performance using primarily processor-oriented measures; courses in every aspect of computing, from programming to computer architecture, often ignore I/O or give it scanty coverage; and textbooks leave the subject to near the end, making it easier for students and instructors to skip it!

This situation doesn't make sense: imagine how you'd like to use a computer without I/O! Furthermore, in an era when machines, from low-end PCs to the fastest mainframes, and even supercomputers, are being built from the same basic microprocessor technology, I/O capability is often one of the most distinctive features of the machines. Lastly, as the importance of networking and the information infrastructure grows, I/O will play an increasingly important role. Remember that machines interact with people through I/O.

If these concerns are still not convincing, our discussion of Amdahl's law in Chapter 2 should remind us that ignoring I/O is dangerous. A simple example demonstrates this.

Impact of I/O on System Performance

Example

Suppose we have a benchmark that executes in 100 seconds of elapsed time, where 90 seconds is CPU time and the rest is I/O time. If CPU time improves by 50% per year for the next five years but I/O time doesn't improve, how much faster will our program run at the end of five years?

Answer

We know that

$$\text{Elapsed time} = \text{CPU time} + \text{I/O time}$$
$$100 = 90 + \text{I/O time}$$
$$\text{I/O time} = 10 \text{ seconds}$$

The new CPU times and the resulting elapsed times are computed in the following table:

After *n* years	CPU time	I/O time	Elapsed time	% I/O time
0	90 seconds	10 seconds	100 seconds	10%
1	$\frac{90}{1.5} = 60$ seconds	10 seconds	70 seconds	14%
2	$\frac{60}{1.5} = 40$ seconds	10 seconds	50 seconds	20%
3	$\frac{40}{1.5} = 27$ seconds	10 seconds	37 seconds	27%
4	$\frac{27}{1.5} = 18$ seconds	10 seconds	28 seconds	36%
5	$\frac{18}{1.5} = 12$ seconds	10 seconds	22 seconds	45%

The improvement in CPU performance over five years is

$$\frac{90}{12} = 7.5$$

However, the improvement in elapsed time is only

$$\frac{100}{22} = 4.5$$

and the I/O time has increased from 10% to 45% of the elapsed time.

How we should assess I/O performance often depends on the application. In some environments, we may care primarily about system throughput. In these cases, I/O bandwidth will be most important. Even I/O bandwidth can be measured in two different ways:

1. How much data can we move through the system in a certain time?

2. How many I/O operations can we do per unit of time?

Which measurement is best may depend on the environment. For example, in many supercomputer applications, most I/O requests are for long streams of data, and transfer bandwidth is the important characteristic. In another environment, we may wish to process a large number of small, unrelated accesses to an I/O device. An example of such an environment might be a tax-processing office of the National Income Tax Service (NITS). NITS mostly cares about processing a large number of forms in a given time; each tax form is stored separately and is fairly small. A system oriented toward large file transfer may be satisfactory, but an I/O system that can support the simultaneous transfer of many small files may be cheaper and faster for processing millions of tax forms.

In other applications, we care primarily about response time, which you will recall is the total elapsed time to accomplish a particular task. If the I/O requests are extremely large, response time will depend heavily on bandwidth, but in many environments most accesses will be small, and the I/O system with the lowest latency per access will deliver the best response time. On single-user machines such as workstations and personal computers, response time is the key performance characteristic.

A large number of applications, especially in the vast commercial market for computing, require both high throughput and short response times. Examples include automatic teller machines (ATMs), airline reservation systems, order entry and inventory tracking systems, file servers, and machines for timesharing. In such environments, we care about both how long each task takes *and* how many tasks we can process in a second. The number of ATM requests you can process per hour doesn't matter if each one takes 15 minutes—you won't have any customers left! Similarly, if you can process each ATM request quickly but can only handle a small number of requests at once, you won't be able to support many ATMs, or the cost of the computer per ATM will be very high.

If I/O is truly important, how should we compare I/O systems? This is a complex question because I/O performance depends on many aspects of the system and different applications stress different aspects of the I/O system. Furthermore, a design can make complex trade-offs between response time and throughput, making it impossible to measure just one aspect in isolation. For example, response time is generally minimized by handling a request as early as possible, while greater throughput can be achieved if we try to handle related requests together. Accordingly, we may increase throughput on a disk by grouping requests that access locations that are close together. Such a policy will increase the response time for some requests, probably leading to a larger variation in response time. Although throughput will be higher, some benchmarks constrain the maximum response time to any request, making such optimizations potentially problematic.

Before discussing the aspects of I/O devices and how they are connected, let's look briefly at some performance measures for I/O systems.

8.2 I/O Performance Measures: Some Examples from Disk and File Systems

Assessment of an I/O system must take into account a variety of factors. Performance is one of these, and in this section, we give some examples of measurements proposed for determining the performance of disk systems. These benchmarks are affected by a variety of system features, including the disk technology, how disks are connected, the memory system, the processor, and the file system provided by the operating system. Overall, the state of benchmarking on the I/O side of computer systems remains quite primitive compared with the extensive activity lately seen in benchmarking processor systems. Perhaps this situation will change as designers realize the importance of I/O and the inadequacy of our techniques to evaluate it.

Before we discuss these benchmarks, we need to address a confusing point about terminology and units. The performance of I/O systems depends on the rate at which the system transfers data. The transfer rate depends on the clock rate, which is typically given in MHz $=10^6$ cycles per second. The transfer rate is usually quoted in MB/sec. In I/O systems, MBs are measured using base 10 (i.e., 1 MB = 10^6 = 1,000,000 bytes), unlike main memory where base 2 is used (i.e., 1 MB = 2^{20} = 1,048,576). In addition to adding confusion, this difference introduces the need to convert between base 10 (1K = 1000) and base 2 (1K = 1024) because many I/O accesses are for data blocks that have a size that is a power of two. Rather than complicate all our examples by accurately converting one of the two measurements, we make note of this distinction and the fact that treating the two measures as if the units were identical introduces a small error. We illustrate this error in section 8.8.

Supercomputer I/O Benchmarks

Supercomputer I/O is dominated by accesses to large files on magnetic disks. Many supercomputer installations run batch jobs, each of which may last for hours. In these situations, I/O consists of one large read followed by writes to snapshot the state of the computation should the computer crash. As a result, supercomputer I/O in many cases consists more of output than input. The overriding supercomputer I/O measure is data throughput: the number of bytes per second that can be transferred between a supercomputer's main memory and disks during large transfers.

Transaction Processing I/O Benchmarks

Transaction processing (TP) applications involve both a response time requirement and a performance measurement based on throughput. Furthermore, most of the I/O accesses are small. Because of this, TP applications are chiefly concerned with *I/O rate*, measured as the number of disk accesses per second, as opposed to *data rate*, measured as bytes of data per second. TP applications generally involve changes to a large database, with the system meeting some response time requirements as well as gracefully handling certain types of failures. These applications are extremely critical and cost-sensitive. For example, banks normally use TP systems because they are concerned about a range of characteristics. These include making sure transactions aren't lost, handling transactions quickly, and minimizing the cost of processing each transaction. Although reliability in the face of failure is an absolute requirement in such systems, both response time and throughput are critical to building cost-effective systems.

A number of transaction processing benchmarks have been developed. The best-known set of benchmarks is a series developed by the Transaction Processing Council (TPC). The most recent versions of these benchmarks are TPC-C and TPC-D, both of which involve processing of queries against a database. TPC-C involves light- and medium-weight queries based on an order-entry environment, but also typical of the type of transactions needed in a reservation system or online banking system. TPC-D involves complex queries typical of decision support applications.

TPC-C is significantly more sophisticated than the earlier TPC-A and TPC-B benchmarks. It involves nine different types of database records, five different types of transactions, and a model of transaction requests meant to simulate real users generating transactions at terminals. The benchmark specification, including the reporting rules, is 128 pages long! Performance on TPC-C is measured in transactions per minute or second (TPM or TPS) and encompasses a complete system measurement including disk I/O, terminal I/O, and computation. An extensive description of the TPC organization and benchmarks is available via the TPC link at *www.mkp.com/books_catalog/cod/links.htm*.

File System I/O Benchmarks

File systems, which are stored on disks, have a different access pattern. For example, measurements of Unix file systems in an engineering environment have found that 80% of accesses are to files of less than 10 KB and that 90% of all file accesses are to data with sequential addresses on the disk. Furthermore, 67% of the accesses were reads, 27% were writes, and 6% were read-modify-write accesses, which read data, modify it, and then rewrite the same location. Such measurements have led to the creation of synthetic file system benchmarks. One of the most popular of such benchmarks has five phases, using 70 files with a total size of 200 KB:

- *MakeDir*: Constructs a directory subtree that is identical in structure to the given directory subtree

- *Copy*: Copies every file from the source subtree to the target subtree

- *ScanDir*: Recursively traverses a directory subtree and examines the status of every file in it

- *ReadAll*: Scans every byte of every file in a subtree once

- *Make*: Compiles and links all the files in a subtree

As we will see in section 8.6, the design of an I/O system involves knowing what the workload is.

Types and Characteristics of I/O Devices

I/O devices are incredibly diverse. Three characteristics are useful in organizing this wide variety:

- *Behavior*: Input (read once), output (write only, cannot be read), or storage (can be reread and usually rewritten).

- *Partner*: Either a human or a machine is at the other end of the I/O device, either feeding data on input or reading data on output.

- *Data rate*: The peak rate at which data can be transferred between the I/O device and the main memory or processor. It is useful to know what maximum demand the device may generate.

For example, a keyboard is an *input* device used by a *human* with a *peak data rate* of about 10 bytes per second. Figure 8.2 shows some of the I/O devices connected to computers.

In Chapter 1, we briefly discussed four important and characteristic I/O devices: mice, graphics displays, disks, and networks. We use mice, disks, and networks as examples to illustrate how I/O devices interface to processors and memories, but before we do that it will be useful to discuss these devices in more detail than in Chapter 1.

Device	Behavior	Partner	Data rate (KB/sec)
Keyboard	input	human	0.01
Mouse	input	human	0.02
Voice input	input	human	0.02
Scanner	input	human	400.00
Voice output	output	human	0.60
Line printer	output	human	1.00
Laser printer	output	human	200.00
Graphics display	output	human	60,000.00
Modem	input or output	machine	2.00–8.00
Network/LAN	input or output	machine	500.00–6000.00
Floppy disk	storage	machine	100.00
Optical disk	storage	machine	1000.00
Magnetic tape	storage	machine	2000.00
Magnetic disk	storage	machine	2000.00–10,000.00

FIGURE 8.2 The diversity of I/O devices. I/O devices can be distinguished by whether they serve as input, output, or storage devices; their communication partner (people or other computers); and their peak communication rates. The data rates span six orders of magnitude. Note that a network can be an input or an output device, but cannot be used for storage. Disk sizes, as well as transfer rates for devices, are always quoted in base 10, so that 1 MB = 1,000,000 bytes, and 10 Mbit/sec = 10,000,000 bits/sec.

Mouse

The interface between a mouse and a system can take one of two forms: the mouse either generates a series of pulses when it is moved (using the LED and detector described in Chapter 1 to generate the pulses), or it increments and decrements counters. Figure 8.3 shows how the counters change when the mouse is moved and describes how the interface would operate if it generated pulses instead. The processor can periodically read these counters, or count up the pulses, and determine how far the mouse has moved since it was last examined. The system then moves the cursor on the screen appropriately. This motion appears smooth because the rate at which you can move the mouse is slow compared with the rate at which the processor can read the mouse status and move the cursor on the screen.

Most mice also include one or more buttons, and the system must be able to detect when a button is depressed. By monitoring the status of the button, the system can also differentiate between clicking the button and holding it down. Of course, the mapping between the counters and the button position and what happens on the screen is totally controlled by software. That's why, for example, the rate at which the mouse moves across the screen and the rate at which single and double clicks are recognized can usually be set by the user.

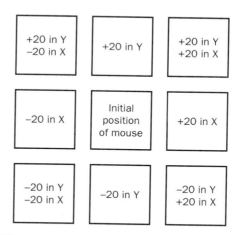

FIGURE 8.3 Moving the mouse in the horizontal direction or vertical direction causes the X or Y counter, respectively, to increment or decrement. Moving it along a diagonal causes both counters to change. Since the ball doesn't move when the mouse is not contacting the surface, it may be picked up and moved without changing the counters. When the mouse uses pulses to communicate its movement, there are four types of pulses: +X, −X, +Y, and −Y. Rather than generate a change in the counter value, the mouse generates the appropriate number of pulses on each of the four pulse signal lines. The value 20 is an arbitrary count that measures how far the mouse has moved.

Similarly, software interpretation of the mouse position means that the cursor doesn't jump completely off the screen when the mouse is moved a long distance in one direction. This method of having the system monitor the status of the mouse by reading signals from it is a common way to interface lower-performance devices to machines; it is called *polling*, and we'll revisit it in section 8.5.

Magnetic Disks

As mentioned in Chapter 1, there are two major types of magnetic disks: floppy disks and hard disks. Both types of disks rely on a rotating platter coated with a magnetic surface and use a moveable read/write head to access the disk. Disk storage is *nonvolatile*, meaning that the data remains even when power is removed. Because the platters in a hard disk are metal (or, recently, glass), they have several significant advantages over floppy disks:

- The hard disk can be larger because it is rigid.

- The hard disk has higher density because it can be controlled more precisely.

- The hard disk has a higher data rate because it spins faster.

- Hard disks can incorporate more than one platter.

For the rest of this section, we will focus on hard disks, and we use the term *magnetic disk* to mean hard disk.

A magnetic disk consists of a collection of platters (1–15), each of which has two recordable disk surfaces, as shown in Figure 8.4. The stack of platters is rotated at 3600 to 7200 RPM and has a diameter from just over an inch to just over 8 inches. Each disk surface is divided into concentric circles, called *tracks*. There are typically 1000 to 5000 tracks per surface. Each track is in turn divided into *sectors* that contain the information; each track may have 64 to 200 sectors, and the sector is the smallest unit that can be read or written. In 1997, sectors are typically 512 bytes in size. The sequence recorded on the magnetic media is a sector number, a gap, the information for that sector including error correction code (see Appendix B, page B-34), a gap, the sector number of the next sector, and so on. Traditionally, all tracks have the same number of sectors and hence the same number of bits.

As we saw in Chapter 1, to read and write information the read/write heads must be moved so that they are over the correct location. The disk heads for each surface are connected together and move in conjunction, so that every head is over the same track of every surface. The term *cylinder* is used to refer to all the tracks under the heads at a given point on all surfaces.

To access data, the operating system must direct the disk through a three-stage process. The first step is to position the head over the proper track. This operation is called a *seek*, and the time to move the head to the desired track is called the *seek time*.

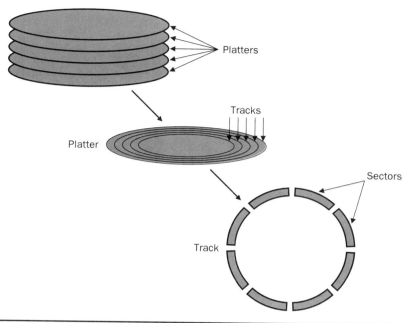

FIGURE 8.4 Disks are organized into platters, tracks, and sectors. Both sides of a platter are coated so that information can be stored on both surfaces. Floppy disks have the same organization, but consist of only one platter.

Disk manufacturers report minimum seek time, maximum seek time, and average seek time in their manuals. The first two are easy to measure, but the average is open to wide interpretation because it depends on the seek distance. The industry has decided to calculate average seek time as the sum of the time for all possible seeks divided by the number of possible seeks. Average seek times are usually advertised as 8 ms to 20 ms, but, depending on the application and scheduling of disk requests, the actual average seek time may be only 25% to 33% of the advertised number, because of locality of disk references. This locality arises both because of successive access to the same file and because the operating system tries to schedule such access together.

Once the head has reached the correct track, we must wait for the desired sector to rotate under the read/write head. This time is called the *rotational latency* or *rotational delay*. The average latency to the desired information is halfway around the disk. Because the disks rotate at 3600 RPM to 7200 RPM, the average rotational latency is between

$$\text{Average rotational latency} = \frac{0.5 \text{ rotation}}{3600 \text{ RPM}} = \frac{0.5 \text{ rotation}}{3600 \text{ RPM} / \left(60 \frac{\text{seconds}}{\text{minute}}\right)}$$

$$= 0.0083 \text{ seconds} = 8.3 \text{ ms}$$

and

$$\text{Average rotational latency} = \frac{0.5 \text{ rotation}}{7200 \text{ RPM}} = \frac{0.5 \text{ rotation}}{7200 \text{ RPM}/\left(60\dfrac{\text{seconds}}{\text{minute}}\right)}$$

$$= 0.0042 \text{ seconds} = 4.2 \text{ ms}$$

Smaller diameter disks are attractive because they can spin at higher rates without excessive power consumption, thereby reducing rotational latency.

The last component of a disk access, *transfer time,* is the time to transfer a block of bits, typically a sector. The transfer time is a function of the sector size, the rotation speed, and the recording density of a track. Transfer rates in 1997 are between 2 and 15 MB/sec. The one complication is that most midrange and high-end disks have a built-in cache that stores sectors as they are passed over; transfer rates from the cache are typically higher, and may be up to 40 MB/sec in 1997. Today, most disk transfers are multiple sectors in length.

The detailed control of the disk and the transfer between the disk and the memory is usually handled by a *disk controller.* The controller adds the final component of disk access time, *controller time,* which is the overhead the controller imposes in performing an I/O access. The average time to perform an I/O operation will consist of these four times plus any wait time incurred because other processes are using the disk.

Disk Read Time

Example

What is the average time to read or write a 512-byte sector for a typical disk rotating at 5400 RPM? The advertised average seek time is 12 ms, the transfer rate is 5 MB/sec, and the controller overhead is 2 ms. Assume that the disk is idle so that there is no waiting time.

Answer

Average disk access time is equal to average seek time + average rotational delay + transfer time + controller overhead. Using the advertised average seek time, the answer is

$$12 \text{ ms} + 5.6 \text{ ms} + \frac{0.5 \text{ KB}}{5 \text{ MB/sec}} + 2 \text{ ms} = 12 + 5.6 + 0.1 + 2 = 19.7 \text{ ms}$$

If the measured average seek time is 25% of the advertised average time, the answer is

$$3 \text{ ms} + 5.6 \text{ ms} + 0.1 \text{ ms} + 2 \text{ ms} = 10.7 \text{ ms}$$

Notice that when we consider average measured seek time, as opposed to average advertised seek time, the rotational latency can be the largest component of the access time.

Disk densities have continued to increase for more than 40 years. The impact of this compounded improvement in density and the reduction in physical size of a disk drive has been amazing, as Figure 8.5 shows. The aims of different disk designers have led to a wide variety of drives being available at any particular time. Figure 8.6 shows the characteristics of three different

FIGURE 8.5 Six magnetic disks, varying in diameter from 14 inches down to 1.8 inches. These disks were introduced over more than a decade ago and hence are not intended to be representative of the best 1998 capacity of disks of these diameters. This photograph does, however, accurately portray their relative physical sizes. The widest disk is the DEC R81, containing four 14-inch diameter platters and storing 456 MB. It was manufactured in 1985. The 8-inch diameter disk comes from Fujitsu, and this 1984 disk stores 130 MB on six platters. The Micropolis RD53 has five 5.25-inch platters and stores 85 MB. The IBM 0361 also has five platters, but these are just 3.5 inches in diameter. This 1988 disk holds 320 MB. In 1997, the most dense 3.5-inch disk has 10 platters and holds 9.1 GB in the same space, yielding an increase in density of about 30 times! The Conner CP 2045 has two 2.5-inch platters containing 40 MB, and was made in 1990. The smallest disk in this photograph is the Integral 1820. This single 1.8-inch platter contains 20 MB and was made in 1992. Photo by Peg Skorpinski.

magnetic disks from a single manufacturer. Large-diameter drives have many more megabytes to amortize the cost of electronics, so the traditional wisdom was that they had the lowest cost per megabyte. But this advantage is offset for the small drives by the much higher sales volume, which lowers manufacturing costs: in 1997, disks cost between $0.10 and $0.20 per megabyte, almost independent of width. The smaller drives also have advantages in power and volume per byte, as Figure 8.6 shows.

Elaboration: Many recent disks have included caches directly in the disk. Such caches allow for fast access to data that was recently read between transfers requested by the CPU. Of course, such capabilities complicate the measurement of disk performance and increase the importance of workload choice. The 5.25-inch Seagate drive shown in Figure 8.6 comes with an integrated cache.

Elaboration: Each track has the same number of bits, and the outer tracks are longer. The outer tracks thus record information at a lower density per inch of track than do tracks closer to the center of the disk. Recording more sectors on the outer tracks than on the inner tracks, called *constant bit density*, is becoming more widespread with

Characteristics	Seagate ST423451	Seagate ST19171	Seagate ST92255
Disk diameter (inches)	5.25	3.50	2.50
Formatted data capacity (MB)	23,200	9100	2250
MTBF (hours)	500,000	1,000,000	300,000
Number of disk surfaces	28	20	10
Rotation speed (RPM)	5400	7200	4500
Internal transfer rate (Mbits/sec)	86–124	80–124	up to 60.8
External interface	Fast SCSI-2 (8–16 bit)	Fast SCSI-2 (8–16 bit)	Fast ATA
External transfer rate (MB/sec)	20–40	20–40	up to 16.6
Minimum seek (track to track) (ms)	0.9	0.6	4
Average seek + rotational delay (ms)	11	9	14
Power/box (watts)	26	13	2.6
MB/watt	892	700	865
Volume (cu. in.)	322	37	8
MB/cu. in.	72	246	273

FIGURE 8.6 Characteristics of three magnetic disks by a single manufacturer. These disks represent the maximum density of the 1997 Seagate product family at each size. The disks shown here either interface to SCSI, a standard I/O bus that we discuss on page 672, or ATA, a standard disk interface for PCs. Compared to the disks shown in the table that appeared in the first edition of this book in 1994, the disks shown above have 25–40 times the MB/watt and 90–450 times the MB/cu. ft.! MTBF stands for mean time before failures—a standard measurement of reliability. The two larger disks contain sector caches that store the contents of sectors as they are passed over. The internal transfer rate is that rate at which bits are read from the disk surface, while the external transfer rate includes that rate at which a sector in the cache that is requested can be transferred. See the link to Seagate at *www.mkp.com/ books_catalog/cod/links.htm* for more information on these drives, as well as some information on modern disk technology.

the advent of intelligent interface standards such as SCSI (see section 8.4). The rate at which an inch of track moves under the head varies: it is faster on the outer tracks. Accordingly, if the number of bits per inch is constant, the rate at which bits must be read or written varies, and the electronics must accommodate this factor when constant bit density is used.

Networks

Networks are the major medium used to communicate between computers. Key characteristics of typical networks include the following:

- *Distance:* 0.01 to 10,000 kilometers
- *Speed:* 0.001 MB/sec to 100 MB/sec
- *Topology:* Bus, ring, star, tree
- *Shared lines:* None (point-to-point) or shared (multidrop)

We'll illustrate these characteristics with three examples.

The RS232 standard provides a 0.3- to 19.2-Kbit/sec *terminal network.* A central computer connects to many terminals over slow but cheap dedicated wires. These point-to-point connections form a star from the central computer, with each terminal ranging from 10 to 100 meters in distance from the computer.

The *local area network* (LAN) is what is commonly meant today when people mention a network, and Ethernet is what most people mean when they mention a LAN. (Ethernet has in fact become such a common term that it is often used as a generic term for LAN.) The basic Ethernet is essentially a 10-Mbit/sec, one-wire bus that has no central control. Messages, or *packets*, are sent over the Ethernet in blocks that vary from 64 bytes to 1518 bytes. Recently, several companies have developed a faster version (usually called Fast Ethernet) that offers rates that are 10 times higher (i.e., 100 Mbit/sec), and a Gigabit Ethernet has been proposed for delivery in 1998.

An Ethernet is essentially a bus with multiple masters and a scheme for determining who gets bus control; we'll discuss how the distributed control is implemented in the exercises. Because the Ethernet is a bus, only one sender can be transmitting at any time; this limits the bandwidth. In practice, this is not usually a problem because the utilization is fairly low. Of course, some LANs become overloaded through poor capacity planning, and response time and throughput can degrade rapidly at higher utilization.

One way in which the limits of the original bus-oriented Ethernet have been overcome is through switched networks. A *switched network* is one in which switches are introduced to reduce the number of hosts per Ethernet segment. In the limit, there is only one host per segment and that host is directly connected to a switch. Switched networks are common in long-haul networks, the next topic, but such networks have recently been popular in local area applications as the use of higher-performance machines and multimedia data has put significant strains on shared Ethernets.

Long-haul networks cover distances of 10 to 10,000 kilometers. The first and most famous long-haul network was the ARPANET (named after its funding agency, the Advanced Research Projects Agency of the U.S. government). It transferred data at 56 Kbits/sec and used point-to-point dedicated lines leased from telephone companies. The host computer talked to an *interface message processor* (IMP), which communicated over the telephone lines. The IMP took information and broke it into 1-Kbit packets, which could take separate paths to the destination node. At each hop, a packet was stored (for recovery in case of failure) and then forwarded to the proper IMP according to the address in the packet. The destination IMP reassembled the packets into a message and then gave it to the host. Most networks today use this *packet-switched* approach, in which packets are individually routed from source to destination.

The ARPANET was the precursor of the Internet. The key to interconnecting different networks was standardizing on a single protocol family, TCP/IP (Transmission Control Protocol/Internet Protocol). The IP portion of the protocol provides for addressing between two hosts on the Internet, but does not guarantee reliable delivery. TCP provides a protocol that can guarantee that all packets are received and that the packets have no transmission errors. These two protocols work together to form a *protocol stack*, where TCP packets are encapsulated in IP packets. The standardization of the TCP/IP packet format is what allows the different hosts and network to communicate.

The bandwidths of networks are probably growing faster than the bandwidth of any other type of device at present. High-speed networks using copper and coaxial cable offer 100 Mbit/sec bandwidths, while optical fiber offers bandwidths up to 1 Gbit/sec. In the future, it appears that Internet-like technologies may be extended up to the 1-Gbit/sec range. These super high-speed networks are likely to be switched rather than using shared links.

Another leader among the emerging network technologies is ATM (Asynchronous Transfer Method). ATM is a scalable network technology (from 155 Mbits/sec to 2.5 Gbits/sec) that originated in long-haul networks switching both voice and data. It is already being deployed in backbone switching applications and, together with Fast Ethernet approaches, is a contender for future desktop connectivity.

The challenge in putting these networks into use lies primarily in building systems that can efficiently interface to these media and sustain these bandwidths between two programs that want to communicate. Meeting this challenge requires that all the pieces of the I/O system, from the operating system to the memory system to the bus to the device interface, be able to accommodate these bandwidths. This is truly a top-to-bottom systems challenge.

**Hardware
Software
Interface**

To allow communication across multiple networks with different characteristics, TCP/IP defines a standard packet format. An IP packet, which contains Internet addressing information, encapsulates a TCP packet that contains both address information interpreted by the host and the data being communicated.

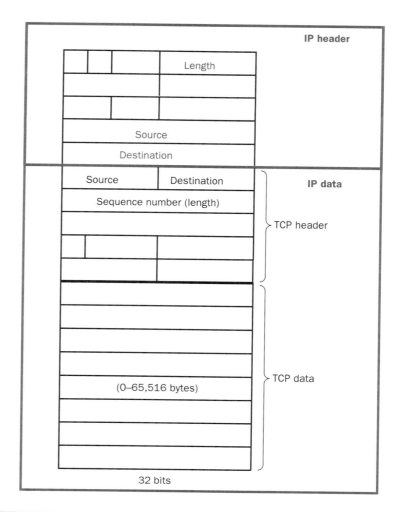

To see the importance of looking at performance from top to bottom, including both hardware and software, consider the following example.

Performance of Two Networks

Example

Consider the following measurements made on a pair of SPARCstation 10s running Solaris 2.3, connected to two different types of networks, and using TCP/IP for communication:

Characteristic	Ethernet	ATM
Bandwidth from node to network	1.125 MB/sec	10 MB/sec
Interconnect latency	15 μs	50 μs
HW latency to/from network	6 μs	6 μs
SW overhead sending to network	200 μs	207 μs
SW overhead receiving from network	241 μs	360 μs

Find the host-to-host latency for a 250-byte message using each network.

Answer

We can estimate the time required as the sum of the fixed latencies plus the time to transmit the message. The time to transmit the message is simply the message length divided by the bandwidth of the network.

The transmission times are

$$\text{Transmission time}_{\text{Ethernet}} = \frac{250 \text{ bytes}}{1.125 \times 10^6 \text{ bytes/sec}} = 222 \text{ μs}$$

$$\text{Transmission time}_{\text{ATM}} = \frac{250 \text{ bytes}}{10 \times 10^6 \text{ bytes/sec}} = 25 \text{ μs}$$

So the transmission time for the ATM network is about a factor of nine lower.

The total latency to send and receive the packet is the sum of the transmission time and the hardware and software overheads:

$$\text{Total time}_{\text{Ethernet}} = 15 + 6 + 200 + 241 + 222 = 684 \text{ μs}$$

$$\text{Total time}_{\text{ATM}} = 50 + 6 + 207 + 360 + 25 = 648 \text{ μs}$$

The end-to-end latency of the Ethrnet is only about 1.06 times higher, even though the transmission time is almost 9 times higher!

8.4 Buses: Connecting I/O Devices to Processor and Memory

In a computer system, the various subsystems must have interfaces to one another. For example, the memory and processor need to communicate, as do the processor and the I/O devices. This is commonly done with a *bus*. A bus is a shared communication link, which uses one set of wires to connect multiple subsystems. The two major advantages of the bus organization are versatility and low cost. By defining a single connection scheme, new devices can easily be added, and peripherals can even be moved between computer systems that use the same kind of bus. Furthermore, buses are cost-effective because a single set of wires is shared in multiple ways.

The major disadvantage of a bus is that it creates a communication bottleneck, possibly limiting the maximum I/O throughput. When I/O must pass through a single bus, the bandwidth of that bus limits the maximum I/O throughput. In commercial systems, where I/O is very frequent, and in supercomputers, where the I/O rates must be very high because the processor performance is high, designing a bus system capable of meeting the demands of the processor as well as connecting large numbers of I/O devices to the machine presents a major challenge.

One reason bus design is so difficult is that the maximum bus speed is largely limited by physical factors: the length of the bus and the number of devices. These physical limits prevent us from running the bus arbitrarily fast. Within these limits, there are a variety of techniques we can use to increase the performance of the bus; however, these techniques may adversely affect other performance metrics. For example, to obtain fast response time for I/O operations, we must minimize the time to perform a bus access by streamlining the communication path. On the other hand, to sustain high I/O data rates, we must maximize the bus bandwidth. The bus bandwidth can be increased by using more buffering and by communicating larger blocks of data, both of which increase the delay to complete the bus access! Clearly, these two goals, fast bus accesses and high bandwidth, can lead to conflicting design requirements. Finally, the need to support a range of devices with widely varying latencies and data transfer rates also makes bus design challenging.

A bus generally contains a set of control lines and a set of data lines. The control lines are used to signal requests and acknowledgments, and to indicate what type of information is on the data lines. The data lines of the bus carry information between the source and the destination. This information may consist of data, complex commands, or addresses. For example, if a disk wants to write some data into memory from a disk sector, the data lines will be used to indicate the address in memory in which to place the data as well as to carry the actual data from the disk. The control lines will be used to indicate what type of information is contained on the data lines of the bus at each point in the transfer. Some buses have two sets of signal lines to separately communicate both data and address in a single bus transmission. In either case, the control lines are used to indicate what the bus contains and to implement the bus protocol. And because the bus is shared, we also need a protocol to decide who uses it next; we will discuss this problem shortly.

Let's consider a typical *bus transaction*. A bus transaction includes two parts: sending the address and receiving or sending the data. Bus transactions are typically defined by what they do to memory. A *read* transaction transfers data *from* memory (to either the processor or an I/O device), and a *write* transaction writes data *to* the memory. Clearly, this terminology is confusing. To avoid this, we'll try to use the terms *input* and *output*, which are always defined from the perspective of the processor: an input operation is inputting data from the device to memory, where the processor can read it, and an output operation is outputting data to a device from memory where the processor wrote it. Figure 8.7 shows the steps in a typical output operation, in which data will be read from memory and sent to the device. Figure 8.8 shows the steps in an input operation where data is read from the device and written to memory. In both figures, the active portions of the bus and memory are shown in color, and a read or write is shown by shading the unit, as we did in Chapter 6. In these figures, we focus on how data is transferred between the I/O device and memory; in section 8.5, we will see how the I/O operation is initiated.

Types of Buses

Buses are traditionally classified as one of three types: *processor-memory buses*, *I/O buses*, or *backplane buses*. Processor-memory buses are short, generally high speed, and matched to the memory system so as to maximize memory-processor bandwidth. I/O buses, by contrast, can be lengthy, can have many types of devices connected to them, and often have a wide range in the data bandwidth of the devices connected to them. I/O buses do not typically interface directly to the memory but use either a processor-memory or a backplane bus to connect to memory. Backplane buses are designed to allow processors, memory, and I/O devices to coexist on a single bus; they balance the demands of processor-memory communication with the demands of I/O device-memory communication. Backplane buses received their name because they were often built into the *backplane*, an interconnection structure within the chassis; processor, memory, and I/O boards would then plug into the backplane using the bus for communication.

Processor-memory buses are often design-specific, while both I/O buses and backplane buses are frequently reused in different machines. In fact, backplane and I/O buses are often *standard buses* that are used by many different

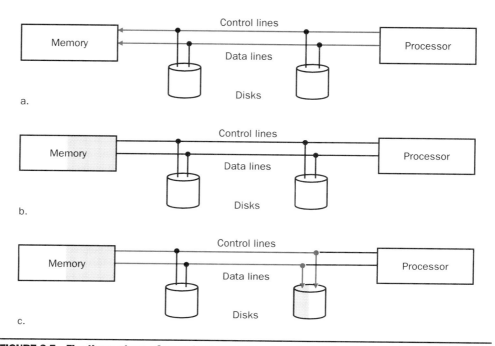

FIGURE 8.7 The three steps of an output operation. In each step, the active participants in the communication are shown in color, with the right side shaded if the device is doing a read and the left side shaded if the device is doing a write. Notice that the data lines of the bus can carry both an address (as in a) and data (as in c). (a) The first step in an output operation initiates a read from memory. The control lines signal a read request to memory, while the data lines contain the address. (b) During the second step in an output operation, memory is accessing the data. (c) In the third and final step in an output operation, memory transfers the data using the data lines of the bus and signals that the data is available to the I/O device using the control lines. The device stores the data as it appears on the bus.

computers manufactured by different companies. By comparison, processor-memory buses are often proprietary, although in many recent machines they may be the backplane bus, and the standard or I/O buses plug into the processor-memory bus. In many recent machines, the distinction among these bus types, especially between backplane buses and processor-memory buses, may be very minor.

During the design phase, the designer of a processor-memory bus knows all the types of devices that must connect to the bus, while the I/O or backplane bus designer must design the bus to handle unknown devices that vary in latency and bandwidth characteristics. Normally, an I/O bus presents a fairly simple and low-level interface to a device, requiring minimal additional electronics to interface to the bus. A backplane bus usually requires additional logic to interface between the bus and a device or between the backplane bus

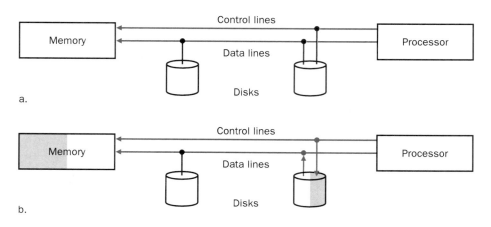

FIGURE 8.8 An input operation takes less active time because the device does not need to wait for memory to access data. As in the previous figure, the active participants in each step in the communication are shown in color, with the right side shaded if the device is doing a read and the left side shaded if the device is doing a write. (a) In the first step in an input operation, the control lines indicate a write request for memory, while the data lines contain the address. (b) The second step in an input operation occurs when the memory is ready and signals the device, which then transfers the data. Typically, the memory will store the data as it receives it. The device need not wait for the store to be completed. In the steps shown, we assume that the device had to wait for memory to indicate its readiness, but this will not be true in some systems that use buffering or have a fast memory system.

and a lower-level I/O bus. A backplane bus offers the cost advantage of a single bus. Figure 8.9 shows a system using a single backplane bus, a system using a processor-memory bus with attached I/O buses, and a system using all three types of buses. Machines with a separate processor-memory bus normally use a bus adapter to connect the I/O bus to the processor-memory bus. Some high-performance, expandable systems use an organization that combines the three buses: the processor-memory bus has one or more bus adapters that interface a standard backplane bus to the processor-memory bus. I/O buses, as well as device controllers, can plug into the backplane bus. The IBM RS/6000 and Silicon Graphics multiprocessors use this type of organization. This organization offers the advantage that the processor-memory bus can be made much faster than a backplane or I/O bus and that the I/O system can be expanded by plugging many I/O controllers or buses into the backplane bus, which will not affect the speed of the processor-memory bus.

Synchronous and Asynchronous Buses

The substantial differences between the circumstances under which a processor-memory bus and an I/O bus or backplane bus are designed lead to two different schemes for communication on the bus: *synchronous* and

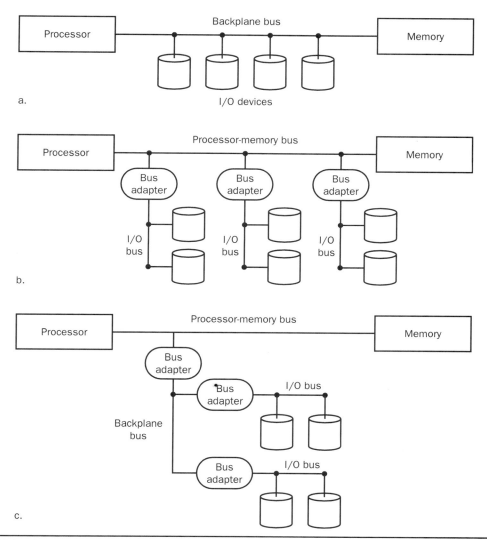

FIGURE 8.9 Many machines use a single backplane bus for both processor-memory and I/O traffic. Some high-performance machines use a separate processor-memory bus that I/O buses plug into. Some systems make use of all three types of buses, organized in a hierarchy. (a) A single bus used for processor-to-memory communication, as well as communication between I/O devices and memory. The bus used in older PCs has this structure. (b) A separate bus is used for processor–memory traffic. To communicate data between memory and I/O devices, the I/O buses interface to the processor-memory bus, using a bus adapter. The bus adapter provides speed matching between the buses. In many recent PCs, the processor-memory bus is a PCI bus (a backplane bus) that has I/O devices that interface directly as well as an I/O bus that plugs into the PCI bus; the latter is a SCSI bus. (c) A separate bus is used for processor-memory traffic. A small number of backplane buses tap into the processor-memory bus. The processor-memory buses interface to the backplane bus. This is usually done with a single-chip controller, such as a SCSI bus controller. An advantage of this organization is the small number of taps into the high-speed processor-memory bus.

asynchronous. If a bus is synchronous, it includes a clock in the control lines and a fixed protocol for communicating that is relative to the clock. For example, for a processor-memory bus performing a read from memory, we might have a protocol that transmits the address and read command on the first clock cycle, using the control lines to indicate the type of request. The memory might then be required to respond with the data word on the fifth clock. This type of protocol can be implemented easily in a small finite state machine. Because the protocol is predetermined and involves little logic, the bus can run very fast and the interface logic will be small. Synchronous buses have two major disadvantages, however. First, every device on the bus must run at the same clock rate. Second, because of clock skew problems, synchronous buses cannot be long if they are fast (see Appendix B for a discussion of clock skew). Processor-memory buses are often synchronous because the devices communicating are close, small in number, and prepared to operate at high clock rates.

An asynchronous bus is not clocked. Because it is not clocked, an asynchronous bus can accommodate a wide variety of devices, and the bus can be lengthened without worrying about clock skew or synchronization problems. To coordinate the transmission of data between sender and receiver, an asynchronous bus uses a *handshaking protocol*. A handshaking protocol consists of a series of steps in which the sender and receiver proceed to the next step only when both parties agree. The protocol is implemented with an additional set of control lines.

A simple example will illustrate how asynchronous buses work. Let's consider a device requesting a word of data from the memory system. Assume that there are three control lines:

1. *ReadReq*: Used to indicate a read request for memory. The address is put on the data lines at the same time.

2. *DataRdy*: Used to indicate that the data word is now ready on the data lines. In an output transaction, the memory will assert this signal since it is providing the data. In an input transaction, an I/O device would assert this signal, since it would provide data. In either case, the data is placed on the data lines at the same time.

3. *Ack*: Used to acknowledge the ReadReq or the DataRdy signal of the other party.

In an asynchronous protocol, the control signals ReadReq and DataRdy are asserted until the other party (the memory or the device) indicates that the control lines have been seen and the data lines have been read; this indication is made by asserting the Ack line. This complete process is called *handshaking*. Figure 8.10 shows how such a protocol operates by depicting the steps in the communication.

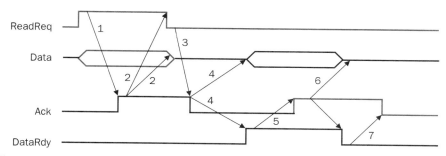

The steps in the protocol begin immediately after the device signals a request by raising ReadReq and putting the address on the Data lines:

1. When memory sees the ReadReq line, it reads the address from the data bus and raises Ack to indicate it has been seen.
2. I/O device sees the Ack line high and releases the ReadReq and data lines.
3. Memory sees that ReadReq is low and drops the Ack line to acknowledge the Readreq signal.
4. This step starts when the memory has the data ready. It places the data from the read request on the data lines and raises DataRdy.
5. The I/O device sees DataRdy, reads the data from the bus, and signals that it has the data by raising Ack.
6. The memory sees the Ack signal, drops DataRdy, and releases the data lines.
7. Finally, the I/O device, seeing DataRdy go low, drops the Ack line, which indicates that the transmission is completed.

A new bus transaction can now begin.

FIGURE 8.10   The asynchronous handshaking protocol consists of seven steps to read a word from memory and receive it in an I/O device. The signals in color are those asserted by the I/O device, while the memory asserts the signals shown in black. The arrows label the seven steps and the event that triggers each step. The symbol showing two lines (high and low) at the same time on the data lines indicates that the data lines have valid data at this point. (The symbol indicates that the data is valid, but the value is not known.)

An asynchronous bus protocol works like a pair of finite state machines that are communicating in such a way that a machine does not proceed until it knows that another machine has reached a certain state; thus the two machines are coordinated.

The handshaking protocol does not solve all the problems of communicating between a sender and receiver that have different clocks. An additional problem arises when we sample an asynchronous signal (such as ReadReq). This problem, called a *synchronization failure*, can lead to unpredictable behavior; it can be overcome with devices called *synchronizers*, which are described in Appendix B.

FSM Control for I/O

Example

Show how the control for an output transaction to an I/O device from memory (as in Figure 8.7) can be implemented as a pair of finite state machines.

Answer

Figure 8.11 shows the two finite state machine controllers that implement the handshaking protocol of Figure 8.10.

If a synchronous bus can be used, it is usually faster than an asynchronous bus because of the overhead required to perform the handshaking. An example demonstrates this.

Performance Analysis of Synchronous versus Asynchronous Buses

Example

We want to compare the maximum bandwidth for a synchronous and an asynchronous bus. The synchronous bus has a clock cycle time of 50 ns, and each bus transmission takes 1 clock cycle. The asynchronous bus requires 40 ns per handshake. The data portion of both buses is 32 bits wide. Find the bandwidth for each bus when performing one-word reads from a 200-ns memory.

Answer

First, the synchronous bus, which has 50-ns bus cycles. The steps and times required for the synchronous bus are as follows:

1. Send the address to memory: 50 ns

2. Read the memory: 200 ns

3. Send the data to the device: 50 ns

Thus, the total time is 300 ns. This yields a maximum bus bandwidth of 4 bytes every 300 ns, or

$$\frac{4 \text{ bytes}}{300 \text{ ns}} = \frac{4 \text{ MB}}{0.3 \text{ seconds}} = 13.3 \frac{\text{MB}}{\text{second}}$$

At first glance, it might appear that the asynchronous bus will be *much* slower, since it will take seven steps, each at least 40 ns, and the step corresponding to the memory access will take 200 ns. If we look carefully at Figure 8.10, we realize that several of the steps can be overlapped with the memory access time. In particular, the memory receives the address at the end of step 1 and does not need to put the data on the bus until the beginning of step 5; steps 2, 3, and 4 can overlap with the memory access time. This leads to the following timing:

Step 1: 40 ns

Steps 2, 3, 4: maximum (3 x 40 ns, 200 ns) = 200 ns

Steps 5, 6, 7: 3 x 40 ns = 120 ns

Thus, the total time to perform the transfer is 360 ns, and the maximum bandwidth is

$$\frac{4 \text{ bytes}}{360 \text{ ns}} = \frac{4 \text{ MB}}{0.36 \text{ seconds}} = 11.1 \frac{\text{MB}}{\text{second}}$$

Accordingly, the synchronous bus is only about 20% faster. Of course, to sustain these rates, the device and memory system on the asynchronous bus will need to be fairly fast to accomplish each handshaking step in 40 ns.

Even though a synchronous bus may be faster, the choice between a synchronous and an asynchronous bus has implications not only for data bandwidth but also for an I/O system's capacity in terms of physical distance and the number of devices that can be connected to the bus. Asynchronous buses scale better with technology changes and can support a wider variety of device response speeds. It is for these reasons that I/O buses are often asynchronous, despite the increased overhead.

Increasing the Bus Bandwidth

Although much of the bandwidth of a bus is decided by the choice of a synchronous or asynchronous protocol and the timing characteristics of the bus, several other factors affect the bandwidth that can be attained by a single transfer. The most important of these are the following:

1. *Data bus width*: By increasing the width of the data bus, transfers of multiple words require fewer bus cycles.

2. *Separate versus multiplexed address and data lines*: Our example in Figure 8.8 used the same wires for address and data; including separate lines for addresses will make the performance of writes faster because the address and data can be transmitted in one bus cycle.

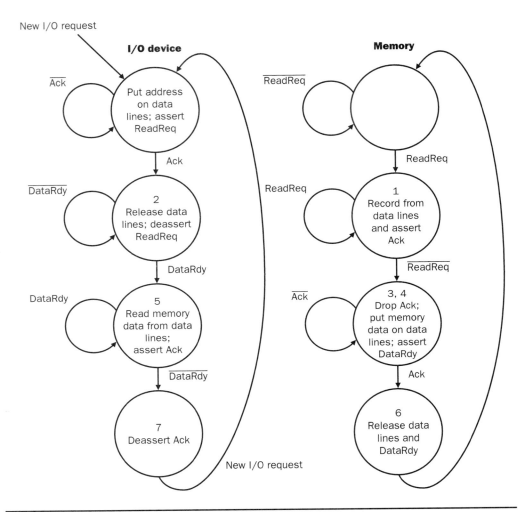

FIGURE 8.11 These finite state machines implement the control for the handshaking protocol illustrated in Figure 8.10. The numbers in each state correspond to the steps shown in Figure 8.10. The first state of the I/O device (upper-left corner) starts the protocol when a new I/O request is generated, just as in Figure 8.10. Each state in the finite state machine effectively records the state of both the device and memory. This is how they stay synchronized during the transaction. After completing a transaction, the I/O side can stay in the last state until a new request needs to be processed.

3. *Block transfers*: Allowing the bus to transfer multiple words in back-to-back bus cycles without sending an address or releasing the bus will reduce the time needed to transfer a large block.

Each of these design alternatives will increase the bus performance for a single bus transfer. The cost of implementing one of these enhancements is one or more of the following: more bus lines, increased complexity, or increased response time for requests that may need to wait while a long block transfer occurs.

Performance Analysis of Two Bus Schemes

Example

Suppose we have a system with the following characteristics:

1. A memory and bus system supporting block access of 4 to 16 32-bit words.

2. A 64-bit synchronous bus clocked at 200 MHz, with each 64-bit transfer taking 1 clock cycle, and 1 clock cycle required to send an address to memory.

3. Two clock cycles needed between each bus operation. (Assume the bus is idle before an access.)

4. A memory access time for the first four words of 200 ns; each additional set of four words can be read in 20 ns. Assume that a bus transfer of the most recently read data and a read of the next four words can be overlapped.

Find the sustained bandwidth and the latency for a read of 256 words for transfers that use 4-word blocks and for transfers that use 16-word blocks. Also compute the effective number of bus transactions per second for each case. Recall that a single bus transaction consists of an address transmission followed by data.

Answer

For the 4-word block transfers, each block takes

1. 1 clock cycle that is required to send the address to memory

2. $\dfrac{200 \text{ ns}}{5 \text{ ns/cycle}} = 40$ clock cycles to read memory

3. 2 clock cycles to send the data from the memory

4. 2 idle clock cycles between this transfer and the next

This is a total of 45 cycles, and $256/4 = 64$ transactions are needed, so the entire transfer takes $45 \times 64 = 2880$ clock cycles. Thus the latency is 2880 cycles $\times$ 5 ns/cycle = 14,400 ns. The number of bus transactions per second is

$$64 \text{ transactions} \times \frac{1 \text{ second}}{14,400 \text{ ns}} = 4.44\text{M transactions/second}$$

The bus bandwidth is

$$(256 \times 4) \text{ bytes} \times \frac{1 \text{ second}}{14,400 \text{ ns}} = 71.11 \text{ MB/sec}$$

For the 16-word block transfers, the first block requires

1. 1 clock cycle to send an address to memory

2. 200 ns or 40 cycles to read the first four words in memory

3. 2 cycles to send the data of the block, during which time the read of the four words in the next block is started

4. 2 idle cycles between transfers and during which the read of the next block is completed

Each of the three remaining 4-word blocks requires repeating only the last two steps.

Thus, the total number of cycles for each 16-word block is $1 + 40 + 4 \times (2 + 2) = 57$ cycles, and $256/16 = 16$ transactions are needed, so the entire transfer takes, $57 \times 16 = 912$ cycles. Thus the latency is 912 cycles $\times$ 5 ns/cycle = 4560 ns, which is roughly one-third of the latency for the case with 4-word blocks. The number of bus transactions per second with 16-word blocks is

$$16 \text{ transactions} \times \frac{1 \text{ second}}{4560 \text{ ns}} = 3.51 \text{M transactions/second}$$

which is lower than the case with 4-word blocks because each transaction takes longer (57 versus 45 cycles).

The bus bandwidth with 16-word blocks is

$$(256 \times 4) \text{ bytes} \times \frac{1 \text{ second}}{4560 \text{ ns}} = 224.56 \text{ MB/second}$$

which is 3.16 times higher than for the 4-word blocks. The advantage of using larger block transfers is clear.

Elaboration: Another method for increasing the effective bus bandwidth when multiple parties want to communicate on the bus is to release the bus when it is not being used for transmitting information. Consider the example of a memory read that we examined in Figure 8.10. What happens to the bus while the memory access is occurring? In this simple protocol, the device and memory continue to hold the bus during the memory access time when no actual transfer is taking place. An alternative protocol, which releases the bus, would operate like this:

1. The device signals the memory and transmits the request and address.

2. After the memory acknowledges the request, both the memory and device release all control lines.

3. The memory access occurs, and the bus is free for other uses during this period.

4. The memory signals the device on the bus to indicate that the data is available.

5. The device receives the data via the bus and signals that it has the data, so the memory system can release the bus.

For the synchronous bus with 16-word transfers in the example above, such a scheme would occupy the bus for only 272 of the 912 cycles required for the complete bus transaction.

This type of protocol is called a *split transaction protocol*. The advantage of such a protocol is that, by freeing the bus during the time data is not being transmitted, the protocol allows another requestor to use the bus. This can improve the effective bus bandwidth for the entire system, if the memory is sophisticated enough to handle multiple overlapping transactions.

With a split transaction, however, the time to complete one transfer is probably increased because the bus must be acquired twice. Split transaction protocols are also more expensive to implement, primarily because of the need to keep track of the other party in a communication. In a split transaction protocol, the memory system must contact the requestor to initiate the reply portion of the bus transaction, so the identity of the requestor must be transmitted and retained by the memory system.

Obtaining Access to the Bus

Now that we have reviewed some of the many design options for buses, we can deal with one of the most important issues in bus design: How is the bus reserved by a device that wishes to use it to communicate? We touched on this question in several of the above discussions, and it is crucial in designing large I/O systems that allow I/O to occur without the processor's continuous and low-level involvement.

Why is a scheme needed for controlling bus access? Without any control, multiple devices desiring to communicate could each try to assert the control and data lines for different transfers! Just as chaos reigns in a classroom when everyone tries to talk at once, multiple devices trying to use the bus simultaneously would result in confusion.

Chaos is avoided by introducing one or more *bus masters* into the system. A bus master controls access to the bus: it must initiate and control all bus requests. The processor must be able to initiate a bus request for memory and thus is always a bus master. The memory is usually a *slave*—since it will respond to read and write requests but never generate its own requests.

The simplest system possible has a single bus master: the processor. Having a single bus master is similar to what normally happens in a classroom—all communication requires the permission of the instructor. In a single-master system, all bus requests must be controlled by the processor. The steps involved in a bus transaction with a single-master bus are shown in Figure 8.12. The major drawback of this approach is that the processor must be involved in every bus transaction. A single sector read from a disk may require the processor to get involved hundreds to thousands of times, depending on the size of each transfer. Because devices have become faster and capable of transferring

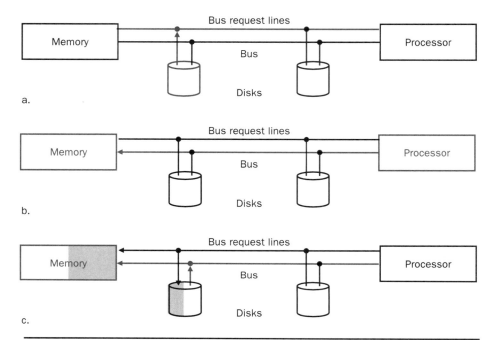

FIGURE 8.12   The initial steps in a bus transaction with a single master (the processor). A set of bus request lines is used by the device to communicate with the processor, which then initiates the bus cycle on behalf of the requesting device. The active lines and units are shown in color in each step. Shading is used to indicate the source of a read (memory) or destination of a write (the disk). After step c, the bus cycle continues like a normal read transaction, as in Figure 8.7. (a) First, the device generates a bus request to indicate to the processor that the device wants to use the bus. (b) The processor responds and generates appropriate bus control signals. For example, if the device wants to perform output from memory, the processor asserts the read request lines to memory. (c) The processor also notifies the device that its bus request is being processed; as a result, the device knows it can use the bus and places the address for the request on the bus.

at much higher bandwidths, involving the processor in every bus transaction has become less and less attractive.

The alternative scheme is to have multiple bus masters, each of which can initiate a transfer. If we want to allow several people in a classroom to talk without the instructor having to recognize each one, we must have a protocol for deciding who gets to talk next. Similarly, with multiple bus masters, we must provide a mechanism for arbitrating access to the bus so that it is used in a cooperative rather than a chaotic way.

Bus Arbitration

Deciding which bus master gets to use the bus next is called *bus arbitration*. There are a wide variety of schemes for bus arbitration; these may involve special hardware or extremely sophisticated bus protocols. In a bus arbitration scheme, a device (or the processor) wanting to use the bus signals a *bus request* and is later *granted* the bus. After a grant, the device can use the bus, later signaling to the arbiter that the bus is no longer required. The arbiter can then grant the bus to another device. Most multiple-master buses have a set of bus lines for performing requests and grants. A bus release line is also needed if each device does not have its own request line. Sometimes the signals used for bus arbitration have physically separate lines, while in other systems the data lines of the bus are used for this function (though this prevents overlapping of arbitration with transfer).

Arbitration schemes usually try to balance two factors in choosing which device to grant the bus. First, each device has a *bus priority*, and the highest-priority device should be serviced first. Second, we would prefer that any device, even one with low priority, never be completely locked out from the bus. This property, called *fairness*, ensures that every device that wants to use the bus is guaranteed to get it eventually. In addition to these factors, more sophisticated schemes aim at reducing the time needed to arbitrate for the bus. Because arbitration time is overhead, which increases the bus access time, it should be reduced and overlapped with bus transfers whenever possible.

Bus arbitration schemes can be divided into four broad classes:

- *Daisy chain arbitration*: In this scheme, the bus grant line is run through the devices from highest priority to lowest (the priorities are determined by the position on the bus). A high-priority device that desires bus access simply intercepts the bus grant signal, not allowing a lower-priority device to see the signal. Figure 8.13 shows how a daisy chain bus is organized. The advantage of a daisy chain bus is simplicity; the disadvantages are that it cannot assure fairness—a low-priority request may be locked out indefinitely—and the use of the daisy chain grant signal also limits the bus speed.

- *Centralized, parallel arbitration*: These schemes use multiple request lines, and the devices independently request the bus. A centralized arbiter chooses from among the devices requesting bus access and notifies the selected device that it is now bus master. The disadvantage of this scheme is that it requires a central arbiter, which may become the bottleneck for bus usage. PCI, a standard backplane bus, uses a central arbitration scheme.

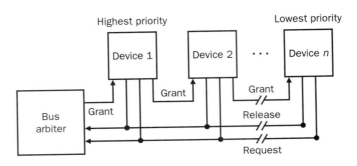

FIGURE 8.13 A daisy chain bus uses a bus grant line that chains through each device from highest to lowest priority. If the device has requested bus access, it uses the grant line to determine access has been given to it. Because the grant line is passed on only if a device does not want access, priority is built into the scheme. The name "daisy chain" arises from the structure of the grant line that chains from device to device. The detailed protocol used by a daisy chain is described in the elaboration below.

■ *Distributed arbitration by self-selection*: These schemes also use multiple request lines, but the devices requesting bus access determine who will be granted access. Each device wanting bus access places a code indicating its identity on the bus. By examining the bus, the devices can determine the highest-priority device that has made a request. There is no need for a central arbiter; each device determines independently whether it is the high-priority requestor. This scheme, however, does require more lines for request signals. The NuBus, which is the backplane bus in Apple Macintosh IIs, uses this scheme.

■ *Distributed arbitration by collision detection*: In this scheme, each device independently requests the bus. Multiple simultaneous requests result in a *collision*. The collision is detected and a scheme for selecting among the colliding parties is used. Ethernets, which use this scheme, are further described in Exercise 8.28 on page 708.

The suitability of different arbitration schemes is determined by a variety of factors, including how expandable the bus must be both in terms of the number of I/O devices and the bus length, how fast the arbitration should be, and what degree of fairness is needed.

Elaboration: The protocol followed by a device on a daisy chain bus is the following:

1. Signal the request line.

2. Wait for a transition on the grant line from low to high, indicating that the bus is being reassigned.

3. Intercept the grant signal, and do not allow lower-priority devices to see it. Stop asserting the request line.

4. Use the bus.

5. Signal that the bus is no longer required by asserting the release line.

By watching for a transition on the grant line, rather than just a level, we prevent the device from taking the bus away from a lower-priority device that believes it has been granted bus access. To improve fairness in a daisy chain scheme, we can simply make the rule that a device that has just used the bus cannot reacquire the bus until it sees the bus request line go low. Since a device will not release the request line until its request is satisfied, all devices will have an opportunity to use the bus before any single device uses it twice. Some bus systems—VME, for example—use multiple daisy chains with a separate set of request and grant lines for each daisy chain and a priority encoder to select from among the multiple requests.

The Big Picture

The different bus characteristics allow the creation of buses optimized for a wide range of different devices, number of devices, and bandwidth demands. Figure 8.14 shows some of the design alternatives we have discussed and what choices might be made in low-cost versus high-performance systems. In general, higher-cost systems use wider and faster buses with more sophisticated protocols—typically a synchronous bus for the reasons we saw in the example on page 662. In contrast, a low-cost system favors a bus that is narrower and does not require intelligence among the devices (hence a single master), and is asynchronous so that low-speed devices can interface inexpensively.

Option	High performance	Low cost
Bus width	separate address and data lines	multiplex address and data lines
Data width	wider is faster (e.g., 32 bits)	narrower is cheaper (e.g., 8 bits)
Transfer size	multiple words require less bus overhead	single-word transfer is simpler
Bus masters	multiple masters (requires arbitration)	single master (no arbitration)
Clocking	synchronous	asynchronous

FIGURE 8.14 The I/O bus characteristics determine the performance of I/O transfers, the number of I/O devices that can be connected, and the cost of connecting devices. Shorter buses can be faster but will not be as expandable. Similarly, wider buses can have higher bandwidth but will be more expensive. Split transaction buses are another way to increase bandwidth at the expense of cost (see the elaboration on page 666).

Bus Standards

Most computers allow users to add additional and even new types of peripherals. The I/O bus serves as a way of expanding the machine and connecting new peripherals. To make this easier, the computer industry has developed several bus standards. The standards serve as a specification for the computer manufacturer and for the peripheral manufacturer. A bus standard ensures the computer designer that peripherals will be available for a new machine, and it ensures the peripheral builder that users will be able to hook up their new equipment.

Machines sometimes become so popular that their I/O buses become de facto standards, as is the case with the IBM PC-AT bus. Once a bus standard is heavily used by peripheral designers, other computer manufacturers incorporate that bus and offer a wide range of peripherals. Sometimes standards are created by groups that are trying to address a common problem. The small computer systems interface (SCSI) and Ethernet are examples of standards that arose from the cooperation of manufacturers. Sanctioning bodies like ANSI or IEEE also create and approve standards. The PCI standard was initiated by Intel and later developed by an industry committee.

Figure 8.15 summarizes the key characteristics of the two dominant bus standards: PCI (a general-purpose backplane bus) and SCSI (an I/O bus). A SCSI bus typically interfaces to a backplane bus or to a processor-memory bus. A SCSI controller coordinates transfers from a device on the I/O bus to the memory via the processor-memory bus. One emerging bus standard is Fibre Channel, proposed as a follow-on to SCSI and based on high-speed point-to-point links, which would be organized as a loop for multiple devices.

Bus bandwidth for a general-purpose bus is not simply a single number. Because of bus overhead, the size of the transfer affects bandwidth significantly. Since the bus usually transfers to or from memory, the speed of the memory also affects the bandwidth.

Buses provide the electrical interconnect among I/O devices, processors, and memory, and also define the lowest-level protocol for communication. Above this basic level, we must define hardware and software protocols for controlling data transfers between I/O devices and memory, and for the processor to specify commands to the I/O devices. These topics are covered in the next section.

Characteristic	PCI	SCSI
Bus type	backplane	I/O
Basic data bus width (signals)	32–64	8–32
Address/data multiplexed?	multiplexed	multiplexed
Number of bus masters	multiple	multiple
Arbitration	centralized, parallel arbitration	self-selection
Clocking	synchronous 33–66 MHz	asynchronous or synchronous (5–10 MHz)
Theoretical peak bandwidth	133–512 MB/sec	5–40 MB/sec
Estimated typical achievable bandwidth for basic bus	80 MB/sec	2.5–40.0 MB/sec (synchronous) or 1.5 MB/sec (asynchronous)
Maximum number of devices	1024 (with multiple bus segments; at most 32 devices/bus segment)	7–31 (bus width − 1)
Maximum bus length	0.5 meter	25 meters
Standard name	PCI	ANSI X3.131

FIGURE 8.15   Key characteristics of two dominant bus standards. Both PCI and SCSI bus standards have been significantly extended. PCI has a double-width version (64 bits vs. 32 bits) and a fast version (66 MHz vs. 33 MHz). The original SCSI bus was asynchronous. Faster, synchronous versions were developed, followed by extensions for a wider bus (16 and 32 bits versus 8, called wide SCSI) and a faster clock (10 MHz, called fast SCSI, vs. 5 MHz for the original synchronous SCSI). Fast, wide SCSI combines the higher clock rate and wider bus. In addition, a 20-MHz version of the SCSI bus (called Ultra) was developed and released in late 1996. The specifications for these standard buses become extremely complex. For example, the PCI standard is 282 pages long, while the SCSI-2 specification, which includes both the faster and wider versions, is over 600 pages long! The SCSI-2 specification, a good overview of SCSI and its development, and the PCI specification are available via links at *www.mkp.com/books_catalog/cod/links.htm.*

8.5   Interfacing I/O Devices to the Memory, Processor, and Operating System

A bus protocol defines how a word or block of data should be communicated on a set of wires. This still leaves several other tasks that must be performed to actually cause data to be transferred from a device and into the memory address space of some user program. This section focuses on these tasks and will answer such questions as the following:

- How is a user I/O request transformed into a device command and communicated to the device?
- How is data actually transferred to or from a memory location?
- What is the role of the operating system?

As we will see when we answer these questions, the operating system plays a major role in handling I/O, acting as the interface between the hardware and the program that requests I/O.

The responsibilities of the operating system arise from three characteristics of I/O systems:

1. The I/O system is shared by multiple programs using the processor.

2. I/O systems often use interrupts (externally generated exceptions) to communicate information about I/O operations. Because interrupts cause a transfer to kernel or supervisor mode, they must be handled by the operating system (OS).

3. The low-level control of an I/O device is complex because it requires managing a set of concurrent events and because the requirements for correct device control are often very detailed.

Hardware Software Interface

The three characteristics of I/O systems above lead to several different functions the OS must provide:

■ The OS guarantees that a user's program accesses only the portions of an I/O device to which the user has rights. For example, the OS must not allow a program to read or write a file on disk if the owner of the file has not granted access to this program. In a system with shared I/O devices, protection could not be provided if user programs could perform I/O directly.

■ The OS provides abstractions for accessing devices by supplying routines that handle low-level device operations.

■ The OS handles the interrupts generated by I/O devices, just as it handles the exceptions generated by a program.

■ The OS tries to provide equitable access to the shared I/O resources, as well as schedule accesses in order to enhance system throughput.

To perform these functions on behalf of user programs, the operating system must be able to communicate with the I/O devices and to prevent the user program from communicating with the I/O devices directly. Three types of communication are required:

1. The OS must be able to give commands to the I/O devices. These commands include not only operations like read and write, but other operations to be done on the device, such as a disk seek.

2. The device must be able to notify the OS when the I/O device has completed an operation or has encountered an error. For example, when a disk has completed a seek, it will notify the OS.

3. Data must be transferred between memory and an I/O device. For example, the block being read on a disk read must be moved from disk to memory.

In the next few sections, we will see how these communications are performed.

Giving Commands to I/O Devices

To give a command to an I/O device, the processor must be able to address the device and to supply one or more command words. Two methods are used to address the device: memory-mapped I/O and special I/O instructions. In memory-mapped I/O, portions of the address space are assigned to I/O devices. Reads and writes to those addresses are interpreted as commands to the I/O device.

For example, a write operation can be used to send data to an I/O device where the data will be interpreted as a command. When the processor places the address and data on the memory bus, the memory system ignores the operation because the address indicates a portion of the memory space used for I/O. The device controller, however, sees the operation, records the data, and transmits it to the device as a command. User programs are prevented from issuing I/O operations directly because the OS does not provide access to the address space assigned to the I/O devices and thus the addresses are protected by the address translation. Memory-mapped I/O can also be used to transmit data by writing or reading to select addresses. The device uses the address to determine the type of command, and the data may be provided by a write or obtained by a read. In any event, the address encodes both the device identity and the type of transmission between processor and device.

Actually performing a read or write of data to fulfill a program request usually requires several separate I/O operations. Furthermore, the processor may have to interrogate the status of the device between individual commands to determine whether the command completed successfully. For example, the DEC LP11 line printer has two I/O device registers—one for status information and one for data to be printed. The Status register contains a *done bit*, set by the printer when it has printed a character, and an *error bit*, indicating that the printer is jammed or out of paper. Each byte of data to be printed is put into the Data register. The processor must then wait until the printer sets the done bit before it can place another character in the buffer. The processor must also check the error bit to determine if a problem has occurred. Each of these operations requires a separate I/O device access.

Elaboration: The alternative to memory-mapped I/O is to use dedicated I/O instructions in the processor. These I/O instructions can specify both the device number and the command word (or the location of the command word in memory). The processor communicates the device address via a set of wires normally included as part of the I/O bus. The actual command can be transmitted over the data lines in the bus. Examples of computers with I/O instructions are the Intel 80x86 and the IBM 370 computers. By making the I/O instructions illegal to execute when not in kernel or supervisor mode, user programs can be prevented from accessing the devices directly.

Communicating with the Processor

The process of periodically checking status bits to see if it is time for the next I/O operation, as in the previous example, is called *polling*. Polling is the simplest way for an I/O device to communicate with the processor. The I/O device simply puts the information in a Status register, and the processor must come and get the information. The processor is totally in control and does all the work.

The disadvantage of polling is that it can waste a lot of processor time because processors are so much faster than I/O devices. The processor may read the Status register many times, only to find that the device has not yet completed a comparatively slow I/O operation, or that the mouse has not budged since the last time it was polled. When the device has completed an operation, we must still read the status to determine whether it was successful.

Polling can be used in several different ways, depending on the I/O device and whether the I/O device can initiate I/O independently. For example, a mouse is an input-only device that initiates I/O independently, when a user moves the mouse or clicks a button. Because a mouse has a low I/O rate, polling is often used to interface to a mouse. Many other I/O devices, such as a floppy disk or a printer, initiate I/O only under control of the operating system. Thus we need only poll such devices when the OS knows that the device is active. As we will see, this allows polling to be used even when the I/O rate is somewhat higher.

Overhead of Polling in an I/O System

Example

Let's determine the impact of polling overhead for three different devices. Assume that the number of clock cycles for a polling operation—including transferring to the polling routine, accessing the device, and restarting the user program—is 400 and that the processor executes with a 500-MHz clock.

Determine the fraction of CPU time consumed for the following three cases, assuming that you poll often enough so that no data is ever lost and assuming that the devices are potentially always busy:

1. The mouse must be polled 30 times per second to ensure that we do not miss any movement made by the user.

2. The floppy disk transfers data to the processor in 16-bit units and has a data rate of 50 KB/sec. No data transfer can be missed.

3. The hard disk transfers data in four-word chunks and can transfer at 4 MB/sec. Again, no transfer can be missed.

Answer

First the mouse:

$$\text{Clock cycles per second for polling} = 30 \times 400 = 12{,}000 \text{ cycles per second}$$

$$\text{Fraction of the processor clock cycles consumed} = \frac{12 \times 10^3}{500 \times 10^6} = 0.002\%$$

Polling can clearly be used for the mouse without much performance impact on the processor.

For the floppy disk, the rate at which we must poll is

$$\frac{50\dfrac{\text{KB}}{\text{second}}}{2\dfrac{\text{bytes}}{\text{polling access}}} = 25\text{K}\frac{\text{polling accesses}}{\text{second}}$$

Thus, we can compute the number of cycles (ignoring the base 2 versus base 10 discrepancy):

$$\text{Cycles per second for polling} = 25\text{K} \times 400$$

$$\text{Fraction of the processor consumed} = \frac{10 \times 10^6}{500 \times 10^6} = 2\%$$

This amount of overhead is significant, but might be tolerable in a low-end system with only a few I/O devices like this floppy disk.

In the case of the hard disk, we must poll at a rate equal to the data rate in four-word chunks, which is 250K times per second (4 MB per second/16 bytes per transfer). Thus,

$$\text{Cycles per second for polling} = 250\text{K} \times 400$$

Ignoring the discrepancy in bases,

$$\text{Fraction of the processor consumed} = \frac{100 \times 10^6}{500 \times 10^6} = 20\%$$

Thus one-fifth of the processor would be used in just polling the disk. Clearly, polling will probably be unacceptable for a hard disk on this machine.

If we knew that the floppy disk and hard disk were active only 25% of the time and we poll only when the device is active, then the average overhead for polling would be reduced to 0.5% and 5%, respectively. Although this reduces the overhead, notice that once the OS initiates an operation on the device, it must poll continuously since the OS does not know when the device will actually respond and want to initiate a transfer.

The overhead in a polling interface was recognized long ago, leading to the invention of interrupts to notify the processor when an I/O device requires attention from the processor. *Interrupt-driven I/O,* which is used by almost all systems for at least some devices, employs I/O interrupts to indicate to the processor that an I/O device needs attention. When a device wants to notify the processor that it has completed some operation or needs attention, it causes the processor to be interrupted.

An I/O interrupt is just like the exceptions we saw in Chapters 5, 6, and 7, with two important exceptions:

1. An I/O interrupt is asynchronous with respect to the instruction execution. That is, the interrupt is not associated with any instruction and does not prevent the instruction completion. This is very different from either page fault exceptions or exceptions such as arithmetic overflow. Our control unit need only check for a pending I/O interrupt at the time it starts a new instruction.

2. In addition to the fact that an I/O interrupt has occurred, we would like to convey further information such as the identity of the device generating the interrupt. Furthermore, the interrupts represent devices that may have different priorities and whose interrupt requests have different urgencies associated with them.

To communicate information to the processor, such as the identity of the device raising the interrupt, a system can use either vectored interrupts or an exception Cause register. When the interrupt is recognized by the processor, the device can send either the vector address or a status field to place in the Cause register. As a result, when the OS gets control, it knows the identity of the device that caused the interrupt and can immediately interrogate the device. An interrupt mechanism eliminates the need for the processor to poll the device and instead allows the processor to focus on executing programs.

Elaboration: To deal with the different priorities of the I/O devices, most interrupt mechanisms have several levels of priority. These priorities indicate the order in which the processor should process interrupts. Both internally generated exceptions and I/O interrupts have priorities; typically, I/O interrupts have lower priority than internal exceptions. There may be multiple I/O interrupt priorities, with high-speed devices associated with the higher priorities. If the exception mechanism is vectored (see section 5.6), the vector address for a fast device will correspond to the higher-priority interrupt. If a Cause register is used, then the register contents for a faster device are set for the higher-priority interrupt.

Transferring the Data between a Device and Memory

We have seen two different methods that enable a device to communicate with the processor. These two techniques, polling and I/O interrupts, form the basis for two methods of implementing the transfer of data between the I/O device and memory. Both these techniques work best with lower-bandwidth devices, where we are more interested in reducing the cost of the device controller and interface than in providing a high-bandwidth transfer. Both polling and interrupt-driven transfers put the burden of moving data and managing the transfer on the processor. After looking at these two schemes, we will examine a scheme more suitable for higher-performance devices or collections of devices.

We can use the processor to transfer data between a device and memory based on polling. Consider our mouse example. The processor can periodically read the mouse counter values and the position of the mouse buttons. If the position of the mouse or one of its buttons has changed, the operating system can notify the program associated with interpreting the mouse changes.

An alternative mechanism is to make the transfer of data interrupt driven. In this case, the OS would still transfer data in small numbers of bytes from or to the device. But because the I/O operation is interrupt driven, the OS simply works on other tasks while data is being read from or written to the device. When the OS recognizes an interrupt from the device, it reads the status to check for errors. If there are none, the OS can supply the next piece of data, for example, by a sequence of memory-mapped writes. When the last byte of an I/O request has been transmitted and the I/O operation is completed, the OS can inform the program. The processor and OS do all the work in this process, accessing the device and memory for each data item transferred. Let's see how an interrupt-driven I/O interface might work for the floppy disk.

Overhead of Interrupt-Driven I/O

Example

Suppose we have the same hard disk and processor we used in the example on page 676, but we use interrupt-driven I/O. The overhead for each transfer, including the interrupt, is 500 clock cycles. Find the fraction of the processor consumed if the hard disk is only transferring data 5% of the time.

Answer

The interrupt rate when the disk is busy is the same as the polling rate. Hence,

$$\text{Cycles per second for disk} = 250\text{K} \times 500$$
$$= 125 \times 10^6 \text{ cycles per second}$$

$$\text{Fraction of the processor consumed during a transfer} = \frac{125 \times 10^6}{500 \times 10^6} = 25\%$$

Assuming that the disk is only transferring data 5% of the time,

$$\text{Fraction of the processor consumed on average} = 25\% \times 5\% = 1.25\%$$

As we can see, the absence of overhead when an I/O device is not actually transferring is the major advantage of an interrupt-driven interface versus polling.

Interrupt-driven I/O relieves the processor from having to wait for every I/O event, although if we used this method for transferring data from or to a hard disk, the overhead could still be intolerable, since it would consume 25% of the processor when the disk was transferring. For high-bandwidth devices like hard disks, the transfers consist primarily of relatively large blocks of data (hundreds to thousands of bytes). So computer designers invented a mechanism for off-loading the processor and having the device controller transfer data directly to or from the memory without involving the processor. This mechanism is called *direct memory access* (DMA). The interrupt mechanism is still used by the device to communicate with the processor, but only on completion of the I/O transfer or when an error occurs.

DMA is implemented with a specialized controller that transfers data between an I/O device and memory independent of the processor. The DMA controller becomes the bus master and directs the reads or writes between itself and memory. There are three steps in a DMA transfer:

1. The processor sets up the DMA by supplying the identity of the device, the operation to perform on the device, the memory address that is the source or destination of the data to be transferred, and the number of bytes to transfer.

2. The DMA starts the operation on the device and arbitrates for the bus. When the data is available (from the device or memory), it transfers the data. The DMA device supplies the memory address for the read or write. If the request requires more than one transfer on the bus, the DMA unit generates the next memory address and initiates the next transfer. Using this mechanism, a DMA unit can complete an entire transfer, which may be thousands of bytes in length, without bothering the processor. Many DMA controllers contain some memory to allow them to deal flexibly with delays either in transfer or those incurred while waiting to become bus master.

3. Once the DMA transfer is complete, the controller interrupts the processor, which can then determine by interrogating the DMA device or examining memory whether the entire operation completed successfully.

There may be multiple DMA devices in a computer system. For example, in a system with a single processor-memory bus and multiple I/O buses, each I/O bus controller will often contain a DMA processor that handles any transfers between a device on the I/O bus and the memory. Let's see how much of the processor is consumed using DMA to handle our hard-disk example.

Overhead of I/O Using DMA

Example

Suppose we have the same processor and hard disk as our earlier example on page 676. Assume that the initial setup of a DMA transfer takes 1000 clock cycles for the processor, and assume the handling of the interrupt at DMA completion requires 500 clock cycles for the processor. The hard disk has a transfer rate of 4 MB/sec and uses DMA. If the average transfer from the disk is 8 KB, what fraction of the 500-MHz processor is consumed if the disk is actively transferring 100% of the time? Ignore any impact from bus contention between the processor and DMA controller.

Answer

Each DMA transfer takes

$$\frac{8 \text{ KB}}{4\dfrac{\text{MB}}{\text{second}}} = 2 \times 10^{-3} \text{ seconds}$$

So if the disk is constantly transferring, it requires

$$\frac{1000 + 500\dfrac{\text{cycles}}{\text{transfer}}}{2 \times 10^{-3}\dfrac{\text{seconds}}{\text{transfer}}} = 750 \times 10^3\dfrac{\text{clock cycles}}{\text{second}}$$

Since the processor runs at 500 MHz,

$$\text{Fraction of processor consumed} = \frac{750 \times 10^3}{500 \times 10^6}$$

$$= 1.5 \times 10^{-3} = 0.2\%$$

Unlike either polling or interrupt-driven I/O, DMA can be used to interface a hard disk without consuming all the processor cycles for a single I/O. In addition, the disk will not be actively transferring data most of the time, and this number will be considerably lower. Of course, if the processor is also contending for memory, it will be delayed when the memory is busy doing a DMA transfer. By using caches, the processor can avoid having to access memory most of the time, thereby leaving most of the memory bandwidth free for use by I/O devices.

Elaboration: To further reduce the need to interrupt the processor and occupy it in handling an I/O request that may involve doing several actual operations, the I/O controller can be made more intelligent. Intelligent controllers are often called *I/O processors* (as well as *I/O controllers* or *channel controllers*). These specialized processors basically execute a series of I/O operations, called an *I/O program*. The program may be stored in the I/O processor, or it may be stored in memory and fetched by the I/O processor. When using an I/O processor, the operating system typically sets up an I/O program that indicates the I/O operations to be done as well as the size and transfer address for any reads or writes. The I/O processor then takes the operations from the I/O program and interrupts the processor only when the entire program is completed. DMA processors are essentially special-purpose processors (usually single-chip and nonprogrammable), while I/O processors are often implemented with general-purpose microprocessors, which run a specialized I/O program.

Direct Memory Access and the Memory System

When DMA is incorporated into an I/O system, the relationship between the memory system and processor changes. Without DMA, all accesses to the memory system come from the processor and thus proceed through address translation and cache access as if the processor generated the references. With DMA, there is another path to the memory system—one that does not go through the address translation mechanism or the cache hierarchy. This difference generates some problems in both virtual memory systems and systems with caches. These problems are usually solved with a combination of hardware techniques and software support.

The difficulties in having DMA in a virtual memory system arise because pages have both a physical and a virtual address. DMA also creates problems for systems with caches because there can be two copies of a data item: one in the cache and one in memory. Because the DMA processor issues memory requests directly to the memory rather than through the cache, the value of a memory location seen by the DMA unit and the processor may differ. Consider a read from disk that the DMA unit places directly into memory. If some of the locations into which the DMA writes are in the cache, the processor will receive

Hardware Software Interface

In a system with virtual memory, should DMA work with virtual addresses or physical addresses? The obvious problem with virtual addresses is that the DMA unit will need to translate the virtual addresses to physical addresses. The major problem with the use of a physical address in a DMA transfer is that the transfer cannot easily cross a page boundary. If an I/O request crossed a page boundary, then the memory locations to which it was being transferred would not be contiguous in the physical memory—the memory locations would correspond to multiple virtual pages, each of which could be mapped to any physical page. Consequently, if we use physical addresses, we must constrain all DMA transfers to stay within one page.

One method to allow the system to initiate DMA transfers that cross page boundaries is to make the DMA work on virtual addresses. In such a system, the DMA unit has a small number of map entries that provide virtual-to-physical mapping for a transfer. The operating system provides the mapping when the I/O is initiated. By using this mapping, the DMA unit need not worry about the location of the virtual pages involved in the transfer.

Another technique is for the operating system to break the DMA transfer into a series of transfers, each confined within a single physical page. The transfers are then *chained* together and handed to an I/O processor or intelligent DMA unit that executes the entire sequence of transfers; alternatively, the operating system can individually request the transfers.

Whichever method is used, the operating system must still cooperate by not remapping pages while a DMA transfer involving that page is in progress.

the old value when it does a read. Similarly, if the cache is write-back, the DMA may read a value directly from memory when a newer value is in the cache, and the value has not been written back. This is called the *stale data problem* or *coherency problem*.

We have looked at three different methods for transferring data between an I/O device and memory. In moving from polling to an interrupt-driven to a DMA interface, we shift the burden for managing an I/O operation from the processor to a progressively more intelligent I/O controller. These methods have the advantage of freeing up processor cycles. Their disadvantage is that they increase the cost of the I/O system. Because of this, a given computer system can choose which point along this spectrum is appropriate for the I/O devices connected to it.

Hardware Software Interface

The coherency problem for I/O data is avoided by using one of three major techniques. One approach is to route the I/O activity through the cache. This ensures that reads see the latest value while writes update any data in the cache. Routing all I/O through the cache is expensive and potentially has a large negative performance impact on the processor, since the I/O data is rarely used immediately and may displace useful data that a running program needs. A second choice is to have the OS selectively invalidate the cache for an I/O read or force write-backs to occur for an I/O write (often called cache *flushing*). This approach requires some small amount of hardware support and is probably more efficient if the software can perform the function easily and efficiently. Because this flushing of large parts of the cache need only happen on DMA block accesses, it will be relatively infrequent. The third approach is to provide a hardware mechanism for selectively flushing (or invalidating) cache entries. Hardware invalidation to ensure cache coherence is typical in multiprocessor systems, and the same technique can be used for I/O; we discuss this topic in detail in Chapter 9.

8.6   Designing an I/O System

There are two primary types of specifications that designers encounter in I/O systems: latency constraints and bandwidth constraints. In both cases, knowledge of the traffic pattern affects the design and analysis.

Latency constraints involve ensuring that the latency to complete an I/O operation is bounded by a certain amount. In the simple case, the system may be unloaded, and the designer must ensure that some latency bound is met either because it is critical to the application or because the device must receive certain guaranteed service to prevent errors. Examples of the latter are similar to the analysis we looked at in the previous section. Likewise, determining the latency on an unloaded system is relatively easy, since it involves tracing the path of the I/O operation and summing the individual latencies.

Finding the average latency (or distribution of latency) under a load is a much more complex problem. Such problems are tackled either by queuing theory (when the behavior of the workload requests and I/O service times can be approximated by simple distributions) or by simulation (when the behavior of I/O events is complex). Both topics are beyond the limits of this text.

Designing an I/O system to meet a set of bandwidth constraints given a workload is the other typical problem designers face. Alternatively, the designer may be given a partially configured I/O system and be asked to balance the system to maintain the maximum bandwidth achievable as dictated by the preconfigured portion of the system. This latter design problem is a simplified version of the first.

The general approach to designing such a system is as follows:

1. Find the weakest link in the I/O system, which is the component in the I/O path that will constrain the design. Depending on the workload, this component can be anywhere, including the CPU, the memory system, the backplane bus, the I/O controllers, or the devices. Both the workload and configuration limits may dictate where the weakest link is located.

2. Configure this component to sustain the required bandwidth.

3. Determine the requirements for the rest of the system and configure them to support this bandwidth.

The easiest way to understand this methodology is with an example.

I/O System Design

Example   Consider the following computer system:

- A CPU that sustains 300 million instructions per second and averages 50,000 instructions in the operating system per I/O operation

- A memory backplane bus capable of sustaining a transfer rate of 100 MB/sec

- SCSI-2 controllers with a transfer rate of 20 MB/sec and accommodating up to seven disks

- Disk drives with a read/write bandwidth of 5 MB/sec and an average seek plus rotational latency of 10 ms

If the workload consists of 64-KB reads (where the block is sequential on a track) and the user program needs 100,000 instructions per I/O operation, find the maximum sustainable I/O rate and the number of disks and SCSI controllers required. Assume that the reads can always be done on an idle disk if one exists (i.e., ignore disk conflicts).

Answer   The two fixed components of the system are the memory bus and the CPU. Let's first find the I/O rate that these two components can sustain and determine which of these is the bottleneck. Each I/O takes 100,000 user instructions and 50,000 OS instructions, so

Maximum I/O rate of CPU =

$$\frac{\text{Instruction execution rate}}{\text{Instructions per I/O}} = \frac{300 \times 10^6}{(50 + 100) \times 10^3} = 2000 \frac{\text{I/Os}}{\text{second}}$$

Each I/O transfers 64 KB, so

$$\text{Maximum I/O rate of bus} = \frac{\text{Bus bandwidth}}{\text{Bytes per I/O}} = \frac{100 \times 10^6}{64 \times 10^3} = 1562 \frac{\text{I/Os}}{\text{second}}$$

The bus is the bottleneck, so we can now configure the rest of the system to perform at the level dictated by the bus, 1562 I/Os per second.

Now, let's determine how many disks we need to be able to accommodate 1562 I/Os per second. To find the number of disks, we first find the time per I/O operation at the disk:

Time per I/O at disk = Seek/rotational time + Transfer time

$$= 10 \text{ ms} + \frac{64 \text{ KB}}{5 \text{ MB/sec}} = 22.8 \text{ ms}$$

This means each disk can complete 43.9 I/Os per second. To saturate the bus requires 1562 I/Os per second, or $1562/43.9 \approx 36$ disks.

To compute the number of SCSI buses, we need to know the average transfer rate per disk, which is given by

$$\text{Transfer rate} = \frac{\text{Transfer size}}{\text{Transfer time}} = \frac{64 \text{KB}}{22.8 \text{ ms}} \approx 2.74 \text{ MB/sec}$$

Assuming the disk accesses are not clustered so that we can use all the bus bandwidth, we can place seven disks per SCSI bus and controller. This means we will need 36/7, or six buses and controllers.

Notice the significant number of simplifying assumptions that are needed to do this example. In practice, many of these simplifications might not hold for critical I/O-intensive applications (such as databases). For this reason, simulation is often the only realistic way to predict the I/O performance of a realistic workload.

Real Stuff: A Typical Desktop I/O System

The emergence of two dominant standards in the desktop personal computer market has led to an enormous degree of commonality among I/O systems. These two standards are PCI, as a backplane bus, and SCSI or SCSI-2, as an I/O bus. Although systems with older buses (ISA or IDE) continue to ship, such systems have rapidly been replaced on all but the least-expensive, lowest-performance machines. Interestingly, the benefits of a single bus standard, in terms of greater availability of devices and lower cost, have led to the adoption of backplane and I/O bus standards across both the IBM-compatible and Macintosh platforms, and a larger fraction of workstation vendors are also adhering to these standards.

Figure 8.16 shows the I/O system of the Macintosh 7200 series, which is typical of the I/O system of midrange to high-end desktop machines in 1997. PCI is used as the backplane bus, with slower devices sharing a lower-performance bus, such as SCSI.

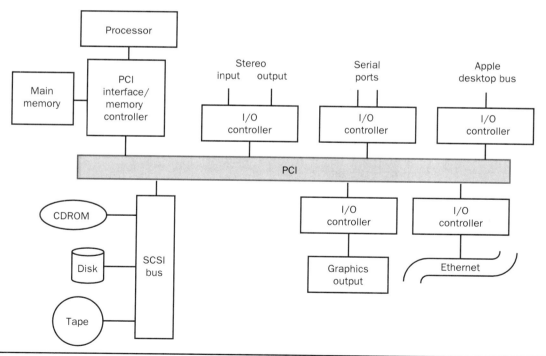

FIGURE 8.16 **Organization of the I/O system on the Apple Macintosh 7200 series.** The PCI backplane bus is used to interface all devices and interfaces to the processor and memory system. Serial ports provide for connections such as low-speed Appletalk network. The desktop bus provides support for keyboards and mice. In reality, several of the slow I/O devices (audio I/O, serial ports, and the desktop bus) share a single port onto the PCI bus, but we show them separately for simplicity.

8.8   # Fallacies and Pitfalls

Fallacy: A 100-MB/sec bus can transfer 100 MB of data in 1 second.

Of course, this is only a fallacy when the definition of a megabyte of storage and a megabyte per second of bandwidth do not agree. As we discussed on page 642, I/O bandwidth measures are usually quoted in base 10 (i.e., 1 MB/sec = 10^6 bytes/sec), while 1 MB of data is typically a base 2 measure (i.e., 1 MB = 2^{20} bytes). How significant is this distinction? The time to transfer 100 MB of data on a 100-MB/sec bus is actually

$$\frac{100 \times 2^{20}}{100 \times 10^6} = \frac{1,048,576}{1,000,000} = 1.048576 \approx 1 \text{ second}$$

A similar, but smaller, error is introduced when we treat a kilobyte, meaning either 10^3 or 2^{10} bytes, as equivalent, while a larger error is introduced when we treat a gigabyte, meaning either 10^9 or 2^{20} bytes, as equivalent.

Pitfall: Using the peak transfer rate of a portion of the I/O system to make performance projections or performance comparisons.

Many of the components of an I/O system, from the devices to the controllers to the buses, are specified using their peak bandwidths. In practice, these peak bandwidth measurements are often based on unrealistic assumptions about the system or are unattainable because of other system limitations. For example, in quoting bus performance, the peak transfer rate is often specified using a memory system that is impossible to build.

A PCI bus has a peak bandwidth of about 133 MB/sec. In practice, even for long transfers, it is difficult to sustain more than about 80 MB/sec for realistic memory systems.

Amdahl's law also reminds us that the throughput of an I/O system will be limited by the lowest-performance component in the I/O path.

Fallacy: Magnetic storage is on its last legs and will be replaced shortly.

This is both a fallacy and a pitfall. Such claims have been made constantly for the past 20 years, though the string of failed alternatives in recent years seems to have reduced the level of claims for the death of magnetic storage. Among the unsuccessful candidates proposed to replace magnetic storage have been magnetic bubble memories, optical storage, and photographic storage. None of these systems has matched the combination of characteristics that favor magnetic disks: nonvolatility, low cost, reasonable access time, and high reliability. Magnetic storage technology continues to improve at the same or faster pace it has sustained over the past 25 years. In fact, the rate of density improvement has increased in the last 10 years, and rotational speeds and seek times have also improved significantly in the past few years.

Pitfall: Moving functions from the CPU to the I/O processor, expecting to improve performance without a careful analysis.

There are many examples of this pitfall trapping people, although I/O processors, when properly used, can certainly enhance performance. A frequent instance of this fallacy is the use of intelligent I/O interfaces, which, because of the higher overhead to set up an I/O, can turn out to have worse latency than a processor-directed I/O activity (although if the processor is freed up sufficiently, system throughput may still increase). Frequently, performance falls when the I/O processor has much lower performance than the main processor. Consequently, a small amount of main processor time is replaced with a larger amount of I/O processor time. Workstation designers have seen both these phenomena repeatedly.

A more serious problem can occur when the migration of an I/O feature changes the instruction set architecture or system architecture in a programmer-visible way. This forces all future machines to have to live with a decision that made sense in the past. If CPUs improve in cost/performance more rapidly than the I/O processor (and this will likely be the case), then moving the function may result in a slower machine in the next computer.

The most telling example comes from the IBM 360. It was decided that the performance of the ISAM system, an early database system, would improve if some of the record searching occurred in the disk controller itself. A key field was associated with each record, and the device searched each key as the disk rotated until it found a match. It would then transfer the desired record. This technique requires an extra large gap between records when a key is present.

The speed at which a track can be searched is limited by the speed of the disk and by the number of keys that can be packed on a track. On an IBM 3330 disk, the key is typically 10 characters; the gap is equivalent to 191 characters if there is a key, and 135 characters when no key is present. If we assume that the data is also 10 characters and that the track has nothing else on it, a 13,165-byte track can contain

$$\frac{13,165}{191 + 10 + 10} = 62 \text{ key-data records}$$

The time per key search is

$$\frac{16.7 \text{ ms (1 revolution)}}{62} = 0.27 \text{ ms/key search}$$

In place of this scheme, we could put several key-data pairs in a single block and have smaller interrecord gaps. Assuming that there are 15 key-data pairs per block and that the track has nothing else on it, then

$$\frac{13,165}{135 + 15 \times (10 + 10)} = \frac{13,165}{135 + 300} = 30 \text{ blocks of key-data pairs}$$

The revised performance is then

$$\frac{16.7 \text{ ms } (1 \text{ revolution})}{30 \times 15} \approx 0.04 \text{ ms/key search}$$

Of course, the disk-based search would look better if the keys were much longer.

As processors got faster, the CPU time for a search became trivial, while the time for a search using the hardware facility improved very little. While the strategy made early machines faster, programs that use the key search operation in the I/O processor run up to six times slower on today's machines!

8.9 Concluding Remarks

I/O systems are evaluated on several different characteristics: the variety of I/O devices supported; the maximum number of I/O devices; cost; and performance, measured both in latency and in throughput. These goals lead to widely varying schemes for interfacing I/O devices. In the low end, schemes like buffering and even DMA can be avoided to minimize cost. In midrange systems, buffered DMA is likely to be the dominant transfer mechanism. In the high end, latency and bandwidth may both be important, and cost may be secondary. Multiple paths to I/O devices with limited buffering often characterize high-end I/O systems. Increasing the bandwidth with both more and wider connections eliminates the need for buffering at an increase in cost. Typically, being able to access the data on an I/O device at any time (high availability) becomes more important as systems grow. As a result, redundancy and error correction mechanisms become more and more prevalent as we enlarge the system.

The design of I/O systems is complicated because the limiting factor in I/O system performance can be any of several critical resources in the I/O path, from the operating system to the device. Furthermore, independent requests from different programs interact in the I/O system, making the performance of an I/O request dependent on other activity that occurs at the same time. Lastly, design techniques that improve bandwidth often negatively impact latency, and vice versa. For example, adding buffering usually increases the system cost and also the system bandwidth. But it also increases latency by placing additional hardware between the device and memory. It is this combination of factors, including some that are unpredictable, that makes designing I/O systems and improving their performance challenging not only for architects but also for OS designers and even programmers building I/O-intensive applications.

> **The Big Picture**
>
> The performance of an I/O system, whether measured by bandwidth or latency, depends on all the elements in the path between the device and memory, including the operating system that generates the I/O commands. The bandwidth of the buses, the memory, and the device determine the maximum transfer rate from or to the device. Similarly, the latency depends on the device latency, together with any latency imposed by the memory system or buses. The effective bandwidth and response latency also depend on other I/O requests that may cause contention for some resource in the path. Finally, the operating system is a bottleneck. In some cases, the OS takes a long time to deliver an I/O request from a user program to an I/O device, leading to high latency. In other cases, the operating system effectively limits the I/O bandwidth because of limitations in the number of concurrent I/O operations it can support.

Future Directions in I/O Systems

What does the future hold for I/O systems? The rapidly increasing performance of processors strains I/O systems, whose physical components cannot improve in performance as fast as processors. To hide the growing gap between the speed of processors and the access time to secondary storage (primarily disks), main memory is used as a cache for secondary storage. These *file caches*, which rely on spatial and temporal locality in access to secondary storage, are maintained by the operating system. The use of file caches allows many file accesses to be handled from memory rather than from disk.

Magnetic disks are increasing in capacity quickly, but access time is improving only slowly. One reason for this is that the opportunities for magnetic disks are growing faster in the low end of the market than in the high end, and the low end is driven primarily by the demand for lower cost per megabyte. This market has helped shrink the size of the disk from the 14-inch platters of the mainframe disk to the 1.3-inch disks developed for laptop and palmtop computers. In fact, the dramatic demand for small disks has led to an accelerated rate of improvement in disk density, so that the density of magnetic disks has been growing faster since about 1990 than it ever did! What is surprising is that this period of growth came at a time when a number of people were predicting the end (or at least a reduction in the use) of magnetic disks!

In addition to increases in density, transfer rates have grown rapidly as disks increased in rotational speed and interfaces improved. In addition, virtually every high-performance disk manufactured today includes a track or sector buffer that caches sectors as the read head passes over them.

One major new disk organization that has emerged in the last few years is an array of small and inexpensive disks. The argument for arrays is that since price per megabyte is independent of disk size, potential throughput can be increased by having many disk drives and, hence, many disk heads. Simply spreading data over multiple disks automatically forces accesses to several disks. (While arrays improve throughput, latency is not necessarily reduced.) Adding redundant disks to the array offers the opportunity for the array to discover a failed disk and automatically recover the lost information. Arrays may thus enhance the reliability of a computer system as well as performance. This redundancy has inspired the acronym *RAID* for these arrays: *redundant arrays of inexpensive disks*. A number of computer companies offer RAIDs for their disk subsystems. For example, IBM has both a RAID offering (see the IBM link at *www.mkp.com/books_catalog/cod/links.htm*), as well as a disk subsystem built from the largest disks they manufacture.

The next level of the storage hierarchy below magnetic disks has also yielded extraordinary increases in capacity in the last several years. This increase has come partly from improvements in magnetic recording that also helped disks, but also from a different recording technology, the *helical scan tape*. Found in VCRs, camcorders, and digital audio tapes, helical scan tape records at an angle to the tape rather than parallel, as in longitudinally recorded tapes. The tape still moves at the same speed, but the fast-spinning tape head records bits much more densely—a factor of about 50 to 100 denser than longitudinally recorded tapes. And because the medium was created for consumer products, the improvement in cost per bit over time has been even greater than for traditional magnetic tapes used solely by the computer industry.

Advances in tape capacity are being enhanced by advances on two other fronts: compression and robots. Faster processors have enabled systems to begin using compression to multiply storage capacity. Factors of two to three are common, with compression of 20:1 possible for certain types of data such as images. The second enhancement that is changing the cost-effectiveness of very large online storage is the emergence of inexpensive robots to automatically load and store tapes, offering a new level in the hierarchy between *online* magnetic disks and *offline* magnetic disks on shelves. This *"robo-line"* storage means access to terabytes of information at the delay of tens of seconds, without the intervention of a human operator. Figure 8.17 is a photograph of a tape robot.

Computer networks are also making great strides. Both 100-Mbit Ethernet and switched Ethernet solutions are being used in new networks and in upgrading networks that cannot handle the tremendous explosion in bandwidth created by the use of multimedia and the growing importance of the World Wide Web. ATM represents another potential technology for expanding even further. To support the growth in traffic, the Internet backbones are being switched to optical fiber, which allows a significant increase in bandwidth for long-haul networks.

FIGURE 8.17 The Exabyte EXB-120 holds 116 8-mm helical scan tapes. Each tape holds 10 GB, yielding a total capacity of over a terabyte. The EXB-120 costs about as much as two to four workstations. Photo courtesy of the Exabyte Corporation.

One of the most interesting storage technologies being explored is holography. One research project under way hopes to demonstrate a storage device with terabyte capacity and with transfer rates of 1 Gbit/sec. This would represent about an order of magnitude improvement in both storage size and transfer rate versus the largest disks in 1997. See the pertinent IBM link at *www.mkp.com/books_catalog/cod/links.htm* for a description of this joint academic-industry research activity.

Such advances offer "computing science fiction" scenarios that would have seemed absurd just a few years ago. For example, if all the books in the Library of Congress were converted to ASCII, they would occupy just 10 terabytes (although the pictures might take even more, depending on their number and resolution). Helical scan tapes, tape robots, compression, and high-speed networks could be the building blocks of an electronic library. All the information on all the books in the world would be available at your fingertips for the cost of a large minicomputer. And parallel processing, discussed in the next chapter, will allow this information to be indexed so that all books could be searched by content rather than by title. Electronic libraries would change the lives of anyone with a library card, and the technology to create them is within our grasp.

8.10   Historical Perspective and Further Reading

The history of I/O systems is a fascinating one. Many of the most interesting artifacts of early computers are their I/O devices. Magnetic tape was the first low-cost magnetic storage and today persists as the lowest-cost storage medium. Early tape drives used reel-to-reel technologies and linear recording, which were eventually replaced by tape cartridges and helical recording. As disks became cheaper, tapes were relegated primarily to archival purposes, causing additional focus on density, as opposed to speed, and on large-scale archival technologies such as tape robots.

The earliest random access storage devices were drums and fixed-head disks. A drum had a cylindrical surface coated with a magnetic film. It used a large number of read/write heads positioned over each track on the drum (see Figure 8.18). Drums were relatively high-speed I/O devices often used for virtual memory paging or for creating a file cache to slower-speed devices. Drums, which had no seek time, survived into the 1970s in higher-speed applications, such as paging or use in high-end machines. Eventually improvements in disk speed and the significant cost advantage of disks eliminated drum technology. Large (2 to 3 feet in diameter) single-platter, fixed-head disks were also in use in the 1950s.

In 1956, IBM developed the first disk storage system with both moving heads and multiple disk surfaces in San Jose, helping to seed the development of the magnetic storage industry in the southern end of Silicon Valley. The IBM 305 RAMAC (Random Access Method of Accounting and Control) could store 5 million characters (5 MB) of data on 50 disks, each 24 inches in diameter. The RAMAC is shown in Figure 8.19.

Moving-head disks quickly became the dominant high-speed magnetic storage, though their high cost meant that magnetic tape continued to be used extensively until the 1970s. The next key development for hard disks was the removable hard disk drive developed by IBM in 1962; this made it possible to share the expensive drive electronics and helped disks overtake tapes as the preferred storage medium. Figure 8.20 shows a removable disk drive and the multiplatter disk used in the drive. IBM also invented the floppy disk drive in 1970, originally to hold microcode for the IBM 370 series. Floppy disks became popular with the PC about 10 years later.

The sealed Winchester disk, which was developed by IBM in 1973, completely dominates disk technology today. (All the disks shown in Figure 8.5 on page 649 are Winchester disks.) Winchester disks benefited from two related properties. First, reductions in the cost of the disk electronics made it unnecessary to share the electronics and thus made nonremovable disks economical.

**FIGURE 8.18   A magnetic drum made by Digital Development Corporation in the 1960s
and used on a CDC machine.** The electronics supporting the read/write heads can be seen on
the outside of the drum. Photo courtesy of the Computer Museum of America.

Since the disk was fixed and could be in a sealed enclosure, both the environmental and control problems were greatly reduced, allowing significant gains
in density. The first disk that IBM shipped had two spindles, each with a 30-
MB disk; the moniker "30-30" for the disk led to the name Winchester. Winchester disks grew rapidly in popularity in the 1980s, completely replacing
removable disks by the middle of that decade.

Recently, low-cost removable drives have been resurrected for use in back-
up and portable locations. These drives typically are available both in floppy

FIGURE 8.19   The RAMAC disk drive from IBM, made in 1956, was the first disk drive with a moving head and the first with multiple platters. The IBM storage technology Web site has a discussion of IBM's major contributions to storage technology. Find the link at *www.mkp.com/books_catalog/cod/links.htm*. Photo courtesy of IBM.

media, storing about 100 MB in 1997, and a removable hard disk format, storing 1–2 GB. These removable disks have lower density and are slower than nonremovable disks, but the removable media are attractive for certain environments.

The 1970s saw the invention of a number of remarkable I/O devices. Perhaps one of the most unusual was a film storage device that stored data optically on small strips of photographic film. These film storage devices could not only read and write film, but actually kept the filmstrips stored in the device (which was about 5 feet by 4 feet by 3 feet), retrieving them mechanically.

The early IBM 360s pioneered many of the ideas that we use in I/O systems today. The 360 was the first machine to make heavy use of DMA, and it introduced the notion of I/O programs that could be interpreted by the device. Chaining of I/O programs was a key feature. The concept of channels introduced in the 360 corresponds to the I/O bus of today.

The trend for high-end machines has been toward use of programmable I/O processors. The original machine to use this concept was the CDC 6600, which used I/O processors called *peripheral processors*.

FIGURE 8.20 **This is a DEC disk drive and the removable pack.** These disks became popular starting in the mid-1960s and dominated disk technology until Winchester drives in the late 1970s. This drive was made in the mid-1970s; each disk pack in this drive could hold 80 MB. Photo courtesy of the Commercial Computing Museum.

The forerunner of today's workstations and personal computers was the Alto, developed at Xerox Palo Alto Research Center in 1973 [Thacker et al. 1982], shown in Figure 8.21. This machine integrated the needs of the I/O functions into the microcode of the processor. This included support for the bit-mapped graphics display, the disk, and the network. The network for the Alto was the first Ethernet [Metcalfe and Boggs 1976]. The Alto also supported the first laser printer, configured as a print server accessible over the Ethernet. Similarly, disk servers were also built. The mouse, invented earlier by Doug Engelbart of SRI, was a key part of the Alto. The 16-bit processor used a writable control store, which enabled researchers to program in support for the I/O devices. The single microprogrammed engine drove the graphics display, mouse, disks, network, and, when there was nothing else to do, ran the user's program.

While today we associate microprocessors with the personal computer revolution, they were originally developed to meet the demand for special-purpose controllers. Since the invention of the microprocessor, designers have developed many I/O controllers that adapt a microprocessor to a specific task. These include everything from DMA controllers to SCSI controllers to complete Ethernet controllers on a single chip.

FIGURE 8.21 The Xerox Alto. Although never sold as a product, Xerox donated a number of these machines to several major universities as well as using them heavily internally. The use of a mouse, a local area network, and a personal graphics display with a window system were key characteristics of the Alto later broadly adopted by workstation and PC companies. Photo courtesy of the Computer History Center.

The first multivendor bus may have been the PDP-11 Unibus in 1970. DEC encouraged other companies to build devices that would plug into its bus, and many companies did. A more recent example is SCSI (small computer systems interface). This bus, originally called SASI, was invented by Shugart and was later standardized by the IEEE. This open system approach to buses contrasts with proprietary buses using patented interfaces, which companies adopt to forestall competition from plug-compatible vendors. The use of proprietary buses also raises the costs and lowers the availability of I/O devices that plug into proprietary buses because such devices must have an interface designed exclusively for that bus.

Ongoing development in the areas of tape robots (see Figure 8.17 on page 693), head-mounted displays, gloves for complete tactile feedback, and computer screens that you write on with pens are indications that the incredible developments in I/O technology are likely to continue in the future.

To Probe Further

Bashe, C. J., L. R. Johnson, J. H. Palmer, and E. W. Pugh [1986]. *IBM's Early Computers*, MIT Press, Cambridge, MA.

Describes the I/O system architecture and devices in IBM's early computers.

Borrill, P. L. [1986]. "32-bit buses: An objective comparison," *Proc. Buscon 1986 West*, San Jose, CA, 138–45.

A comparison of various 32-bit bus standards.

Chen, P. M., E. K. Lee, G. A. Gibson, R. H. Katz, and D. A. Patterson [1994]. "RAID: High-performance, reliable secondary storage," *ACM Computing Surveys* 26:2 (June) 145–88.

A tutorial covering disk arrays and the advantages of such an organization.

Gray, J., and A. Reuter [1993]. *Transaction Processing: Concepts and Techniques*, Morgan Kaufmann, San Francisco.

A description of transaction processing, including discussions of benchmarking and performance evaluation.

Hennessy, J., and D. Patterson [1995]. *Computer Architecture: A Quantitative Approach*, Second edition, Morgan Kaufmann Publishers, San Francisco, Chapters 6 and 7.

Chapter 6 focuses on I/O devices, including an extensive discussion of RAID technologies and more accurate I/O performance modeling. Chapter 7 focuses on interconnection technologies, including buses and an extensive discussion on networking.

Kahn, R. E. [1972]. "Resource-sharing computer communication networks," *Proc. IEEE* 60:11 (November) 1397–1407.

A classic paper that describes the ARPANET.

Levy, J. V. [1978]. "Buses: The skeleton of computer structures," in *Computer Engineering: A DEC View of Hardware Systems Design*, C. G. Bell, J. C. Mudge, and J. E. McNamara, eds., Digital Press, Bedford, MA.

This is a good overview of key concepts in bus design with some examples from DEC machines.

Metcalfe, R. M., and D. R. Boggs [1976]. "Ethernet: Distributed packet switching for local computer networks," *Comm. ACM* 19:7 (July) 395–404.

Describes the Ethernet network.

Smotherman, M. [1989]. "A sequencing-based taxonomy of I/O systems and review of historical machines," *Computer Architecture News* 17:5 (September) 5–15.

Describes the development of important ideas in I/O.

Thacker, C. P., E. M. McCreight, B. W. Lampson, R. F. Sproull, and D. R. Boggs [1982]. "Alto: A personal computer," in *Computer Structures: Principles and Examples*, D. P. Siewiorek, C. G. Bell, and A. Newell, eds., McGraw-Hill, New York, 549–72.

Describes the Alto—forerunner of workstations as well as the Apple Macintosh.

Key Terms

The wide variety of characteristics present in different I/O devices and the corresponding system techniques for adapting to those devices have introduced a number of new terms, summarized below.

asynchronous bus
backplane bus
bus arbitration
bus master
bus request
bus transaction
centralized, parallel
 arbitration
daisy chain arbitration
direct memory access (DMA)
distributed arbitration by
 collision detection

distributed arbitration by self-
 selection
Ethernet
fairness
handshaking protocol
I/O instruction
interrupt-driven I/O
memory-mapped I/O
polling
processor-memory buses
redundant arrays of
 inexpensive disks (RAID)

rotation latency or delay
sector
seek
slave
small computer systems
 interface (SCSI)
split transaction protocol
synchronous bus
track
transaction processing
transfer time

Exercises

8.1 [10] <§§8.1–8.2> Here are two different I/O systems intended for use in transaction processing:

■ System A can support 1000 I/O operations per second.

■ System B can support 750 I/O operations per second.

The systems use the same processor that executes 50 million instructions per second. Assume that each transaction requires 5 I/O operations and that each I/O operation requires 10,000 instructions. Ignoring response time and assuming that transactions may be arbitrarily overlapped, what is the maximum transaction-per-second rate that each machine can sustain?

8.2 [15] <§§8.1–8.2> {Ex. 8.1} The latency of an I/O operation for the two systems in Exercise 8.1 differs. The latency for an I/O on system A is equal to 20 ms, while for system B the latency is 18 ms for the first 500 I/Os per second and 25 ms per I/O for each I/O between 500 and 750 I/Os per second. In the workload, every 10th transaction depends on the immediately preceding transaction and must wait for its completion. What is the maximum transaction rate that still allows every transaction to complete in 1 second and that does not exceed the I/O bandwidth of the machine? (For simplicity, assume that all transaction requests arrive at the beginning of a 1-second interval.)

8.3 [5] <§8.3> The following simplified diagram shows two potential ways of numbering the sectors of data on a disk (only two tracks are shown and each track has eight sectors). Assuming that typical reads are contiguous (e.g., all 16 sectors are read in order), which way of numbering the sectors will be likely to result in higher performance? Why?

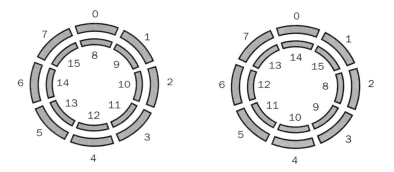

8.4 [5] <§8.3> What size messages would result in ATM outperforming Ethernet by a factor of two, assuming latencies and bandwidths equivalent to those reported in the example on page 654?

8.5 [5] <§8.3> The speed of light is approximately 3×10^8 meters per second, and electrical signals travel at about 50% of this speed in a conductor. When the term *high speed* is applied to a network, it is the bandwidth that is higher, not necessarily the velocity of the electrical signals. How much of a factor is the actual "flight time" for the electrical signals? Consider two computers that are 100 meters apart and two computers that are 5000 kilometers apart. Compare your results to the latencies reported in the example on page 654.

8.6 [5] <§8.3> The number of bytes in transit on a network is defined as the flight time (described in Exercise 8.5) multiplied by the delivered bandwidth. Calculate the number of bytes in transit for the two networks described in Exercise 8.5, assuming a delivered bandwidth of 5 MB/sec.

8.7 [5] <§8.3> A secret government agency simultaneously monitors 100 cellular phone conversations and multiplexes the data onto a network with a bandwidth of 1 MB/sec and an overhead latency of 350 μs per 1-KB message. Calculate the transmission time per message and determine whether there is sufficient bandwidth to support this application. Assume that the phone conversation data consists of 2 bytes sampled at a rate of 4 KHz.

8.8 [10] <§8.3> A program repeatedly performs a three-step process: It reads in a 4-KB block of data from disk, does some processing on that data, and then writes out the result as another 4-KB block elsewhere on the disk. Each block is contiguous and randomly located on a single track on the disk. The disk drive rotates at 7200 RPM, has an average seek time of 8 ms, and has a transfer rate of 20 MB/sec. The controller overhead is 2 ms. No other program is using the disk or processor, and there is no overlapping of disk operation with processing. The processing step takes 20 million clock cycles, and the clock rate is 400 MHz. What is the overall speed of the system in blocks processed per second?

8.9 [10] <§8.3> A transaction processing system utilizes a network and two different message sizes. The transaction request is quite small and consists of a 10-byte message. The transaction response is larger and consists of a 150-byte message. Assume that every transaction consists of a request and a response. Determine which of the two networks described in the example on page 654 would be better for this system.

8.10 [5] <§§8.3, 8.4> Assume that the bus and memory systems described in the example on page 665 are used to handle disk accesses from disks like the one described in the example on page 648. If the I/O is allowed to consume 100% of the bus and memory bandwidth, what is the maximum number of simultaneous disk transfers that can be sustained for the two block sizes?

8.11 [5] <§8.4> The example on page 665 assumed that the memory system took 200 ns to read the first four words, and each additional four words required 20 ns. Redo the example with the assumption that the memory system takes 150 ns to read the first four words and 30 ns to read each additional four words.

8.12 [5] <§8.4> The example on page 665 demonstrates that using larger block sizes results in an increase in the maximum sustained bandwidth that can be achieved. Under what conditions might a designer tend to favor smaller block sizes? Specifically, why would a designer choose a block size of 4 instead of 16 (assuming all of the characteristics are as identified in the example)?

8.13 [15] <§8.4> This question examines in more detail how increasing the block size for bus transactions decreases the total latency required and increases the maximum sustainable bandwidth. In the example on page 665, two different block sizes are considered (4 words and 16 words). Compute the total latency and the maximum bandwidth for all of the possible block sizes (between 4 and 16) and plot your results. Summarize what you learn by looking at your graph.

8.14 [15] <§8.4> This exercise is similar to Exercise 8.13. This time fix the block size at 4 and 16 (as in the example on page 665), but compute latencies and bandwidths for reads of different sizes. Specifically, consider reads of from 4 to 256 words, and use as many data points as you need to construct a meaningful graph. Use your graph to help determine at what point block sizes of 16 result in a reduced latency when compared with block sizes of 4.

8.15 [10] <§8.4> This exercise examines a design alternative to the example on page 665 that may improve the performance of writes. For writes, assume all of the characteristics reported in the example as well as the following:

> 5. The first four words are written 200 ns after the address is available, and each new write takes 20 ns. Assume a bus transfer of the most recent data to write, and a write of the previous four words can be overlapped.

The performance analysis reported in the example would thus remain unchanged for writes (in actuality, some minor changes might exist due to the need to compute error correction codes, etc., but we'll ignore this). An alternative bus scheme relies on separate 32-bit address and data lines. This will permit an address and data to be transmitted in the same cycle. For this bus alternative, what will the latency of the entire 256-word transfer be? What is the sustained bandwidth? Consider block sizes of four and eight words. When do you think the alternative scheme would be heavily favored?

8.16 <20> <§8.4> Consider an asynchronous bus used to interface an I/O device to the memory system described in the example on page 665. Each I/O request asks for 16 words of data from the memory, which, along with the I/O device, has a 4-word bus. Assume the same type of handshaking protocol as appears in Figure 8.10 on page 661 except that it is extended so that the memory can continue the transaction by sending additional blocks of data until the transaction is complete. Modify Figure 8.10 (both the steps and diagram) to indicate how such a transfer might take place. Assuming that each handshaking step takes 20 ns and memory access takes 60 ns, how long does it take to complete a transfer? What is the maximum sustained bandwidth for this asynchronous bus, and how does it compare to the synchronous bus in the example?

8.17 [15] <§§8.3–8.6> Redo the example on page 685, but instead assume that the reads are random 4-KB reads. You can assume that the reads are always to an idle disk, if one is available.

8.18 [20] <§§8.3–8.6> Here are a variety of building blocks used in an I/O system that has a synchronous processor-memory bus running at 200 MHz and one or more I/O adapters that interface I/O buses to the processor-memory bus.

- *Memory system:* The memory system has a 32-bit interface and handles four-word transfers. The memory system has separate address and data lines and, for writes to memory, accepts a word every clock cycle for 4 clock cycles and then takes an additional 4 clock cycles before the words have been stored and it can accept another transaction.

- *DMA interfaces:* The I/O adapters use DMA to transfer the data between the I/O buses and the processor-memory bus. The DMA unit arbitrates for the processor-memory bus and sends/receives four-word blocks from/to the memory system. The DMA controller can accommodate up to eight disks. Initiating a new I/O operation (including the seek and access) takes 1 ms, during which another I/O cannot be initiated by this controller (but outstanding operations can be handled).

- *I/O bus:* The I/O bus is a synchronous bus with a sustainable bandwidth of 10 MB/sec; each transfer is one word long.

- *Disks:* The disks have a measured average seek plus rotational latency of 12 ms. The disks have a read/write bandwidth of 5 MB/sec, when they are transferring.

Find the time required to read a 16-KB sector from a disk to memory, assuming that this is the only activity on the bus.

8.19 [15] <§§8.3–8.5> {Ex. 8.18} For the I/O system described in Exercise 8.18, find the maximum instantaneous bandwidth at which data can be transferred from disk to memory using as many disks as needed; how many disks and I/O buses (the minimum of each) do you need to achieve the bandwidth? Since you need only achieve this bandwidth for an instant, latencies need not be considered.

8.20 [20] <§§8.3–8.5> {Ex. 8.18, 8.19} Assume all accesses in the I/O system described in Exercise 8.18 are 4-KB block reads. If there are a total of six I/O buses, six DMA controllers, and 48 disks, find the maximum number of I/Os the system can sustain in steady state assuming that the reads are uniformly distributed to the disks. What is the sustained I/O bandwidth?

8.21 [15] <§§8.3–8.5> {Ex. 8.18, 8.19, 8.20} With the organization in Exercise 8.20, clearly it is possible to saturate the I/O buses because you have six of them at 10 MB/sec and 48 disks at 5 MB/sec. Compute the minimum block size (which should be a power of two) that will saturate the I/O buses. For this block size, how many I/O operations per second can the system perform and what is the I/O bandwidth?

8.22 [15] <§§7.3, 7.5, 8.4, 8.5> Consider a write-back cache used for a processor with a bus and memory system as described in the example on page 665 (assume that writes require the same amount of time as reads). The following performance measurements have been made:

- The cache miss rate is .05 misses per instruction for block sizes of 8 words.

- The cache miss rate is .03 misses per instruction for block sizes of 16 words.

- For either block size, 40% of the misses require a write-back operation, while the other 60% require only a read.

Assuming that the processor is stalled for the duration of a miss (including the write-back time if a write-back is needed), find the number of cycles per instruction that are spent handling cache misses for each block size. (Hint: First compute the miss penalty.)

8.23 [10] <§8.6> Write a paragraph identifying some of the simplifying assumptions that were made in the analysis described in the example on page 681.

8.24 [2 days–1 week] <§8.5, Appendix A> This assignment uses SPIM to build a simple set of I/O routines that will perform I/O to the terminal using polling. First, you need to build two I/O routines, whose C declarations and descriptions are shown below:

```
void print (char *string);
```

The procedure `print` takes a single argument, which is the address of a null-terminated ASCII string. All of the characters of the string except the null-terminating character should be output by `print`. It should print the characters one at a time, waiting for each character to be output before sending the next one. It should not return until all the characters have been output. The procedure `print` should work for strings of any length. This version of `print` should not use interrupts; just test the ready bit of the transmitter control register continuously until the device is ready.

```
char getchar();
```

The procedure `getchar` takes no arguments and returns a character result. If `getchar` waits until a character has been typed on the terminal, then it should return the character's value in $v0 (the result register). Do not use interrupts; simply test the ready bit continuously until a character has arrived.

Write a main program that uses these two procedures to read a line from the terminal, which will be terminated by a carriage return. Then print the entire line to the terminal, including a carriage return and line feed. All your code should obey the conventions in Appendix A for procedure calling, stack usage, and register usage.

8.25 [3 days–1 week] <§8.5, Appendix A> Your assignment is to build an interrupt-driven mechanism for buffered I/O to and from the terminal. (This exercise handles output only; Exercise 8.26 handles input.)

For the output-only portion, there are three parts to the program:

1. A main program, which repeatedly calls procedure `print` to print the string "I know what I am doing."

2. The procedure `print`, which stores the output characters in a buffer shared by it and the interrupt routine.

3. The interrupt routine, which copies characters from the output buffer to the transmitter.

You need to write all three routines. The routine `print` and the interrupt routine should communicate by using a shared circular buffer with space for 32 characters. The `print` procedure should take a string as argument and add the characters of the string to the output buffer one at a time, advancing as soon as there is space in the buffer. Keep in mind that `print` should not manipulate the terminal device registers directly, except to make sure that transmitter interrupts are enabled. Furthermore, `print` should contain additional code to deal with a full output buffer. The main program generates characters much faster than they can be output, so the buffer will quickly fill up. In a real system, if the output buffer fills up, the operating system will stop running the current user's process and switch to a different process. Your program doesn't need to support multiple users, so `print` can take a simpler approach: it just checks the buffer over and over again until eventually it isn't full anymore. The buffer is full when the next position in which `print` wants to insert a character has not been emptied by the interrupt routine.

After writing print, write the interrupt routine called by `print`. Here is a list of things the interrupt routine must do:

1. If the transmitter is not ready, then the interrupt routine should not do anything. (You shouldn't have received an interrupt in the first place if the transmitter isn't ready, but it's a good idea to check anyway.)

2. If the output buffer isn't empty, copy the next character from the output buffer to the Transmitter data register and adjust the buffer pointers.

3. If the output buffer is empty, turn off the interrupt-enable bit in the Transmitter control register. Otherwise, continuous interrupts will occur. Each time it deposits a character in the buffer, `print` will need to turn this bit on.

4. Don't forget that you must save and restore any registers that you use in the interrupt routine, even temporary registers such as register $t0 and register $t1. This is necessary because interrupts can occur at any time

and those registers may be in use at the time of the interrupt. You must save the registers on the stack. The only exceptions to this rule are registers $k0 and $k1, which are reserved for use by interrupt routines; these registers need not be saved and restored. One of these registers can be used to return from the interrupt routine back to the code that was interrupted.

Test your code by writing the main routine that calls print to print the string. It should output lines continuously, with each line containing the characters "I know what I am doing."

8.26 [3 days–1 week] <§8.5, Appendix A> {Ex. 8.25} Extend the code you've already written to be able to handle interrupt-driven input. This program should do input in the same way as the previous program did output: by using a buffer to communicate between the routine getchar and the interrupt routine. Be aware that getchar returns a character from the buffer, waiting in a loop if no characters are present. Similarly, the interrupt routine will add characters as they are typed, discarding characters if the buffer is full when they arrive. For this, an eight-entry buffer should work well.

Use these two routines to read characters from the terminal and to output them to the terminal. Try typing characters rapidly to make sure your program can handle the output or the input buffer filling up. For example, if you type two or three characters rapidly, the output buffer may fill up. However, no output should be lost: the print procedure will simply have to spin for a bit, during which time additional input characters will be buffered in the input buffer. If you type eight or ten characters very rapidly, then the input buffer will probably fill up. When this happens, your interrupt routine will have to discard characters: the program should continue to function, but there won't be any output of the discarded input characters you typed. Once the output catches up with the input, your program should accept input again just as if the input buffer had never filled up.

8.27 [1 day–1 week] <§§8.2–8.4> Take your favorite computer and write programs that achieve the following:

1. Maximum bandwidth from and to a single disk

2. Maximum bandwidth from and to multiple disks

3. The maximum number of 512-byte transactions from and to a single disk

4. The maximum number of 512-byte transactions from and to multiple disks

What is the percentage of the bandwidth that you achieve compared to what the I/O device manufacturer claims? Also, record processor utilization in each case for the programs that are running separately. Next, run all four together and see what percentage of the maximum rates you can achieve. From this, can you determine where the system bottlenecks lie?

In More Depth

Ethernet

An Ethernet is essentially a standard bus with multiple masters (each computer can be a master) and a distributed arbitration scheme using collision detection. Most Ethernets are implemented using coaxial cable as the medium. When a particular node wants to use the bus, it first checks to see whether some other node is using the bus; if not, it places a carrier signal on the bus, and then proceeds to transmit. A complication can arise because the control is distributed and the devices may be physically far apart. As a result, two nodes can both check the Ethernet, find it idle, and begin transmitting at once; this is called a *collision*. A node detects collisions by listening to the network when transmitting to see whether a collision has occurred. A collision is detected when the node finds that what it hears on the Ethernet differs from what it transmitted. When collisions occur, both nodes stop transmitting and delay a random time interval before trying to resume using the network—just as two polite people do when they both start talking at the same time. Consequently, the number of nodes on the network is limited—if too many collisions occur, the performance will be poor. In addition, constraints imposed by the requirement that collisions be detected by all nodes limit the length of the Ethernet and the number of connections to the network. Although this idea sounds like it might not work, it actually works amazingly well and has been central to the enormous growth in the use of local area networks.

8.28 [3 days–1 week] <§§8.3–8.4> Write a program that simulates an Ethernet. Assume the following network system characteristics:

- A transmission bandwidth of 10 Mbits/sec.
- A latency for a signal to travel the entire length of the network and return to its origin of 15 μs. This is also the time required to detect a collision.

Make the following assumptions about the 100 hosts on the network:

- The packet size is 1000 bytes.
- Each host tries to send a packet after T seconds of computation, where T is exponentially distributed with mean M. Note that the host begins its T seconds of computation only after successfully transmitting a packet.
- If a collision is detected, the host waits a random amount of time chosen from an exponential distribution with a mean of 60 μs.

Simulate and plot the sustained bandwidth of the network compared to the mean time between transmission attempts (M). Also, plot the average wait time between trying to initiate a transmission and succeeding in initiating it (compared to M).

Ethernets actually use an exponential back-off algorithm that increases the mean of the back-off time after successive collisions. Assume that the mean of the distribution from which the host chooses how much to delay is doubled on successive collisions. How well does this work? Is the bandwidth higher than when a single distribution is used? Can the initial mean be lower?

In More Depth

Disk Arrays

As mentioned in section 8.9, one method of organizing disk systems is to use arrays of smaller disks that provide more bandwidth through parallel access. In most disk arrays, all the spindles are synchronized—sector 0 in every disk rotates under the head at the exact same time—and the arms on all the disks are always over the same track. Furthermore, the data are "striped" across the disks in the array, so that consecutive sectors can be read in parallel. Let's explore how such a system might work.

8.29 [20] <§§8.3–8.5> Assume that we have the following two magnetic disk configurations: a single disk and an array of four disks. Each disk has 64 sectors per track, each sector holds 1000 bytes, and the disk revolves at 7200 RPM. Assume that the seek time is 6 ms. The delay of the disk controller is 1 ms per transaction, either for a single disk or for the array. Assume that the performance of the I/O system is limited only by the disks and the controller. Remember that the consecutive sectors on the single disk system will be spread one sector per disk in the array. Compare the performance in I/Os per second of these two disk organizations, assuming that the requests are random reads, half of which are 4 KB and half of which are 16 KB of data from sequential sectors. The sectors may be read in any order; for simplicity, assume that the rotational latency is one-half the revolution time for the single disk read of 16 sectors and the disk array read of 4 sectors. Challenge: Can you work out the actual average rotational latency in these two cases?

8.30 [10] <§§8.3–8.5> {Ex. 8.29} Using the same disk systems as in Exercise 8.29, with the same access patterns, determine the performance in megabytes per second for each system.

9

Multiprocessors

*There are finer fish in the sea than
have ever been caught.*

Irish proverb

The Five Classic Components of a Computer

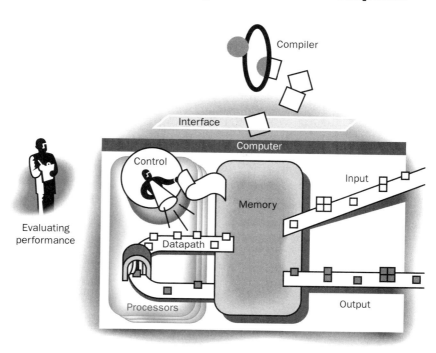

9.1   Introduction

> *"Over the Mountains*
> *Of the Moon,*
> *Down the Valley of the Shadow,*
> *Ride, boldly ride"*
> *The shade replied,—*
> *"If you seek for Eldorado!"*
>
> Edgar Allan Poe, "Eldorado," stanza 4, 1849

Computer architects have always sought the El Dorado of computer design: to create powerful computers simply by connecting many existing smaller ones. This golden vision is the fountainhead of multiprocessors. The customer orders as many processors as the budget allows and receives a commensurate amount of performance. Thus multiprocessors must be scalable: the hardware and software are designed to be sold with a variable number of processors, with some machines varying by a factor of more than 50. Since software is scalable, some multiprocessors can support operation in the presence of broken hardware; that is, if a single processor fails in a multiprocessor with n processors, the system provides continued service with $n-1$ processors. Finally, multiprocessors may have the highest absolute performance—faster than the fastest uniprocessor.

The good news is that the multiprocessor has established a beachhead. Keeping in mind that the microprocessor is now the most cost-effective processor, it is generally agreed that if you can't handle a timeshared workload on a single-chip processor, then a multiprocessor composed of many single-chip uniprocessors is more effective than building a high-performance uniprocessor from a more exotic technology. Moreover, virtually all current file servers can be ordered with multiple processors, and the database industry has standardized on multiprocessors. Consequently, multiprocessors now embody a significant market.

Commercial multiprocessors usually define high performance as high throughput for independent tasks. This definition is in contrast to running a single task on multiple processors. We use the term *parallel processing program* to refer to a single program that runs on multiple processors simultaneously.

Here are key questions that drive the designs of multiprocessors:

- How do parallel processors share data?

- How do parallel processors coordinate?

- How many processors?

The answers to the first question fall in two main camps. Processors with a *single address space*, sometimes called *shared-memory processors,* offer the programmer a single memory address space that all processors share. Processors communicate through shared variables in memory, with all processors capable of accessing any memory location via loads and stores.

As processors operating in parallel will normally share data, they also need to coordinate when operating on shared data; otherwise, one processor could start working on data before another is finished with it. This coordination is called *synchronization*. When sharing is supported with a single address space, there must be a separate mechanism for synchronization. One approach uses a *lock*: only one processor at a time can acquire the lock, and other processors interested in shared data must wait until the original processor unlocks the variable. Locking is described in section 9.3.

Single address space multiprocessors come in two styles. The first takes the same time to access main memory no matter which processor requests it and no matter which word is asked. Such machines are called *uniform memory access* (*UMA*) multiprocessors or *symmetric multiprocessors* (*SMP*). In the second style, some memory accesses are faster than others depending on which processor asks for which word. Such machines are called *nonuniform memory access* (*NUMA*) multiprocessors. As you might expect, there are more programming challenges to get highest performance from a NUMA multiprocessor than a UMA multiprocessor, but NUMA machines can scale to larger sizes and hence are potentially higher performance.

The alternative model to shared memory for communicating uses *message passing* for communicating among processors. Message passing is required for machines with *private memories*, in contrast to shared memory. As an extreme example, processors in different desktop computers communicate by passing messages over a local area network. Provided the system has routines to *send* and *receive* messages, coordination is built in with message passing since one processor knows when a message is sent and the receiving processor knows when a message arrives. The receiving processor can then send a message back to the sender saying the message has arrived, if the sender needs that confirmation.

One recent phenomenon has been to try to take the extreme example above—computers connected over a local area network—and make it act as a single large multiprocessor. Such *clusters* of computers leverage the switch-based local area networks to provide high bandwidth between computers in the cluster.

In addition to two main communication styles, multiprocessors are constructed in two basic organizations: processors connected by a single bus, and processors connected by a network. The number of processors in the multiprocessor has a lot to do with this choice. We will examine these two styles in detail in sections 9.3 and 9.4.

> **The Big Picture**
>
> Figure 9.1 shows the relationship between the number of processors in a multiprocessor and choice of shared address versus message-passing communication and the choice of bus versus network physical connection. Shared address is further divided between uniform and nonuniform memory access. Although there are many choices for some numbers of processors, for other regions there is widespread agreement.

Category	Choice		Number of processors
Communication model	Message passing		8–256
	Shared address	NUMA	8–256
		UMA	2–64
Physical connection	Network		8–256
	Bus		2–32

FIGURE 9.1   Options in communication style and physical connection for multiprocessors as the number of processors varies. Note that the shared address space is divided into uniform memory access (UMA) and nonuniform memory access (NUMA) machines.

One challenge in writing this book is keeping examples up-to-date when the industry is rapidly changing. We decided that in this chapter we could keep electronic pointers to the real examples available via the World Wide Web. See the section for Chapter 9 at *www.mkp.com/cod2e.htm* to find the latest information on machines that demonstrate these ideas.

Let's start by looking at the general issues in programming multiprocessors.

9.2 Programming Multiprocessors

A major concern which is frequently voiced in connection with very fast computing machines . . . is that they will . . . run out of work. . . . It must be considered that . . . [past] problem size was dictated by the speed of the computing machines then available. . . . For faster machines, the same automatic mechanism will exert pressure towards problems of larger size.

John von Neumann, address presented at IBM seminar
on scientific computation, November 1949

The bad news is that it remains to be seen how many important applications will run faster on multiprocessors via parallel processing. The obstacle is not the price of the uniprocessor used to compose multiprocessors, the flaws in topologies of interconnection networks, nor the unavailability of appropriate programming languages; the difficulty has been that too few important application programs have been rewritten to complete tasks sooner on multiprocessors. Because it is even harder to find applications that can take advantage of many processors, the challenge is greater for large-scale multiprocessors.

As a result of the programming difficulty, most parallel processing success stories are a result of software wizards developing a parallel subsystem that presents a sequential interface. Examples include databases, file servers, computer-aided design packages, and multiprocessing operating systems.

But why is this so? Why should parallel processing programs be so much harder to develop than sequential programs?

The first reason is that you *must* get good performance and efficiency from the parallel program on a multiprocessor; otherwise you would use a uniprocessor, as programming is easier. In fact, uniprocessor design techniques such as superscalar and out-of-order execution take advantage of instruction-level parallelism, normally without involvement of the programmer. Such innovation reduces the demand for rewriting programs for multiprocessors.

Why is it difficult to write multiprocessor programs that are fast, especially as the number of processors increases? As an analogy, think of the communication overhead for a task done by one person compared to the overhead for a task done by a committee, especially as the size of the committee increases. Although *n* people may have the potential to finish any task *n* times faster, the communication overhead for the group may prevent it; *n*-fold speedup becomes especially unlikely as *n* increases. (Imagine the change in communication overhead if a committee grows from 10 people to 1000 people to 1,000,000.)

Another reason why it is difficult to write parallel processing programs is that the programmer must know a good deal about the hardware. On a uniprocessor, the high-level language programmer writes the program largely ignoring the underlying machine organization—that's the job of the compiler. But, so far at least, the parallel processing programmer had better know the underlying organization to write programs that are fast and capable of running with a variable number of processors. Moreover, such tailored parallel programs are not portable to other multiprocessors.

Although this second obstacle is beginning to lessen, our discussion in Chapter 2 reveals a third obstacle: Amdahl's law. It reminds us that even small parts of a program must be parallelized to reach their full potential; thus coming close to linear speedup involves discovering new algorithms that are inherently parallel.

Speedup Challenge

Example

Suppose you want to achieve linear speedup with 100 processors. What fraction of the original computation can be sequential?

Answer

Amdahl's law (page 75) says,

Execution time after improvement =

$$\frac{\text{Execution time affected by improvement}}{\text{Amount of improvement}} + \text{Execution time unaffected}$$

Substituting for the goal of linear speedup with 100 processors means the execution time is reduced by 100:

$$\frac{\text{Execution time after improvement}}{100} =$$

$$\frac{\text{Execution time affected by improvement}}{100} + \text{Execution time unaffected}$$

Solving for the unaffected execution time,

$$\text{Execution time unaffected} = \frac{\text{Execution time after improvement}}{100}$$

$$- \frac{\text{Execution time affected by improvement}}{100} = 0$$

Accordingly, to achieve linear speedup with 100 processors, *none* of the original computation can be sequential. Put another way, to get a speedup of 99 from 100 processors means the percentage of the original program that was sequential would have to be 0.01% or less.

Yet there are applications with substantial parallelism.

Speedup Challenge, Bigger Problem

Example

Suppose you want to perform two sums: one is a sum of two scalar variables and one is a matrix sum of a pair of two-dimensional arrays, size 1000 by 1000. What speedup do you get with 1000 processors?

Answer

If we assume performance is a function of the time for an addition, t, then there is 1 addition that does not benefit from parallel processors and 1,000,000 additions that do. If the time before is $1,000,001t$,

Execution time before improvement =

$$\frac{\text{Execution time affected by improvement}}{\text{Amount of improvement}} + \text{Execution time unaffected}$$

$$\text{Execution time before improvement} = \frac{1,000,000t}{1000} + 1t$$

$$= 1001$$

Speedup is then

$$\text{Speedup} = \frac{1,000,001}{1001} = 999$$

Even if the sequential portion expanded to 100 sums of scalar variables versus one sum of a pair of 1000 by 1000 arrays, the speedup would still be 909.

9.3 Multiprocessors Connected by a Single Bus

The high performance and low cost of the microprocessor inspired renewed interest in multiprocessors in the 1980s. Several microprocessors can usefully be placed on a common bus for several reasons:

- Each microprocessor is much smaller than a multichip processor, so more processors can be placed on a bus.

- Caches can lower bus traffic.

- Mechanisms were invented to keep caches and memory consistent for multiprocessors, just as caches and memory are kept consistent for I/O, thereby simplifying programming.

Figure 9.2 is a drawing of a generic single-bus multiprocessor, and Figure 9.3 lists the characteristics of some commercial single-bus computers.

Traffic per processor and the bus bandwidth determine the useful number of processors in such a multiprocessor. The caches replicate data in their faster memories both to reduce the latency to the data *and* to reduce the memory traffic on the bus.

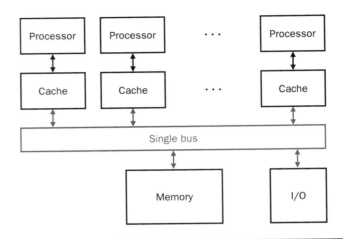

FIGURE 9.2   A single-bus multiprocessor. Typical size is between 2 and 32 processors.

Name	Maximum number of processors	Processor name	Processor clock rate	Maximum memory size/ system	Communi- cations BW/ system
Compaq ProLiant 5000	4	Pentium Pro	200 MHz	2,048 MB	540 MB/sec
Digital AlphaServer 8400	12	Alpha 21164	440 MHz	28,672 MB	2150 MB/sec
HP 9000 K460	4	PA-8000	180 MHz	4,096 MB	960 MB/sec
IBM RS/6000 R40	8	PowerPC 604	112 MHz	2,048 MB	1800 MB/sec
SGI Power Challenge	36	MIPS R10000	195 MHz	16,384 MB	1200 MB/sec
Sun Enterprise 6000	30	UltraSPARC 1	167 MHz	30,720 MB	2600 MB/sec

FIGURE 9.3   Characteristics of multiprocessor computers connected by a single backplane bus that are for sale in 1997. The communication style for these machines is shared memory with uniform memory access times. These machines are generally designed to be used with multiple generations of microprocessors both to allow customers to upgrade their existing machines and to allow companies to amortize their research and development investment. For example, the SGI Power Challenge was first delivered in 1993 with the MIPS R4400 and then again in 1995 with the R8000. Note that the bus and memory system did not change over this time. (See *www.mkp.com/cod2e.htm* for pointers to these and more recent bus-connected multiprocessors.)

Parallel Program (Single Bus)

Example

Suppose we want to sum 100,000 numbers on a single-bus multiprocessor computer. Let's assume we have 10 processors.

Answer The first step again would be to split the set of numbers into subsets of the same size. We do not allocate the subsets to a different memory, since there is a single memory for this machine; we just give different starting addresses to each processor. Pn is the number of the processor, between 0 and 9. All processors start the program by running a loop that sums their subset of numbers:

```
sum[Pn] = 0;
for (i = 10000*Pn; i < 10000*(Pn+1); i = i + 1)
    sum[Pn] = sum[Pn] + A[i]; /* sum the assigned areas*/
```

This loop uses load instructions to bring the correct subset of numbers to the caches of each processor from the common main memory.

The next step is to add these many partial sums, so we divide to conquer. Half of the processors add pairs of partial sums, then a quarter add pairs of the new partial sums, and so on until we have the single, final sum. We want each processor to have its own version of the loop counter variable i, so we must indicate that it is a "private" variable.

In this example, the two processors must synchronize before the "consumer" processor tries to read the result from the memory location written by the "producer" processor; otherwise, the consumer may read the old value of the data. Here is the code (half is private also):

```
half = 10; /* 10 processors in 1-bus multiprocessor*/
repeat
        synch(); /* wait for partial sum completion*/
        if (half%2 != 0 && Pn == 0)
            sum[0] = sum[0] + sum[half-1];
        half = half/2; /* dividing line on who sums */
        if (Pn < half) sum[Pn] = sum[Pn] + sum[Pn+half];
until (half == 1); /* exit with final sum in Sum[0] */
```

We have used what is called a *barrier synchronization* primitive; processors wait at the barrier until every processor has reached it. Then they proceed. Barrier synchronization allows all processors to rapidly synchronize. This function can be implemented either in software with the lock synchronization primitive, described in section 9.3, or with special hardware that combines each processor "ready" signal into a single global signal that all processors can test.

Recall from Chapter 8 that I/O can experience inconsistencies in the value of data between the version in memory and the version in the cache. This *cache coherency* problem applies to multiprocessors as well as I/O. Unlike I/O, which rarely uses multiple data copies (a situation to be avoided whenever possible), as the second half of the example suggests, multiple processors routinely require copies of the same data in multiple caches. Alternatively, accesses to shared data could be forced always to go around the cache to memory, but that would be too slow and it would require too much bus bandwidth; performance of a multiprocessor program depends on the performance of the system when sharing data.

The protocols to maintain coherency for multiple processors are called *cache coherency protocols*. The next few subsections explain cache coherency protocols and methods of synchronizing processors using cache coherency.

Multiprocessor Cache Coherency

The most popular protocol to maintain cache coherency is called *snooping*. Figure 9.4 shows how caches access memory over a common bus. All cache controllers monitor, or *snoop*, on the bus to determine whether or not they have a copy of the shared block.

Snooping became popular with machines of the 1980s, which used single buses to their main memories. These uniprocessors were extended by adding multiple processors on that bus to give easy access to the shared memory. Caches were then added to improve the performance of each processor, leading to schemes to keep the caches up-to-date by snooping on the information over that shared bus.

Maintaining coherency has two components: reads and writes. Multiple copies are not a problem when reading, but a processor must have exclusive access to write a word. Processors must also have the most recent copy when reading an object, so all processors must get new values after a write. Thus,

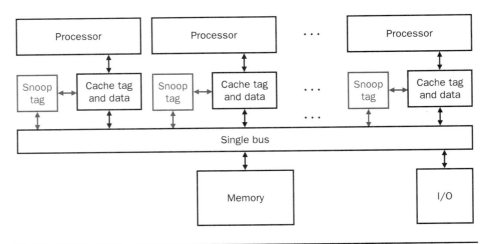

FIGURE 9.4   A single-bus multiprocessor using snooping cache coherency. The extra set of tags, shown in color, are used to handle snoop requests. The tags are duplicated to reduce the demands of snooping on the caches.

snooping protocols must locate all the caches that share an object to be written. The consequence of a write to shared data is either to invalidate all other copies or to update the shared copies with the value being written.

The status bits already in a cache block are expanded for snooping protocols, and that information is used in monitoring bus activities. On a read miss, all caches check to see if they have a copy of the requested block and then take the appropriate action, such as supplying the data to the cache that missed. Similarly, on a write, all caches check to see if they have a copy and then act, either invalidating or updating their copy to the new value.

Since every bus transaction checks cache address tags, you might assume that it interferes with the processor. It would interfere if not for duplicating the address tag portion of the cache (not the whole cache) to get an extra read port for snooping (see Figure 9.4). This way, snooping rarely interferes with the processor's access to the cache. When there is interference, the processor will likely stall because the cache is unavailable.

Snooping protocols are of two types, depending on what happens on a write:

- *Write-invalidate*: The writing processor causes all copies in other caches to be invalidated before changing its local copy; it is then free to update the *local* data until another processor asks for it. The writing processor issues an invalidation signal over the bus, and all caches check to see if they have a copy; if so, they must invalidate the block containing the word. Thus, this scheme allows multiple readers but only a single writer.

- *Write-update*: Rather than invalidate every block that is shared, the writing processor broadcasts the new data over the bus; all copies are then updated with the new value. This scheme, also called *write-broadcast*, continuously broadcasts writes to shared data, while write-invalidate deletes all other copies so that there is only one local copy for subsequent writes.

Write-update is like write-through because all writes go over the bus to update copies of the shared data. Write-invalidate uses the bus only on the *first* write to invalidate the other copies, and hence subsequent writes do not result in bus activity. Consequently, write-invalidate has similar benefits to write-back in terms of reducing demands on bus bandwidth, while write-update has the advantage of making the new values appear in caches sooner, which can reduce latency.

Commercial cache-based multiprocessors use write-back caches because write-back reduces bus traffic and thereby allows more processors on a single bus. To preserve that precious communications bandwidth, all commercial machines also use write-invalidate as the standard protocol.

Measurements to date indicate that shared data has lower spatial and temporal locality than other types of data. Thus shared data misses often dominate cache behavior, even though they may be just 10% to 40% of the data accesses.

**Hardware
Software
Interface**

One insight is that block size plays an important role in cache coherency. For example, take the case of snooping on a cache with a block size of eight words, with a single word alternatively written and read by two processors. The protocol that only broadcasts or sends one word has an advantage over a scheme that transfers the full block.

Large blocks can also cause what is called *false sharing*: When two unrelated shared variables are located in the same cache block, the full block is exchanged between processors even though the processors are accessing different variables (see Exercises 9.5 and 9.6). Compiler research is under way to reduce false sharing by allocating highly correlated data to the same cache block and thereby reduce cache miss rates.

Elaboration: In a multiprocessor using cache coherency over a single bus, what happens if two processors try to write to the same shared data word in the same clock cycle? The bus arbiter decides which processor gets the bus first, and this processor will invalidate or update the other processor's copy, depending on the protocol. The second processor then does its write. Bus arbitration forces sequential behavior from writes on different processors, and this explains how writes from different processors to different words in the same block will work correctly.

The policy of when a processor sees a write from another processor is called the *memory consistency model*. The most conservative is called *sequential consistency*: the result of any execution is the same as if the accesses of each processor were kept in order and the accesses among different processors were interleaved. Some machines use more liberal models to achieve higher memory performance.

An Example of a Cache Coherency Protocol

To illustrate the intricacies of a cache coherency protocol, Figure 9.5 shows a finite state transition diagram for a write-invalidation protocol based on a write-back policy. Each cache block is in one of three states:

1. *Read Only*: This cache block is clean (not written) and may be shared.

2. *Read/Write*: This cache block is dirty (written) and may *not* be shared.

3. *Invalid*: This cache block does not have valid data.

The three states of the protocol are duplicated in the figure to show transitions based on processor actions as opposed to transitions based on bus operations. This duplication is done only for purposes of illustration; there is really only one finite state machine per cache, with stimuli coming either from the attached processor or from the bus.

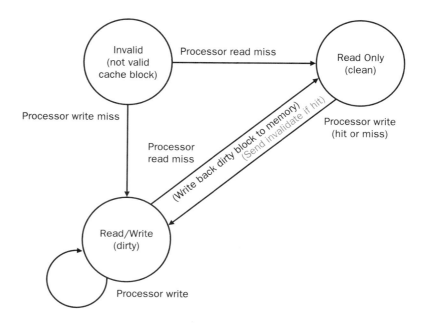

a. Cache state transitions using signals from the processor

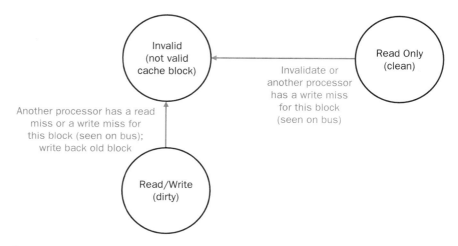

b. Cache state transitions using signals from the bus

FIGURE 9.5 A write-invalidate cache coherency protocol. The upper part of the diagram shows state transitions based on actions of the processor associated with this cache; the lower part shows transitions based on actions of other processors as seen as operations on the bus. There is really only one state machine in a cache, although there are two represented here to clarify when a transition occurs. The black arrows and actions specified in black text would be found in caches without coherency; the colored arrows and actions are added to achieve cache coherency. In contrast to what is shown here, some protocols consider writes to clean data a write miss, so that there is no separate signal for invalidation.

Transitions in the state of a cache block happen on read misses, write misses, or write hits; read hits do not change cache state. Let's start with a read miss. When the processor has a read miss that maps onto a block, it will change the state of that block to Read Only, and then acquire the bus and write back the old block if the block was in the Read/Write state (dirty). All the caches in the other processors monitor the read miss to see if this block is in their cache. If one has a copy and it is in the Read/Write state, then the block is changed to the Invalid state. (Some protocols would change the state to Read Only.) The read miss is then satisfied by reading from memory.

Now let's try writes. To write a block, the processor acquires the bus, sends an invalidate signal, writes into that block, and places it in the Read/Write state. Because other caches monitor the bus, all caches check to see if they have a copy of that block; if they do, they invalidate it.

As you might imagine, there are many variations on cache coherency that are much more complicated than this simple model. The one found on both the Pentium Pro and PowerPC is called *MESI*, a write-invalidate protocol whose name is an acronym for the four states of the protocol: Modified, Exclusive, Shared, Invalid. The Modified state is the same as the Read/Write state in Figure 9.5, and Invalid is the same state too. The Read Only state of Figure 9.5 is divided, depending on whether there are multiple copies (Shared state) or there is just one (Exclusive state). In either case, memory has an up-to-date version of the data. This extra state means that a write to data that is in the Exclusive state does not require an invalidation since there is only one copy of the block. A write to data in the Read Only of Figure 9.5 would require an invalidation, since there may be multiple copies.

Other variations on coherency protocols include whether or not the other caches try to supply the block if they have a copy, whether or not the block must be invalidated on a read miss, as well as whether writes invalidate or update the shared data.

Synchronization Using Coherency

One of the major requirements of a single-bus multiprocessor is to be able to coordinate processes that are working on a common task. Typically, a programmer will use *lock variables* (also known as *semaphores*) to coordinate or synchronize the processes. The challenge for the architect of a multiprocessor is to provide a mechanism to decide which processor gets the lock and to provide the operation that locks a variable. Arbitration is easy for single-bus multiprocessors, since the bus is the only path to memory: the processor that gets the bus locks out all other processors from memory. If the processor and bus provide an *atomic swap operation*, programmers can create locks with the proper semantics. Here the adjective *atomic* means indivisible, so an atomic swap means the processor can both read a location *and* set it to the locked value in the same bus operation, preventing any other processor or I/O device from reading or writing memory until the swap completes.

Figure 9.6 shows a typical procedure for locking a variable using an atomic swap instruction. Assume that 0 means unlocked ("go") and 1 means locked ("stop"). A processor first reads the lock variable to test its state. A processor keeps reading and testing until the value indicates that the lock is unlocked.

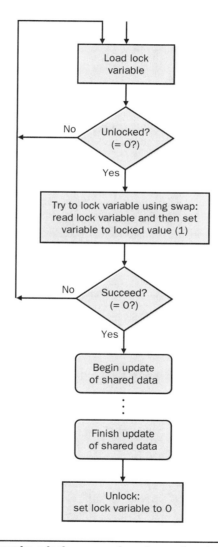

FIGURE 9.6   Steps to acquire a lock or semaphore to synchronize processes and then to release the lock on exit from the key section of code.

The processor then races against all other processors that were similarly *spin waiting* to see who can lock the variable first. All processors use an atomic swap instruction that reads the old value and stores a 1 ("stop") into the lock variable. The single winner will see the 0 ("go"), and the losers will see a 1 that was placed there by the winner. (The losers will continue to write the variable with the locked value of 1, but that doesn't change its value.) The winning processor then executes the code that updates the shared data. When the winner exits, it stores a 0 ("go") into the lock variable, thereby starting the race all over again.

Let's examine how the spin lock scheme of Figure 9.6 works with bus-based cache coherency. One advantage of this algorithm is that it allows processors to spin wait on a local copy of the lock in their caches. This reduces the amount of bus traffic; Figure 9.7 shows the bus and cache operations for multiple processors trying to lock a variable. Once the processor with the lock stores a 0 into the lock, all other caches see that store and invalidate their copy of the lock variable. Then they try to get the new value for the lock of 0. (With write-update cache coherency, the caches would update their copy rather than first invalidate and then load from memory.) This new value starts the race to see who can set the lock first. The winner gets the bus and stores a 1 into the lock; the other caches replace their copy of the lock variable containing 0 with a 1. They read that the variable is already locked and must return to testing and spinning.

This scheme has difficulty scaling up to many processors because of the communication traffic generated when the lock is released.

Step	Processor P0	Processor P1	Processor P2	Bus activity
1	Has lock	Spins, testing if lock = 0	Spins, testing if lock = 0	None
2	Sets lock to 0 and 0 sent over bus	Spins, testing if lock = 0	Spins, testing if lock = 0	Write-invalidate of lock variable from P0
3		Cache miss	Cache miss	Bus decides to service P2 cache miss
4		(Waits while bus busy)	Lock = 0	Cache miss for P2 satisfied
5		Lock = 0	Swap: reads lock and sets to 1	Cache miss for P1 satisfied
6		Swap: reads lock and sets to 1	Value from swap = 0 and 1 sent over bus	Write-invalidate of lock variable from P2
7		Value from swap = 1 and 1 sent over bus	Owns the lock, so can update shared data	Write-invalidate of lock variable from P1
8		Spins, testing if lock = 0		None

FIGURE 9.7 Cache coherency steps and bus traffic for three processors, P0, P1, and P2. This figure assumes write-invalidate coherency. P0 starts with the lock (step 1). P0 exits and unlocks the lock (step 2). P1 and P2 race to see which reads the unlocked value during the swap (steps 3–5). P2 wins and enters the *critical section* (steps 6 and 7), while P1 spins and waits (steps 7 and 8). A critical section is the name for the code between the lock and the unlock.

9.4 Multiprocessors Connected by a Network

Single-bus designs are attractive, but limited because the three desirable bus characteristics are incompatible: high bandwidth, low latency, and long length. There is also a limit to the bandwidth of a single memory module attached to a bus. Thus, a single bus imposes practical constraints on the number of processors that can be connected to it. To date, the largest number of processors connected to a single bus in a commercial computer is 36, and this number seems to be dropping over time.

If the goal is to connect many more processors together, then the computer designer needs to use more than a single bus. Figure 9.8 shows how this can be organized. Note that in Figure 9.2 on page 718, the connection medium—the bus—is between the processors and memory, whereas in Figure 9.8, memory is attached to each processor, and the connection medium—the network—is between these combined nodes. For single-bus systems, the medium is used on every memory access, while in the latter case it is used only for interprocessor communication. Figure 9.9 lists several machines connected via networks.

This brings us to an old debate about the organization of memory in large-scale parallel processors. The debate unfortunately often centers on a false dichotomy: *shared memory* versus *distributed memory*. Shared memory really means a single address space, implying implicit communication with loads

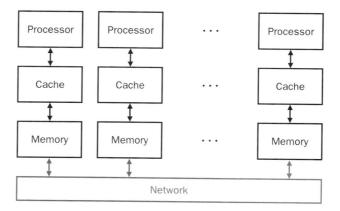

FIGURE 9.8 The organization of a network-connected multiprocessor. Note that, in contrast to Figure 9.2, the multiprocessor connection is no longer between memory and the processor. Multiprocessors have also been built with the network above the memory; the Cray XMP and YMP multiprocessors are perhaps the best-known examples, and the Sun Enterprise 10000 is the most recent example (see Figure 9.9).

and stores. The real opposite of a single address is *multiple private memories,* implying explicit communication with sends and receives.

Distributed memory refers to the physical location of the memory. If physical memory is divided into modules, with some placed near each processor, as in Figure 9.8, then physical memory is distributed. The real opposite of distributed memory is *centralized memory,* where access time to a physical memory location is the same for all processors because every access goes over the interconnect, as in Figure 9.2. This style of machine is sometimes called *dance hall,* with the processors all on one side and the memories all on the other, invoking the image of a school dance with the boys on one side of the floor and the girls on the other. (The Tera Computer is one example; see *www.mkp.com/cod2e.htm* for a pointer to it.)

As we said in section 9.1, single address space versus multiple address spaces, and distributed memory versus centralized memory, are orthogonal issues: multiprocessors can have a single address space and a distributed physical memory. The proper debates concern the pros and cons of a single address space, of explicit communication, and of distributed physical memory.

In machines without a single global address, communication is explicit; the programmer or the compiler must send messages to ship data to another node and must receive messages to accept data from another node.

Name	Maximum number of processors	Processor name	Processor clock rate	Maximum memory size/ system	Communications BW/link	Node	Topology
Cray Research T3E	2048	Alpha 21164	450 MHz	524,288 MB	1200 MB/sec	4-way SMP	3-D torus
HP/Convex Exemplar X-class	64	PA-8000	180 MHz	65,536 MB	980 MB/sec	2-way SMP	8-way crossbar + ring
Sequent NUMA-Q	32	Pentium Pro	200 MHz	131,072 MB	1024 MB/sec	4-way SMP	Ring
SGI Origin2000	128	MIPS R10000	195 MHz	131,072 MB	800 MB/sec	2-way SMP	6-cube
Sun Enterprise 10000	64	UltraSPARC 1	250 MHz	65,536 MB	1600 MB/sec	4-way SMP	16-way crossbar

FIGURE 9.9   Characteristics of multiprocessor computers connected by a network that are for sale in 1997. All these machines have a shared address space with nonuniform memory access time except for the Sun Enterprise 10000, which offers a shared address with uniform memory access time. And all these machines except the Cray Research T3E are cache coherent, with the HP, Sequent, and SGI using directories. The Sun machine uses buses for addresses and a switch for data, so it supports coherency with conventional snooping on the address buses. Communication bandwidth is peak per link, counting all bytes sent including network headers. The bisection bandwidth typically scales with the number of processors. (See *www.mkp.com/cod2e.htm* for pointers to these and more recent network-connected multiprocessors.)

Parallel Program (Message Passing)

Let's try our summing example again for a network-connected multi-processor with 100 processors using multiple private memories.

Since this computer has multiple address spaces, the first step is distributing the 100 subsets to each of the local memories. The processor containing the 100,000 numbers sends the subsets to each of the 100 processor-memory nodes.

The next step is to get the sum of each subset. This step is simply a loop that every execution unit follows; read a word from local memory and add it to a local variable:

```
sum = 0;
for (i = 0; i<1000; i = i + 1) /* loop over each array */
  sum = sum + A1[i]; /* sum the local arrays */ limit = 100;
```

The last step is adding these 100 partial sums. The hard part is that each partial sum is located in a different execution unit. Hence, we must use the interconnection network to send partial sums to accumulate the final sum. Rather than sending all the partial sums to a single processor, which would result in sequentially adding the partial sums, we again divide to conquer. First, half of the execution units send their partial sums to the other half of the execution units, where two partial sums are added together. Then one quarter of the execution units (half of the half) send this new partial sum to the other quarter of the execution units (the remaining half of the half) for the next round of sums. This halving, sending, and receiving continues until there is a single sum of all numbers. Let P_n represent the number of the execution unit, send(x,y) be a routine that sends over the interconnection network to execution unit number x the value y, and receive() be a function that accepts a value from the network for this execution unit:

```
half = 100;/* 100 processors */
repeat
  half = (half+1)/2; /* send vs. receive dividing line*/
  if (Pn >= half && Pn < limit) send(Pn - half, sum);
  if (Pn < (limit/2-1)) sum = sum + receive();
  limit = half; /* upper limit of senders */
until (half == 1); /* exit with final sum */
```

This code divides all processors into senders or receivers and each receiving processor gets only one message, so we can presume that a receiving processor will stall until it receives a message. Thus, send and receive can be used as primitives for synchronization as well as for communication, as the processors are aware of the transmission of data.

Addressing in Large-Scale Parallel Processors

Most commercial, large-scale processors use memory that is distributed; otherwise it is either very difficult or very expensive to build a machine that can scale up to scores of processors with scores of memory modules.

The next question facing distributed-memory machines is communication. For the hardware designer, the simplest solution is to offer only send and receive instead of the implicit communication that is possible as part of any load or store. Send and receive also have the advantage of making it easier for the programmer to optimize communication: It's simpler to overlap computation with communication by using explicit sends and receives rather than with implicit loads and stores.

On the other hand, loads and stores normally have much lower communication overhead than do sends and receives. And some applications will have references to remote information that is only occasionally and unpredictably accessed, so it is much more efficient to use an address to remote data when *demanded* rather than to retrieve it in case it *might* be used. Such a machine has *distributed shared memory* (DSM).

Hardware Software Interface   Adding a software layer to provide a single address space on top of sends and receives so that communication is possible as part of any load or store is harder, although it is comparable to the virtual memory system already found in most processors (see Chapter 7). In virtual memory, a uniprocessor uses page tables to decide if an address points to data in local memory or on a disk; this translation system might be modified to decide if the address points to local data, to data in another processor's memory, or to disk. Although *shared virtual memory*, as it is called, creates the illusion of shared memory—just as virtual memory creates the illusion of a very large memory—since it invokes the operating system, performance is usually so slow that shared-memory communication must be rare or else most of the time is spent transferring pages.

Caches are important to performance no matter how communication is performed, so we want to allow the shared data to appear in the cache of the processor that owns the data as well as in the processor that requests the data. Thus, the single global address in a network-connected multiprocessor resurrects the issue of cache coherency, since there are multiple copies of the same data with the same address in different processors. Clearly the bus-snooping protocols of section 9.3 won't work here, as there is no single bus on which all memory references are broadcast. Since the designers of the Cray T3E (see Figure 9.9) had no bus to support cache coherency, the T3E has a single address space but it is not cache coherent.

A cache-coherent alternative to bus snooping is *directories*. In directory-based protocols, there is logically a single directory that keeps the state of every block in main memory. Information in the directory can include which caches have copies of the block, whether it is dirty, and so on. Fortunately, directory entries can be distributed so that different requests can go to different memories, thereby reducing contention and allowing a scalable design. Directories retain the characteristic that the sharing status of a block is always in a single known location, making a large-scale parallel processor plausible.

Designers of snooping caches and directories face similar issues; the only difference is the mechanism that detects when there is a write to shared data. Instead of watching the bus to see if there are requests that require that the local cache be updated or invalidated, the directory controller sends explicit commands to each processor that has a copy of the data. Such messages can then be sent over the network. Figure 9.9 shows the characteristics of several directory-based, nonuniform access multiprocessors.

Hardware Software Interface

Note that with a single address space, the data could be placed arbitrarily in memories of different processors. This has two negative performance consequences. The first is that the miss penalty would be much longer because the request must go over the network. The second is that the network bandwidth would be consumed moving data to the proper processors. For programs that have low miss rates, this may not be significant. On the other hand, programs with high miss rates will have much lower performance when data is randomly assigned.

If the programmer or the compiler allocates data to the processor that is likely to use it, then this performance pitfall is removed. Unlike private memory organizations, this allocation only needs to be good, since missing data can still be fetched. Such leniency simplifies the allocation problem.

Another possible solution is to add a second level of coherence to the main memory for every processor. This directory would allow blocks of main memory to migrate, relieving the programmer or the compiler of memory allocation. As long as main memory blocks are not frequently shipped back and forth repeatedly, this scheme may achieve the performance of intelligent allocation of memory at the cost of considerably more hardware complexity. This scheme is called *cache-only memory*. This migration can occur at the page level by the operating system, or we can imagine doing it in hardware.

Figure 9.10 summarizes the coherency options for a single address space.

Since the number of pins per chip is limited, not all processors can be connected directly via a network. This restriction has inspired a whole zoo of topologies for consideration in the design of the network. In section 9.6, we'll look at the characteristics of some of the key alternatives of network designs. But first let's look at another way to connect computers by networks.

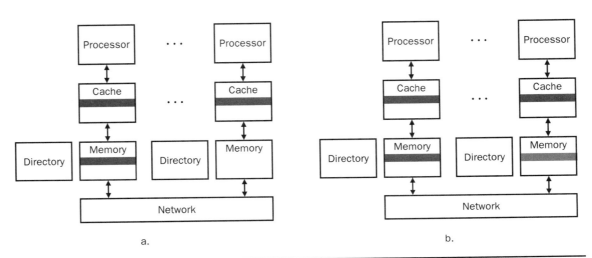

FIGURE 9.10 Options for a single address space in a large-scale parallel processor. The shaded rectangles represent the replicated data. *(a)* Coherence at *cache* level using directories in a network-connected multiprocessor. The original data is in memory, and the copies are replicated only in the caches. *(b)* Coherence at *memory* level using directories in a network-connected multiprocessor. The copies are replicated in remote memory (in color) *and* in the caches. The scheme in *b* is similar to the scheme used in the Kendall Square Research KSR-1. As long as memory is coherent, the data can be safely cached. If the data in a memory is invalidated, then corresponding blocks in the cache must be invalidated as well.

The Big Picture

Figure 9.11 compares cost performance of bus-connected UMA multiprocessors to network-connected NUMA multiprocessors. The network has a smaller initial cost, and then costs scale up somewhat more quickly than the bus-connected machine. Performance for both machines scales linearly until the bus reaches its limit, and then performance is flat no matter how many processors are used. When these two effects are combined, we see that the network-connected NUMA has consistent performance per unit cost, while the bus-connected machine has a "sweet spot" plateau. The plateau suggests that customers need to be more selective with bus-connected than with network-connected multiprocessors, and that bus designers need to be careful to pick a sweet spot that matches the needs of most customers.

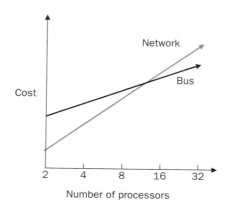

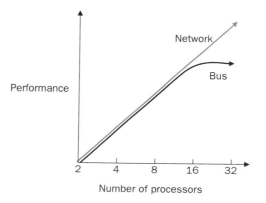

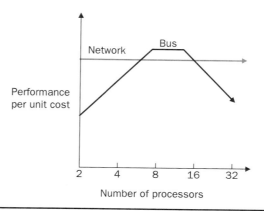

FIGURE 9.11 Cost, performance, and cost/performance of bus-connected and network-connected shared address multiprocessors. The combination of cost and performance suggests a "sweet spot" in 1997 for bus-connected multiprocessors of 8 to 16 processors, shown as a plateau in the cost/performance graph. Network-connected multiprocessors have better cost/performance to the left of the sweet spot because they are less expensive, and better cost/performance to the right of the sweet spot because they have higher performance. A bus designer effectively chooses the sweet spot by the width and the speed of the bus, which determines both the left edge of the plateau (cost) and right edge (scalability). *(page 733)*

9.5 Clusters

Garry [Kasparov] will win, because the computer cannot improve that much in a single year.

Mike Valvo, expert chess commentator before the match between Kasparov and Deep Blue, *Techwire*, May 6, 1997

There are many mainframe applications—such as databases, file servers, Web servers, simulations, and multiprogramming/batch processing—amenable to running on more loosely coupled machines than the cache-coherent NUMA machines of the prior section. These applications often need to be highly available, requiring some form of fault tolerance and repairability. Such applications—plus the similarity of the multiprocessor nodes to desktop computers and the emergence of high-bandwidth, switch-based local area networks—suggests that large-scale processing of the future may use *clusters* of off-the-shelf, whole computers. But the most historic example is the victory of the IBM SP2—a cluster of 32 nodes very similar to the RS/6000 workstation with hardware accelerators for chessboard evaluators—over chess champion Kasparov in 1997.

For example, in 1997 a cluster of 100 UltraSPARC desktop computers at UC Berkeley, connected by 160-MB/sec per link Myrinet switches, was used to set world records in database sort—sorting 8.6 GB of data originally on disk in one minute—and in cracking an encrypted message—taking just 3.5 hours to decipher a 40-bit DES key.

The Berkeley cluster above was constructed by the customers using off-the-shelf components, as is often the case. Figure 9.12 shows clusters sold by computer companies such as the IBM SP2. These company-designed clusters are normally sold to provide scalable, highly available systems—that is, systems whose goal is both to scale across a large number of processors, memory, and disks, *and* to be available 24 hours a day, 365 days a year.

One drawback of clusters has been that the cost of administering a cluster of N machines is about the same as the cost of administering N independent machines, while the cost of administering a shared address space multiprocessor with N processors is about the same as administering a single machine.

Another drawback is that clusters are usually connected using the I/O bus of the computer, whereas multiprocessors are usually connected on the memory bus of the computer. The memory bus has higher bandwidth, allowing multiprocessors to drive the network link at higher speed and to have fewer conflicts with I/O traffic on I/O-intensive applications.

Name	Maximum number of processors	Processor name	Processor clock rate	Maximum memory size/ system	Communi- cations BW/link	Node	Maximum number of nodes
HP 9000 EPS21	64	PA-8000	180 MHz	65,536 MB	532 MB/sec	4-way SMP	16
IBM RS/6000 HACMP R40	16	PowerPC 604	112 MHz	4,096 MB	12 MB/sec	8-way SMP	2
IBM RS/6000 SP2	512	Power2 SC	135 MHz	1,048,576 MB	150 MB/sec	16-way node	32
Sun Enterprise Cluster 6000 HA	60	UltraSPARC	167 MHz	61,440 MB	100 MB/sec	30-way SMP	2
Tandem NonSrop Himalaya S70000	4096	MIPS R10000	195 MHz	1,048,576 MB	40 MB/sec	16-way SMP	256

FIGURE 9.12   Characteristics of clusters commercially available in 1997. All but the IBM SP2 are marketed for high-availability applications. The SP2 is used for number-crunching scientific applications and for data mining. (See *www.mkp.com/cod2e.htm* for pointers to these and more recent clusters.)

A final weakness is the division of memory: a cluster of N machines has N independent memories and N copies of the operating system, but a shared address multiprocessor allows a single program to use almost all the memory in the computer. Thus a sequential program in a cluster has $1/N$th the memory available compared to a sequential program in an SMP.

The weakness of separate memories for program size turns out to be a strength in system availability and expandability. Since a cluster consists of independent computers connected through a local area network, it is much easier to replace a machine without bringing down the system in a cluster than in an SMP. Fundamentally, the shared address means that it is difficult to isolate a processor and replace a processor without heroic work by the operating system. Since the cluster software is a layer that runs on top of local operating systems running on each computer, it is much easier to disconnect and replace a broken machine.

Given that clusters are constructed from whole computers and independent, scalable networks, this isolation also makes it easier to expand the system without bringing down the application that runs on top of the cluster. High availability and rapid, incremental expandability make clusters attractive to service providers for the World Wide Web.

Another difference between the two tends to be the price for equivalent computing power for large-scale machines. Since large-scale multiprocessors have small volumes, the extra development costs of large machines must be amortized over few systems, resulting in higher cost to the customer. Since the same switches sold in high volume for small systems can be composed to construct large networks for large clusters, local area network switches have the same economy-of-scale advantages as small computers.

As is often the case with two competing solutions, each side tries to borrow ideas from the other to become more attractive.

On one side of the battle, to combat the high-availability weakness of multiprocessors, hardware designers and operating system developers are trying to offer the ability to run multiple operating systems on portions of the full machine, so that a node can fail or be upgraded without bringing down the whole machine.

On the other side of the battle, since both system administration and memory size limits are approximately linear in the number of independent machines, some are reducing the cluster problems by constructing clusters from small-scale SMPs. For example, a cluster of 32 processors might be constructed from eight four-way SMPs or four eight-way SMPs. Such "hybrid" clusters—sometimes called *clustered, shared memory*—are proving popular with applications that care about cost/performance, availability, and expandability. Indeed, all but one of the commercially provided clusters in Figure 9.12 are based on SMPs.

The next section describes networks used in both clusters and multiprocessors.

9.6 | Network Topologies

The straightforward way to connect processor-memory nodes is to have a dedicated communication link between every node. Between the high cost/performance of this *fully connected* network and the low cost/performance of a bus are a set of networks that constitute a wide range of trade-offs in cost/performance. Network costs include the number of switches, the number of links on a switch to connect to the network, the width (number of bits) per link, and length of the links when the network is mapped into a physical machine. For example, on a machine that scales between tens and hundreds of processors, some links may be metal rectangles within a chip that are a few millimeters long, and others may be cables that must stretch several meters from one cabinet to another. Network performance is multifaceted as well. It includes the latency on an unloaded network to send and receive a message, the throughput in terms of the maximum number of messages that can be transmitted in a given time period, delays caused by contention for a portion of the network, and variable performance depending on the pattern of communication. Another obligation of the network may be fault tolerance, since very large systems may be required to operate in the presence of broken components.

Networks are normally drawn as graphs, with each arc of the graph representing a link of the communication network. The processor-memory node is shown as the black square, and the switch is shown as a colored circle. In this section, all links are *bidirectional*; that is, information can flow in either direction. All networks consist of *switches* whose links go to processor-memory nodes and to other switches. The first improvement over a bus is a network that connects a sequence of nodes together:

This topology is called a *ring*. Since some nodes are not directly connected, some messages will have to hop along intermediate nodes until they arrive at the final destination.

Unlike a bus, a ring is capable of many simultaneous transfers. Because there are numerous topologies to choose from, performance metrics are needed to distinguish these designs. Two are popular. The first is *total network bandwidth*, which is the bandwidth of each link multiplied by the number of links. This represents the very best case. For the ring network above with P processors, the total network bandwidth would be P times the bandwidth of one link; the total network bandwidth of a bus is just the bandwidth of that bus, or one times the bandwidth of that link.

To balance this best case, we include another metric that is closer to the worst case: the *bisection bandwidth*. This is calculated by dividing the machine into two parts, each with half the nodes. Then you sum the bandwidth of the links that cross that imaginary dividing line. The bisection bandwidth of a ring is two times the link bandwidth, and it is one times the link bandwidth for the bus. If a single link is as fast as the bus, the ring is only twice as fast as a bus in the worst case, but it is P times faster in the best case.

Since some network topologies are not symmetric, the question arises of where to draw the imaginary line when bisecting the machine. This is a worst-case metric, so the answer is to choose the division that yields the most pessimistic network performance; stated alternatively, calculate all possible bisection bandwidths and pick the smallest. We take this pessimistic view because parallel programs are often limited by the weakest link in the communication chain.

At the other extreme from a ring is a *fully connected network*, where every processor has a bidirectional link to every other processor. For fully connected networks, the total network bandwidth is $(P \times P - 1)/2$, and the bisection bandwidth is $(P/2)^2$.

The tremendous improvement in performance of fully connected networks is offset by the tremendous increase in cost. This inspires engineers to invent new topologies that are between the cost of rings and the performance of fully connected networks. The evaluation of success depends in large part on the nature of the communication in the workload of parallel programs run on the machine.

The number of different topologies that have been discussed in publications would be difficult to count, but the number that have been used in commercial parallel processors is just a handful. Figure 9.13 illustrates two of the popular topologies. Real machines frequently add extra links to these simple topologies to improve performance and reliability.

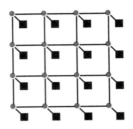 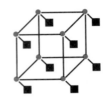

| a. 2-D grid or mesh of 16 nodes | b. n-cube tree of 8 nodes ($8 = 2^3$ so $n = 3$) |

FIGURE 9.13   Network topologies that have appeared in commercial parallel processors.
The colored circles represent switches and the black squares represent processor-memory nodes.
Even though a switch has many links, generally only one goes to the processor. The Boolean n-cube topology is an n-dimensional interconnect with 2^n nodes, requiring n links per switch (plus one for the processor) and thus n nearest-neighbor nodes. Frequently these basic topologies have been supplemented with extra arcs to improve performance and reliability. For example, the switches in the left and right columns of the 2-D grid could be connected through the unused ports on each switch, making four horizontal rings.

An alternative to placing a processor at every node in a network is to leave only the switch at some of these nodes. The switches are smaller than processor-memory-switch nodes, and thus may be packed more densely, thereby lessening distance and increasing performance. Such networks are frequently called *multistage networks* to reflect the multiple steps that a message may travel. Types of multistage networks are as numerous as single-stage networks; Figure 9.14 illustrates two of the popular multistage organizations. A *fully connected* or *crossbar network* allows any node to communicate with any other node in one pass through the network. An *Omega network* uses less hardware than the crossbar network ($2n \log_2 n$ vs. n^2 switches), but contention can occur between messages, depending on the pattern of communication. For example, the Omega network in Figure 9.14 cannot send a message from P0 to P6 at the same time it sends a message from P1 to P7.

Implementing Network Topologies

This simple analysis of all the networks in this section ignores important practical considerations in the construction of a network. The distance of each link affects the cost of communicating at a high clock rate—generally, the longer the distance, the more expensive it is to run at a high clock rate. Shorter distances also make it easier to assign more wires to the link, as the power to drive many wires from a chip is less if the wires are short. Shorter wires are

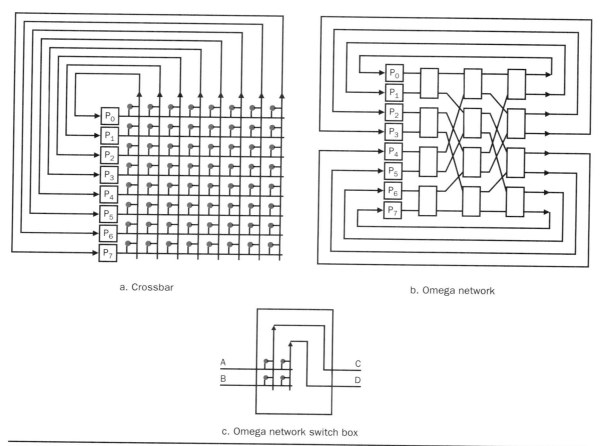

a. Crossbar

b. Omega network

c. Omega network switch box

FIGURE 9.14 Popular multistage network topologies for eight nodes. The switches in these drawings are simpler than in earlier drawings because the links are unidirectional; data comes in at the bottom and exits out the right link. The switch box in c can pass A to C and B to D or B to C and A to D. The crossbar uses n^2 switches, where n is the number of processors, while the Omega network uses $n/2 \log_2 n$ of the large switch boxes, each of which is logically composed of four of the smaller switches. In this case, the crossbar uses 64 switches versus 12 switch boxes, or 48 switches, in the Omega network. The crossbar, however, can support any combination of messages between processors, while the Omega network cannot.

also cheaper than long wires. A final practical limitation is that the three-dimensional drawings must be mapped onto chips and boards that are essentially two-dimensional media. The bottom line is that topologies that appear elegant when sketched on the blackboard may look awkward when constructed from chips, cables, boards, and boxes.

9.7 Real Stuff: Future Directions for Multiprocessors

For over a decade prophets have voiced the contention that the organization of a single computer has reached its limits and that truly significant advances can be made only by interconnection of a multiplicity of computers in such a manner as to permit cooperative solution. . . . Demonstration is made of the continued validity of the single processor approach . . .

> Gene Amdahl, "Validity of the single processor approach
> to achieving large scale computing capabilities,"
> Spring Joint Computer Conference, 1967

Uniprocessor performance is improving at an unprecedented rate, with microprocessors leading the way. Figure 1.20 on page 30 shows that the fastest microprocessors have increased in performance by more than 50% per year every year since 1987. This rapid rate of change does not come free: the estimate of the cost of development of the recent Pentium Pro is $400 million.

Memory capacity has improved at a high rate for a considerably longer time than for processors. Figure 1.14 on page 22 shows that DRAMs have increased their capacity fourfold about every three years. Once again, the tremendous development investment, combined with the low cost of purchasing DRAMs, has led almost all computer manufacturers, including parallel processor companies, to build their memories from DRAMs.

A final technology is the interconnection network. The bandwidth of the interconnection network has improved because of improvements in the speed of logic, improvements in the packaging of parallel processors, and advances in the speed of the physical links. For example, the peak bandwidth per link improved over one decade from 0.5 MB/sec in the Intel iPSC (1986) to 800 MB/sec in the SGI Origin (1996).

Thus the three technologies available to parallel processor designers are fast microprocessors, high-capacity DRAMs, and increasing network bandwidth; interestingly, all are improving at comparable rates.

As mentioned earlier, the rapid change in commercial multiprocessors led us to place the machines that illustrate these ideas on the World Wide Web, so that we could keep the examples from becoming stale. See the section for Chapter 9 at *www.mkp.com/cod2e.htm* to find links to the latest information.

Facts of Life for Large-Scale Parallel Processors

The exciting prospect of building the world's fastest computer is constrained by some facts of life for the parallel processor designer. The first fact of life is that because the nodes are very similar to the core of a desktop computer, the cost of a large-scale parallel processor node is comparable to the cost of a desktop computer.

Most supercomputers cost less than $25,000,000 for processor and memory; since the price of desktop computers has remained between $2500 and $10,000, even if nodes could match desktop computer prices, the largest parallel processors will have no more than 2500 to 10,000 nodes. This estimate does not include the cost of the interconnection network, leading to even fewer nodes. Furthermore, many computers are purchased for scientific applications at a much lower price; thus these machines have far fewer nodes than the practical maximum. Accordingly, while a practical limit of the number of processors is 1000 to 10,000, for many customers and applications, 100 processors will be sufficient.

In 1997, most multiprocessors are in the range of 8 to 16 processors, with the number moving up slowly. If 95% of the machines sold will have less than 100 processors, those 5% of larger machines must carry a larger research and development burden and hence be more expensive per node.

The topology of the interconnection network is important in the construction of a machine that can scale from 100 to 10,000 nodes, and the best topology for 100 to 500 nodes may not be the choice for 1000 to 10,000 nodes. Thus, the topology may vary with the maximum number of nodes and the packaging choices for that machine. The good news is that there are many good interconnection network topologies to choose from; the bad news is that, given these fine alternatives and the importance of the topology to the cost of the machine, there is unlikely to be a single topology that all parallel processor companies will follow.

The second reason for the lesser importance of topologies is that cost-effective fault tolerance is incompatible with topology-dependent algorithms because by definition a broken link or node means that sometimes messages will follow different paths than the programmer would expect from the network topology. Fault tolerance is critical because a machine with 10,000 nodes, each similar to a desktop computer, should have a mean time between failures that is 10,000 times worse than a desktop computer. Thus, with large parallel processors, the question is not *whether* anything is broken at any point in time, but rather *how many* components are broken. Parallel processors must work in the presence of broken network links and broken nodes; hence large parallel processors are not amenable to topology-specific algorithms even if the overhead of communication is reduced.

Hardware Software Interface

The lack of a standard topology is less of an obstacle to portable parallel processor programs than you might first suspect. One reason is that the software overhead to send a message is so large that it masks the effects of the topology. In other words, these overhead costs are so high that the time to send a message to the nearest neighbor node is similar to the time to send to the furthest neighbor. The overhead is high in some cases because the protocols are designed to send large messages, so that sometimes by pipelining them, the latency is seen only once. Other reasons for the high overhead are invoking the operating system on sending or receiving a message and a slow interface between the processor and the network.

Taken in combination, these elements deflate the value of topology-specific algorithms:

- The lack of a standard topology combined with the importance of portable parallel processor programs to the success of the industry

- The high overhead of communication, making the latency virtually the same for messages independent of the distance between nodes

- Operation in the presence of broken links and broken nodes

The Big Picture

A key characteristic of parallel programs is frequency of synchronization and communication. Large-scale parallel machines have distributed physical memory; the higher bandwidth and lower overhead of local memory compared to nonlocal memory strongly rewards parallel processing programmers who utilize locality.

Massive Parallelism

The term *massively parallel* is widely used but rarely defined, but no one would define a computer with less than 100 processors as massively parallel. Even with such a conservative dividing line, parallel processing using more than 100 processors is not yet important in everyday computing. Ideally, we should have a simple model that allows programmers to more easily create portable parallel programs that achieve good performance on real multiprocessors *and* that enables researchers to invent new algorithms that will work well on many multiprocessors. Unfortunately, few theoretical models for parallel computation accurately predict performance of current commercial multiprocessors.

One interesting event for massively parallel processors (MPP) is the Accelerated Strategic Computing Initiative (ASCI), a program to accelerate the development of massively parallel supercomputers by ordering a small number of machines costing $50 million to $100 million. A series of ASCI supercomputers will be built, leading up to a 100-teraFLOPS supercomputer by early next century. Figure 9.15 shows the first three ASCI machines. In December 1996, the distributed-memory, message-passing multiprocessor from Intel (ASCI Red) was the first computer to operate at the rate of 1 teraFLOPS (a million MFLOPS).

Name	Number of processors	Processor	Memory size/ system	Communi- cations BW/link	Node	Topology	Peak perfor- mance (tera- FLOPS)	Year
ASCI Red (Intel)	9216	200-MHz Pentium Pro	580,608 MB	800 MB/sec	2-way SMP	two 2-D grids	1.8	1996
ASCI Blue Pacific (IBM RS/6000 SP)	–	successor to Power2 SC	–	–	–	–	3.0	1998
ASCI Blue Mountain (SGI Origin2000)	3072	successor to MIPS R10000	–	–	–	–	3.0	1998

FIGURE 9.15 Characteristics of ASCI supercomputers. All are distributed-memory machines, but only the SGI machine communicates via a shared address and is cache coherent. The costs of the three machines are $46 million, $93 million, and $110 million, respectively. (See *www.mkp.com/cod2e.htm* for pointers to these and more recent MPPs.)

9.8 Fallacies and Pitfalls

> *Number 9: Quote performance in terms of processor utilization, parallel speedups or MFLOPS per dollar.*
>
> David H. Bailey, "Twelve ways to fool the masses when giving performance results on parallel supercomputers,"
> *Supercomputing Review,* 1991

The many assaults on parallel processing have uncovered numerous fallacies and pitfalls. We cover three here.

Pitfall: Measuring performance of parallel processors by linear speedup versus execution time.

"Mortar shot" graphs—plotting performance compared to the number of processors, showing linear speedup, a plateau, and then a falling off—have long been used to judge the success of parallel processors. Although scalability is one facet of a parallel program, it is an indirect measure of performance. The primary question to be asked concerns the power of the processors being scaled: a program that linearly improves performance to equal 100 Intel 8086s may be slower than the sequential version on a single Pentium Pro desktop computer. Be especially careful of floating-point-intensive programs, as processing elements without floating-point hardware assist may scale wonderfully but have poor collective performance.

Measuring results using linear speedup compared to the execution time can mislead the programmer as well as those hearing the performance claims of the programmer. Many programs with poor speedup are faster than programs that show excellent speedup as the number of processors increases.

Comparing execution times is fair only if you are comparing the best algorithms on each machine. (Of course, you can't subtract time for idle processors when evaluating a parallel processor, so CPU time is an inappropriate metric for parallel processors.) Comparing the identical code on two machines may seem fair, but it is not; the parallel program may be slower on a uniprocessor than a sequential version. Sometimes, developing a parallel program will lead to algorithmic improvements, so that comparing the previously best-known sequential program with the parallel code—which seems fair—compares inappropriate algorithms. To reflect this issue, sometimes the terms *relative speedup* (same program) and *true speedup* (best programs) are used.

Fallacy: Amdahl's law doesn't apply to parallel computers.

In 1987, the head of a research organization claimed that Amdahl's law had been broken by a multiprocessor machine. To try to understand the basis of the media reports, let's see the quote that gave us Amdahl's law [1967, p. 483]:

A fairly obvious conclusion which can be drawn at this point is that the effort expended on achieving high parallel processing rates is wasted unless it is accompanied by achievements in sequential processing rates of very nearly the same magnitude.

This statement must still be true; the neglected portion of the program must limit performance. One interpretation of the law leads to the following lemma: portions of every program must be sequential, so there must be an economic upper bound to the number of processors—say, 100. By showing linear speedup with 1000 processors, this lemma is disproved and hence the claim that Amdahl's law was broken.

The approach of the researchers was to change the input to the benchmark: rather than going 1000 times faster, they computed 1000 times more work in comparable time. For their algorithm, the sequential portion of the program was constant, independent of the size of the input, and the rest was fully parallel—hence, linear speedup with 1000 processors. Simply scaling the size of applications, without also scaling floating-point accuracy, the number of iterations, the I/O requirements, and the way applications deal with error may be naive. Many applications will not calculate the correct result if the problem size is increased unwittingly.

We see no reason why Amdahl's law doesn't apply to parallel processors. What this research does point out is the importance of having benchmarks that can grow large enough to demonstrate performance of large-scale parallel processors.

Fallacy: Peak performance tracks observed performance.

One definition of peak performance is "performance that a machine is guaranteed not to exceed." Alas, the supercomputer industry uses this metric in marketing, and its fallacy is being exacerbated with parallel machines. Not only are industry marketers using the nearly unattainable peak performance of a uniprocessor node (see Figure 9.16), but they are then multiplying it by the total number of processors, assuming perfect speedup! Amdahl's law suggests how difficult it is to reach either peak; multiplying the two together also multiplies the sins. Figure 9.17 compares the peak to sustained performance on a benchmark; the 64-processor IBM SP2 achieves only 7% of peak performance. Clearly peak performance does not always track observed performance.

Machine	Peak MFLOPS rating	Harmonic mean MFLOPS of the Perfect Club benchmarks	Percent of peak MFLOPS
Cray X-MP/416	940	14.8	1%
IBM 3090-600S	800	8.3	1%
NEC SX/2	1300	16.6	1%

FIGURE 9.16 Peak performance and harmonic mean of actual performance for the 12 Perfect Club benchmarks. These results are for the programs run unmodified. When tuned by hand, performance of the three machines moves to 24.4, 11.3, and 18.3 MFLOPS, respectively. This is still 2% or less of peak performance.

| | Cray YMP (8 processors) | | IBM SP2 (64 processors) | |
	MFLOPS	% Peak	MFLOPS	% Peak
Peak	2,666	100%	14,636	100%
3D FFT PDE	1,795	67%	1,093	7%

FIGURE 9.17   Peak versus observed performance for Cray YMP and IBM RS/6000 SP2.

Such performance claims can confuse the manufacturer as well as the user of the machine. The danger is that the manufacturer will develop software libraries with success judged as percentage of peak performance measured in megaflops rather than taking less time, or that hardware will be added that increases peak node performance but is difficult to use.

9.9   Concluding Remarks—Evolution versus Revolution in Computer Architecture

The stumbling way in which even the ablest of the scientists in every generation have had to fight through thickets of erroneous observations, misleading generalizations, inadequate formulations, and unconscious prejudice is rarely appreciated by those who obtain their scientific knowledge from textbooks.

James B. Conant, *Science and Common Sense*, 1951

Reading conference and journal articles from the last 30 years can be discouraging; so much effort has been expended with so little impact. Optimistically speaking, these papers act as gravel and, when placed logically together, form the foundation for the next generation of computers. From a more pessimistic point of view, if 90% of the ideas disappeared, no one would notice.

One reason for this predicament is what could be called the "von Neumann syndrome." By hoping to invent a new model of computation that will revolutionize computing, researchers are striving to become the von Neumann of the 21st century. Another reason is taste: researchers often select problems that no one else cares about. Even if important problems are selected, there is frequently a lack of experimental evidence to demonstrate convincingly the value of the solution. Moreover, when important problems are selected and the solutions are demonstrated, the proposed solutions may be too expensive relative to their benefit. Sometimes this expense is measured as straightforward cost/performance—the performance enhancement does not merit the added cost. More often the expense of innovation comes from being too disruptive to computer users.

Figure 9.18 shows what we mean by the *evolution-revolution spectrum* of computer architecture innovation. To the left are ideas that are invisible to the

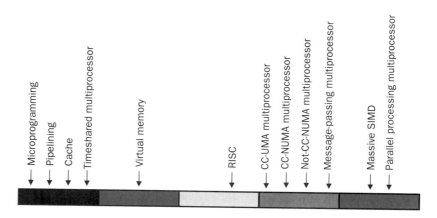

FIGURE 9.18 The evolution-revolution spectrum of computer architecture. The first four columns are distinguished from the last column in that applications and operating systems may be ported from other computers rather than written from scratch. For example, RISC is listed in the middle of the spectrum because user compatibility is only at the level of high-level languages (HLLs), while microprogramming allows binary compatibility, and parallel processing multiprocessors require changes to algorithms and extending HLLs. You see several flavors of multiprocessors on this figure. "Timeshared multiprocessor" means multiprocessors justified by running many independent programs at once. "CC-UMA" and "CC-NUMA" mean cache-coherent UMA and NUMA multiprocessors running parallel subsystems such as databases or file servers. "Not-CC-NUMA" means a shared address but *not* cache-coherent NUMA for similar applications. And the same applications are intended for "message passing." "Parallel processing multiprocessor" means a multiprocessor of some flavor sold to accelerate individual programs developed by users. (See section 9.10 to learn about SIMD.)

user (except presumably better cost, better performance, or both); this is the evolutionary end of the spectrum. At the other end are revolutionary architecture ideas. These are the ideas that require new applications from programmers who must learn new programming languages and models of computation, and must invent new data structures and algorithms.

Revolutionary ideas are easier to publish than evolutionary ideas, but to be adopted they must have a much higher payoff. Caches are an example of an evolutionary improvement. Within five years after the first publication about caches, almost every computer company was designing a machine with a cache. The Reduced Instruction Set Computer (RISC) ideas were nearer to the middle of the spectrum, for it took closer to 10 years for most companies to have a RISC product. Examples of revolutionary computer architecture came from several parallel processing companies in the late 1980s. Every program that runs efficiently on those machines was either substantially modified or written especially for it, and programmers needed to learn a new style of programming for it. The obstacles were too large for most of these companies to survive.

Projects that the computer industry ignores may be valuable if they document the lessons learned for future efforts. The sin is not in having a novel architecture that is commercially unsuccessful, but in neglecting to quantitatively evaluate the strengths and weaknesses of the novel ideas. And failures of past research projects do not mean that the ideas are dead forever. Changes in technology may rejuvenate an idea that previously had the wrong trade-offs or rejuvenate an idea that was ahead of the technology.

When contemplating the future—and inventing your own contributions to the field—remember the evolution-revolution spectrum. Acceptance of hardware ideas requires acceptance by software people; therefore, hardware people must learn more about software. And if software people want good machines, they must learn more about hardware to be able to communicate with and thereby influence hardware designers. Also, keep in mind the principles of computer organization found in this book; these will surely guide computers of the future, just as they have guided computers of the past.

9.10 Historical Perspective and Further Reading

As parallelism can appear at many levels, it is useful to categorize the alternatives. In 1966, Flynn proposed a simple model of categorizing computers that is still useful today. Scrutinizing the most constrained component of the machine, he counted the number of parallel instruction and data streams and then labeled the computer with this count:

1. *Single instruction stream, single data stream* (SISD, the uniprocessor)

2. *Single instruction stream, multiple data streams* (SIMD)

3. *Multiple instruction streams, single data stream* (MISD)

4. *Multiple instruction streams, multiple data streams* (MIMD)

Some machines are hybrids of these categories, of course, but this classic model has survived because it is simple, easy to understand, and gives a good first approximation. It is also—perhaps because of its understandability—the most widely used scheme.

Your first question about the model should be, "Single or multiple compared with what?" A machine that adds a 32-bit number in 1 clock cycle would seem to have multiple data streams when compared with a bit-serial computer that takes 32 clock cycles to add. Flynn chose computers popular during that time, the IBM 704 and IBM 7090, as the model of SISD; today, the MIPS implementations in Chapters 5 and 6 would be fine reference points.

Single Instruction Multiple Data Computers

SIMD computers operate on vectors of data. For example, when a single SIMD instruction adds 64 numbers, the SIMD hardware sends 64 data streams to 64 ALUs to form 64 sums within a single clock cycle.

The virtues of SIMD are that all the parallel execution units are synchronized and they all respond to a single instruction that emanates from a single program counter (PC). From a programmer's perspective, this is close to the already familiar SISD. Although every unit will be executing the same instruction, each execution unit has its own address registers, and so each unit can have different data addresses.

The original motivation behind SIMD was to amortize the cost of the control unit over dozens of execution units. Another advantage is the reduced size of program memory—SIMD needs only one copy of the code that is being simultaneously executed, while MIMD may need a copy in every processor. Virtual memory and increasing capacity of DRAM chips have reduced the importance of this advantage.

Real SIMD computers have a mixture of SISD and SIMD instructions. There is typically an SISD host computer to perform sequential operations such as branches or address calculations. The SIMD instructions are broadcast to all the execution units, each with its own set of registers and memory. Execution units rely on interconnection networks to exchange data.

SIMD works best when dealing with arrays in *for* loops. Hence, for massive parallelism to work in SIMD, there must be massive data, or *data parallelism.* SIMD is at its weakest in *case* or *switch* statements, where each execution unit must perform a different operation on its data, depending on what data it has. Execution units with the wrong data are disabled so that units with proper data may continue. Such situations essentially run at $1/n$th performance, where n is the number of cases.

A basic trade-off in SIMD machines is processor performance versus number of processors. The Connection Machine 2 (CM-2), for example, offers 65,536 single-bit-wide processors, while the Illiac IV had 64 64-bit processors. Figure 9.19 lists the characteristics of some well-known SIMD computers.

Surely the best-known SIMD is the Illiac IV (seen in Figure 9.20), perhaps the most infamous of the supercomputer projects. Although successful in pushing several technologies useful in later projects, the Illiac IV failed as a computer. Costs escalated from the $8 million estimated in 1966 to $31 million by 1972, despite the construction of only a quarter of the planned machine. Actual performance was at best 15 MFLOPS compared to initial predictions of 1000 MFLOPS for the full system (see Falk [1976]). Delivered to NASA's Ames Research in 1972, the computer took three more years of engineering before it was operational. For better or worse, computer architects are not easily discouraged; SIMD successors of the Illiac IV include the ICL DAP, Goodyear MPP (Figure 9.21), Thinking Machines CM-1 and CM-2, and Maspar MP-1 and MP-2.

Institution	Name	Maximum no. of proc.	Bits/ proc.	Proc. clock rate (MHz)	Number of FPUs	Maximum memory size/system (MB)	Communi- cations BW/system (MB/sec)	Year
U. Illinois	Illiac IV	64	64	5	64	0.125	2,560	1972
ICL	DAP	4,096	1	5	0	2	2,560	1980
Goodyear	MPP	16,384	1	10	0	2	20,480	1982
Thinking Machines	CM-2	65,536	1	7	2048 (optional)	512	16,384	1987
Maspar	MP-1216	16,384	4	25	0	256 or 1024	23,000	1989

FIGURE 9.19   Characteristics of five SIMD computers. Number of FPUs means number of floating-point units.

FIGURE 9.20   The Illiac IV control unit followed by its 64 processing elements. It was per-haps the most infamous of supercomputers. The project started in 1965 and ran its first real appli-cation in 1976. The 64 processors used a 13-MHz clock, and their combined main memory size was 1 MB: 64×16 KB. The Illiac IV was the first machine to teach us that software for parallel machines dominates hardware issues. Photo courtesy of NASA Ames Research Center.

FIGURE 9.21 The Goodyear MPP with 16,384 processors. It was delivered May 2, 1983, to NASA Goddard Space Center and was operational the next day. It was decommissioned on March 1, 1991.

Vector Computers

A related model to SIMD is *vector processing*. It is a well-established architecture and compiler model that was popularized by supercomputers, and is considerably more widely used than SIMD. Vector processors have high-level operations that work on linear arrays of numbers, or vectors. An example vector operation is

$$A = B \times C$$

where A, B, and C are each 64-element vectors of 64-bit floating-point numbers. SIMD has similar instructions; the difference is that vector processors depend on pipelined functional units that typically operate on a few vector elements per clock cycle, while SIMD typically operates on all the elements at once.

Advantages of vector computers over traditional SISD processors include the following:

1. Each result is independent of previous results, which enables deep pipelines and high clock rates.

2. A single vector instruction performs a great deal of work, which means fewer instruction fetches in general, and fewer branch instructions and so fewer mispredicted branches.

3. Vector instructions access memory a block at a time, which allows memory latency to be amortized over, say, 64 elements.

4. Vector instructions access memory with known patterns, which allows multiple memory banks to simultaneously supply operands.

These last two advantages mean that vector processors do not need to rely on high hit rates of data caches to have high performance. They tend to rely on low-latency main memory, often made from SRAM, and have as many as 1024 memory banks to get high memory bandwidth.

To get even higher performance, all vector supercomputers offer multiple processors, a transition to our next topic. Figure 9.22 shows several vector machines.

Elaboration: Although MISD fills out Flynn's classification, it is difficult to envision. A single instruction stream is simpler than multiple instruction streams, but multiple instruction streams with multiple data streams (MIMD) are easier to imagine than multiple instructions with a single data stream (MISD).

While it was conceivable to write 100 different programs for 100 different processors in an MIMD machine, in practice this proved to be impossible. Today MIMD programmers write a single source program and think of the same program running on all processors. This approach is sometimes called *single program multiple data* (*SPMD*).

Name	Vector registers	Elements per vector register	Elements computed per clock cycle	Number of functional units	Processor clock rate	Maximum number of processors	Maximum memory size/system
Cray J90	8	64	1	4	100 MHz	32	8,192 MB
Cray T90	8	128	2	8	455 MHz	32	8,192 MB
Fujitsu VPP300	8–256	64–2048	8	4	140 MHz	16	32,768 MB
NEC SX-4 single node	8 + 8192 scratchpad	256 + variable up to 8K	8	16	125 MHz	32	8,192 MB

FIGURE 9.22 Characteristics of four vector computers that are for sale in 1997. All vector computers in this figure but the Cray T90 use CMOS technology to build the processor. To lower main memory latency (but raise system cost), the T90 uses SRAM instead of DRAM.

Multiple Instruction Multiple Data Computers

It is difficult to distinguish the first MIMD: arguments for the advantages of parallel execution can be traced back to the 19th century [Menabrea 1842]! And even the first computer from the Eckert-Mauchly Corporation had duplicate units, in this case to improve reliability.

Two of the best-documented multiprocessor projects were undertaken in the 1970s at Carnegie-Mellon University. The first of these was C.mmp, which consisted of 16 PDP-11s connected by a crossbar switch to 16 memory units. It was among the first multiprocessors with more than a few processors, and it had a shared-memory programming model. Much of the focus of the research in the C.mmp project was on software, especially in the operating systems area. A later machine, Cm*, was a cluster-based multiprocessor with a distributed memory and a nonuniform access time, which made programming even more of a challenge. The absence of caches and a long remote access latency made data placement critical.

Although very large mainframes were built with multiple processors in the 1970s, multiprocessors did not become highly successful until the 1980s. Bell [1985] suggests the key to success was that the smaller size of the microprocessor allowed the memory bus to replace the interconnection network hardware, and that portable operating systems meant that parallel processor projects no longer required the invention of a new operating system. He distinguishes parallel processors with multiple private addresses by calling them *multicomputers*, reserving the term *multiprocessor* for machines with a single address space.

The first bus-connected multiprocessor with snooping caches was the Synapse N+1 in 1984. The mid-1980s saw an explosion in the development of alternative coherence protocols, and Archibald and Baer [1986] provide a good survey and analysis, as well as references to the original papers. The late 1980s saw the introduction of many commercial bus-connected, snooping-cache architectures, including the Silicon Graphics 4D/240, the Encore Multimax, and the Sequent Symmetry.

In the effort to build large-scale multiprocessors, two different directions were explored: message-passing multicomputers and scalable shared-memory multiprocessors. Although there had been many attempts to build mesh- and hypercube-connected multiprocessors, one of the first machines to successfully bring together all the pieces was the Cosmic Cube, built at Caltech [Seitz 1985]. It introduced important advances in routing and interconnect technology and substantially reduced the cost of the interconnect, which helped make the multicomputer viable. Commercial machines with related architectures included the Intel iPSC 860, the Intel Paragon, and the Thinking Machines CM-5. Alas, the market for such machines proved to be much smaller than hoped, and Intel withdrew from the business (with ASCI Red being their last machine) and Thinking Machines no longer exists. Today this space is mostly clusters, such as the IBM RS/6000 SP2 (Figure 9.23).

FIGURE 9.23   The IBM RS/6000 SP2 with 256 processors. This distributed-memory machine is built using boards from desktop computers largely unchanged plus a custom switch as the interconnect. In contrast to the SP2, most clusters use an off-the-shelf, switched local area network. Photo courtesy of the Lawrence Livermore National Laboratory.

Extending the shared-memory model with scalable cache coherence was done by combining a number of ideas. Directory-based techniques for cache coherence were actually known before snooping cache techniques. In fact, the first cache coherence protocol actually used directories and was implemented in the IBM 3081 in 1976. The idea of distributing directories with the memories to obtain a scalable implementation of cache coherence (now called distributed shared memory or DSM) was the basis for the Stanford DASH multiprocessor; it is considered the forerunner of the NUMA computers in Figure 9.9 on page 728. The Kendall Square Research KSR-1—may it rest in peace—was the first commercial implementation of scalable coherent shared memory. It extended the basic DSM approach to implement a concept called COMA (Cache Only Memory Architecture), which makes the main memory a cache (see Figure 9.10 on page 732).

There is a vast amount of information on multiprocessors: conferences, journal papers, and even books seem to be appearing faster than any single person can absorb the ideas. One good source is the Supercomputing Conference, held annually since 1988. Two major journals, *Journal of Parallel and Distributed Computing* and the *IEEE Transactions on Parallel and Distributed Systems,* contain largely papers on aspects of parallel computing. Textbooks on parallel computing have been written by Almasi and Gottlieb [1989]; Andrews [1991]; Culler, Singh, and Gupta [1998]; and Hwang [1993]. Pfister's book [1995] is one of the few on clusters.

To Probe Further

Almasi, G. S., and A. Gottlieb [1989]. *Highly Parallel Computing,* Benjamin/Cummings, Redwood City, CA.

A textbook covering parallel computers.

Amdahl, G. M. [1967]. "Validity of the single processor approach to achieving large scale computing capabilities," *Proc. AFIPS Spring Joint Computer Conf.,* Atlantic City, NJ, (April) 483–85.

Written in response to the claims of the Illiac IV, this three-page article describes Amdahl's law and gives the classic reply to arguments for abandoning the current form of computing.

Andrews, G. R. {1991]. *Concurrent Programming: Principles and Practice,* Benjamin/Cummings, Redwood City, CA.

A text that gives the principles of parallel programming.

Archibald, J., and J.-L. Baer [1986]. "Cache coherence protocols: Evaluation using a multiprocessor simulation model," *ACM Trans. on Computer Systems* 4:4 (November) 273–98.

Classic survey paper of shared-bus cache coherency protocols.

Arpaci-Dusseau, A., R. Arpaci-Dusseau, D. Culler, J. Hellerstein, and D. Patterson [1997]. "High-performance sorting on networks of workstations," *Proc. ACM SIGMOD/PODS Conference on Management of Data*, Tucson, AZ, May 12–15.

How a world record sort was performed on a cluster, including architecture critique of the workstation and network interface. By April 1, 1997, they pushed the record to 8.6 GB in one minute and 2.2 seconds to sort 100 MB.

Bell, C. G. [1985]. "Multis: A new class of multiprocessor computers," *Science* 228 (April 26) 462–67.

Distinguishes shared address and nonshared address multiprocessors based on microprocessors.

Culler, D. E., and J. P. Singh, with A. Gupta [1998]. *Parallel Computer Architecture,* Morgan Kaufmann, San Francisco.

A new textbook on parallel computers.

Falk, H. [1976]. "Reaching for the Gigaflop," *IEEE Spectrum* 13:10 (October) 65–70.

Chronicles the sad story of the Illiac IV: four times the cost and less than one-tenth the performance of original goals.

Flynn, M. J. [1966]. "Very high-speed computing systems," *Proc. IEEE* 54:12 (December) 1901–09.

Classic article showing SISD/SIMD/MISD/MIMD classifications.

Hord, R. M. [1982]. *The Illiac-IV, the First Supercomputer,* Computer Science Press, Rockville, MD.

A historical accounting of the Illiac IV project.

Hwang, K. [1993]. *Advanced Computer Architecture with Parallel Programming,* McGraw-Hill, New York.

Another textbook covering parallel computers.

Menabrea, L. F. [1842]. "Sketch of the analytical engine invented by Charles Babbage," Bibliothèque Universelle de Genève (October).

Certainly the earliest reference on multiprocessors, this mathematician made this comment while translating papers on Babbage's mechanical computer.

Pfister, G. F. [1995]. *In Search of Clusters: The Coming Battle in Lowly Parallel Computing*, Prentice Hall, Upper Saddle River, NJ.

An entertaining book that advocates clusters and is critical of NUMA multiprocessors.

Seitz, C. [1985]. "The Cosmic Cube," *Comm. ACM* 28:1 (January) 22–31.

A tutorial article on a parallel processor connected via a hypertree. The Cosmic Cube is the ancestor of the Intel supercomputers.

Slotnick, D. L. [1982]. "The conception and development of parallel processors—A personal memoir," *Annals of the History of Computing* 4:1 (January) 20–30.

Recollections of the beginnings of parallel processing by the architect of the Illiac IV.

9.11   Key Terms

These terms reflect the key ideas in the chapter. Check the Glossary for definitions of the terms you do not know.

atomic operation	MESI cache coherency protocol	shared memory
barrier synchronization	message passing	single instruction stream, multiple data streams (SIMD)
cache coherency	multicomputer	
cluster	multiple instruction streams, multiple data streams (MIMD)	single instruction stream, single data stream (SISD)
crossbar network		
data parallelism		snooping cache coherency
directory	multiprocessor	symmetric multiprocessor (SMP)
distributed memory	multistage network	
distributed shared memory (DSM)	network bandwidth	synchronization
	nonuniform memory access (NUMA)	uniform memory access (UMA)
false sharing		
fully connected network	parallel processing program	vector processor
lock	receive message routine	write-broadcast
main memory coherence	send message routine	write-invalidate
massively parallel		

9.12   Exercises

9.1 [15] <§9.1> Write a one-page article examining your life for ways in which concurrency is present and mutual exclusion is obtained. You may want to consider things such as freeways going from two lanes to one, waiting in lines at different types of businesses, obtaining the attention of your instructor to ask questions, and so on. Try to discover different means and mechanisms that are used for both communication and synchronization. Are there any situations in which you wish a different algorithm were used so that either latency or bandwidth were improved, or perhaps the system were more "fair"?

9.2 [10] <§9.1> Consider the following portions of two different programs running at the same time on two processors in an SMP. Assume that before this code is run, both x and y are 0.

Processor 1:   ...; x := x + 1;   y := x + y;   ...

Processor 2:   ...; y := x + 1; ...

What are the possible resulting values of x and y, assuming the code is implemented using a load-store architecture? For each possible outcome, explain how x and y might obtain those values. (Hint: You must examine all of the possible interleavings of the assembly language instructions.)

9.3 [10] <§§9.1–9.3> Imagine that all the employees in a huge company have forgotten who runs the company and can only remember whom they work for. Management is considering whether or not to issue one of the following two statements:

- "Today every employee should ask his boss who his boss is, then tomorrow ask that person who *his* boss is, and so forth, until you eventually discover who runs the company."

- "Everyone, please write the name of your boss on a sheet of paper. Find out what name the person on your sheet of paper has on *his* sheet of paper, and tomorrow write that name on your sheet of paper before coming to work. Repeat this process until you discover who runs the company."

Write a paragraph describing the difference between these two statements and the resulting outcomes. Explain the relationship between the two alternatives described above and what you have learned about concurrency and interprocess synchronization and communication.

9.4 [5] <§§9.1–9.3> {Ex. 9.3} Analyze the performance of the two algorithms above. Consider companies containing 100 people, 1000 people, or 10,000 people. Can you think of any ways to improve either of the two algorithms or to accomplish the same task even faster?

9.5 [5] <§9.3> Count the number of transactions on the bus for the following sequence of activities involving shared data. Assume that both processors use write-back caches, write-update cache coherency, and a block size of one word. Assume that all the words in both caches are clean.

Step	Processor	Memory activity	Memory address
1	processor 1	write	100
2	processor 2	write	104
3	processor 1	read	100
4	processor 2	read	104

9.6 [10] <§9.3> False sharing can lead to unnecessary bus traffic and delays. Follow the directions for Exercise 9.5, except change the block size to four words.

9.7 [15] <§9.4> Another possible network topology is a three-dimensional grid. Draw the topology as in Figure 9.13 on page 738 for 64 nodes. What is the bisection bandwidth of this topology?

9.8 [1 week] <§§9.2–9.6> A parallel processor is typically marketed using programs that can scale performance linearly with the number of processors. Port programs written for one parallel processor to the other, and measure their absolute performance and how it changes as you change the number of processors. What changes must be made to improve performance of the ported programs on each machine? What is performance according to each program?

9.9 [1 week] <§§9.2–9.6> Instead of trying to create fair benchmarks, invent programs that make one parallel processor look terrible compared with the others and also programs that always make one look better than others. What are the key performance characteristics of each program and machine?

9.10 [1 week] <§§9.2– 9.6> Parallel processors usually show performance increases as you increase the number of processors, with the ideal being n times speedup for n processors. The goal of this exercise is to create a biased benchmark that gets worse performance as you add processors. For example, one processor on the parallel processor would run the program fastest, two would be slower, four would be slower than two, and so on. What are the key performance characteristics for each organization that give inverse linear speedup?

9.11 [1 week] <§§9.2–9.6> Networked workstations may be considered parallel processors, albeit with slow communication relative to computation. Port parallel processor benchmarks to a network using remote procedure calls for communication. How well do the benchmarks scale on the network versus the parallel processor? What are the practical differences between networked workstations and a commercial parallel processor?

9.12 [1 week] <§§9.2–9.6> *Superlinear* performance improvement means that a program on n processors is more than n times faster than the equivalent uniprocessor. One argument for superlinear speedup is that time spent servicing interrupts or switching contexts is reduced when you have many processors because only one needs service interrupts and there are more processors to be shared by users. Measure the time spent on a workload in handling interrupts or context switching for a uniprocessor versus a parallel processor. This workload may be a mix of independent jobs for a multiprogramming environment or a single large job. Does the argument hold?

9.13 [15] <§9.9> Construct a scenario whereby a truly revolutionary architecture—pick your favorite candidate—will play a significant role. Significant is defined as 10% of the computers sold, 10% of the users, 10% of the money spent on computers, or 10% of some other figure of merit.

9.14 [20] <§§9.1–9.11> This chapter introduced many new vocabulary terms related to the subject of multiprocessors. Some of the exercises in this chapter (e.g., 9.1, 9.3) are based on an analogy in which people are thought of as processors and collections of people as multiprocessors. Write a one-page article exploring this analogy in more detail. For example, are there collections of people who use techniques akin to message passing or shared memories? Can you create analogies for cache coherency protocols, network topologies, or clusters? Try to include at least one vocabulary term from each section of the text.

Assemblers, Linkers, and the SPIM Simulator

James R. Larus
Computer Sciences Department
University of Wisconsin–Madison

*Fear of serious injury cannot alone
justify suppression of free speech
and assembly.*

Louis Brandeis
Whitney v. California, 1927

A.1   Introduction

Encoding instructions as binary numbers is natural and efficient for computers. Humans, however, have a great deal of difficulty understanding and manipulating these numbers. People read and write symbols (words) much better than long sequences of digits. Chapter 3 showed that we need not choose between numbers and words because computer instructions can be represented in many ways. Humans can write and read symbols, and computers can execute the equivalent binary numbers. This appendix describes the process by which a human-readable program is translated into a form that a computer can execute, provides a few hints about writing assembly programs, and explains how to run these programs on SPIM, a simulator that executes MIPS programs. Unix, Windows, and DOS versions of the SPIM simulator are available through *www.mkp.com/cod2e.htm.*

Assembly language is the symbolic representation of a computer's binary encoding—*machine language*. Assembly language is more readable than machine language because it uses symbols instead of bits. The symbols in assembly language name commonly occurring bit patterns, such as opcodes and register specifiers, so people can read and remember them. In addition, assembly language permits programmers to use *labels* to identify and name particular memory words that hold instructions or data.

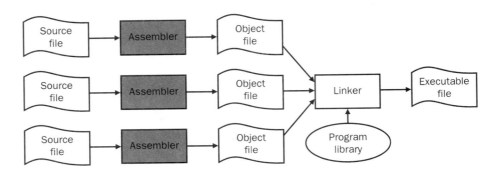

FIGURE A.1 The process that produces an executable file. An assembler translates a file of assembly language into an object file, which is linked with other files and libraries into an executable file.

A tool called an *assembler* translates assembly language into binary instructions. Assemblers provide a friendlier representation than a computer's 0s and 1s that simplifies writing and reading programs. Symbolic names for operations and locations are one facet of this representation. Another facet is programming facilities that increase a program's clarity. For example, *macros*, discussed in section A.2, enable a programmer to extend the assembly language by defining new operations.

An assembler reads a single assembly language *source file* and produces an *object file* containing machine instructions and bookkeeping information that helps combine several object files into a program. Figure A.1 illustrates how a program is built. Most programs consist of several files—also called *modules*—that are written, compiled, and assembled independently. A program may also use prewritten routines supplied in a *program library.* A module typically contains *references* to subroutines and data defined in other modules and in libraries. The code in a module cannot be executed when it contains *unresolved references* to labels in other object files or libraries. Another tool, called a *linker*, combines a collection of object and library files into an *executable file*, which a computer can run.

To see the advantage of assembly language, consider the following sequence of figures, all of which contain a short subroutine that computes and prints the sum of the squares of integers from 0 to 100. Figure A.2 shows the machine language that a MIPS computer executes. With considerable effort, you could use the opcode and instruction format tables in Chapters 3 and 4 to translate the instructions into a symbolic program similar to Figure A.3. This form of the routine is much easier to read because operations and operands are written with symbols, rather than with bit patterns. However, this assembly

```
00100111101111011111111111100000
10101111101111110000000000010100
10101111101001000000000000100000
10101111101001010000000000100100
10101111101000000000000000011000
10101111101000000000000000011100
10001111101011100000000000011100
10001111101110000000000000011000
00000001110011100000000000011001
00100101110010000000000000000001
00101001000000010000000001100101
10101111101010000000000000011100
00000000000000000111100000010010
00000011000011111100100000100001
00010100001000001111111111110111
10101111101110010000000000011000
00111100000001000001000000000000
10001111101001010000000000011000
00001100000010000000000000011101100
00100100100001000000010000110000
10001111101111110000000000010100
00100111011110100000000000100000
00000011111000000000000000001000
00000000000000000001000000100001
```

FIGURE A.2 MIPS machine language code for a routine to compute and print the sum of the squares of integers between 0 and 100.

language is still difficult to follow because memory locations are named by their address, rather than by a symbolic label.

Figure A.4 shows assembly language that labels memory addresses with mnemonic names. Most programmers prefer to read and write this form. Names that begin with a period, for example .data and .globl, are *assembler directives* that tell the assembler how to translate a program but do not produce machine instructions. Names followed by a colon, such as str or main, are labels that name the next memory location. This program is as readable as most assembly language programs (except for a glaring lack of comments), but it is still difficult to follow because many simple operations are required to accomplish simple tasks and because assembly language's lack of control flow constructs provides few hints about the program's operation.

By contrast, the C routine in Figure A.5 is both shorter and clearer since variables have mnemonic names and the loop is explicit rather than constructed with branches. (If you are unfamiliar with C, you may wish to look at Web Extension II at *www.mkp.com/cod2e.htm*.) In fact, the C routine is the only one that we wrote. The other forms of the program were produced by a C compiler and assembler.

```
addiu   $29, $29, -32
sw      $31, 20($29)
sw      $4, 32($29)
sw      $5, 36($29)
sw      $0, 24($29)
sw      $0, 28($29)
lw      $14, 28($29)
lw      $24, 24($29)
multu   $14, $14
addiu   $8, $14, 1
slti    $1, $8, 101
sw      $8, 28($29)
mflo    $15
addu    $25, $24, $15
bne     $1, $0, -9
sw      $25, 24($29)
lui     $4, 4096
lw      $5, 24($29)
jal     1048 812
addiu   $4, $4, 1072
lw      $31, 20($29)
addiu   $29, $29, 32
jr      $31
move    $2, $0
```

FIGURE A.3 The same routine written in assembly language. However, the code for the routine does not label registers or memory locations nor include comments.

In general, assembly language plays two roles (see Figure A.6). The first role is the output language of compilers. A *compiler* translates a program written in a *high-level language* (such as C or Pascal) into an equivalent program in machine or assembly language. The high-level language is called the *source language,* and the compiler's output is its *target language.*

Assembly language's other role is as a language in which to write programs. This role used to be the dominant one. Today, however, because of larger main memories and better compilers, most programmers write in a high-level language and rarely, if ever, see the instructions that a computer executes. Nevertheless, assembly language is still important to write programs in which speed or size are critical or to exploit hardware features that have no analogues in high-level languages.

Although this appendix focuses on MIPS assembly language, assembly programming on most other machines is very similar. The additional instructions and address modes in CISC machines, such as the VAX (see Web Extension III at *www.mkp.com/cod2e.htm*), can make assembly programs shorter but do not change the process of assembling a program or provide assembly language with the advantages of high-level languages such as type-checking and structured control flow.

```
            .text
            .align  2
            .globl  main
main:
            subu    $sp, $sp, 32
            sw      $ra, 20($sp)
            sd      $a0, 32($sp)
            sw      $0,  24($sp)
            sw      $0,  28($sp)
loop:
            lw      $t6, 28($sp)
            mul     $t7, $t6, $t6
            lw      $t8, 24($sp)
            addu    $t9, $t8, $t7
            sw      $t9, 24($sp)
            addu    $t0, $t6, 1
            sw      $t0, 28($sp)
            ble     $t0, 100, loop
            la      $a0, str
            lw      $a1, 24($sp)
            jal     printf
            move    $v0, $0
            lw      $ra, 20($sp)
            addu    $sp, $sp, 32
            j       $ra


            .data
            .align  0
str:
            .asciiz "The sum from 0 .. 100 is %d\n"
```

FIGURE A.4 The same routine written in assembly language with labels, but no comments. The commands that start with periods are assembler directives (see pages A-51–A-53). .text indicates that succeeding lines contain instructions. .data indicates that they contain data. .align n indicates that the items on the succeeding lines should be aligned on a 2^n byte boundary. Hence, .align 2 means the next item should be on a word boundary. .globl main declares that main is a global symbol that should be visible to code stored in other files. Finally, .asciiz stores a null-terminated string in memory.

When to Use Assembly Language

The primary reason to program in assembly language, as opposed to an available high-level language, is that the speed or size of a program is critically important. For example, consider a computer that controls a piece of machinery, such as a car's brakes. A computer that is incorporated in another device, such as a car, is called an *embedded computer*. This type of computer needs to respond rapidly and predictably to events in the outside world. Because a

```
#include <stdio.h>

int
main (int argc, char *argv[])
{
        int i;
        int sum = 0;

        for (i = 0; i <= 100; i = i + 1) sum = sum + i * i;
        printf ("The sum from 0 .. 100 is %d\n", sum);

}
```

FIGURE A.5   The routine written in the C programming language.

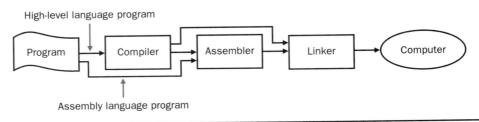

FIGURE A.6   Assembly language either is written by a programmer or is the output of a compiler.

compiler introduces uncertainty about the time cost of operations, programmers may find it difficult to ensure that a high-level language program responds within a definite time interval—say, 1 millisecond after a sensor detects that a tire is skidding. An assembly language programmer, on the other hand, has tight control over which instructions execute. In addition, in embedded applications, reducing a program's size, so that it fits in fewer memory chips, reduces the cost of the embedded computer.

A hybrid approach, in which most of a program is written in a high-level language and time-critical sections are written in assembly language, builds on the strengths of both languages. Programs typically spend most of their time executing a small fraction of the program's source code. This observation is just the principle of locality that underlies caches (see section 7.2 in Chapter 7).

Program profiling measures where a program spends its time and can find the time-critical parts of a program. In many cases, this portion of the program can be made faster with better data structures or algorithms. Sometimes, however, significant performance improvements only come from recoding a critical portion of a program in assembly language.

This improvement is not necessarily an indication that the high-level language's compiler has failed. Compilers typically are better than programmers at producing uniformly high-quality machine code across an entire program. Programmers, however, understand a program's algorithms and behavior at a deeper level than a compiler and can expend considerable effort and ingenuity improving small sections of the program. In particular, programmers often consider several procedures simultaneously while writing their code. Compilers typically compile each procedure in isolation and must follow strict conventions governing the use of registers at procedure boundaries. By retaining commonly used values in registers, even across procedure boundaries, programmers can make a program run faster.

Another major advantage of assembly language is the ability to exploit specialized instructions, for example, string copy or pattern-matching instructions. Compilers, in most cases, cannot determine that a program loop can be replaced by a single instruction. However, the programmer who wrote the loop can replace it easily with a single instruction.

In the future, a programmer's advantage over a compiler is likely to become increasingly difficult to maintain as compilation techniques improve and machines' pipelines increase in complexity (Chapter 6).

The final reason to use assembly language is that no high-level language is available on a particular computer. Many older or specialized computers do not have a compiler, so a programmer's only alternative is assembly language.

Drawbacks of Assembly Language

Assembly language has many disadvantages that strongly argue against its widespread use. Perhaps its major disadvantage is that programs written in assembly language are inherently machine-specific and must be totally rewritten to run on another computer architecture. The rapid evolution of computers discussed in Chapter 1 means that architectures become obsolete. An assembly language program remains tightly bound to its original architecture, even after the computer is eclipsed by new, faster, and more cost-effective machines.

Another disadvantage is that assembly language programs are longer than the equivalent programs written in a high-level language. For example, the C program in Figure A.5 is 11 lines long, while the assembly program in Figure A.4 is 31 lines long. In more complex programs, the ratio of assembly to high-level language (its *expansion factor*) can be much larger than the factor of three in this example. Unfortunately, empirical studies have shown that programmers write roughly the same number of lines of code per day in assembly as in high-level languages. This means that programmers are roughly x times more productive in a high-level language, where x is the assembly language expansion factor.

To compound the problem, longer programs are more difficult to read and understand and they contain more bugs. Assembly language exacerbates the problem because of its complete lack of structure. Common programming idioms, such as *if-then* statements and loops, must be built from branches and jumps. The resulting programs are hard to read because the reader must reconstruct every higher-level construct from its pieces and each instance of a statement may be slightly different. For example, look at Figure A.4 and answer these questions: What type of loop is used? What are its lower and upper bounds?

Elaboration: Compilers can produce machine language directly instead of relying on an assembler. These compilers typically execute much faster than those that invoke an assembler as part of compilation. However, a compiler that generates machine language must perform many tasks that an assembler normally handles, such as resolving addresses and encoding instructions as binary numbers. The trade-off is between compilation speed and compiler simplicity.

Elaboration: Despite these considerations, some embedded applications are written in a high-level language. Many of these applications are large and complex programs that must be extremely reliable. Assembly language programs are longer and more difficult to write and read than high-level language programs. This greatly increases the cost of writing an assembly language program and makes it extremely difficult to verify the correctness of this type of program. In fact, these considerations led the Department of Defense, which pays for many complex embedded systems, to develop Ada, a new high-level language for writing embedded systems.

A.2   Assemblers

An assembler translates a file of assembly language statements into a file of binary machine instructions and binary data. The translation process has two major parts. The first step is to find memory locations with labels so the relationship between symbolic names and addresses is known when instructions are translated. The second step is to translate each assembly statement by combining the numeric equivalents of opcodes, register specifiers, and labels into a legal instruction. As shown in Figure A.1, the assembler produces an output file, called an *object file*, which contains the machine instructions, data, and bookkeeping information.

An object file typically cannot be executed because it references procedures or data in other files. A label is *external* (also called *global*) if the labeled object can be referenced from files other than the one in which it is defined. A label is *local* if the object can be used only within the file in which it is defined. In most assemblers, labels are local by default and must be explicitly declared global. Subroutines and global variables require external labels since they are referenced from many files in a program. Local labels hide names that should not be visible to other modules—for example, static functions in C, which can only be called by other functions in the same file. In addition, compiler-generated names—for example, a name for the instruction at the beginning of a loop—are local so the compiler need not produce unique names in every file.

Local and Global Labels

Example

Consider the program in Figure A.4 on page A-7. The subroutine has an external (global) label `main`. It also contains two local labels—`loop` and `str`—that are only visible with this assembly language file. Finally, the routine also contains an unresolved reference to an external label `printf`, which is the library routine that prints values. Which labels in Figure A.4 could be referenced from another file?

Answer

Only global labels are visible outside of a file, so the only label that could be referenced from another file is `main`.

Since the assembler processes each file in a program individually and in isolation, it only knows the addresses of local labels. The assembler depends on another tool, the linker, to combine a collection of object files and libraries into an executable file by resolving external labels. The assembler assists the linker by providing lists of labels and unresolved references.

However, even local labels present an interesting challenge to an assembler. Unlike names in most high-level languages, assembly labels may be used before they are defined. In the example, in Figure A.4, the label `str` is used by the `la` instruction before it is defined. The possibility of a *forward reference*, like this one, forces an assembler to translate a program in two steps: first find all labels and then produce instructions. In the example, when the assembler sees the `la` instruction, it does not know where the word labeled `str` is located or even whether `str` labels an instruction or datum.

An assembler's first pass reads each line of an assembly file and breaks it into its component pieces. These pieces, which are called *lexemes*, are individual words, numbers, and punctuation characters. For example, the line

```
ble $t0, 100, loop
```

contains 6 lexemes: the opcode `ble`, the register specifier `$t0`, a comma, the number `100`, a comma, and the symbol `loop`.

If a line begins with a label, the assembler records in its *symbol table* the name of the label and the address of the memory word that the instruction occupies. The assembler then calculates how many words of memory the instruction on the current line will occupy. By keeping track of the instructions' sizes, the assembler can determine where the next instruction goes. To compute the size of a variable-length instruction, like those on the VAX, an assembler has to examine it in detail. Fixed-length instructions, like those on MIPS, on the other hand, require only a cursory examination. The assembler performs a similar calculation to compute the space required for data statements. When the assembler reaches the end of an assembly file, the symbol table records the location of each label defined in the file.

The assembler uses the information in the symbol table during a second pass over the file, which actually produces machine code. The assembler again examines each line in the file. If the line contains an instruction, the assembler combines the binary representations of its opcode and operands (register specifiers or memory address) into a legal instruction. The process is similar to the one used in section 3.4 in Chapter 3. Instructions and data words that reference an external symbol defined in another file cannot be completely assembled (they are unresolved) since the symbol's address is not in the symbol table. An assembler does not complain about unresolved references since the corresponding label is likely to be defined in another file.

The Big Picture

Assembly language is a programming language. Its principal difference from high-level languages such as BASIC, Java, and C is that assembly language provides only a few, simple types of data and control flow. Assembly language programs do not specify the type of value held in a variable. Instead, a programmer must apply the appropriate operations (e.g., integer or floating-point addition) to a value. In addition, in assembly language, programs must implement all control flow with *go to*s. Both factors make assembly language programming for any machine—MIPS or 80x86—more difficult and error-prone than writing in a high-level language.

Elaboration: If an assembler's speed is important, this two-step process can be done in one pass over the assembly file with a technique known as *backpatching*. In its pass over the file, the assembler builds a (possibly incomplete) binary representation of every instruction. If the instruction references a label that has not yet been defined, the assembler records the label and instruction in a table. When a label is defined, the assembler consults this table to find all instructions that contain a forward reference to the label. The assembler goes back and corrects their binary representation to incorporate the address of the label. Backpatching speeds assembly because the assembler only reads its input once. However, it requires an assembler to hold the entire binary representation of a program in memory so instructions can be backpatched. This requirement can limit the size of programs that can be assembled.

Object File Format

Assemblers produce object files. An object file on Unix contains six distinct sections (see Figure A.7):

- The *object file header* describes the size and position of the other pieces of the file.

- The *text segment* contains the machine language code for routines in the source file. These routines may be unexecutable because of unresolved references.

- The *data segment* contains a binary representation of the data in the source file. The data also may be incomplete because of unresolved references to labels in other files.

- The *relocation information* identifies instructions and data words that depend on absolute addresses. These references must change if portions of the program are moved in memory.

- The *symbol table* associates addresses with external labels in the source file and lists unresolved references.

- The *debugging information* contains a concise description of the way in which the program was compiled, so a debugger can find which instruction addresses correspond to lines in a source file and print the data structures in readable form.

Object file header	Text segment	Data segment	Relocation information	Symbol table	Debugging information

FIGURE A.7   Object file. A Unix assembler produces an object file with six distinct sections.

The assembler produces an object file that contains a binary representation of the program and data and additional information to help link pieces of a program. This relocation information is necessary because the assembler does not know which memory locations a procedure or piece of data will occupy after it is linked with the rest of the program. Procedures and data from a file are stored in a contiguous piece of memory, but the assembler does not know where this memory will be located. The assembler also passes some symbol table entries to the linker. In particular, the assembler must record which external symbols are defined in a file and what unresolved references occur in a file.

Elaboration: For convenience, assemblers assume each file starts at the same address (for example, location 0) with the expectation that the linker will *relocate* the code and data when they are assigned locations in memory. The assembler produces *relocation information*, which contains an entry describing each instruction or data word in the file that references an absolute address. On MIPS, only the subroutine call, load, and store instructions reference absolute addresses. Instructions that use PC-relative addressing, such as branches, need not be relocated.

Additional Facilities

Assemblers provide a variety of convenience features that help make assembler programs short and easier to write, but do not fundamentally change assembly language. For example, *data layout directives* allow a programmer to describe data in a more concise and natural manner than its binary representation.

In Figure A.4, the directive

```
.asciiz "The sum from 0 .. 100 is %d\n"
```

stores characters from the string in memory. Contrast this line with the alternative of writing each character as its ASCII value (Figure 3.15 in Chapter 3 describes the ASCII encoding for characters):

```
.byte 84, 104, 101, 32, 115, 117, 109, 32
.byte 102, 114, 111, 109, 32, 48, 32, 46
.byte 46, 32, 49, 48, 48, 32, 105, 115
.byte 32, 37, 100, 10, 0
```

The .asciiz directive is easier to read because it represents characters as letters, not binary numbers. An assembler can translate characters to their binary representation much faster and more accurately than a human. Data layout directives specify data in a human-readable form that the assembler translates to binary. Other layout directives are described in section A.10 on pages A-51–A-53.

String Directive

Example

Define the sequence of bytes produced by this directive:

```
.asciiz "The quick brown fox jumps over the lazy dog"
```

Answer

```
.byte 84,  104, 101, 32,  113, 117, 105, 99
.byte 107, 32,  98,  114, 111, 119, 110, 32
.byte 102, 111, 120, 32,  106, 117, 109, 112
.byte 115, 32,  111, 118, 101, 114, 32,  116
.byte 104, 101, 32,  108, 97,  122, 121, 32
.byte 100, 111, 103, 0
```

Macros are a pattern-matching and replacement facility that provide a simple mechanism to name a frequently used sequence of instructions. Instead of repeatedly typing the same instructions every time they are used, a programmer invokes the macro and the assembler replaces the macro call with the corresponding sequence of instructions. Macros, like subroutines, permit a programmer to create and name a new abstraction for a common operation. Unlike subroutines, however, macros do not cause a subroutine call and return when the program runs since a macro call is replaced by the macro's body when the program is assembled. After this replacement, the resulting assembly is indistinguishable from the equivalent program written without macros.

Macros

Example

As an example, suppose that a programmer needs to print many numbers. The library routine `printf` accepts a format string and one or more values to print as its arguments. A programmer could print the integer in register $7 with the following instructions:

```
          .data
int_str:  .asciiz "%d"
          .text
          la   $a0, int_str  # Load string address
                             # into first arg
          mov  $a1, $7       # Load value into
                             # second arg
          jal  printf        # Call the printf routine
```

The .data directive tells the assembler to store the string in the program's data segment, and the .text directive tells the assembler to store the instructions in its text segment.

However, printing many numbers in this fashion is tedious and produces a verbose program that is difficult to understand. An alternative is to introduce a macro, print_int, to print an integer:

```
          .data
int_str:.asciiz "%d"
          .text
          .macro   print_int($arg)
          la       $a0, int_str # Load string address into
                                 # first arg
          mov      $a1, $arg    # Load macro's parameter
                                 # ($arg) into second arg
          jal      printf       # Call the printf routine
          .end_macro
print_int($7)
```

The macro has a *formal parameter*, $arg, that names the argument to the macro. When the macro is expanded, the argument from a call is substituted for the formal parameter throughout the macro's body. Then the assembler replaces the call with the macro's newly expanded body. In the first call on print_int, the argument is $7, so the macro expands to the code

```
la  $a0, int_str
mov $a1, $7
jal printf
```

In a second call on print_int, say, print_int($t0), the argument is $t0, so the macro expands to

```
la  $a0, int_str
mov $a1, $t0
jal printf
```

What does the call print_int($a0) expand to?

Answer

```
la  $a0, int_str
mov $a1, $a0
jal printf
```

This example illustrates a drawback of macros. A programmer who uses this macro must be aware that print_int uses register $a0 and so cannot correctly print the value in that register.

<table>
<tr><td>**Hardware
Software
Interface**</td><td>Some assemblers also implement *pseudoinstructions*, which are instructions provided by an assembler but not implemented in hardware. Chapter 3 contains many examples of how the MIPS assembler synthesizes pseudoinstructions and addressing modes from the spartan MIPS hardware instruction set. For example, section 3.5 in Chapter 3 describes how the assembler synthesizes the `blt` instruction</td></tr>
</table>

from two other instructions: `slt` and `bne`. By extending the instruction set, the MIPS assembler makes assembly language programming easier without complicating the hardware. Many pseudoinstructions could also be simulated with macros, but the MIPS assembler can generate better code for these instructions because it can use a dedicated register ($at) and is able to optimize the generated code.

Elaboration: Assemblers *conditionally assemble* pieces of code, which permits a programmer to include or exclude groups of instructions when a program is assembled. This feature is particularly useful when several versions of a program differ by a small amount. Rather than keep these programs in separate files—which greatly complicates fixing bugs in the common code—programmers typically merge the versions into a single file. Code particular to one version is conditionally assembled, so it can be excluded when other versions of the program are assembled.

If macros and conditional assembly are useful, why do assemblers for Unix systems rarely, if ever, provide them? One reason is that most programmers on these systems write programs in higher-level languages like C. Most of the assembly code is produced by compilers, which find it more convenient to repeat code rather than define macros. Another reason is that other tools on Unix—such as `cpp`, the C preprocessor, or `m4`, a general macro processor—can provide macros and conditional assembly for assembly language programs.

A.3 Linkers

Separate compilation permits a program to be split into pieces that are stored in different files. Each file contains a logically related collection of subroutines and data structures that form a *module* in a larger program. A file can be compiled and assembled independently of other files, so changes to one module do not require recompiling the entire program. As we discussed above, separate compilation necessitates the additional step of linking to combine object files from separate modules and fix their unresolved references.

The tool that merges these files is the *linker* (see Figure A.8). It performs three tasks:

- Searches the program libraries to find library routines used by the program
- Determines the memory locations that code from each module will occupy and relocates its instructions by adjusting absolute references
- Resolves references among files

A linker's first task is to ensure that a program contains no undefined labels. The linker matches the external symbols and unresolved references from a program's files. An external symbol in one file resolves a reference from another file if both refer to a label with the same name. Unmatched references mean a symbol was used, but not defined anywhere in the program.

Unresolved references at this stage in the linking process do not necessarily mean a programmer made a mistake. The program could have referenced a library routine whose code was not in the object files passed to the linker. After matching symbols in the program, the linker searches the system's program libraries to find predefined subroutines and data structures that the program

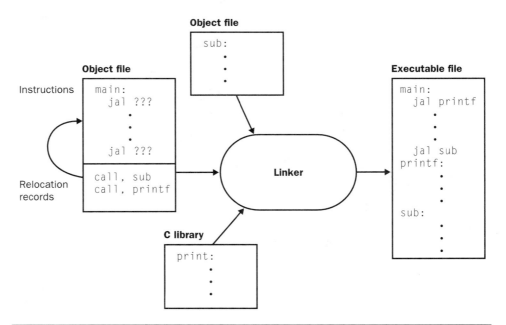

FIGURE A.8   The linker searches a collection of object files and program libraries to find non-local routines used in a program, combines them into a single executable file, and resolves references between routines in different files.

references. The basic libraries contain routines that read and write data, allocate and deallocate memory, and perform numeric operations. Other libraries contain routines to access a database or manipulate terminal windows. A program that references an unresolved symbol that is not in any library is erroneous and cannot be linked. When the program uses a library routine, the linker extracts the routine's code from the library and incorporates it into the program text segment. This new routine, in turn, may depend on other library routines, so the linker continues to fetch other library routines until no external references are unresolved or a routine cannot be found.

If all external references are resolved, the linker next determines the memory locations that each module will occupy. Since the files were assembled in isolation, the assembler could not know where a module's instructions or data will be placed relative to other modules. When the linker places a module in memory, all absolute references must be *relocated* to reflect its true location. Since the linker has relocation information that identifies all relocatable references, it can efficiently find and backpatch these references.

The linker produces an executable file that can run on a computer. Typically, this file has the same format as an object file, except that it contains no unresolved references or relocation information.

Loading

A program that links without an error can be run. Before being run, the program resides in a file on secondary storage, such as a disk. On Unix systems, the operating system kernel brings a program into memory and starts it running. To start a program, the operating system performs the following steps:

1. Reads the executable file's header to determine the size of the text and data segments.

2. Creates a new address space for the program. This address space is large enough to hold the text and data segments, along with a stack segment (see section A.5).

3. Copies instructions and data from the executable file into the new address space.

4. Copies arguments passed to the program onto the stack.

5. Initializes the machine registers. In general, most registers are cleared, but the stack pointer must be assigned the address of the first free stack location (see section A.5).

6. Jumps to a start-up routine that copies the program's arguments from the stack to registers and calls the program's `main` routine. If the `main` routine returns, the start-up routine terminates the program with the exit system call.

A.5   Memory Usage

The next few sections elaborate the description of the MIPS architecture presented earlier in the book. Earlier chapters focused primarily on hardware and its relationship with low-level software. These sections focus primarily on how assembly language programmers use MIPS hardware. These sections describe a set of conventions followed on many MIPS systems. For the most part, the hardware does not impose these conventions. Instead, they represent an agreement among programmers to follow the same set of rules so that software written by different people can work together and make effective use of MIPS hardware.

Systems based on MIPS processors typically divide memory into three parts (see Figure A.9). The first part, near the bottom of the address space (starting at address 400000_{hex}), is the *text segment*, which holds the program's instructions.

The second part, above the text segment, is the *data segment*, which is further divided into two parts. *Static data* (starting at address 10000000_{hex}) contains objects whose size is known to the compiler and whose lifetime—the interval during which a program can access them—is the program's entire execution. For example, in C, global variables are statically allocated since they can be referenced anytime during a program's execution. The linker both assigns static objects to locations in the data segment and resolves references to these objects.

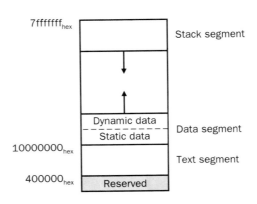

FIGURE A.9   Layout of memory.

Immediately above static data is *dynamic data*. This data, as its name implies, is allocated by the program as it executes. In C programs, the malloc library routine finds and returns a new block of memory. Since a compiler cannot predict how much memory a program will allocate, the operating system expands the dynamic data area to meet demand. As the upward arrow in the figure indicates, malloc expands the dynamic area with the sbrk system call, which causes the operating system to add more pages to the program's virtual address space (see section 7.3 in Chapter 7) immediately above the dynamic data segment.

The third part, the program *stack segment*, resides at the top of the virtual address space (starting at address $7fffffff_{hex}$). Like dynamic data, the maximum size of a program's stack is not known in advance. As the program pushes values on the stack, the operating system expands the stack segment down, towards the data segment.

This three-part division of memory is not the only possible one. However, it has two important characteristics: the two dynamically expandable segments are as far apart as possible, and they can grow to use a program's entire address space.

Hardware Software Interface

Because the data segment begins far above the program at address 10000000_{hex}, load and store instructions cannot directly reference data objects with their 16-bit offset fields (see section 3.4 in Chapter 3). For example, to load the word in the data segment at address 10008000_{hex} into register $v0 requires two instructions:

```
lui  $s0, 0x1000 # 0x1000 means 1000 base 16 or 4096 base 10
lw   $v0, 0x8000($s0) # 0x10000000 + 0x8000 = 0x10008000
```

(The *0x* before a number means that it is a hexadecimal value. For example, 0x8000 is 8000_{hex} or $32{,}768_{ten}$.)

To avoid repeating the lui instruction at every load and store, MIPS systems typically dedicate a register ($gp) as a *global pointer* to the static data segment. This register contains address 10008000_{hex}, so load and store instructions can use their signed 16-bit offset fields to access the first 64 KB of the static data segment. With this global pointer, we can rewrite the example as a single instruction:

```
lw $v0, 0($gp)
```

Of course, a global pointer register makes addressing locations 10000000_{hex}–10010000_{hex} faster than other heap locations. The MIPS compiler usually stores *global variables* in this area because these variables have fixed locations and fit better than other global data, such as arrays.

Procedure Call Convention

Conventions governing the use of registers are necessary when procedures in a program are compiled separately. To compile a particular procedure, a compiler must know which registers it may use and which registers are reserved for other procedures. Rules for using registers are called *register use* or *procedure call conventions*. As the name implies, these rules are, for the most part, conventions followed by software rather than rules enforced by hardware. However, most compilers and programmers try very hard to follow these conventions because violating them causes insidious bugs.

The calling convention described in this section is the one used by the gcc compiler. The native MIPS compiler uses a more complex convention that is slightly faster.

The MIPS CPU contains 32 general-purpose registers that are numbered 0–31. Register $0 always contains the hardwired value 0.

- Registers $at (1), $k0 (26), and $k1 (27) are reserved for the assembler and operating system and should not be used by user programs or compilers.

- Registers $a0–$a3 (4–7) are used to pass the first four arguments to routines (remaining arguments are passed on the stack). Registers $v0 and $v1 (2, 3) are used to return values from functions.

- Registers $t0–$t9 (8–15, 24, 25) are caller-saved registers that are used to hold temporary quantities that need not be preserved across calls (see section 3.6 in Chapter 3).

- Registers $s0–$s7 (16–23) are callee-saved registers that hold long-lived values that should be preserved across calls.

- Register $gp (28) is a global pointer that points to the middle of a 64K block of memory in the static data segment.

- Register $sp (29) is the stack pointer, which points to the last location on the stack. Register $fp (30) is the frame pointer. The jal instruction writes register $ra (31), the return address from a procedure call. These two registers are explained in the next section.

The two-letter abbreviations and names for these registers—for example $sp for the stack pointer—reflect the registers' intended uses in the procedure call convention. In describing this convention, we will use the names instead of register numbers. Figure A.10 lists the registers and describes their intended uses.

Register name	Number	Usage
$zero	0	constant 0
$at	1	reserved for assembler
$v0	2	expression evaluation and results of a function
$v1	3	expression evaluation and results of a function
$a0	4	argument 1
$a1	5	argument 2
$a2	6	argument 3
$a3	7	argument 4
$t0	8	temporary (not preserved across call)
$t1	9	temporary (not preserved across call)
$t2	10	temporary (not preserved across call)
$t3	11	temporary (not preserved across call)
$t4	12	temporary (not preserved across call)
$t5	13	temporary (not preserved across call)
$t6	14	temporary (not preserved across call)
$t7	15	temporary (not preserved across call)
$s0	16	saved temporary (preserved across call)
$s1	17	saved temporary (preserved across call)
$s2	18	saved temporary (preserved across call)
$s3	19	saved temporary (preserved across call)
$s4	20	saved temporary (preserved across call)
$s5	21	saved temporary (preserved across call)
$s6	22	saved temporary (preserved across call)
$s7	23	saved temporary (preserved across call)
$t8	24	temporary (not preserved across call)
$t9	25	temporary (not preserved across call)
$k0	26	reserved for OS kernel
$k1	27	reserved for OS kernel
$gp	28	pointer to global area
$sp	29	stack pointer
$fp	30	frame pointer
$ra	31	return address (used by function call)

FIGURE A.10   MIPS registers and usage convention.

Procedure Calls

This section describes the steps that occur when one procedure (the *caller*) invokes another procedure (the *callee*). Programmers who write in a high-level language (like C or Pascal) never see the details of how one procedure calls another because the compiler takes care of this low-level bookkeeping. However, assembly language programmers must explicitly implement every procedure call and return.

Most of the bookkeeping associated with a call is centered around a block of memory called a *procedure call frame*. This memory is used for a variety of purposes:

- To hold values passed to a procedure as arguments
- To save registers that a procedure may modify, but which the procedure's caller does not want changed
- To provide space for variables local to a procedure

In most programming languages, procedure calls and returns follow a strict last-in, first-out (LIFO) order, so this memory can be allocated and deallocated on a stack, which is why these blocks of memory are sometimes called *stack frames*.

Figure A.11 shows a typical stack frame. The frame consists of the memory between the frame pointer ($fp), which points to the first word of the frame, and the stack pointer ($sp), which points to the last word of the frame. The stack grows down from higher memory addresses, so the frame pointer points above the stack pointer. The executing procedure uses the frame pointer to quickly access values in its stack frame. For example, an argument in the stack frame can be loaded into register $v0 with the instruction

```
lw $v0, 0($fp)
```

A stack frame may be built in many different ways; however, the caller and callee must agree on the sequence of steps. The steps below describe the calling convention used on most MIPS machines. This convention comes into play at three points during a procedure call: immediately before the caller invokes the callee, just as the callee starts executing, and immediately before the callee returns to the caller. In the first part, the caller puts the procedure call arguments in standard places and invokes the callee to do the following:

1. Pass arguments. By convention, the first four arguments are passed in registers $a0–$a3. Any remaining arguments are pushed on the stack and appear at the beginning of the called procedure's stack frame.

2. Save caller-saved registers. The called procedure can use these registers ($a0–$a3 and $t0–$t9) without first saving their value. If the caller expects to use one of these registers after a call, it must save its value before the call.

3. Execute a jal instruction (see section 3.6 of Chapter 3), which jumps to the callee's first instruction and saves the return address in register $ra.

Before a called routine starts running, it must take the following steps to set up its stack frame:

1. Allocate memory for the frame by subtracting the frame's size from the stack pointer.

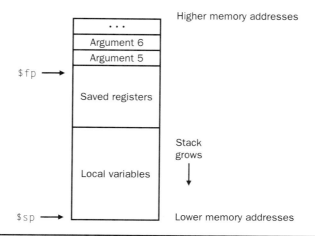

FIGURE A.11   Layout of a stack frame. The frame pointer ($fp) points to the first word in the currently executing procedure's stack frame. The stack pointer ($sp) points to the last word of frame. The first four arguments are passed in registers, so the fifth argument is the first one stored on the stack.

2. Save callee-saved registers in the frame. A callee must save the values in these registers ($s0–$s7, $fp, and $ra) before altering them since the caller expects to find these registers unchanged after the call. Register $fp is saved by every procedure that allocates a new stack frame. However, register $ra only needs to be saved if the callee itself makes a call. The other callee-saved registers that are used also must be saved.

3. Establish the frame pointer by adding the stack frame's size minus four to $sp and storing the sum in register $fp.

Hardware Software Interface

The MIPS register use convention provides callee- and caller-saved registers because both types of registers are advantageous in different circumstances. Callee-saved registers are better used to hold long-lived values, such as variables from a user's program. These registers are only saved during a procedure call if the callee expects to use the register. On the other hand, caller-saved registers are better used to hold short-lived quantities that do not persist across a call, such as immediate values in an address calculation. During a call, the callee can also use these registers for short-lived temporaries.

Finally, the callee returns to the caller by executing the following steps:

1. If the callee is a function that returns a value, place the returned value in register $v0.

2. Restore all callee-saved registers that were saved upon procedure entry.

3. Pop the stack frame by adding the frame size to $sp.

4. Return by jumping to the address in register $ra.

Elaboration: A programming language that does not permit *recursive* procedures—procedures that call themselves either directly or indirectly through a chain of calls—need not allocate frames on a stack. In a nonrecursive language, each procedure's frame may be statically allocated since only one invocation of a procedure can be active at a time. Older versions of Fortran prohibited recursion because statically allocated frames produced faster code on some older machines. However, on load-store architectures like MIPS, stack frames may be just as fast because a frame pointer register points directly to the active stack frame, which permits a single load or store instruction to access values in the frame. In addition, recursion is a valuable programming technique.

Procedure Call Example

As an example, consider the C routine

```
main ()
{
  printf ("The factorial of 10 is %d\n", fact (10));
}

int fact (int n)
{
  if (n < 1)
    return (1);
  else
    return (n * fact (n - 1));
}
```

which computes and prints 10! (the factorial of 10, $10! = 10 \times 9 \times \ldots \times 1$). fact is a recursive routine that computes $n!$ by multiplying n times $(n - 1)!$. The assembly code for this routine illustrates how programs manipulate stack frames.

Upon entry, the routine main creates its stack frame and saves the two callee-saved registers it will modify: $fp and $ra. The frame is larger than required for these two registers because the calling convention requires the minimum size of a stack frame to be 24 bytes. This minimum frame can hold four argument registers ($a0–$a3) and the return address $ra, padded to a double-word boundary (24 bytes). Since main also needs to save $fp, its stack frame must be two words larger (remember: the stack pointer is kept doubleword aligned).

```
        .text
        .globl  main
main:
        subu    $sp,$sp,32      # Stack frame is 32 bytes long
        sw      $ra,20($sp)     # Save return address
        sw      $fp,16($sp)     # Save old frame pointer
        addu    $fp,$sp,28      # Set up frame pointer
```

The routine main then calls the factorial routine and passes it the single argument 10. After fact returns, main calls the library routine printf and passes it both a format string and the result returned from fact:

```
        li      $a0,10          # Put argument (10) in $a0
        jal     fact            # Call factorial function

        la      $a0,$LC         # Put format string in $a0
        move    $a1,$v0         # Move fact result to $a1
        jal     printf          # Call the print function
```

Finally, after printing the factorial, main returns. But first, it must restore the registers it saved and pop its stack frame:

```
        lw      $ra,20($sp)     # Restore return address
        lw      $fp,16($sp)     # Restore frame pointer
        addu    $sp,$sp,32      # Pop stack frame
        jr      $ra             # Return to caller

        .rdata
$LC:
        .ascii  "The factorial of 10 is %d\n\000"
```

The factorial routine is similar in structure to main. First, it creates a stack frame and saves the callee-saved registers it will use. In addition to saving $ra and $fp, fact also saves its argument ($a0), which it will use for the recursive call:

```
        .text
fact:
        subu    $sp,$sp,32      # Stack frame is 32 bytes long
        sw      $ra,20($sp)     # Save return address
        sw      $fp,16($sp)     # Save frame pointer
        addu    $fp,$sp,28      # Set up frame pointer
        sw      $a0,0($fp)      # Save argument (n)
```

The heart of the `fact` routine performs the computation from the C program. It tests if the argument is greater than 0. If not, the routine returns the value 1. If the argument is greater than 0, the routine recursively calls itself to compute `fact(n-1)` and multiplies that value times *n*:

```
        lw      $v0,0($fp)      # Load n
        bgtz    $v0,$L2         # Branch if n > 0
        li      $v0,1           # Return 1
        j       $L1             # Jump to code to return

$L2:
        lw      $v1,0($fp)      # Load n
        subu    $v0,$v1,1       # Compute n - 1
        move    $a0,$v0         # Move value to $a0
        jal     fact            # Call factorial function

        lw      $v1,0($fp)      # Load n
        mul     $v0,$v0,$v1     # Compute fact(n-1) * n
```

Finally, the factorial routine restores the callee-saved registers and returns the value in register $v0:

```
$L1:                            # Result is in $v0
        lw      $ra, 20($sp)    # Restore $ra
        lw      $fp, 16($sp)    # Restore $fp
        addu    $sp, $sp, 32    # Pop stack
        j       $ra             # Return to caller
```

Stack in Recursive Procedure

Example

Figure A.12 shows the stack at the call `fact(7)`. `main` runs first, so its frame is deepest on the stack. `main` calls `fact(10)`, whose stack frame is next on the stack. Each invocation recursively invokes `fact` to compute the next-lowest factorial. The stack frames parallel the LIFO order of these calls. What does the stack look like when the call to `fact(10)` returns?

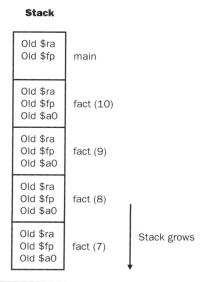

FIGURE A.12   Stack frames during the call of fact(7).

Answer

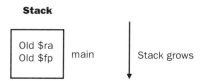

Elaboration: The difference between the MIPS compiler and the gcc compiler is that the MIPS compiler usually does not use a frame pointer, so this register is available as another callee-saved register, $s8. This change saves a couple of instructions in the procedure call and return sequence. However, it complicates code generation because a procedure must access its stack frame with $sp, whose value can change during a procedure's execution if values are pushed on the stack.

Another Procedure Call Example

As another example, consider the following routine that computes the tak function, which is a widely used benchmark created by Ikuo Takeuchi. This function does not compute anything useful, but is a heavily recursive program that illustrates the MIPS calling convention.

```
int tak (int x, int y, int z)
{
  if (y < x)
    return 1+ tak (tak (x - 1, y, z),
      tak (y - 1, z, x),
      tak (z - 1, x, y));
  else
    return z;
}
int main ()
{
  tak(18, 12, 6);
}
```

The assembly code for this program is below. The tak function first saves its return address in its stack frame and its arguments in callee-saved registers, since the routine may make calls that need to use registers $a0–$a2 and $ra. The function uses callee-saved registers since they hold values that persist over the lifetime of the function, which includes several calls that could potentially modify registers.

```
        .text
        .globl  tak

tak:
        subu    $sp, $sp, 40
        sw      $ra, 32($sp)

        sw      $s0, 16($sp)     # x
        move    $s0, $a0
        sw      $s1, 20($sp)     # y
        move    $s1, $a1
        sw      $s2, 24($sp)     # z
        move    $s2, $a2
        sw      $s3, 28($sp)     # temporary
```

The routine then begins execution by testing if y < x. If not, it branches to label L1, which is below.

```
        bge     $s1, $s0, L1     # if (y < x)
```

If y < x, then it executes the body of the routine, which contains four recursive calls. The first call uses almost the same arguments as its parent:

```
        addu    $a0, $s0, -1
        move    $a1, $s1
        move    $a2, $s2
        jal     tak              # tak (x - 1, y, z)
        move    $s3, $v0
```

Note that the result from the first recursive call is saved in register $s3, so that it can be used later.

The function now prepares arguments for the second recursive call.

```
addu    $a0, $s1, -1
move    $a1, $s2
move    $a2, $s0
jal     tak          # tak (y - 1, z, x)
```

In the instructions below, the result from this recursive call is saved in register $s0. But, first we need to read, for the last time, the saved value of the first argument from this register.

```
addu    $a0, $s2, -1
move    $a1, $s0
move    $a2, $s1
move    $s0, $v0
jal     tak          # tak (z - 1, x, y)
```

After the three inner recursive calls, we are ready for the final recursive call. After the call, the function's result is in $v0 and control jumps to the function's epilogue.

```
move    $a0, $s3
move    $a1, $s0
move    $a2, $v0
jal     tak          # tak (tak(...), tak(...), tak(...))
addu    $v0, $v0, 1
j       L2
```

This code at label L1 is the consequent of the *if-then-else* statement. It just moves the value of argument z into the return register and falls into the function epilogue.

```
L1:
    move  $v0, $s2
```

The code below is the function epilogue, which restores the saved registers and returns the function's result to its caller.

```
L2:
    lw      $ra, 32($sp)
    lw      $s0, 16($sp)
    lw      $s1, 20($sp)
    lw      $s2, 24($sp)
    lw      $s3, 28($sp)
    addu    $sp, $sp, 40
    j       $ra
```

The `main` routine calls the `tak` function with its initial arguments, then takes the computed result (7) and prints it using SPIM's system call for printing integers.

```
        .globl  main
main:
        subu    $sp, $sp, 24
        sw      $ra, 16($sp)

        li      $a0, 18
        li      $a1, 12
        li      $a2, 6
        jal     tak                     # tak(18, 12, 6)

        move    $a0, $v0
        li      $v0, 1                  # print_int syscall
        syscall

        lw      $ra, 16($sp)
        addu    $sp, $sp, 24
        j       $ra
```

A.7   Exceptions and Interrupts

Section 5.6 of Chapter 5 describes the MIPS exception facility, which responds both to exceptions caused by errors during an instruction's execution and to external interrupts caused by I/O devices. This section describes exception and interrupt handling in more detail. In MIPS processors, a part of the CPU called *coprocessor 0* records the information the software needs to handle exceptions and interrupts. The MIPS simulator SPIM does not implement all of coprocessor 0's registers, since many are not useful in a simulator or are part of the memory system, which SPIM does not implement. However, SPIM does provide the following coprocessor 0 registers:

Register name	Register number	Usage
BadVAddr	8	register containing the memory address at which memory reference occurred
Status	12	interrupt mask and enable bits
Cause	13	exception type and pending interrupt bits
EPC	14	register containing address of instruction that caused exception

These four registers are part of coprocessor 0's register set and are accessed by the `lwc0`, `mfc0`, `mtc0`, and `swc0` instructions. After an exception, register EPC contains the address of the instruction that was executing when the exception occurred. If the instruction made a memory access that caused the exception, register BadVAddr contains the referenced memory location's address. The two other registers contain many fields and are described below.

Figure A.13 shows the Status register fields implemented by the MIPS simulator SPIM. The interrupt mask field contains a bit for each of the five hardware and three software possible interrupt levels. A bit that is 1 allows interrupts at that level. A bit that is 0 disables interrupts at that level. The low 6 bits of the Status register implement a three-deep stack for the kernel/user and interrupt enable bits. The kernel/user bit is 0 if a program was in the kernel when an exception occurred and 1 if it was running in user mode. If the interrupt enable bit is 1, interrupts are allowed. If it is 0, they are disabled. When an interrupt occurs, these 6 bits are shifted left by 2 bits, so the current bits become the previous bits and the previous bits become the old bits (the old bits are discarded). The current bits are both set to 0 so the interrupt handler runs in the kernel with interrupts disabled.

Figure A.14 shows the Cause register fields implemented by SPIM. The five pending interrupt bits correspond to the five interrupt levels. A bit becomes 1 when an interrupt at its level has occurred but has not been serviced. The Exception code register describes the cause of an exception with the following codes:

Number	Name	Description
0	INT	external interrupt
4	ADDRL	address error exception (load or instruction fetch)
5	ADDRS	address error exception (store)
6	IBUS	bus error on instruction fetch
7	DBUS	bus error on data load or store
8	SYSCALL	syscall exception
9	BKPT	breakpoint exception
10	RI	reserved instruction exception
12	OVF	arithmetic overflow exception

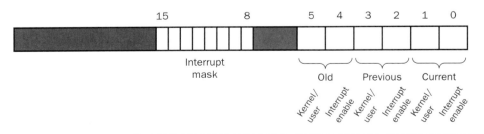

FIGURE A.13 The Status register.

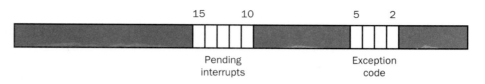

FIGURE A.14 The Cause register. In actual MIPS processors, this register contains additional fields that report: whether the instruction that caused the exception executed in a branch's delay slot, which coprocessor caused the exception, or that a software interrupt is pending.

Exceptions and interrupts cause a MIPS processor to jump to a piece of code, at address 80000080_{hex} (in the kernel, not user address space), called an *interrupt handler*. This code examines the exception's cause and jumps to an appropriate point in the operating system. The operating system responds to an exception either by terminating the process that caused the exception or by performing some action. A process that causes an error, such as executing an unimplemented instruction, is killed by the operating system. On the other hand, exceptions such as page faults are requests from a process to the operating system to perform a service, such as bringing in a page from disk. The operating system processes these requests and resumes the process. The final type of exceptions are interrupts from external devices. These generally cause the operating system to move data to or from an I/O device and resume the interrupted process. The code in the example below is a simple interrupt handler, which invokes a routine to print a message at each exception (but not interrupts). This code is similar to the interrupt handler used by the SPIM simulator, except that it does not print an error message to report an exception.

Interrupt Handler

Example

The interrupt handler first saves registers $a0 and $a1, which it later uses to pass arguments. The interrupt handler cannot store the old values from these registers on the stack, as would an ordinary routine, because the cause of the interrupt might have been a memory reference that used a bad value (such as 0) in the stack pointer. Instead the interrupt handler stores these registers in two memory locations (save0 and save1). If the interrupt routine itself could be interrupted, two locations would not be enough since the second interrupt would overwrite values saved during the first interrupt. However, this simple interrupt handler finishes running before it enables interrupts, so the problem does not arise.

```
    .ktext 0x80000080
sw  $a0, save0    # Handler is not re-entrant and can't use
sw  $a1, save1    # stack to save $a0, $a1
                  # Don't need to save $k0/$k1
```

The interrupt handler then moves the Cause and EPC registers into
CPU registers. The Cause and EPC registers are not part of the CPU register set. Instead, they are registers in coprocessor 0, which is the part of the
CPU that handles interrupts. The instruction mfc0 $k0, $13 moves coprocessor 0's register 13 (the Cause register) into CPU register $k0. Note that
the interrupt handler need not save registers $k0 and $k1 because user
programs are not supposed to use these registers. The interrupt handler
uses the value from the Cause register to test if the exception was caused
by an interrupt (see the preceding table). If so, the exception is ignored. If
the exception was not an interrupt, the handler calls print_excp to print
a warning message.

```
mfc0    $k0, $13        # Move Cause into $k0
mfc0    $k1, $14        # Move EPC into $k1

sgt     $v0, $k0, 0x44  # Ignore interrupts
bgtz    $v0, done

mov     $a0, $k0        # Move Cause into $a0
mov     $a1, $k1        # Move EPC into $a1
jal     print_excp      # Print exception error message
```

Before returning, the interrupt handler restores registers $a0 and $a1.
It then executes the rfe (return from exception) instruction, which restores
the previous interrupt mask and kernel/user bits in the Status register.
This switches the processor state back to what it was before the exception
and prepares to resume program execution. The interrupt handler then returns to the program by jumping to the instruction following the one that
caused the exception.

```
done:
        lw      $a0, save0
        lw      $a1, save1
        addiu $k1, $k1, 4 # Do not reexecute
                          # faulting instruction
        rfe               # Restore interrupt state
        jr      $k1

        .kdata
save0:  .word 0
save1:  .word 0
```

Elaboration: On real MIPS processors, the return from an interrupt handler is more complex. The rfe instruction must execute in the delay slot of the jr instruction (see elaboration on page 444 of Chapter 6) that returns to the user program so that no interrupt-handler instruction executes with the user program's interrupt mask and kernel/user bits. In addition, the interrupt handler cannot always jump to the instruction following EPC. For example, if the instruction that caused the exception was in a branch instruction's delay slot (see Chapter 6), the next instruction may not be the following instruction in memory.

A.8   Input and Output

SPIM simulates one I/O device: a memory-mapped terminal. When a program is running, SPIM connects its own terminal (or a separate console window in the X-window version xspim) to the processor. A MIPS program running on SPIM can read the characters that you type. In addition, if the MIPS program writes characters to the terminal, they appear on SPIM's terminal or console window. One exception to this rule is control-C: this character is not passed to the program, but instead causes SPIM to stop and return to command mode. When the program stops running (for example, because you typed control-C or because the program hit a breakpoint), the terminal is reconnected to spim so you can type SPIM commands. To use memory-mapped I/O (see below), spim or xspim must be started with the -mapped_io flag.

The terminal device consists of two independent units: a *receiver* and a *transmitter*. The receiver reads characters from the keyboard. The transmitter writes characters to the display. The two units are completely independent. This means, for example, that characters typed at the keyboard are not automatically echoed on the display. Instead, a program must explicitly echo a character by reading it from the receiver and writing it to the transmitter.

A program controls the terminal with four memory-mapped device registers, as shown in Figure A.15. "Memory-mapped" means that each register appears as a special memory location. The *Receiver Control register* is at location ffff0000$_{hex}$. Only two of its bits are actually used. Bit 0 is called "ready": if it is 1, it means that a character has arrived from the keyboard but has not yet been read from the Receiver Data register. The ready bit is read-only: writes to it are ignored. The ready bit changes from 0 to 1 when a character is typed at the keyboard, and it changes from 1 to 0 when the character is read from the Receiver Data register.

Bit 1 of the Receiver Control register is the keyboard "interrupt enable." This bit may be both read and written by a program. The interrupt enable is initially 0. If it is set to 1 by a program, the terminal requests an interrupt at level 0 whenever the ready bit is 1. However, for the interrupt to affect the processor,

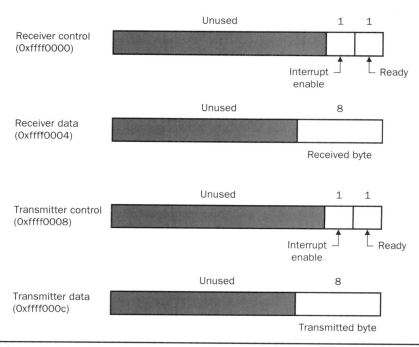

FIGURE A.15   The terminal is controlled by four device registers, each of which appears as a memory location at the given address. Only a few bits of these registers are actually used. The others always read as 0s and are ignored on writes.

interrupts must also be enabled in the Status register (see section A.7). All other bits of the Receiver Control register are unused.

The second terminal device register is the *Receiver Data register* (at address ffff0004$_{hex}$). The low-order 8 bits of this register contain the last character typed at the keyboard. All other bits contain 0s. This register is read-only and changes only when a new character is typed at the keyboard. Reading the Receiver Data register resets the ready bit in the Receiver Control register to 0.

The third terminal device register is the *Transmitter Control register* (at address ffff0008$_{hex}$). Only the low-order 2 bits of this register are used. They behave much like the corresponding bits of the Receiver Control register. Bit 0 is called "ready" and is read-only. If this bit is 1, the transmitter is ready to accept a new character for output. If it is 0, the transmitter is still busy writing the previous character. Bit 1 is "interrupt enable" and is readable and writable. If this bit is set to 1, then the terminal requests an interrupt on level 1 whenever the ready bit is 1.

The final device register is the *Transmitter Data register* (at address ffff000c$_{hex}$). When a value is written into this location, its low-order 8 bits (i.e., an ASCII character as in Figure 3.15 in Chapter 3) are sent to the console. When the Transmitter Data register is written, the ready bit in the Transmitter Control register is reset to 0. This bit stays 0 until enough time has elapsed to transmit the character to the terminal; then the ready bit becomes 1 again. The Transmitter Data register should only be written when the ready bit of the Transmitter Control register is 1. If the transmitter is not ready, writes to the Transmitter Data register are ignored (the write appears to succeed but the character is not output).

Real computers require time to send characters over the serial lines that connect terminals to computers. These time lags are simulated by SPIM. For example, after the transmitter starts to write a character, the transmitter's ready bit becomes 0 for a while. SPIM measures time in instructions executed, not in real clock time. This means that the transmitter does not become ready again until the processor executes a certain number of instructions. If you stop the machine and look at the ready bit, it will not change. However, if you let the machine run, the bit eventually changes back to 1.

A.9 SPIM

SPIM is a software simulator that runs programs written for MIPS R2000/R3000 processors. SPIM's name is just MIPS spelled backwards. SPIM can read and immediately execute assembly language files or (on some systems) MIPS executable files. SPIM is a self-contained system for running MIPS programs. It contains a debugger and provides a few operating system-like services. SPIM is much slower than a real computer (100 or more times). However, its low cost and wide availability cannot be matched by real hardware!

An obvious question is, Why use a simulator when many people have workstations that contain MIPS chips that are significantly faster than SPIM? One reason is that these workstations are not universally available. Another reason is rapid progress toward new and faster computers may render these machines obsolete (see Chapter 1). The current trend is to make computers faster by executing several instructions concurrently. This trend makes architectures more difficult to understand and program. The MIPS architecture may be the epitome of a simple, clean RISC machine.

In addition, simulators can provide a better environment for programming than an actual machine because they can detect more errors and provide more features than an actual computer. For example, SPIM has an X-window interface that works better than most debuggers on the actual machines.

Finally, simulators are a useful tool in studying computers and the programs that run on them. Because they are implemented in software, not silicon, simulators can be easily modified to add new instructions, build new systems such as multiprocessors, or simply to collect data.

Simulation of a Virtual Machine

The MIPS architecture, like that of many RISC computers, is difficult to program directly because of delayed branches, delayed loads, and restricted address modes. This difficulty is tolerable since these computers were designed to be programmed in high-level languages and present an interface appropriate for compilers rather than assembly language programmers. A good part of the programming complexity results from delayed instructions. A *delayed branch* requires two cycles to execute (see elaborations on pages 444 and 502 of Chapter 6). In the second cycle, the instruction immediately following the branch executes. This instruction can perform useful work that normally would have been done before the branch. It can also be a nop (no operation). Similarly, *delayed loads* require two cycles so the instruction immediately following a load cannot use the value loaded from memory (see section 6.2 of Chapter 6).

MIPS wisely chose to hide this complexity by having its assembler implement a *virtual machine*. This virtual computer appears to have nondelayed branches and loads and a richer instruction set than the actual hardware. The assembler *reorganizes* (rearranges) instructions to fill the delay slots. The virtual computer also provides *pseudoinstructions*, which appear as real instructions in assembly language programs. The hardware, however, knows nothing about pseudoinstructions, so the assembler must translate them into equivalent sequences of actual, machine instructions. For example, the MIPS hardware only provides instructions to branch when a register is equal to or not equal to 0. Other conditional branches, such as when one register is greater than another, are synthesized by comparing the two registers and branching when the result of the comparison is true (nonzero).

By default, SPIM simulates the richer virtual machine. However, it can also simulate the bare hardware. Below, we describe the virtual machine and only mention in passing features that do not belong to the actual hardware. In doing so, we follow the convention of MIPS assembly language programmers (and compilers), who routinely use the extended machine. (For a description of the real machines, see Gerry Kane and Joe Heinrich, *MIPS RISC Architecture*, Prentice Hall, Englewood Cliff, NJ, 1992.)

Getting Started with SPIM

The rest of this appendix contains a complete and rather detailed description of SPIM. Many details should never concern you; however, the sheer volume of information can obscure the fact that SPIM is a simple, easy-to-use program. This section contains a quick tutorial on SPIM that should enable you to load, debug, and run simple MIPS programs.

SPIM comes in multiple versions. One version, called `spim`, is a command-line-driven program and requires only an alphanumeric terminal to display it. It operates like most programs of this type: you type a line of text, hit the `return` key, and `spim` executes your command.

A fancier version, called `xspim`, runs in the X-windows environment of the Unix system and therefore requires a bit-mapped display to run it. `xspim`, however, is a much easier program to learn and use because its commands are always visible on the screen and because it continually displays the machine's registers. Another version, `PCspim`, is compatible with Windows 3.1, Windows 95, and Windows NT. The Unix, Windows, and DOS versions of SPIM are available through *www.mkp.com/cod2e.htm*.

Since many people use and prefer `xspim`, this section only discusses that program. If you plan to use any version of `spim`, do not skip this section. Read it first and then look at the "SPIM Command-Line Options" section (starting on page A-44) to see how to accomplish the same thing with `spim` commands. Check *www.mkp.com/cod2e.htm* for more information on using `PCspim`.

To start `xspim`, type `xspim` in response to your system's prompt (%):

```
% xspim
```

On your system, `xspim` may be kept in an unusual place, and you may need to execute a command first to add that place to your search path. Your instructor should tell you how to do this.

When `xspim` starts up, it pops up a large window on your screen (see Figure A.16). The window is divided into five panes:

- The top pane is called the *register display*. It shows the values of all registers in the MIPS CPU and FPU. This display is updated whenever your program stops running.

- The pane below contains the *control buttons* to operate `xspim`. These buttons are discussed below, so we can skip the details for now.

- The next pane, called the *text segments*, displays instructions both from your program and the system code that is loaded automatically when `xspim` starts running. Each instruction is displayed on a line that looks like

```
[0x00400000] 0x8fa40000 lw $4, 0($29)  ; 89: lw $a0, 0($sp)
```

The first number on the line, in square brackets, is the hexadecimal memory address of the instruction. The second number is the instruction's numerical encoding, again displayed as a hexadecimal number. The third item is the instruction's mnemonic description. Everything following the semicolon is the actual line from your assembly file that produced the instruction. The number 89 is the line number in that file. Sometimes nothing is on the line after the semicolon. This means that the instruction was produced by SPIM as part of translating a pseudo-instruction.

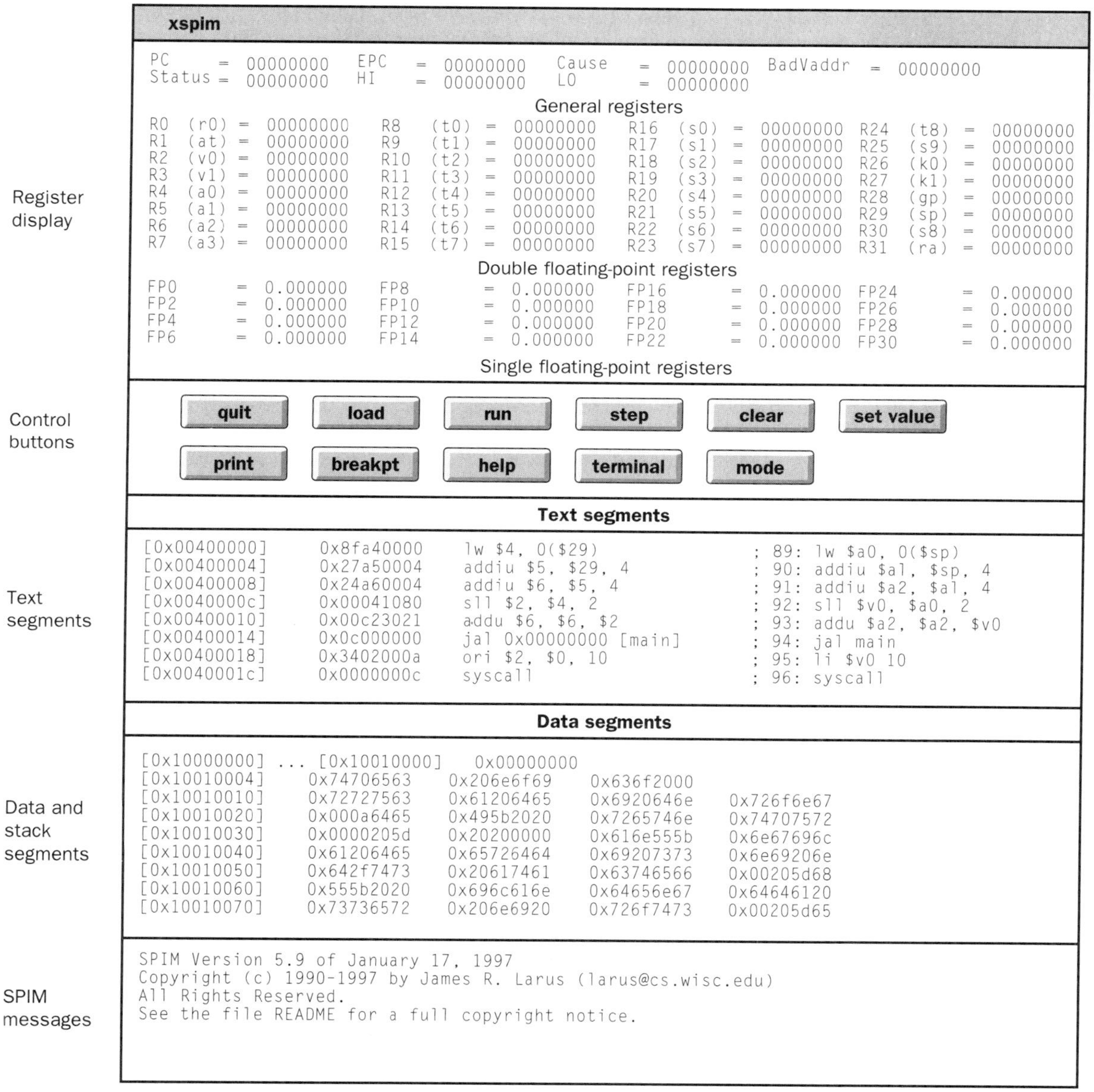

Register display

Control buttons

Text segments

Data and stack segments

SPIM messages

```
xspim

PC      = 00000000   EPC = 00000000   Cause = 00000000   BadVaddr = 00000000
Status  = 00000000   HI  = 00000000   LO    = 00000000
                              General registers
R0  (r0) = 00000000   R8  (t0) = 00000000   R16 (s0) = 00000000   R24 (t8) = 00000000
R1  (at) = 00000000   R9  (t1) = 00000000   R17 (s1) = 00000000   R25 (s9) = 00000000
R2  (v0) = 00000000   R10 (t2) = 00000000   R18 (s2) = 00000000   R26 (k0) = 00000000
R3  (v1) = 00000000   R11 (t3) = 00000000   R19 (s3) = 00000000   R27 (k1) = 00000000
R4  (a0) = 00000000   R12 (t4) = 00000000   R20 (s4) = 00000000   R28 (gp) = 00000000
R5  (a1) = 00000000   R13 (t5) = 00000000   R21 (s5) = 00000000   R29 (sp) = 00000000
R6  (a2) = 00000000   R14 (t6) = 00000000   R22 (s6) = 00000000   R30 (s8) = 00000000
R7  (a3) = 00000000   R15 (t7) = 00000000   R23 (s7) = 00000000   R31 (ra) = 00000000
                          Double floating-point registers
FP0  = 0.000000   FP8  = 0.000000   FP16 = 0.000000   FP24 = 0.000000
FP2  = 0.000000   FP10 = 0.000000   FP18 = 0.000000   FP26 = 0.000000
FP4  = 0.000000   FP12 = 0.000000   FP20 = 0.000000   FP28 = 0.000000
FP6  = 0.000000   FP14 = 0.000000   FP22 = 0.000000   FP30 = 0.000000
                           Single floating-point registers
```

quit   load   run   step   clear   set value

print   breakpt   help   terminal   mode

Text segments

```
[0x00400000]   0x8fa40000   lw $4, 0($29)          ; 89: lw $a0, 0($sp)
[0x00400004]   0x27a50004   addiu $5, $29, 4       ; 90: addiu $a1, $sp, 4
[0x00400008]   0x24a60004   addiu $6, $5, 4        ; 91: addiu $a2, $a1, 4
[0x0040000c]   0x00041080   sll $2, $4, 2          ; 92: sll $v0, $a0, 2
[0x00400010]   0x00c23021   addu $6, $6, $2        ; 93: addu $a2, $a2, $v0
[0x00400014]   0x0c000000   jal 0x00000000 [main]  ; 94: jal main
[0x00400018]   0x3402000a   ori $2, $0, 10         ; 95: li $v0 10
[0x0040001c]   0x0000000c   syscall                ; 96: syscall
```

Data segments

```
[0x10000000] ... [0x10010000]   0x00000000
[0x10010004]   0x74706563   0x206e6f69   0x636f2000
[0x10010010]   0x72727563   0x61206465   0x6920646e   0x726f6e67
[0x10010020]   0x000a6465   0x495b2020   0x7265746e   0x74707472
[0x10010030]   0x0000205d   0x20200000   0x616e555b   0x6e67696c
[0x10010040]   0x61206465   0x65726464   0x69207373   0x6e69206e
[0x10010050]   0x642f7473   0x20617461   0x63746566   0x00205d68
[0x10010060]   0x555b2020   0x696c616e   0x64656e67   0x64646120
[0x10010070]   0x73736572   0x206e6920   0x726f7473   0x00205d65
```

```
SPIM Version 5.9 of January 17, 1997
Copyright (c) 1990-1997 by James R. Larus (larus@cs.wisc.edu)
All Rights Reserved.
See the file README for a full copyright notice.
```

FIGURE A.16 SPIM's X-window interface: xspim.

■ The next pane, called the *data and stack segments*, displays the data loaded into your program's memory and the data on the program's stack.

■ The bottom pane is the *SPIM messages* that xspim uses to write messages. This is where error messages appear.

Let's see how to load and run a program. The first thing to do is to click on the load button (the second one in the first row of buttons) with the left mouse key. Your click tells xspim to pop up a small prompt window that contains a box and two or three buttons. Move your mouse so the cursor is over the box, and type the name of your file of assembly code. Then click on the button labeled assembly file within that prompt window. If you change your mind, click on the button labeled abort command, and xspim gets rid of the prompt window. When you click on assembly file, xspim gets rid of the prompt window, then loads your program and redraws the screen to display its instructions and data. Now move the mouse to put the cursor over the scrollbar to the left of the text segments, and click the left mouse button on the white part of this scrollbar. A click scrolls the text pane down so you can find all the instructions in your program.

To run your program, click on the run button in xspim's control button pane. It pops up a prompt window with two boxes and two buttons. Most of the time, these boxes contain the correct values to run your program, so you can ignore them and just click on ok. This button tells xspim to run your program. Notice that when your program is running, xspim blanks out the register display pane because the registers are continually changing. You can always tell whether xspim is running by looking at this pane. If you want to stop your program, make sure the mouse cursor is somewhere over xspim's window and type control-C. This causes xspim to pop up a prompt window with two buttons. Before doing anything with this prompt window, you can look at registers and memory to find out what your program was doing. When you understand what happened, you can either continue the program by clicking on continue or stop your program by clicking on abort command.

If your program reads or writes from the terminal, xspim pops up another window called the *console*. All characters that your program writes appear on the console, and everything that you type as input to your program should be typed in this window.

Suppose your program does not do what you expect. What can you do? SPIM has two features that help debug your program. The first, and perhaps the most useful, is single-stepping, which allows you to run your program an instruction at a time. Click on the button labeled step and another prompt window pops up. This prompt window contains two boxes and three buttons. The first box asks for the number of instructions to step every time you click the mouse. Most of the time, the default value of 1 is a good choice. The other box asks for arguments to pass to the program when it starts running. Again, most of the time you can ignore this box because it contains an appropriate value. The button labeled step runs your program for the number of instructions in the top box. If that number is 1, xspim executes the next instruction in your program, updates the display, and returns control to you. The button labeled continue stops single-stepping and continues running your program. Finally, abort command stops single-stepping and leaves your program stopped.

What do you do if your program runs for a long time before the bug arises? You could single-step until you get to the bug, but that can take a long time, and it is easy to get so bored and inattentive that you step past the problem. A better alternative is to use a *breakpoint*, which tells xspim to stop your program immediately before it executes a particular instruction. Click on the button in the second row of buttons marked breakpoints. The xspim program pops up a prompt window with one box and many buttons. Type in this box the address of the instruction at which you want to stop. Or, if the instruction has a global label, you can just type the name of the label. Labeled breakpoints are a particularly convenient way to stop at the first instruction of a procedure. To actually set the breakpoint, click on add. You can then run your program.

When SPIM is about to execute the breakpointed instruction, xspim pops up a prompt with the instruction's address and two buttons. The continue button continues running your program and abort command stops your program. If you want to delete a breakpoint, type in its address and click on delete. Finally, list tells xspim to print (in the bottom pane) a list of all breakpoints that are set.

Single-stepping and setting breakpoints will probably help you find a bug in your program quickly. How do you fix it? Go back to the editor that you used to create your program and change it. To run the program again, you need a fresh copy of SPIM, which you get in two ways. Either you can exit from xspim by clicking on the quit button, or you can clear xspim and reload your program. If you reload your program, you *must* clear the memory, so remnants of your previous program do not interfere with your new program. To do this, click on the button labeled clear. Hold the left mouse key down and a two-item menu will pop up. Move the mouse so the cursor is over the item labeled memory & registers and release the key. This causes xspim to clear its memory and registers and return the processor to the state it was in when xspim first started. You can now load and run your new program.

The other buttons in xspim perform functions that are occasionally useful. When you are more comfortable with xspim, you should look at the description below to see what they do and how they can save you time and effort.

SPIM Command-Line Options

Both Unix versions of SPIM—spim, the terminal version, and xspim, the X version—accept the following command-line options:

-bare
: Simulate a bare MIPS machine without pseudoinstructions or the additional addressing modes provided by the assembler. Implies -quiet.

-asm
: Simulate the virtual MIPS machine provided by the assembler. This is the default.

-pseudo
: Allow the input assembly code to contain pseudoinstructions. This is the default.

-nopseudo
: Do not allow pseudoinstructions in the input assembly code.

-notrap
: Do not load the standard exception handler and start-up code. This exception handler handles exceptions. When an exception occurs, SPIM jumps to location 80000080_{hex}, which must contain code to service the exception. In addition, this file contains start-up code that invokes the routine main. Without the start-up routine, SPIM begins execution at the instruction labeled __start.

-trap
: Load the standard exception handler and start-up code. This is the default.

-noquiet
: Print a message when an exception occurs. This is the default.

-quiet
: Do not print a message at exceptions.

-nomapped_io
: Disable the memory-mapped I/O facility (see section A.8). This is the default.

-mapped_io
: Enable the memory-mapped I/O facility (see section A.8). Programs that use SPIM syscalls (see section on "System Calls," page A-48) to read from the terminal *cannot* also use memory-mapped I/O.

-file
: Load and execute the assembly code in the file.

-execute
: Load and execute the code in the MIPS executable file *a.out*. This command is only available when SPIM runs on a system containing a MIPS processor.

-s <seg> size   Sets the initial size of memory segment *seg* to be *size* bytes. The memory segments are named: text, data, stack, ktext, and kdata. The text segment contains instructions from a program. The data segment holds the program's data. The stack segment holds its runtime stack. In addition to running a program, SPIM also executes system code that handles interrupts and exceptions. This code resides in a separate part of the address space called the *kernel*. The ktext segment holds this code's instructions, and kdata holds its data. There is no kstack segment since the system code uses the same stack as the program. For example, the pair of arguments -sdata 2000000 starts the user data segment at 2,000,000 bytes.

-l <seg> size   Sets the limit on how large memory segment *seg* can grow to be *size* bytes. The memory segments that can grow are data, stack, and kdata.

Terminal Interface (spim)

The simpler Unix version of SPIM is called spim. It does not require a bit-mapped display and can be run from any terminal. Although spim may be more difficult to learn, it operates just like xspim and provides the same functionality.

The spim terminal interface provides the following commands:

exit   Exit the simulator.

read "file"   Read *file* of assembly language into SPIM. If the file has already been read into SPIM, the system must be cleared (see reinitialize, below) or global labels will be multiply defined.

load "file"   Synonym for read.

execute "a.out"   Read the MIPS executable file *a.out* into SPIM. This command is only available when SPIM runs on a system containing a MIPS processor.

run <addr>   Start running a program. If the optional address *addr* is provided, the program starts at that address. Otherwise, the program starts at the global label __start, which is usually the default start-up code that calls the routine at the global label main.

step <N>	Step the program for *N* (default: 1) instructions. Print instructions as they execute.
continue	Continue program execution without stepping.
print $N	Print register *N*.
print $fN	Print floating point register *N*.
print addr	Print the contents of memory at address *addr*.
print_sym	Print the names and addresses of the global labels known to SPIM. Labels are local by default and become global only when declared in a .globl assembler directive (see "Assember Syntax" section on page A-51).
reinitialize	Clear the memory and registers.
breakpoint addr	Set a breakpoint at address *addr*. *addr* can be either a memory address or symbolic label.
delete addr	Delete all breakpoints at address *addr*.
list	List all breakpoints.
.	Rest of line is an assembly instruction that is stored in memory.
<nl>	A newline reexecutes previous command.
?	Print a help message.

Most commands can be abbreviated to their unique prefix (e.g., ex, re, l, ru, s, p). More dangerous commands, such as reinitialize, require a longer prefix.

X-Window Interface (xspim)

The tutorial, "Getting Started with SPIM" (page A-39), explains the most common xspim commands. However, xspim has other commands that are occasionally useful. This section provides a complete list of the commands.

The X version of SPIM, xspim, looks different but operates in the same manner as spim. The X-window has five panes (see Figure A.16). The top pane displays the registers. These values are continually updated, except while a program is running.

The next pane contains buttons that control the simulator:

quit	Exit from the simulator.
load	Read a source or executable file into SPIM.

run	Start the program running.
step	Single-step a program.
clear	Reinitialize registers or memory.
set value	Set the value in a register or memory location.
print	Print the value in a register or memory location.
breakpoint	Set or delete a breakpoint or list all breakpoints.
help	Print a help message.
terminal	Raise or hide the console window.
mode	Set SPIM operating modes.

The next two panes display the memory. The top one shows instructions from the user and kernel text segments. (These instructions are real—not pseudo—MIPS instructions. SPIM translates assembler pseudoinstructions into one to three MIPS instructions. Each source instruction appears as a comment on the first instruction into which it is translated.) The first few instructions in the text segment are the default start-up code (__start) that loads argc and argv into registers and invokes the main routine. The lower of these two panes displays the data and stack segments. Both panes are updated as a program executes.

The bottom pane is used to display SPIM messages. It does not display output from a program. When a program reads or writes, its I/O appears in a separate window, called the *console*, which pops up when needed.

Surprising Features

Although SPIM faithfully simulates the MIPS computer, SPIM is a simulator and certain things are not identical to an actual computer. The most obvious differences are that instruction timing and the memory systems are not identical. SPIM does not simulate caches or memory latency, nor does it accurately reflect floating-point operation or multiply and divide instruction delays.

Another surprise (which occurs on the real machine as well) is that a pseudoinstruction expands to several machine instructions. When you single-step or examine memory, the instructions that you see are different from the source program. The correspondence between the two sets of instructions is fairly simple since SPIM does not reorganize instructions to fill delay slots.

Byte Order

Processors can number bytes within a word so the byte with the lowest number is either the leftmost or rightmost one. The convention used by a machine is called its *byte order*. MIPS processors can operate with either *big-endian* or *little-endian* byte order. For example, in a big-endian machine, the directive .byte 0, 1, 2, 3 would result in a memory word containing

Byte #			
0	1	2	3

while in a little-endian machine, the word would contain

Byte #			
3	2	1	0

SPIM operates with both byte orders. SPIM's byte order is the same as the byte order of the underlying machine that runs the simulator. For example, on a DECstation 3100 or Intel 80x86, SPIM is little-endian, while on a Macintosh or Sun SPARC, SPIM is big-endian.

System Calls

SPIM provides a small set of operating-system-like services through the system call (syscall) instruction. To request a service, a program loads the system call code (see Figure A.17) into register $v0 and arguments into registers $a0–$a3 (or $f12 for floating-point values). System calls that return values put their results in register $v0 (or $f0 for floating-point results). For example, the following code prints "the answer = 5":

```
        .data
str:
        .asciiz  "the answer = "
        .text
        li       $v0, 4    # system call code for print_str
        la       $a0, str  # address of string to print
        syscall            # print the string

        li       $v0, 1    # system call code for print_int
        li       $a0, 5    # integer to print
        syscall            # print it
```

The print_int system call is passed an integer and prints it on the console. print_float prints a single floating-point number; print_double prints a double precision number; and print_string is passed a pointer to a null-terminated string, which it writes to the console.

Service	System call code	Arguments	Result
print_int	1	$a0 = integer	
print_float	2	$f12 = float	
print_double	3	$f12 = double	
print_string	4	$a0 = string	
read_int	5		integer (in $v0)
read_float	6		float (in $f0)
read_double	7		double (in $f0)
read_string	8	$a0 = buffer, $a1 = length	
sbrk	9	$a0 = amount	address (in $v0)
exit	10		

FIGURE A.17   System services.

The system calls read_int, read_float, and read_double read an entire line of input up to and including the newline. Characters following the number are ignored. read_string has the same semantics as the Unix library routine fgets. It reads up to $n - 1$ characters into a buffer and terminates the string with a null byte. If fewer than $n - 1$ characters are on the current line, read_string reads up to and including the newline and again null-terminates the string. *Warning:* Programs that use these syscalls to read from the terminal should not use memory-mapped I/O (see section A.8).

Finally, sbrk returns a pointer to a block of memory containing n additional bytes, and exit stops a program from running.

A.10   MIPS R2000 Assembly Language

A MIPS processor consists of an integer processing unit (the CPU) and a collection of coprocessors that perform ancillary tasks or operate on other types of data such as floating-point numbers (see Figure A.18). SPIM simulates two coprocessors. Coprocessor 0 handles exceptions, interrupts, and the virtual memory system. SPIM simulates most of the first two and entirely omits details of the memory system. Coprocessor 1 is the floating-point unit. SPIM simulates most aspects of this unit.

Addressing Modes

MIPS is a load-store architecture, which means that only load and store instructions access memory. Computation instructions operate only on values in registers. The bare machine provides only one memory-addressing mode: c(rx), which uses the sum of the immediate c and register rx as the address. The virtual machine provides the following addressing modes for load and store instructions:

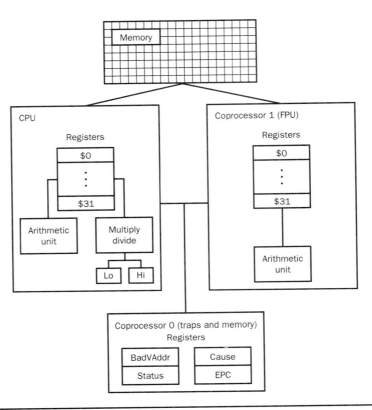

FIGURE A.18   MIPS R2000 CPU and FPU.

Format	Address computation
(register)	contents of register
imm	immediate
imm (register)	immediate + contents of register
label	address of label
label ± imm	address of label + or − immediate
label ± imm (register)	address of label + or − (immediate + contents of register)

Most load and store instructions operate only on aligned data. A quantity is *aligned* if its memory address is a multiple of its size in bytes. Therefore, a half-word object must be stored at even addresses and a full word object must be stored at addresses that are a multiple of four. However, MIPS provides some instructions to manipulate unaligned data (lwl, lwr, swl, and swr).

Elaboration: The MIPS assembler (and SPIM) synthesizes the more complex addressing modes by producing one or more instructions before the load or store to compute a complex address. For example, suppose that the label `table` referred to memory location 0x10000004 and a program contained the instruction

```
ld $a0, table + 4($a1)
```

The assembler would translate this instruction into the instructions

```
lui $at, 4096
addu $at, $at, $a1
lw $a0, 8($at)
```

The first instruction loads the upper bits of the label's address into register $at, which the register that the assemble reserves for its own use. The second instruction adds the contents of register $a1 to the label's partial address. Finally, the load instruction uses the hardware address mode to add the sum of the lower bits of the label's address and the offset from the original instruction to the value in register $at.

Assembler Syntax

Comments in assembler files begin with a sharp sign (#). Everything from the sharp sign to the end of the line is ignored.

Identifiers are a sequence of alphanumeric characters, underbars (_), and dots (.) that do not begin with a number. Instruction opcodes are reserved words that *cannot* be used as identifiers. Labels are declared by putting them at the beginning of a line followed by a colon, for example:

```
        .data
item:   .word 1
        .text
        .globl main  # Must be global
main:   lw    $t0, item
```

Numbers are base 10 by default. If they are preceded by *0x*, they are interpreted as hexadecimal. Hence, 256 and 0x100 denote the same value.

Strings are enclosed in doublequotes ("). Special characters in strings follow the C convention:

- newline\n

- tab \t

- quote\"

SPIM supports a subset of the MIPS assembler directives:

.align n	Align the next datum on a 2^n byte boundary. For example, .align 2 aligns the next value on a word boundary. .align 0 turns off automatic alignment of .half, .word, .float, and .double directives until the next .data or .kdata directive.
.ascii str	Store the string *str* in memory, but do not null-terminate it.

.asciiz str   Store the string *str* in memory and null-terminate it.

.byte b1,..., bn   Store the *n* values in successive bytes of memory.

.data <addr>   Subsequent items are stored in the data segment. If the optional argument *addr* is present, subsequent items are stored starting at address *addr*.

.double d1, ..., dn   Store the *n* floating-point double precision numbers in successive memory locations.

.extern sym size   Declare that the datum stored at *sym* is *size* bytes large and is a global label. This directive enables the assembler to store the datum in a portion of the data segment that is efficiently accessed via register $gp.

.float f1,..., fn   Store the *n* floating-point single precision numbers in successive memory locations.

.globl sym   Declare that label *sym* is global and can be referenced from other files.

.half h1, ..., hn   Store the *n* 16-bit quantities in successive memory halfwords.

.kdata <addr>   Subsequent data items are stored in the kernel data segment. If the optional argument *addr* is present, subsequent items are stored starting at address *addr*.

.ktext <addr>   Subsequent items are put in the kernel text segment. In SPIM, these items may only be instructions or words (see the .word directive below). If the optional argument *addr* is present, subsequent items are stored starting at address *addr*.

.set noat and .set at   The first directive prevents SPIM from complaining about subsequent instructions that use register $at. The second directive reenables the warning. Since pseudoinstructions expand into code that uses register $at, programmers must be very careful about leaving values in this register.

.space n   Allocate *n* bytes of space in the current segment (which must be the data segment in SPIM).

.text <addr>   Subsequent items are put in the user text segment. In SPIM, these items may only be instructions or words (see the .word directive below). If the optional argument *addr* is present, subsequent items are stored starting at address *addr*.

.word w1,..., wn   Store the *n* 32-bit quantities in successive memory words.

SPIM does not distinguish various parts of the data segment (.data, .rdata, and .sdata).

Encoding MIPS Instructions

Figure A.19 explains how a MIPS instruction is encoded in a binary number. Each column contains instruction encodings for a field (a contiguous group of bits) from an instruction. The numbers at the left margin are values for a field. For example, the j opcode has a value of 2 in the opcode field. The text at the top of a column names a field and specifies which bits it occupies in an instruction. For example, the op field is contained in bits 26–31 of an instruction. This field encodes most instructions. However, some groups of instructions use additional fields to distinguish related instructions. For example, the different floating-point instructions are specified by bits 0–5. The arrows from the first column show which opcodes use these additional fields.

Instruction Format

The rest of this appendix describes both the instructions implemented by actual MIPS hardware and the pseudoinstructions provided by the MIPS assembler. The two types of instructions are easily distinguished. Actual instructions depict the fields in their binary representation. For example, in

Addition (with overflow)

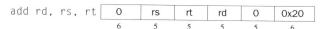

the add instruction consists of six fields. Each field's size in bits is the small number below the field. This instruction begins with 6 bits of 0s. Register specifiers begin with an *r,* so the next field is a 5-bit register specifier called rs. This is the same register that is the second argument in the symbolic assembly at the left of this line. Another common field is imm$_{16}$, which is a 16-bit immediate number.

Pseudoinstructions follow roughly the same conventions, but omit instruction encoding information. For example:

Multiply (without overflow)

mul rdest, rsrc1, src2   *pseudoinstruction*

In pseudoinstructions, rdest and rsrc1 are registers and src2 is either a register or an immediate value. In general, the assembler and SPIM translate a more general form of an instruction (e.g., add $v1, $a0, 0x55) to a specialized form (e.g., addi $v1, $a0, 0x55).

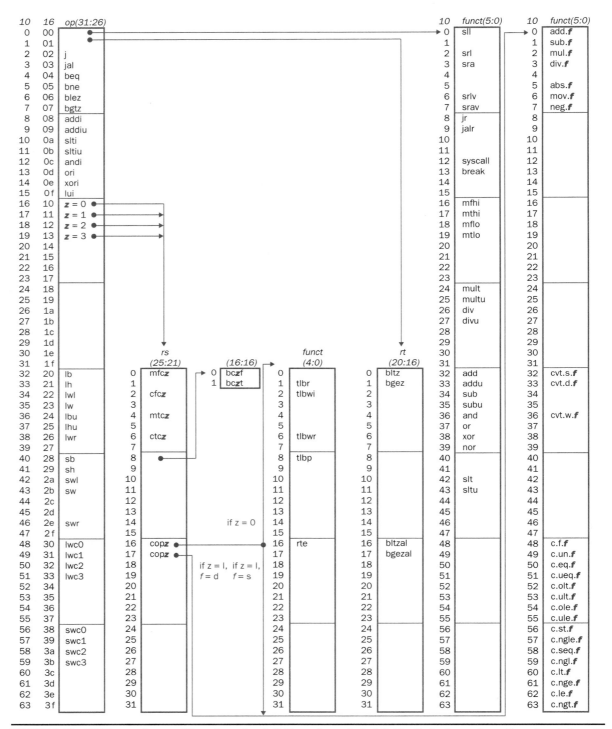

FIGURE A.19 MIPS opcode map. The values of each field are shown to its left. The first column shows the values in base 10 and the second shows base 16 for the op field (bits 31 to 26) in the third column. This op field completely specifies the MIPS operation except for 6 op values: 0, 1, 16, 17, 18, and 19. These operations are determined by other fields, identified by pointers. The last field (funct) uses "f" to mean "s" if rs = 16 and op = 17 or "d" if rs = 17 and op = 17. The second field (rs) uses "z" to mean "0", "1", "2", or "3" if op = 16, 17, 18, or 19, respectively. If rs = 16, the operation is specified elsewhere: if z = 0, the operations are specified in the fourth field (bits 4 to 0); if z = 1, then the operations are in the last field with f = s. If rs = 17 and z = 1, then the operations are in the last field with f = d. *(page A-54)*

Arithmetic and Logical Instructions

Absolute value

abs rdest, rsrc   *pseudoinstruction*

Put the absolute value of register rsrc in register rdest.

Addition (with overflow)

add rd, rs, rt

0	rs	rt	rd	0	0x20
6	5	5	5	5	6

Addition (without overflow)

addu rd, rs, rt

0	rs	rt	rd	0	0x21
6	5	5	5	5	6

Put the sum of registers rs and rt into register rd.

Addition immediate (with overflow)

addi rt, rs, imm

8	rs	rt	imm
6	5	5	16

Addition immediate (without overflow)

addiu rt, rs, imm

9	rs	rt	imm
6	5	5	16

Put the sum of register rs and the sign-extended immediate into register rt.

AND

and rd, rs, rt

0	rs	rt	rd	0	0x24
6	5	5	5	5	6

Put the logical AND of registers rs and rt into register rd.

AND immediate

andi rt, rs, imm

0xc	rs	rt	imm
6	5	5	16

Put the logical AND of register rs and the zero-extended immediate into register rt.

Divide (with overflow)

div rs, rt	0	rs	rt	0	0x1a
	6	5	5	10	6

Divide (without overflow)

divu rs, rt	0	rs	rt	0	0x1b
	6	5	5	10	6

Divide register rs by register rt. Leave the quotient in register lo and the remainder in register hi. Note that if an operand is negative, the remainder is unspecified by the MIPS architecture and depends on the convention of the machine on which SPIM is run.

Divide (with overflow)

div rdest, rsrc1, src2   *pseudoinstruction*

Divide (without overflow)

divu rdest, rsrc1, src2   *pseudoinstruction*

Put the quotient of register rsrc1 and src2 into register rdest.

Multiply

mult rs, rt	0	rs	rt	0	0x18
	6	5	5	10	6

Unsigned multiply

multu rs, rt	0	rs	rt	0	0x19
	6	5	5	10	6

Multiply registers rs and rt. Leave the low-order word of the product in register lo and the high-order word in register hi.

Multiply (without overflow)

mul rdest, rsrc1, src2   *pseudoinstruction*

Multiply (with overflow)

mulo rdest, rsrc1, src2   *pseudoinstruction*

Unsigned multiply (with overflow)

mulou rdest, rsrc1, src2   *pseudoinstruction*

Put the product of register rsrc1 and src2 into register rdest.

Negate value (with overflow)

neg rdest, rsrc   *pseudoinstruction*

Negate value (without overflow)

negu rdest, rsrc   *pseudoinstruction*

Put the negative of register rsrc into register rdest.

NOR

nor rd, rs, rt

0	rs	rt	rd	0	0x27
6	5	5	5	5	6

Put the logical NOR of registers rs and rt into register rd.

NOT

not rdest, rsrc   *pseudoinstruction*

Put the bitwise logical negation of register rsrc into register rdest.

OR

or rd, rs, rt

0	rs	rt	rd	0	0x25
6	5	5	5	5	6

Put the logical OR of registers rs and rt into register rd.

OR immediate

ori rt, rs, imm

0xd	rs	rt	imm
6	5	5	16

Put the logical OR of register rs and the zero-extended immediate into register rt.

Remainder

rem rdest, rsrc1, rsrc2   *pseudoinstruction*

Unsigned remainder

```
remu rdest, rsrc1, rsrc2          pseudoinstruction
```

Put the remainder of register `rsrc1` divided by register `rsrc2` into register `rdest`. Note that if an operand is negative, the remainder is unspecified by the MIPS architecture and depends on the convention of the machine on which SPIM is run.

Shift left logical

```
sll rd, rt, shamt
```

0	rs	rt	rd	shamt	0
6	5	5	5	5	6

Shift left logical variable

```
sllv rd, rt, rs
```

0	rs	rt	rd	0	4
6	5	5	5	5	6

Shift right arithmetic

```
sra rd, rt, shamt
```

0	rs	rt	rd	shamt	3
6	5	5	5	5	6

Shift right arithmetic variable

```
srav rd, rt, rs
```

0	rs	rt	rd	0	7
6	5	5	5	5	6

Shift right logical

```
srl rd, rt, shamt
```

0	rs	rt	rd	shamt	2
6	5	5	5	5	6

Shift right logical variable

```
srlv rd, rt, rs
```

0	rs	rt	rd	0	6
6	5	5	5	5	6

Shift register `rt` left (right) by the distance indicated by immediate `shamt` or the register `rs` and put the result in register `rd`. Note that argument `rs` is ignored for `sll`, `sra`, and `srl`.

Rotate left

```
rol rdest, rsrc1, rsrc2           pseudoinstruction
```

Rotate right

`ror rdest, rsrc1, rsrc2`   *pseudoinstruction*

Rotate register `rsrc1` left (right) by the distance indicated by `rsrc2` and put the result in register `rdest`.

Subtract (with overflow)

`sub rd, rs, rt`
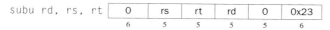

Subtract (without overflow)

`subu rd, rs, rt`
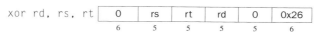

Put the difference of registers `rs` and `rt` into register `rd`.

Exclusive OR

`xor rd, rs, rt`
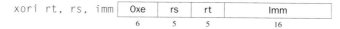

Put the logical XOR of registers `rs` and `rt` into register `rd`.

XOR immediate

`xori rt, rs, imm`
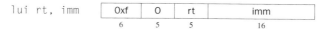

Put the logical XOR of register `rs` and the zero-extended immediate into register `rt`.

Constant-Manipulating Instructions

Load upper immediate

`lui rt, imm`

0xf	0	rt	imm
6	5	5	16

Load the lower halfword of the immediate `imm` into the upper halfword of register `rt`. The lower bits of the register are set to 0.

Load immediate

`li rdest, imm`   *pseudoinstruction*

Move the immediate `imm` into register `rdest`.

Comparison Instructions

Set less than

slt rd, rs, rt

Set less than unsigned

sltu rd, rs, rt

Set register rd to 1 if register rs is less than rt, and to 0 otherwise.

Set less than immediate

slti rd, rs, imm

0xa	rs	rd	imm
6	5	5	16

Set less than unsigned immediate

sltiu rd, rs, imm

0xb	rs	rd	imm
6	5	5	16

Set register rd to 1 if register rs is less than the sign-extended immediate, and to 0 otherwise.

Set equal

seq rdest, rsrc1, rsrc2   *pseudoinstruction*

Set register rdest to 1 if register rsrc1 equals rsrc2, and to 0 otherwise.

Set greater than equal

sge rdest, rsrc1, rsrc2   *pseudoinstruction*

Set greater than equal unsigned

sgeu rdest, rsrc1, rsrc2   *pseudoinstruction*

Set register rdest to 1 if register rsrc1 is greater than or equal to rsrc2, and to 0 otherwise.

Set greater than

sgt rdest, rsrc1, rsrc2   *pseudoinstruction*

Set greater than unsigned

sgtu rdest, rsrc1, rsrc2   *pseudoinstruction*

Set register rdest to 1 if register rsrc1 is greater than rsrc2, and to 0 otherwise.

Set less than equal

sle rdest, rsrc1, rsrc2   *pseudoinstruction*

Set less than equal unsigned

sleu rdest, rsrc1, rsrc2   *pseudoinstruction*

Set register rdest to 1 if register rsrc1 is less than or equal to rsrc2, and to 0 otherwise.

Set not equal

sne rdest, rsrc1, rsrc2   *pseudoinstruction*

Set register rdest to 1 if register rsrc1 is not equal to rsrc2, and to 0 otherwise.

Branch Instructions

Branch instructions use a signed 16-bit instruction *offset* field; hence they can jump $2^{15} - 1$ *instructions* (not bytes) forward or 2^{15} instructions backwards. The *jump* instruction contains a 26-bit address field.

In the descriptions below, the offsets are not specified. Instead, the instructions branch to a label. This is the form used in most assembly language programs because the distance between instructions is difficult to calculate when pseudoinstructions expand into several real instructions.

Branch instruction

b label   *pseudoinstruction*

Unconditionally branch to the instruction at the label.

Branch coprocessor *z* true

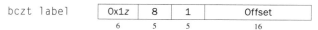

Conditionally branch the number of instructions specified by the offset if *z*'s condition flag is true (false). *z* is 0, 1, 2, or 3. The floating-point unit is $z = 1$.

Branch coprocessor *z* false

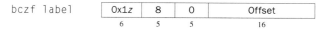

Conditionally branch the number of instructions specified by the offset if *z*'s condition flag is true (false). *z* is 0, 1, 2, or 3. The floating-point unit is $z = 1$.

Branch on equal

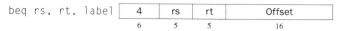

Conditionally branch the number of instructions specified by the offset if register rs equals rt.

Branch on greater than equal zero

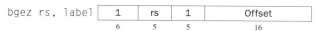

Conditionally branch the number of instructions specified by the offset if register rs is greater than or equal to 0.

Branch on greater than equal zero and link

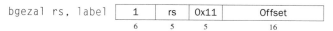

Conditionally branch the number of instructions specified by the offset if register rs is greater than or equal to 0. Save the address of the next instruction in register 31.

Branch on greater than zero

Conditionally branch the number of instructions specified by the offset if register rs is greater than 0.

Branch on less than equal zero

blez rs, label

6	rs	0	Offset
6	5	5	16

Conditionally branch the number of instructions specified by the offset if register rs is less than or equal to 0.

Branch on less than and link

bltzal rs, label

1	rs	0x10	Offset
6	5	5	16

Conditionally branch the number of instructions specified by the offset if register rs is less than 0. Save the address of the next instruction in register 31.

Branch on less than zero

bltz rs, label

1	rs	0	Offset
6	5	5	16

Conditionally branch the number of instructions specified by the offset if register rs is less than 0.

Branch on not equal

bne rs, rt, label

5	rs	rt	Offset
6	5	5	16

Conditionally branch the number of instructions specified by the offset if register rs is not equal to rt.

Branch on equal zero

beqz rsrc, label   *pseudoinstruction*

Conditionally branch to the instruction at the label if rsrc equals 0.

Branch on greater than equal

bge rsrc1, rsrc2, label   *pseudoinstruction*

Branch on greater than equal unsigned

bgeu rsrc1, rsrc2, label   *pseudoinstruction*

Conditionally branch to the instruction at the label if register rsrc1 is greater than or equal to rsrc2.

Branch on greater than

```
bgt rsrc1, src2, label                 pseudoinstruction
```

Branch on greater than unsigned

```
bgtu rsrc1, src2, label                pseudoinstruction
```

Conditionally branch to the instruction at the label if register rsrc1 is greater than src2.

Branch on less than equal

```
ble rsrc1, src2, label                 pseudoinstruction
```

Branch on less than equal unsigned

```
bleu rsrc1, src2, label                pseudoinstruction
```

Conditionally branch to the instruction at the label if register rsrc1 is less than or equal to src2.

Branch on less than

```
blt rsrc1, rsrc2, label                pseudoinstruction
```

Branch on less than unsigned

```
bltu rsrc1, rsrc2, label               pseudoinstruction
```

Conditionally branch to the instruction at the label if register rsrc1 is less than rsrc2.

Branch on not equal zero

```
bnez rsrc, label                       pseudoinstruction
```

Conditionally branch to the instruction at the label if register rsrc is not equal to 0.

Jump Instructions

Jump

Unconditionally jump to the instruction at target.

Jump and link

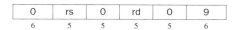

Unconditionally jump to the instruction at target. Save the address of the next instruction in register $ra.

Jump and link register

```
jalr rs, rd
```

0	rs	0	rd	0	9
6	5	5	5	5	6

Unconditionally jump to the instruction whose address is in register rs. Save the address of the next instruction in register rd (which defaults to 31).

Jump register

```
jr rs
```

0	rs	0	8
6	5	15	6

Unconditionally jump to the instruction whose address is in register rs.

Load Instructions

Load address

```
la rdest, address
```                              *pseudoinstruction*

Load computed *address*—not the contents of the location—into register rdest.

Load byte

```
lb rt, address
```

0x20	rs	rt	Offset
6	5	5	16

Load unsigned byte

`lbu rt, address`

0x24	rs	rt	Offset
6	5	5	16

Load the byte at *address* into register `rt`. The byte is sign-extended by `lb`, but not by `lbu`.

Load halfword

`lh rt, address`

0x21	rs	rt	Offset
6	5	5	16

Load unsigned halfword

`lhu rt, address`

0x25	rs	rt	Offset
6	5	5	16

Load the 16-bit quantity (halfword) at *address* into register `rt`. The halfword is sign-extended by `lh`, but not by `lhu`.

Load word

`lw rt, address`

0x23	rs	rt	Offset
6	5	5	16

Load the 32-bit quantity (word) at *address* into register `rt`.

Load word coprocessor

`lwcz rt, address`

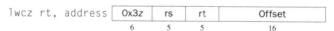

0x3z	rs	rt	Offset
6	5	5	16

Load the word at *address* into register `rt` of coprocessor z (0–3). The floating-point unit is $z = 1$.

Load word left

`lwl rt, address`

0x22	rs	rt	Offset
6	5	5	16

Load word right

`lwr rt, address`

0x26	rs	rt	Offset
6	5	5	16

Load the left (right) bytes from the word at the possibly unaligned *address* into register `rt`.

Load doubleword

ld rdest, address   *pseudoinstruction*

Load the 64-bit quantity at *address* into registers rdest and rdest + 1.

Unaligned load halfword

ulh rdest, address   *pseudoinstruction*

Unaligned load halfword unsigned

ulhu rdest, address   *pseudoinstruction*

Load the 16-bit quantity (halfword) at the possibly unaligned *address* into register rdest. The halfword is sign-extended by ulh, but not ulhu.

Unaligned load word

ulw rdest, address   *pseudoinstruction*

Load the 32-bit quantity (word) at the possibly unaligned *address* into register rdest.

Store Instructions

Store byte

Store the low byte from register rt at *address.*

Store halfword

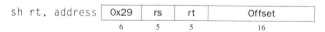

Store the low halfword from register rt at *address.*

Store word

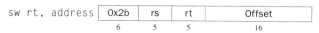

Store the word from register rt at *address.*

Store word coprocessor

swcz rt, address

0x32	rs	rt	Offset
6	5	5	16

Store the word from register rt of coprocessor z at *address*. The floating-point unit is z = 1.

Store word left

swl rt, address

0x2a	rs	rt	Offset
6	5	5	16

Store word right

swr rt, address

0x2e	rs	rt	Offset
6	5	5	16

Store the left (right) bytes from register rt at the possibly unaligned *address*.

Store doubleword

sd rsrc, address   *pseudoinstruction*

Store the 64-bit quantity in registers rsrc and rsrc + 1 at *address*.

Unaligned store halfword

ush rsrc, address   *pseudoinstruction*

Store the low halfword from register rsrc at the possibly unaligned *address*.

Unaligned store word

usw rsrc, address   *pseudoinstruction*

Store the word from register rsrc at the possibly unaligned *address*.

Data Movement Instructions

Move

move rdest, rsrc   *pseudoinstruction*

Move register rsrc to rdest.

Move from hi

mfhi rd

0	0	rd	0	0x10
6	10	5	5	6

Move from lo

The multiply and divide unit produces its result in two additional registers, hi and lo. These instructions move values to and from these registers. The multiply, divide, and remainder pseudoinstructions that make this unit appear to operate on the general registers move the result after the computation finishes.

Move the hi (lo) register to register rd.

Move to hi

Move to lo

Move register rs to the hi (lo) register.

Move from coprocessor z

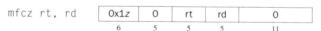

Coprocessors have their own register sets. These instructions move values between these registers and the CPU's registers.

Move coprocessor z's register rd to CPU register rt. The floating-point unit is coprocessor z = 1.

Move double from coprocessor 1

    mfc1.d rdest, frsrc1   *pseudoinstruction*

Move floating-point registers frsrc1 and frsrc1 + 1 to CPU registers rdest and rdest + 1.

Move to coprocessor z

Move CPU register rt to coprocessor z's register rd.

Floating-Point Instructions

The MIPS has a floating-point coprocessor (numbered 1) that operates on single precision (32-bit) and double precision (64-bit) floating-point numbers. This coprocessor has its own registers, which are numbered $f0–$f31. Because these registers are only 32 bits wide, two of them are required to hold doubles, so only floating-point registers with even numbers can hold double precision values.

Values are moved in or out of these registers one word (32 bits) at a time by lwc1, swc1, mtc1, and mfc1 instructions described above or by the l.s, l.d, s.s, and s.d pseudoinstructions described below. The flag set by floating-point comparison operations is read by the CPU with its bc1t and bc1f instructions.

In the actual instructions below, bits 21–26 are 0 for single precision and 1 for double precision. In the pseudoinstructions below, fdest is a floating-point register (e.g., $f2).

Floating-point absolute value double

abs.d fd, fs
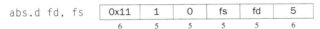

Floating-point absolute value single

abs.s fd, fs
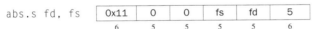

Compute the absolute value of the floating-point double (single) in register fs and put it in register fd.

Floating-point addition double

add.d fd, fs, ft
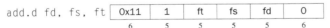

Floating-point addition single

add.s fd, fs, ft
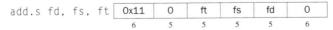

Compute the sum of the floating-point doubles (singles) in registers fs and ft and put it in register fd.

Compare equal double

Compare equal single

Compare the floating-point double in register fs against the one in ft and set the floating-point condition flag true if they are equal. Use the bclt or bclf instructions to test the value of this flag.

Compare less than equal double

Compare less than equal single

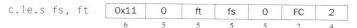

Compare the floating-point double in register fs against the one in ft and set the floating-point condition flag true if the first is less than or equal to the second. Use the bclt or bclf instructions to test the value of this flag.

Compare less than double

Compare less than single

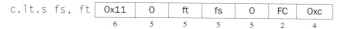

Compare the floating-point double in register fs against the one in ft and set the condition flag true if the first is less than the second. Use the bclt or bclf instructions to test the value of this flag.

Convert single to double

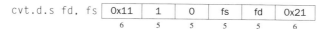

Convert integer to double

cvt.d.w fd, fs

0x11	0	0	fs	fd	0x21
6	5	5	5	5	6

Convert the single precision floating-point number or integer in register fs to a double precision number and put it in register fd.

Convert double to single

cvt.s.d fd, fs

0x11	1	0	fs	fd	0x20
6	5	5	5	5	6

Convert integer to single

cvt.s.w fd, fs

0x11	0	0	fs	fd	0x20
6	5	5	5	5	6

Convert the double precision floating-point number or integer in register fs to a single precision number and put it in register fd.

Convert double to integer

cvt.w.d fd, fs

0x11	1	0	fs	fd	0x24
6	5	5	5	5	6

Convert single to integer

cvt.w.s fd, fs

0x11	0	0	fs	fd	0x24
6	5	5	5	5	6

Convert the double or single precision floating-point number in register fs to an integer and put it in register fd.

Floating-point divide double

div.d fd, fs, ft

0x11	1	ft	fs	fd	3
6	5	5	5	5	6

Floating-point divide single

div.s fd, fs, ft

0x11	0	ft	fs	fd	3
6	5	5	5	5	6

Compute the quotient of the floating-point doubles (singles) in registers fs and ft and put it in register fd.

Load floating-point double

l.d fdest, address   *pseudoinstruction*

Load floating-point single

l.s fdest, address   *pseudoinstruction*

Load the floating-point double (single) at address into register fdest.

Move floating-point double

mov.d fd, fs

0x11	1	0	fs	fd	6
6	5	5	5	5	6

Move floating-point single

mov.s fd, fs

0x11	0	0	fs	fd	6
6	5	5	5	5	6

Move the floating-point double (single) from register fs to register fd.

Floating-point multiply double

mul.d fd, fs, ft

0x11	1	ft	fs	fd	2
6	5	5	5	5	6

Floating-point multiply single

mul.s fd, fs, ft

0x11	0	ft	fs	fd	2
6	5	5	5	5	6

Compute the product of the floating-point doubles (singles) in registers fs and ft and put it in register fd.

Negate double

neg.d fd, fs

0x11	1	0	fs	fd	7
6	5	5	5	5	6

Negate single

neg.s fd, fs

0x11	0	0	fs	fd	7
6	5	5	5	5	6

Negate the floating-point double (single) in register fs and put it in register fd.

Store floating-point double

s.d fdest, address   *pseudoinstruction*

Store floating-point single

s.s fdest, address   *pseudoinstruction*

Store the floating-point double (single) in register dest at address.

Floating-point subtract double

sub.d fd, fs, ft

0x11	1	ft	fs	fd	1
6	5	5	5	5	6

Floating-point subtract single

sub.s fd, fs, ft

0x11	0	ft	fs	fd	1
6	5	5	5	5	6

Compute the difference of the floating-point doubles (singles) in registers fs
and ft and put it in register fd.

Exception and Interrupt Instructions

Return from exception

rfe

0x10	1	0	0x20
6	1	19	6

Restore the Status register.

System call

syscall

0	0	0xc
6	20	6

Register $v0 contains the number of the system call (see Figure A.17) provided
by SPIM.

Break

break code	0	code	0xd
	6	20	6

Cause exception *code*. Exception 1 is reserved for the debugger.

No operation

nop	0	0	0	0	0	0
	6	5	5	5	5	6

Do nothing.

A.11 Concluding Remarks

Programming in assembly language requires a programmer to trade off helpful features of high-level languages—such as data structures, type checking, and control constructs—for complete control over the instructions that a computer executes. External constraints on some applications, such as response time or program size, require a programmer to pay close attention to every instruction. However, the cost of this level of attention is assembly language programs that are longer, more time-consuming to write, and more difficult to maintain than high-level language programs.

Moreover, three trends are reducing the need to write programs in assembly language. The first trend is toward the improvement of compilers. Modern compilers produce code that is typically comparable to the best handwritten code and is sometimes better. The second trend is the introduction of new processors that are not only faster, but in the case of processors that execute multiple instructions simultaneously, also more difficult to program by hand. In addition, the rapid evolution of the modern computer favors high-level language programs that are not tied to a single architecture. Finally, we witness a trend toward increasingly complex applications—characterized by complex graphic interfaces and many more features than their predecessors. Large applications are written by teams of programmers and require the modularity and semantic checking features provided by high-level languages.

To Probe Further

Kane, G., and J. Heinrich [1992]. *MIPS RISC Architecture*, Prentice Hall, Englewood Cliffs, NJ.

The last word on the MIPS instruction set and assembly language programming on these machines.

Aho, A., R. Sethi, and J. Ullman [1985]. *Compilers: Principles, Techniques, and Tools*, Addison-Wesley, Reading, MA.

Slightly dated and lacking in coverage of modern architectures, but still the standard reference on compilers.

Key Terms

A number of key terms have been introduced in this appendix. Check the Glossary for definitions of terms you are uncertain of.

absolute address	interrupt handler	separate compilation
assembler directive	local label	source language
backpatching	machine language	stack segment
callee-saved register	macros	static data
caller-saved register	procedure call or stack frame	symbol table
data segment	recursive procedures	text segment
external or global label	register-use or procedure-call	unresolved reference
formal parameter	convention	virtual machine
forward reference	relocation information	

Exercises

A.1 [5] <§A.5> Section A.5 described how memory is partitioned on most MIPS systems. Propose another way of dividing memory that meets the same goals.

A.2 [20] <§A.6> Rewrite the code for `fact` to use fewer instructions.

A.3 [5] <§A.7> Is it ever safe for a user program to use registers $k0 or $k1?

A.4 [25] <§A.7> Section A.7 contains code for a very simple exception handler. One serious problem with this handler is that it disables interrupts for a long time. This means that interrupts from a fast I/O device may be lost. Write a better exception handler that is interruptable and enables interrupts as quickly as possible.

A.5 [15] <§A.7> The simple exception handler always jumps back to the instruction following the exception. This works fine unless the instruction that causes the exception is in the delay slot of a branch. In that case, the next instruction is the target of the branch. Write a better handler that uses the EPC register to determine which instruction should be executed after the exception.

A.6 [5] <§A.9> Using SPIM, write and test an adding machine program that repeatedly reads in integers and adds them into a running sum. The program should stop when it gets an input that is 0, printing out the sum at that point. Use the SPIM system calls described on pages A-48 and A-49.

A.7 [5] <§A.9> Using SPIM, write and test a program that reads in three integers and prints out the sum of the largest two of the three. Use the SPIM system calls described on pages A-48 and A-49. You can break ties arbitrarily.

A.8 [5] <§A.9> Using SPIM, write and test a program that reads in a positive integer using the SPIM system calls. If the integer is not positive, the program should terminate with the message "Invalid Entry"; otherwise the program should print out the names of the digits of the integers, delimited by exactly one space. For example, if the user entered "728," the output would be "Seven Two Eight."

A.9 [25] <§A.9> Write and test a MIPS assembly language program to compute and print the first 100 prime numbers. A number n is prime if no numbers except 1 and n divide it evenly. You should implement two routines:

- `test_prime (n)`   Return 1 if n is prime and 0 if n is not prime.
- `main ()`   Iterate over the integers, testing if each is prime. Print the first 100 numbers that are prime.

Test your programs by running them on SPIM.

A.10 A.10 [10] <§§A.6, A.9> Using SPIM, write and test a recursive program for solving the classic mathematical recreation, the Towers of Hanoi puzzle. (This will require the use of stack frames to support recursion.) The puzzle consists of three pegs (1, 2, and 3) and n disks (the number n can vary; typical values might be in the range from 1 to 8). Disk 1 is smaller than disk 2, which is in turn smaller than disk 3, and so forth, with disk n being the largest. Initially, all the disks are on peg 1, starting with disk n on the bottom, disk $n - 1$ on top of that, and so forth, up to disk 1 on the top. The goal is to move all the disks to peg 2. You may only move one disk at a time, that is, the top disk from any of the three pegs onto the top of either of the other two pegs. Moreover, there is a constraint: You must not place a larger disk on top of a smaller disk.

The C program on the next page can be used to help write your assembly language program.

```c
/* move n smallest disks from start to finish using extra */
void hanoi(int n, int start, int finish, int extra){
  if(n != 0){
    hanoi(n-1, start, extra, finish);
    print_string("Move disk");
    print_int(n);
    print_string("from peg");
    print_int(start);
    print_string("to peg");
    print_int(finish);
    print_string(".\n");
    hanoi(n-1, extra, finish, start);
  }
}
main(){
  int n;
  print_string("Enter number of disks>");
  n = read_int();
  hanoi(n, 1, 2, 3);
  return 0;
}
```

The Basics of Logic Design

I always loved that word, Boolean.

Claude Shannon
IEEE Spectrum, April 1992
(Shannon's master's thesis showed that the algebra
invented by George Boole in the 1800s could represent the
workings of electrical switches.)

B.1   Introduction

This appendix provides a brief discussion of the basics of logic design. It does not replace a course in logic design nor will it enable you to design significant working logic systems. If you have little or no exposure to logic design, however, this appendix will provide sufficient background to understand all the material in this book. In addition, if you are looking to understand some of the motivation behind how computers are implemented, this material will serve as a useful introduction. If your curiosity is aroused but not sated by this appendix, the references at the end provide several additional sources of information.

Section B.2 introduces the basic building blocks of logic, namely *gates*. Section B.3 uses these building blocks to construct simple *combinational* logic systems, which contain no memory. If you have had some exposure to logic or digital systems, you will probably be familiar with the material in these first two sections. Section B.4 is a short introduction to the topic of clocking, which is necessary to discuss how memory elements work. Section B.5 introduces memory elements; it describes both the characteristics that are important to understanding how they are used in Chapters 5 and 6, and the background that motivates many of the aspects of memory hierarchy design in Chapter 7. Section B.6 describes the design and use of finite state machines, which are sequential logic blocks. If you intend to read Appendix C, you should thoroughly understand the material in sections B.2 through B.6. But if you intend to read only the material on control in Chapters 5 and 6, you can skim the appendices, but you should have some familiarity with all the material except section B.7. Section B.7 is intended for those who want a deeper understanding of clocking methodologies and timing. It explains the basics of how edge-triggered clocking works, introduces another clocking scheme, and briefly describes the problem of synchronizing asynchronous inputs.

B.2 Gates, Truth Tables, and Logic Equations

The electronics inside a modern computer are *digital*. Digital electronics operate with only two voltage levels of interest: a high voltage and a low voltage. All other voltage values are temporary and occur while transitioning between the values. As mentioned in Chapter 3, this is a key reason why computers use binary numbers, since a binary system matches the underlying abstraction inherent in the electronics. In various logic families, the values and relationships between the two voltage values differ. Thus, rather than refer to the voltage levels, we talk about signals that are (logically) true, or are 1, or are *asserted*; or signals that are (logically) false, or 0, or *deasserted*. The values 0 and 1 are called *complements* or *inverses* of one another.

Logic blocks are categorized as one of two types, depending on whether they contain memory. Blocks without memory are called *combinational*; the output of a combinational block depends only on the current input. In blocks with memory, the outputs can depend on both the inputs and the value stored in memory, which is called the *state* of the logic block. In this section and the next, we will focus only on combinational logic. After introducing different memory elements in section B.5, we will describe how *sequential* logic, which is logic including state, is designed.

Truth Tables

Because a combinational logic block contains no memory, it can be completely specified by defining the values of the outputs for each possible set of input values. Such a description is normally given as a *truth table*. For a logic block with n inputs, there are 2^n entries in the truth table, since there are that many possible combinations of input values. Each entry specifies the value of all the outputs for that particular input combination.

Truth Tables

Example

Consider a logic function with three inputs, *A*, *B*, and *C*, and three outputs, *D*, *E*, and *F*. The function is defined as follows: *D* is true if at least one input is true, *E* is true if exactly two inputs are true, and *F* is true only if all three inputs are true. Show the truth table for this function.

Answer

The truth table will contain $2^3 = 8$ entries. Here it is:

Inputs			Outputs		
A	**B**	**C**	**D**	**E**	**F**
0	0	0	0	0	0
0	0	1	1	0	0
0	1	0	1	0	0
0	1	1	1	1	0
1	0	0	1	0	0
1	0	1	1	1	0
1	1	0	1	1	0
1	1	1	1	0	1

Truth tables can completely describe any combinational logic function; however, they grow in size quickly and may not be easy to understand. Sometimes we want to construct a logic function that will be 0 for many input combinations, and we use a shorthand of specifying only the truth table entries for the nonzero outputs. This approach is used in Chapter 5 and Appendix C.

Boolean Algebra

Another approach is to express the logic function with logic equations. This is done with the use of *Boolean algebra* (named after Boole, a 19th century mathematician). In Boolean algebra, all the variables have the values 0 or 1 and, in typical formulations, there are three operators:

- The OR operator is written as +, as in *A* + *B*. The result of an OR operator is 1 if either of the variables is 1. The OR operation is also called a *logical sum*, since its result is 1 if either operand is 1.

- The AND operator is written as · , as in $A \cdot B$. The result of an AND operator is 1 only if both inputs are 1. The AND operator is also called *logical product*, since its result is 1 only if both operands are 1.

■ The unary operator NOT, written as $\overline{A}$. The result of a NOT operator is 1 only if the input is 0. Applying the operator NOT to a logical value results in an inversion or negation of the value (i.e., if the input is 0 the output is 1, and vice versa).

There are several laws of Boolean algebra that are helpful in manipulating logic equations.

■ Identity law: $A + 0 = A$ and $A \cdot 1 = A$.

■ Zero and One laws: $A + 1 = 1$ and $A \cdot 0 = 0$.

■ Inverse laws: $A + \overline{A} = 1$ and $A \cdot \overline{A} = 0$.

■ Commutative laws: $A + B = B + A$ and $A \cdot B = B \cdot A$.

■ Associative laws: $A + (B + C) = (A + B) + C$ and $A \cdot (B \cdot C) = (A \cdot B) \cdot C$.

■ Distributive laws: $A \cdot (B + C) = (A \cdot B) + (A \cdot C)$ and $A + (B \cdot C) = (A + B) \cdot (A + C)$.

In addition, there are two other useful laws, called DeMorgan's laws, that are discussed in more depth on page B-46.

Any set of logic functions can be written as a series of equations with an output on the left-hand side of each equation and a formula consisting of variables and the three operators above on the right-hand side.

Logic Equations

Example

Show the logic equations for the logic function described in the previous example.

Answer

Here's the equation for D:

$$D = A + B + C$$

F is equally simple:

$$F = A \cdot B \cdot C$$

E is a little tricky. Think of it in two parts: what must be true for E to be true (two of the three inputs must be true), and what cannot be true (all three cannot be true). Thus we can write E as

$$E = ((A \cdot B) + (A \cdot C) + (B \cdot C)) \cdot (\overline{A \cdot B \cdot C})$$

We can also derive E by realizing that E is true only if exactly two of the inputs are true. Then we can write E as an OR of the three possible terms that have two true inputs and one false input:

$$E = (A \cdot B \cdot \overline{C}) + (A \cdot C \cdot \overline{B}) + (B \cdot C \cdot \overline{A})$$

Proving that these two expressions are equivalent is the task of Exercise B.7.

Gates

Logic blocks are built from *gates* that implement basic logic functions. For example, an AND gate implements the AND function, and an OR gate implements the OR function. Since both AND and OR are commutative and associative, an AND or an OR gate can have multiple inputs, with the output equal to the AND or OR of all the inputs. The logical function NOT is implemented with an inverter that always has a single input. The standard representation of these three logic building blocks is shown in Figure B.1.

Rather than draw inverters explicitly, a common practice is to add "bubbles" to the inputs or output of a gate to cause the logic value on that input line or output line to be inverted. For example, Figure B.2 shows the logic diagram for the function $\overline{\overline{A} + B}$, using explicit inverters on the left and using bubbled inputs and outputs on the right.

Any logical function can be constructed using AND gates, OR gates, and inversion; several of the exercises give you the opportunity to try implementing some common logic functions with gates. In the next section, we'll see how an implementation of any logic function can be constructed using this knowledge.

FIGURE B.1 Standard drawing for an AND gate, OR gate, and an inverter, shown from left to right. The signals to the left of each symbol are the inputs, while the output appears on the right. The AND and OR gates both have two inputs. Inverters have a single input.

FIGURE B.2 Logic gate implementation of $\overline{\overline{A} + B}$ using explicit inverts on the left and using bubbled inputs and output on the right. This logic function can be simplified to $A \cdot \overline{B}$.

In fact, all logic functions can be constructed with only a single gate type, if that gate is inverting. The two common inverting gates are called NOR and NAND and correspond to inverted OR and AND gates, respectively. NOR and NAND gates are called *universal*, since any logic function can be built using this one gate type. Exercises B.3 and B.4 ask you to prove this fact.

B.3   Combinational Logic

In this section, we look at a couple of basic logic building blocks that we use heavily, and we discuss the design of structured logic that can be automatically implemented from a logic equation or truth table by a translation program. Last, we discuss the notion of an array of logic blocks.

Decoders

Another logic block that we will use in building larger components is a *decoder*. The most common type of decoder has an n-bit input and 2^n outputs, where only one output is asserted for each input combination. This decoder translates the n-bit input into a signal that corresponds to the binary value of the n-bit input. The outputs are thus usually numbered, say, Out0, Out1, . . . , Out$2^n- 1$. If the value of the input is i, then Out$i$ will be true and all other outputs will be false. Figure B.3 shows a 3-bit decoder and the truth table. This decoder is called a *3-to-8 decoder* since there are 3 inputs and 8 (2^3) outputs. There is also a logic element called an *encoder* that performs the inverse function of a decoder, taking 2^n inputs and producing an n-bit output.

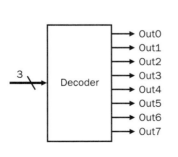

Inputs			Outputs							
I2	I1	I0	Out7	Out6	Out5	Out4	Out3	Out2	Out1	Out0
0	0	0	0	0	0	0	0	0	0	1
0	0	1	0	0	0	0	0	0	1	0
0	1	0	0	0	0	0	0	1	0	0
0	1	1	0	0	0	0	1	0	0	0
1	0	0	0	0	0	1	0	0	0	0
1	0	1	0	0	1	0	0	0	0	0
1	1	0	0	1	0	0	0	0	0	0
1	1	1	1	0	0	0	0	0	0	0

a. A 3-bit decoder   b. The truth table

FIGURE B.3   A 3-bit decoder has 3 inputs, called I2, I1, and I0, and 2^3 = 8 outputs, called Out0 to Out7. Only the output corresponding to the binary value of the input is true, as shown in the truth table. The label 3 on the input to the decoder says that the input signal is 3 bits wide.

Multiplexors

One basic logic function that we saw quite often in Chapters 4, 5, and 6 is the *multiplexor*. A multiplexor might more properly be called a *selector*, since its output is one of the inputs that is selected by a control. Consider the two-input multiplexor. As shown on the left side of Figure B.4, this multiplexor has three inputs: two data values and a selector (or control) value. The selector value determines which of the inputs becomes the output. We can represent the logic function computed by a two-input multiplexor as $C = (A \cdot \bar{S}) + (B \cdot S)$, which is shown in gate form on the right side of Figure B.4.

Multiplexors can be created with an arbitrary number of data inputs. When there are only two inputs, the selector is a single signal that selects one of the inputs if it is true (1) and the other if it is false (0). If there are n data inputs, there will need to be $\lceil \log_2 n \rceil$ selector inputs. In this case, the multiplexor basically consists of three parts:

1. A decoder that generates n signals, each indicating a different input value

2. An array of n AND gates, each combining one of the inputs with a signal from the decoder

3. A single large OR gate that incorporates the outputs of the AND gates

To associate the inputs with selector values, we often label the data inputs numerically (i.e., 0, 1, 2, 3, ... , $n - 1$) and interpret the data selector inputs as a binary number. Sometimes, we make use of a multiplexor with undecoded selector signals.

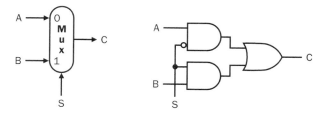

FIGURE B.4 A two-input multiplexor, on the left, and its implementation with gates, on the right. The multiplexor has two data inputs (*A* and *B*), which are labeled *0* and *1*, and one selector input (*S*), as well as an output *C*.

Two-Level Logic and PLAs

As pointed out in the previous section, any logic function can be implemented with only AND, OR, and NOT functions. In fact, a much stronger result is true. Any logic function can be written in a canonical form, where every input is either a true or complemented variable and there are only two levels of gates—one being AND and the other OR—with a possible inversion on the final output. Such a representation is called a *two-level representation* and there are two forms, called *sum of products* and *product of sums*. A sum-of-products representation is a logical sum (OR) of products (terms using the AND operator); a product of sums is just the opposite. In our earlier example, we had two equations for the output E:

$$E = ((A \cdot B) + (A \cdot C) + (B \cdot C)) \cdot (\overline{A \cdot B \cdot C})$$

and

$$E = (A \cdot B \cdot \overline{C}) + (A \cdot C \cdot \overline{B}) + (B \cdot C \cdot \overline{A})$$

This second equation is in a sum-of-products form: it has two levels of logic and the only inversions are on individual variables. The first equation has three levels of logic.

Elaboration: We can also write E as a product of sums:

$$E = \overline{(\overline{A} + \overline{B} + C) \cdot (\overline{A} + \overline{C} + B) \cdot (\overline{B} + \overline{C} + A)}$$

To derive this form, you need to use *DeMorgan's theorems*, which are discussed on page B-46. Exercise B.8 asks you to derive the product-of-sums representation from the sum of products using DeMorgan's theorems.

In this text, we use the more common sum-of-products form. It is easy to see that any logic function can be represented as a sum of products by constructing such a representation from the truth table for the function. Each truth table entry for which the function is true corresponds to a product term. The product term consists of a logical product of all the inputs or the complements of the inputs, depending on whether the entry in the truth table has a 0 or 1 corresponding to this variable. The logic function is the logical sum of the product terms where the function is true. This is more easily seen with an example.

Sum of Products

Example

Show the sum-of-products representation for the following truth table.

Inputs			Output
A	**B**	**C**	**D**
0	0	0	0
0	0	1	1
0	1	0	1
0	1	1	0
1	0	0	1
1	0	1	0
1	1	0	0
1	1	1	1

Answer

There are four product terms, since the function is true (1) for four different input combinations. These are

$$\bar{A} \cdot \bar{B} \cdot C$$

$$\bar{A} \cdot B \cdot \bar{C}$$

$$A \cdot \bar{B} \cdot \bar{C}$$

$$A \cdot B \cdot C$$

Thus, we can write the function for D as the sum of these terms:

$$D = (\bar{A} \cdot \bar{B} \cdot C) + (\bar{A} \cdot B \cdot \bar{C}) + (A \cdot \bar{B} \cdot \bar{C}) + (A \cdot B \cdot C)$$

Note that only those truth table entries for which the function is true generate terms in the equation.

We can use this relationship between a truth table and a two-level representation to generate a gate-level implementation of any set of logic functions. A set of logic functions corresponds to a truth table with multiple output columns, as we saw in the example on page B-5. Each output column represents a different logic function, which may be directly constructed from the truth table.

The sum-of-products representation corresponds to a common structured-logic implementation called a *programmable logic array* (PLA). A PLA has a set of inputs and corresponding input complements (which can be implemented

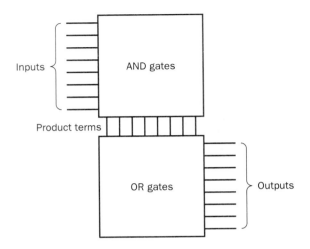

FIGURE B.5   The basic form of a PLA consists of an array of AND gates followed by an array of OR gates. Each entry in the AND gate array is a product term consisting of any number of inputs or inverted inputs. Each entry in the OR gate array is a sum term consisting of any number of these product terms.

with a set of inverters), and two stages of logic. The first stage is an array of AND gates that form a set of product terms (sometimes called *minterms*); each product term can consist of any of the inputs or their complements. The second stage is an array of OR gates, each of which forms a logical sum of any number of the product terms. Figure B.5 shows the basic form of a PLA.

A PLA can directly implement the truth table of a set of logic functions with multiple inputs and outputs. Since each entry where the truth table is true requires a product term, there will be a corresponding row in the PLA. Each output corresponds to a potential row of OR gates in the second stage. The number of OR gates corresponds to the number of truth table entries for which the output is true. The total size of a PLA, such as that shown in Figure B.5, is equal to the sum of the size of the AND gate array (called the *AND plane*) and the size of the OR gate array (called the *OR plane*). Looking at Figure B.5, we can see that the size of the AND gate array is equal to the number of inputs times the number of different product terms, and the size of the OR gate array is the number of outputs times the number of product terms.

A PLA has two characteristics that help make it an efficient way to implement a set of logic functions. First, only the truth table entries that produce a true value for at least one output have any logic gates associated with them. Second, each different product term will have only one entry in the PLA, even if the product term is used in multiple outputs. Let's look at an example.

PLAs

Example

Consider the set of logic functions defined in the example on B-5. Show a PLA implementation of this example.

Answer

Here is the truth table we constructed earlier:

Inputs			Outputs		
A	**B**	**C**	**D**	**E**	**F**
0	0	0	0	0	0
0	0	1	1	0	0
0	1	0	1	0	0
0	1	1	1	1	0
1	0	0	1	0	0
1	0	1	1	1	0
1	1	0	1	1	0
1	1	1	1	0	1

Since there are seven unique product terms with at least one true value in the output section, there will be seven columns in the AND plane. The number of rows in the AND plane is three (since there are three inputs), and there are also three rows in the OR plane (since there are three outputs). Figure B.6 shows the resulting PLA, with the product terms corresponding to the truth table entries from top to bottom.

Rather than drawing all the gates, as we did in Figure B.6, designers often show just the position of AND gates and OR gates. Dots are used on the intersection of a product term signal line and an input line or an output line when a corresponding AND gate or OR gate is required. Figure B.7 shows how the PLA of Figure B.6 would look when drawn in this way. The contents of a PLA are fixed when the PLA is created, although there are also forms of PLA-like structures, called *PALs*, that can be programmed electronically when a designer is ready to use them.

ROMs

Another form of structured logic that can be used to implement a set of logic functions is a *read-only memory* (ROM). A ROM is called a memory because it has a set of locations that can be read; however, the contents of these locations

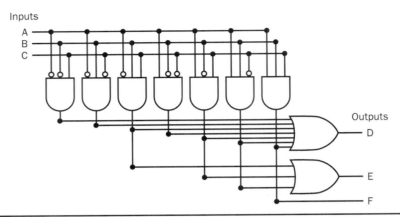

FIGURE B.6   The PLA for implementing the logic function described above.

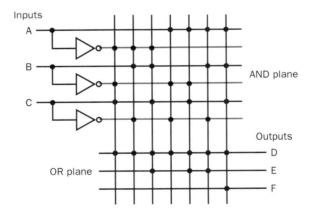

FIGURE B.7   A PLA drawn using dots to indicate the components of the product terms and sum terms in the array. Rather than use inverters on the gates, usually all the inputs are run the width of the AND plane in both true and complement forms. A dot in the AND plane indicates that the input, or its inverse, occurs in the product term. A dot in the OR plane indicates that the corresponding product term appears in the corresponding output.

are fixed, usually at the time the ROM is created. There are also *programmable ROMs* (PROMs) that can be programmed electronically, when a designer knows their contents. There are also erasable PROMs; these devices require a slow erasure process using ultraviolet light, and thus are used as read-only memories, except during the design and debugging process.

A ROM has a set of input address lines and a set of outputs. The number of addressable entries in the ROM determines the number of address lines: if the ROM contains 2^n addressable entries, called the *height*, then there are n input lines. The number of bits in each addressable entry is equal to the number of output bits and is sometimes called the *width* of the ROM. The total number of bits in the ROM is equal to the height times the width. The height and width are sometimes collectively referred to as the *shape* of the ROM.

A ROM can encode a collection of logic functions directly from the truth table. For example, if there are n functions with m inputs, we need a ROM with m address lines (and 2^m entries), with each entry being n bits wide. The entries in the input portion of the truth table represent the addresses of the entries in the ROM, while the contents of the output portion of the truth table constitute the contents of the ROM. If the truth table is organized so that the sequence of entries in the input portion constitute a sequence of binary numbers (as have all the truth tables we have shown so far), then the output portion gives the ROM contents in order as well. In the previous example starting on page B-13, there were three inputs and three outputs. This leads to a ROM with $2^3 = 8$ entries, each 3 bits wide. The contents of those entries in increasing order by address are directly given by the output portion of the truth table that appears on page B-13.

ROMs and PLAs are closely related. A ROM is fully decoded: it contains a full output word for every possible input combination. A PLA is only partially decoded. This means that a ROM will always contain more entries. For the earlier truth table on page B-13, the ROM contains entries for all eight possible inputs, whereas the PLA contains only the seven active product terms. As the number of inputs grows, the number of entries in the ROM grows exponentially. In contrast, for most real logic functions, the number of product terms grows much more slowly (see the examples in Appendix C). This difference makes PLAs generally more efficient for implementing combinational logic functions. ROMs have the advantage of being able to implement any logic function with the matching number of inputs and outputs. This advantage makes it easier to change the ROM contents if the logic function changes, since the size of the ROM need not change.

Don't Cares

Often in implementing some combinational logic, there are situations where we do not care what the value of some output is, either because another output is true or because a subset of the input combinations determines the values of the outputs. Such situations are referred to as *don't cares*. Don't cares are important because they make it easier to optimize the implementation of a logic function.

There are two types of don't cares: output don't cares and input don't cares, both of which can be represented in a truth table. *Output don't cares* arise when we don't care about the value of an output for some input combination. They appear as Xs in the output portion of a truth table. When an output is a don't care for some input combination, the designer or logic optimization program is free to make the output true or false for that input combination. *Input don't cares* arise when an output depends on only some of the inputs, and they are also shown as Xs, though in the input portion of the truth table.

Don't Cares

Example

Consider a logic function with inputs A, B, and C defined as follows:

- If A or C is true, then output D is true, whatever the value of B.
- If A or B is true, then output E is true, whatever the value of C.
- Output F is true if exactly one of the inputs is true, although we don't care about the value of F, whenever D and E are both true.

Show the full truth table for this function and the truth table using don't cares. How many product terms are required in a PLA for each of these?

Answer

Here's the full truth table, without don't cares:

Inputs			Outputs		
A	**B**	**C**	**D**	**E**	**F**
0	0	0	0	0	0
0	0	1	1	0	1
0	1	0	0	1	1
0	1	1	1	1	0
1	0	0	1	1	1
1	0	1	1	1	0
1	1	0	1	1	0
1	1	1	1	1	1

This requires seven product terms without optimization. The truth table written with output don't cares looks like

Inputs			Outputs		
A	**B**	**C**	**D**	**E**	**F**
0	0	0	0	0	0
0	0	1	1	0	1
0	1	0	0	1	1
0	1	1	1	1	X
1	0	0	1	1	X
1	0	1	1	1	X
1	1	0	1	1	X
1	1	1	1	1	X

This truth table can be further simplified to yield

Inputs			Outputs		
A	**B**	**C**	**D**	**E**	**F**
0	0	0	0	0	0
0	0	1	1	0	1
0	1	0	0	1	1
X	1	1	1	1	X
1	X	X	1	1	X

This simplified truth table requires a PLA with four minterms, or it can be implemented in discrete gates with one two-input AND gate and three OR gates (two with three inputs and one with two inputs). This compares to the original truth table that had seven minterms and would require four AND gates.

Logic minimization is critical to achieving efficient implementations. One tool useful for hand minimization of random logic is *Karnaugh maps*. Karnaugh maps represent the truth table graphically so that product terms that may be combined are easily seen. Nevertheless, hand optimization of significant logic functions using Karnaugh maps is impractical, both because of the size of the maps and their complexity. Fortunately, the process of logic minimization is highly mechanical and can be performed by design tools. In the process of minimization the tools take advantage of the don't cares, so specifying them is important. The textbook references at the end of this appendix provide further discussion on logic minimization, Karnaugh maps, and the theory behind such minimization algorithms.

Arrays of Logic Elements

Many of the combinational operations to be performed on data have to be done to an entire word (32 bits) of data. Thus we often want to build an array of logic elements, which we can represent simply by showing that a given operation will happen to an entire collection of inputs. For example, we saw on page B-9 what a 1-bit multiplexor looked like, but inside a machine, much of the time we want to select between a pair of *buses*. A bus is a collection of data lines that is treated together as a single logical signal. (The term *bus* is also used to indicate a shared collection of lines with multiple sources and uses, especially in Chapter 8, where I/O buses were discussed.)

For example, in the MIPS instruction set, the result of an instruction that is written into a register can come from one of two sources. A multiplexor is used to choose which of the two buses (each 32 bits wide) will be written into the Result register. The 1-bit multiplexor, which we showed earlier, will need to be replicated 32 times. We indicate that a signal is a bus rather than a single 1-bit line by showing it with a thicker line in a figure. Most buses are 32 bits wide; those that are not are explicitly labeled with their width. When we show a logic unit whose inputs and outputs are buses, this means that the unit must be replicated a sufficient number of times to accommodate the width of the input. Figure B.8 shows how we draw a multiplexor that selects between a pair of 32-bit buses and how this expands in terms of 1-bit-wide multiplexors. Sometimes we need to construct an array of logic elements where the inputs for some elements in the array are outputs from earlier elements. For example, this is how a multibit-wide ALU is constructed. In such cases, we must explicitly show how to create wider arrays, since the individual elements of the array are no longer independent, as they are in the case of a 32-bit-wide multiplexor.

B.4   Clocks

Before we discuss memory elements and sequential logic, it is useful to discuss briefly the topic of clocks. This short section introduces the topic and is similar to the discussion found at the beginning of Chapter 5. More details on clocking and timing methodologies are presented in section B.7.

Clocks are needed in sequential logic to decide when an element that contains state should be updated. A clock is simply a free-running signal with a fixed *cycle time*; the *clock frequency* is simply the inverse of the cycle time. As shown in Figure B.9, the *clock cycle time* or *clock period* is divided into two portions: when the clock is high and when the clock is low. In this text, we use only *edge-triggered clocking*. This means that all state changes occur on a clock edge. We use an edge-triggered methodology because it is simpler to explain. Depending on the technology, it may or may not be the best choice for a clocking methodology.

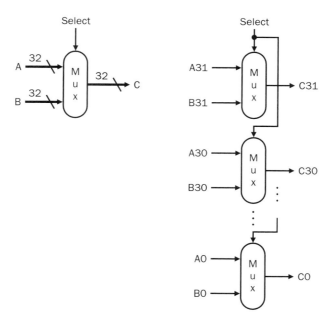

a. A 32-bit wide 2-to-1 multiplexor

b. The 32-bit wide multiplexor is actually an array of 32 1-bit multiplexors

FIGURE B.8   A multiplexor is arrayed 32 times to perform a selection between two 32-bit inputs. Note that there is still only one data selection signal used for all 32-bit multiplexors.

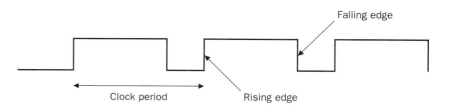

FIGURE B.9   A clock signal oscillates between high and low values. The clock period is the time for one full cycle. In an edge-triggered design, either the rising or falling edge of the clock is active and causes state to be changed.

In an edge-triggered methodology, either the rising edge or the falling edge of the clock is *active* and causes state changes to occur. As we will see in the next section, the state elements in an edge-triggered design are implemented so that the contents of the state elements only change on the active clock edge. The choice of which edge is active is influenced by the implementation technology and does not affect the concepts involved in designing the logic.

The major constraint in a clocked system, also called a *synchronous system*, is that the signals that are written into state elements must be *valid* when the active clock edge occurs. A signal is valid if it is stable (i.e., not changing) and the value will not change again until the inputs change. Since combinational circuits cannot have feedback, if the inputs to a combinational logic unit are not changed, the outputs will eventually become valid. Figure B.10 shows the relationship among the state elements and the combinational logic blocks in a synchronous, sequential logic design. The state elements, whose outputs change only on the clock edge, provide valid inputs to the combinational logic block. To ensure that the values written into the state elements on the active clock edge are valid, the clock must have a long enough period so that all the signals in the combinational logic block stabilize. This constraint sets a lower bound on the length of the clock period. In the rest of this appendix, as well as in Chapters 5 and 6, we usually omit the clock signal, since we are assuming that all state elements are updated on the same clock edge. Some state elements will be written on every clock edge, while others will be written only under certain conditions (such as a register being updated). In such cases, we will have an explicit write signal for that state element. The write signal must still be gated with the clock so that the update occurs only on the clock edge if the write signal is active. We will see how this is done and used in the next section.

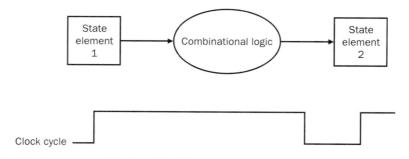

FIGURE B.10   The inputs to a combinational logic block come from a state element, and the outputs are written into a state element. The clock edge determines when the contents of the state elements are updated.

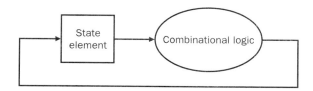

FIGURE B.11 An edge-triggered methodology allows a state element to be read and written in the same clock cycle without creating a race that could lead to undermined data values. Of course, the clock cycle must still be long enough so that the input values are stable when the active clock edge occurs.

One other advantage of an edge-triggered methodology is that it is possible to have a state element that is used as both an input and output to the same combinational logic block, as shown in Figure B.11. In practice, care must be taken to prevent races in such situations and to ensure that the clock period is long enough; this topic is discussed further in section B.7.

Now that we have discussed how clocking is used to update state elements, we can discuss how to construct the state elements.

B.5   Memory Elements

In this section, we discuss the basic principles behind memory elements, starting with flip-flops and latches, moving on to register files, and finally to memories. All memory elements store state: the output from any memory element depends both on the inputs and on the value that has been stored inside the memory element. Thus all logic blocks containing a memory element contain state and are sequential.

The simplest type of memory elements are *unclocked*; that is, they do not have any clock input. Although we only use clocked memory elements in this text, an unclocked latch is the simplest memory element, so let's look at this circuit first. Figure B.12 shows an *S-R latch* (set-reset latch), built from a pair of NOR gates (OR gates with inverted outputs). The outputs Q and $\overline{Q}$ represent the value of the stored state and its complement. When neither S nor R are asserted, the cross-coupled NOR gates act as inverters and store the previous values of Q and $\overline{Q}$. For example, if the output, Q, is true, then the bottom inverter produces a false output (which is $\overline{Q}$), which becomes the input to the top inverter, which produces a true output, which is Q, and so on. If S is asserted then the output Q will be asserted and $\overline{Q}$ will be deasserted, while if R is asserted, then the output $\overline{Q}$ will be asserted and Q will be deasserted. When S and R are both deasserted the last values of Q and $\overline{Q}$ will continue to be stored in the

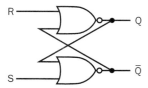

FIGURE B.12 A pair of cross-coupled NOR gates can store an internal value. The value stored on the output Q is recycled by inverting it to obtain $\overline{Q}$ and then inverting $\overline{Q}$ to obtain Q. If either R or $\overline{Q}$ are asserted, Q will be deasserted and vice-versa.

cross-coupled structure. Asserting S and R simultaneously can lead to incorrect operation: depending on how S and R are deasserted, the latch may oscillate or become metastable (this is described in more detail in section B.7).

This cross-coupled structure is the basis for more complex memory elements that allow us to store data signals. These elements contain additional gates used to store signal values and to cause the state to be updated only in conjunction with a clock. The next section shows how these elements are built.

Flip-Flops and Latches

Flip-flops and *latches* are the simplest memory elements. In both flip-flops and latches, the output is equal to the value of the stored state inside the element. Furthermore, unlike the S-R latch described above, all the latches and flip-flops we will use from this point on are clocked, which means they have a clock input and the change of state is triggered by that clock. The difference between a flip-flop and a latch is the point at which the clock causes the state to actually change. In a clocked latch, the state is changed whenever the appropriate inputs change and the clock is asserted, whereas in a flip-flop, the state is changed only on a clock edge. Since throughout this text we use an edge-triggered timing methodology where state is only updated on clock edges, we need only use flip-flops. Flip-flops are often built from latches, so we start by describing the operation of a simple clocked latch and then discuss the operation of a flip-flop constructed from that latch.

For computer applications, the function of both flip-flops and latches is to store a signal. A *D latch* or *D flip-flop* stores the value of its data input signal in the internal memory. Although there are many other types of latches and flip-flops, the D type is the only basic building block that we will need. A D latch has two inputs and two outputs. The inputs are the data value to be stored (called D) and a clock signal (called C) that indicates when the latch should read the value on the D input and store it. The outputs are simply the value of the internal state (Q) and its complement ($\overline{Q}$). When the clock input C is asserted, the latch is said to be *open*, and the value of the output (Q) becomes the value of the input *D*. When the clock input *C* is deasserted, the latch is said to be *closed*, and the value of the output (*Q*) is whatever value was stored the last time the latch was open.

Figure B.13 shows how a D latch can be implemented with two additional gates added to the cross-coupled NOR gates. Since when the latch is open the value of *Q* changes as *D* changes, this structure is sometimes called a *transparent latch*. Figure B.14 shows how this D latch works, assuming that the output *Q* is initially false and that *D* changes first.

As mentioned earlier, we use flip-flops as the basic building block rather than latches. Flip-flops are not transparent: their outputs change *only* on the clock edge. A flip-flop can be built so that it triggers on either the rising (positive) or falling (negative) clock edge; for our designs we can use either type. Figure B.15 shows how a falling-edge D flip-flop is constructed from a pair of D latches. In a D flip-flop, the output is stored when the clock edge occurs. Figure B.16 shows how this flip-flop operates.

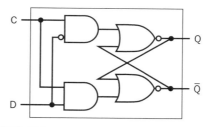

FIGURE B.13 A D latch implemented with NOR gates. A NOR gate acts as an inverter if the other input is 0. Thus, the cross-coupled pair of NOR gates acts to store the state value unless the clock input, *C*, is asserted, in which case the value of input *D* replaces the value of *Q* and is stored. The value of input *D* must be stable when the clock signal *C* changes from asserted to deasserted.

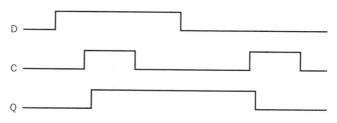

FIGURE B.14 Operation of a D latch assuming the output is initially deasserted. When the clock, *C*, is asserted, the latch is open and the *Q* output immediately assumes the value of the *D* input.

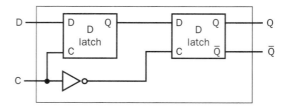

FIGURE B.15 A D flip-flop with a falling-edge trigger. The first latch, called the master, is open and follows the input D when the clock input, C, is asserted. When the clock input, C, falls, the first latch is closed, but the second latch, called the slave, is open and gets its input from the output of the master latch.

Because the D input is sampled on the clock edge, it must be valid for a period of time immediately before and immediately after the clock edge. The minimum time that the input must be valid before the clock edge is called the *set-up time*; the minimum time during which it must be valid after the clock edge is called the *hold time*. Thus the inputs to any flip-flop (or anything built using flip-flops) must be valid during a window that begins at time t_{set-up} before the clock edge and ends at t_{hold} after the clock edge, as shown in Figure B.17. Section B.7 talks about clocking and timing constraints in more detail.

We can use an array of D flip-flops to build a register that can hold a multibit datum, such as a byte or word. We used registers throughout our datapaths in Chapters 5 and 6.

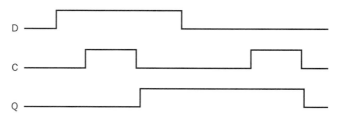

FIGURE B.16 Operation of a D flip-flop with a falling-edge trigger, assuming the output is initially deasserted. When the clock input (C) changes from asserted to deasserted, the Q output stores the value of the D input. Compare this behavior to that of the clocked D latch shown in Figure B.14. In a clocked latch, the stored value and the output, Q, both change whenever C is high, as opposed to only when C transitions.

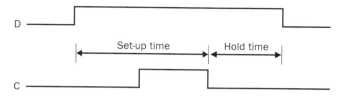

FIGURE B.17 Set-up and hold time requirements for a D flip-flop with a falling-edge trigger. The input must be stable a period of time before the clock edge, as well as after the clock edge. The minimum time the signal must be stable before the clock edge is called the set-up time, while the minimum time the signal must be stable after clock is called the hold time. Failure to meet these minimum requirements can result in a situation where the output of the flip-flop may not even be predictable, as described in section B.7. Hold times are usually either 0 or very small and thus not a cause of worry.

Register Files

One structure that is central to our datapath is a *register file*. A register file consists of a set of registers that can be read and written by supplying a register number to be accessed. A register file can be implemented with a decoder for each read or write port and an array of registers built from D flip-flops. Because reading a register does not change any state, we need only supply a register number as an input, and the only output will be the data contained in that register. For writing a register we will need three inputs: a register number, the data to write, and a clock that controls the writing into the register. In Chapters 5 and 6, we used a register file that has two read ports and one write port. This register file is drawn as shown in Figure B.18. The read ports can be implemented with a pair of multiplexors, each of which is as wide as the number of bits in the register file. Figure B.19 shows the implementation of two register read ports for a 32-bit-wide register file.

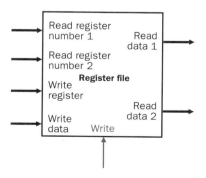

FIGURE B.18 A register file with two read ports and one write port has five inputs and two outputs. The control input Write is shown in color.

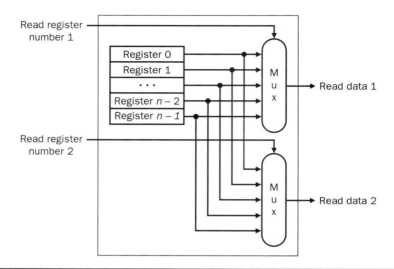

FIGURE B.19   The implementation of two read ports for a register file with _n_ registers can be done with a pair of _n_-to-1 multiplexors each 32 bits wide. The register read number signal is used as the multiplexor selector signal. Figure B.20 shows how the write port is implemented.

Implementing the write port is slightly more complex since we can only change the contents of the designated register. We can do this by using a decoder to generate a signal that can be used to determine which register to write. Figure B.20 shows how to implement the write port for a register file. It is important to remember that the flip-flop changes state only on the clock edge. In Chapters 5 and 6, we hooked up write signals for the register file explicitly and assumed the clock shown in Figure B.20 is attached implicitly.

What happens if the same register is read and written during a clock cycle? Because the write of the register file occurs on the clock edge, the register will be valid during the time it is read, as we saw earlier in Figure B.10. The value returned will be the value written in an earlier clock cycle. If we want a read to return the value currently being written, additional logic in the register file or outside of it is needed. Chapter 6 makes extensive use of such logic.

SRAMs

Registers and register files provide the basic building block for small memories, but larger amounts of memory are built using either *SRAMs* (static random access memories) or *DRAMs* (dynamic random access memories). In this section, we discuss SRAMs, which are somewhat simpler, while the next sec-

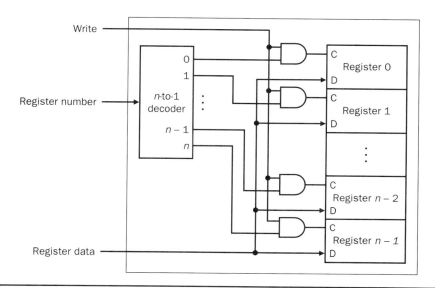

FIGURE B.20 The write port for a register file is implemented with a decoder that is used with the write signal to generate the C input to the registers. All three inputs (the register number, the data, and the write signal) will have set-up and hold-time constraints that ensure that the correct data is written into the register file.

tion discusses DRAMs. SRAMs are simply integrated circuits that are memory arrays with (usually) a single access port that can provide either a read or a write. SRAMs have a fixed access time to any datum, though the read and write access characteristics often differ.

A SRAM chip has a specific configuration in terms of the number of addressable locations, as well as the width of each addressable location. For example, a 256K × 1 SRAM provides 256K entries, each of which is 1 bit wide. Thus it will have 18 address lines (since 256K = 2^{18}), a single data output line, and a single data input line. A 32K × 8 SRAM has the same total number of bits, but will have 15 address lines to address 32K entries each of which holds an 8-bit-wide datum; thus there are eight data output and eight data input lines. As with ROMs, the number of addressable locations is often called the *height*, with the number of bits per unit called the *width*. For a variety of technical reasons, the newest and fastest SRAMs are typically available in narrow configurations: × 1 and × 4. Figure B.21 shows the input and output signals for a 32K × 8 SRAM.

To initiate a read or write access, the Chip select signal must be made active. For reads, we must also activate the Output enable signal that controls whether or not the datum selected by the address is actually driven on the pins. The

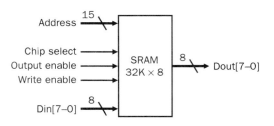

FIGURE B.21   A 32K x 8 SRAM showing the 15 address lines (32K = 2^{15}) and eight data inputs, the three control lines, and the eight data outputs.

Output enable is useful for connecting multiple memories to a single-output bus and using Output enable to determine which memory drives the bus. The SRAM read access time is usually specified as the delay from the time that Output enable is true and the address lines are valid until the time that the data is on the output lines. Typical read access times for SRAMs in 1997 vary from about 5 ns for the fastest CMOS parts to 25-ns parts, which, while slower, are usually cheaper and often denser. The largest SRAMs available in 1997 have over 4 million bits of data.

For writes, we must supply the data to be written and the address, as well as signals to cause the write to occur. When both the Write enable and Chip select are true, the data on the data input lines is written into the cell specified by the address. There are set-up-time and hold-time requirements for the address and data lines, just as there were for D flip-flops and latches. In addition, the Write enable signal is not a clock edge but a pulse with a minimum width requirement. The time to complete a write is specified by the combination of the set-up times, the hold times, and the Write enable pulse width.

Large SRAMs cannot be built in the same way we build a register file because, unlike a register file where a 32-to-1 multiplexor might be practical, the 64K-to-1 multiplexor that would be needed for a 64K × 1 SRAM is totally impractical. Rather than use a giant multiplexor, large memories are implemented with a shared output line, called a *bit line*, which multiple memory cells in the memory array can assert. To allow multiple sources to drive a single line, a *three-state buffer* (or *tri-state buffer*) is used. A three-state buffer has two inputs: a data signal and an Output enable. The single output from a three-state buffer is equal to the asserted or deasserted input signal if the Output enable is asserted, and is otherwise in a *high-impedance state* that allows another three-state buffer whose Output enable is asserted to determine the value of a shared output. Figure B.22 shows a set of three-state buffers wired to form a multiplexor with a decoded input. It is critical that the Output enable of at most one of the three-state buffers be asserted; otherwise, the three-state

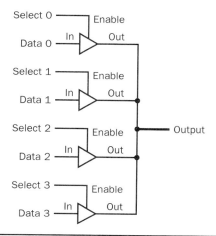

FIGURE B.22   Four three-state buffers are used to form a multiplexor. Only one of the four Select inputs can be asserted. A three-state buffer with a deasserted Output enable, has a high-impedance output that allows a three-state buffer whose Output enable is asserted to drive the shared output line.

buffers may try to set the output line differently. By using three-state buffers in the individual cells of the SRAM, each cell that corresponds to a particular output can share the same output line. The use of a set of distributed three-state buffers is a more efficient implementation than a large centralized multiplexor. The three-state buffers are incorporated into the flip-flops that form the basic cells of the SRAM. Figure B.23 shows how a small 4×2 SRAM might be built, using D latches with an input called Enable that controls the three-state output.

The design in Figure B.23 eliminates the need for an enormous multiplexor; however, it still requires a very large decoder and a correspondingly large number of word lines. For example, in a $16K \times 8$ SRAM, we would need a 14-to-16K decoder and 16K word lines (which are the lines used to enable the individual flip-flops)! To circumvent this problem, large memories are organized as rectangular arrays and use a two-step decoding process. Figure B.24 shows how a $32K \times 8$ SRAM might be organized using a two-step decode. As we will see, the two-level decoding process is quite important in understanding how DRAMs operate.

Recently we have seen the development of both synchronous SRAMs (SSRAMs) and synchronous DRAMs (SDRAMs). The key capability provided by synchronous RAMs is the ability to transfer a *burst* of data from a series of sequential addresses within an array or row. The burst is defined by a starting address, supplied in the usual fashion, and a burst length. The speed advantage of synchronous RAMs comes from the ability to transfer the bits in the

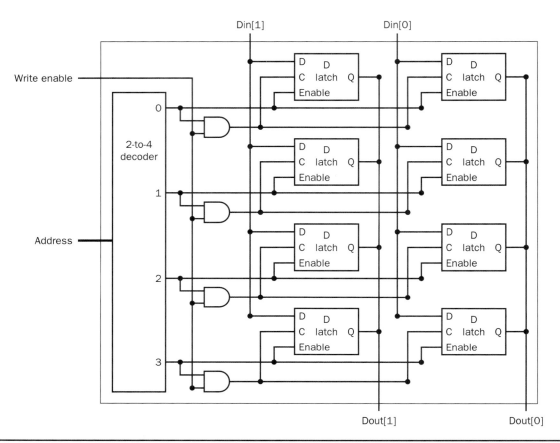

FIGURE B.23   The basic structure of a 4 x 2 SRAM consists of a decoder that selects which pair of cells to activate. The activated cells use a three-state output connected to the vertical bit lines that supply the requested data. The address that selects the cell is sent on one of a set of horizontal address lines, called the word lines. For simplicity, the Output enable and Chip select signals have been omitted, but they could easily be added with a few AND gates.

burst without having to specify additional address bits. Instead, a clock is used to transfer the successive bits in the burst. The elimination of the need to specify the address for the transfers within the burst significantly improves the rate for transferring the block of data. Because of this capability, synchronous SRAMs and DRAMs are rapidly becoming the RAMs of choice for building cache-based systems that naturally do block transfers.

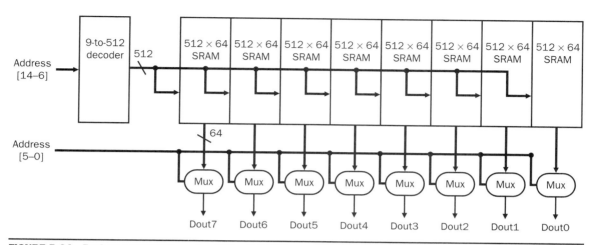

FIGURE B.24   Typical organization of a 32K x 8 SRAM as an array of 512 x 64 arrays. The first decoder generates the addresses for eight 512 × 64 arrays; then a set of multiplexors is used to select 1 bit from each 64-bit-wide array. This is a much easier design than a single-level decode that would need either an enormous decoder (15 to 32K) or a gigantic multiplexor (32K to 1).

DRAMs

In a static RAM (SRAM) the value stored in a cell is kept on a pair of inverting gates, and as long as power is applied, the value can be kept indefinitely. In a dynamic RAM (DRAM), the value kept in a cell is stored as a charge in a capacitor. A single transistor is then used to access this stored charge, either to read the value or to overwrite the charge stored there. Because DRAMs use only a single transistor per bit of storage, they are much denser and cheaper per bit. By comparison, SRAMs require four to six transistors per bit. In DRAMs, the charge is stored on a capacitor, so it cannot be kept indefinitely and must periodically be *refreshed*. That is why this memory structure is called *dynamic*, as opposed to the static storage in an SRAM cell. To refresh the cell, we merely read its contents and write it back. The charge can be kept for several milliseconds, which might correspond to close to a million clock cycles. Today, single-chip memory controllers often handle the refresh function independently of the processor. If every bit had to be read out of the DRAM and then be written back individually, with large DRAMs containing multiple megabytes, we would constantly be refreshing the DRAM, leaving no time for accessing it. Fortunately, DRAMs also use a two-level decoding structure, and this allows us to refresh an entire row (which shares a word line) with a read cycle followed immediately by a write cycle. Typically, refresh operations consume 1% to 2% of the active cycles of the DRAM, leaving the remaining 98% to 99% of the cycles available for reading and writing data.

Elaboration: How does a DRAM read and write the signal stored in a cell? The transistor inside the cell is a switch, called a *pass transistor*, that allows the value stored on the capacitor to be accessed for either reading or writing. Figure B.25 shows how the single-transistor cell looks. The pass transistor acts like a switch: when the signal on the word line is asserted, the switch is closed, connecting the capacitor to the bit line. If the operation is a write, then the value to be written is placed on the bit line. If the value is a 1, the capacitor will be charged. If the value is a 0, then the capacitor will be discharged. Reading is slightly more complex, since the DRAM must detect a very small charge stored in the capacitor. Before activating the word line for a read, the bit line is charged to the voltage that is halfway between the low and high voltage. Then, by activating the word line, the charge on the capacitor is read out onto the bit line. This causes the bit line to move slightly toward the high or low direction, and this change is detected with a sense amplifier, which can detect small changes in voltage.

DRAMs use a two-level decoder, as shown in Figure B.26, consisting of a *row access*, followed by a *column access*. The row access chooses one of a number of rows and activates the corresponding word line. The contents of all the columns in the active row are then stored in a set of latches. The column access then selects the data from the column latches. To save pins and reduce the package cost, the same address lines are used for both the row and column address; a pair of signals called RAS (Row Access Strobe) and CAS (Column Access Strobe) are used to signal the DRAM that either a row or column address is being supplied. Refresh is performed by simply reading the columns into the column latches and then writing the same values back. Thus an entire row is refreshed in one cycle. The two-level addressing scheme, combined with the internal circuitry, make DRAM access times much longer (by a factor of 5 to 10) than SRAM access times. In 1997, typical DRAM access times range from 60 to 110 ns. The much lower cost per bit makes DRAM the choice for main memory, while the faster access time makes SRAM the choice for caches.

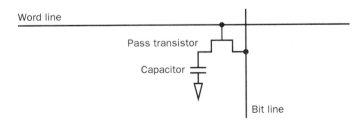

FIGURE B.25   A single-transistor DRAM cell contains a capacitor that stores the cell contents and a transistor used to access the cell.

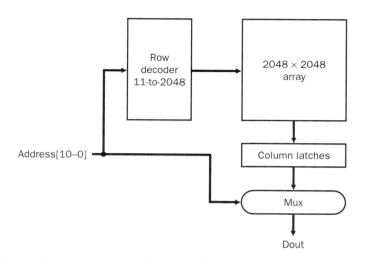

FIGURE B.26   A 4M x 1 DRAM is built with a 2048 x 2048 array. The row access uses 11 bits to select a row, which is then latched in 2048 1-bit latches. A multiplexor chooses the output bit from these 2048 latches. The RAS and CAS signals control whether the address lines are sent to the row decoder or column multiplexor.

You might observe that a 4M × 1 DRAM actually accesses 2048 bits on every row access and then throws away 2047 of those during a column access. DRAM designers have used the internal structure of the DRAM as a way to provide higher bandwidth out of a DRAM. This is done by allowing the column address to change without changing the row address, resulting in an access to other bits in the column latches. *Page-mode* and *static-column-mode* RAMs both provide the ability to access multiple bits out of a row by changing the column address only. (The difference is whether CAS must also be reasserted or not.) *Nibble-mode* RAMs internally generate the next three column addresses, thus providing 4 bits (called a *nibble*) for every row access. EDO (Extended Data Out) represents that latest version in page-mode style RAMs. In 1997, EDO RAMs have become standard for most applications, and provide access times within a row as low as 25 ns. In 1997, SDRAMs are gaining broad acceptance; as stated above, SDRAMs provide even faster access to a series of bits within a row by eliminating the need to specify the column address, instead sequentially transferring all the bits in a burst under the control of a clock signal. As we discussed in Chapter 7, these modes can be used to boost the bandwidth available out of main memory to match the needs of the processor and caches.

Error Correction

Because of the potential for data corruption in large memories, most computer systems use some sort of error-checking code to detect possible corruption of data. One simple code that is heavily used is a *parity code*. In a parity code the number of 1s in a word is counted; the word has odd parity if the number of 1s is odd and even otherwise. When a word is written into memory, the parity bit is also written (1 for odd, 0 for even). Then, when the word is read out, the parity bit is read and checked. If the parity of the memory word and the stored parity bit do not match, an error has occurred. A 1-bit parity scheme can detect at most 1 bit of error in a data item; if there are 2 bits of error, then a 1-bit parity scheme will not detect any errors, since the parity will match the data with two errors. (Actually, a 1-bit parity scheme can detect any odd number of errors; however, the probability of having three errors is much lower than the probability of having two, so, in practice, a 1-bit parity code is limited to detecting a single bit of error.) Of course, a parity code cannot tell which bit in a data item is in error.

A 1-bit parity scheme is an error-detecting code; there are also *error-correcting codes* (ECC) that will detect and allow correction of an error. For large main memories, many systems use a code that allows the detection of up to 2 bits of error and the correction of a single bit of error. These codes work by using more bits to encode the data; for example, the typical codes used for main memories require 7 or 8 bits for every 128 bits of data.

Elaboration: A 1-bit parity code is a *distance-2 code*, which means that if we look at the data plus the parity bit, no 1-bit change is sufficient to generate another legal combination of the data plus parity. For example, if we change a bit in the data, the parity will be wrong, and vice versa. Of course, if we change 2 bits (any 2 data bits or 1 data bit and the parity bit), the parity will match the data and the error cannot be detected. Hence, there is a distance of two between legal combinations of parity and data.

To detect more than one error or correct an error, we need a *distance-3 code*, which has the property that any legal combination of the bits in the error correction code and the data have at least 3 bits differing from any other combination. Suppose we have such a code and we have one error in the data. In that case the code plus data will be 1 bit away from a legal combination and we can correct the data to that legal combination. If we have two errors, we can recognize that there is an error, but we cannot correct the errors. Let's look at an example. Here are the data words and a distance-3 error correction code for a 4-bit data item.

Data	Code bits	Data	Code bits
0000	000	1000	111
0001	011	1001	100
0010	101	1010	010
0011	110	1011	001
0100	110	1100	001
0101	101	1101	010
0110	011	1110	100
0111	000	1111	111

To see how this works, let's choose a data word, say 0110, whose error correction code is 011. Here are the four 1-bit error possibilities for this data: 1110, 0010, 0100, and 0111. Now look at the data item with the same code (011), which is the entry with the value 0001. If the error correction decoder received one of the four possible data words with an error, it would have to choose between correcting to 0110 or 0001. While these four words with error have only 1 bit changed from the correct pattern of 0110, they each have 2 bits that are different from the alternate correction of 0001. Hence the error correction mechanism can easily choose to correct to 0110, since a single error is much lower probability. To see that two errors can be detected, simply notice that all the combinations with 2 bits changed have a different code. The one reuse of the same code is with 3 bits different, but if we correct a 2-bit error, we will correct to the wrong value, since the decoder will assume that only a single error has occurred. If we want to correct 1-bit errors and detect, but not erroneously correct, 2-bit errors, we need a distance-4 code.

Although we distinguished between the code and data in our explanation, in truth, an error correction code treats the combination of code and data as a single word in a larger code (7 bits in this example). Thus it deals with errors in the code bits in the same fashion as errors in the data bits.

While the above example requires $n - 1$ bits for n bits of data, the number of bits required grows slowly, so that for a distance-3 code, a 64-bit word needs 7 bits and a 128-bit word needs 8. This type of code is called a *Hamming code*, after R. Hamming, who described a method for creating such codes.

B.6 Finite State Machines

As we saw earlier, digital logic systems can be classified as combinational or sequential. Sequential systems contain state stored in memory elements internal to the system. Their behavior depends both on the set of inputs supplied and on the contents of the internal memory, or state of the system. Thus a sequential system cannot be described with a truth table. Instead, a sequential system is described as a *finite state machine* (or often just *state machine*). A finite state machine has a set of states and two functions called the *next-state function* and the *output function*. The set of states correspond to all the possible values of the internal storage. Thus, if there are n bits of storage, there are 2^n states. The next-state function is a combinational function that, given the inputs and the current state, determines the next state of the system. The output function produces a set of outputs from the current state and the inputs. Figure B.27 shows this diagrammatically.

The state machines we discuss here and in Chapter 5 are *synchronous*. This means that the state changes together with the clock cycle, and a new state is computed once every clock. Thus, the state elements are updated only on the clock edge. We use this methodology in this section and throughout Chapters

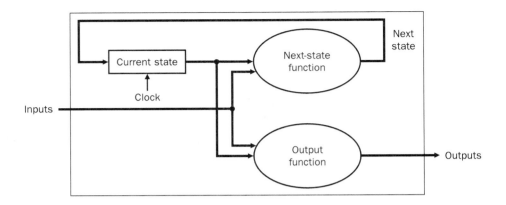

FIGURE B.27 A state machine consists of internal storage that contains the state and two combinational functions: the next-state function and the output function. Often, the output function is restricted to take only the current state as its input; this does not change the capability of a sequential machine, but does affect its internals.

5 and 6, and we do not usually show the clock explicitly. We use state machines throughout Chapters 5 and 6 to control the execution of the processor and the actions of the datapath.

To illustrate how a finite state machine operates and is designed, let's look at a simple and classic example: controlling a traffic light. (Chapters 5 and 6 contain more detailed examples of using finite state machines to control processor execution.) When a finite state machine is used as a controller, the output function is often restricted to depend on just the current state. Such a finite state machine is called a *Moore machine*. This is the type of finite state machine we use throughout this book. If the output function can depend on both the next state and the current input, the machine is called a *Mealy machine*. These two machines are equivalent in their capabilities, and one can be turned into the other mechanically. The basic advantage of a Moore machine is that it can be faster, while a Mealy machine may be smaller, since it may need fewer states than a Moore machine. We discuss this distinction further in Chapter 5 (pages 398–399).

Our example concerns the control of a traffic light at an intersection of a north-south route and an east-west route. For simplicity, we will consider only the green and red lights; adding the yellow light is left for an exercise. We want the lights to cycle no faster than 30 seconds in each direction, so we will use a 0.033-Hz clock so that the machine cycles between states at no faster than once every 30 seconds. There are two output signals.

- *NSlite:* When this signal is asserted, the light on the north-south road is green; when this signal is deasserted the light on the north-south road is red.

■ *EWlite:* When this signal is asserted, the light on the east-west road is green; when this signal is deasserted the light on the east-west road is red.

In addition, there are two inputs: NScar and EWcar.

■ *NScar:* Indicates that a car is over the detector placed in the roadbed in front of the light on the north-south road (going north or south).

■ *EWcar:* Indicates that a car is over the detector placed in the roadbed in front of the light on the east-west road (going east or west).

The traffic light should change from one direction to the other only if a car is waiting to go in the other direction; otherwise, the light should continue to show green in the same direction as the last car that crossed the intersection.

To implement this simple traffic light we need two states:

■ *NSgreen:* The traffic light is green in the north-south direction.

■ *EWgreen:* The traffic light is green in the east-west direction.

We also need to create the next-state function, which can be specified with a table.

Current state	Inputs		Next state
	NScar	**EWcar**	
NSgreen	0	0	NSgreen
NSgreen	0	1	EWgreen
NSgreen	1	0	NSgreen
NSgreen	1	1	EWgreen
EWgreen	0	0	EWgreen
EWgreen	0	1	EWgreen
EWgreen	1	0	NSgreen
EWgreen	1	1	NSgreen

Notice that we didn't specify in the algorithm what happens when a car approaches from both directions. In this case, the next-state function given above changes the state to ensure that a steady stream of cars from one direction cannot lock out a car in the other direction.

The finite state machine is completed by specifying the output function:

Current state	Outputs	
	NSlite	**EWlite**
NSgreen	1	0
EWgreen	0	1

Before we examine how to implement this finite state machine, lets look at a graphical representation, which is often used for finite state machines. In this representation, nodes are used to indicate states. Inside the node we place a list of the outputs that are active for that state. Directed arcs are used to show the next-state function, with labels on the arcs specifying the input condition as logic functions. The graphical representation for this finite state machine is shown in Figure B.28.

A finite state machine can be implemented with a register to hold the current state and a block of combinational logic that computes the next-state function and the output function. Figure B.29 shows how a finite state machine with 4 bits of state, and thus up to 16 states, might look. To implement the finite state machine in this way, we must first assign state numbers to the states. This process is called *state assignment*. For example, we could assign NSgreen to state 0 and EWgreen to state 1. The state register would contain a single bit. The next-state function would be given as

$$\text{NextState} = (\overline{\text{CurrentState} \cdot \text{EWcar}}) + (\text{CurrentState} \cdot \overline{\text{NScar}})$$

where CurrentState is the contents of the state register (0 or 1) and NextState is the output of the next-state function that will be written into the state register at the end of the clock cycle. The output function is also simple:

$$\text{NSlite} = \overline{\text{CurrentState}}$$

$$\text{EWlite} = \text{CurrentState}$$

The combinational logic block is often implemented using structured logic, such as a PLA. A PLA can be constructed automatically from the next-state and output-function tables. In fact, there are computer-aided design (CAD)

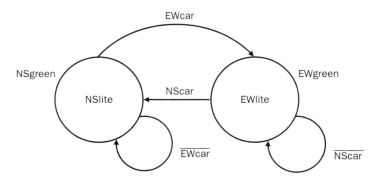

FIGURE B.28 The graphical representation of the two-state traffic light controller. We simplified the logic functions on the state transitions. For example, the transition from NSgreen to EWgreen in the next-state table is $(\text{NScar} \cdot \text{EWcar}) + (\overline{\text{NScar}} \cdot \text{EWcar})$, which is equivalent to EWcar.

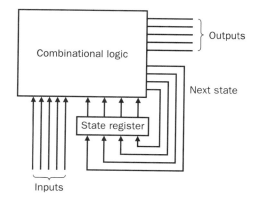

FIGURE B.29 A finite state machine is implemented with a state register that holds the current state and a combinational logic block to compute the next state and output functions. The latter two functions are often split apart and implemented with two separate blocks of logic, which may require fewer gates.

programs that take either a graphical or textual representation of a finite state machine and produce an optimized implementation automatically. In Chapters 5 and 6, finite state machines were used to control processor execution. Appendix C will discuss the detailed implementation of these controllers with both PLAs and ROMs.

B.7 Timing Methodologies

Throughout this appendix and in the rest of the text, we use an edge-triggered timing methodology. This timing methodology has the advantage that it is simpler to explain and understand than a level-triggered methodology. In this section, we explain this timing methodology in a little more detail and also introduce level-sensitive clocking. We conclude this section by briefly discussing the issue of asynchronous signals and synchronizers, an important problem for digital designers.

The purpose of this section is to introduce the major concepts in clocking methodology. The section makes some important simplifying assumptions; if you are interested in understanding timing methodology in more detail, consult one of the references listed at the end of this appendix.

We use an edge-triggered timing methodology because it is simpler to explain and has fewer rules required for correctness. In particular, if we assume that all clocks arrive at the same time, we are guaranteed that a system with edge-triggered registers between blocks of combinational logic can operate correctly without races, if we simply make the clock long enough. A *race* occurs when the contents of a state element depend on the relative speed of different logic elements. In an edge-triggered design, the clock cycle must be long enough to accommodate the path from one flip-flop through the combinational logic to another flip-flop where it must satisfy the set-up time requirement. Figure B.30 shows this requirement for a system using rising edge-triggered flip-flops. In such a system the clock period (or cycle time) must be at least as large as

$$t_{prop} + t_{combinational} + t_{setup}$$

for the worst-case values of these three delays. The simplifying assumption is that the hold-time requirements are satisfied. Satisfying the hold-time requirements in most designs is not a problem, since the propagation time (t_{prop}) is always larger than the hold time for a flip-flop.

One additional complication that must be considered in edge-triggered designs is *clock skew*. Clock skew is the difference in absolute time between when two state elements see a clock edge. Clock skew arises because the clock signal will often use two different paths, with slightly different delays, to reach two different state elements. If the clock skew is large enough, it may be possible for a state element to change and cause the input to another flip-flop to change before the clock edge is seen by the second flip-flop. Figure B.31 illustrates this problem, ignoring set-up time and flip-flop propagation delay. To avoid incorrect operation, the clock period is increased to allow for the maximum clock skew. Thus, the clock period must be longer than

$$t_{prop} + t_{combinational} + t_{setup} + t_{skew}$$

With this constraint on the clock period, the two clocks can also arrive in the opposite order, with the second clock arriving t_{skew} earlier, and the circuit will

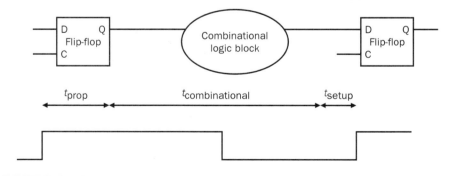

FIGURE B.30 In an edge-triggered design, the clock must be long enough to allow signals to be valid for the required set-up time before the next clock edge. The time for a flip-flop input to propagate to the flip-flip outputs is t_{prop}; the signal then takes $t_{combinational}$ to travel through the combinational logic and must be valid t_{setup} before the next clock edge.

FIGURE B.31   Illustration of how clock skew can cause a race, leading to incorrect operation. Because of the difference in when the two flip-flops see the clock, the signal that is stored into the first flip-flop can race forward and change the input to the second flip-flop before the clock arrives at the second flip-flop.

work correctly. Designers reduce clock skew problems by carefully routing the clock signal to minimize the difference in arrival times. In addition, smart designers also provide some margin by making the clock a little longer than the minimum; this allows for variation in components as well in the power supply. Since clock skew can also affect the hold-time requirements, minimizing the size of the clock skew is important.

Edge-triggered designs have two drawbacks: they require extra logic and they may sometimes be slower. Just looking at the D flip-flop versus the level-sensitive latch that we used to construct the flip-flop shows that edge-triggered design requires more logic. An alternative is to use *level-sensitive clocking*. Because state changes in a level-sensitive methodology are not instantaneous, a level-sensitive scheme is slightly more complex and requires additional care to make it operate correctly.

Level-Sensitive Timing

In a level-sensitive timing methodology, the state changes occur at either high or low levels, but they are not instantaneous as they are in an edge-triggered methodology. Because of the noninstantaneous change in state, races can easily occur. To ensure that a level-sensitive design will also work correctly if the clock is slow enough, designers use *two-phase clocking*. Two-phase clocking is a scheme that makes use of two nonoverlapping clock signals. Since the two clocks, typically called ϕ_1 and ϕ_2, are nonoverlapping, at most one of the clock signals is high at any given time, as shown in Figure B.32. We can use these two clocks to build a system that contains level-sensitive latches but is free from any race conditions, just as the edge-triggered designs were.

One simple way to design such a system is to alternate the use of latches that are open on ϕ_1 with latches that are open on ϕ_2. Because both clocks are not asserted at the same time, a race cannot occur. If the input to a combinational block is a ϕ_1 clock, then its output is latched by a ϕ_2 clock, which is open only during ϕ_2 when the input latch is closed and hence has a valid output. Figure

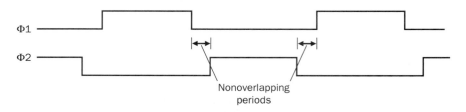

FIGURE B.32   A two-phase clocking scheme showing the cycle of each clock and the non-overlapping periods.

B.33 shows how a system with two-phase timing and alternating latches operates. As in an edge-triggered design, we must pay attention to clock skew, particularly between the two clock phases. By increasing the amount of nonoverlap between the two phases, we can reduce the potential margin of error. Thus the system is guaranteed to operate correctly if each phase is long enough and there is large enough nonoverlap between the phases.

Asynchronous Inputs and Synchronizers

By using a single clock or a two-phase clock, we can eliminate race conditions if clock skew problems are avoided. Unfortunately, it is impractical to make an entire system function with a single clock and still keep the clock skew small. While the CPU may use a single clock, I/O devices will probably have their own clock. In Chapter 8, we showed how an asynchronous device may communicate with the CPU through a series of handshaking steps. To translate the asynchronous input to a synchronous signal that can be used to change the state of a system, we need to use a *synchronizer*, whose inputs are the asynchronous signal and a clock and whose output is a signal synchronous with the input clock.

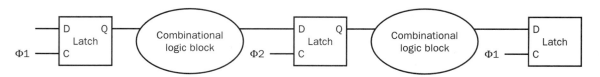

FIGURE B.33   A two-phase timing scheme with alternating latches showing how the system operates on both clock phases. The output of a latch is stable on the opposite phase from its C input. Thus, the first block of combinational inputs has a stable input during ϕ_2 and its output is latched by ϕ_2. The second (rightmost) combinational block operates in just the opposite fashion with stable inputs during ϕ_1. Thus the delays through the combinational blocks determine the minimum time that the respective clocks must be asserted. The size of the nonoverlapping period is determined by the maximum clock skew and the minimum delay of any logic block.

Our first attempt to build a synchronizer uses an edge-triggered D flip-flop, whose *D* input is the asynchronous signal, as shown in Figure B.34. Because we communicate with a handshaking protocol (as we will see in Chapter 8), it does not matter whether we detect the asserted state of the asynchronous signal on one clock or the next, since the signal will be held asserted until it is acknowledged. Thus, you might think that this simple structure is enough to sample the signal accurately, which would be the case except for one small problem.

The problem is a situation called *metastability*. Suppose the asynchronous signal is transitioning between high and low when the clock edge arrives. Clearly, it is not possible to know whether the signal will be latched as high or low. That problem we could live with. Unfortunately, the situation is worse: when the signal that is sampled is not stable for the required set-up and hold times, the flip-flop may go into a *metastable* state. In such a state, the output will not have a legitimate high or low value, but will be in the indeterminate region between them. Furthermore, the flip-flop is not guaranteed to exit this state in any bounded amount of time. Some logic blocks that look at the output of the flip-flop may see its output as 0, while others may see it as 1. This situation is called a *synchronizer failure*. In a purely synchronous system, synchronizer failure can be avoided by ensuring that the set-up and hold times for a flip-flop or latch are always met, but this is impossible when the input is asynchronous. Instead, the only solution possible is to wait long enough before looking at the output of the flip-flop to ensure that its output is stable, and that it has exited the metastable state, if it ever entered it. How long is long enough? Well, the probability that the flip-flop will stay in the metastable state decreases exponentially, so after a very short time the probability that the flip-flop is in the metastable state is very low; however, the probability never reaches 0! So designers wait long enough that the probability of a synchronizer failure is very low, and the time between such failures will be years or even thousands of years. For most flip-flop designs, waiting for a period that is several times longer than the set-up time makes the probability of synchronization failure very low. If the clock rate is longer than the potential metastability period

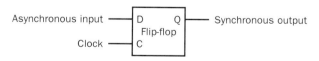

FIGURE B.34 A synchronizer built from a D flip-flop is used to sample an asynchronous signal to produce an output that is synchronous with the clock. This "synchronizer" will *not* work properly!

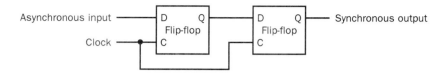

FIGURE B.35 This synchronizer will work correctly if the period of metastability that we wish to guard against is less than the clock period. Although the output of the first flip-flop may be metastable, it will not be seen by any other logic element until the second clock, when the second D flip-flop samples the signal, which by that time should no longer be in a metastable state.

(which is likely), then a safe synchronizer can be built with two D flip-flops, as shown in Figure B.35. If you are interested in reading more about these problems, look into the references.

B.8   Concluding Remarks

This appendix introduces the basics of logic design. If you have digested the material in this appendix, you are ready to tackle the material in Chapters 5 and 6, both of which use the concepts discussed in this appendix extensively.

To Probe Further

There are a number of good texts on logic design. Here are some you might like to look into.

Katz, R. H. [1993]. *Modern Logic Design,* Benjamin/Cummings, Redwood City, CA.

A general text on logic design.

McCluskey, E. J. [1986]. *Logic Design Principles,* Prentice Hall, Englewood Cliffs, NJ.

Contains extensive discussions of hazards, optimization principles, and testability.

Mead, C., and L. Conway [1980]. *Introduction to VLSI Systems,* Addison-Wesley, New York.

Discusses the design of VLSI systems using nMOS technology.

Proser, F. P., and D. E. Winkel [1987]. *The Art of Digital Design,* second edition, Prentice Hall, Englewood Cliffs, NJ.

A general text on logic design.

Wakerly, J. F. [1990]. *Digital Design: Principles and Practices,* Prentice Hall, Englewood Cliffs, NJ.

A general text on logic design.

B.9 Key Terms

This appendix introduces a number of major terms that may be new to you. These key terms are listed below. If you have only browsed this appendix, the key terms should provide a good review. All of these terms are defined in the Glossary at the back of this book.

asserted signal
bus
clock skew
clocking methodology
combinational logic
D flip-flop
deasserted signal
decoder
edge-triggered clocking
finite state machine
flip-flop
gate
hold time

latch
level-sensitive clocking
metastability
minterm or product term
NAND gate
next-state function
NOR gate
page mode
programmable logic array (PLA)
programmable ROM (PROMs)
propagation time

read-only memory (ROM)
register file
selector or control value
sequential logic
set-up time
state element
static random access memory (SRAM)
sum of products
synchronizer failure
synchronous system

B.10 Exercises

B.1 [10] <§B.2> Show that there are 2^n entries in a truth table for a function with n inputs.

B.2 [10] <§B.2> One logic function that is used for a variety of purposes (including within adders and to compute parity) is *exclusive OR*. The output of a two-input exclusive-OR function is true only if exactly one of the inputs is true. Show the truth table for a two-input exclusive-OR function and implement this function using AND gates, OR gates, and inverters.

B.3 [15] <§B.2> Prove that the NOR gate is universal by showing how to build the AND, OR, and NOT functions using a two-input NOR gate.

B.4 [15] <§B.2> Prove that the NAND gate is universal by showing how to build the AND, OR, and NOT functions using a two-input NAND gate.

B.5 [15] <§§B.2, B.3> Prove that a two-input multiplexor is also universal by showing how to build the AND, OR, and NOT functions using a multiplexor.

In More Depth

DeMorgan's Theorems

In addition to the basic laws we discussed on pages B-5 and B-6, there are two important theorems, called DeMorgan's theorems, which are

$$\overline{A + B} = \overline{A} \cdot \overline{B} \quad \text{and} \quad \overline{A \cdot B} = \overline{A} + \overline{B}$$

B.6 [10] <§B.2> Prove DeMorgan's theorems with a truth table of the form

A	B	$\overline{A}$	$\overline{B}$	$\overline{A} + \overline{B}$	$\overline{A} \cdot \overline{B}$	$\overline{A \cdot B}$	$\overline{A + B}$
0	0						
0	1						
1	0						
1	1						

B.7 [15] <§B.2> Prove that the two equations for E in the example starting on page B-6 are equivalent by using DeMorgan's theorems and the axioms shown on page B-6.

B.8 [15] <§§B.2–B.3> Derive the product-of-sums representation for E shown on page B-10 starting with the sum-of-products representation. You will need to use DeMorgan's theorems.

B.9 [30] <§§B.2–B.3> Give an algorithm for constructing the sum-of-products representation for an arbitrary logic equation consisting of AND, OR, and NOT. The algorithm should be recursive and should not construct the truth table in the process.

B.10 [5] <§§4.2, B.2, B.3> Assume that X consists of 3 bits, x2 x1 x0. Write four logic functions that are true if and only if

- X contains only one 1
- X contains an even number of 1s
- X when interpreted as an unsigned binary number is less than 3
- X when interpreted as a signed (two's complement) number is less than –1

B.11 [5] <§§4.2, B.2, B.3> {Ex. B.10} Implement the four functions described in Exercise B.10 using a PLA.

B.12 [5] <§§4.2, B.2, B.3> Assume that X consists of 3 bits, x2 x1 x0, and Y consists of 3 bits, y2 y1 y0. Write logic functions that are true if and only if

- X < Y, where X and Y are thought of as unsigned binary numbers

- X < Y, where X and Y are thought of as signed (two's complement) numbers
- X = Y

B.13 [5] <§§B.2, B.3> Show a truth table for a multiplexor (inputs A, B, and S; output C), using don't cares to simplify the table where possible.

B.14 [5] <§§B.2, B.3> Implement a switching network that has two data inputs (A and B), two data outputs (C and D), and a control input (S). If S equals 1, the network is in pass-through mode, and C should equal A, and D should equal B. If S equals 0, the network is in crossing mode, and C should equal B, and D should equal A.

B.15 [10] <§§B.2, B.5> Construct the truth table for a four-input even-parity function (see page B-34 for a description of parity).

B.16 [10] <§§B.2, B.5> Implement the four-input even-parity function with AND and OR gates using bubbled inputs and outputs.

B.17 [10] <§§B.2, B.3, B.5> Implement the four-input even-parity function with a PLA.

B.18 [5] <§B.5> Which of the following two code fragments better describes a D latch? Which better describes a D flip-flop?

```
repeat
  while (clock==low) do
    {} \* nothing *\
  Q = D;
  while (clock==high) do
    {} \* nothing *\
until (power_goes_off)
```

or

```
repeat
  while (clock==high) do
    Q = D
until (the_battery_wears_out)
```

B.19 [5] <§B.5> Quite often, you would expect that given a timing diagram containing a description of changes that take place on a data input D and a clock input C (as in Figures B.14 and B.17 on pages B-23 and B-25, respectively), there would be differences between the output waveforms (Q) for a D latch and a D flip-flop. In a sentence or two, describe the circumstances (e.g., the nature of the inputs) for which there would not be any difference between the two output waveforms.

B.20 [5] <§B.5> Figure B.19 on page B-26 illustrates the implementation of the register file for the MIPS datapath. Pretend that a new register file is to be built, but that there are only two registers and only one read port, and that each register has only 2 bits of data. Redraw Figure B.19 so that every wire in your diagram corresponds to only 1 bit of data (unlike the diagram in Figure B.19, in which some wires are 5 bits and some wires are 32 bits). Redraw the registers using D flip-flops. You do not need to show how to implement a D flip-flop or a multiplexor.

B.21 [10] <§B.6> A friend would like you to build an "electronic eye" for use as a fake security device. The device consists of three lights lined up in a row, controlled by the outputs Left, Middle, and Right, which, if asserted, indicate that a light should be on. Only one light is on at a time, and the light "moves" from left to right and then from right to left, thus scaring away thieves who believe that the device is monitoring their activity. Draw the graphical representation for the finite state machine used to specify the electronic eye. Note that the rate of the eye's movement will be controlled by the clock speed (which should not be too great) and that there are essentially no inputs.

B.22 [10] <§B.6> {Ex. B.21} Assign state numbers to the states of the finite state machine you constructed for Exercise B.21 and write a set of logic equations for each of the outputs, including the next state bits.

B.23 [15] <§§B.2, B.5> Construct a 3-bit counter using three D flip-flops and a selection of gates. The inputs should consist of a signal that resets the counter to 0, called *reset*, and a signal to increment the counter, called *inc*. The outputs should be the value of the counter. When the counter has value 7 and is incremented, it should wrap around and become 0.

B.24 [20] <§§B.3, B.5> A *Gray code* is a sequence of binary numbers with the property that no more than 1 bit changes in going from one element of the sequence to another. For example, here is a 3-bit binary Gray code: 000, 001, 011, 010, 110, 111, 101, and 100. Using three D flip-flops and a PLA, construct a 3-bit Gray code counter that has two inputs: *reset*, which sets the counter to 000, and *inc*, which makes the counter go to the next value in the sequence. Note that the code is cyclic, so that the value after 100 in the sequence is 000.

B.25 [25] <§§B.2, B.6> We wish to add a yellow light to our traffic light example on page B-36. We will do this by changing the clock to run at 0.25 Hz (a 4-second clock cycle time), which is the duration of a yellow light. To prevent the green and red lights from cycling too fast, we add a 30-second timer. The timer has a single input, called *TimerReset*, which restarts the timer, and a single output, called *TimerSignal*, which indicates that the 30-second period has expired. Also, we must redefine the traffic signals to include yellow. We do this by defining two output signals for each light: green and yellow. If the output NS-green is asserted, the green light is on; if the output NSyellow is asserted, the yellow light is on. If both signals are off, the red light is on. Do *not* assert both the green and yellow signals at the same time, since American drivers will certainly be confused, even if European drivers understand what this means! Draw the graphical representation for the finite state machine for this improved controller. Choose names for the states that are *different* from the names of the outputs.

B.26 [15] <§B.6> Write down the next-state and output-function tables for the traffic light controller described in Exercise B.25.

B.27 [15] <§§B.2, B.6> Assign state numbers to the states in the traffic light example of Exercise B.25 and use the tables of Exercise B.26 to write a set of logic equations for each of the outputs, including the next-state outputs.

B.28 [15] <§§B.3, B.6> Implement the logic equations of Exercise B.27 as a PLA.

Mapping Control
to Hardware

*A custom format such as this
is slave to the architecture of
the hardware and the instruction set
it serves. The format must strike
a proper compromise between
ROM size, ROM-output decoding,
circuitry size, and machine
execution rate.*

Jim McKevit et al.
8086 design report, 1977

C.1   Introduction

Control typically has two parts: a combinational part that lacks state and a sequential control unit that handles sequencing and the main control in a multicycle design. Combinational control units are often used to handle part of the decode and control process. The ALU control in Chapter 5 is such an example. A single-cycle implementation like that in Chapter 5 can also use a combinational controller, since it does not require multiple states. Section C.2 examines the implementation of these two combinational units from the truth tables of Chapter 5.

Since sequential control units are larger and often more complex, there are a wider variety of techniques for implementing a sequential control unit. The usefulness of these techniques depends on the complexity of the control, characteristics such as the average number of next states for any given state, and the implementation technology.

The most straightforward way to implement a sequential control function is with a block of logic that takes as inputs the current state and the opcode field of the Instruction register and produces as outputs the datapath control signals and the value of the next state. The initial representation may be either a finite state diagram or a microprogram. In the latter case, each microinstruction represents a state. In an implementation using a finite state controller, the next-state function will be computed with logic. Section C.3 constructs such an implementation both for a ROM and a PLA.

An alternative method of implementation computes the next-state function by using a counter that increments the current state to determine the next state. When the next state doesn't follow sequentially, other logic is used to determine the state. Section C.4 explores this type of implementation and shows how it can be used for the finite state control created in Chapter 5.

In section C.5, we show how a microprogram representation of sequential control is translated to control logic.

C.2   Implementing Combinational Control Units

In this section, we show how the ALU control unit and main control unit for the single clock design are mapped down to the gate level. With modern CAD systems this process is completely mechanical. The examples illustrate how a CAD system takes advantage of the structure of the control function, including the presence of don't-care terms.

Mapping the ALU Control Function to Gates

Figure C.1 shows the truth table for the ALU control function that was developed in section 5.3. A logic block that implements this ALU control function will have three distinct outputs (called Operation2, Operation1, and Operation0), each corresponding to one of the three bits of the ALU control in the last column of Figure C.1. The logic function for each output is constructed by combining all the truth table entries that set that particular output. For example, the low-order bit of the ALU control (Operation0) is set by the last two entries of the truth table in Figure C.1. Thus the truth table for Operation0 will have these two entries.

ALUOp		Funct field						Operation
ALUOp1	ALUOp0	F5	F4	F3	F2	F1	F0	
0	0	X	X	X	X	X	X	010
X	1	X	X	X	X	X	X	110
1	X	X	X	0	0	0	0	010
1	X	X	X	0	0	1	0	110
1	X	X	X	0	1	0	0	000
1	X	X	X	0	1	0	1	001
1	X	X	X	1	0	1	0	111

FIGURE C.1   The truth table for the three ALU control bits (called Operation) as a function of the ALUOp and function code field. This table is the same as that shown Figure 5.15.

Figure C.2 shows the truth tables for each of the three ALU control bits. We have taken advantage of the common structure in each truth table to incorporate additional don't cares. For example, the five lines in the truth table of Figure C.1 that set Operation1 are reduced to just two entries in Figure C.2. A logic minimization program will use the don't-care terms to reduce the number of gates and the number of inputs to each gate in a logic gate realization of these truth tables.

ALUOp		Function code fields					
ALUOp1	**ALUOp0**	**F5**	**F4**	**F3**	**F2**	**F1**	**F0**
X	1	X	X	X	X	X	X
1	X	X	X	X	X	1	X

a. The truth table for Operation2 = 1 (this table corresponds to the left bit of the Operation field in Figure C.1)

ALUOp		Function code fields					
ALUOp1	**ALUOp0**	**F5**	**F4**	**F3**	**F2**	**F1**	**F0**
0	X	X	X	X	X	X	X
X	X	X	X	X	0	X	X

b. The truth table for Operation1 = 1

ALUOp		Function code fields					
ALUOp1	**ALUOp0**	**F5**	**F4**	**F3**	**F2**	**F1**	**F0**
1	X	X	X	X	X	X	1
1	X	X	X	1	X	X	X

c. The truth table for Operation0 = 1

FIGURE C.2 **The truth tables for the three ALU control lines.** Only the entries for which the output is 1 are shown. The bits in each field are numbered from right to left starting with 0; thus F5 is the most significant bit of the function field, and F0 is the least significant bit. Similarly, the names of the signals corresponding to the 3-bit operation code supplied to the ALU are Operation2, Operation1, and Operation0 (with the last being the least significant bit). Thus the truth table above shows the input combinations for which the ALU control should be 010, 001, 110, or 111 (the combinations 011, 100, and 101 are not used). The ALUOp bits are named ALUOp1 and ALUOp0. The three output values depend on the 2-bit ALUOp field and, when that field is equal to 10, the 6-bit function code in the instruction. Accordingly, when the ALUOp field is not equal to 10, we don't care about the function code value (it is represented by an X). See Appendix B for more background on don't cares.

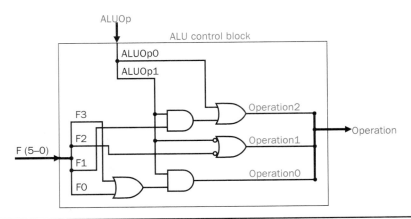

FIGURE C.3 The ALU control block generates the three ALU control bits, based on the function code and ALUOp bits. This logic is generated directly from the truth table in Figure C.2. Only 4 of the 6 bits in the function code are actually needed as inputs, since the upper 2 bits are always don't cares. Let's examine how this logic relates to the truth table of Figure C.2. Consider the Operation2 output, which is generated by two lines in the truth table for Operation2. The second line is the AND of two terms (F1 = 1 and ALUOp1 = 1); the top two-input AND gate corresponds to this term. The other term that causes Operation2 to be asserted is simply ALUOp0. These two terms are combined with an OR gate whose output is Operation2. The outputs Operation0 and Operation1 are derived in similar fashion from the truth table.

From the simplified truth table in Figure C.2, we can generate the logic shown in Figure C.3, which we call the *ALU control block*. This process is straightforward and can be done with a computer-aided design (CAD) program. An example of how the logic gates can be derived from the truth tables is given in the legend to Figure C.3.

This ALU control logic is simple because there are only three outputs, and only a few of the possible input combinations need to be recognized. If a large number of possible ALU function codes had to be transformed into ALU control signals, this simple method would not be efficient. Instead, you could use a decoder, a memory, or a structured array of logic gates. These techniques are described in Appendix B, and we will see examples when we examine the implementation of the multicycle controller in section C.3.

Elaboration: In general, a logic equation and truth table representation of a logic function are equivalent. (We discuss this in further detail in Appendix B.) However, when a truth table only specifies the entries that result in nonzero outputs, it may not completely describe the logic function. A full truth table completely indicates all don't-care entries. For example, the encoding 11 for ALUOp always generates a don't care in the output. Thus a complete truth table would have XXX in the output portion for all entries with 11 in the ALUOp field. These don't-care entries allow us to replace the ALUOp field 10 and 01 with 1X and X1, respectively. Incorporating the don't-care terms and minimizing the logic is both complex and error-prone and, thus, is better left to a program.

Mapping the Main Control Function to Gates

Implementing the main control function with an unstructured collection of gates, as we did for the ALU control, is reasonable because the control function is neither complex nor large, as we can see from the truth table shown in Figure C.4. However, if most of the 64 possible opcodes were used and there were many more control lines, the number of gates would be much larger and each gate could have many more inputs.

Since any function can be computed in two levels of logic, another way to implement a logic function is with a structured two-level logic array. Figure C.5 shows such an implementation. It uses an array of AND gates followed by an array of OR gates. This structure is called a *programmable logic array* (PLA). A PLA is one of the most common ways to implement a control function. We will return to the topic of using structured logic elements to implement control when we implement the finite state controller in the next section.

Control	Signal name	R-format	lw	sw	beq
Inputs	Op5	0	1	1	0
	Op4	0	0	0	0
	Op3	0	0	1	0
	Op2	0	0	0	1
	Op1	0	1	1	0
	Op0	0	1	1	0
Outputs	RegDst	1	0	X	X
	ALUSrc	0	1	1	0
	MemtoReg	0	1	X	X
	RegWrite	1	1	0	0
	MemRead	0	1	0	0
	MemWrite	0	0	1	0
	Branch	0	0	0	1
	ALUOp1	1	0	0	0
	ALUOp0	0	0	0	1

FIGURE C.4 The control function for the simple one-clock implementation is completely specified by this truth table. This table is the same as that shown in Figure 5.27.

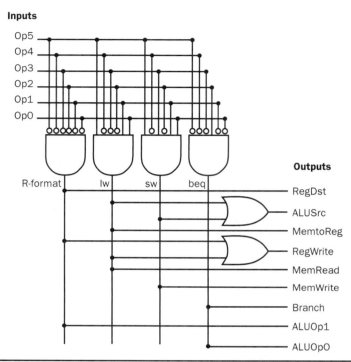

FIGURE C.5 The structured implementation of the control function as described by the truth table in Figure C.4. The structure, called a programmable logic array (PLA), uses an array of AND gates followed by an array of OR gates. The inputs to the AND gates are the function inputs and their inverses (bubbles indicate inversion of a signal). The inputs to the OR gates are the outputs of the AND gates (or, as a degenerate case, the function inputs and inverses). The output of the OR gates is the function outputs.

C.3   Implementing Finite State Machine Control

To implement the control as a finite state machine, we must first assign a number to each of the 10 states; any state could use any number, but we will use the sequential numbering for simplicity as we did in Chapter 5. (Figure C.6 is a copy of the finite state diagram from Figure 5.42 on page 396, reproduced for ease of access.) With 10 states we will need 4 bits to encode the state number, and we call these state bits: S3, S2, S1, S0. The current-state number will be stored in a state register, as shown in Figure C.7. If the states are assigned sequentially, state i is encoded using the state bits as the binary

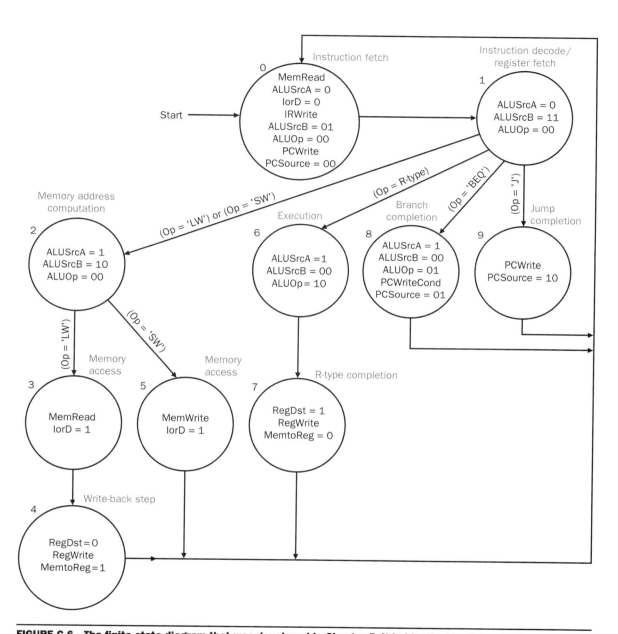

FIGURE C.6 The finite state diagram that was developed in Chapter 5; it is identical to Figure 5.42.

number i. For example, state 6 is encoded as 0110_{two} or S3 = 0, S2 = 1, S1 = 1, S0 = 0, which can also be written as

$$\overline{S3} \cdot S2 \cdot S1 \cdot \overline{S0}$$

The control unit has outputs that specify the next state. These are written into the state register on the clock edge and become the new state at the beginning of the next clock cycle following the active clock edge. We name these outputs NS3, NS2, NS1, NS0. Once we have determined the number of inputs, states, and outputs, we know what the basic outline of the control unit will look like, as we show in Figure C.7.

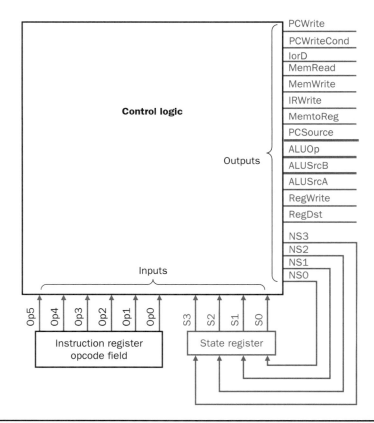

FIGURE C.7   The control unit for MIPS will consist of some control logic and a register to hold the state. The state register is written at the active clock edge and is stable during the clock cycle.

The block labeled "control logic" in Figure C.7 is combinational logic. We can think of it as a big table giving the value of the outputs in terms of the inputs. The logic in this block implements the two different parts of the finite state machine. One part is the logic that determines the setting of the datapath control outputs, which depend only on the state bits. The other part of the control logic implements the next-state function; these equations determine the values of the next-state bits based on the current-state bits and the other inputs (the 6-bit opcode).

Figure C.8 shows the logic equations: the top portion showing the outputs, and the bottom portion showing the next-state function. The values in this table were determined from the state diagram in Figure C.6. Whenever a control line is active in a state, that state is entered in the second column of the table. Likewise, the next-state entries are made whenever one state is a successor to another.

Output	Current states	Op
PCWrite	state0 + state9	
PCWriteCond	state8	
IorD	state3 + state5	
MemRead	state0 + state3	
MemWrite	state5	
IRWrite	state0	
MemtoReg	state4	
PCSource1	state9	
PCSource0	state8	
ALUOp1	state6	
ALUOp0	state8	
ALUSrcB1	state1 +state2	
ALUSrcB0	state0 + state1	
ALUSrcA	state2 + state6 + state8	
RegWrite	state4 + state7	
RegDst	state7	
NextState0	state4 + state5 + state7 + state8 + state9	
NextState1	state0	
NextState2	state1	(Op = 'lw') + (Op = 'sw')
NextState3	state2	(Op = 'lw')
NextState4	state3	
NextState5	state2	(Op = 'sw')
NextState6	state1	(Op = 'R-type')
NextState7	state6	
NextState8	state1	(Op = 'beq')
NextState9	state1	(Op = 'jmp')

FIGURE C.8   The logic equations for the control unit shown in a shorthand form. Remember that "+" stands for OR in logic equations. The state inputs and NextState entries outputs must be expanded by using the state encoding. Any blank entry is a don't care.

In Figure C.8 we use the abbreviation stateN to stand for current state N. Thus, stateN is replaced by the term that encodes the state number N. We use NextStateN to stand for the setting of the next-state outputs to N. This output is implemented using the next-state outputs (NS). When NextStateN is active, the bits NS[3–0] are set corresponding to the binary version of the value N. Of course, since a given next-state bit is activated in multiple next states, the equation for each state bit will be the OR of the terms that activate that signal. Likewise, when we use a term such as (Op = 'lw'), this corresponds to an AND of the opcode inputs that specifies the encoding of the opcode lw in 6 bits, just as we did for the simple control unit in the previous section of this chapter. Translating the entries in Figure C.8 into logic equations for the outputs is straightforward.

Logic Equations for Next-State Outputs

Example   Give the logic equation for the low-order next-state bit, NS0.

Answer   The next-state bit NS0 should be active whenever the next state has NS0 = 1 in the state encoding. This is true for NextState1, NextState3, NextState5, NextState7, and NextState9. The entries for these states in Figure C.8 supply the conditions when these next-state values should be active. The equation for each of these next states is given below. The first equation states that the next state is 1 if the current state is 0; the current state is 0 if each of the state input bits is 0, which is what the rightmost product term indicates.

$$\text{NextState1} = \text{State0} = \overline{S3} \cdot \overline{S2} \cdot \overline{S1} \cdot \overline{S0}$$

$$\text{NextState3} = \text{State2} \cdot (\text{Op[5-0]} = \text{'lw'})$$
$$= \overline{S3} \cdot \overline{S2} \cdot S1 \cdot \overline{S0} \cdot \text{Op5} \cdot \overline{\text{Op4}} \cdot \overline{\text{Op3}} \cdot \overline{\text{Op2}} \cdot \text{Op1} \cdot \text{Op0}$$

$$\text{NextState5} = \text{State 2} \cdot (\text{Op[5-0]} = \text{'sw'})$$
$$= \overline{S3} \cdot \overline{S2} \cdot S1 \cdot \overline{S0} \cdot \text{Op5} \cdot \overline{\text{Op4}} \cdot \text{Op3} \cdot \overline{\text{Op2}} \cdot \text{Op1} \cdot \text{Op0}$$

$$\text{NextState7} = \text{State6} = \overline{S3} \cdot S2 \cdot S1 \cdot \overline{S0}$$

$$\text{NextState9} = \text{State1} \cdot (\text{Op[5-0]} = \text{'jmp'})$$
$$= \overline{S3} \cdot \overline{S2} \cdot \overline{S1} \cdot S0 \cdot \overline{\text{Op5}} \cdot \overline{\text{Op4}} \cdot \overline{\text{Op3}} \cdot \overline{\text{Op2}} \cdot \text{Op1} \cdot \overline{\text{Op0}}$$

NS0 is the logical sum of all these terms.

As we have seen, the control function can be expressed as a logic equation for each output. This set of logic equations can be implemented in two ways: corresponding to a complete truth table, or corresponding to a two-level logic structure that allows a sparse encoding of the truth table. Before we look at these implementations, let's look at the truth table for the complete control function.

It is simplest if we break the control function defined in Figure C.8 into two parts: the next-state outputs, which may depend on all the inputs, and the control signal outputs, which depend only on the current-state bits. Figure C.9 shows the truth tables for all the datapath control signals. Because these signals actually depend only on the state bits (and not the opcode), each of the entries in a table in Figure C.9 actually represents 64 (= 2^6) entries, with the 6 bits named Op having all possible values; that is, the Op bits are don't-care bits in determining the datapath control outputs. Figure C.10 shows the truth table for the next-state bits NS[3–0], which depend on the state input bits and the instruction bits, which supply the opcode.

Elaboration: There are many opportunities to simplify the control function by observing similarities among two or more control signals and by using the semantics of the implementation. For example, the signals PCWriteCond, PCSource0, and ALUOp0 are all asserted in exactly one state, state 8. These three control signals can be replaced by a single signal.

A ROM Implementation

Probably the simplest way to implement the control function is to encode the truth tables in a read-only memory (ROM). The number of entries in the memory for the truth tables of Figures C.9 and C.10 is equal to all possible values of the inputs (the 6 opcode bits plus the 4 state bits), which is $2^{\# \text{inputs}} = 2^{10} = 1024$. The inputs to the control unit become the address lines for the ROM, which implements the control logic block that was shown in Figure C.7 on page C-10. The width of each entry (or word in the memory) is 20 bits since there are 16 datapath control outputs and 4 next-state bits. This means the total size of the ROM is $2^{10} \times 20 = 20$ Kbits.

The setting of the bits in a word in the ROM depends on which outputs are active in that word. Before we look at the control words, we need to order the bits within the control input (the address) and output words (the contents), respectively. We will number the bits using the order in Figure C.7 on page C-10, with the next-state bits being the low-order bits of the control *word* and the current-state input bits being the low-order bits of the *address*. This means that the PCWrite output will be the high-order bit (bit 19) of each memory word,

s3	s2	s1	s0
0	0	0	0
1	0	0	1

a. Truth table for PCWrite

s3	s2	s1	s0
1	0	0	0

b. Truth table for PCWriteCond

s3	s2	s1	s0
0	0	1	1
0	1	0	1

c. Truth table for IorD

s3	s2	s1	s0
0	0	0	0
0	0	1	1

d. Truth table for MemRead

s3	s2	s1	s0
0	1	0	1

e. Truth table for MemWrite

s3	s2	s1	s0
0	0	0	0

f. Truth table for IRWrite

s3	s2	s1	s0
0	1	0	0

g. Truth table for MemtoReg

s3	s2	s1	s0
1	0	0	1

h. Truth table for PCSource1

s3	s2	s1	s0
1	0	0	0

i. Truth table for PCSource0

s3	s2	s1	s0
0	1	1	0

j. Truth table for ALUOp1

s3	s2	s1	s0
1	0	0	0

k. Truth table for ALUOp0

s3	s2	s1	s0
0	0	0	1
0	0	1	0

l. Truth table for ALUSrcB1

s3	s2	s1	s0
0	0	0	0
0	0	0	1

m. Truth table for ALUSrcB0

s3	s2	s1	s0
0	0	1	0
0	1	1	0
1	0	0	0

n. Truth table for ALUSrcA

s3	s2	s1	s0
0	1	0	0
0	1	1	1

o. Truth table for RegWrite

s3	s2	s1	s0
0	1	1	1

p. Truth table for RegDst

FIGURE C.9 The truth tables are shown for the 16 datapath control signals that depend only on the current-state input bits, which are shown for each table. Each truth table row corresponds to 64 entries: one for each possible value of the 6 Op bits. Notice that some of the outputs are active under nearly the same circumstances. For example, in the case of PCWriteCond, PCSource0, and ALUOp0, these signals are both active only in state 8 (see (b), (j), and (l)). These three signals could be replaced by one signal. There are other opportunities for reducing the logic needed to implement the control function by taking advantage of further similarities in the truth tables.

Op5	Op4	Op3	Op2	Op1	Op0	S3	S2	S1	S0
0	0	0	0	1	0	0	0	0	1
0	0	0	1	0	0	0	0	0	1

a. The truth table for the NS3 output, active when the next state is 8 or 9. This signal is activated when the current state is 1.

Op5	Op4	Op3	Op2	Op1	Op0	S3	S2	S1	S0
0	0	0	0	0	0	0	0	0	1
1	0	1	0	1	1	0	0	1	0
X	X	X	X	X	X	0	0	1	1
X	X	X	X	X	X	0	1	1	0

b. The truth table for the NS2 output, which is active when the next state is 4, 5, 6, or 7. This situation occurs when the current state is one of 1, 2, 3, or 6.

Op5	Op4	Op3	Op2	Op1	Op0	S3	S2	S1	S0
0	0	0	0	0	0	0	0	0	1
1	0	0	0	1	1	0	0	0	1
1	0	1	0	1	1	0	0	0	1
1	0	0	0	1	1	0	0	1	0
X	X	X	X	X	X	0	1	1	0

c. The truth table for the NS1 output, which is active when the next state is 2, 3, 6, or 7. The next state is one of 2, 3, 6, or 7 only if the current state is one of 1, 2, or 6.

Op5	Op4	Op3	Op2	Op1	Op0	S3	S2	S1	S0
X	X	X	X	X	X	0	0	0	0
1	0	0	0	1	1	0	0	1	0
1	0	1	0	1	1	0	0	1	0
X	X	X	X	X	X	0	1	1	0
0	0	0	0	1	0	0	0	0	1

d. The truth table for the NS0 output, which is active when the next state is 1, 3, 5, 7, or 9. This happens only if the current state is one of 0, 1, 2, or 6.

FIGURE C.10 The four truth tables for the four next-state output bits (NS[3–0]). The next-state outputs depend on the value of Op[5–0], which is the opcode field, and the current state, given by S[3–0]. The entries with X are don't-care terms. Each entry with a don't-care term corresponds to two entries, one with that input at 0 and one with that input at 1. Thus an entry with n don't-care terms actually corresponds to 2^n truth table entries.

and NS0 will be the low-order bit. The high-order address bit will be given by Op5, which is the high-order bit of the instruction, and the low-order address bit will be given by S0.

We can construct the ROM contents by building the entire truth table in form where each row corresponds to one of the 2^n unique input combinations and a set of columns indicate which outputs are active for that input combination. We don't have the space here to show all 1024 entries in the truth table.

However, by separating the datapath control and next-state outputs, we do, since the datapath control outputs depend only on the current state. The truth table for the datapath control outputs is shown in Figure C.11. We include only the encodings of the state inputs that are in use (that is, values 0 through 9 corresponding to the 10 states of the state machine).

The truth table in Figure C.11 directly gives the contents of the upper 16 bits of each word in the ROM. The 4-bit input field gives the low-order four address bits of each word, and the column gives the contents of the word at that address.

If we did show a full truth table for the datapath control bits with both the state number and the opcode bits as inputs, the opcode inputs would all be don't cares. When we construct the ROM, we cannot have any don't cares, since the addresses into the ROM must be complete. Thus, the same datapath control outputs will occur many times in the ROM, since this part of the ROM is the same whenever the state bits are identical, independent of the value of the opcode inputs.

Outputs	Input values (S[3–0])									
	0000	0001	0010	0011	0100	0101	0110	0111	1000	1001
PCWrite	1	0	0	0	0	0	0	0	0	1
PCWriteCond	0	0	0	0	0	0	0	0	1	0
IorD	0	0	0	1	0	1	0	0	0	0
MemRead	1	0	0	1	0	0	0	0	0	0
MemWrite	0	0	0	0	0	1	0	0	0	0
IRWrite	1	0	0	0	0	0	0	0	0	0
MemtoReg	0	0	0	0	1	0	0	0	0	0
PCSource1	0	0	0	0	0	0	0	0	0	1
PCSource0	0	0	0	0	0	0	0	0	1	0
ALUOp1	0	0	0	0	0	0	1	0	0	0
ALUOp0	0	0	0	0	0	0	0	0	1	0
ALUSrcB1	0	1	1	0	0	0	0	0	0	0
ALUSrcB0	1	1	0	0	0	0	0	0	0	0
ALUSrcA	0	0	1	0	0	0	1	0	1	0
RegWrite	0	0	0	0	1	0	0	1	0	0
RegDst	0	0	0	0	0	0	0	1	0	0

FIGURE C.11   The truth table for the 16 datapath control outputs, which depend only on the state inputs. The values are determined from Figure C.9. Although there are 16 possible values for the 4-bit state field, only 10 of these are used and are shown here. The 10 possible values are shown at the top; each column shows the setting of the datapath control outputs for the state input value that appears at the top of the column. For example, when the state inputs are 0011 (state 3), the active datapath control outputs are IorD or MemRead.

a
s,
na-
le.

Control ROM Entries

Example

For what ROM addresses will the bit corresponding to PCWrite, the high bit of the control word, be 1?

Answer

PCWrite is high in states 0 and 9; this corresponds to addresses with the 4 low-order bits being either 0000 or 1001. The bit will be high in the memory word independent of the inputs Op[5–0], so the addresses with the bit high are 000000000, 0000001001, 0000010000, 0000011001, ..., 1111110000, 1111111001. The general form of this is XXXXX0000 or XXXXX1001, where XXXXX is any combination of bits, and corresponds to the 6-bit opcode on which this output does not depend.

We will show the entire contents of the ROM in two parts to make it easier to show. Figure C.12 shows the upper 16 bits of the control word; this comes directly from Figure C.11. These datapath control outputs depend only on the state inputs, and this set of words would be duplicated 64 times in the full ROM, as we discussed above. The entries corresponding to input values 1010 through 1111 are not used, so we do not care what they contain.

Figure C.13 shows the lower 4 bits of the control word corresponding to the next-state outputs. The last column of the table in Figure C.13 corresponds to all the possible values of the opcode that do not match the specified opcodes.

Lower 4 bits of the address	Bits 19–4 of the word
0000	1001010000001000
0001	0000000000011000
0010	0000000000010100
0011	0011000000000000
0100	0000001000000010
0101	0010100000000000
0110	0000000001000100
0111	0000000000000011
1000	0100000010100100
1001	1000000100000000

FIGURE C.12 The contents of the upper 16 bits of the ROM depend only on the state inputs. These values are the same as those in Figure C.11, simply rotated 90°. This set of control words would be duplicated 64 times for every possible value of the upper 6 bits of the address.

In state 0, the next state is always state 1, since the instruction was still being fetched. After state 1, the opcode field must be valid. The table indicates this by the entries marked illegal; we discuss how to deal with these illegal opcodes in section 5.6.

Not only is this representation as two separate tables a more compact way to show the ROM contents, it is also a more efficient way to implement the ROM. The majority of the outputs (16 of 20 bits) depend only on 4 of the 10 inputs. The number of bits in total when the control is implemented as two separate ROMs is $2^4 \times 16 + 2^{10} \times 4 = 256 + 4096 = 4.3$ Kbits, which is about one-fifth of the size of a single ROM, which requires $2^{10} \times 20 = 20$ Kbits. There is some overhead associated with any structured-logic block, but in this case the additional overhead of an extra ROM would be much smaller than the savings from splitting the single ROM.

Current state S[3–0]	Op [5–0]					
	000000 (R-format)	000010 (jmp)	000100 (beq)	100011 (lw)	101011 (sw)	Any other value
0000	0001	0001	0001	0001	0001	0001
0001	0110	1001	1000	0010	0010	illegal
0010	XXXX	XXXX	XXXX	0011	0101	illegal
0011	0100	0100	0100	0100	0100	illegal
0100	0000	0000	0000	0000	0000	illegal
0101	0000	0000	0000	0000	0000	illegal
0110	0111	0111	0111	0111	0111	illegal
0111	0000	0000	0000	0000	0000	illegal
1000	0000	0000	0000	0000	0000	illegal
1001	0000	0000	0000	0000	0000	illegal

FIGURE C.13   This table contains the lower 4 bits of the control word (the NS outputs), which depend on both the state inputs, S[3–0], and the opcode, Op [5–0], which correspond to the instruction opcode. These values can be determined from Figure C.10. The opcode name is shown under the encoding in the heading. The 4 bits of the control word whose address is given by the current-state bits and Op bits are shown in each entry. For example, when the state input bits are 0000, the output is always 0001, independent of the other inputs; when the state is 2, the next state is don't care for three of the inputs, 3 for lw, and 5 for sw. Together with the entries in Figure C.12, this table specifies the contents of the control unit ROM. For example, the word at address 1000110001 is obtained by finding the upper 16 bits in the table in Figure C.12 using only the state input bits (0001) and concatenating the lower 4 bits found by using the entire address (0001 to find the row and 100011 to find the column). The entry from Figure C.12 yields **0000000000011000**, while the appropriate entry in the table immediately above is 0010. Thus the control word at address 1000110001 is **0000000000011000**0010. The column labeled "Any other value" applies only when the Op bits do not match one of the specified opcodes.

Although this ROM encoding of the control function is simple, it is wasteful, even when divided into two pieces. For example, the values of the Instruction register inputs are often not needed to determine the next state. Thus the next-state ROM has many entries that are either duplicated or are don't care. Consider the case when the machine is in state 0: there are 2^6 entries in the ROM (since the opcode field can have any value), and these entries will all have the same contents (namely, the control word 0001). The reason that so much of the ROM is wasted is that the ROM implements the complete truth table, providing the opportunity to have a different output for every combination of the inputs. But most combinations of the inputs either never happen or are redundant!

A PLA Implementation

We can reduce the amount of control storage required at the cost of using more complex address decoding for the control inputs, which will encode only the input combinations that are needed. The logic structure most often used to do this is a programmed logic array (PLA), which we mentioned earlier and illustrated in Figure C.5. In a PLA, each output is the logical OR of one or more minterms. A *minterm*, also called a *product term*, is simply a logical AND of one or more inputs. The inputs can be thought of as the address for indexing the PLA, while the minterms select which of all possible address combinations are interesting. A minterm corresponds to a single entry in a truth table, such as those in Figure C.9 on page C-14, including possible don't-care terms. Each output consists of an OR of these minterms, which exactly corresponds to a complete truth table. However, unlike a ROM, only those truth table entries that produce an active output are needed, and only one copy of each minterm is required, even if the minterm contains don't cares. Figure C.14 shows the PLA that implements this control function.

As we can see from the PLA in Figure C.14, there are 17 unique minterms—10 that depend only on the current state and 7 others that depend on a combination of the Op field and the current-state bits. The total size of the PLA is proportional to (#inputs × #product terms) + (#outputs × #product terms), as we can see symbolically from the figure. This means the total size of the PLA in Figure C.14 is proportional to $(10 \times 17) + (20 \times 17) = 460$. By comparison, the size of a single ROM is proportional to 20 Kbits, and even the two-part ROM has a total of 4.3 Kbits. Because the size of a PLA cell will be only slightly larger than the size of a bit in a ROM, a PLA will be a much more efficient implementation for this control unit.

Of course, just as we split the ROM in two, we could split the PLA in two PLAs: one with four inputs and 10 minterms that generates the 16 control outputs, and one with 10 inputs and 7 minterms that generates the 4 next-state

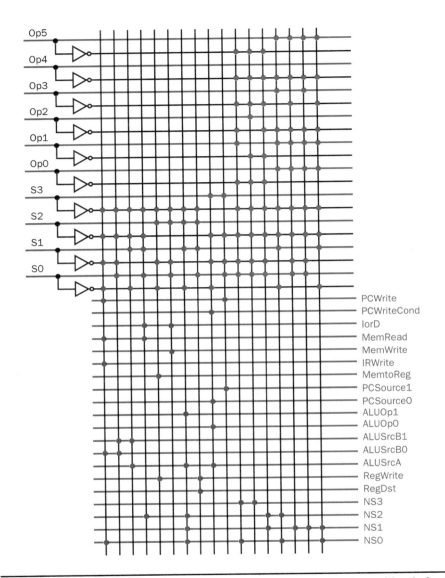

FIGURE C.14   This PLA implements the control function logic for the multicycle implementation. The inputs to the control appear on the left and the outputs on the right. The top half of the figure is the AND plane that computes all the minterms. The minterms are carried to the OR plane on the vertical lines. Each colored dot corresponds to a signal that makes up the minterm carried on that line. The sum terms are computed from these minterms, with each grey dot representing the presence of the intersecting minterm in that sum term. Each output consists of a single sum term.

outputs. The first PLA would have a size proportional to $(4 \times 10) + (10 \times 16) = 200$, and the second PLA would have a size proportional to $(10 \times 7) + (4 \times 7) = 98$. This would yield a total size proportional to 298 PLA cells, about 55% of the size of a single PLA. These two PLAs will be considerably smaller than an implementation using two ROMs. For more details on PLAs and their implementation, as well as the references for books on logic design, see Appendix B.

C.4 Implementing the Next-State Function with a Sequencer

Let's look carefully at the control unit we built in the last section. If you examine the ROMs that implement the control in Figures C.12 and C.13, you can see that much of the logic is used to specify the next-state function. In fact, for the implementation using two separate ROMs, 4096 out of the 4368 bits (94%) correspond to the next-state function! Furthermore, imagine what the control logic would look like if the instruction set had many more different instruction types, some of which required many clocks to implement. There would be many more states in the finite state machine. In some states, we might be branching to a large number of different states depending on the instruction type (as we did in state 1 of the finite state machine in Figure C.6 on page C-9). However, many of the states would proceed in a sequential fashion, just as states 3 and 4 do in Figure C.6.

For example, if we included floating point, we would see a sequence of many states in a row that implement a multicycle floating-point instruction. Alternatively, consider how the control might look for a machine that can have multiple memory operands per instruction. It would require many more states to fetch multiple memory operands. The result of this would be that the control logic will be dominated by the encoding of the next-state function. Furthermore, much of the logic will be devoted to sequences of states with only one path through them that look like states 2 through 4 in Figure C.6. With more instructions, these sequences will consist of many more sequentially numbered states than for our simple subset.

To encode these more complex control functions efficiently, we can use a control unit that has a counter to supply the sequential next state. This counter often eliminates the need to encode the next-state function explicitly in the control unit. As shown in Figure C.15, an adder is used to increment the state, essentially turning it into a counter. The incremented state is always the state that follows in numerical order. However, the finite state machine sometimes "branches." For example, in state 1 of the finite state machine (see Figure C.6 on page C-9), there are four possible next states, only one of which is the sequential next state. Thus, we need to be able to choose between the incremented state and a new state based on the inputs from the Instruction register and

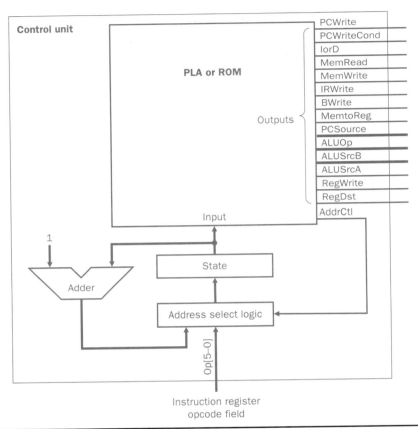

FIGURE C.15 **The control unit using an explicit counter to compute the next state.** In this control unit, the next state is computed using a counter (at least in some states). By comparison, Figure C.7 on page C-10 encodes the next state in the control logic for every state. In this control unit, the signals labeled *AddrCtl* control how the next state is determined.

the current state. Each control word will include control lines that will determine how the next state is chosen.

It is easy to implement the control output signal portion of the control word, since, if we use the same state numbers, this portion of the control word will look exactly like the ROM contents shown in Figure C.12 on page C-17. However, the method for selecting the next state differs from the next-state function in the finite state machine.

With an explicit counter providing the sequential next state, the control unit logic need only specify how to choose the state when it is not the sequentially following state. There are two methods for doing this. The first is a method we have already seen: namely, the control unit explicitly encodes the next-state function. The difference is that the control unit need only set the next-state lines when the designated next state is not the state that the counter indicates. If the number of states is large and the next-state function that we need to encode is mostly empty, this may not be a good choice, since the resulting control unit will have lots of empty or redundant space. An alternative approach is to use separate external logic to specify the next state when the counter does not specify the state. Many control units, especially those that implement large instruction sets, use this approach, and we will focus on specifying the control externally.

Although the nonsequential next state will come from an external table, the control unit needs to specify when this should occur and how to find that next state. There are two kinds of "branching" that we must implement in the address select logic. First, we must be able to jump to one of a number of states based on the opcode portion of the Instruction register. This operation, called a *dispatch*, is usually implemented by using a set of special ROMS or PLAs included as part of the address selection logic. An additional set of control outputs, which we call AddrCtl, indicates when a dispatch should be done. Looking at the finite state diagram (Figure C.6 on page C-9), we see that there are two states in which we do a branch based on a portion of the opcode. Thus we will need two small dispatch tables. (Alternatively, we could also use a single dispatch table and use the control bits that select the table as address bits that choose which portion of the dispatch table to select the address from.)

The second type of branching that we must implement consists of branching back to state 0, which initiates the execution of the next MIPS instruction. Thus there are four possible ways to choose the next state (three types of branches, plus incrementing the current-state number), which can be encoded in 2 bits. Let's assume that the encoding is as follows:

AddrCtl value	Action
0	Set state to 0
1	Dispatch with ROM 1
2	Dispatch with ROM 2
3	Use the incremented state

If we use this encoding, the address select logic for this control unit can be implemented as shown in Figure C.16.

To complete the control unit, we need only specify the contents of the dispatch ROMs, and the values of the address-control lines for each state. We have already specified the datapath control portion of the control word using the

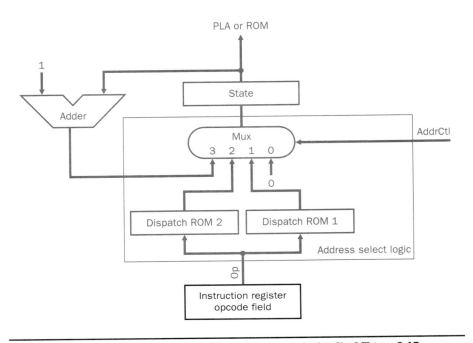

FIGURE C.16   This is the address select logic for the control unit of Figure C.15.

ROM contents of Figure C.12 on page C-17 (or the corresponding portions of the PLA in Figure C.14 on page C-20). The next-state counter and dispatch ROMs take the place of the portion of the control unit that was computing the next state, which was shown in Figure C.13 on page C-18. We are only implementing a portion of the instruction set, so the dispatch ROMs will be largely empty. Figure C.17 shows the entries that must be assigned for this subset. Section 5.6 of Chapter 5 discusses what to do with the entries in the dispatch ROMs that do not correspond to any instruction.

Now we can determine the setting of the address selection lines (AddrCtl) in each control word. The table in Figure C.18 shows how the address control must be set for every state. This information will be used to specify the setting of the AddrCtl field in the control word associated with that state.

The contents of the entire control ROM are shown in Figure C.19. The total storage required for the control is quite small. There are 10 control words, each 18 bits wide, for a total of 180 bits. In addition, the two dispatch tables are 4 bits wide and each has 64 entries, for a total of 512 additional bits. This total of 692 bits beats the implementation that uses two ROMs with the next-state function encoded in the ROMs (which requires 4.3 Kbits).

Dispatch ROM 1		
Op	**Opcode name**	**Value**
000000	R-format	0110
000010	jmp	1001
000100	beq	1000
100011	lw	0010
101011	sw	0010

Dispatch ROM 2		
Op	**Opcode name**	**Value**
100011	lw	0011
101011	sw	0101

FIGURE C.17 The dispatch ROMs each have $2^6 = 64$ entries that are 4 bits wide, since that is the number of bits in the state encoding. This figure only shows the entries in the ROM that are of interest for this subset. The first column in each table indicates the value of Op, which is the address used to access the dispatch ROM. The second column shows the symbolic name of the opcode. The third column indicates the value at that address in the ROM.

State number	Address-control action	Value of AddrCtl
0	Use incremented state	3
1	Use dispatch ROM 1	1
2	Use dispatch ROM 2	2
3	Use incremented state	3
4	Replace state number by 0	0
5	Replace state number by 0	0
6	Use incremented state	3
7	Replace state number by 0	0
8	Replace state number by 0	0
9	Replace state number by 0	0

FIGURE C.18 The values of the address-control lines are set in the control word that corresponds to each state.

State number	Control word bits 17–2	Control word bits 1–0
0	1001010000001000	11
1	0000000000011000	01
2	0000000000010100	10
3	0011000000000000	11
4	0000001000000010	00
5	0010100000000000	00
6	0000000001000100	11
7	0000000000000011	00
8	0100000010100100	00
9	1000000100000000	00

FIGURE C.19 The contents of the control memory for an implementation using an explicit counter. The first column shows the state, while the second shows the datapath control bits, and the last column shows the address-control bits in each control word. Bits 17–2 are identical to those in Figure C.12.

Of course, the dispatch tables are sparse and could be more efficiently implemented with two small PLAs. The control ROM could also be replaced with a PLA.

Optimizing the Control Implementation

We can further reduce the amount of logic in the control unit by two different techniques. The first is *logic minimization*, which uses the structure of the logic equations, including the don't-care terms, to reduce the amount of hardware required. The success of this process depends on how many entries exist in the truth table, and how those entries are related. For example, in this subset, only the lw and sw opcodes have an active value for the signal Op5, so we can replace the two truth table entries that test whether the input is lw or sw by a single test on this bit; similarly we can eliminate several bits used to index the dispatch ROM because this single bit can be used to find lw and sw in the first dispatch ROM. Of course, if the opcode space were less sparse, opportunities for this optimization would be more difficult to locate. However, in choosing the opcodes, the architect can provide additional opportunities by choosing related opcodes for instructions that are likely to share states in the control.

A different sort of optimization can be done by assigning the state numbers in a finite state or microcode implementation to minimize the logic. This optimization, called *state assignment*, tries to choose the state numbers such that the resulting logic equations contain more redundancy and can thus be simplified. Let's consider the case of a finite state machine with an encoded next-state control first, since it allows states to be assigned arbitrarily. For example, notice that in the finite state machine the signal RegWrite is active only in states 4 and 7. If we encoded those states as 8 and 9, rather than 4 and 7, we could rewrite the equation for RegWrite as simply a test on bit S3 (which is only on for states 8 and 9). This renumbering allows us to combine the two truth table entries in part (o) of Figure C.9 on page C-14 and replace them with a single entry, eliminating one term in the control unit. Of course, we would have to renumber the existing states 8 and 9, perhaps as 4 and 7.

The same optimization can be applied in an implementation that uses an explicit program counter, though we are more restricted. Because the next-state number is often computed by incrementing the current-state number, we cannot arbitrarily assign the states. However, if we keep the states where the incremented state is used as the next state in the same order, we can reassign the consecutive states as a block. In an implementation with an explicit next-state counter, state assignment may allow us to simplify the contents of the dispatch ROMs.

If we look again at the control unit in Figure C.15 on page C-22, it looks remarkably like a computer in its own right. The ROM or PLA can be thought of as memory supplying instructions for the datapath. The state can be thought of as an instruction address. Hence the origin of the name *microcode* or *microprogrammed control*. The control words are thought of as *microinstructions* that control the datapath, and the State register is called the *microprogram counter*. Figure C.20 shows a view of the control unit as *microcode*. The next section describes how we map from a microprogram to microcode.

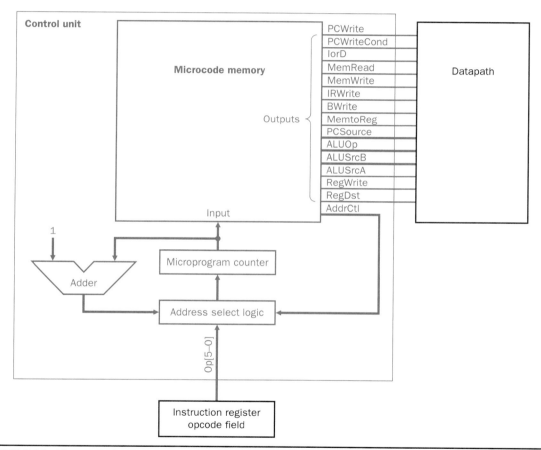

FIGURE C.20   The control unit as a microcode. The use of the word "micro" serves to distinguish between the program counter in the datapath and the microprogram counter, and between the microcode memory and the instruction memory.

C.5   Translating a Microprogram to Hardware

To translate the microprogram of section 5.5 into actual hardware, we need to specify how each field translates into control signals. We can implement the microprogram with either finite state control or a microcode implementation with an explicit sequencer. If we choose a finite state machine, we need to construct the next-state function from the microprogram. Once this function is known, we can map a set of truth table entries for the next-state outputs. In this section, we will show how to translate the microprogram assuming that the next state is specified by a sequencer. From the truth tables we will construct, it would be straightforward to build the next-state function for a finite state machine.

Assuming an explicit sequencer, we need to do two additional tasks to translate the microprogram: assign addresses to the microinstructions and fill in the contents of the dispatch ROMs. This process is essentially the same as the process of translating an assembly language program into machine instructions: the fields of the assembly language or microprogram instruction are translated, and labels on the instructions must be resolved to addresses.

Figure C.21 shows the various values for each microinstruction field that controls the datapath and how these fields are encoded as control signals. If the field corresponding to a signal that affects a unit with state (i.e., Memory, Memory register, ALU destination, or PCWriteControl) is blank, then no control signal should be active. If a field corresponding to a multiplexor control signal or the ALU operation control (i.e., ALUOp, SRC1, or SRC2) is blank, the output is unused, so the associated signals may be set as don't care.

The sequencing field can have four values: Fetch (meaning go to the Fetch state), Dispatch 1, Dispatch 2, and Seq. These four values are encoded to set the 2-bit address control just as they were in Figure C.18 on page C-25: Fetch = 0, Dispatch 1 = 1. Dispatch 2 = 2, Seq = 3. Finally, we need to specify the contents of the dispatch tables to relate the dispatch entries of the sequence field to the symbolic labels in the microprogram. We use the same dispatch tables as we did earlier in Figure C.17 on page C-25.

A microcode assembler would use the encoding of the sequencing field, the contents of the symbolic dispatch tables in Figure C.22, the specification in Figure C.21, and the actual microprogram in Figure 5.46 on page 408 to generate the microinstructions.

Since the microprogram is an abstract representation of the control, there is a great deal of flexibility in how the microprogram is translated. For example, the address assigned to many of the microinstructions can be chosen arbitrarily; the only restrictions are those imposed by the fact that certain microinstruc-

Field name	Value	Signals active	Comment
ALU control	Add	ALUOp = 00	Cause the ALU to add.
	Subt	ALUOp = 01	Cause the ALU to subtract; this implements the compare for branches.
	Func code	ALUOp = 10	Use the instruction's function code to determine ALU control.
SRC1	PC	ALUSrcA = 0	Use the PC as the first ALU input.
	A	ALUSrcA = 1	Register A is the first ALU input.
SRC2	B	ALUSrcB = 00	Register B is the second ALU input.
	4	ALUSrcB = 01	Use 4 as the second ALU input.
	Extend	ALUSrcB = 10	Use output of the sign extension unit as the second ALU input.
	Extshft	ALUSrcB = 11	Use the output of the shift-by-two unit as the second ALU input.
Register control	Read		Read two registers using the rs and rt fields of the IR as the register numbers and putting the data into registers A and B.
	Write ALU	RegWrite, RegDst = 1, MemtoReg = 0	Write a register using the rd field of the IR as the register number and the contents of ALUOut as the data.
	Write MDR	RegWrite, RegDst = 0, MemtoReg = 1	Write a register using the rt field of the IR as the register number and the contents of the MDR as the data.
Memory	Read PC	MemRead, IorD = 0	Read memory using the PC as address; write result into IR (and the MDR).
	Read ALU	MemRead, IorD = 1	Read memory using ALUOut as address; write result into MDR.
	Write ALU	MemWrite, IorD = 1	Write memory using the ALUOut as address, contents of B as the data.
PC write control	ALU	PCSource = 00 PCWrite	Write the output of the ALU into the PC.
	ALUOut-cond	PCSource = 01, PCWriteCond	If the Zero output of the ALU is active, write the PC with the contents of the register ALUOut.
	jump address	PCSource = 10, PCWrite	Write the PC with the jump address from the instruction.
Sequencing	Seq	AddrCtl = 11	Choose the next microinstruction sequentially.
	Fetch	AddrCtl = 00	Go to the first microinstruction to begin a new instruction.
	Dispatch 1	AddrCtl = 01	Dispatch using the ROM 1.
	Dispatch 2	AddrCtl = 10	Dispatch using the ROM 2.

FIGURE C.21 Each microcode field translates to a set of control signals to be set. This table specifies a value for each of the fields that were originally specified in Figure 5.46 on page 408. These 22 different values of the fields specify all the required combinations of the 18 control lines. Control lines that are not set which correspond to actions are 0 by default. Multiplexor control lines are set to 0 if the output matters. If a multiplexor control line is not explicitly set, its output is a don't care and is not used.

tions must occur in sequential order (so that incrementing the State register generates the address of the next instruction). Thus the microcode assembler may reduce the complexity of the control by assigning the microinstructions cleverly.

Microcode dispatch table 1		
Opcode field	**Opcode name**	**Value**
000000	R-format	Rformat1
000010	jmp	JUMP1
000100	beq	BEQ1
100011	lw	Mem1
101011	sw	Mem1

Microcode dispatch table 2		
Opcode field	**Opcode name**	**Value**
100011	lw	LW2
101011	sw	SW2

FIGURE C.22   The two microcode dispatch ROMs showing the contents in symbolic form and using the labels in the microprogram.

Organizing the Control to Reduce the Logic

For a machine with complex control, there may be a great deal of logic in the control unit. The control ROM or PLA may be very costly. Although our simple implementation had only an 18-bit microinstruction (assuming an explicit sequencer), there have been machines with microinstructions that are hundreds of bits wide. Clearly, a designer would like to reduce the number of microinstructions and the width.

The ideal approach to reducing control store is to first write the complete microprogram in a symbolic notation and then measure how control lines are set in each microinstruction. By taking measurements we are able to recognize control bits that can be encoded into a smaller field. For example, if no more than one of eight lines is set simultaneously in the same microinstruction, then this subset of control lines can be encoded into a 3-bit field ($\log_2 8 = 3$). This change saves 5 bits in every microinstruction and does not hurt CPI, though it does mean the extra hardware cost of a 3-to-8 decoder needed to generate the eight control lines when they are required at the datapath. It may also have some small clock cycle impact, since the decoder is in the signal path. However, shaving 5 bits off control store width will usually overcome the cost of the decoder, and the cycle time impact will probably be small or nonexistent. For example, this technique can be applied to bits 14–9 of the microinstructions in this machine, since only 1 bit of the 7 bits of the control word is ever active (see Figure C.19 on page C-25).

This technique of reducing field width is called *encoding*. To further save space, control lines may be encoded together if they are only occasionally set in the same microinstruction; two microinstructions instead of one are then required when both must be set. As long as this doesn't happen in critical routines, the narrower microinstruction may justify a few extra words of control store.

Microinstructions can be made narrower still if they are broken into different formats and given an opcode or *format field* to distinguish them. The format field gives all the unspecified control lines their default values, so as not to change anything else in the machine, and is similar to the opcode of an instruction in a more powerful instruction set. For example, we could use a different format for microinstructions that did memory accesses from those that did register-register ALU operations, taking advantage of the fact that the memory access control lines are not needed in microinstructions controlling ALU operations.

Reducing hardware costs by using format fields usually has an additional performance cost beyond the requirement for more decoders. A microprogram using a single microinstruction format can specify any combination of operations in a datapath and can take fewer clock cycles than a microprogram made up of restricted microinstructions that cannot perform any combination of operations in a single microinstruction. However, if the full capability of the wider microprogram word is not heavily used, then much of the control store will be wasted, and the machine could be made smaller and faster by restricting the microinstruction capability.

The narrow, but usually longer, approach is often called *vertical microcode,* while the wide but short approach is called *horizontal microcode*. It should be noted that the terms "vertical microcode" and "horizontal microcode" have no universal definition—the designers of the 8086 considered its 21-bit microinstruction to be more horizontal than other single-chip computers of the time. The related terms *maximally encoded* and *minimally encoded* are probably better than vertical and horizontal.

C.6 Concluding Remarks

We began this appendix by looking at how to translate a finite state diagram to an implementation using a finite state machine. We then looked at explicit sequencers that use a different technique for realizing the next-state function. Although large microprograms are often targeted at implementations using this explicit next-state approach, we can also implement a microprogram with a finite state machine. As we saw, both ROM and PLA implementations of the logic functions are possible. The advantages of explicit versus encoded next state and ROM versus PLA implementation are summarized below.

> **The Big Picture**
>
> Independent of whether the control is represented as a finite state diagram or as a microprogram, translation to a hardware control implementation is similar. Each state or microinstruction asserts a set of control outputs and specifies how to choose the next state.
>
> The next-state function may be implemented by either encoding it in a finite state machine or by using an explicit sequencer. The explicit sequencer is more efficient if the number of states is large and there are many sequences of consecutive states without branching.
>
> The control logic may be implemented with either ROMs or PLAs (or even a mix). PLAs are more efficient unless the control function is very dense. ROMs may be appropriate if the control is stored in a separate memory, as opposed to within the same chip as the datapath.

C.7 Key Terms

The most important terms for this appendix are listed here and are defined in the Glossary.

horizontal microcode	minimally encoded	state inputs
logic minimization	next-state counter	vertical microcode
maximally encoded	next-state outputs	
microcode assembler	state assignment	

C.8 Exercises

C.1 [10] <§C.2> Instead of using 4 state bits to implement the finite state machine in Figure C.6 on page C-9, use 9 state bits, each of which is a 1 only if the finite state machine is in that particular state (e.g., S1 is 1 in state 1, S2 is 1 in state 2, etc.). Redraw the PLA (Figure C.14 on page C-20).

C.2 [5] <§C.3> {Ex. 5.6} How many product terms are required in a PLA that implements the single-cycle datapath for jal, assuming the control additions described in Exercise 5.6 on page 427?

C.3 [5] <§C.3> {Ex. 5.5} How many product terms are required in a PLA that implements the single-cycle datapath and control for addiu, assuming that the control additions you needed were found in Exercise 5.5 on page 427?

C.4 [10] <§C.3> {Ex. 5.27} Determine the number of product terms in a PLA that implements the finite state machine for jal constructed in Exercise 5.27 on page 431. The easiest method to do this is to construct the truth tables for any new outputs or any outputs affected by the addition.

C.5 [10] <§C.3> {Ex. 5.15} Determine the number of product terms in a PLA that implements the finite state machine for addi in Exercise 5.15 on page 429. The easiest way to do this is to construct the additions to the truth tables for addi.

C.6 [20] <§C.4> {Ex. 5.15} Implement the finite state machine of Exercise 5.15 on page 429 using an explicit counter to determine the next state. Fill in the new entries for the additions to Figure C.19 on page C-25. Also, add any entries needed to the dispatch ROMs of Figure C.22 on page C-30.

C.7 [15] <§§C.3–C.6> Determine the size of the PLAs needed to implement the multicycle machine of Chapter 5 assuming that the next-state function is implemented with a counter. Implement the dispatch tables of Figure C.22 on page C-30 using two PLAs, and the contents of the main control unit in Figure C.19 on page C-25 using another PLA. How does the total size of this solution compare to the single PLA solution with the next state encoded? What if the main PLAs for both approaches are split into two separate PLAs by factoring out the next state or address select signals?

Glossary

absolute address   A variable's or routine's actual address in memory.

abstraction   A model that renders lower-level details of computer systems temporarily invisible in order to facilitate design of sophisticated systems.

activation record   *See* procedure frame.

address   A value used to delineate the location of a specific data element within a memory array.

address mapping   *See* address translation.

address translation   Also called address mapping. The process by which a virtual address is mapped to an address used to access memory.

addressing mode   One of several addressing regimes delimited by their varied use of operands and/or addresses.

aliasing   A situation in which the same object is accessed by two addresses; can occur in virtual memory when there are two virtual addresses for the same physical page.

ALU   *See* arithmetic logic unit (ALU).

Amdahl's law   A rule stating that the performance enhancement possible with a given improvement is limited by the amount that the improved feature is used.

AND gate   Hardware that performs the AND operation on input signals yielding a single signal result.

AND operation   An operation that leaves a 1 in the result only if both bits of the operands are 1.

architecture   *See* instruction set architecture.

arithmetic logic unit (ALU)   Hardware that performs arithmetic and logical operations.

arithmetic mean   The average of the execution times that is directly proportional to total execution time.

assembler   A program that translates a symbolic version of an instruction into the binary version.

assembler directive   An operation that tells the assembler how to translate a program but does not produce machine instructions; always begins with a period.

assembly language   A symbolic language that can be translated into binary.

asserted signal   A signal that is (logically) true, or 1.

asynchronous bus   A bus that uses a handshaking protocol for coordinating usage rather than a clock; can accommodate a wide variety of devices of differing speeds.

atomic operation   An operation in which the processor can both read a location and write it in the same bus operation, preventing any other processor or I/O device from reading or writing memory until it completes.

backpatching   A method for translating from assembly language to machine instructions in which the assembler builds a (possibly incomplete) binary representation of every instruction in one pass over a program and then returns to fill in previously undefined labels.

backplane bus   A bus that is designed to allow processors, memory, and I/O devices to coexist on a single bus.

barrier synchronization   A synchronization scheme in which processors wait at the barrier and do not proceed until every processor has reached it.

base addressing   Also called displacement addressing. An addressing regime in which the operand is at the memory location whose address is the sum of a register and an address in the instruction.

basic block   A sequence of instructions without branches (except possibly at the end) and without branch targets or branch labels (except possibly at the beginning).

biased notation   A notation that represents the most negative value by $00 \ldots 000_{two}$ and the most positive value by $11 \ldots 11_{two}$, with 0 typically having the value $10 \ldots 00_{two}$, thereby biasing the number such that the number plus the bias has a nonnegative representation.

binary bit   *See* binary digit.

binary digit   Also called binary bit. One of the two numbers in base 2, 0 or 1, that are the components of information.

block   The minimum unit of information that can be either present or not present in the two-level hierarchy.

Booth's algorithm   An algorithm based on the observation that the ability to both add and subtract allows for multiple ways to compute a product, so that by looking at multiple bits we potentially save arithmetic operations.

branch delay slot   The slot directly after a delayed branch instruction, which in the MIPS architecture is filled by an instruction that does not affect the branch.

branch hazard   Also called control hazard. An occurrence in which the proper instruction cannot execute in the proper clock cycle because the instruction that was fetched is not the one that is needed; that is, the flow of instruction addresses is not what the pipeline expected.

branch history table   *See* branch prediction buffer.

branch not taken   A branch where the branch condition is false and the program counter (PC) becomes the address of the instruction that sequentially follows the branch.

branch prediction   A method of resolving a branch hazard that assumes a given outcome for the branch and proceeds from that assumption rather than waiting to ascertain the actual outcome.

branch prediction buffer   Also called branch history table. A small memory that is indexed by the lower portion of the address of the branch instruction and that contains one or more bits indicating whether the branch was recently taken or not.

branch taken   A branch where the branch condition is satisfied and the program counter (PC) becomes the branch target. All unconditional branches are taken branches.

branch target address   The address specified in a branch, which becomes the new program counter (PC) if the branch is taken. In the MIPS architecture the branch target is given by the sum of the offset field of the instruction and the address of the instruction following the branch.

bubble   *See* pipeline stall.

bus   In logic design, a collection of data lines that is treated together as a single logical signal; also, a shared collection of lines with multiple sources and uses.

bus arbitration   The process of deciding which bus master gets to use a bus next.

bus master   A unit on the bus that can initiate bus requests.

bus request   A signal on the bus requesting access to a bus.

bus transaction   A sequence of bus operations that includes a request and may include a response, either of which may carry data. A transaction is initiated by a single request and may take many individual bus operations.

bypassing   *See* forwarding.

cache coherency   Consistency in the value of data between the versions in the caches of several processors.

cache memory   A small, fast memory that acts as a buffer for a slower, larger memory.

cache miss   A request for data from the cache that cannot be filled because the data is not present in the cache.

callee   A procedure that executes a series of stored instructions based on parameters provided by the caller and then returns control to the caller.

callee-saved register   A register saved by the routine making a procedure call.

caller   The program that instigates a procedure and provides the necessary parameter values.

caller-saved register   A register saved by the routine being called.

capacity miss   A cache miss that occurs because the cache, even with full associativity, cannot contain all the block needed to satisfy the request.

central processor unit (CPU)   Also called processor. The active part of the computer, which contains the datapath and control and which adds numbers, tests numbers, signals I/O devices to activate, and so on.

centralized, parallel arbitration   A bus arbitration scheme that employs multiple request lines by which the devices independently request the bus and that uses a centralized arbiter to choose from the devices requesting bus access and to notify the selected device that it is now bus master.

chip   *See* integrated circuit.

clock   *See* clock cycle.

clock cycle   Also called tick, clock tick, clock period, clock, cycle. The time for one clock period, usually of the processor clock, which runs at a constant rate. The clock cycle is often used to measure the speed at which hardware can perform basic functions.

clock cycles per instruction (CPI)   Average number of clock cycles per instruction for a program or program fragment.

clock period   *See* clock cycle.

clock rate The speed of the processor or system clock measured as the number of clock cycles per second and usually stated in megahertz or millions of clock cycles per second. The clock rate is the inverse of the clock period. Designers refer to the clock cycle time both as the duration of one clock period, measured as seconds per clock cycle (e.g., 2 ns) and as the clock rate, measured as clock cycles per second (e.g., 500 MHz).

clock skew The difference in absolute time between the times when two state elements see a clock edge.

clock tick *See* clock cycle.

clocking methodology The approach used to determine when data is valid and stable relative to the clock.

cluster A set of computers connected over a local area network (LAN) that function as a single large multiprocessor.

cold start miss *See* compulsory miss.

collision miss *See* conflict miss.

combinational logic A logic system whose blocks do not contain memory and hence compute the same output given the same input.

commit unit The unit in a dynamic or out-of-order execution pipeline that decides when it is safe to release the result of an operation to programmer-visible registers and memory.

compiler A program that translates high-level language statements into assembly language statements.

compulsory miss Also called cold start miss. A cache miss caused by the first access to a block that has never been in the cache.

computer generation A classification of computers often based on the implementation technology used in each generation, originally lasting eight to ten years.

conditional branch An instruction that requires the comparison of two values and that allows for a subsequent transfer of control to a new address in the program based on the outcome of the comparison.

conflict miss Also called collision miss. A cache miss that occurs in a set-associative or direct-mapped cache when multiple blocks compete for the same set and that are eliminated in a fully associative cache of the same size.

context switch A changing of the internal state of the processor to allow a different process to use the processor that includes saving the state needed to return to the currently executing process.

control The component of the processor that commands the datapath, memory, and I/O devices according to the instructions of the program.

control hazard *See* branch hazard.

control signal A signal used for multiplexor selection or for directing the operation of a functional unit; contrasts with a data signal, which contains information that is operated on by a functional unit.

control value *See* selector value.

CPI *See* clock cycles per instruction (CPI).

CPU *See* central processor unit (CPU).

CPU execution time Also called CPU time. The actual time the CPU spends computing for a specific task.

CPU time *See* CPU execution time.

crossbar network A network that allows any node to communicate with any other node in one pass through the network.

cycle *See* clock cycle.

D flip-flop A flip-flop with one data input that stores the value of that input signal in the internal memory when the clock edge occurs.

daisy chain arbitration A bus arbitration scheme in which the bus grant line is run through the devices from highest priority to lowest (the priorities are determined by the position on the bus) so that when the bus is requested the highest priority device sees the bus grant signal first.

data dependencies The need for specific data at a given point in a pipeline.

data hazard Also called pipeline data hazard. An occurrence in which a planned instruction cannot execute in the proper clock cycle because data that is needed to execute the instruction is not yet available.

data parallelism Parallelism achieved by having massive data.

data segment The segment of a Unix object or executable file that contains a binary representation of the initialized data used by the program.

data transfer instruction A command that moves data between memory and registers.

datapath The component of the processor that performs arithmetic operations.

datapath element A functional unit used to operate on or hold data within a processor. In the MIPS implementation the datapath elements include the instruction and data memories, the register file, the arithmetic logic unit (ALU), and adders.

deasserted signal A signal that is (logically) false, or 0.

decoder A logic block that has an n-bit input and $2n$ outputs where only one output is asserted for each input combination.

defect A microscopic flaw in a wafer or in patterning steps that can result in the failure of the die containing that defect.

delay *See* rotation latency.

delayed branch A type of branch where the instruction immediately following the branch is always executed, independent of whether the branch condition is true or false.

delayed load A software format that requires load instructions to be followed by an instruction independent of the load.

die The individual rectangular sections that are cut from a wafer, more informally known as chips.

die area The size of a die.

direct-mapped cache A cache structure in which each memory location is mapped to exactly one location in the cache.

direct memory access (DMA) A mechanism that provides a device controller the ability to transfer data directly to or from the memory without involving the processor.

directory A repository for information on the state of every block in main memory, including which caches have copies of the block, whether it is dirty, and so on.

dispatch An operation in a microprogrammed control unit in which the next microinstruction is selected on the basis of one or more fields of a macroinstruction, usually by creating a table containing the addresses of the target microinstructions and indexing the table using a field of the macroinstruction. The dispatch tables are typically implemented in ROM or programmable logic array (PLA). The term *dispatch* is also used in dynamically scheduled processors to refer to the process of sending an instruction to a queue.

displacement addressing *See* base addressing.

distributed arbitration by collision detection A bus arbitration scheme that allows each device to independently request the bus and that uses a scheme for retrying the arbitration when multiple simultaneous requests occur.

distributed arbitration by self-selection A bus arbitration scheme that gives the devices requesting the bus the ability to determine which device gets the bus by having each requester detect whether it should receive the bus allocation.

distributed memory Physical memory that is divided into modules, with some placed near each processor in a multiprocessor.

distributed shared memory (DSM) A memory scheme that uses addresses to access remote data when demanded rather than retrieving the data in case it might be used.

divisor A number that the dividend is divided by; produces the dividend when multiplied by the quotient and added to the remainder.

DMA *See* direct memory access (DMA).

don't-care term An element of a logical function in which the output does not depend on the values of all the inputs. Don't-care terms may be specified in different ways.

double precision A floating-point value represented in two 32-bit words.

DRAM *See* dynamic random access memory (DRAM).

DSM *See* distributed shared memory (DSM).

dynamic pipeline scheduling A form of scheduling that goes past stalls in order to find later instructions to execute while waiting for the stalls to be resolved.

dynamic random access memory (DRAM) Memory that contains the instructions and data of a program while it is running, which allows faster access than accessing a magnetic disk.

edge-triggered clocking A clocking scheme in which all state changes occur on a clock edge.

Ethernet A computer network whose length is limited to about a kilometer. Originally capable of transferring up to 10 million bits per second, newer versions can run up to 100 million bits per second and even 1000 million bits per second. It treats the wire like a bus with multiple masters and uses collision detection and a back-off scheme for handling simultaneous accesses.

exception Also called interrupt. An unscheduled event that disrupts program execution; used to detect overflow.

exception enable Also called interrupt enable. A signal or action that controls whether the process responds to an exception or not; necessary for preventing the occurrence of exceptions during intervals before the processor has safely saved the state needed to restart.

exclusive OR gate Hardware that performs the exclusive OR operation on input signals yielding a single signal result exclusive OR operation; also, an operation that leaves a 1 in the result only if two bits of the operands are unequal.

executable file A functional program in the format of an object file that contains no unresolved references, relocation information, symbol table, or debugging information.

execution time *See* response time.

exponent In the numerical representation system of floating-point arithmetic, the value that is placed in the exponent field.

external label Also called global label. A label referring to an object that can be referenced from files other than the one in which it is defined.

fairness   A property of an allocation scheme, such as a bus arbitration protocol, that ensures that no device, even one with low priority, ever be completely locked out from the bus.

false sharing   A sharing situation in which two unrelated shared variables are located in the same cache block and the full block is exchanged between processors even though the processors are accessing different variables.

finite state machine   A sequential logic function consisting of a set of inputs and outputs, a next-state function that maps the current state and the inputs to a new state, and an output function that maps the current state and possibly the inputs to a set of asserted outputs.

firmware   Microcode implemented in a memory structure, typically ROM or RAM.

flip-flop   A memory element for which the output is equal to the value of the stored state inside the element and for which the internal state is changed only on a clock edge.

floating point   Computer arithmetic that represents numbers in which the binary point is not fixed.

floppy disk   A portable form of secondary memory composed of a rotating mylar platter coated with a magnetic recording material.

flush (instructions)   To discard instructions in a pipeline, usually due to an unexpected event.

formal parameter   A variable that is the argument to a procedure or macro; replaced by that argument once the macro is expanded.

forward reference   A label that is used before it is defined.

forwarding   Also called bypassing. A method of resolving a data hazard by retrieving the missing data element from internal buffers rather than waiting for it to arrive from programmer-visible registers or memory.

frame pointer   A value denoting the location of the saved registers and local variables for a given procedure.

fully associative cache   A cache structure in which a block can be placed in any location in the cache.

fully connected network   A network that connects processor-memory nodes by supplying a dedicated communication link between every node.

gate   A device that implements basic logic functions, such as AND or OR.

general-purpose electronic computer   A computer that has not been constructed for one specific function.

general-purpose register (GPR)   A register that can be used for addresses or for data with virtually any instruction.

geometric mean $\sqrt[n]{\prod_{i=1}^{n} \text{Execution time ratio}_i}$ A formula useful for summarizing execution times that have been normalized.

gigabyte   Traditionally 1,073,741,824 (2^{30}) bytes, although some communications and secondary storage systems have redefined it to mean 1,000,000,000 (10^9) bytes.

global label   *See* external label.

global miss rate   The fraction of references that miss in all levels of a multilevel cache.

global pointer   The register that is reserved for static data.

GPR   *See* general-purpose register (GPR).

guard   The first of two extra bits kept on the right during intermediate calculations of floating-point numbers; used to improve rounding accuracy.

handshaking protocol   A series of steps used to coordinate asynchronous bus transfers in which the sender and receiver proceed to the next step only when both parties agree that the current step has been completed.

hard disk   A form of secondary memory composed of rotating metal platters coated with a magnetic recording material.

hardwired control   An implementation of finite state machine control typically using programmable logic arrays (PLAs) or collections of PLAs and random logic.

harmonic mean of rates $HM = \dfrac{n}{\sum_{i=1}^{n} \dfrac{1}{\text{Rate}_i}}$ A summary that tracks execution time when the data is given as rates rather than as a times.

hexadecimal   Numbers in base 16.

high-level programming language   A portable language such as C, Fortran, or Java composed of English words and algebraic notation that can be translated by a compiler into assembly language.

hit rate   The fraction of memory accesses found in a cache.

hit time   The time required to access a level of the memory hierarchy, including the time needed to determine whether the access is a hit or a miss.

hold time The minimum time during which the input must be valid after the clock edge.

horizontal microcode Use of microinstructions containing many fields that can control the datapath units in parallel and require little additional decoding. The use of many fields makes the microinstructions wider or more horizontal.

immediate addressing An addressing regime in which the operand is a constant within the instruction itself.

implementation Hardware that obeys the architecture abstraction.

imprecise exception *See* imprecise interrupt.

imprecise interrupt Also called imprecise exception. Interrupts or exceptions in pipelined computers that are not associated with the exact instruction that was the cause of the interrupt or exception.

in-order commit A commit in which the results of pipelined execution are written to the programmer-visible state in the same order that instructions are fetched.

in-order execution A conventional pipelined execution, in which all following instructions must wait when an instruction is blocked from executing.

input device A mechanism through which the computer is fed information, such as the keyboard or mouse.

instruction format A form of representation of an instruction composed of fields of binary numbers.

instruction latency The inherent execution time for an instruction.

instruction mix A measure of the dynamic frequency of instructions across one or many programs.

instruction set The vocabulary of commands understood by a given architecture.

instruction set architecture Also called architecture. An abstract interface between the hardware and the lowest level software of a machine that encompasses all the information necessary to write a machine language program that will run correctly, including instructions, registers, memory size, and so on.

integrated circuit Also called chip. A device combining dozens to millions of transistors.

interrupt An exception that comes from outside of the processor. (Some architectures use the term *interrupt* for all exceptions.)

interrupt-driven I/O An I/O scheme that employs interrupts to indicate to the processor that an I/O device needs attention.

interrupt enable *See* exception enable.

interrupt handler A piece of code that is run as a result of an exception or an interrupt.

I/O instruction A dedicated instruction that is used to give a command to an I/O device and that specifies both the device number and the command word (or the location of the command word in memory).

jump address table Also called jump table. A table of addresses of alternative instruction sequences.

jump-and-link instruction An instruction that jumps to an address and simultaneously saves the address of the following instruction in a register ($ra in MIPS).

jump table *See* jump address table.

kernel benchmark A small, time-intensive code fragment from a real program that is used for performance evaluation.

kernel mode Also called supervisor mode. A mode indicating that a running process is an operating system process.

kilobyte 1024 (2^{10}) bytes.

LAN *See* local area network (LAN).

latch A memory element in which the output is equal to the value of the stored state inside the element and the state is changed whenever the appropriate inputs change and the clock is asserted.

latency (pipeline) The number of stages in a pipeline or the number of stages between two instructions during execution.

least recently used (LRU) A replacement scheme in which the block replaced is the one that has been unused for the longest time.

least significant bit The rightmost bit in a MIPS word.

level-sensitive clocking A timing methodology in which state changes occur at either high or low clock levels but are not instantaneous, as such changes are in edge-triggered designs.

link editor *See* linker.

linker Also called link editor. A systems program that combines independently assembled machine language programs and resolves all undefined labels into an executable file.

load-store machine Also called register-register machine. An instruction set architecture in which all operations are between registers and data memory may only be accessed via loads or stores.

load-use data hazard A specific form of data hazard in which the data requested by a load instruction has not yet become available when it is requested.

loader A systems program that places an object program in main memory so that it is ready to execute.

local area network (LAN) A network designed to carry data within a geographically confined area, typically within a single building.

local label A label referring to an object that can be used only within the file in which it is defined.

local miss rate The fraction of references to one level of a cache that miss; used in multilevel hierarchies.

lock A synchronization device that allows access to data to only one processor at a time.

logic minimization   A technique for reducing the number of gates needed to implement a set of logic functions.

loop unrolling   A technique to get more performance from loops that access arrays, in which multiple copies of the loop body are made and instructions from different iterations are scheduled together.

LRU   *See* least recently used (LRU).

machine language   Binary representation used for communication within a computer system.

macro   A pattern-matching and replacement facility that provides a simple mechanism to name a frequently used sequence of instructions.

macroinstruction   An instruction in the instruction set architecture being implemented, used to distinguish the instructions visible to the programmer from the microinstructions of a microprogrammed control unit.

magnetic disk   A form of nonvolatile secondary memory composed of rotating platters coated with a magnetic recording material.

main memory   *See* primary memory.

main-memory coherence   Consistency in the value of data in memory in a network-connected multiprocessor.

massively parallel   A computer with at least 100 processors.

maximally encoded   Use of encoded forms of control that require multiple levels of decode; vertical microcode is maximally encoded.

megabyte   Traditionally 1,048,576 (2^{20}) bytes, although some communications and secondary storage systems have redefined it to mean 1,000,000 (10^6) bytes.

megaFLOPS   *See* million floating-point operations per second (MFLOPS).

memory   The storage area in which programs are kept when they are running and that contains the data needed by the running programs.

memory hierarchy   A structure that uses multiple levels of memories; as the distance from the CPU increases, the size of the memories and the access time both increase.

memory-mapped I/O   An I/O scheme in which portions of address space are assigned to I/O devices and reads and writes to those addresses are interpreted as commands to the I/O device.

MESI cache coherency protocol   A write-invalidate protocol whose name is an acronym for the four states of the protocol: Modified, Exclusive, Shared, Invalid.

message passing   Communicating between multiple processors by explicitly sending and receiving information.

metastability   A situation that occurs if a signal is sampled when it is not stable for the required set-up and hold times, possibly causing the sampled value to fall in the indeterminate region between a high and low value.

MFLOPS   *See* million floating-point operations per second (MFLOPS).

microcode   The set of microinstructions that control a processor.

microcode assembler   A program that translates microprograms into microinstructions that can be implemented in a ROM or PLA.

microinstruction   A representation of control using low-level instructions, each of which asserts a set of control signals that are active on a given clock cycle as well as specifies what microinstruction to execute next.

microprogram   A symbolic representation of control in the form of instructions, called microinstructions, that are executed on a simple micromachine.

microprogrammed control   A method of specifying control that uses microcode rather than a finite state representation.

million floating-point operations per second (MFLOPS)   Also called megaFLOPS. A measurement of program execution speed based on the number of millions of floating-point operations executed per second. MFLOPS is computed as the number of floating-point operations in a program divided by the product of the execution time and 10^6.

million instructions per second (MIPS)   A measurement of program execution speed based on the number of millions of instructions. MIPS is computed as the instruction count divided by the product of the execution time and 10^6.

MIMD   *See* multiple instruction streams, multiple data streams (MIMD).

minimally encoded   Use of an unencoded control format that can directly control a datapath; horizontal microcode is minimally encoded.

minterms   Also called product terms. A set of logic inputs joined by conjunction (AND operations); the product terms form the first logic stage of the programmable logic array (PLA).

MIPS   *See* million instructions per second (MIPS).

miss penalty   The time required to fetch a block into a level of the memory hierarchy from the lower level, including the time to access the block, transmit it from one level to the other, and insert it in the level that experienced the miss.

miss rate   The fraction of memory accesses not found in a level of the memory hierarchy.

most significant bit   The leftmost bit in a MIPS word.

motherboard   A plastic board containing packages of integrated circuits or chips, including processor, cache, memory, and connectors for I/O devices such as networks and disks.

multicomputer   Parallel processors with multiple private addresses.

multicycle implementation   Also called multiple clock cycle implementation. An implementation in which an instruction is executed in multiple clock cycles.

multilevel cache   A memory hierarchy with multiple levels of caches, rather than just a cache and main memory.

multiple clock cycle implementation   *See* multicycle implementation.

multiple-instruction issue   A procedure in which the instruction fetch unit can send multiple instructions to the next pipeline stage in a single clock cycle.

multiple instruction streams, multiple data streams (MIMD)   A computer classification in Flynn's taxonomy referring to computers that use multiple instruction streams and multiple data streams.

multiprocessor   Parallel processors with a single shared address.

multistage network   A network that supplies a small switch at each node.

NAND gate   An inverted AND gate.

network bandwidth   Informally, the peak transfer rate of a network; can refer to the speed of a single link or the collective transfer rate of all links in the network.

next-state counter   A counter that supplies the sequential next state.

next-state function   A combinational function that, given the inputs and the current state, determines the next state of a finite state machine.

next-state output   An output of the combinational logic that specifies the next-state number.

nonblocking cache   A cache that allows the processor to make references to the cache while the cache is handling an earlier miss.

nonuniform memory access (NUMA)   A type of single-address space multiprocessor in which some memory accesses are faster than others depending which processor asks for which word.

nonvolatile memory   A form of memory that retains data even in the absence of a power source and that is used to store programs between runs. Magnetic disk is nonvolatile and DRAM is not.

nop   An instruction that does no operation to change state.

NOR gate   An inverted OR gate.

normalized   A number in floating-point notation that has no leading 0s.

NUMA   *See* nonuniform memory access (NUMA).

object program   A combination of machine language instructions, data, and information needed to place them properly in memory.

opcode   The field that denotes the operation and format of an instruction.

operating system   Supervising program that manages the resources of a computer for the benefit of the programs that run on that machine.

out-of-order commit   A commit in which the results of pipelined execution need not be written to the programmer visible state in the same order that instructions are fetched.

out-of-order execution   A situation in pipelined execution when an instruction blocked from executing does not cause the following instructions to wait.

output device   A mechanism that conveys the result of a computation to the user.

overflow (floating-point)   A situation in which a positive exponent becomes too large to fit in the exponent field.

page fault   An event that occurs when an accessed page is not present in main memory.

page mode   A mechanism in DRAM that provides the ability to access multiple bits of a row by changing the column address only and, hence, is faster than a normal access cycle that changes row and column addresses.

page table   The table containing the virtual to physical address translations in a virtual memory system. The table, which is stored in memory, is typically indexed by the virtual page number; each entry in the table contains the physical page number for that virtual page if the page is currently in memory.

parallel processing program   A single program that runs on multiple processors simultaneously.

PC   *See* program counter (PC).

PC-relative addressing   An addressing regime in which the address is the sum of the program counter (PC) and a constant in the instruction.

personal computer   A general-purpose computer designed to be manufactured in high volume and at a cost affordable enough to allow for use in the home.

physical address   An address in main memory.

physically addressed cache   A cache that is addressed by a physical address.

pipeline data hazard   *See* data hazard.

pipeline stall   Also called bubble. A stall initiated in order to resolve a hazard.

pipelining   An implementation technique in which multiple instructions are overlapped in execution, much like to an assembly line.

pipelining stage   A step in executing an instruction that occurs simultaneously with other steps in other instructions and typically lasts one clock cycle.

pixel   The smallest individual picture element. Screen are composed of hundreds of thousands to millions of pixels, organized in a matrix.

PLA   *See* programmable logic array (PLA).

polling   The process of periodically checking the status of an I/O device to determine the need to service the device.

precise exception   *See* precise interrupt.

precise interrupt   Also called precise exception. An interrupt or exception that is always associated with the correct instruction in pipelined computers.

prefetching   A technique in which data blocks needed in the future are brought into the cache early by the use of special instructions that specify the address of the block.

primary memory   Also called main memory. Volatile memory used to hold programs while they are running; typically consists of DRAM in today's computers.

procedure   A stored subroutine that performs a specific task based on the parameters with which it is provided.

procedure call convention   *See* register-use convention.

procedure call frame   A block of memory that is used to hold values passed to a procedure as arguments, to save registers that a procedure may modify but that the procedure's caller does not want changed, and to provide space for variables local to a procedure.

procedure frame   Also called activation record. The segment of the stack containing a procedure's saved registers and local variables.

processor-memory bus   A bus that connects processor and memory and that is short, generally high speed, and matched to the memory system so as to maximize memory-processor bandwidth.

product terms   *See* minterms.

program counter (PC)   The register containing the address of the instruction in the program being executed

programmable logic array (PLA)   A structured-logic element composed of a set of inputs and corresponding input complements and two stages of logic: the first generating product terms of the inputs and input complements and the second generating sum terms of the product terms. Hence, PLAs implement logic functions as a sum of products.

programmable ROM (PROM)   A form of read-only memory that can be programmed when a designer knows its contents.

PROM   *See* programmable ROM (PROM).

propagation time   The time required for an input to a flip-flop to propagate to the outputs of the flip-flop.

protection   A set of mechanisms for ensuring that multiple processes sharing the processor, memory, or I/O devices cannot interfere, intentionally or unintentionally, with one another by reading or writing each other's data. These mechanisms also isolate the operating system from a user process.

pseudoinstruction   A common variation of assembly language instructions often treated as if it were an instruction in its own right.

quotient   The primary result of a division; a number that when multiplied by the divisor and added to the remainder produces the dividend.

RAID   *See* redundant arrays of inexpensive disks (RAID).

raster cathode ray tube (CRT) display   A display, such as a television set, that scans an image one line at a time, 30 to 75 times per second.

read-only memory (ROM)   A memory whose contents are designated at creation time, after which the contents can only be read. ROM is used as structured logic to implement a set of logic functions by using the terms in the logic functions as address inputs and the outputs as bits in each word of the memory.

receive message routine   A routine used by a processor in machines with private memories to accept a message from another processor.

recursive procedures   Procedures that call themselves either directly or indirectly through a chain of calls.

redundant arrays of inexpensive disks (RAID)   An organization of disks that uses an array of small and inexpensive disks so as to increase both performance and reliability.

reference bit   Also called use bit. A field that is set whenever a page is accessed and that is used to implement LRU or other replacement schemes.

register addressing   A mode of addressing in which the operand is a register.

register file   A state element that consists of a set of registers that can be read and written by supplying a register number to be accessed.

register-register machine   *See* load-store machine.

register use   *See* register-use convention.

register-use convention   Also called procedure call convention. A software protocol governing the use of registers by procedures.

relocation information   The segment of a Unix object file that identifies instructions and data words that depend on absolute addresses.

remainder   The secondary result of a division; a number that when added to the product of the quotient and the divisor produces the dividend.

rename buffer   Also called rename register. An extra internal register within processors that is used to hold results while waiting for the commit unit to commit the result to one of the real registers.

rename register   *See* rename buffer.

reorder buffer   A register that holds instructions in a dynamic pipelined machine whose results have not yet been committed to programmer-visible registers or memory; machines with out-of-order execution and in-order commit will retire an instruction from the reorder buffer only when the instruction has finished execution and all instructions ahead of it have been completed.

reservation station   A buffer within a functional unit that holds the operands and the operation.

response time   Also called execution time. The total time required for the computer to complete a task, including disk accesses, memory accesses, I/O activities, operating system overhead, CPU execution time, and so on.

restartable instruction   An instruction that can resume execution after an exception is resolved without the exception's affecting the result of the instruction.

return address   A link to the calling site that allows a procedure to return to the proper address; in MIPS it is stored in register $ra.

ROM   *See* read-only memory (ROM).

rotation latency   Also called delay. The time required for the desired sector of a disk to rotate under the read/write head; usually assumed to be half the rotation time.

round   Method to make the intermediate floating-point result fit the floating-point format; the goal is typically to find the nearest number that can be represented in the format.

scientific notation   A notation that renders numbers with a single digit to the left of the decimal point.

SCSI   *See* small computer systems interface (SCSI).

secondary memory   Nonvolatile memory used to store programs and data between runs; typically consists of magnetic disks in today's computers.

sector   One of the segments that make up a track on a magnetic disk; a sector is the smallest amount of information that is read or written on a disk.

seek   The process of positioning a read/write head over the proper track on a disk.

segmentation   A variable-size address mapping scheme in which an address consists of two parts: a segment number, which is mapped to a physical address, and a segment offset.

selector value   Also called control value. The control signal that is used to select one of the input values of a multiplexor as the output of the multiplexor.

semiconductor   A substance that does not conduct electricity well.

send message routine   A routine used by a processor in machines with private memories to pass to another processor.

separate compilation   Splitting a program across many files, each of which can be compiled without knowledge of what is in the other files.

sequential access memory   Memory whose access time differs depending on the location of the data being retrieved because data is stored sequentially so that all data must be passed over to access the final bit of information; contrasts with random access memory, in which any bit may be accessed in the same time.

sequential logic   A group of logic elements that contain memory and hence whose value depends on the inputs as well as the current contents of the memory.

set-associative cache   A cache that has a fixed number of locations (at least two) where each block can be placed.

set-up time   The minimum time that the input to a memory device must be valid before the clock edge.

shared memory   A memory for a parallel processor with a single address space, implying implicit communication with loads and stores.

sign-extend   To increase the size of a data item by replicating the high-order sign bit of the original data item in the high-order bits of the larger, destination data item.

significand   In the numerical representation system of floating-point arithmetic, the value in that is placed in the significand field.

silicon   A substance found in sand that does not conduct electricity well.

silicon crystal ingot   A rod composed of silicon crystal that is between 6 and 12 inches in diameter and about 12 to 24 inches long.

SIMD   *See* single instruction stream, multiple data streams (SIMD).

SIMM   *See* single in-line memory module (SIMM).

single clock cycle implementation   *See* single-cycle implementation.

single-cycle implementation   Also called single clock cycle implementation. An implementation in which an instruction is executed in one clock cycle.

single in-line memory module (SIMM)   A small printed circuit board containing 4 to 24 DRAM integrated circuits. Today's computers use SIMMs to allow main memory to be upgraded and expanded over time by the customer.

single instruction stream, multiple data streams (SIMD) A computer classification in Flynn's taxonomy that refers to computers with single instruction streams but multiple data streams and in which a single instruction operates on many data elements at the same time.

single instruction stream, single data stream (SISD) A computer classification in Flynn's taxonomy that refers to computers with single instruction streams and single data streams. (SISD is the conventional processor covered in the first eight chapters.)

single precision A floating-point value represented in a single 32-bit word.

SISD *See* single instruction stream, single data stream (SISD).

slave A device that responds to read and write requests but does not generate them and hence cannot be a bus master.

small computer systems interface (SCSI) A bus used as a standard for I/O devices.

SMP *See* symmetric multiprocessor (SMP).

snooping cache coherency A method for maintaining cache coherency in which all cache controllers monitor or snoop on the bus to determine whether or not they have a copy of the desired block.

source language The high-level language in which a program is originally written.

spatial locality The locality principle stating that if a data location is referenced, data locations with nearby addresses will tend to be referenced soon.

SPEC benchmark *See* system performance evaluation cooperative (SPEC) benchmark.

speculative execution A pipelining technique that combines dynamic scheduling with branch prediction.

speedup The measure of how a machine performs relative to how it previously performed before an enhancement was implemented. Speedup is equal to the ratio of execution time before the enhancement to execution time after the enhancement.

split cache A scheme in which a level of the memory hierarchy is composed of two independent caches that operate in parallel with each other with one handling instructions and one handling data.

split transaction protocol A protocol in which the bus is released during a bus transaction while the requester is waiting for the data to be transmitted, which frees the bus for access by another requester.

SRAM *See* static random access memory (SRAM).

stack A data structure for spilling registers organized as a last-in-first-out queue.

stack frame *See* procedure call frame.

stack pointer A value denoting the most recently allocated address in a stack that shows where registers should be spilled or where old register values can be found.

stack segment The portion of memory used by a program to hold procedure call frames.

state assignment A control optimization that works by attempting to choose the state numbers such that the resulting logic equations contain more redundancy and can thus be simplified.

state element A memory element.

state input An input to the combinational logic that specifies the current state.

static data The portion of memory that contains data whose size is known to the compiler and whose lifetime is the program's entire execution.

static random access memory (SRAM) A memory where data is stored statically (as in flip-flops) rather than dynamically (as in DRAM). SRAMs are faster than DRAMs, but less dense and more expensive per bit.

sticky bit A bit used in rounding in addition to guard and round that is set whenever there are nonzero bits to the right of the round bit.

stored-program computer A computer whose instructions are represented as numbers, allowing the same memory to contain instructions and data and thus allowing programs to produce programs.

stored-program concept The idea that instructions and data of many types can be stored in memory as numbers, leading to the stored program computer.

structural hazard An occurrence in which a planned instruction cannot execute in the proper clock cycle because the hardware cannot support the combination of instructions that are set to execute in the given clock cycle.

subroutine library A collection of commonly used programs.

sum of products A form of logical representation that employs a logical sum (OR) of products (terms joined using the AND operator).

supercomputer The fastest and most expensive computer, typically used for scientific computation. Supercomputers generally cost between $1 and $30 million.

superpipelining A technique that increases processor speed by lengthening pipelines.

superscalar An advanced pipelining technique that enables the processor to execute more than one instruction per clock cycle.

superscalar pipelining A technique that replicates internal components of the computer in order to launch and execute multiple instructions in every pipeline stage.

supervisor mode *See* kernel mode.

symbol table A table that matches names of labels to the addresses of the memory words that instructions occupy.

symmetric multiprocessor (SMP) Also called UMA machine. A multiprocessor in which accesses to main memory take the same amount of time no matter which processor requests the access and no matter which word is asked.

synchronization The process of coordinating the behavior of two or more processes, which may be running on different processors.

synchronizer failure A situation in which a flip-flop enters a metastable state and where some logic blocks reading the output of the flip-flop see a 0 while others see a 1.

synchronous bus A bus that includes a clock in the control lines and a fixed protocol for communicating that is relative to the clock.

synchronous system A memory system that employs clocks and where data signals are read only when the clock indicates that the signal values are stable.

system call A special instruction that transfers control from user mode to a dedicated location in supervisor code space, invoking the exception mechanism in the process.

system CPU time The CPU time spent in the operating system performing tasks on behalf of the program.

system performance evaluation cooperative (SPEC) benchmark A set of standard CPU-intensive, integer and floating point benchmarks based on real programs.

systems software Software that provides services that are commonly useful, including operating systems, compilers, and assemblers.

tag A field in a table used for a memory hierarchy that contains the address information required to identify whether the associated block in the hierarchy corresponds to a requested word.

temporal locality The principle stating that if a data location is referenced then it will tend to be referenced again soon.

terabyte Originally 1,099,511,627,776 (2^{40}) bytes, although some communications and secondary storage systems have redefined it to mean 1,000,000,000,000 (10^{12}) bytes.

text segment The segment of a Unix object file that contains the machine language code for routines in the source file.

three Cs model A cache model in which all cache misses are classified into one of three categories: compulsory misses, capacity misses, and conflict misses.

tick *See* clock cycle.

TLB *See* translation-lookaside buffer (TLB).

track One of 1000 to 5000 concentric circles that makes up the surface of a magnetic disk.

transaction processing A type of application that involves handling small short operations (called transactions) that typically require both I/O and computation. Transaction processing applications typically have both response time requirements and a performance measurement based on the throughput of transactions.

transfer time The time required to transfer a block of bits, typically a sector, during disk access.

transistor An on/off switch controlled by electricity.

translation-lookaside buffer (TLB) A cache that keeps track of recently used address mappings to avoid an access to the page table.

ulp *See* units in the last place (ulp).

UMA *See* uniform memory access (UMA).

UMA machine *See* symmetric multiprocessor (SMP).

underflow (floating-point) A situation in which a negative exponent becomes too large to fit in the exponent field.

uniform memory access (UMA) Memory access that takes the same amount of time no matter which processor requests the access and no matter which word is asked for.

units in the last place (ulp) The number of bits in error in the least significant bits of the significand between the actual number and the number that can be prepresented.

unresolved reference A reference that requires more information from an outside source in order to be complete.

use bit *See* reference bit.

user CPU time The CPU time spent in a program itself.

vacuum tube An electronic component, predecessor of the transistor, that consists of a hollow glass tube about 5 to 10 cm long from which as much air has been removed as possible.

valid bit A field in the tables of a memory hierarchy that indicates that the associated block in the hierarchy contains valid data.

vector processor An architecture and compiler model that was popularized by supercomputers in which high-level operations work on linear arrays of numbers.

vector supercomputer A supercomputer whose instructions operate on vectors of numbers, typically 64 floating-point numbers at a time.

vectored interrupt An interrupt for which the address to which control is transferred is determined by the cause of the exception.

vertical microcode Use of microinstructions containing many fewer fields that require additional decoding before being used to control the datapath units. The use of fewer fields makes the microinstructions narrower or more vertical.

very large scale integrated (VLSI) circuit A device containing tens of thousands to millions of transistors.

virtual address An address that corresponds to a location in virtual space and is translated by address mapping to a physical address when memory is accessed.

virtual machine A virtual computer that appears to have nondelayed branches and loads and a richer instruction set than the actual hardware.

virtual memory A technique that uses main memory as a "cache" for secondary storage.

virtually addressed cache A cache that is accessed with a virtual address rather than a physical address.

VLSI circuit *See* very large scale integrated (VLSI) circuit.

volatile memory Storage, such as DRAM, that only retains data if it is receiving power.

wafer A slice from a silicon ingot no more than 0.1 inch thick, used to create chips.

weighted arithmetic mean A summary that tracks the execution time of a workload with weighting factors designed to reflect the presence of the programs in a workload; computed as the sum of the products of weighting factors and execution times.

wide area network A network extended over hundreds of kilometers which can span a continent.

word The natural unit of access in a computer, usually a group of 32 bits; corresponds to the size of a register in the MIPS architecture.

workload A set of programs run on a computer that is either the actual collection of applications run by a user or is constructed from real programs to approximate such a mix. A typical workload specifies both the programs as well as the relative frequencies.

write-back A scheme that handles writes by updating values only to the block in the cache, then writing the modified block to the lower level of the hierarchy when the block is replaced.

write-broadcast A snooping protocol scheme in which the writing processor disseminates the new data over the bus, allowing all copies to be updated with the new value.

write buffer A queue that holds data while the data are waiting to be written to memory.

write-invalidate A type of snooping protocol in which the writing processor causes all copies in other caches to be invalidated before changing its local copy, which allows it to update the local data until another processor asks for it.

write-through A scheme in which writes always update both the cache and the memory, ensuring that data is always consistent between the two.

yield The percentage of good dies from the total number of dies on the wafer.

Index

Human Nutrition and Dietetics

R. Passmore
DM(Oxon), FRCP(Edin)
Formerly Lieutenant-Colonel, Indian Medical Service,
Reader in Physiology,
University of Edinburgh

M. A. Eastwood
MB, MSc, FRCP(Edin)
Physician, Western General Hospital, Edinburgh

A. R. Mills
PhD(Edin), FRCP(Edin), FFCM
Formerly of the Colonial Medical Service,
WHO Staff in India and Nepal
Senior Lecturer in Community Medicine, University of Edinburgh

W. A. M. Cutting
MB, FRCP(Edin)
Senior Lecturer, Tropical Child Health, University of
Edinburgh

B. F. Clarke
MB(NZ), FRCP(Edin)
Physician, Royal Infirmary, Edinburgh

Janet M. Knox
SRD
Senior Dietitian, Royal Infirmary, Edinburgh

M. F. Oliver
MD, FRCP(Edin & Lond), FFCM
Professor of Cardiology, University of Edinburgh,
Physician, Royal Infirmary, Edinburgh

J. M. Bone
BSc, MB, FRCP(Edin)
Physician, Royal Liverpool Hospital, Liverpool

Davidson and Passmore Human Nutrition and Dietetics

R. Passmore
M. A. Eastwood

Assisted by the following
members of the
Edinburgh Medical School

A. R. MILLS *Community medicine*
W. A. M. CUTTING *Paediatrics*
B. F. CLARK *Diabetes*
JANET KNOX *Dietetics*
M. F. OLIVER *Cardiology*
J. M. BONE *Renal diseases*

EIGHTH EDITION

CHURCHILL LIVINGSTONE
EDINBURGH LONDON MELBOURNE AND NEW YORK 1986

CHURCHILL LIVINGSTONE
Medical Division of Longman Group Limited

Distributed in the United States of America by
Churchill Livingstone Inc., 1560 Broadway, New York,
N.Y. 10036, and by associated companies, branches
and representatives throughout the world.

First edition 1959
Second edition 1963
Third edition 1966
Fourth edition 1969
Fifth edition 1972
Sixth edition 1975
Seventh edition 1979
Eighth edition 1986

ISBN 0 443 02467 7 (PPR)
ISBN 0 443 02486 3 (CSD)

British Library Cataloguing in Publication Data
Davidson, *Sir* Stanley
   Davidson and Passmore human nutrition and
   dietetics. — 8th ed.
   1. Nutrition
   I. Title   II. Passmore, R.   III. Eastwood, M. A.
   613.2   TX353

Library of Congress Cataloging in Publication Data
Davidson, Leybourne Stanley Patrick, Sir, 1894–
   Davidson and Passmore Human nutrition and dietetics.
   Rev. ed. of: Human nutrition and dietetics/Stanley
Davidson . . . [et al.] 7th ed. 1979.
   Bibliograpy: p.
   Includes index.
   1. Nutritional disorders. 2. Diet therapy.
3. Nutrition.   I. Passmore, R. (Reginald)   II. Eastwood,
M. A. (Martin A.)   III. Title.   IV. Title: Human nutrition
and dietetics. [DNLM; 1. Diet Therapy.   2. Nutrition
Disorders.   WB 400 D252h]
RC620.D38   1985   613.2   85–12762

Produced by Longman Group (FE) Ltd
Printed in Hong Kong

Preface

Nutrition and dietetics have an important role in promoting health and in preventing and treating diseases. This book gives an introductory account of each of these aspects and is related to problems in countries throughout the world. The primary aim is to help undergraduates in colleges and universities, but it is hoped that it will continue to be useful to others. Many people who become interested in nutrition and whose work may have nutritional implications have already a professional knowledge of a part of the subject, but little or none of some of the other aspects. Such people may be doctors, food scientists and manufacturers, educationists, economists, social scientists or administrators. The book should help them to increase the range of their knowledge and broaden their viewpoint.

The whole of the book has been revised and there are references to some 350 articles and books published in 1980 or later. These are the news of the day. Similar previous additions were making the book unwieldly and many dating from 1950 to 1980 have now been deleted. But there are still 200 references to papers and books published before 1950. We hope that students will read some of these. It is not possible to understand nutrition, or indeed any science, without some knowledge of how the masters of the past collected the information and developed the ideas that we use today.

Our first edition appeared in 1959 with Stanley Davidson as the senior author. He conceived the book, took a major part in the production of the first four editions and remained interested in it until the end of his life. Sadly he died in 1981. An appreciation of his contributions to nutrition and a brief account of his life and character follow this preface. Jack Brock, whose wisdom and wide knowledge of nutrition contributed much to the last three editions, died in 1983. He was a personal friend of long standing. Stewart Truswell after his move to Australia found it impossible to continue as an author. Much of what he contributed remains in this edition. Collaboration with him was always pleasant and fruitful and I regret greatly that it is no longer practical.

Fortunately Martin Eastwood was able to take his place and we have prepared this edition with the help of colleagues in the Edinburgh Medical School. These are named on the title page. Others who have helped with advice and material are Dr D. G. D. Barr, Dr Anne Ferguson, Mr L. Gove, Dr J. A. Lorrain, Dr D. S. McLaren, Mr J. N. Mansbridge, Mr N. Thomson, Ms Margaret Sangster, Ms Margaret Stoddard and Mr D. A. K. Waters. Edinburgh Medical School is large and flourishing. Its members travel widely and we have many visitors. It is a good place for conversations which help one to appreciate worldwide problems and new developments. We also have several excellent libraries. This edition owes a great deal to many people, but we alone must take the responsibility for errors of omission and commission.

We owe much to Kit Hamilton and Anne McCarthy for preparing the manuscript for the press and making the index, and to Sylvia Hull of Churchill Livingstone who has given continued support and encouragement over many years.

R. PASSMORE
M. A. EASTWOOD

Edinburgh, 1986

Leybourne Stanley Patrick Davidson (1894–1981)

Stanley Davidson's interest in nutrition arose from his work as a haematologist. Between 1927 and 1940 he contributed 34 papers on his laboratory and clinical studies on pernicious anaemia and iron deficiency anaemia. These papers were useful at the time but his reputation throughout the whole of the English-speaking world rests much more on his textbooks written for students. *The principles and practice of medicine* first published in 1952 was in the 13th edition and had sold a million copies at the time of his death. It has had more readers than William Osler's textbook with the same title first published in 1900. *A textbook of dietetics* with I. A. Anderson as a junior author was published in 1940 with a second edition in 1947. With the help of A. P. Meiklejohn and R. Passmore it was completely rewritten and published in 1959 with the title *Human nutrition and dietetics*. Seven editions of this have been produced, the later ones with the help of J. F. Brock and A. S. Truswell. It has survived longer as a working textbook than any of its three great predecessors, namely Robert Hutchinson's *Food and the principles of dietetics* (1900), Graham Lusk's *The science of nutrition* (1906) and Elmer McCollum's *The newer knowledge of nutrition* (1918).

A series of coincidences generated and maintained his interest in nutrition. In 1914 he was a preclinical medical student at Cambridge. Despite the fact that he had had one kidney removed for hydronephrosis when he was 12 years old, he enlisted in the Gordon Highlanders in August of that year. Then in his own words he 'spent the autumn, winter and spring in the trenches of Northern France under the dreadful conditions of wet and cold . . . In the summer of 1915 he was very severely wounded and developed gas gangrene. His life was seriously endangered by toxaemia, sepsis and cachexia for nearly a year. That his remaining kidney was markedly affected was manifested by the constant passage of albumin, leucocytes and casts in the urine. The diet prescribed and eaten for more than a year after discharge from hospital was low in protein and high in carbohydrate, and alcohol was prohibited. As the albuminuria continued and health was not improved, and because the restriction of food and drink proved extremely irksome, he decided to stop all dietary restrictions and eat and drink what he liked.' His health then improved and his single damaged kidney functioned effectively for more than 60 years. This personal experience gave him a commonsense and empirical attitude to dietetics which remained with him throughout his

professional life and made him critical and careful in the use of all restrictive diets.

The second coincidence arose out of his interest in pernicious anaemia. After qualifying in medicine at Edinburgh he trained both as a bacteriologist and as a clinician and began a general study of the relation of bacteria to disease. This led him to investigate the possible role of gut bacteria in the aetiology of pernicious anaemia. At this time, in Boston, Minot and Murphy were introducing the dietary treatment of the disease with raw liver, and Castle's brilliant investigations were providing a rationale for the good responses to this treatment. Davidson and Castle formed a friendship which was only ended by death. With G. L. Gulland, the Professor of Medicine, and Sister Pybus, the senior dietitian at the Royal Infirmary of Edinburgh, he developed the use of dietary liver for the treatment of the disease. A monograph, *Pernicious anaemia* (1930) by Davidson and Gulland gave a full account of the disease with many practical details of the dietary treatment. This work established his reputation as a young scientifically minded physician and led to his appointment as Regius Professor of Medicine in Aberdeen.

Davidson arrived at Aberdeen at the height of the economic depression when wages were low and the dole did not permit families of the unemployed to purchase sufficient food. Undernutrition was widespread and large numbers of women were anaemic. At that time I was a senior medical student in London and Osler's textbook was my Bible. It described this anaemia under the title chlorosis. The section on aetiology gives the conditions as 'common among the ill-fed, overworked girls of large towns, who are confined all day in close badly lighted rooms. Lack of proper exercise and fresh air with improper food are important factors. Emotional and nervous disturbances may be prominent — so that certain writers regarded the disease as a neurosis'. Significantly there is no mention of iron in this section, though later Blaud's pills are recommended in treatment. Davidson in a series of papers established the role of iron deficiency as the specific factor responsible for the disease and this led to the removal of the word, chlorosis, from medical textbooks. At Aberdeen he was fortunate in being near the Rowett Research Institute where John Boyd Orr was then director: They became friends for life and Orr was a major influence in developing his interests in the wider importance of nutrition throughout the world. Also at the Rowett was Isobella

Leitch, and Davidson and Leitch's review article, *Nutritional anaemias of man and animals* (1934, *Nut. Abst. Rev.* 3, 901–30) is a landmark in the history of nutrition.

In 1938 Davidson returned to Edinburgh as Professor of Medicine. Edinburgh was a much larger medical school than Aberdeen and his responsibilities for teaching and the care of patients, much increased by the outbreak of World War Two, effectively ended his research career. However work on nutritional anaemias was resumed after the war by the staff of his department, notably by R. H. Girdwood.

Stanley Davidson was a man of many sides. I was never a member of his department and can only describe one aspect of his activities. Commonsense and a capacity for hard work seemed his main attributes. Personal experience of severe illness when a young man made him appreciative of the needs of patients. He was always critical of bizarre diets and careful not to impose unnecessary restrictions. He was a good looking man with an athletic figure and had been a keen games player and was reputed to have been first class at tennis. A session on the book was always liable to be postponed because an opportunity for a day's salmon fishing or shooting or golf had arisen, but the work was made up and deadlines met. He had never worked abroad but made long visits to Africa, Asia and Australasia. These were always multi-purpose — to see old friends, to fish, to act as an external examiner or to represent the Royal College of Physicians of Edinburgh which he had served as President from 1953–57. These visits gave him a useful working knowledge of the nutritional problems of developing countries. He was in no sense an intellectual and did not read widely. Unlike many professors, he was unafraid of displaying his ignorance by asking naive questions. I was present many times when he was questioning his junior staff or colleagues from other departments or distinguished visitors. He was a good listener and, when an interview was over, he would quickly and with good judgment separate the wheat from the chaff in what we had heard. In this way and with a large correspondence with doctors in many countries, he kept himself up-to-date. He was not a good writer by nature, but would spend endless time revising drafts of what he and others had written with an unerring eye for a clumsy phrase or a meaningless sentence. A cynical friend once remarked: 'Poor Stanley, he only has 500 words in his vocabulary, but he does know how to use them'. This legitimate exaggeration helps to explain why students have appreciated his books so much.

No account of Stanley Davidson would be complete without reference to money, a continuing preoccupation in both his private and public life. His father had been a successful civil engineer often working abroad — Stanley was born in Ceylon — and left a large estate in Aberdeenshire. To their great regret Lady Davidson and Stanley had no children. They lived modestly and before their deaths almost all their fortune had been given away, mostly to the Universities of Aberdeen and Edinburgh and to the Edinburgh Royal College of Physicians. By contrast to his generosity with large sums, no Scot was ever more careful in spending sixpence, either of his own or of government money. In the nutritional field nothing roused his anger more than the fact that doctors continued to prescribe organic salts of iron when ferrous sulphate was equally effective and so much cheaper: he made many calculations of the cost of this unnecessary extravagance to the National Health Service. Stanley was always extremely generous to me in the financial arrangements for *Human Nutrition*, which was primarily his book, but after he had retired when I was visiting at his home, I used to be asked to bring a bottle of distilled water from the laboratory for his car batteries because his garage was now charging him too much. There are many similar stories.

Stanley Davidson was a man of character, a likeable and infuriating man, but always good company. Those who knew him personally are unlikely ever to forget him. We miss his sense of fun and his good sense. Many more who knew of him only through his books will remain grateful for his help in starting them on their way by providing them with the clearest of guidance in what were often potentially confusing subjects, and with a 'no nonsense' approach to problems.

R. P.

(Reprinted from Human Nutrition: Applied Nutrition 1982 36A: 239–40)

Contents

PART ONE

Physiology

It were well, therefore, that mankind were aware of the tendency which every kind of diet has to produce effects either immediately, or after repetition, unfavourable to health. It would, however, be difficult to give to the bulk of mankind the necessary instruction on this subject, and it would hardly be necessary to render it very universal, as it is not in many cases, and only in particular persons, that diseases arise from errors in diet; but it is absolutely necessary that physicians who have the whole of mankind as objects of their attention, should study this matter; without which they cannot either perceive the causes of diseases, or direct the means of obviating them. In this business, however, I have often found physicians very deficient, from their great ignorance of the nature of aliments, and of the principles which should lead to the proper and necessary distinction of them. To supply this deficiency, and to give the necessary instruction, the foregoing treatise has been attempted; and though in some particulars it may be both imperfect and mistaken, I flatter myself that it gives the necessary principles more fully and justly than they had been given before, and at least points out the necessary speculations that must be entered into for ascertaining the nature of aliments more exactly. In all this I cannot have been too minute; and I cannot be of more service than by engaging physicians in a minute study of the subject.

Cullen W 1798 Treatise of the materia medica. Edinburgh, Vol 1, p 432

1

Historical and Geographical Perspectives

Nutrition as a science can be said to have been founded by Lavoisier towards the end of the eighteenth century, but dietetics is a much older subject. Hippocrates frequently gave his patients advice about what foods they should eat and, since the days of ancient Greece, doctors in all countries have used dietetics as an important part of their treatment. Nutrition is an art and also a science, based on increasingly secure foundations. Only in the twentieth century did governments begin to assume responsibility for seeing that the poorer and underprivileged sections of society receive enough of the right types of food;[1] to carry out this responsibility knowledge of the science of nutrition becomes of great practical importance.

From a nutritional point of view mankind can be divided into four types: (1) primitive hunter-gatherers, (2) peasant agriculturists and pastoralists, (3) urban slum dwellers, and (4) the affluent. There are not many primitive hunter-gathers in the world today, but the major part of the human race are still peasant agriculturists, although increasing numbers are either joining the urban slum dwellers or becoming affluent. In no country is there only one type of community. Britain and the United States of America are affluent, but contain many urban slum dwellers and in each there are still a few peasant agriculturists. India has all four types of communities. She is still predominantly a country of peasants, but the rapidly growing towns have increasing numbers of poor urban slum dwellers and a sizeable affluent society; in the jungles a few primitive hunter-gatherers live their lives outside any civilisation.

In this book the problems of therapeutic dietetics and community nutrition are not sharply separated. Each depends on the same fundamental biochemical and physiological science. Before starting an account of this science, a brief description is given of the main nutritional problems in the four types of society.

HUNTER-GATHERERS

Homo sapiens and his predecessors *Homo erectus* and *Homo habilis* were primarily vegetarians but they have done some hunting for a million years, possibly longer. Hunting slowly developed as man moved away from the other primates; he became omnivorous (whereas other primates are largely vegetarian), skilled in toolmaking and developed social groups, such as hunting bands and large families.

It was only 10 000 years ago that the next stage, the technical development of agriculture, began. Thus for at least 99 per cent of the time that man has been evolving from his primate precursors, he has been a hunter-gatherer so that our bodies have presumably evolved well adapted for doing what hunter-gatherers do and eating what they eat.

It is a common misconception that our forebears lived in the cold and ate nothing but meat. The archaeological evidence indicates that man originated in the sunny parts of the world. Loomis[2] has suggested that man's original skin colour was brown, giving protection from the sun, and that white men evolved after settlement in northern Europe where dark-skinned people would suffer more readily from rickets (p. 305). However, there must have been many differences in diets from place to place and from time to time. For example, Eskimos and Lapps obtain ample vitamin D from marine sources; in some coastal sites the relative amounts of shells in the middens compared with the numbers of bones indicate that shellfish provided the major part of the animal protein intake. Until recently the vegetable part of early man's diet was ignored. Remains of vegetable food in archaeological sites are far less spectacular and much more difficult to identify than the animal bones.

But what were the women doing while their menfolk went out hunting? In rock paintings in southern Africa man the hunter is shown stalking antelopes and shooting at animals with bow and arrow. But the women, with their secondary sex characteristics overemphasised, often have short sticks in their hands, which may be weighted with a stone towards the lower end. These are not weapons. They are sticks used for digging out roots and tubers to eat, the Stone Age forerunners of spade and plough. Thus archaeology gives some understanding of our early ancestors' way of life.

We can also study the hunter-gatherers who are living in the world today. There are only a few groups left and in another generation there may be even fewer. It is not that the people themselves are dying out but their technology is too limited and subtle to stand up to competition from industrial technology. At a symposium on contemporary hunter-gatherers Lee[3] showed that most of them, except in the Arctic, obtain more food from gathering vegetables than from hunting animals. Lee and De Vore of Harvard made a study of Kung Bushmen (also called San) in north-west Botswana. These Bushmen are isolated from the outside world of technology by a waterless belt around them, 80 miles wide. This area appears as a blank on the map, except for Mount Aha which when you get there is not a mountain at all. The strategy of the Harvard study was that two or three social anthropologists lived in their own camp near a Bushmen camp for a year or more at a time. They learnt the click language, made friends with and observed the Bushmen while disturbing their way of life as little as possible.

One researcher made three visits to assess their medical and nutritional states at different seasons.[4] The main conclusions were as follows. First, the Bushmen do not become obese, except for the few who live with Bantu primitive pastoralists in the neighbourhood. At the end of the dry season the Bushmen tend to become somewhat undernourished and energy deficient, and this may contribute to their short adult stature.

Secondly, they showed no malnutrition unless something had gone wrong, e.g. an illness or an injury. There were no clinical or biochemical signs of deficiency of any vitamin.

Thirdly, high blood pressure was not found, and both systolic and diastolic pressures fall with increasing age in male Bushmen. This is in striking contrast to the picture in affluent communities, in which mean systolic and diastolic pressures rise with age in both men and women. The explanation could be that the Bushmen do not eat salt.[5] There is no archaeological evidence that palaeolithic or mesolithic man undertook salt extraction or had any interest in salt deposits. This started in neolithic times, presumably when there were food surpluses, which had to be preserved and stored.

Fourthly, the Bushmen's plasma cholesterol concentration averaged 3.0 mmol/l (120 mg/100 ml), a figure among the lowest in the world. Much higher figures are found in most populations who eat meat, as the high proportion of saturated fatty acids in the fat of domestic animals tends to raise cholesterol concentration. But the meat of wild buck has no fat round it and the small amount of fat in the muscle of wild bovids contains mostly polyunsaturated fatty acids.[6] The Bushmen do not eat only meat; they obtain more than half their energy from vegetable foods. The largest single item in their diet is the mongongo nut, *Ricinodendron rautanenii*, which is a good source of protein and whose oil is rich in linoleic acid. The essential characteristic of the hunter-gatherer's diet is that it is mixed. The men go out hunting but the supply of meat is intermittent and more of it comes from small animals than from the larger antelopes. The women, meanwhile, collect vegetable food. This often involves walking long distances carrying heavy loads of nuts, etc. on their backs, and sometimes a baby as well. The old women stay behind in camp and do the chores like breaking up nuts and fetching water in ostrich egg shells from the well a mile away.

Fifthly, the Bushmen do not have carious teeth though their teeth get worn down by the hard food as they get older. They occasionally enjoy wild honey but have no other concentrated sugar.

Sixthly, their numbers are few and appear to be stationary; One reason for the wide spacing of births could be the delayed resumption of ovulation from the combined effects of breast feeding continuing for about three years and mild seasonal undernutrition.[7] If they do not die from infections or accidents, they live to a good old age. The proportion over 65 years, approximately 7 per cent, is the same as that in Scotland in 1901.

These observations on the Bushmen and other studies on contemporary hunter-gatherers give some insights into nutritional and other aspects of early man, but care is needed in extrapolating because present-day hunter-gatherers may be regressive societies.

Some people would like to go back to the hunter-gatherer's way of life, but this is impossible; there are too many of us and hunter-gatherers need a lot of space.

PEASANT AGRICULTURISTS AND PASTORALISTS

How to grow crops and to domesticate animals was discovered independently in several widely separated centres from about 8000 or 9000 BC, first around Mesopotamia. It was then possible for people to stay in one place, to build homes and cities, and to store treasure. Distribution became uneven, societies became structured and jobs specialised. The population increased greatly. Wars and human epidemics became part of the pattern of life. Great civilisations like the Egyptian, the Mayan and the classical Greek were based on primitive agriculture.

In large areas of rural Africa, South America, Asia and Oceania the people are still at this stage of technical development and obtain their food from subsistence farming. Nutrition in this setting has five striking differences from that of hunter-gatherers.

First, with harvests once a year, food had to be stored. Hunter-gatherers do not store food; they share it.

Secondly, some of the wealthy overeat and become obese. Hunter-gatherers feast now and again after a successful hunt but not regularly.

Thirdly, alcohol is available, made from the ready supply of carbohydrate in cereals. Hunter-gatherers do not have this solace. Perhaps in smaller social groups they have less need for it.

Fourthly, the most dangerous nutritional effects have come from concentrating on a single crop that yields the most energy (calories per acre or joules per hectare). If this crop fails from drought or blight there is famine. The Irish potato famine of 1845–46 was the most terrible example in Europe (p. 556). The Irish peasants at that time had become completely dependent on potatoes. When the crop became infected by epidemic potato blight the effect was devastating. If a crop becomes contaminated with a toxin many people are likely to be poisoned. Ergotism and lathyrism are examples.

Fifthly, there is the liability to develop specific deficiency disease, when a large proportion of the dietary energy comes from a single staple food, e.g. a cereal or starchy root. Children are more likely than adults to suffer from such a disease, because of their extra need of nutrients for growth and because the common infections of childhood increase rates of utilisation. The two most important of such specific deficiency diseases are kwashiorkor, principally due to lack of protein, and keratomalacia, where lack of vitamin A may lead to permanent blindness. Diets based on large quantities of a cereal from which most of the thiamin (vitamin B_1) has been removed by milling may lead to beriberi, a disease once common amongst rice-eaters in the East. Pellagra is still an important disease amongst maize-eaters in Africa and elsewhere. It is due to a lack of niacin and its precursor, the amino acid tryptophan.

Most of the healthy and virile populations of the world have been peasant agriculturists. The Highlands of Scotland and Nepal have for generations produced famous battalions of fighting men, feared and respected by their adversaries throughout the world. Peasant agriculturists are healthy and feed well, as long as they have enough good land and favourable weather; but in Asia and Latin America and to a lesser extent in Africa increases in population, due to decline in mortality from infectious disease, have caused fragmentation of the holdings. It is difficult for a man to provide a good mixed diet for his family on less than 4 hectares (10 acres) of land.

Pastoralists

Pastoralists are at the same technical level as subsistence agriculturists but have a different way of life and are less numerous. In arid grasslands they follow their grazing animals with the seasons, travelling light and living in tents. The life of Lapps is based on reindeer, of Iranian nomads on sheep and goats, and of Tibetan nomads on yaks; in Africa the Tuareg depend on their camels, and the Fulani and Masai on their cattle. Pastoral tribes once had a military advantage with their horses over their sedentary neighbours. (Sedentary is used here in the anthropological sense to mean settled on an area of land, not inactive.) However, now the two groups usually co-exist peacefully in a symbiotic relationship, trading animal for agricultural products. Pastoralists have fallen behind since sedentary groups, in tidy constituencies, have more voting power, more schooling and get on better with administrators.

Pastoral tribesmen do not show the usual relation between income and the quality of the diet (p. 513). Although they are poor in money yet they may eat a diet rich in animal protein. Some consume large quantities of sour milk even as adults; their intestinal lactase persists, as in northern Europeans. They may not eat this rich animal diet all the year round. Nutritionists know far less about the day-to-day way of life of these people than they do about sedentary groups, which are more comfortable to study. Pastoralists deserve sympathetic understanding by officials: there should be a place for them in the ecosystem.

URBAN SLUM DWELLERS

The industrial revolution produced multitudes of a new urban proletariat who were uprooted from their rural origins and packed round the factories in bad housing. Such conditions, so vividly described by Dickens and other novelists, are being repeated today in many countries. But the problems are bigger because the twentieth-century slum and shanty town dwellers have fewer resources and are more numerous. In the industrial countries the growing cities of 100 years ago, for all their grime and misery, had a solid basis of economic life. But the new migrant multitudes are pouring 'into an urban wilderness where opportunities grow less as the millions pile on top of one another and the farms do not feed them or the industries employ them'.[8]

An increasing number of the world's population is crowding in and around the cities of Asia, Africa and Latin America. They tend to have the worst of both worlds. Traditions are lost but not replaced by education. Families are broken up, mothers go out to work and leave their babies inadequately cared for. The food which they buy is likely to be poor value for money and contaminated by pathogens. The problems are often compounded by alcoholism and violence.

In many towns in Africa, Asia and Latin America the

infant mortality (defined on p. 526) is over 100, whereas in prosperous countries with good health services it is below 15. In 1900 infant mortality rates were over 100 in many towns in Europe and North America. A combination of poor hygiene and bad nutrition was and is responsible. In a slum, conditions are ideal for the spread of infections, notably gastroenteritis and respiratory infections. These illnesses diminish food intake and increase the need for nutrients, and so readily precipitate marasmus, a severe and often fatal state of undernutrition in children. Infants prematurely weaned are particularly susceptible. While the infant mortality in a poor community may be 10 times that in a prosperous one, in the 1 to 4 year age-group the mortality may be 50 times higher. Again infections diseases may precipitate severe undernutrition in toddlers on a poor diet with little or no milk. Measles and whooping cough are ubiquitous. Nowadays in Britain these illnesses are usually mild and a death is exceptional. Yet 70 years ago large numbers of young children in Britain died of measles and whooping cough, as they still do in many countries.

In slum conditions adolescents and adults are much less susceptible to deficiency diseases than are children, but such diseases may follow severe infections. In adults a more important cause is drug dependence. Alcohol was the drug most commonly responsible in the past and still is in many places, but nowadays other psychotropic drugs may contribute. Persons dependent on drugs may become malnourished for four reasons: (1) they may spend so much money on the drug that they cannot afford a proper diet, (2) a drug may depress their appetites, (3) a drug habit may upset incentives to healthy living, and (4) a drug may interfere with metabolism in the tissues and organs, notably in the liver. Poor nutrition is but one aspect of urban poverty, albeit a very important one. It sets up a vicious circle, making its victim physically and mentally unfit for work and so driving him and his family deeper into proverty. All contemporary experience shows that programmes for better housing, for clean water, for the control of infectious diseases, for more and better food, and for education in health and nutrition, or the provision of better wages and more jobs, do not alone solve the problems of poverty. A coordinated attack simultaneously along these fronts is needed. Nutritionists cannot work effectively on their own. They require to be in a team with other health and social workers.

AFFLUENT SOCIETIES

Writing in 1984 one can say that North America, Europe, Australia, New Zealand and the cities of Singapore and Hong Kong are affluent societies. People there are free of the fear of crop failure and the great majority of them can afford to eat their favourite dishes all the year round. They have a food industry which provides foods from all parts of the world, preserves them, mainly by canning and refrigeration, and prepares convenience foods that greatly reduce the domestic labour of preparing meals. Affluence is beneficial to health. Mortality rates show that with increasing wealth fewer infants and young people die and that the elderly live longer. Much evidence indicates that the health of the people in affluent countries has never been better than it is in 1984. Nevertheless we worry about our food and our health, perhaps more than ever before. While there is no cause for alarm, it is a fact that many people continue to suffer and die from chronic diseases of the heart and blood vessels, diabetes, cancer and other degenerative disorders before completing the life span determined by their genetic make-up. It is widely and correctly held that diet contributes to the causes of many of these premature deaths.

National statistics show that with increasing wealth there is increased consumption of meat, animal fats and sugar, and decreased consumption of cereals and potatoes. There is also greatly increased use of tobacco and alcohol. A marked reduction in physical activity takes place due to the decreased need for manual work, more private and public transport and the rise of the habit of sitting in front of a television screen, as the main form of recreation at all ages. There is no doubt that none of these changes is beneficial to health. Excessive consumption of tobacco and alcohol are major causes of ill health and deaths which are preventable. If reduced physical activity is not accompanied by reduced dietary intake, obesity follows inevitably; it is widespread in all affluent societies and is a contributory cause of diabetes and hypertension.

The importance of the qualitative changes in diet brought about by affluence are difficult to assess. It has been the subject of much research in the 1960s and 1970s and this will continue throughout the 1980s and 1990s. Progress depends on finding out correlations between the nature of diets and the prevalence of specific diseases. Such research is expensive in both time and money.

As already stated, many people in affluent societies worry about their food. These are ready recipients of nutrition information which pours out on television and radio, in newspaper and magazine articles and in books. Many of the authors have little or no qualifications in nutrition. Advertisers promote the sale of food products without regard to their nutritive value for individual people. There is much nutritional misinformation, some of which is dangerous. Professional nutritionists have the task of correcting this and supplying accurate information. They have to educate individuals at all ages and persons responsible for institutional catering and those who influence governments, as they have a large part in determining the price and availability of foods in the shops. In the past, nutritional education has been directed mainly towards mothers of infants and young children. These are now generally fed well and malnutrition is much more frequently found at the other end of life. More nutrition education is needed for the elderly and for those who care for them in institutions. Adolescents also require education as this is the period when food habits, often lasting for life, are acquired.

Today in hospitals physicians and surgeons save many lives using techniques unknown a generation ago. These techniques impose nutritional stresses and often prevent normal feeding. There have been great advances in providing nutritional support for such patients and these will continue.

Affluence removes the nutritional problems of poor peasants and urban slum dwellers but at the same time creates its own nutritional problems. However, even in the wealthiest cities there are always some very poor people and cases of malnutrition continue to arise. The social and medical services need to be alert to this and to be able to identify individuals and groups who are at risk of malnutrition so as to provide appropriate means of prevention and treatment where necessary.

This account of historical and geographical perspectives attempts to lay a basis for the application of nutritional science to the needs of a varied and evolving world population. The scientific principles are broadly the same whatever cultural group is being considered. The application through nutrition education is vastly different. If this universal science is to bring the best results for the world as a whole we must learn to apply it to all groups, using language and educational techniques which are adapted to regional cultures.

REFERENCES

1. Passmore R 1983 An historical introduction to food, health, and nutrition policies in the United Kingdom. In: McLaren D S (ed) Nutrition in the community. Wiley, London, ch 2
2. Loomis W F 1967 Skin-pigment regulation of vitamin-D biosynthesis in man. Science 157: 501–6
3. Lee R B 1968 What hunters do for a living: a comparative study. In: Lee R B, De Vore I (eds) Man the Hunter. Aldine, Chicago, p 41–3
4. Truswell A S, Hansen J D L 1976 Medical research among the !Kung. In: Lee R B, De Vore I (eds) Kalahari hunter-gatherers. Harvard University Press, Cambridge, Mass, p 166–95
5. Truswell A S, Kennelly B M, Hansen J D L, Lee R B 1972 Blood pressures of !Kung Bushmen in the northern Kalahari, Botswana. Am Heart J 84: 5–12
6. Sinclair A J, Slattery W J, O'Dea K 1982 The analysis of polyunsaturated fatty acids in meat by capillary gas–liquid chromatography. J Sci Food Agric 33: 771–6
7. Wilmsen E N 1978 Seasonal effects of dietary intake on Kalahari San. Fed Proc 37: 65–72
8. Ward B 1969 The poor world's cities. Economist 233: 56–62

POSTSCRIPT

In the Oulé, Massa and Go dialects there was no such word as 'nation', and the tribes were still interested only in their witch-doctors, in magic ceremonies and, of course, in meat. Up to now the only Oulé aspiration he had been able to exploit with any success had been their need for meat — the old need of men in Africa — and indeed of all men. It was a deeper and much more urgent need than that for new political institutions. In his youth he had often seen an animal shot down and eaten where it lay by villagers, the greediest of whom absorbed as much as ten pounds of meat at a sitting. From the Tchad to the Cape the Africans' craving for meat, eternally stimulated by inadequate or ill-balanced diet, was the strongest and most fraternal bond the continent had in common. It was a dream, a longing, an aspiration that never ceased, a physiological cry of the body, stronger and more torturing than the sexual instinct. Meat! It was the oldest, the most truly real and sincere, and the most unanimous aspiration of humanity. He thought of Morel and his elephants, and smiled bitterly. To the white man the elephant had long meant merely ivory, and to the black man it always meant merely meat — the most abundant quantity of meat that a lucky hit with the assegai could procure for him. The idea of the 'beauty' of the elephant, or the 'nobility' of the elephant, was the idea of a man who had had enough to eat, a man of restaurants and of two meals a day and of museums of abstract art.

Gary R 1958 The roots of heaven. (Translation.) Michael Joseph, London

2

Composition of the Body

What are little boys made of?
What are little boys made of?
Slugs and snails and puppy-dogs' tails;
That's what little boys are made of.

What are little girls made of?
What are little girls made of?
Sugar and spice and all things nice;
That's what little girls are made of.

Many carcasses of small animals have been analysed chemically, but the results do not necessarily apply to man. A complete chemical analysis of the human cadaver is a formidable task which has been carried out on a number of occasions, but not sufficiently often to give the range of variations in people of different age and sex.[1] Nevertheless, enough is known to state that the data in Table 2.1 are representative of a normal man.

Table 2.1 A normal chemical composition for a man weighing 65 kg

	kg	Per cent
Protein	11	17.0
Fat	9	13.8
Carbohydrate	1	1.5
Water	40	61.6
Minerals	4	6.1

Most of the material listed in Table 2.1 is part of the essential structure of the body, but a portion represents reserves or stores. Of the 9 kg of fat not more than about 1 kg is essential; the remainder represents a store which can be drawn upon in times of need. In obese people this store may be very much larger and form up to 70 per cent of the body weight. Most of the protein is an essential component of the cells, but probably about 2 kg can be lost without serious results. By contrast, the body can be depleted at most by 200 g of carbohydrate. During starvation the store of carbohydrate is continually replenished by synthesis from the larger reserves of protein and fat. The body can lose up to 10 per cent of its total water and at least a third of the mineral content of the skeleton without serious risk to life. The size of the stores and the factors that determine deposits and withdrawals are important nutritional considerations, amplified in succeeding chapters.

COMPARTMENTS OF THE BODY

At a meeting of the New York Academy of Sciences in 1963 the Professor of Surgery at Harvard, Dr Francis D. Moore, went to the blackboard and wrote the following equation:

$$MAN = CM + EST + FAT$$

This is interpreted as follows. A man can be divided into three compartments. CM is the cell mass which is the active tissue, carrying out all the work of the body. EST is the extracellular supporting tissue which supports the cell mass. This again can be subdivided into two parts: the extracellular fluid, and minerals and protein fibres in the skeleton and other supporting tissue. The extracellular fluid comprises the blood plasma and lymph and the fluid which bathes the cells. The living skeleton is, however, very different from the dead specimens familiar in anatomy museums. It is a cellular organ in which the supporting mineral deposits are laid down. FAT is the energy reserve held in adipose tissue beneath the skin and around the internal organs.

In a healthy body the cell mass may contribute about 55 per cent of the total weight, the extracellular supporting tissue about 30 per cent and the far reserve about 15 per cent. These proportions may be greatly altered by disease. Thus in starvation arising from lack of food or in the emaciation that results from any wasting disease, the cell mass is reduced and the fat reserve may be almost completely utilised. The extracellular supporting tissue is little altered in absolute size and so becomes relatively bigger and may comprise 50 per cent or more of the body weight. In obesity the fat reserve is greatly increased.

8

ELECTROLYTES

An important difference exists between the chemical constitution of the fluid within the cells and that of the extracellular fluid which surrounds them. Cell fluid is primarily a solution of potassium ions and extracellular fluid a solution of sodium chloride. The anions within the cell are provided mainly by phosphates, proteins and organic acids in varying proportions. Table 2.2 shows approximate concentrations of these and other ions in the two fluids. The difference between the concentration of the ions inside and outside the cells is only maintained by the expenditure of energy which is provided by the metabolic processes within the cells. Much of the energy expenditure of the resting body is used to maintain this electrolyte equilibrium. Cellular activity either in muscle, nerve or secretory cell is associated with local disturbances of ionic equilibrium at the cell wall and chemical energy is needed to restore resting conditions.

Table 2.2 A normal distribution of ions in intracellular and extracellular fluids

	Intracellular (mEq/l)	Extracellular (mEq/l)
Cations:		
Na^+	10	145
K^+	150	5
Ca^{2+}	2	2
Mg^{2+}	15	2
	177	154
Anions:		
Cl^-	10	100
HCO_3^-	10	27
SO_4^{2-}	15	1
Organic acids		5
PO_4^{3-}	142	2
Proteins		19
	177	154

CHEMICAL DISSECTION OF THE BODY

It is possible by chemical methods to determine the size of the chief compartments of the human body.[2] The methods are of necessity indirect. Many of them are too complex and time-consuming to be of practical value in routine clinical medicine. They are, however, mostly within the competence of even a small research laboratory. The results obtained, using the methods now to be described, have had a profound effect on our understanding of the changes that take place in the body as a result of nutritional diseases. They make possible quantitative measurements of these changes.

The dilution principle

It is possible to determine the volume (V) of a fluid in an irregular container by adding to it a measured quantity (Q) of a substance which diffuses freely and evenly throughout the fluid. After an interval to allow even distribution of the test substance, its concentration (C) in the fluid is determined. Then the volume can be calculated from the formula

$$V = \frac{Q}{C}$$

This principle has wide applications in human biology.

Total body water

In living man or any intact animal it is possible to estimate the total body water in the following way. A known weight of a substance which is freely diffusible in all the body fluids is given to the subject, either by mouth or by intravenous injection. After sufficient time has been allowed for the substance to diffuse throughout all the tissues, a sample of blood is withdrawn and the concentration of the substance in the plasma determined. The total body water can then be calculated as described above. Corrections have to be made for any excretion or metabolism of the substance during the period of diffusion. Many freely diffusible substances, e.g. urea, antipyrine and ethanol, have been used for this purpose. Today the isotopes deuterium and tritium are usually employed. Consistent results with each have been obtained by experienced workers. As there is the dual assumption not only that the test substance is freely diffusible into all cells of the body, but also that proper corrections have been made for any losses, the prudent sometimes express their results in terms of the size of the 'tritium space' or the 'antipyrine space'. A normal value for the total body water is 40 litres and varies from 50 to 65 per cent of the body weight, or even more widely according to the degree of fatness of the subject.

Extracellular water. A number of substances — sucrose, inulin (a carbohydrate derived from a plant root), sodium thiocyanate, sodium thiosulphate and the bromide ion, which can be labelled isotopically — when injected into the body appear to occupy a 'space' which is much smaller than the total body water and which is probably the same as the extracellular fluid. The 'thiocyanate space' can be measured conveniently in any laboratory without special equipment, and provides a useful measure of the extracellular fluid. (Thiocyanate enters the red blood corpuscles and a correction has to be made in calculating the extracellular fluid from the thiocyanate space.) The extracellular fluid normally comprises 18 to 24 per cent of the body weight. In patients with oedema from starvation or other cause, it may be increased to 50 per cent of the body weight. In dehydration it is markedly reduced.

Cell water and cell mass.   If the total body water and extracellular water are measured as described above, the difference between the two can be taken as the cell water. Thus the reference man whose chemical composition is given in Table 2.1 has a total body water of 40 1. If the extracellular water is 15 1 then

$$\text{Cell water} = 40-15 = 25 \text{ litres}$$

Cells vary in their water content. Muscle cells are about 75 per cent water. Red blood corpuscles, brain cells and cells in tendons and connective tissue contain less water. It is a reasonable approximation to say that 70 per cent of the whole cell mass is water. Hence in our reference man

$$\text{Cell mass} = \text{cell water} \times \frac{100}{70} = 35.7 \text{ kg}$$

This figure represents about 55 per cent of the total body weight of 65 kg. Thus in a healthy lean man the active metabolising tissue comprises little more than half the body weight. In an obese individual the proportion will be much less.

An estimate of the cell mass can also be made by measuring the amount of the natural isotope of potassium, ^{40}K, in the body, using a whole body counter.

Effects of age

The proportion of water in mammalian embryos is higher than in the mature animals. In man water forms about 88 per cent of a 28-week fetus[3] and falls to about 75 per cent in a newborn baby, 65 per cent at the age of 2 months and reaches an adult value of about 60 per cent by the age of 4 months.[4] This is due in part to an increasing proportion of fat in the body, but also extracellular and cell water become relatively less as the body matures. This process probably continues very slowly throughout life and the water content of old men is a little less than that of young adults.[5] Charles Dickens[6] described this when he wrote: 'Anyone may pass, any day, in the thronged thoroughfares of the metropolis, some meagre, wrinkled yellow old man.... This old man is always a little old man. If he were ever a big old man, he has shrunk into a little old man; if he were always a little old man, he had dwindled into a less old man.' To be able to dry up gracefully may be the secret of a happy old age.

Body fat

Determination by underwater weighing

Archimedes was set the problem of finding out how much silver was present in a crown of reputedly pure gold. He solved it by determining the density d (mass/volume) of the crown and of pure gold and of pure silver. Then if x is the fraction of silver in the crown

$$\frac{1}{d(\text{crown})} = \frac{1-x}{d(\text{gold})} + \frac{x}{d(\text{silver})}$$

The proportion of fat in the human body can be determined using the same principle, for it is well known that fat floats. The density of human fat has been measured many times and does not differ significantly from 0.900. The density of the fat-free body, the lean body mass, cannot be accurately determined, but there is much evidence that in health it is close to 1.10. If x be the percentage of fat in the human body

$$\frac{100}{d(\text{body})} = \frac{100-x}{1.10} + \frac{x}{0.90}$$
$$x = \frac{495}{d(\text{body})} - 450$$

The density of the human body can be determined by weighing first in air and then in water. If M is the mass of the body and V the volume, then

$$d = \frac{M}{V}$$

The volume is obtained by displacement. The difference between the weight of the body in air and the weight when submerged in water is the weight of the water displaced. The volume corresponding to this mass of water can be obtained by dividing by the density of water at the time of underwater weighing. The underwater weight has to be corrected for the upthrust of the residual air in the lungs. This in a young person is about 1.2 litres, but increases as the lungs lose their elasticity with age. It can be measured using a nitrogen washout technique. It is impossible to measure the gas in the alimentary tract. The amount is usually small (about 100 ml) and can be neglected.

Attempts to assess the fat content of man from measurements of body density arose as a result of a practical problem. Some men on a draft for recruitment into the US Navy were marked unfit for service by a medical board because their weights exceeded the maximum permissible for their heights. As these men were professional footballers in civil life, it seemed unlikely that they were unfit for naval service because of obesity. A US naval surgeon, Behnke[7] examined the men. They were weighed in air and under water. Their density was calculated and found in some cases to be as high as 1.090 to 1.097, indicating a fat content of 4 per cent or less. From this it was concluded that the excess weight was mainly due to extra muscle and not fat.

The real difficulty in calculating the total fat from the density measurement and body weight in air arises from the impossibility of getting a direct measure of the density of the lean body mass (the body minus its fat content) owing to the varying density of the skeleton. As the bath is around 37°C the procedure is not unpleasant for the subject (as we can vouch from personal experience) and is applicable to active people of either sex.

There are many reports of the fat content of samples of the population in different countries. Some of these have been summarised in a table in previous editions. Table 2.3 gives data for 481 citizens of Glasgow obtained by Durnin & Womersley.[8] This shows three things. First, women have more fat than men, secondly the average fat content of the body rises with age and thirdly the enormous range of individual variation. Body weight does not rise with age in poor peasant agriculturists, but the rising fat content of Glaswegians is typical of all populations where the majority of the people have access to ample food. There is no agreement on how much additional fat constitutes obesity and this is discussed in Chapter 28. By any standard there are many obese people in Glasgow. Heavy physical exercise reduces body fat. In Prague Pařisková[9] reported that trained male runners had an average fat content of 6.3 per cent and young female gymnasts of only 8 per cent. Such an extreme degree of thinness may have adverse effects on health in the long run.

Table 2.3 Fat content of Glasgow citizens calculated from measurements of body density[8]

| Age (years) | Fat as a percentage of body weight | | | |
| | Men | | Women | |
	mean	range	mean	range
16–19	15	7–30	26	14–43
20–29	15	5–38	29	10–54
30–39	23	13–38	33	19–53
40–59	25	11–37	35	24–61
60–69	28	11–50	39	26–52

Determination using the dilution principle
A gas that is much more soluble in fat than in water and quickly dissolves in all the body fat could provide a means of measuring total body fat. An isotope of krypton (^{85}Kr) and cyclopropane have been used.[10,11] However, the method is beset with technical difficulties when applied to man and, as yet, has not yielded reliable results in man.

Subcutaneous fat
A large proportion of the body fat is carried directly beneath the skin. Special calipers have been designed for measuring skinfold thickness. Measurements taken at several sites on the body can be combined to give an index of body fatness and correlate well with determination of total body fat from density measurements.

Skin calipers, if carefully used, provide a simple and practical means of assessing the obesity (Chap. 28).

The skeleton
No reliable method for assessing the size or composition of the skeleton in the living body has been developed. Indeed there have not been sufficient direct analyses of human skeletons to allow accurate statements of the range of variation. It is known that in the USA Negroes have on average a slightly heavier skeleton than whites. Garn[12] gave an excellent summary of what knowledge was available 20 years ago and pointed out how accurate studies of body composition in life are handicapped by lack of methods for study in this compartment. This remains true today. A brief statement on the chemical composition of the skeleton is given on page 104.

GROWTH

Many examples are given in this book of how growth and development may be impaired as a result of a failure of nutrition. A child does not grow like a crystal, and a newborn baby is not a miniature adult. The internal organs, notably the brain and liver, form a much larger proportion of total weight than in the mature body, and there is relatively much less muscle, bone and adipose tissue. Growth of some organs takes place in different stages of childhood. The brain grows rapidly in the first two years of life, when it reaches about 75 per cent of adult size; the uterus remains small for the first ten years and then grows to adult size in two or three years; the lymphatic organs, thymus, tonsils and lymph nodes are small at birth, grow rapidly in the first few years to a maximum size by the age of 10 and thereafter regress. These differential growth rates are controlled over the years by a metabolic clock, set to a time-table which is genetically determined but which may be slowed down for a period by a poor diet and severe or repeated infections. Early in fetal life the control system becomes centred in the brain and it operates principally through the hypothalamus, which itself regulates the trophic secretions of the anterior pituitary gland and hence other endocrine glands. These glands have a major role in the control growth, and in early life disease affecting any one of them disrupts the pattern of growth in various different ways. Cretinism (p. 295) arising from a failure of the thyroid gland to secrete its hormones is a good example.

Growth can occur only if the organs and tissues receive the nutrients needed for the synthesis of their protein and other molecules. It is therefore dependent on an adequate diet. An insufficiency of energy and protein are the commonest causes in man of failure to grow or of disproportional growth except in affluent societies. The effects of this lack on body composition are described on page 283. In theory, a dietary deficiency of any one of the 35 or more nutrients known to be essential for mammals could be responsible for impairment of growth in man. Well-known examples are lack of iron, vitamin D and vitamin A, leading to failure of normal development of red blood corpuscles, bone and epithelial surfaces respectively.

Growth is also impaired when disease of the alimentary tract prevents adequate absorption of nutrients. Examples are repeated attacks of gastroenteritis and coeliac disease. Many disorders of metabolism prevent normal utilisation of nutrients and so retard growth or development. Diabetes and phenylketonuria are well-known examples. Chronic infectious diseases severely retard growth. They may do this by reducing appetite, by preventing normal absorption or utilisation of nutrients and by the increased need for nutrients brought about by fever.

Disturbances in growth occur most commonly in the period immediately after weaning. In the uterus the fetus normally receives an adequate supply of nutrients even if the mother's diet is far from satisfactory. Only when a mother's diet is grossly insufficient or if the placenta is abnormal is fetal growth impaired (p. 575). Similarly lactation supplies the needs of early infancy when the growth rate is most rapid. As a child gets older, growth rate slows and the need for nutrients is relatively less; stores of nutrients may have been built up and infectious diseases are in general less frequent and less severe owing to the buildup of immunity. However, insufficient food for a significant period at any time during childhood and adolescence may prevent an individual from reaching his full potential in height and weight, as judged by accepted standards (p. 519). Chronic undernutrition delays the onset of puberty and the menarche. The trigger that releases the endocrine factors responsible for puberty may be dependent on body fat. The menarche is often delayed in ballet dancers who are very thin as a result of much exercise and a restricted diet.[13]

Animal experiments, mainly on rats and pigs, by McCance & Widdowson[14] show that severe distortions of the pattern of growth follow dietary restriction at various stages of development. Even if a newborn pig is prevented from growing for a year by this means, rapid growth follows when a normal diet is given, although the animal does not quite reach normal size and proportions. In man a short interruption of growth and development arising as a result of nutritional failure can be made good by **catch-up growth** (Fig. 2.1), provided a good diet is given. In general, children below the age of 5 years can make up for a period of retarded growth very well, but thereafter their capacity to do so declines.

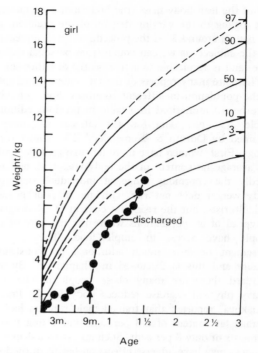

Fig. 2.1 Catch-up growth in a Baganda girl who was admitted to hospital when 9 months old weighing only 2.4 kg. (McCance & Widdowson)[14]

In urbans slums and some peasant communities the usual diet of children may be barely adequate and in such communities a severe nutritional illness may permanently impair growth and development. This is discussed in Chapter 29.

Dr J.M. Tanner of the Institute of Child Health, University of London, is the leading authority on human growth, and two of his recent books[15,16] are strongly recommended to students.

Cell growth

An organ or tissue may enlarge in two ways. The number of cells may increase by multiplication, **cell hyperplasia**, or the individual cells may get bigger, **cell hypertrophy**. In some tissues, hyperplasia ceases early in life. Thus in the brain the number of neurones reaches approximately the adult value during the second year of life. Thereafter if any are destroyed, they cannot be replaced by hyperplasia. During the period of rapid hyperplasia in early life the brain is especially susceptible to damage by any factor disturbing normal nutrition (p. 290). In adults both cardiac and skeletal muscle cells cannot divide. When an athlete goes into training and gains weight by 'putting on muscle', this is due to cell hypertrophy. If the ventricles of the heart have to carry out extra work, either in health due to heavy physical activity or in disease, e.g. hypertension or aortic valve damage, they enlarge due to cell hypertrophy. By contrast the epithelial lining of the gut is replaced by cell hyperplasia every two or three days throughout life. Liver cells retain the power to regenerate and after severe damage with the death or **necrosis** of many cells, hyperplasia may restore liver function to normal levels. Adipocytes also are capable of hyperplasia. As in health adipocytes in fat depots are normally well loaded with fat, they have a limited capacity for hypertrophy and obesity is associated often with hyperplasia. If part of any organ is destroyed by trauma or disease, it is replaced by fibrous tissue formed by fibroblasts, connective tissue cells which proliferate in the damaged area.

The distinction between cell hyperplasia and hypertrophy is very important in considering the effect of nutritional factors on individual organs.

REFERENCES

1. Widdowson E M, McCance R A, Spray C M 1951 The chemical composition of the human body. Clin Sci 10: 113–25
2. Passmore R, Draper M H 1970 The chemical anatomy of the human body. In: Thompson R H S, Wotton I D P (eds) Biochemical disorders in human disease, 3rd edn. Churchill, London, p. 1–14
3. Apte S V, Iyengar K 1972 Composition of the human foetus. Br J Nutr 27: 305–12
4. Foman S J 1967 Body composition of the male reference infant during the first year of life. Pediatrics 40: 863–70
5. Norris A H, Lundy T, Shock N W 1963 Trends in selected indices of body composition in men between the ages 30 and 80 years. Ann NY Acad Sci 110: 623–36
6. Dickens C 1867 Little Dorrit. Chapman & Hall, London, ch 31
7. Behnke A R, Feen B G, Welham J C 1942 The specific gravity of healthy man. JAMA 118: 495–8
8. Durnin J G V A, Womersley J 1974 Body fat assessed from total body density and its estimation from skinfold thickness: measurements on 481 men and women aged 16 to 72 years. Br J Nutr 32: 77–97
9. Pařisková J 1977 Body fat and physical fitness. Martinus Nijhoff, The Hague
10. Hytten F E, Taylor K, Taggart N 1966 Measurement of total body fat in man by adsorption of ^{85}Kr. Clin Sci 31: 111–9
11. Halliday D 1971 An attempt to estimate total body fat and protein in malnourished children. Br J Nutr 26: 147–53
12. Garn S M 1963 Human biology and research in body composition. Ann NY Acad Sci 110: 429–46
13. Frisch R E, Wyshak G, Vincent L 1980 Delayed menarche in and amenorrhea in ballet dancers, N Engl J Med 303: 17–19
14. McCance R A, Widdowson E M 1974 The determinants of growth and form. Proc R Soc Lond (Biol) 185: 1–17
15. Tanner J M 1978 Foetus into man: physical growth from conception to maturity. Open Books, London
16. Tanner J M (ed) 1981 Control of growth. Churchill Livingstone, Edinburgh

3

Energy

Just before the French Revolution Lavoisier and the physicist Laplace carried out experiments in which they placed a guinea-pig in a very small closed chamber surrounded by ice. They measured the amount of ice melted over a 10-hour period and at the same time the amount of carbon dioxide given out by the animal. They demonstrated that there was a relationship between the heat produced by the animal and the respiratory exchange. Lavoisier also measured the oxygen consumption of men, and showed that it increased after food and exercise.

Lavoisier has properly been considered the founder of the modern science of nutrition. For over a hundred years after his death on the guillotine, ingenious and learned men exercised their talents in designing calorimeters in which laboratory animals and men could live for many hours or even a few days whilst their metabolism was studied. In 1849 Reynault and Reiset in Paris carried out numerous experiments on small animals and planned to construct a large human respiration chamber in a hospital. They were unable to get the necessary funds and they had to drop their project. Pettenkofer and Voit were more fortunate. They acquired the patronage of King Maximilian II of Bavaria. By 1886 they had constructed at Munich a chamber in which a man could live for several days and have all his respiratory exchanges measured. After measurements on a fasting man lasting 24 hours, the protein 'burned' was calcu-

lated from the urinary nitrogen and the fat from the respiratory carbon dioxide (after deducting the carbon in the protein burned and assuming no change in the carbohydrate store of the body). A difference of only 6.2 per cent was found between the measured oxygen absorption and that calculated as necessary for the combustion of the body materials metabolised. This accuracy indicates both their experimental skill and the soundness of the assumptions on which their calculations were based.

Rubner in Berlin, Zuntz in Switzerland and Johansson in Sweden were others who from 1880 onwards extended the work of the Munich school and so laid many of the foundations of modern nutritional science. But it was the American, Atwater, a student of Voit in Munich, who carried out the experiments which have established the essential quantitative physiological knowledge on which all assessments of the energy needs of men are based. Atwater returned to the USA from Germany in 1892 and enlisted the help of Rosa, an engineer. Together they constructed a human calorimeter which could measure the heat produced by a man with an accuracy of 0.1 per cent. At the same time the chamber incorporated the respiration apparatus used by Pettenkofer and Voit. Table 3.1 illustrates how accurately Atwater was able to measure the energy exchange of man.

When in 1906 Hopkins at Cambridge carried out his experiments which demonstrated beyond doubt the

Table 3.1 An experiment of Atwater and Benedict[1] (values in megajoules)

		Total 4 days	Average 1 day
(a)	Heat combustion of food eaten	41.22	10.31
(b)	Heat of combustion of faeces	1.26	0.32
(c)	Heat combustion of urine	2.25	0.56
(m)	Heat of combustion of alcohol eliminated	0.35	0.09
(d)	Estimated heat of combustion of protein gained (+) or lost (−)	−1.16	−0.29
(e)	Estimated heat of combustion of fat gained (+) or lost (−)	−2.26	−0.56
(f)	Estimated energy of material oxidised in the body $a - (b + c + m + d + e)$	40.78	10.19
(g)	Heat determined	40.06	10.02
(h)	Heat determined greater (+) or less (−) than estimated $(f-g)$	−0.68	−0.17
(i)	Heat determined greater (+) or less (−) than estimated $(h+f)$ (per cent)	−	−1.6

existence of 'accessory food factors' (later known as vitamins), Atwater had completed his work. A chapter had been written in the textbooks of physiology which has needed no subsequent revision. After Hopkins' discovery, interest shifted sharply from the energy needs to the vitamin needs of both man and animals. The quality rather than the quantity of an individual's food became the foremost interest.

The first part of this chapter gives an account of the classical physiology of energy exchanges. It differs little from accounts written in the early part of the century and it is extremely unlikely that any essential changes will be made in the future. Excellent accounts of the subject have been given by Graham Lusk,[2] who was personally associated with the classical experiments, and by Karl Guggenheim[3] in a new book on the history of nutrition. All serious students of the science of nutrition should read carefully one or other of these books which describes in detail so much of the work that is fundamental to the science.

The second part attempts to appraise the energy needs of contemporary man. It is a guide for those responsible for food planning or for drawing up ration scales. In contrast to the former part it rests on a limited experimental and scientific basis. However, practical policies have often to be decided by judgments based on inadequate data.

PHYSIOLOGY

Forms of energy

The biologist is interested in energy in five forms: (1) solar, (2) chemical, (3) mechanical, (4) thermal, (5) electrical.*

In plants and animals the various forms of energy are quantitatively interchangeable. It has been frequently demonstrated that living creatures, like inanimate matter, can neither create nor destroy energy but can only transform it and so obey the first law of thermodynamics, which states the principle of the conservation of energy.

Animals differ from green plants in that they cannot utilise solar energy directly. Green plants are able to synthesise complicated organic substances such as carbohydrates, proteins and fats from simple inorganic materials, such as CO_2, H_2O, NH_3 and SO_4. In this process, photosynthesis, solar energy is used and converted into chemical energy which is stored by the plant.

* The existence of powerful electric organs in some fish is a clear-cut demonstration that animals can generate electrical energy: most electrical organs in fish are modified muscle end plates. The processes of excitation in both muscle and nerve are dependent on electrical changes on the cell membranes.

Plants, which are independent of other forms of life, are thus distinguishable from all animals, which are wholly dependent on plants.

Animals get their energy from their food in a chemical form, which is derived directly or indirectly from plants. This energy is bound in molecules of carbohydrate, fat, protein and alcohol.

Energy taken in as food is used (1) to perform mechanical work, (2) to maintain the tissues of the body, and (3) for growth.

In the conversion of chemical energy into mechanical energy, man acts as an engine with a measurable thermodynamic efficiency. Most of the energy is dissipated as heat. At best a man can convert 25 per cent of the energy in his food into mechanical work. In this respect he is much more efficient than most steam engines and about on a par with a good internal combustion engine.

Of the energy required for maintenances less than 10 per cent is used for internal mechanical work, e.g. the beating of the heart and the movements of respiratory muscles. Over 90 per cent is used either for the osmotic pumps which maintain the differences in electrolyte concentrations between intra- and extracellular fluids or for the synthesis of protein and other macromolecules. These syntheses take place continuously with the turnover of cell constituents, and at an increased rate in the growing child.

The energy in the food is ultimately converted into heat and its dissipation maintains the temperature of the body. Unless the environmental temperature is very cold, even a small amount of muscular activity produces enough heat to maintain the temperature, especially if the heat is conserved by adequate clothing. The extra heat developed when hard mechanical work is done represents waste that must be eliminated if the temperature of the body is to be kept normal. This is effected by means of sweating.

The unit of energy is the joule (J) and is the energy expended when 1 kilogram (kg) is moved 1 metre (m) by a force of 1 newton (N). Physiologists and nutritionists are concerned with large amounts of energy and the convenient units are the kilojoule ($kJ = 10^3J$) and the megajoule ($MJ = 10^6J$).

Rates of work or energy expenditure are conveniently expressed in watts ($W = J/s$). Twelve people sitting talking in a room produce heat at the rate of about 60 kJ/min and this is equivalent to a one kilowatt electric fire, as many hostesses know.

Formerly energy was always expressed quantitatively in units of heat, the unit used being the kilocalorie (kcal).

The calorie is a derived, not a basic unit. The International Table calorie was defined by the 1956 Steam Conference as 4.1868 J. The 15° calorie is the amount of heat required to raise the temperature of water 1°C from 14.5° to 15.5°; it is 4.1855 J. The thermochemical calorie is based on the heat of combustion of benzoic acid and is 4.184 J. All three conversion factors are in current use and there is some confusion. Either of the first two are appropriate for nutritional work and we follow the Royal Society[4] and use the thermochemical calorie, i.e. 4.184 J (and 1 kcal = 4.184 kJ). In practice 4.2 is close enough as a conversion factor. The error from rounding off is less than the variation in energy content of foods. The calorie has become such a familiar unit that it will be some time before many people become accustomed to the use of the joule. Accordingly in many places we give energy values in both joules and calories.

Energy content of food

If a foodstuff is placed in a small chamber or bomb (Fig. 3.1) and exposed to a high pressure of oxygen it can be ignited by a small electric current. All the organic material is burnt and the heat liberated can be measured. The heats of combustion of the three 'proximate principles' — carbohydrates, proteins and fats — and of alcohol are shown in Table 3.2. There are slight differences in the heats of combustion of the nutrients in different foods. In the animal body, the tissues are able to oxidise carbohydrate and fat completely to carbon dioxide and water, but the oxidation of protein is never complete. Nitrogenous substances derived from protein such as urea, uric acid and creatinine are excreted in the urine. Many observations of the heat of combustion of urine have shown that it contains unoxidised material equivalent to 33.1 kJ (7.9 kcal)/g of nitrogen or 5.23 kJ (1.25 kcal)/g of protein oxidised by the body. It is therefore necessary to subtract 5.23 kJ/g from the heat of combustion of protein. Further corrections are necessary to allow for the incomplete absorption of nutrients in the alimentary canal. Atwater, over 50 years ago, made a large number of experiments in which he analysed the faeces of three young American men for periods lasting for three to eight days, whilst on mixed diets typical of the time. He concluded that 92 per cent of protein, 95 per cent of fat and 99 per cent of carbohydrate were normally absorbed. From this the 'Atwater factors' for the available energy of the three different proximate principles (as given in Table 3.2) have been derived. It is important to remember that these factors make allowance for the energy in the food lost in faeces and urine. They are physiological approximations based on experiments on a limited number of subjects on one kind of diet. Experiments by Southgate and Durnin[5] in Glasgow on young and old persons of both sexes on diets containing varying amounts of vegetables and cereals confirmed that for most practical purposes the Atwater factors can be used to calculate metabolisable energy.

In practice, the energy values of diets are calculated

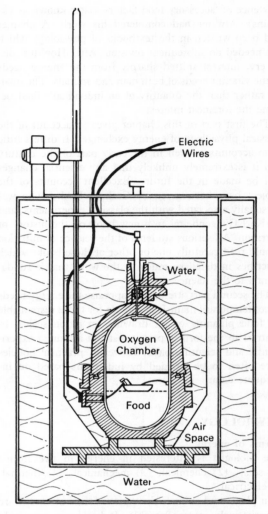

Fig. 3.1 The bomb calorimeter. The bomb is placed inside a vessel of water, the temperature of which can be accurately measured. The foodstuff is placed in a small crucible. The bomb is filled with oxygen at high pressure and the foodstuff ignited by means of electric leads. The material in the bomb burns and the heat produced leads to a rise of temperature in the surrounding water.

from tables of food analyses, of which many are available (Chap. 16). These tables give figures for the carbohydrate, protein and fat content of each food as determined by chemical analysis; the energy value of the food is calculated by multiplying these figures by the Atwater factors or some variant of them. Differences may arise from the methods of calculating the results. The protein content of each food is always determined from its nitrogen content. Most proteins contain about 16 per cent of nitrogen. To calculate the protein content of foods, the nitrogen content has frequently been multiplied by 6.25, but this figure is only an approximation and cer-

Table 3.2 The heat of combustion and the available energy in the three proximate principles in a mixed diet

	Heat of combustion		Loss in urine		Availability %	Atwater factors	
	kJ/g	kcal/g	kJ/g	kcal/g		kJ/g	kcal/g
Protein							
Meat	22.4	5.35	5.23	1.25	92	17	4
Egg	23.4	5.58					
Fat							
Butter	38.2	9.12					
Animal fat	39.2	9.37		—	95	37	9
Carbohydrate							
Starch	17.2	4.12					
Glucose	15.5	3.69		—	99	16	4
Ethyl alcohol	29.7	7.10	trace		100	29	7

tainly too high for cereals and too low for milk. For these 5.7 and 6.4 per cent respectively are better values, and have been used by some authors in the construction of their tables. The heat of combustion of the different carbohydrates varies significantly. In older tables of food analyses the carbohydrate content is calculated by difference, i.e. the carbohydrate content of the food is taken to be the difference between the total weight and the sum of the water, protein, fat and mineral content. It is then mostly starch, which has a higher value than sugars. In some modern tables the amount of glucose, fructose, sucrose, dextrins and starch have been determined and the carbohydrate content expressed in terms of monosaccharide. It does not then include the cellulose and other unavailable carbohydrates (p. 34) and the best conversion factor is 15.7 kJ (3.75 kcal)/g.

In general all these differences and inconsistencies are small in comparison with the variations between different samples of the same food. In particular almost all animal foods have a very varying fat content and this may greatly affect their energy value. On the other hand the chemical composition of a given variety of a cereal is relatively constant.

Despite all these uncertainties the energy values for foods given in tables of food composition are of practical use. They are unlikely to lead to any serious error in making up diets for an individual patient or for prescribing ration scales for institutions, service personnel, etc. They are well tried and practical guides. The intelligent user would, however, be well advised to find out exactly how the energy values in his particular table have been obtained and to keep an eye open for possible anomalies. Excellent accounts of the history of the various factors in use today with full references to the classical papers have been given by Widdowson.[6,7]

The uncertainties inherent in all tables of energy values of food make them of little use to the research worker who wishes to feed diets of accurately known energy content for metabolic balance studies on patients or laboratory animals. For such there is no escape from painstaking analyses of samples of the foods eaten and the urine and faeces excreted.

Alcohol can serve as a source of energy for man. The heat of combustion of ethyl alcohol is 29.7 kJ (7 kcal)/g and under favourable circumstances, as Atwater showed, all this energy can be utilised by man. How much of the alcohol ingested is actually used under different dietary circumstances is a difficult problem, which is considered in Chapter 7.

Sheep and other ruminants are able to derive energy from cellulose and other types of dietary fibre (except lignin), which are broken down by bacteria in the alimentary tract to short-chain fatty acids: these are subsequently absorbed into the circulation and metabolised. There is no evidence that man derives significant amounts of energy from cellulose.

MEASUREMENT OF ENERGY EXPENDITURE

Direct calorimetry is easy in theory, though difficult and costly in practice. If an animal or man is put into a small chamber in which all the heat evolved can be measured, then the total energy expenditure is the sum of that heat plus any mechanical work performed (as on a stationary bicycle). Figure 3.2 is a diagrammatic representation of the Atwater and Rosa chamber. With this they established two quantitative relationships in human metabolism.

1. Total energy expenditure (the sum of the heat produced plus the mechanical work done) was equal to the net energy from the food consumed (the total chemical energy in the food minus the energy lost in the faeces and urine). They left no doubt that man

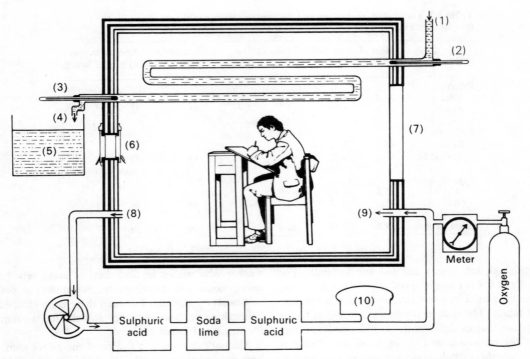

Fig. 3.2 The Atwater and Rosa respiration calorimeter. The walls of this chamber are insulated. Heat produced in it is absorbed by water passing in at (1) and out at (4), its temperature on entering and leaving being recorded on the thermometers (2) and (3). The volume of water that has flowed through the cooling system is measured in the vessel (5). The subject may be observed through the window (7), while food may be introduced and excreta removed through the porthole (6). Air leaves the chamber at (8) and passes through a blower and over sulphuric acid and soda-lime to absorb water and carbon dioxide. Oxygen measured by a gas meter is added to the system before the air passes into the chamber at (9). (10) is a tension equaliser. (From Bell G H, Davidson J N, Scarborough H 1968 *Textbook of Physiology and Biochemistry*, 7th edn. Edinburgh: Livingstone.)

obeys the fundamental law of the Conservation of Energy.

2. Total energy expenditure is quantitatively related to the oxygen consumption.

Indirect calorimetry is the measurement of oxygen consumption and technically a simpler procedure than the measurement of heat. It is based on the fact that when an organic substance is completely combusted either in a calorimeter or in the human body, oxygen is consumed in amounts directly related to the energy liberated as heat. The oxidation of glucose goes quantitatively as follows:

$$\underset{180\ g}{C_6H_{12}O_6} + \underset{\substack{6 \times 22.4 \\ \text{litres}}}{6\ O_2} = \underset{\substack{6 \times 22.4 \\ \text{litres}}}{6\ CO_2} + \underset{6 \times 18\ g}{6\ H_2O} + \underset{2.78\ MJ}{\text{heat}}$$

This equation states that 180 g of glucose yields 2.78 MJ of energy or that the heat of combustion of 1 g of glucose is 2.78/180 = 15. 5 kJ (3.69 kcal). As 6 × 22.4 litres of oxygen are used, 1 litre of oxygen is equivalent to 2.78/(6 × 22.4) = 20.8 kJ (4.95 kcal). The ratio of

the carbon dioxide produced to the oxygen used is known as the respiratory quotient (RQ). The RQ for the oxidation of glucose is 1.0.

Similar equations can be written for the combustion of a fatty acid or a protein. Table 3.3 gives values for the heat of combustion, RQ and energy equivalent of O_2 for fat, protein and starch (the chief carbohydrate in the diet). This table was first set out by the Swiss physiologist Zuntz over 80 years ago. As the energy equivalent of oxygen is much the same, whichever of the three foodstuffs is oxidised, a figure of 20 kJ (4.8 kcal)/litre of oxygen is a good approximation when, as is usual, a mixture of the three is being used.

It is also known that 1 g of urinary nitrogen arises from the metabolism of 6.25 g of protein. If, in addition to the oxygen used (O_{2m}), the carbon dioxide produced (CO_{2m}) and the urinary nitrogen (U_N) are also measured, it is then possible to calculate the amounts of carbohydrate, fat and protein metabolised. This is known as the **metabolic mixture**. The energy used can also be calculated more precisely. Four equations give the means of doing this.

Table 3.3 Energy yields from oxidation of foodstuffs

1 g of —	O_2 required ml	CO_2 produced ml	RQ	Energy developed kJ	kcal	Energy equivalent of 1 l of O_2 kJ	kcal
Starch	828.8	828.8	1.000	17.51	4.183	21.13	5.047
Animal fat	2019.2	1427.3	0.707	39.60	9.461	19.62	4.868
Protein	966.1	781.7	0.809	18.59	4.442	19.26	4.600

Carbohydrate (g) $= 4.12 CO_{2m} - 2.91 O_{2m} - 2.54 U_N$
Fat (g) $= 1.69\, O_{2m} - 1.69\, CO_{2m} - 1.94\, U_N$
Protein (g) $= 6.25\, U_N$
Energy (kJ) $= 15.8\, O_{2m} + 4.86\, CO_{2m} - 12.0\, U_N$

These equations are derived from the values presented in Table 3.3 and the value given above for the protein equivalent of urinary nitrogen.[8] Any reader can check them by solving three simple, if cumbersome equations. Energy expenditure and the metabolic mixture can be calculated rapidly from the equations either by hand, using a proforma, or by a computer. Their use gives the same answer as the classical method described in most textbooks, based on a calculation of the non-protein RQ. The non-protein RQ is an abstraction which has no physiological meaning, as protein metabolism is never zero.

If neither the urinary nitrogen nor the carbon dioxide output have been measured, a useful approximation of the rate of energy expenditure (E) can be derived from measurements of the minute volume of expired air (V) and its oxygen content (O_{2E}) using Weir's[9] formula

$$E \text{ (watts)} = 3.43\, V\, (20.93 - O_{2E})$$

Measurement of oxygen consumption

The oxygen consumption of man has been measured in respiration chambers, where there is the advantage of being able to record it over long periods. However, respiration chambers are expensive and difficult to manipulate (though far less so than calorimeter chambers) and, when within one, the subject's activities are necessarily limited. For these reasons most measurements of oxygen uptake are made when the subject is breathing into some form of apparatus, which can measure the total volume of gas expired (the minute volume) and provide a sample of expired air for analysis. This involves the use of valves which separate the inspired air from the expired air. These valves may be housed in a small metal or plastic box with a rubber mouthpiece which the subject grips between his teeth. Alternatively they may be housed in a rubber mask covering the face. The rubber mouthpiece is most frequently employed. Some people experience an initial difficulty in breathing through valves and require a period of practice or training before reliable results are obtained. Indeed all sub-

jects need a few minutes practice before they breathe naturally through a strange apparatus.

Many different types of apparatus have been designed. The **Benedict Roth spirometer** (Fig. 3.3) is a closed circuit system in which the subject breathes in oxygen from a metal cylinder about 6 litres in capacity, and the expired air passes back through a soda-lime canister (to absorb the carbon dioxide) into the same cylinder. The cylinder floats on water inside a second cylinder. As the oxygen is consumed the inner cylinder falls and the rate of fall is recorded by an ink-writer on a rotating drum. The Benedict Roth apparatus is used in hospitals for measuring the resting or basal metabolism, for which purpose it is eminently suitable. It is very simple to use and the direct reading of oxygen consumption avoids the necessity of gas analyses. As the carbon dioxide is not measured the RQ cannot be cal-

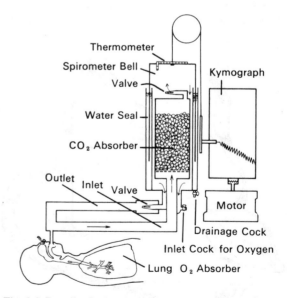

Fig. 3.3 Benedict Roth spirometer. The subject wears a noseclip and breathes through a mouthpiece which is connected to the apparatus by two valves. He breathes in oxygen through the inspiratory valve and breathes out through the expiratory valve into the carbon dioxide absorber. The amount of oxygen used is recorded on the revolving drum by the pen attached to the counter weight

culated and the heat equivalent of oxygen is assumed to be 20 kJ (4.8 kcal)/l. The apparatus is not portable so it can only be used when the subject is at rest either lying or sitting.

The physiologist is usually interested in the carbon dioxide production as well as the oxygen consumption. To measure both, the subject after breathing in ordinary room air breathes out into a **Douglas bag**, which is made of rubber or plastic of 100 litres capacity. The expired air is collected for a period of 3 to 10 minutes. The air in the bag is then passed through a gas meter, measured and a portion set aside for subsequent analysis of the carbon dioxide and oxygen content. The Douglas bag method is the simplest and most reliable means of measuring the respiratory exchanges. It is the method of choice in the laboratory. However, it is cumbersome and clumsy to use for experiments in the field or in industry.

For measurements of energy expenditure during industrial work and everyday life, the procedure was greatly facilitated by the development in Germany of the **Max Planck respirometer**.[10] This apparatus (Fig. 3.4) is a light-weight portable respirometer, which can measure directly the volume of the expired air and simultaneously divert a small fraction into a plastic bladder for subsequent analysis. The instrument weighs only about 2.5 kg and can be worn on the back like a haversack. Its introduction made possible the systematic measurement of the energy used in a variety of normal occupations as diverse as housework and coalmining. An improved model of the Max Planck respirometer, the MISER, has been introduced by Goldsmith.[11]

The Benedict Roth spirometer, the Douglas bag and the Max Planck respirometer are each suitable for undergraduate practical classes. The apparatus is not expensive. For research, especially when studying patients for long periods in a metabolic ward, it is more convenient to use a plastic hood which covers the subject's head and fits loosely over the shoulders. Room air is drawn into the hood by continuous suction and the outgoing air passed through O_2 and CO_2 analysers.

Rates of energy expenditure

Many thousands of measurements of the energy expenditure of men and women undertaking a great variety of activities have been made by indirect calorimetry. These have been collected into a series of tables, which provide estimates of the energy output of man during his various activities in day-to-day life.[12,13] The tables are in some ways complementary to the well-known food tables which provide estimates of dietary energy intake.

There have been many differences of opinion as to what constitutes hard work. A physiological definition would be useful; Table 3.4 presents quantitative definitions of work intensities. It is based on a study of Christensen[14] in the Swedish iron industry, but is generally applicable. The figures given are for men of about 65 kg.

Table 3.4 Energy expenditure in relation to intensity of muscular work (modified from Christensen)[14]

Grade of work		W	kcal/min
Very light	less than	170	<2.5
Light		170–350	2.5–4.9
Moderate		350–500	5.0–7.4
Heavy		500–650	7.5–9.9
Very heavy		650–800	10.0–12.5
Exceedingly heavy	over	800	over 12.5

Table 3.5 is a selection of figures giving the energy expenditure of various physical activites. There are naturally variations in individual efficiency in carrying out the same task, and these affect the energy expenditure. The major part of human work consists in moving the body about and in most activities energy expenditure is closely related to body weight. Obviously the grading of activities can only be approximate. Many measurements indicate that most jobs on a farm involve moderate physical activity, but some are heavy and others, perhaps an increasing number, are light. Similarly when most of us play tennis we are moderately active, but it requires heavy work to win a Wimbledon championship.

Resting and walking together make up a large pro-

Fig. 3.4 The Max Planck respirometer. The subject breathes out through an expiratory valve and the volume is directly measured and recorded on the counter. A portion of the expired air is diverted into the bladder for subsequent analysis

Table 3.5 Examples of the energy expenditure of physical activities

Light work at 170–350 W (2.5–4.9 kcal/min)

    Assembly work
    Light industry
    Electrical industry
    Carpentry
    Military drill
    Most domestic work with modern appliances
    Gymnastic exercises
    Building industry
    Bricklaying
    Plastering
    Painting
    Agricultural work (mechanised)
    Driving a truck
    Golf
    Bowling

Moderate work at 350–500 W (5.0–7.4 kcal/min)

    General labouring (pick and shovel)
    Agricultural work (non-mechanised)
    Route march with rifle and pack
    Ballroom dancing
    Gardening
    Tennis
    Cycling (up to 10 mph)

Heavy work at 500–650 W (7.5–9.9 kcal/min)

    Coal mining (hewing and loading)
    Football
    Country dancing

Very heavy work at 650 W (>10 kcal/min)

    Lumber work
    Furnace men (steel industry)
    Swimming (crawl)
    Cross-country running
    Hill climbing

portion of the total daily energy expenditure. Each is now considered in more detail.

Energy expenditure at rest

When a subject is at complete rest and no physical work is being carried out, energy is required for the activity of the internal organs and to maintain the body temperature, as already discussed. This energy is called the basal or resting metabolism. The **basal metabolic rate (BMR)** is determined experimentally when the subject is lying down at complete physical and mental rest, wearing light clothing in a room comfortably warm and at least 12 hours after the last meal. Table 3.6 gives standard values[15] for the BMR of people of both sexes and of all ages. It is based on a compilation of many hundreds of observations on people in many countries. It will be observed that the results are expressed in W/m^2. Surface area has long been used to standardise measurements of the BMR in individuals of varying size. Rubner showed many years ago that animals so

diverse as the horse, man, the dog and the mouse had very different BMRs if expressed in W/kg of body weight, but the figures for each species are remarkably similar if expressed in W/m^2 of surface area. The surface area of a few men and women has been accurately determined by pasting small pieces of paper all over the body and measuring the area of the paper. From these measurements it was shown that surface area can be predicted from measurements of height and weight. A nomogram has been constructed for this purpose (Fig. 3.5).

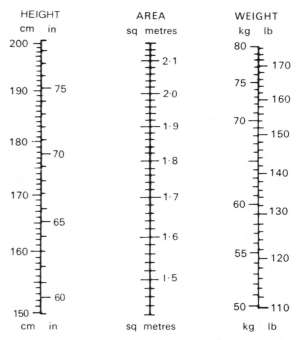

Fig. 3.5 Nomogram for calculating surface area. A line joining the height on the left-hand scale with nude weight on the right-hand scale cuts the centre scale at the predicted surface area

While surface area provides a convenient standard for comparing the BMR of different species, it is not the best standard for assessing the BMR of individual members of the same species. In particular, in people whose body shape and composition depart markedly from the normal, the use of the surface area may mislead. This is certainly so in obese people. The BMR is more closely related to 'lean body mass' than to surface area. When the figures are expressed in relation to the lean body mass the differences between men and women recorded in Table 3.6 disappear. They are not the result of any fundamental differences in the metabolism of the two sexes, but reflect that fact that women are fatter than men (p. 11). Table 3.7 gives normal values for the

Table 3.6 Standards for basal metabolic rates (W/m²)[15]

Age (years)	1	3	5	7	9	11	13	15	17	19	20
Male	61.7	59.7	57.2	55.0	52.5	50.0	49.2	48.6	47.5	45.6	45.0
Female	61.7	59.4	56.4	52.8	49.7	48.9	46.9	44.2	42.2	41.4	41.1

Age (years)	25	30	35	40	45	50	55	60	65	70	75	80
Male	43.6	42.8	42.6	42.2	41.9	41.7	41.1	40.6	40.0	39.2	38.6	38.3
Female	40.8	40.8	40.8	40.6	40.0	39.4	38.6	38.1	37.5	36.9	36.4	35.8

Table 3.7 Normal values for the resting rate of energy expenditure of adults (watts)

Men	Women	Fat per cent	Weight (kg)							
			45	50	55	60	65	70	75	80
Thin		5–	–	68	73	78	83	88	92	97
Average		10–	–	65	70	75	80	85	88	93
Plump	Thin	15–	57	62	67	72	77	82	85	90
Fat	Average	20–	55	58	63	68	73	78	82	86
	Plump	25–	–	55	60	65	70	75	78	83
	Fat	30–	–	–	57	62	67	72	75	80

resting metabolism of adults of different weights related to their body fat. This can be determined from skinfold measurements (p. 271) or assessed clinically. From this table standard values can be obtained more easily than from Table 3.6 and in our experience agreement with measured values obtained both from hospital patients and from students in their practical classes is equally good.

As Table 3.6 shows, the BMR is high in actively growing young children and falls rapidly in the first 12 years of life. Thereafter a steady slow decline sets in.

Many observers have found that the BMR of Asians was about 10 per cent below the standards set up in North America and Europe. The question arose as to whether this was a racial difference or an effect of climate. Eleanor Mason, a pupil of Benedict, investigated the problem during many years when she was a college teacher in Madras and Bombay. A paper[16] giving some of her findings has a full bibliography of the older literature. While some racial differences cannot be excluded, there is now no doubt that the BMR of most, but not all, Europeans falls in a tropical climate. The reverse has not been firmly established. However, the many Asian and African medical students who have measured their BMR in physiology classes in Edinburgh have usually obtained values as high as their European classmates. How climate acts on the BMR is unknown.

When changing from the lying to the sitting or standing position the metabolism may rise by about 20 and 30 per cent respectively. When sitting quietly in a chair throughout the day, metabolism can be taken to be about 20 per cent above the basal rate plus an additional 10 per cent if a meal has been taken in the previous three hours.

When asleep throughout the night, the overall metabolic rate approximates very closely to the BMR. When sleep begins, the effect of the last meal may raise the metabolism slightly, but in the small hours of the morning it is usually a little lower than basal rates. This is probably due to a slight fall in body temperature. These two effects cancel each other and errors introduced in calculating total metabolism throughout the night from the BMR are negligible.

Thermogenic effect of food

This term is used to describe the effect of food in raising the metabolic rate above the value found when fasting. Previously known as the specific dynamic action of food, this effect was much studied by Rubner and others between 1885 and 1910 and their work is summarised by Lusk[2] in his textbook. They established that food might increase metabolism by as much as 30 per cent and 'that meat ingestion raises the metabolism most, fat next and sugar least of all the foodstuffs'.

Later investigators [17,18,19] agree that it is difficult to get consistent quantitative results and they give less emphasis to the specific nature of the effect of different nutrients. The size of the effect is not closely related to the size of the meal. On normal diets the overall effects amount to no more than 5 to 10 per cent of the basal metabolism over 24 hours. It is therefore not a phenomenon of much practical importance and, in particular, there is no case for attempting to adjust obesity diets, so as to maximise the effect.

The causes of the thermogenic effect remain uncertain. The fact that it has been demonstrated[20] within 10 minutes of ingestion of a meal suggests that part of it can be accounted for by the work necessary for the secretion of gastric juice which may contain hydrogen ions at 10^6 times the concentration present in the plasma. However, this cannot account for its continuation, which may be for as long as five to six hours after a heavy meal. Clearly the absorption of food must in some way stimulate metabolism in the cells in general. Observations on malnourished Jamaican children are of interest;[21] a test meal had a maximum effect of 6 per cent. The effect with the same meal was 23 per cent when the children were growing rapidly during nutritional rehabilitation, but the value fell to 6 per cent when recovery was complete. This suggests that the effect is related in some way to protein synthesis but as much heat production may occur after gelatin (of poor biological value) and sucrose as after milk protein.[19] Perhaps in adults the ingestion of food may accelerate protein turnover.

Energy expenditure when walking

This has been extensively studied in many countries. There can be no doubt about the complexity of the factors that may determine energy expenditure, but speed and body weight are the most important. Table 3.8 gives figures for rate of energy expenditure for people of different weights walking on the level at varying speeds. The table can be used as a guide to the amount of physical exercise needed to achieve a given expenditure of energy, when exercise is used as a means of weight reduction.

Table 3.8 Rates of energy expenditure (W) when walking related to speed of walking and gross body weight (modified from Durnin and Passmore)[13]

Speed (mph)	Weight (kg) 45	55	65	75	85	95
2.0	150	185	200	225	250	275
2.5	185	251	240	275	300	335
3.0	215	250	285	315	360	390
3.5	150	290	325	360	410	450
4.0	285	325	365	415	460	510

The figures are converted into kJ/min or kcal/min by multiplying by 0.06 or 0.0144 respectively. A man of 65 kg who spends 30 min walking to his office at 4 mph utilises $365 \times 30 \times 0.06 = 657$ kJ or 158 kcal. This amount of energy could come from about 18 g of either dietary or adipose tissue fat. It is some four times more energy than he would have spent in 25 min in bed and 5 min driving to the office in his car.

ENERGY REQUIREMENTS OF MAN

When in health and with food freely available, each individual meets his own energy needs with remarkable precision (p. 87). In clinical practice the assessment of a patient's energy requirements usually requires a simple experiment which presents no difficulty. For instances, to find out whether 10.5 MJ (2500 kcal)/day will provide sufficient energy for an accountant with diabetes to carry out his business in the office and pursue his usual recreations, all that is necessary is to give him a diet providing 10.5 MJ and observe if he gains or loses weight. There are wide variations in the energy requirements of individuals, even of those following the same occupation and apparently leading similar kinds of lives. If exact knowledge of an individual's requirements is needed, resort to this simple experiment is necessary.

It is much more difficult to determine the energy requirements of large groups of people. Such information is needed by governments to provide a base for national food policies. It is also needed by those responsible for planning diets for the armed forces, schools and other institutions. The problem of assessing how much food is needed, neither too little nor too much, is an old one which presented itself even before Noah began to victual the Ark. It is ever-recurring.

METHODS OF ASSESSMENT

Dietary surveys

Voit in 1881 recorded the food consumed by labourers and artisans in Germany and concluded that the average man needs 12.8 MJ (3055 kcal)/day. Similarly Atwater in 1902 calculated the energy in the diets of farmers in Connecticut and Vermont; he found that they consumed 14.3 and 15.2 MJ (3410 and 3635 kcal)/day respectively. Since then dietary surveys have been carried out on a large scale in many countries and provide the basis of many estimates of human energy requirments. The technique of dietary surveys is discussed on page 524. Their use is subject to two inevitable drawbacks. (1) When food is available in abundance and there is nothing to restrict consumption, more food than is required may be eaten. On the other hand, when supplies are insufficient or purchasing power is low, consumption is likely to be less than optimal requirements. (2) A dietary survey can give no information of how the energy in the diet is expended, how much is needed for occupational activities and how much for off-work and recreational activities. With the changing patterns of life brought about by mechanisation in industry and increased means of mechanical transport, these are often important questions.

On the practical side, the carrying out of family dietary surveys (measuring all the food consumed over a period in one household) is relatively simple. Individual dietary surveys, in which all the food consumed by a single person is measured and which provide much more detailed information, are technically more difficult; a high degree of co-operation on the part of the subject is necessary.

Surveys of energy expenditure
These attempt to overcome the drawbacks inherent in the methods of dietary surveys. Such surveys demand the collection of two distinct types of data, (a) the recording, often minute by minute, of the diverse physical activities in which the subject spends his time, and (b) the assessment of the energy cost of each activity either by direct measurement of oxygen consumption or from previously published tables. The sum of all the products (time spent in each activity multiplied by the energy cost of that activity) equals the total energy expenditure.

The first of such surveys was carried out in workers in all the major industries in Germany during World War II[22] and used as a basis for food rationing. Between 1950 and 1965 many surveys on men and women with different occupations were carried out in the United Kingdom (Table 3.9) and more recently a few have been reported on peasant farmers in various parts of the world (Table 3.10). Both these tables show the enormous variation in energy expenditure of individuals in each occupational category.

RECOMMENDED INTAKES

Tables giving recommended intakes of energy have been drawn up by international and national committees in many countries. The use of these tables is discussed in Chapter 15, in which two of them are reproduced in full.

It is important to remember that the recommendations of all tables apply only to large groups of people. Individual requirements may depart markedly from the figures given. The recommendations are intended to provide a measure of the food sufficient to supply the energy required for a fully productive working life and for active recreations.

The energy requirements of individuals are dependent on four variables: (1) physical activity, (2) body size and composition, (3) age, and (4) climate and environment.

There are also extra needs for growth in childhood and adolescence and for pregnancy and lactation.

Effect of activity
One of the first surveys of energy expenditure was on underground workers and clerks at a coal mine in Scotland.[23] The authors presented a summary of their results with the daily energy divided into three parts, one expended during sleep, one during activities at work and one during non-occupational activities and recreations (Table 3.11). This approach proved useful and is now the basis of the FAO/WHO estimations of the energy (p. 170) requirements of adults. It is certainly convenient for considering the energy needs of men and women employed in industry, but less applicable to peasant agriculturists and to women whose main activities are domestic and in the home. Table 3.12 shows how the approach can be used to estimate the needs of adult men in the United Kingdom today.

Table 3.9 Daily rates of energy expenditure by individuals with various occupations in the United Kingdom between 1950 and 1965 [13]

| Occupation | Energy expenditure (MJ/day) | | |
	Mean	Minimum	Maximum
Men			
Elderly retired	9.7	7.3	11.8
Office workers	10.5	7.6	13.7
Colliery clerks	11.7	9.6	13.8
Laboratory technicians	11.9	9.3	15.9
Elderly industrial workers	11.9	9.1	15.6
Building workers	12.6	10.2	15.7
University students	12.3	9.4	18.5
Steel workers	13.7	10.9	16.6
Farmers	14.4	12.1	16.8
Army cadets	14.6	12.5	16.8
Coal miners	15.4	12.4	19.1
Forestry workers	15.4	12.0	19.2
Women			
Elderly housewives	8.3	6.5	10.1
Middle-aged housewives	8.7	7.4	9.6
Laboratory technicians	8.9	5.6	10.6
Assistants in department store	9.4	7.6	12.0
University students	9.6	5.8	10.5
Factory workers	9.7	8.2	12.4
Bakery workers	10.5	8.2	14.2

Table 3.10 Daily rates of energy expenditure by individuals in peasant communities

			Energy expenditure (MJ/day)			
			Mean			
Men						
Israel[24]	Yemenites	summer	12.8	range	10.0–19.1	
		winter	12.6		9.2–18.3	
	Kurdish	summer	12.8		9.9–17.6	
		winter	13.0		8.4–26.7	
Upper-Volta[25]	dry season		10.1	s.e.	0.25	
	wet season		14.4		0.41	
New Guinea[26]	coastal village		9.8	s.d.	1.64	
	highland village		10.8		1.10	
Women						
Israel[24]	Yemenites	summer	9.6	range	7.7–12.0	
		winter	10.0		6.9–13.5	
	Kurdish	summer	9.4		6.9–16.0	
		winter	10.0		7.2–17.0	
Upper-Volta[27]	dry season		9.7		8.7–11.2	
	wet season		12.1		10.2–15.1	
New Guinea[26]	coastal village		7.7	s.d.	1.08	
	highland village		9.4		0.98	

Table 3.11 Average daily expenditure of energy by 10 clerks (average age 28.3 years, weight 64.6 kg) and by 19 miners (average age 33.6 years, weight 65.7 kg) as measured over a whole week[23]

	Clerks		Miners	
	MJ	kcal	MJ	kcal
Asleep and day-time dozing	2.1	500	2.1	490
Activities at work	3.7	890	7.3	1750
Non-occupational activities and recreations	5.9	1410	5.9	1420
Total	11.7	2800	15.3	3660

Table 3.12 Energy expenditure and range of requirements of food for individuals and recommended intakes for groups of men in different occupational groups in the United Kingdom.

	Sedentary	Moderately active	Very active
	MJ/8 h	MJ/8 h	MJ/8 h
Energy expenditure			
In bed	2.0	2.0	2.0
At work	4.0	5.5	7.5
Non-occupational	3.0–7.0	3.0–7.0	3.0–7.0
	MJ/24 h	MJ/24 h	MJ/24 h
Energy requirement from food	9.0–13.0	10.5–14.5	13.0–17.0
Recommended intake for a group	10.5	12.0	14.0

Energy expenditure in bed approximates closely to the basal metabolic rate and amounts to about 2 MJ/8h.

The occupational energy is taken as 4.0, 5.5 and 7.5 MJ for men following sedentary, moderately active and very active occupations respectively. The difficulty lies in placing a particular group of workers into one of those categories. Many workers in the traditional heavy industries nowadays only do heavy muscular work for short periods and most of their time is spent in work which would be classified as light or moderate (Table 3.5).

Non-occupational energy varies very widely from 3.0 to 7.0 MJ. There is no evidence that those employed in sedentary work are more likely to choose recreations demanding physical activity than those in heavy industry (see Table 3.11). A figure of 4.5 MJ has been taken in calculating the recommended intake for each of the three groups in Table 3.12. It is below the median of the range, but is only a guess based on the impression that more time is being spent in watching television and spectator sports and less in active recreations and games.

For adult women figures of 1.75, 3.5 and 3.75 MJ may be taken as the energy expenditure resting in bed, in occupational activities and in recreations respectively, giving a total daily food requirement of 9.0 MJ.

All these figures are only applicable to large groups. Dietary energy requirements are determined in large part by the extent of the physical activity of individuals. This is continually changing in part by free choice and in part determined by changes in the nature of industrial and domestic work and the opportunities available for different types of recreation.

Table 3.12 is a useful guide for planning food supplies and prescribing diets for large groups in the United Kingdom. As the figures assume a way of life, the table does not set out general physiological standards. For other countries and for this country in the future modifications may be needed.

Effect of body size and composition

A big 80 kg man obviously needs more food than a small 40 kg woman. However, it is difficult to relate quantitatively food requirements and body size. Small animals eat much more food per unit of body weight than large ones. This is because the ratio of surface area to weight increases as size diminishes and consequently more energy is needed to meet heat losses from the relatively large surface. In mammalian species of varying size, food requirements are closely correlated with $W^{0.73}$.

In laboratory studies of rates of energy expenditure (E) during standard tasks by men and women E is directly related to body weight (W) and the correlation is very close for walking (Table 3.8). By contrast in calculations of the daily energy expenditure (Table 3.9), individual values of E correlated poorly with W and no better with $W^{0.73}$. Further individual dietary surveys in Britain show that food intake rises very little with increase in body weight.[28] There is thus a paradox as yet unexplained. Perhaps big people are less physically active than small people.

The recommended energy intakes of FAO/WHO (Table 15.1, p. 170) are for populations with mean weights of 65 and 55 kg for men and women. When mean weights are known to be many kilograms away from these figures, some adjustment is necessary, but it should be small, as high mean weights generally indicate widespread obesity and low mean weights widespread undernutrition.

Effect of age

Age may affect requirements in two main ways. First, as people become older they tend to engage in employment which demands a smaller expenditure of energy, and also to reduce physical exercise not connected with their work. For example, miners tend to leave the heavy jobs at the coal face after the age of 45 and by 60 few remain at this type of work. When older people take lighter employment they need less food. Secondly, in the basal metabolic state and in the 'resting' condition, the expenditure of energy per unit of body weight decreases slowly after the early twenties (Table 3.6). This decline with age is largely due to a reduction in the proportion of metabolically active tissue in the body.

Recommended intakes at various ages are given in Tables 15.1 and 15.2 (pp. 170 and 171).

Effect of climate

It is common opinion that cold weather stimulates appetite and hot weather depresses it. There are, however, few observations of either food intakes or energy expenditures under comparable conditions to support this. Any effect of climate is mainly due to changes in physical activity, but also basal metabolism is lower (p. 22). Both very cold and very hot weather tend to restrict outdoor physical activity and so food requirements. McCance and his colleagues[29] studied a group of British students and a group of Sudanese students first in Cam-

bridge during the winter and later in Khartoum during the summer. In both places the students had a similar programme of laboratory and education work which took up about four to six hours per day and ample opportunity for games and outdoor activities. Table 3.13 gives some of the results and shows that both food intake and energy expenditure were substantially less in Khartoum than in Cambridge. It is difficult to make recommendations for energy requirements in the tropics, but it seems sensible to reduce the recommended intakes given above by 5 to 10 per cent in places where the mean annual temperature exceeds 25°C.

Growth in childhood

The energy intake of children of different ages must obviously allow for satisfactory growth and physical development, and for the high degree of activity characteristic of healthy children. Recommendations (Tables 15.1 and 15.2, pp. 170 to 171) are based on observed intakes of normally growing children. For the first year of life they are related to body weight. The energy requirement per kilogram of body weight is then more than double that of the adult but falls slowly as the rate of growth per unit of body weight falls with age.

The energy required for growth is difficult to assess. The problems are discussed fully by Brody [30] in a book which is one of the classics of the literature on nutrition. Contemporary work is concerned mainly with rates of protein synthesis and turnover and is reviewed by Waterlow and Jackson.[31] They give a value of 4.6 kJ/g for the energy cost of weight gain, after deducting the energy stored.

In children of all ages there are wide individual variations in activity. The energy expenditure of healthy active children can be extremely high, and that of inactive children can be so low that they become obese even when their energy intake is below the recommended amount. In dealing with feeding problems of small groups of children, account must be taken of activity as well as of size and age.

Clearly, it is not always desirable to adjust the energy allowances of growing children to their actual weight.

Table 3.13 Mean daily energy intake and expenditure and weight change during 8 days by British and Sudanese male students in Cambridge in the winter (temperatures 1 to 12°C) and in Khartoum in the summer (temperatures 20 to 35°C)

	Energy intake		Energy expenditure		Weight change
	MJ/day	kcal/day	MJ/day	kcal/day	kg
10 British subjects					
in Cambridge	13.7	3280	13.7	3300	+0.57
in Khartoum	10.1	2420	11.2	2680	−0.73
8 Sudanese subjects					
in Cambridge	13.5	3240	11.5	2760	+0.99
in Khartoum	12.4	2970	10.3	2460	+0.88

Thus if children are below the standard weight for age (pp. 519 to 520) owing to malnutrition, they may need more than the recommended intake per kilogram of body weight to enable them to grow faster. There is however a limit to the extent to which a child can catch up after a period of undernutrition. If a child has been seriously undernourished for a long period, it is inevitable that he will develop into a small adult and giving large amounts of food only has the effect of making him obese.

Pregnancy

Oxygen consumption is increased during pregnancy to meet the needs of the fetus and placenta and of the enlarged uterus and breasts and also for increased cardiac and respiratory work. Serial measurements of resting oxygen consumption throughout pregnancy on 11 Boston women[32] showed an overall increase for the nine months equivalent to 114 MJ (27 100 kcal) of energy. This figure is an average, but there was little individual variation. The diet also has to provide the energy in the fat and protein laid down in the fetus and in increased maternal stores. The increase of of maternal body fat is very variable, but about 4 kg is a normal value.[31] A realistic figure for the total energy cost of a pregnancy is about 335 MJ (80 000 kcal).[33] Little of this is needed in the first trimester and an increased daily intake, spread evenly over the last six months, of 1.6 MJ (380 kcal) covers it. Many women in industrial societies should not increase their food intake so much, because their physical activity is cut down in pregnancy, often markedly when a job is given up for the first baby. On the other hand a poor housewife with a family of young children to care for may need all the extra food, when she becomes pregnant again. With many women, both a reduction in activity and a modest increase in food intake are likely to take place.

Lactation

The quantity of breast milk produced by individual women varies widely and depends on many factors, including the social environment and the physical and mental health of the mother. For the purpose of estimating requirements for lactation for a period of six months, an average daily milk production of 850 ml (equivalent to about 2.4 MJ or 600 kcal) may be assumed. Satisfactory data for assessing the efficiency of human milk production do not exist, but it may be of the order of 80 per cent. To provide milk with a value of 2.4 MJ, a mother would therefore need additional 3.0 MJ/day from food if her body stores are not to be depleted. In fact very few women who are lactating eat an additional 3.0 MJ/day. The extra fat laid down during pregnancy provides a reserve of energy for use in lactation. An additional dietary intake of 2.1 MJ (500 kcal)/day during lactation is recommended in the USA. This is above intakes of lactating Australian women six to eight weeks after the birth of their children.[34]

REFERENCES

1. Atwater W O, Benedict F G 1899 Experiments on the metabolism of matter and energy in the human body. US Dept Agric Bull no 69, p 76
2. Lusk G 1906 The science of nutrition, 4th edn, 1928. Saunders, Philadelphia
3. Guggenheim K Y 1981 Nutrition and nutritonal disease. The evolution of concepts. Heath, Lexington, Mass
4. Royal Society 1972 Metric units, conversion factors and nomenclature in nutritional and food Sciences. London
5. Southgate D A T, Durnin J V G A 1970 Calorie conversion factors. An experimental reassessment of the factors used in the calculation of the energy value of diets. Br J Nutr 24: 517–35
6. Widdowson E M 1955 Assessment of the energy value of human foods. Proc Nutr Soc 14: 142–54
7. Widdowson E M 1978 Note on the calculation of the energy value of foods and of diets. In: Paul A A, Southgate D A T (eds) The composition of foods. HMSO, London, p 322–6
8. Consolazio C F, Johnson R E, Pecora E 1963 Physiological measurements of metabolic functions in man. McGraw-Hill, New York
9. Weir J B de V 1949 New methods for calculating metabolic rate with special reference to protein metabolism. J Physiol 109: 1–9
10. Müller E A, Franz H 1952 Energieverbrauchssungen bei beruflicher Arbeit mit einer verbesserten Respirations-Gasuhr. Arbeitsphysiologie 14: 499–504
11. Eley C, Goldsmith R, Layman D, Tan G L E, Walker E 1978 A respirometer for use in the field for the measurement of oxygen consumption. 'The Miser', a miniature, indicating and sampling electronic respirometer. Ergonomics 21: 153–164
12. Passmore R, Durnin J V G A 1955 Human energy expenditure. Physiol Rev 35: 801–40
13. Durnin J V G A, Passmore R 1967 Energy, work and leisure. Heinemann, London
14. Christensen E H 1953 Physiological evaluation of work in the Hykroppa iron works. In: Floyd W F, Welford A T (eds) Ergonomics Society symposium on fatigue. Lewis, London, p 93–108
15. Fleish A 1951 Le mêtabolisme basal standard et sa determination au moyen du 'metabocalculator'. Helv Med Acta 18: 23–44
16. Mason E D, Jacob M, Balakrishnan V 1964 Racial group differences in the basal metabolism and body composition of Indian and European women in Bombay. Hum Biol 36: 374–96
17. Garrow J S, Hawes S E 1972 The role of amino acid oxidation in causing 'specific dynamic action' in man. Br J Nutr 27: 211–9

18. Swindells Y E 1972 The influence of activity and size of meals on caloric response in women. Br J Nutr 27: 65–73

19. Bradfield R B, Jourdan M H 1973 Relative importance of specific dynamic action in weight-reduction diets. Lancet 2: 640–3

20. Passmore R, Ritchie F J 1957 The specific dynamic action of food and the satiety mechanism. Br J Nutr 11: 79–85

21. Brooke O G, Ashworth A 1972 The influence of malnutrition on the postprandial metabolic rate and respiratory quotient. Br J Nutr 27: 407–15

22. Lehmann G, Müller E A, Spitzer H 1950 Der Calorien bedarf bei gewerblicher Arbeit. Arbeitsphysiologie 14: 166–235

23. Garry R C, Passmore R, Warnock G M, Durnin J V G A 1955 Studies on expenditure of energy and consumption of food by miners and clerks, Fife, Scotland, 1952. MRC Special Rep Ser no 289

24. Edholm O G, Humphrey S, Lourie J A, Tredre B E, Brotherhood J 1973 Energy expenditure and climatic exposure of Yemenite and Kurdish Jews in Israel. Philos Trans Soc Lond (Biol) 266: 127–40

25. Brun T, Bleiberg F, Goihams S 1981 Energy expenditure of male farmers in the dry and rainy seasons in Upper-Volta. Br J Nutr 45: 67–75

26. Norgan N G, Ferro-Luzzi A, Durnin J V G A 1974 The energy and nutrient intake and the energy expenditure of 204 New Guinean adults. Philos Trans R S Lond (Biol) 268: 309–48

27. Bleiberg F M, Brun T A, Goihams S 1980 Duration of activities and energy expenditure of female farmers in dry and rainy seasons in Upper-Volta. Br J Nutr 43: 71–82

28. Thomson A M, Billewicz W Z, Passmore R 1961 The relation between calorie intake and body-weight in man. Lancet 1: 1027–8

29. McCance R A, Hamad El Neil, Nasr el Din, Widdowson E M, Southgate D A T, Passmore R, et al 1971 The responses of men and women to changes in their environmental temperatures and ways of life. Philos Trans R Soc Lond (Biol) 259: 533–65

30. Brody S 1945 Bioenergetics and growth, reprinted 1964. Haffner, New York

31. Waterlow J C, Jackson A A 1981 Nutrition and protein turnover in man. In: Waterlow J C (ed) Nutrition of man. Churchill Livingstone, Edinburgh, p 5–10

32. Emerson K, Saxena B N, Poindexter E L 1972 Caloric cost of normal pregnancy. Obstet Gynecol 40: 786–94

33. Hytten F E 1980 Weight gain in pregnancy. In: Hytten F E, Chamberlain G (eds) Clinical physiology in obstetrics. Blackwell, Oxford, p 193–233

34. English R M, Hitchcock N E 1968 Nutrient intakes during pregnancy, lactation and after the cessation of lactation in a group of Australian women. Br J Nutr 22: 615–24

4

Carbohydrates

Carbohydrates provide a great part of the energy in all human diets. In the diets of poor people, especially in the tropics, up to 85 per cent of the energy may come from this source. On the other hand, in the diets of the rich in many countries, the proportion may be as low as 40 per cent. Neither of these extremes is desirable.

Green plants synthesise carbohydrates from carbon dioxide and water with evolution of oxygen under the influence of sunlight. The primary products are the **sugars** which are readily soluble in water and so easily transported throughout the tissue fluid of both plants and animals to provide the fuels of the cells. Sugars are polymerised to form **polysaccharides**, macromolecules not readily soluble in water that can be stored. Seed grains and root vegetables contain large amounts of the polysaccharide starch, the predominant chemical component of most human diets. Animals also form a storage polysaccharide glycogen, but the amount present in animal tissues are small.

Plants also synthesise other carbohydrate polymers. **Cellulose** and **hemicellulose** are fibrous substances and the main components of their cell walls. As plants mature, the cell walls incorporate **lignin**, the main component of wood, consisting of polymerised alcohols. **Pectins** and **gums** are viscous substances in plant sap. These five substances provide plants with a structure that is stable and partially rigid. Collectively they are known as **dietary fibre** although not all are fibres.

Animal tissues also contain structural carbohydrate. Carbohydrate polymers are present in proteoglycans which are major components of connective tissue and also of viscous secretions. Glycoproteins found in many tissues and with diverse functions are polypeptides containing a few short chains of carbohydrate and also some lipids contain carbohydrate. The amounts relative to protein and fat are small and negligible in dietetics.

Starch and also most of the sugars are broken down by intestinal digestive enzymes into simple sugars, monosaccharides, and then absorbed. These processes are completed in the small intestine, and in health only traces of starch or sugar pass into the large intestine.

Starch and sugars are thus made available to the tissues as a source of energy and are known as **available carbohydrates**. Cellulose, hemicellulose, gums and pectin are not digested by alimentary enzymes. These split the α $(1{\to}4)$ bonds that join the glucose molecules in chains present in starch, but cannot split the β $(1{\to}4)$ bonds linking the glucose molecules in cellulose and hemicellulose. (The α and β forms of glucose differ in the spatial arrangements of the —H and —OH attached to the C_1 atom.) The structural carbohydrates of plants pass through the small intestine virtually unchanged. In the large intestine they are partly fermented by bacteria and partly excreted in the faeces. The products of fermentation are carbon dioxide, hydrogen, methane and volatile fatty acids (acetic, propionic and butyric acid). The gases may be passed as flatus or absorbed and excreted through the lungs. The volatile fatty acids are absorbed and can be utilised; they are a major source of fuel for ruminants in which fermentation takes place in the rumen, but in man the amounts absorbed are small. The structural carbohydrates of plants are known as **unavailable carbohydrates,** or dietary fibre. In dietetics the distinction between available and unavailable carbohydrates is useful and important. However, in various disorders of the alimentary tract available carbohydrate may pass into the large intestine and there be fermented. In some circumstances a part of the unavailable carbohydrate may be made available by bacterial fermentation in the large intestine. The distinction is thus not absolute. Figure 4.1 shows the main differences in diagrammatic form.

AVAILABLE CARBOHYDRATES

Dietary sources (Table 4.1)

Sucrose is the familiar sugar in the home. This has been processed from sugar cane or sugar beet and the commercial product is 99 per cent pure sugar. Now a major source of energy, until the eighteenth century it was available only as a luxury valued for its sweetness.

Table 4.1 Dietary sources of available carbohydrates

Carbohydrate	Natural source	Relative sweetness	Products of digestion	Common daily intake (g)
Sugars (disaccharides)				
Sucrose	Refined from sugar cane and sugar beet	100	Glucose and fructose	100
Lactose	Milk and milk products	30	Glucose and galactose	15
Maltose	Malted foods		Glucose and glucose	Negligible
Trehalose	Fungi and insects		Glucose and glucose	Negligible
Sugars (monosaccharides)				
Glucose	Fruits and honey	50	–	5
Fructose	Fruits and honey	170	–	5
Mannose	Manna		–	–
Polysaccharides				
Starch	Cereal products, root vegetables, beans and other plants	0	Glucose	250
Dextrins	Small amounts in natural starch	0	Glucose	Negligible
Glycogen	Meats	0	Glucose	Negligible

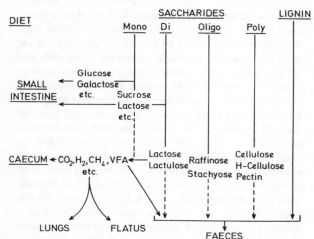

Fig. 4.1 Disposal of available and unavailable carbohydrate by the intestinal canals

It is a disaccharide readily hydrolysed by acids and by the enzyme sucrase in the small intestine into glucose and fructose.

Lactose is the sugar present in milk. It is a disaccharide and readily hydrolysed into glucose and galactose.

Maltose is a disaccharide made up of two molecules of glucose. It is formed by the breakdown of starch in the process of malting and is present in small amounts in malted foods.

Trehalose is a disaccharide composed of two molecules of glucose. It is known as the mushroom sugar, being present in fungi and also in insects. The fact that we still possess the specific enzyme, trehalase, necessary

for its hydrolysis suggests that insects were much more important food for our ancestors than for us now.

Fructose is a monosaccharide found in fruits and vegetables and mainly responsible for their sweetness.

Glucose is a monosaccharide found in fruits and vegetables but is much less sweet than fructose and sucrose. Honey is mainly a mixture of fructose and glucose. Glucose manufactured from starch is sold commercially in a variety of relatively expensive proprietary preparations; these however have no advantage over sucrose as a source of energy for healthy people.

Mannose is a monosaccharide present in manna, which Moses told the Israelites is 'the bread that the Lord has given you to eat' (Exodus 16.16). Manna is the common name for lichens which in drought curl up into light balls that may be blown across a desert and from which bread can be made.

Pentoses are present as constituents of the macromolecules in the cells of all natural foodstuffs, but only in small amounts and so are not important as a source of energy. **Ribose** and **deoxyribose** are components of nucleic acids and, as they are synthesised by all animals, are not essential nutrients. **Arabinose** and **xylose** are components of pectins and gums which may be made available by bacterial fermentation in the colon. Small amounts of pentoses are found in normal urine.

Raffinose, a trisaccharide present in molasses, and **stachyose**, a tetrasaccharide present in beans, become available only after bacterial fermentation in the caecum and large intestine.

Sugar alcohols are found in nature and also prepared commercially. **Sorbitol** is formed from glucose by the enzyme aldose reductase. It is present in some fruits but it is the factory product that has a place in dietetics, being used in the manufacture of 'diabetic' soft drinks, jam and other foods. Sorbitol is only half as sweet as sucrose but it is absorbed from the gut more slowly and converted in the liver into fructose. It thus has less effect on blood sugar than sucrose. Large amounts cause osmolar diarrhoea. Sorbitol is present in nerve and other tissues in small amounts that are increased by hyperglycaemia and this may be responsible for the impaired nerve conduction occurring in some diabetic patients (p. 387).

Mannitol and **dulcitol** are alcohols derived from mannose and galactose. Both have a variety of uses in food manufactures. Mannitol is extracted commercially from a seaweed that grows on the coasts of Britain.

Inositol is a cyclic alcohol with six hydroxyl radicles and allied to glucose. It is present in many foods, especially the bran of cereals. Its hexophosphate ester, phytic acid, impairs absorption of calcium and iron in the small intestine.

Starch is the form in which carbohydrate is stored in granules in the roots and seeds of plants. Starch grains usually contain two polysaccharides derived from glucose. Amylose is a long unbranched chain of glucose units with $\alpha (1\rightarrow4)$ linkages; it is responsible for the blue colour that appears on adding a weak solution of iodine to a suspension or solution of starch. Amylopectin, the major component of most starch grains, is a highly branched molecule with about 12 glucose units in each branch, the branches being joined by $\alpha(1\rightarrow6)$ linkages; it gives a brownish violet colour on the addition of iodine. Some varieties of cereals, such as waxy rice and maize, contain virtually no amylose. Starch grains obtained fresh from plants are insoluble in water. Heating, however, produces a solution that remains fairly stable, although it may gel on cooling. Under the microscope the starch grains of a raw potato can be seen lying in groups within the thin wall of the cells. Moist heat causes the grains to swell; cells may disrupt and the starch become soluble. Thus cooking renders the starch more accessible to digestive enzymes.

Dextrins are degradation products of starch in which the glucose chains have been broken down to smaller units by partial hydrolysis. They are the main source of carbohydrate in proprietary preparations used as oral supplements and for tube feeding (Chap. 52). Liquid glucose is a mixture of dextrins, maltose, glucose and water. These products are a means of giving carbohydrate in an easily assimilated form to patients who are seriously ill. Dextrins being larger molecules than sucrose or glucose have less osmotic effects and so are less likely to cause osmolar diarrhoea. Dextrins should not be confused with **dextran**, a carbohydrate polymer obtained from bacterial cell walls. This has no part in dietetics but is used in medicine as a plasma expander. A 10 per cent solution given intravenously causes an increase in blood volume, with consequent rise in cardiac output and renal blood flow in patients who are in shock following haemorrhage.

Glycogen, the animal equivalent of starch, is present in liver and muscle. Like starch it is readily broken down by pancreatic amylase to glucose. In most foods of animal origin it is a negligible source of dietary carbohydrates, but an oyster (removed from its shell) contains about 6 per cent of its wet weight as glycogen.

DIGESTION AND ABSORPTION

The salivary glands secrete an **amylase** (ptyalin). This is incorporated in the bolus of food that is formed by chewing and then swallowed. The digestion of starch begins in the bolus but when this is broken up in the stomach, the acid gastric juice inactivates the enzyme. Digestion occurs mainly in the small intestine through the action of amylase in the pancreatic juice. This breaks down the starch to short-chain dextrins and maltose. In the brush border of the intestinal epithelium there are hydrolases that split the dextrin, and also specific disaccharidases, **maltase**, **sucrase** and **lactase**, that convert maltose, sucrose and lactose into monosaccharides. The concentrations of these enzymes in a sample of the brush border obtained by biopsy can be measured.

The monosaccharides glucose, fructose and galactose are then transported across the epithelial cells and enter the portal vein. This takes place against a concentration gradient and so requires energy. The active transport system is similar to the one that absorbs glucose from the renal tubules and involves the breakdown of ATP and the presence of Na^+. Different sugars compete for transport and galactose and glucose are absorbed faster than fructose.

After a meal the blood glucose rises to a maximum in about 30 minutes and then returns slowly to the fasting level after 90 to 180 minutes. The height of the maximum and the rate of return to normal vary with the nature of the meal. The glycaemic index of different foods has been calculated from the area under the blood glucose curve after ingestion of a portion of the food containing 50 g of carbohydrate.[1] Values, compared with an arbitrary figure of 100 after ingesting only glucose, range from 60 to 80 for cereal products to below 30 for beans and other pulses. These values may be useful in planning diabetic diets when the aim is to keep the blood sugar as low as possible. However, after a mixed meal of several foods many factors affect the rate of absorption of carbohydrate. The rate of passage through the stomach and upper small intestine is obviously important, and this depends on the amount of peristalsis and the viscosity of the bolus passing.

In health and with a normal diet, available carbohydrate is digested and absorbed virtually completely in the small intestine. If an excess of unabsorbed carbohydrate arises due to a disorder of the absorption mechanism or occasionally to excessive intake, the osmotic effect leads to retention of fluid in the lumen and a watery diarrhoea (osmolar diarrhoea).

A fraud

In 1975 an amylase inhibitor was reported[2] to be present in the kidney bean, *Phaseolus vulgaris*. Soon over 100 commercial preparations had been placed on the market and advertised as starch blockers with the claim that one tablet was able to block the digestion and absorption of 100 g of starch. The appeal to would-be slimmers was great and in 1982 over one billion (1000 000 000) tablets were consumed daily in the USA. Although the tablets inhibit starch digestion by amylase *in vitro*, they are totally ineffective in man, as three independent investigators have shown.[3,4,5]

DISPOSAL OF AVAILABLE CARBOHYDRATES

Monosaccharides after leaving the alimentary tract in the portal vein go first to the liver. The main carbohydrate absorbed is glucose, but there may also be large amounts of fructose, if the diet contains much sugar and fruit, and galactose in amounts depending on the quantity of milk drunk. Carbohydrate is the main sourse of dietary energy and its utilisation for this purpose is described in Chapter 8. Here only the immediate disposal and storage are discussed. As the breakdown of polysaccharides to monosaccharides is a hydrolysis, energy is not required and so virtually all the energy in digestible polysaccharides becomes available to the tissues.

Glucose

The ability of the tissues to dispose of dietary carbohydrate is assessed by the glucose tolerance test, an essential part of the investigation of a diabetic patient and described on page 376. There are three ways in which the tissues dispose of blood glucose (Fig. 4.2). It may be utilised directly as a source of energy (A) or stored either in the form of glycogen (B) or after conversion into fat (C) before subsequent utilisation.

The tissues use as fuel a mixture of glucose and fatty acids, the proportion of fatty acids increasing with time after a meal. But the brain normally uses only glucose and requires some 80 g daily. In starvation this may be provided by gluconeogenesis from amino acids in tissue proteins, mainly from muscle, but fat cannot be converted into glucose. With prolonged starvation the brain adapts and can then utilise fatty acids and ketones (p. 83). The importance of the blood glucose to the brain is shown by the fact that even a small fall, as when

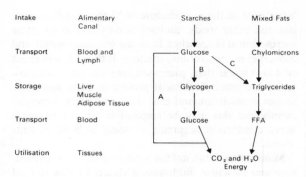

Fig. 4.2 Supply of energy to the tissues

a diabetic patient has received a small overdose of insulin, causes weakness, a feeling of uneasiness and confusion; there may be abnormal behaviour which has led to arrests by the police on a charge of being drunk and disorderly. Severe hypoglycaemia causes coma and, if not treated promptly, death.

The proportions of absorbed glucose disposed of by the three routes can only be determined by the use of complex techniques using isotopes. There have been no large studies in man indicating the variations in the proportion that may arise from the nature of the meal, individual constitution or previous state of nutrition.

Of the three routes of disposal of glucose indicated in Figure 4.2, it is probable that under normal circumstances the greater part goes by route C. The simple measurement of the RQ only indicates relative utilisation of carbohydrate and fat. The theoretical value of the RQ for conversion of carbohydrate to fat is 1.3, compensating for the value of 0.7 for the oxidation of fat. RQs above 1.0 have been found in hedgehogs in the autumn when they are eating large amounts of carbohydrate preparatory to hibernation.[6] Readers can raise their own RQ above 1.0 but only by gorging on carbohydrates for some hours, not a pleasant experience.[7]

Conversion into fat

This takes place in both the liver and adipose tissue. Fatty acids are synthesised from the two carbon units, acetyl CoA, formed from glucose. The glycerol needed for esterification of free fatty acids before they can be stored as triglycerides can also be formed from glucose. The relative importance of the liver and adipose tissue in triglyceride synthesis in man is uncertain, but the greater part may be formed in the liver and then transported as very low density lipoprotein (p. 62) to adipose tissue.

Even when the dietary carbohydrate is not in excess of needs a large proportion of it may be converted into fat, which is then used by the tissues. Stetten & Boxer,[8] using deuterium as an indicator, showed that in rats on a high carbohydrate diet at least 10 times as much glucose was converted into fatty acids as into glycogen. Further isotopic studies have shown that the rate of turnover of glucose in the body is much slower than the rate of turnover of the free fatty acids (FFA). Dole[9] has calculated that FFA can provide energy for the tissues at a rate two and a half times as fast as can glucose. Of the three routes indicated in Figure 4.2 by which glucose can supply energy to the tissues, it now seems probable that under normal circumstances the major part goes by route C.

The synthesis of fatty acids from glucose requires energy, and the immediate source of this is ATP. In subsequent use of the fatty acids as fuel for the tissues, about 16 per cent less energy becomes available than when the glucose is utilised directly (p. 78). The uneconomical use of glucose by prior conversion into triglyceride thus raises dietary needs for energy. A possible partial explanation of how some people who are apparently big eaters remain thin is that in them a higher proportion of dietary glucose goes through this pathway than in those with a tendency to plumpness.

Lessons from a past controversy

Today everyone knows that carbohydrates can be converted into fat and so may be fattening. But this is not obvious and was only established scientifically in 1845 after a bitter controversy had raged for five years in Paris, then the centre of the scientific world. Controversy, still often bitter, is commonplace among nutritionists at the present time and events in Paris many years ago have their lessons for us. The centre of the dispute was Jean Baptiste Dumas, the chemist who had rightly acquired an enormous reputation for his work in establishing the structure of organic compounds and setting out their formulae as we now know them. Although not a biologist he was appointed to the Chair of Organic Chemistry in the School of Medicine in 1838. He was a brilliant lecturer, as the young Louis Pasteur in a letter to his father recorded: 'His course is easy to comprehend; I take it down exactly. You cannot possibly figure what influence on the world the course has. The hall is immense and always full. It is necessary to go half an hour before to get a place, exactly as at the theatre. Likewise there is much applause. There are always 600–700 people present.'

Dumas was an imaginative man and his hero was Lavoisier, whom he considered, on no good evidence, to have shown that 'everything tends to perfection, to truth and to simplicity'. In his lectures he correctly and for the first time described the vegetable kingdom: '[a] vast system of reducers, taking in carbon dioxide and water from the air, converting their carbon and hydrogen into living matter and liberating their oxygen to the atmosphere. By contrast the animal kingdom is a veritable apparatus of combustion which is ceaselessly oxidising living matter and returning their end products, carbon dioxide and water to the air.' He went further: 'It is then in the plants that the true laboratory of organic chemistry resides; ligneous matter, starch, gums and sugars are one part, fibrin, albumin, casein and gluten the other part of the fundamental products of the two kingdoms. These products are formed in plants and in plants only, and transported by digestion in animals.' He thus stated firmly that animals lacked the ability to synthesise organic material. This necessitated accepting an old view that the function of the alimentary canal was confined to making dietary matter soluble and so able to be absorbed. Modern views on digestion were being developed in Germany, and Schwann in 1836 first gave the name pepsin to an extract of stomach which contained digestive properties. However, Dumas was able to dismiss these on chemical grounds, perhaps influenced by national chauvinism — a factor not unknown in science today.

In Germany there was Dumas' great rival in chemistry, Liebeg. He reported that a lean goose, weighing 4 lb, weighed 9 lb and contained 3½ lb of pure fat after feeding for 36 days on 24 lb of maize. This fat, Liebeg argued, could not have come from the maize. Dumas analysed a sample of maize and found it contained 9 per cent of a yellow oil and he claimed that this together with the fat originally present in the goose could account for all the fat present when it was killed. The problem of fat formation was then studied by several workers in French and German laboratories and hotly debated. Here another colourful character must be introduced.

J. B. Boussingault (1801–81) trained in the School of Mining in Paris and then went to South America where he worked as director of a mine, but he studied natural history and for a time was on the staff of the revolutionary, Simon Bolivar. Returning to France after 10 years, he married a rich wife and settled down on her farm in Alsace to study agriculture chemistry. He soon showed that some plants absorbed nitrogen from the air which was used for the synthesis of protein. These experiments interested Dumas and the two became friends, Boussingault being an active supporter of Dumas' views. An experiment on the farm, in which seven cows in producing 17 976 litres of milk had consumed 689 g of fatty substances in their fodder yet produced only 673 g of butter, allowed Dumas to hang on to his position. Boussingault went on to study the fattening of ducks, geese and pigs on experimental diets and measured the total amount of fat in the carcasses. His paper to the Academy of Science in 1845 demonstrated beyond doubt that fat could be synthesised by animals. This long paper with many tables of analyses is a masterpiece and the first example of balance studies, so familiar to us today.

The story of the controversy that enthralled the scientific world of the time is told with style and erudition by Holmes.[10] Clashes between theory and experiment and between personalities continue today. There are two lessons for students today. First always be very critical of the brilliant lecturer, and secondly remember that the establishment is sometimes wrong.

Conversion into glycogen

Glycogen is the storage form of glucose in animals and so analogous to starch in plants. Table 4.2 sets out normal values for the glycogen and sugar content of an adult man. The liver is the organ richest in glycogen; concentrations in skeletal muscles are lower, but owing to the greater bulk of the muscles they contain the major part of the store. This can be mobilised and glucose made immediately available to an individual muscle. The total store is small and in starvation is exhausted in about 24 hours; then blood sugar can only be maintained by gluconeogenesis from protein in the tissues. For this reason it is important that all patients who are seriously ill receive some carbohydrate daily; if for any reason this cannot be given by mouth, intravenous infusion of glucose is needed — about 100 g daily for an adult.

The store of muscle glycogen is raised above the normal when a subject is starved for 24 hours and then fed

Table 4.2 Glycogen and sugar content of normal man. Body weight, 70 kg; liver weight, 1800 g; muscle mass, 35 kg; volume of blood and extracellular fluids, 21 litres (Soskin & Levine)[11]

	g/kg	Total g
Muscle glycogen	7	245
Liver glycogen	60	108
Blood and extracellular fluid sugar	0.8	17
Total body carbohydrate		370

an excess of carbohydrates. This procedure may be useful to some athletes and sportsmen taking part in events requiring a high rate of energy expenditure for 30 minutes or longer and is discussed in Chapter 63.

The discovery of glycogen was made by Claude Bernard in Paris in 1850 in the aftermath of the controversy on the origin of animal fat. The experiments which led to it are a classic in physiology. They paved the way for the young Bernard's subsequent career and his conception of the constancy of the internal environment. Maintenance of the constancy of blood glucose by control of deposition and withdrawal from glycogen stores is a prime example of what is now known as homeostasis.

Fructose

Fructose is absorbed more slowly but utilised more quickly than glucose. Metabolism takes place entirely in the liver where it is converted by fructose kinase into fructose 1-phosphate which is then split into two trioses, dihydroxyacetone phosphate and glyceraldehyde. These can be used for the synthesis of glucose or enter the glycolytic pathway to form lactic acid. As these processes are not dependent on insulin, fructose can be utilised by diabetics. It is much sweeter than sucrose and has for a long time been used to make jam and confectionery for diabetics. However, fructose was commercially expensive and not readily available until 1975 when new technology developed in Finland put large quantities on the European market. In the USA a high fructose corn syrup (55 to 90 per cent fructose) is commercially available. These products have been promoted energetically but physicians, at least in Britain, have not been persuaded that fructose has an important role in diabetic diets. Furthermore, although there is no doubt that in health large amounts of fructose can be metabolised with safety, in severely ill patients fructose, especially when given intravenously to replace glucose solutions, has been associated with the development of lactic acid acidosis. This condition is not common but, when it occurs, it is often severe and sometimes fatal. In liver disease the rate at which fructose is cleared from the blood may be reduced, sometimes markedly. A fuller account of the physiology of fructose is given by Grapo & Olefsky.[12]

Galactose

Galactose is converted into glucose in the liver. It is first phosphorylated and the galactose phosphate is then exchanged for glucose phosphate in uridine diphosphate glucose. The uridine diphosphate galactose is then converted into uridine diphosphate glucose by an epimerase, the net result being the formation of glucose 1-phosphate which may then be readily converted into glycogen.

UNAVAILABLE CARBOHYDRATE OR DIETARY FIBRE

In 1982 the best-selling book in the United Kingdom was a guide to high-fibre diets based on wholemeal cereals with ample vegetables and fruit.[13] The sale of over a million copies in one year demonstrated the popular demand for dietary information. Yet the message of the book had been available for centuries. However, the new study of nutrition in this century, prompted by the discovery of vitamins, overlooked the importance of dietary fibre. In 1956 the dietetics textbook[14] most used in the UK stated 'the value of these unavailable carbohydrates or roughage in the diet has been, and still is, over-rated'.

This orthodox opinion was jolted in 1969 by Burkitt,[15] who pointed out that cancer and other diseases of the large intestine, common in the West, were rarely seen in tropical Africa. He suggested that high intakes of dietary fibre protected Africans against these Western diseases. His interest had arisen from a study of the writings of Cleave,[16] who has for many years advocated natural diets. Interest was further aroused in 1971 by a report that patients with diverticulitis of the colon, previously treated with bland, low-fibre diets, improved greatly when given high-fibre diets.[17] Evidence was also presented that dietary fibre might reduce the risk of coronary heart disease, diabetes, and other common disorders in the West, as well as disorders of the large bowel.

In the 1970s there was much investigation of the chemical and physical properties of fibre, the amounts present in different diets, its physiological effects, and the relation between the quantity and quality of fibre in the diet and various diseases.[18,19]

TYPES OF DIETARY FIBRE*

Plants synthesise from simple sugars several carbohydrate polymers. Starch, a store of energy for the plant, is almost entirely digested and absorbed from the

* This section has been published previously in The Lancet 1983; 2:202–206.

upper small intestine in animals, though a small proportion trapped in fibrous tissue may pass to the caecum. Fibrous or viscous polysaccharides give plants their structure and form; these are not digested in the mammalian small intestine and, in man, pass unchanged into the colon where they are fermented to a variable extent. These polysaccharides, the indigestible components of plant cell walls, make up dietary fibre.[20]

The structure of the plant cell wall changes with growth, stage of differentiation, cell environment, and specialist functions of the cell. The macromolecular components of the wall are fibrillar polysaccharides (mainly cellulose), matrix polysaccharides (pectic substances, hemicelluloses, and glycoproteins), and encrusting substances (mainly lignin). The chemical composition of cell-wall materials from parenchymatous and lignified tissues in dicotyledons and monocotyledons differs. The chemistry of dietary fibre therefore varies from plant to plant and is affected by the growing conditions and age of the plant.[21]

CHEMISTRY OF FIBRE

Cellulose is a polymer of glucose linked by β-$(1\rightarrow4)$ bonds. Cellulose molecules are arranged within the microfibrils in a highly ordered crystalline state in chains 4000–6000 nm long and possibly 4 nm in diameter; each consists of several thousand glucose units.

Hemicelluloses are branched polymers of pentose and hexose sugars (eg. xylose, arabinose, mannose, galactose, and their uronic acid derivatives). The proportions depend on the plant source: for instance, xyloglucans are the predominant hemicelluloses in parenchymal fruit and vegetable tissues.

Lignins are polymers of aromatic alcohols; they encrust the cellulose and hemicelluloses during secondary thickening.

Pectins are a complex mixture of colloidal polysaccharides; they are partly esterified rhamnogalacturonans with an α-$(1\rightarrow4)$-linked D-galacturonan chain interspersed with L-rhamnopyranosyl residues with sidechains which include D-glucuronic and galacturonic acid. Some acidic groups are methylated. Some pectin is extractable from plant tissue by means of aqueous chelating agents, but 20–30 per cent is closely bound to other cell-wall constituents, especially α-cellulose. Pectins readily hold water in an interconnecting network.

Gums are water-soluble viscous polysaccharides of 10 000–30 000 units, mainly glucose, galactose, mannose, arabinose, rhamnose, and their uronic acids, which may be methoxylated and acetylated. Gums commonly used in the food industry are gum arabic, tragacanth, karaya gum, carob gum, and guar gum, which are obtained as exudates from stems or seeds of tropical and semitropical trees and shrubs.

Mucilages are polysaccharides from seeds and seaweeds used in small amounts in the food industry as thickening and stabilising agents by virtue of their water-holding and viscous properties. The mucilages of some seeds (eg. ispaghula husks) are bulk laxatives made up of highly branched arabinoxylans. Alginic acid from seaweed is a polymer of $(1\rightarrow4)$-linked β-D-mannuronic acid or of $(1\rightarrow4)$-linked α-L-guluronic acid or a mixture. There are also polysaccharides containing fucose in seaweed mucilages. The mucilages may be sulphated to a variable degree.

Chemical analysis

The complexities of plant structure and the variable association between constituent polysaccharides cause great difficulties in analysis. Complex studies of cell-wall chemistry[21–23] have yet to be translated into quantitative analytical procedures. Old estimates of crude fibre obtained by difference have been replaced by separate analysis of each component.[24] There are few studies on the reproducibility of dietary fibre analysis, but the yardstick for measurements remains that of Southgate.[24]

PHYSICAL PROPERTIES

Dietary fibre is a biological unit, not a chemical entity. The mixture of polymers should be regarded as a whole. The physical attributes of the fibres in plant cell walls determine the shape and so the function of the plant and also the effects of dietary fibre on digestion and absorption. The proportion of water-soluble and insoluble fibre, fibre chemistry, particle size, and the extent to which the cellular and pore structure of the fibre is affected by processing and cooking all affect digestion and absorption.

Water-holding capacity

Water is a prominent component of young plant cell walls, but as they age they fill with hydrophobic lignins. Water in the cell wall determines the conformation of pectins and other polysaccharides in the cell matrix and also the strength of association by hydrogen bonding between these polysaccharides and so the permeability characteristics of the wall. Cooking, processing, and eating of a plant food destroy the anatomy, but the water-holding characteristics of the fibre persist, though they are modified. Water is present in three phases in fibre passing along the intestine and colon. Phase 1 water, bound by the hydrophilic polysaccharides of the fibre, is unavailable: the amount depends on the chemical composition of the fibre. The availability of phase 2 water, held in the fibre matrix, depends on the matrix pore size. Phase 3 water is additional water physically trapped within the fibre network, which depends on the fibre source and on subsequent processing.[25] Bran, which is very insoluble, contains little bound water, whereas leafy vegetable fibre that is partly water-soluble contains a higher proportion. Less suction pressure is required to remove water from wheat bran than from vegetable fibre, because in the latter water-soluble polysaccharides form gels in which water is an integral part.[26] Small molecules partition themselves between the water phases in a manner explicable by phase systems with one or two continuous phases.[27] Absorption of glucose and water-soluble drugs can be delayed by association with gel water of viscous polysaccharides. The relation between water-holding capacity of fibre in the colon and faecal bulking is very complex.

Cation exchange

The cation-exchange capacity of dietary fibre is a property of the plant cell wall and varies with the plant species from strong and monofunctional to weak and polyfunctional,[28] increasing with the age of the plant. Fibre has no anion-exchange properties. The cation-exchange capacity does not alter electrolyte metabolism, which suggests that it is lost after bacterial fermentation.

Adsorption properties

Dietary fibre, especially lignin, adsorbs organic substances such as bile acids and many drugs. Adsorption is affected by processing, particle size, and bacterial fermentation. It is pH-dependent and greater for more hydrophobic materials (dihydroxy-bile acids are more strongly adsorbed than trihydroxy-bile-acid conjugates). Incorporation of bile acids into micelles retards adsorption, and hence more may be adsorbed on fibre in the colon than in the jejunum.[29] It is not clear whether or not bile-acid adsorption to fibre affects cholesterol metabolism:[30] bran does not lower serum cholesterol, but other bile-acid adsorbents and non-adsorbing gels, such as pectins and gum arabic, do.[18,29]

DIETARY SOURCES

Wholemeal, brown, and white bread provide 8.5, 5.1, and 2.7 g/100 g, respectively, potatoes and most other root vegetables 1–2.5 g/100 g, leafy vegetables 2.5–3.5 g/100 g, and fruits up to 3 g/100 g.[31] Calculations from dietary surveys in Europe and North America[32] indicate that average intake is about 25 g/day but there are great variations. For example, vegetarians may eat 40 g or more, while many people eat only 10 g or less. Of the average 25 g/day about 10 g comes from bread and cereal products, 7 g from potatoes, 6 g from other vegetables, and 2 g from fruit. In the past intakes were higher; the decline from about 40 g/day 100 years ago is due to a fall in the amounts of bread and potatoes eaten, the major change in the diets of the UK and the

USA since 1880. In Africa, especially in maize-eating communities, dietary fibre intakes range from 50 to 150 g/day. Rice diets in Asia and elsewhere are said to have a fibre content intermediate between the African and European diets,[32] but fibre intake in Japan appears similar to that in the UK.[33] The traditional diets of the Masai tribes in East Africa and of Eskimos, which contain no food of vegetable origin, indicate that fibre is not an essential dietary constituent.

PHYSIOLOGICAL ACTIONS

High-fibre diets increase the bulk of the faeces and the rate of passage of material through the large intestine. Components of dietary fibre have differing physiological effects. In many studies an effect of a fibre has been demonstrated satisfactorily only when the fibre has been given as a supplement in amounts far in excess of those found in usual diets. People adapt to changes in fibre intake, and a change observable soon after a change in diet may not persist. For these reasons the study of the physiological actions of dietary fibre, especially possible long-term effects on prevalence of chronic diseases, is beset with difficulties.

Faecal weight

The usual output of faeces by people on western diets is 80–160 g/day, compared with 225 g/day (mean for 24 subjects) in vegetarians and 470 g/day (mean for 15 subjects) in Ugandan villagers.[34] When subjects on low-fibre diets are given supplements of high-fibre foods faecal weight increases (Table 4.3).

Table 4.3 Effect on faecal weight of added dietary fibre

Fibre content of diet (g)		Source of added fibre	Number of subjects	Mean faecal weight (g/day)		
Low	High			Low fibre	High fibre	Ref
12	45	Fruit, vegetables, wholemeal cereals	46	69	185	35
4.1*	7.2*	+16 g bran	8	107	174	36
22	60	+bran	6	95	197	37
22	61	+cabbage extract	5	88	143	37
22	67	+carrot extract	6	117	189	37
22	88	+apple extract	5	141	203	37

*Crude fibre.

Intestinal transit time

Fibre may slow down the passage of food in the mouth and stomach[38] and so help to promote a sensation of satiety and, by delaying entry of food into the small intestine, modify the rate of absorption of nutrients.

Pectins and gums slow down movement in the jejunum by increasing the viscosity of its contents; in this way they may delay the absorption of glucose and other nutrients. Overall intestinal transit time can be measured by means of radiographically opaque pellets taken by mouth. Overall transit time in people on low-fibre diets is between 60 and 90 h and is reduced by adding fibre to the diet; it is only about 30 h in rural Africans. Faster movement through the colon is the cause of most of the reduction in transit time.

Fermentation in the large intestine
Virtually all dietary fibre enters the caecum unchanged. The lignin and most of the cellulose (50–97 per cent) passes out in the faeces unaltered.[39] The remaining cellulose and most of the hemicelluloses and pectins (72–97 per cent) are broken down by bacterial fermentation in the colon. The energy liberated by fermentation is used by the colonic bacterial population for growth. Some of the volatile short-chain fatty acids formed are absorbed and metabolised. The gases formed (hydrogen, methane, or both) are excreted as flatus and, after absorption, through the lungs. The amount of hydrogen in the expired air reflects the amount of fermentation taking place. Fasting levels rise threefold after ingestion of hemicellulose and tenfold after ingestion of oligosaccharides and other sugars not absorbed in the small intestine.[40] Giving fibre on one occasion does not usually increase breath hydrogen,[40] but after ingestion of certain polysaccharides (eg. gum arabic and carrot fibre) for 3 weeks breath hydrogen increases.[41,42] Methane levels in expired air do not rise after ingestion of fibre. Bacteria carry out almost all fermentation in the human colon. A small majority of the bacterial population is anaerobic. Bacteria colonise the colon soon after birth and after some weeks the population is similar to that in adults. The quantity and nature of the dietary fibre may determine the bacterial flora of the colon. However, there was no significant change in the relative numbers of groups of bacteria counted in faeces of four London students when 36 g/day fibre was added to their low-fibre diet, although the total bacterial content of the faeces rose threefold.[43] As yet there is no convincing evidence that the bacterial flora of the colon differs in people on African, European, or North American diets. The bacterial mass in the colon contributes to the total metabolism of the body, like the liver and other organs, but its effects are small and their importance uncertain.

Nature of the faeces
About 70–80 per cent of the faeces is water, a proportion that varies little and is independent of the daily output.[44] Of the solid contents about half is bacterial mass and half dietary fibre with a little undigested food. A greater intake of dietary fibre leads to a larger faecal mass in one

of two ways.[45] If the extra fibre comes from wheat bran, the predictable increase in stool weight is a function of the water-holding capacity of the bran.[46] This capacity depends on particle size and is reduced by cooking, so that more cooked bran needs to be given to obtain the same stool bulking effect.[47] If the extra fibre comes from fruit and vegetables, the effect is less predictable. There is a slight rise in stool weight as a result of increased bacterial proliferation during fermentation of the fibre.[45]

Enterohepatic cycle and cholesterol metabolism
Studies of the faecal output of bile acids and plasma cholesterol concentration in relation to the amounts of dietary fibre eaten have given inconsistent and often contradictory results.[19] Supplementing a typical UK diet with large amounts of pectin increases faecal output of bile acids and reduces plasma cholesterol, but these changes do not occur after supplements of wheat bran (Table 4.4).[48,49]

Table 4.4 Effects of supplements of pectin and wheat bran on faecal bile acid excretion and plasma cholesterol

	Number of subjects	Faecal weight (g/day)	Faecal bile acids (mg/day)	Plasma cholesterol (mmol/day)
Control diet	9	140	265	5.80
Control diet + 15 g pectin	9	168	371	4.92
Control diet	6	125	251	5.26
Control diet + 23 g bran	6	225	233	5.57

THERAPEUTIC USES

Dietary fibre is the most effective means of treating chronic constipation and diverticular disease; it is also valuable in the irritable bowel syndrome (Chap. 46). The best supplement is coarse wheat bran but ispaghula (Fybogel) is effective, more palatable and acceptable to the elderly.

High fibre diets are generally prescribed for patients with obesity and diabetes. Whether an increase in fibre in diets of the general population would decrease the prevalence of these and other diseases of Western civilisation is uncertain. Foods rich in fibre taste good and we recommend them to all.

Possible adverse effects
Anyone changing from a low to a high fibre diet is liable to abdominal discomfort from increased gas production in the colon and sometimes diarrhoea. These symptoms are usually transient.

Excretion of minerals in the stools is increased by a high fibre diet, and this may be followed by mineral deficiency in unusual circumstances, for example high fibre diets predispose to rickets and osteomalacia (Chap. 32).

It can be stated with confidence that people who increase their fibre intake up to 50 g/day, double the amount usually present in British diets, run no risk of any serious adverse effects on their health. But enough is enough. Enthusiasts who pour large quantities of bran on their food gain no benefit from the excess and expose themselves unnecessarily to hazards, known and perhaps unknown.

REFERENCES

1. Jenkins D J A, Thomas D M, Wolever M S, Taylor R H, et al 1981 Glycemic index of foods: a physiological basis for carbohydrate exchanges. Am J Clin Nutr 34: 362–366
2. Marshall J J, Lauda C M 1975 Purification and properties of phaseolin, an inhibitor of amylase from the kidney bean, *Phaseolus vulgaris*. J Biol Chem 250: 8030–8037
3. Bo-Linn G W, Santa Ana C A, Morawski S G, Fordtran J S 1982 Starch blockers — their effect on calorie absorption from a high-starch meal. New Engl J Med 307: 1413–1416
4. Garrow J S, Scott P F, Heels S, Nair K S, Halliday D 1983 'Starch blockers' are ineffective in man. Lancet 2: 60–61
5. Carlson G L, Li B U K, Bass P, Olsen W A 1983 A bean amylase inhibitor formulation (starch blocker) is ineffective in man. Science NY 219: 393–394
6. Pembrey M S 1903 Further observations upon the respiratory exchange and temperature of hibernating mammals. J Physiol 29: 195–212
7. Passmore R, Swindells Y E 1963 Observations on the respiratory quotients and weight gain after eating large quantities of carbohydrate. Br J Nutr 17: 331–339
8. Stetten D, Boxer G E 1944 The rate of turnover of liver and carcass glycogen, studied with the aid of deuterium. J Biol Chem 155: 231–242
9. Dale V P 1965 Energy storage. In: Renold A E, Cahill G F (eds) Handbook of physiology. Section 5: Adipose tissue. American Physiological Society, Washington DC, p 13–18
10. Holmes F L 1974 Claude Bernard and animal chemistry. Harvard University Press, Cambridge, Mass.
11. Soskin S, Levine R 1952 Carbohydrate metabolism, 2nd edn. Chicago University Press, Chicago.
12. Grapo P A, Olefsky J M 1980 Fructose — its characteristics, physiology and metabolism. Nutr Today 15 (4): 10–15
13. Eyton A 1982 F-plan diet. Penguin Books, Harmondsworth, Middlesex
14. Mottram V H, Graham G 1956 Hutchison's Food and the principles of dietetics, 11th edn. Arnold, London, p 19
15. Burkitt D P 1969 Related disease — related cause. Lancet 2: 1229–1231
16. Cleave T L, Campbell G D, Painter N S 1969 Diabetes, coronary thrombosis and the saccharine disease. Wright, Bristol
17. Painter N S 1971 Treatment of diverticular disease. Br Med J 2: 156
18. Spiller G A, Kay R M (eds) 1980 Medical aspects of dietary fibre. Plenum, New York
19. Royal College of Physicians of London 1980 Medical aspects of dietary fibre. Pitman Medical, Tunbridge Wells
20. Trowell H, Southgate D A T, Wolever T M S, Leeds R A, Gassull M A, Jenkins D A 1976 Dietary fibres redefined. Lancet 1: 967
21. Salvendran R R 1983 The chemistry of plant cell walls. In: Birch G G, Parker K J (eds) Dietary fibre. Applied Science Publishers, London, p 95–148
22. Aspinall G O 1970 Pectins, plant gums and other plant polysaccharides. In: Pigman W W, Horton D (eds) The carbohydrates, chemistry and biochemistry, 2nd edn. Academic Press, New York and London, vol IIB, p 515
23. Albersheim P 1965 Biogenesis of the cell wall. In: Bonner J, Valner J E (eds) Plant biochemistry. Academic Press, New York and London, p 298
24. Southgate D A T 1976 Determination of food carbohydrates. Applied Science Publishers, London
25. Robertson J A, Eastwood M A 1981 An investigation of the experimental conditions which could affect water-holding capacity of dietary fibre. J Sci Food Agric 32: 819–825
26. Robertson J A, Eastwood M A 1981 A method to measure the water-holding properties of dietary fibre using suction pressure. Br J Nutr 46: 247–255
27. Nielsen L E 1978 Predicting the properties of mixtures. Marcel Dekker, New York
28. McConnell A A, Eastwood M A, Mitchell W D 1974 Physical characteristics of vegetable foodstuffs that could influence bowel function. J Sci Food Agric 25: 1457–1464
29. Story J A, Kritchevsky D, Eastwood M A 1979 Dietary fiber — bile acid interactions. In: Inglett G E, Falkehag S I (eds) Dietary fibers: chemistry and nutrition. Academic Press, New York and London, p 49–65
30. Oakenfull D G, Fenwick D E 1978 Absorption of bile salts from aqueous solution by plant fibre and cholestyramine. Br J Nutr 40: 299–309
31. Paul A A, Southgate D A T 1978 McCance and Widdowson's The composition of human foods, 4th edn. HMSO, London
32. Bingham S, Cummings J H 1980 Sources and intakes of dietary fiber in man. In: Spiller G A, Kay R M (eds) Medical aspects of dietary fiber. Plenum, New York, p 261–284
33. Minowa M, Bingham S, Cummings J H 1983 Dietary fibre intake in Japan. Human Nutr: Apply Nutr 37A: 113–119
34. Burkitt D P, Walker A R P, Painter N S 1972 Effect of dietary fibre on stools and transit times, and its role in the causation of disease. Lancet 2: 1408–1412
35. Stass-Wolthuis M, Hautvast J G A J, Hermus R J J, et al 1979 The effect of a natural high fiber diet on serum lipids, fecal lipids and colonic function. Am J Clin Nutr 32: 1881–8
36. Eastwood M A, Kirkpatrick J R, Mitchell W D, Bone A, Hamilton T 1973 Effects of dietary supplements of wheat bran and cellulose on faeces and bowel function. Br Med J 4: 392–394

37. Cummings J H, Branch D J A, Southgate D A T, Houston H, James W P T 1978 Colonic response to dietary fibre from carrot, cabbage, apple, bran and guar gum. Lancet 1: 5–9

38. Holt S, Heading R C, Carter D C, Prescott L F, Hothill P 1979 Effect of gel fibre on gastric emptying and absorption of glucose and paracetamol. Lancet 2: 636–639

39. Southgate D A T, Durnin J V G A 1970 Calorie conversion factors. An experimental reassessment of the factors used in the calculation of the energy value of human diets. Br J Nutr 24: 517–535

40. Tadesse K, Eastwood M A 1978 Metabolism of dietary fibre components in man assessed by breath hydrogen and methane. J Nutr 40: 393–396

41. McLean Ross A H, Eastwood M A, Brydon W G, McKay L F, Anderson D M W, Anderson J R 1982 Gum arabic metabolism in man. Proc Nutr Soc 41: 64A

42. Robertson J, Brydon W G, Tadesse K, Wenham P, Walls A, Eastwood M A 1979 The effect of raw carrot on serum lipids and colon function. Am J Clin Nutr 32: 1889–1892

43. Drasar B S, Jenkins D J A, Cummings J H 1976 The influence of a diet rich in wheat fibre on the human faecal flora. J Med Microbiol 9: 423–431

44. Wyman J B, Heaton K W, Manning A P, Wicks A C B 1978 Variability of colonic function in healthy subjects. Gut 19: 146–150

45. Stephen A M, Cummings J H 1980 Mechanism of action of dietary fibre in the human colon. Nature 284: 283–284

46. Smith A N, Drummond E, Eastwood M A 1981 The effect of coarse and fine Canadian red spring wheat and French soft wheat on colonic motility in patients with diverticular disease. Am J Clin Nutr 34: 2460–2463

47. Wyman J B, Heaton K W, Manning A P, Wicks A C B 1976 The effect on intestinal transit time and the faeces of raw and cooked bran in different doses. Am J Clin Nutr 29: 1474–1479

48. Kay R M, Truswell A S 1977 Effect of citrus pectin on blood lipids and fecal steroid excretion in man. Am J Clin Nutr 30: 171–175

49. Kay R M, Truswell A S 1977 The effect of wheat fibre on plasma lipid and faecal steroid excretion in man. Br J Nutr 37: 227–235

Proteins

The contribution made by proteins to the energy value of most well-balanced diets is usually between 10 and 15 per cent of the total and seldom exceeds 20 per cent. Their importance lies in the fact that every cell in the body is partly composed of proteins which are subject to continuous wear and replacement. Carbohydrates and fats contain no nitrogen or sulphur, two essential elements in all proteins. Whereas the fat in the body can be derived from dietary carbohydrates and the carbohydrates from proteins, the proteins of the body are inevitably dependent for their formation and maintenance on the proteins in food. A monograph edited by Munro and Allison[1] now a classic sets out the established information on which all contemporary research on protein metabolism is based.

SOURCES AND CHEMICAL NATURE

Animal proteins can be divided into two kinds, fibrous and globular. Plant proteins are not so easily classified but, broadly speaking, most are glutelins or prolamines.

Fibrous proteins

These consist of long coiled or folded chains of amino acids bound together by peptide linkages. They are found in the protective and supportive tissues of animals such as skin, hair, feathers, tendons and the fins and scales of fish. The fibrous proteins in such tissues are very insoluble in water and for the most part indigestible. Nevertheless they are a valuable byproduct of the food industry since gelatin and other nitrogenous substances can be extracted from them. **Keratin,** the chief protein of hair, has been much studied by the wool industry. It is interesting chemically because it contains 11 per cent of the sulphur-containing amino acid, cystine. Its practical importance lies in its resistance to solution and its elasticity. The latter property is common to all the fibrous proteins. Their contracted molecules can be stretched out straight and, under suitable conditions, will remain stretched; this is the secret of a 'permanent wave' in the hair. Other fibrous proteins include the **collagen** of connective tissue, the **fibrin** of a blood clot and the **myosin** of muscle. The latter is an intracellular protein. All of these consist of long, elastic, molecular chains and although insoluble in water are more digestible than keratin. The Chinese have long known how to extract nourishment out of shark fins and other unpromising sources of fibrous proteins. The prudent housewife with a good stock pot, and particularly with the aid of a pressure-cooker, can do the same.

Globular proteins

These are found in the tissue fluids of animals and plants, in which they readily disperse either in true solution or colloidal suspension. Important from the standpoint of nutrition are **caseinogen** in milk, **albumin** in egg white, and **albumins** and **globulins** of blood. The exact configuration of their rounded molecules is a challenge to molecular biologists. For the nutritionist it is enough to know that they are not only easily digestible but also contain in their structure a good proportion of the essential amino acids (see below).

Glutelins and prolamines

These are the chief plant proteins. Glutelins, which are insoluble in neutral solutions, but soluble in weak acids and alkali, are present in cereals. They include glutenin from wheat, hordenin from barley and oryzenin from rice. These are probably not homogeneous substances. Prolamines are insoluble in water but dissolve in alcoholic solution. On hydrolysis they give large quantities of proline and ammonia. Typical prolamines are gliadin from wheat and zein from maize.

Wheat occupies a unique position in food because of its gluten content. Gluten is a mixture of two proteins, gliadin and glutenin; these two, when mixed with water, give the characteristic stickiness which enables the molecules, present in wheat flour, to be bound together by moderate heat with the production of dough, from which bread is baked. Rye has a small content of gluten and so (with difficulty) can be made into a loaf. Oats, barley, maize, millets and rice cannot be made into bread. The grains may be eaten after boiling or their flour made into porridge, bannocks, tortillas, etc.

Protamines and histones

These are basic proteins of low molecular weight. They are usually associated or combined with nucleic acids. Large amounts of protamine are found in male fish roes and also in cellular nucleoproteins. Protamines have a practical use in the commerical production of delayed-action insulins.

Coagulation and denaturation

Many water-soluble proteins when subjected to heat at about 100°C or above, as in the formal process of cooking, coagulate. The change of the white of an egg on boiling is a familiar example. Once a protein has undergone this change its properties are permanently altered; it can never be brought back into simple solution in water and its specific properties, e.g. enzymic, hormonal or immunological, are permanently destroyed. Proteins also undergo a lesser change, known as denaturation, in which they become less soluble in water. This occurs when they are exposed to a variety of agents such as moderate heat, ultraviolet light or alcohol and mild acids or alkalis. The exact nature of the denaturation process is obscure; it apparently involves some disorganisation of the specific arrangement of the component amino acids. To a certain extent it is reversible, once normal conditions are restored; but most enzymes and allergens lose their specific properties when once denatured. Proteins are most easily denatured at their isoelectric point, i.e. the particular pH at which the electric charges on their NH_2 and COOH groups precisely balance; this varies from one protein to another. It seems probable that many of the finer arts of cooking, such as simmering, the addition of vinegar, lye or wine, depend for their success on securing the proper degree of denaturation in preparation for the final coagulation.

AMINO ACIDS

Proteins consist of large molecules with molecular weights ranging from 1000 to over 1 000 000. In their native state some are soluble and some insoluble in water. They can be broken down by hydrolysis into simple units — the amino acids. These are all characterised by the presence of a carboxyl (COOH) group with acidic properties and an amino (NH_2) group with basic properties, attached to the same carbon atom; the rest of the molecule varies with the particular amino acid. The structure of an amino acid may be represented by the formula.

$$R—\overset{\overset{\displaystyle H}{|}}{\underset{\underset{\displaystyle NH_2}{|}}{C}}—COOH$$

where R represents the remainder of the molecule. It would be reasonable to expect that an infinite variety of compounds of this composition might exist in nature; but in fact only some 20 amino acids are commonly found in biological materials.

The amino acids are linked together in protein molecules by peptide linkages in which the basic (amino) group of one amino acid is linked to the carboxyl group of another, with the elimination of a molecule of water. Any two amino acids can be joined by this linkage to form part of a peptide chain and every amino acid may occur in varying amounts in different positions in the chain. Figure 5.1 lists 20 amino acids in the animal and plant kingdoms which resemble the 26 letters of the alphabet since they can be arranged in sequences to form an infinite number of proteins and sentences respectively. Every species of animal has its characteristic proteins — the proteins of beef muscle, for instance, differ from those of pork muscle. It is the sequence of amino acids in proteins that give each species its specific immunological characters and uniqueness.

Plants can synthesise all the amino acids they need

Name	Standard abbreviation		R
Glycine		Gly	H—
Alanine		Ala	CH_3
Valine	E	Val	$(CH_3)_2CH—$
Leucine	E	Leu	$(CH_3)_2CH—CH_2—$
Isoleucine	E	Ile	$C_2H_5—CH(CH_3)—$
Serine	E	Ser	$CH_2OH—$
Threonine	E	Thr	$CH_3—CHOH—$
Aspartic acid		Asp	$HOOC—CH_2—$
Glutamic acid		Glu	$HOOC—CH_2—CH_2—$
Lysine	E	Lys	$H_2N(CH_2)_4—$
Ornithine		Orn	$H_2N(CH_2)_3—$
Arginine		Arg	$\overset{H_2N}{\underset{HN}{>}}C—NH—(CH_2)_3—$
Histidine		His	$\underset{N}{\overset{NH—C—CH_2—}{HC\quad CH}}$
Phenylalanine	E	Phe	⬡—$CH_2—$
Tyrosine		Tyr	HO—⬡—$CH_2—$
Tryptophan	E	Trp	(indole ring)—$CH_2—$
Cysteine		Cys	$HSCH_2—$
Methionine	E	Met	$CH_3—S—(CH_2)_2—$
Proline		Pro	*Formula* (ring with N—H, COOH)
Hydroxyproline		Hyp	HO (ring with N—H, COOH)

Fig. 5.1 The principal amino acids. Those marked E cannot be synthesised by man and are essential constituents of the diet.

from simple inorganic chemical compounds, but animals are unable to do this because they cannot synthesise the amino (NH$_2$) group; so in order to obtain the amino acids necessary for building protein they must eat plants, or other animals which have in their turn lived on plants.

The human body has certain limited powers of converting one amino acid into another. This is achieved in the liver, by the process of **transamination,** whereby an amino group is shifted from one molecule across to another under the influence of aminotransferases, the coenzyme of which is pyridoxal phosphate (p. 163). However, the ability of the body to convert one amino acid into another is restricted. There are several amino acids which the body cannot make for itself and so must obtain from the diet. These are termed **essential amino acids.**

Essential amino acids

Rose[2] showed that the adult human body can maintain nitrogenous equilibrium on a mixture of eight pure amino acids as its sole source of nitrogen. These eight are isoleucine, leucine, lysine, methionine, phenylalanine, threonine, tryptophan and valine. A ninth essential amino acid was added to the list when histidine was shown to be needed to maintain nitrogen balance over a period of two or three weeks.[3] Histidine is also needed by infants for growth. Inability to synthesise the carbon skeleton of these amino acids is the probable reason why they are essential, since the oxo- and hydroxy- analogues provide an effective substitute for some of them.[4]

The difference between essential and non-essential amino acids is not clear cut. Rapid growth, stress or illness may increase needs beyond the capacity for synthesis. Histidine may become essential in chronic renal failure because of impaired renal synthesis. Other factors that may determine whether or not an amino acid is essential are the availability of its carbon skeleton and how easily it can be transaminated.[26]

Characteristics of individual amino acids

Glycine.   It is the simplest amino acid. During periods of rapid growth the demand for glycine may be enormous. For the young chick, glycine is an essential amino acid since its supply becomes, for a time, a limiting factor to growth. It is an important precursor in many syntheses in the body, such as those of the purine bases porphyrins, creatine and the conjugated bile acids. Many aromatic substances, whether produced endogenously or consumed as drugs or food additives, are conjugated in the liver with glycine. The conjugate is then excreted in the bile or urine.

Glutamic acid.   This dicarboxylic acid easily loses its amino group to keto acids such as pyruvic acid, in this way giving rise to other amino acids in the body. Glu-

tamic acid is the predominant amino acid in wheat protein (gliadin). The strong, meaty flavour of monosodium glutamate gives it commercial value as a flavouring agent for cooking. Glutamic acid also plays an important role in the metabolism of ammonia. It picks up an extra amino group in muscles to form glutamine, which is the source of urinary ammonia. Glutamic acid is the precursor of the neurotransmitter, γ-aminobutyric acid in the brain.

Arginine.   This participates in the formation of urea in the liver, by the process known as the ornithine-arginine cycle, first described by Krebs. The reader is referred to textbooks of biochemistry for details.

Lysine.   As most cereals contain very little lysine, it is the amino acid likely to be deficient in poor vegetarian diets. It is the parent substance of carnitine, which transports fatty acids within the cell.

Cysteine and methionine.   These are the principal sources of sulphur in the diet of man. The body can make cysteine from methionine but not vice versa, so that methionine is the dietary essential. Cystine is formed when two molecules of cysteine are reduced and linked by an S—S bond. It is present in the keratin of hair and in insulin, in each of which it forms about 12 per cent of the whole protein molecule.

Methionine is also concerned with the important process of **transmethylation.** The chief dietary sources of labile methyl groups are methionine and betaine, $(CH_3)_3.N.CH_2.COOH$, which accordingly are called **methyl donors.** Methionine gives up the terminal CH_3 group attached to its sulphur atom. Dietary deficiency of methionine in rats results in a fatty liver which can be cured by restoring this amino acid to the diet, or alternatively by giving the choline which the body would normally form from it. Taurine, which like glycine is conjugated with the bile acids, is derived from the metabolism of cysteine.

Phenylalanine and tyrosine.   These two amino acids which contain a benzene ring in their molecules provide the raw material from which the body makes the hormones adrenaline and thyroxine. They are also the origin of the pigment melanin which occurs in the hair, the choroid lining of the eye and in the skin. The body can convert phenylalanine to tyrosine, but not vice versa, so that the former is the dietary essential.

Histidine.   This amino acid contains an imidazole ring and is readily converted to histamine by an enzyme histidine decarboxylase present in many tissues, notably in the intestinal tract. Histamine is a stimulus for acid secretion in the stomach. It is also stored in granules in mast cells, from which it is released in many allergic reactions. In the skin this gives rise to urticaria or nettle rash, and in the lungs to constriction of the bronchi causing the symptoms of asthma. 3-Methyl histidine is present in the urine and in increased amounts after exercise. Its excretion has been used as an index of the breakdown of muscle protein but the significance of this is uncertain.[5]

Tryptophan. This is the raw material from which synthesis of some nicotinic acid takes place in the body. It is the precursor of 5-hydroxytryptamine (5-HT), also known as serotonin, a physiological substance which causes vasoconstriction and is present in many tissues, especially the argentaffin cells of the intestinal mucosa, and in the blood platelets. When the platelets break up in the formation of a blood clot, they release 5-HT which appears to prevent bleeding by causing vasoconstriction of the neighbouring blood vessels. 5-HT is also a neuro-transmitter in parts of the central nervous system.

Proline and hydroxyproline. These consist essentially of a pyrrole ring. This same ring structure is found in the porphyrins which go to make haemoglobin and the cytochromes. These amino acids are prevalent in the collagen of connective tissue.

Leucine, isoleucine and valine. The carbon atoms in these amino acids are arranged in a branched chain. Dietary sources are taken up mainly not by the liver but by muscles. There they are oxidised and the nitrogen used for the formation of alanine in the glucose-alanine cycle (p. 81).

Amino acid sequences and protein structure

The order and arrangement of the amino acids in a protein can be determined by splitting off fragments of the chain by partial digestion with proteolytic enzymes or acid hydrolysis. Insulin was the first protein to have its amino acid sequence determined. This was done in 1951 by Sanger at Cambridge. Since then, the number of proteins whose amino acid sequence has been reported rose and is now over 1000. Insulin (Fig. 5.2) is composed of two chains containing 21 and 30 amino acids. The chains are held together in two places by S—S bonds of cysteine. The smaller chain has a loop in it. The three amino acids in the loop differ in samples of insulin ob-

tained from different species of animals. The specificity of the order of the amino acids in proteins is remarkable. This is shown by the fact that the protein in the haemoglobin of patients with sickle-cell anaemia differs from normal haemoglobin by only one amino acid; valine replaces glutamine in a sequence of 580 amino acids.

DIGESTION

Proteins undergo hydrolysis by proteolytic enzymes in the gastrointestinal tract, resulting in the release of peptides and amino acids.

Pepsin. This enzyme is secreted by the peptic cells of the mucosa of the stomach. It works best in an acid medium (optimum pH about 1.2) which is normally provided by the hydrochloric acid secreted by the oxyntic cells of the gastric mucosa. Pepsin breaks down proteins to smaller units, polypeptides, also composed of amino acids,. The initial partial digestion of proteins in the stomach is not essential.

Rennin. This is another proteolytic enzyme secreted by the stomach of newborn mammals. It clots the protein of milk (caseinogen) and is the active principle of rennet, an extract from the stomach of animals or from certain plants used to curdle milk. There is no evidence, however, that rennin plays any part in protein digestion in the adult.

Trypsin. This is the chief proteolytic enzyme of the pancreatic juice. It acts best in an alkaline medium (optimum pH about 8) and converts proteins into polypeptides. The pancreatic juice is the principal means whereby proteins are normally digested. When disease of the pancreas obstructs or prevents the flow of the juice, failure of protein digestion is shown by the presence of undigested fibres of meat in the stools and by an increase in the amount of faecal organic nitrogen. At the same time the stools and flatus are foul-smelling, due to the action of bacteria in the large intestine on

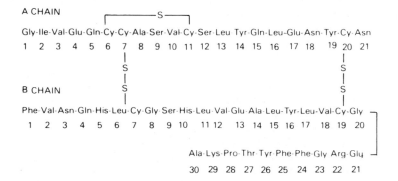

Fig. 5.2 Sequences of amino acids in the insulin molecule. (Sanger F 1964 In: Nobel Lectures. Elsevier, Amsterdam, p 544–56)

undigested protein, producing hydrogen sulphide and other products of putrefaction.

The digestion of proteins may be continued until they are completely broken down to amino acids which are then absorbed. Van Slyke and Meyer[6] in 1912 demonstrated the rise in amino nitrogen in the blood during protein absorption.

Yet there are quantitative difficulties in accounting for protein digestion and absorption entirely in the form of amino acids.[7] There is now good evidence that small peptides containing two to six amino acid residues are absorbed from the gut lumen at least as rapidly as free amino acids and by an independent transport mechanism in the cell.[8]

Measurements of the net absorption of amino acids after a meal containing 15 g of milk protein show that it is 70 to 80 per cent complete in three hours.[9] Patients with the genetic defect known as cystinuria are unable to absorb cysteine, arginine and lysine fully, owing to a failure of a transport system common to these amino acids.

In the first few days of life and in certain disease states traces of undigested protein may be absorbed. For instance a dietary protein occasionally exerts a general allergic response, such as urticaria, in people sensitive to it. Some part of the protein must have passed unchanged through the intestinal mucosa. Simple peptides and amino acids, being common to all species of animals, have no allergic or immunological properties.

It seems likely that, in general, proteins from animal sources are more easily and rapidly absorbed than vegetable proteins, perhaps because vegetable proteins are often enclosed in a cellulose covering. The immediate urinary excretion of protein waste products is larger after a meal containing animal protein than when the same amount of protein is provided by vegetables.[10]

Faecal nitrogen

Most of the protein in foods and in the digestive secretions is hydrolysed and the amino acids are absorbed in the small intestine. The residue that enters the colon, together with the protein in the shed colonic mucosa, is then subject to bacterial metabolism. The faecal nitrogen is made up in part of bacterial proteins and in part of remnants of food proteins that have escaped digestion and absorption.

As stated in Chapter 3, Atwater concluded from his experiments that the net absorption of the nitrogen in protein was 92 per cent. Subsequent experience has shown that among healthy persons eating the usual 'civilised' diets there is little variation from this figure. If the diet consists of unrefined cereals and contains much dietary fibre, digestion may be less complete and faecal losses of nitrogen higher.

Protein synthesis and turnover

The discovery of the roles of DNA and RNA in protein synthesis is one of the great achievements of modern science, comparable with the exploration of outer space. It has established biology alongside physics as a subject which attracts the best intellects in schools and universities. The discovery has been well publicised. Numerous articles in popular journals describe how deoxyribonucleic acids and ribonucleic acids carry codes, which sort a mixture of amino acids into order appropriate for insertion into a specific protein molecule under construction. Textbooks of biochemistry provide the details.

The amount of protein synthesised daily depends on the requirements for growth, for the manufacture of digestive and other enzymes and for replacement of proteins broken down in the cells of the various tissues. The tissues of the body are under continuous repair. The rates at which they are broken down and replaced vary greatly. The mucosa of the small intestine is probably renewed every one to two days. The red blood cells have each a life of about 120 days. The skin is also being shed and replaced continuously. Isotope studies indicate that in the human body plasma albumin is being synthesised at the rate of about 10 g/day and fibrinogen at about 2 g/day. On the other hand collagen persists for a very long time and that laid down in the bones of infant rats has been shown to be still present after 300 days.

As rates of turnover of protein in cells are not easily measured, it is difficult to get an accurate estimate of the daily rate of protein synthesis. It is certainly greater than the daily intake of protein in the diet, and amino acid liberated by the breakdown of old protein can be utilised again for synthesis.

The possibility of using amino acids labelled with ^{15}N as tools for measuring rates of protein turnover and synthesis was suggested by experiments carried by Schoenheimer over 40 years ago.[11] This approach has been much used but is beset with both methodological and technical difficulties. Two papers in Nature[12,13] review the position, and Table 5.1 gives estimates of synthesis rates at various ages. For an adult man synthesis

Table 5.1. Total body protein synthesis rate in humans at various ages

Age group	No. of studies	Body weight (kg)	Age (range)	Total body protein synthesis (g kg^{-1} d^{-1})
Newborn (premature)	10	1.94	1–46 d	17.46
Infant	4	9.0	10–20 mths	6.9
Young adult	4	71	20–23 yr	3.0
Elderly	4	56	69–91 yr	1.9

amounts to over 200 g daily, or about five times the minimum dietary requirement. New techniques are being developed to measure changes in rates of protein synthesis and degradation and to relate these to changes in lean body mass arising from dietary and hormonal imbalances.[14]

Protein as a source of energy

An important process in the metabolism of all amino acids is the removal of the amino group and its replacement by oxygen with the the formation of a keto acid which is then available as a source of energy. The amino group is taken into the ornithine-arginine cycle in the liver and subsequently built up into urea. Most of the oxoacids formed by oxidative deamination are coverted into pyruvic acid and so pass into the citric acid cycle. Alanine is the principal amino acid released from the muscle, and is used for gluconeogenesis when energy intake is insufficient. There are, however, other routes. For example, glutamic acid after deamination yields 2-oxoglutaric acid. This acid is one of the intermediary stages between citric acid and oxaloacetic acid in the cycle.

Glucose may be formed from many amino acids. Over 70 years ago Dakin[15] fed single amino acids to diabetic dogs and in many instances was able to collect corresponding amounts of glucose in the urine. However, leucine, lysine, methionine and tryptophan do not form glucose in these circumstances; nor generally do cystine, isoleucine, phenylalanine and tyrosine. These amino acids may, however, give rise to acetoacetic acid. For this reason they have been called ketogenic amino acids, whereas the other amino acids are glucogenic. Acetoacete and glucose formed from amino acids are important primary fuels of the tissues (Chap. 8).

An excellent account of the intermediary metabolism of amino acids is given by Krebs.[16] Before reading this, it might be advisable to study the chapter on protein metabolism in Lusk.[17] Some young biochemists appear to think that their subject only started when preparations of mitochondria first became available. There was much excellent biochemical work of direct application to nutrition carried out in the first 25 years of this century and for the study of this Lusk is the best guide.

Protein reserves

The amount of protein in the body is not constant, but depends to some extent on the protein content of the diet. If a person on a high protein diet is put on a low protein diet overnight, the daily output of nitrogen (N) in the urine does not drop immediately. It falls slowly and after four to six days reaches a level roughly similar to the amount of N in the diet. If a transfer back to a high protein diet is made the urinary N output rises

slowly and after a few days approximates to the high intake.[18] The excess N excreted or the N retained on changing from a high protein to a low protein diet and back is equivalent to between 175 and 350 g of protein in an adult man. This is called the **labile body protein.**

Addis showed in 1936 that when rats were given a diet deficient in protein, the protein content of the liver fell by 40 per cent and of the alimentary tract and pancreas by 30 per cent; the muscles and skin lost 8 per cent and the brain only 5 per cent of their original protein contents.[19]

There has been much argument as to whether a man or animal benefits from having this labile store full (p. 50).

A well fed human adult contains about 11 kg of protein, of which he can lose about 3 kg without serious loss of function or threat to life. Most of this loss is due to destruction of cell substance and cannot be regarded as a withdrawal from stores.

NITROGEN BALANCE

Nearly all the nitrogen in the diet and in the excreta is present in the form of amino groups ($-NH_2$). Amino N is readily determined by the Kjeldahl method. The material is first digested by heating with concentrated sulphuric acid and a catalyst. This converts the N into ammonium sulphate. After cooling, excess sodium hydroxide is added. The ammonia is then expelled by steam distillation into acid and estimated by titration. When nutritionists talk about urinary N or N balance, they are referring to amino N, not total N.

A subject is said to be in the N balance when the N intake (I) in the diet equals the N output in the urine (U), faeces (F) and by the skin (S):

$$I = U + F + S$$

Table 5.2 shows two examples: in the first the diet was low in protein and the balance is negative, which

Table 5.2 Nitrogen balances of an obese young woman after several days on diets containing 24 and 80 g protein/day

	g N/day	
Intake		
Food	3.9	12.7
Output		
Urine	5.3	9.3
Faeces	0.7	0.6
Skin	(0.2)	(0.2)
	——	——
	6.2	10.1
Balance	−2.3	+2.6

is interpreted as a loss of tissue protein; in the second the protein content of the diet was high, the balance positive and the subject can be presumed to be laying down tissue protein.

The N balance technique is used by physiologists to determine the minimum protein requirements of man. It is also used in the metabolic wards of hospitals to find out whether a patient is gaining or losing tissue protein on a particular therapeutic regime. A reliable estimate of the N balance can only be made if material is collected over a period of days on a constant regime. Five days is usually adequate but some preliminary days should be allowed for adjustment if the N intake on the test diet differs from that on the previous diet. If an accurate balance is required, it is necessary to determine analytically the N in an aliquot of the subject's diet. U can be determined precisely, from an analysis of 24-hour samples of urine. Accurate collection of a 24-hour sample is an important task of the nursing staff in a hospital metabolic unit. The interval between the ingestion of food and the passage of the corresponding faeces is usually about 24 hours, but may vary greatly. For accurate work, it is necessary to mark the food at the beginning and end of the collection period with a dye or other readily detectable marker and to analyse the faecal material collected between the two marks. The output of N in the faeces is normally only a small fraction of the dietary intake. In some circumstances useful estimates of the N balance can be made without collecting faeces and assuming a small figure for faecal N.

It is difficult to measure the cutaneous N loss. In 12 African subjects it was between 188 and 480 mg N/day.[20] Six medical students taking heavy physical exercise for about seven hours daily in Jamaica[21] lost 3 to 4 kg of sweat, containing from 190 to 700 mg N. In laboratory studies[22] the total skin loss of N by subjects in a comfortable environment varied from 90 to 190 mg/ day.

FACTORS AFFECTING N BALANCE

Growth
A 12-year old boy who gains 5 kg in weight in a year adds nearly 1 kg of protein to his body. To do this he must retain 160 g of N and be in positive N balance to the extent of about 0.4 g/day throughout the year. This N retention is controlled by growth hormone secreted by the anterior pituitary gland. Injections of growth hormone produce positive nitrogen balances both in man and in experimental animals. Other hormones which may promote nitrogen retention include insulin and the male sex hormones. The spurt in growth which occurs at puberty, so marked in boys, is associated with the development of the testes.

Injury and stress
After any injury or surgical operation there is an increased urinary excretion of N and a negative N balance (Chap. 51). It is part of a general catabolic response to injury, caused by increased secretion of adrenal cortical hormones, in response to the stimulus of trauma.

Physical exercise
It is common opinion, that those who do hard physical work require plenty of meat in their diets. In many families the working men are given an undue share of a limited supply of meat and eggs at the expense of the young children and mother. To justify this scientifically, it would be necessary to show that muscular activity increased protein metabolism and so would cause a negative N balance unless extra protein was given.

In 1889 two physiologists, Fick and Wislicenus, climbed a Swiss mountain, the Faulhorn, 1956 metres high. On the climb and during a recovery period they excreted in their urine 5.7 and 5.5 g of N/13 hours respectively. This represents a breakdown of protein no greater than would be expected during a day spent in light activities. Since then, several other investigators have failed to demonstrate a rise in urinary N during and following muscular activities. No support is available to justify the view that working men should get an undue proportion of protein from the family ration.

However, an athlete who goes into training may gain weight due to hypertrophy of muscle; this is brought about by synthesis of new protein and necessitates a positive N balance. The dietary needs of athletes are discussed in Chapter 63.

Intestinal bacterial flora
Ruminants can utilise urea to provide amino acids through the action of micro-organisms in their alimentary tract. Monogastric animals do not normally utilise urea. However, when the protein intake is very low, for example in some diets used in the treatment of chronic renal failure[23] and in diets based on sweet potatoes in New Guinea,[24] they may do so. Urea diffuses from the blood into the gut lumen where bacteria may hydrolyse it. The ammonia produced may be used for the synthesis of amino acids either directly by the intestinal bacteria or after absorption into the portal vein by the liver. The suggestion made by Oomen that nitrogen-fixing bacteria can make gaseous nitrogen available has not been confirmed but remains a possibility.[25] The evidence that in some circumstances the bacteria in the gut play a part in maintaining nitrogen balance is well presented in a recent review.[26]

PHYSIOLOGICAL NEEDS

Proteins in the diet supply the amino acids required for

the growth of young animals, infants and children and also those needed for the maintenance of the tissues in adults. The amounts needed for growth are much greater than those for maintenance. The newborn human infant probably needs about five times as much protein as the adult per unit of weight. As the child develops the rate of growth slows down and so the need for protein is progressively reduced, but until after puberty it remains larger than the adult's. Protein deficiency in children is widespread in Africa, Asia and Latin America as kwashiorkor (Chap. 29) but in adults is much less frequently found.

If the energy content of the diet is inadequate, protein is used to supply energy. In consequence protein deficiency is much more likely to occur if a diet is lacking energy.

Obligatory N loss

This is total N loss on a N-free diet providing sufficient energy to meet requirements; it is also known as the endogenous N loss. Measurements indicate that a representative figure for a 65 kg man is 3.5 gN/day (2.4 g in the urine, 0.8 g in the faeces, 0.2 g from the skin and 0.1 g miscellaneous).[27] This is equivalent to 22 g of protein. This is the minimum need for protein under any circumstance.[22]

Protein requirement for N balance

There is much individual variation in the minimum amount of protein that must be fed in order to maintain N equilibrium. Sherman in 1920 reviewing all the evidence from European and American sources, concluded that the range of variation lay between 21 and 65 g /70 kg body weight/day.[28] In many subsequent studies, the values have fallen within this stage. A daily protein intake of 45 g or about 0.7 g/kg, provided it is of good quality (NPU at least 70, see below), is sufficient to keep most adults in N balance for a period of many weeks. This amount is less than adults normally eat. Whether consumption of higher amounts is necessary for health is discussed on page 50.

Protein requirement for growth

The infant grows fastest in the first three months of life and then the daily requirement of protein is 2.4 g/kg. As growth slows down, the need for protein declines, being 1.85, 1.62 and 1.44 g/kg daily at ages of 3 to 6, 6 to 9 and 9 to 12 months respectively. Thereafter protein requirements continue to decline slowly until growth stops. Growing children need more protein of better quality than do adults. However even if the protein intake appears adequate for a child, it cannot be utilised for growth unless the energy intake also meets requirements.

The subject of protein requirements has stimulated many writers. A review by Irvin and Hegsted 1971 has a bibliography of 373 papers.[29]

Dietary sources

The protein content of almost every food used by man has been determined by measuring the total nitrogen by the Kjeldahl method and multiplying the value found by 6.25 or other appropriate factor (p. 16). The protein content is expressed as g/100 g of food in all well-known food tables. This does not relate the protein to the energy content of the food. Table 5.3 gives the protein content of some common foods expressed as the proportion of the energy in the foods provided by protein. Most satisfactory human diets provide from 10 to 15 per cent of the energy in the form of protein. The table enables one to distinguish at a glance foods which are poor, adequate and good as sources of protein in relation to their energy content. The low protein content of cassava and bananas is important. In those countries where these foods are the main source of energy, protein deficiency is widespread.

The quantity of protein in a food, however, may be misleading as a measure of its value for growth or maintenance of tissue. The quality of the protein is also important and is now discussed.

Table 5.3 Protein content of various foods, expressed as their contribution (per cent) to the energy provided by each food

Value of food as a source of protein	Proportion of energy from protein (%)
Poor	
Cassava	3.3
Cooked bananas (plantains)	4.0
Sweet potatoes (*Ipomoea batatas*)	4.4
Taros	6.8
Adequate	
Potatoes	7.6
Rice (home-pounded)	8.0
Maize (wholemeal)	10.4
Millet (*Setaria italica*)	11.6
Sorghum (*Sorghum vulgare*)	11.6
Wheat flour (medium extraction)	13.2
Millet (*Pennisetum glaucum*)	13.6
Good	
Groundnuts (peanuts)	18.8
Cow's milk (3.5% fat)	21.6
Beans and peas	25.6
Beef (lean)	38.4
Cow's milk, skimmed	40.0
Soya bean	45.2
Fish, fatty	45.6
Fish, dried	61.6

QUALITY OF PROTEINS

The nutritive value of a protein depends to an important degree on the relation of the amino acids in its molecule to those required for building new tissues. If the protein of the diet is seriously deficient in one or more of the essential amino acids, N equilibrium cannot be sustained, no matter how complete and excellent the diet may be in all other respects. If, however, another protein containing the missing amino acid in adequate amounts is added to the diet, N equilibrium and normal nutrition can be established. This capacity of proteins to make good one another's deficiencies is known as their **supplementary value.**

It has been known for a long time that proteins differ in quality. As long ago as 1915 the great American nutritionist Mendel divided proteins into two classes: those which when fed to rats 'allowed growth' and those with which there was 'failure of growth'.[30] Soon afterwards proteins were divided into animal and vegetable proteins. Formerly these were known as first and second class proteins respectively. However, many vegetable proteins are little inferior to animal proteins and merit more than a second class label. Much more important is the fact that suitable mixtures of vegetable proteins are 'first-class' and promote growth in both laboratory rats and in children nearly as well as milk proteins. This is due to the proteins of different foods having different proportions of amino acids in their make-up. A relative lack of a particular amino acid in one protein can be made good in a mixture of proteins, provided such a mixture contains a protein which has an adequate amount of that particular amino acid. In any protein the amino acid which is furthest below the standard (see below) is known as the **limiting amino acid.** Tryptophan is the limiting amino acid in maize protein, lysine in wheat protein and the sulphur-containing amino acids (methionine and cysteine) in beef protein.

Many attempts have been made to give a numerical value to the quality of both individual dietary proteins and mixtures of proteins present in various human diets. It cannot be said that these have been entirely successful. Three international expert committees have examined on and a fourth is in the pipeline,[31-33] but their reports have not escaped criticism. A succinct and critical account of the work of these Committees was given by Scrimshaw in a Shattuck lecture to the Massachusetts Medical Society.[34] Readers who only require sufficient knowledge of the quality of different proteins to enable them to advise individual patients can be content with the preceding paragraphs. Anyone responsible for planning diet schedules for hospitals, schools or the armed forces, especially in the tropics, should read on.

BIOLOGICAL TESTS

The protein to be tested can be fed to animals and its capacity to maintain the N balance or to promote growth measured. The design and interpretation of reliable tests is beset with difficulties and a monograph by Pellett and Young is a recommended guide.[35]

The tests are mostly based on estimations of the N balance. The **biological value** (BV) of a protein is defined as

$$\frac{\text{Retained N}}{\text{Absorbed N}} \times 100$$

The protein to be tested is fed to the animal as the sole source of N in the diet and below the level needed for maintenance. The measured urinary and faecal N is corrected by subtracting the quantities lost on a protein-free diet. Then

$$BV = \frac{I - (F - F_m) - (U - U_e)}{I - (F - F_m)} \times 100$$

where I, F and U are the intake and faecal and urinary output of N on the test diet, and F_m and U_e are the faecal and urinary output on a protein-free diet.

The biological value (BV) makes no allowance for losses of N in digestion. This is included in the **net protein utilisation** (NPU) which is defined as:

$$\frac{\text{Retained N}}{\text{Intake of N}} \times 100$$

This is equal to BV × availability. NPU is normally measured with the protein intake at or below maintenance levels. It can be calculated from N balance data in man. In animals, gain of carcass N in weaning rats is more often used. Values determined under other conditions have been termed 'operative' (NPU_{op}).

For a combined measure of both the quantity and quality of the protein in a diet, the net dietary protein value (ND_pV) is used. This is defined as:

$$\text{Intake of N} \times 6.25 \times NPU_{op}$$

As already described, it is often convenient to express the protein content of a food in terms of the percentage of the energy content provided by protein (Table 5.3). The protein content of a diet can be similarly expressed and an additional factor given for the quality of the mixed proteins. The **net dietary protein energy ratio** is defined as:

$$\frac{\text{Protein energy}}{\text{Net dietary intake}} \times NPU_{op}$$

The use of these indices has assisted in the testing of the qualities of many different types of diets.

Standard BV and NPU measurements, which consider only one intake level and zero, tend to overestimate the nutritional quality of some proteins. The best biological estimates of protein quality are provided by the slope of the intake-response line from several points in the range of intakes where the line is linear; it should not include zero protein intake. If carcass N retentions in animals are used in this way, the index is the **relative nutritive value** and the line of the test protein is related to a standard (egg or lactalbumin).

Protein efficiency ratio (PER) is the weight gain per weight of protein eaten. The test is carried out on young rats and has the serious fault that no allowance is made for the protein used in maintenance; hence the values obtained are not related by simple proportion. The test is relatively simple and used for labelling regulations in Canada and the USA.

Many nutritionists find this complex terminology, and indeed all modern literature on the biological testing of protein, difficult to follow. Fortunately a full understanding is not necessary for the dietitians either in the home or in the hospital. They should be able to understand the principles on which the chemical score is based and to apply chemical scores to diets which may be recommended.

CHEMICAL TESTING

Whereas biological methods for testing the quality of proteins have been available for over 60 years, chromatographic and microbiological methods for estimating the amino acid content of proteins only began to be used some 30 years ago. Values for proteins in many foods are now included in tables of food composition used in many countries. Table 5.4 gives figures for the protein in four common foods. Such information is only of value when related to estimates of amino acid requirements (Table 5.5)

Table 5.4 Content of essential amino acids in proteins (mg amino acid/g protein)

	Hen's egg	Cow's milk	Beef muscle	Wheat flour
Isoleucine	54	47	53	42
Leucine	86	95	82	71
Lysine	70	78	87	20
Methionine and cystine	57	33	38	31
Phenylalanine and tyrosine	93	102	75	79
Threonine	47	44	43	28
Tryptophan	17	14	12	11
Valine	66	64	55	42

Table 5.5 Amino acids required to maintain N balance in adults and growth in infants under 6 months[33]

	Man	Woman	Combined adult values	Infant
	(mg d^{-1})		(mg kg^{-1} d^{-1})	
Histidine	—	—	—	28
Isoleucine	700	550	10	70
Leucine	1100	730	14	161
Lysine	800	545	12	103
Methionine and cystine	1100	700	13	58
Phenylalanine and tyrosine	1100	700	14	125
Threonine	500	375	7	87
Tryptophan	250	168	3.5	17
Valine	800	622	10	93

AMINO ACID REQUIREMENTS

It is possible to feed human beings on artificial diets in which a mixture of amino acids is the sole source of nitrogen. If then one of the essential amino acids is omitted from the mixture, an adult subject goes into negative nitrogen balance, and an infant or young child ceases to grow. The missing amino acid can then be replaced in gradually increasing amounts, until the subject is again in nitrogen balance or until normal growth is resumed. In this way an estimate of the human requirements for each of the amino acids can be made.

Such experiments are difficult and tedious, and require much care and patience from both the investigators and their subjects. In the USA estimates of human requirements of amino acids have been made for adult men,[36] for adult women[37] and for infants.[38] Table 5.5 gives a summary of the findings. Comparison of the two right-hand columns of Table 5.5 shows that infants require more of their total protein to be supplied in the form of essential amino acids.

Amino acid scores

A chemical grading of the quality of a protein can be made by comparing its amino acid content with that of a reference protein and for this purpose hen's egg protein is recommended (Table 5.4).

Amino acid score =

$$\frac{\text{mg of amino acid in 1 g test protein}}{\text{mg of amino acid in 1 g reference pattern}} \times 100$$

The score should, in theory, be calculated for all the essential amino acids and the lowest score taken. In practice the scores need be calculated only for lysine, the sulphur-containing amino acids and tryptophan, as one or other of these is the limiting amino acid in common foods.

Table 5.6 The chemical score and net protein utilisation (NPU) of some common foods[33]

Protein	Chemical score	NPU determined on children	NPU determined on rats
Maize	49	36	52
Millet	63	43	44
Rice	67	63	59
Wheat	53	49	48
Soya	74	67	65
Whole egg	100	87	94
Human milk	100	94	87
Cow's milk	95	81	82

Table 5.6 compares the chemical scores and NPU values of proteins from single foodstuffs. It is difficult to obtain NPU values using man as the test animal, but relatively easy using the rat. The Table indicates that the results obtained with the two species agree sufficiently well to justify applying values obtained with rats to human diets. The chemical scores also agree with NPU values.

Most good mixed diets have a NPU value of around 70, and this figure is little affected by the amount of protein of animal origin in the diet. When 70 per cent or more of the dietary proteins come from a single staple food, e.g. maize, cassava or wheat, the NPU value of the food becomes of great importance and may determine whether or not protein requirements are met.

RECOMMENDED INTAKES

In nearly all communities adults eat more protein than is necessary to maintain N balance. Psychological and social factors as well as physiological needs determine intake. Much study has been devoted to three questions:

1. What is the minimum amount of dietary protein on which normal human life and activity can be sustained?
2. What is the desirable or optimal intake of protein for a man who has a free choice of food?
3. Is a high-protein diet beneficial or harmful?

These questions are important, since they raise the practical issue as to whether our present dietary habits provide the right amount of protein for our needs and, were we to increase our protein intake considerably, how would it affect our health?

In 1909 the American physiologist Chittenden attempted to answer the second question by keeping healthy adult males, including himself, on diets containing as little as 40 g of protein daily for periods of up to one year.[39] Chittenden asserted that this regime not only maintained, but often increased physical and mental vigour. He argued that reduction of the protein intake to the low levels used in his experiments is actually beneficial, claiming that the extra work in excreting the nitrogen from higher intakes of protein throws a strain on the kidneys and tends to cause renal and vascular disease.

However, there is good evidence that the kidneys can normally excrete the N end-products from large protein intakes without suffering damage. The Australian rangerider, the gaucho of the South American plains and the Masai warrior of Central Africa all build up and maintain their good physique on diets which contain anything up to 250 or even 300 g of protein daily. A high protein intake seems to be tolerated throughout a lifetime without ill-effects. Nevertheless Chittenden's observation that adults can maintain good health on protein intakes far below current Western European and North American standards still remains true, and is a valuable contribution to knowledge.

In the opposite camp to Chittenden was Carl Voit, the great German pioneer in the scientific study of human nutrition. As early as 1881 he suggested 145 g as a suitable daily allowance of proteins. But the chief exponent of the view that a high protein intake promoted the vigour and physical efficiency of 'superior' men was the physiologist Rubner. In the Germany of 1914 he was a man of influence, and probably did more than any army general to lose the war that then began; for on his advice German agriculture was continued on the old policy of rearing large herds of cattle and sheep. No additional pastures were ploughed. His failure to realise that cereals can yield up to six times more dietary energy per acre than cattle contributed importantly to the defeats which followed in 1917. When food became short in Central Europe as a result of the Allied blockade, it was too late to increase cereal production effectively. This mistake was avoided in Britain during World War II when Drummond was Scientific Adviser to the Ministry of Food.

A study of the diets of different races throughout the world shows that there is a great variation in the amount of protein on which man can subsist. A few, as already mentioned, may provide over 200 g protein. By contrast the diet of many millions of poor people in Asia, Africa and Latin America provides less than 50 g of protein per day. Attempts to relate racial constitution to dietary habits have often tended to support the view that generous intakes of protein are desirable — as for example McCarrison's comparison between the poor physique of rice-eating Bengalis and the good physique of milk-drinking Sikhs.[40]

Animal experiments do not support the view that a high level of labile body protein confers any biological advantage.[41] Laboratory rats kept on low protein diets, which would allow no reserve of protein to accumulate, stand up to stresses such as exercise, unfavourable environmental temperatures, physical and chemical agents, injuries, infections, parasitic infestations and dietary deprivations as well as rats provided with a surplus of protein. It is naturally impossible to test these points experimentally in human subjects.

Recommendation of the League of Nations

In 1935 the League's Technical Committee on Nutrition stated: 'In practice, the protein intake for all adults should not fall below 1 g of protein per kg of body weight. The protein should be derived from a variety of sources, and it desirable that a part of the protein should be of animal origin.'[42]

This compromise between the views of Chittenden and Rubner reflected the practical wisdom of the committee whose members included Elmer McCollum, Boyd Orr, Edward Mellanby and E. P. Cathcart. The figure passed into textbooks of physiology and medicine and is still a useful guide for clinical practice and for food administrators.

Recommendations of national and United Nations (FAO/WHO) committees

Since the League of Nations report appeared, USA, UK and many other governments have issued reports on recommended dietary intakes, which included recommendations on protein, and four FAO/WHO committees have reported on protein (see Chapter 15). The earlier USA recommendation followed the League of Nations but in 1953 the first FAO report introduced a factorial basis for their recommendation. This requires estimates of three different factors: (1) the minimum protein needs, based on obligatory N losses or N balances; (2) protein quality, based on biological values or chemical scores; and (3) a safety factor to allow for individual variations. There have been great difficulties in deciding on the best figures for these factors. Furthermore, most of the resulting recommendations have been lower than that of the League of Nations. Hence they are impracticable since low protein diets based on them would not be acceptable to most people and also they would be likely to contain separated fats and refined carbohydrates in amounts prejudicial to health. The seemingly unending time that committees have spent in laudable attempts to make recommendations that appear scientific demonstrates, so it seems in retrospect, that circumlocution offices (p. 506) continue to flourish.

UK official committees have debated factorial methods at length but ended up with a recommendation that is empirical and based on the observation that diets in which proteins provide 10 per cent of the energy meet the needs for protein. This is certainly true for large populations and provides a practical and simple standard for food administrators in all countries. However, for persons whose energy intake is very low, for example many old women, such a diet may not meet energy needs and requires supplementation with protein-rich food. Also the recommendation overestimates protein needs of those whose occupation demands heavy work and who regularly take a high energy diet.

Recommendations for infants and young children

Protein is needed for growth and the protein intake of a breast fed infant is about 8 g day. In the first month of life this is between 2 and 3 g/kg of body weight. This requirement declines exponentially with age and by the time they are 5 years old most children grow well on an adult diet in which 10 per cent of the energy comes from protein. In human milk protein provides only 7.5 per cent of the energy but this is of high biological value and is sufficient during the first six months of live. Thereafter and at least for the first five years of life a child needs a diet richer in protein than an adult. Young children should have a greater proportion of the protein-rich foods in the family diet than adult members. These are cow's milk, meat, eggs and pulses — the poor man's meat — in all of which 20 per cent of the energy or more comes from protein (Table 5.3).

When a family diet is barely adequate, the distribution of food within the family is all-important. There is ample evidence that if the children do not receive shares of the foods richer in protein than those given to the adults, they fail to develop normally and are at risk of developing protein-energy malnutrition. This is perhaps the most important lesson that a nutritionist has to teach.

Protein deficiency

Protein-energy malnutrition is described in Chapter 29. In the Third World it is a major disorder in children causing failure of normal growth and development in enormous numbers and with a large mortality.

Protein deficiency also occurs in adults and in prosperous countries. It is not infrequently seen in patients in hospital practice and cases may arise in several ways.

1. Chronic alcoholics and other drug addicts may have irregular food habits and their diets may be grossly deficient in proteins.
2. Patients with chronic gastrointestinal disorders may not be able to eat sufficient food or to digest and absorb the protein that is eaten.
3. Surgical patients with severe injuries, especially those with burns, have increased N losses and are often unable to feed normally.
4. Some patients with chronic renal disease lose large amounts of protein in the urine that cannot be replaced from a normal diet.
5. Patients with a damaged liver may be unable to

utilise amino acids for the synthesis of specific proteins, for example plasma albumin.

The conditions are described in the clinical sections and the diagnosis of protein deficiency and its specific treatment is dealt with in chapters 51 and 52.

Adaptions to low protein intakes

The health of most adults would probably be unaffected if they were put on diets providing either 50 or 150 g protein daily. Clearly the tissues of the body can adapt to widely different levels of protein intake. This is in sharp contrast to the effect of varying intakes of energy. The need for energy is fixed by the rate of energy expenditure. If the intake falls below or exceeds this need, then inevitably the subject wastes or becomes obese. The nature of the adaption to varying protein intakes have been much studied in the Tropical Metabolism Research Unit in Jamaica.[43] The liver has a key role in the adaptive processes, for it is only in the liver that nitrogen can be transformed from amino acids into urea. The state of the liver must determine what proportion of nitrogen in the amino acids entering it via the circulation is converted into urea, and what proportion is retained within the amino acid pool and used for synthetic processes in the protein turnover of the tissues. Studies with labelled amino acids indicate that in rats on a low protein diet the turnover of protein is maintained in the liver, but reduced in the muscles and skin. This is probably effected by changes in the activity of liver enzymes. In protein deficiency levels of amino acid activating enzymes are high and levels of argininosuccinase, the enzyme responsible for the formation of urea, are low. Table 5.7 shows the activity of these enzymes in samples of liver obtained by biopsy from Jamaican children a few days after admission to hospital with severe malnutrition and one to two months later when they had recovered well. Many experiments in rats,[45] confirmed by a few observations in man, have established that quantitative aspects of amino acid metabolism in the liver are determined by the dietary protein intake and directed to maintaining protein synthesis.

Alterations of hormone balance play an important part in the different responses of the body to protein deficiency, which may be accompanied by varying degrees of energy deficit. Energy balance determines whether insulin or cortisol predominate.[46] When there is adequate carbohydrate this stimulates insulin secretion, which favours deposition of amino acids in muscle at the expense of the liver. If starvation predominates, insulin secretion is low but cortisol increased. Cortisol produces muscle wasting but deposition of protein in the liver.

SULPHUR
S (at. wt 32)

The greater part of the sulphur in the human body is present in the two sulphur-containing amino acids, methionine and cysteine, or in the double form of the latter, cystine. Several enzyme systems, for example those containing co-enzyme A and glutathione, depend for their activity on free sulphydryl (SH) groups. Sulphate ions are present in the cells and sulphate also occurs bound to various organic molecules. Of these the best known are heparin and chondroitin sulphate.

Two known vitamins, thiamin and biotin, contain sulphur. Sulphate esters of fatty acids are said to occur in the body, although practically nothing is known of their significance. The prefix *thio* (Greek: *theion* = sulphur) is used to denote certain compounds containing sulphur. Thiosulphate and thiocyanate have been detected in body fluids; the latter occurs in saliva, especially of tobacco smokers.

The sulphur-containing amino acids, methionine and cysteine, provide from 20 to 50 mmol (0.6 to 1.6 g) of sulphur daily. The amount depends on the quality and quantity of the dietary proteins. Inorganic sulphate and other sulphur-containing organic substances provide smaller amounts.

About 95 per cent of the dietary sulphur is oxidised to sulphate and excreted in the urine. The remainder appears in the urine as neutral sulphur. e.g. in sulphur-containing amino acids, taurine and thiocyanate. Most of the sulphate is present in the urine as free ions, but about 5 per cent as esters of organic compounds, mainly of hydroxyindole, formed by bacteria in the intestine. On a meat diet and during starvation the ratio of sulphur to nitrogen in the urine is about 1 to 14, the same as in muscle. Sulphur balances have been measured in obese subjects on reducing diets.[47] There is no evidence that sulphur deficiency occurs, except in association with protein deficiency.

Table 5.7 Enzymic activity of the livers of children with malnutrition[44]

	Amino acid activating enzymes	Arginino-succinase
Soon after admission	1.44	1.06
One to two months later	0.91	1.46

The figures for the amino acid activating enzymes are the mean of 18 measurements and expressed in μmol P exchanged/mg protein hourly; for argininosuccinase the figures are the mean of 11 measurements and expressed in μmol urea/mg protein hourly. The changes on recovery are statistically significant.

REFERENCES

1. Munro H N, Allison J H 1964 Mammalian protein metabolism. Academic Press, New York
2. Rose W C 1957 The amino acid requirements of adult man. Nutr Abstr Rev 27: 631–47
3. Kopple J D, Swerseid M E 1975 Evidence that histidine is an essential amino acid in normal and chronically uremic man. J Clin Invest 55: 881–91
4. Boebel K P, Baker D H 1982 Comparative utilization of the α-keto and D- and L-analogs of leucine, isoleucine and valine by chicks and rats. J Nutr 112: 1929–39
5. Harris C I 1981 Reappraisal of the quantitative importance of non-skeletal-muscle source of N-methyl histidine in urine. Biochem J 194: 1011–4
6. Van Slyke D D, Meyer G M 1912 The amino-acid nitrogen of blood: preliminary experiments on protein assimilation. J Biol Chem 12: 399–410
7. Fisher R B 1954 Protein metabolism. Methuen, London
8. Matthews D M 1975 Intestinal absorption of peptides. Physiol Rev 55: 537–608
9. Mawer G E, Nixon E 1969 The net absorption of the amino acid constituents of a protein meal in normal and cystinuric subjects. Clin Sci 36: 463–77
10. Phansalkar S V, Patwardhan V N 1955 Utilization of animal and vegetable proteins: urinary nitrogen excretion in absorptive and early postabsorptive phases. Indian J Med Res 43: 265–76
11. Schoenheimer R S 1942 The dynamic state of body constituents. Harvard University Press, Cambridge, Mass
12. Waterlow J C 1975 Protein turnover in the whole body. Nature 253: 157
13. Young V R, Skeffee W P, Pencharz P B, Winterer J C, Schrimshaw N S 1975 Total human body protein synthesis in relation to protein requirements at various ages. Nature 253: 192–3
14. Reeds P J, James W P T 1983 Protein turnover. Lancet 1: 571–4
15. Dakin H D 1913 Studies on the intermediary metabolism of amino-acids. J Biol Chem 14: 321–3
16. Krebs H A 1964 The metabolic fate of amino acids. In: Munro H N, Allison J B (eds) Mammalian protein metabolism, vol 1. Academic Press, New York, p 125–76
17. Lusk G 1928 The science of nutrition, 4th edn. Saunders, Philadelphia
18. Martin C J, Robison R 1922 The minimum nitrogen expenditure of man and the biological value of various proteins for human nutrition. Biochem J 16: 407–47
19. Addis T, Poo L J, Lew W 1936 The quantities of protein lost by the various organs and tissues of the body during a fast. J Biol Chem 115: 111–6
20. Darke S J 1960 The cutaneous loss of nitrogen compounds in African subjects. Br J Nutr 14: 115–9
21. Ashworth A, Harrower A D B 1967 Protein requirements in tropical countries: nitrogen losses in sweat and their relation to nitrogen balance. Br J Nutr 21: 833–43
22. Calloway D H, Margen S 1971 Variation in endogenous nitrogen excretion and dietary nitrogen utilization as determinants of human protein requirement. J Nutr 101: 205–16
23. Richards P, Ell S, Halliday D 1977 Direct evidence for the synthesis of valine in man. Lancet 1: 112–4
24. Oomen H A P C 1970 Interrelationship of the human intestinal flora and protein utilization. Proc Nutr Soc 29: 197–206
25. Bergersen F J, Hipsley E H 1970 The presence of N-fixing bacteria in the intestines of man and animals. J Gen Microbiol 60: 61–5
26. Jackson A A 1983 Amino acids: essential and non-essential. Lancet 1: 1034–7
27. Young V R, Scrimshaw N S 1968 Endogenous nitrogen metabolism and plasma free amino acids in young adults given a 'protein-free' diet. Br J Nutr 22: 9–20
28. Sherman H C 1920 Protein requirement of maintenance in man and the nutritive value of bread. J Biol Chem 40: 97–109
29. Irvin M S, Hegsted J M 1971 A conspectus of research on protein requirements of man. J Nutr 101: 385–430
30. Mendel L B 1915 Nutrition and growth. JAMA 64: 1539–47
31. FAO 1957 Protein requirements. FAO Nutr Studies no 16
32. FAO/WHO 1965 Protein requirements. WHO Tech Rep Ser no 301
33. FAO/WHO 1973 Energy and protein requirements. WHO Tech Rep Ser no 522
34. Scrimshaw N S 1976 An analysis of past and present recommended dietary allowances for protein in health and disease. N Engl J Med 294: 136–42, 198–203
35. Pellett P L, Young V R 1980 Nutritional evaluation of proteins foods. United Nations University WHTR-3/UNUP-129, Tokyo
36. Rose W C, Wixom R L, Lockhart H B, Lambert G F 1955 Amino acid requirements of man. XV The valine requirement. Summary and final observations. J Biol Chem 217: 987–1004
37. Leverton R M, and others 1956 The quantitative amino acid requirements of young women. J Nutr 58: 59–82 (threonine), 83–112 (valine), 219–29 (tryptophan)
38. Holt L E, György P, Pratt E L, and two others 1960 Protein and amino acid requirements in early life. New York University Press, New York
39. Chittenden R H 1909 The nutrition of man. Heinemann, London
40. McCarrison R 1936 Nutrition and health. Cantor lectures, republished 1953. Faber, London, p 24
41. Holt L E, Halac E, Kajdi C N 1962 The concept of protein stores and its implications in diet. JAMA 181: 699–705
42. League of Nations, Technical Commission of the Health Committee 1935 Report on the physiological bases of nutrition. Series of League of Nations Publications III Health II: 6
43. Waterlow J C 1968 Observations on the mechanism of adaption to low protein intakes. Lancet 2: 1091–7
44. Stephen J M L, Waterlow J C 1968 Effects of malnutrition on activity of two enzymes concerned with aminoacid metabolism in human liver. Lancet 1: 118–9
45. Stephen J M L 1968 Adaptive enzyme changes in liver and muscle of rats during protein depletion and refeeding. Br J Nutr 22: 153–63
46. Coward W A, Whitehead R G, Lunn P G 1977 Reasons why hypoalbuminaemia may or may not appear in protein-energy malnutrition. Br J Nutr 38: 115–26
47. Jourdan M, Glock C, Margen S, Bradfield R B 1980 Sulphate, acid base and mineral balances of obese women during weight loss. Am J Clin Nutr 33: 236–43

6

Fats

Fats provide a convenient and concentrated source of energy. Unfortunately there is some confusion in terms. The housewife, when she goes to buy butter, margarine or lard, has a clear idea of what she means by fat. Biochemists, in an effort to be more precise, invented a new word — lipid which covers all the chemical substances included in the housewife's fat — triglycerides, phospholipids, sterols, etc. Lipids have been defined as substances which are insoluble in water but soluble in organic solvents such as ether, chloroform and benzene. They are actual or potential esters of fatty acids. But these criteria cannot be applied too rigidly or exclusively. The chemist uses the term 'fat' in a restricted sense to mean the 'neutral fats' which are mixtures of esters of fatty acids. The term 'oil' is applied indiscriminately both to liquid, digestible triglycerides (such as olive oil) and to indigestible mineral hydrocarbons (such as liquid paraffin). Hereafter we use the word 'fat' in the housewife's sense when referring to the fat content of foods and diets, but follow the chemical nomenclature when considering the metabolism of lipids in the body.

In practical dietetics it is useful to refer to **visible fats,** meaning butter and margarine, lard and vegetable oils. This is convenient as visible fat can be accurately measured and therefore accurately prescribed. In contrast, many other foods contain different proportions of fat, which are closely associated with the other constituents in an emulsion or as part of the tissue. Hence the **total fat** in a diet is hard to measure, because different samples of the same food may vary widely in fat content, especially in the case of meat. Only approximate figures for total fat content are provided by food tables or nutrition labelling. Accurate assessments of the total fat in a diet require chemical analysis of samples in the diet as actually consumed.

The fats in the body were divided by Terroine, a distinguished French physiologist, into two parts. *L'élément variable* is the fuel store. This depends on the energy content of the previous diet and may be only 5 kg or less after a period of semistarvation and 50 kg or more in an obese person; it is made up mainly of **triglycerides.** *L'élément constant* is part of the essential structure of the cells. The membranes surrounding cells, mitochondria and the intracellular organelles are composed of macromolecules of lipids and protein; the lipid is mainly phospholipid. The amount in the body, between 0.5 and 1.0 kg, is independent of the state of nutrition. **Cholesterol** is another lipid present in cell membranes; it has also an important role in fat transport in the blood and is the precursor from which bile salts and adrenal and sex hormones are made. **Prostaglandins** and related substances are local hormones formed in most tissues from fatty acid precursors. These have been shown to have many powerful actions in pharmacological doses. As they are destroyed very rapidly in the tissues, it is difficult to determine their physiological roles but these are probably diverse and important.

Thus lipids in the body have three roles: (1) in adipose tissue they form the chief store of energy; (2) in all tissues they are a main part of the structure of cell membranes; and (3) they are the precursors from which many hormones are made. Each of these three functions may be affected by the quantity and quality of dietary fats, as may mechanisms for transport of lipids to and from the various organs and tissues in the blood. How much differences of lipid metabolism attributable to diet are responsible for degenerative disorders contributing to morbidity and mortality with advancing age is, as we shall see, a major question in medical research today.

CHEMICAL COMPOSITION AND DISTRIBUTION

TRIGLYCERIDES

Triglyceride is the main form of fats both in foodstuffs and in the storage depots of most animals. They are esters of glycerol and fatty acids, Figure 6.1 being a typical example. In this there is a saturated fatty acid at position 1 on the glycerol molecule and an unsaturated fatty acid in position 2. This is typical of nearly all triglycerides. The fatty acid at position 3 may be either saturated or unsaturated.

$$CH_2-O-\overset{\overset{\displaystyle O}{\|}}{C}-(CH_2)_{14}-CH_3$$
$$CH_3-(CH_3)_7-CH=CH-(CH_2)_7-\overset{\overset{\displaystyle O}{\|}}{C}-O-CH$$
$$CH_2-O-\overset{\overset{\displaystyle O}{\|}}{C}-(CH_2)_{16}-CH_3$$

Fig. 6.1 Structural formula of a typical triglyceride

In natural fats the fatty acids are distributed among the glycerol molecules not by chance but in a biological order. Thus in a mixture of triglycerides, molecules of a single fatty acid (say palmitic acid) are attached first to every molecule of glycerol. Triglycerides containing two molecules of palmitic acid are not found unless palmitic acid provides more than one third of the total fatty acids present. Any fatty acid forming less than a third of the total fatty acids never occurs more than once in any triglyceride.

FATTY ACIDS

Over 40 different fatty acids (FA) are found in nature. These give a diversity and chemical specificity to the complex lipids found in natural fats and oils comparable to that given by the amino acids to proteins.

Fatty acids have the basic formula $CH_3(CH_2)_nCOOH$ where n can be any even number from 2 to 24. Three classes of fatty acids are described according to the number of double bonds between the carbon atoms. In a saturated FA there are none; in an unsaturated FA there may be one (monoenoic acids) or two or more (polyenoic acids). There is now great interest in the

Table 6.1 The more important natural fatty acids

Saturated acids		
Butyric acid	C4:0	short chain
Caproic acid	C6:0	
Caprylic acid	C8:0	
Capric acid	C10:0	medium chain
Lauric acid	C12:0	
Myristic acid	C14:0	
Palmitic acid	C16:0	long chain
Stearic acid	C18:0	
Arachidic acid	C20:0	
Behenic acid	C22:0	
Monounsaturated acids		
Palmitoleic acid	C16:1	
Oleic acid	C18:1	
Erucic acid	C22:1	
Polyunsaturated acids (PUFA)		
Linoleic acid	C18:2	
Linolenic acid	C18:3	
Arachidonic acid	C20:4	

Palmitic acid a hexadecanoic acid

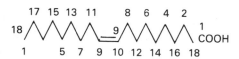

Oleic acid or *cis* 9-octadeconoic acid
or C18:1,*n*-9

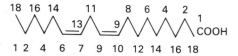

Linoleic acid or *cis* 9,12-octadecadienoic acid
or C 18:2,*n*-6

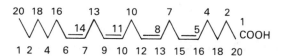

Arachidonic acid or *cis* 5,8,11,14-eicosatetraenoic acid
or C18:4,*n*-6

Fig. 6.2 Structural formulae and systematic names of some fatty acids

latter group and they are commonly referred to by the acronym PUFA (Poly Unsaturated Fatty Acids). PUFA include the essential fatty acids that have to be provided in the diet (p. 65).

Table 6.1 lists the more important fatty acids under their common or trivial names. Figure 6.2 sets out the structure of some of these with their systematic names. Regrettably there are two systems for numbering the carbon atoms, and Figure 6.2 shows one above and the other below the chain. On top the atom in the carboxyl group is numbered 1 and numbers rise with each succeeding atom in the chain up to the terminal methyl group. This is the system used by chemists and provides the basis for official names. Nutritionists and some biochemists number the carbon chains in unsaturated acids the other way round, starting with the methyl carbon atom as 1. The reason for this is as follows. Unsaturated fatty acids undergo further desaturation and chain lengthening in the body. Desaturation enzymes only operate on the bond between the two carbon atoms two places away from a double bond and towards the carboxyl end (to the right in Fig. 6.2). The position of the first double bond in the chain relative to the methyl carbon atom determines the number of double bonds that

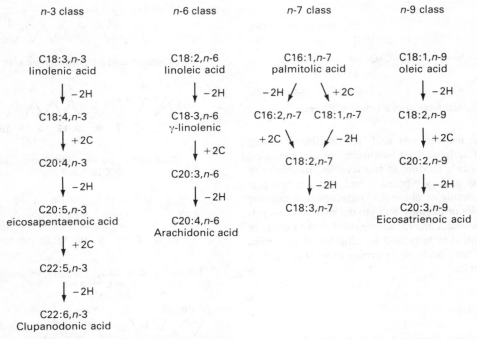

n-3 class	n-6 class	n-7 class	n-9 class
C18:3,n-3 linolenic acid	C18:2,n-6 linoleic acid	C16:1,n-7 palmitolic acid	C18:1,n-9 oleic acid

Fig. 6.3 Desaturation and chain lengthening of fatty acids

can be inserted. The four main dietary unsaturated fatty acids are known as *n*–3, *n*–6, *n*–7 and *n*–9, according to the position of the first double bond relative to the methyl carbon atom. Figure 6.3 shows these acids and the derivatives that may be formed in the metabolism of each of them. The distinction is important because acids in classes *n*–7 and *n*–9 cannot function as essential fatty acids which all belong to the *n*–3 and *n*–6 classes. The physiological importance of the individual acids shown in Figure 6.3 is controversial and considered after an account of the actions of essential fatty acids (p. 65). Biological functions of fatty acids depend on their property of being *amphipathic*. The methyl tail of the chain is *hydrophobic* and the tails tend to agglomerate and so expose a minimum surface to water. The carboxyl group is polar and *hydrophilic* and so maintains maximum contact with surrounding water.

The chemical composition of fatty acids alters their physical properties, and chain lengthening and desaturation may give them advantages as structural components of cell membranes. Water solubility depends on chain length. For practical purposes, only caprylic acid (C8) and those with shorter chains are soluble in water. Longer chain lengths increase the volume of the hydrophobic phase in a membrane. The melting point is related to both chain length and unsaturation. Vegetable oils have more long chain polyunsaturated and fewer short chain acids than hard animal fats. Longer chains and more numerous double bonds in their lipids may help to maintain fluidity in hydrophobic membranes.

Cis and trans isomers. As unsaturated fatty acids contain double bonds between two carbon atoms, they can exist in two geometric isomeric forms. This is because at a double bond there is no freedom of rotation for the two groups on either side of the bond. In *cis* forms of unsaturated fatty acids there is a kink in the chain with an angle of about 25 degrees at each double bond, and in those that have several double bonds, such as linolenic acid the chain is curved and doubles back on itself (Fig. 6.4). This configuration allows such acids to be tightly packed in the macromolecules of complex

Fig. 6.4 Model of a linoleic molecule

structural lipids. In the *trans* form the chain is straight as in unsaturated fatty acids.

The unsaturated fatty acids found in both plants and animals are in the *cis* form. They may, however, be changed into the *trans* forms during manufacturing processes by heat under certain conditions. These are not incorporated into structural lipids and cannot function as essential fatty acids, but they can be oxidised and serve as fuels for the tissues.

Some seed oils contain small amounts of fatty acids with a branched chain or a cyclic structure. These are not known to have any physiological action in animals. However, a cyclopentene derivative, chaulmoogric acid, is the main fatty acid in chaulmoogra oil which for many years was used effectively as a drug to treat leprosy.

Distribution of fatty acids in animal and plant life
The chemical composition of the natural fats is related to the biological species from which they are derived. Organisms which have been classed together by biologists on morphological grounds have been found by chemists to share in general the same fatty acids in approximately similar proportions. Hilditch was a pioneer in finding out the biological distributions of the fatty acids. His book is the classic reference work on the subject.[1]

In fats from all freshwater life, whether plant or animal, the unsaturated C16, C18, C20, and C22 fatty acids predominate. They are present in varying proportions and in different states of unsaturation. The only important saturated acid is palmitic acid, which is usually presents as 10 to 18 per cent of total acids.

In the marine world polyunsaturated C20 and C22 fatty acids, containing up to six double bonds, are most numerous. In highly developed fish and aquatic mammals the fatty acids form esters with other higher alcohols as well as with glycerol. The fats present in salmon and sea-trout, fish which live both in fresh and salt water, have fatty acids which conform to the general picture of other marine animals.

In land animals, and particularly in mammals, the unsaturated oleic acid and the saturated palmitic acid predominate. Palmitic acid forms about 25 to 30 per cent of the fatty acids in the depot fat of all the common mammals and this accounts for their hardness and low iodine value relative to marine oils. Stearic acid is found principally in the fat of ruminants, where it in part replaces oleic acid.

Milk fats, such as butter, differ from other animal fats in containing small amounts of short-chain C4 to C8 fatty acids.

In plant seeds the fatty acids are less varied than in aquatic life. As in land animals, oleic acid and palmitic acid are prominent, but a third acid, linoleic acid, provides a large component. Linoleic and linolenic acids are amongst the most familiar constituents of the numerous seed oils. Coconut oil is an exception in that it is mostly made up of short- and medium-chain saturated fatty acids, with very little oleic and linoleic acid. Olive oil is very rich in oleic acid but contains little linoleic acid. The elucidation of the relationship of the different fatty acid components of the fats with the morphology and natural history of plants and animals from which they come is a fascinating biological problem.

Table 6.2 gives the relative amounts of the different fatty acids in some common foods and vegetable oils.

A diet rich in linoleic and linolenic acid can be obtained by eating plenty of vegetable seed oils. Arachidonic acid seldom occurs in vegetable oils, but animals have no difficulty in synthesising it from linoleic acid.

The proportion of essential fatty acids that remains in vegetable and marine oils after hardening by commercial hydrogenation is important. Completely hydrogenated fats of course contain none. Formerly most margarines contained little or no EFA. With the steady increase in the consumption of margarine during the first 50 years of the present century, national intakes of linoleic acid probably declined. Recently, owing to the interest in the physiological action of these acids, manufacturers have been at great pains to produce margarines containing linoleic acid. Products are now available in which 50 per cent or more of the fatty acids are polyunsaturated. This is achieved by skilful blending of vegetable oils that have not been hydrogenated.

Medium chain triglycerides (MCT)
These are fractionated from coconut oil (Table 6.2) and consist mostly of C8:0 and C10:0. They have been introduced into dietetics because they are hydrolysed by pancreatic lipase more easily than other triglycerides and because, once absorbed, they go direct to the liver in the portal vein in the form of fatty acids. Patients with steatorrhoea often absorb MCT much better than other fats so MCT is a valuable source of energy for such patients.

Erucic acid C22:1
This very long chain monounsaturated acid is the principal fatty acid in rapeseed oil, one of the few vegetable oils that is easily grown in temperate areas of the world such as northern Europe and Canada. It has been found that when large amounts of rapeseed oil (50 per cent of total energy) are fed to experimental animals fatty change occurs in heart muscle. This is because erucic acid enters the myocardial cells but is oxidised more slowly than other fatty acids and so accumulates intracellularly in triglycerides.[2] Geneticists have now produced a variety of rapeseed, Canbra, that contains only 2 per cent of erucic acid.

Table 6.2 Pattern of fatty acids in fats and oils (approximate percentage of total fatty acids)

	C4–12 saturated	C14:0	C16:0	C18:0	C16:1 + C18:1	C18:2	Other PUFAs	Other FAs
Butter, cream and milk	13	11	26	11	30	2	1[b]	12
Beef	—	3	29	16	48	2	1	—
Bacon and pork	—	2	26	14	50	7	1	—
Chicken	—	1	26	7	45	18	2	—
Fish oil	—	5	15	3	27	7	43[a]	—
Coconut oil	58	18	10	3	8	2	—	—
Palm oil	—	1	40	4	45	9	—	—
Cocoa butter	—	—	26	35	36	3	—	—
Rapeseed oil	—	—	3	1	24	15	10[b]	40[c]
Olive oil	—	—	12	2	73	11	1	—
Groundnut oil	—	—	12	3	53	30	1	—
Sesame oil	—	—	9	5	40	43	—	—
Cottonseed oil	—	1	24	2	20	50	1	—
Corn (maize) oil	—	—	12	2	31	53	2	—
Soya bean oil	—	—	10	4	24	53	7[b]	—
Sunflower seed oil	—	—	6	6	33	58	—	—
Safflower seed oil	—	—	7	2	13	74	—	—
Margarine	3	5	23	9	33	12	1	5
Margarine, polyunsaturated	2	1	12	8	22	52	1	—

[a] Long-chain polyunsaturated fatty acids (C20 and C22).
[b] C18:3 (linolenic); [c] C22:1 (erucic).
   Note. The composition of all these fats and oils varies depending on methods of animal husbandry and crop production. In margarines the proportion of fats and oils for the blend are adjusted to world market prices.

A regulation in the UK and EEC now limits the erucic acid in edible oils and fats and in foods containing them to 5 per cent of the fat component.

WAXES

Waxes are fatty acid esters of higher alcohols. They occur widely in the cuticle of leaves and fruit and in the secretions of insects and may be mixed with very long-chain hydrocarbons (C21–35). They replace the triglycerides to some extent in the tissues of aquatic animals (e.g. crustaceans). In some whales, wax esters form the major component of the depot fat. So far waxes have not been shown to be an important constituent of any of the higher land animals, nor do they contribute importantly to normal human diets.

PHOSPHOLIPIDS

Phospholipids, the main structural lipids in cell membranes, are a group of substances which, like the triglycerides, are esters of glycerol with fatty acids but only with two. Instead of the third fatty acid, the carbon atom in position 3 is linked to phosphate to which a nitrogen-containing compound (choline, ethanolamine or serine) or inositol is attached. Figure 6.5 shows the structure of a **lecithin** molecule, a typical phospholipid.

   Lecithin derives its name from the Greek word *lekithos*, egg yolk, and was isolated from this source in 1850. It is not a single substance but a mixture of different fatty acid esters. A saturated FA is usually present at C-1 and an unsaturated one at C-2; this is often polyunsaturated and lecithins contain a higher proportion of these than triglycerides.

$$CH_2-O-\overset{\overset{\textstyle O}{\|}}{C}-(CH_2)_{14}-CH_3$$

$$CH_3-(CH_2)_4-C=C-CH_2-C=C-(CH_2)_7-\overset{\overset{\textstyle O}{\|}}{C}-O-CH$$

$$CH_2-O-\overset{\overset{\textstyle O}{\|}}{P}-O-CH_2-\overset{+}{N}{\Big\langle}{\begin{matrix}CH_3\\CH_3\\CH_3\end{matrix}}$$

Fig. 6.5 Structural formula of a typical phospholipid

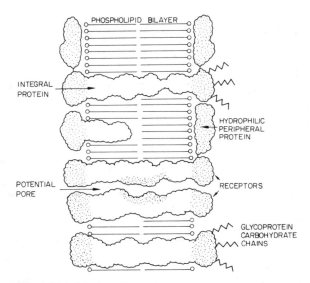

Fig. 6.6 Model of a cell membrane

Phospholipids, in contrast to neutral triglycerides, carry electric charges, a negative one at the phosphate group and a positive one at the amine radical. Thus they have a polar head and non-polar tails (the fatty acid chains). This orientates their molecules in cell membranes, where they are arranged in two layers with the hydrophobic tails directed to the centre of the membrane and the charged heads to the two surfaces. On the outside there are hydrophilic peripheral proteins (Fig. 6.6). Lecithin is a detergent and food manufacturers often add 0.2 per cent of it to fat emulsions in which it acts as a stabiliser.

The **sphingomyelins** found in myelin in the nervous system are phospholipids in which phosphorylcholine is esterified with sphingosine, a complex base, structurally similar to a monoglyceride. **Cardiolipids**, found in the mitochondrial membranes of heart muscle, consist of two phospholipid molecules linked together by a glycerol molecule through their phosphate radicals. The esterified fatty acids are mostly polyunsaturated. **Glycolipids** (cerebrosides and gangliosides) contain sphingosine attached to hexoses and complex carbohydrates; they do not contain phosphorus. Glycolipids are important components of cell membranes. Little is known about their nutritional significance.

STEROLS

These comprise an important and widely distributed class of biological substances, all of which have the same basic ring structure. Sterols are solid alcohols and, like all alcohols, can form esters with fatty acids.

Cholesterol

Cholesterol is found in all animal tissues, so that some is present in all foods of animal origin, but eggs are the only common food rich in cholesterol. It is virtually absent from foods of plant origin. Most Western diets provide about 500 mg/day.

Cholesterol has three distinct roles in the body: (1) as a structural component of all cell membranes, (2) as a precursor of bile acids and (3) as a precursor of adrenal and gonadal hormones and of vitamin D. Cholesterol is also present, often in large amounts, in atheromatous lesions of arterial walls. These can be found at almost all autopsies, increasing in number and severity as age advances. They are an underlying cause of the cardiovascular diseases that are the major cause of death in all countries where there is effective control of infectious diseases. This is the reason why cholesterol arouses so much interest both in professional people and among the lay public.

Chemical and physical properties
The chemical structure of cholesterol is shown in Figure 6.7, the conventional formula above and the conformational formula below. The main feature of the molecule is a steroid ring that is nearly planar. At one end (C-3) there is a polar hydroxyl group and at the other end (C-17) a freely movable hydrocarbon tail, at the side (C-18 and 19) are two methyl groups. The molecular weight is 386.

The hydroxyl group at C-3 is readily esterified with a free fatty acid or with a fatty acid of phospholipid, commonly that in the 2 position of lecithin. In plasma most of the cholesterol, 60 to 70 per cent, is esterified but in the cells most is found free.

Cholesterol is insoluble in water, but readily soluble in ether and chloroform. In the small intestine it is made soluble by association with the amphipathic bile acids (see below): in the blood it is transported bound to soluble lipoproteins.

Formation of bile acids
These are formed in the liver from cholesterol (Fig. 6.7). The first and rate-limiting step is hydroxylation at C-7, followed by oxidation of the side chain with the formation of a — COOH radical. This produces chenodeoxycholic acid. Further hydroxylation at C-12 yields cholic acid. These are the two primary bile acids. They are excreted in the bile as conjugates with taurine or glycine. The polar groups and the shape of the molecules make the bile acids effective detergents and enable them to solubilise fats present in the small intestine.

Synthesis
In addition to a dietary source, the body obtains cholesterol by synthesis. This takes place mainly in the liver

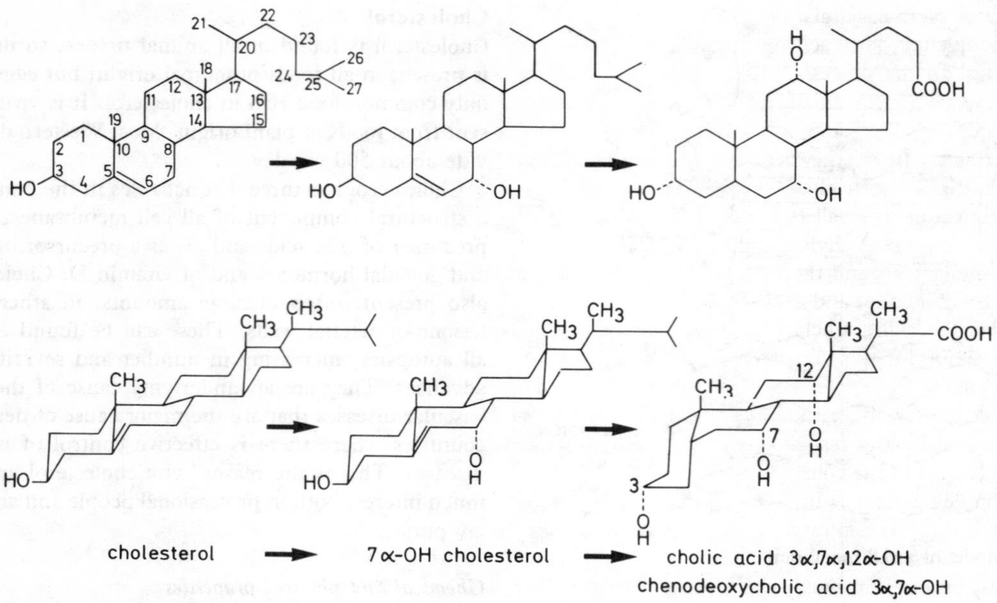

Fig. 6.7 Structural and conformational formulae of cholesterol and a bile acid

but also in all cells of the body. The basic building block is acetate of which three molecules after activation unite; the product is then reduced to mevalonate and this is converted into a five-carbon isoprene unit. Six of these form the 30C squalene from which cholesterol is derived. A feedback control operates on the reduction to mevalonate, the rate-limiting reaction. This maintains cholesterol concentrations in plasma and probably also in cells within a small range for long periods, even when there are wide variations in dietary intake. However, plasma cholesterol rises with very high intakes and usually falls when intake is very low (Chap. 40).

Plant sterols

Plants contain phytosterols, which differ from cholesterol only in having one or two extra carbon atoms in the side chain. A common one, β-**sitosterol**, is 24-ethyl cholesterol. Plant sterols are poorly absorbed. They also interfere with absorption of cholesterol, and β-sitosterol has been used to lower plasma cholesterol. One of the plant sterols, **ergosterol**, is found in yeasts and fungi. Under the influence of ultraviolet light it is converted into vitamin D_2, ergocalciferol.

DIGESTION AND ABSORPTION

The presence of fat in the food delays the emptying of the stomach. This may contribute to the feeling of satiety after a meal rich in fat. The mechanism of the delay may be attributed to the inhibitory action on the movements of the stomach of the hormone secretin liberated when fat enters the duodenum.[3]

EMULSIFICATION AND HYDROLYSIS

Fats have to be reduced to small particles before digestion and absorption are possible. Conditions first become suitable for emulsification in the duodenum, below the point where the pancreatic juice and bile enter. Bile salts, and small quantities of fatty acids and monoglycerides liberated by pancreatic lipase, are then able to emulsify fat either in a slightly acid or alkaline medium (pH range of 6.0 to 8.5), with the formation of droplets or micelles smaller than 0.5 μm. None of the three substances alone is an effective emulsifier under the conditions found in the intestine and the combination of the three is necessary for the digestion of fat.

Pancreatic lipase splits triglycerides into fatty acids, diglycerides, monoglycerides and glycerol. Hydrolysis is slow at the 2-monoglyceride stage. Pancreatic juice also contains phospholipase and cholesterol esterase. The contents of the small intestine are not sufficiently alkaline to allow the fatty acids liberated by hydrolysis to form soaps with alkalis under normal conditions.

The final result is a clear microemulsion of lipids, which is then presented to the microvilli of the mucous membrane of the small intestine.

ABSORPTION

Fatty acids and monoglycerides pass into the cells of the mucous membrane as very small particles or micelles which can be demonstrated by the electron microscope. Within the cells further hydrolysis may take place under the influence of intracellular monoglyceride lipase and then the long-chain fatty acids are re-esterified into new triglycerides. In the processes of digestion and absorption, the fatty acids are mixed, so that the triglycerides of the food lose their identity and new triglycerides partly characteristic of the animal species are formed. After resynthesis the triglycerides enter the lacteals of the small intestine as small particles from 0.1 to 0.6 μm in diameter, known as chylomicrons (see below). These pass into the lacteals and the mesenteric lymph vessels, enter the thoracic duct and thence join the systemic circulation via the right subclavian vein. In experimental animals it is not difficult to make a fistula in the thoracic duct and collect the chyle therefrom. In clinical medicine an occasional opportunity to study the formation of chyle arises; if, as a result of injury, a leak occurs in the thoracic duct in the course of its passage through the thorax, the chyle escapes into the pleural cavity (chylothorax) and can be aspirated through the chest wall.

The fat absorbed enters the circulation via the thoracic duct, except for most short- and medium-chain fatty acids which pass to the liver via the portal vein.

Enterohepatic circulations (Fig. 6.8)
Bile acid conjugates entering the duodenum are mostly absorbed in the ileum, return to the liver and again secreted in the bile. Some of the conjugates enter the colon

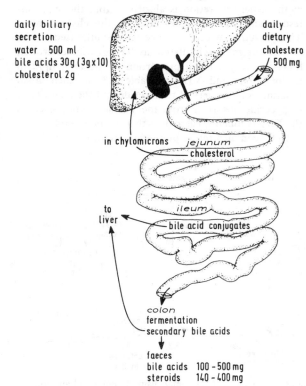

daily biliary secretion
water 500 ml
bile acids 30g (3g x 10)
cholesterol 2g

daily dietary cholesterol 500 mg

in chylomicrons *jejunum*
cholesterol

to liver *ileum*
bile acid conjugates

colon
fermentation
secondary bile acids

faeces
bile acids 100 - 500 mg
steroids 140 - 400 mg

Fig. 6.8 Enterohepatic circulations

where under bacterial action they are deconjugated and the OH groups in the 7 and 12 positions reduced with the formation of deoxycholic acid and lithocholic acid. These secondary bile acids are partly absorbed from the colon to the liver to be reconjugated with taurine and glycine. Some pass through the colon and are excreted as faecal steroids. Figure 6.8 indicates the quantities of bile salts and cholesterol that may be involved in these circulations. The effect of dietary fibre on the cholesterol circulation is discussed in Chapter 4.

Completeness of digestion and absorption
Most fats, when fed to adult subjects in quantities up to 100 g/day, are digested and absorbed to the extent of at least 95 per cent. Much larger quantities, up to 250 g/day or even more, can sometimes be absorbed if the body is short of energy. Arctic explorers and lumberjacks frequently consume and digest such large amounts. In constitutionally thin people there is no evidence of a failure to digest or absorb fats. Normally, fats never form more than 10 per cent of the dry weight of the stools and the amount present is largely independent of the dietary intake. With a fat intake of 100 g/day or less, the presence of more than 7 g of fat daily in the faeces (taken as an average over a period of at least five days) constitutes evidence of some failure of fat absorption and justifies a diagnosis of steatorrhoea. Steatorrhoea is found whenever there is a failure of secretion either of the bile salts or the pancreatic juice. It also occurs in the malabsorption syndrome (Chap. 46).

LIPID TRANSPORT

Whereas for transport of carbohydrate glucose serves as a convenient currency, being a simple chemical and readily soluble in water, transport of lipids is complex, since different forms have to pass between the various organs and tissues and all are insoluble in water. Lipids are carried in the blood bound to protein in complex macromolecules known as **lipoproteins**. These continue to be the subject of much research. A review by Havel et al[4] has 900 references and runs to 101 pages. The summary that follows here gives a broad outline of findings that can be taken as established, but many details, especially of the quantitative aspects and of control mechanisms, have yet to be elucidated.

Four classes of lipoprotein are characterised by their density and electrophoretic mobility (Table 6.3). Each contains triglycerides, phospholipid and cholesterol bound to protein carriers (apoproteins) in large molecular complexes. In each of the four classes the proportion of these components in the complexes varies slightly but differs markedly from that in the other classes.

Table 6.3 Properties and composition of plasma lipoprotein (modified from Lewis)[5]

	Chylomicrons	Very low density lipoproteins (VLDL)	Low density lipoproteins (LDL)	High density lipoproteins (HDL)
Density	<0.96	0.96–1.006	1.006–1.063	>1.063
Electrophoretic mobility	–	pre-β	β	α
Diameter of particle (nm)	75–600	28–75	17–28	17
Approximate composition (per cent)				
Triglycerides	86	55	10	3
Phospholipids	8	20	20	22
Cholesterol–free	1.5 ⎫	10 ⎫	10 ⎫	5 ⎫
–esters	2.5 ⎬ 4	5 ⎬ 15	35 ⎬ 45	15 ⎬ 20
Protein	2 ⎭	10 ⎭	25 ⎭	55 ⎭
Main function	Transport of triglycerides From small intestine to liver	From liver to peripheral tissues	Transport and control of cholesterol	

Apoproteins

These are large complexes made up of several units of relatively small proteins of molecular weight 7000–35 000. Over 10 of these have been identified, the most prevalent being known as A, B and C. Details of these units are incompletely known and there is as yet no agreed terminology. They are synthesised by parenchymal cells of the liver and mucosal cells of the small intestine.

Chylomicrons

These are the main vehicle for carrying triglycerides from the alimentary canal to the liver and they also carry phospholipids, cholesterol and fat soluble vitamins in relatively small amounts. They are cleared from the circulation, usually in 2 to 4 hours after a meal, by lipoprotein lipases on the surface of endothelial cells of the capillary bed of muscle, adipose tissue and liver. These enzymes hydrolyse the triglycerides and the free fatty acids formed are taken up by the cells. The chylomicrons are progressively reduced in size to small particles, known as remnants; from these LDL may be formed in the plasma or they may be taken up by the liver and metabolised.

Very low density lipoproteins (VLDL)

These are the carriers of endogenous triglycerides from the liver to peripheral tissues. After assembly in the liver they enter the blood stream. Like the chylomicrons they are then subject to the action of lipoprotein lipases in the extrahepatic capillary beds. Fatty acids and monoglycerides are liberated and absorbed into the cells. The protein portions of the complex with a little remaining lipid stay in the circulation where they are known as remnants, and from these the low density lipoproteins are formed subsequently. The plasma concentration of VLDL changes little and, unlike that of the chylomicrons, is not closely related to ingestion of fats.

Fasting plasma triglyceride concentration reflects VLDL concentration. After an overnight fast normal values range from about 0.3 to 1.7 mmol/l (25 to 150 mg/100 ml).

Low density lipoproteins (LDL) and cholesterol metabolism (Fig. 6.9)

Cholesterol is carried in the blood mainly on LDL and in the esterified form. Cholesterol in the diet and also in the biliary secretion is absorbed from the small intestine and carried to the liver in the chylomicrons. Then together with any cholesterol synthesised in the liver it enters the circulation as VLDL. Cholesterol is, however, only a small proportion of the total lipid in chylomicrons and VLDL (Table 6.3) as their main function is as carriers of triglyceride and the quantity of triglyceride absorbed from the gut and synthesised in the liver is much greater than that of cholesterol.

LDL contains much more cholesterol than triglycer-

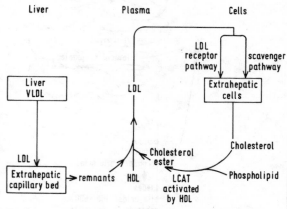

Fig. 6.9 Aspects of the metabolism of cholesterol and low density lipoproteins

ide and is formed in the plasma from remnants and also from cholesteryl esters, made available from phospholipids through the action of an enzyme, **lecithin-cholesterol acyl transferase** (LCAT). This enzyme is activated by another lipoprotein, **high density lipoprotein** (HDL), formed in the liver. HDL appears to determine the rate of formation of LDL and so to regulate cholesterol metabolism, but its mechanism of action is not as yet known.

LDL is taken up by specific receptors on cell membranes. It is then broken down and its cholesterol used to restructure the membranes which are being continuously turned over and renewed. LDL appears to function as a mobile reserve of cholesterol from which cells can draw through their specific receptors at a rate determined by the need for structural renewal. LDL is also taken up by cells by a route independent of the receptors and known as the scavenger pathway. Free cholesterol may also leave the cells and then is esterified and taken up into LDL through the action of HDL.

The cholesterol content of most mammalian tissues lies between 1 and 3 g/kg of wet weight and in the body of an adult human male there is altogether about 140 g.[6] Of this a little over 3 g circulates in the plasma LDL. The turnover of this mobile pool in healthy subjects is about 1.5 g daily and indirect evidence indicates that about two thirds of this goes through specific receptor sites and one third through the scavenger pathway.[4] Study of the quantitative aspects of the kinetics of cholesterol metabolism, essential for understanding of its control, is beset with technical difficulties and requires much more research.

Plasma cholesterol in healthy people ranges from 3.6 to 7.8 mmol/l (140 to 300 mg/100 ml). It is independent of the dietary intake, unless this is very high, and reflects closely plasma LDL concentration.

Carriage of free fatty acids (FFA)

FFA liberated from triglycerides in adipose tissue is carried in the plasma to other tissues bound to albumin. The complex is much smaller and simpler than the other lipoproteins. On each albumin molecule there are seven binding sites. Plasma concentration of FFA soon after a meal is about 0.5 mmol/l; in prolonged starvation it may rise to 4.0 mmol/l. The molar ratio of FFA/albumin. in plasma then approaches 7, showing that carrying capacity is saturated.

ADIPOSE TISSUE

Dietary fat is brought to the adipose tissues direct from the intestine in the form of chylomicrons and from the liver as VLDL or pre-β-lipoproteins. Dietary glucose is also transported to adipose tissue and there converted into triglycerides.

It was once thought that adipose tissue was an inert store in which the surplus energy of the diet was kept in the form of fat until needed. Two Israeli scientists, Wertheimer & Shapiro, in a classical review,[7] were mainly responsible for dispelling this idea and demonstrating that adipose tissue has considerable metabolic activities. A major portion of the dietary energy, both as fat and carbohydrate is taken to adipose tissue and deposited as triglycerides. The fatty acid pattern of these triglycerides partly reflects that of the individual's customary dietary fat, notably in the proportion of linoleic acid which cannot be synthesised in the body. Between meals, when the adipose tissue reserves are drawn upon to provide fuel for the muscles and other tissue, the triglycerides are subsequently broken down to free fatty acids (FFA), which enter the blood and supply the tissues with energy. The deposition and mobilisation of fat in adipose tissue proceeds at rates which are ever varying, depending upon the supply of energy at the last meal and the immediate needs of the tissues, particularly those determined by muscular activity. These rates are controlled by endocrine factors and the autonomic nervous system. Insulin stimulates the synthesis of adipose tissue trigycerides from glucose and the uptake of plasma triglycerides into adipose tissue by the agency of lipoprotein lipase. Most other hormones, such as catecholamines and glucagon which appear in plasma in increased amounts during fasting, have the opposite effect and favour lipolysis.

ANATOMICAL CONSIDERATIONS

Adipose tissue is a large organ and very variable in size. In a healthy man it may amount to some 8 to 15 kg and in a healthy woman from 10 to 20 kg. In a very emaciated patient it is reduced to about 1 kg, and some very obese people carry around over 100 kg. Its distribution in the body is also uneven.

Distribution of adipose tissue.

Male connoisseurs of the female form are reputed to start their visual inspection at the ankle and work upwards. This traditional guide is generally reliable, but sometimes the amount of subcutaneous fat over the ankles and legs bears little relation to the amount of fat elsewhere. This is perhaps a relatively common but minor manifestation of the process responsible for the rare disease lipodystrophy, in which the fat disappears from the face, arms and legs and accumulates around the hips and thighs. As middle-age advances, especially in the male, many people acquire a greatly increased layer of fat over the abdomen and at the same time their limbs become thin.

The internal adipose tissue has an important role in

providing protective cushions for the various viscera. The external fat acts as an insulator, conserving body heat.

Adipose tissue consists of mesenchymal connective tissue cells (adipocytes). Triglyceride is stored within these, usually as a single large droplet. The cells are supplied by a capillary network. Adipose tissue also receives nerves from the autonomic nervous system, the fibres of which appear to terminate in close relation to both cells and blood vessels.

CHEMICAL COMPOSITION

Punch biopsy through the skin, a minor procedure, provides samples of adipose tissue for analysis. Most contain about 80 to 85 per cent fat, the remainder being cell material and supporting tissue. Protein and water form about 2 and 10 per cent respectively. The results of analyses vary widely, even of samples taken from one individual, but at different sites. In obese subjects the fat content is seldom more than 90 per cent. Increased fat storage is associated with increases in both the size and number of adipocytes, but it is difficult to quantitate the changes.

The amount of cellular material in adipose tissue is not generally appreciated. Thus if a healthy man carries 10 kg of adipose tissue, of which 85 per cent is fat, he has 1.5 kg of fat-free adipose tissue. This is about the weight of his liver and contains about 200 g of protein.

Table 6.4 shows the fatty acid pattern (measured by gas-liquid chromatography) of adipose tissue obtained by needle biopsy from the buttocks of healthy men and women in London. Oleic acid was the major fatty acid and there were slightly more monounsaturated acids and less palmitic acid in women than men, making their fat softer. Patterns like these have been reported from different parts of the world. In general the human species has a characteristic pattern of fatty acids in adipose tissue, but it may be modified by diet. C12:0 and C14:0 fatty acids are 11 and 16 per cent respectively in Polynesians who consume much of their fat as coconuts[9]

Table 6.4 Mean percentage of fatty acids in subcutaneous samples of adipose tissue from healthy adults[8]

Fatty acid	Men (8)	Women (8)
12:0	0.9	0.7
14:0	4.2	3.5
14:1	1.1	1.1
15:0	0.6	0.6
16:0	23.3	20.0
16:1	10.1	10.7
18:0	4.4	3.4
18:1	48.4	53.0
18:2	7.2	7.1

while C18:2 fatty acid may be as high as 35 per cent in patients taking diets high in corn oil to reduce their plasma cholesterol.[10]

DEPOSITION OF FAT IN THE STORES

Triglycerides reaching adipose tissue in the form of chylomicrons and VLDL are hydrolysed by lipoprotein lipase at the luminal surface of the capillary endothelial cell; the free fatty acids liberated then pass across the endothelial cell into the adipose tissue cells. Endogenous heparin may have a role in this clearing of fat from the blood. Within the cells the fatty acids are again resynthesised into triglycerides. For this process to be complete an additional source of glycerol is needed. This is provided by the breakdown of carbohydrate within the cell. The deposition of fat within the cell is thus determined in part by the available carbohydrate.

Fat is also formed in adipose tissue from glucose in the blood. When fat is being laid down rapidly there is always an increase in the small amount of glycogen present in adipose tissue cells. Fat formation by adipose tissue is dependent on insulin which markedly increases the uptake of glucose by adipose tissue incubated in vitro. A failure to form fat from glucose is a characteristic feature of insulin deficiency.

Fat formation is of course dependent on the supply of nutrients provided by the diet. Under certain circumstances fat formation is greatly increased; for instance, during pregnancy it is normal for a woman to increase her fat stores by about 4 kg,[11] presumably as an insurance to meet the future demands of lactation. Other animals, notably marine mammals, lay down much bigger stores. When suckling her young the mother seal cannot feed. Lactation only lasts about two weeks and the mother is reputed to lose 90 kg of weight, mostly fat, in the process. This fat has to be deposited by the mother in advance during pregnancy. The seal is born weighing about 14 kg and after two weeks weighs about 40 kg. Spawning salmon, migratory birds, hedgehogs and other hibernating animals lay down large stores of fat, which are accurately adjusted to meet future needs for energy. More knowledge about how this extra deposition of fat is controlled to meet physiological requirements might elucidate the problem of obesity in man.

ADIPOSE TISSUE AS AN ELECTRIC BLANKET

Starving people frequently complain of feeling cold. It is easy to appreciate that the subcutaneous adipose tissue acts like a good blanket and prevents heat loss. Under certain circumstances adipose tissue may also generate heat and thus act in the manner of an electric blanket.

Mammals react to cold by muscular activity, typically by shivering, which produces heat. Heat may also be a product of cyclic chemical reactions in which no work is done. Non-shivering thermogenesis occurs when triglycerides are hydrolysed and the liberated fatty acids at once re-esterified. This cycle can proceed in **brown adipose tissue** (BAT), a specialised form of adipose tissue in which the cells contain many small droplets of lipid, numerous mitochondria and a high content of cytochrome pigments. The cycle is activated by noradrenaline and sympathetic nerve stimulation.

In most newborn mammals BAT is conspicuous, especially in the thorax around the thymus gland and in the dorsal subcutaneous fat in the neck and between the scapulas. Because in most species myelination of nerves is very incomplete at birth, heat production by shivering in response to cold is ineffective and activation of BAT is the chief mechanism for controlling body temperature in a cold environment. This has been described in newborn rabbits in a classical paper by Hull & Segall.[12] Babies in the first months of life raise their oxygen consumption markedly in response to a cold environment with no obvious increase in muscular activity.[13]

BAT persists into adult life in hedgehogs and other hibernators and is responsible for warming them up at the time of arousal; it also persists in rats and other rodents; but in most species it atrophies early in life. In adult man it is not conspicuous, but small amounts may be present. As yet there has been no systematic anatomical study in man. For many years textbooks have stated that non-shivering thermogenesis occurs in response to cold but the crucial demonstration, an increase in oxygen consumption after exposure to cold in subjects paralysed by curare and given artificial respiration is only recent.[14] A suggestion that activation of BAT may be a means of disposal of excess dietary energy and that some obese patients may lack this mechanism has received much publicity on television and in the popular press. The evidence for this is controversial (Chap. 9).

ESSENTIAL FATTY ACIDS

In 1929 a classical paper by Burr & Burr[15] showed that young rats when put on a fat-free diet continued to grow normally for up to 8 weeks, but growth then slowed and had stopped altogether by 12 weeks. A squamous dermatitis developed and was most marked over the tail. This could be prevented by adding very small amounts of fat to the diet. Subsequent work showed that a group of polyunsaturated long chain fatty acids were essential for growth and to prevent the skin condition, and these became known as essential fatty acids (EFA).

Physiologically the most important EFA is arachidonic acid (C20:4,$n-6$), but this is readily formed in the tissues from linoleic acid (C20:2,$n-6$) which is the main dietary source. EFAs are present in all lipid macromolecules but are relatively much more numerous in the storage fats of plants than of animals; most vegetable oils are therefore good dietary sources. EFAs are the predominant fatty acids in the phospholipids and cholesteryl esters that are the main component of the membranes surrounding cells and intracellular organelles such as mitochondria. The EFAs with their relative low melting points may help to make the membranes less rigid and their greater chain length increases the volume of the hydrophobic phase. These properties may explain how in EFA deficiency capillary permeability is increased and swelling of mitochondria occur. Saturated fatty acids (e.g. those in hydrogenated coconut oil) oppose the action of EFA and, if added to an EFA-deficient diet, growth stops sooner and the skin lesions develop earlier.

Deficiency in man

Most of the early work on EFA deficiency was on rats, but it was soon shown that they were an essential dietary factor for many other mammals and they are probably needed by all animal species. The demonstration of EFA deficiency in man was, however, delayed for a long time. In 1938 one volunteer male lived for six months on an experimental low fat diet, containing only about 2 g butterfat daily,[16] He remained in good health throughout and no skin lesions developed, but he lost a little weight and the linoleic and arachidonic acid content of his serum lipids fell. It can be concluded that his requirement of EFA was very small in relation to the stores in his depot fat.

In 1958 a report described how some cases of infantile eczema benefited from EFA therapy.[17] This led to large numbers of luckless young children with this disease being dieted with vegetable oil preparations rich in EFA with no apparent benefit; most of these cases would now be diagnosed as atopic dermatitis, an immunological disorder in which EFA could not be expected to be beneficial. However, Hansen's cases that responded had very low birth weight and were subsequently fed on skimmed milk, then orthodox dietary treatment for such infants. Thus they had not been able to lay down a normal store of EFA before birth and then been given a virtually EFA-free diet; hence their skin condition can be attributed to EFA-deficiency. Today great care is taken to see that the feeds of babies of very low birth weight contain all essential nutrients and EFA deficiency in infants is rare and the result of inadequate care.

In 1971 the first unequivocal case of EFA deficiency in an adult was reported.[18] The patient, a man of 44 years, had had all but 60 cm of his small bowel removed surgically. Then he was given only intravenous feeding with preparations containing no fat, and after 100 days he developed a scaly dermatitis. Several similar cases were reported in North America. A biochemical test that allows early diagnosis of EFA deficiency before the appearance of skin changes depends on a failure in production in the tissues of arachidonic acid (C20:4,$n-6$) and excess production of eicosatrienoic acid (C20:3,$n-9$) (see Fig. 6.3). As a result the relative portion of the latter in body fats rises. This can be measured in plasma lecithin and is known as the triene/tetraene ratio. In health the ratio is 0.1, rising to 1.0 in severe EFA deficiency. Using this ratio as a diagnostic criterion three patients with chronic disease of the small bowel who had been treated with low fat diets, but not given intravenous feeding were found in London.[19] These patients also had fatty degeneration of the liver, anaemia and thrombocytopenia.

Such cases can now be prevented by the intravenous feeding with EFA. Intralipid is a preparation of soya oil that contains 56 g/l of linoleic acid; its use both prevents and cures EFA deficiency. That several severe cases occurred in North America is attributable to a ban placed on Intralipid for safety reasons by the US Food and Drug Administration, whose characteristic excess of caution had discounted many years of its use without significant adverse effects in France and other European countries.

Essential fatty acids, prostaglandins and thrombosis
Research since 1975 has shown that arachidonic acid derived from the EFA linoleic acid is the precursor of prostaglandins in the tissues and that one of these, prostaglandin H_2, is readily converted into two substances, prostacylin and thromboxane A_2, the former inhibiting and the latter stimulating a part of the clotting mechanism in the blood. Figure 6.10 shows the metabolic pathways.

The first stage in the formation of a thrombus is aggregation of platelets in the blood. This is most likely to occur at the site of damage to the endothelium lining a vessel, for example an atheromatous lesion in a coronary artery. Prostacylin is formed in vascular endothelial cells from prostaglandin H_2 by the action of an endoperoxide. It is a powerful vasodilator and its main physiological function may be to promote active hyperaemia in a tissue. It is also a potent inhibitor of platelet aggregation. Thromboxane A_2 is also formed from prostaglandin H_2 in membranes of platelets. It is a vasoconstrictor and also a stimulus to platelet aggregation. Both these substances are very unstable and rapidly destroyed in the tissues. An imbalance between synthesis and destruction of these two substances may be responsible for thrombus formation. Details of these new discoveries of the formation and properties of prostacylin and thromboxane A_2 are given

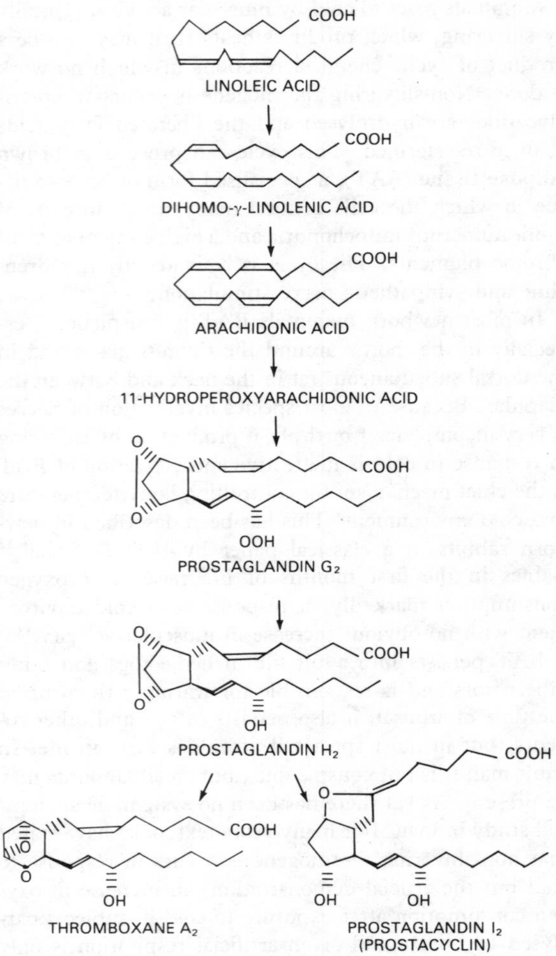

Fig. 6.10 Formation of prostacyclin and thromboxane A_2 from linoleic acid

in a review by Vane,[20] the discoverer of prostacyclin.

These substances are metabolites of $n-6$ unsaturated fatty acids of which linoleic acid is the main dietary source. In the $n-3$ class linolenic acid is the parent substance and eicosapentaenoic acid (Fig. 6.3) the derivative corresponding to arachidonic acid. Thromboxane A_3 is a metabolite of $n-3$ class but, unlike thromboxane A_2, it does not promote platelet aggregations. In most dietary fats the predominant essential fatty acids belong to the $n-6$ class, but in marine oils the $n-3$ class, especially eicosapentaenoic acid, are predominant.

There is evidence that in man marine oils, either in the diet or fed as a supplement, may alter the coagulability of the blood and thereby possibly reduce the risk of thrombus formation. In Greenland the Eskimos may eat as much as 400 g of fatty whale and seal meat daily. Their blood lipids contain a higher proportion of eicosapentaenoic acid and a lower proportion of arachidonic acid than those of Danes, and their bleeding times are nearly twice as long; they also have a low death rate from coronary thrombosis.[21,22] Sinclair, who as long ago as 1956 suggested that coronary thrombosis was related to a relative EFA deficiency,[23] took part in these studies; later he went for 100 days on a diet rigidly limited to seal and other animal food, mainly fish. He remained well on this regime but his bleeding time rose markedly.[24] Seven German men went on an experimental diet with 500–800 g of mackerel, providing 7–11 g of eicosapentaenoic acid daily. After 9 days the ratio of $C20:5,n-3/C20:4,n-6$ in plasma lipids rose from below 0.2 to 1.5 and platelet aggregation and thromboxane synthesis fell.[25] Fortunately such heroic dietary measures are not necessary, as similar effects on platelets followed after giving a daily supplement of 20 ml of a fish oil preparation to patients with ischaemic heart disease.[26] There is now a need for studies over long periods to find out whether those marine oils that are rich in $n-3$ fatty acids reduce the risk of thrombosis in susceptible persons, and also to determine whether they have any adverse effects, for example, the fat necrosis reported in young pigs.[27] A concentrated preparation of fish lipids is commercially available and known as Maxepa (Maximum Eicosa Pentaenoic Acid).

Today the role of essential fatty acids in nutrition is uncertain but exciting. Most Western diets provide from 8–15 g of essential fatty acids daily and each of us has a reserve of 0.5–1.0 kg in adipose tissue. Prostaglandins and thromboxane are active in the tissues at concentrations measured in ng/ml and the total production of prostaglandins, as assessed by the urinary excretion of the chief metabolite, is of the order of 100 μg daily. Although patients with evidence of a recent thrombosis are commonplace in hospital wards, the majority of us live and die without ever a sign of thrombus formation. If dietary deficiency of essential fatty acids is responsible for thrombus formation, as some evidence suggests may well be the case, it is difficult to relate it in quantitative terms with changes in lipid metabolism in the tissues which could lead to the event.

Further information about the biology of essential fatty acids and on the effects arising when a diet does not supply them in sufficient amounts is available in two reviews.[28,29]

Recommended intake

Overt evidence of EFA deficiency is seen only when they provide less than 1 to 2 per cent of total dietary energy, or less than 2 to 5 g of linoleic acid daily for an adult. The effects of higher intakes in reducing coagulability of the blood and in reducing plasma concentrations of cholesterol suggest that a higher intake is desirable. A recommendation[30] that people should take over 10 per cent of their dietary energy as polyunsaturated fatty acids, not all of which function as EFA, has received much support, but to implement it many people would have to alter their dietary habits greatly. The quantitative aspects of the physiological roles of EFA in the tissues are not yet sufficiently known to justify precise recommendations of requirements. Like most nutritionists, we ourselves choose our foods so that our diets provide much more linoleic acid than is needed to prevent overt signs of EFA deficiency but do not eschew all animal fats or make a fetish of vegetable oils.

DIETARY NEEDS FOR FAT

The amount of fat in diets varies greatly. In most prosperous countries fat usually contributes 35 to 45 per cent of the total energy. In some poor countries the figure is 15 per cent or even lower. It is very difficult to state what represents too much or too little fat for health. However, in all civilisations, Eastern or Western, old or new, fat has always been a necessity for the preparation of good meals. There is almost no country where a housewife can prepare the meals which she would like for her family without materials in which fat supplies at least 20 per cent of the energy. That the average figure in several countries is far below this reflects the wide prevalence of poverty. Many people cannot enjoy their traditional diet through lack of fat. In Britain in 1934–38 fat provided 38 per cent of the total energy in the diet. As a result of wartime rationing and restrictions on food this figure fell gradually and reached a minimum of 33 per cent in 1947. Thereafter it rose steadily and in 1982 was 41 per cent. This small wartime restriction of the fat intake caused much publicly voiced discontent. Many of the ailments of the time were ascribed to a shortage of fat in the diet, not only by harrassed housewives but also by some physicians. A national diet containing 33 per cent of fat certainly supplies far more fat than is necessary to meet physiological needs. Hence no conceivable physical harm could have arisen from this restriction. In retrospect it seems clear that the true explanation of the discontent was that many articles of food cooked with inadequate amounts of fat are unpalatable to traditional British tastes. In any country social requirements of fat for good living are far higher than physiological requirements for physical health. In the present state of knowledge it is difficult to state a minimum fat requirement for man. Human diets low in fat are almost always also low in other nutrients necessary for the maintenance of health. It is thus difficult to ascribe any disease arising in these conditions specifically to a deficiency of fat.

Minimal requirements for fat may indeed be very low. Mitra[31] made a study of the dietary habits of the Hos, an aboriginal tribe in Bihar, India. He investigated 250 families and found that 200 made no use of any kind of fat in their cooking. This was not due to poverty, for many of the Hos had acquired some money by collecting forest products and they visited bazaars in nearby towns where they could have purchased fats had they so wished. They did not do so because they were ignorant of the use of fats and oils in cooking; their culinary practices were limited to boiling and — very occasionally — baking. The Hos possessed cattle but used them only as beasts of burden; they drank no milk and ate no meat. The total daily fat intake of different families was estimated as varying from 2.4 to 3.8 g/head, which would provide at most 2 per cent of the total energy, but might contain 1 g or so of EFA. Although the health and nutrition of these aborigines were by no means ideal, they presented no signs or symptoms which could be attributed to fat deficiency, their general level of nutrition and physique being no worse than that of neighbouring villagers who regularly consumed vegetable oils.

High fat diets are almost always also high in energy and so — except in those physically active — lead to obesity. High fat diets are also usually associated with high plasma cholesterol and LDL concentrations and this may be a factor contributing to a variety of diseases, but this effect may be due to a low P/S ratio in the fatty acids of the diet rather than to the total amount of fat.

PRACTICAL RECOMMENDATIONS

Although scientific precision is lacking for making such recommendations, two seem sensible. First any community which wishes to feed well and in a civilised tradition (either Eastern or Western) should obtain at least 20 per cent of its energy from fat. Secondly, individuals in prosperous communities who lead sedentary lives and have reached middle age would be well advised to limit their fat intake to 35 per cent of their total energy.[32] The possible value of reducing intakes of animal fats and the use of vegetable oils in the prevention and treatment of atherosclerosis are discussed in Chapter 41.

A high fat intake is essential for very active people spending over 17 MJ(4000 kcal/day). Lumberjacks in the sub-Arctic and workers on polar expeditions often require this amount of energy and would have to spend much of their working day eating to obtain such a high energy intake solely from bulky carbohydrate sources. Fats give them the necessary energy quickly, so that they can get on with their job in the short time allotted to them.

REFERENCES

1. Hilditch T P, Williams P N 1964 The chemical composition of natural fats, 4th edn. Chapman & Hall, London.
2. Abdellatif A M M, Vles R O 1973 Pathological effects of dietary rapeseed oil in rats. Nutr Metab 15: 219
3. Valenzuela J E, Defilippi C 1981 Inhibition of gastric emptying in humans by secretin, the octapeptide of cholecystokinin and intraduodenal fat. Gastroenterology 81: 898–902
4. Havel R J, Goldstein J L, Brown M S 1980 Lipoproteins and lipid transport. In: Bondy P K, Rosenburg L E (eds) Metabolic control and disease. Saunders, Philadelphia, p 393–494
5. Lewis B 1976 The hyperlipidaemias. Clinical and laboratory practice. Blackwell, Oxford
6. Cook R P 1958 Distribution of sterols in organisms and tissues. In: Cook R P (ed) Cholesterol. Academic Press, New York, p 145–180
7. Wertheimer E, Shapiro B 1948 The physiology of adipose tissue. Physiol Rev 28: 451–464
8. Heffernan A G A 1964 Fatty acid composition of adipose tissue in normal and abnormal subjects. Am J Clin Nutr 15: 5–10
9. Shortland F B, Czochanska Z, Prior I A M 1969 Studies on fatty acid composition of adipose tissue and blood lipids of Polynesians. Am J Clin Nutr 22: 594–605
10. Albutt E C, Chance G W 1969 Plasma and adipose tissue fatty acid of diabetic children on long-term corn oil diets. J Clin Invest 48: 139–145
11. Hytten F E, Leitch I 1971 The physiology of pregnancy, 2nd edn. Blackwell, Oxford
12. Hull D, Segall M M 1965 The contribution of brown adipose tissue to heat production in the new-born rabbit. J Physiol (Lond) 181: 449–457
13. Hey E N 1969 The relation between environmental temperature and oxygen consumption in the new-born baby. J Physiol (Lond) 200: 589–603
14. Jesson K, Rabol A, Winkler K 1980 Total body and splanchnic thermogenesis in curarised man during a short exposure to to cold. Acta Anaesthesiol Scand 24: 339–344
15. Burr G O, Burr M M 1929 A new deficiency disease produced by rigid exclusion of fat from the diet. J Biol Chem 82: 345–367
16. Brown W R, Hansen A E, Burr G O, McQuarrie I 1938 Effects of prolonged use of extremely low-fat diet on an adult human subject. J Nutr 16: 511–524
17. Hansen A E, Haggard M E, Boelsche A N, Adam D J D, Wiese E F 1958 Essential fatty acids in infant nutrition: clinical manifestions of linoleic acid deficiency. J Nutr 66: 565–576
18. Collins F D, Sinclair A J, Royle J P, Coats D A, Maynard A T, Leonard R F 1971 Plasma lipids in human linoleic acid deficiency. Nutr Metab 13: 150
19. Press M, Kikuchi H, Shimoyama T, Thompson G R 1974 Diagnosis and treatment of essential fatty acid deficiency in man. Br Med J 2: 247–250
20. Vane J R 1982 Prostacylin in health and disease. Publication No. 58. Royal College of Physicians of Edinburgh
21. Dyerberg J, Bang H O 1979 Haemostatic function and platelet polyunsaturated fatty acids in Eskimos. Lancet 2: 433–435

22. Bang H O, Dyerberg J, Sinclair H M 1980 The composition of the Eskimo food in north Greenland. Am J Clin Nutr 33: 2657–2661

23. Sinclair H M 1956 Deficiency of essential fatty acids and atherosis, etcetera. Lancet 1: 381–383

24. Sinclair H M 1980 Prevention of coronary heart disease: the role of essential fatty acids. Postgrad Med J 56: 579–584

25. Siess W, Roth P, Scherer B, Kurzmann I, Böhlig B, Weber P C 1980 Platelet-membrane fatty acids, platelet aggregation, and thromboxane formation during a mackerel diet. Lancet 1: 441–444

26. Hay C R M, Durber A P, Saynor R 1982 Effect of fish oil on platelet kinetics in patients with ischaemic heart disease. Lancet 1: 1269–1272

27. Ruiter A, Jongbloed A W, van Gent C M, Dansa L H J C, Mott S H M 1978 The influence of dietary mackerel oil in the condition of organs and on blood lipid composition in the young growing pig. Am J Clin Nutr 31: 2159–2166

28. Willis A L 1981 Nutritional and pharmacological factors in eicosanoid biology. Nutr Rev 39: 289–301

29. Sinclair H M 1984 Essential fatty acids in perspective. Human Nutr Clin Nutr 38C: 245–60

30. Vergroesen A J, de Deckere E A M, ten Hoor F, Hornstra G, Houstmuller U M T 1975 In: Hawkins W W (ed) The essential fatty acids. Miles symposium. Nutrition Society of Canada, Ontario.

31. Mitre K 1942 Observations on the diet and nutritional state of an aboriginal (Hos) tribe. Indian J Med Res 30: 91–97

32. Committee on Medical Aspects of Food Policy 1984 Diet and cardiovascular disease. DHSS Report on Health and Social Subjects no 28. HMSO, London

POSTSCRIPT

A leading article on fish, fatty acids, and human health in the New England Journal of Medicine comments on three studies reported in the same issue. These raise important questions about the metabolic effects of fish fatty acids.

(Glomset J A 1985 Fish, fatty acids, and human health. N Engl J Med 312: 1253–4)

7

Alcohol

Ethyl alcohol (ethanol, C_2H_5OH) is formed in nature by the fermentation of sugar and used by man for several purposes. It may serve as a disinfectant, a drug, a food or a preservative. In classical experiments with a human calorimeter Atwater and Benedict[1] showed that the energy liberated by oxidation of ethanol can be utilised by the body and that its use replaces similar amounts of energy derived from carbohydrate and fat. As a source of fuel for the body ethanol differs from carbohydrate and fat in two important respects. First, ethanol cannot be utilised by muscle directly and is mainly metabolised in the liver. Secondly, ethanol is metabolised at a fixed rate which is unaffected by its concentration in the blood.

ABSORPTION, DISTRIBUTION AND DISPOSAL

Ethanol being soluble in both water and lipids diffuses rapidly through cell membranes and into cells. Hence an oral dose is soon absorbed from the alimentary canal, part of it from the stomach, and distributed throughout the total body water. Indeed it can be used as a measure of total body water. Thus in a 65 kg man with a total body water of 40 litres a dose of 30 g (about 4 fl. oz of whisky), given on an empty stomach, quickly raises the ethanol concentrations in all body fluids, including the blood, to about 750 mg/1; such a concentration certainly impairs judgment and may or may not lead to symptoms of intoxication. Most people are drunk at blood levels over 1500 mg/1. Absorption is delayed if alcohol is taken slowly throughout the course of a meal. Some Russians are said to prepare themselves for a drinking session of vodka with a litre of milk. Most people would have difficulty taking so much and in a study in New Zealand blood alcohol rose only marginally less when 240 ml of milk was taken before 90 ml of whisky.[2]

After absorption ethanol appears in both expired air and in urine in concentrations related directly to the blood concentration, since ethanol is not actively secreted by the lungs and kidneys but simply diffuses out from them. The amounts of ethanol disposed of in these ways is small and over 90 per cent of an ingested dose is metabolised in the liver. The rate of metabolism varies widely in individuals and ranges from 60 to 200 mg/kg an hour. The hourly rate is usually about 100 mg/kg and this means that a 65 kg man after a 30 g dose of ethanol clears his blood in about $(30 \times 1000)/(65 \times 100) = 4.6$ hours.

Metabolism in the liver

Ethanol is metabolised almost entirely in the liver. The first step is oxidation to acetaldehyde. There are two enzyme systems that may carry out this reaction.

Alcohol dehydrogenase is a non-specific enzyme present in the liver of all mammals. Its natural substrates are alcohols produced in intermediary metabolism, for example in steroid and bile acid metabolism. It also oxidises ethanol and methanol when these are ingested. The enzyme is present in the cell cytoplasm. Its co-factor is NAD; NADH is produced, and the oxidation is linked to the formation of high energy bonds in ATP.

$$CH_3CH_2OH + NAD^+ \rightarrow CH_3CHO + NADH + H^+$$
alcohol dehydrogenase

The microsomal ethanol-oxidising system (MEOS) is not present normally in liver, but may be induced by repeated ingestion of ethanol. It is included in the mixed function oxidase system which is induced by many drugs. The system is dependent on NADPH and cytochrome P-450, and catalyses the direct utilisation of molecular oxygen without formation of ATP.

$$CH_3CH_2OH + NADPH + H^+ + O_2$$
$$\rightarrow CH_3CHO + NADP + 2H_2O$$

Acetaldehyde formed by these enzymes is converted into acetyl CoA by aldehyde dehydrogenase. The acetyl CoA may then be used as a source of energy in the citric acid cycle or enter a synthetic pathway, e.g. for fatty acids or cholesterol. As the acetyl CoA can pass into the blood stream and be metabolised elsewhere, ethanol may serve as a source of energy for other tissues, including muscle. However, as the rate-limiting reaction is the formation of acetaldehyde which occurs only in the liver, the rate of clearance of ethanol alcohol from the blood cannot be increased by muscular exercise.

When, as in normal persons, ethanol is disposed of by alcohol dehydrogenase and acetaldehyde dehydrogenase, all the energy is utilised in the tissues; ethanol then spares isoenergetically the metabolism of carbohydrate and fat. When ethanol is first converted to acetaldehyde by MEOS, part of the energy liberated cannot be utilised and is dissipated directly as heat. It is not known how much ethanol has to be taken or for how long before MEOS activity is induced in man. However it is certain that part of the energy in the ethanol taken in by some heavy drinkers is not available for utilisation in the tissues.

When ethanol is oxidised by alcohol dehydrogenase, NAD is converted to NADH. The NAD may be reformed in a reaction which is coupled with the formation of lactic acid from pyruvic acid and subsequent lactic acid acidosis.

Many substances, both nutrients and drugs, e.g. caffeine, have been tested to see if they accelerate the removal of ethanol from the blood. Positive results have been obtained only with fructose. In patients with a blood ethanol over 1500 mg/l who received an intravenous infusion of 200 g of fructose (500 ml of a 40 per cent solution), the rate of ethanol clearance was 23 per cent higher than in untreated controls.[3] This effect may be due to more rapid reoxidation of $NADH_2$ by glycerate derived from fructose. If fructose is used to treat anyone in an alcoholic coma, the risk of inducing a dangerous lactic acid acidosis should be appreciated.

Two therapeutic points arise from the nature of the enzymic mechanisms for the removal of ethanol. First, methanol is far more dangerous than ethanol because the formaldehyde formed by its oxidation damages the retina irreversibly and a single dose may cause permanent blindness. As ethanol and methanol are oxidised by the same enzyme and compete for it, ethanol slows down the oxidation of methanol and the production of its toxic product. Hence ethanol should be administered to a patient who has ingested methanol. Secondly, acetaldehyde does not normally accumulate in the tissues after taking ethanol, because it is removed by acetaldehyde dehydrogenase as fast as it is formed. This enzyme can be inhibited by a drug, disulfiram (Antabuse). If after the administration of this drug a patient takes a drink he rapidly develops unpleasant symptoms, nausea, giddiness and headache, due to the accumulation of acetaldehyde in the blood. This may help a chronic alcoholic to give up drinking.

Most of the above account of enzymic mechanisms for the metabolism of alcohol has been established for a long time. The role of the MEOS system is fully discussed by Pirola and Lieber.[4] Contemporary interest is in hepatic acetaldehyde dehydrogenase.[5] The cytosol fraction of this enzyme is reduced in alcoholics and remains low after a period of abstention, unlike alcohol dehydrogenase. This may be part of an underlying genetic effect contributing to alcoholism.

INTAKE

The amount of ethanol and energy value in various alcohol beverages is given in Table 21.1 Beers, wines, fortified wines and spirits contain about 30, 100, 150 and 300 g/l, respectively. Assuming an hourly clearance rate of 100 mg/kg, a 65 kg man could in 24 hours dispose of 156 g, i.e. the ethanol in 9 pints (5.2 litres) of beer, 1.5 litres of table wine or half a bottle (0.5 litre) of whisky. This calculation provides one basis for the poster that appeared in the Paris Metro, 'Les prescription de l'Académie de Médecine; Jamais plus qu'un litre de vin par jour!' Another is the steep rise in the incidence of cirrhosis seen when daily consumption of alcohol regularly exceeds 80 g in men (less in women).

The energy content of ethanol is normally 29.7 kJ (7.1 kcal)/g. Its density is 0.794 g/ml. Allowing for a small loss, excreted directly in the urine, the energy provided by alcoholic drinks can be quickly calculated by the formula:[6]

6.7 (or 1.6) × percentage of alcohol in drink (by volume)
× fluid ounces drunk
= energy provided in kJ (or kcal)

Two 4-oz glasses of wine with an alcohol content of 12 per cent would supply

6.7 (or 1.6) × 12 × 8 = 540 kJ (or 155 kcal)

A litre of wine, containing about 100 g ethanol, provides nearly 3 MJ or 710 kcal, about half the basal metabolism for 24 hours.

Ethanol can be given in small divided doses up to this total amount to patients, if liver function is not impaired. It provides a source of energy which is readily absorbed and utilised; it is also suitable for intravenous nutrition (p. 497). Given in repeated small doses ethanol usually has a pleasant sedative effect and is not intoxicating.

Data provided by Customs and Excise indicate that in 1975 consumption of alcoholic beverages per head of population in the UK was 206 pints of beer, 11.3 pints of wine and 4.8 pints of spirits. The ethanol in these beverages accounted for 5.6 per cent of the total energy available in the national food supply. This figure has been increasing steadily and was only 3.0 per cent in 1950.

Nevertheless the United Kingdom is a relatively small consumer of alcohol. The *Encyclopaedia Britannica* gives an international league table of alcohol consumption for 1970. The data are expressed in litres of ethanol consumed each year per head of population over 15 years of age. France tops the list with 22.6 litres, followed by Italy 15.0, Austria 14.4, West Germany 13.5, Portugal 13.4, Switzerland 13.0, Spain 12.8, Australia 11.8, Hungary 11.1, Belgium 10.9, New Zealand 10.8, Czechoslovakia 10.5, USA 10.1, Denmark 8.7, Canada 8.4 and the UK and Sweden 7.2. Other countries are relatively sober, but no figure is given for the USSR. There is very little data about individual consumption in any of these countries, but in all of them there must be many people who get far more dietary energy from ethanol than from protein. One individual dietary survey of the crew of a British oil tanker sailing to the Persian Gulf showed that they took on average 13 per cent of their energy as ethanol[7] Clearly it is important to record intakes of alcoholic beverages in any dietary survey. If this is not done energy intake is likely to be underestimated, perhaps by a large amount. However, in individuals with a high intake of ethanol, part of it is likely to be oxidised by MEOS and then the energy is not all physiologically available. For such persons a figures of 22 to 25 kJ (5 to 6 kcal)/g may be appropriate for calculating the energy value of ethanol consumed.

The increasing consumption of alcohol in Britain in the 1970s has been put in historical perspective by Spring and Buss,[8] who analysed the unique records of HM Customs and Excise, which go back to 1684. Then ethanol consumption, almost all as beer, was more than double what it is today. The trend of consumption after 300 years has in general been downwards, except for a peak in the prosperous late Victorian era and a more recent but still relatively small increase in the 1970s (Fig. 7.1). Spring and Buss describe how beer has been partly replaced by spirits and wine as well as by tea and coffee and how economic and social factors and taxes have affected the consumption of different alcoholic beverages.

In taking a dietary history the number of drinks may be recorded in units. One unit is half a pint of beer, one measure of spirits, one glass of wine (4 oz) or one glass of sherry or port (2 oz). Each of these units contains 8–10 g of alcohol. A regular daily intake of not more than 4 units can be considered moderate and is unlikely to have adverse effects on health in most people.

Other constituents

There is more to beers, wines and spirits than ethanol and sugar. They contain negligible protein or vitamins except for a little nicotinic acid and less riboflavin in beer; thus they provide 'empty calories'. Some wines contain appreciable amounts of iron; 13 mg/l is an average figure for Medoc wines, and haemosiderosis can occur in people who habitually consume large quantities of certain wines or kaffir beer (see p. 222).

Associated with ethyl alcohol are congeners — higher alcohols, fused oil, etc — which are present in larger amounts in some drinks than others. Much of the discomfort of a hangover is due to the congeners rather than to ethanol itself. When the same dose of ethanol in eight different drinks was given at weekly intervals to healthy volunteers, hangovers were most distressing after brandy, then came red wine, rum, whisky, white wine and gin in descending order; after vodka and pure ethyl alcohol the subjects only suffered a little tiredness and thirst.[9]

EXCESSIVE INTAKES

Many of us take alcoholic drinks when with friends on convivial occasions or to reduce feelings of shyness, stress or fatigue. Such **social drinking** in moderation has no adverse effect on physical health, and most social drinkers consider it a psychological benefit. However, a social drinker is exposed to two hazards. First, they may go on binges and, secondly, they can become dependent on alcohol, having to take large amounts every day. They have then become an alcoholic. Women tolerate repeated large intakes much less well than men.

A binge may last several hours and involve very large intakes of ethanol, up to 500 g, with very little food. The blood concentration rises to a high figure and there are gross signs of intoxication, the liver removes the ethanol at the usual slow hourly rate of about 100 mg/kg, and it may take two or more days after drinking has ceased to clear the blood. Then, provided the binger has not driven a car or got otherwise involved with the police, or developed acute gastric erosion or hypoglycaemia, he may be little the worse for the episode. If the binges are not repeated too frequently, general health and nutrition remain good. Regular weekend bingers run a risk of developing pancreatitis.

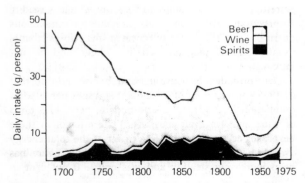

Fig. 7.1 Average daily intakes of alcohol from beer, wine and spirits in Britain from 1684 to 1975. Calculated from the records of HM Customs and Excise

Alcoholism

An alcoholic is a person who cannot stop drinking when there is good reason for doing so. They may need a shot in the morning to start the day. Tolerance of the drug increases and consumption may rise to two to three bottles of wine or more than one bottle of spirits a day; thus the daily intake of ethanol is more than a normal liver can metabolise. In regular heavy drinkers the liver clears ethanol from the blood more rapidly than normal and the brain is more tolerant of its effects. Such persons may seldom show signs of intoxication, but never be completely sober.

In almost all alcoholics, family life and personal relationships are disturbed. Though they may retain their job, their competence is greatly reduced. Many, especially in the professional and managerial classes, keep up their position because they have the support of long-suffering wives or colleagues.

Some alcoholics retain their physical health surprisingly well for many years and may appear well nourished. Others become malnourished. Because of their social and financial problems, feeding arrangements are usually unsatisfactory. Appetite is poor, sometimes as a result of a chronic gastritis induced by their drug. As a result they may be in a state of partial starvation or develop signs of deficiency of one or more specific nutrients. Impairment of judgment and coordination from intoxication make alcoholics liable to trauma; poor nutritional and social status may increase their susceptibility to infections. Any of these illnesses may necessitate admission to hospital.

Removal of the supply of alcohol may precipitate in about two days **delirium tremens**, characterised by mania, hallucinations and tremor. This acute withdrawal syndrome occurs when blood alcohol approaches zero in a person who has become habituated to having alcohol constantly in his blood.

Alcoholics are at greater risk than other persons of developing cirrhosis of the liver (p. 448), peripheral neuropathy (p. 315), Wernicke's encephalopathy (p. 316), carcinoma of the oesophagus and stomach (p. 568), pancreatitis (p. 456) and cardiomyopathy (p. 369). To what extent each of these conditions is directly due to the toxic action of ethanol or the indirect effect of deficiencies of nutrients in a poor diet is discussed in the appropriate section of the book.

There are no reliable figures for the prevalence of alcoholism in any country. Various indices, like hospital admission rates for alcoholism and death rates from cirrhosis of the liver, only show the tip of the iceberg. The mortality rates of men who are heavy drinkers are much higher than normal both in Britain[10] and in Sweden.[11] Although the physical aspects of the disease are usually easily recognised, its social and economic manifestations are often overlooked. Many alcoholics do not recognise that they are ill. In Europe and North America the abuse of alcohol by middle-aged persons is a much more serious problem than the use of marihuana, LSD or heroin by young people, but it receives less publicity.

The outlook for an alcoholic who continues drinking is inevitably progressive social, psychological and physical deterioration. If they give up the use of the drug and becomes a total abstainer, in a large proportion of cases there is a marked improvement in health and often a return to normal life. Total abstinence is advised and an ex-alcoholic should not risk social drinking. It can seldom be achieved by the patient's unaided effort and expert professional case and supervision is needed, often at first in an institution.

There are no specific nutritional measures during rehabilitation. All patients need a good mixed diet and may require vitamin supplements for a period to build up depleted reserves.

REFERENCES

1. Atwater W O, Benedict F G 1902 An experimental enquiry regarding the nutritive value of alcohol. Mem Natl Acad Sci 8: 231–397
2. Janus E D, Sharman J R 1972 Milk and blood alcohol New Z Med J 75: 339–42
3. Brown S S, Forrest J A H, Roscoe P 1972 A controlled trial of fructose in the treatment of acute alcoholic intoxication. Lancet 2: 898–900
4. Pirola R C, Lieber C S 1976 Hypothesis: energy wastage in alcoholism and drug abuse: the possible role of hepatic microsomal enzymes. Am J Clin Nutr 29: 90–93
5. Thomas M, Halsall S, Peters T J 1982 Role of hepatic aldehyde dehydrogenase in alcoholism: demonstration of a persistent reduction of cytosolic activity in abstaining patients. Lancet 2: 1057–9

6. Gastineau C F 1976 Nutrition note: alcohol and calories. Mayo Clin Proc 51: 88
7. Eddy T P, Wheeler E F, Stock A L 1971 Nutritional and environmental studies on an ocean-going oil tanker. Br J Indus Med 28: 342–52
8. Spring J, Buss D H 1977 Three centuries of alcohol in the British diet. Nature 270: 567–72
9. Pawan G LS 1973 Alcoholic drinks and hangover effects. Proc Nutr Soc 32: 15A
10. Marmot G M, Rose G, Shipley M J, Thomas B J 1981 Alcohol and mortality: a U-shaped curve. Lancet 1: 580–3
11. Petersson B, Krantz P, Kristensson H, Trell E, Sternby N H 1982 Alcohol-related death: a major contributor to mortality in urban middle-aged men. Lancet 2: 1088–90

8

Fuels of the Tissues

The energy supplied in the diet is mostly in the form of complex macromolecules of carbohydrate, protein and fat. This energy cannot be utilised by the tissues until these have been broken down into smaller molecules, monosaccharides, free fatty acids (FFA) and amino acids (AA). An account of the energy present in foods and of the small losses that occur in making it available to the tissues has been given in Chapter 3. Chapters 4, 5 and 6 describe how the digestive processes break down the large molecules into smaller ones which can be transported in the blood and may be utilised by the tissues. The tissues are not dependent on a continuous supply of energy from the digestive tract. Much of the energy that is absorbed, often the greater part, is not used directly but only after the smaller molecules have been converted back into macromolecules, glycogen, triglycerides and proteins. These then form stores or reserves that can be mobilised to meet the continuing but varying needs of the tissues for energy. Ethyl alcohol is an additional source of energy, as described in Chapter 7. In the present chapter the fuels of the tissues are discussed. Table 8.1 lists substances that circulate in the blood stream and which the tissues can utilise directly. These fuels are utilised in varying proportions dependent on the dietary supply and the needs of individual tissues. The metabolic mixture is regulated by feedback mechanisms dependent on concentrations of the fuels in the blood and is controlled mainly by endocrine secretions.

The immediate sources of energy for metabolism in cell tissues are compounds with high energy phosphate bonds. Of these, adenosine triphosphate (ATP) is the most important. It is formed in cells from adenosine diphosphate (ADP) and inorganic phosphate (P_i), and the energy needed for its formation comes from the fuels in oxidative reactions which are coupled with phosphorylation. The hydrolysis of ATP to ADP and P_i provides the cells with the energy required for mechanical work, organic syntheses and for the ionic pumps which maintain the gradient of electrolytes between intracellular and extracellular fluids.

Table 8.1 Substances which circulate in the blood and are utilised by tissues as a source of energy

Fuel	Source
Prime fuels	Dietary carbohydrate
Glucose	Glycogen stores
	Gluconeogenesis in the liver from certain amino acids and glycerol
Free fatty acids	Triglycerides in adipose tissue
Secondary fuels	Free fatty acids and certain
Ketones*	amino acids; formed in the liver
Lactic acid	Formed in tissues from glucose when the supply of oxygen is inadequate
Glycerol	Triglycerides
Additional fuels	Dietary
Ethyl alcohol	Dietary carbohydrate
Fructose	Dietary carbohydrate
Galactose	

* Ketones is a collective term for acetoacetic acid and its derivatives 3-hydroxybutyric acid and acetone.

High-energy phosphate compounds

ATP is not the only phosphorylated intermediate involved in the transfer of energy. Phosphocreatine, which serves as an energy-rich store in muscle, can be used to regenerate ATP. Guanosine triphosphate (GTP) is generated in the citric acid cycle at the stage where succinate is formed from succinyl-CoA; it then readily donates a phosphate group to ADP to form ATP. GTP is involved in gluconeogenesis by phosphorylating malate and in the synthesis of DNA and RNA. Glycerol phosphate is required in its phosphorylated form both for the conversion of fatty acids to triglycerides and for the shuttle of electrons across mitochondrial membranes. There are a range of energy-rich phosphorylated intermediates in the flow of energy within a cell, but ATP forms a link between them and, for simplicity, we can think of food energy as being converted into ATP energy.

The free energy change ($\triangle$ G) for the oxidation of glucose to CO_2 and water is -2870 kJ mol^{-1} (-686 kcal mol^{-1}). In cells the oxidation is linked with the formation of ATP from ADP and P_i, a reaction for which $\triangle G$ is + 36.8 kJ mol⁻¹. Oxidation of 1 mol of glucose usually leads to the formation of 36 mol ATP, in which 36 × 36.8 (1385) kJ are made available for use by the cells. This is just under half the value of $\triangle G$ for the total oxidation, the remainder of the energy being dissipated as heat. This thermodynamic efficiency of conversion compares favourably with that for the use of fuels in combustion engines. When the ATP is hydrolysed to ADP, this energy is utilised either for work or for synthesis of new materials and ultimately dissipated as heat.

Production of ATP

Figure 8.1 shows the various stages in the breakdown of glucose at which ATP is produced. Detailed descriptions of these metabolic pathways and those for fatty acid and amino acid oxidation can be obtained from textbooks of biochemistry, e.g. McGilvery and Goldstein.[1] Glucose occurs in the cytoplasm of cells; pyruvate undergoes oxidative decarboxylation to form acetyl-CoA, which is then oxidised in the citric acid cycle by enzymes present in mitochondria. The greater part of the transduction of energy in glucose to ATP occurs in the citric acid

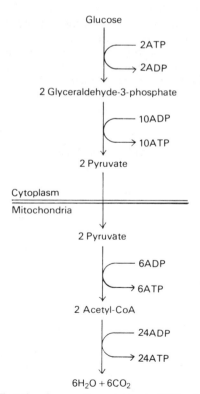

Fig. 8.1 Transfer of energy from glucose to ATP under aerobic condition. Net production of ATP is 36 mol from 1 mol of glucose

cycle, but some occurs during glycolysis and this is important because it does not depend on oxygen.

Glycolysis

The first stage in glycolysis is the conversion of one molecule of glucose to two molecules of glyceraldehyde-3-phosphate (GAP). This requires two molecules of ATP. Under aerobic condition the conversion of 2 GAP to two pyruvate molecules produces 8 ATP molecules, so that there is a net yield of 6 ATP from the conversion of glucose to pyruvate. Anaerobic glycolysis is the only source of energy for the ionic pumps in red blood corpuscles which do not contain mitochondria and is also a main source in cells of the renal tubules. Cells of malignant tumours also get most of their energy by aerobic glycolysis.

Anaerobic glycolysis. Under anaerobic conditions pyruvate is reduced to lactate, and this utilises six molecules of ATP for two molecules of pyruvate. Hence when one molecule of glucose is converted to lactate, the net yield of ATP is only two molecules. For this reason much more glucose has to be utilised to provide a given amount of energy to a tissue under anaerobic conditions than when it is supplied with oxygen. Lactate diffuses out of anaerobic tissues into the blood stream whence it is taken up by the liver and converted back into glucose (**the Cori cycle**). It may also be taken up by other tissues and serve as a fuel for them. In health, anaerobic conditions occur only in muscle during moderately severe exercise (p. 85). In a fit person lactate begins to appear in the blood when oxygen consumption rises above 1.5 l/min, i.e. brisk walking at 4.5 miles/hour or over. In heavy exercise blood lactate rises rapidly because production in muscle greatly exceeds the liver's capacity for uptake and gluconeogenesis in the Cori cycle. Unless we are physically very active, only a very small part of our daily energy is utilised anaerobically.

In pathological conditions where the supply of oxygen to a tissue is reduced, anaerobic glycolysis is an important additional source of energy. In this respect it is unique, as metabolism of both free fatty acids (FFA) and amino acids (AA) is dependent on oxidations. Disorders of the circulation, either local or generalised, reduce the supply of oxygenated blood to a tissue and so may make it dependent on anaerobic glycolysis. Lactate then diffuses into the blood stream and may cause a metabolic acidosis. This commonly accompanies acute circulatory failure, e.g. in shock after a severe haemorrhage or a coronary thrombosis. Severe burns are a special case because regenerating cells, which form the granulomatous mass in a healing wound, have a high need for energy and, as the blood supply has inevitably been damaged by the burn, they depend on anaerobic glycolysis. The glucose for this has to be provided from the liver by gluconeogenesis from either lactate (the Cori cycle) or amino acids. These considerations help to explain the rapid weight loss that often occurs in patients with severe burns.

Oxidations

Of the 36 molecules of ATP that may be formed from the breakdown of one molecule of glucose, 24 arise from the oxidation of two molecules of acetyl-CoA in the citric acid cycle. Most of the energy in FFA is also transduced in the cycle. Thus one molecule of palmitic acid can yield 129 molecules of ATP, of which 96 arise in the oxidation of eight molecules of acetyl-CoA; the corresponding figures for other fatty acids differ slightly (see Table 8.2) and depend on the chain length and degree of unsaturation of each acid. Amino acids after deamination are also oxidised in the cycle, but the intermediary metabolism and the point of entry into the cycle (Fig. 8.2) of individual acids varies greatly.

OVERALL PRODUCTION OF ATP IN THE HUMAN BODY

Table 8.2 shows how the carbohydrate, fat, protein and ethanol in a diet which provides 10.8 MJ might generate 142 moles of ATP. The energy equivalence of ATP under the conditions found in the body is uncertain and not quite the same as the standard free energy but may be taken as 33 kJ (7.8 kcal) mol^{-1}. On this basis a man who is in energy balance on a diet providing 10.8 MJ converts about 4.5 MJ, or 44 per cent of the dietary

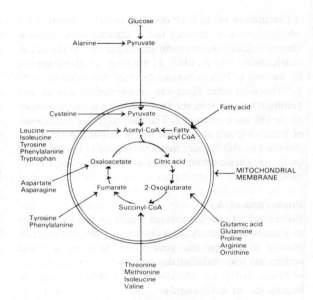

Fig. 8.2 Points of entry of derivatives of dietary carbohydrate, fat and protein into the enzyme systems of the citric acid cycle situated in the mitochondria of cells

energy into ATP energy, the remainder appearing directly as heat. The ATP produced varies a little with the exact fatty acid composition of the diet and the nature of the carbohydrate also affects the yield. The energy conversion of protein hydrolysis and oxidation depends on the AA composition of the protein and about 30 per cent of the protein energy is excreted as urea.

Table 8.2 Estimated daily production of ATP from the energy ingested by a subject on a Western diet

Food eaten	Amount		Energy content		ATP generated in moles per mol	
	g	mmol	kJ/g	total kJ	substrate	total
Carbohydrate as glucose (mol wt 180)	300	1667	16	4 800	36	60.0
Fat as triglyceride (mol wt av. 861.5)	100	116	37	3 700		
yielding on hydrolysis						
Glycerol (mol wt 92)	10.7	116			20	2.3
Fatty acids						
saturated, e.g. palmitic acid (mol wt 254)	22.1	87			129	11.2
monounsaturated, e.g. oleic acid (mol wt 282)	49.1	174			144	25.1
polyunsaturated, e.g. linoleic acid (mol wt 280)	24.4	87			142	12.4	51.0
Protein as amino acid (mol wt av. 110)	80	727	17	1 360		
Oxidation in deamination to urea					1.4	
as glucose		288			10.4	
as 3-hydroxybutyric acid		145			3.7	
as acetoacetate		61			1.4	16.9
Alcohol as ethyl alcohol (mol wt 46)	35	761	29	1 020	18	13.7
				10 800		141.6

The production of ATP does not proceed at a constant rate but varies in response to the demand for energy by the cells. The concentration of ATP in the cell fluid is small, amounting to about 1 mmol kg^{-1} in tissues such as the liver or brain, but can be as high as 6 mmol kg^{-1} in skeletal muscle. Hence an adult may have only 200 millimoles of ATP in the body, despite a production of about 140 moles each day. The ATP pool is turning over extremely rapidly and for the whole body would only last about a minute; rapidly metabolising tissues such as the brain may only have enough ATP for 2 to 3 seconds. This dependence on a continuous supply of fuel and oxygen for the maintenance of brain tissues accounts for the almost instantaneous loss of consciousness when the blood supply to the brain stops and the rapid irreversible damage which occurs after 2 minutes when the small amount of oxygen and glucose in the cerebral blood stream has been exhausted.

Regulation of ATP supply

The need for a continuous supply of ATP demands that its production is geared closely to energy requirements of the cells. This integration of supply and use depends mainly on the ATP/ADP ratio within the cell. Under resting conditions, in metabolically active tissues such as the liver it is held at about 2 with the low concentration of ADP limiting oxidation of fuels until the work output of the cell rises and converts more ATP to ADP. In muscle the ratio is 20 and this markedly inhibits the rate of glycolysis. The low [ADP] also affects the type of fuel consumed by the cell since the lower the [ADP] the greater the likelihood of FFA being oxidised in preference to glucose. This relationship holds in part because oxidation of NADH in mitochondria depends on three steps requiring ADP; as [ADP] falls NADH oxidation is reduced, [NADH] rises and therefore [NAD^+] falls. This fall limits glycolysis at the step from glyceraldehyde-3-phosphate to diphosphoglycerate (the first intermediary en route to pyruvate) and also conversion of pyruvate to acetyl-CoA. During the oxidation of FFA to acetyl-CoA half the electrons bypass the NADH step and are transferred to flavoproteins, which are more powerful reducing agents than NAD^+ and less affected by ADP. Thus resting muscles consume predominantly FFA and no glucose; [ATP] is high, [ADP] low and [NADH] high. Most other tissues at rest also consume FFA since the ATP/ADP ratio is sufficiently high to limit glycolysis.

Organs and tissues increase their demand for glucose as energy output increases. This is readily seen in exercising muscle which, despite continued oxidation of FFA, increases its consumption of glucose as [ATP] falls. In unusual circumstances, when the demand for glucose cannot be met, e.g. in patients with burns, life is threatened. Then not only is Cori cycle activity high

but, as [ADP] falls, glucose oxidation is increased and thereby reduces [NADH] as much as is compatible with the supply of oxygen. Thus the balance of ADP and ATP has a key role in determining not only the rate of oxidation of fuels by cells but even the type of fuel used. Inorganic phosphate (P_i) does not exert a regulatory role since [P_1] is about 10 mmol l^{-1} (20 times that of ADP) and so does not usually limit rephosphorylation of ADP.

Assimilation

Energy is needed for the digestion and absorption of nutrients. Carbohydrates, fats and protein are broken down by hydrolytic reactions that do not require energy, but energy is needed to synthesise the enzymes present in the secretions of the alimentary tract. Sugars and amino acids need to be actively transported across the intestinal mucosa; the cost of transport for sugars is about 2.5 per cent of their energy content, but for amino acids may be more expensive if the γ-glutamyl cycle is involved; absorption of lipids does not require energy. Gastric and pancreatic digestion are unlikely to utilise more than 5 per cent of ingested energy, since the rise in energy expenditure in response to a meal varies from 10 to 20 per cent of the energy ingested, and this includes metabolic costs involved in the distribution and storage of the fuels.

Storage

Glucose

Glucose is stored as glycogen in the liver at a small cost since only 1 mole of ATP is needed for 1 mole of glucose. When liver glycogen is used as a reserve to provide glucose for the rest of the body, the energy cost doubles since glucose must then be reformed for transport to the tissues. When glucose is stored as fat the energy cost is much greater since the fatty acids have to be synthesised and then esterified with glycerol phosphate derived from glucose. The overall equation for the synthesis of tripalmitate from glucose is

$$4.5 \text{ glucose} + 4O_2 + 5(\text{ADP} + P_i) \rightarrow \text{palmitate} + 11 \text{ CO}_2 + 5 \text{ ATP}$$

It is an oxidation with a very high respiratory quotient and in the tissues is coupled with the net formation of about 18 moles of ATP. Subsequent oxidation of the palmitate produces only 129 moles of ATP compared with 162 which can be derived from the 4.5 moles of glucose by direct oxidation. Thus the storage of glucose as fat involves the loss of 20 per cent of the ATP equivalents of glucose. The intermediary steps in the synthesis of palmitate from glucose are numerous and details of their complex energetics are given by McGilvery and Goldstein.[1]

Triglyceride

The storage of dietary fat as triglyceride (TG) is much less costly than that of dietary carbohydrate since the energy cost of the repeated hydrolysis and re-esterification is small. For re-esterification a fatty acid has to be converted to its coenzyme-A derivative at the cost of two high-energy phosphate bonds. Thus in the epithelium of the small intestine the recombination of two fatty acids with a monoglyceride requires 4 ATP. In adipose tissue 2 ATP are needed to form glycerol phosphate from glucose and 6 ATP to esterify it with three fatty acids. Thus a total of only 12 ATP are required for the esterifications needed to convert a dietary into a storage triglyceride. A total of 437 ATP can be provided by the oxidation of the triglyceride. The additional energy needed for the synthesis of lipoprotein carriers is minute so that the overall cost of fat storage is only about 3 per cent of the total energy ingested as fat.

Amino acids

The energy cost of storing amino acids is greater than that of dietary fat since approximately four energy-rich phosphate bonds are needed for each peptide bond synthesised. The cost of this depends on the source of the ATP used but, if it comes from direct oxidation of glucose with the generation of 36 mol ATP/mol glucose, then the storage of 1 gram of tissues protein would cost 2.9 kJ, approximately 17 per cent of the protein's metabolisable energy. This cost does not include the energy involved in the synthesis of the nucleotides needed for synthesis of the peptide bonds and this may require an additional 10 per cent of energy. The energy needed for AA transport into cells may be much higher but the cost is uncertain since only some amino acids are actively transported into cells. Nevertheless the cost of storing AA as protein is substantially higher than that of storing carbohydrate as glycogen or fat as TG.

ENERGETIC DIFFERENCES IN SUBSTRATE OXIDATION

The loss of energy available from glucose when it is first stored as fat has already been explained, but the route of substrate oxidation may also affect the yield of ATP. This is illustrated by comparing the energy derived from FFA oxidised via ketone body production rather than directly in the citric acid cycle.

Energetics of fatty acid and ketone body metabolism

Fatty acid oxidation starts with successive cleavages from the chain of two carbon units of acetyl-CoA. In the liver a small part of the acetyl-CoA is normally converted to acetoacetic acid. Acetoacetic acid together with its derivatives 3-hydroxybutyric acid and acetone, collectively known as ketone bodies, enter the blood and serve as fuel for other tissues.

Table 8.2 gives a figure of 51 mol ATP generated from 100 g of dietary fat. This was calculated on the assumption that all of the fatty acids underwent cleavage into two carbon units. If the fatty acids were broken down into acetoacetate before oxidation, net production of ATP would be 49 mol. Taking the energy equivalence of ATP as 33 kJ mol^{-1} and the total energy of the triglyceride as 3700 kJ, the efficiencies of conversion in direct oxidation of fatty acids and in oxidation via ketones are 45 and 43 per cent respectively. The corresponding figure in the utilisation of glucose given in Table 8.2 is 43 per cent. All of these calculations are too uncertain to allow precise comparisons, but they do show that the thermodynamic efficiency of the formation of ATP is high and substantially the same whether glucose, FFA or acetoacetate is the primary fuel.

The state of metabolism may affect the distribution of different fuels between tissues. Thus in starvation peripheral utilisation of fuels changes and ketone body production plays a crucial role in providing energy to the brain. The mechanisms and control of ketone body production are set out later.

If the liver generates 3-hydroxybutyrate from acetoacetate, this deprives it of a NAD-linked step for energy production; but energy becomes available in the peripheral tissues from the oxidation of 3-hydroxybutyrate back to acetoacetate. Hence there is some advantage in the transfer of additional energy from the liver to the peripheral tissues in the form of 3-hydroxybutyrate rather than acetoacetate. If 80 per cent of the ketones produced are 3-hydroxybutyrate (i.e. a 3-hydroxybutyrate/acetoacetate ratio of 4:1), then there is a shift in energy distribution; less becomes available to the liver during the preliminary oxidation to ketone bodies and more is available from the ketone bodies going to peripheral tissues. This extra energy more than compensates for a 3 per cent loss of energy in regenerating acetyl-CoA from ketone bodies in the periphery. This loss is, as we shall see, a small price to pay for the chance of producing for the brain a fuel which is derived from fat rather than from protein.

Substrate cycling

The body expends energy not only on the distribution and storage of fuels but also in making these fuels readily available for use by different tissues. The main fuel of the tissues is FFA, which is continually released into the blood stream from the fat depots and circulates at concentrations which permit rapid uptake by the tissues. Not all the fatty acid entering the circulation is removed for immediate oxidation; most is recycled by the liver and returned as TG in very low density lipoproteins to

Table 8.3 The energetic significance of substrate cycling

Cycle	ATP used (mol/ mol substrate)	Substrate ATP energy lost (per cent)	Estimated substrate turnover (mmol/day)	Energy used in turnover (kJ /day)
Glucose-lactate (Cori cycle)	4	11.1	200	65
Triglyceride adipose tissue re-esterification	8	1.8	150	45
Protein turnover	4	17.2	2500	804
Glucose 6-phosphate-glycogen	1	2.8	2000	161

the adipose tissue for release once more as FFA and glycerol. This process provides in the blood a continuous supply of fatty acids which can be boosted by lipolysis when the demand for energy increases. The continuous recycling of fuel, however, imposes an additional energy cost, of about 40–50 kJ/day (Table 8.3). A rather higher cost of about 65 kJ may be involved in the Cori cycle where approximately 36 g glucose recycles from lactate in those tissues which have to rely on glycolysis for their fuel supply. These two substrate cycles are inexpensive but they play a crucial role in the distribution of fuel to the tissues.

A more expensive process is the turnover of about 275 g protein which is synthesised and degraded each day throughout the day. This turnover is crucial since the continuous release of amino acids allows cells in the liver and other tissues to respond to sudden metabolic demands by synthesising enzymes in amounts appropriate for the new requirements. Thus an inflow of excess AA leads to the rapid induction of enzyme responsible for catabolising AA. An inflow of carbohydrate also leads to rapid induction of enzymes for glycogen storage and glucose oxidation. The presence of an infection may cause reprogramming of protein synthesis in the liver with the secretion of fibrinogen, transferrin and many glycoproteins but a fall in synthesis of albumin. Turnover of muscle protein is also essential to allow the body to respond to fasting and to maintain prolonged exercise, since muscle protein is a source of AA for gluconeogenesis in the liver. In severe exercise the rate of efflux of AA from muscle corresponds to the rate of protein breakdown and matches the large increase in the hepatic requirements for glucose (see below).

Turnover of protein is an integral part of the body's capacity to adjust its fuel supply to needs imposed by the environment, and the cost of protein turnover is substantial. Table 8.3 includes only the cost of synthesising the peptide bonds of 275 g protein a day and excludes any cost associated with protein breakdown, ribosomal synthesis or AA transport and recycling. If the cost of AA recycling is high, then the cost of protein turnover rises and may account for over 25 per cent of the resting metabolic rate.

Energy has to be provided at varying rates for many different metabolic processes; of these, the most expensive is probably the maintenance of the electrochemical gradients across cell membranes by the energy-demanding sodium pumps. The cost of sodium pumping is difficult to estimate but it may be as much as 50 per cent of the resting metabolic rate.

Two cycles are present in the early stages of glucose metabolism. The conversion of glucose to glucose 6-phosphate by hexokinase utilises ATP and it is reversed by glucose 6-phosphatase. Similarly the conversion of fructose 6-phosphate to fructose 1,6-diphosphosphate utilises ATP and is reversed by hexose diphosphatase. Both these cycles appear to accomplish nothing and all the energy from the breakdown of ATP is dissipated as heat. Hence they have been called **futile cycles**. They may be present either as a flaw in biological design or as a subtle form of control of metabolic processes. Hexokinase is inhibited by some substances lower down on the glycolytic pathway; a fall in concentration of one of these might increase the rate of cycling and so lower ATP/ADP ratio in the cell. In this way the activity of the cycle could be a factor in controlling the rate of oxidation of glucose.

The amount of energy expended in these continuously operating substrate cycles is uncertain and difficult to measure. They are ways in which the body can change its rate of fuel combustion without changing its work output. How much any of these cycles contributes to the variability in the resting metabolic rate of different individuals and of one individual from day to day is unknown.

FLOW OF ENERGY BETWEEN ORGANS

Quantitative estimates of the utilisation of different fuels by the different organs of man and of the flux of fuels between organs depend on measurements of blood flow and of differences in arterial and venous concentrations of the fuels. Until techniques were available for catheterising the veins draining the principal organs of the human body and so obtaining repeated samples of venous blood, conclusions had to be drawn from animal experiments. Although the same fuels are used by all higher animals there are marked species differences in the mixtures used under differing circumstances. Catheterisation of large veins requires a meticulous technique, experience and, for physiological studies, a supply of willing volunteers. Much of what follows is derived from catheterisation studies carried out since 1970.

Glucose absorption and distribution

A normal meal containing about 100 g starch is absorbed over a 2–3 hour period. During this time the liver extracts about 50 g of the glucose, having quickly shut down its own production of glucose from AA. Insulin concentration rises in the portal vein in response to rises in blood glucose and amino acids and secretion of gut hormones. The liver stores a large part of the glucose as glycogen, uses the glucose as its own fuel and allows additional glucose to pass into the main circulation where it supplies both the brain and muscle with energy and restocks the muscle with glycogen. Glucose uptake by the liver differs from that in peripheral tissues in that the liver has both a specific transport system for glucose with a large capacity and a kinase for phosphorylating glucose with a low affinity for glucose. This ensures that phosphorylation responds to the concentration of glucose without the need for insulin. Thus the rate of glucose extraction by the liver responds to the concentration of glucose in the portal blood without the need for insulin or other hormonal controls. In contrast, muscle and adipose tissue have a rate-limiting step at the transport stage of uptake and this is insulin-sensitive; once uptake has occured the hexokinase has a very high affinity for glucose so it is rapidly stored as glycogen or metabolised. The peripheral distribution of glucose is thus finely controlled by the plasma insulin.

Storage of glucose as fat

Most of the glucose stored after a starchy meal may be converted at first to glycogen rather than fat. Glycogen is, however, a temporary store whereas fat is a long-term store of energy. Some glucose is converted to fat in both the liver and adipose tissue. The relative importance of these two organs for fat synthesis in man is uncertain, but the liver is probably the dominant site. Glucose contributes to TG synthesis both by providing the glycerol for the esterification of FFA and by being converted into FFA. The three-carbon unit glycerol phosphate needed for the re-esterification is generated in both the liver and fat cells during glycolysis, but in the liver glycerol phosphate can also be synthesised from glycerol itself. The glycerokinase needed for this conversion is absent or of low activity in fat cells. Glucose generates FFA via the two-carbon unit, acetyl-CoA. When [ATP] is high, ac-

tivity of the citric acid cycle is limited and so accumulating acetyl-CoA is then used for synthesising FFA rather than for oxidation. After a meal glucose flowing directly to the fat cells is used mainly for synthesis of glycerol phosphate rather than FFA, but in the liver it is used for synthesis of FFA and subsequent conversion to TG.

Triglyceride distribution after a meal

Digestion and absorption of fat is much slower than that of starch and protein because fat delays gastric emptying and enters the circulation mainly through lymphatic channels as chylomicrons (p. 61). After a meal containing fat, chylomicrons may enter the blood faster than they are removed and the plasma is then opalescent. Lymphatic absorption delays the influx of fat into the blood and channels it past the liver to peripheral tissues. Chylomicron TG is broken down in adipose tissue, muscle and liver, where FFA and glycerol are released by lipoprotein lipase. The FFA is re-esterified with newly formed glycerol phosphate and then stored as TG. Thus there are two hydrolyses with re-esterification before dietary fatty acids are stored, but this is accomplished with little loss of energy.

Most of the ingested fat is probably taken up from the blood by adipose tissue but some is removed by the liver and muscle. This distribution depends on lipoprotein lipase activity in the tissues. Activity varies during the day, and after a meal rises in adipose tissue and falls in muscle. Between meals this is reversed so that muscle then becomes the preferential site of storage of TG. Control of this cyclical variation directs the energy flow from one organ to another. The maximum clearance rate of TG is about 15.5 g h⁻¹ in a 70 kg man.[2] Thus after a meal containing 50 g of fat it takes more than three hours to clear the blood. Clearance is rarely at a maximum since the rate is proportional to plasma [TG]. At the normal fasting value of 1 mmol l⁻¹ clearance is 7 g h⁻¹ and reaches the maximum rate when the concentration exceeds 5 mmol l⁻¹. Hence after a meal clearance of fat from the blood proceeds slowly and it is necessary for a patient to fast for 12 hours before his basal plasma [TG] can be measured.

The daily turnover of TG in the fat depots is about 140 g, or 6 g h⁻¹,[2] and greater than the normal dietary intake.[2] Hence the fatty acid composition of adipose tissue TG is only slowly affected by the type of fat in the diet. But when American subjects were given diets in which corn oil or linseed oil was the only source of fat, after a year or more the proportion of polyunsaturated fatty acids in their adipose tissue fatty acids rose markedly.[3] When coconut oil is the major source of dietary fat, medium chain fatty acids never reach the fat stores since being water-soluble they pass in the portal blood to the liver, where they are oxidised.

Amino acid absorption and distribution

Proteins like starch are rapidly digested in the duodenum and jejunum and after a meal concentrations of amino acids and glucose rise in the blood at about the same time. Once absorbed, AAs pass to the liver in both plasma and red blood cells. About 25 per cent of the alanine and an appreciable proportion of serine, threonine, methionine, leucine, isoleucine and tyrosine are carried from one tissue to another in red blood cells.

After a meal concentrations of all amino acids rise in the systemic circulation but the greatest increases are in leucine, isoleucine and valine. The liver extracts from the portal blood most of the excess AA, but relatively less of those with branched chains, valine, leucine and isoleucine; these, which contribute 20 per cent of the weight of non-collagen proteins, account for 50 per cent of the increased output of AA from the liver. Within 30 min of ingesting a protein-rich meal there is an appreciable increase in the uptake of valine, leucine and isoleucine by muscles and a smaller increase of other AAs.

Glutamate and aspartate form about 20 per cent of ingested protein but do not appear in appreciable quantity in the portal blood because they are rapidly converted to alanine in the intestine. Alanine has a key role in integrating protein and carbohydrate metabolism since it is readily extracted by the liver, provides the carbon skeleton for gluconeogenesis and carries nitrogen for excretion as urea.

Studies of protein absorption and AA distribution in normal man showed that the greater part of the branched chain AAs reach the systemic circulation and are not oxidised in the liver.[4] After a meal of 47 g of beef protein containing about 10 g of branched chain AAs, only 1 g of these passed each hour into the systemic circulation, but plasma [AA] was raised by 50–100 per cent for up to 8 hours. This prolonged output into the systemic circulation is not due to slow digestion of proteins; the intestines and to a lesser extent the liver moderate the flow of AAs to the rest of the body. As the AA supply to the liver increases there is a surge in the synthesis of export proteins, including albumin, and breakdown of hepatic cell proteins is slowed. The result is an increase in the mass of hepatic protein. Subsequent rapid turnover of both gut and liver proteins maintains the outflow of AAs to the periphery for several hours.

Dietary amino acids mix in the blood with those recycling from the tissues; the total daily turnover of AA is about 350 g, i.e. about 15 g h^{-1}. Entry of AA from the intestine may double their flow in the portal blood for 3 hours following a meal. After entry into liver and muscle cells a proportion of the AAs is metabolised to provide either substrate for gluconeogenesis or energy in the citric acid cycle (Fig. 8.2). Over 24 hours the rate of oxidation of AA by the tissues approximately matches the amount ingested but there is a surge in oxidation after each meal. The liver is the major site for oxidation and the only site for generating urea.

Although the liver acts as a temporary store of AAs in the form of protein, the main long-term store is in muscle. Muscle protein increases during the day, as AAs flow from the gut, and AAs are released when there is a need for gluconeogenesis. This cyclical net movement of AA does not involve alanine, which passes to the liver from muscle even in the postprandial phase. Alanine is then serving as a nitrogen carrier, the alanine carbon coming from blood glucose and muscle glycogen, and the nitrogen from the oxidation of other AA especially the branched chain ones. The alanine carbon is used once more for glucose synthesis in the liver. In this way a **glucose-alanine cycle** transfers nitrogen from muscles to the liver.

Plasma alanine concentrations remain unchanged after a meal despite the large inflow of alanine from three sources, ingested alanine, intestinal metabolism of glutamate and aspartate, and the glucose-alanine cycle. Therefore net synthesis of glucose from alanine is unlikely after a meal. Muscle nitrogen can be transferred to 2-oxoglutarate to form glutamate and to pyruvate to form alanine, but the latter is the major carrier. Glutamine serves as a nitrogen source for AA production in the kidneys, particularly when ketosis develops during starvation (see below) and there is a need for ammonium production to balance the ketones excreted in the urine. Blood glutamine concentrations after a meal may actually fall, especially in red blood cells,[5] reflecting the dominance of the pyruvate-alanine transamination systems in muscle.

The sequence of changes in AA metabolism after a meal is closely regulated by hormones. There is an increase in both plasma insulin and glucagon concentrations. Insulin stimulates the uptake of AA by peripheral tissues and glucagon ensures that the liver continues to put out the glucose needed by the brain. Without glucagon the insulin-stimulated liver would immediately inhibit glucose output and this would be a serious problem after a low carbohydrate meal. An increase in both glucagon and insulin secretion is therefore necessary after ingesting protein.[6]

Much information about amino acid metabolism, both in health and disease, can be found in a review by Abumrad and Miller.[7]

FUEL RESERVES IN MAN

When food is unavailable the body has to rely on its own stores of fuel; these are summarised in Table 8.4. The store of carbohydrate is small and mostly as glycogen in muscle and liver. Muscle glycogen is usually considered to be available for energy production in the muscle only.

Table 8.4 Available fuel reserves in an adult man (modified from Cahill)[8]

Tissue (weight in kg)	Glucose and glycogen		Mobilisable proteins		Triglycerides	
	g	kJ	g	kJ	g	kJ
Blood (10)	15	255	100	1 700	5	185
Liver (1)	100	1700	100	1 700	50	1 850
Intestines (1)	0	0	100	1 020	0	0
Brain (1.4)	2	34	40	680	0	0
Muscle (30)	300	5100	4000	68 000	600	22 200
Adipose tissue (15)	20	340	300	5 100	12 000	444 000
Skin, lung, spleen (4)	13	220	240	4 080	40	1 480
Total	450	7649	5000	82 280	12 695	469 715

In muscle it plays a key role in maintaining a subject's capacity to remain active (see below). When fasting, the crucial provision of glucose for the brain depends initially on liver glycogen and, after 12 to 18 hours, on synthesis of glucose by both the liver and kidneys. The glucose is derived at first mainly from AA coming from muscle protein. The total mass of body protein amounts to about 12 kg in a 65 kg man and of this about 50 per cent is in muscle. Not all of this protein is available, however, since studies in Jamaica have shown that collagen proteins, constituting 25 per cent of muscle and total body proteins, are not depleted in severe malnutrition.[9] The non-collagen protein in muscle, in the form of myofibrillar proteins and the enzymes of the muscle sarcoplasm, can provide under extreme condition up to 4 kg of protein for gluconeogenesis (see also p. 79). Other tissues, including the liver, intestine, skin, brain and adipose tissue, lose protein as starvation develops and contribute about another 1 kg of amino acids. However, simple starvation, unaccompanied by infection or the provision of a protein-deficient diet, seems to deplete muscle protein selectively, and muscles bear the brunt of a poor energy intake. In time, other tissues contribute their amino acids for glucose production, but this is clinically less obvious in patients with marasmus.

Triglycerides are stored without water, unlike protein or glycogen, which are deposited within cells with five times their weight of water. TG have a lower specific gravity, but twice the energy value of protein and carbohydrate. This high energy density makes fat a highly economical fuel for storing for use in times when food is scare. On the other hand, when excess fat is deposited in obesity, large energy stores accumulate for only a moderate increase in weight.

Transition of fuel supplies during fasting
As glucose absorption slows after a carbohydrate meal, plasma insulin falls and plasma glucagon rises. This altered glucagon/insulin ratio ensures continued hepatic

glucose output of glucose for the brain and other glycolytic tissues. Glucagon stimulates gluconeogenesis as well as hepatic glucose output but insulin also has an important role; as plasma insulin falls, glycogen synthesis declines and glycogenolysis increases, and when blood glucose also falls muscle and adipose tissue reduce their uptake of glucose. At the same time the hormone-sensitive lipase in adipocytes is activated and increases FFA output rapidly, so providing fuel for most of the body's tissues. If the interval between a meal is longer than 12 hours, e.g. in those who do not eat breakfast, then liver glycogen reserves become depleted and additional glucose has to be produced, mainly from AA.

Muscle glycogen falls progressively during the first five days of starvation, and may contribute 140 g of glucose to the brain during this crucial period when hepatic glycogen reserves are exhausted and circulating blood ketones are still at too low a concentration to supply the brain.[10] Muscle glycogen could yield 25–30 g glucose for the brain each day during early starvation by generating pyruvate which enters the Cori cycle. If fasting continues, blood glucose falls slightly, plasma insulin falls markedly and plasma glucagon rises. The lower insulin leads to decreased uptake of AA by muscle, but a lower rate of protein synthesis increases their concentration within muscle. Then there is an efflux of AA from muscle to the liver. In starvation, muscle changes from a state of net synthesis to one of net catabolism of protein.

Muscle is the major reserve of AA in the body but the amounts of each AA released from muscle do not reflect their proportions in the muscle proteins. Catabolism releases mainly alanine and glutamine (Table 8.5). Alanine is the preferred substrate for gluconeogenesis in the liver, and glutamine contributes to gluconeogenesis in the kidneys as starvation progresses. The carbon skeletons of the alanine and glutamine effluxing from muscle are derived from several sources: some pyruvate and 2-oxoglutarate is derived from AA metabolism and can then be transaminated to alanine and glutamate. Ad-

Table 8.5 The pattern of release of some amino acids from the human forearm and their contribution to muscle protein (data from Ruderman)[10]

Amino acid	Percentage of all amino acids released	Percentage of muscle protein
Alanine	28.0	6.4
Glutamine	23.0	6.6
Lysine	8.7	12.6
Glycine	7.9	4.0
Histidine	2.8	3.1
Valine	2.8	3.5
Leucine	2.0	6.2
Isoleucine	2.0	3.9
Aspartate	0	7.0
Glutamate	−7.9 (net uptake)	11.7

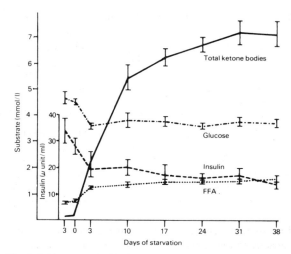

Fig. 8.3 Concentrations of blood total ketone bodies and glucose, serum insulin and plasma free fatty acids (FFA) in 37 obese subjects during prolonged starvation. Values are means ± SE. (Owen and Richard)[11]

ditional glutamate is taken up by muscle from blood and used for glutamine synthesis.

In prolonged starvation the flow of alanine from muscle falls and this is reflected in a steady decline in urea synthesis and excretion. Glutamine output tends to persist since, after 10 days of fasting, ammonia becomes the main nitrogen product in the urine.

Ketone body production

The increases in plasma FFA and glucagon during fasting both promote synthesis of ketone bodies from fatty acids in the liver. These are used by most tissues, including the brain, as fuels and reduce the need for glucose. Initially production of ketones is small, but, as fasting continues, it rises progressively until they become the substrate with the highest concentration in the blood (Fig. 8.3). After comparing the concentration of the different circulating fuels, it is not surprising that ketones come to dominate the fuel economy of some tissues during starvation. The change from glucose oxidation to FFA oxidation with the addition of ketone body metabolism occurs within a matter of three days of fasting and subsequently further changes occur until ketone bodies become the major fuel for the brain (Table 8.6).

For many years the state of ketosis was considered undesirable because severe ketosis develops rapidly in a poorly controlled diabetic and may cause a fatal acidosis. Yet the development of ketosis in a normal subject is a beneficial physiological response to both starvation and a low carbohydrate diet. In these circum-

Table 8.6 Fuel supplies and utilisation during a short fast and prolonged starvation (adapted from Cahill)[8]

Tissue	Fuel	Fasting 3 days (g/day)	Starvation 6 weeks (g/day)
Energy supplies from			
Adipose tissue	FFA	180	180
Liver	Ketones	150	150
	Glucose	150	80
	Glycerol	20	20
	Lactate + pyruvate	40	40
	Amino acids	70	20
Muscle	Glycogen	20	0
	Amino acids	75	20
Energy utilised by			
Brain	Glucose	100	40
	Ketones	50	100
Liver	Amino acids	70	20
Muscle	Amino acids	75	20
Other tissues	Glucose	50	40
	FFA	30	30
	Ketones	100	50

stances ketogenesis is controlled and does not become excessive. The advantages of switching to metabolise ketones rather than free fatty acids are many. First, the transformation of FFA into ketone bodies produces a fuel which can be used by the brain; without this source of energy the brain would need 120 g of glucose daily and this would have to be provided by tissue proteins. The demand for glucose would soon put an intolerable strain on the tissues and the survival time in starvation would be severely limited. Another advantage of ketones is that they readily pass across cell membranes without the need for specific transport systems or binding proteins, as required for glucose and FFA. Being water-soluble the ketones readily reach a concentration where they are oxidised in preference to glucose without the need for additional regulatory mechanisms at the cell level. Ketones also reduce the rate of oxidation of branched chain AA in muscle and thereby reduce the efflux and loss of AA from muscle.

Ketone body synthesis

The three ketone bodies acetoacetate, 3-hydroxybutyrate and acetone are generated from acetyl-CoA only in the liver, but the reactions are readily reversible in all tissues, where the acetyl-CoA can be oxidised in the citric acid cycle. The generation of NADH during fatty acid oxidation also favours the conversion of acetoacetate to 3-hydroxybutyrate. The reverse of these reactions predominates in the peripheral tissues because of the continuous use of acetyl-CoA by the citric acid cycle.

Normally only acetoacetate and 3-hydroxybutyrate are measured in blood; acetone is readily formed by decarboxylation of acetoacetate and is excreted in the breath where it is responsible for the characteristically sweet odour of a ketotic subject. The ratio 3-hydroxybutyrate to acetoacetate varies in part because of changes in the ratio of NAD/NADH in the liver. In the blood the ratio may rise from 2 up to 5 or even 10 under conditions of rapid fatty acid oxidation. The reduction of acetoacetate to 3-hydroxybutyrate has the advantage of transferring reducing equivalents from the liver to the peripheral tissues where they yield an additional three molecules of ATP for each molecule of 3-hydroxybutyrate oxidised.

Two major events seem to determine the development of ketosis. First there is a rise in plasma [FFA]. This occurs when plasma insulin falls and provides the liver with the substrate for ketogenesis. An acute rise in plasma [FFA], however, produces only a small increase in ketone body production in well-fed individual,[12] so that a further major change in liver metabolism must occur to ensure that FFA is converted to ketone bodies rather than re-esterified to TG. Ketogenesis is activated by an increase in the ratio of plasma glucagon to insulin but the relative importance of glucagon and insulin is uncertain. The control of ketogenesis seems to be exerted at the carnitine acyltranferase step and may depend on the availability of carnitine. This step is responsible for the movement of FFA from the cytoplasm into the mitochondria and, if this is blocked, FFA is re-esterified in the cytoplasm and do not enter the mitochondria for oxidation to acetyl-CoA.[13] Subsequent conversion of acetyl-CoA to acetoacetate appears to be increased if liver glycogen stores are low, as would be expected during starvation, but the mechanism accounting for this effect is uncertain. Once the liver has been primed for ketogenesis then the availability of FFA determines the rate of ketone body production; a fall in plasma [FFA] in response to a glucose-induced release of insulin leads to a very rapid fall in the concentration of ketone bodies in blood.

Changes in ketone body metabolism during starvation

The concentration of ketone bodies in the blood reflects the balance between their rate of production in the liver and their rate of oxidation in the three principal tissues metabolising ketones, brain, kidneys and muscles. The rate of oxidation is proportional to blood concentrations during the first few days of starvation as ketone body concentrations rise from the normal value of 0.5 to 1 up to 3 mmol l^{-1}. At this stage they are oxidised at near maximal rate and provide 30–40 per cent of total energy requirements. Ketones contribute about 10 per cent of the energy for muscle after an overnight fast but this proportion rises to 50–80 per cent after 3–7 days of starvation.[11]

The increase in plasma ketones during prolonged fasting results from a reversal in the progressive changeover in muscle from FFA to ketone body oxidation. After 6 weeks of fasting perhaps only 10 per cent of the muscle's fuel comes from ketone bodies but the brain and kidneys are now almost totally dependent on ketones. Muscle continues to take up acetoacetate but releases 3-hydroxybutyrate, this reductive step signifying the increased consumption of fatty acids and the ready availability of NADH within muscle. Thus the late switch in fuel consumption by muscle boosts and the supply of ketones for the brain and so reduces the need for muscle protein to be used for gluconeogenesis. This extraordinary survival mechanism is futher helped by the effect of both ketones and FFA in reducing oxidation of branched chain AA in muscle. Conservation of these, particularly leucine, enhances synthesis of muscle proteins and tends to limit the rate of muscle protein breakdown.

The complex physiological roles of ketone bodies are discussed fully in a review by Robinson and Williamson.[14]

Urinary ketone bodies

Normally from 1–3 mmol of ketones are excreted in the

urine daily, about 1 per cent of the amount produced. At low plasma concentrations the greater part of the urinary ketones is acetoacetate, but when plasma 3-hydroxybutyrate rises to about 2 mmol l^{-1} its urinary output begins to increase exponentially.[15] When in starvation plasma ketones reach 5 mmol l^{-1} the predominant urinary ketone is 3-hydroxybutyrate. The ability of the kidneys to conserve ketones is nutritionally significant, since an equimolar amout of amino acids is needed to generate ammonia to balance the excretion of acid; 3-hydroxybutyric acid is a weaker acid than acetoacetic acid. During starvation this action of the kidneys protects the body from being depleted of up to 8 g of nitrogen daily.

Fuel supply during exercise

Measurements of arteriovenous glucose differences show that at rest muscle uses very little glucose. The total amount for all the muscles of an adult man is only 20–25 mg/min, about one quarter of the rate at which the brain uses glucose. The RQ of resting muscle is close to 0.7, reflecting the dominance of fat as a fuel.[16] Most of this is in the form of FFA and is derived from endogenous triglyceride within the muscles. When exercise starts, the immediate source of additional energy is ATP but, as we have seen, the supplies are very small; they can be generated rapidly from the small store of phosphocreatine which provides enough energy to run for about 100–200 metres. This supply is also soon exhausted and then glycolysis of muscle glycogen provides energy anaerobically but only in small amounts. If work is to continue, the muscles must soon shift to oxidation of a mixture of carbohydrate and fat.

Glucose is the major fuel at first during muscular work but as exercise proceeds there is a greater proportion of fat in the mixture. Yet carbohydrate still provides 40 per cent of the fuel, even if heavy exercise is continued for nearly 3 hours (Table 8.7). Studies of samples of blood obtained from the femoral artery and vein confirm this finding and show also the proportions of the fuel provided by blood glucose and muscle glycogen (Fig. 8.4). More details of the fuels used by muscles are given in a report of a seminar at Yale University.[17]

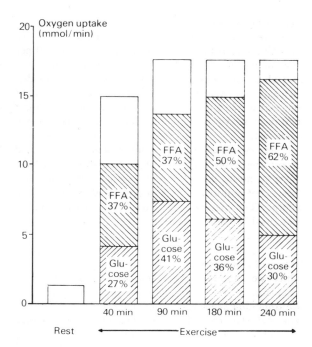

Fig. 8.4 Uptake of oxygen and substrates by the legs during prolonged exercise. Hatched areas represent the proportion of total oxygen uptake contributed by oxidation of FFA and blood glucose. Open portions indicate oxidation of non-bloodborne fuels (muscle glycogen and intramuscular lipids). (From Ahlberg et al)[20]

During continued exercise exogenous glucose for the muscles has to come from glycogen stores in the liver and, once these are depleted, from AA catabolism and gluconeogenesis. Alanine output from muscle increases rapidly in response to exercise and in proportion to the intensity of the work. At the same time branched chain AAs pass into the muscles for oxidation and their concentration in blood falls. With the increased need for glucose production the hepatic extraction of alanine goes up progressively from 40 to 90 per cent. During the exercise the brain continues to demand its usual supply of glucose so the additional demand for glucose by the muscle must be met at the cost of muscle proteins. All these changes are associated with a fall in plasma insulin.

A failure of carbohydrate supply may in some circumstances be a limiting factor in exercise. For example, in a study of the effect of prolonged exercise and starvation on secretion of growth hormone,[18] two medical students offered to walk 28 miles in 7 hours with no breakfast. One of them after 23 miles collapsed suddenly; he was given oral glucose and after 30 min he had recovered fully. Measurements of his respiratory exchanges indicated that he had utilised 150 g of carbohydrate during the walk and the proportion of carbohydrate in his metabolic mixture had fallen from 65 to 35 per cent. The

Table 8.7 Relative proportions of carbohydrate and fat in the fuel mixture during prolonged heavy work with energy expenditure at 900–1000 W (Christensen and Hansen)[19]

Time (min)	Respiratory Quotient	Percentage of energy from Carbohydrate	Fat
0–30	0.910	69	31
30–60	0.890	63	37
60–90	0.875	57	43
90–120	0.855	50	50
120–150	0.840	45	55
150–162	0.825	40	60

other student, who completed the walk without apparent difficulty, was estimated to have utilised only 125 g of carbohydrate and at the end of the walk only 10 per cent of his metabolic mixture was carbohydrate. The three highly trained Scandinavian athletes who provided the data for Table 8.7 may be calculated to have used on average 325 g of carbohydrate during their prolonged period of heavy exercise, but they had probably eaten breakfast.

These estimates of the amount of carbohydrates used in prolonged physical work indicate a need for a large store of muscle glycogen before taking part in any athletic event requiring a high or prolonged expenditure of energy. The dietary means to ensure such a store are described in Chapter 63.

Recovery from exercise

Once exercise has stopped, muscles continue to extract circulating glucose at three to four times the resting rate for some time, and this presumably helps to restore their stock of glycogen. However, the rate is far less than during severe exercise, and so gluconeogenesis in the liver drops to about twice the pre-exercise rate. Much of this glucose comes via the Cori cycle from circulating lactate which increases to concentrations of 10 mmol l^{-1} towards the end of exhausting exercise.

At the end of exercise insulin concentrations rapidly increase, particularly in the portal blood. This increase may depend on a fall in catecholamine output as well as a tendency for blood glucose to rise as glucose extraction by muscle falls. Despite the rise in plasma insulin, plasma glucagon remains high for some time and this may help to replenish hepatic glycogen stores.

The changes in amino acid metabolism are equally rapid after exercise. During the exercise period muscle is in negative nitrogen balance and urea production rates may rise by 60 per cent in trained athletes. After exercise, however, the increasing insulin aids uptake of amino acids from protein supplied in the next meal and athletes usually remain in nitrogen balance on the day of an event. In this way the well-known absence of a marked negative nitrogen balance during heavy and prolonged exercise is explained.

REFERENCES

1. McGilvery R W, Goldstein G 1981 Biochemistry, a functional approach. Saunders, Philadelphia
2. Kissebah A H, Adams P W, Wynn V 1974 Plasma free fatty acid and triglycerides transport kinetics in man. Clin Sci 47: 259–78
3. Hirsch J 1965 Fatty acid patterns in human adipose tissues. In: Handbook of physiology, section 5: Adipose tissue. American Physiological Society, Washington, p 181–9
4. Wahren J, Felig P, Hagenfeldt J 1976 Effect of protein ingestion on splanchnic and leg metabolism in normal man and in patients with diabetes mellitus. J Clin Invest 57: 987–99
5. Aoki T T, Brennan M F, Muller W A, et al 1976 Amino acid levels across normal forearm muscles and splanchnic bed after a protein meal. Am J Clin Nutr 29: 340–50
6. Felig P, Wahren J, Sherwin R, Hendler R 1976 Insulin, glucagon, and stomatostatin in normal physiology and diabetes mellitus. Diabetes 25: 1091–9
7. Abumrad N N, Miller B 1983 The physiologic and nutritional significance of plasma-free amino acid levels. J Parenter Nutr 7: 163–70
8. Cahill G F 1976 Starvation in man. Clin Endocrinol Metab 5–2: 397
9. Picou E, Halliday D, Garrow J S 1966 Total body protein, collagen and non-protein collagen in infantile protein malnutrition. Clin Sci 30: 345–51
10. Ruderman N B 1975 Muscle amino acid metabolism and gluconeogenesis. Annu Rev Med 26: 245–58
11. Owen O E, Reichard G A 1975 Ketone body metabolism in normal, obese and diabetic subjects. Isr J Med 11: 560–70
12. Grey N J, Karl I, Kipnis D M 1975 Physiologic mechanisms in the development of starvation ketosis in man. Diabetes 24: 10–16
13. McGarry J D, Foster D W 1977 Hormonal control of ketogenesis. Arch Intern Med 137: 495–501
14. Robinson A M, Williamson D M 1980 Physiological roles of ketone bodies as substrates and as signals in mammalian tissues. Physiol Rev 60: 143–87
15. Johnson R E, Passmore R 1961 Multiple factors in experimental human ketosis. Arch Intern Med 107: 43–50
16. Andres R, Cader G, Zierler K L 1956 The quantitatively minor role of carbohydrates in oxidative metabolism by skeletal muscle in the basal state. J Clin Invest 35: 671–82
17. Felig P, Wahren J 1975 Full homeostatis in exercise. N Engl J Med 293: 1078–84
18. Fonseka C C, Hunter W M, Passmore R 1965 The effect of long-continued exercise on plasma growth hormone levels in human adults. J Physiol (Lond) 182: 26–27P
19. Christensen E H, Hansen O 1939 Untersuchunger uber die Verbrennungsborgänge bei langdauernder, schewer Muskelarbeit. Skand Arch Physiol 81: 152–9
20. Ahlberg G, Felig P, Hagenfeldt L, Hendler R, Wahren J 1974 Substrate turnover during prolonged exercise in man. J Clin Invest 53: 1080–90

Energy Balance and the Regulation of Body Weight

For large numbers of people the regulation of body weight is a continuing struggle throughout life. Others maintain their weight within narrow limits and without effort. This is a familiar observation but scientific explanation of this difference, despite much study, remains elusive.

The chief factor determining body weight in adults is the size of the energy store in the form of fat, and this depends on the balance between the energy (E) balance

$$\triangle E_S = \pm (E_I - E_O)$$

where S is the store, mainly in the adipose tissue, I is the intake in the food and O is the output of which the main variable is the amount of physical activity. The use of mathematical symbols emphasises that the balance is constrained by the laws of thermodynamics within which all exchanges of energy in living matter operate.

The balance is also determined in part by the mind and especially by the various appetites. These were defined in 1855 by Alexander Bain,[1] an Aberdeen philosopher, who was one of the first to adopt a vigorous scientific approach to psychology.

> The appetites commonly recognised are a select class of volitional sensations and feelings; and circumscribed by the following property — namely they are the craving produced by the recurring wants and necessities of our bodily or organic life . . . sleep, exercise, repose, thirst, hunger and sex are the appetites most universally present throughout the animal tribes.

Satisfaction of these appetites affects the energy balance. Psychological factors are probably more often responsible for prolonged upsets of the balance with consequent large losses or gains in weight than are disturbances of the underlying physiological control mechanism — at least in prosperous communities with an assured supply of food.

The physiological mechanism regulates the energy balance through controlling inputs and outputs of energy from centres in the central nervous system in a manner similar in many ways to the mechanisms that regulate body temperature, blood pressure and plasma osmolality.

Technical factors

Experimental study of the energy balance is made difficult by a number of technical constraints. First $\triangle E_S$ can be measured with precision only in groups of animals by carcass analysis. In man it is nearly always necessary to rely on changes in body weight which may be due to losses or gains in either fat or water. The methods available for measuring body fat (Chap. 2) are not precise enough to determine the nature of a gain or loss of weight occurring in as few days on an experimental regime. A change in weight of 1 kg, if entirely due to fat, is $\triangle E_S$ 37 MJ but, if entirely due to water, $\triangle E_S$ is 0. The difference is the equivalent of at least 3 days normal food intake.

Both E_I and E_O can be measured with an accuracy of about ± 1 per cent on a subject in a human calorimeter, but this is not a normal life and experiments rarely last more than one week. Measurements of E_I and E_O can be carried out on subjects living an almost normal life and for longer periods, but even with the most conscientious subjects and competent collecting, and analysis of data, the error is larger; also the effect of any single error in either collection or analysis is cumulative. The longer an experiment is continued in order to increase the accuracy of the value of $\triangle E_S$, the greater will be the error in $(E_I - E_O)$. In practice, it is very difficult to get an accurate measurement of E_O in a man or woman leading a normal life over a long period.

ACCURACY AND TIME-SCALE OF THE REGULATION

Anyone who gets on the scales each morning after emptying the bladder, but before breakfast, finds variations in weight from day to day. In a careful study on young women in New Zealand[2] a gain or loss of more than 0.5 kg each day was found in 13 per cent of the daily weighings and of more than 1.0 kg in nearly 2 per cent. A gain or loss of as much as 2 kg is unusual except in association with the cyclical changes in a woman's water balance during the menstrual cycle. The daily changes are not cumulative; they compensate one another and reflect primarily changes in water balance from day to day and have a standard deviation of about 0.5 per cent of body weight.[3]

Nan Taggart of Aberdeen provided a good example of how appetite can regulate food intake to maintain the body weight accurately over a week, but not on a day-to-day basis. For 11 consecutive weeks she weighed every item of food that she ate.[4] During this period she also weighed herself accurately under standard conditions each morning, except on Sundays when she did not go to the laboratory. She did not analyse her results until all the figures were collected. She was surprised to find that her average intake of food on Monday to Friday provided 9.6 MJ/day; whereas on Saturdays it provided 10.8 MJ/day and on Sundays 12.8 MJ/day. During the weekdays she lost on average 480 g which she regained at the weekend. Until the results had been analysed she did not realise that she ate more at the weekends, and at no time was she conscious of undue hunger or repletion. It would appear that during the first five days of the week she was about 2.9 MJ deficient and this was responsible for the loss of weight. Yet she was not hungry on Friday night, nor was she aware that she ate much more on Sundays than on other days.

A deficit of 2.9 MJ is the equivalent of one meal. An examination of daily records of energy intake and expenditure[5] suggests that some people may be either in energy excess or deficit by as much as three good meals before an adjustment of food intake is made.

Measurements of the food intake of a group of Edinburgh students who undertook a period of five days of hard exercise between two periods of artificially restricted sedentary life, showed that in none of the students did the food intake change abruptly with the changes in energy expenditure.[6] During this experiment one of the subjects developed mumps, which restricted

his food intake for four days. Figure 9.1 shows that for this subject over a period of 13 days, energy intake equalled energy expenditure despite large daily fluctuations in the energy balance.

On a larger time-scale, the weights of 1277 men and 1690 women were recorded every two years over 18 years in a study of health at Framingham, Massachusetts.[7] For both sexes the average of the difference between the highest and lowest weight of each individual was 21.2 lb, just under 10 kg. In only seven was it less than 5 lb. Clearly in most of us, weight varies substantially over the years, but in some it stays remarkably constant. In 1930, as an undergraduate, R.P..had a tail-coat made to enable him to attend a cousin's 21st birthday party. He still wears the coat occasionally and it still fits. Since the coat was made, he has eaten more than 20 tons of food, enough to fill two or three lorries, and his weight has never varied by more than 2.5 kg. A contemporary who has slowly acquired by middle-age a modest spread amounting to some 10 kg has not been a glutton. The energy equivalent of adipose tissue gained is about 26 kJ/g, so his total dietary excess is 260 MJ. If this was spread over 20 years, it amounts to only about 35 kJ, or 8 kcal, a day.

Slow changes in weight may indicate changes in lean tissue as well as in fat. With ageing, the amount of lean tissue declines even when body weight stays the same. Conversely, a footballer training for a new season may lose weight as his body fat content falls, but this decrease is minimised by an increase in muscle mass as training progresses. Overeating, however, leads to an increase in weight as both lean tissue and fat are deposited.

CONTROL CENTRES IN THE BRAIN

That there are areas in the brain that affect the energy balance was suggested when Fröhlich in 1901 described the case of a 14-year-old boy in Vienna who had rapidly become obese; he had symptoms of a tumour localised at the base of the brain, but no evidence of disturbance of the endocrine function of the pituitary gland. Obesity has also been reported as a consequence of a head injury with damage to the base of the skull but this, like Fröhlich's syndrome is rare.

Experimental study followed the introduction of stereotactic instruments for making localised lesions in the brain. At Yale in 1948 Brobeck[8] showed that destruction of the medial hypothalmic nuclei in rats was followed by overeating (hyperphagia) and obesity. Lesions of the lateral nuclei often lead to hypophagia but this may be only temporary. These findings were soon repeated in many species, including primates.

These nuclei have been considered to operate as sa-

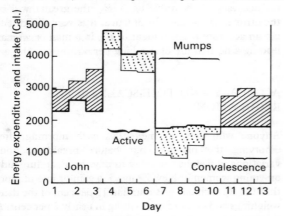

Fig. 9.1 Energy balance of a young man. (—) Daily energy intake, (—) daily energy expenditure, ▨ excess intake over expenditure, ▨ excess expenditure over intake

tiety and feeding centres respectively, but this is over-simplification. The effect of damage to these centres may be slight unless adjacent axons in nerve pathways from lower parts of the brain are also damaged.

The nature of these pathways has been studied in rats by observing the effect on feeding behaviour of injecting through cannulas permanently implanted into specific areas in the hypothalamic region chemical neurotransmitters. These pharmacological experiments indicate that there are both α– and β-adrenoreceptors and also dopamine receptors on neurones in the hypothalamus which are activated by nerve impulses in pathways from the midbrain and medulla. Thus the neuronal regulatory mechanism is probably widespread in the brain and not confined to small discrete areas, as earlier experiments had suggested. Details are given in a review by Bray & York.[9]

Much research is now undertaken that attempts to relate biochemical changes in the brain with behavioural activities, such as feeding. The catecholamines and other amines such as 5-hydroxytryptamine and histamine are distributed unevenly in the brain with high concentrations in some areas, especially the hypothalamus. These concentrations and also those of amino acids may be determined in part by dietary factors. Many biologically active peptides, such as the endomorphins and the gut hormones, are also present in brain and concentrated at specific sites. At the time of writing there is no clear picture of how any of these active substances determine behaviour and other factors that regulate the energy balance, but one may well emerge soon. Two reviews[10,11] give summaries of the large and growing literature on this subject.

INPUTS TO THE CONTROL CENTRES

Nervous stimuli

A hungry man can sometimes feel his stomach contracting. If a small balloon attached to a catheter is swallowed and attached to a manometer, contractions of the stomach can be recorded in most of us just before a meal and cease when food is taken. These contractions may be presumed to signal that the stomach is empty and probably play a role in initiating feeding. However, this signal is not essential and a dog whose stomach has been completely denervated feeds normally. In man the gastric nerves are cut extensively in many operations on the stomach and the vagus nerve is often cut to reduce acid secretion in patients with peptic ulcer. Usually, none of these procedures affect food intake.

Chemical stimuli

A fall in blood glucose, as after a small dose of insulin, causes hunger and the cessation of eating after a meal is associated with a rise in blood glucose. However, since a diabetic may be ravenously hungry when his blood sugar is high, this cannot be a direct cause of satiety. In 1953 Mayer[12] showed that hunger and satiety were associated with small and high differences between glucose concentrations in arterial and venous blood respectively, and suggested that satiety was due to a high insulin-dependent rate of transport of glucose into cells in the hypothalamus. An analogue of glucose, 2-deoxyglucose, which enters the cells but is not metabolised, promotes feeding. It is presumed that it blocks intracellular glucose receptors which otherwise would be signaling satiety. As the inhibitory effect of the analogue is increased when it is injected into the portal vein, glucose receptors may also be present in the liver. The effect on the liver is abolished by vagotomy. Glucose receptors may therefore pass information via the vagus to the brain about a fall in glucose supply to the liver arising from a fall in blood glucose or in liver blood flow or perhaps in hepatic glycogen. How important these peripheral receptors are in comparison with central receptors is uncertain.[13]

After a meal a rise in blood glucose is associated with a fall in free fatty acids (FFA) in the blood and during starvation concentration of FFA rises. Sensations of hunger and satiety are closely associated with blood FFA which may well be a signal determining feeding behaviour.

Biogenic amines, active peptides and amino acids may also have effects on feeding behaviour, but, as indicated previously, their roles are at present ill-defined.

Thermal stimuli

When we are cold we often feel hungry and on a very hot day appetite may be markedly depressed. Central mechanisms for regulation of body temperature are situated in the hypothalamus close to the feeding and satiety centres. In 1948 Brobeck[14] showed that the amount of food eaten by rats was closely related to the temperature at which the animal house was maintained, and suggested that we eat to keep warm. Civilised man protects himself against changes in temperature in the environment by means of clothing, heating and air conditioning. Obese tissue provides extra insulation against cold and thin people feel cold more intensely than others.

Stimuli from adipose tissue

The neural, chemical and thermal stimuli described above may all have an important role in determining feeding behaviour of wild animals and sometimes of man. Each can initiate feeding. But each acts on a short time scale and as has been shown food intake by man is not adjusted rapidly to changes in energy expenditure. Several days may elapse before appropriate changes in behaviour restore the energy balance and so maintain body weight. In 1953 Kennedy[15] suggested that there is a long-term regulating mechanism which depends on information on the size of the fat stores. The nature of the signal is not known, but a natural steroid with a high fat: water partition coefficient could monitor the amount of fat in the body by the dilution principle. Administration of progesterone to rats increases food intake and in certain circumstances decreases energy expenditure and leads to gain in weight and fat.[16]

OUTPUTS FROM THE CONTROL CENTRES

The energy balance is obviously mainly determined by the relation between food intake, physical activity and rest. Unlike the responses in a reflex action, they are neither fixed nor predictable. They are behavioural responses and involve both body and mind.

Feeding behaviour

This is a motor activity initiated or suppressed by sensations or perceptual states arising from incoming stimuli. Feeding may be initiated by hunger, which is a complex sensation arising from physiological changes in the state of the body's store of energy, and inhibited by fullness, a sensation arising in the alimentary canal. Feeding behaviour is also markedly influenced by appetite and satiety. These depend on the nature and quality of the food and the immediate physical and social environment and they are also influenced by habits, family customs and indeed by education and cultural background. One man's food may appear as another man's poison.

Physical activity

Hunger causes wild animals to go and search for food and may stimulate civilised men and women to activity needed to prepare a meal at home or go out to a restaurant. In circumstances when food is not available continuous hunger suppresses spontaneous activity. This occurs in experimental animals and in man. Thus when only about half the normal food supply is provided, as in prisoner of war camps in the Far East and in the famous Minnesota experiment (Chap. 27) all unnecesary movements are curtailed and in this way, together with a fall in the resting metabolic rate, energy expenditure is so reduced that survival is possible. This is an important adaptive change.

To what extent satiety promotes a drive to exercise in affluent societies is uncertain and has been little studied. On more than one occasion after a long session preparing this book we have gone out and climbed to the top of Arthur's Seat in Edinburgh before returning to work and a good evening meal. Is this an example of a physiological drive to exercise initiated by a high food intake in those whose work is sedentary? Such a drive may be an important control on body weight in some persons.

Metabolic changes

When food intake is reduced, the resting metabolic rate falls slowly. This can be attributed in part to wasting of tissues and a reduction of cell mass. This is one of the factors that permits survival when the food supply is reduced greatly.

Is there a metabolic mechanism which protects some people from the usual consequence of continuing dietary excesses? It is a common observation that some people eat heartily, never worry about their diet and yet remain thin.

The concept of a regulatory mechanism which limited increase in the energy store following dietary excess by dissipating the excess as heat was put forward long ago in the German literature and known as *Luxuskonsumption*.[17] It was based on observations of both dogs and men where the gains in weight following periods of excess eating were less than expected. Since then several studies, the most thorough on volunteers amongst the prisoners in Vermont State gaol,[18] appear to support the concept. However, none of them has convinced the sceptics, aware of the technical difficulties in measuring the energy balance in man over long periods (p. 24).

The metabolic rate is well-known to rise after a meal. This rise, formerly known as the specific dynamic action of food but now as diet-induced thermogenesis (DIT), is variable even in any one individual, but is roughly related to the size of the meal. Most of it can be accounted for by the energy required to secrete the digestive enzymes and to transport and store the absorbed nutrients (Chap. 3). Even after a big meal the metabolic rate usually has returned to the basal level within 4 hours. If DIT is more than an expression of the energy used for disposal of nutrients and has a regulatory role, it would be expected to persist in an overfed subject. In Edinburgh measurements of the resting metabolic rate early in the morning have been made on many subjects before and during periods of overfeeding lasting for four or more days.[19] After the digestion and disposal of the nutrients in the meal on the previous evening, the metabolic rate returned to normal and there was no sign of increased stores of energy raising the basal metabolic rates. Others have confirmed this and there is no convincing evidence to the contrary.[20]

The elucidation of the role of brown adipose tissue (BAT) in regulation of body temperature in the newborn and in adults of some species (p. 65) led to the hypothesis that regulation of energy balance could be effected by the generation of DIT in BAT. This received much publicity in the media, probably because it carries the implication that obesity arises from a lack of BAT and so provides slimmers with a physical explanation of their problems. Scientific support has come mainly from experiments on cafeteria-fed rats, given free access to a number of palatable foods. The rats then increased their dietary energy intake by about 80 per cent and it was claimed that most of this was dissipated by thermogenesis.[21] Others have not confirmed this and the experiments have been criticised on technical grounds.[22] Two reviews[23, 24] set out the case for and against luxuskonsumption. The advocates have not as yet persuaded the critics that any experiments providing sound evidence of its role in disposing of excess dietary energy have been carried out.

The concept of luxuskonsumption has been around for over 80 years, and has received recently new life and a new name — the acronym DIT. Its appeal lies in that it offers a plausible explanation for obesity in metabolic terms. But if energy stores were regulated by an increase of metabolism after overfeeding, this would have been unequivocally demonstrated by now. Luxuskonsumption appears an idea of no substance — a straw in the wind that has been chased by many without profit.

Habit and pleasure

The affluent seldom eat primarily because they are hungry. Meals are prepared at certain times by custom in our homes, canteens and restaurants and we eat when we know that they are ready. The initiating of feeding is therefore in our society more in response to custom and habit than to physiological stimuli. For most people the variable that determines energy balance is not the times when we start eating but what makes us stop. What determines whether we have one or two pieces of toast at breakfast? Why on some occasions are we unable to eat a whole helping of potatoes, which is normally enjoyed? There is no easy answer to these questions. Often we have finished eating before products of digestion can have entered the blood in significant amounts; though we may feel full the stomach is seldom distended to its capacity. Eating is associated with pleasure and we stop when it ceases to be pleasant. Cabanac[25] pointed out that a feeling of pleasure in response to a sensory input depends on the state of the body as well as the nature of the stimulus. Thus putting the hand into water at 20°C is very pleasant when immersed in a hot bath, but very unpleasant when in a cold bath. Similarly he found that a sweet-tasting and an orange-smelling stimulus were rated as very pleasant when fasting, but unpleasant and neutral respectively one hour after ingesting 50 g of glucose. The regulating system may be reset at different levels in different individuals and this may account for the difficulty in preventing a relapse in obesity.

GENERAL CONSIDERATION

Mammals and other higher animals evolved in an environment where food was usually scarce. They had to work for it and to get enough to meet their energy needs and to maintain a store of energy in the form of fat for when food was not available easily. This store had the additional use of providing insulation against heat losses in a cold environment, but it had to be kept within limits so as not to impede movements or by its weight increase their energy cost. The size of the store that migratory birds build up before their departure is a critical factor for the success of their journey.[26] Seals and other aquatic mammals build up a large store during pregnancy to meet energy needs during lactation when they are on land and cannot get their normal food. How the sizes of these stores are monitored so that they are just sufficient to meet the specific energy requirements of migration and lactation is unknown. They are examples of how physiological adaptations have evolved to meet special circumstances with precision. For most of the three million years of his existence *Homo* has lived in an environment where food is scarce. He is adapted to be able to withstand long periods of a restricted energy supply.

Eating is a pleasure which all higher animals appear to enjoy. Overindulgence, except for brief occasions, was impossible until a continued assured food supply from the cultivation of cereals became available about 7000 years ago. Because of the uncertainties of agriculture the great majority of the population worked hard

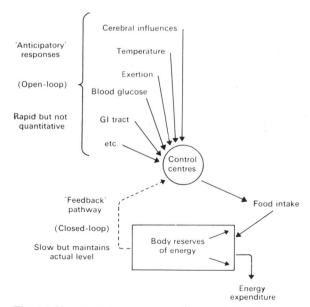

Fig. 9.2 Hypothetical organisation of the regulation of energy balance. GI = Gastrointestinal. (Professor Hervey)[16]

in the field and only a minority of people, mostly the wealthy, could overeat regularly. Only since the beginning of the nineteenth century has there been large industrial communities with assured food supplies and at first the cost of food in relation to wages acted as a brake on consumption. Only very recently have there been large communities with an abundant and varied food supply which most of the members could afford to purchase. There has been so short an experience of abundant food that the processes of evolution have not had time to produce effective adaption. Attitudes to food change slowly, not always for the better. Ancient reli-

gions lay down occasions for feasting and fasting. Contemporary man is good at feasting but seldom fasts. It is not surprising that the energy balance is often upset or that the physiological, psychological and social factors that determine it in each individual are poorly understood. Of all the regulatory mechanisms in the brain, that which determines and fixes the reserve of energy as body fat is perhaps the most complicated. Figure 9.2 indicates relations of the inputs and outputs already discussed, but it is no more than a sketch of possibilities. Neither the exact nature nor the relative quantitative importance of the various components of the diagram can be stated.

REFERENCES

1. Bain A 1855 The senses and the intellect. Parker, London, p 249
2. Robinson M F, Watson P E 1965 Day-to-day variations in body-weight of young women. Br J Nutr 19: 225–235
3. Garrow J S 1978 Energy balance and obesity in man, 2nd edn. Elsevier, Amsterdam
4. Taggart N 1962 Diet, activity and body-weight. A study of variations in a woman. Br J Nutr 16: 223–235
5. Durnin J V G A 1961 'Appetite' and the relation between expenditure and intake of calories in man. J Physiol (Lond) 156: 294–309
6. Passmore R, Thomson J G, Warnock G M 1952 A balance sheet of the estimation of energy intake and energy expenditure as measured by indirect calorimetry. Br J Nutr 6: 253–264
7. Gordon T, Kannel W B 1973 The effect of overweight on cardiovascular disease. Geriatrics 28(8): 80–88
8. Brobeck J R, Teppermann J, Long C N H 1943 Experimental hypothalmic hyperphagia in albino rat. Yale J Biol Med 15: 831–853
9. Bray G A, York D A 1979 Hypothalamic and genetic obesity in experimental animals: an autonomic and genetic hypothesis. Physiol Rev 59: 719–809
10. Bray G A 1982 Regulation of energy balance. Proc Nutr Soc 41: 95–108
11. Morley J E, Levine A S 1983 The central control of appetite. Lancet 1: 398–400
12. Mayer J 1953 Genetic, traumatic and environmental factors in the etiology of obesity. Physiol Rev 33: 472–508
13. Russek M 1981 Current status of the hepatostatic theory of food intake control. Appetite 2: 137–143
14. Brobeck J R 1948 Food intake as a mechanism of temperature regulation. Yale J Biol Med 20: 545–552
15. Kennedy G C 1953 The role of depot fat in the hypothalamic control of food intake in the rat. Proc R Soc Lond (Biol) 140: 578–592
16. Hervey G R 1971 Physiological mechanisms for the regulation of energy balance. Proc Nutr Soc 30: 109–116
17. Grafe E, Graham D 1911 Über die Anpassungsfäkigkeit des tierischen organismus und überreichliche Nahrungszufuhr (Nach Versuchen am Hunde). Hoppe Seylers Z Physiol Chem 73: 1–67
18. Sims E A H, Goldman R F, Gluck C M, Horton E S, Kelleher P C, Rowe D W 1968 Experimental obesity in man. Trans Am Assoc Physns 81: 153–170
19. Strong J A, Shirling D, Passmore R 1967 Some effects of overfeeding for four days in man. Br J Nutr 21: 909–919
20. Passmore R 1983 Luxuskonsumption, brown fat and human obesity. Br Med J 287: 362–363
21. Rothwell N J, Stock M J 1979 A role for brown adipose tissue in diet-induced thermogenesis. Nature 281: 31–35
22. Hervey G R, Tobin G 1982 The part played by variation of energy expenditure in the regulation of energy balance. Proc Nutr Soc 41: 137–153
23. Rothwell N J, Stock M J 1983 Luxuskonsumption, diet-induced thermogenesis and brown fat: the case in favour. Clin Sci 64: 19–23
24. Hervey G R, Tobin G 1983 Luxuskonsumption, diet-induced thermogenesis and brown fat: a critical review. Clin Sci 64: 7–18
25. Cabanac J 1971 Physiological role of pleasure. Science NY 173: 1103–1107
26. Weis-Fogh T 1967 Metabolism and weight economy in migrating animals, particular birds and insects. In: Nutrition and physical activity. Swedish Nutrition Symposium no. 5, p 84–97

10

Water and Electrolytes

A 65 kg man contains about 40 litres of water. Of this, about 25 litres is intracellular and 15 litres extracellular. The principal cation in the cell water is potassium (concentration about 150 mmol/l) and in the extracellular fluids sodium (concentration about 140 mmol/l). These fluids are continuously being turned over and both their amounts are kept constant by a balance between intake and output. Intake is from the diet and sometimes in patients intravenous therapy; output is mainly in the urine. The kidneys control outputs so as to keep the composition of the cell water and extracellular fluid constant. Disturbances of these balances are common and rectifying them is of great importance in clinical practice. It is essential to be familiar in quantitative terms with the amounts of Na and K likely to be present in the diet, in the excreta and in the body fluids.

WATER BALANCE

The water intake comprises the fluid drunk and the water in the food eaten. The water formed by the oxidation of carbohydrate, protein and fat is also available (metabolic water). The output consists of the urine, the water in the faeces and the water evaporated from the skin and lungs. Table 10.1 shows a normal water balance in a young man leading a sedentary life. The data can only be obtained if the facilities of a metabolic ward are available. The table shows that the liquid drunk is roughly equal to the urine output. These are easily measured and form the basis of a **fluid balance chart**, which can be kept by the nursing staff in any ward. It is a useful guide to the water balance, provided that there are not large losses from the alimentary tract or from sweating caused by fever or a hot environment.

Measurement

If the facilities of a metabolic ward are available, the complete water balance can be determined by established methods.[2]

In brief, the fluid consumed is easily measured and the water in the solid components of the diet can be estimated by homogenising and drying a duplicate sample of the whole day's food.

The metabolic water can be calculated, since the oxidation of the proximate principles yields water in the following amounts:

1 g starch	0.60 g water
1 g protein	0.41 g water
1 g fat	1.07 g water

If the subject is neither losing nor gaining weight, the composition of the diet provides a measure of the nutrients actually oxidised. If the subject is losing weight, an addition must be made for the water produced by the oxidation of protein and tissue fat; conversely, if the subject is gaining weight the excess nutrients laid down do not yield water. The metabolic water is usually small in proportion to the total intake of water and any error is of little significance in calculating the water balance.

The urine volume is easily measured, as is the faecal water by weighing the faeces before and after drying. The evaporative water loss is determined from the invisible weight loss.

The invisible weight loss = weight of food and liquid consumed ± any change in body weight − the weight of urine and faeces.

Table 10.1 The daily water balance of a young man leading a sedentary life on a diet providing 8.8 MJ (2110 kcal)/day[1]

(Mean of five daily measurements)	Water ml/day
Intake:	
Water content of solid food	1115
Liquid drunk	1180
Metabolic water	279
	2574
Output:	
Urine	1295
Faecal water	56
Evaporative water loss	1214
	2565
Water balance	+9

These are all simple measurements.

The evaporative water loss = the invisible weight loss − weight of CO_2 expired + weight of O_2 absorbed.

Under normal circumstances the evaporative water loss is about 93 per cent of the invisible weight loss. The exact figure depends on the RQ and may vary from 90 to 102 per cent.

Water intake

In normal life the intake of fluids is largely determined by social custom and habit. The kidney is the principal organ regulating the amount of water in the body. Thirst is normally an additional physiological regulating mechanism. It was at one time thought that thirst was produced by dryness of the mouth and throat. More probably the sensation of thirst arises as a result of the concentration of sodium in the blood. An increase of 1 per cent in the osmolality of the blood causes thirst. The sensory receptors for thirst are in the hypothalamus and the thirst centre is closely connected with the feeding centres. Thirst is predominantly associated with water depletion, but not with salt depletion. Indeed if there is an associated salt depletion such as may occur in the tropics as a result of losses in the sweat, the thirst mechanism may not operate adequately. For this reason heavy manual workers, and also febrile patients, may easily become dehydrated and salt depleted without complaining of thirst. Such people may have to be persuaded to drink sufficient water, to which salt has been added. Fitzsimmons[3,4] has reviewed the physiological mechanisms involved in thirst.

In medical practice fluids can be given in other ways than by mouth — into the veins, subcutaneously or into the peritoneal cavity.

Water output

From the skin.   Water is commonly lost from the skin by sweating. Rates as high as 2500 ml/h have been recorded in hot climates, both in the tropics and in hot industrial occupations. A loss of 500 ml/h is not uncommon. Unless this water is replaced by increased intake, the body becomes dehydrated. Severe symptoms result from dehydration when about 10 per cent of the total body water has been lost.

From the lungs.   The expired air is saturated with water vapour at 37°C. Under normal conditions only about 300 ml/day are lost in this way. When the inspired air is very dry, losses may be considerable. On the slopes of Mount Everest, for instance, the cold dry air draws off much more moisture from the lungs than is lost in a temperate climate. The losses are exaggerated by the increased ventilation of the lungs necessitated by the low oxygen content of the inspired air. It is probable that earlier Everest climbers became dehydrated from this cause which impaired their fitness for the final assault.

In Sir John Hunt's first successful expedition this was appreciated and special attention was paid to the water intake of every member of the expedition. Each was made to drink 5 to 7 pints (3 to 4 litres) daily.[5] This apparently small point in physiology may have made the difference between success and failure in the final assault on the summit.

From the gastrointestinal tract.   The small loss of water in the faeces is the balance of large exchanges which take place in the intestines. The saliva, the gastric secretions, the bile and the secretions of the pancreas and glands of the small intestine may together add up to 8 litres or more fluid daily. All but a small proportion of this is normally reabsorbed in the gut. If, however, there is diarrhoea, vomiting or an intestinal fistula, fluid losses may be large and cause dehydration. In infants and small children particularly, gastroenteritis with diarrhoea and vomiting may cause a rapid and dangerous reduction in the total body water.

From the kidneys.   The volume of the urine is very variable and in general reflects the fluid intake but the minimum volume is determined by the nature of the diet.

The urine is normally more concentrated than the blood and to achieve this concentration the kidneys must do work. The concentrating power of the kidneys can be assessed from simple measurements of its specific gravity. A more precise assessment is obtained from measurements of osmolality, usually obtained by determining the effect of the urinary solutes in lowering the freezing point. Osmolality is expressed in terms of osmoles. One gram molecule in 1 kg of water of any un-ionised substance is equal to 1 osmol. When a substance is ionised forming cations and anions, both exert an osmotic effect. For monovalent ions 1 equivalent weight has an osmolality of 1 osmol, but for divalent ions one equivalent weight is equal to only 0.5 osmol. The fluids of the body are dilute and contain several ions, so it is convenient to express their concentration in terms of milliosmoles (mosmol).

The osmolality of the blood is normally just under 300 mosmol/kg and the healthy human kidney can produce urine with an osmolality of 1200 mosmol/kg, i.e. it can concentrate the blood plasma four times. The concentrating power of the kidneys of many animals is much higher than this, particularly those who live in deserts and have to survive on a very limited water intake. The relation between the specific gravity and osmolality of the urine varies slightly, depending on the constituents of the urine. For a healthy subject on a good mixed diet the relationship is approximately as follows.

Sp.gr.	1.007	1.015	1.020	1.025	1.030	1.035
mosmol	400	600	800	1080	1200	1400

The main constituents of the urine are nitrogenous end products, of which over 80 per cent is usually urea, and sodium chloride. Although there are over 100 other substances present in urine, the amounts are normally so small that they contribute no more than about 15 per cent of the osmolality. As the amounts of urea and sodium chloride in the urine depend on the dietary intake of protein and salt, the osmolar load on the kidneys depends mainly on the dietary intake. Thus the diet determines the amount of work that the kidneys have to do.

Osmolar load of a diet

Consider a diet providing 100 g of protein and 10 g of salt. The protein contains 16 g of nitrogen which must be excreted, mostly as urea. The molecular weight of urea is 60 of which 28 comes from its two atoms of nitrogen. Thus every gram of dietary nitrogen leads to the formation of just under 2 g of urea and the urine of the subject eating 100 g/day of protein contains about 30 g of urea. As the mol. wt of urea is 60, this is equivalent to 0.5 osmol or 500 mosmol. The 10 g of salt yield Na^+ and Cl^-, both in amounts of $(10 \times 1000)/58.5 = 170$ mmol, and their combined osmolar load is 340 mosmol. Thus the protein and salt in the diet produce an osmolar load of 840 mosmol. This figure may be arbitrarily raised to 1000 to take in the other urinary constituents. As the kidneys cannot concentrate urine normally to more than 1200 mosmol/kg, the subject must pass $1000/1200 = 830$ ml of urinary water. This is known as the **obligatory water** and is required to enable the kidneys to clear the dietary osmolar load. All people normally drink far more water than is essential for renal function. If the daily water intake of a person on the above diet was 1500 ml, then 670 ml of this can be described as **free water**. The conception of the division of the urinary water into obligatory and free portions, the obligatory being determined by the osmolar load of the diet, is useful under two circumstances. The first is when disease of the kidneys reduces their power of concentration. The second is when the supply of water is limited, as it may be to survivors of shipwreck in a lifeboat and to other castaways.

The normal control of the urine volume depends on a regulatory mechanism, which involves a nerve centre in the hypothalamus and the antidiuretic hormone (ADH) secreted by the posterior pituitary gland, regulating fluid absorption in the renal tubules. The hypothalamus contains cells — osmoreceptors — which are sensitive to changes in concentration of the solutes in the plasma. A dilution of the plasma (as after drinking a glass of water) is sensed by the receptor cells which are connected by nerve fibres with the posterior pituitary gland. The secretion of ADH by the gland is inhibited, and a diuresis sets in. Conversely, if the plasma becomes concentrated, the osmoreceptors are stimulated and signal the posterior pituitary to increase the secretion of ADH and a diminished urine flow results. If the hypothalamus or posterior pituitary gland is injured by disease, secretion of the hormone may be impaired or stopped. Very large volumes of dilute urine are passed. This conditions is known as diabetes insipidus.

Water balance in infancy

At birth the full function of the kidneys is not developed, and for the first two or three days of life the daily urinary volume is only about 20 ml. The volume of the colostrum may be little more than this. Kidney function improves simultaneously with the development of lactation. At 2 weeks the urinary volume is usually about 200 ml and the volume of milk ingested about 500 ml. At 3 months the volume of milk may be 800 to 900 ml and the urine volume about 300 ml daily. The excess water is eliminated by evaporation, at a higher rate than is usual in adults. Naturally there are great variations. Infants are particularly liable to lose large quantities of fluid by diarrhoea and vomiting. Indeed dehydration is a common and dangerous feature of many febrile illnesses in infancy and early childhood.

SODIUM AND POTASSIUM

Understanding of the quantitative aspects of sodium and potassium metabolism and especially their relation to osmolality is much easier if all values are expressed in terms of millimoles rather than units of weight. The latter, however, are still used in most food tables and often in the literature. The appropriate conversion factors are

1 g NaCl	=	17.1 mmol Na^+
1 g Na^+	=	43.5 mmol Na^+
1 g KCl	=	13.4 mmol K^+
1 g K^+	=	25.6 mmol K^+

Normal values are given in Table 10.2

Body content. The total amounts of sodium and potassium are similar but the distribution is very different. Most of the Na is in the extracellular fluid, whereas nearly all the K is in cell water. There is a large amount of sodium in the bone minerals but this is not freely exchangeable with Na and so does not act as a short-term store, but in prolonged sodium deficiency it may be drawn upon.

Diet. There is a wide range of intakes of both sodium and potassium. High intakes of sodium occur when salt is added at the table and in cooking and when large quantities of processed foods to which salt has been added by manufacturers are a feature of the diet. The possible hazards from a high intake are discussed later in this chapter. Natural diets, consisting mainly of cereals and vegetables, contain much less sodium and in poor communities in the tropics often barely sufficient

Table 10.2 Sodium and potassium metabolism

	Sodium	Potassium
Body content (mmol)		
Extracellular fluid	2000	80
Cell water	400	3500
Bone	1500	—
Total	3900	4300
(Values for a 65 kg man)		
Plasma concentration (mmol/l)	140	4
Range in health	132–145	3.5–5
Intake and output (mmol/day)		
Diet	70–250	50–150
Urine	A little less than dietary intake	
Faeces	5	10
Sweat (mmol/l)	20–80	5–15

to meet the losses in sweat and in repeated attacks of diarrhoea. The usual intake of potassium is about 65 mmol daily but may be much greater if large quantities of fresh vegetables and meat are eaten.

Output

Very little of either sodium or potassium is lost in the faeces and from the skin, except when there is diarrhoea or prolonged sweating. Normally the urine output approximates to fluid intake. Indeed a 24 hour sample of urine provides a more reliable measure of intake than calculations using food tables and a dietary study.

Table 10.3 Causes of water depletion (modified from Lambie and Robson)[6]

Reduced intake	
Water unavailable	At sea after shipwreck
	In a desert when lost
Inability to obtain water	Infants
	Elderly and debilitated patients
	Unconscious patients
Inability to swallow	Diseases of mouth and oesophagus
Increased losses	
From the skin	Hot environment, excessive exercise, fever, hyperthyroidism
From the lungs	Hyperventilation
	Fever, high altitudes
From the alimentary tract	Prolonged vomiting
	Diarrhoea
	Enteritis, dysentery, cholera
	Fistulas
In the urine	Osmotic diuresis
	In diabetes mellitus
	Too concentrated food, e.g. with tube feeding and infant milk powders
	Drinking sea water
	Various kidney disorders
	Diabetes insipidus

The kidneys conserve Na^+ and K^+ and regulate their plasma concentrations. They do this by controlling renal tubular reabsorption under the influence of adrenal cortical hormones, especially aldosterone. The complex mechanisms involved are described in textbooks of physiology. Conservation of Na^+ is very effective and virtually Na^+-free urine can be excreted. If the body sodium is depleted as by excessive sweating, reabsorption may be almost complete and sodium chloride can no longer be detected in the urine by adding silver nitrate, which normally yields a white precipitate of silver chloride. This test is useful in clinical practice in hot climates. Renal conservation of K^+ is less complete and the urine always contains at least 10 mmol/l.

Healthy kidneys have no difficulty in excreting any quantity of salt that may be taken in the diet, provided there is sufficient excretion of water. As already stated, the kidneys cannot concentrate the urine above a specific gravity of about 1.035. This limit to the kidneys' capacity to excrete salt is of practical importance for survival after shipwreck when fresh water is unavailable (Chap. 64).

DEFICIENCY STATES

Tables 10.3, 10.4 and 10.5 set out the more common and important causes of water, sodium and potassium depletion but they are by no means complete. Serious depletion may arise suddenly or insidiously and is easily overlooked by the unwary. Thus even in Scotland a healthy teenager may collapse with dehydration after a single hot day of intense activity. In tropical countries towards the end of the hot season it is wise to assume that all patients admitted to hospital as medical or surgical emergencies are dehydrated to the extent of at least 2 litres. An infant may have severe and even fatal dehydration after only one or two days of diarrhoea and vomiting in an attack of gastroenteritis. The mental confusion of an old lady may be due to potassium deficiency

Table 10.4 Causes of sodium depletion (modified from Lambie and Robson)[6]

Losses in sweat
   As for water depletion (Table 10.3)

Losses from the alimentary tract
   As for water depletion (Table 10.3)

Losses in the urine
   In diabetes mellitus due to osmotic diuresis
   In Addison's disease due to adrenal cortical insufficiency
   Excessive doses of diuretic drugs
   Renal tubular damage in chronic renal failure and in the diuretic phase of acute renal failure

Losses in transudates and exudates
   Ascites and other peritoneal exudates
   Severe burns and extensive dermatitis

Table 10.5 Causes of potassium depletion (modified from Lambie and Robson)[6]

Losses from the alimentary tract
    As for water depletion (Table 10.3)
    Chronic abuse of purgatives

Losses in the urine
    In wasting diseases and starvation due to breakdown of tissues
    Due to overdosage with drugs; common with diuretics and corticosteroids but also with many others
    Aldosterone excess
        In Cushing's syndrome and disease
        Secondary in some cases of malignant hypertension,
    Cirrhosis of the liver and the hephrotic syndrome
    In renal disease
        Chronic pyelonephritis, renal tubular acidosis and some others

from faecal losses caused by the mild laxative that she has taken for many years. In these four examples, as in nearly all cases of deficiency of water, sodium and potassium, serious effects can be avoided by early recognition of risk and suitable preventive action or by prompt replacement therapy.

SOME QUANTITATIVE ASPECTS

Sweating

After losing 2 litres of body water in a short period, a person is very thirsty, after losing 4 litres very weak and in danger of collapse, and after losing 8 litres probably dead. These figures should be seen against sweat rates. Up to 3 litres/hour may be lost during continuous hard physical activity in any climate. In hot weather with only light and intermittent activity, up to 1 litre an hour may be lost and daily losses of 4 litres by sedentary persons and 8 litres by active workers are commonplace. The maximum loss recorded in the *Guinness Book of Records* is 14 litres in 24 hours. Thus it is easy to see how rapidly serious effects can arise from dehydration due to sweating. When dehydration arises slowly from water loss by any route, greater losses can be sustained before there is danger of circulatory collapse or death.

The Na content of sweat varies from 20 to 80 mmol/l. Persons acclimatised to heat, either by residence in a hot climate or by hard exercise with sweating in a cold climate, conserve Na by secreting sweat with only about 30 mmol/l. With his figure and a daily sweat rate of 4 litres, 120 mmol of dietary sodium are required to meet losses in sweat during the hot weather in the tropics. The sweat glands do not concentrate K and sweat contains little more than is present in plasma. Sweating does not therefore significantly deplete body K.

Alimentary tract losses

About 10 litres of water and large amounts of Na and K enter the alimentary tract daily from the diet and the alimentary secretions. The greater part of this is absorbed and only about 150 ml of water, and 5 mmol of Na and 10 mmol of K are lost in the faeces daily. The losses increase when absorption is impaired by diarrhoea. In the extreme case of severe cholera, absorption is stopped completely and plasma pours out through the epithelium of the gut into the lumen. Up to 18 litres of stool may be passed in 24 hours. This is almost isotonic with plasma and contains large amounts of Na and also K. If these losses are not immediately replaced by intravenous therapy, death after a few hours is inevitable. In a moderately severe case of diarrhoea from any cause 3 litres of water with corresponding amounts of Na and K may be lost in one day. Without effective replacement therapy such a patient is soon seriously depleted and very ill. The cumulative effects of mild chronic diarrhoea are less obvious and symptoms arising from depletion, especially of potassium, are easily overlooked.

Tissue wasting

This is an important cause of potassium deficiency in diabetes, in underfeeding and after injury. Most of the wasting is from muscle and a reduction of muscle mass of 1 kg is a loss of 105 mmol of K and 210 g of protein (34 g of N). The K/N ratio of the tissue lost is therefore 3.0. If nitrogen and potassium balance are both carried out, the K/N ratio of the cellular material lost or gained can be calculated. This may be a useful guide to what is happening in the cells.

CLINICAL FEATURES

Water depletion

Evidence of dehydration is sunken features, particularly the eyes which recede into the orbit. The skin and tongue are dry. The skin becomes loose and lacks elasticity. On pinching, it stands away from the subcutaneous tissues. This sign may be obscured by obesity and especially in a fat infant. The patient is usually, but not always thirsty.

When dehydration is severe (a loss of extracellular fluid of over 4 litres in a 65 kg man), signs of oligaemic shock are likely to be present. There is peripheral vasoconstriction, the pulse rate is high and systolic blood pressure low; there is oliguria. Apathy and weakness are marked.

Sodium depletion

The early symptoms are mainly psychological and behavioural in nature and so not specific. In clinical practice, sodium depletion is usually seen associated with either water depletion or other general metabolic disorders. The best description of pure sodium depletion is by McCance in a classic paper.[7] He and three of his medical students went on a low sodium diet and exposed themselves daily to a radiant heat bath to induce sweat losses of 2 to 3 litres/day. Soon foods, even fruit, seemed tasteless. There was anorexia and nausea that was not associated with food. All suffered from excessive fatigue and a general sense of exhaustion. They also had cramps that were mild, but any sudden movement was liable to cause muscle spasm, for example in the fingers when trying to use a pipette or pair of forceps. Pulse rates were raised slightly but no changes in blood pressure were detected. In one of the subjects a balance study indicated a sodium deficit after 11 days of just over 1000 mmol, nearly 80 per cent of this being due to losses in the sweat.

More severe depletion associated with other metabolic disturbances leads to reduced extracellular fluid, oligaemia and a marked fall in blood pressure.

Potassium depletion

The chief features of potassium deficiency are muscular weakness and mental confusion. The weakness is well illustrated by a rare disease, familial periodic paralysis. The patient is subject to recurrent attacks of muscular weakness and paralysis which last for several hours. The attacks are associated with low levels of plasma potassium. They are probably caused by a periodic over-secretion of aldosterone by the adrenal cortex.

The absence of characteristic symptoms makes it difficult to recognise potassium deficiency clinically. The concentration of potassium in the plasma may bear little relation to the amount in the tissues. When tissues are breaking down and losing potassium, plasma concentration may be higher than normal.

The cardiac muscle is involved in the general muscular weakness. The electrocardiogram commonly shows S–T depression and a broad low T wave. Sudden death is a possible consequence.

The smooth muscle of the small intestine may become paralysed, **paralytic ileus**; this leads to abdominal distension, which may be an important early sign of potassium deficiency, especially in children.

REPLACEMENT THERAPY

When possible, it is best to use oral rehydration solutions (ORS) described on page 436. If there are large deficits and the patient is seriously ill or cannot drink sufficient amounts, intravenous therapy is needed and described in Chap. 51. The infusion fluid has to be isotonic with blood. For this purpose, either sodium chloride or glucose may be used. Water depletion is usually greater than sodium depletion and it is important not to overload the patient with Na. A mixture of NaCl and glucose solutions is therefore given.

Potassium replacement is with KCl. A 4 g tablet provides 53 mmol K^+. There is always a danger of potassium excess (see below). It is safe to give two tablets by mouth on one day or to infuse intravenously 53 mmol slowly over 4 hours. If larger doses are used, repeated measurements of plasma $[K^+]$ are necessary and the treatment stopped if it rises significantly above the upper limit of the normal value (5 mmol/l).

EXCESSES IN THE TISSUES

Water and sodium

Oedema, an increase in extracellular fluids, is common in many conditions. It arises whenever there is an increase in venous pressure. Local oedema is due to obstruction of either the venous or lymphatic drainage of a tissue. Generalised oedema occurs in heart failure when the heart cannot empty the ventricles effectively and there is a rise in central venous pressure. Generalised oedema also occurs in starvation (p. 263) and in liver disease, associated with diminished formation of plasma albumin. In liver disease obstruction of the portal vein also leads to large accumulations of fluid in the peritoneal cavity, a condition known as ascites (p. 452). Generalised oedema is also associated with some kidney diseases, especially the nephrotic syndrome (p. 403) when large losses of protein in the urine lead to a low plasma albumin. Oedema causes tissues to swell and can be detected in subcutaneous tissues by the pitting which forms after pressure has been applied with a finger. This simple clinical test is not very sensitive since oedema is not usually apparent until limb volume is increased by 10 per cent or more.[8]

At one time it was usual to see in any medical ward two or more patients in whom the tissues of all the organs were waterlogged by severe oedema. Attempts to remove the fluid by giving a strict low sodium diet and so causing sodium depletion with consequent dehydration had only very limited success. Such diets are unpleasant to take and their use added to patients' discomfort and distress with little real benefit. The situation changed completely with the introduction of frusemide and other thiadiazine diuretics that inhibit the action of carbonic anhydrase in the renal tubules and so prevent reabsorption of sodium and increase its urinary output. These new diuretics are one of the great marvels of modern medicine and nowadays a waterlogged patient is a rare sight. With their use, a low sodium diet is seldom necessary but it is sensible not to overload the body with sodium by taking a high sodium diet. There are large numbers of patients taking diuretics regularly for an indefinite period; they all need dietary advice to curtail their use of table salt and the use of cooking salt and to eat sparingly of highly salted processed foods (see below).

Water excess

Overhydration with a reduced plasma $[Na^+]$ and plasma osmolality may occur with an excessive intake. This may happen if large quantities of water are drunk to quench thirst in a hot climate when at the same time there are additional sodium losses in sweat. It also occurs in beer drinkers[9] in whom it may be not uncommon. Overhydration may also arise in conditions where water excretion by the kidneys is impaired, e.g. in the nephrotic syndrome, in cardiac failure, and owing to many common drugs including benzodiazepines, and inappropriate secretion of ADH by carcinoma of the lungs and other tumours.

Overhydration leads to an increase in intracellular water and is a potentially dangerous and even lethal condition. The symptoms are non-specific. In early cases there is difficulty in concentrating, drowsiness and giddiness, sometimes associated with headache and nausea. In severe cases there may be confusion, behavioural disturbances, convulsions and coma. When these symptoms are present, a low plasma $[Na^+]$ makes the diagnosis likely. Treatment is primarily by reducing the fluid intake which should not exceed the urinary output by more than 600 ml, except when sweating is marked.

Sodium excess

This is usually associated with excess water giving rise to oedema. Pure sodium excess may arise from infusion of too much hypertonic solutions of sodium salts. Normally this induces thirst, but patients receiving such treatment are usually very ill and may be unable to drink. It also arises in infants whose mothers have repeatedly made up their milk powder with insufficient water. The infant is then, of course, thirsty but cannot drink without the mother's aid; further, the full capacity to excrete Na^+ only develops some weeks after birth. With a high plasma $[Na^+]$ there is irritability, overbreathing and often fever, followed in severe cases by convulsions: in infants fontanelle tension is increased. Lowering plasma $[Na^+]$ should proceed slowly and take 2 to 3 days. In infants peritoneal dialysis may be used.

Potassium excess

Healthy kidneys excrete potassium readily and poisoning does not arise from an oral intake. However, a dangerous rise of plasma $[K^+]$ may follow an intravenous infusion especially when, as is often the case, renal function is impaired by a diminished blood flow owing to shock. A raised plasma $[K^+]$ causes typical changes in the electrocardiogram with a high T-wave and a shortened Q–T interval and an accompanying risk of cardiac arrest.

In acute renal failure this can be prevented by giving a potassium-free diet for a few days; this means no fruit juices. It may also sometimes be necessary to restrict dietary potassium in cases of chronic renal failure.

SODIUM AND POTASSIUM CONTENTS OF FOODS

Values for large numbers of individual foods can be found in the tables of food analysis listed in Chapter 16. Table 10.6 gives values for 10 common foods that might be bought from the stalls of a country market and compares them with processed products sold in supermarkets. It can be seen readily that the ratio of Na/K which is about 2:3 in the combined extra- and intracellular fluids of the body (Table 10.2) is much lower than this in the unprocessed foods and much higher in the processed ones. Three important lessons can be learnt from this table. The first is that all foods (except separated fats and oils, sugars and alcoholic beverages) are good sources of potassium. This is due to the fact that cells of both plants and animals that form the basis of natural foods are rich in potassium. The second lesson is that all diets based on natural foods are inevitably low in sodium unless a liberal use is made of salt in the kitchen and at the table. Thirdly, diets containing large amounts of processed foods are inevitably high in sodium.

SALT

Salt has had a major role in the evolution of the higher animals and man. Life began in the salt-rich environment of the sea. Within primitive cells a potassium-

Table 10.6 Comparison of the sodium and potassium content of some natural and processed foods (values taken from Paul and Southgate[10] and expressed in mmol/100 g)

	Na	K
Natural foods		
Wheat flour, whole meal	0.1	9.2
Rice, raw polished	0.3	2.8
Beef, lean	2.7	9.0
Pork, lean	3.3	9.5
Herring, fresh	2.9	8.7
Milk (cow's)	2.2	3.8
Potatoes, new boiled	1.7	8.5
Carrots, young boiled	1.0	6.1
Beans, haricot boiled	0.4	8.2
Tomatoes, raw	0.1	8.7
Processed foods		
White bread	23	2.6
Rice Krispies	48	4.1
Beef sausages	35	3.8
Bacon, lean	81	9.0
Kipper	43	13.3
Butter, salted	38	0.4
Cheese, cheddar	27	3.1
Potatoes, instant powder made up	11	8.7
Carrots, young canned	12	2.2
Beans, canned	21	7.7
Tomato ketchup	49	15.1

rich, sodium-poor fluid was separated by the cell walls from the sodium-rich environment. Movement of these ions across the membranous cell walls is one of the fundamental processes of life and an essential part of cell excitability, especially in cells of the nervous system. The colonisation of estuaries, rivers and later land was a move to a sodium-poor environment. The rocks and soils of the earth contain little sodium, except for the rock-salt deposits that originated from the evaporation of sea water in remote geological time. Although these deposits are numerous and found in all continents, they are dispersed widely and not generally available to land animals. These continued to have their cells bathed in the salt-rich environment of the blood and lymph, but to maintain this internal environment an effective method of conserving sodium was needed. The development of the capacity of the renal tubules to reabsorb sodium enables mammalian kidneys to secrete a virtually sodium-free urine. The importance of this will be realised when it is appreciated that the dietary intake of sodium by primitive adult man living entirely on plant foods would have been less than 10 mmol daily; this would be substantially raised by the extent to which he was carnivorous. The urge to hunt and trap was probably determined as much by a need for sodium as a need for protein.

There is no archaeological evidence that primitive man utilised salt. The art of panning salt from sea water was probably not discovered before the development of the first civilised agricultural societies less than 12 000 years ago and the greater part of the evolution of *Homo* took place on a salt-free diet. The first known salt mines, found in the Austrian Tyrol, date from the late Bronze Age, about 1000 BC. In a scholarly review Kaunitz[11] has pointed out that it is not known accurately when man first began to use salt. Sanskrit and its daughter languages have no common root for salt, so perhaps the Indo-Europeans at the time of their first migrations did not know of its use. However, salt was certainly available in the early civilisations and Homer called it 'divine'. For at least 3000 years sodium chloride has played 'an amazingly important part in the lives of men. Wars have been fought over its sources, and for centuries its trade was more important than that of any other material'.[11] The salaries which we draw are in lineal descent from the salt money paid to the Roman soldiers. Imperial governments, such as those in the Roman provinces and in British India, have found a salt tax a convenient source of revenue; everyone paid it. This was because salt was the best food preservative available. Salted meat and fish were an important part of the diet in early times.

It is impossible to state with any precision human physiological requirements of sodium or the need for salt. In the middle of this century there were still iso-

lated communities in South East Asia, Africa, Polynesia and the Amazon basin who had not discovered the use of salt. There may be still some today, but most have now a limited access to salt which they prize greatly. Man can live with the sodium present in natural foods and does not need salt for survival. But there may be a need for salt to allow the operation of the higher functions of the central nervous system required to construct civilisations. Lack of initiative is a striking feature of early experimental human sodium deficiency.[7]

There may be adverse effects from too much salt. There are many reports showing that in communities with no or very limited access to salt blood pressure does not rise with age. Gleibermann in an extensive review[12] has shown a positive correlation of daily salt intake, ranging from 1 to 27 g, with both diastolic and systolic blood pressure in 27 human populations. This and the fact that blood pressure falls when a high sodium intake is reduced suggest that excess sodium is an important cause of hypertension. However, a correlation between individual salt intake and blood pressure has not, as yet, been demonstrated in a population with access to ample salt. The relation of sodium intake to hypertension and the place of reducing sodium intake in treatment of the disease are discussed in Chapter 41.

We are now exhorted by health educators in governments and elsewhere to reduce our salt intakes. There is no doubt most of us consume more salt than we need and some of us very much more. This advice is sensible, for to follow it will bring no harm and possibly the benefit of a reduced risk of developing hypertension, a major cause of premature death. But it should not be carried to extremes as was done in 1977 by the US Senate Select Committee on Nutrition and Human Needs in their first report on *Dietary Goals for the United States*, where a goal of 3 g of salt a day was recommended. As the estimated range of salt intakes in the country at this time was from 6 to 18 g a day, achievement of this goal would have involved a total change of food habits. This the American people, who like their food and are healthy relative to most other countries, rejected and quite rightly.

Salt and sodium are fascinating subjects with their roles in the physiology of all mammals and in the history, economics and sociology of *Homo sapiens*. All of these aspects are discussed fully and in a very readable, yet scholarly, manner in a monograph by Denton.[13]

DIETS LOW IN SODIUM

A reduced sodium intake is beneficial in all patients with sodium retention from whatever cause. A moderate reduction can be achieved by not using table salt, reducing cooking salt to a minimum and avoiding or eating spar-

Table 10.7 Approximate daily intake of sodium on different regimes (1 mmol Na = 23 mg Na or 58.8 mg NaCl)

	Sodium expressed as		
	mmol	g Na	g NaCl
A normal diet	150	3.5	9.0
Restricted salt regime	100	2.3	6.0
Low sodium diet, moderate	50	1.2	3.0
Low sodium diet, strict	25	0.6	1.5

ingly salt-rich foods. Such a restricted sodium regime is usually well tolerated and suitable for most patients. When a more severe reduction is indicated a low sodium diet using special salt-free foods is required. Table 10.7 gives the approximate sodium intake of a restricted regime and two low sodium diets. As the sodium content of all foods is subject to wide variation, calculations of intake based on values given in food tables are liable to error of 15 per cent or more. The regime and the diets are described here to avoid repetition; indications for their use are given in several other chapters in the clinical sections of the book.

Restricted sodium regime

This allows the diet to be chosen from normal foods, but the foods which are rich sources of sodium should be excluded as far as possible or reduced to a minimum.

For most patients a restricted salt regime is a hardship, but one which can be undertaken for weeks or months with self-discipline. The regime does not exclude the sharing of meals with one's family or friends, but it does involve the selection of suitable articles of food.

The following points must be firmly impressed on patients and may be given to them as a printed list.

1. No table salt is permitted.
2. Salt used in cooking and baking powder must be reduced to a minimum.
3. Sodium-rich foods, such as ham and bacon, sausages, all tinned meats and fish, shellfish, cheese, all sauces (except special home-made ones) and all biscuits, scones and shop cakes must be avoided.
4. The maximum amount of ordinary bread allowed is five thin slices daily and the maximum amount of butter is 30 g daily.
5. Helpings of fresh meat and fish, should be small, and some vegetables naturally contain moderate amounts of sodium, e.g. beetroot, carrots, celery, radish, turnip and watercress. Potatoes are low in sodium if cooked without added salt, e.g. in their skins.
6. One egg and 250 ml ($\frac{1}{2}$ pint) of milk daily are allowed.
7. All fruits and nuts are permitted.
8. Sugar and jams, rice and sago are freely allowed.

Low sodium diets

With the use of special foods and dietary measures, the daily sodium intake can be greatly reduced (Diets No. 12 and No. 13). Strict adherence to such diets is necessary if these low intakes are to be achieved; the use of special salt-free bread and butter is essential. The provision of a low sodium diet is usually only possible for patients in hospital. If taken at home, expert dietary supervision and instruction are necessary. Salt-free bread and butter are not easy to obtain in many places.

By restricting the diet to washed rice, fruit and fruit juices, as first advocated by Kempner[14], it is possible to reduce the sodium intake to below 10 mmol/day. Patients find this diet monotonous and unappetising. Hence it is seldom recommended.

Uraemia may develop in a patient with cardiac or renal disease who is on a low sodium diet. The doctor must keep this danger in mind.

ACID-BASE BALANCE

Human life is possible only if the blood is kept with a narrow range of alkalinity. In health the blood is maintained between pH 7.35 and 7.45. This precise equilibrium is maintained by two mechanisms. First, the rate of excretion of carbonic acid (a weak acid) through the lungs acts as a very fine adjustment. Secondly, the kidneys are able to excrete urine with either an acid or an alkaline reaction. In disease of the lungs or of the kidneys, these controlling mechanisms may no longer work normally and an acidosis or alkalosis results. Such effects are of great interest to the physiologist and of much practical importance to the physician, but are outside the scope of this book. Here we shall be concerned only with the dietary aspect of acid-base balance which, compared with the renal and respiratory aspects, is very minor.

It has long been known that the urine of the rabbit is normally alkaline and the urine of the dog acid. This is related to the nature of their diets. The fresh urine of an omnivorous animal is usually slightly acid, but in vegetarians it is often neutral, and in large meat-eaters more strongly acid. This is chiefly because sulphuric acid is produced by metabolic oxidation of the sulphur amino acids in protein, and phosphoric acid is formed from the oxidation of nucleoproteins and phospholipids. The hydrogen ion produced in this way on a mixed diet is around 70 mmol/day. Except when kidney function is seriously impaired (Chap. 44) the pH of the blood is easily maintained by the kidneys excreting a correspondingly more or less acid urine.

Fruits and vegetables are alkali-producing foods, but they may taste acidic and are often thought to be 'acid' foods. Many food faddists and some physicians (who should know better) have made much of the 'acidity' of fruits and vegetables. This acidity is due to the presence in plant tissues of a variety of organic acids — citric acid (citrus fruits, pineapple, tomato and most summer fruits), malic acid (apples, plums and tomatoes), benzoic acid (cranberry and bilberry), tartaric acid (grapes), oxalic acid (strawberries, unripe tomatoes, rhubarb and spinach). Sinclair and Hollingsworth[15] give some details of the amount of acid present in fruits and vegetables. They state that very few foods are ever as acid as gastric juice. Further, the body can easily oxidise malic and citric acid. Benzoic acid is excreted by the kidney as hippuric acid. Tartaric acid is hardly absorbed at all. Oxalic acid forms insoluble calcium salts and so is not easily absorbed from the intestines; nevertheless it can also be oxidised and excreted. Intake of these acids, even from large quantities of fruits and vegetables, is well within the capacity of the body to deal with them.[15] They do not cause acidosis. The digestive disturbances from which young gentlemen are known to suffer after an illicit visit to an orchard are attributable to sudden intake of large quantities of indigestible dietary fibre.

However, there are two organic acids produced within the body which can give rise to acidosis. These are lactic and acetoacetic acid. Large quantities of lactic acid may accumulate in the blood after severe muscular exercise (up to 10 mmol/l). The rapid breathing during recovery from exercise helps to restore the acid-base balance by blowing off carbonic acid.

In many pathological states the tissues are inadequately oxygenated and then lactic acid accumulates, e.g. in heart failure. A serious form of **lactic acidosis** arises as a medical emergency in some patients with diabetes and liver disorders in the absence of tissue hypoxia. It is precipitated by drugs, especially biguanides, and by intravenous infusion of fructose.

Acetoacetic acid and its derivative β-hydroxybutyric acid are produced in excess in diabetes that has been inadequately treated. These acids accumulate in the blood and as both are stronger acids than carbonic acid, they displace the bicarbonate in the blood. As a result the dangerous condition of **ketoacidosis** develops (p. 384). These ketone bodies also accumulate in the tissues and plasma when fat metabolism predominates, as in fasting and in any patient whose dietary intake is not meeting energy needs. The subsequent acidosis is seldom severe.

REFERENCES

1. Passmore R, Meiklejohn A P, Dewar A D, Thow R K 1955 Energy utilization in overfed thin young men. Br J Nutr 9: 20–27
2. Consolazio C F, Johnson R E, Pecora L J 1963 Physiological measurements of metabolic function in man. McGraw-Hill, New York
3. Fitzsimmons J T 1972 Thirst. Physiol Rev 52: 468–561
4. Fitzsimmons J T 1979 The physiology of thirst and sodium appetite. Cambridge University Press, Cambridge
5. Hunt J 1953 The ascent of Everest. Hodder & Stoughton, London, p 275
6. Lambie A T, Robson J S 1974 Disorders of water and electrolyte metabolism. In: Passmore R, Robson J S (eds) Companion to medical studies. Blackwell, Edinburgh, vol 3, pt 49, p 1–57
7. McCance R A 1936 Medical problems in mineral metabolism. III: Experimental human salt deficiency. Lancet 1: 823–830
8. Drury A N, Jones N W 1927 Observations on the rate at which oedema forms when the veins of the human limbs are congested. Heat 14: 55–70
9. Hilden T, Svendson T L 1975 Electrolyte disturbances in beer drinkers. Lancet 2: 245–246
10. Paul A A, Southgate D A T 1978 McCance and Widdowson's The composition of human foods, 4th edn. HMSO, London
11. Kaunitz H 1956 Causes and consequences of salt consumption. Nature 178: 1141–1144
12. Gleibermann L 1973 Blood pressure and dietary salt in human populations. Ecology Food Nutr 2: 143–156
13. Denton D 1982 The hunger for salt: an anthropological, physiological and medical analysis. Springer, Berlin
14. Kempner W 1948 Treatment of hypertensive vascular disease with rice diets. Am J Med 4: 545–577
15. Sinclair H M, Hollingsworth D F 1969 Hutchison's Food and the principles of nutrition, 12th edn. Arnold, London, p 133

11

Bone Minerals

Man's food, whether of vegetable or animal origin, is derived from the soil or the sea. The chemical composition of both depends on the rocks that lie beneath them. These are composed of minerals, all of which have a regular arrangement of atoms that has some geometrical symmetry. Over 3000 minerals are known and most of them are complex salts. All of the 103 elements, except some of the gases, occur in one or more of these minerals. Living matter is composed mainly of 11 elements (C, H, O, N, P, S, Na, K, Cl, Ca, Mg) but most of the other elements can be detected in the tissues of plants and animals. Another 12 elements (Fe, Zn, Cu, Co, I, F, Cr, Mn, Mo, Se, V) are known to have a role in one or more metabolic processes in higher animals, including man. They are therefore essential nutrients, but as the daily dietary requirements of man are less than 100 mg, they are known as **trace elements.** Trace amounts of most of the remaining elements are also found in living tissues, but as far as is known none of them are essential nutrients for man, but future research may well add to the list of those that are.

Salts of Na, K, I and F are in general soluble in water and these elements when ingested are usually readily absorbed. Salts of the other elements are relatively insoluble in water and only a small proportion of the dietary intake is absorbed. Furthermore, as these elements are present in the blood mostly bound to plasma proteins, little or none can be excreted in the urine. Control of the amounts present in the body is effected by regulation of absorption in the small intestine.

Primary dietary deficiencies of trace elements are well known to veterinarians and occur where cattle, sheep and horses graze on pastures where the soil is deficient in one of these elements. Because of his varied diet they are uncommon in man, except for iron deficiency. All customary human diets contain amounts of iron which are only marginally adequate to make good the loss of blood that occur in menstruation and to supply the needs of the fetus. Consequently iron deficiency is common in women between the ages of 15 and 50 years in all societies. Secondary deficiencies of mineral elements arise when there are excessive losses from the body as a result of chronic diarrhoea or repeated haemorrhages.

Mechanisms regulating absorption normally protect the tissues against adverse effects from too high a concentration of any of the elements. These mechanisms may be overwhelmed by an excessive intake. The best-known example is siderosis arising from a large dietary intake of iron. Excessive intakes of many elements notably lead, mercury and cadmium arise from the pollution of water and food due to the use of these substances in industry. Toxic amounts of some elements, e.g. lead and mercury, may be absorbed through the lungs, when the atmosphere is polluted with their vapours. The skin is also a possible route of absorption, and toxic effects may arise from contact with chemicals in industry or from the medicinal use of ointments and lotions. It has long been known that the body cannot readily remove the iron administered as part of a blood transfusion and that repeated blood transfusions lead to excessive storage. Now that it is possible to maintain patients for long periods on intravenous feeding, it is important to see that the infusion fluids contain sufficient, but no excess, of each of the mineral elements that are essential nutrients.

Knowledge of the amounts of trace elements in foods and tissues was rudimentary until about 1965 owing to the difficulties of analysis by orthodox chemical methods. The introduction of atomic absorption spectrometry revolutionised analytical procedures. New information has been pouring in and there is no sign that the flow is ceasing. The interpretation of these data in terms of dietary requirements and the risks of deficiency or toxic effect is always difficult, and it is seldom wise to jump to any conclusion from a single set of data. Four editions of Underwood's textbook[1] provide a continuing account of our knowledge of trace elements.

Each of the essential minerals is a component of one or more of the enzyme systems that together make up the metabolism of an organism. As cations they interact with charged groups on proteins and membranes and this electrostatic binding changes the structural configuration of macromolecules and so their biochemical activity. In the most primitive organisms Fe has an

Table 11.1 Some data on calcium in the human body

Present in the skeleton of a young adult male	1200 g	30 mol
Present in the skeleton of a newborn baby	30 g	750 mmol
Concentration in blood and extracellular fluid		
Total	8.5–10.5 mg/dl	2.1–2.6 mm
Ionic	about 4 mg/dl	about 1mm
Concentration in cells and intracellular fluid		
Total	about 8 mg/dl	about 2 mm
Ionic	about 4μg/dl	about 1μm
Daily intake by adults in countries with good dairy herds	1000 mg	25 mmol
Concentration in milk		
Cow's	120 mg/dl	30 mm
Human	34 mg/dl	8.2 mm
Daily turnover in adult skeleton	400–600 mg	10–15 mmol
Oaily urinary output in an adult	50–350 mg	2.5–9 mmol
Daily faecal output in an adult	650–900 mg	16–22.5 mmol

essential role in oxidation and reduction, P in the storage and utilisation of energy and Ca in excitability. These roles were probably established at the very beginning of life in the sea where the three elements were available from the rocks below. These three fundamental processes operate in all living tissues today and, though modifications and adaptations have arisen during evolution, they remain essentially unchanged. Two of these elements, Ca and P, together with Mg, are main components of the exoskeletons of lower animals and of the cartilage and bone of vertebrates. This chapter deals with the bone minerals and the next chapter with iron and other trace elements.

CALCIUM
Ca (at. wt 40)

Calcium salts are the main component of igneous rocks and about 3.6 per cent of the earth's crust consists of the element. They are for the most part insoluble in water but soluble in strong acids. Water from rivers, springs and wells contains calcium in small amounts depending on its acidity and on the calcium content of the rocks and soil with which it has been in contact. Plants take up some of this calcium and all foods of vegetable origin contain small but useful amounts, unless they have been highly processed, e.g. refined sugars and separated oils and fats. Animals concentrate calcium in milk and the only important foods rich in calcium are milk and milk products. In communities who keep good dairy herds about half the dietary calcium comes from milk. Communities who drink little or no milk have relatively low calcium intakes.

The skeletons of all animals consist of a protein matrix upon which insoluble calcium salts are deposited. Large amounts of dietary calcium have to be absorbed during the growing period and smaller amounts in adult life to maintain the bones. There are small but very closely controlled concentrations of calcium in the extra- and intracellular water, and calcium ions have a major role in excitation of muscle and of cells in the glandular organs and nervous system. Table 11.1 sets out some quantitative data on calcium in the human body.

CALCIUM IN THE SKELETON

In life the skeleton is not made up of dry bones, as seen in a museum. In a young adult man the weight of the bones is about 9 kg, or 14 per cent of body weight. The chemical composition of the skeleton is shown in Table 11.2. Most of the protein is collagen, but there is a small amount of proteoglycans containing carbohydrate. Most of the mineral is hydroxyapatite, $3Ca_3(PO_4)_2,Ca(OH)_2$, and there are also small amounts of other salts containing magnesium, sodium, carbonate and citrate. The total amount of calcium in the skeleton of a young adult male is about 1.2 kg, or 30 mol.

The skeleton is not a fixed structure and each bone is continuously being replaced and reorganised. This process was studied in the eighteenth century, notably by the anatomist John Hunter. He fed animals madder,

Table 11.2 Composition of the skeleton of a young adult in life

	kg
Total weight	9.0
Protein	1.8
Water	2.25
Fat	0.45
Minerals	4.50

a natural red dye which was taken up by newly formed bone after absorption, and studied the subsequent fate of the stained bone. When after 1935 radioisotopes became available, it was possible to label bone, first with ^{32}P and later with [45]Ca. Measurements could then be made of the amounts of calcium deposited and reabsorbed daily. In adult man the calcium turnover is normally from 400 to 600 mg daily, or about 0.05 of the total calcium. At this rate about seven years are needed for the total turnover of skeletal mineral. In children whose bones are growing the turnover rate is faster and the calcium may be replaced completely in one year.

Bone growth in early life

From estimates of the size of the skeleton at different ages, the net accretion of calcium by the bones can be calculated. Figure 11.1 shows that it is about 150 mg daily in early infancy and then falls to about 100 mg, rising to 400 mg at puberty during the adolescent growth spurt. These rates of accretion are reduced when the protein matrix on which the calcium salts are deposited is deficient (e.g. in protein-energy malnutrition) and when the supply of calcium is reduced by impaired alimentary absorption (e.g. in vitamin D deficiency, rickets). Giving calcium supplements alone to children on diets low in calcium in controlled clinical trials has produced only small and occasional increases in growth rate,[3,4] much less than can readily be obtained by giving such children supplements of milk or a vegetable protein mixture, not rich in calcium. In the many parts of the world where poor diets prevent the normal growth of children, lack of protein and energy to form the cellular matrix is the factor limiting bone growth, and the bone which is formed is calcified normally except when inadequate exposure to sunlight causes a deficiency of cholecalciferol and subsequent rickets. It would be much easier and cheaper to give children a calcium salt rather than milk or other protein supplement, but unfortunately this would be of little benefit.

During pregnancy a mother has to supply the fetus with up to 30 g of calcium, and when she is lactating her milk provides up to 300 mg daily. If her diet is deficient in calcium, she draws upon the reserves in her bones. Repeated pregnancies with long lactations in a women whose diet contains little or no milk and so is low in calcium leads to demineralisation and softening of her bones (**osteomalacia**).

Bone atrophy with age

Before the age of 40 years bone begins to atrophy. There is little change in the chemical composition and histological structure, but the mass of the skeleton shrinks. In advanced old age it is normally only about 70 per cent of its size in the prime of life. Like greying of the hair and hardening of the lens of the eye, this is part of the normal process of ageing. The bones become less dense and this can be detected by radiography, but routine radiographs only detect gross changes. For epidemiological studies the ratio of the area of cortical bone to the total bone area in a metacarpal bone is usually measured (Fig. 11.2). The figure shows a sharp decline in bone density in women about the time of the menopause and

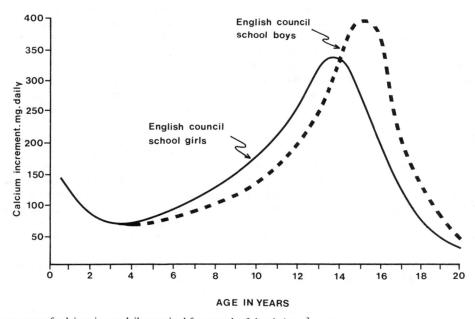

Fig. 11.1 Increments of calcium in mg daily required for growth of the skeleton[2]

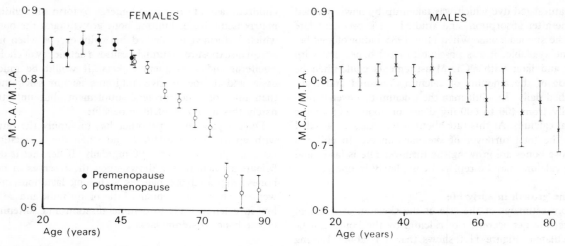

Fig. 11.2 Metacarpal cortical/total area ratios in normal men and women (mean ± SD). (Redrawn from Nordin)[5]

a much more gradual decline in men. It also shows that there are wide individual variations. The data in Figure 11.2 was obtained in England,[5] but similar data are available from the USA[6] and South Africa.[7]

When the bone density is much less than expected for the subject's age, the condition of **osteoporosis** is said to exist. In most cases there is no obvious cause and the terms postmenopausal and senile osteoporosis are frequently used. Osteoporosis, however, may arise from chronic gastrointestinal and endocrine disorders that disturb calcium absorption from the gut and its deposition in bone. Osteoporotic bones break more easily than normal bones. When the condition is advanced, trivial injuries may cause a fracture. An old lady may break the neck of her femur when she falls after tripping up on a carpet. Such fractures in the old are common and not only cause much suffering and disability, but are also an economic problem to the community owing to the number of hospital beds and staff required for their care.

Osteoporosis, like other degenerative changes of old age, cannot be prevented, but it may be possible to slow down its rate of progress, especially in those in whom this is more than usually rapid. Three methods may be useful in appropriate patients.

Exercise. Confinement to bed leads to a negative calcium balance and immobilisation is known to cause osteoporosis at any age; it is sensible to encourage all old people, and especially those with radiological evidence of osteoporosis, to be as physically active as possible. The more that they are on their feet, the less the risk of pathological fractures of the femur and spine.

Dietary therapy. An osteoporotic bone has lost both calcium and protein and so it is not unreasonable to think that a diet low in calcium and protein might accelerate the osteoporotic process. There is no epidemiological evidence to support this view. Osteoporosis

is not more common in those parts of Asia and Africa where diets are low in these nutrients than in the well fed countries of Europe and North America.[8] Indeed in the USA osteoporosis is probably more common in the white than in the black population, who in general eat poorer diets. In South Africa changes in bone density with advancing age is similar in the white and black communities,[9] although the latter have much poorer diets. Also in the USA no correlation has been found between dietary calcium and density of bone in middle-aged subjects.[10] Furthermore, for 40 years the population of the UK had a daily intake of calcium some 200 mg more than that of other countries because our bread and flour were fortified with calcium. There is no evidence that, as a result of this measure, the bones of our old people are less brittle than those of old people elsewhere.

The above evidence indicates that no policy designed to increase the calcium intake of a whole population would be likely to reduce the incidence of osteoporosis in old people. It is, however, sensible for old people to take a diet with ample calcium, i.e. to drink a glass of milk regularly. The case for giving calcium salts to patients with osteoporosis is unproven. Many patients when receiving large doses of calcium go into positive calcium balance but this has not been shown to be accompanied by an increase in bone density. On the other hand, some old people have a markedly reduced capacity to absorb calcium from the gut,[11] and in such patients therapeutic doses of a calcium salt might be of benefit.

Hormonal therapy. There is no doubt that normal bone structure depends on a balance of endocrine secretions. Osteoporosis is a feature of hyperparathyroidism, hyperthyroidism, Cushing's disease and the prolonged use of corticosteroids for therapeutic purposes. Bilateral oophorectomy in a premenopausal woman leads at once to an increased urinary excretion of calcium and subsequently to osteoporosis. This can be prevented by oestrogen replacement therapy which is always indicated in such cases. There is some epidemiological evidence from Newhaven, Connecticut[12] that women who receive postmenstrual oestrogens are at reduced risk of fractures of the hip and radius. The routine and prolonged use of oestrogens after the menopause carries dangers as well as benefits and has long been a controversial subject[13] and is outside our scope.

Androgens have frequently been prescribed for men with osteoporosis, but the benefits have seldom been obvious.

The above summary indicates present lack of knowledge of the mechanisms underlying atrophy of bone with advancing age. Alvioli[14] has written a major review of this difficult subjec with over 500 references.

CALCIUM OUTWITH THE SKELETON

Of total body calcium only about 1 per cent is not present in the skeleton, but this small fraction has a major role in cell biology. Calcium ions are readily bound by electrostatic forces to proteins inside and outside the cells and to cell membranes. Proteins which bind Ca^{2+} include albumin, myosin, troponin C, modulator and transport proteins, extracellular hydrolytic enzymes and prothrombin.[15] The binding alters the shape and configuration of the protein molecules and this determines their biological activity. Thus changes at a neuromuscular junction, initiated by the arrival of nerve impulses, cause calcium bound to the sarcoplasmic reticulation to be liberated. The resultant free Ca^{2+} are then bound to troponin molecules, and this is the internal trigger which leads to shortening of myofibrils and so to contraction of muscle. Several hormones may stimulate metabolic changes by increasing uptake of Ca^{2+} by cells; within the cell Ca^{2+} is bound to enzymic proteins, changes their configuration and so activates them. For example, adrenaline promotes glycolysis by activating phosphorylases in this way. In the blood Ca^{2+} is needed to activate prothrombin and other clotting factors. Removal of Ca^{2+} by binding to citrate or other chelating agents prevents the clotting of blood.

The normal concentration of calcium in the plasma is between 8.5 and 10.5 mg/dl (2.1 to 2.6 mmol/litre). About half of this is present as free ions and half is bound to plasma albumin. Ionic calcium is difficult to measure and clinical laboratories normally report only values for total calcium. If plasma albumin is low, this value is also low, but there may be no reduction in ionic calcium. Plasma calcium may then be adjusted by an addition of 0.02 (40-plasma albumin) mg/dl.

The calcium content of cells is not as easily measured as that of blood. The total calcium is of about the same order as that in blood, but ionic calcium is very much less and in the resting state the concentration may be as low as 1 μM. There are thus very high ionic gradients between extra- and intracellular calcium. It is the modulation of this gradient that controls many cellular activities.

CALCIUM INTAKE

The average daily intake of calcium varies from 350 to 1200 mg in different countries and is closely related to the milk supply. In most European countries and in North America milk provides about half of the dietary calcium. Table 11.3 gives the calcium content of some common foods.

Views on the importance of dietary calcium have changed markedly in the last 60 years. Sherman's popular American textbook,[16] which appeared in six editions between 1920 and 1950, stated that 'the ordinary mixed diet of Americans and Europeans, at least amongst dwellers in cities and towns, was more often deficient in calcium than in any other chemical element'. Sherman, who was a professor at Columbia University, had a great influence on the teaching of nutrition. Americans of all ages were often advised to drink a quart rather than a pint of milk daily, advice which many followed.

Sherman's conclusion was based on two experimental findings. First the calcium intake was often the factor limiting the growth of rats on experimental diets. Secondly adult men and women often went into negative calcium balance when put on diets containing moderate amounts of calcium (500–700 mg). Second thoughts began to arise when it was found, as already described, that in countries with a poor milk supply and consequently a low calcium intake, human bones were calcified normally and had no increased liability to fracture. The beneficial effect of milk on the growth of undernourished children was well known in Sherman's time, but it was not clear then that this could be attributable to its protein content and not primarily to its calcium. In 1939 Nicholls & Nimalasuriya[17] showed that growing children in Sri Lanka often maintained a positive calcium balance on very low intakes of calcium (about 200 mg daily). Children were shown to be different from young rats in their need for calcium.

Adaptation to low calcium intakes
In 1952 Hegsted & his colleagues[18] showed that Peruvians on different levels of calcium intake excreted less calcium than would have been expected from reports in

Table 11.3 Calcium content of some common foods (selected values from various food tables)

Food	Description	Range (mg/100 g or 100 ml)
Cheese	Hard — from whole or skimmed milk	400–1200
Cheese	Soft — from whole or skimmed milk, and processed	60–725
Milk	Cow's — fresh whole	120
Milk	Human	35
Nuts	Various — without shells	13–250
Pulses	Raw — dried	40–150
Herring	Raw — edible parts	33
Roots, gourds and stems	Raw — various, except potato	20–80
Vegetables*	Raw — green, leafy	25–250
Eggs	Fresh, whole	50–60
Oatmeal	Raw, 65 per cent extraction	55–60
Whole wheat	100 per cent extraction	30–40
Wheat flour†	70 per cent extraction	13–20
Millets	Most varieties	20–50
Fruits	Various — raw, fresh	3–60
Fish‡	Fresh	17–32
Beef, mutton, pork and poultry	Raw — edible portions	3–24
Maize	Various millings	5–18
Rice	Raw, polished	4
Potatoes	Raw — all seasons	7–10

* Green vegetables most commonly used in temperate climates all fall in the lower part of the range and therefore contribute little to the calcium content of the diet.
† In Britain this is fortified and Ca is 140 mg/100 g.
‡ Sardines and other small fish eaten whole provide anything up to 400 mg Ca/100 g and may therefore be important sources of calcium.

the North American and European literature. Their subjects had been accustomed to diets low in calcium. At about the same time Walker & Arvidsson[19] reported from Johannesburg that the bones of adult Bantus whose regular diet provided no more than 300 mg of calcium contained normal amounts of the element. In 1958 Malm[20] made a thorough study of the adaptation of 26 Norwegian prisoners to diets low in calcium. The subjects were healthy men aged 20 to 69 years, some of whom were investigated continuously for a year or longer. Table 11.4 illustrates a metabolic study of a man in whom, after several months on a low calcium diet, the faecal loss was so reduced that he was virtually in balance. Of the 26 subjects, 22 adapted satisfactorily, 10 rapidly and 12 slowly as in the example. One man made a slight adaptation, but in three there was no adaptation. Adults who have grown accustomed over a long period to a calcium intake greatly in excess of their true needs, may no longer absorb enough calcium to keep themselves in equilibrium when their dietary intake is reduced. Table 11.4 shows that when adaptation has occurred, a much smaller proportion of the dietary calcium is present in the faeces, i.e. alimentary absorption is increased.

Alimentary absorption

Calcium is transported across the intestinal mucosa bound to a specific carrier protein. The formation of this protein in the epithelial cells is dependent on cholecalciferol (vitamin D) and its metabolism. Insufficiency of cholecalciferol leads to a failure of absorption and calcium deficiency.

Calcium has to be present in the soluble ionic form before it can be bound to the carrier protein. There are many substances commonly present in the lumen of the gut which are capable of binding or reacting with calcium ions and so rendering them insoluble. To what extent these substances impair calcium absorption is not fully known — at least in quantitative terms.

Phytic acid. In 1925 Mellanby[21] showed that puppies developed rickets when fed a diet poor in vitamin D and calcium, and containing large amounts of bread. The puppies that ate the most bread grew fastest and developed the most severe rickets. Mellanby at first attributed this to the growth-promoting properties of the bread, which allowed the puppies to grow faster than their bones could lay down calcium. He soon found, however, that the effect was not due solely to the quantity of bread eaten; there were also qualitative dif-

Table 11.4 An example of adaptation by a Norwegian to a low calcium diet.[20] (All figures in mg/day)

Days observed	Intake	Urine	Faeces	Balance	Total gain or loss
210	942	238	605	+100	+21 g
210	436	200	323	−88	−18.5 g
196	454	209	252	−7	−1.3 g

ferences. Whole wheat flour was more rachitogenic than white flour, and oatmeal worse than either. The story was completed[22] by the finding that there is a substance in cereals that prevents calcium absorption and this was identified as phytic acid, the hexaphosphoric ester of inositol.

In 1942 McCance & Widdowson[23] showed that these findings were applicable to human diets, and Table 11.5 gives a summary of the experiments on one of their subjects. It was then a critical time in World War II when the outcome of the Battle of the Atlantic still lay in the balance. Food from North America was vital, but there were not enough ships to transport it; consequently a change from white bread to bread containing more of the whole grain became essential. The experiments led to the decision to fortify the new bread with calcium.

Table 11.5 Intake and absorption of calcium on diets largely composed of bread[23]

Bread	Intake mg/day	Absorption mg/day	% of intake
Brown	550	89	16
Dephytinised brown	590	231	39
White	488	250	51

Although many experiments have shown that a sudden change to a diet containing much phytic acid adversely affects calcium absorption, this is not likely to be permanent. There are many communities whose habitual diet is based on whole or lightly milled cereals and contains sufficient phytic acid to be able, in theory, to precipitate all the calcium that it contains.[24] Clearly this does not occur under the conditions present in the human intestine, where the ability to break down phytic acid is developed when the diet is rich in unrefined cereals. There is little reason to think that calcium absorption is influenced by the amounts of phytic acid commonly present in human diets. However, it is probable that, when chapattis made of wholemeal flour are a major item in the diet, as in many Asian communities, the large intake of phytic acid by diminishing absorption of calcium predisposes to rickets and osteomalacia (Chap. 32).

Dietary fibre. Dietary fibre binds calcium in proportion to its uronic acid content (Chap. 4). Uronic acids can be digested by bacteria in the colon and absorption from the colon may help to maintain calcium balance when on a high fibre diet.

Phosphate. Before the discovery of phytic acid it was generally believed that phosphate intake had a crucial influence on calcium absorption. This belief originated from experiments showing that a high dietary Ca/P ratio caused rickets in rats.

Subsequent human experiments show that phosphate intake has little or no influence on calcium absorption, at least within the range within which these normally occur in foodstuffs. Six Norwegian men given phosphate by mouth in amounts sufficient to provide an extra 250 to 1000 mg P/day for four to eight weeks maintained their normal calcium balance.[26] In breast-fed babies, a supplement of phosphates did not hinder absorption of calcium.[27]

Ca/P ratios in food can therefore be forgotten, along with other once popular but now outmoded scientific fashions. This firm dictum appeared in the first edition. We see no reason to modify it, as regards normal diets, and it is supported by a later study.[28] However, the absorption of calcium in the first few weeks of life from artificial milks presents special problems.[29] In such preparations the Ca/P ratio may be important.

Fats. Fatty acids form insoluble soaps with calcium. Thus fatty acids, and particularly those that are saturated, may carry into the faeces significant amounts of calcium. They may also carry with them fat-soluble vitamin D. Hence it is understandable how patients with chronic intestinal disorders leading to increased fat in the faeces (steatorrhoea) may develop osteomalacia after a time.

Oxalic acid. This can inhibit the absorption of calcium because calcium oxalate is insoluble. Soluble oxalates are present in certain fruits and vegetables, but the amounts of these consumed are seldom sufficient to have any practical influence on calcium absorption.

CALCIUM OUTPUT

Lactation

A lactating mother commonly loses 150 to 300 mg of calcium daily in her milk. The mammary glands withdraw this amount from the blood, which is simultaneously replenished from the calcium pool, and so the plasma concentration is maintained, though at a somewhat lower level probably because of the reduced plasma albumin concentration. If the diet is grossly deficient in calcium, the bones must provide the calcium for the milk. However, in the whole period of lactation the total amount of calcium secreted would never exceed 100 g, which is small by comparison with the total amount normally present in the bones. Furthermore, there is evidence that calcium absorption is enhanced in late pregnancy and during lactation. Prolactin increases the rate at which vitamin D is converted to the active 1,25 dihydroxy form.[30] It is understandable, therefore, why there is usually no radiographic evidence of loss of calcium salts from the bones during lactation, although in women previously seriously depleted of calcium, breastfeeding may precipitate the clinical features of osteomalacia.

Excretion

In the faeces.   Most of the calcium found in the stools is that part of the dietary intake which, for one reason or another, never gets absorbed. The remainder comes from shed epithelial cells and the digestive juices daily poured into the intestinal tract. Assuming this quantity to be about 8 litres and also that these juices have the same content of ionised calcium as the blood serum, 400 mg Ca/day is likely to secreted into the lumen of the bowel. The amount ultimately reabsorbed depends on the various factors mentioned above which influence calcium absorption.

In the urine.   The urine normally contains 100 to 350 mg Ca/day. The amount varies greatly from person to person[31] and is higher in the summer.[32] In women the fasting overnight level of calcium excretion increases after the menopause.[33] This may provide an explanation for postmenopausal osteoporosis. A milk drink before going to bed might reduce nocturnal bone loss. Urinary excretion of calcium falls when dietary protein is reduced and rises when it is increased.[34] The calcium loss is usually greater than any increased absorption on moderate and high protein intakes. This phenomenon helps to explain how people in developing countries have no more osteoporosis than those in Europe and North America, despite lower calcium intakes.

In the sweat.   Men working in extreme heat may lose over 100 mg/h of calcium in the sweat.[35] Under these conditions the sweat may contribute 30 per cent of the total calcium output. Normally this loss is about 15 mg/day and insignificant.

CALCIUM BALANCE

An adult on a normal mixed diet is usually in a state of calcium equilibrium, i.e. the amount lost in the faeces and urine is approximately equal to the amount present in the food. Table 11.6 give the data of the measured calcium exchanges of healthy individuals living on very different diets.

In growing children the body is normally in positive balance, with calcium being steadily retained for the for-

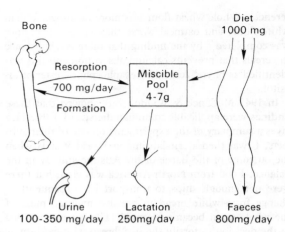

Fig. 11.3 Calcium exchanges in the body

mation of new bone. As the table clearly shows, when the need of the bones is great, net absorption of dietary calcium via the intestinal mucosa can be much greater than normal.

Figure 11.3 shows the main features of calcium balance. A miscible pool, mainly in the blood and extracellular fluids, provides for the slow turnover in bones. This pool is replenished by dietary calcium and losses occur in urinary excretion. The concentration of plasma calcium is finely regulated and controls the size of the pool.

RECOMMENDED DIETARY ALLOWANCE

The recommended dietary allowance of calcium for an adult male in the first report of the US Food and Nutrition Board[40] was 1000 mg. In arriving at this figure, the Board relied on balance studies and in 1943, when the report appeared, data from the study of nearly 100 subjects were available and these confirmed Sherman's early findings. When in 1962 FAO/WHO considered calcium requirements, they suggested that an intake between 400 and 500 mg was a practical allowance.[24] By that time the data from balance studies in Peru and

Table 11.6 Examples of calcium balances in healthy individuals. (All figures in mg/day)

Subject	Diet	Intake	Urine	Faeces	Total excretion	Balance
South African male[36]	Normal mixed European	1008	135	858	993	+ 15
Bengali male[37]	Rice and fish	536	80	395	475	+ 61
German boy aged 11[38]	Orphanage diet: wholemeal bread and vegetables	944	43	509	552	+392
South Indian children[39]	Orphanage diet: wheat, pulses and vegetables	204	26	101	127	+ 77

in other countries with an habitually low intake of calcium were available. Since then, many committees in many countries have spent innumerable hours debating calcium requirements and come up with various figures between these two. As primary calcium deficiency has never been reported in man on any normal diet, debating a recommended dietary allowance now seems of no practical value. Indeed the resulting figure can be misleading as, when a diet survey shows that the calcium intake of a community is less than that recommended, it may be concluded, wrongly, that calcium deficiency is present. A real difficulty in that we cannot diagnose a mild calcium deficiency.

The causes of error are interesting and it is worthwhile considering how they arise. In the case of calcium requirements it was not because the experimental findings were wrong. Human beings whose normal intake of calcium is high do go into negative balance when their intake is reduced. A high intake of phosphate in rats and of phytic acid in puppies does lead to calcium deficiency. In man a sudden increase in intake of phytic acid does lead to diminished calcium absorption. However, it was not appreciated that the human experiments lasted only a few weeks and that man takes time to adapt to changes in diet. Rats and puppies, especially under strict laboratory conditions, do not always respond in the same way as man. Further, those who were responsible for these findings, notably Sherman, Mellanby and McCance & Widdowson, were experimentalists of high repute and deservedly so. It is perhaps normal for lesser men to read into the findings of the masters more than is there. Evidence is also often overestimated by the prosecution, and at the time of these studies there was much enthusiasm for incriminating lack of individual nutrients as causes of disease. Finally then, as now, the value of laboratory experiments was overestimated relative to the study of the natural history of diseases. Insufficient attention was paid to the lack of clinical evidence of calcium deficiency. All these factors continue to lead intelligent men and women into errors, and these are liable to get into textbooks which should always be read with the mind open to suspicion.

PLASMA CALCIUM

Regulation

This is by hormonal mechanisms operating at three sites, the bones, the kidney and the gut, and independent of the nervous system. Three hormones are responsible, parathyroid hormone, calcitonin and metabolites of vitamin D.

The parathyroid glands that are in the neck, either embedded in or close to the thyroid gland, respond directly to a fall in plasma calcium by increased secretion.

This immediately reduces renal calcium excretion and also promotes calcium absorption from the gut. Parathyroid hormone also releases calcium from bone, but its action on turnover and remodelling of bone is slower.

Calcitonin is secreted by C cells of the thyroid gland in response to a raised plasma calcium. Its main action, which is rapid, is to reduce calcium output from bone and it is probably a fine control.

Vitamin D and its metabolites increase calcium absorption from the small intestine as described in Chapter 13. Vitamin D metabolites also increase reabsorption of calcium by bones and kidney.

Plasma ionised calcium is also affected by pH. It is decreased by alkalosis and raised by acidosis.

Hypocalcaemia

Hypocalcaemia may occur after operations on the thyroid gland, if too much parathyroid tissue is removed, causing diminished mobilisation of calcium from bone. It is usually due to impaired alimentary absorption because of vitamin D deficiency and is a common feature of rickets and osteomalacia; it may also occur in patients with the malabsorption syndrome.

When plasma ionic calcium is reduced, nerve and muscle become more readily excitable. Sensation of tingling and numbness may be present and on the motor side twitching of muscles, known as **tetany**, which may be followed by spasm. The face, hands and feet are mainly affected; characteristically the wrist and metacarpophalangeal joints are flexed and the interphalangeal joints extended. This is known as *le main d'accoucheur*. The larynx may be affected and this causes a coarse stridor.

Hypercalcaemia

In infants

Idiopathic hypercalcaemia of infants was first described in 1952 at St Mary's Hospital, London.[41] Soon after, it was reported in many other parts of Britain and in Northern Europe, though infrequently in the USA. It became rare after 1957 when the amounts of vitamin D in cod liver oil in infant foods were reduced.

The disease usually starts between the ages of 5 and 8 months. Infants affected suffer from loss of appetite, vomiting, wasting, constipation, flabby muscles and a characteristic facial appearance. The concentration of calcium in the plasma is raised, as may be that of urea and cholesterol, and also the blood pressure. Calcification may occur in the heart and kidneys. Mental retardation may be marked and the damage to brain and other organs irreparable. The infants not infrequently die. The aetiology is not always clear. Excessive absorption of calcium results from overdosage with cholecalciferol, and many of the infants had received excessive amounts of vitamin D preparations. In others there was no evidence of such overdosage. It is to this latter group of cases that the name idiopathic hypercalcaemia should be restricted. Perhaps these infants had some idiosyncrasy or hypersensitivity to the vitamin. For further information two reviews[42, 43] are recommended.

Treatment consists in providing a diet as low as possible in calcium, and free from vitamin D. The commercial product, Locasol (Trufood Ltd), is satisfactory since on reconstitution with water to a 12.5 per cent (1 in 8) solution, it provides a fluid which is similar to breast milk except that it contains rather less calcium and no vitamin D. It can be used as a beverage suitably flavoured and also in preparing soups, puddings and dishes permitted in the low calcium diet.

In adults

Hypercalcaemia occurs in adults as a result of hyperparathyroidism or excessive doses of vitamin D. It has also been reported in patients with peptic ulcer with impaired renal function treated with a milk diet and large doses of alkali — the milk–alkali syndrome. It may also occur in patients with cancer of the lung and at other sites due to 'inappropriate' secretion of a parathyroid hormone-like substance by tumour cells. Hypercalcaemia can be reduced by treatment with calcitonin.

A slow increase in plasma calcium, as is usual in hyperparathyroidism, may not at first cause any symptoms. Calcium excretion in the urine is increased and this may lead to formation of stones and renal colic is often the first symptom. A rapid increase, as may occur with acute poisoning from overdoses of cholecalciferol, may cause a variety of symptoms, mainly attributable to disturbed activity of the peripheral and central nervous systems.

THERAPEUTIC USES OF CALCIUM

In tetany and when the bones are decalcified due to poor calcium absorption, as in rickets, osteomalacia and the malabsorption syndrome, or when excessive calcium has been lost from the body, as in hyperparathyroidism or chronic renal disease, calcium lactate or gluconate should be given by mouth. A level teaspoonful of calcium lactate weighs about 2 g and provides 400 mg of absorbable calcium. An effective therapeutic dose is three teaspoonfuls given three times a day in water before meals (providing about 3.6 g of calcium). Proprietary effervescent tablets are available. Calcium gluconate can be given intravenously in aqueous solution for the immediate relief of tetany.

PHOSPHORUS
P (at. wt 31)

As phosphate is a major constituent of all plant and animal cells, phosphorus is present in all natural foods. Food manufacturers also use it as a food additive for various reasons. Total food supplies in the United Kingdom provide 1.5 g P/head daily of which about 10 per cent is added artificially.

Primary dietary deficiency of phosphorus is not known to occur in man, though it may arise in cattle grazing on land lacking in phosphates. In people taking large quantities of aluminium hydroxide antacids dietary phosphate is bound and not absorbed. This can lead to secondary phosphate depletion. Occasional cases have been reported. There is muscle weakness and bone pains. Plasma inorganic phosphate is very low and urinary phosphorus only about 15 mg/day.[44]

Most of the phosphate in the body is present in bones which contain from 600 to 900 g P. Bone ash was a component of many ancient and mediaeval remedies and later glycerophosphates have had a great vogue as a tonic. Now with all other tonics it is in disrepute.

Phosphate metabolism may be disturbed in many types of disease, notably those affecting the kidneys and bone. The plasma concentration of phosphate is controlled mainly by renal excretion, and normally falls within the range 0.8 to 1.4 mmol/l (2.5 to 4.5 mg P/100 ml) in the fasting state. Foods rich in calcium and protein are generally rich in phosphorus and dietitians are seldom asked to provide diets with a specified content. There is no recommended intake in Britain. The US recommended intake (p. 171) of P is equal to that for calcium except in infancy: 800 mg/day for adults is a generous allowance for most circumstances.[45]

The effects on young infants fed on preparations of cow's milk with a much higher phosphate content than human milk are discussed on page 582.

MAGNESIUM
Mg (at. wt 24)

All human tissues contain small amounts of magnesium. The whole adult body contains about 25 g or 1 mol of the metal. The greater part of this amount is present in bones in combination with phosphate and bicarbonate. Bone ashes contain rather less than 1 per cent magnesium. It seems likely that the bones provide a reserve supply of magnesium, as of calcium and sodium, which is available when there is a shortage elsewhere in the body.

About one-fifth of the total magnesium in the body is present in the soft tissues, where it is apparently mainly bound to protein. The plasma normally contains

0.6 to 1.0 mmol/l (1.4 to 2.4 mg/100 ml). Next to potassium, magnesium is the predominant cation in living cells. The concentration in cell water is about 10 mmol/l and so there is a large gradient across the cell membranes. Inside the cells the metal is concentrated within the mitochondria where it is a co-factor for cocarboxylase and co-enzyme A and concerned with energy transfer.

Fortunately, from the standpoint of the nutritionist, most foods contain useful amounts, particularly those of vegetable origin, because magnesium is an essential component of chlorophyll. A typical British diet contains 200 to 400 mg or 8 to 17 mmol/day,[45] which should be ample to maintain normal reserves. Cereals and vegetables between them normally contribute more than two-thirds of the daily magnesium intake. The US recommended intake for adults is 350 mg (15 mmol)/day. Vitamin D appears to increase Mg absorption from the intestine.

It is unlikely therefore that magnesium deficiency would arise in man from simple lack of foods containing it.

Magnesium deficiency

Excessive losses of magnesium in the faeces or urine occur in many diseases and the resulting magnesium deficiency leads to apathy and muscular weakness and sometimes to tetany and convulsions. These features are not characteristic and diagnosis is made by finding a low plasma Mg.

Diarrhoea even for a few days in young children may cause magnesium deficiency which is commonly found in children admitted to hospital with protein-energy malnutrition. In adults it may arise in patients with prolonged diarrhoea from any cause, with intestinal fistulae or with the malabsorption syndrome.

Increased urinary losses occur in various renal disorders, in diabetic ketoacidosis, where it follows osmotic diuresis and muscle wasting, in hyperparathyoidism and sometimes in hyperthyroidism and in hyperaldosteronism. Many alcoholics have a low plasma Mg.

Magnesium salts given by mouth are poorly absorbed and tend to cause diarrhoea. For patients with diarrhoea receiving intravenous fluids a daily addition of 20–30 mmol of Mg to the infusion prevents deficiency.

The dose for children is 10 mmol/kg. To replace established depletion larger doses are needed, but plasma Mg should be repeatedly checked to avoid hypermagnesaemia.

STRONTIUM
Sr (at. wt 88)

In 1798 Hope,[46] who was professor of medicine in Glasgow, described a mineral found in the ore from the lead mines of Strontian in Argyllshire. He wrote: 'Considering it a peculiar earth, I thought it necessary to give it a name. I have called it strontites from the place where it was found, a mode of derivation, in my opinion, fully as proper as any quality it may possess.'

Although widely distributed in nature and present in foods and in the skeleton, strontium is probably not an element essential for human life and aroused little medical interest until the start of atomic explosions. These produce the radioactive isotope of the element ^{90}Sr which is widely dispersed in the fallout. The isotope subsequently may become incorporated into plants and animals and so into human food.

Strontium, like calcium and magnesium, is a divalent metal and its biological behaviour is in many ways similar to that of calcium. In general strontium is present in those foods which are rich in calcium, especially milk and to a lesser extent fresh vegetables; it is also stored in bone. Concentrations of strontium in biological material tend to be about one thousand times less than those of calcium. Balance studies have been made on babies.[47] Cow's milk is richer than human milk in strontium as it is in calcium. The intake of strontium was four to eight times greater in bottle-fed babies than in breast-fed babies, and the amount of strontium retained was dependent on the quantity of milk ingested. Breast-fed babies excreted more strontium than they were receiving, due to a large urinary output. The urinary output of strontium was slightly reduced, when supplementary phosphate was given. In all infants, the ratio strontium: calcium was higher in the urine and faeces than in the bones. The body thus appears to discriminate against strontium in favour of calcium, especially in the breast-fed infant.

REFERENCES

1. Underwood E J 1977 Trace elements in human and animal nutrition, 4th edn. Academic Press, New York
2. Leitch I, Aitken F C 1959 The estimation of calcium requirements: a re-examination. Nutr Abstr Rev 29: 393–407
3. Aykroyd W R, Krishnan B G 1938 Effect of calcium lactate on children in a nursery school. Lancet 2: 153–155
4. Rajalaksini R, Merchant G V, Gandhi V H 1973 Effects of calcium and/or vitamin D supplementation on skeletal status of children, school boys and adults. Baroda J Nutr 4: 51–69
5. Nordin B E C 1971 Clinical significance and pathogenesis of osteoporosis. Br Med J 1: 571–576
6. Garn S M, Rohmann C G, Wagner B 1967 Bone loss as a general phenomenon. Fed Proc 26: 1729–1736

7. Solomon L 1979 Bone density in ageing Caucasian and African populations. Lancet 2: 1326–1330
8. Nordin B E C 1966 International patterns of osteoporosis. Clin Orthop 45: 17–30
9. Solomon L 1979 Bone density in ageing Caucasian and African populations. Lancet 2: 1326–1329
10. Garn S M 1972 The course of bone gain and the phases of bone loss. Orthop Clin N Am 3: 503–520
11. Bullamore J R, Gallagher J G, Wilkinson R, Nordin B E C, Marshall D H 1970 Effect of age on calcium absorption. Lancet 2: 535–537
12. Hutchinson T A, Polansky S M, Feinstein A R 1979 Post-menopausal oestrogens protect against fractures of hip and distal radius. Lancet 2: 705–708
13. Kerr M G, Parboosingh I J T 1974 Climacteric and menopause. In: Passmore R, Robson J S (eds) Companion to medical studies. Blackwell, Edinburgh, vol 3, pt 28, p 13–15
14. Alvioli L V 1977 Osteoporosis: pathogenesis and therapy. In: Alvioli L V, Krane S M (eds) Metabolic bone disease. Academic Press, New York, vol 1, p 307–385
15. Wiliams R J P 1979 Cation and proton interactions with proteins and membranes. Biochem Soc Trans 7: 481–508
16. Sherman H C 1920–50 (6 edns) Chemistry of food and nutrition. Columbia University Press, New York
17. Nicholls L, Nimalasuriya A 1939 Adaptation to a low calcium intake in reference to the calcium requirements of a tropical population. J Nutr 18: 563–577
18. Hegsted D M, Moscaso I, Collazos C 1952 A study of the minimum calcium requirements of adult man. J Nutr 46: 181–201
19. Walker A R P, Arvidsson U B 1954 Studies on human bone from South African Bantu subject. Metabolism 3: 385–391
20. Malm O J 1958 Calcium requirement and adaptation in adult man. Scand J Clin Lab Invest 10: suppl 36
21. Mellanby E 1925 Experimental rickets. Spec Rep Ser Med Res Coun Lond no. 93
22. Mellanby E 1934 Nutrition and disease. Oliver & Boyd, Edinburgh
23. McCance R A, Widdowson E M 1942 (a) Mineral metabolism of healthy adults on white and brown bread dietaries. (b) Mineral metabolism on dephytinised bread. J Physiol (Lond) 101: 44–85, 304–313
24. Food and Agricultural Organisation/World Health Organisation 1962 Calcium requirements. WHO Tech Rep Ser no. 230
25. James W P T, Branch W J, Southgate D A T 1978 Calcium binding by dietary fibre. Lancet 1: 638–639
26. Malm O J 1953 On phosphates and phosphoric acid as dietary factor in the calcium balance of man. Scand J Clin Lab Invest 5: 75–84
27. Widdowson E M, McCance R A, Harrison G E, Sutton A 1963 Effect of giving phosphate supplements to breast-fed babies on absorption and excretion of calcium, strontium, magnesium and phosphorus. Lancet 2: 1250–1251
28. Spencer H, Kramer L, Norris C 1975 Calcium absorption and balances during high phosphorus intake in man. Fed Proc 34: 888
29. Widdowson E M 1965 Absorption and excretion of fat, nitrogen, and minerals from 'filled' milk by babies one week old. Lancet 2: 1099–1105
30. Boass A, Toverud S U, McCain T A, Pike J W, Haussler M R 1977 Elevated serum levels of Ca 25-dihydroxycholecalciferol in lactating rats. Nature 267: 630–632
31. Davis R H, Morgan D B, Rivlin R S 1970 The excretion of calcium in the urine and its relation to calcium intake, sex and age. Clin Sci 39: 1–12
32. Robertson W G, Gallagher J C, Marshall D H, Peacock M, Nordin B E C 1974 Seasonal variations in urinary excretion of calcium. Br Med J 4: 436–437
33. Nordin B E C 1971 Clinical significance and pathogenesis of osteoporosis: Br Med J 1: 571–579
34. Chu J W, Margen S, Costa F M 1975 Studies in calcium metabolism. II: Effects of low calcium and variable protein intake on human calcium metabolism. Am J Clin Nutr 28: 1028–1035
35. Consolazio C F, Matoush L O, Nelson R A, Hackler L R, Preston E E 1962 Relationship between calcium in sweat, calcium balance and calcium requirement. J Nutr 78: 78–88
36. Walker A R P, Fox F W, Irving J T 1948 The effects of bread rich in phytate phosphorus on the metabolism of certain mineral salts with special reference to calcium. Biochem J 42: 452–462
37. Basu K P 1946 Studies on protein, fat and mineral metabolism on Indians. Indian Res Fund Ass Special Rep no. 15
38. Widdowson E M, Thrussel L A 1951 Studies of undernutrition Wuppertal 1946–49. The absorption and excretion of nitrogen, calcium, magnesium and phosphorus. Spec Rep Ser Med Res Coun Lond no. 275, p 296–312
39. Begum A, Pereira S M 1969 Calcium balance studies on children accustomed to low calcium intakes. Br J Nutr 23: 905–911
40. Food and Nutrition Board 1943 Recommended dietary allowances. National Research Council Reprint and Circular Series no. 115
41. Lightwood R 1952 Idiopathic hypercalcaemis with failure to thrive: nephrocalcinosis. Proc R Soc (Med) 45: 401
42. Forfar J O, Tompsett S L 1959 Idiopathic hypercalcaemia of infancy. Adv Clin Chem 2: 167–200
43. Mitchell R G 1967 Modern views on rickets and hypercalcaemia in infancy. World Rev Nutr Diet 8: 207–243
44. Dent C E, Winter C S 1974 Osteomalacia due to phosphate depletion from excessive aluminium hydroxide ingestion. Br Med J 1: 551–552
45. Marshall D H, Nordin B E C, Speed R 1976 Calcium, phosphorus and magnesium requirements. Proc Nutr Soc 35: 163–173
46. Hope T C 1798 Account of a mineral from Strontian, and of a peculiar species of earth which it contains. Trans R Soc Edin 4(2): 3–39
47. Widdowson E M, McCance R A, Harris G E, Sutton A 1963 Effect of giving phosphate supplements to breast-fed babies on absorption and excretion of calcium, strontium, magnesium and phosphorus. Lancet 2: 1250–1251

12

Iron, Zinc and Other Trace Minerals

The body contains small amounts of many minerals, some of which are essential nutrient since they are components of many enzyme systems. There are about 4 g of iron and 2 g of zinc in an adult body and these two elements are involved in many metabolic mechanisms. The other essential minerals are present in smaller amounts and have more limited roles. Traces of many mineral elements from the earth's crust can be detected in the human body and appear to have no physiological role. When mankind learnt to mine and concentrate ores, we became at risk of mineral poisoning. Lead is the major hazard and lead poisoning was common in Roman times. Mercury poisoning has also been known for a long time.

IRON
Fe (at. wt 56)

Iron has two major roles in human physiology. First the four iron atoms in the haemoglobin molecule combine loosely with O_2 in amounts varying with the partial pressure of the gas and in this way act as the carrier of O_2 from the atmosphere to the tissues; O_2 is similarly attached to the iron atoms in myoglobin and this provides a small store of O_2 in muscles. Secondly ferrous and ferric iron present in cytochromes and in many proteins in all cells interchange with gain or loss of an electron

$$Fe^{2+} \rightleftharpoons Fe^{3+} + e$$

This reaction is an essential part of the electron chain responsible for the oxidation of many substances in intermediary metabolism and for the reductions necessary in the synthesis of larger molecules from their components.

Both Fe^{2+} and Fe^{3+} readily form complexes by ligand bonds with many organic and inorganic ions. Hence ionic iron is virtually absent from tissues and indeed is very toxic (see below). The absence of ionic iron from the blood and so from the glomerular filtrate prevents the kidneys from excreting Fe.

Iron is present in the earth's crust in amounts greater than any other mineral except aluminium. Because they can be easily either oxidised or reduced, iron-containing substances played an essential role in the evolution of living matter and of the present atmosphere of the planet.[1] Both of the these processes began about three aeons (3000 million years) ago. Then the atmosphere consisted mainly of water vapour with small amounts of CO, CO_2, N_2 and H_2, but contained virtually no O_2. When such an atmosphere is irradiated by ultraviolet light, the energy in the photons promotes the synthesis of hydrogen cyanide (HCN), formaldehyde (HCHO) and ammonia (NH_3). From these substances amino acids, nucleotides, sugars and lipids can be synthesised, provided they are protected from oxidation. The earliest forms of life must have been viruses and protista, and so prokaryotic and distinguishable from the eukaryotic cells of higher forms by a less organised structure and the absence of nuclei.

Three aeons ago the greater part of the iron in the earth's crust and in the hydrosphere was in the reduced or ferrous form, mainly as FeO. This would act as an oxygen acceptor and so maintain the anaerobic conditions necessary for the formation of complex organic molecules. The build-up of O_2 in the atmosphere began about two aeons ago as a consequence of the development by prokaryotic algae in the hydrosphere of photosynthesis with the reduction of H_2O and the liberation of its O_2 into the atmosphere. Photosynthesis depends on the green pigment chlorophyll, and an iron-containing protein, ferridoxine, is part of the electron chain involved in its synthesis.

Land plants first appeared only about 0.4 aeons ago and the atmosphere probably attained its present form a little later. As aerobic conditions became established much of the iron in the earth's crust and in the hydrosphere became converted from the ferrous to the ferric state. Today the greater part of our environmental iron and almost all the iron in plants is in the ferric state. This is important in nutrition, since ferric iron complexes are much less readily solubilised than ferrous ones. Hence their iron is less available for absorption in the small intestine.

Table 12.1 Iron in the body of an adult male

	Chemical form	Approximate amount (mg)	
In the blood	Haemoglobin		2500
In the tissues	Myoglobin	320	
	Haem enzymes	80	
	Non-haem enzymes	100	500
Stores mainly in	Ferritin	700	
liver, spleen and	Haemosiderin	300	1000
bone marrow			
		Total	4000

IRON EXCHANGES IN THE BODY

An adult male contains about 4 g of iron in his body and a female a little less. Table 12.1 shows its distribution. In a classic paper in 1937 McCance & Widdowson[2] set out the view that little or no iron was excreted either by the intestines or the kidneys, and that the amount of iron in the body was kept constant by controlled absorption in the small intestine of sufficient to replace the iron lost in dead cells, desquamated from the surfaces. Iron is also lost whenever there is bleeding, and in women menstrual loss is approximately the same as the loss in desquamation. In pregnancy iron is needed for the fetus and placenta and there is inevitably some loss of blood in labour. In consequence women during their reproductive life have to absorb about twice as much iron from the diet as men. When isotopes of iron, ^{55}Fe and ^{59}Fe, became available, Moore was a pioneer in using them to study iron exchanges in the body, and in 1961 he summarised his findings in a diagram,[3] reproduced with minor modifications as Figure 12.1.

Anaemia due to iron deficiency is the commonest nutritional disorder throughout the world. It occurs mainly in women with excessive menstrual losses, and also in both sexes in those areas of the tropics where there is widespread infestation with hookworms (ancylostomiasis), which suck blood from the intestines. Iron deficiency also arises from acute and chronic haemorrhage and from a variety of disorders of the gut interfering with absorption. A monograph, *Iron metabolism in man*, by Bothwell et al,[4] gives a full account of the subject and its 2600 references are a mine of detailed information.

OUTPUT

The loss of iron in the urine is less than 100 µg daily. Some of this is present in erythrocytes, leucocytes and epithelial cells in the sediment and the remainder probably comes from these cells after disintegration.

The suggestion has often been made that iron loss in sweat might be partly responsible for anaemia in the tropics. However, in a study[5] in Dar es Salaam on active young men, such losses amounted to only 250–500 µg daily.

Measurements of the rate of decline of specific activity of body iron after giving a radioisotope indicated a daily loss of iron from the body of up to 1 mg in healthy men.[6] Absorption of this amount of iron from the diet is now accepted as sufficient to meet the needs of the body in the absence of any blood loss.

Measurements have been made of the menstrual blood loss of British[7] and Swedish women.[8] In most women it is from 20 to 40 ml at each period. This is a loss of about 2.5 to 5 g of haemoglobin with 8.6 to 17.2 mg of iron. To make good this loss, 0.3 to 0.6 mg extra iron has to be absorbed from the diet daily. However, the distribution of the amount of menstrual loss is markedly skewed to the right, and about 10 per cent of women lose more than 80 ml of blood at each period. These need to absorb daily an extra 1.2 mg of iron or more.

INTAKE

The diet of most people provides from 10 to 14 mg of iron daily. Meat, meat products, cereals, vegetables and fruits all contain iron (Table 12.2) but amounts vary greatly in different samples. This is partly due to the iron content of soils which varies more than 100-fold. Lower intakes only occur with diets composed mainly of refined cereals, sugars and fats, as for example in the economic depression in the 1930s when poor women in Aberdeen were estimated to be getting only 7.7 mg.[9] Milk is a poor source and in the first few months of life infants rely on stores of iron laid down in the liver before birth. Infants for whom mixed feeding is not started at the age of 6 months inevitably become iron-deficient,

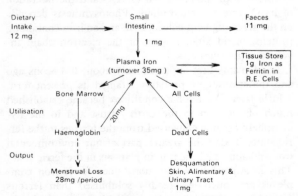

Fig. 12.1 Summary of daily iron metabolism in man (adapted from Moore)[3]

Table 12.2 Iron content of some common foods

Food	Description	Range (mg/100 g)
Black (blood) sausage		20
Liver	Raw	6.0–14.0
Beef	Raw, fresh	2.0–4.3
Fish	Raw	0.5–1.0
Eggs	Whole, fresh	2.0–3.0
Pulses	Various	1.9–14.0
Millets	Various, raw	3.8–8.0
Wheat flour	Whole meal	4.0
Wheat flour	White flour	1.5
Chocolate	Plain	2.8–4.4
Treacle		9.2–11.3
Dried fruit	Various	2.0–10.6
Green leafy vegetables*	Raw	0.4–18.0
Potatoes and other root vegetables	Raw	0.3–2.0
Fruits	Tinned and fresh	0.2–4.0
Milk	Cow's, fresh whole	0.1–0.4
Wines	Red and white	0.5–1.2

*Green vegetables commonly used in the tropics all fall in the upper part of the range and may therefore be useful sources of iron, while the vegetables (less green) most commonly used in temperate climates are generally from the lower part of the range and are consequently less important in their contribution to the iron content of the diet.

as did patients kept for long periods on a milk diet for peptic ulcers. If iron vessels are used for cooking or processing of foods, the amount of iron in the product may be increased greatly and so lead to iron overload (see below).

As less than 10 per cent of dietary iron has to be absorbed to balance daily losses (up to 20 per cent in menstruating and pregnant women), the factors determining absorption are more important than the total intake of iron.

Absorption

The amount of iron which is absorbed from food depends on the form of iron and on other constituents of the diet.[10] In animal foods nearly all the iron is present as haem iron and so is present in the Fe^{2+} form. Haem iron is absorbed very much better than inorganic iron from vegetable foods and is little affected by other constituents in the diet. Haem absorption increases in iron deficiency and is reduced when the body is overloaded with iron. The iron in vegetable foods is present as non-haem complexes in which Fe^{3+} is bound in an insoluble form to proteins, phytates, oxalates, phosphates and carbonates. The absorption of inorganic iron can be studied by mixing a radioactively labelled ^{55}Fe or ^{59}Fe salt with a food or meal. The inorganic iron in the meal acts as a single pool so the same rate of absorption is found when the labelled iron is added as a salt or when the isotope has been incorporated into the ingested vegetables by growing them in isotope-enriched nutrient

solutions. By using these isotope techniques Larisse & Martinez-Torres[11] were able to show the range in absorption of inorganic iron from a variety of vegetable foods fed to 87 Venezuelan peasants (Fig. 12.2). The iron present in animal foods, labelled for example by injecting chickens and rabbits with the isotope, is better absorbed as it is in the haem state. The use of animal foods also improves the absorption of inorganic iron by forming soluble complexes of amino acids and iron in the intestine and thus facilitating its absorption. Other food substances, e.g. sugars, citric acid and amines, also increase inorganic iron uptake, the most important dietary promotor of iron absorption being ascorbic acid.[4] The amount of iron absorbed is related to the ascorbic acid content of an artificial diet,[12] and this is in part due to the reducing action of ascorbic acid which favours the conversion of Fe^{3+} to Fe^{2+}.

Whole cereals are rich in iron, but it is poorly absorbed perhaps because of the phytate present. In communities where 70 per cent or more of the energy intake comes from whole wheat, maize or sorghum, daily intakes of iron may be up to 20 mg and yet iron deficiency is widespread. The addition of small quantities of green vegetables, fruits and meat to such unbalanced diets is perhaps more valuable in promoting the absorption of inorganic iron than in preventing possible scurvy or increasing the protein intake.

The consumption of common beverages may affect iron absorption. It is decreased by tea, at least in Indian women in Durban.[13] This may be due to binding of iron by tannin. Alcohol may promote absorption. Thus the iron in beer in Johannesburg brewed from maize and sorghum is better absorbed than when these cereals are made into gruels.[14]

Gastrointestinal factors. Gastric HCL facilitates absorption of non-haem iron by converting ferric to ferrous iron. Achlorhydria and iron deficiency anaemia are epidemiologically associated although all patients with achlorhydria are not anaemic; yet it has been demonstrated that achlorhydria reduces absorption of ferric iron administered with food by about 50 per cent.[15] On the other hand prolonged iron deficiency may lead to gastric atrophy which is sometimes reversible with iron therapy.

Other gastrointestinal conditions can influence iron absorption. Patients who have had partial gastrectomy are liable to develop iron deficiency anaemia. Any cause of malabsorption or intestinal hurry is usually associated with iron deficiency. Both an acute fever and a chronic infection may reduce iron absorption and lead to anaemia.

Mechanisms and regulation
Porphyrins with their haem iron cross the brush border of epithelial cells in the small intestine unchanged.

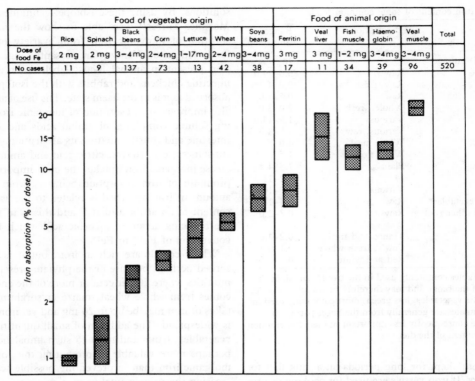

Fig. 12.2 Iron absorption from food. The hatched areas are between the antilogs of the log standard error on each side of the geometric mean. Scatter of individual cases is considerably greater. (From Larisse and Martinez-Torres)[11]

Within the cells the iron is liberated enzymatically. Non-haem iron is taken up from the gut lumen by border membranes at specific receptor sites which are probably glycoproteins. Iron crosses the epithelial cells bound to a carrier protein, as yet unidentified, and then passed into the plasma where it is attached to the protein transferrin (see below). Absorption is mostly in the duodenum and proximal jejunum, and does not normally take place against a concentration gradient.

Iron absorption is greatly increased when new red cells are being rapidly formed in the bone marrow, e.g. after a haemorrhage, and when the iron store in the lymphoreticular system is reduced. Moore[16] summarised his measurements of iron absorption in man by stating that the average in 218 normal subjects approximated to 10 per cent and in 148 iron-deficient patients to 20 per cent. These averages cover wide individual variations.

The control of absorption through the activity of the bone marrow and through the amount of iron in the stores appear to be independent of each other. In pernicious anaemia, iron stores are not usually reduced, yet absorption is at once increased when red cell production is increased by administration of vitamin B12. On the other hand in normal pregnancy uncomplicated by anaemia, iron absorption increases to meet the needs of the

fetus. Iron stores, as assessed by serum ferritin, fall progressively throughout pregnancy,[17] and this fall may be the stimulus to increased absorption. The nature of the signals which convey information from the erythropoietic marrow and from the storage organs to the intestinal mucosa are unknown.

TRANSPORT

Iron is absorbed into the blood stream and not into the lymph. It is carried in the plasma bound to **transferrin**, a globulin (mol. wt about 88 000), formed mainly in the liver. Its concentration in the plasma is 3–4 g/l (22–45 mol/l). One molecule can bind two molecules of iron, so the total iron binding capacity (TIBC) of plasma is 3.1–5.1 mg/l (68–90 mol/l). TIBC is raised in pregnancy and in iron-deficiency anaemia. Plasma transferrin is reduced when protein synthesis is impaired and its value is used as an index of malnutrition (p. 491).

Normally TIBC is not fully saturated and in health plasma iron varies from 0.8 to 1.6 mg/l, tending to be lower in women than in men. It is much lower in patients with anaemia due to iron deficiency.

TURNOVER

As the life of a red blood cell is about 120 days, 1/120 of body haemoglobin is broken down and resynthesised daily. In this process about 20 mg of iron have to be transported from the spleen, liver and other lymphoreticular tissue, where the old red cells are broken down, to the bone marrow where the new ones are formed. Intracellular tissue iron (about 500 mg) is also being continuously replaced, as is the iron lost in desquamated cells. The iron turnover in these processes is about 15 mg daily, giving a total body turnover of about 35 mg daily. This is, of course, much greater than the 1 mg or less absorbed from the diet daily.

STORES

Iron is stored in the cells as **ferritin**, soluble complexes of a core of Fe^{3+} compounds surrounded by a coat of proteins (apoferritins) and as **haemosiderin**, insoluble complexes, probably formed from ferritin. The total store in the body is normally about 1 g, mostly as ferritin. Some ferritin is present in all cells, but most is in the fixed phagocytes of the liver, spleen and bone marrow. When the stores are increased, haemosiderin can be seen by the naked eye in the liver and spleen after the addition of ferricyanide which stains it a deep Prussian blue. A condition known as **siderosis**. The amount of storage iron in the body can be assessed by measuring plasma ferritin by immunoassay. In a healthy man with Hb 15 g/dl, it was 80 µg/l, six weeks later after seven venesections Hb was 11 g/dl and plasma ferritin less than 12 µg/l.[18] In another study[19] mean plasma ferritin concentrations were 159, 51 and 6 µg/l respectively in healthy men, in those with reduced stores and in those with no visible haemosiderin in bone marrow.

Iron overload

The classic example is **haemochromatosis**, a rare genetic disorder. The primary defect is a failure to control iron absorption from the small intestine. The excess iron is then deposited in the tissues. As the daily excess is small compared with storage capacity, patients do not usually present themselves until middle age, when large amounts of fibrous tissues has formed in many organs as a reactive response to the excess iron. The characteristic features are an enlarged and cirrhotic liver, pancreatic diabetes, a slate-grey discoloration of the skin and hypogonadism, probably secondary to iron deposition in the pituitary. The disease is fatal in a few years if the iron in the body cannot be reduced.

Iron overload may occur, but usually to a much smaller extent, when there is a haemolytic anaemia, for example in any of the diseases due to genetic defects of red blood cells, briefly described on page 467. This is due to an inability of the body to excrete the iron liberated by the increased rate of breakdown of red blood cells. Repeated blood transfusions also lead to iron overload since the extra iron given cannot be excreted.

Nutritional iron overload. This condition, also known as siderosis, follows high iron intakes, usually over 40 mg daily. Such intakes are usually due not to iron originally present in the food, but to adventitious iron from iron vessels used in cooking and more frequently in the preparation of alcoholic preparations. The condition is common in the Bantu population of Johannesburg who drink beer brewed from maize or sorghum in iron vessels, and most of our knowledge comes from studies in that city.[4,14] However, nutritional iron overload has been reported from many places and it may be much more common, at least in its minor forms, than is generally supposed. It has been prevalent in Boston[20] amongst the poor wine-drinking population. Although most wines contain less than 10 mg/l of iron, many cheap wines contain up to 40 mg/l and higher values have been reported. Samples of Normandy cider have contained 16 mg/l and many litres of this can be drunk on hot days.

In Johannesburg alcoholics often present with a syndrome of cirrhosis of the liver, scurvy and osteoporosis and in such cases at autopsy the iron content of the liver is usually much higher than normal. Then it is not possible to assess the relative importance of iron overload and alcohol in causing cirrhosis. Scurvy is not common in black South Africans except in association with alcoholism and iron overload. However, in subjects with these disorders, increased catabolism of ascorbic acid with a high urinary excretion of oxalate has been demonstrated.[21] Deficiency of ascorbic acid may be responsible for the osteoporosis, as it is necessary for the formation of bone collagen.

An assessment of the degree of iron overload in a population can be made from measurements of the iron content of samples of liver obtained at routine post mortems. The upper limit of normal is about 0.25 mg/g. In Johannesburg in 1959 the mean for those aged 20–29 years was 0.5 mg/g and rose to 1.9 mg/g at ages over 60. In 1976 the rise with age was still present, but concentrations had fallen to 0.25 and 1.3 mg/g in the age groups 20 to 29 and over 60.[22] The reduction in overload is attributable to partial replacement of home-brewed beer by beer from commercial breweries. Iron overload also occurs in other communities in Africa who use iron vessels for cooking and brewing, but its prevalence is not known. A minor degree of overload probably has no adverse effect on health, but it might be a contributory cause of liver cirrhosis.

Treatment

Desferrioxamine is a polyhydroxamic acid that chelates Fe^{3+}. It is prepared from the chelated form (ferrioxamine) which occurs naturally in a mould. Iron in the tissues is chelated by the drug and then can be excreted by the kidneys. The usual dose of 1 g daily raises the urinary output of iron up to 15 mg daily. Desferrioxamine is used mainly to prevent iron overload after repeated transfusions. It is also useful in reducing iron overload in children with thalassaemia. When overloading has been going on for years and the liver has become enlarged, the only effective way to remove the large amounts of iron is by venesection.

Taking 500 ml of blood removes about 250 mg of iron. As the excess iron may be as much as 50 g, bleeding has to be repeated weekly for many months. Fortunately patients with liver cirrhosis due to nutritional overload or haemochromatosis tolerate this well and the prognosis is improved.

RECOMMENDED INTAKES

Most national committees have recommended 10 mg iron/day for men and postmenopausal women. This is based on a need for 0.5 to 1.0 mg to replace tissue losses and absorption of up to 10 per cent of intake. Women during their reproductive life need more iron, but usually absorb it more efficiently. For them the FAO/WHO and USA recommendation (Tables 15.1 and 15.2) is 18 mg or more/day. This aims to cover the iron losses through menstruation of almost all women, and to maintain a store sufficient to make iron therapy during pregnancy unnecessary. Family diets do not normally provide this amount, and the recommendation could only be implemented by a policy of fortifying foods with iron. Bread has been fortified in some countries but this has been generally ineffective, as the iron added is poorly absorbed. However, salt fortified with iron has reduced the prevalence of anaemia in some parts of India (p. 462).

The British recommendation for menstruating women is 12 mg/day,[23] sufficient to meet the iron needs of 90 per cent of them. The small minority with large menstrual losses causing anaemia should be identified by the health services and given daily doses of medicinal iron.

THERAPEUTIC USES

Fortunately the treatment and prevention of iron deficiency anaemia does not depend only on dietary means. Ferrous salts are cheap and effective when given orally (p. 462). In some conditions (e.g. the malabsorption syndrome) they may be ineffective by mouth. Then iron sorbitol may be given intramuscularly or iron dextrin by slow intravenous infusion.

TOXIC EFFECTS

Iron salts in large doses are very toxic and they are second to aspirin as a cause of accidental poisoning in young children. This arises when their mother's medicinal iron tablets are mistaken for sweets. Within an hour there is nausea and vomiting and diarrhoea. In severe cases this is followed by gastrointestinal bleeding and circulatory collapse and later by liver necrosis and then is often fatal. Treatment is by washing out the stomach with desferrioxamine, which is then left in the stomach to prevent absorption. In severe cases desferrioxamine is given intravenously to chelate iron already absorbed. Prevention depends on mothers being aware of the importance of storing medicines in cupboards inaccessible to small children.

Possible adverse effects of medicinal doses of iron are discussed on page 463.

ZINC
Zn (at. wt 65)

The total body content of zinc in an adult is over 2.0 g (30 mmol). This is half the body content of iron and much higher than the corresponding figures for any other trace element. Zinc is a component of over 50 enzymes, including carbonic anhydrase, alcohol dehydrogenase, alkaline phosphatase, lactate dehydrogenase, superoxide dismutase and pancreatic carboxypeptidase. The tissues that contain the highest concentrations of zinc are the choroid of the eye and the prostrate. Semen has 100 times the concentration of blood plasma. Relatively high concentrations are present in the skin but most of the body zinc is in the bones, where the concentration is 3 μmol/g (200 μg/g), compared with an average of 0.5 μmol/g (30 μg/g) in fat-free tissues of the body.

Normal plasma concentrations range from 12 to 17 μmol/l (80–110 μg/dl); red cells contain 200 μmol/l (13 μg/ml); hair contains 2–4 μmol/g (125–250 μg/g) in newborns and adults. Urinary excretion ranges from 6–9 μmol (0.4–0.6 mg) daily. The main route of excretion is the faeces, which contain both endogenously zinc excreted in pancreatic and intestinal juices and unabsorbed zinc from the diet.

The zinc content of the body is regulated by homostatic mechanisms, mainly through control of absorption from the gut.

DIETARY INTAKE

Good dietary sources of zinc are meats (3–5 mg/100 g), whole grains and legumes (2–3 mg/100 g). Oysters (70 mg/100 g) are outstandingly rich in zinc. White bread, fats and sugar are poor sources. Human milk at first contains about 1 mg/100 ml but the concentration later falls.

Human diets provide from 7 to 17 mg daily and the USA recommended intake for adults is 15 mg. Only about 20 per cent of this is absorbed. Phytate and other components of dietary fibre bind zinc and increase faecal excretion.[24] High fibre diets, as normally recommended, do not lead to zinc depletion but this may be a hazard in poor countries where a very high proportion of dietary energy comes from unrefined cereals and for cranks who dose themselves with excessive amounts of bran.

Zinc deficiency

Zinc deficiency is established as responsible for clinical disorders in two circumstances, both very rare. **Acrodermatitis enteropathica** is a congenital disorder characterised by a pustular and bullous dermatitis, alopecia and diarrhoea. It occurs in early childhood and was always fatal until the discovery that daily doses of zinc sulphate were effective treatment.[25] A few patients who have been on total parenteral nutrition for long periods have developed bullous eruptions of the skin that responded promptly to zinc.

In many patients with chronic disorders the zinc content of the plasma and hair is below the normal range, strongly suggesting depletion of reserves which are mainly in the bones. These patients often improve after administration of zinc. However, it is difficult to establish that any of their symptoms are attributable to zinc deficiency for three reasons. First the skin lesions, the characteristic feature of established zinc deficiency, are absent. Secondly a large part of the plasma zinc is bound to albumin and, as many of these patients are malnourished, their plasma albumin is low which automatically lowers plasma zinc; the zinc content of hair is also not a reliable guide. Thirdly controlled clinical trials of zinc supplementation are difficult to carry out and interpret because in chronic disorders improvement is slow and it is difficult to be sure that observed changes are not due to dietary improvement or other therapeutic measures.

Evidence suggesting zinc deficiency has often been reported in patients with protein-energy malnutrition, the malabsorption syndrome, chronic alcoholism, diabetes, the nephrotic syndrome, chronic febrile illness and stress from surgery and burns; urinary zinc output increases in response to injury. Plasma zinc is often low in patients on dialysis for renal failure; affected men may suffer from impotence but a report that sexual potency could be restored by adding zinc to the dialysis fluid has not been confirmed.[26] Chronic ulcers, especially those associated with varicose veins, may heal better if the patient is given a zinc supplement, and zinc is one of the nutrients essential for optimum wound healing. Both the fetus and young infant may suffer from zinc insufficiency in the mother. It may be a part cause of the malformations occurring in some infants of alcoholic mothers (p. 577). Human milk is not a rich source of zinc and during lactation an infant depends on a reserve laid down in the last three months of intrauterine life and hence preterm infants are at risk of insufficiency.[27]

The above are examples of disorders that may either diminish the supply of zinc to the tissues or increase the need. There is no convincing evidence that the clinical features present in any of them are directly due to zinc deficiency, but it is good practice to give a zinc supplement, 200 mg zinc sulphate (40 mg Zn) daily, to any patient whose plasma zinc is below the normal range.

Zinc deficiency does not arise in healthy persons living on any of the diets commonly consumed in any country. However, the claim has been made that it is responsible for a clinical syndrome seen in some poor peasant communities in Iran and elsewhere in the Middle East where the diet consisted mainly of unleavened bread, *toonok*. Older children and adolescents are affected and the main features are small stature, mild anaemia, hypogonadism and delayed puberty with a low plasma zinc[28] Zinc supplementation has been followed by puberty and accelerated growth.[29] The diets in the villages where these young people lived was generally poor and whether or not any of the clinical features is attributable specifically to zinc deficiency is uncertain.

The speculations of distinguished scientists always merit careful attention. The Australian immunologist F.M.Burnet[30] has pointed out that zinc metalloenzymes are concerned with DNA replication, repair and transcription. He suggests that senile dementia may follow upon the cascading effects of error-prone or ineffective DNA-handling enzymes in neurones which have an age-associated loss of ability to make zinc available for insertion into newly synthesised enzymes and that this might be equivalent to an Orgel error catastrophe. While admitting that the evidence for this is wholly indirect, he suggest that supplementary zinc could prevent or delay the onset of dementia in subjects genetically at risk.

Toxicity

Zinc is much less toxic than most metals, but nausea, vomiting and fever have followed the use for renal dialysis of water stored in a galvanised tank.[31] Inhalation of zinc oxide fumes in industry may cause a similar acute illness.

IODINE
I (at. wt 127)

The adult body contains 20 to 50 mg (160 to 400 μmol) of iodine, about 8 mg of this is concentrated in the thyroid gland. Since the thyroid normally weighs only 0.05 per cent of the whole body it is evident that this concentration is intense. Iodine is contained in the hormones stored and secreted by the gland.

HISTORY

Iodine was discovered in 1811 by Courtois, who was working in Paris to keep Napoleon supplied with gunpowder. He used kelp (dried seaweed) as a source of lye for the manufacture of nitre and found the iodine in it. The chemical properties of the new element were investigated by Gay-Lussac and by Humphry Davy who — by the personal permission of Napoleon — was passing through Paris on his way to Italy at the time. In 1820 the Geneva physician, Coindet, successfully treated goitrous patients with tincture of iodine. This was enthusiastically pursued by several French and Swiss investigators, notably by Chatin of Paris. He made extensive and surprisingly accurate analyses of iodine in foodstuffs and drinking waters and came to the conclusion that although the element is universally distributed in nature, it is relatively deficient in areas where goitre is endemic. This was the first scientific backing for the belief that goitre is due to deficiency of iodine. In 1860 Boussingault instigated the use of iodine in the prevention of goitre among school children in three areas of France. Unfortunately the dose given was far too large and toxic effects were observed. This brought discredit on the whole idea. Soon afterwards the mounting enthusiasm for bacteriology, engendered by Pasteur, sent the medical profession on a false trial in pursuit of an infective cause for goitre.

After 1900 Americans began to take up the trail. Marine found that goitre in trout could be prevented with iodine and in 1920 published the results of a classic experiment in school children in Akron, Ohio.[32] This succeeded in proving what the French had failed to show a generation before — that sodium iodide in suitable doses reduces the incidence of goitre in children. Their results were confirmed and enthusiastically supported by numerous doctors in Switzerland.

Meanwhile Kendall & Osterberg[33] in America, after much painstaking work, succeeded in isolating from thyroid glands a crystalline iodine-containing compound which they called 'thyroxin'.

PHYSIOLOGY

All vertebrate animals require iodine and they all possess thyroid tissue in some parts of the body. This tissue has the specific property of taking up iodine, storing it, and subsequently releasing it in controlled amounts in the form of thyroid hormones. Iodine is unique among the mineral elements in that it is an essential component of specific hormones.

The iodine in food and water is quickly absorbed from the alimentary canal, mostly as inorganic iodide; a proportion of this is taken up by the thyroid gland, the amount depending on the activity of the gland. In the gland the iodide is oxidised to iodine, which is immediately bound to tyrosine with the formation of mono- and diiodotyrosines. These substances are subsequently converted into the hormones triiodothyronine (T_3) and thyroxine (T_4). This takes place in the epithelial cells of the gland. Thyroxine is then bound to a globulin to form thyroglobulin in which form it is stored in the vesicles of the gland. From the gland it is released, as required, into the blood stream loosely bound to an α-globulin. With a normally active gland plasma concentrations of T_4 range from 75–150 mmol/1 and of T_3 from 1.1–2.2 mmol/1. The output of thyroid hormones is controlled from the pituitary gland by means of the thyrotropic hormone.

The thyroid secretions determine the level of metabolism in many cells. If the secretion is deficient, basal metabolism falls, the circulation is reduced and the whole tempo of the patient's life is slowed down.

The secretions also control in some way the state of the connective tissues. A lack of the hormone causes accumulation of mucinous material under the skin and in other organs. This coarsens the features and gives the patient suffering from thyroid deficiency a characteristic appearance (myxoedema).

The part played by lack of iodine and other dietary factors in causing enlargement of the thyroid gland (goitre) is discussed in Chapter 30.

SOURCES

The iodide content of plants and animals is determined by the environment in which they grow. As most soils contain little iodide, most foodstuffs are poor sources. Fruits, vegetables, cereals, meat and meat products may contain up to 100 μg/kg, but the amount varies greatly in different samples and is usually between 20 and 50 μg/kg. The only rich source of iodide is sea food. The following analyses were obtained on fish in Glasgow by Wayne:[34] haddock 6590, whiting 650 to 3610, and herring 210 to 270 μg/kg. Diets in Glasgow provided from 40 to 1000 μg/kg. If sea-fish is eaten at one or two meals in a week, this provides an intakes of about

150 μg/day which is sufficient to prevent goitre in normal circumstances.

Much attention has been directed in the past to the iodide content of drinking waters in areas where goitre occurs, as compared with the waters in goitre-free districts. As a result there has been a tendency to regard drinking water as an important source of iodide. But fresh water usually contains only small amounts of iodide, e.g. 1 to 50 μg/1 in Britain, so that it contributes little to the needs of the body. The iodide content of the water in a locality is more important as an index of the amount of iodide that is likely to be provided by the cereals and vegetables that grow in the soil which the water irrigates. Among people who do not live largely on home grown food it is a matter of little consequence.

RECOMMENDED INTAKES

Various figures, ranging from 50 to 300 μg/day, have been proposed for the requirements of adults but are based on scant evidence; moreover they may be unrealistic, since the physiological need for iodine is influenced by many dietary and environmental factors such as the amount of cabbage and other *brassicae* eaten, the hardness of the drinking water, the climate, the age and sex of the people and their exposure to infections or other stress. These factors are discussed in connection with goitre in Chapter 30.

PROPHYLACTIC AND THERAPEUTIC USES

Small doses of iodine are of great value in the prevention of goitre in areas where it is endemic, and are of value in treatment, at least in the early stages. Larger doses have a temporary value in the preparation of patients with hyperthroidism for surgical operation.

FLUORINE
F1 (at. wt 19)

In 1805 Gay-Lussac first detected fluorine in the animal body. Traces of this element are regularly present in human tissues, notably in the bones, teeth, thyroid gland and skin. There is now no doubt that traces of fluorine in the teeth help to protect them against decay, and traces of fluorine are needed for normal growth in rats.

SOURCES

The chief source is usually drinking water, which, if it contains 1 part per million (p.p.m.) of fluoride, supplies 1 to 2 mg/day. Soft waters may contain no fluorine, whilst very hard waters may contain over 10 p.p.m.

Compared with this source, the fluoride in foodstuffs is of little importance. Very few foods contain more than 1 p.p.m. The exception is sea-fish which may contain relatively large amounts of the order of 5 to 10 p.p.m. Another significant source is tea, particularly China tea, which in the dry state may contain as much as 100 p.p.m. In Britain and Australia, where people are addicted to tea, the adult intake from this source may be as much as 1 mg daily.

METABOLISM

Ingested fluorides are completely ionised and rapidly absorbed and distributed throughout the extracellular fluid, in a manner similar to chloride. Levels in the blood and tissues are so low that it has been difficult to make reliable analyses. Fluoride is rapidly excreted in the urine, even by those with severe kidney disease. The relation of urinary output to the total intake is complicated and related to the state of the bones. Fluoride is a bone seeker. In rats, 60 per cent of a dose of radio-fluoride can be found in the skeleton after two hours. It is also deposited in dental enamel. The study of both storage and mobilisation of fluoride is technically difficult. Reports by WHO and the Royal College of Physicians, London give good accounts of available knowledge.[35,36]

Fluorosis in animals
This may occur in cattle and sheep whenever the vegetation on which they graze is contaminated by fluoride-containing dust. A notable outbreak was caused by the eruption of Mount Hekla in Iceland in 1845.[37] Smoke from brick kilns in England and from the aluminium works at Fort William in Scotland have likewise caused fluorosis in livestock. The first sign is usually seen in the teeth of young growing animals, which are mottled with white patches and present a rough enamel surface. In adult animals the first effect is generally the development of bony changes. The surfaces of the long bones and lower jaw become thickened and densely calcified, often with bony outgrowths (exostoses). The animals become weak and their milk yield is reduced.

Fluorosis in man
In many parts of the world where the fluoride content of the water is high (over 3 to 5 parts per million) mottling of the teeth is common. The enamel loses its lustre and becomes rough. Bands of brown pigmentation separate patches as white as chalk. Small pits may be present on the surface (Fig. 12.3). All the teeth may be affected, but mottling is usually best seen on the incisors of the upper jaw. Dental fluorosis is not usually associated with any evidence of skeleton fluorosis or indeed with any impairment of health.

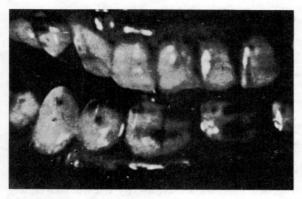

Fig. 12.3 Fluorosis in a Sudanese man. (Courtesy of Professor D A Smith)

Severe fluoride poisoning has been reported in several localities in India, China, Argentina and the Transvaal, where the water supply contains over 10 p.p.m. fluoride. Fluoride poisoning has also occurred as an industrial hazard among workers handling flouride-containing minerals such as cryolite, used in smelting aluminium. The effects are much the same as in animals; there is a loss of appetite and an increased density (sclerosis) of the bones of the spine, pelvis and limbs. In addition the ligaments of the spine becomes calcified, producing a 'poker back'. There may also be ossification of the tendinous insertions of muscles, producing characteristic 'rose-thorn' shadows in the radiograph. Neurological disturbances secondary to the changes in the vertebral column can occur. Jolly et al[38] give a full account of the clinical features of fluorosis in North India where, in localised areas, the water may contain 14 p.p.m. of fluoride.

Fluoride and osteoporosis

As osteosclerosis is a consequence of excess fluoride, it is reasonable to speculate that osteoporosis might be promoted by a deficiency of fluoride.[39] Lack of knowledge of the factors that determine the progress of the osteoporosis, which occurs in all of us when middle age is reached, and the uncertainties of measuring its rate of progress, make attempts to verify this hypothesis extremely difficult.

COPPER
Cu (at. wt 64)

DIETARY INTAKES

Some pastures lack copper, so cattle grazing on the herbage may develop anaemia due to Cu deficiency. In other species osteoporosis or ataxia (swayback) can occur. However, primary Cu deficiency has never been reported in adult man, presumably because his diet usually comes from a variety of lands. Normal adult diets provide 15–45 μmol (1–3 mg)/day and the estimated daily requirement for children is 0.8 μmol/kg. Green vegetables, many species of fish, oysters and liver are good sources, providing 4 μmol/MJ or more, whereas most other foods, e.g. milk, meats, bread, provide less than 2 μmol/MJ. As milk is a poor source, some infants are at risk of Cu deficiency, which has been reported when feeds contain less than 1.6 μmol/MJ (42 μg/100 kcal). All medicinal iron preparations contain traces of Cu.

EXCRETION AND METABOLISM

The major portion of the dietary Cu appears in the faeces and very little in the urine. The low urinary output is due to almost all the Cu in plasma being bound to a specific protein, caeruloplasmin, which is not excreted; the remainder is loosely bound to albumin. The total body Cu in an adult is about 2 mmol (100 to 150 mg). There is a higher concentration in the liver than in other tissues; in the later months of pregnancy Cu is transferred from the maternal to the fetal liver, where a reserve is built up for use when the infant is on a milk diet. Lack of this reserve makes premature infants more prone to Cu deficiency.

Copper is a component of many enzyme systems, e.g. cytochrome oxidase, dopamine hydroxylase, superoxide dismutase and lysyl oxidase. Cu depletion in experimental animals leads to a failure to use ferritin iron, which accumulates in the liver. This may be due to a decline in caeruloplasmin activity. Iron metabolism is closely dependent on Cu, and in animals it is difficult to distinguish between the anaemias arising from deficiencies of the two elements.

Deficiency states

Anaemia responding to copper is occasionally found in preterm infants, in protein-energy malnutrition and in patients on prolonged total parenteral nutrition. Plasma Cu and caeruloplasmin concentrations are low.

Menkes' syndrome is a rare genetically determined failure of Cu absorption, leading to progressive mental retardation, failure to keratinise hair, which becomes kinky, hypothermia, low concentrations of Cu in plasma and liver, skeletal changes and degenerative changes in aortic elastica.[40] Formerly the children always died within three years of birth, but there is now hope that with adequate Cu therapy they may thrive.

Toxicity

Copper sulphate is widely used for killing algae and bacteria in swimming baths and is potentially dangerous to man and animals. Concentrations should not be allowed to exceed 12 µmol/l in drinking water.

Excess Cu accumulates in the tissues in a rare genetically determined condition, **Wilson's disease** or hepatolenticular degeneration. Deficient synthesis of caeruloplasmin in the liver leads to Cu being transported in plasma loosely bound to albumin. There appears to be a positive Cu balance throughout life, and the excess Cu is deposited in the tissues, mainly in the liver and basal nuclei of the brain. This leads to cirrhosis of the liver and brain disturbances, e.g. coarse tremor and personality changes. The outlook was hopeless until the discovery that the chelating agent, D-penicillamine, promotes Cu excretion. Now, provided that the diagnosis is made early and treatment continued for life, the outlook is fairly good.

Indian childhood cirrhosis is an uncommon fatal disorder of children aged 1 to 3 years which occurs in families, mainly middle-income, in rural areas. Its causes has for long been a mystery. High copper concentrations have now been found in the liver and it is suggested that this may come from brass and copper household utensils in which milk is boiled and stored.[41] If this hypothesis is substantiated, the disease should be preventable by education but this would be formidable task.

COBALT
Co (at. wt 59)

Cobalt is a constituent of vitamin B12, an essential nutrient for man and many other animals (p. 158). No other role for the element in human nutrition has been identified. Vitamin B12 is the only compound of cobalt that is nutritionally effective in man and other monogastric animals. In cattle and sheep, bacteria in the rumen are able to use metallic Co to synthesise vitamin B12 and are thus the ultimate source of the vitamin in human diets.

When Co salts have been used as a non-specific bone marrow stimulus in the treatment of certain refractory anaemias, doses of 500 µmol/day produced serious toxic effects including goitre, hypothyroidism and heart failure. An outbreak of severe cardiomyopathy with a high mortality affecting heavy beer-drinkers in Quebec was traced to Co deliberately added to the beer to improve its head.[42] The beer contained up to 25 µmol/l of Co, and some of the men were said to be drinking 12 litres daily.

CHROMIUM
Cr (at. wt. 52)

Chromium is present in all organic matter and appears to be an essential nutrient. Only the trivalent form is biologically active, and it cannot be oxidised to the hexavalent form in the tissues. Analytical methods are still difficult and uncertain, and this makes interpretation of the literature hazardous. Dietary intakes in the USA vary from 0.1 to 2 µmol (5 to 100 µg)/day; most of this is not absorbed and urinary excretion is low. Plasma concentrations are usually between 0.4 and 1.0 µmol/l and a lower figure may suggest a deficient intake. The total body content in adults is 100 to 200 µmol (5 to 10 mg). The concentration of Cr in hair ranges from 3 to 6 µmol/kg and low values may be an index of deficiency.[43]

In experimental animals, Cr deficiency leads to a reduced rate of removal of ingested glucose, due to a low sensitivity of peripheral tissues to insulin. An organic compound of Cr, termed 'glucose tolerance factor' (GTF) is much more active than inorganic chromium salts. The richest source of GTF is brewer's yeast; black pepper, liver, wholemeal bread, even beer appear to be moderate sources. Its chemical composition has still to be elucidated but it contains nicotinic acid in combination with trivalent Cr.

Jeejeebhoy et al[44] reported the case of a woman who was maintained on total parenteral nutrition for $3\frac{1}{2}$ years after complete removal of the small intestine for mesenteric thrombosis. She then lost weight, her glucose tolerance was impaired and she had to be given insulin. Cr concentrations in her blood and hair were one-tenth and one-quarter of normal respectively. When 250 µg $CrCl_3$ was added daily to the intravenous fluid, glucose tolerance returned to normal, insulin was stopped and she remained well. Children with protein-energy malnutrition often have impaired glucose tolerance and in some areas this improves when a Cr supplement is given.

A review, *Chromium in Biological Systems*,[45] runs to 70 pages and 265 references. Yet there is still little hard knowledge and no certainty about the role of chromium in human nutrition.

MANGANESE
Mn (at. wt 55)

Manganese deficiency has not been described in man but can be produced in many laboratory animals and in poultry has been of commercial importance. The features in all species are deformities of bone, poor growth and ataxia of the newborn from abnormal formation of otoliths in the inner ear. Manganese is a co-factor in phosphohydrolases and phosphotransferases involved in the synthesis of proteoglycans in cartilage.

Human diets provide from 20–150 µmol (1–8 mg)/day. The average British diet is calculated to contain

4.6 mg/day, half coming from tea.[46] Unrefined vegetarian diets can provide more. About 5 per cent is absorbed. The body of an adult man contains 12–20 mg with higher concentrations in bones, liver and kidneys. Excretion is via the bile. Foods rich in Mn are whole cereals, legumes and leafy vegetables; tea is very rich. Meat, milk and refined cereals are poor sources. Infants before weaning may have a low intake.

Manganese is relatively non-toxic to laboratory animals and poisoning of man due to food contamination is unknown. Mineworkers in Chile have developed 'Manganese madness' with severe psychotic symptoms and Parkinsonism.

SELENIUM
Se (at. wt 79)

This element is irregularly distributed in soils; some contain too much and some too little. In North America, soil concentrations are too high in parts of Wyoming and the Dakotas. Certain plants, Grey's vetch and locoweed, thrive on such soils and accumulate Se in their leaves and seeds. Two diseases of the livestock grazing on these plants, 'blind staggers' and 'alkali disease', were shown in 1935 to be caused by acute and chronic selenium intoxication respectively.[47] In alkali disease animals' hooves become deformed and they loose hair.

That selenium is an essential nutrient was discovered later. Schwarz was investigating dietary causes of liver necrosis in rats. This could be produced by a diet in which the source of protein was Torula yeast. Brewer's yeast would prevent the necrosis and Schwarz recognised three nutritional components with this activity — cystine, vitamin E and a third factor, an organic derivative of selenium.[48] Soon after this it was discovered that white muscle disease of lambs in New Zealand could be prevented by selenium treatment.

There is an overlap between selenium deficiency and vitamin E deficiency in different animal species. Most of the deficiency syndromes can be prevented or cured by either Se or vitamin E, e.g. liver necrosis in rats and white muscle disease of lambs. But fetal resorption in rats responds only to vitamin E and pancreatic atrophy in chicks responds only to Se. The reason for the interchangeability of vitamin E and Se is that Se is an integral part of glutathione peroxidase, which destroys lipid hydroperoxides and guards against oxidative damage to lipid membranes.

The soil contains very little selenium in the South Island of New Zealand, and residents of Dunedin have a mean blood concentration of 0.86 μmol/1 compared with 1.3 to 4.3 μmol/1 in the USA and Britain, and up to 10 μmol/1 in parts of Venezuela with high Se levels in soil. Some New Zealanders have suboptimal activity of blood glutathione oxidase, but there is no excess of human liver or muscle disease in the country.[49]

In some areas of China the soil is poor in selenium and a cardiomyopathy occurs in children (Keshan's disease). It has been reported that children can be protected against this by sodium selenite[50] but this has yet to be confirmed.

In the British diet most of the Se comes from cereals and meat (mean content 110 and 120 μg/kg), but fish is richer (mean content 320 μg/kg). Milk, vegetables and fruits contain little. The estimated daily intake of Se is about 60 μg, less than estimates in North America and other European countries but more than in New Zealand.[51] The availability of Se in foods is discussed in a long review.[52]

MOLYBDENUM
Mo (at. wt 96)

There is no evidence that deficiency of Mo is responsible for any disorder of man. However, it is an essential nutrient. Animals on a low Mo diet do not grow normally and the element forms an essential part of several enzyme systems, e.g. xanthine oxidase.

The amount of Mo present in plants varies greatly depending on the soil, being relatively high in those grown on neutral or alkaline soils with a high content of organic matter and low in those grown on acid sandy soils. Consequently dietary intakes vary, but are usually within the range 0.5 to 2.0 mg/day. Concentrations in human whole blood ranging from 30 to 700 nmol/1 have been reported in different geographical areas. The output in the urine may be up to half the total daily intake.

A very high incidence of gout in some areas of Armenia, USSR, has been attributed to very high intakes of Mo (10–15 mg/day) from local plants growing on the Mo-rich soil. Molybdenum has a cariostatic effect in animals, and it has been reported that dental caries rates are lower than average in children brought up in areas where the soil has a high Mo content.

VANADIUM
V (at. wt 51)

That vanadium was a component of a respiratory pigment in some tunicates (sea squirts) has been known to the erudite for a long time, but the element aroused no interest in nutritionists until 1977. Then two commercial preparations of ATP gave quite different results in experiments. One was found to contain an inhibitor of Na-K ATPase (the sodium pump) and this was identified as vanadium at a molar concentration 1 : 3000 that of ATP.[53] That this inhibition might be important in mammalian physiology was indicated by the finding that vanadium was a powerful diuretic. The question then arises — could vanadium deficiency be responsible for the sodium and water retention in nutritional oedema? This cannot be answered as yet.

Vanadium is widespread in small amounts in most human foods and American diets probably provide about 25 μg daily. The concentration in human blood is of the order of 100 ng/ml and is regulated homeostatically. An outburst of papers on vanadium has started and a review by Golden & Golden[54] gives the background to these.

NICKEL
Ni (at. wt 59)

Traces of Ni are present in human tissue and there is evidence that it is an essential nutrient for rats, chicks and swine. However it is difficult to produce Ni deficiency in animals and there is no evidence of its existence in man. Nickel alloys are widely used for lining cooking vessels and pasteurisation equipment, and in the food industry but this has not led to poisoning, as far as is known. In animals the toxic dose is high relative to normal intakes.

SILICON
Si (at. wt 28)

Silica is second only to oxygen in abundance in the biosphere. The element and its salt are poorly soluble in water and only trace amounts are present in tissues. It is an essential nutrient for the growing chick and rats; abnormalities occur in the bones of deficient animals. Silicon may be an integral part of proteoglycans of cartilage and of the ground substance of connective tissue.

LITHIUM
Li (at. wt 7)

Lithium is not an essential element for animals or man, as far as is known. It has a place in psychiatry and is used in the prevention of recurrent attacks of mania and depression. These effects are regarded as pharmacological. The dose is regulated so that the plasma concentration lies close to 1.0 mmol/1, which does not alter concentrations of sodium and potassium; adverse effects are liable to arise if the concentration rises above 2 mmol/1.

BORON
B (at. wt 11)

Boron was shown to be an essential nutrient for plants as long ago as 1910, but there is no evidence that the element plays a role in any aspect of animal metabolism. Human diets provide about 2 mg/day; most of this is absorbed from the gut and appears in the urine. The dose producing toxic symptoms in man is about 50 times this amount and it is not likely that boron presents a problem in human nutrition. Boric acid was formerly used as a food preservative, but has been declared unsafe as a food additive by an FAO/WHO Expert Committee.

TIN
Sn (at. wt 119)

Rats raised in an all-plastic isolator system with a highly purified diet did not grow normally until they received a supplement of stannic sulphate, 1 p.p.m. of diet. This suggests that tin is an essential nutrient, but the experiments await confirmation. Naturally occurring Sn deficiency is unknown either in animals or man.

The widespread use of tin and tinfoil in cans and in packages of food presents potential hazards to man. Although in most countries cans are now coated with lacquer, which greatly reduces food contamination by tin, many canned foods contain higher concentrations of tin than unprocessed food. Human diets have been reported as containing from 30 to 40 μmol (3.5 to 17 mg)/day, more than would be present in unprocessed food. Such intakes have a high safety margin, as the toxic dose for man is about 40 to 60 μmol/kg of body weight. Ingested tin is poorly absorbed and is mainly excreted in the faeces. Apart from rare reports of gastrointestinal symptoms, there is no good evidence of human toxicity from inorganic tin in foods. The upper limit permissible in a canned food is usually taken as 2.1 mmol (250 mg)/kg. As 1 kg of such a food would constitute a toxic dose for a 65 kg man, this limit seems to allow too small a safety margin.

ALUMINIUM
Al (at. wt 27)

Aluminium is the third most abundant element in the earth's crust and its compounds are widespread in soils. Although present in trace amounts in biological material it does not appear to be an essential element. Al cooking vessels are much used, but the metal is too insoluble for these to be a hazard. Aluminium hydroxide is used therapeutically as an antacid. Aluminium poisoning is an important potential hazard to patients with chronic renal failure on haemodialysis. Their tissues are exposed to very large quantities of water from which traces of aluminium may be absorbed and in time cause a variety of symptoms (p. 412).

LEAD
Pb (at. wt 207)

As far as is known, lead has no essential role or beneficial effect on the tissues. Ever since lead was first mined and smelted, people have been at risk of absorbing toxic amounts in their drinking water, in their food and in the air. Lead poisoning may lead to anaemia, a peripheral neuropathy or an encephalopathy. It is now mainly an industrial hazard of lead workers, but there are still homes where the water supply comes through lead pipes, people who make home-made wines using pewter vessels, and lead toys and paints which children suck. Children are more susceptible than adults to comparable degrees of exposure to lead. The atmosphere may be a danger in the vicinity of an industrial plant, and in a town where there is much traffic pouring out lead in exhaust fumes.

A blood concentration above 1.4 μmol/l (30 μg/dl) suggests undue exposure, and higher concentrations are associated with the risk of developing lead poisoning. In industrial societies from 1 to 2 μmol (200 to 400 μg) are ingested in the food daily; 90 per cent of this is unabsorbed and appears in the faeces, most of the remainder being excreted in the urine. Thus a faecal specimen containing more than 4 μmol or a urine specimen containing more than 400 nmol/l suggest excess contamination of the food. The concentration of lead in the atmosphere of Los Angeles in 1969 was found to be 22 nmol (4.5 μg)/m³. This indicates that citizens would be inhaling about 400 nmol/day, a significant additional lead load. In spite of an increase in atmospheric lead, the lead content of contemporary hair in the USA is lower than that of locks of hair preserved from 50 to 100 years ago.[55]

Although the amounts of lead of concern to biologists are measured in micromoles and nanomoles, industry in the United States processes over one million tons per year. Continuing surveillance of the lead hazard is necessary in all industrial communities.

ARSENIC
As (at. wt 75)

Minute amounts of arsenic may have an essential role in animals, but the element is better known to all readers of detective stories as a poison. It is present in soil and water and in many plant and animal foods. The diet of an adult man contains normally from 6 to 50 μmol (0.4 to 3.9 mg)/day, and 43 μmol/day has been suggested as an acceptable upper limit. Shellfish contain much more arsenic than other foods. Organic arsenicals are sometimes added to poultry and pig diets, in the belief that they stimulate growth, possibly by modifying intestinal flora. This may raise As concentrations in muscle and liver to 6.5 and 26 μmol/kg. However, the As in such foods is organically bound and appears to be rapidly excreted without significant retention of elemental As.

MERCURY
Hg (at. wt 201)

Mercury is not known to have any essential role in the metabolism of living tissues. However, Hg compounds have a number of important uses in industry and elsewhere. Most of the Hg that may contaminate the environment is in metallic or inorganic form. Mercury poisoning produces tremors and stomatitis, but the symptoms are reversible when the patient is removed from further exposure to Hg. Nearly all of us have mercury in our mouth in the form of dental amalgam but this is a stable alloy; the Hg is not absorbed and causes no trouble.

The dangerous forms of Hg are the alkyl derivatives, methylmercury and ethylmercury which produce an encephalopathy, often irreversible. Alkyl mercury derivatives are taken into the body in the food and poisoning has occurred after eating carnivorous fish from polluted waters and seed grain previously treated with mercurial fungicide.

When waters are contaminated with inorganic Hg, microorganisms convert it into methylmercury which then moves up the food chain, becoming more concentrated as it passes through plant-eating small fish to carnivorous large fish like tuna, swordfish and pike. Severe cases of poisoning occurred in fishermen and their families round Minimata Bay in Japan when it was polluted by effluent from a factory. In Sweden and parts of North America it was subsequently discovered that fish in inland lakes contained amounts of mercury up to 25 μmol/kg and the sale of fish from these lakes was banned. Even some deep-sea tuna have contained appreciable amounts of mercury. The dangers were taken up by the world press, and governments made arrangements to monitor the amounts of mercury in fish. In Britain the mercury in canned tuna ranged from 0.5 to 4 μmol/kg, about half as methylmercury. Most of the deep-sea fish landed contain very small amounts, e.g. cod average 400 nmol/kg, while in coastal fish from a few estuaries receiving effluents from large chemical plants the content averaged 2.5 μmol/kg. WHO set the provisional tolerable weekly intake of mercury at 1.5 μmol (300 μg), of which no more than 1.0 μmol should be methylmercury. Hg poisoning from fish appears to be a potential rather than a real hazard. However, a case has been reported in New York: the patient was a lady who ate 0.5 kg of swordfish daily.[56]

Tragic outbreaks of a different method of poisoning have occurred in Pakistan, Guatemala and Iraq after illiterate peasant families have eaten seed grains dressed with an alkyl mercury compound to prevent fungal disease, despite a red dye on the grain and warnings on the sacks. After a latent period of 2 to 5 weeks ataxia and visual disturbances develop and may lead to permanent paralysis or death. In the 1972 Iraq epidemic 6500 cases were admitted to hospital and there were 459 deaths.[57]

In surveillance of populations for evidence of mercury ingestion, blood or hair can be examined. Concentrations below 100 nmol (20 μg)/1 of whole blood are satisfactory.

CADMIUM
Cd (at. wt 112)

Cadmium is not an essential nutrient. It is present in the geosphere and the body accumulates it slowly, as the small amounts in water and food are poorly absorbed. By the age of 50 years there may be 200 to 300 μmol (20 to 30 mg) in the body with the highest concentration in the kidney.

Cadmium poisoning is well known as an industrial hazard. In acute cases bronchitis is the main feature but in chronic cases the kidneys are most affected with proteinuria and other signs of renal dysfunction. Blood Cd is raised above 50 nmol/litre, taken as the upper limit of normality.

There has been two instances of a local population being exposed to excess Cd through their food. In Japan 200 people who were living on rice irrigated by waste water from a mine above their land developed a painful and severe osteomalacia (itai-itai disease).[58]

In Shipham, a Somerset village situated near a long-disused zinc and lead mine, the Cd content of the soil and vegetables was high. Some of the garden produce had pale transparent leaves, attributed to Cd poisoning. The village became headline news, but the health records of the villagers was satisfactory and their mortality rates over the previous 40 years was below the national average.[59]

COMMENT

Because until recently accurate analysis of trace elements in biological material was either impossible or extremely difficult, precise knowledge of the ranges of concentrations in tissues that may be essential for health or be toxic is available in very few cases. Now that better analytical methods are available there has been an upsurge of research in the biological role of these elements. Though it would be unwise to predict what this will reveal and what practical effects will follow in the prevention and treatment of disease, there are several fields in which valuable results may be obtained.

The first is infant feeding. Infants have a less varied diet than adults and their main food, milk, is a poor source of some of the trace elements. There are reports of low concentrations of some elements in children suffering from various forms of protein-energy malnutrition. There is now a good case for studying in detail intake and tissue concentrations of trace elements in relation to the growth and development of children. It is not known to what extent manufacturing processes either add to or reduce the amounts present in foods for infants and young children. These are not normally analysed for trace elements, nor are they subject to any satutory controls in this respect. Research might show that both upper and lower limits for the concentrations of certain elements in infant foods are desirable.

In some countries, an association has been demonstrated between the softness of the drinking water and an increased mortality from cardiovascular diseases. Research may show that a deficiency of one element or an excess of another, or the combination of the two, has an adverse effect on the myocardium or other tissues. There are other diseases in which trace elements could well be involved, for example dental caries (p. 422) and types of cancer that have a high prevalence in localised areas.

There are also the continuing hazards of pollution of the environment by industrial processes. It has long been known that traces of lead and mercury can enter the body after contamination of the food, the drinking water or the air, and have severe toxic effects. The ways in which inorganic mercury can be converted to the more dangerous alkyl mercury and contaminate foods have been worked out in the last 10 years. Cadmium is now under suspicion in this respect. Clearly there is a need to keep a close watch on the environment to ensure that it is not contaminated by dangerous amounts of any of these elements.

Agricultural scientists know well that there are many antagonisms and synergisms between the different trace elements and with other nutrients. In plant nutrition they cannot be considered in isolation, nor can they in human nutrition, as a story from India shows.[60,61] There are living near the Nagarjunasagar dam in Andhra Pradesh men whose spines have become stiff early in life and their legs bent at the knees with the deformity known as genu valgum. The fluorine content of the water in the area is high and this accounts for the os-teosclerosis of the spine; it also probably increases the effects of a mild copper deficiency to induce osteoporosis in the legs. The copper deficiency arises because their main dietary source is their staple cereal, sorghum. The lack of copper in the cereal arises from increased molybdenum in soil, due to increased alkalinity, following a rise in subsoil water.

Wordsworth provides a fitting final comment to this chapter:

'Dust as we are, the immortal spirit grows
Like harmony in music; there is a dark
Inscrutable workmanship that reconciles
Discordant elements.'

REFERENCES

1. Enclopaedia Britannica 1973 Atmosphere, development of. 15th edn, Macropaedia vol 2, p 313–319
2. McCance R A, Widdowson E M 1937 Absorption and excretion of iron. Lancet 2: 680–684
3. Moore C V 1959–60 Iron metabolism and nutrition. Harvey Lect Series 55: 67–101
4. Bothwell T H, Charlton R W, Cook J D, Finch C A 1979 Iron metabolism in man. Blackwell, Oxford
5. Wheeler E F, El-Neil H, Willson J O C, Weiner J S 1973 The effect of work level and dietary intake on water balance and the excretion of sodium, potassium and iron in a hot climate. Br J Nutr 30: 127–137
6. Green R, Charlton R W, Seftel H, et al 1968 Body iron excretion in man. A collaborative study. Am J Med 45: 336–353
7. Jacobs A, Butler E B 1965 Menstrual blood loss in iron-deficiency anaemia. Lancet 2: 407–409
8. Hallberg L, Högdahl A-M, Nilsson L, Rybo G 1966 Menstrual blood loss — a population study. Acta Obstet Gynecol Scand 45: 320–351
9. Fullerton H W 1936 Anaemia in poor class women. Br Med J 2: 523–528
10. Halberg L 1982 Iron absorption and iron deficiency. Hum Nutr Clin Nutr 36C: 259–278
11. Layrisse M, Martinez-Torres C 1971 Food iron absorption. Prog Haematol 7: 137–160
12. Cook J D, Monsen E R 1977 Vitamin C, the common cold and iron absorption. Am J Clin Nutr 30: 235–241
13. Disler P B, Lynch S R, Charlton R W, et al 1975 The effect of tea on iron absorption. Gut 16: 193–200
14. Derman D P, Bothwell T H, Torrance J D, et al 1980 Iron absorption from maize (*Zea mays*) and sorghum (*Sorghum vulgare*) beer. Br J Nutr 43: 271–279
15. Jacobs P, Bothwell T H, Charlton R W 1964 Role of hydrochloric acid in iron absorption. J Appl Physiol 19: 187–188
16. Moore C V 1973 In: Goodhart R S, Shils M E (eds) Modern nutrition in health and disease, 5th edn. Lea & Febiger, Philadelphia, p 302
17. Fenton V, Cavill I, Fisher J 1977 Iron stores in pregnancy. Br J Haematol 37: 145–149
18. Jacobs A, Miller E, Worwood M, Beamish M R, Wardrop C A 1972 Ferritin in the serum of normal subjects and patients with iron deficiency and iron overload. Br Med J 4: 206–208
19. Lipschitz D A, Cook J D, Finch C A 1974 A clinical evaluation of serum ferritin. New Engl J Med 290: 1213–1216
20. MacDonald R A 1964 Hemochromatosis and hemosiderosis. Thomas, Springfield, Ill
21. Lynch S R, Seftel H C, Torrance J D, Charlton R W, Bothwell T H 1967 Accelerated oxidative catabolism of ascorbic acid in siderotic Bantu. Am J Clin Nutr 20: 641–647
22. MacPhail A P, Simon M O, Torrance T D, et al 1979 Changing patterns of dietary iron overload in black South Africans. Am J Clin Nutr 32: 1272–1278
23. Department of Health and Social Security 1979 Recommended daily amounts of food energy and nutrients for groups of people in the United Kingdom. Report on Health and Social Subjects no. 15. HMSO, London
24. Solomon N 1982 Biological availability of zinc in humans. Am J Clin Nutr 35: 1048–1075
25. Moynahan E J 1974 Acrodermatitis enterohepatica: a lethal inherited human zinc disorder. Lancet 2: 399–400
26. Brook A C, Johnson D G, Ward M K, et al 1980 Absence of a therapeutic effect of zinc in the sexual dysfunction of haemodialysed patients. Lancet 2: 618–621
27. Meadows N J, Ruse W, Smith M R, et al 1982 Zinc and small babies. Lancet 2: 1135–1137
28. Prasad A S, Miale A, Farid Z, Sandstead H H, Shubert A R 1963 Zinc metabolism in patients with the syndrome of iron deficiency anaemia, hepatosplenomegaly, dwarfism and hypogonadism. J Lab Clin Med 61: 537–549
29. Hambidge K M, Hambidge C, Jacobs M, Barum J D 1972 Low levels of zinc in hair, anorexia, poor growth and hypogensia in children. Pediatric Res 6: 868–874
30. Burnet F M 1981 A possible role of zinc in the pathology of dementia. Lancet 1: 186–188
31. Gallery E D M, Bloomfield J, Dixon S R 1972 Acute zinc toxicity in haemodialysis. Br Med J 4: 331–333
32. Marine D, Kimball O P 1920 Prevention of simple goiter in man. Arch Intern Med 25: 661–672
33. Kendall E C, Osterberg A E 1919 The chemical identification of thyroxin. J Biol Chem 40: 265–334
34. Wayne E J, Koutras D A, Alexander W D 1964 Clinical aspects of iodine metabolism. Blackwell, Oxford
35. World Health Organization 1970 Fluorides and human health WHO Monogr Ser no. 59
36. Royal College of Physicians 1976 Fluoride, teeth and health. Pitman, London
37. Roholm K 1937 Fluorine intoxication. Nyt Nordisk Forling, Copenhagen
38. Jolly S S, Singh B M 1969 Endemic fluorosis in Punjab (India). Am J Med 47: 553–563
39. Riggs B L, Seeman E, Hodgson S F, Taves D L, O'Fallon W M 1982 Effect of the fluoride/calcium regime on vertebral fracture occurrence in postmenopausal women. New Engl J Med 306: 446–450
40. Danks D M, Stevens B J, Campbell P E, et al 1972 Menkes' kinky-hair syndrome. Lancet 1: 1100–1102

41. Tanner M S, Kantarjian A H, Bhave S A, Pandit A N 1983 Early introduction of copper-contaminated animal milk feeds as a possible cause of Indian childhood cirrhosis. Lancet 2: 992–995

42. Morin Y, Daniel P 1967 Quebec beer-drinkers cardiomyopathy: etiological considerations. Can Med Assoc J 97: 926–928

43. Hambidge K M 1974 Chromium nutrition in man. Am J Clin Nutr 27: 505–514

44. Jeejeebhoy K N, Chu R C, Marliss E B, Greenberg G R, Bruce-Robertson A 1977 Chromium deficiency, glucose and neuropathy reversed by chromium supplementation in a patient receiving long-term total parental nutrition. Am J Clin Nutr 30: 531–538

45. Mertz W 1969 Chromium occurrence and function in biological systems. Physiol Rev 49: 163–239

46. Wenlock R W, Buss D H, Dixon E J 1979 Trace nutrients. 2: Manganese in British food. Br J Nutr 41: 253–261

47. Krehl W A 1970 Selenium, the maddening mineral. Nutr Today 5: 26–32

48. Schwartz K, Foltz C M 1957 Selenium as an integral part of factor 3 against dietary necrotic liver degeneration. J Am Chem Soc 79: 3292–3293

49. Thomson C D, Robinson M F, Campbell D R, Rhea H M 1982 Effect of prolonged supplementation with daily supplements of selenomethionine and sodium selenite on glutathione peroxidase activity in New Zealand residents. Am J Clin Nutr 36: 24–31

50. Anonymous 1979 Selenium in the heart of China. (Editorial.) Lancet 2: 889–890

51. Thorn J, Robertson J, Buss D H, Bunton M G 1978 Trace nutrients. Selenium in British food. Br J Nutr 39: 391–396

52. Young V R, Nahapetian A, Janghorbani M 1982 Selenium bioavailability with reference to human nutrition. Am J Clin Nutr 35: 1076–1088

53. Cantley L C, Josephson L, Warner R, et al 1977 Vanadate is a potent (Na, K)-ATPase inhibitor found in ATP derived from muscle. J Biol Chem 252: 7421–7423

54. Golden M H N, Golden B E 1981 Trace elements. Br Med Bull 37: 31–36

55. Weiss D, Whitten B, Leddy D 1972 Lead content of human hair (1871–1971). Science NY 178: 69–70

56. Korns R F 1972 The frustrations of Batlye Russow. Nutr Today 7: 21–23

57. Bakir F, Damluji S F, Amin-Zaki L, et al 1973 Methylmercury posioning in Iraq. Science NY 181: 230–241

58. Anonymous 1971 Cadmium pollution and itai-itai disease. (Editorial.) Lancet 1: 382–383

59. Inskip P, Beral V, McDowall M 1982 Mortality of Shipham residents: 40-year follow-up. Lancet 1: 896–899

60. Krishnamachari K A V R, Krishnaswamy K 1973 Genu valgum and osteoporosis in an area of fluorosis. Lancet 2: 877–879

61. Agarwal A K 1975 Crippling cost of India's big dam. New Scientist 65: 260–261

13

Fat-soluble Vitamins

The vitamins are organic substances which the body requires in small amounts for its metabolism, yet cannot make for itself at least in sufficient quantity. They are not related chemically and differ in their physiological actions.

NOMENCLATURE OF VITAMINS

As the vitamins were discovered, each was first labelled with a letter, but once a vitamin had been isolated and its chemical structure identified, it was given a specific name. It is entirely correct to use this specific name provided it is applied only to a single chemical substance. However, there are advantages in certain circumstances for retaining some of the original letters as labels for the following reasons.

1. Many of the vitamins, such as vitamins A, D, K, E and B12, consist of several closely related compounds with similar physiological properties.

2. It is useful still to talk about the 'vitamin B complex' because the vitamins concerned in it (though unrelated chemically) often occur together in the same foodstuffs.

FACTORS INFLUENCING UTILISATION

Availability. Not all of the vitamin may be in absorbable form. For instance most of the nicotinic acid in cereals is bound in such a way that it is not absorbed from the gut. Fat-soluble vitamins may fail to be absorbed if the digestion of fat is impaired.

Antivitamins. These are present in some natural foods (Chap. 25). Several synthetic analogues of vitamins have proved to be highly poisonous (e.g. aminopterin, desoxypyridoxine), because they block the true vitamins at their site of action in enzyme systems. Some drugs antagonise a particular vitamin. Examples are given under individual vitamins.

Provitamins. Substances occur in foods which are not themselves vitamins but are capable of conversion

into vitamins in the body. Thus the carotenes are provitamins of vitamin A and to some extent at least the amino acid tryptophan can be converted to nicotinic acid. Vitamin D is synthesised in the skin by the action of sunlight on a derivative of cholesterol (p. 138).

Biosynthesis in the gut. The normal bacterial flora of the gut is capable of synthesising significant amounts of certain vitamins (e.g. vitamin K, nicotinic acid, riboflavin, vitamin B12, folic acid). Bacteria may also extract vitamins from the ingested food and retain them until excreted in the faeces. In health the small intestine of man is for the most part sterile. The large intestine carries a heavy load of bacteria, but usually absorption from the large intestine is limited to water and salts. It is unlikely that bacterial activity significantly affects the amounts of vitamins available to a healthy human body. When intestinal disease is present, and particularly if there is diarrhoea (a common concomitant of nutritional disorders), the small intestine may harbour large numbers of bacteria. These are more likely to reduce than to increase the amounts of available vitamins as is clearly demonstrated in the blind loop syndrome.

Interactions of nutrients. If the diet is rich in carbohydrates or alcohol, more thiamin is needed for metabolism. The requirement for vitamin E is increased when the intake of polyunsaturated fats is high. There are several other interactions of nutrients like this. For this reason the nutritive value of a diet in respect of a given vitamin may differ from the chemical analysis of its vitamin content.

Several monographs on vitamins have been published. The most recent one, *Vitamins in Medical Practice*, vol 1 1980 and vol 2 1982, edited by B M Barker and D A Bender, is recommended for reference and further reading. It contains good bibliographies of all the vitamins. A monograph by H E Sauberlich, J H Skala and R P Dowdy, *Laboratory Tests for the Assessment of Nutritional Status*, 1974 (CRC Press, Cleveland), is recommended for details of laboratory techniques. The figures in this and the next chapter giving the vitamin contents of foods are mostly taken from *The Composition of Foods* by A A Paul and D A T Southgate. They are illustrative only and readers should use data from one of the tables listed on p. 179, appropriate for their country.

VITAMIN A OR RETINOL

HISTORY

In experiments carried out between 1906 and 1912 Hopkins showed that young rats fed on a diet of casein, starch, sugar, lard and inorganic salts failed to grow and finally died. The addition to the diet of only 3 ml of milk daily, supplying not more than 4 per cent of the total energy, enabled the rats to thrive. He thus demonstrated the existence of an 'accessory food factor' in milk. In 1913 two groups of American workers extracted this growth factor with ether, thus showing that it was fat-soluble. Osborne and Mendel[1] extracted it from butter, and McCollum and Davis[2] from butter, egg yolk and cod-liver oil. Two years later the latter workers proposed the name 'fat-soluble A' to distinguish it from 'water-soluble B' which they had detected in whey, yeast and rice polishings. Vitamin A, as it came to be called, was further distinguished from fat-soluble vitamin D following the demonstration that it was ineffective in the cure of rickets produced experimentally in puppies by Mellanby in 1918.

The relationship of vitamin A to the plant pigment carotene was demonstrated in 1920 by Rosenheim and Drummond.[3] They showed that the vitamin A potency of vegetable foods was closely related to their content of carotene — a pigment that had been isolated from carrots nearly a century before. The final proof that carotene is the precursor of vitamin A was largely due to the subsequent work of Moore[4] at Cambridge, whose monograph on the vitamin is a classic.

CHEMISTRY OF RETINOL

The retinol molecule consists of a hydrocarbon chain with a β-ionone ring at one end and an alcohol group at the other (Fig. 13.1). It is the main form of vitamin A in foods and was formerly known as vitamin A_1. Pure crystalline retinol is the reference standard for vitamin A activity. The usual form is the *all-trans* stereoisomer. Isomers with *cis* configuration at the 11 or 13 position occur less commonly and have somewhat lower biological activity. Vitamin A_2 is 3-dehydroretinol; it has about half the biological activity of retinol but is of little biological importance, only occurring in the livers of some Indian fish.

The terminal alcohol group can be oxidised in the body to an aldehyde, retinal, or a carboxylic acid group, retinoic acid. In foodstuffs the alcohol is usually esterified with fatty acids (retinyl esters).

Retinol itself is a pale yellow, almost colourless compound, soluble in fats and fat solvents but not in water. It is stable to heat at ordinary cooking temperatures but liable to oxidation and destruction if the fats that contain it turn rancid. Vitamin E, if present, protects it from oxidation. Retinol is also destroyed by exposure to sunlight.

CONVERSION OF β-CAROTENE INTO RETINOL

There are about 100 naturally occurring pigments, the carotenoids, which are chemically similar in structure to β-carotene (Fig. 13.1). They are responsible for most of the yellow-red colour of vegetables and some fruits. The most important, β-carotene, has a widespread distribution in association with chlorophyll, the green pigment necessary for photosynthesis; it can be split in the

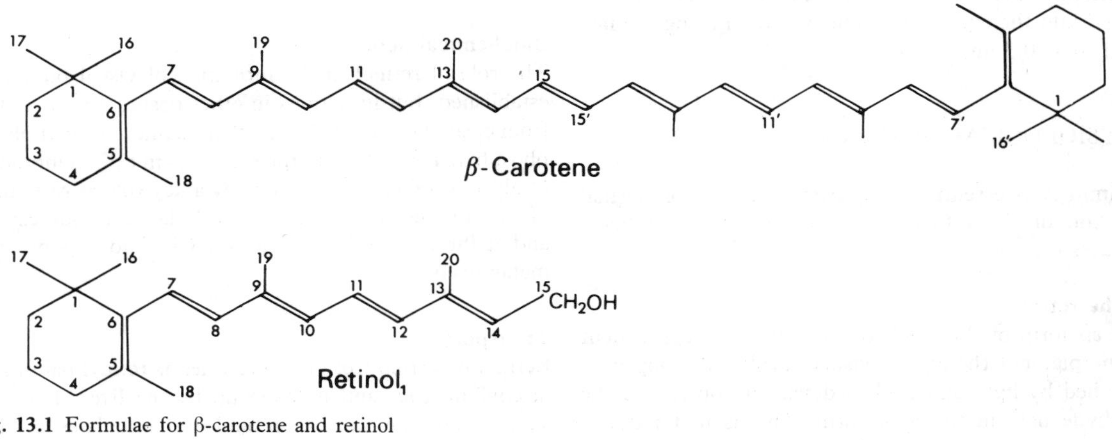

Fig. 13.1 Formulae for β-carotene and retinol

middle of its long hydrocarbon chain by an enzyme in the small intestinal mucosa, β-carotene-15, 15'-oxygenase, to yield two molecules of retinol. β-Carotene is therefore a provitamin A. It is the only carotenoid which has a structure identical with retinol in both halves of the molecule. Most of the other carotenoids, such as xanthophyll, the other yellow pigment associated with chlorophyll, and lycopene, the red pigment of tomatoes, have no provitamin A activity. The biochemistry of carotenoids is discussed in two reviews.[5,6]

Dark-green leaves are a good source of β-carotene, carrots are an excellent source, and red palm oil is very rich in α-carotene. In many parts of the world where animal foods are seldom eaten almost all the vitamin A intake comes from such vegetable sources. Even in Europe and North America about half the vitamin A comes from β-carotene.

Absorption of β-carotene from the diet is very variable and depends on the quantity and quality of the dietary fat. The conversion of β-carotene to retinol takes place mainly in the intestinal mucosa in man and most animals, but the liver and probably other tissues are alternative sites. Many studies have shown that 6 μg of β-carotene has the biological activity of 1 μg of retinol. Most of this difference is due to the poor absorption of carotene. The vitamin A activity of a diet is usually expressed in retinol equivalents. This is calculated by adding to the retinol content one-sixth of the β-carotene content.

Formerly vitamin A activity was expressed in terms of international units (iu). Carotene was available in pure form before vitamin A and by definition 1 iu of vitamin A was made equal to 0.6 μg of β-carotene and all values of vitamin A were expressed in this unit. Since crystalline retinol became available there is no longer a need for an international unit; the term 'retinol' should be used to mean vitamin A alcohol, while the term 'vitamin A' should be used to include all compounds with vitamin A activity. All values for vitamin A expressed as international units in the old literature may be converted into the equivalent value of retinol using the factor 1 iu = 0.3 μg of retinol.

PHYSIOLOGICAL ACTION

Vitamin A is essential for growth and also for normal function of the retina and development of epithelial surfaces.

In the retina

The *cis* form of the aldehyde of retinol is a component of the pigment rhodopsin (visual purple). Rhodopsin is bleached by light and broken down into opsin and the aldehyde now in the *trans* form. This is first reduced back into the vitamin which is subsequently converted to the *cis* form and then into the *cis* aldehyde. This visual cycle was elucidated by Wald,[7] who was awarded a Nobel Prize for the work.

Vitamin A deficiency reduces the rhodopsin in the rods of the retina and in this way leads to night blindness. The ability to see in the dark, dark adaptation, can be tested using an apparatus described by Dow and Steven[8] and this is useful in the early diagnosis of deficiency.

In epithelial surfaces

In vitamin A deficiency epithelial cells undergo squamous metaplasia. They are flattened and heaped one upon another and the surface becomes keratinised.[9] This process is most easily seen on the conjunctiva covering the sclera and cornea of the eye, producing the condition known as xerophthalmia (Chap. 31). When severe this leads to softening destruction of the cornea and permanent blindness. Xerophthalmia is the most serious deficiency disease in the world today.

In the skin keratinisation blocks the sebaceous gland with horny plugs, a condition known as follicular keratosis (p. 332).

Similar changes occur in the epithelial linings of the respiratory, gastrointestinal and urogenital tracts, at least in experimental animals. There they are not so well marked, probably because the surfaces are not exposed to the external environment. Vitamin A deficiency has not been established as a contributory cause of any disease of the internal organs of man. However, the metaplasia that it produces resembles that seen in known precancerous conditions and, in experimental animals, high doses of the vitamin can prevent the development of skin cancers after the application of cancer-producing agents.[10] In this way support is given to those who claim on epidemiological evidence that vitamin A deficiency may be a contributory cause of human cancer (Chap. 60).

Biochemical action

The role of retinol in the formation of visual purple is established, but its actions in other tissues are as yet far from clear. DeLuca[11] showed that mannose retinyl phosphate is involved in the synthesis in cell membranes of glycoproteins. These may play a key role as receptors of specific hormones, in intercellular communication and adhesion and in cell growth and lipoprotein metabolism.[12]

Transport

Retinol is carried from the intestines as retinyl palmitate in chylomicrons and is taken up by the liver. It is released from the liver as retinol and circulates in the blood bound to a specific transport protein, retinol-binding protein (RBP), which forms a complex with plasma prealbumin (PA). Both RBP and PA can be measured by immunoassay and concentrations of both are low in malnourished children.[13,14] After ingestion of retinol, 80 per cent is absorbed. Usually 30 to 50 per cent is stored in the liver, 20 to 60 per cent is conjugated and excreted in bile as the glucuronide.

Storage

The livers of people killed accidentally in Britain contain on average 270 µg/g of retinol, or about 400 mg in the whole liver.[15] This is sufficient to meet requirements for many months or years with no dietary intake. Liver stores are not inexhaustible and in postmortem surveys in Canada and the USA it has been found that some 20 to 30 per cent of people have had liver vitamin A in the low range of 0 to 40 µg/g by the time of death.[16,17] In Bangladesh 78 per cent of people had low concentrations (< 40 µg/g) in the liver.[18]

HUMAN DEFICIENCY

Vitamin A deficiency was induced in 16 human volunteers in an experiment carried out in Sheffield from 1942 to 1944. Anyone with a special interest in vitamin A should study the account of this investigation.[19] It is noteworthy that although night blindness and some follicular keratosis resulted, there was no xerophthalmia. The clinical effects of vitamin A deficiency are usually seen only in people whose diet has been deficient for a long time both in dairy produce and vegetables. Deficiency of vitamin A occasionally develops from faulty absorption, caused by a variety of diseases of the alimentary tract. Owing to the large store of the vitamin this is very rare and could only occur in a previously healthy man after many months of severe illness.

Diagnosis

In the Sheffield experiment the most sensitive test of retinol deficiency was the measurement of dark adaptation.

Retinol can be measured in the blood by means of the blue colour that it develops in the presence of antimony trichloride or trifluoracetic acid (Carr-Price reaction). There is also a fluorimetric procedure. The level in the blood does not begin to fall until the body's reserves are severely depleted. Mean values for plasma retinol and carotenoids are given in Table 13.1. The lower limits which can be considered satisfactory are 200 and 800 µg/litre for retinol and carotenoids respectively. The concentration of carotenoids reflects the recent dietary intake of the precursor.

When an individual regularly consumes very large amounts of foods rich in carotenoids, the plasma can become distinctly orange-yellow and the skin can become tinged with the same colour. This is called **hypercarotenaemia**. Unlike jaundice, in which bile pigments accumulate in the body, the eyes do not become yellow. Hypercarotenaemia is a benign condition; vitamin A is not formed in toxic amounts and the skin reverts to its normal colour on changing to an ordinary diet.

DIETARY SOURCES

Retinol is chiefly found in milk, butter, cheese, egg yolk, liver and some of the fatty fish. The liver oils of fish are the richest natural sources of vitamin A, but these are used as nutritional supplements rather than foods.

Carotenes are found chiefly in green vegetables in association with chlorophyll, so that the green outer leaves of vegetables are good sources of carotene, while the white inner leaves contain little. Other useful sources are

Table 13.1 Plasma concentrations of retinol and carotenoids (µg/l) and retinol-binding protein and prealbumin (mg/l)

Country	Retinol	Carotenoids	RBP	PA
Britain[20]				
Adults	450 (150–900)	1330 (150–3700)	—	—
Canada[21]				
Adults	650	1130	—	—
South India[22]				
Healthy children	240	500	—	—
Children with vitamin A deficiency	100	180	—	—
Cairo[13]				
Healthy children	224	—	23.7	143
Children with kwashiorkor	101	—	15.2	75

Table 13.2 Dietary sources of vitamin A activity (typical values)

Source	µg retinol equivalent/ 100g edible portion
Supplying preformed retinol	
Fatty fish and their oils	
Halibut-liver oil	900 000
Cod-liver oil	18 000
Shark-liver oil	180 000
Herring and mackerel	50
Sardine	trace
Dairy produce	
Butter	830
Margarine, vitaminised	900
Eggs, fresh, whole	140
Milk, fresh, whole	40
Cheese, whole, fatty type	320
Meats	
Liver, sheep and ox	15 000
Beef, mutton, pork	0–4
Supplying carotene	
Fruit and vegetables	
Red palm oil	30 000
Carrots	2000
Leafy vegetables	685
Tomatoes	100
Apricots, fresh	250
Bananas	30
Sweet potatoes, white	50
Sweet potatoes, red and yellow	670
Orange and juice	8

Negligible sources
Lard and vegetable oils, white fish, cereals (except maize), potatoes, sugar, jams and syrups

yellow and red fruits and vegetables, particularly carrots (Table 13.2). All vegetable oils are devoid of vitamin A activity, with the exception of red palm oil which is extensively produced in West Africa and Malaysia. Vitamin A is added artificially to margarine to provide the same concentration as that of good summer butter.

The yellow colour usually present in dairy products, cheese, butter and eggs, is due to carotenoids, but gives no indication of the amount of vitamin A present.

Losses in the preparation and handling of food
Both retinol and carotene are stable to ordinary cooking methods, though some loss may occur at temperatures above 100°C as when butter or palm oil is used for frying. Fruits and other foods that are dried in the sun lose much of their vitamin A potency. Considerable losses of retinol may occur in fish liver oils bottled in colourless glass and displayed in shop windows before being sold to the public. The stability of carotene in tinned foods was dramatically shown when it was found that cooked carrots that had been sealed in air-tight containers in 1824 for the Arctic voyage of *HMS Hecla* had much the same carotene content as fresh carrots when the containers were opened more than 100 years later.[23]

RECOMMENDED INTAKES

Hume and Krebs[19] showed that an intake of 440 ug/day given to depleted human volunteers slowly restored dark adaptation to normal, and concluded that the minimum protective intake was no greater than this. They also showed that volunteers receiving 880 µg/day maintained normal dark adaptation for a year. The FAO/WHO recommended intake for adults of 750 µg/day is based mainly on these findings. British diets on average provide about 1300 µg retinol equivalents/day, of which about two-thirds comes from carotenes.

The recommended intake for infants is based on measurements of intake of retinol by breast-fed infants. As vitamin A is essential for growth, children might be expected to need more than adults per weight of body weight. There is no experimental or field data from which requirements of children and adolescents can be calculated and the recommendations in Table 15.2 are based on interpolation from infant and adult requirements.

THERAPEUTIC USES

Retinol is invaluable in the treatment of xerophthalmia. It should also be given to patients with the malabsorption syndrome or obstructive jaundice, and to malnourished people who show Bitôt's spots (p. 335) or follicular keratosis.

Where vitamin A deficiency is prevalent, minor disorders of the eyes and skin often improve more rapidly if children are given prophylactic doses of the vitamin. A total dosage of 7.5 mg of retinol given in capsules over a period of one week should achieve the maximum therapeutic benefit. There is also the clinical impression that this often improves their growth and well-being. The prescription of vitamin A or its sale over the counter for trivial conditions like sunburn is not justified by any reliable clinical trial.

Pharmaceutical preparations of vitamin A and their dosage for prevention and treatment of xerophthalmia are described on page 300.

The use of retinol and retinoids in the treatment of skin diseases is described in Chapter 49.

TOXICITY

The early explorers of the Arctic learnt from the Eskimos that it is unwise to eat the liver of the polar bear; it causes drowsiness, headache, vomiting and extensive peeling of the skin. Polar bear and seal liver may contain nearly 600 mg retinol/100 g.[24] Husky dogs' livers contain half this amount; death and disease have occurred in Antarctic explorers who were forced to eat their dogs.[25]

A few cases of children under 3 years old with retinol poisoning have been described in the USA. Usually they have been the victims of misguided maternal enthusiasm, receiving a daily dose between 30 to 150 mg for several months. Some concentrated preparation has usually been given in large doses, in the mistaken belief that if a little does good, more should do better. The characteristic changes observed were anorexia, irritability, a dry itching skin, coarse, sparse hair and swellings over the long bones due to bony exostoses. The liver was sometimes enlarged. Plasma retinol concentrations were about 900 µg/l. Rapid recovery followed withdrawal of the vitamin.

In adults 17 cases have been reviewed.[26] Most were women who had taken 14 to 90 mg/day of retinol for over 8 years for chronic skin diseases. The clinical features were skin changes, headache, muscular stiffness and enlarged liver. Plasma retinol concentrations were from 0.8 to 20 mg/l. At least one death has occurred in a food faddist.

VITAMIN D OR CHOLECALCIFEROL

HISTORY

Cod-liver oil was used in Scotland as a traditional folk remedy at least as early as the eighteenth century. The famous French physician Trousseau began to use it in 1860 for the treatment of rickets. Mellanby[27] first clearly showed by his classical studies on puppies that rickets is a nutritional disease responding to a fat-soluble vitamin present in cod-liver oil. The vitamin was prepared in pure form in 1931 simultaneously in Britain and Germany.

CHEMISTRY (Fig. 13.2)

A number of distinct but closely related compounds possess rickets-preventing (antirachitic) properties. These are all sterols. Certain sterols on exposure to ultraviolet irradiation undergo a small structural change which makes them antirachitic. Only two 'activated' sterols are of importance in nutrition and therapeutics. These were first described as vitamin D_2 and D_3 and are still known by these labels. The material originally described as vitamin D_1 was subsequently shown to be an impure mixture of sterols.

Cholecalciferol, vitamin D_3

This substance is the natural form of vitamin D. It is produced by the ultraviolet irradiation of 7-dehydrocholesterol, a sterol widely distributed in animal fats, such as the oily secretions in mammalian skin and the oil of the preen glands of birds.

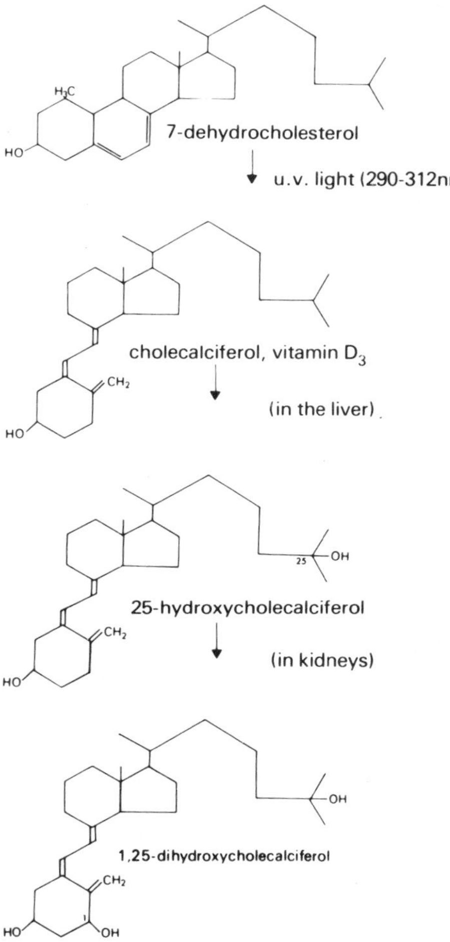

Fig. 13.2 The metabolism of vitamin D. Ergocalciferol undergoes the same 25- and 1-hydroxylations

Ergocalciferol, vitamin D_2

Ergocalciferol is manufactured by exposing ergosterol, a sterol found in fungi and yeasts, to the action of ultraviolet light. Irradiation of egosterol gives rise to several related substances — some toxic — of which only ergocalciferol has marked antirachitic properties. The irradiation has to be carefully controlled so that toxic substances are not present, except in traces, in the final product.

Although ergocalciferol is widely used in therapeutics, it occurs very rarely in nature. It is absent in almost all plant and animal tissues. Ergocalciferol differs from cholecalciferol only in an extra methyl group at C-24 and a double bond between C-22 and C-23, and undergoes the same hydroxylations in the body.

SOURCES

Only a very few foods provide the vitamin (Table 13.3).

Table 13.3 Vitamin D in foods (1 µg is equal to 40 of the old international units)

Food	Mean vitamin D (µg/100g)
Naturally containing the vitamin	
Cod liver oil	210
Herrings, kippers	22
Sardines, pilchards (canned)	8
Tuna (canned)	6
Eggs	1.75
Butter	0.75
Liver	0.75
Cheese (cheddar)	0.25
Cream (double)	0.25
Milk, unfortified (summer)	0.03
Fortified with vitamin D	
Margarine	8.8
Infant milks (after dilution)	about 1.1
Some yogurts	about 2.2
Milk in USA, Canada	1.1

Cereals, vegetables and fruit contain no vitamin D. Meat, poultry and white fish contribute insignificant amounts.

The only rich sources are the liver oils of fish, which obtain the vitamin by ingesting plankton living near the surface of the sea and so exposed to sunlight. Many people obtain little or no vitamin from their diet and get their supply by synthesis from 7-dehydrocholesterol, which takes place in the stratum granulosum of the skin through the action of ultraviolet light.

Since in man cholecalciferol is formed in one organ of the body (the skin) and it acts on distant target organs (the gut and the bones), it could be classified as a hormone rather than a vitamin, as suggested by Loomis.[28] The rate of synthesis in the skin is determined by the degree of exposure to ultraviolet light and probably by the amount of pigment. Loomis points out that *Homo sapiens* evolved in a tropical environment where he was exposed heavily to sunlight. His skin was probably brown, containing large amounts of melanin which protects against solar damage. When such early men migrated north, the sunlight was less intense and they were also less exposed to it, owing to the necessity to clothe themselves in furs against the cold. A heavily pigmented child is probably more susceptible to rickets because the melanin reduces penetration of u.v. light and less 7-dehydrocholesterol is irradiated, and natural selection would have favoured the evolution of a people with fair skins. This attractive hypothesis for the evolution of the white races is by no means proven.

Loomis has estimated that the pink cheeks of a European infant (area about 20 cm²) can synthesise daily about 10 µg of vitamin D if adequately exposed; this is enough to prevent rickets. The $25(OH)D_2$ and $25(OH)D_3$ in plasma can be distinguished by immunoassay. This makes it possible to see how much of the circulating form of the vitamin comes from sunlight and

fish oils as $25(OH)D_3$, and how much as $25(OH)D_2$ from pharmaceutical preparations and fortified milk. In the USA, where milk is fortified, five times as much $25(OH)D_3$ was found in normal adults in St Louis, Missouri, which shows that sunlight is the principal source of their vitamin D.[29]

Breast milk contains 0.06–1.2 µg/dl of vitamin D and this may be insufficient for normal bone mineralisation in some infants.[30]

PHYSIOLOGY (Fig. 13.3)

Vitamin D in food is absorbed in the small intestine only when fat digestion and absorption are normal. It is carried in chylomicrons to the liver. Here vitamin D of cutaneous or dietary origin is converted in the microsomes to $25(OH)D$, the circulating form of the vitamin which is carried on a special transport globulin. The plasma $25(OH)D$ concentration is normally above 5 µg/l (12 nmol/l). The amount of vitamin D stored in the human body is not as large as that of vitamin A. More is stored in the adipose tissue than the liver.[31] It is excreted in the bile as more polar hydroxylated metabolites, some in the form of glucuronides.

The active form of vitamin D is $1,25(OH)_2D$, which is formed only in the kidney by the action of a specific mitochondrial hydroxylase on $25(OH)D$. The dihydroxy metabolite is about 10 times more active than vitamin D_3, itself on the target tissues and acts more quickly. It was the 10 to 12 hour delay before vitamin D stimulated intestinal calcium absorption that prompted the search for active intermediates. These were discovered in the laboratories of Kodicek[32] in Cambridge, England and of DeLuca[33] in Wisconsin.

$1,25(OH)_2D$ functions as a hormone which, along

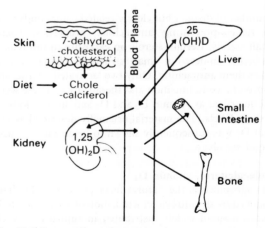

Fig. 13.3 Intermediary metabolism of vitamin D

with parathyroid hormone and calcitonin, regulates calcium and phosphate metabolism. Three effects of $1,25(OH)_2D$ are now well established. (1) It promotes calcium absorption in the upper small intestine by inducing the synthesis of a specific calcium-binding protein in the epithelial cell. It appears to pass to the nucleus of the cell and there stimulate production of a specific messenger RNA. (2) It acts on bone to mobilise calcium into the circulation. This effect requires the presence of parathyroid hormone. (3) It facilitates phosphate absorption by stimulating a separate phosphate transport mechanism in intestinal epithelial cells. This is independent of the calcium transport system and is easiest to demonstrate in the distal small intestine where little calcium is absorbed.

A fall in plasma calcium is monitored by the parathyroid glands which then secrete more parathyroid hormone. Parathyroid hormone stimulates the hydroxylase in kidney mitochondria and secretion of $1,25(OH)_2D$ increases. By its actions on the intestine and bone it increases plasma calcium. But if plasma calcium rises synthesis of $1,25(OH)_2D$ shuts off.

PATHOLOGY

Vitamin D deficiency alters the processes involved in the growth of bones. Growth in length of the long bones normally occurs at the band of epiphyseal cartilage lying between the shaft (or diaphysis) and the epiphysis. New cartilage is continuously formed at the epiphyseal end, while at the diaphyseal end the cartilage degenerates and is invaded by capillaries and osteoblasts, forming osteoid tissue in which calcium salts are deposited. The formation of new cartilage keeps pace with its degeneration and with the simultaneous formation of new bone at the end of the diaphysis, so that the bone grows in length. Growth ceases when no further new cartilage is formed and the diaphyseal bone meets and fuses with the epiphysis.

Experiments on animals have shown that in vitamin D deficiency the epiphyseal cartilage grows, but the normal degeneration of this cartilage becomes defective, so that there is widening of the zone between diaphysis and epiphysis. At the diaphyseal end the cartilage is irregularly invaded by excessive osteoid tissue in which little calcification takes place. Calcification is also reduced beneath the periosteum which covers the outer surface of the bones; there is an overgrowth of osteoid tissue below the periosteum and delay in the normal outward thickening.

These anatomical lesions in animals deprived of vitamin D are accompanied by the biochemical effects of calcium depletion and the general manifestations of rickets (Chap. 32).

INTERACTION WITH DRUGS

Some drugs, notably phenobarbitone, induce the synthesis of hydroxylating enzymes in the microsomes of the liver cells. In this way the metabolism of vitamin D may be accelerated and this may account for the development of rickets and osteomalacia in some patients on prolonged treatment with sedatives and anticonvulsants.

RECOMMENDED INTAKES

Most authorities have recommended a daily dietary intake of 10 μg (400 iu) for children. A dietary supply may not be essential, and children in many tropical countries do not develop rickets despite negligible quantities in their food. In northern countries and also in those tropical communities where it is the custom not to expose infants and young children to sunlight, rickets occurs frequently in infants unless the vitamin is available in the diet. Experience has shown that 10 μg daily is sufficient to protect a child against rickets and this intake involves no risk of hypervitaminosis. The vitamin should also be provided, about 2.5 μg/day, for older children and adults who are deprived of sunlight for long periods for any reason. Intakes above the recommended levels are potentially dangerous and should be avoided.

PROPHYLACTIC AND THERAPEUTIC USES

The uses of vitamin D in the prevention and treatment of rickets and of osteomalacia are discussed in Chapter 32.

Synthetic $1,25(OH)_2D$ and analogues such as $1,\alpha$-hydroxy vitamin D are effective in the treatment of hypocalcaemic states caused by diseases, such as hypoparathyroidism and vitamin D-resistant rickets (Chap. 32).

TOXICITY

A daily dose of 50 μg, only five times the recommended intake, may be toxic if taken over prolonged periods. Overdosage is recognised by hypercalcaemia and plasma calcium rises from 2.75 up to 4.5 mmol/litre. The common symptoms are anorexia and loss of weight, nausea, headache, depression and irritability, but these may be absent. In more severe cases there is confusion and stupor which may suggest meningitis. Renal failure may follow and this can be fatal.

The condition was first recognised in young children when cod liver oil began to be replaced by halibut liver oil and other concentrated preparations. A mother accustomed to giving her child cod liver oil might mistake instructions and give a similar dose of a concentrate. It is now seen in adults prescribed large doses of vitamin D for metabolic bone disease, associated with kidney or liver disease or the malabsorption syndrome; 20 such cases have been reported from Dundee,[34] of whom two died and three had persisting renal impairment. Clearly, all patients receiving vitamin D therapy should have their plasma calcium checked regularly. All mothers should be warned of the danger of overdosage.

VITAMIN K AND RELATED SUBSTANCES

HISTORY

In 1934 Dam and Schönheyder in Denmark described a nutritional disease of chickens characterised by bleeding which was not due to vitamin C deficiency. Bleeding could be prevented by giving a variety of foodstuffs: lucerne (alfalfa) and decayed fish meal were particularly effective. The active principle in these materials could be extracted with ether and thus a new fat-soluble vitamin was discovered. Dam[35] named it vitamin K (Koagulations-vitamin). With the aid of the Swiss chemist Karrer and his colleagues, Dam finally isolated the vitamin in 1939. In the same year, and only a few months later, the successful synthesis of vitamin K was announced from three different laboratories in the USA.

CHEMISTRY

The vitamin, a naphthoquinone, exists in nature in two forms. Vitamin K_1, originally isolated from lucerne, is the only form that occurs in plants. It is called phytylmenaquinone or phylloquinone by nutritionists but in the British and US pharmacopoeias its name is phytomenadione. It has a 20-carbon phytyl side-chain attached to 2-methyl-1,4-naphthoquinone (menadione or menaquinone). Figure 13.4 gives its chemical structure. It is a yellow oil, soluble in fat solvents, but only slightly soluble in water.

Vitamin K_2, originally isolated from putrid fish meal, is one of a family of homologues produced by bacteria, with 4 to 13 isoprenyl units in the side-chain (Fig. 13.4). They are called menaquinone-4 to menaquinone-13, according to the number of isoprenyl units.

PHYSIOLOGICAL ACTIVITY

Absorption of vitamin K_1 requires bile and pancreatic juice. It is transported from the intestine in chylomicrons and in the blood on β-lipoproteins.

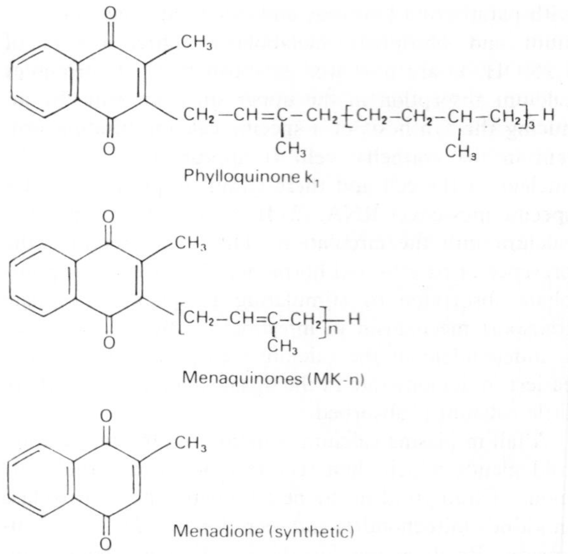

Phylloquinone k_1

Menaquinones (MK-n)

Menadione (synthetic)

Fig. 13.4 Structures of vitamin K

The only known function of vitamin K is as a cofactor for the synthesis in the liver of four proteins which participate in the coagulation cascade — prothrombin or factor II, and factors, VII, IX and X. Vitamin K acts after the constituent amino acids of these proteins have been strung together on the ribosomes.

It is essential for the carboxylation of glutamic acid moieties on the chain to γ-carboxyglutamide (Gla). These then provide sites for the binding of calcium and phospholipids necessary for the formation of thrombin. In the process the vitamin passes through a cycle.[36] It is first reduced to the hydroquinone form (KH_2); the reduced form is dependent on thiol groups and is inhibited by warfarin (see below). KH_2 then reacts with the peptide chain, CO_2 and O_2 to form peptide-Gla and the epoxide KO_2. This is enzymatically converted to K, the reaction requiring a thiol group and inhibited by warfarin. Reduced lipoic acid may be the source of the thiol groups. Since Gla is not metabolised, its urinary excretion is a measure of vitamin K activity. In vitamin K deficiency the clotting time is prolonged and so is the prothrombin time; activities of factors VII, IX and X, but not of other coagulation factors, are much reduced.[37]

Vitamin K_1 normally comes into the body in the diet. Vitamins K_2 are synthesised by bacteria in the lumen of the large intestine. Rats deprived of the vitamin in their diet only develop deficiency if coprophagy is prevented. Probably about half of our vitamin normally comes from gut bacteria, and vitamin K deficiency may occur in patients given antibiotics that reduce the intestinal bacterial flora. Body stores of vitamin K are not large but there are modest amounts in the liver.

Proteins containing Gla formed by the action of vitamin K are found in most tissues and notably in bone. There 10 to 20 per cent of the non-collagenous protein contains Gla and, as it binds calcium, has been named osteocalcin.[36] The role of this specialised protein, whose synthesis depends on vitamin K, is unknown.

HUMAN DEFICIENCY

Primary deficiency

Primary deficiency may arise in infants but is very rare in adults. Newborn babies have a sterile intestinal tract and are fed on foods relatively free from bacterial contamination. Cow's milk contains small amounts of vitamin K but breast milk is a very poor source. Infants in the first week of life have less prothrombin in their blood than normal adults and sometimes have a prolonged prothrombin time. There is spontaneous improvement within a few days. At one time bleeding in the newborn was attributed solely to hypoprothrombinaemia due to lack of vitamin K but even if the vitamin has been provided an immature liver may be slow in starting synthesis of prothrombin, and there are other causes of haemorrhage in the newborn which do not involve prothrombin.

Conditioned deficiences

Defects in absorption
As vitamin K is fat-soluble, it is not surprising that any defect in absorption of fats may result in vitamin K deficiency.
   Biliary obstruction. The secretion of bile salts is as necessary for the normal absorption of vitamin K as for other fat-soluble substances. Severe bleeding during or, more frequently, a day or two after an operation for the relief of jaundice due to obstruction of the common bile duct was a complication much feared by surgeons. Today this danger can be reduced by giving vitamin K by injection before operation.
   Malabsorption. In coeliac disease and other conditions in which fats are not effectively absorbed, bleeding due to deficiency of vitamin K may occur.
   Intestinal antibiotics. If antibiotics which reduce colonic flora are given for more than a week to a patient who has been eating poorly, vitamin K deficiency, hypoprothrombinaemia and bleeding can occur, especially in those who are ill with other disease.[37]
   Liver disease. In severe disease of the liver synthesis of prothrombin may fail and bleeding result even if an ample supply of vitamin K is given.

Antagonists: anticoagulants

Cattle develop a tendency to bleed if they are fed on spoilt sweet clover. The substance, dicoumard, respon-

sible for this effect was isolated and synthesised as dicoumarol by Stahmann, Huebner and Link in Wisconsin.[38] It prolongs the prothrombin time of the blood; this discovery opened up a new field in the treatment of thrombosis.

Dicoumarol itself has now been replaced in clinical use by other synthetic analogues such as warfarin and phenindione. They antagonise the actions of vitamin K and inhibit synthesis of prothrombin and factors VII, IX and X in the liver.

LABORATORY DIAGNOSIS

The effects of vitamin K deficiency can be detected by determining the 'prothrombin time'. Freshly drawn blood that has been prevented from clotting by the addition of oxalate (which precipitates calcium) is centrifuged. To the separated plasma, an excess of calcium salts is then added to overcome the effect of the oxalate, and also a source of thromboplastin (generally derived from brain tissue). The time it then takes for the plasma to clot is taken as an inverse measure of its prothrombin content.

DIETARY SOURCES

Vitamin K is present in fresh green leafy vegetables, such as broccoli, lettuce, cabbage and spinach. Beef liver is a good source but most other animal foods, cereals and fruits are poor sources unless they have undergone extensive bacterial putrefaction. Testing the response of prothrombin time to intravenous vitamin K_1 in a patient not absorbing the vitamin because of obstructive jaundice showed that the adult dietary requirement is about 40 μg/day.[39]

THERAPEUTIC USES

   In haemorrhagic disease of the newborn. In about 1 of every 800 infants born, bleeding occurs between the second and fifth days of life somewhere in the body either into the skin, nervous system, peritoneal cavity or alimentary tract (melaena neonatorum). Vitamin K deficiency is not always the cause and trauma at birth is undoubtedly responsible in some cases. Because of the low incidence of bleeding in the newborn and the improved efficacy of vitamin K in its treatment, most obstetric units in Britain no longer give vitamin K as a routine prophylactic measure either to infants or expectant mothers shortly before delivery. They confine its use to the prevention of bleeding in newborn infants who have suffered from trauma at birth or who show signs of bleeding. Water-soluble analogues of vitamin K should not be used in the newborn, especially if premature, because they may cause hyperbilirubinaemia. In some Third World countries haemorrhagic disease of the newborn is more common. Then there may be a case for giving every baby a prophylactic dose of 1 mg of vitamin K_1 intramuscularly. This preventive measure rarely has an adverse effect but may be a significant addition to the budget of the health service.

In biliary obstruction and fistula, and in malabsorption. Vitamin K preparations are invaluable in cases where its absorption has been impaired by lack of bile salts, pancreatic secretion or by other causes of malabsorption. This is an essential preoperative measure if surgery is contemplated in such cases. Phytomenadione should be given preoperatively for three days in a dose of 10 to 20 mg daily intramuscularly. The plasma prothrombin time is usually restored to normal within a week. When there is severe damage to the liver, little or no improvement in the prothrombin time can be expected unless a transfusion of blood or a concentrate of clotting factors is given.

In anticoagulant therapy. When patients are treated with warfarin, phenindione or similar drugs, overdosage may lead to bleeding. If this is severe, 20 mg of phytomenadione can be injected intravenously. In less severe cases the drug can be given by mouth (10 to 20 mg every eight hours).

VITAMIN E (TOCOPHEROLS)

Vitamin E was discovered in 1923 by Evans and Bishop[40] in California. They found that rats fed on a diet of casein, cornstarch, lard, butter and yeast fail to reproduce. Female rats aborted, while male rats became sterile. This could be corrected by the administration of certain vegetable oils. It was not until 1936 that Evans and his colleagues finally isolated pure vitamin E from the unsaponifiable fraction of wheat-germ oil. They called it tocopherol. The synthesis of α-tocopherol was accomplished in 1938 by Karrer in Switzerland and by Smith in the USA.

CHEMISTRY

Eight tocopherols and tocotrienols with vitamin E activity have been identified, differing from each other in the number and position of the methyl groups round the ring of the molecule (Figs. 13.5 and 13.6). All have the same physiological properties; α-tocopherol, which is synthesised commercially, is the most potent. Relative to it the biological activities of β- and γ-tocopherol and α-tocotrienol are 40, 8 and 20 per cent. Other forms

Naturally occurring tocopherols

Tocol	Tocotrienol	Methyl Positions
α -(alpha)	ζ -(zeta)	5, 7, 8
β -(beta)	ε -(epsilon)	5, 8
γ -(gamma)	η -(eta)	7, 8
δ -(delta)	8 -(methyl-tocotrienol)	8

Fig. 13.5 The tocotrienols are designated in accordance with methyl positions corresponding to the tocopherols. In descending order they are called α-, β-, γ-, and δ-tocotrienols respectively

Fig. 13.6 d-α-Tocopherol

have little activity. The tocopherols are yellow, oily liquids, freely soluble in fat solvents and remarkably stable to heat, even at temperatures above 100°C. The term vitamin E is useful as a name for any mixture of biologically active tocopherols.

BIOCHEMICAL ROLE

Being fat-soluble, vitamin E is found in all cell membranes. Here it may prevent the destructive nonenzymic oxidation of polyunsaturated fatty acids by molecular oxygen. This action is similar to that of antioxidants used in the food industry to prevent fats going rancid (p. 229). The products of oxidative deterioration of fat may appear in the tissues as pigments, which can be estimated by fluorimetric methods, and are associated with cell damage. They are likely to be found in the tissues of old animals and of those on diets lacking vitamin E. Hence it seems sensible to guess that the vitamin may have a role in preventing a large number of degenerative disorders. Yet there is no evidence to support this view (see below). In 1973 Tappel,[41] in giving a good account of the cellular action of the vitamin, states: 'The more research is done on the substance, the more intriguing it appears. Thus there is a nagging suspicion that there is a very important use for the vitamin and we are just not smart enough to see it'. Anyone listening to the 61 contributions to a symposium[42] in New York in 1982 would probably consider that this was still true.

DIETARY SOURCES

The richest sources are vegetable oils, in descending order wheat germ, sunflower seed, cotton seed, safflower, palm, rapeseed and other oils. In consequence margarine and shortening are major sources in Western diets. The average intake in household diets in the UK is 6.0 mg per person daily of which 26 per cent come from fats and oils, mainly margarine, and 12 per cent from vegetables and 9 per cent from cereals.[43] This total excludes the vitamin E in tea, a rich potential source from which little is extracted in the infusion.

The USA recommended intakes have been reduced and are now 8 mg of α-tocopherol equivalents for adult women and 10 mg for men. These figures still carry a high safety margin. Requirement increases with the polyunsaturated fat content of the diet, but this is not of practical importance as foods rich in polyunsaturated fat are also rich in vitamin E.

Vitamin E is so widely distributed in human foods that a primary deficiency has arisen only in patients on total parental nutrition and never in a healthy person on a natural diet.

Deficiency in experimental animals

In animals a bewildering array of different diseases are produced on regimes deficient in vitamin E. Fetal resorption occurs in female rats and other rodents; degeneration of the seminiferous epithelium of the testis occurs in rabbits, dogs and some monkeys; muscular dystrophy occurs in herbivores, affecting voluntary, cardiac and smooth muscle; nutritional encephalomalacia occurs in chicks; haemorrhages and exudative diathesis in turkeys; liver cell necrosis can occur in rats and pigs if the diet is also deficient in selenium. In monkeys a haemolytic anaemia occurs and the red cells show increased sensitivity to peroxide *in vitro*. In general, high intakes of polyunsaturated fat make animals more susceptible to deficiency and non-toxic intakes of selenium are protective, though there are exceptions.

Deficiency in man[44]

This has been established in three circumstances.

Malabsorption.   When absorption of fat is impaired, so is that of vitamin E. An extreme example is the rare hereditary disorder, abetalipoproteinaemia, in which a failure to form chylomicrons prevents fat absorption. Affected children fail to thrive, have fatty diarrhoea and become progressively weak and ataxic due to degenerative changes in sensory and motor tracts in the spinal cord and also in the cerebellum; retinol changes impair vision. A low fat diet and supplements of vitamin E may delay development of the neurological lesions.[45] Biochemical evidence of vitamin E deficiency (see below) is not uncommon in patients with the malabsorption syndrome and in a few cases of cystic fibrosis affecting the pancreas and of biliary cirrhosis neurological features similar to those of abetaliproteinuria have been reported.

Genetic blood disorders.   In two hereditary disorders, glucose-6-phosphate dehydrogenase deficiency (p. 467) and glutathione synthetase deficiency, anaemia arises from decreased survival of red blood cells, as is known to occur in experimental vitamin E deficiency. The vitamin, acting as an antioxidant, protects cells from lysis caused by lipid peroxidation and sulphydryl group oxidation, and its administration to patients with these disorders increases the life span of their red blood cells.[46]

Premature infants.   These are at increased risk of developing haemolytic jaundice and also internal haemorrhages. The risks have been reported to be reduced by administration of vitamin E.[47,48] As all milk formulae now available contain adequate amounts of the vitamin, it is not necessary to give supplements as a routine but they may be needed in some circumstances. One of these is when a very small baby is nursed in an incubator and supported by high concentrations of oxygen in the inspired air. An excess of oxygen may cause vasoconstriction and epithelial proliferation in the vessels of the retina and vitreous humor (retrolental fibroplasia). This may be followed by retinal detachment and permanent blindness. The risk of this can be reduced by vitamin E administration.[49]

Other conditions.   As severe deficiency in experimental animals led to disorders of every system of the body, patients with a great variety of diseases have been given high doses of the vitamin. Benefit has often been reported but has not been established by a controlled clinical trial except in those described above. Claims that it is of value in common conditions such as the menopausal syndrome, infertility, fibrositis and various diseases of skin and muscle have not been confirmed. It has been much used for intermittent claudication due to vascular disease in the legs. Here reports of trials have been conflicting. Some patients have been able to walk longer distances after prolonged use of the vitamin but whether this is due to any improvement in their arteries or to a placebo effect is uncertain. Vitamin E therapy is safe and when patients think that improvement follows its use, there is no need to disillusion them. Some athletes are dosed with the vitamin by their coaches and this is modern black magic.[50]

LABORATORY DIAGNOSIS

Plasma α-tocopherol concentration provides an index of vitamin E status. A value below 0.5 mg/dl should be unacceptable and an indication for a dietary supplement.

As the vitamin is carried bound to plasma lipids, a value may need correction if plasma lipids are abnormal. Low values, below 0.1 mg/dl, are often found in cystic fibrosis.[51]

Increased susceptibility of erythrocytes to haemolysis *in vitro* and decreased erythrocyte survival *in vivo* also provide a measure of deficiency but these tests are not in routine use.

THERAPEUTIC DOSE AND TOXICITY

The British Pharmacopoeia preparation is α-tocopherol

acetate and the usual dose is 50 mg daily. Many proprietary preparations are available. Babies of very low birth weight may be given a daily intramuscular injection of 10 mg/kg body weight for 1–4 days and thereafter a daily supplement. Transient nausea, flatulence and other minor symptoms have been reported after administration of the vitamin but it is one of the least toxic of drugs. It is now a common practice to give high doses to very small babies and this seems potentially dangerous.

REFERENCES

1. Osborne T B, Mendel L B 1913 The relation of growth to the chemical constituents of the diet. J Biot Chem 15: 311–326
2. McCollum E V, Davis M 1913 The necessity of certain lipids in the diet during growth. J Biol Chem 15: 167–175
3. Rosenheim O, Drummond J C 1920 On the relation of the lipochrome pigments to the fat-soluble accessory food factor. Lancet 1: 862–864
4. Moore T 1957 Vitamin A. Elsevier, New York
5. Goodwin T W 1983 Developments in carotenoid biochemistry over 40 years. Trans Biochem Soc 11: 473–483
6. Simpson K L 1983 Relative value of carotenes as precursors of vitamin A. Proc Nutr Soc 42: 7–17
7. Wald G 1968 Molecular basis of visual function. Science NY 162: 230–239
8. Dow D J, Steven D M 1941 An investigation of simple methods for diagnosing vitamin A deficiency by measurements of dark adaptation. J Physiol (Lond) 100: 256–262
9. Wolbach S B, Howe P R 1925 Tissue changes following deprivation of fat-soluble vitamin A. J Exp Med 42: 753–778
10. Bollag W 1983 Vitamin A and retinoids: from nutrition to pharmacology in dermatology and oncology. Lancet 1: 860–863
11. DeLuca L M 1977 The direct involvement of vitamin A in glycosyl-transfer reactions of mammalian membranes. Vitam Horm 35: 1–57
12. Weber F 1983 Biochemical mechanisms of vitamin A action. Proc Nutr Soc 42: 31–41
13. Smith F R, Goodman D S, Zaklama M S, et al 1973 Serum vitamin A, retinol-binding protein and prealbumin concentrations in protein calorie malnutrition. Am J Clin Nutr 26: 973–981
14. Large S, Neal G, Glover J, Thamangkul O, Olson R E 1980 The early changes in retinol-binding protein and prealbumin concentrations in plasma of protein-energy malnourished children after treatment with retinol and an improved diet. Br J Nutr 43: 393–402
15. Huque T, Truswell A S 1979 Retinol content of human livers from autopsies in London. Proc Nutr Soc 38:41A
16. Hoppner K, Phillips W E J, Murray T K, Campbell J S 1968 Survey of liver vitamin A stores of Canadians. Can Med Assoc J 99: 983–986
17. Raica N J, Scott J, Lowry L, Sauberlich H E 1972

Vitamin A concentrations in human tissues collected from five areas in the United States. Am J Clin Nutr 25: 291–296
18. Abedin Z, Hussain M A, Ahmad K 1976 Liver reserve of vitamin A from medico-legal cases in Bangladesh. Bangladesh Med Res Coun Bull 2: 43–51
19. Hume E M, Krebs H A 1949 Vitamin A requirements of adults: an experimental study of vitamin A deprivation in man. Spec Rep Ser Med Res Coun Lond no. 264
20. Leitner Z A, Moore T, Sharman I M 1952 Vitamin A carotenoids and tocopherol levels in the blood of two different classes of patients. Br J Nutr 6:x-xi
21. Phillips W E J, Murray T K, Campbell J S 1970 Serum vitamin A and carotenoids in Canadians. Can Med Assoc J 102: 1085–1086
22. Chandra H, Venkatachalam P S, Belavadi B, Reddy V, Gopalan C 1960 Some observations on vitamin A deficiency in Indian children. Indian J Child Hlth 9: 589–595
23. Drummond J C, Macarra T 1938 The examination of some tinned foods of historical interest. Part 3: Chemical investigations. Chem Indust 57: 828–833
24. Rodahl K, Moore T 1943 The vitamin A content and toxicity of bear and seal liver. Biochem J 37: 166–168
25. Shearman D J C 1978 Vitamin A and Sir Douglas Mawson. Br Med J 1: 283–285
26. Muenter M D, Perry H O, Ludwig J 1971 Chronic vitamin A intoxication in adults. Am J Med 50: 129–135
27. Mellanby E 1918 The part played by an accessory factor in the production of experimental rickets. J Physiol Lond 52:xi
28. Loomis W F 1967 Skin pigment regulation of vitamin D synthesis in man. Science NY 157: 501–506
29. Haddad J G, Hahn T J 1973 Natural and synthetic sources of circulating 25-hydroxy vitamin D in man. Nature 244: 515–517
30. Tang G 1983 The quandary of vitamin D in the newborn infant. Lancet 1: 1370–1372
31. Mawes E B, Backhouse J, Holman C A, Lumb B, Stanbury S W 1972 The distribution and storage of vitamin D and its metabolites in human tissues. Clin Sci 43: 413–431
32. Kodicek E 1974 The story of vitamin D from vitamin to hormone. Lancet 1: 325–329
33. De Luca H F 1982 Metabolism and molecular mechanism of action of vitamin D: 1981. Trans Biochem Soc 10: 147–158

34. Paterson C R 1980 Vitamin-D poisoning: survey of causes in 21 patients with hypercalcaemia. Lancet 1: 1164–1165

35. Dam K 1935 The antihaemorrhagic factor of the chick. Biochem J 29: 1273–1285

36. Gallop P M, Lian J B, Hauscha P V 1980 Carboxylated calcium-binding proteins and vitamin K. N Engl J Med 302: 1460–1466

37. Colvin B T, Lloyd M J 1977 Severe coagulation defect due to a dietary deficiency of vitamin K. J Clin Path 30: 1147–1148

38. Stahmann M A, Huebner C F, Link K P 1941 Studies on the hemorrhagic sweet clover disease. V: Identification of the hemorrhagic agent. J Biol Chem 138: 513–527

39. Barkham P, Shearer M J 1977 Metabolism of vitamin K_1 (phylloquinone) in man. Proc R Soc Med 70: 93–96

40. Evans H M, Bishop K S 1923 Existence of a hitherto unknown dietary factor essential for reproduction. JAMA 81: 889–892

41. Tappel A L 1973 Nutr Today 8(4): 4–12

42. Lubin E, Machlin L J (eds) 1982 Vitamin E: biochemical, hematological and clinical aspects. Ann N Y Acad Sci 393: 1–504

43. Bull N L, Buss D H 1982 Biotin pantothenic acid and vitamin E in the British household food supply. Hum Nutr Appl Nutr 36A: 190–196

44. Bieri J G, Corash L, Hubbard Van S 1983 Medical uses of vitamin E. New Engl J Med 308: 1063–1071

45. Muller D D R, Lloyd J K, Bird A C 1977 Long-term management of abetalipoproteinuria. Arch Dis Child 52: 209–21

46. Corash L, Spielberg S, Bartsocas D, et al 1980 Reduced chronic hemolysis during high-dose vitamin E administration in Mediterranean-type glucose-6-phosphate phosphatase deficiency. N Engl J Med 303: 416–420

47. Gaeber J E, Williams M L, Oski F A 1977 The use of intramuscular vitamin E in premature infants. J Pediatr 90: 282–284

48. Chiswick M, Johnson M, Woodhall C, et al 1983 Protective effect of vitamin E (DL-alpha-tocopherol) against intraventricular haemorrhage in premature babies. Br Med J 287: 81–84

49. Kittner H M, Godis L B, Rudolph A J, et al 1981 Retrolental fibroplasia: efficacy of vitamin E in a double-blind clinical study of preterm infants. N Engl J Med 305: 1365–1371

50. Sharman I M, Down M G, Sen R N 1971 The effects of vitamin E and training on physiological function and athletic performance in adolescent swimmers. Br J Nutr 26: 265–276

51. Farrell P. M, Bieri J G, Fratantoni J F, Wood R E, DiSant'Agnese P A 1977 The occurrence and effects of human vitamin E deficiency. J Clin Invest 60: 233–241

14

Water-soluble Vitamins

VITAMIN C

Deficiency of vitamin C, now known as ascorbic acid, is the cause of scurvy. As ascorbic acid is widely distributed in the tissues of all plants and animals, with the notable exception of the dried seeds of cereals and pulses, scurvy is not a disease that occurs in people on natural diets containing fresh foods. Scurvy was classically a disease of sailors. On long sea voyages in the sixteenth, seventeenth and eighteenth centuries, beginning with Vasco da Gama's journey round the Cape of Good Hope to India in 1497. A brief history of scurvy is in Chapter 35. The history of vitamin C began in 1907 when Holst & Fröelich[1] in Christiania, now Oslo, first produced scurvy in an experiment animal, the guinea pig. It was soon shown to be caused by a lack of an accessory food factor, which was termed vitamin C. Ascorbic acid was identified as vitamin C in 1932 by Glen King,[2] an American who had worked in Hopkins laboratory at Cambridge. Previously in 1928, Szent-Györgyi,[3] a Hungarian also working in Hopkins laboratory, had isolated ascorbic acid from adrenal glands, oranges and cabbages and shown it to be a powerful reducing substance, but had not recognised it as a vitamin. Nearly 50 years later, Szent Györgyi,[4] by then an American citizen and a Nobel Prize winner, was still worrying about ascorbic acid. 'I think ascorbic acid is fundamental; it is involved in the simplest processes on which life is built.' Unfortunately neither he nor anyone else can define precisely its role in these processes.

CHEMISTRY

Ascorbic acid (AA) is a simple sugar with molecular weight 176. It is a white crystalline substance which is stable when dry but easily oxidised when in solution in water, especially in an alkaline medium and on exposure to heat, light and traces of metals especially copper. In a cold acid solution it is fairly stable. The first stage of oxidation to dehydroascorbic acid (DHA) is readily reversible (Fig. 14.1), but subsequent oxidation to dioxo-

Fig. 14.1 Reversible oxidation of ascorbic acid

gulonic acid cannot be reversed.

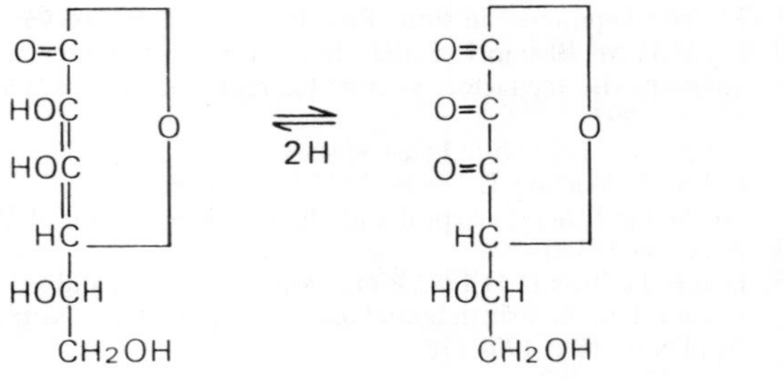

Ascorbic acid is a powerful reducing agent. It readily gives up an electron to convert Fe^{3+} into Fe^{2+}. This conversion takes place in the lumen of the gut and, as most of the dietary iron is in the ferric state and only ferrous iron can be absorbed, it may be critical in getting sufficient iron absorbed to prevent anaemia.[5] Ascorbic acid is present in all tissues and through its reducing action may have important effects on synthetic processes and energy exchanges, but these have not been defined and in this respect ascorbic acid resembles glutathione.

Most plant and animal tissues can synthesise ascorbic acid from glucose via L-gulonic acid and L-gulonolactone. This takes place in the liver of all higher animals except primates, the guinea-pig, an Indian fruit-eating bat, the red-vented bulbul and some other birds. In these species a mutation has probably been responsible for the loss of an enzyme on the synthetic pathway for ascorbic acid; such a defect is the cause of many of the diseases known as Inborn Errors of Metabolism. Scurvy differs from these diseases only in that the defect appears to be present in all members of an affected species. However, it is possible that the defect is not absolute and that synthesis may occur in some humans. Some lactating women in India appeared over long periods to lose more ascorbic acid in milk and urine than they took in their diet.[6] Not all of Vasco da Gama's crew developed scurvy; a few survived and the object of his voyage was achieved.

DISTRIBUTION, UTILISATION AND EXCRETION IN THE HUMAN BODY

Ascorbic acid is readily and rapidly absorbed in the small intestine and little or none is lost in the faeces with a normal diet.

After absorption it is distributed in the blood but taken up unevenly by the tissues. The classical studies of Hodges and his colleagues[7,8] on nine volunteers in the Iowa State Penitentiary using isotopically labelled ^{14}C ascorbic acid showed that when the subjects received 75 mg of ascorbic acid daily, the average size of the pool in which this was distributed was 1500 mg. The pool fell to 300 mg after 55 days on an ascorbic acid-free diet (Fig. 14.2). It was calculated that on a diet providing 30 mg daily the size of the pool would be 1000 mg.

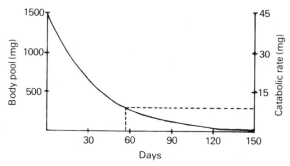

Fig. 14.2 Curve of ascorbate pool derived from data on nine men whose body pool of ascorbate was labelled with [14]C L-ascorbic acid. They were then fed on a diet devoid of vitamin C. Initially the body pool averaged 1500 mg. The average daily rate of catabolism was 3 per cent of the existing body pool. Thus the maximal rate approximated to 45 mg/day. When the body pool fell below 300 mg total and the catabolic rate below 9 mg/day, signs of scurvy began to appear (about 55 days). From this curve one can estimate the approximate body pool size from the dose. Thus with a daily intake of 30 mg the pool size should be about 1000 mg. (Data of Hodges and Baker)[13]

Plasma concentrations. This is related to the dietary intake and is about 1.2 mg/dl (68 μmol/l) on a diet containing about 100 mg. It falls to 0.1 mg/dl after about four weeks on diets containing less than 10 mg of ascorbic acid. Depletion studies have shown that a plasma concentration below 0.1 mg/dl indicates a high risk of developing scurvy and between 0.1 and 0.2 mg/dl a moderate risk. Values above 0.2 mg/dl are acceptable. White blood cells normally contain over 15 mg/dl and a value below 7 mg/dl indicates a high risk of scurvy. The amount in the white blood cells provides a better index of depletion of ascorbic acid than does the amount in the plasma, but the estimation is technically more difficult.

Concentration in organs All organs and tissues have a higher concentration than plasma. Concentrations are high in glandular organs, especially the adrenal glands where it may be 50 times more than in plasma. There is much data about the ascorbic acid content of guinea-pig organs but relatively little in man. Table 14.1 gives data obtained from autopsies in Pittsburgh in 1934. The figures are averages and there were wide individual variations, but it was not possible to relate the finding to dietary intakes or plasma concentrations in life. The figures show very high concentrations in early life and a steady fall with increasing age. As the weights of the glandular organs are small, the brain and liver — each of which weighs about 1.5 kg — contain the major amount of ascorbic acid and presumably provide a store which is available when the dietary intake is reduced. The total ascorbic acid in all the organs listed in Table 14.1 falls some way short of the 1500 mg found in the ascorbic acid pool. There must also be some in muscle. In guinea-pig muscle concentrations are usually between 30 and 40 mg/kg. Values for human muscle are certainly lower. If a figure of 20 mg/kg is taken, then a 70 kg man with 30 kg of muscle would have 600 mg of ascorbic acid in his muscles. This would be the largest store of the vitamin in his body.

Table 14.1 Average values (mg/kg) for the ascorbic acid content of human organs obtained at autopsy (from Yavorsky et al)[9]

Organ	Age group 1–30 days (11)	1–10 years (11)	11–45 years (17)	46–77 years (19)
Adrenal gland	581	550	393	230
Brain	460	433	n.m.	110
Pancreas	365	225	152	95
Thymus	304	190	n.m.	46
Spleen	153	157	127	81
Kidney	153	98	98	47
Liver	149	163	135	64
Lung	126	58	65	45
Heart	76	42	42	21

Number of subjects are shown in parenthesis. n.m. = not measured.

The aqueous humour of the eye also has a much higher concentration than the plasma. Kinsey[10] found values of from 20–25 mg/dl in rabbits whose plasma concentration ranged from 0.5–2.0 mg/dl. The aqueous humour supplies the nutrition of the lens which is also rich in ascorbic acid.

The ascorbic acid content of human connective tissue has been measured in samples of the anterior rectus sheath obtained during abdominal operations.[11] Amounts between 30 and 60 mg/kg were found in patients with plasma concentrations ranging from 0.4 to 1.3 mg/dl whose dietary intake may be presumed to have been satisfactory. Values from 0 to 15 mg/kg were found in 12 patients with plasma concentrations below 0.1 mg/dl.

Urinary excretion.   How the kidneys deal with ascorbic acid was worked out by Friedman, Sherry and Ralli.[12] Ascorbic acid passes into the glomerular filtrate in the same concentration as in the plasma but, provided the plasma concentration is below 1.4 mg/dl, almost all is reabsorbed in the renal tubules. Thus the kidneys conserve the vitamin well and very little appears in the urine with normal dietary intakes. Estimations of the urinary output of ascorbic acid are of no value in assessing the risk of scurvy for this reason. If, however, the plasma concentration is raised above 1.4 mg/dl by giving preparations of ascorbic acid, renal clearance of ascorbic acid rapidly rises and almost all the dose is lost in the urine.

Rate of utilisation.   In the Iowa studies the urine, faeces and expired air were analysed for their content of labelled carbon after injection of ^{14}C ascorbic acid. Less than 2 per cent of the label was found in the faeces, showing the completeness of absorption, and only about 2 per cent in the carbon dioxide of the expired air. Nearly all was present in the urine and most of it not in ascorbic acid itself or in the first two products of its oxidation, dehydroascorbic acid and dioxogulonic acid, but in unidentified metabolic products. From the output of the label the rate of utilisation of the vitamin was calculated. This was 45 mg/day when the body pool was at a maximum of 1500 mg. When after depletion the body pool fell to 300 mg and signs of scurvy began to appear, the catabolic rate was below 9 mg/day (Fig. 14.2). The rate of utilisation thus appears to be determined by the size of the pool and so is related to the dietary intake and not to any specific physiological need.

Ascorbic acid and extracellular connective tissue

The characteristic feature of scurvy, both the natural disease in man and the experimental disease in guinea-pigs, is an 'inability of the supporting tissues to produce and maintained intercellular substances'. These are the words of Burt Wolback, a Boston pathologist who studied the histological lesions in scurvy for many years and presented a beautifully illustrated paper presented at the Lind bicentenary symposium in Edinburgh[14] The capillary haemorrhages are due to a defect in the basement membrane that lines the capillaries and the intracellular cement that joins the endothelial cells together. The failure of wounds to heal is due to a defect in the formation of scar tissue. In children and young guinea-pigs the failure of cartilage, bone and dentine to develop normally is due to a defect in the extracellular matrix in which the chondroblasts, osteoblasts and ondontoblasts, lay down the hard minerals. This matrix is composed of the protein collagen which forms about one-fifth of the wet weight of both bone and cartilage. Changes in the matrix prevent the osteoblasts laying down new bone and lead to demineralization. This is responsible for the breakdown of old fractures as was graphically described by Walter[15] in his account of Anson's voyage round the world.

> But a most extraordinary circumstance, and what could be scarcely credible upon any single evidence, is that the scars of wounds which had been for many years healed were forced open again by this virulent distemper. Of this there was a remarkable example in one of the invalids on board the *Centurion*, who had been wounded about fifty years before at the Battle of the Boyne, for though he was cured soon after, and had continued well for a great number of years past, yet on his being attacked by the scurvy, his wounds, in the progress of the disease, broke out afresh and appeared as if they had never healed: nay, what is still more astonishing, the callus of a broken bone which had been completely formed for a long time, was found to be hereby dissolved, and the fracture seemed as if it had never been consolidated.

The defect is in the formation of collagen, the protein forming the basement membrane of capillaries, the fibrous tissue in scars and the matrix of the hard tissues. The collagen molecule, which is very large, is assembled outside the cells from smaller units of procollagen which are synthesised by connective tissue cells and secreted into the extracellular spaces. Not all collagens are identical in their molecular structure, but all are characterised by a unique combination of amino acids in their makeup. The procollagen chain is a coil with many repeating units of —glycine—hydroxyproline—proline—. Hydroxyproline is not found in proteins other than collagen and it is formed from proline by the action of proline hydroxylase, present in fibroblasts (Fig. 14.3). In the absence of ascorbic acid this enzyme is not activated and production of hydroxyproline is neglible.[16]

Ascorbic acid, the adrenal cortex and stress

In the eighteenth century Lind[17] and many others reported that scurvy was more likely to break out in ships when the crews were exposed to cold, damp and rough seas, fatigued by hard work or debilitated by other diseases. Non-specific stresses clearly predisposed the men to the disease. The first association of vitamin C with

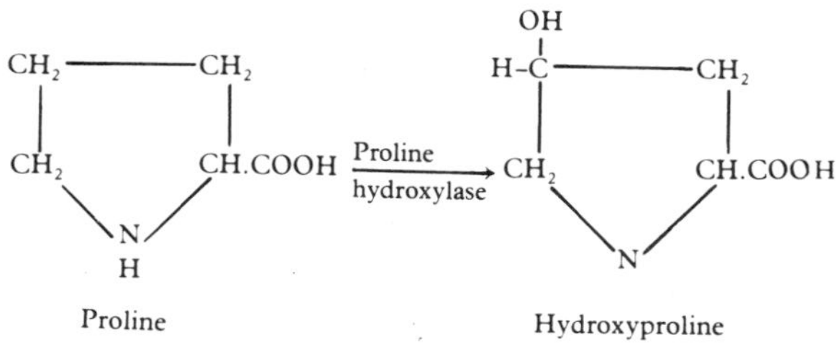

Fig. 14.3 Action of proline hydroxylase

the adrenal glands was the observation of McCarrison[18] that they were hypertrophied in scorbutic guinea-pigs. The high concentration of ascorbic acid in adrenal glands was shown to be depleted by fatigue and by infections.[19]

Soon after the discovery of the role of the pituitary hormone, ACTH, in promoting secretion of adrenocortical hormones in conditions of stress, injections of ACTH were shown to deplete the adrenal cortex of ascorbic acid and to increase the concentration of ascorbic acid in the adrenal veins. These findings lead to the view that a major physiological role of ascorbic acid was in the synthesis of steroid hormones in the adrenal cortex in response to stresses of various kinds. However, this attractive theory failed to explain the fact that, when the adrenal glands are destroyed, as in Addison's disease, the patient's signs and symptoms, mainly extreme muscular weakness, in no way resemble those found in scurvy. It has been disproved by the finding that isolated adrenal cells, in which almost all the ascorbic acid had been removed during preparation, were still able to synthesise adrenocortical hormones in response to stimulation by ACTH.[20] Adrenal function tests, e.g. plasma cortisol before and after ACTH, are normal in scurvy.

It is difficult to believe that the high concentrations of ascorbic acid in the adrenal glands serve no biological purpose. A new theory is that ascorbic acid has a continuous inhibitory effect either on the synthesis of adrenocortical hormones or on their release from the gland into the blood stream. The role of ACTH would then be to reverse this inhibition by releasing ascorbic acid from the cells which could then secrete the hormones.

Other actions

In addition to its established roles in preventing scurvy and in stress, ascorbic acid has been implicated in lipid metabolism and atherogenesis, immunity reactions, detoxications, development of cancers and cerebral functions. Each of these is reviewed in a small monograph by Hughes[21] which has a good bibliography, but most of his references can be criticised as 'soft' science. They provide no convincing evidence that deficiency of ascorbic acid is responsible for any clinical conditions that might arise from the changes discussed.

ASCORBIC ACID AS A DRUG

Ascorbic acid is a cheap and safe drug. There have been many claims that it is useful in the treatment of a large number of diseases. Its most enthusiastic advocate is Linus Pauling (1976), whose book *Vitamin C and the Common Cold and the Flu* has had a great influence. Pauling became interested in ascorbic acid in 1966 when he received a letter from Irwin Stone, the successful novelist, advising him to take large doses of it daily. He and his wife then began to take 1 g or more daily and at once 'noticed an increased feeling of wellbeing, and especially a striking decrease in the number of colds that we caught and in their severity.' He then began to study the literature on ascorbic acid and the first edition of his book appeared in 1970 and soon had large numbers of readers.

Pauling was greatly respected by scientists for his work as a chemist on the structure of large molecules and especially by biologists for his explanation of how a small change in the chemical composition of haemoglobin was responsible for the sickle cell phenomenon in red blood corpuscles. He was also well known to the general public for his work to promote peace and had the rare distinction of receiving two Nobel prizes, one for science and one for peace. Furthermore, his book on vitamin C was beautifully written and easily read by the general public despite the fact that it contained complicated scientific argument and many references to the literature. As a result of his advocacy, very large numbers of the public in America and other countries began to take tablets of ascorbic acid regularly.

Pauling's hypothesis was based on a study of the evolution of the diet of primates. He calculated the average content of ascorbic acid in 110 natural plant foods, as might be eaten by a gorilla, and showed that a human adult eating a diet made up of these foods would obtain 2.3 g of the vitamin, some 50 times the USA recommended intake. Furthermore, he showed that the potential rate of synthesis of ascorbic acid, as reported in several species of animals, if extrapolated to man, indicated a human daily requirement of up to 10 g.

Pauling's book has stimulated at least 15 clinical trials of the use of ascorbic acid in prophylaxis or treatment of the common cold. Not all of these were technically good. The largest and best of these were carried out in Toronto,[22] in which 1349 subjects out of 3520 who enrolled completed the three months of study. The subjects were divided into eight groups who received a placebo or a dose of ascorbic acid both prophylactically throughout the trial and during episodes of infection. Table 14.2 shows the treatment schedules and an abstract of their results. One of the placebo groups had fewer episodes and of less severity than any of the other groups. None of the groups receiving ascorbic acid had

Table 14.2 Ascorbic acid in the prophylaxis and treatment of the common cold

Treatment (g ascorbic acid/day) Prophylactic	Therapeutic	Mean number of episodes	Mean days of symptoms	Mean days off work
Placebo	Placebo	1.53	5.40	1.18
Placebo	Placebo	1.47	4.16	0.94
0.25	Placebo	1.53	4.77	1.11
1.0	Placebo	1.51	5.04	1.09
2.0	Placebo	1.51	4.87	1.29
Placebo	4	1.52	4.82	0.97
Placebo	8	1.58	4.52	1.05
1	4	1.57	5.38	1.13

a sickness experience that was statistically different from the placebo groups. Pauling has supported claims from a hospital in Scotland that large doses of ascorbic acid given to patients with terminal cancer prolongs their life and improves its quality.[23] This study lacked adequate controls, and in a well-designed trial from the Stanford Medical School patients with advanced cancer got no benefit from large doses of the vitamin.[24]

Toxicity. Ascorbic acid in large doses has been taken by many thousands of persons for long periods without untoward effect and must be one of the safest of drugs. Yet it is known to increase the urinary output of oxalic acid and of uric acid, and intestinal absorption of iron. Large doses are therefore dangerous to those with a liability to urinary stones or to iron-storage disease. The Canadian workers found that after an abrupt withdrawal of a high dose, blood concentrations of ascorbic acid were abnormally low, and this might be dangerous. For these reasons we cannot recommend that large doses should be taken for long periods for prophylactic purposes. The risk of taking up to 4 g daily for a few days for therapeutic purposes should be acceptable.

Orthomolecular medicine. Pauling claims in his book that large doses of ascorbic acid may be beneficial in cancer, heart disease, schizophrenia and other diseases. This view is derived from his concept of orthomolecular medicine which '. . . is the preservation of good health and the treatment of disease by varying the concentrations in the human body of substances that are normally present in the body and are required for health . . . . To achieve the best of health, the rate of intake of essential foods should be such as to establish and maintain optimum concentrations of essential molecules, such as those of ascorbic acid. There is no doubt that a high concentration of ascorbic acid is needed to provide the maximum protection against infection, and to permit the rapid healing of wounds. I believe that in general the treatment of disease by the use of substances such as ascorbic acid, that are normally present in the human body and are required for life is to be preferred to the treatment by the use of powerful synthetic substances or plant products, which may, and usually do,

have undesirable side effects.'

Orthomolecular medicine is an attractive idea, but the principle appears to work only in those very rare cases of heredity disorders caused by enzymic defects which respond to pharmacological doses of a vitamin (p. 350).

DIETARY SOURCES

Fresh fruit and fruit juices are usually the richest sources (Table 14.3), but amounts vary greatly from species to species and in different samples of the same species. Blackcurrants and guavas are particularly rich. Green leafy vegetables are also good sources. Potatoes are not a rich source, but as large amounts may be eaten they provide the major intake of ascorbic acid in some countries, e.g. Scotland.

Losses of ascorbic acid due to oxidation are inevitable during cooking. They can be kept to less than 50 per cent if the fresh food is put straight into boiling water from which the oxygen has been driven off and, when frying potatoes, by rapid immersion in hot deep fat. As traces of copper and an alkaline medium facilitate oxidation, copper pots and baking soda should not be used. Losses continue when vegetables are kept warm on hot plates, so vegetables should be served as soon after cooking as possible.

Losses also occur on storage, especially if the fruit or vegetables are damaged. Manufacturers of canned and frozen fruits and vegetables take good care to use only material of high quality which is processed quickly. Such foods may contain more ascorbic acid than reputedly fresh foods which have been lying in markets or shops for some days before being sold.

Fresh early potatoes contain about 30 mg/100 g of ascorbic acid before cooking and over 75 per cent of this may be lost after 9 months storage. This and the additional losses on cooking probably account for the occasional cases of scurvy seen in old people in Edinburgh. These usually occur in April and May and never in the months immediately after the fresh crop has become available.

Table 14.3 Some good sources of ascorbic acid

Food	Ascorbic acid (mg/100g edible) Raw	Cooked *
Fruits		
Blackcurrants	200	140
Guavas (canned)	—	180
Strawberries	60	—
Citrus fruits — orange, grapegruit, lemon juice	40–50	—
Redcurrants and gooseberries	40	28
Raspberries, loganberries and blackberries	20–25	14–26
Melons and pineapple	25	—
Bananas	10	—
Cooking apples	—	12
Peaches and apricots	7–8	—
Dessert apples, pears, plums, grapes, figs, cherries	2–5	—
Salads		
Green peppers	100	—
Watercress, mustard and cress	40–60	—
Radish, lettuce, tomato	15–25	—
Onions	10	6
Carrots	6	4
Celery	7	—
Parsley	150	—
Vegetables		
Broccoli tops and brussels sprouts	(100)	35
Cauliflower, cabbage and spinach	50–60	15–25
Asparagus, leeks	—	18–20
Peas	25	14
Parsnips and turnips	—	10–17
New early potatoes	—	18
Main crop potatoes	—	9
Sweetcorn	—	9
Runner beans	—	5
Animal foods		
Liver	(23)	15
Milk	2	1

* Usually stewed fruit and boiled vegetables.

Liver is good source of ascorbic acid and fresh milk contains some. Fresh meat provides only traces but with offal supplies sufficient to prevent scurvy, as many Arctic explorers know. An example of the protective role of meat was when the Indian Third Cavalry division was besieged by the Turks in Kut-el-Amara in Mesopotamia in December 1915. When the garrison surrendered in April 1916, scurvy had broken out in the Indian sepoys, but not in the British soldiers who had eaten their horses.[25]

RECOMMENDED INTAKES

These vary greatly from country to country. For an adult man the present recommendation in the USA is 60 mg and in the UK 30 mg a day. The higher American figure is aimed at tissue saturation and is practical for a country with a plentiful supply of fruit juices and canned fruits. It is not a physiological necessity and lower intakes should not be taken as evidence of deficiency of the vitamin.

There are communities living in arid deserts and in cold climates high up in the Andes and Himalayas who are vigorous and healthy despite intakes little more than sufficient to prevent scurvy, less than 10 mg a day; among them are to be found many physically active very old people (Chap. 62). In the past such low intakes of ascorbic acid were commonplace in the long cold winters of northern America and Europe. Yet the people were capable of great exertions. The Mormon community who trekked thousands of miles from the east to settle in Utah in the cold winters of 1845–47 and beset by hostile Indians showed rare courage and endurance, despite intakes of vitamin C far below the present American recommendations. During the nineteenth century when Britannia did 'rule the waves', rations for the Royal Navy contained little ascorbic acid and sickness records provide no evidence of the existence of what has been called subclinical scurvy.[26] Surgeon Admiral Sheldon Dudley, a critical scientist who was a Fellow of the Royal Society, after studying the records concludes that the evidence favours those 'who believe a maintenance dose of ascorbic acid for a healthy adult is rather below than above 15 mg a day'. This makes sense.

THIAMIN — VITAMIN B

HISTORY

In 1897 the Dutch physician Eijkmann,[27] working in a military hospital in Java, fed some domestic fowls on the food provided for his patients suffering from beriberi. He noticed that they developed weakness of the legs and head retraction. Their food consisted mainly of polished rice; a new head cook at the hospital discontinued this supply of 'military' rice, so that the birds had to be fed on whole-grain 'civilian' rice, with the result that they recovered. Many great advances in science have started from such chance observations pursued by men of inspiration. Eijkman won the Nobel Prize many years later for showing that there was something existing in very small amounts in the germ and pericarp of rice that protected fowls from a disease resembling beriberi, and for recognising that it was an unknown nutrient. He extracted it from rice polishings with water and alcohol.

Thirty years later Jansen & Donath,[28] working in the same laboratory, succeeded in isolating this factor (thiamin) in crystalline form. They used small rice birds (*Munia maja*) instead of fowls for testing the activity of the different fractions which they prepared in the course of isolating the vitamin. Thiamin deficiency, they found, could readily be produced in this bird; it was also produced in pigeons, rats and mice by numerous other workers who were seeking in the 1920s to identify and isolate the vitamin.

In 1936 the structure of the vitamin was finally elucidated (Fig. 14.4) and its synthesis accomplished by R R Williams & Cline.[29] Williams began his search for the vitamin in 1913 in the Philippines, under the guidance of E B Vedder, a pioneer in the clinical study of beriberi.

Thiamin deficiency in birds

The condition produced in birds by acute thiamin deficiency is characterised by head retraction and convulsions indicating a disorder of the nervous system. These features are due to an acute biochemical lesion in the brain, not necessarily associated with any anatomical lesion of the brain or peripheral nerves. The giving of pure synthetic thiamin rapidly relieves this biochemical lesion.

CHEMISTRY

Thiamin hydrochloride is a white crystalling substance. The molecule consists of a pyrimidine ring joined to a sulphur-containing thiazole ring. It is readily soluble in water, but not in most fat solvents nor in fats. It is rapidly destroyed by heat in neutral or alkaline solutions; in acid solution, however, it is resistant to heat up to 120°C. Thiamin can be converted by controlled oxidation into an inactive product, thiochrome, which is strongly fluorescent in ultraviolet light. The property is used for the chemical estimation of the vitamin in biological materials. It is also measured microbiologically.

PHYSIOLOGICAL ACTIVITY

Thiamin was the first vitamin whose precise activity in the body was stated in biochemical terms. This was achieved at Oxford between 1928 and 1935. Peters[30] has written an historical account of the work. It was first demonstrated that lactic acid accumulates in the brains of thiamin-deficient pigeons. It was then found that minced brain tissue from such birds took up less oxygen than brain tissue from normal birds in the presence of added glucose or lactic acid *in vitro*. This failure of oxidation could be corrected by adding thiamin in catalytic amounts to the brain tissue. It was thus established for the first time that a vitamin could be an essential part of an enzyme system. At the start it seemed likely that thiamin was specifically concerned with lactic acid, but it was found that pyruvic acid also accumulated in the brain and blood of such birds and that thiamin is specifi-

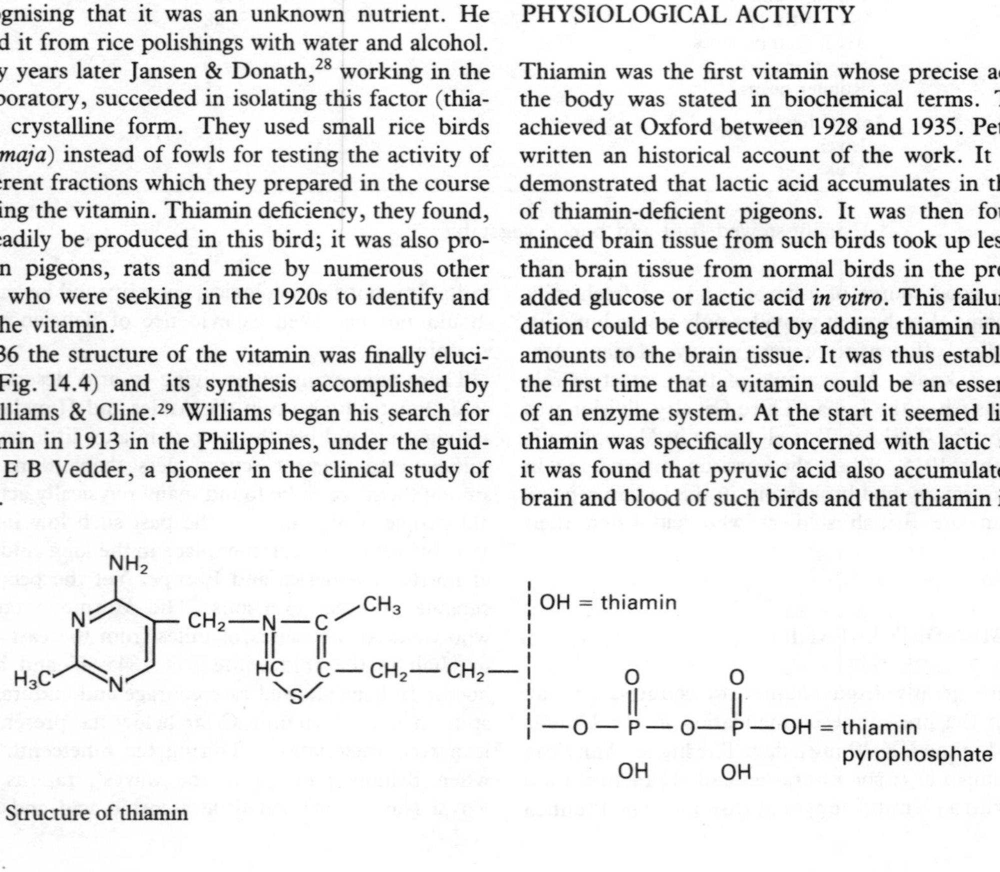

Fig 14.4 Structure of thiamin

cally concerned with its removal. It is now known that thiamin pyrophosphate (TPP) is the coenzyme of carboxylase, the enzyme concerned with the oxidative decarboxylation of pyruvic acid.

The fact that thiamin is concerned with a stage in the breakdown of carbohydrate explains how signs of deficiency of the vitamin develop most rapidly in animals fed diets rich in carbohydrates. The onset of deficiency is delayed by a diet rich in fat. There is evidence from dietary surveys that the same may also be true in man.

The brain and nerves have a respiratory quotient of unity, which shows that their energy is derived mostly from the oxidation of carbohydrate. The role of thiamin in the breakdown of carbohydrate explains how deficiency in animals leads rapidly to a biochemical lesion in the brain. TPP is also required for the decarboxylation of 2-oxoglutarate in the citric acid cycle and of the keto acids formed after deamination of the branched chain amino acids, leucine, isoleucine and valine; it is also needed in the transketolase reaction in the hexose monophosphate pathway. Thiamin is present in the body mostly as TPP but about 10 per cent is thiamin triphosphate.

Thiamin is absorbed from the small intestine by an active process which is impaired in alcoholics with folate deficiency.[31]

The total amount of thiamin in the wellnourished human body is small, in all to about 25–30 mg. Concentrations in the heart, brain, liver and skeletal muscles are about 2.7, 1.2, 1.0 and 0.7 $\mu g/g$ respectively.[32] The body has no means of storing any excess so that no benefit derives from taking large doses; the excess in lost in the urine.

Experimental deficiency in man. Human volunteers have been fed on diets deficient in thiamin but adequate in other respects.[33] The first symptoms have usually been loss of appetite and mental changes resembling anxiety states, with irritability and easy exhaustion. To what extent these are specific effects of the deficiency is open to question. They may be the nonspecific result of an unaccustomed regime and a distasteful diet.

Laboratory diagnosis

The amount of thiamin in the urine reflects recent intake but is no reliable test of deficiency, since it falls to low levels before the tissues are depleted. The point at which a dietary deficiency of the vitamin becomes important is when it is sufficiently severe to cause a biochemical lesion. The rise in the level of pyruvic acid in the blood of patients with beriberi was first shown in 1936 by Platt & Lu.[34] This test is made more sensitive by measuring the accumulation of pyruvic acid in the blood following an oral dose of glucose. However, thiamin deficiency is

by no means the sole cause of an elevated blood pyruvic acid.

A more specific test is the measurement of the transketolase activity in the red blood corpuscles with and without the addition of TPP *in vitro*. If TPP increases activity by more than 25 per cent, this indicates thiamin deficiency.[35]

DIETARY SOURCES

All animal and plant tissues contain thiamin and it is therefore present in all whole natural foods; but the only important stores in the biological world are in the seeds of plants. The germ of cereals, nuts, peas, beans and other pulses and in addition yeast are the only rich sources. All green vegetables, roots, fruits, flesh foods and dairy produce (except butter) contain significant amounts of the vitamin, but none are rich sources. As the vitamin is not soluble in fats, it is not found in butter or in any separated vegetable or animal oil. Pork resembles human flesh in having a higher content of thiamin than beef or mutton. In the refining of sugar and many cereal products all the naturally occurring vitamin may be removed: there is also none in distilled spirits. The labile thiaminase present in certain uncooked fish may also decrease the thiamin content of rice diets in the Far East. The distribution of the vitamin within cereal grains and the effect of milling and other food processing are discussed on pages 184 and 189. The thiamin content of some common foods is given in Table 14.4.

As thiamin is readily soluble in water, large amounts may be lost when rice or vegetables are cooked in an excess of water which is afterwards discarded. It is relatively stable to temperatures up to boiling point, provided that the medium is slightly acid, as in baking with yeast. But if baking powder is used, or if soda is added in the cooking of vegetables, almost all the vitamin may be destroyed. The loss of thiamin in the cooking of an ordinary mixed diet is usually about 25 per cent. Modern processes for freezing, canning and dehydrating food result in only small losses.

RECOMMENDED INTAKES

While there is a relationship between the utilisation of thiamin and the amount of carbohydrate in the diet, it is more practical to relate thiamin intake to total dietary energy. Williams & Spies[36] calculated the thiamin/energy ratio of 100 diets, of which 66 were associated with beriberi. Beriberi did not occur when the ratio was greater than 62 $\mu g/MJ$. This can be taken as the minimum protective intake. FAO/WHO recommend a daily intake of 96 $\mu g/MJ$ (0.4 mg/1000 kcal) for all classes of

Table 14.4 Sources of thiamin

Source	Description	μg/MJ	Thiamin mg/1000 kcal	mg/100 g
Satisfactory or rich sources not usually associated with beriberi				
Whole wheat	—	290	1.2	0.4
Pulses	Various	290	1.2	0.4
Millets	Sorghum	290	1.2	0.4
Rice	Home pounded	84*	0.35*	0.08–0.14*
Rice	Parboiled and milled	76*	0.32*	0.11*
Poor sources associated with beriberi				
White bread †	70 per cent extraction flour	48	0.20	0.05–0.07
Rice	Raw, milled	36	0.15*	0.02–0.04*
Sugars and jams	—	0	0	—
Alcoholic beverages	—	0	0	—
Moderate sources protective against beriberi if consumed in large amounts				
Fruits and vegetables	Fresh	120–290	0.5–1.2	0.02–0.20
Pork	Fresh	240–360	1.0–1.5	0.6–0.9
Beef and mutton	Fresh	70–120	0.3–0.5	0.05–0.15
Milk	Cow's	170	0.7	0.04
Eggs	Whole	150	0.6	0.09
Rich sources used in the treatment of beriberi				
Yeast ‡	Brewer's, dried	—		6–24
Bran	Rice or wheat	—		2–4
Marmite	Yeast extract	—		3.0

Note. Butter, vegetable oils and other fats contain no thiamin, but as the vitamin is not needed for their metabolism they are not beriberi-producing.
* Assuming losses of 50 per cent in washing and cooking.
† Unfortified.
‡ Baker's yeasts have much less thiamin than brewer's yeast and are unreliable for therapeutic purposes.

consumers, including nursing mothers. This provides a sufficient margin of safety.

Thiamin–energy relationships in foods

It should be emphasised that beriberi is not a disease of famines. Indeed cardiovascular beriberi may occur among people with good supplies of polished rice and good appetites to eat it. It results from a poorly balanced diet. The thiamin/energy ratios of foods indicate those which protect against beriberi and those which are liable to produce the disease, if consumed in excessive amounts. Thus pulses and most whole cereals have a ratio of about 290 μg/MJ (1.2 mg/1000 kcal) and are actively protective against beriberi. Raw polished rice has a value of about 36 μg/MJ (0.15 mg/1000 kcal) and is beriberi-producing. Most fruits, vegetables and flesh foods have a ratio just above a critical level of about 60 and are weakly effective in preventing beriberi.

THERAPEUTIC USES

Thiamin is life-saving in the treatment of cardiovascular and infantile beriberi (p. 314), in Wernicke's encepha-

lopathy (p. 316) and in some forms of cardiomyopathy (p. 369). It may be given, though without expectation of dramatic results, in cases of nutritional neuropathy. There is no reliable evidence that it is useful in any other disorder of the nervous system. The prescription of synthetic thiamin, either alone or in combination with other vitamins, as a general tonic or appetiser, is supported by no scientific evidence and is now discredited.

In prescribing thiamin it should be remembered that the healthy human body contains only about 25 mg of the vitamin. Furthermore, it has no means of storing any excess taken in the diet; the excess is lost rapidly in the urine. The human body is certainly an effective machine for dissolving thiamin pills and transferring the solution to the urinal.

NICOTINIC ACID (NIACIN) AND NICOTINAMIDE

HISTORY

Nicotinic acid has been known to organic chemists since 1867. As early as 1913 Funk isolated it from yeast and rice polishings in the course of an attempt to identify the water-soluble anti-beriberi vitamin. But interest in the acid was lost when it was found ineffective in curing pigeons of beriberi and did not arise again until 1935, when its amide was found to be a component of the respiratory coenzyme NAD.

Nicotinic acid was shown to be the 'pellagra-preventing' (P-P) vitamin in the following manner. In the 1920s Goldberger and his colleagues in the US Public Health Service recognised that human pellagra and also black tongue in dogs responded not only to treatment with animal protein but also to boiled extracts of yeast almost devoid of protein.[37] This naturally led to the supposition that the P-P factor was identical with 'heat-stable vitamin B$_2$' present in yeast. In 1937 Elvehjem[38] isolated nicotinamide from liver as the factor that would cure black tongue in dogs. Reports of the dramatic therapeutic effects of nicotinic acid in human pellagra quickly followed.

CHEMISTRY

Nicotinic acid is a simple derivative of pyridine (Fig. 14.5). Although related chemically to nicotine, it possesses very different physiological properties. It is a white crystalline substance readily soluble in water and resistant to heat, oxidation and alkalis: it is in fact one of the most stable of the vitamins. Nicotinic acid is easily synthesised commercially. It occurs naturally in the body in the form of the amide, nicotinamide (niacinamide).

COOH = nicotinic acid
CONH$_2$ = nicotinamide
(niacinamide)

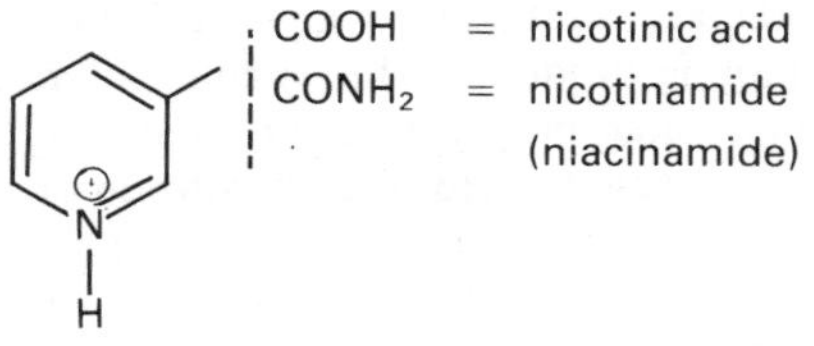

Fig. 14.5 Structure of nicotinic acid

PHYSIOLOGICAL ACTIVITY

Nicotinamide is a component of the respiratory coenzymes NAD and NADP. Lack of NAD in pellagra may account for the inflammatory changes that occur in the skin and gastrointestinal tract, though the precise mechanism involved is still obscure. In pharmacological doses nicotinic acid inhibits lipolysis in adipose tissue, but this is probably not a physiological action.

Laboratory diagnosis of deficiency
Attempts to diagnose deficiency by measuring nicotinic acid itself in body fluids have proved disappointing.

Blood normally contains about 5 mg/l mainly as NAD, but in states of manifest deficiency the amount is not greatly reduced.

The urinary excretion of the nicotinic acid metabolite, N'-methylnicotinamide, is used as a measure of reserves of nutritional status (p. 524).

DIETARY SOURCES

The human body is not entirely dependent on dietary sources of nicotinic acid, as it may also be synthesised from trytophan (Fig. 14.6). Observations on a large group of patients[39] suggest that on average about 60 mg of tryptophan are needed to replace 1 mg of dietary nicotinic acid. The nicotinic acid equivalent (the nicotinic acid content plus one-sixtieth of the tryptophan content) of a food or diet is a better measure than the nicotinic acid content alone. Its use removes one anomaly: milk and eggs are poor sources of nicotinic acid, although they have long been recognised as beneficial to patients with pellagra; each of these foods has a high nicotinic acid equivalent.

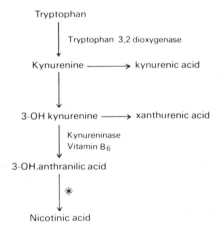

Fig. 14.6 The conversion of tryptophan to nicotinic acid. In deficiency of vitamin B6, kynurenic acid and xanthurenic acid appear in the urine in increased amounts.
*Several intermediary steps.

Nicotinic acid is widely distributed in plant and animal foods, but only in small amounts, except in meat (especially offal), fish, wholemeal cereals and pulses (Table 14.5). Table 14.6 gives the nicotinic acid equivalent of some foods and shows the important contribution that may come from tryptophan. In many cereals, especially maize, and perhaps also in potatoes, the greater part may be in a bound unabsorbable form.[40] Nicotinic acid can be liberated from the bound form, niacytin, by treatment with alkali. For a long time in

Table 14.5 Nicotinic acid and nicotinamide in foods

Food	mg/100g edible part
High content	
Liver and kidney	7.0–17.0
Beef, mutton, pork	3.0–6.0
Fish	2.0–6.0
Brewer's yeast	30–100
Bovril	82
Marmite	60
Groundnuts	16
Coffee (instant)	30
Wheat bran (outer only)	25–46*
Wheatgerm meal	3.0–7.0*
Rice (lightly milled)	2.0–4.5*
Wheat, wholemeal flour	4.0–5.5*
Sorghum	2.5–3.5*
Millets (various)	1.3–3.2*
Moderate content	
Pulses	1.5–3.0
Nuts	1.0–2.0
Dried fruit	0.5–5.0
Oatmeal	1.0*
Rice (highly milled) raw	1.5*
Wheat flour 70 percent extraction†	0.7*
Low content	
Maize meal, potato, vegetables, fresh fruits, eggs, milk and cheese	

* Much of the nicotinic acid in some, possibly all, cereals is in bound form, not biologically available. † Unfortified.

Mexico *tortillas* have heen made from maize treated with lime water. This practice may account for a low incidence of pellagra in Mexico (Chap. 34).

Cooking causes little destruction of nicotinic acid but it may be lost in the cooking water and 'drippings' from cooked meat if these are discarded. In a mixed diet, from 15 to 25 per cent of the nicotinic acid of the cooked foodstuffs may be lost in this way. Commercial processing and storage of foodstuffs cause little loss.

RECOMMENDED INTAKES

The Joint Committee of FAO/WHO (1967) recommended an intake of 1.6 mg/MJ (6.6 mg/1000 kcal)

nicotinic acid equivalents in the diet. Most authorities base their recommendations on this figure.

In pregnancy larger than normal amounts of nicotinamide metabolites are excreted in the urine on ordinary diets and after a load of 2 g L-tryptophan. Administration of oestrogens and oral contraceptives containing oestrogens likewise increase nicotinamide metabolites in urine.[41] The first enzyme on the kynurenine pathway, tryptophan dioxygenase, is induced by oestrogens. This suggests that more tryptophan is converted to NAD during pregnancy so 60 mg tryptophan in the diet may than be equivalent to more than 1 mg nicotinic acid.

THERAPEUTIC USES

Nicotinic acid and nicotinamide have specific and dramatic effects in pellagra and Hartnup disease (Chap. 34) The acid, though not the amide, causes transient vasodilation when taken by mouth, resulting in flushing, burning and tingling, especially round the neck, face and hands. Nevertheless nicotinic acid has been widely used as a vasodilator drug in chilblains and other vascular disorders.

Pharmacological doses (1 g thrice daily) of nicotinic acid are sometimes used to lower plasma lipids in patients with hyperlipidaemia.

RIBOFLAVIN

HISTORY

Riboflavin was discovered in the course of the search for the hypothetical 'heat-stable vitamin B_2'. In 1933 Kuhn was attempting to identify this vitamin by means of its growth-promoting properties in rats and finally isolated riboflavin from eggs.[42] However, riboflavin did not have all the properties previously ascribed to vitamin B_2, e.g. it did not cure black-tongue in dogs. Evidently, therefore, riboflavin was only one of several factors present in the heat-stable fraction of the vitamin B complex.

An important clue to the nature of Kuhn's crystals

Table 14.6 The nicotinic acid equivalents in some common foods

Food	Nicotinic acid (all values in mg/MJ)	Tryptophan	Nicotinic acid equivalent
Milk — cow's	0.3	162	3.0
human	0.6	106	2.4
Wheat, white flour	0.6*	71	1.8
Maize	1.2*	25	1.6
Maize grits	0.4*	17	0.7
Beef	5.9	306	11.0
Eggs	0.1	275	4.8

* Nicotinic acid in cereals is mostly unavailable.

was that they were yellow. In 1932 Warburg & Christian[43] had described their 'yellow enzyme', a respiratory catalyst. They obtained it from extracts of yeast and went on to show that it consisted of a protein component combined with a yellow pigment, neither of which alone was enzymically active, though effective in combination. It was an inspired guess that the yellow pigment of Warburg's enzyme was identical with the new vitamin, for so it proved to be. In 1935 riboflavin was synthesised by two independent groups of workers under Kuhn in Heidelberg and Karrer in Basle.

CHEMISTRY

Riboflavin is a yellow-green fluorescent compound, soluble in water but not in fats, composed of an alloxazine ring linked to an alcohol derived from the pentose sugar ribose (Fig. 14.7). Though stable to boiling in acid solution, in alkaline solution it is readily decomposed by heat. It is also destroyed by exposure to light.

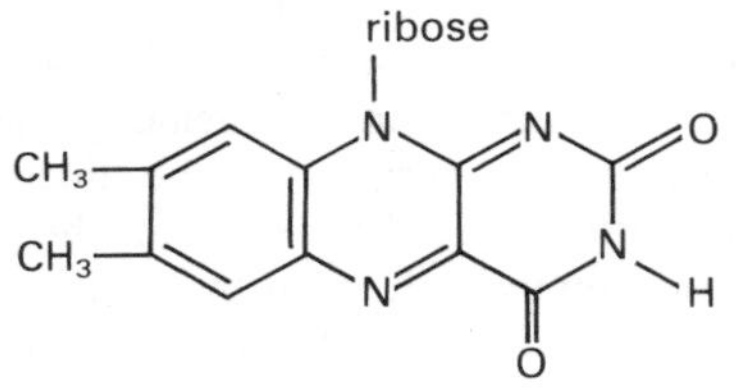

Fig. 14.7 Structure of riboflavin

In plant and animal tissues riboflavin is linked with phosphoric acid to form flavin mononucleotide (FMN). This with adenosine monophosphate forms flavin adenine dinucleotide (FAD). FMN and FAD are the prosthetic groups of the flavoproteins enzymes involved in oxidation-reduction reactions.

DIETARY SOURCES

The best sources of riboflavin are liver, milk and cheese, eggs and some green vegetables (Table 14.7). Riboflavin differs from other components of the vitamin B complex in that it occurs in good amounts in dairy produce, but is relatively lacking in cereal grains. It is also present in beer. Polished rice and other refined cereals contain very little. Ordinary methods of cooking do not destroy the vitamin apart from losses that occur when the water in which green vegetables have been boiled is discarded. If foods, especially milk, are left exposed to sunshine, large losses may occur. Especially good sources of the natural vitamin are yeast extract (e.g. Marmite) and meat extract (e.g. Bovril).

Table 14.7 Main dietary sources of riboflavin

Food	Range (mg/100g edible portion)
Liver and kidneys	2.0–4.0
Egg	0.47
Milk (fresh cow's)	0.20
Cheeses	0.25–0.80
Whole cereals	0.1–0.3
Pulses	0.1–0.3
Beef, mutton, poultry and pork	0.1–0.3
Green leafy vegetables	0.03–0.3
Beer	0.02–0.06
Yeast extract (Marmite)	11.0
Meat extract (Bovril)	7.4
Wheat bran	0.36

Green vegetables and fruits in tropical countries are, in general, richer in riboflavin than those in temperate regions.

Effects of deficiency in animals

Riboflavin deficiency in animals always results in a failure to grow. A great variety of lesions have been reported in animals; these include dermatitis, loss of hair, conjunctivitis, corneal vascularisation and opacities, impaired reproduction with congenital malformations in the offspring, anaemia with hypoplastic bone marrow, neuropathy and fatty liver.

Effects of deficiency in man

In 1938 Sebrell & Butler [44] described the clinical effects of feeding human subjects for four months on a diet providing about 0.5 mg/day of riboflavin. Their subjects developed angular stomatitis, cheilosis and nasolabial seborrhoea (p. 333) which responded to the administration of riboflavin. Two years later Sydenstricker[45] first described among pellagrous patients in southern USA an invasion of the cornea by capillary blood vessels similar to that seen in rats suffering from riboflavin deficiency. This ocular lesion, accompanied by lachrymation and photophobia was often associated with angular stomatitis and other features of the orogenital syndrome (p. 334). These lesions responded to the administration of riboflavin. However, other factors besides riboflavin deficiency can cause angular stomatitis and circumcorneal vascularisation.

In view of the importance of riboflavin in cell respiration it seems surprising that the clinical changes attributed to its deficiency are minor and do not by themselves threaten life. Even though riboflavin has a wide distribution in the foodstuffs used by man there are still many people who live for long periods on a very low intake and consequently minor signs of deficiency are common in many parts of the world. Why these conditions do not progress and lead to serious illness remains a mystery.

Laboratory diagnosis

In the presence of ultraviolet light riboflavin has a brilliant greenish-yellow fluorescence which provides a means of detecting and estimating small quantities in extracts of biological materials. It can also be estimated by microbiological assay. These methods have been of value in measuring the riboflavin in foodstuffs, in human urine and faeces, and in the tissues of animals.

Urinary riboflavin reflects the recent intake. It tends to increase when the nitrogen balance is negative. An established test for quantifying any functional effect of deficiency in the tissues is the measurement of activity of glutathione reductase in erythrocytes, with and without added FAD. An activation coefficient of over 1.30 with added FAD indicates inadequate riboflavin in the tissues.[46]

RECOMMENDED INTAKES

FAO/WHO recommended an intake of 130 µg/MJ (0.55 mg/1000 kcal) in the diet, and this is the basis of most other recommendations.

THERAPEUTIC USES AND TOXIC EFFECTS

Synthetic riboflavin, both for oral and parenteral administration, is readily available, but its therapeutic uses are not well supported by objective clinical evidence. It may be tried empirically in cases of angular stomatitis and the other lesions that sometimes co-exist, especially if they occur in cases of the malabsorption syndrome, in which the absorption of riboflavin may be impaired. Those who wish to prescribe this vitamin may give it by mouth in doses of 5 mg three times daily. There is no evidence that larger doses produce any further benefit.

Thus far, no one seems to have been adversely affected by treatment with synthetic riboflavin.

THE ANAEMIA-PREVENTING VITAMINS

HISTORY

Pernicious anaemia, described by Addison in 1849, occurs sporadically in most human races, apparently without relation to dietary habits. A constitutional or genetic predisposition to the disease was early recognised and in many cases it has now been shown to be the result of autoimmune reactions. As its name implies, the disease was fatal and feared until in 1926 Minot & Murphy[47] demonstrated the value of whole liver by mouth in its treatment. This was followed by the classic experiments of Castle[48] who showed that beef muscle mixed with normal gastric juice caused new blood formation in patients with pernicious anaemia, though neither was effective alone. He called the unknown factor in gastric juice 'intrinsic factor' and that in beef 'extrinsic factor', suggesting at the same time that the two interact to produce the remedial substance present in liver. Later it was found that the need for intrinsic factor could be circumvented, not only by giving large amounts of liver by mouth but also by injecting extracts of liver intramuscularly. Thereafter the search for the hypothetical 'anti-PA' vitamin was directed towards its isolation from extracts of liver. Each new concentrate of liver could only be tested by therapeutic trials on human patients with Addisonian anaemia. The lack of a suitable animal to assist in laboratory trials delayed the discovery of vitamin B12.

VITAMIN B12 — CYANOCOBALAMIN AND RELATED SUBSTANCES

The discovery that protein-free extracts of liver, given by injection, were effective in pernicious anaemia, led to many attempts over a period of 20 years to isolate from liver the active principle concerned. Progress was necessarily slow through lack of any easy means of detecting the vitamin until Mary Schorb discovered that liver extracts effective in pernicious anaemia had growth-promoting properties for the micro-organism *Lactobacillus lactis dorner*. The search for the growth factor proceeded rapidly and, aided by the fact that it was found to have a red colour, the isolation of crystalline vitamin B12 was achieved almost simultaneously in Britain[49] and the USA.[50] Proof soon followed of its effectiveness in the treatment of both the haematological and neurological manifestations of pernicious anaemia.

Chemistry

About 1 ton of fresh liver was needed for the isolation of 20 mg of the red crystals. These were found to have a molecular weight of about 1350 and to contain, surprisingly, 4 per cent of the mineral element cobalt, which previously was known to be an essential nutrient for sheep and cattle. The crystalline material was named cyanocobalamin. It is freely soluble in water and resistant to boiling in neutral solution though unstable in the presence of alkalis. It was subsequently found that the cyano-group in the molecule was an artefact of the extraction procedure.

The cobalt is contained in a porphyrin-like ring which is linked to a nucleotide containing a base, ribose and phosphoric acid (Fig. 14.8). In nature, vitamin B12 usually occurs in combination with protein.

Vitamin B12 is present in the body in several forms, including 5'-deoxyadenosylcobalamin, the major coenzyme form, methylcobalamin and hydroxocobalamin. The last is available commercially and is even more effective therapeutically than cyanocobalamin. The vit-

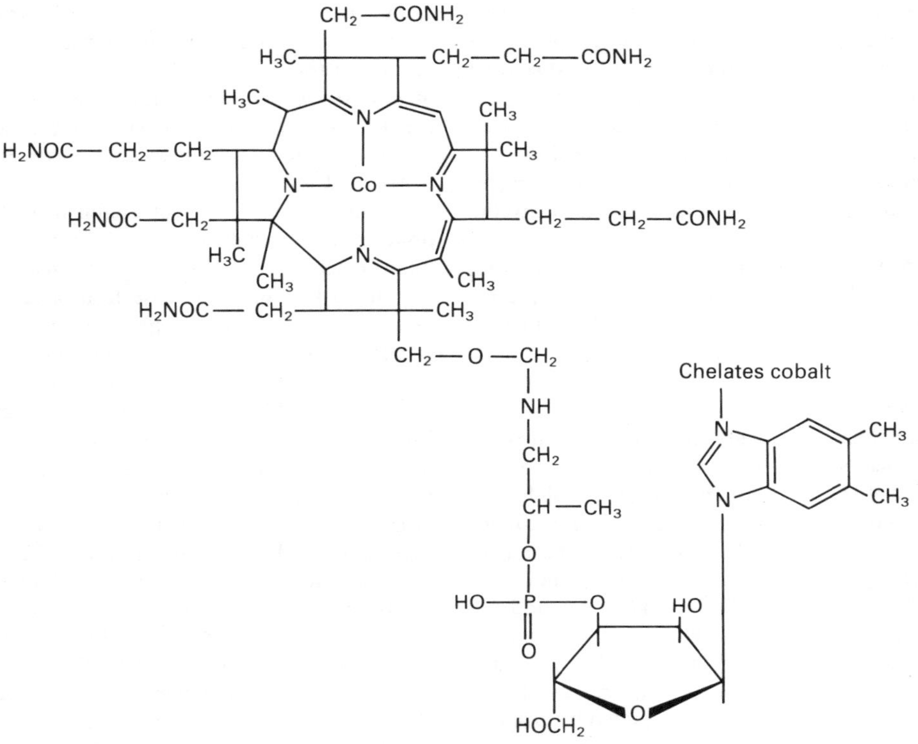

Fig. 14.8 Structure of vitamin B12

amin is produced commercially as a cheap by-product of the cultivation of *Streptomyces griseus* used in the preparation of the antibiotic streptomycin.

Physiological action

On development of erythrocytes
Deficiency of vitamin B12 is most severely felt in tissues where the cells are normally dividing rapidly, e.g. in the blood-forming tissues.

Biopsies of bone marrow show abnormal cells — megaloblasts — which are larger than the nucleated cells that give rise to normal red blood corpuscles and have characteristic large reticulated nuclei. When megaloblasts are present in the bone marrow the circulating erythrocytes are bigger than normal (macrocytic) though usually carrying a normal concentration of haemoglobin (normochromic).

Megaloblastosis occurs because DNA formation is limited but that of RNA is not. As the cells develop they synthesise RNA normally but DNA synthesis does not keep pace. The consequence is slower replication of cells which have more nuclear chromatin than normal, but not enough for division, and a larger cytoplasm than nucleus. The defect is due to impaired synthesis of thymine, the characteristic base of DNA, from deoxyuri-dine. The metabolic mechanisms responsible for this synthesis depend on both vitamin B12 and folate and are discussed on p. 161. Deficiency of vitamin B12 and of folate each produce megaloblastic anaemia and the two conditions cannot be distinguished by microscopic examination of bone marrow or peripheral blood.

On the nervous system
Vitamin B12 plays a separate biochemical role, unrelated to folate, in the maintenance of myelin in the nervous system. This is probably due to dependence of propionate catabolism on vitamin B12. The normal sequence is from propionyl coenzyme A via methylmalonyl coenzyme A to succinyl coenzyme A, which is metabolised in the citric acid cycle. Deoxyadenosyl vitamin B12 is essential for the last step. In vitamin B12 deficiency 15- and 17-carbon fatty acids and branched fatty acids appear in nervous tissue. It is likely that the odd-numbered fatty acids are formed when propionyl coenzyme A is used instead of acetyl coenzyme A for fatty acid synthesis and that branched chain fatty acids result when methylmalonyl coenzyme A substitutes for malonyl coenzyme A. Patients with vitamin B12 deficiency usually excrete methylmalonic acid in their urine. This has been used as a test for deficiency; it does not occur in folate deficiency. An animal model for subacute com-

bined degeneration of the spinal cord (p. 329) has been found, the fruit bat *Rousettus aegypticus*. Coprophagy has not been observed in these animals; their usual sources of vitamin B12 are presumed to be from stagnant water and insect pests on fruit. When kept in cages and given fruit and distilled water, after 200 days their plasma B12 fell and their pattern of flying was disturbed, presumably because they had become ataxic due to demyelination of the spinal cord.[51]

Hydroxocobalamin has an affinity for cyanide; this appears to be a detoxication mechanism in people exposed to repeated small amounts of cyanide in food or in tobacco smoke.

Dietary intake

Vitamin B12 is unique amongst vitamins in that it is not found in any plants. The dietary intake varies according to the amount of animal products consumed. High cost, low cost and poor American diets have been estimated to provide 32, 16 and 3 μg/day respectively and a poor Asian diet 0.5 μg/day.[52] Vitamin B12 is present in several forms in foods. The main ones are adenosyl- and hydroxocobalamin, of which 34 and 55 per cent are absorbed. Methylcobalamin is found in egg yolk and cheese, and sulphitocobalamin in some canned foods. Little or no cyanocobalamin occurs in foods. Vitamin B12 activity is usually stable during food preparation but boiling in an alkaline medium can lead to losses. Most vegetarians will drink milk and so get a modest supply. Cow's milk contains about 0.3 μg/100 g. How strict vegetarians, who eat no animal product, get the vitamin remains a mystery. There may be traces in microorganisms and mould which contaminate their food.

Alimentary absorption

There is now no doubt that vitamin B12 is the 'extrinsic factor' postulated by Castle, but it still remains to be explained exactly why normal gastric secretion is needed for its absorption. As Castle himself[53] has said: 'It can be stated with assurance that pernicious anaemia is usually an example of highly specific isolation of the affected person from his alimentary environment. Thus his disease would not develop if the patient could effect daily the transfer of a millionth of a gram of vitamin B12 the distance of a small fraction of a millimetre across the intestinal mucosa and into the blood stream. This he cannot do, principally as a result of failure of his stomach to secrete into its lumen some essential but still unknown substance.' We now know that intrinsic factor is a glycoprotein secreted by the parietal cells of the stomach. Vitamin B12 is absorbed in the distal part of the ileum and not in the jejunum.

The normal requirements of an adult to prevent signs of deficiency are probably about 1 μg/day. When micrograms of vitamin B12 are given to patients with pernicious anaemia by mouth, little absorption, if any, occurs. When milligrams are given, a very small percentage of the dose is absorbed but probably a sufficient quantity to prevent deficiency. This may be due to simple diffusion. For the absorption of physiological doses and also of the vitamin present in foods, intrinsic factor is essential. Neither the nature nor the mode of action of intrinsic factor is as yet established. The failure to produce it in pernicious anaemia arises from an autoimmune reaction, which destroys the secretion glands in the stomach. This may arise from a genetically determined defect in immunological tolerance.

The tapeworm *Diphyllobothrium latum* infects many species of freshwater fish. Human infection occurs round the world wherever raw or insufficiently cooked fish is eaten. The adult worms which may reach a length of 15 metres assimilate the vitamin from the food and make it unavailable to the host (p. 466). In a variety of intestinal diseases, e.g. the malabsorption syndrome, especially the blind loop syndrome, an increased bacterial flora may affect absorption of vitamin B12 because the bacteria assimilate it from the food. In ileal disease vitamin B12 cannot be absorbed and after total gastrectomy intrinsic factor is lost. Some drugs, e.g. *p*-aminosalicylic acid, biguanides, slow-release potassium and colchicine, interfere specifically with the absorption of vitamin B12. In each of the above ways anaemia due to secondary vitamin B12 deficiency may arise.

Transport, excretion and storage

Cobalamin is carried in the blood attached to three proteins, transcobalamins I, II and III. II is the functionally more important carrier and it gives up its vitamin B12 to the tissues rapidly. The other two transcobalamins bind the vitamin more permanently. Some vitamin B12 is excreted in the bile but this is partly reabsorbed in normal people, in an enterohepatic cycle. Up to 2 μg daily may be excreted in the faeces and less in the urine. Loss of endogenous, as well as exogenous, vitamin explains why deficiency develops more rapidly in malabsorption than on an inadequate diet. Excess intake is stored, mostly in the liver. Total body cobalamin in normal adults is 2 to 5 mg of which half or more is in the liver. This is about 1000 times the estimated daily utilisation and losses.

Primary deficiency in man

A completely vegetarian diet, containing no milk, eggs or other foods of animal origin, is practically devoid of cobalamins, provided that all its components are fresh and free from fermentation by microorganisms. People who follow such a diet have occasionally developed megaloblastic anaemia or more commonly developed neurological manifestation of vitamin B12 deficiency (p. 329).

Laboratory diagnosis

The plasma concentration in healthy persons normally lies between 200 and 960 pg/ml. A value below 80 is diagnostic of vitamin B12 deficiency. Values between 80 and 200 are equivocal. The capacity of the bowel to absorb vitamin B12 is a valuable test used in the investigation of complex cases of megaloblastic anaemia. If a 1 μg dose of radioactive B12 is given to healthy persons, only about 30 per cent is recovered in the faeces, whereas over 70 per cent is recovered in patients with pernicious anaemia and in malabsorbtion. The two may be differentiated by giving another dose of radioactive B12 this time with intrinsic factor which corrects absorption in pernicious anaemia. The measurement of the urinary excretion of the isotope (Schilling test) is now in general use as a test. To ensure prompt urinary excretion of the absorbed radioactive B12 a 'flushing' dose of 1000 μg 'cold' vitamin is often given.

Recommended intakes

The USA official recommendation is 3 μg a day. This can only be tentative, but two things are certain: a remission can be brought about in pernicious anaemia by the daily injection of 1 μg of vitamin B12; people in apparent health may get only 0.5 μg/day in their diet.

Therapeutic uses

Vitamin B12, given by injection, provides complete and satisfactory treatment in cases of pernicious anaemia. The general practice is to give 1000 μg of hydroxocobalamin by injection twice weekly until the haemoglobin is normal. Subsequently an injection of 1000 μg every six weeks is all that is needed to keep the patient in health. The blood should be examined every six months. A similar dose schedule is required in subacute combined degeneration of the cord and in vitamin B12 deficiency due to other causes.

FOLATE (FOLIC ACID, FOLACIN)

History

In 1931 Dr Lucy Wills[54] in Bombay drew attention to the importance of nutritional megaloblastic anaemia in pregnant women (Chap. 48). She reproduced this anaemia in monkeys by means of a diet composed chiefly of polished rice and white bread, similar to that eaten by her patients. This anaemia did not respond to any vitamin known at that time, nor to purified liver extract (presumably containing vitamin B12). Yet good clinical responses were obtained with an autolysed yeast preparation[55] which was generally ineffective in pernicious anaemia. Therefore yeast contained an antianaemic principle (the 'Wills' factor') that was different from the factor present in purified liver extract.

Then an unexpected clue came from an unrelated field of biochemistry. A preparation was obtained from spinach and called folic acid.[56] It was a growth factor for *Lactobacillus casei*. This preparation would cure a dietary anaemia in chicks. The isolation of a crystalline active principle was announced in 1945 by a large team of American industrial chemists, who soon accomplished its synthesis. The substance was pteroylglutamic acid (PGA), a complex containing a pterin.

It was soon found that synthetic folic acid would cure dietary anaemia in chicks and also in monkeys. Hence it was reasonable to try it empirically in pernicious anaemia; dramatic responses occurred comparable to that produced by liver extract. However, the neurological lesions were not improved and were often made worse.[57] Some time was to elapse before it was shown that the real therapeutic role of folic acid lay in the treatment of the megaloblastic anaemias of malnutrition, pregnancy and malabsorption (Chap. 48). Thus Lucy Wills' original observation that there are at least two different dietary factors concerned with megaloblastosis was shown to be correct.

Chemistry

Folic acid, often referred to as folacin in the USA, consists of a pterin ring attached to *p*-aminobenzoic acid and conjugated with one molecule of glutamic acid. It is a yellow crystalline substance, sparingly soluble in water and stable in acid solution. When heated in neutral or alkaline media, however, it undergoes fairly rapid destruction, so it may be destroyed by some methods of cooking (see below). Several closely allied compounds have been identified in living matter:

1. Up to six additional molecules of glutamic acid may be attached through the γ-carboxyl group to pteroylmonoglutamic acid. The test organism, *Lactobacillus casei* can utilise pteroyltriglutamic acid but not compounds with more than three glutamic acid residues, the pteroylpolyglutamates.

2. Two reduced forms of folate, 7,8-dihydrofolate and 5,6,7,8-tetrahydrofolate (THF), may be present in the tissues.

3. In the course of its numerous metabolic functions folate, usually in the tetrahydroform, may have active one-carbon groups on the N-5 or N-10 positions or bridging the two. The most important of these are 5-methyl-THF, 5,10-methylene-THF, 5,10-methenyl-THF, 5-formyl-THF and 10-formyl-THF and 5-formimino-THF. The structural relation between folic acid and THF is shown in Figure 14.9.

Metabolic roles of folate and vitamin B12

The methyl group required to convert deoxyuridine into thymine (p. 159) is provided by 5,10-methylene-THF, which has to be made from THF. For this the main

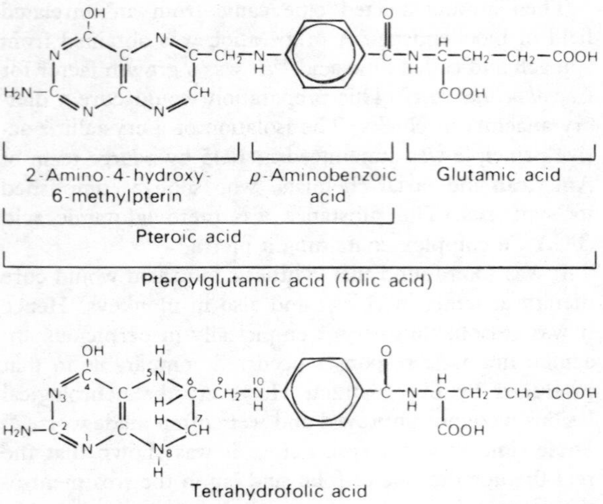

Fig. 14.9 The structure of folic acid and THF. The N-5 and N-10 nitrogen atoms participate in the transfer of one-carbon groups

source of methyl groups is methionine formed from homocysteine by methionine synthetase. This enzyme has both vitamin B12 and folate polyglutamate as co-factors. Methionine is a source of formate as well as methyl groups. Formate is a single carbon atom unit and is needed to form folate polyglutamate from folate. Vitamin B12 may thus regulate folate metabolism by the supply of folate.[58]

Absorption, excretion and storage
About three-quarters of the folate in foods is in poly-glutamyl forms. These are normally hydrolysed to free folate by a conjugase (a γ-L-glutamyl carboxypeptidase) present in small intestinal epithelium. Free folate is actively absorbed from the upper small intestine. At some stage during absorption it appears to be reduced and methylated to methyl-THF.

Folic acid is stored mainly in the liver which normally contains 5 to 15 mg/kg. Small amounts are excreted in faeces and urine, but additional amounts are presumed to be metabolised and some is lost by desquamation of cells from body surfaces.

Deficiency
Folate deficiency may arise in four ways.
1. As a dietary defect. This is common among poor people in the tropics where it often gives rise to megaloblastic anaemia. It is unusual in prosperous countries, except in pregnancy when the need for the vitamin is increased.
2. From malabsorption. It occurs in coeliac disease and other disorders of the upper small intestine where folate is absorbed.
3. Excess demands. This occurs when cell proliferation is very active as in leukaemias and in some other cancers and in haemolytic anaemia.
4. Interference with folate metabolism by drugs. Almost all anticonvulsants used to treat epilepsy reduce plasma folate,[59] as do some other drugs. These include oral contraceptives and ethanol but the reduction is seldom large and anaemia is uncommon.

There are also at least six errors of folate metabolism arising from hereditary defects in specific enzymes.[60] All are very rare. They usually present early in life and the children may be mentally retarded as well as anaemic. Megadoses of the vitamin may lead to clinical improvement.

Laboratory diagnosis
Folate may be estimated in fluids by microbiological assay. The normal plasma concentration is between 6 and 20 µg/l. Folate deficiency is possible if the plasma concentration is below 6 and certain if below 3. Erythrocytes contain much more (160–650 µg/l) and provide a means of measuring tissues stores, which is now used in diagnosis. Various folate absorption tests are in use. A dose of folate is given by mouth and plasma concentrations determined at intervals thereafter. These are of special value in doubtful cases of the malabsorption syndrome.

Dietary sources
Folic acid is present in foods in several different forms. The methods used for analysis of foodstuffs and body fluids are microbiological. The organism most used is *Lactobacillus casei* which responds to all forms of folic acid with up to three glutamic acid residues: this is free folate. To demonstrate the pteroylpolyglutamates, foods are treated with a conjugase obtained from chicken liver and again microbiologically analysed for folate: this is total folate. Absorption of polyglutamates is not as complete as that of free folate.

Some indications of the relative folic acid content of foods is given in Table 14.8. The richest source is liver, in which most of the folate is 5-methyl-THF and well absorbed. Other foods contain most of the folate as poly-glutamates and are less reliable as dietary sources (FAO/WHO, 1970). Table 14.8 shows free and total folate in a selection of uncooked foods. There is uncertainty about the reliability of the methods used for analysis and figures in present tables may be too low. There is a need for new analyses and until these are available folate intakes cannot be estimated with confidence.[61]

When different forms of folate, labelled with isotopes, were given to healthy volunteers,[62] the heptaglutamate was shown to be split to monoglutamate during digestion and about 55 per cent of it was absorbed. The avail-

Table 14.8 Folate in foods

Food	Folate (mg/100g) Free	Folate (mg/100g) Total
Good sources		
Liver (ox)	180	290
Broccoli tops	89	130
Spinach	30	140
Cabbage (savoy)	60	90
Beans (runner)	57	60
Peanuts	28	110
Hazel nuts	23	72
Fair sources		
Bread (wholemeal)	21	39
Bread (white)	6	27
Rice (polished)	15	29
Oranges	30	37
Bananas	14	22
Eggs	25	25
Poor sources		
Potatoes (new)	3	10
Apples	3	6
Milk (cow's)	4	5
Beef, mutton, poultry and pork	<5	<15

Values are for fresh (uncooked) foods: cooking losses can be considerable.

ability of five pure forms of folate including THF and pteroylheptaglutamate, and of the folate in 12 natural foods was assessed by measuring urinary folate with an assay of *Lactobacillus casei*.[63] Availability appeared to be low, 25 to 50 per cent, from lettuce, egg, orange and wheat germ, but 50 to 96 per cent for lima beans, liver, brewer's yeast and bananas. This suggests that factors in foods as well as the forms of folate may influence absorption.

Food preparation can cause serious losses of folic acid — in canning, in prolonged heating, when cooking water is discarded, and from reheating. Reducing agents in food tend to protect the folic acid.

Recommended intakes

For non-pregnant adults the USA and UK recommendations are 400 and 300 µg daily.

In normal adults 100 µg of pteroylglutamic acid have prevented or cured folate-deficient megaloblastic anaemia[64] but is not always sufficient to maintain or restore plasma folate concentration. The safe requirement appears to be 200 µg/day as available folate. This would correspond to 300 µg/day as total folate if it is assumed that conjugated forms are 50 per cent utilised and make up 50 per cent of the total. For infants, human milk provides 5 µg folate/100 ml, and 5 µg folate/kg body weight meets the daily requirement. In pregnancy there is an additional requirement of about 100 µg of available folate. Many doctors in the UK prescribe a daily supplement containing 400 µg during pregnancy.

Therapeutic uses and toxicity

Folic acid is required for the treatment of nutritional megaloblastic anaemia, the megaloblastic anaemias of pregnancy and infancy, and in some cases of the malabsorption syndrome. A daily dose of 5 to 10 mg by mouth is usually sufficient. It should never be used in Addisonian anaemia because it may make the neurological features of the disease worse. A small daily dose (400 µg) is often given during pregnancy.

Folic acid normally has no adverse effects. However, when it is used to treat megaloblastic anaemia secondary to the use of antiepileptic drugs, the epilepsy may be aggravated.[59] Certain synthetic analogues are highly poisonous, notably methotrexate which is used as an antimetabolite in the treatment of leukaemia.

VITAMIN B6 — PYRIDOXINE AND RELATED COMPOUNDS

The vitamin was first identified as the factor in the vitamin B complex, distinct from thiamin and riboflavin, that would cure a specific nutritional dermatitis in rats. Birch & György[65] concentrated the vitamin in 1936; soon after, it was isolated and synthesised. György has recalled the history.[66]

BIOCHEMICAL ACTION

Vitamin B6 is present in foods in three forms which are readily interconverted in the tissues and of equal biological value (Fig. 14.10). The aldehyde, pyridoxal, and the amine, pyridoxamine, function as co-enzymes after phosphorylation. A synthetic preparation of the alcohol, pyridoxine hydrochloride, is used in clinical medicine.

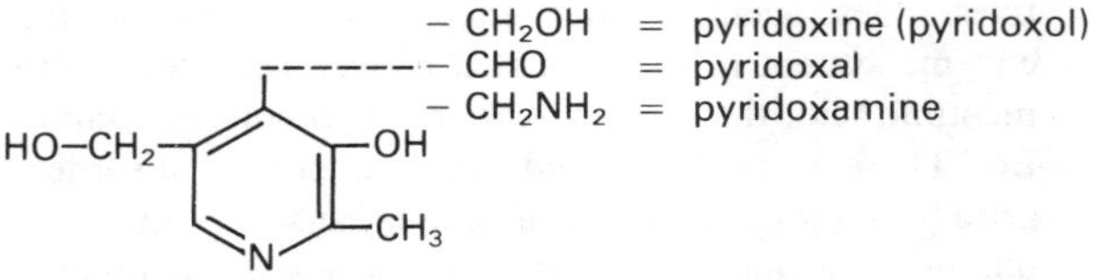

$$- CH_2OH = \text{pyridoxine (pyridoxol)}$$
$$- CHO = \text{pyridoxal}$$
$$- CH_2NH_2 = \text{pyridoxamine}$$

Fig. 14.10 Structure of vitamin B6

Vitamin B6 provides the co-enzyme for over 60 different decarboxylation and transamination reactions involving amino acids. Some of these have been used as clinical tests of vitamin B6 status. Transaminase activity in erythrocytes can be measured with and without added pyridoxal phosphate. As the enzyme is not normally saturated with the co-factor, its activity rises after the addition. The rise is much greater in vitamin B6 deficiency. More often the tryptophan loading test is used. After a dose of 2 g of tryptophan, the urinary excretion of xanthurenic acid is measured. This is increased in vitamin B6 deficiency, because kynurine cannot be converted to nicotinic acid and is diverted to xanthurenic acid (Fig. 14.6).

Deficiency in experimental animals

The obvious feature of severe deficiency in rats is a dermatitis, known as acrodynia. There is hyperkeratosis affecting the paws, the ears and nose with underlying oedema. Desquamatous follows, leaving raw pink areas. There are other widespread abnormalities. In pigs anaemia is a main feature due to a failure in the synthesis of the porphyrin, haem, as the enzyme that synthesises amino-laevulinic acid is dependent on pyridoxal phosphate. Dogs develop convulsions and monkeys obstructive lesions in arteries due to proliferating smooth muscle cells.

Human deficiency

Primary dietary deficiency.   This has not been reported in adults and the widespread distribution of the vitamin in foods prevents its occurrence on any natural diet. In infants a minor epidemic of convulsions in the USA was attributed to a milk formula that provided little vitamin B6 due to a manufacturing error.[67]

Drug induced.   In 1952 the introduction of **isoniazid** was a revolution in the treating of tuberculosis. However, it was soon reported that some patients on the drug developed a peripheral neuropathy and that this could be prevented by pyridoxine. It is now standard practice to give patients receiving 300 mg or more isoniazid a daily dose of 10 mg of pyridoxine. Isoniazid is a hydrazide and inactivates pyridoxal phosphate by forming a hydrazone with it.

Other drugs have also been reported to reduce vitamin B6 status, notably oestrogens and oral contraceptives. Oestrogens induce increased activity of the enzyme system in the liver that converts tryptophan to nicotinic acid; this may increase requirements of vitamin B6. There is no good evidence that clinical disorders arise from reduced vitamin B6 status caused by endogenous or exogenous oestrogens. Nevertheless pyridoxine, often in very large doses, is taken by many women for depression and other symptoms associated with menstrual and gynaecological disorders. The vitamin may be prescribed by physicians or taken on the advice of health magazines. This does at least no harm when the dose of pyridoxine is restricted to 10 mg a day, and at this level pyridoxine is one of the safest of drugs.

However, some patients have been prescribed or taken as much as from 2 to 6 g daily. In seven such patients, these doses caused a sensory neuropathy that was incapacitating.[68] This experience shows that megadoses of vitamins are potentially dangerous and serves as a warning to those who follow the precepts of orthomolecular medicine (p. 150).

Pyridoxine dependency

Two conditions, both very rare, are known in which the clinical features can be relieved by doses of pyridoxine up to 100 mg a day, many times the normal intake. The first is convulsions occurring in a well-nourished infant.[69] The second is hypochromic anaemia in an adult with normal or increased iron reserves.[70] These can be presumed to be due to hereditary or other defects in specific enzyme systems.

Dietary intake

Cereals, meats, fruits, leafy and other vegetables each contain moderate amounts of vitamin B6, usually in the range of 0.1 to 0.3 mg/100 mg. Among common foods the only rich source is liver (0.5 mg/100 g). Processed foods such as fats, oil, sugar and alcoholic spirits contain none. Most adult diets provide 1.5 to 2 mg daily.

The USA recommended intakes for adult men and women are 2.2 and 2.0 mg a day, with an additional 0.6 mg in pregnancy. For infants it is 0.3 mg a day. As human milk is reported to contain only 0.01 mg/100 ml, it is difficult to see how this could be met. The recommendations are of practical use in the prescription of formula for total parental nutrition.

PANTOTHENIC ACID

Pantothenic acid is a constituent of coenzyme A and present in all living matter; its distribution in natural foodstuffs is so widespread that deficiency of the vitamin is unlikely to occur in man.

After the discovery of riboflavin, nicotinic acid and pyridoxine it was soon realised that there was still at least one other factor left in materials containing the hypothetical 'vitamin B2'. This 'filtrate factor' was recognised by its ability to prevent a dermatitis that develops round the eyes and beak of chicks fed on a diet deficient in it, and to prevent grey hair in black rats similarly fed. Attempts to isolate this factor were proceeding along orthodox lines using rats and chicks when, as in the case of folic acid, the microbiological approach unexpectedly revealed the vitamin. In 1939 R J Williams[71] isolated the vitamin, using the growth of yeast at a test of its presence, and later achieved its synthesis. He called it pantothenic acid because of its apparently universal distribution in living matter.

CHEMISTRY

Pantothenic acid is a dimethyl derivative of butyric acid

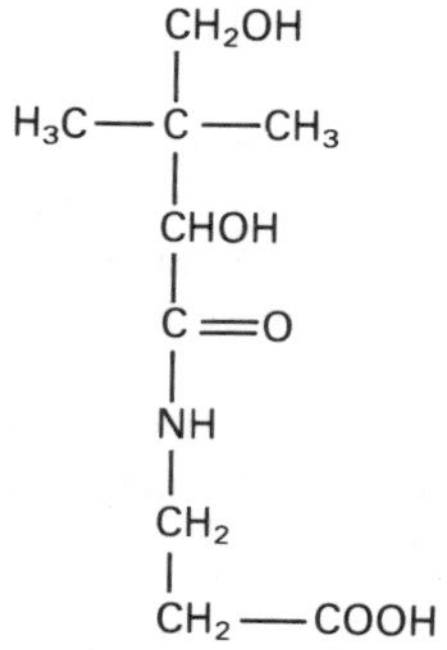

Fig. 14.11 Structure of pantothenic acid

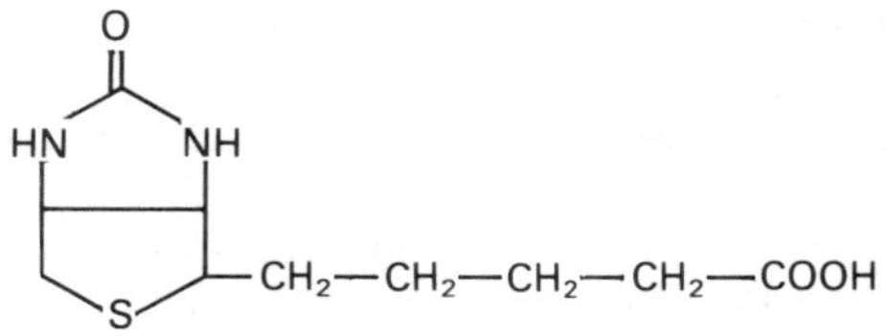

Fig. 14.12 Structure of biotin

joined by a peptide linkage to the amino acid β-alanine (Fig. 14.11). The vitamin itself is a pale yellow oily liquid that has never yet been crystallised, but its calcium salt crystallises readily and this is the form in which it is generally available. Though stable in neutral solution, it is easily destroyed by heat, both on the acid and alkaline side of neutrality.

HUMAN REQUIREMENTS

Most human diets provide 3–10 mg daily, derived from a variety of natural foods, and this is ample to meet needs. For adult patients on total parenteral nutrition 15 mg is an adequate daily dose and 1 mg daily is sufficient for infants.

Concentrations in blood and urinary excretion may be below normal in lower socioeconomic groups,[72] but no clinical features attributable to deficiency of the vitamin have been established. The claim that pantothenate relieves the burning foot syndrome has not been confirmed (Chap. 36) but some physicians continue to use it and doses of 10 mg daily of the calcium salt by intramuscular injection may be tried. Although administration of the vitamin brings back the pigment to the grey hairs of experimentally deficient rats, those who advertise it for grey-haired men and women are 'out for a fast buck'.

BIOTIN

Biotin deficiency does not occur in man except under extraordinary circumstances; yet it is a vitamin of such physiological interest that it merits some mention.

Rats fed on the raw white of eggs as their sole source of animal protein develop a dermatitis and become emaciated. Raw egg-white contains a particular protein (avidin) which combines with biotin rendering it unavailable to the rat. By cooking the eggs the avidin is denatured and the biotin liberated. The vitamin was synthesised in 1943. Figure 14.12 shows its structure.

Biotin is one of the most active biological substances known; extremely small amounts have marked effects on the growth of yeast and certain bacteria. This provides the means by which it can be measured in foodstuffs. It is a co-factor for the acetyl CoA, proprionyl CoA and pyruvate carboxylase systems. These incorporate dissolved CO_2 in equilibrium with bicarbonate into metabolic pathways for the synthesis of fatty acids and for gluconeogenesis.

Deficiency in man

Sydenstricker and his colleagues[73] produced biotin deficiency by feeding four volunteers a diet very poor in all the vitamins of the B group. This diet was composed largely of dried egg-white which supplied 30 per cent of the energy in the diet. Other known components of the B complex except biotin were added in synthetic form. After 10 weeks on the diet the subjects were fatigued, depressed and sleepy, with nausea and loss of appetite. Muscular pains, hyperaesthesiae and paraesthesiae developed, without reflex changes or other objective signs of neuropathy. As the authors point out, these features could not be distinguished from those previously attributed to thiamin deficiency. The tongue became pale with loss of papillae. The skin became dry, 'crackled', with fine scaly desquamation (p. 333) and anaemia and hypercholesterolaemia developed. All of these signs and symptoms were relieved by the injection of a concentrated preparation containing 150 to 300 μg of biotin daily. The authors concluded: 'The phenomena observed were similar to some of those observed in spontaneous avitaminoses.'

Biotin deficiency has been described in an eccentric man who lived on a diet consisting mainly of six dozen raw eggs weekly, washed down with 4 quarts of red wine daily.[74] He had a severe dermatitis which responded to injections of the methyl ester of biotin. A second case was in a boy with bulbar poliomyelitis who had received six raw eggs daily by gastric tube for 18 months.[75] He developed scaly dermatitis and loss of hair. A third case was a man with cirrhosis of the liver who consumed raw eggs.[76]

Human milk contains 0.7 μg/100 ml of biotin, only a third of the content of cow's milk. If the mother is malnourished, the intake can become critical and cases of severe seborrhoeic dermatitis have been reported in breast-fed infants that improved when biotin was given to their mothers.[77]

A number of cases of carboxylase deficiency responding to large doses of biotin have been reported.[78,79] The clinical features are loss of hair, an erythematous rash, keratoconjunctivitis, ataxia and lactic acidosis.

It is extremely unlikely that the reader will ever see a patient with biotin deficiency. The story of it is bizarre but bizarre happenings are a feature of nutrition. When a patient presents with a skin rash for which no explanation is apparent, remember biotin deficiency. You may bring off a diagnostic coup.

DIETARY SOURCES AND THERAPEUTIC USES

Yeasts and bacteria of many species either make or retain biotin; it seems probable that human needs can be met by a supply from the numerous microorganisms that are present in his food or inhabit his large intestine. Moreover, biotin is present in a variety of bacteria-free foods. Liver, kidney and yeast extract are good sources. Pulses, nuts, chocolate and some vegetables (e.g. cauliflower) are fair sources. Other meats, dairy produce and cereals are relatively poor.

For adult patients on total parenteral nutrition 300 μg is an adequate daily dose and 30 μg is sufficient for an infant. A therapeutic dose is 10 mg daily.

REFERENCES

1. Holst A, Fröelich T 1907 Experimental studies relating to ship beri-beri and scurvy. J Hyg (Lond) 7: 634–671
2. Waugh W A, King C G 1932 Isolation and identification of vitamin C. J Biol Chem 97: 325–331
3. Szent-Györgyi A 1928 Observations on the function of peroxidase systems and the chemistry of the adrenal cortex: description of a new carbohydrate derivative. Biochem J 22: 1387–1409
4. Anderson T W, Passmore R, Szent-Györgyi A, Paulin L C 1978 To dose or megadose: a debate about vitamin C. Nutr Today 13(2): 6–33
5. Cook J D, Monsen E R 1977 Vitamin C, the common cold and iron absorption. Am J Clin Nutr 30: 235–251
6. Rajalakshmi R, Desdar A D, Ramakrishnam C V 1965 Vitamin C secretion during lactation. Acta Paediatr Scand 54: 375–382
7. Hodges R E, Hood J, Canham J E, Sauberlich H E, Baker E M 1971 Clinical manifestations of ascorbic acid deficiency in man. Am J Clin Nutr 24: 432–443
8. Baker E M, Hodges R E, Hood J, Sauberlich H E, March S C, Canham J E 1971 Metabolism of ^{14}C- and ^{3}H-labelled L-ascorbic acid in human scurvy. Am J Clin Nutr 24: 444–454
9. Yavorsky M, Almaden P, King C G 1934 The vitamin C content of human tissues. J Biol Chem 106: 525–527
10. Kinsey V E 1947 Transfer of ascorbic acid and related compounds across blood–aqueous barrier. Am J Ophthalmol 30: 1262–1266
11. Crandon J H, Mikal S, Landeau B R 1953 Ascorbic acid deficiency in experimental and surgical subjects. Proc Nutr Soc 12: 273–279
12. Friedman G J, Sherry S K, Ralli E P 1940 The mechanism of the excretion of vitamin C by the human kidney at low and normal plasma levels of ascorbic acid. J Clin Invest 19: 685–689
13. Hodges R E, Baker E M 1973 In: Goodhart R S, Shils M E (eds) Modern nutrition in health and disease, 5th edn. Lea & Febiger, Philadelphia, p. 252
14. Wolbach S B 1953 Experimental scurvy. Its employment for the study of intercellular substances. Proc Nutr Soc 12: 247–255
15. Walter R 1748 Lord Anson's voyage round the world (1740–1744). Abridged and annotated by Pack S W C (1947). Penguin Books, London
16. Levene C I, Bates C J 1975 Ascorbic acid and collagen synthesis in cultured fibroblasts. Ann N Y Acad Sci 258: 288–305
17. Lind J 1753 A treatise of the scurvy. Reprinted by the Edinburgh University Press, 1953
18. McCarrison R 1919 Studies in deficiency diseases. Medical Publications, Oxford
19. Harris L J, Passmore R, Pagel W 1937 Vitamin C and infection: influence of infection on the vitamin C content of the tissues of animals. Lancet 2: 735–737
20. Kitabchi A E, West W H 1975 Effect of steroidogenesis on ascorbic acid content and uptake in isolated adrenal cells. Ann N Y Acad Sci 258: 422–431
21. Hughes R E 1981 Vitamin C: some current problems. British Nutrition Foundation, London
22. Anderson T W, Suranyi G, Beaton G H 1974 The effect on winter illness of large doses of vitamin C. Can Med Assoc J 111: 31–42
23. Cameron E, Pauling L 1976 Supplemental ascorbic acid in the supportive treatment of cancer. Prolongation of survival time in terminal human cancer. Proc Natl Acad Sci USA 73: 3685–3689
24. Creagan E T, Moertel C G, O'Fallon M J, et al 1979 Failure of high-dose vitamin C to benefit patients with advanced cancer. N Engl J Med 301: 687–690
25. Hehir P 1922 Effects of chronic starvation in the siege of Kut. Br Med J 1: 865–868
26. Dudley S 1953 James Lind: laudatory address. Proc Nutr Soc 12: 202–209
27. Eijkman C 1897 Ein Versuch zür Bekampfung der Beriberi. Virchows Arch (Pathol Anat Physiol) 149: 187–194
28. Jansen B P C, Donath W F 1926 Antineuritisch Vitamine. Chem Weekblad 23: 201
29. Williams R R, Cline J K 1936 Synthesis of vitamin B₁. J Am Chem Soc 58:1504
30. Peters R A 1953 Significance of biochemical lesions in the pyruvate oxidase system. Br Med Bull 9: 116–122
31. Thomson A D, Leevy C M 1972 Observations on the mechanism of thiamine hydrochloride absorption in man. Clin Sci 43: 153–163
32. Ferrebee J W, Weissman N, Parker D, Owen P S 1942 Tissue thiamin concentrations and urinary thiamin excretion. J Clin Invest 21: 401–408
33. Keys A, Henschel A, Taylor H L, Mickelsen O, Brozek J 1945 Experimental studies on man with a restricted intake of the B vitamins. Am J Physiol 144: 5–42

34. Platt B S, Lu G D 1936 Chemical and clinical findings in beri-beri. Q J Med 5: 355–373
35. Brin M 1962 Erythrocyte transketolase in early thiamine deficiency. Ann N Y Acad Sci 98: 528–541
36. Williams R R, Spies T 1938 Vitamin B₁ in medicine. Macmillan, New York
37. Goldberger J, Wheeler G A, Lillie R D, Rogers L M 1926 A further study of butter, fresh beef, and yeast as pellagra preventives, with considerations of the relation of factor P–P of pellagra (and black tongue of dogs) to vitamin B. Public Health Rep 41: 297–318
38. Elvehjem C A, Madden R J, Strong F M Wooley D W 1937 Relation of nicotinic acid and nicotinic acid amide to canine black tongue. J Am Chem Soc 59: 1767
39. Horwitt M K, Harvey C C, Rothwell W S, Cutler J L, Haffron D 1956 Tryptophan–niacin relationships in man. J Nutr 60: suppl 1, 1–43
40. Mason J B, Gibson N, Kodicek E 1973 The chemical nature of the bound nicotinic acid of wheat bran: studies of nicotinic acid-containing macromolecules. Br J Nutr 30: 297–311
41. Horwitt M K, Harvey C C, Dahm C H 1975 Relationship between levels of blood lipids, vitamins C, A and E, serum copper compounds and urinary excretions of tryptophan metabolites in women taking oral contraceptives. Am J Clin Nutr 28: 403–412
42. Kuhn R, György P, Wagner-Jouregg T 1933 Über ovoflavin, den farbstaff des Eiklars. Ber dt Chem Ges 66:576
43. Warburg O, Christian W 1932 Über ein neuco Oxydationferment und sein Adsorptionspektrum. Biochem Z 254:438
44. Sebrell W H, Butler R E 1938 Riboflavin deficiency in man. Public Health Rep 53: 2282–2284
45. Sydenstricker V P, Sebrell W H, Cleckley H M, Kruse H D 1940 The ocular manifestations of aribinoflavinosis. JAMA 114: 2437–2445
46. Thurnham D I, Rathaketle P 1982 Incubation of NAD(P)H₂: glutathione oxidoreductase (EC 1.6.4.2) with flavine adenine dinucleotide for maximum stimulation in the measurement of riboflavin status. Br J Nutr 48: 459–466
47. Minot G R Murphy W P 1926 Treatment of pernicious anaemia with a special diet. JAMA 87: 470–476
48. Castle W B 1929 Observations on the etiologic relationship of achylia gastrica to pernicious anaemia. I: The effect of the administration of the contents of the normal human stomach after the ingestion of beef muscle. Am J Med Sci 178: 748–764
49. Smith E L, Parke L F J 1948 Purification of the anti-pernicious anaemia factor. Biochem J 43: viii
50. Rickes E L, Brink N G, Koniuszy F R, Wood T R, Folkers K 1948 Crystalline vitamin B₁₂. Science NY 107: 396–397
51. Green R, van Tonder S V, Oettle G J, Cole G, Metz J 1975 Neurological changes in fruit bats deficient in vitamin B₁₂. Nature 254: 148–150
52. Chung A S M, Pearson W N, Darby W J, Miller O N, Goldsmith G A 1961 Folic acid, vitamin B₆, pantothenic acid and vitamin B₁₂ in human dietaries. Am J Clin Nutr 9: 573–582
53. Castle W B 1953 Development of knowledge concerning the gastric intrinsic factor and its relation to pernicious anaemia. N Engl J Med 249: 603–614
54. Wills L 1931 Treatment of 'pernicious anaemia of pregnancy' and 'tropical anaemia' with special reference to yeast extract as a curative agent. Br Med J 1: 1059–1064
55. Wills L 1953 The nature of the haemopoietic factor in Marmite. Lancet 1: 1283–1286
56. Mitchell H K, Snell E E, Williams R J 1941 The concentration of folic acid. (Letter.) J Am Chem Soc 63:2284
57. Davidson L S P, Girdwood R H 1947 Folic acid as a therapeutic agent. Br Med J 1: 587–591
58. Chanarin I, Deacon R, Lumb M, Perry J 1980 Vitamin B₁₂ regulates folate metabolism by the supply of formate. Lancet 2: 505–507
59. Reynolds E H 1973 Anticonvulsants, folic acid and epilepsy. Lancet 1: 1376–1378
60. Charnarin I 1980 In: Barker B M, Bender D A Vitamins in medicine. Heinemann, London, vol 1, p 281–283
61. Phillips D R, Wright A J A, Southgate D A T 1982 Values for folates in food (Letter.) Lancet 2:605
62. Godwin H A, Rosenberg H I 1975 Comparative studies of intestinal absorption of (³H)pterylmonoglutamate and (³H)pterylhepaglutamate. Gastroenterology 69: 364–373
63. Tamura T, Stokstad E L R 1973 Availability of food folate in man. Br J Haematol 25: 513–532
64. Herbert V 1968 Folic acid deficiency in man. Vitam Horm 26: 525–535
65. Birch T W, György P 1936 A study of the chemical nature of vitamin B₆ and methods for its preparation in a concentrated state. Biochem J 30: 304–315
66. György P 1971 Developments leading to the metabolic role of vitamin B₆. Am J Clin Nutr 24: 1250–1256
67. Coursin D B 1954 Convulsive seizures in infants with pyridoxine deficient diet. JAMA 154: 406–408
68. Schaumburg H, Kaplan J, Windebank A, et al 1983 Sensory neuropathy from pyridoxine abuse. N Engl J Med 309: 445–448
69. Scriver C R 1967 Vitamin B₆ deficiency and dependency in man. Am J Dis Child 113: 109–114
70. Mason D Y, Emmerson P M 1973 Primary acquired sideroblastic anaemia: response to treatment with pyridoxal-5-phosphate. Br Med J 1: 389–390
71. Williams R J 1939 Pantothenic acid — vitamin. Science N Y 89:486
72. Kerrey E, Crispin S, Fox H M, Kies C 1968 Nutritional status of preschool children. I: Dietary and biochemical findings. Am J Clin Nutr 21: 1274–1279
73. Sydenstricker V P, Singal S A, Briggs A P, DeVaughn N M, Isbell H 1942 Observations on the 'egg white' injury in man. JAMA 118: 1199–1200
74. Williams R H 1973 Clinical biotin deficiency. N Engl J Med 228: 247–252
75. Scott D 1958 Clinical biotin deficiency (egg white injury). Acta Med Scand 162: 69–70
76. Baugh C M, Malone J H, Butterworth C E 1968 Human biotin deficiency induced by raw egg consumption in a cirrhotic patient. Am J Clin Nutr 21: 173–182
77. Nisenson A 1969 Seborrheic dermatitis of infants: treatment with biotin injection for the nursing mother. Pediatrics 44:1014
78. Thoene J, Baker H, Yoshino M, Sweetman L 1981 Biotin-responsive carboxylase deficiency associated with subnormal plasma and urinary biotin. N Engl J Med 304: 817–822
79. Tanaka K 1981 New light on biotin deficiency. (Editorial.) N Engl J Med 304: 839–840

15

Dietary Standards

Food supplies and diets often have to be planned. Ration scales for soldiers and for schools and institutions had to be drawn up from estimates of requirements based on observations of the amounts of food eaten by healthy persons. The Romans sometimes gave their legionaries a ration of one librum of wheat. The librum became the European pound. One pound of wheat flour or other cereal is now known to provide the energy needed for the resting metabolism of an adult man and is still a practical unit for planning food supplies when a cereal provides a greater part of the dietary energy.

In the nineteenth century, when knowledge of the chemical constituents of foods was first available, it became possible to state dietary requirements in terms of nutrients rather than foods. Since about 1925, when quantitative knowledge of requirements for vitamins began to be accumulated, it has become possible to give estimates of human dietary requirements for an increasing number of nutrients.

These are now set out in tables of recommended dietary intakes or allowances (RDI or RDA). There are many of these prepared by nutritionists in different countries. The terms RDI and RDA are not distinguishable. Two well-known ones[1,2] are reproduced here as Table 15.1 and Tables 15.2a and b. These are used in five different ways.

How recommended dietary intakes are used

Assessment of dietary surveys
RDIs provide a standard against which the nutrients in the food eaten by different sections of the community or a whole country can be assessed. In the annual reports of the British National Food Survey the diets of samples of different sections of the population are compared against the RDI of the Department of Health and Social Security.[3] In this way it is possible to detect any group with a low intake of one or more nutrients. Any such group may then be investigated and, if clinical or biochemical evidence of deficiency (Chap. 55) is found, steps are taken to improve their diet or provide a supplement of nutrients.

RDIs should not be used to assess the diet of an individual patient as they are designed to be higher than average requirements.

Planning diets
Authorities planning diets of ordinary food for institutions, e.g. boarding schools, old people's homes and prisons, and for the armed services and special therapeutic diets for individuals, should ensure that the diet meets the RDI. Caterers in institutions usually derive their menus from traditional wisdom, but if a complaint about under-feeding arose RDIs would be used in the enquiry.

Planning food supplies
International agencies use RDIs in planning long-term aid for underdeveloped regions and for calculating food supplies needed for famine relief. All national governments should, in forming agricultural policies, use RDIs as the common ground between economic planners and nutritionists. However, it is not possible to diagnose the nutritional deficiencies present in a country by comparing average food available per head against the RDI, because the distribution of available foods in various sections of the population is often very uneven.

Nutritional labelling
For canned and packed foods the amounts of important nutrients in an average serving may be given on the label, expressed as a proportion of the recommended intake for the intended consumer (Chap. 26).

Nutrient density
The nutrient value of any food may be expressed in terms of its content of nutrients and of energy, each related to RDI. This is the nutrient density and for any one nutrient in a food is

$$\frac{(\text{Nutrient in 100 g})/(\text{energy in 100 g})}{(\text{RDI of nutrient})/(\text{RDI of energy})}$$

This concept is especially useful for new types of manufactured foods and foods enriched with synthetic foods.

Thus the nutrient density of thiamin in bread made from 70 per cent extraction white flour (thiamin 0.08 mg and energy 1.43 MJ/100 g) in the diet of a sedentary man (RDI, thiamin 1.1 mg and energy 11.3 MJ/day) is

$$\frac{0.08}{143} \times \frac{11.3}{1.1} = 0.57$$

As the value is far below 1.0, the bread is a poor source of thiamin and other richer sources are needed in the diet to meet the RDI. If the flour is enriched with thiamin so as to contain 0.24 mg/100 g, as is the law in the UK, then its nutrient density is 1.7. Bread made from such flour is a good source of thiamin. Even if eaten with a thick covering of butter or jam, providing extra energy but little or no thiamin, the nutrient density would be above 1.0 and thus satisfactory.

How recommended dietary intakes are derived

Committees produce RDIs. Their first step is to decide whether a compound is an essential nutrient for man. If an organic compound, it must cure a deficiency disease. If an inorganic element, it must be found regularly in the body and shown to have a function. The next decisions are how low the intake of the nutrient can fall before disease occurs and how much of it prevents or cures the deficiency disease. For most nutrients the minimum requirement needed to prevent deficiency disease can be stated with some precision.

Persons who show no evidence of deficiency disease may not be in full health. Amounts of a nutrient greater than the minimum requirement may be utilised physiologically and this may promote health. Some biochemical studies are aimed at defining criteria of optimal nutrition and here there are possibilities for different opinions. Thus the US Food and Nutrition Board was concerned that the tissues should be saturated with vitamin C while in Britain the Department of Health and Social security consider that 'in the UK few of us are saturated with the vitamin but we do not appear to suffer any ill effects as a result.' The RDA for ascorbic acid for adults was 70 mg in the USA and only 30 mg in the UK.

Safety factors have to be added to average minimum requirements to deal with three variables. The first is the range of physiological requirements, which is very wide for some nutrients; the safety factor covers the majority (about 95 per cent) of individuals. The second is the possible increase in the requirements caused by the minor stresses of everyday life; however, RDIs do not allow for infections, injuries and other illnesses. A third variable sometimes considered is the different availability of a nutrient in various foods. For example FAO/WHO recommendations for iron (Table 15.1) are adjusted for the proportion of animal food in the diet, because haem iron is more readily absorbed than iron in vegetable foods (Chap. 11).

RDIs for energy contrasted with those for nutrients

That the RDI for nutrients and for energy are presented in separate tables in the USA emphasises a fundamental difference. It is not possible to recommend exactly how much energy an individual requires to get from his food. It depends on how physically active he is at work and at leisure, and varies from time to time. If all of a class of 100 students were to eat exactly their RDI of energy for two weeks, about half would lose and half would gain weight. If the students were forced to continue this experiment for a year, then a few of them would be seriously undernourished and some would have become obese. RDIs for energy are a catering average; individuals take more or less according to appetite which follows their energy expenditure. On the other hand, RDIs for protein, vitamins and minerals supply the needs of the great majority of people and without causing adverse effects from overdosage in any.

RDIs in different countries

In some countries figures for the RDI of some nutrients, e.g. protein, ascorbic acid, calcium and iron, have changed over the years. For these nutrients there is uncertainty how to define both adequate and optimal nutritional status. Foods rich in good quality protein or ascorbic acid or calcium or iron are usually expensive, and it is impractical to set RDIs for these nutrients as high as they are in some richer countries. When the American RDIs were first published in 1943, a practical Indian nutritionist remarked to R.P., 'They are a beautiful dream.' For other nutrients which are less controversial or have not attracted as much research interest by nutritional scientists, the dietary standards change little with time or place. Examples are thiamin and nicotinamide.

A report[4] by the Committee on International Dietary Allowances of the International Union of Nutritional Sciences (1975) compares RDIs in 41 countries, groups of countries and international agencies.

The RDIs of 15 European countries and WHO/FAO are compared by Wretlind.[5] For adult males RDIs for protein range from 60 to 120 g, for calcium from 500 to 1500 mg and for ascorbic acid from 30 to 100 mg. Clearly the committees were not interpreting in the same way established knowledge of physiological needs, and perhaps they were sometimes more concerned with social wants. In this critical and entertaining essay, Wretland balances himself delicately on the fence. He quotes France and Switzerland as two countries with no official RDIs or other dietary standards and the reader may suspect that he considers them sensible. He suggests that all that is wanted are statements of desirable nutrients densities, applicable to all diets, and of minimum physiological needs below which symptoms of deficiencies may be expected.

Table 15.1 World Health Organization Recommended Intakes (Passmore et al)[1]

Age	Body weight (kg)	Energy (kcal)	Energy (MJ)	Protein[a] (g)	Vitamin A[b] (µg)	Vitamin D[c] (µg)	Thiamin (mg)	Riboflavin (mg)	Niacin (mg)	Folic acid (µg)	Vitamin B12 (µg)	Ascorbic acid (mg)	Calcium (g)	Iron[d] (mg)
Children														
<1	7.3	820	3.4	14	300	10.0	0.3	0.5	5.4	60	0.3	20	0.5–0.6	5–10
1–3	13.4	1360	5.7	16	250	10.0	0.5	0.8	9.0	100	0.9	20	0.4–0.5	5–10
4–6	20.2	1830	7.6	20	300	10.0	0.7	1.1	12.1	100	1.5	20	0.4–0.5	5–10
7–9	28.1	2190	9.2	25	400	2.5	0.9	1.3	14.5	100	1.5	20	0.4–0.5	5–10
Male adolescents														
10–12	36.9	2600	10.9	30	575	2.5	1.0	1.6	17.2	100	2.0	20	0.6–0.7	5–10
13–15	51.3	2900	12.1	37	725	2.5	1.2	1.7	19.1	200	2.0	30	0.6–0.7	9–18
16–19	62.9	3070	12.8	38	750	2.5	1.2	1.8	20.3	200	2.0	30	0.5–0.6	5–9
Female adolescents														
10–12	38.0	2350	9.8	29	575	2.5	0.9	1.4	15.5	100	2.0	20	0.6–0.7	5–10
13–15	49.9	2490	10.4	31	725	2.5	1.0	1.5	16.4	200	2.0	30	0.6–0.7	12–24
16–19	54.4	2310	9.7	30	750	2.5	0.9	1.4	15.2	200	2.0	30	0.5–0.6	14–28
Adult man (moderately active)	65.0	3000	12.6	37	750	2.5	1.2	1.8	19.8	200	2.0	30	0.4–0.5	5–9
Adult woman (moderately active)	55.0	2200	9.2	29	750	2.5	0.9	1.3	14.5	200	2.0	30	0.4–0.5	14–28
Pregnancy (later half)		+350	+1.5	38	750	10.0	+0.1	+0.2	+2.3	400	3.0	50	1.0–1.2	e
Lactation (first 6 months)		+550	+2.3	46	1200	10.0	+0.2	+0.4	+3.7	300	2.5	50	1.0–1.2	e

a As egg or milk protein.
b As retinol.
c As cholecalciferol.
d On each line the lower value applies when over 25 per cent of calories in the diet come from animal foods, and the higher value when animal foods represent less than 10 per cent of calories.

e For women whose iron intake throughout life has been at the level recommended in this table, the daily intake of iron during pregnancy and lactation should be the same as that recommended for non-pregnant, non-lactating women of childbearing age. For women whose iron status is not satisfactory at the beginning of pregnancy, the requirement is increased; and in the extreme situation of women with no iron stores, the requirement can probably not be met without supplementation.

Table 15.2a USA Recommended Daily Dietary Allowances.[2] These are designed for the maintenance of good nutrition of practically all healthy people in the USA. (In the original report this table has long footnotes setting out how values for fat-soluble vitamins and niacin are expressed and other explanatory notes. These have been omitted as most of this information can be found in earlier chapters of the book)

	Age (years)	Weight (kg)	Weight (lb)	Height (cm)	Height (in)	Protein (g)	Fat-Soluble Vitamins Vit A (µg RE)	Vit D (µg)	Vit E (mg α-TE)	Water-Soluble Vitamins Vit C (mg)	Thiamin (mg)	Riboflavin (mg)	Niacin (mg NE)	Vit B6 (mg)	Folacin (µg)	Vit B12 (µg)
Infants	0.0–0.5	6	13	60	24	kg × 2.2	420	10	3	35	0.3	0.4	6	0.3	30	0.5
	0.5–1.0	9	20	71	28	kg × 2.0	400	10	4	35	0.5	0.6	8	0.6	45	1.5
Children	1–3	13	29	90	35	23	400	10	5	45	0.7	0.8	9	0.9	100	2.0
	4–6	20	44	112	44	30	500	10	6	45	0.9	1.0	11	1.3	200	2.5
	7–10	28	62	132	52	34	700	10	7	45	1.2	1.4	16	1.6	300	3.0
Males	11–14	45	99	157	62	45	1000	10	8	50	1.4	1.6	18	1.8	400	3.0
	15–18	66	145	176	69	56	1000	10	10	60	1.4	1.7	18	2.0	400	3.0
	19–22	70	154	177	70	56	1000	7.5	10	60	1.5	1.7	19	2.2	400	3.0
	23–50	70	154	178	70	56	1000	5	10	60	1.4	1.6	18	2.2	400	3.0
	51+	70	154	178	70	56	1000	5	10	60	1.2	1.4	16	2.2	400	3.0
Females	11–14	46	101	157	62	46	800	10	8	50	1.1	1.3	15	1.8	400	3.0
	15–18	55	120	163	64	46	800	10	8	60	1.1	1.3	14	2.0	400	3.0
	19–22	55	120	163	64	44	800	7.5	8	60	1.1	1.3	14	2.0	400	3.0
	23–50	55	120	163	64	44	800	5	8	60	1.0	1.2	13	2.0	400	3.0
	51+	55	120	163	64	44	800	5	8	60	1.0	1.2	13	2.0	400	3.0
Pregnant						+30	+200	+5	+2	+20	+0.4	+0.3	+2	+0.6	+400	+10
Lactating						+20	+400	+5	+3	+40	+0.5	+0.5	+5	+0.5	+100	+1.0

Minerals

Calcium (mg)	Phosphorus (mg)	Magnesium (mg)	Iron (mg)	Zinc (mg)	Iodine (µg)
360	240	50	10	3	40
540	360	70	15	5	50
800	800	150	15	10	70
800	800	200	10	10	90
800	800	250	10	10	120
1200	1200	350	18	15	150
1200	1200	400	18	15	150
800	800	350	10	15	150
800	800	350	10	15	150
800	800	350	10	15	150
1200	1200	300	18	15	150
1200	1200	300	18	15	150
800	800	300	18	15	150
800	800	300	18	15	150
800	700	300	10	15	150
+400	+400	+150		+5	+25
+400	+400	+150		+10	+50

Table 15.2b Mean heights and weights and recommended energy intakes for the USA[2]

Category	Age (years)	Weight (kg)	Weight (lb)	Height (cm)	Height (in)	Energy needs (with range) (kcal)		Energy needs (with range) (MJ)
Infants	0.0–0.5	6	13	60	24	kg × 115	(95–145)	kg × 0.48
	0.5–1.0	9	20	71	28	kg × 105	(80–135)	kg × 0.44
Children	1–3	13	29	90	35	1300	(900–1800)	5.5
	4–6	20	44	112	44	1700	(1300–2300)	7.1
	7–10	28	62	132	52	2400	(1650–3300)	10.1
Males	11–14	45	99	157	62	2700	(2000–3700)	11.3
	15–18	66	145	176	69	2800	(2100–3900)	11.8
	19–22	70	154	177	70	2900	(2500–3300)	12.2
	23–50	70	154	178	70	2700	(2300–3100)	11.3
	51–75	70	154	178	70	2400	(2000–2800)	10.1
	76+	70	154	178	70	2050	(1650–2450)	8.6
Females	11–14	46	101	157	62	2200	(1500–3000)	9.2
	15–18	55	120	163	64	2100	(1200–3000)	8.8
	19–22	55	120	163	64	2100	(1700–2500)	8.8
	23–50	55	120	163	64	2000	(1600–2400)	8.4
	51–75	55	120	163	64	1800	(1400–2200)	7.6
	76+	55	120	163	64	1600	(1200–2000)	6.7
Pregnancy						+300		
Lactation						+500		

The data have been assembled from the observed median heights and weights of children, together with weights for adults given by life insurance companies. The energy allowances for the young adults are for men and women doing light work. The allowances for the two older age groups allow for a decrease in resting metabolic rate and reduction in activity. Energy allowances for children through age 18 are based on median energy intakes of children of these ages followed in longitudinal growth studies. The values in parentheses are 10th and 90th percentiles of energy intake to indicate the range of energy consumption among children of these ages.

The WHO/FAO report[1] condenses judgments on energy and nutrient requirements by a series of expert committees convened in the 1960s or early 1970s. The values given provide a basis for assessment of nutrient intakes but in some cases they would be unacceptably low for prescription of diets in affluent populations. The US report[2] gives the best-known recommendations from an industrial country. The report explains how the recommendations have been derived and how they are meant to be used.

THE FUTURE: A NEED FOR TWO DIETARY STANDARDS

Committees have long been aware that their recommendations are used both for assessment and planning, and aware also of the difficulties in providing figures suitable for both purposes. The chief difficulty is that diets customary in many countries, and accepted as good, often provide far more of some nutrients, especially protein, calcium and vitamin A, than appears to be needed to meet physiological requirements. This difficulty and others are considered by Hegsted[6] in a critical review. He suggested the need for two standards. The first, based on estimates of nutrient needs, would be for use in assessment or evaluation of diets. The second, for which food supplies, food habits and the aims of nu-

trition education would be considered, would be for use in planning.

This approach was used at the Round Table Discussion on Recommended Intakes at the Second European Nutrition Conference in Munich in 1976.[7] Two levels of dietary standards were suggested. 'The **group physiological requirement**, or "safe level", is useful for evaluating diets or diagnosing an unsatisfactorily low intake of one or more nutrients. The **recommended intake**, or **desirable range**, is intended for teaching, for menu planning by housewives, dietitians, caterers, and ultimately for agricultural economic planning. These prescriptive values are higher than the requirements and may be expressed in foods . . . . Where a country's recommended intake for protein is generous — say 65 g for an adult — this cannot be used as a criterion for assessing if a diet is adequate; a low standard has to be found such as the FAO/WHO value of 37 g or the British "minimum" of 45 g/day'. A third standard, an upper limit above which undesirable toxic effects may be expected, would be useful. This could be stated with some confidence for vitamins A and D and for several trace elements, but not for vitamin C.

Recommendation might be more useful and practical if based on available food supplies, rather than on estimates of physiological needs. An estimate of what foods constitute an average British diet, based on data in reports of the National Food Survey and expressed in terms of 12 classes of foods has been made.[8] Changes are then suggested that could lead to a Better British Diet. The health of the population might be improved if consumption of oils and fats, sugar and alcoholic beverages were reduced. Economic factors might reduce consumption of meat but this would have no adverse effect on health. The loss of energy from decreased consumption of these foods could be made good by increased consumption of grain products, potatoes, fruit and vegetables. Figures are suggested for the amounts of these changes which might be practical over 10 years. None of the changes is revolutionary but most of them reverse trends in consumption in recent years. This suggestion for an improved national diet could be used as a basis for recommended intakes for purposes of planning, as indicated at the Munich discussion.

REFERENCES

1. Passmore R, Nicol B M, Rao M N, and two others 1974 Handbook on human nutritional requirements. FAO Nutr Stud no 28. WHO Monogr Ser no 61
2. Committee on Dietary Allowances, Food and Nutrition Board 1980 Recommended dietary allowances, 9th revised edn. National Academy of Sciences, Washington DC
3. Department of Health and Social Security 1979, reprinted with revision 1981 Recommended daily amounts of food energy and nutrients for groups of people in the United Kingdom. Report by the Committee on Medical Aspects of Food Policy. HMSO, London
4. Truswell A S, and 10 others 1983 Recommended dietary intakes around the world. Nutr Abstr Rev 53: 1075–119
5. Wretlind A 1982 Standards for nutritional accuracy of the diet: European and WHO/FAO viewpoints. Am J Clin Nutr 36: 366–75
6. Hegsted D M 1975 Dietary standards J Am Diet Assoc 66: 13–21
7. Wretlind A, Hedja S, Isakasson B, Kübler W, Truswell A S, Vivanco F 1977 Round table on comparison of dietary recommendations in different European countries. Nutr Metab 21: 210–49
8. Passmore R, Hollingsworth D, Robertson J 1979 Prescription for a better British diet. Br Med J 1: 527–31

PART TWO

Food

It is not easy to ascertain the exact quantity and quality of food proper for every age, sex, and constitution: But a scrupulous nicety here is by no means necessary. The best rule is to avoid all extremes. Mankind were never intended to weigh and measure their food. Nature teaches every creature when it has enough of food, and a very small degree of reason is sufficient for the choice of it. Men seldom err in this respect through ignorance. The most knowing are generally the most guilty.

Tho' MODERATION *be the only rule necessary with respect to the quantity of food, yet the quality of it merits further attention. Many people, if they can satisfy the appetites of hunger and thirst, are very indifferent what they eat or drink. The following observations will show the danger of such conduct.*

Provisions may be rendered unwholesome various ways. Bad seasons may either prevent the ripening of grain, or damage it afterwards. Wet and cold summers seldom bring the fruits of the earth to maturity; and if the harvest likewise prove rainy, they are often so damaged as to be very hurtful. These indeed are acts of Providence; it is therefore our duty to submit to them: But surely no punishment can be too severe for those who suffer provisions to be spoilt, by hoarding them on purpose to enhance the price. The soundest grain, if kept too long, must become unfit for use.

The poor are generally the first who suffer by unsound provisions: But the lives of the labouring poor are of the greatest importance to the state. Besides, diseases occasioned by unwholesome food often prove infectious, and by that means reach people in every station.

Buchan W 1769 Domestic medicine. Edinburgh, p 64

16

Foods and Food Composition Tables

The physiological roles of the essential nutrients, carbohydrates, fats, proteins, minerals and vitamins have now been considered. Next it is necessary to describe the principal foods of man in terms of these nutrients. Foods are conveniently classified in ten categories: (1) cereals, (2) starchy roots, (3) sugars and syrups, (4) pulses, nuts and seeds, (5) vegetables, (6) fruits, (7) meat, fish eggs and novel proteins, (8) milk and milk products, (9) oils and fats, and (10) beverages. First a brief account is given of food tables, which describe individual foods in terms of their content of nutrients.

It is now 100 years since the first food composition tables were published in 1878 by König in Germany.[1] These were followed in 1896 by the classic American tables compiled by Atwater and Woods.[2] Some of the many tables now available are listed in Table 16.1. Every dietitian and nutritionist should be in possession of one of these or some other suitable table of food values, for it is these tables that enable dietetics to be a science as well as an art.

Widdowson and McCance[3] have aptly stated: 'There are two schools of thought about food tables. One tends to regard the figures in them as having the accuracy of atomic weight determinations; the other dismisses them as valueless on the grounds that a foodstuff may be so modified by the soil, the season or its rate of growth than no figure can be a reliable guide to its composition. The truth, of course, lies somewhere between these points of view.' To understand the information that tables provide, and to assess their reliability and accuracy it is necessary to read the introductions which describe how they have been compiled. If this is not done the tables may be abused by improper application.

Applications

Clinical practice
Accurate prescribing of diets containing known amounts of some of the important nutrients is essential for the treatment of certain diseases. Diets low in energy for obese patients, diets containing known amounts of carbohydrate and fat for diabetics, diets rich in protein for the nephrotic syndrome, and diets with a low sodium content for patients with congestive heart failure are well-known examples.

Accurate interpretation of a dietary history may be a valuable aid to diagnosis. For example, an estimate of the amount of ascorbic acid in a patient's previous diet may assist in deciding whether a purpuric rash is a manifestation of scurvy or of some blood disease. Many problems of this nature arise in clinical medicine.

Community health
In a dietary survey after intakes of the different foods have been measured, tables have to be used to calculate intakes of the various nutrients; then comparisons with recommended intakes (Chap. 15) allow judgements to be made as to whether these intakes are or are not sufficient to maintain the group in good health. From statistics of national agricultural production and of imports and exports of food and census data, food tables are used to calculate the amounts of nutrients per head of population in a country. In this way Ministries of Agriculture make use of food tables in planning national diets. The food industry also uses food tables in planning and promoting the use of new foods.

In prescribing diets for closed communities such as the armed services, boarding schools, old people's homes, prisons, etc. it is important to make sure that any recommended ration scale is compared with acceptable standards and that its use is not likely to cause deficiency disease.

The large number of calculations required, even for an individual patient, let alone a community sample, make the use of a computer very helpful. Food tables are now available as input material for computers.

Clinical research
Tables are useful as a guide in the planning stages, but they rarely provide information about intake of nutrients which is precise enough to allow an accurate balance to be drawn up.

Limitations

How far can food tables help to provide answers to the practical problems discussed above? There is the drawback that each figure in the table can only be an average of the analysis of a limited number of samples of each food. Laboratory errors are small for most methods and can be minimised by replication. Sampling error is very important, especially when whole dishes or meals are analysed. For any single plant or animal foodstuff there are small individual genetic variations; there are large possibilities of differences in composition due to the variety or strain, and equally large effects from conditions of culture or husbandry and maturity or freshness. The effect of cooking is considered in Chapter 23. For this reason it is best to use tables based on analyses of local foods. A few principles can be set out which indicate the significance of these variations and so allow an intelligent use of the tables.

Water

Variation in the water content of foods is the main cause of variation in the content of other nutrients. Thus figures for the composition of foods containing large amounts of water are always uncertain. Cereal grains contain relatively little water and, although there are variations in the nutrient content of different varieties of the same cereal, these are relatively small. Cereals have been extensively analysed and tables give reliable figures for most of them. Diets with a high cereal content are usually eaten by poor people. Thus the error involved in calculating the nutrients consumed by a farm worker in Kenya, living mainly on maize and sorghum, is much less than the error in making a similar calculation for a business executive in Chicago with his varied diet.

Proximate principles

Perhaps the least variable of the chemical constituents of foods is protein. On numerous occasions when the protein content of a diet has been calculated from tables and simultaneously determined by analyses of aliquot portions of the diet, there has been very good agreement. The error in using tables to calculate the protein content of a diet is not likely to be more than 7 per cent.

The error in estimating carbohydrate and fat from the tables is also not very great — with one important exception. This is the calculation for meat. There are large variations in the fat content of different helpings of beef, mutton or pork and people vary greatly in the amount of fat on meat they eat or reject. These greatly affect the calculated energy value.

Energy

The energy value of a diet can usually be calculated with an accuracy sufficient for practical purposes. However,

it is necessary to know the way in which the energy values given in a table have been calculated in order not to make invalid comparisons with other data. The error introduced by the use of tables should not be more than 10 per cent unless the diet contains large quantities of meat. Thus estimates can be made with the help of the tables, which suffice for most clinical and public health purposes. The tables have sufficient accuracy for use in prescribing for obese and diabetic patients. The error will be minimal in assessing simple diets based on cereals and at a maximum with rich mixed diets. Error of up to 10 per cent are too great for most metabolic studies, and tables of food analyses are of little use to clinical scientists and physiologists, who must make their own analyses on aliquot samples of their subjects' diets.

Vitamins

The variations in the vitamin content of foods is very much greater than the variations in proximate principles. They are especially large in all classes of vegetables and fruits and particularly for vitamin A activity and ascorbic acid content. These variations are so great that the use of tables to give a quantitative assessment of the vitamin content of a diet may produce a set of figures that have no factual basis. With poor diets containing only small amounts of foods rich in vitamins, the errors are less. For instance food tables should enable a statement to be made as to whether a diet contains less or more than 5 mg of ascorbic acid, i.e. whether or not it is likely to be associated with scurvy. Similar assessments can be made for vitamin A activity and the principal vitamins of the B group.

Minerals

For minerals the tables are of limited value. There are enormous variations in the iron content of different samples of the same food. Different tables can give very different values for the iron content of a diet. This is due mainly to the fact that foods are readily contaminated with iron during preparation. For calcium and trace elements, the value of the figures is limited by uncertainty as to how much of the element is available for absorption.

Sampling and other problems

Those who prepare food tables have difficulty in ensuring that the foods actually analysed are a representative sample of the foods eaten. Their difficulty arises with simple agricultural products, such as cereals, fresh meat and vegetables, but is much greater with manufactured foods. Representative sampling of foods such as cakes, ice cream, meat pies and other made-up dishes is impossible. The more these foods contribute to a diet, the less accurate is an estimate of intake of nutrients based on tables. Two reports[4,5] compare the nutrient content of diets determined by chemical analysis and calculated from tables.

The preparation of each of the tables listed below was a major task, and inevitably they soon become out of date. For example the 1978 British tables give figures for energy and some 33 nutrients for all common foods together with appendices showing 18 amino acids, 16 fatty acids, cholesterol, etc. for selected foodstuffs. New foods appear in every country, and nutritionists become interested in new components of diets. Thus most tables at present available provide inadequate information about amounts of fibre and trace elements in foods —

subjects of great current interest. Those who use food tables should not grumble too much about their inadequacies; rather they should be grateful to those who prepare the tables for their immense efforts which provide so much useful information.

The Group of European Nutritionists set up a working party to study the general principles which have to be considered in the preparation of national food composition tables. The report[6] considers the selection of food items and of nutrients, sampling procedure, statistical expression and the best chemical methods.

Table 16.1 A selected list of food tables

Food tables	Source
AFRICA *Food Composition Table for Use in Africa* Woot-Tsuen Wu Leung *et al.* (1968)	Obtainable from FAO *or* Nutrition Program, National Center for Chronic Disease Control, Public Health Service, US Department of Health, Education and Welfare, 9000 Rockville Pike, Bethesda, Md
WEST AFRICA *Aliments de l'ouest Africain — Tables de Composition* Toury, J., Giorgi, R., Favier, J. C. and Savina, J. F. (1965)	Organisation de Coordination et de Cooperation pour la lutte contre les grandes Endemies-Organisme de Recherches sur l'Alimentation et la Nutrition Africaines, Dakar, Senegal
ETHIOPIA *Food Composition Table for Use in Ethiopia* Ågren, G. and Gibson, R. (1968)	Obtainable from Children's Nutrition Unit, Addis Ababa, PO Box 1768
GHANA *Food Composition Table* (1969)	Food Research Institute — Food Research and Development Unit, Accra
SOUTH AFRICA *Studies on the Chemical Composition of Foods Commonly Used in Southern Africa* Fox, F. W. (1966)	South African Institute for Medical Research, Johannesburg
ASIA	
EAST ASIA *Food Composition Table for Use in East Asia* (1972)	US Department of Health, Education and Welfare (National Institute of Arthritis, Metabolism and Digestive Diseases, National Institutes of Health, Maryland 20014) *or* FAO, Food Policy and Nutrition Division, Rome
INDIA *Nutritive Value of Indian Foods* Gopalan, C., Rama Sastri, B. V. and Balasubramanian, S. C. (1976)	National Institute of Nutrition, Indian Council of Medical Research, Hyderabad 7
JAPAN *Standard Tables of Food Composition in Japan* (1982)	Resources Council, Science and Technology Agency Report No. 87, Tokyo
PAKISTAN *Nutritive Value of Foodstuff and Planning of Satisfactory Diets in Pakistan. Part I, Composition of Raw Foodstuffs* Chughtai, M.I.D. and Waheed Khan, A. (1960)	Division of Biochemistry, Institute of Chemistry, Punjab University, Lahore
PHILIPPINES *Food Composition Table Recommended for Use in the Philippines. Handbook I* 3rd revision (1964)	The Food and Nutrition Research Center, National Science Development Board, Manila
AUSTRALIA *Tables of Composition of Australian Foods*, revised edition Thomas, S. and Corden, M. (1977)	Australian Commonwealth Department of Health, Nutrition Section, Canberra

Table16.1(contd.)

Food tables	Source
EUROPE	
DENMARK *Fodevare-og ernaeringstabeller* Rich Ege-Nyt. (1969)	Nordish Forlag, Arnold Busck, Copenhagen
FINLAND *Ruoka-Aine-Taulukko* Turpeinen, O. and Roine, P. (1967)	Department of Biochemistry, College of Veterinary Medicine, Hameentie 57, Helsinki
FRANCE *Tables de Composition des Aliments* Randoin, L., Legallic, P., Dupuis, Y. and Beradin, A. (1961)	Institut Scientific d'Hygiene Alimentaire, Centre National de la Recherche Scientifique, Paris
HUNGARY *Food Composition Tables*, 7th edition Tarján, R. and Lindner, K. (1972)	Medicinakonyvkiado, Budapest
ITALY *Composizione in alcuni principi nutritiv e valore calorico degli alimenti comunemente in Italia* (1968)	National Institute of Nutrition, Rome (for internal use of the Institute, not published)
NETHERLANDS *Nederlandse Voedingsmiddeln Tabel*, 30th edition (1977) (revised regularly)	Voorlichtingsbureau voor de Voeding, Laan Copes van Cattenburch 44, Den Haag-2011
NORWAY *Naerings Middel Tabell*, 3rd edition (1966)	Pub. Landsforeningen for Kosthold of Helse, Oslo
POLAND *Tabele skladu I wartosci odzywczych produktow spozywczych* Szczygla, A. (ed) (1972)	Panstwowy Zaklad Wydawrietw Lekarskich, Warsaw
SWEDEN *Fadoämnes-Tabeller* Abramson, E. (1971)	Svenska Bokförlaget, Bonniers, Stockholm
WEST GERMANY *Die Zusammensetzung der Lebensmittel: Nährwerttabellen* Souci, S. W., Fachmann, W. and Kraut, H. (1981)	Wissenschaftliche Verlagsgesellschaft MBH, Stuttgart
UNITED KINGDOM *McCance and Widdowson's The Composition of Foods*, 4th revised edition Paul, A. A. and Southgate, D. A. T. (1978)	H.M. Stationery Office, London
USSR *Tabulky Kalorickych a biologickych Kudnor potravin*, 2nd edition Muller, S. (1969)	SPN, Bratislava, Czechoslovakia
NEAR EAST *Food Composition Tables for the Near East* FAO Food and Nutrition Paper no. 26/1982)	Obtainable from the Food and Agricultural Organisation of the United Nations, Rome
ISRAEL *Tablaoth Herkev Hamsonoth* Guggenheim, K. (1964)	College of Nutrition and Home Economics, Ministry of Education and Culture, Jersualem
TURKEY *Gida Komposizyon Cetvelleri* Koksal, O. and Baysal, A. (1966)	School of Public Health, Ankara
AMERICA	
USA *Composition of Foods. Raw, Processed, Prepared* Agriculture Handbook No. 8 Watt, B. K. and Merrill, A. L (1963) Revision 8–1: *Dairy and Egg Products* Posati, L. P. and Orr, M. L. (1976) Revision 8–2: *Species and Herbs* Marsh, A. C., Moss, M. K. and Murphy, E. W. (1977)	Obtainable from Superintendent of Documents, US Government Printing Office, Washington, DC 20402
CANADA *Nutrient Value of Some Common Foods* Health and Welfare, Canada (1971)	Nutrition Division, Department of National Health and Welfare, Ottawa

Table 16.1(contd.)

Food tables	Source
LATIN AMERICA	
INCAP-ICNND Food Comsumption Table for Use in Latin America Woot-Tsuen Wu Leung and Flores, M (1961)	Obtainable from INCAP, Apartado Postal No. 11–88, Guatemala City, Guatemala, C.A.
CARIBBEAN	
Food Composition Tables for Use in the English Speaking Caribbean (1974)	Caribbean Food and Nutrition Institute, Kingston, Jamaica
OTHERS	
TROPICAL COUNTRIES	
Tables of Representative Values of Foods Commonly Used in Tropical Countries (MRC Special Series No. 302) Platt, B. S. (1962)	HM Stationery Office, London

FAO Updated Annotated Bibliography of Food Composition Tables (Food Composition Section, Food Consumption and Planning Branch, Nutrition Division, Rome, 1975) lists food tables from 72 countries.

REFERENCES

1. König J 1878 Chemie der menschlichen Nahrungs-und Genussmittel. Springer, Berlin. (Quoted in Kaser et al 1947)
2. Atwater W O, Woods C D 1896 The chemical composition of American food materials. US Dept Agriculture Office Experiment Stations Bull no 28. (The revised edition 1899 by Atwater W O and Bryant A P was much bigger, being based on 4000 analyses, and became better known)
3. Widdowson E M, McCance R A 1943 Food tables, their scope and limitations. Lancet 1: 230–2
4. Kaser M M, Steinkamp R C, Robinson W D, and two others 1947 A comparison of the calculated and determined caloric and vitamin content of mixed diets. Am J Hyg 46: 297–325
5. Stock A L, Wheeler E F 1972 Evaluation of meals cooked by large-scale methods: a comparison of chemical analyses and calculations from food tables. Br J Nutr 27: 439–48
6. Southgate D A T 1974 Guidelines for the preparation of food tables. Karger, Basel

17

Cereals

Cereal grains are the seeds of domesticated grasses. Stable civilisations have arisen only when primitive hunting communities have learned how to raise successive cereal crops from cultivated land. Without the use of cereals man is reduced to an uncertain and unsettled nomadic life. They have been modified and improved by centuries of cultivation and selective breeding.

In many rural areas, including large parts of Asia and Africa, cereals provide more than 70 per cent of the energy in the common diet. As a country becomes more prosperous this proportion falls, but cereals remain the most important single food. In the national diet of the UK bread and flour products provide about 29 per cent of the energy, about 15 per cent coming from bread. Only isolated people, such as the Eskimos and a few pastoral tribes, are almost entirely carnivorous and do not cultivate cereals or root crops.

World cereal production in 1980 was about 1.6×10^9 metric tons. Of this wheat, maize, rice and barley, the main cereals, provided 27, 25, 24 and 11 per cent respectively. With a world population of about 4×10^9 people about 1.0 kg a head was available daily — equivalent to 14 MJ of energy. However, most of the maize and barley is used as animal food and also for brewing and malting. The resulting meat, milk, eggs and alcoholic drinks when consumed by man provide him with only a small part of the energy that went into their production. Present-day cereal production could probably meet the needs of double the present work population, if everyone became a vegetarian and teetotal. In the decade 1970–79 cereal production increased faster (2.8 per cent annually) than growth in population (1.7 per cent annually). Although world cereal production is adequate and cereals can be readily stored and traded, serious shortage often follows a local failure of production when economic factors prevent sufficient imports. North America produces about 1.4 kg a head daily. The large surplus is exported to meet the regular needs of many other countries and is the world's main insurance agains the disasters that can arise from local famines.

Wheat is the cereal of choice in temperate or dry climates and rice in damp tropical climates. Rice grows best in the deltas of the great rivers since it is essentially a mud plant requiring an abundant water supply. Maize is a poor man's food, being hardy, easily cultivated and relatively immune from the predation of birds. Millets grow in hot climates, on poor soil with limited water supply. They are the principal crops in many dry areas in the tropics. Oats are a hardy crop and at one time the staple food of the people of Scotland, but now are grown chiefly for cattle fodder. Rye grows in poor soil in cold climates. In the last five hundred years it has been progressively replaced by wheat.

The name 'corn' is generally used in the English-speaking world to mean the most familiar local cereal — whatever the species. Thus 'corn' in Scotland means oats, in England, wheat, and in the USA, maize. The choice depends largely on climate and economic factors, but custom and precedent are also important. All cereals can be ground into flour for cakes or porridge, but only wheat and rye bake into bread.

The whole grains of all cereals have a similar chemical constitution and nutritive value. They provide energy and protein, which is usually of good quality. They contain appreciable amounts of calcium and iron, but the value of these minerals is partly discounted by the presence of phytic acid which may interfere with their absorption. Cereals are totally devoid of ascorbic acid and practically devoid of vitamin A activity. Yellow maize is the only cereal containing significant amounts of carotene. Whole cereal grains also contain useful amounts of the water-soluble B group of vitamins.

Table 17.1 shows how similar are the nutritive values of the whole grains of all the principal cereals, although their limiting amino acids differ. To ensure adequate intakes of minerals and vitamins A and C, a diet based on cereals requires supplementation with milk, fruits and vegetables. When cereal grains are consumed in their entirety an adequate supply of the B group of vitamins is ensured except in the case of maize, in which the niacin is not biologically available. If, however, the grains are first milled and outer portions of the seed, including the germ and scutellum, discarded, there is

Table 17.1 Nutritive value of the main whole cereal grains (values per 100 g)

	Energy MJ	kcal	Protein (g)	Limiting amino acid	Fat (g)	Calcium (mg)	Iron (mg)	Thiamin (mg)	Niacin (mg)	Riboflavin (mg)	Carotene (μg)	Ascorbic acid (mg)
Wheat (whole meal)	1.40	334	12.2	Lysine	2.3	30	3.5	0.40	5.0	0.17	Trace	0
Rice (husked)	1.49	357	7.5	Lysine (threonine)	1.8	15	2.8	0.25	4.0	0.12	Trace	0
Maize (whole meal)	1.19	356	9.5	Tryptophan (lysine)	4.3	12	5.0	0.33	1.5	0.13	Up to 800	0
Millet (sorghum)	1.44	343	10.1	Lysine	3.3	30	6.2	0.40	3.5	0.12	Trace	0
Oats (rolled)	1.61	385	13.0	Lysine	7.5	60	3.8	0.50	1.3	0.14	Trace	0
Rye	1.34	319	11.0	Lysine	1.9	50	3.5	0.27	1.2	0.10	Trace	0

a grave risk that there will be an insufficiency of the B group of vitamins. Fortunately oats, barley, millets and rye are usually only lightly husked and most of the whole grain is eaten. Wheat and rice, however, are invariably subjected to some degree of milling. The extent to which the milling process removes the vitamins is of importance. For a proper understanding of the nutritive value of the cereals and of the changes they undergo in preparing them as food for man it is necessary to consider the structure of the cereal grain and the composition of its parts.

WHEAT

Wheat is the most important crop in the world. There are 14 species, wild or cultivated, of the genus *Triticum*. *Triticum aestivum* or *vulgare*, the common bread wheat, contains three sets of chromosomes, i.e. 21 in its reproductive cells. Archaeological evidence indicates that it originated from relatives of einkorn (seven chromosomes) and emmer (14 chromosomes) around 8000 BC in western Asia. The genetics of wheat is a highly specialised and an important branch of science. New varieties of wheat are being developed in the main wheat-growing countries.

Hard wheats giving a strong flour, relatively rich in gluten, are the best for making bread. Soft wheats giving a weak flour with less gluten are better for making biscuits and confectionery. Flours may be blended to suit a baker's purpose.

Anatomy of the grain. A readable monograph on *Wheat in Human Nutrition* by Aykroyd and Doughty[1] elaborates many of the points mentioned below. The grain is a seed with the structure shown in Fig. 17.1. The outer coverings are the pericarp and testa which are hard, and contain much indigestible fibre. Beneath them

is the aleurone layer, which is an envelope of cells rich in protein. These outer layers form about 12 per cent of the weight of the grain. Inside is the endosperm, comprising about 85 per cent of the weight of the grain, and consisting of an inner and outer portion. The germ (or embryo) — situated at the lower end of the grain — consists of the shoot and root. The embryo is attached to the grain by a special structure, the scutellum. The embryo and scutellum are only just visible to the naked eye and form about 3 per cent of the total weight of the grain.

Distribution of nutrients in the grain. This is not uniform. The germ is relatively rich in protein, fat and several of the B vitamins. So also is the scutellum, which contains about 50 times more thiamin than the whole grain, perhaps as much as half of the total thiamin in the grain. The outer layers of the endosperm and the aleurone layer contain a higher concentration of protein, vitamins (especially niacin) and phytic acid than the inner endosperm. The inner endosperm contains most of the starch and protein in the grain.

Wheat is usually ground into flour before being prepared as food. Flour containing the whole grain may be used but usually the germ and a varying proportion of the outer layers are separated from the central portion of the grain and discarded as bran. The proportion of the whole grain that is utilised to make flour is known as the **extraction rate**. Thus an 85 per cent extraction rate flour contains 85 per cent by weight of the whole grain and 15 per cent is discarded as bran. It is important to remember that the extraction rate refers to the proportion of the original grain in the flour and not in the bran. Thus flour of a 'high extraction rate' has lost little of the aleurone layer and outer endosperm.

Nutritive value of flour
Tables 17.2 and 3 show the effects of milling at different extraction rates on the composition of the resulting

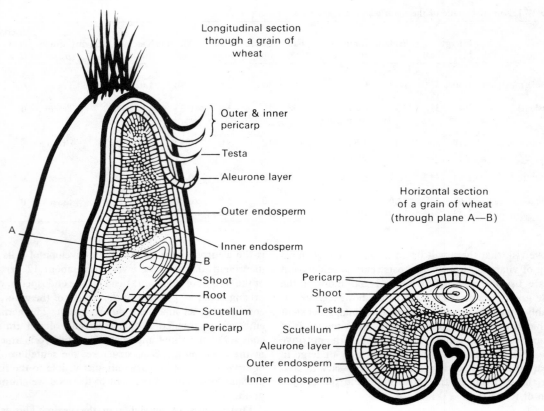

Fig. 17.1 Structure of the wheat grain (from McCance)[3]

flours. The nutritional significance of these changes have to be considered against the background of the diet. Whole wheat is devoid of vitamins A, D and C and contains very little fat and these have to supplied by other items in the diet. There are many records of healthy communities who get up to 70 per cent of their dietary energy from wheat. In an experiment which is now a classic Widdowson and McCance[4] showed that children in orphanages in Germany were healthy and grew well on diets in which 75 per cent of the energy was provided by wheat, about 20 per cent by vegetables and only about 5 per cent by foods of animal origin. Furthermore there was no difference between groups of children whose bread was made from flour of 100, 85 and 70 per cent extraction. This experiment confirmed common observation that bread made from flour was a nutritious food, even if the extraction rate was as low as 70 per cent as in most white bread.

Significance of milling losses for health

Protein. In the sample of 72 per cent extraction for which the data is given in Table 17.2, protein provides about 13 per cent of the energy. This proportion in the whole diet is more than enough to meet the needs of growth and maintain N balance provided the quality of the protein is satisfactory. Weanling rats whose sole source of protein was 75 per cent extraction flour did not gain weight as fast as those fed whole wheat flour[5] but did so when lysine was added to their white flour.[6] Lysine is the first limiting amino acid in wheat protein. However, in older rats, who grow more slowly, and also in children wheat protein contains sufficient lysine for growth provided the energy need is met, and there is no need for supplementation with lysine in ordinary circumstances. Contrary to much old-fashioned teaching bread is a good source of protein no matter what kind of flour it is made from.

Water-soluble vitamins. In low extraction flours large losses of these occur during milling, as Table 17.3 shows. When white bread made from 70 per cent extraction flour provides no more than 30 per cent of the dietary energy and the other foods are varied and of good quality, requirements of all the known vitamins in this group are likely to be met. This is the situation in prosperous industrial countries where primary dietary deficiencies due to lack of any known vitamin are uncommon. Yet the loss of the vitamins in milling in-

Table 17.2 Nutritive value of some unfortified wheat flours (values per 100 g)

Percentage extraction	Energy MJ	kcal	Protein (g)	Fat (g)	Dietary fibre (g)	Calcium (mg)	Total phosphorus (mg)	Phytate P (mg)
100	1.35	318	13.2	2.0	9.6	35	340	240
85	1.39	327	12.8	2.0	7.5	20	270	100
72	1.43	337	11.3	1.2	3.0	15	130	30
40	1.48	347	10.8	1.3	3.0	11	90	15

Table 17.3 Some micronutrients in whole wheat flour ond in flours of different extraction rate (values per 100 g) (Paul and Southgate)[2]

Percentage extraction	Thiamin (mg)	Riboflavin (mg)	Niacin (mg)	Pyridoxine (mg)	Total folate (μg)	Vitamin E (mg)	Iron (mg)	Zinc (mg)
100	0.46	0.08	5.6	0.50	57	1.0	4.0	3.0
85	0.30*	0.06	1.7*	0.30	51	trace	2.5	2.4
72	0.10*	0.03	0.7*	0.15	31	trace	1.5	0.9
40	0.10*	0.02	0.7*	0.10	10	trace	1.5	0.7

* Before fortification

creases the risk of deficiency in individuals whose diets are otherwise poor and lacking in these vitamins. For this reason white flours are often fortified with thiamin and nicotinic acid and sometimes with riboflavin. Thus in Britain without such fortification the average diets in households with low incomes would only just meet thiamin requirements. Hence there is a good reason for fortifying all low extraction flours with thiamin. Average intakes of other vitamins in this group are satisfactory without fortification. There is no evidence at present that losses of vitamins in milling cause a significant hazard to health in prosperous communities. Yet under exceptional circumstances they may be dangerous and outbreaks of beriberi have occurred in communities living mainly on white bread, e.g. in British troops beseiged in Kut, Mesopotamia, in 1915[7] and in isolated fishing communities in Newfoundland.[8]

Nearly all the vitamin E present in whole wheat is removed by milling but other dietary sources usually produce adequate amounts.

Dietary fibre. Whole wheat flour contains three times as much dietary fibre as white flour (Table 17.2). This gives it a mild laxative effect, which a few people find disagreeable. Other beneficial effects of wheat bran and of dietary fibre in general are discussed in Chapter 4.

Minerals. Whole wheat flour contains amounts of calcium, iron and zinc which would be nutritionally valuable if they were absorbed, but this is greatly impeded by binding to dietary phytate. Low extraction flours have lost much of these minerals (Tables 17.2 and 17.3) but what remains may be better absorbed because of the loss of phytate. All wheat flours are thus an un-

reliable source of minerals. White flour is often fortified with iron preparations, but it is uncertain whether significant amounts of these are absorbed and no benefit to health has been demonstrated.[9,10] Calcium was added to flour in Britain in 1942 (p. 109), but after nearly 40 years there is no evidence that our bones are any stronger as a result of the addition. The impairment of zinc absorption by unleavened wholemeal bread is described in Chapter 11.

Selection of flour

In poor rural communities in which over 60 per cent of dietary energy comes from wheat flour, the extraction rate should be high to ensure an adequate supply of B vitamins. Such flour is usually made into unleavened bread.

Increasing prosperity always leads to a more varied diet and a decreasing consumption of cereals. A great variety of breads and flour products (cakes, pastries and biscuits or cookies) are made by bakers who have to suit their customers' choices and their purses. In exercising their craft skills bakers have to select their raw material from an enormous variety of flours whose baking qualities depend on the strain of wheat, its condition of growth and the extraction rate during milling. Plant geneticists and agronomists contribute greatly to the efficiency of production of wheat and much to the baking properties of its flour[11] but relatively little to its nutritive value. The protein content of the wheat grain may be a little below 10 g/100 g or, in a few selected strains, as high as 20 g/100 g, but all wheats are satisfactory sources of protein. It is the millers who most affect the nutritive value of the final product.

Milling

In prehistoric times wheat was crushed and ground with a large stone quern. Drawings indicate that this was usually a woman's job in Egypt, where the first mention of millers was about 1500 BC.[12] Most of the flour consumed was whole meal but white flour, perhaps 80 per cent extraction, could be obtained by using sieves made from papyrus, rushes, flax or horsehair. To use white bread in a household was a sign of prestige amongst the wealthy in Athens and Rome. For some classical writers, e.g. Plato and Cato, wholemeal flour appeared to have an appeal as a symbol of the simple and good life of the countryside (McCance and Widdowson);[13] this view has been held by some people throughout history and persists today. Throughout the Middle Ages in Europe wheat was ground between large stones frequently in watermills. The flour was mostly of high extraction but white flour could be produced and was used by the rich. Thus Chaucer's prioress ate white loaves, but the poor widow in the Nun's Tale could afford only brown.

In the eighteenth century new sources of power and new machinery began to improve milling techniques. The price of white flour fell, and by the beginning of the nineteenth century it was the accepted food of the poor in Europe and North America. Millstones were replaced by steel rollers in about 1870, when there were also great improvements in techniques for sieving and bolting flour.

At this time various chemicals began to be added as flour improvers and preservatives (p. 230). The former are needed to give flours good baking qualities. Since pure vitamins became commercially available in about 1940 some of these have been added as has iron, and in Britain, calcium.

The quality of flours is regulated by laws. In the UK there are the Bread and Flour Regulations (1984). In drawing up these the Government is advised by the Food Standards Committee, whose report[14] on *Bread and Flour* gives a full account of the considerations on which the law is based. There is a list of permitted additives and limits are set to the amounts allowed in flours. Low extraction flours have to be enriched by the addition of thiamin, niacin, iron and calcium. It was recommended by the DHSS[15] that these additions be no longer mandatory but this was not accepted in drawing up the new regulations.

In the United States most low extraction flours are enriched with thiamin, riboflavin, nicotinamide and iron up to 0.44, 0.26, 3.5 and 2.9 mg/100 g respectively. Calcium and vitamin D may also be added. The law varies in different states and the additions are not usually compulsory but are needed to satisfy labelling regulations for enriched bread.

Millers have to produce the flour which their customers, whether they be commercial or home bakers, demand. Two other factors have influenced the production of white flour. First, because most of the fat in the whole grain is removed, white flour is less likely than whole meal to go rancid and so is a better commercial product. Secondly, in the Middle Ages millers kept the bran as payment for the milling and sold it as cattle fodder. The amount of bran retained could not be controlled by the customer, and both of Chaucer's millers were rogues:

A theef he was for sothe of corn and mele,
And that a sly and usaunt for to stele.

The lower the extraction rate, the more the bran that the miller can sell. We would not presume to say to what extent, if any, these factors influence the commercial policy of millers today.

Baking

This is one of the most ancient of human crafts. Early in classical times there were large numbers of professional bakers in Rome, and in most cities bread-making has always been carried out by bakers; but it is also a domestic art and before modern means of transport were available much of the bread eaten by country folk was baked in the home. Nowadays in Great Britain there are only a few housewives — and an occasional man — who like to bake their own bread but the number may be increasing.

Wheaten flour has the property that, after being mixed with water and made into dough, it rises if gas is liberated in the dough either by natural yeast fermentation or from the addition of artificial baking powder.

The protein complex gluten (a mixture of gliadin and glutelin) present only in wheat and rye gives the dough the viscid property which keeps it together and so lets it rise when distended by gas. Good bread has a firm, strong texture and the loaf stands up well. Flours made from hard wheats such as those grown in the USA and Canada have this property of 'strength' and make good bread. British wheat is 'weak' and not good for bread-making though ideal for biscuits or crackers.

Cultivated yeasts are generally used for the fermentation process. Young growing yeast is first mixed with sugar and a little flour. Fermentation soon begins and the yeast culture is then added to the dough and kneaded thoroughly. Salt, about 2 per cent, is added that toughens the gluten and makes the dough less sticky and also for its flavour. For home baking, dried yeast preparations are available. These are mixed with the flour and then water added. Fermentation is allowed to proceed until the carbon dioxide has blown the dough up to one and a half times its original size. This may take from one to four hours, depending on the nature of the yeast culture added. The dough is then kneaded again, shaped into loaves and baked in ovens at about 230°C.

The Chorleywood Bread Process, introduced in 1961, is a mechanical process which eliminates the need for the traditional and lengthy bulk fermentation of dough. High-speed mixers develop the dough in less than five minutes. As they have a high cost and high consumption of power, they can be used only by large bakeries. About 200 plants belonging to the major milling groups now produce about 70 per cent of British bread by this process. The nutritive value of the flour is not altered.[16]

Activated Dough Development is another process introduced in 1962 in the USA. In this the changes in the physical properties of the dough brought about by fermentation or mechanical mixing are achieved by chemical reducing agents. Of these the most used is L-cysteine, now a permitted additive in the United Kingdom. This confers some of the advantages of the Chorleywood process without the need for expensive equipment.

Bread

Bread has the same nutritive properties as the flour from which it was baked, but the nutrients are diluted by the water added to make the dough and the sodium content is increased from 300 to over 500 mg/100 g. In the final product the water content should not be outside the range of 35 to 40 per cent. The energy content of breads lies within the range 0.9 to 1.05 MJ (215 to 250 kcal)/100 g and the content of other nutrients is correspondingly reduced from the figures given for flours in Tables 17.2 and 3.

The flour used in bread-making is nearly always solely wheat flour, but sometimes other cereal flours and soya bean flour may be added in small amounts. Bread made from mixtures of wheat and rye are well known. There are also many speciality breads which may contain milk and milk products. There are three main types of bread.

White bread. This is made from low extraction flours which may contain additives and additional nutrients as already described.

Brown bread. By law in Britain this has to contain crude fibre in amounts of not less than 0.6 g/100 g. It is usually made from a mixture of whole wheat and white flours with a minimum of about 50 per cent whole wheat, which corresponds to an extraction rate of 85 per cent. Caramel may be added for colouring.

Wholemeal bread. This has to be made from whole wheat flour. Bleaching and improving agents are not permitted, but preservatives are.

These three breads provide respectively about 78, 12 and 10 per cent of the market in Britain. Consumption of brown bread has been rising slowly and steadily for over 20 years. Consumption of wholemeal bread was falling but is now rising. These proportions reflect consumers' choices, but may be partly determined by availability. Wholemeal bread is made mostly by small bakers and is less widely available, though shops selling a variety of wholemeal bread can be found easily in most towns.

There is no doubt that white bread is a good commercial product. It is the bread that is best suited for making sandwiches. Yet those of us who appreciate the taste of wholemeal and brown breads, as well as their additional nutritive properties, wonder why we are in such a small minority. To eat good wholemeal bread is one of the pleasures of living which many seem not to know about. The bigger millers appear to be content to manufacture a second-rate product and to make no attempt to promote their goods of quality.

High protein breads. Persons wishing to lose weight have to reduce their intake of energy but still require protein. For such people bread with more than the normal amount of protein, 13.0 to 13.5 g/100 g of dry matter, may be useful. Such breads are made by adding protein to flour, and this protein may be wheat gluten, skimmed milk or soya flour The law now permits the terms 'protein bread' and 'high protein bread' to apply to breads containing 16 and 22 per cent of protein respectively. Such breads have been described as 'starch reduced', but this is misleading and it is recommended that this term should not be permissible.

As lysine is the limiting amino acid in wheat flour, the addition of this amino acid has been suggested. However, lysine is not the limiting amino acid in British diets, which usually provide sufficient from other foods.

Biscuits. These are made from flours which are baked with very little water. Sometimes a small amount of baking powder is added. In the days of sailing ships, biscuits were consumed in large quantities at sea. In making modern fancy biscuits, sugar, fat, chocolate and flavouring agents may be added. Some biscuits such as Scottish shortbread contain up to 30 per cent fat. British wheats are very well suited for biscuit manufacture. Biscuits made in Edinburgh, Reading and other towns have acquired an international reputation for quality, and large quantities are exported. In the USA British biscuits are called 'crackers'.

Cakes and confectionery. These are made by baking wheaten flour with sugar and fat, to which eggs are sometimes added. Fruit and nuts may also be incorporated. Until sugar became regularly available and cheap, cakes were a luxury and, in the Middle Ages, were usually made only for feasts and festivals. Flour of high-extraction rate is not suitable for cake-making. Rich cakes may contain large amounts of fat and sugar and so are of high energy value.

Breakfast cereals. These only became popular in the twentieth century.[17] They are prepared from a number of cereals, including wheat, maize and rice and are not usually eaten in large amounts, but people appreciate their palatability, their ready cooked state and the attractive packages. Their chief nutritive value is that they are always eaten with milk. Some products are fortified (voluntarily) with B vitamins and even iron. There are many children who do not like milk as a drink, but consume a good amount with their daily breakfast cereal.

Other products

Toast.   Toast is made by applying dry heat to bread. This drives off some of the moisture. There are also changes in the starch grain and the brown colour is due to the Maillard reaction between protein and sugar from the starch. As water is driven off, the content of nutrients — expressed as a proportion of weight — rises. Patients on accurately prescribed diets should weigh their bread before toasting.

Macaroni, spaghetti and vermicelli.   These and other forms of Italian 'pasta' are made from a very hard variety of wheat (*Triticum durum*), high in protein, which flourishes in the warm, dry Italian climate. Only the endosperm is used for making flour for 'pasta'; consequently it is not rich in the B group of vitamins. Their very high gluten content enables the characteristic mouldings to be made.

Thus far we have described European methods of preparing wheat. In Asia and North Africa wheat is often eaten as unleavened bread. The flour used is usually of high extraction, often milled in the home.

Chapattis.   These are the common form in which wheat is eaten in India, Pakistan and Iran. They are made from wholemeal flour (atta). Coarse sieves remove some of the fibre and bran. This may amount to 5 to 7 per cent of the total weight so Indians usually eat 93 to 95 per cent extraction flour. One method of making a chapatti is as follows: the dough is first prepared by mixing the atta with water and kneading. Usually salt and a little oil are added. A portion of the dough is rolled on a wooden board until it is flat, thin and circular. It is then placed on a flat iron pan over a open fire and slowly cooked. When one side is done, the chapatti is turned over and the other side cooked. There are many minor variations in technique and chapatti-making is a subtle art. Those made by an expert are soft and tasty with the delicious flavour of whole wheat.

RICE

Rice is second to wheat in global importance as a staple food for man. It gives a higher yield per hectare but requires warm conditions. There are two cultivated species, *Oryza sativa*, Asian rice, is the major one; *O. glaberima*, African rice, is grown in parts of West Africa. The earliest archaeological remains of rice from around

Fig. 17.2 Thailand. Replanting the rice (FAO photo by Eric Schwab)

3000 BC were found in China. Most rice is grown under semi-aquatic conditions in paddy fields, but there are varieties which grow on dry land. The International Rice Research Institute (IRRI), set up in 1962 in the Philippines, has bred high yielding, semidwarf varieties, starting with IR8. Two crops of rice a year of this and other varieties can be grown under favourable conditions. A picture of rice cultivation is shown in Fig. 17.2.

The rice grain has a botanical structure similar to the wheat grain.[18] Microdissection of individual grains has enabled analyses to be made of the thiamin content of their components (Table 17.4).[18] Pericarp, aleurone and the scutellum together contain 79 per cent of the total thiamin present in the grain, although constituting only 6.2 per cent of the weight. By contrast the endosperm, which represents 92 per cent of the grain by weight, contains only 8.8 per cent of the thiamin.

Changes similar to those already described for wheat occur when rice is milled. These changes are important because rice so often forms such a large proportion of the total food of rice-eaters. The chemical properties of rice in relation to the nutritive value of rice diets are given in two monographs.[19, 20].

From time immemorial a variety of methods have been used for husking 'paddy' — the rice grain in the husk. The domestic labour of preparing rice by hand-pounding is still undertaken in parts of the East. The paddy is placed in a stone or wooden mortar, about 6 inches in diameter and 8 inches deep, and pounded with wooden pestles about 6 foot long. Usually two or more people pound together. The pounding breaks the outer husk and allows it to be separated by winnowing. Some of the germ and part of the pericarp is removed, the

Table 17.4 Thiamin content of fractions of the rice grain

Part of grain	Proportion of grain (per cent)	Thiamin content (μg/g)	Proportion of the total thiamin of the grain (per cent)
Pericarp and aleurone	5.95	31	32.5
Covering to germ	0.20	12	
Epiblast	0.27	78	3.9
Coleorhiza	0.20	94	3.5
Plumule	0.31	46	2.7
Radicle	0.17	62	2.0
Scutellum	1.25	189	43.9
Outer endosperm	18.80	1.3	
Inner endosperm	73.10	0.3	8.8

amount depending on the vigour and duration of the pounding. It is possible to produce a refined white rice almost totally devoid of vitamins by home-pounding. Yet home-pounded rice normally retains over half of the outer layers of the grain, thus conserving the greater part of the vitamins. It is essentially a high-extraction cereal grain and a satisfactory source of B vitamins. However, pounding is a wearisome domestic drudgery even if, as in many parts of Bengal and Thailand, a simple mechanical device enabling the mortar to be worked by the feet is used. It is therefore not surprising that mechanical rice mills have spread among the rice-eating people. The housewife is relieved of domestic labour, at no financial cost, since many mills are content to retain as their fee the bran removed, which is sold as cattle fodder. Mills can produce a highly refined rice, almost devoid of vitamins as Table 17.5 shows.

Table 17.5 Thiamin content of rice at different stages of milling (Aykroyd et al)[19]

	μg/g of rice
Husked only	4.0
Once polished	1.8
Twice polished	1.0
Thrice polished (ready for market)	0.7

Parboiling. There is, however, one process which is widely applied both in the home and the mill in the preparation of rice, which has a profound effect upon the content of the B group of vitamins in the final product. Parboiling is the steaming or boiling of unhusked rice after preliminary soaking. This splits the woody outer husk and renders its subsequent removal easier. Small quantities of paddy may be parboiled in domestic vessels before pounding. In the bigger mills it is steamed under pressure in large cylinders, in a process known as conversion.[21] The parboiling either drives the vitamin into the interior of the grain or may fix the scutellum so that it is less readily removed in the milling process.

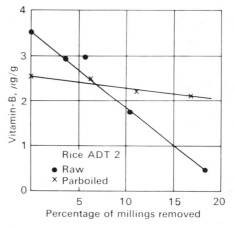

Fig. 17.3 The effect of milling in the raw and parboiled states on thiamin content of rice (Aykroyd et al)[19]

Then the vitamins are not removed with the bran and remain behind in the milled grain. Figure 17.3 shows the effect of varying degrees of milling upon the two samples of the same paddy, one parboiled and one raw; even in very highly milled samples of parboiled rice the major portion of the thiamin is still present. Similar results are obtained for nicotinic acid.

This is important for in all parts of the world where rice forms the staple article of diet beriberi has been liable to break out, except where it was the custom to parboil the rice. The parboiling of rice is the simplest preventive measure against beriberi.

In addition to milling, the rice grain is subject to another severe loss of vitamins in the washing and cooking of the cereal. Rice, purchased in the bazaar, must be washed in the home before cooking, which itself involves the use of water. Much of the water is often subsequently discarded. The B group of vitamins are all very soluble in water and heavy losses may thus result in the home. Experiments conducted under cooking conditions common in South India showed that half the thiamin and nicotinic acid that escaped the mills might be thrown away as domestic waste. Even higher losses may occur. Such losses can be reduced, first by seeing that rice reaches the home as clean as possible; this requires clean and good storage conditions in shops and bazaars. Secondly, within the home a minimum of water should be used for cooking, and all surplus should not be discarded but taken as the drink known as 'congie'.

Enrichment of rice. A field trial in the Philippines indicated that rice enriched with thiamin and other nutrients could prevent beriberi. An enrichment programme presents many technical difficulties, especially the problem of enforcement,[22] and has seldom been undertaken.

Protein content. Most samples of milled rice contain 6.5 to 8.0 g/100 g of protein, providing 7.0 to 8.5 per cent of the energy. This is less than in other cereals, but no other cereal protein is of such good quality. Lysine is the limiting amino acid. A variety has been bred with 14 g/100 g of protein which was well utilised in nitrogen balance experiments on man.[23]

MAIZE

Maize (*Zea mays*) is second to wheat in world food production. Most of this is used as feed for livestock but maize is the staple food of man in Central America and in many parts of Africa, South America and elsewhere. It is also used in the food industry in the manufacture of corn starch, glucose and some whiskies.

Maize originated in Central America and cobs have been found in archaeological material dated 5000 BC and it was the staple food of Mayan and Aztec civilisations. Columbus found maize growing in Cuba in 1492 and brought some to Europe where it quickly became established in Mediterranean countries and later in other parts of Africa and also in some places in Asia. The Pilgrim Fathers were given seeds of Indian corn by the Indians and corn was a central part of the first Thanksgiving dinner in 1621. Today nearly half of the world's maize is grown in the corn belt stretching from South Dakota to Ohio.

Maize differs from other cereals in that its numerous kernels are attached to a rigid stem and the entire ear is enclosed by the modified leaf sheath. This impedes the dispersal of grain and maize is dependent on man for its propagation.

Maize is in general much more resistant to drought than either wheat or rice. In addition it gives a high yield per acre and is relatively free from the predation of birds. It matures rapidly so that a good crop can be grown in a short season. For these reasons maize has acquired a well-deserved reputation as a poor man's cereal.

The maize grain has the same general structure as that of rice and wheat. The following preparations are used as human food.

Sweetcorn ('corn on the cob') is a type with short maturing season. It is eaten before the sugar in the endosperm has been converted to starch.

Whole maize grain. This is the whole grain which is removed from the cob after drying, usually in the sun.

Whole maize meal. Whole maize grain is ground to meal fineness either by hand-pounding or by modern techniques. The meal is not subjected to any 'bolting' and contains 97 to 100 per cent of the original grain.

Decorticated maize meal. This is the wholemeal with most of the pericarp, but none of the germ, removed by sieving or simple fanning. It usually contains 90 to 96 per cent of the original grain.

Degerminated maize meal. The wholemeal is passed through finer sieves, which remove most of the pericarp and germ. It usually contains about 85 per cent of the original grain.

Hominy or samp. This is the starchy portion of the endosperm, left after the whole grain has been softened by steaming, the pericarp removed and the germ loosened by a handling machine. In the USA hominy has acquired culinary prestige and its nutritive deficiencies are made up by other foods. In southern Africa where it may contribute a large part of the dietary energy among the poor, samp contributes to protein malnutrition.

Maize may be boiled and made into a porridge. This is the usual method in Europe and Africa. Maize may also be made into flat bread, as in tortillas. Maize itself will not make leavened bread, but it can be mixed with wheat flour and baked into good loaves.

The nutrient value of maize resembles that of other cereals in general, but differs in some important respects. Yellow maize contains a mixture of carotenoids some of which, β-carotene, cryptoxanthin and β-zea-carotene, have provitamin A activity. Values range from 100 to 800 μg/100 g (expressed as β-carotene). The principal protein in maize is zein, which forms about half the total protein in the whole grain. Zein is an imperfect protein, lacking lysine and tryptophan. This defect is important in the relation of maize to pellagra (Chap. 34). Truswell and Brock[24] measured the nutritive value of maize protein in human adults. The biological value is about 57 — not so low as was once thought. A supplement for maize protein should contain both lysine and tryptophan and possibly isoleucine. Opaque-2 is a strain of maize, homozygous for a recessive gene, which is relatively rich in lysine and tryptophan. This quality of its protein allowed the nitrogen balance to be maintained in adult men with no other significant source of protein in their diet.[25] Opaque-2 maize has been effective in preventing pellagra in an endemic area in northwest China.[26]

The niacin present in maize is in a bound form and does not become available. For this and other reasons pellagra is associated with maize eating (see p. 318). In preparing Mexican *tortillas*, the grains are softened by heating in lime-water and then ground directly into a dough and cooked on a hot iron plate. Treatment with lime-water makes the niacin available.[27]

MILLETS

Millets are cereals very resistant to drought and so have been extensively cultivated in arid regions. They are the staple food of many people in Africa and also in some areas of Asia and Latin America. With the spread of irrigation and the introduction of drought-resistant varieties of wheat, millet cultivation is tending to decline, notably in India. Ripening millets need to be watched to protect them from birds. Millets have always been regarded as a poor man's food and there are social prejudices against their use. Although this is understandable (they are much less tasty than wheat or rice) it is unfortunate, for they have good nutritive value and their protein is a valuable addition to rice protein in predominantly rice diets.

There are a variety of different millets which have an even greater variety of names. Common millets are: (1) *Sorghum vulgare*, often known as the large millet, or sorghum. In India, where it is widely grown. it is known as *juar* in the north and *cholam* in the south. (2) *Eleusine coracana* is known as *finger millet* in Africa and as *ragi* in South India. (3) *Pennisetum typhoideum* is widely grown in India and known as *bajra* in the north and *cambu* in the south. There are a variety of names for it in use in Africa; it is often referred to in scientific literature simply as 'millet'. In Ethiopia teff (*Eragrotis abyssinia*), a small millet, is the staple food. In South America quinoa (*Chenopodium quinoa*) is a hardy millet which is widely grown in the cold arid countryside on the altiplano. Many other species of millets are grown locally.

Millets, like other cereals, have to be husked. The grains may then be soaked and boiled and made into a porridge or ground into a meal. These processes are usually carried out in the home since millet-eaters are mostly simple peasants. Refined millet products have not yet appeared on any international market on an appreciable scale.

OATS

In Scotland oats became the staple food of the people in the seventeenth and eighteenth centuries, gradually replacing barley and rye. In the nineteenth century oats were in turn gradually replaced by wheat. Oatcakes and brose (oatmeal stirred into boiling water to which milk and whisky may be added) ceased to be common daily foods, while porridge survived chiefly as a breakfast dish. In the twentieth century oats have been largely ousted even from this limited position by the ubiquitous breakfast cereals; few Edinburgh people today eat porridge for breakfast.

In the milling of oats only the fibrous pericarp is usually removed and the germ is retained. Most forms of oatmeal are thus not highly refined. Oatmeal contains more protein (12 g/100) and more oil (8.5 g/100 g) than other common cereals. Frequently nowadays the grains are not ground, but crushed flat between rollers. Heat is applied during the process and the grains are thus partially cooked. The resulting 'rolled oats' are the basis of several convenient breakfast preparations.

The decline in the consumption of oatmeal is probably attributable in the main to a change in cooking habits. Porridge as traditionally cooked in Scotland is prepared the night before and left to warm on the hob of the kitchen fire overnight, or in the haybox. The introduction of gas and electric cookers has abolished this traditional practice, and although proprietary brands of rolled oats can be made into porridge in a few minutes before breakfast, a ready-cooked breakfast cereal or a loaf of wheaten bread is less trouble for the housewife working with one eye on the clock. Oatmeal is making a small come-back in the form of 'muesli' a nutritious breakfast dish of Swiss origin in which it is mixed with fruit and sometimes honey and taken with milk.

BARLEY

Barley is widely grown in almost all parts of the world. It was once much used as a human food. It produces the most satisfactory malt for brewers and is the basis of the best beers and much whisky in many countries. It is widely used as a cattle food.

RYE

Rye (*Secale cercele*) was once a common crop all over Europe and is still grown extensively in the north and east. The crops are resistant to cold. Many people like rye bread, which is tasty, rich in the B group of vitamins and also contains dietary fibre.

TRITICALE

Triticale is a new cereal, the result of crossing two genera, *Triticum* (wheat) and *Secale* (rye). The aim is to combine the winter hardiness of rye with the properties of wheat that are commercially valuable. Some promising varieties are being developed by geneticists in Canada and Mexico.

REFERENCES

1. Aykroyd W R, Doughty J 1970 Wheat in human nutrition. FAO Nutr Stud no 23
2. Paul A A, Southgate D A T 1978 The composition of foods. HMSO, London
3. McCance R A 1946 Bread. Lancet 1: 77–81
4. Widdowson E M, McCance R A 1954 Studies on the nutritive value of bread and on the effect of variations in the extraction rate of flour on the growth of undernourished children. Spec Rep Ser Med Res Coun Lond no 287
5. Chick H 1942 Biological value of the proteins contained in wheat flours. Lancet 1: 405–8
6. Hutchison J B, Moran T, Pace J 1956 Nutritive value of the protein of white and wholemeal bread on relation to the growth of rats. Proc R Soc Lond (Biol) 145: 270–9
7. Hehir P 1922 Effects of chronic starvation during the siege of Kut. Br Med J 1: 865–8
8. Aykroyd W R 1930 Beriberi and other food-deficiency diseases in Newfoundland and Labrador. J Hyg Cambridge 30: 357–86
9. Callender S T, Warner G T 1968 Iron absorption from bread. Am J Clin Nutr 21: 1170–4
10. Elwood P C, Waters W G, Sweetnam P 1971 The haematinic effect of iron in flour. Clin Sci 40: 31–7
11. Spicer A (ed) 1975 Bread, social, nutrition and agricultural aspects. Applied Science, London
12. Darby W J, Ghaliounghui P, Grivetti L 1977 Food: the gift of Osiris. Academic Press, New York
13. McCance R A, Widdowson E M 1956 Breads white and brown. Pitman, London
14. Food Standards Committee 1974 Report on bread and flour. HMSO, London
15. Department of Health and Social Security 1981 Nutritional aspects of bread and flour. Report on health and social subjects no 23. HMSO, London
16. Knight R A, Christie A A, Orton C R, Robertson J 1973 Comparison of the nutrient content of retail white bread made conventionally and by the Chorley Wood process. Br J Nutr 30: 181–8
17. Collins E J T 1976 Changing patterns of bread and cereal-eating in Britain in the twentieth century. In: The making of the modern British diet Oddy D T, Miller D S (eds) Croom Helm, London, p 26–43
18. Hinton J J C 1948 The distribution of vitamin B_1 in the rice grain. Br J Nutr 2: 237–41
19. Aykroyd W R, Krishnan B G, Passmore R, Sundararajan A R 1940 The rice problem in India. Indian Med Res Memoirs no 32
20. Food and Agricultural Organization 1954 Rice and rice diets. Nutritional Studies no 1. FAO, Rome
21. Kent N L 1978 Technology of cereals, with special reference to wheat. Pergamon Press, Oxford
22. Food and Agricultural Organization 1954 Rice enrichment in the Philippines. Nutritional Studies no 12. FAO, Rome
23. Clark H E, Howe J M, Chung-Ja Lee 1971 Nitrogen retention of adult human subjects fed on high protein rice. Am J Clin Nutr 24: 324–8
24. Truswell A S, Brock J F 1962 The nutritive value of maize protein for man. Am J Clin Nutr 10: 142–52
25. Clark H E, Allen P E, Meyers S M, and two other 1967 Nitrogen balances of adults consuming Opaque-2 maize protein. Am J Clin Nutr 20: 825–33
26. Chen Xue-Cum, Yen Tai-An, Tong Xiu-Zhen, and four others 1983 Opaque-2 maize in the prevention and treatment of pellagra. Nutr Res 3: 171–80
27. Laguna I, Carpenter K J 1951 Raw versus processed corn in niacin-deficient diets. J Nutr 45: 21–8

18

Foods from the Vegetable Kingdom

Plants are the source of many other types of food beside cereals. These are considered in this chapter under the headings starchy roots, sugars and syrups, legumes, nuts, vegetables and fruits.

STARCHY ROOTS

The potato is the most important food of this class in temperate climates. In the tropics cassava (also known as manioca, yuca and tapioca), the yams, the sweet potato and taro are all important foods. Sago, as it is very rich in starch, is usually classified with these foods, though in fact it is derived from the pith of a palm. Arrowroot and a large number of other roots are also eaten in small quantities in the tropics. Such roots all contain large quantities of starch and so are good sources of energy. For the most part they are poor in protein, minerals and vitamins.

Table 18.1 gives values for the principal nutrients in starchy roots. They are easily cultivated, often giving high yields even on poor soil, and so have been widely used by peasants in many parts of the world. The common garden root vegetables contain much less starch

and are discussed on page 201 under Vegetables. Figure 18.1 shows a typical cassava plantation in the tropics and Figure 18.2 a market.

COMMON POTATO (*Solanum tuberosum*)

This is a native of the New World. It flourished and continues to flourish on the *altiplano* in the Andes and was the staple food of the peasants under the Inca civilisation. It was introduced into Europe by the early explorers, at first as a curiosity. Cultivation spread rapidly throughout the European continent in the second half of the seventeenth century and in the eighteenth century. The introduction of the potato was initially a great blessing since it provided the peasants with a cheap alternative crop to cereals. Until the eighteenth century the history of all European countries was marked by famines due to failure of the main cereal crops as a result of drought or disease. Potato cultivation provided a second crop which allowed a population to survive a failure of the cereal harvests. The last serious famines in Scotland were during the 'six dear years' of William III's reign at the end of the seventeenth century, before the

Table 18.1 Starchy roots (potato, sweet potato, yams, taro). Composition in terms of 100 g of the retail weight, as purchased

	Range	Selected value	Notes
Moisture, per cent	65–85	—	—
Energy kJ	210–510	330	—
Energy kcal	50–125	80	—
Carbohydrate, g	10–25	18	—
Protein, g	1.5–2.5	2.0	Tapioca and sago as sold in Europe, 0.3–0.4
Fat, g	Trace	0	—
Calcium, mg	10–30	20	—
Iron, mg	0.5–2.0	0.8	—
Carotene, μg	0	0	Sweet potato: most varieties 300; deep yellow and red up to 4500
Ascorbic acid, mg	5–25	15	—
Thiamin, mg	0.05–0.10	0.075	—
Ribofalvin, mg	0.03–0.08	0.05	—
Nicotinic acid, mg	0.5–1.5	1.0	—

Fig. 18.1 Plantation of yuca (cassava or manioca)

Fig. 18.2 Cassava market

extensive cultivation of potatoes. In Ireland the potato flourished exceedingly and completely ousted cereal crops. The peasants became entirely dependent on one food crop again, and they paid the inevitable penalty. The potatoes were attacked by the blight (*Phytophthora infestans*); the harvest failed for three years from 1845 to 1847 and the people suffered one of the most disastrous famines in history. The population fell frem 8.2 million in 1841 to 6.6 million in 1851. Probably over one million died and many were forced to emigrate. Ireland has not yet recovered her former population and Boston, Glasgow and many other cities owe a large part of their present population to the potato blight.

The potato has two remarkable properties. First, it is the cheap food that can best support life when fed as the sole article of diet. In 1913 Hindhede[1] described how a man lived on a diet of 2 to 4 kg of potatoes daily with a little margarine as the only other source of food for 300 days. Secondly, potatoes yield more energy per acre than any cereal crop. The importance of this fact to an eighteenth-century peasant can be illustrated by some calculations from data collected by Young in 1771 of yields on English farms (Table 18.2).[2]

Table 18.2 Average yields from English farms in the eighteenth century

	Average annual yield per acre Bushels*	kg	Energy value of crop MJ	Acres required to provide 42 MJ
Wheat	23	650	8 900	1.7
Barley	32	820	11 400	1.4
Oats	38	690	9 300	1.6
Potatoes	427	109 000	31 900	0.5

* Young's figures for 1771. With modern agricultural techniques all yields per acre are higher, but the difference between potatoes and cereals still holds.

The first column gives Young's data in bushels, a measure of volume. The second column gives the weight of the crops and the third their approximate energy value. The last column gives the amount of land required to provide the total energy needs of a family of a man and wife with three young children (estimated at 42 MJ or 10 000 kcal/day). Thus the peasant needs less than half as much land to feed his family if he grows potatoes in place of cereals as his main crop. He also needs less land for his subsidiary crops to provide protective foods. These conditions are ideal for the landlord. Salaman in his classic book on the history of the potato has pointed out that in 'potato civilisations' the peasants have been at the mercy of their landlords. Seldom in history has man been reduced to more misery and abject poverty than the South American peasants under their Inca rulers and the Irish under their English landlords.[3]

An example of the benefit that potatoes can bring to peasant agriculturists is the story of their introduction into the Khumbu valley in Nepal, some 15 miles from Mount Everest and the homeland of the Sherpas.[3a] This occurred in about 1860 and the first potatoes probably came from the garden of the British Residency in Katmandu. They gave much higher yields in the light sandy soil than the buckwheat, previously the staple food of the Sherpas. This led to a much larger food supply and also, because the potato is easier to cultivate than buckwheat, more leisure time. As a result the population grew. In 1856 there were only 169 households in the valley and the number increased to 596. Although

Buddhism had been established in the valley for at least 300 years, the foundation of monasteries and nunneries and the building of village temples and religious monuments took place after 1860. The introduction of the potato was soon followed by a flowering of religious life.

Potatoes contain 75 to 80 per cent of water and yield from 290 to 380 kJ (70 to 90 kcal)/100 g. Of the energy, 7.6 per cent comes from protein, a negligible amount from fat and most from starch. The protein content is low, about 2 g/100 g, but it has a biological value equal to that of egg proteins when fed as a sole source of protein to man.[4] Potatoes are a useful source of protein, especially if large amounts are eaten, and of dietary fibre[5].

Potatoes contain small but not very important amounts of minerals and the B group of vitamins. They are a good source of potassium. Potatoes are not rich in ascorbic acid, but when they are eaten in large quantities they often provide a considerable proportion of the ascorbic acid in the diet. However, their ascorbic acid content is very variable; figures ranging from 4 to 50 mg/100 g are given in the literature. This wide variation is due, in part at least, to losses in storage. A figure of 30 or over is only found in freshly dug potatoes, whereas from March in the northern hemisphere until the new harvest values are usually below 10 mg. This seasonal variation can be important. In Edinburgh for instance, where patients with scurvy are occasionally seen, they appear usually in the spring and early summer and in old people living alone. The disease is seldom found after the new potatoes arrive in the shops; they probably serve to prevent scurvy throughout the autumn and winter.

The effect of cooking on the ascorbic acid content of potatoes is discussed in Chapter 22.

Potatoes are easily digested and well absorbed and are thus a good food for invalids. They are a valuable and useful food with an important place in the British diet. Their reputation for being fattening is undeserved. They do, of course, form fat if eaten in amounts sufficient to make the energy value of the diet greater than the daily energy expenditure. But so do all other foods. The energy density of potatoes is only 26 per cent that of beef steak, for example, and 10 per cent that of butter.

Potatoes contain an alkaloid solanine that is potentially toxic to man (p. 244).

CASSAVA (*Manihot esculenta*)

These shrubs, of which there are several species, are native to South America, but are now widely grown in tropical Africa and some parts of Asia. Cultivation is easy, new trees being propagated from stem cuttings. When they have grown to a height of 6 to 12 feet they are dug up and the tubers or thickened roots cooked.

Cassava is the principal food of many people in the tropics. The fresh root contains 50 to 75 per cent of water, less than 1 per cent of protein and the remainder mostly starch. Only about 3 per cent of the energy is derived from protein: this is less than half of the proportion of energy derived from protein in potatoes, yams and taro. This low-protein content places cassava in a different nutritional class from the other starchy roots. Kwashiorkor is common in communities dependent on cassava. As an easily cultivated food providing energy it is a valuable crop for many people; but it should only be cultivated along with other crops which can provide additional protein.

The leaves and outer parts of the roots contain a glyceride, linamarin, from which hydrogen cyanide is released by enzymic action. This is removed by grating the roots and then drying them in the sun. There is in West Africa a close association between the consumption of cassava and the prevalence of neuropathies (p. 329) and the patients often have a raised plasma concentration of thiocyanate, to which cyanide is converted by a detoxicating mechanism.[6] It is likely that the consumption of cassava contributes to the aetiology of these neuropathies through its cyanide. However, this can only be a subsidiary factor since they also occur in patients who have never eaten cassava. Thiocyanate diminishes the secretory capacity of the thyroid gland and cassava eaters are at increased risk of developing goitre.

Tapioca as sold in western countries is a preparation of cassava from which most of the protein is removed: it is almost pure starch.

YAMS

The two most important cultivated varieties are the greater yam (*Dioscorea alata*) and the lesser yam (*D. esculenta*). Both are climbing tropical plants. The tubers take 4 to 12 months to develop. Those of the larger species are big and may be as large as a football. The lesser yam has clusters of smaller tubers. Several wild yams may also serve as a source of food.

Like potatoes, yam tubers are rich in starch, but also contain significant amounts of protein.

SWEET POTATO (*Ipomoea batatas*)

This herbaceous plant with starchy tubers is extensively cultivated in the southern states of the USA and other hot climates. The crop is propagated from stem cuttings, and the tubers weigh up to 0.5 kg each. They have the same general properties as the potato and when fresh may contain up to 30 mg/100 g of ascorbic acid. Many varieties are coloured yellow or red. The pigments are carotenoids and anthocyanins and the sweet potato can be a useful source of vitamin A activity in the diet.

TARO (*Colocasia esculenta*)

This is widely grown in the Pacific Islands and in parts of Africa and Asia. It is also known by various local names such as *dasheen, eddo, keladi* and *cocoyam*. The *Colocasia* plant is a herbaceous perennial with tubers 15 to 30 cm long, which are used for propagation. They have the same general nutritive properties as yams and potatoes. The young leaves and stalks are also eaten as fresh vegetables.

SAGO

This is obtained from the pith of the sago palm (*Metroxylon sagu*) which is widely grown in Malaya, Indonesia and other parts of the Far East. The tree has to be felled and split before the starch is washed out. The commercial preparations ('pearl sago') are almost devoid of protein.

INVALID FOODS

Sago, tapioca, arrowroot and ground rice have each some reputation as 'invalid foods'. The commercial preparations on sale in temperate countries are almost pure starch. Provided it is realised that these foods are almost devoid of proteins, minerals and vitamins, they are useful as easily assimilated sources of energy. Taken with a suitable source of protein, as in milk puddings, they are valuable foods for the sick and also for young growing children.

SUGARS AND SYRUPS

Sugar consumption in the UK was 35 g/head daily in 1855 and rose steadily, interrupted only by rationing in the two world wars, to 138 g/head daily in 1958. Since then it has fallen to around 120 g (Fig. 18.3). Thus although sugar was cheap, consumption rose with increasing affluence, but there appears to be a maximum which has now been reached in some countries.

During the Middle Ages cane sugar was part of the spice trade that came from the East to Venice and so into Europe. In the thirteenth and fourteenth centuries the price of sugar lay between one to two shillings a pound — more than a week's wages for a servant. It was much in demand by apothecaries for making their confections. The supply increased with the development of the sugar colonies — the West Indies and the Atlantic Islands. The cultivation of sugar was closely associated with the growth of slavery. The history of both is well told by Aykroyd in a book entitled *Sweet Malefactor*, which can be recommended to anyone interested in the background of West Indians.[7]

In the middle of the seventeenth century sugar was discovered in beetroot by the German chemist Nargraf, and during the Napoleonic Wars much sugar beet was planted in France with a view to achieving independence from outside sources. During the nineteenth century sugar beet cultivation was greatly extended in Germany and France and more recently in Great Britain. There was also a great increase in imports of sugar from cane grown in the colonies.

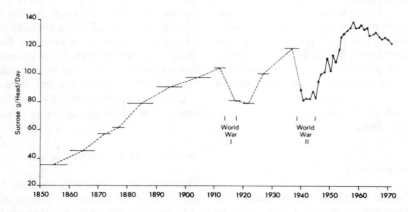

Fig. 18.3 Total amount of refined sugar available for daily consumption in the UK (g/head). Since 1970 it has been about 120 g/head, varying slightly mainly due to difficulties in supply

Sugar is readily preserved and so is suitable as an article of trade. This, together with its cheapness and usefulness as a flavouring agent, made it popular with the new industrial urban populations. As a cheap and easily digested form of energy, sugar is a valuable food; but as it lacks every nutrient save carbohydrate, its very attractiveness is a danger in that it tends to displace other more nutritious foods from the diet. With increased sugar consumption there is usually an increase in the incidence of dental disease.

Crystalline table sugar is one of the purest chemicals produced in large quantities by modern industry. It is practically 100 per cent sucrose and contains no other nutrients, nor any potentially toxic compounds. 'Brown sugar' is less highly refined sucrose containing traces of other sugars and minerals, and colouring matter; perhaps for this reason it has a better flavour and is esteemed for use in coffee. Public demand for brown sugar has sometimes tempted the manufacturers to produce a spurious imitation of it by simply adding a synthetic brown dye. The raw sugar cane that is chewed — especially by children — in the sugar-growing areas of the tropics contains only traces of protein, vitamins and minerals.

Syrups are highly concentrated solutions in which the sugar is unable to crystallise out owing to the presence of small quantities of other substances. They include molasses, treacles and golden syrup which are by-products of the manufacture of crystalline cane sugar. These contain 20 to 30 per cent of water in addition to sugar. They may also contain nutritionally significant amounts of calcium and iron, some of which probably comes from the vessels in which they have been processed. Molasses are popular remedies for the treatment of several diseases; there is no scientific support for their use.

Various natural syrups exist of which perhaps the most famous is the maple syrup obtained from the sap of the maple in Canada and New England. It contains about 20 per cent of water and the remainder carbohydrate.

Honey is a pleasant attractive food. At many times and places it has acquired a special reputation either as a medicine or as a nutritious food. Unfortunately this reputation is undeserved. Most honeys consist of about 20 per cent water and about 75 per cent of sugars, mostly fructose and glucose, with only traces of other nutrients. However, despite these dismal chemical analyses, honey and maple syrup continue to be appreciated by all who enjoy pleasant and attractive food.

Jams are made by boiling either fresh fruit or a pulp preserved with SO_2 (sulphited pulp) with sugar. Pectin may or may not be added, dependent on the amount present in the raw material. The minimum fruit content in Britain varies from 30 to 40 per cent for different fruits, but is only 20 per cent for citrus fruits (marma-

lades). Most jams contain about 65 per cent of sugar. On the continent of Europe the term marmalade refers to any jam made from a fruit purée.

Confectionery (candy)   The ingredients of most toffees (candy) are a mixture of sugar, a syrup and a little fat; they may contain up to 70 per cent of carbohydrate. Boiled 'sweeties' are often about 50 per cent sucrose and 40 per cent glucose. Plain chocolate consists of cocoa, other fats and sucrose. A typical analysis, with figures in g/100 g, is cocoa butter 20, non-fat cocoa solids 15, other fats 25, sucrose 40, but there are wide variations. In milk chocolate, non-fat milk solids and butter may constitute about one-fifth of the ingredients.

LEGUMES

Peas, beans and lentils are the seeds of plants of the family *Fabaceae*, formerly known as *Leguminosae*. The family is large and contains species that can grow in most soils and climates, and throughout the world legumes make some contribution to the diets of most people. They are also known as pulses, a word introduced into the English language from Norman French some 700 years ago and derived from the Latin *puls*, meaning a thick paste or pottage. Lentils and allied pulses are usually eaten in this form. A monograph *Legumes in Human Nutrition* by Doughty and Walker[8] is recommended as a good account of their history, of the species grown as food for man and of their role in nutrition. The chemical composition of pulses (Table 18.3) is similar to that of cereals, except that fresh peas and most fresh beans contain much more water. But there are differences that give pulses an invaluable place in diets consisting mainly of cereals, especially rice and maize.

Protein content

Table 18.4 compares the proteins present in cereals, pulses and meats. Pulses are the richest source. The percentage of total energy provided by protein in pulses is higher than in meats and much higher than in cereals. The quality of the proteins may be judged by their content of three essential amino acids, methionine, lysine and tryptophan. Pulse proteins as a sole source of dietary nitrogen would be unsatisfactory because of their low content of methionine. Their lysine content is much higher than that of cereals and approaches that of meats. Though pulses are not in general as rich in tryptophan as are cereals, they are richer than maize, and the figures in Table 18.4 illustrate why maize eaters need beans. They also show that a cereal diet supplemented by pulses may provide more protein than a diet supplemented by meats and that the quality of the proteins in such diets is comparable.

Table 18.3 Pulses (peas, beans and lentils). Nutrient in 100 g of dry weight

	Range	Selected value	Notes
Moisture, per cent	8–15	—	—
Energy kJ	1340–1460	1400	—
Energy kcal	320–350	340	—
Carbohydrate, g	55–65	60	Soya bean, 20
Protein, g	17–25	20	Soya bean, 38
Fat, g	1–5	4	Soya bean, 18
Calcium, mg	100–200	150	—
Iron, mg	2–8	6	—
Carotene, μg	12–120	60	—
Ascorbic acid, mg	0	0	When sprouted, 10–15
Thiamin, mg	0.2–0.6	0.4	—
Riboflavin, mg	0.1–0.3	0.2	Soya bean, 0.75
Nicotinic acid, mg	1.5–3.0	2.0	—

The figures in Table 18.4 provide a contemporary explanation, based on chemical analyses, of what was known empirically at least 3000 years ago. Pulses are the poor man's meat, and they promote good health. This is illustrated by an Old Testament story (Daniel I).

Table 18.4 Comparison of the quantity and quality of the es proteins present in cereals, pulses and meats

	Quantity Percentage of energy from protein	Quality Amino acids (mg/g nitrogen)		
		Met	Lys	Trp
Wheat	14.4	100	230	70
Rice	8.4	130	150	80
Maize	10.6	120	170	40
Haricot beans	31	70	450	60
Lentils	31	50	450	50
Beef	22	170	570	80
Lamb	18	160	610	80

After Nebuchadnezzar, the King of Babylon, had captured Jerusalem, he decided to take Daniel and three other young Jews into his household. He 'appointed them a daily provision of the King's meat, and of the wine which he drank'. Daniel refused this offer and petitioned Melzar, one of the household staff thus: 'Prove thy servants, I beseech thee, ten days; and let them give us pulse to eat and water to drink. Then let our countenances be looked upon before thee, and the countenance of the children that eat of the portion of the King's meat: and as thou seest, deal with thy servants.' This offer was accepted and 'at the end of ten days their countenances appeared fairer and fatter in flesh than all the children which did eat the portion of the King's meat'. This may be the first controlled experiment in human nutrition. Nowadays we would continue the ob-

servations longer, but the message is clear and was learnt. In many Jewish and Christian circles sensible men modified canonical orders to fast to orders to give up meats for which legumes could be substituted. This was common practice during Lent in mediaeval Europe.

Early in the present century Mendel began the scientific study of the quality of the dietary proteins (p. 48). This led to animal proteins being classified as first class and vegetable proteins as second class, a lesson taught to all students for many years. It is indeed true when a single protein is fed as the sole source of nitrogen, but there is nothing second class about suitaable mixtures of vegetable proteins. Since 1970 food manufacturers have been diluting in increasing amounts the poor man's meats with textured vegetable proteins (p. 210). In most of these a legume is one of the main ingredients and the substitution does not diminish the quality of the protein in the diet.

Today all concerned with nutrition education have to inform those who are vegetarian by choice and those whom economic necessity forces to be vegetarians on most days of the importance of a good daily intake of legumes. This is of especial importance for infants and growing children. Preparations of cereals and legumes, made either commercially or in the home, have been demonstrated to be effective substitutes for the milk of cows and other domestic animals.

Vitamins

Pulses as a class are good sources of the B group of vitamins (except riboflavin). More important, the greater part of these vitamins present in the harvested seeds is actually consumed. There are no losses comparable with those that may arise in the milling and cooking of rice. Pulses have therefore a deserved reputation as a food which protects against beriberi.

Although pulses, except peas and garden beans, like cereal grains are devoid of any vitamin C activity, large amounts of ascorbic acid are formed on germination; sprouted pulses are an excellent preventive against scurvy (p. 327).

Hospitals dietitians in Asia and Africa find sprouted pulses a useful item for their menus, especially when fresh vegetables and fruits are scarce and expensive. The sophisticated may find them useful at cocktail parties — for guests like them; they are cheap, and supplement the nutritive value of the other refreshment.

Digestibility

Pulses have a reputation for being indigestible. This was acquired at the time of Galen or even earlier. It is only partially deserved. In health, the digestion of pulses and the absorption of their principal nutrients is practically complete and about as effective as is the assimilation of cereals. However, even in minor gastrointestinal disorders their digestion may be incomplete. Flatulence may be assessed objectively by measuring flatus volume or breath hydrogen. It appears to be largely due to stachyose and verbascose (p. 30).

Toxins

Some pulses may sometimes contain toxic substances. The effects of those associated with the lathyrus pea are described on page 242, with groundnuts contaminated by a fungus on page 246 and favism from broad beans on page 468.

THE LEGUMES IN HUMAN DIETS

Peas

The word *pease* comes from Sanskrit and modified forms are found in most Indo-European languages. The Mediterranean countries, the Near East, Central Asia and India are the natural habitat of 'the common pea' (*Pisum sativum*). Archaeologists have found cultivated peas in Neolithic villages. They were usually eaten dry, and fresh green peas first became popular in the seventeenth century in Paris where Madame de Maintenon, the secret wife of Louis XIV, described them as a 'fashion and a madness'. However, the fashion stayed and peas continue as a favourite crop of gardeners. Large-scale cultivation, mostly by mechanical means, and preservation by canning and freezing have made peas readily available at all seasons of the year. The best canned and frozen peas are as good nutritionally as fresh peas. They also taste good, but every gardener knows not quite so good as the peas that he grows.

Beans

The broad bean, *Vicia faba*, also known as the horse bean, probably originated in Asia Minor. It was grown extensively in ancient Egypt, but was not eaten by the priests or the upper classes for reasons that remain obscure.[9] It is now grown extensively and is an important component of diets in the Mediterranean region, where it is associated with favism (p. 468), and also in highlands in Africa, Asia, and Central and South America. A variety, sometimes known as the Windsor bean, is a crop popular with European gardeners.

The haricot bean, *Phaseolus vulgaris*, is of Mexican origin. It is one of the foods acquired by the Old World from the New in the sixteenth century. Also known as kidney beans and French beans, they are not grown in most parts of the world, but mainly in the Americas. They can be preserved by drying or by canning. A can of baked beans is a popular basis for a cheap and nutritious meal that has to be prepared hurriedly. Many varieties are grown. Some are harvested immature and the whole pod eaten (the French *haricot vert*).

The Lima bean, *Phaseolus lunatus*, originates from Peru. Also known as the butter bean, it grows only in a hot, humid climate. It is a valuable part of the diet of many communities in the tropics.

The scarlet runner bean (*Phaseolus coccineus*) also originates from tropical America. Popular with gardeners, the green pods are sliced and eaten before the seed matures. Hence its nutritive properties are those of a green vegetable and not of a legume.

The locust bean (*Parkia biglobosa*) comes from a leguminous tree which grows in West Africa. There the seeds may be fermented and used as condiment.

Lentils and similar pulses

Lentils are the seeds of *Lens esculenta* of which many varieties are known. The plants are small, about 25 to 50 cm high, with small leaves and pale blue flowers. The plant originated in the Mediterranean countries and has been an important crop there for a long time. Esau sold his birthright to his brother Jacob 'for bread and pottage of lentils' (Genesis XXV, 34). Later lentils were introduced into many countries in Europe and Asia; in India large areas were planted, especially in Bengal. There are several varieties: the Indian and Egyptian kinds are orange-red in colour and these are the lentils most commonly imported into Europe. A green variety also exists. Lentils may be made into soups or ground into a flour.

Besides the lentils several similar pulses are widely cultivated in tropical and semitropical countries. In India they are named dhals. There the best known are Bengal gram (*Cicer arietinum*), black gram (*Vigna mungo*), green gram (*V. radiatus*) and red gram or pigeon pea (*Cajanus cajan*). A pulse, khesari dhal (*Lathyrus sativus*), was once sown widely in Central India. Its special value was that it was very resistant to drought. Even if the main cereal crop failed in a dry season, some khesari could be harvested. However, it was found that if large amounts of khesari dhal were eaten, paralysis of the lower limbs commonly followed. This condition, lathyrism, is discussed on page 330.

Soya beans

The soya bean (*Glycine max*) has been eaten in China for several thousand years. The whole dry grain contains about 40 per cent of protein (twice as much as in most other pulses) and also up to 20 per cent of fat. Soya forms the basis of a great variety of the sauces and pastes with which Chinese cooks garnish their food. To the Chinese peasant subsisting on rice, the extra protein and fat, and incidentally B vitamins, provided by even a small amount of soya, can be of immense nutritional value. For the Chinese gourmet, soya is one of the raw materials out of which the cooks create their delicious works of art.

No other people have acquired the Chinese taste for soya, but the bean has become an important raw material for the international food industry. Production in the USA rose between 1935 and 1973 from 2 to 45 million tons per year. Soya bean oil is a major raw material of modern margarine. Soya bean cake is used in animal husbandry as a good source of protein, and is fed to cattle, pigs and poultry. Soya flour is being increasingly used in human foods. The lists of ingredients on the packs in a supermarket show that it is present in many sausages, biscuits, breakfast foods and other cereal products and in made-up dishes. Human consumption of soya protein is increasing with the development of textured vegetable proteins and other artificial meat (p. 209). Soya protein is an important constituent in some infant foods and milk substitutes.

Groundnuts

Also known as peanuts and monkey nuts, groundnuts (*Arachis hypogaea*) are in fact the seeds of a leguminous plant. They are therefore properly pulses and not nuts. The plants originated in Brazil, but are now grown widely all over the tropics. After flowering, the ends of the flower stalk bend down and the young pods are forced into the ground by the direction of growth. They ripen underground and have to be dug up at harvest.

Groundnuts resemble other pulses in general nutritive value, except that they are rich in fat. The whole seed contains about 40 per cent of fat, twice the amount in soya beans.

As most children know, peanuts are good to eat, but few would care to eat a lot of them. The cultivation of groundnuts is seldom intended as a primary source of human food. The chief product is the oil, which can be used either as cooking oil or for making margarine and soap. The secondary product is the residue or cake left after the expression of the oil. Groundnut cake is excellent cattle food. It is also in theory an excellent protein-rich food for man. However, it is difficult to overcome the unpleasant taste. Experience has shown that as a diluent of flours from millets, wheat or other sources up to 10 per cent can be well tolerated; in higher proportions the mixture becomes nauseating and unpalatable.

NUTS

We know of no record of any people who regularly consumed large quantities of nuts, except for some bushmen in Botswana. In Great Britain during the last war it was possible to register as a vegetarian, surrender one's meat ration and receive in return up to 2 lb of nuts weekly. In 1941 there were only 16 000 registered vegetarians, but the numbers rose to 70 000 by 1947.

However, nuts are an occasional small luxury which everyone enjoys. As the different popular nuts grow in many parts of the world there is a small but flourishing international trade. Most of the imported nuts go direct to the manufacturers of confectionery and biscuits and to bakers.

Most nuts have a high content of fat and protein, but as they are eaten in such small amounts their nutritive value is generally insignificant, compared with their flavouring properties. A variety of different kinds of nuts are described in the Glossary.

Coconuts (*Cocos nucifera*)

This palm contributes to human needs in many ways. As its fruit is not botanically a nut but rather a stone-fruit or loupe, coconuts are a little out of place here. Coconut palms grow on low-lying land often near the sea, and their graceful leaves and the curves of their trunk give great charm to many tropical landscapes. To the hot and thirsty traveller there is no more refreshing drink than the water inside a green coconut and it is also hygienic. However, coconut water is of little nutritive value; it is a minor luxury of the tropics and available to any small boy who can climb a palm unseen by the owner. The white flesh inside the nut, when dried, is known as 'copra'. It has a high content of oil, and coconut oil is the most valued product of the palm. It is widely used as a cooking oil in the tropics and is exported for soap making. The residual cake after the oil has been extracted is known as 'poonac' and is used as a cattle food. Copra itself is a good food and can be eaten either dried or fried. It is rich in fat (over 30 per cent). Dried coconut is imported into temperate countries and used by confectioners and cake makers, who value its flavour.

The fresh sap of the palm (sweet toddy) is a pleasant drink but it contains few nutrients. Sweet toddy is readily fermented by yeasts and this product has been the chief alcoholic drink in many parts of the tropics.

OTHER SEEDS

Many other miscellaneous seeds play a small part in various diets. On the music-hall stage no Russian peasant is complete unless he is chewing **sunflower seeds**. These have a composition similar to groundnuts and are cultivated widely in Russia and elsewhere as a source of oil. Chewing the seeds of these and similar plants no doubt provides an additional small source of nutrients to many peasants.

VEGETABLES

There are hundreds of 'common vegetables' eaten in different parts of the world. Everyone knows what 'vegetables' are and yet they defy exact classification or description. Some vegetables, like spinach, cabbage and lettuce are leaves; others — onions, turnips and radishes — are roots; egg-plants (brinjals or aubergines), gourds and marrows are fruits; celery is a stalk and cauliflower and globe artichokes are flowers. Clearly there is no biological structure common to 'vegetables' and largely determining their chemical composition, as in the case of cereal grains.

Nevertheless, despite the great variety of botanical structure, vegetables all possess the same general nutritive properties.

Social factors

Before discussing the nutritive properties of vegetables it is proper to state that man should eat vegetables because he likes them; vegetables may also be good for him, as nutrition education posters proclaim, but this should be a secondary consideration. In the Middle Ages few people ate vegetables regularly. Only the religious houses kept vegetable gardens and these were very poorly stocked. An interest in gardening arose at the time of the Reformation in Europe. It has spread to England in the seventeenth century and to Scotland in the eighteenth. Many new vegetables were introduced, not a few coming from the New World. Both landowners and merchants began to take pride in their vegetables gardens and the produce greatly improved the quality of the table which they kept. The poor followed their example. It was soon demonstrated that a small well cared for cottage garden could provide a varied supply of vegetables for a family. English cottage gardeners acquired a well deserved reputation for their skill as vegetable growers; any tourist in rural England today will see that this skill is still maintained. This is less true in Scotland.

With the industrial revolution many who moved from the country to the town were cut off from their supply of fresh vegetables. To meet the needs of the cities large commercial market gardens were started. These have been for the most part well run and they continue to produce a great number of excellent varieties of vegetables. Some delay in the passage of the vegetables from the market gardens to the greengrocers' shops in the cities is inevitable. This may be extended, sometimes to days, by a complicated trade with too many middlemen.

In industrial countries there is nowadays a satisfactory variety of canned and frozen vegetables. The keen gardener will claim that these do not taste quite so good as the produce he brings straight into his own kitchen. Nevertheless the quality and nutritional value are excellent. The food technologist has taken over from the housewife much of the drudgery of cleaning, preparing and even the cooking of vegetables. A regular supply of vegetables, either fresh, frozen or canned, should be an essential part of good living and good feeding. Vegetables add to the elegance and attractiveness of a meal. In many underdeveloped tropical countries the need for vegetables for health reasons is particularly important. Modern methods both for growing and marketing require to be developed on a large scale. The picturesque vegetable market of small tropical towns cannot be adapted to meet the needs of big cities.

Nutritive properties

These are shown in Tables 18.5 and 18.6.

The value of vegetables as a source of energy is very small. Most provide from 40 to 200 kJ (10–50 kcal)/100 g. To obtain 4.2 MJ (1000 kcal) it would be necessary to eat 2 to 3 kg of vegetables. The large bulk of vegetables helps to promote satiety and this, with their low-energy value, makes them useful in the prevention and treatment of obesity. Vegetables are also of little value as a source of proteins and essential amino acids. All vegetables contain dietary fibre. This increases the bulk of the faeces. In this way vegetables, by increasing the size of the stool, have a mild laxative effect.

Most vegetables contain amounts of calcium and iron that are probably physiologically significant. However, it is doubtful if the actual figures given for these minerals in food tables are of much value. The mineral content of different samples of the same vegetable may vary greatly. Oxalic acid in some leafy vegetables may interfere with calcium absorption. [10] Even though much of the iron present in vegetables may not be absorbed, the ascorbic acid which they also contain may aid its absorption (p. 146).

All vegetables contain small amounts of the B group of vitamins, but their contribution to the total intake is seldom great. Most leafy vegetables are fair sources of riboflavin. In the tropics a small supply of greens may reduce the incidence of angular stomatitis, often attributed to an insufficiency of riboflavin.

The chief nutritive value of vegetables is as a supply

Table 18.5 Green leafy vegetables: (a) (cabbage, brussels sprouts, lettuce, spinach, parsley, amaranth, coriander, fenugreek, neem, etc.) Composition in terms of 100 g of the retail weight, as purchased

		Range	Selected value	Notes
Moisture, per cent		75–80	—	—
Energy	kJ	40–200	80	—
	kcal	10–50	20	—
Carbohydrate, g		1–12	3	—
Protein, g		1–4	2	—
Fat, g		Trace	0	—
Calcium, mg		25–500	100	In temperate zones, 75 In tropical zones, 250
Iron, mg		1–25	5	—
Carotene, µg		600–6000	1800	In the higher range in the tropics
Ascorbic acid, mg		10–200	50	In temperate zones, 30 In tropical zones, 180
Thiamin, mg		0.03–0.08	0.05	—
Riboflavin, mg		0.03–0.25	0.08	Kale and spinach up to 0.5
Nicotinic acid, mg		0.2–1.0	0.5	—
Folic acid, µg		20–100	50	—

Table 18.6 Other vegetables: (b) (onions, turnips, cauliflower, leeks, egg plants, pumpkins, gourds, etc.). Composition in terms of 100 g of the retail weight, as purchased

		Range	Selected value
Moisture, per cent		70–90	—
Energy	kJ	40–200	100
	kcal	10–50	25
Carbohydrate, g		2–10	5
Protein, g		0.5–2.5	1.5
Fat, g		0–0.4	
Calcium, mg		20–100	65
Iron, mg		0.5–4.0	1.5
Carotene, µg		0–180	90
Ascorbic acid, mg		5–100	25
Thiamin, mg		0.05–0.20	0.07
Riboflavin, mg		0.01–0.20	0.05
Nicotinic acid, mg		0.1–1.0	0.5
Folic acid, µg		2–30	10

of β-carotene, ascorbic acid and folate. Cereals and pulses in general lack all these vitamins. So vegetables are able to make good deficiencies likely to arise on diets containing excessive amounts of cereals. It is in this way that vegetables balance a diet.

The β-carotene content of vegetables is very variable. The great majority have good vitamin A activity. There is a rough relation between colour and β-carotene content. All green leafy vegetables are rich and some, such as kale, very rich. Cucumber, cauliflower, some of the gourds and other pale vegetables may contain very little.

All vegetables contain valuable amount of ascorbic acid, but the quantities are variable and losses in cooking and preparation may be great. However, a single helping of vegetables (3 oz: 90 g) daily, even if it has been badly treated by the cook, will usually provide at least 10 mg of ascorbic acid, an amount known to prevent scurvy. Losses in cooking and preserving are discussed in Chapter 23.

In many tropical countries it is impossible to overemphasise the improvement in health that is likely to arise from even a small increase in the vegetable supply. A poor woman with insufficient iron, vitamin A and ascorbic acid in her diet may find great improvement in her health as a result of taking one helping of good garden vegetables a day. In Africa and Asia there are few keen and competent gardeners; some are schoolmasters who set an excellent example to their pupils, but their numbers are few in relation to the need. A single enthusiast in a village or small town, by giving instruction and encouragement to his neighbours in the art of gardening, can carry out first-class preventive medicine in his spare time. Oomen and Grubben have produced a beautifully illustrated book to encourage consumption of leafy vegetables in the tropics.[11] Many grow wild and are not familiar to expatriate health educators.

Other types of 'vegetables' which may serve as food for man deserve brief mention.

Seaweed and marine algae have been used as a human food by the Chinese for many centuries and today seaweeds are eaten regularly in significant amounts by Japanese communities. Carrageen 'moss' is a seaweed still eaten on the west coasts of Scotland, South Wales and Ireland. A preparation known as lava was formerly in frequent use in London as an accompaniment of roast mutton. As already described (p. 35), agar and alginic acid are polysaccharides derived from seaweeds which are used by food technologists to alter the texture and consistency of foods, especially in making jellies.

The chief carbohydrates in seaweeds are mannitol and the polysaccharides alginic acid and laminarin. Seaweeds contain less than 1 per cent of fat, but appreciable amounts of protein, and a high content of minerals. An account of the nutritional properties of seaweed with a bibliography is given by Black.[12] There are several million tons of seaweed round the shores of the British islands that could be harvested. So far attempts to make a palatable food have met with little success.

FUNGI

A good account of the use of mushrooms and toadstools as food is given by Ramsbottom.[13] The British appear to be uniquely conservative in their fear of toadstools. Only certain species are poisonous, notably the Death Cap (*Amanita phalloides*) which has been responsible for nearly all the deaths. Many British toadstools are excellent eating. In other parts of the world a great variety of fungi are eaten. Fungi are for the most part delicious food and are eaten for their flavour. As they only contain up to 3 per cent protein, less than 1 per cent fat and about 2 per cent carbohydrate, their nutritive value is small. Mushrooms contain unusual amounts of trehalose (p. 30).

Fungi are valuable as one of the few luxury foods that are freely available to poor countrymen. Commercial cultivation has now made them available to townsmen. They are much appreciated by all who love good food.

FRUITS

Since the beginning of civilisation men of ingenuity who have had a little land to spare have used it to cultivate orchards and fruit gardens. In this art there has been a steady and progressive increase in skill and technical knowledge. The modern grower can provide fruit of great variety and excellent quality.

No other class of foods has such a variety of pleasant and attractive flavours. By delicacy of colouring, fruits attract the eye as well as the palate. For thousands of years vintners have been preserving the best and most delicate flavours in wines and liqueurs. Housewives have been similarly engaged for about three hundred years in preserving and jam making. In the last hundred years they have been greatly assisted by food technologists. All these skills have contributed beyond measure to the pleasures of the table and the art of living.

The nutritive value of fruits is much less important. The only essential nutrient in which fruits are rich is ascorbic acid. Almost all fruits contain physiologically significant amount of this vitamin and some are very rich. As fruits are often eaten raw, large intakes of the vitamin may be provided. Table 14.3 gives the ascorbic acid content of some fruits. How important fruit is in a national diet depends on one's opinion as to man's requirements of ascorbic acid.

Fruits, of course, like vegetables contain dietary fibre and add bulk to the stools; they are thus mild natural laxatives. A few people with sensitive colons can take fruit only in small quantities; if larger amounts are taken diarrhoea follows. Prunes contain derivatives of hydroxyphenylisatin, which stimulates the smooth muscle of the colon. Pectin present in fruit assist in the formation of jellies and is of great value to jam-makers.

Most fruits contain small quantities of carotene and the B group of vitamins. The amounts present are not usually great enough to increase significantly the intake of these nutrients by people who are already living on a good mixed diet, but under certain circumstances they may be very valuable. In many parts of the tropics there is a sudden and obvious improvement in the health of the children coincident with the mango or jack-fruit season. Children may eat enormous quantities of these fruits which are rich in carotenoids with provitamin A activity.

Fruits contain little or no protein or fat. Most contain 5 to 20 per cent of carbohydrate. Ripe fruits contain no starch. Fructose and glucose are the chief sugars found. These two sugars are often present in equal proportions. Apples and pears contain much more fructose, while apricots and peaches contain sucrose.

Fruits contain a great variety of organic acids. They are responsible for the sourness of unripe fruit. During ripening the concentration of these acids falls and that of the sugars rises. As already described, the body readily disposes of these acids; most are easily oxidised, some excreted in the urine and a few are not absorbed from the gut. They do not give rise to acidosis.

Bananas are a fruit which requires special mention. They contain much larger amounts of carbohydrate than most fruits and so can act as a useful source of energy. There are about 50 varieties of bananas. They vary widely in composition, but may contain carbohydrate 20 g, protein 1 g, fat 0.2 g with an energy value of about 335 kJ (80 kcal)/100 g. In some parts of the tropics they may be the staple food of children and are often eaten together with large quantities of cassava. As a consequence the consumption of carbohydrate is high, while that of protein is low and kwashiorkor may occur.

The staple diet of many Africans is matoke (*Musa species*), a banana usually eaten green. This contains a high concentration of 5-hydroxytryptamine (5-HT), which has widespread actions on the circulatory and nervous systems. A suggestion that large intakes of 5-HT from matoke might be responsible for endomyocardial fibrosis, common in parts of Africa, has received only little support.[14]

In small quantities bananas are a pleasant and attractive food and have acquired a well merited reputation in temperate climates. They are very easily digested. In ripe bananas 15 to 20 per cent of the pulp consists of sucrose, fructose or glucose and 1 to 2 per cent is starch.[15] It is important that bananas given to children

be fully ripe. They can be digested by babies as early as the third month. Bananas contain no gluten hence their value in coeliac disease. They are also a food for convalescence.

REFERENCES

1. Hindhede M 1913 Studien über Eiweissminimum. Skand Arch Physiol 30: 97–182
2. Young A 1771 The farmer's tour through the east of England. London, vol 4, p 120
3. Salaman R N 1949 The history and social influence of the potato. Cambridge University Press
3a. Fürer-Haimendorf C von 1964. The Sherpas of Nepal. Murray, London, p 7–11
4. Koffanyi E, Jekat F, Müller-Wecker H 1970 The minimum protein requirement of humans, tested with mixtures of whole egg plus potato and maize plus beans. Hoppe-Seylers Z Physiol Chem 351: 1485–91
5. Flynn J F, Beirn S F O, Burkitt D P 1977 The potato as a source of fibre in the diet. Ir J Med Sci 146: 285–8
6. Osuntokun B O, Monekosso G L, Wilson J 1969 Relationship of a degenerative tropical neuropathy to diet. Br Med J 1: 547–550
7. Aykroyd W R 1967 Sweet malefactor. Sugar, slavery and human society. Heinemann, London
8. Doughty J, Walker A 1982 Legumes in human nutrition. FAO Food and Nutrition Paper no 20

9. Darby W J, Ghaliouigui P, Grivetti L 1977 Food: the figt of Osiris. Academic Press, New York, p 682
10. Pingle U, Ramasastri B V 1978 Absorption of calcium from a leafy vegetable rich in oxalates. Br J Nutr 39: 119–25
11. Oomen H A P C, Grubber G J H 1977 Tropical vegetables in human nutrition. Konüklijk Institute voor de Tropen, Amsterdam
12. Black W A P 1953 Seaweeds and their value in foodstuffs. Proc Nutr Soc 12: 32–39
13. Ramsbottom J 1953 Mushrooms and toadstools. Proc Nutr Soc 12: 39–44
14. Crawford M A, Gales M M, Somers K, Hansen I L 1970 Studies on plasma amino acids in East African adults in relation to endomyocardial fibrosis. Br J Nutr 24: 393–403
15. Palmer J K 1971 The biochemistry of fruits and their products. In: Hulme A C (ed) Academic Press, New York, vol 2, p 65

19

Meat, Fish and Eggs; Novel Proteins

MEAT AND MEAT PRODUCTS

Meat was an important part of the hunter-gatherer's diet. Today in many parts of the world peasants have little or no meat to eat, along with the urban poor. By contrast annual consumption in the USA is about 200 lb/head. Protein of animal origin is not essential for man as has been amply demonstrated by many vegetarians who have led full and active lives. Yet as soon as the income of a family or community rises, there is nearly always an increase in the amount of meat they consume.

MEAT PRODUCTION

The flesh of more than 100 species of animals is eaten by man. Production of beef and mutton is the responsibility of stockmen and butchers who over the generations have developed a *mystère* of what determines the quality of meat. To their traditional wisdom there is now added *meat science*. This is a growing subject and a systematic account of it is given in a textbook by Lawrie.[1] Genetics and physiology are being applied to improve the live animal and biochemistry and electron microscopy to understand changes in the muscle tissues after slaughter.

We are now in the middle of a revolution in meat production and a significant proportion of our supply is no longer produced on a farm but in a factory. In western countries, this applies to nearly all of the poultry, much of the pork and a small but increasing proportion of beef cattle. Factory farming converts protein unacceptable to man into an acceptable form; but it is an inefficient means of supplying energy, because of the large areas of arable land needed to produce the animal feeds.

There is a natural concern that factory meat may be of poorer quality and of less nutritive value than farm meat. So far there is little justification for such fears. No significant differences were found in the amounts of the important nutrients present in samples of 'barley beef' from stall-fed cattle and in beef from farm animals.[2]

QUALITY OF MEAT

Meat is appreciated for its digestibility, tenderness and flavour..

Digestibility
The muscle proteins are more rapidly and easily digested than the connective tissue proteins, mostly collagen, and fat. As an animal ages there is relatively more connective tissue and the meat of an old ewe is tougher than that of a young lamb. The collagen content varies with cut. Thus it may be as low as 2.5 per cent in a fillet of beef and as high as 23.6 per cent in skin meat.[3]

Fat delays the emptying of the stomach and the proportion of fat in a helping of meat may vary from 8 to 50 per cent and more for bacon. Cuts of pork often contained large amounts of fat and this probably explains why pork acquired the reputation of being indigestible.

Tenderness
We like our meats to be tender and perceive its tenderness through three sensory components: first, the ease of initial penetration by the teeth; next, the ease with which the meat breaks into fragments; and, lastly, the amount of unchewable residue. The ultimate measurement must be semiquantitative rating of tenderness given by a reliable taste panel but several workers have devised tests to try and express this by physical laboratory methods. Tenderness varies with species, breed and age of the animal. Coarse muscle fibres are less tender and connective tissue, especially elastin, is associated with toughness. Marbled meat with fat between the muscle fibres is usually more tender. After slaughter the proportions of these structures do not change but there can be large variations in tenderness, depending on how the meat is handled. Rigor mortis follows interdigitation of the actin and myosin filaments in the

muscle fibres as the ATP is used up in anaerobic glycolysis. Conditions which retard or reduce the degree of muscle fibre shortening in rigor mortis give more tender meat. The tenderness of beef and venison improves if it is stored at temperatures just above freezing for 10 to 14 days, called 'conditioning'. Tenderness first decreases with the onset of rigor mortis and then slowly improves. The detailed biochemical explanation of this second phase is still being worked out. It appears to result from the local action of muscle proteases or cathepsins, with some weakening of the attachment of actin filaments and increased water-holding capacity of the non-fibrous, sarcoplasmic proteins.

Cooking make meat more tender; slow cooking hydrolyses collagen to gelatin.

Flavour

The flavour of meat is a complex sensation. Much of it is due to water-soluble substances such as inosinic acid, hypoxanthine derived from ATP, glycopeptides and amino acids such as glutamic acid. Meat with very little fat tastes insipid. There is a gradual loss of flavour during storage, even frozen, due to evaporation of volatile substances. The flesh of full-grown male pigs contains trace of an unpleasant 'boar odour'. Substances in animals' feeds can sometimes give undesirable flavours in the meat and volatile taints can be absorbed during frozen storage.

NUTRITIVE PROPERTIES (Table 19.1)

The energy value of meat depends on its fat content, which as already stated varies greatly. For this reason, the use of food tables to calculate the energy content of diets containing much meat is subject to large errors.

However, meat is a good source of energy as lean muscle contains about 20 per cent of protein and 5 per cent of fat.

The protein of meat is of high biological value, but this may be somewhat reduced when the proportion of connective tissue protein is high. Cooking denatures the natural proteins and makes them more susceptible to digestive enzymes.

Meats are usually rich in iron and also in zinc, but contain little calcium. They are an important source of nicotinic acid and riboflavin. Indeed in most British and American diets about half the total nicotinic acid and one-quarter of the total riboflavin come from meat. Meats also contain some thiamin; pork contains the most. There is very little vitamin A or ascorbic acid in muscle meats but they provide moderate amounts of vitamin B12.

The fat in beef and mutton contains little polyunsaturated fatty acids. This is because these acids are hydrogenated in the rumen of cattle and sheep. The fat in chicken and turkey meat contains much more, depending on the amount of these acids in the poultry food.

Offal

This curious word — a corruption of off-fall — is defined by the Meat Inspection Regulations 1963 as 'any part of a dead animal removed from the carcase in the process of dressing it, but does not include the hide or skin'. Some offals, e.g. liver, kidney, heart and tongue, are foods of repute found on the menus of the best restaurants. Others, e.g. sweetbreads (pancreas and thymus), tripe (dressed stomach of ox or sheep), feet (pigs' and calves'), brains, chitterlings (pigs' intestines), maws (pigs' stomach), lambs' fries (testicles) and udders, are often regarded as local delicacies, but are more likely to be found in back street eating houses. Nevertheless all

Table 19.1 Meat and offal (composition in terms of 100 g of the retail weight, as purchased) (based on Paul and Southgate)[4]

	Chicken	Beef (rump steak)	Lamb chop (inc. fat)	Liver	Notes
Moisture, per cent	74	67	49	67–70	
Energy kJ	508	821	1558	567–748	
Energy kcal	121	197	377	135–180	
Carbohydrate, g	0	0	0	0.6–2.2	
Protein, g	20	19	15	20	Duck 11
Fat, g	4*	14	35	6.3–10.3	
Calcium, mg	14	6	7	7	Tongue and blood sausage 32–35
Iron, mg	0.7	2.3	1.2	7–21	Blood sausage 20; kidney 6; heart 4
Retinol equiv., μg	trace	trace	trace	9300–18 100	Kidney 100–150
Ascorbic acid, mg	0	0	0	10–23	Kidney 7–14; heart 6
Thiamin, mg	0.1	0.08	0.09	0.21–0.31	Pork 0.9; bacon 0.6
Riboflavin, mg	0.16	0.26	0.16	2.7–3.3	Kidney 2; heart 1
Nicotinic acid equiv., mg	11.6	8.2	7.1	14–19	Kidney 7–14
Vitamin B12/μg	trace	2	1	56–110	Kidney 14–55

* Fat 18 g if skin eaten as well.

offal is of good nutritional value. Carnivorous animals in custody do not thrive on 'muscle meat' alone. Bone and offal contribute greatly to the nutritional value of their diet. Liver contains more vitamins and absorbable iron than muscle and so is a valuable food. At one time lightly cooked liver was the only means of saving the lives of patients with pernicious anaemia. Liver nowadays plays a very small part in hospital dietetics. Liver, kidneys and pancreas, being rich in cells, contain more nucleic acids than muscle. For this reason patients with gout have been advised to avoid them.

Sausages

These have been used throughout historical times as a convenient form in which meat can be preserved and transported. Odysseus, waiting to revenge himself on the suitors, sat impatiently like 'a man before a great fire taking a sausage full of fat and blood, turning it this way and that and longing to have it roasted more speedily'. Cities like Cambridge, Bologna, Frankfurt and Hamburg have achieved fame from their sausages as well as from their universities. The basis of all sausages is a mixture of meat and flour and their quality depends on the proportion and quality of the meat. In Britain the best sausages contain pork and the cheaper varieties beef.

Germany has a great reputation for the variety of its sausages, many made from liver and offal. A variety of seasonings are used; chipolata sausages contain chives; saveloys, pigs' brains. With such varied recipes, any general statement of the nutritive value of sausages would be liable to a large error. In the absence of any precise knowledge of the composition, protein 12 g, fat 20 g, carbohydrate 12 g and energy 1.2 MJ (280 kcal)/100 g is a reasonable estimate.

Meat extractives, beef tea, soups, etc.

Meat extracts like Bovril have been used for generations. They contain the freely water-soluble substances of muscle — potassium, phosphates, peptides, nucleotides, creatine, vitamin B12 and other vitamins. When reconstituted with hot water, 'beef teas' have a very low concentration of solids and do not supply significant amounts either of energy or protein, but commercial preparations usually contain large amounts of sodium. However, they stimulate appetite and hence may be useful in the feeding of convalescents.

Slugs and snails and puppy-dogs' tails' or chacun a son goût

Those of us who have been brought up as members of one of the great religions of the world — particularly caste Hindus, but to a lesser extent all Mohammedans, Jews and Christians — seldom realise the extent to which our daily diet is artificially restricted. Religious taboos are partly responsible, but custom and tradition are much more important. There are many foods which would cause any 'civilised' man to revolt at the very thought of eating them; yet some of these foods are very palatable and many are nutritious. They can play an important part in the diet of unsophisticated people. Nicol has recorded how the Isoko tribe in Nigeria may obtain up to 20 g of protein/head daily from mud-fish, monkeys, pangolin, porcupine. cane-rat, Gambian rat, snails, palm weevils and frogs.[5] Without the addition of these luxuries to their diet, the Isoko would be very poorly off. Young boys show much ingenuity in hunting and trapping such animals.

Bristowe gives an interesting account of the insects that may be eaten in Vietnam and Thailand.[6] Even wealthy and well-bred people consider the larvae of a coffee-boring moth (*Zeuzero coffeae*) delicious when roasted and eaten with rice and salt. Properly cooked and served, locusts can be an attractive and nourishing food. Flying ants cooked in butter are considered to be a delicacy in parts of Africa.

Many South Americans rear guinea-pigs especially for the table, and they are reputed to be very tasty. Some Polynesians regard dog-flesh as a delicacy. These practices seem particularly distasteful to laboratory-trained nutritionists.

There are many records of the inhabitants of besieged cities in Europe eating cats, dogs and even rats with avidity. Man's range of foods is much wider than social conventions normally permit. Amongst primitive people these foods may contribute significantly to the total protein content of the diet and so improve health — particularly of small boys. A visiting nutritionist may well fail to be informed about these foods, unless special enquiries are made. Few of these foods have been analysed and little is known about their nutritive value.

Wild animals are a large potential source of food in some countries. It used to be thought that the inhabitants of certain parts of Africa would be better off nutritionally if the wild animals were exterminated and the grazing lands used for cattle, sheep and goats. But the yield of meat from game such as blesbok, eland, wildebeest and springbok, if properly protected and culled, is likely to be greater than that obtained from domestic animals grazed on the same land. Talbot has provided a useful review of wild animals as a source of food.[7]

FISH AND OTHER SEA FOODS

Fish are an important source of animal protein for some people. Lean or white fish contains less than 1 per cent of fat and about 10 per cent of protein with energy values ranging from 220 to 330 kJ (50 to 80 kcal)/100 g. Familiar white fish on the British coast are cod, haddock, pollack, saithe, brill, ling, whiting, John Dory, sole, plaice and turbot. These fish have a reputation — for the most part well merited — as being a light and easily digested food, suitable for invalids. Oily fish contain 8 to 15 per cent of fat and so have a higher energy value — 330 to 660 kJ (80 to 160 kcal)/100 g. Oily fish eaten in Great Britain are herring (including the preserved forms, kippers and bloaters), pilchards, salmon, whitebait, eel, sardines and sprats. Intermediate species — usually with 2 to 7 per cent of fat — are hake, halibut, mackerel, mullet and trout.

Fish proteins have a high biological value similar to the proteins of land animals. Yet, although many fish are delicious, on the whole fish are less tasty than meat, and a fish diet tends to be monotonous. Good cooks have a great variety of sauces and garnishes by which they make fish more interesting and appetising. In the Middle Ages, housewives used the herb garden with skill to flavour the flesh of coarse fish such as carp, pike, perch, roach, dace and chub, which came out of the fishponds kept by the great manor houses. The monosyllabic names of these fish indicate that they were familiar to the earliest users of the English language. The art of cooking them is now all but lost.

The content of protein in fish is somewhat less than in meat and there is often a large waste in the scales and bones. This should be remembered in calculating the relative cost of proteins of different origin.

The only fish offal commonly eaten is the roe, both the hard roe and the soft roe or milts. Cod roe and herring roe contain 20 to 25 per cent of protein and are rich in nucleic acids. True caviare is the roe of the sturgeon; many imitations are produced by colouring other fish roes. This rich and tasty food contains about 30 per cent of protein and 20 per cent of fat.

Fish oils are rich sources of the fat-soluble vitamins A and D. Marine fish are the richest source of iodine in the diet and a good source of fluoride. Small fish — such as sprats and sardines — may be a useful source of calcium when eaten whole, together with the bones. In the great river deltas of the East, where there is extensive cultivation of rice (a cereal poor in calcium) and few or no dairy cattle, the general level of calcium intake is always low. This can be improved by proper use of the small fish which abound in the ditches, tributaries and irrigation canals that lead off from the big rivers.

Shellfish

Lobsters, crayfish, crabs, shrimps and other crustaceans have little fat and an energy value of about 200 kJ (50 kcal)/100 g. They are very tasty and have become an expensive 'prestige' food. As the demand for them is high, many natural breeding grounds are overfished

and becoming exhausted. But the coarse, big muscle fibres of the larger species are not easily digested. Some people are sensitive to the proteins of these creatures and develop a variety of allergic reactions from eating them.

Oysters, mussels and other molluscs contain rather more protein (15 per cent) than most fish. They also contain about 5 per cent of the carbohydrate glycogen, but little fat. Oysters have acquired a reputation as an expensive luxury food, whereas the other molluscs are often regarded as poor man's fare; all can be attractive and useful foods. Oysters are the richest food source of zinc. They accumulate this and related metals from their water environment and can contain up to 100 mg/100 g.

These shellfish live on seashores and are sometimes gathered near the output of urban sewage. Unfortunately they may harbour bacteria, particularly those of the Salmonella group. Proper supervision is necessary both of sewage disposal and the collection of shellfish, to prevent the danger of infection. Though shellfish such as mussels and winkles are safe if properly cooked, it is well to be sure that those eaten raw — such as oysters — come from a pure source. Mussels occasionally cause neurotoxic poisoning (p. 244).

Fish-meal and fish-flour

These two products of the fishing industry are used as feeds for dairy animals and poultry and so add to the world's supply of protein-rich foods. But they can be used with greater nutritional efficiency directly as food for man. They can be incorporated in stews and staple starches or scattered on cooked foods such as porridge. Prepared from small whole fish, they have excellent nutrient content. Objections have been raised on grounds of hygiene (the alimentary contents), flavour, keeping quality and simple fastidiousness. All of these objections can and should be overcome. Care must be taken that the processes for preparing fish-flour from fish-meal do not destroy any amino acids in the crude fish-meal.

An increase in the consumption of sea food requires improved methods of conservation. Many offshore waters — notably the North Sea and the waters around Iceland and the Faeroes — have been overfished. Very rich fishing grounds are available in deeper and less accessible waters, though in many parts of the world such as Africa, South America and South-east Asia the traditional methods of fishing — the nets and the boats — are ill-adapted for exploiting these fields. Modern methods of fishing with motor trawlers and drifters have been greatly extended in tropical seas. Previously unfamiliar species of deeper water fish will be exploited.

Marine fishing is the most expensive in use of energy of any type of food production. Only about 5 per cent of the energy put into power boats and refrigerators is got back as food energy. For most farming operations in affluent countries the yield of food energy is 1 to 5 times the total energy put in.

We are becoming aware that the living resources of the sea are not unlimited. The prospects of greatly increasing the world's catch of marine fish, some 60 million tons a year, do not seem very bright at present. Several species are threatened by overfishing. The catch of whales gets less each year and the Peruvian anchovy (*Engraulis ringens*) which had reached 20 per cent of the total world catch by 1970 completely failed in 1972, with disastrous effects on the price of fish-meal for animal feedstuffs. Landings of herring from British coastal waters have been falling steadily since 1963. Too many ships from several different countries have been fishing in the North Sea. It is hoped that the international agreements on 200 mile limits of fishing rights off the shores of maritime countries will allow better control of tonnage, size and species of fish caught. Fish populations should be managed as a national resource in a more rational and conservative way.

Instead of hunting haphazardly ocean fish whose population size and rates of replacement are little known, an alternative approach is fish farming. The supply of fresh-water fish can be increased by systematic cultivation with proper stocking and the use of mineral and nitrogen fertilisers added to the fishponds. In the tropics much progress along these lines has been made, often stimulated by the Fisheries Divisions of FAO. In Europe the fish ponds which in medieval times supplied fish in winter to the monasteries and other great houses have long been in disuse. Nowadays trout served in restaurants is likely to have come from a fish farm. Floating marine fish farms in Scottish lochs are producing commercial quantities of salmon. Marine fish farming is never likely to be cheap. As well as containing the fish and protecting them from contamination, they have to be fed, often on fish-meal.

EGGS

Since the egg forms a complete food for the embryo chick, it is naturally rich in essential nutrients. An average hen's egg, weighing about 2 oz or 60 g, contains 6 g of protein and 6 g of fat and yields about 330 kJ (80 kcal). The proteins — most of which are albumins in the white of the egg — have the highest biological value for human adults of all food proteins. The amino acids composition of whole hens' eggs is sometimes used as a standard against which the chemical score of other proteins is compared. Values of the amino acid pattern of egg proteins are given on p. 49. A hen's egg contains about 30 mg of calcium and 1.5 mg of iron; however, the iron is bound, possibly to the protein conalbumin,

and poorly absorbed in man.[8] The yolk is a fair source of vitamin A and also contains significant amounts of thiamin, nicotinic acid and riboflavin; most of the yellow colour of yolks is xanthophyll (lutein) which is a carotenoid but not a vitamin A precursor. There is no ascorbic acid. Tolan and colleagues[9] compared the nutrients in eggs from free-range and battery hens; eggs from free-range hens contained more folate and vitamin B12.

Eggs have been described as nature's 'convenience food', since they come in an hygienic pack, are easily stored and readily opened and cooked. For this reason and also because of their nutritive value they are well suited to the needs of old people who usually like them. An egg contains about 250 mg of cholesterol and when eaten in large numbers may raise the plasma cholesterol.

The eggs of many other species of birds are eaten in various parts of the world and all have approximately the same nutritive value as eggs of domestic hens.

NOVEL PROTEIN FOODS

Attempts to find new foods rich in protein arise from two main motives. There is the need for new infant foods suitable for preventing protein-energy malnutrition, so prevalent in many countries, and also for a cheap alternative to meat. Everywhere prices of meat have been rising for many years and in some countries the supply has declined. A suitable alternative to meat might obtain an established place in our diets, just as 100 years ago the manufacture of margarine provided a valuable alternative to butter. There is also the fear that world population will outgrow its supply of conventional foods. The term 'novel protein' is used to describe several different types of product and no definition is generally acceptable. Defatted soya flour and fish proteins concentrates are products of food technology which have been available for many years, and the former is widely used in the food industry. In as much as they are not conventional foods, they can be described as novel.

Plankton, algae and leaves

It is possible to extract and concentrate an edible material from biological sources which themselves cannot be used as human food because of their high content of indigestible material. The Japanese have been pioneers in preparing foods from plankton, the mass of small crustacea and coelenterates that abound on the surface waters of the sea, and from chlorella, the green alga which forms the scum on top of many pools. In England Pirie has devised a process on a small factory scale for extracting protein from green leaves and grasess.[10] He has entertained his friends with the product which has the consistency of a friable cheese and only a slight taste which is not unpleasant. These are three potential sources of novel protein, which a hungry world may need some day, but for which no one shows much enthusiasm at present.

Protein-rich material from microorganisms

Large industrial firms are using their resources to develop new foods from microorganisms. Protein-rich foods can be obtained from yeasts grown in mineral oils, from bacteria grown in methanol, manufactured from methane and other hydrocarbons in natural gas, and from a fungus, *Fusarium graminearum*, grown on hydrolysed bean starch. Some of these products have been used as protein concentrates for animal feeding. It is likely to be a long time before any one of them is shown to be safe and acceptable as a human food.

Proteins from legumes and oil seeds

There are available in the USA and Britain vegetable protein products which have been textured and flavoured to resemble meat. Textured vegetable protein (TVP) is a registered name in the USA. Stews, meat pies and goulashes have been prepared from these products and their resemblance to the real thing is as close as that of good margarine to butter. A TVP preparation from soya bean is in use in school meal programmes in the USA and is on sale in Britain. In as much as the raw materials of these products are conventional foods, and as there is no reason to think that the physical changes brought about in the texturing and spinning have harmful effects, there seem to be no new problems of toxicity.

Just as margarine is now enriched with vitamins A and D to give it a nutritive value similar to that of butter, it is sensible to make new foods as nutritious as meat. It has been suggested that they should contain in 100 g of dry matter a minimum of 50 g protein, 1.3 g methionine, 10 mg iron, 2 mg thiamin, 0.6 mg riboflavin and 5 μg vitamin B1. The natural ingredients contain no vitamin B12 and this would have to be added. Vegetable proteins in general have less methionine than animal proteins and most products would require enrichment with this amino acid to bring their biological value up to approximately that of most meat. Artificial additions of iron, thiamin and riboflavin might or might not be needed. With these safeguards there is no reason to think that the substitution of meat by such foods in a mixed diet would have any adverse affect on nutrition.

These new products should be welcomed as nutritious cheap alternatives to meat with an appeal to families, schools, homes for old people and others whose purchases of meat are restricted by small incomes. Yet it is important that no one should be deceived into thinking that they are eating meat when they are not. There are no special difficulties in ensuring that manufacturers of novel protein foods label their containers with the appropriate description of their contents. Caterers who buy these products and use them to prepare 'meat pies', 'meat stews', etc., either for consumption in restaurants and canteens or for outside sale, are under the same legal obligations as manufacturers to inform their customers by correct labelling of their products. Many articles of food are likely to be prepared from mixtures of meat and novel proteins, but as yet there are no regulations regarding the proportion of meat in the mixture necessary to ensure that the article can still be described as a meat product.

The introduction of novel protein foods thus poses problems concerning their safety, nutritive value, labelling and composition. These are discussed in reports by the Food Standards Committee,[11] Department of Health and Social Security.[12]

REFERENCES

1. Lawrie R A 1974 Meat science, 2nd edn. Pergamon Press, Oxford
2. Harries J M, Hubbard A W, Alder F E, and two others 1968 The nutritive value of beef from intensively reared animals. Br J Nutr 22: 21–31
3. Bender A E, Zia M 1976 Meat quality and protein quality. J Food Tech 11: 495–8
4. Paul A A, Southgate D A T 1978 The composition of foods. HMSO, London
5. Nicol B M 1953 Protein in the diet of the Isoko tribe of the Niger delta. Proc Nutr Soc 12: 66–69
6. Bristowe W S 1953 Insects as foods Proc Nutr Soc 12: 44–8
7. Talbot L M 1964 Wild animals as sources of food. Proceedings of the Sixth International Congress of Nutrition. E & S Livingstone, Edinburgh, p 243–51
8. Callender S T, Marney S R, Warner G T 1970 Eggs and iron absorption. Br J Haematol 19: 657–65
9. Tolan A, Robertson J, Orton C R, and three others 1974 The chemical composition of eggs produced under battery, deep litter and free range conditions. Br J Nutr 31: 185
10. Pirie N W 1975 Leaf protein: a beneficiary of tribulation. Nature 256: 239–41
11. Food Standards Committee. 1980 Report on meat products. HMSO, London
12. Department of Health and Social Security 1980 Food which simulate meat. Report on Health and Social Subjects no 17

20

Milk and Milk Products; Oils and Fats

MILK AND CHEESE

Milk is the sole natural food for the human infant for the first few months of life. After about 3 to 6 months it is desirable to give supplementary foods and gradually wean the infant on to a good mixed diet. In this process milk slowly loses its dominant place in the infant's diet, but for the first two years of life it is important that milk should remain the largest single item of food.

From the age of 2 years and until growth ceases, children grow more rapidly and reach maturity sooner if given ample quantities of milk. Increased growth rates are generally associated with improved health and vitality and with relative freedom from disease. All nutritionists agree that a regular intake of milk is beneficial to growing children. There are, however, many people who have doubts as to whether large quantities (more than 2 pints or 1 litre daily) are desirable. It is not proven that the unusually rapid growth promoted by such large intakes is beneficial. In many tropical countries little milk is available and a few children are intolerant of milk (Chap. 50). European children can grow well on a diet composed almost entirely of wheaten bread and vegetables, with no milk.[1] The same has been found in Guatemala, India and other countries with well-balanced combinations of vegetable foods.

As a complete food easily given, readily digested and absorbed milk is good for invalids, especially for patients with acute illnesses. There is no evidence, however, that milk is an indispensable food for adults. As a good source of the principal nutrients it can be recommended for those who like it.

CHEMICAL COMPOSITION OF MILK

This chapter is concerned with milk as a food for adults and for children after weaning from the breast or bottle. Human breast milk is considered only incidentally and its composition and that of the various infant milk preparations are discussed in Chapter 61.

Typical values for the carbohydrate, protein, fat and energy content of milks consumed by man are given in Table 20.1. The values for human milk are taken from analyses of pooled samples in Britain.[2] Reindeer, red deer, moose, musk-ox, eland and Bali cattle are other potential sources of milk for man.[3]

Protein
Cow's milk contains much more protein than human milk. About 80 per cent of this protein is casein. The rest, whey proteins, broadly resemble those found in plasma and include lactalbumin and various immunoglobulins which have a role in defence mechanisms in early life (p. 582).

Fat
The fat in freshly secreted milk is present in fine globules, many of which are as small as 0.5 μm in diameter.

Table 20.1 Typical analyses of milk from various species

	Carbohydrate (g/dl)	Protein (g/dl)	Fat (g/dl)	Energy	
				kJ/dl	kcal/dl
Human	7.3	1.07	4.2	293	70
	(7.1–7.8)	(0.95–1.20)	(3.7–4.8)	(272–314)	(65–75)
Cow	5.0	3.5	3.5	275	66
	(4.2–6.8)	(2.5–4.0)	(3–6)		
Buffalo	4.5	4.3	7.5	430	103
Goat	4.5	3.7	4.8	320	76
Ewe	4.9	6.5	6.9	450	109
Mare	5.7	1.3	1.2	160	29
Camel	4.1	3.7	4.2	290	69

Fat in this form is easily digested. When milk is left to stand these globules run together to form cream. The fat content of both human and cow's milk varies greatly.

The fatty acid composition of the fat in human and cow's milk is given on p. 581 where the possible significance of the differences is discussed.

In some mammals the fat content of the milk is very high. The milk of whales and sea lions, for instance, contains over 40 g/dl of fat. In these animals lactation lasts for a very short period, during which the mothers cannot feed. The milk transfers an enormous quantity of fat from the mother to the young in the course of a few days. Elephant's milk contains 20 g of fat and reindeer milk 17 g/dl.

Carbohydrate

The carbohydrate in all milks is lactose. This sugar is much less sweet than sucrose. Human milk contains more lactose than cow's milk. Cow's milk is frequently 'humanised' by diluting and then adding sucrose or glucose. The young infant thus becomes accustomed to an unnaturally sweet food at an early age.

Minerals

Calcium is present in all milks in good quantities. Human milk usually contains between 25 and 35 mg/dl. Cow's milk contains about 120 mg/dl. The calcium is present chiefly in combination with caseinogen and is more readily absorbed than that in other foods, probably because calcium salts of amino acids are soluble. Milk is thus a most valuable food for the formation of bone.

Milk contains very little iron. All milks provide 0.1 to 0.2 mg/dl. Young mammals depend for their initial supply of iron on stores accumulated during intrauterine life. In the human infant these stores are sufficient for only four to six months, and if iron is not then provided in the diet anaemia is likely to follow. Infants born prematurely have smaller reserves of iron in the liver, and so are more liable to develop anaemia.

Vitamins

Table 20.2 gives normal values for the vitamin content of cow's whole milk and human milk. If the dietary intake of any vitamin is high some of the excess is likely to appear in the milk, especially vitamin A and riboflavin.

Cow's milk is a useful but not rich source of vitamins. Its riboflavin may be especially valuable to children on poor diets and its nicotinic acid may help to prevent pellagra in maize-eaters. Cow's milk contains little vitamin D mostly as the aqueous-soluble sulphate and unless enriched cannot be relied on to prevent rickets. The ascorbic acid content is also not high and it is destroyed by pasteurisation, boiling or allowing the milk to stand in sunlight.

Table 20.2 Normal values for the vitamin content of cow's milk (whole raw) and human milk[2,4]

	Cow's milk /dl	Human milk /dl
Vitamin A (µg) summer	43	50
winter	30	
Vitamin D (µg)	0.15	0.8
Thiamin (µg)	40	20
Riboflavin (µg)	190	30
Nicotinic acid (µg)	80	220
Ascorbic acid (µg)	1.5	3.8

DIGESTION OF MILK

Milk clots when it enters the stomach. This is due to the action of an enzyme — rennin. The clotting converts the caseinogen into insoluble casein. The clot contracts and is subsequently digested. Infants secrete little pepsin in the stomach; the clot is digested by trypsin and other proteolytic ensymes in the small intestine. The biological significance of this clotting is not known; it is reputed to make milk less easily digested. It can be partially prevented by diluting the milk with water, thus reducing the concentration of calcium which is necessary for the formation of the clot. Clotting can also be prevented by the addition of sodium citrate. Both of these means have been much used, but whether they increase the digestibility of milk is doubtful. Milk is readily digested and absorbed by infants and growing children.

Cow's milk — owing to its high protein content and its content of phosphate and citrate — exerts a strong buffering action, thus lowering the acidity of the gastric juice. It is perhaps for this reason that milk is often so effective in reducing the discomfort caused by a peptic ulcer and the associated hyperacidity.

MILK PRODUCTS

Soured and fermented milks

In many countries, milk is drunk sour or curdled. Various bacteria are used for this purpose — *Lactobacillus acidophilus* found in man, *L. bifidus* found in the alimentary tract of infants and *L. bulgaricus* found in cows. All these bacteria cause a breakdown of the lactose in the milk with the formation of lactic acid (up to 3 per cent). The natural method of preparation is to boil the milk and somewhat reduce its volume. After cooling it is inoculated with a small portion of the previous day's milk as a starter. The souring takes about 24 hours. Condensed and reconstituted dried milk can be used for the purpose. Commercial preparations of the bacterial cultures are also available as starters. Sour milk (yogurt) contains all the protein, fat, calcium and vitamins of the original milk. It is a safe preparation in countries where

MILK AND MILK PRODUCTS; OILS AND FATS   213

standards of dairy hygiene are low, for the original milk is sterilised by boiling and the subsequent profuse growth of *L. acidophilus* overgrows any chance pathogenic contaminant. There are many traditional forms of sour milk which are appreciated as national drinks.

Yogurt originated in South-east Europe and Turkey. If the milk has been much concentrated by boiling, the yogurt is diluted with water for drinking and is then known as *doogh* in Afghanistan and Iran, or *eyran* in Turkey. If souring is allowed to take place when the milk is warm (about 55°C), a preparation known as *laban* is formed, which may contain a little alcohol from yeast fermentation. *Kefir* is a sour milk made in the Caucasus with lactobacilli and a lactose-fermenting yeast, which may have an alcohol content of 1 per cent. *Koumiss* is a popular Russian drink prepared from mares' milk, which is rich in lactose. It may contain up to 3 per cent alcohol.

Consumption of commercially produced yogurt increased greatly in Britain and the USA in the 1960s. The organisms most used for the processing are *L. bulgaricus* and *Streptococcus thermophilus*. Composition varies greatly and a draft prepared for the *Codex Alimentarius* suggests a minimum content of non-fat milk solids of 8.5 g/dl and of milk fat 3 g/dl. Skimmed yogurts are also popular and for these a maximum fat content of 0.5 g/dl is suggested.

The great Russian scientist Metchnikoff at the end of the nineteenth century conceived the idea that yogurt was an elixir of life. His theory was that the putrefactive bacteria present in the large intestine produce toxins that shorten life. He thought that by taking yogurt, the milk-souring bacilli would become dominant in the intestine and oust the usual putrefactive bacteria. He himself took yogurt regularly and established it as a fashion in many European cities. Metchnikoff was mistaken: *L. bulgaricus* cannot proliferate in the human bowel. But yogurt is a nutritious and convenient food.

Dahi is a sour milk preparation made in innumerable Indian homes. Whole milk is brought to the boil and then allowed to cool to about body temperature and kept at this heat in an earthen vessel. A small amount of yesterday's dahi is added as a starter. When cool, dahi is a delicious drink, especially in the hot weather, although perhaps an acquired taste for Europeans. The butter fat may be removed from dahi by churning and used to make *ghee*. The remaining sour milk is known as *lassi* and is also a popular drink.

Curds (junket)
Curds are the clotted proteins formed when fresh milk is artificially inoculated with rennet (a commercial preparation of rennin, prepared either from calves' stomachs or vegetable sources). Sweetened and flavoured forms are junket.

Whey
Whey is the fluid that separates from the clot in making cheese. It contains most of the lactose in the original milk and a little lactalbumin, but almost no casein or fat. Whey is often wasted and efforts are being made to find economic ways to concentrate the lactalbumin, a good quality protein, which could be a useful protein supplement.

Butter
This is discussed later in this chapter.

Cream
Cream contains all the fat and usually from one-third to half of the protein and lactose in milk. The standards for cream have varied in different countries and from time to time. In the UK the Food Standards Committee recommend that cream should contain 20 per cent butterfat with double cream 18 per cent and half cream 12 per cent. These figures are mathematically inconsistent and it would be more logical to to have single cream with 24 per cent fat. The present recommendation is that whipping cream should contain 35 per cent fat but the consumer may be confused by the distinction between this and 'whipped' cream, i.e. that already prepared and which by the judicious use of sugar and other food products, e.g. gums, can be presented as an already prepared cream of much lower fat content. The regulations are currently under review.

The famous Devonshire cream or clotted cream is prepared by heating the milk in special pans. This brings about a rapid and effective separation of the fat. Devonshire cream may contain 60 per cent of fat.

Evaporated and condensed milk
Evaporated milk is the liquid product obtained by the partial removal of water from milk or skimmed milk. Condensed milk is the product obtained in the same way, but with the addition of sugar. The first came into use to meet the needs of the people in the new industrial towns in Europe and North America in the nineteenth century, and both products are now finding new markets in the greatly increased urban populations of Asia, Africa and South America. Clearly, legal composition standards are needed and those in force in Britain are shown in Table 20.3. There are also important labelling requirements, including the statement, 'should not be used for babies except under medical advice', on partly skimmed milk products and 'unfit for babies' on skimmed milk products. In some countries infants fed on these products have become blind, due to the development of keratomalacia.

Skimmed milk
This is milk from which the fat has been removed in the

Table 20.3 Compositional standards laid down in Britain for evaporated and condensed milk

	Percentage of milk fat	Minimum percentage of milk solids including fat
Evaporated full cream milk	9.0*	31.0
Condensed full cream milk	9.0*	31.0
Evaporated partly skimmed milk	4.5*	26.5
Condensed partly skimmed milk	4.5*	26.5
Evaporated skimmed milk	0.5†	22.0
Condensed skimmed milk	0.5†	

* Minimum permitted.
† Maximum permitted.

making of butter or cream. It is a by-product of the butter industry and since it is readily dried, large quantities of the dried product are available on the world market. In Great Britain skimmed milk has been traditionally fed to pigs and is despised as a human food. This is unfortunate, since it contains most of the protein and nearly all the calcium in the original milk. It also contains the B group of vitamins. Skimmed milk is thus a good food. Largely through the good offices of the United Nations Children's Fund (UNICEF) many thousands of tons of dried skimmed milk have been distributed to children in countries which are short of dairy cattle. The improvement in health of children receiving this milk has been demonstrated in controlled experiments and vast numbers of children have benefited.

Dried skimmed milk from the USA has been enriched with vitamin A but milk donated by European countries has not. Because xerophthalmia is reported in many developing countries, dried skimmed milk used in aid programmes should be enriched with vitamin A.

In modern industrial societies milk processing factories are adept at handling and mixing milks to maintain a product of standard fat content despite the seasonal variations with lower fat contents in the natural product during the winter seasons. In the United States and Europe milk is sold in a variety of grades with the fat content clearly labelled. Britain is unusual not only in maintaining a daily milk delivery service to each household, which is claimed to account for the high milk consumption, but also for the limitations imposed on the pasteurisation and fat content of milk. Thus the standard milk has to contain 3.75 per cent fat and the creamier Jersey milk 4.75 per cent fat. Skimmed milk is also delivered to households on request but this product has to be sterilised rather than pasteurised so that the taste is considered by most people to be unsatisfactory. In the USA and on the Continent a pleasant skimmed milk product is commercially available, and additional products with 1.5–2.0 per cent milk fat are sold as substi-

tutes for the standard milk. There is resistance to their introduction in Britain.

The fat in whole milk if taken in large amounts, may have an adverse effect was shown in one experiment.[5] Healthy male students were asked to drink 2 litres of milk a day and to restrict their usual diet so as not to gain weight. In this they succeeded, but the milk raised their mean plasma cholesterol from 4.6 to 5.1 mmol/l after one week. In two subsequent weeks it fell slightly but not to the initial value.

Casein

Various preparations of casein are on the market. Casilan, a calcium caseinate is one which is well known. These preparations have little taste and provide a most convenient and effective means of enriching diets with protein in dietetic practice, as in the treatment of burns, prolonged fevers and in convalescence from severe illnesses. They can be added to soups, puddings, milk drinks, cocoa, etc.

Cheese

Milk production is inevitably subject to large seasonal variations. In the summer months when pastures are good, cows yield more milk than in the winter; a surplus in summer is therefore common. Cheese-making is an effective method of preserving some of this surplus and has been a traditional occupation of European farmers' wives for generations. There are over 400 varieties.

The basic process in cheese-making is the clotting of the milk. The milk may or may not be soured first. Rennet is used to form the clot, usually at a temperature of about 30°C. The clot, which contains almost all the protein in the milk, also entangles the fat and many of the other nutrients. The clot is then gently separated from the whey and salted. It is pressed to remove moisture and a firm cake is made. The cheese is then put in cheese bags and kept in a cool room to ripen. During ripening bacterial fermentation takes place; the particular bacteria and moulds responsible give the cheese its characteristic texture and flavour. Many variations in the details of cheese-making exist. Cow's milk is usually employed, but Roquefort cheese comes from ewe's milk and some Norwegian cheeses from goat's milk. The blue colour characteristic of Stilton, Gorgonzola and Roquefort is produced by moulds developing during the ripening process. The most famous English cheeses are Cheddar, Cheshire, Wensleydale and Stilton. France produces the greatest variety: Camembert, Brie, Livarot and Pont l'Eveque are famous French soft cheeses; Roquefort, Saint Paulin and Port-du-Salut are semi-soft cheeses. Italy produces the blue Gorgonzola, semi-soft Bel Paese and the hard Parmesan. Limburger is a soft, strongly flavoured Belgian cheese. Holland produces many notable Dutch cheeses — particularly the round red Edam — and Denmark the famous Danish blue. Gruyère, with its characteristic holes, comes from Switzerland. These and many other cheeses are described by Eekhor-Stork.[6] France has the highest cheese consumption of any country (daily average 40 /head) followed by Israel.

Those who will not eat cheese forego a food which is not only tasty but also nutritious. Most cheeses contain 25 to 35 per cent of protein and this protein is of high biological value. The fat content usually varies from 16 to 40 per cent. Cheeses are also rich in calcium, vitamin A and riboflavin. There are also dietetic cheeses made from skimmed milk; cottage cheese contains 4 per cent fat.

The cheese reaction. Many cheeses contain tyramine, the amine of the amino acid tyrosine. The amounts vary greatly, but a portion of Cheddar may contain 20 mg. Tyramine stimulates the sympathetic system by inhibiting uptake of noradrenaline at the synaptic junctions where its concentration increases, causing a big rise in blood pressure. The tyramine naturally present in foods is normally destroyed very quickly in the tissues by monoamine oxidases (MAO). However, drugs such as phenelzine and tranylcypromine which are used for the treatment of depression, inhibit MAO. If patients on these drugs eat a large portion of cheese, the tyramine present is not destroyed and may produce alarming reactions. Headache, severe nausea and dizziness frequently occur, with severe hypertension, followed occasionally by cerebral haemorrhage or cardiac failure. Patients taking MAO inhibitors have to be careful with other food, drinks and medicines containing amines.

Khoa, rabri, churkom, dried reindeer milk and other delicacies

Cheese-making is characteristically a European art. There are, however, a number of ways in which surplus milk can be concentrated, sometimes into forms which may be preserved for a long time. In India, *khoa* or *mawa* is made by boiling milk briskly in an open pan until about two-thirds of the water has been evaporated and it has the consistency of dough; *rabri* is made by skimming off successive layers of cream from simmering milk and adding sugar when the liquid residue is greatly reduced; the skimmed-off clots are then blended back into the liquid residue to make a sweet concentrate. In the Himalayas the Sherpas heat any excess *lassi* and the clot formed, mainly casein, is strained through bamboo baskets and then dried before an open fire to make *churkom*. In Lapland reindeer milk is put in a reindeer stomach over an open smoking fire. As the water evaporates and the milk is 'cured', more milk is added and it may

take two or three weeks before the stomach is filled with grains of dried milk. This quantity may last a Lapp family for the winter.

Nearly all indigenous soured milk products have the advantage that they are much less likely to be contaminated with pathogenic organisms than fresh milk. They can therefore be strongly recommended in places where the standards of dairy hygiene are low.

OILS AND FATS

These are valuable foods as they provide a concentrated source of energy and they are also essential to the art of good cooking in all civilised societies. Most plants bearing oil seeds are tropical. African and Asian societies early in their civilisation learnt how to express the oil from the local crop and to use it for cooking. Olive trees are a feature of the Mediterranean landscape and olive oil was much used in ancient Greek, Hebrew and Roman societies. Northern Europeans were mainly dependent on animal fats until the twentieth century. These included lard (pig fat), suet (perirenal fat of cattle and sheep) and beef dripping. Table 20.4 lists the principal world sources of oils and fats. They were not only used as foods but also as fuel for heating and lighting (now almost entirely replaced by mineral oils) and also for soap-making, which still continues.

Margarine was invented in 1869 by the French chemist, Mège-Mourie, and its production stimulated by the shortage of butter during the Franco-Prussian war. Thereafter production increased steadily and a large

Table 20.4 The principal oil and fats. The vegetable oils are listed twice: first in order of world production and secondly in order of the export trade which approximates to their use by the food industry in the manufacture of margarine and other products

Production	Exports
Vegetable oils	
Soya bean oil	Soya bean oil
Sunflower seed oil	Coconut oil
Groundnut oil	Palm oil
Cottonseed oil	Groundnut oil
Rapeseed oil	Rapeseed oil
Palm oil	
Olive oil	
Sesame oil	
Maize (corn oil)	
Marine oils	
Whale oil	
Fish oils	
Animal fats	
Butter	
Lard (from pigs)	
Suet (from ruminants)	

industry was built up. At first animal fats were the main raw material; in the 1930s whale oil was much used, but today these have been largely replaced by vegetable oils. Soya bean oil from USA crops is now the main raw material, but the industry is adaptable and price and availability determine which oils are used. The order in which the exports are set out in Table 20.4 approximates to the order of use by manufacturers. The development of supplies and international trade in vegetable oils was largely due to Lord Leverhulme, who acquired a small soapworks in 1884 and by 1925 had a world market with 250 associated companies and was a pioneer of 'multinationalism'.

Oil seed crops are grown on plantations, but production is still mainly in the hands of farmers, both large and small. To celebrate the centenary of margarine, van Stuyvenberg[7] edited a book giving an excellent account of its economic, social and scientific history.

NUTRITIONAL VALUE

Oils and fats consist predominantly of triglycerides and contain little water. Vegetable oils and animals fats have an energy value of about 3700 kJ (900 kcal)/100 g. Butter and margarines are a little lower, about 3000 kJ (730 kJ)/100 g, because they contain some water. Diets containing little or no oils and fats or foods into which they had been incorporated are of low nutritional density and hence so bulky as to be unsuitable for active men and women needing more than 12.6 MJ (3000 kcal) daily. They provide not only energy but essential fatty acids in varying amounts (Table 6.1). However, they are not essential articles of diet, since natural unprocessed foods provide adequate amounts of these (p 68). Those vegetable oils with a high content of polyunsaturated fatty acids, particularly corn oil and sunflower seed oil, are useful in diets for the treatment of patients with familial hypercholesterolaemia (Chap. 40). One vegetable oil, rape seed oil, contains erucic acid in amounts which may be toxic and regulations in EEC countries limit the level of erucic acid in edible oils and fats to 5 per cent. Regrettably edible oils and fats may be criminally adulterated with toxic oils with disastrous consequences and examples are given in Chapter 25.

Oils and fats may be a source or potential source of fat-soluble vitamins. Most vegetable oils contain significant amounts of vitamin E; none contain vitamin D and most are devoid of vitamin A activity. Red palm oil is a rich source of β-carotene and children in Nigeria re-

ceiving red palm oil have been shown to be in better health than those that had none.[8] Corn oil contains small amouts of carotene. Animal fats contain small but nutritionally significant amounts of vitamin D and retinol. Butter, however, is a good source of retinol and has some vitamin D. The amounts depend on the quality of the cow's diet. Good summer butter may contain up to 1300 μg of retinol/100 g, but winter as little as 500 μg. The enrichment of margarines with retinol and vitamin D (first made statutary in the United Kingdom at the start of World War II) was a major advance in public health. By law margarine must contain 700 μg of retinol and 8 μg of vitamin D/100 g. This measure is an important part of the continuing campaign to prevent rickets.

In India, Pakistan and other eastern countries butter fats are clarified by heating and the resulting product is known as *ghee*. Ghee may be made in the home or as an industrial product. Processes vary. Good ghee may contain almost all the vitamins present in the original milk fat, but losses may be up to 50 per cent.

ROLE IN DIETS

Separated oils and fats are essential for good cooks and food manufacturers to practise their arts. They have been part of good living since the beginning of history. They are also expensive compared with cereals and cereal products. With increasing prosperity consumption rises and in many countries about 40 per cent of the dietary energy comes from fat. In many individuals the proportion is higher. There is a consensus among nutritionists that this proportion is too high, except for the now small minority who are very active physically. A reduction would be likely to lower the prevalence of obesity and heart disease. But how great a reduction is practical or desirable is uncertain. A major cause of complaint about the British diet in World War II and after was the small ration of fat. Annual consumption of oils and fats before the war was 45.3 lb/head and fell to 37.9 lb in 1943 and 33.9 lb in 1947. Such a reduction would only be acceptable in a national emergency. In poorer countries both peasants and urban slum dwellers prize oils and fats as essentials to allow preparation of traditional diets. Very few diets would be rated good if at least 20 per cent of the energy did not come from fat. Oils and fats are one of the many examples of the good things in life, which many of us take to excess when opportunity is presented.

REFERENCES

1. Widdowson E M, McCance R A 1954 Studies on the nutritive value of bread and on the effect of variations in the extraction rate on the growth of under-nourished children. MRC Spec Rep Ser no. 287
2. Department of Health and Social Security 1977 The composition of mature human milk. Report on Health and ·Social Subjects no 12. HMSO, London
3. Arman P 1979 Milk from semi-domesticated ruminants. World Rev Nutr Diet 33: 198–227
4. Paul A A, Southgate D A T 1978 The composition of food. HMSO, London
5. Roberts D C K, Truswell A S, and six others 1982 Milk, plasma cholesterol and controls in nutritional experiments. Atherosclerosis 42: 323–5
6. Eekhof-Stork N 1976 The world atlas of cheese. Paddington Press, London
7. van Stuyvenberg J H (ed) 1969 Margarine. An economic, social and scientific history. Liverpool University Press, Liverpool
8. Nicol B M 1952 The nutrition of Nigerian peasants with special reference to the effects of deficiencies of the vitamin B complex, vitamin A and animal protein. Br J Nutr 6: 34–55

21

Beverages; Herbs and Spices

BEVERAGES

The needs of the human body for water have already been discussed (p. 94). To meet them man must drink. *Homo sapiens* is not very fond of plain water and prefers flavoured fluids such as beer, wine, spirits, tea, coffee, cocoa, fruit juice, or even synthetic 'colas' and 'lemonades'. Americans encourage the consumption of plain water by serving it iced.

Beverages are appreciated for their flavour and for the pharmacological action of certain ingredients which many contain. Some are also a source of energy and a few provide small amounts of micronutrients.

Flavours are provided by the essential oils in the herbs, berries, and other fruit and grains which go to form the basic ingredients of many drinks. In tea and coffee gardens, in orchards, hop fields and vineyards, cultivators use the experience of generations to produce the best raw materials. Tea blenders, vintners, distillers, housewives and many others use traditional skills to refine and concentrate the basic ingredients. All humanity is grateful for the labours of such skilled craftsmen. To the epicure with a trained palate, the appreciation of well-made tea and coffee — of fine wines and spirits — is one of the privileges of living in a civilised society. The chemistry of 'Bouquet and Essence' was discussed many years ago in a learned editorial in the *Lancet*[1] with references to appropriate French and German literature. Chemists have not yet replaced professional tea and wine tasters[2] and the supreme qualities of 'Scotch' still remain a mystery, immune from science.

SOFT DRINKS

These include any fruit squash, crush and cordial (as distinct from fruit juice), colas, soda water, tonic water, sweetened artificially carbonated water that may or may not be flavoured, and ginger beer. They may be sold as concentrates or powders requiring dilution or ready to drink. Those that are sold at final volume for drinking are usually carbonated and thus fizzy. Cola drinks orig-

inated in 1886 in the United States and contained extracts from the kola nut, prepared by a pharmacist, John Pemberton. They are now manufactured throughout the world by many companies who use cola essences mostly provided by two American companies. The precise formulation of these essences is a closely guarded secret even within the companies. Large amounts of soft drinks are consumed, the total production in the UK in 1974 being 816 imperial gallons or 66 litres per head of population. The corresponding figure for the USA is just over 100 litres per head.

Soft drinks have little value in nutrition except that they encourage people to drink water. Some citrus squashes contain significant amounts of natural vitamin C or may be enriched with it, when claims are made on the label. Most soft drinks are sweetened. If sugar is used, this may contribute to obesity and the drink is unsuitable for diabetics. In one British product the content of glucose has been advertised as especially valuable for giving energy; but in fact glucose taken by mouth is no better than sucrose as a source of energy. Cola drinks usually contain caffeine in concentrations from 50 to 200 mg/l. Table 21.1 gives the electrolyte content and osmolality of some popular soft drinks, often seen at the bedside of hospital patients.

Fruit juices

Fruit juices are obtained from fruit by mechanical processes. After removal of a portion of the water, they may

Table 21.1 Analysis of popular soft drinks[3]

Brand	pH	Osmolality (mosmol/kg)	Electrolytes (mmol/l) Sodium	Potassium
'Coca-Cola'	2.8	469	3.0	0.1
'Pepsi-Cola'	2.7	576	1.0	0.1
'Seven-Up'	3.5	388	4.0	0.0
'Lucozade'	3.0	710	18.0	0.5
Orange juice	4.0	587	1.0	46.0
Apple juice	3.6	694	0.0	27.4
'Ribena'* diluted 1:3	3.0	1180	4.0	8.0

* Blackcurrant cordial.

be sold as a concentrated juice. Fruit juice has become an almost essential component of an American breakfast. This is a pleasant habit which is spreading slowly into Europe. Fruit juices contain approximately the same nutrients as whole fruit but have lost most of the pectin. The most important nutrient is vitamin C. This varies greatly depending on the fruit from which the juice was prepared. Citrus fruit juices may be expected to contain between 30 and 50 mg dl and pineapple and tomato juices about half as much. Apple juices contain little of the vitamin. Fruit juices are also useful for patients on low sodium diets or receiving diuretic drugs for any reason, as their content of potassium is high and of sodium low. A reasonable assumption is that juice contains not more than 2.5 mmol/l of Na and not less than 30 mmol/K and that K/Na ratio is at least 20.1.

Tea, coffee and cocoa

These beverages contain small amounts of three drugs, caffeine, theobromine and theophylline. These are methyl derivatives of xanthine. Caffeine is the most active; it is a stimulant to the nervous system and often prevents fatigue; many people find that caffeine appears to facilitate mental work. Most people in western countries are habituated to caffeine; they are accustomed to take it, but they do not become addicted to it. The British housewife, who is so frequently 'dying for a cup of tea', may feel tired and frustrated if she does not get it, but otherwise suffers no serious symptoms.

An excessive intake of caffeine can cause sleeplessness and so may aggravate emotional instability and mental illness. In some persons caffeine appears to sensitise the heart and increase the incidence of ventricular premature beats but this alone is not a reason to forbid its use. Both contain tannin, which is a weak protein precipitant and astringent. Tea and coffee do not impair digestion when taken in moderate amounts and not excessively strong, whether by healthy people or patients.

Caffeine is a weak diuretic. It is of little medicinal value for this purpose, nor are tea and coffee contraindicated for this reason.

Tea

Tea has been drunk in China for thousands of years. It was introduced into Europe in the seventeenth century and was at first a great luxury. After the discovery that tea could be grown easily on large estates in Sri Lanka and India, enormous quantities were imported into Great Britain, where for nearly a hundred years it has been a cheap and popular beverage.

Several varieties of the shrub are cultivated. Fertile soil, a warm climate and a good rainfall are necessary conditions for growth and these are found in Sri Lanka, Assam and the hill districts of South India. The shrubs are allowed to grow up to a height of about 4 ft and are pruned each year. The young and tender leaves, 'two leaves and a bud' of each shoot, are picked by hand, usually by women. After picking, the leaves are taken to a factory, usually on the estate, where they are withered, mashed or rolled and allowed to ferment. They are then dried. Most Indian and Ceylon tea sold in Great Britain is blended by mixing samples grown in different gardens.

Green teas commonly consumed by the Chinese are withered at high temperatures, so that the enzymes responsible for the fermentation are destroyed and this process in the manufacture is omitted.

The great variety of teas on the market are of interest to the connoisseur, but not to the physician or dietitian. They can be recommended as an attractive drink to all except a few unfortunates, in whom tea appears to cause indigestion probably owing to the tannin present. Robert Hutchison, a distinguished physician at the London Hospital, used to give lectures to medical students on food at dietetics at the end of the nineteenth century. In his book (1900)[4] based on these lectures he reported his analyses of many types of tea; he found the tannin content of a cup (150 ml) of infusion to vary from 60 to 280 mg. Caffeine contents varied from 50 to 80 mg. The mild stimulating effect of caffeine has already been described. Its pharmacopoeial dose is 60 to 300 mg, so that many cups have to be drunk before this maximum is exceeded.

Tea contains flavenols which after infusion polymerise to form tannins with an astringent flavour. This process is inhibited by acids as when lemon juice is added, and the polymers are absorbed by milk proteins. The British custom of adding milk and sugar (not practised by connoisseurs) masks the flavour and also adds significantly to the dietary energy of some people.

Coffee

Coffee beans are the seeds of coffee trees that are widely cultivated in the tropics. They have been grown in Ethiopia and Arabia for hundreds of generations. There are large plantations in India, Indonesia, Africa and especially in Brazil.

A variety of trees are grown. Most are 10 to 15 ft high with evergreen leaves. Shade trees are necessary to protect them from excessive sun. They bear clusters of white flowers which develop into the beans. A tree provides the best crop when between 6 and 14 years old; it requires regular and skilful pruning.

The beans have to be roasted and ground before the infusion is made. Hutchison[4] found about 100 mg of caffeine and 200 mg of tannin in a cup of coffee, made by infusing 2 oz (60 g) in a pint (450 ml) of water. Analyses of cups of coffee and tea[5] showed that today's Londoners may get from 58 to 168 mg of caffeine in a cup of coffee and from 43 to 92 mg in a cup of tea. Coffee made at home was slightly weaker than that served in cafés (averages 92 and 99 mg/cup respectively), but homemade tea was stronger (averages 70 to 56 mg/cup).

Coffee rapidly loses some of its flavour after grinding; the best coffee is made from beans ground in the home. Preparations of dried ground coffee are convenient but lack bouquet. Instant coffee is a modern form of coffee prepared in a factory; an infusion from coffee beans is spray dried and the powder sold in airtight containers. In the home it is conveniently made into a drink by simply adding warm water. Instant coffees have overtaken traditional ground beans in popularity in many industrial countries. They contain 20 to 40 mg of caffeine per gram of powder.

Coffee is a popular drink and in moderate amounts a mild cerebral stimulant and diuretic. People habituated to several cups of coffee during the day feel tired if this is stopped and may have headaches. But coffee is not inert. Too much can produce anxiety symptoms, cardiac arrhythmias, gastrointestinal discomfort or insomnia. Some people are more sensitive to the pharmacological actions of coffee or are allergic to it. Decaffeinated coffee has most of the taste without most of the pharmacological effects. There is much evidence that caffeine is one of the safest of drugs[6] and reports that it increased the risk of developing coronary heart disease and cancer of the pancreas are not confirmed.

Roasted coffee beans and instant coffee powder contain 10 to 40 mg nicotinic acid/100 g; the darker the roast the more nicotinic acid. One cup of instant coffee provides around 0.6 mg of the vitamin.[7]

Coffee may be adulterated and — especially in times of scarcity — a great variety of substances are used for this purpose. The most important is chicory which is frequently added to French coffee. Chicory is the root of a wild endive. It is dried, partly caramelised and then added to coffee in proportions varying from 10 to 80 per cent. Chicory's great attraction is its cheapness. There is no reason to think that it is in any way injurious to health.

Cocoa

Cocoa is made from the fruit of a tree indigenous in Central and South America. It is a small tree — about 20 ft high — and grows only in damp tropical lands. Cultivation has spread from tropical America to West Africa, Sri Lanka and other parts of Asia. West Africa now provides the greater part of the world's supplies. The fruit is a gourd in which the numerous seeds are embedded. The seeds are removed from the pulp, placed in heaps and allowed to dry in the sun for several days. During this process they lose their bitterness and acquire the pleasant taste characteristic of cocoa. The seeds are then roasted and ground.

The chief xanthine derivative in cocoa is theobromine, but it also contains some caffeine and tannin.

Natural waters

The most important quality of a natural water is that it should be free from pathogenic organisms. Cholera and typhoid are the classical water-borne diseases and there are many others. Lead water pipes and storage vessels were once an important cause of lead poisoning, and there are still homes in which these have not been replaced. The constant vigilance of water engineers and public health authorities is necessary to protect civilised communities from these diseases. So accustomed have many of us become to the services of these experts that they are often too readily taken for granted. In countries where clean water is not available everywhere, much ill-health is attributable to water-borne diseases.

Natural waters may contain too little iodine and too little or too much fluoride with effects discussed in Chapter 12. Soft waters contain little or no calcium, but very hard waters may contain 200 mg calcium per litre or more and so may provide a useful proportion of the daily intake of this mineral. Communities' drinking water can sometimes become accidentally contaminated by industrial effluents such as cadmium (p. 129) and mercury (p. 128) and where the water is collected off heavily fertilised agricultural land its content of nitrate needs to be monitored because of the possibility of nitrosamine formation (p. 567).

Mineral waters

Natural springs of water with a strong odour or taste have always excited the imagination of man. From time immemorial healing powers have been attributed to such mineral waters; and indeed in more credulous times many were accredited with miraculous properties. All over the world there are watering-places and spas whither many resort to drink the waters in search of health. There is no doubt that large numbers of patients have benefited from visits to spas. Such benefit, however, can usually be attributed to a change of regime and a new and more regular habit of life rather than to any special medicinal property of the water. Indeed the mineral salts present in many spa waters are in such low concentrations as to be virtually devoid of physiological or pharmacological action.

Mineral waters contain small quantities of sodium chloride, sodium carbonate and bicarbonate, also salts of calcium and magnesium and sometimes iron or hydrogen sulphide. They are usually mildly alkaline. The total mineral content is seldom as high as 8 g/l and is often much less. Many of these waters are naturally aerated with carbon dioxide.

The best-known waters come from France and Germany. Perrier, Contrexéville, Vichy, Apollinaris and Evian waters are bottled on a large scale and have a world-wide sale. Their pleasant sharp taste makes them refreshing to drink and for this they can be recommended. Inasmuch as their use may restrict the intake of other less desirable beverages, they may promote health.

The popular modern taste for carbonated water as a diluent or 'mix' for alcoholic drinks or fruit juices no doubt derives from the earlier taste for naturally aerated waters. 'Soda water' in its traditional siphon is simply water from any wholesome source, with carbon dioxide forced into it under pressure. It has no medicinal properties.

ALCOHOLIC DRINKS

Alcohol is a drug which depresses the higher nerve centres. Its first effect is to reduce the sense of worry and so to promote a feeling of well-being. It also loosens the imagination. Men and women come out of themselves, are more sociable and generally less intolerant of their fellow beings. For these reasons alcohol promotes good fellowship. If not abused, it is a valuable social stimulant which has been appreciated by many civilised men.

Alcohol, even in small doses, impairs the judgment and inhibits the skills necessary for fine movements. Euphoria usually prevents the subject from appreciating this loss. It is in this way that alcohol is so specially dangerous for motorists, even in small amounts. The other dangers of the misuse of alcohol are discussed in Chapter 7.

For these reasons many thoughtful people are total abstainers and advocate total abstinence for others. Of the four men who have had the greatest influence on human thought, two — Jesus Christ and Socrates — are reputed to have been wine-drinkers. The other two, Gautama Buddha and Mohammed, are said to have been abstainers. Lesser men are similarly divided, though the divisions do not always follow religious lines. Whatever one's personal views, it is important to appreciate the sincere opinions of others. We ourselves believe that alcohol has a valuable role in promoting social intercourse and thereby health. In certain circumstances alcohol is a valuable drug in the treatment of disease; it can stimulate appetite, act as a useful bedtime sedative — especially for elderly or injured people — and it is a good source of energy.

From the earliest times man has used yeasts to ferment carbohydrates and so to produce ethyl alcohol (ethanol). A great variety of carbohydrate sources have been used. The best alcoholic drinks are made from fruit or cereal grains. But there are many other sources, ranging from the sap of palm trees used in Africa to the fermented milk of mares of the Tartars.

Ethanol is seldom the only product of fermentation when microorganisms grow in a carbohydrate medium; given a good supply of oxygen they generally yield acetic acid instead, with the production of vinegar. The cellulose contained in wood pulp when fermented yields a high proportion of methyl alcohol which is highly toxic and can cause permanent blindness. Many fermented liquors contain small amounts of congeners, higher alcohols (fusel oils), aldehydes, ethers and volatile acids which can have toxic effects; they are partly responsible for the 'hangover'.[8] By their traditional art, the brewer, vintner and distiller — aiming at a benign and beneficient drink — generally managed to exclude these toxic products.

Beer, ale and stout

The best brews are made from malted barley. The barley grains are moistened and allowed to sprout for a few days in a warm atmosphere. This activates the enzyme diastase which begins to split the starch in the grains. At the proper moment the activity of the enzyme is stopped by heating ('malting') the sprouting grains in kilns. The temperature at which the malting is carried out determines the final appearance of the brew. For dark beers and stout (also known as 'porter' in London), the heat is sufficiently intense to produce some caramel which gives the colour. The dried malt is ground and then mixed with water to produce the 'mash'. The quality of the water is most important; the waters of Edinburgh, Dublin and Burton-on-Trent have each been the foundation on which large brewing industries have been built. The fluid from the mash is called 'wort'. The wort is boiled with the result that a further enzymic action is stopped and intruding microorganisms are killed. Generally hops are added during the boiling to impart the distinctive bitter flavour to the brew. The chemical substances responsible in the essential oil of hops are now known and synthetic isohumulones are increasingly used, to many people's regret.

The wort, once cooled, is piped off into vats where it is inoculated with a pure culture of yeast. The maintenance of a good yeast culture is one of the most carefully guarded and unpredictable secrets of good brewing. In the making of British-type ales, selected strains of *Saccharomyces cerevisiae* and a temperature of 15–20°C are used. Much of the multiplying yeast rises to the top. In the making of lager-type beers, a cooler temperature and selected strains of *Saccharomyces carlsbergensis (uvarum)* are used. Fermentation occurs at the bottom of the vessel so that carbon dioxide rises up thorough the wort. Prolonged cool storage follows. This type of beer orginated in Munich and *lager* is the German word for a storage cellar. When the fermentation has reached the proper stage the wort is filtered off into casks where some further fermentation may take place. Various clearing agents are usually added, such as gelatin, isinglass or tannin — sometimes with additional hops.

Most beers, ale and stout contain from 3 to 7 g ethanol/100 ml, though some 'special brews' may contain much more. Their energy value is usually between 125 and 250 kJ (30 and 60 kcal)/100 ml — about the same as milk. But they differ from milk in that they contain no protein, fat or useful amounts of calcium. The only vitamins present in beer are small amounts of nicotinic acid and riboflavin. The Food Standards Committee (1977) *Report on Beer*[9] is recommended for a readable introduction to the science of making beer.

Country beers and toddies

In many parts of the world country beers are made by fermenting cereals such as maize, millets or rice. Where palm trees grow, toddy can be made by fermenting the sweet sap. In Japan sake is made from rice, in Mexico pulque from the agave plant, and in Africa beers are usually made from sorghum. Wild yeasts are generally used for the fermentations. Such beers and toddies are usually produced for their intoxicating effects. Their alcohol content varies greatly, and they may contain as little as 1 g or as much as 7 g/100 ml. This alcohol is, of course, a source of energy, and country beers and toddies may also contain thiamin, riboflavin, nicotinic acid and ascorbic acid in amounts which are nutritionally significant. Thus these beverages are sometimes useful foods[10] and they have a traditional place in many peasant diets in Africa and Latin America. In some villages, excessive amounts are drunk and this may be responsible for much poverty and ill-health. Elsewhere, the beer may be a valuable supplementary food and a useful 'cement' to the cultural life of the village. In Africa, as elsewhere, alcoholism is an old problem, but reformers should not condemn these country beers hastily, without a knowledge of the social circumstances and the amounts of alcohol and vitamins usually derived from them by the local people.

Mead, cider, country 'wines'

Mead made from honey was perhaps the first alcoholic drink. Homer and the writers of the Norse sagas were familiar with it. The Roman conquerors of Britain tried hard to introduce wine in its place; relics of their efforts remain in the terraced hillsides overlooking the Severn river. Wine-making continued on a small scale in the mediaeval monasteries in order to provide for the Eucharist. But in our cold and uncongenial climate, the only fruit that could be depended on to produce fermentable sugars was the apple. Cider made from fermented apple juice was the *vin ordinaire* of the British.

A few people in Britain still make their own home brews, such as elderberry, cowslip and dandelion 'wine'. The wild yeasts present in these materials, mixed with raisins or some other good source of sugar, generally produce a benign and sometimes potent brew.

Wines

The grape is unique among fruits in that no additional sugars need be added to enable wild yeasts present on the fruit to carry out a satisfactory fermentation. In the making of wine the French are pre-eminent; the great clarets, sauternes, burgundies and champagnes — Château Lafite, Châteu d'Yquem, Richebourg, Veuve Clicquot — are names to conjure with. Then there are the German wines of the Rhine and Moselle — the Schloss Johannisberg and Berncastler Doktor. All these are the proper delight and solace of civilised Europeans. Other countries also produce some fine wines and every gourmet has his favourite. Italian, Greek, Hungarian, South African, Australian, Chilean and Californian wines all have their special virtues. Taken with a meal they are excellent adjuvants to appetite. *The World Atlas of Wine* gives maps and descriptions of the vineyards from which the world's wines are produced.[11]

But there is also a dark side to the story of wine. In the grape-growing areas of the world *vin ordinaire* is the common drink of the people and is used to quench thirst. Two wine-growing countries, France and Italy, have the highest alcohol consumption in the world and also a high incidence of cirrhosis of the liver. Natural wines contain 8 to 13 g of ethanol/100 ml and some unfermented sugars, but no other nutrients in significant amounts. One bottle (650 ml) of *vin ordinaire* provides about 1.9 MJ (450 kcal). They may also contribute to iron overload (p. 119).

French wines contain very variable amounts of histamine — from 0.1 mg/l in the best champagnes to 30 mg/l in some burgundies. As little as 20 μg of histamine if injected intravenously produces headache and it is possible that histamine contributes to the after effects of too much cheap wine.

Fortified wines, such as sherry, port and madeira, have alcohol added to raise the concentration up to 20 g/100 ml.

Spirits

The art of concentrating ethanol by distillation from fermented liquors was probably discovered by one of the great Arabian physicians despite their traditional abstinence. The word 'alcohol' is derived from the Arabic — *al Kohl* (the powder). Most likely it was first prescribed solely as a drug.

The number and variety of distilled spirits used by modern man is legion. Only the most notable can be mentioned here.

Whisky.   The name derives from the Gaelic *uisgebeatha* (water of life) and certainly much of life in the Scottish Highlands still revolves round it. In a similar way the French call brandy *eau-de-vie*, the Italians *acquavite*, whilst the Danes call their spirits *akvavit*.

Most Scotch whisky now on sale is 'blended' from a mixture of pot-stilled 'malt' whisky with 'patent-still' grain spirit. The unique flavour and aroma of pure malt whisky is probably due to the fact that the wort from which it is distilled is made from barley, malted over peat fires. The method of distillation in potstills — based on the principle of the alchemists' retort — also adds something to its quality. Potentially toxic substances present in the first distillate and those remaining in the pot are discarded. Pure malt whisky is the best way to 'treat' a Highlander.

Patent 'Coffey-still' whisky is produced by spraying wort into a tall wooden chamber into which superheated steam is introduced from below. The various alcohol-containing fractions are drawn off by pipes placed at different levels in the chamber. The alcohol so produced forms the body of most exported 'Scotch'.

The best Scotch is matured for at least seven years in oak casks which have previously contained sherry. From them it acquires the characteristic colour and loses its initial rawness by esterification of its higher alcohols. For the visitor to Scotland, Brander is a good guide to the national drink.[12]

The strength of a whisky is generally stated in terms of 'proof'. 'Proof' spirit is traditionally of such a strength that gunpowder will ignite when mixed with it in a teaspoon. Nowadays the meaning of 'proof' is more precisely defined. At 51°F proof spirit contains 57.07 per cent alcohol by volume or 48.24 per cent by weight. Whisky sold in Great Britain is almost uniformly 70 per cent proof, i.e. the alcoholic strength is approximately 30 per cent. A standard bottle of whisky containing 700 ml therefore provides about 230 g of ethanol, which at 30 kJ/g amounts to 6.9 MJ (1600 kcal). But apart from its energy value, whisky has no other purely nutritional virtues.

Other whiskies.   *Irish.* Irish whiskey has much the same qualities as Scotch, though most is kept for home consumption and little is exported. 'Poteen' is the traditional name for the product of the illicit stills, at one time commonly hidden in the hills.

Bourbon.   This is 'the water of life' for gentlemen of Scottish ancestry living in the Southern States of the USA. It was first produced in Bourbon County, Kentucky. The mash consists chiefly of maize ('corn') to which some malted barley or wheat is added. Originally it was matured in casks that had been used to import molasses. Nowadays the casks are deliberately burnt on the inside to reproduce the traditional flavour.

Rye.   Rye whiskey is made in Canada and the USA. The brands are distilled from mashes of combinations of cereals, including rye.

Other distilled spirits.   *Brandy.* 'Une fine champagne' — a brandy distilled from champagne grapes — is the perfect ending to a gourmet's meal. No other distilled spirit has such a fine aroma or is prepared with so much care. The names of Cognac and Armagnac, the two producing areas, are justly celebrated by *bon-viveurs* throughout the world.

Rum.   Molasses provide the carbohydrate from which this distilled spirit is prepared. It was the crude drink of those who had traffic among the sugar islands of the West Indies, such as British sailors and New England slavers. Nowadays some well-matured and gentle rums are produced.

Gin.   This is essentially a Dutch drink. It arrived in Britain when William of Orange succeeded to the British throne at the end of the seventeenth century. Properly made, it is an almost pure aqueous solution of ethanol, derived from a variety of sources, but deliberately flavoured by the addition of various vegetable agents, of which juniper (*geniévre* in French — hence 'Geneva') is the principal ingredient. Gin thus differs from the spirits so far mentioned in that its flavour is due to additives rather than the materials from which it is made. In eighteenth-century Britain almost any crude distilled spirit was cheaply and freely sold as 'gin' with tragic consequences to the desperate inhabitants of the verminous city slums. Nowadays gin is a civilised drink and the heart of a good cocktail.

Vodka.   This is another neutral spirit distilled from fermented rye or potatoes. Vodka is the nearest to pure aqueous ethanol of all these beverages, colourless and contains very little congeners. It is the standard liquor of the Russians, but has lately been adopted in the West. It may yet help to smooth our differences of opinion!

Calvados.   This is the traditional liquor of the Celts in the westermost parts of France. It is made by distilling cider which in turn is made from apples. A similar liquor is called 'applejack' in the USA. Vermont farmers make it for their own use, not by distillation, but by leaving the cider barrels outside in the depth of winter. The unnecessary water in the barrels turns to ice, but the ethanol-containing fraction — having a lower freezing point — can be siphoned off into smaller barrels. This process is repeated at each major frost. Thus a hard winter produces a real 'hard' liquor.

Slibovitz.   This is a distinctive drink made in Yugoslavia by distilling fermented plums.

Ouzo.   In Greece may be any kind of spirit with added flavourings.

Table 21.2 Alcohol content, sugar and energy value of common alcoholic beverages (figures taken from Paul and Southgate)

	Alcohol g/dl	Sugars g/dl	Energy kJ	(kcal)/dl
Beers				
Brown ale, bottled	2.2	3.0	117	(28)
Draught ale, mild	2.6	1.6	104	(25)
Draught ale, bitter	3.1	2.3	132	(32)
Lager, bottled	3.2	1.5	120	(29)
Strong ale	6.6	6.1	301	(72)
Ciders				
Dry	3.8	2.6	152	(36)
Sweet	3.7	4.3	176	(42)
Vintage	10.5	7.3	421	(101)
Wines				
Red	9.5	0.3	284	(68)
White, dry	9.1	0.6	275	(66)
White, sweet	10.2	5.9	394	(94)
Champagne	9.9	1.4	315	(76)
Fortified wines				
Sherry, dry	15.7	1.4	481	(116)
Sherry, sweet	15.6	6.9	568	(136)
Port	15.9	12.0	655	(157)
Spirits (70 per cent proof) Brandy, gin, rum, whisky	31.7	trace	919	(222)

Arak. Once out of Europe or North America the names of distilled liquors and their origins become confused. The word *arak* or *raki* applies throughout most of the East to any distilled spirit. It is usually made by distilling 'toddies' produced from fermented palm sap and can be very toxic.

Liqueurs. For centuries monks and other skilled people have worked to produce the perfect ending to a good meal. The best French brandy has obvious pride of place, but after it follow the great liqueurs, made by adding sugar to ethanol, with secret and subtle flavouring agents.

Table 21.2 gives the alcohol content and energy value of alcoholic beverages commonly taken in Britain today.

HERBS AND SPICES

In all parts of the world herbs and spices are used to flavour food and so make it more attractive and appetising. Large numbers of plants have been cultivated for this purpose. Their flavour resides in essential oils, or oleo resins, often in specialised parts of the plant. In Britain in the Middle Ages, mint, balm and basil, sage and thyme, chives, garlic and fennel, marjoram, horse radish, parsley and rosemary were grown in herb gardens. Spices are the exotic products of tropical lands. Herbs are usually leafy and spices often seeds, fruit or flower parts, bark or roots. In tropical countries, chillies, turmeric, coriander seeds, pimento, cumin, pepper, capsicum, cinnamon, cloves, nutmeg, vanilla and ginger are grown and commonly used. From time immemorial there has been a profitable trade in spices between the East and Europe. Two good sources of information on the varieties of spices, their nature and the history and extent of their world trade are Rosengarten[13] and the Encyclopaedia Britannica.[14]

In any part of the world, even in the poorest homes, it is unusual to find neither condiments nor spices. They are essential to the culinary art and promote appetite, good feeding and thus health. In communities without refrigerators herbs and spices may have some preservative action on meat and certainly counteract the taste of spoiled or monotonous food. Several such as cardamon, dill, peppermint and anise are claimed to have a carminative action, helping to bring up wind after a heavy meal. Nevertheless they have little direct nutritional value. Individual daily intakes in India may vary from 7 to 30 g. The energy value and protein content of this is negligible. Some condiments such as green chillies are rich in ascorbic acid (100 mg/100 g); they may contribute significantly to the ascorbic acid content of the diet. Most herbs and spices contain the B group of vitamins and minerals such as calcium and iron in appreciable concentrations, but the quantities eaten are too small to be significant.

Some herbs contain substances which are poisonous to man. Most of these are well known locally and tradition assures that they are avoided. Toxic effects of nutmeg, wormwood oil and Worcester sauce are described on page 245. In Jamaica herbal teas may be responsible for liver disease (p. 450).

In industrial countries natural flavouring agents are being replaced to a considerable extent by artificial chemical ones. A variety of artificial sauces is a feature of the table in most cheap restaurants and indeed in many homes.

REFERENCES

1. Anonymous 1961 Bouquet and essence. Lancet 2: 1391–2
2. Davidoff J, Gaskell G 1980 Palatable truths: what makes a wine taster? New Scientist 88: 790–2
3. Head J, Hogarth M, Pårsloe J, Broomhall J 1983 Soft drinks, electrolytes and sick children. Lancet 1: 1450
4. Hutchison R 1900 Food and the principles of dietetics. Arnold, London, p 306
5. Al-Samarrac W, Ma M C F, Truswell A S 1975 Methylxanthine consumption from coffee and tea. Proc Nutr Soc 34: 18–9A

6. Nutrition Reviews 1979 Workshop on caffeine. Nutr Rev 37: 124–6

7. Okungbowa P, Ma M C F, Truswell A S 1977 Niacin in instant coffee. Proc Nutr Soc 36: 26A

8. Pawan G L S 1973 Alcoholic drinks and hangover effects. Proc Nutr Soc 32: 15A

9. Food Standards Committee 1977 Report on beer. HMSO, London

10. Platt B S 1955 Some traditional alcoholic beverages and their importance in indigenous African communities. Proc Nutr Soc 14: 115–23

11. Johnson H 1971 The world atlas of wine. Mitchell Beazley, London

12. Brander M 1975 A guide to Scotch whisky. Johnston & Bacon, Edinburgh

13. Rosengarten F 1969 The book of spices. Livingstone, Philadelphia

14. Encyclopedia Britannica, 15th edn 1974 Spices, herbs, and flavourings. Macropedia 17: 502–8

22

Food Processing

Many species of animals collect and store food, but only *Homo sapiens* processes it. They have acquired techniques for preserving and cooking their food and developed arts which give it taste and flavour. The techniques of food processing use both physical and chemical methods, the application of heat and the addition of salt being prototypes. Any chemical that is added to a food deliberately for any of the above purposes is known as a food additive.

Traditional methods for preserving and processing food in the kitchen were the base on which food manufacturies grew, at first slowly. Today the food industries provide a more varied and secure diet than was formerly possible and generally made up of items of good quality. They employ an advanced technology based on **food science**. This science continues to be developed, mainly in the laboratories of the big manufacturers but also in colleges and universities where it is established as an academic subject with many excellent journals, monographs and textbooks. No textbook on nutrition could hope to give an adequate account of food science even at an elementary level. We consider only some aspects where technological processes may affect either the nutritive value or safety of food products.

DEVELOPMENT OF FOOD TECHNOLOGY

Apart from fruits and salads, man seldom eats food that is fresh and raw. The preservation, preparation and cooking of foods are domestic arts, which have been practised since before the time that man learnt to write and to record his history. The study of the utensils used for these purposes, which have been found at prehistoric sites of human habitations, is an important part of archaeology. Meat, fish and fruits were preserved by drying, vegetables by pickling, and many foods by salting. Excess milk was converted into cheese, and barley was malted and brewed into beer. The basic arts of cooking (boiling, roasting, baking and frying) have been practised since time immemorial. The use of herbs and

spices as flavouring agents is also very ancient, and natural colouring agents, e.g. cochineal, have been used for a long time to make foods appear pleasing to the eye. In the traditional farmhouses of Europe, the farmer's wife processed and prepared a large variety of foods.

The industrial revolution drew large numbers of people into towns, away from the countryside where their food was grown. Women were increasingly employed in factories and offices and so were less available for their traditional roles of preparing food in the home. At the same time, many new chemicals and physical processes were introduced, e.g. refrigeration on a large scale. In industrialised countries between 1850 and 1950 a steadily increasing proportion of food was prepared in factories and after 1950 the food industry expanded rapidly. In the United Kingdom in 1970, it employed 8.1 per cent of the population in industry, a proportion exceeded only by the the construction industry, mechanical engineering and electrical engineering. Supermarkets selling ready prepared foods and precooked meals increasingly continue to replace the shops of traditional grocers, greengrocers, butchers and fishmongers. In the USA in 1975, about 40 per cent of all meals, whether eaten in the home, in restaurants or in food service-stations, were prepared and cooked outside the home. This proportion is likely to increase. The preparation of food has become food technology, which is based on food science.

New foods have been developed which serve as substitutes for traditional foods that may have become scarce or too expensive. Margarine is the classical example. Margarines are an acceptable alternative to butter (p. 215); they are fortified with vitamins A and D, and some contain large amounts of polyunsaturated fatty acids, which are almost absent from butter. Meat substitutes, prepared from novel proteins of vegetable origin (p. 209), are rapidly becoming acceptable alternatives in many meat dishes. Many new food preparations play a big part in the diets of infants and young children.

The food industry is, however, not without its critics. There is a large and widespread demand for **health foods**, and there are advocates for compost-grown vegetables and free-range chickens. Such people believe that fresh foods and those grown without the use of artificial fertilisers have mysterious beneficial properties. If you are lucky enough to be asked to dinner by a friend in the country, you may be given chicken from his backyard, new potatoes, peas and pears picked in his garden that morning. He may tell you that the supermarket sells nothing that tastes so good. He may well be right and it would be ungracious to argue. You have enjoyed a luxury. Yet the supermarket foods are also good, can be enjoyed all the year round and are generally cheaper. That canned foods are nutritious is shown by an experiment carried out many years ago.[1] For 18 months one colony of rats were fed entirely on canned foods and another colony on foods brought fresh from shops or grown locally. The growth of the animals, their breeding performance and the chemical composition of their bones, teeth and soft tissues were the same in the two colonies. There was no indication that dependence on canned foods had any adverse effects on health. A similar conclusion can be drawn from the excellent health of several Antarctic expeditions whose members have lived entirely on processed foods for many months.

A food industry is essential to feed the large population of modern towns, whose needs could not be met from markets of the traditional rural type. Further, the food industry continues to grow and is commercially successful because most consumers like its products. In prosperous countries people living in rural areas choose to eat much the same foods as those living in towns. The advantages of modern processed foods are numerous. First, their use greatly reduces the domestic work involved in preparing traditional dishes, and many products are aptly referred to as **convenience foods**; the use of such foods transfers some of a housewife's chores from the home to the factory. Secondly, they provide consumers with a much more varied choice of foods than formerly and choice is no longer restricted by the seasons of the year. Some foods which were once eaten only by the wealthy or on special occasions are now commonplace articles of diet, for example oranges, tomatoes and poultry. Travellers and those who work in foreign countries can in most places obtain foods from their native land and may, if they wish and have the money, feed as they would if they were at home.

FOOD PRESERVATION

Fresh foods may be decomposed by autolysis due to the lytic enzymes which they contain and by the action of putrefactive bacteria and fungi, the spores of which abound in the atmosphere. The ancient methods of food preservation — heating, drying, salting and pickling — are still the basis of modern food technology. Perhaps the most important new factor in determining present diets is the great developments in domestic and commercial refrigeration. In Britain in 1974, 84 per cent of households had a refrigerator and 15 per cent a deep freezer. Canning of food was successfully carried out early in the nineteenth century and has evolved slowly and steadily. The range of foods that are now preserved in cans or in plastic and other synthetic packets is very large, and developments in packaging make many more foods available to consumers.

Chemical preservatives

Sodium chloride, acetic acid, ethyl alcohol and sucrose are preservatives which have been used in the home for generations. Their value is undisputed and they are much used in industry. In the nineteenth century new chemicals were introduced; many of these, such as borate and formaldehyde, have been discarded as they were shown to be potentially toxic in the amounts used. Table 22.1 lists permitted preservatives in the UK. Certain salts and alternative forms of these substances are also permitted. Other countries have similar but not necessarily identical lists. As described in Chapter 25, legislation controls the concentrations of permitted preservatives and ensures a wide margin of safety. Permitted concentrations are usually less than one-hundredth of that which might have toxic effects. Sulphur dioxide and the hydroxybenzoates are the most used preservatives and are frequently added to fruit and vegetable products, beer, meat products, sauces and spices. Propionic acid is used mainly for bread and flour confectionery. Sodium nitrate and nitrite are used in cured meats, including bacon and ham, but are not permitted in most other foods.

Table 22.1 Permitted preservatives (UK Preservatives in Food Regulations 1975)

Benzoic acid	Sodium nitrite
Methyl 4-hydroxybenzoate	2-Hydroxybiphenyl
Ethyl 4-hydroxybenzoate	Propionic acid
Propyl 4-hydroxybenzoate	Sorbic acid
Biphenyl	Sulphur dioxide
Nisin	2-(Thiazol-4-yl) benzimidazole
Sodium nitrate	Hexamine

Although preservation by chemical means is often satisfactory, in general it is better to use physical methods such as heat and refrigeration.

Irradiation of food

Putrefactive bacteria and fungi, as well as pathogenic organisms, are readily killed by gamma rays, which also inhibit sprouting and delay ripening of seeds and fruits. As irradiation is carried out in bulk and on packaged foods, this method of preservation has great commercial potential (Table 22.2).

Table 22.2 Examples of applications of irradiation in food preservation[2]

General application	Specific examples	Dose (Mrad)
Decontamination of food ingredients	Various spices Onion or cocoa powder Dyes Mineral supplements	1.0 (10 kGy)
Inactivation of Salmonella	Meat and poultry Egg products Shrimps and frog legs Meat and fish meal	0.30–1.0 (3–10 kGy)
To extend refrigerated storage (0–4°C)	Prepackaged meat and fish	0.25–0.50 (2.5–5 kGy)
Prolonged storage of fruit etc.	Strawberries Mangoes Papayas	0.20–0.50 (2.5–5 kGy)
Control of insects	Wheat and rice Dates Cocoa beans	0.02–0.30 (0.20–3 kGy)
Inhibition of sprouting or growth	Potatoes Onions Garlic Mushrooms	0.01–0.30 (0.1–3 kGy)

Only small doses of radiation that neither destroys nutrients nor produces toxic substances are required. Irradiation has been in use since 1962 to sterilise foods for laboratory animals and no adverse effects have arisen; yet its use for human foods has been very slow. In 1983 there was still prohibitive legislation against it both in the UK and the USA, the only exemption being for the preparation of sterile diets for patients in hospital with severe damage to their immunity system; for example patients on large doses of immunosuppressive drugs after an organ transplant. The Netherlands has been in the forefront of development and at least 14 irradiated foods have been put on the market there, but economic reasons have limited their use. Japan, Canada, the USSR, Italy and Israel have all allowed distribution of irradiated foods. UN expert committees assess the safety and value of varying doses of radiation for specific foods.[3]

A comment on this conservative approach to a new technology made as long ago as 1964 is: 'The treatment of food by irradiation is as new and strange to most people as the cooking of food must have been to our early forefathers. At present the evidence that food treated by irradiation is never harmful is not so complete as might ideally be required, but had we assembled at the Dawn of Time to consider the safety of cooked foods the available evidence would have been much less satisfactory and indeed is still incomplete.'[4]

COOKING

Most foods of animal origin could probably be digested raw by man but raw meats are unpalatable and seldom consumed; yet in a crisis a hungry person readily eats the raw flesh of any beast, bird or fish. The cooking of meat makes it easy to chew and so allows the digestive juices a more rapid access to the protein. The heat of cooking coagulates the muscle proteins, which actually thus become less readily digested by proteolytic enzymes *in vitro*. But the tough collagen fibres of connective tissues are converted by heat into gelatin and this increases the tenderness of the meat. The elastic tissue in tendons and sinews is insoluble and virtually indigestible.

Fruits and green vegetables may be eaten raw in limited amounts. Cereals, roots and legumes, however, cannot easily be digested by man unless cooked. Most plant cells are surrounded by a rough cellulose wall which is little disrupted by mastication and through which the digestive enzymes cannot readily pass. The heat in cooking causes the starch within the cells to swell. This bursts the cell walls, and the starch and other nutrients within become accessible to digestive enzymes. Cooking improves the nutritive value of legumes such as soya beans and groundnuts by destroying trypsin inhibitors.

Cooking is, of course, much more than making food more digestible through the action of heat. Ingredients have to be mixed to give the product the correct texture; some foods have to be firm and crisp, others smooth, bland and fluid. Tenderness and succulence are important and above all taste and flavour. A good cook can achieve all these aims using as ingredients only natural foods from the countryside and two artificially purified chemicals, sodium chloride and sucrose. This is seldom practical except in remote rural areas. Elsewhere many ingredients and foods are products of the food industry and contain chemicals added by manufacturers which facilitate a cook's work and improve the quality of the meal when it is served.

Cooks use the same processes whether they are preparing foods at home or in the kitchen of a restaurant or in the plant of a large food manufacturer. Methods vary according to the scale of the operation, but fundamental principles are the same.

FOOD ADDITIVES

The food industry could not provide us with satisfactory food products without using a large number of chemical additives. The types of additives needed and the benefits that they provide are set out in a small monograph *Why Additives?*[25] Here we give only a brief outline of the main classes of additive. In Chapter 25 the principles of testing additives are described and the reasons why some additives formerly used are no longer permitted. Chapter 26 gives a brief account of the legal and other measures that protect consumers against possible dangers.

Preservatives

Chemicals which are permitted preservatives have already been listed in Table 22.1.

Colouring agents

The art of cooking includes making food attractive to the eye. Cooks have long been familiar with some natural colouring agents such as cochineal (from crushed insects), caramel (from burnt sugar) and saffron (a plant pigment). Tomatoes, parsley, mustard and cress and cherries are used to give colour to a dish. It would be difficult nowadays to sell a food product unless the colour was pleasing. This applies especially to cakes and sweets. Large numbers of organic dyes have been used to colour foods. Many have been discarded after prolonged tests have shown that they may cause cancers in experimental animals. Thirty-one colours, which have been shown to be harmless in exhaustive animal tests, are permitted colouring matter under the UK Colouring Matter in Food Regulation 1973 (amended 1976) and may be added to foods. Most of these are synthetic organic dyes, but products of natural origin such as chlorophyl, caramel, several carotenoids and beetroot red are included. The Regulations also state permitted concentrations. Other countries have similar but not identical lists.

Flavouring agents

The flavour of most common fruits and many vegetables may be mimicked by synthetic chemicals. Examples are benzaldehyde, *n*-propyl acetate and diethyl sulphite with the flavour of almond, pear and peppermint respectively. Such substances are much used in the food industry, particularly in the manufacture of sweets. Monosodium glutamate, the salt of a natural amino acid, is also much used because it brings out the flavour of the meat in stews, meat pies, etc. Hence it is an ingredient of many sauces.

Flavouring agents make up the largest number of permitted food additives. Over 2000 are on the EEC list. The reasons why there are so many are: (1) these are mostly extracted or synthesised natural flavour components or closely related chemically, (2) natural food flavours consist of many different chemical components, and (3) the amounts concerned are minute and varied.

Sweetening agents

Sucrose from cane or beet is the classical sweetener but, as it is a rich source of energy, intake has to be restricted especially by persons liable to put on weight. Of artificial sweeteners saccharin is the most used; it is 400 times as sweet as sucrose and provides no extra energy. Diabetic patients and weight-watchers sweeten their drinks with it, but it is not used extensively by the food industry because it is destroyed by heat. Cyclamate, which is 30 times as sweet as sucrose, is heat-resistant and formerly provided an alternative to sugar in pastries, canned foods, jellies, sauces pickles and other foods. Its use was banned in 1969 in the USA, UK and other countries, following a report that some rats receiving very large doses had developed tumours of the urinary bladder. There are those who think that the ban was inadvisable, as the benefit derived from cyclamate far outweighed the possible hazard from the amounts likely to be consumed by any individual. The dipeptide L-aspartyl-L-phenylalamin, aspartame, is 180 times sweeter than sugar; it is broken down in the body to its two constituent amino acids, which are then metabolised in the normal way. In 1974 its use as a food additive was approved in the USA but with certain restrictions. In 1982 an official report in the UK[6] recommended that the ban on cyclamate should stay but the use of aspartame be permitted. Since then theoretical doubts about the safety of aspartame,[7] widely publicised, have not led to any change in the law and, in our opinion, this is right.

The search for new sweeteners goes on. The fruit of the climbing vine *Dioscoreophyllum cumminsii*, which grows in tropical forests, contains a substance reported to be 1500 times sweeter than sucrose.[8] It is known as the serendipity berry. As yet is has not found a place in western diets.

Emulsifiers and stabilising agents

A number of substances, of which the best known is glyceryl monostearate, are used in the manufacture of cakes, ice-cream and salad creams. They enable fats to be used more economically, and act by allowing fat to be emulsified with more water and by making the emulsions more stable. Glyceryl monostearate is a normal product of digestion in the human small intestine.

Antioxidants

Most natural fats and oils contain substances which prevent the slow oxidative changes leading to rancidity. The best known of these are the tocopherols (vitamin E). Such substances may be removed or destroyed in manufacturing processes. Hence artificial antioxidants are added to the refined products in order to prevent rancidity. Fats used for making biscuits and cakes often contain gallic acid or butylated hydroxyanisole (BHA) or butylated hydroxytoluene (BHT) added for this purpose. Antioxidants are important in the oils used for frying potato crisps.

Flour improvers

These have an effect on the rheological properties of doughs and batters similar to what occurs when flour is stored for some weeks. They are said to 'strengthen' the flour and allow the baking of bread which is well risen and stays fresh longer. For this purpose chlorine dioxide is added to flour used for making bread in the UK and USA. L-Cysteine hydrochloride is an improver added to flour for making cakes. Benzoyl peroxide may be used as a bleaching agent for white flour.

Miscellaneous food additives

Acids give a sour or tart taste and in some foods are needed to achieve the optimal pH for technical purposes. They are compounds which occur in nature, such as citric, tartaric or malic acids or hydrochloric.

REFERENCES

1. Godden W 1939 Nutritive value of canned foods. J Soc Chem Indus Lond 58: 81–6
2. Ley F J 1983 Food irradiation makes progress. Br Nutr Found Bull 37: 37–45
3. World Health Organization 1981 Wholesomeness of irradiated food. Report of a joint FAO/IAEA/WHO Expert Committee. WHO Tech Rep Ser no 659
4. Ministry of Health 1964 Report of the working party on irradiation of food. HMSO, London
5. British Nutrition Foundation 1977 Why additives? Forbes, London
6. Food Additives and Contaminants Committee 1982 Report on the review of sweeteners in food. HMSO, London.

Humectants prevent foods from drying out. Sorbitol and glycerine are examples.

Thickeners, including pectins, vegetable gums and gelatins, give foods their uniform texture and desired consistency, as in ice-cream.

Polyphosphates are used to process meats, especially poultry meat and fish, because some taste panels have found that this improves the flavour of the product and makes it more tender and juicy. Many manufacturers do not use phosphates as they are not satisfied that these confer benefits. The treatment carries no toxicological hazard, but inevitably increases the water content of the product.

Micronutrients are sometimes added to restore losses during processing. Some manufacturers add ascorbic acid to dehydrated potato powder or to fruit-based drinks. Enrichment of foods with nutrients is discussed on page 537.

7. Wurtman R J 1983 Neurological changes following high dose aspartame with dietary carbohydrate. N Engl J Med 309: 429–30
8. Inglett G E, May J F 1969 Serendipity berries: source of a new intense sweetner. J Food Sci 34: 408–11

POSTSCRIPT

A recent article gives a good summary of the present state of the art of food processing in North America.
(Levine A S, Labuza T P, Morley J E 1985 Food technology: a primer for physicians. N Engl J Med 312: 628–34)

23

Losses of Food and Nutrients in Food Processing

WASTAGE

Physiologists who attempt to assess human needs for nutrients naturally use as their data measurements of amounts of food that are actually eaten. On the other hand the data for administrators, whose duty it is to see that a country or district has sufficient food to satisfy requirements, are the statistics of the size of the crops in the fields and of the amounts of food in the holds of ships in the ports and in trucks at the frontiers. These two sets of data cannot be directly compared, for it is inevitable that a proportion of the crop in a field or of a cargo of food in a ship is never eaten but is wasted.

In some countries, two sets of figures are available. The first is the amount of food moving into consumption and derived from records of foodstuffs leaving the farms and arriving in the ports, less the food that is exported. The second is from measurements of actual consumption of samples of families or individuals. For example, in Britain for the five years 1972–76 the food moving into consumption daily per head of population ranged between 12.2–12.8 MJ (2910 and 3060 kcal) with an additional 0.59–0.67 MJ (140–160 kcal) from alcohol. Together they add up to 12.8–13.5 MJ (3070–3200 kcal). However, over the same period the National Food Survey showed that the food brought into the home in a large sample of families averaged 9.6–10.4 MJ (2290–2490 kcal)/head, excluding alcohol and meals consumed outside the home. The weighted physiological requirement for energy calculated from the recommended daily intakes for the different categories of people in the UK is 9.7 MJ (2325 kcal) per person. This is only 74 per cent of the food moving into consumption. Thus about 25 per cent of food leaving the farms and imported is unaccounted for. There is no reason to suppose that the gap would be smaller in any other industrial country. Some is eaten in catering establishments. Where does the rest of this food go?

It is not possible to give exact figures partly because this is an unglamorous and neglected field of research.

Losses of food vary greatly with the food and the circumstances. The Ministry of Agriculture, Fisheries and Food has set up a Food Waste survey unit to try and obtain more figures. Roy[1] suggests that **waste** should be used for a potential source of food that has, knowingly, been discarded or destroyed (kitchen scraps, food not sold in shops or restaurants and food discarded in factories) while **loss** is used for potential food that has inadvertently been destroyed or spoiled, e.g. stored grain eaten by rats, meat spoiled by bacterial growth and nutrients destroyed or going into solution in vegetable canning. These suggested usages seem sensible but are not yet generally adopted; there are overtones of guilt to the word 'waste'.

If we start at the farm gate or port, food may be lost during storage. In Britain this is small for milk and cereals but about 10 per cent for potatoes and more for some vegetables. Some potential food is wasted in processing e.g. parts of vegetables and fruit, trimmings of meat and fish, whey in making cheese and blood in abattoirs. Food is also wasted in markets and shops, particularly fruit and vegetables.

Once the food has been brought into the premises where it will be cooked and eaten, waste can occur in the kitchen, from food not used during serving and from food left on the plate. In large-scale catering like school meals overall losses are usually about 10 per cent but caterers are often reluctant or unable to discuss detailed figures. Larger losses are to be expected in expensive restaurants and in hospitals. Platt[2] in a classic study of hospital catering found 25 to 35 per cent of food sent from the kitchen was leftover in serving dishes, and plate waste averaged an additional 10 per cent.

Food waste has been measured in 672 households in Britain in 1980.[3] A random sample of 1000 households throughout the country had been asked to take part. The weekly waste amounted to 11.7 MJ (2790 kcal) per household in summer and 10.1 MJ (2410 kcal) in winter. These averages were 6.5 and 5.4 per cent of expected energy usage in the home. Waste was less in larger households with children, but did not appear to be related to income or geographical regions. The above figures include waste fed to pets. Details of this large survey are given in 10 tables in the original paper.

When an investigator is scrutinising a family in this way its behaviour is likely to be distorted. The Anthropology Department at the University of Arizona set up a Garbage Project, in which they examined household refuse in Tucson 'as a non reactive measure of behaviour', a sort of instant archaeology.[4] Households in 1974 threw on average $100 worth of food into their garbage bins. More meat, fish and vegetables were discarded than other foods. Average estimates of waste of different types of food ranged from 1 to 12 per cent. Food poured down the drain, put on compost heaps or fed to household pets was not counted.

In communities living at or near the hunger level there is virtually no waste. Anyone who has been a prisoner-of-war can relate elaborate precautions taken to prevent any loss of the meagre rations and may describe how men habitually licked their plates clean. Similarly in many poor homes, especially in Africa and Asia, nothing is wasted.

Food fed to pets
In the USA it has been estimated that 22 million dogs and 30 million cats eat food equivalent to 5 per cent of the total human energy requirement and 14 per cent of the protein requirement. In Britain 4.8 million dogs and nearly 5 million cats may eat 3 per cent of human energy requirement and 2 per cent of protein requirement. In 1970 the pet-food market was estimated to be worth one billion dollars in the USA and £40 million in Britain. It would be improper to suggest that this food was wasted and some of it would legally be 'unfit for human consumption'. Yet these rough estimates do indicate that a significant proportion of the food supplies available for man are diverted to another use in these countries.

LOSSES OF NUTRIENTS DURING FOOD PROCESSING AND COOKING

Wastages of food are obvious to all who witness them, if seldom measured. They are the responsibility of the community, the management or the individual. Invisible chemical losses of nutrients that occur during food processing and cooking are the special responsibility of, and common ground between, nutritionists and food scientists.

PROTEINS, FAT AND CARBOHYDRATES

Many changes in the chemical structure of molecules of proteins, fats and carbohydrates are brought about by heat; some of these may diminish nutritive value, others may lead to the formation of potentially toxic substances. In general there is little difference except in scale between heating processes in industry, in catering and in traditional domestic preservation and preparation of food.

Proteins
The flavour and aroma of roast meat and the golden-brown crust of freshly baked bread are delicious but the complicated chemical reaction underlying these culinary delights reduce the availability of one or more essential amino acids in the food protein. This is the Maillard reaction between reducing sugars and amino acids (Fig. 23.1). In food proteins most amino groups are taken up in peptide bonds, but there are free amino groups on the dibasic lysine and these may react with sugars and the amino acid is then no longer biologically available. With mild heat treatment causing only a little browning the loss of available lysine is small; but with severe heat, causing pronounced browning, it may be

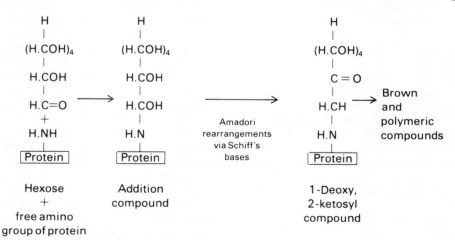

Fig. 23.1 Simplified outline of the Maillard reaction

large and accompanied by small reductions of availability of other amino acids.[5] During the baking of bread, biscuits and breakfast cereals, 10 to 15 per cent of the available lysine is lost; spray-drying of skimmed milk reduces it less than 10 per cent but roller-drying can produce losses up to 40 per cent. The total lysine, measured by amino acid column chromatography, after hydrolysis of the protein may be little changed. However, reactive lysine, measured by dye-binding, may fall markedly.[6]

Fats

Changes occur in frying oils and fats when they are used repeatedly or overheated. Part of the fatty acids are oxidised or form cyclic compounds or polymers, and more than a hundred different monomeric components have been found by multiple chromatography in heated cottonseed oil. Most of these are present in tiny amounts and the question arises whether any of them have deleterious biological effects. Overheated or 'abused' frying oils depress the growth of rats. There is also some loss of linoleic acid and of vitamin E when oils are used for frying. All these changes can be minimised by avoiding high temperatures, frying for short times and not repeatedly using an oil. Antioxidants are often incorporated in oils used to manufacture snack foods. Olive oil has a reputation for quality in cooking. Unrefined olive oil does not undergo oxidative deterioration on moderate heating because $\triangle^5$-avenasterol, a minor sterol in the unsaponifiable fraction, acts as a natural antioxidant.[7]

Carbohydrate

The effects of heating on carbohydrates are predominantly beneficial in that it breaks down cell walls, solubilises starch and makes it more easily digested. Raw potato starch produces lethal caecal enlargement in rats but this effect does not occur with heated potato starch. The Maillard reaction involves sugars as well as amino acids. Another browning reaction, caramelisation, affects sugars alone and fructose is the most sensitive. The

loss of food energy from this is negligible with a careful cook.

VITAMINS AND MINERALS

Losses occur in two ways. First, nutrients may be leached out of the tissues of either plant or animal foods and discarded in the cooking water. Losses of minerals and water-soluble vitamins may result. Secondly, heat may destroy some of the vitamins present.

Table 23.1 summarises the lability or stability of selected vitamins in different conditions. The most sensitive vitamins are ascorbic acid, folate and thiamin but losses of riboflavin, vitamin A, pyridoxine, vitamin B12 and vitamin E occur in particular conditions. Nicotinic acid is the most stable of the vitamins and information about vitamin D is incomplete.

Ascorbic acid

Losses in the kitchen may be large and significant. It is readily oxidised and, if this proceeds beyond the stage of dehydro-ascorbic aicd, all vitamin activity is permanently lost. Oxidation may be accelerated by enzymic action, by heat, by an alkaline medium, by traces of copper and by free access to atmospheric oxygen. These facts have practical application in preserving and cooking food.

In most plant tissues there is an enzyme, ascorbic acid oxidase, which is separated from ascorbic acid in the intact cells. When leaves or fruits are bruised, pounded or chopped, cell structures are damaged and the enzyme gains access to the vitamin and begins to destroy it. However, the enzyme is rapidly inactivated at temperatures of 60°C and above. The destruction of ascorbic acid is minimal when fruits and vegetables are immediately placed in boiling water, but maximal if they are placed in cold water and slowly brought to the boil. Some loss of the vitamin is inevitable in cooking, but can be reduced if the cooking is carried out for the shortest possible time. Access to oxygen is reduced greatly if the water is first boiled to drive off dissolved

Table 23.1 Stability of vitamins in different conditions

	pH <7	pH ±7	O_2	Light	Heat	Metals	Reducing agents
β-Carotene	L	S	L	L	L		
Thiamin	S	L	L	S/L	L	L	L
Riboflavin	S	S	S	L	S/L	L	L
Nicotinic acid	S	S	S	S	S	L	
Pyridoxine	S	S	S/L	L	S	S	L
Folate	L	S	S/L	L	S/L		L
Vitamin B12	S/L	S	S/L	L	S/L		L
Ascorbic acid	S	L	L	L	L	L	S

L, labile; S, stable.

oxygen and if a lid is placed on the saucepan to exclude air. Copper pots should not be used for cooking vegetables nor baking soda added to preserve their colouring. Similarly when potatoes are fried, losses of ascorbic acid are less if they are rapidly immersed in hot deep fat than if they are fried slowly in a shallow pan. Losses due to heat continue if vegetables or fruit are kept on a hot-plate after cooking and not served immediately. Ascorbic acid is very soluble in water, and the more cooking water used, the greater the amounts of the vitamin leached out and discarded.

If all these rules are disobeyed, as they frequently are in many homes and even more often in canteens, vegetables and fruits may be served almost devoid of vitamin C. This applies particularly to potatoes, often the most important source of ascorbic acid in the diet. Less than 30 per cent of the vitamin that survives cooking may be retained after a period on a hot-plate in a canteen.[8] However, if the proper precautions are all taken, it is possible to preserve as much as 70 per cent of the ascorbic acid. In the absence of any accurate knowledge of the cooking methods used, it is advisable to assume a destruction of 50 per cent of the vitamin.

In small domestic pressure-cookers the temperature is raised well above the normal boiling point, but the time of exposure to heat is greatly reduced. These two effects tend to cancel out. Potatoes cooked in a pressure cooker may retain 80 per cent of the ascorbic acid, and such cookers can be used with confidence.

Vitamin C keeps well in frozen vegetables but about 25 per cent is lost in the preliminary blanching and the next step down occurs after the frozen storage period, during the final cooking. In the canning sequence losses may be comparable but are often greater.[9] Dehydration of potatoes in making instant potato granules destroys most of the vitamin C.

Thiamin

Losses in the preparation of rice are important. In parts of Asia where the diet is predominantly rice the method of preparation may determine whether the cooked product retains sufficient thiamin to prevent beriberi. Rice, as purchased in any bazaar, has to be washed and this washing water is then discarded. The rice is then cooked in water and this cooking water is usually discarded, though it is sometimes consumed. About 50 per cent of the thiamin (and other B vitamins) that has escaped the miller can be lost. If the rice is clean it does not need to be washed before cooking; the minimum of cooking water should be used and consumed.

In other foods thiamin is sensitive to heat at neutral and alkaline pH though less labile than vitamin C. Losses are usually around 10 to 20 per cent but can be

greater. They are hastened by alkaline baking powder and the preservative sulphite (or SO_2).

Other vitamins

Riboflavin is sensitive to light. About 50 per cent of the vitamin in milk can be destroyed in 2 hours by exposure to bright sunlight and 20 per cent on a dull day.

Vitamin B6 is sensitive to heat and activity is substantially reduced in canning and sterilisation or drying of milk. Loss of pyridoxal and pyridoxamine are greater than those of pyridoxine.

Folate is rapidly destroyed by heat in alkaline or neutral conditions. About 50 per cent is lost in canning and after cooking of vegetables; most of the total folate loss is free folate. Losses in cooking meat and eggs are usually less.

Vitamin B12 is stable when meat or liver are cooked under ordinary conditions but it can of course dissolve into cooking water or drip. In milk, pasteurisation destroys 7 per cent, boiling for 3 minutes destroys 30 per cent and ultraheat treatment 20 per cent of the vitamin activity.

Vitamin A and carotenes are stable during mild heat treatment but are oxidised at high temperatures in the presence of oxygen. Antioxidants in foods are protective. Only a small proportion of the carotenes pass into cooking water because they are not water-soluble.

Vitamin E is slowly destroyed by heat during frying and is sensitive to light. It is also, unlike other vitamins, unstable in fried foods during frozen storage.

Minerals, including trace elements may be dissolved out in cooking water, but such losses are usually small. During canning, small amounts of trace elements may be lost or acquired from contact with metal surfaces.[10]

COMMENT

Bender puts the losses of nutrients during food processing into perspective.[11]

1. Some loss is inevitable, but for most nutrients losses are small.

2. Manufacturing losses, when they occur, are often in place of similar cooking losses at home.

3. The importance of the losses in a particular food has to be considered in relation to the whole diet. If a food makes only a small contribution to the intake of nutrients, processing losses are not of practical significance. On the other hand changes in any food which makes a major contribution to nutrient supply, e.g. milk and cereal products for babies, and cereals in many countries, need continual vigilance.

4. There are beneficial effects — destruction of trypsin inhibitor in legumes and liberation of bound niacin in cereals.
5. Other advantages of food processing are protection from pathogenic organisms, better flavour and cheaper price. Often the ultimate choice is between dried, canned or frozen peas (say) in mid-winter or no peas at all.

REFERENCES

1. Roy R 1976 Wastage in the UK food system. Earth Resources, London
2. Platt B S, Eddy T P, Pellett P L 1963 Food in hospitals. Oxford University Press
3. Wenlock R W, Buss D H, Derry B J, Dixon E J 1980 Household food wastage in Britain. Br J Nutr 43: 53–70
4. Harrison G G, Rathje W L, Hughes W W 1975 Food waste behaviour in an urban population. J Nutr Educ 7: 13–16
5. Hurrell R F, Carpenter K J 1977 Maillard reactions in foods. In: Hoyem T, Kvale O (eds) Physical, chemical and biological changes in foods caused by thermal processing. Applied Science, London p 168–84
6. Hurrell R F, Carpenter K J 1975 The use of three dye-binding procedures for the assessment of heat damage to proteins. Br J Nutr 33: 101–15
7. Morton I D 1977 Physical, chemical and biological changes related to different time-temperature combinations. In: Hoyem T, Kvale O (eds) Physical, chemical and biological changes in foods caused by thermal processing. Applied Science, London p 135–51
8. Thompson J C 1946 Lossess of nutrients in the preparation of foodstuffs. Proc Nutr Soc 4: 171–4
9. Benterud A 1977 Vitamin losses during thermal processing. In: Hoyem T, Kvale O (eds) Physical, chemical and biological changes in foods caused by thermal processing. Applied Science, London, p 185–201
10. Schroeder H A 1971 Losses of vitamins and trace minerals resulting from processing and preparation of food. Am J Clin Nutr 24: 562–73
11. Bender A E 1977 Biological changes — a consensus. In: Hoyem T, Kvale O (eds) Physical, chemical and biological changes in foods caused by thermal processing. Applied Science, London, p 185–201

24

Infective Agents in Food

The dangers from pathogenic organisms in food far exceed those of toxic agents, either natural poisons or man-made chemicals. There are at least 30 species of worms, protozoa, bacteria and viruses which may gain access to food and so enter the body and cause a well-defined disease.

Meats, eggs and milk from infected animals may contain pathogens and, when eaten, can cause disease in man. Helminth infections, e.g. tapeworms, brucellosis (undulant fever), tuberculosis and salmonella infections are familiar examples of diseases of both animals and man.

There are more than 1600 types of Salmonella which have been identified and distinguished by their serological reaction. These are the commonest cause of **bacterial food poisoning.** They infect most species of vertebrates and are especially widespread in poultry. *Salmonella typhimurium* (mouse typhoid) is the type most frequently responsible for human infections. Salmonella may enter the blood stream and invade the tissues, causing an enteric fever like typhoid, but usually they are confined to the intestines where they cause an acute gastroenteritis with diarrhoea and vomiting as the main features. Mice and rats infected with *S. typhimurium* commonly excrete the organism in their faeces and urine and so many infect human food to which they have access.

Many pathogenic bacteria and viruses are excreted in human faeces and some in urine. Infection may spread by transfer of the pathogen by flies or the human hand to foods or food utensils. Infections spread in this way are known as **faecal-oral diseases.** They include the dysenteries and acute gastroenteritis which are often caused by infection with various viruses and serotypes of *Escherichia coli.*

All pathogens are destroyed by heat, and food which has been properly cooked and handled is safe. However, in cooking, the heat may not penetrate the food sufficiently; particularly a large joint of meat, and undercooked foods are dangerous. Furthermore, food may be contaminated after cooking. Meat, milk and eggs are excellent growth media for bacteria; foods which have been cooked, improperly stored and then warmed up are especially dangerous.

Prevention of infections spread by food and the faecal-oral route depends on scrupulous attention to cleanliness along the whole food chain — abattoirs, food manufacturers, warehouses, retail shops, catering establishments, restaurants, and domestic kitchens and larders. In all these places care is required to prevent small rodents and flies from getting access to food. All food handlers should be scrupulously clean in their personal habits and be provided with clean lavatories and opportunities for washing their hands. Some persons harbour a pathogen and excrete it continuously in either faeces or urine without having any symptom of disease. Such **carriers** are particularly dangerous and have been responsible for many outbreaks of disease.

Food-borne infections and faecal-oral diseases are especially prevalent in poor urban communities with poor facilities for storing foods, inadequate water supplies and lavatories. In such circumstances infections are common and contribute to the high death rates, especially in young children. But the wealthy are by no means assured of protection. Anyone who thinks that only the poor are exposed to dirty foods should read George Orwell's *Down and Out in Paris* and find out what may go on in an expensive restaurant out of sight of the patrons.

In the prevention of outbreaks of bacterial food poisoning it is valuable to identify accurately the responsible bacteria and to demonstrate the presence of a specific bacterium both in the patients and in the food responsible for the outbreak. The public health laboratory services have the expertise for precise bacteriological diagnosis.

Public health authorities also have the duty to inspect abattoirs, the premises of food manufacturers, wholesale and retail shops that sell food, and all catering establishments and restaurants. They have the legal right to close any premises that are not up to acceptable standards of hygiene. Unfortunately, few public health departments have sufficient staff to carry out adequate inspections.

BACTERIAL FOOD POISONING

This produces an acute gastroenteritis which is usually short and self-limiting. Between 8000 and 12 000 cases are notified each year in England and Wales, but many are unreported. The incidence rises in years when there is prolonged hot weather. There are between 20 and 50 deaths each year, resulting from severe dehydration and loss of electrolytes; these deaths occur mainly in the very young and very old and in those with debilitating diseases.

Salmonella infections. These account for over 70 per cent of reported cases of food poisoning. *Salmonella typhimurium* is the organism most commonly responsible, but over 1600 serotypes of Salmonella are now known. Many of these are very rare, but two formerly rare, *S. agona* and *S. virchou*, have now become established in the food chain in Britian. An accurate bacteriological diagnosis of the cause of an outbreak is essential to establish its source. This is usually meat or poultry. Imported raw eggs and egg powders have also been responsible. Salmonella may multiply in foods which have been inadequately cooked, but usually infection follows contamination of cooked foods from a raw food via food handlers or kitchen utensils. The incubation period is usually 12 to 36 hours and the disease lasts for 1 to 7 days, being nearly always accompanied by fever.

Clostridial infections. *Clostridium welchii*, known as *Cl. perfringens* in the USA, is responsible for about 20 per cent of infections in Britain. This is an anaerobic organism which forms spores resistant to heat. Spores are widespread in soil and dust. Infection occurs typically after eating meat which has been cooked on the previous day and allowed to cool under conditions which enable surviving spores to form vegetative forms. The victim then ingests what is a broth culture of the bacteria, which then multiply in the gut and produce an enterotoxin. The incubation period of the disease is 8 to 24 hours. Diarrhoea is often accompanied by abdominal pain, but vomiting and fever are uncommon.

Staphylococcal infections. *Staphylococcus aureus* is widespread. Up to 30 per cent of healthy people are carriers and it is frequently recovered from nasal swabs. But it is potentially pathogenic and responsible for many skin infections and may enter the blood stream to form abscesses in deep tissues. Foods are readily contaminated by carriers and may, under suitable conditions, provide a good culture medium for growth of the organism. Some strains produce a powerful enterotoxin which is resistant to heat. Ingestion of a contaminated food may be followed very quickly in 2 to 4 hours by vomiting and diarrhoea, which may be severe and accompanied by collapse due to dehydration.

Other bacterial infections. The three types of infection described above have been well known for 50 years or more. However, in a large majority of outbreaks of gastroenteritis, none of the three can be identified: other bacterial species shown to have been responsible for outbreaks of gastroenteritis are now briefly described.

Escherichia coli, one of the predominant members of the normal bacterial flora of the gut, was formerly considered to be non-pathogenic. However, some serotypes have been shown to produce an enterotoxin or have a local cytotoxic effect and these are often responsible for acute gastroenteritis in young children and also for traveller's diarrhoea (p. 435). In these instances the victim may not have built up a specific immunity to a particular serotype not previously encountered.

Bacillus cereus is a saprophytic spore-bearing organism widely found in nature. It can be recovered from many samples of uncooked rice. The spore may survive normal cooking and produce vegetative forms during cooling. These produce an enterotoxin which causes severe vomiting one hour after ingestion or diarrhoea later. Infection occurs usually in those who eat in Chinese restaurants. Incidence is unknown as it is often not reported. Fortunately, recovery is usually rapid.

Vibrio parahaemolyticus is an organism related to the cholera vibrio which grows in sea water. It is responsible for profuse diarrhoea and dehydration which may follow the consumption of raw or undercooked seafoods.

Campylobacter are a group of vibrio-like organisms responsible for infectious abortion of cattle and ewes (*C. fetus*) and for attacks of acute diarrhoea in man (*C. jejuni*). Several outbreaks have been reported in Europe and the USA associated with infected milk or drinking water. Infection may also be spread from person to person, especially in children, or from infected poultry and dogs.

Yersinia enterocolitica under its old name of *Pasteurella pseudotuberculosis* has long been known to cause various disorders in many species of animals. Chinchillas have been much infected and spread from a farm may have been responsible for the first reports of human cases in 1963. Gastroenteritis and mesenteric adenitis due to this organism have now occurred many times.

VIRAL INFECTIONS CAUSING GASTROENTERITIS

More than 25 different viruses are known to infect man through the alimentary tract and can be isolated from faeces. Rotavirus and norwalk virus are established as major causes of gastroenteritis,[1] others may also be responsible. Viruses unlike bacteria, cannot multiply in foods, but food handlers and dirty utensils are means whereby small doses may be transferred to foods and subsequently ingested. Then they may multiply in the intestinal tract. To what extent viruses are responsible for attacks of acute gastroenteritis is uncertain. It would seem probable that they are a common cause of attacks in young children when often no bacteria can be held responsible. In early life there is not the immunity to the common viruses which is built up by repeated exposure. For technical reasons the isolation and culture of viruses is a long way behind that of bacteria, but it is catching up fast. The future may show that viruses have an important role in gastrointestinal disease.

OTHER BACTERIAL DISEASES SPREAD BY FOOD

Botulism. This is a severe, often fatal form of food poisoning, fortunately now very rare. First described in Germany in 1817 as 'sausage' poisoning (Latin *botulus*, sausage), it has followed eating canned meats, liver and other pastes and also large hams. These foods under certain circumstances are an ideal medium for the growth of *Clostridium botulinum*. This is a saprophyte which is widespread and found in soils. It forms heat-resistant spores. If these are not destroyed by adequate heat in cooking, vegetative forms may grow anaerobically, and these produce one of the most potent toxins known, the lethal dose for mammals being less than 1 μg/kg. It blocks transmission at the neuromuscular junctions. Early symptoms of poisoning are weakness of the eye muscles and difficulty in swallowing; paralysis of the muscles of respiration leads to death. The food industry is well aware of the dangers of botulism and uses nitrites as a preservative which prevents anaerobic growth. No case had occurred in Britain for over 20 years until 1978, when four members of a family in Birmingham became ill after eating tinned salmon. In the USA cases continue to occur occasionally through eating home-canned meat.

Brucellosis. Infection in man gives rise to a continued fever in which remissions and relapses are common (undulant fever). The responsible organisms, *Brucella melitensis* and *B. abortus*, affect goats and cows respectively and are found in their milk. Bruce was an army doctor who first isolated the former species in 1886 from soldiers suffering from 'Malta fever' who had been drinking goat's milk. Eradication of the disease in cattle has proved very difficult. Effective pasteurisation makes milk safe, but cream and cheese made from unpasteurised milk may contain *Brucella*, and those who buy these products from small farmers run a risk of infection. Several hundred cases are notified yearly in Britain; many patients are stockmen or veterinary surgeons for whom the disease is an occupational risk.

Bovine tuberculosis. Cattle are readily infected with tuberculosis and excrete the organism in their milk. *Mycobacterium bovis*, if ingested by man, causes enlargement of the cervical and mesenteric lymph nodes. It may then enter the blood stream and lead to tuberculous lesions in any organ and especially in bones and joints. Fifty years ago, when the drinking of raw milk in Britain was widespread (in part due to opposition to pasteurisation on spurious nutritional grounds), human infection was common in children. Today many elderly people have scars in their necks and some have orthopaedic deformities, as reminders of past illnesses. Tuberculosis has now been almost eradicated from cattle in Britain and all milk is pasteurised. As a result, this dangerous disease is now almost unknown in man. Continual watchfulness is necessary. In south-west England there is a focus of infection in badgers which has been held to be responsbile for some occasional cases in cattle. Steps have been taken to control the spread.

HELMINTH INFECTIONS

Many helminths have complicated life cycles in which they live as parasites in more than one host. Man may be infected by eating undercooked pork and beef and raw salads.

Undercooked pork and beef

The pig and beef tapeworms, *Taenia solium* and *T. saginata*, form cysts which are present in muscle. If these are eaten by man, the adult worms develop in the gut. Segments of the worm may be passed in the faeces and cause alarm, but the adult worms are not responsible for any symptoms. If a person harbours *T. solium*, he may infect himself with ova passed in the faeces. These may then develop into larval forms which penetrate into muscles and other tissues where they form cysts. The condition is known as **cysticercosis** and may lead to epilepsy and other neurological disorders if cysts are in the brain. Fortunately this is very rare.

Undercooked pork may also contain larvae of *Trichinella spiralis*, which after ingestion can penetrate the tissues and cause a febrile illness with muscle pain and other symptoms of **trichinosis,** which is usually mild and brief.

Undercooked and raw fish

A fish tapeworm, *Diphyllobothrium latum*, has a worldwide distribution in freshwater fish. Man may be infected by raw fish. The adult worm is very long, up to 15 metres. It competes with the host for limited supplies of ingested vitamin B12, and infection may lead to megaloblastic anaemia. This is not uncommon in Finland and in some other countries.

Raw fish and crabs are sometimes eaten in the Far

East and may be considered a delicacy by some Chinese. Visitors are warned not to partake, as they become infected by two flukes. Metacercaria of *Clonorchis sinesis* enter the biliary tract, where they may survive for many years and lead to a variety of symptoms and liver disorders, **clonorchiasis.** Larvae of *Paragonimus westermanii* burrow through the intestinal wall and in the lungs develop into adult worms which form fibrous cysts; they may communicate with a bronchiole and sputum containing ova may be coughed up. The condition is known as **paragonimiasis.**

Raw salads

The liver fluke *Fasciola hepatica* is common in sheep. Human cases occur occasionally and five small outbreaks of **fascioliasis** have been reported in England after eating watercress. The adult flukes live in the liver and biliary system, where they may be responsible for a variety of symptoms. Salads may be responsible for infection with roundworms, *Ascaris lumbricoides*, whipworms, *Trichuris trichura*, and the protozoon *Giardia lamblia*. These parasites spread by the faecal-oral route (see below). In the East the practice of Chinese and other gardeners of using human night soil as fertiliser had led to heavy contamination of lettuce and other salad crops. An article in *The Guardian* (22 April 1978) reports that 9000 tons of human manure leave Shanghai daily for surrounding rural areas. As the population of Shanghai is only 6 million, this is an example of Chinese statistics overestimating the productivity of the people, but it serves as a warning to visitors that they should avoid salads and all uncooked foods.

Raw salads carry saprophytic bacteria that are normally present in soil and water. Examples are various species of *Escherichia*, *Pseudomonas* and *Klebsiella*. They often colonise the human intestine where they normally do no harm and form part of the bacterial flora. In patients whose immune responses are impaired by anti-inflammatory drugs, radiation therapy or any severe illness, these opportunist organisms can invade tissues and cause serious infection. For this reason it is advisable not to include salads in the diets of patients who are seriously ill, especially when a low white cell count indicates impaired immunity.[2]

FAECAL-ORAL INFECTIONS

In these diseases the infective agent is excreted in the faeces and enters the body via the mouth. Mechanisms for transfer of the agent from faeces to mouth vary widely and are often not known. Contamination of drinking water with sewage is a well-known means and food may be contaminated by flies and food handlers. Amoebic and bacillary dysentery are faecal-oral diseases and their incidence is high in many tropical countries where flies abound, and outbreaks often occur in temperate climates when a spell of hot weather allows the fly population to increase. As already mentioned, rota- and other viruses may cause gastroenteritis. Two major diseases, poliomyelitis and infectious hepatitis, are caused by viruses which are excreted in the faeces. In both diseases the virus is excreted by symptom-free carriers, and it has been estimated that a million people in the USA are carriers of hepatitis virus. How these two diseases spread is unknown. Large outbreaks of hepatitis occurred in troops in World Wars I and II and in the Vietnam war. It is not unlikely that these outbreaks were due to poor hygienic conditions in army cookhouses.

CONCLUSION

Brief summaries have been given of common pathogens that may be spread by foods and of the more serious diseases that may arise. A fuller account of the diseases can be found in medical textbooks, e.g. Passmore & Robson[3] and of how their spread can be prevented by food hygiene in a monograph by Hobbs & Gilbert.[4] Enough should have been said to have impressed on the reader the potential dangers of infection from foods. Prevention depends on 'clean food handled by clean people in clean premises with clean equipment and protection from flies and vermin.' 'Cleanliness is, indeed, next to Godliness,' as John Wesley said in a sermon. It is a virtue which many try to achieve in the domestic life and yet remain all too tolerant of, or unaware of, dirt in public places.

REFERENCES

1. Blacklow N R, Cukor G 1981 Viral gastroenteritis. N Engl J Med 304: 397–406
2. Remington J S, Schimpff S C 1981 Please don't eat the salads. N Engl J Med 304: 433–434
3. Passmore R, Robson J S (eds) 1974 A companion to medical studies. Blackwell Scientific, Edinburgh, vol 3, p 12.36–12.64
4. Hobbs B C, Gilbert R J 1978 Food poisoning and food hygiene, 4th edn. Arnold, London

25

Food Toxicity

At a very early age a child learns from his parents that he cannot eat everything and that certain substances are poisonous. An older child hears and reads stories of romance in which kings and courtiers, afraid that their enemies may poison them, employ food tasters at banquets. It is not surprising that many adults have an ingrained fear of poisons in food nor that the widespread dissemination of chemicals in an industrial society and their deliberate addition to food, though proper causes of concern, raise irrational fears and emotions.

A poison is difficult to define and many substances present in food would have adverse or toxic effects if taken in large doses, but the amounts normally present in foods are harmless.

Table 25.1 Toxic substances in foods

NATURAL	
Inherent	Usually present in the food and affects everyone if they eat enough, e.g. solanine in potatoes, and lathyrus toxin (p. 242)
Toxin resulting from abnormal conditions of animal or plant used for food	For example, neurotoxic mussel poisoning (p. 244), honey from bees feeding on Rhododendron or Azalea nectar
Consumer abnormally sensitive	Constitutional, e.g. coeliac disease from wheat gluten (p. 437), favism from broad beans (p. 468), allergy to particular food (p. 477), or drug-induced, e.g. cheese reaction (p. 215)
Contamination by pathogenic bacteria	Acute illness, usually gastrointestinal, e.g. toxins produced by *Staphylococcus aureus* or *Clostridium botulinum;* food may not appear spoiled
Mycotoxins	Food mouldy or spoiled, e.g. aflatoxin B_1 from *Aspergillus flavus* is a liver carcinogen
ACCIDENTAL CHEMICAL CONTAMINATION OR POLLUTION	
Unintentional additives — man made	
Chemicals used in agriculture and animal husbandry	For example, fungicides on grain, insecticides on fruit, antibiotics or hormones given to animals
Environmental pollution	For example, organic mercury (p. 128), cadmium (p. 129), PCB and PBB (p. 248) and radioactive fall-out can affect any stage of food chain
Intentional food additives	
Preservatives, emulsifiers, flavours, colours, etc.	Some have been in use for centuries; many are naturally based and used in small amounts; the most thoroughly tested and monitored of all chemicals in food

Table 25.1 gives a classification of the ways by which toxic substances may be present in foods.

Toxins naturally present in plant foods, and infection of food by pathogenic bacteria have caused more human disease and mortality than the other categories. Accidental chemical contamination and environmental pollution have been responsible for local disasters from time to time. The intentional additives used in food processing today in well-organised countries are those considered safe by authoritative bodies. Standards of safety are strict and may be getting stricter. The public and their food safety administrations tend to set higher standards of safety for pure synthetic chemicals than for the complex of substances present in natural foods.

As Magnus Pyke[1] has put it, the tests for new foods and additives are now so stringent that if Sir Walter Raleigh turned up now with the potato, as a new and unknown food, he would never stand a chance of having it accepted because of the solanine which it contains.

Disposal of ingested foreign substances

As foreign substances differ greatly in their chemical nature, their fate in the body varies. In general a substance may follow one of five possible sequences, each of which has variants.

1. It may pass through the gastrointestinal tract and not be absorbed. Pectin and other food thickeners are examples. It may, however, be digested by enzymes in the upper gastrointestinal tract or broken down by bacteria in the colon. Even if a substance is not absorbed it can affect the motility of the gastrointestinal tract and cause vomiting, diarrhoea or constipation. It can also irritate the mucous membrane and produce ulceration. Chronic irritation, if caused by a substance ingested over a long period, could lead to cancer formation. Cancer of the gastrointestinal tract occurs at sites where movement is slowed down and gut contents are in prolonged contact with the mucous membrane, e.g. the lower end of the oesophagus, the pyloric end of the stomach and the colon.

2. A substance may be absorbed and pass into the portal vein to the liver. Here it may be metabolised and then excreted back into the gastrointestinal tract in the bile. This sequence may be repeated, in an enterohepatic cycle. The substance or its metabolites can be recovered in the faeces but it has been inside the body and could damage the liver.

3. Water-soluble substances may be absorbed and pass through the liver into the general circulation. In the blood the substance may be partly bound to one of the plasma proteins, but it is excreted by the kidneys and passes into the urine. An example of a substance which follows this sequence is saccharin, which is excreted unchanged. If such a substance should be

oncogenic, the organ most likely to be affected is the urinary bladder.

4. Fat-soluble substances after absorption reach the liver. There they are often metabolised in two stages and usually the metabolites are more water-soluble and so more easily excreted and less toxic. The first stage is oxidation by the non-specific microsomal enzyme oxidising system (MEOS) in the hepatocytes. Cytochrome P-450 is an integral part of this system. The second stage is conjugation of the oxidation product, usually with glucuronic acid or sulphate. Some substances wholly or partly bypass the first stage and are conjugated directly. The metabolites are then excreted in the urine or the bile. An example is the antioxidant BHT (butylated hydroxytoluene); its three butyl groups are partly oxidised and it is excreted in the urine as glucuronic acid conjugates.

5. A substance may be absorbed but neither metabolised nor excreted; it stays in the body and accumulates. Even if harmless in small amounts in acute or subacute tests, it may lead to long-term harmful effects. Toxicologists are naturally concerned about substances that behave in this way. Examples are fat-soluble compounds like DDT (p. 247) and PBB (p. 248). These are not only stored in the adipose tissue but pass into the milk fat in lactating women. Substances handled like calcium can stay in bone for a long time, e.g. fluoride and radioactive strontium.

Toxicity testing

Safety is always relative. Despite numerous statutory safety regulations, travellers on land, sea and air are still killed by accidents, and no food can be guaranteed safe. The most an authority can do is to define an acceptable risk. In general, authorities permit substances to be present in foods when the maximum amount likely to be consumed daily is 100 times less than the minimum amount shown to have an adverse effect on experimental animals with due allowance for the body weight of the animals. Experimental animals are used for toxicity testing of pharmaceuticals, including cosmetics, and foods; such tests form the large majority of over 4 million vivisections carried out annually in the UK. Antivivisectionists protest strongly against this use of animals. The tests are also expensive and add to the price of many products. Hence attempts are being made to find alternative tests which use tissue cultures or isolated cells. These tests may be the main method of testing for toxicity in the future, but cannot wholly replace animal testing until much more is known about their reliability.

Species differ in their tolerance of many poisons, and an equivalent dose of a chemical shown to be harmless in one species of experimental animal may not be safe for man. Most substances are first tested on rats, but none is considered safe for man until the tests have been repeated on a species which is not rodent: rabbits, cats and dogs are most commonly used. Preferably, tests should also be carried out on a primate.

The signs of acute poisoning are usually obvious and it is not difficult to determine the maximum amount of a single dose of a substance that can be taken with safety. Since a potential food toxin is likely to be consumed throughout the life span of consumers, it has to be tested for long periods in animals and over at least two generations. The fetus is especially sensitive to some toxins, as is the ability of mature animals to reproduce. Malignant disease frequently does not arise until an animal has been exposed to an oncogenic agent for a major portion of its life span. A WHO report[2] outlines procedures for investigating intentional and unintentional food additives.

Examples are now given of poisoning in man due to natural and artificial toxins in foods. The accounts are of necessity anecdotal and many, it is hoped, are only of historical interest. Characteristically the illnesses present with an unusual combination of symptoms and signs in a community over a considerable time, and the possibility of their being due to a food toxin has been overlooked at first. In any outbreak of an unusual disease, it is wise to consider this possibility.

NATURAL FOOD TOXINS

There are people who are so alarmed at the possible chemical hazards from eating foods grown and prepared with the aid of modern chemical industry that they wish to return to a simple life and eat only natural foods. Unfortunately the chemical hazards in the fields and woods are also numerous. Table 25.2 gives a list of foods containing pharmacological agents known to have adverse effects on man. The list is far from complete and monographs are available prepared by the Committee on Food Protection of the US Food and Nutrition Board[3] and by Liener.[4,5] These contain much curious information and are very readable. Here it is only possible to give a brief account of a few somewhat arbitrarily selected toxins which appear of special interest in medicine.

Table 25.2 indicates that there are natural poisons which have a great variety of acute and chronic pharmacological effects. Presumably many of these evolved in plants as protective mechanisms against animals feed-

Table 25.2 Some possible toxic effects of foods

Source	Active agent	Effects
Bananas and some other fruits	5-Hydroxytryptamine; adrenaline; noradrenaline	Effects on central and peripheral nervous system
Some cheeses	Tyramine	Raises blood pressure; enhanced by monoamine oxidase inhibitors
Almonds, cassava and other plants	Cyanide	Interferes with tissue respiration
Quail	Due to consumption of hemlock	Hemlock poisoning
Mussels	Due to consumption of dino-flagellate, *Gonyaulax*	Tingling, numbness, muscle weakness, respiratory paralysis
Cycad nuts	Methylazoxymethanol (cycasin)	Liver damage; cancer
Some fish, meat or cheese	Nitrosamines	Cancer
Mustard oil	Sanguinarine	Oedema (epidemic dropsy)
Legumes	Haemagglutinins	Red cell and intestinal cell damage
Some beans	Vicine β-Aminopropionitrile β-*N*-Oxalyl-amino-L-alanine	Haemolytic anaemia (favism) Interferes with collagen formation Toxic effects on nervous system, lathyrism
Ackee fruit	α-Amino-β-methylene Cyclopropane propionic acid	Hypoglycaemia, vomiting sickness
Brassica seeds and some other Cruciferae	Glucosinolates, thiocyanate	Enlargement of thyroid gland (goitre)
Rhubarb	Oxalate	Oxaluria
Green potatoes	Solanine; possibly other sapotoxins	Gastrointestinal upset
Many fish	Various, often confined to certain organs or seasonal	Mainly toxic effects on nervous system
Many fungi	Various mycotoxins	Mainly toxic effects on nervous system and liver

ing on them. Animals in turn have evolved elaborate biochemical reactions and cellular responses for disposing of the toxins or of at least partially neutralising their effects. Man and many other animals have also learnt by experience to avoid eating some of the foods containing potent toxins. Some of the most potent toxins are found in fungi which may contaminate otherwise healthy foods.

LATHYRUS POISONS

Tares is the traditional English name for the vetches and an old word used loosely for various pulses and legumes. In Biblical times they were poorly regarded. 'But while men slept, his enemy came and sowed tares among the wheat' (St Matthew, xiii. 25). Why the sowing of tares was regarded as an unfriendly act is not wholly clear. The tendrils by which these plants climb up the wheat stalks certainly hamper reaping. But they may also have been known to be nutritionally unsatisfactory.

For a long time one species of tare (*Lathyrus sativus*: *Khesari dhal* in Hindustani) has been deliberately sown with the wheat by farmers in dry districts of many countries in Asia and North Africa where the rainfall is uncertain. If the rains are good, the wheat overgrows the lathyrus, of which little is harvested. If the rains fail and there is a poor crop of wheat, a useful harvest of lathyrus may be reaped. Eaten in small quantities, lathyrus seeds are a valuable food. But if they are the main source of energy (providing more than 50 per cent), a severe disease of the spinal cord (lathyrism, p. 330) may result, causing crippling and permanent paralysis. An excellent account of the disease and the circumstances under which it arises has been given by a soldier, General Sleeman.[6]

After many failures to find a neurotoxin, two were isolated in succeeding years. In 1962 in the USA β-N-oxalyl-amino-L-alanine (BOAA) was isolated and identified in the common vetch (*Vicia sativa*), which frequently grows as a weed in lathyrus crops.[7] The next year in India β-N-oxalyl-L-α,β diaminopropionic acid was isolated from seeds of *Lathyrus sativus*.[8] Both of these can cause neurological lesions in primates, but over 20 years later the relation between intakes of the two toxins and the incidence and nature of the neurological lesions in man has not been worked out.

Allied vetches, notably the sweet pea, *Lathyrus odoratus*, when fed to rats, readily give rise to a severe disturbance of collagenous structures throughout the body, notably in skin and bones, known as osteolathyrism.[9] This is not a natural disease of either man or animals but can be readily produced in laboratory animals. The neurotoxin responsible, β-aminoproprionitrile, is a much used tool in the experimental study of collagen formation.

SEAWATER FISH

Ciguatera

This is an old Portuguese word introduced in 1787 to describe poisoning that arose after eating fish from the Pacific Ocean and the Caribbean Sea. The clinical features are those of an acute neuromuscular disorder with weakness and sensory changes. Most attacks are of moderate severity and the symptoms clear up in a few days, but itching may persist for several weeks and occasionally widespread paralysis is followed by coma and death. Captain Cook (1777) describes a typical attack.[10]

5 September, 1774, Cape Colnet, New Caledonia. This afternoon a fish being struck by one of the natives near the watering-place, my clerk purchased it, and sent it to me after my return on board. It was of a new species, something like a sunfish with a large, long, ugly head. Having no suspicion of its being of a poisonous nature, we ordered it to be dressed for supper: but, very luckily, the operation of drawing and describing took up so much time that it was too late, so that only the liver and roe were dressed, of which the two Mister Forsters and myself did but taste. About three o'clock in the morning we found ourselves seized with an extraordinary weakness and numbness all over our limbs. I had almost lost the sense of feeling; nor could I distinguish between light and heavy bodies, of such as I had strength to move; a quart pot full of water and a feather being the same in my hand. We each of us took an emetic, and after that a sweat, which gave us much relief. In the morning, one of the pigs which had eaten the entrails was found dead. When the natives came on board and saw the fish hang up, they immediately gave us to understand it was not wholesome food.

A large number of species of fish may be poisonous. Some of these are always poisonous and others may usually be eaten with safety, but are poisonous at certain times of the year. Poisonous fish have usually been feeding on a coral reef; deep-sea fish are generally safe. The toxin or toxins responsible have not been identified. Fish becomes poisonous because of factors in their environment which get into their food supply. Jardin[11] has suggested that the toxins may be organo-minerals. It is possible that natural disturbances in ocean beds may affect the amounts of trace elements in rocks and sediment, which become incorporated into organic material and so into the algae and other basic components of the food of fishes.

Scombrotoxic poisoning

This results from bacterial spoilage of tunny, mackerel and related fish. Disrupted muscle liberates histidine from which histamine is formed, and this together with other toxins produce headache, palpitation, flushing and diarrhoea a short time after ingestion. This is not prevented by cooking the fish. An outbreak, affecting over 200 people, from canned tuna occurred in the USA.[12] Other toxins may be present in seawater fish.[13]

Mussel poisoning

A toxin, saxitoxin, may be present in plankton, particularly the dinoflagellate *Gonyaulax tamarensis* which is ingested by bivalves such as mussels. The toxin is stable and remains in the tissues of the shellfish which appear to be resistant. It is not destroyed by cooking. Dinoflagellates at times multiply to such an extent that they may colour the sea and such 'red tides' cause a heavy mortality among seabirds, especially shags. Mussels, a delicacy usually safe to eat, may then become toxic. These conditions occur occasionally off the eastern seaboard of the USA and Canada,[14] and more rarely during summer off the coast of Britain between Aberdeen and Yorkshire.[15,16] People who are unfortunate enough to eat mussels at such a time develop, within 30 minutes paraesthesiae, weakness of limbs, ataxia and vomiting. Death can occur from respiratory paralysis.

FRESHWATER FISH

Fishermen and their families around the Koenigsberg Haff in East Germany during the period between World Wars I and II suffered outbreaks of acute paroxysmal myoglobinuria, preceded by severe pain in all muscles. Always on the day before an attack fish, usually eel or burbot, had been eaten. The condition became known as Haff disease, and German investigators concluded that the fish eaten contained a toxin which had entered the Haff with the effluent from nearby industrial works. However, a small outbreak in Sweden affected persons who had eaten burbot from a lake uncontaminated by industrial waste. Berlin[17] suggested that thiaminase present in the fish might be the cause, but this seems unlikely. Haff disease is rarely reported nowadays and the toxin responsible remains unidentified.

MISCELLANEOUS TOXINS IN FOODS

Argemone contamination of edible oils

In Bengal and Bihar mustard oil is the chief cooking fat. In the same part of the world epidemic dropsy has been endemic for a long time. In a series of investigations in which the clues were analysed in the best detective manner, Lal and his colleagues[18,19] showed that mustard oil was responsible for this disease. The toxin was not present in the oil from the mustard seeds themselves, but in oil from the seeds of a poppy weed (*Argemone mexicana*). This weed commonly grows in the mustard crops. Its seeds contain a toxic alkaloid, sanguinarine.[20] Sanguinarine inhibits the oxidation of pyruvic acid and, as in wet beriberi, cardiomyopathy may follow (p. 313). Other edible oils, such as groundnut oil, can be contaminated with argemone oil.

Ackee fruit (*Blighia sapida*)

The fruit grows profusely in Jamaica and is eaten by large numbers of people, especially children. Yet it is widely credited with being responsible for a form of food poisoning, 'vomiting sickness'.[21] Dr Cicely Williams undertook an investigation of the disease for the Jamaican Government.[22] She was able to study numerous patients and a few outbreaks in detail. In some, the symptoms could be attributed to other diseases. Yet there were several patients in whom no definite cause could be found, despite thorough investigation. A specific poison from the ackee fruit could not be excluded. She concluded that if such poison were indeed responsible, large amounts would have to be consumed, and the patients must be peculiarly susceptible to the poison, probably because of their undernourished state. Ackee fruit contains a water-soluble substance, α-amino-β-methylene cyclopropyl-propionic acid, that causes accumulation of branched short-chain fatty acids and acute hypoglycaemia and is known as hypoglycin.[23] This substance is now believed to be responsible for the clinical features of vomiting sickness.

Brassica species

Brassica is a large genus which includes cabbages, mustards and rapes. Rabbits and other laboratory animals fed large amounts of raw leaves develop goitre, which may also occur after feeding the seeds. This is due to the presence of glucosinolates and thiocyanates. Glucosinolates act on the thyroid gland like thiouracil by preventing the synthesis of thyroxine. Thiocynates reduce the concentration of iodine in the thyroid gland. Some of the brassicas, notably cabbage, are common human foods, but there is no evidence that when eaten in normal amounts, as part of a balanced diet, they are anything but beneficial. Goitrogens in foods are further considered in Chapter 30.

Potatoes

It has been known for a long time that potatoes contain an alkaloid, solanine, that is potentially toxic. In normal potatoes there is about 7 mg/100 g, mostly in the skin, but also in eyes and sprouts. Potato poisoning is very rare, but an outbreak occurred in a London school affecting 78 boys.[24] The main symptoms were headache, vomiting and diarrhoea. Fever and circulatory collapse led to 17 of the boys being admitted to hospital, of whom three were dangerously ill with neurological disturbances, stupor and hallucinations. A sample of the potatoes that had been served at the school, when peeled and boiled, contained 33 mg of solanine per 100 g. There is little doubt that solanine poisoning was responsible for the outbreak, but how these particular potatoes came to have such a high solanine content is a mystery.

A suggestion that solanine in potatoes eaten by mothers in early pregnancy might be responsible for spina bifida and other abnormalities of the central nervous system received much publicity in the lay press. There is no epidemiological or other evidence to support it.

Cycads

There has been a high incidence of a form of motor neurone disease and of a disease known as Parkinsonism dementia among the Chamorro people on the island of Guam and the neighbouring Mariana islands. It has been suspected that the traditional high consumption of the seeds of the cycad, *Cycas circinalis*, might be responsible. Certainly cycad seeds contain a toxin, cycasin, which in experimental animals is a potent hepatotoxin and also carcinogenic (p. 567). Yet hepatic disease, including carcinoma, is only slightly more common in Guam than in the USA; feeding adult animals with cycasin has not produced neurological damage, and it has not been shown that the victims of the motor neurone disease have eaten more cycad seeds or prepared them in a different way from unaffected islanders.[25]

Spices

Spices and flavouring agents contain volatile and essential oils and hydrocarbons which stimulate glandular secretion and may have a weak action on the nervous system. Many of them if taken in large doses have toxic actions. For instance nutmeg, mace and dill contain myristicin. In 1832, the Czech physiologist Purkinje ate three nutmeg seeds and became delirious and went into a deep stupor. Smaller amounts of nutmeg may cause vomiting and colic.

Wormwood oil obtained from an African tree, *Artemisia absinthium* with a sweet-smelling wood is used as a flavouring agent in the liqueur absinthe and in vermouth and other wines. Its active principle, thujone, stimulates the nervous system and may cause convulsions.

Worcester sauce contains acetic acid, black pepper, garlic and other spices. Several patients who had acquired the habit of consuming up to one bottle a day have developed renal failure, and in some cases renal calculi.[26] Complete recovery may occur when the habits is given up. The toxin has not been identified.

Oestrogens

Some plant foods, including soya bean, contain traces of oestrogens, but the amounts are so small that no adverse effects follow the consumption of such foods. Larger amounts may be present in meat from animals previously dosed with oestrogens to promote growth. This practice is now not permitted in most countries.

Carcinogens

Many natural foods have been shown to contain substances which produce tumours in experimental animals. The extent to which they may be responsible for malignant disease in man is discussed in Chapter 60.

Antivitamins

Attention was first drawn to the antivitamins in veterinary practice. Cattle fed on spoiled sweet clover develop a haemorrhagic disease. This is due to the presence in the clover of dicoumarol, a substance chemically related to vitamin K.[27] It produces haemorrhages by causing vitamin K deficiency in the tissues. Synthetic analogues of dicoumarol are used in clinical practice to reduce the liability to coagulation.

Natural substances can act an antivitamins by preventing their absorption or by destroying them in the gut. For example in 1936 an outbreak of paralysis, 'Chastek paralysis', developed in silver foxes on a farm in the USA belonging to Mr Chastek. The foxes had been fed on carp. The presence of a thiaminase was demonstrated in the flesh and viscera of these fish.[28] Additional thiamin both prevented and cured the disease. Thiaminase has been found in several species of fish. A different substance (3, 4-dihydroxy cinnamic acid) with thiaminase activity occurs in bracken and other plants. Thiamin deficiency due to consumption of thiaminase has not been reported in man. Fish is used as a food in zoos and nature reserves, as well as in commercial animal production, and those who use it should be aware of the hazard from thiaminase.

Hallucinogenic substances

In 1676 British soldiers engaged in putting down a rebellion in Virginia ate a salad containing the Jimson weed *Datura stramonium*. Some of them were reported to have been turned into natural fools performing many simple tricks, but they remembered nothing of this when they recovered. The weed contains alkaloids, such as scopolamine, which produce hallucinations. Cases of poisoning have been reported in 'beatniks' who have eaten the weed for its psychic effects and in children who have tasted its fruits out of curiosity.

The Mexican plant peyote, which contains mescaline, and the hemp plant, *Cannabis indica*, widespread in Asia and Africa, are two examples of plants which have been consumed deliberately for their psychic effects.

The fly toadstool, *Amanita muscaria*, contains muscarin, but only in small amounts and the characteristic symptom of poisoning is cerebral excitement, which is due to mycetoatropine. An example of its action was a young man admitted to a Glasgow hospital in a confused and drowsy state.[29] By occupation he was a salmon poacher, and he and his brother used to eat deliberately *A. muscaria* because they enjoyed the feeling of unreality and detachment which gave. Others have become addicted, including apparently the Russian Empress Catherine the Great.

TOXINS OF FUNGAL ORIGIN

Mushrooms

Some mushrooms and many other species of fungi are excellent eating but others are poisonous. The mushroom commonly responsible for poisoning in Britain is *Amanita phalloides* and in America *Amanita serna*. Each contains two types of toxin. Phallotoxins are heptapeptides that act quickly, causing vomiting, diarrhoea and abdominal pain. Amatoxins are octopeptides and act after they have been taken up by hepatocytes and renal tubular cells. Oliguria and other evidence of renal failure may appear only after the gastrointestinal symptoms have subsided. Damage to the kidney may be fatal unless haemodialysis is available. Treatment is by washing out the stomach repeatedly and replacing losses of fluid and electrolytes. Haemodialysis should be started early in severe cases. Antidotes that may be useful are penicillin in large doses, silymarin and thioctic acid.

The dangers of eating any unfamiliar mushroom is illustrated by the story of three young people on holiday in the north of Scotland.[30] They had gathered and eaten mushrooms with orange gills (*Cortinarius speciosissimus*). Gastrointestinal symptoms of varying severity followed and 10 days later all three were admitted to the Edinburgh Royal Infirmary. One of the party showed evidence of only slight renal damage and recovered fully. The other two are now also alive and well, thanks to haemodialysis and subsequent renal transplantation.

Ergot

Epidemics of the disease known as St Anthony's fire was described in France in the eleventh century. The disease was called 'fire' because of the intolerable burning pain in the limbs, which became black, shrivelled and dropped off. Convulsions, palsies and disordered movements affected some patients, indicating that the central nervous system as well as the peripheral vascular system were affected. Epidemics were frequent in many countries in Europe, but it was not until the beginning of the eighteenth century that it was associated with eating rye infected by a fungus, *Claviceps purpura*. The disease, especially the convulsive form, was severe in Germany in the eighteenth century and persisted in Poland and Russia until well into the twentieth century. A classic book by Barger[31] describes the features of the disease and his work with Dale on the ergot alkaloids present in the fungus and responsible for its toxicity.

Occasional outbreaks are reported today. Thus in Ethiopia five cases of gangrenous ergotism occurred, associated with eating wild oats infected with *Claviceps*

species.[32] In India outbreaks have occurred associated with the millet (*Pennisetum typoides*), known as bajra, infected with *Claviceps fusiformis*.[33] This fungus produces alkaloids of the clavine group, which are different from the ergot alkaloids. The clinical features of poisoning are severe nausea and vomiting, accompanied by giddiness and drowsiness, but recovery is rapid and complete. Hence it is a much less serious disease than classical European ergotism.

Aflatoxins

In 1960 a widespread outbreak of a fatal disease characterised by acute enteritis and hepatitis occurred in England among young turkeys which had been fed a ration containing imported groundnut meal.[34] The groundnuts concerned had been harvested, stored and processed under conditions of high humidity. The toxic factors were produced by *Aspergillus flavus*, a mould contaminating the nuts. They are brightly fluorescing furanocoumarin compounds known as 'aflatoxins'. Aflatoxins are now known to contaminate human foods. Nuts and grains produced and stored in warm moist climates are most likely to be affected. Aflatoxins damage the liver and lead to carcinoma in many animals. Aflatoxin B1 is the most potent known natural hepatocarcinogen, at least in susceptible species such as the rat and duckling. The toxic dose in primates is about 0.05 mg/kg daily. There has been much conjecture about the possible role of aflatoxins in primary carcinoma of the liver in man in Africa and Asia (p. 567).

Maize contaminated with aflatoxin appeared to be responsible for an epidemic of an acute illness which occurred in 1974 and affected 200 villages in Gjarat and Rajasthan, India. The clinical features were jaundice, ascites, portal hypertension and a high mortality. It was estimated that patients had consumed from 2 to 6 mg of aflatoxin daily for one month.[35] Aflatoxins have also been detected in autopsy liver samples from some cases of the Reye-Johnson syndrome, acute encephalopathy with fatty liver.[36] Aflatoxins are of great importance in animal husbandry, and a monograph is available.[37]

Other mycotoxins

The discovery of aflatoxins means that mouldy food and fodder is not merely unattractive; it may be dangerous. Other potentially dangerous mycotoxins may be produced by moulds that can grow on foods. Sterigmatocystin from *Aspergillus versicolor* on maize is carcinogenic in animals but much less potent than the aflatoxins. Patulin from *Penicillium expansum*, found in rotten apples, may occur in apple juice and cider, is also carcinogenic.

The trichothecenes, produced by species of *Fusarium* on mouldy cereals, appear to be responsible for a human disease, alimentary toxic aleukia, in Russia. Ochrotoxin from *Aspergillus ochraceus* on mouldy barley has been responsible for kidney disease in swine in Denmark. Evidence is accumulating that Balkan nephropathy, a slowly progressive nephropathy without hypertension which is endemic in parts of the Danube valley, may be due to toxins from *Penicillium cyclopium* on stored maize.[38] The list of mycotoxins is long and still being added to. It will take a long time to work out which are of importance in human disease. Meanwhile all mouldy food should be regarded with caution. It would be salutary for the enthusiasts for natural foods to ponder that mycotoxins are more likely to contaminate foods grown and processed without fungicides, preservatives and chemical additives.

AGRICULTURAL CHEMICALS

A farmer has to worry about his crops. Weeds, insects, fungi, bacteria and viruses can all seriously reduce the yield in the fields. After harvest, rodents, moulds and putrefying bacteria may cause further loss. His animals may suffer from external parasites, ticks, lice and maggots in the skin and many species of worms and other organisms in the alimentary canal and internal organs. These dangers can be prevented or at least reduced by chemical agents which, if improperly used, can reach a final food product in amounts which may be toxic to consumers. Modern farming is a highly technical business which depends on the chemical industry. The very high yields now obtainable (Table 50.1) would be impossible without the use of chemicals.

PESTICIDES AND WEED KILLERS

The danger from these is mainly to manufacturers, distributors and farm workers; acute poisoning is well known to occur amongst them and has been responsible for several deaths. Only very rarely has the residue left on a crop been responsible for acute poisoning. Two such outbreak are now described.

One evening in 1959, 13 children and one adult were admitted to a hospital in Singapore.[39] They had been taken ill suddenly and most of them had collapsed. Examination showed signs of overactivity of the parasympathetic system — sweating, dilated pupils, excessive salivation and increased secretions in the lungs. Many had fits and those severely affected became unconscious; four children died. Acting with commendable speed, the medical staff of the hospital suspected organophosphate poisoning and warned the public health authority. Early on the next morning, after it had been discovered that all the patients had eaten barley recently imported from Europe , instructions were issued making 'barley poisoning' notifiable. Subsequently the barley

was found to be contaminated with the insecticide Parathion, which is a powerful anticholinesterase agent. Prompt action contained the outbreak to 38 cases with nine deaths.

Another dramatic story comes from Sri Lanka 22 years later.[40] Young Tamil girls from tea estates complained of pain in the calves and weakness of the feet and hands; they had absent ankle jerks, wrist drop and other signs suggesting a toxic polyneuropathy. In all cases the symptoms had first appeared two to four weeks after the menarche. At this time it was the custom to prohibit meat and fish and to give the girls raw eggs and gingili oil. This cooking oil was used sparingly in the community but the girls after eating a raw egg were served the oil in the shell, filled to the brim. This ritual continued for two weeks and ended with a ceremonial bath. Enquiries at the oil merchants revealed that oil had been stored in metal drums originally used for mineral oils. The insecticide tri-cresyl phosphate was detected in the samples of oil. It was calculated that during the two weeks the girls had each received 2.8 to 5.6 g of the poison, a dose probably sufficient to cause neuropathy.

There are over 100 pesticides in use in the UK. Chief interest lies in the organochlorine insecticides, DDT (dichlorodiphenyl trichlorethane) and dieldrin. These substances or their degradation products persist on agricultural products and so find their way into our food. As they are very slowly eliminated from the body and are fat-soluble, they accumulate in adipose tissue. In 1972 in the UK, samples of human fat contained about 2.5 mg/kg of DDT and its derivatives and about 0.2 mg/kg of dieldrin. Substantially higher figures have been found in the USA and other countries. Thus modern man carries around in his adipose tissue a few milligrams of pesticide. We know of no evidence that this does us any harm. The government chemist reviewing the situation in Britain wrote, 'The facts do not give cause for complacency; neither do they merit alarm.' Since then, dietary intakes of pesticides have fallen substantially.

In 1970 the US Department of Agriculture restricted the use of DDT for livestock, food crops and ornamental plants and gardens. This decision was reached when it was judged that the benefits derived from its use in the USA did not justify a risk to health. In countries where DDT is part of a malaria control programme, the benefits from DDT might be judged to far outweigh the risk.

The widespread use of DDT has had adverse effects on hawks, eagles and other birds that live on the flesh of small animals. In some areas many of their eggs have not hatched and this has lead to a reduction in numbers. The eggs may be defective due to a deficiency of oestrogens which may be metabolised at an increased rate by microsomal enzymes of the liver induced by DDT.

ANTIBIOTICS

Antibiotics are used to treat infectious diseases in farm animals. They have also been incorporated into animal foodstuffs because in some way, not yet fully explained, they promote growth; thus they are of economic value in the rearing of pigs and poultry. They have also been used in food preservation. In these ways foods may become contaminated, but there is no evidence that this has had any direct adverse effect on man.

A serious indirect effect of the indiscriminate use of antibiotics in animal husbandry is the development of bacterial resistance to their action. Strains of *Salmonella typhimurium* and *Escherichia coli* which may infect both man and livestock are liable to acquire such resistance. This is carried in the genetic material of the bacteria and may be transferred to different bacteria, which then become resistant, although not previously exposed to the antibiotic.

Acquired bacterial resistance is a complex phenomenon of the utmost importance to animal husbandry and human medicine. In 1969 it was considered in detail by a government committee and their report[41] (known as the Swann report after the chairman) fascinating reading. While appreciating the great value of antibiotics in veterinary practice and in some circumstances in animal husbandry, the committee makes detailed recommendations for preventing their abuse. It is now illegal to add antibiotics to animal foodstuffs but unfortunately strains of *Salmonella* resistant to antibiotics continue to be found. This is in part due to bad animal husbandry and also to the misuse of antibiotics by the veterinary and medical professions.[42]

HORMONES

Steroid sex hormones act as anabolic agents in beef cattle. **Diethylstilboestrol** (DES) was used in the USA between 1954 and 1972. It hastened growth, reducing feed requirements and produced animals with more protein and less fat in the carcass. Anxiety grew about its use because by 1971 radioactive techniques became sensitive enough to detect DES at 2 µg/kg in livers from a small minority of animals. At the same time in cases of the rare adenocarcinoma of the vagina occurring in young women, it was found that their mothers had been treated with DES in large dosage during pregnancy. It was used then to reduce the risk of miscarriage. The ban on oestrogens in beef production is not really logical. Comparable amounts of oestrogens are naturally present in soya beans and in eggs; endogenous production in women and the amounts used in oral contraceptives are much larger. The ban is being challenged but meanwhile hormonal feed additives are not permitted in the EEC except for a combined DES/androgen preparation still used in pig feeds in Britain.

FUNGICIDES ON SEED GRAIN

Several tragic accidents have affected peasant farmers who were supplied with new types of seed grain that had been treated with chemicals to prevent fungus disease of the young wheat plant. If the previous harvest was small and instructions poor, people have eaten some of the seed grain. Alkyl mercury poisoning in Iraq in 1972 is described on page 129. In Turkey hexachlorobenzene was used as the fungicide. Ingestion of treated grain led to 3000 cases of porphyria with skin lesions precipitated by sunlight in the late 1950s.[43]

INDUSTRY

Foods may be contaminated by industrial poisons in various ways — improper disposal of industrial waste and accidents and crime at a plant. Fortunately all of these are rare but, as the scale of industrial processing gets bigger, the wider the effect when something goes wrong.

Industrial waste
Outbreaks of poisoning by food contaminated by failure to dispose of industrial waste containing mercury and cadmium in a safe manner are described in Chapter 12.

Accident
Widespread poisoning of farm animals with lesser effects on man occurred in the USA in 1973. An illiterate truck driver in Michigan delivered 2000 lb of Firemaster, a fire retardant made of **polybrominated biphenyls** (PBB), instead of Neutromaster, a magnesium oxide supplement, from a chemical firm to an animal feed depot. Here the employees assumed it was an improved version of the feed supplement. In consequence, poisoned grain was delivered to hundreds of farms and fed to many thousands of animals. Animals became ill but it took a year before the poison was identified. By that time much farm and dairy produce had become contaminated with PBB, which is metabolised extremely slowly and tends to accumulate in the body. Some people in the area lost weight and became disorientated. Three years later PBB could be detected in most samples of mother's milk in Michigan State.[44]

CRIMINAL ADULTERATION

A mysterious new disease broke out in Spain in May 1981. There were 13 000 cases admitted to hospital and over 100 deaths. People in the poorer quarters of Madrid were most affected but some cases occurred in the provinces. The agent responsible was soon identified as a cooking oil, sold fraudulently by doorstep traders in unlabelled bottles as pure olive oil. In fact it was mostly rapeseed oil with some other oils as ingredients. It contained aniline, which is used to denature rapeseed oil for industrial purposes.[45] However, the nature of the chemical poison remains unknown.

The clinical features were diverse and not explicable by any known pathology.[46] In May acute cases presented with fever, rashes, myalgia and respiratory distress; most of the deaths were due to a pneumonopathy. Although the oil was quickly identified as the responsible agent and ceased to be used, cases continued to present in June and July but with new features. Intense muscular pain and numbness of the arms and legs were common. Thromboembolism was a serious but uncommon complication. The disease changed again in August and September when patients presented with scleroderma-like skin lesions, Raynaud's phenomenon, dysphagia, severe motor weakness with muscular atrophy and weight loss. Some died of respiratory failure. In each of these stages there was no consistent change in laboratory findings. At autopsy vascular changes with endothelial swelling and cellular infiltration of the vessel wall was seen in all organs.

Crime will always be with us but this strange and tragic consequence of it could have been averted by rapid enforcement of the law. The lesson is that local authorities should have the staff to detect promptly all breaches of food safety laws and regulations, together with the power to enforce them strictly.

RADIOACTIVE FALL-OUT

For 18 years from 1945 when an atomic bomb was dropped on Hiroshima until 1963 when the Nuclear Test Ban was signed by the governments of the United States, the Soviet Union and the United Kingdom, atomic explosions periodically liberated radioactive dust into the atmosphere. This dust rose into the stratosphere, where it might drift for many hundreds of miles before sinking into the lower atmosphere and finally to the earth's surface. After each nuclear explosion, fall-out contaminated a large area determined mainly by local meteorological conditions. In an affected area, cereal crops, vegetables and fruits which may be eaten by man were contaminated, and also grasses and herbage eaten by cattle. Their milk and meat then contains radioactive material. In general, foods of animal origin become more dangerous to man than those of plant origin because the radioactive material is concentrated in milk and meat.

The main potentially dangerous radioisotopes in fall-out are iodine-131 (^{131}I), strontium-90 (^{90}Sr) and caesium-137 (^{137}Cs). ^{131}I has a half life of only 8 days and so most of that liberated by an explosion becomes inactive in the upper atmosphere. Nevertheless, unacceptable amounts were found in some samples of milk. ^{90}Sr and ^{137}Cs have half lives of 28 and 30 years respectively and so are potentially greater dangers. The absorption, storage and excretion of strontium is similar to that of calcium and so ^{90}Sr is concentrated in milk. The body deals with caesium as it deals with potassium and so caesium is concentrated in muscle and all meats may be contaminated. ^{90}Sr is especially dangerous because it is stored in bone, and the adjacent bone marrow is very susceptible to damage by radiation. The concentration of ^{90}Sr in milk makes it especially dangerous to infants and children.

Before 1963 radioactive fall-out caused significant contamination of foods in many countries and was a real cause of concern. An account of the situation in the United Kingdom at that time is given by Hawthorn.[47] The Nuclear Test Ban Treaty in 1963 was an event of major importance to the world but the protection provided by the ban is as secure, and no more, as any other international treaty.

An accident in a nuclear power station can also be followed by contamination of foods produced in its vicinity. Such accidents have happened, e.g. at Windscale in the north of England in 1957, but are fortunately rare.

In 1969 WHO and the International Atomic Energy Agency (IAEA) established an International Reference Centre for Environmental Radioactivity at Le Vesignet, France. This assists national governments in collecting information about all forms of radiation in the environment which are a potential danger to health and gives advice on control measures. It publishes periodically reports on the concentrations of ^{90}Sr and ^{137}Cs in samples of milk from various countries.

In an emergency, it is safe to eat foods which have been stored or packed in airtight tins or jars or otherwise protected from atmospheric dust. Tinned foods which have been exposed to intense radiation do not become radioactive. Other remedial measures are uncertain. Since calcium and strontium use the same transport mechanism, increasing the dietary calcium might be expected to reduce intestinal absorption of ^{90}Sr.

FOOD ADDITIVES

No chemical can be deliberately added to foods until it has been through extensive tests for toxicity. Yet, experience may lead to reassessment. Three examples are given.

Agene

For many years nitrogen trichloride, known as agene, was added as an improver to most of the flour used to make bread in the United Kingdom. There was no suspicion that it was in any way toxic. Mellanby in 1946 investigated a neurological disorder then prevalent in fox hounds and known as canine hysteria.[48] He was able to show that the disorder affected only dogs whose diet consisted mainly of bread; he then showed that it was agene in the bread which damaged the nervous system. As a result, the use of agene as a flour improver was no longer allowed and it was replaced by chlorine diozide. Nitrogen trichloride is an example of a substance which is much more toxic for one species, the dog, than for most other species including man. Nevertheless, the decision to ban its use in human foods seems wise.

Cyclamate

The Soft Drinks Regulations (1964) permitted the use of cyclamate as an artificial sweetener. The maximum amount that could be added to soft drinks was 1.35 g/litre. The Regulation was based on the advice of the Food Additives and Contaminants Committee, who were aware that cyclamates were already permitted in the USA and in a report published in 1966 they give extensive evidence based on tests on rats, mice, cats, dogs, rabbits and man that cyclamate is not toxic. In 1969 it was reported that in tests in the USA eight out of 240 rats who were given cyclamate in daily doses of over 2 g/kg body weight developed tumours of the urinary bladder. As a result, cyclamate was banned immediately in the USA and soon after in the UK. The dose shown to be carcinogenic in the rats was very high. To achieve it, a 12 year old boy weighing 40 kg would have to drink daily about 60 litres of a soft drink containing the maximum permitted amount of cyclamate. The ban was the result of a hasty decision and further more careful appraisal seems to be needed. Diabetics, who would be expected to take more cyclamate than the general population, have not shown any excess of cancer of the urinary bladder.[49]

Monosodium glutamate

In 1968 Dr Kwok[50] reported that for several years he had suffered 'from numbness of the back of the neck, gradually radiating to both arms and back, general weakness and palpitation'. The symptoms came on while eating in a Chinese restaurant, lasted two hours and left no hangover. The syndrome is now well known and presumed to be due to monosodium L-glutamate (MSG). The Chinese have used seaweeds and soya beans, both of which contain sodium glutamate, as natural condiments for generations. MSG is a permitted flavouring enhancer widely used for savoury foods in the food industry. There is no certainty that it is responsible for the symptoms, but the evidence against it is strong. As the symptoms are transient, only affect a minority of consumers, lead to no permanent damage, are early associated by the sufferer with excess consumption of highly flavoured foods and so can be avoided, there seems no case for banning the use of glutamate as a flavouring agent — at least for adults. Glutamate has been added to many infants foods, but most manufacturers of these foods have now ceased to use it. This seems a wise decision until more is known about its possible actions.

The stories of agene, of cyclamate and of monosodium glutamate are worth pondering on for they have several messages for nutritionists. First, they show the uncertainty of contemporary knowledge; reports of new observations may at any time challenge accepted opinions of the day. They illustrate the value of a careful study of unusual and unexplained symptoms when these appear either in man or in any other animal species. The difficulty in making a decision as to what is an acceptable risk, and the need to proceed slowly before making a judgment on any chemical, is well demonstrated. Consumers may take comfort from the fact that we are unable to provide evidence that any human being has suffered in health in any serious way as a consequence of taking a permitted food additive, although occasionally an individual is found to be allergic to one of them (Chap. 50). This, of course, must not be used as an excuse for relaxing present standards of toxicity testing. The need to make present tests more precise and to devise better tests continues.

REFERENCES

1. Pyke M 1971 Food and society. Murray, London, p 102
2. World Health Organisation 1967 Procedures for investigating intentional and unintentional food additives. WHO Tech Rep Ser no. 348
3. Committee on Food Protection, Food and Nutrition Board, National Research Council 1973 Toxicants occurring naturally in foods, 2nd edn. National Academy of Sciences, Washington DC
4. Liener I E (ed) 1969 Toxic constituents in plant foodstuffs. Academic Press, New York
5. Liener I E (ed) 1974 Toxic constituents of animal foodstuffs. Academic Press, New York
6. Sleeman W H 1844 Rambles and reflexions of an Indian official. (New edition 1893 Smith V A (ed).) Westminster Press, London
7. Ressler C 1962 Isolation and identification from common

vetch of the neurotoxin β-cyano-l-alanine, a possible factor in neurolathyrism. J Biol Chem 237: 733–735

8. Adiga P R, Rao S L N, Sarma P S 1963 Some structural features and neurotoxic action of a compound from *L. sativus* seeds. Curr Sci 32: 153–155

9. Weaver A L 1967 Lathyrism: a review. Arthritis Rheum 10: 470–478

10. Cook J 1777 A voyage towards the south pole and round the world. Strahan & Cadell, London, vol 2, p 112

11. Jardin C 1972 Organo-minerals and ciguatera. FAO Nutr Newsletter 10(3): 14–25

12. Merson M H, Baine W B, Gangarosa E J, Swanson R C 1974 Scomboid fish poisoning: outbreak traced to commercially canned tuna fish. JAMA 228: 1268–1269

13. Bagnis R, Berglund F, Eliam P S, van Esch G J, Halstead W B, Kojima K 1970 Problems of toxicants in marine food products. Bull WHO 42: 69–88

14. Meyer K F 1953 Food poisoning. N Engl J Med 249: 843–852

15. Gemmil J S, Manderson W G 1960 Neurotoxic mussel poisoning. Lancet 2: 307–309

16. McCollum J P K, Pearson R C M, Ingham H R, Wood P C, Dewar H A 1968 An epidemic of mussel poisoning in north-east England. Lancet 2: 767–770

17. Berlin R 1948 Haff disease in Sweden. Acta Med Scand 129: 560–572

18. Lal R B, Roy S C 1937 Investigations into the epidemiology of epidemic dropsy. Indian J Med Res 25: 163–259

19. Lal R B, Makherji S P, Das Gupta A C, Chatterji S R 1940 Quantitative aspects of the problem of toxicity of mustard oil. Indian J Med Res 28:163

20. Sarkar S N 1948 Isolation from argemone oil of disanguinarine and sanquinarine: toxicity of sanguinarine. Nature 162: 265–266

21. Jelliffe D B, Stuart K L 1954 Acute toxic hypoglycaemia in the vomiting sickness of Jamaica. Br Med J 1: 75–77

22. Williams C D 1954 Report on vomiting sickness in Jamaica. Government Printer, Jamaica

23. Holt C von, Chang J, Holt M von, Böhm H 1964 Metabolism and metabolic effects of hypoglycin. Biochim Biophys Acta 90: 611–613

24. McMillan M, Thompson J C 1979 An outbreak of suspected solanine poisoning in schoolboys. Q J Med 48: 227–243

25. Kurland L T 1972 An appraisal of the neurotoxicity of cycad and the etieology of amyotrophic lateral sclerosis in Guam. Fed Proc 31: 1540–1542

26. Murphy K J 1971 Worcestershire sauce and the kidney. Med J Aust 1: 1119–1121

27. Link K P 1945 The anticoagulant 3,3'-methylene bis(4-bis(4-hydroxycourmanin). Fed Proc 4: 176–182

28. Green R G, Carlson W E, Evans C A 1942 The inactivation of vitamin B₁ in diets containing whole fish. J Nutr 23: 165–174

29. Horne C H W, McCluskie J A W 1963 The food of the gods. Scot Med J 8: 489–91

30. Short A I K, Watling R, MacDonald M K, Robson J S 1980 Poisoning by *Cortinarius speciosissimus*. Lancet 2: 942–944

31. Barger G 1931 Ergot and ergotism. Gurney & Jackson, London

32. King B 1979 Outbreak of ergotism in Wollo, Ethiopia. Lancet 1:1411

33. Krishnamachari K A V R, Bhat R V 1976 Poisoning by ergoty bajra (pearl millet) in man. Indian J Med Res 64: 1624–1628

34. Allcroft A, Carnaghan R B A, Sargeant K, O'Kelly J 1961 A toxic factor in Brazilian groundnuts. Vet Rec 73: 428–429

35. Krishnamachari K A V R, Bhat R V, Nagaragan V, Tilak T B G 1975 Hepatitis due to aflatoxicosis: an outbreak in western India. Lancet 1:1061

36. Chaves-Carballo E, Ellefson R D, Gomez M R 1976 An aflatoxin in the liver of a patient with Reye-Johnson syndrome. Mayo Clin Proc 51: 48–50

37. Goldblatt L E (ed) 1969 Aflatoxins. Academic Press, New York

38. Barnes J M, Austwick P K C, Carter R L, Flynn F V, Peristianis G C, Aldridge W N 1977 Balkan (endemic) nephropathy and a toxin-producing strain of *Penicillium verrucosum* var *cyclopium*: an experimental model in rats. Lancet 1: 671–675

39. Karagaratnam K, Bron W K, Hoh T K 1960 Parathion poisoning from contaminated barley. Lancet 1: 538–542

40. Senanayake N, Jeyaranam J 1981 Toxic polyneuropathy due to gingili oil contaminated with tri-cresyl phosphate affecting adolescent girls in Sri Lanka. Lancet 1: 88–89

41. Report of the Joint Committee on the use of Antibiotics in Animal Husbandry and Veterinary Medicine 1969 HMSO, London

42. Anonymous 1979 Salmonellosis — an unhappy turn of events. (Editorial) Lancet 1: 1009–1010

43. Peters H A 1976 Hexachlorbenzene poisoning in Turkey. Fed Proc 35: 2400–2403

44. Brilliant L B, Wilcox K, Amburg G V, Eyster E, Isbister J, Bloomer A W, et al 1978 Breast-milk monitoring to measure Michigan's contamination with polybrominated biphenyls. Lancet 2: 643–646

45. Tabuenca J M 1981 Toxic-allergic syndrome caused by ingestion of rapeseed oil denatured with aniline. Lancet 2: 567–568

46. Toxic Epidemic Syndrome Study Group 1982 Toxic epidemic syndrome, Spain, 1981. Lancet 2: 697–702

47. Hawthorn J 1959 The occurrence of radiostrontium in foodstuffs. Proc Nutr Soc 18: 44–49

48. Mellanby E 1946 Diet and canine hysteria: experimental production by treated flour. Br Med J 2: 885–887

49. Armstrong B, Lea A J, Adelstein A M, Donovan J W, White G C, Ruttle S 1976 Cancer mortality and saccharin consumption in diabetics. Br J Prev Soc Med 30: 151–157

50. Kwok R H M 1968 Chinese-restaurant syndrome. N Engl J Med 278:796

26

Consumer Protection

The records of history show that there have always been men who are ready to make a fast buck by trick or fraud. Short weight and the dilution of milk with water are ancient practices and almost everywhere there have been laws against them; these practices still continue in countries which lack adequate means of enforcement. In Europe in the Middle Ages pepper and other costly spices imported from the East were frequently adulterated by mixing with local seeds, leaves or flour or even with sand. Sugar, coffee and tea were similarly diluted. There were also old laws against the sale of unsound meat and other foods.

In the period 1750–1850 the Industrial Revolution caused large numbers of people to leave the countryside and work in the new towns. Separated from the fields where their food was grown and from the local markets and shops where they could purchase it, industrial workers became increasingly dependent on food manufacturers, some of whom were fraudulent. Foods were often adulterated and some of the adulterants were new chemicals which were poisonous. The medical profession then knew little about toxicology, and analytical methods for detecting and identifying adulterants did not exist. In Britain the problem came to a head in 1851 when Dr Wakley, the owner and first editor of the *Lancet*, published the names of over 3000 tradesmen whose wares had been found by private investigators to be adulterated. Many people thought that libel actions would kill the *Lancet*, but it was never sued, probably because it had the support of the medical profession. Instead, his crusade led to the passage by Parliament of the 1860 Adulteration of Food and Drink Act and, when this proved ineffective, of the 1875 Sale of Food and Drugs Act, the basis from which our modern laws have developed. By 1875 new chemical knowledge had enabled the science of food analysis to develop, and the appointment of public analysis to local government authorities enabled the law to be enforced. Similar laws were passed in other countries and fraudulent adulteration of food on a large scale ceased. The same situation has, however, arisen again since 1950 with the rapid growth of towns in Africa and Asia where many countries lack suitably trained inspectors and analysts who are needed to ensure that laws and regulations are enforced.

In 1875 knowledge of bacteriology was rudimentary, but the next 25 years was a golden age and by 1900 most of the bacteria commonly causing food poisoning had been identified, together with useful knowledge of how they may spread and the nature of the diseases which they cause. Food hygiene then became a science and this made possible the control of the spread of food poisoning by inspection of slaughterhouses, food warehouses, retail shops and kitchens in restaurants, hotels and other public institutions. Today this control is only partially effective and, as shown in Chapter 24, many infective agents continue to contaminate food. Together they constitute far and away the greatest danger to health from food, against which consumers need protection.

The twentieth century has seen the rise of new chemical hazards from food. As already described, food manufacturers deliberately add chemicals to foods to assist manufacture and storage, and farmers use pesticides, weedkillers and antibiotic agents on their crops and animals, some of which may carry over into the final food product. From these practices consumers derive much benefit; without them, food supplies would be less secure, more monotonous and of poorer quality. However, they are and will always remain a potential hazard. The chemical contamination of foods by industrial wastes which pollute our atmosphere and water supplies is probably increasing, and some examples have already been given in Chapters 12 and 25. As will be described later in the present chapter there are government agencies in the larger countries which ensure that there is toxicological testing and assessment of the risks involve in these hazards. It is our opinion that the risks run at present are slight and acceptable.

In an agricultural community food is bought and sold in local markets and small shops. The customer can see what he or she is purchasing and judge its quality. Formerly retail shops bought most of their food in bulk from wholesalers and a purchase was weighed and wrapped before the customer's eyes. Now the housewife shopping in a supermarket sees nothing of what she buys, and can only get information by reading the label on the pack. It is therefore essential that this information be accurate and not misleading. This is particularly important when a pack contains a food preparation with many ingredients or consists of a whole meal. Customers are also greatly influenced in their choice by advertisements and especially those on television. A main concern of contemporary food legislation to protect consumers is with the control of labelling and advertisement.

Although fraudulent tradesmen and manufacturers were responsible for the introduction and growth of food legislation, their modern counterparts must not be cast in this role. Big manufacturers and retail stores are concerned with the quality of their goods, and in a competitive market any disclosure of an unsatisfactory product would have disastrous consequences for the firm. Modern legislation arises out of continuing dialogues between trade associations, consumer associations and enforcement authorities. These dialogues are in general harmonious because each party is concerned that foods should be safe and of good quality.

In a country the size of Britain there are tens of thousands of people whose work in one way or another ensures the quality of our food. Most of these have specialist knowledge and some have experience in judging complex issues. The rest of this chapter is a brief résumé of how their work is organised. There are many large books which deal with technical aspects. One small book which can be recommended to the general reader and to all students of nutrition is *Food Quality and Safety: a Century of Progress* (Ministry of Agriculture, Fisheries and Food, 1977). It records a symposium to celebrate the centenary of the Sale of Food and Drugs Act 1875. Papers were prepared by workers with experience in several countries, and the discussions in which many joined were lively and informative.

LEGISLATION

The Sale of Food and Drugs Act 1875 was replaced in turn by the Food and Drugs (Adulteration) Act 1928 and later by the Food and Drugs Acts of 1938 and 1955, which later is still in force. The drugs aspects of the 1955 Act were superseded by the passing of the Medicines Act in 1968. Discussions are now taking place which will lead to a new Act concerned only with food. The 1955 Act is amplified by regulations and orders which cover most of the common foods or groups of food, e.g. the Bread and Flour Regulations, the Condensed and Dried Milk Regulations, the Soft Drinks Regulations. There are also separate Food Hygiene Regulations. All of these have been reviewed and amended at intervals. Proposals for new legislation are put before Parliament by the Minister of Agriculture, Fisheries and Food. Before legislation is drawn up, the Minister takes advice from interested parties, and since 1948 this has been channelled through a Foods Standards Committee, in respect of composition labelling, advertising, additives and contaminants.

Foods Standards Committee

The members of this committee are appointed by the Minister of Agriculture, Fisheries and Food on behalf of all ministries concerned with foods, but they are not civil servants. There are ten members and at present three come from the food industry, three are drawn from consumer and enforcement interests, and four, including the Chairman, are from the scientific field. The composition of the Committee changes slowly and many members have served for over 10 years and so have acquired much general experience. Officials of the Ministry adminster the Committee and provide expert advice on legislative matters. The Committee receives advice on health and nutritional matters from the Department of Health and Social Security and its advisory committees. Assessors may be appointed from the food industry and scientific institutes to give technical advice on particular subjects. The Committee is asked periodically by ministers to review existing legislation or to consider new areas and make recommendations for changes on specific subjects. Recent reports have been on Bread and Flour (1974), Novel Protein foods (1974), Yogurt (1975), Soft Drinks (1976), Beer (1976) and Water in Food (1978). Labelling (1979), Claims and Misleading Descriptions (1980), Meat and Meat Products (1980), Infant Foods and Table Spreads and Margarine are being prepared.

Before starting a report the Committee invites interested organisations and individuals to submit written evidence and some of these later give oral evidence. Committee reports are published and interested parties may send comments to the Minister. After receiving these, the Minister draws up new legislation which does not always follow the recommendations of the Committee. Reports now provide a general account of manufacturing processes and of the nutritive value of the various products and aim to be of general educational value. They are recommended reading for students of nutrition.

Food Additives and Contaminants Committee

This was set up as a body independent of the Foods Standards Committee in 1964 and has since operated in a similar way to carry out duties previously under the single committee but following the Government's on-slaught on quangos the two committees are again amal-gamated. Reports have been on Emulsifiers and Stabilisers (1970), Packaging (1970), Preservatives (1972), Solvents (1974), Antioxidants (1975), Lead (1975), Flavourings (1976) and Additives and Processing Aids in Beer (1978). As regards food additives the Com-mittee operates by recommending permitted lists of those that may be used for specific purposes, and these lists are reviewed at intervals.

Two criteria are considered before a substance is put on the permitted list. The first is its safety and the sec-ond the technical need in the manufacturing process. The first criterion is overriding, and no substance is con-sidered safe until the Committee is satisfied that it has been tested for toxicity in an elaborate series of trials using several species of animals and that it has no ad-verse effects on growth and reproduction.

As regards contaminants the Committee aims to en-courage good agricultural, manufacturing and handling techniques, so as to reduce possible contamination at all stages of food production to a minimum. For example, there are legal limits to the amounts of arsenic and lead that may be present in a food.

Enforcement

Enforcement of food legislation is in the hands of local government authorities. They inspect, analyse and take legal action. Inspection is by environmental health of-ficers, who are derived from the old sanitary inspectors under the Medical Officer of Health, and by consumer protection officers, formerly known as inspectors of weights and measures. It is the duty of these officers of district councils to inspect regularly all premises hand-ling food in their district, to obtain samples of foodstuffs offered for sale and have them analysed, and to inves-tigate complaints made by individual members of the public. Complaints about composition, labelling and ad-vertising are made to local authorities, who either have their own analytical laboratories run by public analysts or use consultant public analysts. Cases are brought be-fore a magistrate's court.

Local government organisation evolves slowly and usually haphazardly. With the reorganisation of local government in the UK following the 1972 Act, it is too early to say how effective enforcement is at the moment. The general impression is that in many areas it works but that regionalisation might be more sensible. One criticism is that magistrates who for a long time have dealt competently with cases of short weight and other simple frauds have not sufficient knowledge and experi-ence to deal with the complex law on labelling and advertising (see below). It has been suggested that special new courts be set up by central government to deal with such cases.

EUROPEAN COMMON MARKET

The Treaty of Rome established the European Econ-omic Community (EEC) whose members are bound by Article 2 of the Treaty to establish a common market. A common market implies that goods can move freely in it and that their sale throughout the market is not restricted by regional regulations governing their nature and composition or the methods of manufacture, pack-aging and labelling. Although all the member countries have such regulations with the same aim of protecting consumers, it is surprising how much they differ in de-tail. Many of these differences arise from long-estab-lished preferences by consumers in different countries for particular products. There are, for instance, well-known differences in the bread, beer, chocolate and jam commonly consumed in the various countries. It is not the intention to prohibit the sale of any local product in its country of origin, but to ensure that products can be sold freely within the market. This in practice means that all products are adequately defined and sold with the appropriate label. This process of removing trade barriers is known as **harmonisation**.

The decision-making body in the EEC is the Council of Ministers. Suggestions for legislation are orginally put up by the Commission. There are 13 commissioners ap-pointed by national governments and Britain appoints two. They are assisted by some 5000 administrative staff who work in Brussels and are divided into 19 director-ate-generals. The European Assembly is an advisory body whose members are elected democratically. It con-siders and comments on suggestions put up by the Com-mission to Council. Its headquarters are in Strasbourg.

The Commission has produced over 20 draft direc-tives affecting specific classes of foods. When these have been approved by the Council, which only follows de-tailed argument in committee by government represen-tatives, each member government has to amend its national laws if they are at variance with the directive. These new rules are then part of each national law and affect all member countries. In contrast the Council may make 'regulations' which have immediately the force of law throughout the EEC. These are often introduced for new foods. There are already regulations relating to the grading of eggs and of fruit and vegetables, water in fro-zen chicken and to the categories and labelling on wine. There are directives on chocolate, honey and sugar which have or should soon become national regulations. Most of the draft directives are still under discussion and some have been withdrawn. There are also directives on food additives, most of which are now national regulations.

The process of harmonisation is slow and involves endless committees who receive evidence and infor-mation from manufacturers, trade associations and consumers. Imagination, patience and a progmatic outlook are needed. However, there can be little doubt that as a result of this great expenditure of time and money individual customers in Common Market countries will have better information of the nature of the foods which they purchase and more assurance that whatever their origin they are of good quality.

UNITED STATES

The first settlers soon had to take action against fraud, and in 1630 the Massachusetts Bay Colony prosecuted Nicholas Knopp from Holland 'for taking upon him to cure the scurvy by a water of noe worth nor value which he sold at a very deare note.' He was fined £5 and declared liable to prosecution by his defrauded customers. Various laws were passed modelled on those in the home countries and these include many ordinances to ensure that flour and other foods for export were not adulterated.

Insistence on States' rights delayed the first federal Food and Drugs Act until 1906. This followed a crusade by the chief food chemist to the Department of Agriculture, Dr Harvey W. Wiley. He had a 'poison squad' of volunteers, who were fed for five days large doses of borax, formaldehyde, salicylic acid, copper sulphate and sulphurous acid with the aim of finding the dose sufficient to produce symptoms. The great depression of the 1930s showed up the weaknesses of the Act and led to the Federal Food, Drug and Cosmetic Act (1938). The deaths of at least 73 persons in 1937 from a drug sold as Elixir Sulfanilamide was the final factor in the passage of the Act. The Act set up the Food and Drug Administration (FDA), which is still responsible to the Secretary of the Department of Health, Education and Welfare for protecting public health. The FDA is divided into six sections, one of which is the Bureau of Health.

In the 1938 Act the FDA had to prove that a drug or additive was harmful before it could be removed from the market. But the 1958 Food Additives Amendment changed the responsibility. The onus now lies with the manufacturer to prove the safety of a new additive before it receives clearance for marketing. Additives that may be used are on a list of 'generally recognised as safe' (GRAS) substances. This numbers several hundred and includes natural and traditional additives that have been used for many years, but never subjected to intensive toxicological scrutiny, like sugar, pepper, mustard, cinnamon as well as more modern compounds like MSG, BHA and sulphur dioxide which appear to be safe after multiple animal tests and short-term human studies. The largest number of substances are flavour ingredients, which are mostly natural derivatives and used in very tiny amounts. If new evidence suggests a compound is not safe, it may be removed from the GRAS list. This happened with cyclamate, amaranth and saccharin.

For many fresh foods e.g. meat, poultry, dairy products, fruit and vegetables, the US Department of Agriculture is the regulatory authority.

A feature of modern US food laws, known as the Delaney Clause, is a proviso in the 1958 Food Additive Amendment which states: 'No [food] additive shall be deemed safe if it is found to induce cancer when ingested by man or animal.' This clause is a veto which prevents the FDA from exercising its judgment and was directly responsible for the ban on cyclamates when a few of the rats receiving huge doses developed cancer of the bladder. Americans will probably have to live with the Delaney Clause for some time as any Congressman who tried to repeal it would be interpreted as asking for a vote for cancer and this would not help his political career.

The main risk against which the American public have to be protected is that of food-borne infections. As in Britain, the true incidence is not known because many instances are not reported. In America a higher proportion of meals are eaten outside the home than in Britain, these have been prepared and cooked in restaurants, and although the proportion of these that are unhygienic may be small, the total number is large. Further, botulism, unknown in Britain for decades, continues to occur and causes deaths in the USA although this usually arises from errors in home canning.

The second major concern of FDA is with food labelling owing to the great increase in sales of packaged precooked meals. Enthusiasm for nutritional labelling is much greater in America than in Britain.

DEVELOPING COUNTRIES

The great increase in the growth of cities in Africa, Asia and Latin America in the last three decades has led to problems in food hygiene and adulteration similar to those in Europe and North America in the nineteenth century. It is much easier to pass legislation than to train and support the large staff of skilled people needed to enforce it.

Another factor is that a large part of the exports of many of these countries consists of food products. Importing countries properly require that these conform with their own standards. To facilitate international trade and to assist the advance of food technology in developing countries, FAO and WHO started jointly in 1963 preparing a *Codex Alimentarius*. This is concerned with standards for the composition of all major foods and also with provisions concerning food hygiene, food additives, pesticides and residues, methods of sampling and analysis and labelling. The Codex aims to set standards for some 200 foods. In this immense task most progress has been made with milk and milk products. A Code of Principles dealing with the use of proper designations and ethical practices in the international trade of milk products has been accepted by more than 70 countries. Codex standards have to be considered and adopted by each country. Agreement on a Codex Standard does not compel any country to adopt it.

Labelling

A housewife often cannot see the goods, which she wishes to purchase, because they are ready packed in the shop. She has to select her goods by using the information on the labels. Consumers in Britain are protected against false information by the Trades Description Act which applies to all goods and, more specifically in the case of foods, by the Labelling of Food Regulations (1983). The latter is based on the Foods Standards Committee report on Labelling (1979)

With a few exceptions all foods have to be labelled with an 'appropriate designation' defined in the regulations as a 'name and description sufficiently specific, in each case, to indicate to an intending purchaser the true nature of the food to which it is applied and, as respect of any ingredient or any constituent, a specific (and not generic) name or description.' When a food contains more than one ingredient the appropriate designation of each ingredient must be given in a list, setting out the ingredients in the order of the amounts present in the food. Food additives have to be included in the list of ingredients, usually by a category name, e.g. preservative, flavour enhancer or colouring agent. This may be followed by additive's chemical name and serial number. The serial numbers of some 170 permitted additives can be obtained from the Ministry of Agriculture, Fisheries and Food, Lion House, Alnwick, Northumberland NE66 2PF.

It is now statutory for the label on most prepacked foods to be date marked. This is a statement 'Sell by' or 'Best before' followed by the day, month and year.

It is not necessary for a manufacturer to give the amounts of nutrients present in a product, but some like to do so, notably for breakfast cereals. This information is useful and educative for consumers with some knowledge of nutrition but may easily mislead the ignorant, by implying falsely that there is a specific benefit from the amount of a particular nutrient in the product. The advantages and dangers of 'nutritional labelling' are now the subject of much discussion in many countries.

In Britain there is a list of scheduled vitamins and minerals for which claims can be made. At present these are vitamin A, thiamin, riboflavin, nicotinic acid, vitamin C and vitamin D and the minerals calcium, iodine and iron.

The labelling of foods designed for those who wish to reduce weight presents problems. In the UK it is illegal to refer to them solely as slimming foods but they may be described as foods useful as part of a slimming diet. A food may only be described as 'starch-reduced' when its starch content is substantially less than that of a similar natural food and its total carbohydrate content is less than 50 per cent of the dry matter. A claim that a food is a source of protein may not be made unless 12 per cent of the energy from such food comes from protein.

Pictures on labels and advertisements may be misleading. They may show fresh fruit when the product contains only fruit flavouring or depict other foods commonly consumed with the product without explicitly stating that these are not present in the container. Adjectives such as 'natural', 'fresh', 'pure' and 'homemade' may be misused. Language is continuously changing and such words as butter, cream, cutlet, steak and chop are now used to describe products different from the original. Some of these extended uses seem legitimate and others appear deliberately misleading. Legislation in these fields is difficult and control is effected mainly by manufacturers and advertisers using codes of practice. Fortunately the big manufacturers are concerned with the good name of the food industry as a whole and through their associations can apply pressure on any manufacturer whose labels and advertisements might bring the industry into disrepute.

Labelling in the USA

In the labelling system introduced between 1973 and 1975 the rules about what is fair description of the product and its ingredients are complex but similar to those in Britain already described. For most foods nutrition labelling is optional but it is mandatory whenever nutritional claims are made or a nutrient is added to a food. When it is used, the manfacturer must put on the label the measurement that he is taking as a serving, how many servings there are in the container and the calories, protein, carbohydrate and fat (all in grams) per serving. This is followed by eight nutrients that all have to be listed, expressed as a percentage of the recommended daily allowance in a serving — protein, vitamin A, thiamin, riboflavin, niacin, vitamin C, iron and calcium. When a serving contains less than 2 per cent, no figure is given for this nutrient. there are three recommended daily allowances that may be used as denominators, one for infants and another for children under 4 years, but the one commonly used is for adults, the US RDA of the Food and Drug Administration. It uses the highest figures for any adult group in the Recommended Dietary Allowances of the Food and Nutrition Board of the National Academy of Sciences.

In addition to these nutrients that must be listed, there are another 15 optional pieces of nutritional information, any number of which can be shown if the manufacturer wishes. These are the content of saturated and polyunsaturated fat, dietary cholesterol, sodium, vitamins D, E, B6, B12, folacin, biotin and pantothenic acid, and the minerals phosphorus, iodine, magnesium, zinc and copper. All values have to be expressed as the percentage of the US RDA per serving. When the type of fat or cholesterol is put on the label there must be a footnote saying that, 'This information is provided for individuals who, on the advice of a physician, are modifying their total dietary intake of fat (or cholesterol).'

The American system can only be used by an informed public. A book to educate laymen, *Nutrition Labeling: How It Can Work For You*, has been written by the National Nutrition Consortium of six scientific societies concerned about nutrition. Its address is 9650 Rockville Pike, Bethesda, Maryland 20014. Even for those people who can understand it the present system is cumbersome, it gives unnecessary information, e.g. riboflavin deficiency is rare in the USA, and labels may fail to list dietary components that could be important.

ADVERTISING

All advertising in Britain including that of food is supervised by the Code of Advertising Practice (CAP) Committee, which is made up of representatives of advertisers, advertising agencies and the media. The Committee, whose address is 15–17 Ridgmount Street, London WC1E 7AW, has a code of practice, regularly updated. It advises advertisers, checks copy and deals with complaints from consumers. The Advertising Standards Authority is a higher authority and about 50 per cent of its members are independent. The Authority deals with the government departments and other outside organisations and with complaints from firms and trading authorities and those from consumers which the CAP Committee may pass on. Advertising on television and radio is the responsibility of the Independent Broadcasting Authority, 70 Brompton Road, London SW3.

SUMMARY

Consumers in the industrialised countries are protected by complicated systems involving government, manufacturers, advertisers and the media, and operating through statutory regulations and voluntary codes of practice. It involves a series of compromises, in many of which the balance may change over the years. The government and manufacturers in general work well together and are rarely at loggerheads on major issues. Manufacturers like to have some guidelines laid down by statute, but prefer details to be left in voluntary hands. They continuously and rightly oppose any proposed change in the law which might restrict technical developments. Consumers may be assured that the system protects them adequately against hazards to health which might arise from chemicals added to foods and from loss of nutrients in foods as a result of processing. Labels and advertisements may not always be as informative as they might be, and on occasions are still positively misleading. However, in this respect they are better than formerly; the system of control is not fixed, but subject to continuing review and we may hope for improvements. It still remains true that the most frequent hazards to health arise not from additives or from processing but from poor hygiene and its associated microbiological risks, which can arise in shops, in restaurants, cafés and canteens in institutions and, all too frequently, in the home.

Primary Nutritional Diseases

PART THREE

Primary Nutritional Diseases

27

Starvation and Anorexia Nervosa

Starvation arises (1) when there is not enough food to eat, for instance in times of famine, (2) when there is severe disease of the digestive tract, preventing the absorption of nutrients, as in the malabsorption syndrome and cancer of the oesophagus, (3) when there is a disturbance which either reduces appetite or interferes with the normal metabolism of the nutrients by the tissues, such a disturbance might be metabolic in origin (e.g. in renal or hepatic failure) or due to severe and long-continued infection, and (4) in patients who greatly reduce their food intake for psychological reasons (e.g. anorexia nervosa). In all these circumstances there is wasting of the body with much loss of both muscle and fat. This gives rise to a clinical picture with an underlying morbid anatomy and chemical pathology which is essentially similar whatever the primary cause.

This chapter is concerned primarily with the clinical features, pathology and treatment of starvation in adults. Its effects in children are described in Chapter 29, and the metabolic changes are discussed from a different viewpoint in Chapter 8. Other relevant material is the effects of diseases of the digestive tract (Chap. 46), special feeding methods (Chap. 52), the numerous causes of a failure in food supply (Chap. 54) and some administrative measures in famine relief (Chap. 58).

HISTORY

Starvation must have been a common experience of primitive man during the three million years of his evolution from simian ancestors. Mankind was not able to secure his food supply until he learnt to cultivate cereals, only about 12 000 years ago. Until then, human communities were small and scattered. The main causes of death that kept numbers down were probably starvation and violence, the latter often due to tribal warfare.[1] The great infectious diseases, a dominant cause of death in historical times until recently, probably only spread in large communities and so were a relatively small cause of mortality in prehistoric man. Infectious diseases are not a common cause of death in wild animals. Millions

of years of experience of starvation has allowed time for the evolution of adaptive changes, favouring survival during periods when sufficient food was not available. In contrast for only a few thousand years have any human communities had experience of an ample secure food supply, permitting the development of obesity. Hence contemporary man is much better adapted to resist a shortage than a surplus of food.

There have been three distinct phases in the scientific investigation of undernutrition and starvation during this century. In the period before World War I there were several professional fasting men. These strange creatures were prepared to go for periods up to 30 days without food. They were much studied by physiologists and from their experiments valuable information was obtained, especially in regard to the importance of the obligatory protein losses; this was ably summarised by Lusk in successive editions of his classic book.[2] Between the two wars the subject attracted little attention; in this period vitamins dominated nutritional research. World War II brought about widespread undernutrition and starvation in many parts of the world. They became matters of practical importance to many doctors and much valuable new information was obtained. Five excellent monographs are available. Smith & Woodruff[3] (1951) and Helweg-Larsen et al[4] describe their own experiences in Japanese and Nazi prison camps; Burger et al[5] report on starvation in Holland during the winter of 1944–45, and the workers in the Department of Experimental Medicine, Cambridge,[6] give an account of the undernutrition in Germany in the immediate post-war years. Keys et al[7] describe a laboratory experiment in which 32 young men volunteered to live for six months on a diet providing only 7.7 MJ (1600 kcal)/day. As a result they became severely undernourished, losing about 25 per cent of their body weight.

Since 1945 the concept of the division of the body into compartments (Chap. 2) has been increasingly useful. Measurements of their size in relation to the state of nutrition have led to a clearer understanding of the chemical pathology of undernutrition. As a result more precise methods of treatment are available for patients who are undernourished following serious medical and surgical disorders. It is significant that an important book dealing with undernutrition comes from the department of surgery at Harvard.[8]

MORBID ANATOMY

Wasting of the tissues is the most characteristic feature of starvation. At autopsy a patient who has died of starvation may have little or no remaining adipose tissue. As a result the skin is loose. There is also marked atrophy of the skeletal muscles. Superficial oedema is usually present; its distribution is largely determined by gravity. Fluid may also be found in the peritoneal and pleural cavities.

There is also atrophy of all the viscera except the brain, which is spared. Atrophy of the heart is marked. In an adult man in health the heart weighs about 350 g. Porter[9] who performed 459 autopsies on victims of an Indian famine in 1899 found that in 45 per cent of the men the heart weighed less than 170 g and in some cases no more than 100 g. This atrophy, if severe, is often irreversible and the subsequent failure of the circulation is a frequent cause of death. Atrophy of the small intestine, which affects both the mucous membrane and the muscular walls, is always present and may be very severe. Donovan (1848), writing of his experiences in the great Irish famine, states that he observed: 'Total disappearance of the omentum, and a peculiarly thin condition of the small intestines which (in such cases) were so transparent that if the deceased had taken any food immediately before death, the contents could be seen through the coats of the bowel.'[10] In 1945 Stanley Davidson saw a similar picture in persons dying of starvation in Belsen concentration camps. The virtual loss of the power to absorb nutrients by the atrophied intestinal mucous membrane greatly prejudices the chances of recovery. Ramalingaswami[11] gives an account of autopsies on victims of the 1966–67 Bihar famine which emphasises the extent of the cardiac atrophy.

A monograph by Jackson[12] reviews past literature on the effect of starvation on the organs of man and experimental animals, and one by Follis[13] the pathological changes.

ADAPTIVE CHANGES

The wasting and loss of weight are at first rapid if food supplies are suddenly reduced, but gradually slow down even though there is no change in the amount of food eaten. There are three reasons for this slowing down:
1. With the wasting of the body, the cell mass of actively metabolising tissue is reduced and therefore requires less energy to maintain its activities.

2. The body, being lighter, requires less mechanical work to move it about.
3. All unnecessary voluntary movements are curtailed.

In these ways the body is able to achieve an important degree of biological adaptation to a restricted food supply. Indeed were it not for this adaptability, the human species might well have become extinct long since.

Twenty-five per cent of the weight of a healthy, non-obese body can usually be lost without immediate danger to life. With greater losses the hold on life is slender, but some have survived losses up to 50 per cent of their initial weight.

An excellent review of the adaptive changes in response to starvation is by Grande[14]

Changes in body composition
The wasting of tissues during starvation greatly affects the chemical composition of the body. Table 2.1 (p. 8) sets out the chemical composition of the body of a normal man. In Table 27.1 the alterations which may occur after he has lost 25 per cent of his original weight are given. The most obvious change is the disappearance of over 70 per cent of the body fat. The loss of intracellular water is also large.

Stores of energy and survival
Table 27.1 indicates that a normal man may lose about 3 kg of protein, 6.5 kg of fat and 200 g of carbohydrate. These amounts of protein, fat and carbohydrate represent a reserve or store of about 310 MJ (75 000 kcal). It must be emphasised that these figures apply to a normal man. In an obese subject the reserve is much greater and in a small thin person much less. If the normal healthy man is deprived of all food, but not required to take any exercise, energy expenditure is at about 6 MJ/day and at this rate the reserve lasts for just over 50 days. Political hunger strikers have seldom survived

Table 27.1 The changes in body composition of a man who in health weighed 65 kg-and then lost 25 per cent of this weight as a result of partial starvation

	In health (kg)	After starvation (kg)
Protein	11.5	8.5
Fat	9	2.5
Carbohydrate	0.5	0.3
Water:		
Extracellular	15	15
Intracellular	25	19
Minerals	4	3.5
	65.0	48.8

These figures describe what might occur to the hypothetical man described in Chapter 2. For reported changes see references 7 and 8.

for more than 60 days. Women have a larger reserve of fat and this may account for the fact that in severe famines they have often survived better than men.

A man does not die quickly of starvation. Many healthy people have taken no food for 14 days. The experience is unpleasant, but involves no serious impairment of physiological function and leaves no permanent effect on health.

Table 27.1 shows that the reserves of carbohydrate are insufficient to meet energy needs even for a day. Wherever possible it is desirable to provide a starving man with at least 100 g of carbohydrate daily. This will prevent the onset of ketosis and also reduce the breakdown of endogenous protein. Measurements of the differences between the O_2, CO_2 and glucose content of the arterial and venous blood of the brain indicate that normally it only utilises carbohydrate and not protein and fat. The oxygen consumption of the human brain is about 45 ml/min. This involves the combustion of 80 to 90 g/day of glucose. During complete starvation part of this comes from the conversion of protein to carbohydrate, i.e. gluconeogenesis in the liver.

Of the 310 MJ reserve in the example quoted above, about 17 per cent is provided by endogenous protein. This corresponds to the breakdown of 66 g/day of protein, and amounts of protein of this order are catabolised during brief fasting (Table 27.2). But in prolonged fasting or starvation adaptive mechanisms come into play which slow down the breakdown of protein to only about 20 g/day after 5 or 6 weeks.[15] Adaptation occurs in the brain so that it can utilise keto acids, particularly β-hydroxybutyric acid.[16] This spares the need for glucose. Gluconeogenesis in the liver falls off because the amount of alanine coming from muscle is reduced. Meanwhile the kidney has to continue to form ammonia from amino acids to maintain acid-base homeostasis and in the process glucose is produced. Thus the major share of the reduced gluconeogenesis takes place in the kidney.

Changes in body water

Table 27.2 shows estimates of the substances lost from the bodies of young men submitted to partial dietary restriction for two to three weeks, while a regime of physical activity involving an expenditure of about 10.9 MJ (2600 kcal)/day was maintained.

There is a large loss of body water, about 1.5 kg, in the first three days. This is a characteristic immediate response to dietary carbohydrate restriction and is responsible for the greater part of the weight loss that occurs in the first week, when dietary intake is restricted, either by illness or voluntarily at the start of a reducing regime. It is due to water bound to glycogen being freed, as the glycogen store is depleted, and then excreted. One gram of glycogen binds 3–4 g of water.

Famine oedema. Table 27.2 also shows that in the second week of restriction losses of body water were small and had stopped altogether by the end of the third week. Table 27.1 showed that after six months of partial starvation, the water content of the body had fallen much less than the body weight; the loss was of intracellular water and the amount of extracellular water remained virtually unchanged. Thus as the tissues waste, the size of the extracellular compartment becomes relatively greater, and this gives rise to oedema. Famine oedema is a characteristic feature not only in victims of famine, but also in patients severely undernourished as a result of disease. It has been known and studied since the time of Hippocrates, and McCance's review[18] has over 500 references; its cause is still not properly understood.

Protein deficiency, always associated with starvation, may cause the concentration of plasma albumin to fall and this contributes to the oedema in some cases. However, there is no correlation between the severity of the oedema and the plasma albumin concentration[19] and this cannot be the main cause. There is surprisingly little disturbance of renal function, although the excretion of a large water load may be delayed. This is probably the consequence of a slight reduction in glomerular filtration rate resulting from a reduced cardiac output. Again this might be a contributory factor in some cases of famine oedema, but is not the main cause.

A possible explanation, first suggested by Youmans,[20] is a fall in interstitial fluid pressure. When fat is lost and the tissues shrink, the skin is not sufficiently elastic to contract to the new body size. This may lead to a fall

Table 27.2 Losses of body weight and fat, protein and water on low energy diets, (a) 4.3 MJ (1020)kcal)/day (13men) and (b) 2.4 MJ (580 kcal)/day (6 men) (data from reference17)

Days	Mean daily loss in grams							
	Weight		Fat		Protein		Water	
	a	b	a	b	a	b	a	b
1–3	800	733	200	198	40	66	560	469
4–6	—	500	—	200	—	50	—	250
7–13	233	367	161	194	28	48	44	125
22–24	167	—	142	—	25	—	0	—

in tissue tension with seepage of water from the blood into the interstitial spaces. The body may be said to get too small for its skin. This explanation could account for the fact that famine oedema is most common and severe in old people, whose skin is less elastic than the young. Pressure in the interstitial tissue is normally sub-atmospheric and about minus 6 mmHg. A vacuum of over 15 mmHg has to be applied to the arm before oedema occurs.[21]

Associated with the constancy of the extracellular fluid volume, there is little change in the amount of sodium in the body. The total exchangeable sodium may be over 2000 mmol and within the normal range. Thus there is an excess of sodium relative to the reduced size of the body.

With the shrinkage of the cells and loss of intracellular water, there is loss of total body potassium. The potassium deficiency may amount to more than one-third of the 3500 mmol normally present in the body.

Unless the period of starvation has been very long, many months or even years, there is only a small loss of minerals from the skeleton.

Hormone production

Secretion of pituitary gonadotrophins is impaired and plasma concentrations of testosterone and urinary 17-oxosteroids fall. Plasma insulin is low during fasting because glucose and amino acids, which stimulate its secretion, are not being absorbed. In prolonged fasting plasma insulin falls and plasma glucagon rises during the first few days and then both stay steady at the new levels.[22] Secretion of pituitary growth hormone tends to be increased and this favours fat mobilisation. In prolonged starvation the plasma concentration of the active form of the thyroid hormone 3,5,3'-triiodothyronine falls and that of its inactive metabolite 3,5',3'-T_3 rises.[23] This may be an adaptive change, partly responsible for the fall in metabolism. Other endocrine changes associated with marasmus in children are discussed in Chapter 29.

CLINICAL FEATURES

The patients are thin and the lax skinfolds give evidence of recent loss of weight. The hair is dry and lustreless. The eyes are dull and sunken, yet wasting of the orbital tissues may make them appear unduly prominent, particularly since the sclerae are unusually avascular. The skin is thin, dry, inelastic; often there is peripheral cyanosis, even in warm weather. Dirty brown splotches of pigmentation may appear over the face and trunk; these were recognised during the last century as one of the stigmata of famine.

Polyuria at night is a frequent and troublesome symptom of impending famine oedema. When oedema begins to appear it is usually first noticed in the face if the patient is lying down, giving the patient a puffy appearance which may falsely suggest adequate nutrition. When the patient gets up and walks about, the fluid gravitates to the legs, causing ankle oedema.

The blood pressure is low; the diastolic pressure may be impossible to estimate, while the systolic pressure may be as low as 70 mmHg. The pulse rate usually falls progressively during prolonged partial starvation. In severe cases it is often below 40/min. When wasting becomes marked, the heart appears small on a radiograph.

Although hydraemia and a mild anaemia (Hb 9 to 12 g/dl) are common, severe anaemia is not a feature of starvation. If found, it is an indication of other co-existent disease. Associated vitamin deficiencies seldom give rise to clinical signs in starving people; the need for vitamins is probably reduced when the metabolism of the body is lowered by starvation.

Clinical evidence of hormonal disturbance is not lacking in starvation. Amenorrhoea and delayed puberty are common features but lactation is sometimes maintained. Men lose their libido and may become impotent; they may develop enlargement of the breasts (gynaecomastia). In children there is often a growth of lanugo hair, especially over the forearms and back, as may be seen in other gross endocrine disorders.

Psychological disturbances

Symptoms related to the psychological state of starving people are of practical importance. Although the intellect is usually clear, the personality may be seriously deranged. The mind is never fixed for long on a single subject, except the desire for food. Mental restlessness is combined with physical apathy. The patient becomes self-centred and indifferent to the troubles of others, even those of his dearest friends and relatives. He worries and becomes hypochondriacal, even hysterical, about his own disability. He is sensitive to noise and other petty irritations which may make him quarrelsome. These symptoms may intensify rather than diminish in the early stages of treatment; consequently the starving patient is difficult to manage. This feature of the disorder should be remembered and treated objectively by people engaged in famine relief, otherwise they may lose sympathy with those whom they are trying to help. They must never expect thanks for their kindness.

In the last stages of starvation, the personality may disintegrate completely. A mother may steal from her child. Donovan[10] in 1848 described in elegant language the horrible results of breakdowns in family ties which occurred in a small town during the great Irish famine. Cannibalism has been reported in many countries of the world (including Scotland) in times of famine.

Infections

Starvation patients often suffer from infections — malaria, cholera, typhus, relapsing fever, pneumonia, gastroenteritis — to name only a few. Tuberculosis may add to the clinical signs present, often in unusual ways, for infection in starvation may give rise to little or no fever. These infections further aggravate the plight of a starving person. Their relationship to famine is discussed in Chapter 58.

Cancrum oris, an infective gangrene of the mouth eroding the lip and cheeks, is a dreadful catastrophe which occasionally occurs in famines both among children and adults. The sufferers are usually not only malnourished but also severely dehydrated by diarrhoea or lack of nursing care. Large areas of the mouth and face may be destroyed before the patient succumbs. The only possible treatment is surgical excision of the dead tissues after a period of refeeding and medical care.

The terminal event in starvation is usually intractable diarrhoea. The atrophied intestinal glands and the paper-thin walls of the digestive tract are unable to digest and absorb properly even a bland diet, much less the kind of food on which people during famine may hope to survive, such as roots, leaves, and bread made from coarse grain. In almost all famines, outbreaks of diarrhoea have been reported, but bacteriologists have seldom found organisms that could be held responsible. Once diarrhoea has begun, it is a serious sign.

Diagnosis

In times of famine the signs of starvation may be all too obvious, so much so that other causes of emaciation can be overlooked. However, a similar clinical picture may be produced by tuberculosis, dysentery or other severe chronic diseases. In the early stage of anorexia nervosa the psychogenic origin of weight loss is easily overlooked. overlooked.

Famine oedema has to be distinguished from other primary causes of oedema — cardiac, renal or hepatic.

TREATMENT

In simple undernutrition, all that is needed is suitable food. Its management is more an administrative than a medical problem. When the patient suffering from starvation is seriously ill the nature of the treatment depends essentially on the facilities available. Here only measures possible under famine conditions, when the nursing staff is inevitably limited, are described. Under these circumstances methods such as intravenous feeding are often impractical. This and other special feeding methods which may be used when the number of patients is limited, the nursing staff sufficient and well trained and when expert laboratory help is available are described in Chapter 52.

Most famine victims, because of alimentary dysfunction, cannot deal with large quantities of food. The patient's desire for food is often immense and no guide to his digestive capacities. Limitation of the food intake may be necessary. This is essential if there is diarrhoea or severe cachexia.

The choice of food is difficult. Many starving people in the prison camps of World War II died from diarrhoea and collapse after the well-meaning attentions of those who rescued them. They were given any food that happended to be available — bully-beef, baked beans — which they could not readily digest. Only bland foods can be tolerated by the thin-walled intestines lacking essential digestive enzymes.

Frequent small feeds of skimmed milk, 100 ml or so at a time — as often as the patient is willing and able to take them — is a good way to avert death from starvation. This requires constant personal attention and nursing care. It is entirely impractical to prescribe for the needs of the patient in terms of calculated energy needs. Skimmed milk powders are normally reconstituted to give a mixture of 10 to 15 per cent strength. However, if the patient is very weak a more dilute mixture may be preferable. A variety of mild flavouring essences may be useful to stimulate the appetite. Slightly sour foods are usually acceptable; yogurt or other kinds of curdled milk may be tried. There is a possibility of lactose intolerance if large amounts of skimmed milk are given. Starving patients may tolerate moderate amounts of fat or edible oils, which provide a larger energy intake. In an Ethiopian famine a mixture of 42 per cent dried skimmed milk, 32 per cent edible oil, 25 per cent sugar, plus potassium, magnesium and vitamins gave good results in children.[24] As the patient begins to recover he should be encouraged gradually to take semi-solid foods, along the lines followed in weaning a baby. With refeeding there may be a temporary increase in oedema, and so the intake of salt should be restricted.

There may come a time in severe starvation when the patient, although still fully rational, refuses all food. The outlook is then very grave. Nasogastric or parenteral feeding (Chap. 52) provides the only hope. Spectacular improvement may follow, but some patients are beyond recovery.

PROGNOSIS

Most people with primary undernutrition recover rapidly, once they have a free access to food. Appetites may be enormous. Over 21 MJ (5000 kcal)/day may be consumed and be associated with a weekly gain in weight of 1.5 to 2 kg. In some patients, despite careful nursing and a good diet, low blood pressure and diarrhoea may persist. If, after one or two weeks, they show little improvement, this suggests strongly that irreversible changes in the myocardium or small intestine have developed and that the prognosis is poor. After any severe famine there are some who may linger on in this condition for many months if supported by good medical and nursing skill. But death rather than recovery is the usual end.

ANOREXIA NERVOSA

This is a psychiatric disease arising from a refusal to eat which often leads to severe emaciation. It was first described in 1874 by Sir William Gull of Guy's Hospital, London, who attributed it to a 'morbid mental state'. The disease characteristically occurred in young women aged 15 to 25 years and was uncommon. Since about 1970 it has become much more prevalent. There is now a large literature. Two monographs, one from Texas by Bruch[25] and one from London by Crisp[26] describe the disease as it presents today. The former, entitled *The Golden Cage*, helps the families and friends of patients to get the understanding of the nature of the disease which they need to support the patient. Crisp describes anorexia nervosa as a distorted biological solution to an existential problem with crippling effect on physical, psychological and social development.

Patients are usually middle class and often above average intelligence. They come from homes where plenty of food is available and taken for granted, and often some of the family are obese. The disease affects mainly adolescent girls and young women, but cases are seen in older women and also in men.

PSYCHOPATHOLOGY

The central abnormality is a desire to obtain and then maintain a low body weight. The patient may have been through a phase of obesity early in adolescence. Often she has been an obedient and compliant child, but is intelligent, highly strung and insecure. A history of psychological disturbance and conflict with one or both parents during puberty is common, but there is no specific setting which precipitates the onset of the disease. Both the patient's and the family history may be difficult to obtain, as there may be denial that there is anything wrong or abnormal.

Whether the patients are truly anorexic, i.e. without desire for food, is uncertain. It is more probable that they repress the sensation of hunger or fail to act on it. Some are tormented by their physiological need and

haunted by the thought of food. Insatiable appetite **bulimia** may lead to occasional orgies of eating when large quantities of any food that is available are consumed. Some patients deliberately induce vomiting and others purge themselves repeatedly. Information about these habits may be deliberately withheld from the family and the physician.

A pathognomic feature is 'the vigour and stubbornness with which the often gruesome emaciation is defended as normal and right and the only possible protection against the dreaded fate of being too fat'.[27] There is a distortion of the body image. This can be measured using an apparatus in which two lights on a screen are moved various distances apart. The patient is asked to state the distance which she thinks corresponds to the width of her body at various sites. Hips, waist and bust are often overestimated by 50 per cent. The extent of the overestimation may be so great that it constitutes a delusion.

An important question is whether the compulsive starvation which reduces the body to its size before puberty is due to fear of fatness or fear of feminity. When Freud's influence was dominant, the retreat from sexual maturity was attributed to early sexual trauma or even a confusion between oral sexuality and eating. Today a well-rounded shape is unfashionable among young girls and large numbers of them attempt to slim by controlling their carbohydrate intake. Patients have often subsisted on a diet based on fruit, vegetables, cheese or yogurt and black coffee, a diet commonly chosen by girls who wish to slim. In anorexia nervosa has the fashionable wish to slim turned into a pathological obsession?

CLINICAL FEATURES

The weight may be reduced to 35 kg or less and the loss of subcutaneous fat sharply delineates underlying muscles. These may be maintained by restless activity. This may be promoted by a high intelligence and take various forms, including sports at which some patients have excelled. Gull remarked of one patient, 'It seemed hardly possible that a body so wasted could undergo the exercise which seemed so agreeable.' Patients often deny all normal sense of fatigue.

Nutritional state
All the usual features of starvation may be present. The pulse is slow, the blood pressure, peripheral blood flow and skin temperatures are all low. These changes have been accurately measured in 33 subjects under controlled conditions.[28] There is usually no anaemia and no hypoalbuminaemia. There may be fine downy hair, lanugo, over the body. Amenorrhoea is a characteristic fea-

ture but secondary sexual characteristics are present. Urinary excretion of gonadotrophins and oestrogens (testosterone in males) is diminished. Plasma oestradiol is low; plasma luteinising hormone (LH) is low in the day and high at night, the opposite of the normal. The response to LH-releasing hormone depends on the patient's weight and the critical figure is about 47 kg, depending on height. Menstruation starts at puberty when weight rises above this, and stops in anorexia nervosa when it falls below.[29] The plasma potassium may be abnormally low and this is an indication that the patient may have been taking purgatives or may have been inducing vomiting.

Diagnosis
Anorexia is common in patients with an anxiety state, a depressive illness and some forms of schizophrenia. It may arise from a focal lesion of the pituitary-hypothalmic axis caused by trauma, haemorrhage or a neoplasm, but such lesions are very rare. Occasionally it is the presenting feature of tuberculosis or other general infections. In all of these conditions the obsessional concern with food and the physical and mental overactivity, characteristic of anorexia nervosa, are normally absent. However, the differential diagnosis may be difficult and the pitfalls are fully described by Crisp.[26] The diagnosis should always be considered in an underweight adolescent girl with unusual symptoms.

TREATMENT

The primary aim is to get the patient to eat. Severe cases should be treated by a psychiatrist and under close supervision in hospital until a satisfactory weight has been achieved. The nursing staff and dietitian have to be skilled and forebearing, for these patients are notoriously slow eaters and many cunningly get rid of food by forced vomiting or concealment. It is unrealistic to expect a patient to eat a large diet at once. Diet No. 2 (p. 609), appropriately modified to the patient's tastes, may be tried at the start. Many patients have eaten no bread, potatoes or cereal products for a long time and it may be difficult to persuade them to try these foods again.

Chlorpromazine in doses up to 150 to 200 mg three times daily makes the patient more amenable, counteracts vomiting and is claimed to increase appetite. The doctor's efforts should be directed to exploring the manner of life, and in particular events immediately antedating the onset, and to supplying explanations and reassurance. In no condition is it more important to have only one therapist in direct charge who must be prepared to follow up the patient over a long period of time.

Disturbed relationships within the family need attention. It is often easy but unhelpful to blame a parent for expressing exasperation or a patient for misinterpreting the concern of others. Regular interviews with relatives conducted by a psychiatric social worker over many months should reduce guilt, misunderstanding and intolerance.

Prognosis
Recovery, which implies restoration of weight and menstruation occurs within several months in favourable cases. Those who had been previously obese reach their target weight sooner than other patients.[30]

A disquietingly high proportion, estimated at 50 per cent, make only a partial recovery, continuing to restrict their diet and remaining abnormally thin. There is a mortality of about 5 per cent from suicide or inanition in the five years from first diagnosis.

REFERENCES

1. McKeown T 1979 The role of medicine; dream mirage or nemesis. Blackwell, Oxford, p 73
2. Lusk G 1928 The science of nutrition, 4th edn. Saunders, Philadelphia
3. Smith D A, Woodruff M F A 1951 Deficiency diseases in Japanese prison camps. MRC Spec Rep Ser. no. 274. Medical Research Council, London
4. Helweg-Larsen P, Hoffmeyer H, Kieler J, et al 1952 Famine disease in German concentration camps. Acta Med Scand suppl 274
5. Burger J C E, Drummond J C, Sandstead H R 1948 Malnutrition and starvation in western Netherlands, September 1944 to July 1945. General State Printing Office, The Hague
6. Department of Experimental Medicine, Cambridge 1951 Studies of undernutrition, Wuppertal 1946-9. MRC Spec Rep Ser no. 275
7. Keys A, Brezek J, Henschel A, Mickelsen O, Taylor H L 1950 The biology of human starvation, University of Minnesota Press, Minneapolis
8. Moore F O 1959 The metabolic care of the surgical patient. Saunders, Philadelphia
9. Porter A 1889 The diseases of the Madras famine 1877-78. Government Press, Madras
10. Donovan G 1848 Observations on the peculiar diseases to which the famine of last year gave origin, and on the morbid effects of insufficient nourishment. Dublin Med J 19: 67-8
11. Ramalingaswami V 1971 Studies of the Bihar famine 1966-67. In: Famine. Symposia of the Swedish Nutrition Foundation no. 9
12. Jackson C M 1925 The effects of inanition and malnutrition upon growth on structure. Churchill, London
13. Follis R H 1958 Deficiency diseases. Thomas, Springfield
14. Grande F 1964 Man under caloric deficiency. In:

Handbook of physiology — adaptation to the environment. American Physiological Society, Washington DC, p 911–37

15. Cahill G F 1970 Starvation in man. N Engl J Med 282: 668–75

16. Owen O E, Morgan A P, Kemp H G, Sullivan J M, Herrava H G, Cahill G F 1967 Brain metabolism during fasting. J Clin Invest 46: 1589–95

17. Brozek J, Grande F, Taylor H L, Anderson E R, Bushkirk E R, Keys A 1957 Changes in body weight and body dimensions in men performing work on a low calorie carbohydrate diet. J Appl Physiol 10: 412–20

18. McCance R A 1951 The history, significance, and aetiology of hunger oedema. MRC Spec Rep Ser no. 275, 21–82

19. Beattie J, Herbert P A, Bell D J 1948 Famine oedema. Br J Nutr 2: 47–65

20. Youmans J B 1936 Nutritional oedema. Int Clin 4: 120–45

21. Guyton A C, Harris J G, Taylor A E 1971 Interstitial fluid pressure. Physiol Rev 51: 527 63

22. Marliss E B, Aoki T T, Unger R H, Soeldner J S, Cahill G F 1970 Glucagon levels and metabolic effects in fasting man. J Clin Invest 49: 2256–70

23. Vagenakis A G, et al 1975 Diversion of peripheral thyroxine metabolism from activating to inactivating pathways during complete fasting. J Clin Endocrinol Metab 41: 191–4

24. Mason J B, Hay R W, Levesche J, Peel, Darley S 1974 Treatment of severe malnutrition in relief camps. Lancet 1: 332–5

25. Bruch H 1978 The Golden Cage, the enigma of anorexia nervosa. Open Books, London

26. Crisp A H 1980 Anorexia nervosa. Academic Press, London

27. Bruch H 1974 Eating disorders, obesity, anorexia nervosa and the person within. Routledge & Kegan Paul, London

28. Fohlin H 1977 Body composition, cardiovascular and renal function in adolescent patients with anorexia nervosa. Acta Paediatr Suppl 268

29. Frisch R E, McArthur J W 1974 Menstrual cycles: fatness as a determinant of minimum weight for height necessary for their maintenance or onset. Science NY 185: 949–51

30. Stordy B J, Marks V, Kalucy R S, Crisp A H 1977 Weight gain, thermic effect of glucose and resting metabolic weight during recovery from anorexia nervosa. Am J Clin Nutr 30: 138–46

28

Obesity

Every year books and innumerable articles on slimming appear in the popular press. Slimming has become big business and there is no lack of charlatans. Much of the information so widely dispersed is irrelevant and so misleading, and some of it is false and dangerous. Not surprisingly many patients and some of their professional advisers often become confused. They then think that the causes of obesity and its treatment are complex. Obesity is an inevitable result of eating more than is needed and the only one way to slim is by reducing the amount of food eaten. This may be simple in theory, but for many people is difficult in practice. Before giving a professional account of obesity and its treatment, a brief dogmatic summary is given, using only commonplace words. This, it is hoped, will enable the reader to keep a clear picture of the wood in mind when considering later the complexities of some of the trees.

Obesity, the most prevalent nutritional disorder in prosperous communites, is the result of an incorrect energy balance leading to an increased store of energy, mainly as fat. The physiological regulation of energy stores is complex and not understood fully (Chap. 9). Fortunately all that a patient needs to know, and indeed must know, is that obesity arises only as consequence of taking in more energy in their food than is expended in the activities of their daily life, and furthermore if the diet is restricted so as to supply less energy than is being used, then the body has to draw upon the stores in adipose tissue and weight is lost.

Eating and physical exercise are behavioural activities and so controllable by will power and hence obesity is a behavioural disorder. Only rarely can its onset be attributed to a metabolic disease or other organic cause.

Obesity is rare in primitive societies and in wild animals, but wherever civilisation has provided a plentiful supply of appetising foods, there have been fat men and women, and also fat cats and dogs and fat pigs and cattle. In the twentieth century, new sources of power in industry, in homes and for transport has greatly reduced the necessity to use human muscle power. In Europe and North America today much less food is needed to meet the energy requirements of daily life than in the times of our grandfathers and great grandfathers. We have inherited their food habits and customs, and the food industry now provides many new foods that are rich and appetising, so it should be no surprise that obesity is widespread among us.

Obesity increases the risk of developing many diseases. This it does partly through the mechanical effects of the mass of extra tissues on the functions of various organs and systems, and partly as a consequence of changes in metabolism that it induces. When obesity is severe, one or more of these diseases is likely to impair health and life expectancy is greatly reduced. Obesity is therefore a disorder that should be taken seriously. On the other hand most people who have gained only a little weight feel well, have no signs of any disease and there is no good evidence that their life expectancy is reduced. Such people may be described better as plump rather than as obese. Very many of them wish to lose weight for social reasons or because their clothes have become too tight or to make themselves fitter for sports and active recreations. They should be encouraged to reduce, if only to lower the risk of their subsequently becoming seriously obese. However, they should not allow consideration of their weight to become a fetish.

Obesity can be prevented and cured only by changing a patient's way of life. Effective treatment is impossible unless the patient is well motivated and able and willing to take full responsibility for carrying it out. Dietitians and doctors have no cure for obesity, but they can help patients to cure themselves by giving advice on diet and exercise, and by supporting them in their resolution to carry on with a new way of life which is usually hard and difficult for a long time.

DEFINITION AND ASSESSMENT

Obesity is a state in which an excess of fat has accumulated. In most cases it can be detected by visual inspection and this usually suffices for diagnosis. It is also important to assess the degree of obesity, so as to be able to monitor progress and regulate treatment. This is customarily done by weighing the patient and relating weight to height.

Weight and height

The weight of an individual in relation to height depends not only on the amount of fat present but also on the frame or build of the body. Large bones and bulky muscles may be responsible for a relatively large weight. Acceptable weights for height of adult men and women are given in Table 55.2 (p. 521) and may be used as standards. It is common to consider persons whose weight is more than 10 per cent of the standard as overweight and those more than 20 per cent as obese.

More than 100 years ago Quetelet, a Belgian mathematician interested in statistics and sociology, suggested that the ratio W/H^2 was a useful index for classifying people of different sizes.[1] His index, forgotten by all but a few anthropometricians, has now been recalled into use as an **obesity index**, and a chart based on the index that is simple to use for grading obesity has been devised by Garrow[2] (Table 28.1 and Fig. 28.1). The index is easily calculated and requires no judgment of the size of the body frame but does not distinguish between

Table 28.1 Grading of obesity by weight W (kg) and height (H) (m)

Grade III	W/H^2	>40
Grade II	W/H^2	30 to 40
Grade I	W/H^2	25 to 29.9
Not obese	W/H^2	< 25

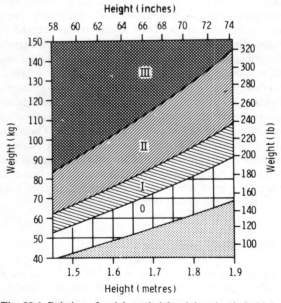

Fig. 28.1 Relation of weight to height giving the desirable range (0) and the grades of obesity defined by the W/H^2 ratio in Table 28.1. (From Garrow)[2]

overweight due to obesity and to muscle hypertrophy. A full discussion of this and other indices of adiposity is in a review by Garrow.[3]

Measurement of body fat

Unfortunately determinations of body fat based on measurements of body water, body potassium or body density (Chap. 2) are not possible in clinical practice. However, an assessment can be made from measurements of skinfold thicknesses. For this purpose various calipers are available. The Harpenden calipers (British Indicators Ltd, St Albans, Herts) or the Holtain calipers (Holtain Ltd, Crymmych, Dyfed, Wales) are recommended. Measurements should be made at four sites:

1. Triceps, at a point equidistant from the tip of the acromion and the olecranon.
2. Subscapular, just below the tip of the inferior angle of the scapula.
3. Biceps, at the mid-point of the muscle with the arm hanging vertically.
4. Suprailiac, over the iliac crest in the mid-axillary line.

Durnin & Womersley[4] made measurements of skinfold thickness at these four sites and of body density by underwater weighing on 209 men and 272 women aged from 16 to 72 years. The relations between the sum of the four skinfolds and the percentage of body fat, derived from density were calculated from regression equations. Table 28.2 gives the results. The higher body fat corresponding to a given skinfold in women than in men is attributable to a higher proportion of the total fat being over the thighs and hips. Durnin & Womersley conclude that the use of their table 'for assessing total body fat with relative ease and reasonable accuracy on men and women of widely differing age should make it of common use in many fields of medicine, physiology, nutrition and anthropology.' Our experience in practical classes with students confirms this view. Skinfold calipers quantitate pinching the skin, as a sphygmomanometer quantitates feeling the pulse.

To make the measurements at four sites, the patients have to be undressed; for survey work in which large numbers of people are being studied, this may be impractical. Then a single measurement over the triceps is useful. A table of normal values is given in Chapter 55 p. 522.

EPIDEMIOLOGY

Obesity is common wherever there is an abundant supply of appetising foods, as anybody can verify in the streets of a prosperous town or holiday resort. Numer-

Table 28.2 The equivalent fat content, as a percentage of body weight, for a range of values for the sum of four skinfolds (biceps, triceps, subscapular and suprailiac) of males and females of different ages[4]

Skinfolds (mm)	Males (age in years)				Females (age in years)			
	17–29	30–39	40–49	50+	16–29	30–39	40–49	50+
20	8.1	12.2	12.2	12.6	14.1	17.0	19.8	21.4
30	12.9	16.2	17.7	18.6	19.5	21.8	24.5	26.6
40	16.4	19.2	21.4	22.9	23.4	25.5	28.2	30.3
50	19.0	21.5	24.6	26.5	26.5	28.2	31.0	33.4
60	21.2	23.5	27.1	29.2	29.1	30.6	33.2	35.7
70	23.1	25.1	29.3	31.6	31.2	32.5	35.0	37.7
80	24.8	26.6	31.2	33.8	33.1	34.3	36.7	39.6
90	26.2	27.8	33.0	35.8	34.8	35.8	38.3	41.2
100	27.6	29.0	34.4	37.4	36.4	37.2	39.7	42.6
110	28.8	30.1	35.8	39.0	37.8	38.6	41.0	43.9
120	30.0	31.1	37.0	40.4	39.0	39.6	42.0	45.1
130	31.0	31.9	38.2	41.8	40.2	40.6	43.0	46.2
140	32.0	32.7	39.2	43.0	41.3	41.6	44.0	47.2
150	32.9	33.5	40.2	44.1	42.3	42.6	45.0	48.2
160	33.7	34.3	41.2	45.1	43.3	43.6	45.8	49.2
170	34.5	34.8	42.0	46.1	44.1	44.4	46.6	50.0
180	35.3	—	—	—	—	45.2	47.4	50.8
190	35.9	—	—	—	—	45.9	48.2	51.6
200	—	—	—	—	—	46.5	48.8	52.4
210	—	—	—	—	—	—	49.4	53.0

In two-thirds of the instances the error was within ± 3.5 per cent of the body-weight as fat for the women and ± 5 per cent for the men.

ous surveys have recorded its prevalence in selected samples of communities. As the condition is not notifiable, there is no reliable information on prevalence in any country. A sensible guess[2] is that among adults in the UK and USA between 25 and 33 per cent have Grade I obesity, about 4 per cent Grade II and 0.05 per cent Grade III. The first are the multitude providing the support for the huge slimming industry; the second present an enormous problem to the medical services; the third fortunately are much less common, but a general practitioner with 2500 patients on his list is likely to have one such case.

Obesity occurs at all ages and commonly affects the health of infants, adolescents and the elderly.

Fashion determines much of human behaviour, especially that of young ladies. The voluptuous curves on the nude bodies of so many of these in the pictures by Rubens and Renoir suggest that in Belgium around 1630 and in France around 1880 there was much admiration for a figure which today would send its owner rushing off to join a slimming club. In Edinburgh we often have opportunity to contrast the neat slim figure of an elderly American lady visitor with that of her portly husband. She clearly has made great efforts to conform to fashion as we see it in the *New Yorker*; he poor man is, we suspect, the victim of too many business luncheons, the occupational risk to health to which successful managers are so often exposed.

There are other occupations which carry a risk of obesity. In a market in a small town in rural Africa or Asia, it is unlikely that any case of obesity can be seen among the peasants who are buying and selling goods, but one or more may well be found among the cooks in the nearby eating house and behind the counter in the money-lender's shop. These are but a few illustrations of the many circumstances that may determine the prevalence of obesity in different sections of a community.

AETIOLOGY

Traditional textbooks of medicine usually place obesity in the section on metabolic disorders and alongside that on endocrine diseases. This may be misleading. The metabolic and endocrine changes found commonly in patients with grade II or grade III obesity (see below) in all probability are the consequence and not the cause of the obesity. In only a very small minority of patients is there evidence of a physical condition or metabolic disturbance that might be held responsible. In contrast eating to an extent that is inappropriate to the patient's physical activities is always the direct cause. Obesity is thus a behavioural disorder and so could be classified along with other psychiatric disorders. This, of course, does not make the difficult problem of aetiology any easier. However, to have a clear understanding of where the main problem lies helps patients, as well as dietitians and doctors, in their approach to management.

Nibbling between meals contributes to the obesity of some housewives who are fond of the cooking and of others who work in kitchens. On the other hand, in Prague those who ate only three times a day were more likely to be overweight than those who ate five or six times.[5] Laboratory rats who like to nibble all through the night also become obese, if their access to food is limited to a short period in the 24 hours.

An ingenious set of experiments has been carried out by Schachter[6] in which the food consumed by subjects who were overweight and by those of normal weight were measured in various artificial situations. Compared with the controls, the amounts eaten by obese subjects were little affected by previous food intake, i.e. by hunger and satiety, and depended more on the taste and appearance of the food and on psychological and physical factors in the environment in which the food was served. Schachter postulates that feeding is determined by internal or physiological cues, to which the obese are relatively insensitive, and by external cues, to which they are more sensitive than normal persons. He supports his theory with observations in real-life circumstances, e.g. the factors which affect how well obese subjects keep a religious fast.

This theory appears convincing, except for reservations about its general applicability. Schachter's subjects were New Yorkers, most of them university students or graduates and many of them Jews. Thus, like the Viennese subjects on whose experiences Freud built his theories of psychoanalysis, they were not typical representatives of mankind. It would be interesting to see if similar results were obtained with middle-aged working-class women in Glasgow or with the shopkeepers of East Africa. Cultural factors may contribute to obesity in various ways. Thus in parts of Africa and the West Indies moderate obesity in women is desired by their menfolk and admired by their sisters. The Sumo wrestlers of Japan weigh 120 kg or more, not all of this muscle.

Another behavioural difference that has been reported between obese and normal people is that the obese eat faster and spend less time chewing each mouthful of food.[7] This, too, needs confirmation.

Children and all young mammals play naturally and in this they expend much energy. Our food habits first develop at a time of life when we are physically very active. Most schools, colleges and universities pay little attention to physical education. Facilities for games are usually inadequate and students get little encouragement to take part in them regularly. The views of Francois Rabelais written in 1535 are worth consideration. He was both a physician and an educationlist and a bitter opponent of the Schoolmen at the Sorbonne in Paris who concentrated on the intellect and took no notice of the body. This is how in his book he describes the education of Gargantua.[8]

'In the morning, for three solid hours his teachers would read to him. When this was over, they would go out, still talking about what they had just read, and find some sport at Bracque or in the meadows, playing ball, tennis or three-cornered tossball, briskly exercising their bodies as they, before, had exercised their souls. . . . They ordinarily stopped when they were sweating all over or when they were exhausted. Then they would be very thoroughly rubbed and dried, would change their shirts, and would stroll leisurely back to see if dinner was ready. While they were waiting, they would recite, clearly and eloquently, such sentences as they had remembered from their morning's reading. In the meanwhile, Monsignor Appetite would put in an appearance, and they would all sit down, in orderly fashion at the table.'

The source of much of the obesity in towns and cities of today may be a failure to instil into young people orderly habits at the table and to provide playing fields and the opportunities to use them.

Genetic defects

A defect in a single gene leads to obesity in some species, for example the ob/ob strain of mice and the Zucker strain of rats. These have been much studied with a large literature.[9] In man obesity often runs in families, but it is difficult to separate genetic from environmental factors. No single gene is responsible for human obesity. Some groups of people that have had to struggle to obtain enough food in harsh environments and had repeated famines in their history are unusually liable to become obese when they move to a sedentary surburban way of life. Australian Aborigines, the islanders of Nauru and Indians in Natal in South Africa are examples. Natural selection may have favoured metabolically 'thrifty genotypes' in these groups.[10] There are rare genetic disorders in which obesity is a clinical feature. The best known is the Prader-Willi syndrome, characterised by muscle hypotonia, mental retardation, diabetes and obesity.

Endocrine factors

Obesity frequently accompanies hypothyroidism, hypogonadism, hypopituitarism and Cushing's syndrome, but it is not an essential feature of these conditions. The fact that in women obesity commonly begins at puberty, during pregnancy or at the menopause suggests an endocrine factor. Yet the overwhelming majority of obese patients show no clinical evidence of an endocrine disorder and the function of their endocrine glands is normal on routine tests.

There are certain well-defined changes in metabolism associated with obesity which are described below. It is probable that these changes are a result of obesity and not its cause. Yet tests of endocrine function have been crude until recently. It is possible that new methods may lead to the discovery of small, but important deviations of endocrine or metabolic functions that contribute to obesity.

Trauma
Obesity may follow damage to the hypothalamus and its connections after a head injury or other localised lesion. Such cases are clinical curiosities and uncommon.

In obesity energy stores continue to be regulated but the neuronal control in the brain is offset. In a like manner body temperature is still regulated during fever but at a different level. Genetic defects, endocrine factors and habits alter the setting and may reduce the sensitivity of the control system. Of these, habits are overwhelmingly the more important as a cause of obesity. Habits arise from purposeful psychological drives and can be subjected to will power. The problems of the relation between mind and brain that have fascinated learned men for centuries and remain unresolved underlie the aetiology of obesity.

Metabolism
More than 50 years ago it was reported[11] that basal or resting metabolism of obese people was within normal limits. All subsequent work has confirmed this. The resting metabolic rate (RMR) is closely related to lean body mass (p. 21) which is increased in most obese people. When an obese person loses weight, RMR falls rapidly in the first few days and thereafter steadily.

Obesity is associated with both hyperplasia and hypertrophy of adipocytes. Adipose tissue is a metabolic organ with manifold activities and these have been concisely reviewed.[12]

Table 28.3 shows metabolic changes commonly found in obese patients. They are probably a consequence and not a cause of the obesity. The most important are the first three, which show that many obese people are in a prediabetic state. Obese people develop much less ketonuria in response to starvation than those of normal

Table 28.3 Metabolic changes commonly present in obese patients

Glucose tolerance	decreased
Sensitivity to insulin	decreased
Plasma insulin	increased
Response to starvation	
production of ketone bodies	decreased
plasma free fatty acids	increased
Plasma triglycerides	increased
Plasma cholesterol	increased
Plasma uric acid	increased
Sensitivity to growth hormone	decreased
Urinary 17-hydroxycorticoids	increased

weight; when they are given very low energy diets for several weeks, significant ketoacidosis does not arise.[13] Perhaps the most important change is the hyperinsulinaemia;[14] this may be due to inadequate feedback inhibition of insulin secretion or reduced numbers of insulin receptors associated with obesity.[14a]

CLINICAL FEATURES

Obesity grade I
Most of the 'do-it-yourself' slimmers are in this grade. Their overweight has not affected their health and they are able to lead their normal lives. Life insurance statistics indicate that their life expectancy is but little above normal (Fig. 28.2).

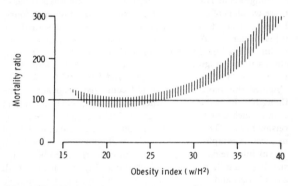

Fig. 28.2 Relation of obesity index (W/H²) to mortality ratio. Average mortality = 100. Data from American life insurance companies. (From Garrow)[2]

Obesity grade II
Patients in this grade form the majority of cases treated by doctors and dietitians. Although some of them appear to be in good health and leading normal lives, they are likely to have a reduced exercise tolerance with shortness of breath on exertion and to be unduly fatigued by continuing physical activity. This is due to the burden of the increased weight that they carry always and to reduced capacity of the circulatory and respiratory systems that work under handicaps imposed by masses of internal fat and fatty infiltration of muscle.

For mechanical and metabolic reasons these patients are at increased risk of one or more of the disorders listed in Table 28.4. They often first seek medical advice because of symptoms that have arisen from one of these, and it may be only then that they realise that their obesity is something to be taken seriously. Mortality rates rise with increasing weight and life expectation becomes reduced to from a half to a third of the normal number of years (Fig. 28.2). They are also at increased risk when under anaesthesia; surgical operations are more difficult and post-operative complications are more likely.

Obesity grade III

These patients are pathetic creatures. Their everyday activities are seriously restricted by their enormous mass, and they are likely to be suffering from many of the disorders listed in Table 28.4. Life expectation is low. Usually they have serious psychological disturbances. These may have been present in the initial stages of the disease and contributed to its development.

An account of an extreme case was given by the explorer Speke in 1883. On his journey to the source of the Nile he stayed with an African tribe whose men greatly appreciated the charms of fat women and saw a girl whose obesity was literally man-made. His diary[15] records:

> After a long and amusing conversation with Rumarika in the morning, I called on one of his sisters-in-law. She was another of those wonders of obesity, unable to stand excepting on all fours. I was desirous to obtain a good view of her and actually to measure her . . . After getting her to sidle and wiggle into the middle of the hut, I took her dimensions: round arm 1 ft 11 in; chest 4 ft 4 in; thigh 2 ft 7 in; calf 1 ft 8 in; height 5 ft 8 in. All of these were exact except the height, and I believe I could have obtained this more accurately if I could have laid her on the floor. Not knowing what difficulties I should have to contend with in such a piece of engineering, I tried to get her height by raising her up. This after infinite exertions on the part of both of us, was accomplished, when she sank down again fainting. Meanwhile the daughter, a lass of 16, sat stark naked before us, sucking at a milk pot, on which the father kept her at work with a rod in his hand, for as fattening is the first duty of a fashionable female life, it must be duly enforced by the rod, if necessary. I got up a bit of flirtation with missy and induced her to rise and shake hands with me. Her features were lovely, but her body as round as a ball.

Self inflicted obesity of a similar order, if rarely quite so severe, is seen in hospitals in Europe and North America today.

TREATMENT

Treatment is simple in principle. If a patient eats a diet providing 500–1000 kcal (1–4 MJ) less than is needed for the activities of daily life, then and only then will the excess reserves of energy in adipose tissue be drawn upon and weight lost at a rate of 0.5–1 kg (1–2 lb) each week.

In practice this is for most patients very difficult, since it requires changes in long established habits with a new discipline, similar to that which an athlete imposes on himself when going into training. Besides restricting food intake, physical fitness should be improved by taking as much exercise as is possible. For many obese patients, handicapped by the load of extra

Table 28.4 Diseases with increased prevalence in obese subjects

Diabetes
Hypertension
Gall bladder diseases
Fatty liver
Gout
Pulmonary disorders
Osteoarthritis
Hernias (diaphragmatic and abdominal)
Varicose veins
Intertriginous dermatitis

weight that they must carry with them and by reduced capacity of the circulation and respiratory systems, this is at first a new and hard challenge. Only with strong motivation maintained over many months or years can patients lose weight and sustain the loss. They need continuing support for morale and this can be given by doctors, dietitians and by mutual exchanges in a slimming club. All three may co-operate. As well as this support most patients need practical advice on food and health based on hard science. False ideas of no practical value, often bizarre and sometimes dangerous, circulate widely and are taken up readily by despairing patients.

A target weight and a realistic time to reach this target should be settled by agreement between patient and adviser at the start of treatment. For some patients it is unrealistic to aim at reduction to a theoretically ideal weight, but it is always possible to set a target which would ensure a marked improvement in health and sense of fitness. For example, if the aim is to lose 15 kg (about 30 lb, or 2 stone), this can be achieved in 30 weeks, if dietary energy intake is maintained at 500 kcal below daily needs. This is the minimum rate of loss that should be accepted and the necessary dietary restriction need not be harsh. The aim could be achieved in 15 weeks, if the dietary energy is 1000 kcal below needs; this requires much stricter dieting and so is more difficult for the patient.

Once the target has been fixed, progress has to be checked regularly. This is by weighing which should be at least once every four weeks, but not more than once a week. Too frequent weighings may lead to an obsession for the scales; inappropriate depression or elation may arise if for two or three days no weight is lost or if there is a marked drop. Daily variations in body weight, as in normal persons, are to be expected. With even a slight dietary restriction up to 3 kg is usually lost in the first week. This is largely due to utilisation of the carbohydrate store and loss of water bound to glycogen. Patients should not be depressed when the first week's progress is not repeated. The effectiveness of treatment is indicated by the slope of the line on the weight chart over many weeks.

Dietary advice

This has to be tailored to the patients previous food habits. A dietary history has to be elicited in detail and more than one session may be needed to get a full picture. This usually indicates that energy intake could be reduced sufficiently to meet the target by cutting down on or eliminating from the diet the food items listed in Appendix 2, p. 611. Snacks between meals and excessive consumption at too frequent feasts to mark social occasions or as adjuncts to business meetings may also have to be curtailed. In these ways energy intake may be adjusted without the necessity of going on to a diet with prescribed amounts of specific items. Diet sheets handed out without explanation and discussion should play no part in the treatment of obesity.

Some patients, however, may find it easier to cut down on food intake by taking a strictly defined diet. Diet no. 3 (p. 610) is an example of one which provides only 1000 kcal (4.2 MJ) and which, if adhered to, ensures a satisfactory weight loss. A few patients may like to have in their homes a small dietitian's balance and for a week or so weigh helpings of all foods. Thereafter they can rely on their eyes for judging the size of helpings, but should make occasional weighings to check their visual judgment.

Any curtailment of food intake is liable to reduce intakes of essential nutrients. All reducing regimes should include ample fruit and vegetables and preferably wholemeal bread. These should supply ample vitamins and minerals. They also supply dietary fibre and this may help to promote a sense of satiety and so make the inevitably small meals more satisfying; it also prevents constipation. There is normally no need for patients to take supplements of minerals and vitamins. However, the risk of developing iron deficiency is at least as great as with normal diets. If there is any evidence to suggest that a patient is becoming anaemic, haemoglobin should be measured and, if this is low, an iron supplement given. Diet No. 3, although providing only 1000 kcal, contains 60 g protein, ample for normal needs. In order to accelerate weight loss, further restriction is sometimes prescribed. Then to prevent depletion a protein supplement should be given.

Slimmers are bombarded with information and advice in magazines and daily newspapers and by radio and television. They see in shops shelves loaded with artificial foods claiming to be able to help them. They should know and understand that there is no such thing as a specific slimmers diet. The diet that we recommend (Diet No. 3) is no more than a scaled down version of the diets recommended for normal people (Diets 1 and 2). Much publicised low carbohydrate diets and advice such as 'eat fat and get slim' are both potentially dangerous. So is severe dietary restriction. Patients should not reduce their diet below 1000 kcal, except on medical advice and with close supervision.

Patients should appreciate that there are no slimming foods; all foods are fattening if taken in excess. Foods legitimately advertised as aiding in a slimming diet are modified forms of conventional foods and beverages, usually with a lower energy density. Those who like these products may enjoy them in moderation. They are only gimmicks, but few of us go through life without the aid of a number of gimmicks.

Formula diets providing all the nutrients that a slimmer needs are easily obtainable in many shops. Most of these are manufactured by reliable companies and based on the best scientific information available. Patients who wish to make a complete break with previous bad dietary habits may find a period subsisting on one of these a help. This can do no harm as an experiment, but because of our ignorance of requirements of trace elements and perhaps of other essential micronutrient, it is not one that should be continued for more than a few weeks.

A few patients have found that one day of total starvation each week has helped them to slim. This practice can do no harm, but it is a gimmick; in many people it would be followed by insatiable appetite next day leading to loss of all the benefit.

Exercise and physical fitness

While it is easy, at least in theory, to curtail energy intake by 500 kcal by reducing food intake, it is much more difficult to increase energy output a similar amount by increasing physical activity. This is due to constraints upon our time imposed by modern ways of life and in many obese people to reduced capacity for even moderate exercise resulting from their disorder. If the reader in the evening after supper goes out and takes a brisk walk lasting for an hour, energy expenditure will be only some 200 kcal more than that spent in a chair in front of a television box. To make this change occasionally may be enjoyable, but to do so seven days a week throughout the year in all weathers is another matter. Considerations such as these help to explain why physicians continue to put much less emphasis on exercise than on diet in their advice to obese patients.

Even if the exercise contributes only a little to a negative energy balance, it benefits by promoting physical fitness. Exercise prevents atrophy of muscle. Insufficient use of the muscles of the trunk and limbs of the respiratory system and of the myocardium increases the risk of patients to orthopaedic, respiratory and circulatory disorders.

Obese patients may be advised to walk, when possible, rather than use their cars or public transport, to climb stairs rather than use an elevator and to take up one or more hobbies demanding physical exercise. Examples of these suitable for the middle aged and elderly are dancing, swimming, golf and gardening. If the garden is small, it is better to mow the grass and cut the hedges by hand and not to misspend money on an electric mower and shears. The above are only small aids to slimming and cannot replace dietary restrictions. But they are positive and enjoyable, whereas dieting is negative and inevitably dreary.

Patients need to know that purchase of a massage machine, vibrator or other physical device, some of which are advertised widely will not remove excess weight; the only loss will be that of money. Excessive sweating in a Turkish bath causes loss of water, which is soon replaced, but does not remove fat.

Psychological support and management

Slimming requires resolution and an effort of the will to carry on against continuing discomfort. In this respect it resembles training for athletic events. Athletes depend on coaches and trainers for support and encouragement. Although individual physicians and dietitians have provided this successfully for many patients, the medical and dietetic professions as a whole have a poor record. In the past the records of hospital obesity clinics that have been published have told a dismal story, failures and relapses far outnumbering successes. There is no reason to think that general practitioners have done any better. Since 1970 slimmers have been turning in increasing numbers to slimming clubs whose members provide self-help. These have differing organisations; many are run by past patients who have themselves reduced successfully and are on a commercial basis with members paying for attendance at meetings. The clubs provide what psychiatrists call group behavioural therapy. That such clubs are prospering and that one or more can be found in most large towns suggests that they are having more successes than the older hospital clinics.

Although the main difficulty in treatment, sustaining the patient's resolution and will power, is a psychological one, psychiatrists have in the past played only a small part in treatment. Only a small minority of the obese have a well defined psychiatric disorder and so are obvious cases for referral to a psychiatrist.

Management takes time and patients can be very demanding. The interval between visits to a clinic and the amount of a doctor's or dietitian's time required at each visit may vary greatly with different patients. Some may require at first frequent visits to learn from a dietitian the nutritive values of different foods and how to plan a diet; others may have health problems which they need to discuss with a doctor. When weight loss has been steady, the interval between visits can be lengthened. Failure to attend for an appointment may be due to disappointment and disillusion following a failure to keep to the diet. All such failures should be followed up.

The general principles described above are relevant for all who wish to slim whatever their grade of obesity. Their manner of application differs with the different grades and additional forms of treatment may be useful for those in grades II and III.

Obesity grade I

This includes the vast majority of would-be slimmers. The data of the life insurance companies indicates that they have a normal or almost normal life expectation. They are mostly healthy and wish to lose weight for psychological or social reasons. These people are plump rather than obese. They should be encouraged in their resolve to reduce, as this reduces their risk of developing obesity grade II with its many health hazards. Some of them, especially young women, should be warned of the dangers of excessive loss weight and of the risk of anorexia nervosa. The number in this group make up armies of 'do it yourself' slimmers who maintain the slimming industries in all prosperous countries. So great are their numbers relative to the numbers of dietitians and physicians that it would be impossible for most of them to be given individual professional treatment; indeed the majority do not require this. Those who do seek such advice should be reassured about their health, if necessary, given a brief outline of general principles, as described above, and encouraged in their resolve to slim.

Visitors to Edinburgh can see in the National Gallery of Scotland an excellent example of grade I obesity. Titian's lass is better described as plump (Fig. 28.3). Who would want to make her any different?

Fig. 28.3 Venus Anadyomene by Titian (Courtesy of The National Gallery of Scotland)

Obesity grade II

This includes the majority of obese patients with whom doctors and dietitians are concerned both in hospitals and in general practice. Many have first gone to the medical service on account of symptoms of disorders commonly associated with obesity. Others are detected at a routine medical examination or on a visit for a minor complaint and may claim to be fit and well. They need first a thorough medical examination with an assessment and treatment, if indicated, of any disorders that are found. Then a programme, along the lines already discussed, should be initiated for the treatment of their obesity. In addition drug therapy may help some patients in certain circumstances.

Anorectic drugs

Amphetamine and its derivatives have been much used as 'slimming agents'. They are psychomotor stimulants and also have an anorectic action. By stimulating higher cortical centres they may overcome feelings of fatigue and depression and create a sense of well-being. They may also cause insomnia, irritability, increased heart rate, raised blood pressure and severe psychotic reactions. Patients rapidly become habituated to them and sometimes develop dependence. Serious withdrawal symptoms may occur on discontinuing the drug. For these reasons amphetamine should not be prescribed.

Diethylpropion, phenmetrazine and fenfluramine are three drugs which have some chemical resemblance to amphetamine. They are also psychomotor drugs, but safer than amphetamine. They have some anorectic action but physicians' assessments of their value in a reducing regime vary greatly. They may be prescribed for cases of refractory obesity for periods of up to six weeks. After this period their appetite-suppressing effect usually wears off. Patients with a history of depression or other psychological disturbance should not be treated thus unless they can be supervised carefully.

Anorectic drugs are no substitute for a dietary regime and radical alteration of food habits. At best they are an aid which may help some patients to adhere more strictly to their diets.[16] It is never justified to use these drugs at the beginning of treatment.

Other drugs

Thyroxine stimulates metabolism and for this reason it has had an extensive trial in the treatment of obesity. However it is contraindicated except in those rare cases in which obesity is associated with evidence of hypothyroidism. In euthyroid people thyroxine produces no increase in metabolism unless given in doses which cause tremor, diarrhoea, palpitation and tachycardia. The latter is particularly undersirable in elderly patients with myocardial weakness. Hence the administration of thyroxine to obese euthyroid patients is not only useless but potentially dangerous.

Methyl cellulose is indigestible and adds bulk to the diet. In clinical trials it has had little if any effect in promoting weight loss, and it is very doubtful if it is of any value as an adjunct to dietary therapy. However, it is quite harmless.

Sedatives and tranquillisers can play no part in the treatment of obesity *per se* but they may be useful for some obese patients who suffer from an anxiety state.

Diuretics have been extensively tried in the treatment of obesity. They are potentially dangerous and are of no value in promoting weight loss unless the patient has oedema due to cardiac failure or other organic disease.

Obesity grade III

The regime of dietary restriction and increased activity already described aims at a weight loss of about 1 kg (2 lb) a week. Patients in this grade could not expect to return to normal weight at this rate in much under a year and for some not until after a far longer time. In addition to the treatment advocated for grade II obesity there are two other forms of therapy, intensive dieting and various surgical operations. However, the prognosis is poor as, even if a large amount of weight is lost, it is usually soon regained. It is generally unkind to add to sufferings of these unfortunate people by submitting them to the discomforts and dangers of these procedures.

Intensive dietary treatment

Diets providing only 500 kcal daily or a period of total starvation are justifiable in some patients who are not responding well to less vigorous restrictions. Patients should be under close medical supervision and for total starvation in hospital. In selected patients with no orthopaedic or cardiovascular complication, it is possible to increase physical activities. Patients have been kept for up to six weeks on diets providing only 400 kcal, whilst they walked 10 miles daily.[17] Negative energy balances of up to 3000 kcal/day and weight losses of up to 3 kg (7 lb) a week followed. This regime can be beneficial for some carefully selected patients.

If dietary intake is below 1000 kcal/day, a multivitamin supplement is required and mineral supplements may also be necessary. Excessive losses of potassium and nitrogen may occur and urinary outputs of these should be checked regularly. During therapeutic total starvation the urinary nitrogen excretion can be reduced from the usual level of 6–8 g/day to 2–3 g/day by giving DL-3-hydroxybutyrate (18 g/day) and this was more effective in sparing protein than a similar dose of glucose.[18] Administration of hydroxybutyrate did not affect the rate of weight loss, but seemed to increase the fat/lean ratio of the tissue lost.

Surgical treatment

Surgical interference with the gastrointestinal tract aiming to reduce food intake may be considered in patients in whom medical treatment has failed and whose life has been made miserable by severe obesity. Various forms of jejunoileostomy which by creating a bypass of the small intestine, lead to malabsorption have been carried out. After the operation food intake has to be reduced to prevent the diarrhoea, flatulence and abdominal discomfort. The operation is unphysiological and carries a mortality of up to 4 per cent. Complications with features of the malabsorption syndrome and the blind loop syndrome frequently arise. These often make the patient worse off than before. After extensive trials such operations are now seldom carried out.

An alternative approach is to reduce the size of the stomach and then the discomfort caused by a normal meal forces the patient to reduce food intake.

Gastroplasty is an operation in which the stomach is reduced to a small reservoir, about 60 ml in capacity, in the fundus which drains through a narrow channel, about 12 mm in diameter, along the greater curvature and into the duodenum.[19] In a study in Denmark[20] in which 27 patients were operated on and compared with 30 patients treated with a conventional low energy diet, those who had gastroplasty lost only a little more weight than the controls but they maintained their loss over two years much better. Two patients developed subphrenic abscesses but there were no other serious postoperative complications. Operations to reduce the capacity of the stomach are much more safe and less unphysiological then those that restrict access of food to the small intestine.

A surgical procedure that reduces food intake, does no permanent harm, and is readily reversible, is to wire the jaws together with a dental splint. The patient can then speak and drink but not eat. He is limited to a liquid diet based on milk with a low energy density. The procedure has been effective in some patients, but many have returned to former eating habits and regained weight when their jaws were unwired.

Surgical removal of large masses of fat from the abdomen, thighs or arms is contraindicated. It is likely to be followed by the appearance of irregular ugly lumps of fat at the operation sites. However, plastic operations to reduce and resuspend enlarged pendulous breasts may be of psychological benefit in some cases.

Neurosurgeons are able to modify human behaviour by making discrete lesions in the brain using a specific site identified by stereotatic techniques. Some years ago in Denmark a few obese patients had operations at which lesions were made in the hypothalamus at sites similar to those in rat brain where lesions are known to produce aphagia.[21] These have been discontinued, but it is possible that, as neurosurgeons gain more experience with these techniques, this approach to the problem of intractable obesity will be explored again.

REFERENCES

1. Quetelet L A J 1869 Physique sociale. Muquardt, Brussels, vol 2, p 92
2. Garrow J S 1981 Treat obesity seriously. Churchill Livingstone, Edinburgh
3. Garrow J S 1983 Indices of adiposity. Nutr Abst Rev 53: 697–708
4. Durnin J G V A, Womersley J 1974 Body fat assessed from total body density and its estimation from skinfold thickness. Br J Nutr 32: 77–97
5. Fabry P 1967 Metabolic consequences of the pattern of food intake. In: Handbook of physiology. Section 6: Alimentary canal. American Physiology Society, Washington DC, p 31–49
6. Schachter S 1968 Obesity and eating. Science NY 161: 751–6
7. Wagner M, Hewitt M I 1975 Oral satiety in the obese and nonobese. J Am Diet Assoc 67: 344–6
8. Rabelais F 1946 The essential Rabelais. Selected, translated and edited by Putman S. Chatto & Windus, London, p 125–6
9. Bray G A, York D A 1979 Hypothalmic and genetic obesity in experimental animals: an autonomic and endocrine hypothesis. Physiol Rev 59: 719–809
10. James W P T, Trayburn P 1976 An integrative view of the metabolic and genetic basis for obesity. Lancet 2: 770–2
11. Strang J M, Evans F A 1929 The energy exchange in obesity. J Clin Invest 6: 277–89
12. Galton D J, Wallis S 1982 The regulation of adipose cell metabolism. Proc Nutr Soc 41: 167–73
13. Kekwick A, Pawan G L S, Chalmers T M 1959 Resistance to ketosis in obese subjects. Lancet 2: 1157–9
14. Elahi D, Nagulesparan M, Hershopf R J, et al 1983 Feedback inhibition of insulin secretion by insulin: relation to the hyperinsulinaemia of obesity. New Engl J Med 306: 1192–202
14a. Olefsky J M 1981 Insulin resistance and insulin action: an in vitro and in vivo perspective. Diabetes 30: 148–62
15. Speke J H 1863 Journal of the discovery of the source of the Nile. Blackwood, Edinburgh, p 231
16. Douglas J G, Gough J, Preston P G, et al 1983 Long-term efficacy of fenfluramine in the treatment of obesity. Lancet 1: 384–6
17. Strong J A, Passmore R, Ritchie F J 1958 Clinical observations on obese patients during a strict reducing regimen. Br J Nutr 12: 105–22
18. Pawan G L S, Semple S J G 1983 Effect of 3-hydroxybutyrate in obese subjects on very-low-energy diets and during total starvation. Lancet 1: 15–7
19. Gomes C A 1979 Gastroplasty in morbid obesity. Surg Clin North Am 59: 1113–20
20. Andersen T, Backer O G, Stokholm K H, Quaade F 1984 Randomized trial of diet and gastroplasty compared with diet along in morbid obesity. N Engl J Med 310: 352–6
21. Quaade F 1974 Sterotaxy for obesity. Lancet 1:267

29

Protein-Energy Malnutrition

Protein-energy malnutrition (PEM) describes a range of clinical disorders. At one end, marasmus is due to a continued restriction of both dietary energy and protein, as well as other nutrients. At the other end is kwashiorkor, due to a quantitative and qualitative deficiency of protein, but in which energy intake may be adequate. These two syndromes are the extremes. Between them are forms in which the clinical features are due to varying combinations of deficiency of protein and energy together with deficiences of minerals and vitamins and with associated infections. These less well-defined forms provide the majority of cases. PEM is the most important public health problem in underdeveloped countries in the world today. It is largely responsible for the fact that in some areas up to half the children born do not survive to the age of 5 years. Death rates in these children may be 20 to 50 times the rate in rich and prosperous communities in Europe and North America.

This chapter describes PEM as it occurs in children. It is much less common and usually less severe in adults. This is because adults do not need protein for growth and in most adult diets proteins provide 10 per cent of the energy. Typical kwashiorkor may occur in an adult secondary to malabsorption and following surgical resections of the gut. Evidence of PEM can be found in patients in both the medical and surgical wards of hospitals in North America and Europe, if it is looked for carefully (p. 491).

HISTORY

Cicely Williams introduced the word kwashiorkor into modern medicine. It is the name used by the Ga tribe, who live around Accra in Ghana, for the 'sickness the older child gets when the next baby is born'; this indicates the circumstances in which the disease most commonly develops, namely an ignorance of the best foods to give children during the weaning period, or an inability to provide them for one reason or another.

Her first report on kwashiorkor was in the 1931 Annual Medical Report of the Gold Coast colony, which has now been reprinted. This was only read locally, but a paper soon followed in an international journal.[1]

There was a long incubation period before the disease became generally recognised. This was partly because international communication was disrupted during World War II, but Dr Williams had been transferred to Malaya in 1936, and in Africa the disease was confused with pellagra. At the first session of the FAO/WHO Expert Committee on Nutrition in 1949 there was no place for protein malnutrition on the agenda. The subject was raised indirectly under the heading of pellagra; the committee asked WHO to conduct an enquiry into the various features of kwashiorkor. To this end Brock and Autret toured Africa and wrote a report[2] which drew together the common features in different countries and set out questions that required research. In 1954 Trowell, Davies & Dean wrote a monograph[3] on kwashiorkor based on their experience in Uganda. Only after this did kwashiorkor start to appear in the textbooks, and in a few years protein malnutrition was being considered the most important nutritional disease in the world. In 1959 Jelliffe[4] introduced the term 'protein-calorie malnutrition' because of the close association between kwashiorkor and marasmus. Marasmic children have also received low protein intakes; in kwashiorkor anorexia leads to inadequate energy intake. In 1977 a monograph by Alleyne and his colleagues[5] gave a full account of the clinical features and pathology, then fully established.

AETIOLOGY AND EPIDEMIOLOGY

PEM occurs characteristically in children under 5 years, wherever the diet is poor in protein and energy. No age is immune, but in older persons the disease is much less frequent and the clinical manifestations not so obvious and usually less severe.

Typically the marasmic form of the syndrome occurs in infants under 1 year and more frequently in towns; kwashiorkor is mainly a disease of rural areas occurring in the second year of life. Figure 29.1 emphasises these distinctions, which are often far from clear cut.

Marasmus

During the nineteenth century in the industrial towns in Europe and North America marasmus, resulting from the poor diets and numerous infections, took a toll of infant lives probably as large as it is taking in many Asian, African and South American towns today. The urban influences which predispose to marasmus are a rapid succession of pregnancies and early and abrupt weaning, followed by dirty and unsound artificial feeding of the infants with very dilute milk products, given in inadequate amounts to avoid expense. Thus the diet is low in both energy and proteins. In addition poor houses and lack of equipment make the preparing of clean food almost impossible. Repeated infections develop, especially of the gastrointestinal tract; these the mother often treats by starvation for long periods, the infant receiving water, rice water or other non-nutritious fluid.

In marasmus, weaning has often been early. The mother may be induced to stop breast feeding for various reasons, including the presence of infections in herself or in the infant. Unfortunately she may have been influenced unwisely by advertisements in the press or on the radio which advocate, for commercial reasons, the advantages of artificial food products. A frequent reason for stopping breast feeding is the beginning of another pregnancy. There appears to be a widespread belief among poor, uneducated women that the milk of a pregnant woman is bad for her child. A common reason in towns is the necessity or desire to return to paid work.

Kwashiorkor

Kwashiorkor arises when, after a prolonged period on the breast, the child is weaned onto the traditional family diet; this may be low in protein because of poverty, insufficient land and poor agricultural practice. There is no supplement of milk or a totally inadequate one. Custom, sometimes reinforced by taboos, determines that the limited supply of foods of animal origin is given mainly to the men of the family. In many rural areas, where kwashiorkor is endemic, the food supply becomes scarce each year before the harvest; at this 'hungry season' the incidence of kwashiorkor and other nutritional diseases increases.

If the customary diet of a population is limited in protein and in energy to around the minimum requirements, a child may be in moderate health until protein and energy needs are raised by an infection. Kwashiorkor is frequently precipitated in epidemic

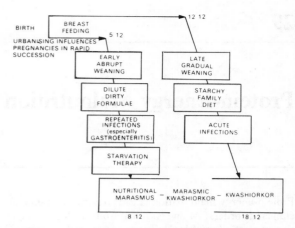

Fig. 29.1 Paths leading from early weaning to nutritional marasmus and from protracted breast feeding to kwashiorkor (McLaren)[6]

proportions by outbreaks of febrile illnesses such as malaria, measles or gastroenteritis. A heavy load of intestinal helminths also contributes to the disease.

Both marasmus and kwashiorkor arise as a result of poverty and ignorance. Even if food is available and there is the money to buy it, many mothers have received no satisfactory instruction in infant feeding. Eggs, fish, meat and sometimes milk may not be given to children because custom or taboos do not allow them. Unsuitable commercial food preparations may be purchased or good preparations misused.

In parts of many underdeveloped countries between 0 and 5 per cent of children have severe PEM and up to 50 per cent have moderate forms, which usually means underweight children. The type of severe PEM differs greatly. In large cities, in South America and in Asia, marasmus is generally commoner than kwashiorkor, but in Africa south of the Sahara kwashiorkor is often commoner. There traditional children's diets are often based on cassava and have a low protein/energy ratio. Accurate figures for the incidence of severe PEM can be obtained only by special surveys, as neither kwashiorkor nor marasmus are notifiable.

Associated nutrients deficiencies. Deficiencies of retinol, folate, iron, magnesium and potassium are commonly found in PEM and may be the presenting clinical feature. Deficiency of retinol is the most important as it may lead to keratomalacia and permanent blindness. Research reports suggest that lack of zinc, copper, chromium, selenium, pyridoxine, vitamins E and K and essential fatty acids may each be important in some circumstances. Thus in individual cases the cause of the child's disease and the clinical features may vary greatly.

Table 29.1 Classification of PEM (FAO/WHO)[7]

	Body weight as percentage of standard	Oedema	Deficit in weight for height
Kwashiorkor	80–60	+	+
Marasmic kwashiorkor	<60	+	++
Marasmus	<60	0	++
Nutritional dwarfing	<60	0	minimal
Underweight child	80–60	0	+

CLINICAL FEATURES

The clinical presentation depends on the type, severity and duration of the dietary deficiencies. The five forms summarised in Table 29.1, are described separately, but each is part of the whole PEM spectrum. When describing the metabolic disorders and morbid anatomy, and the treatment, and prevention of the disease, the different forms are considered together.

Nutritional marasmus

There is a failure to thrive, irritability, fretfulness or, alternatively, apathy. Diarrhoea is frequent. Many infants are hungry, but some are anorexic. The child is wizened and shrunken and there is little or no subcutaneous fat (Fig. 29.2). There is often dehydration. The weight is much below the standard for age. The temperature may be subnormal. If the disease is of long duration, the length of the child is also below the standard, but less so than the weight. There is usually watery diarrhoea with acid stools. If infective gastroenteritis is added, the diarrhoea is severe. The abdomen may be shrunken or distended with gas. Because of the thinness of the abdominal wall, peristalsis may be easily visible. The muscles are weak and atrophic and this, together with the lack of subcutaneous fat, makes the limbs appear as skin and bone.

The skin and mucous membranes may be dry and atrophic, but the characteristic changes found in kwashiorkor are not usually present. Evidence of vitamin deficiencies may or may not be found.

Nutritional marasmus presents a clinical picture similar to marasmus produced by infections or other wasting diseases. Indeed in any infant with PEM there is usually more than one cause and each must be diagnosed if treatment is to be successful.

Psychological disturbances, resulting from a lack of a mother's love and care, can depress the appetite, and hence may be a factor in the causation of marasmus.

Kwashiorkor

There is oedema together with failure to thrive, anor-

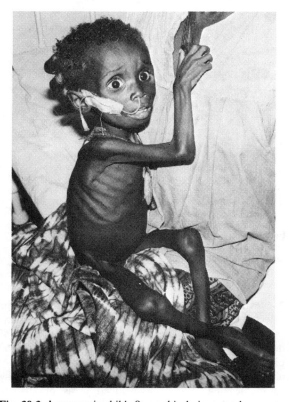

Fig. 29.2 A marasmic child. Some skin lesions can be seen on the shoulders, and the hair is thinned over the temples. Tube used for nasogastric feeding is strapped to the cheek. (Photo by Dr. R. G. Whitehead)

exia, diarrhoea and a generalised unhappiness or apathy. An infection often precipitates the onset and may be the reason for bringing the child to the doctor.

Failure of growth is an early sign, though oedema and the presence of some subcutaneous fat make the weight loss less striking than in marasmus.

Oedema may be slight or gross depending partly on the amount of salt and water in the diet. It may be distributed over the whole body, including the face, but is usually more marked on the lower limbs (Fig. 29.3).

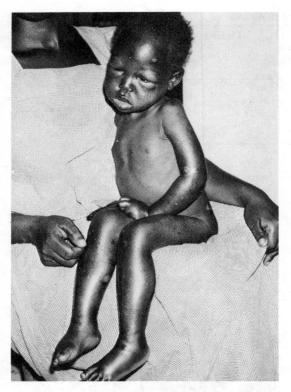

Fig. 29.3 A child with kwashiorkor in Uganda, showing oedema of face, feet and hands, and skin lesions. (Photo by Dr R. G. Whitehead)

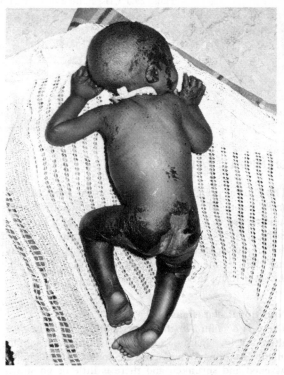

Fig. 29.4 A child with kwashiorkor, showing pigmented skin lesions especially over the buttocks, thighs, side of head and backs of hands. (By courtesy of Professor Walter Gordon)

Ascites and pleural effusions are usually slight and, if detected clinically, suggest the presence of an infection.

The characteristic **dermatosis** consists of areas of desquamation and areas of both hypo- and hyper-pigmentation. The skin first becomes thickened as if varnished. This then peels and appears like 'flaky paint', leaving cracks or denuded areas of shallow ulceration. In moderate cases the dermatosis resembles crazy paving; when severe, the desquamated part of the child's body looks as if there has been a burn. The lower limbs, buttocks and perineum are usually most affected but ulcers can occur over pressure points and deep cracks in skinfolds. The lesions are determined in part by associated skin infections and trauma. In maize-eating areas pellagrous features may also be present in parts of the skin that are exposed to light. The skin lesions heal with areas of depigmentation. Figure 29.4 shows moderately severe skin lesions on the buttocks which are starting to heal.

The **hair** is sparse, soft and thin. Negro children lose their characteristic curl. There may be changes in pigmentation with diffuse patches or streaks which may be red, blond or grey in colour. This is seen more often in Negro than in Asian children. Because hair takes time to grow it reflects the child's nutrition one to three months earlier. It is easy to pull out with forceps a few hairs from the occipital region and to examine them later under the microscope. Changes in the structure of the hair root, such as a reduced diameter of the bulb, provide an index of the nutritional state which may be useful in population at risk of protein-energy malnutrition.[8]

Angular stomatitis, cheilosis and a smooth atrophic tongue are commonly seen, as is ulceration around the anus.

Watery diarrhoea or large semisolid, acid stools are usual. The liver can generally be palpated and is firm and not tender. The hepatomegaly is sometimes marked.

The muscles are always wasted and as a result many children regress in their physical development and may no longer be able to walk or crawl.

Some degree of anaemia is always present and may be severe, though this is unusual. Every variety of haematological picture may be found. As discussed on page 467, protein deficiency itself may give rise to anaemia, but the diets of the children have often been lacking in iron and folic acid and in addition there may be impaired absorption of these nutrients from the gut.

Apathy is a characteristic feature and the child appears constantly unhappy. Neurological features are unusual, but some children during recovery have unexplained tremors resembling Parkinsonism.

Kwashiorkor has to be distinguished from marasmus and from oedema arising from renal or hepatic disease, heart failure or severe anaemia. A careful history and clinical examination including examination of the urine for protein should suffice to exclude these.

Marasmic kwashiorkor

In areas where PEM is endemic, many patients coming to a hospital or clinic show a mixture of some of the features of both marasmus and kwashiorkor. These children are sometimes said to have marasmic kwashiorkor, but their condition is often referred to simply as protein-energy malnutrition. As already explained, this is due to the varying nature of the dietary deficiency and the social factors responsible for the disease and the presence or absence of infections.

Nutritional dwarfing or stunting

Some children adapt to prolonged insufficiency of food — energy and protein — by a marked retardation of growth. Weight and height are both reduced and in the same proportion, so they appear superficially normal. When weight or height is checked against standards for normal children it is seen that they resemble children a year or more younger.

The underweight child

For every florid case of kwashiorkor or marasmus there are usually several children with mild to moderate PEM. Like an iceberg, there is more malnutrition below the surface than is visible above. Children with subclinical PEM can, however, be detected by their weight for age or weight for height which are significantly below normal. In areas where kwashiorkor is the predominant form of PEM, they may have reduced plasma albumin and sometimes other biochemical signs of protein deficiency. These children are growing up smaller than their genetic potential and, of greater importance, in many environments they are at risk of gastroenteritis, respiratory and other infections, which can precipitate frank malnutrition. Mild to moderate PEM is probably the major reason why the mortality in children from 1 to 4 years of age in some parts of Africa, Asia and Latin America is 30 to 40 times higher than in Europe or North America.

For the above reasons doctors, medical assistants and nurses should recognise growth retardation in its early phase. Failure to appreciate its presence and significance, when a child is brought to a clinic for what may be at first a minor ailment, leads to ineffective therapy. This may be followed by repeated outpatient visits, subsequent hospitalisation and all too often a fatal outcome.

Growth retardation can be recognised by weighing and measuring the child and referring to standard charts or tables (p. 519). Nutritional dwarfing must be distinguished from other causes of dwarfing such as renal disease, endocrine disorders, various forms of the malabsorption syndrome and congenital metabolic disorders. In the majority of cases, the dietary and clinical history and a physical examination suffice to make the diagnosis clear.

BIOCHEMICAL AND METABOLIC DISORDERS

The clinical features of PEM are a consequence, direct or indirect, of an insufficient supply of energy and of amino acids to the tissues, which need them for protein synthesis. As a result there is a failure of function of the different organs. Effective treatment of the disorder depends on some understanding of the biochemical lesions and of the effects of associated vitamin and mineral deficiencies.

Body composition

A high body water content, loss of the fat stores and loss of protein from the wasted muscles and other tissues greatly alter the chemical composition of the child. Table 29.2 illustrates the differences which may be found. Children with PEM are not only underweight, but their tissues are abnormal in composition. With treatment dramatic gain of weight is associated with a return to normal body composition.

A further point has been brought out by careful chemical analysis of the bodies of children who had died of PEM.[9] The total protein in the body amounted to 62 per cent of the expected value in a normal child. Of this protein 42 per cent was collagen. In a normal child collagen amounts to 27 per cent of the total protein.

Table 29.2 The chemical composition which might be found in a normal child and in one severely ill with PEM, marasmic-kwashiorkor, each aged 1 year

| | Normal | | PEM | |
	(kg)	(%)	(kg)	(%)
Body weight	10.0	100	5.0	100
Water	6.2	62	4.0	80
Protein	1.7	17	0.6	12
Fat	1.5	15	0.1	2
Minerals	0.6	6	0.3	6

Table 29.3 Mean daily intakes of energy and protein and percentage of feed refused by 8 children aged 10 to 36 months during recovery from PEM[10]

	Energy kJ/kg	kcal/kg	Protein (g/kg)	Feed refused (%)
Period of rapid recovery	670	160	3.7	0.5
Intermediary period	636	152	3.5	3
Full recovery	485	116	2.7	27

Hence the collagen protein, which turns over very slowly, is mostly retained, but a large part of the cellular protein is lost.

General metabolism

The metabolic rate is reduced but probably no more than cell mass; there is no evidence of any economy in the utilisation of energy by the cells. Adaptive changes in the utilisation of protein are described on page 52. The tissues have a full capacity to utilise both energy and protein, once these become available. This is well shown by the high intake of both energy and protein when children in Jamaica with PEM were given free access to food and encouraged to eat (Table 29.3).[10] The figures after recovery are representative of a normal child, but during the period of rapid recovery energy utilisation was nearly 40 per cent above normal. Children did not begin to refuse feeds until body weight approached the normal for their age, a good example of the regulatory mechanism for control of body weight. The recovery process has a thermodynamic efficiency of about 20 per cent.

In an acute case in an infant or young child, provided electrolyte disturbances are corrected and infections are treated, the cells are well able to utilise nutrients to restore the lost tissues. The above figures provide background information for drawing up dietary schedules for use in treatment (p. 287)

Protein metabolism

The disorder in the supply of amino acids is illustrated by characteristic changes in the pattern of plasma amino acids.[11] Plasma concentrations of essential amino acids, especially branched chain amino acids and tyrosine are low, but those of some non-essential amino acids may be higher than normal. As soon as treatment with protein starts, the concentration of amino acids in the plasma rises and there may be an overflow aminoaciduria.

The plasma albumin concentration is low, owing to a failure of synthesis in the liver. In patients with severe kwashiorkor it is usually below 20 and sometimes below 10 g/l. In marasmus the concentration is also lowered, but not to the same extent, and values around 25 g/l are common. A rise in plasma albumin is a useful sign of recovery. A low concentration certainly is in part responsible for the oedema which is often present.

Plasma IgG is often raised if infections are present, but other immunoglobulins are usually normal. Plasma transferrin is lowered, especially in severe cases, and may be a better guide to prognosis than plasma albumin. Plasma retinol-binding protein is also lowered and this may be a contributory cause of keratomalacia.

Concentrations of some plasma enzymes are reduced, reflecting depletion of these enzymes in the tissues and organs. Low values for cholinesterase, alkaline phosphatase, amylase and lipase have been reported.

The blood urea is usually low and may fall to 1 mmol/l (6 mg/100 ml). This reflects a reduced protein intake rather than a lowered rate of protein catabolism. Urinary creatinine is also reduced, reflecting decreased muscle mass.

Lipid metabolism

A fatty liver is characteristic of kwashiorkor but is unusual in marasmus. The excess fat in the liver is triglyceride. In kwashiorkor, but not in marasmus, plasma triglyceride and plasma cholesterol are low, due to a decreased ability of the liver cells to mobilise lipid in the form of lipoproteins.

In all forms of PEM, concentrations of FFA in the plasma tend to be high. This probably is a result of the state of partial starvation.

Carbohydrate metabolism

Blood glucose is usually normal. However, hypoglycaemia may occur and is a complication that should be kept in mind when caring for patients in hospital. Glucose tolerance is also usually normal but may be impaired. In some countries, but not in others, it has improved after giving 0.25 mg of chromium chloride.[12]

Electrolyte and water metabolism

A deficiency of potassium arises as a result of the diarrhoea and losses in the stools can amount to 20 to 30 mmol/day. Plasma [K+] is often below normal, and very low values, less than 2.5 mmol/l may be found. Measurements of the natural isotope ^{40}K with a total body counter in Jamaican children have indicated a total body K of 35 mmol/kg body weight, rising to 45 in three to four weeks on treatment with a daily potassium supplement of 6 to 8 mmol/kg.[13] This made good K depletion in the tissues and thereafter the concentration in the tissues remained constant, but the total body content rose further in the next 8 to 10 weeks as the wasted muscle and other tissue were replaced.

A deficiency of magnesium also arises from increased losses in the stools, and plasma magnesium concentrations are generally low.

Plasma [Na⁺] is usually normal. Low values are found if there have been large losses in sweat or stools and when intake of salt is diminished but intake of water is large. In this last circumstance the kidney's ability to conserve sodium may be insufficient to prevent depletion. Thus sodium deficiency is a possible complication of PEM, but is not a usual feature. If the water intake has been restricted and dehydration is marked, plasma [Na⁺] may be above normal.

Plasma [H⁺] may be either raised or lowered. Acidosis is probably due to poor circulation and consequent tissue hypoxia. Alkalosis is known to be associated with potassium depletion and a failure of the kidneys to excrete bicarbonate.

The total body water may increase from 60 per cent of body weight in normal children to 80 per cent.[14] The very high values occur in marasmic children, whose body fat had been greatly reduced. The increase is mainly in extracellular water but the cells are also overhydrated. The direct effects of PEM on body water and electrolytes may be complicated by acute or chronic diarrhoea, leading to dehydration.

The severity of clinical oedema is not closely associated with the size of the increase in total body water or with the level of plasma albumin. The cause and nature of the oedema still remains in part a mystery. Increases of urinary aldosterone, of antidiuretic hormone and of plasma renin have been reported by different investigators. The oedema may shift from one part of the body to another. Indeed, clinical dehydration and shock may be found in a child, associated with gross oedema in parts of the body. It is of interest that on therapy there may be an increase in oedema coincident with marked improvement in the general clinical condition. It is often several days before diuresis sets in and the oedema disappears.

Drug metabolism

Malnourished children are likely to have infections and may have other complications requiring drug treatment. With each drug that is given, no matter how well known it is, the question should be asked: 'How is this drug metabolised and in what way may it be altered in a malnourished child?' Some antibiotics and antimalarials act by interfering with nutrition more in the microorganism than in the human host, and they need to be used with care in PEM. The antibiotics streptomycin, chloramphenicol and the tetracyclines inhibit protein synthesis by interfering with the action of messenger or

transfer RNA. The antimalarial trimethoprim is a folate antagonist. The therapeutic action of these drugs depends on their acting on the bacterial and protozoan pathogens in much lower concentrations than on mammalian cells, which they may not enter readily owing to a permeability barrier. However, they should be used with caution in PEM.

Some drugs are carried in the circulation bound to plasma proteins. Kwashiorkor plasma with a low albumin content has a reduced binding capacity for salicylates, digoxin and the barbiturate thiopentone. After a standard dose, higher concentrations of the free form of the drug increase the risk of toxic effects. Many drugs are detoxicated in the liver by the microsomal enzyme-oxidising system and its function may be impaired in PEM. Then the half-life of the drug is prolonged and a standard dose may be toxic.

Present knowledge of how PEM affects the pharmokinetics of drugs is limited[15] and more research is needed. Meanwhile all drugs should be used with caution and standard doses based on body weight are often too high.

CHANGES IN THE ORGANS AND SYSTEMS OF THE BODY

Digestive organs

The cells of the pancreas and of the intestinal mucosa atrophy and cannot produce digestive enzymes in normal amounts. Aspirates of duodenal contents contain reduced amounts of amylase, trypsin and lipase.[16] Biopsy specimens of jejunal mucosa show that the activity of many enzymes, especially the disaccharidases, lactase, sucrase and maltase, are greatly reduced in the atrophic mucosa.[17] The mucosal atrophy is associated with impaired absorption of nutrients. Although activities of most enzymes rise with treatment, it may take many months before that of lactase returns to normal.

Liver

The clinical and biochemical features of the fatty liver found in kwashiorkor have already been described. The fat first accumulates in small droplets within liver cells, situated at the periphery of the lobules. The droplets increase in size and extend from the periphery to the centre of the lobules. In severe cases all the liver cells may be filled, each with a big fat droplet, pushing aside the cell nucleus and reducing the cytoplasm to a narrow rim.

Despite the marked structural change liver function is well maintained and severe liver failure is unusual. Plasma bilirubin is usually normal; prothrombin concentrations are often reduced, but return to normal on treatment with vitamin K. Plasma concentrations of alanine aminotransferase and isocitric dehydrogenase are usually normal and, if found raised, suggest the presence of damage from a bacterial or viral infection.

With proper treatment the lipid accumulated in the liver cells is all cleared with return to a normal structure. This is the usual course of events. The possible development of cirrhosis is discussed on page 290.

Endocrine organs

There is no evidence of primary hypofunction of the endocrine glands in PEM. Indeed the reverse may be the case. Plasma concentrations of growth hormone may be raised in kwashiorkor, as the pituitary responds effectively to the stimulus of protein depletion.

Many studies have shown that plasma concentrations of cortisol and other adrenocorticosteroids are normal or raised. Children with PEM respond to stimulation with corticotrophin with higher concentrations of plasma cortisol than normal but the half-life of cortisol in the plasma is prolonged, indicating impairment of cortisol metabolism in the tissues.[18] Several of the metabolic disturbances found in PEM may be related to the high concentration of circulating cortisol.

There is no specific disturbance of thyroid function. Owing to reduced plasma concentrations of thyroxine-binding protein and prealbumin in kwashiorkor total plasma thyroxine is often low, but free T_4 is usually normal or raised. In marasmus it is normal or low.

Impaired insulin secretion after glucose tolerance tests has already been described. A low insulin:cortisol ratio in the plasma is an adaptive change to chronic under-nutrition and is strongly correlated with retarded growth rates.[19]

Cardiovascular system

Atrophy of the heart, as found in starvation (p. 262), may be seen at autopsy or on radiographs of children with severe chronic PEM. This leads to a reduced cardiac output and a poor circulation. In many severe cases the extremities are cold and cyanosed and the pulse small or impalpable. The signs are associated with a high mortality but recovery may occur and, when it does, no cardiac disabilities remain.

The electrocardiogram shows low-voltage changes in the QRS complex and the T-wave may be depressed or inverted. Some of these changes are rapidly reversed by potassium therapy. In the myocardium of fatal cases, there is usually cellular infiltration and necrosis of individual fibrils, and the histological picture is similar to myocarditis.[20]

Kidneys

Mild albuminuria may be found but there is no specific structural or functional abnormality of the kidneys. The glomerular filtration rate may be low, but this is probably due to dehydration or reduced cardiac output. The concentrating power of the kidneys is often poor, but this may be the result of depression of tubular function by electrolyte deficiencies. Aminoaciduria occurs when protein is fed. These signs of renal dysfunction are not severe enough to complicate the clinical picture and are not responsible for the oedema. They are all reversible by treatment.

Immunological system

The immune responses of the body are produced by cells arising in the thymus, lymph nodes and spleen, the lymphoreticular organs. These are very immature at birth and develop rapidly in the first two years of life. A large literature on the effects of inanition and malnutrition in man and experimental animals was reviewed as long ago as 1925 by Jackson.[21] In young malnourished animals, atrophy of the thymus is marked and often greater than that of other organs. Atrophy of the lymph nodes and spleen is usually less obvious except when inanition has been severe and prolonged.

In both marasmus and kwashiorkor the thymus, tonsils, spleen and other lymphoid tissues are atrophied.[22] These changes are accompanied by a delayed or absent tuberculin response and other skin hypersensitivity reactions; reduced complement activity in the serum, especially the C3 component; reduced numbers of thymus-dependent lymphocytes (T cells) in the blood; reduced lymphocytes transformation in response to phytohaemoglutinin. The bactericidal action of neutrophil leucocytes is also impaired.[23] These signs of reduced cell-mediated immunity are in contrast to a usually unimpaired humoral immunity; the response to injected antigens is often normal and plasma IgG may be higher than normal.

The depression of cell-mediated immunity is attributable mainly to protein deficiency but lack of zinc, folate and other nutrients are sometimes in part the cause. That it is responsible for the high mortality from measles, gastroenteritis and other common infections in malnourished young children seems beyond doubt. Once the immunological system has reached maturity it is much less susceptible to malnutrition, and the evidence that in adults the state of nutrition has a major effect on the course of infectious diseases is controversial (see Chap. 59).

TREATMENT

Children who are seriously ill require treatment in hospital as their recovery depends on high standards of clinical skill and nursing care, with some laboratory support. When the acute phase of the illness is over, they need several weeks of special feeding and some medical supervision before recovery is complete.

Table 29.4 Milk feeds suitable for children with severe PEM

| | Composition | | | | | |
	Cow's milk (ml)	Water (ml)	Sugar (g)	Oil (g)	Energy (kJ(kcal)/dl)	Protein (g/dl)
Half strength	500	500	25	—	180 (38)	1.7
Full strength	1000	—	50	—	360 (75)	3.3
High energy	900	—	70	55	560 (133)	3.0

Circumstances frequently make it difficult to provide this in the home. In areas where PEM is common special rehabilitation centres for patients after discharge from hospital and also for children who are chronically undernourished but have not required admission to hospital have been shown to facilitate full recovery.

Resuscitation

Most children admitted to hospital have had repeated attacks of diarrhoea and often of vomiting and as a result are dehydrated. Some of these respond to oral rehydration therapy (p. 436), but, if the response is not prompt or the dehydration is severe, intravenous fluids should be given at once.

The infusion fluids that may be used, precautions necessary in their administration and biochemical monitoring are described in Chapter 52. The amount of fluid given depends on the clinical progress and less may be needed if there is oedema. The composition of the fluid requires modification if acidosis is marked and if there is either hypo- or hypernatraemia. The latter is uncommon but potentially dangerous. A small infusion of plasma is beneficial when there is severe peripheral circulatory failure and of whole blood or red cells when there is severe anaemia. As in these conditions the myocardium may be damaged by hypoxia and there is a risk of acute heart failure, infusion should be slow and a fast diuretic (frusemide) given at the start.

Many patients have malaria, pneumonia, dysentery, staphylococcal and other infections and require the appropriate chemotherapy. In the malnourished, infections often do not cause fever and so may easily be overlooked. It is recommended that all severely malnourished children be given a short course of procaine benzylpenicillin and ampicillin. If ampicillin is not available, alternatives are chloramphenicol and tetracycline.

Hypothermia is often present and needs urgent treatment. At night infants may miss the heat from their mother's body and it is often wise to let their mothers sleep with them in hospital. Hypoglycaemia is also a common emergency; it is less likely to occur when a child is fed every two hours.

Feeding

From the first or second day the child should be given a dilute milk feed with added sugar. When this is accepted, the strength can be increased and a vegetable oil added to give extra energy. Table 29.4 gives the composition of suitable feeds, as recommended by WHO.[24]

Milk from goats, ewes or buffaloes can be used. Buffalo's milk contains 7.5 per cent fat, more than twice that of cow's milk. As fat is poorly tolerated by seriously ill children, it should at first be diluted with up to an equal part of boiled water.

When fresh milk is not available, milk preparations may be used. Evaporated milk (500 ml), full cream milk powder (150 g), skimmed milk powder (75 g) and K-MIX2 (100 g) may be substituted for one litre of milk. K-MIX2 is a formula produced for and distributed by UNICEF for initiation of treatment of severe PEM. It is made up of calcium caseinate (3 parts), skimmed milk powder (5 parts) and sucrose (10 parts) with added retinol palmitate.

The fluid needs of young children are about 150 ml kg⁻¹ daily. These are met by giving one of the above feeds, the total daily amount being determined by body weight. At first this is divided amongst 12 feeds given every 2 hours. When this is well tolerated, eight feeds can be given every 3 hours and later six feeds every 4 hours. If a child is at first too weak to suck, the feeds can be given through a nasogastric tube as described in Chapter 52.

Infants who are seriously ill improve when given 1 g protein kg⁻¹ body weight daily. Good recovery can be obtained with 2 g and recovery is not accelerated by giving more than 3.5 g. With any of the above foods, protein intake is satisfactory.

The supply of energy presents a more difficult problem. A high energy diet is required and this can only be made up by including large amounts of fat. Impaired fat absorption is characteristic of severe PEM and some infants cannot at first tolerate the amount of fat in whole cow's milk. Feeds then have to be made up from skimmed milk powder or K-MIX2 formula. With these alone improvement should occur but is slow. A vegetable oil can then be incorporated into the feeds in gradually increasing amounts. A high energy feed based on skimmed milk powder or K-MIX2 requires 85 g of vegetable oil in one litre of feed.

All the figures given above are to be taken as guidelines and not as part of a rigid schedule. For some children they are too much or too little, or a too concentrated or a too dilute feed. When a child is not making the progress anticipated, the clinical condition should be reviewed and in the light of this changes in makeup and amounts of feeds considered.

All children in hospital with severe PEM should receive a daily supplement of vitamins and minerals. Many of those who had previously had repeated attacks of diarrhoea are depleted of magnesium and zinc.

As soon as children are able to take normal food and any infection or other complication is under control, it is economical for the medical services to discharge them to a centre where their nutritional rehabilitation can be supervised.

A full account of the clinical management of severe PEM with details of how feeds can be made up is given in a WHO publication.[24]

Rehabilitation

'Is hospital the place for the treatment of malnourished children?' This question was the title of a review by Cook in 1971.[25] He showed that when children who had been treated in hospital for PEM were followed up the results were frequently disastrous. In several series about one third were dead within a year from the very disease for which they had been 'successfully treated' in hospital and many others were still seriously malnourished. There were causes for these sad outcomes which still persist. The first is poverty of the families and the second is failure to involve parents, particularly mothers, in the treatment and recovery. About the first there is little that the health services can do but nutritional rehabilitation is a practical approach to the second.

In children who are not desperately ill with complicated PEM, and those who are recovering after resuscitation, management should combine appropriate nourishment and nutrition education. The concept of nutrition rehabilitation is based on practical nutrition training for mothers, in which they learn by feeding their children back to health, under sympathetic supervision and using local foods. The principles can be carried out in three settings, now described.

Residential units

In these, mothers are admitted with their children. Under the guidance of a nutrition demonstrator they work as a group, and prepare a suitable therapeutic diet of available foods and feed their children. The whole of their time is a practical learning experience, and the fact that they are involved in their child's recovery makes a significant impact.

Day care centres

In these, mothers only help with the cooking and feeding on one or two days a week though the children attend daily. It therefore takes longer for mothers to appreciate the essential messages about better feeding, but it involves less domestic disruption than admission.

Domicilliary rehabilitation

This is done in the home and is more personal, as nutrition advice and help is given on a one-to-one basis by a nutrition demonstrator or specially trained health worker. Instruction and help can be precise, relating to the individual child and the particular home circumstances, but it is relatively more costly in personnel time and lacks the beneficial effects of mutual encouragement and group dynamics.

Successful nutrition rehabilitation requires detailed knowledge about local foods, cooking and feeding practices. The cost, seasonal availability and nutritive values of local foods is fundamental. Based on this knowledge, a diet shoud be designed which supplies enough nourishment for a significant improvement in the malnutrition, but is economical enough to be possible for even poor families. The smaller the changes from the normal patterns of cooking and feeding, the better the prospects that the dietary regime will be accepted and used. This requires a blend of biochemical and anthropological knowledge, and various compromises are necessary. Another key element is sympathetic and effective communication of these messages, and an appropriately trained nutrition demonstrator from the same cultural group is probably the most effective agent. There should be no use of nutritional terminology, but an emphasis on feeding children more frequently and effectively with mixtures of the local foods. Mothers who take an active part in preparing the food, feeding their children and watching them recover their health and vitality are more likely to retain the ideas and continue with a similar regime at home.

Figures 29.5 and 29.6 show schematically the roles of residential and day care nutrition rehabilitation units in relation to the health services and the community. They are taken from a review by Cutting.[26] Every medical, health and nutrition service which is regularly treating malnourished children is wasting effort and resources if it does not include a practical training component in the management regime. Some form of nutrition rehabilitation is essential.

Concentration food supplements

For rapid replacement of lost tissues and catch-up growth, children need a high energy diet (up to 840 kJ (200 kcal) kg^{-1} body weight daily) with ample protein.

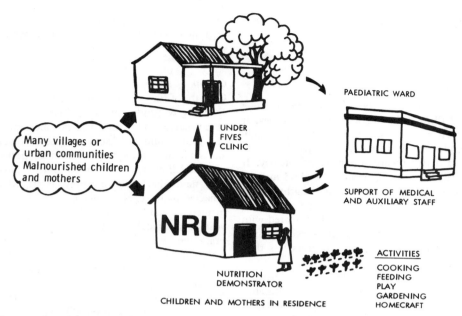

Fig. 29.5 Influences of nutrition rehabilitation units

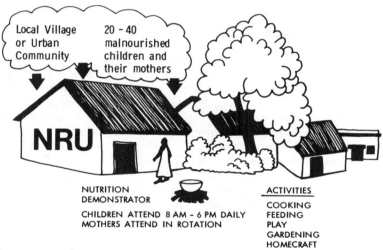

Fig. 29.6 Day care rehabilitation

It is often difficult to get a child to eat such large amounts when the energy density of the family foods is low, especially if rice or bananas are the staple food. Malnourished children need supplements of concentrated foods. These can be made locally from available sources but commercially manufactured supplements are valuable and even essential in many circumstances.

The 1975 edition of this book gave a table setting out the composition, protein content and price of 40 protein food mixtures used in different countries for the re-habilitation of children with PEM. The prototype was Incaparina, which was developed in Guatemala and made up from maize, cotton seed flour, vitamin A, lysine and calcium carbonate. A contemporary list would probably contain over 100 such mixtures. They are prepared either by government agencies or commercial firms, most of them are used only in the country of origin. Two that were developed in the USA are widely used internationally and distributed free by UNICEF and other charities. They are known as CSM, a corn (maize), soya, milk mixture and WSB, a wheat soya blend.

PROGNOSIS

A child may suffer for a short period of its life from one of the forms of PEM and make a complete recovery. If growth has been retarded for a short period or only slightly, the child may reach the normal size for its age quickly, provided the dietary supply is satisfactory. If growth is retarded for a long period, the child may be stunted and develop into a small, but healthy adult. Kruger[27] measured 154 children treated in Kampala six to 11 years earlier and found them small compared with a control group of Baganda children. Bone age, assessed by X-ray of the wrist, was one or two years less than chronological age.

If the disease is so severe as to demand treatment in hospital, the prognosis is uncertain and often bad. Thus out of 343 children admitted to hospital in Jamaica, 15 per cent died, 12 per cent recovered slowly, 30 per cent at an intermediate rate and 43 per cent rapidly.[28] When these children returned home and ate the usual diet for poor Jamaican families, they gained height and weight between the ages of 2 and 10 years comparable to controls in the same families and not greatly below Boston standards for height but less for weight.

Two aspects of prognosis merit further discussion.

The liver disorder

The fatty degeneration of the liver heals completely without fibrosis in the vast majority of cases. However, cirrhosis and other disorders of the liver in adolescents and adults are relatively common in many parts of the tropics where PEM is endemic. It is possible that an infection, e.g. virus hepatitis, a mycotoxin or a chemical toxin, e.g. alcohol or iron, is more likely to lead to progressive liver disease if it is acting on a liver damaged by chronic malnutrition.

Mental retardation

The possibility that severe early malnutrition may permanently impair mental development is of great importance. In pigs and rats severe underfeeding early in postnatal life leads to a permanent decrease in myelination of nerve cells, and reduced DNA content and other biochemical changes in the brain. This may be associated with impaired learning ability and poor performance in tests of behavioural activity.

There are dangers in extrapolating from these results, well established in animals, to man. The time relationship between brain development, birth and weaning differs in babies, piglets and young rats. In studying the processes of learning in man it is inevitably difficult to separate the effects of malnutrition from those of deprivation of parental and other social care.

Growth of the brain

Growth of the human brain has been measured by Dobbing & Sands[29] by comparisons of a large number of normal brains obtained at postmortem from fetuses and young children. Rapid increase of total cell number starts at midgestation and continues past one year of postnatal life; neurones appear during intrauterine life and neuroglial cells multiply later. Myelination is reflected by the cholesterol content of the brain. It starts to increase before birth and continues past the second year of postnatal life. Compared with the rest of the brain the cerebellum has a more rapid growth spurt, which all takes place in the first year after birth.

Children in Cape Town who had been severely malnourished in the first year of life had at the age of 7 years a smaller head circumference, reflecting reduced brain growth, and a lower IQ than a control group.[30] The brains of children in Jamaica who died in the first year of life weighed less than normal and had proportional reductions of DNA and cholesterol.[31] However, a small brain in a wasted child may be capable of catch-up growth.

Intellectual development

Many observers have reported that children who had survived severe PEM in early childhood performed less well in intelligence tests than controls. However, a poor performance could be due to their growing up in an unfavourable pyschological environment rather than to a short period of malnutrition in early life.

The severe famine in Dutch cities from December 1944 to April 1945 (p. 526) affected the nutrition of large numbers of infants during their last months *in utero* and early months after birth. Subsequently cohorts of Dutch males born between March 1943 and February 1946 were examined at the age of 19 years, when they had to register for military service. No effect of the famine was found on either the incidence of mental retardation or the distribution of measurements of the IQ in any cohort.[32]

In a sibling study of Jamaican children IQs at ages 6 to 10 were lower in children who had been admitted for malnutrition in their first two years, and these children tended to be withdrawn in their behaviour.[33] In Uganda a follow-up of children admitted to hospital with acute kwashiorkor showed no correlation between the severity of the disease and subsequent intelligence tests, but those admitted with chronic malnutrition scored less well than controls[34] Two monographs[35,36] review the whole subject of early malnutrition and mental development.

In the present state of knowledge it is proper to warn governments that failure to provide adequate nutritional services for mothers and young children may well lead to a school population with a diminished capacity for learning. On the other hand, a mother whose child has for any reason suffered a period of severe malnutrition and made a good recovery may be reassured that subsequent mental development is not likely to be impaired seriously, if at all.

PREVENTION

Prevention of PEM is the fight against poverty and ignorance and this is discussed in Chapter 56.

REFERENCES

1. Williams C D 1933 A nutritional disease of childhood associated with a maize diet. Arch Dis Child 8: 423–33
2. Brock J F, Autret M 1952 Kwashiorkor in Africa. WHO Mongr Ser no. 8. WHO, Geneva
3. Trowell H C, Davies J N P, Dean R F A 1954 Kwashiorkor. Arnold, London
4. Jelliffe D B 1959 Protein-calorie malnutrition in tropical preschool children. J Pediatr 54: 227–56
5. Alleyne G A O, Hay R W, Picou D I, Stanfield J P, Whitehead R G 1977 Protein-energy malnutrition. Arnold, London
6. McLaren D A 1966 A fresh look at protein-calorie malnutrition. Lancet 2: 485–8
7. FAO/WHO 1971 Expert Committee on Nutrition, 8th report. WHO Tech Rep Ser no. 477
8. Bradfield R B 1974 Hair tissue as a medium for the differential diagnosis of protein-calorie malnutrition. J Pediatr 84: 294–6
9. Picou E, Halliday D, Garrow J S 1966 Total body protein, collagen and non-collagen protein in infantile protein malnutrition. Clin Sci 30: 345–51
10. Ashworth A 1969 Growth rates in children recovering from protein-calorie malnutrition. Br J Nutr 23: 835–45
11 Saunders S J, Truswell A S, Barbezat G O, Wittman W, Hansen J D L 1967 Plasma free aminoacid pattern in protein calorie malnutrition. Lancet 2: 795–7
12. Gürson C T, Saner G 1971 Effect of chromium on glucose utilization in marasmic protein-calorie malnutrition. Am J Clin Nutr 24: 1313–9
13. Alleyne G A O, Viteri F, Alvarado J 1970 Indices of body composition in infantile malnutrition: total body potassium and urinary creatinine. Am J Clin Nutr 23: 875–8
14. Garrow J S, Fletcher K, Halliday D 1965 Body composition in severe infantile malnutrition. J Clin Invest 44: 417–24
15. Buchanan N 1984 Effect of protein-energy malnutrition on drug metabolism in man. World Rev Nutr Diet 43: 129–39
16. Barbezat G O, Hansen J D L 1968 The exocrine pancreas and protein calorie malnutrition. Pediatrics 42: 77–92
17. James W P T 1968 Intestinal absorption in protein-calorie malnutrition. Lancet 1: 333–4
18. Alleyne G A O, Young V H 1967 Adrenocortical function in children with severe protein-calorie malnutrition. Clin Sci 33: 189–200
19. Coward W A, Lunn P G 1981 The biochemistry and physiology of kwashiorkor and marasmus. Br Med Bull 37: 19–24
20. Wharton B A, Balmer S E, Somers K, Templeton A C 1969 The myocardium in kwashiorkor. Q J Med 38: 107–16
21. Jackson C M 1925 The effects of inanition and malnutrition upon growth and structure. Churchill, London, p 261–99
22. Smythe P M, Brereton-Stiles G G, et al 1971 Thymolymphatic deficiency and depression of cell mediated immunity in protein calorie malnutrition. Lancet 2: 939–44
23. Chandra R K 1983 Nutrition, immunity, and infection: present knowledge and future directions. Lancet 1: 688–91
24. World Health Organization 1981 The treatment and management of severe protein-energy malnutrition. WHO, Geneva
25. Cook R 1971 Is hospital the place for the treatment of malnourished children? J Trop Pediatr 17: 15–25
26. Cutting W A M 1983 Nutritional rehabilitation. In: McLaren D A (ed) Nutrition in the community. Wiley, Chichester, p 321–37
27. Kruger R H 1969 Some long term effects of severe malnutrition in early life. Lancet 2: 514–7
28. Garrow J S, Pike M C 1967 The short-term prognosis of some primary infantile malnutrition. Br J Nutr 21: 155–65
29. Dobbing J, Sands J 1973 Quantitative growth and development of human brain. Arch Dis Child 48: 757–67
30. Stock M B, Smythe P M 1963 Does undernutrition during infancy inhibit brain growth and subsequent intellectual development? Arch Dis Child 38: 546–52
31. Rosso P, Hormozabal J, Winick M 1970 Changes in brain weight, cholesterol, phospholipid and DNA content in malnourished children. Am J Clin Nutr 23: 1275–9
32. Stein Z, Susser M, Saenger G, Marrolla F 1972 Nutrition and mental performance: prenatal exposure to the Dutch famine of 1944–1945 seems not related to mental performance at age 19. Science NY 178: 708–13
33. Hertzig M E, Birch H G, Richardson S A, Tizard J 1972 Intellectual levels of school children severely malnourished during the first two years of life. Pediatrics 49: 814–24
34. Hoorweg J, Stanfield J P 1976 The effects of protein energy malnutrition in early childhood on intellectual and motor abilities in later childhood and adolescence. Dev Med Child Neurol 18: 330–50
35. Winick M 1976 Malnutrition and brain development. Oxford University Press, New York
36. Lloyd-Still J D 1976 Malnutrition and intellectual development. MTP Press, Lancaster

30

Endemic Goitre

Julius Caesar was impressed by the enlarged necks of people living in some Alpine regions. In Renaissance paintings the Madonna and court ladies were often painted with necks which suggest moderate enlargement of the thyroid glands. The British anatomist Thomas Wharton, who gave the thyroid gland its name, thought that it served to beautify the neck particularly in women, to whom for this reason a larger gland had been assigned. But Paracelsus in the fifteenth century pointed out that in areas where goitres were large and frequent some of the children were cretins.

The term 'goitre' is used to denote enlargement of the thyroid gland of whatever kind. Simple goitre is said to be present when the gland is visible and palpable, but the subject has no symptoms either of hypothyroidism or hyperthyroidism. It is endemic in many parts of the world and in these areas it is estimated that 200 million people are affected. Such goitres do not usually affect health, but they sometimes result in complications which may have serious consequences. Environmental rather than hereditary factors determine the prevalence of most simple goitres — especially dietary factors, of which iodine deficiency is the major one. A history of iodine and its relation to the thyroid gland is given on page 122.

A comprehensive account of the epidemiology, pathogenesis and prevention is given in a monograph by Stanbury & Hetzel.[1]

GEOGRAPHICAL DISTRIBUTION

Endemic goitre occurs chiefly in three types of terrain:
1. In mountainous areas of Europe, Asia, the Americas and Africa, such as the Alps, Himalayas, Andes, Rockies and Cameroon mountains and the Highlands of New Guinea.
2. On alluvial plains that were recently covered by glaciers, such as the area round the Great Lakes of North America and in some areas of New Zealand.
3. In isolated localities where the water in common use is obtained from wells or springs originating in limestone, as in Derbyshire and the Cotswolds in England.

The condition has always been most prevalent in remote rural areas where there is much poverty and sanitation and water supplies are primitive. In many endemic areas in underdeveloped countries goitres and their associated complications are still a major public health problem, but in prosperous communities, although small goitres may still be found in moderate numbers, the severity of the condition is much less than formerly.

It used to be thought that goitre occurred only in areas remote from the sea. It was even suggested that iodine vapour was carried inland by sea breezes to fertilise the neighbouring land. This idea is now discredited. First, the sea itself contains a very low concentration of iodine; secondly, edible plants grown near the sea have been found to contain no more iodine than those grown elsewhere; thirdly, goitre is quite common is some seaboard regions. It is true, however, that seafoods, fish and shellfish, are the richest food sources of iodine; so also is seaweed, from which iodine was first isolated. Carrigeen 'moss' a seaweed still used as food on the west coast of Scotland, may have unsuspected nutritive value in this regard; also in some parts of the Orient seaweed is used as food.

Derbyshire neck found a place in textbooks of medicine in the nineteenth century because goitre was so prevalent in the rural population of the Peak district, who at that time were greatly impoverished. In 1966 the West Derbyshire Medical Society[2] found that in a total population of 30 000, simple goitres with symptoms were present in 6.6 per cent of the females and that 2.5 per cent had been treated for thyroid abnormalities, mostly on account of evidence of hyperthyroidism. Endemic goitre is thus still a problem in Derbyshire, though much less than formerly. The decline probably began with the arrival of railways in the valleys, which made the people less dependent on locally grown foods.

Simple goitre may occur sporadically in persons born and raised far from areas where goitre is endemic. This can be caused by inherited dyshormonogenesis, by autoimmune or infective thyroiditis or by goitrogenic substances, or drugs, as well as by a low intake of iodine in a susceptible individual.

AETIOLOGY

The important of iodine in relation to the thyroid gland is discussed on page 122. The normal thyroid gland contains about 8 mg of iodine. In simple goitre this amount may be reduced to about 1 mg, even though the gland is larger. The essential cause of simple goitre is an inability of the thyroid gland to make sufficient thyroxine, which contains 64 per cent of iodine. Simple goitre arises most commonly at those periods in life when there is a general alteration in hormonal activity in the body, notably during adolescence and pregnancy. In endemic areas if the prevalence is low, only the women have goitres; but if the prevalence is high, the men may be almost equally affected.

Iodine deficiency. Marine[3] in the USA carried out experiments on trout in which the addition of iodine to the water prevented enlargement of the thyroid gland. He was the first to use iodised salt to prevent the appearance of goitre in schoolgirls living in an endemic area. The evidence that he collected focused attention on the iodine intake and proved that endemic goitre is essentially a deficiency disease. In general, the distribution of endemic goitre in the world goes hand in hand with signs of low iodine intake; these are a low iodine in water, low urinary excretion or low plasma concentrations of inorganic iodine. But the correlation is incomplete. Some individuals and some areas have less or more goitre than would be expected from indices of iodine intake. Evidently dietary and other factors can interfere with the availability of iodine for the thyroid gland.

Dirty water. An early advocate of the belief that simple goitre results from multiple causes, including iodine deficiency, was Sir Robert McCarrison.[4] In Gilgit, in the foothills of the Himalayas, there were eight villages in series, each deriving its water supply from the same stream — progressively contaminated with sewage from the village above. The incidence of goitre was highest in the lowest village. But a neighbouring village was entirely free from goitre; this village had an independent water supply from a spring. McCarrison himself and some army volunteers drank the filtered silt in the polluted water from the goitrous villages.[5] A third of them developed goitre in one to two months, whereas others who drank the silt after it had been boiled failed to do so. McCarrison's investigations suggest that faecal bacteria can produce a goitrogenic substance. The occurrence of goitre in the same valley was reinvestigated over 60 years later by an Anglo-Pakistan team.[6]

They did not confirm a correlation between goitre and bacterial counts in the water. They suggest that the silt McCarrison drank adsorbed the small amount of iodine in the water. It is still hard to see how the goitres could have appeared in such a short time.

Goitrogenic substances in food. In 1928 Chesney and his colleagues[7] at Johns Hopkins Hospital made the chance observation that rabbits raised in the laboratory for the study of syphilis and fed largely on cabbage developed goitres. This observation was followed up by Sir Charles Hercus[8] in New Zealand, who established the goitrogenic properties of cabbages, turnips and particularly the seeds of cabbage, mustard and rape.

Most of the goitrogens identified in plants are organic compounds containing sulphur, such as thioglycosides, isothiocyanates and thiocyanates.[9] These may be present in the plant as inactive forms that are converted into goitrogens in the plant or after ingestion in animal tissues. Thus in cabbage (*Brassica*) a thioglucoside, progoitrin, is converted by rats into 5-vinyl-2-thio-oxalidine, the active goitrin. The ability of plants and animals to convert these inactive forms into goitrogens varies. As yet none of these plant goitrogens has been shown unequivocally to be responsible for outbreaks of goitre in man.

Cattle may consume large amounts of brassica, depending on the forage, and some of the goitrogen passes into the milk. In Tasmania the incidence of goitre among children increased despite the distribution of potassium iodide tablets. At the same time the consumption of milk increased, and 'many-headed kale' was introduced to feed the dairy herds. It was thought that milk from these cows carried with it goitrogens derives from the kale[10] but attempts to isolate from the milk a substance with sufficiently strong goitrogenic properties were unsuccessful.[11]

In tropical Africa, notably Zaire, goitre is present in some districts but not in others and a goitrogen in cassava, a staple food, may be responsible. Cassava contains a glucoside, limarin, which yields thiocyanate on hydrolysis. The ratio of urinary iodine/urinary thiocyanate was found to correlate with the presence or absence of goitre.[12,13]

Simple goitre in non-endemic areas

In all parts of the world, patients can be found with simple goitres. Glasgow for instance is not an endemic areas, but many patients are seen with non-toxic goitres, for which there is no obvious cause. There is convincing evidence[14] that iodine deficiency was at least a contributory cause of the goitre in these patients. Their estimated dietary intake of iodine was only 60 per cent of the intake of controls and their urinary iodine excretion was only 50 per cent of the control level. Some of the other aetiological factors discussed above may also be operative in individual cases, but there is little doubt that the customary diet of most communities contains iodine in amounts which provide only a small margin of safety and that iodine deficiency, particularly in adolescents and young women, can occur in any locality.

CHEMICAL PATHOLOGY

Iodine is well absorbed from food and after absorption about half of it is normally taken up by the thyroid gland and the rest is excreted in the urine. If dietary iodine is insufficient, plasma inorganic iodide falls; urinary excretion falls too and may be used to indicate iodine intake. The pituitary responds by increasing the secretion of the thyrotrophin (TSH) and plasma TSH concentration is abnormally high in endemic goitre. This stimulates increased uptake of iodine by the gland and usually leads to enlargement of the gland. In mild cases normal plasma concentrations of thyroid hormones (T_3 and T_4) are maintained, but the proportion of T_3 to T_4 may be increased. This may be due to an adaptive change with increased synthesis of T_3.[15]

PATHOLOGY

The normal thyroid gland is composed of a multitude of follicles filled with eosin-staining colloid. This material consists of thyroglobulin, an iodine-containing protein, from which the normal hormonal secretions of the gland are derived. Each follicle is surrounded by a layer of cells which synthesise the hormones.

Simple goitre. The enlargement of the gland is due to both overgrowth (hyperplasia) of the cells lining the follicles and to an excess of colloid. The hyperplasia and accumulation of colloid in the iodine-deficient gland can perhaps be compared with the overgrowth of osteoblasts and accumulation of osteoid tissue that take place as a result of lack of calcium at the growing points of the bones in rickets.

Colloid goitre. Simple goitres that have been present for years may become very large, due to a massive accumulation of colloid in thin-walled follicles, and interfere with breathing. However, goitres which appear superficially to be small may cause serious respiratory embarrassment and other pressure effects by retrosternal growth. To most people a prominent goitre is unsightly, but in certain areas of Africa where the condition is endemic such tumours are considered a sign of beauty.

Nodular goitre. In long-standing cases of simple goitre another change sometimes takes place: the development of nodules which are localised areas of cellular proliferation within the gland. Similar nodules some-

times occur — perhaps for other reasons — in people who have never lived in a goitre area. Hyperthyroidism and malignant changes occur in rare instances in patients with nodular goitre.

CLINICAL SIGNS

The thyroid is the only endocrine organ apart from the testes that is readily accessible to clinical examination. The normal gland in an adult weighs 20 to 25 g. A very large goitre is obvious to everyone; recognition of small goitres is also simple and reproducible between observers. Difficulty arises in grading the size of goitres that lie between the just detectable and the very large. In field studies the following classification is recommended,

Grade O a   Thyroid not palpable or if palpable not larger than normal.

Grade O b   Thyroid distinctly palpable but usually not visible with the head in a normal or raised position; considered to be definitely larger than normal, i.e. at least as large as the distal phalanx of the subject's thumb.

Grade I   Thyroid easily palpable and visible with the head in either a normal or a raised position. The presence of a discrete nodule qualifies for inclusion in this grade.

Grade II   Thyroid easily visible with the head in a normal position.

Grade III   Goitre visible at a distance

Grade IV   Monstrous goitres

Observer variation is considerable and can make comparisons of grades meaningless, e.g. in a group of peopl   fore and after prophylactic iodine. In Derbyshire one family doctor recorded three small goitres and 78 of medium size and his neighbour 14 small ones and 12 of medium size.[2] Anyone planning a goitre survey needs to take steps to minimise the observer error. It is preferable to have two examiners. Some workers mark the outline of the thyroid on the skin (Fig. 30.1). Before going into the field examiners should have some training from a specialist in thyroid diseases.

CLINICAL EFFECTS AND COMPLICATIONS

In the great majority of cases of simple goitre there are no clinical manifestations due to hypofunction or hyperfunction of the thyroid gland. Simple colloid goitre may require surgical treatment either for aesthetic reasons or because of pressure effects on the adjacent structures. The following complications occur rarely: (1) hypothy-

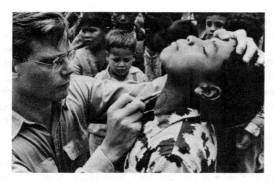

Fig. 30.1 A goitre survey in Guatemala

Fig. 30.2 Endemic goitre in children at an oasis in Egypt.
(By courtesy of Dr I. Abdou)

roidism, (2) hyperthyroidism, (3) cretinism, and (4) deaf-mutism. Such complications are more likely to be encountered in regions where endemic goitre is prevalent. These undesirable clinical effects and complications can be greatly reduced by the appropriate prophylactic measures described below. Figure 30.2 shows grades I and II goitres in Egyptian children.

TREATMENT

A simple goitre in a non-endemic area rarely requires treatment. The patient may be assured that no harm is likely to arise and that in time it will probably get smaller. If this does not occur and the goitre becomes disfiguring, iodine therapy is seldom effective, but thyroxine 0.2 to 0.3 mg/day may be given. This inhibits production of TSH by the pituitary gland and so reduces the size of the thyroid gland. If there is no response to thyroxine and the goitre continues to be disfiguring, thyroidectomy should be considered, and this is indi-

cated if the size of the goitre leads to obstruction of the trachea or if there is retrosternal extension.

Endemic cretinism
In places where endemic goitre is severe, cretinism may affect up to 5 per cent of the population. Endemic cretinism presents in two types.[16] In **nervous cretinism** there is mental deficiency, deaf mutism, spasticity and ataxia but features of hypothyroidism are hard to find. In **myxoedematous cretinism** there is dwarfism, signs of myxoedema and no goitre. The nervous type predominates in most areas of endemic goitre, but the myxoedematous type is a common in Zaire. Congenital cretinism occurring occasionally in Europe and North America is myxoedematous in type.

Nervous cretinism[17] can be prevented by giving a single injection of iodised poppy-seed oil to the women of childbearing age but it must be given before pregnancy starts. It thus appears that iodine is required for the early development of the nervous system before the fetal thyroid appears in the third month of gestation. In myxoedematous cretins the nervous system develops normally in the critical early months but the thyroid gland fails to adapt adequately by hypertrophy to severe iodine deficiency. The thyroid glands are small and uptake of radioiodine very low. Consequently such cretins have low plasma T_3 and T_4 with clinical signs of hypothyroidism, including dwarfism. Both types of cretinism are seen in endemic areas but the proportion of the two varies from region to region.

PREVENTION

Iodine prophylaxis when carried out effectively abolished endemic goitre.

Iodisation of table salt greatly reduced the prevalence of goitre in many countries, including the USA, Switzerland, Yugoslavia, New Zealand and countries in South America. In the USA iodised salt must contain 76 µg of iodine/g salt and daily consumption of salt by most people is between 2 and 6 g. Lower levels of iodisation are used in most other countries and are effective. Salt is not iodised in the UK. On account of its stability potassium iodate is preferable to potassium iodide for the iodisation of the crude moist salt consumed in many countries.

Where goitre is endemic daily intakes of dietary iodine are likely to be less than 50 µg. The aim is to increase this to the normal range of from 100 to 300 µg. The amount of iodine added to the salt should be related to the usual consumption of salt in the community so that individual iodine intakes fall within this range. Iodine given for medical purposes may cause allergic skin rashes and induce hyperthyroidism, but the risk of these adverse effects from iodised salt is minimal. Although iodised salt is used widely in the USA, not a single case of allergy to iodine has been reported.[18] Hyperthyroidism is known to have followed the introduction of iodised salt in only one instance. This was in Tasmania[10] where the number of patients with hyperthyroidism seen at the Launceston hospital increased and was unusually high in elderly men.[19] This was regarded as an acceptable price to pay for the eradication of endemic goitre.

Iodised oil injections provide an alternative means of prevention in parts of the world where the use of iodised salt is not possible and where endemic goitre is most severe and accompanied by cretinism. These are isolated communities with few if any roads and no large markets. The mountainous regions of Boliva and Ecuador, many parts of Nepal and the highlands of New Guinea are examples. There a vicious circle exists. Goitres are not merely a cosmetic problem, but impair the vitality of many of the people by causing hypothyroidism, and cretinism retards the intellectual development of children. The people are unable to do much to help themselves to break out of their bondage to iodine deficiency and the poverty that goes with it. It is for such communities that iodised oil injections offer promise as a medical measure to be applied to vulnerable groups, e.g. young adult women. In the mountainous regions of New Guinea, a single injection of iodised poppy-seed oil has been shown to correct the deficiency for a period of two to three years.[20] It also produced significant regression of goitre in a high proportion of cases within three months of the injection. Iodised oil has now been used successfully in many countries.[21]

Iodisation of the water supply in a remote village in Malaysia, where distribution of iodised salt and injection of iodised oil were impractical, reduced the prevalence of goitre from 61 to 30 per cent in nine months.[22] Iodinators consisting of cannisters containing iodine crystals were connected to main water pipes and a fraction of the water diverted through them.

Programmes for goitre control require continuous **surveillance** as the sad story from India shows.[23] In the early 1960s it was estimated that the population exposed to endemic goitre was about 120 million, nearly all in remote rural areas. Twelve plants for the iodisation of salt were set up. Surveys carried out 15 to 20 years later showed that these had had little impact. In 10 districts prevalence that had been between 20 and 50 per cent remained substantially unchanged. Falls in some were offset by increases in others. Production capacity in the plants was underused and distribution of the iodised salt was impeded by a failure to supply railway wagons and lack of supervision by state health authorities. The report concludes that 'goitre and similar health and nutritional problems are diseases of the poor and underprivileged and, therefore, apparently looked upon as their problems not ours. Unless health, nutrition and welfare programmes are executed in all seriousness, with a sense of urgency and dedication, the present drift will continue.'

REFERENCES

1. Stanbury J B, Hetzel B S (eds) 1980 Endemic goitre and endemic cretinism. Wiley, New York
2. West Derbyshire Medical Society 1966 Derbyshire neck: thyroid abnormalities in the Derbyshire Peak district. Lancet 2: 959–61
3. Marine D 1924 Etiology and prevention of simples goitre. Medicine 3: 453–79
4. Sinclair H M 1953 The work of Sir Robert McCarrison. Faber, London
5. McCarrison R 1908 Observations on endemic cretinism in the Chitral and Gilgit valleys. Lancet 2: 1275–80
6. Chapman J A, Grant I S, Taylor G, Mahmud K, Sardur-ul-Mulk, Shadid M A 1972 Endemic goitre in the Gilgit Agency, West Pakistan with an appendix on dermatoglyphics and taste-testing. Philos Trans R Soc Lond (Biol) 263: 459–90
7. Chesney A M, Clawson T A, Webster B 1928 Endemic goitre in rabbits. I: Incidence and characteristics. Bull Johns Hopkins Hosp 43: 261–77
8. Hercus C E, Purves H D 1936 Studies on endemic and experimental goitre. J Hyg (Camb) 36: 182–203
9. Gaitan E 1980 Goitrogens in the etiology of endemic goitre. In: Stanbury J B, Hetzel B S (eds) Endemic goitre and endemic cretinism. Wiley, New York, p 219–36
10. Clements F W, Wishart J W 1956 A thyroid-blocking agent in the etiology of endemic goiter. Metabolism 5: 623–39
11. Clements F W, Gibson H B, Howeler-Coy J F 1970 Goitre prophylaxis by addition of potassium iodate to bread. Lancet 1: 489–92
12. Delange F, Ahluwalia R (eds) 1983 Cassava toxicity and thyroid research and public health issues. Publication 207e. International Development Research Centre, Ottawa, Canada.
13. Anonymous 1982 Dietary goitrogens. (Editorial.) Lancet 1: 1394–5
14. Wayne E J, Koutras D A, Alexander W D 1964 Clinical aspects of iodine metabolism. Blackwell, Oxford
15. Karmarkar M G, Deo M G, Kochupillai N, Ramalingaswami V 1974 Pathophysiology of Himalayan endemic goiter. Am J Clin Nutr 27: 96–103
16. Pharoah P, Delange F, Fierro-Benitez R, Stanbury J B 1980 Endemic cretinism. In: Stanbury J B, Hetzel B S (eds) Endemic goitre and endemic cretinism. Wiley, New York, p 395–421
17. Pharoah P O D, Buttfield I H, Hetzel B S 1971 Neurological damage to the fetus resulting from severe iodine deficiency during pregnancy. Lancet 1: 308–10
18. Talbot J M, Fisher K D, Carr C J 1976 A review of the

significance of untoward reaction to iodine in foods. Life Sciences Research Office, Federation of American Societies for Experimental Biology

19. Steward J C, Bidor G I, Buttfield H S, Hertzel B S 1971 Epidemic thyrotoxicosis in northern Tasmania: studies of clinical features and iodine nutrition. Aust NZ J Med 3: 203–11

20. Buttfield I H, Black M L, Hoffman M J, Mason E K, Hetzel B S 1965 Correction of iodine deficiency in New Guinea natives in iodised oil injection. Lancet 2: 767–9

21. Hetzel B S, Thilby C H, Fierro-Benitez R, Pretell E A,

Buttfield I H, Stanbury J B 1980 Iodized oil in the prevention of endemic goitre and cretinism. In Stanbury J B, Hetzel B S (eds) Endemic goitre and endemic cretinism. Wiley, New York

22. Maberly G F, Eastman C J, Corcoran J M 1981 Effect of iodination of a village water-supply on goitre size and thyroid function. Lancet 2: 1270–2

23. Nutrition Foundation of India. 1983 The national goitre control programme. A blueprint for its intensification. Scientific Report no. 1

31

Xerophthalmia

Xerophthalmia (Greek *xeros*, dry; *ophthalmos*, eye) is a condition caused by vitamin A deficiency. In its mild form it is confined to the conjunctiva and this is very common in many countries. At this stage there is no disability, but it is a clear warning of the probability of vitamin A deficiency. When it spreads to the cornea there is danger of corneal ulceration and a permanent defect in vision. In severe cases there is softening of the cornea, keratomalacia, which, if not immediately treated, soon leads to permanent blindness. Keratomalacia is frequently associated in young children with protein-energy malnutrition. When this occurs, the mortality is high even with the best treatment.

For fuller accounts of all aspects of xerophthalmia monographs by McLaren[1] and Sommer[2] and a WHO report[3] are recommended.

HISTORY

Night blindness and its cure by liver, rich in vitamin A, was mentioned in Egyptian and Chinese writings going back to 1500 BC. It was well known to Greek and Roman physicians. European mediaeval literature has many accounts of the condition.

Keratomalacia was described many times in the nineteenth century by physicians and ophthalmologists, as occurring in children in the industrial slums of Europe. The first account of the condition in the tropics is a description in 1866 of an outbreak in the children of Negro slaves on a coffee plantation in Brazil.

The outbreak of xerophthalmia in Denmark from 1916 to 1920 is instructive. Some 700 children were affected and over 400 had keratomalacia despite the fact that Denmark had many large dairy herds, and ample supplies of vitamin A should have been available. However, in the early years of World War I most of the butter was exported to Germany where it fetched a high price. Consequently the price of butter and whole milk rose in Denmark. The poor could only obtain separated milk and vegetable margarine (at that time not enriched with vitamins). Oatmeal gruel and vegetable broth from

barley were the main items of the diet of many poor children. In 1918 rationing of butter was introduced and a weekly allowance of 0.25 kg of butter/head abolished the disease. When rationing was lifted prematurely, prices again rose and the disease returned.[4,5,6]

EPIDEMIOLOGY

The disease is widespread in South East Asia and most of the cases occur in Indonesia, Bangladesh, India and the Philippines. After extensive surveys in Indonesia and reviewing the literature from the other three countries, Sommer[2] concludes that roughly 500 000 preschool children develop corneal xerophthalmia each year and that one third to one half become permanently blind as a result. Figure 31.1 shows one of these tragedies. The incidence of milder cases is probably 10 times as great. Most of the cases occur in the villages. With increasing prosperity xerophthalmia is no longer seen in Singapore, Hong Kong and Japan, but it is still an important cause of blindness in some parts of China.[3]

Xerophthalmia is common in parts of the Middle East, where it may be overlooked because trachoma is widespread. In Africa there are endemic areas in Benin,

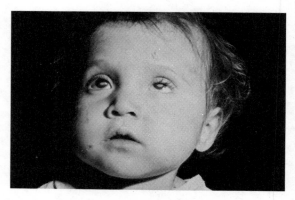

Fig. 31.1 Child blinded in infancy by keratomalacia. (By courtesy of Dr D S McLaren)

Kenya, Malawi, Upper Volta and Zambia.[3] Vitamin A deficiency is widespread in Latin America and the Caribbean but the incidence of xerophthalmia is not reported to be high.

The disease is unknown in Europe today. Occasional cases have arisen in the USA in unfortunate children reputedly allergic to cow's milk and fed on milk substitutes with no vitamin A activity.

Keratomalacia is frequently associated with PEM and infections. In Africa the measles virus commonly affects the eyes causing a severe keratoconjunctivitis and leading to blindness. Vitamin A deficiency may well make this complication more likely.

AETIOLOGY

Xerophthalmia arises when the diet contains practically no whole milk and butter and very limited amounts of fresh vegetables and fruit and so lacks both retinol and carotenes. Xerophthalmia and keratomalacia both occur in the first year of life amongst artifically fed infants but are rare amongst the breast fed. Children in poorly nourished communities are born to mothers who have had small intakes of vitamin A and consequently their liver stores are small at birth. Protein-energy malnutrition further aggravates the partial deficiency because absorption and plasma transport of vitamin A are impaired.

PATHOLOGY

When vitamin A deficiency is produced in experimental animals the epithelial cells of the cornea undergo the squamous metaplasia characteristic of vitamin A deficiency (p. 134). There have been no reports of the histopathology of the condition in man for many years. This is probably due to the difficulty in getting permission for autopsies in those countries where xerophthalmia is common.

CLINICAL FORMS

Five clinical manifestations of vitamin A deficiency and three associated conditions are described by WHO[3] and these have been given code numbers to assist reporting (Table 31.1).

Conjunctival xerosis

The bulbar cunjunctiva is dry, thickened, wrinkled and pigmented, due to a failure to shed the epithelial cells, and consequent keratinisation. The pigmentation gives the conjunctiva a peculiar 'smoky' appearance. The pigment is diffuse and especially marked in the

Table 31.1 Forms of xerophthalmia and associated conditions

Code	
X1A	Conjunctival xerosis
X1B	Conjunctival xerosis with Bitôt's spots
X2	Corneal xerosis
X3A	Corneal ulceration/keratomalacia < 1/3 corneal surface
X3B	Corneal ulceration/keratomalacia > 1/3 corneal surface
XN	Night blindness
XF	Xerophthalmia fundus
XS	Corneal scars

interpalpebral fissure. Dryness, thickening and pigmentation, characteristic of the condition, are also caused by long periods of exposure to glare, dust and infections. It is extremely common in older children and adults in the tropics, in whom it often has no nutritional significance, or only reflects a past deficiency of vitamin A. In children under 5 years it is more likely to be due to a dietary deficiency.

Bitôt's spots are commonly associated with conjunctival xerosis. In children under 5 years of age they are usually due to vitamin A deficiency. However, they are often found in older children and adults in whom there is no evidence of vitamin A deficiency. They are described on page 335.

Corneal xerosis

When dryness spreads to the cornea, this takes on a dull, hazy, lacklustre appearance. This is due to the keratinisation which is the result of vitamin A deficiency on all epithelial surfaces. The cornea often becomes insensitive to touch with a wisp of cotton wool. Slit-lamp examination may show cellular infiltration of the cornea, which intensifies the haziness and may have a bluish, milky appearance; it is usually most marked in the lower central portion.

Corneal ulceration may occur from many causes and be unrelated to vitamin A deficiency. The characteristic feature is a loss of substance (erosion) of a part or the whole of the corneal thickness. Unless there is secondary infection, there are no signs of inflammation. The lesion only heals by scarring.

Corneal xerosis may progress suddenly and rapidly to keratomalacia.

Keratomalacia

Softening and dissolution of the cornea follow and are known to ophthalmologists as colliquative necrosis. This presents a grave emergency. When the process involves only part of the cornea, there is ulceration but the inflammatory reaction is mild. Effective treatment at this stage is followed by corneal scarring and opacity.

If the process is not stopped by treatment, perforation of the cornea leads to prolapse of the iris, extrusion of the lens and infection of the whole eyeball which almost invariably occurs (Fig. 31.2). The chances of saving any useful vision are slight. Healing results in scarring of the whole eye and frequently in total blindness.

The retinol content of the plasma is below 200 µg/1, the lower limit of the range (p. 135). Reserves of retinol are exhausted and none may be detectable in the liver at autopsy.

Fig. 31.2 Keratomalacia in a child from Jordan. (By courtesy of Dr D S McLaren)

Night blindness
The role of retinol in night vision has been described on page 134. Night blindness is an early symptom of vitamin A deficiency and is often present without any signs of xerophthalmia. The symptom is also caused by several other conditions and is discussed on page 335.

Xerophthalmia fundus
In schoolchildren or young adults with prolonged vitamin A deficiency ophthalmoscopic examination may show lesions appearing as spots, either white or yellow, scattered along the sides of the blood vessels. The spots may fuse and the lesions are most numerous on the periphery of the fundus and never appear on the macula.

Corneal scars
These are white, opaque patches on the cornea and the result of healing of an older ulcer. Vision may be seriously affected, depending on the size of the scars. There are other possible causes of corneal scars but, in an area where vitamin A deficiency is known to have existed, their prevalence is an indication of its severity.

DIAGNOSIS

Keratomalacia must be distinguished from other diseases causing corneal lesions such as repeated exposure to dust, trauma, bacterial infections, measles and trachoma. Trachoma usually begins on the conjunctival surface of the upper lid and later extends to the cornea. The opacity (pannus) comes down like a window blind from above.

The child often has some other illness at the time, like gastroenteritis, kwashiorkor, measles or respiratory infection, which can distract attention from the eyes unless they are examined. Measles may precipitate or aggravate xerophthalmia in a malnourished child. If in doubt about the eyes of a malnourished child, it can do no harm to give a course of treatment with vitamin A.

TREATMENT

The administration of vitamin A in a dose of 30 mg of retinol (100 000 i.u.) daily for three days should be started immediately the diagnosis is made or strongly suspected. It is recommended that half the dose should be given orally in the form of halibut oil or other oil solution and half intramuscularly as water-miscible retinol palmitate. An oil solution should not be injected as the retinol is then absorbed very slowly from the injection site. The practice of instilling cod-liver oil directly into the eye is not recommended. During convalescence 9 mg of retinol in the form of a fish liver oil orally is adequate. It is also essential to ensure that the diet is satisfactory in regard to other nutrients.

For the prevention and treatment of secondary bacterial infection, antibiotics are of great value. Local treatment of the eye will only be required if disorganisation is already present, in which case the services of an ophthalmic surgeon should be obtained.

PREVENTION

Professional training
Medical students in Britain cannot learn to recognise xerophthalmia with confidence by the traditional clinical method of being shown a patient, because the last case reported was in 1938. However, doctors planning to work in underdeveloped areas and medical students in countries where xerophthalmia occurs must be trained to recognise it. Thirty pictures of the different stages of the disease are shown in a colour atlas of nutritional disorders[8] which should be in the library of all medical schools. The Nutrition Section of the Royal Tropical Institute, Amsterdam in the Netherlands, has made two sets of colour slides of xerophthalmia for this purpose, which they have offered to supply at moderate cost. Colour photographs, 'Know the signs and symptoms of xerophthalmia', are obtainable free by health workers who write to the American Foundation for Overseas Blind, 22 West 17th Street, New York, NY10011, USA.

Training the doctors is only the start of prevention because most cases occur in urban poor and rural peasants in under-doctored areas, and keratomalacia develops without the children being seen by a doctor. Therefore to extend prevention, nurses, midwives, and other paramedical staff associated with maternal and child health clinics should be trained.

Dietary advice

First, pregnant women should be advised to eat dark supplements rich in vitamin A in prophylactic doses. This helps to build up stores of retinol in the fetal liver and should be continued during lactation. Secondly, mothers should be advised to include in the weaning foods dark green leafy vegetables or yellow and orange fruits, which are locally available, cheap and known to be good sources of β-carotene. Bangladesh issued two postages stamps in 1976 which show an eye and foods to prevent xerophthalmia, with the caption: 'Foresight prevents blindness.'

Prophylactic retinol

Where blindness from keratomalacia is a major public health problem single large prophylactic doses of retinol in oily solution are recommended. This is given as a capsule to be taken by mouth. Table 31.2 sets out dosages. Large-scale trials of this procedure started in 1970 and are going on in India, Bangladesh, Indonesia, the Philippines and other countries with varying degrees of success. The dose is safe and adverse effects are rare. The main difficulty and expense is in obtaining and training personnel, and operational costs may be high. Where possible, existing health staff should be used. All prophylactic programmes should be evaluated by periodic field surveys of the prevalence of xerophthalmia. The benefits from such programmes in India and Indonesia have now been reported.[10,11]

A community should be considered at serious risk of keratomalacia if more than 2 per cent of the children have conjunctival xerosis or if in more than 5 per cent plasma retinol is below 100 µg/l. Constant surveillance is essential to see that a programme continues to be effective and also to ensure that it continues to be needed and that there is no unnecessary expense.

In Guatemala a different approach is being tried: fortification of table sugar with water-miscible vitamin A. Preliminary studies by INCAP have shown that this is technically feasible. In the Philippines fortification of monosodium glutamate with vitamin A is being tested because MSG is consumed by the whole population, including children.

A newsletter, the Xerophthalmia Club Bulletin, has been started, to keep those working to prevent xerophthalmia in touch with what is being done in other countries. The bulletin's secretary is Mrs A Pirie, Nuffield Laboratory of Ophthalmology, Oxford, England.

The finding that children with mild xerophthalmia have a greatly increased mortality[9] is additional justification for vigorous community programmes to prevent vitamin A deficiency.

Blindness

Nutritional disorders of the eye are only one of several causes of blindness. There are probably more than 10 million blind people in the world. That most of these became blind before the age of 5 and that probably in two-thirds of the cases the blindness is preventable makes the situation the more tragic. We feel that a far more energetic attack on the problem should be made, especially in the underdeveloped countries. In India there are over two million blind people; in Bangladesh, Vietnam and Indonesia there are very large numbers; in parts of West Africa 90 per cent of the population have eye disease. Throughout much of Latin America eye diseases and blindness are widespread.

Causes of blindness common in some parts of the world are as follows. Trachoma, a virus infection, is still the most important eye disease in the world. The countries around the Mediterranean Sea are severely affected. It is common in children and, if untreated, often causes progressive loss of vision and blindness. Smallpox often affected the eyes and was reputed to be responsible for one-fifth of the blindness in India. Onchocercosis is

Table 31.2 Prophylactic doses of retinol palmitate[2]

Individual	Oral dose		Timing
	mg	iu	
Children			
Up to the age of 1 year	55	100 000	Once every 4–6 months
above the age of 1 year	110	200 000	Once every 4–6 months
Newborn	27.5	50 000	At birth
Women			
not pregnant	165	300 000	Not normally repeated
pregnant or lactating	2.75	5 000	Daily
	11	20 000	Weekly

caused by a filarial worm which is transferred from man to man by flies. It causes nodules in the skin and thence microfilaria invade the eye which leads to blindness. The disease commonly affects people in Central America and in Central Africa who live beside rivers. In some villages, all the adult population are blind. Venereal diseases, congenital syphilis and gonococcal ophthalmia neonatorum are important causes of blindness in parts of the world where the maternity services are inadequate or totally lacking. Accidents in the home and at work are common causes of blindness. Many young children lose their sight in this way. Diabetes, cataract and glaucoma are important causes of blindness in elderly people.

Vitamin A deficiency is thus one of seven important causes of blindness and the most easily preventable. A former Director-General of WHO has stated: 'If one-tenth of the money we now spend to support unnecessary blindness was spent to prevent it, society would gain in terms of cold economy, not to mention considerations of the happiness of humanity.'

REFERENCES

1. McLaren D S 1980 Nutritional ophthalmology. Academic Press, London
2. Sommer A 1982 Nutritional blindness: xerophthalmia and keratomalacia. Oxford University Press, Oxford and New York
3. World Health Organisation 1982 Control of vitamin A deficiency and xerophthalmia. WHO Tech Rep Ser no. 672
4. Block C E 1921 Clinical investigation of xerophthalmia and dystrophy in infants and young children. J Hyg (Camb) 19: 283–304
5. Block C E 1924 Blindness and other diseases in children arising from deficient nutrition (lack of fat-soluble vitamin A factor). Am J Dis Child 27: 139–48
6. Block C E 1924 Further clinical observations into the diseases arising in consequence of a deficiency in the fat-soluble A factor. Am J Dis Child 28: 659–67
7. Sommer A, Tarwotjo I, Hussaini G, Susanto D, Soegiharto T 1981 Incidence, prevalence and scale of blinding malnutrition. Lancet 1: 1407–8
8. McLaren D S 1981 A colour atlas of nutritional disorders. Wolfe, London
9. Sommer A, Tarwotjo I, Hussaini G, Susanto T 1983 Increased mortality in children with mild vitamin A deficiency. Lancet 2: 585–8
10. Vijayaraghavan K, Rameshwar Sarma K V, Pralhad Rao N, Reddy V 1984 Impact of massive doses of vitamin A on incidence of nutritional blindness. Lancet 2: 149–51
11. Ministry of Health, Jakarta 1984 Xerophthalmia surveillance. Prevalence of xerophthalmia in Lombok. Wkly Epidemiol Rec 17: 129–30

32

Rickets and Osteomalacia

Rickets, a word derived from the Anglo-Saxon *wrikken* to twist, is a disease of children in which the bones are softened and deformed. It arises as a result of deficiency of vitamin D and a failure to absorb calcium from the small intestine. Osteomalacia, which means softening of bone, arises when there is vitamin D deficiency in adults. The resultant calcium deficiency leads to demineralisation of the bones.

The severe forms of both diseases with gross deformities of the skeleton are now rare but cases may be seen occasionally in hospitals in most countries. Only a few foods are good sources of vitamin D and the major part, about 90 per cent, of the vitamin in our bodies comes from photosynthesis in the skin. Minor forms of the disease leading to impairment of bone growth in children and demineralisation in adults, especially old people, continue to be found in sections of the community in all countries. The prevention of rickets and osteomalacia remains an important problem for all public health authorities. The means have been known for nearly 100 years, but effective application is still difficult.

HISTORY

Although rickets was described in ancient times, it was not well known until the seventeenth century. The first clinical description in Britain was that of Daniel Whistler, an Oxford man who wrote his DM thesis on rickets in 1645. This was followed in 1650 by the better known description of Glisson, a Cambridge graduate and physician in London. Contemporary writers described the thick pall of smoke that began to overcast London in the seventeenth century. Industrial smoke and high tenement buildings together shut out the sunlight and, as industrial cities grew, so rickets spread. Although rickets may occur in children living in the country, it is never widespread unless local custom confines them indoors. Prior to 1900, in many industrial cities, up to 75 per cent of the children of the poorer classes were affected. Rickets came to be known as a disease of 'poverty and darkness'. Glasgow, Vienna and Lahore each acquired an unenviable reputation as homes of the disease. In Lahore, as in many other eastern cities, the purdah system confined women and children in narrow courtyards where the sun seldom penetrated.

After 1900 the severity of rickets began to decline, probably mainly due to more exposure to sunlight as legislation for smoke abatement began to be enforced effectively, and also to the increasing empirical use of cod-liver oil for personal prophylaxis. The discovery of vitamin D and the study of the large outbreaks of both rickets and osteomalacia in Vienna in 1919 after the end of World War I elucidated the dual roles of diet and sunshine in preventing the diseases.[1,2] After her hundredth birthday Dame Harriette Chick presented a paper[3] to the British Nutrition Foundation in which she relates the chemical, clinical and sociological aspects of the disease as they had presented in Vienna. This is a masterpiece which all nutritionists can enjoy reading.

Thereafter the incidence of rickets declined in Europe and North America and by 1945 it had all but been eradicated from the United Kingdom. This was due in part to wartime nutrition policies; provision of vitamin D supplement for all children and pregnant women and the enrichment of margarine and National Dried Milk with the vitamin. In 1952 cases of hypercalcaemia in infants and young children (p. 112) were reported. Although not numerous, they were often fatal and attributable to vitamin D toxicity. To prevent this the vitamin D contents of cod-liver oil, infants milks and cereals were reduced. This measure effectively prevented hypercalcaemia but allowed rickets to return, although on nothing like the scale of earlier years. Today a small residue of rickets remains in some urban communities as is described below.

EPIDEMIOLOGY

The epidemiology of rickets and osteomalacia is important because the diseases can be prevented by good educational and administrative services. These require much effort and cost money, and so should be directed specifically at sections of a population at real risk. Epidemiological data are useless unless diagnosis is accurate. Diagnosis of established cases is easy because these have well-defined clinical and radiological features and characteristic changes in blood chemistry. However in the much more common early stages of the diseases, these criteria for diagnosis are equivocable. The new methods for measuring plasma concentrations of vitamin D and its metabolites now make assessments of vitamin D status much more precise and should allow field surveys to detect the prevalence of early vitamin D deficiency much more reliably.

Rickets is characteristically most severe in children between the ages of 1 and 3 years when they are growing rapidly and the limb bones have to support an increasing weight. It often becomes more pronounced at puberty, associated with the growth spurt. Vitamin D deficiency is now recognised in very young infants (neonatal rickets), especially those born with low birth weights; it is attributable to a mother being unable to supply sufficient vitamin to the fetus or subsequently in her milk.

Osteomalacia is classically a disease of multiparous women who through lack of vitamin D have been unable to replace calcium from their bones lost to the fetus *in utero* and in lactation. Fortunately this condition is now very rare in most countries. However, osteoporosis, an inevitable consequence of ageing, is often accompanied by osteomalacia. Elderly people who for many reasons may be restricted in their physical activity may not get sufficient exposure to sunlight to meet their needs for vitamin D. Vitamin D deficiency has always been considered mainly a problem for paediatricians and in some places for obstetricians; today in many countries it may occur most frequently in geriatric practice.

Now that it is realised that normal diets do not meet the body's needs for vitamin D and that we depend on exposure to sunlight for its synthesis, there can be no surprise that all communities in northern latitudes are at risk of rickets and osteomalacia. The short hours of daylight during the long winter and the necessity of covering the whole body with clothing as protection against the cold limit severely synthesis in the skin. The seasonal variation in vitamin D status in Sunderland in the north of England, latitude 55 °, was shown by measurement of the plasma concentration of 25-hydroxy vitamin D (25(OH)D) in old people.[4] In July–August the mean value was 25.3 nmol/l and in December–February it fell to 8.8 nmol/l. There were only 23 subjects in the survey and the winter mean, although no cause for action in an individual, suggests that there might be a substantial number of old people in the town with lower values who needed a vitamin D supplement.

What is surprising is that vitamin D deficiency occurs where sunlight is abundant. Thus in the Indian subcontinent there are reports of rickets in young children in Calcutta[5] and in Hyderabad[6] and of osteomalacia in young women in Delhi[7] and Karachi[8]. Rickets in older children is seen in Jamaica[9] and in Cape Town and Johannesburg. (Professor John Hansen, personal communication). In none of these places is there any lack of sunlight. Cases of rickets and osteomalacia probably arise in all countries, but as they are seldom severe are usually overlooked. The purdah system and the traditional dress of Muslim women, now being enforced in Iran and widespread in Saudi Arabia, is responsible for some cases. Some mothers in Africa and Asia deliberately keep their young son out of the sun because they do not want him to become 'a black man' and colour prejudice is not restricted to those of European descent.

RICKETS AND OSTEOMALACIA IN THE UNITED KINGDOM

Vitamin D deficiency persists in the United Kingdom but predominantly in immigrant families of Asian origin. The epidemiology and aetiology has been much studied and is reviewed in a government report.[10] Although rickets was often referred to as the English disease, it was more prevalent and more severe in Scotland, especially in Glasgow. Professor Arneil and his colleagues at the Royal Hospital for Sick Children have studied the problem for many years and presented their results in a series of papers. The latest[11] summarises their main findings. The number of cases of florid rickets admitted to the hospital over the years is shown in Figure 32.1.

There was a marked increase after 1962 following measures to reduce the vitamin D content of infant foods. Most of the cases then were in Scottish children, but these declined and there have been none since 1975. However the numbers in Asian children rose reaching a peak in 1973 and although there has now been a decline, cases are still seen. Out of 200 Asian children surveyed in 1979, blood analyses (see below) indicated subclinical rickets in nine. A similar decline has also occurred in Manchester.[12] Surveys in several other towns in 1970–80 showed that rickets continued to occur in children and adolescents and predominantly in the Asian population.[10]

Cases of frank osteomalacia in adults are also seen in small numbers, again predominantly in Asians. Thus 45 patients were admitted to the Royal Orthopaedic Hospital which covers Greater London in 1974–79. Of these 43 were Asian, 39 aged 10–50 years and 35 female.[13] Histological examination of bone samples obtained by biopsy indicate that osteomalacia is not

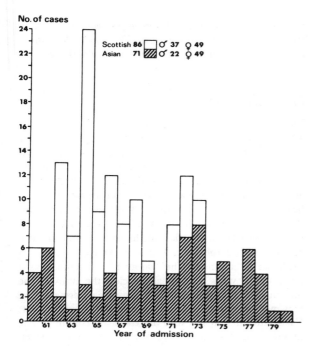

Fig. 32.1 Number of children with florid rickets admitted annually to Royal Hospital for Sick Children, Glasgow, 1960–80

uncommon in the elderly of all races; it may be present in up to 35 per cent of patients with fractures of the femur. Studies in Edinburgh,[14] Leeds[15] and London[16] leave no room for doubt that mild osteomalacia, not easily detectable, is a preventable factor contributing to the disabilities of large numbers of the elderly in the United Kingdom.

RISK FACTORS

Inadequate exposure to sunlight. In northern latitudes long winters with only a few hours of daylight greatly reduce exposure to ultraviolet radiation. Vitamin D deficiency is then a risk for all children and adolescents, as they have greater need for the vitamin than adults, and also for all elderly people and others with disabilities restricting outdoor activity. But insufficient exposure to sunlight cannot account for all the epidemiological findings and other risk factors may be present. A full discussion of these based on studies in the Asian community in Glasgow is given by Dunnigan.[17]

Unrefined cereals. The classic experiments of Mellanby[18] in 1919 showed that puppies developed rickets when white bread in their diet was replaced by unrefined oatmeal. Asian communities whose staple food is chapattis made from high extraction wheat flour

appear to be at increased risk of both rickets and osteomalacia.

Vegetarianism. Strict Hindus and others who eat no animal food provide an increased proportion of cases of osteomalacia seen in Britain. This complete exclusion of vitamin D from the diet does not normally lead to rickets or osteomalacia but increases the risk. In London Asians, Hindus have lower plasma concentrations of 25(OH)D than Moslems and Christians.[19]

Prolonged breast feeding. When an infant is fed exclusively on milk from a vitamin D deficient mother for more than three months, the risk of infantile rickets rises.

Skin pigmentation. Heavy pigmentation reduces synthesis of vitamin D in the skin. This can only be a minor risk factor since in Britain rickets is much less common in the darker West Indian than in the lighter Asian communities.

SECONDARY OSTEOMALACIA AND RICKETS

Gastrointestinal disease. Osteomalacia may arise in patients with the malabsorption syndrome (p. 437) after many months. This is due to impaired calcium absorption.

Renal disease. Osteomalacia and other bone disorders arise in patients with chronic renal failure (p. 407). Impaired formation of $1,25(OH)_2D$ in the kidney may be responsible.

Liver disease. Osteomalacia is sometimes found in patients with cirrhosis of the liver due to failure to form 25(OH)D.

Inborn errors of metabolism. Five different genetic defects that lead to rickets are known.[20] All are uncommon. The main features of these are listed in Table 32.1.

CHEMICAL PATHOLOGY

The primary defect of reduced calcium absorption from the gut causes plasma calcium to fall from the normal value of about 2.5 mmol/l. It may fall as low as 1.3 mmol/l or even less, which usually causes tetany (see below).Compensatory secretion of parathyroid hormone counteracts this fall, but increases output of inorganic phosphorus in the urine. As a result plasma phosphorus falls from the normal value in childhood of over 1.3 mmol/l. However, in mild cases plasma calcium and phosphorus are usually within normal limits. A more constant early change is an increase in plasma alkaline phosphatase, an enzyme formed by osteoblasts in the osteoid tissue of growing bones. The normal plasma concentration of the enzyme in the first three years of

Table 32.1 Inborn errors of metabolism leading to rickets

X-linked hypophosphataemia
X-linked dominant defect of phosphate absorption in renal tubules; plasma Pi markedly decreased; previously known as vitamin D-resistant rickets; rickets in early childhood; later bow legs; healthy, short stocky; treatment with phosphate supplements and large doses of vitamin D

Hypophosphataemic bone disease
Autosomal dominant defect of phosphate absorption in renal tubules; clinical features similar to the above; very rare

Fanconi syndrome
Autosomal recessive general defects of absorption in renal tubules; often associated with cystinosis; urine contains greatly increased phosphate and also amino acids and glucose; disturbances of electrolyte and acid base balance; failure to thrive, polyuria and dehydration; mild to severe rickets; treatment with phosphate and potassium supplements, sodium bicarbonate, vitamin D

Vitamin D-dependency type I
Autosomal recessive defect in conversion of vitamin D to 1,25(OH)$_2$D; plasma Pi and Ca both decreased; onset in infancy with irritability and tetany; severe deformities; treatment with 1,25(OH)$_2$D

Vitamin D-dependency type II
Autosomal recessive defect making the target tissues resistant to 1,25(OH)$_2$D; features similar to type I, but may occur later and be less severe; alopecia common; treatment with large doses of vitamin D or 1,25(OH)$_2$D

life is between 120 and 250 King-Armstrong units/l. Values of 300–400 are found in early mild cases of rickets. However, high values are sometimes found in children receiving vitamin D supplements and with no clinical or radiological evidence of rickets.[21] All of the above changes in the plasma are found in advanced cases, but they are not reliable guides to the detection of early vitamin D deficiency or subclinical rickets.

The new methods for measuring plasma concentrations of vitamin D and its metabolites, 25(OH)D and 1,25(OH)$_2$D, has changed the situation.[22] Concentrations of all three fall in early vitamin D deficiency. Measurement of plasma 25(OH)D is technically the easiest. Values below 20 nmol/l (8 ng/ml) are now commonly taken as evidence of deficiency and an indication for a dietary supplement of the vitamin.

MORBID ANATOMY

The histological changes in the bones in active human rickets are essentially the same as those experimental animals described on page 139. In osteomalacia, progressive decalcification leads to replacement of bony substance with soft osteoid tissue. Seams of this, which do not constitute more than 6 per cent of total bone area

in normal adults, are widespread in sections of bone from patients with osteomalacia. The whole skeleton is affected, most markedly the spine, pelvis and legs.

CLINICAL FEATURES

Rickets

The infant with rickets has often received sufficient dietary energy and may appear well nourished. Indeed it used to be a commonplace that the fat, flabby child, 'crammed with distressful bread', which won the prize at the local baby show by virtue of being so much heavier than its competitors, was usually rachitic. But the child is restless, fretful and pale, with flabby and toneless muscles which allow the limbs to assume unnatural postures ('acrobatic rickets'). Excessive sweating on the head is common. The abdomen is distended as a result of the weak abdominal muscles, the atony of the intestinal musculature and the intestinal fermentation that may arise from excessive carbohydrates in the diet. Gastrointestinal upsets with diarrhoea are common. The infant or child is prone to respiratory infections. Development is delayed so that the teeth often erupt late and there is failure to sit up, stand, crawl and walk at the normal ages.

The bony changes are the most characteristic and easily identifiable signs of rickets. There is extension and widening of the epiphyses at the growing points, where cartilage meets bone. The earliest bony lesion are usually enlargement of the epiphyses at the lower end of the radius and at the costochondral junctions of the ribs, the latter producing the clinical sign known as 'beading' of the ribs or 'rickety rosary', an early and important diagnostic feature. Later features seen in British children with rickets are 'bossing' of the frontal and parietal bones and delayed closure of the anterior fontanelle. Later too, there may be deformities of the chest such as undue prominence of the sternum ('pigeon chest') and a transverse depression, passing outwards from the costal cartilages towards the axillae which deepens with inspiration. This was very familiar to us in our student days as Harrison's sulcus. It was apparently caused by the sucking in of the softened ribs on inspiration during whooping cough, or other respiratory infections to which rachitic children are prone. Even today in unusually severe cases, respiratory function can be seriously impaired by the combination of respiratory infection and a rachitic chest. Twenty such cases with acute heart failure, aged 1 to 2 years have been described from Ethiopia.[23]

If rickets continues into the second and third year of life, these signs may persist or be magnified. Deformities such as kyphosis of the spine develop as a result of the new gravitational and muscular strains, caused by

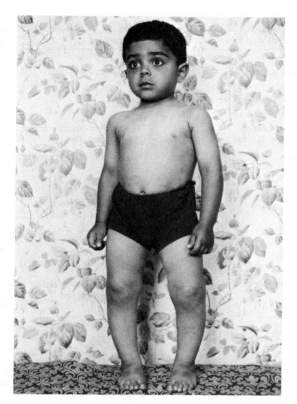

Fig. 32.2 Rickets in a child from the Asian community in Glasgow. Note the marked bowing of the tibiae. (By courtesy of Dr M G Dunnigan)

sitting up and crawling. At the same time there may be enlargement of the lower ends of the femur, tibia and fibula. When the rachitic child begins to walk, deformities of the shafts of the leg bones develop, so that 'knock knees' or 'bow legs' are added to the clinical picture. Anterolateral bowing of the tibiae at the junction of the middle and lower thirds is frequently noted in young children with rickets (Fig. 32.2). The spinal kyphosis is often replaced by lordosis. Pelvic deformities may follow and lead years later to serious difficulties at childbirth.

When ionised calcium in the plasma is reduced, infantile tetany may result, with spasm of the hands and feet and of the vocal cords. The latter causes a high-pitched, distressing cry and great difficulty in breathing. In bygone days — when florid rickets was common — tetany was sometimes associated with alarming general convulsions.

DIAGNOSIS

In a fully developed case this is easy. But in countries where the disease is now rare and medical students and family doctors are no longer familiar with it, there is an increasing likelihood that mild cases will be missed. A flabby baby towards the end of its first year, unable to pull itself up, fretful and easily irritated, with too few teeth showing and liable to profuse sweats, should always be suspected of having rickets. Early evidence of rickets may be overlooked in a child ill with bronchopneumonia or diarrhoea, especially in the first year of life. If there is any doubt, a radiograph of the wrist may show characteristic changes at the epiphyses; the outline of the joint is blurred and hazy, and the epiphyseal line becomes broadened. Later, in older children, as a result of decalcification of the metaphysis and the effects of movements and stresses the classical concave 'saucer' deformity is clearly shown radiographically. The opinion of an experienced radiologist may be needed to distinguish the picture from that of scurvy. The diagnosis is supported by a raised plasma alkaline phosphatase and confirmed if plasma 25(OH)D is low.

It is sometimes necessary to distinguish rickets from other rare disorders involving the bones, such as congenital syphilis, achondroplasia and osteogenesis imperfecta. Radiographs of the bone are helpful in differentiating these disorders.

Osteomalacia

Deformities of the spine, pelvis and legs are now rarely seen. For full accounts of these, as they appeared in Vienna, Peking and Kashmir, the classical papers[2,24,25] should be consulted. Today the common presenting features are pain and muscular weakness. Pain ranges from a dull ache to severe pain. Sites frequently affected are the ribs, sacrum, lower lumbar vertebrae, pelvis and legs. Bone tenderness on pressure is common. Muscular weakness is often present and the patient may find difficulty in climbing stairs or getting out of a chair. A waddling gait is not unusual. Tetany may be manifested by carpopedal spasm and facial twitching. Spontaneous fractures may occur, independent of the pseudofractures described below.

Radiographic features

There is rarefaction of bone and commonly translucent bands (pseudofractures, Looser's zones), often symmetrical, at points submitted to compression stress. Common sites are the ribs, the axillary borders of the scapula, the pubic rami and the medial cortex of the upper femur. Looser's zones are diagnostic of osteomalacia.

Diagnosis

The early symptoms may resemble those present in osteoporosis and rheumatic disorders. Table 32.2 lists the distinctions from osteoporosis. In mild cases these

Table 32.2 The differential diagnosis of osteomalacia and osteoporosis

	Osteomalacia	Osteoporosis
Clinical features		
Skeletal pain	A major complaint usually persistent	Episodic and usually associated with a fracture
Muscle weakness	Usually present and producing disability and, when severe, a characteristic gait	Absent
Fractures	Relatively uncommon; healing delayed	The usual presenting feature; heals normally
Skeletal deformity	Common, especially kyphosis	Only occurs where there is a fracture
Radiographic features		
Loss of density of bone	Widespread	Irregular and often most marked in the spine
Loss of bone detail	Characteristic	Not a feature
Looser's zones	Diagnostic	Absent
Biopsy		
Histological changes	Excess osteoid tissue with bone present in normal quantity	Bone reduced in quantity but fully mineralised
Biochemical changes		
Plasma Ca and P	Often low	Normal
Plasma alkaline phosphatase	Often high	Normal
Urinary calcium	Often low	Normal or high
Response to treatment		
Vitamin D	Dramatic	None

may not be clear. Then measurement of plasma 25(OH)D should clinch the diagnosis.

TREATMENT

A daily oral dose of 25–125µg (1000–5000 i.u.) of vitamin D cures rickets and osteomalacia. Because of the risk of toxicity this should be reduced to 10 µg, the prophylactic dose, when plasma alkaline phosphatase has returned to normal and radiographs show that healing is established. Children can be given halibut-liver oil in a very small dose (1 ml) since it contains 30 to 40 times the concentration of vitamin D of cod-liver oil. Many proprietary preparations are available which contain standard amounts of vitamins A and D dispensed as capsules or palatable syrups. For severe cases needing 125 µg/day, synthetic calciferol is useful. One millilitre of the BP solution contains about 75 µg of vitamin D.

In times of social upheaval, such as may be occasioned by war, floods or pestilence, when an infant or young child may be seen once by an emergency medical service and perhaps not again for months, a single massive dose of vitamin D, e.g. 3.75 mg (150 000 i.u.) (three strong calciferol tablets, BP), can be given by mouth with reasonable safety and curative effects. The single dose can be given by intramuscular injection, but this has no proved advantage over the oral route. A daily small dose is recommended for normal practice because of the danger of overdosage.

Treatment of osteomalacia is essentially the same as for rickets when it is primarily due to a defective intake of vitamin D, namely 25 to 125 µg (1000 to 5000 i.u.) daily. If there is evidence of malabsorption the dose should be up to 1.25 mg (50 000 i.u.) daily and it may have to be given intramuscularly at weekly or monthly intervals. If the disease is secondary to kidney or liver disease large doses and either $1,25(OH)_2D$ or $25(OH)D$ are indicated.

Advice on diet and general hygiene is needed. An adequate intake of calcium is essential. The best source is milk and at least 500 ml should be drunk daily. When this is not practical and in severe cases, calcium lactate, taken by mouth, should be prescribed. An egg daily and butter or fortified margarine increase the dietary intake of vitamin D and are recommended. Mothers of young children require tactful education in feeding and general care, as do elderly patients. Unnecessary clothing should be removed and every opportunity to go out and enjoy the sunshine taken.

PROGNOSIS

Rickets is not a fatal disease *per se*, but the untreated rachitic child is a weakling with an increased risk of infections, notably bronchopneumonia. The skeletal changes usually tend to heal spontaneously as the child gets older. The bony deformities, if mild, usually right themselves as growth proceeds, but in severe cases pigeon chest, contracted pelvis, knock knees or bow legs may persist. With early and sufficient treatment these changes are entirely avoided.

In osteomalacia vitamin D quickly relieves the pain and muscular weakness but it takes many weeks or months to restore the bones to their normal strength.

PREVENTION

All people at risk of rickets can be protected by a supplement of 10 μg of vitamin D daily. This dose is effective and safe; any health professional can recommend it to any individual person. All public health authorities have to decide whether it is advisable for the whole of any section of the community. There is general agreement that supplements are necessary in all countries with long dark winters for all children up to 5 years of age, and for their mothers during pregnancy and lactation. Whether or not to continue this policy throughout childhood and adolescence depends on information about their vitamin D status and the incidence of clinical rickets. All children on anticonvulsive drugs should continue to receive a supplement. In some communities there is now evidence suggesting that large numbers of the elderly require extra vitamin D to protect them against osteomalacia.

It is not sufficient to make supplements of vitamin D freely available. Rickets occurs predominantly in families which are poor and where the mother lacks education and is often feckless. An intensive programme of health education is needed to ensure that the supplements are taken regularly; this should also provide advice on diet, clothing and general hygiene. Health education has been shown to be effective in the Asian community in Glasgow.[26]

In countries with abundant sunlight children should not normally need a vitamin D supplement. Where rickets is known to be present, teaching of mothercraft, emphasising that young children must not be excessively protected from the sun, should suffice. However protein-energy malnutrition is sometimes associated with rickets and routine dietary supplements may be needed in some circumstances.

In Britain vitamin D is available as a Welfare Food in the form of drops, and five of these daily provide a protective dose. Many suitable commercial preparations are also available. Cod-liver oil is effective but now seldom used. One teaspoonfull (about 4 ml) of the BP preparation contains not less than 9 μg of vitamin D. In tropical countries other fish-liver oils may be more easily obtained and do not require foreign currency; they also contain useful amounts of vitamin A. Sometimes it may be advantageous to give children a single massive dose (1–2 mg) of vitamin D. This is stored in the liver, liberated slowly and protects a child for several months. As there is a slight risk of symptoms of hypervitaminosis, it is recommended only in exceptional circumstances.

Smoke abatement, slum clearances and provision of open-air playgrounds were mainly responsible for the marked fall in the prevalence of rickets in the early part of the present century. The great improvements in these matters have to be maintained and extended where necessary. That these are public health measures of major importance must never be forgotten.

REFERENCES

1. Chick H, Dalyell E J, Hume E M, Mackay H M M, Henderson Smith H, Wimberger H 1923 Studies of rickets in Vienna, 1919–1922. MRC Spec Rep Ser no. 77. HMSO, London
2. Dalyell E J, Chick H 1921 Hunger-osteomalacia in Vienna 1920. Lancet 2: 842–53
3. Chick H 1976 Study of rickets in Vienna 1919–1922. Med Hist 20: 41–51
4. Lawson D E M, Paul A, Black A E et al 1979 Relative contributions of diet and sunlight to vitamin D state in the elderly. Br Med J 2: 303–5
5. Chaudhuri M K 1975 Nutritional profile of Calcutta pre-school children. Indian J Med Res 63: 189–95
6. Raghuramulu N, Reddy V 1982 Studies on vitamin D metabolism in malnourished children. Br J Nutr 47: 231–4
7. Matthew R, Rizvi S N, Rao M B, Vaishnava R 1975 The role of phytate in the pathogenesis of nutritional osteomalacia. J Assoc Physicians India 23: 871–8
8. Rab S M, Baseer A 1976 Occult osteomalacia amongst healthy and pregnant women in Pakistan. Lancet 2: 1211–3
9. Miller C G, Chutkan W 1976 Vitamin D deficiency in Jamaican children. Arch Dis Child 51: 214–8
10. Department of Health and Social Security 1980 Rickets and osteomalacia. Report on Health and Social Subjects no. 19. HMSO, London
11. Goel K M, Sweek E M, Campbell S, Allenburrow A, Logan R W, Arneil G C 1981 Reduced prevalence of rickets in Asian children in Glasgow. Lancet 2: 405–7
12. Stephens W P, Klimuk P S, Warrington S, Taylor J L, Berry J L, Mawer E B 1982 Observations on the natural history of vitamin D deficiency amongst Asian immigrants. Q J Med 51: 171–88

13. Stamp T C B, Walker P G, Perry W, Jenkins M V 1980 Nutritional osteomalacia and late rickets in Greater London 1974–1979: clinical and metabolic studies in 45 patients. Clin Endocrinol Metab 9(1): 81–105

14. Chalmers J, Conacher W D H, Gardner D L, Scott P J 1967 Osteomalacia — a common disease of elderly women. J Bone Joint Surg (Br) 49: 403–23

15. Aaron J E, Gallagher J C. Anderson J, et al 1974 Frequency of osteomalacia and osteoporosis in fractures of the proximal femur. Lancet 1: 229–33

16. Faccini J M, Exton-Smith A N, Boyde A 1976 Disorders of bone and fracture of the femoral neck — evaluation of computer image analysis in diagnosis. Lancet 1: 1089–92

17. Dunnigan M G, McIntosh W B, Ford J A, Robertson I 1982 Acquired disorders of vitamin D metabolism. In: Heath D, Marx S J (eds) Calcium disorders. Butterworth, London

18. Mellanby E 1922 Discussion on the etiology of rickets. Br Med J 2: 849–52

19. Hunt S P, O'Riordan J L H, Windo J, Truswell A S 1976 Vitamin D status in different subgroups of British Asians. Br Med 2: 1351–4

20. Scriver C R, Fraser D, Kooh S W 1982 Hereditary rickets. In: Heath D, Marx S J (eds) Calcium disorders. Butterworth, London, p 1–46

21. Stephen J M L, Stephenson P 1971 Alkaline phosphatase in normal infants. Arch Dis Child 46: 185–8

22. Mawer E B 1980 Clinical implication of measurements of circulating vitamin D metabolites. Clin Endocrinol Metab 9(1): 63–79

23. Marian T W, Sterky G 1973 Severe rickets in infancy and childhood in Ethiopia. J Pediatr 82: 876–8

24. Miles L M, Chih Tung Feng 1925 Calcium and phosphorus metabolism in osteomalacia. J Exp Med 41: 137–57

25. Wilson D C 1929 Osteomalacia (late rickets) studies. Clinical symptoms in relation to bone changes as shown by X-ray examination. Indian J Med Res 17: 339–47

26. Dunnigan M G, McIntosh W B, Sutherland G R, Gardee R, Glenkin B, Ford J A, Robertson I 1981 Policy for prevention of Asian rickets in Britain: a preliminary assessment of the Glasgow rickets campaign. Br Med J 282: 357–60

33

Beriberi and the Wernicke-Korsakoff Syndrome

Beriberi is a nutritional disorder formerly widespread in the rice-eating people of the East. The etymology of the word 'beriberi' is obscure; it probably comes from a word in a Malay dialect, *beri*, meaning weak. The epidemiology, chemical pathology and response to therapy all suggest that its main features are due to deficiency of thiamin, but that factors in a poor diet contribute. Three forms of the disease occur: (1) wet beriberi, characterised by oedema often associated with high-output cardiac failure, (2) dry beriberi, a polyneuropathy, and (3) the infantile form. Characteristically beriberi has occurred in outbreaks or epidemics in a community, whose members are all eating similar diets based on the same type of rice.

Thiamin deficiency is also an aetiological factor in three conditions not uncommon in chronic alcoholics in all parts of the world. These are (i) alcoholic polyneuropathy clinically indistinguishable from dry beriberi, (ii) a thiamin-responsive cardiomyopathy, and (iii) an encephalopathy, the Wernicke-Korsakoff syndrome.

Classical oriental beriberi is first described and then thiamin deficiency as it presents in non-rice eaters.

ORIENTAL BERIBERI

HISTORY AND AETIOLOGY

A Japanese naval surgeon, Takaki,[1] was the first to demonstrate that beriberi is essentially a nutritional disease arising when the proportion of polished rice in the diet is excessive. After studying the disease for a number of years he persuaded the Japanese authorities in 1883 and 1884 to replace a part of the rice in the ration by wheaten bread and to increase the allowance of vegetables and milk.

There was a striking reduction in the incidence and mortality of the disease as shown in Table 33.1. Takaki himself attributed this improvement to an increase in protein intake.

Further observations in the Far East also showed that beriberi was associated with the consumption of rice that

Table 33.1 Beriberi in the Japanese Navy

Year	Force	Cases of beriberi	Deaths from beriberi
1878	4528	1485	32
1879	5081	1978	57
1880	4956	1725	27
1881	4641	1163	30
1882	4769	1929	51
1883	5346	1236	40
1884	5638	718	8
1885	6918	41	0
1886	8475	3	0
1887	9106	0	0

had been highly polished in the raw state and that it could be prevented either by adding other foods, as Takaki had done, or by substituting parboiled rice for raw-milled rice. Table 33.2 illustrates this. Beriberi was endemic in the Philippine Scouts as described in Vedder's classic monograph.[3] In 1909 there were 618 cases; then 20 oz of polished rice in their rations was changed to 16 oz of unpolished rice and 1.6 oz of dried beans. In 1911 there were only three cases of beriberi and in 1913 none. Numerous other reports have described the spectacular reduction of beriberi in China, Japan, the Philippines, Thailand, Malaysia, Singapore, Indonesia and Burma amongst people living on diets composed chiefly of highly milled rice. In India, beriberi was an important endemic disease only in the coastal region between Madras City and Vishakhapatnam where rice is usually raw-milled. In all other parts of India, Pakistan and Sri Lanka rice is usually parboiled before

Table 33.2 Observations on patients in Kuala Lumpur asylum in 1907 by Fletcher[2]

Diet	Number of patients	Cases of beriberi	Deaths
East ward: mainly raw polished rice	124	34	18
West ward: mainly par-boiled rice	123	2	0

milling and this conserves the vitamin B complex (p. 189) and so prevents beriberi.

Although beriberi is usually associated with a rice diet, this is not invariably the case. The disease may occur in groups consuming highly milled wheat. A striking example of this was described in the fishermen of Newfoundland and Labrador by Aykroyd.[4] These men and their families were often cut off through the long winter from all sources of fresh provisions. When their winter stores consisted mainly of large quantities of refined wheat flour, beriberi used to be common. Another example of the disease afflicting wheat-eaters occurred in 1916 when the Third Indian Division was besieged by the Turks at Kut-el-Amara.[5] During the siege the Indian sepoys ate whole-wheat chapattis and did not develop beriberi. The British troops ate white bread made from refined wheat flour and beriberi broke out among them.

The present position
Beriberi is much less common in South-East Asia than formerly. The disease has virtually disappeared from prosperous Asian countries such as Japan, Taiwan and Malaysia, as well as in the big cities such as Hong Kong, Singapore, Manila, Bangkok, Rangoon and Jakarta and their surrounding countryside.

The position is not so clear in the remote country areas. Here accurate information is difficult to obtain. Infants and young children who are ailing from any cause but without fever, are sometimes reported to have beriberi but the diagnosis has seldom been made by a doctor. It is seen in remote villages in Thailand but seldom in hospitals. Eating raw fermented fish, which contains thiaminase, and chewing fermented tea leaves both reduce the availability of the small amount of thiamin in the diet.[6]

Several factors are responsible for the disappearance of beriberi from many places. These are discussed on page 314.

CHEMICAL PATHOLOGY

In wet beriberi a specific biochemical lesion arises as a result of the dietary deficiency of thiamin. Carbohydrates are incompletely metabolised because thiamin pyrophosphate (TPP) is an essential coenzyme for the decarboxylation of pyruvate to acetylCoA, which is the bridge between anaerobic glycolysis and the citric acid cycle. TPP is also the coenzyme for transketolase in the hexose monophosphate pathway and for decarboxylation of 2-oxoglutarate to succinate in the citric acid cycle. Consequently pyruvic acid and lactic acid accumulate in the tissues and body fluids. In wet beriberi local accumulation of these metabolites dilates peripheral

blood vessels especially in the muscles, as in normal subjects during exercises. In beriberi this vasodilation may be extreme and so lead to capillary leakage. To maintain the circulation the cardiac output is increased. This adds a burden on the heart muscle which is already impaired through lack of thiamin. As the disease progresses the heart dilates and congestive heart failure accentuates the oedema. This is an example of 'high output' failure. Sudden death may result from myocardial failure.

The best method of detecting thiamin deficiency in the tissues is by measurement of transketolase activity in the erythrocytes (p. 153).

In chronic dry beriberi the blood pyruvate is usually within normal limits.

MORBID ANATOMY

In wet beriberi the heart at autopsy is greatly dilated; there is general oedema of the tissues and serous effusions into the body cavities, often most marked in the pericardium. Microscopic examination usually shows loss of striation of myocardial fibres, which are also finely vacuolated and often fragmented.

In dry beriberi there is severe wasting of muscle. In long-standing cases there is degeneration of peripheral nerves, both sensory and motor, with extensive demyelination and destruction of the axons. The vagus and other autonomic nerves may be affected. Degenerative changes both in the tracts and in grey matter of the cord may be found.

CLINICAL FEATURES

The early symptoms and signs are common to wet and dry beriberi. The onset is usually insidious, though sometimes precipitated by unwonted exertion or a minor febrile illness. At first there is anorexia and ill-defined malaise, associated with heaviness and weakness of the legs. This may cause some difficulty in walking. There may be a little oedema of the legs or face and the patient may complain of precordial pain and palpitations. The pulse is usually full and moderately increased in rate. There may be tenderness of the calf muscles on pressure and complaints of 'pins and needles' and numbness in the legs. The tendon jerks are usually sluggish, but occasionally slightly exaggerated. Anaesthesia of the skin, especially over the tibiae, is common. Such a condition may persist for months or even years with only minor alterations in the symptoms. In areas where beriberi is endemic it is often extremely common. Patients are only mildly incapacitated and may continue to earn their living even as manual labourers, but at a low level of efficiency. At any time this chronic malady may develop into either of the severe forms.

Wet beriberi

Oedema is the most notable feature and may develop rapidly to involve not only the legs but also the face, trunk and serous cavities. Palpitations are marked and there may be breathlessness. Anorexia and dyspepsia are commonly present. There may be pain in the legs after walking, similar to the pain that results from ischaemia in muscle. The calf muscles are frequently tense, slightly swollen and tender on pressure.

The neck veins become distended and show visible pulsations. The apex beat of the heart is displaced outwards. In the arteries there is often a lowered diastolic pressure and systolic pressure is disproportionately higher; hence on auscultation over the femoral and other large arteries, a curious 'pistol shot' sound may be heard. The pulse is generally fast and bounding as in aortic regurgitation. If the circulation is well maintained, the skin is warm to the touch owing to the associated vasodilation. When the heart begins to fail the skin becomes cold and cyanotic, particularly on the face. Electrocardiograms often show no changes but in some cases there are low voltages of the QRS complex, inverted T waves or evidence of disturbed conduction. The volume of the urine is diminished, but there is no albuminuria. The mind is usually clear. The patient is in danger of sudden increase in the oedema, acute circulatory failure, extreme dyspnoea and death.

Dry beriberi

The essential feature is a polyneuropathy. The early symptoms and signs are described above. The muscles become progressively more wasted and weak, and walking becomes increasingly difficult. The thin, even emaciated patient needs at first one stick, then two, and may finally become bedridden. The disease is a chronic malady, which may be arrested at any stage by improving the diet. Bedridden patients and those with severe cachexia are very susceptible to infections. Then dysentery or tuberculosis are often fatal unless prompt and efficient treatment is given.

The older accounts of beriberi record that cerebral manifestations are uncommon. However, amongst the British prisoners of war in Japanese camps, where beriberi was endemic, there were many cases of Wernicke's encephalopathy (p. 316).

Infantile beriberi

This occurs in breast-fed infants, usually between the second and fifth months. The mothers may have no clinical signs of beriberi although they must have been eating a diet and secreting milk with a low thiamin content. However, frank beriberi can develop in late pregnancy and the puerperium. The clinical features in infants differ somewhat from the adult disease. It exists in an acute and chronic form. In the former cardiac failure may develop abruptly; the mother may have noticed that the infant is restless, cries a lot, is passing less urine than normal and shows signs of puffiness. The infant then may suddenly become cyanosed with dyspnoea and tachycardia and die within 24 to 48 hours. Other serious signs are convulsions and coma. One characteristic sign, usually encountered only in severe cases, is partial or complete aphonia; the infant's cry becomes thin with a plaintive whine.

In the chronic form, which is much less common, the main symptoms are due to gastrointestinal disturbances. There is obstinate constipation and vomiting, repeated irregularly throughout the day and unrelated to meals. The child is fretful and sleeps poorly. The muscles are soft and toneless, but not markedly wasted. There is often intense pallor of the skin with cyanosis round the mouth. Cardiac failure and sudden death are common.

Infantile beriberi has been the chief cause of death between the ages of 2 and 5 months in rice-eating rural areas, and may still be an important cause in remote parts of Burma and northern Thailand.

DIFFERENTIAL DIAGNOSIS

A large number of diseases may closely resemble the various forms of beriberi. In endemic areas the diagnosis is usually not difficult. Outside these areas it is unwise to make the diagnosis unless there is a history of a poor diet based on polished rice or other refined cereal or of alcoholism and poor food intake (see below).

In mild and chronic cases there may be few or no physical signs and the diagnosis may have to depend on the interpretation of symptoms and the dietary history, often inaccurately described. In prisons and labour forces, such patients may be accused of malingering. The symptoms also closely resemble the manifestations of anxiety states.

The oedema of wet beriberi has to be distinguished from that associated with hepatic and renal disease and heart failure. The warm extremities in cardiac beriberi and the absence of protein in the urine are useful diagnostic points. Famine oedema should seldom be a diagnostic difficulty if a proper dietary history is taken. In the past there has been much confusion with epidemic dropsy (p. 244).

Cardiovascular beriberi has to be distinguished from other causes of high output cardiac failure, notably hyperthyroidism and severe anaemia.

In all doubtful cases of wet beriberi the therapeutic response to thiamin usually settles the diagnosis.

The features of dry beriberi are sometimes indistinguishable on clinical examination from other forms of polyneuropathy (p. 315). The diagnosis is based mainly on the dietary history, and the absence of other aetiological factors. In endemic areas the disease may be confused with neuritic leprosy, but this is characterised by palpable, cord-like superficial nerves and areas of skin anaesthesia. These two diseases not infrequently occur together and when they do, dry beriberi, if mild, may be overlooked.

The diagnosis of infantile beriberi may be difficult. Neither oedema nor paralysis is an early sign and sudden death may occur before either is present. In cases of doubt the presence of minimal signs or symptoms of beriberi in the mother may decide the issue. A history of the sudden death of a previous child between the ages of 2 and 5 months is suggestive. In public health practice among a rice-eating community a rise in death-rate of infants of this age group should suggest the possibility that infantile beriberi has become endemic. Infantile beriberi may be confused with PEM and the two may occur together.

TREATMENT

Wet beriberi. Treatment must be started as soon as the diagnosis is made, because fatal heart failure may be sudden. Complete rest is essential and thiamin should be given at once, intramuscularly, 25 mg twice daily for three days. Thereafter an oral dose of 10 mg two or three times a day should be continued until convalescence is established. Smaller amounts would probably be adequate. Many prisoners of war in Malaysia during World War II responded excellently to a daily dose of 5 mg allotted from the short supply.

The prompt response of a patient with cardiovascular beriberi to thiamin is one of the most dramatic events of medicine. Within a few hours the breathing is easier, the pulse-rate slower, the extremities cooler and a rapid diuresis begins to dispose of the oedema. Within a few days the size of the heart is restored to normal. Muscular pain and tenderness are also dramatically improved. The ECG may show characteristic paradoxical changes while the patient improves. In a typical case the tracing is normal while heart failure is severe, then as recovery starts T-wave inversions appear in some precordial leads for a few days.

During convalescence and rehabilitation a good mixed diet with less rice is needed. Another cereal should, if possible, be substituted for part of the rice in the diet. Pulses have a well-deserved reputation for curing and preventing beriberi, e.g. 120 g (4 oz) of beans or lentils.

Dry beriberi. Thiamin should be given in the same doses as for wet beriberi in order to refill the depleted tissue stores of the vitamin. However, no spectacular improvement is likely to follow. Patients are generally undernourished and, if they take sufficient of a good mixed diet to enable them to gain weight, slow improvement may be expected. Provided the dietary intake is adequate, there is no need to continue with supplementary thiamin. Infections and intercurrent disease should be treated and appropriate physiotherapy given.

Infantile beriberi. The simplest way to treat infantile beriberi is via the mother's milk. The mother should receive 10 mg thiamin twice daily — in severe cases this should be by injection. In addition the infant should be given thiamin in doses of up to 10 to 20 mg intramuscularly once a day for three days. This should be followed by 5 to 10 mg orally twice a day. With severe heart failure or convulsions and coma the initial dose may be increased to 25 to 50 mg given intravenously very slowly.

PREVENTION

Beriberi can be prevented by the use of undermilled, home pounded or parboiled rice, by the fortification of rice with thiamin or by increased use of pulses and other foods containing thiamin. Medicinal preparations of thiamin are also available and cheap.

It is difficult to say which of these factors has been responsible for the widespread decline in the disease. Changed milling practices are probably the most important and in many areas rice is not so highly polished as to remove all the bran. There are government regulations controlling milling in several countries, but these are largely ineffective owing to the difficulty of enforcing them. There is a move to replace the steel rollers in mills with ones made of rubber or other soft material, which prevents a high degree of polishing, but this is likely to be resisted by the millers.

There is no evidence of a increased use of home pounded or parboiled rice. Indeed the increasing number of small village mills has reduced home pounding. Such mills are potentially dangerous as they can produce a highly polished product and since the millers usually retain the bran as commission and sell it for cattle food, they have an incentive to produce an overmilled polished rice.

Fortified rice is available in Japan; it is supplied to the armed forces in Taiwan, but not to the civilian population. In the Philippines the only manufacturer of fortified rice has gone out of business. In Papua/New Guinea, there is a law that only fortified white rice may be imported, but this may not be enforced. In northern Thailand a trial programme of rice enrichment is in progress.[7] In other countries there is no programme of fortification.

Improvement in social and economic conditions and

the consequent consumption of a better diet with more thiamin-containing foods has certainly occurred in Japan, Taiwan and Malaysia, and in the larger cities, where beriberi was formerly common.

Medicinal thiamin is more widely used owing to the extension of medical services. The establishment of Maternal and Child Health Centres has led to many pregnant and lactating women getting good advice on diet as well as vitamin supplements; infants may also receive them or extracts of rice bran (in the Philippines).

The reasons for the decline of beriberi remain obscure. Clearly no single preventive measure has been applied effectively over a wide area. In most rice-eating countries, levels of thiamin intake appear to provide little margin of safety. There is no cause for complacency among public health authorities and efforts to increase thiamin intake by the measures described above should be pursued energetically.

THIAMIN DEFICIENCY IN THOSE WHOSE STAPLE DIET IS NOT RICE

Thiamin deficiency in countries where rice is not the staple food arises in the great majority of cases in persons whose diet has been greatly restricted usually as a result of chronic alcoholism. It also arises, but rarely, secondary to carcinoma of the stomach and other conditions associated with prolonged partial starvation. Hence there is always a lack of other essential nutrients and this together with the effects of the primary disease affects the clinical picture, seldom as clear-cut as in oriental beriberi.

It is important to realise, both in the pathogenesis and the management of these syndromes of thiamin deficiency, that intravenous infusions of dextrose can precipitate or aggravate the condition unless thiamin is given as well.

Alcoholic neuropathy

Alcoholics who have restricted their food intake for many weeks often develop a disorder of peripheral nerves sometimes indistinguishable from dry beriberi. In the days when the US Navy was supplied with liberal amounts of spirits, alcoholic neuritis was often diagnosed in ratings, but not in officers, who suffered from beriberi. This social distinction was not supported by any differences in the clinical and laboratory findings. Strauss[8] showed conclusively that alcohol was not the direct cause of the nerve lesions. These may improve on dietary therapy without altering the intake of ethanol. Biochemical tests on the blood when the patient is seen do not necessarily reflect the nutritional state of the peripheral nerves when the condition was developing.

Treatment is as for dry beriberi. The administration of thiamin leads to no dramatic improvement, but if the patient takes a good diet and gives up alcohol completely a slow diminution of the symptoms may be expected.

Alcoholic neuropathy is often clinically indistinguishable from other types of neuropathy, in which more than one nerve is involved. The lesions are symmetrical and the nerves of the lower limbs are affected more severely than those in the upper limbs. Usually there is dysfunction of both sensory and motor fibres. The effects on sensory nerves may be paraesthesiae (pins and needles) or sometimes severe nerve pains, as in the burning feet syndrome; there may be loss of sensation, either numbness of the extremities or loss of position sense. Signs of motor nerve involvement are foot drop, muscle wasting and impaired knee and ankle jerks.

Other causes of polyneuropathy are as follows.

1. Deficiency diseases — pellagra (p. 321), subacute combined degeneration (p. 329), burning feet syndrome (p. 328), and pyridoxine deficiency (p. 164).

2. Metabolic diseases — diabetes mellitus (p. 386), uraemia, porphyria, etc.

3. Chemical poisoning — heavy metals (lead, arsenic and mercury), tri-o-cresylphosphate, and some drugs, e.g. large doses of isoniazid (over 300 mg/day) for the treatment of tuberculosis.

4. Infective — Guillain-Barré syndrome, diphtheria, leprosy, etc.

5. In association with carcinoma.

6. Rare genetic types, e.g. Refsum's disease (p. 349).

Occidental beriberi heart disease

Cardiac failure with generalised oedema, pulmonary congestion and dyspnoea sometimes develops in chronic alcoholics in western countries. Damage to the myocardium may be due to direct action of ethanol or to thiamin deficiency. As usually the condition arises gradually and there are no signs of a high cardiac output or dramatic response to thiamin, it differs from acute wet beriberi. In haemodynamic studies of a small series of patients[9] the cardiac output was in some well above and in others well below the normal range, but total peripheral resistance was always low; the authors suggest that some of their patients had chronic beriberi. Views on alcoholic heart disease have been summarised in a recent editorial.[10]

Less frequent is a sudden circulatory collapse with lactic acidosis, first described in Japan and known as shoshin beriberi (*sho*, acute damage; *shin*, heart). This has now been reported in alcoholics in many western countries and the diagnosis is probably often overlooked.[11]

It would seem wise to give all alcoholics with evidence of heart failure sufficient thiamin to replenish their tissues; in most cases no benefit is likely but it will do no harm and in few may be life-saving.

WERNICKE-KORSAKOFF SYNDROME

Wernicke in 1881 described a neurological disorder occurring in three patients, two of them alcoholics and the third a seamstress who had persistent vomiting after ingestion of sulphuric acid. It is characterised by weakness of eye muscles (ophthalmoplegia), so that the patient cannot look upwards or sideways, and a state of disorientation and apathy. Sometimes there are jerky, rhythmical movements of the eyes (nystagmus) and if the patient can stand he is unsteady (ataxia). The mortality was very high until thiamin became available, when it was found that many of the cases recovered dramatically after large doses.

Korsakoff in 1887 described a psychosis, also occurring in alcoholics, characterised by a severe defect in memory and learning, but with other thought processes relatively little affected. Confabulation is a characteristic feature, though not always present. The patient can remember past events with verifiable accuracy. He cannot remember what he did earlier in the same day but tends to provide a superficially convincing tale rather than say he has forgotten.

A monograph[12] describing 245 patients in Boston concluded that Wernicke's disease and Korsakoff's psychosis are manifestations of the same pathological process and attributable to thiamin deficiency. They were able to carry out postmortems on 82 cases. There were symmetrical lesions in various parts of the brain stem, diencephalon and cerebellum, the areas commonly affected being the mamillary bodies, the nuclei of the thalamus and the periaqueductal grey matter. In the most advanced lesions there was virtually complete tissue necrosis; the less severe lesions were characterised by destruction of myelin with less damage to neurones. Small haemorrhages are characteristic but not always present.

The same histological features were seen in cases of Wernicke's disease and of Korsakoff's psychosis. Most of the patients who recovered from the acute confusional state subsequently developed some memory defect; patients with Korsakoff's psychosis had nearly always had some ocular and ataxic signs. It is postulated that Korsakoff's psychosis develops later in a patient who has recovered from Wernicke's encephalopathy. As Victor et al[12] put it, 'The response of the Korsakoff's psychosis to thiamin is slow and in almost 80 per cent of cases is incomplete. This does not necessarily mean that the pathogenesis of the memory defect is different from that of the ophthalmoplegia and ataxia but may simply reflect the fact that the structural changes in the diencephalon which are responsible for the memory defect are more severe (and less reversible) than those in the ocular and vestibular nuclei and the cerebellum.'

Incidence appears to be increasing, as consumption of alcohol rises in many countries, and the diagnosis is often missed clinically and made by the pathologist.[13] This oversight is serious, as treatment with thiamin is usually effective when given promptly. Large doses, as for wet beriberi, are needed. Diagnosis is confirmed by a quick response to thiamin therapy or demonstrating thiamin deficiency by the RBC transketolase test. The TPP effect is very high in Wernicke's encephalopathy[14] but in suspected cases thiamin should be given as soon as blood has been taken, without waiting for the result.

Although the syndrome usually occurs in alcoholics, it may arise, as already mentioned, secondary to any disorder which seriously impairs nutrition. It is perhaps the human counterpart of the severe brain disturbances that occur in pigeons fed on polished rice. It is strange that the syndrome is not described by early writers in the Orient; there is no mention of it by Vedder.[3] However, there were 52 cases in Europeans on rice diets in prisoner of war hospitals in Singapore, where outbreaks of beriberi were occurring.[15]

COMMENT

Thiamin deficiency can thus lead to an encephalopathy or a cardiomyopathy or a peripheral neuropathy. Two, or rarely all three, diseases can occur together in a patient but it is surprising how often they do not. We cannot yet explain why the brain is affected in one person, the heart in another and the peripheral nerves in a third. Because alcoholism is widespread and body stores of thiamin in alcoholics are likely to be small, all doctors should be aware of thiamin deficiency. It is treatable if not left too late. There are still many unsolved problems in the relation between ethanol, thiamin and brain damage.[16]

REFERENCES

1. Takaki K 1906 The preservation of health among the personnel of the Japanese Navy and Army. Lancet 1: 1369–74, 1451–5, 1520–3
2. Fletcher W 1907 Rice and beriberi: preliminary report on an experiment conducted at the Kuala Lumpur Lunatic Asylum. Lancet 1: 1776–9
3. Vedder E B 1913 Beriberi. Bale & Davidson, London
4. Aykroyd W R 1930 Beriberi and other food-deficiency diseases in Newfoundland and Labrador. J Hyg (Camb) 30: 357–86
5. Hehir P 1922 Effects of chronic starvation during the siege of Kut. Br Med J 1: 865–8

6. Vimokesant S, Kunjara S, Rungruangsak K, Nakornchai S, Panijpan B 1982 Beriberi caused by antithiamin factors in food and its prevention. Ann NY Acad Sci 378: 123–36

7. Thanangkul O, Whitaker J A 1966 Childhood thiamine deficiency in northern Thailand. Am J Clin Nutr 18: 275–7

8. Straus M B 1935 The etiology of 'alcoholic neuritis'. Am J Med Sci 189: 378–82

9. Blacket R B, Palmer A J 1960 Haemodynamic studies in high output beriberi. Br Heart J 22: 483–501

10. Portal R W 1981 Alcoholic heart disease. Br Med J 283: 1202–3

11. Majoor C L, Hillen H F 1982 Cardiac beriberi with lactic acidosis and cardiovascular collapse (shoshin), a disease condition not rare in alcoholics but easily misdiagnosed. Ned Tijdschr Geneeskd 126: 749–57

12. Victor M, Adams R D, Collins G H 1971 The Wernicke-Korsakoff syndrome. Davis, Philadelphia

13. Anonymous 1981 Alcoholic brain damage. Lancet 1: 477–8

14. Truswell A S, Konno T, Hansen J D L 1972 Thiamine deficiency in adult hospital patients. S Afr Med J 46: 2079–82

15. De Wardener H E, Lennox B 1947 Cerebral beriberi (Wernicke's encephalopathy): review of 52 cases in a Singapore prisoner-of-war hospital. Lancet 1: 11–7

16. Thomson A D, Ryle P R, Shaw D K 1983 Ethanol, thiamine and brain damage. Alcohol Alcoholism 18: 27–43

34

Pellagra

Pellagra is a nutritional disease endemic among poor peasants who subsist chiefly on maize, among whom it is chronic and relapsing, with a seasonal incidence. The typical clinical features are loss of weight, increasing debility, an erythematous dermatitis characteristically affecting parts of the skin exposed to sunlight, gastrointestinal disturbance especially diarrhoea and glossitis, and mental changes. Pellagra has been called the disease of the three Ds: 'dermatitis, diarrhoea and dementia'. This is a useful mnemonic for medical students but diarrhoea and mental changes are not always present in mild and early cases and the mental symptom is usually depression and not dementia.

Pellagra is now rarely seen in most parts of the world, but in the nineteenth and first part of the twentieth century there were periodic outbreaks affecting thousands of people in many countries. Throughout this long period many field observations and epidemiological studies led to learned arguments about its aetiology before it was finally established as a dietary deficiency disease. Over the years five major books[1-5] on pellagra have been written and it is the best example of how prolonged epidemiological studies can finally elucidate the aetiology of a common endemic disease with many social ramifications.

HISTORY

Pellagra was unknown to classical and mediaeval physicians. After the introduction of maize into Europe from the Americas, it was first described by Casal as occurring in Spain in 1735. An Italian physician Frapolli named it in 1771 (*pelle* = skin; *agra* = rough). The disease spread with the cultivation of maize. In the nineteenth century it was common in Spain, Italy, France, Serbia (Yugoslavia), Romania, Bulgaria and the Ukraine. Great epidemics occurred in North Africa, especially in Egypt. Later it spread to other parts of Africa. Thus in 1897 there was a large epidemic of rinderpest in South Africa which decimated the cattle. Before this disaster milk, and especially 'amasi', a sour milk preparation, were important items of the Bantu diet. With the loss of this milk the children had to be weaned on to maize paps; the reduced supply of meat led to a much bigger proportion of maize in the diet. Large numbers of children and adults began to suffer from pellagra.

The disease first became prominent in the USA in 1907, affecting many Negro and poor white families in the southern states. This coincided with the commercial degermination of maize. Pellagra was so widespread that it was held to be an infectious disease. The Federal Government sent a physician, Goldberger, to investigate the outbreaks and much of the credit for demonstrating that pellagra is a deficiency disease belongs to him. An edited selection of his papers written between 1913 and 1928 is now available.[3] Pellagra remained an important disease in many southern states until the USA entered World War II; then consequent upon full employment and the rise in wages, poverty and the dietary dependence on maize were reduced. Maize meal has subsequently been enriched with nicotinamide in the USA. A good account of the factors that led to the disappearance of endemic pellagra from the USA is given by Davies.[6]

EPIDEMIOLOGY TODAY

Africa appears to be the only continent where there are areas in which it remains an important public health problem. In parts of southern Africa, it remains endemic and there are large outbreaks in the spring and summer months. More than half the patients who attend clinics in some Bantu homelands have pellagrous skin lesions, and pellagra accounts for a proportion of the admissions to the Bantu Mental Hospital in Pretoria. The prevalence of pellagra in South Africa is probably due to the maize being machine-milled in factories and not pounded by the women in their villages. Refined machine-milled maize flour contains less tryptophan and much less nicotinic acid than wholemeal maize flour. Pellagra is endemic in Lesotho. The people have their own name for it, 'Lefula-pone', which means the disease of the mealies (maize). In Egypt, Sudan, Kenya and Tanzania pellagra is much less common than formerly, but still occurs in some areas.

In India sporadic cases are seen in maize eaters: however, pellagra occurs mainly where sorghum is the staple cereal and in Hyderabad it is responsible for up to 10 per cent of admissions to mental hospitals in some seasons. Gopalan and Srikantia were the first to report this in 1960 and suggested that the pellagragenic action of sorghum was due to the fact that its proteins contained a higher proportion of leucine than those of other cereals and millets.[7] It has been difficult to confirm this hypothesis, but Bender[8] has now shown that a dietary excess of leucine in rats inhibits kynurinase and increases activity of picolinate carboxylase in the pathways of tryptophan metabolism. Both of these effects would result in reduced formation of nicotinamide.

AETIOLOGY

The history of the search for the cause of pellagra well illustrates how the growth of knowledge can bring together apparently opposing theories and shows in the end that each has a substance of truth.

Toxic theory
Early in the nineteenth century it was observed that outbreaks of pellagra in southern Europe often followed the consumption of mouldy maize and it was suggested in Italy that, as in ergotism, a toxic product from the mould was responsible.[1] This hypothesis received support for several decades and has now been revived, at least in part, by Schoental.[9] She points out that T-2 mycotoxins from mouldy grains have been responsible for outbreaks of lethal poisoning in livestock and also in man. There is as yet no contemporary evidence associating the symptoms of pellagra with any of these toxins.

Bacterial infection
At the end of the nineteenth century, bacteriology was a new subject and it was common to ascribe a bacterial origin to any disease for which there was no obvious cause. When in 1914 Goldberger went from Washington to begin his experiments on pellagra in Jackson, Mississippi, it was commonly thought to be an infection disease.

Protein deficiency theory
The diet of impoverished pellagrins was poor in protein and this deficiency was first suggested as the cause of the disease nearly a century ago. This theory gained support when Wilson[10] in Egypt showed how closely pellagra was linked to the intake of zein, a protein known to be of poor quality. Goldberger showed that small quantities of milk prevented pellagra.

Vitamin deficiency theory
The above concept of the cause of the disease was altered by the discovery that extracts of yeast and liver contained a heat-stable, non-protein factor that would cure both human pellagra and black-tongue in dogs. The investigation of black-tongue in dogs ultimately led to the identification of nicotinic acid as the pellagra-preventing (P-P) factor (p. 155).

Reconciliation of the three theories.
The dramatic therapeutic effects of nicotinic acid in pellagra at first seemed the final proof of the last of these theories, with the result that the alternatives were temporarily forgotten, until revived by the results of subsequent research.

It still remained to be explained why the disease is so closely associated with maize. Maize actually contains more nicotinic acid than oats, rye and white bread though less than whole wheat. Aykroyd and Swaminathan[11] pointed out that maize diets in a part of India where pellagra was endemic contained more nicotinic acid than poor rice diets in other regions where it was rare.

Two complementary explanations became available. First, most of the nicotinic acid in maize is present in a bound form that is not absorbed in the gut and so unavailable to the tissues, a discovery made by Kodicek.[12] Secondly, nicotinamide is synthesised in the body from tryptophan present in ample amounts in most dietary proteins but not in zein, the chief protein in maize. Hence milk, a poor source of nicotinic acid, is pellagra-preventive.

Absence of pellagra in Aztec society
The high incidence of pellagra in maize eaters in southern Europe, contrasted with absence of the disease in Central America and Mexico from where the maize had come, was an old problem. A young Mexican physician, Ismael Salas, in a thesis presented in Paris in 1863 and quoted extensively by Roussel[1] provided an explanation, now known to be correct. The main article of the diet of Mexican peasants was and still is the *tortilla*, as opposed to bread made from maize flour eaten by pellagrins in France and Italy. Salas describes in detail how tortillas were made. Maize grains were mixed with a thin paste of slaked lime and heated for 18 hours. Then they were washed with water and put on a round stone with a stone cylinder placed on top. The pressure reduced the grains to a malleable paste from which round pancakes could be cut. These were then cooked on a hot iron plate and turned over frequently. Gas was formed in the process and made the tortilla as

'light and savoury as the best bread'. We now know that the prolonged heat used in the making of tortillas liberates the bound nicotinic acid and makes the vitamin available to the tissues.

Pellagra in non-maize eaters

It has long been known that symptoms of pellagra occasionally arise in Europeans and North Americans who do not eat maize and they were said to have pseudo-pellagra. Most patients are alcoholics, but it is now uncommon and much less frequent than manifestations of thiamin deficiency in alcoholics. Pellagrous skin rashes have occurred in patients after severe partial starvation, e.g. in the malabsorption syndrome, and in those on very low protein diets for the treatment of chronic renal failure.

An inborn error of metabolism. A rare disorder, closely resembling pellagra, occurs in children. There is a good description of two English schoolboys, brothers aged 8 and 11 years, seen at St Thomas's Hospital, London, in 1913.[13] Both had pellagrous rashes and neurological lesions and died soon after. Understanding of this condition has followed a study from the Middlesex Hospital in 1956.[14] This showed that, besides the skin lesions, there is usually cerebellar ataxia and biochemical abnormalities, notably aminoaciduria. It is now called **Hartnup's disease** after the first family investigated. The underlying defect is in the transport of tryptophan and affects absorption of the amino acid in the small intestine as well as in the renal tubules. Now over 50 cases have been reported, most of whom have responded well to treatment with nicotinamide.

CLINICAL FEATURES

The patient is often underweight, and presents the general features of undernutrition.

Skin

The diagnosis is generally first suggested by the appearance of the skin. Characteristically, there is an erythema resembling severe sunburn, appearing symmetrically over the parts of the body exposed to sunlight, especially the backs of the hands, the wrists and forearms, face and neck. Exposure to trauma or mechanical irritation of the skin, especially over bony prominences, may also determine the site of the lesion. The skin in the affected areas is at first red and slightly swollen; it itches and burns. In acute cases the skin lesions may progress to vesiculation, cracking, exudation and crusting with ulceration and sometimes secondary infection; but in chronic cases the dermatitis occurs as a roughening and thickening of the skin with dryness,

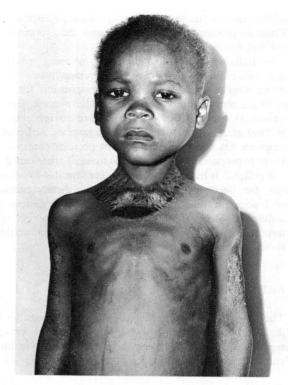

Fig. 34.1 Pellagra in a child, showing Casal's collar and also skin lesions on the arms. (Patient of J. D. L. Hansen and A. S. Truswell)

scaling and a brown pigmentation (Fig. 34.1). This is the only symptom or sign in many people in endemic areas in Africa.

Digestive system

Complaints of digestive upset are usual, and diarrhoea is common but not always present. There may be nausea, a burning sensation in the epigastrium, and sometimes constipation in chronic cases. The digestive symptoms may be aggravated by the presence of intestinal parasites. The mouth is sore and often shows angular stomatitis and cheilosis. The tongue characteristically has a 'raw beef' appearance — red, swollen and painful, though usually without loss of papillae. Secondary infection of the mouth with Vincent's organisms is common. A non-infective inflammation followed by mucosal atrophy may involve the gastrointestinal tract and account for the diarrhoea which is characteristically profuse and watery, sometimes with blood and mucus in the stools, and accompanied by tenesmus. The rectum and anus are frequently affected and chronic gastritis with reduction or absence of acid secretion is a common finding. Vaginitis and amenorrhoea may occur.

Nervous system

In mild cases the symptoms consist of weakness, tremor, anxiety, depression and irritability; in severe acute cases delirium is common and dementia occurs in the chronic form. Because of these changes, chronic pellagrins may be admitted to mental hospitals. In chronic cases there may be decreased sensation in the feet to touch and loss of vibration and position sense, often accompanied by hyperaesthesia and paraesthesia. The loss of position sense may give rise to ataxia. Spasticity and exaggerated tendon reflexes give evidence of involvement of the pyramidal tracts. These features are those of subacute combined degeneration of the cord and may be due to associated vitamin B12 deficiency. Alternatively there may be footdrop and impairment of tendon reflexes, indicating a perpheral nerve lesion.

DIAGNOSIS

The classical case is easily diagnosed if a careful dietary and social history is taken and the typical clinical signs are present. The skin lesions are of diagnostic importance since they are only found in pellagra, whereas the gastrointestinal and mental features may be present in many other diseases. It is the occasional case in a non-maize eater that may present difficulties. A variety of erythemas and exfoliative skin lesions may mimic pellagra. The two characteristic features of cutaneous pellagra are its symmetrical distribution, determined by the clothes of the patient and exposure to sunlight, and the therapeutic response to nicotinic acid. A nutritional glossitis identical with the tongue changes seen in pellagra may occur without the other signs of the disease in people who have been all the time indoors, out of sunlight. In any unexplained delirium or dementia in a person who has been taking a poor diet for a prolonged period, the possibility of pellagra should be remembered.

Pellagra is a disease affecting poor people on bad diets. Hence it is often accompanied by signs of protein-energy malnutrition, by anaemia and by deficiencies of thiamin and other vitamins. These together with chronic infections may complicate the clinical picture.

LABORATORY FINDINGS

N-Methylnicotinamide, a normal excretory product of nicotinic acid, appears in reduced amounts in the urine. A level of urinary excretion below 0.2 mg/6 h or 0.5 mg/g of creatinine indicates a deficiency of the vitamin, but not necessarily a diagnosis of pellagra. Reproducibility of the method is not very satisfactory, as other substances sometimes interfere with the fluorimetric procedure. The fasting plasma tryptophan ranges from 1.0 to 4.8 mg/l in pellagrins and from 6.5 to 8,8 mg/l in healthy adults.[15] Plasma tryptophan may prove to be a convenient test for confirming a diagnosis of pellagra.

Examination of the blood may show anaemia and hypoalbuminaemia due to the associated dietary deficiencies. The anaemia may be macrocytic or microcytic, depending on the predominant associated deficiency.

PROGNOSIS

In endemic areas the majority of patients are mild cases, improving in the winter and relapsing with the increased sunshine in the spring. Mental symptoms, especially dementia, are perhaps the most serious feature and may be permanent. Occasionally a fulminating form develops, with fever and severe prostration which can be fatal. In the past many deaths were due to secondary infections (notably tuberculosis and dysentery) or to emaciation due to general dietary failure, intensified by the diarrhoea.

TREATMENT

Specific vitamin therapy

For quick relief of symptoms nicotinic acid or nicotinamide are the standard treatment. Nicotinamide is to be preferred because it does not cause the unpleasant flushing and burning sensations that often result from taking nicotinic acid. These are transitory and harmless, but may alarm the patient. A suitable dose for either nicotinamide or nicotinic acid is 100 mg 4-hourly by mouth, although a smaller dose is likely to be effective. The vitamin is rapidly absorbed from the stomach, despite severe digestive disorders. There is therefore no need to give intravenous or intramuscular injections. The immediate response to nicotinamide is usually dramatic; within 24 hours the erythema diminishes, the tongue becomes paler and less painful and the diarrhoea ceases. Often there is striking improvement in the patient's behaviour and mental attitude. But nicotinamide alone is usually insufficient to restore health, because of other associated deficiencies, notably of protein and other components of the vitamin B complex. Preparations of vitamin B complex should be given as a routine and if there are signs of peripheral neuropathy or subacute combined degeneration of the cord larger doses of thiamin or vitamin B12 are indicated.

Diet

The first aim should be to make good qualitative and quantitative deficiencies of the previous diet. To restore the patient to normal weight, the diet should provide ample energy and good quality protein, as is present in milk, eggs, meat or fish. In severely ill patients it is necessary to climb the dietetic ladder cautiously. The food should be low in bulk at first in order to avoid further diarrhoea. The diet may be poorly tolerated because of the mental state of the patient and the sore mouth which may make eating difficult. Alcohol should be forbidden.

General measures

Rest in bed and sedation are necessary for severely ill pellagrins, especially those with marked mental symptoms; they are often troublesome patients who need understanding. If the dermatitis is associated with much crusting or secondary infection, gentle washing with a bland solution is indicated.

PREVENTION

That pellagra has vanished from the southern states of America, where formerly it afflicted tens of thousands of poor country folk, demonstrates in a dramatic way that the disease is preventable. This came about with the general improvement in the economic state, the education and the nutrition of the population.

Enrichment of maize meal with vitamins is technically simple and inexpensive but is difficult to implement for subsistence farmers who grow their own maize.

From the standpoint of agricultural policy, it is clearly wise to avoid dependence on a single cereal crop, such as maize, or to devote too great an acreage of fertile land for the cultivation of cash-crops, such as cotton or tobacco. Animal husbandry should be encouraged in all areas where pellagra is endemic so that the production of milk and milk products and meat is increased. Encouraging the planting of opaque-2 maize (p. 190) may help. It contains about three times as much tryptophan and twice as much lysine as conventional maize.

REFERENCES

1. Roussel T 1866 Traité de la pellagra et des pseudo-pellagres. Bailliére, Paris
2. Harris H F 1919 Pellagra. Macmillan, New York
3. Terris M 1963 Goldberger on pellagra. State University Press, Baton Rouge, Louisiana
4. Roe D A 1973 A plague of corn: the social history of pellagra. Cornell University Press, Ithaca
5. Carpenter K J (ed) 1981 Pellagra. Benchmark papers in biochemistry, vol 2. Hutchinson Press, Stroud, Pa
6. Davies J N P 1964 The decline of pellagra in the southern United States. Lancet 2: 195–6
7. Gopalan C, Srikantia S G 1960 Leucine and pellagra. Lancet 1:954–7
8. Bender D A 1983 Effects of a dietary excess of leucine on tryptophane metabolism in the rat: a mechanism for the pellagragenic action of leucine. Br J Nutr 50: 25–32
9. Schoental R 1980 Mouldy grain and the aetiology of pellagra: the role of toxic metabolites of *Fusarium*.

Biochem Soc Trans 8: 147–50
10. Wilson W H 1921 The diet factor in pellagra. J Hyg (Camb) 20: 1–59
11. Aykroyd W R, Swaminathan M 1940 Nicotinic acid content of cereals and pellagra. Indian J Med Res 27: 267–77
12. Kodicek E, Braude R, Kon S K, Mitchell K G 1956 The effect of alkaline hydrolysis of maize on the availability of its nicotinic acid to the *pig*. Br J Nutr 10: 51–67
13. Box C R 1913 Fatal pellagra in two English boys. Br Med J 2: 2–4
14. Baron D N, Dent C E, Harris H, Hart E W, Jepson J B 1956 Hereditary, pellagra-like skin rash with temporary cerebellar ataxia, constant renal amino-aciduria and other bizarre biochemical features. Lancet 1: 421–8
15. Truswell A S, Hansen J D L, Wannenburg P 1968 Plasma tryptophan and other amino acids in pellagra. Am J Clin Nutr 21: 1314–20

35

Scurvy

Scurvy is a nutritional disease which results from prolonged subsistence on diets practically devoid of fresh fruit and vegetables. Lack of ascorbic acid causes a disturbance in the structure of connective tissue, leading to swollen, bleeding gums, and haemorrhages into the skin and elsewhere.

HISTORY

Scurvy was not clearly recognised by Greek, Roman or mediaeval physicians. In 1453 Constantinople was sacked by the Turks, so that Venice lost naval control of the Eastern Mediterranean, and the overland trade route between Europe and Asia was blocked. This disaster for Christian merchant adventurers stimulated the Portuguese to find a sea route to India. In 1497 Vasco de Gama sailed round the Cape of Good Hope and established a trading centre on the Malabar coast. Scurvy broke out among his crew on the voyage and 100 out of his 160 men died. For the next 300 years scurvy was a major factor determining the success or failure of all sea ventures, whether undertaken for purposes of war, trade or exploration. As early as 1535 the French explorer Jacques Cartier, whose crew was severely affected in Newfoundland, discovered that the juice of the leaves of a certain tree had remarkable antiscorbutic properties. An account of this discovery, as recorded in Hakluyt's *The Principall Navigations* (1600), was reproduced in earlier editions of our book.

Later Canadian explorers, suffering from scurvy, attempted to identify the curative Ameda tree without success, probably because the Indians by then were less communicative. The tragedy was that as they died of the disease the tree was probably standing right beside them; for as Lind suggested, it was probably the spruce fir. The value of a decoction of spruce or pine needles as an antiscorbutic remedy was well known to the Swedes at least as early as the sixteenth century, and subsequently used by the Russians in their repeated attempts to find an Arctic sea-route to the Pacific.

Curiously the antiscorbutic value of pine needles was rediscovered in the USSR in 1943.

The subsequent history of scurvy is of great interest. Many writers showed that the disease could be cured by a variety of fresh fruits and vegetables, but medical learning was so constricted by Galen's classical pathology of 'humours' that the conception of a deficiency disease was not realised till long after. In 1753 Lind, a Scots naval surgeon, published *A Treatise of the Scurvy*,[1] in which he showed not only that the disease could be cured by fresh oranges and lemons, but also that it could be prevented by adequate dietary and other hygienic measures. His own account of the first controlled therapeutic trial ever undertaken is as follows:

On the 20th of May 1747, I took twelve patients in the scurvy, on board the *Salisbury* at sea. Their cases were as similar as I could have them. They all in general had putrid gums, the spots and lassitude, with weakness of their knees. They lay together in one place, being a proper apartment for sick in the forehold; and had one diet common to all . . . Two of these were ordered each a quart of cyder a-day. Two others took twenty-five gutta of *elisir vitriol* three times a-day, upon an empty stomach; using a gargle strongly acidulated with it for their mouths. Two others took two spoonfuls of vinegar three times a day, upon an empty stomach; having their gruels and their other food well acidulated with it, as also the gargle for their mouth. Two of the worst patients, with the tendons in the ham rigid . . . were put under a course of sea-water. On this they drank half a pint every day, and sometimes more or less as it operated, by way of gentle physic. Two others had each two oranges and one lemon given them every day. These they eat with greediness, at different times, upon an empty stomach. They continued but six days under this course, having consumed the quantity that could be spared. The two remaining patients, took the bigness of a nutmeg three times a-day, of an electuary recommended by an hospital-surgeon, made of garlic, mustard-seed, *rad. raphan.*, balsam of Peru, and gum myrrh; using for common drink, barley-water well acidulated with tamarinds . . .

The consequence was, that the most sudden and visible good effects were perceived from the use of the oranges and lemons; one of those who had taken them, being at the end of six days fit for duty . . . The other was the best recovered of any in his condition; and being now deemed pretty well, was appointed nurse to the rest of the sick.[1]

Lind was aware that an adequate supply of fresh vegetables or a suitable fruit juice could prevent the occurrence of scurvy. He states that abstinence from them is 'the occasional (i.e. apparent) cause of the evil' but other factors such as exposure to cold and wet, drunkenness, putrid air and overcrowding below decks were 'predisposing causes'. Such factors, often today loosely called 'stress', are now known to have important effects on ascorbic acid metabolism (p. 148).

Captain James Cook was the first person to demonstrate that a long voyage could be undertaken without the crew developing scurvy. In his voyage round the world from 1772 to 1775 in which he explored Australia and New Zealand, none of his men developed the disease, thanks to the care with which he seized every opportunity to provide them with fresh vegetables and fruit (including oranges and lemons) whenever they touched land. But it was not until 1795, 42 years after the publication of Lind's treatise, that his pupil Sir Gilbert Blane persuaded the Lords of the Admiralty to put his precepts into practice and thus immediately abolished scurvy from the Royal Navy. This was at the beginning of the Napoleonic wars when Great Britain's command of the sea was of paramount importance to her. The application of Lind's teaching doubled the fighting force of the Navy at sea without adding a penny to the naval estimates.[2] For a further 50 years however, the disease lingered on in the merchant navies of the world. The long interval between the discovery of the new knowledge and its application to the benefit of humanity makes a sad story in history.

When scurvy ceased to be an important disease of sailors, it developed in another section of the community; the knowledge of the chemistry of food obtained in the nineteenth century enabled a variety of preserved and artificial milks to be manufactured. These provided an adequate substitute for the protein, fat and carbohydrate in human milk and so removed the wet nurses from our society. But these substitutes for human milk contained little or no ascorbic acid, so scurvy in infants became an important disease. The heyday of infantile scurvy was in the last 20 years of the nineteenth century.

EPIDEMIOLOGY

Fortunately scurvy is now an uncommon disease, but cases occur in all countries in persons who for one reason or another have dropped out of society. In Britain they are usually old men who have been living alone and cases usually occur in the spring when potatoes, the chief source of ascorbic acid in poor diets, have lost most of the vitamin during winter storage. Infantile scurvy is now very rare in Britain, but isolated cases, presenting problems in diagnosis, are reported from many countries. Alcoholics and other drug addicts may also suffer from scurvy, but considering their number and the poor diets on which many of them exist, cases are surprisingly few. Scurvy is also sometimes seen in dietary cranks and in patients with chronic diseases, especially of the gastrointestinal tract, when food intake is impaired.

Outbreaks of scurvy occur in poor nomadic and peasant populations in arid or semi-desert districts, when the rains fail and there is a threat of famine. Scurvy is still a danger for civil populations in besieged cities, but owing to the ease with which ascorbic acid can be supplied even in wartime it should not arise.

AETIOLOGY

Scurvy results from the prolonged consumption of a diet devoid of fresh fruit and vegetables. Lack of ascorbic acid is responsible for the characteristic features of the disease, but such diets are likely to lack other nutrients such as iron, folate, vitamin A and sometimes protein. Thus although ascorbic acid relieves the predominant signs of the disease it does not always completely cure the patient. Further, although a diet may seem from the history to contain adequate amounts of ascorbic acid, it may in fact be scorbutic if practically all the vitamin has been destroyed in its cooking. Another factor may be the influence of stress which increases the utilisation of ascorbic acid.

PATHOLOGY

Haemorrhages either large or microscopic may be found anywhere in the body. They are most common in the gums if the teeth are still present, in subcutaneous tissues, and beneath the periosteum of bones and the synovia of joints. These are sites of minor trauma. Haemorrhages into the brain or heart muscle may cause sudden death. Haemorrhages are due to defective collagen formation in the basement membranes of capillaries arising from lack of ascorbic acid needed to convert proline to hydroxyproline. There is also a failure of wound healing and old wounds which have healed may break down (p. 148).

As deaths from scurvy are now rare, there is seldom an opportunity for a postmortem and the classical account of autopsy findings is by Aschoff & Koch.[3]

CLINICAL FEATURES

The best clinical account of scurvy is that given by Lind, who had greater experience of the disease than any modern physician and described his observations with the clarity and elegance characteristic of his time.

Lind said that the pathognomonic sign of the disease was the appearance of the gums and certainly the characteristic gingivitis often first suggests the diagnosis. The gums are swollen, particularly in the region of the papillae between the teeth, sometimes producing the appearance of 'scurvy buds' (Fig. 35.1). These may be so extensive that they project beyond the biting surface of the teeth and almost completely conceal them. The spongy gums are livid in colour and bleed on the slightest touch. There is always some infection; indeed this seems necessary for the production of the scorbutic gingival appearances since human volunteers suffering from ascorbic acid deficiency did not develop it if their gums were previously healthy. Associated with the infection there is an offensive foetor. In patients without teeth the gums appear normal.

The first sign of cutaneous bleeding is often to be found on the lower thighs, just above the knees. These haemorrhages are perifollicular — tiny points of bleeding around the orifice of a hair follicle. For some time beforehand the follicle can be seen to be raised above the general surface of the skin, giving the appearance of folliculosis, which is quite commonly seen in varying degrees in people apparently well supplied with ascorbic acid. The condition in scurvy can be distinguished by its appearance from the follicular keratosis sometimes associated with vitamin A deficiency. In the latter condition there is usually a horny plug of keratin projecting from the orifice of the hair follicle. In scurvy there is a heaping up of keratin-like

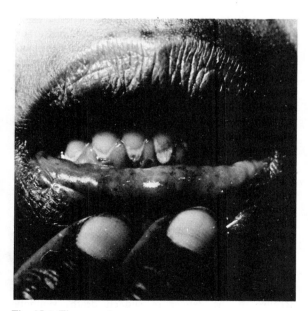

Fig. 35.1 The gums in scurvy

material on the surface around the mouth of the follicle, through which a deformed 'cockscrew' hair characteristically projects. Perifollicular haemorrhages may subsequently appear on the buttocks, abdomen, legs and arms; they are often followed by petechial haemorrhages, developing independently of the hair follicles, due to rupture of capillary vessels. Such purpuric spots are usually first seen on the feet and ankles. Thereafter large spontaneous bruises (ecchymoses) may arise almost anywhere in the body, but usually first in the legs. In dark skins these changes are not always easily seen and may be overlooked. African patients often present with pain in a leg due to haemorrhage into intermuscular septa in the thigh or calf. In volunteers with experimental scurvy several additional clinical features have been described.[4] These include (1) ocular haemorrhages, especially in the bulbar conjunctiva; (2) Sjögren's syndrome, i.e. loss of secretion of salivary and lacrimal glands and swelling of the parotid glands; (3) femoral neuropathy; (4) oedema of the lower limbs with oliguria; and (5) psychological disturbances, hypochondria and depression.

Anaemia is present in most patients and the causes have been much discussed.[5,6] It is not due directly to ascorbic acid deficiency, since anaemia is not found in experiment scurvy in man. In patients the bone marrow may be normoblastic or megaloblastic and associated deficiency of iron or folate is often responsible, but there may be other unidentified factors. Destruction of erythrocytes in muscle haematomata may lead to bilirubinaemia and mild jaundice.

Osteoporosis may occur in scurvy, not surprisingly since ascorbic acid is necessary for the synthesis of collagen in all parts of the body, including the bones. The most severe cases have been reported in Johannesburg in young and middle-aged man, some of whom have had compression fractures of vertebrae, unusual except in the elderly. These men are usually alcoholics with evidence of excess iron storage.[7] The mechanisms relating siderosis to increased ascorbic acid metabolism and consequent scurvy are not yet understood (p. 119).

Examination of a patient with scurvy usually reveals no abnormal physical signs of disease except gingivitis and cutaneous haemorrhages and hence the gravity of his condition may not be appreciated. However, haemorrhages into any of the internal organs may occur and a patient die suddenly and without warning, apparently from cardiac failure. Lind himself described how a sailor afflicted with scurvy fell dead while working at a windlass.

Scurvy in infants

Until the teeth have erupted, scorbutic infants do not develop gingivitis. When this occurs the gums have the classical appearance of 'scurvy buds' described above,

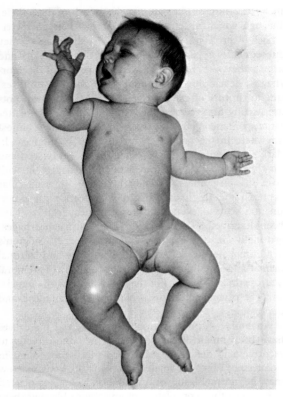

Fig. 35.2 Infantile scurvy. The frog-like position is due to large painful subperiosteal haemorrhages in both femurs. There are haematomata in the scalp and also beading of the costochondral junctions. (Patient of J. D. L. Hansen)

a diagnostic feature. The first sign of bleeding is usually a large subperiosteal haemorrhage immediately over-lying one of the long bones — frequently the femur — producing the characteristic 'frog-legs' position (Fig. 35.2). This gives rise to intense pain, especially on movement. The infant may cry continuously and agon-isingly, and scream even louder when lifted.

DIAGNOSIS

The distinctive appearance of the gums must be distinguished from other causes of gingivitis, the commonest of which is periodontal disease (p. 422). In the latter condition there are usually accumulations of calculus on the teeth, with retraction of the gum margin. The inflamed rim of the gums is bright red in colour, in contrast to the cyanotic appearance in scurvy, and there is usually much less swelling. In Vincent's angina the gums are acutely inflamed, ulcerated and painful, but here again the bright red appearance of the lesions is distinctive. Poisoning with heavy metals, particularly

lead and mercury, produces a gingivitis in which the gum margin is stained blue; but there is usually little swelling and the appearance is easily distinguished from scurvy. Phenytoin, a drug used in epilepsy, may cause marked swelling of the gums, but they preserve their normal colour and do not bleed.

The perifollicular haemorrhages of scurvy are distinctive in appearance. But if only petechiae are visible, other causes of purpura must be excluded, e.g. blood dyscrasias, drug poisoning or prothrombin deficiency. If ecchymoses are the chief manifestations, the patient may be seen first by a surgeon, on the suspicion of some undisclosed trauma.

Scurvy in infants and children may sometimes be mistaken for rheumatic fever or osteomyelitis, because of the pain caused by a subperiosteal haemorrhage. The refusal of the child to use one leg may cause the disease to be mistaken for poliomyelitis.

The dietary and social history establishes the diagnosis in doubtful cases. Old solitary people may insist that they fend very well for themselves, but careful questioning shows that they do not bother to buy fresh fruit or vegetables. In other instances the proper foods may be purchased but they are so badly cooked that the diet is made scorbutic.

Special investigations. Capillary fragility may be increased. This can be shown by the application of a sphygmomanometer cuff to the arm and leaving it inflated for five minutes, half-way between the systolic and diastolic blood pressure. A shower of petechia then appears over the area of skin below the cuff. But this is not a specific test for scurvy.

Ascorbic acid can be estimated with relative ease either in blood plasma or whole blood. This is useful only in excluding the diagnosis, since if any measurable amount of ascorbic acid can be detected in the blood, the case is not one of scurvy. The absence of detectable ascorbic acid, however, does not necessarily indicate that the patient has scurvy, since the blood level of the vitamin falls to unmeasurable levels long before the disease develops. A better index of the body reserves of the vitamin is its concentration in the white blood corpuscles. If none can be measured, the diagnosis of scurvy is practically certain.

The estimation of ascorbic acid in the urine provides no reliable aid to diagnosis, because small amounts of the vitamin or some other substance reducing 2,6-dichlorophenolindophenol, continue to be excreted in the urine, even in manifest scurvy.

TREATMENT

Because of the danger of sudden death, synthetic ascorbic acid should be given at once and in adequate amounts. The vitamin is very soluble and rapidly absorbed from the digestive tract. It can be given intravenously, but a large part of the dose is immediately lost in the urine. The aim should be to saturate the body with ascorbic acid with as little delay as possible. The fully saturated body contains about 5 g of the vitamin, so that a dose of 250 mg by mouth four times daily should achieve this within a week, despite some loss in the urine.

It sometimes happens that scurvy arises among people far removed from supplies of synthetic ascorbic acid (e.g. among prisoners of war); in such situations valuable therapeutic effects are obtained by the use of natural sources of the vitamin such as fresh fruit and vegetables, sprouting peas or extract of pine needles.

Once the danger of sudden death is averted by giving ascorbic acid, attention should be paid to correcting the general deficiencies of the patient's former diet. A liberal diet, including fresh fruit and as much properly cooked vegetables as are available and the patient will accept, should be given. If the patient is anaemic, ferrous sulphate and folate tablets by mouth are indicated.

With adequate treatment no patient dies of scurvy; but if treatment is delayed he may die. If the measures recommended above are applied, recovery is usually rapid and complete.

PREVENTION

Scurvy tends to occur at the two extremes of age. The prevention of scurvy in infants has been accomplished by the better education of mothers and helped by the distribution of cheap, concentrated orange juice of standard ascorbic acid content.

For old people living alone, the provision of proper meals is the best means of preventing scurvy. This should be the responsibility of their family. If there are no relations or these are unable or unwilling to care for the old person, responsibility falls on the social services. So far, however, the Welfare State has failed to find any simple administrative means of preventing scurvy among the old and solitary, who are often unresponsive to education. In cases where an old person is unwilling or unable to eat foods containing the vitamin, ascorbic acid tablets may be prescribed.

Scurvy is seldom a hazard for those who travel or work in arid and barren lands or make long sea voyages now that cans of fruit juice of good quality are readily available. In case their supply is destroyed or cannot be replaced, all such people should have with them some ascorbic acid.

In times of drought and famine, when fresh vegetables are not available, ascorbic acid can be obtained by the germination of pulses or cereals. A well-tried recipe that has prevented many cases of scurvy in India is: 'A sufficient quantity of whole (unsplit) dhal or gram (say $1\frac{1}{2}$ to 2 oz per man) is soaked in water for 12 to 24 hours. A container big enough to allow for expansion and holding sufficient water should be used. Then pour off the water, remove the grains and spread on a damp blanket in a layer thin enough to allow access of air, and cover with another damp blanket. Keep the blankets damp by sprinkling with water. In a few hours small shoots will appear, and when these are $\frac{1}{2}$ to 1 inch long the process is complete. Vitamin C content is maximal after about 30 hours of germination.' Pulses normally contain no ascorbic acid but 30 g of dried pulse on germination yield 9 to 15 mg, sufficient to prevent scurvy.

On his solo sailing voyage around the world (1966–67) Sir Francis Chichester grew mustard and cress in trays and avoided scurvy by eating this. Visitors to his 54-foot yacht, *Gipsy Moth IV*, can still see mustard and cress growing in the galley.

REFERENCES

1. Lind J 1973 A treatise of the scurvy. Reprinted 1953 by Edinburgh University Press
2. Dudley S F 1953 The Lind tradition in the Royal Navy medical service. In: Lind J A treatise of the scurvy. Reprint 1953 by Edinburgh University Press, p 369–86
3. Aschoff L, Koch W 1919 Scorbut: eine Pathologisch-Anatomische Studie. Fischer, Jena
4. Hodges R E, Hood J, Canham J E, Sauberlich H E, Baker E M 1971 Clinical manifestations of ascorbic acid deficiency in man. Am J Clin Nutr 24: 432–43
5. Bronte-Stewart B 1953 The anaemia of adult scurvy. Q J Med 22: 309–29
6. Cox E V 1968 The anaemia of scurvy. Vitam Horm 26: 635–52
7. Seftel H C, Malkin C, Schmaman A, et al 1966 osteoporosis, scurvy and siderosis in Johannesburg Bantu. Br Med J 1: 642–6

36

Other Nutritional Disorders of the Nervous System

In addition to conditions due mainly to thiamin deficiency, there are other primarily neurological disorders directly attributable to dietary factors. With the exception of vitamin B12 neuropathy, the precise cause is unknown. Most patients have been on poor diets deficient in many nutrients and sometimes in addition there may be evidence of a toxic factor in the food. These disorders are described in this chapter. The relation of diet to neurological and psychiatric disorders in general is discussed in Chapter 49.

Burning feet syndrome

Outbreaks of this distinct clinical syndrome have occurred at various times in Europe, Central America, Africa and India among people living on very poor diets. It was common during the Spanish Civil War[1] and among European prisoners in the Far East during World War II.[2,3] It is sometimes seen in elderly people in Britain.

The earliest symptom is aching, burning or throbbing in the feet. This becomes more intense and is followed by sharp, stabbing, shooting pains, which may spread up as far as the knee like an electric shock, causing excruciating agony. They come on in paroxysms and are usually worse at night. Most patients get some relief by walking about, and sufferers may spend the night limping up and down outside their quarters. Some manage to get relief by wrapping their feet in cold wet cloths or sitting with their feet in a pail of cold water. Continuous pain and loss of sleep produce a thin, exhausted, irritable patient.

In contrast to the striking symptoms, objective signs of neuropathy are seldom marked unless the polyneuropathy of beriberi co-exists. The tendon jerks are usually normal but may be exaggerated. In the great majority of cases there is no demonstrable sensory change; indeed there is some doubt whether the syndrome should properly be classified as a neuropathy. It may be due chiefly to peripheral vascular changes[3] or to lesions of the dorsal root and sympathetic ganglia.[2]

The syndrome has been associated with the prolonged consumption of a diet deficient in protein and the B group of vitamins. Patients who suffer from it may also develop the orogenital syndrome (p. 334) or nutritional amblyopia, see below, but rarely beriberi. World War II prisoners improved when given yeast, Marmite, rice polishings and other foods rich in the vitamin B complex and a well-balanced high protein diet. The nutrient responsible was not identified. Subsequently improvement of the symptoms was reported after giving pantothenic acid to patients in India,[4] but this was not confirmed in Sri Lanka.[5]

The syndrome can be seen sometimes in chronic alcoholics and patients with diabetic and other neuropathies, and rarely in other disorders.

Nutritional amblyopia
(Nutritional retrobulbar neuropathy)

A progressive failure of vision attributable to a retrobulbar neuropathy occurred among prisoners of war in World War II. They were a number of cases in British and Indian soldiers admitted to military hospitals in India after release from Japanese camps.[6] In Egypt also, about a hundred cases occurred among German prisoners of war who had suffered for some time previously from chronic dysentery. Many cases were seen in Nigeria between 1930 and 1940.[7] Disturbances of vision, however, are seldom mentioned in accounts of pellagra and beriberi. The incidence of the condition in prisoners of war aroused renewed interest and discussion, though little new was learned about its aetiology.

All the patients appear to have had one feature in common — a period of many months on diets grossly deficient in respect of many essential nutrients. There are thus good reasons for thinking that the disorder is nutritional in origin. The nature of the diets held to be responsible has been very variable. It would appear unlikely that a deficiency of any single nutrient is responsible.

A typical history is that over a period of three weeks or so there is a growing inability to see the colours of small objects. A mist obscures the central field of vision and gradually becomes so intense that it is impossible to recognise acquaintances. There may be retrobulbar pain, but this is often absent. Sometimes the eyes smart. Tinnitus, deafness and dizziness — apparently due to associated involvement of the eighth nerve — may occur. In Japanese camps none became completely blind, but several were severely incapacitated.

A central or paracentral scotoma is always present but there is little or no peripheral contraction of the visual fields. The visual acuity varies greatly; in some there is little impairment; in others it may be as low as 6/60. In mild cases the retinae appear normal on examination with an ophthalmoscope. When the loss of vision is severe, temporal pallor of the optic discs is usually present.

Nutritional amblyopia is always a result of a poor diet and associated with lack of one or more vitamins of the B complex but the precise cause is not known. When the symptoms are not severe they are relieved rapidly by a good diet supplemented by yeast or Marmite, but when vision is markedly affected little or no improvement results from any form of treatment. A full account of the disease with a large bibliography is given in a monograph by McLaren.[8]

Optic atrophy also occurs in heavy smokers and then is often effectively treated with hydroxocobalamin. It probably arises from the neurotoxic effect of cyanide present in tobacco.

Retrobulbar neuropathy and spinal ataxia occur together in Western Nigeria among people who subsist largely on cassava. The syndrome, called tropical ataxic neuropathy, appears to be caused primarily by chronic ingestion of small amounts of cyanide from the cassava. It is dealt with more fully in the following section.

Spinal ataxia

Patients who have been living for long periods on unbalanced diets occasionally develop neurological signs which indicate that the principal lesion is in the dorsal columns of the spinal cord, involving particularly proprioceptive sensation. The gait is unsteady and the patient is unable to stand upright without swaying when the eyes are closed (Romberg's test). Vibration sense in the legs is often lost. The condition has been described in association with nutritional amblyopia in Malaysia[9] and in prisoners of war.[10] We ourselves have seen two cases in strict vegetarians who ate no foods of animal origin and in such cases the essential dietary abnormality is lack of vitamin B12, which occurs only in foods of animal origin or in foods fermented by microorganisms. In other words, the disease may be a form of subacute combined degeneration of the cord, but due to a direct dietary deficiency of vitamin B12, in contrast to the conditioned deficiency that occurs in pernicious anaemia.

In tropical ataxic neuropathy, as seen in Western Nigeria[11] and Tanzania,[12] vitamin B12 plays only a secondary role. In the fully developed syndrome there is sensory spinal ataxia, retrobulbar neuropathy or optic atrophy and sometimes bilateral nerve deafness. Signs indicating mild involvement of the lateral or pyramidal tracts may be found. Epidemiologically the condition is found in people who regularly consume large amounts of cassava.[13] Cassava contains a cyanogenic glycoside, linamarin, which can be broken down to yield free hydrogen cyanide by enzymes in the plant tissue if it is crushed or left standing in water. Ingested cyanide is detoxified by sulphur-containing amino acids, which convert it to thiocyanate, and by hydroxocobalamin which forms cyanocobalamin. Patients with tropical ataxic neuropathy have increased plasma concentrations and urinary excretion of thiocyanate[10] with increased vitamin B12 and reduced cystine in the plasma.[14] These findings strongly suggest that this nutritional neuropathy results from chronic ingestion of small amounts of cyanide from cassava in people whose diet does not contain sufficient sulphur-containing amino acids and vitamin B12 to detoxify it. The condition can be prevented in part by cooking methods which wash out the glycoside or boil off the HCN.

Cerebellar cortical degeneration

This condition in which the characteristic clinical feature is ataxia of the legs arises from degenerative changes limited to the anterior superior part of the vermis of the cerebellum. It is associated with alcoholism and poor nutrition but the response to vitamin therapy and nutritional rehabilitation is less consistent than in the Wernicke-Korsakoff syndrome.

Vitamin B12 neuropathy

This was commonly associated with pernicious anaemia before the introduction of treatment with vitamin B12. Known as subacute combined degeneration of the cord it affected mainly the dorsal and lateral columns and was often severe and incapacitating. The full clinical picture of the disease is now rarely seen but some evidence of involvement of the spinal cord is not uncommon when a patient first presents with pernicious anaemia and is occasionally found before anaemia develops. Vitamin B12 neuropathy also arises from lack of vitamin B12 in the diet, e.g. in some castes of strict Hindus and in vegans. In such people anaemia is characteristically not seen, presumably because a vegetable diet supplies sufficient folic acid.

Clinical features. Early symptoms are tingling, coldness and numbness in the extremities due to peripheral neuropathy. Motor weakness and ataxia appear later and become increasingly severe as the cord is involved. The physical signs depend on the relative involvement of the peripheral nerves and the dorsal and lateral columns of the cord. In severe cases ataxia is the outstanding feature with loss of reflexes especially in the lower limbs. Sometimes the pyramidal tracts are involved and spasticity, increased reflexes and an extensor plantar response are present. If the brain is affected there may be an organic psychosis and this may be the first evidence of vitamin B12 deficiency.

Treatment and prevention This is the same as for pernicious anaemia and is described on page 465. If treatment is begun early, recovery is complete, but in severe cases the damage is irreparable.

Spastic paraplegia

Lathyrism. *Lathyrus sativus*, or Kesari dhal, is a drought-resistant pulse, widely grown in parts of the Indian subcontinent (p. 199). If eaten in excessive amounts and for a long period, it gives rise to lathyrism.

The onset of lathyrism is usually sudden and is often preceded by exertion or exposure to cold. A patient may go to bed well and wake up paralysed; or he may fall down at the plough. Sometimes backache and stiffness of the legs precede the onset of the paralysis by a few days. The condition is a spastic paralysis of the lower limbs, due presumably to a precisely localised lesion of the lower parts of the pyramidal tracts. The motor nerves to the muscles of the trunk, upper limbs and sphincters are spared. The sensory nervous system is not involved. In mild cases there is only stiffness and weakness of the legs and exaggerated knee and ankle jerks. In more severe cases the patient walks with bent knees on tiptoe. The legs are often crossed; a 'scissors gait' develops and walking is only possible with the aid of sticks. In severe cases paraplegia in flexion follows, and walking becomes impossible. The patient can only move about by pushing himself along, supporting his body on his hands, buttocks and heels. The paraplegia is typi-cally spastic with greatly increased ankle and knee jerks, and with clonus. The final stage of the disease is completely incapacitating and the sufferers may move to the cities where they are easily recognised amongst the beggars.

The toxic factors responsible for lathyrism are discussed on page 242.

Epidemic lathyrism was mainly a disease of famine, but numerous cases continue to occur in Madhya Pradesh state in India.[15] There *Lathyris sativus* continues to be sown as an insurance against a partial failure of the wheat crop. When the price of wheat rises, many of the poor increase their consumption of the pulse and cases of lathyrism arise. Prevention requires changes in agricultural and economic policies. The toxin can be extracted from kesari dal by heating it in four volumes of water for an hour, and education could make this an effective means of prevention.

There is no specific treatment. All patients need a good diet. Minor cases may make a complete recovery following satisfactory dietary and physical rehabilitation. In most cases the pathological changes are irreversible and, as already stated, the patients drift into beggary.

Other forms of spastic paraplegia

In the late 1930s one of us (RP) on visits to hospitals in India was often shown an isolated case of spastic paralysis in a young adult for which no cause had been found. Several papers from tropical countries described the condition. It continues to occur and authors from India, Malaysia, Singapore, Ghana, Nigeria and Jamaica writing in Spillane's monograph[16] provide evidence that spastic paraplegia of unidentified origin is much commoner in tropical countries than elsewhere. Some of the patients are malnourished but the majority are not. No association with a natural food poison has been established. The disease remains an unresolved mystery, and it is possible that some dietary factor may be responsible.

REFERENCES

1. Peraita M 1942 Neuropathien infolge mangelhafter Ernahrung. Arch Psychiat Nervenkr 114: 611–48
2. Smith D A, Woodruff M F A 1951 Deficiency diseases in Japanese prison camps. MRC Spec Rep Ser no. 274
3. Cruickshank E K 1952 Dietary neuropathies. Vitam Horm 10: 1–45
4. Gopalan G 1946 The burning feet syndrome. Indian Med Gaz 81:22
5. Bibile S W, Lionel N D W, Dunuwille R, Perara G 1957 Pantothothenol and the burning feet syndrome. Br J Nutr 11: 434–9
6. Denny-Brown D 1947 Neurological conditions resulting from prolonged and severe dietary restrictions. Medicine 26: 41–113
7. Fitzgerald Moore D G 1937 Retrobulbar neuritis cum avitaminosia. W Afr Med J 9: 35–40
8. McLaren D S 1980 Nutritional ophthalmology. Academic Press, London, p 150–79
9. Landor J V, Pallister R A 1935 Avitaminosis B2. Trans R Soc Trop Med Hyg 29: 121–34
10. Spillane D, Scott G I 1945 Obscure neuropathy in the Middle East: report on 112 cases in prisoners-of-war. Lancet 2: 261–4
11. Osuntokun B O 1968 An ataxic neuropathy in Nigeria. Brain 91: 215–48
12. Makene W J, Wilson J 1972 Biochemical studies in Tanzanian patients with a toxic tropical neuropathy. J Neurol Neurosurg Psychiatry 35: 31–3

13. Osuntokun B O, Monekosso G L, Wilson J 1969 Relationship of a degenerative tropical neuropathy to diet: report of a field survey. Br Med J 1: 547–50

14. Osuntokun B O, Durowoju M E O, McFarlane H, Wilson J 1968 Plasma amino-acids in the Nigerian nutritional ataxic neuropathy. Br Med J 3: 647–9

15. Nutrition Foundation of India 1982 The lathyrism problem: current status and new dimensions. Scientific Report no. 2.

16. Spillane J D (ed) 1973 Tropical neurology. Oxford University Press, London

37

Lesser Nutritional Disorders

In this chapter an account is given of a variety of clinical conditions which are commonly found in malnourished people. For the most part they do not result in severe disability and are rarely a primary cause of complaint. They are usually found on the routine examination of school children, the medical inspection of a labour force, or at maternity and child welfare clinics.

Much has been written about the aetiology of each of these conditions. In general it may be said that the majority can arise from a variety of causes, both dietary and otherwise. The practical importance of these stigmata is that their presence should draw attention to the diet. A single case found in a prosperous community is likely to be due to a cause other than a dietary deficiency. When many cases are found in a poor community the diet is probably responsible, but accurate diagnosis can only be made by biochemical studies and the results of appropriate therapeutic trials.

DISORDERS OF THE SKIN

Follicular hyperkeratosis

The normal human skin contains pores, which are the openings of microscopic follicles. The secretions of the sebaceous and sweat-producing glands enter the follicles and reach the surface through these pores. Hairs emerge from their roots through the same follicles. In follicular hyperkeratosis the follicles become blocked with plugs of keratin derived from their epithelial lining which has undergone squamous metaplasia (Fig. 37.1). This pathological change has been attributed to vitamin A deficiency. Therapeutic trails in the East and in Africa have repeatedly shown that halibut-liver oil, red-palm oil or other oils rich in vitamin A or carotene may produce a striking clinical improvement. Vegetable oils are also likely to be rich in essential fatty acids and vitamin E, and the condition has responded to vitamin E therapy.[1] Other factors may contribute to its development, such as exposure to sunlight and lack of cleanliness. Follicular keratosis was not a regular feature in experimentally induced vitamin A deficiency in British adults.[2] It is

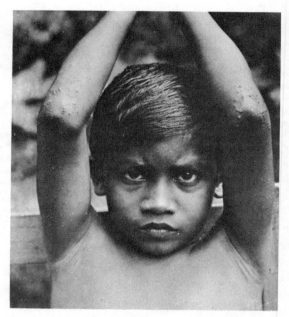

Fig. 37.1 Follicular hyperkeratosis. (By courtesy of Dr K. Mahadeva)

rarely seen in very young children, the vulnerable age for xerophthalmia. A further difficulty is that slight follicular keratosis may be found in people who are adequately nourished in respect of vitamin A. Thus the condition is not a specific or constant feature of vitamin A deficiency.

The typical distribution is over the backs of the upper arms and the fronts of the thighs, but it may extend over the buttocks and indeed over the whole trunk. Only the feet, hands, and face may be spared. Some degree of xeroderma (see below) is commonly associated. The horny plugs that project from the follicular orifices can often be pulled out with a fine pair of forceps; they give the skin a characteristic feeling of roughness, like that of a nutmeg grater. Because of its appearance, the condition has been called 'toad-skin' or phrynoderma. The appearance is distinct from the condition sometimes seen in scurvy, in which the hyperkeratosis is superficial and perifollicular — often with a small underlying haemorrhage — but without any projecting horny plug (Chap. 35).

Folliculosis This is sometimes mistaken for follicular hyperkeratosis. The follicles are raised above the surface, but no horny plug projects from the follicular orifices. It is common on the backs of the arms of well-nourished British school children, and although its cause is unknown, there is no evidence that it has any nutritional significance.

Xeroderma

This means dryness of the skin. Instead of the normal smooth, moist, velvet texture, the skin feels dry and often rough. On uncovering the legs, a cloud of fine, branny dandruff is often seen. Xeroderma is commonly but not constantly associated with follicular keratosis and 'crackled skin'.

Crazy-paving skin

In this condition the appearance suggests a layer of lacquer painted on the surface, which on drying has broken up into individual islands of varying size (Fig. 37.2). There is often some desquamation from the borders of each island, while the intervening gaps may become fissured. The commonest site for this lesion is the shins, and it seems probable that exposure to dirt and alternate heat and moisture is often responsible.

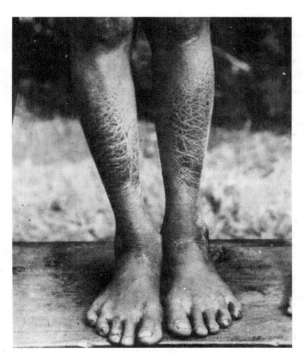

Fig. 37.2 Crazy-paving skin

Flaky paint dermatosis

This is characteristic of PEM. The skin becomes hyperpigmented and keratin separates in flakes which are larger than those in crazy-paving skin. It is common in the napkin area and often secondarily infected. Cure has been effected by an amino acid mixture devoid of vitamins.

Pachyderma (elephant skin)

This word was introduced by Nelson[3] to describe a condition common in malnourished people. The areas of skin affected are thick, rough and thrown into folds like the skin of an elephant. It starts as a roughness of the skin on the back of the hands and feet, and the skin of the whole body may be affected. The changes are most marked at the back of the elbows and front of the knees. Fissures may occur round the heels. The condition is seen most often in boys and in the dry season.

It is obviously unwise to suggest that 'elephant skin', 'crazy-paving' and xeroderma are due solely to poor nutrition. On the other hand Nicol[4] demonstrated their probable nutritional significance by showing that these condition are less common among Nigerians who eat red-palm oil (rich in vitamin A activity) than among those who do not.

Dyssebacea (nasolabial seborrhoea)

This term has been given to the appearance of enlarged follicles around the sides of the nose and sometimes extending over the cheeks and forehead. The follicles are plugged with dry sebaceous material which often has a yellow colour, for which reason Stannus originally coined the name 'sulphur flake' in describing the condition in malnourished Sudanese. It is commonly found in Africans with pellagra and may be related to riboflavin deficiency.

Atrophy of skin

In starving people and those suffering from serious undernutrition as a result of debilitating disease, the skin may be thin and inelastic. Over the front of the legs it appears shiny and tightly stretched. This is due to a general failure in the nutrition of the cells that are normally concerned with maintaining the skin in health and replacing losses of epithelium from the surface. It cannot be ascribed to dietary deficiency of any single nutrients.

Pigmentary changes and colour

Nutritional failure can affect the colour of the skin in many different ways. The dirty brown pigmentation of the skin in chronic undernutrition has already been described, as well as the patchy hyperpigmentation and depigmentation often associated with kwashiorkor. In pellagra there is typically an erythema with subsequent desquamation and pigmentation. The areas of skin especially involved are those exposed to sunlight or affected by friction. In anaemia the skin may be unduly pale. The hands of underfed children are often cyanosed, even in warm weather; while in cold, damp climates they may be affected by chilblains.

Chilblains, once common in Great Britain in wintertime, are seldom seen in North America where the houses are centrally heated. Nutritional deficiencies have often been blamed for chilblains, on no good grounds. Calcium, nicotinic acid, vitamin K and others have all been recommended for their treatment. Nicotinic acid may help by its vasodilator properties.

Tropical ulcer

Tropical ulcers were once of considerable interest to nutritionists but are now rarely discussed, probably because their prevalence is much reduced. They are chronic ulcers, affecting chiefly the lower limbs, occurring in hot, damp climates among people whose tissues are vitiated by malnutrition. They are often caused by minor injuries in people living in poor hygienic surroundings, debilitated by diseases such as dysentery and malaria. They used to be common in coolies employed on plantations; European prisoners of war working on the Burma-Siam railway were severely affected. *Fusobacterium fusiformis* and *Borrelia vincenti* are commonly present in the lesions. Tropical ulcers are not attributable to lack of a single nutrient, but their presence in any community or labour force is an indication that the diet and hygienic conditions are unsatisfactory.

Angular stomatitis

This is an affection of the skin at the angles of the mouth, characterised by heaping-up of greyish-white sodden epithelium into ridges, giving the appearance of fissures radiating outwards from the mouth (Fig. 37.3). Secondary infection and staining by food may give the lesion a yellowish colour. It may extend across the mucocutaneous boundary and produce whitish patches on the mucous membrane lining the cheeks. In differential diagnosis it must be distinguished from other lesions in the same site, notably herpes labialis, syphilitic rhagades and lichen planus.

Angular stomatitis often responds rapidly to large doses of riboflavin and sometimes to pyridoxine. It occurs in association with iron deficiency anaemia and other debilitating diseases. The most common cause in Britain is ill-fitting dentures.

Cheilosis. This is a zone of red, denuded epithelium at the line of closure of the lips. It is frequently seen in pellagrins and is often associated with angular stomatitis. Both lesions may have a seasonal incidence and only appear during periods of drought and lack of fresh

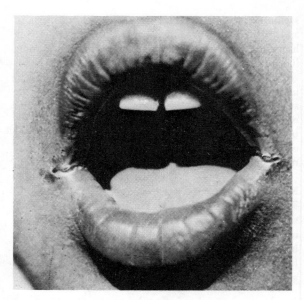

Fig. 37.3 Angular stomatitis. (By courtesy of Dr K. Mahadeva)

foods; but it is unlikely that lack of any one specific vitamin or nutrient is the sole cause. The condition overlaps with chapped lips, seen in healthy people who have been exposed to cold winds or excessive sunlight.

Orogenital syndrome

In this condition there is angular stomatitis, but in addition there are changes in the epithelium of the mouth, tongue and lips, and other mucocutaneous junctions are affected. The earliest sign is oedema and milky opacity of the buccal mucosa which goes on to patchy or diffuse desquamation of the lips, tongue and sometimes soft palate. These areas are red and sensitive. Capillary oozing, with crusted blood on the lips and secondary infection with superficial ulceration may occur. Soggy, whitish patches at the outer angles of the eyes, within the ears, at the vulva or prepuce of the penis, and around the anus are often present. Associated with these changes there is often corneal vascularisation and a scaly, greasy eczema at the angles of the nose, on the lips, chin and behind the ears. A dry, intensely itching, erythematous dermatitis, with a well-defined edge, may appear on the genitalia — the scrotum or mons pubis, over the perineum and down the inner sides of the thighs. There is often secondary infection. The syndrome caused much distress among British prisoners of war in Japanese hands. It responds well to natural preparations of the vitamin B complex such as yeast extract (e.g. Marmite), though not to any single synthetic vitamin.

DISORDERS OF THE HAIR AND NAILS

In health the hair is sleek and glossy, often with a natural wave or curl. In malnourished or undernourished people the hair frequently becomes dull and lustreless; it is not easily brushed and tends to stand up straight ('staring hair'). At the same time the colour of the hair may change. In fair people it may turn to a dirty brown, while in black-haired people there may be loss of pigment, with a change of colour ranging from brown, rusty red to almost white. This occurs in kwashiorkor (p. 282). The depigmentation is sometimes seen in bands across the length of each individual hair, corresponding to previous alternating periods of poor and relatively satisfactory nutrition — the flag sign.

Dietary factors such as deficiency of pantothenic acid (p. 165) or biotin can change the colour of the hair of black rats to grey, but the white or grey hair of human middle age has no nutritional significance. Nor is baldness a manifestation of nutritional failure.

In chronic iron deficiency anaemia the fingernails may be spoon-shaped (koilonychia). In other forms of malnutrition the nails may be brittle or thickened or lined on the surface, either transversely or longitudinally; but these changes may also be seen in well-nourished people. Severe protein deficiency may result in transverse white bands in the nails, occurring symmetrically on both hands.[5]

COMMENT

Until more is known about the chemical pathology of the skin, hair and nails it will continue to be difficult to assess the significance of certain clinical changes in these structures which are sometimes seen on examination of underfed or malnourished people.

DISORDERS OF THE EYE

Night blindness

It has already been explained in Chapter 13 that retinol plays an essential part in the mechanism of vision in dim light. Night blindness is a frequent complaint in underdeveloped communities who have no night lights and where the diet is grossly lacking in retinol and β-carotene. Children who stray from home after dark may get lost, or fall down a well or injure themselves in other ways. However, many factors besides retinol deficiency may contribute to complaints of night blindness. These include fatigue, emotional disturbances associated with acute danger and also chronic anxiety states. Moreover, there are organic causes such as retinitis pigmentosa. Night blindness arising from vitamin A deficiency always responds to suitable vitamin therapy and it is unwise to make the diagnosis before adequate therapeutic trials have been carried out.

In the past, night blindness has been a common complaint of the malingerer and is quickly learnt by others unless promptly dealt with. Unless the diet is known to be grossly deficient, or therapeutic trials have been carried out, it is best to assume that the cause is not nutritional.

Conjunctival xerosis

This has already been discussed as a manifestation of vitamin A deficiency (p. 299).

Bitôt's spots

Charles Bitôt was a French physician who first described, over 100 years ago, greyish or glistening white plaques formed of desquamated thickened conjunctival epithelium, usually triangular in shape and firmly adherent to the underlying conjunctiva. Sometimes the spots are covered with material resembling-dried foam which can be scraped away but forms again. It consists of epithelial debris, fatty globules and often masses of xerosis bacilli. The spots are generally bilateral, on the temporal sides of the cornea, and in coloured races are often surrounded by dense brown pigmentation. In the past Bitôt's spots have often been associated with vitamin A deficiency and they are frequently present in children whose diet has been grossly lacking in this vitamin. However there is good evidence[6,7] that the condition can be present when there are no other signs of lack of vitamin A, including no impairment of dark adaptation, and the diet provides ample quantities of the vitamin or its precursor, β-carotene.

Pigmentation of the conjunctiva is frequently associated with xerophthalmia. Pigment may be deposited (1) round the cornea (pigmented ring), (2) in the lower eyelid (pigmented gutter), and (3) over the sclera equatorially in the area commonly occupied by Bitôt's spots. The nutritional significance of this pigment formation is uncertain. Various forms of irritation appear to play a major role in its causation.

Corneal vascularisation

The essential lesion in this condition is an invasion of the normally avascular cornea by capillary blood vessels. These vessels cannot be seen with the naked eye, nor with an ordinary hand lens. A slit-lamp microscope in the hands of an experienced observer is needed for positive identification. Small greyish-white opacities may also be seen on the surface of the cornea. The patient usually complains of a burning sensation in the eyes, misty vision, lachrymation and photophobia — the latter symptom may make slit-lamp examination difficult. Associated with the condition there is often injection of the conjunctiva with dilated blood vessels which are easily visible on simple inspection, without the use of a slit-lamp. However, the presence of an injected conjunctiva should not allow the assumption that a vascular cornea is also present. Corneal vascularisation may be associated with the orogenital syndrome, with keratomalacia and with ariboflavinosis.

Nutritional amblyopia (p. 328) is a major nutritional disorder of the eyes.

DISORDERS OF THE MOUTH

Angular stomatitis and cheilosis are described earlier in this chapter.

Nutritional glossitis
Deficiencies of nicotinic acid, riboflavin, vitamin B12, folic acid and iron may all give rise to glossitis. It is a feature of pellagra, sprue and the various types of nutritional anaemias. The tongue seems to be particularly susceptible to metabolic disorders of all kinds. When a sudden and severe restriction in the supply of one or other of the above nutrients occurs, acute glossitis develops. If the deficiency is partial and extends over months or years, chronic atrophic glossitis is more often seen. In acute glossitis the tongue is swollen, sometimes to such an extent that it is continually pressed against the lower jaw and well-marked dental impressions are visible. The papillae are usually very prominent. The colour of the tongue is characteristically red, but in some cases it may have a purplish blue. The mucous membrane sometimes desquamates in patches leaving areas of red raw surface. Deep irregular fissuring is common and shallow ulcers may occur, especially on the sides or tip (Fig. 37.4). The tongue may be extremely painful, so much so that fear of pain may prevent the patient from eating.

There are those who claim to be able to distinguish the appearance of the tongue in nicotinic acid deficiency from that of vitamin B12, folic acid or riboflavin deficiency; the last is said to be magenta in colour. But the distinction is not important as in nearly all cases there has been a multiple dietary deficiency of vitamins.

In chronic atrophic glossitis the tongue is small, with an atrophic mucous membrane and small or absent papillae so that its surface appears smooth, moist and abnormally clean. Fine fissuring may be present. It is usually not painful.

In pellagra the tongue responds dramatically to nicotinic acid, as is the case with the acute glossitis of pernicious anaemia treated with vitamin B12 or the glossitis of the sprue syndrome treated with folic acid.

The tongue of different individuals varies consider-

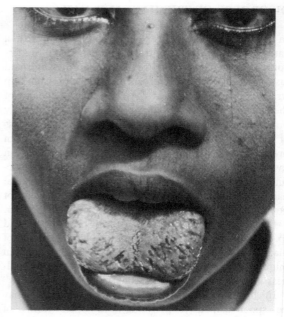

Fig. 37.4 Nutritional glossitis

ably. Some healthy people have patches on the tongue where the filiform papillae are absent. This geographical tongue is not related to disease. Others have a fissured or pigmented tongue. These normal variations can be confused with nutritional glossitis by inexperienced observers. The tongue is affected too by prolonged or severe dehydration.

Parotid gland enlargement
Swelling of the parotid glands is found among children in some parts of Africa and Asia. An extensive study of the condition in French West Africa produced convincing evidence that the swellings are nutritional in origin, and lack of adequate protein a probable cause.[8] The swellings may increase slowly and persist for years; on the other hand, with an improvement in the diet they may disappear quickly. The condition may readily be confused with mumps. Histological examination of the swollen gland shows hypertrophy of the acini. In the final state, fibrosis develops with cystic dilation of the ducts — a parotid cirrhosis.

The parotid glands are sometimes enlarged temporarily during the refeeding of people who have been severely undernourished.

COMMENT

The observing and recording of the signs described in this chapter is a useful aid to nutritional assessment of children and others in poor communities.

REFERENCES

1. Nadiger H A 1980 Role of vitamin E in the aetiology of phrynoderma (follicular dermatosis) and its relationship with B-complex vitamins. Br J Nutr 4: 211–4
2. Hume E M, Krebs H A 1949 Vitamin A requirements of human adults. MRC Spec Rep Ser no. 264
3. Nelson J W 1952 Pachyderma: the natural history. Trans R Soc Trop Med Hyg 46: 538–42
4. Nicol B M 1949 Nutrition of Nigerian peasant farmers, with special reference to the effects of vitamin A riboflavin deficiency. Br J Nutr 3 25–43
5. Muehrcke R C 1956 The finger-nails in chronic hypoalbuminaemia: a new physical sign. Br Med J 1: 1327–8
6. Darby W J, McGarrity W J, McLaren D S, Paton D, Alemu Z, Medhen M G 1960 Bitôt's spots and vitamin a deficiency. Public Health Rep (Wash) 75: 738–43
7. Rodger F C, Saiduzzafast H, Grover A D, Fazel A 1963 A reappraisal of the ocular lesions in Bitôts spots. Br J Nutr 17: 475–85
8. Raoult A, Thomas J, Thiery G, Perrin G, Perrellon G 1957 Les parotidoses de malnutrition en AOF. Bull Méd Afr Occid Fr (NS) 2: 5–72 (Trop Dis Bull 1957; 54: 1454–5, abstract)

Diet and Other Diseases

38

Nutritional Aspects and Dietetic Treatment of General Diseases

Part III deals with nutritional diseases which are called primary because the principal or most obvious causation is the consumption of a diet with insufficient or excess sources of energy or lacking a proper balance of protein or other nutrients. In Part IV a number of diseases, many of which are common and well-known, are considered for one or both of two reasons: (1) the nature of the previous diet may play some part in aetiology which is multiple and complex, and (2) modification of the usual diet or the provision of a special diet reduces the metabolic burden on disordered organs or relieves symptoms and other manifestations of disease.

DIET AND DISEASES OF MULTIPLE AETIOLOGY

Most of the diseases described in Part IV cannot be attributed to a single major cause. Figure 38.1 may help understanding of the complexities of their aetiology. Its essence is a triad, inheritance (the genotype), favourable environmental influences (nurture) and unfavourable environmental influences (stress). The genotype represents inheritance which is complete at the moment of conception. From then onwards, including the intrauterine period, the constitution evolves under the continuing interaction of favourable and unfavourable factors in the environment. The nutritionist and dietitian should notice that the first item in the left-hand column of favourable environmental influences (nurture) is food. While it is true that 'we are what we eat' it is also true that 'we are what we are born' or in the language of biology 'we are what our environment allows our genotype to become'. Here the role of nutrition in the promotion of health and the role of malnutrition in the causation of a number of diseases are stressed, because these are the themes of the book. The perspective shown in Figure 38.1 is discussed more fully by Brock in a Croonian lecture.[1]

Another feature shown in the figure is that the actions of nurture, and of stress, including bad diet, often operate over very long periods of time before their effects become evident in an unhealthy constitution or a recognisable disease. Constitution is never fixed; in the same individual it may be healthy in one decade and unhealthy in another. Over short periods of time, the patient may fluctuate between health and disease, even if he has a healthy constitution but, of course much more readily if he has an unhealthy constitution.

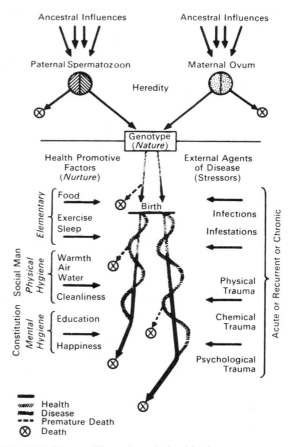

Fig. 38.1 Diagram illustrating relationships between genotype and environment, both favourable and unfavourable, in determining the development of constitution and life expectation, and of experience of health and disease

In the diseases known as **inborn errors of metabolism** (Chap. 39), a term introduced by Garrod in 1908, the major cause is a deficiency or error in a single gene. This is usually the result of spontaneous or induced mutation in one or both of the parents and becomes part of the genotype of the fetus. These diseases are therefore at least potentially present at the moment of conception. A concept '*one gene, one enzyme*' evolved from Garrod's ideas.

Several hundred such inborn errors of metabolism have since been described and probably many hundreds more remain to be discovered. Some of these undoubtedly account for idiosyncrasies of food preference, digestion and assimilation which come within the notice of dietitians. Although theoretically one enzyme is deficient because of one gene error, in many of the inborn errors there is evidence of aberration of several enzymes and presumably more than one gene is involved. These inborn errors of metabolism have to be sharply distinguished from **acquired congenital diseases** which though present at the time of birth are not due to genetic errors but to defects of the intrauterine environment exerted through the maternal tissues. Examples are the defects which have arisen when during pregnancy a mother has contracted rubella or received thalidomide.

Congenital defects can be produced in animals by feeding grossly defective diets during pregnancy. There are tenfold differences between different populations in the incidence of births of babies with severe structural defects of the nervous system. These differences are unexplained and dietary factors might be responsible (p. 576).

HABITUAL DIETARY PATTERNS

The habitual dietary patterns of a community or a family have a complex but important role in diseases of multiple aetiology. At one extreme of a range of nutritional relevance to the causation and management of disease lies the classical inborn error of metabolism, galactosaemia (p. 348), in which an inherited lack of a single enzyme makes it impossible for the newborn child to develop normally on nature's diet, human breast milk, or on the traditional substitute, cow's milk. If diagnosed early, satisfactory development may be ensured by feeding the infant on a galactose-free diet.

In the other half of the range lies coronary heart disease (Chap. 41), common in prosperous communities. Diets customary in such communities are one of a number of unfavourable environmental causes. Other responsible environmental factors include lack of exercise, emotional stress and cigarette smoking. All these should be given consideration in assessing causation and prevention. Certain families suffer more heavily than others which suggests that there may be an inherited basis, probably polygenic, rendering some members of susceptible families unable to metabolise normally high intakes of certain foods such as saturated fats. This metabolic defect leads over several decades to accumulation of cholesterol and the development of atherosclerosis in the coronary arteries.

Between the two extremes of this spectrum there lies a great range of diseases of multiple and uncertain origin in which conditioning may occur over decades in subjects who are rendered vulnerable by their inherited gene pattern (genotype); susceptible, that is, to the effects of unfavourable factors in their environment which would be better resisted by another genotype. The resultant phenotype or constitution is a diathesis or state of undue susceptibility to later events which precipitate a disease. The constitutional diathesis leads to few if any symptoms until the disease is precipitated, which may be in early childhood, in middle life, or only late in life.

The aetiology of gout (Chap. 43) might be represented somewhere in the middle of the range of nutritional relevance. Gout is clearly based on an inherited metabolic aberration which permits excessive endogenous purine synthesis. This aberration often does not become manifest until the fifth decade of life or later. It may be suggested by a family history of gout and diagnosed while still asymptomatic by a high concentration of plasma uric acid. It may remain undetected throughout life if the environment is favourable. If, on the other hand, this gouty constitution or diathesis is taxed by high intakes of exogenous purines, as in repeated overindulgent eating of rich protein meals and by much consumption of alcohol, an attack of acute gout is precipitated. If the dietary overindulgence is continued or periodically repeated, chronic gout may follow.

It is difficult to place diabetes mellitus (Chap. 42) at an appropriate point in the spectrum of relevance of diet to causation, although diet is of outstanding importance in management. It would appear that diabetes mellitus in its common juvenile and adult forms is a constitutional disease of multiple aetiology. There is evidence that, in the common clinical type associated with obesity in middle age, an important provoking cause is long-continued overconsumption of energy-yielding foods in relation to energy expenditure. This hypothesis underlies orthodox advice to people to avoid obesity particularly if they have a family history of diabetes. In juvenile diabetes it is likely that constitutional susceptibility (diathesis) is more important than habitual diet.

The common anaemias (Chap. 48) fit well into the principles represented by Figure 38.1. Dietary deficiency of the more important haemopoietic nutrients, iron, folate and vitamin B12 may be absolute or may be conditioned by other environmental factors. Chronic blood loss and repeated pregnancies drain the iron stores of the body and increase the need for dietary iron. In idiopathic chronic iron-deficiency anaemia there is evidence of constitutionally impaired ability to absorb iron from the intestine. In classical pernicious anaemia there is a failure of intestinal absorption of vitamin B12. This is constitutional; it has inherited roots and develops over decades in the form of gastric mucosal atrophy, probably the result of autoimmune mechanisms. Folate deficiency may be dietary or follow impaired digestion and absorption, and lead to megaloblastic anaemia. Increased demands arising from a constitutional disorder (sickle-cell trait) or in pregnancy may contribute in varying proportions to folic acid deficiency.

The figures given for recommended intakes of nutrients (Chap. 15) should not be taken to imply that the dietary needs of all men are alike if physiological and other stresses allowed for in the tables are the same. Such an assumption is of course demonstrably wrong in the case of some inborn errors of metabolism where 'one man's meat may be another man's poison'. Moreover there are among apparently healthy people many variations in response to daily diets which fulfil 'recommended intakes' of nutrients. Some grow fat and some stay thin (Chap. 25). Some are flatulent and some comfortable after meals. With further knowledge it may well appear that constitutional idiosyncrasies of digestion, assimilation and metabolism are responsible for a variety of unidentified symptoms and minor ill-health and eventually contribute to chronic and degenerative diseases of middle age.

PROPHYLACTIC DIETARY REGIMES

Table 38.1 lists some constitutional aberrations, in which the expression of the genotype may be prevented or mitigated and the individual enjoy good health if he lives within certain dietary restrictions.

Emphasis is laid, because this is a book on nutrition and diet, on those dietary measures which can prevent or delay the onset of the symptoms of the disease.

Table 38.1 Constitutional aberrations of which the effect may be neutralised or prevented by a diet, dietary modification or nutrient therapy

Aberration	Recommendation
Phenylketonuria	Low phenylalanine intake
Galactosaemia	No milk
Lactose intolerance	Limited milk
Sickle cell trait	Iron and folic acid supplements
Glucose-6-phosphate deficiency (favism)	No broad beans
High blood uric acid	Moderation at all times and especially at feasts
High plasma cholesterol	Low saturated fat
High blood pressure	Salt restriction
Gluten sensitivity	No wheat or wheat products
Various hypersensitivity states	No shellfish, eggs, milk or wheat etc.
Obesity	Low energy

However, in dealing with any of these constitutional abnormalities the physician should correct any apparent overemphasis on food and diet against the general perspective of other environmental or inherited factors which determine the development of healthy and unhealthy constitutions. In other words habitual dietary patterns, although important, constitute only a part of the total environment which shapes the constitution towards susceptibility to manifestations of disease. Prophylactic diets nevertheless constitute an important responsibility of physicians, paediatricians, nutritionists and health administrators. The nature of the diet probably contributes to the length of the life span in millions of people; this is one example of the potential value of the diet in prophylaxis.

THERAPEUTIC DIETARY REGIMES

Table 38.2 lists some disturbances of physiological function imposed upon the organs and tissues of the body by organic diseases. In each of these conditions the functional state of the organs and the patient's health can be

Table 38.2 Disturbances of physiological function that may be mitigated by a dietary regime

Disturbance of physiological function	Disease	Therapeutic diet
Uraemia	Renal failure	Low protein
Excess protein loss in urine	Nephrotic syndrome	High protein
Oedema, generalised	Heart failure, renal disease, liver failure	Salt restriction
Failure to digest and absorb fat	Pancreatic disease, biliary obstruction, malabsorption syndromes	Low fat
Diminished glucose tolerance	Diabetes mellitus	Low sugar, often low energy
Excess acid and pepsin secretion by stomach	Peptic ulcer	Bland regime
Gluten enteropathy	Coeliac disease	No wheat or wheat products

Table 38.3 Symptoms that may be relieved by dietary modifications

Symptom	Diseases present in	Recommendations
Dysphagia	Various diseases of the pharynx and oesophagus	Semifluid diet
Dyspepsia	Many causes, including peptic ulcer	Bland regime
Nausea	Liver disease, gallbladder disease etc.	Low fat
Chronic constipation	Dyschezia	High fibre
Chronic diarrhoea	Many causes	Bland regime
Loss of weight	Wasting diseases, burns, trauma	High energy

made better or worse by the nature of the diet. Table 38.3 lists some symptoms which may be relieved by appropriate changes in diet. The elaboration and application of the above dietary regimes is particularly the sphere of dietitians. These diets and regimes have wide application but opinions have changed greatly about the value of some of them in the last three decades. For example, in many disorders of the gastrointestinal tract, such as peptic ulcer, therapeutic diets are now thought to have a limited place in the relief of symptoms rather than in the cure of the disease. On the other hand, interest in therapeutic diets in chronic renal disease has grown following the success of haemodialysis and transplantation in prolonging the lives of many patients.

Whereas medical and nutritional science has provided a firm basis for some aspects of dietetic therapy, there remains much that is empirical. It is tempting to reject certain diets as having no scientific validity but the art of medicine is wider than the science. A patient is sometimes benefited by a remedy which has little or no scientific basis. The diets listed in Table 38.1 and 38.2 all rest on some scientific basis. Some of those in Table 38.3 are used empirically.

GENERAL DIETETIC CONSIDERATIONS

When prescribing a diet it is essential to bear in mind the following points.

1. Be sure that the diet is well balanced and satisfactory in relation to energy, carbohydrates, protein and fat, with adequate minerals and vitamins. The recommended daily intakes of nutrients vary with age, sex, physiological state and activity. The energy intake has to be adjusted to the individual if the patient is not to gain or lose weight. Remember that if attention is directed solely to the dietetic treatment of a particular symptom, e.g. diarrhoea or gastric pain, the general nutrition of the patient may suffer.
2. Consider the patient's economic status and occupation and see that the dietary regime is suitable for each case. Obviously different schemes will be required for an office worker, a miner and a night watchman.
3. The diet may need to be adjusted for the patient's religious practice. It is no use prescribing a midday meal

for a Muslim during Ramadan, or pork for an orthodox Jew or a chicken curry for a strict Hindu.

4. Give due consideration to the individual's likes and dislikes for different articles of food and for different flavours. Never prohibit an article from a diet unless there is a clear history of a personal idiosyncrasy to it, or unless there is adequate clinical or experimental evidence for its exclusion.
5. The dietetic requirements of acute and chronic disease may be very different. Thus, in intense diarrhoea, excessive vomiting or infections which are severe in degree but short in duration (e.g. acute food poisoning and lobar pneumonia) the essential need is for fluids, glucose and salt to prevent or correct dehydration, ketosis and loss of electrolytes. In long-continued diseases, such as ulcerative colitis, the diet should be adequate both in quantity and quality, and if possible in variety.
6. Foods consumed away from home must be taken into account. This includes alcoholic drinks, sweets and confectionery and advice about eating in a restaurant.

Food idiosyncrasy

In medicine idiosyncrasy is a term used to describe an unusual effect not met with in a normal person. Idiosyncrasies to individual drugs and foods are common. Established causes of food idiosyncrasy are immunological disorders or allergies described in Chapter 50 and genetic abnormalities of specific enzyme systems described in Chapter 39. Some of these are serious disorders and major modifications of a patient's diet is necessary to prevent them.

Patients often say that a particular food does not agree with them. In most cases a dietitian drawing up a therapeutic diet should respect this view and may be able to plan a diet that excludes the food, and elaborate investigations of the cause of its adverse effect are not needed. While in some cases there may be an underlying organic disorder, often the patient simply dislikes the food and any symptoms which may arise from taking it are psychological in origin.

DIET SHEETS

The details of prophylactic and therapeutic dietary

regimes are given in an appendix (p. 607); in various parts of the text the reader is referred to a numbered diet as one example of a type diet. Such type diets require to be modified by dietitians to suit the needs of individual patients in different parts of the world. The diets are based on British or North American foodstuffs which may be too expensive, unavailable or not appreciated in other countries; then it is the task of dietitians to adapt the specimen diets to comparable local foodstuffs. A glossary on page 602 is designed to help dietitians and doctors to talk to patients who come from other areas or parts of the world and to understand diet sheets from the other side of the Atlantic.

In general, strict and rigid adherence to a dietary regime with accurate weighing of all foods is seldom needed except for short periods. As it requires close supervision by a dietitian, it is usually best done in hospital. A short period in hospital on a strict diet is often beneficial in that it teaches a patient what foods to avoid and how to judge the weight of a helping of food by eye. Thereafter a less severe regime may be followed easily at home. This gradation is exemplified in diets for diabetes. Many patients who require dietary treatment have chronic diseases and the treatment may have to continue for a long time and often for life. Dietary restrictions are always irksome, but to a varying degree depending on the personality of the patient. When patients are seriously ill and cannot be expected to survive for a long period, it is seldom justifiable to add to their trouble by imposing a rigid adherence to a strict diet.

Therapeutic diets have an important role in modern medicine. Many patients do not get adequate advice and instruction, and as a result they may fail to derive full benefit from other forms of treatment. On the other hand therapeutic diets should always be used with common sense. The benefit likely to arise from improvement in the patient's physical condition should outweigh the tedium of the restrictions on enjoyment of food.

'There's many a slip twixt cup and lip.' Merely to hand a printed diet sheet to a patient across a desk is no guarantee that there will be any change in what the patient eats. Good communication is essential in the complex and difficult task of persuading patients to change dietary habits. Diet sheets are only one tool in this task and should be supported by talks, demonstrations, sometimes group sessions and home visits, and then reinforced by arrangements for follow-up at suitable intervals.

FOOD IN HOSPITALS

The quality of food served in a hospital affects the morale of the patients and also of resident staff and of those who take meals in its canteens. Even in the best

hospitals standards may slip and complaints arise and regrettably in many hospitals they are set too low.

A classic report[2] based on an investigation in 1963 on the feeding arrangements and nutritive value of meals served in 152 hospitals in England and Wales is a distressing tale of deficiencies uncovered. The report showed that large hospitals were more likely to provide an unsatisfactory service than small ones in which in many cases the food was excellent. Many of the deficiencies arose in old hospitals where the kitchens and their equipment had not been modernised and the staff worked under great difficulties.

There is no doubt that today in many hospitals throughout the world meals are poorly served and often inadequate. A study in an Oxford hospital in 1984 showed that many patients did not eat sufficient food to meet baseline requirements of energy, protein, iron and vitamins.[3]

Hospital budgets are now becoming less and less able to meet all the needs of patients. It is important for the kitchen to get its due share and sufficient money for staff and new equipment, as well as for food. Poor equipment and insufficient trained staff are mainly responsible for the outbreaks of food poisoning that continue to occur all too frequently among hospital patients and staff.

Caterers, nurses, doctors and dietitians share the responsibility for patients' food. Caterers purchase the foods and supervise the preparation, cooking and transport from kitchen to wards. Nurses organise its distribution and ensure that, as far as possible, all patients get food that they like. They also have to coax many patients to eat. Doctors order special diets for patients who need them. Dietitians supervise the preparation of these diets and see that they are adjusted to the individual needs of patients. Doctors and dietitians frequently overlook that they have a responsibility to see that all patients in the wards have a good diet, since this is an essential part of their management whatever the nature of their disease. All nurses should remember that Florence Nightingale emphasised that an essential part of a nurse's duty was to see that each of her patients was properly fed.

Patients often get poor food when there is a poor liaison between doctors, dietitians, nurses and caterers. These separate professions share a responsibility for the food in a hospital. This responsibility becomes effective when there is mutual understanding and discussions of practical problems as these arise.

REFERENCES

1. Brock J F 1972 Nature, nurture, and stress in health and disease. Lancet 1: 701–4
2. Platt B S, Eddy T P, Pellett P L 1963 Food in hospitals. Oxford University Press
3. Todd E A, Hunt P, Crowe P J, Royle G T 1984 What do patients eat in hospital? Hum Nutr Appl Nutr 38A: 294–7

39

Inborn Errors of Metabolism

Sir Archibald Garrow in the Croonian lectures to the Royal College of Physicians in 1908[1] described four conditions, albinism, alcaptonuria, cystinuria and pentosuria, characterised by being genetically determined, present at birth and not constituting a disease, although persons with cystinuria were at increased risk of developing renal stones. He called these conditions inborn errors of metabolism and distinguished them from metabolic diseases, determined in part by genetic constitution, of which he gave gout, diabetes and obesity as examples.

This distinction is no longer made. Steadily increasing knowledge of biochemistry and genetics has shown that there are over 200 conditions in which a genetically determined defect in a single enzyme system impairs its activity and leads to a metabolic disorder. In many of these the nature of the enzymic defect has now been fully described and in a few the locus or position of the aberrant mutant gene on a specific chromosome is known. The change in the genetic constitution, or genotype, is expressed in the physical and mental characteristics of the individual, the phenotype. In most of these disorders expression of the phenotype is readily detectable at or soon after birth by clinical or biochemical examination. In some it only becomes manifest later in life as a result of interaction between the phenotype and the environment, which includes the nature of the diet. The clinical consequences of these errors in metabolism vary enormously. In a few instances, as in those described by Garrod, they are compatible with good health and a normal life span. In many the defect is so severe that an affected infant can only survive for a few days or weeks. In others there is survival with varying degrees of physical or mental disabilities and a shortened life span, and in some of these conditions dietary treatment is of great value.

Some of these disorders are commonly seen in clinical practice. Examples are the hyperlipidaemias, diabetes and gout and these are described in the next three chapters; in each of these disorders diet plays a part in the expression of the phenotype. The haemoglobinopathies, common in some racial groups, are briefly discussed in Chapter 48. That genetic defects can give rise to obesity in experimental animals is well known, but there is little evidence that they are a causative factor in most cases of human obesity (Chap. 28).

Other inborn errors of metabolism are uncommon. Most doctors and dietitians who have spent their working life in a general hospital or community practice have not been responsible for the care of a single case. The incidence of phenylketonuria is about 1 in 20 000 births and of others, such as maple-syrup urine disease, of the order of 1 in 100 000. Some are so rare that they have only been identified in one or two families.

Only two of these uncommon disorders, phenylketonuria and galactosaemia, are described in this chapter. In both, dietary treatment has revolutionised the outlook for the affected child. Brief notes are given on some other conditions which may be responsive to diet. Information about the remainder can be obtained from a textbook by Stanbury et al[2] that weighs over 3 kg or from a paediatrician in a large hospital for children who is a specialist in these disorders.

PHENYLKETONURIA (PKU)

PKU is caused by a defect in metabolism of the amino acid phenylalanine. In affected children physical development is usually normal but mental development is impaired to a varying degree. If untreated, many of the children become mentally defective adults who have to be cared for in institutions. Dietary treatment started soon after birth allows normal or nearly normal development.

The biochemical and genetic defects
PKU acquired its name when it was first identified by the finding of a ketone, phenylpyruvic acid, in the urine. This, however, is only incidental and the primary defect is in the phenylalanine hydroxylating system that converts the amino acid into tyrosine.

When this system cannot convert all of the ample

amounts of phenylalanine derived from the protein in a mother's milk, the concentration in the blood rises and this is responsible for the impaired development of the nervous system. Some of the excess phenylalanine is deaminated to phenylpyruvic acid which is excreted in the urine.

Hydroxylation is effected by phenylalanine hydroxylase (PH) and a coenzyme 5,6,7,8-tetrahydrobiopterin (BH_4). In the process the coenzyme is oxidised to dihydrobiopterin (BH_2) from which it is reformed by another enzyme, dihydrobiopterin reductase (DHPR). BH_2 is provided by synthesis from guanosine triphosphate. Hydroxylation may be impaired by genetic defects in production of PH, of DHPR and of an enzyme responsible for the formation of BH_2 (Fig. 39.1). A defect in production of PH is responsible for the usual classical form of PKU but other defects lead to variant forms of the disorder.

The clinical manifestations (the phenotype) depend not only on which of several genes is defective but also on the severity of the defect. The genes responsible for the control of the hydroxylation are not closely linked and may be on different chromosomes. The defects are transmitted by autosomal recessive inheritance. Often several members of a family are affected and these are homozygous. Unaffected heterozygous individuals act as carriers.

There is still much to learn about the biochemistry and genetics of PKU and they are now subject to much research. It is hoped that this will lead to more precise diagnosis and so to better management of individual cases and also, possibly, to a method of prevention. PKU is also of great general scientific interest and in a long review Scriver & Clow[3] aptly call it an 'epitome of human biochemical genetics'.

Classical phenylketonuria

An affected baby at first progresses normally. At the age of 8 to 10 months the parents may become anxious because their child is slow in learning to sit and handle things and is generally unresponsive. About one quarter of the children develop eczema. After the first birthday the retarded development becomes obvious and there may be signs of severe birth damage, such as myoclonic epilepsy and marked hyperactivity. Most affected children grow up to become physically sound but are mentally defective. Now that there is early biochemical diagnosis and effective dietary management, this clinical picture is rarely seen.

Plasma phenylalanine is usually 10 times or more above the upper limit of normality (2.0 mg/100 ml, or 1.2 mmol/l).

Variant forms

Besides classical PKU, other forms of hyperphenylalaninaemia are known and at least nine types have been listed.[2] In one, plasma phenylalanine is high at birth but falls progressively to normal and it is probably due to delayed maturation of PH. In another, plasma phenylalanine though above normal is much less than in classical PKU and usually there are no clinical manifestations; it is probably due to a limited defect in the synthesis of PH. Deficiencies of DHPR and BH_2 are also described.[3]

DIETARY MANAGEMENT

Clinical manifestations do not arise if an affected infant is put on a low phenylalanine diet soon after birth and kept on it for a long period. An entirely artificial diet

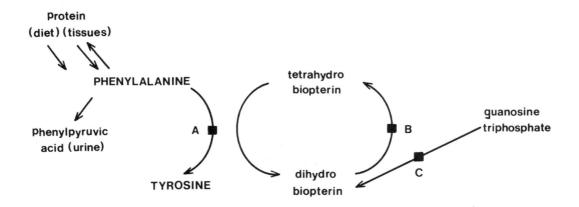

Fig. 39.1 A simplified scheme of enzyme defects leading to phenylalanaemia. Defects occur in phenylalanine hydroxylase (A), in dihydropterin reductase (B) and in dihydropterin synthetase (C). Classical phenylketonuria is due to defect A

imposes a severe emotional strain on a young child and clearly should be continued no longer than is absolutely necessary. It is sensible to compromise and stop at about the age of 8 years[4] when the risk of subsequent mental deterioration is certainly slight, though not as yet fully assessed.

As soon as the diagnosis is made, breast feeding should be stopped and the infant bottle-fed with a low phenylalanine milk substitute; Minafen (Cow & Gate) and Lofenalac (Mead Johnson) are preparations readily available. Greater difficulty arises when the baby has to be weaned. A mother then has to prepare a low phenyl-alanine diet for her child from five lists of foods. For this she needs continuing help from a dietitian. The lists are (1) basic foods containing negligible phenylalanine which can be used freely (these include sugar, jams, sweets, solid vegetable oils and cooking oils), (2) fruits and vegetables which can be taken freely, since they provide neglible phenylalanine and protein in a normal helping, and fruits and vegetables which, if taken in large quantities, add a significant amount of phenylala-nine, but may be used in small quantities in vegetable stews, sauces and salads, (3) a basic list of 50 mg phenyl-alanine exchanges of foods, (4) manufacturers foods of neglible phenylalanine content and (5) exchanges of foods containing 50 mg of phenylalanine (by calculation taking 1 g of protein as 50 mg phenylalanine). These lists, which are revised yearly, can be obtained from the National Society for Phenylketonuria and Allied Dis-orders, 26 Towngate Grove, Mirfield, West Yorkshire.

Maternal PKU

Until recent years most adult women with PKU were feeble minded and few of them became pregnant. Now a generation of baby girls have grown up into women who are healthy in body and mind and whose fertility is also normal. An international review[5] covering 524 pregnancies in 155 women has shown that these have resulted in an abnormally high number of spontaneous abortions and of babies with mental retardation, micro-cephaly and congenital heart disease. It is not clear whether dietary treatment begun during pregnancy has any benefit. A high phenylalanine content in the maternal blood may well have many adverse effects on the fetus during the first 8 weeks of its life during which the structural organisation of the body is laid down. There is thus a strong case for starting a low phenyla-nine diet before conception. This is a difficult decision for a healthy woman and she will be helped by professional advice in making it and in carrying it out.

THE CHALLENGE TO COMMUNITY HEALTH SERVICES

Phenylketonuria was first described in 1934. In the subsequent 50 years sufficient knowledge of the defect has been obtained to make it possible that no child born with the defect becomes mentally retarded. To ensure this is a challenge to a community. The first problem is early detection. This in theory is simple. All that is needed is a drop of the baby's blood on a filter paper and an assessment by bioassay of its phenylala-nine content (the Guthrie test). But to ensure that blood is obtained from every baby soon after birth is an administrative task requiring great effort and money. Although the analysis is easy, a laboratory has to be provided capable of examining and reporting on a large number of samples accurately and quickly, and this also requires effort and money. The second problem is the provision of an artificial diet for the first years of a child's life. The ingredients are now easily obtained but are expensive. Regular surveillance is required to ensure that the mother understands the dietary instructions and is carrying them out; this again requires administrative effort and money. Cost-benefit analyses are now fashion-able in medicine. It is difficult to draw up an econ-omic balance sheet for PKU, but it is probable that the financial burden of providing effective services for the detection of the defect and for treating the children is less than the cost that would otherwise be necessary to maintain them in an institution for the many years of a normal life span. Furthermore, treatment allows those with PKU to lead a full and productive life. Economics plays an important part in medical practice but fortu-nately in our society it is only secondary. The wonder or miracle is that, as a result of the scientific study of PKU, many families can now be saved from the tragedy of having one or more members who are feeble minded.

GALACTOSAEMIA

A hereditary defect causing diminished activity of glucose-1-phosphate uridyl transferase impairs the metabolism of galactose (p. 34), causing its concen-tration in the blood to rise. Toxic signs appear soon after birth when an infant begins to take milk and are due to accumulation of galactose-1-phosphate within the cells. The defect is less common than phenylketonuria and was found in only six out of 530 000 babies examined in Scotland,[6] a prevalence of 1 in 88 000.

CLINICAL FEATURES

The clinical picture varies in severity from case to case. In its severe form the disorder may be manifest in infants within two or three weeks after birth, as indi-cated by vomiting, difficulty in feeding, loss of weight and the onset of jaundice. In such patients the spleen may be palpable and the liver greatly enlarged and very firm, and ascites may be present. Examination of the urine shows the presence of sugar (galactose) and also protein. Without immediate dietetic treatment of such severe cases death rapidly occurs. In mild to moderate cases the diagnosis may be missed because of the failure of the doctor to examine the urine of an infant who has infrequent vomiting and who is not thriving. If the disorder is allowed to continue for months, cataracts are likely to develop and these may lead in time to blindness. Mental and physical retardation are also likely to occur.

A much rarer form is due to lack of galactokinase. In this, mental development is normal and the liver is not damaged but severe cataracts leading to blindness occur early in childhood.

DIAGNOSIS

This is made by demonstrating raised blood galactose in a sample of blood obtained at the same time as a sample for the Guthrie test for PKU. It is confirmed by demonstrating reduced glucose-1-phosphate uridyl transferase activity in erythrocytes.

TREATMENT

Breast feeding should be stopped immediately and the infant given a milk powder in which lactose has been replaced by dextrin, dextrose and maltose. Commercial preparations available are Galactomin (Cow & Gate). Subsequently milk, milk products and food preparations containing these should be excluded from the diet. These measures at once relieve symptoms and ensure that they do not recur. It is usually necessary to continue these restrictions throughout life. Compliance with such a regime is difficult and can be tested by showing the absence of galactosuria and, more precisely, by measuring the concentration of galactose-1-phosphate in packed lysed red cells, which should not exceed 2 mg/100 ml. Further restrictions to reduce the intake of galactosides, present in small quantities in most foods, and widely used in the food industry as a filler or flavouring agent, have been advocated but this is impractical and almost certainly unnecessary.[7] Lactose is used in the pharmaceutical industry in the formulation of many drug products. Such preparations can normally be taken with safety but when a patient requires large doses for a long time it may be wise to use an alternative drug.

The dietary treatment of galactosaemia, like that of phenylketonuria, is a story of success for scientific medicine. But success depends on the health services

ensuring early diagnosis and providing the surveillance necessary to see that patients comply with the dietary restrictions.

OTHER HEREDITARY DEFECTS RESPONSIVE TO DIETARY THERAPY

Refsum's disease. This is due to a defect in the enzyme systems responsible for the metabolism of phytanic acid (3,7,11,15-tetramethyl-hexadecanoic acid) which accumulates in the plasma and tissues. Phytanic acid is derived from phytol, a product of the hydrolysis of chlorophyl. The main clinical features are peripheral neuropathy, cerebellar ataxia, nerve deafness and retinitis pigmentosa. Symptoms usually first appear in childhood and progress slowly, patients becoming severely disabled between the age of 20 to 30 years. An account of the biochemical and clinical features in three patients seen in London gives a fuller picture of the disease.[8] Patients may be greatly improved by removing phytanic acid by plasma exchange and by a diet low in chlorophyl. This requires exclusion or restriction of many fruits and vegetables, butter and ruminant fat. Lists of foods suitable for a low phytanic acid diet are available.[9]

Abetalipoproteinaemia. In this rare, autosomal and recessive disorder there is a failure to form low density lipoprotein. Plasma cholesterol is very low and chylomicrons do not appear in the blood after a fatty meal. It presents in early childhood when there is a failure to thrive, steatorrhoea and characteristic spiky red blood cells. Later, neurological degeneration causes ataxia and failure of vision. Absorption of fat-soluble vitamins is impaired and early treatment with vitamin E delays or may prevent development of neurological complications.[10]

Maple-syrup urine disease. A defect in the oxidative deamination of the branched-chain amino acids, leucine, isoleucine and valine, leads to accumulation in the blood of their oxoacids; these are excreted in the urine, to which they impart an odour of maple syrup. Soon after birth the infant has difficulty in feeding; loss of reflexes, convulsions and coma follow and in severe cases death within a month. Those who survive longer are mentally defective unless fed with a formula diet low in leucine, isoleucine and valine. A few children have been reared successfully and when they are older require a low protein diet based on gelatin, gluten-free flour, butter, margarine, sugar and fruits.

Homocystinuria. The sulphur-containing essential amino acid methionine is metabolised by demethylation to form homocystein which is coupled with serine by cystathione synthetase. A defect in this enzyme leads to increased concentrations of homocystein, homocystine and methionine in plasma and urine. Affected children are mentally retarded. Dislocation of the lenses is common and abnormalities of bone and other tissues may be present. A low methionine diet based on a soya protein formula has allowed some children to develop normally for several years. Homocystinuria may follow other enzymic defects and then mental retardation does not follow invariably and other abnormal effects are rare. The value of a low methionine diet in such cases is doubtful.

Defects in urea synthesis.   Inherited deficiencies of each of the five enzymes in the urea cycle have been described. In affected infants ammonia accumulates in the blood and causes vomiting, lethargy, respiratory distress, seizures and coma. The prognosis is very poor but a few children are surviving after 6 years with a diet very low in protein supplemented with citrulline or arginine where appropriate, and given sodium benzoate and sodium phenyl acetate.[11] The latter two are excreted after conjugation as hippuric acid and phenylacetylglutamine and so provide an alternative to urea as a means of excreting nitrogen.

Hypertyrosinaemia.   This is not uncommon but usually transient and due to slow maturation of *p*-hydroxyphenyl pyruvic acid (*p*-HPPA) oxidase, an enzyme responsible for the oxidative deamination of tyrosine. The hypertyrosaemia is accentuated by deficiency of vitamin C and for this reason it is important to see that all preterm babies have a supplement of the vitamin. By the age of 4 months, blood tyrosine is normal and there are no clinical features. Partial *p*-HPPA oxidase deficiency is a very rare but serious disorder leading to failure to thrive and disorders of the liver and kidneys. There may be a good response to a low tyrosine, low phenylalanine diet.

Fructose intolerance.   This is due to lack of the aldolase which converts fructose-1-phosphate to dihydroxyacetone phosphate and glyceraldehyde. When fructose is ingested, fructose-1-phosphate accumulates in the liver; this interferes with release of glucose from the liver and leads to severe hypoglycaemia. Infants are free of symptoms unless given sugar (sucrose). Then there may be vomiting and hypoglycaemic fits, and a series of episodes may lead to jaundice and enlargement of the liver. Treatment consists of excluding sucrose and fruit from the diet. This is easy in an infant, but is a formidable problem for a mother as her child grows up. Fortunately the condition is very rare. It has been noticed that the teeth of patients with fructose intolerance do not show caries.

Von Gierke's disease (glycogen storage disease, type I).   The defect is a low activity of glucose-6-phosphatase so that mobilisation of glycogen is impaired and large amounts accumulate in the liver. Although very rare, it is well known because most patients survive into adult life. Growth is retarded and there is marked enlargement of the liver so that the abdomen is protruded. Hypoglycaemia and ketoacidosis may occur in the newborn and attacks may continue throughout life, often brought on by an infection or temporary starvation. Mental development is retarded only if episodes of hypoglycaemia have been frequent and severe. Dietary management consists in preventing such attacks, which arise as a result of inability to maintain the concentration of blood sugar by mobilising glycogen. A diet high in protein promotes gluconeogenesis from amino acids and so helps to maintain blood sugar. In severe cases frequent feeds, every 3 to 4 hours may be required. A moderate amount of carbohydrate is permissible, but this should be in the form of glucose or its polymer, starch. Both sucrose and lactose should be avoided, because fructose and galactose are readily converted to glycogen in the liver. As the child grows up attacks of hypoglycaemia become less severe.

Disorders responding to pharmacological doses of vitamins

Some 25 disorders are known that respond to doses of a vitamin that is 10 to 100 times or more greater than the normal dietary intake.[12] In these disorders the consequences of an hereditary defect in an enzyme system can be partially or completely prevented by providing a high concentration of a coenzyme in the tissues or by bypassing a block in a transport system. The best known are the various forms of hereditary rickets (p. 306) and hereditary pellagra, known as Hartnup's disease (p. 320). Some of the others have been briefly described earlier in the book in accounts of individual vitamins. All are rare and only one or two cases of some have been reported. The benefit of megavitamin therapy in these disorders is established. Enthusiasts for megavitamin therapy have sometimes used this to support their claims that it promotes health and is of benefit in diseases such as cancer and the common cold. This has no justification. An editorial[13] discusses with sense and clarity the proper use of megavitamin therapy for these very rare disorders, and its misuse and potential dangers when patients are persuaded to try it for common complaints as well as serious disorders which it does not benefit.

REFERENCES

1. Garrod A 1908 Inborn errors of metabolism. Lancet 2: 1–7, 73–9, 142–8, 214–20
2. Stanbury J B, Wyngaarden J B, Fredrickson D S 1978 The metabolic basis of inherited disease, 4th edn. McGraw-Hill, New York
3. Scriver C R, Clow C L 1980 Phenylketonuria: epitome of human biochemical genetics. N Engl J Med 303: 1336–42, 1394–1400

4. Smith I, Wolff O H 1974 Duration of treatment of phenylketonuria. (Letter.) Lancet 1:1229
5. Lenke R R, Levy H L 1980 Maternal phenylketonuria and hyperphenylalaninaemia. N Engl J Med 303: 1202–8
6. Stevenson J S, Kennedy R 1978 Phenylketonuria screening in Scotland 1965–77. Health Bull 36: 277–9
7. Clothier C M, Davidson D C 1983 Report on galactosaemia workshop. Hum Nutr Appl Nutr 37A: 483–90
8. Billimoria J D, Clemens M E, Gibberd F B, Whitelaw M N 1982 Metabolism of phytanic acid in Refsum's disease. Lancet 1: 194–6
9. Masters-Thomas A, Bailes J, Billimoria J D, et al 1980 Heredopathia atactica polyneuritiformis (Refsum's disease). 2: Estimation of phytanic acid in foods. J Hum Nutr 34: 251–4
10. Muller D P R, Lloyd J K, Wolff O H 1983 Vitamin E and neurological function. Lancet 1: 225–8
11. Msall M, Batshaw M L, Suss R, Brusilow S W, Mellits E D 1984 Neurologic outcome in children with inborn errors of urea synthesis. N Engl J Med 310: 1500–5
12. Scriver C R 1973 Vitamin-reponsive inborn errors of metabolism. Metabolism 22: 1319–44
13. Rudman D, Williams P J 1983 Megadose vitamins. Use and misuse. N Engl J Med 309: 488–90

40

Hyperlipidaemia

The role of lipoproteins in the transport of lipide in the blood has been described in Chapter 6. Great interest in these lipoproteins arose in about 1950 when it become generally known that a high concentration of those rich in cholesterol was associated with vascular disorders and especially with ischaemic heart disease, or coronary heart disease (CHD) as it is commonly called. Before considering the clinical features and management of patients with hyperlipoproteinaemia (conveniently contracted to hyperlipidaemia), the range of normal values is discussed and how this can be modified by the nature of the diet in apparently healthy persons.

Normal values and diagnosis
Hyperlipidaemia may arise from an increased concentration of either cholesterol or triglycerides and frequently both are raised.

Cholesterol. Plasma cholesterol values in an apparently healthy population are scattered over a wide range and distribution is skewed to the left (Fig. 40.1). The position of the median and the skew varies in different populations. There is a slow rise with age starting at 20 years but ceasing at about 60 years when it may be followed by a slight fall. This does not occur in some individuals and is not seen in primitive societies. The rise is less steep in women until the menopause when it may increase abruptly. After 60 years there is little or no difference between the sexes.

Mortality from CHD rises with increasing levels of plasma cholesterol and the rise is continuous and curvilinear. However, there appears to be a threshold at about 5.4 mmol/litre (210 mg/dl). Above this the risk of death from CHD rises sharply and is high in the upper fifth quintile of plasma cholesterol values in an affluent society (Fig. 40.2). Below the threshold, deaths may

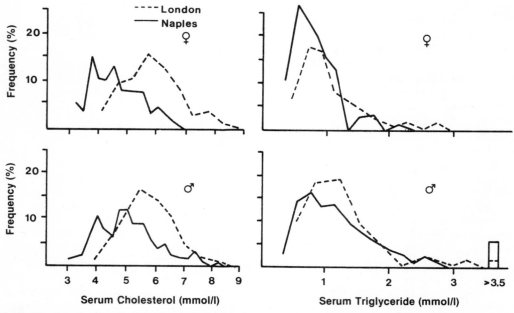

Fig. 40.1 Distribution of serum cholesterol and trigylcerides in apparently healthy subjects aged 20–69 years in London and Naples. (Data from Lewis)[1]

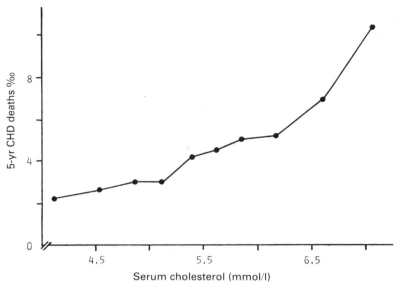

Fig. 40.2 Five year age-related CHD mortality rates per 1000 and serum cholesterol in American men. (Modified from data of the Multiple Risk Intervention Trial)[2]

occur but the risk is relatively low and not closely related to plasma cholesterol.

Usually only total plasma cholesterol is measured, but it is often useful to determine its distribution in the different lipoprotein fractions (Table 6.3). The main fractions are the very low density lipoproteins (VLDL) which are triglyceride-rich, the low density lipoproteins (LDL) which are rich in cholesterol and the high density lipoproteins (HDL) which also carry a good deal of cholesterol in conjunction with lecithin. It is the LDL and HDL fractions which are of particular importance in atherosclerosis and coronary heart disease. The LDL fraction is responsible for the transfer of most of the cholesterol from the liver to tissues where it is taken up by LDL receptors. When there is too great a concentration of LDL with a deficiency in LDL receptors, cholesterol accumulation can occur. The HDL fraction, on the other hand, is a scavenger lipoprotein responsible for removal of excess cholesterol from tissues. Thus the LDL/HDL ratio is a convenient quick method of assessing the extent of atherogenicity of an individual's plasma lipoproteins.

Triglycerides Plasma triglyceride in apparently healthy people is subject to variations. Fasting values commonly range from 0.4–1.5 mmol/litre (35–130 mg/dl) but may be higher and only those over 3.0 mmol/litre (270 mg/dl) suggest hypertriglyceridaemia. Plasma triglyceride rises after a meal containing fats and so blood samples have to be taken after an overnight fast. A high fasting plasma triglyceride is often associated with a high plasma cholesterol, but is not by itself a risk factor for CHD.[3]

EFFECT OF DIET ON PLASMA LIPIDS

Fat (triglycerides) intake
Many experiments on human volunteers were made in the 1960s to study the effects on different dietary fats on plasma lipids.[4,5] These showed plasma cholesterol was raised by saturated fatty acids (S), lowered by polyunsaturated ones (P) and little affected by monosaturated ones. Figure 40.3 shows one such experiment. Keys and his colleagues[6] collated the results into a mathematical formula, now simplified into

$$\Delta \text{ Plasma cholesterol} = 1.35 \, (2\Delta S - \Delta P)$$

where ΔS and ΔP are changes in the percentages of dietary energy derived from saturated and polyunsaturated fatty acids. The saturated fatty acids raise plasma cholesterol twice as much as polyunsaturated ones lower it.

In an experiment reported in 1983 the effect of substituting polyunsaturated fatty acids for monounsaturated fatty acids in the diet was much less than predicted by the Keys equation.[7] This may have been due to the initial levels of plasma cholesterol in the US volunteer subjects being lower than those in the subjects of the earlier experiments.

In practice, plasma cholesterol falls if the percentage of dietary energy provided by fats is reduced. The saturated fatty acids, palmitic (C16:0) and myristic acid (C14:0) raise plasma cholesterol more than those with shorter and longer chains.[8]

The polyunsaturated fatty acids predominating in marine oils (C20:5 and C22:6) and those in vegetable oils (C18:2 and C20:4) have similar effects in lowering LDL

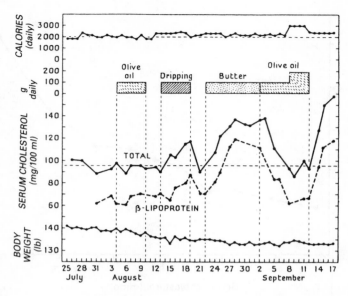

Fig. 40.3 Changes in the serum cholesterol levels in a male Bantu, aged 37, coincided with changes in the intake of animal fat. On a basic diet low in protein and fat and free from cholesterol a supplement of olive oil did not raise the serum cholesterol level or maintain the raised level when substituted for butter. Even when the olive oil supplement was doubled so that it provided over 60 per cent of the total calories, the serum cholesterol level did not rise again until a 'full diet' consisting of beef and vegetables (fat content about 140 g) was given. The mean serum cholesterol level before fat feeding was 95.6 ± 5.5 mg/100 ml. (Data from Bronte-Stewart et al)[4]

and, perhaps unfortunately HDL. This effect is increased if the P/S ratio of the fats is above 0.6.

After a change in diet it takes 10–14 days to establish the new level of plasma cholesterol which is not affected by the immediate past food intake. In general changes in the amount and nature of the dietary fat affect plasma triglyceride in the same manner as they do plasma cholesterol, but less markedly and consistently.

Cholesterol intake

Dietary cholesterol has little effect on plasma cholesterol over the range of intake usual in prosperous societies (300–500 mg daily) since increasing intake inhibits endogenous production. Very high intakes, only obtainable by eating two or more eggs daily, however, raise plasma concentration and this can be lowered significantly by eliminating from the diet all the main sources — eggs, meat and offal. Dietary cholesterol is much less important than dietary fat in determining plasma cholesterol.

Carbohydrate intake

Fasting plasma triglyceride increases when either starch or sugar is added to an experimental diet and also when carbohydrate replaces fat isoenergetically.[9] The rise on changing from a 40 to an 80 per cent carbohydrate diet

averaged 1.1 mmol/litre (100 mg/dl) in normal people but was two to three times as great in patients with hyperlipidaemia.[10] The lipoprotein which increases is VLDL with more triglyceride per unit of protein and a larger particle size. Hepatic synthesis of triglyceride is probably increased.

The effect does not last for more than a few months. People who subsist on diets high in starchy foods, like rice or maize, do not have high plasma triglycerides unless they are obese.

Sucrose in large amounts may have a greater effect than starch in raising plasma triglycerides in some susceptible individuals.[11]

Plasma cholesterol usually falls with increasing carbohydrate in the diet.

Alcohol intake

Generous intakes of ethanol may lead to hypertriglyceridaemia in predisposed individuals. Alcoholism was the commonest cause of hypertriglyceridaemia in patients admitted to the Hammersmith Hospital.[12] Alcohol favours hepatic lipogenesis, and this stimulates the synthesis of VLDL as well as leading to a fatty liver (Chap. 7). In some persons even small amounts increase plasma triglyceride while on the other hand some alcoholics do not have hyperlipidaemia.

CLASSIFICATION OF HYPERLIPIDAEMIAS

The hyperlipidaemias were classified in 1967 by Fredrickson[13] on the basis of abnormalities in plasma lipoproteins into five types with two subtypes. This classification was approved by WHO and used widely. However, only type I, which is very rare, and type IIA, which is relatively uncommon, are well-defined clinical entities; each is due to a genetic disorder. The other four Fredrickson types have no unique distinguishing clinical features, and differences in lipoprotein patterns are not clear cut. They arise either as a result of a manner of life, including the nature of the diet, or secondary to a number of diseases; genetic factors are also present in many cases.

Three groups of hyperlipidaemic patients are now described. These are (1) primary genetic disorders, (2) hyperlipidaemia of affluence and (3) hyperlipidaemia secondary to established diseases.

This classification simplifies discussion of the important problem of management of individual patients.

PRIMARY GENETIC DISORDERS

Familial hypercholesterolaemia

This is a disorder transmitted as an autosomal polymorphic dominant gene. It consists of an increase in low density lipoproteins (LDL), the main carrier of cholesterol in the blood, and is due to genetic failure of LDL receptors. Plasma cholesterol may be over 30 mmol/litre in homozygous adults. The usual range in heterozygous adults is 10–20 mmol/litre. Prevalence of the disorder has been estimated at from 0.25 to 0.5 per cent of a population and it accounts for about 2 per cent of all cases of hypercholesterolaemia. The biochemical abnormality can be detected at birth.

Clinical features

There is a greatly increased risk of coronary heart disease. A heart attack due to myocardial infarction before the age of 30 is not uncommon and 50 per cent of patients present evidence of CHD before they are 50 years old. Thus the disorder greatly reduces life expectancy.

Xanthomata, swellings or small tumours containing cholesterol and sometime triglyceride, commonly occur and may be the presenting feature. Common sites are tendons, especially the Achilles tendon and tendons on the back of the hands and skin, and around the eye where they are known as xanthelasmata.

Corneal arcus occurs early and when seen in someone under 40 years is probably due to the disorder.

Management

This aims at preventing coronary heart disease by keeping plasma LDL cholesterol as low as possible throughout life and beginning in early childhood. This involves lifelong dietary restriction and the use of drugs. Although there is as yet no strong evidence that dietary restriction alone is effective, reduction of plasma cholesterol by the use of intestinal resins has been shown to be effective. Nevertheless, the prognosis is so poor that there is ethical justification for also advising and encouraging adherence to a restricted dietary regime.

Since clinical manifestations of the disorder rarely arise before the patient is an adult, early diagnosis depends on examination of the blood. Whenever the diagnosis is made in a new adult patient, a biochemical examination of the blood should be made on as many of the near relatives as possible, especially the children.

All affected members of the family should then be advised to begin lifelong dietary restrictions to reduce plasma cholesterol and often prolonged periods on a drug. Compliance with this advice is a great strain on patients and their families and they need all the encouragement that they can get from doctors and dietitians.

Since the disorder is not common and management requires much special expertise and has to be lifelong, it is best for patients to attend a centre in a large hospital. Some of these now have special lipid clinics. It is from such clinics that new knowledge of the effectiveness of treatment will come.

The diet should be low in saturated fats and cholesterol, but polyunsaturated fats from vegetable oils and in other foods are permitted. Detailed dietary instruction are given with Diet No. 14 on page 628.

Two drugs lower plasma cholesterol effectively. Cholestyramine is an anion exchange resin that absorbs bile salts and increases their excretion in the stools. Although this leads to increased synthesis of cholesterol, plasma cholesterol falls. Gastrointestinal side effects may be severe. Nicotinic acid in pharmacological doses (3–6 g/day) inhibits lipolysis and mobilisation of free fatty acids from adipose tissue and also reduces plasma VLDL. Both drugs have been shown to be very safe in the short term. Nicotinic acid has vasodilator effects which cause hot flushings in some individuals but these are not serious. Reduction of plasma cholesterol for long periods increases the risk of stone formation in the bile and the incidence of gall bladder disease.

A third drug, clofibrate, that lowers plasma cholesterol is no longer prescribed since its continued use has been shown to be associated with an increased number of deaths from a variety of causes.

Primary hypertriglyceridaemia

The alimentary lipaemia, seen after a meal containing

fat, is not cleared at the normal rate and chylomicrons persist in the blood on an ordinary diet. This rare disease usually presents in childhood and appears to be the homozygous form of an autosomal mutant. The child may present with abdominal pain, and pancreatitis can occur. The liver and spleen are enlarged. Eruptive xanthomata, small yellow skin nodules on a faintly erythematous base, may appear when the plasma triglycerides are very high and though cholesterol may be moderately elevated the TG:cholesterol ratio is about 10:1. Post-heparin lipolytic activity of the plasma is grossly defective. Treatment is with a very reduced fat intake, usually 25 to 30 g/day or sufficiently low to keep the patient asymptomatic (e.g. Diet 10). Medium chain triglycerides can help make the diet more palatable because they do not form chylomicrons. However, they are expensive and there is little knowledge of their long-term effect. No drugs are effective. The hyperlipidaemia is not associated with diabetes and does not predispose to atherosclerosis. Affected children appear to grow out of the disturbance to some extent as they get older.

HYPERLIPIDAEMIA OF AFFLUENCE

In affluent societies a large minority of adults, often more than a third, have plasma cholesterol concentrations above the ranges found in peasant agriculturists and urban slum dwellers. The hyperlipidaemia is not due to a single biochemical defect and plasma VLDL and LDL are frequently both raised in the same individual, so there may be hypertriglyceridaemia as well.

Most individuals are in good health and the only specific clinical feature of the disorder may be the presence of xanthomata, but these appear only rarely. More commonly corneal arcus is present prematurely.

The importance of the condition is the association of high plasma cholesterol with coronary heart disease. But it has little or no assocation with plasma triglycerides alone.

Although the association of high plasma cholesterol, coronary heart disease and affluence is clear in epidemiological studies of communities, it is much less obvious in individual members of an affluent community. A person with a low plasma cholesterol may have a severe heart attack and many, particularly women, with a high one live to a ripe age.

Several factors known to increase the risk of CHD are discussed in the next chapter. A high plasma cholesterol is one of these.

Diet is clearly a cause of hyperlipidaemia but it is not the only one. As many individuals in affluent societies do not become hyperlipidaemic, there is a constitutional factor, but the genetics of the disorders are complex and not worked out. Other unknown factors may be contributory.

There has now been many field trials in each of which the effect on the incidence of CHD following lowering of plasma cholesterol, either by drugs or the changes in the diet, has been compared with controls. In four large prospective trials in which all of those in the treated and control groups were initially healthy, the results show unequivocally that lowering an initially raised plasma cholesterol can lower the incidence of CHD (Table 40.1). But in these trials the subjects were selected from large numbers of men (480 000 in the Lipid Research Clinics) with very high plasma cholesterol. Even with these selected men, incidence of CHD though less was still high after treatment. It is uncertain whether any of the treatments would have a similar effect on the much larger proportion of the population with only a moderately raised plasma cholesterol. Also, in all these studies there was no change or an increase in total mortality. Trials, in which the subjects had had a previous heart attack and recurrences were recorded, have suggested that reduction of hyperlipidaemia at this late stage is of little value.

The use of drugs to maintain a low plasma cholesterol is associated with long-term risks to health and is not justified except in patients with familial hypercholesterolaemia.

Table 40.1 Primary prevention trials of cholesterol lowering and incidence of coronary heart disease

	Treatment	Follow-up (years)		Number	Cases of CHD	Annual incidence of CHD/1000 men
Lipid Research Clinics USA[14]	Cholestyramine	7	Treatment	1906	155	11.6
			Control	1900	187	14.1
WHO, Europe[15]	Clofibrate	5	Treatment	5331	167	6.2
			Control	5296	208	7.8
Los Angeles Veterans[16]	Diet	8	Treatment	424	52	15.3
			Control	422	65	19.2
Oslo study group[17]	Diet, cessation of smoking	5	Treatment	604	19	6.3
			Control	628	36	11.3

Severe and lifelong dietary restrictions are also only justifiable for those with this disorder, but all persons with hyperlipidaemia of affluence require dietary advice. This has to be tailored to each individual and depends on previous dietary habits and the presence or absence of other diseases. Advice given is for a lifetime and is useless unless there is patient compliance. Foods are to be enjoyed and all foods taken in moderation and at appropriate times may be 'good for you'. Rigid bans and severe restrictions will not be observed and, in any case, are unnecessary.

For the overwhelming majority of persons with hyperlipidaemia, with or without evidence of CHD, it is sufficient if they follow the seven dietary guidelines recommended by American Government health authorities and set out on page 529. Adherence to these is likely to cause plasma lipids to fall significantly and maintain them at a lower level.

The guidelines enable patients to enjoy their food with their families and friends in homes and restaurants. But patients do need to know what 'moderation' and 'too much' mean. Most require expert advice from a dietitian who can amplify the guidelines.

Screening

Most individuals with hyperlipidaemia are diagnosed only when they go to a hospital or clinic with symptoms suggestive of CHD or other disorder. If doctors, both in general practice and in hospitals, included a measurement of plasma cholesterol along with taking blood pressure and testing urine in routine general examinations of patients, many more people with high values would be detected. These could then be given appropriate advice and treatment where necessary. More families with genetic hypercholesterolaemia would be detected early. The costs, both in time and money, would be small in relation to likely benefit. Whether screening of the whole population should be undertaken, as some advise, is more debatable. The costs of all programmes of mass screening are high and have to be considered carefully, as well as probable benefits.

HYPERLIPIDAEMIA SECONDARY TO ESTABLISHED DISEASES

Hypercholesterolaemia is a feature of hypothyroidism and the nephrotic syndrome. Hypertriglyceridaemia commonly and hypercholesterolaemia sometimes accompany obesity, diabetes and gout and occur occasionally in many other disorders of metabolism. No special features are associated with these raised concentrations, which tend to fall as the underlying disorders are brought under control.

REFERENCES

1. Lewis B 1976 The hyperlipidaemias: clinical and laboratory practice. Blackwell, Oxford, p 131
2. Neaton J D, Kuller L H, Wentworth D, Borhani N O 1984 Total and cardiovascular mortality in relation to cigarette smoking, serum cholesterol and diastolic blood pressure among black and white males followed up for five years. Am Heart J 108: 759–69
3. Hulley S B, Rosenman R H, Bawol R D, Brand R J 1980 Epidemiology as a guide to clinical decisions. The association between triglyceride and coronary heart disease. N Engl J Med 302: 1383–9
4. Bronte-Stewart B, Antonis A, Eales L, Brock J F 1956 Effects of feeding different fats on serum cholesterol level. Lancet 1: 521–6
5. Ahrens E H, Insull W, Hirsch J, et al 1959 The effect on human serum lipids of a dietary fat, highly unsaturated but poor in essential fatty acids. Lancet 1: 115–9
6. Keys A, Anderson J T, Grande F 1965 Serum cholesterol responses to changes in the diet. I: Iodine value of dietary fat versus 2S-P. Metabolism 14: 747–58
7. Becker N, Illingworth D R, Alaupovic P, Connor W E, Sundberg E E 1983 Effects of saturated, monounsaturated and ω-6 polyunsaturated fatty acids on plasma lipids, lipoproteins and apoproteins in humans. Am J Clin Nutr 39: 355–60, 497–9 (correspondence)
8. McGandy R B, Hegstead D M, Meyers M L 1970 Use of semisynthetic fats in determining effects of specific dietary fatty acids on serum lipids in man. Am J Clin Nutr 23: 1288–98
9. Ahrens E H, Hirsch J, Oetta A, Farquahar J W, Stein Y 1961 Carbohydrate induced and fat induced lipaemia. Trans Assoc Am Physicians 74: 134–46
10. Glueck C J, Levy R I, Fredrickson D S 1969 Immunoreactive insulin, glucose tolerance and carbohydrate inducibility in types II, III, IV and V hyperlipoproteinaemia. Diabetes 18: 739–47
11. Macdonald I, Braithwaite D M 1964 The influence of dietary carbohydrates on the lipid pattern in serum and in adipose tissue. Clin Sci 27: 23–30
12. Chait A, Mancini M, February A, Lewis B 1972 Clinical and metabolic study of alcoholic hyperlipidaemia. Lancet 2: 62–6
13. Fredrickson D S, Levy R I, Lees R S 1967 Fat transport in lipoproteins — an integrated approach to mechanisms and disorders. N Engl J Med 276: 148–56
14. Lipid Research Clinics Program 1984 Coronary prevention trial results. 1. Reduction in incidence of coronary heart disease. 2. The relation of incidence of coronary heart disease to cholesterol lowering. JAMA 251: 351–64, 365–74
15. Committee of Principal Investigators, WHO Clofibrate Trial 1978 A cooperative trial in the primary prevention of ischaemic heart disease using clofibrate. Br Heart J 40: 1069–118
16. Dayton S, Pearce M L, Hashimoto S, Dixon W J, Tomiyasu U 1969 A controlled clinical trial of a diet high in unsaturated fat in preventing complications of atherosclerosis. Am Heart Assoc Monogr no. 25
17. Hjermann I, Velve Byre K, Holme E, Leren P 1981 Effect of diet and smoking intervention on the incidence of coronary heart disease. Lancet 2: 1303–10

41

Diseases of the Cardiovascular System

Diseases of the cardiovascular system account for half or more of all deaths in countries where measures for the prevention and treatment of infectious diseases are generally effective. Cancers account for about one fifth of deaths and the remainders are due to diseases of other systems, accidents, violence and poisoning.

We all have to die and, in the absence of infections, natural death in old age is due to the wearing out and failure of one or more of the systems of the body (Chap. 62). Arteries tend to wear out sooner than other tissues and failure of the blood supply to the heart muscle and to the brain are the major causes of death. A heart attack (coronary heart disease) and a stroke (cerebrovascular disease) are by no means always fatal. Many survive with varying degrees of disability; some are able to take up again their old activities and there is little change in their manner of life; others remain invalids and some may be totally incapacitated.

Cardiovascular diseases thus take up a large proportion of the resources in time and money of a health service. With more and more people living to an advanced age, their relative importance is likely to increase. What it is hoped can be prevented is their occurrence in middle-age and sometimes early in adult life.

EPIDEMIOLOGY

Figures 41.1, 2 and 3 show death rates in men and women aged 55–64 years from heart disease, from cerebral vascular disease and from all causes in 26 countries of varying degree of affluence and the changes between 1958 and 1976. Many points that may indicate causes and so means of prevention are clear from these figures.

1. There is a wide range of death rates from country to country, especially from heart disease in men.
2. In women rates in all countries are lower, often much lower, than in men.
3. Between 1958 and 1976 almost all death rates in women fell.
4. In this period death rates from heart disease in men

rose in 18 out of the 26 countries, in many substantially. Only in Canada and the USA was there a substantial fall.
5. Although all countries in the tables are prosperous compared with Third World countries, their order in the table is not closely related to their relative affluence.
6. The order of the countries differs markedly in the tables. Thus Japan and Portugal come first and third with the highest death rates from cerebrovascular disease in men and 24th and 26th with the lowest death rates from heart disease in men.

From the international data it can be concluded that there are risk factors in the environment, including possibly the nature of the diet, that determine the death rates from both heart disease and cerebrovascular disease. When these risk factors can be identified, preventive measures become possible.

Much progress has been made in identifying risk factors by epidemiological studies in communities in many countries. As these have been found to be different for heart disease and cerebrovascular disease, they are considered separately and later in the chapter after a brief account of two pathological processes commonly occurring in the blood vessels of both heart and brain.

PATHOLOGY

There are two separate processes that determine the clinical manifestation of vascular diseases. The first is atheromatous degeneration which slowly and insidiously may narrow the lumen of an artery and reduce the elasticity of its walls. Progressive atheroma of the coronary and cerebral vessels limits the functional capacity of heart and brain but seldom is solely responsible for a heart attack or stroke. These usually follow upon an intravascular clot (thrombosis) or haemorrhage. These are sudden events arising at a focal point, though they are much more likely to occur in an atheromatous vessel.

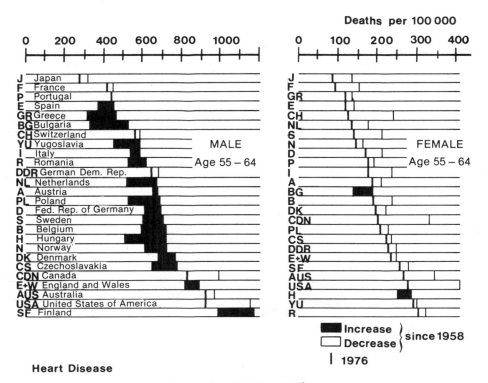

Heart Disease

Fig. 41.1 Mortality rates from heart disease in 26 countries in 1958 and 1976[1]

Cerebrovascular Disease

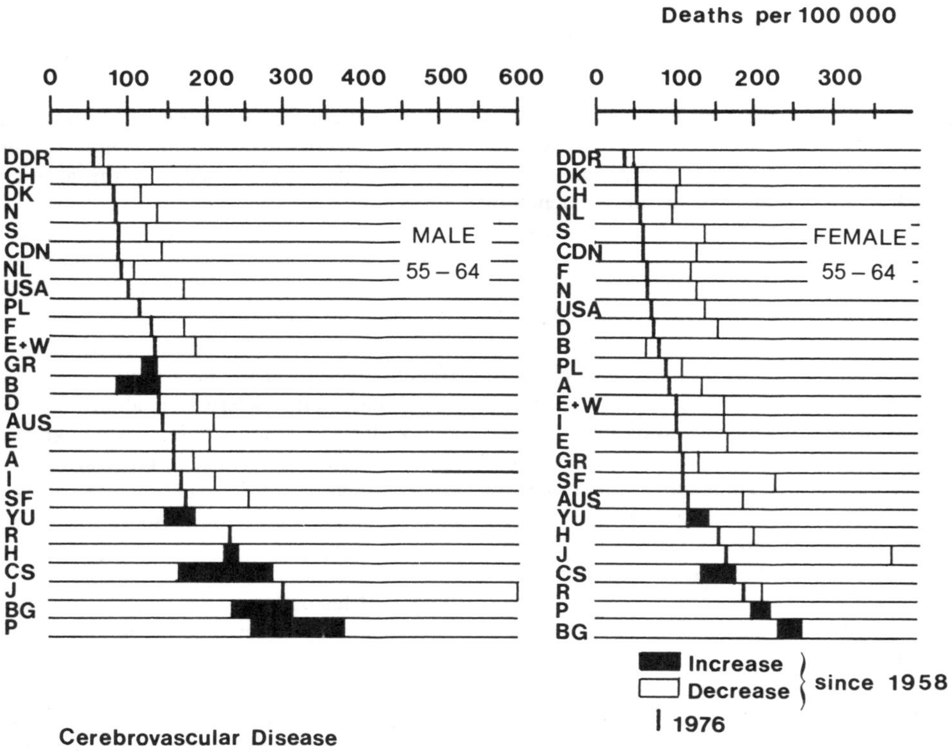

Fig. 41.2 Mortality rates from cerebral vascular diseases in 26 countries in 1958 and 1976[1]

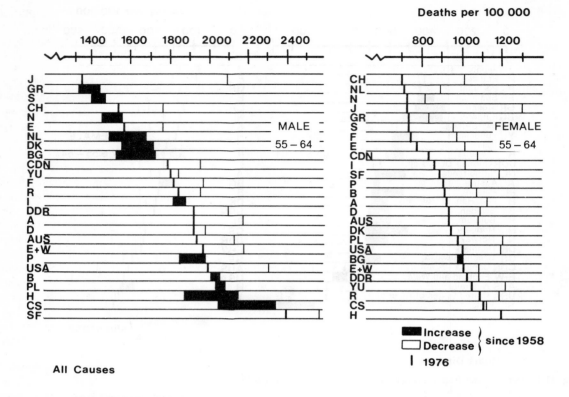

Fig. 41.3 Mortality rates from all causes in men and women in 26 countries in 1958 and in 1976[1]

This distinction between the slow ongoing and sudden acute pathological processes is important in considering risk factors and preventive measures. Epidemiological studies are nearly all related only to the incidence of sudden appearance of clinical symptoms, obvious to both patient and doctor. It is difficult to study the epidemiology of atheroma which is invisible to the naked eye except in the postmortem room. Arteriography, which outlines the lumen of a vessel after injection of a radio-opaque material, permits assessment of the amount of atheroma present. Improved methods are making it increasingly useful in the study of individual patients and in clinical trials, but such an invasive technique could not be used for epidemiological studies on healthy people. Non-invasive methods, such as Doppler techniques, are becoming more sensitive and specific and may be of value for such studies in the future.

ATHEROSCLEROSIS

Atherosclerosis, the most important of the degenerative diseases of arteries, consists of focal accumulation in the intimal lining of arteries of a variable combination of

lipids, complex carbohydrates, blood and blood products, fibrous tissue and calcium deposits; there are associated changes in the media of the arteries. Arterioles are relatively unaffected.

The three major clinical forms of atherosclerotic disease arise from narrowing of the coronary arteries, the cerebral arteries and the femoral artery and its branches, but other arteries can be affected, such as the renal or mesenteric, with the possible consequences of disease in the organ supplied by the artery.

Coronary atherosclerosis is almost invariably associated with aortic atherosclerosis. Although it also tends to be associated with disease in other arteries, most of the epidemiological and experimental work has been concerned with atherosclerosis in the coronary rather than other arteries.

Types of lesion
It is customary to separate the lesions of atherosclerosis into fatty streaks, plaques and complicated lesions (Fig. 41.4).

Fatty streaks are short, thin, slightly raised yellow lines running longitudinally along the internal surface of arteries and consist of an intracellular accumulation

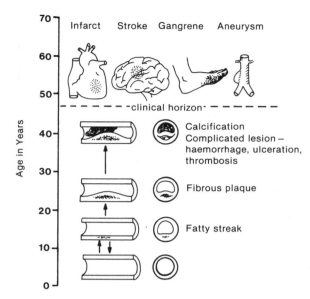

Fig. 41.4 Scheme showing the natural history of atherosclerosis. (From McGill)[2]

of lipids within the intima. Electron microscopy has shown that the affected cells are probably smooth muscle cells. Fatty streaks differ somewhat in their anatomical and epidemiological distribution from plaques and it would seem that, while they may progress to plaques in some situations, they may be reversible in others.

Plaques are the established lesions of atherosclerosis. They are raised, focal, circumscribed lesions up to 1 cm in diameter, consisting of various amounts of fibrous tissue and lipid. The lipid accumulates mostly in extracellular amorphous masses; plaques in which this process is prominent are called **soft** or **atheromatous plaques**. In others fibrous tissue is prominent and lipid is widely scattered or localised to the deeper portions of the lesion; these are called **hard** or **fibrous plaques**. The plaques increase the thickness of the intima and thus encroach on the lumen of the artery. As individual plaques become larger they tend to coalesce. Large lesions destroy the internal elastic lamina and involve the inner layer of the media.

Four other processes may now occur to complicate the lesions. First, the endothelium may be lost so that the surface ulcerates and the fatty contents may be exposed to the blood stream. Secondly, fibrin is commonly deposited and thrombosis occurs on the plaque surface, probably because of the roughening produced by ulceration. Organisation of the thrombus is followed by its incorporation into the plaque and it may become eventually covered by endothelium. Thirdly, free blood can be found in a plaque. It is often difficult for the pathol-

ogist to decide whether this has come from rupture of small vessels deep in the lesion or from the lumen of the artery through a surface fissure. Finally calcification may occur.

Development with ageing

Some atherosclerotic lesions can be found at almost all postmortems. A few small lesions are seen in most adolescents and they increase in number and size throughout life. In some communities there are fewer lesions than in others and within a community some individuals have accelerated atherosclerosis while the arteries of others are relatively spared. Atherosclerosis does not usually lead to clinical disease until middle age.

Chemical pathology

That atherosclerotic lesions contain large amounts of fatty material, a big proportion of which is cholesterol, has been known since the time of Virchow in the middle of the nineteenth century. Detailed chemical characterisation of the lipids in individual lesions obtained by microdissection is now possible.[3]

An established plaque covered by endothelium contains a large amount of cholesterol esters in which the fatty acid pattern resembles that of plasma cholesterol esters, linoleate being the most abundant. It is therefore a reasonable speculation that the cholesterol comes from the plasma. Understanding of how cholesterol crosses the endothelial barrier would be valuable. These observations are consistent with the **filtration theory** of the formation of atheroma. As plasma cholesterol concentration is in part dependent on the nature of the diet, dietary factors could promote and also prevent atheroma formation by filtration.

Whereas in plaques the lipid is mainly extracellular, in fatty streaks it is intracellular, lying in smooth muscle cells. Further, the cholesterol esters have a bizarre fatty acid pattern and do not resemble those in plasma. Thus it is unlikely that fatty streaks seen in children and commonly in young adults develop into plaques.

Thrombogenesis

The complex system that ensures that blood stays fluid when in the circulation and clots immediately when there is haemorrhage is described in physiology textbooks. Although thrombosis in slow-flowing blood in peripheral veins is not uncommon, arterial thrombosis obstructing a coronary or cerebral artery is a rare event and a disaster which is unlikely to happen to most of us before reaching an advanced age. The immediate cause of this disaster is not known. Although an arterial thrombus almost always forms at the site of an atheromatous plaque, these are present in most of us from an early age.

Interest is now centred on the opposing effects of

prostacylin and thomboxane A_2 on platelet aggregation (p. 66). These substances are all derived from arachidonic acid and the possibility that dietary polyunsaturated fats influence platelet aggregation and reduce the tendency to thrombosis is discussed in Chapter 6. Polyunsaturated fats include the essential fatty acids (EFA), and the hypothesis that EFA deficiency is an important cause of coronary heart disease has for long been advocated by Sinclair.[4]

It is possible, even likely, that small thrombi form frequently in the circulation. These microthrombi are then attached to the arterial wall where they are rapidly lysed. A failure of the fibrolytic mechanism could in this way allow a thrombus to grow. This is the basis of the **thrombogenic theory** of the formation of atheroma put forward as long ago as 1842 by Rokitansky, the famous Viennese pathologist. It is based on the view that atheroma is derived from material deposited on the intimal wall from the blood. Duguid[5] placed the theory on a more secure basis. In its simplest form it postulates that a minute lesion of the intimal surface occurs, perhaps as a result of mechanical trauma. At this point platelet aggregation forms a small thrombus which sticks to the vessel wall. If this is not lysed at once the fibrin in it becomes organised; fibrous tissue is formed, it eventually becomes covered with endothelium and the lipid in the thrombus becomes the lipid of the atherosclerotic lesion. An extension of the theory is that minute lesions of the intima, followed by local mural thrombosis, are common but are normally cleared by fibrinolysis. Hence one of the primary faults responsible for atherosclerosis might lie in an increased tendency to thrombosis or in an inefficient fibrinolytic mechanism.

CORONARY HEART DISEASE (CHD)

Coronary heart disease or ischaemic heart disease (IHD) are synonymous terms for a group of syndromes arising from failure of the coronary arteries to supply sufficient blood to the myocardium. These syndromes are in most cases associated with atherosclerosis of the coronary arteries. They include myocardial infarction, angina pectoris and sudden death without infarction.

Myocardial infarction. This is necrosis or destruction of part of the heart muscle due to failure of the blood supply (ischaemia). It may lead to sudden death or heal, leaving a scar. Patients with healed lesions may be severely disabled or may be able to return to their normal life with little or no restriction of their physical activities, but they carry an increased risk of a second infarct. The infarction is usually due to a thrombus forming in an atherosclerotic coronary artery and blocking the lumen. Sometimes there is no thrombus and the infarct arises because the lumen of a coronary artery has been so narrowed by atherosclerosis that the blood flow is insufficient to supply the oxygen needed to maintain the cardiac muscle. However, occasional cases of myocardial infarction are seen in which neither thrombosis nor significant narrowing of the lumen can be recognised.

Angina pectoris (Latin, pain in the chest). In this condition exercise or excitement provokes severe chest pain and so limits the patient's physical activities. Patients may live for many years and remain free of further disability, so long as they keep within the limits of their exercise tolerance. However, they carry an increased risk of sudden death or myocardial infarction, especially if they undertake any unusual exertion. Emotional stress may also bring on angina.

Sudden death. A proportion of cases of sudden death occur in people who have had angina pectoris or myocardial infarction. Their death is presumed to be due to CHD. In most death is unexpected but autopsy shows evidence of old myocardial infarction or extensive atheroma of the coronary arteries; they are also presumed to have died of CHD. In a third group the cause remains unexplained after autopsy. Some of these may be due to ventricular fibrillation, possibly the result of a sudden disturbance of the electrical stability of the heart due to overactivity of sympathetic nerves.

CLINICAL FEATURES

The dominant symptom is a severe, pressing or constricting pain, poorly localised deep in the centre of the chest and characteristically radiating down the left or both arms. In angina pectoris this pain comes on with exertion or excitement; it forces the patient to stop and when he does so the pain passes off in a few minutes. Patients with angina can suffer several attacks of pain in a day and they can go on like this for long periods of time.

In myocardial infarction the pain often comes on at rest; it is very severe, lasts for hours and is only relieved by strong opiates like morphine. It is accompanied by general symptoms such as weakness, collapse, cardiac arrhythmias and circulatory shock.

The pain is not always typical. Some patients have a mild myocardial infarction without noticing pain ('silent coronary'). On the other hand there are several other causes of pain in and around the chest which can mimic CHD, such as pericarditis, pulmonary embolism, oesophageal and respiratory disease.

While the electrocardiogram often changes temporarily during an attack of angina, it is usually normal between attacks. But soon after the onset of myocardial infarction the ECG may undergo a permanent change and show the infarct pattern. In the first few days after an infarct raised plasma concentrations of creatine kinase and other myocardial enzymes are of diagnostic value.

Patients with angina or who have had a myocardial infarct are liable to develop cardiac failure or arrhythmias.

RISK FACTORS

These may be constitutional or environmental (nature and nurture) or due to the presence of various diseases and metabolic abnormalities. They have been identified in two ways.

In **retrospective studies** findings in a series of patients are compared post hoc with those in a matched series of controls. Doubts about whether the controls match the patients in all respects, except the presence of CHD, often lead to uncertainty about any conclusions drawn.

In **prospective studies** a large number of apparently healthy people are first screened and then followed up for many years during which all attacks of CHD are recorded.

The most famous prospective study has been conducted in the small town of Framingham, Massachusetts, in the USA.[6] Over 5000 healthy men and women over 30 years of age were taken into the study in 1949. They were questioned about their way of life and examined clinically and a number of biochemical and other investigations were carried out. Thereafter they were reexamined every two years, and the staff of the study, who maintained a permanent office in the town, made careful records of all illnesses. As the years passed some developed one of the forms of CHD, others had other illnesses and some died. The accumulated records of these have been related to the habits and findings noted in the earlier examinations. From this and other studies[7] we now have quantitative information about several risk factors for CHD — and for some other diseases of later life as well — which provide a basis for preventive measures.

A number of risk factors are well established (Table 41.1), some are obviously interrelated and others apparently independent; clearly many factors contribute to the aetiology of CHD.

Sex and age
It is well known that men are more prone to CHD than women (see Fig. 41.2) and that in both sexes incidence rises with age.

After the menopause there is a greatly increased incidence in women, and by the age of 70 there is no difference between the sexes. The relative immunity of women during their reproductive life is almost certainly due to the secretion of the ovarian hormones. The

Table 41.1 Risk factors in coronary heart disease (modified from Brusis & McGandy)[8]

Factors known to increase the risk of coronary heart disease but not necessarily 'abnormalities' *per se* and not amenable to preventive intervention.
  1. Maleness
  2. Increasing age
  3. A family history of premature vascular disease
  4. Endomorphic body build
  5. Certain behaviour patterns and personality traits.

Factors known to increase the risk of coronary heart disease which are, or merge into, disease entities *per se*.
  1. Hyperlipidaemias
  2. Hypertension
  3. Diabetes mellitus
  4. Obesity
  5. Hyperuricaemia and gout
  6. Certain electrocardiographic abnormalities.

Factors known to increase the risk of coronary heart disease which are primarily due to culture and environment.
  1. Cigarette smoking
  2. Dietary habits (high intakes of saturated fats, etc.)
  3. Lack of physical exercise
Less well demonstrated
  4. Emotional stress and tension
  5. Soft drinking water.

concentration of plasma total cholesterol is lower in women aged 20 to 45 years than men of the same age group but HDL cholesterol is higher. If both ovaries are removed before the age of 35, this is often followed by a rise in plasma total cholesterol and the incidence of CHD is greatly increased.

Family history
Some families are more susceptible to CHD than others. Family clustering of any disease may be due either to inherited susceptibility or family sharing of environmental experience, e.g. an atherogenic diet. More than 50 per cent of plasma cholesterol is genetically determined. In families susceptible to CHD there is often a high incidence of other diseases which have multiple aetiology, e.g. hypertension, diabetes mellitus, gout and hyperlipidaemia.

Knowledge of the genetic basis of CHD and its relationships to the associated diseases is still fragmentary.

Somatotypes or body build
Endomorphs are most susceptible, followed by mesomorphs and ectomorphs in that order.

Behaviour patterns and personality traits
Friedman & Rosenman[9] have claimed that people with what they call Behaviour Pattern A have an increased incidence and prevalence of CHD. Such people show an excessive sense of time urgency, a preoccupation with

vocational deadlines and enhanced aggressiveness and competitive drive. This behaviour pattern is probably constitutional, i.e. it results from the interaction of inheritance and environment.

Hyperlipidaemia

The relation between plasma cholesterol and incidence of CHD is discussed in the previous chapter. In summary, a patient with a very high plasma cholesterol is at high risk of developing the disease at an early age but for the majority with values not greatly raised the increased risk is small.

Hypertension

In the Framingham study, the incidence of CHD in men aged 45 to 65 years with blood pressures exceeding 160/95 was more than five times that in normotensive men (blood pressure 140/90 or less). Elevations in both diastolic and systolic pressures correlate positively with CHD, the diastolic pressure perhaps being more important in younger people.

Obesity

Mortality statistics show that obesity is associated with an increased risk of death from heart disease but perspective studies indicate that this risk is not a high one.

While a moderately increased plasma cholesterol or mild hypertension or grade 1 obesity (plumpness), each by itself, carries only a small risk of CHD, a combination of any two of them increases it much more, and in a patient with all three the prognosis is very uncertain unless they are reduced by appropriate treatment.

Diabetes mellitus

This disorder is an important risk factor both in its clinically recognised and latent forms. This association is not due solely, or evenly mainly, to blood lipid disturbances. Diabetics are particularly prone to hypertension and proliferative lesions of the small blood vessels.

Hyperuricaemia and gout

There is a positive association between these abnormalities and CHD (Chap. 43), although not all hyperuricaemia represents pre-gout. The mechanisms are unknown.

Electrocardiographic abnormalities

Persons with an abnormal ECG or with ECG changes of left ventricular hypertrophy have an increased risk of developing CHD. If the changes are present when the patient is at rest, they may represent early CHD rather than predisposing factors. Abnormalities which appear on exercise usually indicate relatively advanced ischaemia.

Cigarette smoking

Peripheral vascular disease and CHD, particularly myocardial infarction, occur much more frequently in heavy cigarette smokers than in those who do not smoke.[7,10] There is a clear relationship between CHD and the amount of smoking. The mechanism(s) by which nicotine or some other constituent of tobacco causes this adverse effect is not clear. It may be due to the vasoconstrictor action of nicotine, to inhalation of carbon monoxide, or to some undesirable effect on the coagulability of the blood. Alternatively, heavy smoking may be a manifestation of a susceptible personality and a reaction to stress and strain. What is clear, however, is that patients with CHD should give up smoking.

Diet

A high intake of saturated fatty acids may raise plasma cholesterol and so promote the formation of atheroma, a low intake of polyunsaturated fatty acids may modify platelet function and so promote the formation of thrombi, an intake of energy above requirements leads to obesity and a high intake of salt may lead to hypertension in susceptible individuals (see below). For all these reasons, diet is important in relation to CHD. But dietary differences do not alone explain the wide variations in incidence of the disease in different countries (Fig. 41.1) nor how it is that some individuals suffer a heart attack early in life. Diet is less important than genetic hypercholesterolaemia or cigarette smoking in the aetiology of coronary artery disease.

The dietary hypothesis when it was put forward in the 1950s led to much enthusiasm since it indicated a means of prevention. Innumerable articles in popular newspapers and magazines and talks on the radio and television have presented it as established. The enthusiasts have included many physicians in all countries and these have formed committees, published reports and written articles in the medical press. Enthusiasm is infectious. Critical scientists are much less eager to appear in print. Now many scientists, Ahrens,[11] Harper,[12] McMichael,[13] Mann,[14] Oliver[15] and Olson,[16] have set out deficiencies in the theory and questioned whether major changes in national diets could reduce significantly the incidence of coronary heart disease.

Recommendations of the COMA report. The British Government's committee on medical aspects of food policy, known as COMA, published in 1984 a report on diet and coronary heart disease.[17] This recommends that the national intake of fat should be reduced from just over 40 per cent of food energy, the level in previous years, to 35 per cent. This recommendation is unchanged from that in a COMA report in 1974. It is also recommended that no more than 15 per cent of food energy should come from saturated fatty acids. Individuals whose intakes are in excess of these levels are advised to reduce them accordingly. No specific recommendation about intake of cholesterol is made. It is also recommended that intakes of sugar and salt should not be increased further and that excessive intake of alcohol is to be avoided.

To put these recommendations into practice a higher proportion of dietary energy would have to come from bread, potatoes and other vegetables and a lower proportion from separated fats and fatty meats. This requires a reversal of changes that have been occurring slowly but steadily in our national diet since World War II rationing ended. The recommendations are practical in that they could be carried out without revolutionary changes in our diet or in our methods of food production and manufacture. The changes are in line with all nutritional teaching and would be likely to be of benefit to the general health of the people. The evidence presented by the COMA report that these dietary changes by themselves would produce a significant fall in the incidence of coronary heart disease is unconvincing.

Lack of exercise
Prosperity certainly leads to a reduction in the amount of manual work done by members of a community. As the wealth of a country increases, the 'pick and shovel' men decline and are replaced by those who flick switches and occupy office chairs. An increase in private cars and public transport reduces the number who rely on walking and the push bicycle to get them from place to place. There is some evidence that physical activity protects against CHD. There are occupations in which the risk of developing CHD is less than in others. Thus Morris and his colleagues[18] showed that London bus conductors (on double-decker vehicles) have a lower incidence than bus drivers, and postmen who deliver letters have a lower incidence than telephonists and post-office clerks. Further, when the disease was present in conductors and postmen, it was less severe. In a national survey in Britain the extent of the atherosclerosis found in coronary arteries at autopsy correlated with previous occupation.[19] It was concluded that physical activity at work was a protection against CHD. 'Men in physically active jobs have less coronary heart disease during middle age, what disease they have is less severe, and they develop it later than men in physically inactive jobs'.

Active recreations are also important. In middle-aged Harvard alumni, the incidence of heart attacks was lower in those who had been physically active.[20]

Emotional stress and tension
It is often suggested that the stress and strain of modern life predispose to coronary heart disease, but this is difficult to establish. The stress and strain to which the prosperous business executive or professional man is exposed are well known. A cartoon in the *New Yorker* showed two middle-aged men in shorts on the verandah of a luxurious holiday hotel. One says to the other 'If I were the type to relax could I afford to be here?' The stress and strain of poverty receive much less publicity. It is difficult to be certain that the modern prosperous communities suffer from more stress and strain than their less wealthy predecessors. Increased risk of myocardial infarction could be due to acute or chronic adrenergic overdrive caused by stress. Possible mediating factors include plasma noradrenaline and FFA. The stress of racing driving raised plasma triglycerides and FFA but not plasma cholesterol.[21] The same reaction probably occurs in some urban drivers.

However, there is no doubt that once coronary heart disease is established, emotion can be the immediate cause of clinical symptoms.[22] Long ago the great anatomist, John Hunter, who suffered from angina pectoris, said that he was at the mercy of any knave who chose to enrage him. President Eisenhower described how his symptoms of coronary thrombosis developed on the golf course when for the third time in one morning he was recalled to the clubhouse to answer an unnecessary telephone call from the State Department.

Drinking water
In at least nine countries a significant negative association between the hardness of the drinking water and mortality from all cardiovascular diseases has been reported. The harder the drinking water the lower the death rate from cardiovascular disease.[23] No explanation of this extraordinary finding is as yet established. Calcium or magnesium in hard waters could have a protective action and there are several trace elements in hard waters that might be beneficial. On the other hand, soft waters, being more acidic, are more likely to dissolve potentially toxic trace elements like lead and cadmium from pipes or rocks. However, no association between the quality of the water supply and the incidence of CHD has now been reported in many countries. Heyden[24] lists these reports and after reviewing the evidence in favour of the 'water story' concludes that, because of the inconsistencies and controversies, it would be premature to advise modification of water supplies in the hope of preventing cardiovascular diseases.

Coffee and alcohol
Reports that myocardial infarction was associated with high consumption of coffee have not been confirmed. Moderate alcohol consumption is not a risk factor, and in patients with disorders directly attributable to alcohol the incidence of CHD is no higher than normal.

PREVENTION AND MANAGEMENT

As the causes of coronary heart disease are not established, specific programmes for prevention are not practical. This does not mean that nothing can be done. It is certain that it is a disease of affluence, and increasing affluence makes it less easy to keep some of the simple rules of health set forth by wise physicians repeatedly since the time of Hippocrates. These are discussed in Chapter 56 together with how individuals can be helped to follow them by means of health education and by Government action. There can be no doubt that if these rules, which include eating a prudent diet, were more generally followed the incidence of CHD would fall. A fall has been reported in many countries when wartime restrictions forced people to lead a more simple life.

The one single factor that would certainly reduce the incidence of CHD is a reduction in cigarette smoking.

Patients who have been admitted to hospital after a myocardial infarction or other evidence of CHD require advice before discharge. All are worried about their future. Although this is uncertain, in many cases they can be reassured that they can resume their previous work and recreations and can look forward to a good life for many years. Three specific pieces of advice should be given.

1. Stop smoking.
2. Moderate the diet so as to prevent being overweight.
3. Take as much physical exercise as possible without causing undue breathlessness or fatigue.

CEREBROVASCULAR DISEASE

Cerebrovascular disease is second only to heart disease as a cause of premature deaths (Fig. 41.2). The epidemiology of the two differ in important respects. In cerebrovascular disease mortality in women is only a little less than in men, and in most countries has been falling in both sexes. There is the same wide range of mortality in countries but the order is very different.

While underlying atherosclerosis is common to both conditions, the overwhelming risk factor is a high blood pressure. Cerebrovascular disease has little association with hypercholesterolaemia, but much more with obesity than does CHD.

HYPERTENSION

Some degree of hypertension in the systemic arteries is a common finding in middle age when the pressure in the brachial artery is measured with the sphygmomanometer. Because hypertension can be asymptomatic for many years, because it is an important predisposing cause of several major diseases and because it is amenable to treatment, measurement of the blood pressure is a part of all routine clinical examinations of adults.

The pathological changes which accompany established hypertension are a thickening of the arterioles with hyaline material and, later, hypertrophy of the myocardium of the left ventricle. If untreated, moderate hypertension eventually leads to cardiac failure, with dilation of the left ventricle and congestion of the pulmonary or systemic veins. It also causes ischaemic changes in the kidney, nephrosclerosis. However, before these direct consequences of prolonged hypertension develop the patient may suffer from vascular accidents to which hypertension is an important predisposing factor. It is one factor increasing the risk of coronary atherosclerosis (as discussed above) and is a strong risk factor for cerebral vascular disease.

In a minority of patients blood pressure is very high. This is called **malignant hypertension**. The heart, kidneys, retinal and other arteries are quickly affected; there is an immediate risk of a dangerous vascular accident; thus vigorous treatment is required.

In about 80 per cent of cases clinical examination and special investigation do not demonstrate a cause for the condition. This is called **essential hypertension**. Treatment has to be symptomatic. In the remaining cases the hypertension is usually secondary to renal disease, e.g. glomerulonephritis or pyelonephritis (Chap. 44), and less commonly, to an endocrine disorder, e.g. Cushing's syndrome, phaeochromocytoma, primary aldosteronism or acromegaly, or to the rare congenital malformation, coarctation of the aorta. Pregnancy also predisposes to hypertension.

Criteria for diagnosis. In healthy young adults the systolic blood pressure is about 120 mmHg and the diastolic pressure about 80. There is usually a gradual rise of blood pressure as age advances and at 65 years the mean figure is about 160/90. The rise with age is very variable. In some people it is more rapid and reaches a higher level than the above figure. It is difficult to state at what point the level ceases to be normal and hypertension begins. The diastolic pressure is a more reliable guide to the presence or absence of hypertension than the systolic pressure. Without qualifications, e.g. age, obesity and the circumstances in which the blood pressure is recorded, blood pressure figures *per se* are often of little value. Nevertheless the following figures may be used as a rough guide to severity, if present persistently.

A diagnosis of hypertension is usually made in a patient under 25 years of age when the diastolic pressure is 90 or above, but in a patient aged 70 years or more not unless it is over 100. Unless diastolic pressure is above 105, hypertension may be said to be mild or moderate and when it exceeds 120 to be severe.

RISK FACTORS

The rise in blood pressure as age advances is a feature of affluent Western societies and is much less marked in peasant communities. In some primitive people, for example in New Guinea and the bushmen in Botswana, there is no rise. The rise cannot therefore be an inevitable part of the process of ageing but rather a response to the environment that occurs in industrialised countries in the majority of people, but not in a sizable minority. Three factors certainly determine whether or not the rise occurs in an individual and there may be others. A full account of these risk factors based on experience at Framingham is given by Castelli.[25]

Heredity

Hypertension frequently affects several members of a family and there is a high correlation between the blood pressures of identical twins. In the 1960s there was a prolonged but amicable dispute between two much respected professors of medicine in England. Platt in Manchester claimed that hypertensive patients formed a distinct group of the population who carried a dominant gene, albeit of low penetration. This view was based on observations claiming to show that the distribution of blood pressure in adults was bimodal. Pickering in Oxford produced convincing evidence that the distribution was a single Gaussian curve, skewed to the right and so resembling the distribution of height. This implies that hypertension is a graded characteristic and the result of polygenic or multifactorial inheritance. This dispute and much else about hypertension is recorded in a classic monograph by Pickering.[26]

A new hypothesis is that individual susceptibility to hypertension is related to decreased activity of (Na^+, K^+) ATPase, the enzyme that through the sodium pump maintains intracellular concentrations of Na^+ and K^+. The activity of the enzyme is genetically determined and differs in various ethnic groups.[27,28]

Obesity

Hypertension commonly accompanies obesity though it may occur in thin people. When obese patients with hypertension reduce their weight to the normal value, their blood pressure frequently returns to normal without any other treatment. This indicates that in susceptible individuals obesity is a direct cause of hypertension.

High salt intake

That a sudden restriction of salt intake reduces blood pressure in normal people, that a very low sodium diet causes a dramatic fall in blood pressure in patients with severe hypertension and that feeding rats large amount of salt induced hypertension has been known for a long time. Yet the association between dietary salt and hypertension did not stimulate interest among physicians, epidemiologists and the general public in a manner comparable to that aroused by dietary fats and coronary heart disease. Fashion is always fickle and unreliable whether in ideas or in clothes. A review article by Dahl[29] in 1972 had a great influence in directing attention to the role of excess dietary salt in causing hypertension, and this now appears to offer an opportunity for preventive measures with greater potential for benefit than those concerned with dietary fats and coronary heart disease.

It is difficult to get reliable estimations of salt intakes by a population group, but the literature contains records, not all reliable, of mean salt intake and mean blood pressure of 27 populations scattered throughout the world.[30] The data indicate that there is a direct positive correlation between the two variables, and in some culturally homogeneous groups in Japan and Taiwan salt intake appears as the major environmental factor affecting blood pressure. In Europe and North America much salt is added to foods in manufacturing processes and salt intakes are generally high. However, it is even more difficult to get reliable information about the salt intakes of individuals in a population. The data from Framingham, based only on a dietary history, show no increase in incidence of high blood pressure with a high salt intake.[25] In Framingham, as elsewhere in North America and Europe, intakes of salt are four to five times higher than in countries with a low salt intake and a low incidence of hypertension. It seems probable that there is a threshold for salt intake, as yet undefined, above which hypertension commonly arises in susceptible individuals and that susceptibility is genetically determined.

Other possible risk factors[31]

Stress, either mental or physical, raises the blood pressure immediately but this is only temporarily. It has not been established that repeated stresses lead to a sustained higher blood pressure at rest. Reviews of epidemiological evidence that environmental stresses may contribute to hypertension and of the theory that individuals with a poor capacity for relaxation are more prone to hypertension indicate that stress is not a major risk factor.[32]

Many reports comparing the blood pressure of athletes and non-athletes and of those whose occupations require heavy and light work have given conflicting results. Inactivity may be a risk factor but, if so, is only a minor one.[33,34]

Treatment

Drugs. Hypotensive agents are numerous and each lowers blood pressure by differing actions on the cardiovascular system. They relieve the symptoms in most patients and their widespread use is probably mainly responsible for falling death rates from hypertension. However, all have adverse effects, though patients vary in susceptibility to these, and it is sometimes difficult to find a drug which is effective in a dose that a patient can tolerate.

Diuretics are given along with hypotensive agents and act by increasing sodium output in the urine. They also increase potassium output, and their long-term use tends to cause potassium depletion unless a supplement is given.

Diet. If a patient is overweight, dietary restriction lowers the blood pressure. In many patients with mild hypertension this is the only treatment required. When weight and blood pressure have both returned to normal, if weight is kept down, blood pressure is unlikely to rise again.

Salt restriction was shown to be effective in lowering the blood pressure of patients with severe hypertension as long ago as 1948. However, the Kempner diet used were very low in salt (p. 101) and not acceptable for continual use by patients. At this time new diuretic drugs were introduced and most physicians were content to use these to promote sodium excretion and did not advise their patients to worry about dietary restriction of intake. Since then, reports[35,36] have shown that moderate reductions of sodium intake, along the lines of a restricted salt regime (p. 101), is of benefit to patients. This regime involves no hardship and can be prescribed for all patients in addition to any drugs that are needed.

In the manifestations of hypertension, as in most other diseases, there is a strong psychological component. Many patients need much support to enable them to change old habits and eat a sensible diet and lead a sensible life. Daily periods of relaxation and regular holidays are good for hypertensives, as for all of us.

Prevention

A reduced intake of salt is part of the dietary guidelines now widely recommended in affluent countries. Measures to achieve this involve action by individual consumers, by food manufacturers and perhaps by Government. Enthusiasts for action should appreciate that present dietary habits and the nature of the foods readily available in shops and supermarkets lead to a high salt intake and that these are not easily changed. Recommendations for changes that are too restrictive are liable to be counterproductive.

Individual health education. Advice not to use table salt and to use a minimum of salt in home cooking is sound and already acceptable to many. Salt added in the home is, however, only a small part of total intake. More important for the public to know is the fact that prepared meats (corned beef, luncheon meat, bacon, sausages, etc.) contain about 20 times as much salt as was present in the original fresh meat. Chips and crisp potatoes are very rich sources of salt compared with potatoes cooked at home with little salt. Kippers and other salted fish and also canned fish are fine for an occasion but if eaten frequently may increase salt intake greatly. Many snack foods eaten by children are rich in salt. By a suitable choice of foods any individual or family can reduce their salt intake by about one third.

Manufacturers. Salt is added to manufactured foods as a preservative and because customers like it. Restricted legislation of the amount of salt permitted in a food, unless the permitted level was set so high as to be ineffective, would be strongly opposed by both manufacturers and consumers. Manufacturers are not unresponsive to medical opinion and have greatly reduced the previously high salt content of infant foods when it was shown that this was a cause of hyperosmolar dehydration, a serious disorder in infants (p. 584). A significant part of the salt in our diet is that added to bread, butter and cheese. Low salt bread, butter and cheese are obtainable but not in most shops and they tend to be looked upon as medicinal products. If there was a popular demand for low salt foods of all sorts, manufacturers would produce and advertise them.

Governments. Legislation to restrict the addition of salt to foods or to make statutory declaration of salt content on the labels of food products would be difficult to enforce. A more practical approach would be to provide more money and support for appropriate health education.

When the above was away to the typesetters, a letter appeared in *The Lancet*[37] signed by 13 people from reputable medical centres in Scotland, England, the USA, Sweden and New Zealand querying the widespread advice that dietary salt intake should be reduced. The letter points out correctly that there is no evidence from selected populations that this would produce any benefit and also that the long-term effect of reduced dietary sodium intake in man is not known. The idea (or likelihood) that salt in the diet has some positive value has been totally ignored. The letter produced 10 replies in subsequent issues of *The Lancet* and most of these were critical of its viewpoint and advocated national policies for reducing intakes of salt. Salt intake is a contentious subject.

CARDIOMYOPATHIES

These are a group of disorders characterised by an impairment of the ventricular pump leading to congestive heart failure arising from pathological changes in the myocardium not attributable to coronary heart disease. They are mentioned briefly, because, as in many other disorders of unknown aetiology, there has been speculation that they may be nutritional in origin but this appears unlikely in the great majority of cases.

Cardiomyopathies are not uncommon in all parts of the world.[38] Although many factors have been held responsible in individual cases, usually no cause is identified. Thiamin deficiency is responsible for the rare form known as Soshin's disease (p. 315) and selenium deficiency is the probable cause of Keshan's disease, common in some parts of China (p. 126). In Europe and North America chronic alcoholism is the commonest cause. A form known as endomyocardial fibrosis occurs widely in tropical Africa, where it was suggested that a large intake of bananas, with their high content of 5-hydroxytryptamine might be responsible. This is no longer tenable and the condition may be due to hypersensitivity to malaria or other chronic infection.

HEART FAILURE

Whatever the cause of heart disease, it will, unless very mild, lead to some impairment of the efficiency of the heart as a pump. In severe CHD and in cardiomyopathies the heart fails because its muscle is weakened; in hypertension and valvular disease it fails because the muscle is working against an increased load. In mild degrees of heart failure the only manifestation is an inability to increase the cardiac output in response to strenuous exertion and the patient has dyspnoea on exertion. In moderate grades there is venous congestion, either in the pulmonary circulation causing dyspnoea or in the systemic veins causing oedema and hepatic enlargement. Acute and severe cardiac failure causes pulmonary oedema and cardiogenic shock.

Treatment
As already indicated heart failure may occur in hypertensive, coronary, valvular, pulmonary or other cardiac disease. Irrespective of the cause, the aim of treatment is to secure the maximum of rest for the heart and to remove the oedema. The basis of treatment is (a) complete rest, (b) the administration of diuretics, (c) a diet low in sodium, and also in energy if the patient is obese and (d) in special circumstances a digitalis preparation.

It is important to realise that when heart failure first presents this is often not a terminal event. It has usually been precipitated by a respiratory infection, arrhythmia or some other complication. If these are diagnosed and effectively treated at the same time as symptomatic treatment is given for the heart failure, the patient may well get over the episode and be able to lead a relatively normal life, sometimes for years before heart failure becomes incapacitating.

Dietary management
The diet should be constructed on the following principles.
1. As the oedema fluid has the same sodium concentration as plasma, oedema is always associated with retention of sodium. In severe oedema the excess fluid retained may amount to 10 litres or more, containing 1400 mmol of sodium, equivalent to over 80 g of sodium chloride. The removal of this is greatly facilitated if the sodium intake is reduced. Details of how to reduce the sodium intake are given on page 101.
2. Rigid restriction of the fluid intake, as was formerly recommended, is not necessary if the intake of sodium is adequately reduced and its excretion increased. Sufficient fluid to quench thirst and make the patient comfortable, i.e. 1.5 to 2 litres daily, may be allowed.
3. Owing to the congestion of the digestive organs, each feed must be small in quantity and easily digestible. In the initial treatment, fluid or semifluid food is advisable for patients who are seriously ill.
4. In patients who are seriously ill, as after a severe myocardial infarction, it is important to prevent ketosis arising and for this purpose ample glucose or other carbohydrate should be given.

For most patients with mild or moderate degrees of cardiac failure the restricted salt regimen described on page 101 is suitable.

For the severe grades of failure, the Karell fluid diet has been recommended. This is simple and effective. It consists of 800 ml of milk, given in four feeds each of 200 ml (one small glass). No other food or fluid is given. It provides about 2.2 MJ (550 kcal), 28 g protein and about 0.45 g (20 mmol) of sodium. This diet should only be employed for two or three days as the patient will complain of monotony and thirst.

Alternatively the patient can start with a light diet (Diet No. 13) which provides about 3.8 MJ, 40 g protein and 1 g (45 mmol) of sodium. No table salt should be added. Care should be taken not to prescribe medicines containing sodium, e.g. stomach powders, and to avoid baking powder in cooking.

With improvement in the clinical condition a light ward diet can be given and the protein intake increased, but the salt intake must still be restricted. The restricted salt regimen keeps the sodium intake to about one-third of normal. If a diuretic is prescribed for a long period, a potassium supplement is needed.

Compensated heart disease. When recovery has taken place or in less severe cases, the patient may be up and about and able to continue his normal occupation. Heart disease, however, always involves some curtailment of physical activities, and the more arduous recreations must be given up. This reduction in energy expenditure should always be balanced by a corresponding reduction in food intake. If the diet is not reduced appropriately, obesity will inevitably follow. Obesity is common in patients with heart disease and requires to be treated in the usual way.

Chronic congestive failure. Some patients, especially those with hypoxia from respiratory disease, become pathetically thin and undernourished. This cardiac cachexia is largely the result of poor appetite, resulting from hypoxaemia, compression of the stomach by the congested liver and the tendency of high doses of digitalis to produce nausea. In addition specific deficiencies of nutrients may arise in patients with chronic congestive cardiac failure — for example, hypoalbuminaemia, malabsorption of fat and subclinical folate deficiency. Thus, even if the prognosis is hopeless, protein, potassium and vitamin deficiencies should be looked for and corrected.

REFERENCES

1. Junge B, Hoffmeister H 1982 Civilization — associated diseases in Europe and industrial countries outside of Europe: regional differences and trends in mortality. Prev Med 11: 117–30
2. McGill H C (ed) 1968 The geographic pathology of atherosclerosis. Williams & Wilkins, Baltimore
3. Smith E B, Staples E M, Dietz 1979 Role of endothelium in sequestration of lipoprotein and fibrinogen in aortic lesions, thrombi, and graft pseudointimae. Lancet 2: 812–6
4. Sinclair H M 1980 Prevention of coronary heart disease: the role of essential fatty acids. Postgrad Med J 56: 579–84
5. Duguid J B 1954 Diet and coronary disease. Lancet 1: 891–4
6. Dawber T R 1980 The Framingham study. The epidemiology of atherosclerotic disease. Harvard University Press, Cambridge, Mass
7. The Pooling Project Research Group 1978 Relationship of blood pressure serum cholesterol, smoking habit, relative weight and ECG abnormalities to incidence of major coronary events. J Chronic Dis 31: 201–306
8. Brusis O A, McGrandy R B 1971 Nutrition and man's heart and blood vessels. Fed Proc 30: 1417–20
9. Friedman M, Rosenman R H 1959 Association of specific overt behaviour pattern with blood and cardiovascular findings. JAMA 169: 1286–96
10. Doll R, Hill A B 1964 Mortality in relation to smoking: ten years' observations of British doctors. Br Med J 1: 1399–1410, 1460–7
11. Ahrens E H 1985 The diet-heart question in 1985: has it really been settled. Lancet 1: 1085–7
12. Harper A E 1983 Coronary heart disease — an epidemic related to diet? Am J Clin Nutr 37: 669–81
13. McMichael J 1979 Fats and atheroma: an inquest. Br Med J 1: 173–5
14. Mann G V 1977 Diet — heart: end of an era. N Engl J Med 297: 644–50
15. Oliver M F 1982 Diet and coronary heart disease. Hum Nutr Clin Nutr 360: 413–27
16. Olson R E 1980 Statement to the House Agriculture Subcommittee on Domestic Marketing Consumer Relations and Nutrition. Nutr Today 15(3): 12–9
17. Department of Health and Social Security 1984 Diet and cardiovascular disease. Rep Health Soc Subj (Lond) no. 28
18. Morris J N, Heady J A, Raffle P A B, Roberts C G, Parks J W 1953 Coronary heart disease and physical activity of work. Lancet 2: 1053–7, 1111–20
19. Morris J N, Crawford M D 1958 Coronary heart disease and physical activity of work. Br Med J 2: 1485–96
20. Paffenbarger R S, Wing A L, Hyde R T 1968 Physical activity as an index of heart attack risk in college alumni. Am J Epidemiol 108: 161–75
21. Taggart P, Carruthers M 1971 Endogenous hyperlipidaemia induced by the stress of racing driving. Lancet 1: 363–6
22. Crisp A H, Queenam M, D'Souza M F 1984 Myocardial infarction and emotional climate. Lancet 1: 616–9
23. Crawford M D, Gardner M J, Morris J N 1968 Mortality and hardness of local water supplies. Lancet 1: 827–31
24. Heyden J The hard facts behind the hard-water story and ischaemic heart disease. J Chronic Dis 29: 149–57
25. Castelli W P 1982 Hypertension: a perspective from the Framingham experience. In: Sleight P, Freis E D (eds) Hypertension. Butterworth, London, p. 1–13
26. Pickering G W 1968 High blood pressure. Churchill, London
27. Garay R P, Nazaret C, Dagher G, et al 1982 Approche génétique de l'épidémiologie geographlique de l'hypertension artérielle. Trop Cardiol 8: 49–53
28. Beutler E, Kuhl W, Sacks P 1983 Sodium-potassium-ATPase is influenced by ethnic origin and not by obesity. N Engl J Med 309: 756–60
29. Dahl L K 1972 Salt and hypertension. Am J Clin Nutr 25: 231–44
30. Gliebermann L 1973 Blood pressure and dietary salt in human populations. Ecol Food Nutr 2: 143–55
31. Gutman M C, Benson H 1971 Interaction of environmental factors and systemic arterial blood pressure: a review. Medicine 50: 543–55
32. Benson H 1977 Systematic hypertension and the relaxation response. N Engl J Med 296: 1152–6
33. Leon A S, Blackburn H 1982 Physical activity and hypertension. In: Sleight P, Freis E D (eds) Hypertension. Butterworth, London, p. 14–36
34. Paffenbarger R S, Wing A L, Hyde R T, Jung D L 1983 Physical activity and incidence of hypertension in college alumni. Am J Epidemiol 117: 245–57
35. Morgan T, Adams W, Gillies A, et al 1978 Hypertension treated by salt restriction. Lancet 1: 227–30
36. MacGregor G A, Markandu N D, Best F E, et al 1982 Double-blind randomised crossover trial of moderate sodium restriction in essential hypertension. Lancet 1: 351–8
37. Brown J J, et al 1984 Salt and hypertension. Lancet 2: 456
38. WHO Expert Committee 1984 Cardiomyopathies. WHO Tech Rep Ser no 697

42

Diabetes Mellitus

Diabetes mellitus is a syndrome due to a variety of underlying diseases characterised by a raised glucose concentration in the blood, due to deficiency or diminished effectiveness of insulin. The disorder is chronic and also affects the metabolism of fat and protein. Glucose usually spills over into the urine and this is associated with polyuria and loss of weight. There is in some patients the hazard of the acute complication of keto-acidosis, which is a dangerous, but treatable, medical emergency. Diabetics have an increased risk of athero-sclerotic diseases and of certain obstetrical difficulties. In longstanding cases specific changes can occur in the eyes, feet, nerves and kidneys. A textbook by Oakley et al[1] gives a full account of the disorder.

EPIDEMIOLOGY

Diabetes mellitus is the commonest endocrine disorder. There are two major types. Type 1 insulin dependent diabetes was formerly known as juvenile onset diabetes as its incidence is at a peak between 10 and 12 years of age. Type 2 non-insulin diabetes contains the great majority of diabetics who first become ill in middle age or later. For this reason the frequency of diabetes in different communities can only be compared when rates are standardised for age. Because the onset is often insidious, in any large group of people there are some who know they have diabetes and others with mild or early diabetes who are as yet unaware that they have it; these cases can be detected by finding glucose in the urine and a high blood glucose. In Britain about 1 per cent of the population have 'known' diabetes and a similar proportion may be 'discovered' by biochemical screening. Criteria for diagnosis have been standardised by WHO[2] (p. 376) and there are now sufficient comparable surveys to show that the prevalence of type 2 diabetes varies greatly between different populations.

The large numbers of reports on the prevalence of diabetes in many parts of the world have been put together and discussed with erudition in a monograph by West.[3] In general in peasant communities prevalence is low and of the order of 0.1 per cent. Most of the cases are of type 1. The onset of this type is usually in childhood. Cases may occur in the first two years of life but the highest incidence is between 10 and 12 years of age. Thereafter incidence falls but a few cases arise in middle age.

With urbanisation and increasing prosperity prevalence rises but most of the cases are of type 2 and occur in the middle-aged and the elderly. As life expectancy increases, prevalence also increases and is commonly of the order of 1 to 3 per cent in many countries today. Diabetes thus becomes an increasingly important clinical problem.

There are a few communities where prevalence is very high. These include Indian communities in South Africa (10) and Fiji (14), Australian Aborigines (14), American Indians, Cherokee (29) and Puri (35) and the inhabitants of the Pacific island of Nauru (34).[4] The figures are percentage prevalence in the adult population. All of these have gone through prolonged periods in their history when food was scarce, and it has been suggested that natural selection led to survival of a thrifty genotype which predisposes to obesity and diabetes in conditions of relative affluence.[5]

AETIOLOGY

In the great majority of patients diabetes is a primary disorder, but it may arise secondary to other diseases that impair the function of the pancreas or destroy its structure.

Genetic and dietary factors, infections and possibly stress may each increase the risk of an individual developing diabetes.

Genetic factors
As long ago as 1689 a family in which four children had diabetes was described[6] and since then there have been other families with many diabetic members. However,

families share the same diet as well as the same genes, and the role of heredity is far from clear despite over 300 papers which West reviews.[3]

Many separate genetic mechanisms increase the risk of diabetes and its various manifestations, and these differ in type 1 and type 2 diabetes. All communities with a low prevalence have also a low prevalence of obesity. Obesity is common in all racial and ethnic groups with a high prevalence of type 2 diabetes, but not all type 2 diabetics are obese.

Many attempts have been made to identify genetic markers, but as yet the results are of no practical value either in epidemiological studies or in identifying potential patients.

Dietary factors

Obesity. A close association between obesity and diabetes has long been recognised. Although most type 2 diabetics are obese, only a minority of obese patients develop diabetes. Whether or not an obese individual develops diabetes probably depends on genetic factors.

The view that obesity is diabetogenic in those genetically predisposed to the disease is based on the fact that in simple obesity there is insulin resistance, particularly in muscle, and hyperinsulinaemia. The mechanisms which induce this increased secretion of insulin and resistance to its action are being investigated. It is postulated that there is impaired insulin uptake by receptors in target tissues.

Estimates of plasma insulin in patients with symptoms of diabetes immediately after diagnosis support this concept. Although some of those who are obese have an abnormally high plasma insulin, most show some degree of insulin deficiency.[7] In general, the more carbohydrate tolerance is impaired in obese diabetics, the more deficient the insulin secretory response to various stimuli.

Obese people in general are less physically active than those whose weight is normal. It is possible that physical exercise may reduce the risk of diabetes in susceptible individuals.

Dietary restrictions. Restrictions on the food supply of a community affect diabetes. This is well illustrated by rationing in the United Kingdom from 1940 to 1947. During this period mortality from diabetes was reduced by nearly 50 per cent.[8] Mortality rates do not necessarily reflect prevalence rates but there is no doubt that rationing was beneficial to individuals susceptible to diabetes.

Sugar intake. A large consumption of sugar may predispose to diabetes and West[3] lists 21 papers supporting this claim, but also 22 papers which do not. A high intake of sugar is certainly associated with a high prevalence of obesity. It is unlikely that sucrose has a specific diabetogenic effect, though the very high intake

in some Indian communities in South Africa may contribute to the high prevalence of diabetes among them.[9]

Dietary fibre. In many African countries the fibre content of the diet is high and prevalence of diabetes low. In prosperous communities this relationship tends to be reversed. This led to the hypothesis[10] that a low fibre diet was part of the aetiology of diabetes, but it is difficult to see how a deficiency of fibre could cause the disorder. Most diets now recommended for diabetics are high in fibre but this is for the general benefits from such diets and not for a specific effect on the disorder.

Infections

Diabetes is frequently first diagnosed by finding glucose in the urine of a patient with an acute staphylococcal or other infection. Types 1 and 2 diabetes both present in this way. Infections cause a non-specific outpouring of catabolic hormones which antagonise insulin action and this may trigger the onset of the disorder.

There is now increasing evidence[11] that type 1 diabetes especially in younger patients follows a Coxsackie or other virus infection. There is sometimes a long interval between the infection and the onset of symptoms. The virus may trigger an autoimmune reaction in the pancreatic islets and this impairs insulin secretion and ultimately destroys the beta cells.

Stress

Physical injury, surgery and emotional distress sometimes precede the first symptoms of diabetes. Like infection, these each cause a sudden increase in secretion of catabolic hormones which may precipitate the disorder. However, stress probably does not cause diabetes in people who otherwise would never have developed it.

There is no single cause of primary diabetes. The disorder follows impaired secretion by pancreatic islet cells or utilisation of insulin by peripheral tissues. Many environmental factors may lead to such impairment in susceptible individuals. Genetic factors appear as the main determinant of susceptibility to such environmental factors, those leading to overweight and obesity being the most important in type 2 diabetes and viral infections in type 1.

Secondary diabetes

A minority of cases of diabetes occur as the result of diseases which destroy the pancreas and lead to impaired secretion of insulin, e.g. pancreatitis, haemochromatosis, carcinoma of the pancreas and pancreatectomy.

Diabetes may also accompany endocrine disorders which increase concentrations of catabolic hormones or modify the regulation of insulin receptors.

Growth hormone. This, if administered to dogs,

produces permanent diabetes and about 30 per cent of patients with acromegaly are diabetic.

Adrenocortical hormones. Cortisol and other corticosteroids raise the blood glucose by increasing protein breakdown and by inhibiting utilisation of glucose by peripheral tissues. Thus many patients with Cushing's syndrome show impaired carbohydrate tolerance; conversely increased sensitivity to insulin is an important feature of Addison's disease and hypopituitarism, and this can be corrected by corticosteroids.

Adrenaline. This raises blood glucose by increasing breakdown of liver glycogen and by suppressing secretion of insulin. Patients with a phaeochromocytoma frequently show a diabetic glucose tolerance test and the incidence of these rare tumours is relatively high among diabetic patients.

Thyroid hormones. Thyroxine if given in excess aggravates the diabetic state and some patients with hyperthyroidism show impaired glucose tolerance.

Gestational diabetes. This refers to the hyperglycaemia which may occur temporarily during pregnancy in women with an inherited predisposition to type 1 or type 2 diabetes. During normal pregnancy there is an increased production of hormonal antagonists to insulin which leads to increased rates of secretion and release of insulin. A failing pancreas may be unable to meet this demand.

Drugs, for example the adrenocortical steroids and thiazide diuretics, may precipitate diabetes, especially in those genetically susceptible.

Liver disease, particularly cirrhosis and hepatitis, may be associated with impaired glucose tolerance.

CHEMICAL PATHOLOGY

The hyperglycaemia results from the insulin secreted by the pancreas being either insufficient in amount or ineffective in action, possibly as a result of receptor abnormalities, for one or more reasons. Hence there is an underlying intracellular lack of glucose, leading to increased proteolysis and lipolysis as compensatory reactions under the influence of such catabolic hormones as growth hormone and cortisol. Thus the hyperglycaemia arises from two main sources, a reduced rate of removal of glucose from the blood by the peripheral tissues and an increased release of glucose from the liver into the circulation. Although significant amounts of insulin can often be detected in the plasma of cases of type 1 and type 2 diabetes, its concentration is lower than in normal subjects whose blood glucose is raised to comparable heights. It seems likely that the abnormalities in carbohydrate tolerance and lipid metabolism result directly from the lack of insulin. However, the sequence of events which culminate in the development

of this insulin-deficient state is still uncertain. It may arise from a primary disorder of insulin secretion. Alternatively the primary defect may not be in the pancreas but due to insulin resistance as a consequence of a receptor defect in the target tissue.

Consequences of hyperglycaemia and glycosuria. When the glucose concentration in the blood exceeds the capacity of the renal tubules to reabsorb it from the glomerular filtrate, glycosuria occurs. In the majority of people the level of blood glucose at which this happens is approximately 10 mmol/l (180 mg/dl). Glucose increases the osmolality of the glomerular filtrate and thus prevents the reabsorption of water as the filtrate passes down the renal tubules. In this way the volume of urine is markedly increased in diabetes, and polyuria and nocturia occur. This in turn leads to loss of water and electrolytes which results in thirst and polydipsia. In acute cases, or in more slowly progressive cases if the fluid intake has been low, e.g. because of mental confusion or for other reasons, severe depletion of water and electrolytes may occur. As the blood glucose rises the extracellular fluid becomes hypertonic, and water leaves the cells. In the early stages, before the volume of the extracellular fluid is grossly reduced the patient shows few clinical signs, but if the loss of water and electrolytes continues, depletion of extracellular fluid leads to the clinical features of severe dehydration.

Consequences of poor glucose utilisation. Impaired utilisation of carbohydrate results in a sense of fatigue, and two compensatory mechanisms operate to provide alternative metabolic substrate. Both lead to loss of body tissue and wasting may occur in spite of a normal or even increased intake of food. This is added to any loss of weight resulting from loss of fluid.

Increased glycogenolysis and gluconeogenesis. Glycogen and protein are present in cells associated with water and intracellular electrolytes. As glycogen and protein are catabolised, glucose, water and electrolytes, particularly potassium, are released into the extracellular space. An increased urinary excretion of potassium, magnesium and phosphorus therefore occurs in uncontrolled diabetes.

Increased lipolysis. This is seen as a raised fasting plasma concentration of free fatty acid (FFA) in response to a carbohydrate load. The extent to which lipolysis occurs is proportional to the degree of insulin deficiency. If the latter is marked, the normal response to feeding may be completely lost and the plasma concentration of FFA may remain three or four times above the normal level.

Fatty acids are taken up by the liver and degraded through stages to acetyl CoA. Normally most of these molecules enter the citric acid cycle, but in severe diabetes more is formed than the cycle can handle.

Instead acetyl coenzyme A is converted to acetoacetic acid. Most of this is then reduced to β-hydroxybutyric acid, while some is decarboxylated to acetone. These **ketone bodies** are oxidised and utilised as metabolic fuel, but their rate of utilisation is limited. When the rate of production by the liver exceeds that of removal by the peripheral tissues, then blood concentration rises. Ketone bodies are strong acids which dissociate readily and release hydrogen ions into the body fluids. This causes a decrease in plasma bicarbonate and an increase in P_{CO_2} in the arterial blood. This state is called **ketoacidosis**.

The extent to which the clinical features of dehydration and ketoacidosis are seen in individual cases depends on the speed at which the condition develops and the extent to which patients increase their intake of fluid, as well as on the degree of insulin deficiency present.

MORBID ANATOMY

The pancreas. Abnormalities in the islets of Langerhans are found at autopsy in most cases of clinical diabetes. However, these are mostly of a quantitative nature and nearly all the types of lesion in the islets in diabetes also occur in non-diabetics, although they are much less common.

In type 1 diabetics there are marked changes in the islet tissue. The abnormality consists essentially of degeneration of the islet tissue, from which the β cells have largely disappeared, leaving behind α cells and small undifferentiated cells. The remaining β cells show evidence of excessive activity; the nuclei are commonly enlarged with degranulation of the cytoplasm. Antibodies to islet cells are usually found in the blood of young diabetics soon after the onet of their disease.

In type 2 diabetics a moderate reduction in the mass of islet tissue is commonly seen which does not appear to account for the degree of impaired carbohydrate tolerance. On the other hand, in many cases the β cells, despite prolonged hyperglycaemia and their reduced number, fail to develop cytological signs of hyperactivity, which suggests that in these diabetics the β cells may be insensitive to the stimulus of a rise in blood glucose.

Extrapancreatic tissues. Diabetes is commonly associated with a disorder of small blood vessels (microangiopathy) which is seen as an abnormal thickening of the basement membrane and changes in the endothelium of the capillaries throughout the body. Its development seems to be mainly related to the duration of clinical diabetes, glycaemic control and possibly as yet other unidentified factors. The widespread involvement of small blood vessels appears to be the common denominator of a large group of complications associated with long-term diabetes. The main impact of this microangiopathy is on the retina and the kidneys.

CLINICAL FEATURES

Type 1 diabetes
This usually appears before the age of 40 years in patients of normal or less than normal weight. Symptoms are usually severe and develop rapidly. Without insulin treatment severe ketoacidosis occurs and is often fatal. Since insulin is required for their survival, an alternative name for this group of patients is **insulin-dependent**.

Type 2 diabetes
This usually appears in middle age or later in patients who are often obese and in whom hyperglycaemia can usually be controlled by dietary means alone or, if not, by an oral hypoglycaemic drug. Some insulin is detectable in the plasma of nearly all patients in this category, and they are therefore less prone to develop ketosis. In this sense type 2 is a less severe disease than type 1; however, the long-term complications occur in both types. Many type 2 patients have a long history of mild symptoms which may be ignored or misdiagnosed for years.

SYMPTOMS AND PRESENTATION

Diabetes may be discovered in several ways.

1. Some patients present complaining of some or all of the classical symptoms which are thirst, polydipsia, polyuria, nocturia, tiredness, loss of weight, reduced visual activity, white marks on clothing, pruritus vulvae or balanitis. The severity of the symptoms is related to the severity of glycosuria. If mild hyperglycaemia has developed slowly over many years, glycosuria may be slight, and the symptoms of diabetes correspondingly trivial.
2. Many patients are first found to have glycosuria in the course of some routine examination, for insurance, for employment purposes, or preoperatively. They may have had few or no symptoms.
3. Diabetes may first present as a fulminating ketoacidosis. This may have been precipitated by an acute infection but there may be no obvious cause. Epigastric pain and vomiting may be the presenting complaints. These are acute medical emergencies and are usually type 1.

4. Patients may present with symptoms which are due to one of the complications of diabetes e.g. failing vision; paraesthesiae in the limbs or pain in the legs owing to diabetic neuropathy or peripheral vascular disease; impotence; infection of the skin, lungs or urinary tract. Many of these patients also admit to symptoms attributable to glycosuria.

Physical signs

Cases without complications usually show no signs attributable to diabetes. Vulvitus or balnitis may be found, since the external genitalia are prone to infection by fungi (Candida) which flourish on skin and mucous membranes contaminated by glucose.

In a fulminating case there is dehydration, with loose dry skin, and a dry furred tongue with cracked lips, and the intraocular pressure may be obviously reduced. Usually the pulse is rapid and blood pressure low. Breathing may be deep and rapid; the sweet smell of acetone may be noticeable in the breath. Apathy and confusion may be present or there may be stupor or even coma.

Evidence of complications of diabetes may be noted. Ophthalmoscopy may show diabetic retinopathy. Early signs of diabetic neuropathy are depression of the ankle jerks and impaired vibration sense in the legs. The presence of nephropathy may be indicated by proteinuria.

DIAGNOSIS

When the classical symptoms are present, the diagnosis is often beyond doubt by the time the history taking and physical examination are complete, and it may then be confirmed by the finding of marked glycosuria, with or without ketonuria, and a random blood glucose greater than 11.0 mmol/l (200 mg/dl). However, in many patients, particularly those with diabetes of later onset who have few if any symptoms, and where glycosuria is frequently discovered by chance, the diagnosis is less obvious and a glucose tolerance test is required.

Urine testing

Glycosuria. Glucose-specific dip-stick methods are best. Diastix (Ames and Co.) consists of a paper stick impregnated with an enzyme preparation which gives a semiquantitative estimate of glycosuria (0.25 to 2.0 per cent) when dipped in urine containing glucose. No other urinary constituent gives this reaction; it therefore provides a rapid and specific test for glucose. Quantitative measurement of urinary reducing activity can be obtained using copper reduction methods, with Clinitest tablets (Ames and Co.) but is a non-specific and less convenient technique.

It is common practice to examine overnight specimens of urine for glucose. Mild cases of diabetes may be missed in this way but are detected if a sample collected during the two hours following a meal is examined.

Some undoubtedly diabetic people have a negative test owing to a raised renal threshold, and non-diabetics with a low renal threshold may give a false positive test. In order to distinguish cases of this type from patients with mild diabetes, a glucose tolerance test is required.

Ketonuria. The amounts of ketone bodies normally excreted by healthy persons are not detected by routine side-room methods, but clinically important amounts are detected by the nitroprusside reaction which is conveniently carried out using Acetest tablets or Ketostix paper sticks (Ames and Co.). Ketonuria may be found in normal people who have been fasting for long periods, who have been vomiting repeatedly or who have been eating a diet high in fat and low in carbohydrate. Ketonuria is therefore not pathognomic of diabetes, but if both ketonuria and glycosuria are found, the diagnosis of diabetes is practically certain.

Random blood sugar

In many cases diabetes can be diagnosed by a single blood glucose estimation, which may be used as a confirmatory test when the classical symptoms suggest the diagnosis. A random blood glucose exceeding 11.0 mmol/l (200 mg/dl) is almost certain to indicate diabetes. However, a lower random blood glucose does not exclude it, and some degree of standardisation of the conditions under which the blood glucose is measured is necessary. In practice, the oral glucose tolerance test is the cornerstone of the diagnosis.

The oral glucose tolerance test (Fig. 42.1)

The patient, who should have been on an unrestricted carbohydrate intake of at least 150 g and normal physical activity for three days or more, fasts overnight. Outpatients should rest for at least half an hour before the test, and should remain seated and not smoke during the test. A sample of blood is taken to measure the fasting blood glucose level and 75 g glucose dissolved in about 200–300 ml of flavoured water is then given by mouth. Thereafter samples of blood are collected at half-hourly intervals for two hours, and their glucose content estimated.

Criteria for diagnosis

Although clinical symptoms and urine tests usually provide a strong indication that a patient has diabetes,

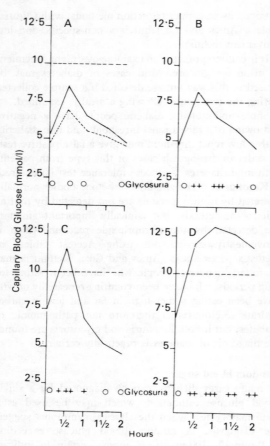

Fig. 42.1 The glucose tolerance test: blood glucose curves after 75 g glucose by mouth, showing (A) normal curve, (B) renal glycosuria, (C) alimentary (lag storage) glycosuria and (D) diabetes mellitus of moderate severity. The broken line indicates the renal threshold for glucose

a firm diagnosis usually requires a glucose tolerance test. The types of response to the test are illustrated in Figure 42.1. Table 42.1 gives diagnostic criteria for diabetes and for impaired glucose tolerance. These are taken from a WHO report[2] and recommended for international use.

Formerly glucose was usually measured in whole venous or capillary blood. It is now common practice to use venous plasma in which glucose concentration is a little higher than in whole blood. The figures in Table 42.1 have been rounded off.

Differential diagnosis of glycosuria

Renal glycosuria. If glucose appears in the urine when the blood glucose level is less than 10 mmol/l (180 mg/dl), the individual has a low renal threshold for glucose or renal glycosuria. This is a benign condition which may run in families and which commonly occurs temporarily in pregnancy.

Renal glycosuria is a much more frequent cause of glycosuria than diabetes in young persons, particularly in the age group 20 to 30 years, when they are commonly examined prior to entering the armed services, professions and industry. In the older age groups the reverse holds, and hyperglycaemia in excess of 10 mmol/l can occur without any glycosuria. Hence if urine tests for glucose are used as a method of screening for diabetes, some cases will be missed.

Alimentary (lag storage) glycosuria. In some individuals an unusually rapid but transitory rise of blood glucose follows a meal and the concentration exceeds the normal renal threshold and during this time glucose is present in the urine. Although the peak blood glucose is abnormally elevated, the value two hours after oral

Table 42.1 Diagnostic values for oral glucose tolerance test under standard conditions. Load 75 g glucose in 250–350 ml of water for adults or 1.75 g/kg body weight (to a maximum of 75 g) for children, using specific enzymatic glucose assay. Two classes of response are identified — diabetes mellitus and impaired glucose tolerance

	Glucose concentration		
	Venous whole blood	Capillary whole blood	Venous plasma
Diabetes mellitus			
Fasting	>7.0 mmol/l (>1.2 g/l)	>7.0 mmol/l (>1.2 g/l)	>8.0 mmol/l (>1.4 g/l)
and/or			
2 hours after glucose load	>10.0 mmol/l (>1.8 g/l)	>11.0 mmol/l (>2.0 g/l)	>11.0 mmol/l (>2.0 g/l)
Impaired glucose tolerance			
Fasting	<7.0 mmol/l (<1.2 g/l)	<7.0 mmol/l (<1.2 g/l)	<8.0 mmol/l (<1.4 g/l)
and			
2 hours after glucose load	(>7.0–<10.0 mmol/l (>1.2–<1.8 g/l)	>8.0–<11.0 mmol/l (>1.4–<2.0 gl/l)	>8.0–<11 mmol/l (>1.4–<2.0 g/l)

glucose is within normal limits (Fig. 42.1). This response to a meal or to a dose of glucose is traditionally known as 'lag storage', although alimentary glycosuria is a better term. It is not uncommon as a cause of symptomless glycosuria and may occur in otherwise normal people or after a partial gastrectomy, when it is due to rapid absorption, or in patients with hyperthyroidism or liver disease. This type of blood glucose curve is usually regarded as benign and unrelated to diabetes.

Starvation. Carbohydrate deprivation can lead to the development of a diabetic type of blood glucose curve with associated glycosuria in normal people. However, the carbohydrate intake has to be less than about 50 g/day before it has a notable effect and there is no glycosuria. This may be important in interpreting a glucose tolerance test in a person on a reducing diet or with a low intake of food during an acute illness.

MANAGEMENT

Diabetic patients no longer die in ketoacidosis in any number as they once did, but treated diabetic patients still have an overall mortality two and a half times that of the non-diabetic population, largely due to an increased death rate from coronary heart disease. Moreover, many of those whose duration of life has been extended are chronic invalids. They may live for many years with cerebral, coronary or peripheral vascular disease, or with renal disease or serious visual impairment.

LONG-TERM AIMS

The ideal treatment for diabetes would allow the patient to remain not only symptom-free but in good health with a normal metabolic state and to escape the long-term complications.

Although the relation between the degree of control and the development of serious complications is not simple, it would appear that the vascular abnormalities are secondary to the metabolic abnormalities, since they are found in both primary and secondary diabetes and in experimental diabetes in animals. The increased death rate from coronary heart disease is only partly accounted for by increased prevalence of obesity, hyperlipidaemia and hypertension amongst diabetics.

The incidence of diabetic microangiopathy is related to age at diagnosis and duration of diabetes and almost certainly results from metabolic abnormalities present in the majority of patients undergoing treatment.[12] It is therefore important to strive to achieve and maintain a normal metabolic state. Unfortunately the degree of metabolic control achieved in most patients by conven-

tional treatment is poor when monitored on a 24-hour basis and compared with normal subjects. Techniques are now being developed to achieve more physiological control.

IMMEDIATE AIMS

These are (1) abolition of symptoms while avoiding hypoglycaemia, (2) correction of hyperglycaemia and glycosuria and other metabolic abnormalities, and (3) attainment and maintenance of a desirable body weight.

Patients should realise as early as possible that it is upon them that success or failure will depend. The doctor can only advise. As adherence to a diabetic regime demands self-discipline and a sense of purpose, time should be spent on the education of each patient, so that they understand the object of each aspect of their treatment and have sufficient knowledge to undertake the day-to-day management of their diabetes.

As soon as the diagnosis is certain, patients should be told that they have diabetes, be reassured, and instruction and treatment begun forthwith. Many patients have an anxiety reaction on being told that they have diabetes. If they understand what is wrong with them, why they have certain symptoms, and what they should do to correct the abnormalities present, then they are likely to be less afraid and much more co-operative in carrying out the regimen prescribed.

Types of treatment
There are three methods of treatment and each involves an obligation for the patient to adhere to a dietary regimen for the remainder of life.

Diet alone

Diet and oral hypoglycaemic drugs

Diet and insulin.

Approximately 40 per cent of new cases of diabetes can be controlled adequately by diet alone, about 30 per cent require insulin and another 30 per cent will need an oral hypoglycaemic drug. Insulin is needed for juvenile-onset cases; older patients often do not require insulin except when control of their diabetes is disturbed by an illness, infection or operation.

Diet
In all diabetics the amount and time of food intake, particularly the carbohydrate, should be controlled so as to prevent, as far as is possible, fluctuations of blood glucose beyond the normal range. Intake of refined sugars should be low because their consumption is followed by absorption and a high peak of blood glucose. Patients should avoid feasting or fasting; their intake from day to day should be maintained with adjustments

for exercise and appetite; they should not miss a meal or over-indulge.

Type 1 patients require insulin and their food, especially carbohydrate, should be adjusted to match the time of action of their insulin. This depends on the type of insulin being used and whether the patient is having a single injection or more than one each day. The balance between insulin and meals has to be adjusted from time to time. These patients may still be growing and often start treatment below normal weight. They usually want to take moderate and sometimes strenuous exercise. They therefore require a generous amount of dietary energy.

Type 2 patients are usually obese. Being middle aged or elderly they may not take much exercise. For both of these reasons the daily energy intake should be restricted to about 4.2 MJ (1000 kcal). For them, Dr Arnold Bloom's dictum is sound advice: 'If you are overweight it doesn't matter what you eat as long as you don't eat it!' Such patients, if they can only bring their weight down to the desirable range (p. 521) can nearly always be managed on diet alone and seldom require insulin or oral hypoglycaemic drugs. The difficulty is to motivate the patient. Airline pilots succeed because their flying career depends on avoiding insulin or drugs.[13] Results are excellent where both doctors and dietitians recommend reducing diets with enthusiasm.[14]

Nature of the diet. Before insulin was available diabetic diets were very low in carbohydrate and so the proportion of fat was high, and this changed only slowly. In 1931 in the diets used at the London Hospital percentages of energy from carbohydrate, fat and protein were 15, 68 and 17 per cent respectively.[15] But in 1928 Joslin in his influential textbook[16] wondered: 'Can it be that the prevalence of arteriosclerosis in diabetes is to be attributed to the high fat diets we have prescribed and more especially if these diets have been rich in cholesterol? I suspect this may be the case. At any rate it is reasonable to maintain the cholesterol in the blood of our patients at a normal level and I shall strive to do.'

In 1935 Rabinowich[17] in Montreal reported that with a high carbohydrate–low energy diet good diabetic control could be obtained. Subsequently many diabetic clinics found that blood glucose was no higher and plasma cholesterol lower when the fat provided no more than 40 per cent of the dietary energy. Today it is orthodox to recommend the same proportions of dietary carbohydrate, fat and protein for diabetic patients as for healthy people. Old ideas die hard and in the 1970s many British clinics were still using diets unnecessarily low in carbohydrate and so high in fat.[18]

The nature of the carbohydrate is, however, important. Sucrose should be eliminated or greatly restricted. Starchy foods rich in dietary fibre are beneficial for diabetics as for all of us. For diabetics there is the additional benefit that the gums in legumes and other vegetable foods by increasing the viscosity of the intestinal contents reduce the postprandial peak in blood glucose. In this way they improve diabetic control.[19] Guar gum is especially effective and can be incorporated into crispbreads.[20] Oxford workers report that these can be a useful component of a diabetic diet, but it is uncertain whether they will be widely acceptable to patients.

There are two essential points about a diabetic diet. First, energy intake should be adjusted to maintain ideal body weight. Secondly, all patients taking insulin should follow a regular pattern of meals, matched to the injected insulin.

Exchange systems

Most British diabetic clinics divide foods into three categories — forbidden, freely allowed and foods that may be exchanged on the basis of carbohydrate content. The British Diabetic Association has a List of Carbohydrate Exchanges (p. 618); each item contains 10 g of carbohydrate. Thus 7 oz (200 ml) milk can be exchanged with one orange or half a thick slice of bread (20 g). A difficulty is that these foods are not equivalent in their pattern of other nutrients, and even their carbohydrates are not qualitatively the same.

In the USA the exchange unit for bread contains 15 g carbohydrate. This is the amount in a full slice of bread. The exchange system is extended to all types of food and, in the 1976 revision, six exchanges are used — for milk, vegetables (non-starchy), fruit, bread (including pasta, other cereals and starchy vegetables,) meat (with fish and other protein-rich foods) and fats. For each group the carbohydrate, fat and protein of the exchange unit are different. The exchange unit for each food group is based on the composition of average servings of foods in the group. From these six food exchanges the American Diabetic and Dietetic Associations have made nine standard diet plans. The diets for growing children provide more milk. Where the physician wants to take steps to reduce plasma cholesterol, milk is replaced by skimmed milk and diary fats replaced by polyunsaturated oils and margarines. The exchanges are shown on page 623.

Method of constructing a daily diet

As the daily intake of nutrients should be fixed, some kind of exchange system is necessary to avoid the monotony of a static diet sheet; this is the basis for the construction of nearly all diets.

The first step in preparing any dietary regimen is to map out a timetable of the patient's day including a description of their usual meals. The daily requirement of energy is next decided. This should be adequate for the patient's needs, and is determined for each patient after considering such factors as age, sex, actual weight in relation to desirable weight, occupation and other physical activities. An approximate range for various groups might be (1) an obese, middle-aged or elderly patient with mild diabetes, 4.2 to 6.7 MJ (1000 to 1600 kcal) daily; (2) an elderly diabetic but not overweight, 5.8 to 7.5 MJ (1400 to 1800 kcal) daily; (3) a young and active diabetic, 7.5 to 12.5 MJ (1800 to 3000 kcal) daily. The importance of maintaining the body weight at or slightly below the ideal for the patient's height cannot be overemphasised. The energy range of group 2 may have to be extended if the diet is not sufficient to maintain weight, and young patients in group 3 who are overweight may have to reduce temporarily their daily intake to below 7.5 MJ (1800 kcal).

Next, the proportion of energy derived from carbohydrate, protein and fat must be allocated. The average in British household diets is about carbohydrate 46 per cent, protein 12 per cent and fat 42 per cent. In most diabetic diets the proportion of energy from carbohydrate should be 50–55 per cent, from protein between 10 and 15 per cent and from fat less than 35 per cent. Most clinics in Third World countries and some in affluent countries manage their patients with a higher proportion of carbohydrate, as starch and associated fibre but not as sugar.

Carbohydrate. A minimum of 100 g is needed to prevent ketonuria. With higher intakes it may be difficult to achieve satisfactory blood glucose concentrations throughout 24 hours. If the daily intake of carbohydrate has to be as high as 240 g to meet energy needs, about 50 g is usually provided in each of the three main meals, 20 g in three snacks and 30 g in 600 ml of milk. Experience shows that it is difficult to prevent an excessive rise in blood glucose after each meal with amounts larger than this. Foods rich in sucrose and other sugars should be kept to a minimum.

The British Diabetic Association allows diabetics to take up to 2 oz (60 g) of fructose a day. Sorbitol, used for making diabetic jams, is not restricted on the ground that large intakes cause diarrhoea and so are self-limiting. As fructose and sorbitol have the same energy value as other sugars, obese diabetics should not use them. These allowances enable British diabetics to include fruit in their diets but fruit containing (say) 30 g fructose is likely to have a more favourable effect on glucose and insulin metabolism than pure fructose. Though fructose may not raise blood glucose as much as sucrose or glucose, it may raise plasma triglycerides more.

Protein. The consumption of foods rich in protein is largely determined by social and economic considerations and may be lower than desirable. If this is the case, every effort should be made to ensure that some is eaten at each meal. As amino acids stimulate insulin secretion, in both normal subjects and in those with type 2 diabetes, a smaller rise in blood glucose occurs when carbohydrate is consumed along with protein. A minimum amount, about 50 g, of protein should therefore be specified in all diabetic diets but, unless the patient is obese, more may be taken if desired.

Fat. Because diabetic patients have an increased risk of death from coronary heart disease, and because this may be related to the amount of saturated fat in the diet, the total amount of fat should be restricted even in those who are not obese.

When the patient's total requirements have been assessed the figures must be translated into practical and comprehensible instructions, using one of the types of diet prescription sheets (Appendix 2).

Each patient should be given a list of carbohydrate exchanges (p. 618) with instructions regarding the meals at which they may be taken. The diet sheet and exchanges should be discussed with the patient repeatedly and with a relative if necessary.

Types of diet

There are two types of diet: (1) measured diet, in which the amount of food to be eaten at each time of the day is specified, and (2) unmeasured diet, in which the patient is supplied with a list of foods grouped in three categories — foods with a high concentrated carbohydrate content which are to be avoided altogether, foods with a relatively stable unconcentrated carbohydrate content which are to be eaten in moderation only, and non-carbohydrate foods which may be eaten as desired. Examples are shown on page 620.

Measured diets. In these diets the portions of food may be measured either by weighing with scales or more simply by using household measures. Measured diets are required for patients who are being treated with insulin, and also for some of those who are overweight and on a reducing regimen.

The former should, if at all possible, weigh out the portions of food initially and should be provided with a simple balance (available on NHS prescription). After a few weeks most patients are capable of assessing the weight of portions with sufficient accuracy by eye, and regular weighing becomes less necessary. However it is important to check visual assessments by weighing from time to time.

Diabetics who are obese should be urged to accept a reducing regimen. The method of achieving reduction in weight is the same for obese diabetic patients as for those with simple obesity. Diet No. 3 (p. 610) meets the needs of many. The portions in the diet can be weighed out with scales but usually household measures suffice. It should be explained that such a strict diet has to be followed only until the standard weight is reached;

thereafter the diet may be increased, and advice can then be given on how to avoid monotony by using the list of exchanges for diabetic diets.

Unmeasured diets. If insulin is not required and obesity is not marked, it may not be necessary for the patient to follow such an accurate diet. Sometimes it may be impractical to do so because of the patient's mental, visual or other physical incapacity or unwillingness to cooperate. Many patients develop the disease when they are already middle-aged or elderly and have a mild type of diabetes often associated with moderate obesity. For such patients an unmeasured diet of the type described on page 622 is used.

Alcohol. Patients need advice regarding the consumption of alcohol. There is no medical objection to taking alcoholic drinks in moderation provided patients realise that they must take account of their energy value and sometimes of their carbohydrate content. Beer for example may contain 10 to 30 g of carbohydrate per half litre (1 pint approx.) and with the alcohol this provides 630 to 1700 kJ (150 to 400 kcal), depending on the strength of the beer. Sweet wines and cider all have a high sugar content, and spirits such as whisky and gin, while free of carbohydrates, provide about 300 kJ (70 kcal)/30 ml.

Sweetening agents. Advice may also be asked about sweetening agents and diabetic foods and drinks. Saccharin and aspartame may be used and have no energy value.

DRUGS

Oral hypoglycaemic drugs

A number of compounds reduce hyperglycaemia in patients who would otherwise require insulin. The sulphonylurea compounds, tolbutamide and chlorpropamide and the newer generation of agents such as glibenclamide, glipizide, gliquidone, and to a lesser extent the biguanide, metformin, have a place in the management of about 30 per cent of diabetic patients. Although their mechanism of action is different, the action of both groups depends upon a supply of endogenous insulin, and it is therefore futile and dangerous to attempt to control juvenile-onset diabetes with these compounds.

Sulphonylureas. Tolbutamide is the mildest, and probably also the safest, of the sulphonylureas. Since its effective action does not exceed six to eight hours it should be taken two or three times a day. The dose varies between 1 and 2 g/day. It is well tolerated and toxic reactions such as skin rashes rarely occur. Unfortunately, the relapse rate is relatively high.

Chlorpropamide has a biological half-life of about 36 hours, and an effective concentration can be maintained in the blood by a single dose at breakfast. The usual maintenance dose is between 100 and 375 mg/day; larger doses should not be used on a long-term basis, since there is an increased risk of toxic effects, such as jaundice, drug rashes, and blood dyscrasia. Two other effects should be noted. If alcohol is taken following chlorpropamide an unpleasant flushing of the face occurs in some patients. Chlorpropamide may lead to severe hypoglycaemia, which can be refractory to treatment. Care should be taken to avoid this in elderly patients, and once glycosuria has been abolished and symptoms relieved, the dose should be reduced to the minimum. Many patients who require 375 to 500 mg/day initially can later be maintained on 100 mg or less/day.

The newer sulphonylureas are active at lower dosage levels and have a relatively short plasma half-life of up to approximately six hours. Sulphonylureas are valuable in the treatment of patients with type 2 diabetes who fail to respond to simple dietary restriction and who are not overweight. They should not be given to obese patients since they act by stimulating the production of endogenous insulin and this leads in turn to an increase in weight with a consequent reduction in life expectancy.

Biguanides. These have a higher incidence of adverse effects than the sulphonylureas, particularly lactic acidosis, and only metformin is now acceptable. It is valuable in two situations. First, as it does not lead to an increase in weight, it is preferred for a patient with diabetes who is overweight but in whom hyperglycaemia persists despite efforts to adhere to a diet and reduce weight. Secondly, as its hypoglycaemic effect appears to be synergistic with that of the sulphonylureas, there is a place for combining the two when the sulphonylureas alone have proved inadequate (primary failure), and when, as happens with 5 to 10 per cent of patients, initial success is followed after several months or even one or two years by loss of control (secondary failure).

Unlike the sulphonylureas, metformin does not produce hypersensitivity reactions or hypoglycaemia in therapeutic doses, and is given with food in two or three daily doses of 0.5 to 1.0 g each.

Clinical uses

Patients of normal weight may be started on an oral hypoglycaemic drug as soon as it is clear that dietary measures alone are inadequate. It is usually possible to reach a decision on the success or failure of these drugs within a week, though occasionally a full response may not be apparent for much longer. Diabetics treated successfully in this way for prolonged periods may later need an alteration of dose or a change of regimen temporarily or permanently; in particular they may require insulin to meet the needs created by severe infection, an operation or other stress.

A report from America[21] suggesting that those taking tolbutamide and phenformin are at increased risk of dying from cardiovascular disease has not been confirmed.

Insulin

A single dose of the original soluble insulin cannot keep the blood glucose within the normal range for more than six hours. Diabetics had to give themselves several injections daily until the introduction of depot insulins. With these insulin is realised slowly from the site of injection and the effect of a single injection is prolonged. Most diabetics now manage with two injections daily, one before breakfast and one before the evening meal, each containing soluble and depot insulin. This usually keeps the blood glucose within reasonable limits for 24 hours without undue risk of hypoglycaemia.

More physiological control could be obtained by a continuous infusion. A portable insulin pump driven by electric batteries was introduced in 1978 by a team based on Guy's Hospital, London, who have now reported on their experience after some years.[22] The pumps are expensive but several models are on sale in the USA. It is difficult to say what role these insulin pumps will play in the future. Most patients will probably wish to continue with their injections but those who like gadgets may prefer a pump and some of them have now been under good control with no adverse effects after using one for several years.

Soluble insulin. This is a clear solution in contrast to the depot insulins which are cloudy. When injected subcutaneously, soluble insulin begins to lower the blood glucose in 30 minutes; the effect is maximal in 4 to 6 hours and ends after 6 to 10 hours. A patient stabilised on soluble insulin alone would therefore need at least two injections in the day.

Soluble insulin is essential in the following circumstances:

1. For new cases with severe dehydration or ketoacidosis.
2. For emergencies associated with ketosis, such as acute infection, gastroenteritis or some surgical operations.
3. For the treatment of nearly all young patients.

Depot insulins. The action of a single injection of insulin can be prolonged by delaying its release from the site of injection into the circulation. For this purpose there are insulin zinc preparations suspended in acetate buffer. Release of insulin in the tissues depends on the size of the insulin particles. Insulin in the presence of zinc can be absorbed onto a foreign protein (protamine or globin). A protein–zinc insulin complex forms which breaks up slowly in the subcutaneous tissues. Slow onset/long duration depot insulins do not lower blood sugar before 4 to 6 hours; the effect is maximal at 8 to 14 hours and only ends after 20 to 30 hours. With intermediary depot preparations, the corresponding times are 2 to 3 hours, 6 to 10 hours and 10 to 14 hours, but with one preparation, isophane, the effect continues for 12 to 22 hours. Some. but not all, soluble and depot preparations are miscible and then a single injection of the mixture can be given and provides better control. A small number of cases can be adequately controlled by a single morning injection of depot insulin. These patients are usually elderly with mild diabetes. Most insulin-requiring diabetics, however, do best on a depot insulin with one or two supporting doses of soluble insulin. The choice of depot insulin is determined by consideration of the patient's way of life, e.g. his meal pattern, occupation, hours of work and recreation, in relation to the time of action of the various depot insulins. More insulin is required to cover main meals and periods of inactivity, and vice versa.

Highly purified insulins. Most conventional insulin preparations are made from beef pancreas and contain polypeptides other than insulin which are antigenic. Antigenicity depends above all on the purity of a preparation. Highly purified insulins have in the last few years become increasingly available. With these there is usually a fall in insulin requirements and cases of severe insulin resistance are rare; further local and general allergic reactions are less frequent. It is possible that they may give better control and so reduce the incidence of the complications of diabetes.

Human insulin. This has become available since 1979 and is prepared either by enzymatic modification of porcine insulin or biosynthetically from bacteria using recombinant DNA techniques. At present there are no discernible advantages over highly purified porcine insulin.

In practice, combinations of the various insulin preparations should be tried, and the time of their administration varied in the light of urine tests and blood glucose estimations at different times of the day until control is smooth over the 24-hour period. It is impossible to forecast the response of a patient to insulin, and the daily dose required varies from 10 to 100 units or more.

A practical point, worth mentioning since it may give rise to distress if not anticipated, is that blurring of vision (which may occur in a severe diabetic before treatment) may become noticeably worse after starting treatment with insulin. It is due to transitory osmotic abnormalities in the eye, especially the lens, and may persist for several weeks.

CHOICE OF THERAPEUTIC REGIMEN

The regimen eventually adopted in each case is chosen by a process of trial and error, and changes may be needed as more is learnt about the patient and the kind of diabetes which he or she has.

The indications for the types of regimen are as follows.

1. Practically all young patients who develop diabetes before the age of 40 years require treatment with insulin. The majority are best controlled by a combination of a short-acting and intermediate-acting (depot) insulin injected twice daily, before breakfast and before the evening meal.

2. Most patients developing the disease over the age of 40 years can, and should, be controlled by diet alone. This applies particularly to obese patients, but others may do well on dietary therapy alone. Obese patients should be treated by dietary restriction and weight reduction rather than by insulin or other hypoglycaemic agent. The advent of insulin obscured the remarkable improvement in glucose tolerance which usually results from reduction in weight. Insulin and the sulphonylureas increase the appetite, and thus may increase weight and intensify disability.

3. Those over the age of 40 who are not controlled by dietary measures alone usually respond well to sulphonylurea if they are not obese, or to a biguanide if they are obese. If adequate control is not achieved by one drug, a combination of sulphonylurea and biguanide may be tried. If this fails insulin is needed.

4. Elderly patients who require insulin often do well with a small dose (20 units) of a depot insulin alone. A few, particularly those who would otherwise require more than 40 units a day, should be given soluble insulin in addition.

INITIATION OF TREATMENT

It is seldom necessary to admit new diabetic patients to hospital. It is desirable that they learn to manage all aspects of their disorder as quickly as possible, while leading a normal existence at home and at work and this can best be done as an outpatient. However, patients need to be seen daily at first and if this is not otherwise possible, admission to hospital is necessary. Hospital admission is also needed if there is severe ketoacidosis.

As soon as the diagnosis is made, a careful search is needed for early evidence of complications such as coronary heart disease and hypertension, obliterative arterial disease, peripheral neuropathy, cataract, retinopathy, nephropathy, pulmonary tuberculosis and other infections, particularly of the skin and urinary tract.

Patient's education
1. All patients capable of learning should be taught how to test urine with a Diastix or Clinitest set (and sometimes with Acetest tablets also), to keep a record of the results in a notebook and to understand their significance.

2. All patients requiring insulin should learn to measure the dose accurately with an insulin syringe (BS 1619), to give their own injections and to adjust their dose on the basis of urine tests and factors such as illness, unusual exercise and insulin reactions. They should be made to experience an insulin reaction at the earliest possible stage, so that they can recognise the early signs and take appropriate action.

3. All patients should have a working knowledge of diabetes, i.e. be able to recognise the symptoms associated with marked glycosuria and to understand their significance. They should be told that many drugs have undesirable effects on the diabetic state, as may also an illness of any kind or an emotional upset. They should be advised to come to the doctor or the clinic at once, without prior appointment, as soon as they are aware of any deterioration in health or urine tests not responding rapidly to simple measures.

4. All patients should know how to take care of their feet, and to respect any infected lesion.

Education of the patient is time-consuming and repeated practical demonstrations may be required, supplemented by appropriate booklets. If the patient is a child, or is blind, mentally defective or otherwise incapable, instructions in these matters should be given to a parent or guardian.

Diabetics who are taking insulin or oral hypoglycaemic drugs should carry a card at all times stating their name and address, the fact that they are diabetic, the nature and dose of insulin or other drugs they may be taking, and giving the name, address and telephone number of their family doctor and their diabetic clinic. Suitable cards are provided by the British Diabetic Association.

SUPERVISION AND ASSESSMENT OF CONTROL

Diabetics should be seen at regular intervals for the remainder of their lives. The object of these visits is to check the degree of control and to watch for complications. The frequency of visits is determined by the biochemical control achieved and the reliability of the patient. At the patient's regular visit to the diabetic clinic or to their general practitioner, the degree of control should be assessed by considering their weight, the results of urine tests, a the presence or absence of symptoms of hyper- or hypoglycaemia. Fasting plasma lipids should also be checked from time to time.

Glycosylated haemoglobin. Like most other proteins haemoglobin may be glycosylated, the glucose molecule being attached to valine at the end of the β chain. The percentage of Hb molecules glycosylated is related to the time of exposure of erythrocytes to glucose and to the ambient glucose concentration. It is therefore an integrated index of blood glucose over a period of time and so a measure of control of diabetes over the previous three or four weeks. In a diabetic the percentage may be 15 or more, whereas in non-diabetics it is about 6 per cent. A single estimation is of limited value but a series of estimations over a long period is a useful index of whether or not a patient has been maintaining reasonable control of blood glucose.

Urine testing

Proper assessment of control is impossible unless in the course of their normal activity patients test samples of urine regularly. By selecting suitable times for the tests and tabulating the results, it is easy for the doctor or the experienced patient to decide whether the dose of insulin or hypoglycaemic drug should be adjusted, or whether the carbohydrate content of the diet or the time when it is taken should be altered.

Diabetics taking insulin should test samples of urine obtained before breakfast, before the midday and evening meals, and at bedtime. Tests at each of these times should be carried out two or three times a week, not necessarily all on any one day. Before a test they should empty the bladder and discard this urine about 30 minutes before passing the specimen for the test. Otherwise the premeal specimen includes urine passed into the bladder after the previous meal and gives the impression that the blood glucose before meals is higher than it really is.

Urine testing in such patients can be usefully supplemented with blood glucose testing, using capillary blood obtained by finger prick and a sensitive chemical strip read either directly or with a portable meter.

Patients treated by diet alone or with oral hypoglycaemic agents should test the first morning specimen and samples passed two or four hours after the main meals of the day; the majority of specimens should be either free of or contain only a trace of glucose.

Insulin reactions and hypoglycaemia

If soluble insulin is injected into a normal person the blood glucose falls, producing symptoms that may begin to appear when the concentration is about 2.8 mmol/l (50 mg/dl) and are fully developed at about 2.2 mmol/l. In diabetes who are constantly hyperglycaemic, the same symptoms may develop at much higher concentrations, e.g. 7 mmol/l.

The symptoms of hypoglycaemia are a feeling of being weak and empty, hunger, sweating, palpitation, tremor, faintness, dizziness, headache, diplopia and mental confusion. Abnormal behaviour, leading occasionally to arrest by the police on a charge of being drunk and disorderly, may also occur. Alternatively, and particularly in children, there may be lassitude and somnolence, muscular twitching, convulsions and deepening coma.

Hypoglycaemia causes secretion of adrenaline which leads to tachycardia and tremor and, by mobilising liver glycogen, combats the hypoglycaemia. This homoeostatic reaction partly explains why patients rarely die of hypoglycaemic coma from too much soluble insulin. By contrast, coma is dangerous when it arises from a large dose of depot insulin or from an overdose of sulphonylurea. Repeated profound hypoglycaemia may lead to permanent mental changes because the brain is dependent on the blood glucose for its energy. For this reason, recurrence of hypoglycaemia should be prevented by prompt reduction of the dose of insulin or of sulphonylurea.

Hypoglycaemia due to overdosage with soluble insulin comes on rapidly, at the time when the insulin is having its maximum effect, and usually passes off soon. Reactions from intermediate-acting depot insulins given before breakfast usually occur in the late afternoon and when given before the evening meal at night or early next morning. These reactions begin gradually with little adrenaline response and can become persistent and profound unless treated vigorously.

Treatment of hypoglycaemic reactions

Since hypoglycaemia can easily be corrected if recognised early, it is useful for diabetic patients to experience the condition under supervision. In this way they learn to recognise the early symptoms. They should be advised that the most frequent causes of the condition are unpunctual meals and unaccustomed exercise, and try to avoid both or make adjustments to meet these circumstances. They should always carry some tablets of glucose or a few lumps of sugar for use in an emergency. Unless an attack of hypoglycaemia is accounted for adequately, the patient should reduce the next and subsequent dose of insulin by 20 per cent, and seek medical advice.

If the patient is so stuporous that he cannot swallow, he should be given glucagon (1 mg) subcutaneously or intramuscularly. This can be administered by a relative. Recovery should follow within about five to ten minutes. If this fails an intravenous injection of 25 g of glucose (50 ml of a 50 per cent solution) which may have to be repeated.

As soon as the patient is able to swallow, 30 g of sugar by mouth should be given. Full recovery may not occur immediately, especially if the patient has been in a coma for some time.

COMPLICATIONS

Ketoacidosis

Before the discovery of insulin more than 50 per cent of diabetic patients ultimately died of ketoacidosis. Today this complication is preventable and accounts for less than 2 per cent of diabetic deaths. However, both the incidence and the mortality rate are still regrettably high. Failure of patients to understand their disease, and failure to appreciate the significance of symptoms of poor control are the common causes. A clear understanding of the biochemical disorders involved is essential for its efficient treatment which should aim at having the patient out of danger within 24 hours. A full review with 91 references to recent papers by Foster & McGarry[23] is recommended further reading.

Water and electrolyte depletion. The deficit of total body water in a severe case may be about 6 litres. About half of this is derived from the intracellular compartment and occurs early in the development of acidosis when there are few clinical features; the remainder represents loss of extracellular fluid sustained largely in the later stages. Marked contraction of the size of the extracellular space occurs, with haemoconcentration, a decrease in plasma volume, and finally a fall in blood pressure with oliguria.

The concentrations of sodium and potassium in plasma give little indication of total body losses, and may even be raised due to disproportionate losses of water. Sodium loss, mainly from the extracellular space, may amount to as much as 500 mmol. Potassium loss from the cells may be 400 mmol or more. Treatment with insulin is likely to cause a precipitous fall in the plasma potassium. This is due to (1) dilution of extracellular potassium by the administration of potassium-free fluids, (2) movement of potassium into the cells as the result of insulin therapy and (3) continued renal loss of potassium.

Acidosis is assessed by measuring the plasma bicarbonate and is severe if the concentration is less than 12 mmol/l. Arterial pH is a more valuable guide but its measurement may not be readily available. There are no rapid quantitative methods for the determination of plasma ketones but a Ketostix strip dipped in plasma indicates whether significant ketonaemia is present or not.

Clinical features

Any form of stress, particularly an acute infection, can precipitate severe ketoacidosis in even the mildest case of diabetes. The most common cause is neglect of treatment due to carelessness, misunderstanding or illness, and failure to adjust the therapeutic regimen in the event of an acute infection.

There is intense thirst and polyuria. Constipation,

muscle cramps and altered vision are common. Sometimes, there is abdominal pain, with or without vomiting. Hence diabetic ketoacidosis is important in the differential diagnosis of the acute abdomen. Weakness and drowsiness are commonly present but the state of consciousness is variable and a patient with dangerous ketosis requiring urgent treatment may walk into hospital. For this reason the term diabetic ketoacidosis is to be preferred to the traditional 'diabetic coma', which suggests that there is no urgency until unconsciousness occurs. In fact it is imperative that energetic treatment is started at the earliest possible stage.

The signs include a dry tongue, soft eyeballs due to dehydration, hyperventilation indicated by rapid, deep, sighing respirations and a rapid, weak pulse, with low blood pressure and acetone may be smelt in the breath. Sometimes there is abdominal rigidity and tenderness. Ultimately coma supervenes.

Laboratory tests show heavy glycosuria and ketonuria, blood glucose usually between 20 and 40 mmol/l (360 and 720 mg/100 ml), and low plasma bicarbonate and blood pH.

The degree of hyperglycaemia and ketoacidosis do not always correlate well. Even at a level of blood glucose as low as 20 mmol/l (350 mg/dl), life-threatening acidosis may be present; on the other hand coma can occur, usually in elderly patients, with extreme hyperglycaemia and dehydration but no ketoacidosis, **hyperosmolar diabetic coma**.

Treatment

This condition should be treated with the utmost urgency in hospital. Intravenous therapy is required since , even when the patient is able to swallow, fluids given by mouth may be poorly absorbed. Extracellular fluid is repleted first with sodium chloride infusions. It is now conventional treatment to give low dose insulin starting with 6 to 8 units per hour and halving the dose when the blood glucose has returned to normal. In the majority of cases potassium therapy, approximately 13–20 mmol per 0.5 litre infusion fluid, should be started from the·outset. Intracellular fluid is replaced once the blood glucose has fallen below 14 mmol/l (250 mg/100 ml) by infusing glucose solution. Intensive medical care is needed and the blood glucose, pH, electrolytes and ketones have to be monitored, hourly at first. Details of management are given in textbooks of medicine.

Differential diagnosis of coma in a diabetic. Confusion between coma due to hypoglycaemia and that associated with ketosis should seldom arise; the distinction is usually clear (Table 42.2), but diabetic coma may occasionally pass undetected into hypoglycaemic coma through too enthusiastic treatment; likewise, vomiting induced by hypoglycaemia by a depot insulin may continue until diabetic coma develops.

Table 42.2 Differential diagnosis of coma in a diabetic

	Hypoglycaemic coma	Coma with ketosis
History	No food Too much insulin Unaccustomed exercise	Too little or no insulin An infection Digestive disturbance
Onset	In good health immediately before Related to time of last injection of insulin	Ill-health several days before
Symptoms	Of hypoglycaemia; occasional vomiting from depot insulins	Of glycosuria and dehydration; abdominal pain and vomiting
Signs	Moist skin and tongue Sweating Normal or raised blood pressure Shallow or normal breathing Brisk reflexes Plantar responses usually extensor	Dry skin and tongue Low blood pressure Reduced intraocular tension Hyperventilation ('air hunger') Diminished reflexes Plantar responses usually flexor
Urine	No ketonuria No glycosuria, provided that the bladder has been recently emptied	Ketonuria Glycosuria
Blood	Hypoglycaemia Normal plasma bicarbonate	Hyperglycaemia Reduced plasma bicarbonate

Vascular disorders

Vascular disease, arterial, arteriolar and capillary, is the largest and most intractable problem in clinical diabetes. Arterial disease is much the commonest cause of death in diabetics over the age of 50 years, and the mortality rate is far higher than in the general population. Strict control probably offers the best chance of delaying the onset and progress of the vascular complications of diabetes. Unfortunately, however, they may develop despite every effort by both patient and doctor to maintain precise control of the diabetes.

Atherosclerosis occurs commonly and extensively in diabetics. The pathological changes in diabetics are not specific in a qualitative sense but they occur earlier and are more widespread than in non-diabetics. Thus diabetics are more prone, at an earlier age than other people, to myocardial infarction, intermittent claudication and gangrene of the toes and feet.

The peripheral pulses in the legs are often diminished or impalpable, and particularly in elderly patients, ischaemic changes in the feet are frequently apparent. Defective circulation in the legs resulting in poorly nourished tissues predisposes to the dangerous complication of gangrene. If a painless peripheral neuropathy is present, this may also be of aetiological importance, since the patient tends to ignore or neglect injuries and other damage to the tissue. Diabetic gangrene usually starts in one foot, following a trivial injury — the cutting of a corn, or a burn from a hot-water bottle. Toxic absorption from necrotic tissue and secondary infection may kill the patient unless the limb is amputated. Amputation of a toe, a foot or even a whole leg is sometimes necessary to save life.

Much can be done to prevent this serious complication by instructing diabetics with a poor circulation to wear properly fitting shoes, to use bedsocks rather than hot-water bottles, never to cut their own corns and to 'keep their feet as clean as their face'. The services of a skilled chiropodist are invaluable.

Diabetic nephropathy. A specific type of renal lesion may occur as a result of the changes in the basement membrane of the glomerular capillaries. This is known as **diabetic glomerulosclerosis**, and there are two types, diffuse and nodular: the former is the more common and consists of a generalised thickening glomerular capillary walls. The nodular type is a development of this, and in these cases rounded masses of acellular, hyaline material are super-imposed upon the diffuse lesion in the glomeruli. These are sometimes called Kimmelstiel–Wilson nodules. Diabetic glomerulosclerosis can be seen by light microscopy in about 70 per cent of diabetic patients at autopsy. In the early stages of diabetes there may be little or no clinical evidence of renal involvement, and even with well-established diabetic glomerulosclerosis there may be only slight to moderate proteinuria. In some cases, however, there is marked proteinuria and the nephrotic syndrome with increasing renal failure and uraemia.

There is no way of preventing or modifying the progress of nephropathy once it is apparent as proteinuria. Management is similar to that for other forms of chronic renal disease.

Pancreatic transplants

Patients with severe renal failure due to diabetic nephropathy may require a kidney transplant. Then a pancreatic transplant, using the same donor, may be given and some of these have functioned well. Until organ transplantation and the necessary accompanying immunosuppressive measures become much safer, which it is hoped they will, it seems improper to advise a young diabetic to undergo the risks of a transplant for a disease for which there is already safe and effective treatment.

Diabetic retinopathy. Various elements go to make up retinopathy as viewed with the ophthalmoscope. These are micro-aneurysms of the capillaries; abnormalities of the retinal veins, particularly dilatation and tortuosity; haemorrhages; waxy exudes; new vessel formation; fibrous proliferation, occurring mainly in association with new vessels; and vitreous detachment. They are seen in varying combinations in different patients.

Micro-aneurysms, abnormalities of the veins, and new vessels do not of themselves interfere seriously with vision, but the other elements of retinopathy may do so. Retinal or preretinal haemorrhages seriously affect vision if they involve the macula, or if they break through into the vitreous, when sudden severe visual loss is usual. Exudates are also associated with symptoms if the macula is involved. Unfortunately all these lesions occur most frequently in the vicinity of the disc. New vessels appear most commonly at the disc, but can originate anywhere except at the macula. The new vessels in themselves do little harm, but they leak irritative serous products which cause vitreal–retinal adhesions and vitreous contraction. The latter puts traction on the friable new vessels so that vitreous haemorrhage and retinal detachment may occur and cause blindness.

Patients with only micro-aneurysms, retinal haemorrhages and exudates are classified as having background diabetic retinopathy; those with preretinal haemorrhages, new vessel formation or fibrous proliferation are classified as having proliferative diabetic retinopathy.

As with nephropathy, duration of diabetes and the degree of metabolic control are probably the important factors influencing the occurrence of retinopathy, the course of which is very variable. However in general, prognosis for vision is good for patients with background retinopathy, especially if they are young, and bad for those with proliferative retinopathy, of whom half are blind within five years. This poor visual prognosis has now been improved by photocoagulation treatment, especially if given at an early stage of the proliferative retinopathy. The variable nature of the natural course makes assessment of the effectiveness of any treatment extremely difficult.

Cataract

The prevalence of cataract in old people is much higher in those who have diabetes. Rarely a specific type of opacity of the lens occurs in diabetic children whose disease has not been adequately controlled.

Infections

Lowered resistance to infection is associated with poor control of diabetes. The following forms are especially important.

Carbuncle. The development of a carbuncle may unmask diabetes and may even precipitate ketosis and coma. The diabetic state brought on by a carbuncle is not invariably permanent; glucose tolerance may return to normal (at least temporarily) when the infection

subsides. Cleanliness is a special virtue in the prevention of skin infection in diabetes. Once infection has occurred a suitable antibiotic is needed.

Urinary tract infections. The presence of glucose in the urine provides a favourable medium for the growth of bacteria. Intractable infections of the urinary tract frequently occur, and for this reason catheterisation should be avoided. Once infection has occurred treatment consists of controlling the glycosuria and the administration of suitable antibiotics.

Vulvitis. Pruritus vulvae is very commonly associated with moniliasis in the diabetic woman. *Candida albicans* is nearly always present. In the majority, the treatment is abolition of glycosuria which brings rapid relief. In a few cases local treatment with vaginal pessaries and nystatin cream may be required.

Pulmonary tuberculosis. In countries where this is prevalent all new diabetic patients should have a chest radiograph. Elsewhere one is not necessary unless a patient is losing weight for no apparent reason.

Diabetic neuropathies

Peripheral neuropathy is a frequent complication of diabetes at any stage, which in the majority of cases may be unnoticed by the patient, but in some gives rise to troublesome symptoms. Motor, sensory or autonomic nerves may be involved, usually in a symmetrical manner. The most common types are as follows.

1. Acute peripheral neuropathy occurs usually in poorly controlled severe diabetes and involves one or many nerves. The clinical features are described on page 315. Pain is prominent, especially in the legs at night. This type of neuropathy appears to be metabolic in origin since it often improves rapidly when the diabetes is controlled.

2. Chronic peripheral neuropathy may be due to a combination of both metabolic and ischaemic changes. It is usually seen in older diabetics with long-standing disease. The clinical features are those of a painless neuropathy affecting the legs, with diminished tendon jerks and vibration sense. In severe cases there may be trophic changes in the feet; ulceration may follow trivial trauma and disorganisation of joints can occur.

3. Involvement of autonomic nerves may cause nocturnal diarrhoea, overflow incontinence of urine, impotence or postural hypotension. This complication occurs in long-standing cases and is unresponsive to treatment.

4. Diabetic amyotrophy is a predominantly motor form and consists of bilateral weakness and wasting of muscles of the pelvic girdle. With good control of the diabetes slow recovery usually takes place.

Aldose reductose inhibitors

Treatment of severe neuropathy with aldose reductase inhibitors (sorbinil) is now being investigated.[24,25] The pathway for the formation of sorbitol from aldose sugars such as glucose is dependent on a rate-limiting enzyme, aldose reductase. This enzyme has a low affinity for glucose and significant amounts of sorbitol are formed only when the concentration of intracellular glucose is high. The enzyme is present in Schwann cells of peripheral nerves and epithelial cells of the lens, and it is in these two tissues that the highest concentrations of sorbitol are found. In diabetics local formation and accumulation of sorbitol may be partly responsible for peripheral neuropathy and also for cataract. It is likely to be some time before it is established that administration of a specific inhibitor of the enzyme confers significant benefit in these chronic disorders and that any risks from its use are acceptable.

PROBLEMS IN MANAGEMENT

Children

Fortunately diabetes is not common in childhood, but when it occurs it is relatively severe and always requires treatment with insulin. The therapeutic problem of matching the dose of insulin to the food intake raises practical difficulties.

Food. Since children should be growing, their energy requirements are large in proportion to their size and difficulties may be experienced in meeting them. In children, likes and dislikes for particular foods are often fickle and unpredictable. It is important to make sure that the child does not become too fat; hypoglycaemia due to too much insulin can lead to excessive appetite and hence to obesity. A diabetic child must not have sugar or sweets, but otherwise the composition of the diet need differ little from that of their friends. Everything possible should be done to avoid making them appear different from their contemporaries. As early as possible they should be encouraged to take responsibility for their own care and, once properly trained, they can take part in all normal activities. However, they should swim only in supervised pools, and avoid lonely cross-country walks. The British Diabetic Association runs special summer camps for diabetic children.

Insulin. Day-to-day requirements for insulin are often very variable. Children cannot be expected to lead the steady life of a business man or housewife; their emotions and activities fluctuate unexpectedly — sometimes wildly active and sometimes sulking. This affects their daily needs for insulin; excessive activity may result in hypoglycaemia, and lethargy in hyperglycaemia. The latter may also be caused by one of the numerous infectious diseases to which all children are prone. A combinations of one of the depot insulins and soluble insulin before breakfast and usually a second dose of soluble insulin before supper is usually a suitable arrangement.

Pregnancy

If a diabetic woman wishes to have a child there is no reason why she should avoid pregnancy, provided that she suffers from none of the more serious complications and is under close medical care.

Nevertheless pregnancy in a diabetic woman carries certain risks; in the later stages she may develop an excessive accumulation of amniotic fluid (hydramnios); in addition the fetus is sometimes unusually large, leading to difficulty in labour. Moreover the chances that she may lose her baby either from a stillbirth or in the neonatal period are greater than those of a non-diabetic mother, even with the most careful supervision. There is also an increased risk of her baby having a neural tube defect or other error in development. As the main organs of the body are formed in the early weeks of uterine life, good metabolic control should be established before conception. A planned pregnancy reduces the risk.

A pregnant diabetic patient requires close supervision by a team consisting of physician, obstetrician, anaesthetist, nurse and dietitian. The sooner the pregnancy is diagnosed the better. An expectant mother should spend a week as an ambulant in-patient in hospital towards the end of the third month of pregnancy. This enables her and the team to get to know each other and her diabetes can be brought under the best possible control; she may need further education in the management of her diet and insulin while at home. If her diabetes was previously well controlled, at first her diet need not differ from that to which she is accustomed, but later she may need more milk. Practical problems may be created by bouts of vomiting and food fads that commonly occur in the early stages of any pregnancy.

After the diagnosis of pregnancy, the patient should be seen at first fortnightly and later at weekly intervals. Continued control of the diabetes may be complicated by other factors. First, the renal threshold for glucose often falls as pregnancy advances. This leads to no ill effect but it means that tests for glycosuria at home may cease to be a reliable index of diabetic control. Further, in the later stages of pregnancy, lactosuria occasionally occurs and may lead to confusion. This can be overcome by self-monitoring of glucose in blood obtained by finger-prick. If excessive losses of glucose in the urine occur due to lowered renal threshold, additional carbohydrate feeds may be given between meals and sometimes at night, covered by suitable amounts of soluble insulin. Requirements for insulin often increase as pregnancy advances. Frequent measurements of blood glucose are needed to ensure that extra insulin is not producing hypoglycaemia; or alternatively, that hyperglycaemia is not insidiously building up.

'Pregnancy should seldom, if ever, be allowed to proceed to term. The infant has a much better chance of survival if it is delivered between the thirty-sixth and thirty-eighth weeks by induction of labour or by Caesarian section.' These sentences were written in 1959 for the first edition of our book and have been orthodox teaching for over 25 years. Today with improved glycaemic control many pregnancies are allowed to go on to full term and Caesarian section is less used. For carefully selected patients early Caesarian section has become unnecessary. Following delivery the insulin requirements of the mother fall. Frequent blood glucose estimations and co-operation between the physician and dietitian are needed to ensure an uneventful return to the former regimen.

Diabetes and surgery

Any surgical operation, however minor, and the accompanying anaesthetic, cause a metabolic stress which the diabetic is less well able to meet than the normal person. The stress is temporary and is not aggravated by a mild hyperglycaemia, but an accompanying acidosis prejudices normal recovery. The position is worse if there is tissue wasting with much breakdown of fat and protein. Two points should be kept in mind: first is the need to provide an adequate supply of energy for the tissues, and secondly, the need to be on the alert for acidosis.

In practice there are two separate problems. The first is the management of a stabilised diabetic who has to undergo an operation at a time which can be chosen by the surgeon and physician. The second is that of a diabetic whose disease may not be well controlled and who has to undergo an emergency operation; diabetes is sometimes first diagnosed when the urine is tested before an operation.

Elective surgery in a stabilised diabetic

All diabetics should be admitted to hospital about three days before an operation, even a minor one. During this period the control of the diabetes can be checked thoroughly. Provided they go to the theatre in good condition, there is unlikely to be any significant change in the blood glucose, plasma bicarbonate or ketone levels during the operation. In fact, hypoglycaemia is more likely to occur than acidosis so it is generally advisable to give no insulin immediately before operation. During the day before the operation the usual diet and morning dose of soluble insulin should be given but doses of depot insulin of more than 20 units should be reduced by half and a supplementary dose of soluble insulin given later that day instead. It is usually possible to arrange for the operation to take place in the morning. The patient should receive no breakfast and nothing by mouth before operation. Before being transferred to the theatre the fasting blood glucose level should be determined. If this lies between 7 and 11 mmol/l (120 to 200 mg/dl) then no glucose or insulin need be given. If the level is below 7 then about 25 to 40 g of glucose should be given intravenously, preferably in hypertonic solution, in order to prevent possible hypoglycaemia during the operation. No insulin is necessary. If the fasting blood glucose is over 11 mmol/l which is infrequent, then some soluble insulin is required. About one-third of the usual total daily dose is indicated, but its administration can usually be postponed until after operation.

Recovery from the anaesthetic should be carefully supervised. The sooner patients return to their usual diet the better. This interval may be a few hours or several days, depending on the nature and severity of the operation. Within a few hours after an anaesthetic many patients are able to take a fluid or semifluid feed containing 25 g of carbohydrate at three- to four-hourly intervals, covered by suitable doses of soluble insulin. Examples of feeds which may be given are: (1) 100 ml fruit juice plus 15 g sucrose; (2) 200 ml milk plus 10 g cereal plus 7 g sugar; and (3) 200 ml milk plus 20 g Ovaltine, Horlicks or similar preparation.

Some insulin-dependent diabetics after a major operation may need to have most of their energy requirements supplied as glucose, either intravenously or by mouth. If all has gone well, a single determination of the fasting blood glucose each morning suffices. If recovery is stormy, measurements may be necessary at four-hourly intervals or even more frequently.

Each specimen of urine should be tested for glucose and ketone bodies. Determination of the plasma bicarbonate and electrolytes in the blood are also helpful. The insulin dosage depends on these findings, and until stability has been regained only soluble insulin should be used.

Surgical emergencies.   Circumstances vary so much that it is impossible to consider them except in the most general way. The essentials are to maintain the oxidation of glucose by the tissues at a sufficient rate and to combat acidosis and electrolyte disturbances when they occur. This can only be done effectively if the state of the diabetic control is assessed continuously and accurately. A laboratory service that can provide rapid results is thus essential. As long as the surgical condition remains untreated and the metabolic stress continues, the diabetic condition is likely to get worse. Once the surgical condition is under control they may be expected to respond promptly to the appropriate therapy for diabetes.

PROGNOSIS

The prognosis in diabetes has improved steadily since the introduction of insulin, but even with its use the expectation of life is still less than that of a non-diabetic. It is difficult to estimate the prognosis of an individual patient because so many variable factors have to be considered. Thus the child of parents poor in means and education, who is first seen in coma, obviously has a very different future compared with the middle-aged lady in easy circumstances who complains of nothing but a little thirst and pruritus. and can afford the time and the means to follow precisely the diet prescribed. The incidence of the complications of diabetes is mainly related to the duration of the disease but probably also to the precision with which it has been controlled.

PREVENTION

Diabetes is a disease of the prosperous, and in wealthy countries it is one of the major health problems. The hardships of World War II were associated with a marked decline in the incidence of diabetes in European countries; rationing of both food and petrol was probably responsible. The importance for health of sufficient exercise and of avoiding dietary excess has been stated repeatedly. Diabetes, like obesity and atherosclerosis, is likely to arise in predisposed persons who eat too much and exercise too little.

SCREENING

It is much easier to control the disease and to maintain the health of the patient if the diagnosis is made early. In many patients, the biochemical changes can be detected before symptoms make them seek medical advice. Any screening technique is expensive and should only be used if it is likely that a significant number of new diabetics will be recognised. Groups at high risk are first-degree relatives of known diabetics, the obese and mothers of babies weighing more than 4.5 kg at birth. The prevalence of diabetes in different communities varies from less than 0.5 to 5 per cent and sometimes more. About half of the cases may be unaware that they have the disease. These figures vary widely according to the social and economic state of the people and the educational and medical services available.

Urine testing has been used as a screening procedure but is wasteful since up to 3 per cent of people may have renal glycosuria and so have to be recalled for blood tests. Estimation of the blood glucose two hours after 75 g glucose orally is recommended and autoanalysers enable large numbers of samples to be tested daily.

GENETIC COUNSELLING

Diabetic patients often consult their doctor about the advisability of having children and sometimes it is a duty to warn them of the dangers. They can be told that the risks of pregnancy and delivery are little greater for a diabetic mother than for a normal woman, provided she submits to the strict discipline required. The chances that she will produce a healthy baby are also good, but not quite so good as for a normal mother. The chances that her child will eventually develop diabetes are higher than normal. If both parents have diabetes, the probability is that about 25 per cent of their children will develop the disease at some stages in life. The risk is about half this if only one parent is affected. Many diabetics have healthy children, and how strongly a doctor should word these necessary warnings is a matter for judgment in each case.

CONCLUSION

The management of a patient with diabetes mellitus offers an opportunity for good medical and dietetic practice, there being few other chronic diseases in which efficient management makes so much difference to a patient's life. The problems presented by the aetiology of diabetes and its long-term complications continue to offer some of the most demanding and fascinating challenges in medical research today.

REFERENCES

1. Oakley W G, Pyke D A, Taylor K G 1980 Diabetes and its management, 3rd edn. Blackwell, Oxford
2. World Health Organization 1980 Report of an expert committee on diabetes. WHO Tech Rep Ser no. 646
3. West K M 1978 Epidemiology of diabetes and its vascular lesions. Elsevier, New York
4. Zimmet P 1982 Type 2 (non-insulin-dependent) diabetes — an epidemiological overview. Diabetologia 22: 399–411
5. Neel J V 1962 Diabetes: a 'thrifty' genotype rendered detrimental by 'progress'. Am J Hum Genet 14: 353–62
6. Morton R 1689 Phthisiologia. London, p. 44

7. Olefsky J M 1981 Insulin resistance and insulin action. Diabetes 30: 148–62

8. Himsworth H P 1949 Diet in the aetiology of human diabetes. Proc R Soc Med 42: 323–6

9. Cleave T L 1974 The saccharine disease. Wright, Bristol

10. Trowell H 1975 Dietary-fibre hypothesis of the etiology of diabetes mellitus. Diabetes 24: 762–5

11. Gamble D R 1980 An epidemiological study of childhood diabetes affecting two or more siblings. Diabetologia 19: 341–4

12. Tchobroutoky G 1978 Relation of diabetic control to development of vascular complications. Diabetologia 15: 143–52

13. Krall L P 1969 In: Masek J, Osankova K, Cuthbertson D P (eds) Proceedings of the eighth international nutrition congress. Excepta Medica, Amsterdam, p. 376

14. Hadden D R, Montgomery D A D, Skelly R J, et al 1975 Maturity onset diabetes: response to intensive dietary management. Br Med J 3: 276–8

15. Simmonds R 1931 Handbook of diets. Heinemann, London

16. Joslin E P 1928 The treatment of diabetes mellitus, 4th edn. Lea & Febiger, Philadelphia

17. Rabinowich I M 1935 Effects of the high carbohydrate–low calorie diet upon carbohydrate tolerance in diabetes mellitus. Can Med Assoc J 33: 136–44

18. Truswell A S, Thomas B J, Brown A M 1975 Survey of dietary policy and management in British diabetic clinics. Br Med J 4: 7–11

19. Simpson H C R, Simpson R W, Lousley S, et al 1981 A high carbohydrate leguminous fibre diet improves all aspects of diabetic control. Lancet 1: 1–5

20. Jenkins D J A, Wolever T M S, Nineham R, et al 1978 Guar crispbread in the diabetic diet. Br Med J 2: 1744–6

21. University Group Diabetes Program 1970 A study of the effects of hypoglycemic agents on vascular complication in patients with adult-onset diabetes. Diabetes 19: 789–830

22. Pickup J C, Viberti G C, Bilious R W, et al 1982 Safety of continuous insulin infusion: metabolic deterioration and glycaemic autoregulation after deliberate cessation of infusion. Diabetologia 22: 175–9

23. Foster D W, McGarry J D 1983 The metabolic derangements and treatment of diabetic ketoacidosis. N Engl J Med 309: 159–69

24. Young R J, Ewing D J, Clarke B F 1983 A controlled trial of sorbinil, an aldose reductase inhibitor, in chronic painful diabetic neuropathy. Diabetes 32: 938–42

25. Judzewitsch R G, Jaspan J B, Polonsky K S, et al 1983 Aldose reductase inhibition improves nerve conduction velocity in diabetic patients. N Engl J Med 308: 119–25

43

Gout and Hyperuricaemia

Gout is a characteristic arthritis which affects single joints, often the big toe, in painful episodes that last only a few days but are liable to recur. Middle-aged men are chiefly afflicted. It is caused by deposition in the joint of urate crystals, associated with an increased concentration of urate in the plasma, **hyperuricaemia.**

Gout is thus a clinical entity and hyperuricaemia its biochemical basis. Gout was known to the physicians of ancient Greece and Rome. The classical description was written in 1663 by Sydenham, himself a lifelong sufferer, who clearly differentiated it from other joint disorders. Hyperuricaemia was first demonstrated in gouty patients in 1848 by Sir Alfred Garrod, who should not be confused with Sir Archibald Garrod (p. 346). Subsequent research showed that it results from abnormal purine metabolism which is usually primary and then partly of genetic origin. Less commonly it occurs secondary to renal and certain metabolic diseases.

Hyperuricaemia may be, and often is, asymptomatic. Such individuals, however, carry a greatly increased chance of the clinical complications, gouty arthritis, or uric acid stones in the urinary tract. Those who have recurrent gout and hyperuricaemia over a long time are liable to develop tophi, accumulations of urate in tendons or cartilage. Epidemiological studies also show significant associations between hyperuricaemia and several of the common degenerative diseases of affluent societies, such as hypertension and atherosclerotic diseases.

AETIOLOGY

Table 43.1 shows data for a small North American town and probably reflects the prevalence in most Western countries, 3.0 per cent of all men over 30 years and 0.4 per cent of women. The prevalence of gout was directly related to the plasma urate concentration and most cases occurred in association with concentrations over 420 μmol/l (7.0 mg/100 ml) in men and 355 μmol/l (6.0 mg/100 ml) in women.

That primary gout is a disease in which both genetic and environmental factors play is illustrated by the Maoris (Table 43.2). There is a high prevalence amongst the Maoris on the remote Pacific island of Puka Puka, who live today under the same conditions as their forefathers have for at least 2000 years. The prevalence is nearly twice as high in the Maoris in New Zealand who originally emigrated from islands like Puka Puka and now lead a Westernised life. The European population of New Zealand has a lower prevalence, similar to that in Framingham, USA.

The Maoris and others around the Pacific — Filipinos, Marianas Islanders and the Blackfoot and Pima Indians of the United States — have high plasma urates. In other parts of the world such as Africa the frequency of gout and hyperuricaemia appears to be less than in Western communities.

Gout tends to be familial and about 25 per cent of the relatives of patients have hyperuricaemia. In some

Table 43.1 Serum uric acid concentrations and the prevalence of gouty arthritis in men and women aged 30 years or over in Framingham, Massachusetts[1]

| Serum uric acid | | Men | | | Women | | |
μmol/l	mg/dl	Number examined	Gouty arthritis Number	Per cent	Number examined	Gouty arthritis Number	per cent
<355	<6	1281	8	0.6	2665	2	0.1
355–410	6–6.9	790	15	1.9	151	5	3.3
420–475	7–7.9	162	27	16.7	23	4	17.4
480–535	8–8.9	40	10	25.0	4	0	—
535+	9+	10	9	90.0	1	0	—

Table 43.2 Prevalence of gouty arthritis in Maori and Causasian men and women over 30 years of age[2]

Race	Habitat	Prevalence of gouty arthritis (per cent)	
		Men	Women
Maori	Puka Puka	7.0	0
Maori	New Zealand	13.3	1.4
Caucasian	New Zealand	2.4	0

families transmission patterns suggest an autosomal dominant inheritance with low penetrance, especially in females.

Gout is rare in boys before puberty and in women until after the menopause. Hippocrates noted this and added that eunuchs were not affected. The concentration of plasma urate is low in children. It rises in boys at puberty so that the average value is about 90 μmol/l (1.5 mg/dl) higher in men than women. In women plasma urate falls during pregnancy. It goes up at the menopause and thereafter runs only a little below the male average. Plasma urate is lowered by oestrogens, and gout may occur in women given androgen therapy.

It was recognised in the eighteenth century that large enjoyable meals and the consumption of alcoholic drinks were often the prelude to an attack of gout. Doctors often imposed some sort of dietary discipline on their gouty patients. When Garrod showed that gout was characterised by an increase in blood urate this provided an apparent rational basis for dietetic treatment. For a time it was assumed that this increase in urate was derived directly from the diet and patients were advised to restrict meat and other food rich in purines. We now know that dietary nucleoproteins contribute, at most, only 50 per cent of the urate present in the blood of normal people and cannot account for the high concentrations found in gout. Most of the urate is formed endogenously. When effective uricosuric drugs were introduced, starting with probenecid in the 1950s, dietary treatment for patients with gout came to take very much of a second place, and patients were only advised to avoid excessive intake of food rich in purines.

The fact remains, however, that gout is a disease of the wealthy and disappears in times of need. At the end of the Second World War it was exceedingly rare in Germany. Epidemiological and metabolic information

has accumulated which shows several ways in which diet can contribute to underlying hyperuricaemia or precipitate an attack of gout.

Overweight. Many patients who first develop gout in middle life are overweight. Table 43.3 shows how the mean blood urate increases as relative weight creeps up in British business executives. At the other end of the world, obesity is thought to be an important factor accounting for the higher plasma urates and frequency of gout in New Zealand Maoris compared with primitive Polynesian islanders.

Alcohol. In an earlier age doctors observed empirically that an acute attack of gout might be precipitated by over-indulgence in alcohol. Port and Madeira wine were thought to be especially dangerous. This was probably because of associated social and dietary habits. It is now known that plasma urate is higher in men who habitually consume too much alcohol in any form and that it is raised by a binge. The mechanism is probably that the associated increase in plasma lactate inhibits renal excretion of urate.

Dietary purines. When gouty subjects are put on a low purine diet, plasma urate may fall by 1.0 mg/dl or even more. Not all purines have the same effect on plasma urate, and RNA raises it more than DNA.[4] Old tables giving the purine content of vegetables varies greatly and some low purine foods may contain more purine per unit of energy than meat.

Starvation. Plasma urate rises, starting after only one day, and can reach 10 mg/dl. The hyperuricaemia coincides with the development of ketosis and comes about because ketoacids reduce the renal excretion of urate. Attacks of gout have been reported in obese patients treated by total starvation. This is important when someone with a tendency to gout stops eating because of an acute illness or an operation.

Fructose. A temporary increase in plasma urate occurs after an infusion or oral dose of fructose, due to rapid phosphorylation of fructose causing instability of AMP in the liver. The unstable AMP breaks down to adenosine and ultimately to uric acid.[5]

Many famous men in history suffered from gout, including Alexander the Great, Luther, Newton, Milton, Harvey, Dr Johnson, Franklin and Louis XIV. To Sydenham it seemed that 'more wise men than fools are victims', though there are many exceptions. In our

Table 43.3 Mean blood urate and weight, as percentage of expected weight, in British male business executives[3]

	Relative weight							
	80	80–	90–	110–	100–	120–	130+	Total
Number of men	114	616	1996	2660	1415	463	180	7444
Mean blood urate (mg/100 ml)	5.16	5.39	5.72	6.01	6.27	6.46	6.66	5.96
(μmol/l)	300	325	345	360	375	390	400	355

own times its frequency in university professors and business executives has prompted the hypothesis that a moderately high concentration of urate may be a cerebral stimulant. Caffeine, the stimulant in coffee and tea, only differs chemically from uric acid in having three extra methyl groups on the purine ring.

Normal man and the primates are hyperuricaemic compared to most mammals, whose serum urate is about 12 to 18 μmol/l (0.2 to 0.3 mg/dl). This is because during evolution primates have lost the liver enzyme uricase, which breaks uric acid down to allantoin.

Secondary gout

In some cases gout occurs secondary to another disease, either one which impairs renal excretion such as chronic renal failure, or a condition which leads to overproduction of urate such as proliferative haemopoietic disorders like leukaemia, polycythaemia or myelofibrosis, and the skin disease, psoriasis. A few drugs have the side-effect of reducing urate excretion, the most important being the thiazide diuretics. The Lesch-Nyhan syndrome[6] is a rare inborn error of metabolism in which an affected boy has choreoathetosis, mental deficiency, and a strikingly aggressive personality associated with gout and urate stones.

CHEMICAL PATHOLOGY

Uric acid is 2,6,8-trioxypurine (Fig. 43.1). It ionises weakly at N-9. Its pK is 5.8 so that at the pH of plasma, it is almost completely dissociated and circulates as the monovalent urate ion. In urine, which usually has a lower pH, it is excreted for the most part as the free acid.

Uric acid is the ultimate oxidation product of the purine bases, adenine and guanine. The enzyme for the last step, xanthine oxidase, contains molybdenum.

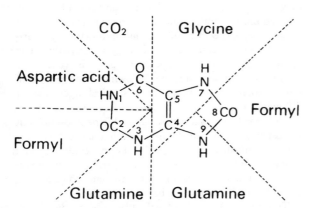

Fig. 43.1 Uric acid and the origins of the purine ring

Adenine and guanine are synthesised as part of the body's nucleoproteins from the simple precursors indicated in Figure 43.1. This summarises the many chemical steps in building up AMP and GMP. Thus purines are synthesised from three non-essential amino acids, glycine, aspartic acid and glutamine, and from one-carbon units, which are all freely available in the body's metabolic pools. The formyl units are supplied by THFA (folic acid) derivatives.

Studies with ^{15}N-glutamine indicate that the miscible pool of urate in body fluids is normally about 70 mmol (1.2 g). There are two sources of this pool, exogenous and endogenous. The exogenous source is the diet; a good Western diet contains sufficient purines to provide 30 to 60 mmol (0.5 to 1.0 g) of urate/day. About 20 per cent of the dietary purines are destroyed in the process of digestion; but the greater part goes to form urate in the body's miscible pool. The endogenous source is from breakdown of purines made in nucleoprotein synthesis. The extent of endogenous urate production can be judged by the fact that on a purine-free diet the excretion of uric acid is 18 to 60 mmol (0.3 to 0.5 g)/day.

The amount of urate destroyed in the body is small. Studies with ^{15}N-urate show that about 15 per cent of the miscible pool is catabolised daily and this takes place by bacterial action in the gut. Gouty patients may break down rather more than normal people. But the major way in which urate is lost from the body is by excretion in the urine, normally around 45 per cent of the miscible pool daily.

In gout the miscible pool of urate is enlarged and ranges from 120 to 1800 mmol (2 to 30 g). But in tophaceous gout only the peripheral layers of the tophi are readily exchangeable and the body's total urate can therefore be even larger. At least one-third of patients with gout are overproducers of urate with a high urinary excretion on low purine diets. In them there appears to be some acceleration of the first, rate-limiting step in purine synthesis;

5-Phosphoribosyl-1-pyrophosphate+glutamine
→ 5-phosphoribosylamine+glutamic acid
  + pyrophosphate

Whether or not they are overproducers of urate, gouty subjects have a somewhat lower rate of uric acid excretion at any given plasma urate concentration than have non-gouty subjects.

CLINICAL FEATURES

The first attack of gout is often a dramatic and alarming experience. The patient has usually enjoyed good health until his early forties, and then suddenly (often in the middle of the night) has an agonising, stabbing pain in one joint, generally the metatarsophalangeal joint of the big toe. The joint attacked is thought to be determined by its susceptibility to minor injury; the big toe is easily stubbed or injured by an ill-fitting shoe. The wrists, ankles and knees are much less common sites. As a rule it is peripheral rather than central joints that are affected; the spine is practically immune.

The joint is swollen and exquisitely tender; pain is aggravated by the least movement. The overlying skin is tense, red and shiny with distended veins and may later show oedema. Fever, malaise, loss of appetite, gastrointestinal upset and scanty highly coloured urine are common accompaniments. The patient may with good reason be very irritable. Blood examination often shows a raised erythrocyte sedimentation rate and a polymorph leucocytosis.

Even without treatment the natural tendency is for the attack to pass off after a few days. As the inflammation subsides the skin over the joint becomes scaly and itches. The joint recovers completely. There may be no further episodes for years but if the underlying hyperuricaemia is high and not regulated, attacks tend to occur with increasing frequency and to last longer. Eventually a stage may be reached where there is chronic, persistent, though generally less painful arthritis of several joints. During this phase **tophi** begin to appear; these are crystalline deposits of sodium urate which develop in the lobes of the ear, at the base of the big toe, in other toes or fingers, in the olecranon bursa behind the elbow or in tendon sheaths on the back of the hand. A tophus may vary in size from a pin head to a golf ball. It is usually painless. When tophi develop in joints they erode the neighbouring bone and appear on radiographs as clear, punched-out areas, since sodium urate is not radio-opaque.

Production of arthritis

Acute gouty arthritis is a non-infective inflammation with a polymorphonuclear exudate in the joint and intense congestion around it. Sudden changes in the plasma urate are likely to provoke an attack, whether the concentration is rising or falling from a previously high level. A careful search of fluid from gouty joints usually shows needle-shaped, birefringent crystals of sodium urate. Injection of urate microcrystals into the knees of healthy volunteers brought on in two hours acute arthritis that closely resembled gout in both its local and general effects. Faires and McCarty[7] who did these courageous experiments on one another were both prostrated with excruciating pain after four hours. When their joints were aspirated many of the urate crystals in the fluid were found to be inside polymorphs. In the pathogenesis of acute gout there appears to be a vicious cycle in which precipitation of sodium urate

crystals from supersaturated body fluids evokes a polymorph response. The polymorphs phagocytose the urate crystals and this raises their metabolic activity, increases the local lactate concentration and lowers the pH, which favours further crystal formation in the joint.

Complications

People with hyperuricaemia have a greatly increased liability to form **uric acid stones** in the urinary tract. These can present with renal colic and are one cause of the chronic renal disease that is an important late complication in gout. Uric acid stones are seen in hyperuricaemic patients who excrete normal amounts of uric acid as well as in the overexcretors. The reason appears to be that the urine is unusually acid, thus reducing the solubility of uric acid and this acidity is related to reduced NH_4^+ excretion. The NH_4^+ which is excreted has been formed in the kidneys mostly from glutamine. In gout the kidneys may receive decreased amounts of glutamine because more has been diverted into purine synthesis.

The Framingham study showed increased incidence of coronary heart disease in persons with asymptomatic hyperuricaemia. Hyperuricaemia is associated with hypertriglyceridaemia, but not with hypercholesterolaemia.

There is also an association between hyperuricaemia and hypertension, which is only partly explicable by the action of some drugs used for hypertension, like thiazide diuretics, that are known to decrease urate excretion. Degenerative renal disease occurs in patients with chronic gout, and hypertension itself appears to reduce uric acid clearance. It is not surprising that raised plasma urates have been reported in patients with cerebral vascular disease.

DIAGNOSIS

When the classic site, the big toe, is affected, clinical diagnosis is usually straightforward and is confirmed by a raised plasma urate. But when other joints are affected it must be borne in mind that asymptomatic hyperuricaemia can coincide with non-gouty arthropathy. The clinical setting for an attack of gout is sometimes confusing. It may come on following some period of stress, such as an injury or a surgical operation or following a myocardial infarction. Response of monoarticular arthritis to a course of colchicine is useful, but not infallible evidence of gout. If tophi are present, urate can be confirmed chemically by the murexide test in a biopsy; tophi and punched out translucent juxta-articular lesions on radiographs are late changes and gout should be diagnosed before this stage.

There is another type of arthritis caused by deposition of crystals of calcium pyrophosphate in joints, sometimes called 'pseudogout'. Large joints are usually involved, especially the knees, which show calcification of articular cartilage. It does not respond to colchicine and the plasma urate is normal.

TREATMENT

Some patients, after a single attack, remain in a state of natural remission for years without further disability. They do not need drugs, but require advice about diet and way of life and arrangements for periodic follow-up of the plasma urate. In other patients attacks of gout are frequent and plasma urate is high. Regular and continued medical treatment is needed both to relieve the arthritis and to reduce the risk of late complications.

Drugs

These are used for two purposes. First there are drugs which relieve the acute arthritis, but do not affect plasma urate concentrations. The oldest effective remedy for acute gout is colchicine, the alkaloid from the autumn crocus (*Colchicum autumnale, L.*). This plant has been used as specific treatment for over 200 years and was introduced into America for this purpose by Benjamin Franklin. It appears to act by inhibiting the polymorph response to urate crystals and so breaking the vicious cycle. The dose is 0.5 mg every hour or 1 mg two-hourly until relief is obtained (usually at 4 to 8 mg total dose) or diarrhoea supervenes. If the response to colchicine is too slow or diarrhoea too troublesome, it may be reinforced with or replaced by a short course of phenylbutazone or of corticotrophin or one of the adrenal corticosteroids. During the acute attack the patient gets little rest from pain, which is always worse at night. He should be in bed and the joint made as comfortable as possible by supporting it on pillows and protecting it from pressure and knocks.

The second group of drugs reduce the pool of urate in the body and hence deal with the underlying biochemical abnormality. They have to be given for months or years. Probenecid, introduced in 1952, is a uricosuric agent, i.e. it impairs the reabsorption of uric acid by the renal tubules and so increases uric acid excretion in the urine usually by 30 to 50 per cent. As its administration is continued, plasma urate falls and later the frequency of arthritis decreases and tophi regress. Sulphinpyrazone is another drug of this type. Aspirin should not be given at the same time as uricosuric agents because it interferes with their action on the renal tubules.

The use of uricosuric drugs is difficult if patients already have renal damage or a history of uric acid stones. Ample fluids should be given to reduce the risk of further stone formation. In such patients and when there is gross overproduction of uric acid the newer drug allopurinol is the preferred treatment. It acts by inhibiting xanthine oxidase so that uric acid production is reduced and the patient excretes instead xanthine and hypoxanthine, which are more soluble.

Neither probenecid nor allopurinol have any direct effect on gouty arthritis; indeed when treatment to reduce the body's pool of urate is started attacks of gout are liable to occur, and prophylactic doses of colchicine, 0.5 mg three times a day, should be given for the first two or three months. Other adverse effects are unusual with these drugs.

Diet

The dietary advice for a patient who has had one or more attacks of primary gout should be based on the following principles, which arise from the epidemiological and metabolic findings discussed earlier.

If the patient is overweight, he should be advised to bring his weight down by a gentle dietary regimen. This has been demonstrated to produce a moderate reduction of plasma urate.[8] But fasting, even for short periods, is likely to do more harm than good and may induce an attack of gout.

Feasting should equally be avoided. Heavy, rich meals high in purines or fat are likely to raise the plasma urate and may be followed by an acute attack.

Excessive alcohol is sometimes the underlying stress which precipitates gout. People are prone to understate their alcohol consumption, and the patient should be told that all types of alcoholic drinks need to be restricted. A compromise prescription of 'reasonable amounts' can all too easily be interpreted by the patient with too much latitude. Men who take more than two drinks a day have plasma urate concentrations higher than normal.[3]

For the small minority of patients with severe gout who respond poorly or are intolerant to uricosuric drugs a strict low-purine regimen along the lines recommended by Zöllner[4] may be valuable. But for the majority of patients urate-lowering drugs are so effective and so easy to take that the only modification of dietary purine necessary is to avoid foods rich in purine, e.g. liver, kidneys, sweetbreads, sardines, anchovies, fish roes and meat extracts.

Because of the increased risk of stone in the urinary tract patients should maintain a good intake of non-alcoholic fluids, and take a drink of water before going to bed. Coffee and tea, although they contain methyl-xanthines such as caffeine, can be drunk because caffeine is not converted into uric acid in the body.

Lastly it is wise to check fasting plasma lipids and treat hyperlipidaemia if present, and to give gouty subjects some advice on dietary and other measures which may reduce the risk of coronary heart disease.

REFERENCES

1. Hall A P, Barry P E, Dawber T R, McNamara P M 1967 Epidemiology of gout and hyperuricemia. Am J Med 42: 27–37
2. Prior I A M 1971 The price of civilization. Nutr Today 6(4): 2–11
3. Phoon W H, Pincherle G 1972 Blood uric acid in executives. Br J Biol Med 29: 334–7.
4. Zöllner N 1973 Influence of various purines on uric acid metabolism. Bibl Nutr Dieta 19: 34–43
5. Woods H F, Alberti K C M 1972 Dangers of intravenous fructose. Lancet 2: 1354–7
6. Lesch M, Nyhan W L 1964 A familial disorder of uric acid metabolism and central nervous system function. Am J Med 36: 561–70
7. Faires J S, McCarty D J 1962 Acute arthritis in man and dogs after intrasynovial injection of sodium urate crystals. Lancet 2: 682–4
8. Nicholls A, Scott J T 1972 Effect of weight-loss on plasma and urinary levels of uric acid. Lancet 2: 1223–4

44

Diseases of the Kidneys and Urinary Tract

The dietetic treatment of patients with renal disease has undergone many changes as a result of the widespread availability of artificial kidneys (dialysis) and kidney transplantation. In many centres patients who would have died from terminal renal failure now have a reasonable chance of living for years in good health. With improvements in the use of the artificial kidney, patients on regular dialysis have been liberated from some of the dietary restrictions that were previously thought necessary. The recipient of a successful, well-functioning renal transplant can usually eat normally with few restrictions on food and fluid intake. While these developments have made the task of the dietitian easier in some respects, her role in the treatment of other renal disorders remains unchanged. Dietetics still forms the cornerstone of treatment when renal function is modified or impaired by disease.

PHYSIOLOGY

The management of patients with renal disorders is firmly grounded on an understanding of how the kidneys work in health and how their function is disturbed by disease processes.

The kidneys are each composed of approximately one million similar functional units called nephrons. Each nephron consists of a glomerulus which is a tuft of capillaries invaginated into an epithelial sac (Bowman's capsule), from which arises a tubule. The blood flow through the kidneys is large, amounting to about one-quarter of the cardiac output at rest, i.e. 1300 ml/min. Branches of the renal artery give rise to afferent arterioles which divide to form the glomerular capillaries. These unite to form the efferent arterioles which supply blood to the renal tubules.

The hydrostatic pressure within the glomerular capillaries results in the filtration of fluid into Bowman's capsule. This fluid is similar in composition with plasma, except that it normally contains no fat and very little protein.

The filtrate, formed at the glomerulus at a rate of 100 ml/min, passes first into the proximal convoluted tubule and from there through the loop of Henle and distal convoluted tubule to the collecting ducts. It is modified according to the needs of the body by the selective reabsorption of its constituents and of water, and by tubular secretion. Of the 150 000 ml of water and 22 500 mmol of sodium filtered through the glomerular capillaries during the course of a day, only about 1500 ml of water and 100–200 mmol of sodium remain to be excreted as urine.

The kidneys are essential for maintaining many aspects of the internal chemical environment of the body. Their main functions are indicated in Table 44.1. As excretory organs they remove such waste products of nitrogen metabolism as urea, uric acid and creatinine, as well as hydrogen ions and sulphates which arise from degradation of sulphur-containing amino acids. They also excrete surplus quantities of water, sodium, potassium, calcium, phosphate, magnesium and other ions.

The kidneys regulate the amounts of water, sodium, hydrogen ions and several other electrolytes in the body. By modifying the composition of the urine they maintain not only the volume of the body fluids but also their electrolytic composition within very narrow limits. In the healthy adult, for example, extreme responses to dehydration and overhydration are produced by a change in either direction of only 2 per cent in the water content of the body. The daily urinary volume can be reduced from the usual 1500 ml to only 500 ml, following water deprivation, and increased to approximately 20 litres following the ingestion of a sufficiently large volume of water.

The kidneys are the exclusive site for the production of 1,25-dihydroxy vitamin D, the most active metabolite of the vitamin which acts on the intestine to increase calcium absorption, and maintains normal mineralisation of bone. They also produce erythopoietin and renin. Erythopoietin acts on the bone marrow to increase production of red blood cells. Renin is released from the kidneys in response to a low blood pressure or sodium deficiency; it enhances the production of angiotensin which increases the blood pressure directly and

Table 44.1 Functions of kidneys

	Daily load for an adult	Effects of renal failure
EXCRETION		
Nitrogenous metabolites		
Urea	(dietary protein × ⅓) g	Increased plasma
Uric aicd	4 mmol	concentrations,
Creatinine	10 mmol	uraemia
Other metabolites		
Sulphate	25–40 mmol	Acidosis
Hydrogen ions	40–80 mmol	
Surplus nutrients		
Water	1500–5000 ml*	Hypertension,
Sodium	100–200 mmol	oedema.
Potassium	60–80 mmol	Hyperkalaemia
Calcium	2–7 mmol	—
Chloride	100–200 mmol	As for sodium
Phosphate	20–40 mmol	Hyperparathyroidism
REGULATION		
Water — total body content, osmolality		
Sodium — extracellular fluid volume, blood pressure		Loss of
Potassium — plasma concentration, neuromuscular excitability		homeostasis and flexibility in
Hydrogen — level of acidity in cells and plasma		extreme conditions
Magnesium — plasma concentration		
METABOLIC		
Vitamin D — 1α-hydroxylation		Bone disease
Erythropoietin synthesis		Anaemia
Renin synthesis		?
Hormone degradation		?

*Including 'one over the eight' on Saturday night.

also stimulates production of aldosterone. Several polypeptide hormones, including parathyroid hormone, calcitonin, insulin and gastrin are degraded by the kidneys.

ASSESSMENT OF RENAL FUNCTION

Clinical observation and biochemical analysis of plasma and urine can be used in conjunction to provide a reliable assessment of renal function and the patient's needs. Used in isolation they can be misleading. Many symptoms and signs are not specific, but are often valuable guides to therapy. Thirst, polyuria and polydipsia are features of diabetes mellitus and insipidus as well as of chronic renal failure. In all three conditions they indicate not only that the kidneys are unable to conserve water, but also that the patient has an increased requirement for water which must be satisfied if fluid balance is to be maintained. Peripheral oedema and pulmonary oedema indicate that the extracellular fluid volume is increased by at least 2 litres in adults with a corresponding increase in total body sodium. Both arise from failure of renal regulation of sodium homeostasis, which

can result from cardiac failure as easily as from intrinsic renal disease. Whatever the cause, the patient benefits from measures designed to promote net loss of sodium from the body. The absence of oedema, hypertension and polyuria in a patient with biochemical signs of advanced renal failure sometimes indicate the presence of excessive renal sodium loss due to defective tubular reabsorption of sodium. This condition often responds to an increase in sodium intake, with restoration of total body sodium, extracellular fluid and plasma volumes, and with improvement in renal blood flow, **glomerular filtration rate** (GFR) and overall renal function.

Measurement of plasma concentrations of urea, creatinine, sodium, potassium, bicarbonate, calcium, inorganic phosphate and alkaline phosphatase provides inexpensive and convenient biochemical indices of renal function.

Changes in the excretory function of the kidney are reflected in plasma urea and creatinine concentrations. If their production rates remain unchanged, their concentrations double when GFR is halved. In patients with established renal failure these measurements provide a simple guide to the progress of disease.

A substance that is neither secreted nor reabsorbed

in the tubules, e.g. creatinine, can be used to measure GFR. If U and P are the concentrations in the urine and plasma respectively and V is the volume of urine excreted in 1 min, then UV/P is the **clearance** of the substance. GFR is conveniently estimated by measuring creatinine clearance. Its value is about 125 ml/min in healthy young men; it is related to the size of the kidneys, which are related to the size of the body, and so is usually a little less in young women. GFR falls slowly with age and at 70 years is about 75 per cent of the value in youth. There is a large reserve of glomerular function. Kidney failure rarely produces symptoms until the GFR falls below 30 ml/min.

The regulatory function of the kidneys with respect to potassium and phosphate ions is reflected directly in their plasma concentrations, whereas the renal contribution to hydrogen ion homeostasis is reflected in the plasma bicarbonate concentration. The secondary effects of renal dysfunction on vitamin D and bone metabolism are often indicated by changes in plasma calcium and alkaline phosphatase concentrations.

Paradoxically, the plasma sodium concentration reflects a change in body water as often as a change in sodium balance, being increased in dehydration and decreased in overhydration or in water intoxication. Since sodium is an important determinant of extracellular and plasma volumes, changes in body sodium are more reliably assessed clinically in terms of the presence or absence of peripheral oedema and by measurement of arterial blood pressure.

The volume of the urine is variably increased, normal, or decreased at different stages of acute and chronic renal failure. While the urine volume is often the most important factor in determining water balance, other sensible and insensible losses must be taken into account when assessing the fluid requirements of a patient. Since 1 litre of water weighs 1 kilogram, an invaluable guide to changes in body water is to weigh the patient at the same time each day or at each clinic visit under standard conditions.

Abnormal urinary constituents such as blood and protein do not always indicate the presence of kidney disease, but call for further investigation of the kidneys and urinary tract. In glomerulonephritis both the activity of the disease process and the response to treatment can be followed by measuring the quantity of protein excreted in a 24 h collection of urine. The same sample can be used to measure creatinine clearance. The excretion rates of sodium and potassium can be easily measured, and can be used to assess either the response to diuretic therapy or requirements for dietary supplements. In certain primary and secondary disorders of the renal tubules, there may be excessive loss of electrolytes such as sodium, potassium or magnesium. which can be diagnosed only by giving the patient a diet

low in one of these substances and observing whether the urinary excretion is reduced appropriately.

PRINCIPLES OF DIETETICS IN RENAL DISORDERS

Diseases affecting the kidneys disturb renal function in a limited number of ways. Frequently prescription of appropriate dietetic therapy is a logical way to help a patient compensate for the altered pattern of renal excretion and regulation.

As can be seen in Table 44.1, a major task of the kidneys is the elimination from the body of surplus nutrients taken in by mouth. When renal function is greatly reduced, homeostasis may often be maintained by reducing oral consumption of water, sodium, potassium and magnesium to no more than minimum requirements. In addition, by reducing intake of protein, the production of urea, the principal nitrogenous waste metabolite, is reduced substantially. These dietetic measures form the basis for the conservative management of severe acute and chronic renal failure.

In other renal disorders the capacity of the kidney to excrete sodium is impaired, with little or no loss of other excretory and regulatory functions. This can be treated by reducing the dietary intake of sodium.

Certain diseases, e.g. the nephrotic syndrome, damage the glomerular capillaries and result in massive loss of albumin and other proteins from the plasma into the urine. Increasing dietary intake of protein allows increased hepatic synthesis of albumin which compensates in part for the urinary losses.

Diseases affecting the renal tubules can result in excessive urinary losses of water, sodium, potassium, phosphate and other substances, either alone or in combination. These losses can usually be replaced by an appropriate increase in oral intake.

Dietetic principles are still of major importance in the successful management of the patients with renal disease, despite the introduction of effective diuretic agents which inhibit tubular reabsorption of sodium and water, and the use of the artificial kidney. In sodium-retaining states, for example, the therapeutic effect of diuretics in increasing the urinary excretion of sodium is enhanced if the oral intake of sodium is also limited. In many patients who appear to have refractory oedema, the effectiveness of the diuretic regimen may have been lost by the continued consumption of an unlimited quantity of sodium chloride by mouth. In these circumstances, the only additional measure required for therapy to be successful is to reduce oral sodium intake. Even when renal function is lost completely, dietetic measures alone may hold the patient in reasonable homeostasis for several days before artificial kidney treatment becomes necessary to sustain life and health. Such conservative treatment may be sufficient in a metabolically stable patient with a short self-limiting disturbance in renal function.

Unfortunately, severe constraints upon eating habits are poorly tolerated, not only for social reasons but also because they affect the supply of essential nutrients, and patients often feel hungry. In practice, the need to sustain general nutrition becomes a major consideration. Dietetic measures cannot compensate for other aspects of disordered renal function, and in both acute and chronic renal failure many of the roles played by the dietitian have been taken over by the artificial kidney.

THE ARTIFICIAL KIDNEY

Peritoneal dialysis and haemodialysis refer to the two different ways in which urea, creatinine and other water-soluble substances of small molecular weight can be removed from the blood by diffusion across a semipermeable membrane into fluid that can be drained away. In peritoneal dialysis fluid is introduced into the peritoneal cavity where it is separated from the blood capillaries by the natural cellular peritoneal membrane. In haemodialysis the blood is taken from the patient and passed through a haemodialyser in which the blood is separated from the dialysis fluid by an artificial cellophane membrane.

Peritoneal dialysis

The first demonstration that peritoneal lavage might benefit humans with renal failure as well as animals was in 1923. Sterile dialysis fluid containing sodium, calcium, magnesium and chloride in approximately the same concentrations as in normal plasma is run into the peritoneal cavity through an indwelling cannula. Urea, creatinine, potassium, phosphate, toxic metabolites and certain drugs diffuse from the blood into the fluid and are drained away after a suitable equilibration period. Acidosis can be corrected by including lactate in the dialysis fluid. Lactate diffuses from the dialysis fluid into the plasma and is metabolised with the consumption of one hydrogen ion for each molecule of lactate. Surplus water is removed osmotically. Glucose is added to the dialysis fluid to increase the osmotic pressure and to draw water across the peritoneal membrane from the plasma. Sodium is removed simultaneously, since the water drawn into the peritoneal cavity dilutes the dialysis fluid and causes a fall in the sodium concentration; this generates a concentration gradient for the diffusion of sodium from plasma into dialysis fluid. Sodium can also be removed by using dialysis fluid in which the sodium concentration is somewhat lower than in the plasma.

Peritoneal dialysis is now a standard treatment for both acute and chronic renal failure, but two contrasting approaches have evolved regarding the delivery of dialysis fluid into the peritoneal cavity, and the time taken for treatment.

Intermittent peritoneal dialysis. Used for many years as standard maintenance treatment for patients with chronic renal failure, this is now more commonly reserved for treatment in acute renal failure when haemodialysis cannot be used. It is less efficient than haemodialysis and takes longer to perform, but has the valuable advantage for small hospitals in being simpler. In addition the equipment is relatively inexpensive and does not require special installation.

The dialysis fluid is usually stored in vats above the patient and run in by gravity. A simple timing device controls clamps on the tubing to regulate the flow of fluid into the peritoneal cavity and drainage into a large vat at the bedside. For stable patients with no recent abdominal surgery, 2 litres of fluid can be used for each exchange, on an hourly cycle which incorporates an equilibration period of 30 minutes. For patient with chronic renal failure 20–30 litres of dialysis fluid would be required, taking 10–15 hours and usually carried out

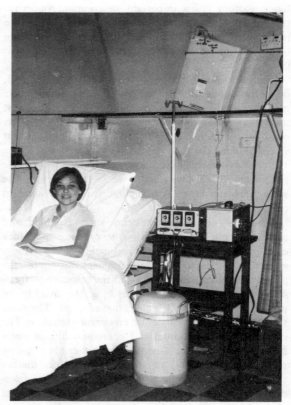

Fig. 44.1 A patient with chronic failure on maintenance peritoneal dialysis

overnight three to five times per week. Strict asepsis is necessary to avoid peritonitis. A patient on intermittent peritoneal dialysis is shown in Figure 44.1. Seriously ill patients tolerate smaller volumes of dialysis fluid better, and a shorter cycle may be needed for longer periods.

Continuous ambulatory peritoneal dialysis (CAPD) has revolutionised treatment for many patients with chronic renal failure. Two litres of dialysis fluid are run into the peritoneal cavity by gravity from a plastic bag which is then rolled up and tucked into a belt or pocket. The patient then stands up and walks away. Six to eight hours later, after a period of continuous dialysis, which allows complete equilibration between the peritoneal fluid and plasma for small molecules such as urea and creatinine, potassium and phosphate, the bag is unrolled and the fluid drained back. The bag with its 'uriniferous' load is disconnected and replaced by a fresh bag with two more litres of sterile dialysis fluid. The process is repeated three or four times daily, seven days weekly for as long as the patient needs treatment.

The advantages are that no special equipment is needed, and the bag change can be carried out by the patient unaided at home, at work, or indeed anywhere within reach of a wash-basin and clean horizontal surface to lay out the bag and sterile dressings. A patient preparing for a bag change is shown in Figure 44.2. Since the process of dialysis takes place without interruption, there are no lengthy intervals when metabolites and surplus nutrients accumulate and have to be regulated dietetically. In particular salt and water can be removed continuously, and thus few restrictions need be placed on their consumption.

The principal disadvantage is that even greater care is needed if micro-organisms are not to be introduced into the peritoneal cavity from the air or from dirty fingers, since the sterile contents of the dialysis tubing are exposed at each bag change between 21 and 28 times weekly. Not surprisingly the risk of peritonitis is much greater and not all patients with renal failure can maintain the requisite standard of hygiene at all times.

Haemodialysis

A haemodialysis machine to purify the blood continuously in an extracorporeal circuit was first used successfully by Dr Willem J. Kolff in occupied Holland in 1943. Since then, haemodialysis equipment has been modified extensively with a considerable reduction in size and a corresponding rise in efficiency. The disposable device shown in Figure 44.3 brings the patient's blood and dialysis fluid together on opposite sides of a cellophane membrane and has an excretory capacity for urea and creatinine of between two and three normal human kidneys. Since blood is pumped through the extracorporeal circuit at a rate of 200 ml/min, the patient has to be protected against the hazards which would arise if a leak developed, a clot formed, or if air was drawn into the system. This is effected by a series of monitors controlled electronically and incorporated into the dialysis machine. This machine also produces dialysis fluid by mixing tap-water in a fixed proportion with a concentrated solution of salts. The fluid is warmed to blood temperature, drawn through the dialyser and pumped off to waste with its additional load of urea and creatinine and other metabolites removed from the blood. Figure 44.4 shows the dialyser and supporting equipment. It can be truly regarded as an artificial kidney, producing a continuous supply of artificial urine!

Haemodialysis works in a comparable fashion to peritoneal dialysis. The dialysis fluid is similar in composition, except that acetate is used instead of lactate for correction of acidosis. Sodium and water are removed by applying a hydrostatic rather than an osmotic pressure differential across the semipermeable membrane.

With improvements in dialyser design, haemodialysis is now much more efficient than peritoneal dialysis.

Fig. 44.2 A patient on peritoneal dialysis preparing for a bag change

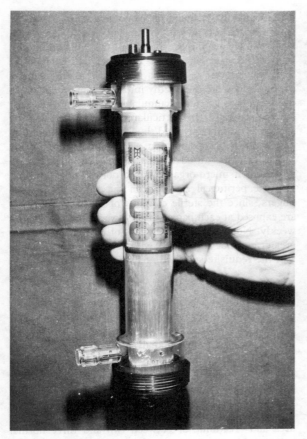

Fig. 44.3 A disposable dialyser

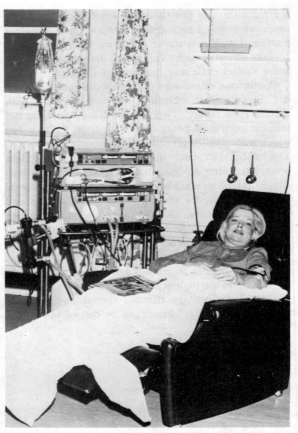

Fig. 44.4 A patient with chronic renal failure on maintenance haemodialysis

Many patients with chronic renal failure require no more than four hours on dialysis repeated three times a week. The procedure is somewhat more complex for the patient to understand and to learn to use unaided, and the capital costs of the machine and its installation are greater. Access to the blood stream is gained either by the insertion of indwelling cannulae into a peripheral artery and a neighbouring vein or by the surgical creation of a subcutaneous arteriovenous fistula. In a patient with chronic renal failure this can last for many years. The veins are dilated with blood under arterial pressure and are thus more accessible for repeated venepuncture. Patients soon learn to insert their own needles under local anaesthesia and to carry out their own dialysis treatment with little or no assistance.

Peritoneal dialysis and haemodialysis are not without disadvantages. Patients on CAPD must exchange their dialysis fluid several times every day and risk peritonitis if they are not meticulously careful. Patients on haemodialysis are tied to a kidney machine for hours at a time, and treatments must be repeated. No patient on dialysis is more than 7–10 days away from death if their regimen is interrupted. Amino acids and water soluble vitamins are removed from the plasma as readily as other small molecules and lost in the dialysis fluid. The peritoneal membrane is not impermeable to plasma proteins, and large quantities of proteins and smaller peptides may be lost from the body. Both forms of treatment replace renal function in terms of the excretion of nitrogenous metabolites and the correction of acidosis to the extent that patients can enjoy a normal intake of protein. Their capacity for the excretion of drugs and surplus quantities of water, sodium, potassium and phosphate is limited, if used intermittently rather than continuously. Thus some limitation of dietary intake is often necessary and nutrients removed during dialysis must be replaced (p. 412). Neither form of dialysis can replace metabolic functions of the kidney such as the synthesis of erythropoietin and the conversion of 25-hydroxy vitamin D to 1,25-dihydroxy vitamin D. Nevertheless, renal function is sufficiently replaced by these artificial means to enable most patients to stay not only alive but well and able to continue their normal employment and family life for many years.

DIETETICS IN RENAL DISORDERS

In the management of patients with diseases affecting the kidneys, dietetics is of greatest value when renal function is impaired. There is little or no need to interfere with the eating habits and way of life of patients when the kidneys continue to preserve homeostasis, as they usually do in acute and chronic pyelonephritis, asymptomatic glomerulonephritis, mild proteinuria or hypertension. Tubular disorders, such as the Fanconi syndrome, which can result in abnormal losses of phosphate, sodium, potassium or magnesium, may appear to invite dietetic intervention but in most cases can be treated by giving supplements of the appropriate salts on top of a normal food intake.

While the kidneys are affected by many different diseases, the ways in which renal function can be impaired are relatively few and disorders requiring the specialised help of a dietitian are included in four clinical syndromes, (1) acute glomerulonephritis, (2) the nephrotic syndrome, (3) acute renal failure and (4) chronic renal failure.

Acute glomerulonephritis

Acute glomerulonephritis is characterised by acute inflammation of the glomeruli with congestion, cellular proliferation and infiltration of polymorphs. Renal blood flow and glomerular filtration rate are reduced by 50 per cent or more and the damaged glomerular capillaries exude plasma proteins and cellular elements of the blood into Bowman's space. The urine volume falls to between 500 and 1000 ml/day and sodium excretion is greatly reduced. The urine contains moderate amounts of protein, with red and white blood cells in abundance, and casts of the renal tubules formed by precipitation of protein and red cells in the tubular system.

Since the patient continues to ingest normal quantities of sodium and water, oedema develops and the blood pressure rises, leading to complaints of malaise, headaches and swelling of the face and hands in the morning and of the ankles at night. Plasma concentrations of urea and creatinine rise in proportion to the fall in glomerular filtration rate, but acidosis and hyperkalaemia are usually mild and only require treatment if renal failure ensues.

In the past, acute glomerulonephritis was common, frequently following infection with β-haemolytic streptococci in children and young adults with tonsillitis or scarlet fever. Today troublesome streptococci are usually rapidly obliterated by penicillin, and acute glomerulonephritis is less common, but it can still follow infection of the upper respiratory tract. In poststreptococcal glomerulonephritis glomerular damage is caused not by direct infection of the kidney but by deposition of soluble immune complexes of streptococcal antigen with antibody formed in response to the foreign organisms.

A similar syndrome with a comparable pathogenesis can develop in patients with bacterial endocarditis, and in patients with other manifestations of disordered immunity, e.g. Henoch Schönlein purpura and systemic lupus erythematosus.

In almost all patients the disease is self-limiting. The glomerular inflammation resolves spontaneously and usually full renal function is restored in one to three weeks. In a few patients proteinuria persists and the nephrotic syndrome develops. Infrequently there is a progressive decline in renal function, leading ultimately to chronic renal failure.

Treatment

There are no specific agents known to reverse the glomerular lesion. Dietetics forms the mainstay of treatment, although drugs may be indicated to control hypertension and diuretics are often used to increase urinary excretion.

Fluid intake should be restricted to a volume calculated from the volume of urine passed plus the estimated insensible water loss, usually 500 ml daily. During the first few days of treatment, the fluid given should be less than the requirements to allow for dispersal of oedema fluid. Daily weighing provides a useful monitor of overall fluid balance.

At first it is wise to restrict the sodium intake to 40–60 mmol/day and the protein intake to 40 g/day, although the latter is often unnecessary. Diet No. 6 can be used for this purpose. Restriction of sodium intake can be relaxed when oedema resolves and the blood pressure falls. Restriction of protein is only needed when the blood urea is raised. Diuretics are sometimes used to increase urinary sodium and measurements of the daily output are useful. In the great majority of patients the glomerular lesion resolves completely within three weeks and no further treatment is needed.

A few patients develop severe renal failure and require dialysis. The dietary protein can then be restored to normal or may be increased if there has been heavy proteinuria. If facilities for dialysis are not available, a very low protein diet (Diet No. 4) may be needed. The theoretical and practical difficulties with these measures are discussed in the section on chronic renal failure.

Nephrotic syndrome

The nephrotic syndrome is characterised by heavy proteinuria, hypoalbuminaemia and peripheral oedema. It occurs when damage to glomerular capillaries results in greatly increased losses of plasma proteins from the body into the urine. Normally only small amounts of protein are filtered through the glomerular basement membrane and these are totally reabsorbed by the tubules. Proteinuria develops when the leakage of protein from the glomeruli exceeds the reabsorptive capacity of the renal tubules. The nephrotic syndrome ensues when the loss of protein in the urine exceeds the capacity of the liver to compensate by increasing synthesis of albumin. Daily losses of up to 5 g in the adult and up to 0.1 g/kg in children can usually be tolerated. If the loss of protein is greater or if protein synthesis in the liver is impaired, plasma concentration of albumin falls. The balance of hydrostatic and colloid osmotic pressures across the capillaries throughout the body is altered, favouring the movement of water and solute from the circulating blood plasma to the interstitial fluid. The plasma volume falls and in compensation sodium is reabsorbed avidly from the renal tubules. Sodium is retained in the body and the plasma volume restored at the expense of a greatly increased extracellular volume which is evident clinically as peripheral oedema. Of the plasma proteins albumin with its relatively small molecule escapes most readily through the leak in the glomerular membrane. Plasma globulins with a higher molecular weight appear in the urine in much smaller amounts. In fact, plasma concentrations of lipoproteins are increased and hyperlipidaemia is a feature of the nephrotic syndrome.

The syndrome can arise from diseases affecting the glomeruli alone, and from diseases in which the glomeruli are affected secondarily to changes elsewhere in the body. Indeed, in the world as a whole, the commonest cause of the nephrotic syndrome may be quartan malaria. In temperate climates a frequent cause in children is **minimal lesion glomerulonephritis** in which the glomeruli are primarily involved mysteriously with little or no abnormality to be seen on light microscopy and no sign of damage to the glomerular basement membrane on electron microscopy. In **membranous glomerulonephritis** there is thickening of the basement membrane with deposition of immunoglobulins and complement. In **proliferative glomerulonephritis** there is also deposition of immunoglobulins in the basement membrane and elsewhere in the glomeruli with an increase in the number of cells in a manner similar to that found in acute glomerulonephritis. Minimal lesion glomerulonephritis is distinguished by the consistency with which the proteinuria responds to treatment with corticosteroids and other immunosuppressive drugs. The treatment of membranous and proliferative glomerulonephritis with these agents is much more controversial.

The nephrotic syndrome can arise secondarily from damage to the glomerular capillaries in diabetes mellitus, amyloidosis, multiple myeloma and disseminated lupus erythematosus.

Treatment

Dietetics plays a major part in treatment. The two renal defects are loss of plasma proteins and retention of sodium. All patients benefit from a limitation in sodium intake and an increase in dietary protein, even when the glomerular lesion can be expected to respond to prednisolone. These symptomatic measures are often necessary both before diagnosis can be made by renal biopsy and also while waiting for the kidneys to respond to more specific therapy.

In practical terms the simultaneous manipulation in opposite directions of two prominent constituents of the diet presents a considerable challenge. A daily protein intake of 90–120 g for adults and of 2–3 g/kg for children is recommended to replenish depleted stores and to enhance hepatic synthesis of albumin. This could be achieved by taking double helpings of meat and fish, at least two and preferably four eggs daily (each contains approximately 7 g of protein), an extra half to one pint of milk and cream-cheese in abundance. Unfortunately these foods are moderately rich sources of sodium even before the addition of salt in cooking or at table.

For many patients, in whom the renal tubules are responsive to diuretic drugs, extreme degrees of salt restriction are not required. Salt should not be added at table and only small quantities added during cooking. Fresh meat and fish can be used to supplement the protein intake, but tinned products and foods preserved with salt, such as ham, sausages and kippers must be avoided. Eggs can be used freely but cheese other than cream-cheese should be reserved for special occasions. There is usually no difficulty in meeting the increased protein requirements of the mild nephrotic by these dietetic means, apart from the ability of the patients to pay for a richer style of living.

Difficulties arise if the patient is refractory to diuretic therapy. Frequently the albuminuria is of greater magnitude, often in excess of 10 g/day and the plasma albumin is reduced to less than 20 g/l. Then tubular reabsorption of sodium is so avid, that even by using combinations of diuretics that act at different sites along the nephron the excretion of sodium in the urine may not exceed 50 mmol/day. Under these conditions salt should be avoided in cooking as well as at the table. This can be achieved at home without subjecting the rest of the family to a restricted salt regimen, if the food for the family is cooked together without added salt and the portion for the patient separated before adding salt to the rations for the rest. Food cooked without salt is impalatable. Moreover, at very low salt intakes, even food containing only moderate amounts of salt may need to be restricted. This at once jeopardises attempts to increase protein intake. It may be necessary to use salt-free bread and salt-free butter to allow sodium to be taken in more proteinaceous forms. The good domestic cook can do much to provide a large range of tasty salt-free foods. Herbs, curry powder, paprika and other peppers, onions and garlic can be used to flavour savoury dishes containing meat and fish. Potassium glutamate can be used in cooking and table salt substitutes such as Selora which also contains potassium can be used freely unless renal failure supervenes. Salt-free tinned foods such as baked beans and processed peas are available and salt-free tomato ketchup and salad dressing can be obtained from Health Food stores. Salt-free pickles and chutney can be made at home. Salt-free baking powder containing potassium bicarbonate and bitartrate instead of the sodium salts can be used at home to provide salt-free breads, scones and cakes. Recipes and more detailed advice can be found in *Cooking for Special Diets* by Bee Nilson (Penguin).

Frequently the protein intake cannot be sustained by these manipulations and protein concentrates are needed. Salt-free casein, derived from milk, is available in powder form. Casilan and Edosol are preparations which can be added to milk drinks, milk puddings and sauces, or sprinkled on porridge. These must be distinguished from other milk preparations, such as Complan and Build Up, which provide a palatable protein supplement but contain sodium in abundance. The effectiveness of these measures in sustaining the prescribed level of dietary protein can be assessed by measuring the urinary urea excretion rate as well as the total urinary protein. The same 24 h collection of urine can be used to measure sodium and potassium excretion and thus to monitor the effectiveness of the diuretic therapy. Unless the patient is losing abnormally large quantities of nitrogen in the faeces, or is in a strongly anabolic or catabolic state, the urinary urea excretion should reflect changes in the intake of protein by mouth. Thus a daily intake of 90–120 g protein should result in the urinary excretion of approximately 600 mmol (36 g) of urea daily.

Dietary salt restriction is aided by the use of diuretics to increase loss of sodium in the urine. There is always an associated increase in potassium excretion and so a supplement of potassium chloride should be given to all patients on diuretic therapy. Excessive use of diuretics may reduce the plasma volume and renal blood flow and so can precipitate acute renal failure.

Patients whose oedema remains refractory to dietary measures and diuretics usually respond to infusions of salt-poor albumin derived from fractionation of human plasma proteins. The albumin infusion is accompanied by an appropriate cocktail of diuretics, and is an important safeguard against the calamity of acute renal failure.

In nephrotic patients with slowly deteriorating renal function a dilemma arises. Should they be given a high protein diet to supplement losses or a low protein diet to mitigate the uraemia? Usually a compromise is reached by moderating the degree of protein restriction. Often the patient solves his own problem when his abnormally permeable glomeruli are obliterated by advancing disease and the urinary loss of protein falls.

A daily intake of 90–120 g protein, 80–120 mmol sodium and 10 MJ (2400 kcal) is suitable for most patients with the nephrotic syndrome of mild to moderate severity. Diet No. 7 illustrates how this can be achieved.

Acute renal failure

Acute renal failure is a catastrophic event. When it occurs in a patient whose kidneys were previously healthy, the kidneys can recover functionally provided that the patient can be kept alive during the period when their excretory function is lost and homeostasis is impaired and that the patient does not die from the causative injury or disease. Keeping a patient alive for the two or three weeks needed for recovery is one of the most satisfactory achievements of modern medicine. Unfortunately, acute renal failure has a depressingly high mortality as it is often a complication of an illness which itself presents a grave threat to life.

Acute renal failure was not described in early textbooks of medicine. It was first recognised in 1940 in the London Blitz when it was a common complication of crush injuries and shock caused by falling masonry. Causes found today are:

1. *Loss of blood* from any cause including complications of pregnancy, trauma or gastrointestinal bleeding.
2. *Loss of plasma* as in burns and crush injuries.
3. *Loss of fluid* — (a) *from the gut* in severe vomiting, diarrhoea, acute intestinal obstruction, paralytic ileus and fistulous drainage, (b) *in the urine* in diabetic coma, (c) *from the skin* in excessive sweating (heat stroke).
4. *General anaesthetics and surgical operations* which reduce renal blood flow and may precipitate renal failure in those whose blood volume is precariously balanced.
5. *Serious infections*, especially septicaemia from *Escherichia coli*, may produce shock, and reduce renal blood flow.
6. Acute haemolytic disorders.
7. *Nephrotoxins* which may be drugs, industrial chemicals or natural substances. Examples of these are paracetamol, paraquat and mushrooms.

A common factor in many of these conditions is a prolonged episode of hypotension with systolic blood pressure less than 90 mmHg for one hour or more.

The susceptibility of the kidney to ischaemic damage may be related to the high renal blood flow which amounts to one-fifth of the resting cardiac output, and to the critical balance between arterial, venous and capillary pressures which determines the glomerular filtration rate. Blood loss is not the only cause of peripheral circulatory failure. Severe infection and septicaemia can result in shock in various ways. A fall in plasma volume can arise from excessive loss of plasma proteins in inflammatory exudates and from a generalised increase in capillary permeability. The plasma proteins are consumed at an increased rate in catabolic states, following infection and trauma, especially when the supply of exogenous fuel to provide energy is inadequate for the increased needs.

The serious nature of the underlying condition may explain why the overall mortality in acute renal failure is around 50 per cent, varying from less than 10 per cent in obstetrical cases to over 80 per cent in patients with multiple injuries or abdominal sepsis. Despite these gloomy statistics, there is every reason to expect that the kidneys will recover with little or no residual damage in the great majority of patients, if only the patient can survive and recover from the underlying illness. Rarely infarction of the kidney causes necrosis of the renal cortex and then there is no chance that normal renal function will ever return.

The disturbance in renal function passes through phase of total renal failure with oliguria, followed by a phase of recovery characterised by diuresis. The oliguric phase immediately follows the precipitating event and can last for a few days or for several weeks. The patient is often very ill with the metabolic disturbances of uraemia superimposed on his underlying condition. Some of the consequences of acute renal failure can be inferred from Table 44.1. The urine volume is low. The excretion of water, sodium, potassium and nitrogenous waste products are all diminished. Patients are at risk from overloading with fluid and electrolytes by both oral and intravenous routes. They cannot respond to an increased intake which may be given in the mistaken belief that the kidneys need encouraging. Hyperkalaemia is common and threatens life. Its prominence in acute renal failure may result from the increased breakdown of damaged tissues and extravasated blood with release of intracellular potassium. Acidosis and tissue hypoxia which accompany peripheral circulatory failure may also have a part to play. The blood urea can rise alarmingly, at a daily rate approaching 15 mmol/l. This results both from the breakdown of damaged tissues and also from an exaggeration of the catabolic response to trauma.

The diuretic phase is welcomed like rain after a long drought. After passing little or no urine for two weeks or longer the day arrives that all have been waiting for and a moderate amount of urine is passed. In succeeding days the urine volume reaches supernormal quantities. The patient has now entered the diuretic phase of the illness, which indicates that the tubular epithelium is starting to regenerate. But the quality of the urine is at first subnormal. It contains too little urea and too much sodium and potassium. When diuresis is established, the urine volume increases progressively to between 3 and 5 litres per day and the excretion of sodium, potassium,

urea and other solutes increases in parallel. The blood urea falls to normal over seven to ten days, reflecting the restoration of effective glomerular filtration.

Although the excretory function of the kidney is restored, the regulatory function of the tubules recovers more slowly. The internal environment of the patient is still at risk, but from excessive losses of water, sodium, potassium, bicarbonate and magnesium, rather than from the retention of these substances, as in the oliguric phase. Residual defects of tubular function can sometimes be detected long after the blood urea has returned to normal.

Treatment

During the phase of oliguria or anuria, protein metabolism should be reduced to a minimum, by giving only 20 g/day of protein and appropriate treatment to reduce endogenous protein metabolism to the lowest possible level. A daily intake of 100 g of sugar has a marked protein-sparing effect. If more sugar can be given, e.g. up to 300 g, this helps to reduce the inevitable loss in weight which occurs during the anuric phase. Such large quantities of sucrose and glucose are unpleasantly sweet, but glucose polymers such as Maxijul or Hycal are better tolerated. They are given in about 500 ml of water which is administered daily by mouth. If the patient is vomiting, dextrose in water has to be given intravenously. This amount of water roughly meets the daily obligatory loss of water through the skin and lungs. During the diuretic phase electrolytes are given only to replace losses. The diet should contain potassium chloride by mouth. Usually 2 to 3 g/day are required. With further improvement in renal function a gradual return to a normal diet is made.

The above old orthodox treatment is in some places the only one available. Where there are the facilities, it has been replaced by haemodialysis for the more serious cases, but not all patients with acute renal failure need dialysis. When the precipitating event is short-lived and the disturbance rapidly corrected with incomplete loss of renal function lasting only a few days the above regimen suffices. It is also often advisable in elderly patients who tolerate dialysis poorly. Patients with oliguria lasting from one to three weeks were often treated successfully in the ten to fifteen years before dialysis became readily available and many owed their lives to the above regimen and others based on the same principles.

Haemodialysis. The introduction of haemodialysis has changed the dietetic management of patients in acute renal failure. The dictum 'feed and dialyse' has replaced attempts to reduce protein turnover by restricting dietary protein. There are many reasons for wishing to support protein stores. The most common cause of death in acute renal failure is infection, and protein deficiency is well-known to lower the resistance of the body to invading micro-organisms. Many patients have surgical wounds to heal and damaged tissues to repair. The hypercatabolic patient whose blood urea rises by daily increments of 10–15 mmol/l consumes body protein at rates approaching 100 g/day. There may be additional protein losses into pleural and peritoneal exudates, or from open wounds. Peritoneal dialysis can impose another drain on protein reserves. The failure of earlier approaches to treatment was acknowledged in the traditional expectation that ill patients with acute renal failure would lose lean body weight at rates of 0.5 to 1 kg daily and in the comment that this weight loss should be taken into account when assessing fluid requirements.

The main purposes of dietetic treatment are to maintain stores of protein and to provide an optimal environment for wound healing and the defence against infection. Sufficient energy should be provided to minimise catabolism of body protein and to allow dietary amino acids to be used for protein synthesis. Sufficient protein must be given to balance metabolic and exudative losses. Between 9 and 12 MJ (2000 and 3000 kcal) and 50–100 g protein are usually required. The problems in providing such a regimen vary with the stage of the illness.

During the oliguric phase, the patient is acutely ill and has little appetite for food. Feeding by mouth may not be possible following abdominal surgery, if the bowel has been damaged or if there is peritonitis. Initially intravenous feeding may be the only way to provide nutrients in sufficient quantity. Solutions of amino acids, glucose and other carbohydrates are available in varying concentrations, as well as fat emulsions suitable for intravenous administration. One litre of 25 per cent dextrose given together with 1 litre of a solution of a balanced mixture of essential and non-essential amino acids, equivalent to 58 g protein, provides 9.4 MJ (2200 kcal). Insulin is often needed to control blood glucose. Even to supply these basic requirements a potential hazard can be seen immediately in the 2000 ml of water which it provides. The solution to this problem is daily haemodialysis, often necessary in any case to remove nitrogenous waste. For patients maintained by parenteral nutrition for periods longer than a week, attention should be given to the need for essential fatty acids which can be met by intravenous infusion of a suitable fat emulsion. In addition supplements of minerals and vitamins and ultimately trace elements are needed (Chap. 51).

As uraemia and infection come under control, feeding by mouth can be resumed. Initially provisions from the hospital kitchen may need to be supplemented at the bedside with imagination and flexibility. A wide variety of different preparations, both new and old, can be tried. Milk forms a useful basis. One or two eggs whipped into half a pint of milk with brandy to taste is surprisingly well accepted. Milk products such as Complan and Build Up can be made up with a wide range of flavours. Ice-cream is usually well tolerated. The supply of non-protein energy can be increased by adding cream to desserts and breakfast cereals and by the use of starch hydrolysates such as Hycal and Maxijul. Unfortunately, these may give rise to diarrhoea if misused.

In patients with prolonged oliguria the dietetic regimen and dialysis treatment more closely resemble the approach to patients with stable chronic renal failure (see below). The frequency of haemodialysis can often be reduced to three times weekly and normal food can be taken. A normal to high protein intake is encouraged and the diet is limited only with respect to sodium, fluids and foods rich in potassium.

The diuretic phase indicates a return of renal function. Nonetheless, dietetic treatment is still important although the problems are reversed. The patient is at risk from excessive loss of water, sodium, potassium, chloride, bicarbonate, phosphate and magnesium. Normal food and a free fluid intake may need to be supplemented by salts given in tablet or capsule form. As before, the fluid and electolyte status should be monitored by daily weighing, clinical examination and measurements of plasma electrolytes. Analysis of the urine for sodium and potassium provides a useful guide to replacement therapy.

CHRONIC RENAL FAILURE (URAEMIA)

Chronic renal failure is the final common pathway in many different diseases (Table 44.2). The two commonest causes are glomerulonephritis and pyelonephritis (infection of the urinary tract). Polycystic disease is a congenital disorder, the effects of which are often not manifest until adult life. Analgesic nephropathy follows prolonged use of phenacetin and possibly aspirin and other drugs. **Uraemia** is a term used to describe general

Table 44.2 Causes of chronic renal failure

	Relative* incidence
Pyelonephritis	30
Glomerulonephritis	28
Hypertension	10
Polycystic kidneys	7
Obstruction of the urinary tract	5
Analgesic nephropathy	5
Diabetic nephropathy	3
Miscellaneous disorders	12

* Based on a survey of 500 cases in Scotland[1]

renal failure from any cause. As renal function becomes impaired many complex biochemical changes occur some of which are probably more responsible for the clinical features than the elevation of blood urea. These changes include disturbances in hydrogen ion concentration and abnormalities in water and electrolyte balance. In addition, renal failure is accompanied in the majority of cases by arterial hypertension, and this complicates still further the clinical picture.

The kidneys have a large functional reserve, and the body can tolerate a considerable accumulation of waste metabolites. In consequence few patients develop symptoms of renal failure until the glomerular filtration rate has fallen below 10 ml/min and some 90 per cent of the capacity for eliminating urea and creatinine has been lost. Depending on the activity of the original disease process, renal function may be lost slowly or rapidly and the end stage of renal failure may develop over many years or only a few months.

CLINICAL FEATURES

Clinical features depend on the stage of the disease. At first patients may have symptoms and signs of their original disorder. Patients with glomerulonephritis may be hypertensive or nephrotic. In others with analgesic nephropathy the blood pressure may be low from excessive salt loss. An early sign in many patients is loss of renal reserve. As the patient loses the capacity to concentrate urine, the urine volume rises and the requirement for water increases. The normal diurnal variation in urine volume disappears and the patient has to rise at night to pass urine. He has increased thirst and spontaneously increases his fluid intake to compensate for the loss in renal flexibility.

The failing kidney is equally unable to compensate for large fluctuations in salt intake and for other increased metabolic demands. The patient with mild renal failure tolerates poorly intercurrent medical and surgical illnesses which increase urea production and interfere with the normal intake of water and sodium or which cause increased losses of water and sodium from the gastrointestinal tract. Uncompensated losses of water and sodium result in dehydration and salt depletion, with a fall in plasma volume, arterial blood pressure, renal blood flow and glomerular filtration rate. Renal function is lost in proportion and mild renal failure progresses to severe uraemia. It is not uncommon for mild chronic renal failure to present for the first time as acute renal failure following a chest infection or an acute abdominal surgical emergency.

When more than 90 per cent of functioning renal tissue has been destroyed, uraemic symptoms become more prominent (Table 44.1). Tiredness and breath-lessness on exertion may arise from anaemia. A tendency to bleed due to abnormal platelet function is common. Anorexia, nausea and vomiting may result from the accumulation of urea, creatinine or an unknown uraemic 'toxin'. When GFR falls below 5 ml/min the kidneys may be unable to excrete even normal quantities of sodium and water. Many patients at this stage develop hypertension, oedema and features of water intoxication. The excretion of hydrogen ions is impaired, the plasma bicarbonate concentration falls and an observer may notice compensatory hyperventilation of which the patient is often unaware (Kussmaul's respiration). Potassium homeostasis is usually maintained until the urine volume falls below 1000 ml/24 h, after which hyperkalaemia can be rapidly fatal. Plasma phosphate rises and plasma calcium falls; the parathyroid glands hypertrophy to compensate for these biochemical changes and the plasma concentration of parathyroid hormone is increased. Metabolic bone disease may lead to bone pain and pathological fractures in patients with renal failure of several years duration.

Hyperlipidaemia is a characteristic feature of chronic renal disease and occurs early in the nephrotic syndrome. The main abnormality is increased plasma concentrations of triglycerides and VLD lipoproteins. This reflects a general metabolic disorder, but the mechanisms responsible for the change in blood lipids are not known. The abnormality persists on dialysis and after a renal transplant, and is associated with an increased risk of cardiovascular disease.

In the final stages death can result from hypertensive encephalopathy, uraemic coma, pulmonary oedema, gastrointestinal haemorrhage, pericardial effusion, hyperkalaemia or severe infection. Many of these events can be predicted from Table 44.1 and almost all can be prevented by rational therapy based on an understanding of the excretory and homeostatic tasks of the kidney.

TREATMENT

Treatment of chronic renal failure varies according to the stage of the illness. In mild cases, active steps should be taken to control hypertension, to correct salt and water imbalance and to treat active urinary tract infection. During the course of an illness in which oral feeding cannot be maintained, fluids and electrolytes should be given intravenously. Protein restriction may not be necessary in the absence of symptoms (see below). Indeed, a high protein diet is usually indicated in nephrotic patients with excessive losses of protein in the urine. Sodium restriction may be necessary in some patients, but others may need extra salt to compensate for urinary losses. Sodium bicarbonate may be needed for treatment of acidosis. $1,25\text{-}(OH)_2$ Vitamin D can be used for the treatment and prevention of metabolic bone disease. There is a real risk, however, that an increase in plasma calcium may damage the kidney and accelerate loss of renal function.

As renal failure progresses and the patient develops symptoms of uraemia, more active measures become necessary to compensate for the loss of renal function. Patients may be treated conservatively by dietetic measures alone, by regular haemodialysis or peritoneal dialysis or by renal transplantation.

Conservative treatment

One hundred years ago the patient with renal failure was cupped and bled, and the activity of the bowels and skin promoted by saline purges, hot baths and Dover's powder, which increased the elimination of 'excrementititous substances' by alternative routes. He was advised to travel south in winter and to take the mineral waters at Vichy and other spas in order to flush out the urinary passages. He was instructed always to wear flannel next to the skin and to abstain totally from the use of alcohol. Few of these measures survive today, apart from venesection which is still practised, but used for investigative purposes rather than for therapy. By contrast, some aspects of the dietetics practised in Victorian times may still be valid in the treatment of uraemia, although perhaps for different reasons.

Failing kidneys, like tuberculous lungs, were thought to need rest. Thus treatment was directed towards relieving the kidneys as much as possible from 'the labour of elimination'. The volume of the urine and the urea excretion rate were measured and taken as guides to fluid replacement and to the quantity of protein given by mouth. Dietary protein was limited and the patient advised to take meat only once daily. Acute illnesses were treated with milk fortified by arrowroot, but the quantity limited to 1–2 pints daily since greater volumes of fluid and the dissolved mineral elements were felt to make dropsical conditions more difficult to treat. The convalescent patient was weaned from beef-tea and mutton broth to fish and fowl and not allowed red meats such as mutton and beef.

Now, as then, in both severe and mild renal failure, regular attention should be given to the state of water and sodium balance, to the correction of acidosis and to control of blood pressure. The principal additional measure as renal failure progresses is to reduce dietary protein, in the first instance to 0.5 g/kg bodyweight, which corresponds to 30–40 g/day in most adults. This leads to a fall in urea production and in the blood urea. Gastrointestinal symptoms such as anorexia and vomiting are often relieved. This may result from a reduction in the diffusion of urea from the plasma into the intestinal lumen where it is hydrolysed by bacterial

urease to ammonium carbonate. Ammonia released in the gut is reabsorbed and taken to the liver in the portal circulation where it is either recycled to urea or used for synthesis of non-essential amino acids. This provides an important metabolic pathway which is exploited in patients on very low protein diets and other experimental regimens in the treatment of severe chronic renal failure.

Diet No. 6 (p. 614) provides 40 g of protein and 40 mmol sodium. Protein restriction of this order usually has little effect on the supply of energy or on the provision of essential nutrients. For patients expending more than 8.4 MJ (2000 kcal)/day additional energy can be provided by increasing the consumption of fat and sugar, or by the use of polymeric glucose preparations derived from hydrolysis of starch such as Caloreen and Hycal.

It is customary to restrict protein when the blood urea rises above 30 mmol/l and the plasma creatinine above 500 μmol/l, especially if the patient has symptoms. Moreover there is now some evidence that a reduction in dietary protein may delay progression to renal failure when introduced at this stage or even earlier.[2] The effect, if it can be confirmed, may be unrelated to the fall in nitrogen intake. Many proteinaceous foods contain phosphate in abundance, and the consumption of this important nutrient falls as protein is restricted. The concentration of phosphate in plasma, interstitial fluid and the glomerular filtrate is also reduced, and the risk of kidney damage from precipitation of calcium phosphate around the tubules minimised. Other burdens on the kidney are relieved when protein is restricted: the metabolic breakdown of sulphur-containing amino acids to sulphuric acid falls, and any harmful effects of sulphate and acidosis reduced.

The adverse effects of unnecessary protein restriction should not be ignored. This is illustrated by the experience of Sir Stanley Davidson. He had a kidney removed for hydronephrosis at the age of 12. Despite this handicap he managed to enlist in the infantry in August 1914 and spent the autumn, winter and spring in the trenches in northern France under the dreadful conditions of wet and cold that existed during that period of World War I. In the summer of 1915 he was very severely wounded and developed extensive gas gangrene. His life was endangered from sepsis and cachexia for nearly a year. That his remaining kidney was markedly affected was manifested by the constant passage of albumin, leucocytes and casts in the urine. The diet prescribed and eaten for more than a year after discharge from hospital was low in protein and high in carbohydrate, and alcohol was prohibited. As the albuminuria continued and health was not fully restored, and because the restriction of food and drink proved extremely irksome, he decided to stop all dietary restriction and eat and drink whatever he liked. For more than 70 years and until shortly before his death at the age of 87 the function of the one remaining kidney was satisfactory, as judged by the sense of well-being, a normal blood pressure and pyelogram and the absence of abnormal constitutents in the urine and the blood.

Very low protein diets. On a diet totally devoid of protein but supplying adequate quantities of other essential nutrients and energy, the body continues to produce urea and other nitrogenous metabolites from the breakdown of endogenous protein. In theory, nitrogen balance should be maintained and loss of lean body mass prevented if just sufficient protein is given by mouth to balance these basal endogenous losses, which correspond to approximately 0.25 g of protein/kg body weight, or 15–20 g protein daily in the average adult.

Giovannetti and Maggiore[3] in 1964 demonstrated that uraemic patients could be sustained on a basal protein-free diet when this was supplemented with a mixture of essential amino acids or a single protein of high biological value, e.g. egg protein. Another Italian, Giordano, argued that with such a regimen the patient could be induced to utilise his own waste urea nitrogen for synthesis of non-essential amino acids through the entero-hepatic cycle of urea. These Italian regimens were soon adapted to British tastes.[4] Patients who would otherwise have required dialysis could be kept well, symptom-free, and even rehabilitated at work for several months. The modified Giovanetti/Giordano diet is illustrated in Diet No. 5. Supplements of methionine, the first limiting amino acid in the diet, and of vitamins are needed and a major problem is the supply of sufficient energy. In practice many patients feel hungry and find it difficult to tolerate large quantities of cream, butter or margarine, cooking oil and sugar. Polymeric glucose preparations, such as Hycal and Maxijul, can be used but, as unabsorbed polysaccharide may cause an osmotic diarrhoea, they are often poorly tolerated.

These dietetic measures can sustain patients in whom the GFR has fallen to 2–4 ml/min long after dialysis would have been necessary if protein intake had not been reduced. Not surprisingly, in patients with less than 5 per cent of their original functioning kidney tissue, other steps have to be taken in addition to protein restriction to preserve fluid and ionic balance. In many ways doctor and dietitian can be regarded as a pair of artificial organs themselves functioning on behalf of the patient to maintain 'renal' homeostasis.

Thus fluid balance needs even more careful attention than before and the patient should be advised to limit fluid intake when the urine volume falls below 1000 ml/day. Varying degrees of sodium restriction become necessary to control hypertension and to prevent peripheral and pulmonary oedema. Hyperkalaemia, often a problem as urine volume falls, can be treated by

the oral or rectal administration of cation exchange resins such as Resonium A (Winthrop) (in the sodium and hydrogen phase) or Calcium Resonium (Winthrop) (in the calcium phase). Potassium ions are exchanged for sodium and hydrogen ions with Resonium A, and for calcium ions with Calcium Resonium. In some patients this replaces one problem with another. Acidosis can be corrected by giving sodium bicarbonate by mouth, but dietary sodium may need restricting even further. The rise in plasma phosphate can be limited by using the gastrointestinal tract as a substitute for the artificial kidney. Aluminium hydroxide given by mouth in the form of tablets, capsules, or an antacid gel removes phosphate in direct combination as aluminium phosphate. In some patients it may cause flatulence and a sensation of epigastric fullness, as well as producing constipation. Unfortunately, these measures cannot prevent death in terminal uraemia from gastrointestinal haemorrhage, pericarditis and pericardial tamponade or uraemic coma. Despite the best dietetic attention, it is difficult to avoid depletion of protein and other essential nutrients. Patients' resistance to infection is often lowered and wounds heal poorly following surgery and there are a variety of biochemical abnormalities. Previously these features were attributed to the effects of uraemia, but many are found in protein depletion from other causes and it is difficult to exclude the possibility that the dietetic treatment may have a contributory role. This may help to explain why a patient taken on for treatment by dialysis and transplantation after a period of severe protein restriction often has a long uphill struggle to climb out of the grave that almost buried him.

Experimental 'no-protein' diets. Amino acids can be synthesised in the body by transamination of 2-oxo-acid precursors which supply the analogous carbon skeleton of the amino acid. The oxo-acid precursors of the non-essential amino acids can be synthesised in the body but not those of the essential amino acids. When the precursor of valine was fed to healthy persons and to patients with uraemia, 25–50 per cent was converted into the essential amino acid.[5]

$$CH_3\!\!\diagdown$$
$$\qquad\quad CHCOCOOH$$
$$CH_3\!\!\diagup$$

2-Oxoisovaleric acid

$$CH_3\!\!\diagdown$$
$$\qquad\quad CHCHNH_2COOH$$
$$CH_3\!\!\diagup$$

Valine

In theory, a patient given the oxo-acid analogues of all the essential amino acids in correct proportion should be able to utilise his own waste amino groups to synthesise both essential and non-essential amino acids, and thus could replace endogenous protein losses entirely from waste amino nitrogen. In this way a patient with total renal failure and no loss of urea in the urine could be made self-sustaining with respect to nitrogen and independent of exogenous protein.

There are many practical difficulties facing the patient who attempts to feed on his own flesh and blood in this way. The problems of very low protein diets would be intensified. Moreover, the cost of the synthetic oxo-acid precursors is high. Nonetheless the idea is attractive, and may find a place in future regimens for patients with advanced uraemia.

Dialysis treatment
In the early 1960s when dialysis facilities were scarce and almost experimental, patients were taken on for treatment only when life was threatened and conservative measures had been unsuccessful. Today it is generally accepted that dialysis treatment is best started when the patient can no longer be maintained on moderate protein restriction, and long before the effects of protein depletion become apparent.

Both peritoneal dialysis and haemodialysis rapidly relieve the patient not only from uraemic symptoms such as tiredness and anorexia but also from many dietary restrictions. The residual limitations depend to some degree on the treatment used and to some extent on the patient.

Haemodialysis. Treatment with the disposable device shown in Fig. 44.3 for four to eight hours three times weekly removes all the urea generated by a normal dietary intake of protein, and all the creatinine and uric acid produced from the metabolic turnover of a normal lean body mass. Oedema in all patients and hypertension in almost all patients can be corrected by the removal of fluid by ultrafiltration at the time of dialysis. In most patients, however, the urine volume falls below 500 ml daily within the first week of regular treatment, and thereafter the excretion of sodium and potassium in the urine makes little or no contribution towards homeostasis. If dietary intake of sodium and water is not limited in the 2–3 day intervals between treatments, oedema fluid accumulates and the blood pressure rises.

The two criteria of successful management are the control of hypertension and the social rehabilitation of the patient. Unfortunately few patients can walk out of the dialysis unit and return to work unaided after losing more than 2 litres of fluid over a single treatment period. For the majority of patients this means drinking no more than 500 to 1000 ml of fluid and restricting sodium intake to 50 mmol daily. Patients become thirsty if more salt is taken and find it difficult to comply with fluid restrictions.

If blood pressure is normal and oedema absent, the amount of fluid removed in dialysis is determined from the change in body weight between treatments. An increase in weight of 1 kg indicates the consumption of 1 litre of water over requirements. The patient rapidly learns both to adjust the ultrafiltration pressures across the dialyser to remove this fluid and also to regulate his fluid intake to maintain his 'dry' weight stable over weeks and months of regular treatment.

Patients also lose lean body mass and adipose tissue when appetite is impaired during an intercurrent illness and regain their weight during their recovery. These longer term changes have to be distinguished carefully by patient, dietitian and doctor from short-term changes due to indiscretion of salt and water. Patients adapt to severe fluid restriction in various ways. One Scot was happy with his regimen as long as he could take his fluid allowance entirely in the form of neat whisky.

In the past, potassium intake was controlled rigorously and ion exchange resins given to prevent plasma potassium rising to dangerous levels before dialysis. Today the patient should still be cautioned severely against the consumption of large quantities of foods very rich in potassium, e.g. bananas, fresh oranges and dried fruits. However, even these foods may be allowed in small amounts at long intervals and there is no reason to limit dietary intake of potassium below 80–100 mmol/day, which is the average for the general population. This more liberal policy has resulted from a reduction in the potassium concentration of the dialysis fluid, from the use of better dialysers and from more frequent dialysis which gives better control of acidosis. Most of the potassium in the body is located in the cells, and the balance between intracellular and extracellular fluid concentrations of potassium is governed by the prevailing state of acidosis or alkalosis. Between dialysis treatments hydrogen ions accumulate causing a slight shift of potassium from the cells and a substantial rise in plasma potassium. The degree of hyperkalaemia is quite out of proportion to the 10–15 per cent increase in total body potassium represented by the 200–300 mmol ingested over the 3–4 day period between dialysis treatments.

Aluminium hydroxide is required by most patients to maintain plasma phosphate concentrations below 2.0 mmol/l. Above this level calcium and phosphate salts precipitate in extraskeletal tissues, ultimately causing irritation of the conjunctiva and red eyes, vascular calcification, unsightly periarticular swellings and pseudogout. On the other hand, too much aluminium hydroxide and too little dietary phosphorus, which can result from excessive limitation of protein intake, can result in phosphate depletion and skeletal demineralisation resembling osteomalacia. Hyperparathyroidism, which previously was resistant to all medical treatment, can now be controlled in most patients by daily doses of $1-2$ μg of $1,25$-$(OH)_2$ vitamin D.

Iron requirements are increased by blood losses in the dialyser, from cannulation sites and from medical curiosity. It is usually sufficient to give a daily iron supplement by mouth. In most patients haemoglobin concentration is low, between 6 and 10 g/dl, due to deficiency in erythropoetin, but would be lower without iron.

Peritoneal dialysis. Patients on CAPD can drink freely and enjoy a much more liberal dietary regimen than patients on haemodialysis or intermittent peritoneal dialysis, simply because surplus water and electrolytes are removed from the plasma continuously, and the process of dialysis is not interrupted for long periods. Indeed a high protein intake is needed to maintain plasma protein concentrations and lean body mass as amino acids and protein are lost in the dialysis fluid. Most patients are encouraged to take at least 100 g of protein daily, using eggs, milk and meat to supplement their normal diet. Restriction in salt and water intake may become necessary if blood pressure is difficult to control. In some patient, the rate of ultrafiltration across the peritoneal membrane falls with time, making it difficult to remove large quantities of fluid. This can follow repeated episodes of peritonitis, and may ultimately result in failure of treatment. Obesity may develop if dialysis fluid containing glucose in high concentration has to be used frequently in order to remove surplus fluid and sodium.

Some limitation in the consumption of foods high in potassium may be needed but, as for patients on haemodialysis, a normal daily intake of potassium can be allowed. Some patients still require aluminium hydroxide for control of phosphate, and all need water-soluble vitamins to replace losses on dialysis (see below). Since there are no losses of blood on dialysis, the requirements for iron are less and supplements not essential. Anaemia is rarely a problem in patients on CAPD.

Unwanted losses and gains from dialysis fluids. The natural peritoneal and artificial cellophane membranes used for dialysis are permeable not only to unwanted ions and waste metabolites but also to water-soluble nutrients which could be lost from the plasma. Excessive quantities of mineral salts present in haemodialysis fluid prepared from domestic water may diffuse in the opposite direction. Patients on haemodialysis can be exposed each week to 900 litres of dialysis fluid by contrast with more modest requirements of patients on CAPD ($42-54$ litres) and normal individuals who rarely ingest more than 15 litres weekly.

Loss of glucose is readily prevented by including it in the dialysis fluid. Amino acids and small peptides are lost by diffusion but the combined loss rarely exceeds

30 g weekly on either peritoneal or haemodialysis, and is readily replaced if the patient has a normal protein intake. Patients on peritoneal dialysis lose on average 60 g of plasma proteins each week and require a high protein diet. Even then their albumin is usually slightly reduced.

Vitamins. Plasma concentrations of ascorbic acids, folate and pyridoxine are reduced by dialysis. Losses of 80 to 280 mg of ascorbic acid have been reported in a single haemodialysis treatment As plasma concentrations fall, so does removal by diffusion across the dialyser membrane. Nevertheless, to maintain normal plasma concentrations daily oral supplements of 100 mg of ascorbic acid, 1 mg of folic acid and 5 mg of pyridoxine are recommended.

Thiamin, riboflavin, pantothenic acid, nicotinic acid and biotin are also lost on dialysis, but in quantities no greater than urinary losses in patients with normal renal function, and plasma concentrations are normal. Supplements are usually given routinely in the form of a multivitamin pill.

Although vitamin B12 is a large molecule and bound to plasma proteins, significant losses may occur. Plasma concentrations are usually normal, but there may be a slight downward trend in patients maintained on dialysis for several years. As in malabsorption syndromes, plasma concentration may be kept within the normal range at the expense of hepatic stores; the need for supplements may become apparent in the future when more patients have been on dialysis for many years.

Plasma concentrations of vitamins A and D are normal in patients on haemodialysis. Losses across the cellophane membrane would be unlikely in view of their low solubility in water and their binding to plasma proteins. Losses on peritoneal dialysis might be greater in view of the losses of plasma proteins, but there is no evidence to confirm this.

Minerals. Under normal circumstances the dialysis patient neither gains nor loses excessive amounts of copper, molybdenum, lead, cobalt, nickel, zirconium, manganese or bromine. An increased tissue content of fluorine, tin, strontium and cadmium and a loss of rubidium have been reported, but the clinical significance of these changes is not known. In the early days of dialysis copper tubing was used and adverse effects occurred from copper leached into the dialysis fluid. Reports of zinc toxicity and accumulation have been followed by the conflicting suggestion that zinc deficiency may be more prevalent and indeed may be responsible for symptoms of sexual inadequacy. The risks of lead intoxication are greatly reduced by replacing lead in piping by plastic or stainless steel.

A far greater problem is the accumulation of aluminium, now recognised as a potential cause of disability and death in patients on haemodialysis. All dialysis patients are given aluminium hydroxide by mouth to bind phosphate in the gastrointestinal tract for treatment of hyperphosphataemia. A far more important source of unwanted aluminium is the water used for making dialysis fluid. Alum is used extensively for the treatment of drinking water, but not all water authorities take steps to ensure the removal of surplus aluminium. Transfer from dialysis fluid to the patient is enhanced by the very low concentrations in plasma water which result from the protein binding of the metal and its rapid dispersal to the tissues, particularly to brain, bone and muscle. The clinical effects are consistent with this distribution. Patients initially develop disturbances of speech and progress to severe dementia and death within months. Skeletal demineralisation, in the form of intractable osteomalacia resistant to treatment even with $l\alpha$-hydroxycholecalciferol, may complicate the picture. There was a wide variation in the incidence of these disorders between different centres, which correlates with aluminium concentrations in the water supply. Dialysis dementia disappears when dialysis fluid made from highly purified water is used. In one hospital with a very high incidence of dialysis dementia, the aluminium content of the water delivered to the dialysis unit was 1 part per million, compared with a concentration of less than 0.06 p.p.m. in ordinary tap-water. The source of the aluminium was traced to two anodes of aluminium weighing 32.4 kg in the water heating system, which completely disappeared over a two-year period. Most of the aluminium was precipitated at the bottom of the hot-water tank as aluminium hydroxide, but enough was dissolved in the water passing through to intoxicate fatally six patients. No other patients were affected after the unit was transferred to another hospital where the aluminium content of the water was low, despite the continued administration of aluminium hydroxide by mouth.

Transplantation

There are many advantages in having a built-in kidney that works on its own. This is obvious at social gatherings of patients with chronic renal failure. Those with transplanted kidneys look pink, drink beer and have to use the lavatory. By contrast, haemodialysis patients are pale, drink spirits only and usually have to wait until their next dialysis to achieve salt and water homeostasis.

Unfortunately the body has a built-in reaction to a kidney that once belonged to someone else. Even after great care has been taken to get a compatible donor and with powerful drugs which can suppress the immune response, there is only a 70 per cent chance that a transplanted kidney will be functioning two years after the operation. These depressing statistics are tolerable only because the chances of a kidney, which has survived two years, working for another ten years there-

after are high, and because with careful attention to diet and drugs the mortality and morbidity from the operation is now very low. Many patients come back for a second operation which carries no worse a prognosis than the first.

The most important role for the dietitian is to support the general nutrition of the patient before, during and after the transplant operation in order to counterbalance the side-effects of the drugs, azathioprine, prednisolone and more recently cyclosporin A, given to prevent rejection. Immunosuppressive drugs as a group impair the resistance of the body to infection. Most of the problems in the transplanted patient arise from the use of prednisolone, often given in very high dosage during the first few weeks after the operation and also when acute rejection threatens the graft. Corticosteroid drugs even in moderate dosage have pronounced catabolic effects, accelerating protein breakdown and hepatic gluconeogenesis from amino acids. In patients unsupported by an adequate dietary protein, muscle wasting and depletion of tissue proteins results, with delayed healing of wounds and failure to localise infections. While some of these effects on underlying protein metabolism are probably unavoidable, they can be prevented to a large extent by providing sufficient dietary energy and protein to match catabolic losses and maintain tissue protein.

Patients are best prepared for transplantation by regular dialysis for several weeks with restoration of a healthy appetite and a normal way of life. Since the transplanted kidney is placed in the iliac fossa outside the peritoneal cavity, the activity of the gastrointestinal tract is impaired for no more than a few hours after the operation and feeding by mouth should be resumed as soon as possible. Management of the patient thereafter depends on what the kidney does next.

If the kidney functions immediately, the patient can eat normally with free fluids and an unrestricted salt intake. Subsequently the onset of rejection is usually accompanied by a reduction in the urine volume and sodium excretion, then by a deterioration in renal excretory function. The fluid allowance and sodium intake should be reduced to maintain homeostasis. However, it is unwise to restrict protein, since the dosage of prednisolone has to be greatly increased in an attempt to reverse the rejection process; it is better to dialyse the patient if the rejected kidney is unable to meet the metabolic demands of a full diet. Many transplanted kidneys undergo at least one rejection episode of variable severity, but with prompt treatment there is a good chance of full recovery.

If the transplanted kidney does not function immediately, the patient should be fed and dialysed in the manner to which he has been accustomed, until renal function recovers sufficiently to make dialysis unnecessary. Kidneys from cadaver donors have often undergone a period of ischaemic damage between clamping the renal vessels and perfusion with ice-cold preservative. Renal ischaemia following a fall in arterial blood pressure is a common cause of acute tubular necrosis, so it is not surprising that many transplanted kidneys pass little urine in the early days following anastomosis with a different set of blood vessels situated several miles from their original supply. Frequently the onset of recovery is characterised by a diuretic phase, in which supplements of sodium chloride, sodium bicarbonate and potassium may be required.

The functioning transplanted kidney produces erythropoetin and the red cell count and haemoglobin concentration usually rise to normal within 1–3 months. Haematinics such as iron and folic acid should be given to maintain stores and to support the increased activity of the bone marrow. Another metabolic function resumed by the transplanted kidney is the synthesis of $1,25\text{-}(OH)_2$ vitamin D. In most patients bone lesions heal and hyperparathyroidism resolves. In some patients the plasma phosphate concentration falls to abnormally low levels in the first few weeks after kidney function is restored. This may be due to residual hyperparathyroidism or renal tubular damage. Phosphate supplements may be needed if plasma concentrations are very low, so as to ensure normal bone mineralisation. In most patients, however, a full normal diet is sufficient in itself.

After the first month with a new kidney, the most prominent nutritional problem is one of surfeit, resulting from the high doses of prednisolone. As in Cushing's disease, fat stores are increased, partly at the expense of the lean body mass and partly from an increased appetite. Few patients can voluntarily limit their food intake and so do not lose weight until the dosage of prednisolone is reduced even with encouragement from doctor and dietitian. Often control of weight gain is as much as can be expected. The occasional patient is overtly diabetic, requiring insulin in the early stages and subsequently oral hypoglycaemics or carbohydrate restriction alone as the dosage of steroids is reduced.

Treatment of diabetics in chronic renal failure

Many young diabetics have died from chronic renal failure. Recent experience shows that they can benefit from dialysis and transplantation, providing there are no overt signs of ischaemic heart disease. Most of the difficulties in management arise not from the increased complexity of having two metabolic disturbances to treat, but from technical problems relating to vascular access and from other complications such as diabetic retinopathy. Patients on haemodialysis require an anticoagulent, heparin, to prevent the blood from clotting in the extracorporeal circuit. This is a risky

business in diabetics who have fragile retinal capillaries that bleed easily. In diabetics with widespread degenerative vascular disease, moreover, surgeons may not be able to establish an arteriovenous fistula needed for haemodialysis without jeopardising the circulation to the rest of the limb.

For these reasons, CAPD has become very popular with diabetic patients in renal failure. Heparin is not normally required, and in any case does not cross the peritoneal membrane from the dialysis fluid to the blood. An added advantage is that insulin can be added to the dialysis fluid and is absorbed continuously into the plasma, providing better control of the blood glucose. The additional glucose load from the dialysis fluid can be covered with an increased dose of insulin.

In patients on dialysis with little urine and even less glomerular function, the urinary glucose is a poor guide to the state of the diabetes and control depends on measurements of blood glucose. Ketoacidosis is rarely a problem, and patients with little or no renal function are largely immune from excessive urinary losses of sodium and water.

After renal transplantation the same principles should be followed as for the surgical diabetic (p. 388). An increased insulin requirement can be expected when the high doses of prednisolone are given. Subsequently insulin should be reduced in parallel with the dosage of prednisolone.

It is now possible in some centres to transplant the pancreas as well as the kidney from the same donor. The grafted islet cells maintain homeostatis from the moment the blood vessels have been joined up, and respond normally to changes in the blood glucose by secreting insulin or glucagon. Not only should the grafted kidney be protected from the risk of developing diabetic nephropathy, but the patient can at last eat freely and no longer needs exogenous insulin. While there are still many problems to overcome, this is an area of great promise for the future.

STONES IN THE URINARY TRACT

Stones may form in the bladder (vesical calculi) or the kidney (renal calculi). Whereas renal calculi are ubiquitous, vesical calculi are now endemic in only a few rural areas, mostly in the tropics. Epidemiologically they are two separate diseases, but each arises from changes in the chemistry of the urine predisposing to stone formation.

CHEMISTRY OF CALCULUS FORMATION

At least 95 per cent of stones are made up of calcium salts. About 3 per cent are uric acid salts and about 1 per cent are cystine. Most stones are a mixture, calcium oxalate, calcium phosphate and magnesium ammonium phosphate being the main constituents, but about one third are pure calcium oxalate. Stones form more readily infected urine in which bacteria have converted urea into ammonia so making the urine more alkaline.

The solubility of a salt in a solvent depends on the product of the concentrations of its cation and anion or more correctly of the ion activities. These are difficult to measure, and are determined in part by the presence of other ions in the solvent. These may allow a salt solution to become supersaturated. Crystals of calcium oxalate are present in all urines and are probably the result of precipitation from a supersaturated solution of these ions. The crystals are small and normally washed out when the urine is voided.

Crystal growth is determined by the chemical constituents of the urine which may be altered by metabolic derangements and also by diet; these are risk factors and some of these are discussed later. There are also present in urine substances that inhibit crystal growth. These include citrate, pyrophosphate and, possibly the most important, glycosoaminoglycans. What determines the amounts of the latter normally present in urine and what may cause a deficiency are questions as yet unanswered.[6]

VESICAL CALCULUS

Bladder stones usually occur either in boys, in young men or in old men (in whom it is generally associated with prostatic obstruction or other cause of urinary stagnation). Formerly it was common in young boys in Britain, but now it is very rare. A similar decline has taken place in all prosperous countries of Europe and North America.

Excruciating pain often led the sufferers to desperate measures. Relief by operation was sought long before the era of anaesthetics and aseptic surgery. Accredited surgeons fought shy of the risks of the operation. Indeed cutting for the stone was expressly forbidden in the earliest forms of the Hippocratic oath. In consequence many sufferers availed themselves of the services of 'stone-cutters', or lithotomists. These men flourished in Europe between 1500 and 1800. Their craft was often handed down from father to son as a closely guarded secret. Eight generations of the Collot family practised in France, and some by attendance on the King or his family acquired the title 'Royal Lithotomist'. Many lithotomists travelled widely seeking patients or perhaps avoiding the relatives of their less fortunate patients. During the nineteenth century the incidence of stone in the bladder began to decline in Europe. It is now a rare disease (except in elderly men). A fascinating history of bladder stone has been written by Ellis.[7]

In most parts of the tropics stone in the bladder is also uncommon, but there are well-defined 'stone areas' in southern China, Thailand, Pakistan, Iran and other countries. In such areas the visitor may find a surgeon who has a cupboard full of an assortment of bladder stones of every variety of chemical composition.

One of us had the opportunity to visit such as area in the Ubon province of Thailand.[8] The surgeon-in-charge of the hospital at the capital of the province kindly gave access to the hospital records. During four years he had removed 610 bladder stones. This corresponded to a yearly rate of 1.8 operations per 10 000 inhabitants of the province, but this gives a false impression of the incidence. The disease, in fact, is largely confined to young boys. Between the ages of 4 and 6, the operation rate among boys was over 10 per 10 000 boys. The relative immunity of young girls is probably attributable to their anatomy; it is easier for them to pass small stones *per urethram*. The epidemiology of the stone in Thailand has now been studied in much more detail (see below).

Dietary factors. The great fall in the incidence of vesical calculus among children and young adults in Britain coincided roughly with improvement in nutrition: the disease affected predominantly the poorer classes. In all the 'stone areas' in Asia the diet is far from ideal and is generally of a poor vegetarian nature. These facts suggest a dietary cause.

Nevertheless there are other facts that are not consistent with this view. In former times prosperous men sometimes suffered from stone. Samuel Pepys was 'cut for the stone' in 1658 when he was 25, and we know from his *Diary* that he lived well. In the 'stone areas' of Thailand the nutritional state of the children is not good, when judged by modern European or American standards. Yet the children compare favourably with those in other parts of Asia, especially in many parts of rural Madras, where deficiency diseases are common, but stone in the bladder is rare.

McCarrison[9] studied the relation between diet and stones in India and also produced both renal and vesical calculi in rats by feeding diets low in vitamin A and rich in calcium. These diets had little resemblance to human diets and so his results must be interpreted with caution.

Unfortunately all these observations leave the problem of the 'stone areas' in the tropics unsolved. However, at least in Thailand there is evidence that the diet may contribute. A team led by Halstead and Valyasevi studied the problem and between 1963 and 1973 published 10 papers in the *American Journal of Clinical Nutrition*. The team found marked differences between the diets consumed by 16 farm families resident in a small village in which bladder stone was epidemic, compared to that consumed by 15 families who were predominantly shopkeepers and government workers in

Ubol, a town of 27 000 inhabitants in which the incidence of stone was 14-fold lower. The town families consumed ordinary rice predominantly, while the villagers ate glutinous rice. Village diets were monotonous and consisted of rice, vegetables and uncooked 'fermented' fish, with infrequent supplements of fruits and animal protein, while the town families ate rice with cooked fermented fish, a great variety of fruits and other animal protein prepared in a variety of ways. Village children have many more crystals of oxalate in their urine than children in the town. These disappeared when orthophosphate was given. The village diets may contain an excess of oxalate and oxalate precursors and be deficient in phosphate.

Other factors. Stagnation and infection of urine and prolonged confinement to bed each predispose to stone formation. One or more of these is almost always present in a patient with a bladder stone in a non-endemic area.

RENAL CALCULUS

Renal colic, the excruciating pain caused by the passage of stones down the urinary tract, is well known in all countries. It stops when the stone is passed naturally or removed by a surgeon. A patient may never have another attack or attacks may recur at irregular and sometimes long intervals. Some patients have frequent attacks when they pass many small stones or gravel.

Most stones remain in the kidney and then they often produce no symptoms (silent stones). There they may grow, sometimes to a very large size. Infection may lead to pyelonephrosis, the commonest cause of chronic renal failure (Table 44.2).

Epidemiology

It is difficult to get a true picture of the prevalence of renal calculi. In England in 1976, 17 general practices with 64 454 people on their lists reported 67 stone episodes in 53 patients, and annual incidence of 85/100 000.[10] On the other hand in the Glasgow area a full radiographic examination of a random sample of 2000 of the population revealed 79 stone cases, a prevalence of 38/1000.[11] These stones were present in the kidneys and most of them were not producing symptoms.

Admissions to hospital for renal calculi have been increasing steadily in all industrialised countries, especially in men in social classes I and II.[6] No environmental cause has been established but diet, especially a low intake of vegetable fibre and a high intake of animal protein, have been incriminated. Both national and regional studies show a correlation between hospital discharges for renal stone disease and animal protein intake.[12]

Aetiology and pathogenesis

Bacteria infecting the kidney may provide a nidus on which a crystalline deposit may grow. Such a deposit is less likely to be washed away if the flow of urine is diminished. Infection and stagnation of urine predispose to formation of stones but are responsible for only a small proportion of cases. High urinary excretion of calcium, oxalate, uric acid and cystine each increase the risk of stones and the various causes of these are now briefly described. However, in the majority of patients suffering from renal stones no chemical or other abnormality can be detected. They are said to be idiopathic, a euphemism meaning that no cause has been found.

Increased urinary calcium. A daily urinary excretion of calcium above 300 mg in men and 250 mg in women has been called 'hypercalciuria' and is present in about 8 per cent of the healthy population but in less than half of patients who form stones.[13] It is due to high intestinal absorption of dietary calcium, perhaps caused by a high plasma concentration of $1,25\text{-}(OH)_2$ vitamin D.

Hypercalciuria with increased risk of stone formation occurs in hyperparathyroidism, which is the cause of 5 to 10 per cent of all calcium stones. Hypercalciuria also occurs after prolonged use of corticosteroids, in renal tubular acidosis, sarcoidosis and malignant disease of bone and these are causes of stone.

The urinary calcium output is normally unrelated to the dietary intake and there is no evidence that a patient who has passed a calcium stone reduces the risk of a recurrence by going on a low calcium diet. But it seems sensible for such a person not to have a high intake and this can be ensured by taking milk, yogurt and cheese only in small helpings — no great hardship.

Increased urinary oxalate. The greater part of the urinary oxalate is endogenous and comes from the metabolism of glycine in the tissues. Most of the dietary oxalate is unabsorbed and excreted in the faeces. Increased absorption is, however, the commoner cause of hyperoxaluria and this is liable to occur when the functions of the small bowel is impaired by disease.[14] Patients with Crohn's disease (regional enteritis) are known to be at increased risk of stone formation.

Primary hyperoxaluria arises from an inborn error of metabolism. Two types are known arising from two separate enzyme defects in the metabolism of glycine. Stone formation occurs in childhood, recurrences are common and often damage the kidneys and lead to chronic renal failure.

A typical English diet contains about 120 mg of oxalic acid of which 75 mg comes from five cups of tea.[15] It is sensible for anyone who has passed a stone containing oxalate to avoid tea, and also rhubarb and spinach (oxalic acid content 250–800 mg/100 g). This is not difficult. A low oxalate diet requires a severe restriction in choice of foods as many of vegetable origin contain up to 30 mg/100 g. It should be tried only in patients who have formed stones repeatedly at short intervals and with marked hyperoxaluria, shown by an oral oxalate loading test to be exogenous in origin.[14]

Increased urinary uric acid. This is a consequence of hyperuricaemia and stones are a common complication of gout (Chap. 43). Urate stones can also occur when there is no detectable abnormality in uric acid metabolism. The diet may need to be modified to reduce the purine intake as for patients with gout.

Increased urinary cystine. Cystinuria is due to an inborn error of metabolism. The renal tubules fail to reabsorb the amino acids, cystine, lysine, arginine and ornithine. These pass in large amounts into the urine where cystine, the least soluble amino acid, tends to precipitate out and form stones.

Prevention

Fluid intake. This is by far the most important prophylaxis against all forms of stone. A good flow of urine washes out particles of gravel. Normally urine flow is at its lowest during the night and so water should be drunk before going to bed. All patients who have suffered from stone should drink sufficient to produce at least 2.5 litres of urine daily. Occcasional measurements of urinary output is a useful reminder of this necessity.

The fluid intake is especially important for those who live in the tropics or work in a hot environment, as the urinary output is diminished by the amount of water lost in sweating. Europeans in the tropics have a higher incidence of stone disease than those who live at home. However, those who have suffered one or more attacks of renal colic can visit a tropical country, either to take up an appointment or for a holiday, with no increased risk of a recurrence, provided they always drink sufficient to get a high output of urine.

Diet. Only rarely does a patient who suffers from stone need a special diet. Nonetheless all patients should consider their dietary habits and alter them, if necessary, so that they drink only moderate amounts of milk and tea and eat only moderate amounts of milk products, meat and fish. They should forego spinach and rhubarb, but other vegetables and fruits may be of benefit by increasing fibre intake.

Drugs. The following drugs may be useful in some circumstances but patients who take them for long periods should be under medical supervision.

Bendrofluazide reduces urinary calcium by about 30 per cent; the mechanism of action is unknown but probably renal.

Pyridoxine in megadoses may be given to patients who form oxalate stones in the hope of diverting glycine metabolism towards serine and away from oxalate.

Penicillamine given by mouth is useful in cystinuria, as it combines with cystine which is then excreted in a more soluble form.

REFERENCES

1. Pendreigh D M, Heasman M A, Howitt L F, et al 1972 Survey of chronic renal failure in Scotland. Lancet 1: 304–7
2. Brenner B M, Meyer T W, Hostetter T H 1982 Dietary protein intake and the progressive nature of kidney disease. N Engl J Med 307: 652–9
3. Giovannetti S, Maggiore Q 1964 A low-nitrogen diet with proteins of high biological value for severe chronic uraemia. Lancet 1: 1000–3
4. Berlyne G M, Bazzard F J, Booth E M, Janabi K, Shaw A B 1967 The dietary treatment of acute renal failure. Q J Med 36: 59–83
5. Halliday D, Madigan M, Chalmers R A, et al 1981 The degree of conversion of α-keto acids to valine in health and uraemia. Q J Med 50: 53–62
6. Peacock M, Robertson W G 1982 Medical aspects of urolithiasis. In: Symposium on renal disease. R Coll Physicians Edin Publ no 57, p 109–38
7. Ellis H 1969 A history of bladder stone. Blackwell, Oxford
8. Passmore R 1953 Observations on the epidemiology of stone in the bladder in Thailand. Lancet 1: 638–40
9. Sinclair H M (ed) 1953 The work of Sir Robert McCarrison. Faber, London, p 244–60
10. Currie W E, Turner P 1979 The frequency of renal stones within Great Britain in a gouty and non-gouty population. Br J Urol 51: 337–41
11. Scott R, Freeland R, Mowat W, et al 1977 The prevalence of calcified upper urinary tract stone disease in a random population. Br J Urol 49: 589–95
12. Robertson W G, Peacock M, Heyburn P J, Hanes F A 1980 Epidemiological risk factors in calcium stone disease. Scand J Urol Nephrol (suppl) 53: 15–28
13. Parfit A M, Higgins B A, Nassim J R, Collins J A, Hill A 1964 Metabolic studies in patients with hypercalciuria. Clin Sci 27: 463–82
14. Rampton D S, Kasidas G P, Rose G A, Sarner M 1979 Oxalate loading test — screening test for steatorrhea. Gut 20: 1089–94
15. Zarembski P M, Hodgkinson A 1962 The oxalic acid content of English diets. Br J Nutr 16: 627–34

45

Dental Disease

The teeth are a living memorial to the defects of the previous diet. Too often by middle age a few crumbling and unstable tombstones are all that remain to commemorate past errors. This is a misfortune, since there can be no question that good teeth and gums are important for maintaining health. Furthermore the appearance of bad teeth, and the foetor that may come from them, are undesirable for aesthetic reasons.

Two closely associated pathological processes need to be considered: dental caries (decay of the enamel of the teeth) and periodontal disease of the gums (pyorrhoea alveolaris).

HISTORY AND GEOGRAPHICAL DISTRIBUTION

Both caries and periodontal disease occur among people of British ancestry throughout the world and among other people who have adopted their dietary habits. Rickets used to be called 'the English disease', but dental caries has at least as much title to that name. A German visitor to the Court of Elizabeth I left a personal impression of the Queen; he remarked on her hooked nose; narrow lips and black teeth; the last he explained as a defect the English seem subject to from their too great use of sugar. George Washington (a man of impeccable British ancestry) was one of the first ever to wear false teeth.

Although the British have long been prone to bad teeth, the evidence of mediaeval graveyards suggests that dental health was once much better. Drummond and Wilbraham[1] concluded that the decline in dental health that took place in the last century was due to the altered eating habits of country people coming into the new industrial towns. The changes which they thought important were: (1) the decline in the consumption of milk, (2) the general use of refined sugar which had previously been an aristocratic delicacy, and (3) the introduction of roller-milled white flour which was softer than the traditional wholemeal stone-ground wheat. Certainly by 1900 the general state of dentition

in Britain was deplorable; bad teeth was one reason that led to a high rejection of recruits for the army at that time.

By contrast, good dentition is the rule in primitive (though not necessarily uncivilised) people. The Eskimos who live in isolated settlements have excellent teeth with less than 5 per cent affected by caries. Their traditional diet is based on raw walrus meat and fish. In those who live in trading stations where they can buy canned food prevalence of caries is high. The Masai in Kenya, who live almost entirely on milk, meat and raw blood, have little caries. Their neighbours, the Kikuyu, whose diet is rich in carbohydrates and who take readily to European dietary habits, are prone to caries.[2] In many countries such foodstuffs as refined wheat flour and sugar and sweetened soft drinks nowadays form a regular part of the diet of the people, particularly in the towns, where the prevalence of caries and periodontal disease is often very high.

The study of populations during a war and when living in isolation often throws light on nutritional problems, as the following examples show.

In Norway[3] the dental health of children actually improved in World War II during the German occupation, despite the cruel restriction of food supplies. Sugar and sweets were, of course, almost impossible to obtain; the people reverted to the traditional short commons of the European peasantry — wholemeal bread and such vegetables as they could grow for themselves. Though the supply of milk for children was deficient, they nevertheless developed good teeth.

For many years the people of Tristan da Cunha lived in almost complete isolation in the Atlantic. They were poor, but several investigators who visited the island reported on their excellent dental health. In 1942 a meteorological station was set up on the island. The regular visits of ships and the establishment of a fish canning factory led to a great increase in prosperity, the introduction of imported foods and a rapid decline in dental health. When the islanders were evacuated in 1961, a dental survey showed that both caries and periodontal disease were widespread.[4]

DENTAL STRUCTURE

The substance of the teeth is mainly composed of a bone-like material, dentine, which is protected on its outer surface by a thin layer of very hard enamel. Inside is the soft pulp cavity, supplied by a nerve and an arteriole (Fig. 45.1). Enamel is formed by cells known as ameloblasts, which are ectodermal in origin; dentine is formed by odontoblasts derived from mesoderm.

Dentine resembles bone in that it is composed of a cellular, protein-containing matrix in which calcium salts are deposited. Whereas bone consists of about 40 per cent of inorganic salts and 60 per cent of matrix, dentine contains about 80 per cent of inorganic salts. Enamel is even more dense, with less than 5 per cent of non-cellular matrix which nevertheless plays an essential part in maintaining its structure. Even the enamel surface of a tooth is a living tissue.

DENTAL HYPOPLASIA

The growth of teeth, like that of any other organ or structure in the body, may be impaired by adverse factors in fetal life, infancy or early childhood. A defective diet or a severe infection which impairs growth may lead to hypoplasia of either enamel or dentine or both.

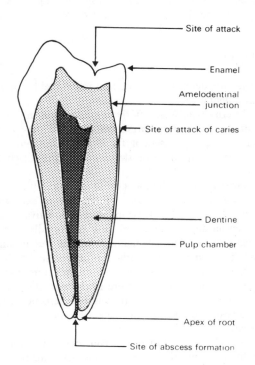

Fig. 45.1 The structure of a tooth showing sites of attack of carries

Site of attack

Enamel

Amelodentinal junction

Site of attack of caries

Dentine

Pulp chamber

Apex of root

Site of abscess formation

Two types of hypoplasia of the permanent teeth have been described

G-hypoplasia (gross hypoplasia). In this the enamel surface is seen to be deeply pitted. The pitting is often present in a regular line affecting most of the teeth. This hypoplasia can often be ascribed to an illness in early childhood — such as whooping cough — at the time when the permanent teeth were developing.

M-hypoplasia. This less familiar kind was first described by Lady Mellanby and called after her. There is a general defect in development of the enamel so that the surface of the tooth, instead of being perfectly smooth and hard, has an irregular 'washboard' texture, which is often more easily felt than seen, by running a fine probe over the posterior surface of the tooth. In a long series of investigations, a close association was demonstrated between the incidence of M-hypoplasia and of caries in London school-children.[5]

Linear hypoplasia of the incisors of the primary dentition has been reported in several underdeveloped parts of the world. It is more common in children with PEM.[6] Intrauterine development of the enamel may be impaired by maternal vitamin D deficiency.[7]

DIETARY FACTORS AND DENTAL DEVELOPMENT

Vitamin D deficiency. Dentine and bone are analogous structures of similar origin and in the absence of vitamin D neither develop normally. The relation between vitamin D deficiency, dental hypoplasia and caries is not clear cut and surveys in the United States and Canada have given conflicting answers.[8] Very few of the chidren in London studied by the Mellanbys would have had clinical rickets, but for many of them the supply of vitamin D would at best have been only marginally adequate. The much greater prevalence of caries in northern countries than in tropical countries may be in part due to smaller exposure to sunlight and the consequent diminished synthesis of the vitamin in the skin. Eruption of the teeth is delayed in children with clinical rickets.

Protein-energy malnutrition. The relation between eruption of the deciduous teeth and PEM was examined in a symposium which contained reports from fifteen different countries. In general, dental eruption is usually little delayed in mild or moderate PEM but may be in children with severe growth retardation.[9]

DENTAL CARIES

Dental caries results in the destruction of the hard structures of the teeth. Initially, the enamel outer covering of the crown becomes decalcified, the area usually appearing as a small white spot. As the destructive process continues discoloration becomes more pronounced, the tooth surface softens and decay penetrates deeper into the enamel structure. Once caries penetrates through the enamel into the dentine, it spreads laterally as well as in depth and cavitation occurs. As the lesion deepens, the pulp becomes affected and before it is irreversibly damaged it reacts to certain substances, particularly sweets, and to temperature with sensitivity and pain. At a certain point, the cellular structure becomes damaged beyond repair and the pulp dies. Bacteria proceed down the root canal, out through the apex of the tooth and into the surrounding structures, causing either acute or chronic abscesses. This process may be free of discomfort or agonisingly painful.

EPIDEMIOLOGY

The major index used to measure the occurrence of caries is DMF (decayed, missing, filled) index for permanent teeth, and its counterpart the d.e.f. (decayed, indicated for extraction, or filled) index for deciduous teeth. Relatively few teeth are congenitally missing, lost due to trauma or removed for reasons other than caries up to early adulthood. Therefore, the M, or missing, component can be assumed to be due to caries at least until the early twenties.

By about age 35 years the number of teeth extracted for periodontal reasons begins to exceed that for caries, so the index loses its power as a measure of the prevalence of caries. Studies on reasons for tooth loss are generally based on subjective judgments without the use of X-rays and are not very reliable. Measures of caries experience, therefore, become more and more inaccurate as age increases and the data should be viewed accordingly. However, despite the various reasons that may make epidemiological measurements inexact, the data show a staggering amount of disease in all communities that have adopted Western dietary habits (Table 45.1). Females have higher DMF scores than males. At virtually all ages they have more filled and fewer decayed teeth than males, and starting in the teenage years more missing teeth. This disparity appears to be the result of differential receipt of dental services. Correlations of DMF with income and education have been weak, although, as expected, the F component is

higher and the D and M components are lower for upper socioeconomic groups. There are still throughout the Third World many rural communities with little or no caries.

PATHOGENESIS

Production of dental caries depends on bacteria. Streptococci normally reside on and between the teeth and produce lactic acid by fermenting sugars ingested as food and drink. When a sufficient concentration of acid (about pH 5) is in contact with a dental surface for a long enough time, the crystalline material in the enamel starts to dissolve because calcium phosphate is soluble in acid. Unlike bones the enamel of teeth has little or no capacity for regeneration; once a hole is established, it remains and is likely to enlarge because bacteria can lodge in it more securely than on the biting or brushed surfaces of the teeth.

As well as breaking down sugars to lactic and similar organic acids, some bacteria, e.g. *Streptococcus mutans*, possess enzymes which can build up extracellular accumulations of insoluble polymers of glucose and fructose (dextrans and levans). These adhere to the teeth and form a **plaque** in which the bacteria are protected from the cleansing action of the tongue. After feeds containing sugar, acid is produced in the plaque next to the enamel but inaccessible to neutralisation by saliva.

AETIOLOGY

Four factors determine whether an individual has much or little dental caries.

1. Micro-organisms.   Without micro-organisms caries cannot occur. By fermenting carbohydrate they bring about the acidity essential for demineralisation. The major agents appear to be streptococci, particularly *S. mutans*.

2. Host factors.   These include saliva and the teeth. Decreased salivary secretion, usually due to decreased chewing, leads to an increase in caries. The saliva's buffering action and its ability to raise pH rapidly aids in reducing caries. Saliva contains lysozyme but its antibacterial action in the mouth is probably slight. Both morphology and composition of a tooth affect its susceptibility to caries. Caries is more likely to occur in pits and fissures as well as in teeth where the enamel is less mineralised and lacking in trace elements, especially fluorine.

3. Time.   The frequency of consumption of refined carbohydrates and the length of time they remain in the mouth are directly related to caries activity. In adddition it takes at least 24 hours and possibly longer for dental

Table 45.1 Data from USA 1971–74[10]

Age	Decayed	Missing	Filled	DMF
6–11	0.7	0.1	0.8	1.7
12–17	1.8	0.6	3.7	6.2
18–44	1.7	4.9	8.3	14.9

plaque to organise to the point where destructive activity can take place. Good oral hygiene can counteract this.

4. Substrates for acid production. These are determined by the diet.

DIET

Carbohydrates
Human and animal studies show that refined carbohydrates particularly sucrose, are necessary for the production of caries.[11] Bacteria ferment the carbohydrates into acids which demineralise the tooth structure. Sugar is the principal cause of dental caries, a diseases that affects over 95 per cent of dentate adults in Britain. Each year over 30 million teeth are filled and 5 million extracted by 20 000 dentists at a cost of over £400 million. In Third World countries the prevalence of dental caries is increasing rapidly because of rising sugar consumption. The importance of the sugary foods and the time at which they are eaten was demonstrated at a mental hospital in Vipeholm, Sweden.[12] Sucrose in solution with meals had little cariogenic effect, but sticky toffees and caramels between meals produced a sharp increase in dental caries. At the end of wartime rationing in the UK, children in institutions were given extra sugar, but only at meal times, and this caused no increase in caries.[13]

Several sugars can cause caries but sucrose causes most damage for two reasons: it is the sugar most commonly eaten and it encourages the colonisation and growth in dental plaque of *S. mutans*. Other sugars have a similar property but to a lesser extent. Xylitol is as sweet as sucrose, and in a controlled trial a group of young adults who used confectionery sweetened with xylitol developed less caries than two groups who used sucrose or fructose as sweeteners.[14]

Demineralisation occurs when the pH falls to 5.5 or less. The rapidity of the drop of pH, the level to which it drops, and the time taken for it to return to the resting level depend on the type and concentration of the sugars and the form, and particularly the frequency, of ingestion. If foods and confections containing refined sucrose are eaten more frequently than three times a day the chances of caries attack are greatly increased because the pH of the plaque remains below the critical level for demineralisation for more than three hours a day. If sucrose is consumed infrequently and in very low concentrations, demineralised enamel can remineralise. Remineralisation of early carious lesions, without a break in the outer enamel but advanced enough to show clinical and radiographical changes occurs frequently. The process is enhanced by fluoride. Thus sucrose plays a dominant part in the aetiology of caries, and other sugars are incriminated to a lesser extent.

Other dietary components
Strongly acid drinks taken frequently can dissolve and wear down enamel. Fibrous foods like apples have a scouring action and when they are eaten after a meal this reduces plaque formation. Some foods such as cheese are protective, as they increase the flow of saliva and also have an inhibiting effect on dental plaque by raising pH and increasing the calcium content.[15] Dietary fibre may also be beneficial in this way. Chewing betel reduces the chance of dental caries. The lime content of pan, used in India, raises the pH.

Fluoride
The salts present in dentine and enamel normally contain, besides calcium phosphate and bicarbonate, traces of other elements including fluoride. A concentration of fluoride in drinking water between 0.5 and 1 part per million (p.p.m.) protects against caries; fluoride ions replace hydroxyls in the hydroxyapatite lattice of the mineral in the enamel. In areas where the fluoride content of the water is low, addition of fluoride may more than halve the incidence of caries.

This was demonstrated in a classic experiment in the United Kingdom. Fluoridation of the water supply up to 1 p.p.m. was begun in three areas, Anglesey, Kilmarnock and Watford, in 1956. Three neighbouring areas in which the water was unchanged served as controls. A dental survey of the children was carried out then and again in 1961.[16] Table 45.2 summarises the results. There can be no doubt that in the three areas where fluoride was added to the water, a substantial reduction in caries followed. Similar findings have been recorded from all over the world. Furthermore, in the Scottish burgh of Kilmarnock fluoridation which was started in 1956 was discontinued six and a half years later because of a reversal of opinion of the Burgh Council. Careful studies of the children's teeth showed a substantial reduction of caries in 1961 and 1963 but an increase of caries was quite apparent by 1968.[17]

The benefit of adding traces of fluoride to the public water supply in areas where it is deficient in fluoride was described in 1970 in a monograph from the World

Table 45.2 Effect of fluoridation of the water supply of the district on the prevalence of caries (average number of carious teeth per child)

Children's ages	Control areas		Areas with water to which fluoride was added		Percentage reduction
	1956	1961	1956	1961	
3 years	3.53	3.32	3.80	1.29	66
4 years	5.18	4.83	5.39	2.31	57
5 years	5.66	5.39	5.81	2.91	50
6 years	6.32	6.22	6.49	4.81	26
7 years	7.08	6.89	7.06	6.05	14

Health Organisation.[18] It is now an established practice. In North America over 100 million people are drinking artificially fluoridated water, as are large numbers in many other countries.

If the drinking water in a locality contains more than 2 p.p.m. of fluoride, mottling of the teeth occurs (Fig. 12.3, p. 124). At higher levels (5 p.p.m.) every tooth may be affected and the enamel surface is often irregular and stained brown at gum margins. These levels of fluoride occur naturally in parts of Africa and India. Such teeth are softer than normal and yet unusually resistant to dental decay.

Other trace elements

In Heliconia, an isolated village in the Andes in Colombia, the prevalence of dental caries is unusually low. The water is low in fluoride and the population consume plenty of sugar. A team from the Forsyth Dental Center, Boston, examined trace elements in water, saliva, teeth and dental plaques. Compared with a control village, where the incidence of caries was high, the water of Heliconia contained more calcium, magnesium, molybdenum and vanadium and less copper, iron and manganese.[19] Hardness of water is often associated with a high fluoride content but here they are separated. There have been reports from other countries which suggest that molybdenum may protect against caries. In 21 villages in Papua-New Guinea analyses of soil and food for minerals and trace elements were compared with the number of carious teeth, which ranged from 0 to 30 per cent. Caries was negatively related with alkali and alkaline earth elements in soils, including magnesium, calcium and lithium, and in staple foods with molybdenum and vanadium. Copper and lead in soils and foods were associated with caries.[20]

For further reading, a monograph on dental caries by Silverstone and colleagues[21] with excellent bibliographies is recommended.

PERIODONTAL DISEASE

The term periodontal disease designates a variety of diseases which affect the supporting structures of the teeth. The two most frequently occurring forms are gingivitis and periodontitis. Gingivitis is limited to the gingiva or soft tissue, surrounding the teeth. It is an inflammatory condition that results in bleeding from the gums and may lead to changes in their colour, shape, size, surface texture and consistency. Gingivitis is reversible and does not result in destruction of the tissues that support the teeth. Restoration of oral hygiene can control the condition without permanent damage.

Periodontitis is an extension of the inflammatory process from the gingiva to the supporting periodontal tissues and a destruction of these tissues. Thus periodontitis can at best be only controlled since irreversible tissue destruction has already occurred. The most significant result of chronic periodontitis is the loss of bone supporting the teeth which in turn can lead to mobility and eventual tooth loss.

EPIDEMIOLOGY

Accurate data on prevalence are difficult to obtain. Diagnosis requires (1) an assessment of changes in colour, shape, and surface texture of the gingiva, (2) probing of the gingival sulcus to determine if a periodontal pocket is present and (3) the assessment of tooth function; all of these are difficult to quantitate. There are indices to measure gingivitis, periodontitis, amount of plaque, amount of calculus, or some combination of these factors, but there is not one epidemiological index such as the DMF index for caries that is generally accepted and widely used.

Data from the National Center for Health Statistics in the USA[22] indicate that periodontal disease is a major disorder. Prevalence of periodontitis increases with age and affects about 15, 36 and 50 per cent of age groups 18 to 44, 45 to 64 and 65 to 74 years respectively.

Gingivitis has been found in 32.2 per cent of children aged 12 to 17 years, with an additional 1.3 per cent having periodontitis. Studies of large groups of children in Canada[10] reported from 79 to 96 per cent of 13 to 14 year olds as having gingivitis with periodontitis approaching 3 per cent. There is much variation in the prevalence of gingivitis in adolescents, but periodontitis is less common.

Epidemiological studies show a strong positive correlation between the presence and amount of plaque and calculus and the prevalence and severity of periodontal disease.

In the South Pacific periodontal disease is widespread and not confined to those in close contact with Western civilisation. The Nauruan people, for example, live almost entirely on imported foods, but the Pukapukans in the Cook Islands depend on native foods, yet both communities were grossly affected.[23] Surveys in New Guinea and Pukapuka have shown that caries is present among natives not affected by civilisation. However, when Western foods are introduced, prevalence shows a marked increase.

PRESERVATION OF DENTAL HEALTH

Dental health requires action both by individuals and by communities. Health education is necessary for each to be effective.

Fluoridation of water supplies

The discovery of the role of fluoride in preventing dental caries is a classical contribution of epidemiology to community health. The optimum concentration of fluoride in drinking water is between 0.7 and 1.2 p.p.m. In areas where the water supply contains less than 0.7 p.p.m. addition of sufficient fluoride to raise the concentration to this range may more than halve the incidence of caries. The cost of this varies from as low as $0.14 per head yearly in large cities to $1.73 in small communities in the USA.

There is a wide safety margin. In Africa and in India there are many areas where the fluoride content of the water is so high as to cause widespread mottling of the teeth with no apparent effect on general health. In Bartlett, Texas, the natural drinking water contained 8 p.p.m.; but the incidence of general diseases was no different from that in neighbouring towns where the water supply was low in fluoride.[24] The claim that fluoridation of water causes cancer has been shown to be false.[25]

There has always been and still is strong opposition to this community action. This is based on the grounds that it is mass medication and, as an individual cannot avoid drinking the water, an interference with individual liberties. It is difficult for a scientifically trained person to appreciate this argument. Local water supplies are treated with chlorine and by other means to make them bacteriologically safe and this is done without objection. Fluoride is not a foreign chemical and is only added to water supplies deficient in it.

The antifluoridation lobby gets members elected to local councils who control water supplies. By blocking fluoridation schemes proposed by the dental and medical services, they have been responsible for much unnecessary dental disease. They have also caused much public money to be misspent. In 1983 the Court of Session in Glasgow upheld the claim by an edentulous woman that Strathclyde Regional Council had no right in law to add fluoride to the water in order to combat tooth decay. The case cost the taxpayer £1 million and extended over 201 court days and resulted in a 120 000 word judgment. There have also been expensive lawsuits in Dublin and Pittsburg.

It is tragic that dental caries remains so prevalent in many areas because local authorities refuse to implement the most cost-effective measure for its prevention.

Professional dental care

Dentists preserve carious teeth by filling cavities; they prevent diseases of the teeth and gums by removing calculus and cleaning; they also give orthodontic treatment for overcrowded teeth. They and dental nurses may apply concentrated solutions of fluoride to the teeth; this could not be done in the home because of possible toxic effects if the solution is accidently swallowed. Mature enamel does not incorporate fluoride as readily as that on newly erupted teeth, so topical application is much more effective in children. When done repeatedly in early childhood, it has been shown to reduce the incidence of caries. A sealant consisting of an adhesive resin can be applied to the surfaces of teeth containing pits and fissures. This may remain on a tooth for several years and can be very effective in preventing caries[26] but for this a very careful technique has to be followed.

All the above measures are part of a good school dental service. The provision of such a service and taking steps to see that all children use it regularly is a community responsibility. Appreciation of the value of the service depends on education of parents, teachers and children. In Scotland there is a statutory duty to examine the teeth of primary and secondary school children once yearly, and statistics are based on a yearly inspection in January. The majority of children are in fact seen every six months although this is difficult in the large inner city schools. For those at risk a three times yearly examination is carried out. Sealants and topical fluoride application are used in the service. That the dental health services for schools have been successful in reducing the incidence of caries has been shown by Mansbridge[27] who has studied schoolchildren of 5, 8 and 14 years in Edinburgh and Ayr in 1952, 1959, 1969 and 1983.

Over the period in both areas there has been a marked increase in the percentage of children who are caries free and these increases have been most marked in those children with good oral hygiene.

Reduction of sugar intake

Evidence that the prevalence of caries is related to the amount of sugar eaten in a community has led to the suggestion[11] that government ministries and food and confectionery manufacturers should adopt a common policy to reduce sugar consumption. The measures advocated are (1) no sugar should be added to infant and baby foods, paediatric medicines, fruit juices or vitamin preparations, (2) the levels of added sugars in commonly used foods, such as breakfast cereals and jams should be reduced and more foods with no added sugar should be made available, and (3) the sugar content of confections and drinks should be reduced and sugar-free snacks and drinks made available.[11]

Manufacturers now make many products in line with these recommendations and their use should be encouraged by health education. But they are in business to sell high quality goods that the public like. The high quality of British jams depends on a high sugar content. Governments restrictions on the use of sugar are acceptable only in emergencies, such as war. Manufacturers should not be prevented from making the sweet things that many of us enjoy at times. We should all learn and teach our children to use them in strict moderation. Sweets are excellent as a treat. A survey in the north of England found that children aged 11–12 years consumed daily on average 118 g of sugar, 21 per cent of their energy intake.[28] This is not moderation.

Individual actions

Individuals can care for their teeth in three ways (1) by keeping then clean, (2) by restricting their intake of sweets and sugar and (3) by regular visits to the dentist.

Brushing of the teeth twice daily is strongly recommended and for children a fluoride toothpaste is best. In theory a clean tooth does not decay. A plaque is a potential precursor of caries and of periodontitis and

brushing the teeth limits their formation. Toothpicks of wood or quill are useful for removing debris from between the teeth. Together with massage of the gums they help to prevent gingivitis.

Snacks between meals containing sucrose and sticky sweets should be avoided. The latter prolong the time of contact of sugar between the teeth and this is probably a key factor in the production of caries. Eating salted crisps instead of sweets is switching evils.

After leaving the care of a school dental service, everyone should chose a personal dentist who is visited regularly at intervals determined by their advice.

Reports by WHO,[18] the American Nutrition Foundation,[29] the British Dental association[30] and the Royal College of Physicians[31] provide further information on dental health and are recommended to health educators.

REFERENCES

1. Drummond J C, Wilbraham A 1959 The Englishman's food (edn revised by Hollingsworth D M). Cape, London, p 164–6
2. Orr J B, Gilks J L 1931 Studies on nutrition. The physique and health of two African tribes. MRC Spec Rep Ser no. 155
3. Toverud G 1957 The influence of war and post-war conditions on the teeth of Norwegian school children. III: Discussion of food supply and dental condition in Norway and other European countries. Milbank Mem Fund Q 35: 357–459
4. Holloway P J, James P M C, Slack G L 1963 Dental disease in Tristan da Cunha. Br Dent J 115: 19–25
5. Mellanby M, Mellanby H 1954 Dental structure and caries in 5-year-old children attending LCC schools (1949 and 1951). Br Med J 2: 944–8
6. Sweeney E A, Saffir A J, de Leon R 1971 Linear hypoplasia of deciduous teeth in malnourished children. Am J Clin Nutr 24: 29–31
7. Purvis R J, Barrie W J McK, MacKay G S, et al 1973 Enamel hypoplasia of the teeth associated with neonatal tetany: a manifestation of maternal vitamin D deficiency. Lancet 2: 811–4
8. Shaw J H, Sweeney E A 1973 Nutrition in relation to dental medicine. In: Goodhart R S, Shils M E (eds) Modern nutrition in health and disease, 5th edn. Lea & Febiger, Philadelphia, p 733–69
9. Jelliffe E F P, Jelliffe D B (eds) 1973 Deciduous dental eruption, nutrition and age assessment. J Trop Pediatr Environ Child Hlth 19: 193–248
10. Schoen M H, Freed J R 1981 Prevention of dental disease: caries and periodontal disease. Annu Rev Public Health 2: 71–92
11. Sheiham A 1983 Sugars and dental decay. Lancet 1: 282–4
12. Gustafsson B E, Quensel C E, Larnke L S, et al 1954 The Vipeholm dental caries study. The effect of different levels of carbohydrate intake on caries activity in 436 individuals observed for five years. Acta Odontol Scand 11: 232–364
13. King J D, Mellanby M, Stones H M, Green H N 1955 The effect of sugar supplements on dental caries in children. MRC Spec Rep Ser no 288

14. Scheinin A; Mäkinen K K, Ylitalo K 1974 Turku sugar studies. I: An intermediate report on the effect of sucrose, fructose and xylitol diets on the caries incidence in man. Acta Odontol Scand 32: 383–412
15. Rugg-Gunn A J, Edgar W M, Geddes D A M, Jenkins G N 1975 The effect of different meal patterns upon plaque pH in human subjects. Br Dent J 139: 351–6
16. Ministry of Health, Scottish Office 1962 The conduct of the fluoridation studies in the United Kingdom and the results achieved after five years. Rep Public Health Med Subj no 105
17. Department of Health and Social Security 1969 The fluoridation studies in the United Kingdom and the results achieved after eleven years. Rep Public Health Med Subj no 122
18. World Health Organization 1970 Fluorides and human health. WHO Monogr Ser no 59
19. Glass R L, Rothman K J, Espinal F, Velez H, Smith N J 1973 The prevalence of human dental caries and water-borne trace elements. Arch Oral Biol 18: 1099–1104
20. Barnes D E, Adkins B L, Scharmschula R G 1970 Etiology of caries in Papua-New Guinea. Bull WHO 43: 769–84
21. Silverstone L M, Johnson M W, Hardie J M, Williams R A D 1981 Dental caries: aetiology, pathology and prevention. Macmillan, London
22. Kelly J E, Harvey C R 1979 Basic data on dental examination findings of persons 1–74 years. United States, 1971–1974. National Health Survey ser 11, no 214
23. Davies G N 1956 Dental conditions among the Polynesians of Pukapuka (Danger Island). II: Prevalence of periodontal disease. J Dent Res 35: 734
24. Leone N C, Shimkin M B, Arnold F A, et al 1955 Medical aspects of excessive fluoride in a water supply. Public Health Rep 69: 925–36
25. Erickson J D 1978 Mortality in selected cities with fluoridated and non-l:fluoridated water supplies. N Engl J Med 298: 1112–6
26. McCune R J, Bojanini J, Abodeely R A 1979 Effectiveness of a pit and fissure sealant in the

prevention of caries: three year clinical results. J Am Dent Soc 99: 619–23

27. Mansbridge J N 1985 Community Dent Health (in press)

28. Hackett A F, Rugg-Gunn A J, Appleton D, Allison M, Eastoe E 1984 Sugar eating habit of 405 11- to 14-year-old English children. Br J Nutr 51: 347–56

29. Nutrition Foundation 1980 Report on the relationship between diet nutrition and dental caries. Nutrition Foundation, New York

30. British Dental Association 1969 Fluoridation of water supplies: questions and answers. London

31. Royal College of Physicians 1976 Fluoride, teeth and health. Pitman, London

46

Diseases of the Gastrointestinal Tract

Some aspects of the applied physiology of the gastrointestinal tract are discussed before the nutritional and dietetic aspects of clinical syndromes and diseases are described.

1. The lumen of the gut from the mouth to the anus is outside the body. Those nutrients that are large molecules have to be broken down or digested before they can be absorbed and assimilated into the tissues. Until this happens a nutrient is physiologically outside the body.

2. The intestinal contents are moved along the small intestine by peristaltic waves. The onward movement is delayed by sphincters, the pylorus between the stomach and the duodenum, the ileocaecal valves and the anal sphincters.

3. The absorption of most nutrients depends on active (energy-dependent) transport across the intestinal epithelium. Most nutrients are absorbed from the upper small intestine (jenunum) but vitamin, B12 and also bile acids are absorbed from the distal ileum and large amounts of water and electrolytes from the colon.

4. Exchange between the body proper and the lumen of the tract through the intestinal mucosa is a two-way process. The tract is not only a mechanism for digestion and assimilation but also for exchange and elimination. Here it has much in common with renal tubular secretion and reabsorption.

5. Metabolic activity of the bacterial flora in the caecum and colon modifies organic compounds which have come through the small intestine, notably those secreted into it by the liver. Some of these are then absorbed and so form an enterohepatic circulation; others pass out in the faeces.

6. The functions of the gastrointestinal tract depend on exocrine glands which discharge into the lumen, e.g. the parotid glands, pancreas and liver. They also depend on hormones secreted into the blood stream by the upper part of the tract which influence other parts of the tract.

7. These hormones are peptides. The main physiological actions of three of them, gastrin, secretin and cholecystokinin are well known. Many other gastrointestinal hormones are now identified,[1] but their physiological roles are not yet well defined, and it is not known whether over- or underproduction of any of them is responsible for any gastrointestinal disorder.

8. The amount of water and electrolytes secreted into the lumen is large (Table 46.1) so that diarrhoea or vomiting may cause large negative balances requiring oral or parenteral replenishment.

9. Protein enters the gastrointestinal tract not only in the diet but also in the digestive juices and in the shed mucosal epithelium. The daily output of digestive enzymes is equivalent to up to 50 g of protein and the

Table 46.1 Estimates of quantities of water and Na, K and Cl entering the human intestine daily[2]

	Volume (ml)	Concentration (mmol/l)			Electrolyte load (mmol/24 h)		
		Na	K	Cl	Na	K	Cl
Saliva	1500	30	20	35	45	30	52
Gastric juice	3000	50	10	150	150	30	450
Bile	500	160	5	50	80	3	25
Pancreatic juice	2000	160	5	30		10	60
Internal load	7000				595	73	587
Dietary intake	1500				170	65	110
Grand total	8500				765	138	697

whole mucosa is replaced or turned over every three or four days. Hence usually only about half of the protein entering the lumen is of dietary origin.

10. The intestinal mucosa contains cells which produce antibodies, including the immunoglobulins IgA and IgM. Dysfunction of these cells is a possible basis for gluten enteropathy and may be part of the mechanism leading to pernicious anaemia.

11. Some primary nutritional diseases, e.g. protein-energy malnutrition, lead to atrophy of the gastrointestinal tract and impair absorption of nutrients, so setting up a vicious circle.

12. The gastrointestinal tract through its autonomic nerve supply is closely related to centres in the limbic system of the brain concerned with expression of emotion. Worry and anxiety can be expressed as dyspepsia, which is also one feature of depressive illness. Eating is not only a physiological necessity but also a mode of expression of the emotions and social, cultural and religious attitudes. A diet may need to be modified to relieve symptoms in many organic and psychosomatic disorders of the alimentary tract. Every patient with a disorder of the digestive system should be carefully questioned about his dietary and social habits.

DIETARY HISTORY

The dietary history includes information about the number and time of the meals taken daily, whether they are taken regularly, if they are hurried and if the food is adequately chewed. A description should be obtained of the various foods eaten and of their effects in alleviating or producing symptoms. Enquiries should be made about the use of alcohol, tobacco and medicines. Some drugs may irritate the gastric mucosa and disturb the neuromuscular function of the gastrointestinal tract. Self-medication with proprietary preparations, especially those containing aspirin, may cause dyspepsia. Questions should be directed to finding out whether the patient is living in a state of anxiety induced by social relations at home or at work. We have repeatedly seen dyspepsia, diarrhoea or other abdominal symptoms developing when a love affair is not proceeding on a satisfactory course, when an employee is being bullied by an employer or when some financial misfortune is causing undue worry. It is also important to question whether the patient has been abroad recently, which may give a clue to the nature of an infection of the gastrointestinal tract.

METHODS OF INVESTIGATION

The oesophagus, stomach, duodenum and small intestine can be visualised by radiography after a barium meal and the colon and rectum after a barium enema. Aspiration of gastric juices allows the secretory activity of the stomach in response to pentagastrin and other stimuli to be measured. The rectum and sigmoid colon can be examined through a sigmoidscope. These are established techniques in use for more than 50 years.

The upper and lower parts of the gastrointestinal tract can now be examined using a flexible fibre optic gastroscope or colonoscope. With these instruments the mucosa of the oesophagus, stomach, duodenum and colon can be observed directly and the image projected on a television screen for consultation and teaching. Biopsies can be taken for histological examination. In skilled hands the procedures are now easy and safe. Biopsy material from the small intestine can be obtained using a Crosby capsule. This is attached to a thin plastic tube and swallowed by the patient. It contains a rotating knife which is triggered by suction applied by a syringe to the end of the tube.

DISEASES OF THE MOUTH

Examination of the mouth may show lesions due to local causes or be indicative of general disease. Lesions primarily nutritional in origin are angular stomatitis, cancrum oris, nutritional parotitis and nutritional glossitis (Chapter 37). Glossitis is often a presenting feature in pellagra, the sprue syndrome, pernicious anaemia and iron-deficiency anaemia of long standing. Primary disease of the oral cavity may cause serious malnutrition and dehydration.

The tongue
Doctors have examined the tongues of their patients since the earliest times. The tongue may be dry in mouth breathers and coated with whitish yellow fur in those persons who smoke excessively. A clean red tongue, which is inflamed and painful (acute glossitis), suggests an acute primary deficiency of some member of the vitamin B complex. A clean pale and smooth tongue (chronic atrophic glossitis) suggests pernicious anaemia in remission or a long-standing iron-deficiency anaemia. Treatment includes a well-balanced diet, supplemented by iron or the appropriate vitamin when indicated. A local ulcer may be due to an ill-fitting denture or malignant disease, but rarely nowadays syphilis or tuberculosis.

The teeth, gums and mouth
Nutrition and dental disease are discussed in Chapter 45. While dental sepsis is no longer considered important as a cause of disease, it stands to reason that infections of the teeth and gums should be treated.

A bad taste in the mouth may be due to pyorrh ea

and is rarely due to disease. It often coincides with emotional problems and discussion of these may help.

Inflammatory and haemorrhagic lesions in the mouth and gums can result from many causes, e.g. infections with Vincent's organisms, haemolytic streptococci, *Candida albicans* (thrush), drug reactions and blood diseases (acute leukaemia, agranulocytosis, aplastic anaemia).

Recurrent aphthous ulcers are the commonest form of mouth ulcers. These are small (2 or 3 mm in diameter), superficial and painful. They may begin as vesicles and crops may come and go for no apparent reason, healing spontaneously. Occasionally this unpleasant condition is the first sign of coeliac disease. Therefore if the ulcers persist or recur repeatedly examination of the jejunal mucosa may be considered.

Any inflammatory condition of the mouth may contribute to a nutritional disorder, for the pain and difficulty in swallowing may restrict the intake of food.

TREATMENT

The treatment of angular stomatitis, glossitis and other primary nutritional disorders of the mouth has already been described in Chapter 37. There is no satisfactory evidence that any of the other lesions of the mouth mentioned above are improved by dietary therapy, with the exception of aphthous ulcers of the mouth associated with coeliac disease which may resolve with a gluten-free diet. If lesions are causing pain on chewing or swallowing, a fluid or semiliquid diet (Diet No. 16) might be given until the condition is brought under control.

DISEASES OF THE SALIVARY GLANDS

Parotitis

The enlargement of the parotid glands common in Asia and Africa associated with inadequate intakes of protein is described on page 336.

Inflammation of the parotid gland may be due to the virus of mumps (virus parotitis) or to bacterial infection of the glands which tends to develop during severe febrile illnesses and after major surgical operations if adequate attention is not given to oral hygiene.

Acute parotitis from any cause is often so severe as to make chewing and swallowing painful and difficult. A fluid diet, based on Diet No. 16, should be given until the inflammation subsides.

DISEASES OF THE OESOPHAGUS

Diseases of the oesophagus are much less common than diseases of the stomach or intestine. Difficulty in swallowing (dysphagia) is the main feature and may lead to choking and even inhalation of food, causing pneumonia or death. Inhalation may occur, particularly at night. Dysphagia results from a functional defect, with failure of onward movement of the peristaltic waves; alternatively the wave may be adequate but a block caused by spasm, inflammation or malignant disease prevents the food from getting through the affected area.

Swallowing is under voluntary control in the upper third of the oesophagus and is automatic thereafter. The stomach and oesophagus are kept separate by a combination of the muscle fibres of the diaphragm, the oblique entry of the oesophagus into the stomach and contraction of the smooth muscle fibres at the gastro-oesophageal junction, known as the cardia. A peristaltic wave which moves a bolus of food down the oesophagus relaxes the cardia temporarily. Thus appropriate relaxation and contraction of the smooth muscle at the cardia allow food to enter the stomach and prevent regurgitation of stomach contents into the oesophagus. If this neuromuscular mechanism is disturbed, dysphagia or heartburn may ensue.

Dysphagia may be produced by any neurological disorder, which damages the motor pathway between the cerebral cortex and peripheral muscle. Common causes are a stroke and achalasia. Possibly the commonest cause is achalasia.

Achalasia

The difficulty in swallowing is probably due to failure of the muscular relaxation of the lower end of the oesophagus which normally precedes the advancing peristaltic wave. Peristalsis itself is also abnormal as a result of degenerative changes in the neurones of Auerbach's plexus in the wall of the oesophagus.

Dysphagia is at first intermittent, but may become more and more persistent. In time the oesophagus becomes dilated and later, as a result of the stagnation of food, an oesophagitis develops and causes substernal pain. Diagnosis depends on characteristic changes in radiology and on manometery, i.e. pressure recordings along the oesophagus.

In early cases relief may be obtained by the use of a bland diet (Diet No. 17). This is often ineffective and then mechanical dilation using a balloon may be tried, but finally surgical myotomy may be needed.

Sideropenic dysphagia (Patterson-Kelly or Plummer-Vinson syndrome)

Most patients are women of middle age who have been living on poor diets. It was common in Britain 50 years ago when malnutrition was much more frequent than it is now. Dysphagia is due to degenerative changes at the junction of the pharynx and the oesophagus which may eventually lead to deformity in the form of a mucosal web in the upper oesophagus. These changes are attributed to iron deficiency because almost all patients have iron-deficiency anaemia. The syndrome may predispose to carcinoma. Treatment consists in improving the diet and giving medicinal iron and thereafter keeping the patient under periodic review.

Stricture

This may be either fibrous or malignant. Difficulty in swallowing, first of solid foods and later of semi-solids and liquids, is the presenting feature. Diagnosis is confirmed by oesophagoscopy using a flexible fibre optic endoscope and taking a biopsy or brushings for histological examination. Aspiration of swallowed fluid remaining in the oesophagus, each night and morning, reduces the risk of inhaling regurgitated matter. Relief may be obtained by gentle dilation and the introduction using an endoscope of a plastic tube (Celestin tube). This is valuable in maintaining food intake when radiotherapy is given. Both radiotherapy and surgical resection are used for malignant strictures. Before the operation it is important to restore the patient to a good nutritional state by pre-operative feeding, e.g. by intravenous feeding or by a tube passed through the strictured area with the help of an endoscope. In an inoperable case tube feeding through the stricture may prolong life in a merciful way. A high energy low fibre diet is given, as fibrous foods do not run easily down the tube. Homogenising the food is seldom necessary.

A common complication following dilation of a benign stricture of the lower oesophagus is heartburn, a symptom resulting from reflux of gastric contents into the oesophagus.

Hiatus hernia and reflux oesophagitis

These are common causes of dyspepsia and dysphagia and occur more frequently in women than in men. The diaphragm has several openings through which abdominal viscera can herniate and enter the thorax. Of these the most important is the oesophageal opening, or hiatus, to which the oesophagus is loosely attached. In middle age this attachment weakens so that thereafter the oesophagus and stomach readily herniate. This occurs more commonly in the obese as the increased bulk of their abdominal contents exerts more pressure on the hiatus. Pregnancy and chronic cough may act in the same way. Many of these hernias are symptomless and discovered accidentally by radiologists. Hiatus hernia usually gives rise to symptoms only in so far as the cardia of the stomach ceases to act as a sphincter and allow acid peptic juice to regurgitate into the oesophagus. This produces **reflux oesophagitis**. The cardinal symptom is heartburn which is felt substernally and may be accompanied by regurgitation of acid fluid into the mouth. Periodicity of the symptoms is an important

diagnostic point. Heartburn may occur after meals but typically follows bending, lifting or straining. It may occur when asleep in bed and wake the patient, who may obtain relief by sitting up. Few other pains produced in the alimentary tract are so closely linked to change of posture. The patient may also complain of a more severe pain or the sensation of food sticking. Chronic bleeding is not infrequent and a hiatus hernia should be suspected in any obscure iron-deficiency anaemia. Peptic ulceration of the oesophagus frequently occurs when a hiatus hernia impairs the sphincter and allows acid contents of the stomach to reflux into the oesophagus.

Patients can usually be kept free from symptoms by medical treatment. If there is obesity, weight reduction usually leads to a marked improvement; knowledge of this should motivate the patient to persist with a reducing diet. Corsets and other tight garments should not be worn. Patients distressed with pain at night should sleep with a pillow under the chest and the head of the bed raised on blocks; they should not take solid food before going to bed.

If the pain is severe the regimen should be of the ulcer type with the use of liquid antacids and cimetidine or other histamine (H_2)-receptor antagonist.

Anaemia due to bleeding should be treated with oral iron; if severe, blood transfusion may be needed. If pain persists despite medical treatment, there is probably ulceration and some degree of stricture, and surgical treatment is often required. As a result of newly devised operations more patients who fail to respond adequately to medical treatment are being submitted to surgery than in the past and good results may be expected.

Carcinoma of the oesophagus

The clinical features are those of a stricture. Such carcinomas are either squamous cell carcinomas, which are treated by radiotherapy, or adenocarcinomas arising from the vault of the stomach. Adenocarcinoma may be treated by surgery. Symptomatic relief may be given by passing a Celestin tube into the stomach. The epidemiology is discussed on page 568.

DYSPEPSIA

Dyspepsia is a word of Greek derivation, meaning indigestion or difficulty in digestion. Any gastrointestinal symptom associated with the taking of food is called dyspepsia, e.g. nausea, heartburn, epigastric pain, discomfort or distension. Dyspepsia may be present when there is no structural change in any part of the alimentary canal, in which case it is described as 'functional' and the symptoms may be psychological in origin or due to intolerance of a particular food. On the other hand dyspepsia may be a symptom of any organic disorder of the alimentary canal. It may also be caused reflexly by disease or disorder of structures outside the alimentary tract, e.g. the gall-bladder, pancreas, etc. Dyspepsia may be a symptom of a general disease, e.g. chronic nephritis and cardiac failure.

DYSPEPSIA AND ACID SECRETION

There is a great variation both in the quantity and concentration of acid secreted by the gastric glands. It was once thought that dyspepsia frequently arose as a result of too little or too much acid secretion. However, good digestion may be associated with the whole range of gastric acidity. For instance, patients with pernicious anaemia always have complete absence of acid secretion and yet seldom suffer from dyspepsia when the anaemia has been corrected by treatment with vitamin B12. It is very doubtful if lack of acid alone is ever responsible for digestive disturbances. When dyspepsia occurs with achlorhydria, it is probably due to coincidental conditions such as chronic gastritis, cancer of the stomach or disease of the gall-bladder, or to emotional states.

Likewise, high rates of acid secretion (hyperchlorhydria) may be found in people who have never suffered from dyspepsia. Hyperchlorhydria is frequently found in patients with duodenal ulcer, yet such patients may continue to secrete excessive amounts of acid, not only when they are having symptoms, but during long intervals when they are symptom-free. Hydrochloric acid may be partially responsible for the pain and dyspepsia of the acute stage of peptic ulcer, but this is by no means certain, because these symptoms may be due to hypermotility which so frequently accompanies hypersecretion.

MANAGEMENT OF DYSPEPSIA

A careful enquiry into the dietary history and social habits and a general physical examination are necessary. In young people, unless there is reason to suspect organic disease, it is unnecessary and probably unwise to investigate the stomach by radiography, endoscopy or the response to pentagastrin. Usually the patient has been overworking or overworrying, or is bolting his meals or eating his meals when excessively tired, or has been smoking immoderately or taking too much alcohol. The patient should be assured that if he gives up such habits, his symptoms will probably clear up rapidly. However, dyspepsia occurring for the first time in middle age, especially if accompanied by weight loss, should be carefully investigated without delay.

Patients with functional dyspepsia need dietary advice based mainly on common sense, with no rigid rules. Help is needed to prevent them becoming hypochrondriacs.

Patients may find that certain foods bring on their symptoms whereas others can be taken with impunity. Hence bland diets have been prescribed. However, there is no evidence that any foods are generally irritant and it is important not to restrict a patient's diet unless a particular food has been shown to bring on symptoms in his case. On page 632 a list of ten types of foods that may cause trouble is given, together with a list of foods that can usually be recommended. These lists together with general advice may be helpful in discussing with a patient what he should and should not eat.

PEPTIC ULCER

Peptic ulcer is one of the most common diseases, probably occurring in from 2.5 to 15 per cent of people sometime in their life, but incidence varies greatly in different communities. The term is used for an ulcer in any part of the digestive tract exposed to acid gastric juice, but the common sites are the stomach (gastric ulcer) and duodenum (duodenal ulcer) above the point of entry of the alkaline pancreatic juice.

The term peptic ulcer is used because it appears to develop from a loss of ability of the mucosa to withstand the digestive action of pepsin and HCl. How the healthy mucous membrane is protected from the action of gastric juices is little understood. Obviously a balance exists between acid pepsin secretion and mucosal resistance. In patients with gastric ulcer the secretion of acid is often within normal limits, but patients with duodenal ulcer nearly always have a high output of acid. This is probably accounted for in most cases by a larger than normal number of acid secreting parietal cells in the gastric mucosa. The great importance of gastric hypersecretion is supported by the intractable peptic ulceration of the Zollinger-Ellison syndrome in which gastrin, produced by a tumour of the non-β islet cells of the pancreas stimulates excessive gastric secretion by day and by night.

Less attention has been paid to the response of the gastric mucosa to its own secretion of enzymes and acid. One probable protective agent is the mucoprotein, mucin, which adheres to the stomach wall as a thin but resistant coating. Mucin is secreted in response to local, nervous and hormonal influences. Florey[3] in a Croonian lecture to the Royal Society in 1954 reviewed what little was then known about its protective action. Unfortunately not much more is known now, except for details of the chemical structure of its constituent glycoproteins.[4] Mucin possesses no appreciable buffering power against hydrochloric acid and has no inhibitory effect on pepsin digestion. Hence any protective action which it possesses probably depends on its acting, when gelled by contact with hydrochloric acid, as a physical barrier. Such a barrier would impede the mechanical mixing which brings the gastric juice in contact with surface cells. The lubricant properties of mucin may also help to protect the mucosa from mechanical trauma.

EPIDEMIOLOGY

Accurate estimates of either incidence or prevalence of this common chronic disease with most patients not being treated in hospital is difficult to obtain. Mortality rates and figures for hospital admissions give only a partial picture. The information available is critically reviewed in monographs by Langman[5] and Cook.[6]

In Britain over the last 150 years peptic ulcer has changed gradually from a disease mainly affecting the stomach in young women to one of the duodenum in middle-aged men. Gastric ulcer is now less common than duodenal ulcer. Today duodenal ulcer is three to four times more common in men than in women, and gastric ulcer slightly commoner. Formerly there were marked social gradients. Gastric ulcer affected mainly the poor, and duodenal ulcer the more wealthy. Now there is little difference between the social classes for either. Peptic ulcers occur at all ages and most commonly arise first in middle life. Deaths from complications are mostly in later life. In England and Wales there are about 3000 deaths annually but this is less than 1 per cent of all deaths. Both incidence and death rate are probably declining slowly, the latter partly due to continuing improvements in the surgical management of complications.

In north western Europe and in North America the picture is broadly the same as in Britain but in the USA the disease may be slightly less common. Regional surveys in different parts of the same country have often shown two or threefold differences in incidence.

In the tropics peptic ulcer is less common than in temperate regions but there are areas of high incidence, notably in southern India, especially Kerala State, and in Assam, in West Africa in coastal regions and in East Africa in the Nile–Congo watershed. In these areas duodenal ulcer is the predominant form.

AETIOLOGY

The epidemiological findings suggest strongly that environmental factors are partly responsible for peptic ulcers. As yet, no such factor has been identified. At the turn of the nineteenth century, when the concept of deficiency diseases was new and gastric ulcer was a common disease amongst poor and often malnourished people in the western world, it was natural to speculate that it might be due to a dietary lack. There is no evidence to support this. Gastric ulcer is not common in those parts of the tropics where malnutrition is widespread and often severe. It has not been produced in experimental animals fed on poor diets; such diets may produce acute gastric erosions but these lesions do not penetrate the walls of the stomach and become surrounded by fibrous tissue, the characteristics of human peptic ulcer.

In India and West Africa where the incidence of peptic ulcer is high, the staple food is usually either rice or cassava; incidence is generally low where wheat or millet is the staple. This suggests that a high fibre diet may be protective but there is little evidence to either confirm or refute this.

Potentially irritant substances

Four drugs in common use and with direct actions on the gastric mucosa — caffeine, ethanol, aspirin and nicotine — have each been subject to claims that they promote peptic ulcers. These and counter claims are reviewed by Langman.[5] There is little evidence that any of them is an important factor in inducing ulcers, but each taken in excess may delay healing. Aspirin is the most immediately important as a high proportion of those patients who have had a severe haemorrhage from their ulcer have been taking aspirin previously. The effect of smoking on ulcer patients is discussed below.

Genetic factors

Peptic ulcers occur more frequently in persons with blood group O than in those in other groups, and possibly in those with HLA-B5 antigens.

The factors that make a large minority of mankind periodically susceptible to autodigestion of the epithelium of stomach and duodenum continue to elude us.

CLINICAL FEATURES AND DIAGNOSIS

The commonest symptom is pain or discomfort in the upper central abdomen. It is usually described as burning or gnawing in character. Characteristically the pain comes and goes and is related to meals. In duodenal ulcer it usually occurs when the stomach is empty and is relieved by meals if they are not too large; the pain of gastric ulcer often comes on shortly after eating. Other symptoms which may occur are loss of weight, heartburn or vomiting. In some patients an ulcer causes no symptoms until a complication such as haemorrhage occurs. Should an ulcer bleed slowly, there is melaena (black stools) and anaemia. With a larger haemorrhage there is usually haematemesis; the blood which is vomited is altered to a dark brown colour.

In addition to the symptoms which are ascribable to

acid, spasm of the pyloric canal (pylorospasm) can give rise to a characteristic feeling of sickness and distension; this prevents some patients from taking food which would relieve their symptoms. In addition there may be heart-burn, due to reflux of acid into the oesophagus.

The cardinal investigations for peptic ulcer are radiographic examination with a barium meal and endoscopy. Fibre optic endoscopes have transformed the diagnosis of ulcers, as biopsy of the affected areas is easy and rewarding. These techniques usually demonstrate the ulcer, but even an experienced operator may fail to detect one which is small or in a site where it is difficult to see, e.g. the cardia of the stomach. Intubation of the stomach and measurement of maximal acid output after stimulation by pentagastrin is a useful further investigation if surgery is contemplated. Acid output is usually above the normal range in patients with duodenal ulcer, and low or absent in patients with carcinoma of the stomach.

MEDICAL TREATMENT

Before discussing the medical and dietetic treatment of peptic ulcer it is necessary to indicate the types of cases for which a surgeon should always be called into consultation.
These are:

1. Perforation of a peptic ulcer.
2. Ulcers which, despite medical treatment, cause recurrent attacks of dyspepsia.
3. Any gastric ulcer in middle-aged patients which does not show satisfactory signs of healing within four weeks while on medical treatment; this is because carcinoma of the stomach in its early stages can masquerade as a simple ulcer. Duodenal ulcers on the other hand are never malignant.
4. Any ulcers suspected of malignancy at gastroscopy.
5. Ulcers which show a persistent tendency to bleed in spite of repeated courses of medical treatment, particularly if the patient is over 60 years of age.
6. Old, indurated duodenal ulcers which are producing pyloric stenosis and marked gastric retention, and gastric ulcers on the lesser curvature producing hourglass contraction of the stomach and obstruction.

Aims of medical treatment

Relief of symptoms. In the absence of complications such as pyloric stenosis or penetration of the ulcer into an adjacent organ, it is usually easy to secure relief of symptoms. In many patients the symptoms disappear spontaneously without any medical treatment; yet medical treatment usually leads to a more rapid and complete relief.

Prevention of recurrence. This is more difficult. Patients have remissions and relapses with or without any treatment. The relapse rate for duodenal ulcer may be as high as 80 per cent in a 5 to 10 year period despite medical treatment, including bed rest. Many of the relapses are mild and can be controlled easily.

Principles of treatment

The traditional principles are: (1) rest, both physical and psychological; (2) a bland diet, given in small amounts at frequent intervals; (3) drugs — antacids and secretory inhibitors; (4) giving up smoking.

These principles, long established and clearly stated in 1959 in the first edition of this book, are still applicable, but their relative importance is now changed. The introduction of the histamine (H$_2$) receptor antagonists, cimetidine and ranitidine, has been a revolution in treatment. With these drugs the number of patients requiring admission to hospital and also those needing surgery has been much reduced both in Britain[7] and in the USA.[8]

Drugs. Cimetidine and allied drugs by blocking the H$_2$ receptors in the gastric mucosa reduce acid secretion. This relieves symptoms and may promote healing. The drug is given throughout the day for one to three months. Some physicians keep patients on the drugs for longer in the hope of preventing recurrence. Very large numbers of patients have now been taking these drugs for a long time and adverse effects are uncommon.

Insoluble antacid powders (aluminium hydroxide, magnesium oxide or trisilicate) usually bring immediate relief of pain and continue to be taken by millions of people.

Many drugs formerly used, with little or no evidence that they produced any significant effect either in promoting healing or preventing recurrence, have now been discarded.

Giving up smoking. The need to advise patients to give up smoking is greatly strengthened by a study of the subsequent history of 779 men who had received surgical treatment for peptic ulcer between 1947 and 1965 in Edinburgh.[9] These men had an excess mortality with a mean shift of 9.1 years in the survival curve. The early deaths were not due to surgery or disease of the stomach but mainly to diseases known to be associated with smoking (carcinoma of the lung, chronic bronchitis and coronary heart disease). Eighty-three per cent of the patients were heavy smokers at the time of operation.

Diet. As a student in the early 1930s one of us had to learn the pros and cons of difficult strict dietary regimens which were imposed on patients with ulcers at that time. Some 35 years later he was admitted suffering from the effect of a gastric ulcer to a medical ward in a teaching hospital and later to a surgical ward in another teaching hospital. In both he was given a selection from the ordinary ward diet which he enjoyed and did well on. This remarkable change in the therapeutic practice was not entirely due to the whims of fashion.

A generation ago doctors thought, quite reasonably, that strict dietary regimens could reduce excess gastric secretion of acid. Only after many years of experience was it realised that any reduction of secretion brought about in this way was insufficient to accelerate the healing of an ulcer or to prevent its recurrence. Further, too rigid an adherence to a strict diet sometimes led to the patients becoming undernourished. To Meulengracht[10] of Copenhagen belongs the main credit of liberating patients from the old restrictive diets. Nevertheless some lessons have been learned from them.

Although patients may now eat normal foods, they should avoid large meals. By spreading out their food intake, they reduce the risk of exposing the gastric and duodenal mucosa to excessive amounts of acid. Also many patients find that their symptoms are aggravated by certain foods. These they learn by experience to avoid. A regimen for patients with dyspepsia or peptic ulcer is given in Diet No. 17. While a bland diet usually relieves dyspeptic symptoms, it did not appear to accelerate healing in five clinical trials.[11] We agree with the advice of Ingelfinger,[12] 'Let the ulcer patient enjoy his food.'

When a patient has severe symptoms with pylorospasm or has had a haemorrhage he should be given several small meals daily. Milk, eggs and fruit juice should be the main ingredients. It is important to ensure a good intake of vitamin C since some patients have low reserves as a result of previous self-imposed dietary restrictions.

Rest. Symptoms are often relieved when a patient curtails his business and social activities. Both physical and mental rest appear to promote healing of an ulcer. The great majority of patients with duodenal ulcer and gastric ulcer do not require admission to hospital but, because of anxiety and emotional difficulties, they often need simple psychological support.

Complications of medical treatment
Excessive treatment may cause undesirable results. Scurvy has resulted from too strict adherence for long periods to milk diets prescribed for adults. A rigid dietary regimen may in obsessional persons give rise to emotional disturbances and so aggravate the symptoms. An excess of soluble alkalis can lead to alkalosis with tetany. A condition known as the milk alkali syndrome has occurred in patients who have taken large amounts of milk (more than 1 litre daily) and soluble alkali usually over long periods. Weakness, anorexia and lethargy are the characteristic features and there may be psychological disturbances. Hypercalcaemia is always found and may give rise to calcification in the kidneys and else-

where. Deaths have been reported. Fortunately all of these undesirable effects are very rare.

SURGICAL TREATMENT

Indications of when surgery may be needed have been given on p. 432. The principal operations are shown diagrammatically in Figure 46.1. The selective vagotomy is now the treatment preferred by many surgeons.

After an operation some surgeons keep the stomach empty by continuous suction until the daily aspirate is less than 250 ml/24 hours, during which time patients are fed intravenously. Thereafter they are given water, 30 ml hourly, for the second and third day and then weaned on to a solid diet over the next 2 to 3 days. Once a patient is free of symptoms and there is no evidence of active ulceration they no longer need drugs. They should avoid taking alcohol on an empty stomach and tobacco consumption should be reduced.

As soon as convalescence is established, a patient may return to a full normal diet. A follow-up is necessary to see that they do not suffer from any nu-

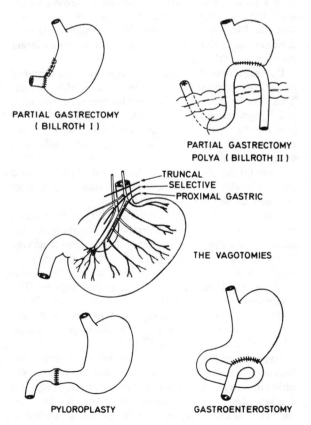

PARTIAL GASTRECTOMY
(BILLROTH I)

PARTIAL GASTRECTOMY
POLYA (BILLROTH II)

TRUNCAL
SELECTIVE
PROXIMAL GASTRIC

THE VAGOTOMIES

PYLOROPLASTY

GASTROENTEROSTOMY

Fig. 46.1 Operations for peptic ulceration

tritional deficiency. Many patients have lost weight prior to operation and, if this is not made good, it is important to take a careful dietary history and to ascertain the cause if they are not eating properly. This may be mental depression or other coexisting disease.

Iron-deficiency anaemia is common after partial gastrectomy, perhaps due to loss of acid which converts the iron to the ferrous state. Megaloblastic anaemia may arise due to loss of intrinsic factor and a failure to absorb vitamin B12. Owing to the large reserves in the liver, deficiency of this vitamin may not be apparent for two or three years.

Evidence of deficiency of riboflavin and nicotinic acid (glossitis), of thiamin (peripheral neuropathy) and of vitamin D (osteomalacia) may occur after major gastrectomies and the prolonged use of restricted diets, but are unusual.

Complications of surgical treatment
After any operation on the stomach many patients complain of symptoms after meals. These **post-cibal syndromes** may occur singly or in combination.

Small stomach syndrome. About 50 per cent of patients feel distended and uncomfortable during or after a meal. This occurs not only after partial gastrectomy but also after vagotomy and drainage. The symptoms tend to lessen with time. Management consists of dividing the individual's usual daily intake into a larger number of smaller meals.

Postvagotomy diarrhoea. This occurs in a minority of patients, typically in episodes, and is often severe. This may be due in part to malabsorption of bile acids and is then treated by cholestyramine. In a few patients it is due to bacteria becoming established in the small intestine and these need treatment with antibiotics, often for a long time.

Food intolerance. About 5 per cent of patients find they are unable to eat particular foods such as eggs, milk or tomatoes without discomfort.

Dumping syndrome. This is a feeling of drowsiness, muscular weakness and sometimes palpitations that occurs after a meal. It is probably due to rapid emptying of the stomach and dumping of its contents into the small intestine; there osmosis may move extracellular fluid into the lumen and so reduce plasma volume. The syndrome can be avoided by measures to slow down gastric emptying, e.g. taking small or dry meals and eating them slowly. Pectin, 20 g dissolved in water, taken before a meal is also helpful.

Hypoglycaemia. Signs of weakness, tremor and faintness, associated with hunger and an empty sensation in the epigastrium sometimes occurs between 1 and 2 hours after a meal. This is due to reactive hypoglycaemia; it is less common than the dumping syndrome.

Jejunal ulceration may result when the jejunum is anastomosed to the stomach and thus becomes exposed to effects of acid gastric juice and pepsin. Cimetidine usually relieves the symptoms and further surgery is now not often needed.

Bilious vomiting. This may arise shortly after an operation and persist. Further surgery is then often needed.

GASTRITIS

The introduction of the flexible gastroscope and improvements in radiological technique have shown that gastritis occurs more frequently than was formerly thought. Yet it is a somewhat imprecise diagnosis. The inflammatory lesion may be either an acute erosive gastritis or a chronic atrophic gastritis. It is rarely due to the direct effect of infection by a pathogenic organism. The cause is often unknown but ingestion of alcohol, drugs or other chemical irritants may be responsible. The commonest drug causing gastritis is aspirin, often taken for headaches and menstrual pain. Atrophic gastritis may be due to an autoimmune reaction and this is responsible for the failure to secrete intrinsic factor and HCl in pernicious anaemia. It is also present in half of the patients with severe iron-deficiency anaemia. Gastritis may also be present in metabolic disorders, e.g. uraemia, and an area of gastritis often surrounds peptic ulcer or carcinoma of the stomach.

Clinical features of gastritis vary from mild anorexia, vague discomfort, nausea and heartburn to severe and repeated vomiting accompanied by diarrhoea if there is associated enteritis. Sometimes the clinical picture may simulate acute peptic ulcer and massive gastric haemorrhage may occur. Nausea, abdominal fullness, heartburn and pain occurring before breakfast and improving as the day goes on are frequently present in chronic alcoholics. Secretory studies indicate an outpouring of mucus and a reduction in the secretion of hydrochloric acid during acute attacks and also in most cases of chronic gastritis.

Acute gastritis
The symptoms are nausea, pain and vomiting and commonly follow an excess of alcohol, aspirin or other drugs, e.g. arsenic formerly used by murderers. They may also follow ingestion of plant or bacterial toxins but are rarely due to infection of the gastric mucosa. The diagnosis is often obvious from the history. Treatment consists of stopping alcohol or the drug, sometimes washing out the stomach and giving alkalis. Water and electrolyte losses can be replaced by an oral rehydration fluid or, if necessary, intravenously as described in the treatment of diarrhoea (see below). With improvement of the condition the patient is given small feeds of milk

and gradually returns to a normal diet within 1 to 2 days.

CARCINOMA OF THE STOMACH

Epidemiology and aetiology are discussed on page 568. Permanent cure can only be achieved by radical surgical resection before metastasis has occurred. Unfortunately early diagnosis is difficult and many cases are diagnosed too late for radical surgery. Then treatment consists of letting them eat such food as they can enjoy and giving iron for the anaemia. If sufficient food cannot be given by mouth, intravenous feeding or jejunostomy feeding, as described in Chapter 51, may be used.

DISORDERS OF THE INTESTINE

The small intestine is the main site of absorption of nutrients. Normally absorption of all nutrients begins in the jejunum and is completed in the ileum, except that of water and electrolytes which is completed in the colon. **Diarrhoea** leads to depletion of water and electrolytes and may be due to disorders of the small or large intestine. The **malabsorption syndrome** arises when there is failure of digestion and absorption due to disorders of the small intestine. This may affect absorption of all nutrients or sometimes only one or two. Failure to absorb fat is often the main feature and leads to **steatorrhoea**. Disorders of the colon lead to **constipation**. These are the main conditions resulting from diseases of the intestine for which modification of the diet and the administration of nutrients parenterally may be required.

ACUTE DIARRHOEAL DISEASES

This term is used by the World Health Organization for a group of diseases caused by infections of the small and large intestine by pathogenic viruses, bacteria or protozoa. The term covers illnesses such as **acute gastroenteritis, bacterial food poisoning, traveller's diarrhoea, infantile diarrhoea** and **weanling diarrhoea**, as well as the specific infections, **bacillary dysentery** and **cholera**. In all of these conditions infection is normally confined to the gastrointestinal tract and is self-limiting. They are dangerous because the losses of water and electrolytes in the diarrhoea and also in associated vomiting lead to dehydration of the body. If the diarrhoea is severe, death from dehydration may occur within one or two days, especially in young children, in the very old and in those previously undernourished. The important new discovery is that serious dehydration can be prevented by giving an **oral rehydration solution** (ORS) early in the disease. The solutions used consist mainly of common salt, sodium bicarbonate and glucose or other source of carbohydrate. They are cheap and can be administered safely by any mother in a primitive home. Their use reduces greatly the need for intravenous fluid replacement which is much more expensive and requires trained medical staff, often available only in hospitals.

EPIDEMIOLOGY

All these diseases are spread by the faecal–oral route, and incidence is closely related to standards of hygiene. Where these are low, the diseases are very common, but those of us living in a comparatively clean environment seldom avoid an occasional attack.

There has been in all countries, and still is in poor communities, an enormous mortality in young children. In 1900 the death rates from dysentery, diarrhoea and enteritis among infants aged under 1 year in New York and London were 5630 and 3982 per 100 000 respectively. In a classic paper Gordon et al[13] analysed their findings of incidence and mortality in Punjab villages and compared them with past and present records in Europe and North America. In the Punjab they found that incidence remained high in the second year of life. Their data indicate that children are at greatest risk immediately after weaning when they are exposed to greater numbers and a greater variety of microorganisms in their food and water at a time when their immune mechanisms are still immature. They coined the term weanling diarrhoea, which is more aptly descriptive than infantile diarrhoea. Today deaths from weanling diarrhoea still occur in Europe and North America but are less than one thousandth of the number in former years. In large areas of the world, especially in the tropics, mortality from weanling diarrhoea is of the same high order as in New York and London in 1900.

Bacterial food poisoning remains all too common in Britain, as described in Chapter 24. The diarrhoea usually lasts for less than 48 hours and deaths are uncommon. Outbreaks in homes for old people are more dangerous and in some there have been several deaths.

Traveller's diarrhoea is now a well-recognised hazard of modern life. Seldom a serious disease, it causes much inconvenience and may spoil a holiday or business trip. Between a quarter and a half of the three million US citizens who visit Mexico each year suffer an attack[14] and the figures, if available, for UK citizens visiting Mediterranean countries might well be similar. The organisms chiefly responsible are enterotoxic strains of *Escherichia coli*, *Shigella sonnei* (the main cause of mild dysentery) and various viruses, especially rotavirus, but in many cases the exact cause cannot be found.

DIAGNOSIS

Accurate microbiological diagnosis is not needed for the treatment of a simple case of acute diarrhoea. In the management of an outbreak it is essential, as only in this way can the source of infection be identified with certainty.

CLINICAL FEATURES

The diarrhoea is usually accompanied by abdominal discomfort and nausea and often by vomiting. Fever, if present, is seldom high. In mild cases these are the only symptoms. When there is severe dehydration, there is circulatory collapse with a marked fall in blood pressure (oligaemic shock). This in itself may be fatal or lead to death later from acute renal failure.

The dehydration follows mainly from the diarrhoea. Infections not only interfere with intestinal absorption but the cholera toxin, and possibly other toxins, causes active secretion of chloride by the intestinal mucosa. Then with the chloride, sodium and water flow out from the tissues into the lumen of the gut. In an extreme case (severe cholera) as much as 1 litre of fluid may be lost in an hour. This explains how death from cholera may arise within a few hours of the onset of the disease. An adult human body contains about 40 litres of water. Loss of 10 per cent leads to circulatory collapse and few patients survive a rapid loss of 15 per cent. Sodium is lost in the diarrhoeal fluid. In severe cholera sodium concentration in the stools is almost the same as in the blood plasma. Although in most cases of diarrhoea it is much less, sodium deficiency may occur rapidly. Losses of potassium in the stools leads to potassium deficiency; signs of this may not occur for a few days but are commonly found in chronic diarrhoea.

Vomiting when present also increases the fluid loss and the accompanying loss of acid leads to an alkalosis, often present and a cause of apathy and drowsiness.

Sweating may lead to a loss of a litre or more during the course of a hot day in the tropics by an adult, even when at rest. Losses in children are proportionately greater due to their relatively larger surface area. Fever also leads to sweating.

These considerations help to explain how severe dehydration can arise in a very short time.

An attack of diarrhoea inevitably reduces food intake, but the deficiency is usually made up quickly once the attack is over. Repeated attacks in a young child whose normal diet is barely adequate for growth is a common cause of protein-energy malnutrition, as described in Chapter 29. In this way these infections are responsible for retarded growth and development of young children in poor communities and also for a large part of the deaths from malnutrition.

TREATMENT

Oral rehydration

A solution recommended by WHO[15] is:

Sodium chloride (table salt)	3.5 g
Sodium bicarbonate (baking soda)	2.5 g
or trisodium citrate, dihydrate	2.9 g
Potassium chloride	1.5 g
Glucose	20 g
Dissolve in 1 litre of potable water	

The solution was first developed in Bangladesh for the treatment of cholera and subsequently used for weanling diarrhoea; there its value for both these conditions is now firmly established. A paediatric colleague has told us that he benefited from it during an attack of traveller's diarrhoea while on a visit to Bangladesh. Solutions of slightly different composition may be used. Thus in Bangladesh the glucose may be replaced by 30 g of rice powder which is cheaper and as effective.[16] The sodium concentration of the WHO solution is 90 mmol/l; this is suitable for countries where natural foods are low in sodium and sodium deficiency is common, as in Bangladesh. In proprietary preparations available in the USA and UK, the sodium concentration is usually lower, about 35 mmol/l. Such solutions have been shown to be effective in controlled trials in the USA.[17] A carbohydrate is included in the powder because glucose is needed to facilitate absorption of sodium.

The composition of the powder becomes of relatively little importance if it is not mixed with the appropriate amount of water. A measuring cylinder has to be provided and the powder packaged for a set amount of water. Alternatively a measuring scoop may be provided. Packaging and the provision of simple instructions for use are a problem for the health services, which in the poor communities, where the need for oral rehydration therapy is greatest, are inevitably short of money.

Intravenous fluids

Absorption of oral fluids depends on a good blood supply to the alimentary canal. Circulatory collapse, detected by a fall in blood pressure, indicates a need to replace fluid intravenously. This is also necessary when vomiting is severe. Except in cholera, losses of water are relatively greater than those of sodium; a solution of 50 mmol of NaCl with 5 per cent glucose may be used. In young children a lower concentration of NaCl may be desirable to avoid any risk of hypernatraemia. Intestinal loss of potassium should be replaced and $NaHCO_3$ may be needed to correct acidosis arising from starvation; rarely NH_4Cl may be required to correct alkalosis caused by vomiting. Details are given in Chapter 52.

Other therapy
Most physicians do not prescribe any antibiotic drug or chemotherapeutic agent for an attack of acute diarrhoea. These are reserved for cases which do not clear up quickly, and after a microbiological diagnosis has been made when it is possible to select the appropriate drug.

Opiates and bismuth preparations are much used to relieve symptoms. Their value is perhaps more often due to a placebo effect than to a pharmacological action. In the recommended doses they have no adverse effects.

MALABSORPTION SYNDROME

Lack of digestive secretions and injury to the epithelial surface of the small intestine impair absorption of nutrients. A number of common diseases listed in Table 46.2 that arise from very different causes produce similar clinical features of undernutrition and malnutrition, known for a long time as the malabsorption syndrome.

CLINICAL FEATURES

Loss of weight is usually present and in cases of long standing there is marked emaciation with oedema. Chronic diarrhoea with accompanying symptoms of abdominal discomfort and distension is the second characteristic feature.

Steatorrhoea, increased fat in the faeces, is frequently present, its severity depending on the amount of fat in the diet and the nature of the underlying lesion. It is diagnosed when the daily output of faecal fat, measured

Table 46.2 Causes of malabsorption that may lead to severe undernutrition

---

Lack of pancreatic and bile secretions
Chronic pancreatitis
Chronic liver disease
Biliary tract disease
(discussed in Chapter 46)

Injury to the mucosa of the small intestine
Gluten enteropathy (coeliac disease)
Tropical enteropathy and sprue
Regional enteritis (Crohn's disease)
Surgical resections
Bacterial overgrowth
Radiation injury

---

over 3–5 days, exceeds 7 g. There is usually diarrhoea with a bulky stool that has an offensive smell and floats on water, so that it is flushed only with difficulty from a water closet. Medium chain fatty acids (p. 452) are useful in the treatment of severe cases.

Vitamin and mineral deficiencies. Anaemia is usually present due to impaired absorption of iron and folic acid. Nutritional glossitis, angular stomatitis and peripheral neuropathy arise from deficiency of the B group of vitamins, the first two commonly in early cases, the latter usually only in cases of long standing. Prolonged failure of calcium absorption may lead to evidence of osteomalacia and to tetany. Haemorrhages attributable to vitamin K deficiency may be present. Clinical evidence of vitamin A deficiency is rare.

DIAGNOSIS

This is obvious in an advanced case but is easily overlooked in the early stages. In any patient presenting with unexplained loss of weight or with evidence of a vitamin or mineral deficiency with no obvious dietary cause, malabsorption should be considered. Then the clinical history has to be considered carefully, together with laboratory tests of nutritional status and appropriate tests to detect possible underlying causes.

Gluten enteropathy (coeliac disease)
Gluten enteropathy arises in individuals who are sensitive to gluten, a main constituent of wheat flour and also present to a small extent in rye, barley and oats but not in rice. Such persons develop lesions of the small intestine which lead to diarrhoea and malabsorption. Symptoms usually arise within the first three years of life, but may first present at any age, even in the elderly. They are relieved if gluten is excluded completely from the diet. This means that many common foods cannot be eaten and, for most patients, lifelong commitment to a special diet.

The discovery that an idiosyncrasy or sensitivity to gluten is the cause of coeliac disease was made in 1950 by a young Dutch doctor, Dicke.[18] Gluten is a mixture of proteins (p. 40) and gliadin is the component responsible for coeliac disease.

Epidemiology
The Coeliac Society estimate that there are about 25 000 patients in the United Kingdom, i.e. prevalence is about 1 in 2000. Prevalence is probably of the same order in all countries with diets based on European traditions with wheat as the staple cereal. It is higher, 1 in 300, in the west of Ireland.[19] This may be due to heredity as the disease has a tendency to run in families. It is uncommon in most parts of Africa and Asia, where

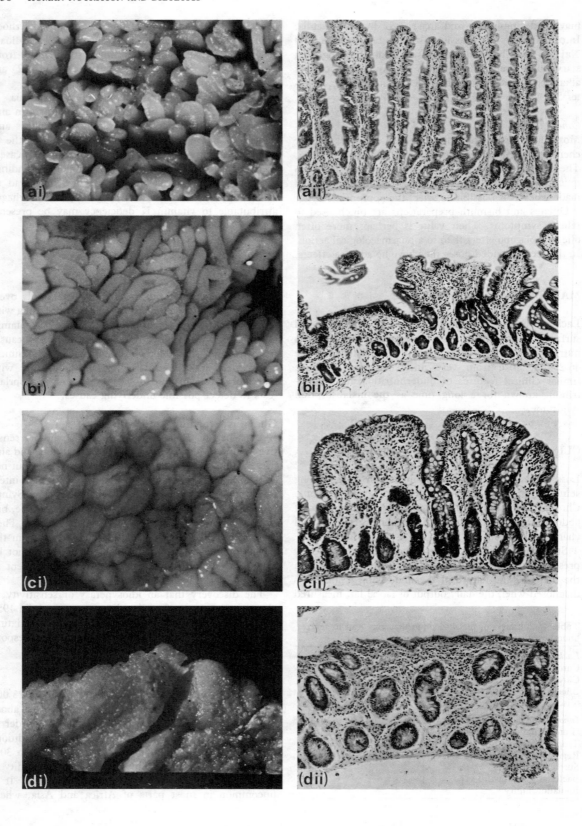

wheat is not the staple food. Formerly it was considered as a disease of children and most cases still present before the age of 2 years and soon after the introduction of wheat in the diet. Now many cases are diagnosed in adults and some not until late in life. Some of these may have had a mild and symptomless disorder since childhood but it is likely that sensitivity may develop at any age.

Pathology

Endoscopy and biopsy of the small intestine show a patchy atrophy of the mucosa. In mild cases the surface appears flat and the villi are blunted. The epithelial cells are flat instead of columnar. The crypts are enlarged and tortuous and the epithelium infiltrated with lymphocytes. In severe cases there are large areas of the jejunum in which there are virtually no villi (Fig. 46.2). While the striking feature of the histology of the mucosa is atrophy, there is also an increase in lymphocytes and lymphoreticular cells, suggesting a low grade immunological reaction.

The lesions are probably due to a local immunity reaction to a small peptide fraction of gliadin. As there is no characteristic increase in IgE antibodies, it is not a simple allergy and, despite much study over the last 15 years, its nature remains unknown. A paper by Simpson and colleagues[20] gives an introduction to recent literature and is an example of the new approaches to the problem.

Fig. 46.2 Dissecting microscope and histological appearances of the jejunal mucosa (courtesy of Professor R H Girdwood).

(ai) Normal villous pattern, a mixture of 'fingers' and 'leaves'. ($\times$ 24)

(aii) Normal mucosa with finger-like villi and a narrow basal portion. Villi have scalloped margins characteristic of jejunum. The cell infiltrate in the delicate stroma is sparse. (Haematoxylin & eosin, $\times$ 95)

(bi) Partial villous atrophy, showing 'leaves', ridges and convolutions. ($\times$ 24)

(bii) Jejunal mucosa with partial villous atrophy. The pattern is irregular and the ratio of the villous portion of the mucosa to the basal portion is decreased. The number of inflammatory cells in the lamina propria is increased. (Haematoxylin & eosin, $\times$ 95)

(ci) Advanced villous atrophy showing a mosaic pattern. ($\times$ 24)

(cii) Advanced villous atrophy showing a further stage towards total liver atropy. (Haematoxylin & eosin, $\times$ 95)

(di) Total villous atrophy with a flat mucosa. ($\times$ 24)

(dii) Total villous atrophy in a patient with untreated gluten enteropathy. The surface of the mucosa is flat, the crypts are irregular and their cell nuclei are hyperchromatic. Numerous plasma cells infiltrate the lamina propria. (Haematoxylin & eosin, $\times$ 95)

Clinical features

The characteristic feature is a fatty diarrhoea. Children fail to thrive and adults usually lose weight, mainly due to malabsorption of fat. Malabsorption of iron, folate and vitamin B12 may lead to anaemia, of vitamin D to rickets and osteomalacia and of vitamin K to haemorrhages. There is a wide range in the severity of the disease. Characteristically an untreated child presents a pathetic picture of severe undernutrition, but in some cases the disease is mild and anaemia or bone pain from osteomalacia may be the main feature.

Before the work of Dicke in 1950 coeliac disease was known only as a disease of children. About one-third of the cases died of malnutrition after a varying period, a third survived into adult life as chronic invalids and about a third appeared to recover. The disease was not known to arise in adults but, with hindsight, we can be sure that many adults diagnosed as 'idiopathic steatorrhoea' were suffering from coeliac disease which had presented for the first time after childhood. Thus the disease, if untreated, varies greatly in intensity and patients are subject to exacerbations and remissions. It may be presumed that patients presenting first in adult life have had the disorder since early childhood but in so mild a form as to escape detection until some factor, nearly always unidentified, provoked symptoms. Although a few patients may revert to a normal diet with apparent impunity, some abnormality of the jejunal mucosa probably always returns and some biochemical evidence of poor absorption of one or more nutrients usually persists. They are also at risk of further exacerbations and complications.

Several diseases may be associated with coeliac disease. In children those include IgA deficiency, diabetes mellitus, allergy to cow's milk, lactose intolerance and dermatitis hepatiformis. Adults are more prone to autoimmune disorders and may be infertile; they are also at increased risk of developing lymphoma and carcinoma of the small intestine.

Diagnosis

The diagnosis should be suspected when any of the above clinical features are present. Confirmation is provided when there is a marked improvement following withdrawal of gluten-containing foods from the diet. It should be firmly established by endoscopy and biopsy, if possible, but this procedure requires experience and in young children is difficult and not without danger.

Treatment

The disease can be completely relieved if gluten is excluded from the diet. This is a formidable task for wheat flour is present in bread, many breakfast cereals, biscuits, cakes, pastries, sausage, macaroni and spaghetti; it is added to many soups, sauces and puddings and to some proprietary milk preparations.

Diet No. 15 sets out a sample menu for a day and on the same page there is a list of foods containing gluten which are forbidden, and a list of foods free of gluten (p. 629) which can be included in the diet. The Coeliac Society supplies a comprehensive list of gluten-free products available commercially.

Children who have suffered from coeliac disease for a short time respond to the gluten-free diet within a few weeks. Patients who have been ill for years, particularly adults, may have a badly damaged mucous membrane. They may require up to three to six months dietetic treatment before full recovery.

Anaemia is usually present. In more than 90 per cent of children it is due to iron deficiency. Folic acid deficiency is also usually present as shown by low plasma levels, but megaloblastic anaemia is uncommon. In adult coeliac disease, a megaloblastic anaemia due to folic acid deficiency is frequently present. Correction of both types of anaemia occurs coincidentally with the improvement in absorption which results from the gluten-free diet. Until this recovery is complete, it is advisable to give iron orally and in some cases parenterally to those patients with hypochromic anaemia, and folic acid by mouth. These preparations will cure not only anaemia but the glossitis and stomatitis which may also be present. present.

The remarkable success which results from the gluten-free diet in both children and adults suffering from coeliac disease can only be obtained if every trace of gluten is eliminated from the diet.

Once the diagnosis has been firmly established, it is recommended that every patient stays on a gluten-free diet for life, because of the risk of the disease recurring or of malignant disease arising if there is a return to a normal diet.[21] These risks have not yet been and may never be stated in accurate quantitative terms, but tragic cases occur of patients who, after giving up the diet, develop severe osteomalacia or die of one of the complications of the disease. If a patient returns to a normal diet and finds that they remain well, they may decide that the benefit from eating normal foods outweighs the risks of further disease. Such cases should be seen at yearly intervals and examined carefully for clinical and biochemical evidence of the return of the disorder.

Tropical sprue
Sprue is the name which the Dutch in Java gave to a tropical disease in which the presenting features are sore mouth, fatty diarrhoea and associated secondary manifestations of undernutrition and malnutrition. The cause is unknown.

Although delayed and defective absorption of fat is the abnormality most easily recognised, the absorption of water, electrolytes, glucose, vitamins and minerals is also impaired. These defects are associated with atrophy of the jejunal villi, which is a non-specific change similar to that seen in gluten enteropathy.

Sprue is a serious disease, and without proper medical and dietary care may prove fatal. Remissions and relapses are common. With proper treatment the majority of patients make a full recovery and seldom relapse, particularly if they leave the tropics. Nevertheless a few fail to respond to all forms of therapy and become chronic invalids.

Treatment
Treatment is with a low fat diet and Diet no. 11 is suitable for a case of moderate severity. Appropriate supplements of vitamins and minerals are required when there is clinical evidence of specific deficiencies. If there is no response to dietary measures, improvement usually follows the administration of a wide-spectrum antibiotic such as tetracycline, 1 g daily by mouth.

Sprue was a common disease amongst Europeans in India and the Far East, but those in Africa were not affected. Many cases occurred during World War II but since then incidence has declined and it is now uncommon. Many studies failed to identify either an infective agent or a dietary toxin[22] and the cause was, and remains, a mystery.

Although the full picture of sprue and, especially the severe steatorrhoea, is seldom seen in natives of the topics, intestinal malabsorption is common and this is now discussed.

Tropical enteropathy
Patients with intermittent chronic diarrhoea who are underweight and anaemic are commonly seen in the tropics. Though the symptoms are usually mild, severe secondary malnutrition may occur which can be fatal. At postmortem marked atrophy of the small intestine is seen. This condition occurring in the indigenous population resembles sprue as seen in Europeans in many ways, but a sore mouth and tongue and steatorrhoea, prominent features in sprue, are much less evident. Biopsy studies on apparently healthy people in several tropical countries have shown villi in the jejunal mucosa to be blunt and shortened with apparent reduction in the absorptive surfaces. Tropical enteropathy appears to be common and often subclinical.[6]

The cause is unknown. Many patients have suffered from attacks of dysentery, malaria and other tropical diseases, but the diarrhoea is not usually associated with severe, recent infections. Examinations of the faeces often shows a number of protozoal and helminth parasites. The significance of these is uncertain but opinion is growing that Strongyloides stercoralis, a nematode worm, and Giardia lamblia, a flagellated protozoa, may be responsible for malabsorption by mechanisms at present unknown. The plasma albumin is often low, perhaps due to increased loss of protein in the faeces. Anaemia may be due to defective absorption of iron and folic acid and not uncommonly of both.

When the symptoms are not severe the diarrhoea may cease and the patient's general condition improve greatly after a few days in hospital on a good diet, with deworming, the treatment of any identified infections and supplements of iron and folate. Some patients do not respond to these simple measures and the diarrhoea persists. The intestinal atrophy is then irreversible and the prognosis poor.

Chronic pancreatitis and failure of bile secretion due to liver disease are also important causes of the malabsorption syndrome in the tropics.

Surgical resections of the small intestine

Irreversible damage occasionally makes it necessary to remove surgically a large part of the small intestine. This may be due to vascular disease and obstruction of the mesenteric vessels by thrombosis and embolism, or severe Crohn's disease (see below), and less commonly to perforations and peritonitis caused by chronic ulceration or penetrating abdominal wounds. Sometimes the whole small intestine has to be removed and then the patient must be fed entirely by the intravenous route (Chap. 52). There are now several patients with no small intestine who have been able to lead active lives despite being wholly dependent on total parenteral nutrition, It is possible to maintain good nutrition with surprising little small intestine, in some cases no more than 4 to 6 feet. In such cases a normal meal soon provokes diarrhoea and frequent small feeds with a low fat content are required. An artificial diet of easily assimilable foods, such as casein hydrolysate, sucrose and medium chain fatty acids is often of benefit and may promote weight gain. The glucose electrolyte solution used in the treatment of acute diarrhoea (p. 436) helps to maintain fluid balance when necessary. Diarrhoea may be due to irritation by unabsorbed bile salts and can be relieved by cholestyramine, an anion exchange resin which binds these. In all such patients regular checks are required to detect early signs of mineral or vitamin deficiencies, as they are at greatly increased risk of developing a nutritional anaemia or nutritional bone disease.

Bacterial overgrowth

The small intestine normally carries only a small population of commensal bacteria, but overgrowth readily occurs when there are structural abnormalities and disturbances of motility. Clinical features of malabsorption may then occur, especially steatorrhoea and vitamin B12 deficiency. The terms **blind loop** or **stagnant loop syndrome** are used to describe the condition. The syndrome may follow any surgical operation that disturbs the normal motility of the gut and most commonly those that leave a blind loop, such as Billroth II partial gastrectomy (Fig. 46.1).

Radiation injury

Radiotherapy is liable to damage epithelial cells in the small and large intestine and also to cause endarteritis and inflammatory reactions. Partial villous atrophy results and commonly leads to malabsorption and diarrhoea; in more severe cases abscesses form and are followed by sinuses and fistulae. These effects are most likely to follow radiotherapy for cancer of the uterus and vagina and other pelvic organs. The folic acid antagonist methotrexate and other drugs used in the chemotherapy of cancer also damage the intestinal mucosa and frequently cause diarrhoea. Patients undergoing intensive treatment for malignant disease are thus at considerable risk of becoming undernourished.

Carbohydrate intolerance

The sugars, sucrose, maltose and lactose, are hydrolysed by specific disaccharidases present in the brush border of the epithelium of the small intestine. Damage to this epithelium from any cause may impair production of these enzymes. Then the sugars enter the colon unhydrolysed and the water that goes with them may cause an osmotic diarrhoea. In the colon they are fermented and the gases produced cause flatulence and abdominal discomfort and cramp. Volatile fatty acids produced by bacterial action make the stools acid and they have a foul sour smell. These symptoms are often associated with acute and chronic diarrhoea arising from any cause. Carbohydrate intolerance may also be due to lack of specific disaccharidases in the brush border.

Lactase deficiency. Lactose is not present in any food except milk and after weaning is absent from the diet of all mammals except man. Adult mammals have little or no lactase in their intestinal epithelium. Most of the human species are in line with other mammals and cease to produce lactase in significant amounts after weaning. However, lactase production persists in some adults, probably due to an autosomal dominant gene. This gene is present in most people of European origin and also in those of Hamitic ancestry in Africa and Asia, but is absent in the majority of people in these continents. The evidence supporting this story is strong.[6,23]

In Britain studies of intestinal mucosa obtained by biopsy indicate that just under 5 per cent of those of European stock are lactase deficient but as many as 75 per cent of the non-white population.[24] Lactase deficiency does not necessarily mean that modest amounts of milk are not tolerated. Kittens by the age of four months no longer produce lactase[25] but we all know that an old cat likes a saucer of milk. Most Indians like milk and those that can afford it drink it regularly; yet 38 of them in Vellore, who volunteered for biopsy, all had negligible amounts of lactase in their intestinal epithelium.[26] Traditional Hindu culture gives milk a prominent place in good diets; school teachers and doctors in India know from experience that milk is good for children and for convalescent patients. The finding that most Hindus are lactase-deficient appears at first as a paradox. This may be explained by considering dosage. In tests for lactose tolerance, it has been customary to give 50 g of the sugar, the content of 1 litre of milk, an amount recommended for the daily intake of children and adults by American nutritionists in the 1930s. The rapid ingestion of so much lactose causes symptoms of intolerance in anyone who is lactase deficient. With ingestion of 5 to 10 g of lactose, the amount usually obtained from milk at any one time, gas production is not usually sufficient to cause symptoms, and the osmotic effect may soften the stools without producing diarrhoea.

In practical medicine, it has to be remembered that large numbers of people are lactase-deficient. In any patient who complains of long-standing abdominal discomfort for which there is no obvious cause, the possibility of milk intolerance should be considered, but this is not due to lactase deficiency.

Sucrase deficiency. This is a rare defect inherited through an autosomal recessive gene. On weaning the infant suffers from chronic diarrhoea and fails to thrive, until sucrose is excluded from the diet.

Intestinal obstruction

Intestinal obstruction may arise in many different ways. It is essential to decide in every case whether the cause of the obstruction is mechanical or due to paralysis of the intestinal muscle (paralytic ileus), as treatment in each type is entirely different. It is also important to determine whether the obstruction is high, i.e. in the jejunum or upper ileum, or low, i.e. in the lower ileum or colon, and whether strangulation of the bowel has occurred.

The common causes of mechanical obstruction are external hernias, volvulus, tumours of the colon, bands or adhesions due to previous inflammatory disease or operation and, in children, intussusception. Paralytic ileus is usually a consequence of peritonitis, resulting from any cause, e.g. a gastric or intestinal perforation or an abdominal operation.

The chief features of intestinal obstruction are vomiting, complete constipation and colicky pain which may be absent or slight in paralytic ileus. A serious loss of water and electrolytes results from the vomiting and from the stagnation of intestinal secretions in the dilated paralysed loops. The loss of fluid from the circulation from this latter source may be several litres in the 24 hours and this may lead to prerenal uraemia. The loss of potassium contributes to the apathy, mental confusion and muscular weakness, which usually follows intestinal obstruction.

Intestinal obstruction is always serious and so it should be treated only in a hospital where surgical and biochemical help are available. Immediate operation is required for the relief of mechanical obstruction, while it is strongly contraindicated in paralytic ileus. In the latter the distension of the paralysed gut must be treated by continuous suction through a tube passed into the stomach or jejunum, and continued until the bowel recovers from its paralysed state. In both types of obstruction the loss of fluid and electrolytes must be made good by appropriate infusions and intravenous feeding is often needed.

Chronic regional enteritis (Crohn's disease)

This is a chronic inflammatory disease which may arise anywhere along the alimentary tract but classically, the ileocaecal region is most frequently affected, then the colon and, less commonly, the small intestine. The inflammatory process is focal, with normal tissue between affected areas, and may contain granulomas. The disease usually presents in early adult life with chronic ill-health, diarrhoea, abdominal pain, anaemia and weight loss. There may be chronic intermittent obstruction and even fistula to the skin, bladder or vagina. Systematic manifestations are arthritis, iritis, skin lesions (erythema nodosum) and liver disease.

This disease undermines health and disrupts the life of its victims, who are often in the prime of life. Medical science is under challenge to discover its cause and an effective remedy. Each patient is also a challenge to those who provide care, comfort and support. The disease was first described by Crohn in 1933, and its pathological and clinical features are so characteristic that it is very unlikely to have been overlooked previously and highly probably that it is a new disease. Furthermore the disease appears to be becoming more common, though reported incidence rates are still only of the order of 1 to 5 per 100 000 of populations and its nature is changing, in that formerly the pathological process was limited usually to the ileocaecal region but is now often widespread. Despite much investigation no infective agent, immunological disorder or dietary factor has been established as a cause. It is a racial disorder, seldom arising except in persons of European stock; among them it is three to five times more common in Jews, but it is rarely seen in Israel in Sephardic Jews. There is some evidence that it may run in families.

Anti-inflammatory and immunosuppressive drugs and antibiotics such as prednisone, azathioprine and metronidazole often bring about marked clinical improvement, as does sulphasalazine, but their mode of action is unknown. When the disease is limited to a small section of the bowel, surgical resection is effective. Relief obtained after the use of drugs or surgery is often only temporary and most patients require further surgery. Mortality is about twice that in the general population.

Dietary support

Diet is an important part of the management as patients are usually unwell and off their food. They should be given a diet which provides sufficient energy, protein, essential fatty acids, vitamins and minerals. Good nutrition is essential in a disease which is characterised by malabsorption. A recurrent problem is that of intermittent obstruction. When obstruction occurs, the fruit and vegetables in the diet should be stopped immediately and omitted for up to a week after the attack has ended. It is not necessary to reduce intake of fruit and vegetables in intervals between attacks of obstruction.

When fistulae develop or the small intestine is affected, there is a case for placing the patient on a formula diet, or intravenous feeding. There are two arguments for this. First, it reduces losses of nutrients through the fistula. Secondly, it reduces potential allergenic materials in the intestinal tract. There is no doubt that those patients who have recurrent obstruction feel better for such a diet in the short term. It is yet to be proven that they benefit in the long term as most of them ultimately require surgical excision of the affected area of the gut. Before operation a few days on a formula diet cleanses the bowel and helps to restore nutrition.

Crohn's disease is a chronic, remitting disease; it is important to follow up all patients and assess regularly their state of nutrition by clinical examination and biochemical tests.

Ulcerative colitis

This is a common cause of chronic diarrhoea in temperate climates. There is blood and mucus in the stool due to an inflammatory reaction and ulcers in the mucosa of the large intestine. The ulcerations are superficial in contrast with Crohn's disease. Colitis is most frequently situated in the rectum and may extend as far as the caecum but this is uncommon. No cause is known, though there are many theories. No microbial pathogen has been identified.

The tendency of this disease to remit and relapse has become somewhat less frequent since the introduction of effective treatment with sulphasalazine. In the acute stage treatment is with corticotrophin and corticosteroids, and in the long term, sulphasalazine. The complication of toxic dilation is dangerous since it may be followed by perforation of the gut wall. Then the only treatment is to remove the entire colon and fashion an ileostomy. This operation is also recommended for some patients who have much diarrhoea and in whom conventional therapy has proved ineffective. Occasionally, patients who have had the entire bowel affected by colitis from their youth may develop cancer of the colon, but this is much less frequent since safe and effective drugs became available. Mild cases confined to the rectum may be treated by corticosteroid enemata. The very sick patient requires skilled nursing and medical care with replacement of fluid, electrolytes and blood. In general, a patient who is mobile yet passing several stools a day and who is under control with drugs, does not need dietary constraints and should eat a diet which is adequate in all usual ways. When there is associated diverticulosis or, curiously, constipation, the diet may have to be modified appropriately.

Diet and gastrointestinal fistulae

These are treated by surgery supported by control of infection, skin care, electrolyte replacement and maintenance of nutrition. This can be either by oral feeding or parenteral nutrition. Fistulae often close more quickly if total parenteral nutrition is used.

Diet and ileostomies and colostomies

At operation the proximal part of the gut is sutured to the skin of the abdominal wall. This artificial stoma serves as a passage for the removal of unabsorbed material which has passed through the ileum.

Patients with an ileostomy can usually eat a normal or nearly normal diet fairly soon after operation. It is important that a patient who has been troubled by diarrhoea for a long period of time or has been ill from toxic dilation should be encouraged to eat exactly what he likes as soon as possible. Where patients find that particular items of food, for example rhubarb, alcohol, onions, lettuce, fried fish or soup cause trouble, that item should be removed from the diet. At some later time — say, after one or two weeks — this item of food can be returned to the diet to see whether this coincides with recurrence of symptoms. One problem is that of flatulence, and eating beans and onions may cause an unpleasant smell. Each patient must, however, judge for himself by trial and error. Because of the risk of water and sodium depletion, plenty of water and an increased salt intake are advisable. Most patients with an ileostomy now keep good health and have adjusted socially and psychologically to their condition.[27] Some practical advice for them is given by Bingham.[28]

Colostomies are the result of a portion of the large bowel being brought up onto the surface and the faecal material passing out into a bag at that point. Usually such an operation is for cancer of the colon or for complicated diverticular disease. A low-residue diet is sometimes advised postoperatively but it is again important to achieve a normal diet rapidly. Some patients find loose stools may be caused by certain vegetables but this is variable and each patient must experiment for himself. After either an ileostomy or a colostomy it is important that patients should never resort to eating or drinking less than they require in an attempt to alter the functioning of the stoma.

Diverticulosis and diverticular disease

Diverticula are blind pouches which may be present in the oesophagus, stomach and small and large intestines. They may be congenital in origin or be acquired during life. They are found most frequently in the colon, and especially in the sigmoid section. The presence of diverticula is known as diverticulosis; when they cause symptoms the condition is called diverticular disease. About 30 per cent of all persons over the age of 60 in Britain and America have diverticulosis, but only 5 to 10 per cent of these develop symptoms or complications. Diverticulosis is less common in many of the countries of the Third World. Painter and Burkitt,[29] suggest this is because people in affluent societies eat too little fibre in their diets. Symptoms usually arise from spasm of the colon. Occasionally if stagnation in diverticula is followed by infection, an inflammatory reaction occurs. Repeated attacks of these result in a chronically inflamed bowel, with narrowing of the lumen and pericolic adhesions.

Treatment

If symptomless diverticula are discovered during routine radiological examination, no treatment is required, except to advise the patient to include more dietary fibre in their diet. This should be on the same lines as the diet recommended for patients liable to constipation. The addition of wheat bran to an ordinary Western diet improves bowel habits[30] and reduces colonic pressures in patients with symptomatic diverticular disease.[31]

Many patients have periodic attacks of mild left-sided abdominal pain, fever and irregularity of the bowels. These should be treated medically by giving two tablespoons of bran at breakfast to increase the bulk of the stools and eating a high fibre diet (Diet No. 18). When there are signs of active inflammation a broad-spectrum antibiotic may be given. Pain may be relieved by giving antispasmodic drugs. Purgative should not be used.

A few cases require surgery because of obstruction, perforation or abscess formation, or for severe and extensive involvement of the intestine.

Irritable bowel syndrome

Mucomembranous colic, spastic constipation, spastic colon, 'mucous colitis' and nervous diarrhoea are probably all manifestations of the syndrome of the 'irritable bowel'. The term 'mucous colitis' is particularly unfortunate, as the condition is emphatically not an inflammation of the colon.

The syndrome is characterised by the passage of loose or pellet stools, often preceded by lower abdominal pain. Sufferers may become so conscious of and so obsessed with their condition that visits to a theatre or travel in a train without access to a toilet become impossible. The patient may appear tense with signs of general reactivity such as tachycardia and brisk reflexes and the descending colon may be tender and palpable. Examination by barium enema and sigmoidoscopy are normal.

All these disturbances of the function of the colon may be regarded as abnormal responses to emotional stimuli and so are psychosomatic disorders. The irritable bowel syndrome is a group of symptoms that reflect a limited repertoire of gut responses. Three factors may contribute to its aetiology, deficiency of dietary fibre, psychological constitution, and stress or what may be called life-theatening events. One patient may eat little fibre, a second have a nervous disposition, a third be beset with domestic worries. In others all three contribute. The first essential is to see that the symptoms are not due to simple constipation and then to exclude an inflammatory disorder or cancer. Psychotherapy is needed; often simple reassurance and explanation of the nature of the symptoms is all that is required, but sometimes expert psychiatric treatment is required. The patient should be helped to develop regular bowel habits by following the regimen recommended for patients liable to constipation (see below). The regular use of drugs should be avoided. Circumstances may require the use of tranquillisers, laxatives or drugs to control diarrhoea, but these should be discontinued as soon as possible and the patient should not be allowed to become dependent on any drug.

Carcinoma of the colon and rectum

The causes are discussed in Chapter 60. The only treatment of value is resection of the tumour, preceded if necessary by colostomy for the immediate relief of colonic obstruction.

The diagnosis may be missed when there has been longstanding constipation or other chronic disease of the colon. It should always be considered when there is a change of bowel habits in a middle-aged or elderly person.

Constipation

Constipation is delay in passage of the faeces. Defeacation is a reflex action, stimulated by distension of the rectum with faeces, but it is under voluntary control and normally takes place only when time and circumstances are suitable. The presence of food in the stomach is a stimulus to a gastrocolic reflex which causes movements of the colon, and these may lead to faeces entering the rectum. The reflex usually occurs after the first meal of the day. In some people the presence of liquid in the stomach initiates the reflex and a drink on rising may be sufficient to stimulate defaecation. Some healthy people do not defaecate every day and a few do so only once or twice a week. They should not be considered constipated, and constipation should only be diagnosed when delay in defaecation causes discomfort and indigestion.

The two common causes of constipation are a small faecal bulk and persistent neglect of the call to defaecate. Many diseases are associated with constipation.

The daily faecal output ranges normally from 75 to 200 g of which 50 to 175 g is water. The bulk of the faeces is mainly water, and the amount of water depends on the amount of dietary fibre present and the capacity of the fibre to bind water. Low fibre diets predispose to constipation.

If the call to defaecate is persistently neglected, the reflex mechanism becomes less sensitive and constipation results. This is likely to happen when there are insufficient toilets or the toilet is cold, dirty or inaccessible. Children are readily put off from going to the toilet, and parents should see that they do. Going to the toilet should become a habit early in life.

Gastrointestinal diseases that commonly give rise to constipation are diverticular disease and the irritable bowel syndrome. Carcinoma of the colon and rectum sometimes present as constipation and, when a middle-aged or elderly person develops constipation for the first time, it is essential to make a thorough examination of the large bowel. Constipation is common in psychiatric disorders which cause depression. Any neurological disease causing lesions in the lumbar cord may affect the reflex centres responsible for defaecation and lead to constipation.

Pregnant women and old people are often constipated. The reasons for this are not known. Perhaps the pressure of the gravid uterus on the colon may delay movements of the contents. In old people the sensitivity of the neuromuscular reflexes in the colon may be impaired or they may become less aware of the presence of faeces in the rectum.

When constipation is due to a low intake of dietary fibre, there is often pain in the left side of the abdomen along the line of the descending colon, and the faeces may be passed as hard pellets. Passage of faeces relieves the pain. When the call to defaecate has been repeatedly ignored, a mass of inspissated faecal matter may accumulate in the descending colon. Then fluid contents of the colon may run down the side of the mass and cause a watery diarrhoea.

Treatment

Diet. The intake of dietary fibre should be increased by eating whole cereals and increasing consumption of fruit and vegetables. The most important factor is the water-holding capacity of the fibre (Chap. 4). Coarse bran has a capacity of 6 g water/g of fibre, but fine bran holds only 2–3 g water/g. Patients should be encouraged to take coarse bran as a breakfast cereal. One table-spoonful of bran may be taken in the first week and two thereafter. The bran may be made more palatable by adding cooked fruits. Fruits and vegetables whose fibre hold waters effectively are oranges, apples, carrots and the cabbage family. The diet should contain a helping of vegetables and two such fruits each day. These measures increase faecal weight and reduce transit time in subjects on controlled diets. As these fibres also bind metallic cations, faecal loss of these may be increased, but the danger of deficiency arising is slight. Diet No. 18 is suitable for patients with constipation and incorporates the advice above. When obesity is present, Diet No. 3 may be prescribed.

Correction of faulty habits. It is important to see that a young child goes to the toilet at a regular time each day. An adult may lose the habit from laziness, hurry or a lack of suitable accommodation. Once the reflex has been lost, it can only be regained by persistent and unhurried attempts to move the bowels at the same time each day. Worry, anxiety, fatigue and change of occupation may each effect the normal rhythm of evacuation, and a patient may need advice on his whole way of life. Sufferers from constipation have often been exhorted to drink more water and take more outdoor exercise; these are two healthy practices but may not relieve constipation.

Drugs. Many laxatives are available. Their continued use may lead to excessive losses of potassium, sodium and water in the faeces and is not recommended. Two mild laxatives that are recommended for short periods on occasions are lactulose and senna. Lactulose is a sugar which is not absorbed in the small intestine but passes to the colon where it may be partially broken down by bacteria. It reduces absorption of water from the colon by increasing the osmolality of its contents, and so increases the bulk of the faeces. Senna is a glycoside which is broken down in the small intestine to emodin; this is absorbed into the blood stream and stimulates the muscles of the colon for 6 to 12 hours after administration of the senna.

A new remedy, effective in two cases of long standing, is the opioid antagonist, naloxone.[32] Opioid peptides are now known to be present in neuroendocrine cells in the intestinal wall and opium preparations have been used for over 2000 years to reduce gut movements.

REFERENCES

1. Gregory R A (ed) 1982 Regulatory peptides of gut and brain Br Med Bull 38: 219–318
2. Parsons D S 1967 Sodium chloride absorption by the small intestine and the relationships between salt transport and the absorption of water and some organic molecules. Proc Nutr Soc 26: 46–55
3. Florey H W 1954 Mucin and the protection of the body. Proc R Soc Lond (Biol) 143: 147–58
4. Piper D W 1980 Mucus: chemistry and characteristics. In: Sircus W, Smith A N (eds) Scientific foundations of gastroenterology. Heinemann, London, p 333–43
5. Langman M J S 1979 The epidemiology of chronic digestive diseases. Arnold, London
6. Cook G C 1980 Tropical gastroenterology. Oxford University Press, Oxford
7. Wyllie J H, Clark C G, Alexander-Williams J, et al 1981 Effect of cimetidine on surgery for duodenal ulcer. Lancet 1: 1307–8
8. Finberg H V, Pearlman L A 1981 Surgical treatment of peptic ulcer in the United States. Trends before and after the introduction of cimetidine. Lancet 1: 1305–7
9. Ross A H M, Smith M A, Anderson J R, Small W P 1982 Late mortality after surgery for peptic ulcer. N Engl J Med 307: 519–22
10. Meulengracht E 1939 The medical treatment of peptic ulcer and its complications. Br Med J 2: 321–4
11. Anonymous 1969 Diet and duodenal ulcer. (Editorial.) Br Med J 3: 727–8
12. Ingelfinger F J 1966 In: Ingelfinger F J, Relman A S, Finland M (eds) Controversy in internal medicine. Saunders, Philadelphia, p 171
13. Gordon J E, Chitkara I D, Wyon J B 1963 Weanling diarrhoea. Am J Med Sci 245: 345–77
14. Gorbach S L 1982 Traveller's diarrhoea. N Engl J Med 307: 881–2
15. World Health Organization 1984 A manual for the treatment of acute diarrhoea. Document WHO/CDD/SER/80.2(rev 1)
16. Molla A M, Sarkar S A, Hossain M, Molla A, Greenhough W B 1982 Rice-powder electrolyte solution as oral therapy in diarrhoea due to *Vibrio cholera* and *Escherichia coli*. Lancet 1: 1317–9
17. Santoshan M, Daum R S, Dillman L, et al 1982 Oral rehydration therapy of infantile diarrhoea. A controlled study of well nourished children in the United States and Panama. N Engl J Med 306: 1070–5
18. Dicke W K 1950 Coeliac disease: investigation of harmful effects of certain types of cereal on patients. Doctoral thesis, University of Utrecht
19. Mylotte M, Egan-Mitchell B, McCarthy C F, Nicholl B 1973 Incidence of coeliac disease in the West of Ireland. Br Med J 1: 703–5
20. Simpson F G, Field H P, Howdle P D, Robertson D A F, Lesowsky M S 1983 Leucocyte migration inhibition test in coeliac disease — a reappraisal
21. McCrae W M, Eastwood M, Martin M R, Sircus W 1975 Neglected coeliac disease. Lancet 1: 187–90
22. Strong R P 1942 Still's tropical diseases, 6th edn. H K Lewis, London, p 1023–5
23. Johnson J D 1981 The regional and ethnic distribution of lactose malabsorption. Adaptive and genetic hypotheses. In: Paige I M, Bayless T M (eds) Lactose digestion. Johns Hopkins Univ Press, Baltimore, p 11–22
24. Ferguson A, MacDonald D M, Brydon W G 1984 Prevalence of lactase deficiency in British adults. Gut 25: 163–7
25. Morris J G, Trudell J, Pencovie T 1977 Carbohydrate digestion by the domestic cat (*Felix catus*). Br J Nutr 37: 365–73
26. Swaminathan N, Nathan V I, Baker S J, Radhakrishnase H N 1970 Disaccharidase levels in jejunal biopsy specimens from American and South Indian control subjects and patients with tropical sprue. Clin Chim Acta 30: 707–12
27. Kennedy H J, Lee E C G, Claridge G, Truelove H S 1982 The health of subjects living with a permanent ileostomy. Q J Med 51: 341–57
28. Bingham S, McNeil N I, Cummings J H 1977 Diet for the ileostomist. J Hum Nutr 31: 365–6
29. Painter N S, Burkitt D P 1971 Diverticular disease of the colon: a deficiency disease of Western civilisation. Br Med J 2: 450–4
30. Painter N S, Almeida A Z, Coleburne K W 1972 Unprocessed bran in treatment of diverticular disease of the colon. Br Med J 2: 137–40
31. Findlay J M, Smith A N, Mitchell W D, Anderson A J B, Eastwood M A 1974 Effects of unprocessed bran on colonic function in normal subjects and in diverticular disease. Lancet 1: 146–9
32. Kreek M J, Schaefer F E, Hahn E F, Fishman J 1983 Naloxone, a specific opioid antagonist, reverses chronic idiopathic constipation. Lancet 2: 261–2

47

Diseases of the Liver, Biliary Tract and Pancreas

The liver is a barrier through which nutrients and other substances absorbed from the alimentary canal into the portal veins pass before entering the systemic circulation. It is responsible for over 25 per cent of the resting metabolism, although weighing less than 2.5 per cent of the whole body, and has been aptly described as the body's chemical workshop.

The liver is damaged and its function impaired in many disorders and diseases. Damage of moderate severity often becomes manifest as jaundice. Minor and reversible damage is common in many nutritional disorders when the proportion of fat in the metabolic mixture becomes unusually high. Serious damage to the liver is caused by many infections and toxic chemicals. Of these, viral hepatitis and ethyl alcohol are by far the commonest in most countries. Persistent infection and continuing exposure to a toxin both cause progressive structural changes and impairment of function leading to liver failure. This is usually soon followed by death unless these changes can be reversed.

Dietary therapy is an important part of the treatment of liver failure and of its serious complications.

Table 47.1 Summary of the functions of the liver

Intermediary metabolism	Gluconeogenesis from amino acids, conversion of glucose into fatty acids, ketone body formation, interconversion of monosaccharides
Synthetic	Plasma albumin, alpha-globulins, lipoproteins, transferrin and other carrier proteins, coagulation factors
Excretory	Cholesterol and other steroids, including steroid hormones, bile salts and pigments, many drugs and toxins
Storage	Glycogen, vitamins A and D, vitamin B12, iron
Immunological	As an important part of the lymphoreticular system
Haematopoiesis	Main site of formation of erythrocytes in early fetal life; after birth a potential but rarely used site

LIVER FUNCTION AND STRUCTURE

Table 47.1 and Fig. 47.1 are aide-mémoires which summarise the main points. In the acinus the liver cells, or hepatocytes, are arranged in zones around a central portal tract made up of small branches of the portal vein, hepatic artery and bile duct. Blood flows from here through capillary sinusoids between the hepatocytes into branches of the hepatic vein lying in the periphery; bile formed in the hepatocytes flows through canaliculi into the branch of the bile duct in the portal tract.

The development of a technique for isolating hepatocytes from the different zones has made it possible to begin to study differences in functions of the zones.[1] Cells in zone 1 which surround the portal tract are active in gluconeogenesis, glygogen storage and in transport and secretion of bile salts. Cells in zone 3 in the periphery around hepatic venules are active in glycoly-

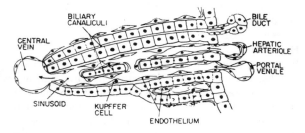

Fig. 47.1 Half a liver acinus. Blood enters the sinusoids at the equator of the acinus and percolates past the plates of hepatocytes to enter the central vein. The hepatocytes secrete bile into the intercellular network of canaliculi which drain into biliary ductules

sis, glycogenolyis and in the synthesis of bile salts. The zones also differ in their susceptibility to damage by different pathogenic agents. For example, cells in zone 3 are most damaged by hypoxia, to which the liver is peculiarly susceptible because only about one fifth of its blood supply comes from the hepatic artery and is fully saturated with oxygen, the remainder being relatively unsaturated portal blood.

LIVER DAMAGE

The successive stages in liver damage can be understood by following the effect of continuing high intakes of alcohol. Other damaging agents have the same general effects though the extent of the damage and the time course may differ markedly.

Fatty globulation
Large doses of ethanol quickly cause fat droplets to become visible in the cytoplasma of hepatocytes. This was obvious in biopsy specimens of liver taken from healthy human volunteers who had been given 200 g of alcohol daily for 18 days.[2] The fat present in healthy cells is not visible because the water-insoluble triglycerides are present linked to phospholipids and other substances to form amphipathic molecules that are dispersed as micelles in the cell water. The complex physicochemical environment that permits micelle formation is readily disturbed by any factor affecting the nutrition of the cell. Droplets of triglycerides are then formed and these are seen easily under the lower power of a light microscope. The physicochemical factors underlying this fatty globulation are discussed fully by Dixon.[3]

This process is readily reversed if the damaging factor is removed. If not, the droplets persist and grow. Whereas a healthy liver is usually less than 10 per cent fat, the fat content of a severely damaged liver may be 70 per cent or more. Such a liver has a histological appearance resembling adipose tissue and its function is greatly impaired.

Hepatitis
Following continued excessive alcohol intake, the liver may become tender and enlarged, being easily palpable below the costal margin, and the patient may become jaundiced. This is due to an inflammatory reaction provoked by necrosis or death of hepatocytes due to excessive fatty globulation or, in other cases, to a direct toxic effect. The histological picture shows small widely scattered necrotic areas with aggregation of mononuclear cells, often a few polymorphs and increased activity of Kupffer cells.

The hepatitis usually resolves completely if alcohol intake is stopped or greatly reduced. If it is continued, acute liver failure may arise with deep jaundice and severe cerebral symptoms (fulminant hepatitis and encephalopathy) and this has a high mortality. Much more commonly it becomes chronic. Then patients may complain of general malaise, anorexia and a variety of digestive disturbances and become progressively undernourished. Others may be remarkably well and unaware of their condition. The range of incapacity is very wide.

During the course of chronic hepatitis there is a slow progressive fibrosis leading eventually in some cases to major disturbances of liver structure and function.

Cirrhosis of the liver
This term was introduced by Laennec in 1826 and refers to the colour (Greek *kirrhos*, tawny) of nodules of hepatocytes regenerating between strands of fibrous tissue. It is used now to refer to any diffuse chronic disease of the liver in which necrosis has caused collapse of the reticulin framework that supports each acinus and its replacement with fibrous tissue. Fibrous tissue contracts with time and then may obstruct the branches of the portal vein and bile duct within the liver.

Intrahepatic obstruction causes a rise in pressure in all branches of the portal vein (portal hypertension). Venous congestion leads to enlargement of the spleen which can usually be detected by palpation. More important it leads to varicosities which may bleed. Oesophageal bleeding is a common and serious consequence of cirrhosis of the liver. Increased venous pressure impedes the return of interstitial tissue fluid into the capillary circulation; it leaks into the peritoneal cavity where it accumulates in large amounts, up to 10 litres or more, and this is known as **ascites**. Ascitic fluid sequesters a large amount of sodium.

Damage to liver cells leads to jaundice that may be severe and also to encephalopathy. In this the clinical features are disordered sleep rhythm, restlessness or drowsiness, impaired intellectual function with confusion and, in severe cases, stupor and coma. The onset may be insidious or sudden. Sometimes these features are the first manifestations of liver failure to appear and then they may be mistaken for a psychiatric disorder. The condition is due to unidentified toxic substances reaching the brain in the systemic circulation. These may arise from disturbances of intermediary metabolism or to substances absorbed from the gut that the damaged hepatocytes are unable to detoxify.

The damaging effects of alcohol on the liver vary greatly from individual to individual, both in severity and in the time taken for symptoms to appear. Some alcoholics drink themselves to death before reaching the age of 25 years. Others who may drink similar large amounts live to draw an old age pension without becoming seriously incapacitated. This variability is well illustrated in a report giving the history of the development of the clinical features of 510 patients with alcoholism treated in Scottish hospitals.[4] There is also marked variability in individual responses to other liver toxins and infective agents.

Tests of liver function

Many biochemical tests have been used to assess liver function. Table 47.2 lists those that are widely used, generally in combination.

Jaundice

This is a result of an increase in the bilirubin in the blood. The skin and sclera of the eyes appear yellow and the urine is usually dark yellow or brown. Jaundice is not detectable until the plasma bilirubin rises above 34 μmol/l. The upper limit of normal is 13.6 μmol/l (8 mg/l). When the plasma concentration is between these two figures, a patient is said to have subclinical jaundice.

There are three types of jaundice. **Hepatocellular** jaundice is due to damage to hepatocytes by toxic or infectious agents interfering with the uptake and conjugation of bilirubin by the cells or to blocking of the bile canaliculi (cholestatic jaundice). **Prehepatic** (haemolytic) jaundice is due to increased bilirubin from excessive destruction of red blood cells. A healthy liver can handle a bilirubin load six times greater than normal. Hence except in the newborn, haemolytic jaundice is usually mild. It may arise from congenital defects causing the erythrocytes to be unduly fragile (spherocytosis, sickle cell anaemia, thalassaemia) or from the action of extracorpuscular factors (some drugs, incompatible blood transfusions). **Posthepatic** jaundice is due to an obstruction of bile flow between the liver and duodenum. Common causes are impacted gall-stones and cancer of the head of the pancreas. The excess bilirubin in the plasma is then in the conjugated form, whereas in prehepatic jaundice it is unconjugated.

Table 47.2 Some tests of liver function

	Normal range	
Plasma bilirubin	3.4–13.6 μmol/l 2–8 mg/l	A measure of ability to transport bile
Plasma albumin	>45 g/l	A measure of synthetic ability
Plasma aspartate Plasma alanine aminotransferase	10–40 i.u./l 2–15 i.u./l	Damage to hepatocytes liberates these enzymes which then enter the blood
Plasma alkaline phosphatase	20–90 i.u./l	An index of biliary obstruction and cholestasis
Prothrombin time	expressed as a ratio after comparison with a control sample of blood	A measure of ability to synthesis coagulation factors

Jaundice is sometimes accompanied by itching (pruritus) and this may be severe. The cause is retention of bile salts in the blood and it may be relieved by cholestyramine. This is an anion exchange resin which binds bile salts in the gut and so interrupts the enterohepatic circulation and increases faecal excretion of bile salts.

AGENTS DAMAGING THE LIVER

Dietary deficiencies

Soon after the discovery of insulin, it was observed that depancreatised dogs treated with insulin developed fatty livers and that this could be prevented by feeding raw beef pancreas. In a long series of experiments Best and others[5] showed that this was due to the action of choline which they established as a lipotropic factor. Himsworth[6] produced fatty livers in rats fed on diets low in protein and, if the diet was also deficient in vitamin E, acute necrosis of the liver occurred in some animals and this could go on to cirrhosis. Protection against this effect of vitamin E deficiency could be provided by adequate doses of selenium. The fatty changes in these rats may have been due to a lack of choline arising from dietary deficiency of methionine which provides the methyl groups needed for its synthesis. Fatty changes in the livers of monkeys have been produced by low protein diets[7] and accompanied by a reduced capacity of the liver to synthesise and secrete lipoproteins. In these monkeys there was no subsequent liver fibrosis.

In man the fatty changes seen in the liver in kwashiorkor (p. 285) may be attributed to a low protein intake. Here there is evidence of reduced capacity to secrete β-lipoproteins[8] but, as the plasma phospholipids contain normal amounts of choline,[9] not of choline deficiency. Choline deficiency has never been shown to be responsible for liver damage in man.

Fatty changes in the liver are common whenever there is a high proportion of fat in the metabolic mixture, for example in uncontrolled diabetes, in starvation, in some cases of obesity and when too much carbohydrate has been infused during intravenous feeding (p. 499). In these cases, as in kwashiorkor, the changes are easily reversible and not followed by fibrosis.

Infective agents

Viral hepatitis

This is by far the commonest cause of liver disease and infection is ubiquitous in all countries.

Hepatitis A virus is excreted in the stools and spread by the faecal–oral route. Where standards of hygiene are low, few escape infection in childhood or adolescence. In a typical attack, the initial symptoms are loss of appetite, nausea and malaise and usually mild fever. After four to seven days jaundice appears and the liver is enlarged and tender. The symptoms usually last from two to six weeks, but complete clinical and biochemical recovery may take many months. Minor attacks in which there is no jaundice are not easily diagnosed and probably very common, especially in children, and confer a life-long immunity.

Very rarely there is a fulminant hepatitis with symptoms of acute liver failure and then death usually occurs within 10 days. Good nutrition is no protection. Most physicians who work in the tropics have had experience of a tragic case in a healthy young individual recently arrived without immunity in an area where infection is widespread and the local inhabitants have acquired immunity in childhood from infections that were mild, despite widespread malnutrition.

Recovery from a typical infection is complete and not followed by fibrosis and cirrhosis. Some apparently healthy people, who may or may not have a history of a clinical attack of the disease, excrete the virus in their faeces. Such carriers are a focus from which an epidemic may arise. It is possible that some of the cases of cirrhosis in which no cause can be found may be due to long continuing exposure of the liver to the virus.

Hepatitis B virus produces a disease known as homologous serum jaundice because it arises after transfusion of blood or blood products obtained from a donor who is a carrier. It can also be spread by the use of one needle to give injections to a series of patients without effective sterilisation. Thus it was identified as a hospital infection and it is now common in drug addicts. The virus is rarely or never spread by the faecal–oral route and natural infection probably arises from close personal contact, as between sexual partners. Infection causes an illness similar to that caused by hepatitis A virus, but fulminant cases and death are much more common. Chronic cases also occur and some become asymptomatic carriers of the disease. They are a potential danger to a community, especially to drug addicts and homosexuals. A carrier can be detected by the presence of the e antigen of the virus (HBeAg) in the serum.

Infection with hepatitis A and B viruses leads to production of several antibodies which appear in the serum. Many of these have a short life but the IgG antibodies to hepatitis A capsid protein (HAA) and to a surface protein of hepatitis B virus (HBs) persist for long periods, probably for life. Their presence indicates past infection that may have been asymptomatic.

Gamma-globulin preparations that confer temporary passive immunity against both A and B viruses are available and can be given to members of health services and others who may be at increased risk of infection at their work. Vaccines for protection against hepatitis B infection are now available but are costly.

Non-A and non-B viruses have been identified recently but to what extent they are responsible for viral hepatitis is not yet known.

Yellow fever virus, like the hepatitis viruses, has a specific affinity for hepatocytes. It is much more virulent and in many of the great epidemics in tropical countries, more than 20 per cent of patients died of acute liver failure. Yellow fever is now very rare, as the mosquito, *Aëdes aegypti*, the vector responsible for its transmission from man to man, is a domestic species and easily controlled. Reservoirs of infection persist in monkeys in tropical Africa and South America and these are a potential threat to man.

Other infective agents
Many infections are associated with some impairment of liver function and focal lesions may occur in some, for example pyaemic and typhoid abscesses. In three diseases the liver is especially involved. In Weil's disease leptospira invade all organs and tissues but markedly the liver and jaundice is the common presenting feature. Amoebiasis is primarily a disease of the large intestine but protozoa may migrate up the portal vein and cause amoebic hepatitis and liver abscesses. In schistosomiasis with infection of the large intestine by *Schistosoma mansoni*, ova frequently move up the portal vein and cause multiple granulomata in the liver; these become fibrosed and are a common cause of cirrhosis of the liver in many parts of Africa and the Middle East.

Toxic agents

Alcohol
The progressive damage to the liver that may follow continuing large intakes from alcohol has already been described. There is an association between national consumption of alcohol and deaths from cirrhosis (Table 47.3), but many of these deaths, up to half in some countries, occur in patients who did not take alcohol. Also many alcoholics do not develop cirrhosis. What makes the liver of some individual more susceptible to damage by alcohol is not known. In parts of Africa and Asia, cirrhosis of the liver is probably commoner than in Europe and North America and cases occur at a younger age and are not so frequently associated with alcoholism.[11] The reason for these differences is a mystery. Possibly alcohol, other undetected toxic chemicals and infective agents not detected clinically may act synergistically to produce progressive liver damage.

Toxic substances in natural foods
Senecio (ragwort) contain an alkaloid which damages the liver in experimental animals and in horses and cattle. Such herbs are frequently consumed as bush teas and herbal remedies in Jamaica, where there is strong

Table 47.3 Cirrhosis mortality and alcohol consumption in different countries[10]

	Mortality (deaths from cirrhosis per 100 000 of population over 25 years old)	Alcohol consumption (as litres of absolute alcohol/head yearly)
France	27	16
Portugal	55	14
Italy	52	14
West Germany	40	11
Spain	39	12
USA	29	5.8
Canada	20	6.5
Sweden	16	5.7
Holland	7.4	4.8
UK	5.7	6.2

evidence that they are responsible for a form of cirrhosis known as **veno-occlusive disease of the liver (VOD)**. In this condition degenerative processes start around the hepatic veins in the centre of the lobule. Occlusion of the hepatic veins may occur owing to thickening of the intimal lining; venous drainage is thus impaired. Cirrhosis may follow with scarring distributed around the central veins in the lobules and its pathology is quite different from that of portal cirrhosis.[12] Clinically VOD resembles other forms of cirrhosis and patients who are often children present with hepatomegaly and ascites. There is a high mortality. Cases closely resembling, if not identical to VOD, have been reported in several African and Asian countries. In Afghanistan an outbreak arose after a drought when the wheat was contaminated with seeds of a heliotrope present in the crop as a weed.[13] Other substances present in natural foods and potential liver poisons are discussed in Chapters 25 and 60. Foods may be contaminated by moulds that produce toxin. Aflatoxins are known to cause liver disease in domestic animals (Chapter 25). They are commonly found on human foods in many parts of Africa and are probably responsible for some cases of cirrhosis.

Drugs

Many drugs can damage the liver in susceptible individuals and produce a clinical and biochemical picture similar to acute viral hepatitis. Examples are paracetamol, a much used analgesic, phenelzine and tranylcypromine, sometimes used in the treatment of depression, and the general anaesthetic halothane. Cholestatic jaundice may follow the use of methyltestosterone and very rarely oral contraceptives. A hypersensitivity reaction leading to cholestasis and jaundice

may follow the use of chlorpropamide and tolbutamide for diabetes and of other drugs.

Industrial chemicals

Workers in the chemical industry may be exposed to many chemicals that damage the liver and produce jaundice. Examples are organic hydrocarbons, carbon tetrachloride, tetrachlorethylene, trinitrotoluene and arsenic.

Storage diseases and congenital disorders

Excess stores of iron (p. 119), copper (p. 125), galactose (p. 348) and glycogen (p. 350) may accumulate in the liver and in time lead to cirrhosis. These conditions are usually due to hereditary defects. Hereditary defects in the transport and conjugation of bilirubin may lead to jaundice. Four have been described, three very rare. The best known is Gilbert's disease in which uptake of unconjugated bilirubin by hepatocytes is impaired. Those people affected usually have no symptoms but jaundice, anorexia, nausea and abdominal pain may arise during a period of stress, such as an infection, fasting or strenuous exercise. Their life span is normal and they need no treatment except occasionally a sedative to relieve itch or abdominal discomfort.

DIETETIC MANAGEMENT AND TREATMENT

Acute hepatitis

There is as yet no antiviral agent for use against the hepatitis virus but metronidazole is very effective in amoebic hepatitis. Patients with viral hepatitis do well with rest, which should be in bed while they are febrile, and abstinence from alcohol.

No specific dietary treatment is needed but, as most patients lack appetite and suffer from nausea, meals should be well cooked and attractively served. Several small meals may be better tolerated than three large ones.

There is no evidence that the course of the disease is influenced by the fat content of the diet. But when jaundice is marked, fat and fatty foods are poorly tolerated. In addition, the absorption of fat from the intestine is impaired because of the lack of bile salts. Under these circumstances the intake of fat should be restricted temporarily to 20 to 50 g daily. Energy then has to be provided mainly from carbohydrate, but an ample intake of protein is indicated to prevent any possible adverse effect of protein malnutrition. Diets Nos. 10 and 11 are suitable. Fried foods and the articles of food likely to cause dyspepsia, listed in Diet No. 17, should be avoided. When the appetite has returned, milk and butter are usually well tolerated. Diet No. 1, with its high protein content, is suitable for convalescence.

Provided the patient is taking adequate amounts of fruit, vegetables and milk there is no need to give supplements of any vitamin or mineral. It is orthodox to prohibit alcohol for six months after the jaundice has disappeared. Even when the attack has been mild and there has only been slight jaundice for a few days, patients should follow this advice.

Fulminant hepatic failure

Sudden massive destruction of liver cells due to acute viral hepatitis or poisoning by alcohol or drugs (halothane and paracetamol are well known causes), leads to severe disturbances in other organs and systems. Each of the complications has to be treated with intensive supportive therapy in the hope of keeping the patient alive for sufficient time to allow some regeneration of hepatocytes. Haemorrhages as result of lack of clotting factors synthesised by the liver lead to oligaemia, shock and renal failure. Profound hypoglycaemia and potassium depletion occur. Intravenous infusion of hypertonic glucose and electrolytes is required with repeated monitoring of blood concentrations. Sedatives may be needed for delirium but, owing to state of the liver, are potentially dangerous. Plasma exchange transfusion and heroic measures such as excorporeal transfusion of the patients blood through a pig's liver and liver transplantation have been tried. Despite all treatment the majority of patients die.

Chronic hepatitis

This is common in alcoholics and occasionally follows viral hepatitis. When it is due to alcohol most patients do very well when alcohol intake is stopped and do not require dietary or other treatment. If after six months of total abstinence a patient feels well and liver function tests have improved, alcohol can be allowed in moderation — not more than 15 g daily.

Some chronic alcoholics are malnourished because they eat irregularly and seldom take a proper meal. They need to change their dietary habits and require professional advice, support and supervision from a dietitian.

Cirrhosis

Many patients with cirrhosis are seriously malnourished, especially those who are alcoholic, and require nutritional rehabilitation with a high energy, high protein diet. This may be difficult to achieve on account of poor appetite, and admission to hospital is then necessary. The protein intake can be supplemented by 20 to 40 g of Casilan or Lonalac daily, which may be given in milk, soups or ice cream (p. 492). A high protein diet carries the risk of precipitating encephalopathy. When tolerance of normal dietary fat is low, preparations of medium chain triglycerides containing C8 and C10 fatty

acids may be given, as these are digested and absorbed in the absence of bile salts. The fat-soluble vitamins are also poorly absorbed and supplements may be needed. A monthly intramuscular injection of vitamin K (10 mg), of vitamin A (30 mg) and of vitamin D (2.5 mg) provides for maintenance. As bleeding is common and often severe, vitamin K should be given at once and continued. Osteomalacia is a well-known complication of chronic liver disease, and also reserves of vitamin A in the liver have been shown to be low, though clinical evidence of deficiency is rare. Vitamins A and D should be given in the doses recommended above at first. If these doses are continued for many months, it should be remembered that these vitamins can be toxic even in relatively small doses.

Alcohol should be forbidden entirely. If the patient can take and digest a high energy, high protein diet as indicated above, temporary improvement can be anticipated in most cases. When the condition is due to alcoholism, if the damage is not too far advanced, excellent therapeutic results can confidently be expected provided the patient accepts strict abstinence. The treatment of the principal complications, namely ascites, portal hypertension and hepatic coma, requires to be considered separately.

Ascites

Fluid accumulates in the peritoneal cavity because of increased capillary pressure in the portal vessels and decreased oncotic pressure owing to a failure of the liver to synthesise plasma albumin. Sodium is retained in the fluid, partly owing to failure of the liver to inactivate aldosterone.

The ascitic fluid often amounts to 10 litres and contains protein in concentrations of 10 to 20 g /l. Tapping the abdomen to remove the fluid (paracentesis) is not desirable except for diagnostic purposes. It depletes the body of plasma proteins and carries a risk of introducing infection. Treatment consists of a diet rich in protein and low in sodium, and also diuretics to increase urinary output of sodium and fluid. A wide variety of diuretics have been used with success. With all of them there is a danger of electrolyte imbalance. Overdosage may lead to sodium deficiency and also to potassium depletion. The latter can be prevented by giving a potassium supplement. Spironolactone which antagonises the action of aldosterone on the distal renal tubular cells is the diuretic of choice. It is particularly effective when given with chlorothiazide, because spironolactone reduces the absorption of sodium from the distal and chlorothiazide from the proximal renal tubules.

The construction of a high protein diet which is also low in sodium is difficult because the protein-rich foods (meat, eggs, dairy products) have a high sodium content. Diets Nos. 7 or 12 are suitable. The former provides a high protein intake from a variety of sources but contains more sodium than Diet No. 12. The latter can be increased in protein by adding a proprietary preparation of casein such as Casilan, which is practically free from sodium. Fluid need not be restricted. The assessment of control of ascites and oedema is best made by weighing the patient.

As a result of these measures the accumulation of ascitic fluid decreases and may finally cease, and the level of plasma albumin usually increases. Thereafter the sodium intake can be gradually increased, but the patient should not add table salt to his food. Salt-rich foods should also be avoided.

Portal hypertension

Bleeding from oesophageal and gastric varices is common and often serious and a cause of death. Even small haemorrhages may precipitate encephalopathy by loading the gut with protein. The anaemia that follows is treated with iron and repeated blood transfusions are often necessary. Pressure in the veins can be relieved by a surgical operation that shunts the portal vein into the inferior vena cava or the splenic vein, after splenectomy, to the left renal vein. Such operations are dangerous and increase the risk of death from liver failure and are carried out only when the risk of death from haemorrhage is high.

Hepatic encephalopathy

This may develop in acute or subacute hepatocellular failure or more frequently as a late feature of cirrhosis of the liver. The clinical features are disordered sleep rhythm, restlessness or drowsiness, as well as impaired intellectual function, confusion, stupor and, in severe cases, coma. A slow 'flapping' tremor and a characteristic odour to the breath (foetor hepaticus) are diagnostic signs.

The provision of adequate nutrition during this emergency may be very difficult because there is usually a marked loss of appetite, and nausea and vomiting readily occur. In addition the decision in regard to the degree and duration of restriction of protein is difficult since too much protein precipitates hepatic coma, while too little may prolong the illness.

Knowledge of the nature of the metabolic changes responsible for the disturbances of cerebral function might lead to dietetic therapy becoming more effective. How much protein can be given with safety? Does the type of protein and its amino acids constituents matter? These are still matters of controversy.[14] Formerly the view was that ammonia and amines produced from dietary amino acids by intestinal bacteria were not adequately removed from the portal circulation; increased amounts reached the arterial circulation and so impaired the function of the brain. Concentration of

NH_4 in arterial blood, and of glutamine in the CSF is often raised when there is liver failure, but it is unlikely that this is the sole cause of the cerebral disorders. The pattern of amino acids in the blood is altered. Concentrations of aromatic amino acids and methionine, normally metabolised in the liver, are raised and of branch chain amino acids, metabolised mainly in muscle, lowered. Entry of aromatic amino acids into brain cells may be facilitated. These amino acids are precursors of noradrenaline and 5-hydroxytryptamine, neurotransmitters in the central nervous system. The suggestion was made in 1975 that increased availability of these amino acids might be responsible for the cerebral symptoms,[15] but this is not yet established. The clinical observation that encephalopathy is more likely to occur in patients who bleed into the gastrointestinal tract lead to the theory that animal protein in the gut might be dangerous. However, clinical trials of animal and vegetable proteins in the diets of patients at risk of encephalopathy provided no evidence that the type of dietary protein is important.[16]

In practice it is important to prevent starvation and minimise the risk of hypoglycaemia and so ample carbohydrate is needed. It is also necessary to provide ample fluids and to preserve electrolyte balance which may be gravely upset, especially if vomiting is severe.

All dietary protein is stopped and 6.2 MJ (1600 kcal) daily is given in the form of glucose or glucose polymer drinks flavoured with fruit juice by mouth in small feeds at one-hour or two-hour intervals. If the patient's level of consciousness does not permit this, intravenous feeding with glucose solutions should be given. Fructose causes severe acidosis and should not be used. The amount of saline used as carrier for the carbohydrate should be adjusted daily, taking into account the urinary output and the state of electrolyte balance. A preparation of B vitamins and ascorbic acid is added to the fluid or given by intramuscular injection. Even in the absence of dietary protein the bacteria in the gut appear to contribute to the clinical picture, probably by producing toxic nitrogenous compounds. Because of this, oral neomycin, 1.0 g six-hourly, is recommended to kill off the major intestinal bacterial flora. Lactulose, a non-absorbable sugar which is fermented in the colon producing lactic acid, has been used with success and may constitute the basis for the supposed value of yogurt. Both of these measures probably act by increasing lactobacilli in the colon at the expenses of Gram-negative bacilli which possess urease and produce ammonia.

As soon as signs of recovery from hepatic failure are noted, e.g. a reduction in the degree of mental confusion or apathy, 20 g of protein should be added to the diet. If there is no mental deterioration, further additions of protein to the diet may be tried; 500 ml of skimmed milk contains approximately 20 g of protein and this can be given in small feeds several times a day as a supplement to the glucose drinks. It may be possible to increase the consumption of skimmed milk to 1.5 l/day which provides about 60 g of protein. The ideal is for the patient to take a balanced convalescent diet with sufficient protein to prevent deterioration of hypoalbuminaemia. However, in the late stages of cirrhosis it is usually necessary to keep the patient indefinitely on a restricted protein intake (45 to 50 g), otherwise mental symptoms tend to recur.

Biliary cirrhosis

Stagnation of bile in the canaliculi of the liver may lead to hepatitis and subsequently to cirrhosis. This may be a consequence of unrelieved obstruction of the bile duct and then secondary bacterial infection is often an additional factor. Biliary cirrhosis also arises from an autoimmune reaction causing cholangitis within the liver. This disease occurs most commonly in middle-aged women.

Prompt surgical treatment of obstructive jaundice usually prevents any damage to the liver from progressing. The outlook for patients with the auto-immune disorder is poor and few survive more than five years. Portal hypertension and ascites are less frequent than in other forms of cirrhosis. Jaundice fluctuates in intensity as does pruritis which is often severe and then may be relieved by cholestyramine.

The dietary measures described for other forms of cirrhosis are indicated and, as dietary fat is usually poorly tolerated, there is more often a need for medium chain triglycerides and also for intramuscular injections of fat-soluble vitamins as maintenance therapy.

DISEASES OF THE GALL-BLADDER AND BILE DUCTS

The function of the gall-bladder and bile ducts is to concentrate, store and deliver bile into the duodenum at appropriate times to assist digestion; hormonal and nervous factors play a part in this process. The stimulus for this activity is the entry of food into the small intestine; this causes the mucosa of the duodenum and jejunum to secrete a hormone, cholecystokinin, which is carried in the blood to the gall-bladder and causes it to contract. Fats and foods rich in fats are especially effective for this purpose. The gall-bladder and the sphincter of Oddi appear to be reciprocally innervated. Thus vagal stimulation causes contraction of the gall-bladder and relaxation of the sphincter, while stimulation of the sympathetic nerves produces the reverse effects. Disturbance of these reciprocal effects and of the

hormonal mechanism may be responsible for initiating both organic disease and functional disorders of the biliary tract. The latter include biliary achalasia (failure in relaxation of the sphincter of Oddi), biliary dyskinesia (spasm of the sphincter of Oddi) and bilious vomiting associated with such conditions as migraine.

Gall-stones (cholelithiasis)

The bile is concentrated in the gall-bladder and when it is supersaturated gall-stones are likely to form. Supersaturation arises when there is an insufficient amount of solubilising agents such as bile acids and, to a lesser extent, lecithin to keep cholesterol and bile pigments in solution. By far the most common gall-stones are mixed stones composed of cholesterol, bile pigment and various calcium salts including calcium palmitate. In the centre there is often a protein nidus. This suggests an infective origin, but it is more likely that the protein is a mucoprotein and part of the bile secretion. The stones are usually multiple and their surfaces are faceted. Much rarer in the western world are multiple small stones of almost pure bile pigment and single large stones of almost pure cholesterol are found. Pigment gall-stones are more prevalent in the eastern world and may be due to increased haemolysis arising from the sickle cell trait and thalassaemia.

Gall-stones are found in about 20 per cent of autopsies and are more common in women than in men. Prevalence is higher in some ethnic groups, notably the Pima Indians in Arizona, where nearly 50 per cent of adults can be shown to have gall-stones by cholecystography.[17] Prevalence appears to be increasing and the cause of this is not known. Advancing age, repeated pregnancies and a sedentary life and the use of oral contraceptives have been claimed to be contributing factors.

The effect of diet is unclear. Dietary factors have been shown to influence bile lipid composition in different ways in several species of animals but there are no consistent data.[18] In man it has been suggested that high cholesterol diets, lack of dietary fibre and an insufficiency of polyunsaturated fats predispose to gall-stones but this has yet to be proven.

The formation of cholesterol gall-stones depends on the concentration in the bile of cholesterol relative to that of the conjugated bile acids and lecithin (phospholipid) which keep cholesterol in a micellar soluble phase. Bile with a relative high cholesterol concentration is said to be lithogenic and this may arise from either excess of cholesterol or lack of bile acids. Excess cholesterol could be due to increased activity of the rate limiting enzyme in its synthesis (hydroxymethylglutaryl-coenzyme A reductase, HMGCoA reductase). Deficiency of bile acid could be due to deficiency of the enzyme that controls their formation (cholesterol 7α-hydroxylase). However, changes in enzyme activities alone cannot explain the formation of supersaturated bile. A more likely explanation is an increased cycling of bile salts within the enterohepatic circulation.

Gall-stones that are causing symptoms are usually removed surgically. Often a stone causes no symptoms and then there is no strong case for its removal. A follow-up of 123 faculty members of the University of Michigan with silent stones revealed that the 15-year cumulative probability of the development of biliary pain or complications was only 18 per cent.[19]

Some gall-stones can be dissolved in the gall-bladder by administration of the bile acid, chenodeoxycholic acid, or the related ursodeoxycholic acid. In a large trial complete dissolution occured in 13.5 per cent of cases after two years but at a cost of some adverse effects — diarrhoea and a slight rise of plasma cholesterol.[20] The treatment is thus of very limited value but may be used for selected patients who know the likelihood of benefit and the risks. Ursodeoxycholic acid is of very limited value but may be used for selected patients. However, it often relieves the symptoms of gall-stones and seldom causes diarrhoea. So it is of value for patients who are elderly, frail or who are losing weight before operation.

Acute cholecystitis

Acute cholecystitis is rarely due primarily to infection of the gall-bladder but almost always occurs in association with obstruction to the cystic duct or neck of the gall-bladder, upon which infection is usually superimposed. In most cases gall-stones are the cause of obstruction.

Treatment

Cholelithiasis with accompanying cholecystitis is primarily the province of the surgeon who may prefer to postpone operation until the acute infection has subsided. The treatment at the onset is that of any acute febrile illness. The patient should be in bed and given suitable analgesics and antibiotics. Heat should be applied to the gall-bladder region and ample fluids given intravenously if the patient is vomiting. So long as the gall-bladder is acutely inflamed, it is advisable to keep the organ at rest as far as possible. To this end fat, which causes contraction of the gall-bladder, should be excluded from the diet. For acute cases an entirely fluid diet of at least 2 to 3 litres daily, given in small feeds at hourly or two-hourly intervals is advisable for a few days.

When the condition settles down, as it usually does within two or three days, clear soups, beef tea, milk, fruit jellies, and cereals may be added, and the diet is rapidly built up to normal or to that recommended for chronic cholecystitis (see below). After recovery if there are gall-stones or a non-functioning gall-bladder, cholecystectomy should be advised.

Chronic cholecystitis

Pending the decision to remove the gall-bladder or if for any reason operation is contraindicated, dietetic treatment along the following lines should be given. The principles are the same for the small minority of cases without stones as for the majority who have them.

Foods which precipitate or aggravate the symptoms should be avoided. These are likely to include cooked meats rich in fat and fried foods. Since biliary stasis predisposes to the formation of gall-stones, a moderate intake of uncooked fat, e.g. in milk, butter and cream cheese is permitted, and may promote drainage of the gall-bladder. Eggs may be permitted in moderation, if they do not cause symptoms. The diet should be bland and contain adequate protein.

Care should be taken to avoid large meals and indigestible articles of food because of the ease with which dyspepsia occurs, and ample quantities of fluids should be taken first thing in the morning, last thing at night and between meals. If, as is frequently the case, the patient is obese, Diet No. 3 should be prescribed.

Obstructive jaundice

When jaundice is due to obstruction of the main bile passages by stone, stricture or malignant disease, the liver cells are, at least for some time, relatively uninjured and hence if the obstruction is removed in time, no permanent cellular damage occurs. Nevertheless, it is advisable to ensure that the patient takes an ample supply of carbohydrate and protein of good quality in the form of skimmed milk and skimmed milk powder. This is particularly desirable as a preoperative measure to prevent the toxic effects of general anaesthesia. Since the flow of bile is reduced, a low intake of fat is indicated.

Laparotomy should be carried out in all cases if the jaundice does not subside within a few weeks, unless the history and biochemical tests strongly suggest that the patient has acute hepatocellular disease with superimposed intrahepatic obstruction.

Diet No. 10 is suitable for most cases of obstructive jaundice. When the patient's appetite improves Diet No. 11 can be used. If the obstruction is suddenly produced, as by impaction of a gall-stone, colic, vomiting and fever may temporarily necessitate a fluid diet, as for acute cholecystitis. If jaundice continues for more than a few days supplements of the fat-soluble vitamins A, D and K should be given parenterally. In long-continued obstructive jaundice there is a risk of osteomalacia developing and an oral supplement of calcium should be given. If the obstructive jaundice cannot be relieved and continues for many months or years, the condition terminates in hepatocellular failure.

DISEASES OF THE PANCREAS

The external secretion of the pancreas may be impaired by inflammatory disease and this leads to failure of digestion and absorption.

The flow of pancreatic juice reaches a maximum between one to two hours after a meal. Secretion is stimulated partly by nervous mechanisms acting through the vagus nerves but chiefly in response to the hormones, secretin and pancreozymin, which are formed when acid chyme comes into contact with the mucosal cells of the duodenum. The volume of pancreatic juice secreted daily is probably about 2 litres, which may contain 300 mmol of sodium and up to 40 g protein, most of which is absorbed.

Acute pancreatitis

This is a serious disorder which may lead to haemorrhagic necrosis of the pancreas, peritonitis and death. It usually occurs in middle-aged and elderly persons. Its aetiology is far from clear but in at least 60 per cent of cases there is an association with biliary tract disease. In some of these cases obstruction by gall-stones or oedema or spasm of the sphincter of Oddi causes a reflux of bile along the pancreatic duct. This activates the pancreatic enzymes which results in autodigestion of the cells and blood vessels of the pancreas. As a consequence a serosanguinous exudate is liberated into the peritoneal cavity with the production of peritonitis and hydrolysis of the fat in the omentum and mesentery. About a quarter of the cases give a history of alcoholism in Britain, but this proportion is much higher in some other countries.

The main symptom is the sudden onset of agonising pain in the epigastrium which may radiate to the back; it may follow a heavy meal or an excess of alcohol. Nausea and vomiting are frequently present. Moderate fever occurs and jaundice may develop. In addition there are signs of peritonitis and profound shock.

The plasma amylase rises and when activity is above 7500 Somogyi units/l a diagnosis of acute pancreatitis is virtually certain.

Treatment

When the diagnosis of acute pancreatitis has been established, medical management consists of the relief of pain and the control of shock. Continuous gastrointestinal suction is essential to reduce vomiting and distension. It also removes acid gastric juice, a stimulus to pancreatic secretion. Production of gastric juice is inhibited by cimetidine and ranitidene and in these ways

the pancreas is rested. Antibiotics should be administered to prevent secondary infection of damaged tissues.

When the acute stage has settled down, diet therapy as for chronic pancreatitis should be instituted and surgery considered.

Subacute recurrent pancreatitis

In some parts of the world recurrent attacks of subacute pancreatitis are common and are usually associated with intermittent heavy drinking. Unless the subject abstains completely these attacks, any one of which may be fatal if not properly treated, lead to a final picture of inanition, diabetes and malabsorption. With abstinence the prognosis is good. Relapsing subacute pancreatitis may sometimes be due to an undiagnosed stone in the common bile duct.

Chronic pancreatitis

This may follow repeated attacks of acute or subacute pancreatitis or be associated with chronic inflammation of the biliary tract or with the penetration of a chronic duodenal ulcer into the pancreas. In these conditions fibrosis is marked between the lobules of acinar tissue and destroys the epithelial cells. The islet cells are spared for a long time. In many cases the pathogenesis is not understood. The disease occurs most commonly in males in the fifth and sixth decades and is often associated with alcoholism.

In the tropics the disease usually presents at an earlier age and commonly there is diabetes and a radiograph shows calcification of the pancreas. Cook[21] reviews 15 reports from countries in Africa and Asia. The cause is not established. Alcohol does not seem to be important and viral infections or dietary toxins acting on an organ previously damaged by protein-energy malnutrition may be responsible.

Clinical features

The main features are recurrent attacks of mid-abdominal and lumbar pain, often relieved by a crouching position, lasting for three or four days and accompanied by nausea, vomiting and pyrexia. In milder cases there may be chronic diarrhoea with undigested fat and muscle fibres in the stools and loss of weight may be prominent. The association of these findings and a diabetic type of glucose tolerance curve is virtually diagnostic. Plain radiographs of the abdomen may show a fine stippled calcification of the pancreas. Plasma amylase estimations are of little value. There may be a slowly progressive and painless jaundice with enlargement of the liver, and a history of chronic cholecystitis and gall-stones is not uncommon. Ultimately the full picture of the malabsorption syndrome and diabetes may develop.

Treatment is mainly medical. When exacerbations of

pain, colic and vomiting occur, the measures described under acute pancreatitis may be required. Surgery may be needed to relieve obstructive jaundice. Stones at the lower end of the bile duct may be diagnosed and removed with a flexible endoscope.

Dietetic regimen

Alcohol must be prohibited. This is of the greatest therapeutic importance. The dietetic treatment of the diarrhoea and loss of weight may be difficult; defects in the digestion of carbohydrate and protein are usually present in addition to failure of fat digestion. Nevertheless it is mainly from carbohydrate and protein that the diet has to be constructed, because the principal defect is a failure of fat digestion. Fried and greasy food and foods rich in fats should be prohibited. Only skimmed milk should be given. Small helpings of chicken, white fish or very lean meat are allowed with any vegetable (except fried potatoes). Fruits (fresh or stewed), jams, jelly and sugar should be taken plentifully. Diet No. 11, which contains 45 g of fat daily, is suitable for the initial treatment of cases of moderate severity. If the patient is not able to take this diet it may be necessary to omit for a few days some of the solid foods and give extra protein; Casilan or Lonalac, preparations of dried milk proteins, can be added to the milk or other beverage. Medium-chain fatty acids may also be given. Supplements of the fat-soluble vitamins and calcium should be given to all cases with a long history of steatorrhoea.

The deficient secretion of the pancreas should be supplemented by active pancreatic extracts. These should be taken at each main meal sprinkled on the food, sipped in a liquid vehicle or as tablets. Response to substitution therapy is assessed by improvement in the character and frequency of the stools. Insulin or hypoglycaemia drugs may be necessary when diabetes mellitus supervenes.

Surgery may be required for the relief of obstructive jaundice.

Cystic fibrosis

This is an hereditary disorder of exocrine glands, transmitted by an autosomal recessive gene. The clinical features arise early in childhood and are a consequence of damage to the pancreas and lungs, arising from blockage of their ducts by tenacious, sticky secretions. The children fail to thrive and previously few survived into adult life, death being due mainly to chronic pulmonary disease. However, with improved methods of treatment the outlook is becoming less gloomy. The pancreatic disorder leads to the malabsorption syndrome with steatorrhoea. The sweat glands secrete a fluid with an abnormally high sodium content and this together with diarrhoea may lead to sodium deficiency.

Dietetic regimen

Children have poor appetites and are frequently undernourished. Time and patience are needed to see that they eat sufficient to meet their energy needs. Some can manage with normal food and a restricted fat intake; in others supplements of protein (e.g. Casilan), glucose polymers and medium chain fatty acids are needed. In severe cases an elemental diet given by nasogastric tube is required.

Most patients need long-term treatment with a pancreatic extract. Supplements of vitamins, especially A and D, and of salt may be indicated.

REFERENCES

1. Gumucio J J, Miller D L 1981 Functional implications of liver cell heterogeneity. Gastroenterology 80: 393–403
2. Rubin E, Lieber C S 1968 Alcohol-induced hepatic injury in nonalcoholic volunteers. N Engl J Med 278: 869–76
3. Dixon K C 1982 Cellular defects in disease. Blackwell, Oxford, p 350–74
4. Hislop W S, Bouchier I A D, Allan J G, et al 1983 Alcoholic liver disease in Scotland and northeastern England: presenting features in 510 patients. Q J Med 52: 232–43
5. Best C H, Lucas C C, Ridout J H 1956 Vitamins and the protection of the liver. Br Med Bull 12: 9–13
6. Himsworth H P 1950 The liver and its disease, 2nd edn. Blackwell, Oxford
7. Ramalingaswami V, Deo M G, Sood S K 1961 Protein deficiency in the Rhesus monkey. In: Progress in meeting protein needs of infants and preschool children. Proceedings of an international conference. Publication No. 843. National Academy of Science, Washington DC
8. Truswell A S, Hansen J D L 1969 Fatty liver in protein-calorie malnutrition. South Afr Med J 43: 280–3
9. Truswell A S, Hansen J D L, Wittman W, et al 1966: Serum lipoproteins and phospholipids in relation to fatty liver in kwashiorkor. South Afr Med J 40:887
10. Sherlock S 1981 Diseases of the liver and biliary system, 6th edn. Blackwell, Oxford, p 334
11. Ramalingaswami V, Nayak N C 1970 Liver disease in India. Prog Liver Dis 3: 222–35
12. Bras G, Hill K R 1956 Veno-occlusive disease of the liver: essential pathology. Lancet 2: 161–9
13. Mohabbat O, Srivasta R N, Younos M S, et al 1976 An outbreak of hepatic veno-occlusive disease in northwestern Afghanistan. Lancet 2: 269–71
14. Anonymous 1983 Diet and hepatic encephalopathy. (Editorial.) Lancet 1: 625–6
15. Munro H N, Fernstrom J D, Wurtman R J 1975 Insulin, plasma amino acid imbalance, and hepatic coma. Lancet 1: 722–4
16. De Bruijn K M, Blendis L M, Zilm D H, Carlen P L, Anderson G H 1983 Effect of dietary protein manipulations in subclinical portal-systemic encephalopathy. Gut 24: 53–60
17. Sampliner R E, Bennett P H, Comess L J, Rose F A,

Burch T A 1970 Gall-bladder disease in Pima Indians: demonstration of high prevalence and early onset by cholecystography. N Engl J Med 283: 1358–64

18. Dam H 1971 Determinants of cholesterol cholelithiasis in man and animals. Am J Med 51: 596–613

19. Gracie W A, Ransohoff D F 1982 The natural history of gallstones: the innocent gallstone is not a myth. N Engl J Med 307: 798–800

20. Schoenfield L J, Lachin J M 1981 The Steering Committee, The National Cooperative Gallstone Study Group. Chenodiol (chenodeoxycholic acid) for dissolution of gallstones. A controlled trial of efficiency and safety. Ann Intern Med 95: 257–82

21. Cook G C 1980 Tropical gastroenterology. Oxford University Press, p 195–9

48

The Anaemias

Haemoglobin concentrations in healthy persons vary widely. Figure 48.1 presents their cumulative frequency in a large population.[1] It can be seen that the distribution is skewed to the left and that there are no sharp cut-off points below which anaemia can be stated to be present. However, standards below which anaemia is likely to be present have been set out by WHO[2] and are presented in Table 48.1. In practice they serve as useful guides. Most persons who are only slightly anaemic by these necessarily arbitrary standards are free of symptoms and may appear in good health; it is a mistake to assume that minor symptoms arising in a person who is only mildly anaemic by the above standards are necessarily due to the anaemia. Yet their capacity for hard physical work may be reduced and they are at increased risk of serious consequences if they suffer a haemorrhage as a result of any accident, during childbirth or from any disease.

There are three main causes of anaemia.

1. Loss of blood from the circulation, i.e. external or internal haemorrhage.
2. Haemolysis, i.e. increased destruction of red blood cells (erythrocytes).

Table 48.1 Haemoglobin concentrations below which anaemia is likely to be present at sea level

	Age	Hb g/dl
Children	6 months to 6 years	11
	6 years to 14 years	12
Adults	Men	13
	Women	12
	Pregnant women	11

3. Reduced production of erythrocytes and haemo-globin — dyshaemopoiesis.

The life of the erythrocyte is about 120 days. The bone marrow replaces them at a rate which enables their number to be maintained. Ingredients of the effete erythrocytes are used so that the call on haemopoietic nutrients in the diet is minimised. The nutritional anaemias are dyshaemopoietic anaemias in which marrow activity is limited by deficiency of erythrocyte and haemoglobin building blocks.

For the production of erythrocytes, many nutrients are needed. The most important are iron, folic acid and vitamin B12, but others are protein, pyridoxine, ascorbic acid, copper and vitamin E. It is unusual for anaemia to arise in an otherwise healthy person solely as a direct result of a poor diet. However the diet often contains insufficient of one or more of the essential nutrients to meet increased needs caused by chronic haemorrhage, infection and genetic defects affecting the red blood cell. Disorders of the alimentary tract often lead to impaired absorption of the essential nutrients and so to anaemia. Hence secondary anaemias are exceedingly common and treatment has to be aimed not only at removing the primary cause, but also at meeting increased demands of nutrients.

Reviews of nutritional anaemias by WHO deal with the public health aspects.[2,3]

HAEMATOLOGICAL FINDINGS

If there is an insufficiency of iron for the formation of

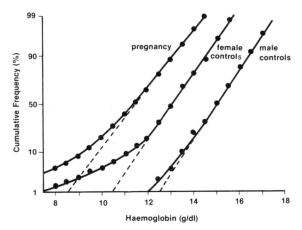

Fig. 48.1 Probability plots of cumulative frequency distributions for haemoglobin (From Bothwell et al)[1]

haemoglobin, the red blood corpuscles are pale and small and the anaemia is said to be **hypochromic** and **microcytic**. If the maturation of the red blood corpuscles in the bone marrow is impaired by lack of folate or vitamin B12, the cells which enter the blood stream are irregular in size and shape, but usually on average larger than normal, and contain their full complement of haemoglobin. Such anaemia is **orthochromic** and **macrocytic**. However, it is usually referred to as **megaloblastic**, after the typical immature precursor of the red blood corpuscles, the megaloblast, which is seen in the bone marrow. Samples of bone marrow are obtained by sternal or iliac puncture. This procedure is safe and carried out with a local anaesthetic.

Occasionally in Britain and very often in the tropics, the bone marrow lacks both iron and either folate or vitamin B12. This gives rise to a hypochromic macrocytic or **dimorphic anaemia**.

A measurement of the Hb concentration in the blood does not distinguish between these types of anaemia. Two additional measurements made on peripheral blood are useful. The first is the haematocrit or packed cell volume (PCV) obtained by centrifuging blood under standard conditions and reading the height of the column of packed red cells. The second additional measurement is the red cell count (RBC).

Three ratios derived from these measurements help differentiate the types of anaemia. Hb/PCV gives the **mean corpuscular haemoglobin concentration** (MCHC), expressed in g/dl. If the value is below 30, the red cells are lacking in haemoglobin and the anaemia is hypochromic. This finding is an indication for iron therapy.

Hb/RBC × 10 gives the **mean corpuscular haemoglobin** (MCH) in picograms (10^{-12} g). This is also low in hypochromic anaemia.

PCV/RBC gives the **mean corpuscular volume** (MCV) in femtolitres (10^{-15} l). A value of over 95 fl indicates that the erythrocytes are on average larger than normal. This suggests that there may be a deficiency of either folate or vitamin B12.

The Hb concentration and PCV can be measured accurately with simple apparatus by persons with limited laboratory experience. The RBC count is a more difficult and time consuming procedure, and reliable results can be obtained only by persons with experience of the method. In many laboratories it is now mechanised (e.g. the Coulter counter). Table 48.2 gives the normal range of findings in women and typical values found in patients deficient in iron or folate.

An additional measurement in peripheral blood is the **reticulocyte count**. Reticulocytes are immature erythrocytes, which can be easily identified by the presence of small granules on staining with cresyl blue. Normally they are less than 1 per cent of the total number of erythrocytes, but they increase when the bone marrow is more than normally active. For example in a patient responding to vitamin B12 therapy, they may amount to 20 per cent or more.

CLINICAL FEATURES OF ANAEMIA

Anaemias give rise to the same general clinical features whatever the cause. As the partial pressure of oxygen in the blood is not reduced, symptoms only arise when the transport of oxygen by the blood is insufficient to meet the needs of the body. As the need for oxygen is related to physical activity, a person leading a sedentary life may have a moderate degree of anaemia and yet be entirely free of symptoms, though these develop if unaccustomed exercise is taken. Any significant degree of anaemia is always associated with an inability to make sustained physical effort. As anaemia often develops very slowly, the patient may gradually and unknowingly reduce physical activity to a lower level. Thus it is not unusual to find a woman undertaking her normal

Table 48.2 Typical findings in peripheral blood in anaemia due to deficiencies of iron and folate

	Normal range in women	Deficiency Iron	Folate
Basic measurements			
Haemoglobin (Hb) g/dl	12–16	7	7
Packed cell volume (PCV) per cent	36–47	28	22
Red blood cells (RBC) × 10^{-12}/l	3.9–5.6	3.5	2.0
Derived values			
Mean corpuscular haemoglobin concentration (MCHC) per cent	30–36	25	32
Mean corpuscular haemoglobin (MCH) pg	27–32	20	35
Mean corpuscular volume (MCV) fl	75–95	80	110

housework with a haemoglobin level of less than 7.5 g/dl, but doing it slowly.

The severity of the clinical features is dependent not only on the degree of anaemia, but on the rapidity of its development. Common symptoms are general fatigue and lassitude, breathlessness on exertion, giddiness, dimness of vision, headache, insomnia, pallor of the skin, palpitation, anorexia and dyspepsia, tingling and 'pins and needles' in the fingers and toes (paraesthesiae). Angina pectoris (due to myocardial hypoxia) is sometimes present. Physical signs include pallor of mucous membranes and fingernails, tachycardia, functional systolic murmurs, evidence of cardiac dilation and, in severe cases, oedema of the ankles and crepitations at the bases of the lungs. In addition to these general features of anaemia there may be signs of nutritional deficiency, particularly angular stomatitis, koilonychia and glossitis. Atrophy of the papillae and mucous membranes gives the tongue a smooth glazed appearance (chronic atrophic glossitis). The atrophy begins at the edges and later affects the whole tongue. As a result the tongue appears moist and exceptionally clean. Koilonychia is the name given to certain changes in the nails; first there is brittleness and dryness: later there is flattening and thinning and finally concavity (spoon-shaped nails).

HYPOCHROMIC ANAEMIA DUE TO IRON DEFICIENCY

This is by far the most common variety of anaemia

throughout the world, affecting mainly women in their reproductive years, infants and children. Figure 48.2 shows the average haemoglobin concentrations in members of the poor families in Aberdeen during the economic depression in the 1930s.[4] Probably today in many cities of the world where there is much poverty, haemoglobin concentrations are similar to those in Aberdeen 50 years ago. In Britain today iron deficiency is still common, but much less severe than formerly. In South Wales Elwood[6] found that 120 out of 1080 women had haemoglobin concentrations below 12 g/dl.

In both rural and urban areas in the tropics this type of anaemia is extremely common. Losses of iron occur not only in menstruation and pregnancy but also as a result of infection with hookworms. Many tropical diets do not contain sufficient absorbable iron to make good these losses.

Iron deficiency anaemia is much less common in men than in women. When found in a male in Britain, it should not be assumed to be nutritional in origin unless all sources of pathological bleeding and organic disease have been excluded.

Iron deficiency may reduce storage iron without causing anaemia. Plasma ferritin reflects the size of the iron stores. Mean values for men and women in the USA were 94 and 34 μg/l respectively,[7] but there were wide variations. Each microgram per litre in the plasma may reflect 8 mg of storage iron.[1] Values of plasma ferritin below 32 μg/l indicate that the stores of iron are greatly reduced. When this occurs without anaemia, the condition is analogous to hypovitaminosis C and hypo-

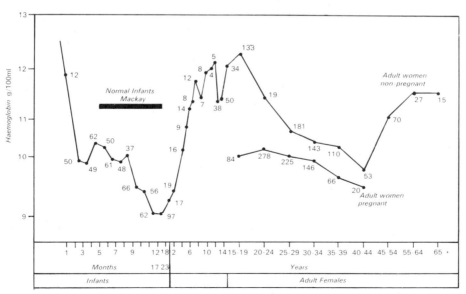

Fig. 48.2 Mean haemoglobin concentrations of poor women in Aberdeen[4] and of children in London[5] during the economic depression in the 1930s. These findings stimulated Stanley Davidson to give a course of lectures on nutrition to medical students in Aberdeen which were the origin of our book

vitaminosis D and the person is at increased risk of developing anaemia.

Women of child-bearing age

The main cause is the increased need for iron which is a direct consequence of menstruation and pregnancy. A secondary cause is a failure of iron adsorption often associated with a diminished secretion of hydrochloric acid by the stomach.

Menstrual losses.   The amounts of iron that may be lost in menstruation have been given on p. 116. All menstruating women have to absorb extra iron from the diet and in about 5 per cent the extra amount needed is over 2 mg daily. Few normal diets could meet this requirement.

Pregnancy and lactation.   The loss of iron involved in a normal pregnancy (iron content of fetus, 400 mg), delivery (iron content of placenta, uterus and blood loss, 325 mg) and lactation (iron content of milk during six months of lactation, 175 mg) may total approximately 900 mg. This entails an extra demand for absorption of about 2 mg Fe/day for a period of 460 days. Even if we deduct an estimated saving from the omission of menstruation during pregnancy, the negative iron balance is still large.

It is obvious that menstruation and pregnancy greatly increase a woman's requirements for iron; it is not surprising that diet alone is often unable to meet the deficit.

Failure of absorption.   The factors determining absorption of dietary iron are discussed on page 117. As haem-bound iron (in meats) is well absorbed and phytates and phosphates in coarse foods of vegetable origin impair iron absorption, it is easy to explain the high incidence of iron deficiency anaemia in women in poor tropical communities.

Clinical features

The anaemia is often well advanced, e.g. haemoglobin level 7.5 g/dl, before significant symptoms are apparent. These have been described on page 460. In addition dysphagia occurs occasionally in severe cases (p. 428) and sometimes koilonychia. While paraesthesiae are common, objective signs of disease of the central nervous system are never found in iron deficiency anaemia. If untreated the condition follows a chronic course. Then atrophic gastritis and a failure to secrete HCl are common; this may further impair iron absorption from a poor diet. The importance of the syndrome is not that it is dangerous to life but that it leads to a loss of efficiency and impaired general health and vitality.

Prophylaxis and treatment

For the prophylaxis of iron deficiency anaemia in women, the butcher and the greengrocer are of particular importance. Once anaemia has developed it is both unwise and uneconomic to try to correct it by dietary means alone, and it is to the chemist that one should turn for help.

Diet

Every doctor should have some knowledge of the iron content of foods (Table 12.2) so that he may give sensible advice on which foods are of value as cheap sources of iron. The most valuable dietary sources of iron are meats and liver; they should preferably be eaten once a day. Eggs also have a high iron content but this is poorly absorbed possibly because of phospholipid inhibitors in the yolk. Less expensive sources of iron are beans, especially soya beans, and nuts. Dark green vegetables such as spinach and watercress and certain fruits, especially dried apricots, peaches, prunes and raisins, are useful sources of iron, but in general fresh fruits and vegetables are of greater value because of their ascorbic acid content, which facilitates iron absorption. Cereals cannot be relied upon to contribute greatly to the iron intake, since the phytates and phosphates reduce its absorption. Milk is a poor source of dietary iron.

Intake of iron may be increased by enrichment of a common food. Thus iron is added to bread in some countries (p. 186). Common salt is another possible vehicle. In a trial in India, 13 villages were provided with salt containing 1 mg/g of elemental iron, and this raised the mean haemoglobin concentration of the blood in both sexes and at all ages, and reduced the prevalence of anaemia.[8]

Yet many women with large menstrual losses become anaemic despite a good diet and these women require medical iron. Anaemia is common in pregnancy when the following prophylactic measures are recommended: (1) routine estimation of the haemoglobin in all women at their first antenatal visit and (2) iron therapy for those with a haemoglobin below 11 g/dl. Because mild anaemia is so common in the third trimester, many doctors prescribe a preparation of iron and folate for all women from the twenty-fourth week until term. This is sound practice where attendances at antenatal clinics are uncertain or irregular, but many women do not need the supplement.

Medicinal iron

There are over 40 oral preparations of iron available on prescription in the United Kingdom. Ferrous sulphate is the preparation of choice. It is made up in tablets, either 200 mg of the exsiccated salt or 280 mg of $FeSO_4.7H_2O$. Each of these contains about 60 mg of elemental iron. The recommended dose is one tablet three times a day after food. If 20 per cent of the iron is absorbed, an additional 35 mg becomes available to the tissues. This should lead to a rise of haemoglobin of 1 g/dl per week provided sepsis, toxaemia or haemorrhage are absent. Treatment should be continued for 10 weeks after the haemoglobin has returned to normal to allow the stores to be refilled.

For the exceptional patient who is unable to swallow tablets, a liquid preparation containing ferrous sulphate should be prescribed. The efficacy of ferrous salts is rapidly reduced if oxidation to the ferric state occurs. Accordingly they must not be prescribed in simple watery solution but should be mixed with 50 per cent glucose and ascorbic acid which retard oxidation. The British Pharmacopoeia preparation, ferrous sulphate mixture (NF), is a suitable liquid preparation since it meets this requirement. One tablespoonful is equivalent to one 200 mg tablet of ferrous sulphate and should be given three times a day well diluted with water.

Rarely oral iron therapy is unacceptable and then injections of a parenteral iron preparation should be given. Medicinal iron is not well absorbed if there is deficiency of ascorbic acid, but provided the patient is getting a good balanced diet, it is not necessary to give a supplement of ascorbic acid or of any other nutrient.

Adverse effects. Gastrointestinal effects, such as nausea, heartburn and epigastric discomfort, are commonly reported after iron medication. Preparations of iron other than ferrous sulphate, such as ferrous succinate, ferrous fumarate and ferrous gluconate, are promoted on the ground that they are less likely to cause these effects. There is good evidence that absorption of iron from them is no better than from ferrous sulphate. In a controlled clinical trial in Edinburgh 93 young women were given five different 'iron pills', one contained ferrous sulphate, three other ferrous salts and one a placebo.[9] Between 16 and 23 subjects complained of symptoms after each of the iron preparations and 20 with the placebo. It can be concluded that in most cases the symptoms were psychological in origin. There is now little doubt that genuine intolerance of ferrous sulphate and of other iron preparations occurs but is uncommon. As ferrous sulphate is much cheaper than any of the other iron preparations, it should be prescribed first. Sir Stanley Davidson never tired of preaching that this was a means of economising in the health services that lay solely in the hands of individual doctors.

Experience in Sweden. In 1965 between 25 and 30 per cent of women of child-bearing age were anaemic. Ten years later the figure had fallen to 6 to 7 per cent.[10] During this period increased use of oral contraceptives probably decreased menstrual blood losses. The fortification of all types of flour was increased from 30 to 75 mg/kg. Sales of iron preparations increased and reached over 17 000 kg, equivalent to 5.8 mg per head daily and more than five times the amount in the United Kingdom. Sales of ascorbic acid increased markedly. The authors discuss the relative effects of these changes and conclude that increased use of medicinal iron accounted for a reduction of 10 per cent in the prevalence of anaemia, and the higher rate of fortification of flour for a reduction of 7 to 8 per cent. To set against these findings, in 1978 four men out of 347 persons screened in Sweden were found on biochemical evidence to have stores of iron greatly in excess of normal.[11]

Infants and children

Aetiology
The following factors help to explain the frequency of anaemia in early life.

Prolonged milk feeding. Breast-fed and particularly artificially fed infants may be kept too long on milk alone without supplements of iron-containing foods.

Low birth weight. At birth the full-term baby has a haemoglobin level of approximately 17 g/dl. After birth a haemolysis occurs and by the sixth to eighth week the haemoglobin falls to 11 g/dl. The iron set free is stored, principally in the liver, and utilised during the period of milk feeding. At the end of nine months the haemoglobin should have risen to 13 g/dl. Premature and full-term infants of low birth weight, for example twins, have a small blood volume and hence smaller stores of iron to tide them through the milk-feeding period. Moreover, their rate of growth is greater and hence the requirements for iron are increased.

Nutritional anaemia in the mother. When a mother is suffering from nutritional iron deficiency anaemia her child's antenatal stores of iron may be inadequate.

Infections. The common infections of infancy and childhood often depress the bone marrow.

Malabsorption. Gluten enteropathy is an occasional cause.

Clinical features
In infants the symptoms of anaemia are not so easily recognised as in adults, but there is always impairment of general health and vitality.

Prevention
The prophylactic measures may be summarised as follows:
1. The prevention and treatment of iron deficiency anaemia in pregnant women and those suffering with menorrhagia.
2. Efficient treatment of infections in infants.
3. The provision of supplementary feeds of broth, minced meat, vegetable purées and other easily digested sources of iron from the age of 4 to 6 months onwards.

4. The administration of prophylactic doses of iron to infants of low birth weight from the third month of life onwards.

Treatment

Once anaemia has developed, dietetic measures cannot be relied on to cure the anaemia and hence must be supplemented with medicinal iron in a dose of about 6 mg/kg. For this purpose the ferrous sulphate mixture for infants (BPC) is a suitable preparation. One to two teaspoonfuls well diluted with water three times a day is the usual dose depending on the age of the child.

Hypochromic anaemia due to haemorrhage

Acute haemorrhage. The sudden loss of a large volume of blood, 1 litre or more, from trauma or intestinal bleeding produces peripheral circulatory failure (shock).

The rapid loss of 2 to 3 litres of blood is usually fatal, whereas an even greater quantity may be lost without causing death if it is spread over a period of 24 to 48 hours. During this period restoration of the circulating blood volume is proceeding by the withdrawal into the blood of tissue fluid. This haemodilution, which takes some hours to develop, is reflected by a fall in the haemoglobin level and red cell count. Hence, immediately after a haemorrhage of 1 litre in a normal person, the haemoglobin may be 15 g/dl, but fall to 12 g some hours later when dilution has occurred. When the circulating blood volume is partially restored, the acute symptoms of shock subside. Treatment of acute haemorrhage, if large, requires blood transfusion.

Chronic haemorrhage. This results from persistent or repeated loss of small amounts of blood. The most frequent causes are menorrhagia, and bleeding from the alimentary canal due to a carcinoma, peptic ulcer or, especially in children, a Meckel's diverticulum and occasionally haemorrhoids. Alimentary bleeding from the taking of aspirin must be remembered. Such persistent blood loss causes a progressive fall in haemoglobin.

Diagnosis depends upon the finding of a blood picture of hypochromic anaemia and the discovery of a source of chronic haemorrhage. It is important to test the faeces for occult blood and, if found, to do a sigmoidoscopy and a radiographic examination of the alimentary tract. Endoscopy of the upper alimentary tract may show the source of blood loss.

Treatment involves the arrest of the haemorrhage by appropriate means where possible and the administration of iron and a good diet.

Hypochromic anaemia due to malabsorption of iron

Iron deficiency anaemia is common in the malabsorption syndrome and after gastrointestinal operations. As months or years may elapse before the anaemia becomes manifest, the patient will have left the charge of the surgical specialist and be under the care of the general practitioner, who should be on the lookout for this development.

ANAEMIAS DUE TO DEFICIENCIES OF VITAMIN B12 AND FOLATE

Deficiency of these vitamins leads to megaloblastic anaemia. This may be due either to dietary lack or, much more commonly in Europe and North America, a defect in intestinal absorption. Pregnant women are especially liable to develop this type of anaemia. In all countries megaloblastic anaemia is much less common than iron-deficiency anaemia and, from the viewpoint of public health, is relatively less important.

Pernicious anaemia

The term pernicious anaemia should be limited to the group of megaloblastic anaemias which is due to a failure in secretion of intrinsic factor by the stomach other than from surgery. The history of the discovery of vitamin B12 is given on page 158.

Aetiology

There is failure to absorb dietary vitamin B12 owing to lack of production of intrinsic factor in the gastric mucosa. Antibodies against gastric mucosa can often be detected in the serum and are probably responsible for destroying the mechanism for producing intrinsic factor. The disease thus arises as an autoimmune disorder. It often has a family incidence.

Morbid anatomy

In the stage of relapse there is extension of red bone marrow into the shafts of the long bones. The marrow shows the presence of many megaloblasts and a great reduction in the number of normoblasts. There is evidence of increased blood destruction — enlargement of the spleen, hyperbilirubinaemia and increased deposition of iron (haemosiderin) in the liver, spleen, kidneys and bone marrow. The gastric mucosa is thin and atrophic. Gastric analysis invariably shows complete achlorhydria. In inadequately treated cases degenerative changes in the dorsal and lateral tracts of the spinal cord may be found (subacute combined degeneration).

Clinical features

This disease is rare before the age of 30 and affects females more than males between 45 and 65 years of age. The onset is insidious and the degree of anaemia is often great before the patient consults a doctor. The patient generally appears well nourished despite the fact that weight loss is a common feature. The skin and mucous membranes are pale, and in severely anaemic cases the skin may show a faint lemon-yellow tint. When the tongue is painful it often has a red, raw appearance; later the mucous membrane becomes smooth and atrophic. In about 80 per cent of cases in relapse paraesthesiae occur in fingers and toes — numbness, tingling, 'pins and needles'. Occasionally there are objective signs of involvement of the spinal cord (vitamin B12 neuropathy), which may rarely develop before the anaemia. Psychiatric symptoms may occur associated with low levels of vitamin B12 in the plasma, but in the absence of other signs of neuropathy.

Diagnosis

The differential diagnosis of pernicious anaemia from other forms of megaloblastic anaemia depends upon the age of the patient, the finding of histamine-fast or pentagastrin-fast achlorhydria, upon the absence of pregnancy and the lack of evidence of malnutrition, malabsorption or structural change in the small intestine. Plasma vitamin B12 is below 160 ng/l while plasma folate is usually normal. The Schilling test, with oral vitamin B12 labelled with radioactive cobalt, shows subnormal absorption which is corrected if intrinsic factor is given at the same time.

Treatment

General. The decision to give a blood transfusion depends on the clinical state of the patient. When the haemoglobin level is so low as to endanger life. e.g. under 4 g/dl, it should always be given. Physical activity should be at a minimum until the haemoglobin is above 7 g/dl.

Specific. Hydroxocobalamin should be given in a dosage of 1000 μg intramuscularly twice during the first week, then 250 μg weekly until the blood count is normal. Folic acid should never be used alone in the treatment of pernicious anaemia as it does not prevent the development of neurological complications, and may precipitate them.

Within 48 hours of the first injection of a cobalamin the bone marrow shows a striking change from a megaloblastic to a normoblastic state. Within two to three days the reticulocyte count begins to rise, reaching a maximum about the fourth to seventh day.

In some cases the rapid regeneration of the blood depletes the iron reserves of the body so that the haemoglobin fails to rise above 10 to 11 g/dl. To prevent this, ferrous sulphate, 200 mg thrice daily, should be given.

When subacute combined degeneration of the cord is present the dose of a cobalamin should be 250 μg twice weekly and continued at this high level for at least six months.

Maintenance. Patients should continue to receive regular doses of a cobalamin for the rest of their life. The dose is so regulated that the haemoglobin level is maintained at the normal level. The dose of hydroxocobalamin recommended is 1000 μg given by intramuscular injection every four to six weeks. Regular blood counts are therefore essential every six months and the assessment should never be made solely on clinical impression or on the haemoglobin level alone. Only thus can the appearance of subacute combined degeneration of the cord be prevented.

Prognosis

If a case is properly treated with vitamin B12 the prognosis is excellent and the neurological complications are prevented, arrested or cured. Prior to the discovery of liver therapy the disease ran a progressive downhill course, death occurring usually within three years. Hence the title, pernicious.

Nutritional megaloblastic anaemia in adults

Folate deficiency. The classical studies of Wills p. 161 in Bombay drew attention to this disease. Her patients were mainly pregnant women who had been living for long periods on poor diets consisting mainly of rice and lacking foods of animal origin and vegetables. They mostly responded well to Marmite, a yeast product.

Nutritional megaloblastic anaemia occurs commonly in underdeveloped countries and was formerly known as tropical macrocytic anaemia. It may occur at any age, but adult women, infants and young children are affected much more frequently than men. It is often made manifest by pregnancy. It is seldom important in a population which eats meat and green vegetables regularly. In Britain and other Western countries nutritional megaloblastic anaemia due to dietary deficiency is uncommon and occurs most frequently in pregnancy (see below), but has been reported in Indian women.[12] Very occasionally it occurs in housebound old people living alone and eating a very poor diet.

The disease also arises as a result of a failure to absorb folic acid in gastrointestinal disorders which lead to the malabsorption syndrome. The condition may develop when the dietary folate is unable to meet demands for increased erythropoiesis caused by other diseases, e.g. the haemoglobinopathies (p. 467), and other haemolytic anaemias. After prolonged treatment with antiepileptic drugs plasma folate is often low and megaloblastic anaemia sometimes occurs. Oral contraceptives may impair folate absorption in some women.[13,14]

Clinical features and diagnosis

The disease progresses slowly and, if untreated, the haemoglobin concentration is likely to fall very low (2 to 4 g/dl). Loss of weight and signs of various vitamin deficiencies are frequently but not always observed. Glossitis is often present. Paraesthesia is a common complaint.

The peripheral blood shows a macrocytic anaemia and the bone marrow a megaloblastic reaction. Plasma folate is less than 3 ng/ml and red cell folate under 100 ng/ml. There is free hydrochloric acid in the gastric juice.

Treatment

Folic acid in a dose of 5 to 10 mg daily is effective. Patients who are seriously ill (haemoglobin level less than 5 g/dl) need blood transfusion to tide them over until the folic acid has acted. Iron is often required before a full haematological response can occur. The patient should be given a well-balanced diet, and continue on it. If poverty or custom makes this impossible the patient should be advised to change her habits so as to include some good sources of folate (Table 14.8) every day. Pregnant and lactating women have greater needs for folate than anyone else in the community. A follow-up clinic is invaluable for detecting relapses in their earliest stages and also for periodic dietetic advice which can help to prevent a return to the defective diet.

Vitamin B12 deficiency. Vitamin B12 is found only in animal foods so that strict vegetarians, or vegans, who regularly avoid eating dairy products and eggs as well as meat, are at risk of developing deficiency. Because liver stores of the vitamin are normally large, it takes several years for a previously well-nourished person to develop clinical manifestations on an inadequate diet. In Britain dietary vitamin B12 deficiency disease is very rare among Caucasians. In most vegans the plasma vitamin B12 is often moderately reduced and there may be a sore mouth and tongue but anaemia is unusual. Severe anaemia developed in a 6-month-old baby, fed only at the breast by a vegan mother in California.[15]

Because pure dietary deficiency is an uncommon cause of vitamin B12 deficiency anaemia, other conditions need to be ruled out before the diagnosis is established. Vitamin B12 absorption and gastric and intestinal function should be shown to be normal and the patients should not be on drugs such as biguanides which can impair vitamin B12 absorption.

Tapeworm anaemia

The tapeworm, *Diphyllobothrium latum*, absorbs vitamin B12 from the small intestine and so infection may lead to anaemia. Although the distribution of the worm in fishes is widespread, human infection has been studied mainly in Finland. There about 2 per cent of the adult population harbour the worm.[16] Only a small proportion of carriers develop megaloblastic anaemia, but many have low plasma concentrations of vitamin B12.

Megaloblastic anaemia of pregnancy

A temporary macrocytic anaemia with megaloblastic reaction in the bone marrow sometimes occurs during pregnancy or the puerperium. The clinical features are the same as those of nutritional megaloblastic anaemias. The factors involved in its causation include increased demands and dietary deficiency, especially of folic acid and much more rarely of vitamin B12.

Cases of megaloblastic anaemia of pregnancy usually respond dramatically to the oral ingestion of 10 mg of folic acid daily. If the anaemia is very severe and is not discovered until close to full term, blood transfusion is indicated. Megaloblastic anaemia may recur in subsequent pregnancies. A co-existing deficiency of iron is frequent, and this leads to a dimorphic blood picture. Iron therapy is indicated in such cases. Since there is biochemical evidence of folic acid depletion in about 20 per cent of pregnant women in Britain and because pernicious anaemia is rare in this age group, it is reasonable to give folic acid as a prophylactic. A dose of 300 μg daily is ample for this purpose and this may be given with iron in a suitable preparation during the last trimester of pregnancy. Since megaloblastic anaemia occurs more frequently in pregnant women in tropical underdeveloped countries, they have a special need for a folic acid/iron supplement.

Megaloblastic anaemia of infancy and childhood

Megaloblastic anaemia is not uncommon in association with protein-energy malnutrition and usually responds to folic acid. It is rare in full-term infants in Britain and other wealthy countries except in association with infection and malabsorption. Low plasma folate is common in premature babies, and a few of these develop overt megaloblastic anaemia.

In Germany and in Italy it has arisen in infants fed exclusively on goat's milk, which has an exceptionally low folate content.[17]

Megaloblastic anaemia associated with the malabsorption syndrome

Megaloblastic anaemia is commonly seen in the syndrome due to failure of absorption of folic acid, of vitamin B12 or of both. It may also occur subsequent to resection or short-circuiting of a large segment of the small intestine.

The clinical features are those of the underlying alimentary disease together with the general symptoms of anaemia. Symptoms and signs of various vitamin and mineral deficiencies are also frequently present.

In gluten enteropathy and tropical sprue there is usually an excellent haematological response to folic acid, given intramuscularly for the first two or three days and orally in a dosage of 10 to 20 mg a day thereafter. It is wise to supplement this with 1000 μg of hydroxocobalamin by injection every four to six weeks, and, particularly in the tropics, iron by mouth may also be required. When megaloblastic anaemia is associated with blind or stagnant loops of the small intestine there is likely to be a response to cobalamin therapy, but surgical correction should be undertaken if possible.

OTHER NUTRITIONAL CAUSES OF ANAEMIA

The production of the protein portion of the framework of the red corpuscles and the synthesis of globin are affected by a diminished intake of amino acids. However, the deficiency must be severe and long continued because the protein requirement for the synthesis of haemoglobin takes precedence over that required for the manufacture of plasma proteins.

The role of protein-energy malnutrition in the causation of tropical nutritional anaemia has been extensively studied. In kwashiorkor the anaemia is usually moderate in degree. As there is often an associated dietary deficiency of iron, ascorbic acid, folic acid or, more rarely, vitamin B12, and one or more of a variety of infections may be present, it is not surprising that no consistent haematological picture is found or that the anaemia is sometimes severe.

Patients who have lost weight from a simple insufficiency of food are often mildly anaemic. In the Minnesota experiment p. 261 when volunteers had lived for 24 weeks on an inadequate diet and lost about 25 per cent of their body weight the haemoglobin was reduced to an average of 11.7 g/dl. The cause of this anaemia is that all the organs of the body — with the exception of the skeleton and nervous system — shrink when the body is short of energy, yet the total volume of water in the body is little changed. The red cell population, or 'erythron', is no exception. So one effect of weight loss from lack of dietary energy is a smaller red cell population in a normal plasma volume. If the patient has lost 25 per cent of his lean body mass, the haemoglobin concentration in his blood is likely to be 75 per cent of normal.

The anaemias of scurvy and pyridoxine deficiency are discussed on pages 325 and 164 respectively.

GENETIC DEFECTS OF RED BLOOD CELLS

There are hereditary defects of red blood corpuscles that make them more susceptible to haemolysis and persons who carry these genes are liable to become anaemic. Homozygotes are relatively uncommon and this is

fortunate as in them anaemia is often severe and may be fatal. Heterozygotes are much more numerous and at least 100 million persons carry one or other of these genes which have become dispersed by migration all over the world. In them, anaemia, if present, is slight and there are usually no clinical features. Dietitians and nutritionists should know a little about these conditions because heterozygotes are at increased risk of becoming severely anaemic if exposed to nutritional or other haematological hazards. Brief notes are given below on the four commonest of these genetic defects.

Thalassaemia
The genotype originated in Mediterranean countries (Greek *thalassa*, sea) but has spread especially to the East across Asia. It is defined by a defect in synthesis of part of the polypeptide chain of haemoglobin A, which is partially compensated by persisting synthesis of fetal haemoglobin (Hb-F). There are also abnormalities of the red cell membrane. Homozygotes have thalassaemia major, a severe haemolytic anaemia and rarely survive into adult life. Heterozygotes may or may not have a mild anaemia, thalassaemia minor.

Sickle cell trait
This is common in African Negroes and is due to an abnormal haemoglobin, haemoglobin S, differing only in having a single molecule of valine instead of one of glutamic acid in one of the polypeptide chains. The configuration of the molecules of Hb-S distort the red blood corpuscles into a characteristic sickle shape. Such corpuscles are abnormally sensitive to hypoxia. Persons with the sickle cell trait are at risk of a haemolytic crisis when flying and cabin pressure is reduced. Heterozygotes have the sickle cell trait and are only occasionally anaemic. Homozygotes have a severe anaemia, sickle cell disease.

Spherocytosis
This is the commonest congenital defect of red blood corpuscles in northern Europe. The abnormality lies in the cell membranes which are more than normally permeable to sodium ions. The cells assume the shape of spheres which are more easily trapped in the microcirculation of the spleen, where haemolysis takes place, than the normal biconcave discs. The defect is inherited as an autosomal dominant. In most cases the increased loss of cells by haemolysis is slight and can be made good by increased production in the bone marrow. When anaemia develops, removal of the spleen reduces haemolysis and cures the anaemia but does not change the underlying defect.

Glucose-6-phosphate dehydrogenase deficiency
The genotype is found in all races and is present in up to 35 per cent of some Mediterranean populations and

in 10 per cent of American Negroes. It is due to an incomplete dominant gene, and is fully expressed in males and in homozygous females. Glucose-6-phosphate is oxidised by a dehydrogenase linked to the conversion of NADP to $NADPH_2$ which in some way maintains the stability of red cell membranes. Persons with the defect are liable to develop anaemia when treated with oxidant drugs. More than 40 drugs are known to produce haemolysis and these include commonly used anti-malarials, sulphonamides, antipyretics and analgesics. It is also produced by ingesting the broad bean, *Vicia faba*, or inhaling its pollen. Continued ingestion leads to severe anaemia as was recognised many years ago in Mediterranean countries where it was known as **favism**.

A survey in Glasgow[18] showed abnormal haemoglobins in the blood of 38 out of 380 children whose parents came from Africa, the Indian subcontinent and China, but none in 99 children of Scottish parents. However, the incidence of mild anaemia, usually due to iron deficiency, was only a little higher (20 per cent) in the children of immigrant parents than in those with Scottish parents (16 per cent). Thus these genetic defects are common in immigrant populations and, though they seldom affect health, their presence in a community is a potential cause of severe anaemia.

ANAEMIA IN TROPICAL COUNTRIES

In tropical countries the causes of the different types of anaemia, their clinical features and their treatment are similar to those occurring in temperate climates. There are, however, additional factors which are not present in temperate climates. Thus the demands for iron may be greatly increased by the loss of haemoglobin in the faeces and urine resulting from haemorrhage due to parasitic diseases such as hookworm and schistosomiasis. In addition significant amounts of iron may be lost in the sweat and shed epithelial skin cells during muscular work in hot climates. The role of malaria and hookworm in the production of anaemia requires special emphasis (see below). Other protozoal and helminthic infections as well as bacterial infections which are common in the tropics may be responsible for anaemia. When these additional factors operate in persons who live on diets deficient in iron and protein, it is not surprising that anaemia in tropical countries is both frequent and severe.

The nutritional megaloblastic anaemias of tropical climates are always associated with diets poor in animal protein and fresh vegetables, and hence low in vitamin B12 and especially folate. Requirements of these substances are increased during periods of growth, in pregnancy, as a result of infections including malaria, and when increased red cell formation occurs as in

haemolytic anaemias. It is therefore wise to add folic acid (up to 5 mg daily) to the therapeutic regime for infants and toddlers with protein-energy malnutrition and for all patients suffering from malnutrition, chronic infections or haemolytic anaemias.

Malaria

An attack of malarial fever, especially when due to *Plasmodium falciparum*, is always accompanied by haemolysis, and in a severe or prolonged attack severe anaemia may ensue. After the parasites have been removed from the blood, haemolysis may continue, due to a complement-mediated immune response, and there may also be a mild depression of erythropoiesis.[19] When malarial infection is associated with pregnancy and malnutrition, the anaemia may present as megaloblastic anaemia due to folate deficiency, but is more usually hypochromic and microcytic because of iron deficiency. Since the blood destruction is intravascular, most of the iron liberated from the destroyed red cells is retained in the body and can be used again for synthesis of haemoglobin. If it were not for this conservation of iron, the incidence and severity of the anaemia would be much greater than it is. The treatment of malaria in the individual and its eradication from areas of low or moderate endemicity are thus prerequisites for the treatment and prevention of anaemia.

A vicious circle develops in communities suffering from chronic malaria — sickness, weakness and anaemia, economic inefficiency, poverty, malnutrition, bad housing and social conditions, reinfection. Experience has shown how effective malarial control can be in eradicating the disease from large areas and how remarkable are the benefits which ensue.

Hookworm infection

Infection with hookworm is a common cause of anaemia where there is 'wet' cultivation of the land. The clinical and haematological features are similar to those of chronic hypochromic anaemia. A heavy infection with hookworms is always associated with anaemia. Smaller loads may be carried without ill-effect. Haemorrhages occur at the site of the attachment of the worms to the intestinal mucous membrane. These are certainly in part responsible for the anaemia. It has been calculated that each worm may ingest from 0.03 to 0.15 ml of blood daily. A patient with a heavy infection, namely about 1000 worms (which would give a stool count of about 20 000 ova/g faeces) would sustain a heavy loss of blood and anaemia would quickly develop. Detailed studies of hookworm load, blood loss and anaemia have been made in Venezuela[20] and in West Africa.[21]

Heavy hookworm infection usually occurs in populations whose dietary intake of iron is unsatisfactory. The hypochromic anaemia is then in part due to a poor diet and in part to the worms. This combination causes much ill-health; it may reduce greatly the working capacity of both men and women and is thus directly responsible for the poverty of many families in the tropics.

Experience has shown that in treating anaemia due to hookworm, whether in a single patient or in a large community, satisfactory results can only be obtained by the use of a combination of vermifuges, dietary improvement and the administration of medicinal iron.

Heavy infection may cause severe anaemia with haemoglobin levels below 4 g/dl. In such seriously ill patients, before administering a vermifuge, blood transfusions should be given and the general condition of the patient improved by bed rest, diet and medicinal iron.

OTHER CAUSES OF ANAEMIA

Anaemia may arise from a number of disorders where there is no evidence that nutritional deficiency is of primary aetiological importance. They include the following:

Infection. A mild or moderate normochromic anaemia may develop secondary to chronic infection, particularly if fever is present. A mild degree of iron deficiency may be found. The response to iron therapy, both oral and parenteral, is usually unsatisfactory unless the primary cause of the anaemia is removed.

Drugs. Many drugs can cause anaemia by impairing red cell formation, by causing haemolysis or by leading to bleeding. Small repeated haemorrhages in the stomach due to aspirin is a common example.

Uraemia. In chronic renal disease anaemia is common but the bone marrow remains cellular until renal damage is marked, when hypoplasia may be found. Deficiency of erythropoietin is a possible cause.

Hepatic cirrhosis. Here the anaemia is usually macrocytic or normocytic. If megaloblastic anaemia occurs this is probably due to primary malnutrition, and is found particularly in chronic alcoholics with cirrhosis. The occurrence of iron deficiency anaemia suggests gastric or oesophageal haemorrhage.

Malignant disease. The causes of anaemia in widespread malignant disease are numerous. They include impaired appetite, malabsorption or blood loss from the alimentary tract, multiple deposits in the bone marrow, and occasionally increased haemolysis.

Sideroblastic anaemia. Abnormal utilisation of iron by the marrow may cause a refractory anaemia. Some cases respond to pyridoxine therapy.

REFERENCES

1. Bothwell T H, Charlton R W, Cook J D, Finch C A 1979 Iron metabolism in man. Blackwell, Oxford, p 223
2. World Health Organization 1972 Nutritional anaemias. WHO Tech Rep Ser no. 503
3. World Health Organization 1975 Control of nutritional anaemia with special reference to iron deficiency. WHO Tech Rep Ser no. 580
4. Davidson L S P, Fullerton H W, Campbell R 1935 Nutritional iron deficiency anaemia. Br Med J 2: 195–8
5. Mackay H M 1933 The normal haemoglobin level during the first year of life. Arch Dis Child 8: 221–5
6. Elwood P C 1968 Some epidemiological problems of iron deficiency anaemia. Proc Nutr Soc 27: 14–23
7. Cook J D, Lipschitz D A, Miles L E M, Finch C A 1974 Serum ferritin as a measure of iron stores in normal subjects. Am J Clin Nutr 27: 681–7
8. National Institute of Nutrition, Hyderabad 1980 Community studies using common salt fortified with iron. Annual Report: 166–9
9. Kerr D N S, Davidson L S P 1958 Gastrointestinal intolerance to oral iron preparations. Lancet 2: 489–92
10. Hallberg L, Bengtsson C, Garby L, Lennartsson J, Rossander L, Tibblin E 1979 An analysis of factors leading to a reduction in iron deficiency in Swedish women. Bull WHO 57: 947–54
11. Olsson K S, Heedman P A, Stangard F 1978 Preclinical hemochromatosis in a population on a high-iron-fortified diet JAMA 239: 1999–2000
12. Britt R P, Harper C, Spray G H 1971 Megaloblastic anaemia among Indians in Britain. Q J Med 40: 499–520
13. Chanarin I 1980 The folates. In: Barker B M, Bender D A (eds) Vitamins in medicine. Heinemann, London, p 298
14. Hettiarachchy N S, Kantha Sachi S, Corea S M X 1983 The effect of oral contraceptive therapy and of pregnancy on serum folate levels of rural Sri Lankan women. Br J Nutr 50: 495–501
15. Higginbottom M C, Sweetman L, Nyhan W L 1978 A syndrome of methylmalonic aciduria, homocystinuria, megaloblastic anaemia and neurologic abnormalities in a vitamin-B12 deficient breast-fed infant of a strict vegetarian. N Engl J Med 299: 317–23
16. Saarni M, Palva I, Ahrenberg P 1977 (Correspondence.) Lancet 1:806
17. Wintrobe M M 1967 Clinical haematology, 6th edn. Kimpton, London, p 834
18. Goel K M, Logan R W, House F, Connell M D, Strevens E, Watson W H, Bulloch C B 1978 The presence of haemoglobinopathies, nutritional iron and folate deficiencies in native and immigrant children in Glasgow. Health Bull 36: 176–83
19. Woodruff A W, Ansdell V E, Pettit L E 1979 Causes of anaemia in malaria. Lancet 1: 1055–7
20. Layrisse M, Roche M 1964 The relationship between anaemia and hookworm infection. Am J Hyg 79: 279–301
21. Gillies H M, Watson Williams E J, Ball P A J 1964 Hookworm infection and anaemia. Q J Med 33: 1–24

49

Diseases of the Nervous, Locomotor and Respiratory Systems and of the Skin

NERVOUS SYSTEM

The brain is responsible for about one-fifth of the basal metabolism and its need for glucose and oxygen has long been recognised. Nitrogenous and lipid material are also required for the growth and regeneration of myelin sheaths and axis cylinders and for the enzyme systems needed for cellular metabolism. Imbalances of sodium and potassium and other electrolytes affect the cerebrospinal fluid and the excitability of nerve cells. Vitamins, especially those belonging to the B complex, must be available in adequate amounts since they are essential for the utilisation of carbohydrate which plays such a predominant role in the metabolism of the nervous system. Neurological diseases in which malnutrition is of primary aetiological importance are the nutritional encephalopathies and neuropathies associated with pellagra (nicotinic acid deficiency), Wernicke's encephalopathy (thiamin deficiency), beriberi (thiamin deficiency), and subacute combined degeneration of the cord (vitamin B12 deficiency). The clinical features and treatment of these diseases and other primary nutritional disorders affecting the brain, spinal cord and peripheral nerves are described in Part III. Many of the inborn errors of metabolism (Chap. 39) also affect the nervous system. Severe undernutrition may follow a reduced intake of food due to psychiatric causes or neurological disease affecting the muscles and making feeding difficult. Anorexia nervosa (Chap. 27) is the classic example of the former and motor neurone disease of the latter.

The possible roles of nutrition in some of the major neurological and psychiatric disorders are now discussed.

NEUROLOGICAL DISORDERS

Cerebrovascular disease

This is numerically the most important of all diseases of the central nervous system. More people die or are disabled by a stroke than by coronary heart disease. Atherosclerosis of the cerebral vessels and hypertension are the main causes and the possible role of dietary factors in their aetiology is discussed in Chapter 41.

Nutrition has a role in the complex problems arising in the rehabilitation of patients after a stroke. Difficulties in feeding due to either physical or psychological disability may lead to undernutrition. Some patients are helped in their immediate problems by a period of tube feeding. On the other hand, many patients are overweight and a reducing diet might lower the blood pressure and so decrease the risk of a second stroke. A dietitian has therefore an important place in a rehabilitation team.

Multiple sclerosis

This disease which affects about 1 in 2000 people in Britain usually starts early in adult life. It is characterised by relapses and remissions and leads to severe disability after a varying number of years. The symptoms are manifold and may include double vision, weakness of one or more limbs, sensations of numbness or pins and needles (paraesthesia), inco-ordination of movement (ataxia), nystagmus and loss of control of the bladder. The symptoms are caused by lesions disseminated in the central nervous system, consisting of areas of demyelination.

The cause of the disease remains unknown and there have been many theories. Current views are that it may be due to the action of an unidentified slow virus or that it is an immunological disorder related to an attack of measles in early life.

Two observations have suggested that nutritional factors might be responsible. First, in swayback, a disease of lambs characterised by demyelination, affected areas of brain show a loss of lecithin and other cerebral lipids, but the proportion of saturated to unsaturated fatty acids in cerebral lecithins is increased. Secondly, in the human disease there is a reduction in plasma linoleate, and the phospholipids in both red blood corpuscles and platelets have a reduced proportion of linoleate. These findings have suggested the use of linoleic acid in treatment and in a controlled clinical trial with 80 patients observed over two years, relapses were reported to be less severe and less prolonged in patients receiving daily a dose of a sunflower seed oil emulsion containing 8.6 g of linoleic acid than in those receiving an olive oil emulsion with only 0.2 g of linoleic acid.[1] This finding has not been confirmed though in some cases relapses appeared to be less severe in patients receiving supplements.[2] In the past the hopes of patients have often been falsely raised by new remedies, which have subsequently been shown to be ineffective and it would be unwise to promise too much benefit from the ingestion of sunflower seed oil.

The final stages of the disease may be very distressing. Severe tremor of the hands and of the head may make feeding difficult, as it also may in Parkinson's disease. Then patients may benefit from tube feeding.

Epilepsy

Epilepsy is a common disorder and about 1 in 200 people are affected. They are liable to periodic attacks usually associated with a disturbance of consciousness and commonly manifest as fits. In a small minority of cases a local lesion in the brain or a generalised metabolic disturbance is responsible. In the great majority of patients the cause is unknown and they are said to have idiopathic epilepsy.

Antiepileptic drugs are very effective in preventing the seizures. Before these were available many bizarre remedies were advocated to stop the fits, or, in the language of the past, to drive out the devils. A period of starvation was sometimes seen to reduce their frequency. Such benefit may have been due to a depression of the brain by the accompanying ketoacidosis. Ketogenic diets are advocated when the fits cannot be controlled by drugs.[3,4] Childhood myoclonic epilepsy is a rare form of the disease occurring in young children which is often resistant to drugs; it is usually associated with brain damage and patients have many attacks throughout the day. It is not good for a growing child to be ketoacidotic and a ketogenic diet should only be tried after thorough tests have shown that the fits cannot be controlled by drugs. Less than 1 in 100 epileptic children fail to respond to drugs. For this small minority a diet low in carbohydrate and high in fat may help to control the fits. Medium chain triglycerides are useful in designing such a diet.

Antiepileptic drugs induce changes in liver metabolism which may increase requirements of vitamin D and folic acid. Patients taking large doses over the years should be checked regularly for signs of anaemia and rickets or osteomalacia.[5]

Patients with epilepsy should take normal well-balanced meals at regular intervals. Epileptic children should not be allowed to take very large meals as these may predispose them to fits.

Migraine

The term migraine is now loosely applied to different types of headaches and a more precise definition is needed.[6] **Classical migraine** is a disease characterised by periodic paroxysmal headaches. The headache is usually preceded by a vague malaise that warns the patient of its impending arrival. The onset is sudden and accompanied by visual or other sensory disturbances. The headache usually begins in one temporal region and spreads to involve the whole of one side of the head. The attacks often first appear at the time of puberty and decline in frequency and severity when middle-age is past. Usually there is a family history. There is seldom any suggestion that an attack is related to any article of diet.

The term migraine is also applied to headaches that lack the above characteristics and are often accompanied by nausea, vomiting and other gastrointestinal features. Such symptoms commonly occur in children and are sometimes referred to as 'bilious vomiting'. Many reports provide evidence that such attacks can be brought on by ingestion of specific articles of diet to which the patient is intolerant or allergic. The nature of these foods and the reactions to them are described in Chapter 50.

The symptoms of classical migraine are attributable to cerebral vasospasm and ischaemia followed by cerebral and extracerebral vasodilation and hyperaemia. Measurements of cerebral blood flow have shown that these changes do not occur in the common migraine attack[7] and the two forms differ in pathophysiology.

Hyperkinesis and hyperactivity

The term hyperkinesis has an established use to describe a syndrome in children characterised by sustained activity, impulsiveness, distractibility, inability to concentrate and aggressiveness. Typically it occurs in children with organic brain damage sustained at birth or early in life, but it is sometimes seen in epileptic children and in others with no evidence of cerebral pathology. In such cases there is no evidence that the symptoms are related to diet or any article of food.

In the 1960s there was much interest in the USA in a condition called minimal brain dysfunction in children with learning difficulties and other problems in behavioural development, including symptoms of overactivity. Conflicting views were presented at a New York Academy of Science Conference.[8] There are no reliable criteria for either clinical or pathological diagnosis and widely different views as to its incidence; some observers thought that at least 5 per cent of children were affected and there were sceptics who doubted the existence of the syndrome. The subject attracted wide interest in the lay press and television after the publication of a book, *Why your child is hyperactive* by an allergist, B. F. Feingold.[9] He claimed that children with behavioural problems and learning difficulties benefited from a diet in which all foods containing additives were eliminated; he also claimed that the incidence of hyperactivity was increasing with the greater use of food additives in the food industry.

There is no doubt that food additives, notably artificial colouring agents, may cause symptoms in susceptible persons who are intolerant of one or more of them (see Chapter 50). There is no convincing evidence that such symptoms, including hyperactivity, are common in children. Nevertheless many American parents have imposed a Feingold diet on their difficult children. Such severe dietary restrictions inevitably add to the problems that already beset a family. The decision to put a child on a Feingold diet is not one for amateurs and should only be made after consultation with an experienced allergist and a paediatric neurologist. The Feingold diet is a good example of how enthusiasts for nutrition may misuse a little knowledge. Good critical accounts of hyperactivity and food additives have been given by two American paediatricians.[10,11]

PSYCHIATRIC DISORDERS

Deficiencies of thiamin, nicotinic acid and vitamin B12 may each be associated with psychological disorders, as described elsewhere. Occasionally the psychological symptoms are so marked and other symptoms and signs of the deficiency so slight that the correct diagnosis may be overlooked and the patient at first is treated as if he was a neurotic or had a psychotic disorder. Some of these patients appear to have requirements for a vitamin in excess of the recommended intake. Pauling's concept of orthomolecular medicine (p. 150) has appealed to some psychiatrists who have become enthusiastic advocates of megavitamin therapy for schizophrenia.[11] Their claims were examined by the American Psychiatric Association,[12] who could find no evidence to justify them. Claims that schizophrenia may sometimes be due to gluten sensitivity have also not been substantiated.[13]

Although schizophrenia may eventually be shown to be a metabolic disorder, or a collection of several differing ones, the nature of the underlying biochemical disturbances is at present largely unknown. There is no evidence from studies either of its chemical pathology or its epidemiology that dietary factors contribute in any way to its aetiology, or indeed that they are responsible for more than a small fraction of psychiatric disorders.

Psychiatric disorders may lead to abnormal feeding behaviour and so to anorexia nervosa (Chap. 27) and obesity (Chap. 28).

LOCOMOTOR SYSTEM

Diseases of the bones, joints, muscles and ligaments include a variety of disorders, often loosely grouped together under the heading of 'rheumatism'. The cause of these disorders is seldom simple and often obscure. They differ from one another widely in their aetiology, pathology and clinical course. They are often chronic, painful, disabling illnesses from which there is frequently little relief except by palliative measures such as physiotherapy and the prescription of analgesic drugs and corticosteroids. It is not surprising that numerous patients and their doctors have resorted to every possible method of treatment, including special diets. Various dietary regimes have been prescribed in the past, but have been founded on false hopes and mistaken theory. For a time it was widely believed that 'rheumatism' was due to an accumulation of acids in the body; efforts were made to avoid 'acid' foods, or to prescribe a diet that would keep the urine permanently alkaline. However, there is no evidence to associate rheumatism with 'acidity', which is an outworn notion as explained on page 101. A diet low in meat was often recommended to maintain an alkaline urine and also because of the erroneous belief that rheumatism is due to disordered purine metabolism, which is only true of gout.

CHRONIC RHEUMATIC DISEASES

The principal members of this group are rheumatoid arthritis, osteoarthrosis and non-articular rheumatism. They account for a very important proportion of temporary or permanent disablement in temperate climates. The rheumatic group of diseases is second only to bronchitis in men and holds first place among women as a reason for seeking medical advice.

Rheumatoid arthritis

Rheumatoid arthritis occurs in people of all ages. The peak incidence in both men and women is approximately at the age of 40. It occurs in women at least three times as frequently as in men. It is mainly a disease of temperate climates which are associated with cold and damp. The principal tissue affected is the synovial membrane of joints, which becomes inflamed and thickened. A characteristic antibody, the rheumatoid factor is usually demonstrable in the plasma and the cause of the disease appears to be an autoimmune disorder.

The onset is usually insidious. Muscular stiffness develops first and is followed later by pain and swelling of many joints, starting frequently with the small joints of the hands and feet. During the active stage of the disease the patient suffers from general malaise and fatigue; fever is sometimes present and the appetite is poor. In such patients loss of weight usually occurs. There is frequently some degree of anaemia.

Treatment

Successful treatment depends on the co-ordinated efforts of the physician, orthopaedic surgeon, physiotherapist, occupational therapist and social worker. The programme of treatment should be carefully co-ordinated to meet the needs of each individual case. All factors likely to have an adverse influence on the patient should be dealt with, and recommendations as to future activity based on an accurate knowledge of functional capacity. These ends can best be achieved in special units devoted to the study and treatment of the chronic rheumatic diseases.

Although diet has no specific curative value, common sense dictates that an attempt should be made to correct anaemia and loss of weight by diet and other measures.

To improve the state of nutrition the whole art of the dietitian may be needed. Any foods that tempt the patient to eat may be tried, but in general those rich in protein, iron and ascorbic acid should be offered first. Additional vitamin and mineral concentrates are often prescribed, although their value is doubtful. In the acute stage, when loss of weight, anorexia and continued fever are present, the instructions for the dietetic treatment of pyrexia (p. 487) are indicated. Marked clinical improvement is often associated with a better state of nutrition.

Osteoarthrosis

Osteoarthrosis is characterised by degeneration of the articular cartilage and the formation of bony outgrowths at the edges of the joints. A generalised form of the disease occurs normally in middle-aged women in whom the small joints of the fingers, the carpometacarpal joint of the thumb and the interfacetal joints of the spine are particularly affected. The more localised form, in which only one or two of the larger joints are involved, occurs amongst elderly people of both sexes. There is no impairment of general health.

Osteoarthrosis is an exaggeration of normal ageing in the joints. When one joint is particularly affected, there is frequently a history of an injury to that joint some years before. Malalignment following fractures of the long bones gives rise to osteoarthrosis in adjacent joints. Symptoms are prone to develop in the weight-bearing joints or those joints subjected to excessive strain at work. Obesity predisposes to osteoarthrosis of the weight-bearing joints in the lower half of the body.

The joints most frequently involved are those of the spine, the hips, knees, elbows and the terminal joints of the fingers. The symptoms are gradual in onset. Pain is at first intermittent and of an aching character, appearing especially after the joint has been used, and relieved by rest. As the disease progresses, movement in the affected joints becomes increasingly limited, at first by muscular spasm and later by the loss of joint

cartilage and the formation of osteophytes. General health is usually excellent.

Treatment

The pathological changes in osteoarthrosis are irreversible, but much can be done to alleviate the symptoms. For this purpose, rest, graduated physical exercises and physiotherapy, including hydrotherapy, are of particular value. Analgesics should be prescribed according to the patient's needs. In selected cases orthopaedic operations are indicated. Diet has a limited, though useful, part to play in treatment. There is no evidence that deficiency of any nutrient is responsible for the primary defect, the degeneration of the articular cartilage. On the other hand obesity, by placing an extra strain on the joints, may hasten the onset. In addition, once the disease is established, pain and joint deformity reduce the patient's capacity for physical exercise and this renders him more liable to become obese unless he takes the necessary dietary precautions. Hence the prevention and correction of obesity is a valuable aid in management.

A form of widespread osteoarthrosis which affects children occurs in Siberia, China and Korea; it is called **Kashin-Beck disease** after its discoverers.[14] Degeneration of joint cartilage is probably due to toxins from a fungus *Fusaria sporotrichiella* which infects local cereal crops.

Non-articular rheumatism

'Non-articular rheumatism', 'muscular rheumatism' and 'fibrositis' are terms which describe a number of conditions characterised by pain and stiffness, often of sudden onset, affecting mainly the neck, shoulders, back and gluteal regions. Usually no cause can be found but exposure to cold and damp, excessive or unaccustomed muscular activity, injury to muscles and tendons and poor posture may each be held responsible. Muscular pain and stiffness arise often as a result of strain or injury to ligamentous or articular structures. Thus most cases of brachial neuralgia, lumbago and sciatica may result from degenerative changes in the intervertebral discs, either from prolapse of the nucleus pulposus or from narrowing of the intervertebral foramina, leading to pressure on spinal nerve roots.

In the acute stage the patient may be severely incapacitated by pain and stiffness. In the more chronic stage pain is felt most often after rest and improves with moderate activity. Muscular spasm may be marked and movement limited.

Treatment

In the acute attack of muscular rheumatism such as lumbago, rest in bed is essential, together with heat to the affected part and analgesics in ample amounts. At a later stage physiotherapy (heat, massage and graduated exercise) is essential. In cases with lesions of the intervertebral disc causing pressure, operation should be considered.

Diet has no specific part to play in curative treatment but if the patient is obese, reduction in weight may be of value in the relief of symptoms.

FRACTURED FEMUR

Elderly people are liable to trip and fall and break the neck of their femur. This then requires surgical pinning. The length of time before they become mobile again and can return home varies greatly. A controlled clinical trial[15] showed that in thin patients who may be undernourished the period in hospital can be reduced by tube feeding at night. This is valuable when a poor appetite limits the amount of food eaten in the day.

RESPIRATORY SYSTEM

The main causes of disease in the respiratory system are (1) infection (2) inhaled irritants, (3) allergy, (4) vascular accidents, and (5) malignant disease.

Infection. This is by far the most important cause of disease in the respiratory tract. Infection may be caused by a virus, as in the case of coryza, influenza and virus pneumonia, or by bacteria, as in bronchitis, bronchopneumonia, lobar pneumonia and tuberculosis. The complex problems of the part which the state of nutrition plays in preventing infections are discussed in Chapter 59, and also the contribution which diet makes to helping the patient to overcome an infection once it has been acquired.

Irritants. Exposure to tobacco smoke, industrial pollution or other inhaled irritants over many years leads to chronic bronchitis. When severe and prolonged and complicated by heart failure, this may lead to severe undernutrition and a state of cachexia. This is probably due to anorexia caused by chronic hypoxaemia.

Allergy. Certain respiratory diseases are allergic in origin, the most obvious example being hay fever. Another disease in which allergy plays an important role is bronchial asthma. Besides inhaled dust or pollen, ingested foods such as eggs, milk, wheat, shellfish, etc. can be responsible for asthma. The detection of a food allergen and it subsequent exclusion from the diet may be an important factor in the treatment of asthma. The role of food allergy in the causation of disease is discussed in Chapter 50.

Vascular accidents. The most common vascular accident in the lung is embolism from a thrombosis formed usually in the veins of the lower limb or pelvis. If this dislodges it travels through the right side of the heart and obstructs one of the pulmonary arteries. It occurs especially in elderly people confined to bed, e.g.

after an operation. There is no good evidence that nutritional factors play a part in the aetiology.

Malignant disease. Malignant disease of the bronchial tree and lungs has greatly increased in frequency in recent years. Tobacco smoke and pollution of the atmosphere with smoke and fumes are of great aetiological importance. There is little evidence that nutritional factors play any part in the causation of bronchial carcinoma or that dietetic treatment influences the course of the disease.

SKIN DISEASES

The skin manifestations of scurvy and pellagra have already been described, and Chapter 37 gives an account of various conditions of the skin commonly found in malnourished communities. The skin manifestations of linoleic acid deficiency and Refsum's disease respond to appropriate nutritional therapy.

Since there are several skin diseases of which the cause is unknown and which persist for long periods and respond poorly to treatment, it is not surprising that both patients and doctors have sometimes attributed their origin to dietary errors and attempted to cure them by dietetic means. Krehl[16] gives references going back to 1912 for claims of the therapeutic value of various low fat and low protein diets in the treatment of **psoriasis**. None of these has stood up to critical evaluation. Chronic psoriasis is a distressing condition and patients should not be asked to take on the additional burden of dietary restrictions, for which there is no scientific justification.

Acne, so common in teenagers, has been attributed to eating excessive amounts of sweets and chocolates. There is no evidence to support this view or that dietary factors are in any way responsible for the disease. In severe cases not responding to local treatment, a synthetic analogue of vitamin A, 13-*cis*-retinoic acid, has produced prolonged remissions.[17] Since 1982 it has been on the market in the USA as isotretinoin. The dose recommended is 2 mg/kg daily by mouth. This is a large amount in relation to daily intake of retinol and evidence of hypervitaminosis A has appeared after prolonged administration of the drug.[18] Hence it should be used with caution in selected cases and it is not a panacea for a common disease.

The one chronic skin disorder that may be improved by dietary measures is **dermatitis herpetiformis**. Over 70 per cent of these patients have varying degrees of atrophy of the jejunal mucosa and are sensitive to gluten. They benefit greatly from a gluten-free diet, though it may take many months before the skin lesions clear up completely. Dermatitis herpetiformis appears to be one manifestation of coeliac disease and should be managed as such.

REFERENCES

1. Millar J H D, Zilkha K J, Langman M J S, et al 1973 Double-blind trial of linoleate supplementation of the diet in multiple sclerosis Br Med J 1: 765–8
2. Bates D, Fawcett P R W, Shaw D A, Weightman D 1978 Polyunsaturated fatty acids in treatment of acute remitting multiple sclerosis Br Med J 2: 1390–1
3. Livingston S 1972 Comprehensive management of epilepsy Thomas, Springfield, Ill
4. Bower B D, Schwartz R H, Eaton J, Aynesley Green A 1982 The use of ketogenic diets in the treatment of epilepsy In: Wharton B (ed) Topics in perinatal medicine 2. Pitman, London
5. Hahn T J 1980 Drug-induced disorders of vitamin D and mineral metabolism. Clin Endocrinol Metab 9(1): 107–129
6. Blau J N 1984 Towards a definition of migraine headaches. Lancet 1: 444–5
7. Olesen J, Tfelt-Hansen P, Henriksen L, Larsen B 1981 The common migraine attack may not be initiated by cerebral ischaemia. Lancet 2: 438–40
8. De la Cruz FF, Fox B H, Roberts R H (eds) 1973 Minimal brain dysfunction. Ann N Y Acad Sci 205: 1–396
9. Feingold B F 1975 Why your child is hyperactive. Random House, New York
10. Wender E H 1981 Hyperactivity and the food-additive-free diet. In: Barness L A (ed) Nutrition and medical practice. Ari Publ, Westport, Conn, p 248–57
11. Schechter N L 1982 The baby and the bathwater: hyperactivity and the medicalization of child rearing. Perspect Biol Med 25: 406–16
12. American Psychiatric Association 1973 Megavitamin and orthomolecular medicine in psychiatry. Task Force Rep no. 87. Washington DC
13. Anonymous 1983 Gluten in schizophrenia. (Editorial.) Lancet 1: 744–5
14. Nesterov A I 1964 The clinical course of Kashin-Beck disease. Arthritis Rheum 7: 29–40
15. Barstow M D, Rawlings J, Allison S P 1983 Benefits of supplementary tube feeding after fractured neck of femur: a randomised control trial. Br Med J 287: 1589–92
16. Krehl W A 1973 In: Goodhart R S, Shils M E (eds) Modern nutrition in health and disease, 5th edn. Lea & Febiger, Philadelphia, p 948
17. Pack G L, Olsen T G, Yoder F W, et al 1979 Prolonged remissions of cystic and conglobate acne with 13-cis-retinoic acid. N Engl J Med 300: 329–33
18. Pittsley R A, Yoder R W 1983 Retinoid hyperostosis: skeletal toxicity associated with long-term administration of 13-cis-retinoic acid for refractory icthyosis. N Engl J Med 308: 1012–4

50

Idiosyncrasies, Food Intolerance and Food Allergies

I am of a constitution so general, that it consorts and sympathiseth with all things. I have no antipathy, or rather idiosyncrasy, in diet, humour, air, anything.

Thomas Browne, 1643

Men are of different constitutions with respect to their powers of digestion, nor less different with respect to the irritability of their system, and are consequently variously affected by the same aliments; and this so much so as to have produced the vulgar observation that *one man's meat is another man's poison*. This indeed does not apply in many cases, and only remarkably in the case of the idiosyncrasies of some particular persons.

William Cullen, 1789

In medical parlance the name idiosyncrasy is commonly applied to exceptional responses, on the part of exceptional individuals, to stimuli which are insufficient to produce any conspicuous effects in the great majority of members of the human race. Such stimuli are often applied in the forms of articles of diet or particular drugs, the pollen of particular plants, or the exhalations of particular animals.

Archibald Garrod, 1931

The quotations[1,2,3] come from the writings of a country doctor who was one of the fathers of English literature and of two physicians, eminent in the long lines of professors of medicine at Edinburgh and Oxford universities. These men give authority to the use of **idiosyncrasy** to describe any unusual response of the body to any substance in the external environment, including a food. This authority needs restating firmly, because a group of British physicians[4,5] have given the word a new and restricted meaning. They failed to recognise that idiosyncrasy, a Greek word used by the physician Dioscorides in the first century AD, has been established in the English language for over 300 years. Change is not required and can only be confusing. Otherwise their publications can be recommended strongly for the clear accounts given of the prevalence, diagnosis and management of clinical disorders arising from idiosyncrasies to foods.

These disorders are conveniently described as **food intolerance** and, when attributable to immunity reactions, as **food allergy**. That such disorders exist has never been in dispute but there has always been uncer-tainty as to how common they are. Orthodox teaching in medical schools has in general followed Cullen[2] in his view that 'one man's meat is another man's poison . . . does not apply in many cases'. There have always been enthusiasts who think otherwise, but their views have not been generally accepted because their dietary studies have been poorly controlled and their diagnoses based on ill-defined clinical criteria. Some of these enthusiasts, who may have charged high fees for advice that appeared little better than quackery, brought the subject into disrepute.

Yet the old medical orthodoxy is now under challenge, notably from ecologists who claim that chemicals present in diets from environmental pollution or as additives used by food manufacturers are responsible for many common clinical disorders. In as much as it is now established that some of these chemicals can cause clinical symptoms in a few susceptible individuals, this challenge is a benefit to medical practice. But ecologists have as yet failed to demonstrate that chemical contaminants of foods in amounts below the maxima permitted by law have had widespread adverse effects on the health of any community.

Psychological factors

Food and sex, both essential for the survival of a species, depend on behavioural activity that is often accompanied by strong emotions. It is therefore not surprising that adverse responses to particular foods sometimes arise in the mind. In one American study a history of food intolerance could not be confirmed by a controlled test in over half of the patients.[6] This is probably not unusual and the majority of patients with symptoms which they attribute to food require psychological aid, not dietary advice.

Allergy has been given much publicity in popular newspapers and on radio and television, and unfortunately much of the information is inaccurate. This has made it easier for emotionally disturbed adults and parents of emotionally disturbed children to seek an explanation and a way out of their difficulties through allergy. They fall an easy prey to quack 'allergists', many of whom now flourish. Some of them after receiving a sample of hair and a large fee will send by post a list of offending foods and a prescription for a restricted diet.

Unfortunately there are also many uncritical doctors who go along with their patients in the diagnosis without the time-consuming and difficult investigations that may be needed to establish the diagnosis. An example is the vogue for Dr Feingold's treatment of hyperactive children by diets which exclude food additives, especially colouring agents. There is little doubt that these have been associated with hyperactivity in a few children, but established cases are rare. Hyperactivity is a behavioural disorder for which there are at present no agreed diagnostic criteria. It is an easy escape from the problems presented by a difficult child to label him as hyperactive. Child rearing is subject to fashions and hyperactivity has now become a vogue, as is well described in a thoughtful essay by an American paediatrician.[7]

PATHOGENESIS

Food intolerance in an individual may be due to three organic causes: (1) a genetic defect leading to deficiency of a specific enzyme, (2) hypersensitivity to a chemical present in a food, similar to the intolerance shown by some individuals to common drugs, and (3) the development of an allergic state.

Genetic defects

Genetically determined deficiencies of a specific enzyme may make a patient intolerant of a specific food. An example is glucose-6-phosphate deficiency which may lead to severe anaemia if the patient eats broad beans (favism, p. 468). Another is galactose-1-phosphate uridyl transferase deficiency which leads to metabolic disturbance if galactose is ingested (p. 348). Such defects are uncommon causes of food intolerance.

Hypersensitivity to chemicals in foods

Many natural foods contain pharmacologically active substances such as the amines histamine and tyramine. The headache and other symptoms occurring in the well-known cheese reaction (p. 215) are attributable to tyramine. Many amines have powerful vasomotor actions on the cerebral blood vessels and food containing them may in susceptible individuals be responsible for 'sick headaches', a layman's diagnosis, and sometimes difficult to distinguish from classical migraine (p. 471). Only a small proportion of sufferers from classical migraine claim that their attacks are brought on by specific foods. It is also possible that pharmacologically active substances present in foods affect motility and the

local circulation in the small intestine, and so may be responsible for symptoms such as abdominal discomfort and pain. There are as yet no authoritative tables giving the range of content of these amines and similar substances in natural foods. A few people can take coffee only in very small amounts because the caffeine in it causes irregularities of the heartbeat and palpitations.

The Chinese restaurant syndrome (p. 250) is the classical example of intolerance of a food additive, in this case monosodium glutamate. Some susceptible people are intolerant of other food additives, such as the artificial colouring agent tartrazine, and preservatives such as sodium benzoate. This may be a direct chemical effect or an allergic response after binding of the additive to a protein.

Allergy

The word was coined in 1905 by Von Pirquet, a Viennese paediatrician, who was studying the responses of experimental animals to tuberculin and other foreign substances. He used the word, derived from the Greek, *allos*, other and *ergon* work, to describe the altered reactivity of tissues that arises after exposure to a foreign protein or antigen. At first it was used to cover both protective and hypersensitivity reactions but was soon restricted to the latter.

Four distinct types of hypersensitivity reactions, arising under differing circumstances, are recognised by immunologists. Only type I, which includes the food allergies, is of direct concern to nutritionists. This type depends on a reaction in which an antigenic allergen combines with a particular antibody, immunoglobulin IgE, within the tissues. IgE is synthesised and secreted by plasma cells in response to stimulation by specific allergens; IgEs then move through the circulation and are bound to the membranes of mast cells in the tissues, particularly in the skin, the respiratory passages and the digestive tract. At these sites they can combine with circulating allergen and this damages the mast cells, which then release histamine and other factors that are responsible for the clinical features. These are usually due to **local reactions** which cause urticaria (hives), asthma, rhinitis, hay fever, and gastrointestinal disturbances, the common manifestations of allergy. Allergic individuals appear to be more liable to form IgE in response to exposure to antigenic allergens in small amounts, and this tendency is often inherited.

A generalised reaction, fortunately very uncommon, is often fatal. It is known as **anaphylactic shock**. The mechanism underlying is illustrated by the following experiment. A guinea-pig is made sensitive to the serum of another animal by a single small injection of the serum. This produces a small amount of specific antibody. If later a second but larger dose of the serum is given, profound and often fatal collapse follows due to fall in blood pressure and bronchospasm consequent upon a sudden release of large amounts of histamine into the circulation. Anaphylactic shock is most frequently encountered in people who receive a therapeutic or prophylactic injection containing some foreign protein to which they have been made sensitive by a previous injection of the same material. It is very rare for it to occur after ingestion of a food. An account[8] of the complex subject of immunology, specially tailored for nutritionists, and given to them recently in Glasgow, is recommended.

CLINICAL FEATURES

Tables 50.1, 2 and 3 give data from 100 patients investigated at Guy's Hospital, London.[9] They were not a random sample of the London population, and attendance at the hospital is determined in part by the special interests of the physicians. Many allergy clinics would have a higher proportion of young children, but other reports from Europe and North America convey the same general message with only small variations in detail.

Foods commonly associated with intolerance

Table 50.1 lists the foods to which the patients were found to be intolerant. Many patients were intolerant of more than one food. There are few foods to which intolerance has not been reported. The first six foods in the table in the same order are responsible for most cases of food intolerance in clinics throughout the world. In over 70 per cent of these patients there was evidence of an allergic reaction.

Table 50.1 Foods causing intolerance in 100 patients at Guy's Hospital, London[9]

Food	Number of patients affected
Milk	46
Egg	40
Nuts/peanuts	22
Fish/shellfish	22
Wheat/flour	9
Chocolate	9
Artificial colours	7
Pork/bacon	7
Chicken	6
Tomato	6
Soft fruits	6
Cheese (but not milk)	5

Also yeast (3 cases); banana, beef, cucumber, onion, pineapple, sweetcorn, tea/coffee (2 each); apple, celery, cream, ginger, Marmite, pear, potato, quails, soya, sultanas (1 each).

Age incidence

Intolerance to food may arise at any age, but most commonly in early childhood. Table 50.2 shows the age ranges of the 100 patients studied in London. After the age of 5 years food allergies tend to disappear spontaneously but allergies to inhaled substances such as pollens, dusts, animal hair and dander often first develop in later childhood.

Table 50.2 Age incidence of 100 patients with food intolerance at Guy's Hospital, London[9]

Age group	Number of patients affected
0–10 years	30
11–20 years	20
21–30 years	16
31–40 years	9
41–50 years	17
51–60 years	6
61–70 years	2

Common symptoms

Table 50.3 gives the prominent symptoms and their incidence in 100 patients. Incidence adds up to more than 100 as many patients had two or more symptoms. Only six patients complained of headache. Some of the symptoms were not related to food and could be ascribed to inhaled allergens. These are commoner than food allergies but the two are often associated together. The gastrointestinal symptoms were nausea, abdominal discomfort, and also diarrhoea and vomiting. Angiooedema is a form of acute localised urticaria affecting usually the eyelids and lips, and sometimes the hands and feet and other sites.

The symptoms usually arise soon after ingestion of the offending food — lip swelling, rhinorrhea and vomiting within a few minutes, asthma and urticaria within an hour. Diarrhoea occurs later. All of these are transitory. They may subside within an hour and normally within 24 hours in the absence of a second challenge. Eczema often develops insidiously, sometimes after other symptoms have subsided or after several days of repeated

Table 50.3 Prominent symptoms in 100 patients with food intolerance at Guy's Hospital, London[9]

Symptom	Number of patients affected
Asthma	58
Gastrointestinal	41
Eczema	37
Urticaria (hives)	35
Rhinorrhea	31
Angio-oedema	8

challenge. It may then persist for many days or even weeks, even if the offending food is not eaten again.

A family history of allergy is common. When both parents suffer severely from asthma or hay fever, it is often advisable to warn them that their child is at a greatly increased risk of developing a food allergy.

DIAGNOSIS

Dietary history

A careful dietary history should always be taken. In some cases of food allergy the symptoms develop so rapidly and dramatically, almost immediately after eating the offending food, that the patient is able to make his own diagnosis. More often it is not so easy to associate symptoms with any particular food, especially if there is a delay of some hours between the eating of the suspected food and the onset of symptoms. A particular food may be wrongly believed by a patient to be the cause of their allergy, because it happened to be eaten immediately before an attack, when in fact it was due to some other cause. In cases of doubt, a patient should be given a diary in which to record with great care and detail, over a period of many days or even weeks, all the foods eaten and the times of meals. The diary should record any disturbances which might be due to food allergy, stating the nature and intensity of the symptoms and the time of their occurrence. If a careful study of the diary suggests a relationship between the intake of a certain food and the onset of allergic manifestations the following tests should be carried out.

Provocative food test

Patients are given a small quantity of a suspected food in a made-up dish, so that they are unaware that they are eating the food that they suspect and dread. If the patient notes in a diary any typical symptoms at the appropriate interval after the meal, this strongly suggests that the food is responsible. Alternatively a suspected food may be given through a nasogastric tube. Owing to the variability of allergic responses, the test should be repeated two or preferably three times before either a positive or negative result is accepted. If a negative result is obtained on three occasions, it can be concluded that the symptoms are not due to the suspected food. If the tests are positive, then appropriate treatment should be undertaken as discussed below. A provocative test should be done only when a patient is asymptomatic and preferably after periods when the suspected substances have been eliminated from the diet. Tests should not be made in patients who develop severe allergic reactions immediately after the ingestion of a recognised article of food; then the test is unnecessary and may be dangerous.

Strict elimination diets

If the history, skin tests (see below) and trial and error with restricted diets fail to provide a clue to the diagnosis, strict elimination diets may be helpful. With infants and young children this is easier than with adults, because of the limited variety of foods which they eat. It is not too difficult to eliminate from a child's diet milk, eggs and wheat, the common causes of children's food allergy. In adults the procedure is much more difficult because of the greater number of foods to which sensitivity may develop. Various types of elimination diets have been devised with the object of discovering the offending article. Patients may have to be fed on such diets for many weeks before the offending article of food is discovered and, as the diets are complicated, they are normally only suitable for the investigation of patients in a hospital with a dietetic department and by a physician experienced in the subject of allergy. As such elimination tests are tedious and time consuming for both patient and doctor, they should be undertaken only when symptoms believed to be due to food sensitivity are seriously inconveniencing the patient.

Skin tests

Minute quantities of extracts containing suspected antigens are pricked into the skin over the forearm. A well-defined wheal (5 mm in diameter), surrounded by an area of vasodilation is taken as a positive result. Skin tests have been in use for 80 years but are still a subject of controversy. False positives are common, and a positive test may persist long after a childhood food allergy has subsided. However, they correlate well with RAST tests (see below) and can be useful in establishing whether or not an individual has the capacity to make IgE antibodies when challenged by common environmental antigens. Their practical value in diagnosis may be increased with the use of purer and better standardised extracts.

Radioallergosorbent (RAST) tests

These are skin-prick tests that aim to detect the presence of IgE antibodies. They attempt to measure the binding of IgE to allergens such as those present in milk, eggs and fish. An arbitrary score from 0 to 4 is given. Allergic patients usually have a score above 2. Tests are expensive and not as yet very informative. While certainly a useful research tool, the tests are not established in routine clinical practice.

TREATMENT

Elimination of the causative food

If a food can be identified and eliminated from the diet, then the symptoms will not recur. For example, if the responsible article of food is one which is not consumed regularly (e.g. shellfish), it can easily be avoided: it is far more difficult in the case of eggs, milk and wheat, which are present in so many foods — cakes, puddings, sauces and gravies, soups, etc.

A clinical trial showed that the incidence of eczema in infants whose mother or father had a history of allergy was greatly reduced by following an allergen-avoiding regimen for six months.[10] The dietary aspects of the regimen were continuation of breast feeding for six months; if supplements were needed, a soya bean preparation, Velactin, was used and all cow's milk preparations, dairy products, fish and eggs were excluded from the diet. Older children with eczema have benefited from exclusion of eggs and cow's milk from their diet and substitution of soya milk.[11]

Denaturation of the protein
Sometimes if a protein is denatured by heat it ceases to act as an allergen. Thus a patient sensitive to raw milk or lightly boiled eggs may be able to take with impunity boiled milk or an egg which has been boiled for at least 10 minutes. Patients who are sensitive to eggs may be able to take the yolks, especially if well cooked, although the whites may continue to cause symptoms.

Hyposensitisation
For over 50 years some physicians have been trying to help patients by giving repeatedly small doses of allergen, either by injection or by mouth, in the hope that their sensitivity may disappear. While this appears to have been sometimes effective in cases of hay fever, success in food allergy has never been demonstrated in a controlled trial. The method continues to have a vogue in the treatment of food allergies in the USA but is generally discredited by physicians and is not even mentioned in most orthodox textbooks.

Drugs
A number of drugs that may mitigate the symptoms of allergy are available. Antihistamines are often effective in controlling local forms of allergy such as urticaria and angio-oedema. Somnolence is sometimes an inconvenience if they have to be taken regularly. Bronchodilator drugs are used to treat bronchial spasm in attacks of asthma. Corticosteroids are highly effective in preventing attacks, but their adverse effects limit their long-term use, especially in children. The prescription of tranquillisers and sedatives may be indicated because of the close association with psychological disturbances.

Sodium cromoglycate, chemically related to a substance present in an umbelliferous plant once used as a herbal remedy, inhibits secretion from mast cells, but only if given before they are challenged by an antigen. It may be given as a single dose before intake of a known allergen; in this way it may allow a child to take school meals. Alternatively it may be used continuously for patients on restricted diets for whom it allows more freedom.

In experimental animals, factors that suppress IgE synthesis and so prevent allergies have been demonstrated.[12] It is likely that these are present in man and that their effects can be potentiated by drugs. If this turns out to be true, the outlook for sufferers from all forms of allergy will be greatly improved in the future.

General advice
Every patient proved to be allergic to a particular food should be advised to avoid it, at least for a time. Some years later it may be tried cautiously, especially if it is an important article of diet. All people with a well-defined food allergy should know about it and inform their doctor; otherwise they may suffer a severe or even fatal reaction from a therapeutic injection given for the treatment of some other disease. For instance, a patient sensitive to eggs may react badly to immunising injections prepared on an egg medium, such as those for poliomyelitis, influenza or yellow fever. Similarly patients who are sensitive to pork may develop an allergic response to soluble or zinc protamine insulin (prepared from the pancreas of pigs) should they develop diabetes mellitus and require insulin injections. Insulin zinc suspensions are useful in this respect since they are uncontaminated by species-specific proteins. Injections of ACTH derived from cattle may cause shock in patients allergic to beef.

Maintaining the nutrition of the patient
Many intelligent allergic patients, knowing something of the nature of their disease, go to great lengths to avoid any food that may aggravate it. Some avoid so many kinds of food that they become severely undernourished. A similar result may follow from unwise advice from their doctors. This is particularly true in the case of growing children. It must be stressed that allergic patients should not be subjected to dietary restrictions without good evidence that their symptoms are due to a food allergen. In many cases this can only be determined in a clinic where the appropriate tests can be carried out.

Further information can be found in an excellent report[13] on *Food intolerance and food aversion* by the Royal College of Physicians and the British Nutrition Foundation.

REFERENCES

1. Browne T 1643 Religio medici. Everyman edition 1931, part II, para 1. Dent, London
2. Cullen W 1789 A treatise of the materia medica, vol 1, p 431. Edinburgh
3. Garrod A E 1931 The inborn factors in disease. Clarendon Press, Oxford, p 133
4. Food Allergy Workshop (Coombes R R A, chairman) 1980 Proceedings of the first food allergy workshop. Medical Education Services, Oxford
5. Lessof M H (ed) 1983 Clinical reactions to food. Wiley, Chichester
6. Bock S A, Lee H Y, Renigis L K, May C D 1978 Studies of hypersensitivity reactions to foods in infants and children. J Allergy Clin Immunol 62: 327–34
7. Schechter N L 1982 The baby and the bathwater: hyperactivity and the medicalization of child rearing. Perspect Biol Med 25: 406–16
8. Bleumink E 1983 Immunological aspects of food allergy. Proc Nutr Soc 42: 219–31
9. Lessof M H, Wraith D G, Merritt T G, Merrritt J, Buisseret P D 1980 Food allergy and intolerance in 100 patients — local and systemic effects. Q J Med 49: 259–71
10. Matthew D J, Taylor B, Norman A P, Turner M W, Soothill J F 1977 Prevention of eczema. Lancet 1: 321–4
11. Atherton D J, Sewell M, Soothill J F, Wells R S 1978 A double blind crossover trial of an antigen-avoidance diet in atopic eczema. Lancet 1: 401–3
12. Katz D H 1980 Recent studies on the regulation if IgE antibody synthesis in experimental animals. Immunology 41: 1–24
13. Royal College of Physicians and British Nutrition Foundation 1984 Food intolerance and food aversion. J R Coll Physicians 18: 1–41

51

Injury, Surgery and Fever

The meals were at first irregular, and throughout the patients scrambled for them. It occurred frequently that the bad cases, when unable to feed themselves, were not fed at all, except by the women; that a great mess of cold arrowroot and wine stood by the bedside the whole day, till it was thrown away; that the poultices were put on cold, or left on till they were hard, and then not washed off; that the bedsores were unattended to till they had become so bad that the medical officers' attention was called to them.

Florence Nightingale used these words to describe the hospital at Scutari to which the wounded were taken after the battle of Balaclava. Death rates in the hospital in January, February and March 1855 were 321, 427 and 315 per 1000 patients.[1] Walt Whitman's[2] account of the plight of the wounded in hospitals around Washington after the battle of Gettysberg in 1863 is perhaps the most harrowing of all great literature in the English language. But conditions at Washington were slightly less appalling than at Scutari because Florence Nightingale's influence crossed the Atlantic quickly and a few trained women were available as nurses. Today many must die as a consequence of sepsis and malnutrition among the wounded in the relatively small wars that occur in many parts of the world. Millions would die in this way if a nuclear war broke out.

Surgery is an ancient craft but its practice was limited mainly to the treatment of injuries and wounds until after 1850 when anaesthetics had come into general use. Successive technical advances — antisepsis, asepsis, blood transfusions, antibiotics, artificial respiration and life-support systems — enable surgeons to do operations that were not even in their dreams a few years ago. Major operations are now possible on the very young, the very old and the very sick. The trauma associated with surgery always increases the need for nutrients, and the circumstances attending operation usually restrict food intake at least temporarily. Table 51.1. lists factors that lead to undernutrition in surgical patients.

Any patient who has surgical treatment in hospital inevitably undergoes a period of partial starvation but its extent varies greatly. For a straightforward operation, such as repair of a hernia or removal of the uterus

Table 51.1 Factors which lead to undernutrition after an injury or operation

Increased need for nutrients
Raised metabolism
    Metabolic response to injury
    Fever

Replacement of extraneous losses
    Haemorrhage
    Serous exudates, especially after burns
    Fistulae and sinuses

Reduced intake of nutrients
Difficulty in feeding
    Inability to sit up or use arms
    Damage to CNS and impaired consciousness
    Damage to upper alimentary tract
    Iatrogenic starvation[a]

Reduced appetite[b]
    Anxiety
    Infection and sepsis
    Drugs — anaesthetics, chemotherapy for cancer, etc.
    Radiotherapy

[a] For explanation, see text p. 485.
[b] These factors are especially liable to reduce food intake in elderly patients.

without complications, the overall energy deficit is likely to be between 2000 and 4000 kcal (5–10 MJ). The effect of this on a well-nourished person is negligible and it can soon be made good by a normal hospital diet; but if this is of poor quality or unattractively served, the patient's morale may be low, appetite poor and convalesence prolonged. On the other hand, the removal of an abdominal cancer with complications requiring further surgical procedures under anaesthesia and when the patient develops an infection resistant to antibiotics or is receiving chemotherapy or radiothery for cancer, undernutrition or malnutrition may seriously impair recovery and threaten life. Such patients require nutritional support from nasogastric or intravenous feeding, as described in the next chapter, often for a long time. Indeed without such support, many of the new surgical procedures would be impossible.

A generation ago most surgeons had little knowledge

and not much interest in nutrition. They were content to leave the feeding of their patients in the hands of the ward sister. The position changed radically in 1959 with the publication of a monograph, *The metabolic care of the surgical patient* by Francis Moore,[3] the Professor of Surgery at Harvard. This book is now a classic. Moore has written an updated but abbreviated version of his book as a long chapter in an established textbook of surgery,[4] and this is recommended reading. Today surgeons in the major hospitals are well informed about nutrition and work closely with dietitians, on whom they depend. For dietitians, work in a surgical ward is a demanding challenge to their professional skill.

The factors leading to undernutrition set out in Table 51.1 are now discussed.

THE METABOLIC RESPONSE TO INJURY

Any injury to the body as a result of either an accident or surgery leads to metabolic changes that ensure an increased supply of energy to the tissue and limit fluid losses. Effects that can be readily measured are: (1) increased resting oxygen consumption, (2) increased urinary output of nitrogen, (3) increased urinary output of potassium, (4) reduced urinary output of water, and (5) reduced urinary output of sodium.

This catabolic phase lasts for about 24 hours after a simple repair of a hernia and for about 4 to 5 days after a major resection of the colon. Complications that delay healing, such as sepsis and the need for additional surgical interventions, may prolong it, sometimes for several weeks. In such circumstances, increased protein catabolism is met by breakdown of muscle protein and loss of weight. This may be as much as 20 kg in a prolonged illness. Then death from inanition is likely unless the patient is fed intravenously.

An anabolic phase follows when wound healing is fully established. Losses of muscle and other tissue proteins are replaced and the fat depots restored. This is quickly achieved after most operations and injuries, but when the catabolic phase has lasted weeks or even months a similar period of anabolism is needed before convalescence is complete.

In individual patients the metabolic response to injury is often compounded with the effects of shock, fever and partial starvation.

Water and electrolytes

Trauma is followed by a fall in urinary volume to about 30 ml/hour or 700 ml/day and at the same time urine concentration is raised to about 1000 mOsm/litre, three times the plasma concentration and near the maximum that the kidneys can achieve. This is brought about by increased secretion of vasopressin by the posterior pitu-

itary gland in response to painful stimuli, visceral traction and also to reduced blood volume and plasma osmolality when there is oligaemic shock.

Table 51.2 shows the water balance that may be anticipated in a patient in bed soon after an operation with no extraneous fluid losses. The metabolic water is that produced by the oxidation of 60 g of protein and 150 g fat, the probable metabolic mixture in a fasting man. As the protein comes mainly from muscle about 240 ml of intracellular water becomes available from tissue breakdown. An intake of about 1 litre a day is therefore needed, but this is increased when insensible loss is increased by fever, sweating and by hypernoea and when there is a fistula or other external losses. If this amount cannot be taken by mouth, it should be given intravenously as an isotonic solution of glucose or saline. If water is given in excess, overhydration of the tissues with oedema of the lungs and signs of water intoxication, such as drowsiness, headache, nausea and vomiting, may occur.

Potassium. Breakdown of muscle and other cells leads to a loss of potassium, and 240 ml of cell water contains about 35 mmol. This is mostly excreted in the urine, and within 24 hours of injury urinary potassium usually rises to about 100 mmol/24 hour (Fig. 51.1). If this loss continues for several days and is not made good by dietary or intravenous supplements, severe potassium deficiency may develop. This is not usually reflected by a fall in plasma concentration which may be unchanged when one third of total body potassium or over 1000 mmol has been lost. Repletion of cell potassium is an important part of convalescence from a severe operation or injury.

Sodium. After an operation urinary excretion of sodium falls, sometimes to as low as 10 mmol/24 h and there is marked sodium retention (Fig. 51.1). The cause of this is not fully understood. It leads to retention of extracellular water, which is always increased relative to total body water, and may be manifest in clinical oedema. Overprovision of saline is dangerous, so glucose and saline infusions are normally given postoperatively in a ratio of 2:1.

Injury is thus followed by a period of deficiency of potassium and of excess of body sodium and water.

Table 51.2 Water balance after a simple operation over 24 hours

Output (ml)		Input (ml)	
Urine	700	Metabolic water	180
Faeces	50	Water available from tissue breakdown	240
Insensible loss from skin and lungs	750	Required intake	1060
	1500		1500

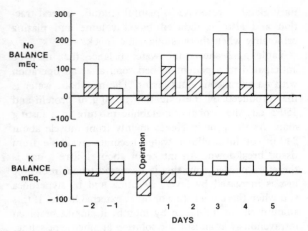

Fig. 51.1 Sodium and potassium balances following a major operation. The intake is plotted from the baseline upwards; the output is plotted from the intake downwards: the shaded area therefore represents the balance between intake and output. In positive balance this lies above the baseline while in negative balance it lies below the baseline

These are obligatory changes that it is neither possible nor desirable to prevent entirely. After a simple operation they are readily made good in convalesence. Fruit juices, which are relatively rich in potassium and low in sodium, help in this. When the injury is severe and healing is delayed by complications, these changes persist and may seriously impede recovery and threaten life. In all such cases it is necessary to monitor accurately water and electrolyte metabolism and to make appropriate adjustments, usually by intravenous therapy (Chap. 52).

Protein metabolism
After an operation there is an increase in urinary nitrogen and a rise in the resting metabolic rate by 10 per cent or more. This reaction to injury will always be associated with the name of Sir David Cuthbertson. In 1930 and 1932 he published two papers[5, 6] that established it as an important physiological adaptation. The mobilisation of protein serves two functions; it provides first an endogenous source of energy for the tissues, and secondly amino acids and nucleotides that are used in wound healing.

At that time Cuthbertson was a postgraduate student of E. P. Cathcart, the Professor of Physiology in Glasgow. Cathcart's main interest was in nutrition and as a young man he had been a pupil of Carl Voit in the Institute of Hygiene in Munich (p. 14). So Cuthbertson's pàpers are in a main historical stream of nutritional research. He continued to work on this subject when he became the Director of the Rowett Institute for Agricultural Research in Aberdeen and after his retire-

ment in Glasgow. Fifty-two years after his first paper, he wrote an extensive review of the subject with a bibliography of 98 references.[7] The following extract from this sets out the main features of the response.

I introduced the term 'ebb' to characterise the period of depressed metabolism associated with the initial phase of the reaction to moderate or severe trauma and which is described in the classical literature on trauma as the period of shock. This is a period of general inhibition of protein synthesis though certain acute phase reactant proteins increase in the blood. I then used the term 'flow' for the phase of increase in metabolic rate denoted by increased oxygen uptake and heat production which occurs in some 36 to 48 hours in those that recover from the 'ebb' phase. This is also sometimes referred to as the period of 'traumatic inflammation' and is characterised by the increased urinary losses of nitrogen, sulphur, and phosphorus-containing metabolites. In general, the more well-built and nourished the patient prior to his injury the greater the effect, and the more severe the accidental injury the greater the hypercatabolism, which generally reached a peak between the 4th to 8th day after injury. The total loss of nitrogen in one case during the first 10 days was 137 g, a reduction of the body's N content by 7.7 per cent. Accidental injuries exhibited greater effects than elective operations.

This loss of nitrogen is obligatory and cannot be prevented by diet or intravenous feeding. But it has to be made good, and this is one of the major aspects of the management of convalesence after a major operation or severe injury. This is achieved by encouraging patients to eat large quantities of normal foods and Diet No. 1 presents a sample menu.

Fat metabolism
After an operation the small reserves of carbohydrate in the body are soon expended. Then if, as is common, a patient cannot eat normally, endogenous stores of fat are drawn upon to meet energy needs. With the raised oxygen consumption, a patient in bed may use from 150 to 200 g of fat daily. This is associated with a rise in plasma concentrations of free fatty acids and mild ketosis but not, in the absence of other factors, to severe ketoacidosis. If there are complications after an operation, the raised metabolism persists and over 1 kg of fat may be lost weekly; then severe emaciation may follow. This can be in large part prevented by parenteral or intravenous feeding when a patient cannot eat a high energy convalescent diet. However this should be supervised so that it does not lead to obesity.

Endocrine responses
All the above changes are effected by the endocrine system with some assistance from the autonomic nervous system. As already mentioned, increased secretion of vasopressin by the posterior pituitary is mainly responsible for the water retention. The anterior pituitary response to trauma is increased secretion of

ACTH and its plasma concentration rises within 30 minutes of the start of an abdominal operation. At the same time plasma cortisol rises and the adrenal glands respond to trauma directly and are not dependent on stimulation by ACTH. The increased secretion of cortisol promotes glucogenesis in the liver and so increases the rate of breakdown of protein. Aldosterone secretion also increases after surgery and appears mainly responsible for the changes in excretion of sodium and potassium. Secretion is stimulated by the renin — angiotensin system that is activated by reduced renal blood flow in response to blood loss and oligaemia. Plasma thyroxine rises immediately after injury, indicating that increased oxygen consumption is due to increased activity of the thyroid gland. Marked rises in the urinary excretion of adrenaline and noradrenaline indicate increased production of those catechol amines. After an operation, plasma concentrations of growth hormone and glucagon are often high and of insulin often low. These changes occur in partial starvation and may not be a direct consequence of trauma. A large study of endocrine responses after injury is reported by Stoner.[8]

All of these changes arise immediately or very soon after an operation and persist until recovery is well under way. They are obligatory and serve to preserve homeostasis but, if they continue to operate for several days, adverse effects arise. The risk of these is minimised by careful surgery, replacement of blood losses and correcting disturbances of water and electrolyte balance, together with maintaining an adequate intake of energy and protein by intravenous feeding when the oral intake is insufficient.

Fever

The adverse nutritional effects that arise after operation or injury are greatly aggravated by the presence of fever due to infection. In those countries where the spread of the major infectious diseases is well controlled, severe and prolonged fever is nowadays seen most frequently in the surgical wards. The nutritional effect and dietary management of fever is the same in surgical patients as in those with infectious diseases and described at the end of this chapter.

EXTRANEOUS LOSSES OF NUTRIENTS

The most serious of these is haemorrhage. A loss of two litres of blood, by no means unusual in a major road accident, is a loss of about 400 g of protein and other nutrients are lost as well. This, if not made good by blood transfusion, is a major deficit. Of more practical importance is a repeated daily loss of blood. In 100 ml of blood there is some 20 g of protein and nearly 2 mg of iron, and a daily loss of this amount puts up dietary requirements significantly. Repeated blood samples taken for laboratory analysis may cause loss of nutrients approaching this order of magnitude.

Serous exudates from burns contain protein and, when large areas of skin have been burnt, this loss contributes to the nutritional problems presented by these patients who are seriously ill and whose recovery is inevitably protracted.

Fistulae in the alimentary tract and sinuses from abscess cavities in internal organs, bones or joints may discharge matter containing large amounts of protein, sodium and potassium. As these lesions are often slow to heal, patients are at considerable risk of becoming undernourished.

REDUCED INTAKE OF NUTRIENTS

Difficulties in feeding

These arise in many circumstances after an operation. Patients may be unable to sit up or to use one or both arms or be confused. If such a condition persists for any length of time undernutrition may develop. It is the responsibility of nursing staff to see that patients are able to feed themselves easily and to help them when necessary.

Patients who are unconscious and many of those who have had operations on the mouth or the upper alimentary tract have to be fed by one of the methods described in the next chapter.

Iatrogenic starvation may follow when investigations requiring prolonged and repeated visits to the radiology department or a laboratory are ordered, and these coincide with normal meal times in the ward. Then it is important to see that food is put aside until the patient returns to the ward and that meals are not missed.

Loss of appetite

Anxiety. Patients may worry that recovery from an injury or operation will not be complete; sometimes there is fear of cancer arising from lack of information about the nature of their illness. Many are worried about money and about how their family or business will get on in their absence. All these anxieties, whether or not there is justification for them, are likely to reduce appetite.

Sepsis and fever. These are both likely to depress appetite, although how they interfere with the functions of the nervous system to bring this about is not clear.

Drugs. Many drugs depress appetite, often by irritating the gastrointestinal epithelium, leading to nausea, and sometimes by depressing the central nervous system. These effects nearly always follow the use of drugs for the treatment of malignant disease since experience has shown that the drugs at present available only control tissue growth when given in large doses carrying a high risk of secondary adverse effects.

Radiotherapy. Like chemotherapy for cancer, this has to be given in doses with a high risk of adverse effects. In acute radiation sickness the main effects are on the central nervous system, the bone marrow and the gastrointestinal system. Lethargy and depression and nausea and vomiting are common symptoms. These are liable to occur in all patients receiving radiotherapy and to lead to a marked loss of appetite. When the radiation is specifically directed at any part of the gastrointestinal tract, damage to the epithelium is likely to be so severe as to cause a reduction of food intake with a high risk of developing serious undernutrition.

PRACTICAL CONSIDERATIONS

Diets in surgical wards

In most surgical wards only a small minority of patients require a special diet or special feeding. Surgical wards should have the best food that a hospital can provide and patients should be given as much opportunity as is practical to eat what they fancy. Caterers, dietitians and ward sisters share the responsibility of seeing that all patients are presented with adequate amounts of foods that they like, at the right temperature and attractively served, and of ensuring that each patient eats sufficiently.

Supplements

Surgical patients do not need dietary supplements, provided that they can take a good ward diet. The three nutrients in which they are most likely to be deficient are iron, protein and vitamin C. Medicinal iron is required only when iron deficiency anaemia is present. A protein supplement is required when for any reason a patient is not able to eat sufficient of the ward diet to meet energy needs, and also in some elderly women who eat little because their energy needs are very low. There are now many proprietary protein preparations that can be used to enrich common foods (Chap. 52). Wounds do not heal readily unless the tissues have an ample supply of vitamin C. This is best provided by fresh vegetables, fruits and fruit juices. If these are not available, ascorbic acid should be given.

Other supplements may be needed when absorption of nutrients is impaired. Thus in patients with jaundice due to biliary obstruction, failure of the bile salts to reach the duodenum causes malabsorption of fats and fat-soluble vitamins; parenteral vitamin K is then needed before operation to ensure that bleeding is not excessive. Some operations on the stomach remove the area where intrinsic factor is produced; then parenteral vitamin B12 is needed to prevent megaloblastic anaemia;

vitamin B12 is also needed after ileal resection, e.g. for Crohn's disease. After any extensive intestinal resections great care is needed to ensure that deficiencies of vitamins and minerals do not arise.

Diet at time of operation

If the patient is undernourished it is advisable to attempt to correct this, provided the need for the operation is not urgent. A diet rich in energy and protein should be given. But gain in weight is slow, and when the malnutrition is directly attributable to disease or an injury it is wrong to postpone an operation, since it is difficult, if not impossible, to achieve dietary rehabilitation until the surgical condition has been corrected.

Obese patients are poor anaesthetic risks. If the need for an operation is not urgent, it is usually wise to postpone it until some reduction in weight has been achieved by dietetic treatment. This may help the surgeon and anaesthetist in their immediate technical tasks and perhaps improve the patient's ability to recover more quickly. The management of obese patients who are also diabetics and who require an operation is described on page 388.

While it is unwise to starve a patient before operation, it is also dangerous to anaesthetise a subject whose stomach is full of food. This risk can be obviated by making the patient fast overnight. If the operation is to take place in the afternoon, a very light breakfast may be given. If for any reason the start of the operation has to be postponed, the patient should be given small quantities of sweetened fruit juices in water. This helps to maintain his reserves of energy and prevent dehydration.

Postoperative

Neither fluid nor food should be given until the patient is fully recovered from the anaesthetic. Otherwise there is a risk that they will be inhaled into the lungs with the subsequent danger of aspiration pneumonia. This risk is also present if attempts are made to give the patient food or fluids when recumbent. If a patient cannot sit up after recovery from the anaesthetic or cannot eat and drink normally because of being seriously ill or for any other reason, e.g. continuous gastric suction after operations on the stomach and duodenum, they should be fed intravenously (Chap 52).

With modern anaesthetics a patient is likely to be hungry and able to eat as soon as consciousness is fully recovered. At first, small frequent feeds should be given. After gastrointestinal operations 30 ml of fluid is given hourly until the presence of bowel sounds indicates the return of bowel movements. If postoperative convalesence proceeds normally and there are no complications, the patient's appetite is usually a reliable guide to requirements; there is no need to force food in the early stages of convalesence. As the patient has to make good the losses of potassium and nitrogen, the convalescent diet should contain ample fruit and milk, meat, pulses or other good sources of protein, but there is no need for a special diet.

FEVER

During fever basal metabolism increases by about 10 per cent for every degree centigrade rise in body temperature.[9] Associated with the general increase of metabolism, there are increased nitrogen losses in the urine. For these reasons and because there is usually a loss of appetite and diminished food intake, a febrile patient loses weight and, if the fever is prolonged, may become severely emaciated. The metabolic responses to fever have also been studied experimentally by inducing self-limiting infections in healthy human volunteers. Sandfly fever produces a sharp and uncomfortable fever lasting a few days but complete recovery is invariable. US army volunteers given the infection experimentally showed a negative nitrogen balance, decreased plasma concentrations of all amino acids except phenylalanine and decreased plasma iron and zinc.[10]

In a long-continued fever, therefore, an effort should be made to prevent undue loss of body protein by the prescription of a diet in which the protein intake is in excess of the maintenance requirement in health. There is no ground for the old belief that a high protein intake increases the height of the fever.

Apart from these theoretical considerations, the arrangement of the diet is made difficult by the anorexia, present in most fevers, which may be complicated by nausea and vomiting. Much can be done to help by ansuring that the mouth is kept clean. If the tongue is furred and sordes are allowed to accumulate, it is not surprising that the patient has a distaste for food. The mouth should be washed or swabbed out with a weak solution of sodium bicarbonate or other mouthwash before and after every meal.

The introduction of antibiotics and chemotherapeutic agents has greatly reduced the length of most febrile illnesses. Formerly in diseases like enteric fever, pyrexia frequently persisted for three or four weeks, but now it is usually restricted to a few days as a result of treatment. Likewise, in pulmonary tuberculosis pyrexia was present for months prior to the introduction of chemotherapeutic agents which now bring it under control in days or weeks. Yet there are still febrile illnesses in which the infection cannot be brought under control for a considerable time. These are often caused by commensal bacteria, yeast and fungi, widespread in healthy persons and in the environment, that become pathogenic only in patients whose natural immunity is grossly im-paired, often as a result of the use of immunosuppressive drugs. Such infections are liable to occur in patients subjected to the high technology of modern medicine and surgery. Often difficult to treat, they may lead to severe undernutrition.

DIET IN FEVER

It is best to consider diet in fever under two headings: (1) fevers of short duration, e.g. influenza and pneumonia; (2) long-continued fevers, when the infection does not respond to antibiotics.

Short febrile illnesses

In fevers of short duration such as influenza and pneumonia, which last a matter of days, not weeks, the diet should be constructed with the chief object of saving the patient from all possible exertion in the taking of his food; the actual amount of nourishment given is of less importance.

For the first two or three days the diet should be fluid or semifluid and given in the form of small feeds at frequent intervals, usually every two to three hours. Milk is the mainstay of the diet and about 2 pints (1 litre) should be given daily. This provides about 40 g protein and about 3.0 MJ (700 kcal). Some of the milk feeds should be flavoured with cocoa, coffee or tea, or given as an egg switch. Two or three eggs may be given daily, switched in milk or an egg and fruit drink. Liquid cooked cereals such as a gruel or any of the proprietary preparations, served with cream, and custards may be given at some of the feeds to vary the diet. Fresh fruit juice should be given in ample amounts for its sugar content and also as a flavouring agent for the water, which should be supplied to the patient between feeds in liberal quantities. At least 2 to 3 litres of fluid should be taken daily. Diet No. 16 meets these requirements.

As soon as the temperature falls and the patient's appetite improves, a bland diet containing ample protein and energy should be given. Within another two or three days the patient should be taking a good well-balanced diet suitable for convalescence (Diet No. 1). Due attention should be given to the instructions in Diet No. 17 for the prevention and treatment of dyspepsia which is liable to occur in patients recovering from febrile illnesses and from the effects of chemotherapeutic agents on the gastrointestinal tract.

Long-continued fever

If in seven days a fever is not responding to antibiotics, it is necessary to see that the dietary intake, and particularly the intake of protein and energy, is sufficient to meet the extra requirements imposed by the fever. The object of dietetic treatment is to reduce mortality by providing the nutrients required for the body's immune mechanisms, to prevent or curtail the weakness and loss of weight which is so noticeable in long-continued fevers, and to accelerate convalescence. The principles governing the construction of the diet in these circumstances are as follows.

1. The diet should have a high energy value — up to 50 per cent more than the normal maintenance intake for a person in bed. This means that the diet should yield at least 10 MJ (2400 kcal)/day.

2. A liberal protein quota is needed to make good the loss of body protein. Owing to the anorexia and the necessity for providing food in liquid or semisolid form, it may not be possible to give more than 70 to 90 g of protein daily, but this covers the protein loss except in the most severe fevers.

3. A large proportion of the food ingested should be in the form of carbohydrate. This prevents ketosis, which may arise if patients are burning their own body fat in increased amounts owing to the raised metabolism. The protein sparing property of a high carbohydrate diet is also of practical importance.

4. Food should be served initially in liquid or semisolid form and must be easily digestible, well cooked and appetising. Large meals should be avoided and small feeds should be given every two or three hours.

5. Fluids should be given in abundance. Owing to the loss of fluid in sweat and the disinclination of patients to take fluids and food, dehydration may develop in fever. Fluids require to be given in greater amounts than are usually ingested, but excessive amounts should not be forced on the patient. A daily total fluid intake of about 2½ to 3 litres is ample. If vomiting and diarrhoea are prominent features, parenteral treatment may be required.

Salt depletion occurs from sweating and this should be made good by adding sodium chloride to suitable feeds and to glucose lemonade drinks. Diet No. 16 is a semifluid one, which may be used in the early stages of a long continued fever.

As the patient improves and can take solid food, this diet should be modified by the addition of toast or bread with butter or margarine, milk puddings, custards and stewed or fresh fruit, pureed vegetables, eggs, cream of chicken and fish. It is advisable to supplement the diet with vitamins if the patient is eating poorly.

Fever in infants and children

Children are more susceptible to the ill-effects of fever than adults. Feverish children should be nursed in a cool room, wear light clothing and have plenty of fresh air. The principles of the dietetic treatment of adults as described above are applicable for infants and children and are even more important since they are particularly susceptible to dehydration and protein malnutrition. This is especially the case in tropical countries where nutritional diseases are common. For example, a child with pre-kwashiorkor who contracts measles may become extremely ill in a short time and develop severe protein-energy malnutrition rapidly.

CONVALESCENCE

Diet has an important part to play in determining the speed with which a patient recovers from a surgical operation, fever or any serious illness, and hence in the length of time that a hospital bed is occupied. Ample amounts of protein are needed to make good the drain on the body's reserves of protein and, if the patient is under-weight, plenty of energy to build up tissues. Routine hospital diets are often inadequate for these purposes. Furthermore, the patient's appetite may be fickle. Every art of the dietitian may be needed to tempt a jaded appetite.

Once normal feeding has been re-established, a regimen such as Diet No. 1 is satisfactory for most adult patients. Medicinal iron may be needed if the patient is still anaemic from previous bleeding.

Finally it should be remembered that many patients are necessarily confined to bed for long periods during convalescence, e.g. those recovering from multiple injuries involving fractures of bone and those requiring repeated skin grafts for extensive burns. Prolonged immobilisation in bed often leads to extensive demineralisation of the bones. Physiotherapy and occupational therapy can do much to check this process by keeping the movable parts of the body active; at the same time a good calcium intake, provided by plenty of milk, is desirable, to assist remineralisation. The calcium lost from the bones is excreted in the urine and, if the flow or urine is sluggish, calcium stones may develop in the urinary tract. A high fluid intake (2 to 3 litres daily) should be encouraged, to ensure that the urine is sufficiently dilute to keep calcium salts in solution.

REFERENCES

1. Nightingale F 1859 Notes on hospitals: evidence given to the Royal Commissioners on the state of the army in 1857. John Parker, London, p 53
2. Whitman W 1963 Specimen days. In: Stovall F (ed) Prose works 1892, vol 1. New York University Press, p 34–88
3. Moore F D 1959 The metabolic care of the surgical patient. Saunders, Philadelphia

4. Moore F D 1977 Homeostasis: bodily changes in trauma and surgery. The responses to injury in man as the basis for clinical management. In: Sabiston D C (ed) Davis-Christopher Textbook of surgery, 11th edn. Saunders, Philadelphia, p 26–64

5. Cuthbertson D P 1930 The disturbance of metabolism produced by bony and non-bony injury with notes on certain abnormal conditions of bone. Biochem J 24: 1244–63

6. Cuthbertson D P 1932 Observations on the disturbance of metabolism produced by injury to the limbs. Q J Med 1: 233–46

7. Cuthbertson D P 1982 The metabolic response to injury and other related explorations in the field of protein metabolism: an autobiographical account. Scot Med J 27:158–71

8. Stoner H B, Frayn K N, Barton R N, Threlfall C J, Little R A 1979 The relationships between plasma substrates and hormones and the severity of injury in 277 recently injured patients. Clin Sci 56: 563–73

9. Du Bois E F 1948 Fever and the regulation of body temperature. Thomas, Springfield, Ill

10. Wannamacher R W, Pekarek R S, Bartelloni P J, Vollmer R T, Beisel W R 1972 Changes in individual plasma amino acids following experimentally induced sand fly fever. Metabolism 21: 67–76

52

Special Feeding Methods

Three types of special feeding are described in this chapter.

1. **Supplementary feeding**. Normal foods can be enriched by suitable supplements and taken by mouth. Alternatively normal foods may be replaced by preparations of protein or amino acids, fats and carbohydrates in easily assimilable forms. Such preparations are known as **elemental diets**.
2. **Tube feeding**. Normal foods and preparations of nutrients are given by a tube. A tube may be passed into the stomach or duodenum through the nose, **nasogastric feeding**, or directly by surgical operation, **gastrostomy** and **jejunostomy** feeding
3. **Intravenous feeding**. Nutrient preparations are given directly into a vein. This method may be used to supplement normal feeding by mouth but can provide all the nutrients necessary to meet a patient's requirements. Then it is known as **total parenteral nutrition**, or **TPN**.

Tube feeding is an old method of giving nutrients but its use was restricted until cumbersome rubber tubes could be replaced by thin, pliable, plastic ones. Glucose, water and electrolytes have been given intravenously for a long time but safe preparations of amino acids and lipids were not available before about 1960. Since then technical advances in the manufacture of tubing and of preparations of nutrients have revolutionised the treatment and prevention of undernutrition of patients seriously ill in hospital. This is perhaps the greatest advance in practical nutrition in our time.

WHO TO FEED?

Patients requiring special feeding are found mainly among those with gastrointestinal disorders and in the surgical wards, and Chapters 46 and 51 describe many circumstances when it is needed. However, patients with neurological and renal disorders, continued fevers, diabetes and many other conditions may sometimes require such feeding. It may be used for children of all ages, including babies of very low birth weight. Hence

it is best for a hospital to have a central team that provides advice, materials and technical assistance to all wards in the management of patients on special feeding. Details of how such a team functions are given later in the chapter.

The benefits from special feeding are potentially so great that there is a natural tendency for enthusiasts to use it unnecessarily. This should be avoided for three reasons. First, supplementary, tube and intravenous feeding are each more expensive than normal feeding; so they should not be used when a patient can get adequate nourishment from an appetising diet, well served and with coaxing to eat it. Secondly, tube and intravenous feeding inevitably cause inconvenience and some discomfort to a patient. Thirdly, although tube feeding is safe, at least in comparison with a prescription for most drugs, parenteral nutrition carries risks of adverse effects, some of which may be dangerous.

Special feeding methods are needed only when a patient is either seriously undernourished or at risk of becoming so, and when they are unable to eat normal foods in sufficient quantities or cannot digest and absorb it. Hence, before starting, a patient's nutritional status should be assessed.

Nutritional assessment

This is based on a dietary history, clinical examination and weight, to which may be added anthropometric measurements and laboratory analyses of blood and urine. The methods used in hospital practice are essentially the same as those for nutrition surveys in community medicine, as described and discussed in Chapter 55.

Dietary history

This can tell whether a patient was eating a good or poor diet before admission to hospital and so indicate the likelihood of previous undernutrition. When a patient is unable for any reasons to give a history, an attempt should be made to get it from someone in their home. If this is impossible, for example when the patient is old, emaciated and confused and living alone, it is wise to assume that the previous diet was poor.

Clinical examination

A complete examination of all systems is necessary, with special attention paid to evidence of recent wasting of fat or muscle and to those physical signs known to arise from or be frequently associated with malnutrition. A nutritional assessment chart on which the presence or absence of these signs can be ticked off is often useful. A full list of such signs, published by WHO for international reference, is given on p. 517. Many are attributable to vitamin deficiencies not commonly seen in Europe and North America. A chart containing only those signs known to be prevalent in the local hospital community should be designed.

Anthropometry

A patient should be weighed before starting treatment whenever this is possible. Bedridden patients can be weighed in bed on a special balance but these balances are expensive and not generally available. Height should also be measured. Comparison with reference standards for adults (Table 55.5), infants and young children (Fig. 55.1) and older children and adolescents (Fig. 55.2) gives some guide as to a patient's nutritional status, always provided there is no oedema. An apparently normal weight may also mask severe tissue wasting in a patient who was previously obese. The initial weight is most useful as a firm base for comparison with future weights and this is a good index of subsequent progress.

Midarm circumference and triceps skinfold thickness are two measurements easy to take and now much used in hospital practice. Their value is discussed in Chapter 55. Although they are crude indices of nutritional status and there are no reliable standards for initial assessments, both are useful in checking visual impressions and in following a patient's progress.[1]

Laboratory investigations

Blood haemoglobin and plasma albumin concentrations should be measured as a routine in all patients suspected of being undernourished. If there is anaemia, further blood examinations as described in Chapter 48 are necessary. If plasma albumin is below 35 g/l, there is a probability of protein deficiency. In 1974 a paper from Boston[2] drew general attention to the fact that cases of protein-energy malnutrition (PEM) could be found in adults in surgical and other wards of hospitals in prosperous communities. Since then, there has been much study of the value of measurements of plasma concentrations of albumin and other proteins in detecting and assessing PEM in adult hospital patients. Table 52.1 sets out figures for the lower limit of normality below which protein deficiency may be said to be present, and others

Table 52.1 Concentrations of some plasma proteins in relation to protein deficiency

	Lower limit of normality	Values indicating severe deficiency	Half-life (days)
Albumin (g/l)	35	25 or below	20
Transferrin (g/l)	2.0	1.0 or below	11
Thyroxine-binding prealbumin (mg/l)	250	100 or below	2

below which it is severe. Most patients in whom the concentrations are below normal benefit from a protein supplement to a hospital diet. Concentrations suggesting that protein deficiency is severe are an indication of a need for intravenous amino acid feeding. Table 52.1 also gives the half-life of each of the proteins.

The turnover rate for albumin is the slowest and so it is the least sensitive index of changes in protein metabolism. Other plasma proteins with a relatively short half-life are retinol-binding protein, complement component C3 and fibronectin.[3] There is as yet no consensus on which of these many plasma proteins are the best to use for routine assessment.

Assessment of the nutritional status of patients in surgical wards is now a fashionable subject for research. It is not possible to foretell what the future will bring, but precision usually has its cost. Money is required for apparatus and for technical staff; treatment may be delayed and patients inconvenienced. To be practical the methods in routine use have to be simple and readily applicable to patients who are often seriously ill. A review by an experienced Canadian team[4] concludes: 'General clinical assessment is a reproducible and valid technique for evaluating nutritional status before surgery. Unless further studies show that laboratory measurements of nutritional status are more accurate than clinical evaluation or provide better prognostic information, we suggest that carefully performed history taking and physical examination are sufficient for nutritional assessment.'

ORAL SUPPLEMENTS

Increased intakes of energy and protein can be obtained by enriching ordinary foods such as milk, milk preparations, soups, soufflés, jellies, cakes and ice creams with casein, fat emulsions or sugars. Proprietory preparations of casein and of fat are available and can be incorporated readily into these foods. They vary in their acceptability which depends very much on the patient's preference and the dietitian's skill in incorporating them into other foods. Complan (Glaxo Ltd) is a preparation of milk proteins; 100 g provides 31 g of protein, 44 g carbohydrate and 16 g of fat, and it is also rich in minerals and vitamins though low in sodium. Casilan (Glaxo Ltd) and Lonalac (Mead-Johnson) are preparations of milk protein, low in fat, carbohydrates and sodium. The nutrient content of these and other proprietary preparations suitable as oral supplements is given in Appendix 3.

These preparations can be mixed with sugar and vegetable oil in any proportion and a number of recipes concocted. Flavouring agents, coffee, vanilla, strawberry etc. may be added. Cane sugar and glucose make any mixture very sweet. Hence patients may prefer dextrins as a source of carbohydrate. The components can be made up with a varying quantity of water to different consistencies and served either as a hot drink or as ice cream. If a little gelatin is added the whole mixture can be made to set as a jelly.

Many convalescent patients and those with cancer receiving radiotherapy or cytotoxic drugs are often depressed and have little appetite; they benefit from appetising foods of high nutrient density.

TUBE FEEDING

In the early part of the century tube feeds consisted of milk to which sugar was added. When in about 1950 kitchen homogenisers came on the market, liquidised food that was more nutritionally complete could be easily prepared. Commonly used ingredients were milk, eggs, sugar and vegetable oil, but many other foods were added. However, today it is usual to give proprietary preparations made up wholly or in part of pure chemicals, and these are listed in Appendix 3. They are the ultimate convenience foods and necessarily expensive. Money can be saved by making up preparations from normal foods in the kitchen, but at the expense of staff time. Contraindications are disorders in the small intestine, such as fistulae, obstruction, paralytic ileus and intractable vomiting.

Tube feeding should not be used when with coaxing and encouragement a patient can be persuaded to take by mouth normal food with supplements sufficient to meet their requirements of nutrients.

The tubes

Fine bore pliable tubes first came on the market in 1975 and they have revolutionised tube feeding. Because of their pliability and small diameter, patients are virtually unaware of their presence and tolerance is excellent. They are of particular value for a patient with an oesophageal stricture where there is only a tiny space available through which a tube can pass. A disadvantage is that the tube is relatively easily dislodged through coughing or vomiting.

A further development is a mercury weighted small bore tube made of polyurethane. This has the great advantage that it passes through the stomach into the duodenum and remains there since the mercury tip acts as an anchor. Though unsuitable for patients with very narrow nasal passages, it is the best tube for general use at the present time.

The older Ryle's tube is still of value in certain situations but is uncomfortable. Its main advantage is the ease with which correct placement can be ascertained by aspiration without the need for radiography. This is a major factor for consideration in a patient whose tube may be more often up than down, since overexposure to X-rays is avoided. In addition the time between the repassing of the tube and radiography is lost for feeding. Because aspiration is so easy to carry out, a Ryle's tube is indicated for patients (1) in whom there is a doubt about gastric emptying, (2) who are confused or agitated, and (3) who are unconscious or have no cough reflex.

Regular replacement of the tube is required since within ten days the PVC becomes rigid. If a patient is being encouraged to have an oral intake, then this tube is far from ideal. It also affects the efficiency of the cardiac sphincter, thereby increasing the risk of gastric reflux. Table 52.2 summarises the advantages and disadvantages of the three types of tube in common use.

Table 52.2 Advantages and disadvantages of three types of tube in common use

	Standard Ryle tube	Fine bore tube	Mercury weighted small bore tube
Material	PVC	PVC	Polyurethane
Diameter — internal	2.5 mm	1.0 mm	2.0 mm
— external	4.0 mm	1.8 mm	3.0 mm
Period of time after which tube should be replaced	5 days	10 days	6 months
Aspiration	Very easy	Difficult	Easy
Tendency to displace through vomiting or suction	Unlikely	Frequently	Unlikely
Radiographic confirmation of position	Not needed	Essential	Only if aspiration proves difficult
Suitability for patients with oesophageal stricture or narrow nasal passages	Unsuitable	Suitable	Unsuitable

Feeding routes

Solutions can be administered by tubes via the following routes; nasogastric, nasoduodenal, nasojejunal, gastrostomy, and jejunostomy. Nasal passage of a tube is used in most cases to avoid surgical insertion, but is contraindicated in a patient with upper gastrointestinal obstruction, or in an uncooperative patient for whom long-term feeding is anticipated.

Intragastric feeding is still used to a large extent but the passage of a long tube into the duodenum or jejunum is becoming common. The action of the pyloric sphincter minimises regurgitation and tube displacement. Passage is carried out either with a long fine bore tube under radiographic control or by passing a mercury weighted tube into the stomach. By peristalsis it reaches the duodenum.

When feeding directly into the small intestine is carried out correctly, digestion and absorption take place normally. Intolerance and the dumping syndrome may occur due to poor feed selection or inappropriate administration.

When serious disease in the mouth, oesophagus or stomach makes the passage of a tube difficult or undesirable, it can be put directly in the stomach or jejunum by a surgeon under local anaesthesia. Surgeons can easily insert a tube at the end of an abdominal operation. The tube is kept in position by suturing to the abdominal wall. Care has to be taken to prevent sepsis at this point. Feeding procedures are similar to those with a nasogastric or nasojejunal tube.

Feeding requirements

For an individual patient these have to be considered in relation to a previous nutritional assessment. The nutrients to be given by tube feeding also depend on whether this is to be the sole intake or only a supplement to oral foods. The recommendations give below are guidelines which may require modification; there can be no fixed rules.

Fluid. Most adult patients require 30 ml kg^{-1} body weight. This may need to be increased to 45 ml kg^{-1} in patients who are severely stressed to allow excretion of the excess urea and other products of tissue catabolism. An increase, perhaps as much as 500 to 1500 ml, may be needed to replace fluid loss in sweating due to fever or high environmental temperature; surgical wards in hospitals in temperate climates are often kept at near tropical temperatures, as this makes blankets unnecessary and so facilitates dressings and nursing care. The fluid used to irrigate the tube should be included as part of the total requirement. This is especially relevant to bolus feeding (see below). The daily volume of urine reflects the fluid intake and if it is between 900 and 2500 ml, intake is probably satisfactory.

Energy. A daily intake of 130 kJ (32 kcal) kg^{-1} body weight usually meets requirement. For a 65 kg man this is 8.5 MJ (2100 kcal) daily, allowing for an overall of energy expenditure of 100 W. This is 25 per cent above the normal rate of resting energy metabolism (p. 21). If this rate is raised by a catabolic response to injury, intake should be raised up to 210 kJ (50 kcal) kg^{-1} body weight, or 13.7 MJ (3250 kcal) daily for a 65 kg man.

Whether or not energy intake is meeting requirements can be checked by measuring oxygen uptake while the patient is in bed. If V_{O_2} is 250 ml min^{-1}, the rate of energy expenditure is 82W. To meet this for 24 h the diet should supply 7.1 mJ (1700 kcal). Measurement of V_{O_2} is now much easier technically and it causes less inconvenience to a patient than many technical procedures in routine use.

Protein. The normal protein requirement of 1 g kg^{-1} body weight is met when 12 per cent of the energy comes from protein. Hypermetabolic and stress patients may need from 1.5 to 3 g kg^{-1} body weight, but it is wasteful to provide a high protein intake without adequate energy from fat and carbohydrate, as then the protein is used as a source of energy.

The protein requirement can be checked periodically by measuring the nitrogen content of a 24 hour sample of urine. If this is equal to 90 per cent or more of the nitrogen in the diet, it can be assumed that the patient is in N balance and that the need for protein is being met.

Sodium and potassium. A daily sodium intake of 30–40 mmol is sufficient even for very ill patients, provided there are no extrarenal losses. If these are present, they can be made good by adding to the feeds appropriate amounts of 1 mmol.ml^{-1} NaCl solution. This can also be done when, as happens occasionally, hyponatraemia is found in a tube-fed patient. However, in most such cases this is due to water overload and the treatment is restriction of fluid intake. This raises the osmolality of the feed, but a hyperosmolar feed can be tolerated when given at a slow and regular rate.

The potassium content of a feed should be related to its protein content. At least 1 mmol should be given for every gram of protein.

Vitamins and minerals. Requirements can be met by giving a daily supplement. Proprietary solutions vary greatly in their content but in general more than meet recommended intakes. However, requirements of most trace elements are not known accurately. When a patient has been on an entirely artificial diet for more than 4 weeks, plasma concentrations of trace elements should be determined to give early warning of a deficiency or toxic state.

Nutrient solutions

A prescription for a solution suitable for a patient who

weighs 60 kg and has not lost much weight and who is not in a hypermetabolic state is

Complan	300 g
Caloreen	85 g
Prosparol	75 ml
Water	1500 ml

To this should be added a vitamin and mineral supplement. Table 52.3 gives its nutrient content. Protein provides 12 per cent of the energy. Emaciated patients who are in a hypermetabolic state need more protein and Table 52.4 describes a suitable solution in which 17 per cent of the energy comes from protein. The ingredients are proprietary preparations of elemental foods and the solution may be made up either in the hospital pharmacy or a ward kitchen. There is no reason why they should not be ordinary articles of diet put through a kitchen homogeniser. In the early days of tube feeding, milk with bouillon and beaten eggs were the main ingredients. Natural ingredients are cheaper but now seldom used, probably because of the extra labour required to make up the solution.

Solutions, like drinking water, should be 'clean' but do not always have to be sterile, though this may be necessary in patients whose immunity is impaired by disease or immunosuppressive drugs. Sterilising can be by boiling, by filtration, by autoclaving or by irradiation. The latter method is safe, effective and convenient for large bulks and so its present limited use may be extended.

The ingredients given in Table 52.4 are suitable only when the digestive mechanisms of the small intestine are functioning more or less normally. In many patients this is not the case and then preparations of short-chain peptides or amino acids, medium-chain triglycerides and dextrins of small molecular weight are required. Such ingredients are much more expensive and so should not be used unnecessarily. Solutions may have to be modified for patients with diabetes or renal failure (Chaps. 42 and 44).

Introduction of the tube

The first requirement is to explain the procedure to the patient. This is of paramount importance, as a patient may be disconcerted or frightened by the prospect. A combination of kindness and resolve ensures that the tube passes down readily. It is also necessary to make sure that the nasal passages are free from mucoid secretions. The patient should be placed in a comfortable semirecumbent position and a protective towel placed in position. It may be necessary to shrink the nasal mucous membrane with a decongestant. The tube should be lubricated and then passed through either nostril. Weighting the end of a tube with mercury facilitates its passage from the nasal passages to the soft palate and into the pharynx. Then a simple swallow with or without sips of water aids passage into the stomach. A guide mark on the tube shows when the length in the stomach is sufficient to allow the tip to pass through the pylorus and duodenum and into the proximal jejunum. Fine bore tubes are provided with a guide wire which facilitates passage and this is withdrawn carefully by simple traction when the stomach is reached. The tube is then taped to the patient.

If the tube enters the trachea or a bronchus, dyspnoea and coughing occur and it should be withdrawn. It is essential to make sure the tube has passed into the oesophagus and not into the trachea, since introduction of fluid into the lungs causes intense discomfort and is potentially dangerous. When the guide mark indicates that the tube is in the stomach, a little fluid should be withdrawn; if litmus paper shows that this is acid, it can be concluded that the tube is in the stomach. An additional test is to place a stethoscope in the left upper quadrant of the abdomen and to hear air forced through the tube with a 50 ml syringe. Any doubt on the position of a tube can be dispelled if a radiograph is taken.

The rate of flow of nutrient solutions may be controlled by using an enteral feeding pump. If the

Table 52.3 A nutrient solution to meet the daily requirements of a 60 kg patient who has not lost much weight and is not in a hypermetabolic state

	Energy (MJ)	(kcal)	Protein (g)	Fat (g)	CHO (g)	Na$^+$ (mmol)	K$^+$
Complan 300 g	5.53	1300	60	48	165	46	64
Caloreen 85 g	1.42	340	–	–	85	–	–
Prosparol 75 ml	1.39	335	–	37	–	–	–
	8.34	2005	60	85	250	46	64

Table 52.4 A nutrient solution to meet the daily requirements of an emaciated patient weighing 40 kg who is in a hypermetabolic state

	Energy (MJ)	(kcal)	Protein (g)	Fat (g)	CHO (g)	Na$^+$ (mmol)	K$^+$
Complan 300 g	5.53	1330	60	48	165	46	64
Caloreen 60 g	1.00	240	–	–	60	–	–
Prosparol 75 ml	1.37	330	–	37	–	–	–
Casilan 25 g	0.37	90	22	–	–	–	–
KCl solution 1 mmol/ml						–	20
	8.27	1990	82	85	225	46	84

solution is run in by gravity, a trip should be fixed to a stand above the level of the patient and the rate of flow controlled by a screw clamp.

A mercury-ended tube should not be disposed of in the general rubbish, as the mercury is both expensive and potentially toxic.

Feeding procedures

For the first 2 to 4 hours a clear sterile solution of 5 per cent glucose in water should be run in at the rate of 50 ml an hour or slower to establish that it is tolerated by the patient and that there is no block. Occasionally a tube becomes blocked and then it should be flushed out with water using a 2 ml syringe. If feeds are given intermittently during the day, the tube should be flushed through at the end of each feed and before the start of the next. Due to the movements of the patient a tube may become partially withdrawn. Then the guide wire should be used to reposition it and the position checked as before. A fine bore tube should be changed every 7 to 10 days, as it becomes hardened.

Occasionally nausea occurs and this may be relieved by a syrup containing metoclopramide (10 mg) given three times a day. If there is vomiting and it is clear that the tube is in the stomach, the patient should be fed lying on the right side to allow the stomach to empty by gravity. In the event of a patient requiring regular turning because of the danger of bed sores, feeding can be discontinued when on the left side.

Initiation

It is important not to cause osmotic diarrhoea by giving a feed that is too concentrated. Generally feeds are started at quarter strength, then increased each day to half, three quarters and full strength. However, if as with many commercial preparations the osmalility of the solution can be calculated, a full strength feed of up to 400 mosmol/litre can be given from the start.

Bolus feeding

This is the rapid administration of 300–400 ml of solution at intermittent periods. In general this practice is becoming obsolete since a poor tolerance giving rise to diarrhoea, distension and nausea is frequent. However, it may be necessary for patients receiving continuous physiotherapy such as those in a neurosurgical unit. If bolus feeding is adopted, the gastric residuum should be checked before each feed is given and this should always be returned to prevent electrolyte imbalance. If more than 150 ml is aspirated, gastric emptying is delayed and the regime should be reviewed.

Continuous drip feeding This is the more successful and better tolerated method of delivery and essential when feeding directly into the duodenum or jejunum.

The optimum hourly rate is less than 150 ml. Gravity drip flow rates can be inconsistent and require to be checked frequently; the use of a regulatory pump reduces variation in flow rate which it is essential to keep constant if tube feeding is to be a success.

Care of the solutions

Feeding solutions have to be treated with full hygienic precautions during the preparation, storage and administration. Feeds should be stored in a refrigerator to avoid bacterial growth and taken out before administration in time to reach room temperature; very cold feeds are not tolerated. A feed should be discarded when it has been more than 24 hours out of storage. Feeding reservoirs and tubing should be changed every day. Reservoirs should be of a size to minimise the number of refillings, and kept clean to reduce the risk of bacterial growth.

Documentation

Nursing staff should accurately record (1) the time when a feed is started and completed, (2) the volume administered, (3) water used to irrigate the tubing and (4) the patient's output of urine. Careful monitoring is needed to see that the patient is in fluid balance.

The patient

For tube feeding to be a success, patients have to accept it and co-operate, and they need and appreciate encouragement. The staff should explain the procedure and ultimate benefit to patients who are often worried because they feel that they have little control over their feeding. When an oral intake is permitted, foods of their choice should be offered. When this is contraindicated, the mouth and lips have to be kept clean and moist. When possible, patients should be allowed to move around freely, and when medically stable, they can continue tube feeding at home, provided they are adept at its management. Some patients find overnight feeding convenient.

Monitoring

The following checks should be carried out as a routine:
1. Initially, measurement of plasma urea, electrolytes and blood glucose.
2. Every eight hours, a record of fluid intake and output with a report if urine output falls to 30 ml/h.
3. Daily, calculation of actual intakes of energy, protein, fat and carbohydrate.
4. Every second day, weighing early in the morning, wearing the same clothes and on the same scales. If the patient is in fluid balance and weight is decreasing, extra protein and energy should be added to the regime.

5. Weekly, collection of urine for 24 hours for a rough estimation of nitrogen balance, a full blood count and measurements of midarm circumference and triceps skinfolds.

Complications

These usually arise from technical errors and with scrupulous attention to details are seldom serious. Careful monitoring detects them in an early stage when appropriate action can be taken.

Dehydration and overhydration from a too small or too large fluid intake arise commonly. The fluid balance gives early warning and allows the necessary adjustments to be made quickly.

Diarrhoea follows when an iso-osmolar feed is given too rapidly and when a hyperosmolar one is used. Hyperosmolar diarrhoea may also be due to too much lactose. As most tube feeds do not contain dietary fibre, defaecation is much less frequent than normal. Patients who are worried and think that they are constipated can be assured that a bowel movement once a week is normal in their circumstance. Diarrhoea may also be due to gastroenteritis caused by bacterial or viral infection.

Cough and dyspnoea arise when fluid enters the lungs from an improperly placed tube. Pneumonia may then follow and also when vomit is aspirated. This is a dangerous and sometimes fatal complication.

Oesophageal ulceration and stricture and gastric erosion caused by the presence of the tube have occurred but with the thin tubes now used are very rare.

INTRAVENOUS INFUSION OF WATER AND ELECTROLYTES

Infusion of fluid into a peripheral vein is a simple and much used procedure for the prevention and treatment of dehydration that can arise from many causes (Table 10.3, p. 96). The fluid used should be iso-osmolar with the plasma and both 5 per cent glucose and 0.9 per cent NaCl solutions are used. These are made up in bottles or plastic bags of 500 ml capacity. A patient who cannot take fluids by mouth needs two bags a day for maintenance. If dehydration is already present, at least two more bags are needed to restore the tissue fluids and in severe cases up to 12 bags may be needed.

Such large amounts are safe provided that they are given slowly so that the circulation is not overloaded. Several days may be needed for full restoration. The risk of overloading the circulation is increased when a patient is elderly or feeble and also in infants.

For maintenance one bag of saline solution providing 150 mmol of Na^+ is sufficient to meet sodium requirements, and a second bag to meet water requirements

should be 5 per cent glucose. The ratio of the two solutions to be used for replacement depends on the cause of the depletion. If it is due to excessive sweating, either from fever or exposure to a hot environment, and the patient has not been able to drink, water depletion is relatively greater than sodium depletion; then more glucose solution than saline solution is needed. On the other hand if the losses are from the alimentary tract and if the patient has previously been drinking freely, sodium depletion may be more severe than water depletion. Then plasma $[Na^+]$ falls, sometimes markedly, and it may be advisable to give in addition small quantities of a hyperosmolar saline solution. The classical example of this is severe cholera. Repeated measurements of plasma $[Na^+]$ are a guide as to whether sodium replacement is insufficient, adequate or excessive. The urine volume is a similar guide for water replacement.

Water and sodium depletion are often associated with disturbances of the acid–base balance. If the kidneys are functioning normally, this imbalance is usually corrected by excretion of a more acid or more alkaline urine. When acidosis is severe, a sodium bicarbonate solution should be given. The classical example is diabetic ketoacidosis. A patient in diabetic coma might require two to three bags of iso-osmolar $NaHCO_3$ and six to eight bags of iso-osmolar saline.

Potassium depletion is treated by addition of 50 mmol to a bag of saline solution. As a sudden rise of plasma $[K^+]$ can cause dangerous disturbances of cardiac rhythm, this should be infused slowly over 4 hours. It may then be repeated but regular monitoring of plasma $[K^+]$ is essential.

PARENTERAL NUTRITION

When by 1965 solutions of amino acids and fine emulsions of lipids were first freely available together with the technique of inserting a catheter into a large central vein, it became practical to infuse directly into a vein essential nutrients in quantities sufficient to meet all the daily needs of a patient. Since then, parenteral nutrition has been increasingly used and shown to be a safe procedure with acceptable risks when carried out by an experienced team. Its most spectacular success has been in patients who have had surgical removal of the greater part of the small intestine. Many of such patients are now alive and in good health several years after the operation.

Parenteral nutrition is now indicated in any disease or circumstance when the digestive and absorptive functions of the small intestine are seriously impaired. This occurs commonly in patients with an intestinal fistula and in those receiving radiotherapy and chemotherapeutic drugs for cancer. Parenteral nutrition is also used after major abdominal and thoracic surgery, severe burns and accidents causing multiple injuries. It is also used for infants of very low birth weight and for some patients with severe malnutrition.

In all of these circumstances it should be used only when tube feeding is impractical or has been shown to be ineffective. Tube feeding is much less dependent on the technical skill of the staff and so carries less risk of serious mishaps.

SUPPLY OF NUTRIENTS

These are provided by infusion of an amino acid solution, a glucose solution and a solution containing an emulsion of lipids. These solutions are obtained from manufacturers and contain electrolytes. Amino acid solutions and lipid emulsions contain small amounts of glucose. Usually two solutions and sometimes three are infused concurrently. A concentrate of vitamins and essential minerals is added to one of them. The solutions are run in slowly over at least 12 hours of the day. Table 52.5 gives requirements of nutrients for adults and infants.

Energy

At most, only up to 6.3 MJ (1500 kcal) can be infused daily into a peripheral vein, because a concentrated solution of glucose causes thrombophlebitis in small veins and the use of a dilute solution would overload a patient with water. This is barely enough to meet the basal metabolism of an adult man. Surgical patients need from 20 to 100 per cent more to cover the increased metabolism due to injury and sepsis. Medical patients who are not confined to bed need sufficient to cover their daily physical activities and sometimes more to allow weight lost to be regained. No patient's energy needs can be met fully by infusion into a peripheral vein and so effective parenteral nutrition requires the use of a central vein (see below).

The energy provided by amino acids (protein), carbohydrate and fat should be in approximately the same proportions as recommended for a normal diet, namely 12, 58 and 30 per cent respectively. However, adverse effects may arise from infusing too much glucose or lipid (see below) and much latitude is permissible. A patient who is malnourished and requires to gain weight may need a higher proportion of energy from amino acids, but it is useless and potentially dangerous to raise this above 20 per cent.

Commercial preparations of amino acids contain all the essential amino acids in approximately the proportions needed to meet requirements and also non-essential ones, such as alanine and glycine. The molar

proportion of essential to non-essential acids should be at least 1 to 2.

Intralipid, the most used fat preparation, is made from vegetable oils and is rich in essential fatty acids. At least 10 g is needed daily to prevent essential fatty acid deficiency.

Other sources of energy that have been infused are fructose and sorbitol, which is converted in the liver to fructose, and ethanol. As fructose is not dependent on insulin for its metabolism, it was thought that it might be more readily utilised than glucose but no advantage has been shown to follow its use, and as the risk of severe lactic acidosis is increased it is not recommended. Up to 100 g of ethanol can be utilised daily and this meets about half of the basal requirements of an adult man. If this amount is infused slowly over 24 hours,

Table 52.5 Tentatively recommended daily allowances of energy and nutrients for patients on complete intravenous nutrition. The allowances cover resting metabolism, some physical activity and specific dynamic action but for trauma, burns, pyrexia and other conditions that increase metabolism and/or losses extra nutrients are needed[5].

Nutrient	Allowance/kg body weight Adults	Neonates and infants
Water, ml	30	120
Energy, MJ	0.13	0.4–0.5
kcal	30	90–110
Amino acid N, g	0.09	0.3
Glucose, g	2	12
Fat, g	2	1–4
Sodium, mmol	1–1.4	2
Potassium, mmol	0.7–0.9	2
Calcium, mmol	0.11	0.5–1
Magnesium, mmol	0.04	0.15
Iron, μmol	0.25–1	2
Manganese, μmol	0.1	0.3
Zinc, μmol	0.7	1
Copper, μmol	0.07	0.3
Chromium, μmol	0.015	0.01
Selenium, μmol	0.006	0.04
Molybdenum, μmol	0.003	0.012
Chloride, mmol	1.3–1.9	3
Phosphorus, mmol	0.15	1
Fluoride, μmol	0.7	3
Iodide, μmol	0.015	0.04
Thiamin, mg	0.02	0.05
Riboflavin, mg	0.03	0.1
Niacin, mg	0.2	1
Vitamin B6, mg	0.03	0.1
Folate, μg	3	20
Vitamin B12, μg	0.03	0.2
Pantothenate, mg	0.2	1
Biotin, μg	5	30
Vitamin C, mg	0.5	3
Vitamin A, μg	10	100
Vitamin D, μg	0.04	2.5
Vitamin K, μg	2	50
Vitamin E, IU	0.5	1

concentration in the blood does not rise enough to cause symptoms of intoxication and has a sedative effect that may be beneficial. In the 1950s some surgeons frequently administered intravenous alcohol but since lipid preparations became available, it has seldom been used.

Water and electrolytes

About 30 ml kg^{-1} body weight of water is needed to meet invisible loss and allow adequate renal excretion. If more than 100 ml kg^{-1} is given, there is danger of overloading. For most patients a normal output of urine is obtained with infusions of 2 litres of solutions daily. These should contain 100–150 mmol of sodium and about 60 mmol of potassium, the amounts provided in a normal diet.

Minerals

Requirements are less than on a normal diet as only small proportions of the dietary intake are absorbed in the small intestine. Furthermore all are potentially toxic in doses that are not much greater than requirements. Table 52.5 gives suggested intakes. In all patients on long-term parenteral nutrition regular monitoring of plasma concentrations ensures that enough of each and no more is given. They may be given as a separate supplement or combined with a vitamin preparation.

Vitamins

A concentrated supplement containing vitamins in at least the amounts recommended for a normal diet should be added daily to one of the bags (Table 52.5). Surgical patients often require additional vitamin C and may need extra vitamin K. Additional folate or vitamin B12 may be necessary to prevent or treat anaemia.

Preparation of the infusion

Solutions come from manufacturers with a predetermined composition and each contains predominantly amino acids or glucose or lipid. Patients differ in their needs for these and other nutrients, so parental nutrition has to be flexible. A prescription for nutrients written by a physician or surgeon for a particular patient can be prepared by a pharmacist from the commercial solutions available.

The infusion for the day can be made up conveniently in a plastic bag of 3 litre capacity. This reduces the number of times that a nurse has to change the giving set to once a day and so lowers the risk of infection. The pharmacist mixes solutions of amino acids and glucose together with any supplements of electrolytes, minerals or vitamins into this bag. This is done in a laminar flow cabinet, thereby reducing greatly the risk of bacterial and other contamination. In the past lipid solutions have been infused separately, though often simultaneously with the main mixed solution, using a Y-shaped junction for attachment of the two lines to the extension tube of the of the catheter. It is now possible under some conditions to add the lipid to the 3 litre bag and it is hoped that further developments make this generally practical.

The techniques for parenteral nutrition are new and still developing. It is not yet clear what are the best solutions for manufacturers to provide for pharmacists so that they have the flexibility to meet the different prescriptions of doctors, necessary because of the varying requirements of patients.

Insertion and maintenance of the catheter

The first thing is to talk to the patient. Inability to eat adds inevitability to anxiety due to a serious disease and being trapped in a hospital. The nature of the procedure should be explained and assurance given that it is a safe and effective substitute for normal feeding.

A silicon catheter is inserted into a large central vein under local anaesthesia and with strict asepsis. This should be done by an experienced operator in a surgical theatre. The common practice is to enter the subclavian vein through an incision below the clavicle and then to pass the catheter into the superior vena cava. The catheter is made to pass through a subcutaneous tunnel about 10 cm long, which greatly reduces the risk of subsequent sepsis, and is then secured by sutures. A chest radiograph is taken to ensure that it is in the correct position and that there is no pneumothorax.

Subsequent movements of the catheter are minimised by attaching an extension tube to it. This reduces the risk of sepsis and the rare possibility of a catheter breaking. The tube is changed every three days using a strict aseptic protocol and this is also needed for changing dressings. The catheter should not be used for taking samples of blood, injecting drugs or measuring central venous pressure.

The infusions are run in using a pump and positive pressure or under gravity with a reliable flow control. It is important to control the flow rate accurately and to ensure that a large volume is not infused rapidly.

When the catheter has to be disconnected from the infusion line, the patient should be tipped head down and the breath held in full expiration to prevent sucking in of air. If the catheter is disconnected for any time longer than needed for the immediate change from one line to another, a heparin lock, 2 ml of solution containing 2000 units of heparin, is fitted. When a patient is at home, this can be done by the district nurse or by the patient but strict aseptic precautions are necessary. A heparin lock should be replaced if it has remained in position for 24 hours.

Complications of the infusion

The list of these given below is long and formidable and serves as a warning that parental nutrition should not be undertaken by those who work in small district hospitals where the necessary experience cannot be gained. Fortunately, except for sepsis, complications are minimal when an experienced team is in charge of the procedures. Patients can be assured that they are safe with their catheters.

Complications of insertion are (1) pneumothorax and haemopneumothorax, (2) puncture or thrombosis of the subclavian artery and (3) damage with subsequent infection spreading to the trachea, oesophagus, pericardium and large vessels and nerves. Complications of maintenance are (1) sepsis, (2) a large venous thrombosis, (3) a catheter may block, migrate or break, (4) cardiac tamponade and (5) air embolism.

Metabolic complications

Electrolyte disturbances, dehydration and fluid overload commonly arise. They can be detected by appropriate monitoring (see below) and the necessary adjustments in the composition of the infusion made in time to prevent serious consequences.

As most patients on parenteral nutrition are confined to bed or can take only limited physical activity, it is easy to overfeed them. Deficiencies of specific vitamins and trace elements and of essential amino acids arise in time when these are not included in the infusion. These nutritional disorders arise in many circumstances and they present no special features when due to parenteral nutrition. Allergic and toxic reaction may occur but are uncommon.

When food is taken by mouth, most nutrients enter the systemic circulation after passing through the liver, but with parenteral nutrition all enter directly. Bypassing the liver may have metabolic consequences. Immediate disposal of blood glucose is mainly in the liver. Rapid infusion of a concentrated glucose solution into systemic vessels may cause hyperglycaemia, leading to hyperosmolar dehydration. Large doses of insulin may be needed to control the blood glucose. Much of this is then converted into fat and an enlarged fatty liver may result. Conversion of glucose to fat raises the respiratory quotient; the excess CO_2 in the blood is a stimulus to respiration and the increased ventilatory effort required to remove it may be a critical factor in a patient who is dangerously ill.

The lipid emulsion that is absorbed from the gut enters the lymphatic channels that drain via the thoracic duct directly into a subclavian vein; the emulsion is then cleared from the plasma mainly in the lungs. An emulsion given parenterally, when infused slowly is usually cleared from the plasma within 4 hours, as after a normal fatty meal. But this does not always happen and periodically a sample of plasma taken 6 hours after the end of an infusion should be examined to see that the opalescence has cleared.

Microscopic fat emobli in the main organs of patients with severe injuries are common. These may occur more frequently in patients receiving parenteral lipids, but the extra risk is slight.

Infection

The source of local sepsis, often caused by *Staphylococcus albus*, may be difficult to trace. Commensal bacteria from the patient or an attendant are common causes. But dressings may sometimes be responsible and these should be checked for sterility if there is the slightest reason to suspect them.

Continued fever suggests bacteriaemia and possibly septicaemia. Then total parenteral nutrition should be stopped for 48 hours and a heparin lock inserted.

Supervision of patients

At the start of parenteral nutrition a patient requires close clinical supervision in hospital. This should include (1) daily measurement of fluid intake and output, recorded on a fluid balance chart, (2) daily testing of the urine for glucose and ketones, (3) thrice weekly weighing and (4) weekly measurements of skinfold thicknesses and midarm circumference.

Biochemical monitoring is the main means for ensuring that the infusion accurately meets a patient's need and for making adjustments in its composition appropriate to the patient's progress. Table 52.6 is a schedule for monitoring suitable from the start of parenteral feeding. If a patient has serious disturbances of water and electrolyte metabolism or acid–base balance, some of these analyses should be made more frequently. Blood should be sent to the laboratory immediately after the sample has been taken and the analyses completed and results sent to the ward as soon as possible. It is useful to have results by midday so that if they indicate a need for changes in the prescription, the new one can be made up in the afternoon.

When a patient has been stable for some time, biochemical monitoring may be reduced to once weekly. After 6 weeks plasma concentrations of trace elements should be checked and this is repeated monthly.

PARENTERAL NUTRITION FOR INFANTS

The very young can be fed by parenteral nutrition but this is a dangerous procedure for preterm infants weighing only 1500 g or less because of the risk of infection, pneumonia and septicaemia. It is best to feed these

Table 52.6 A schedule for biochemical monitoring during parenteral nutrition

	Condition of patient		
	Unsteady	Steady first 3 weeks long term	Steady
Plasma			
Na, K, Cl, urea	1–2 times daily	Thrice weekly	Weekly
Glucose	Thrice weekly	Thrice weekly	Weekly
Albumin or transferrin, osmolality	Twice weekly	Twice weekly	Weekly
Ca, Mg, Zn	–	–	Once in 8 weeks
Trace elements	Once monthly	Once monthly	Once monthly
Folate and vitamin B12	Twice weekly	Twice weekly	Weekly
ASAT, ALAT, ALP*, bilirubin			
Blood	Twice weekly	Twice weekly	Weekly
Hb, PVC, platelet count, thrombotest	Up to 6 times daily	Daily	Twice weekly
Urine			
Na, K, Cl	Daily	Twice weekly	–
Glucose, urea, osmolality	Thrice weekly	Twice weekly	Weekly
Acid–base balance	Daily	–	–

* ASAT and ALAT, asparagine and alanine aminotransference; ALP, alkaline phosphatase.

infants by a tube passed beyond the pylorus and only to resort to parenteral feeding if this becomes ineffective due to an intestinal disorder such as necrotising enterocolitis.

The nutrients required for parenteral nutrition in infants are given in Table 52.5 and a practical manual is available.[7] As a peripheral vein is preferable to a central one, only small amounts of glucose can be given and much of the energy has to come from fat. Lipid may be infused in amounts up to 4 g kg^{-1} of body weight, but large amounts should not be given when there is jaundice. Fat clearance has to be checked regularly and accurately and the opacity of the plasma should be measured using a nephelometer.

With both tube and parenteral feeding it is important to maintain fluid balance. The daily water requirement of an infant is about 150 ml kg^{-1} body weight. This may be increased greatly by diarrhoea and vomiting and by increased losses from the skin and lungs due to sweating or rapid breathing. These losses have to be estimated as accurately as is practical and appropriate amounts of extra fluid given. Both over- and underhydration are readily detected by frequent weighing on a balance accurate to ± 5 g.

HOME PARENTERAL NUTRITION

The usual indication is intestinal failure due to inflammatory disease or extensive resection of the small bowel. In Britain about 10 new patients start on parenteral nutrition at home each year. It is an area fraught with ethical and economic controversies, but few would deny the right of young adults to live by parenteral nutrition. The quality of their lives can be extremely good, as most of the infusion is given at night. One patient in Canada has completed a medical degree while receiving home parenteral nutrition. Patients need hospital support from a dedicated team and a well-organised supply of nutrients and containers. They have to be trained in aseptic techniques. Patients and their home circumstances must be carefully assessed before embarking on this new way of life. A 10 week training period is usually necessary before a patient goes home. It is important that a nurse trained in parenteral nutrition should be readily available to visit the home.

ASSOCIATED DISEASES

Parenteral nutrition is a flexible technique that can be adjusted to meet the nutrient requirements of patients seriously ill with any disease or injury that makes both normal or tube feeding impossible or very difficult. It is not contraindicated for patients with acute or chronic kidney or liver diseases or diabetes. Prescriptions can be adjusted in relation to constraints on intakes of particular nutrients that the metabolic disturbances in these diseases may impose.

A PARENTERAL NUTRITION TEAM

Parenteral nutrition requires the skills of the nurse, pharmacist, dietitian, biochemist and doctor. A team approach is essential. No unit or ward in a hospital is likely to have sufficient patients requiring parenteral nutrition to justify a unit or ward approach. It is better to have one team, acceptable throughout a hospital, who are responsible for all patients.

The nurse looks after the asepsis of the feeding line, administers the solutions order, supervises the general nursing care of the patient and keeps records of fluid balance and urine analyses. The appointment at the Middlesex Hospital, London, of a nutrition nurse who was responsible for dressings and catheter care of patients in all wards reduced the incidence of catheter sepsis from 25 to 4 per cent.[8]

The pharmacist supplies sterile solutions, preferably made to a prescription in the pharmacy, and in one bag with all added vitamins, electrolytes and trace elements.

The dietitian advises and reviews patients during their time on parenteral nutrition and when they come off it.

The biochemist is responsible for the analyses needed for monitoring patients and for investigating the metabolic problems that may arise.

The doctor has overall responsibility for the patient and provides the surgical skill for the insertion of the feeding lines, orders the solutions after assessing the patient's fluid balance, catabolism and clinical state, and the exercise undertaken daily.

The team should meet regularly two to three times a week to review patients' progress in the light of clinical changes and biochemical measurements. At these meet-ings decisions can be made on individual patients and on the working of the nutrition service.

Such a team is now working in Edinburgh in a general hospital with 800 beds. Even though most patients are admitted because of an acute illness, it is rare for more than five patients to be on parenteral nutrition at any one time. These may be in many different wards and it would be impossible for the staff in each ward to become familiar with the many practical problems of parenteral nutrition. The team reviews daily the feeding regimes of all patients. It goes round the wards twice a week and sees each patient. Practical working relations have been developed for meeting the various problems as they arise. The work is advisory and to support the doctors and nurses who are primarily responsible for the care and treatment of each patient. It would be unwise to stray from this supportive role.

COMMENT

Tube feeding needs little equipment, is safe and relatively easy. All medical staff can be trained to carry it out and it should be available for patients in small hospitals in any part of the world. Total parenteral nutrition, by contrast, is a complex technology. It is expensive and all who use it require specialist training; even in the hands of experts there are hazards, some of which may be very dangerous. Hence it should be used only in large central hospitals.

REFERENCES

1. Young G A, Hill G L 1978 Assessment of protein-calorie malnutrition in surgical patients from plasma proteins and anthropometric measurements. Am J Clin Nutr 31: 429–35
2. Bistrian B R, Blackburn M D, Hallowell E, Heddle R 1974 Protein status of general surgical patients JAMA 230: 858–60
3. Chadwick S J D, Sim A J W , Dudley H A F 1984 Plasma fibronectin changes during acute nutritional deprivation in healthy human subjects. Proc Nutr Soc 43:43A
4. Baker J P, Detsky A S, Wesson D E, et al 1981 Nutritional assessment: a comparison of clinical judgment and objective measurements. N Engl J Med 306: 969–72
5. Hallberg D, Hallgren B, Schuberth O, Wretlind A 1982 Parenteral nutrition: goals and achievements Nutr Support Services 2: 15–24
6. Glass E J, Hume R, Lang M A, Forfar J O 1984 Parenteral nutrition compared with transpyloric feeding. Arch Dis Child 59: 131–5
7. Kerner J A (ed) 1983 Manual of pediatric parenteral nutrition. Wiley, Philadelphia.
8. Keshane P P, Jones B J M, Attrill H, et al 1983 Effect of catheter tunnelling and a nutrition nurse on catheter sepsis during parenteral nutrition: a controlled trial. Lancet 2: 1388–90

PART FIVE

Public Health

I took every opportunity of leaving the official hygiene caravan to take an unconducted stroll through the working-class district of the town we were visiting. Observations made in this way tell one more about the real hygienic level of the population than the inspection of selected hospitals and institutions made to look pretty beforehand. One must watch the little children in the streets and courts of the poor districts, look at children as they enter and leave the school buildings with an eye to their state of health, stroll attentively through the courts and alleys, have an eye on the country folk coming to the market and assess their physical quality. I am accustomed never to enter or leave a railway station outside Berlin without spending a few minutes in waiting rooms of lower railway classes and looking at the people there . . .. Anybody who has given his attention to this can soon make instructive comparisons, and receive impressions not to be had from reports, descriptions and statistical tables.

Grotjahn J 1932 Erlebst und Erstrebts. Herbig, Berlin, p 266. Quoted by Greenwood M 1946 British Medical Journal 1:118

53

Community Nutrition

A nutritionist may be consulted about the diet of institutions such as orphanages and prisons, about the feeding of special groups of a population such as mothers and young children or old people, about the feeding of various occupational groups such as night shift workers in industry, plantation labourers or members of the armed services. They may also be asked to advise on the food supply of small, local communities, for example a remote island, or a district or whole province, a country or through the United Nations and other international agencies of a whole continent or even the world.

Whatever the size or nature of a problem in community nutrition there are three aspects to be considered: (1) the causes that lead to its arising, (2) assessment of its extent and severity, and (3) the means of prevention. They are the subjects of the next three chapters. These correspond to the sections on aetiology, diagnosis and prevention in textbooks of clinical medicine.

Aetiology is the study of causes. The cause of a poor food supply may be a failure of agricultural production or a failure of distribution. The latter may be due to social, economic or political factors and ignorance and poverty are the most important.

Assessment is based on the findings of surveys. These may consist of clinical examinations, laboratory investigations of blood, urine and other tissues, anthropometric measurements, vital statistics which include birth and death rates and the incidence or prevalence of specific diseases and diet surveys in which the actual amounts of food consumed are recorded. A single survey can only give information about the state of nutrition of a group of people at a particular period of time. Much more valuable information is obtained by a series of continuing surveys, which go on over the years, a process known as **surveillance**.

Prevention may depend on changes in agricultural methods, in the introduction of new crops or improvements in animal husbandry. It may require changes in economic policy and in budgeting, new developments in industry and new wage policies. Always it necessitates a large educational programme.

From the nature of these problems nutritionists do not work alone. They have to co-operate with people in many walks of life and must be able to converse with agriculturalists, economists, sociologists, politicians, members of the medical and educational professions, works managers and many other people. A nutritional policy, whether for a small institution or a large country, is always based on collective decisions, formed after considering many factors. Nutritionists can only give advice; they do not make the final decisions.

Nutrition policies always depend on the climate of political opinion. In every country there are people who believe that social and economic problems, including the food supply, are primarily the responsibilities of governments, and others who believe that these problems are best left to the free enterprise of private individuals. In practice a compromise is always reached, though the point of compromise differs markedly in various countries. There is no doubt that excessive government action stifles initiative and reduces efficiency, for example in Russian agriculture after the revolution, and also that all problems cannot be resolved by free enterprise, however capable and well-intended individuals may be. In the nutrition field famine relief is an example where, since the time of Joseph and Pharoah, government action has always been necessary.

A nutritionist should also remember that in any society there are both rich and poor and that they have very different nutritional problems, all of which are important. In the affluent cities of North America and Western Europe, there is a small minority of very poor people. Many of these have nutritional problems, unknown to the majority, which are difficult to resolve. In Africa, Asia and Latin America, beside the poor peasant agriculturalists and urban slum dwellers there are many rich families, who have the same nutritional problems as wealthy North Americans and Europeans. Experience shows that the rich, like the poor, are not very good at looking after themselves nutritionally. Any nutritional programme should cover all sections of a community and pay particular attention to minority groups. Small minorities are easily overlooked by enthusiasts studying masses of statistics obtained from large populations.

Much good work can be done locally in community nutrition by harnessing and directing the enthusiasms of men and women of good will. Indeed, nutrition programmes, like all health programmes, are successful only if they receive the support of enthusiastic leaders of the local community. It is a task of nutritionists to seek out and direct such leaders.

In most countries, including the United Kingdom today, nutrition suffers from the lack of clear government policy. This is attributable to the fact that decisions affecting national nutrition are made in several different ministries. Ministries of Agriculture, Health, Education and Trade and above all the Treasury each determine nutrition policy in various ways. Some of these have nutritional advisers. Ministerial decisions are based on many sectional interests and not infrequently conflict with nutritional policies. Innumerable schemes to co-ordinate nutrition policy by means of interdepartmental government committees have been put on paper, and many have been tried out in practice in different countries. In general, it can be said that their successes have been small and limited. The role of governments in promoting good nutrition is discussed in the final section of Chapter 56. Prime ministers and other men of power are in general ignorant of the importance of nutrition in relation to health, and of individual health to the well-being and effectiveness of the community as a whole. That the educated section of a community is in general very poorly informed about human nutrition is attributable to its low prestige in the academic world. Most science and arts graduates of the leading universities of the world have acquired no knowledge of the fundamentals of nutrition nor, indeed, of general self-health care.

Experience shows that programmes aimed solely at raising the nutritional status of a community are seldom successful. All nutrition work should be part of a broader programme aimed at raising the general well-being of a community. The larger programme may include control of infectious diseases, better education, better housing, improved agriculture or better wages and higher production in industry. A nutritionist has to work with experts in these fields and should learn to communicate with them and understand their problems.

Anyone contemplating going into nutritional work should be warned to expect frustration. Their good advice will often be neglected or misinterpreted. They are more likely to get satisfaction from work in a small community and, if they move up to national and international fields, their sense of frustration is likely to increase. But the challenge is there. Every community, large or small, needs a nutrition programme although in most cases its members do not appreciate the need.

Nutritionists in the trials of their career may take comfort from considering three attributes of *Homo sapiens* which greatly influence the effectiveness of their work.

First, he is charitable and many men and women by giving their services and money to a community, either their own or in a foreign country, find the opportunity to follow the injunction of the evangelist, 'Beloved, let us love one another; for love is of God' (I John 4.7). It is a great experience to work with such people.

Secondly, man is susceptible to bureaucracy. The classical description of this disease is the account of the Circumlocution Office in *Little Dorrit*. 'Whatever was required to be done, the Circumlocution Office was beforehand with all the public departments in the art of perceiving how not to do it.' If Charles Dickens were alive today, he would find many circumlocution offices in Whitehall, Washington and other national government headquarters and especially in the various United Nations agencies.

Thirdly, man is corrupt. Sir Robert Walpole, a practical and successful British Prime Minister, is now best remembered for his saying in 1739: 'All those men have their price.' Many nutrition programmes depend on food contracts and it should be no surprise that money and goods, collected by the charitable to aid the needy, often go into venal hands. This is a factor which has often mitigated the hopes of those engaged in international aid to poor people in many countries.

Nowadays, people often appear surprised when they hear of charitable, bureaucratic or corrupt behaviour, but they are of the essence of human nature. The effectiveness of many community nutrition programmes depend on the blend of these essences in the men and women responsible for carrying them out.

COMMUNITY DIETITIANS

Most dietitians work in hospitals but since the 1970s an increasing number have held posts in community medicine.[1,2] In the UK there are appointments in district health services with the aim of promoting health by making local populations more aware and better informed about nutrition. A community dietitian may have attachments to a general practice, to clinics (antenatal, infant welfare or dental) and to a school. In such attachments she works closely with the nurses, especially with health visitors (public health nurses), and with social workers. She can give information, expert advice, literature and audiovisual material to all who work in the health service and to local organisations such as the Regional Community Council, The British Diabetic Association and other voluntary bodies. She is also available for talks and discussion with groups such as mothers and babies, the elderly, the physically or the mentally handicapped, members of slimming clubs and ethnic minorities, who may be vegetarians or have other food preferences. Help may be given in the training of cooks and matrons for residential homes and of home helps.

Community dietitians have many roles and activities, and these require to be modified continuously to meet changing needs and conditions in local areas. It is thus a challenging career which many are now finding rewarding and enjoyable.

REFERENCES

1. Burman G 1982 Nutrition education and its application in the community. Hum Nutr Appl Nutr 36A: 5–10
2. Angore R 1984 The role of the community dietitian in a multidisciplinary approach to nutrition education in an area of multiple deprivation. Hum Nutr Appl Nutr 38A: 5–16

54

Aetiology of Nutritional Disorders

Good health depends on an adequate food supply and this in turn on a sound agricultural policy and a good system of food distribution. The social, economic and agricultural factors that determine the food supply also determine the state of health and the incidence of disease amongst a population. These are the basic aetiological factors causing nutritional disease and they are closely linked with the dangers which arise from failure to control an excessive increase in the population. Even a good food supply and distribution system may fail if there is not proper selection and preparation of food in the home. Lack of health education is responsible for much malnutrition, especially in poor rural areas and urban slums.

The medical and dietetic professions should help to shape public opinion so that people demand sensible nutritional programmes — both national and international. Only by the wide propagation of a sound knowledge of health principles is it possible to create the demand for proper health policies. For these reasons doctors and dietitians should be familiar with the broad outlines of the social, economic and agricultural factors which determine food supply.

INSUFFICIENT FOOD PRODUCTION

The dependence of a satisfactory food supply upon a flourishing agriculture is self-evident. It is a fact which has been realised from the earliest times, and has formed the basis of policy for innumerable wise rulers and leaders of mankind throughout history. Nevertheless the importance of a sound agricultural economy was generally overlooked throughout the industrial revolution in the ninteenth century. Then in the Americas, Africa, Asia and Oceania an apparently inexhaustible supply of land, fresh to agriculture, was available for producing the foods necessary for the urban populations. Although much underfeeding and malnutrition was present in the poor of both industrial and agricultural communities throughout the world, the wealth and prosperity of the successful or privileged minority at the top prevented all

but a few of the clear-sighted from realising the extent and severity of underfeeding among the masses at the bottom of the economic scale. The world wars, with their interference first with food distribution and then with food production, gradually awakened the people of most countries to the importance of the relationships between food, agriculture and population.

At the end of the fighting in World War II, many countries had serious deficiencies in their food supply and some were on the verge of famine. Both agriculture and the international food trade recovered rapidly. By 1955 throughout the world food supplies were at least as good as before the war. Yet in many countries this level was far below estimates of physiological needs. In these countries malnutrition and undernutrition were still widespread, but it was hoped that the pace of agricultural development could be increased and that levels of nutrition would soon be raised.

This hope has not been fulfilled because of the staggering increase in population. The Food and Agricultural Organisation of the United Nations publishes annually estimates of national food production related to population and expressed as an index, the mean value for the years 1961–65 being taken as 100. Since then indices for most countries in Africa, the Near East, the Far East and Latin America have varied little, but those for countries in Western Europe, North America and Oceania have risen markedly. These crude statistics confirm a general impression that in those countries where the majority of the poor and malnourished live, agriculture is barely keeping up with the growth of population; the overall food supply is only marginally better than it was 25 years ago. In contrast, in many wealthy countries the disposal of agricultural surpluses now poses difficult problems, e.g. the 'butter mountain' in Europe.

In most of the poor countries of the world, agricultural production has risen, although to a lesser extent than in the rich countries, and death rates have fallen, often markedly, but there has been as yet little fall in birth rates. As a result the growth of agriculture is barely keeping up with the growth of population, and there has been little change in the amount of food available per head. Undernutrition and malnutrition remain widespread. While in some areas production has increased due to the green revolution (p. 534), the situation generally remains today similar to the picture presented in 1946 by Low. His cartoon illustrates the difficulty experienced by a prosperous and obese American in getting his surplus crops to the thin and hungry Asian (Fig. 54.1). He is studying a book on economics. For 40 years a whole generation of economists, sustained by much goodwill and humanitarianism, have attended innumerable conferences, but the 'surplus of cereals' remains and there are still 'no dollars'. In fact it now appears that any economic solution is unlikely. The poor agricultural countries have in the past obtained much of their foreign exchange by exporting agricultural products. Rich countries are now less dependent on these exports; since synthetic substitutes are now used in place of rubber, natural fibres and drugs of plant origin. The prices of agricultural products are in general less well maintained than those of industrial goods. This leads to a series of economic crises, adversely affecting health and nutrition. In many poor countries these can only be improved by a great increase in agricultural production and a slowing down of the growth of population. Both depend on higher standards of education. Population problems are discussed in Chapter 57. In this chapter

some of the causes of agricultural unproductiveness are discussed and also economic and other factors which prevent the proper distribution and use of the food available in a country.

Agricultural unproductiveness may due to:
    Climatic irregularities and catastrophes
    Soil erosion
    War
    Inefficient farming.

Climatic irregularities

It is a curious anomaly of nature that in Britain, where the daily variations in the weather are so marked and unpredictable as to colour general conversation and social planning, the seasonal variations from year to year are small. British farmers may have good or bad harvests, but their 'bad years' bear no relationship to the catastrophes which regularly afflict farmers in the large continents as a a result of variations in rainfall. In parts of Africa, the Americas, Australia, India and China there are areas many hundreds of miles in extent subject to periodic failure of the annual rain supply. In years of failure the total rainfall may be less than 20 per cent of the average seasonal supply. Such years may alternate with years of floods when mammoth continental rivers, swollen by excessive rain in the mountains, burst their banks and so destroy the crops. Water engineers play

Fig. 54.1 'From land to mouth.' Lord Boyd Orr, first Director-General of FAO. (With acknowledgements to the *Evening Standard*, 26 August, 1946)

an important part in determining the health of the people. The husbanding of water in dams and artificial lakes, its controlled distribution through irrigation canals and the management and control of huge rivers in flood are technical problems, intimately bound up with nutrition, world health and civilisation.

Irrigation may be from a village well, worked by age-old devices like the Persian wheel (Fig. 54.2). At the other extreme there are huge river dams, as on the Nile, requiring capital expenditure of many millions of pounds which bring fertility to great tracts of desert and improve the nutrition of hundreds of thousands of people. A modern feature is the link-up between irrigation and hydroelectric power. Dams of similar magnitude harness many great rivers in America, Asia and Africa.

In 1983 the weather throughout the world was exceptional. The rains failed in Africa from Ethiopia in the north to Zimbabwe and South Africa, and they were very heavy in parts of Peru, Brazil and India. The consequent droughts and floods led to famine conditions in many countries.

Soil erosion

The next most important problem in food production is the prevention of soil erosion and the recovery of land previously degraded by bad agriculture. The immediate agencies of erosion are wind and water, following removal or damage to the pre-existing plant cover. The cause of this damage is usually improper exploitation of land in grazing, ploughing, firing, felling or the collection of domestic fuel. This improper or too violent exploitation itself results from pressures — financial or biological.

A common sequence of events in many districts now barren has been as follows. Originally forest existed. Men came, exploited the forest wealth too rapidly and cut down too many trees. Small areas of arable land were interspersed with areas of waste, broken by large tree stumps. At this stage or earlier, goats were introduced. These beasts are the antithesis of good animal husbandry. Goats differ from cattle and sheep in their ability to grub up the roots of plants and consume them. Goats also eat the leaves and bark of trees and so kill them. Thus the soil is loosened and in succeeding rains washed away, leaving an arid desert or a barren hillside. One of the most striking examples of this process is to be seen in the deserts of North Africa. This barren land was once the glory of the Roman Empire; rich and fertile — a main source of grain and olive oil to metropolitan Rome. After the collapse of the Empire, instead of a numerous peasant population who understood the land and tilled it industriously, nomads wandered through the desert with their flocks of goats, sheep and camels. It is not that the climate had changed, though it may have done a little, but in destroying the Roman Empire in North Africa the Berber and Arab tribes nearly destroyed the land itself. The dams and reservoirs in which the Romans had hoarded the precious water were broken or filled with sand. As a result the winter rains poured down the wadis and into the sea, taking with them much of the fertile top soil. By recklessly grazing their flocks the nomads destroyed the natural forest and vegetation so that the sun and wind and rain

Fig. 54.2 Irrigation by Sakia, one of the most ancient types of water-wheels, can still be seen in many parts of the world. (FAO photo by P. Morin)

stripped the earth from the hills. With nothing to stop it the desert, which can move like an army, slowly crept down to the coast.

In Nepal today the need for fuel in mountain villages compels the villagers to cut the forest at higher and higher levels. Soil erosion in these situations causes landslides which not infrequently carry away whole villages with considerable loss of life.

There are few countries in the world where land degradation in one form or another is not of major importance for the health of future generations. South Africa, Australia, Pakistan, India and many of the new African states are all afflicted. Vigorous counter-measures have begun in the USA, the country of pioneers both in land spoilage and eventual costly cures.

War

War has always been a potent cause of nutritional diseases. It acts by interfering with food distribution, by taking away many of the young men from their normal task of agriculture, and sometimes by destruction of crops and livestock on a large scale. Civil wars have wrought the most havoc in this respect. The Thirty Years War in Europe, the Mahratta Wars in India, the civil wars that set up the Communist regimes in Russia, in China and in Vietnam have all led to disruption of agriculture and so to famine. It should now be abundantly clear that these are the inevitable concomitants of all wars. The deliberate destruction of rice crops by herbicides carried out by the US armed forces in Vietnam[1] is one of novel horrors of war. Militarily such action is not likely to be effective; when there are food shortages, fighting men are usually able to get food for themselves and they have seldom been starved into submission. It is the women, the children and the old people who die.

With so much of modern agriculture, market gardening and animal husbandry depending on electricity, fossil fuels and piped water any act of war destroying power stations, oil refineries or water supplies would rapidly jeopardise food supplies.

Inefficient farming

Ideally, farmers throughout the world should have enough basic education and capital to profit from the enormous developments of scientific knowledge. As yet the majority of the world's farmers possess neither of these essentials to reap the benefits of such knowledge. In underdeveloped countries new methods and techniques have been introduced much more readily into medical than into agricltrual practice.

A majority of the peoples of the world live in underdeveloped agricultural regions where they struggle for existence under conditions that have changed but little for thousands of years and they still face the elemental problem of getting enough to eat. Readers who have not had opportunities for travel can get a good picture of farming conditions at present existing in large parts of the world from a study of the Old Testament. In many countries conditions have changed but little from the time of the Pharaohs. Cairo is a fine modern city; yet within a few miles of the Mohamet Ali Mosque there are villages in which one can see all the simple features of primitive agriculture, which are familiar to the reader of the Bible: the threshing floor, the oxen ploughing, the old men, the asses, the camels. A similar picture can be painted in many parts of the world — India, the East and West Indies, South America and parts of Southern Europe, and an even more primitive one, without wheel or plough in most countries of tropical Africa. Where agriculture remains stagnant, the cause is often rapacious landlords and money-lenders. A peasant farmer may have to mortgage his crops in the field and then one bad harvest puts him into debt from which he never extricates himself. A fair system of land tenure and equitable facilities for obtaining credit are essential for the development of agriculture and these the peasant farmers lack all too frequently.

UNEQUAL DISTRIBUTION OF FOOD

POVERTY

That poverty is responsible for underfeeding and malnutrition, especially in children, is obvious to anyone who today visit the shanty towns on the outskirts of the rapidly growing cities of Africa, Asia and Latin America or who reads *Oliver Twist* and other novels by the great writers who described conditions in European and North American cities in the nineteenth century. Yet all poverty is relative, as Malthus said in 1798. This is illustrated by two newspaper items in 1983. A sister who works with Mother Theresa in Calcutta is reported to have said: 'Conditions in Calcutta have improved. You do not now get people dying and rotting in the streets and you do not get young children simply thrown on rubbish dumps.' In contrast, a survey in the UK was reported as showing that 7 million people are so poor that they do not know where the money for the next instalment for their colour television set is coming from. Poverty means something quite different in Calcutta and in Britain and needs to be defined. Two very different definitions were used in major surveys in the UK, the first by Rowntree[2] in 1899 and the second by Townsend[3] in 1968/69.

Poverty in the UK 1900–39

Rowntree studied 16 362 families in the city of York. He defined a poverty line as the minimum sum of money needed to pay rent and for food, clothing, fuel and a few sundries, and 'nothing must be bought but that which is absolutely necessary for the maintenance of physical health and what is bought must be of the plainest and most economical description'. Money for rail or bus fares, newspapers, postage stamps and sweets was excluded. For a family of man and wife with three children the poverty line was an income below £1 1s 6d a week. With this harsh standard necessitating a way of living that would be intolerable for us today, 15 per cent of the population were living in primary poverty. Rowntree[4] repeated his survey twice and by 1936 the figure had fallen to 6.8 per cent. He commented that this 'represents a great improvement but it must be qualified by a serious sense of concern that so large a proportion of the workers are living below a poverty line which few, if any, will regard as being fixed at too high a level'.

That those living in poverty during the industrial depression in the 1930s were not getting sufficient food to meet physiological needs and that their health was suffering in consequence was demonstrated in two studies that are now classics.

Food, health and income is the title of a book by Orr[5] which had a great influence on the development of nutrition policies in Britain. It contained the results of a survey of 1152 families, in each of which the total food consumption was weighed for one week and a correlation made between food consumption per head and available income in each family. Those in the lowest economic groups, which was believed to comprise $4\frac{1}{2}$ million people (10 per cent of the total population), were living on diets which failed to reach proper standards in almost every respect, especially in energy, proteins, vitamins A and C, and the minerals, iron and calcium. In the next two economic groups, 40 per cent of the population, although the energy and protein intakes were satisfactory, intakes of vitamins and minerals were below standard. No serious student of nutrition has contradicted Orr's principal conclusion that between 1930 and 1935, 10 per cent of the population of Britain had insufficient money to purchase sufficient food for themselves; these people were underfed.

Poverty and public health by M'Gonigle and Kirby[6] records observations made at Stockton-on-Tees on social groups at the bottom of the economic scale, a large proportion of the wage-earners concerned being unemployed. In 1927 an unhealthy slum (Housewife Lane) was demolished and the population moved into a new housing estate. It was possible to keep separate figures for mortality rates for this population both before and after the move and to compare them with a control population remaining in a slum (Riverside) area. Table 54.1 shows that the move from the unhygienic slum into an apparently healthy environment did not result in an improvement in health, but was unexpectedly followed

Table 54.1 Mortality in Stockton-on-Tees (Standardised quinquennial death rate: deaths per 1000 population)

	Total for the borough	Housewife Lane population	Riverside population
1923–27	12	23 (in a slum)	26 (in a slum)
1928–32	12	34 (in a housing estate)	23 (in a slum)

by an increase in the death rate of the people above both their former level and the level of their neighbours who remained in the Riverside slum. The estate itself could not be blamed for the higher mortality, the houses being well constructed and possessing good sanitary arrangements. The deterioration in health was directly attributed to an increase in the rents in the new estate. This of necessity caused a corresponding reduction in the amount of money available for buying food. The amount of money spent on food fell and was much less than that spent by the controls in the slums. The benefits to health, which might have resulted from improved hygiene in the external environment, were more than neutralised by higher rents, which reduced the money available for the purchase of food.

These brief summaries of the main conclusions from the books by Orr, and M'Gonigle and Kirby show in outline the striking effect of poverty on health. It is important to remember that at this time the overall food supply of Great Britian was satisfactory. Estimates agree that the total available food, as retailed in the shops, was equivalent to 12.6 MJ (3000 kcal)/head daily which was ample for the people if it had been properly distributed.

The system of distribution was so unsound that 1 in 10 of the people were underfed; this is a major indictment of the economic structure of our society between the two world wars. Only when the imagination has grasped the full implications of this failure upon individual families and homes is it possible to appreciate the new quality of British society. In 1939 the emergency of war soon led to measures for food production and distribution that ensured for all but a tiny minority of the population sufficient food to meet physiological requirements. These measures are described on page 541.

Poverty and inequality in the UK 1960–80

In 1969 Townsend[3] organised a survey of 3260 households with 10 048 individuals, using a questionnaire 39 pages long, and his report has the title, *Poverty in the United Kingdom*. Poverty is defined in terms of relative deprivation: 'Individuals, families and groups in the population can be said to be in poverty when they lack the resources to obtain the type of diet, participate in the activities and have the living conditions and amenities which are customary, or at least widely encouraged or approved, in the societies to which they belong.' By this standard he found that 25.9 per cent of the population, or 14 million people, were living in poverty. There are no figures today indicating the number of people who are so poor that they cannot get sufficient food to eat. But the low incidence of patients suffering from primary undernutrition and primary deficiency diseases seen in clinics and hospitals suggests that they are numbered in thousands and not in millions as they were at the end of the last century. What Townsend has called poverty is utterly different from the poverty that afflicted millions of people in Europe and North America in the nineteenth century and afflicts hundreds of millions in the Third World today. Thus he confuses our history and, more important, he may obscure our sense of obligation and duty to help many other less fortunate countries.

Inequalities that have serious effects on health and especially on the health of children are present in the UK today.[7,8] The Black Report was written by a group commissioned by the DHSS with Sir Douglas Black, a president of the Royal College of Physicians as chairman and with Townsend as a member. The Government did not publish the report because they could not accept its financial recommendations and, after a delay, it was produced by a commercial publisher. The main conclusions of the report are based on analyses of mortality rates in relation to social class. In the three decades since 1950 mortality rates in general fell but the rates for the poorer classes remained markedly higher than those for the more prosperous and in some instances this difference was increased. 'If mortality rates of occupational class I (professional workers and members of their families) had applied to classes IV and V (partly skilled and unskilled manual workers and their families) during 1970–72, 74 000 lives of people aged under 75 would not have been lost. This estimate includes nearly 10 000 children.' The adverse effect of inequalities of social conditions and income on health in the UK today is now proven and well documented. The ways in which these inequalities operate are not so well established. The poor smoke more and use the health services less effectively than the more prosperous, but this accounts for only a part of the differences. There must be many other factors and inadequate or unsuitable diets may be one of these. The yearly surveys of *Household food consumption and expenditure*, published by the Ministry of Agriculture, Fisheries and Food, have not shown differences between the diets of the social classes that could explain the established differences in mortality rates. Much more investigation is needed and this will be very difficult. However, there is no doubt that inequalities persist in the UK that should not be acceptable to a civilised society, and the Black Report

has done a great service in establishing that these inequalities have serious adverse effects on health.

Poverty is an emotive word very loosely used by the press and politicians. Good health and diet are in the interests of all. Dietary inadequacy should be eliminated as far as possible and where this is due to inadequate income, assistance should be given. So long as poverty is defined by what people consider as an income necessary for a decent standard of living, it will never be eliminated. Today's luxury is tomorrow's necessity.

Income and the quality of diets

The nature of the foods eaten and the quality of diets is related to income. Figure 54.3 shows an analysis of the sources of dietary energy based on agricultural and trade statistics correlated with economic estimates of the value of gross domestic products per head. In all countries, rich and poor alike, protein provides just over 10 per cent of the dietary energy, but the proportion of animal origin rises with income. Whereas in the poorest countries carbohydrate provides over 75 per cent of the energy, in the richest the figure is only 50 per cent and nearly 20 per cent comes from sugar. As income rises, the consumption of cereals falls and of sugar rises. Whereas the poorest countries get little more than 10 per cent of their energy from fat, mostly as unsaturated vegetable fat, wealthy countries get 40 per cent. Neither of the two extremes is to be recommended dietetically. Even if there is enough to eat in the poorest countries, which is unlikely, the supplies of vitamins A and C are almost certainly insufficient and, if most of the protein comes from a single vegetable source, the supply of one or more amino acids is probably insufficient to meet the needs of growing children. The diets in the wealthiest countries are likely to contain saturated fatty acids and sucrose in amounts which predispose to atherosclerosis, dental caries and diabetes. Perhaps the countries with incomes in the middle of the scale feed best, but these figures represent national averages and in most countries the distribution of food is according to social class.

Lack of time

A secondary cause of inadequate nutrition may be lack of leisure. Proper nutrition demands time for the preparation of meals and for their consumption. The housewife who is doing a full day's work outside the home may lack time for shopping and for preparing meals. The increasing employment of women in industry in large towns in the tropics is an important contributory cause of malnutrition in young children. People who live far away from their place of work may leave home at an early hour without a proper breakfast. Children are often sent to school with a hastily prepared lunch of

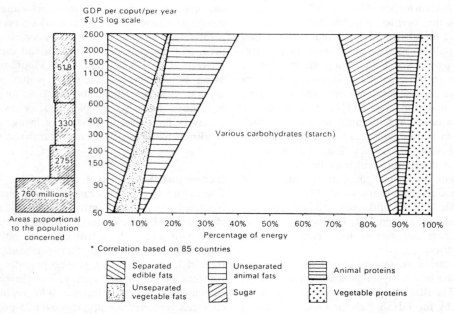

Fig. 54.3 Dietary energy derived from fats, carbohydrate and protein as percentage of total energy related to the incomes or gross domestic products (GDP) of countries. The figures in the shaded area show the population living in countries within each range of GDP[9]

poor nutritional quality. Many workers are still not provided with adequate breaks for their meals and suitable places for eating them. Restaurants and canteens may be so inadequately staffed that they are unable to provide meals in the time available to their patrons.

Ignorance

In most agricultural communities the people are usually adequately nourished provided the harvest has not failed, disease has not destroyed their livestock, the farms have not been plundered by soldiers or rapacious landlords and money lenders have not forced them to sell their crops. Experience of what constitutes a good diet is passed from one generation to another.

The situation is very different when a family moves into a city. Many customary foods are not available. New and strange foods are present in the markets and shops. The housewife may receive false or misleading information from advertisements and shopkeepers. Ignorance of the nutritional value of foods is widespread especially in the rapidly growing urban populations in developing countries. This is responsible for much nutritional disease especially in young children.

Important points on which education is frequently needed include proper methods of cooking vegetables, the nutritional value of fish, the deleterious effects of overmilled cereals, the value of vegetable gardens, and the special needs of children for milk, fruit juices and sunlight.

In prosperous countries ignorance leads to faulty habits, which certainly contribute to the onset of obesity and diabetes and probably to degenerative disorders. The need for nutritional education is discussed on page 530.

Religious customs

The effect of these on food habits may be important. In simple rural communities, all religions commemorate important events in the lives of saints and prophets; these and the ceremonies associated with marriage and death are celebrated either by feasts or fasts. The feasts often provide an excuse for the slaughter of an animal and the comsumption of much extra animal protein. A variety of other delicacies may be set aside for use on these occasions only and these may not be without hazard. For example, excessive consumption of pig-meat at feasts in Papua New Guinea leads to acute necrotic enteritis, well known locally as pig-bel.[10] Feasts are of value in supplementing a monotonous and inadequate day-to-day diet and in many communities dietary surveys, which omit such occasions, may be misleading. Fasts are generally fewer in number, and there is no evidence that an occasional day's fast ever did a healthy individual any harm. They may be of benefit to the richer members of community, but impair the health of people whose day-to-day food consumption is limited by inadequate supplies or low purchasing power. During Ramadan, which lasts for one lunar month in every year, many orthodox Muslims neither eat food nor drink water between sunrise and sundown. Even if the food intake during the hours of darkness is satisfactory, lack of sleep by night and lack of water by day make it difficult for a man to maintain working efficiency throughout a long and hot day, for four weeks, under these conditions. In Khartoum blood concentrations of uric acid and triglycerides rise during Ramadan.[11] Whatever the religious and spiritual significance of the fast may be, most people who have had to work with Muslims during Ramadan agree that it causes loss of stamina and working efficiency. In most Christian communities fasting is limited to replacing a meat dish by fish on Fridays and giving up one item of food in Lent. However, in Ethiopia there are over 100 fast days during the year, in which the intake of energy, protein and other nutrients falls in vulnerable groups.[12]

Religions also enforce many food taboos. Jews and Muslims are forbidden the flesh of the pig, but more important is Hindu prohibition of the consumption of beef and slaughter of cattle. In India the health of the cattle is the crux of the whole economic system. They plough the land, fertilise the soil, carry the crops to market, provide milk for the family and fuel for the hearth. A well-fed, healthy cattle population is a *sine qua non* of a well-fed and properous human community. The origin of the taboo on the slaughter of cattle is uncertain, but it was not a part of the Dravidian and earliest Hindu cultures. No doubt the prohibition arose as a practical expediency under certain acute local circumstances and thereafter received general sanction. A ban on slaughtering cattle might have little effect if abundant cattle fodder were available, enabling the community to pension off old animals. In modern India such conditions do not exist. The pressure on the land by both man and beast is great; sufficient food is at present grown for neither. It has been estimated that half of India's enormous number of cattle have no economic value. They neither provide milk nor pull the plough, but use land needed for the production of human food.

In tribal Africa,[13] and in Polynesia[14] many food taboos have been described which are often strict during pregnancy and lactation. These taboos may reduce the nutritional value of a mother's diet and so affect her health and that of her child. Jelliffe describes how religious customs in West Bengal may delay the onset of mixed feeding and so be a factor in the causation of protein-energy malnutrition. Irrational views and prejudices about food are not confined to undeveloped countries and food myths, fads and fallacies are held tenaciously in all communities.[15,16]

REFERENCES

1. Mayer J, Sidel W 1966 Crop destruction in South Vietnam. Christian Century 83: 829–32
2. Rowntree B S 1901 Poverty: a study of town life. Macmillan, London
3. Townsend P 1979 Poverty in the United Kingdom: a survey of household resources and standards of living. Penguin Books, London
4. Rowntree B S 1918 Poverty: a study of town life, new edn 1937. Longmans Green, London
5. Orr J B 1936 Food, health and income. Gollanz, London
6. M'Gonigle G M C, Kirby J 1936 Poverty and public health. Gollanz, London
7. Field F 1981 Inequality in Britain. Fontana, London
8. Townsend P, Davidson N (eds) 1982 Inequalities in health. The Black Report. Penguin Books, London
9. Périssé J, Sizaret F, François P 1969 The effect of income on the stricture of diet. FAO Nutr Newsletter 7: 1–9
10. Murrell T G C 1966 Some epidemiological features of pig-bel. Papua New Guinea Med J 9: 39–59
11. Gumaa K A, Mustafa K Y, Mahmoud N A, Gader A M A 1978 The effect of fasting in Ramadam. I: Serum uric acid and lipid concentrations. Br J Nutr 40: 573–81
12. Knutson K E, Selinus R 1970 Fasting in Ethiopia: an anthropological and social study. Am J Clin Nutr 23: 956–69
13. Trant H 1954 Food taboos in East Africa. Lancet 2: 703–5
14. Jelliffe E F P, Jelliffe D A 1964 Children in ancient Polynesian Hawaii Clin Pediatr (Phila)3: 604–13
15. Jelliffe D A 1967 Parallel food classifications in developing and industrial countries. Am J Clin Nutr 20: 279–81
16. Pyke M 1970 The development of food myths. In: Food cultism and nutritional quackery. Symposia of the Swedish Nutrition Foundation no. 8, p 22–9

55

Assessment and Surveillance

Assessment of the nutritional status of a hospital patient has been discussed in Chapter 52. Four methods are used: (1) the dietary history, (2) clinical examination, (3) physical measurements and (4) biochemical and other laboratory tests. The same four methods are used in community medicine for the study of the nutritional status of large numbers of people. Assessments have been made by generations of doctors in the school medicine service to identify children needing dietary supplements, and in the armed services at recruiting depots to reject those unfit for enlistment. Today most assessments are made to identify sections of a community at increased risk of nutritional disorders with a view to introducing specific measures to reduce such risks. Such measures form the nutritional component of ‘public health policies of all governments in rich and poor countries alike.

Nutrition policies, whether for a small local community or a whole country, require continuing supervision to see that they are being carried out effectively and also because changes in availability of food and in dietary habits may lead to either new measures being required and others being no longer necessary. Such continuous assessment is now known as surveillance. This term has come into wide use since 1976, following publication of a United Nations report.[1] Whereas nutritional assessment uses the methods of the medical sciences only, nutritional surveillance uses in addition a great variety of sources of information, such as economics (wages and international trade), sociology, agriculture and metereology. Forecasts can then be made of future changes in food supplies.

CLINICAL SURVEYS

These usually consist of three parts: (1) physical examination, (2) making anthropometric measurements and (3) collecting samples of blood or urine for laboratory examination. A form or card, on which all the observations on each subject of the survey is recorded, is required. This form should have space for some demo-

graphic, social and economic data, for example, age, sex, family size, social class, literacy, age of leaving school, family income, size of house, water supply, etc. The nature and number of items on a form is based on a preliminary assessment of what are likely to be relevant and significant findings.

PHYSICAL EXAMINATION

Table 55.1 gives a classified list of signs used in nutrition surveys. Published by WHO and designed as an international reference, it provides a ‘shopping list’ from which individual items can be chosen for observation and recording of their presence or absence. The chosen list is likely to be much longer for a survey of a poor community in the tropics, where physical signs of vitamin deficiencies are common, than for one of a relatively prosperous community in Europe or North America. In some areas, it is relevant to record evidence of infectious disease, for example splenomegaly as evidence of malaria and obvious signs or a history of schistosomiasis, leprosy and onchoceriasis. Although desirable, it is not necessary for the physical examination to be done by a medically qualified doctor; indeed this is often impractical. After some instruction a nurse or a medical auxiliary can carry it out competently.

Sampling. A trap into which an inexperienced team can fall in an unfamiliar place is to examine a sample of the people who are accessible, e.g. those who crowd round when the team arrives in its truck. These are usually teenage boys and middle-aged men, the section of the community least likely to be malnourished. Sickly babies, pregnant women and frail old people are not apparent at first. But the survey will be of little value unless the team establishes sufficient rapport with the people to be allowed to examine its womenfolk and infants.

In times of severe food shortage the clinical state of those walking about in the streets may be no guide to the real situation. Those weak with undernutrition may be unable to leave their homes. This source of error

Table 55.1 Classified list of signs used in nutrition surveys (modified from Jelliffe)[2]

	Group 1* Signs known to be of value in nutrition surveys	Group 2† Signs that need further investigation	Group 3‡ Some signs not related to nutrition
Hair	Lack of lustre Thinness and sparseness Straightness (in Negroes) Dyspigmentation Flag sign Easy pluckability		Alopecia Artificial discoloration
Face	Diffuse depigmentation Nasolabial dyssebacea Moon-face	Malar and supraorbital pigmentation	Acne vulgaris Acne rosacea Chloasma
Eyes	Pale conjunctiva Bitôt's spots Conjunctival xerosis Corneal xerosis Keratomalacia Angular palpebritis	Conjunctival injection Conjunctival and scleral pigmentation Corneal vascularisation Circumcorneal injection Corneal opacities and scars	Follicular conjunctivitis Blepharitis Pingueculae Pterygium Pannus
Lips	Angular stomatitis Angular scars Cheilosis	Chronic depigmentation of lower lip	Chapping from exposure to harsh climates
Tongue	Abnormally smooth or red Oedema Atropic papillae	Hyperaemic and hypertrophic papillae Fissures Geographic tongue Pigmented tongue	Aphthous ulcer Leucoplakia
Teeth	Mottled enamel	Caries Attrition Enamel hypoplasia Enamel erosion	Malocclusion
Gums	Spongy, bleeding gums	Recession of gum	Pyorrhoea
Glands	Thyroid enlargement Parotid enlargement	Gynaecomastia	Allergic or inflammatory enlargement of thyroid or parotid
Skin	Xerosis Follicular hyperkeratosis Petechiae Pellagrous dermatosis Flaky-paint dermatosis Scrotal and vulval dermatitis	Mosaic dermatosis Thickening and pigmenta- tion of pressure points Intertriginous lesions	Ichthyosis Acneiform eruptions Miliaria Epidermophytoses Sunburn Onchocercal dermatosis
Nails	Koilonychia	Brittle, ridged nails	
Subcutaneous tissue	Odema Amount of subcutaneous fat		
Skeletal system	Craniotabes Frontal and parietal bossing Epiphyseal enlargement (tender or painless) Beading of ribs Persistently open anterior fontanelle Deformities of thorax		Funnel chest
Muscles and nervous system	Muscle wasting Motor weakness Sensory loss Loss of ankle and knee jerks Loss of position sense Loss of vibration sense Calf tenderness	Winged scapulae Condition of ocular fundus	

Table 55.1 (Cont'd overleaf)

	Group 1* Signs known to be of value in nutrition surveys	Group 2† Signs that need further investigation	Group 3‡ Some signs not related to nutrition
Gastrointestinal	Hepatomegaly		Splenomegaly
Cardiovascular	Cardiac enlargement Tachycardia	Blood pressure	
Psychological	Listlessness and apathy Mental confusion		

* Group 1   *Signs that are considered to be of value in nutritional assessment*, as, according to present evidence, they indicate with considerable probability deficiency of one or more nurients in the tissues in the recent past.

† Group 2   *Signs that need further investigation*, but in whose causation malnutrition, sometimes of a chronic nature, may play some part, together with other factors. They are found more commonly in people with low standards of living than among more privileged groups.

‡ Group 3   *Signs not related to nutrition*, according to present knowledge, but which, in some instances, have to be differentiated from signs of known nutritional value (Group 1).

misled some of those who accompanied the liberating armies into Holland in 1945 into underestimating the extent of the famine. The error of overlooking those who are housebound is easily made, especially in surveys in the Third World today.

Limitations. Clinical examination for signs of malnutrition is relatively cheap and easy to organise. It does not require elaborate apparatus and reagents. However, there are important limitations. Only a few of the signs listed in Table 55.1 are pathognomonic of a nutritional disorder. Changes in the conjunctiva, lips and skin can be caused by non-nutritional factors like cold, dryness, heat, irritation, infections, smoke, dust, pressure and insect bites. Even if a sign like angular stomatitis can be established as of nutritional origin there are several deficiencies that can cause it (Chap 37). These clinical signs have diminishing frequency as the state of nutrition improves. In a well-nourished community signs of malnutrition are infrequent and so more easily overlooked or misinterpreted. It is in such communities that biochemical tests are of special value.

ANTHROMETRY

HEIGHT AND WEIGHT

These simple measurements are a means of assessing growth of children and of detecting moderate to severe undernutrition and obesity in adults. For infants, children and adolescents heights and weights related to age are given in Figures 55.1 and 55.2. They are recent WHO recommendations,[3] based mainly on measurements of healthy children in Boston[4] which differ little from similar measurements in Edinburgh[5] and London.[6] WHO recommends their worldwide use for measuring nutritional status.

For adults acceptable weights for height are given in Table 55.2. This table is now recommended for clinical use by both USA and UK authorities. It is preferred to the Life Insurance Company tables,[7] widely used for many years, because it does not require an arbitrary assessment of the size of the body frame.

There can be no doubt that these standards are reliable for populations of Caucasian origin; there is also no evidence that they are not reliable for the vast majority of African and Asian people. Besides food intake, other environmental factors associated with poor hygiene may determine height and weight. In individuals the genetic constitution fixes the potential for growth. However, in group surveys the effect of racial and ethnic differences is small compared to that of the environment.[8,9] Hence the standards are applicable internationally with very few exceptions.

There are difficulties involved in the use of such a simple piece of apparatus as a weighing machine. Every balance needs regular checking and, if necessary, recalibration. Lever balances made by firms of repute are reliable and a yearly check is all that is necessary. Spring balances are unreliable and, if used regularly, need repeated checks. Indeed they cannot be recommended for accurate work. It is seldom practical to weigh people naked; a correction is usually needed for the articles of clothing worn. They may vary greatly from season to season and according to fashion. Men usually wear heavier underclothing than women. A rough estimate of a man's clothes in Britain without shoes or jacket is about 2.5 kg. Women's clothes usually weigh about 1.5 kg. In comparing individual weights with standards, it is important to make certain that the standards were obtained in the subjects wearing comparable clothing.

Height should be measured against a flat, vertical surface and the subject must stand as upright as possible on firm level ground without raising the heels from the ground. A sliding headpiece is necessary for accurate work. Infants and very young children are measured

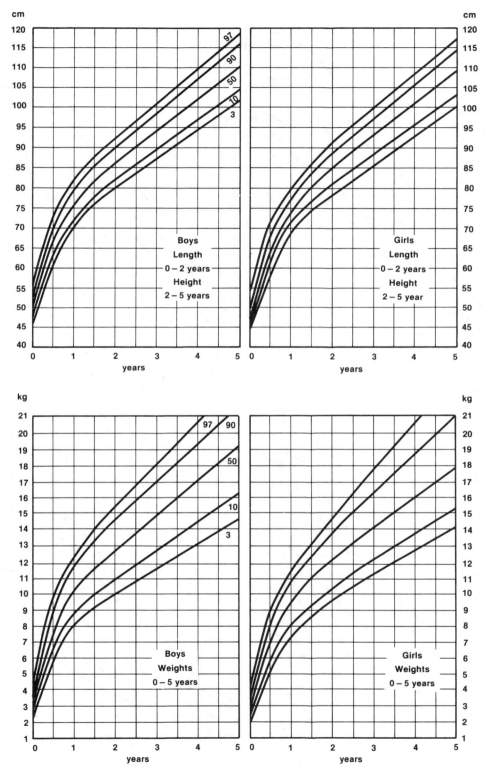

Fig. 55.1 Standard heights and weights of boys and girls 0–5 years old

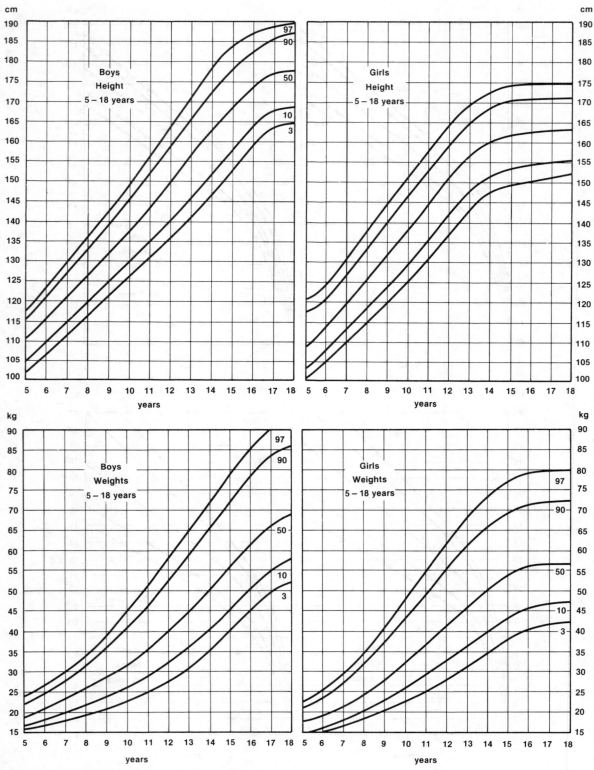

Fig. 55.2 Standard heights and weights of boys and girls 5–18 years old

Table 55.2 Acceptable weights as recommend‌‍ Royal College of Physicians, 1983

Height without shoes (m)	MEN Weight without clothes (kg) Acceptable average	Acceptable weight range	
1.45			
1.48			
1.50			
1.52			
1.54			
1.56			
1.58	55.8	51–?	
1.60	57.6	52–	
1.62	58.6	5?	
1.64	59.6	⸚	
1.66	60.6		
1.68	61.7		
1.70	63.5		
1.72	65.0	59–?⸱	
1.74	66.5	60–75	
1.76	68.0	62–77	
1.78	69.4	64–79	95
1.80	71.0	65–80	96
1.82	72.6	66–82	98
1.84	74.2	67–84	101
1.86	75.8	69–86	103
1.88	77.6	71–88	106
1.90	79.3	73–90	108
1.92	81.0	75–93	112

522 HUMAN NUTRITION AND DIETETICS

Table 55.3 Percentiles of upper arm circumfere‍‌ Survey 1 of 1971 to 1974. (Modified from Fris‍‌

Males

Arm circumference (mm)

Age group	5	10	25
1–1.9	142	146	150
2–2.9	141	145	153
3–3.9	150	153	160
4–4.9	149	154	16‍
5–5.9	153	160	
6–6.9	155	159	
7–7.9	162	167	
8–8.9	162	170	
9–9.9	175	17‍	
10–10.9	181		
11–11.9	186		
12–12.9	193		
13–13.9	194		
14–14.9	22‍		
15–15.9			
16–16.9			
17–17.9			
18–18.‍			
19–2‍			
25–3‍			
35–‍			

lying down, using a sliding head rack. In older children and adults the measurement is subject to considerable daily variation, and is usually greater in the morning than in the afternoon due to effects arising from fatigue and faulty posture. For these reasons measurements of recumbent length are better, especially for children up to 2 years of age. Over the range 110–180 cm (42–71 in) recumbent length exceeds height by an average of 0.5 cm (0.20 in) for boys and 1.1 cm (0.42 in) for girls.

In children it is necessary to record age accurately. In some parts of the world, children and their parents have no recollection of their age. There is no easy way round this difficulty but weight for height ratios are useful.[10]

As in all other methods of nutritional assessment accurate sampling is necessary. Most children attend schools and it is usually easy to get a fair sample of the child population. But it is always difficult to get a random sample of an adult population. For instance during the food shortages in some central European cities after World War II, the occupying military authorities thought that a regular sample of the weights of the civilian population would provide an index of the adequacy of civilian food supplies and thus be a measure of the success of food policies. In this they were probably right. But they proceeded to station a sergeant and a military orderly with a weighing machine at vantage points in the cities with instruction to weigh every tenth passer-by. These records, on examination, were found to produce data heavily biased numerically in favour of the female sex and the age group 15 to 25 years.

MIDARM CIRCUMFERENCE AND TRICEPS SKINFOLD THICKNESS

These two measurements, now commonly used in assessment both in hospital and public health practice, are easy to make. The first reflects muscle mass and the second body fat. As there are no international standards, local ones are used. These are often modified from measurements made on large numbers of US citizens (Tables 55.3 and 4). It can safely be said that a midarm circumference at or below the 10th percentile indicates significant underdevelopment or wasting of muscle, and that a triceps skinfold at or above the 90th percentile indicates obesity.

Midarm circumference, of course, depends on the amount of fat and bone, as well as muscle, in the arms. Attempts have been made to allow for these, so as to get a more precise index of muscle mass.[12] The value of this is doubtful; the two measurements can provide only crude assessments, but these are useful if their obvio‍ limitations are recognised.

Midarm circumference is usually measured ‍

Age group	Males 50	75	90	95	Females 5	10	25	50	75	90	95
	159	170	176	183	138	142	148	156	164	172	177
	162	170	178	185	142	145	152	160	167	176	184
	167	175	184	190	143	150	158	167	175	183	189
	171	180	186	192	149	154	160	169	177	184	191
	175	185	195	204	153	157	165	175	185	203	211
	179	188	209	228	156	162	170	176	187	204	211
	187	201	223	230	164	167	174	183	199	216	231
	190	202	220	245	168	172	183	195	214	247	261
	200	217	249	257	178	182	194	211	224	251	260
	210	231	262	274	174	182	193	210	228	251	265
	202	223	244	261	280	185	194	208	224	248	276	303
	214	232	254	282	303	194	203	216	237	256	282	294
	228	247	263	286	301	202	211	223	243	271	301	338
	237	253	283	303	322	214	223	237	252	272	304	322
	229	244	264	284	311	320	208	221	239	254	279	300	322
	248	262	278	303	324	343	218	224	241	258	283	318	334
	253	267	285	308	336	347	220	227	241	264	295	324	350
	260	276	297	321	353	379	222	227	241	258	281	312	325
.9	262	272	288	308	331	355	372	221	230	247	265	290	319	345
54.9	271	282	300	319	342	362	375	233	240	256	277	304	342	368
-44.9	278	287	305	326	345	363	374	241	251	267	290	317	356	378
5-54.9	267	281	301	322	342	362	376	242	256	274	299	328	362	384
55-64.9	258	273	296	317	336	355	369	243	257	280	303	335	367	385
65-74.9	248	263	285	307	325	344	355	240	252	274	299	326	356	373

Table 55.4 Percentiles for triceps skinfold for whites of the United States Health and Nutrition Examination Survey 1 of 1971 to 1974. (Modified from Frisancho)[11]

Age group	Males Triceps skinfold percentiles (mm²) 5	10	25	50	75	90	95	Females 5	10	25	50	75	90	95
1–1.9	6	7	8	10	12	14	16	6	7	8	10	12	14	16
2–2.9	6	7	8	10	12	14	15	6	8	9	10	12	15	16
3–3.9	6	7	8	10	11	14	15	7	8	9	11	12	14	15
4–4.9	6	6	8	9	11	12	14	7	8	8	10	12	14	16
5–5.9	6	6	8	9	11	14	15	6	7	8	10	12	15	18
6–6.9	5	6	7	8	10	13	16	6	6	8	10	12	14	16
7–7.9	5	6	7	9	12	15	17	6	7	9	11	13	16	18
8–8.9	5	6	7	8	10	13	16	6	8	9	12	15	18	24
9–9.9	6	6	7	10	13	17	18	8	8	10	13	16	20	22
10–10.9	6	6	8	10	14	18	21	7	8	10	12	17	23	27
11–11.9	6	6	8	11	16	20	24	7	8	10	13	18	24	28
12–12.9	6	6	8	11	14	22	28	8	9	11	14	18	23	27
13–13.9	5	5	7	10	14	22	26	8	8	12	15	21	26	30
14–14.9	4	5	7	9	14	21	24	9	10	13	16	21	26	28
15–15.9	4	5	6	8	-11	18	24	8	10	12	17	21	25	32
16–16.9	4	5	6	8	12	16	22	10	12	15	18	22	26	31
17–17.9	5	5	6	8	12	16	19	10	12	13	19	24	30	37
18–18.9	4	5	6	9	13	20	24	10	12	15	18	22	26	30
19–24.9	4	5	7	10	15	20	22	10	11	14	18	24	30	34
25–34.9	5	6	8	12	16	20	24	10	12	16	21	27	34	37
35–44.9	5	6	8	12	16	20	23	12	14	18	23	29	35	38
45–54.9	6	6	8	12	15	20	25	12	16	20	25	30	36	40
55–64.9	5	6	8	11	14	19	22	12	16	20	25	31	36	38
65–74.9	4	6	8	11	15	19	22	12	14	18	24	29	34	36

spring tape at a point midway between the tip of the acromion and the ulnar process with the arm hanging vertically and the forearm supinated. In children from 1 to 5 years of age, strips of cord has been used with red, yellow and green bands marked on them in distances of 70–125, 125–135 and 135–175 mm respectively from a black starting mark.[13] These colours then represent definite malnutrition, possible mild malnutrition and normality. They at once alert the observer, as traffic lights alert a motorist. The use of skinfold calipers is described on p. 270.

Other anthropometric methods

Much ingenuity has been expended on attempts to construct formulae based on anthropometric measurements which provide an index of nutritional status. Early editions of this book gave references to several indices or formulae which had been tried out and, under certain circumstances, had proved useful as an aid to nutritional diagnosis. In the hands of the enthusiastic inventors, they provided useful information, but others found them less satisfactory and they are now seldom used. The devising of anthropometric formulae and the testing of their usefulness is an occupation that has fascinated many able minds. If the results have proved disappointing, this does not mean that the problem is insoluble — only that it is very difficult.

LABORATORY EXAMINATIONS

Two biochemical measurements are much used in nutritional assessments. The first is plasma albumin; the concentrations of this and other plasma proteins in relation to protein deficiency are discussed in Chapter 52. The second is blood haemoglobin as a measure of anaemia; lower limits of normality are given in Chapter 47. Tests used for detecting deficiencies of individual

Table 55.5 Biochemical methods for assessing nutritional status

| Nutrient | Principal methods | | Supplementary methods |
	Indicating reduced intake	Indicating impaired function (IF) or cell depletion (CD)	
Vitamin A	Plasma retinol Plasma carotene		
Thiamin	Urinary thiamin	RBC transketolase and TPP effect (IF)	Plasma pyruvate and lactate
Riboflavin	Urinary riboflavin	RBC glutathione reductase and FAD effect (IF)	RBC riboflavin
Nicotinamide	Urinary N'-methylnicotinamide and 2-pyridone		Fasting plasma free tryptophan
Pyridoxine	Urinary 4-pyridoxic acid	RBC glutamic oxalacetic transaminase and PP effect (IF)	Urinary xanthurenic aicd after tryptophan load
Folic acid	Plasma folate (*Lactobacillus casei*)	RBC folate (CD) Haemoglobin, PCV and smear (IF)	Bone marrow morphology
Vitamin B12	Plasma vitamin B12 (*Euglena gracilis*)	Haemoglobin PCV and smear (IF)	Schilling test. Bone marrow morphology
Ascorbic acid	Plasma ascorbic acid	Leucocyte ascorbic acid (CD)	Urinary ascorbic acid
Vitamin D	Plasma 25-hydroxycholecalciferol	Plasma alkaline phosphatase (IF)	Plasma calcium and inorganic phosphorus
Vitamin E	Plasma tocopherol	RBC haemolysis with H_2O_2 *in vivo*	
Vitamin K		Plasma prothrombin (IF)	
Sodium	Urinary sodium	Plasma sodium	
Potassium		Plasma potassium	
Iron	Plasma iron and TIBC	Haemoglobin, PCV and smear	Bone marrow morphology and stainable iron
Calcium		Plasma calcium	
Iodine	Urinary iodine	Plasma thyroxine and T_3	

Table 55.6 Plasma concentrations and urinary outputs which may be useful in assessing the nutritional state of a patient. Values below those given in the table suggest an inadequate intake or a failure of absorption or an increased requirement. (Mainly from Sanstead et al)[15]

Plasma; all values/litres		Urine; all values/g urinary creatinine	
Albumin	35 g	Iodine	50 μg
Iron	700 μg	N'-Methylnicotinamide	1.6 μg
Retinol	200 μg	Riboflavin	80 μg
Carotene	800 μg	Thiamin	66 μg
25-OH vitamin D	3.5 μg		
Ascorbic acid	3 μg	*In children under six years*	
Vitamin B12	70 μg	Riboflavin	300 μg
Folic acid	7 μg	Thiamin	120 μg

vitamins and nutrients are listed in Table 55.5. In communities where clinical evidence of frank deficiency disease is unusual, these tests by demonstrating a low reserve of a nutrient in the tissues can show an increased risk of a deficiency disease arising in the event of a deterioration of the diet. Table 55.6 gives some figures below which such risks are likely to be present. A full account of methods and of interpretation is given in a book by Sauberlich and his colleagues.[14]

Some of these tests are not suitable for use in the field. It is seldom practical to try to collect a 24-hour sample of urine, but analyses of spot samples can be useful when related to excretion of creatinine.

Samples of urine and blood can be collected by field workers but analyses have to be carried out in a distant laboratory. They have to be transported and stored in a manner which prevents deterioration. This requires planning and discussion between field workers and laboratory staff before the beginning of a survey. Preliminary trial runs are necessary. Packaging is important, as well as facilities for refrigeration, when samples are sent by commercial transport.

DIETARY SURVEYS

Quantitative information about the food eaten by a people or a community, if compared with physiological standards of human needs, has enabled assessments of nutrition to be made that have proved both useful and practical. Data can be collected covering a whole nation, from families of different economic classes or from individuals of special age groups or occupations. Each type of survey can provide valuable information. For sound government planning, nationwide data covering all socioeconomic and age groups are required. In all cases the technique demands care and is time-consuming and exacting. First, some considerations common to all dietary studies require discussion.

A comparison can be made between the amounts of food consumed and a chosen physiological standard only after the data collected have been converted into quantities of energy, carbohydrate, protein, fat, minerals and vitamins. This requires the use of food tables and here errors are inevitably introduced (Chap. 16).

Another difficulty is to reach agreement on the physiological or other standards with which to compare the results of dietary surveys. If repeated dietary surveys are carried out systematically in a country, it is possible to tell whether the quantity or quality of the food consumed is improving or declining. This information is often more useful than a comparison with a physiological standard, which must always be arbitrary.

FAMILY SURVEYS

Most surveys have the family as the basic unit. A trained investigator with the co-operation of the housewife attempts to measure all the food consumed by a family over a period of time, usually a week. A log-book is kept for each family. The investigator visits the housewife at the start of the survey and weighs all the food in her stores. Each day, either the investigator or the housewife weighs all the food purchased and enters this in the log-book. The food wasted is also weighed and entered. At the end of the survey period all food remaining in the store is weighed. Thus all the food eaten in the household is recorded. The age, sex and occupation of members are also noted. The number of visitors eating occasional meals and number of meals eaten outside the home by members of the family are also noted and arbitrary corrections made for them. Measured intakes of nutrients can then be compared with recommended standards.

The family survey is useful for determining the food consumed by different economic and social groups. Experience has shown that it is usually sufficient to survey between 20 and 30 families in a group. As far as possible the families should be chosen by random selection, and every effort should be made to get a representative sample. Success depends on the tact and social skill of the organisers and investigators. Some housewives never co-operate, but with care it should be possible to get the goodwill and help of at least four out of five.

A survey should cover four to seven days and include the weekend when in most countries families change their daily dietary habits. To prolong a survey more than a week is irksome to the housewife.

In some countries there are marked seasonal variations in food intake and hence it may be necessary to repeat surveys at different times of the year. This is less necessary in towns than in country districts, for in the former the diet often changes little throughout the year.

There are two major sources of error in a family survey. The housewife may, through ignorance or carelessness, fail to record or report all her purchases. Alternatively the housewife may put on a show for the survey and feed her family better than usual. With good investigators the second error is the more probable and so surveys tend to overestimate normal consumption. A skilful investigator can often check up on these points and the record of any unreliable housewife should be discarded.

A valuable adjunct to a family dietary survey is often provided by an enquiry into the housewife's budget and the amount of money that she has available to spend on food. A comparison between this and local food prices serves as a check on the dietary assessment and sometimes provides clear evidence that the family concerned cannot possibly afford to purchase an adequate diet.

Institutional surveys are carried out on similar lines and usually are relatively easy.

An inherent drawback to family surveys is that no information is provided about how the food is distributed within the family. It does not distinguish between the food consumed by the housewife, the breadwinner, the children and other dependants.

INDIVIDUAL SURVEYS

The principle is the same as that of family surveys. The selected individuals, assisted and supervised by investigators, weigh and measure everything consumed at each meal. This is a much more exacting task than a family survey, for a great deal of co-operation and a modest degree of intelligence on the part of the subject is needed. Nevertheless, many excellent individual surveys have been undertaken. Children of different age groups, old people, miners, soldiers, housewives and people in various occupations have been studied. A properly conducted series of individual dietary surveys gives a good assessment of nutritional status. However, it should never be assumed that an individual is deficient in a nutrient on the basis of a short dietary study. Clinical and biochemical examination are required to confirm any suspicions raised by the intake data.

Short-cut methods of estimating dietary intake by recall have been devised. The subject is asked either what he ate the day before or what he eats on a typical day. These methods are subject to many inaccuracies but are useful to compare different groups and, when repeated, may indicate important trends. The techniques of making individual dietary surveys are described by Marr[16] and practical details of planning by Black.[17]

NATIONAL SURVEYS

United Kingdom. The National Food Survey Committee has published reports[18] since 1940 that record food consumption in about 8000 households each year. The sample is selected to be representative of the different regions of the country and of families of different size and with different incomes. It does not record the increasing amounts of food eaten outside the home.

United States. The Federal Government organised in 1967 a National Nutrition Survey 'to determine the prevalence of malnutrition and related health problems among low income populations in the United States'. Some 40 000 individuals were examined in 10 states and the sample was weighted to include more of the age, income and ethnic groups believed to be at risk of malnutrition. Clinical examination revealed few signs of malnutrition. Anthropometry showed that black children were in general taller than white children. Sizable minorities of children and teenagers were underweight and many adults were obese. The most common positive findings were in the laboratory tests, especially evidence of low haemoglobin and low plasma vitamin A; some groups showed biochemical evidence of low intakes of protein, riboflavin and vitamin C. The findings are set out in a 940-page report extending to five books.[19] This is by far the largest nutrition survey ever carried out.

Canada. Dietary, biochemical and anthropometric data were obtained in 1970–72 on 19 000 people, a representative sample of all the different groups in the country.[20] The commonest type of malnutrition appeared to be iron deficiency. There was also biochemical evidence of low folate reserves; some cases of goitre and scurvy were found, especially in Eskimos; biochemical evidence of insufficient riboflavin was unusual; obesity and high plasma cholesterol concentrations were common.

The Netherlands. A novel study of a national diet uses a 'market basket' approach.[21] During a period of two years, every two months 126 different items of food were purchased. These were then put into 12 food groups (cereal products, dairy products, etc.) in amounts based on a study of the diet of male adolescents — the most voracious eaters. Samples of of each group were then homogenised and analysed. The results indicate that intakes of eight food additives were each far below the maximum acceptable. Intakes of fat and cholesterol were above and of dietary fibre and linoleic and linolenic acid below those advised by the Dutch Bureau for Nutrition Education.

DEMOGRAPHY

Most countries keep at least some vital statistics and from them it is usually possible to draw certain inferences about the nutrition of the people. The most used for this purpose has been the **infant mortality rate** (the number of babies dying in the first year of life per 1000 live births). In the period 1901–05 the rate for Scotland was 120 and most of the other countries had similar or even higher rates at that time. Since then there has been a fall in most countries, partly attributable to improvements in infant feeding. However, there are still parts of the world where rates range from 75 to 150. In most prosperous countries the rate lies between 10 and 20 and is determined by the quality of the obstetric and paediatric services and not by nutrition.

It has been suggested that the **perinatal mortality rate** (deaths of infants under 1 month and stillbirths per 1000 total births) may give an index of maternal nutrition. Many factors determine survival or death just before and after birth, eg. the nutritional status of the mother, the genetic or constitutional make-up of both mother and child, the degree of exposure to infections and the standard of medical care available. Baird's analysis of trends in perinatal mortality in Britain is now a classic.[22] He concluded that the wartime fall in the rates was due to the special supplementary rations which pregnant women received.

The manifestations and effects of malnutrition are well known to be severe in toddlers (children aged 1 to 4 years). Whereas in Europe and North America the death rate in this age group is usually around 1 per 1000,

in many poor countries the figure is over 20. It may even rise to 100 and then only half the children born may survive to reach the age of 5 years. Although death certificates may record gastroenteritis or respiratory infections, malnutrition contributes to many of the deaths. Thus while infant mortality rates in underdeveloped countries are five to 10 times those of industrial countries, **toddler (1 to 4 years) mortality rates** are up to 50 times as great.

If in any community the perinatal, infant and toddler mortality rates are all falling, then it can be inferred that the general level of nutrition of the people is improving. On the other hand, a rise in any one of these rates should suggest the possibility that there has been a serious decline in standards of child care and probably in nutrition.

In times of food scarcity, daily, weekly and monthly crude death rates may give valuable information about changes from conditions of hardship to conditions in famine. During World War II the Dutch had four years of food shortage and scarcity. These were very unpleasant conditions but they did not constitute a major hazard to health. They were followed from December 1944 to April 1945 by five months of real famine. Table 55.7 shows the effect of these on crude death-rates in some of the principal cities of Holland. In Amsterdam, Rotterdam and the Hague during the worst week of the famine, crude death-rates of about 40 per 1000 (calculated on a yearly basis) were recorded. Such figures are useful to famine administrators in gauging the extent of the disaster and the success of relief measures.

Had similar crude death-rates had been available from rural Bengal early in 1943, the extent of the famine there would have been realised sooner, relief organisations would have started earlier and the mortality figure of 1.5 million from starvation might have been much less.

SURVEILLANCE

Surveillance is a new and fashionable word amongst nutritionists but it has a long history in medicine. It would probably have been used in the discussions in

Table 55.7 Number of deaths in four cities in Western Holland[23]

City	Population	Number of deaths in the first 6 months of			Number of deaths per 1000 inhabitants calculated as mortality in 1 year		
		1939	1944	1945	1939	1944	1945
Amsterdam	800 000	3655	4393	9735	9.2	11.3	25.2
Rotterdam	640 000	2616	3260	7827	8.5	10.7	25.8
The Hague	520 000	2419	2940	6458	9.7	13.0	28.7
Utrecht	170 000	776	1120	2065	9.3	13.0	24.3

Venice in the fourteenth century that led to the quarantine laws for ships as a protection against plague, and in Paris in 1851 at the *Conférence Sanitaire Internationale*, assembled to suggest measures against the threat of cholera. This was the first international health conference and the seed from which the World Health Organisation has grown.[24] WHO has a section of communicable diseases that collects and scrutinises data on all aspects of the occurrence and spread of infectious diseases that are pertinent to effect control. Such data includes morbidity and mortality rates, field investigations of epidemics, isolation of infective agents and the supply and use of vaccines and other immunising agents. Reports are distributed widely to local, national and other international bodies concerned in the public health services.

The first WHO committee to consider nutritional surveillance met in 1975 and its report sets out objectives and discusses methods.[1] Surveillance is a system that is aimed at improving the food supply of people so as to prevent malnutrition. The people may be the whole population of a country or region or the population of only a small minority group. The system is ongoing with its parts closely related (Fig. 55.3) and the stages have to be planned together. It is useless to collect data that cannot be processed and interpreted in a meaningful way. Both planning and responses usually depend on government action and it is futile to begin when the Government is unlikely to act. In general, better nutrition and social equity go together and many élitist governments pay no more than lip service to social equity. Education of public opinion and of government is then needed before starting to plan a system of surveillance.

Small surveillance programmes which may be concerned with only a single nutrient and a minority group of the population are relatively easy and often successful. An example is the study since 1950 of the prevalence of rickets and osteomalacia in the Asian

Table 55.8 Factors affecting the food supply of two different types of communities (WHO)[1]

SETTLED SUBSISTENCE FARMING

Ecology
Meteorology: rainfall, water availability periods
Land: cultivable capacity
Demography: cultivable area per family member (nutritional density)

Resources and production
Cultivation requirements: seed, draft animals, equipment
Crop progress, predicted yield, crop production
Food, stocks and losses
Fuel

Consumption
Food consumption, pattern of food choice, household distribution

MARKET ECONOMY

Ecology
Meteorology: rainfall
Land: patterns of land utilization (cash versus food crop)
Demography: rural/urban division

Resources and production
Food stocks, imports and exports
Food losses
Price of inputs
Fuel

Income and consumption
Market data: selling prices for produce, buying prices for food (especially staples)
Demand: employment, income
Cost-of-living
Income and price-elasticity
Food consumption, pattern of food choice, household distribution

community of Glasgow (Chap. 32). Larger studies are more difficult. The food supply of a whole community depends on many factors not normally the concern of the health services. Table 55.8 lists such factors for two very different populations.

A contemporary review of nutritional surveillance[25] discusses the methodology and emphasises the many practical difficulties. There are as yet very few examples of programmes that have been carried out effectively in large communities. However we can end this chapter on a more hopeful note.

FAO global information and early warning system for food and agriculture[26]

The world food crisis at the beginning of the 1970s made governments, international organisations and the general public feel the necessity for continuous information on prospects for the foods and provisions indispensable for human survival. FAO responded in 1974 by creating a worldwide system of information and rapid alert on food and agriculture. The system has been in operation since

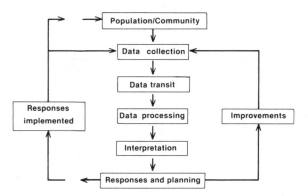

Fig. 55.3 Design for a system of national surveillance. (WHO)[1]

1975 and over 100 countries participate in its activities. It surveys continuously the changing situation and the prospects for food supplies. On numerous occasions, notably in Africa in 1980, it has been an essential element in the security of a country's food supply. The system has two objectives:

1. to survey continuously the supply of and demand for foodstuffs and fertilisers in order to aid governments to take appropriate and timely action.
2. to identify countries or regions where grave deficiencies in food are imminent, and to evaluate eventual needs for urgent food aid.

Over 100 countries provide information and have access to the analyses and forecasts sent out by the system. The worldwide demand for and supply of the following products are monitored: rice, wheat and other cereals, oil seeds, fats, milk, meat, sugar, beans etc., also fodder and fertilisers. Estimates and forecasts of production and consumption and of stocks and export needs are made and also of disposable funds, pledges and despatches of food aid.

Special alerts are given whenever the situation in a country of region is at risk of deteriorating. Donors who assist the Sahel of sub-Saharan Africa are informed every three weeks of the state of affairs in those countries during the rainy or 'hungry season'. Similarly in Asia during the monsoon constant monitoring is carried out. The system has proved effective. In 21 out of 23 requests for food aid due to bad harvests, the alert was given at least two months in advance. For example in the Sahel between September 1980 and August 1981 in 26 countries, 2 million tons of cereals were received. Sometimes alerts are given but the situation improves. Since the system began to operate in 1975 no major catastrophe ensued until the Ethiopian famine of 1984–85. The system gave ample warning of this, but effective action was not taken for reasons not clear to us at the time of writing.

REFERENCES

1. FAO/UNICEF/WHO Expert Committee 1976 Methodology of nutritional surveillance. WHO Tech Rep Ser no. 593
2. Jelliffe D B 1966 The assessment of the nutritional status of the community. WHO Monogr Ser no. 53
3. World Health Organisation 1983 Measuring change in nutritional status. WHO, Geneva
4. Nelson W E 1971 Textbook of pediatrics, 9th edn. Saunders, Philadelphia, p 45
5. Provis H S, Ellis R W B 1955 An anthropomorphic study of Edinburgh school children. Arch Dis Child 30: 328–37
6. Tanner J M, Whitehouse R H, Tahaishi M 1966 Standards from birth to maturity for height, weight, height velocity, and weight velocity: British children 1965. Arch Dis Child 41: 454–71
7. Society of Actuaries and Association of Life Insurance Medical Directors of America 1980 1979 Body build study
8. Habicht J P, Martorell R, Yarbrough C, Malina R A, Klein R E 1974 Height and weight standards for preschool children. How relevant are ethnic differences in growth potential? Lancet 1: 611–5
9. Graiteer P L, Gentry E M 1981 Measuring children: one reference for all. Lancet 2: 297–9
10. Waterlow J C 1973 Note on the assessment and classification of protein-energy malnutrition in children. Lancet 2: 87–9
11. Frisancho A R 1981 New norms of upper limb fat and muscle areas for assessment of nutritional status. Am J Clin Nutr 31: 2540–5
12. Hall J C, O'Quigley J, Giles G R, Appleton A, Stocks H 1980 Upper limb anthropometry: the value of the study of variance. Am J Clin Nutr 33: 1846–51
13. Shakir A, Morley D 1974 Measuring malnutrition. Lancet 1: 758–9
14. Sauberlich H E, Dowdy R P, Skala J H 1977 Laboratory tests for the assessment of nutritional status, 2nd edn. CRC press, Cleveland
15. Sandstead H H, Carter J P, Darby W J 1969 How to diagnose nutritional disorders in daily practice. Nutr Today 4: 20–6
16. Marr J E 1971 Individual dietary surveys: purposes and methods. World Rev Nutr Diet 13: 105–64
17. Black A E 1982 The logistics of dietary surveys. Hum Nutr Appl Nutr 36A 85–94
18. National Food Survey Committee Annual reports Household food consumption and expenditure. HMSO, London
19. US Departments of Health, Education and Welfare 1972 Ten-States Nutrition Survey, 1968–70. DHEW Publication no. (HSM) 72–8134. Center for Disease Control, Atlanta, Georgia
20. Sabry S I, Campbell J A, Campbell M E, Forbes A S 1974 Nutrition Canada. Nutr Today 9(1): 5–13
21. Van Dokkum W, De Vos R H, Cloughley F A, Hulshof K F A M, Dukel F, Wijsman J A 1982 Food additives and food components in total diets in the Netherlands. Br J Nutr 48: 223–31
22. Baird D 1960 The evolution of modern obstetrics. Lancet 2: 557–64
23. Burger J C E, Drummond J C, Sandstead H R 1948 Malnutrition and starvation in western Netherlands, September 1944 to July 1945. General State Printing Office, The Hague
24. Goodman N M 1952 International health organisations. Churchill, London
25. Habicht J-P, Mason J 1983 Nutritional surveillance: principles and practice. In: McLaren D S (ed) Nutrition in the community, 2nd edn. Wiley, Chicester
26. Food and Agriculture Organisation 1983 World System of information and rapid alert on food and agriculture. FAO, Rome

56

Prevention of Nutritional Disorders

Nutritional disorders do not arise when there is ample food production, when the people know how to make the best use of available foods and when steps are taken to ensure that the needs of the very poor and of mothers and young children and others who may be especially liable to malnutrition (vulnerable groups) are met. Agriculture, nutrition education and nutritional support are considered in three separate sections in this chapter. Each of these depends on governments policies for food and nutrition, or the lack of them, and the chapter ends with a general discussion of the role of governments.

NUTRITION EDUCATION

A way of life that wise mothers and fathers have taught their families by example and precept for generations in all parts of the world includes:

1. A diet of bread or other cereals, vegetables and fruits with milk, eggs, fish and limited amounts of meat, eaten to satisfy a natural appetite;
2. Daily exercise in the open air;
3. Temperance with alcohol and other drugs;
4. Daily periods of rest and relaxation, preferably after meals;
5. Ample sleep, especially when young;
6. Cleanliness, both personal and domestic.

Physicians since the time of Hippocrates in ancient Greece have advised their patients that such a regime promotes health and prevents disease. The message is simple and clear. Originally based on observation and experience, the advice in general is consistent with modern science. However, many specific points of detail remain 'unproven'. Health educators should know and distinguish between what appears sensible and facts established by scientific experiment. The science of nutrition has been brilliantly successful in establishing the causes of deficiency diseases, but knowledge and understanding of the role of excess consumption of specific foods in determining the prevalence of common degenerative disorders is uncertain.

Is the world civilised?

Deficiency diseases are still present on a scale that should horrify all of us. In the world each year millions of young children die of protein-energy malnutrition, hundreds of thousands become permanently blind through lack of vitamin A and tens of thousands are born only to become cretinous deaf mutes through lack of iodine. Each of these family tragedies could be prevented. The nutrients needed are known and could be available to all mothers in those parts of the world where the diseases are endemic. The mothers of these children are both ignorant and poor. They need educational services and access to appropriate foods at prices that they can afford. This requires money and effort but in amounts trivial to expenditure in the manufacture of weapons of war or in putting men and women into outer space. The money will not become available and the effort will not be made until we realise that a world in which these family disasters are permitted cannot be called civilised. Society, that is each of us, needs education about the state of the poor and malnourished in the world, and this education is needed especially for those who are in positions to influence public opinion and who choose to serve in governments.

HOW TO CHOOSE A GOOD DIET

In prosperous countries

Choosing a good diet becomes more difficult as large stores and supermarkets replace grocers, greengrocers, butchers, fishmongers and bakeries, which in turn have replaced gardens, orchards, fields and country markets as the places where most families buy their foods. The US Departments of Agriculture and of Health, Education and Welfare have given seven dietary guidelines that help us to make a sensible choice.[1] These are:

1. Eat a variety of foods.
2. Maintain ideal body weight.
3. Avoid too much saturated fat and cholesterol.
4. Eat foods with adequate starch and fibre.
5. Avoid too much sugar.

6. Avoid too much salt.
7. If you drink alcohol, do so in moderation.

Nutritionists everywhere approve these guidelines, except that many consider that healthy citizens do not need to worry about their cholesterol intake. While there is no doubt that dietary excesses of all kinds should be avoided from childhood onwards, there are no specific diets or food prohibitions to help people to live to an active old age with a minimum of the disabilities due to degenerative changes that occur inevitably as age advances. Enthusiasts for a role for diet among the causes for coronary heart disease have propagated the view, now held widely, that butter, whole milk, eggs, fatty bacon and beef are all bad for us. These are foods that we like and experience has shown that they can be eaten in moderation with safety. Vegetable oils and fatty fish, advocated by enthusiasts, are also good foods but there may be dangers in eating too much of them.

In poorer countries
The American dietary guidelines are totally irrelevant to peasant farmers and the masses who now live in shanty towns in Africa, Asia and Latin America. Hesitatingly, because we know how wrong it is to preach to the poor, we suggest for them the following guidelines:

1. Ensure that infants after weaning and toddlers get a daily supplement of a concentrated food, such as a mixture of a cereal and beans or pulses.
2. If your water supply is not safe, boil your drinking water. If in any doubt, boil that given to infants and toddlers.
3. Eat a varied diet and include beans or pulses, green leafy vegetables daily and fruit in season.
4. Take milk, eggs, and fish or meat whenever possible.
5. See that the kitchen is clean.
6. Store food away from flies, rats and mice.

There is no question that the two top priorities in many poor communities are good foods for young children and safe drinking water. Education can help a family to provide these but, of course, community and government action is also required.

FOOD HABITS AND BEHAVIOUR

Food habits are dependent on attitudes, prejudices, general culture and taboos acquired early in life, and form a pattern of behaviour which is characteristic of a group. This is true for prosperous urban communities as well as for poor rural agriculturalists. Nutrition is a behavioural science. The nature of foods produced and their processing and packaging have changed rapidly owing to the scientific revolutions taking place in agriculture and food technology. Since World War II in European countries immigrants have brought in new foods and opened many shops and restaurants. Much better facilities for travel have enabled large numbers of people to become familiar with foods in foreign countries in Africa, Asia and Europe. There is now a supply and a demand for a much greater range of foods than formerly. In Africa and Asia Western foods are available in all towns and most rural areas. New foods and a diversity of choice bring new food habits and these may be good or bad for health.

Simple cause and effect no longer suffice to explain the prevalence of many common diseases and have been partially replaced by the concept of risk factors. Four such factors, diet, physical activity and the use of tobacco and alcohol, commonly appear to act synergistically to determine health and liability to disease. Risk depends on individual behaviour and habits. The certainties of past precepts in health education have been replaced by probabilities that every substance consumed or every pleasure enjoyed has a small or large chance of being harmful. Furthermore the methods of affecting behaviour have developed far beyond the provision of knowledge. It is not productive only to increase knowledge of the relationship between smoking and lung cancer and other diseases among young people. The predisposing, enabling and reinforcing factors of behaviour change have to be brought into action where advertising, economics and group pressures are frequently at odds with health promotion. The protection of economic interests in cigarette consumption have prevailed over health interests, even in China, Yugoslavia and the USSR. The way ahead for reduction in rates for acute myocardial infarction, lung cancer, hypertension, alcoholism and related road accidents and drug abuse is better understanding and better methods of education, coupled with social support and legislation.

Sources of information
The main sources of information about nutrition are now radio, television, newspapers, magazines and popular books and advertisements associated with them. All of these are important vehicles of nutrition education. Programmes and articles on cooking are numerous and can introduce important concepts of nutrition. The women's magazines have an enormous circulation in prosperous countries and local ones, often of good standard, are now circulating in Asia and Africa. They frequently contain articles on food and nutrition. Advertising by the food industry may be educational but most advertisements in magazines and on television are designed to sell the product rather than to educate. It is against this background that teachers in the educational and health services have to work.

Fads and cults

Taboos are not confined to dark Africa, and prescriptions for elixirs did not end in the seventeenth century. A few doctors today put a taboo on eggs because of their cholesterol content and a few prescribe large doses of vitamins as an elixir against all manner of disorders. A great part of nutrition education has to be directed at correcting erroneous and unsubstantiated ideas. Fortunately we have a free press and a price for this is that much rubbish, sometimes potentially dangerous, is published. Journalists like to tell a good story and many of them are prepared to bend the facts for this purpose.

In 1984 in Britain there were at least 20 small volumes on sale giving advice on how to slim. Most of the authors have no scientific, dietetic or medical qualification. There are also popular books on food allergies written by amateurs. While much in these books may be helpful, some tend to advocate unnecessary dietary restrictions and regimes that may be bizarre. Following these may lead to unpleasant neuroses in susceptible people. Two regimes widely advertised in the USA, the Atkins and the Cambridge diets, are potentially dangerous and there are others. Dieting on unsound regimes has been responsible for some deaths.

Quasireligious cults now flourish and some of these impose severe dietary restrictions. Rastafarianism is an example[2] and some followers of the cult have developed deficiency diseases.

Vegetable oils, good and useful foods, are sometimes promoted as elixirs. Many millions of pounds are spent each year on vitamin preparations taken as a tonic, but extra vitamins are not required to supplement a good diet and they have no tonic action.

The USA is the land of extremes and cults, and a book by a distinguished American nutritional scientist provides the scientific details and the insights of people that is needed to debunk quackery arising from false or distorted nutritional knowledge.[3]

Foods before nutrients

Amanda Woyke's farm kitchen popularised, along with West Prussian soup, other simple dishes: manna grits boiled with bits of bacon rind; sorrel cooked like spinach; millet cooked in milk; potatoes in their jackets with curds and caraway seeds; oatmeal sausage on mashed potatoes; natural potato dumplings, Bavarian as well as Bohemian; and fried potatoes accompanied by one thing and another; herring, fried eggs, meatballs, jellied pork?

Gunter Grass[4]

Our forefathers knew the value of good foods and could eat well long before there was a science of nutrition. To choose a good diet it is not necessary to know the words calorie, protein and vitamin. But it is necessary to understand the qualities of different classes of foods and how these combine to form a good diet, and this has to be taught.

Foods are classified by their origin in agriculture and animal husbandry. Cereals, root vegetables, leafy vegetables, fruits, meats, milk and dairy products, fish and eggs, are raw materials that all of us know about. We have to be taught how they are processed by cooks, butchers and bakers, brewers and vintners and by the new manufacturers into the foods that we eat and how to combine foods so as to make a good diet. Classifications based on function, for example into energy producing, body building and protective foods, were formerly much used in elementary teaching. Their imprecision is now seen to make them misleading.

Meals and snacks

A feature of modern life is that much more food is now eaten in snacks and less at proper meals. Snack foods, if well chosen, provide good nutrition and there is no evidence that it matters much how nutrient intake is distributed in time. Many of us, who may be old-fashioned, think that it is best to eat three good meals a day but we cannot find scientific support for this view.

Meals have an important social function. They are where we learn good manners, using this word in its broadest sense. A child learns a way of life from the behaviour and conversation of the family at the meal table. The character of a school or college may be determined by the quality of the meals provided and the setting in which they are served. Visitors to Oxford and Cambridge see that the mediaeval founders of colleges, in which the pupils were then young teenagers, built for them a dining hall, as well as a library and a chapel. Adolescents today get much of their food in snacks. Perhaps if educational authorities today built more dining halls and provided the discipline to ensure that pupils and teachers took meals there, teenagers would be less at odds with the world and more easily see themselves as members of a worthwhile society.

EDUCATION IN MOTHERCRAFT

A mother has dual responsibilities for feeding the young infant and for preparing food for older children and adult members of the family. Education in the former is the task of the Maternity and Child Health services. The latter falls within the scope of Home Economics, which is now realised to be increasingly important especially in underdeveloped countries.

Maternity and Child Health (MCH) centres

These are designed to supervise the health of normal pregnant women and their babies and pre-school children. They are an established part of the medical services, although in many countries their number is far below that necessary to cover even a fraction of the population.

All babies and young children are liable to minor ailments and injuries for which they need treatment. At a visit to a clinic, a few words of advice from a doctor or nurse who has treated the ailment is more likely to be effective than instruction through other educational channels. In the words of Dr Cicely Williams, a centre 'should give individual patients whatever treatment is necessary and whatever prevention they can take'.

Public health nurses, known as health visitors in the UK, are on the staff of MCH centres and visit the homes of the people. This enables them to see the family background, appreciate special difficulties and to tailor instruction to the needs of individual circumstances.

The extension of the MCH services is an urgent problem for the medical services in all countries where malnutrition is widespread. A good arrangement is to have a trained nursing sister in charge of a centre, backed up by a doctor who makes periodic visits and can be consulted by telephone or radio. The sister is assisted by health workers or assistant nurses, recruited from the local population.

In the UK, mothers in social classes IV and V tend to underuse the MCH services, and ways to bring them in have to be found. There are always some feckless mothers: it is among their children that cases of rickets are still occasionally seen.

The MCH services are the proper channel for the education of mothers in the feeding of infants and pre-school children. They have the professional competence and the means of getting the goodwill and respect of the people. However, now and for some time to come they are not sufficiently developed in many countries. The assistance of other organisations is needed. These include community centres, youth clubs, rural service centres, etc. These are in touch with the people and can use the enthusiasm of voluntary workers. Much valuable education comes from such organisations and the case for their extension is strong. When there is urgent need for a job to be done, it does not matter who does it. However, there are dangers. All the above organisations need financial help — for training local workers, for administrative assistance and for some full-time trained staff. Too many competing organisations do not lead to efficiency. Indeed at the village level a series of rival organisations, each giving different advice to mothers (as has been known to happen), is worse than useless.

EDUCATION IN SCHOOLS

Good general education promotes health and good nutrition. A deficient secondary education is an independent risk factor for some disorders; lack of it in a mother prejudices the outcome of a pregnancy and the health of her infant. In India, Kerala is the poorest of all the states economically and so might be expected to have the poorest health records. In fact Kerala has some of the best, and this is attributed to it having the highest level of literacy. It also has the highest proportion of Christians and of Communist voters.

Formal nutrition education in schools is part of courses in **home economics**. Teachers are handicapped because their subject comes low in the academic pecking order and many of their better pupils drop it at the earliest opportunity. They need encouragement and support. Community dietitians can help them, especially in the difficult task of keeping up-to-date with rapidly changing ideas. Possibilities for improvements of nutritional teaching in secondary schools are discussed in papers from London[5] and Vancouver.[6]

Biology courses might be an opportunity for imparting knowledge of the principles of nutrition. Regrettably biology is a much less popular science with pupils than physics and chemistry, and teachers and textbooks nowadays seem to put a disproportionate emphasis on its molecular aspects.

While throughout the world increasing numbers of children leave school with some knowledge of the domestic arts related to nutrition, the proportion of those going on to higher education at universities or elsewhere who have any understanding of the science of nutrition remains very small. This makes the implementation of sensible food policies in a country or community difficult.

PROFESSIONAL TRAINING

Medical students

Nutrition is not a clinical speciality in the way that cardiology or endocrinology is. In medical schools nutrition is taught as part of the undergraduate courses in biochemistry, physiology, pharmacology, pathology, medicine, paediatrics, obstetrics, surgery, community medicine and dentistry. Teaching is diffuse and thus uneven. Important aspects may be omitted, notably the nutritive value of foods and the impact of food technology. There has been much discussion of how this can be remedied by the International Union of Nutritional Science (IUNS)[7] and in the USA[8] and the UK.[9] This is reviewed by Wahlquist & Isaksson.[10]

The proposal of IUNS that 'a medical school should found a Chair of Nutrition, with responsibility to propose an integrated and full teaching programme in nutrition' is an ideal that is seldom practical. A consensus is being reached that a medical school should appoint a co-ordinator for nutrition training who would be a member of a department with active interests in nutrition. A gastroenterologist with a special interest in tube feeding and parenteral nutrition could fill such a role, as could a diabetologist and many others.

Elective periods are now a feature of the curriculum in many schools. Some students have been able to use these to get a good knowledge of nutrition. However, many students manage to complete their medical training and be abysmally ignorant of nutrition. They have not the knowledge to give advice on the dietary problems that patients are increasingly likely to put to them.

Nurses

Nursing schools have the same general problems in teaching nutrition as medical schools. All nurses should have a sound elementary knowledge of nutrition and dietetics. In hospitals they have the responsibility of feeding patients and they may also be asked for dietary advice.

Dietitians

Today in most countries dietitians take a Bachelor of Science (BSc.) course in dietetics or nutrition at a polytechnic or university, which includes or is followed by an attachment to the dietetic department of a general hospital. Dietitians have traditionally been trained to plan and prepare diets for individual patients. Modern courses also prepare them to act as consultants and to give advice to patients, doctors and others on a wide range of subjects related to food. Details of courses in the UK can be obtained from the Secretary, British Dietetic Association, Daimler House, Paradise Street, Birmingham B1 2BJ.

Nutritionists

Besides the BSc. courses, taken in the UK mainly by those intending to practise as dietitians, there are BSc. and Master of Science (MSc.) courses in nutrition that train students to work in the food industry and government and other agencies concerned with nutrition.

For those working or intending to work on field projects in the Third World, there are short courses on nutrition in some North American universities and also in London University, where students with very different backgrounds are accepted. The National Institute of Nutrition, Hyderabad, India has provided regular courses for many years. Two United Nations organisations (FAO and WHO) and various foundations organise ad hoc courses in many countries to meet a specific need.

Comment

Those who organise and take part in nutrition education have to choose their messages and aim them accurately at the group whicb they hope to influence. They have

to decide what to teach and how to teach it. In general this is easier for those working in Third World countries where many persons, especially young children, are obviously undernourished and deficiency disorders are widespread. Three books, each strongly recommended, are available to help them. Jean Richie, a dietitian who has spent much of her life teaching in countries in Africa and Asia has written a monograph full of know-how.[11] A textbook by Morley, a paediatrician with much experience in Africa, shows how important it is to combine education on nutrition and on prevention of infectious diseases.[12] Latham, a community physician, writes with wisdom about nutrition in tropical Africa.[13] Those taking part in a programme of nutrition education in a small community may hopefully look forward to seeing obvious improvement in the well-being and health in the children and sometimes in adults after one or two years.

Nutrition education is much more difficult in communities where the main problems in health are associated with overconsumption and develop insidiously, with the underlying causes and chemical pathology far from clear. In Britain the National Advisory Council for Nutrition Education (NACNE) report published in 1983[14] has led to much discussion. The general guidelines proposed, which are not new, are widely accepted but the report can be criticised for not distinguishing clearly enough between what is established science and what is still only theory. It leaves uncertainties about what to teach and also offers little help on the educational problems of how to teach. The seven dietary guidelines put out by US government departments and quoted earlier in this chapter are simple and cover all established knowledge in the prevention of disorders of overconsumption. The difficulty facing educationalists is that of persuading young people to adopt these dietary habits, when the results of a failure to do so will usually not be apparent for many years.

AGRICULTURE

To prevent widespread undernutrition in a world with a continuing increasing population there has to be a corresponding increase in food production. This could come about by bringing more land into food production or using land already cultivated more efficiently.

Constraints of land

Large areas of the earth's land is either covered by snow or is desert and so cannot produce food. About 3.2 billion hectares are potentially suitable for agriculture and about half of this land is already cultivated. Most of the remainder is either semidesert or not readily accessible, and would require immense investment of capital for road building, clearances, irrigation and fertilisers before it could be used for cultivation. Opening it up would not be economically feasible as an FAO report states:[15]

In southern and in eastern Asia and in certain parts of Latin America and Africa there is almost no scope for expanding the arable area. In the drier regions it will even be necessary to return to permanent pasture the land which is marginal or submarginal for cultivation. In most of Latin America and Africa south of the Sahara there are still considerable possibilities for expanding the cultivated area but the costs of development are high and it will often be more economical to intensify the utilisation of areas already settled.

Furthermore, industrialisation and the new megacities all over the world pave arable land with roads, airports, houses, factories and power stations, steadily making less good land available for cultivation.

Something can be done in the other direction and deserts may be made to bloom, as a visitor to Israel may see. The deserts of Libya and Iraq once provided the food to support large civilisations and could probably do so again, if the will was there, and the revenues from oil made available. However, it would be optimistic to look for cultivation of fresh lands for a major contribution to world food production.

Constraints of energy

All our food energy is derived from the sun. The relation between solar energy and agricultural production was the subject of Sir Kenneth Blaxter's presidential address to the Royal Society of Edinburgh in 1981.[16] The solar energy impinging on Britain in one year is about 33×10^{12} J per hectare and it is this that agriculture traps. The efficiency of solar energy transduction by green plants is about 10 per cent; that of the best solar cells used to generate electrical power is about 18 per cent. Plants have to use energy to synthesise the organic constituents in roots, leaves, straw and seed and their overall efficiency of use of solar energy is about 3 per cent. From this figure it is calculated that the maximum potential yields of wheat and herbage are 13 and 29 tonnes per hectare respectively. In 1981 a farmer in the Lothians near Edinburgh harvested a wheat crop with this maximum yield, and grassland farmers in Northern Ireland have nearly achieved theirs.

This is not the whole energy story. For every joule of food energy produced by modern agriculture, some 10 J of fossil fuel energy is expended by tractors and in the manufacture of agricultural machinery, fertilisers and pesticides. Reserves of fossil fuel are fixed and not renewable and so are a constraint that is likely to limit agricultural production increasingly in the future. Animals are an alternative to tractors as a source of power for agriculture and their relative efficiency is an old problem discussed in Brody's classic book.[17]

Human constraints

While one farmer has obtained from his land the maximum potential yield of wheat, 13 tonnes per hectare, average yields recorded in some countries in the 1970s were

Tonnes/hectare		Tonnes/hectare	
Netherlands	4.6	India	1.2
UK	4.2	Pakistan	1.1
USA	2.1	Iraq	0.6
USSR	1.4	Libya	0.3

These differences are only partly due to natural difficulties of cultivation. More important is the extent to which modern science is applied to agriculture. If it is applied effectively throughout the world, enough food would be provided to meet the needs of an increasing population for the foreseeable future. World hunger can be prevented.

Science was first applied to farming early in the eighteenth century by a few English and other European farmers who increased greatly their crops. Thereafter scientific knowledge grew steadily but slowly and its practical applications even more slowly. It was not until the middle of the twentieth century that a sudden increase of knowledge has made it possible for most arable lands and grazing pastures to give yields that approach their theoretical potential. That in general yields remain far below this is due to two human failures.

First, society does not give farmers in many countries either an equitable system of land tenure or adequate and fair means of obtaining the credit that all need to finance their operations. Without these they lack confidence to use new methods. Secondly most farmers are conservative, usually for good reasons based on past experience. Education and persuasion is needed to overcome this. These factors operate throughout the farming world and affect both great landlords and poor peasants; in the latter they are of overwhelming importance.

The science of economics has not yet solved the problems of world farmers, perhaps because, as T. W. Schultz said in his address on receiving the Nobel Prize for Economics in 1979, 'most economists overrate the importance of land and greatly underrate the importance of the quality of human agents'. Three examples of this are now given.

SOME ECONOMIC PROBLEMS

The green revolution

Research sponsored by the Rockefeller and Ford Foundations led to the production of new varieties of wheat and rice with yields up to four times that of varieties commonly used. These were first sown on a large scale in 1967 in India and Pakistan and later in many other countries. Their immediate success was aptly and hopefully called the green revolution. Unfortunately the revolution has been halted in its tracks. The new seeds gave high yields only if they were properly cultivated. They made heavy demands for water and fertilisers, and weeds and insect and plant pests had to be controlled. Thus cultivation is more expensive. The bigger farmers with money make good profits from their use but most peasant farmers cannot benefit from this great discovery of applied science because they lack cash or credit.

Agribusiness

New techniques in agriculture are exploited much more effectively by large international corporations than by peasant farmers. Land in poor countries where undernutrition is widespread is used too often to grow cattle food and raise stock to provide steaks and even cut flowers for New Yorkers, Londoners and Parisians. This agribusiness may benefit a few landowners and entrepreneurs in the poor countries but not the peasants.[18,19] It promotes rural unemployment since modern agricultural methods require a much smaller labour force than traditional farming. Economic factors divert land from production of beans, which the poor need, to production of food for export to wealthy countries for consumption to people who are already overfed. The gross national income of the country in which the extra food is grown may rise but this is a paper statistic which does not feed the poor, who are often worse off.

The indictment of agribusiness by Susan George, Francis Moore Lappé and Collins is well presented and convincing. It raises political questions about the organisation of society. American capitalists have failed to help the poor in Latin America, Africa and Asia to utilise the new agricultural knowledge to grow the foods they need, but the USA is able to export huge quantities of grain to make good the deficiencies caused by the failure of Russian Communists to organise agriculture in their country. It is easy to condemn those responsible for these failures, but well to remember that among the men who sit on the boards of the giant corporations and on the Soviet committees there is probably a mixture of altruism and roguery similar to that familiar to most of us in our little committees.

Cultivation of drugs

In some countries a real problem has been created by the cultivation of addiction drugs such as hemp and opium. Hemp can be cultivated and prepared by old people and children and its cash yield is more than 10 times the next best cash crop. There is a strong financial incentive to grow it on land that could be used to grow foods. To convert back land used in this manner to normal agriculture is very difficult.

No country can allow itself to be permanently and greatly dependent on others for its foodstuffs and, of these, grain is the most important. Grain has become a powerful weapon of economic warfare and the hungry millions of Africa, Asia and Latin America are pawns in the battles of international politics.

APPLIED NUTRITION PROGRAMMES

These are made up of 'interrelated educational activities aimed at the improvement of local food production, consumption and distribution in favour of local communities, particularly mothers and children in rural areas, in which the guiding principles are co-ordination among different agencies and institutions, and the active participation of the people themselves'. Such programmes began to be initiated by UN agencies and large foundations in villages in Africa, Asia and Latin America in 1960 and there has been over 25 years of experience of them.[20,21,22] A common mistake in the early years was not to recognise the futility of introducing a programme into a country where there were not sufficient resources and staff to continue to run it. Outsiders can provide a community with a stimulus and with material and expert help at the start but only local enterprise can maintain it. The programmes have, however, been the means of interesting national governments in nutrition and have motivated large numbers of local staff. Programmes are now more related to economic realities and more flexible. They take in other aspects of health, especially the control of infectious diseases, besides nutrition.

Programmes are now co-ordinated with primary health services, and the development of these is a prime aim of WHO. They are not the monopoly of the UN and international foundations. Initiative can come from local governments and from private individuals. We ourselves know something of the work of the Valley Trust, which has run for 35 years a sociomedical project at Botha's Hill in Natal, South Africa, designed to promote the health and well-being of the local Zulu community, in which great emphasis is placed on nutritional problems related to agriculture and the educational needs of the people. The trust was started by a few energetic helpers led by Dr H. H. Stott[23] and publishes an annual report. The government provides the medical staff and expenses of the Health Centre at the settlement.

Any scheme for community education is bound to fail unless it has the enthusiastic support of the leaders of the community. These people are almost inevitably conservative in outlook, often with little conception of the need for change. The first task of the organisers, and often the most difficult one, is to persuade such leaders that the scheme is worthwhile.

NUTRIENT QUALITY OF FARM PRODUCE

Agricultural improvements are mostly aimed to increase yields. This in itself tends to improve the overall quality of farm products, since increase in yields of cereals and other staple foods frees land for growing legumes, leafy vegetables and fruit. Efforts of plant geneticists to introduce varieties with higher nutrient content have not met with much practical success, although the new opaque maizes may prove valuable (p. 190).

There is now pressure on farmers to produce milk, cattle, sheep and pigs with a lower fat content, but there are better ways to reduce our dietary fat intake. It would also reduce the taste and flavour for which milk, beef, mutton, bacon and ham are appreciated. Many of us do not want to drink skimmed milk and we like meats of good quality. Let us hope these new puritans will not get their way.

ESSENTIALS FOR GOOD FARM PRACTICES

Farmers require certain essentials if they are to produce sufficient foods and in the variety needed to provide good diets. These are:

1. A good system of land tenure;
2. Facilities for credit;
3. Access to good markets;
4. Access to irrigation where rainfall is uncertain;
5. Supplies of seeds of good quality;
6. Supplies of implements and machines;
7. Supplies of fertilisers and pesticides;
8. Guidelines on what crops are required and motivation to grow them;
9. Educational services to keep them abreast with new knowledge of agriculture and animal husbandry.

These essentials may read like a list of platitudes, but in many countries peasant farmers lack all of them. Even in prosperous countries big farmers are often handicapped by insufficiency of one or more of them. Economic and social organisations everywhere have to be such as ensure the availability of these essentials to farmers, if the people are to be well fed.

NUTRITIONAL SUPPORT

FOOD SUBSIDIES

Artifically lowering the price of foods by means of government subsidies helps families with low incomes to purchase an adequate diet. During World War II the British Government lowered and controlled the prices of beef, mutton, bacon, bread, sugar, milk, potatoes, margarine, butter, cheese and eggs by means of subsidies. These varied from 20 to 50 per cent of the true cost of the food. There is little doubt that this policy contributed to the improvement in the nutrition of the nation that occurred during the war.

Subsidies to agriculture in the form of government guarantees to farmers of prices for their products continue. These aim to provide foods at prices that the people can afford and to secure for farmers adequate incomes. However, in the European Economic Community (EEC) they have got out of hand and lead to large surpluses for which there is no market, the butter mountains and wine lakes. The fair adjustment of these essential subsidies is a critical problem facing all European governments.

The problem is one of 'supply management' or to adjust levels of production to levels of requirements and export opportunities, while safeguarding the legitimate interests of food producers and also, if possible, making room for a larger quantity of food imports from developing countries. The cutting of production is painful but it is no use producing food for which there is no market. Supply management lies at the heart of the present controversies in the EEC.

RATIONING SCHEMES

Rationing is simple in principle and applicable to any food which may be available only in limited amounts. In Britain, during World War II, it was considered necessary to ration the following foods: butcher's meat, bacon, milk, cheese, sugar, fats, and in addition during 1946–48 bread and in 1947–48 potatoes. Such elaborate controls are only possible when the people have the necessary discipline and administrative aptitude. In countries with a simpler dietary pattern and a limited administrative machinery, it is unnecessary and impractical to attempt so much. For instance, during threats of famine in India, it is usual to ration only the staple grain of the district. This has proved to be practical, that is within the scope of the administration, and yet effective in preventing serious deterioration of health in threatened areas. By contrast, in Germany after the war schemes for rationing of bread, cereals, potatoes, fats, sugar, meat, cheese, milk, fish and dried fruits were drawn up and put into operation. The German authorities were unable to enforce these regulations and large black markets thrived. Any rationing scheme should be related to the normal dietary habits of the population, their probable reaction to discipline and the efficiency of the administration.

Black markets. A proportion of goods supposed to be rationed always reaches consumers by channels independent of government control. Such distribution of rationed goods through illegal channels is known throughout the world as a 'black market'. The size of black markets is a measure of the efficiency of the administration and the extent to which the government represents the will of the people. Human nature necessitates that in time of scarcity some exchange of primary products and services must occur without the use of the medium of money and outside any state control. Experience has shown that, as long as this barter of services and products is limited to exchanges between principals for their personal use, it has little effect on the efficient working of a rationing system. No government can hope to prevent such exchanges. Once, however, such exchanges become organised by intermediaries, who themselves produce no goods and perform no essential services, then chaos results. In postwar Germany and in the Bengal famine this was very apparent. Black marketeers should receive the severest penalties of the law.

FOOD ENRICHMENT

Foods may be enriched or fortified by the addition of nutrients. Such additions may be statutory under the law or made voluntarily by food manufacturers, and many examples have been given in previous pages. The addition of vitamins A and D to an artificial food, margarine, to make it comparable with the natural food, butter, was a major advance in nutrition. The addition of thiamin to white flour to replace loss of the vitamin in milling is sensible and a widespread practice. The additions of iodine to salt and of iron to flour are examples of mass medication. The value of the former in preventing goitre is proven, but there is as yet no satisfactory evidence that the latter is of any benefit in preventing anaemia. Many dried and concentrated preparations of milk have vitamins added and this certainly helps to prevent rickets, although there is a danger from excess of vitamin D. Enrichment is now an established practice in wealthy countries with a good food industry and there is little doubt of its value in appropriate cases. No benefit from some additions commonly made or advocated, eg. those of iron, calcium and lysine to wheat flour, has been demonstrated.

Enrichment is used much less in underdeveloped countries, where the need for it is potentially greater. Although it is possible to enrich rice with thiamin and other vitamins this is seldom done, and with the marked decline in the prevalence of beriberi the need for it is now much less. There is strong case for enriching maize with nicotinamide in areas where pellagra is endemic; this is done in the USA but would be of much more benefit in southern Africa. As with rice the big problem is that much of the maize is grown by subsistence farmers. There is the possibility that addition of excess of a vitamin to a diet already unbalanced may uncover a deficiency of another nutrient. Fortification of common salt with iron has been shown in large field trials to reduce the prevalence of severe anaemia in two rural areas in India, but was of little benefit in Madras City.[24] Enrichment policies should always be accompanied by general measures to improve the diet. Guidelines for those responsible for advising food manufacturers or governments have been prepared by the American Medical Association's Council on Food and Nutrition.[25]

WELFARE FOODS

The growing child needs protein, calcium and iron, and vitamins A and D in larger proportions than does the adult. Children and expectant and nursing women constitute a 'vulnerable group', particularly prone to develop nutritional disorders. Welfare foods and school meals are two established methods whereby the extra needs of this vulnerable group are met.

Old people also form a vulnerable group in which nutritional disorders are liable to occur. This is not because they have any extra need for nutrients but is due to the fact that for social and medical reasons they may be unable to obtain or prepare an adequate diet.

Since time immemorial religious people have felt themselves under obligation to help to feed the children of the poor. Such help has usually been sporadic and not always well-directed to physiological needs. In the 1920s experiments carried out by Auden[26] in Birmingham and by Corry Mann[27] were of great importance in showing that even a comparatively good diet might not supply all the specific needs of growing children. Corry Mann carried out experiments on groups of boys in institutions near London. The basic diet was considered satisfactory at the time, though we now know that it was far from ideal; there was no evidence of any nutritional disorders among the boys. A group aged 7 to 11 years were given a supplementary ration of a pint (600 ml) of milk a day; these boys grew 0.8 in taller and 3.13 lb heavier in a year than a control group receiving no supplement of milk. Supplements of sugar, butter, watercress and other foods did not produce the same beneficial effects. In the opinion of the schoolmasters the milk improved the general alertness and vitality of the children. Similar experiments have now been carried out in many parts of the world and draw the attention of health authorites and the public to the special needs of children.

In 1940 when the food situation in Britain caused grave anxiety, an extensive system of Welfare Foods was introduced to protect the vulnerable group of women and children. In the next five years the health of children of all ages and of mothers improved markedly, despite a marked decline in the standards of housing and the hazards of health associated with the evacuation of large numbers of children and the disruption of families. The wartime welfare food services were a notable contribution to child health.

The service consisted of a free issue to all pregnant and lactating women and to children under 5 years of age of free milk, orange juice and cod liver or other vitamin supplement. It has now been curtailed and only families on supplementary benefit or with a disabled child are eligible for free milk and vitamins.

Welfare food services have an especially important role in poor communities throughout the world where the vulnerable groups have a great need for extra protein and vitamins. International organisations such as United Nations Children's Fund (UNICEF) and many voluntary organisations have distributed large amounts of skimmed-milk powder — the surplus of the butter industry. In some underdeveloped countries it is possible to increase the local production of milk and also the facilities for processing it. FAO and UNICEF have helped governments greatly in these respects. In other countries, where pasture is extremely limited or the tsetse fly prohibits the existence of dairy herds, such an increase will be impossible for many years.

Mixtures of vegetable proteins can replace satisfactorily the animal protein in the diet of the young child. The production of suitable mixtures of vegetable proteins from plants which can be grown locally is essentially a problem for regional research.

SCHOOL MEALS

There are few, if any, countries which do not have some school meals services although, on account of the high cost of running them, many are but little more than demonstrations. Great Britain had a large and comprehensive system of school meals which, like many of our social services, had its roots in history. As in most European countries, our centralised services were financed by public money, but evolved out of small private charities. Thus in 1864 the Destitute Children's Dinner Society was founded and, five years later, had 58 dining-rooms open in London. Other charities, notably the London School Dinner Association, followed and spread to other big industrial cities. Elementary school teachers and others soon realised that the work of these charities was not sufficiently extensive to meet the needs of the great number of children in nineteenth-century Britain, who got too little food at home to derive full benefit from their education. The extent of malnutrition amongst the population, disclosed during the recruiting drives for the South African War, disturbed the social conscience and prepared public

opinion for an Act of Parliament in 1906, which permitted local authorities to provide free meals for certain pupils from public funds. At first only destitute children received help, but the service gradually expanded (with many ups and downs) and by 1939 about a quarter of a million children were having midday meals at school.

The outbreak of war in 1939 saw a complete transformation of policy. It was realised that growing children needed foods rich in protein, minerals and vitamins above the normal ration of the adult community and increased employment of women in industry prevented many mothers from finding the time to prepare their children's meals. Bombing and the subsequent movements of population led to the establishment of canteens all over the country and especially in the schools. At the end of 1946, 2.25 million children in England and Wales were receiving school meals. After the war this policy did not change; the aim of the British Government was to provide a midday meal for every school child.

In 1976 in England and Wales 4.8 million children were eating school meals. About 10 per cent of the children in school received them free of charge; for all the other children the charge was less than a comparable meal would cost even at home. The school meals service aimed to provide one-third of the recommended daily energy and between a third and a half of the recommended daily protein intake.[28] The usual meal has two courses and children can ask for extra helpings. Regular amounts of meat and milk are included so that a child whose school lunch was the main meal of the day was well provided for.

In 1980 the legal obligation on local education authorities to provide school meals was removed. Most authorities continue to provide meals or a canteen service but at increased prices, although children whose parents are in receipt of supplementary benefit get them free. More and more children are bringing with them a packed lunch that may or may not be nutritionally satisfactory or eating at snack bars near their schools. Pressure of central government on local governments to effect economies has made the midday meal of many of our children a shambles.

A good school provides lunches for pupils and staff. This is part of a general education. It is ironic that teachers, who long ago provided the initiative for school meals because they could not teach hungry children, now often refuse to supervise the school meal as a first step in 'industrial action'. Perhaps if they took more interest in the school meals service, they would be less frustrated by truancy and other forms of delinquency.

School meals in the USA. There are widespread programmes for school meals in the USA and these have recently been evaluated nationally in a long report.[28a] This was commissioned by the US Government, who asked the question: 'School lunch, is it working?' The authors' answer is, 'Clearly yes on two important dimensions, namely nutritional impact and agricultural support.' At the beginning of the report the editor, who is a professor of paediatrics, makes the guess 'that there would have been no school lunch program unless it promised to help to create stable markets for the abundance that flowed from America's remarkably adept and productive farms and farmers'. EEC farmers, please note.

School meals in tropical countries. An elaborate school meals service is only possible in a country in which the people are prepared to pay to provide health services for children. In many countries school meal services often have to be cut to a much smaller pattern. A committee from the rice-eating countries of Asia recommended the following type of free meal.[29]

		oz	g
1.	Cereals (cereals available, such as lightly milled rice, high extraction wheat, millets or other cereals)	2½	75
2.	A pulse (eg. peas or beans)	½	15
3.	Small fish of which the whole body is eaten (such fish provide calcium)	¼	7
4.	Vegetable (green leafy vegetables preferred)	1	30
5.	Oil (preferably an oil containing carotene)	¼	7
6.	Salt	⅝	5

The committee added: 'A meal of this kind will provide about 400 kcal (1.7 MJ) and will contain all the essential nutrients. It should be regarded as illustrating the general pattern of a cheap school meal, and may of course be modified in various ways in accordance with local conditions and the availability of various foods. For example, a greater amount of vegetables might be included, or fruits might be supplied as an alternative to vegetables. When facilities are not available for the distribution of full meals, specially prepared buns, cakes, *chapattis* made from flour, food yeast, and other ingredients such as powdered small fish may be found satisfactory'. Such meals provide a valuable supplement of protein, vitamins and minerals.

In 1982 a meal similar to the above was being given to 6.2 million young children in the state of Tamil Nadu in India. A report describing the administration of this large programme and its contribution to child health is available.[30]

School milk. Formerly every child in Britain got one-third of a pint (200 ml) of free milk at school. This was withdrawn from secondary schools in 1968 and from primary schools in 1971. A child may, however, still receive free milk at school if the school medical officer certifies that this is necessary for his health. This de-

cision was taken by the Government not because they considered that children do not need milk, but because in their opinion parents rather than taxpayers should pay for it.

Whether or not the loss of this milk has had an adverse effect on child health is uncertain. In one trial[31] half of 600 children aged 7, 8 and 9 years, selected from families with four or more children, were given 200 ml of milk each schoolday for two years. These grew faster than the other half of the sample, who received no supplement. Children whose parents were unemployed or separated appeared to get most benefit.

Even if there were no adverse effects, in our opinion free school milk is justified on educational grounds. A child needs a richer diet than does an adult and milk is the most effective means of enrichment, and free school milk was one of the fundamental preventive measures of our public health service. Its distribution provided a lesson which all could learn, including, it may be added, the teaching profession.

INDUSTRIAL CANTEENS

Those who perform heavy physical work must of necessity consume large amounts of foods of high energy value. Workers in heavy industry, if a choice is available, often prefer to take a proportion of this extra energy in the form of animal protein, although there is no evidence that this is a physiological necessity. In many industrial firms the managers have for long realised the importance of satisfying midday meals to the working man's efficiency and have provided canteens and restaurants for their employees. On the outbreak of World War II and the introduction of rationing in Great Britain, what had previously been the policy of a few enlightened firms was made compulsory by law. In 1945 there were 18 900 industrial canteens of various types and these were serving 8 million meals a day.

Although no longer a statutory obligation, industrial canteens are still a feature of contemporary life in Britain and also in most other countries. They are a convenience to workers and managements usually subsidise them. Whenever there is a national shortage of food or in circumstances that make it difficult for a workforce to get supplies, they are a valuable means of nutritional support.

ROLE OF GOVERNMENTS

Historical perspective
The idea that governments have a responsibility for planning and distribution of food supplies, now widespread, only arose in the present century, although governments

have always had an effect on food supplies through taxes on agriculture.

Land taxes were a main source of government revenue in many early civilisations. Tithe, a tax on agricultural production, was in use in Palestine and neighbouring countries in Biblical times. Jesus in castigating the Pharisees (St Matthew 23:23) said, 'Woe unto you . . . for ye pay tithe of mint and anise and cummin.' Tithe was a main source of income for the Christian Churches; it became part of ecclesiastical law in the sixth century and was made obligatory under secular law in the eighth century. The tax, a tenth part of all agricultural production, was paid either in cash or in crops or livestock. It remained a major tax for centuries, but was not taken to America by the early settlers.

When American wheat became a major source of the bread eaten by the growing populations of European industrial cities, this depressed the price of home-grown wheat. To protect farmers the British Government introduced in 1815 the Corn Law, a tax on imported wheat. The price of bread rose, causing much industrial unrest and contributing to malnutrition in the cities. The Corn Law was at the centre of British political argument until it was repealed in 1846. Governments, however, were not relieved of the responsibility for holding a balance between the interests of agriculturists and consumers. Today agricultural prices are the main cause of contention between member countries of the EEC and the agricultural lobby is one of the most powerful pressure groups influencing US governments. In the nineteenth century and even today nutritional considerations have played only a small part in government bargaining with farmers.

Since the time of the Pharoahs, most governments have accepted responsibility for providing and distributing food to the people in times of famine and other disasters, but in normal times there has been no food strategy related to nutritional needs. The laws of economics set the limits on the food supply of each family. The relief of the poor and needy depended on charity, and in Europe mainly on the Church. In England under the Tudors the State began to accept some responsibility and a series of Poor Laws were enacted. These were aimed mainly at providing work for the indigent so that they could get money to buy food for their families.[32]

Human rights

The conception that charity is not enough and that every individual has a right to receive food sufficient in both quantity and quality to maintain health has developed slowly and is not yet accepted everywhere. However, it was incorporated in the United Nations' *Universal Declaration of Human Rights*, issued in 1948, Article 25 of which reads:

1. Everyone has the right to a standard of living adequate for the health and well-being of himself and of his family, including food, clothing, housing and medical care and necessary services, and the right to security in the event of unemployment, sickness, disability, widowhood, old age or other lack of livelihood in circumstances beyond his control.
2. Motherhood and childhood are entitled to special care and assistance. All children, whether born in or out of wedlock, shall enjoy the same social protection.

Article 25 sets out in writing the ideas which are the basis of the work of WHO. Like Magna Carta in 1215, the Virginia Declaration of Rights in 1771 and the Declaration of the Rights of Man and of the Citizen, adopted in Paris in 1789, the Declaration of the United Nations is an expression of hope. Noble ideas are not easily converted into legal codes that are enforceable. Even slavery, now universally condemned, continues to exist.

Development of government interest in health and nutrition

Governments' interest in health was stimulated by the outbreaks of cholera in Europe and North America which first occurred in 1832 and continued for the next 40 years. These led to the appointment by local authorities of medical officers of health, and the effective separation of the systems for water supply and sewage disposal. The work of Pasteur (1822–95) and Koch (1843–1910) led to the discovery of the bacterial origin of tuberculosis and many other infectious diseases. The problems of preventing the spread of these infections became the main preoccupation of health authorities and diverted attention from the problems of malnutrition. The discovery of vitamins and the general recognition of the importance of the quality of the foods in the diet followed a generation later.

The first of many International Sanitary Conferences was held in Paris in 1851 and was concerned mainly with cholera. There was no international establishment of health workers until 1907, when the Office International d'Hygiène Publique was set up. This was followed in 1921 by the establishment of the Health Committee of the League of Nations with a small full-time staff. The organisation became actively interested in nutrition, and a report on the physiological bases of nutrition[33] was a landmark in stimulating the interests of national governments in nutrition.

A member of the staff of the health division of the League of Nations and a main author of their nutrition report, W. R. Aykroyd, was appointed Director of the Nutrition Laboratory of the Government of India in 1935; at the same time a distinguished agriculturalist, the Marquess of Linlithgow, was appointed Viceroy. There were high hopes of a 'marriage between Health and Agriculture', but the marriage did not take place;

the agricultural partner's interest and energy were diverted by the political problems arising from nationalists fighting for independence. But nutritionists in India were the first to collect systematically the data necessary for a national food strategy. They continue to do so, but their effect on agriculture is still piecemeal and uncoordinated.

In 1943 the National Research Council of the USA published a report on Recommended Dietary Allowances, now in its tenth edition. The report dealt with vitamins and minerals quantitatively, whereas the League of Nations' report had been able to give only general qualitative statements about protective foods. The US report was intended 'as a measure in planning diets and food supplies.' At once it had, and continues to have, a great influence in the USA and also in other countries. Much legislation providing nutritional support for vulnerable groups is based on it. Its effect on agriculture has been small. Food production in North America continues to be determined more by the interests of 'agribusiness' (p. 535) rather than by nutritional considerations.

Two success stories

Nutrition planning has had two outstanding successes, both in emergency situations. The first was the feeding of the people of Britain during World War II, and the second the prevention of famine arising in Europe after the end of World War II by the United Nations Relief and Rehabilitation Administration (UNRAA)

Feeding Britain in World War II

Mortality and morbidity statistics and the records of the growth and development of children indicate that the health and nutrition of the people of Britain improved between 1939 and 1945. Yet during this period of war much of the necessary imports of food from North America was sunk by German submarines in the continuous battle of the Atlantic; large numbers of the population of the industrial cities were evacuated from their homes as a result of air raids; the civilian health services were depleted of doctors, nurses and others who joined the armed services.

That the food supply of the people was maintained and its nutritive value improved was due to the setting up of a Ministry of Food at the start of hostilities in September 1939. The country was fortunate in that the Minister, Lord Woolton, an industrialist, and his chief scientific adviser, Sir Jack Drummond, a former professor of biochemistry, were two men of exceptional ability who served throughout the war. Churchill was also fully aware of the importance of nutrition, as is shown by his statement in a speech in 1943 in the House of Commons: 'There is no finer investment for any

community than putting milk into babies.' The Ministry of Food was responsible for an elaborate scheme of rationing and also for a great expansion of the welfare food services for mothers and children, of school meals and of community feeding in industrial and other canteens, as already described in this chapter. Administrative action was also taken to improve the quality of bread and flour and to fortify margarine with vitamins A and D. The food supply was maintained by the planning of agriculture and the control of imports; the administrative means by which this was done are admirably described in a small book by Fenelon.[34]

Many of these measures, especially the rationing, called for marked changes in food habits and were therefore unpopular. They succeeded because the people realised that they were fair and had the discipline and administrative ability needed for their enforcement.

UNRRA

The United Nations Relief and Rehabilitation Administration was set up when the tide of World War II began to turn against the Axis Powers. Plans for bringing immediate relief to the invaded countries awaiting liberation were drawn up by representatives of 44 nations, who met in the White House, at the invitation of President Roosevelt. The countries that had not been invaded agreed to contribute 2 per cent of their annual income to the resources of UNRRA. The largest contributions were from the USA, £675 million; Britain, £155 million; and Canada, £35 million. With these vast resources — three times more than was spent on relief after the first world war — UNRRA poured supplies into Albania, Austria, Byelorussia, China, Czechoslovakia, Italy, Greece, Poland, the Ukraine and Yugoslavia. Limited aid was also given to seven other countries. Beginning in March 1945, 25 million tons of goods costing £750 million were shipped overseas by UNRRA in more than 6000 ships. The goods included locomotives, trucks and freight cars, more than 300 000 farm animals, thousands of tractors and ploughs and many tons of seed grains, all necessary for restarting agriculture in devastated areas; in addition, UNRRA provided fully equipped hospitals, and much-needed medical supplies and personnel. But agriculture could not be set on its feet overnight and the people had to be fed; the most vital part of UNRRA's work was therefore the provision of food; the foodstuffs were of every kind including hundreds of tons of dried milk for children, and vast quantities of cereals. In all, UNRRA shipped enough grain to make about 12 000 million 1 lb loaves, enough to give five such loaves to every man woman and child in the world. The result was that at least three famines were prevented and untold misery, hardship and underfeeding among many millions of people were alleviated. It was a condition of UNRRA aid that the supplies sent in should be distributed without regard to politics, race or religion. It is a pleasure to recall that these conditions were effectively observed.

UNRRA was wound up when its immediate task was done, but its story is a reminder of what effective international cooperation can do.

The position today
All countries have laws and regulations which affect nutrition. In Britain, the USA and other countries with large government departments, ministries of health, agriculture, industry, education and others each pass legislation that affects nutrition, but there is no overall policy. Only a few countries now have a ministry of food and, where there is one, it is usually of limited influence and the minister is low down in the pecking order of his government colleagues. Many countries now have tables of recommended allowances or intakes of nutrients which are officially recognised and these are used in drafting regulations, eg. for school meals and the enrichment of foods. Departments of health and medical organisations lay down guidelines for the diet of the general population, aimed mainly at reducing the prevalence of cardiovascular disease and obesity. They influence government departments but except in Norway (see below) are not a formal basis for a national food and nutrition policy.

The United Kingdom
After World War II the Ministry of Food was merged with the Ministry of Agriculture. Successive ministers have had an impossible task in representing the legitimate interests of both farmers and consumers, inevitably often at variance. There is an alliance between the Ministry of Agriculture and the nutrition division of the Department of Health which, although always amicable, is uneasy, wasteful of time and has not led to an overall policy. A good case can be made out for a separate Ministry of Food and Nutrition that could give coherence to planning and legislation, but it is unlikely that one will be created and there is no public demand. The NACNE report[14] was issued by the Health Education Council and is not a government publication. The case for a food policy has been well put by Whitehead[35] in a lecture to the Royal Society for the Encouragement of Arts.

The United States
In the USA there is much more popular concern with food and nutrition than in Britain. A large White House conference on Food, Nutrition and Health was assembled in 1969. This led to the appointment of a Senate Select Committee of Nutrition and Human Needs. Their report, *Dietary Goals for the United States*, was issued in 1977. Known as the McGovern report, after the prestigious chairman of the committee, it provoked widespread comment, both favourable and unfavourable. Those who liked the report attempted to get the goals established as national nutrition policy, but the US Senate did not concur and that committee was disbanded.

The McGovern report was reproduced in full in *Nutrition Today* together with lengthy comments from twenty leading authorities on health and nutrition (*Nutrition Today* 1977, volume 12, parts 5 and 6). Criticisms are also summarised by Harper.[36] While large parts of the report received general approval, the recommendations to reduce cholesterol consumption to 300 mg a day and a salt consumption to 3 g a day were criticised as impractical and insufficiently supported by scientific evidence.

In 1980 the Food and Nutrition Board of the National Academy of Science[37] made recommendations for healthy diets, and the US Government issued a small free booklet.[1] These are guidelines for individuals and for nutrition education and do not provide an overall policy on food and nutrition. Policies are determined separately by the Departments of Agriculture and Health. Of these, the Department of Agriculture is by far the more powerful. In 1984 its secretary was a farmer and the interests of the farming lobby often do not coincide with those of nutritionists, as we have seen.

Norway
Norway has a smaller population than the USA and the UK and so has fewer nutrition 'experts'. This may be the explanation of why the Norwegian Government was in 1975 the first to set out a national food and nutrition policy.[38] This appears as a model for other governments to study.

The proposal has four major goals:

1. To stimulate the consumption of healthy foodstuffs;
2. To develop guidelines for food production in accordance with the recommendation of the World Food Council;
3. To increase domestic independence from the importation of food supplies by encouraging increases in the production and consumption of domestic foodstuffs that both satisfy health requirements in terms of nutritional value and agricultural requirements in terms of the specific natural conditions delimiting the potential for food production;
4. In response to the general economic aim of strengthening outlying districts, agricultural production is to be promoted in districts and regions with otherwise poor industrial bases.

The more specific objectives of the Government's policy are:

1. To maintain the existing advantageous nutritional aspects of current agricultural production and patterns of consumption. It is recognised that taste cannot be altered significantly through policy, and it is also recognised that variations in consumption patterns differ both regionally and with regard to different population groups. It is the aim

of the policy to work within the limitations imposed by those differences;

2. To improve the nutritional quality of the overall national diet, it is the aim to reduce the overall intake of fats as a source of energy. The reduction in fats should eventually be to about 35 per cent of the total diet;
3. To substitute for the decline in fat consumption, it is the aim to increase the intake of foodstuffs with heavy concentrations of starches, especially grains and potatoes. Sugar as a source of energy ought to be reduced.
4. In terms of total fat consumption it is the aim to increase the proportion of polyunsaturated fats and decrease the proportion of saturated fats.

A second report[39] indicates that publication of the policy has been followed by improvement in the national diet (a fall in the fat intake from 41 to 38 per cent of the energy), a slight fall in mortality from myocardial infarction and probably a reduced prevalence of obesity and dental caries.

United Nations

Adequate food is on the United Nations list of human rights for everyone (p. 540) and its **Food and Agricultural Organisation** (FAO) was one of the first of UN special agencies and set up in 1945 on the following premises.

The world has never had enough to eat. At least two-thirds of its people are ill-nourished in spite of the fact that two-thirds of the world's people are farmers.

The modern science of production shows that it is entirely possible to produce enough of the right kinds of foods.

The modern science of nutrition proves beyond doubt that if all people could get enough of the right kinds of foods, the average level of health and well-being could be raised much higher than it is now.

But production alone is not enough. Foods must be so distributed that the levels of consumption of those who do not have enough are progressively raised.

This implies an expanding world economy, in which each nation will play its own part, but all will act together.

FAO owes much to the first Director-General, Lord Boyd Orr, who brought to his office the traditions of an Aberdeen farmer and the experience of a lifetime of work in medical and agricultural research, these being mixed and leavened by a spirit and eloquence characteristic of an ancient Hebrew prophet.

In the early days of FAO many people, including the Director-General, hoped that the organisation would become an effective executive agency; they wanted FAO to acquire the surplus food from the crops of the richer agricultural countries and to distribute these, as need arose, amongst countries afflicted with grave food deficiencies or famine. However, under its original constitution such power was not given. FAO could not order the adoption of particular policies nor embark on 'the executive functions of purchase and procurement in order to stimulate output and equalise distribution.' It can only recommend, demonstrate and discuss, and in all countries its work has to be channelled through the ministries of national government.

The **World Health Organisation** (WHO) was established in 1948 and its nutrition division cooperates closely with FAO. A joint FAO/WHO Expert Committee on nutrition first met in 1949 and has now produced many reports. These lay down the broad policy of both organisations; they recommend and encourage work on assessment of nutritional status, standards of requirements for nutrients, protein-energy malnutrition, nutritional anaemia, endemic goitre, xerophthalmia, food technology and toxicology.

Any reader of this book who looks at the list of references will see how much we owe to FAO and WHO. The bringing together of experts of repute and the preparation of international reports does much to facilitate the use of new knowledge.

The nutrition divisions of FAO and WHO, whose headquarters are in Rome and Geneva respectively, have established reputations as educationalists. Besides producing technical reports, they arrange conferences in many countries and have selected and financed many hundreds of men and women from underdeveloped countries for fellowships that enable them to study for long periods abroad. They have also sent almost as many consultants to aid national nutrition programmes in many countries. Many of the consultants and fellows, after their return home, have been able to influence governments to initiate and carry out nutrition programmes. Thanks largely to FAO and WHO there are now throughout the underdeveloped parts of the world a large number of people with a sound professional knowledge of nutrition.

The work of FAO and WHO has been, and continues to be, assisted by the United Nations Children's Fund (UNICEF), which was set up in 1947 when UNRRA had completed its immediate tasks (p. 541) and closed down. UNICEF aids governments to provide essential needs for children. Food, medicines, trained children's nurses, diapers, shoes, etc. have been made available in many parts of the world. At first the greater portion of the resources of the Fund was devoted to the provision of children's meals. For long periods, some four million children were receiving each day a meal partly provided by UNICEF. This effective organisation of material aid of every sort for needy children and their mothers led the UN to establish it on a more permanent basis. UNICEF remains a non-technical organisation and works in conjunction with FAO, WHO and other UN agencies, including the Bureau of Social Affairs and the Educational Scientific and Cultural Organisation (UNESCO). Many joint projects for the control of diseases such as malaria, tuberculosis and yaws have been successfully carried out. UNICEF continues to undertake the purchase and free distribution of milk powder to needy children and others throughout the world and cooperates with FAO in the development of milk-processing plants and dairies. Any UNICEF contribution to a country has to be matched in value by a contribution from the government of the assisted country.

International finance

FAO and WHO can improve food production and distribution only indirectly through their influence on national governments. They are advisory bodies only, and to follow their advice national governments need money or credit. These are notably lacking in most Third World countries.

As a result of a famous conference in 1944 at Bretton Woods, New Hampshire, two organisations came into being, the **World Bank** and the **International Monetary Fund**. The bank obtains funds from subscriptions of member countries and makes loans to governments or private enterprises guaranteed by governments. The fund aims to stabilise currencies and so promote international trade. After 40 years both the bank and the fund continue to operate.

Since 1974 successive increases in oil prices have exacerbated the difficulties of many poorer countries, as one statistic shows. In 1982 in Latin America, Asia, Africa and the Middle East there were 21 countries with collective debts of 500 billion dollars; annual interest on this was equal to 70 per cent of the value of their exports. It is naive to expect that the governments of these countries could operate food and nutrition policies that ensured a good diet for most of their people. Trade and finance are the backbone of a country's economy and so effect the food supply. For readers who are interested in their international aspects a paperback by two economists is recommended.[40] Maynard Keynes was at Bretton Woods and he and many other distinguished economists have served the World Bank and the International Monetary Fund. That these have not, as yet, achieved more success is due to the support that they get from governments of the richer countries being half-hearted.

The future

It cannot be assumed that the techniques which have revolutionised agriculture in Europe and North America in the last 40 years can be exported to peasant farmers in Africa, Asia and Latin America, provided sufficient money is made available. Critics who doubt this assumption point out that much of the money that has already been given for agriculture development has benefited mainly importers, merchants, landowners and corrupt government officials, and that too little has gone to benefit peasant farmers. It is also claimed that the existence of international aid on a large scale stifles local enterprise and initiative.

An analogous situation exists in medicine. There are few large cities in the developing countries which do not have a modern hospital with a competent staff, trained abroad, and adequate equipment, provided by international aid. Yet in these countries most of the people live in villages with no safe water supply and almost no access to trained health workers and essential drugs. WHO now directs its resources in underdeveloped countries to primary health care in the villages. In a statement of policy the Director-General, Halfdan Mahler, includes the passage:

Malnutrition is probably the single most important health problem in developing countries. The national and international health sectors must now come to grips with their responsibilities in nutrition, identify their proper political strategies, define realistic policies and strategies, generate appropriate technologies, and formulate applicable programmes. If we do not succeed in making effective and realistic nutritional activities a cornerstone of primary health care, we are hardly worth our salt as health managers. Once more we seem to have the knowledge but neither the political will nor the social imagination to apply it.

Mahler, like Boyd Orr, has flair and enthusiasm. We hope that his enthusiasm will be infectious and spread ideas for food and nutrition policies and strategies throughout the world, in rich and poor countries alike. In this way a true marriage of health and agriculture will be possible. Agribusiness does not even flirt with nutrition.

Most of the decisions which have to be made by government in the field of nutrition involve financial benefit or loss to sections of the community. Farmers' lobbies want subsidies and higher prices; consumers want cheaper and better food. Industrial lobbies press for additives in food products; the public fear the word additive. The choice is usually determined by those politicians who have the loudest or biggest lobby. In our fallible world this kind of judgment (or misjudgment) will continue to be a feature of all systems of government. Enlightened decisions on programmes for health and nutrition require an educated people and just, forward-looking leaders. The 'keys to the solutions of problems' of health and nutrition throughout the world lie in education.

REFERENCES

1. US Department of Agriculture/US Department of Health, Education and Welfare 1980 Nutrition and your health. Government Printing Office, Washington DC
2. Springer L, Thomas J 1983 Rastafarians in Britain: a preliminary study of their food habits and beliefs. Hum Nutr Appl Nutr 37A: 120–7
3. Herbert V 1980 Nutrition cultism: facts and fiction. Stickley, Philadelphia
4. Grass G 1977 The flounder: a celebration of life, food and sex. Penguin Books, London, p 333
5. Moody R 1982 Priorities for nutrition education in the secondary school. Hum Nutr Appl Nutr 36A: 18–21
6. Schwartz N E, Clampett D M 1983 Evaluation of a nutrition innovation in secondary school home economics education. Human Nutr Appl Nutr 37A: 180–8
7. IUNS Committee on Nutrition Education in Medical Faculties 1971 Report on nutrition education in medical faculties. Proc Nutr Soc 30: 191–3
8. White P L, Mahan L K, Moore M F 1972 Conference on Guidelines for Nutritional Education in Medical Schools and Postdoctoral Training Programs. Available from: American Medical Associates, Chicago
9. Gray J (ed) 1983 Nutrition in medical education. British Nutrition Foundation, London
10. Wahlquist M L, Isaksson B 1983 Training in clinical nutrition: undergraduate and postgraduate. Lancet 2: 1295–7
11. Ritchie J A S 1983 Nutrition and families. Macmillan, London
12. Morley D 1973 Paediatric priorities in the developing world. Butterworth, London
13. Latham M C 1980 Human nutrition in tropical Africa, 2nd edn. FAO Food Nutr Ser no. 11
14. National Advisory Council for Nutrition Education (NACNE) 1983 Proposals for nutrition guidelines for health education. Health Education Council, London
15. Food and Agriculture Organisation 1970 The state of food and agriculture. FAO, Rome
16. Blaxter K 1982 Food and power. In: Yearbook. Royal Society of Edinburgh, p 5–11
17. Brody S 1945 Bioenergetics and growth. Reinhold, New York. (Reprinted 1964 by Hafner, New York, chap 24)
18. George S 1976 How the other half dies. Penguin Books, London
19. Moore Lappé F, Collins J 1977 Food first. Houghton Mifflin, Boston
20. McNaughton J W, Sabry Z I 1983 The role of the food policy and nutrition division of FAO. In: McLaren D S (ed) Nutrition in the community. Wiley, Chichester, p 261–76
21. Ghassemi H, Tepley L J 1983 Nutrition strategies in UNICEF's perspective. In: McLaren D S (ed) Nutrition in the community. Wiley, Chichester, p 277–98
22. Pyle D F 1983 Evaluation of the role of voluntary agencies in nutritional interventions. In: McLaren D S

(ed) Nutrition in the community. Wiley, Chichester, p 299–320
23. Stott H H 1977 The Valley Trust socio-economic project for the promotion of health in a less developed rural area. MD thesis, Edinburgh University
24. Working Group on fortification of Salt with Iron 1982 Use of common salt fortified with iron in the control and prevention of anaemia — a collaborative study. Am J Clin Nutr 36: 1442–51
25. American Medical Association, Council on Food and Nutrition 1973 Improvement of the nutritive quality of foods: general policies. JAMA 225: 1116–1118
26. Auden G A 1923 An experiment in the nutritive value of an extra milk ration. J R Sanit Inst 44: 236–47
27. Corry Mann H C 1926 Diets for boys during the school age. MRC Spec Rep Ser no. 106
28. Department of Education and Science 1975 Nutrition in schools: report of the working party on the nutritional aspects of school meals. HMSO, London
28a. Rush D (ed) 1984 National evaluation of the school nutrition program. Am J Clin Nutr 40 (suppl): 363–464
29. Food and Agriculture Organisation 1948 Nutrition problems of rice-eating countries in Asia. FAO Nutr Mtg Rep Ser no. 2
30. Devadas R P 1983 Nutritious meal programme for children of Tamil Nadu. Bull Nutr Found India January: 1–3
31. Department of Health and Social Security 1981 Report of the subcommittee on nutritional surveillance. Rep Health Soc Subj no. 21
32. Passmore R 1983 An historical introduction to food, health and nutrition policies in the United Kingdom. In: McLaren D S (ed) Nutrition in the community. Wiley, Chichester, p 19–49
33. League of Nations, Technical Commission of the Health Committee 1935 Report on the physiological basis of nutrition. Series of League of Nations Publications III, Health III:6, Geneva
34. Fenelon F G 1952 Britain's food supplies. Methuen, London
35. Whitehead R G 1978 Food policy and health. J R Soc Encouragement of Arts 76: 552–63
36. Harper A E 1978 Dietary goals — a skeptical view. Am J Clin Nutr 31: 310–21
37. Food and Nutrition Board 1980 Towards healthful diets. National Academy of Science, Washington DC
38. Royal Norwegian Ministry of Agriculture 1977 On Norwegian nutrition and food policy. Report to the Storting (1975–1976) no. 32
39. Royal Ministry of Health and Social Affairs, Norway 1983 On the follow-up of Norwegian nutrition policy. Report to the Storting (1981–1982) no. 11
40. McBean A I, Snowden P N 1981 International institutions in trade and finance. Studies in economics no. 18 Allen & Unwin, London

57

The Population Problem

Every second of the day and night — somewhere in the world — four babies are born. Every 24 hours there are 20 000 more births than deaths (FAO, 1974).

HISTORICAL PERSPECTIVES

Malthus

In 1798 Malthus published his famous *Essay on the Principles of Population as it Affects the Future Improvements of Society with Remarks on the Speculation of Mr Godwin, Mr Condorcet and other Writers*. Mr Godwin achieved some fame as the father-in-law of the poet Shelley, over whom he had considerable influence. At the end of the eighteenth century Godwin had seen the results of the great improvements that had recently taken place in British agriculture and had a prophetic glimpse of the possibilities for wealth that the Industrial Revolution was to bring forth. He considered that with these material aids the perfecting of human society was a practical proposition. Malthus' father, a Surrey squire, was a disciple of Godwin and the essay on the principles of population is perhaps a reaction against excessive paternal optimism. The main argument is that any temporary or local improvement in human living conditions will increase a population faster than corresponding agricultural developments can increase the food supply. Hunger and starvation with their associated war and pestilence will then automatically set back the advance and check the population growth: these disasters are inescapable features of human society, which by its very nature can never be stable. Such, in brief, is the Malthusian dilemma. It is today a major problem in most countries and has a large literature. Monographs by Ehrlich,[1] Loraine[2] and Brown[3] are recommended.

Death, births and population growth

Table 57.1 gives population data for the world in 1983. It was drawn up by the Population Reference Bureau, Inc., 1337 Connecticut Avenue NW, Washington DC, USA. The data come from national statistics, and their accuracy depends on the reliability of the census and of the notification of births and deaths in the various countries. For countries in Europe, North America and Oceania the order of accuracy is high, but the figures for most countries in Africa and for many in Asia are little more than intelligent guesses. China and India contain about two-fifths of the inhabitants of the world.

In some countries birth rates still lie between 40 and 50 per 1000. Death rates vary widely, but in some countries have fallen below 10 per 1000. The world population is increasing by 84 million a year and in the absence of major catastrophes, by the year 2000, only 15 years ahead, there will probably be up to 1500 million extra mouths to feed.

It has been pointed out in Chapter 55 that agricultural expansion in many countries is barely keeping pace with the present growth of population. If the above forecast is accepted, the agricultural problem becomes extremely serious. To what extent is it possible to control the numbers of the world population by active social and health policies? To what limits can agricultural production be increased? Before attempting to answer these very important questions, it is necessary to consider briefly some of the factors affecting death rates and birth rates.

Populations with high death rates and high birth rates

For about a thousand years — from the beginning of the Middle Ages to the middle of the eighteenth century — the population of Europe probably remained more or less constant. There is also no evidence of any important permanent changes in the number of inhabitants of Asia during this period. This stability existed because birth rates in all countries were probably over 40 per 1000 of the population yearly. This rate of reproduction probably represents the maximum of which the human species is capable. Yet it was only just sufficient to make up the losses due to war, famine and disease. For the biological survival of man, it was necessary that every adult woman should be as fertile as possible. The organisation of society in all countries, both in the East and in the West, was such as to encourage fertility. In

Table 57.1 World population 1983 (from Data Sheet of the Population Reference Bureau, Washington DC, USA)

Region or Country	Population estimate mid-1983 (millions)	Crude birth rate	Crude death rate	Natural increase (annual, %)	Population doubling time in years (at current rate)	Population projected to 2000 (millions)	Population projected to 2020 (millions)	Infant mortality rate	Total fertility rate	% Population under age 15 years/ over age 64 years	Life expectancy at birth (years)	Urban population (%)	Per capita Calorie supply as % of requirements	Per Capita GNP, 1981 (US$)
WORLD	4 677	29	11	1.8	39	6 130	7 810	84	3.9	34/6	62	39	109	2 754
MORE DEVELOPED	1 158	15	10	0.6	118	1 273	1 342	19	1.9	23/11	73	70	134	8 657
LESS DEVELOPED	3 519	33	12	2.1	32	4 857	6 468	93	4.5	38/4	58	29	101	728
LESS DEVEL (Excl. China)	2 496	37	13	2.4	29	3 613	5 042	105	5.2	41/3	54	33	99	916
AFRICA	513	46	16	3.0	23	851	1 399	120	6.5	45/3	50	27	100	783
NORTHERN AFRICA	120	44	13	3.1	23	188	278	109	6.4	43/3	55	42	110	1 165
Algeria	20.7	46	14	3.2	22	36.5	57.0	116	7.0	47/4	56	52	100	2 129
Egypt	45.9	43	12	3.1	22	65.5	90.8	102	6.0	39/4	57	44	117	654
Libya	3.3	47	13	3.4	20	6.1	9.9	99	7.3	47/2	57	52	144	8 560
Morocco	22.9	44	13	3.1	22	37.3	56.2	106	6.6	46/3	57	41	109	869
Sudan	20.6	47	17	3.0	23	33.2	51.5	123	6.6	44/3	48	25	100	380
Tunisia	6.8	35	10	2.5	28	9.6	12.4	98	5.6	40/4	59	52	115	1 417
WESTERN AFRICA	155	49	18	3.1	23	266	455	139	6.8	47/3	47	22	96	681
Benin	3.8	49	19	3.0	23	6.6	12.0	153	6.7	46/3	47	14	100	326
Cape Verde	0.4	28	9	1.8	38	0.4	0.5	81	3.0	34/4	61	20	—	—
Gambia	0.6	49	28	2.1	33	1.0	1.7	197	6.4	45/3	42	18	94	348
Ghana	13.9	48	16	3.2	21	24.1	41.1	102	6.7	47/3	60	36	87	402
Guinea	5.4	46	21	2.5	28	8.8	15.1	164	6.2	44/3	45	19	83	298
Guinea-Bissau	0.8	40	21	1.9	36	1.2	1.8	147	5.4	39/4	42	24	—	185
Ivory Coast	8.9	47	18	2.9	24	14.8	24.5	126	6.7	45/2	47	38	113	1 174
Liberia	2.1	47	15	3.2	22	3.8	6.7	153	6.9	48/3	54	33	107	536
Mali	7.3	47	21	2.6	26	12.1	21.4	153	6.7	46/3	43	17	84	185
Mauritania	1.8	50	22	2.8	25	3.0	5.4	142	6.9	46/3	43	23	88	484
Niger	6.1	51	22	2.9	24	10.5	19.0	145	7.1	47/3	43	13	94	336
Nigeria	84.2	50	17	3.3	21	148.2	255.5	134	6.9	48/3	49	20	99	873
Senegal	6.1	48	22	2.6	27	9.7	15.4	146	7.1	45/3	43	33	100	499
Sierra Leone	3.8	45	19	2.6	26	6.1	9.8	206	6.1	44/3	47	25	91	319
Togo	2.8	48	18	3.0	23	4.8	7.9	108	6.5	47/3	47	17	91	391
Upper Volta	6.8	48	22	2.6	27	10.9	17.2	210	6.5	45/3	43	9	85	237

Table 57.1 (Cont'd)

Region or Country	Population estimate mid-1983 (millions)	Crude birth rate	Crude death rate	Natural increase (annual, %)	Population doubling time in years (at current rate)	Population projected to 2000 (millions)	Population projected to 2020 (millions)	Infant mortality rate	Total fertility rate	% Population under age 15 years/over age 64 years	Life expectancy at birth (years)	Urban population (%)	Per capita Calorie supply as % of requirements	Per Capita GNP, 1981 (US$)
EASTERN AFRICA	146	48	17	3.1	23	249	430	111	6.6	45/3	48	14	88	305
Burundi	4.5	46	22	2.4	28	7.0	11.7	121	5.9	39/6	42	2	92	235
Comoros	0.4	46	17	2.9	24	0.7	1.1	92	6.2	44/5	47	19	105	313
Djibouti	0.3	49	23	2.7	26	0.5	0.6	—	—	—	—	74	—	476
Ethiopia	31.3	48	23	2.5	27	50.6	79.6	146	6.7	43/5	40	14	74	142
Kenya	18.6	54	13	4.1	17	37.1	72.8	86	8.0	50/3	55	13	88	432
Madagascar	9.5	46	16	3.0	23	15.2	24.2	70	6.4	44/3	47	18	107	332
Malawi	6.8	51	18	3.3	21	12.0	20.8	171	6.9	48/3	47	9	95	200
Mauritius	1.0	26	7	1.9	37	1.2	1.5	35	3.1	34/4	65	43	119	1 342
Mozambique	13.1	45	18	2.7	26	21.5	37.2	114	6.1	44/3	47	9	80	240
Reunion	0.5	23	6	1.7	41	0.7	0.8	16	3.1	32/4	65	41	—	—
Rwanda	5.6	49	18	3.1	22	9.9	18.3	106	6.9	47/3	47	4	94	250
Seychelles	0.1	29	7	2.2	32	0.1	0.1	24.0	4.2	40/6	65	25	—	1 797
Somalia	5.3	46	21	2.6	27	7.2	12.0	146	6.1	44/4	43	30	92	282
Tanzania	20.5	46	14	3.2	22	35.4	60.0	102	6.5	46/3	52	13	87	299
Uganda	13.8	46	15	3.1	22	24.2	43.7	96	6.1	45/3	54	7	79	356
Zambia	6.2	48	16	3.2	22	11.0	19.1	105	6.9	47/3	50	43	86	586
Zimbabwe	8.4	47	13	3.4	20	15.0	26.2	73	6.6	48/3	53	20	79	815
MIDDLE AFRICA	58	45	19	2.7	26	92	148	121	6.0	44/3	46	30	95	483
Angola	7.6	47	22	2.5	27	12.2	20.9	153	6.4	44/3	42	21	89	790
Cameroon	9.1	44	18	2.7	26	14.0	21.7	108	5.7	42/4	47	35	105	793
Central African Republic	2.5	45	20	2.5	28	3.9	6.6	147	5.9	43/3	43	41	95	328
Chad	4.7	45	23	2.1	33	7.1	11.1	147	5.9	42/4	40	18	75	—
Congo	1.7	44	18	2.6	26	2.7	4.6	128	6.0	44/3	47	37	99	1 108
Equatorial Guinea	0.3	35	18	2.5	28	0.4	0.7	142	5.7	42/4	47	54	—	175
Gabon	0.7	35	20	1.5	45	0.9	1.3	116	4.7	34/6	45	36	121	3 909
Sao Tome and Principe	0.1	39	10	2.9	24	0.1	0.1	72	—	—	—	33	—	382
Zaire	31.3	46	18	2.8	25	50.7	81.5	111	6.1	45/3	47	30	96	225

SOUTHERN AFRICA	34	37	11	2.6	26	55	88	97	5.2	42/4	60	46	115	2 349
Botswana	0.9	51	17	3.4	20	1.6	3.0	82	6.5	50/3	50	29	—	902
Lesotho	1.4	41	13	2.9	24	2.2	3.4	114	5.9	40/4	52	5	—	538
Namibia	1.1	43	14	2.9	24	1.8	3.0	119	5.9	44/3	52	45	—	—
South Africa	30.2	36	10	2.6	27	48.5	76.6	95	5.1	42/4	61	50	115	2 509
Swaziland	0.6	49	16	3.3	21	1.0	1.7	134	6.5	46/3	47	15	—	844
ASIA	2 730	30	11	1.9	36	3 564	4 391	89	4.1	36/4	60	27	100	968
SOUTHWEST ASIA	108	37	11	2.6	26	169	246	99	5.5	41/4	60	53	113	3 865
Bahrain	0.4	20	9	2.9	24	0.6	0.8	53	7.6	39/3	66	78	128	7 490
Cyprus	0.7	49	9	1.1	63	0.7	0.8	18	2.3	25/10	72	48	—	3 759
Gaza	0.5	46	13	3.6	20	0.7	0.9	—	—	45 /3	—	90	109	—
Iraq	14.5	24	12	3.4	20	24.2	37.4	77	6.9	46/3	56	72	118	5 450
Israel	4.1	47	7	1.7	41	5.4	6.9	14.6	3.5	33/8	72	89	97	1 623
Jordan	3.6	37	11	3.6	19	6.5	10.3	68	7.2	48/3	61	60	100	25 850
Kuwait	1.6	30	4	3.4	21	2.9	4.5	31.1	6.1	46/2	70	90	—	—
Lebanon	2.6	48	9	2.1	32	3.7	4.9	41	4.0	37/5	66	78	—	5 924
Oman	1.0	31	17	3.1	22	1.7	2.6	127	7.1	45/3	49	8	—	27 790
Qatar	0.3	44	9	2.2	32	0.4	0.6	53	6.8	32/2	58	87	119	12 720
Saudi Arabia	10.4	46	13	3.1	22	18.5	29.5	112	7.2	44/3	54	70	113	1 569
Syria	9.7	31	8	3.8	18	18.0	28.9	61	7.3	48/3	65	48	117	1 511
Turkey	49.2	31	10	2.1	33	70.7	95.2	121	4.3	38/4	62	45	117	25 660
United Arab Emirates	1.4	48	7	2.3	30	2.1	3.1	53	6.8	31/2	63	74	93	459
Yemen, North	5.7	48	21	2.7	26	9.1	13.9	160	6.8	45/3	43	12	93	512
Yemen, South	2.1	48	19	2.9	24	3.4	5.3	144	6.9	46/3	45	38	87	—
MIDDLE SOUTH ASIA	1 011	38	15	2.3	30	1 391	1 790	124	5.2	41/3	50	22	91	251
Afghanistan	14.2	48	23	2.5	27	21.9	32.4	205	6.9	45/2	40	15	75	—
Bangladesh	96.5	49	18	3.1	22	149.4	210.4	135	6.2	45/3	47	10	84	144
Bhutan	1.4	41	19	2.3	31	2.0	3.0	149	6.1	42/3	44	3	—	—
India	730.0	36	15	2.1	33	966.0	1 194.8	122	5.0	39/3	50	22	90	253
Iran	42.5	43	13	3.1	23	66.0	94.7	106	6.4	45/3	55	50	120	—
Maldives	0.2	43	13	3.0	23	0.3	0.4	120	—	41/3	—	11	—	391
Nepal	15.8	44	21	2.3	30	23.1	32.5	149	6.5	42/3	44	5	86	156
Pakistan	95.7	43	15	2.8	25	141.5	196.5	124	6.3	45/3	51	29	99	349
Sri Lanka	15.6	28	6	2.2	32	20.9	25.7	37.1	3.6	35/4	66	24	101	302
SOUTHEAST ASIA	382	33	12	2.1	33	517	654	85	4.6	39/3	54	24	103	663
Brunei	0.2	31	4	2.7	26	0.3	0.4	17.5	5.1	35/3	66	76	—	—
Burma	37.9	38	14	2.4	28	55.0	76.6	99	5.3	41/4	54	29	105	183
Democratic Kampuchea	6.0	38	19	1.9	36	8.9	11.2	201	4.7	35/3	37	15	80	—
East Timor	0.5	44	21	2.3	30	0.7	1.0	211	6.0	42/3	44	11	—	519
Indonesia	155.6	32	15	1.7	41	198.7	238.4	92	4.4	38/3	49	21	106	—
Laos	3.6	44	20	2.4	29	5.2	7.1	128	6.1	42/3	45	15	83	1 817
Malaysia	15.0	31	7	2.4	29	21.1	27.3	31	4.3	39/4	64	30	118	789
Philippines	52.8	34	8	2.7	26	76.5	101.7	54	4.8	41/3	62	39	102	5 220
Singapore	2.5	17	5	1.2	58	3.0	3.3	11.7	1.8	26/4	71	100	101	769
Thailand	50.8	26	7	2.0	36	69.4	87.4	54	3.9	40/3	61	17	103	—
Vietnam	57.0	37	9	2.8	25	78.3	100.1	99	5.2	40/4	54	19	93	—

Table 57.1 (Cont'd)

Region or Country	Population estimate mid-1983 (millions)	Crude birth rate	Crude death rate	Natural increase (annual, %)	Population doubling time in years (at current rate)	Population projected to 2000 (millions)	Population projected to 2020 (millions)	Infant mortality rate	Total fertility rate	% Population under age 15 years/ over age 64 years	Life expectancy at birth (years)	Urban population (%)	Per capita Calorie supply as % of requirements	Per Capita GNP, 1981 (US$)
EAST ASIA	1 229	22	8	1.4	48	1 488	1 700	41	2.7	31/6	69	29	106	1 396
China	1 023.3	23	8	1.5	46	1 244.6	1 426.1	44	2.8	32/6	69	21	105	304
Hong Kong	5.2	17	5	1.2	58	6.6	7.4	9.8	2.3	25/7	76	92	—	5 460
Japan	119.2	13	6	0.7	100	129.7	132.3	7.1	1.8	23/9	76	78	123	10 330
Korea, North	19.2	32	8	2.4	29	27.3	35.8	34	4.3	39/4	64	33	127	—
Korea, South	41.3	25	8	1.7	41	51.8	61.1	34	2.6	33/4	64	57	124	1 720
Macao	0.3	26	8	1.8	39	0.4	0.5	—	—	34/4	—	98	—	—
Mongolia	1.8	37	8	2.9	24	2.7	3.7	54	5.2	42/3	64	51	—	—
Taiwan	18.9	23	5	1.8	38	24.6	33.3	9.1	2.5	32/5	72	66	—	2 360
NORTH AMERICA	259	16	8	0.7	94	302	333	11	1.8	23/11	74	74	187	12 405
Canada	24.9	15	7	0.8	85	33.8	36.2	10.4	1.8	23/9	74	76	126	11 230
United States	234.2	16	9	0.7	95	268.0	296.3	11.4	1.8	23/11	74	74	138	12 530
LATIN AMERICA	390	31	8	2.3	30	564	801	65	4.3	39/4	64	65	108	2 063
MIDDLE AMERICA	100	34	7	2.7	26	234	331	58	4.9	44/3	65	61	115	1 953
Belize	0.2	32	8	2.4	28	0.2	0.2	—	—	49/4	—	52	—	1 110
Costa Rica	2.4	29	4	2.5	27	3.4	4.6	19.1	3.7	37/4	70	44	117	1 476
El Salvador	4.7	36	10	2.6	27	7.8	12.3	53	6.3	45/3	64	41	94	636
Guatemala	7.9	42	10	3.2	22	12.7	19.8	65.9	5.7	44/3	59	37	94	1 159
Honduras	4.1	45	10	3.5	20	7.0	12.0	87	6.5	47/3	58	36	96	591
Mexico	75.7	32	6	2.6	27	115.1	162.4	55	4.7	44/4	66	67	120	2 250
Nicaragua	2.8	47	11	3.6	19	4.8	8.2	89	6.4	48/2	56	53	101	874
Panama	2.1	29	6	2.3	31	2.9	3.8	34	3.9	39/4	70	51	99	1 908
CARIBBEAN	31	26	8	1.8	38	41	55	61	3.5	36/5	66	54	103	—
Antigua and Barbuda	0.1	17	6	1.1	64	0.1	0.2	31.5	2.6	—	—	34	—	3 632
Bahamas	0.2	20	5	1.6	45	0.3	0.4	31.9	3.5	44/4	69	54	—	3 500
Barbados	0.3	17	8	0.9	81	0.3	0.3	22.7	2.1	28/9	71	65	—	—
Cuba	9.8	14	6	0.8	87	11.6	13.2	18.5	1.8	29/8	72	65	117	750
Dominica	0.1	21	5	1.6	43	0.1	0.1	19.6	—	—	—	—	—	—
Dominican Republic	6.2	35	9	2.6	27	9.1	13.2	67	4.7	43/3	61	51	94	1 338

Grenada	0.1	25	7	1.8	39	0.1	0.2	15.4	—	—	71	—	—	872
Guadeloupe	0.3	19	6	1.3	54	0.3	0.4	25	2.7	29/7	70	44	—	—
Haiti	5.7	41	14	2.7	26	8.9	14.9	113	5.5	44/4	52	27	83	297
Jamaica	2.3	27	6	2.1	33	2.9	3.6	28	3.7	38/6	71	50	114	1 182
Martinique	0.3	18	7	1.1	64	0.3	0.4	22	2.7	31/7	70	66	—	—
Netherlands Antilles	0.2	29	7	2.2	32	0.3	0.4	25	—	38/5	—	90	—	—
Puerto Rico	3.4	23	6	1.6	42	4.4	5.2	18.5	2.7	31/6	73	74	—	—
St. Lucia	0.1	28	7	2.2	32	0.2	0.2	30.1	4.8	50/5	—	40	—	—
St. Vincent and the Grenadines	0.1	27	6	2.1	34	0.2	0.2	60.2	—	—	67	—	—	—
Trinidad and Tobago	1.2	25	6	1.9	36	1.5	1.7	26.4	2.7	31/5	70	49	111	5 267
TROPICAL SOUTH AMERICA	216	32	9	2.4	29	316	461	73	4.5	39/4	62	65	103	2 065
Bolivia	5.9	43	16	2.7	26	9.5	17.1	130	6.6	44/3	50	42	87	601
Brazil	131.3	31	8	2.3	30	187.7	268.6	76	4.4	38/4	63	68	105	2 214
Colombia	27.7	28	8	2.0	35	38.2	49.5	56	3.6	38/4	63	60	106	1 334
Ecuador	8.8	41	10	3.2	22	14.6	23.3	81	5.7	44/4	61	45	91	1 171
Guyana	0.8	28	7	2.0	34	1.1	1.4	43	3.9	38/4	70	30	109	723
Paraguay	3.5	35	8	2.7	25	5.5	8.1	46	4.9	42/4	65	40	125	1 557
Peru	19.2	37	11	2.6	26	30.7	50.2	87	5.0	42/3	58	67	92	1 122
Suriname	0.4	28	8	2.0	34	0.6	0.9	36	—	49/4	68	45	109	2 950
Venezuela	18.0	33	5	2.8	24	28.4	41.5	41	4.3	42/3	67	76	107	4 170
TEMPERATE SOUTH AMERICA	44	23	8	1.5	47	53	61	39	2.7	29/8	69	82	122	2 578
Argentina	29.1	24	9	1.5	46	34.5	39.6	41	2.8	28/9	70	82	127	2 560
Chile	11.5	22	7	1.6	45	14.7	17.8	33	2.4	32/6	66	81	112	2 560
Uruguay	3.0	18	10	0.9	79	3.4	4.0	34.1	2.8	27/11	70	84	107	2 820
EUROPE	489	14	10	0.4	199	511	508	16	1.9	22/13	72	69	135	10 025
NORTHERN EUROPE	82	13	11	0.2	391	84	83	11	1.9	20/15	73	74	130	9 935
Denmark	5.1	10	11	-0.1	—	5.1	4.7	8.0	1.4	20/15	74	84	130	12 790
Finland	4.8	13	9	0.4	178	5.0	4.7	7.6	1.7	23/12	73	62	—	10 380
Iceland	0.2	19	7	1.2	60	0.3	0.3	7.7	2.5	26/10	76	88	—	12 550
Ireland	3.5	21	9	1.2	60	4.1	4.9	11.2	3.2	31/11	73	58	149	5 350
Norway	4.1	13	10	0.3	239	4.1	4.0	8.1	1.7	21/15	75	44	122	13 800
Sweden	8.3	11	11	0.0	3 465	8.0	7.4	7.0	1.6	19/17	75	83	117	14 500
United Kingdom	56.0	13	12	0.1	533	56.9	56.3	12.1	1.9	20/15	73	77	131	8 950
WESTERN EUROPE	155	12	11	0.2	436	156	143	10	1.7	19/14	73	81	134	12 704
Austria	7.6	13	12	0.0	3 465	7.4	6.9	12.6	1.7	19/15	72	54	132	10 250
Belgium	9.9	13	11	0.1	495	9.9	9.3	11.7	1.7	19/14	72	95	149	11 980
France	54.6	15	10	0.5	151	56.7	56.9	9.6	2.0	22/13	74	78	134	12 130
Germany, West	61.5	10	12	-0.2	—	59.9	49.3	11.6	1.4	17/14	72	85	132	13 520
Luxembourg	0.4	12	11	0.1	770	0.4	0.3	11.0	1.6	17/14	72	68	149	13 900
Netherlands	14.4	13	8	0.4	158	14.9	14.2	8.2	1.6	21/12	74	88	129	11 140
Switzerland	6.5	12	9	0.2	315	6.3	5.7	9.1	1.5	19/14	75	58	131	17 150

Table 57.1 (Cont'd)

Region or Country	Population estimate mid-1983 (millions)	Crude birth rate	Crude death rate	Natural increase (annual, %)	Population doubling time in years (at current rate)	Population projected to 2000 (millions)	Population projected to 2020 (millions)	Infant mortality rate	Total fertility rate	% Population under age 15 years/over age 64 years	Life expectancy at birth (years)	Urban population (%)	Per capita Calorie supply as % of requirements	Per Capita GNP, 1981 (US$)
EASTERN EUROPE	111	17	11	0.6	125	120	127	21	2.2	23/11	71	60	136	4 571
Bulgaria	8.9	14	11	0.3	231	9.5	9.8	19.5	2.0	22/12	72	62	145	4 413
Czechoslovakia	15.4	16	12	0.4	182	16.5	17.9	16.8	2.1	24/12	70	67	140	5 610
Germany, East	16.7	14	14	0.0	—	16.8	15.3	12.3	1.9	19/15	72	76	142	7 286
Hungary	10.7	13	14	0.0	—	10.8	10.9	20.6	1.9	22/13	70	53	134	4 187
Poland	36.6	19	9	1.0	71	41.0	44.8	20.6	2.3	25/10	71	58	135	—
Romania	22.7	18	10	0.8	91	25.6	28.3	29.3	2.4	26/10	71	49	128	2 546
SOUTHERN EUROPE	141	14	9	0.5	141	151	156	19	1.9	23/12	72	59	139	5 385
Albania	2.9	27	7	2.0	34	3.9	4.8	47	4.2	36/5	69	34	117	—
Greece	9.9	15	9	0.6	110	10.6	11.3	17.9	2.3	22/13	73	65	145	4 540
Italy	56.3	11	10	0.1	495	56.3	53.2	14.1	1.6	21/14	73	69	144	6 830
Malta	0.4	15	9	0.6	108	0.4	0.4	13.1	2.1	23/11	71	83	122	3 970
Portugal	9.9	16	10	0.6	108	11.2	12.2	26.0	2.1	25/11	71	31	130	2 534
Spain	38.4	14	8	0.7	107	43.2	47.3	10.3	2.0	25/11	73	64	135	5 770
Yugoslavia	22.8	17	9	0.8	90	25.1	26.1	30.6	2.0	24/9	70	39	138	2 789
USSR	272	19	10	0.8	83	309	345	33	2.3	25/10	70	62	132	4 701
OCEANIA	24	21	8	1.2	57	29	34	38	2.7	29/8	70	72	122	8 864
Australia	15.3	16	7	0.9	82	18.1	19.9	10.0	1.9	25/10	73	86	120	11 190
Fiji	0.7	29	4	2.5	27	0.8	0.9	36	3.6	36/3	72	37	—	1 884
French Polynesia	0.2	30	7	2.3	30	0.2	0.3	—	—	—	—	39	—	—
New Zealand	3.2	16	8	0.8	83	3.8	4.3	11.7	2.0	29/9	73	83	132	7 580
Papua-New Guinea	3.1	41	16	2.5	28	4.6	6.7	103	6.3	43/3	52	13	—	815
Samoa, Western	0.2	37	7	3.0	23	0.2	0.2	40	5.3	48/3	65	22	—	—
Solomon Islands	0.3	44	9	3.5	20	0.4	0.7	78	6.2	48/3	—	9	—	619
Vanuatu	0.1	45	17	2.8	25	0.2	0.3	101	—	—	—	23	—	—

this, all the great religions of the world, Confucianism, Hinduism, Judaism, Christianity and Islam, have co-operated. An early marriage and a large family was the avowed aim for every girl. Those who achieved this aim received both social and religious approval. The infertile woman was an object of scorn and derision. This attitude to women was all but universal until 200 years ago. Under the circumstances it was sensible — indeed essential — if mankind was to survive. However, now under very different circumstances, it still persists to some extent in all countries and in many it wrongly remains the dominant concept of woman's role in society.

Fall of death rates in Europe in the eighteenth century

In the middle of the eighteenth century the death rate in most European countries began to fall and has for the most part fallen steadily ever since. The reasons for the start of this fall are uncertain. Popular opinion, and even eminent historians such as Trevelyan,[4] often ascribed it to the benefits of the new medical science. In fact therapeutics only advanced sufficiently to have a significant effect on death rates within the last 50 years. Indeed it is only in the last four decades, with the widespread use of antibiotics and insecticides, that medical science has seriously affected demographic processes and so caused renewed interest in the Malthusian dilemma. The fall in death rates in Europe in the eighteenth century can be attributed in part to the spread of religious toleration. Toleration put an end to the lethal civil wars of religions in the previous centuries. Then law and order could be more easily maintained and so roads and communications opened up. In addition, new improved agricultural methods and the introduction of the potato from America markedly reduced the effects of bad agricultural seasons and virtually abolished European famines which had hitherto caused heavy losses of life in most countries.[5] Further, both bubonic plague and smallpox, which caused so many deaths in the sixteenth and seventeenth centuries, declined in Europe and were no longer such important factors in the population equilibrium. The effect of a natural decline in the virulence of smallpox was increased by the discovery of vaccination by Jenner.

Fall of death rates in Asia and Africa

In Asia a similar fall began in the middle of the nineteenth century, often following a period of colonial rule. Law and order gradually replaced civil war; there were enormous increases in transport facilities and by the end of the nineteenth century famine, plague, smallpox and cholera were in large measure controlled. These factors all operated most markedly in the countries which became subjugated to European or Japanese metropolitan powers. Whatever the demerits of colonialism, it was always associated with a fall in the death rate and a rise in the numbers of the colonial peoples.

In most underdeveloped countries, including Africa, death rates fell slowly during the first half of this century but a dramatic drop in many countries first occurred after World War II brought about by the increased economic prosperity, and the widespread use of insecticides and antibiotics.

POPULATION PROBLEMS 1985–2025

In all countries of the Third World, birth rate exceeds death rate and the population is expanding. Many poor countries are already overpopulated and agricultural production is barely increasing sufficiently to keep pace with growth of population. Low standards of nutrition are likely to fall lower, unless radical changes occur soon. Disastrous famines and the accompanying chaos may then follow. More food and fewer new mouths are equally urgent problems.

In forecasting the population changes likely to occur in any country in the next 40 years to 2025, two figures are essential. The first is the number of women of child-bearing age (15–45 years) present in each year. All of these are here right now and losses by death can be predicted with reasonable accuracy. The second is their fertility rate — the annual number of births per 1000 women aged 15–45 years. This figure is subject to marked variation and may be affected by the state of the economy and by feminine fashion. Thus in the USA it fell from about 120 in 1920 to 75 at the depth of the economic depression in 1933. It then rose steadily and by 1960 was back to 120 and this has been called the 'baby boom'. It then began to fall and in 1980 was down to only 70. We can only guess what it will be in future years. We also cannot know with any certainty how emigration and immigration will affect numbers in any country. Hence it is easy to understand how population projections have often in the past been very wrong. It is essential to continue to make these forecasts but to remember that in this, as in all things, the future is uncertain.

The increase in the population in both rich and poor countries alike has been only occasionally associated with a rise in the birth rate. It has been caused almost entirely by a decrease in the death rate. In recent years this has resulted from advances in medical and ancillary sciences and in the medical and social services which make this new knowledge available. Since medical science is partly responsible for creating the problems of overpopulation, it should assume responsibility for solving them. This it could do if it were not for the fact that modern methods of family planning and contraception are not generally or easily applicable in underdeveloped countries. Even in prosperous countries such as the United States and the United Kingdom, birth control has only recently become part of the 'establishment' and formerly received little support either from government or organised medical bodies. However, times are changing. The year 1974 was noteworthy for being nominated World Population Year by the UN and for the holding of a World Population Conference in Bucharest. In the UK it saw provision made for family planning within the National Health Service.

Attitudes only change slowly. In Western medicine, the treatment of an individual patient continues to attract more prestige and money than has attention to the health of the population as a whole. The control of the birth rate by family planning is considered a far less urgent medical problem than heart disease or cancer.

The official Roman Catholic Church still considers contraception to be morally wrong and forbids research and teaching in contraception and the sale of contraceptives, though many of its members dissent from this view. This attitude is responsible for much ill health in poor families in many countries, especially in Latin America.

The International Planned Parenthood Federation, founded in 1948, supports family planning associations in about 100 developing countries. In 1985 it was expecting an income of $55 million. Its plans have now to be restricted because $15 million, the contribution from the United States, has been cancelled. This appears to be the result of President Reagan's bowing to pressures from fundamentalist religious groups. The result will be that great numbers of poor women in many countries will not get the help that they need urgently and in desperation many will turn to abortion. It is to be hope that this decision will be reversed. Fortunately there are compassionate men and women in the USA who agree with us that the widespread distribution of modern contraceptive knowledge is an urgent necessity and this presents a major public health problem.

Community health approach

Exhortation to uneducated women to limit their families is unlikely to be effective. Particularly in areas where the infant mortality rates are high, it is quite useless to preach birth control. It is natural for men and women to desire healthy children to take their place in life and to provide for their parents in old age. In societies where the women are ignorant of the elementary laws of hygiene and cannot manage either to raise their children properly or to protect them against the common infectious diseases associated with dirt and squalor, a woman must produce many children if she is to expect to rear even two or three up to adult life. Children are often considered to be a source of social security. In most countries, both in the East and in the West, it is prob-

able that most women who have successfully produced two, three or four healthy children seek ways and means to prevent the arrival of more. If women can be shown how to raise a small healthy family, then many of them will actively seek advice as to how to prevent more arrivals. It is easy to teach people who desire knowledge.

If this reasoning is accepted, it follows that a first step in any attack on the birth rates must be through the Maternity and Child Health Centres. In these Centres women can be taught mothercraft; nutritional education is, of course, a most important part of such teaching. When the Public Health Nurses have successfully educated the majority of the women in a community how to rear healthy children, then the demand for advice on contraception will inevitably and automatically follow. As in the case of so many other aspects of preventive medicine, the Maternity and Child Health Centres can provide centres from which new ideas must spread out amongst a people. A practical way in which Family Planning can be linked with Child Health Services is by explaining to the mother how a longer birth interval improves the prospects for the present baby and by planning the time to start and discontinue contraceptive measures on the present baby's growth chart. However, the women have to win their husbands over to new ideas; in many communities failure of arrival of another child after two years is regarded as evidence of lack of virility in the husband.

A most important factor, which restricts the birth rate, is the delay in the age of marriage. A girl who is married at 13 or 14 is likely to have more children than one whose marriage is delayed until after she is 20 years of age. The extension of higher education to women has already had an important effect on birth rates in many countries and this influence is spreading. Family Planning and nutrition services are each part of community health. Many women need help from both. Nutritionists should be aware of the Family Planning Service and be ready to work with its members in their community.

Modern contraceptive techniques

Methods of contraception such as the rhythm method and coitus interruptus have been employed since time immemorial. Unfortunately such simple methods have proved either unsatisfactory or ineffective. More modern methods involving the placing of some kind of barrier, either mechanical or chemical, between the sperm and the ovum have not proved suitable for use on a large scale by people who are both poor and ignorant. Now oral contraceptives, intrauterine contraceptive devices (IUCD) and voluntary male sterilisation by vasectomy are being extensively tried in underdeveloped countries. Female sterilisation by tubectomy is also used. The merits of the different methods and the problems arising in their use in Family Planning programmes in several countries are discussed by Mills.[6] The difficulties in carrying out a national contraceptive programme in a very poor country such as Bangladesh are as yet unresolved.

COMMENT

Comparison of Table 57.1, which is mainly 1983 data, with the similar table in our last edition, mainly 1976 data, shows that estimated world population has gone up in the seven years by 468 million, an annual rate of increase of 1.6 per cent. High rates of increase in countries in Africa, Asia and Latin America have not changed greatly. In India and Bangladesh the rates of increase remain at about 2 and 3 per cent. If agriculture production does not continue to increase by at least 2 per cent annually, available food supplies cannot be maintained.

In North America the annual rate of increase is now only 0.7 per cent. In Europe there are six countries in which the population has now ceased to rise. There are 18 other countries in Europe and also Australia, New Zealand, Japan and Singapore that are approaching zero growth and should reach it within the lifetimes of our younger readers. This is good news, but only for some 20 per cent of the world population who live in rich countries. We believe that only if both contraception and scientific agriculture are practised on a worldwide scale can disasters be avoided.

REFERENCES

1. Ehrlich P R 1971 The population bomb. Pan Books, London
2. Loraine J A 1972 The death of tomorrow. Heinemann, London
3. Brown L R 1981 Building a stable society. Norton, New York
4. Trevelyan G M 1942 British social history. Longmans, Green, London, p 341
5. Salaman R N 1948 History and social influence of the potato. Cambridge University Press
6. Mills A R 1974 The population problems and family planning. In: Passmore R, Robson J S (eds) Companion to medical studies. Blackwell, Oxford, vol 3: 71.1–11

58

Famine

As far back as history records, mankind has suffered at irregular intervals from great famines. In many the disaster has been so great that a million or more people have perished. Enormous advances in agriculture and in methods of transport, notably the introduction of potatoes to Europe in the seventeenth century and of railways to India in the nineteenth century, made the prevention and relief of famine technically very much easier. During the first half of the twentieth century great famines appeared to belong to the past and there was little interest in famine relief. This optimism was rudely shattered in 1943 when at least a million people died in the Bengal famine. Severe famine conditions arose again in Bihar in India in 1965–66 and in the civil wars that preceded the establishment of the states of Zaire and Bangladesh and kept Nigeria politically intact. Since 1980 there have been famines in countries south of the Sahara where the desert is spreading, in Ethiopia and in Kampuchea. The problems of famine are very much alive today.

The worst disasters have occurred when the famine has not been foreseen and the government has lacked the administrative experience to organise relief. On the other hand there are many examples of foresight which have enabled relief measures to be planned ahead. A well-planned and organised relief service can help a people to survive a period of famine, not without hardship and suffering but at least with no great increase in the number of deaths. Although there are many books giving excellent historical accounts of particular famines, there are few devoted primarily to the scientific aspects of the prevention and relief of famine. Monographs by Masefield,[1] the Swedish Nutrition Foundation[2] and Aykroyd[3] are recommended.

Since 1975 surveillance by UN organisations, described on page 527, has given early warning of impending famine. This has allowed international aid to reach several countries in time to prevent disaster.

This chapter attempts to give only a broad outline of conditions and to set out a few general principles. Based on experience of famine in India[4] it has been changed little since the first edition. Throughout the nineteenth century governments of Indian provinces had a series of severe famines to deal with and a Famine Code was evolved. It has on many occasions been the means of preventing excess mortality, if not hardship. The success of the relief measures in the Bihar famine 1966–67[2] followed the application of its principles incorporated in Famine Codes of the previous century. An account of the administrative organisation needed for famine relief today applicable to any country is given by Ifekwunigwe.[5] If a Punjab civil servant of 100 years ago could have read his paper, he would have appreciated its clarity but not have been surprised.

CAUSES OF FAMINE

Drought
In tropical and subtropical countries large numbers of people have lived and continued to live under the yearly threat of drought. Failure of the rains, often in successive seasons, has been a frequent cause of famine. The importance of the science of irrigation in the husbanding and control of natural water has been discussed on page 510. In Asia and in Africa irrigation schemes, often on a vast scale, have made large areas of land practically independent of yearly variations in rainfall. Yet much remains to be done and in many districts throughout the tropics and subtropics failure of the rains can bring the people to the verge of disaster.

Crop diseases and pests
The great Irish famines of the nineteenth century were caused by the destruction of the potato crops by a fungus, which produces a disease known as 'the blight'. A good account of this famine has been given by Woodham-Smith.[6] Whenever people are largely dependent on a single crop for their main source of food, there is always the risk that the crop may be destroyed by disease, and famine conditions follow. Plagues of locusts can cause great destruction of all crops and, in some parts of the world, these greedy insects are a potential cause of famine.

Great natural disturbances

Floods and earthquakes are a constant natural threat to man in many parts of the world. They can destroy crops, food stores and communications and so cause famine.

Man-made causes: war, civil commotion and economic factors

Wars and especially civil wars have been directly responsible for many famines throughout history. Food shortages are an inevitable result of all wars and these can readily lead to famine conditions. Nuclear warfare on a large scale in an industrial country might quickly lead to famine amongst the survivors, through destruction of transport, docks and warehouses. Poor social organisation, poverty and lack of transport can prevent the proper distribution of a food supply which is potentially adequate, and so bring about famine.

Each of these four primary causes is still operative.

Many parts of the world are still dependent on an uncertain seasonal rainfall. Small, but locally devastating wars, continue to be a feature of world history.

EFFECTS OF FAMINE

Literature contains many moving accounts of human suffering during famines. Two of these are given below. The first is a letter from Ireland addressed to the Duke of Wellington on 17 December 1846.[7]

Having for many years been intimately connected with the western portion of the county of Cork, and possessing some small property there, I thought it right, personally, to investigate the truth of the several lamentable accounts which had reached me of the appalling state of misery to which that part of the country was reduced . . . . Being aware that I should have to witness scenes of frightful hunger, I provided myself with as much bread as five men could carry, and on reaching the spot I was surprised to find the wretched hamlet deserted. I entered some of the hovels to ascertain the cause, and the scenes that presented themselves were such as no tongue or pen can convey the slightest idea of. In the first, six famished and ghastly skeletons, to all appearance dead, were huddled in a corner on some filthy straw, their sole covering what seemed a ragged horse-cloth and their wretched legs hanging about, naked above the knees. I approached in horror, and found by a low moaning they were alive, they were in fever — four children, a woman, and what once had been a man. It is impossible to go through the details, suffice to say, that in a few minutes I was surrounded by at least 200 of such phantoms, such frightful spectres as no words can describe. By far the greater number were delirious either from famine or from fever. Their demoniac yells are still ringing in my ears, and their horrible images are fixed upon my brain . . . the same morning the police opened a house on the adjoining lands, which was observed shut for many days, and two frozen corpses were found lying upon the mud floor *half devoured by the rats*. A mother, herself in fever, was seen the same day to drag out the corpse of her child, a girl about 12, perfectly naked; and leave

it half covered with stones. In another house . . . the dispensary doctor found seven wretches lying, unable to move, under the same cloak — one had been dead for many hours but the others were unable to move either themselves or the corpse. To what purpose should I multiply such cases? If these be not sufficient, neither would they hear who have the power to send relief and do not, even though "one came from the dead".

The second[8] describes from contemporary letters the scene in Western Bengal in 1770, when it is estimated that 10 million people — or a third of the population — died.

All through the stifling summer the people went on dying. The husbandmen sold their cattle; they sold their implements of agriculture; they devoured their seed grain; they sold their sons and daughters, till at length no buyer of children could be found; they ate the leaves of trees and the grass of the field; and in June 1770, the Resident at the Durbar affirmed that the living were feeding on the dead. Day and night a torrent of famished and disease-stricken wretches poured into the great cities. At an early period of the year pestilence had broken-out. In March we find smallpox at Moosshedabad, where it glided through the vice-regal mutes, and cut off the Prince Syfut in his palace. The streets were blocked with promiscuous heaps of the dying and the dead. Interment could not do its work quick enough; even the dogs and jackals, the public scavengers of the East, became unable to accomplish their revolting work, and the multitude of mangled and festering corpses at length threatened the existence of the citizens.

Of the many effects of famine, it is practical for the purposes of administrating relief to keep three constantly in mind.

Deaths from starvation

It is of prime importance to procure and distribute sufficient food to prevent such deaths. Their number is the measure of the severity of the famine and the effectiveness of the relief organisation. Old people and young children are particularly liable to die of starvation. Adolescents often manage to survive. Women usually survive better than men.

Panic and social disruption

It is natural for starving people, if there is no food in their immediate neighbourhood, to leave home and go in search of something to eat. If such wandering takes place on a large scale, social chaos is inevitable and all relief work becomes many times more difficult. Families are easily disrupted and only with great difficulty later reunited. If parents die, infants and young children may be found helpless with no knowledge of their family name or the whereabouts of their home or of other relations. Adolescents, if separated from their families, readily form gangs, which are actively opposed to all forces of law and order. Such gangs may be a source of much mischief and the subsequent rehabilitation of the members very difficult.

Spread of epidemics

Louse-borne typhus was the great famine disease in Europe, and cholera and smallpox in Asia. But large epidemics of relapsing fever, influenza, tuberculosis, enteric fever — or indeed of any infectious disease — may be associated with famine. In malarious countries famine usually occurs in times of drought and so conditions are unsuitable for the mosquitoes which transmit the disease. When the rains do come, often in excessive amounts, malaria may spread rapidly among the enfeebled survivors of the famine. On some occasions there have been more deaths in the malaria epidemic subsequent to a famine than in the famine itself.

It is unusual to find epidemics of any of the diseases attributable to vitamin deficiencies in a famine, though scurvy may afflict the inhabitants of a besieged city or a desert people.

The rapid spread of infectious diseases among a starving people is attributable to the ease with which the infecting organisms can pass from person to person as a result of overcrowding and the breakdown of normal sanitary arrangements. It is the absence of all hygienic precautions that is responsible for epidemics rather than an increased susceptibility of the starving body to infective micro-organisms. In many famines far more people have died of infectious diseases than of starvation.

Priorities

These three effects of famine, deaths from starvation, social disruption and the spread of epidemics, should be constantly in the mind of relief workers. It is important to repeat and emphasise this; for in a famine there is always more to do than can be done. The time and energy of the workers must be disciplined, for it is easy to be distracted by a charitable heart to a task which may be very worthy yet of secondary importance.

FAMINE RELIEF

Procurement and distribution of food

Transport problems. Fortunately for mankind the causes of famine are local. A district, a province or even occasionally a whole country may be involved, but never a whole continent. Stores of surplus food have always been available — somewhere. How to get the food to the right place fast enough is always the fundamental problem. Modern methods of transport have greatly mitigated the effects of famine. The rapid development of railways throughout India in the middle of the nineteenth century facilitated the organisation of relief and was the means of saving many lives.

Ships, trains, aeroplanes, lorries and sometimes bullock carts, camels and other pack animals may be needed. The procurement and organisation of these is the first and most important problem of a relief organisation.

Quantities of food required. The urgent need is for energy foods; the correction of vitamin and mineral deficiencies in the diet may have to wait until the peak of the famine is past. For infants and children a source of good protein is desirable and can sometimes be provided by dried skimmed milk. The minimum amount of food necessary to preserve human life has been much debated in the past. FAO in 1946 set out recommendations for subsistence and maintenance levels of energy intake, which are given in Table 58.1. These figures represent a compromise between physiological needs and practical difficulties. Nutritionists must warn governments that unless food is available at this emergency subsistence level, deaths from starvation and civil unrest are likely. The figures in Table 58.1 have to be converted into tons of cereal grain. One ton of cereals provides about 15 million MJ. This will suffice for about 1850 sedentary males for a day at the emergency subsistence level. To calculate the total food that must be imported into a famine area, it is also necessary to know or estimate (1) the number of people in the area, (2) the amount of physical labour that is required of them, (3) the proportions of women and children, (4) the stores of food already in the area, and (5) the probable duration of the emergency. With these data, tables of physiological needs can be converted into statements of cargo space required.

Such estimates can be nothing more than intelligent guesses unless a recent and reliable census is available. The importance of a census can never be overestimated.

Table 58.1 Scales of energy allowances suitable for use in time of famine (megajoules/day)

Category	Emergency subsistence level*	Temporary maintenance level†
0–2	4.2	4.2
3–5 years	5.3	6.3
6–9 years	6.3	7.4
10–17 years	8.4	10.5
Pregnant and nursing women	8.4	10.5
Normal consumers (sedentary)		
Male	8.0	9.5
Female	6.8	9.2
Moderate workers	8.4	10.5
Heavy workers	10.5	12.5
Very heavy workers	12.5	14.6

* *Emergency subsistence level* needed to prevent the most serious undernutrition leading to disease and the danger of civil unrest.

† *Temporary maintenance level* sufficiently high to maintain populations in fairly good health but not sufficient for rapid and complete recovery.

Public works. The growth of the British Empire throughout the eighteenth century compelled civil servants to consider ways and means of distributing food to famine victims. They were greatly influenced by two principles. The first was that trade was the natural and proper means for the distribution of all goods, including food, and that governments should interfere with trading operations as little as possible. The second was that charity ultimately degrades the recipient, who should if possible pay for the relief which he receives. In the formulation of these principles the influence of Adam Smith was great. His book *The Wealth of Nations* was published in 1776 and his laissez-faire economic doctrines were widely accepted at the beginning of the nineteenth century. They greatly affected the organisation of famine relief. It was concluded that the real need of famine victims was for money. If they were provided with money, food would become available through the channels of normal trade, which would be developed to meet needs. They could get money if they had the opportunity to work. The solution to the problem was thus the setting up of public works. There has been much experience of the public works system of relief, but it is difficult either to condemn or approve the system wholeheartedly.

In Ireland in 1846–47 and in Bengal in 1943, the system failed to prevent the deaths of hundreds of thousands. It must be added that in both these countries it was administered by local civil servants who were without experience of famine and who were not adequately forewarned. Time and experience are needed to plan and organise public works.

On the other hand, in several parts of India where famine conditions arise owing to failure of the rains, relief works have frequently been the means of helping people through an emergency period without loss of life, but not without hardship and suffering. Here there has been the advantage that the probability of famine was usually foreseen, and experienced local staff available to plan ahead and administer relief work.

Even under the best conditions the system has its disadvantages. The food requirements of the people are increased by the physical work involved and also by the walk from their homes to the work sites. Even with the best planning, it is impossible to organise work for all the immediate neighbourhood. Furthermore, the old and those physically handicapped may be unable to work and so get no relief. Pride may prevent members of the middle classes from undertaking manual labour. Often the work itself is of little value. Road-making has been commonly undertaken and many of the roads have led from 'nowhere in particular to nowhere at all', in the words of Salaman, an historian of the Irish famine.[9] 'Useless physical work may be demoralising. Well-planned public works have their place in famine relief under many circumstances, but it is unwise to rely too

heavily on them, especially if an experienced supervisory staff is not available.

Public kitchens

Cooked food may be distributed from public kitchens. This is usually essential in a severe famine. Only in this way is it possible to ensure that food reaches those too old, too young or so severely handicapped that they cannot work. Further, it is often impossible to bring into a famine area the foods to which the people are accustomed. The introduction of strange foods, which the people may not know how to cook or prepare, has presented great difficulties in the past. This can be overcome in part by the distribution of meals at special centres.

Price control

It is essential that the prices of such foods as are available be kept within the means of the famine victims. There are always some merchants who are willing to exploit the sufferings of others to their own financial gain. Legislation to prevent any excessive rise in prices is essential, and direct subsidies on cereal grains and other foods may be desirable. The extent to which prices are kept down is a measure of the efficiency of the government.

ORGANISATION OF FOREIGN AID

A threat of famine evokes much public sympathy and people wish to give aid to the victims through private charities, their national government and the UN agencies. Two factors operate to prevent this goodwill being turned into effective relief.

First the number of agencies seeking to help may be large and their efforts lack coordination. Administrators and field workers of different agencies may differ in their opinions as to how best to give relief. As famine rouses the emotions, it is not surprising that there are stories of personal animosity between relief workers. Government officials in the country receiving relief have had to deal with many foreign helpers who are at loggerheads. There is need for international planning to channel all foreign aid through a single administrative machinery in the country receiving the aid.

Secondly famine conditions often arise in times of war and especially of civil war. It is a common view that it is possible to win a war by starving the enemy out and military policy has often been directed to this aim. Such a policy has seldom been successful and Mayer gives many examples of its ineffectiveness.[2] When food is scarce, the young men in the armed forces get enough to keep them an effective fighting force and they still have to be defeated in battle before a war is won. It is civilians who suffer from such a policy and the children and old people who starve to death. There is a widespread move amongst governments to outlaw all chemical and bacteriological means of waging war. Such a ban should be extended to include starvation. In the Nigerian civil war, in Kampuchea and now in Ethiopia, relief work for the civilian population was much hindered by the military authorities on both sides. In times of war the Geneva Convention permits the International Red Cross to care for the wounded and sick of both sides and this has been the means of saving much suffering and countless lives. There is need for a similar international organisation for the care of victims of starvation. The practicability of this important idea has been discussed by the Swedish Nutrition Foundation[2] and merits serious study.

The difficulties of international relief organisations in distributing food to civilian populations during a civil war are described by Shawcross[10] in a moving book, *The quality of mercy*, with the subtitle *Cambodia, holocaust and modern conscience*.

MEDICINE IN A FAMINE

The problem before every member of the medical services engaged in famine relief is not 'What is there for me to do?' but rather 'Of the many jobs to be done, which will save most lives?' In a famine there are never enough doctors or nurses; hospital beds and equipment are insufficient; drugs and vaccines are scarce.

Assessment of the state of the famine
The efficient organisation of relief depends upon accurate assessments of the course of the famine. The number of people likely to be in need of relief in the near future must be forecast. This is never an easy matter and there are always those who, for political reasons, seek either to minimise or exaggerate the extent of the distress. Great disasters seldom arise suddenly and without warning. A Public Health Service that can give week-by-week reports on the numbers of deaths and the numbers seeking admission to hospital is invaluable. If possible, the causes of death and the nature of the diseases requiring hospital treatment should be stated; even if the diagnosis cannot always be precise and accurate, the information is still useful, especially as an indication of the appearance of a new infectious disease. The organisation of accurate medical statistics is thus of first importance. An example of this in the Kampuchean disaster is given in a report of a Red Cross epidemiological unit.[11]

Observation of the state of nutrition of the people is also valuable. As discussed in Chapter 55, there is no single simple method of assessing nutritional status.

Nevertheless an observant medical staff, who can move freely over the whole of a famine area, will be able to detect quickly any signs of deterioration in the health of the people.

Prevention of epidemics
An adequate supply of sanitary stores, including vaccines, insecticides and disinfectants, should be available, with sufficient reserves kept in medical stores to meet any further emergency. Most epidemic diseases can be readily controlled by prompt action in the first few days after their appearance; once they are established, control may become impossible before a large toll of mortality has been taken.

The Public Health Service must be maintained and, as far as possible, expanded, even at the expense of the clinical staff. Any breakdown in this service can be the direct cause of innumerable deaths.

Organisation of famine hospitals
Small hospitals widely dispersed amongst the people are more valuable than large institutions. A nearby hospital will help to maintain confidence and so prevent wandering and social disruption. In such hospitals elaborate diagnostic equipment is of secondary importance. Sufficient blankets, kitchen and sanitary equipment, simple drugs and enough staff to allow rapid expansion in an emergency, are essential. Relief workers, if healthy and intelligent, can be rapidly trained to perform hospital duties, even if previously quite inexperienced in hospital work. At Belsen, medical students made excellent workers and their energy, enthusiasm and common sense more than compensated for any deficiencies in technical training. It is the first duty of a medical superintendent to recruit and train a staff sufficiently large to meet any foreseen emergency. In selecting recruits enthusiasm, intelligence and health are the essentials: deficiencies in technical knowledge can rapidly be made good.

Treatment in a famine hospital
The treatment of starvation has been described in Chapter 27. In the early stages rapid recovery frequently follows a few days feeding and attention to minor ailments. If treatment is neglected at this stage the condition of the patient may deteriorate rapidly. Once appetite is lost and strength is so feeble that standing is no longer possible, the prognosis is uncertain and recovery always slow, even with the best medical and nursing care. Hence more lives are saved if the minor sick receive priority in medical care.

Feeding arrangements must be simple and there is no place for elaborate dietary regimes. In a famine hospital the first essential is the preparation of simple, well-cooked meals. The provision of suitable kitchen and dining-room accommodation and equipment may be difficult and should command the doctors' attention. A large staff of nurses and orderlies are necessary when many patients are too week to go to the dining rooms.

Experience has shown that even a small medical service, if well run, will have a beneficial effect in maintaining public confidence. A shortage of doctors, nurses and orderlies is inevitable and every individual doctor must train his assistants to accept the work delegated to them. A doctor's chief task is thus administration and supervision. The ability to foresee needs for simple remedies and equipment is essential, and for success it is necessary to be a master of improvisation.

CONCLUSION

Famine relief inevitably presents may and diverse problems. It is often difficult for a worker on the spot to sort out what is essential from what is only desirable. It is hoped that this chapter will stimulate thought on the principles of relief, for in famine forethought is the best antidote to disaster.

REFERENCES

1. Masefield G B 1967 Food and Nutrition procedures in times of disaster. FAO Nutr Studies no. 21
2. Swedish Nutrition Foundation 1971 Famine: a symposium dealing with nutrition relief operations in times of disaster. Blix G, Hofvander Y, Vahlquist B (eds). Almquist & Wiksell, Stockholm
3. Aykroyd W R 1974 The conquest of famine. Chatto & Windus, London
4. Passmore R 1951 Famine in India: an historical survey. Lancet 2: 303–6
5. Ifekwunigwe A E 1967 Failure of the food distribution system: dealing with famine. Ann N Y Acad Sci 300: 69–86
6. Woodham-Smith C 1962 The Great Hunger: Ireland 1845–9. Hamish Hamilton, London
7. Edwards R D, Williams T D 1956 The Great Famine. Brown & Nolan, Dublin, p 274
8. Hunter W W 1868 Annals of rural Bengal. London, p 26
9. Salaman R N 1948 History and social influence of the potato. Cambridge University Press
10. Shawcross W 1984 The quality of mercy. Deutsch, London
11. Glass R I, Cates W, Nieburg P, Davies C, et al 1980 Rapid assessment of health status of newly arrived Kampuchean refugees, Sa Koes, Thailand. Lancet 1: 868–72

59

Nutrition and Infection

The recorded history of mankind demonstrates repeatedly the close association between war, pestilence, famine and death. They are represented as the four horsemen of the apocalypse in St John's allegory (Revelation, Chap. 6). Fevers, poverty and poor nutrition went together in the slums of industrial cities. Famines have been associated with outbreaks of disease such as typhus, relapsing fever, smallpox and cholera. The great tropical diseases, especially malaria, dysentery and ankylostomiasis were most prevalent among the poverty-stricken. Eighty years ago in the cities of Europe fatal respiratory infections were common in poor children with rickets in the overcrowded slums. Rheumatic fever following streptococcal infection was more frequently found in the children of the poor than of the well-to-do. Wherever in the world there has been hunger and poverty, victims of pulmonary tuberculosis have been numerous. However, poverty is also associated with inadequate houses, overcrowding and insufficient sanitary services. Overcrowding facilitates the passage of micro-organisms from person to person (cross-infection). This is so whether a disease is spread as an air-borne infection or by food or water, or transmitted by insects.

There is no doubt that severe or repeated infections are a common cause of malnutrition. The extent to which malnutrition itself contributes to the incidence and severity of infections is much more difficult to assess.

INFECTIONS AS A CAUSE OF MALNUTRITION

Infections increase the rate of metabolism and the breakdown of tissues (p. 487) and so create a need for extra nutrients. Accompanying fever usually reduces appetite, and when the infection affects the function of the gastrointestinal tract, as is frequent, absorption of nutrients is impaired. In these ways an infection increases requirements of nutrients and at the same time may reduce their supply. These effects may be of trivial significance, if the infection lasts only a few days and the patient was previously well-nourished. If the infection is prolonged or there are repeated attacks or the patient's previous diet was only just adequate, severe malnutrition may arise. How attacks of gastroenteritis, measles and whooping cough frequently precipitate severe and fatal protein-energy malnutrition is described in Chapter 29. These three diseases are ubiquitous and few children escape attacks. In prosperous countries where the children are well fed, the illness is only occasionally serious; in countries where many children have a poor diet these infections carry a high mortality rate (Table 59.1). Most of these deaths would be ascribed more accurately as due to malnutrition than to the infections. Similar high mortality rates have been found in the Caribbean islands,[1] West Africa[2] and Bangladesh.[3] Less seriously infections slow down the growth, and in a Gambian village a close association was found between attacks of gastro-enteritis and of malaria with weight gain in children under 3 years of age.[4] Infectious diseases also contribute to malnutrition by reducing the working capacity of individuals. This is illustrated by malaria. The peasant farmer afflicted with it has an attack of fever when the rains come, and so cannot sow his seed at the right time. His family suffer the next winter from his incapacity, and nutritional troubles result. In a more general way, whenever the breadwinner is struck down by a prolonged infection nutritional failure is likely to affect his dependants.

NUTRITION AND IMMUNITY

Immunity depends on two types of responses by the tissues. **Humoral responses** are the production of antibodies in response to the stimulus of foreign proteins in the invading organisms (antigens). Antibodies are immunoglobulins which may circulate in the blood where they may be detected about a week after injection of an antigen. Antibodies react specifically with antigens of the invader and thereby may destroy it. Antibody may also be formed in response to stimulation by a bacterial toxin; such antibody may neutralise the effect

Table 59.1 Mortality from gastroenteritis, measles and whooping cough, in children under 5 years (from National and WHO reports by Dr J. M. Bengoa)

	Gastroenteritis, 1964		Measles, average 1963–64		Whooping cough, 1964	
	under 1 year (rate per 100 000 liveborn)	1–4 years (rate per 100 000 population	under 1 year (rate per 100 000 liveborn)	1–4 years (rate per 10 000 population)	under 1 year (rate per 100 000 liveborn)	1–4 years (rate per 100 000 population)
Austria	139.0	6.8	4.5	2.2	2.2	1.0
Denmark	40.8	1.7		1.0	2.4	0.3
England and Wales	42.0	3.5	2.1	1.5	3.7	0.3
Chile	1588.0	69.3	413.2	137.6	68.3	8.1
Guatemala	1275.9	704.2	248.0	310.0	589.4	309.2
Mexico	1224.0	267.4	71.0	103.7	112.7	75.8
Philippines	521.0	149.6	58.4	25.6	12.3	2.6

of the toxin. After many specific infectious diseases antibodies persist in the blood for years and prevent or mitigate a second infection. **Cellular responses** are responsible for the mobilisation and production of macrophages, polymorphs and other connective tissue cells. These accumulate at local sites of infection where they may ingest and destroy invading microorganisms (phagocytosis). Different types of cell are evoked by different microorganisms: polymorphs by staphylococci and other pyogenic bacteria, lymphocytes by viruses and tubercle bacilli, and eosinophils by helminths. They may also form a fibrinous exudate which may seal off a local infection and prevent the invaders spreading via the blood and lymph vessels.

The cells responsible for both the humoral and cellular immune responses arise in the lymphoreticular organs and tissues, such as the lymph nodes, thymus, spleen and tonsils. There is a large literature on the effects of inanition in man and experimental animals on the morphology of the lymphoreticular organs which is reviewed and summarised by Jackson.[5] In the young, atrophy of the thymus is marked and often greater than that of other organs. Lymph nodes and the spleen certainly atrophy when inanition is severe and prolonged; in less severe cases the findings are very variable. They have sometimes been reported to be enlarged. The effect of malnutrition on the immunity system is much greater in childhood than in later life.

In childhood
At birth the lymphoreticular system is very immature and its functional capacity limited. Maturation is slow and is completed only after several years. In this respect it resembles the brain and is unlike other organs and systems which are fully functional shortly after birth or in a few weeks. Malnutrition and undernutrition delay the development of immunity responses and of the central nervous system and their adverse effects are much greater in childhood than in adult life.

Cellular immune responses are impaired, often markedly, in protein-energy malnutrition as described on page 286. This is largely responsible for the high mortality from gastroenteritis, measles and whooping cough in countries where PEM is widespread (Table 59.1). These infections are common in all countries but seldom end fatally where the children are well fed.

In adults
The effect of poor nutrition on immunity to infection is much less obvious in adults. Epidemics of the great infectious diseases, such as malaria, smallpox, yellow fever and cholera, spread when conditions for transmission of the infection are favourable among the well fed and hungry alike. Good nutrition is no protection against a high mortality. In the world pandemic of influenza in 1918–19 in which 15–25 million people died, mortality in the USA and many other countries was highest in healthy young adults.[6]

Tuberculosis had long been associated with malnutrition which was thought to reduce immunity to the infection. This view had to be revised after observations in Madras among an urban population living in very poor houses on deficient diets. There the disease can be arrested and its spread from 'open' cases to their families and other close contacts can be controlled if the infection is adequately treated with chemotherapeutic drugs.[7] This was effective without the necessity of isolating the patients in sanatoria and with no change in the poor diet, housing and other hygienic circumstances of the community.

When patients are in a critical condition, survival depends on the capacity of organs and systems of the body to meet the stresses imposed by their illness and its complications. Malnutrition reduces their functional reserves and this may be as important as its effect on the immunity reactions directed against the invading microorganism.

Suppression of infections in malnutrition

Some infections, notably malaria, have appeared to be less virulent in malnourished populations. The severe form of malaria caused by *Plasmodium falciparum* is often fatal due to large numbers of red blood cells containing the parasites becoming sludged and blocking capillaries in the cerebral cortex. Malaria is endemic in the Sahel area of Africa and observations have been made on its manifestations under famine conditions by Murray et al.[8] They observed that during the height of the famine the severe form of the disease was suppressed and cerebral malaria was not seen. After the famine cerebral malaria reappeared especially in settled communities where the diet of the children was mainly cereal grain; its incidence was much less in normal communities where milk was available. The authors discuss their findings in relation to observations of experimental malaria in animals. They suggest that the sludging of the blood may be part of the immune responses of the tissues and does not take place where these are impaired by malnutrition; on the other hand, the malarial parasites themselves are dependent on nutrients and their multiplication may be reduced when the supply, which is dependent on the host's diet, is impaired.

In Tanzania patients with iron-deficiency anaemia were found to have fewer bacterial infections, but not less malaria, than patients with other forms of anaemia.[9] It is suggested that iron deficiency may increase resistance to bacterial infections. Riboflavin deficiency by reducing the life span of erythrocytes may make it more difficult for malarial parasites to survive in the blood and so reduce the chances of transmission.[10]

Invading organisms have their requirements for essential nutrients and these may perhaps be obtained more readily from well fed than from malnourished hosts. Fever is accompanied by loss of appetite and Mann suggests that this anorexia is a defence mechanism that reduces the supply of nutrients essential for the parasitic invader.[11] If this hypothesis was substantiated it would be necessary to think carefully before adopting the modern practice of supplementary feeding and parenteral nutrition for febrile patients and returning to orthodox eighteenth century medicine. 'Much solid food in a fever is in every way hurtful. It oppresses nature, and instead of nourishing the patient, serves only to feed the disease.'[12]

Controlled field studies

There have been two field trials in which the effects of improvements in nutrition, medical care and sanitation have been studied independently in separate villages in the tropics. In the one in Guatemala, which was on a small scale, the results were inconclusive.[13] In a much larger trial in the Punjab four groups of children aged 0 to 3 years were studied. One group received nutritional care, another medical care with emphasis on the treatment and prevention of infectious diseases, a third group received both nutritional and medical care, and a fourth group acted as a control. Each group consisted of all the children (200 to 380) in two or three villages. Analyses of the growth rates, morbidity and mortality rates at different ages shows the benefits derived from both the nutritional and the medical care, but does not show clearly which was the greater.[14,15] In this trial the methods and health staff used were those that could be made available throughout India and Pakistan. The results indicate the practical possibilities of combined attacks on malnutrition and infectious diseases.

CONCLUSION

Fortunately the uncertainties of the precise relation of nutrition to infection do not affect public health policy. In countries where severe malnutrition is uncommon, resistance to infection or recovery from infection is probably little influenced by nutritional and dietetic factors. In other countries where malnutrition is common and often severe, nutritional factors are of great importance in both the prevention and the treatment of infections.

Much practical experience has shown that one-sided public health programmes, aimed solely at improving diets or eradicating a single infectious disease, are relatively unsuccessful in raising the health of a community. This can best be improved by an attack on a broad front against all the factors that contribute to disease. Public health programmes must be well balanced and the activities of individual health workers integrated. Isolated programmes may do more harm than good by diverting money and distracting attention from other more important problems. Nutrition workers must always be in active collaboration with those whose duty it is to control infectious diseases and must make themselves acquainted with the problems and difficulties of other health workers. Similarly all the staff of a public health department, especially those concerned with the control of infectious diseases, must appreciate the ill-effects of a poor diet on health and know something of the methods available for improving the nutrition of a community.

REFERENCES

1. Ashworth A, Waterlow J C 1974 Nutrition in Jamaica. University West Indies Press
2. McGregor I A, Billewicz W Z, Thomson A M 1961 Growth and mortality in children in an African village. Br Med J 2: 1661–6
3. Chen L C, Huq E, Huffman S L 1981 A prospective study of the risk of diarrhoea diseases according to nutritional status of children. Am J Epidemiol 114: 284–92
4. Rowland M C M, Cole T J, Whitehead R G 1977 A quantitative study into the role of infection in determining nutritional status in Gambian village children. Br J Nutr 37: 441–50
5. Jackson C M 1925 The effects of inanition and malnutrition upon growth and structure. Churchill, London, p 261–99
6. Beveridge W I B 1977 Influenza the last great plague: an unfinished story of discovery. Heinemann, London, p 31
7. Fox W 1962 The chemotherapy and epidemiology of tuberculosis. Lancet 2: 413–7, 473–7
8. Murry M J, Murry A B, Murry N J, Murry M B 1978 Diet and cerebral malaria: the effect of famine and refeeding. Am J Clin Nutr 31: 57–61
9. Masawe A E J, Muindi J M, Swai G B R 1974 Infections in iron deficiency and other types of anaemia in the tropics. Lancet 2: 314–7
10. Thurnham D I, Oppenheimer J J, Bull R 1983 Riboflavin status and malaria in infants in Papua New Guinea. Trans R Soc Trop Med Hyg 77: 423–4
11. Mann G V 1980 Food intake and resistance to disease. Lancet 1: 1237–9
12. Buchan W 1769 Domestic medicine: a treatise on the prevention and cure of diseases by regimen and simple remedies
13. Ascoli W, Guzman M A, Scrimschaw N S, Gordon J E 1967 Nutrition and infection field study in Guatemalan villages, 1959–64. Arch Environ Health 15: 439–49
14. Taylor C E, Kielmann A A, DeSweemer C, et al 1978 The Narangwal experiment on interactions of nutrition and infections. Indian J Med Res 68: suppl 1–20
15. Kielmann A A, Taylor C E, Parker R L 1978 The Narangwal nutrition study: a summary review. Am J Clin Nutr 31: 2040–52

60

Food, Nutrition and Cancer

Cancer is a term used by both laymen and the medical profession to refer to malignant neoplasms or tumours. However, the term has no precise meaning and is not used by pathologists. Neoplasia or new growth is said to occur when cells in a tissue or organ proliferate without the normal controls on growth. In malignant neoplasms the cells spread to adjacent tissues by direct invasion or to distant organs by passage through blood or lymph vessels. Then a secondary tumour or metastasis forms. In benign neoplasms growth is limited to the organ of origin, and the tumour may have a well-defined capsule. Benign neoplasms usually cause symptoms only as a result of increasing size and the pressure which they may exert on other tissues. The distinction between benign and malignant neoplasms is usually, but not always, clear cut. Some benign neoplasms have a tendency to become malignant and there are certain hyperplastic states in which neoplasia is liable to arise; these are known as precancerous states. Many neoplasms are called by the name of the tissue together with the suffix '-oma'.

A malignant tumour arising in an epithelial tissue is known as a carcinoma and one arising in connective issue as a sarcoma. Leukaemia is a malignant condition in which the abnormal cells are in the blood and bone marrow.

The Greek word for a tumour is *onkos* and the study of neoplasia is known as oncology. Substances known to produce tumours are said to be carcinogenic or oncogenic.

The rate at which malignant neoplasms grow and their liability to form metastatic tumours varies from one type of neoplasm to another, and also in different individuals with the same neoplasm. For instance, one patient may be dead with metastases all over the body within a few weeks of the discovery of a neoplasm; another patient with an apparently similar tumour may be alive and well many years later. In many neoplasms there are intervals in which growth ceases or is very slow. Although it is most unusual, there are many well documented cases of spontaneous cure. There are immunological processes which may protect a patient against the spread of cancer but their nature is not well understood. Nutritional factors may contribute to this protection.

Neoplastic tissue may be removed by surgery or destroyed by radiation or chemotherapeutic agents. The effectiveness of these methods varies greatly depending on the site and nature of the tumour. Thus, provided the diagnosis is made early, the outlook for a patient with carcinoma of the colon or cervix uteri is good; it is at best very uncertain for a patient with carcinoma of the lung or stomach.

ONCOGENIC AGENTS

In the nineteenth century chimney sweeps, cotton spinners and shale oil workers were known to have a high incidence of skin cancer attributed to prolonged exposure to soot or oil. In 1928 Kennaway first showed that a pure chemical, dibenzanthracene, when repeatedly applied to the skin of animals, produced a squamous carcinoma. Many chemicals applied to the skin, inhaled or taken by mouth, are known to be potentially oncogenic. Some of these have been responsible for cancers arising in workers in the chemical and other industries. Often there has been exposure for a long period, sometimes 20 years before a tumour has developed. Excessive exposure to radiations, electromagnetic or ultraviolet, is oncogenic. Several viruses have been shown to be oncogenic in experimental animals and much evidence suggests that they are a cause of leukaemia in man. Thus there are many known causes of cancer, but in the great majority of patients the agent responsible cannot be identified. Tobacco is far and away the commonest known cause of cancer in man. Oncogenic agents may be present in a diet as a constituent of a natural food and as a chemical food additive or contaminant (see below).

EPIDEMIOLOGY

The geographical distribution of cancer has been studied for many years, but has been beset by difficulties in standardising diagnostic criteria and methods of reporting. Partly as a result of the work of the International Union against Cancer, a reliable picture of the situation throughout the world is emerging. Richard Doll of the Imperial Cancer Research Fund and formerly Regius Professor of Medicine at Oxford has been a pioneer in this work. He has two important messages[1, 2, 3] and both of them are helpful.

First, the great majority of cancers are due to environmental causes and so are potentially preventable. The evidence suggesting this is the variation in the incidence of cancer of all parts of the body throughout the world. The incidence of many cancers differs from country to country by factors ranging from x10 to x50. Only a small part of this variation can be attributed to genetic factors and it is estimated that 80 per cent of human cancers are environmentally determined.

Secondly there has been little or no increase in the overall incidence of cancer in the UK and USA since the 1930s. There has been a marked increase in cancer of the lung and attributable to increased use of tobacco. This has been offset by a decrease in many cancers, including those of the stomach, rectum, uterus and prostate. During these 50 years both populations have been exposed to increasing amounts and varieties of industrial chemicals, yet cancer would have declined markedly if there had not been an increased use of tobacco. The trend is encouraging. The message about cigarette smoking appears to be getting across, though all too slowly among young people and in government circles, and mortality from lung cancer has ceased to rise and may even be falling. We need to know much more about the relation between cancers at other sites and environmental factors. Such knowledge can only come from critical examination of carefully collected epidemiological data.

Dietary factors

There is little to suggest that the incidence of cancer at such common sites in the body as the lung or the cervix uteri is in any way related to dietary habits. On the other hand, there is much to suggest that the wide variation in incidence of cancer at various sites in the alimentary canal and in the liver may be due to oncogenic factors in the diet. The segments of the gastrointestinal tract where cancer usually occurs are those in which the passage of contents down the lumen is slowed. These are the lower end of the oesophagus, the pyloric end of the stomach, the region of the ileocaecal valve and the left side of the large intestine. At these places there is more time for contact between an oncogenic agent derived from food and the mucous membrane. Once absorbed, an oncogenic agent passes to the liver, which is exposed to higher concentrations of it than other tissues. The agent or a water-soluble metabolite may be excreted by the kidneys and then comes in prolonged contact with the mucosa of the urinary bladder. The above are sites where repeated and prolonged chemical irritation may be oncogenic.

Known dietary oncogens

Aflatoxins. These are a group of complex difuranocoumarins formed by some strains of the mould *Aspergillus flavus*, which may grow on groundnuts and other foods when stored in damp warm conditions after harvesting. In animals a single dose of aflatoxin causes acute poisoning with severe liver damage; and aflatoxin B_1 is the most potent hepatic carcinogen known. Only 0.2 μg/day in the diet for 470 days induces liver tumours in 100 per cent of rats. In some parts of the world human foods have been found to be contaminated with small amounts of aflatoxins and this may contribute to a high incidence of hepatoma in some areas (see below).

Pyrrolizidine alkaloids. These substances are present in many species of the herbs *Senecio* and *Crotalaria* and they have been shown to produce hepatoma in rats. These herbs are sometimes used for making bush teas and this practice may be responsible for some human cases of hepatoma.

Cycad nuts. Cycads are an ancient family of tree-ferns grown in many parts of the tropics. Their nuts, which have been much used both as food and medicine in some countries, contain the glycoside, cycasin, which cases tumours of the liver in rats and guinea pigs, but is not known to do so in man.

Nitrosamines. Nitrites may react with secondary amines in the gut to form a class of compounds known as nitrosamines. Some of these, e.g. dimethylnitrosamine, have been shown to be oncogenic in experimental animals. Nitrates are widespread in the soil and present in small amounts in plant and animal tissues, where they may be reduced to nitrites. Nitrates and nitrites are added to foods for their preservative action, especially against clostridial infections of meats. Nitrosamines have been found in several foods in concentrations of the order of 0.1 to 5 μg/kg and also in gastric juice. It is not certain to what extent they arise from added or naturally occurring nitrites.[4] Although there is evidence consistent with the view that ingested nitrate could be a contributory cause of carcinoma of the stomach (see below), nitrates are permitted food additives. The FAO/WHO acceptable daily intake is up to 125 mg/kg body weight.

Food additives. The dye, butter yellow, and the sweetener, cyclamate, were formerly added to foods, but are no longer permitted since they have been shown to produce tumours in experimental animals. All food additives have to undergo rigorous tests for oncogenic activity in animals before they are permitted to be used in foods.

The above observations show that oncogenic agents may be present in the food of all classes of people. Primitive rural and industrialised urban communities may each be at risk. However, the risks, except in a few well known cases, appear to be small. The possible role of dietary oncogenesis in the aetiology of specific tumours is now discussed.

TUMOURS OF THE ALIMENTARY TRACT AND LIVER

Tongue, buccal mucosa and pharynx

These are the commonest sites for tumours in Bombay and such tumours are also common in many parts of south-east Asia, south-east Africa and Puerto Rico; they are uncommon in Europe and the USA. The relative incidence may differ by a factor of 30. Many more males than females are affected in Bombay where the tumours are associated with chewing *pan*, a green vine leaf in which are rolled sliced betel nut, tobacco, slaked lime and some small amounts of other spices.

Oesophagus

Incidence varies greatly. Standardised rates per 100 000 persons aged 35 to 64 years are low (below 6) in most European countries, in the white population of the USA and South Africa, in Australia, in Nigeria and in Uganda. They are moderately high (from 15 to 30) in Switzerland, France, the non-white population of the USA, India and Japan, and very high (over 60) in the African population of southern and eastern Africa. Rates over 100 have been reported in some USSR and Iranian towns bordering on the Caspian Sea.

Carcinoma of the oesophagus is frequently associated with alcoholism and excessive smoking or chewing of tobacco, but this does not explain the wide variations in incidence. In Africa it is associated with drinking maize beer. Incidence varies greatly around the Caspian Sea, and very high rates are found in the south-east corner, where the soil is dry and salty[5] (Joint Iran/IARC Study Group, 1977). The people are Muslim and do not take alcohol or tobacco. Their diet is monotonous and consists of coarse wheat bread, tea, milk and a little meat; fruit and vegetables are lacking; oncogens have not been found in local foods. Urinary metabolites of morphine were found and it appears that opium is eaten. The area of high incidence extends over the border of Iran to south central USSR and right across Asia to parts of northern China. The high incidence in northern Iran appears to go back to antiquity, but in southern Africa carcinoma of the oesophagus was rare 40 years ago.

Stomach

Standardised incidence rates for carcinoma of the stomach vary from over 160 per 100 000 in Japan to less than 10 in some African countries. Other areas with high rates are Iceland, Costa Rica, Chile and parts of Colombia and Eastern Europe. In most parts of Europe it ranges from 30 to 60. In the USA it is 36 in the non-white population, but only 15 in the whites. In India it is 17 and in Australia 23. In South Africa the rate is a little lower in the African than in the white population, a marked contrast to the rates for carcinoma of the oesophagus. In general, the rate falls from east to west as one goes from the USSR to the USA. Rates in immigrant groups tend to correspond more closely to those of the host country than to their country of origin; this particularly applies to Japanese. Clearly, an environmental factor plays a major part in aetiology and it is a reasonable guess that this enters the body with the diet.

The incidence of carcinoma of the stomach is highest in the lower socioeconomic classes but has been falling for the last 20 years or more in most industrial countries, including the USA and Japan. There is a slightly greater incidence in people of blood group A, which reflects the genetic contribution, and an increased risk in patients with chronic atrophic gastritis.

Dietary studies show positive associations of carcinoma of the stomach with salted or pickled foods, e.g. dried salted fish or cured meats and with environmental nitrate (in well water, soil fertilisers, etc.). But negative associations have been found with salad vegetables, citrus fruit and milk comsumption.[6] The most plausible hypothesis at present to link all these features is that dietary nitrates may be reduced to nitrites and react in the stomach with secondary amines (from fermented foods) to form nitrosamines. Conditions are suitable for nitrosamine formation in patients with atrophic gastritis.[7] But vitamin C inhibits the nitrosation reaction and refrigeration probably reduces production of secondary amines.

Small intestine

Tumours of the small intestine are rare in all countries. This might be because the contents are not in contact with the mucous membrane for as long as in the stomach and the large intestine.

Large intestine

Standardised incidence rates for carcinoma of the colon are low (0 to 5 per 100 000) in most African countries, higher (5 to 15) in Asian countries, including Japan, and much higher (15 to 35) in Europe, North America and Australia. Japanese migrants to the USA acquire the higher incidence in the first generation. The disease is associated with affluence and coronary heart disease. Comparisons between countries show a positive correlation ($r = +0.6$) between incidence and both total fat and meat consumption.[14] Three hypotheses, not mutually exclusive, may help to explain these dietary associations.

High fat intake. This is accompanied by increased secretion of bile acids. Some of their desaturated metabolites present in the faeces are oncogenic when tested on animals. These are formed by the action of bacterial flora of the colon and possibly changes in the bacterial flora induced by diet may increase production of oncogens.[8] In several studies cancer of the colon and at other sites has been associated with low values of plasma cholesterol, but this association has not always been found to be present. There is no convincing evidence that hypocholesterolaemia is causally related to any cancer. Nor is there any knowledge of cellular mechanisms from which a causal relationship might be predicted.[9]

High meat intakes. Meat and total fat intakes are usually correlated, but in Copenhagen meat intake is higher and fat consumption lower than in rural Finland; and yet incidence of carcinoma of the colon is four times higher in Copenhagen.[10] Meat itself is unlikely to contain oncogens but they might be formed during roasting and grilling.

Low fibre intakes. Increasing the fibre intake shortens the transit time of food in the gut and makes the contents of the colon more watery (see Chap. 4); therefore, if any exogenous or endogenous oncogen is present, the mucosa is exposed to it for a shorter time and at a lower concentration. The weights of the stools, an index of the fibre content of the diet, were found to be higher in rural Finland than in Copenhagen and are in general much higher in African than in European populations. In this way a high fibre diet might protect against carcinoma of the colon.

Carcinoma of the rectum is commoner in men than women and may be correlated with beer consumption,[11] but not so closely as to cause the authors to change their habits.

Liver

Whereas primary carcinoma of the liver is rare in Europe and North America, it is commonly seen in many parts of Africa. Aflatoxins are probably in part responsible. In Kenya measurement of the aflatoxin content of 2400 samples of food in one district indicated that dietary intakes ranged from 1 to 21 μg/kg body weight daily.[12] Carcinoma of the liver accounted for about half of the total number of cases of malignant

disease in the community. Carcinoma of the liver was rarely found in areas where dietary intakes of aflatoxins were less than 5 μg/kg body weight daily. Similar geographical association of aflatoxins in food and primary cancer of the liver is found in other African countries, especially Mozambique which has the highest incidence in the world, and also in Thailand. Outbreaks of acute hepatitis due to aflatoxin poisoning continue to occur in Kenya.[13] There in association with viral hepatitis are the likely causes of the high incidence of liver cancer.

TUMOURS AT OTHER SITES

Breast

Carcinoma of the breast has a similar geographic distribution to carcinoma of the colon. A high incidence (100 or more per 100 000) is found in the USA, Canada, north-west Europe, Australasia and the white population of South Africa. It is commoner in the higher socioeconomic classes and in unmarried and nulliparous women. The protective effect of pregnancy is greater when it has occurred before the age of 25 years. Lactation has only a small protective effect, but oophorectomy and an early artificial menopause reduces the risk. Migrants from Japan, where the incidence is low, to the USA develop a high rate but only after two generations. The environmental factors responsible for the differences between countries therefore appear to operate early in life. Obesity is a little more common in patients with the disease than in control groups. Comparisons between countries show that the dietary component with the strongest correlation with incidence of the disease is total fat intake.[14] It is the commoner post-menopausal type of the disease which differs between countries and appears to show partial relationship to the diet. It has been suggested that high fat intakes lead to patterns of hormone secretion, more oestradiol and oestrone, less oestriol, which favour oncogenesis. Differences in the patterns of urinary oestrogens of Japanese and Caucasian women are in keeping with this view.[15] There is speculation that 'the present affluent diet from childhood onward may over-stimulate the endocrine system, producing the same effects that one would obtain running a diesel engine on high-octane airplane fuel.'[16] In well-nourished populations the onset of menstruation is earlier and there is a higher incidence not only of neoplasms of the breast but also of the ovary and endometrium of the uterus, organs which depend on sex hormones for their normal function.

Urinary bladder

The artificial sweeteners cyclamate and saccharin have induced bladder tumours in animals when given in very high dosage. However, in a study in the USA of 3010 patients with bladder cancer and 5783 controls, no association between the use of artificial sweeteners and cancer was found.[17]

The relationship between diet and cancer is an important and growing field of research. Components of food or drink may contain exogenous oncogens or stimulate production of endogenous oncogen or hormones that favour oncogenesis. Further, a dietary factor may be protective (e.g. fibre) or a dietary deficiency may predispose to cancer. For example, two papers present evidence that a low dietary intake of vitamin A increases the risk of tobacco-induced lung cancers.[18, 19] At first sight they appear impressive, perhaps due to the elaborate statistical analyses, but cynics may doubt the reliability of the dietary data on which the calculations have been made. Old hands may remember that in 1931 vitamin A was prematurely named as 'the anti-infective vitamin' by an eminent nutritional scientist.[20] Many more studies will be needed before it can justifiably be called an 'anti-cancer' vitamin. Although the cause of most human cancers is unknown, many oncogenic agents have been identified and their actions are known to be affected by genetic factors and by environmental factors, which include the diet. Methods for recording the food intake of populations for studies on the epidemiology of cancer need to be different from those for investigating the prevalence of malnutrition. Up to now they have mostly been inadequate or inappropriate but they are improving as there is more dialogue between epidemiologists and nutritional scientists.

DIET AND TUMOUR GROWTH

Tumours, like the tissues of the body, need nutrients which are derived ultimately from the diet. In theory, it might be possible to devise a diet on which the tissues could survive and a tumour cease to grow. There are many reports describing how reducing the energy content of a diet or the amount of an essential nutrient inhibited the growth of tumours in experimental animals.[21] Unfortunately, in humans, malignant tumours grow rapidly in an emaciated and malnourished body.

Two attempts to interfere with the nutrition of a tumour have met with some success. A folic acid antagonist, methotrexate, which reduces production of RNA and DNA, had an established place in the treatment of chorion carcinoma and leukaemia. The amino acid asparagine can be synthesised by mammalian cells, but not by some malignant cells. A preparation of the enzyme, asparaginase, produced by bacteria *Escherichia coli* produces remissions in some types of leukaemia.

MALIGNANT DISEASE AS A CAUSE OF MALNUTRITION

Severe emaciation and malnutrition follow an untreated malignant tumour of the alimentary tract at any site from the lips down to the pyloric sphincter. This is readily explainable by mechanical interference with eating, swallowing or the passage of food from stomach to duodenum.

With neoplasms at other sites, some patients do not lose weight and appear well nourished despite the presence of a large tumour and sometimes numerous secondaries. However, a cancer patient usually loses some weight and may become extremely emaciated. This is sometimes due to secondary bacterial infection or pressure on a vital structure, but often there is no obvious cause. When a middle-aged or elderly person loses weight for no apparent reason, he should have a thorough clinical and radiological examination for the presence of a neoplasm.

The loss of weight in patients with malignant neoplasm may sometimes be explained by loss of appetite. Anorexia is often marked, but why this should be so is far from clear. Possibly severe cachexia may be the result of metabolic disturbances brought about by the tumour. Some neoplasms are known to produce kinins and hormones, which have marked effects on other tissues of the body. The best-known example is the Zollinger-Ellison syndrome in which there are multiple peptic ulcers arising from excess secretion of gastrin by a carcinoma in the pancreas or duodenal wall. There may be a loss of tissue amino acids due to the catabolic action of a neoplasm. It is also possible that some neoplasms produce a lipid-mobilising factor. It is not humane to ask patients with severe malignant cachexia to undergo the inconveniences and discomforts of an elaborate metabolic investigation, from which there is little hope that they will derive benefit. This is why so little is known about malignant cachexia.

DIETARY THERAPY

Doctors and dietitians should be constantly aware of the diagnostic significance of loss of weight, anorexia and food aversions as early signs of malignant disease. When the diagnosis has been made and a programme of ablative surgery, radiation or treatment with cytotoxic drugs laid down, a supportive diet should be carefully drawn up. This should be higher than normal in energy and nutrient content, and in a form which is acceptable and appetising to the patient while avoiding any food aversions he may have. Many patients require supplementary and tube feeding and some parenteral nutrition, as described in Chapter 52. Dietary modifications may be necessary as a result of ileostomy and colostomy. There is no evidence that a good diet can cure any type of cancer, but there is no doubt that it can add greatly to the comfort of the patient. Since the ultimate hope for the patient may lie in a strong immune reaction to the invading tumour cells, and since there is evidence that a good diet supports the immune system, a rational basis for diet therapy is at least dimly perceptible.

For the most part, however, good diet therapy supports the patient's morale; it provides normal pleasurable gratifications of the body and mind when these are being restricted by advancing disease. Great care should therefore be taken about the aesthetic aspects of the diet, such as arrangement, appearance, odour or bouquet, and taste of the foods. Wine and other alcoholic liquors in moderation may be of great help, although occasionally, as in a few cases of Hodgkin's disease, they may bring on pain.

Finally, there comes a time when the battle is lost. Henceforth there is no point in prolonging life by fussy and uncomfortable attentions. The dietitian should accept the verdict of the doctor and feed the patient in whatever way is most comfortable and least distasteful. Their nutrition no longer matters; what matters is to keep up as far as possible their morale and whatever enjoyment remains in the sight and taste of food.

Cancer nostrums — laetrile

When a patient is going downhill with an apparently incurable disease, they and their relatives may catch at any straw. Innumerable cancer nostrums have been promoted by well-meaning enthusiasts and by rogues wanting to make a fast buck.[22] Laetrile, which has caused a legal furore in the USA, is a cycanogenic glucoside obtained from apricot pips. Its promoters claim that it is a vitamin which is untrue. There is now good evidence from controlled clinical trials that in patients with cancer the course of their disease is not altered by laetrile.[23, 24] However, the manufacturers have since made an effort to market it in the UK and there are many others with spurious cancer cures who take good money from unfortunate sufferers and give them only false hopes.

REFERENCES

1. Doll R 1973 Cancer in its geographical perspective. Proc R Soc Med 66: 307–12
2. Doll R, Peto R 1981 The causes of cancer: quantitative estimates of avoidable risks of cancer in the United States today. J Natl Cancer Inst 66: 1193–308
3. Doll R 1983 Cancer control. In Passmore R (ed) The medical management of malignant disease. R Coll Physns Edin publication no. 59
4. Tannenbaum S R 1983 N-Nitroso compounds: a perspective on human exposure. Lancet 1: 629–32
5. Joint Iran-IRAC Study Group 1977 Esophageal cancer studies in the Caspian litteral of Iran: results of population studies. J Natl Cancer Inst 59: 1127–38
6. Haenszel W, Correa P 1975 Developments in the epidemiology of stomach cancer over the past decade. Cancer Res 35: 3452–9
7. Ruddell W S J, Bone E S, Hill M J, Blendis L M, Walters C L 1976 Gastric juice nitrites: a risk factor for cancer in hypochlorhydric stomach. Lancet 2: 1037–9
8. Hill M J 1983 Bacteria, bile acids and large bowel cancer. Biochem Soc Trans 11: 256–8
9. Lewis B 1983 Plasma lipids and cancer. Biochem Soc Trans 11: 252–4
10. International Agency for Research on Cancer 1977 Dietary fibre, transit time, faecal bacteria, steroids and colon cancer in two Scandinavian populations. Lancet 2: 207–10
11. Breslow N, Enstrom J E 1974 Geographic correlations between cancer mortality rates and alcohol-tobacco consumption in the USA. J Natl Cancer Inst 53: 631–9
12. Peers F G, Linsell C A 1973 Dietary aflatoxins and liver cancer — a population based study in Kenya. Br J Cancer 27: 473–84
13. Ngindu A, Johnson B K, Kenya P R, et al 1982 Outbreak of acute hepatitis caused by alfatoxin poisoning in Kenya. Lancet 1: 1346–8
14. Armstrong B K, Doll R 1975 Environmental factors and cancer incidence and mortality in different countries with special reference to dietary practices. Int J Cancer 15: 617–31
15. Dickinson L E, MacMahon B, Cole P, Brown J B 1974 Estrogen profiles of oriental and caucasian women in Hawaii. N Engl J Med 291: 1211–3
16. Berg J W 1975 Can nutrition explain the pattern of international epidemiology of hormone-dependent cancers? Cancer Res 35: 3345–50
17. Hoover R N, Strasse P H 1980 Artificial sweeteners and human bladder cancer. Lancet 1: 837–40
18. Wald N, Idle M, Boreham J, Bailey A 1980 Low serum vitamin A and subsequent risk of cancer. Lancet 2: 813–5
19. Shekelle R B, Lepper M, Liu S, et al 1981 Dietary vitamin A and risk of cancer in the Western Electric study. Lancet 2: 1185–90
20. Green H N, Pindar D, Davis G, Mellanby E 1931 Diet as a prophylactic agent against puerperal sepsis with special reference to vitamin A as an anti-infective agent. Br Med J 2: 595–8
21. Alcantara E N, Speckman E W 1975 Diet, nutrition and cancer. Am J Clin Nutr 29: 1035–47
22. Ingelfinger F J 1977 Laetrilomania. N Engl J Med 296: 1167–8
23. Moertel M D, Fleming T R, Rubin J, et al 1982 A clinical trial of amygolalin (laetrile) in the treatment of human cancer. N Engl J Med 306: 201–6
24. Relman A S 1982 Closing the books on laetrile. N Engl J Med 306:236

PART SIX

Diet and Physiological Status

61

Pregnancy, Lactation and Infancy

PREGNANCY

An expectant mother needs a good mixed diet both before and during pregnancy. A poor diet may have adverse effects on herself and on her child in many ways.

DIET PRIOR TO PREGNANCY

Size and shape of the pelvis Labour is much more difficult and dangerous when the pelvis is small and flattened. Undernutrition during childhood and adolescence stunts growth and the pelvis is then smaller than normal. The brim of the pelvis is normally round but in a growing girl with rickets it becomes flattened and even kidney shaped, due to projection of the promontary of the sacrum downwards. Good nutrition and the prevention of rickets greatly reduce the hazards of childbirth. In the 1930s in Britain about 400 mothers out of 100 000 died in childbirth; now the number is about 25. This great reduction is due in large part to the fact that a difficult and prolonged labour due to a contracted pelvis, once commonplace, has become a rarity in obstetrical practice. This is one of the great benefits that have followed from improved nutrition of our children.

Fertility. Undernutrition reduces fertility but only if it is very severe. In famine conditions, as existed in Leningrad[1] during the siege in 1942 and in the Netherlands[2] in 1944, conception rates were low. However, in Third World countries today in which the diet is notoriously defective in many nutrients birth rates are usually high. Neither undernutrition nor malnutrition affect the growth of population by reducing the birth rate.

DIET DURING PREGNANCY

Birth weight of infants

The birth weights of infants of well-fed mothers in the upper socioeconomic classes are higher on average than those of poorer mothers. A low birth weight may be due to a baby being born prematurely or to retarded intra-uterine growth. The latter is the common cause in poor mothers. There is good statistical evidence from Scotland[3] and South India[4] that birth weights are related to energy intakes of mothers during pregnancy. When a baby's birth weight is less than 2500 g the chances of survival are much reduced. WHO[5] estimate that in 1979 there were 122 million live births in the world and that 21 million of the infants weighed less than 2500 g. These low weight babies formed 20 per cent of all live births in Asia and 15 per cent in Africa where large numbers of mothers are obviously undernourished. The numbers are smaller in North America and Europe (7 and 8 per cent of live births) where prematurity is the more common cause.

In 1985 a report[5a] on 2456 births in a maternity hospital in Dakar, West Africa, is at odds with the classical hypothesis that a maternal energy deficit limits fetal growth. Anthrometric measurements of the mothers were similar to those observed in affluent societies, but the mean birth weight of their babies was only 3.02 kg. Moreover the fatter women had smaller babies.

Maternal undernutrition is only one of several causes of low birth weight of babies. Other causes are smoking[6] and alcohol consumption, but unless a mother has been drinking heavily the effect is small.[7] In Ethiopia birth weights were low when mothers were undertaking heavy physical work[8] or were infected with leprosy.[9] Other chronic or severe maternal infections and maternal drug abuse are likely to lower birth weights.

Supplementation of maternal diets. This has been shown to reduce the incidence of low birth weights. In a trial in villages in Guatemala[10] fewer babies with low birth weights were born to mothers who were given either of two supplements, a gruel or a refreshing drink containing no protein. Extra energy, but not extra protein, appeared responsible for the increases of birth weight. In another trial in England Asian mothers whose babies are often small were given supplements of energy, protein and vitamins. Mean birth weights were then 3000 g or more. The authors conclude that it would be inappropriate to give supplements to all Asian mothers.[11]

In all communities mothers who do not gain weight normally during pregnancy should be given dietary advice in the second trimester and for some a supplement may be indicated.

Weight gain in pregnancy

It is normal for a woman to gain 3.5 kg (8 lb) in weight by the end of the first 20 weeks of pregnancy and thereafter to gain about 0.5 kg or 1 lb a week until term, when the total gain is 12.5 kg (28 lb). Table 61.1 gives an analysis of how these weight gains are made up. Besides the products of conception and increased size of the reproductive organs, blood volume expands; as the plasma increases a little more than the red cells, it is normal for the haemoglobin concentration in the blood to fall slightly by the end of the pregnancy. In the last 10 weeks there is an increase in the extracellular water, additional to the increase in plasma. The extra fat deposited is about 4 kg. This is an energy store of 150 MJ (36 000 kcal), enough to supply the needs of the body for two to three weeks in an emergency. This fat is deposited throughout pregnancy, but especially in the period between 10 and 20 weeks.

When obesity is present, pregnancy is more likely to be attended by pregnancy hypertension, and other undesirable complications. Emerson[13] reviews the literature and gives the findings in his studies of 1145 cases. An average gain in weight of a little less than 0.5 kg per week during the second half of pregnancy is associated with the lowest overall rates for pregnancy hypertension, prematurity and perinatal mortality. With higher rates of gain, the chances of developing pregnancy hypertension are increased, whereas with lower rates there is an increase of prematurity.[14] Yet there is no satisfactory evidence that overnutrition is the primary cause of pregnancy hypertension.

Some women, mainly in the USA, have been led by fashion to restrict their diets so as to reduce their gain in weight to less than 7 kg. This practice may lead to the delivery of babies of low birth weight with increased risk of perinatal death.

These are average figures and wide variations are compatible with health. If the weight gain is less than half that anticipated, a careful search for the cause should be made. This may be either an inadequate dietary intake or excessive physical activity. If these two are excluded, the possibility of a major physical disorder should be considered. An excessive gain in weight, more than 50 per cent above the figure given, many be due to accumulation of oedema fluid as well as fat.

Stillbirth and perinatal mortality

Poor maternal nutrition increases the risk of stillbirth and of death of a baby within a week after birth. In this way between 60 and 70 out of every 1000 mothers in the UK lost their babies in the 1930s. By 1945 the losses were between 40 and 50. This rapid fall took place when wartime food policy provided extra food rations for pregnant women at subsidised prices and free supplements of vitamins. Losses are now very much lower in prosperous countries due mainly to great improvements in the treatment which obstetric and paediatric services can provide.

Congenital defects

The birth of a baby with a congenital defect in the formation of one or more of its organs is a hazard of pregnancy for which it is possible that factors in maternal diets may be responsible. There are many different types of defect. Those involving the nervous system, anencephalus and spina bifida, have been studied most and a monograph by Elwood & Elwood gives a full account of their epidemiology.[15]

Table 61.2 gives figures for the incidence of anencephalus in different parts of the world and shows the enormous variation.

Incidence in Bogota, Manilla, Santiago, Calcutta, Jamaica, and Bombay is relatively low. As these are places where large numbers of pregnant women would be expected to have poor diets, the epidemiological evidence is strongly against a dietary deficiency being a cause of the malformation. However, Smithells and his colleagues in 1980 reported that when women who had previously given birth to an infant with a neural tube defect were given a multivitamin supplement, starting before conception, the incidence of defects in subse-

Table 61.1 Analysis of the weight gain in pregnancy (modified from Hytten & Leitch)[12]

| | Increase in weight | | | |
	Up to 10 weeks (g)	20 weeks (g)	30 weeks (g)	40 weeks (g)
Fetus, placenta and liquor	55	720	2530	4750
Uterus and breasts	170	765	1170	1300
Blood	100	600	1300	1250
Extracellular water	—	—	—	1200
Fat (by difference)	325	1915	3500	4000
Total gain	650	4000	8500	12500

Table 61.2 The incidence of anencephalus per 1000 births. Data selected from Elwood & Elwood[15]

Bogota	0.11	Sydney	0.74
Turin	0.13	Munich	0.83
Manilla	0.15	Boston	0.98
Santiago	0.30	Holland	1.03
Calcutta	0.36	Bombay	1.15
Uganda	0.36	Quebec	1.19
Sweden	0.37	London	1.41
Jamaica	0.41	Edinburgh	2.83
Japan	0.43	Naples	4.00
Paris	0.45	Dublin	4.23

quent babies was much less than in unsupplemented controls.[16] Large field trials of supplements of vitamins are now in progress in the UK and USA. One may guess that the answers will be inconclusive since there are no records of a high incidence of anencephalus in places where vitamin deficiencies are common. In particular in Bombay where Lucy Wills first established folate deficiency as a common cause of severe anaemia in pregnancy, a high incidence of congenital defects has never been reported.

A dietary toxin acting on a susceptible mother seems a much more likely cause of congenital defects than vitamin deficiencies. Evidence that consumption of blighted potatoes was closely asssociated with defects appeared at first convincing[17] but has not been substantiated.[18] There are many other potential environmental toxins and these are discussed in a review with 231 references.[19] The prevention of congenital malformations remains a challenge to medical science.

Drugs in pregnancy

Many drugs taken by a mother may have adverse effects on her baby. Some drugs are potentially dangerous because they have been shown to be teratogenic (to produce fetal deformities) when given to animals in large doses. Thalidomide is the only drug commonly teratogenic in women in therapeutic doses but this can no longer be prescribed.

A pregnant woman should be told to stop all self-medication and take only drugs prescribed by her doctor, who will use only those of proven benefit to her and carrying a minimum of risk to her baby. Two drugs commonly taken with food require special mention.

Alcohol. Mothers who are alcoholic are at risk of having babies with the **fetal alcohol syndrome**. This consists of a low birth weight, low intelligence and congenital defects, especially of the face. It is an important public health problem in some communities.[20] There is much uncertainty on what constitutes moderate drinking and on its effect on a fetus.[21] We recommend a pregnant woman to take no alcohol but, if she enjoys a drink, we know of no evidence that one only, taken on no more than two occasions in the day, has any effect on her baby.

Caffeine. In 1980 the US Food and Drug Administration advised pregnant women to avoid caffeine-containing food and drugs or to use them sparingly. But those who enjoy a cup of coffee can take heart. Among 12 505 mothers in the USA the risk of having a baby with either a low birth weight or a malformation has now been shown to be quite unrelated to how much coffee they drank.[22] British mothers can assume that their cups of tea are equally safe.

Diet in pregnancy

A mother who before conception was eating a good mixed diet does not need to change her habits when she becomes pregnant. She needs to eat more and her appetite is usually a sound guide as to how much more. But appetite is fickle in pregnancy and she should check her weight periodically and, if she is gaining too much or too little, modify her intake accordingly.

As the iron content of most diets is only marginally adequate for women and as pregnancy increases requirements for folate, nutritional anaemia is common in pregnancy and can be prevented by giving a **haematinic supplement**. This is not needed when the blood haemoglobin is normal but where attendances at antenatal clinics tend to be irregular and so haemoglobin is not checked regularly, it is wise to prescribe ferrous sulphate (200 mg thrice daily) and folate (300 μg once daily) for all mothers after the 24th week of pregnancy.

A mother's diet has to provide the large amount of calcium present in the bones of her baby. Milk is the best source and a daily intake of up to half a litre (600 mg of calcium) ensures an adequate intake. Vitamin D is required for adsorption of the calcium and when there is any doubt about exposure to sunlight supplements of the vitamin should be given. This is especially important for Muslim women in purdah and for women living in regions where the hours of daylight are short in winter and when exposure to sunlight is limited.

The needs for protein are normally met when the diet provides sufficient energy. Rats store protein in the maternal tissues in early pregnancy and transfer it in later pregnancy to the rapidly growing fetus.[23] In this way the protein cost of pregnancy is distributed over the whole period of pregnancy. It would be difficult, if not impossible, to demonstrate these changes in pregnant women but it has long been known that blood urea falls in women early in pregnancy.[24] This indicates that a greater proportion of dietary amino acids are used for protein synthesis and less for gluconeogenesis and as a tissue fuel.

General advice

Pregnancy, especially a first pregnancy, is likely to change the manner of life, including eating habits. All women at their first attendance at an antenatal clinic should be asked about their diet and, if they appear not to be eating well, given simple practical advice. This may need to include discussion about the costs of different foods.

Some women develop voracious appetites early in pregnancy and this may lead to obesity and its ill effects. They should be told to control this and avoid an excessive gain in weight. Others may have a longing for some unusual food. The explanation for these whims is uncertain, but their effects are not serious and they should not be allowed to disturb normal meals and good manners.

Heartburn and other symptoms of indigestion are common and sometimes troublesome, especially in the last trimester, when pressure from the enlarged uterus on the stomach may be responsible. Often there is no obvious cause and no treatment is necessary beyond advising the patient to avoid foods commonly associated with indigestion (see Diet No. 17), to take frequent small meals, to use insoluble antacids as required and to avoid bending or lying flat. Constipation and also haemorrhoids are common minor complications of pregnancy. To minimise this, women should be advised to eat plenty of dietary fibre as wholemeal bread or bran products as well as the fruit and vegetables. Advice to avoid excess of table salt and of salty foods, given to all people, applies during pregnancy.

All pregnant women should be strongly advised to give up smoking and to take alcohol only moderately if at all. They should be encouraged to take outdoor exercise and to continue with active recreations.

DISORDERS OF PREGNANCY

Morning sickness

In the early weeks of pregnancy most women suffer a little from nausea especially in the early morning, and there may be vomiting. The cause of this is not known. 'Morning sickness' is certainly not psychological in origin, although psychological factors often aggravate the symptoms. It may be presumed that these arise from some metabolic or endocrine change brought about by the presence of the fetus or placenta, to which adjustment is usually quickly made.

There are innumerable 'old wives' remedies for morning sickness, but unfortunately no scientific treatment. The patient should be reassured that the condition will shortly disappear. Occasional morning sickness in early pregnancy may be relieved by taking a light snack before rising. Psychological disturbances may require treatment. If the vomiting persists, an anti-emetic drug, e.g. cyclizine 50 mg/day by mouth, may be given.

In some women, both primigravidas and multigravidas, morning sickness and nausea become progressively worse. Vomiting may persist throughout the day so that neither fluid nor food is retained. The resulting metabolic changes may be severe and then she should be admitted to hospital; in many cases this measure alone stops the vomiting. It is necessary to correct the dehydration, ketosis, haemoconcentration and the electrolyte imbalance which are the consequence of vomiting and nausea; the patient should receive ample amounts of fluid, electrolytes and carbohydrates. These can be given by mouth in mild cases, or intravenously in severe cases. With improvement of the patient's condition, which usually occurs within a day or two of admission to hospital, the diet can be gradually increased.

Pregnancy hypertension

The terms 'toxaemia of pregnancy' and pre-eclampsia were formerly used to describe a group of disorders characterised by a raised blood pressure, oedema and albuminuria which develops for the first time during pregnancy. As no toxin has been identified and the condition seldom leads to eclampsia, these terms are unsuitable and the condition is best referred to as pregnancy hypertension. It is convenient to describe two forms.

Mild pregnancy hypertension. The patient feels well but the blood pressure is slightly raised, i.e. over 140/90 mmHg. There may be slight oedema of the ankles and a trace of albumin in the urine. The urinary output is well maintained and the specific gravity is normal. The condition is common and was found in 24 per cent of primigravida and 10 per cent of multigravida in a survey in Scotland. With good antenatal care the prognosis is excellent.

Severe pregnancy hypertension. The blood pressure is over 160/100 mmHg. In addition the oedema is increased in degree and may extend to the hands, face and abdominal wall. Albuminuria exceeds 250 mg/24 hours. In very severe cases other serious features are headache, disturbances of vision, vomiting and oliguria. This condition is relatively rare, occurring in the Scottish survey in 5 per cent of primigravidae and 1 per cent of multigravidae, but is associated with greatly increased risk to both the mother and fetus.

Treatment

For mild cases modified rest, i.e. two hours rest in bed in the afternoon, and adequate sleep, achieved if necessary by the use of a sedative or hypnotic drug, are of prime importance. It is unnecessary to restrict fluids or protein foods, since renal function is satisfactory.

Severe cases and mild cases which do not respond to

the above treatment should be admitted to hospital. In addition to complete bed rest, and the administration of adequate amounts of sedative and hypnotic drugs, the protein intake should be reduced. Antihypertensive drugs should seldom be used as they may reduce utero-placental blood flow and so jeopardise the fetus. If vomiting is a marked feature, the patient may be able to take only small amounts of milk and diluted fruit juice at two-hourly intervals until improvement occurs. If as is usual, the patient improves in hospital, she may be allowed home, but should be kept under close obser-vation. When there is no improvement the pregnancy should be terminated.

Eclampsia

This condition may follow severe pregnancy hyperten-sion and is recognised by the development of epilepti-form convulsions. Medical treatment is the same as that described for severe pregnancy hypertension and in addition, the fits should be treated by suitable sedative drugs such as intravenous magnesium sulphate. If severe oliguria (less than 200 ml/day) or anuria occurs, treat-ment consists in giving glucose 100 to 300 g daily and fluid in limited quantities (500 to 1000 ml daily) intra-venously or by intragastric drip as for patients suffering from acute renal failure. Delivery by Caesarian section is advisable in most cases.

LACTATION

Peasant women, like all mammals, lactate 'with nae bother at all', to use a common Scottish term of speech. For them it is a part of life and a natural experience which gives emotional satisfaction. Urban life and the acquisition of wealth each bring distractions and for many women make lactation difficult and sometimes distasteful. The decline in breast feeding has been marked. In the decade 1960–70 no more than 15 per cent of infants in Scotland got a significant amount of breast milk,[25] and this figure probably applied to most European and North American communities,[26] and to the wealthy in Africa and Asia. It is probable that in some countries this decline has stopped and may even have been reversed. Thus in 1980 in Great Britain 65 per cent of babies were put to the breast at birth, 41 per cent were being breast fed at 6 weeks and 26 per cent at 4 months; a baby's chance of being breast fed was greater the higher the social class of its mother and the longer her period of full-time education.[27] Breast feeding practices in many other countries are reviewed in a WHO report.[28]

After this chapter had been sent to the printers a major report on infant feeding in India was published.[28a] It is based on interviews with 4296 mothers with infants under 1 year of age. The mothers lived in rural areas, small towns and big cities; some were very poor and a few had ample means and could live well. The majority fed their infants in the traditional manner with prolonged breast feeding and without the use of commercial milk formulae and infant foods. These are now widely avail-able and being used on a small scale by both rich and poor mothers. The report is of value outside India be-cause it gives a picture of a country in transition and dis-cusses both the dangers and benefits that arise when these new foods are first introduced.

Causes of failure

The main reasons given by British mothers for stopping breast feeding prematurely were insufficient milk, pain in the breasts or nipples and that breast feeding takes too long. Psychological and social factors underlie these personal explanations. Successful lactation depends on effective ejection of milk. Sensory receptors in the nipple when stimulated by a suckling infant send impulses up the spinal cord to the hypothalamus. There they trigger the release from the posterior pituitary gland of oxytocin. Oxytocin circulating in the blood stimulates myoepithelial cells in the alveoli of the breast and milk is then ejected. This suckling reflex like most neuroendocrine mechanisms is markedly affected by emotions and other psychological factors.

Lactation is effective and pleasurable when a mother is relaxed and free from worry. Worries about domestic, social and personal problems inhibit the flow of milk and are the main cause of failure to lactate satisfactorily.

It is uncommon for an organic disorder to be respon-sible. Local conditions such as cracked and infected nipples, mastitis or breast abscess, if severe, may make it necessary to stop. With most generalised diseases a mother, unless she is seriously ill, can continue to lactate and this is usually best for her baby.

Know-how

Lactation is an art and in common with other domestic arts the necessary know-how was traditionally trans-ferred from one generation of women to another in the home. Where there are fewer babies and many of them are bottle fed, knowledge of the art becomes less wide-spread. Many mothers now require instruction from the health service, during the lying in period from an attendant midwife and later from a health visitor in her home or at a clinic. Advice is also often given in women's magazines and on radio and television programmes. For those who have to give such advice two small books, one from London[29] and one from Oslo[30] and a report from the USA[31] are recommended. Parents self-help groups are being formed. By focusing attention on the mother rather than the baby, they enhance her confidence and sense of self-worth.[32]

How much milk and for how long?

When a baby's only source of food is mother's milk, this has to meet energy needs. Human milk provides about 290 kJ (70 kcal)/100 g. Energy needs depend on body weight and is estimated to vary from 500 to below 420 kJ (120 to 100 kcal)/kg declining as age advances. Each of these figures is subject to wide variation. Whitehead, using the best available figures, estimates that healthy infants at 2, 4 and 6 months need about 780, 880 and 1000 ml of milk daily.[33] A mother can be expected to produce about 800 ml daily but again yields vary greatly. These figures indicate that most mothers, but not all, could meet the needs of their baby at 4 months but only a minority at 6 months. They support the practice of advising mothers to start supplementary feeding when their baby is between 3 and 4 months old.

In many communities, mostly in tropical countries, it is the custom to feed infants solely at the breast for much longer. Waterlow[34] has shown that in some of these countries growth rate is the same for the first four months as for babies in the UK, but thereafter falls below markedly. This, he says, poses the suckling's dilemma. If an infant is not given supplements at the age of 4 months, there is a risk of undernourishment. On the other hand, in communities where levels of hygiene are usually low giving supplements greatly increases the risk of attacks of gastroenteritis, a major cause of ill health and infant mortality. There is no general answer to this dilemma. Advice has to be tempered to the circumstances of individual mothers and of the communities in which they live.

In some communities it is the custom for mothers to continue to suckle their children until they are 2 years of age or more. This is not always to be condemned and there are two possible benefits. Although the child may get little milk from the breast, this may be a valuable addition, especially of high quality protein, to the food that it gets from a poor family diet. Further prolonged suckling tends to inhibit ovulation. Although a far from reliable method of contraception, the practice does lead to longer intervals between pregnancies, and in poor countries this is of great benefit to the health of mothers, to their families and to the community in general.

MATERNAL DIET DURING LACTATION

The energy present in milk and that needed for its production has to be provided by the mother. The energy content of 800 ml of milk is 2300 kJ (560 kcal). The efficiency of milk production is about 80 per cent,[35] so she has to make available some 2300 kJ (700 kcal). Some of this should come from the extra fat laid down during pregnancy and the remainder from an increased dietary intake. The amount of extra food required above

her normal intake may also be affected by changes in physical activity. A mother can tell that she is eating enough and not too much if her weight falls gradually to what it was before she became pregnant and then remains unchanged.

When the diet before and during pregnancy has been good, changes during lactation are not needed, but the old advice to drink some extra milk is sound as this ensures sufficient calcium for the mother's milk without drawing on reserves in her bones. A supplement of vitamin D is also advisable, especially when exposure to sunlight is restricted. Supplements of other vitamins are not needed.

Ample fluids should be taken but more milk is not produced by forcing a large intake. Tea and coffee, as well as beer and wines, may be drunk in moderation. Most drugs in common use are excreted in the milk and many are potentially dangerous for an infant. Mothers should therefore avoid self-medication. Antithyroid and anticoagulant drugs and sedatives and analgesics, when necessary, should be prescribed with care and breast feeding should usually be discontinued when large doses of anticonvulsants are needed to control epilepsy.

When a mother's diet is inadequate, her milk yield is usually well maintained by drawing on her own reserves of nutrients and evidence of malnutrition is likely to appear in a mother before it does in her child. Many women in poor communities have a remarkable ability to breast feed their infants for long periods. This is probably due to repeated stimulation of the neurohumoral reflex by frequently putting the baby to the breast and letting it suckle at night.

Dietary supplements

As already stated most women do not produce sufficient milk to meet the needs of an infant more than 4 months old. Where breast feeding is prolonged and supplementary feeding of the infant at an early age carries a high risk of infection, supplementary feeding of the mother has been thought might improve her milk yield and maintain it over a long period. 'Feed the nursing mother and thereby the infant' became a widely quoted slogan.

A trial to test this hypothesis has now been carried out in a village in Gambia.[36,37] For two successive years all lactating women in the village, about 130, had their home food intake and their breast milk measured each month. During the second year they were given each morning except on Sundays a food supplement providing about 3.5 MJ (830 kcal) of energy. Throughout both years in each month, including the dry months of August and September when home food intake fell, the mean output of breast milk was unchanged at any stage of lactation from 0–3 months up to 12–15 months. This very thorough and competent trial shows beyond any doubt that giving extra food to these mothers did not increase the milk that their infants received.

The trial raised a problem of general nutritional interest. What happened to the energy in the supplement? It did not go into the milk. Through the year of supplementation the women were heavier than in the previous year but in no month was the mean increase as much as 2 kg. Only a small part went into adipose tissue. Home food consumption fell slightly from 6.58 to 6.13 MJ (1570 to 1460 kcal). These two factors account for only a small fraction of the extra energy. The women, who all felt themselves to be in better health on the supplement, thought that it was expended in increased farming activities. The more sophisticated research team, influenced no doubt by contemporary ideas on energy control (Chap. 9), suggest that the supplement might have made the women less metabolically efficient, but their metabolic studies provide little support for this view.[38] Maybe this is an example of how the Lord 'giveth understanding unto the simple' (Psalm 119 verse 130).

BOTTLE FEEDING

Methods of chemical analysis, introduced between 1825 and 1850, showed the quantitative differences between human and cow's milk and that addition of water and sugar to cow's milk allowed it to be used for feeding infants from birth. This scientific advance saved the lives of many infants whose mothers had died in childbirth or been too ill to lactate. Previously the only hope for such infants had been that another mother who was suckling would take on a second baby. It was difficult to find such a wet nurse unless one was wealthy. However, poor women were exploited by rich mothers unwilling to suckle their baby and this became a fashion in which Parisian women led the way.[39] The wet nurse's baby was usually put at a great disadvantage. The introduction of bottle feedling killed this practice.

Comparison of human and cow's milk

Table 61.3 shows that cow's milk contains much more protein and much less carbohydrate than human milk. There is a little less fat and about the same amount of

Table 61.3 Energy, protein, fat and carbohydrate in human and cow's milk (typical values in 1 dl when lactation is well established)

	Human milk	Cow's milk
Energy (kJ)	290	290
(kcal)	70	70
Protein (g)	1.0	3.5
Fat (g)	4.0	3.8
Carbohydrate (g)	7.4	4.5

energy. The simplest modification is therefore dilution and the addition of carbohydrate.

Variations of up to ± 10 per cent of the figures in the table are common and of up to ± 25 per cent not unusual. The composition of milk from the two breasts is not always identical, and for the first 5 to 10 minutes of a feed the milk from each breast may be thin and watery.

Protein. About 20 per cent of the energy in cow's milk comes from protein, but a little less than 7 per cent in human milk. Thus human milk is not a rich source of protein, but the amino acid mixture which it provides contains ample quantities of all the amino acids essential for growth (p. 49).

Fatty acids. Table 61.4 gives typical values for the main fatty acids present in the two milks. Cow's milk also contains about 150 mg/dl of short-chain fatty acids, of which only traces are found in human milk.

The main difference is the much greater amount of linoleic acid present in human milk. Cow's milk can be made to resemble human milk more closely by removing the cream and replacing it with vegetable oils rich in linoleic acid. The benefit from this is uncertain. Premature infants thrived on a formula in which linoleic acid provided only 0.5 per cent of the energy,[40] a little less than the proportion provided in human milk.

Carbohydrates. Lactose is the main carbohydrate in both human and cow's milk. Sucrose rather than lactose was formerly added to meet cow's milk preparations because it was much cheaper but now lactose is generally used. Two groups of babies with low birth weights fed on a cow's milk formula, one with added lactose and the other with added sucrose, did equally well.[41] Whether in the long term the use of sucrose has any adverse metabolic effects is unknown, but in this way a 'sweet tooth' may be acquired very early in life.

Minerals and electrolytes. Concentration of sodium

Table 61.4 Fatty acids g/100 g of total fatty acids in human and cow's milk (Paul and Southgate, 1978)

Fatty acids	Human milk	Cow's milk
Saturated		
C4:0	0	3.2
C8:0	0	2.0
C10:0	trace	1.2
C10:0	1.4	2.8
C12:0	5.4	3.5
C14:0	7.3	11.2
C15:0	26.5	26.0
C18:0	9.5	11.2
Monounsaturated		
C16:1	4.0	2.7
C18:1	35.4	27.8
Polyunsaturated		
C18:2	7.2	1.4
C18:3	0.8	1.5

Table 61.5 Normal values for the electrolyte and mineral content of human and cow's milk

	Human milk	Cow's milk
Sodium (mmol/litre)	7	25
Potassium (mmol/litre)	15	35
Calcium (mg/d)	34	120
Magnesium (mg/dl)	3	12
Phosphorus (mg/dl)	14	95
Iron (μg/dl)	70	50
Copper (μg/dl)	40	20
Zinc (μg/dl)	28	35

and potassium are much higher in cow's milk than in human milk (Table 61.5). Unmodified cow's milk, if given to very young children, would lead to an osmolar load greater than the excretory capacity of their immature kidneys. Cow's milk also contains much more calcium and phosphorus than human milk, but has a much lower Ca/P ratio. The relatively high phosphorus content may reduce calcium absorption for the intestine and produce hypocalcaemia (p. 111). All recommended formulae prepared from cow's milk have, when reconstituted with water, much lower concentrations of Na, K, Ca and P than the original milk.

Vitamins. Both human and cow's milk are normally good sources of all the vitamins, except vitamin D. However, amounts depend on the maternal diet and, reflecting plasma concentrations, are very variable.

The normal amount of ascorbic acid in human milk is about 3 to 4 mg/dl. Even if a mother's diet is very poor her milk provides enough to prevent scurvy, which is practically unknown in breast-fed infants. As the vitamin is readily destroyed by heat, preparations of cow's milk are a poor source unless it is added artificially and infantile scurvy was formerly a common hazard of bottle feeding.

Amounts of thiamin normally range between 10 and 20 μg/dl in human milk, but values below 6 μg/dl have been reported in the Far East where infantile beriberi may occur (p. 313).

All milks are a poor and uncertain source of vitamin D. The richest summer cow's milk contains only about 0.03 μg/dl, as does human milk. This contrasts with a recommended daily intake of 10 μg for infants. Unless an infant is exposed adequately to sunlight or given a supplement of vitamin D or a milk fortified with the vitamin, signs of rickets are likely to appear before the age of 1 year.

Human milk contains about 30 μg/dl of riboflavin, adequate for infants. Cow's milk contains much more, up to 230 μg/litre, and so is very effective in preventing riboflavin deficiency in older infants and young children. However, the vitamin is rapidly destroyed in milk exposed to sunlight in glass bottles.

ANTIMICROBIAL FACTORS

Human milk contains immunoglobulin A, lactoferrin and lysozyme (Table 61.6). The antimicrobial action of these substances probably help to protect breast-fed infants against infection. The output of IgA falls rapidly as lactation becomes established, although the total amount of IgA transferred in the milk remains substantial. Nevertheless, since the infant's own intestine starts to produce IgA after one or two weeks, the protection given by milk IgA probably has greatest importance in very young infants. Immunoglobulins G and M and small amounts of complement components are also present in milk, but in very much smaller concentrations than IgA. IgE is rarely detectable in milk. Colostrum and early milk also contain substantial numbers of viable macrophages and lymphocytes, but it is not known whether these cells are of any benefit to the infant.

Antimicrobial factors originally present in cow's milk are likely to be destroyed by the heat treatment necessary to make it safe for infants. Hence bottle-fed babies get little or none of these factors. Where hygienic conditions are good, there is little or no difference between the incidence of infection in breast and bottle-fed infants; so their practical importance is uncertain (see below, p. 584).

Cow's milk preparations

In prosperous countries liquid cow's milk has been almost entirely replaced for infant feeding by preparations of dried milk powders and evaporated milks. In poorer countries liquid cow's milk may still be used in rural areas, but the increasing urban populations depend more and more on manufactured preparations.

Liquid milk

Cow's milk cannot be given to very young infants until it has been processed. First it has to be diluted to reduce

Table 61.6 Antimicrobial factors in human milk (from McClelland et al)[42]

	Day of lactation	Concentration (mg/dl)	Output (mg/24h)
IgA	2	4400	3516
	5	250	1369
	8–28	137	1061
	50–200	73	668
Lactoferrin	2	1741	1351
	5	673	3173
	8–28	294	2407
	50–200	112	1094
Lysozyme	2	39	37
	5	14	75
	8–28	14	48
	50–200	11	113

the protein concentration. About one part of water should be added to two parts of milk. Then as the carbohydrate content is lower than that of human milk, sugar is added. If 3.5 g of sugar is added to 100 ml of diluted feed (one level teaspoonful to just over 3 oz), then 100 ml of the feed contains about 2.2 g protein, 2.5 g fat and 7.0 g carbohydrate and has an energy value of 300 kJ (76 kcal). An infant's normal requirement of such a feed is the same as for breast milk namely 160 ml/kg daily. Finally, irrespective of whether the original milk was pasteurised, the mixture is boiled. After boiling it is covered to protect it from pathogens in the atmosphere and from flies. It is kept until use in as cool a place as possible.

Infant milk formulae
These are prepared by manufacturers from products of the dairy industry to which are added lactose and vegetable oils and sometimes other carbohydrates or fats. Whole or skimmed cow's milk are common basic ingredients, but whey is now much used. Whey is milk from which the fat and casein has been removed and so does not curdle. Its mineral content may be reduced by electrodialysis or other means. Table 61.7 shows types of formulae now available. All are fortified with vitamin D.

Instructions for making up the feeds are given with each tin, which includes a scoop for measuring out the powder. Mothers often make up feeds incorrectly and excessive amounts of powder may be used. Overconcentrated feeds carry the risks of hypernatraemia and obesity. Mistakes may be made because scoops are not standardised, but of various sizes. When bottle-feeding was usually with liquid milk, doctors, nurses and midwives made a point of instructing mothers carefully in how to prepare feeds. Preparation is much easier with milk powders and this personal instruction appears to be often omitted. But it is still needed as there are many mothers who cannot or do not follow the written instructions accurately and there are variations in the method and volume of fluid to be added.

Evaporated milk
This is defined on page 213. Like dried milk powders, it is convenient, readily available and sterile. Instructions for adding water are provided. Most evaporated milks are fortified with vitamin D but not with ascorbic acid, a supplement of which is necessary.

Ready-to-feed milk
These are preparations of milk powders or evaporated milks which have been diluted. Hence they can be given to a baby without further preparation. At present in Britain they are only in use in hospitals.

BREAST VERSUS BOTTLE

Breast feeding provides a baby with its natural nourishment and helps to promote the bonding of mother and infant, so important in development of the young in all mammals. It is also cheap, clean and safe. For these reasons health authorities everywhere advocate it strongly.

Table 61.7 Constitution, selected compositional details and examples of infant formulae available in Britain which are intended for normal babies. (From Wharton)[43]

Details	Types of formula				
	Added carbohydrate only	Substituted fat	Demineralised whey	Cow's milk	Human Milk
Whey: casein ratio	20:80		60–70: 40–30	20: 80	60–40
Carbohydrate	Lactose and often others — maltodextrin, sucrose		Usually lactose only	Lactose	
Fat	Cow's milk	Blend of vegetable oils and (often) cow's milk fat, or (less commonly) animal fat		Cow's milk	Human milk
Typical Composition					
Protein g/dl	1.8–2.0	1.5–1.9	1.5–1.8	3.4	1.3
Phosphorus mg/dl	40–55	40–55	30–35	95	15
Sodium mmol/dl	1.5	1.2	0.6	2.2	0.6
Examples in Britain		Cow & Gate Plus. Milumil. Ostermilk Complete. SMA Regular.	Aptamil. Cow & Gate Premium. Osterfeed. SMA Gold Cap.		

However, many millions of adult men and women in the world today had little or no breast milk and do not appear to be less healthy than those who had it. Bottle feeding is an acceptable alternative to breast milk provided three conditions are met. These are that the mother has (1) the money to purchase sufficient of the milk preparation, (2) education and intelligence to follow instructions for making up the preparation and (3) facilities in the home for making up the preparation and washing the utensils in a clean room and with safe water. When, as in many communities throughout the world these conditions are not met, a mother's decision to give up the breast and use a bottle is all too often a death sentence for her baby (see below).

When in prosperous communities these conditions are met, the case for breast feeding is not strong and mothers have a choice. Incidences of illnesses and growth rates of infants were found to be no different in breast and bottle-fed babies in two large carefully conducted studies in Sweden[44] and Kuala Lumpur.[45] Professional women and others may have activities outside their homes that they would have to give up while lactating and this might have far-reaching effects on them and on their families. Doctors and nurses have a duty to advise mothers of the advantages of breast feeding and to encourage them to do so. However, the choice is hers. If she is unable or unwilling to do so, she should not be made to feel guilty. In our society kindly persuasion is more likely to promote the cause of breast feeding than militant advocacy.

HAZARDS OF BOTTLE FEEDING

In poor communities the cost of artificial milks relative to income is high. To save money a mother may over-dilute the preparation and so underfeed her baby. Poor hygenic conditions for making up and storing the preparation inevitably lead to repeated attacks of gastroenteritis. These make an ideal prescription for the development of protein-energy malnutrition and inevitably lead to a large infant mortality. In such circumstances it is unrealistic to hope that conditions for satisfactory artificial feeding will become available to the majority of mothers in the near future, the reversal of the present trend away from breast feeding is essential for reducing a high infant mortality. To re-establish the custom of breast feeding is a main task of many health services. It requires not only a full use of all the techniques of health education, but also social and economic changes to permit women who work to have the time to feed their babies.

In prosperous communities where protein-energy malnutrition rarely occurs, it is uncommon for bottle feeding to be responsible for an illness and such that

occur are usually minor. However, the first to be described may have a serious, even fatal consequence.

Hypertonic dehydration

Sodium concentration in human milk is 7 mmol/l. It is between 20 and 25 mmol/l in cow's milk and in most preparations of cow's milk which have been reconstituted according to the instructions. Healthy infants can excrete this extra load of sodium, but have to secrete a more concentrated urine. In 1972 Taitz and Byers[46] found the mean osmolalities of the urine were 105 and 380 mosmol/kg in breast fed and bottle fed babies. Three common circumstances may prevent them excreting the load and lead to a rise in plasma sodium. These are an attack of diarrhoea, fever or a failure of the mother to make up the feed according to the instructions. Diarrhoea and fever increase water losses from the gut and from the skin and lungs, and so reduce the amount available for excreting solutes in the urine. Taitz and Byers measured the sodium concentration of 32 feeds obtained from mothers attending their clinic. In 21 of the samples it was over 30 mosmol/l and in 4 over 40. Many mothers give their babies overconcentrated feeds by not levelling the powder in the scoop as the instructions indicate.

The clinical features of hypertonic dehydration are anorexia and irritability; there may be convulsions. If the condition is allowed to continue, permanent damage to the brain may follow. The diagnosis is made by finding a plasma sodium concentration above 150 mmol/l. Treatment is effected by attending to the underlying cause and, if the condition is severe, by giving dextrose and water or hypotonic saline intravenously. The nature and dosage of the intravenous fluids required is determined by careful monitoring of plasma electrolytes.

The number of babies admitted to hospital for hypertonic dehydration has now fallen, probably because the salt content of infant formulae has been reduced. Doctors and nurses have a duty to see that all mothers using artificial milks understand how to make up feeds accurately. Whereas formerly mothers were given much instruction in the art of breast feeding and in modifying liquid cow's milk, it is now often assumed that the written instructions provided with milk preparations suffice.

Neonatal tetany

This consists of twitches and spasms occurring between the third and fourteenth day of life. It is very rare in breast fed infants. The plasma concentration of calcium is usually low and sometimes also that of magnesium. Alimentary absorption of these elements may be impaired by the high phosphate content of the feeds or by steatorrhoea, owing to inability to absorb fully the fatty acids present in cow's milk. Immaturity of the parathyroid glands is probably a contributory factor and the spasms cease spontaneously by about the fourteenth day or earlier. Treatment by giving calcium gluconate (10 ml of a 10 per cent solution) by mouth with each feed is usually effective. Whether or not there is hypomagnesaemia, magnesium sulphate (50 per cent solution) given intramuscularly in a dose of 0.2 mg/kg of body weight is equally effective and may be the treatment of choice.

Infection

With good hygiene the incidence of infection should be no greater in bottle- than in breast-fed infants. However, those who are bottle fed appear more likely to develop diarrhoea in the neonatal period. Interest has now centred on rotavirus infection,[47,48] but many other microorganisms may be responsible.

Nurses and other attendants in lying-in wards may be carriers of the virus and it may spread from infant to infant. Those infected may have no symptoms, a mild diarrhoea or sometimes severe gastroenteritis which may lead to necrotising enterocolitis. It is possible, though the evidence is not strong, that antimicrobial factors in the colostrum may protect against rotavirus and also other infections.

It is sensible for every mother, whenever possible, to feed her baby at the breast for at least 10 days. Nurses and doctors should encourage strongly all mothers to do so.

Obesity

Bottle-fed babies tend to be heavier than those who are breast fed and not infrequently they become obese. A possible reason for this is that a breast feed is usually terminated by the baby stopping suckling when loss of appetite has indicated that enough milk has been taken. On the other hand a mother makes up a bottle feed with the amount of milk that she thinks her baby needs. She may then keep the teat of the bottle in her baby's mouth and persuade it to continue to feed until the bottle is empty. Long ago when baby competitions were common, judges often awarded first prize to the biggest baby. Tradition dies hard and some mothers still do not appreciate that a big baby is not a better baby.

THE INFANT FOOD INDUSTRY

Manufacturers of milk preparations for infants have since 1970 taken a lot of stick. This has to be considered in relation to the benefit that they have been able to confer upon mankind. For over 100 years manufacturers have provided preparations of continuously improving quality that have been the means of allowing babies, whose mothers could not or were unwilling to give them

breast milk, to develop normally and in full health. In terms of human history this is a great achievement.

Infant milk preparations are manufactured by large companies which trade internationally. Competition between them is keen and this has ensured that, when a customer buys a preparation bearing the brand name of one of the well-known firms, she is getting a good and reliable product. The firms are, however, not only competing with themselves but with manufacturers of breast milk. The promotion and advertising of their products has been an important factor in the decline of breast feeding. The consequences have been disastrous for poor mothers in many countries who have neither the money to buy sufficient quantities for their babies nor a home environment where the milk can be reconstituted with safety. Firms have been castigated as 'baby killers' by enthusiastic proponents of breast feeding. This led to a long legal action for libel in a Swiss court, and in the USA firms have been sued for improper practices. There is substance in many of the criticisms of the sales techniques of some firms and this led to a WHO/UNICEF meeting and the issue of recommendations for marketing and distribution of infant formulae and weaning foods.[49] This was followed by the issue of an International Code of Marketing of Breast-Milk Substitutes.[50] The Code is a most welcome advance but, with so many different firms and countries involved, uncertainties about its effectiveness must remain. Most countries have not introduced legislation, and implementation of the Code depends on good will and cooperation between manufacturers and voluntary bodies.

The fault does not lie all with food manufacturers. Apathy and lack of knowledge among doctors, nurses and nutritionists have also been responsible for large numbers of mothers using artificial milks, unnecessarily and without adequate facilities. Breast feeding versus bottle feeding is a controversy which arouses strong emotions, but the issues are not simple. Social, psychological, educational and economic factors determine the sales of infant milk preparations. All of these and the nutritional factors are discussed in a large book by Jelliffe and Jelliffe.[51] The authors have an unrivalled experience of infant feeding practice in many parts of the world and set out the case for breast feeding with enthusiasm.

PATTERNS OF FEEDING

Feeds from breast or bottle may be given at fixed hours, the once popular Truby King method, or haphazardly and on demand, which also may become a vogue. Life is easier if a routine is followed but a flexible timetable is recommended. Most infants do well with five feeds daily, the first at about 06.00 hours (6 am) and the last at 22.00 hours (10 pm). A feed can be put forward if a baby seems hungry and a mother may give the breast to comfort her child. If for any reason a feed is delayed for an hour or so, the baby may show annoyance but comes to no harm.

Supplementary foods

As already indicated most mothers do not produce enough milk to meet fully the needs of their infants for growth when they are about four months old. Then supplements should be started. Many mothers nowadays give them earlier. This is not necessary if the baby is gaining weight normally. When a mother is in doubt about whether her milk yield is sufficient, she may test weigh her baby before and after a feed without changing the napkin. As milk yield is apt to vary greatly throughout the day, it is best to test weigh all feeds over 24 hours. This is much easier with modern electronic balances. A daily yield of 500 ml is satisfactory and sufficient for the baby at first and this should rise slowly to 700–800 ml. But babies' needs also vary greatly; some grow well on 600 ml or even less and others require more than 800 ml before they are 4 months old.

The first solid food is usually a cereal gruel. This can be soon followed by minces, boiled vegetables and stewed fruit. It is not necessary to sieve the food, but hard particles should be removed. Preparations of supplements in the home is time-consuming and mothers can use the many baby foods prepared by food manufacturers, readily available in shops. It is unnecessary and probably unwise to give these preparations before the age of 2 months. Immature kidneys may not be able to deal with an extra sodium load, arising from the salt that many of them contain. It is also possible that early introduction of cereals containing gluten may make a predisposed infant more likely to develop coeliac disease, a condition which appears to be becoming more prevalent.

Where manufactured infant foods are not available or mothers cannot afford to buy them, as in most peasant communities in the tropics, supplements can be made up in the home using locally available foods. A small monograph by Cameron and Hofvander indicates how this can be done and contains much other good practical advice on infant feeding.[52]

Weaning

There are no physiological constraints that determine when a baby should be weaned from the breast or bottle. Mothers usually find it convenient to do so when the baby is about 6 months old. Weaning should be gradual but is usually completed within seven to 14 days. During this period the infant has to learn to drink cow's milk from a cup and to become accustomed to more solid foods of greater variety.

Where safe cow's milk is not available, breast feeding should be continued much longer. Many poor women continue to suckle their children for two years or more and, as already described, this prolonged lactation may benefit the child and possibly the mother.

Feeding in the second half of infancy

During this period the infant gradually adapts towards an adult pattern of feeding. The first meal is given later in the morning and the last meal earlier in the evening. Three main meals in the day may suffice towards the end of the period but these are usually supplemented with biscuits, milk or other snacks. Milk should be a main feature of the diet and up to a half litre given daily.

Appetite is the best guide to how much food is needed. Provided weight gain is satisfactory, an infant should not be coaxed to eat. Infants, like adults, readily become obese. A theory that infantile obesity leads to hyperplasia of adipocytes and so predisposes to obesity later in life has not been generally supported.[53] Increased physical activity in the second year of life usually removes any excess 'baby fat'.

Sugar should be added only sparingly or not at all to an infant's food. It encourages a 'sweet tooth' and so leads to excessive intakes, predisposing to dental caries later in life. It is also unwise to salt their food as this may habituate them to a high intake with possible adverse consequences later in life.

Infants enjoy their food. Their meals should be a pleasure but consistent with good manners. It is better to terminate a meal at once rather than create a scene by trying to force on a child food that is not wanted or not liked. Here writes an experienced grandfather.

REFERENCES

1. Antonov A N 1942 Children born during the siege of Leningrad in 1942. J Pediatr 30: 250–9
2. Stein, Susser M, Saenger G, Marolla F 1975 Famine and human development: the Dutch hunger winter of 1944–1945. Oxford University Press, New York
3. Thomson A M 1959 Diet in pregnancy. 3 Diet in relation to the course and outcome of pregnancy. Br J Nutr 13: 509–25
4. Belavady B 1969 Nutrition in pregnancy and lactation. Indian J Med Res 57: suppl p 63
5. WHO Division of Family Health 1980 The incidence of low brith weight; a critical review of available information. WHO Stat Q Rep 33(3): 197–224
5a. Briend A 1985 Do maternal energy reserves limit fetal growth? Lancet 1: 38–40
6. Committee of Action on Smoking and Health 1980

Mothers who smoke and their children. Practitioner 224: 735–40

7. Ouellette E M, Rosett H L, Rosman, N P, Weiner L 1977 Adverse effects on the offspring of maternal alcohol abuse during pregnancy. N Engl J Med 297: 528–30

8. Tafari N, Naeye R L, Gobezie A 1980 Effects of maternal undernutrition and heavy physical work during pregnancy on birthweight. Br J Obstet Gynaec 87: 222–6

9. Duncan M E 1980 Babies of mothers with leprosy have small placentae, low birth weights and grow slowly. Br J Obstet Gynaec 87: 471–9

10. Lechtig A, Delgado H, Lasky R E, et al 1975 Maternal nutrition and fetal growth in developing societies. Am J Dis Child 129: 434–7

11. Viegas O A C, Scott P H, Cole T J, et al 1982 Dietary protein energy supplementation of pregnant Asian mothers at Sorento, Birmingham. I Unselected during the second and third trimesters. II Selected during third trimester only. Br Med J 285: 589–92, 592–5

12. Hytten F E, Keitch I 1971 The physiology of human pregnancy. Blackwell, Oxford

13. Emerson R G 1962 Obesity and its association with the complications of pregnancy. Br Med J 2: 516–8

14. Thomson A M, Billewicz W Z 1957 Clinical significance of weight trends during pregnancy. Br Med J 1:243

15. Elwood J M, Elwood J H 1980 Epidemiology of anencephalus and spina bifida. Oxford University Press

16. Smithells R W, Sheppard S, Schoral C J, et al 1980 Possible prevention of neural-tube defects by preconceptional vitamin supplements. Lancet 1: 339–40

17. Renwick J H 1972 Anencephaly and spina bifida are usually preventable by avoidance of a specific unidentified substance present in certain potato tubers. Br J Prev Soc Med 26: 67–88

18. Nevin N C, Merrett J D 1975 Potato avoidance during pregnancy in women with a previous infant with either anencephaly and/or spina bifida. Br J Prev Soc Med 29: 111–5

19. Kalt R H, Warkany J 1983 Congenital malformations: etiological factors and their role in prevention. N Engl J Med 308: 424–31, 491–7

20. Kessel N 1977 The fetal alcohol syndrome from the public health standpoint. Health Trends 9: 86–88

21. Edwards G 1983 Alcohol and advice to the pregnant woman. Br Med J 286: 247–8

22. Linn S, Schoenbaum S C, Monson R R, et al 1983 No association between coffee consumption and adverse outcomes of pregnancy. N Engl J Med 306: 141–5

23. Naismith D J 1977 Protein metabolism during pregnancy. In: Philipp E E, Barnes J, Newton M (eds) Scientific foundations of obstetrics and gynaecology. Heinemann, London, p 503–10

24. Peters J P, van Slyke D D 1946 Quantitative clinical chemist: interpretations, 2nd edn. Bailliére, Tindal & Cox, London, vol 1, p 666

25. Arneil G C 1967 Dietary studies of 4365 Scottish infants. Scottish Health Services Studies no. 6

26. Fomon S J 1971 A paediatrician looks at early nutrition. Bull NY Acad Med 47: 569–78

27. Martin J, Monk J 1983 Infant feeding 1980. Office of Population Censuses and Surveys. HMSO, London

28. World Health Organisation 1981 Contemporary patterns of breast-feeding. Report on the WHO collaborative study on breast-feeding. WHO, Geneva

28a. Gopujkar P V, Chauduri S N, Ramaswami MA, Gore M S, Gopalan C 1984 Infant feeding practices with special references to the use of commercial feeds. Nutrition Foundation of India Scientific Report no. 4. (Editorial in Lancet 1984 2: 614–5)

29. Gunther M 1973 Infant feeding. Penguin Books, London

30. Helsing E, King F S 1982 Breast feeding in practice. Oxford University Press

31. Ogra P L, Greene H L 1982 Human milk and breast feeding: an update on the state of the art. Pediatr Res 16: 266–71

32. Cutting W A M, Ludlam M 1984 Making the best of breast feeding. Fam Practice 1: 69–78

33. Whitehead R G 1983 Nutritional aspects of human lactation. Lancet 2: 167–9

34. Waterlow J C 1981 Observations on the sucklings dilemma. J Hum Nutr 35: 85–98

35. Thomson A M, Hytten F E, Billewicz W F 1970 The energy cost of human lactation. Br J Nutr 24: 565–72

36. Prentice A M, Whitehead R G, Roberts S B, et al 1980 Dietary supplementation of Gambian nursing mothers and lactational performance. Lancet 2: 886–8

37. Prentice A M, Roberts S B, Prentice A, et al 1983 Dietary supplementation of lactating Gambian women. I Effect on breast-milk volume and quality. Hum Nutr Clin Nutr 37C: 53–64

38. Prentice A M, Lunn P G, Watkinson M, Whitehead R G 1983 Dietary supplementation of lactating Gambian women. II Effect on maternal health, nutritional status and biochemistry. Hum Nutr Clin Nutr 37C:65–74

39. Badinter E 1981 The myth of motherhood: an historical review of the maternal instinct. Souvenir Press, London, p 73

40. Combes M A, Pratt E L, Wiese H F 1962 Essential fatty acids in premature infant feeding. Pediatrics 30: 136–44

41. Fosbrooke A S, Wharton B A 1975 'Added lactose'and 'added sucrose' cow's milk formulae in nutrition of low birthweight babies. Arch Dis Child 50: 409–18

42. McClelland D B L, McGrath J, Samson R R 1978 Antimicrobial factors in human milk. Acta Paediatr Scand suppl 271: 1–20

43. Wharton B A 1984 Infant formulae. Br Nutr Found Bull 9: 83–93

44. Mellander O, Vahlquist B, Mellbin T 1959 Breast feeding and artificial feeding; a clinical, serological and biochemical study in 402 infants, with a survey of literature; the Norbotten study. Acta Paediatr Scand (Suppl) 116: 1–108

45. Dugdale A E 1971 The effect of the type of feeding on weight gain and illnesses in infants. Br J Nutr 26: 423–432

46. Taitz L S, Byers H D 1972 High calorie/osmolar feeding and hypertonic dehydration. Arch Dis Child 47: 257–60

47. Cutting W A M 1979 Viral gastroenteritis in children. Tropical Doctor January: 16–30

48. Dearlove J, Latham P, Dearlove B, et al 1983 Clinical range of neonatal rotavirus gastroenteritis. Br Med J 286: 1473–5

49. Joint WHO/UNICEF meeting on infant and young child feeding 1979 WHO, Geneva

50. International Code of marketing of breast-milk substitutes 1981 WHO, Geneva

51. Jelliffe D B, Jelliffe E F P 1978 Human milk in the modern world: psychological, nutritional and economic significance. Oxford University Press

52. Cameron M, Hofvander Y 1983 Manual on feeding infants and young children, 3rd edn. Oxford University Press

53. Hawk L J, Brook C G D 1979 Influence of body fatness in childhood on fatness in adult life. Br Med J 1: 151–2

62

Childhood, Youth and Old Age

CHILDHOOD

After their first birthday children are able to share in a family meal and eat most of the dishes prepared for adults. Appetite is normally a sound guide to requirements. Children's feeding behaviour is far less a matter of habit than adults. A child may eat voraciously for a day or two and then lose all interest in his food for a while. This is natural and there is no necessity to restrict meals in one phase or to attempt to force food during another. Many children occasionally develop specific appetites for one food. This may make the diet temporarily quite unbalanced. This again does no harm, for it is soon rectified naturally, and so need not be checked unless it offends against good manners.

The best guide that the food intake is satisfactory is provided by the weighing machine. It is sound practice to weigh and measure the height of a child every three months. Provided the increase in weight and height is satisfactory (the charts on p. 519), are useful guides) there is no need to worry about a child's diet.

Tables of recommended intakes of energy and nutrients (Chap. 15) are useful for persons responsible for planning the feeding of children in boarding schools and other institutions but the figures, except those for energy, are above most children's needs. The recommendations for energy intake cannot be applied to individuals since children vary so much in their physical activities.

Vitamins

Requirements for vitamins are relatively increased in childhood and it is well known that children are more liable than adults to many deficiency diseases. If the family diet is not satisfactory, then it is desirable to provide daily for the child extra vitamins C, A and D, either in a concentrated supplement or in the form of fruit juice and a fish-liver oil. The beneficial effect of these welfare foods has been repeatedly demonstrated and a great increase in their use is needed in many countries. After the age of 2 years, provided the child is healthy and eats a good mixed diet including fruit and vegetables, there is no necessity for these extra vitamins, except in northern countries where there is little sunshine in winter. In these circumstances a supplement of vitamin D should be continued up to the age of 5 years or longer if cases of rickets have occurred in older children in the community.

Milk

The value of milk as a food for children has been established by practical experience and put on a scientific basis by Corry Mann (p. 537) and many others in controlled field trials. It is desirable that every child up to the age of 5 years should have 500 ml milk daily, and after the age of 5 until growth ceases at least 250 ml. Milk is chiefly valuable as a source of good quality protein and of calcium needed for growth. In practice, growth and development are usually slow in children who receive poor diets containing little or no milk. This need not be so, for Widdowson and McCance[1] showed that if a good mixture of vegetable proteins is provided excellent growth rates are obtained, despite the virtual absence of milk from the diet.

Larger amounts of milk have sometimes been recommended. These may accelerate growth further and, less certainly, increase adult size, but there is no evidence that either is desirable or contributes to health and well being.

The management of children's diets

A child's diet is best taken equally divided between three main meals. Breakfast is usually taken with the family. It is a meal which is frequently skimped by adults, who may indeed do well with very little food in the morning. It is, however, important for children to go to school with a good breakfast inside them. The midday meal may be taken either at home or, more often, at school. If the school does not provide a satisfactory meal, a packed lunch is needed. Young children under 5 years should go to bed early and it is best for them to have their evening meal separately before the rest of the family. If the main family evening meal is taken after 7 o'clock, children under 10 years will also need a meal earlier.

In many countries it is customary to give school children a glass of milk at the mid-morning break and this is sound practice. If the evening meal is late, children want something in the middle of the afternoon. This is permissible. Otherwise children are best without snacks between meals.

Some children readily become obese and there is need to watch that weight gain is not excessive.

Sweets and candies. An excessive consumption of these spoils the appetite for the main meal and predisposes to dental caries. Nevertheless, taken in moderation, especially after meals, they do no harm and are a legitimate pleasure of childhood. The danger of excessive consumption is always present and there is need for discipline.

Good dietary habits can be acquired when young and often persist throughout life. They are more likely to arise from example than from any form of health education. Society in Britain today and probably in many other countries has become so organised that many children only occasionally sit down to a regular meal either at home with their parents or at school with their teachers. They are, in contemporary jargon, deprived kids.

ADOLESCENCE

Adolescents have additional requirements for nutrients due to the spurt in growth that occurs at puberty. In boys this is responsible for a gain of about 20 cm (8 in) in height and 19 kg (40 lb) in weight. In girls the gains are usually less. An increase in appetite occurs and normally ensures that increased food intake meets the additional need for nutrients. More interesting and perhaps more important than this physiological change are the changes that occur in food habits at adolescence and these are determined by psychological factors and social customs.

Adolescence is the period when the independent character of an individual is established. Parental authority and patterns of living are challenged, leading often to friction and acrimony. The characteristic behavioural changes were described by Socrates, as Plato reported.[2]

It becomes the thing for father and son to change places, the father standing in awe of his son, and the son neither respecting nor fearing his parents, in order to assert what he calls his independence . . . . The teacher fears and panders to his pupils, who in turn despise their teachers and attendants; and the young as a whole imitate their elders, argue with them and set themselves up against them, while their elders try to avoid the reputation of being disagreeable or strict by aping the young and mixing with them on terms of easy good fellowship.

After 2500 years the vagaries of youth remain unchanged, and today many young people have additional freedom from parents in that educational grants are paid by the state and unemployment benefit is available for them.

Adolescent eating patterns are part of this behaviour. Meals are missed and snacks, sweets and carry-out foods substituted. Often unconventional meals are taken at unconventional times. This is the period when experimentation with alcohol and sometimes other drugs begins. The pressures of peer groups, advertising and television encourage conformity to non-conformity.

Surveys on teenagers in the USA[3,4] and the UK[5,6] show a wide range of patterns of eating and intake of energy and nutrients; all are apparently compatible with health. Comparisons of measured intakes of nutrients with recommended intakes are of little use to assess the nutritional status of teenagers in affluent societies.

Fewer meals appear to be eaten by teenagers under the social discipline imposed by a family, by a school or college or by a works canteen than formerly. There is no evidence that this is impairing physical health. But an organised meal wherever held helps to give those who take part in it a sense of belonging to a group. A lack of organised meals may thus encourage undesirable deviant behaviour. Claims that the poor quality of teenagers' diets contributes to the prevalence of juvenile delinquency have been publicised widely in the USA. These do not stand up to critical evaluation[7] and the Californian Council against Health Fraud has issued a statement that they are false.

Teenagers in immigrant families often have problems because of differences in the food habits of their family and of the country where they live. These are aggravated by a rigid conservative outlook of either parents or school authorities. Such young people need help and advice.

Despite their problems adolescents in prosperous countries are healthy and lively. Many, but not enough, take an active part in sport and recreations and not a few records are held by teenage athletes.

The greatest danger to health in youth is violence. In countries where infectious diseases are controlled, it is far and away the commonest cause of death in early life. All too often alcohol has been a cause of the fatal accident. The young need education in the correct use of alcohol as an adjunct to a good meal.

Obesity, anorexia nervosa and, in girls, iron deficiency are the important nutritional disorders in adolescence. In countries where goitre is endemic, adolescent girls are most likely to be affected. Dietary and other measures for the prevention of dental health are important at this period of life. All these problems have been discussed in previous chapters.

In conclusion the words of a wise American

nutritionist written in 1968 continue to be true for the United Kingdom in 1984.[8]

It is common practice today to believe that many teenagers have atrocious food habits and are on the brink of a nutritional disaster. The basis for such a generalisation is questionable. We point with pride to our youth — their size, their attainments, and their vitality, even though we view with alarm their food habits. Are we implying that food has no relation to fitness, or do we have a distorted picture of their food choices and eating patterns?

OLD AGE

Life expectation

Few animals survive naturally into old age. They die as a result of starvation or trauma, often from the teeth or claws of predators. The hunter-gatherers who were our primitive ancestors must have died mainly from these causes.[9] Not until *Homo sapiens* acquired the skills needed to raise and store foodcrops and to protect these against rival tribes and began to provide altruistic care for the injured and sick were men and women, together with some of their domestic animals, able to live out their potential physiological life span. For mankind this has been traditionally taken as 70 years. 'The days of our years are threescore years and ten, and by reason of strength they be fourscore, yet is their strength labour and sorrow; for it is soon cut off, and we fly away.' (Psalm 90 verse 10.)

This figure is certainly an underestimate. The mean potential life expectation of both men and women is probably 85 years with individual variations from 70 to 100 years.[10] The evidence to support this view comes from the study of survival rates in countries where mortality from infectious diseases has been progressively reduced. Figure 62.1 shows the percentage survival rates of US citizens to various ages in 1900 and again in 1980. In 1980 the percentage surviving fell very slowly to the age of 50 years and sharply at the age of 65 years. Projecting this curve forward and assuming continuing improvement in the health services, it is possible to draw an ideal curve with the sharp fall beginning at 70 years and 50 per cent surviving at 85 years. There are less than 7000 centenarians in the USA and the odds that any one of us reaches this age is of the order of 33 000 to 1 against. There is no evidence to suggest that a significant fall in these odds is possible.

Shangri-la

This is the name of an imaginary valley in the Himalayas that is an earthly paradise. There are several remote areas of the world in which many people are reported to live to a healthy old age and where centenarians are numerous. Thus in the Hunza province of Pakistan, in parts of Georgia and Azerbaijan in southern USSR and in Vilcabamba in Ecuador high in the Andes, centenarians have been reported to number from 30 to 60 per 100 000 of the populations — about 10 to 20 times the USA rates. However, these figures are suspect as they cannot be supported by birth certificates, except in Vilcabamba where there are baptismal records, but these are unreliable. Leaf, a professor of medicine at Harvard, visited all of these areas and found large numbers of active and healthy old people in each.[11] The one factor common to all of them, men and women alike, was that they had led and continued to lead a hard life in the fields as peasant agriculturalists, usually in a harsh environment. The remarkable absence of chronic degenerative disease might perhaps be attributed to a simple diet, but some of them, particularly in Georgia, lived well and ate meat, dairy products and sugar and were not averse to feasts, alcohol and tobacco. Dr Leaf obviously enjoyed his visit and was well entertained. If there is any message for us from these people, perhaps it is that the secret of a long and healthy old age is not a life of abstinence but one of hard physical labour. After studying 10 Russian publications, Medvedev is doubtful whether very old people are more numerous in Georgia than elsewhere; he suggests that there is a cult of old people there and they may be used for State propaganda.[12]

Hebrew writers in the Old Testament and others after them have made extravagent statements about the ages of old people. Many of these have been scrutinised by Fries and Crapo,[10] who accept the view of the 1980 *Guinness Book of World Records* that there is documentary evidence for only five people reaching the age of 112 years and that the world record of 114 years goes to Shigechiyo Izumi of Japan.

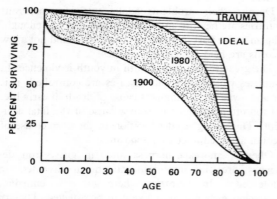

Fig. 62.1 Survival rates of the US population in 1900 and in 1980 and the ideal which would follow elimination of premature death. (US Bureau of Health data quoted by Fries & Crapo)[10]

Running down of organs

Physiology textbooks give many examples of quantitative data that can be used to assess the functional capacity of organs and tissues. These are almost invariably given for young adults alone. Figure 62.2 gives examples of how some decline with age. The capacities of the central nervous, skeletal, reproductive, haemostatic and immune systems also fall with age. The haemopoietic and digestive systems are exceptions. Cells of the bone marrow and epithelial lining of the gut are continuously replaced and the new ones function normally. In the absence of disease old people do not become anaemic and continue to enjoy their food. The digestive capacity of old people was demonstrated by Widdowson[14] in Germany after the end of World War II. She arranged for 19 men all of whom were severely undernourished to have unlimited access to food for up to 6 weeks. Six old men, three of them over 75 years, consumed and digested on average 23.6 MJ (5600 kcal) daily, only very little less than their younger colleagues in the experiment.

The running down of the organs and systems is a gradual process, except for the abrupt cessation of ovarian function at the menopause. It begins soon after the age of 20 years. An obvious demonstration of this is that by the age of 30 the radiance of the hair in youth has gone and in many of us there are incipient signs of baldness and perhaps a few grey hairs. This and the decline of other organs is determined by our genes and so inevitable. At some point between the ages of 70 and 100 years homeostatic mechanisms are no longer able to respond effectively to stress. Death may then follow minor infections and injuries from which earlier in life rapid recovery could be expected. Vascular damage

leading to thrombosis or internal haemorrhage is a common cause of death in old people. In earlier life such lesions may be repaired rapidly and often before they have become sufficiently large to cause symptoms.

It is a reasonable assumption that the survival rate of a population would reach the ideal presented in Figure 62.1 if four conditions were met. Three of the conditions are a collective responsibility of society; these are (1) economic measures to relieve the poor unable to obtain the necessities of life, (2) safe environmental conditions in all places, especially in the homes.and where people work, and (3) access to medical services for the prevention and treatment of infectious and other diseases and for the treatment of trauma. The fourth and perhaps most important responsibility is an individual one; it is to choose a way of living that includes a prudent diet, sufficient physical activities, rest and recreations, and not to be dependent on alcohol, nicotine or other drugs. Attention to these factors should not only reduce the number of premature deaths but also maintain the health of the elderly and limit the period of incapacity and terminal illness before the inevitable end. Figure 62.1 shows that in 80 years the USA has gone a long way towards the ideal and this gives hope for further progress.

Can life span be prolonged?

McCay and his colleagues at Cornell University fed young rats a good diet which promoted rapid growth and development when there was free access to it.[15,16] When the animals were given only limited amounts of the food, growth was delayed, but subsequently they lived longer than those that had grown faster. Similar results have been obtained with insects, fish and other mammalian species and there is no reason to think that *Homo sapiens* would not respond in the same way. However, no one would wish to keep a child permanently hungry for their first 15 years or so in the expectation that they would then live longer. So these animal experiments have no practical application in human nutrition, except that they raise the question of whether maximum growth rates are desirable. When growth has ceased there is no evidence to suggest that the genetically determined life span can be increased by dietary manipulation or by any other means.

NUTRITIONAL REQUIREMENTS OF THE ELDERLY

As age advances, physical activity tends to decline and so less dietary energy is required. Committees that have drawn up tables of recommended intake attempt to quantify this reduction in energy need (Chap. 15).

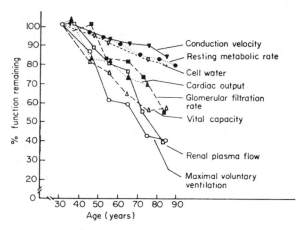

Fig. 62.2 Average values of human functions or capacities related to age, taking values at age 30 years as 100. (Data redrawn from Shock)[13]

While their figures are a useful guide to the needs of large groups of old people, they are not applicable to individuals. There are many men and women over 70 years of age who are as physically active as they were 20 or even 40 years previously and they need as much food as then. The majority who gradually become more sedentary need correspondingly less food and, if they continue their past eating habits, they become obese.

There are no special requirements for specific nutrients in old age. If old people meet their energy requirements by taking a good mixed diet, similar to that which they ate when they were younger, their needs for nutrients are met. Supplements of vitamins and minerals are not needed. Two exceptions to this generalisation arise. First some old people lead such sedentary lives that their energy requirement is very low. Dietary surveys show that a few men and many women aged between 75 and 90 years take less than 6.3 MJ (1500 kcal) daily.[17] Intakes of protein, minerals and vitamins may then be inadequate unless the diet contains a greater proportion of milk, eggs, meat, fruit and vegetables and less of separated fats and sugar than is present in normal adult diets. Eggs are a convenience food, especially valuable for such old people. Secondly a supplement of vitamin D is indicated for those old people who for one reason or another are little exposed to sunlight, especially when they live in northern latitudes with long dark winters (Chap. 32).

Extreme old age

Readers of this book may well appreciate that no one has contributed more and in such varied fields to the science of nutrition in the last 50 years than Dr Elsie Widdowson of Cambridge. Yet when she looks after her centenarian mother, it is art rather than science that is used, as she reports:[18]

In my own series of one old lady, my mother, now aged 105, I can see processes of ageing without the complications of disease. Sight, hearing and memory fail, but not interest in food or processes of digestion. My recipe for nutrition in extreme old age is well-fitting dentures, portions of ordinary meals, milk to drink with all of them, and anything the individual particularly fancies, whether it be fish, fruit, cake or chocolate. Again activity within the person's capacity is very important, especially in the sunshine out of doors. I am sure that tender loving care is as important in extreme old age as it is in infancy in promoting well-being and health.

Nutritional disorders

In Western society obesity is by far the commonest nutritional disorder found in old people. Diabetes frequently accompanies it and in most cases the symptoms are relieved on reduction of weight and there is no need for insulin or other drugs.

In many surveys of selected groups of old people low blood concentrations of a nutrient or other evidence of low tissue reserves have been found. Deficiencies of ascorbic acid, folate and iron are most likely to occur.

In a thorough survey of 879 men and women over 65 years of age chosen at random in the UK, 27 subjects (3.2 per cent) were diagnosed as malnourished.[19] Of these two had frank scurvy and eight angular stomatitis, and the reason given for the diagnosis was in most cases excessive thinness. In 12 of the subjects there were major medical disorders which may have contributed to the malnutrition and in seven cases there were socio-economic causes. In eight cases there was no clear reason for the finding. The incidence of malnutrition is certainly higher in old people than in younger age groups. This can be attributed to a higher proportion of old people living in poverty and a greater prevalence of diseases leading to malnutrition.

The report of a more recent dietary survey[20] in Sydney found that intakes of nutrients by old people were similar to those recorded in the UK.[19] The authors conclude that 'a significant proportion of this population may be at risk', and that this was particularly so for males receiving meals-on-wheels.

Old people in institutions

About 4 per cent of those aged 65 years or over in the UK are resident in institutions[21] and probably a similar percentage in most European countries, in North America and in Australasia. Though the proportion is small, the total numbers are large and inevitably increasing as more of the population survive into old age. Institutions which may be known as geriatric hospitals, eventide homes or simply nursing homes vary in size and organisation. There are small homes with less than 10 beds run privately for profit and government hospitals with hundreds of beds. Some inmates pay nothing, others meet the full cost of their keep. Setting standards of care and seeing that these are maintained is a problem that no government in any country has as yet solved. In most institutions the inmates are well fed, but any expanding enterprise is likely to attract some rogues and idle bureaucrats which no country lacks. Unfortunately but not surprisingly there have been examples of institutions whose inmates have become malnourished.

Many old people in institutions are fussy about their food and have numerous likes and dislikes; others have physical disabilities that make eating difficult. If all are to be well fed, competent administration, dedicated catering and nursing staffs and ready access to expert advice from dietitians are necessary. Supplementary feeding, using the methods described in Chapter 52, is often required.

The picture of old age, too often presented on British television as a period of misery with severe disability and chronic malnutrition is misleading. Most people can now look forward to retirement and old age as a time when they can enjoy themselves, free of many of the responsibilities of former years, and be good company to others. But to achieve this requires the effort to keep going up to the limits of one's physical and mental capacities, however much these may have been reduced by time. *Vitality and Aging* is the title of a cheerful small book which comes from California. Its authors, Fries and Crapo, who work in the medical school of Stanford University, set out concisely what is known about the science of gerontology and given practical guidance on how to keep going.[10] It is good reading both for old people and for those who care for them.

REFERENCES

1. Widdowson E M, McCance R A 1954 Studies on the nutritive value of bread and on the effect of variations in the extraction rate on the growth of undernourished children. MRC Spec Rep Ser no. 287
2. Plato c370 BC The Republic. Penguin Books, London, 2nd edn, revised 1974, p 383
3. Huenemann R L, Shapiro L R, Hampton M C, Mitchell B W 1968 Food and eating practices of teenages. J Am Diet Assoc 53: 17–24
4. Kaufman N A, Poznanski R, Guggenheim K 1981 Eating habits and opinions of teenagers on nutrition and obesity. J Am Diet Assoc 66:244
5. Darke S J, Disselduff M M, Try G P 1980 Frequency distribution of mean daily intakes of food energy and selected nutrients obtained during nutrition surveys of different groups of people in Great Britain between 1968 and 1971. Br J Nutr 44: 243–52
6. Cresswell J, Busby A, Young H, Inglis V 1983 Dietary patterns of third year secondary school girls in Glasgow. Hum Nutr Appl Nutr 37A: 301–6
7. Gray G E, Gray L K 1983 Diet and juvenile delinquency. Nutr Today 18(3): 14–7; (6): 33–6 (Correspondence)
8. Leverton R M 1968 The paradox of teenage nutrition. J Am Diet Assoc 53: 13–6
9. McKeown T 1979 The role of medicine. Blackwell, Oxford, p 71
10. Fries J F, Crapo L M 1981 Vitality and aging. Freeman, San Francisco
11. Leaf A 1973 Observations of a peripathetic gerontologist. Nutr Today 8(5): 4–12
12. Medvedev Z A 1975 Aging and longevity: new approaches and new perspectives. Gerontologist 15: 196–201
13. Shock N W 1957 Age changes in some physiologic processes. Geriatrics 12: 40–8
14. Widdowson E M 1951 The response to unlimited food in Studies of undernutrition, Wuppertal, 1946–9. Dept Exp Med, Cambridge. MRC Spec Rep Ser no. 275: 313–45
15. McCay C M, Crowell M F, Maynard L A 1935 The effect of retarded growth upon the length of the life span and upon the ultimate body size. J Nutr 10: 63–79
16. McCay C M 1949 Diet and aging. Vitam Horm 7: 147–70
17. Lonergan M E, Milne J S, Maule M M, Williamson J 1975 A dietary survey of older people in Edinburgh. Br J Nutr 1975 34: 517–27
18. Widdowson E M 1983 Age, sex and nutrition. Nutr Bull, 8: 117–32
19. Department of Health and Social Security 1972 A nutrition survey of the elderly. Rep Health Soc Subj no. 3
20. Stuckey S J, Darnton-Hill I, Ash S, Brand J C, Hain D L 1984 Dietary patterns of elderly people living in inner Sydney. Hum Nutr Appl Nutr 38A: 255–64
21. Clarke M, Hughes A O, Dodd K J, et al 1979 The elderly in residential care: patterns of disability. Health Trends 11: 17–20

POSTSCRIPT

The possibilities that life expectancy will not be increasing at an 85-year limit are discussed by Schneider and Reed in a review with 166 references.

(Schneider E L, Reed J D 1985 N Engl J Med 312: 1159–67.)

63

Exercise, Sports and Athletics

Joggers of both sexes and all ages are now a familiar sight in and around our towns. They have many opportunities to enter for marathon races which attracts hundreds of competitors. Some aim to cover the 26 miles course in $2\frac{1}{2}$ hours or less and others in 4 hours, while some are satisfied if they just complete it and may take 6 to 8 hours to do so. At the time of writing there is great interest in selecting and training the national teams for the 1984 Olympic Games in Los Angeles where it may be predicted that many new world records will be set. Never before have there been so many people actively taking part in athletics and other sports, nor have the standards of performance at the top ever been so high.

Motivation. Many people take part in athletics and other sports because this helps them to keep fit and they feel better as a result. Others enjoy the challenge of competition or of attaining a defined standard of competence. Most get pleasure from the active movements of their muscles, a continuation into adult life of the romping and play of children.

Benefits. Apart from providing a sense of well-being, regular physical activity has benefits to health. It reduces the risks of obesity and coronary heart disease. The latter in part because it lowers plasma cholesterol.[1] It also probably slows down the inevitable demineralisation of bones which begins in middle age. Perhaps most important of all it prevents the many and serious disorders associated with excessive smoking, since all who enjoy sports know that heavy smoking impairs performance.

Dangers. There are no serious adverse effects of active exercise at any age provided, it is kept within the limits of physical ability. Excessive or inappropriate activity has, however, its dangers.

Some serious athletes, particularly runners and gymnasts and also ballet dancers, develop a psychological state similar to anorexia nervosa.[2] In young women subjected to heavy training programmes, delayed puberty and amenorrhoea often occur. Obsessional coaches, too eager to produce top class performers, may seriously impair both the psychological and physical health of their protégés by imposing too vigorous training regimes.

Unfortunately physical exercise is sometimes associated with sudden death. In 10 years there were 56 such deaths among soldiers aged 19 to 53 years in the British Army, and incidence of 3.5 per 100 000 man years.[3] Of these, 35 were attributable to coronary heart disease. Clearly anyone with symptoms suggestive of coronary heart disease should restrict their activities to those within their capacity and take advice from their physician. Of the other deaths, 10 were due to subarachnoid haemorrhage but these may not have been a result of the exercise. In three of the deaths, all in men under 30 years, no cause was found at postmortem examination.

Athletes and sportsmen are, of course, at risk of a great variety of sports injuries, but sporting authorities make rules and regulations designed to minimise these.

The risks associated with physical exercise are far outweighed by the benefits at all ages. But common sense is needed to tailor ambition to physical capacity. Most people with a physical handicap or a chronic disorder benefit from physical exercise but they all should take medical advice and not exceed any limits that may be imposed.

DIET

In the past athletes and sportsmen have often followed bizarre dietary advice. In no branch of dietetics have so many crackpot diets and food fads been recommended. Two distinguished American nutritionists have separated established facts from the large volume of fiction in reviews of nutrition and athletic performance.[4,5] The dietary requirements of athletes are based on the same principles that govern the nutrition of human beings in general.

It can be stated categorically: (1) that none of the ordinary foods eaten by man are either of special value or contraindicated in athletic training; (2) that preparations of vitamins and minerals, given in addition to a good mixed diet, do not improve athletic performance; (3) that alcoholic drinks taken in small quantities by people accustomed to them have no effect on training. Some practical points are now considered.

Training

This usually involves heavy work for which the energy must come from the diet. Some athletes in training consume diets providing up to 20 MJ (5000 kcal) daily, though intakes are usually lower. Many athletes like meat and eat a lot of it. This is not necessary and some top class athletes are vegetarian. Protein does not provide more than 12 per cent of the energy during heavy work and a normal diet with this proportion of energy from protein meets protein needs. High energy diets have a large and inconvenient bulk, if they do contain a higher proportion of fat than now recommended for sedentary people. Physical activity prevents the disturbances in plasma lipids commonly associated with high fat diets, and a large fat intake does no harm to men and women who are training hard.

At the beginning of training most people lose weight, as excess fat in adipose tissue is removed. Later and more slowly there may be a gain in weight as muscles hypertrophy under the influence of repeated exercise. Most people know their ideal weight when fully fit. The use of the weighing machine, with the above facts in mind, helps individuals to assess whether they have been eating too much or too little.

Types of muscle fibre. Physiologists distinguish two types of muscle fibre by the response to stimulation of their motor nerves. In type 1 it is a slow twitch (ST) with prolonged contraction and in type 2 a fast twitch (FT). ST fibres predominate in crustacea and are adapted to maintaining posture. FT fibres predominate in frog legs and are suited to rapid rhythmic movements. There are also biochemical differences. FT fibres have higher activity of myosin ATPase and the ATP is derived more from glycolysis and less from oxidation of fat. ST fibres contain more myoglobin and appear red. Histochemical examination of small samples of muscle, obtained by needle biopsy, allow the relative amounts of these two main types to be determined.

Human muscles are made up of a mixture and most contain between 35 and 70 per cent of ST fibres.[6] Leg muscles of top class sprinters are reported to contain more FT fibres, and those of long distance runners more ST fibres than in their arm muscles or in muscles of untrained subjects. In muscles of weight lifters and high jumpers the proportion is usually within normal limits. A high proportion of FT fibres may facilitate very rapid movements and of ST fibres, that are less easily fatigued, longer periods of activity.

Popular instruction on training now distinguishes between running and other rhythmic activities (aerobic exercises) and weight lifting and static exercises (anaerobic exercises) with the implication that different types of muscle fibre are required. In fact the amount of anaerobic metabolism depends more on the intensity than on the nature of the exercise. In training for all types of sports and athletic events and in keeping fit, exercises of both types should be carried out but the proportion of time alloted to each in a training schedule adjusted to ultimate goals. Both types aim to build up muscle. No dietary manipulation favours the build up of particular groups up muscles. Dietary advice during training should take into account the intensity and duration of the exercises but is qualitatively the same in all circumstances.

Hypertrophy of muscle. This takes place when muscles are used regularly for additional work. To achieve the build up that they need, top class athletes have to work long hours over many weeks at or near their maximum capacity. The benefit of training is temporary and soon lost if the additional exercise is stopped. For the ordinary person who wishes to keep fit, training is a life long commitment. However once achieved, fitness can be maintained by exercising muscles to full capacity daily for a few minutes.

During the build up there is, of course, a positive nitrogen balance but, as it takes a long time, the positive balance on any one day is small. The protein in a good high energy diet, for example Diet No. 1, is sufficient to meet it and supplements of meat of other high protein foods are not needed.

Anabolic hormones. Hypertrophy of muscle is dependent on hormonal control. In experimental animals it can be promoted by giving testosterone or its analogues, the so-called anabolic hormones. Although all Athletic Associations ban these drugs, they are widely used especially by weight lifters, shot putters and others whose success depends on very powerful muscles. It is difficult to study experimentally in man the long term effect of the use of these hormones. In subjects in whom they have appeared to have promoted weight gain, it has not been possible to demonstrate unequivocally whether this was due to increase of muscle or extracellular fluid. Large doses of these hormones taken over a long time are likely to inhibit the natural secretion of testosterone and many induce permanent adverse effects on the functions of the testes and possibly other endocrine organs. It is possible that these changes may shorten the life span. These effects are discussed by the American College of Sports Medicine.[7]

Diet immediately before an event

There is usually no need to alter the training diet in the days immediately before an event, but the pattern of the meals should be adjusted to allow an interval of two to three hours after a meal and before an event.

Glycogen store in muscle

Physiologists have shown that the glucogen stores in muscles can be raised above the normal level by dietary means. The main fuel for heavy exercise is carbohydrate (p. 85) and if an event requires continuous work at near maximum capacity for more than 30 minutes, depletion of muscle glycogen may become a factor limiting performance. These discoveries followed the introduction of a punch technique for taking samples of deep muscle for analysis, and depended on a supply of athletes willing to provide repeated samples of their quadriceps femoris, the great extensor muscle of the legs which covers the front and sides of the femur.

Normally the glycogen content of this muscle is about 15 g/kg. During running to exhaustion it fell to about 7.5 g after 30 minutes and to about 1 g after an hour, when the subjects had to reduce their work rate. The initial glycogen content of muscle was shown to be of decisive importance in determining how long an individual can sustain heavy exercise.[8] That the glycogen content of muscle could be raised above the usual value was shown in an experiment in which two men working to exhaustion on the same bicycle ergometer, one using his right leg and one his left leg; their other two legs were resting. At the start of the experiment the glycogen content of the muscles of all four legs was about 25 g/kg; at the end of the exercise it was about 1 g/kg in the exercised legs and little changed in the rested pair. The subjects were then given a high carbohydrate diet for three days during which the glycogen in the muscles of the exercised legs rose up to 35 g/kg but there were only very small rises in the two rested legs.[9]

The unusually high store of glycogen depends on giving a high carbohydrate diet after the store has been completely depleted by exercise. The highest values, up to 50 g/kg, were obtained when the depleted state had been maintained by a diet of protein and fat only for three days, followed by carbohydrate for three days.

Such a regimen is quite unnecessary for the great majority of athletes, but might be useful for some long distance races whether running, swimming, cycling or skiing.

During an event

Competitors in a marathon or in any sport where heavy exercise is continued for more than an hour need to be provided with plenty of water. Especially in hot weather, they are at risk of collapse from serious dehydration with salt losses and also from hyperthermia. Their drinks should be sweetened with sugar to prevent hypoglycaemia. This is liable to occur after two or three hours and leads to fatigue, poor performance and ultimately collapse. Dehydration, hyperthermia and hypoglycaemia are potentially fatal. Organisers of events where they are liable to occur have a responsibility to see that all competitors have ample supplies of water and sugar readily available. In British marathons competitors are advised to drink 500 ml of water before starting. Solutions containing glucose and salt are available at staging posts arranged to give all runners an opportunity to drink at least every 30 minutes. The solutions should not be hypertonic, as this delays gastric emptying.

In top-class athletics and other sporting events the difference in performance between the winner and the second is small and more likely to be the result of psychological than physiological factors. Many distinguished athletes are more than normally sensitive people. A wise trainer humours their dietary fancies and sees that they have the food that they like and they think suits them best. He should not impose his or any other dietary theories and remember that individual requirements vary greatly.

There is now a large literature on sports and health. A monograph by Shepherd gives a full account of the physiology of muscles, the fuels that these use and the role of the cardiovascular and respiratory systems in the transport of these fuels and oxygen.[10] A book edited by Pařízková and Rogozkin with contributions from 16 countries discusses many aspects of nutrition, health and exercise from different viewpoints.[11] An American book gives an acount of the synergism of diet and exercise in maintaining health.[12]

In countries where ample food is available and people have the money to buy it, over consumption commonly impairs health and contributes to many diseases. Good health and freedom from disease depends on a sensible way of life with diet balanced to physical activity. Both the general public and individual patients have to be helped to realise this. Present enthusiasms for exercise and sports at all levels of performance are encouraging and should be supported by dietitians and nutritionists.

REFERENCES

1. Rauramaa R, Salonen J T, Kukkonen-Harjula K, et al 1984 Effects of mild physical exercise on serum lipoproteins and metabolites of arachidonic acid: a controlled randomised trial in middle-age men. Br Med J 288: 603–6
2. Yates A, Leekey K, Shisslak C M 1983 Running — an analogue of anorexia? N Engl J Med 308: 251–5
3. Lynch P 1980 Soldiers, sport and sudden death. Lancet 2: 1235–7
4. Mayer J, Bullen B 1960 Nutrition and athletic performance. Physiol Rev 40: 369–97
5. Consolazio F 1983 Food intake and performance. Prog Food Nutr Sci 7: 29–42
6. Saltin B, Henrikson J, Nygaard E, Anderson P 1975

Fiber types and metabolic potentials of skeletal muscles in sedentary man and in endurance runners. Ann NY Acad Sci 301: 3–29

7. American College of Sports Medicine 1977 Position statement on the use and abuse of anabolic-androgenic steroids in sport. Med Sci Sport 9: 11–13

8. Hermansen L, Hultman E K, Slatin B 1967 Muscle glycogen during prolonged severe exercise. Acta Physiol Scand 71: 129–39

9. Bergström J, Hultman E 1966 Muscle glycogen synthesis after exercise: an enhancing factor localised to the muscle cells in man. Nature 210: 309–10

10. Shepherd R J 1982 Physiology and biochemistry of exercise. Praeger, New York

11. Pařizková J, Rogozkin V A (eds) 1978 Nutrition, physical fitness and health. University Part Press, Baltimore

12. White P L, Mondeika T (eds) 1982 Diet and exercise: synergism in health maintenance. American Medical Association, Chicago

64

Climate; Survival Rations

CLIMATE

The climate of a region determined the animals that were hunted and the vegetables and fruits gathered by primitive man. When civilisation began, it determined the crops that were sown and the animals reared for food. Mediterranean people, desert Arabs and Eskimos had and still have very different diets. Irrigation and to a much lesser extent protective buildings (greenhouses) allowed foods to be produced where they did not grow naturally. Trade between regions made mankind less dependent on local agriculture, and modern food processing and manufacture now enables us to eat the foods to which we are accustomed in our native land in cities throughout the world. A book on *Food, and climate nutrition*[1] discusses at length how climate affects food production but has only one short chapter on how climate affects the needs for nutrients. In very hot climates there is an increased need for water and salt but, apart from this, climate imposes no important changes in physiological requirements.

WATER AND SALT

In hot climates the body can only be maintained at an even temperature by sweating. The amount of sweat lost will be determined by the environmental temperature, the humidity and the air movement, and also by the amount of physical work done. A man engaged in double labour in the tropics may readily lose 4 litres NaCl/litre a day and under exceptional circumstances about 240 ml. Sweat contains from 20 to 80 mmol on a hot day in concentration being lower in the is done. It is essential object. The body may lose should be made good a day or about 14 g of salt of heat ... ore if heavy work ... ting, or ... water and salt

is due to vasodilation in the skin expanding the vascular bed. When the compensatory mechanisms are inadequate, blood flow to the brain diminishes and causes fainting. This is not due to the direct effect of sunlight on the head and neck, a myth which gave rise to the use of pith helmets or topees.

Three syndromes are responsible for the severe cases. The first is caused directly by **salt and water depletion**. As in mild cases there is evidence of circulatory shock, but low blood pressure and tachycardia persist; loss of appetite, nausea, headache and emotional changes are common. The muscle cramps characteristic of salt deficiency may occur. The output of urine is always greatly diminished and it is of high specific gravity. The diagnostic test is the absence of salt from the urine; there is no white precipitate of silver chloride on the addition of silver nitrate after acidification with nitric acid.

Anhidrotic heat exhaustion. Is attributable to failure of the sweat glands to secrete, due to fatigue. This loss of ability to sweat may follow many weeks or months in excessive heat. The principal clinical features are dizziness, palpitation, breathlessness and lack of sleep. It has often been preceded by prickly heat, in which the sweat glands get blocked and inflamed.

The dangerous state is **heat hyperpyrexia**. Coma, convulsions or delirium are very likely to occur at a body temperature over 41 °C (106°F) and may do so at temperatures between 39.5 and 41 °C (103 and 106°F). Even with the best medical care renal failure and other fatal complications may occur.

Prevention

It is important to reduce exposure as far as possible. Shade and shelter against the sun are obviously desirable. It is also important to arrange that no unnecessary physical work is carried out and that, as far as possible, men do not have to work in the midday heat. However, even with the best of management, men will always be exposed to excessive heat and its consequent risks.

It is essential that all exposed men should know these risks and how they can best be avoided. All newcomers the tropics need such education and should be taught to respect the heat. They should learn that thirst is not always a reliable guide to water requirements, nor is the natural appetite for salt always reliable. Liberal amounts of drinking water must be available not only in canteens, but in places of work. It is important to see that this water is cool. While men readily drink cool water, they may neglect to drink tepid water, even if there is a physiological need. Each individual can judge whether he is taking enough water by his urine output. If there is not a good flow of urine at least four times in the 24 hours, he is not taking enough. Ample salt should be available on the table at all meals and people told to use it. Cooks should be instructed to salt the food well. As much as 30 g of NaCl may be necessary to make good the losses in the sweat, i.e. at least double a normal intake. It may be desirable to add salt to the drinking water. Amounts up to 0.1 per cent are barely perceptible. This is provided by the addition of $\frac{1}{2}$ oz (2 teaspoonsful) to one gallon. There is a risk that men may not drink water in which they can taste salt; provided adequate table salt is available and the men use it, there should be little need to add salt to the drinking water.

OTHER NUTRIENTS

The effects of climate on the need for the remaining nutrients are small and unimportant in comparison with the extra need for salt and water in the tropics. They are briefly set out below.

Energy. As discussed in Chapter 3, the chief factor determining energy needs is the amount of physical activity undertaken. This is generally little affected by climate except by extremes of heat or excessive cold. Both of these restrict activity, especially by making active physical recreations unpleasant or impossible.

There is some indication that the energy cost of performing a standard task of physical work falls with rise of environmental temperature, but the effect, if it exists, is small and probably negligible. In cold climates, the cost of physical work may be increased by up to 5 per cent by the 'hobbling' effect of the protective clothing. This may weigh 6 kg or more and of necessity restricts the ease of movement, besides involving extra energy for carrying it about.

Fat. When undertaking hard work such as sledging in very cold climates, up to 20 MJ (5000 kcal)/day may be needed. If the diet is not to be very bulky, large quantities of fat (up to 250 g or even more) are required and can be digested and absorbed. A high intake of fat is probably essential if hard physical exercise is undertaken in any climate.

Protein. Reduction in protein intake in ' has been stated to be desirable, owing to ' liberated by the specific dynamic actior

liberal intake of protein does not disturb the heat balance or cause discomfort and there is no good reason to reduce the intake of meat or other protein-rich foods below what is customary in a mixed diet.

Minerals. The sweat contains very small amounts of minerals, but the losses of iron may be significant and contribute to the causation of anaemia, which is so common in many countries with hot climates.

Vitamins. No significant losses occur in the sweat. There is no evidence that the recommended intakes for vitamins need be in any way altered on account of climate, except perhaps in the case of vitamin C. Lind reported that scurvy was much more common and severe in winter than in summer, and in ships going to Greenland and the Baltic than in those going to Southern latitudes. On the other hand, Eskimos appear to have managed with their traditional diets, which contained few sources of ascorbic acid in the long winter months. In cold climates it is certainly important to see that intakes of vitamin C in the food are satisfactory.

Alcohol. Europeans and Americans working in the tropics are much more prone to alcoholism than at home. Alcohol is readily used as an escape from the annoyances and discomforts caused by excessive heat, insects, the absence of family and friends, the lack of customary recreations and the necessity to work with strange people, whose way of life is not fully appreciated. The expatriate man or woman in the tropics who is unable to make adjustments and to develop new interests, readily falls a victim to alcoholism. Nevertheless, despite its dangers, we would not be without alcohol in the tropics. Taken in moderation, it is a valuable sedative and helps to distract from obsessional attention to duty, and to promote social life. Midday drinking is especially dangerous and the old adage, 'never drink before sunset', is to be recommended. It is also necessary to have the strength of mind to withstand the pressure to have rounds of drinks when in convivial and congenial company.

GENERAL CONSIDERATIONS

An adverse climate, whether very hot ... imposes considerable strains, both ... logical, on an individual. I ... he is less able to s ... a satisfactor ... supplice of good catering and good cooking ...

for men and women who have to live and work in a harsh climate cannot be overstressed. Apart from their effect on physical health, they sustain morale. The changes imposed by climate in the physiological requirements of nutrients are negligible (except for the increased requirements for salt and water in hot climates), compared with the need to provide a good mixed diet and to ensure that it is well cooked and attractively served.

SURVIVAL RATIONS

Lifeboats have long been provided with rations for those who survive the immediate disaster of shipwreck. Many civilian and military aeroplanes also carry emergency rations for use in the event of a forced landing in an isolated place. In military planes the pilot can, in an emergency, eject himself and his seat from the plane and descend by parachute. Attached to the undersurface of the seat are rations and equipment for survival. There has been much study of the most suitable type of emergency ration for these and other purposes.[2]

Castaways are usually rescued, if at all, within a period of 14 days. It is not generally considered practical to plan for any longer period of survival. Rescue equipment must provide many other things besides food and, in selecting what articles to include, it is necessary to keep the total bulk of the supplies to a minimum. Food, in fact, receives a very low priority: for no healthy man will die of starvation in 14 days; nor will he suffer any permanent adverse effect from the experience, although his physical efficiency will be somewhat reduced at the time. However, within 14 days he can readily die of lack of water or from exposure to extremes of heat or cold. Water and protection against the environment have, therefore, priority over food, as also has radio equipment which enables the survivor to get in touch with rescue parties. Nevertheless all emergency equipment contains some food which will, in part, prevent the physical deterioration consequent upon total fasting and, perhaps more important, sustain the morale of the survivors. Before discussing these rations it is proper to s the more essential problem of water supply.

Min

A man
ml of w **requirements**
lungs. This equable climate loses at least 800
necessity to d aporation from the skin and
ment. The mini fourfold or more by the
must pass is a little may
essential losses oxidat or in a hot environ-
produced by the tissues. Under that his kidneys
fat in the ainst these
water

this amounts to about 200 ml daily. Thus to prevent a loss of body water the minimum daily intake must be 1 litre, but much more is needed if physical work is undertaken or the weather is hot. As stated in Chapter 2, the body of a healthy man contains about 40 litres of water. A loss of 2 litres or more will usually cause discomfort and inefficiency, a loss of 4 litres is disabling and a loss of 8 litres will rapidly lead to death. Thus even with everything else in their favour, few men would survive 10 days without water.

It is rarely possible to provide emergency water which would be sufficient to cover the losses that might arise under very hot conditions. Small solar stills have been designed which can meet in part the extra needs of castaways on a tropical sea. In such conditions it is essential to attempt to minimise water losses by the provision of tents or other material which give shade; survivors must be warned of the adverse effects of unnecessary physical activity. In great heat, sea water can be used to keep the body cool.

The danger of drinking sea water. Sea water has a concentration of sodium ions of 420 mmol/l and 470 mmol/l of chloride ions. The corresponding concentrations in the blood plasma are about 142 and 104. Sea water is thus much more concentrated than the body fluids. Moreover, the human kidney is not normally able to concentrate either sodium or chloride to as high a level as in the sea.[3] Experiments in which small quantities of sea water have been drunk have given equivocal results. There may be some temporary retention of water, but this is associated with an increased tonicity of the body fluids. This may be expected to give rise to an osmotic diuresis in a short time when the water retained will be lost. In experimental studies on man, it has proved difficult to demonstrate either a beneficial or an adverse effect of drinking small quantities up to 250 ml of sea water. The heroic experiment of Bombard (1953) showed only that one man could drink a lot of sea water and survive.[4] Critchley, however, studied carefully the records of castaways during World War II and showed that the drinking of large amounts of sea water was usually fatal.[5] It is wise to forbid the drinking of any sea water. However, when there is heavy rain, the surface water is nearly fresh and may be drunk.

COMPOSITION OF SURVIVAL RATIONS

The first consideration is that the salt intake should be as low as possible, for the necessity to excrete salt will increase the need for water. Proteins also produce nitrogenous end-products which require water for their elimination and so it is desirable that the protein intake should not be high. Deprivation of protein for a temporary period of 14 days will cause no harm, nor will a similar temporary restriction of the intake of minerals and vitamins. Survival rations have been devised in which the foods are restricted to a mixture of carbohydrate and fats which can be made up in sweets and toffees. Fat has the advantage over carbohydrate that it provides over twice the amount of energy for a given unit of weight. The more fat in the rations, the less is their bulk. On the other hand, dietary carbohydrate is more effective than fat in 'sparing' endogenous nitrogen metabolism and so will reduce the loss of body protein and also the urine volume. Carbohydrate also prevents the ketosis that arises when an excess of fat is metabolised. Johnson & Sargent carried out on a large scale realistic field trials of various emergency rations in different climates for periods of 14 days.[6] In many of these trials the daily water intake was limited to 900 ml. Their results indicated that men survived best if provided with an emergency ration in which the proteins, carbohydrates and fats were distributed in the normal manner (15 per cent of energy from protein, 52 per cent from carbohydrate and 33 per cent from fat).

Whatever the nature of the ration, it is essential that it be provided in a compact form, that requires no cooking or other preparation and that it does not deteriorate on storage even under adverse conditions. Various forms of boiled sweets, candies, toffees and meat bar can be used for this purpose.

REFERENCES

1. Baxter K, Fowden L (eds) 1982 Food, nutrition and climate. Applied Science Publishers, London & New Jersey
2. Hervey G R, McCance R A 1954 Emergency rations. Proc Nutr Soc 13: 41–5
3. Hervey G R, McCance R A 1952 The effects of carbohydrate and sea water on the metabolism of men without food or sufficient water. Proc R Soc Lond (Biol) 139: 527–45
4. Bombard A 1953 The Bombard story. Deutsch, London
5. Critchley M 1953 The shipwreck survivor — a medical study. Churchill, London
6. Johnson R E, Sargent F 1958 Some quantitative interrelationship among thermal environment, human metabolism and nutrition. Proc Nutr Soc 17: 179–86

Appendix 1. Glossary of Foods

(Prepared by Dr Ruth Kay)

Abalone. A mollusc resembling a large scallop which may be served in a salad or soup or fried; other names are **muttonfish** (Australia) and **ormer** (Channel Is.).

Ackee (*Blighia sapida*). Popular in Jamaica, about 3 cm long, red in colour and opens naturally when ripe to expose the edible portion of fleshy cream-coloured aril which surrounds each of the three seeds. The other tissues of the fruit are poisonous, as is under- or over-ripe fruit. The aril is usually eaten fried or boiled.

Almond (*Prunus dulcis var dulcis*). A close relative of the peach and plum, grown in southern Europe and California, mainly for confectionery, notably marzipan. Also eaten as a nut.

Angelcake (N. Am.). A light, spongy, fat-free cake, leavened by air by stiffly beating a large number of egg-whites.

Aubergine (*Solanum melongena*). A glossy, firm fruit, oval or oblong in shape from 10 to 50 cm in length, white or deep purple in colour; other names are **egg plant** and **brinjal** (India); eaten as a cooked vegetable, sliced and fried, or incorporated into curries and other dishes.

Bannock (Scot.). A flat, round cake made from oatmeal, rye, barley or wheat: may take the place of bread in the diet.

Bap (Scot.). A soft breakfast roll, similar in appearance to an American hamburger bun.

Barbecue. A method of grilling (broiling) food on a grid over a flameless heat from charcoal briquettes to produce a distinctive flavour; popular in North America.

Barcelona nut (*Corylus* spp.). A Spanish variety of hazelnut.

Bass. Fresh- and salt-water fish similar in shape and colouring to the salmon; the flesh is firm, lean and delicately flavoured.

Beetroot (*Beta vulgaris*). A crimson spherical root, which is boiled and eaten fresh or pickled; known simply as **beet** in North America.

Betty (N. Am.). A simple pudding: consists of layers of sliced fruit and breadcrumbs baked in a deep, buttered dish, e.g. apple betty.

Bilberry (*Vaccinium myrtillus*). Also known as **blaeberry** and **whortleberry**, a small fruit, blue in colour similar in appearance to a small American blueberry, used mainly for jam or tarts.

Biscuit (N. Am.). A small, soft unsweetened cake, similar in composition to a scone; leavened with baking powder and frequently served as a hot bread in the southern USA.

Biscuit (UK). A crisp, semisweet cracker or a sweetened, flat cookie which is shaped and flavoured. A much wider term than in North America.

Blackberry (*Rubus ulmifolius*). Found wild in most parts of the British Isles; bears a black, seedy berry, eaten fresh or, with apples, stewed or made into jam; also known as **bramble** (Scot.) and **thimbleberry** (N. Am.).

Blackbun (Scot.). A rich fruitcake, enclosed in a pastry case.

Black pudding (**blood sausage**). A sausage made with pig's blood, ground pork, fat, onions, herbs and oatmeal; different versions are found throughout Europe and North America.

Blueberry (*Vaccinium corymbosum*). Native of North America, where blueberry pie is a traditional dessert; a delicious, bluish-black fruit, 7 mm across with a smooth skin. Larger than a bilberry.

Boiled sweets (UK). Any type of hard sugar candy, made without fat.

Bologna. A large round cooked sausage with a mild flavour.

Boston brown bread (N. Am.). A moist, dark bread made from a variety of cereal flours including cornmeal, mixed with butter-milk, molasses, raisins, and steamed; an excellent accompaniment to 'Boston baked beans'.

Boxty (Eire). A type of Irish potato pancake.

Brawn. A cold aspic, made with the trimmings of a pig and may include parts of the head, gristle and feet; cooked with onions and herbs. **Head cheese** is a type of brawn.

Brazil nut (*Bertholletia excelsa*). As the name implies, these nuts flourish in the tropical forests of Brazil; following harvest, the nuts have to be 'humoured' carefully so that they dry slowly and arrive in overseas shops in fine condition just before Christmas.

Breadfruit (*Artocarpus communis*). A starchy fruit, up to 20 cm in diameter, with a thick warty skin; usually eaten roasted and an important item of diet in many parts of the tropics.

Brinjal. See **Aubergine**.

Broad beans (*Vicia faba*). Consumed in Britain as the freshly shelled bean, also called **fava bean** (N. Am.). A hardy crop, it has been suggested as a substitute for soybeans, in areas where the latter do not grow well (see favism, p. 468).

Brownie (N. Am.). A rich chocolate cake, dense and chewy; usually containing walnuts.

Bubble and squeak (UK). A dish of leftover potatoes and cabbage, cooked and fried together; the name derives from the cooking noises.

Bun. In Britain the term refers to a sweetened, light yeast roll, often containing currants; varieties include Bath bun, Chelsea bun and the hot cross-bun (to symbolise the crucifixion, and eaten on Good Friday). In America, a variety of soft, plain rolls such as the hamburger bun; also several types of sweet rolls.

Butter beans (*Phaseolus lunatus*). Large white, mature seeds also known as **lima beans** (N. Am.); most commonly eaten boiled as a vegetable, or in soups and stews.

Buttermilk. A cultured milk, made by adding *Streptococcus lactis* to pasteurised milk (usually skim milk in North America) until the lactic acid content is 0.9 per cent; it has a characteristic tangy flavour and smooth rich body.

Canadian bacon (N. Am.). Also known as **back bacon**, a lean oval-shaped cut from the back of the pig.

Candy (N. Am.). Generic name for any type of concentrated sweets; may refer to a range of confections from chocolate to boiled sweets. In UK, has a more limited meaning.

Cape gooseberry (*Physalis peruviana*). Similar in appearance but less sweet than the ground cherry, found in South Africa and elsewhere and also known as **goldenberries**.

Caramel. A product of indefinite composition, formed when sugars of any kind are partially broken down by heat; its brown colour, slightly burnt flavour and sticky consistency make it a valuable adjunct to the art of the good cook.

Cashew nut (*Anacardium occidentale*). A South American nut with a unique and delicious flavour, spread by the Portuguese to other parts of their former Empire; India is now a major producer of these popular dessert nuts.

Catfish. In Europe includes a number of fish such as the **seawolf** and **dogfish**. The American 'catfish' refers to members of the *Letalarus* family, which is widespread and includes varieties from 1 to 150 lb in weight. The small members of the species are particularly popular in the southern states where catfish and hushpuppies (fried cornmeal puffs) are traditional.

Catsup (N. Am.). Also known as **ketchup**; a mildly seasoned tomato purée, used as table condiment.

Celeriac (*Apium graveolens* var *repaceum*). An irregular-shaped root resembling a turnip; the flavour is similar to that of celery.

602

Chapatti (India). A thin cake of unleavened bread.

Char (N. Am.). Member of the salmon family; a medium-fat fish, cooked like trout.

Chard (*Beta vulgaris*). Sometimes known as the **seakale beet** and **spinach beet**; grown mainly for its leaves which are similar to but less acid than spinach; the broad white stalk may also be eaten.

Cheesecake. More common in North America than elsewhere, a rich dessert consisting of a sweetened cream cheese custard over a biscuit or pastry base; sometimes topped with fruit or preserves.

Chick pea (*Cicer arietinum*). A hard, round yellow-white legume used extensively in India and also popular in Spain and Mexico, where it is given the name **garbanzo**; may be used in a variety of soups and curries or served as a vegetable.

Chicory (*Cichorium intybus*). A compact head of large leaves; most frequently used as a salad vegetable in the same way as endive; it may also be served as a cooked vegetable. The roots of some varieties may be dried, roasted and blended with coffee.

Chinese water chestnut (*Eleocharis tuberosa*). A tuber, valued for its crisp texture; eaten in the East Indies and China and Japan and canned for export to Europe and North America.

Chips (potato) (UK). Long, square-section pieces of potato, deep fried. Very popular in Britain. Traditionally eaten with fish fried in batter, but some British enthusiasts like chips with everything (the title of a play by Arnold Wesker).

Chipolata (Italy). A very small sausage, often seasoned with chives.

Chipped beef (N. Am.). Lean top round which has been corned, dried and sliced very thin.

Chitterlings. Small intestines of any animal but usually the pig, sometimes used as sausage casings; also the trimmings from a freshly killed pig; popular in southern USA.

Chowder. A thick soup, often with a milk base, made with a variety of foods, frequently fish, e.g. clam chowder (N. Am.) and bouillabaise (Fr.); from the French word *chaudiere* — a large, heavy soup pot.

Clam. A bivalve mollusc, common on the Atlantic coast of North America; may be fried, pickled, steamed, or made into a thick soup or chowder.

Clementine. A variety of tangerine or an orange-tangerine hybrid; intermediate between the two in size and colour, peels easily.

Clod (UK). Often 'clod and sticking'; **clod** is the front chest cut of beef and **sticking** the coarse part of the neck; these are cheaper cuts, which contain much gristle and fat, mainly used for stews. Clod is known as **chuck** in North America.

Cloudberry (*Rubus chamaemorus*). A golden berry similar to a raspberry which grows in the northern regions of Canada and Europe.

Cockles (UK). A small mollusc with a delicate flavour, boiled and eaten with a variety of condiments.

Coffeecake (N. Am.). A scone-like cake covered with a crumbly mixture of sugar, flour, and butter, often containing fruit.

Collard (*Brassica oleracea*) (N. Am.). A smooth-leaf variety of cabbage, the leaves of which may be boiled and served like spinach.

Collop. A piece of meat made tender by beating.

Cookie (N. Am.). Any sweetened, flat biscuit; made in a variety of shapes and flavours.

Corn. The North American term for maize (*Zea mays*). In Britain, it may refer to a variety of cereal grains, usually wheat but also oats and maize.

Cornbread (N. Am., especially southern states). A large number of breads made with maize meal, including corn pone, johnny cake, shortening bread, and hoecake. Egg bread and spoon bread are baked from a cornmeal, milk and egg batter and served as a main meal accompaniment.

Cornflour (UK). British for **cornstarch**.

Corn-on-the-cob (N. Am.). The cooked, freshly picked maize cob; when in season, a popular adjunct to the main meal throughout North America.

Cornish pasty (UK). A small, pastry-enclosed pie, containing meat, potato and vegetables; a portable meal which may be eaten hot or cold.

Courgette (*Cucurbita pepo*). A French marrow developed for early cutting, like the Italian **zucchini**, when only a few inches long. The mature courgette is no different from other vegetable marrows. Cooking methods include steaming or frying with garlic and tomato.

Cowpea (*Vigna unguiculata*). An annual legume, used as the dried white seeds; mostly grown in Africa and the United States; it is also an important animal feed.

Cracker (N. Am.). A crisp, flaky, non-sweet biscuit; low-fat varieties include **saltines** and **soda crackers**, which are usually sprinkled with course salt but are otherwise similar to the British cream cracker or water biscuit. Other types may be flavoured, contain more fat and be made from an assortment of cereal flours, e.g. **Graham crackers** which are made from wholemeal flour.

Crackling. The scored skin or rind of a roast of pork after it has been baked crisp.

Cream. A milk product containing at least 18% fat. ★ Single cream (UK), light cream, table or coffee cream (N. Am.) is 18–30% fat; double cream (UK) or heavy cream (N. Am.) contains 36–48% milk fat; whipping cream is 30–36% fat; half cream (N. Am.) is 12% fat; Devonshire cream (UK) is 60% fat and plastic cream (N. Am.) 65–83% milk fat. Dairy sour cream (N. Am.) is a thick, tangy-flavoured cream made by adding a bacterial culture to cream which contains 18% or more of fat.

Cream cracker (UK). A square unsweetened biscuit, the equivalent of an unsalted soda cracker.

Cream of wheat (N. Am.). Coarsely ground particles of refined, hard wheat; usually served as a hot breakfast cereal.

Crisp (potato) (UK). See **Potato chips**.

Crispbreads. The original Swedish crispbreads are made with rye flour but now many varieties are made with wheat. As the water content is lower and the energy correspondingly higher than in ordinary bread, they have no advantage in reducing diets but are pleasant and convenient alternatives to ordinary bread.

Crumpet (UK). A round, flat breadlike teacake, studded with holes, similar to, but spongier than what Americans term an **English muffin**; toasted and served hot with butter and jam.

Custard (UK). A sweet sauce prepared from milk and eggs, flavoured with sugar and vanilla and served with a variety of desserts; eggs may be replaced by custard powder, which consists largely of cornflour.

Damson (*Prunus damascena*). Soft purple fruit with a rich, sour flavour; smaller than plum, native in Britain.

Dandelion greens (*Taraxacum officinale*). Leaves of the common dandelion; sometimes used as a salad vegetable like endive or chicory in North America; however in Britain the dandelion is regarded only as a noxious weed.

Dripping. Beef fat extracted as the meat is cooked; formerly much used for baking and frying.

Dumplings. A main-meal accompaniment, in Britain, made from a stiff dough of flour and suet, often boiled in beef broth. The American variety is made with flour, milk and baking powder and contains less fat.

Eccles cake (UK). A flat, oval pastry with a filling of spiced currants. Related forms include Banbury cakes and Chorley cakes; also known as 'flies' graveyards' to English schoolboys.

Egg plant. See **Aubergine**.

Endive (*Cichorium endivia*). A salad plant with leaves which are characteristically divided and curled. As the green leaves are bitter, they may be blanched to a pale yellow colour by covering to exclude the light for 5 to 10 days before cutting. Sometimes termed **chicory** or **Belgian endive** in America.

Escarole (*Cichorium endivia*). A variety of endive.

Faggots (N. Eng.). Also known as **savoury ducks**, a spiced mixture of ground offal, pork, breadcrumbs and herbs, which are baked and eaten hot or cold.

Fat back (S. USA). The fatty, cheaper scraps of bacon, used to flavour stews and vegetable or cereal dishes.

Filbert (*Corylus maxima*). A robust variety of hazelnut.

Filled milk. Milk in which the cream has been replaced by a vegetable fat; those containing polyunsaturated oils are useful in cholesterol-lowering diets.

Finnan haddie (Scot.). Smoked haddock, cooked in a milk sauce.

Flan (UK). A shallow shell of pastry or sponge, usually filled with jellied fruits or custard. Savoury flans contain various mixtures of cheese, onions and tomatoes.

Fool (UK). A thick, chilled pudding, made with fruit and sugar, mixed with cream or custard, e.g. gooseberry fool.

Fortified milk (N. Am.). Whole or skim milk to which has been added one or more of the nutrients normally present in milk, usually vitamins A, D or skim-milk solids.

★ Figures are approximate only; legal requirements vary in different states and countries.

Frankfurter. A long thin cooked sausage often served in a roll as a **hot dog**; also known as a wiener.

French beans (*Phaseolus vulgaris*). The immature medium-length soft green pods are popular as a boiled vegetable. If allowed to mature the seeds vary in colour and shape from the purple **kidney bean** to the white or multicoloured **haricot bean**, which is used for the ubiquitous 'baked beans'.

French fries (N. Am.). The American word for deep-fried potato sticks, which are familiar to the British as **chips**.

French toast (N. Am.). Bread which is dipped in a mixture of beaten egg and milk and fried until crisp on the outside; may be served with sugar, syrup or bacon.

Gammon (UK). A cut from the hind leg of a pig, cured in the same manner as bacon, while still on the side of the animal.

Gelatin desserts (N. Am.). Commonly referred to by trade names such as 'Jell-O', these are fat-free puddings made from gelatin, sugar and fruit flavouring; known as **jellies** in Britain.

Ghee (Indian). Butter-fat clarified by heating.

Gigot (Scot., Fr.). Leg of mutton.

Golden syrup (UK). A light refined treacle similar to American **corn syrup**.

Gooseberry (*Ribes grossularia*). The European gooseberry bears large yellowish-green or red berries, with a downy skin and a tart but distinctive flavour. Usually made into jam; when mature, many varieties are sweet and excellent to eat raw. The American gooseberry (*R. divaricatum*) is similar but smaller. In England, gooseberry pie is traditional fare for Whitsuntide.

Graham flour (N. Am.). Another name for wholemeal flour.

Granadilla. See **Passion fruit**

Greengage (*Prunus italica*). Several varieties of soft, yellow-green plums, grown in Europe and North America.

Griskin (UK). Lean bacon from the loin of pork.

Ground beef (N. Am.). See **Hamburger**.

Ground cherry (*Physalis pruinosa*). A native of parts of Europe and North America, a yellow, round berry, 2 cm in diameter, enclosed within a lantern-like calyx; flavour is sweet and slightly acid.

Guava (*Psidium guajava*). Light-yellow fruit of the tropics and subtropics; has a sharp flavour, is often stewed or made into jam or jelly; a particularly rich source of vitamin C.

Gumbo (S. USA). A dish or soup thickened with okra; often contains seafood, other ingredients vary.

Haggis (Scot.). The ground liver, heart and lungs of a sheep mixed with suet, oatmeal and herbs, encased in a sheep's stomach; steamed and traditionally accompanied by Scotch whisky.

Hake (UK). A large, round fish caught off the west coast of Britain; cooked in same way as cod or haddock.

Hamburg(er) (N. Am.). Raw, ground meat, usually beef, which may be incorporated into numerous dishes; also a cooked patty of ground meat which is served on a split roll with various garnishes. In Britain, hamburger or ground beef is known as **mince**.

Hazelnut (*Corylus avellana*). Ovoid nut in a hard, brown shell; grows in the hedges in Britain; eaten as a dessert nut and used in confectionery; also known as the **cobnut**.

Head cheese. See **Brawn**.

Herring. Fish with oil flesh, trawled round the shores of Britain and USA; may be served fried, grilled, smoked or pickled. See **Kippers**.

Hominy (N. Am.). The starchy portion of the endosperm of maize, left after the whole grain is softened by steaming and the bran and germ removed, popular in some parts of the USA. **Grits** are a coarsely ground form.

Hot dog. A hot frankfurter sausage in a long, split roll.

Hot pot (UK). An oven-baked casserole, consisting of layers of meat and vegetables topped with sliced potatoes; popular in Lancashire.

Hough (Scot., N. Eng.). Shin and foreleg of beef; gelatinous cuts, which require a long cooking time, also sometimes used for ground beef. The same portion of beef is termed **shank** in North America.

Hovis (UK, a trade name). Bread made from wheat flour, to which extra germ has been added; a good source of the B-vitamins.

Huckleberry (*Solanum intrusum*). A black, smooth-skinned berry, rather flavourless, used in pies and preserves in North America.

Humble pie (UK). Originally 'umble pie', umbles being the offal of a deer which were traditionally huntsman's fare (this type of deer haggis is now rated much higher).

Ice cream. A range of milk-based frozen desserts. The fat may be of milk or vegetable origin but is usually saturated. An exception is

Mellorine, an American product, which contains a substantial amount of polyunsaturated fat. Ice cream may contain 8–20% fat by weight and 5–12% milk solids. **Ice milk** is a low-fat product containing 2–5% fat.

Ices (**water ices**). A frozen confection made from water, sugar and fruit juice or flavouring; known to children in America as **popsicles** and in Britain as **ice lollies**.

Jambalaya (S. USA). A traditional Creole dish, consisting of rice, with tomatoes, meat, fish or shell-fish to give it a characteristic flavour.

Jelly (UK). Usually a gelatin dessert (*q.v.*), less often made by boiling cuts of meat rich in collagen, e.g. calve's foot jelly.

Joint (UK). In Britain, this term refers to a portion of the carcass of an animal, such as a roast of meat. Traditional for main course of Sunday dinner.

Kale (*Brassica oleracea*). A large-leaved vegetable sometimes crimped and curled; used as **winter-greens** In Britain.

Kasha. The Russian name for **buckwheat** (*Polygonum* spp.); seeds hulled and cracked for quick preparation, usually as a side dish with meat or in stews and casseroles; has a distinctive hearty flavour.

Kedgeree (UK). Derives from an Indian recipe **Khichi** which consisted of rice, lentils, onion and spices. The English added fish (often smoked), parsley and eggs to produce a famous dish.

Kippers (UK). Split, salted and smoked herring.

Kohlrabi (*Brassica oleracea*). The turnip-like swollen base is green or purple in colour; usually served as a boiled vegetable.

Kumquat (*Fortunella* supp.). Similar in appearance to a small orange, has an acid taste and is used mainly for preserves or pickled whole.

Lard. A soft, animal fat from the pig, a non-ruminant; used in home-baking.

Leek (*Allium ampeloprasum* var *porrum*). A member of the onion family, the blanched, elongated bulb is used in soups and stews or as a separate vegetable. National emblem of Wales.

Lemon curd (UK). A smooth, thickened mixture of sugar, eggs, lemon juice and butter; used as a spread or as a filling for tarts. Also called **lemon cheese**.

Lentils (*Lens culinaris*). One of the oldest leguminous crops, the orange-coloured seeds are usually sold split and decorticated; may be used in a variety of dishes.

Loganberry (*Rubus loganobaccus*). A dull-red, acid fruit, developed in California by a cross between the blackberry and the raspberry; named after its originator; grown commercially for canning. The **boysenberry** is a similar hybrid.

Lotus root (*Nelembium nuciferum*). The sacred lotus of India and China, a water plant used more in times of food scarcity; the rhizomes may be roasted or steamed and when young have a flavour similar to that of artichokes.

Macadamia nut (*Macadamia ternifolia*). A crisp, sweet nut, white in colour, with a high fat content, native to Australia where it is sometimes known as the **Queensland nut**; also cultivated in Hawaii.

Malted milk. Whole or partly skimmed milk, combined with the liquid extract from a mash of barley and wheat, and dried. This is combined with sugar to form the basis of a number of commercial beverages, such as Ovaltine and Horlicks.

Mango (*Mangifera indica*). A native of India, oval-shaped fruit with greenish-yellow skin and a delicious, sweet-sour, orange-coloured pulp.

Maple syrup (N. Am.). A uniquely flavoured syrup made by concentrating the sap of the sugar maple; delicious on pancakes and waffles and also used to flavour confectionery and ice-cream; now, many commercial brands consist of sucrose syrup with maple flavouring.

Marzipan. Confectionery made from powdered almonds, and eggs.

Matzo. A Jewish unleavened, unsalted bread, made from flour and water; eaten especially during Passover.

Medlar (*Mespilus germanica*). A fruit the size of a small apple, with brown, firm skin; edible only when 'bletted', i.e. aged until soft and brown. Its chief use in Britain is for making jam.

Melba toast (N. Am.). Very thin slices of bread baked in an oven until crisp.

Melon (*Cucumis melo*). Includes several varieties of medium to large-sized fruit: **musk** melon has a netted, yellow-green skin with aromatic flesh and grows in Britain and other temperate regions; **cantaloupe** is a round, rough-skinned variety with sweet, orange flesh; **winter melons** require a longer ripening season but store well and are grown mainly in Mediterranean countries and southern USA, the **honeydew**, a light, smoothed-skinned variety, with sweet, greenish flesh, belonging to this class; **watermelon** is a large melon, commonly cultivated in hot countries and very refreshing.

Mince (UK). See **Hamburger**.

Mincemeat (UK). A spiced preserve, consisting of chopped apples, dried fruit and peel, eggs, sugar and suet; used as a filling for pies and tarts; in America it usually contains cooked ground meat; may be matured in rum or brandy.

Mince pies (Eng.). Pies of short or flaky pastry filled with mincemeat, and traditionally eaten at Christmas.

Mince pies (Scot.). Raised water pastry filled with minced beef or mutton. Also known as **Scotch pies**.

Miso (Japan). A paste, made from soybeans, salt, wheat or barley and water; may be used as a spread or condiment.

Molasses (N. Am.). A dark syrup, drained from sugar during refining; known as **black treacle** in Britain.

Muesli (Switz.). A mixture of dry cereals, notably oat or wheat flakes, combined with dried fruit and nuts; a popular and nutritious breakfast cereal, taken with milk.

Muffin. A British muffin is a light, spongy, unsweetened yeast-cake, toasted, and served hot. The American varieties are more numerous and are a type of small, round quick bread, leavened with baking power. Favourites are bran-, corn-, and blueberry muffins.

Mulberry (*Morus nigra*). A native of Europe and Asia, bears a delicate, purple-red fruit, which is delicious when eaten fresh and full-ripe; easily damaged; also used for making wine and jam. Silkworms are reared on the leaves.

Mullet (UK). A small, round fish with a white flesh.

Mush (N. Am.). A cornmeal porridge served with milk and brown sugar.

Nectarine (*Prunus persica* var *nectarina*). A smooth-skinned peach with a rich flavour, smaller and more brightly coloured than other varieties of peaches.

Oatcakes (UK). The true variety originated in Scotland and consists of a crisp flat, unsweetened biscuit made with oatmeal.

Offal (UK). The word derives from 'off-fall', the parts of an animal removed in the dressing process; offal includes the brains, sweetbreads, stomach and intestines of an animal as well as the organ meats.

Okra (*Hibiscus esculentus*). Immature pods, also known as **lady's fingers** or **gumbo**; mucilaginous in texture, are often used in tropical cookery to thicken soups and stews.

Palm kernel oil. A pale fat from the inner kernel of the oil palm; more expensive than red-palm oil; used for margarine.

Palm oil. An orange oil extracted from the fibrous pulp of the fruit of the oil palm (*Elaeis guineensis*); used in West Africa as food; exported for industrial purposes, used for margarine after refining to remove carotene.

Papaya (*Carica papaya*). Also known as **paw paw**, tropical fruit the shape of a small elongated melon, usually yellow-orange in colour; the flesh is succulent, orange to pink, with a mass of seeds in the central cavity. The plant is the source of the enzyme, papain.

Parkin (UK). A flat cake made from oatmeal, ginger, syrup and treacle in the north of England.

Passion fruit (*Passiflora edulis*). A purple, egg-shaped fruit of the tropics and subtropics; the sweet juicy pulp may be eaten fresh or the juice extracted and bottled; also known as **granadilla**.

Pasta (Ital.). Now popular all over the world in several forms including macaroni, spaghetti, vermicelli and noodles; made from a variety of hard wheat (*Triticum durum*) which is high in gluten.

Pecan (*Carya illinoensis*). Similar to the walnut with a mild sweet flavour; popular in North America where they are sometimes called **hickory nuts**; little known in Britain.

Persimmon (*Diospyros* spp.). The Japanese varieties are 5 to 7 cm in diameter, yellow-red in colour and similar in appearance to a tomato. American varieties are smaller and dark red in colour. The ripe fruit is very sweet and often eaten fresh with lemon or used in sauces, jams or compotes.

Pie (UK). A broad term which refers to (1) a deep dish filled with fruit or meat and vegetables, covered with a pastry top, (2) pork, fruit or custard surrounded by pastry and eaten cold in individual-size pies, (3) **Shepherd's pie**, a meat and vegetable dish covered with mashed potato which has been lightly browned.

Pie (N. Am.). A shallow fruit and pastry tart; the British 'pie' is termed a 'deep-dish' pie.

Pigeon pea (*Cajanus cajan*). A tropical legume; widely grown in India where it is known as **red gram**; also popular in the West Indies.

Pilchards. Fully grown sardines, smaller than herrings; usually canned in oil, brine or tomato sauce.

Pistachio (*Pistacia vera*). Nuts cultivated in Asia, the Mediterranean countries, and southern United States, green kernels with a pleasant, mild flavour; commonly eaten salted or used in confectionery and ice cream.

Plaice (UK). A flat fish low in fat, usually served fried.

Plantain (*Musa* spp.). Green plantains are a type of banana used for cooking. Higher in starch and lower in sugar than dessert bananas, they are picked when the flesh is too hard to be eaten raw; dietary staple in parts of East Africa.

Polenta (Ital.). A maize porridge, to which cheese, barley and chestnuts may be added.

Pomegranate (*Punica granatum*). A yellow-purple fruit about the size of an orange, with thick leathery skin; the seeds are enclosed in a pulpy flesh which is bright red, delicious and juicy.

Popcorn (N. Am.). A variety of maize which is heated in a covered pan until the starch granules swell to four times their size and the kernels burst; may be served salted and buttered. The traditional movie-theatre snack.

Popover (N. Am.). Somewhat similar to a Yorkshire pudding; baked from a flour, milk, and egg batter in lightly greased, individual dishes in a hot oven until the mixture puffs and becomes crisp on the outside.

Porgy. Several species of salt-water fish, in Europe, members of the Pagrus family; in the United States 'porgy' includes the **scup** and **menhaden** fishes. Porgy is prepared and cooked like catfish.

Potato chips (N. Am.). The American term for thinly sliced potatoes, which have been fried, dried and salted before packaging. They are known as **potato crisps** in Britain.

Prawn. A small crustacean, similar to but larger than a shrimp.

Pressed beef. Boned, salted and pressed brisket.

Pretzel. Rings of a flour and water paste, baked in a very hot oven and then glazed and sprinkled with coarse salt; popular as a snack in Germany and North America.

Pudding (UK). Usually used to refer to the sweet or dessert course of a meal; also encompasses a variety of dishes made from a flour base or enclosed in pastry; these contain anything from custard and fruit to meat and vegetables. There are hundreds of English puddings, among the more famous are 'steak and kidney pudding' and the traditional Christmas pudding.

Puris (India). Made by rolling a small flat piece of dough and then frying it in deep butter fat. As butter is expensive, puris are regular food for the rich only and are reserved for festive occasions by other classes.

Quince (*Cydonia vulgaris*). A hard, acid fruit, similar in appearance to a pear or apple; is used mainly for jams and jellies in Britain.

Ragoût. A spicy stew made with meat, fish or poultry, with or without vegetables; from the French *ragoûter*, to awaken the taste.

Rasher (UK). A slice especially of bacon.

Red snapper. An important food fish caught off the eastern seaboard of the United States. The flesh is white, flaky and low in fat.

Rissole (Fr.). A patty of ground meat or fish coated in breadcrumbs and fried; the American equivalent is a **croquette**.

Roe. Refers to both the **milt** (soft roe) of the male fish and the eggs (hard roe) of the female, usually from cod or herring; **caviar** is the roe of the sturgeon. Roes are rich in nucleic acids and cholesterol.

Romaine (*Lactuca sativa*) (N. Am.). Long-leaved lettuce corresponding to cos lettuce in Britain.

(Scarlet) runner bean (*Phaseolus coccineus*). A popular green bean or **string bean** in Britain; grows up to 10 feet in height and produces long, wide pods, often over a foot in length. Scarlet refers to the colour of the flower. An exceptionally tall plant featured in the fairy story 'Jack and the Beanstalk'.

Rutabaga (*Brassica* spp.). A variety of turnip.

Sago. A starch extracted from the sago palm tree (*Metroxylon sagu*), used to thicken soups and puddings.

Saltine. See **Cracker**.

Salsify (*Tragopogon porrifolius*). A white, elongated root eaten as a winter vegetable, boiled, baked, or in soups; the young leaves may be used for salad.

Satsuma. This name, which originates from a cream-coloured Japanese pottery, is now applied to a particular type of tangerine (*Citrus reticulata*) and also to some types of plum.

Sausage. Ground meat, often mixed with cereal, which is enclosed in a thin skin, varieties are numerous and may be raw, cooked or smoked; often highly seasoned. Spicier varieties include **salami** (Ital.) and **bratwurst** (Ger.). See **Bologna** and **Frankfurter**.

Savoury duck. See **Faggot**.

Scampi. A very large prawn.

Scone (UK). A teacake similar in composition to the American baking-powder biscuit.

Scotch collop. Minced meat garnished with tomatoes.

Scrag (end) (UK). The bony part of an animal's carcass; usually refers to the neck of mutton.

Scrapple (N. Am.). Made with the cooked scraps of meat from the head of a pig, combined with salt, spices and cornmeal, cooked and pressed into tins; termed **ponhaws** by Pennsylvania German settlers.

Seakale (*Crambe maritima*). Native to the coasts of Western Europe, the blanched leaf-stalks are boiled like asparagus and are noted for their nutty, slightly bitter flavour.

Semolina. Coarsely ground particles of refined durum wheat, used to make sweetened puddings or to thicken soups; also the basis of several pastas including macaroni.

Seville orange (*Citrus aurantium*). A bitter-flavoured orange used for making marmalade; popular in Britain.

Shallot (*Allium* spp.). A variety of onion, which produces several lateral bulbs, used fresh or for pickling.

Sherbet. A frozen dessert made from a mixture of fruit juice, milk and sugar; fat content is low ranging from 1.2% in North American varieties to 3% in British products; word of Arabic origin.

Shortbread (Scot.). A brittle dry cake, made from flour, and much butter and sugar; may contain 30% fat.

Sillabub (syllabub) (UK). A light, frothy dessert, consisting of whipped cream, wine, spices and sugar.

Silverside (UK). The outer part of the round of beef, usually salted and boiled.

Snap beans. See **French beans**.

Soda bread (Eire). An Irish bread leavened with baking soda.

Sole, Dover (UK). A flat white fish with dark rough skin, also known as **black sole**; noted for the excellency of its fine firm flesh.

Sole, Lemon (UK). Distinguishable from Dover sole as it is more oval and has smooth sandy-brown skin; flesh is good but inferior to that of the Dover sole.

Squab pie (UK). Neck of mutton with thinly sliced apples, baked in a casserole.

Squash (drink) (UK). A fruit-flavoured, sweetened liquid concentrate to which about 3 parts of water or soda water are added, e.g. orange squash, lemon squash.

Squash, Summer (*Cucurbita pepo*). Several varieties which include the warty, orange-coloured **summer crookneck** and the **zucchini**, a long, thin, green marrow.

Squash, Winter (*Cucurbita maxima*). Popular in North America; require a longer ripening season than do the summer squashes. Familiar varieties are the green, warty, **Hubbard squash** and the green, smooth-skinned **acorn squash**; they keep well, the texture being firm and floury and the water content lower than that of summer squashes, they are also a rich source of vitamin A.

Streaky bacon (UK). Term for fatty bacon, similar to **side bacon** in America.

Suet. Shredded beef fat used in steamed puddings.

Sugar. Sucrose, chiefly derived from the sugar cane (*Saccharum officinarum*) and the sugar beet (*Beta vularis* subsp. *cicla*). Less refined products contain traces of other sugars and have a flavour and texture which may be preferred for certain purposes. The terminology in Britain differs from that used in North America; **caster sugar** (UK) is superfine white (N. Am.); **icing sugar** (UK) is confectioner's; **Demerara** is crystallised light brown sugar and **Barbados** is soft, moist, brown sugar.

Sultana (*Vitis vinifera*). A seedless, goldern raisin, made by drying a variety of wine grapes with a firm flesh and high sugar content.

Swede (*Brassica napus* var *napobrassica*). Resembles a turnip and is similarly used in stews or mashed and served as a separate vegetable.

Sweetbreads. The pancreas and thymus glands of an animal, usually a calf.

Sweet chestnut (*Castanea sativa*). A glossy, brown nut 2 to 5 cm wide and enclosed in a spiny, green capsule; may be eaten whole, after boiling or roasting or ground into flour for use in stuffings and other dishes; native to southern Europe; also known as **Spanish chestnuts**.

Tangelo. Sweet-tart hybrid of the tangerine and grapefruit; an example is the **ugli** which resembles a sweet, easily peeled grapefruit.

Tart (UK). A shallow, round pastry shell of any diameter with a sweet, usually fruit filling; known as **pie** in North America.

Tenderloin (N. Am.). Fillet of beef or pork, the tenderest part of an animal.

Timbale (Fr.). A small pastry shell with a variety of sweet or savoury fillines.

Toad in the hole (UK). Pieces of meat or sausages baked in a batter.

Tofu (Japan). A curd or cheese, made from fresh soybeans, rich in protein, has a soft texture and bland flavour and may be incorporated into a number of recipes.

Topside (UK). The top of the round of beef, this is a lean, boneless fine-grained cut, suitable for roasting.

Tortilla (Mex.). A thin, flat pancake made from ground maize; the grains are softened by heating in limewater and then ground directly into a dough and cooked on a hot, iron plate. The lime may provide an important contribution to the calcium intake. A **taco** is a tortilla filled with a mixture of meat, beans and chilli and is a popular snack in the southwest USA.

Tripe. The first and second stomachs of a ruminant, more familiar in Europe and Britain than in North America. Tripe is cooked with milk and onions and requires a long cooking time to tenderise.

Turbot. A large white fish, low in fat; ranks with sole in culinary excellence.

Vanaspatti (India). A vegetable substitute for ghee.

Vegetable marrow (*Cucurbita pepo*) (UK). Same species as many pumpkins and summer squash; the fruit is green, white or striped; the varieties most common in Britain produce large oval or cylindrical fruits, eaten as a boiled vegetable or stuffed with a savoury mixture of meat, onions and tomatoes.

Waffle (N. Am.). Made from a light, spongy batter, which contains more fat than a pancake batter, cooked on an iron grid until it puffs up crisp and golden brown; served hot with syrup.

Walnut (*Juglans regia*). Known to the classical Greek and Hebrew writers and now grown in many parts of Europe and America; used extensively in biscuits and cakes. Its fat is the most polyunsaturated of the dessert nuts.

Water chestnut (*Trapa natans*). Also known as **caltrops**, the edible seed is eaten raw, roasted or baked in Central Europe and Asia; floury in texture with an agreeable flavour. See **Chinese water chestnut**.

Wax beans (*Phaseolus vulgaris*). Yellow podded, stringless beans which may be eaten like French beans, when young and tender. The mature black seeds, which have earned it the name **Mexican black**, are also eaten and have a mushroom-like flavour.

Whitebait (UK). The young of herring, sprats or pilchard, small silver fish caught in the estuaries of rivers around the coast of Britain; usually served fried whole.

White currant (*Ribes sativum*). Variety of redcurrant lacking the pigment; less acid than the red kind.

Whiting (UK). A light, low-fat fish of the cod family. In North America, the name applies to a number of other small fish.

Wineberry (*Rubus phoenicolasius*). A variety of raspberry originating in North China; the fruit is golden orange and pleasantly flavoured.

Yeast extract. A salty preparation used as a savoury spread or to flavour meat dishes; rich in B vitamins and salt but only used in small amounts; often referred to by trade names, e.g. 'Marmite' (UK).

Yorkshire pudding (UK). Made from a batter of flour, milk and eggs, cooked in meat drippings or other fat and traditionally served hot with roast beef. In Yorkshire eaten on its own with gravy as a first course.

Zucchini (*Cucurbita pepo*). A long, thin, Italian marrow developed for cutting while immature.

Zwieback (Germ.). A type of rusk, German in origin, the word literally means 'twice-baked'.

Appendix 2. Diet Sheets

DIETS

The diet sheets that follow have been constructed to illustrate quantitative and qualitative aspects of diets required for the treatment of various diseases. Quantities require modification in relation to the size, age, sex and occupation of a patient. In the dietetic treatment of most diseases it is unnecessary to weigh the amounts of the different foods eaten. Sufficient accuracy will be secured by the use of the terms 'small', 'medium' or 'large helping'. A small helping weighs approximately 30 to 60 g, a medium helping 60 to 90 g and a large helping 120 g or more.

Some diet sheets can best be described as dietary regimens. They are confined to elucidating principles in the selection, preparation and consumption of the meals for a day. Quantities may be left to the patient's choice.

The main meal is usually shown at midday, with a lighter meal in the evening. These can, however, be interchanged.

To facilitate reference to the diets a summary table is given.

SUMMARY OF DIET SHEETS

No.	Titles	Purpose
1	High energy, well balanced	Convalescence and underweight
2	Moderate energy, well balanced	A normal diet
3	Low energy, well balanced	Weight reduction, including diabetes
4	Very low protein, low-to-moderate energy	Acute glomerulonephritis or hepatic encephalopathy
5	Very low protein, moderate energy (modified Giovannetti)	Severe chronic renal failure
6	Low protein	Moderate chronic renal failure, subacute hepatic encephalopathy
7	High protein, restricted sodium	Nephrotic syndrome, hypoalbuminaemia
8	Diabetic diets	Diabetes mellitus
9	Diabetic diets in the USA	Diabetes mellitus
10	Very low fat, high carbohydrate	Nausea, hepatitis, primary hypertriglyceridaemia
11	Low fat, high energy	For malabsorption and steatorrhoea
12	Low sodium, moderate energy	Intractable oedema, e.g. in chronic heart failure, cirrhosis and hypertension
13	Restricted sodium, low energy	Acute cardiac failure
14	Reduced saturated, increased polyunsaturated fat	To lower plasma cholesterol
15	Gluten-free	Coeliac disease
16	Semi-liquid	Upper gastrointestinal obstruction and irritable states
17	Bland regimen	Dyspepsia and peptic ulcer
18	High fibre (roughage)	Constipation and diverticulosis

Diet No. 1	HIGH ENERGY, WELL BALANCED

Indications   For convalescent patients (medical and surgical) and those with wasting diseases, or who are undernourished.

Nutrients   Energy 12.6–14.7 MJ (3000–3500 kcal); protein 100–120 g; adequate in all other nutrients.

Food for the day

Milk	750–1000 ml	Fruit	2–4 servings
Meat and 'protein'	3–5 servings	Fat	90g
Bread and cereal	8–12 servings	Desserts	1–2 servings

Sample daily menu

Early morning   Tea or coffee with sugar, and biscuits.

Breakfast   Fruit or fruit juice.
Cereal with milk and sugar.
Egg, bacon or sausage.
Toast or roll with 30 g butter and jam, jelly, marmalade or honey.
Beverage with cream or milk.

Mid-morning   Milky beverage or fruit juice with snack.

Midday meal   Soup or fruit.
120 g meat, fish or poultry.
Potato or substitute.
Vegetable or salad with dressing if desired.
Dessert or pudding.
Biscuits or roll with butter and cheese.
Beverage with milk.

Mid-afternoon   Sandwiches with filling.
Cake or biscuit.
Tea with milk and sugar.

Evening meal   Fruit juice or soup.
90 g meat, fish or cheese or 1–2 eggs.
Vegetable, and salad with dressing if desired.
Bread or roll with butter.
Dessert or pudding.
Beverage with milk.

Bedtime   Milk drink or eggnog and biscuits or sandwich.

Management

Appetite and food tolerance are often poor, requiring extra consideration and individual attention. Wavering appetites may respond best to small servings at first; amounts may then gradually be increased.

Between meal snacks.   Fruit or fruit drinks which may be taken with milk or ice cream; milk drinks (flavoured milks, eggnog, malted milk, yogurt, milk shake, hot milk); biscuits (crackers), sandwiches (filled with egg, cheese, meat, sardines, dates, banana, meat or yeast extract, honey, jam or peanut butter), toast; nuts; desserts containing milk and eggs.

Diet No. 2   MODERATE ENERGY, WELL BALANCED

Indications   A normal diet suitable for a patient in bed.

Nutrients   Energy 8.4–10.5 MJ (2000–2500 kcal); protein 75–100 g; adequate in all other nutrients.

Food for the day

Milk	450–680 ml	Fruit	2–3 servings
Meat and 'protein'	3–4 servings	Fat	60–75 g
Bread and cereal	6–10 servings	Desserts	1–2 servings

Sample daily menu

Breakfast
Fruit or fruit juice.
Cereal with milk.
Egg, bacon or sausage.
Toast or roll with 20 g butter.
Marmalade, jelly or honey.
Beverage with milk.

Midday meal
120 g meat, fish or poultry.
Potato or substitute.
Vegetable or salad with dressing if desired.
Bread or roll with 30 g butter or biscuits and cheese.
Dessert or pudding.
Beverage with milk.

Mid-afternoon
1 serving of fruit.

Evening meal
Fruit juice or soup.
60–90 g cheese, fish or meat or an egg.
Vegetable or salad, with dressing if desired.
Bread or roll with butter.
Dessert or fruit.
Beverage with milk.

Bedtime
Milky drink and biscuit.

Management

The energy intake may need to be adjusted. It is too much for a small female and may not be enough for a patient who is febrile or undernourished.

Diet No. 3
LOW ENERGY, WELL BALANCED

Indications	For patients with obesity, with or without maturity onset diabetes.
Nutrients	Energy 4.2 MJ (1000 kcal), protein 60 g, fat 35 g; adequate in all other nutrients.

Sample daily menu

Breakfast $\frac{1}{2}$ grapefruit or small glass unsweetened fruit juice.
1 egg (boiled, scrambled or poached) or grilled bacon.
20 g unsweetened breakfast cereal or 120 g porridge with milk from allowance
or 20 g bread with butter from allowance.
Coffee or tea (no sugar) with milk from allowance.

Mid-morning Coffee or tea (no sugar) with milk from allowance.

Midday meal Bouillon or clear soup.
Sandwiches made from 2 thin slices of bread, 60 g chicken or tuna
or 30 g cheese, and butter from allowance.
Small salad (see vegetable list).
1 serving of fruit.

Mid-afternoon Tea or coffee (no sugar) with milk from allowance.

Evening meal 120 ml tomato juice.
60 g chicken or lean meat or 90 g steamed or grilled white fish.
Salad or boiled vegetable (see list).
2 small boiled potatoes.
2 wafers of crispbread with butter from allowance.
1 serving of fruit.
Coffee (no sugar) and milk from allowance.

Allowance for day 300 ml skim milk or whole milk allowed to stand with the cream poured off.
15 g butter or margarine.

Diet No. 3 (Cont'd)

Management

Foods which may be taken as desired

Vegetables: Asparagus, aubergine (egg plant), French, runner or string beans, beetroot, broccoli, Brussels sprouts, cabbage, carrots, cauliflower, celery, chicory, courgettes, cucumber, kale, leeks, lettuce, mustard and cress, mushrooms, okra, onion, parsley, peppers, pumpkin, radishes, sauerkraut, seakale, spinach, summer squash, swede, tomatoes, turnips, turnip tops, watercress. Small portions of peas, parsnip, sweetcorn, haricot, lima and broad beans, and lentils.

Drinks: Water, soda water, tea, coffee (ground or instant), sugar-free lemonade, sugar-free carbonated drinks, diabetic fruit drinks, meat and yeast extracts.

Miscellaneous: Saccharine and aspartame preparations, salt, pepper, vinegar, mustard, herbs, spices, pickles, relish and soy sauce, unthickened gravy.

Foods to be avoided

Sugar (white or brown), glucose, sorbitol. Sweets, toffees, chocolates, candies, cornflour, custard powder. Jam, marmalade, jelly, lemon curd, honey, syrup, molasses. Canned or frozen fruits (unless preserved without sugar).

Dried fruits, e.g. dates, figs, apricots, raisins. Cakes, pastries, puddings and rich desserts. Sweet or chocolate biscuits.

Ice cream and gelatine dessert (table jelly). Condensed or evaporated milk, cream. Nuts, unless used in place of meat or fish dish.

Salad dressing and mayonnaise. Thick and cream sauces. Fatty meats, sausages and fatty fish. All fried foods.

Sweetened fruit juices, fruit squashes. Carbonated beverages. Beer, wine, sherry, spirits — all alcoholic drinks.

The items in the sample daily menu can be exchanged in the same way as diabetic exchanges. People who need to take this diet should be advised where to find low energy recipes and to build up a file of these. There are several suitable books on the market, e.g. Good Housekeeping *Slimmers' Cook Book* (London: Ebury Press).

It is usually wise not to get too hungry. Sometimes a snack between meals saves overdoing it at a meal. No meal should be missed.

Diet No. 4	VERY LOW PROTEIN, LOW-TO-MODERATE ENERGY
Indications	For patients with acute glomerulonephritis or with hepatic encephalopathy.
Nutrients	Protein 20 g, fluids 1200 ml, energy 6.7 MJ (1600 kcal), sodium restricted.

Food for the day

Double cream	60 ml
with water	150 ml
Unsalted butter	35 g
Sugar and glucose	60 g
Jam, jelly, marmalade or honey	45 g
Bread (salt-free may be required)	90 g
Fruit	300 g

Sample daily menu

Breakfast
150 g fruit juice with glucose.
20 g cornflakes or similar breakfast cereal and sugar.
Cream mixture.
30 g bread, toast or roll.
Unsalted butter.
250 ml tea or weak coffee.

Mid-morning
125 ml tea or coffee.
Sugar and cream mixture.
2 biscuits or cookies.

Midday meal
30 g meat or 1 egg.
90 g potato, mashed (no salt) with butter or 60 g boiled rice.
60 g grilled tomato or other vegetable.
Fruit — fresh, stewed or canned.
125 ml tea or carbonated beverage.

Mid-afternoon
30 g bread and unsalted butter.
Jam, jelly or honey.
125 ml tea with cream mixture.

Evening meal
30 g bread toasted or low salt crackers with unsalted butter.
Vegetable salad with oil dressing, if desired.
Water ice or fruit.
125 ml coffee with cream mixture and sugar.

Bedtime
125 ml tea with cream mixture and sugar.
Biscuit or cookie.

Managment
Fluid intake may need to be adjusted depending on fluid balance.

Fruits and potatoes are relatively rich in potassium; if plasma K is rising, potassium intake can be restricted by replacing natural fruit juice by a proprietary fruit squash, by using rice instead of potato and by using only fruits relatively low in potassium, especially pears and apples. (This is not necessary in hepatic encephalopathy.)

Table salt should not be used (no salt on tray). Biscuits and cookies should be low in salt and baking soda. To restrict the sodium further salt-free bread may be used or food may be cooked without salt.

Diet No. 5
Indications

VERY LOW PROTEIN, MODERATE ENERGY (Modified GIOVANNETTI)
For patients with severe chronic renal failure.

Nutrients

Protein 17 g (of high biological value), energy approx. 9.2 MJ (2200 kcal), fluid about 500 ml, Na 12 mmol and K 15 mmol/day. This diet is low in B vitamins, iron and calcium.

Sample daily menu

Breakfast

Oatmeal porridge (5 g oats, 50 ml double cream, 40 ml water).
Glucose or sugar.
30 g salt-free protein-free bread, toasted.
Salt-free butter.
Jam, jelly, marmalade or honey.
80 ml tea with glucose and 10 ml milk.

Mid-morning

50 ml liquid glucose polymer.

Midday meal

25 g chicken (dry weight).
30 g boiled rice (dry weight).
Salt-free butter.
30 g very low protein vegetable.
30 g very low protein fruit and cream.

Mid-afternoon

40 ml grapefruit juice and glucose.
10 g salt-free, protein-free biscuit or rusk.

Evening meal

1 egg, scrambled on toasted, salt-free, protein-free bread with salt-free butter.
Plain ice cream*.
30 g very low protein fruit.

Bedtime

90 ml milk with glucose or sugar.
10 g salt-free, protein-free biscuit.

Management

Salt-free, protein-free bread, biscuits and rusks are baked from wheatstarch flour and obtainable in the UK from Welfare Foods, Stockport.

Proprietary preparations of liquid glucose polymer are Hycal, Caloreen and Maxijul; they are very low in electrolytes.

Very low protein vegetables are tomatoes, egg plant, pumpkins, carrots, onions and green beans.

Very low protein fruits are pears, apples, pineapple, mandarins and grapefruit.

The diet does not meet requirement for the B vitamins, iron and calcium and supplements of these should be given; 500 mg of methionine should also be given daily (250 mg tablet twice daily with meals).

Extra fluid, e.g. tea with cream and a little milk or a liquid glucose drink or a little beer or wine, may be given depending on the urine output.

* Made from 25 ml cream, 25 ml oil, 25 g glucose, 10 ml water, colour and flavour.

Diet No. 6 LOW PROTEIN

Indications For patients with chronic renal failure of moderate severity or with subacute hepatic encephalopathy.

Nutrients Protein 40 g, energy 7.6–8.4 MJ (1800–2000 kcal), Na 40 mmol and K 60 mmol. Adequate in other nutrients but iron and calcium need to be supplemented, if used for a long time.

Food for the day

	Protein (g)
Milk: 120 ml	4
Meat, protein foods: 90 g	21
Fruit or juice: 5 to 6 servings	5
Low protein vegetables: 2 servings	4
Bread, cereals: 3 to 4 servings	6

Cream, fat, sugar, jelly, syrup, hard candy, water ice, tea, coffee and seasonings except salt, as desired.

Sample daily menu

Breakfast Fruit or fruit juice.
Breakfast cereal with milk.
1 slice of toast with salt-free butter and jelly or marmalade.
Coffee with sugar and cream.

Mid-morning Fruit juice with sugar.

Midday meal 60 g meat, poultry or 90 g fish.
Vegetable salad with oil dressing.
1 slice of toast.
Salt-free butter, jam or jelly.
Water ice or
Tea with sugar and cream, or carbonated beverage.

Evening meal 1 egg or 30 g meat.
Potato or rice with butter.
Cooked low protein vegetable with butter.
Fruit.
Coffee or tea with sugar and cream.

Bedtime Fruit juice with sugar or tea with cream.

Management

A variety of cakes and cookies containing 2 g protein can be substituted for 1 slice of bread.

Suitable low protein vegetables and salads are green beans, beetroot, cabbage, carrots, cauliflower, celery, cucumber, egg plant, lettuce, mushrooms, onions, pumpkin, radishes, summer squash, tomatoes and turnips.

Most fruits are suitable except dried fruits.

Diet No. 7   HIGH PROTEIN, RESTRICTED SODIUM

Indications   For patients with nephrotic syndrome or hypoalbuminaemia.

Nutrients   Protein 90–120 g, energy 10 MJ (2400 kcal), Na 80–120 mmol; adequate in
                                    other nutrients.

Sample daily menu
Breakfast   Fruit or fruit juice.
                                    Breakfast cereal.
                                    2 eggs (poached, boiled or scrambled).
                                    1 slice of bread or toast.
                                    Salt-free butter and marmalade, jelly or jam.
                                    Tea or coffee with milk.

Mid-morning   Tea or coffee, with milk.

Midday meal   90–120 g chicken, unsalted meat or fish or 2 eggs as omelet.
                                    Vegetable or salad.
                                    Potato or bread with salt-free butter.
                                    Milk dessert with fruit.

Mid-afternoon   2 slices of bread as sandwiches filled with egg, meat or chicken.
                                    Tea with milk and sugar.

Evening meal   150–180 g meat, poultry or fish.
                                    Bread with salt-free butter or potato.
                                    Vegetable or salad.
                                    Dessert made with milk and fruit.
                                    Coffee with milk and sugar.

Bedtime   Drink of malted milk.

Allowance for day   600 ml milk or more.
                                    45 g salt-free butter.

Management
Sodium intake is restricted by using no table salt and avoiding all highly salted foods, e.g. ham, bacon, sausages, corned beef, smoked fish, cheese, most ketchups and commercial sauces, canned and convenience foods, margarine and salted butter. Some patients may find difficulty in eating so much meat with little salt for flavour. Spices and herbs may be used to enhance flavour. Extra protein may be given by incorporating Casilan or a similar product into various dishes. 30 g Casilan provides 26 g protein.

DIABETIC DIETS

Diabetic diets aim to restrict carbohydrate intake while meeting normal needs for protein and providing just sufficient energy to maintain normal weight in adults and to allow for growth in children. A moderate to high intake of dietary fibre is also advocated. Diets are made up from lists of exchanges, quantitatively defined. Different systems of exchanges are used by the British and American Dietetic and Diabetic Associations. The British Associations use carbohydrate exchanges; formerly protein and fat exchanges were also used but these are no longer recommended officially. The American Associations use bread, meat, milk, fruit and vegetable exchanges.

The planning of diabetic diets is illustrated below in the following stages.

1. A method is given for calculating the nature and number of the exchanges required to make up a diet in which amounts of energy and carbohydrate have been prescribed.
2. A diet plan sets out how these exchanges may be apportioned among each of the day's meals.
3. The British exchange system is described.
4. A diet (No. 8a) based on the above plan is drawn up.
5. An unmeasured regimen (No. 8b) suitable for mild diabetics who are not overweight is described.
6. Diabetic diets based on the American exchange system are summarised.

CONSTRUCTING THE DIET

Nutrients   Energy 7.5 MJ (1800 kcal), carbohydrate 180 g.

Each **carbohydrate exchange** contains approximately 10 g carbohydrate, with an energy value of about 210 KJ (50 kcal) (equivalent to 20 g bread).

One pint of milk contains approximately 30 g carbohydrate, with an energy value of about 1.59 MJ (380 kcal). Thus a diet prescription for 180 g carbohydrate, 7.5 MJ (1800 kcal), would be calculated as follows:

1. The daily intake of carbohydrate (180 g) represents 18 carbohydrate exchanges.
2. The daily allowance of milk is decided either on the basis of the patient's food habits or on his special requirements. In this example it is 1 pint, which contains 3 carbohydrate exchanges, leaving 15 for distribution throughout the day.
3. These provide 4.74 MJ (1130 kcal) and the remainder of the energy is provided by protein and fat. At least 10 per cent of the energy has to come from protein.
4. Finally the carbohydrate exchanges are distributed throughout the day according to the eating habits and daily routine of the patient, and the insulin regimen.

PLAN OF DISTRIBUTION into meals

Exchanges provide   Energy 7.5 MJ (1800 kcal), carbohydrate 180 g.

Breakfast
4 carbohydrate exchanges.
Butter and milk from allowance.
Tea or coffee (no sugar).

Mid-morning
1 carbohydrate exchange.
Butter and milk from allowance.
Tea or coffee (no sugar).

Midday meal
Clear soup if desired.
4 carbohydrate exchanges.
Vegetables if desired (permitted list, p. 619).
Butter and milk from allowance.

Mid-afternoon
1 carbohydrate exchange.
Butter and milk from allowance.
Tea (no sugar).

Evening meal
4 carbohydrate exchanges.
Vegetables if desired (permitted list, p. 619).
Tea or coffee (no sugar).

Bedtime
1 carbohydrate exchange.
Remainder of butter and milk from allowance.

Allowance for day
1 pint (560 ml) whole milk.
30 g butter or margarine.

CARBOHYDRATE EXCHANGES

These are the recommendations of the British Diabetic Association. All the literature prepared for patients by the Association is based on these exchanges.

Each item on this list = 1 carbohydrate exchange (10 g CHO).
The energy value is approximately 210 kJ (50 kcal)

	Raw or cooked	Measure	oz	g
Bread				
White or brown	Plain or toasted	½ slice of thick cut sliced large loaf	⅔	20
		⅔ slice of a thin cut sliced large loaf	⅔	20
		1 slice of a small sliced loaf	⅔	20
Cereal Foods				
All Bran		3 level tablespoons	⅔	20
Biscuits	Plain or semi-sweet	2 biscuits	½	15
Chapattis		made with fat	⅔	20
Cornflakes or other un-sweetened breakfast cereal		3 heaped tablespoons	½	15
Cornflour	Before cooking	2 heaped teaspoons	½	15
Cornmeal		1 level tablespoon	½	15
Custard powder	Before cooking	2 heaped teaspoons	½	15
Flour		1 level tablespoon	½	15
Macaroni	Before cooking	1 heaped tablespoon	½	15
Noodles	Before cooking	1 heaped tablespoon	½	15
Oatcakes			⅔	20
Porridge	Cooked with water	4 level tablespoons	4	120
Rice	Before cooking	2 heaped teaspoons	½	15
Rye crispbread		1½ biscuits	½	15
Sago	Before cooking	2 heaped teaspoons	½	15
Semolina	Before cooking	2 heaped teaspoons	½	15
Spaghetti	Before cooking	1 heaped tablespoon	½	15
Tapioca	Before cooking	2 heaped teaspoons	½	15
Miscellaneous				
Cocoa powder		5 heaped teaspoons	1	30
Horlicks and Ovaltine		2 heaped teaspoons	½	15
Coca Cola or Pepsi Cola			3 fl oz	90 ml
Milk	Fresh		7 fl oz	200 ml
Milk	Evaporated	6 tablespoons	3 fl oz	90 ml
Milk	Sweetened, condensed	1½ tablespoons	⅔	20 ml
Ice cream	Plain		2	60
Sausages			3	90

CARBOHYDRATE EXCHANGES (Cont'd)

	Raw		Stewed (without sugar)	
	oz	g	oz	g
Dried Fruits				
Apricots	1	30	2½	75
Figs	⅔	20	1½	45
Prunes (with stones)	1	30	2	60
Dates (without stones)				
Currants	½	15		
Sultanas				
Raisins				
Fresh fruits*				
Apples (with skin)	4	120	5	150
Bananas (with skin)	2	60		
Cherries	3	90	4	120
Damsons	4	120	6	180
Grapes	2	60		
Greengages	3	90	4	120
Oranges and tangerines				
—with skin	6	180		
—without skin	4	120		
Orange juice	4	120		
Peaches (with stones)	4	120		
Pears	4	120	5	150
Pineapple (fresh)	4	90		
Plums (dessert)	4	120	7	210
Raspberries	6	180	7	210
Strawberries	6	180		
Vegetables†				
Potatoes (raw or boiled)	2	60		
Potatoes (roast or chipped)	1	30		
Potato crisps	⅔	20		
Baked beans				
Butter beans				
Haricot beans	2	60		
Sweet corn				
Tinned peas				
Parsnips	3	90		

The following contain only a small quantity of carbohydrates and may be eaten in moderate quantity (if unsweetened) without being counted in the diet.

* *Fruits*: Avocado pear, blackberries (brambles), blackcurrants, grapefruit, gooseberries, lemons, loganberries, redcurrants, whitecurrants and rhubarb.

†*Vegetables*: Asparagus, beetroot, Brussels sprouts, cabbage, carrots, cauliflower, celery, cucumber, French beans, leeks, lettuce, marrow, mushrooms, mustard and cress, onions, parsley, runner beans, spinach, swede, tomatoes, turnips, watercress, and fresh or frozen garden peas.

DIABETIC DIETS

Permitted and prohibited foods

Foods which may be taken in any quantity
Tea, coffee (milk from allowance, no sugar), meat and yeast extracts.
Energy-free aerated drinks.
Tomato juice, lemon juice.
Diabetic fruit squashes.
Saccharine and aspartame preparations.
Clear soup.
Herbs, seasonings and spices.
Low carbohydrate vegetables and fruits (see p. 619).

Foods to be taken in moderation
Meats, fish, cheese, eggs; butter, margarine, cream and vegetable oils.

Foods to be taken in strict moderation in consultation with the doctor
Spirits, dry wines, dry sherries.

Foods not allowed
Sugar, glucose, sweets, chocolate, honey, syrup, treacle, jam, marmalade, cakes, biscuits (except those specified), pies, fruit tinned in syrup, fruit squash, lemonade or similar aerated drinks, sweet sherries and wine, beer.

Diet No. 8a

A DIABETIC DIET BASED ON THE DISTRIBUTION OF CARBOHYDRATE EXCHANGES IN THE PLAN ON page 617.

Sample daily menu

120 g porridge with milk from allowance.
60 g wholemeal bread with butter from allowance. Tea or coffee with milk from allowance.

Mid-morning

15 g low sugar biscuits(s) or crispbread.
Tea or coffee with milk from allowance.

Midday meal

Clear soup with shredded vegetables.
Lean meat or fish or egg or cheese.
120 g boiled potatoes.
Salad or other unrestricted vegetables if desired.
120 g orange (peeled weight).
Small carton of low fat yogurt.
Milk from allowance with coffee or ½ small carton fruit yogurt.

Mid-afternoon

15 g wheatmeal biscuits.
Tea or coffee with milk from allowance.

Evening meal

Meat or fish or egg or cheese.
Unrestricted vegetables.
60 g wholemeal bread with butter from allowance.
120 g raw apple.
Tea or coffee with milk from allowance.

Bedtime

Remainder of milk from allowance and 15 g Ovaltine
or 20 g bread and butter from allowance.

Allowance for day

500 ml milk.
30 g butter or margarine.

Note — Most 'Diabetic' foodstuffs on sale at Chemists and Health Food Stores *do* contain some carbohydrate and must therefore *not* be taken without consulting your doctor or dietitian.

A cookery book for diabetics, *Measure for Measure*, and carbohydrate values of proprietary foods, *Carbohydrate Countdown*, are obtainable from The British Diabetic Association, 10 Queen Anne Street, London W1M 0BD.

Diet No. 8b   UNMEASURED DIABETIC REGIMEN

Indications   Mild diabetics, who are not obese and patients who are unable to weigh their diet
                              may be given a list of foods which are grouped into three categories.

I. *Foods to be avoided*
1. Sugar, glucose, jam, marmalade, honey, syrup, treacle, fruits in syrup, sweets, chocolate, lemonade, glucose
   drinks, proprietary milk preparations and similar foods which are sweetened with sugar.
2. Cakes, sweet biscuits, chocolate biscuits, pastries, pies, puddings, thick sauces.
3. Alcoholic drinks unless permission has been given by the doctor.

II. *Foods to be eaten in moderation only*
1. Breads of all kinds (including so-called 'slimming' and 'starch-reduced' breads, brown or white, plain or toasted).
2. Rolls, scones, biscuits and crispbreads.
3. Potatoes, peas and baked beans.
4. Breakfast cereals and porridge.
5. All fresh or dried fruit.
6. Macaroni, spaghetti, custard and foods with much flour.
7. Thick soups.
8. Diabetic foods.
9. Milk.

III. *Foods to be eaten as desired*
1. All meat, fish, eggs.
2. Cheese.
3. Clear soups or meat extracts, tomato or lemon juice.
4. Tea or coffee.
5. Cabbage, Brussels sprouts, broccoli, cauliflower, spinach, turnip, runner or French beans, onions, leeks, carrots,
   mushrooms, lettuce, cucumber, tomatoes, spring onions, radishes, mustard and cress, asparagus, parsley,
   rhubarb.
6. Herbs, spices, salt, pepper and mustard.
7. Saccharine or aspartame preparations for sweetening.

For mild diabetics who are obese Diet No. 3 or a similar regimen is used.

Diet No. 9   DIABETIC DIETS IN THE USA

The American Diabetes and Dietetic Associations have meal plans for nine diets for diabetics, providing from 1200 to 3000 kcal. Each diet is made up of a varying number of standard exchanges of six food groups.

FOOD EXCHANGES PER DAY IN SAMPLE MEAL PLANS

Diet	Milk	Vegetables	Fruits	Bread exchanges	Meat exchanges	Fat exchanges	Energy MJ	kcal
1	455 ml	1	3	4	5	1	5.0	1200
2	455 ml	1	3	6	6	4	6.3	1500
3	455 ml	1	3	8	7	5	7.5	1800
4	455 ml	1	4	10	8	8	9.2	2200
5	910 ml	1	3	6	5	3	7.5	1800
6	910 ml	1	4	10	7	11	10.9	2600
7	910 ml	1	6	17	10	15	14.7	3500
8	455 ml	1	4	12	10	12	10.9	2600
9	455 ml	1	4	15	10	15	12.6	3000

Whole milk 455 ml = 1 US pint and 910 ml = US quart.
In fat-controlled diabetic diets, this fat is polyunsaturated and the milk is skim milk.
These diets contain more milk and are especially suitable for children.

Milk includes yogurt. *Vegetables* include most vegetables, but starchy vegetables (legumes, potatoes, etc.) are put among *bread exchanges* while lettuce, parsley, radishes and watercress may be taken ad lib. *Fruits* cover all fruits as long as no sugar is added. *Meat exchanges* include fish and cheese, also peanut butter. *Fat exchanges* include avocados, olives and some fat-rich nuts as well as butter, margarine, cooking oils, cream and salad dressings.

COMPOSITION OF FOOD EXCHANGES

Food	Household measures	Weight g	CHO g	Protein g	Fat g	Energy kJ	kcal
Milk exchanges	½ pint (8 oz)	240	12	8	10	710	170
Vegetable exchanges	½ standard cup	100	5	2		105	25
Fruit exchanges	Varies		10			168	40
Bread exchanges	Varies		15	2		285	68
Meat exchanges	1 oz	30		7	5	305	73
Fat exchanges	1 tsp.	5			5	190	45

Standard cup has a volume of 8 oz.

Further information may be obtained from The American Diabetes Association, 1 West 48th Street, New York, NY 10020, USA.

Diet No. 10	VERY LOW FAT, HIGH CARBOHYDRATE
Indications	For patients with nausea due to hepatitis or obstructive jaundice and with primary hypertriglyceridaemia.
Nutrients	Fat 20–25 g, protein 80–90 g, carbohydrate 400 g, energy 8.4–9 MJ (2000–2300 kcal); other nutrients adequate with possible exception of iron.

Food for the day

Milk, skim	750 ml
Lean meat, poultry and fish	two 90 g portions
Bread and cereal	8–12 slices or equivalent
Vegetables, salad	2–3 servings
Fruit and juice	4–7 servings
Fat	0
Sweets and dessert	Any with no fat

Sample daily menu

Early morning	Glass of fruit juice with glucose or sugar.
Breakfast	Porridge or breakfast cereal with skim milk. Fruit. Bread or toast with marmalade, jelly or jam. Coffee or tea with skim milk and sugar.
Mid-morning	Coffee or tea with skim milk and sugar or fruit juice.
Midday meal	Clear soup or fruit juice. 60 g very lean meat, poultry or white fish (steamed or boiled). Potato or rice (boiled) or bread or roll. Vegetable or salad. Pudding made with cereal or gelatine and skim milk and sugar. Fruit and sugar. Coffee or tea with skim milk and sugar.
Mid-afternoon	2 thin slices of bread with jam or jelly or plain biscuits (low fat). Tea with skim milk and sugar or carbonated beverage.
Evening meal	Similar to midday meal but with items varied.
Bedtime	Coffee or tea with skim milk and sugar.

Management

Avoid butter, margarine or cream. No cooking fat or oil should be used and the following foods should be avoided: whole milk, egg yolk, cheese, ice cream, cakes, potato crisps, pastries and cookies; sweets containing fat, e.g. fudge and milk chocolate; bacon, organ meat, fatty fish, e.g. herrings, mackerel, sardines and salmon; and all canned meat.

Boiled sweets, fruit, fruit juice and carbonated drinks may be taken.

Diet No. 11	LOW FAT, HIGH ENERGY

Indications   For patients with malabsorption and steatorrhoea.

Nutrients   Fat 45–50 g, protein 120 g, energy approx. 11.7 MJ (2800 kcal); adequate in all nutrients.

Food for the day

Milk, skim	680–1360 ml
Lean meat, poultry, fish	200–230 g
Bread, cereal	8–12 slices or equivalent
Vegetables	2–3 servings
Fruit	Any with no fat

Sample daily menu

Breakfast
Fruit or fruit juice.
Cereal or porridge with skim milk.
1 egg.
Toast or rolls with jelly, jam or marmalade.
7 g margarine.
Coffee or tea with skim milk and sugar.

Mid-morning
Fruit juice.

Midday meal
Fruit juice or meat soup.
90 g lean meat or fish.
Vegetables or salad.
Bread or roll or potato.
Fruit or fat-free dessert made from cereal, skim milk and sugar.
Coffee or tea with skim milk and sugar.

Mid-afternoon
Tea with skim milk and sugar.

Evening meal
Same as midday.

Bedtime
Skim milk (flavoured) with crackers and jelly or jam.

Management

The following foods should be avoided: all fried foods, organ meats, whole milk, cheese, cream and cream substitutes, ice cream, milk chocolate, cream soup, gravies, commercial cakes, pies and cookies.

Medium-chain triglycerides can be used to increase energy intake without causing steatorrhoea. Proprietary preparations are Portagen (Mead Johnson) and MCT Oil (Cow and Gate, Liquegen). Recipes for incorporating these into food are obtainable from the manufacturers.

Boiled sweets, fruit, fruit juice and carbonated drinks may be taken.

Diet No. 12   LOW SODIUM, MODERATE ENERGY

Indications   For patients with oedema from congestive heart failure, nephrotic syndrome,
                         chronic glomerulonephritis and cirrhosis of the liver with ascites; may also be
                         used for hypertension.

Nutrients   Sodium 40 mmol, protein 60–90 g, energy 6.7–8.4 MJ (1600–2000 kcal); adequate
                         in other nutrients.

Sample daily menu

Breakfast   Fruit or fruit juice, sweetened as desired.
                         Low-salt cereal (e.g. Puffed Wheat, Shredded Wheat).
                         Milk from allowance
                         1 egg (unsalted).
                         Low sodium bread or toast.
                         Butter from allowance.
                         Jelly or marmalade.
                         Coffee or tea with milk from allowance.

Midday meal   Fruit or fruit juice.
                         90 g unsalted meat, poultry or fresh white fish, which may be grilled or fried in
                         oil.
                         Potato or rice or pasta, cooked without salt.
                         Permitted fresh or frozen vegetable.
                         Salad with low sodium dressing.
                         Low sodium bread with butter from allowance.
                         Fruit and sugar.
                         Tea or coffee with milk from allowance.

Evening meal   Fruit or fruit juice.
                         60 g unsalted meat or fish or 1 egg.
                         Permitted vegetable and salad if desired.
                         Low sodium bread or roll with butter from allowance.
                         Tea or coffee with milk from allowance.

Bedtime   Cup of milk.

Allowance for day   250 ml milk.
                         30 g salt-free butter or margarine.

Management

No salt to be used in cooking or at table.

Avoid all cured meat and fish, e.g. bacon, ham, tongue, pickled brisket and silverside, smoked haddock, kippers, sardines, pilchards, smoked salmon; all canned meats, fish and vegetables and soups; cheeses, bottled sauces, pickles, sausages, and all foods made with bicarbonate of soda or baking powder, e.g. cakes and biscuits; seasoned salts. Check labels of processed foods carefully to see if salt, sodium bicarbonate, sodium benzoate or monosodium glutamate are mentioned among the contents.

To increase the energy intake the following may be added: sugar, fruit, jam, marmalade and boiled sweets and pastilles.

The sodium intake can be reduced further to about 20 mmol/day by the use of low sodium milk, e.g. Lonalac, Loso or Edosol.

A low sodium diet is unappetising and many patients can only take it for a short period. If the low sodium bread and salt-free butter is replaced by normal bread and butter, sodium intake is increased to 60–80 mmol/day. For many patients such a restricted sodium diet is tolerable and therapeutically useful.

Diet No. 13   RESTRICTED SODIUM, LOW ENERGY

Indication   For patients with severe, acute heart failure.

Nutrients   Sodium 40 mmol, protein 40 g, energy 3.8 MJ (900 kcal).

Sample daily menu

Breakfast   1 thin slice of crisp toast.
Butter and milk from allowance.
Weak tea.

Mid-morning   Small glass of fruit juice.

Midday meal   Small helping of white fish, chicken or lean meat.
1 tablespoonful vegetable.
Small helping of milk pudding made with milk from allowance.

Mid-afternoon   1 thin slice of very crisp toast.
Butter and milk from allowance.
Weak tea.

Evening meal   Small helping lean meat, chicken or white fish.
Small helping of fruit.

Bedtime   Milk drink made with remainder of milk from allowance.

Allowance for day   500 ml milk.
15 g butter.

Management

No salt to be used in cooking or at table. Low energy drinks may be taken.

Diet No. 14   REDUCED SATURATED, INCREASED POLYUNSATURATED FAT

Indications   To lower plasma cholesterol.

Nutrients   Reduced saturated fats and cholesterol; increased polyunsaturated fats. Adequate in
                       nutrients, with possible exception of iron. Energy and protein determined by
                       individual needs.

Sample daily menu

Breakfast   Fruit or fruit juice.
                       Cereal or porridge with skim milk.
                       Toast.
                       Polyunsaturated margarine and marmalade or jelly.
                       Coffee or tea with skim milk.

Mid-morning   Coffee or tea with skim milk.

Midday meal   Sandwiches made from bread and polyunsaturated margarine and filled with lean
                           meat, poultry or cottage cheese.
                       Salad.
                       Fruit or allowed dessert.
                       Tea with skim milk.

Mid-afternoon   Fruit.

Evening meal   Cooked poultry, fish or lean meat, which may be fried in polyunsaturated oil.
                       Potatoes or rice or pasta.
                       Vegetables, raw or cooked.
                       Bread or plain roll and polyunsaturated margarine.
                       Fruit or allowed dessert.
                       Coffee with skim milk.

Bedtime   Tea with skim milk or juice.
                       Crackers with a little peanut butter.

Management

   Foods to be avoided: Butter and hydrogenated margarine. Lard, suet and shortenings; cakes, biscuits and
pastries made with these. Fatty and marbled meat and visible fat on meat; meat pies, sausages and luncheon meats.
Whole milk and cream and commercial cream toppings. Chocolate and ice cream. Cheese, except low fat cottage
cheese. Coconut, coconut oil and Coffee Mate. Eggs: no more than 2 eggs per week, including those used in
cooking. Organ meats: liver, kidneys and brain. Fish roes, caviar and shrimps. Fried foods, unless fried in polyunsaturated oil. Potato chips (crisps) and most nuts. Gravy, unless made with polyunsaturated oil, and canned soups.
Salad dressing unless made with polyunsaturated oil
   Foods allowed: Bread, white and wholemeal, toast, crispbreads and plain biscuits. Breakfast cereals and
porridge. Pasta, potatoes and rice. All vegetables and pulses, salads and fruit (fresh, canned and dried). Fish, white
and fatty, which may be baked or fried in polyunsaturated oil. Lean meat, preferably chicken or veal. Condiments
and spices and clear soups. Tea, coffee and fruit drinks. Polyunsaturated oils, e.g. sunflower, maize, cottonseed
and soya. Polyunsaturated margarines. Walnuts and pecans. Skim milk, low fat yogurt. Cottage cheese and skim
milk cheese. Cakes and biscuits made with egg white, skim milk and polyunsaturated fat. Alcohol with discretion.
   For baking only polyunsaturated fats or oils, egg whites and skim milk may be used.
   If the patient is obese, it is important to adjust the energy intake so that the body weight is reduced, and then
maintained at the normal level or a little below.
   Jam, jelly, marmalade, honey, sugar, boiled sweets, pure sugar candy, gum drops, marshmallow are allowed for
patients with familial hypercholesterolaemia, but concentrated sweets should be avoided by patients with hyperlipidaemia of affluence.

Diet No. 15

GLUTEN-FREE

Indications

For patients with coeliac disease or gluten-induced enteropathy. Also for patients with dermatitis herpetiformis.

Nutrients

Energy and protein intake according to age and activity. All cereals containing gluten, i.e. wheat, rye, barley and buckwheat, must be omitted.

Sample daily menu

Breakfast

Fruit or fruit juice.
Cornflakes or puffed rice with milk.
Egg or bacon.
Gluten-free bread (toasted) with butter and marmalade or jelly.
Coffee or tea with milk.

Midday meal

Soup made with meat or vegetable stock and thickened with gluten-free flour; rice, peas or lentils may be added.

Meat or fish; any gravy is thickened with cornflour or other gluten-free flour.
Potato or rice.
Vegetables, avoiding those prepared with mayonnaise or sauce (e.g. canned baked beans). Salad with dressing made without flour.
Fruit or permitted dessert/pudding; special brands of ice cream.
Coffee or tea, with milk.

Evening meal

Fruit or fruit juice.
Main dish with an egg, cheese, fish or meat.
Potato or rice.
Vegetables.
Gluten-free bread or roll with butter.
Fruit or permitted dessert.
Tea with milk.

Diet No. 15 (Cont'd)

Management

Forbidden foods: Bread, biscuits, cakes, cookies, crackers, crispbreads, doughnuts, flour (white or wholemeal), muffins, pancakes, pastry, pies, pretzels, rolls, rusks, scones, toast and waffles. Breakfast cereals made with wheat or oatmeal, e.g. All Bran, Wheat Flakes, Puffed Wheat, Shredded Wheat, Weetabix, Shreddies, Sugar Smacks, Grapenuts, oatmeal, wheat germ. Macaroni, noodles, spaghetti, semolina, vermicelli and other pasta. Meat pie, luncheon meat, canned meat, meat loaf, commercial hamburgers, sausages, bologna and frankfurters. Canned soups and soup mixes. Vegetables with cream sauces or crumbs, e.g. baked beans. Proprietary sauces and ketchups, gravies, commercial salad dressings. Packet and pudding mixtures, pastry mixtures, patent infant foods. Malted milk, Ovaltine, postum and beer, commercial milk flavouring. Baking powder. Cheese spreads. Most ice creams. Commercial chocolates and liquorice sweets.

Foods that may be used freely: Milk (all kinds) and yogurt; may be flavoured with home-made syrup or unprocessed cocoa. Fresh meats and poultry and bacon, fish (fresh or canned), shellfish, organ meats. Gravies made with cornstarch or rice flour. Cheese and egg (boiled, poached, scrambled, omelet and in mixed dishes). Vegetables (fresh, frozen, canned), raw or cooked. Potatoes and rice. Nuts. All fruits and fruit juices. Bread and flour made from wheatstarch, arrowroot, cornmeal, soyabean, rice or potato flour. Breakfast cereals made from rice and maize. Cream, butter, margarine, peanut butter, cooking fats and oils. Sugar, jam, jelly, marmalade, honey, syrup, boiled sweets, hard candies, home-made candy, plain chocolate. Desserts and puddings made with gelatine, tapioca, sago, rice and cornstarch. Cakes and cookies made with gluten-free flour. Coffee, tea and carbonated beverages. Salt, pepper, mustard, spices, garlic and vinegar. Gluten-free manufactured products as listed by the Coeliac Society. Gluten-free bread, biscuits, pasta, flour as provided by pharmaceutical companies, e.g. Welfare Foods (Stockport). Ltd, G.F. Dietary Supplies.

Successful treatment depends on not eating wheat starch containing more than 0.3 per cent protein. Many mixed and manufactured foods contain small amounts of wheat flour, and lists of forbidden and permissible foods should be continuously checked and brought up to date. A current list of gluten-free manufactured products and recipes can be obtained from the Coeliac Society, P.O. Box No. 181, London NW2 2QY.

Diet No. 16   SEMI-LIQUID

Indications   For patients with difficulty in chewing or swallowing or who are severely ill with
                     ulcerative or malignant disease of the gastrointestinal tract.
Nutrients   Energy 6.3–8.4 MJ (1500–2000 kcal), protein 50–75 g.

Sample daily feeds
Early morning   Fruit juice.

Breakfast   Strained porridge with milk and sugar.
                     Tea or coffee with milk and sugar.

Mid-morning   Milk shake drink.

Midday meal   Strained soup.
                     Liquidised meat with gravy or fish with sauce.
                     Sieved vegetables.
                     Mashed potato.
                     Milk pudding with sugar and sieved fruit.
                     Tea or coffee with milk and sugar.

Mid-afternoon   Fruit juice or milk drink.

Evening meal   Liquidised cheese or egg dish.
                     Sieved fruit and ice cream or milk pudding with sugar.
                     Tea or coffee with milk and sugar.

Bedtime   Milk drink.

Allowance for day 500–1500 ml milk.

Management

Foods that may be used: Milk in all forms, including chocolate- and other-flavoured milks, eggnog, yogurt, malted milk and cream. Meat, strained in broth or cream soups; finely minced poultry, meat and fish. Eggs in eggnog and soft-cooked eggs (boiled, poached, scrambled or omelet). Vegetables strained in cream soups. Fruit juices. Cereal gruels. Dessert: flavoured gelatine, junket, custard, ice cream, sherbet and simple puddings. Milk, tea, coffee and cocoa. Sugar and syrups and glucose.

This diet may be inadequate in energy, iron, vitamin A, thiamin and nicotinamide. It is a transition diet used until more adequate oral feeding is possible and may need to be supplemented by nasogastric or parenteral feeding.

Energy can be increased by using more cream, butter and glucose; some patients may not tolerate large intakes of milk and for them the cereal gruel and cream can be increased, and combinations of a glucose polymer (e.g. Maxijul, Caloreen, Hycal), Casilan and cream used.

Diet No. 17   BLAND REGIMEN

Indications   The advice given below is likely to relieve symptoms in patients with peptic ulcers, gastritis and some other gastrointestinal disorders. How many points in the advice are used depends on the physician's judgment and on the patient's individual sensitivity to particular food items.

General Advice
1. Take four meals a day.
2. Take your meals at regular times each day.
3. Eat your meals slowly and chew your food carefully.
4. Avoid rush and hurry before and after meals; if possible rest for a few minutes before and after eating.
5. Do not smoke or drink alcohol before meals, when the stomach is empty.
6. Avoid large, heavy meals and any articles of food which you find disagree with you.
7. Remember that anxiety and worry can upset digestion.
8. See that you get sufficient sleep at night.
9. Consult your dentist at regular intervals.

The following foods should be avoided during the acute stage of dyspepsia or peptic ulcer, and taken sparingly during intermissions by those liable to frequent attacks. By trial and error the patient can find out which of the articles listed below should be avoided thereafter.
1. Alcohol, strong tea and coffee, cola beverages, gravies and soups made from meat extracts.
2. Pickles, spices, curries and condiments.
3. All fried foods.
4. Tough, twice-cooked or highly seasoned meats, sausages, bacon and pork.
5. Salted fish and some fatty fish such as herring, mackerel and sardines.
6. New bread and scones, wholemeal bread, crispbreads, pastry and cakes containing dried fruit or peel.
7. Rich, heavy puddings.
8. Excess sugar and sweets.
9. Raw and unripe fruit and dried fruits, nuts and the pips, skins and peel of all fruits.
10. Raw vegetables, celery, cucumber, onions, radishes and tomatoes.

The following foods are recommended.
1. Dairy products, i.e. milk, cream, butter, mild cheese and eggs (not fried).
2. White fish, steamed, baked or grilled.
3. Bland meats — chicken, tender beef and lamb, sweetbreads, and tripe.
4. White bread and toast, macaroni and rice.
5. Butter and margarine on bread and in cookery.
6. Plain biscuits and cakes; honey, syrup and jellies.
7. Refined and well-cooked cereals, e.g. cornflour, semolina, ground rice and oatflour porridge.
8. Puddings — junket, jellies, custards, blancmange, soufflé, mousse and plain ice cream.
9. Vegetables — potatoes, creamed or mashed, and green and yellow vegetables which may be sieved and puréed with butter.
10. Fruits, stewed and preferably sieved and served as purées or fools and ripe raw bananas.
11. Weak tea, decaffeinated coffee and malted milk drinks.

Diet No. 18   HIGH FIBRE (ROUGHAGE)

Indications   For patients with diverticulosis and constipation.

Nutrients   Energy and protein according to individual needs; increased fibre.

Sample daily menu

Early morning   Fruit juice, tea or coffee.

Breakfast   Orange juice or ½ grapefruit.
Oatmeal porridge or bran cereal (e.g. All Bran) or muesli (oatmeal, chopped fruit
and nuts) with milk.
Wholemeal bread (may be toasted), oatcakes or crispbread.
Chunky marmalade or jam.
Coffee or tea with milk

Midday meal   Vegetable soup, including plenty of chopped fresh vegetables, dried peas, lentils
and barley. Sandwiches made from wholemeal bread and filled with salad,
including raw carrots or celery and cheese.
Tea or coffee with milk.

Mid-afternoon   Oatcakes, wholemeal wheat biscuits or crispbread.
Tea or coffee with milk.

Evening meal   Serving of any kind of meat or fish.
Baked potatoes (in jackets).
Vegetable or salad.
Fruit.
Coffee or tea with milk.

Bedtime   Wholemeal bread or biscuit.
Tea or coffee with milk.

Management

Liberal use should be made of unrefined cereals, e.g. wholemeal bread and flour, of fresh fruit, vegetables and nuts. One tablespoonful of an unprocessed bran may be taken with the breakfast cereal. Refined cereals and flours, e.g. white bread, rice, pasta, cakes and pastries, should be avoided.

People vary in their response to a high fibre diet, and in some individuals amounts of foods high in fibre should be small at first and increased gradually.

Appendix 3. Oral or Tube Feeds

A selection of commercially available preparations

	Composition per 100 ml or 100 g					
	Energy kcal	Protein g	Fat g	CHO g	Na mmol	K mmol
Oral supplements						
COMPLAN-NATURAL (Glaxo) Skim milk, maltodextrin, hydrogenated vegetable oil, sugar. Flavours available: strawberry, chocolate, butterscotch.	444	20	16	55	15	22
BUILD-UP — VANILLA (Carnation) Skim milk, sucrose, glucose syrup solids, lactose. Flavours available: strawberry, chocolate, coffee.	346	22	0.5	68	14	26
FORTIMEL — VANILLA (Cow & Gate) Protein enriched modified skim milk, sucrose, corn oil, lecithin, maltodextrin. Flavours available: strawberry, chocolate, coffee.	100	10	2	10	2	5
EXPRESS SUPPLEMENT — BUTTERSCOTCH (Express Nutrition) Skim milk solids, maltodextrin, vegetable oils, sucrose, dextrose, permitted emulsifier.	159	6	6	20	4	5
CLINIFEED FLAVOUR — NEUTRAL (Cassenne) Maltodextrin, sodium caseinate, soya protein isolate, glucose, maize oil, MCT, soya oil. Also available: coffee.	100	4	3	14	3	3
Liquid enteral feeds						
The taste of some of these makes acceptable for oral feeds.						
ISOCAL (Mead Johnson) Glucose syrup solids, soy oil, caseinate solids, MCT, soy protein isolate, corn oil.	98	3	4	13	2	2
ENSURE (Abbott) Hydrolised cornstarch, sucrose, caseinates, corn oil, soya protein isolate.	106	4	4	15	4	4
ENSURE PWS (Abbott) As above.	150	5.5	5	20	5	6
CLINIFEED ISO (Cassenne) Milk, maltodextrin, whey proteins, vegetable oils, butter fat, glyceryl monostearate. Also available: Clinifeed 400, protein rich and select.	100	3	4	13	2	3
NUTRAVXIL (Kabivitrum) Maltodextrin, sucrose, sunflower oil, sodium and calcium caseinate, soya protein isolate, MCT	100	4	3	14	3	3

634

A selection of commercially available preparations

	Composition per 100 ml or 100 g					
	Energy kcal	Protein g	Fat g	CHO g	Na mmol	K mmol
EXPRESS ENTERALFEED STANDARD (Express Nutrition) Also available: Introductory, high energy.	103	3	5	13	3	3
Chemically defined formulae						
VIVONEX STANDARD (Eaton) Glucose, 17 amino acids, safflower oil.	375	8	0.5	86	14	11
VIVONEX HIGH NITROGEN (Eaton) As above.	375	16	0.3	79	13	7
NUTRANEL (Cassenne) Maltodextrin, whey protein hydrolysate, vegetable oil.	394	16	4.0	74	8	14
TRIOSORBON (Merck) Maltodextrin; mono, oligo and polysaccharides, MCT, sunflower oil, whey, casein, L-cystine.	470	19	19	56	20	20
PEPTISORBON (Merck) Maltodextrin, lactalbumin hydrolysate, MCT.	400	18	5	70	24	12
Carbohydrate supplements						
MAXIJUL (S.H.S.) Low osmolar glucose polymer.	375	—	—	96	2	trace
CALOREEN (Cassenne) Low osmolar glucose polymer.	400	—	—	96	trace	trace
HYCAL (Beecham) Demineralised glucose syrup, demineralised water, citric acid. Flavours available: orange, lemon, raspberry, blackcurrant.	244	—	—	50	trace	trace
FORTICAL (Cow & Gate) Demineralised water, malto dextrin, citric acid. Flavours available: neutral, apple, apricot.	246	—	—	62	trace	trace
Fat supplements						
PROSPAROL (Duncan Flockhart) Water, arachis oil in 50% emulsion.	450	—	50	—	trace	trace
CALOGEN (S.H.S.) Arachis oil, water.	450	—	50	—	trace	trace
LIQUIGEN (S.H.S.) MCT oil, water.	400	—	52	—	2	trace
PREGESTIMIL (Mead Johnson) Glucose, tapioca starch, corn oil, MCT, Lecithin, casein hydrolysate.	462	13	18	62	9	13
Carbohydrate/fat supplements						
DUOCAL (S.H.S.) Maxijul, Liquigen, Calogen, linoleic acid monoglyceride.	470	—	22	73	trace	trace
Protein supplements						
MAXIPRO HBV (S.H.S.) Supplemented whey protein.	388	88	4	—	10	11.5
CASILAN (Karley) Calcium caseinate.	377	90	2	<0.5	7	trace
FORCEVAL (Unigreg) Low sodium protein powder.	370	55	3	30	trace	trace
COMMINUTED CHICKEN (Cow & Gate) Chicken meat. Finely ground chicken meat in water.	60	7.5	3	—	trace	trace

A selection of commercially available preparations

	Composition per 100 ml or 100 g					
	Energy kcal	Protein g	Fat g	CHO g	Na mmol	K mmol
Lactose-free milk						
NUTRAMIGEN (Mead Johnson)	460	15	18	60	9	12
Sucrose, tapioca starch, corn oil, casein hydrolysate.						
PROSOBEE (Mead Johnson)	520	16	28	51	7	13
Glucose syrup, coconut oil, corn oil, soy protein isolate.						

2nd July 1985

Appendix 4. Weights and Measures

Weights   *Approximate equivalents*

1 ounce (oz)	= 28.35 g	30 g
1 pound (lb)	= 453.6 g	
1 stone (14 lb)	= 6.35 kg	
1 gram (g)	= 0.0353 oz	
1 kilogram (kg)	= 2.205 lb	2.2 lb

Fluid measures

1 fluid ounce (fl oz) (Imperial)	= 28.41 ml	30 ml
1 fluid ounce (fl oz) US	= 29.57 ml	
1 Imperial pint (20 fl oz)	= 568.3 ml	600 ml
1 US pint (16 fl oz)	= 473.0 ml	
1 Imperial gallon (160 fl oz)	= 4.546 litres	
1 US gallon (128 fl oz)	= 3.785 litres	
1 millilitre (ml)	= 0.0352 fl oz (Imperial)	
1 litre (l)	= 1.760 Imperial pints	2 pints
	= 2.11 American pints	

Length

1 inch (in)	= 2.54 cm	
1 foot	= 30.48 cm	30 cm
1 mile	=1.609 km	
1 centimetre (cm)	= 0.394 in	
1 kilometre (km)	= 0.621 miles	

Kitchen measures

*In Britain**   *In North America*

1 teaspoonful	= $\frac{1}{8}$ fl oz = about 4 ml
1 dessertspoonful	= $\frac{1}{4}$ fl oz = about 10 ml
1 tablespoonful	= $\frac{1}{2}$ fl oz = about 18 ml

1 teaspoonful = 4.7 ml

1 tablespoonful = 3 teaspoonsful = 14 ml
1 standard cup = 8 fl 0z = 237 ml

* Teaspoons, dessertspoons and tablespoons vary greatly in Britain.

Index